Presented to

_____

_by_ _____

date _____

"The man who hears my word
and has faith in him who sent me
possesses eternal life."

JOHN 5,25

The New American Bible

Translated from the Original Languages
with Critical Use of All the Ancient Sources
by Members of the
CATHOLIC BIBLICAL ASSOCIATION
OF AMERICA

Sponsored by
The Bishops' Committee
of the Confraternity of
Christian Doctrine

THE CATHOLIC PRESS, Publishers
Distributed by
THE WORLD PUBLISHING COMPANY
Cleveland and New York

𝕹ihil 𝕺bstat	Stephen J. Hartdegen, O.F.M., S.S.L. Christian P. Ceroke, O. Carm, S.T.D.
𝕴mprimatur	✠ Patrick Cardinal O'Boyle, D.D. *Archbishop of Washington* JULY 27, 1970

FIRST EDITION

Library of Congress Catalog Card Number: 77-132629
International Standard Book Number: 8326-1206-5

Table of Contents

The Old Testament

TABLE OF CONTENTS

The New Testament

THE BOOKS OF THE BIBLE IN ALPHABETICAL ORDER

The Old Testament

The New Testament

Preface

ON SEPTEMBER 30, 1943, His Holiness Pope Pius XII issued his now famous encyclical on Scripture studies, *Divino afflante Spiritu*. He wrote: "We ought to explain the original text which was written by the inspired author himself and has more authority and greater weight than any, even the very best, translation whether ancient or modern. This can be done all the more easily and fruitfully if to the knowledge of languages be joined a real skill in literary criticism of the same text."

Early in 1944, in conformity with the spirit of the encyclical, and with the encouragement of Archbishop Cicognani, Apostolic Delegate to the United States, the Bishops' Committee of the Confraternity of Christian Doctrine requested members of the Catholic Biblical Association of America to translate the Sacred Scriptures from the original languages, or from the oldest extant form of the text, and to present the sense of the biblical text in as correct a form as possible.

The first English Catholic version of the Bible, the Douay-Rheims (1582-1609/10), and its revision by Bishop Challoner (1750) were based on the Latin Vulgate. In view of the relative certainties more recently attained by textual and higher criticism, it has become increasingly desirable that contemporary translations of the sacred books into English be prepared in which due reverence for the text and strict observance of the rules of criticism would be combined.

THE NEW AMERICAN BIBLE has accomplished this in response to the need of the Church in America today. It is the achievement of some fifty biblical scholars, the greater number of whom, though not all, are Catholics. In particular, the editors-in-chief have devoted twenty-five years to this work. The collaboration of scholars who are not Catholic fulfills the directive of the Second Vatican Council, not only that "correct translations be made into different languages especially from the original texts of the sacred books," but that, "with the approval of the Church authority, these translations be produced in cooperation with separated brothers" so that "all Christians may be able to use them."

The text of the books contained in THE NEW AMERICAN BIBLE is a completely new translation throughout. From the original and the oldest available texts of the sacred books, it aims to convey as directly as possible the thought and individual style of the inspired writers.

The better understanding of Hebrew and Greek, and the steady development of the science of textual criticism, the fruit of patient study since the time of St. Jerome, have allowed the translators and editors in their use of all available materials to approach more closely than ever before the sense of what the sacred authors actually wrote.

Where the translation supposes the received text—Hebrew, Aramaic, or Greek, as the case may be—ordinarily contained in the best-known editions, as the original or the oldest extant form, no additional remarks are necessary. But for those who are happily able to study the original text of the Scriptures at first hand, a supplementary series of textual notes pertaining to the Old Testament is added in an appendix to the typical edition published by the St. Anthony Guild Press. These furnish a guide in those cases in which the editorial board judges that the manuscripts in the original languages, or the evidence of the ancient versions, or some similar source, furnish the correct reading of a passage, or at least a reading more true to the original than that customarily printed in the available editions.

The Massoretic text of 1 and 2 Samuel has in numerous instances been corrected by the more ancient manuscripts Samuel a, b, and c from Cave 4 of Qumran, with the aid of important evidence from the Septuagint in both its oldest form and its Lucianic recension. Fragments of the lost Book of Tobit in Aramic and in Hebrew, recovered from Cave 4 of Qumran, are in substantial agreement with the Sinaiticus Greek recension used for the translation of this book. The lost original Hebrew text of 1 Maccabees is replaced by its oldest extant form in Greek. Judith, 2 Maccabees, and parts of Esther are also translated from the Greek.

The basic text for the Psalms is not the Massoretic but one which the editors considered closer to the original inspired form, namely the Hebrew text underlying the new Latin Psalter of the Church, the *Liber Psalmorum* (1944[1], 1945[2]). Nevertheless they retained full liberty to establish the reading of the original text on sound critical principles.

The translation of Sirach, based on the original Hebrew as far as it is preserved and corrected from the ancient versions, is often interpreted in the light of the traditional Greek text. In the Book of Baruch the basic text is the Greek of the Septuagint, with some readings derived from an underlying Hebrew form no longer extant. In the deuterocanonical sections of Daniel (3, 24-90; 13, 1—14, 42), the basic text is the Greek text of Theodotion, occasionally revised according to the Greek text of the Septuagint.

In some instances in the Book of Job, in Proverbs, Sirach, Isaiah, Jeremiah, Ezekiel, Hosea, Amos, Micah, Nahum, Habakkuk, and Zechariah there is good reason to believe that the original order of lines was accidentally disturbed in the transmission of the text. The verse numbers given in such cases are always those of the current Hebrew text, though the arrangement differs. In these instances the textual notes advise the reader of the difficulty. Cases of exceptional dislocation are called to the reader's attention by footnotes.

The Books of *Genesis to Ruth* were first published in 1952; the Wisdom Books, *Job to Sirach*, in 1955; the Prophetic Books, *Isaiah to Malachi*, in 1961; and the Books of *Samuel to Maccabees,* in 1969. In the present edition of *Genesis to Ruth* there are certain new features: a general introduction to the Pentateuch, a retranslation of the text of Genesis with an introduction, cross-references, and revised textual notes, besides new and expanded exegetical notes which take into consideration the various sources or literary traditions.

The revision of *Job to Sirach* includes changes in strophe division in Job and Proverbs and in titles of principal parts and sections of Wisdom and Ecclesiastes. Corrections in the text of Sirach are made in 39, 27—44, 17 on the basis of the Masada text, and in 51, 13-30 on the basis of the occurrence of this canticle in the Psalms scroll from Qumran Cave 11. In the typical edition published by St. Anthony Guild Press, new corrections are reflected in the textual notes of Job, Proverbs, Wisdom, and Sirach. In the Psalms, the enumeration found in the Hebrew text is followed instead of the double enumeration, according to both the Hebrew and the Latin Vulgate texts, contained in the previous edition of this book.

In the Prophetic Books *Isaiah to Malachi*, only minor revisions have been made in the structure and wording of the texts, and in the textual notes.

The spelling of proper names in THE NEW AMERICAN BIBLE follows the customary forms found in most English Bibles since the Authorized Version.

The New Testament translation has been approached with essentially the same fidelity to the thought and individual style of the biblical writers as was applied in the Old Testament. In some cases, however, the problem of marked literary peculiarities must be met. What by any Western standard are the limited vocabularies and stylistic infelicities of the evangelists cannot be retained in the exact form in which they appear in the originals without displeasing the modern ear. A compromise is here attempted whereby some measure of the poverty of the evangelists' expression is kept and placed at the service of their message in its richness.

Similarly, the syntactical shortcomings of Paul, his frequent lapses into anacolouthon, and the like, are rendered as they occur in his epistles rather than "smoothed out." Only thus, the translators suppose, will contemporary readers have some adequate idea of the kind of writing they have before them. When the prose of the original flows more smoothly, as in Luke, Acts, and Hebrews, it is reflected in the translation.

The Gospel according to John comprises a special case. Absolute fidelity to his technique of reiterated phrasing would result in an assault on the English ear that would be almost unendurable. Yet the softening of the vocal effect by substitution of other words and phrases would destroy the effectiveness of his poetry. Again, resort is had to compromise. This is not an easy matter when the very repetitiousness which the author deliberately employed is at the same time regarded by those who read and speak English to be a serious stylistic defect. Only those familiar with the Greek originals can know what a relentless tattoo Johannine poetry can produce. (A similar observation could be made regarding other New Testament books as well. Matthew and Mark are given to identical phrasing twice and three times in the same sentence. As for the rhetorical overgrowth and mixed figures of speech in the letters of Peter, James, and Jude, the translator must resist a powerful compulsion to tidy them up if only to enable him to render these epistles intelligibly.)

Without seeking refuge in complaints against the inspired authors, however, the translators of THE NEW AMERICAN BIBLE here state that what they have attempted is a translation rather than a paraphrase. To be sure, all translation can be called paraphrase by definition. Any striving for complete fidelity will shortly end in infidelity. Nonetheless, it must be pointed out that the temptation to improve overladen sentences by the consolidation or elimination of multiplied adjectives, or the simplification of clumsy hendiadys, has been resisted here. For the most part, rhetorically ineffective words and phrases are retained in this translation in some form, even when it is clear that a Western contemporary writer would never have employed them.

One other matter should be mentioned. Despite the arbitrary character of the divisions into numbered verses (a scheme which in its present form is only four centuries old), the translators have made a constant effort to keep within an English verse the whole verbal content of the Greek verse. At times the effort has not seemed worth the result since it often does violence to the original author's flow of expression, which preceded it by so many centuries. If this translation had been prepared for purposes of public reading only, the editors would have forgone the effort at an early stage. But since they never departed from the threefold objective of preparing a translation suitable for liturgical use, private reading, and the purposes of students, the last-named consideration prevailed. Anyone familiar with Greek should be able to discover how the translators of the New Testament have rendered any given original verse of Scripture, if their exegetical or theological tasks require them to know this. At the same time, the fact should be set down here that the editors did not commit themselves in the synoptic gospels to rendering repeated words or phrases identically.

This leads to a final consideration: the text used by the translators of the New Testament. Here, punctuation and verse division are at least as important as variant readings. In general, Nestle-Aland's *Novum Testamentum Graece* (25th edition, 1963) was followed. Additional help was derived from *The Greek New Testament* (editors Aland, Black, Metzger, Wikgren), produced for the use of translators by the United Bible Societies in 1966. However, the editors did not confine themselves strictly to these texts; at times, they inclined toward readings otherwise attested. The omission of alternative translations does not mean that the translators think them without merit, but only that in every case they had to make a choice.

Poorly attested readings do not occur in this translation. Doubtful readings of some merit appear within brackets; public readers may include such words or phrases, or omit them entirely without any damage to sense. Parentheses are used, as ordinarily in English, as a punctuation device. Material they enclose is in no sense textually doubtful. It is simply thought to be parenthetical in the intention of the biblical author, even though there is no such punctuation mark in Greek. The difficulty in dealing with quotation marks is well known. Since they do not appear in any form in the original text, wherever they occur here they constitute an editorial decision.

The work of translating the Bible has been characterized as "the sacred and apostolic work of interpreting the word of God and of presenting it to the laity in translations as clear as the difficulty of the matter and the limitations of human knowledge permit" (A. G. Cicognani, Apostolic Delegate, in *The Catholic Biblical Quarterly*, 6, [1944], 389f). In the appraisal of the present work, it is hoped that the words of the encyclical *Divino afflante Spiritu* will serve as a guide: "Let all the sons of the Church bear in mind that the efforts of these resolute laborers in the vineyard of the Lord should be judged not only with equity and justice but also with the greatest charity; all moreover should abhor that intemperate zeal which imagines that whatever is new should for that very reason be opposed or suspected."

Conscious of their personal limitations for the task thus defined, those who have prepared this text cannot expect that it will be considered perfect; but they can hope that it may deepen in its readers "the right understanding of the divinely given Scriptures," and awaken in them "that piety by which it behooves us to be grateful to the God of all providence, who from the throne of his majesty has sent these books as so many personal letters to his own children" (*Divino afflante Spiritu*).

Acknowledgments

THE PUBLISHERS wish to acknowledge their indebtedness to the Bishops' Committee of the Confraternity of Christian Doctrine, which sponsored this new, epochal translation of the Bible, and to the many editors and translators—all members of the Catholic Biblical Association of America—who labored for over a quarter of a century in the preparation of the text.

BISHOPS' COMMITTEE OF THE
CONFRATERNITY OF CHRISTIAN DOCTRINE

Most Rev. Charles P. Greco, D. D., *Chairman*

Most Rev. Vincent S. Waters, D. D.

Most Rev. Joseph T. McGucken, S. T. D.

Most Rev. Romeo Blanchette, D. D.

Most Rev. Christopher J. Weldon, D. D.

EDITORS IN CHIEF

Rev. Louis F. Hartman, C. SS. R., S. S. L., Ling. Or. L.
(† 1970) *Chairman, Editorial Board for the Old Testament*

Rev. Msgr. Patrick W. Skehan, S. T. D., LL. D.
Vice-chairman, Editorial Board

Rev. Msgr. Myles M. Bourke, S. T. D., S. S. L.
Chairman, Editorial Board for the New Testament

Rev. Stephen J. Hartdegen, O. F. M., S. S. L.
Secretary, Editorial Board

Rev. Gerard S. Sloyan, S. T. L., Ph. D.
English Editor for the New Testament

ASSOCIATE EDITORS AND TRANSLATORS

Rev. Edward P. Arbez, S. S., S. T. D. (†1967)

Rev. Msgr. Edward J. Byrne, Ph. D., S. T. D. (†1952)

Rev. Edward A. Cerny, S. S., S. T. D. (†1962)

Rev. Christian P. Ceroke, O. Carm., S. T. D.

Rev. John J. Collins, S. J., S. S. L.

Sr. M. Emmanuel Collins, O. S. F., Ph. D.

Prof. Frank M. Cross, Jr., Ph. D.

Rev. Patrick Cummins, O. S. B., S. T. D. (†1968)

Rev. Antonine A. DeGuglielmo, O. F. M., S. T. D., S. S. L., S. S. Lect. Gen.

Rev. Alexander A. Di Lella, O. F. M., S. T. L., S. S L., Ph. D.

Most Rev. John J. Dougherty, S. T. L., S. S. D.

Rev. William A. Dowd, S. J., S. T. D., S. S. L.

Rev. Joseph A. Fitzmyer, S. J., S. T. L., S. S. L., Ph. D.

Prof. David Noel Freedman, Ph. D.

Rev. Michael J. Gruenthaner, S. J., S. T. D., S. S. D. (†1962)

Rev. Thomas P. Halton, Ph. D.

Rev. Hilary Hayden, O. S. B., S. T. L.

Rev. Msgr. Maurice A. Hofer, S. S. L.

Rev. John Knox, Ph. D., S. T. D.

Rev. Justin Krellner, O. S. B., S. T. D. (†1949)

Rev. Richard Kugelman, C. P., . S. T. L., S. S. L.

Rev. Joseph L. Lilly, C. M., S. T. D., S. S. L. (†1952)

Rev. Roderick F. MacKenzie, S. J., M. A., S. S. D.

Rev. Edward A. Mangan, C. SS. R., S. S. L. (†1955)

Rev. Daniel W. Martin, C. M., S. T. L., S. S. L.

Rev. William H. McClellan, S. J. (†1951)

Rev. James M. McGlinchey, C. M., S. T. D. (†1961)

Rev. Frederick Moriarty, S. J., S. S. L., S. T. D.

Rev. Richard T. Murphy, O. P., S. T. D., S. S. D.

Rev. Roland E. Murphy, O. Carm., S. T. D., S. S. L.

Rev. Msgr. William L. Newton, S. S. D.

Rev. Eberhard Olinger, O. S. B. (†1967)

Rev. Charles H. Pickar, O. S. A., S. T. L., S. S. L.

Rev. Jerome D. Quinn, S. T. L., S. S. L.

Rev. Christopher Rehwinkel, O. F. M., S. T. D., S. S. Lect. Gen.

Rev. Msgr. John F. Rowan, S. T. D., S. S. L. (†1953)

Prof. J. A. Sanders, Ph. D.

Rev. Raymond Schoder, S. J., Ph. D.

Rev. Edward F. Siegman, C. PP. S., S. T. D., S. S. L. (†1967)

Rev. Kevin Smyth, O. F. M. Cap., S. T. D., S. S. L.

Rev. David M. Stanley, S. J., S. T. L., S. S. D.

Rev. Msgr. Matthew P. Stapleton, S. T. D., S. S. L.

Rev. Msgr. John E. Steinmueller, S. T. D., S. S. L.

Rev. John Ujlaki, O. S. B., S. T. D., Litt. D. (†1964)

Rev. Bruce Vawter, C. M., S. T. L., S. S. D.

Rev. John P. Weisengoff, S. T. D., S. S. L.

Introductions to the Books of the

OLD TESTAMENT

THE PENTATEUCH

THE PENTATEUCH, which consists of the first five books of the Bible (Genesis, Exodus, Leviticus, Numbers, Deuteronomy), enjoys particular prestige among the Jews as the "Law," or "Torah," the concrete expression of God's will in their regard. It is more than a body of legal doctrine, even though such material occupies many chapters, for it contains the story of the formation of the People of God: Abraham and the patriarchs, Moses and the oppressed Hebrews in Egypt, the birth of Israel in the Sinai covenant, the journey to the threshold of the Promised Land, and the "discourses" of Moses.

The grandeur of this historic sweep is the result of a careful and complex joining of several historical traditions, or sources. These are primarily four: the so-called Yahwist, Elohist, Priestly and Deuteronomic strands that run through the Pentateuch. (They are conveniently abbreviated as J, E, P and D.) Each brings to the Torah its own characteristics, its own theological viewpoint—a rich variety of interpretation that the sensitive reader will take pains to appreciate. A superficial difference between two of these sources is responsible for their names: the Yahwist prefers the name *Yahweh* (represented in translation as LORD) by which God revealed himself to Israel; the Elohist prefers the generic name for God, *Elohim*. The Yahwist is concrete, imaginative, using many anthropomorphisms in its theological approach, as seen, e.g., in the narrative of creation in Gn 2, compared with the Priestly version in Gn 1. The Elohist is more sober, moralistic. The Priestly strand, which emphasizes genealogies, is more severely theological in tone. The Deuteronomic approach is characterized by the intense hortatory style of Dt 5—11, and by certain principles from which it works, such as the centralization of worship in the Jerusalem temple.

However, even this analysis of the Pentateuch is an oversimplification, for it is not always possible to distinguish with certainty among the various sources. The fact is that each of these individual traditions incorporates much older material. The Yahwist was himself a collector and adapter. His narrative is made up of many disparate stories that have been reoriented, and given a meaning within the context in which they now stand; e.g., the story of Abraham and Isaac in Gn 22. Within the J and P traditions one has to reckon with many individual units; these had their own history and life-setting before they were brought together into the present more or less connected narrative.

This is not to deny the role of Moses in the development of the Pentateuch. It is true we do not conceive of him as the author of the books in the modern sense. But there is no reason to doubt that, in the events described in these traditions, he had a uniquely important role, especially as lawgiver. Even the later laws that have been added in P and D are presented as a Mosaic heritage. Moses is the lawgiver *par excellence*, and all later legislation is conceived in his spirit, and therefore attributed to him. Hence, the reader is not held to undeviating literalness in interpreting the words, "the Lord said to Moses." One must keep in mind that the Pentateuch is the crystallization of Israel's age-old relationship with God.

In presenting the story of the birth of the People of God, the Pentateuch looks back to the promises made to the patriarchs, and forward to the continuing fulfillment of these promises in later books of the Bible. The promises find their classic expression in Gn 12, 1ff. The "God of the Fathers" challenges Abraham to believe: the patriarch is to receive a people, a land, and through him the nations will somehow be blessed.

The mysterious and tortuous way in which this people is brought into being is described: Despite Sarah's sterility, Isaac is finally born—to be offered in sacrifice! The promises are renewed to him eventually, and also to the devious Jacob, as if to show that the divine design will be effected, with or without human cunning. The magnificent story of Joseph is highlighted by the theme of Providence; the promise of a people is taking shape.

Israel is not formed in a vacuum, but amid the age-old civilizations of Mesopotamia and the Nile. Oppression in Egypt provokes a striking intervention of God.

Yahweh reveals himself to Moses as a savior, and the epic story of deliverance is told in Exodus. This book also tells of the Sinai covenant, which is rightfully regarded as the key to the Old Testament. Through the covenant Israel becomes Yahweh's people, and Yahweh becomes Israel's God. This act of grace marks the fulfillment of the first promise: that Abraham will be the father of a great nation, God's special possession. The laws in Exodus and Leviticus (P tradition) are both early and late. They spell out the proper relationship of the federation of the twelve tribes with the Lord. He is a jealous God, demanding exclusive allegiance; he cannot be imaged; he takes vengeance upon the wicked, and shows mercy to the good. Slowly the Lord reveals himself to his people; with remarkable honesty, Israel records the unsteady response—the murmurings and rebellions and infidelities through the desert wanderings up to the plains of Moab.

This sacred history was formed within the bosom of early Israel, guided by the spirit of God. It was sung beside the desert campfires; it was commemorated in the liturgical feasts, such as Passover; it was transmitted by word of mouth from generation to generation—until all was brought together in writing, about the sixth century B.C., when the literary formation of the Pentateuch came to an end.

The Book of Deuteronomy has a history quite peculiar to itself. Its old traditions and law code (12—26) are put forth in the form of "discourses" of Moses before his death. The extraordinarily intense and hortatory tone fits the mood of a discourse. The book contains possibly the preaching of the Levites in the northern kingdom of Israel before its fall in 721 B.C. If this book is situated in its proper historical perspective, its true impact is more vividly appreciated. It is the blueprint of the great "Deuteronomic" reform under King Josiah (640–609 B.C.). This was an attempt to galvanize the people into a wholehearted commitment to the covenant ideals, into an obedience motivated by the great commandment of love (Dt 6, 4ff). Israel has yet another chance, if it obeys. The people are poised between life and death; and they are exhorted to choose life—today (26, 16–19; 30, 15–20).

THE BOOK OF GENESIS

GENESIS, the first book of the Bible, opens with the Hebrew word *bereshit*, which means "in the beginning." The title "Genesis" was given to the Septuagint (Greek) translation of the book because of its concern with the origin of the world (Gn 1, 1; 2, 4), of the human race, and, in particular, of the Hebrew people.

Eleven structural units (*toledoth*), of unequal length and importance, present the unity and purpose of the book in terms of God's universal sovereignty, his dealings with men, and his choice and formation of a special people to be the instrument of his plan of salvation.

The tracing of the direct descendance from Adam to Jacob constitutes the major part of the book, while the genealogical tables of lateral branches are not so developed nor of such interest as those that pertain to the story of the Israelite people. In fact, these lateral branches gradually disappear from the narrative. And with the introduction of Abraham and his covenant with God, the history of humanity as such becomes contracted to the story of the descendants of Abraham through Isaac and Jacob—the chosen people.

Despite its unity of plan and purpose, the book is a complex work, not to be attributed to a single original author. Several sources, or literary traditions, that the final redactor used in his composition are discernible. These are the Yahwist (J), Elohist (E) and Priestly (P) sources, which in turn reflect older oral traditions (see Introduction to the Pentateuch).

In Genesis, the Yahwist source is the most important by

reason of its teaching, its antiquity, and the continuity it gives the book. It constitutes a sacred history, continually drawing attention to the working out of God's design through his interventions in the affairs of men. The Elohist source, less well preserved, is found in fragmentary form only, depicting God's manifestations through visions and dreams rather than theophanies. Angels are God's intermediaries with men. Moreover, there is a solicitude for the divine transcendence and greater sensitivity toward the moral order. The Priestly source contains those elements—chronological data, lists, genealogies—that construct the framework of Genesis and bind its contents together. To the J and E sources it adds such legal institutions as the sabbath rest, circumcision, and the alliances between God and Noah and God and Abraham.

The interpreter of Genesis will recognize at once the distinct object that sets chapters 1—11 apart: the recounting of the origin of the world and of man (primeval history). To make the truths contained in these chapters intelligible to the Israelite people destined to preserve them, they needed to be expressed through elements prevailing among that people at that time. For this reason, the truths themselves must therefore be clearly distinguished from their literary garb.

With the story of the patriarchs Abraham, Isaac and Jacob (11, 27—50, 26), the character of the narrative changes. While we do not view the account of the patriarchs as history in the strict sense, nevertheless certain of the matters recounted from the time of Abraham onward can be placed in the actual historical and social framework of the Near East in the early part of the second millennium B.C. (2000–1500), and documented by non-biblical sources.

Genesis contains many religious teachings of basic importance: the preexistence and transcendence of God, his wisdom and goodness, his power through which all things are made and on which they all depend; the special creation of man in God's image and likeness, and of woman from the substance of man; the institution of marriage as the union of one man with one woman; man's original state of innocence; man's sin of pride and disobedience; its consequences for the protoparents and their posterity. Despite the severity of their punishment, hope of reconciliation is offered by God through the first as well as the subsequent promises of salvation and blessing. Abraham is blessed for his faith and obedience, and he is to be a blessing for all nations through his offspring, Isaac, Jacob, and Jacob's sons (Gn 12, 3; 18, 18; 22, 18), of whom the Messiah, mankind's greatest blessing, will eventually be born (Gal 3, 8).

Frequent references to Genesis are found in the New Testament. Christ becomes the antithesis of Adam: sin and death come to mankind through Adam, justification and life through Jesus Christ (Rom 5, 12.17ff). Noah's ark becomes the symbol of the Church, by which men are saved from destruction through the waters of baptism

(1 Pt 3, 20ff); Abraham's faith is the model for all believers; the sacrifice of his son Isaac typifies the sacrifice of Christ, Son of the Father. The Liturgy, too, relates the persons of Abel, Abraham and Melchizedek to Christ in his act of sacrifice.

The Book of Genesis is divided as follows:
I: The Primeval History (1, 1—11, 26)
II: The Patriarch Abraham (11, 27—25, 18)
III: The Patriarchs Isaac and Jacob (25, 19—36, 43)
IV: Joseph and His Brothers (37, 1—50, 26)

THE BOOK OF EXODUS

THE SECOND BOOK of the Pentateuch is called Exodus from the Greek word for "departure," because the central event narrated in it is the departure of the Israelites from Egypt. It continues the history of the chosen people from the point where the Book of Genesis leaves off. It recounts the oppression by the Egyptians of the ever-increasing descendants of Jacob and their miraculous deliverance by God through Moses, who led them across the Red Sea to Mount Sinai where they entered into a special covenant with the Lord.

These events were of prime importance to the chosen people, for they became thereby an independent nation and enjoyed a unique relationship with God. Through Moses God gave to the Israelites at Mount Sinai the "law": the moral, civil and ritual legislation by which they were to become a holy people, in whom the promise of a Savior for all mankind would be fulfilled.

The principal divisions of Exodus are:
I: The Israelites in Egypt (1, 1—12, 36)
II: The Exodus from Egypt and the Journey to Sinai (12, 37—18, 27)
III: The Covenant at Mount Sinai (19, 1—24, 18)
IV: The Dwelling and Its Furnishings (25,1—40, 38)

THE BOOK OF LEVITICUS

THE NAME "Leviticus" was bestowed on the third book of the Pentateuch by the ancient Greek translators because a good part of this book consists of sacrificial and other ritual laws prescribed for the priests of the tribe of Levi.

Continuing the legislation given by God to Moses at Mount Sinai, Leviticus is almost entirely legislative in character; the rare narrative portions are subordinate to the main legislative theme. Generally speaking, the laws contained in this book serve to teach the Israelites that they should always keep themselves in a state of legal purity, or external sanctity, as a sign of their intimate union with the LORD. Accordingly, the central idea of Leviticus is contained in its oft-repeated injunction: "You shall be holy, because I, the LORD, am holy."

The main divisions of Leviticus are:
I: Ritual of Sacrifices (1–7)
II: Ceremony of Ordination (8–10)
III: Laws regarding Legal Purity (11–16)
IV: Code of Legal Holiness (17–26)
V: Redemption of Offerings (27)

THE BOOK OF NUMBERS

THE BOOK OF NUMBERS derives its name from the account of the two censuses of the Hebrew people taken, one near the beginning and the other toward the end of the journey in the desert (chapters 1 and 26). It continues the story of that journey, begun in Exodus, and describes briefly the experiences of the Israelites for a period of thirty-eight years, from the end of their encampment at Sinai to their arrival at the border of the Promised Land. Numerous legal ordinances are interspersed in the account, making the book a combination of law and history.

The various events described clearly indicate the action of God, who punishes the murmuring of the people by prolonging their stay in the desert, at the same time preparing them by this discipline to be his witnesses among the nations.

In the New Testament Christ and the Apostles derive useful lessons from such events in the Book of Numbers as the brazen serpent (Jn 3, 14f), the sedition of Korah and its consequences (1 Cor 10, 10), the prophecies of Balaam (2 Pt 2, 15f), and the water gushing from the rock (1 Cor 10, 4).

The chief divisions of the Book of Numbers are as follows:
I: Preparations for the Departure from Sinai (1, 1—10, 10)
II: From Sinai to the Plains of Moab (10, 11—22, 1)
III: On the Plains of Moab (22, 2—36, 13)

THE BOOK OF DEUTERONOMY

THE FIFTH and last book of the Pentateuch is called Deuteronomy, meaning "second law." In reality, what it contains is not a new law but a partial repetition, completion and explanation of the law proclaimed on Mount Sinai. The historical portions of the book are also a résumé of what is related elsewhere in the Pentateuch.

The chief characteristic of this book is its vigorous oratorical style. In a series of eloquent discourses Moses presents the theme of covenant renewal in a vital liturgical framework. He exhorts, corrects and threatens his people, appealing to their past glory, their historic mission, and the promise of future triumph. His aim is to enforce among the Israelites the Lord's claim to their obedience, loyalty and love.

The events contained in the Book of Deuteronomy took place on the plains of Moab (1, 5) between the end of the wanderings in the desert (1, 3) and the crossing of the Jordan River (Jos 4, 19), a period of no more than forty days.

The Book of Deuteronomy, written after the Israelites had for centuries been resident in the Land of Promise, takes the form of a testament of Moses, the great leader and legislator, to his people on the eve of his death. At the time of our Lord's coming, it shared with the Psalms a preeminent religious influence among the Old Testament books.

The Savior quoted passages of Deuteronomy in overcoming the threefold temptation of Satan in the desert (Mt 4; Dt 6, 13.16; 8, 3; 10, 20), and in explaining to the lawyer the first and greatest commandment (Mt 22, 35–39; Dt 6, 4).

The book is divided as follows:
  I: Historical Review and Exhortation (1, 1—4, 43)
  II: God and His Covenant (4, 44—11, 32)
  III: Exposition of the Law (12, 1—26, 19)
  IV: Final Words of Moses (27, 1—34, 12)

THE BOOK OF JOSHUA

THE BOOK OF JOSHUA derives its name from the successor of Moses, with whose deeds it is principally concerned. The purpose of the book is to demonstrate God's fidelity in giving to the Israelites the land he had promised them for an inheritance (Gn 15, 18ff; Jos 1, 2ff; 21, 41ff; 23, 14ff).

Their occupation of the country is begun with the crossing of the Jordan and the conquest of Jericho (ch 1—6), in both of which the Lord intervenes on their behalf. This is followed by a first foothold on the Palestinian mountain range, at Ai, Bethel, and Gibeon (ch 7—9), and two sweeping campaigns against the city states in the south of the country (ch 10) and in the north (ch 11), with a summary in ch 12. The broad claim to total sovereignty thus established is spelled out by a combined list of tribal boundaries and of the towns contained within each area or administrative district (ch 13—19), including cities of asylum and cities for the Levites (ch 20, 21). The book closes with a narrative about the tribes east of the Jordan (ch 22), a warning speech by Joshua (ch 23), and a renewal at Shechem (ch 24) of the covenant with the Lord, already affirmed there near the beginning of the conquest (8, 30–35).

Like the books which precede it, the Book of Joshua was built up by a long and complex process of editing traditional materials. Both Jewish and Christian believers have always regarded it as inspired.

The entire history of the conquest of the Promised Land is a prophecy of the spiritual conquest of the world through the Church under the leadership of Jesus the Messiah.

The Book of Joshua may be divided as follows:
  I: Conquest of Canaan (1, 1—12, 24)
  II: Division of the Land (13, 1—21, 45)
  III: Return of the Transjordan Tribes and Joshua's Farewell (22, 1—24, 33)

THE BOOK OF JUDGES

THE BOOK OF JUDGES derives its title from the twelve heroes of Israel whose deeds it records. They were not magistrates, but military leaders sent by God to aid and to relieve his people in time of external danger. They exercised their activities in the interval of time between the death of Joshua and the institution of the monarchy in Israel. Six of them—Othniel, Ehud, Barak, Gideon, Jephthah and Samson—are treated in some detail and have accordingly been styled the Major Judges. The other six, of whose activities this book preserves but a summary record, are called the Minor Judges. There were two other judges, whose judgeships are described in 1 Samuel—Eli and Samuel, who seem to have ruled the entire nation of Israel just before the institution of the monarchy. The twelve judges of the present book, however, very probably exercised their authority, sometimes simultaneously, over one or another tribe of Israel, never over the entire nation.

The purpose of the book is to show that the fortunes of Israel depended upon the obedience or disobedience of the people to God's law. Whenever they rebelled against him, they were oppressed by pagan nations; when they repented, he raised up judges to deliver them (cf 2, 10–23).

The accounts of various events, whether written shortly after their occurrence or orally transmitted, were later skillfully unified according to the moral purpose of the redactor some time during the Israelite monarchy.

The book is divided as follows:
  I: Palestine after the Death of Joshua (1, 1—3, 6)
  II: Stories of the Judges (3, 7—16, 31)
  III: The Tribes of Dan and Benjamin in the Days of the Judges (17, 1—21, 25)

THE BOOK OF RUTH

THE BOOK OF RUTH is named after the Moabite woman who was joined to the Israelite people by her marriage with the influential Boaz of Bethlehem.

The book contains a beautiful example of filial piety, pleasing to the Hebrews especially because of its connection with King David, and useful both to Hebrews and to Gentiles. Its aim is to demonstrate the divine reward for such piety even when practiced by a stranger. Ruth's piety (2, 11), her spirit of self-sacrifice, and her moral integrity were favored by God with the gift of faith and an illustrious marriage whereby she became the ancestress of David and of Christ. In this, the universality of the Messianic salvation is foreshadowed.

In the Greek and Latin canons the Book of Ruth is placed just after Judges, to which it is closely related because of the time of its action, and just before Samuel, for which it is an excellent introduction, since it traces the ancestry of the Davidic dynasty. One might characterize the literary form of this book as dramatic, since about two-thirds of it is in dialogue. Yet there is every indication that, as tradition has always held, it contains true history.

There is no certainty about the author of the book. It was written long after the events had passed (4, 7), which took place "in the time of the judges" (1, 1).

THE HISTORICAL BOOKS

THE HISTORICAL BOOKS include 1 and 2 Samuel, 1 and 2 Kings, 1 and 2 Chronicles, Ezra, Nehemiah, 1 and 2 Maccabees. To these are added the special literary group of Tobit, Judith and Esther.

The books of Tobit, Judith, and 1 and 2 Maccabees, as well as parts of Esther, are called deuterocanonical: they are not contained in the Hebrew canon but have been accepted by the Catholic Church as canonical and inspired.

By means of a series of episodes involving the persons of Samuel, Saul, and David, a century of history unfolds in 1 and 2 Samuel from the close of the period of Judges to the rise and establishment of the monarchy in Israel. Most important is God's promise to David of a lasting dynasty (2 Sm 7), from which royal messianism in the Bible developed.

In 1 and 2 Kings the religious history of Israel extends another four centuries, from the last days of David to the Babylonian captivity and the destruction of Jerusalem (587 B.C.). The various sources for these books are woven into a uniform pattern based on the principle of fidelity to Yahweh for rulers and people alike. The sequence or regnal chronicles in both books is interrupted by a cycle of traditions surrounding the prophets Elijah (1 Kgs) and Elisha (2 Kgs).

Chronicles, Ezra and Nehemiah form a historical work, uniform in style and basic ideas. Chronicles records the long period from the reign of Saul to the return from exile not so much with exactitude of detail as with concern for the meaning of the facts which demonstrate God's intervention in history. The Ezra-Nehemiah chronicle constitutes the most important source for the formation of the Jewish religious community after the Babylonian exile; the two persons most responsible for the reorganization of Jewish life were Ezra and Nehemiah.

1 and 2 Maccabees contain independent accounts of partially identical events which accompanied the attempted suppression of Judaism in Palestine in the second century B.C. Vigorous reaction to this attempt established for a time the religious and political independence of the Jews. 1 Maccabees portrays God as the eternal benefactor of the Jews and their unfailing source of help. The people are required to be devoted to his exclusive worship and to observe exactly the law he has given them. 2 Maccabees, besides supplementing the former volume, gives a theological interpretation of the history of the period and contains teaching on the resurrection from the dead, intercession of the saints, and suffrages for the dead.

Tobit, Judith, and Esther are examples of free composition—the religious novel used for purposes of edification and instruction. Interest in whatever historical data these books may contain is merely intensified by the addition of vivid details. Judith is a lesson in Providence: a pious reflection on the annual Passover observance to convey the reassurance that God is still the master of history who saves Israel from her enemies. Esther's purpose is the glorification of the Jewish people and the explanation of the origin, significance, and date of the feast of Purim. It is a literary development of the principle of reversal of fortune through punishment of the prosperous rich and reward for the virtuous who are oppressed.

SAMUEL TO MACCABEES demonstrates that before as well as during the millennium of history with which it is concerned, Israel was a covenanted people, bound to Yahweh, Lord of the universe, by the ties of faith and obedience. This required observance of the law and worship in his temple, the consequent rewards of which were divine favor and protection. In this way these books anticipate and prepare for the coming of him who would bring type and prophecy to fulfillment, history to term, and holiness to perfection: Christ, the Son of David and the promised Messiah.

THE BOOKS OF SAMUEL

ORIGINALLY but one book, the scroll of Samuel was early divided into two. The Greek translators called these the first and second Books of Kingdoms, a title St. Jerome later modified to "Kings." The Hebrew title, "Samuel," alludes to the leading figure in the first book, who was responsible for the enthronement of David. It is David's history that the second book recounts.

This sacred work thus comprises the history of about a century, describing the close of the age of the Judges and the beginnings of monarchy in Israel under Saul and David. It is not a complete and continuous history, nor a systematic account of the period, but rather a series of episodes centered around the persons of Samuel, Saul and David, the principal figures leading up to the establishment of the royal dynasty of David.

The final editor is unknown, nor are we certain of the time at which the various strands of the narrative were put together, though one may think of the period, perhaps late in the seventh century B.C., when the other volumes of the "Former Prophets," from Joshua through Kings, were built into a more or less continuous historical corpus. The Samuel-Saul-David narratives clearly depend on several written sources: a Samuel cycle, two sets of stories about Saul and David, and a family history of David. This last (2 Sm 9–20; 1 Kgs 1–2), one of the most vivid historical narratives surviving from ancient times, probably originated early in the reign of Solomon.

One of the most significant theological contributions of the Old Testament is found in 2 Samuel 7, the oracle of Nathan. David is here promised an eternal dynasty, and this becomes the basis for the development of royal messianism throughout the Bible. With this promise to David one should compare 2 Chr 17; Pss 89, 20–38 and 132, 11ff; Acts 2, 30; and Heb 1, 5.

The contents of this work may be divided as follows:
I: History of the Last Judges, Eli and Samuel (1 Sm 1, 1—7, 17)
II: Establishment of the Monarchy in Israel (1 Sm 8, 1—12, 25)
III: Saul and David (1 Sm 13, 1—2 Sm 2, 7)
IV: Reign of David (2 Sm 2, 8—20, 26)
V: Appendixes (2 Sm 21, 1—24, 25)

THE BOOKS OF KINGS

THE TWO BOOKS of Kings were originally, like 1 and 2 Samuel, a single historical work. In conjunction with the Books of Samuel, they extend the consecutive history of Israel from the birth of Samuel to the destruction of Jerusalem in 587 B.C. This combined work is designed as a religious history; hence in Kings the temple, which is the chosen site for the worship of Yahweh, occupies the center of attention.

The Books of Kings show clearly the theological bent of a Deuteronomic editor. In them, as already in Judges, material from various sources, such as the "book of the acts of Solomon" (1 Kgs 11, 41) and the "book of the chronicles of the kings of Israel" (1 Kgs 14, 19), is forged into structural unity by an editor whose principal interest is in the fidelity to Yahweh of rulers and people. The reigns of individual kings are adapted to an editorial framework consisting of a presentation and an obituary notice for each, in stereotyped formulas. In between, the achievements of the kings are reported—above all, his fidelity or lack of fidelity to Yahweh. The faithful prosper; the unfaithful pay for their defections. Since this is basically a narrative of sin and retribution, it would not be inappropriate to entitle the Books of Kings "The Rise and Fall of the Israelite Monarchy."

Without minimizing the complexity of the process by which this material was transmitted for many centuries, one may speak of two editions of the Books: the first at some time between 621 B.C. and 597 B.C., and the second, final edition during the Exile; probably shortly after Jehoiachin was released from his Babylonian prison (561 B.C.).

1 Kings carries the history of Israel from the last days and death of David to the accession in Samaria of Ahaziah, son of Ahab, near the end of the reign of Jehoshaphat, king of Judah. Judgment is passed on Ahaziah's reign but the details are given only later, in 2 Kings. We should note the two large cycles of traditions which grew up around the great prophetic figures of Elijah and Elisha, the former in 1 Kings and the latter chiefly in 2 Kings. These cycles, which interrupt the sequence of regnal chronicles, were very probably preserved and transmitted by the prophetic communities to which there are references in the same traditions. The Elijah cycle is the more important since it dramatically underscores Israel's critical struggle with the religion of Canaan.

The principal divisions of the Books of Kings are:
I: The Reign of Solomon (1 Kgs 1, 1—11, 43)
II: Judah and Israel to the Time of Ahab (1 Kgs 12, 1—16, 34)
III: Stories of the Prophets (1 Kgs 17, 1—22, 54)
IV: The Kingdoms of Israel and Judah (2 Kgs 1, 1—17, 41)
V: The Kingdom of Judah after 721 B.C. (2 Kgs 18, 1—25, 30)

THE FIRST BOOK OF CHRONICLES

ORIGINALLY the two books of Chronicles formed, with the Books of Ezra and Nehemiah, a single historical work, uniform in style and basic ideas. The Greek title, *paraleipomena*, means "things omitted, or passed over (in Samuel and Kings)." The Books of Chronicles, however, are more than a supplement to Samuel and Kings; a comparison of the two histories discloses striking differences in scope and purpose. The Books of Chronicles record in some detail the lengthy span from the reign of Saul to the return from the Exile. Unlike the exact science of history today, wherein factual accuracy and impartiality of judgment are the standards for estimating what is of permanent worth, ancient biblical history, with rare exceptions, was less concerned with reporting in precise detail all the facts of a situation than with explaining the meaning of those facts. Such history was primarily interpretative and, in the Old Testament, its purpose was to disclose the action of the living God in the affairs of men. For this reason we speak of it as "sacred history"; its writer's first concern was to bring out the divine or supernatural dimension in history.

This is apparent when we examine the primary objective of the Chronicler in compiling his work. In view of the situation which confronted the Jewish people at this time (the end of the fifth century B.C.), the Chronicler realized that Israel's political greatness was a thing of the past. It would be a people under God, or nothing. Yet Israel's past held the key to her future. The Chronicler proposed to establish and defend the legitimate claims of the Davidic monarchy in Israel's history, and to underscore the place of Jerusalem and its divinely established temple worship as the center of religious life for the Jewish community of this day. If Judaism was to survive and prosper, it would have to heed the lessons of the past and devoutly serve Yahweh in the place where he had chosen to dwell, the temple of Jerusalem. From the Chronicler's point of view, David's reign was the ideal to which all subsequent rule in Judah must aspire.

The Chronicler was much more interested in David's religious and cultic influence than in his political power. There is little of royal messianism in his book. He apparently regarded as something of the distant past the prophet Zechariah's abortive attempt to have the Davidic kingdom reestablished in the time of Zerubbabel at the end of the sixth century B.C. (Zec 6, 9–15). He saw David's primary importance as deriving from the establishment of Jerusalem and its temple as the center of the true worship of the Lord. Furthermore, he presented David as the one who had authorized the elaborate ritual (which, in point of fact, only gradually evolved in the temple built by Zerubbabel) and who had also appointed Levites to supervise the liturgical services there.

There are good reasons for believing that originally the Books of Ezra and Nehemiah formed the last part of a single literary work that began with 1 and 2 Chronicles. Some authors even regard Ezra himself as having been the anonymous Chronicler. In any case, the Chronicler's Hebrew as well as his religious and political outlook points to c. 400 B.C. as the time of composition of this work.

The Chronicler used sources in writing his history. Besides the canonical Books of Genesis, Exodus, Numbers, Joshua and Ruth, and especially the Books of Samuel and Kings, he cites the titles of many other works no longer extant. "The books of the kings of Israel," or "the books of the kings of Israel and Judah," "the history of Samuel the seer," "the history of Nathan the prophet," "the history of Gad the seer," "the commentary on the Books of Kings," are some of the documents mentioned as historical sources.

In addition, the Chronicler's work contains early preexilic material not found in the Books of Kings. At one time scholars discounted the value of this material, but modern research has shown that, even though the Chronicler may have at times treated the material rather freely, he derived it from authentic and reliable sources.

The principal divisions of 1 Chronicles are as follows:
  I: Genealogical Tables (1, 1—9, 34)
 II: The History of David (9, 35—29, 30)

THE SECOND BOOK OF CHRONICLES

THE SECOND BOOK of Chronicles takes up the history of the monarchy where the First Book breaks off. It begins with the account of the reign of Solomon from the special viewpoint of the Chronicler. The portrait of Solomon is an idealized one; he appears as second only to David. The great achievement of the building of the temple and the magnificence of Solomon's court are described in detail while the serious defects of his reign are passed over without comment. All this is in keeping with the Chronicler's purpose of stressing the supreme importance of the temple and its worship. He wishes to impress on his readers the splendor of God's dwelling and the magnificence of the liturgy of sacrifice, prayer and praise offered there. Judah's kings are judged by their attitude toward the temple and its cult. To this ideal of one people, united in the worship of the one true God at the temple of Jerusalem founded by David and Solomon, the restored community would have to conform.

In treating the period of divided monarchy, the Chronicler gives practically all his attention to the kingdom of Judah. His omission of the northern Israelite kings is significant. In his view, the northern tribes of Israel were in religious schism as long as they worshiped Yahweh in a place other than the temple of Jerusalem. The Chronicler makes no mention of the important sanctuaries of Yahweh at Dan and Bethel—as though they had never existed. Nevertheless he retains the ancient ideal of "all Israel" (a phrase occurring forty-one times in Chronicles) as the people of God. The condition he places for a united people is that "the whole congregation of Israel" worship the Lord only in his temple at Jerusalem. This explains his praise of Kings Hezekiah and Josiah for striving, after the fall of Samaria, to unite the remnants of the northern tribes of Israel into the kingdom of Judah.

At the end of the fifth century B.C., during the Chronicler's own time, "the people of the land" were the descendants of the people of all the tribes (including Judah) who had not gone into exile. These had become intermingled with aliens and had evolved a religion of Yahweh very different from the Judaism that developed during the Babylonian exile. Thus, religious and political cooperation between the returned exiles and these "people of the land" was out of the question for the Chronicler. This he clearly shows in the last part of his work, the Books of Ezra and Nehemiah.

The Second Book of Chronicles is divided as follows:
  I: The Reign of Solomon (1, 1—9, 31)
 II: The Monarchy before Hezekiah (10, 1—27, 9)
III: Reforms of Hezekiah and Josiah (28, 1—36, 1)
IV: End of the Kingdom (36, 2–23)

THE BOOK OF EZRA

THE LAST four books of the Hebrew canon are Ezra, Nehemiah, 1 and 2 Chronicles, in that order. Originally, however, Ezra and Nehemiah followed the Books of Chronicles, and formed with them a unified historical work so homogeneous in spirit that one usually speaks of a single author for the four books. He is called "the Chronicler." The treatment of Ezra-Nehemiah as a single book by the earliest chroniclers was undoubtedly due to the fact that in ancient times the two books were put under the one name—Ezra. The combined work Ezra-Nehemiah is our most important literary source for the formation of the Jewish religious community after the Babylonian exile. This is known as the period of the Restoration, and the two men most responsible for the reorganization of Jewish life at this time were Ezra and Nehemiah.

In the present state of the Ezra-Nehemiah text, there are several dislocations of large sections so that the chronological or logical sequence is disrupted. The major instances are pointed out in the footnotes. Although Ezra appears before Nehemiah in this work, it seems probable that Nehemiah's activity preceded his.

What is known of Ezra and his work is due almost exclusively to Ezra 7—10 (the "Ezra Memoirs") and to Neh 8—9. Strictly speaking, the term "Ezra Memoirs" should be used only of that section in which Ezra speaks in the first person, i.e., 7, 27—9, 15. Compare the "Nehemiah Memoirs" in Neh 1, 1—7, 72a; 11, 1f; 12, 27–43; 13, 4–31. The Chronicler combined this material with other sources at his disposal. The personality of Ezra is less known than that of Nehemiah. Ben Sirach, in his praise of the fathers, makes no mention of Ezra. The genealogy of Ezra (7, 1–5) traces his priesthood back to Aaron, brother of Moses. This was the accepted way of establishing the legality of one's priestly office. He is also called *a scribe, well-versed in the law of Moses* (7, 6), indicating Ezra's dedication to the study of the Torah, which he sought to make the basic rule of life in the restored community. It was in religious and cultic reform rather than in political affairs that Ezra made his mark as a postexilic leader. Jewish tradition holds him in great honor; the Talmud even regards him as a second Moses, claiming that the Torah would have been given to Israel through Ezra had not Moses preceded him.

Ezra is sometimes accused of having been a mere legalist who gave excessive attention to the letter of the law. His work, however, should be seen and judged within a specific historical context. He gave to his people a cohesion and spiritual unity which prevented the disintegration of the small Jewish community. Had it not been for the intransigence of Ezra and of those who adopted his ideal, it is doubtful that Judaism would have so effectively resisted Hellenism, then or in later centuries. Ezra set the tone of the postexilic community, and it was characterized by fidelity to the Torah, Judaism's authentic way of life. It is in this light that we can judge most fairly the work of Ezra during the Restoration.

The Book of Ezra is divided as follows:
 I: The Return from Exile (1, 1—6, 22)
 II: The Deeds of Ezra (7, 1—10, 44)

The following list of the kings of Persia, with the dates of their reigns, will be useful for dating the events mentioned in Ezra-Nehemiah:

Cyrus .... 538–529 B.C.
Cambyses .... 529–521 B.C.
Darius I .... 521–485 B.C.
Xerxes .... 485–464 B.C.
Artaxerxes I .... 464–423 B.C.
Darius II .... 423–404 B.C.
Artaxerxes II .... 404–358 B.C.
Artaxerxes III .... 358–337 B.C.
End of the Persian Empire (Defeat of
 Darius III) .... 331 B.C.

THE BOOK OF NEHEMIAH

PROBLEMS common to the combined Books Ezra-Nehemiah have been pointed out in the Introduction to the Book of Ezra. The achievements of the two men were complementary; each helped to make it possible for Judaism to maintain its identity during the difficult days of the Restoration. Nehemiah was the man of action who rebuilt the walls of Jerusalem and introduced necessary administrative reforms. Ezra in turn was the great religious reformer who succeeded in establishing the Torah as the constitution of the returned community.

The biblical sources for Nehemiah's life and work are the autobiographical portions scattered through the book. They are called the "Memoirs of Nehemiah," and have been used more extensively and effectively by "the Chronicler" than the "Memoirs of Ezra." No competent scholar questions the authenticity of Nehemiah's memoirs. From these and other sources, the picture emerges of a man dedicated to the single purpose of the welfare of his people. Despite temperamental shortcomings, Nehemiah was a man of good practical sense combined with deep faith in God. In view of his selfless service to a community capable of severely testing any leader, we can be indulgent toward his numerous appeals to God to credit him with the work he had done. Nehemiah was a layman, and his generous dedication of talents to the service of God and of God's people remains an example of undiminished force for laymen today.

The Book of Nehemiah is divided as follows:
 I: The Deeds of Nehemiah (1, 1—7, 72)
 II: Promulgation of the Law (8, 1—13, 31)

THE BOOK OF TOBIT

THE BOOK OF TOBIT, named after its principal hero, combines specifically Jewish piety and morality with oriental folklore in a fascinating story that has enjoyed wide popularity in both Jewish and Christian circles. Prayers, psalms, and words of wisdom, as well as the skillfully constructed story itself, provide valuable insights into the faith and the religious milieu of its unknown author. The book was probably written early in the second century B.C.; it is not known where.

Tobit, a devout and wealthy Israelite living among the

captives deported to Nineveh from the northern kingdom of Israel in 721 B.C., suffers severe reverses and is finally blinded. Because of his misfortunes he begs the Lord to let him die. But recalling the large sum he had formerly deposited in far-off Media, he sends his son Tobiah there to bring back the money. In Media, at this same time, a young woman, Sarah, also prays for death, because she has lost seven husbands, each killed in turn on his wedding night by the demon Asmodeus. God hears the prayers of Tobit and Sarah, and sends the angel Raphael in disguise to aid them both.

Raphael makes the trip to Media with Tobiah. When Tobiah is attacked by a large fish as he bathes, Raphael orders him to seize it and to remove its gall, heart, and liver because they make "useful medicines." Later, at Raphael's urging, Tobiah marries Sarah, and uses the fish's heart and liver to drive Asmodeus from the bridal chamber. Returning to Nineveh with his wife and his father's money, Tobiah rubs the fish's gall into his father's eyes and cures them. Finally, Raphael reveals his true identity and returns to heaven. Tobit then utters his beautiful hymn of praise. Before dying, Tobit tells his son to leave Nineveh because God will destroy that wicked city. After Tobiah buries his father and mother, he and his family depart for Media, where he later learns that the destruction of Nineveh has taken place.

The inspired author of the book used the literary form of religious novel (as in Jonah and Judith) for the purpose of instruction and edification. There may have been a historical nucleus around which the story was composed, but this possibility has nothing to do with the teaching of the book. The seemingly historical data—names of kings, cities, etc.—are used merely as vivid details to create interest and charm.

Although the Book of Tobit is usually listed with the historical books, it more correctly stands midway between them and the wisdom literature. It contains numerous maxims like those found in the wisdom books (cf 4, 3–19.21; 12, 6–10; 14, 7.9) as well as the customary sapiential themes: fidelity to the law, the intercessory function of angels, piety toward parents, the purity of marriage, reverence for the dead, and the value of almsgiving, prayer, and fasting. The book makes Tobit a relative of *Ahiqar*, a hero of ancient Near Eastern folklore.

Written in Aramaic, the original of the book was lost for centuries. The Greek translation, existing in three different recensions is our primary source. In 1955, fragments of the book in Aramaic and in Hebrew were recovered from Cave IV at Qumran. These texts are in substantial agreement with the Greek recension that has served as the basis for the present translation.

The divisions of the Book of Tobit are:
  I: Tobit's Ordeals (1, 3—3, 6)
 II: Sarah's Plight (3, 7–17)
III: Tobiah's Journey and Marriage to Sarah
     (4, 1—9, 6)
 IV: Tobiah's Return; Cure of Tobit's Blindness
     (10, 1—11, 18)
  V: Raphael Reveals His Identity (12, 1–22)
 VI: Tobit's Song of Praise (13, 1–18)
VII: Epilogue (14, 1–15)

THE BOOK OF JUDITH

THE BOOK OF JUDITH is a vivid story relating how, in a grave crisis, God delivered the Jewish people through the instrumentality of a woman. The unknown author composed this edifying narrative of divine providence at the end of the second or the beginning of the first century B.C. The original was almost certainly written in Hebrew, but the Greek text shows so much freedom in adapting from the Septuagint the language of older biblical books that it must be regarded as having a literary character of its own. It is this Greek form of the book, accepted as canonical by the Catholic Church, which is translated here. St. Jerome, who prepared (with some reluctance) a Latin text of Judith, based his work on a secondary Aramaic text available to him in Palestine, combined with an older Latin rendering from the Greek. The long hymn of chapter 16 he took in its entirety from that earlier Latin text.

Since it is no longer possible to determine with any precision the underlying events which may have given rise to this narrative, it is enough to note that the author sought to strengthen the faith of his people in God's abiding presence among them. The Book of Judith is a tract for difficult times; the reader, it was hoped, would take to heart the lesson that God was still the Master of history, who could save Israel from her enemies. Note the parallel with the time of the Exodus: as God had delivered his people by the hand of Moses, so he could deliver them by the hand of the pious widow Judith (see note on 2, 12).

The story can be divided into two parts. In the first (cc 1—7), Holofernes, commander-in-chief of the armies of Nebuchadnezzar, leads an overwhelming Assyrian force in a punitive campaign against the vassals who refused to help in the Assyrian war against the Medes. The Jewish people stubbornly resist the enemy at Bethulia, guarding the route of access to Jerusalem. Despite the warning of Achior that the Jews cannot be conquered unless they sin against God, the proud general lays siege to the town and cuts off its water supply. After a siege of thirty-four days, the exhausted defenders are desperate and ready to surrender.

At this point, the climax of the story, Judith (the name means "Jewess") appears and promises to defeat the Assyrians. The rest of the story is too well known to repeat in detail. Having fasted and prayed, Judith dresses in her finest garments and proceeds to the Assyrian camp, where she succeeds in killing Holofernes while he lies in a drunken stupor. The Assyrians panic when they discover this, and the Jews are able to rout and slaughter them. The beautiful hymn of the people honoring Judith (15, 9–10) is often applied to Mary in the liturgy.

Any attempt to read the book directly against the backdrop of Jewish history in relation to the empires of the ancient world is bound to fail. The story was written as a pious reflection on the meaning of the yearly Passover observance. It draws its inspiration from the Exodus narrative (especially Ex 14, 31) and from the texts of Isaiah and the Psalms portraying the special intervention of God for the preservation of Jerusalem. The theme of God's hand as the agent of this providential activity, reflected of old in the hand of Moses and now in the hand of Judith, is again exemplified at a later time in Jewish synagogue art. God's hand reaching down from heaven appears as part of the scene at Dura-Europos (before A.D. 256) in paintings of the Exodus, of the sacrifice of Isaac (Gn 22), and of Ezekiel's valley of dry bones (Ez 37).

The Book of Judith is divided as follows:
I: Peril of the Jews (1, 1—7, 32)
II: Deliverance of the Jews (8, 1—14, 10)
III: Victory (14, 11—16, 25)

THE BOOK OF ESTHER

THE BOOK OF ESTHER is named after its Jewish heroine. It tells the story of the plot of Haman the Agagite, jealous and powerful vizier of King Xerxes (Ahasuerus) of Persia (485–464 B.C.), to destroy in a single day all the Jews living in the Persian Empire. He is moved to this out of hatred for the Jewish servant Mordecai, who for religious motives refuses to render him homage. The day of the proposed massacre is determined by lot. Meanwhile Esther, niece and adopted daughter of Mordecai, is chosen queen by King Xerxes in place of Vashti. She averts the pogrom planned against her people and has the royal decree of extermination reversed against Haman and the enemies of the Jews. Mordecai replaces Haman, and together with Esther, works for the welfare of their people. The event is celebrated with feasting and great joy, and the memory of it is to be perpetuated by the annual observance of the feast of Purim (lots), when the lot of destruction for the Jews was reversed for one of deliverance and triumph by Queen Esther and her uncle Mordecai.

The purpose of the book is didactic: the glorification of the Jewish people and the explanation of the origin, significance and date of the feast of Purim on the fourteenth and fifteenth of Adar (February–March). The book was intended as a consolation for Israel, a reminder that God's providence continually watches over them, never abandoning them when they serve him faithfully or turn to him in sincere repentance. There is no justification for interpreting the story in mythological or cultic terms, as though Mordecai and Esther represented

Marduk and Ishtar in their mythological triumph over two Elamite deities.

The Hebrew text of Esther is found in the Hebrew Bible, where it is the last of the five *megilloth* (scrolls) read on special feasts of the Jewish liturgical year.

The book is a free composition—not a historical document, despite the Achaemenian coloring of the narrative. Its time of composition may well have been at the end of the Persian Empire, toward the close of the fourth century B.C. The author shows skill in developing his story and in using the art of contrast for instruction and edification. The solution to the difficulties of the book is to be found in its literary presentation rather than in a forced attempt to square detailed data of the narrative with facts. The evident literary motif of the reversal of fortune of the prosperous wicked and the oppressed virtuous through eventual punishment of the former and triumph of the latter, finds parallels in the story of Joseph (Gn 37; 39—45) and of Judith (8—16). The book is vindictive, but it should be remembered that the precept of love of enemies had not yet been taught by the word and example of Christ.

The text of Esther, written originally in Hebrew, was transmitted in two forms: a short Hebrew form and a longer Greek version. The latter contains 107 additional verses, inserted at appropriate places within the Hebrew form of the text. A few of these seem to have a Hebrew origin while the rest are Greek in original composition. It is possible that the Hebrew form of the text is original throughout. If it systematically omits reference to God and his Providence over Israel, this is perhaps due to fear of irreverent response (see note on 4, 14). The Greek text with the above-mentioned additions is probably a later literary paraphrase in which the author seeks to have the reader share his sentiments. This standard Greek text is pre-Christian in origin. The Church has accepted the additions as equally inspired with the rest of the book.

In the present translation, the portions preceded by the letters A through F indicate the underlying Greek additions referred to above. The regular chapter numbers apply to the Hebrew text.

The book may be divided as follows:
I: Prologue (A, 1–17)
II: Elevation of Esther (1, 1—2, 23)
III: Haman's Plot against the Jews (3, 1–13; B, 1–7; 3, 14–48; B, 8; 4, 9–17; C, 1—D, 16; 5, 1–14)
IV: Vindication of the Jews (6, 1—8, 12; E, 1, 24; 8, 13—10, 3)
V: Epilogue (F, 1–11)

The order of the Vulgate text in relation to the order of the Greek text is as follows:
Vulg. 11, 2—12, 6 = A, 1—17 at the beginning of the book.
    13, 1–7 = B, 1—7 after 3, 13.
    13, 8—15, 3–19 = C, 1—D, 16 after 4, 16.
    15, 1–2 = B, 8.9 after 4, 8.
    16, 1–24 = E, 1–24 after 8, 12.
    10, 4—10, 13 = F, 1–10 after 10, 3.

THE FIRST BOOK OF MACCABEES

THE NAME Maccabee, probably meaning "hammer," is actually applied in the Books of Maccabees to only one man, Judas, third son of the priest Mattathias and first leader of the revolt against the Seleucid kings who persecuted the Jews (1 Mc 2, 4.66; 2 Mc 8, 5.16; 10, 1.16). Traditionally the name has come to be applied to the brothers of Judas, his supporters, and even to other Jewish heroes of the period, such as the seven brothers (2 Mc 7).

The Two Books of Maccabees, placed last in the Douai version of the Old Testament, contain independent accounts of events in part identical which accompanied the attempted suppression of Judaism in Palestine in the second century B.C. The vigorous reaction to this attempt established for a time the religious and political independence of the Jews.

1 Maccabees was written about 100 B.C., in Hebrew, but the original has not come down to us. Instead, we have an early, pre-Christian, Greek translation full of Hebrew idioms. The author, probably a Palestinian Jew, is unknown. He was familiar with the traditions and sacred books of his people and had access to much reliable information on their recent history (from 175 to 134 B.C.). He may well have played some part in it himself in his youth. His purpose in writing is to record the salvation of Israel which God worked through the family of Mattathias (5, 62)—especially through his three sons, Judas, Jonathan, and Simon, and his grandson, John Hyrcanus. Implicitly the writer compares their virtues and their exploits with those of the ancient heroes, the Judges, Samuel, and David.

There are seven poetic sections in the book which imitate the style of classical Hebrew poetry: four laments (1, 25–28.36–40; 2, 8–13; 3, 45), and three hymns of praise of "our fathers" (2, 51–64), of Juda (3, 3–9), and of Simon (14, 4–15).

The doctrine expressed in the book is the customary belief of Israel, without the new developments which appear in 2 Maccabees and Daniel. The people of Israel have been specially chosen by the one true God as his covenant-partner, and they alone are privileged to know him and worship him. He is their eternal benefactor and their unfailing source of help. The people, in turn, must be loyal to his exclusive worship and must observe exactly the precepts of the law he has given them.

There is no doctrine of individual immortality except in the survival of one's name and fame, nor does the book express any messianic expectation, though messianic images are applied historically to "the days of Simon" (14, 4–17). In true deuteronomic tradition, the author insists on fidelity to the law as the expression of Israel's love for God. The contest which he describes is a struggle, not simply between Jew and Gentile, but between those who would uphold the law and those, Jews or Gentiles, who would destroy it. His severest condemnation goes,

not to the Seleucid politicians, but to the lawless apostates among his own people, adversaries of Judas and his brothers, who are models of faith and loyalty.

1 Maccabees has importance also for the New Testament. Salvation is paralleled with Jewish national aspirations (1 Mc 4, 46—14, 41), in contrast to the universal reign of God taught by Christ in the Gospel (Mt 13, 47–50; 22, 1–14). Also, destruction of the wall of the temple separating Jew from Gentile is an act of desecration in 1 Mc 9, 54, but in Eph 2, 14, an act of redemption and unification of both through Christ. On the other hand, association, in 1 Mc 2, 52, of Abraham's offering up of Isaac (Gn 22) with his justification by God (Gn 15, 6) is reflected in Jn 2, 21f, just as the Scriptures are regarded as a source of consolation in 1 Mc 12, 9 and in Rom 15, 4.

The Books of Maccabees, though regarded by Jews and Protestants as apocryphal, i.e., not inspired, Scripture, because not contained in the Palestinian Canon or list of books drawn up at the end of the first century A.D., have nevertheless always been accepted by the Catholic Church as inspired, on the basis of apostolic tradition.

1 Maccabees is divided as follows:
  I: Introduction: Hellenism in Asia Minor (1, 1–9)
  II: The Maccabean Revolt (1, 10—2, 70)
  III: Leadership of Judas Maccabeus (3, 1—9, 22)
  IV: Leadership of Jonathan (9, 23—12, 54)
  V: Simon, High Priest and Ethnarch (13, 1—16, 24)

THE SECOND BOOK OF MACCABEES

ALTHOUGH this book, like the preceding one, receives its title from its protagonist, Judas Maccabee (or Maccabeus), it is not a sequel to 1 Maccabees. The two differ in many respects. Whereas the first covers the period from the beginning of the reign of Antiochus IV (175 B.C.) to the accession of John Hyrcanus I (134 B.C.), this present book treats of the events in Jewish history from the time of the high priest Onias III and King Seleucus IV (c. 180 B.C.) to the defeat of Nicanor's army (161 B.C.).

The author of 2 Maccabees states (2, 23) that his one-volume work is an abridgment of a certain five-volume work by Jason of Cyrene; but since this latter has not survived, it is difficult to determine its relationship to the present epitome. One does not know how freely the anonymous epitomizer may have rewritten his shorter composition, or how closely he may have followed the wording of the original in the excerpts he made. Some parts of the text here, clearly not derived from Jason's work, are the Preface (2, 19–32), the Epilogue (15, 37–39), and probably also certain moralizing reflections (e.g., 5, 17–20; 6, 12–17). It is certain, however, that both works were written in Greek, which explains why the Second Book of Maccabees was not included in the canon of the Hebrew Bible.

The book is not without genuine historical value in supplementing 1 Maccabees, and it contains some apparently authentic documents (11, 16–38). Its purpose, whether intended by Jason himself or read into it by the compiler, is to give a theological interpretation to the history of the period. There is less interest, therefore, in the actual exploits of Judas Maccabeus than in God's marvelous interventions. These direct the course of events, both to punish the sacrilegious and blasphemous pagans, and to purify God's holy temple and restore it to his faithful people. The author sometimes effects his purpose by transferring events from their proper chronological order, and giving exaggerated figures for the size of armies and the numbers killed in battle; he also places long, edifying discourses and prayers in the mouths of his heroes, and inclines to elaborate descriptions of celestial apparitions (3, 24–34; 5, 2ff; 10, 29f; 15, 11–16). He is the earliest known composer of stories that glorify God's holy martyrs (6, 18—7, 42; 14, 37–46).

Of theological importance are the author's teachings on the resurrection of the just on the last day (7, 9.11.14.23; 14, 46), the intercession of the saints in heaven for people living on earth (15, 11–16), and the power of the living to offer prayers and sacrifices for the dead (12, 39–46).

The beginning of 2 Maccabees consists of two letters sent by the Jews of Jerusalem to their coreligionists in Egypt. They deal with the observance of the feast commemorating the central event of the book, the purification of the temple. It is uncertain whether the author or a later scribe prefixed these letters to the narrative proper. If the author is responsible for their insertion, he must have written his book some time after 124 B.C., the date of the more recent of the two letters. In any case, Jason's five-volume work very likely continued the history of the Jews well into the Hasmonean period, so that 2 Maccabees would probably not have been produced much before the end of the second century B.C.

The main divisions of 2 Maccabees are:
  I: Letters to the Jews in Egypt (1, 1—2, 18)
  II: Author's Preface (2, 19–32)
  III: Heliodorus' Attempt To Profane the Temple (3, 1–40)
  IV: Profanation and Persecution (4, 1—7, 42)
  V: Victories of Judas and Purification of the Temple (8, 1—10, 8)
  VI: Renewed Persecution (10, 9—15, 36)
  VII: Epilogue (15, 37–39)

THE WISDOM BOOKS

THE BOOKS of Job, Psalms, Proverbs, Ecclesiastes, the song of Songs, Wisdom, and Sirach. All of these books are all versified by the skillful use of parallelism, that is, of the balanced and symmetrical phrases peculiar to Hebrew poetry. With the exception of the Psalms, the majority of which are devotional lyrics, and the Song of Songs, a nuptial hymn, these books belong to the general class of wisdom or didactic literature, strictly so called because their chief purpose is instruction.

The wisdom literature of the Bible is the fruit of a movement among ancient oriental people to gather, preserve and express, usually in aphoristic style, the results of human experience as an aid toward understanding and solving the problems of life. In Israel especially, the movement concerned itself with such basic and vital problems as man's origin and destiny, his quest for happiness, the problem of suffering, of good and evil in human conduct, of death, and the state beyond the grave. Originating with oral tradition, these formulations found their way into the historical books of the Old Testament in the shape of proverbs, odes, chants, epigrams, and also into those psalms intended for instruction.

The developed compositions of this literature form the sapiential books. The Book of Proverbs is a collection of sentences or practical norms for moral conduct. The Book of Job is an artistic dialogue skillfully handling the problem of suffering though only from the standpoint of temporal life. Ecclesiastes examines a wide range of human experience only to conclude that all things are vanity except the fear of the Lord and observance of his commandments, and that God requites man in his own good time. Sirach gathers and presents the fruits of past experience, thus preparing for the Book of Wisdom, which sees for the just man seeking happiness the full hope of immortality (Wis 3, 4).

Those who cultivated wisdom were called sages. Men of letters, scribes, skilled in the affairs of government, and counselors to rulers, they were instructors of the people, especially of youth (Sir 51, 13–30). In times of crisis they guided the people by revaluating tradition, thus helping to preserve unity, peace and good will. The most illustrious of the sages, and the originator of wisdom literature in Israel, was Solomon. Because of his fame, some of the wisdom books of which he was not the author bear his name.

Despite numerous resemblances, sometimes exaggerated, between the sapiential literature of pagan nations and the wisdom books of the Bible, the former are often replete with vagaries and abound in polytheistic conceptions; the latter remained profoundly human, universal, fundamentally moral, and essentially religious and monotheistic. Under the influence of the law and the prophets, wisdom became piety and virtue; impiety and vice were folly. The teachers of wisdom were regarded as men of God, and their books were placed beside the law and the prophets. The highest wisdom became identified with the spirit of God through which the world was created and preserved (Prv 8, 22–31), and mankind was enlightened.

The limitations of Old Testament wisdom served to crystallize the problems of human life and destiny, thus preparing for their solution through New Testament revelation. Ecclesiastes' vain search for success and happiness on earth ends when the Savior assures these things to his followers, not in this world but in the bliss of heaven. The anxiety in the Book of Job over reconciling God's justice and wisdom with the suffering of the innocent is relieved by the account of the crucified and risen Redeemer in the gospel. By fulfilling all that the Psalms foretold concerning him, Jesus makes the Psalter his prayer book and that of the Church for all time. The love of God for the chosen people which underlies the Song of Songs is perfected in the union of Christ with his church. The personification of the wisdom of Proverbs, Wisdom and Sirach shines forth in resplendent reality in the Word who was with God, and who was God, and who became incarnate to dwell among us; cf Jn 1, 2.14.

THE BOOK OF JOB

Tʜᴇ ʙᴏᴏᴋ ᴏꜰ ᴊᴏʙ, named after its protagonist, is an exquisite dramatic poem which treats of the problem of the suffering of the innocent, and of retribution. The contents of the book, together with its artistic structure and elegant style, place it among the literary masterpieces of all time.

Job, an oriental chieftain, pious and upright, richly endowed in his own person and in domestic prosperity, suffers a sudden and complete reversal of fortune. He loses his property and his children; a loathsome disease afflicts his body; and sorrow oppresses his soul. Nevertheless, Job does not complain against God. When some friends visit him to condole with him, Job protests his innocence and does not understand why he is afflicted. He curses the day of his birth and longs for death to bring an end to his sufferings. The debate which ensues consists of three cycles of speeches. Job's friends insist that his plight can only be a punishment for personal wrongdoing and an invitation from God to repentance. Job rejects their inadequate explanation and calls for a response from God himself. At this point, the speeches of a youth named Elihu (chs 32—37) interrupt the development.

In response to Job's plea that he be allowed to see God and hear from him the cause of his suffering, God answers, not by justifying his action before men, but by referring to his own omniscience and almighty power. Job is content with this. He recovers his attitude of humility and trust in God, which is deepened now and strengthened by his experience of suffering.

The author of the book is not known; it was composed some time between the seventh and fifth centuries ʙ.ᴄ. Its literary form, with speeches, prologue and epilogue disposed according to a studied plan, indicates that the purpose of the writing is didactic. The lesson is that even the just may suffer here, and their sufferings are a test of their fidelity. They shall be rewarded in the end. Man's finite mind cannot probe the depths of the divine om-niscience that governs the world. The problems we encounter can be solved by a broader and deeper awareness of God's power, presence (42, 5) and wisdom.

The divisions of the Book of Job are as follows:
    I: Prologue (1, 1—2, 13)
  II: First Cycle of Speeches (3, 1—14, 22)
 III: Second Cycle of Speeches (15, 1—21, 34)
 IV: Third Cycle of Speeches (22, 1—28, 28)
  V: Job's Final Summary of His Cause (29, 1—31, 37)
 VI: Elihu's Speeches (32, 1—37, 24)
VII: The Lord's Speeches (38, 1—42, 6)
VIII: Epilogue (42, 7—17)

THE BOOK OF PSALMS

Tʜᴇ ʙᴏᴏᴋ ᴏꜰ ᴘsᴀʟᴍs, or Psalter, is a collection of religious songs, traditionally listed as 150. This number, however, is only approximately correct, for several psalms contain two or more originally independent songs, while others, which were originally a single unit, have been broken up into two or more psalms. Moreover, certain psalms and parts of psalms occur more than once in this collection.

The present collection is divided into five "books," perhaps in imitation of the five Books of the Pentateuch. But internal evidence shows that there existed at an earlier period more numerous, smaller collections which were gradually gathered together to form the present Psalter.

In form and subject matter the psalms are most varied. Some were composed for liturgical use in the temple, others, for recitation elsewhere. In some psalms the singer is an individual; in others, the community. One of the most common types is that of supplication to God for his help in various spiritual and temporal needs. But hymns of thanksgiving and of praise are also numerous. Less frequent are poems written primarily to discuss some problem or to teach some lesson.

Prefixed to most of the psalms are certain words and phrases which offer traditional information about the psalm, such as the tone in which it is to be sung, the musical instruments which are to accompany its singing, the historical circumstances connected in some way with its composition, the name of its author, and so forth. These "titles," as they are called, were added, at least in most cases, by later writers. It cannot be proved that they were divinely inspired. They have some value, however, as representing ancient tradition. They are printed here in smaller type.

About half of the psalms are attributed in these "titles" to David. The Davidic authorship of some of these is taken for granted in the New Testament. Some other psalms are attributed to certain groups of temple singers known as "the sons of Korah" and "the sons of Asaph." One psalm each is ascribed to Moses, Solomon, Heman and Ethan. About a third of the psalms have no author's name prefixed to them. Although some of the psalms appear to have been composed during the early postexilic period (the fifth and fourth centuries B.C.), it cannot be demonstrated that any psalms are as late as the Maccabean age.

THE BOOK OF PROVERBS

THE FIRST word of this book, *Mishle*, has provided the title by which it is generally designated in Jewish and Christian circles. The name "Proverbs," while not an exact equivalent of *Mishle*, describes the main contents satisfactorily, even though it is hardly an adequate designation for such parts as 1, 1—9, 18 or 31, 10–31. Among some early Christian writers the book was also known by the name of "Wisdom," and in the Roman Missal it is referred to as a "Book of Wisdom."

The Book of Proverbs is an anthology of didactic poetry forming part of the sapiential literature of the Old Testament. Its primary purpose, indicated in the first sentence (1, 2f), is to teach wisdom. It is thus directed particularly to the young and inexperienced (1, 4); but also to those who desire advanced training in wisdom (1, 5f). The wisdom which the book teaches, covers a wide field of human and divine activity, ranging from matters purely secular to most lofty moral and religious truths, such as God's omniscience (5, 21; 15, 3–11), power (19, 21; 21, 30), providence (20, 1–24), goodness (15, 29), and the joy and strength resulting from abandonment to him (3, 5; 16, 20; 18, 10). The teaching of the entire book is placed on a firm religious foundation by the principle that "the fear of the LORD is the beginning of knowledge" (1, 7; cf 9, 10).

To Solomon are explicitly ascribed parts II and V of the book; he is the patron of Hebrew wisdom. Of Agur (part VI) and Lemuel (part VIII), nothing further is known. Parts III and IV are attributed to "the wise." The remaining parts are anonymous.

The manner of compilation is conjectural. Parts II and V may have circulated first as independent collections, compiled before the fall of Jerusalem, as the references to Solomon (10, 1) and Hezekiah (25, 1) suggest. Parts III, IV and VII would seem to belong together as a third collection of a similar kind.

The author of the first nine chapters, a religious sage familiar with the earlier books, was the editor of the whole as we have it, probably in the early part of the fifth century B.C.

Christ and the Apostles often expressly quoted the Proverbs (Jn 7, 38; Rom 12, 20; Jas 4, 6) or repeated their teaching; compare Lk 10, 14, and Prv 25, 7; 1 Pt 4, 8; Jas 5, 20 and Prv 10, 12. The book has an important place in the Latin and Greek liturgies.

On the basis of titles, subject matter, and poetic structure the Book of Proverbs may be divided as follows:

- I: Introduction: The Value of Wisdom (1, 1—9, 18)
- II: First Collection of the Proverbs of Solomon (10, 1—22, 16)
- III: Sayings of the Wise (22, 17—24, 22)
- IV: Other Sayings of the Wise (24, 23–34)
- V: Second Collection of the Proverbs of Solomon (25, 1—29, 27)
- VI: The Words of Abur (30, 1–6)
- VII: Numerical Proverbs (30, 7–33)
- VIII: The Words of Lemuel (31, 1–9)
- IX: The Ideal Wife (31, 10–31)

THE BOOK OF ECCLESIASTES

THE TITLE *Ecclesiastes* given to this book is the Greek translation of the Hebrew name Qoheleth meaning, perhaps, "one who convokes an assembly." The book, however, does not consist of public addresses, but is a treatise, more or less logically developed, on the vanity of all things. Reflections in prose and aphorisms in verse are intermingled in Ecclesiastes, which contains, besides, an introduction and an epilogue.

The book is concerned with the purpose and value of human life. While admitting the existence of a divine plan, it considers such a plan to be hidden from man, who seeks happiness without ever finding it here below (3, 11; 8, 7.17). Ecclesiastes applies his "Vanity of vanities" to everything "under the sun," even to that wisdom which seeks to find at least a semblance of good in the things of the world. Merit does not yield happiness for it is often tried by suffering. Riches and pleasures do not avail. Existence is monotonous, enjoyment fleeting and vain; darkness quickly follows. Life, then, is an enigma beyond human ability to solve.

While Ecclesiastes concedes that there is an advantage for man in the enjoyment of certain legitimate pleasures lest he lapse into pessimism and despair, he nevertheless considers this indulgence also vanity unless man returns due thanks to the Creator who has given him all. Under this aspect, earthly wisdom would rise to the higher level of true spiritual wisdom. This true wisdom is not found "under the sun" but is perceived only by the light of faith, inasmuch as it rests with God, who is the final Judge of the good and the bad, and whose reign endures forever. The Epilogue gives the clue to this thought (12, 13f).

The moral teaching of the book is imperfect, like the Old Testament itself (Heb 7, 19), yet it marks an advance in the development of the doctrine of divine retribution. While rejecting the older solution of earthly rewards and punishments, Ecclesiastes looks forward to a more lasting one. The clear answer to the problem was to come with the light of Christ's teaching concerning future life.

The author of the book was a teacher of popular wisdom (12, 9). Qoheleth was obviously only his literary name. Because he is called "David's son, king of Jerusalem," it was commonly thought that he was King Solomon. Such personation, however, was but a literary device to lend greater dignity and authority to the book—a circumstance which does not in any way impugn its inspired character. The Epilogue seems to have been written by an editor, probably a disciple of Qoheleth. The entire work differs considerably in language and style from earlier books of the Old Testament. It reflects a late period of Hebrew, and was probably written about three centuries before Christ.

THE SONG OF SONGS

THE SONG OF SONGS, meaning the greatest of songs (1, 1), contains in exquisite poetic form the sublime portrayal and praise of the mutual love of the Lord and his people. The Lord is the Lover and his people are the beloved. Describing this relationship in terms of human love, the author simply follows Israel's tradition. Isaiah (5, 1–7; 54, 4–8), Jeremiah (2, 2f.32), and Ezekiel (16, 23) all characterize the covenant between the Lord and Israel as a marriage. Hosea the prophet sees the idolatry of Israel in the adultery of Gomer (1–3). He also represents the Lord speaking to Israel's heart (2, 16) and changing her into a new spiritual people, purified by the Babylonian captivity and betrothed anew to her divine Lover "in justice and uprightness, in love and mercy" (2, 21).

The author of the Song, using the same literary figure, paints a beautiful picture of the ideal Israel, the chosen people of the Old and New Testaments, whom the Lord led by degrees to an exalted spiritual union with himself in the bond of perfect love. When the Song is thus interpreted there is no reason for surprise at the tone of the poem, which employs in its descriptions the courtship and marriage customs of the author's time. Moreover, the poem is not an allegory in which each remark, e.g., in the dialogue of the lovers, has a higher meaning. It is a parable in which the true meaning of mutual love comes from the poem as a whole.

While the Song is thus commonly understood by most Catholic scholars, it is also possible to see in it an inspired portrayal of ideal human love. Here we would have from God a description of the sacredness and the depth of married union.

Although the poem is attributed to Solomon in the traditional title (1, 1), the language and style of the work, among other considerations, point to a time after the end of the Babylonian Exile (538 B.C.) as that in which an unknown poet composed this masterpiece. The structure of the Song is difficult to analyze; here it is regarded as a lyric dialogue, with dramatic movement and interest.

The use of marriage as a symbol, characteristic of the Song, is found extensively also in the New Testament (Mt 9, 15; 25, 1–13; Jn 3, 29; 2 Cor 11, 2; Eph 5, 23–32; Rv 19, 7ff; 21, 9ff). In Christian tradition, the Song has been interpreted in terms of the union between Christ and the Church and, particularly by St. Bernard, of the union between Christ and the individual soul. Throughout the liturgy, especially in the Little Office, there is a consistent application of the Song of Songs to the Blessed Virgin Mary.

THE BOOK OF WISDOM

THE BOOK OF WISDOM was written about a hundred years before the coming of Christ. Its author, whose name is not known to us, was a member of the Jewish community at Alexandria, in Egypt. He wrote in Greek, in a style patterned on that of Hebrew verse. At times he speaks in the person of Solomon, placing his teachings on the lips of the wise king of Hebrew tradition in order to emphasize their value. His profound knowledge of the earlier Old Testament writings is reflected in almost every line of the book, and marks him, like Ben Sira, as an outstanding representative of religious devotion and learning among the sages of post-exilic Judaism.

The primary purpose of the sacred author was the edification of his co-religionists in a time when they had experienced suffering and oppression, in part at least at the hands of apostate fellow Jews. To convey his message he made use of the most popular religious themes of his time, namely the splendor and worth of divine wisdom (6, 22—11, 1), the glorious events of the Exodus (11, 2—16; 12, 23—27; 15, 18—19, 22), God's mercy (11, 17—12, 22), the folly of idolatry (13, 1—15, 17), and the manner in which God's justice is vindicated in rewarding or punishing the individual soul (1, 1—6, 21). The first ten chapters especially form a preparation for the fuller teachings of Christ and his Church. Many passages from this section of the book, notably 3, 1–8, are used by the Church in her liturgy.

The principal divisions of the Book of Wisdom are:
  I: Reward of Justice (1, 1—6, 21)
 II: Praise of Wisdom by Solomon (6, 22—11, 1)
III: Special Providence of God during the Exodus
     (11, 2—16; 12, 23—27; 15, 18—19, 22) with
     digressions on God's mercy (11, 17—12, 22)
     and on the folly and shame of idolatry (13, 1—
     15, 17)

THE BOOK OF SIRACH
(Ecclesiasticus)

THE BOOK OF SIRACH derives its name from the author, *Jesus, son of Eleazar, son of Sirach* (50, 27). Its earliest title seems to have been "Wisdom of the Son of Sirach." The designation "Liber Ecclesiasticus," meaning "Church

Book," appended to some Greek and Latin manuscripts was due to the extensive use which the Church made of this book in presenting moral teaching to catechumens and to the faithful.

The author, a sage who lived in Jerusalem, was thoroughly imbued with love for the law, the priesthood, the temple, and divine worship. As a wise and experienced observer of life he addressed himself to his contemporaries with the motive of helping them to maintain religious faith and integrity through study of the holy books, and through tradition.

The book contains numerous maxims formulated with care, grouped by affinity, and dealing with a variety of subjects such as the individual, the family, and the community in their relations with one another and with God. It treats of friendship, education, poverty and wealth, the law, religious worship, and many other matters which reflect the religious and social customs of the time.

Written in Hebrew between 200 and 175 B.C., the text was translated into Greek sometime after 132 B.C. by the author's grandson, who also wrote a Foreword which contains information about the book, the author, and the translator himself. Until the close of the nineteenth century Sirach was known only in translations, of which this Greek rendering was the most important. From it the Latin version was made. Between 1896 and 1900, again in 1931, and several times since 1956, manuscripts were discovered containing in all about two thirds of the Hebrew text, which agrees substantially with the Greek. One such text, from Masada, is pre-Christian in date.

Though not included in the Hebrew Bible after the first century A.D., nor accepted by Protestants, the Book of Sirach has always been recognized by the Catholic Church as divinely inspired and canonical. The Foreword, though not inspired, is placed in the Bible because of its antiquity and importance.

The contents of Sirach are of a discursive nature, not easily divided into separate parts. Chapters 1—43 deal largely with moral instruction; chapters 44, 1—50, 24 contain a eulogy of the heroes of Israel and some of the patriarchs There are two appendices in which the author expresses his gratitude to God, and appeals to the unlearned to acquire true wisdom.

The Church uses the Book of Sirach extensively in her liturgy.

THE PROPHETIC BOOKS

THE PROPHETIC books bear the names of the four major and twelve minor prophets, besides Lamentations and Baruch. The terms "major" and "minor" refer merely to the length of the respective compositions and not to any distinction in the prophetic office. Jonah is a story of the mission of the prophet rather than a collection of prophecies. Lamentations and Daniel are listed among the hagiographia in the Hebrew Bible, not among the prophetic books. The former contains a series of elegies on the fate of Jerusalem; the latter is apocalyptic in character. Daniel, who lived far removed from Palestine, was not called by God to preach; yet the book is counted as prophecy. Baruch, though excluded from the Hebrew canon, is found in the Septuagint version, and the Church has always acknowledged it to be sacred and inspired.

The prophetic books, together with the oral preaching of the prophets, were the result of the institution of prophetism, in which a succession of Israelites chosen by God and appointed by him to be prophets received communications from him and transmitted them to the people in his name (Dt 18, 15–20). The prophets were spokesmen of God, intermediaries between him and his people. The communications they received from God came through visions, dreams, and ecstasies and were transmitted to the people through sermons, writings, and symbolic actions.

The office of prophet was due to a direct call from God. It was not the result of heredity, just as it was not a permanent gift but a transient one, subject entirely to the divine will. The prophets preserved and developed revealed religion (1 Sm 12, 6–25), denounced idolatry (1 Kgs 14, 1–13), defended the moral law (2 Sm 12, 1–15), gave counsel in political matters (Is 31, 1ff), and often also in matters of private life (1 Sm 9, 6–9). At times miracles confirmed their preaching, and their predictions of the future intensified the expectation of the Messiah and of his kingdom.

The prophetic literature in this volume contains the substance of the prophets' authentic preaching, résumés, and genuine samples of such preaching. Some parts were recorded by the prophets themselves, some by persons other than the prophets who uttered them.

The prophecies express judgments of the people's moral conduct, on the basis of the Mosaic alliance between God and Israel. They teach sublime truths and lofty morals. They contain exhortations, threats, announcements of punishment, promises of deliverance, made with solemn authority and in highly imaginative language. In the affairs of men, their prime concern is the interests of God, especially in what pertains to the chosen people through whom the Messiah is to come; hence their denunciations of idolatry and of that externalism in worship which excludes the interior spirit of religion. They are concerned also with the universal nature of the moral law, with personal responsibility, with the person and office of the Messiah, and with the conduct of foreign nations.

In content, the literary genre of prophecy uses warning and threat besides exhortation and promise to declare in God's name events of the near and distant future (Is 8—9). In form, the divine source of prophetic declaration appears in: "The word (or oracle) of the Lord," or "Thus says the Lord," followed by the announcement of a coming event and its moral cause (Hos 4, 7–10). Divine exhortation and promise are introduced by such forms as: "Hear this word, O men of Israel, that the Lord pronounces over you" (Am 3, 1). Kindly and persuasive tones pervade the promises of reward and even the threats of punishment (Am 5, 14–15).

Disregard for exact chronological perspective in the prophecies is an additional characteristic. Predictions of the immediate and distant future are often interrelated, not on the basis of years separating the events but on the analogy of the pattern joining present with very distant, though similar, conditions and circumstances. This is prophetic compenetration, idealization in which persons and things of the more immediate present, in the prophet's day, fade into a wider and more perfect order of persons and things of the future; the former are figures and types of the latter. Thus, some details of what the Psalmist said of the kingdom of David and Solomon (Ps 72) went beyond what was fulfilled in these men, as St. Thomas points out, and found their realization only in the kingdom of Christ. St. Jerome before him, and still earlier the apostles themselves—Peter (Acts 2, 14–36) and Paul (Gal 4, 21–31)—taught us that through anticipation in types we discover in Sacred Scripture the truth of things to come.

Thus the universal blessing for mankind, often promised by God through the mouths of his prophets in figures and types, was in time to become personalized and to confer its full benefit on us through the Word made flesh, who became for us the New Covenant through his life, death, and resurrection, as the prophets had foretold.

THE BOOK OF ISAIAH

THE GREATEST of the prophets appeared at a critical moment of Israel's history. The second half of the eighth century B.C. witnessed the collapse of the northern kingdom under the hammer-like blows of Assyria (722), while Jerusalem itself saw the army of Sennacherib drawn up before its walls (701). In the year that Uzziah, king of Judah, died (742), Isaiah received his call to the prophetic office in the Temple of Jerusalem. Close attention should be given to chapter 6, where this divine summons to be the ambassador of the Most High is circumstantially described.

The vision of the Lord enthroned in glory stamps an indelible character on Isaiah's ministry and provides the key to the understanding of his message. The majesty, holiness and glory of the Lord took possession of his spirit and, conversely, he gained a new awareness of human pettiness and sinfulness. The enormous abyss between God's sovereign holiness and man's sin overwhelmed the prophet. Only the purifying coal of the seraphim could cleanse his lips and prepare him for acceptance of the call: "Here I am, send me!"

The ministry of Isaiah may be divided into three periods, covering the reigns of Jotham (742–735), Ahaz (735–715), and Hezekiah (715–687). To the first period belong, for the most part, the early oracles (1—5) which exposed the moral breakdown of Judah and its capital, Jerusalem. With the accession of Ahaz, the prohet became adviser to the king, whose throne was threatened by the Syro-Ephraimite coalition. Rejecting the plea of Isaiah for faith and courage, the weak Ahaz turned to Assyria for help. From this period came the majority of Messianic oracles found in the section of Immanuel prophecies (6—12).

Hezekiah succeeded his father and undertook a religious reform which Isaiah undoubtedly supported. But the old intrigues began again, and the king was soon won over to the pro-Egyptian party. Isaiah denounced this "covenant with death" and again summoned Judah to faith in Yahweh as her only hope. But it was too late; the revolt had already begun. Assyria acted quickly and her army, after ravaging Judah, laid siege to Jerusalem (701). "I shut up Hezekiah like a bird in his cage," boasts the famous inscription of Sennacherib. But Yahweh delivered the city, as Isaiah had promised: God is the Lord of history, and Assyria but an instrument in his hands.

Little is known about the last days of this great religious leader, whose oracles, of singular poetic beauty and power, constantly reminded his wayward people of their destiny and the fidelity of Yahweh to his promises.

The complete Book of Isaiah is an anthology of poems composed chiefly by the great prophet, but also by disciples, some of whom came many years after Isaiah. In 1—39 most of the oracles come from Isaiah and faithfully reflect the situation in eighth-century Judah. To disciples deeply influenced by the prophet belong sections such as the Apocalypse of Isaiah (24—27), the oracles against Babylon (13—14), and probably the poems of 34—35.

Chapters 40—55, sometimes called the Deutero-Isaiah, are generally attributed to an anonymous poet who, prophesied toward the end of the Babylonian Exile. From this section come the great Messianic oracles known as the songs of the Servant, whose mysterious destiny of suffering and glorification is fulfilled in the passion and glorification of Christ. Chapters 56—66 contain oracles from a later period and were composed by disciples who inherited the spirit and continued the work of the great prophet.

The principal divisions of the Book of Isaiah are the following:

A: *The Book of Judgment*

  I: Indictment of Israel and Judah (1, 1—5, 30)
  II: Immanuel Prophecies (6, 1—12, 6)
  III: Oracles against the Pagan Nations (13, 1—23, 18)
  IV: Apocalypse of Isaiah (24, 1—27, 13)

THE BOOK OF JEREMIAH

THE BOOK OF JEREMIAH combines history, biography, and prophecy. It portrays a nation in crisis and introduces the reader to an extraordinary leader upon whom the Lord placed the heavy burden of the prophetic office. Jeremiah was born about 650 B.C. of a priestly family from the little village of Anathoth, near Jerusalem. While still very young he was called to his task in the thirteenth year of King Josiah (628), whose reform, begun with enthusiasm and hope, ended with his death on the battlefield of Megiddo (609) as he attempted to stop the northward march of the Egyptian Pharaoh Neco.

The prophet heartily supported the reform of the pious King Josiah, which began in 629 B.C. Nineveh, the capital of Assyria, fell in 612, preparing the way for the new colossus, Babylon, which was soon to put an end to Judean independence.

After the death of Josiah the old idolatry returned. Jeremiah opposed it with all his strength. Arrest, imprisonment, and public disgrace were his lot. Jeremiah saw in the nation's impenitence the sealing of its doom. Nebuchadnezzar captured Jerusalem and carried King Jehoiachin into exile (22, 24).

During the years 598-587, Jeremiah attempted to Counsel Zedekiah in the face of bitter opposition. The false prophet Hananiah proclaimed that the yoke of Babylon was broken and a strong pro-Egyptian party in Jerusalem induced Zedekiah to revolt. Nebuchadnezzar took swift and terrible vengeance; Jerusalem was destroyed in 587 and its leading citizens sent into exile. About this time Jeremiah uttered the great oracle of the "New Covenant" (31, 31-34) sometimes called "The Gospel before the Gospel." This passage contains his most sublime teaching and is a landmark in Old Testament theology.

The prophet remained amidst the ruins of Jerusalem, but was later forced into Egyptian exile by a band of conspirators. There, according to an old tradition, he was murdered by his own countrymen. The influence of Jeremiah was greater after his death than before. The exiled community read and meditated the lessons of the prophet, and his influence can be seen in Ezekiel, certain of the psalms, and the second part of Isaiah. Shortly after the Exile, the Book of Jeremiah as we have it today was published in a final edition. It is divided as follows:

THE BOOK OF LAMENTATIONS

THE SIXTH CENTURY B.C. was an age of crisis, a turning point in the history of Israel. With the destruction of the temple and the interruption of its ritual, the exile of the leaders and loss of national sovereignty, an era came to an end. Not long after the fall of Jerusalem (587) an eyewitness of the national humiliation composed these five laments. They combine confession of sin, grief over the suffering and humiliation of Zion, submission to merited chastisement, and strong faith in the constancy of Yahweh's love and power to restore. This union of poignant grief and unquenchable hope reflects the constant prophetic vision of the weakness of man and the strength of God's love; it also shows how Israel's faith in Yahweh could survive the shattering experience of national ruin.

As a literary work, the Book of Lamentations is carefully constructed according to a familiar structural device. The first four poems are acrostics in which the separate stanzas begin with successive letters of the Hebrew alphabet from the first to the last. Far from destroying the spontaneous pathos of the songs, this literary feature permits a symbolic and disciplined expression of the profound grief, the sinful responsibility and the enduring hope of the suffering community. The figure of Israel as the bride of Yahweh, familiar from the prophets, appears here again; but now Zion is a desolate widow, the *Judaea Capta* of Titus' memorial coins, sustained only by the faith that God's chastisement will eventually give place to his infinite compassion.

THE BOOK OF BARUCH

THE OPENING verses of this book ascribe it, or at least its first part, to Baruch, the well-known secretary of the prophet Jeremiah. It contains five very different compositions, the first and the last in prose, the others in poetic form. The prose sections were certainly composed in Hebrew, though the earliest known form of the book is in Greek.

An observance of the feast of Booths with a public prayer of penitence and petition (1, 15—3, 8), such as is supposed by the introduction (1, 1-14), would not have been possible during the lifetime of Baruch after the fall of Jerusalem; this indeed is suggested in the prayer itself (2, 26). The prayer is therefore to be understood as the pious reflection of a later Jewish writer upon the circumstances of the exiles in Babylon as he knew them from the Book of Jeremiah. He expresses in their name sentiments called for by the prophet, and ascribes the wording of these sentiments to the person most intimately acquainted with Jeremiah's teaching, namely, Baruch. The purpose of this literary device is to portray for his own and later generations the spirit of repentance which prompted God to bring the Exile to an end.

The lesson thus gained is followed by a hymn in praise of Wisdom (3, 9—4, 4), exalting the law of Moses as the unique gift of God to Israel, the observance of which is the way to life and peace. The ideal city of Jerusalem is then represented (4, 5–29) as the solicitous mother of all exiles, who is assured in the name of God that all her children will be restored to her (4, 30—5, 9).

The final chapter is really a separate work, with a title of its own (6, 1). It is patterned after the earlier letter of Jeremiah (Jer 29), in the spirit of the warnings against idolatry contained in Jer 10 and Is 44. Its earnestness is impressive, but in restating previous inspired teachings at a later day, it does so with no special literary grace.

Thus the principal divisions of the book are seen to be:
  I: Prayer of the Exiles (1, 1—3, 8)
  II: Praise of Wisdom in the Law of Moses (3, 9—4, 4)
  III: Jerusalem Bewails and Consoles Her Captive Children (4, 5–29)
  IV: Jerusalem Consoled: The Captivity about To End (4, 30—5, 9)
  V: The Letter of Jeremiah against Idolatry (6, 1–72)

THE BOOK OF EZEKIEL

EZEKIEL'S complex character makes him one of the most interesting figures in Israelite prophecy. In many ways he resembles the more primitive type of prophet represented by Elijah and Elisha; yet he clearly depends on all his predecessors in prophecy, and his teaching is a development of theirs. His unique contribution to the history of prophetism lies in his manifest interest in the temple and the liturgy, an interest paralleled in no other prophet—even Jeremiah who, like Ezekiel, was also a priest. Particularly because of this interest, Ezekiel's influence on post-exilic religion was enormous, and not without reason has he been called "the father of Judaism." This has resulted in his prophecies reaching us with the evident marks of editing and addition by the post-exilic circles that shared his intense interest. However, we may be sure that in this book we have throughout what is in substance the prophet's own work.

Ezekiel became a prophet in Babylon—the first prophet to receive the call to prophecy outside the Holy Land. As one of the exiles deported by Nebuchadnezzar in 597, his first task was to prepare his fellow countrymen in Babylon for the final destruction of Jerusalem, which they believed to be inviolable. Accordingly, the first part of his book consists of reproaches for Israel's past and present sins and the confident prediction of yet a further devastation of the land of promise and a more general exile. In 587, when Nebuchadnezzar destroyed Jerusalem, Ezekiel was vindicated before his unbelieving compatriots.

After this time, Ezekiel's message changes. From now on his prophecy is characterized by the promise of salvation in a new covenant, and he is anxious to lay down the conditions necessary to obtain it. Even as Jeremiah had believed, Ezekiel thought that the exiles were the hope of Israel's restoration, once God's allotted time for the Exile had been accomplished. His final eight chapters are a utopian vision of the Israel of the future, rid of its past evils and re-established firmly under the rule of the Lord. The famous vision of the dry bones in chapter 37 expresses his firm belief in a forthcoming restoration, Israel rising to new life from the graveyard of Babylon. But Ezekiel's new covenant, like Jeremiah's, was to see its true fulfillment only in the New Testament.

Perhaps no other prophet has stressed the absolute majesty of God as Ezekiel does. This appears not only in the tremendous vision by the river Chebar with which his prophecy opens, but throughout the book. Ultimately, says Ezekiel, whatever God does to or for man is motivated by zeal for his own holy name. The new heart and the new spirit which must exist under the new covenant cannot be the work of man; they too must be the work of God. By such teachings he helped prepare for the New Testament doctrine of salvation through grace.

The Book of Ezekiel is divided as follows:
  I: Call of the Prophet (1, 1—3, 27)
  II: Before the Siege of Jerusalem (4, 1—24, 27)
  III: Prophecies against Foreign Nations (25, 1—32, 32)
  IV: Salvation for Israel (33, 1—39, 29)
  V: The New Israel (40, 1—48, 35)

THE BOOK OF DANIEL

THIS BOOK takes its name, not from the author, who is actually unknown, but from its hero, a young Jew taken early to Babylon, where he lived at least until 538 B.C. Strictly speaking, the book does not belong to the prophetic writings but rather to a distinctive type of literature known as "apocalyptic," of which it is an early specimen. Apocalyptic writing enjoyed its greatest popularity from 200 B.C. to 100 A.D., a time of distress and persecution for Jews, and later, for Christians.

Though subsequent in time to the prophetic, apocalyptic literature has its roots in the teaching of the prophets, who often pointed ahead to the Day of the Lord, the consummation of history. For both prophet and apocalyptist Yahweh was the Lord of history, and he would ultimately vindicate his people.

This work was composed during the bitter persecution carried on by Antiochus IV Epiphanes (167–164) and was written to strengthen and comfort the Jewish people in their ordeal.

The Book contains stories originating in and transmitted by popular traditions which tell of the trials and triumphs of the wise Daniel and his three companions. The moral is that men of faith can resist temptation and conquer adversity. The characters are not purely legendary but rest on older historical tradition. What is more important than the question of historicity, and closer to the intention of the author, is the fact that a persecuted Jew of the second century B.C. would quickly see the application of these stories to his own plight.

There follows a series of visions promising deliverance and glory to the Jews in the days to come. The great nations of the ancient world have risen in vain against Yahweh; his kingdom shall overthrow existing powers and last forever. Under this apocalyptic imagery are contained some of the best elements of prophetic teaching: the insistence on right conduct, the divine control over events, the certainty that the kingdom of God will ultimately triumph. The arrival of the kingdom is a central theme of the Synoptic Gospels, and Jesus, in calling himself the "Son of Man," reminds us that he fulfills the destiny of this mysterious figure in the seventh chapter of Daniel.

The added episodes of Susanna, Bel, and the Dragon, found only in the Greek version, are edifying short stories with a didactic purpose.

These three sections constitute the divisions of the Book of Daniel:
I: Daniel and the Kings of Babylon (1, 1—6, 29)
II: Daniel's Visions (7, 1—12, 13)
III: Appendix (13, 1—14, 42)

THE BOOK OF HOSEA

HOSEA BELONGED to the Northern Kingdom and began his prophetic career in the last years of Jeroboam II (786–746 B.C.). Some believe that he was a priest, others that he was a cult prophet; the prophecy, our only source of information concerning his life, gives us no certain answer in this matter. The collected oracles reveal a very sensitive, emotional man who could pass quickly from violent anger to the deepest tenderness. The prophecy pivots around his own unfortunate marriage to Gomer, a personal tragedy which profoundly influenced his teaching. In fact, his own prophetic vocation and message were immeasurably deepened by the painful experience he underwent in his married life.

Gomer, the adulteress, symbolized faithless Israel. And just as Hosea could not give up his wife forever even when she played the harlot, so Yahweh could not renounce Israel, who had been betrothed to him. God would chastise, but it would be the chastisement of the jealous lover, longing to bring back the beloved to the fresh and pure joy of their first love.

Israel's infidelity took the form of idolatry and ruthless oppression of the poor. No amount of mechanically offered sacrifices could atone for her serious sins. Chastisement alone remained; God would have to strip her of the rich ornaments bestowed by her false lovers and thus bring her back to the true lover. A humiliated Israel would again seek Yahweh. The eleventh chapter of Hosea is one of the summits of Old Testament theology; God's love for his people has never been expressed more tenderly. Hosea began the tradition of describing the relation between Yahweh and Israel in terms of marriage. This symbolism appears later on in the Old Testament; and, in the New, both St. John and St. Paul express in the same imagery the union between Christ and his Church.

The Book of Hosea is divided as follows:
I: The Prophet's Marriage and Its Lesson (1, 1—3, 5)
II: Israel's Guilt and Punishment (4, 1—14, 10)

THE BOOK OF JOEL

THIS PROPHECY is rich in apocalyptic imagery and strongly eschatological in tone. It was composed about 400 B.C. Its prevailing theme is the Day of the Lord.

A terrible invasion of locusts ravaged Judah. So frightful was the scourge that the prophet visualized it as a symbol of the coming Day of the Lord. In the face of this threatening catastrophe, the prophet summoned the people to repent, to turn to the Lord with fasting and weeping. They were ordered to convoke a solemn assembly in which the priests would pray for deliverance. The Lord answered their prayer and promised to drive away the locusts and bless the land with peace and prosperity. To these material blessings would be added an outpouring of the spirit on all flesh. St. Peter, in his first discourse before the people at Pentecost (Acts 2, 16–21), sees in the coming of the Holy Spirit the fulfillment of this promise (1, 1–3, 5).

The concluding poem pictures the nations gathered in the Valley of Jehoshaphat, where the Lord is about to pass judgment. Israel's enemies are summoned to hear the solemn indictment; their evil deeds are at last requited. The tumultuous throng assembled in the valley of decision is made up of the enemies of God and they face inevitable destruction. The oracle changes abruptly from the terrifying image of judgment to a vision of Israel restored and forever secure from her enemies. God is both the vindicator of his people and the source of their blessings (4, 1–21).

THE BOOK OF AMOS

AMOS was a shepherd of Tekoa in Judah, who exercised his ministry during the prosperous reign of Jeroboam II (786–746 B.C.). He prophesied in Israel at the great cult center of Bethel, from which he was finally expelled by the priest in charge of this royal sanctuary. The poetry of Amos, who denounces the hollow prosperity of the northern kingdom, is filled with imagery and language taken from his own pastoral background. The book is an anthology of his oracles and was compiled either by the prophet or by some of his disciples.

The prophecy begins with a sweeping indictment of Damascus, Philistia, Tyre, and Edom; but the forthright herdsman saves his climactic denunciation for Israel, whose injustice and idolatry are sins against the light granted to her. Israel could indeed expect the Day of Yahweh, but it would be a day of darkness and not light. When Amos prophesied the overthrow of the sanctuary, the fall of the royal house, and the captivity of the people, it was more than Israelite officialdom could bear. The priest of Bethel drove Amos from the shrine—but not before hearing a terrible sentence pronounced upon himself.

Amos is a prophet of divine judgment, and the sovereignty of Yahweh in nature and history dominates his thought. But he was no innovator; his conservatism was in keeping with the whole prophetic tradition calling the people back to the high moral and religious demands of Yahweh's revelation. In common with the other prophets, Amos knew that divine punishment is never completely destructive; it is part of the hidden plan of God to bring salvation to men. The perversity of the human will may retard, but it cannot totally frustrate, this design of a loving God. The last oracle opens up a perspective of restoration under a Davidic king.

The Book of Amos may be divided as follows:
  I: Judgment of the Nations (1, 1—2, 16)
  II: Words and Woes for Israel (3, 1—6, 14)
  III: Symbolic Visions: Threats and Promises (7, 1—
    9, 8b)
    Epilogue: Messianic Perspective (9, 8c–15)

THE BOOK OF OBADIAH

THE TWENTY-ONE VERSES of this book contain the shortest and sternest prophecy in the Old Testament. Nothing is known of the author, although his oracle against Edom, a long-standing enemy of Israel, indicates a date of composition sometime in the fifth century B.C. During this period the Edomites had been forced to abandon their ancient home near the Gulf of Aqaba and had settled in southern Judah, where they appear among the adversaries of the Jews returning from exile.

The prophecy is a bitter cry for vengeance against Edom for its heinous crimes. The mountain of Esau will be occupied and ravaged by the enemy but Zion shall remain inviolate. Judah and Israel shall again form one nation; and that triumphant refrain of Israelite eschatology will be heard once more: "The Kingdom is the Lord's!" Many of the verses in this prophecy can be paralleled in Jer 49, 7–22, but it is difficult to determine the precise relationship between these similar passages.

THE BOOK OF JONAH

WRITTEN in the post-Exilic era, probably in the fifth century B.C., this book is a didactic story with an important theological message. It concerns a disobedient prophet who attempted to run away from his divine commission, was cast overboard and swallowed by a great fish, rescued in a marvelous manner, and sent on his way to Nineveh, the traditional enemy of Israel. To the surprise of Jonah, the wicked city listened to his message of doom and repented immediately. All, from king to lowliest subject, humbled themselves in sackcloth and ashes. Seeing their repentance, God did not carry out the punishment he had planned for them. Whereupon Jonah complained to God about the unexpected success of his mission; he was bitter because Yahweh, instead of destroying, had led the people to repentance and then spared them.

From this partly humorous story, a very sublime lesson may be drawn. Jonah stands for a narrow and vindictive mentality, all too common among the Jews of that period. Because they were the chosen people, a good many of them cultivated an intolerant nationalism which limited the mercy of God to their nation. It was abhorrent to their way of thinking that nations as wicked as Assyria should escape his wrath.

The prophecy, which is both instructive and entertaining, strikes directly at this viewpoint. It is a parable of mercy, showing that God's threatened punishments are but the expression of a merciful will which moves all men to repent and seek forgiveness. The universality of the story contrasts with the particularistic spirit of many in the post-Exilic community. The book has also prepared the way for the Gospel with its message of redemption for all, both Jew and Gentile.

THE BOOK OF MICAH

MICAH was a contemporary of Isaiah. Of his personal life and call we know nothing except that he came from the obscure village of Moresheth in the foothills.

His were the broad vistas of the Judean lowland and the distant sea on the western horizon. With burning eloquence he attacked the rich exploiters of the poor, fraudulent merchants, venal judges, corrupt priests and prophets. To the man of the countryside the vices of the nation seemed centered in its capitals, for both Samaria and Jerusalem are singled out for judgment. An interesting notice in Jer 26, 17f informs us that the reform of Hezekiah was influenced by the preaching of Micah.

The prophecy may be divided into three parts:

I: The impending judgment of the Lord, followed by an exposition of its causes, Israel's sins. Censure of Judah's leaders for betrayal of their responsibility. (1, 1—3, 12)

II: The glory of the restored Zion. A prince of David's house will rule over a reunited Israel. (St. Matthew's Nativity narrative points to Christ's birth in Bethlehem as the fulfillment of this prophecy.) A remnant shall survive the chastisement of Judah and her adversaries shall be destroyed. (4, 1—5, 14)

III: The case against Israel, in which the Lord is portrayed as the plaintiff who has maintained fidelity to the covenant. The somber picture closes with a prayer for national restoration and a beautiful expression of trust in God's pardoning mercy. (6, 1—7, 20)

It should be noted that each of these three divisions begins with reproach and the threat of punishment, and ends on a note of hope and promise.

THE BOOK OF NAHUM

SHORTLY before the fall of Nineveh in 612 B.C., Nahum uttered his prophecy against the hated city. To understand the prophet's exultant outburst of joy over the impending destruction it is necessary to recall the savage cruelty of Assyria, which had made it the scourge of the ancient Near East for almost three centuries. The royal inscriptions of Assyria afford the best commentary on the burning denunciation of "the bloody city." In the wake of their conquests, mounds of heads, impaled bodies, enslaved citizens, and avaricious looters testified to the ruthlessness of the Assyrians. Little wonder that Judah joined in the general outburst of joy over the destruction of Nineveh!

But Nahum is not a prophet of unrestrained revenge. God's moral government of the world is asserted. Yahweh is the avenger but he is also merciful, a citadel in the day of distress. Nineveh's doom was a judgment on the wicked city. Before many years passed, Jerusalem too was to learn the meaning of such a judgment.

The Book is divided as follows:
The Lord's Coming in Judgment (1, 2—2, 1.3)
The Imminent Fall of Nineveh (2, 2—3, 19)

THE BOOK OF HABAKKUK

THIS PROPHECY dates from the years 605–597 B.C., or between the great Babylonian victory at Carchemish and Nebuchadnezzar's invasion of Judah which culminated in the capture of Jerusalem. The situation of Judah was desperate at this time, with political intrigue and idolatry widespread in the small kingdom. The first two chapters consist of a dialogue between the prophet and the Lord. For what may be the first time in Israelite literature, a man questions the ways of God, as Habakkuk calls him to account for his government of the world. To this question God replies that he has prepared a chastising rod, Babylon, which will be the avenging instrument in his hand. There is added the divine assurance that the just Israelite will not perish in the calamities about to be visited on the nation.

The third chapter is a magnificent religious lyric, filled with reminiscences of Israel's past and rich in literary borrowings from the poetry of ancient Canaan, though still expressing authentic Israelite faith. God appears in all his majestic splendor and executes vengeance on Judah's enemies. The prophecy ends with a joyous profession of confidence in the Lord, the Savior.

THE BOOK OF ZEPHANIAH

THE TITLE of the prophecy informs us that the ministry of Zephaniah took place during the reign of Josiah (640–609 B.C.). The protest against the worship of false gods, and the condemnation of the pro-Assyrian court ministers who served as regents during Josiah's minority, allow us to place the work in the first decade of the reign. Accordingly, the prophecy of Zephaniah comes rightly before that of Jeremiah, who was probably influenced by it in both language and ideas.

The age of Zephaniah was a time of religious degradation, when the old idolatries reappeared and men worshiped sun, moon, and stars. Rites completely alien to the pure monotheism taught by Moses flourished in Jerusalem. To the corrupt city Zephaniah announced the impending judgment, the Day of the Lord. The prophecy may be divided into three sections, corresponding to the three chapters of the book:

The Day of the Lord: A day of doom. The last few verses of this oracle give the classic description of the Day of the Lord as an overwhelming disaster. The Christian hymn *Dies Irae* is based on this passage (1, 2–18).

The Day of the Lord: A day of judgment of the nations, traditional enemies of God's people (2, 1–15).

Reproach and Promise for Jerusalem: Despite Judah's infidelities, the Lord in his mercy will spare a holy remnant, which will finally enjoy peace. The prophecy closes with a hymn of joy sung by the remnant restored to Zion (3, 1–20).

THE BOOK OF HAGGAI

POST-EXILIC prophecy begins with Haggai, who received the word of the Lord in the second year of Darius (520 B.C.). The Jews who returned from the Exile in Babylonia had encountered formidable obstacles in their efforts to re-establish Jewish life in Judah. The Samaritans had succeeded in blocking the rebuilding of the temple; but after Darius acceded to the throne (522), permission was given to resume the work. At this critical moment, when defeatism and a certain lethargy had overtaken his repatriated countrymen, Haggai came forward with his exhortations to them to complete the great task. The first oracle, an appeal to the Jews, is contained in chapter 1. To this appeal Haggai added a short oracle of encouragement (2, 1–9) for the sake of those who gloomily contrasted the former magnificence of Solomon's temple with the second temple: the Lord would be present in this new abode, and its glory, enhanced by the offerings of the Gentiles, would surpass the ancient splendor.

The prophecy may be divided into five oracles:

The call to rebuild the temple. The economic distress so apparent in Judah is due to the Jews' neglect of the Lord while they provide for their own needs (1, 1–15).
The future glory of the new temple, surpassing that of the old (2, 1–9).
Unworthiness of a people who may be the Samaritans, to offer sacrifice at the newly restored altar. This oracle is cast in the literary form of a *torah*, an instruction given the people by a priest (2, 10–14).
A promise of immediate blessings, which follows upon the undertaking (chapter 1) to rebuild the temple (2, 15–19).
A pledge to Zerubbabel, descendant of David, repository of the Messianic hopes (2, 20–23).

THE BOOK OF ZECHARIAH

ZECHARIAH's initial prophecy is dated to 520 B.C., the same year as that in which Haggai received the prophetic call. The first eight chapters of the Book of Zechariah contain oracles which certainly belong to him while the last six (sometimes called "Deutero-Zechariah") represent the work of one or more unknown authors. In the prophecies proper to Zechariah eight symbolic visions are recorded, all meant to promote the work of rebuilding the temple and to encourage the returned exiles, especially their leaders, Joshua and Zerubbabel. In the final chapter of this first division Zechariah portrays the Messianic future under the figure of a prosperous land to which the nations come in pilgrimage, eager to follow the God of Israel.

The second part of Zechariah is divided into two sections, each with its own introductory title. The first (9–11) consists of oracles whose historical background, date and authorship are extremely difficult to determine. With 9, 9 begins the Messianic vision of the coming of the Prince of Peace. The verses describing the triumphant appearance of the humble king are taken up by the four Evangelists to describe the entry of Christ into Jerusalem on Palm Sunday. Chapter 12 is introduced by an oracle proclaiming the victory of God's people over the heathen. The prophecy closes by describing, in apocalyptic imagery, the final assault of the enemy on Jerusalem, after which the Messianic age begins.

THE BOOK OF MALACHI

THIS WORK was composed by an anonymous writer shortly before Nehemiah's arrival in Jerusalem (445 B.C.). Because of the sharp reproaches he was leveling against the priests and rulers of the people, the author probably wished to conceal his identity. To do this he made a proper name out of the Hebrew expression for "My Messenger" (Malachi), which occurs in 1, 1 and 3, 1. The historical value of the prophecy is considerable in that it gives us a picture of life in the Jewish community returned from Babylon between the period of Haggai and the reform measures of Ezra and Nehemiah. It is likely that the author's trenchant criticism of abuses and religious indifference in the community prepared the way for these necessary reforms.

The chosen people had made a sorry return for divine love. The priests, who should have been leaders, had dishonored God by their blemished sacrifices. In his first chapter, the writer foresees the time when all nations will offer a pure oblation (1, 11)—a prophecy whose fulfillment the Church sees in the Sacrifice of the Mass. The author then turns from priests to people, denouncing their marriages with pagans and their callous repudiation of Israelite wives. Imbued with the nationalist and critical spirit of the times, many had wearied God with the question, "Where is the God of justice?" To this question the prophet replies that the Day of the Lord is coming. But first the forerunner must come, who will prepare the soil for repentance and true worship. The Gospel writers point to John the Baptist as the forerunner ushering in the Messianic age, the true Day of the Lord. When the ground is prepared God will appear, measuring out rewards and punishments and purifying the nation in the furnace of judgment. He will create a new order in which the ultimate triumph of good is inevitable.

THE GOSPEL ACCORDING TO MATTHEW

MATTHEW'S GOSPEL in its present form was written in a Jewish milieu, probably after the destruction of Jerusalem in 70 A.D. There are evidences of the fulfillment of the Mosaic law (1, 19; 5, 18), and also references to violence (21, 38–41), to the burning of a city (22, 7), and to punishment in the wake of Jesus' death (27, 25).

There is also the anti-Pharisee and anti-scribe polemic in Matthew which indicates a fairly complete rift between Christians and official Judaism. By the year 85 A.D. Christians were unwelcome in Jewish synagogues—called *their synagogues* by Matthew to distinguish Jewish from Christian worship (4, 23; 9, 35; 12, 9; 13, 54).

There is thus an ambivalence between Matthew's earlier Jewishness, reflected in the elements of the gospel as they were in the process of formation, and his alienation from Jewish tradition even before these elements were incorporated into the finished gospel.

Ignatius, bishop of Antioch (†110), in his letters to certain churches of Asia Minor, uses several sayings of Jesus found only in this gospel (12, 35; 15, 13; 19, 12). Papias, bishop of Hierapolis in Phrygia, wrote (c 135) that Matthew had compiled a collection of sayings of the Lord "in the Hebrew tongue" (most likely Aramaic), "and each person translated them as he was able." This seems to indicate that various Greek versions of the early collection attributed to Matthew were in existence; one of them may have been the apocryphal gospel of the Hebrews.

Besides the sayings of the Lord, it is certain that the author of Matthew had access to the present Gospel of Mark because of the Marcan verses he uses in chapters 3, 8f, 12–17, 19–22, 24, 26ff. Matthew is obviously an expanded version of Mark, considered the first gospel form to be written. Very few scholars hold that Mark is a condensed version of Matthew.

Both Matthew and Luke, neither of whom can be proved to have copied from the other, seem to have had, besides the Gospel of Mark, another source of some 240 verses which Mark does not include. This source, not found but deduced, is designated simply as Q from Quelle, the German term for "source."

Beginning with a series of reflections relating Jesus and his parentage to the messianism of the Old Testament (1, 1–25), the gospel places his birth in the hostile political environment of the time (2, 1–23). Like the other gospels, Matthew introduces the public ministry of Jesus with a summary of the mission of John the Baptizer (3, 1–17). After the account of the temptation of Jesus (4, 1–11), the gospel reports his teaching and miracles, locating all these in Galilee and its vicinity, exclusive of Jerusalem (4, 12—20, 34). It concludes with the final events and teaching of Jesus, locating them in Jerusalem, and centering them around his passion, death and resurrection (21, 1—28, 20). For this general outline of a gospel, see Acts 1, 21f; 10, 37–41.

The Gospel of Matthew is distinctive for its practice of citing the Old Testament in connection with Jesus' activity and teaching, and for a structured presentation of his doctrine in the form of sermons or discourses (5, 1–7, 29; 10, 5–42; 13, 1–52; 18, 1–35; 24, 1—25, 46). The discourses are followed by collections of miracle-accounts and incidents which reflect Jesus' doctrinal teaching. They are presented by the evangelist in such a way as to be meaningful to the Christian communities of this time.

The gospel as a whole revolves around the concept, no doubt originally developed in Judaeo-Christian circles, that Jesus is the expected Messiah-king of Israel, mysteriously unacceptable to his own people, but no less mysteriously acceptable to many Gentiles.

The universal importance of Christ in this gospel does not derive from the notion of messianic kingship alone, but more especially from his divinity (1, 23; 16, 16; 28, 18). This makes possible his presence in Christian communities in word and sacrament (18, 19; 26, 29) and constitutes him the divine teacher of all nations (28, 19). The bond in Matthew between christology and ecclesiology portrays the mediating mission of the Christian community, that of giving witness to Christ in the world. In the judgment of modern scholars this mission is a theological development within the gospel tradition that requires a date for the Gospel of Matthew later than that of Mark and Luke. Current and more common opinion dates the composition of the Gospel of Matthew between 80–100 A.D., or roughly, 85 A.D. There is also the compelling evidence for the dependence of Matthew on Mark: namely, the 600 of Mark's 661 verses found in Matthew, as well as the relationship of language and order in these two gospels.

The principal divisions of the Gospel of Matthew are as follows:

   I: Prologue: The Coming of the Savior
      (1, 1—2, 23)
  II: Promulgation of the Reign of God
      (3, 1—7, 29)
 III: Preaching the Reign of God (8, 1—11, 1)

THE GOSPEL ACCORDING TO MARK

THE GOSPEL OF MARK is invaluable for grasping the essential characteristics of Jesus' public ministry. The gospels of Matthew and Luke are better understood in the light of the data provided by Mark because of their direct dependence on him. Like the other evangelists, Mark, in addressing himself to Christian readers, places his gospel within the framework of Christian tradition on the identity of Jesus which developed during the course of the apostolic teaching. In Mark's day, the title "Christ" had already become part of Jesus' proper name; for the Gentile Christian it had the religious implication of "savior" or "redeemer" rather than "Messiah," which would be meaningless to all but Jews; cf Rom 9, 5. The title "Son of God" had become the most characteristic name of Jesus, designating him as the God-man; cf Rom 1, 1–4.

The gospel of Mark revolves around the two titles "Christ" and "Son of God." The evangelist shows how the Christian community's faith in Jesus as Savior harmonized with his own knowledge of his divine destiny to suffer, die, and rise again. The miraculous powers of Jesus which so mystified his contemporaries find their satisfactory explanation in the doctrine of Jesus' divinity, which the Christian community grasped only after his resurrection. Although the gospel of Mark was developed in connection with Christian faith in Jesus as redeemer and Son of God, its contents indicate the historical reality of the person and ministry of Jesus in a manner less refined by theological reflection than the accounts of the other evangelists. In Mark, the person of Jesus is depicted with an unaffected naturalness. He reacts to events with authentic human emotion: apprehension (1, 44), anger (3, 5), triumph (4, 40), sympathy (5, 36; 6, 34), surprise (5, 30; 6, 6), admiration (7, 29), sadness (14, 33f), indignation (14, 48f). His disciples take positions toward him that are critical (4, 38; 5, 31; 6, 37; 8, 4.32) or inattentive (7, 16f) He acknowledges that there are things he does not know, e.g., the appointed time for the end of the world, known only to the Father (13, 32); cf also 5, 30; 6, 38.

From a literary standpoint this gospel is divided into clearly distinguishable parts: the title (1, 1), the prologue (1, 2–13), the ministry of Jesus (1, 14—13, 37), his passion, death, and burial (14, 1—15, 47), his resurrection, the commission of the apostles, and his ascension (16, 1–20). The account of the ministry is doctrinal rather than chronological or geographical. The reader's attention is fixed on the mystery of Jesus' person. The average man recognizes in the teaching of Jesus something authentically new (1, 22), and he is thoroughly impressed by Jesus' curative powers (1, 37f; 3, 8–11). The religious leaders are disconcerted when Jesus challenges them on their own ground (2, 16—3, 6). The relatives of Jesus fear for his safety (3, 20f), and his disciples discover that their understanding of him is deficient (4, 36–40; 6, 47–52). Jesus accepts the title of prophet, but he lays no explicit claim to the role of Messiah; he even imposes silence concerning his miracles (1, 44; 5, 43; 7, 36; 8, 26).

At Caesarea Philippi Jesus departs from his reticence and elicits two admissions from his disciples: one is that popular opinion concedes him the role of prophet; the other is that the disciples themselves consider him to be the Messiah (8, 27–30). At this point Mark's gospel reaches its first climax concerning the identity of Jesus, to which it has been building up. Jesus proceeds beyond the messianic confession of his disciples to state clearly his own prophetic understanding of his role: it is the divine will that he should suffer and die at the hands of the Sanhedrin. The mystery of the crucified Messiah, which is a stumbling block to the Jews (1 Cor 1, 23), is traced by Mark to Jesus' self-awareness throughout his ministry. Though the remainder of the gospel incorporates an occasional miracle story (9, 17–27; 10, 46–52; 11, 12ff.20f), and much of Jesus' teaching, it is dominated by his self-revelation as the chosen instrument who is to suffer, die, and rise again (9, 9f.31f; 10, 32ff; 12, 1–12; 14, 1—16, 8). Within the passion narrative, the second and chief climax of Jesus' self-revelation occurs when, in the inquest before the high priest, he is shown by Mark to express the church's faith that he is both Messiah and Son of God (14, 62).

Mark's geographical framework places the ministry of Jesus not only in the Galilean area (1, 14—6, 13), but outside it as well (6, 30—10, 31). The journey to Jerusalem begins in 10, 32 and ends in 11, 1 near that city, where the final days of the ministry are to be spent (11, 1—15, 37).

According to Papias (†135 A.D.), the author of the second gospel was Mark who served as Peter's "interpreter" (editor of Petrine material?). Irenaeus (c 202), Clement of Alexandria (c 215), Tertullian (c 220), and Origen (c 254) attest a similar relationship. There is no need to reject the identification of the author with that John Mark whom the New Testament associates with St. Paul (Acts 12, 25; 15, 37.39; Col 4, 10; 2 Tm 4, 11; Phlm 24), and with St. Peter (Acts 12, 12; 1 Pt 5, 13).

The Petrine influence on Mark should not be exaggerated. Modern scholarship has shown quite clearly that Mark's sources cannot be explained solely in terms of Peter's preaching. On the basis of manuscript and stylistic evidence, Mk 16, 9–20 derives from a hand other than Mark's. The gospel originally ended at 16, 8. The so-called longer ending (vv 9–20), which the Council of

Trent declared to be inspired and canonical, was known to Justin Martyr (c 165), Tatian (c 170), and Irenaeus (c 202).

Data in the gospel clearly indicate that it was intended for Gentile Christian readers (7, 3f.11), or at least readers unfamiliar with Jewish customs; nonetheless, the place of composition is uncertain. Following the suggestion of Clement of Alexandria and Origen, the majority of modern scholars consider the gospel to have been written in Rome. The date of composition is c 70 A.D.

It is true that the gospel of Mark is used less than the others in liturgical worship; nevertheless it has contributed much to these gospels for the Christian understanding of Jesus and his ministry.

> The principal divisions of the Gospel of Mark are as follows:
> I: Prologue: Preparation for the Ministry of Jesus (1, 1–13)
> II: The Mystery of Jesus (1, 14—8, 26)
> III: The Mystery Begins To Be Revealed (8, 27—9, 32)
> IV: The Full Revelation of the Mystery (9, 33—16, 20)

THE GOSPEL ACCORDING TO LUKE

IN ACCORDANCE with the custom of Greek writers of the time, Luke introduces his gospel narrative with a brief preface (1, 1–4) probably intended to cover the Acts of the Apostles as well. Luke here alludes to his predecessors and stresses the care with which he has collected and judged his material. He regards those who wrote the gospel message before him as comprising two groups: "eye-witnesses and ministers of the word," i.e., the Twelve, who were the fundamental source of the gospel tradition (1, 2; Acts 1, 21f; 10, 39); and the "many," who attempted to arrange the preaching and teaching of the Twelve in narrative form (1, 1). Luke places himself in the latter group (1, 3)—not eyewitnesses like the Twelve, but catechists and writers who had familiarized themselves with the traditions about Jesus (the gospel) and the experiences of the Christian communities (Acts of the Apostles).

Luke dedicates his two books to a certain Theophilus (1, 3; Acts 1, 1)—a common name in the Greek world meaning "God's friend." This personage, whether a literary figure signifying Gentiles as such, or a historical individual with some degree of political importance, has received information on Christian teaching. Luke sees him either as a person of influence favorably disposed toward Christian teaching and worthy of more information, or as a Christian seeking more knowledge concerning the practical implications of his faith (1, 4). Perhaps this ambiguity concerning the religious status of Theophilus is deliberate; compare Lk 1, 4 with Acts 18, 25; 21, 21.24.

Many scholars discern in the Lucan gospel and Acts an apologetic strain presumably directed against unfounded criticisms of Christian teaching. Written after the persecution of Nero that began in 64 A.D., and caused hostility toward Christians throughout the empire, Luke-Acts reveal that Jesus himself was accounted innocent by the Roman governor Pontius Pilate (Lk 23, 4.15.22), and that St. Paul, founder of many Christian communities in the empire, was often acquitted by the Roman magistrates of charges against him (Acts 16, 36; 18, 12–17; 25, 26; 26, 32).

The evangelist portrays Christianity, not as a political movement, nor as a sect organized for an initiated few, but as a religious faith open to all men. His portrait of Jesus, drawn from the gospel tradition, manifests the Savior's concern for humanity (10, 25–37; 13, 10–16; 14, 12ff; 15, 11–32), and his identification with the poor (9, 57f; 12, 13–21), the outcast (15, 1f; 17, 11–19), and the criminal (19, 1–10; 23, 39–43). Although the apologetic thought in Luke's writings must be acknowledged, it was nevertheless not his chief purpose to produce an apology for Christianity.

Unlike the other evangelists, Luke presents no main thesis. He is content to let the material of the gospel narrative speak for itself without any argumentative intrusion of his own. The correct understanding of the importance of the Christian gospel is delicately introduced into the traditional material. By aligning Jesus' birth (2, 1ff) and the preaching of John the Baptizer (3, 1f) with the facts of secular history, the evangelist indicates that the gospel tradition did not originate in a myth about gods, but was lived out by Jesus of Nazareth in the real world wherein all men are born, struggle over the meaning of their existence, and die. He depicts Jesus as resolutely facing the reality which that world had in store for him (9, 51). Luke also, in harmony with the growing realization of the Christian communities of his time, removes the concept of the proximate parousia so prominent in Mark 13. But neither these concepts nor any particular aspects of Jesus' teaching that Luke chooses to emphasize are presented in any but a serene fashion. His reverence extends, not only to Jesus as God's Son (1, 35), and to the invisible persons of the Father (11, 2) and the Holy Spirit (11, 13), but also to humanity itself as the fruitful recipient of God's word.

No other evangelist has placed such emphasis on the prophetic word of Jesus; no other is so optimistic over the favorable response it is destined to receive. Nothing that the divine word enacts in history can fail (1, 37). The word of Jesus on love of enemies (6, 27–42) is seen as the only weapon which the small Christian communities of Luke's time possess to combat the forces of persecution. The word of God is the teaching of Jesus, to be planted in the hearts of men (8, 11). And it is the function of the Christian community (24, 27) to confront humanity with this word, which undergoes vicissitudes but inevitably finds out those who will hear, believe, and act (8, 15.21; 11, 28).

Most scholars agree that Luke made use of Mark's gospel as one of his sources; some even consider it to be Luke's principal source, to which he added other material (Lk 1–2; 6, 20—8, 3; 9, 51—18, 14) including an independently derived passion-narrative (22, 1—24, 53). In the view of others, Luke used Mark only as a supplementary source for rounding out the material he took from other traditions. Certainly, Luke's aim was not to improve upon Mark's account of the public ministry of Jesus, but rather to provide material for those like Theophilus, God's friends, desirous of living out the message of Jesus in the world.

Early Christian tradition ascribes the companion volumes of the Lucan gospel and Acts of the Apostles to approximately 75 A.D., and identifies the author with Luke the physician, friend of St. Paul, mentioned in Col 4, 14; Phlm 24; and 2 Tm 4, 11.

The Gospel of Luke is divided as follows:
Preface (1, 1–4)
  I: The Infancy Narrative (1, 5—2, 52)
 II: Preparation for the Public Ministry
     (3, 1—4, 13)
III: The Ministry in Galilee (4, 14—9, 50)
 IV: The Journey Through Perea (9, 51—19, 27)
  V: The Jerusalem Ministry (19, 28—21, 38)
 VI: The Passion of Jesus (22, 1—23, 56)
VII: Appearances after the Resurrection (24, 1–53)

THE GOSPEL ACCORDING TO JOHN

THE REPUTED author of the fourth gospel was John, son of Zebedee, who published it at Ephesus in the last years of his life. Within the Christian community, this is the only important tradition that has come down from antiquity concerning this gospel. In its essentials the tradition is found in Irenaeus ("Adversus Haereses," 3:1, 1) toward the close of the second century. He claims to have had it from Polycarp of Smyrna, who knew John. Thus "the beloved disciple" himself becomes identified as the source of the tradition (19, 35; 21, 24); cf 19, 26f.

While the attestation of this tradition is impressive, it should be remembered that for the ancients authorship was a much broader concept than it is today. In their time a man could be called the "author" of a work if he was the authority behind it, even though he did not write it. Modern critical analysis makes it difficult to accept that the fourth gospel as it now stands was written by one man. Chapter 21 seems to have been added after the gospel was completed (20, 30f); it exhibits a Greek style somewhat different from the rest of the work. The Prologue (1, 1–18) was apparently an independent hymn, subsequently adapted to serve as a preface to the gospel. Within the gospel itself there are signs of some disorder;

e.g., there are two endings to Jesus' discourse at the Last Supper (14, 37; 18, 1).

To solve these problems, scholars have proposed various rearrangements that would produce a smoother order. However, more and more students of this gospel are coming to believe that the inconsistencies were probably produced by subsequent editing in which homogeneous materials were added to a shorter original. Other difficulties for the theory of eyewitness authorship are presented by the gospel's highly developed theology, and by certain elements of its literary style. For instance, some of the miracles of Jesus have been worked into highly dramatic scenes (ch 9); there has been a careful attempt to have the miracles followed by discourses which explain them (chs 5 and 6); the sayings of Jesus have been woven into long discourses of a quasi-poetic form resembling the speeches of personified Wisdom in the Old Testament.

How can the ancient tradition about the authorship of the fourth gospel be reconciled with modern bibilical scholarship? Many scholars, Protestant and Catholic, are coming to accept a theory which tries to do justice to both. This proposes that behind the fourth gospel there was an ancient tradition of the words and deeds of Jesus, a tradition of real historical value, similar in general to, but independent of, the traditions that underlie the synoptic gospels. Thus, just as the name "Peter" has been associated with one of the traditions behind the synoptic gospels, so the name "John, son of Zebedee," may well be attached to the tradition behind the fourth gospel. John, as one of the three privileged disciples who were closest to Jesus, may have preserved and preached this basic tradition about Jesus.

The theory further proposes that it was one of John's disciples who actually developed the tradition into the pattern of the gospel as we know it. Perhaps, under John's guidance, this disciple was the real evangelist: an artistic and theological genius, who gave to the tradition the distinctive literary features which we call "Johannine," and who used the gospel message to respond to the pressing theological needs of his time. All of this would have required the selection and reworking of details from the tradition, and would probably have been based on a long history of Johannine preaching.

Later, the theory continues, still another disciple of John was responsible for the editing of the evangelist's original gospel. He is often called the disciple-redactor, or editor, to distinguish him from the disciple-evangelist. This man added other material which had come down from the wide circle of Johannine disciples (the Prologue and chapter 21), and seems to have included a large body of material from the disciple-evangelist which had not been incorporated into the original edition of the gospel. For instance, if the Last Discourse of Jesus in the original edition came to an end at 14, 31, the redactor added three more chapters of Last Discourse material (15—17), quite like the material in chapter 14 and even duplicating it. But since he did not wish to tamper with the original gospel, he let the original conclusion of 14, 31 stand.

Such a theory respects the ancient tradition that John the Apostle was the authority behind the gospel. It also explains, on the basis of critical analysis, that a disciple of John, here called the disciple-evangelist, was not an eye-witness, and that more than one hand was involved in the writing of the gospel. Moreover it teaches us how to evaluate what we find therein. This gospel contains many valid historical details about Jesus not found in the synoptic gospels: e.g., that after his baptism by John, Jesus was engaged in a baptizing ministry before he changed exclusively to preaching (3, 22); that Jesus' public ministry lasted for several years (see note on 2, 13); that he traveled to Jerusalem on various feasts and met serious opposition long before his death (2, 14ff; chs 5 and 7–10); that he was put to death on the day before Passover (18, 28). These events are not always in order, however, because of the development and editing that ensued.

The fourth gospel is not simply history; the narrative has been organized and adapted to serve the evangelist's theological purposes as well. Among them are: opposition to the synagogue and to such of John the Baptizer's sectarians as tried to exalt their master at Jesus' expense; desire to show that Jesus was the Messiah; desire to convince Christians that their religious belief and practice must be rooted in Jesus. Such theological purposes have caused the evangelist to bring to the fore motifs which, as can be seen by comparison with the synoptic gospels, were not so clear in the synoptic account of Jesus' ministry, e.g., the explicit emphasis on his divinity.

The polemic between the synagogue and the church influenced Johannine language toward harshness especially by reason of the hostility toward Jesus manifested by the authorities—Pharisees and Sadducees—who are referred to frequently as "the Jews" (see note on Jn 1, 19). Such opponents are even described in Jn 8, 44 as springing from their father the devil, whose conduct they imitate in opposing God by rejecting the One whom God has sent. Today, there is a very real effort by Christians and Jews to understand and respect one another and thus to eliminate all embittered criticism.

The final editing of the gospel and arrangement in its present form most probably dates between A.D. 90 and 100. Ephesus is still favored by most scholars as the place of composition, though some have proposed the Syrian city of Antioch.

The chief divisions of the Gospel of John are as follows:
  I: Prologue 1, 1–18
  II: The Book of Signs (1, 19—12, 50)
  III: The Book of Glory (13, 1—20, 31)
  IV: Appendix: The Resurrection Appearances in Galilee (21, 1–25)

THE ACTS OF THE APOSTLES

LUKE is the only one of the evangelists who supplements his gospel with a second volume describing the origin and spread of the Christian communities in New Testament times. He attributes the establishment of these churches to the action of the Holy Spirit, specifically upon Peter (2, 14–18; 4, 8; 15, 8) and Paul (13, 2ff; 16, 6; 20, 22f). Peter was the leading member of the Twelve (1, 13.26) and the recognized authority over the Judaeo-Christian communities (12, 17; 15, 6–12). Paul eventually joined the church at Antioch (11, 25f), which subsequently commissioned him and Barnabas to undertake the spread of the gospel to Asia Minor. This missionary venture generally failed to win the Jews of the diaspora to the gospel, but enjoyed a measure of success among the Gentiles (13, 14—14, 27). Paul's refusal to impose the Mosaic law upon his Gentile converts provoked very strong objection among the Judaeo-Christians of Jerusalem (15, 1), but both Peter and James supported his position (15, 6–21). Paul's second and third missionary journeys (16, 36—21, 16) resulted in the same pattern: of failure among the Jews generally but of some success among the Gentiles.

In Acts, Luke has provided a broad survey of the church's development from the resurrection of Jesus to Paul's first Roman imprisonment, the point at which the book ends. Originally a Judaeo-Christian community in Jerusalem, the church was placed in circumstances impelling it to include within its membership people of other cultures: the Samaritans (8, 4–25), at first an occasional Gentile (8, 26–40; 10, 1–48), and finally the Gentiles on principle (11, 20f). Fear on the part of the Jewish people that Christian messianism, particularly as preached to the Gentiles, threatened their own cultural heritage caused them to be suspicious of Paul's gospel (15, 1–5; 13, 42–45; 28, 17–24). The inability of Christian missioners to allay this apprehension inevitably created a situation wherein the gospel was preached more and more to the Gentiles. Toward the end of Paul's career, the Christian communities, with the exception of those in Palestine itself (9, 31), were mainly of Gentile membership.

In the development of the church from a Judaeo-Christian origin in Jerusalem, with its roots in Jewish religious tradition, to a series of Christian communities among the Gentiles of the Roman Empire, Luke perceives the action of God in history laying open the hearts of all mankind to the divine message of salvation. His approach to the history of the church is predominantly theological. He conceives of the church as a mystery of God introduced into history through the apostolic preaching (1, 21f), which was forced to adapt itself to circumstances and so to carry forward the predestined spread of God's word among men, again in history. His preoccupation with the mystery of the church as the bearer of the word of salvation rules out of his book detailed histories of the various members of the Twelve as well as of the churches founded by Paul. Only the main lines of the roles of Peter and Paul serve Luke's interest. Nonetheless, the historical data he utilizes are of value for the understanding of the church's early life and development and as general background to the Pauline epistles. In the interpretation of Acts, care must be exercised to determine Luke's theological aims and interests and to evaluate his historical data without either exaggerating their literal accuracy or underestimating their factual worth. Concerning the date of Acts, see Introduction of the Gospel according to Luke.

The book of the Acts of the Apostles is divided as follows:
  I: Prologue (1, 1-14)
 II: The Community in Jerusalem Finds Maturity in the Spirit (1, 15—5, 42)
III: Spread of the Church through Persecution in Jerusalem (6, 1—8, 3)
 IV: The Community Carries the Message to Samaria, Syria and Cyprus (8, 4—12, 24)
  V: Mission of Barnabas and Saul (12, 25—15, 35)
 VI: Paul's Mission to the Gentiles (15, 36—21, 14)
VII: Paul the Prisoner Bears Witness to the Resurrection in Jerusalem, Caesarea and Rome (21, 15—28, 31)

THE EPISTLE OF PAUL TO THE ROMANS

CHRISTIANS in Rome seem to have become numerous first among the Jewish population of the city. The Roman historian Suetonius mentions an edict of the Emperor Claudius (died c 49 A.D.) ordering the expulsion of Jews from Rome in connection with a certain "Chrestus," probably an error for "Christus." According to Acts 18, 2, Aquila and Priscilla (or Prisca, as in this epistle) were affected by this edict; cf Rom 16, 3. Since neither early Christian tradition nor Paul's letter to the Romans mentions a founder of the Christian community in Rome, it may be concluded that the Christian faith came to that city through members of the Jewish community of Jerusalem who were Christian converts. About 57 A.D., when Paul wrote the letter, most probably from Corinth, Christians in Rome were predominantly Gentile, with a Judaeo-Christian minority, a circumstance which the majority of scholars see reflected in the letter itself.

At this time Paul was considering a missionary journey to Spain and desired to make Rome his headquarters for the project (15, 22f.28) He was informed about the Roman community (14, 1-11), perhaps by Aquila and Prisca, and it may be assumed that he in turn was known to the Christians there. It would be difficult to explain why he should have written this lengthy letter to them

unless they were unaware of his apostolic role and his whole remarkable history, and would receive his reflections with corresponding interest.

The principal theme of the letter is the relationship between Judaism and Christianity, a topic which Paul judged to be much in the minds of the Roman Christians. Each of these religious faiths claimed to be the way of salvation which established a covenant between God and man and made man the beneficiary of divine gifts. But Christianity regarded itself as the prophetic development and fulfillment of the faith of the Old Testament, declaring that the preparatory Mosaic covenant must now give way to the new and more perfect covenant in Jesus Christ. Paul himself had been the implacable advocate of freedom from the laws of the Mosaic covenant, and he refused to impose them on Gentile converts to Christianity. He had witnessed the personal hostilities that developed between the adherents of the two faiths, and had written his strongly worded letter to the Galatians against those Judaeo-Christians who were persuading Gentile Christian communities to adopt the religious practices of Judaism. For him, the purity of the religious understanding of Jesus as the source of salvation would be seriously impaired if Gentile Christians were obliged to amalgamate the two religious faiths.

Although Paul expressed his grief over Israel's failure to accept Christian messianism (9, 1-8), he remained unsympathetic toward both Jewish and Gentile unbelievers (2 Thes 1, 8ff). This need not seem startling if Paul in fact considered the parousia or second coming of Christ to be a distinct possibility in his own lifetime. His attitude would thus reflect the urgency of conversation and the imminence of the judgment of the world. See notes on 1 Thessalonians 4, 13-18, and on Mark 13, 1-37.

The implication of Paul's exposition of justification by faith rather by the law is that the divine plan of salvation works itself out on a broad theological plane to include the whole of humanity despite the differences in the content of the given religious system to which a human culture is heir.

The Epistle to the Romans contains a powerful exposition of the doctrine of the supremacy of Christ and of faith in him as the source of salvation. It is an implicit plea to the Christians of Rome to hold fast that faith. They are to resist any pressure put on them to accept a doctrine of salvation through works of the law. At the same time they are not to exaggerate Christian freedom through repudiation of law itself.

Romans is a well-constructed epistle. It is divided as follows:
  I: Introduction (1, 1-17)
 II: Humanity without Christ (1, 18—3, 20)
III: Salvation through Faith in Christ (3, 21—5, 21)
 IV: Justification and the Christian Life (6, 1—8, 39)

V: Israel's Present Rejection (9, 1—11, 36)
VI: The Duties of Christians (12, 1—15, 13)
VII: Conclusion (15, 14—16, 27)

THE FIRST EPISTLE OF PAUL TO THE CORINTHIANS

SAINT PAUL established a Christian community in Corinth about the year 50, on his second missionary journey. According to his own testimony in this epistle (written c 56), he began his work in Corinth in "fear and trepidation" (2, 3) because of the city's extreme moral depravity and its pagan cult, which included the practice of religious prostitution. Moderate success attended his efforts among the Jewish Corinthians at first, but they soon turned against him (Acts 18, 1–8). More fruitful was his year-and-a-half mission among the Gentiles (Acts 18, 11), which won to the faith many of the city's poor and unprivileged (1, 26). After his departure, the eloquent and fervent Apollos, an Alexandrian Judaeo-Christian, rendered great service to the Corinthian community. He expounded "from the Scriptures that Jesus is the Messiah" (Acts 18, 27f).

While Paul was in Ephesus on his third missionary journey (16, 8; Acts 19, 1–20), he received disquieting news about Corinth. The community there was displaying open factionalism, certain members identifying themselves with, respectively, the teaching of Paul, of Apollos, of Cephas and others apparently claiming a relationship with Jesus peculiar to themselves alone (1, 12). Christian teaching was being interpreted as a superior wisdom for the initiated few, rather than as the divine means for the humble opening of all hearts to the prophetic word of God in Christ (1, 10—4, 21). The community lacked the moral power to take appropriate action against one of its members who was living publicly in an incestuous union (5, 1–13). Other members engaged in legal conflicts, presenting in pagan courts of law a disedifying portrait of their fellows (6, 1–11); still others had even revived the old practice of religious prostitution (6, 13–20) and participated in sacrifices in the temples of the gods (10, 14–22). Some in the community questioned Paul's apostolic authority and pressed the point that, unlike the other apostles, he did not use the rights of apostleship since he did not accept financial support from the community (9, 15–18). Women appeared at the liturgical assembly without the customary head-covering (11, 2–16), and quarreled over their right to address the assembly (14, 34f).

The community's ills were reflected in the celebration of the eucharistic liturgy itself, when some members behaved clannishly, drank too freely at the agape, and denied Christian social courtesies to the poor among the membership (11, 17–22). Charisms, such as ecstatic prayer and messages, presumed to be due to the impulse of the Holy Spirit, were more highly prized than works of charity (13, 1f.8), and were used at times in a dis-

ordered and even ridiculous way (14, 1–40). There were also members who, despite their belief in the resurrection of Christ, had accepted the opinion of certain peripatetic philosophers against the possibility of general bodily resurrection (15, 1–57).

The lesser problems Paul had to deal with in this epistle concerned matters of conscience discussed among the faithful members of the community: the eating of meats that had been offered to idols (8, 1–13); the use of sex in marriage (7, 1–7); and the attitude to be taken by the unmarried toward marriage in view of the possible nearness of Christ's second coming (7, 8–40). The introductory section of the epistle shows that this general group was in the majority (1, 19), and that it was actually on its behalf that Paul wrote against the threat posed to the community by the views and conduct of the minority.

The epistle illustrates well the mind and character of Paul. He does not stigmatize people by mentioning names. He always treats the questions at issue on the level of the purity of Christian teaching and conduct. Though impelled to insist on his God-given office as founder of the community, and generously including Apollos in this capacity, he nevertheless evaluates his own leading role as that of a servant of God (3, 5–8). On the other hand, he does not hesitate to exercise his authority accordingly as his judgment dictates in every situation, even going so far as to promise a direct confrontation with the recalcitrant should the abuses he scores remain uncorrected (4, 18–21).

Paul writes with confidence in the authority of his apostolic mission. He presumes that the Corinthians will recognize and accept it, despite the deficiencies of their faith. Certain passages in the epistle are of the greatest importance for an understanding of the early Christian teaching on the Eucharist (10, 14–22; 11, 17–34) and on the resurrection of the body (15, 1–57).

THE SECOND EPISTLE OF PAUL TO THE CORINTHIANS

THIS EPISTLE contains Paul's reflections on events that occurred after his first letter had been sent to the Corinthians. He had changed his plan to stay with that community, an intention he had previously announced (1 Cor 16, 5ff), and was criticized by the Corinthian Christians for this; one of them had even publicly reviled him (2, 5). Their attitude caused Paul much anxiety (2, 3f) and greatly strained the relationship between himself and the community he had founded and knew so well (6, 11f Acts 18, 11). It directly impeded his work of ministry at Troas, where he was to be joined by Titus (2, 12f) to receive his personal report on the state of the church at Corinth. Not finding him there, Paul left Troas for Macedonia in search of him. When they finally met, he was greatly relieved, for the letter of reproof Titus had carried to the Corinthians from Paul had won the day at Corinth (7, 5–9). Accordingly, Paul wrote the present letter to confirm the Corinthians' renewed acceptance of his apostolic authority and to prepare them for his coming visit (12, 14; 13, 1).

Although these data do not constitute a complete reconstruction of events in Corinth between the writing of the two Corinthian letters, they are adequate to account for the nature of this second letter, the most subjective of all the Pauline epistles.

The themes of the epistle must be understood in terms of this general background: Paul's suffering and consolation (1, 3–11); his sincerity (1, 12ff); his honesty (1, 15—2, 4); his forgiveness of the offender (2, 5–11); his past anxiety and present relief (2, 12–17); his confidence in the apostolic office despite its hardships (3, 1—6, 10); his plea for frankness (6, 11ff; 7, 2ff); Titus' report upon the effect of the reproachful letter he had brought to the community from Paul (7, 5–16); the appeal concerning the collection for the poor Christians of Jerusalem, delayed because of the troubles within the community (8, 1—9, 15); the reaffirmation of Paul's apostolic authority (10, 1—13, 10).

Many scholars have felt that the lack of continuity in the Second Epistle to the Corinthians and the repetition of material on the same topic (e.g., 2, 14—6, 3 and 10, 1—13, 10; 8, 1–24 and 9, 1–15) are evidence that the epistle was formed from several Pauline letters, including perhaps the letter to the Corinthians written before First Corinthians (1 Cor 5, 9), and the second, severe letter which preceded Second Corinthians (2 Cor 7, 8). However, no theory fragmenting Second Corinthians into several Pauline letters has proved convincing. A satisfactory explanation of the degree of discontinuity and repetition in the letter would be Paul's own state of mind when he composed it. As new thoughts on the themes of his letter occurred to him, he recorded them in the hope that the outpouring of his own heart (6, 11) would ensure the community's faithfulness to him.

The Second Epistle to the Corinthians was written in Macedonia (2 Cor 2, 12f; 7, 5f; 8, 1–4; 9, 2ff), probably in the autumn of 57 A.D., during the course of Paul's third missionary journey (Acts 20, 1f).

THE EPISTLE OF PAUL TO THE GALATIANS

UNTIL the nineteenth century it was assumed that the Epistle to the Galatians was addressed to Christian communities which Paul founded in the interior of Asia Minor on his second missionary journey (Acts 16, 6) and visited on his third (Acts 18, 23). The epistle would then have been written at some time during these journeys between the years 52 and 57. Since the last century, however, many scholars have advanced what is called the South Galatian theory, contending that the epistle was actually written to the communities founded on Paul's first missionary journey in the area of Asia Minor extending from the seacoast inland (Acts 13, 13—14, 27). This premise has also been adopted here. If valid, it places the epistle among Paul's earliest writings, possibly in 48 A.D., or even before, but more probably after the Council of Jerusalem, 49 or 50 A.D. The meeting with James, Cephas, and John on which Paul reports in 2, 1–10 would then be the meeting described by Luke in Acts 15 as the Council itself.

The background facts regarding the Epistle to the Galatians provide a needed explanation of the complex data relative to it in the epistle itself and in Acts. They help to account for the passionate intensity with which Galatians is written.

Paul shows no knowledge of any limitation of the freedom of Gentile Christians in respect to Mosaic law (2, 9). This suggests that Luke's account of the Council of Jerusalem in which that freedom is limited by the provisions of the apostolic decree (Acts 15, 23–29) is a theological construct. After Paul had left Galatia, Judaeo-Christians from Jerusalem came there, and urged the Galatian communities to adopt the practices of the Mosaic law. The "false claimants to the title of brother" (2, 4), as Paul names these preachers who followed him, did not reject Christ as Savior in favor of the law. But, holding to the Christian doctrine of his central role, they nevertheless advocated the law as a highly beneficial addition to Christian living, and appealed for precedent to the actual practice in Palestine under Cephas (2, 1–10). They made light of Paul's apostolic role, holding him to be less informed than the Twelve (1, 11–24) because he had not been a disciple of Jesus during the ministry. They succeeded in disturbing and confusing the consciences of the Galatians, who were tending more and more to follow their teaching as a surer way of salvation (3, 1).

This subtle form of religiosity evoked from Paul a resounding declaration of the true nature of justification by faith in Christ, which frees the conscience from the Mosaic law as a principle of man's justice before God. The process thus begun in Galatians, of reflecting intensively on the meaning of the Christian gospel, eventually led Paul to his more far-reaching and profound exposition in the Epistle to the Romans.

The Epistle to the Galatians is divided as follows:
  I: Introduction (1, 1–10)
  II: Paul's Defense of His Authority and Doctrine (1, 11—2, 21)
  III: Christian Faith and Liberty (3, 1—4, 31)
  IV: Exhortation to Christian Living (5, 1—6, 10)
  V: Conclusion (6, 11–18)

BOOKS OF THE NEW TESTAMENT

THE EPISTLE OF PAUL TO THE EPHESIANS

EARLY CHRISTIAN tradition, beginning with Irenaeus and Clement of Alexandria in the late second century, unhesitatingly ascribed this epistle to St. Paul. Since the early nineteenth century, however, critical scholarship has considered the word-usage, style, comparison with Colossians, the epistle's concept of the church, as well as the doctrine put forward by the writer, to be the basis for strong doubts about its Pauline authorship. This divergence between the two capital sources of opinion on the origin of Ephesians makes it impossible to give a categorical pronouncement for or against authorship by Paul. He was probably not the author of Ephesians in the same sense as of other epistles such as Romans, Galatians, 1 and 2 Corinthians. Whatever the epistle's literary origin, however, the author considered its teachings to be in the Pauline tradition (1, 1; 3, 1); and for purposes of interpreting the text itself, it is practical to adopt the clear implication therein that Paul is its author. If Ephesians is analyzed within the context of Pauline writings, the question of its relationship to the thought of Colossians and other letters of Paul may be fruitfully studied.

It seems certain that this epistle was not specifically addressed to the Christians of Ephesus. Paul had labored there for well over two years (Acts 19, 10), and would hardly have written so impersonally to a community with which he was intimately acquainted. Important early manuscripts (Vaticanus and Sinaiticus) omit the words *at Ephesus* in 1, 1. If Ephesians is the letter referred to in Colossians 4, 16, it may well have been addressed to a number of Christian communities, a possibility that would account for its impersonal character. What is called the letter to the Ephesians is traditionally regarded as having been written by Paul from prison—Colossians, Philippians, Philemon, and Ephesians are in fact known as the "captivity epistles." If the letter is authentically Pauline, it was probably written, as tradition has held, during Paul's first (?) Roman imprisonment, 61–63 A.D.

Ephesians consists of a greeting (1, 1f); a doxology of the greatest importance for the cosmic significance it attaches to Christ (1, 3–14); reflections on the Christian mystery of salvation (1, 15–22) as well as the mystery of the church (2, 22—3, 13); a prayer for the Christian community (3, 14–21); a discussion of the practical implications of the Christian mysteries (4, 1—6, 20), with special attention to family life and a famous reflection on the theology of Christian marriage (5, 22–23); and a friendly conclusion (6, 21–24).

THE EPISTLE OF PAUL TO THE PHILIPPIANS

THE CHRISTIAN community at Philippi dates from about 50 A.D., when Paul, apparently in the company of Luke (Acts 16, 10–40), visited the city on his second missionary journey. On his third journey he again visited Philippi (Acts 20, 1f). The city had a proud history. It was founded by Philip of Macedonia, father of Alexander the Great, and was the scene of the defeat of Mark Antony by Octavian in 42 B.C. After this event it became a Roman colony, and its citizens were granted the right of Roman citizenship. Their esteem for this privilege is reflected in Luke's account of Paul's treatment in Philippi (Acts 16, 35–40).

Describing himself in the present epistle as a prisoner (1, 7.17) facing a possibly unfavorable outcome to his trial (1, 19–26), he three times warns the Philippians against the enemies of their faith (1, 28; 3, 2.18f). He also gives them news of Epaphroditus, one of their number, who had become extremely ill while attending to Paul's needs (2, 25–30). He expresses his own deep affection for the Philippians (1, 3–11), and thanks them warmly for the donations they have sent him (4, 11–20). He exhorts them to be faithful to their vocation (2, 12–18), and to maintain their present unity of belief (2, 1f; 3, 15f; 4, 1), mentioning only one instance of disharmony (4, 2). He ponders the favorable effect his imprisonment has had on the spread of the gospel (1, 12–26), and points to the disinterested sacrifice of Christ as the transcendent formative rule for every Christian action (2, 1–11); proposing his own complete abnegation for the sake of Christ as the example to be followed against the false teaching of the Judaizers (3, 3–18).

The somewhat rambling quality of the epistle has led certain scholars to suggest that several brief letters of Paul to the Philippians were formed into this single composition. The alternative view is that the apostle dictated portions of the letter on separate occasions. Traditionally, Philippians has been assigned to the period of Paul's first Roman imprisonment (61–63 A.D.). In recent years Ephesus has been proposed by a growing number of scholars as the place of composition. It is known to have had a praetorian guard (alluded to in Philippians 4, 22), and therefore probably a judicial authority. It can readily be assumed that Luke did not record all of Paul's imprisonments in Acts; cf 2 Cor 6, 5. Others, however, consider the prison at Caesarea to have been the place (Acts 23, 23.31ff). If the epistle was written in Ephesus, it is to be dated about the year 53; if in Caesarea, about five years later; if in Rome, about 62. Its famous passage on the *kenosis* or emptying of Christ (2, 5–11), probably taken from a Christian hymn, was of inestimable value for the early Christian understanding of the mystery of the incarnation.

The Epistle to the Philippians is divided as follows:
Greetings (1, 1f)
  I: The Example of Paul (1, 3–26)
 II: Pleas for Christian Heroism (1, 27—2, 18)
III: Paul's Assistants and Plans (2, 19–30)
 IV: Christian Dedication (3, 1–21)
  V: Exhortations to Virtue (4, 1–23)

THE EPISTLE OF PAUL TO THE COLOSSIANS

THE CHRISTIAN community at Colossae was not established by Paul, who had never visited there (1, 4; 2, 1), but by Epaphras (1, 7; 4, 12; Phlm 23), to whom Paul refers as a member of the Colossian group. He was probably one of Paul's Ephesian converts. A second likely inference is that he had requested the apostle's aid in the matter of certain religious tenets of non-Christian origin which were influencing the Colossian community. The epistle's two christological passages (1, 15–20; 2, 9–15) are set in contexts suggesting that certain doctrines having to do with angelic spirits (1, 16) and ascetical practices (2, 16) were being advocated at Colossae in a way that detracted from the person of Christ (1, 17.20) and distorted the nature of the Christian life (2, 16–23).

Without entering into debate over the existence of angelic spirits or their function, Paul simply affirms that Christ possesses the sum total of redemptive power (1, 19) and that the spiritual renewal of the human person occurs through contact in baptism with the person of Christ, who died and rose again for man's justification (2, 9–14). It is unnecessary for the Christian to be concerned about placating spirits (2, 15) or avoiding imagined defilement through ascetical practices in regard to food and drink (2, 20–23). True Christian asceticism consists in the conquering of personal sins (3, 5–10) and the practice of love of neighbor in accordance with the standard set by Christ (3, 12–16).

Paul commends the community as a whole (1, 3–8), which seems to indicate that, though the Colossians have been under a certain pressure to adopt the false doctrines, they have not yet succumbed. The apostle expresses his prayerful concern for them (1, 9–14). His preaching has cost him persecution, suffering, and imprisonment, but he regards these as the completion of the sufferings of Christ (i.e., the church?), a required discipline for the sake of the gospel (1, 24—2, 4). His instructions to the Christian family and to slaves and masters require a new spirit of reflection and action. Love, obedience, and service are to be rendered *in the Lord* (3, 18—4, 1).

Paul wrote the letter to the Colossians while in prison, but his several imprisonments leave the specific place and date of composition uncertain. On this point the same problem of determination exists as with Ephesians and Philippians (see the Introduction to these epistles). The highly developed Christology of Colossians would seem to indicate a later imprisonment, most likely the traditional Roman house arrest in which he enjoyed a certain restricted freedom in preaching (61–63 A.D.).

The Epistle to the Colossians is divided as follows:
  I: Introduction (1, 1–14)
 II: The Preeminence of Christ (1, 15—2, 3)
III: Warnings against False Teachers (2, 4–23)

IV: The Ideal Christian Life in the World
  (3, 1—4, 6)
 V: Conclusion (4, 7–18)

THE FIRST EPISTLE OF PAUL TO THE THESSALONIANS

PAUL'S formation of a Christian community at Thessalonica on his second missionary journey (Acts 17, 1–9) produced a considerable disturbance among the Jews residing there. To prevent further disorder he and his companion, Silas, agreed to leave the city (Acts 17, 10). However, he revisited the community on his third journey (Acts 20, 1f). Indications from 1 Thessalonians itself and from Acts permit the almost certain conclusion that the epistle was written only a short time after Paul's departure from Thessalonica (1 Thes 2, 17). In that interval he had been in Athens (3, 1; Acts 17, 16), and from there had sent Timothy to the Thessalonians (3, 2). He now writes to them from Corinth (1, 7; Acts 18, 1–18). Gallio is mentioned as proconsul of Achaia (Acts 18, 12–17) during Paul's Corinthian sojourn of more than a year; and since Gallio assumed the office in 51 or 52 A.D., the letter is to be dated at that time.

Paul writes after receiving Timothy's report on the Thessalonian community (3, 6). Deeply grateful for the information it conveys (1, 2f), he is also moved to declare how valuable to his own work the news of their conversion has been (1, 4–10). Probably to offset slanders uttered against him from outside the community after his departure from Thessalonica, he recalls his undemanding manner of life among them (2, 1–12). He reminds them of the prophetic character of the Christian message and relates it to the harassment they continue to suffer at the hands of the Jews (2, 14ff). He is satisfied of their firm adherence to the gospel, and prays that he may be able to visit them soon (3, 6–10). He exhorts them to greater care in carrying out the gospel precepts, particularly those pertaining to right sexual conduct (4, 1–8). He urges them to live peaceably and to avoid idleness (4, 11f).

Paul next turns his attention to the most serious problem which Timothy's visit to the community has brought to light: their excessive sorrow over the death of members of the community, who are thought to be deprived thereby of the joy of the second coming of Christ. Paul appeals to his own knowledge of Christ's teaching to affirm that the resurrection of the dead is to occur before the parousia, so that Christians living at the time are to have no advantage over those who have died (4, 13–18). He reminds them of Christ's words on the suddenness of the parousia and on the need of constant spiritual readiness for it (5, 1–11). He concludes with a request that they esteem those who occupy positions of authority in the community (5, 12f), and show the proper attitude toward one another in the Christian spirit

(5, 14f). His final words are a prayer that they may be ready at the glorious coming of Christ (5, 23f).

The epistle is of great doctrinal value, revealing as it does the faith of the community. It also manifests the care and labor which were expended in instructing the Christian communities in New Testament times.

The principal divisions of 1 Thessalonians are as follows:
  I: Introduction (1, 1–10)
 II: Relations with the Thessalonians (2, 1—4, 12)
III: The Lord's Second Coming (4, 13—5, 28)

THE SECOND EPISTLE OF PAUL TO THE THESSALONIANS

MOST SCHOLARS accept the authenticity of the second letter to the Thessalonians, as being written in Paul's characteristic language and style. Both letters were written from Corinth, and within a short time of each other, since they show that the apostle is still accompanied by his companions of the second missionary journey, Silas and Timothy (2 Thes 1, 1; Acts 18, 5).

Despite the remarkable literary similarities in the letters, however, the second is the more impersonal, its approach to the subject being somewhat set and formal in tone. The explanation may well lie in the apostle's own less serene circumstances and state of mind, as well as in the disturbing news he had received from Thessalonica after the first letter was written.

He himself is experiencing the difficulties caused by *confused and evil men* (2 Thes 3, 1ff). Meanwhile, persecution against the Thessalonian Christians has intensified (2 Thes 1, 3–10), and the situation among them is worsened by idleness due to the spreading expectation of the parousia (2 Thes 3, 6–12), despite Paul's admonitions in his first letter. He now repeats that the community's life is not to be guided by the false belief that the second coming is imminent, i.e., a day-to-day possibility, whether the alleged source of the belief be the oracular utterance of a self-styled prophet or a letter supposedly written by himself (2 Thes 2, 1ff). He originally taught the Thessalonians, he reminds them, that certain religious events must occur before the parousia can be expected (2 Thes 2, 3–12). Finally, he knows that the community has its refactory members from whom he cannot anticipate simple acquiescence to his teaching, and he gives directions regarding them (2 Thes 3, 14).

The letters to the Thessalonians present incontrovertible evidence that the expectation of the parousia played a capital role in the development of New Testament thought. There is no evidence that this expectation attained in other communities the strength it came to exert in Thessalonica; but the data of 1 and 2 Thessalonians compel its recognition as a conditioning element in the presentation of doctrine while the literature of the New Testament developed.

The principal divisions of 2 Thessalonians are as follows:
  I: Introduction (1, 1–12)
 II: The Lord's Second Coming (2, 1–17)
III: Exhortation (3, 1–18)

THE FIRST EPISTLE OF PAUL TO TIMOTHY

THE THREE LETTERS, 1 and 2 Timothy, and Titus, were first named "pastoral epistles" in the eighteenth century. From the late second century to the nineteenth, their Pauline authorship went unchallenged. Since then, discussion of that question has reached an impasse. Some scholars are convinced that Paul could not have been responsible for the vocabulary and style of the letters, their concept of church organization, or the theological expressions found in them. Others believe just as firmly that, on the basis of statistical evidence, the vocabulary and style are Pauline, even if at first sight the contrary appears to be the case; that the concept of church organization in these epistles is not as advanced as the opponents of Pauline authorship make it out to be, the notion of a hierarchical order in a religious community having existed among the Jews even before the time of Christ, as the scrolls of Qumran indicate; and, finally, that there are affinities between the theological thought of the pastorals and that of unquestionably genuine letters of Paul. A third group, while conceding a degree of validity to the position of the other two, suggests that either the apostle made use of a secretary (possibly Luke; see 2 Tm 4, 11) who was responsible for the composition of the letters, or that they are the work of an anonymous writer compiling traditions about Paul in his later years.

The problem of the literary authorship of the pastorals has not disproved the authenticity of their content. If Paul is considered their more immediate author, they are to be dated between the end of his first Roman imprisonment (Acts 28, 16) and his execution under Nero (63–67 A.D.); if they are regarded as only more remotely Pauline, their date may be as late as the early second century.

The first of the pastorals, 1 Timothy is presented as having been written from Macedonia. Timothy, whom Paul converted, was of mixed Jewish and Gentile parentage (Acts 16, 1ff). He was the apostle's companion on both the second and third missionary journeys (Acts 16, 3; 19, 22), and was often sent by him on special missions (1 Thes 3, 2; 1 Cor 4, 17; Acts 19, 22). In 1 Timothy (1, 3) he is described as the administrator of the entire Ephesian community. The epistle instructs him on his duty to restrain false and useless teaching (1, 3–11; 4, 1–5; 6, 3–16); proposes principles pertaining to his relationship to the older members of the community

(5, 1f) and to the presbyters (5, 17–25); gives rules for aid to widows (5, 3–8), and their selection for charitable ministrations (5, 9–16); deals with liturgical celebrations (2, 1–15), the selection of men for the offices of bishop and deacon (3, 1–13), the relations of slaves and their masters (6, 1f), and the obligations of the wealthier members of the community (6, 17ff). It also reminds Timothy of the prophetic character of his office (1, 12–18), and encourages him in his exercise of it (4, 6–16). The central passage of the letter (3, 14ff) expresses the chief motive that should guide the conduct of Timothy—preservation of the purity of the church's doctrine. On this same note the epistle concludes (6, 20–21).

THE SECOND EPISTLE OF PAUL TO TIMOTHY

THE AUTHORSHIP and date of this epistle are discussed in the Introduction to the First Epistle of Paul to Timothy. The letter portrays Paul as a prisoner (1, 8.16; 2, 9) in Rome (1, 17), and indicates that Timothy is in Ephesus (4, 12). It reveals that, with rare exceptions, Christians have not rallied to Paul's support (1, 15–18), and takes a pessimistic view of the outcome of his case (4, 16). It describes Paul as fully aware of what impends, looking to God, not to men, for his deliverance (4, 3–8.18). It recalls with affectionate remembrance his mission days with Timothy (1, 3ff; cf Acts 16, 1–4). It points to his preaching of the gospel as the reason for his imprisonment and offers Timothy as a motive of steadfastness his own example of firmness in faith despite adverse circumstances (1, 6–14). The epistle suggests that Timothy should prepare others to replace himself as Paul has prepared him for his own replacement (2, 1f), urging him not to desist out of fear from preserving and spreading the Christian message (2, 3–7). It presents the resurrection of Jesus and his messianic role as the heart of the gospel for which Paul has been ready to lay down his life (2, 8f), not only to express fully his own conviction but to support the conviction of others (2, 10–13).

This letter, like the preceding one, urges Timothy to protect the community from the inevitable impact of false teaching (2, 14—3, 9), without fear of the personal attacks which may result (3, 10–14). It recommends that he rely on the power of the Scriptures and on the positive proposal of the doctrine (3, 15—4, 2) without being troubled by those who do not accept him (4, 3ff). The epistle observes in passing that Paul has need of his reading materials and his cloak (4, 13), and what will be best of all, a visit from Timothy.

THE EPISTLE OF PAUL TO TITUS

THE AUTHORSHIP and date of the Epistle to Titus are discussed in the Introduction to 1 Timothy. Titus was a Gentile Christian, apparently from Antioch (Gal 2, 1).

According to 2 Corinthians (2, 13; 7, 6.13f), he was with Paul on his third missionary journey; there is, however, no mention of him in Acts. Besides being the bearer of Paul's severe letter to the Corinthians (2 Cor 7, 6ff), he had the responsibility of taking up the collection in Corinth for the Christian community of Jerusalem (2 Cor 8, 6.16.23). In the present letter (1, 5), he is mentioned as the administrator of the Christian community in Crete, charged with the task of organizing it through the appointment of presbyters and bishops (1, 5–9; here the two terms refer to the same personages).

The letter instructs Titus about the character of the men he is to choose in view of the pastoral difficulties peculiar to Crete (1, 5–16). It suggests the special individual and social virtues which the various age groups and classes in the Christian community should be encouraged to acquire (2, 1–10). The motives for improving one's personal character are to be found preeminently in the mysteries of the incarnation and the second coming of Christ (2, 11–15; 3, 5ff). The community is to be fashioned into a leaven for Christianizing the social world about it (3, 1ff). Good works are to be the evidence of their faith in God (3, 8); those who engage in religious controversy are, after suitable warning, to be ignored (3, 9ff).

The material in Titus is similar to that in 1 Timothy; it is, however, differently oriented.

The principal divisions of the Epistle to Titus are as follows:
I: Introduction (1, 1–4)
II: Pastoral Charge (1, 5–16)
III: Teaching the Christian Life (2, 1—3, 15)

THE EPISTLE OF PAUL TO PHILEMON

THE DATE OF this epistle is discussed in the Introduction to Ephesians. Its Pauline authorship is considered to be incontestable. The interesting fact is that this very personal and undoubtedly private letter was conserved and made public by the second century in a society in which human slavery was an accepted part of the culture.

The letter concerns Onesimus, slave of Philemon, a well-to-do Christian of Colossae (Col 4, 9). Onesimus escaped Philemon's service (v 15), and was guilty of theft in the process (v 18). Paul converted Onesimus to the gospel (v 10) and persuaded him to return to his fomer condition (v 12); this had been his teaching concerning slaves from the first; cf 1 Cor 7, 21. Evidently Onesimus was fearful of the possible punishment that would be meted out to him, but Paul was confident both of Philemon's understanding of Christian teaching (15f) and of his own influence over Philemon (19f). The apostle promised to visit Philemon, meanwhile placing him under a telling kind of moral pressure to accede to his request and receive back his slave with nothing but kindness.

The delicate tone of this letter reflects, against the legal fact of slavery at the time, the incipient Christian insight into its injustice. Paul does not attack the institution, for the small Christian communities were in no position to raise such an issue in a dictatorial political structure. Also, the fact that they regarded the second coming of Christ as an occurrence possible within their lifetime lessened the impulse to any abrupt amd widespread change. That Onesimus the slave was "brother" to Philemon, his legal master (v 16), was a revolutionary idea in the context of the times.

THE EPISTLE TO THE HEBREWS

THERE ARE numerous features of this epistle that indicate authorship other than that of St. Paul the apostle. There is the high quality of its style, which makes Hebrews one of the distinguished works of the New Testament. Its literary structure intermingles doctrinal teaching and moral exhortation. The manner of citing the Old Testament is different, and the system of exegesis it follows reflects Hellenistic rather than Palestinian Judaism.

As early as the end of the second century the Eastern churches had accepted Hebrews as an inspired work composed by Paul, but until the second half of the fourth century the churches of the West questioned its Pauline authorship. Since the letter of Clement of Rome to the Corinthians, written about 96 A.D., cites the Epistle to the Hebrews, it is necessary to date the letter before that time. The identity of its author is a matter of pure speculation. Among those considered, Apollos seems more likely than Luke and Barnabas (cf Acts 18, 24), although nothing is known of his history beyond his activity in Corinth (1 Cor 1, 12; 3, 5). The data of the epistle indicate that its author wrote to a specific Christian community, or at least to communities in a particular area (13, 23; 6, 11f; 10, 19–25), but the allusions are insufficient to permit a judgment on their location. Commentators today are sharply divided on whether the addressees of the epistle were Judaeo-Christian or predominantly Gentile Christian, although the latter view is regarded with slightly more favor. The title "To the Hebrews" may merely represent an inference of the late second century: that the epistle's extensive use of the Old Testament points to its having been addressed to Judaeo-Christians.

The letter seeks to strengthen the practical faith of its recipients, and appeals to them for perseverence (6, 11f) despite harassment (12, 7–13) from forces outside the community (13, 3). Their knowledge and love of Christ hardly support the opinion of those who, on the basis of 6, 4–8, consider them to have been Judaeo-Christians on the point of reversion to Judaism.

The author begins with a reminder of the mysteries of the incarnation and exaltation of Jesus (1, 3), which proclaimed him the culminator of God's word to humanity (1, 1ff). He dwells upon the dignity of the Person of Christ, superior to the angels who, according to Old Testament tradition, appeared in order to make God's plans known to men (1, 4—2, 2). Christ is God's final word of salvation, communicated (in association with accredited witnesses to his teaching: 2, 3f; cf Acts 1, 2ff) not merely by word but through the suffering humanity common to Jesus and to the rest of men (2, 5–16). This enactment of salvation went beyond the pattern known to Moses, faithful prophet though he was of God's word; for Jesus as high priest personally expiated sin and was faithful to God with the fidelity of God's own Son (2, 17—3, 6).

Just as the infidelity of the people thwarted Moses' effort to save them all, so the infidelity of any Christian thwarts God's plan in Christ (3, 6—4, 13). Christians are to reflect that it is their humanity which Jesus assumed with all its defects except its sinfulness, and that he bore the burden of it to his death out of obedience to God. This work of his Son God declared to be the cause of salvation for all (4, 14—5, 10). Although Christians recognize this fundamental doctrine, they may grow weary of its repetition and therefore require other reflections to stimulate their faith (5, 11—6, 20).

The author of Hebrews presents to his Christian readers for their reflection the everlasting priesthood of Christ (7, 1–28), a priesthood which fulfills the promise of the Old Testament (8, 1–13). It also provides the meaning God ultimately intended in the sacrifices of the Old Testament (9, 1–28): these were symbols of the unique sacrifice of Christ which alone obtains forgiveness of the sins of mankind (10, 1–18). Any trial of faith the readers of the epistle may have should resolve itself through consideration of the reality of Jesus' actual existence in the heavenly sanctuary, his foreordained parousia, and the fruits they have already enjoyed through their faith (11, 19–39). It is in the nature of faith to trust the intangible (11, 1ff) which in God's providence one day becomes reality, as the Old Testament itself demonstrates (11, 4–40). This truth shines forth throughout the life of Christ. Despite the afflictions of his ministry, he remained confident of God's final intervention to ensure his resurrection and triumph (12, 1ff). Life's difficulties have meaning when they are accepted as God's discipline (12, 4–13). The message of the gospel is the word of Christ (12, 18–29), advocating peace among men (12, 14–17) and reverence toward all (13, 1–4), respect for authority (13, 7f), and complete reliance upon Christ for holiness of life (13, 9–17).

The principal divisions of the Epistle to the Hebrews are as follows:
I: Introduction (1, 1–4)
II: The Son Higher than the Angels (1, 5—2, 18)

THE EPISTLE OF JAMES

THE TITLE "catholic" gradually came into use to designate seven New Testament epistles: JAMES; 1, 2 and 3 JOHN; 1 and 2 PETER; and JUDE. It first appears in reference to 1 John in the writings of Apollonius about 197 A.D., and later in reference to all these epistles in the church historian Eusebius (260–340 A.D.). The title supposes the epistles in question to lack specific addressees and therefore to be directed to the whole church. This, however, is not the case for 2 and 3 John. With the exception of 1 Peter and 1 John, the inspired character of these catholic epistles was disputed in the early church, and finally settled in their favor only at the beginning of the fifth century.

The Epistle of James has a general addressee: *To the twelve tribes in the dispersion* (1, 1). Its content, however, affords no evidence that the author wrote to non-Christian Jews outside Palestine. Scholarly opinion concerning addressees is undecided between Judaeo-Christian communities outside Palestine and Christians generally. The author concerns himself entirely with Christian conduct. He writes in the spirit of Old Testament wisdom literature (Proverbs, Sirach, Wisdom) and of the moral teaching of Tobit. He is influenced by the tradition of moral exhortation within Judaism, as is indicated by similarities between his letter and extra-canonical Jewish literature, e.g., *The Testament of the Twelve Patriarchs; 1 Enoch; The Manual of Discipline* discovered at Qumran.

Some forty-eight verses in James reveal the influence of sayings of Jesus, especially those in Matthew's Sermon on the Mount. However, except for two allusions to Jesus (1, 1; 2, 1) and one to the parousia (5, 7), the epistle does not relate its moral exhortation to Christology or to the authoritative teaching of Jesus. The force of its teaching is made to rest on the reputation of its author, *James, a servant of God and of the Lord Jesus Christ* (1, 1). The author is a known figure and possesses a standing enabling him to speak with authority.

Of the various personages in the New Testament bearing this name, the James mentioned by Paul in Galatians 2, 9 as one of the pillars of the church in Palestine well meets the requirements for the authorship of this epistle. He is designated by Paul, not as one of the Twelve, but as *the brother of the Lord* (Gal 1, 19). The risen Christ made a significant appearance to him (1 Cor 15, 7). James was the administrator of the Jerusalem community (Acts 12, 17), and for this reason played a leading role in the apostolic Council (Acts 15, 13–21). He was the adviser of Paul on the latter's arrival in Jerusalem after the third missionary journey (Acts 21, 17–25). He is probably to be identified as one of the relatives of Jesus who did not believe in him during the ministry; cf Mk 6, 13; Jn 7, 2–5.

Though not all scholars are satisfied that James, leader of the Jerusalem community, is the author, it must be conceded that the epistle is datable before 62 A.D., when, according to Josephus, James was executed in Jerusalem. Nevertheless, scholars who do not admit James of Jerusalem as the author of the epistle select a date for it toward the end of the first century.

The Epistle of James has acquired special prominence in Christendom because of Martin Luther's claim that its emphasis on good works does not agree with St. Paul's doctrine of justification by faith, and because the Council of Trent declared that James 5, 14f pertains to the promulgation of the sacrament of the Anointing of the Sick.

THE FIRST EPISTLE OF PETER

THERE IS abundant evidence in this epistle that *scattered strangers* in 1, 1 refers to Gentile Christian communities (1, 14.18; 2, 9f; 4, 3f; cf Introduction to James). They are envisioned as the new people of God, aliens in the pagan world. The place-names in 1, 1 indicate that the epistle was intended for Christian communities in Asia Minor, but it is uncertain whether those founded by Paul are also included.

Early Christian tradition, starting with Irenaeus at the beginning of the third century, unhesitatingly ascribed the epistle to Peter. Since the early nineteenth century, however, many scholars have considered it a pseudonymous work. Those who defend its Petrine authorship hold that certain data in the epistle favor the traditional view: its allusions to the sufferings of Jesus (2, 21–24; 3, 18; 4, 1); its recollections of his sayings (1, 6–12; Jn 1, 10f; 16, 20; Mt 5, 10; 13, 17); and its relationship to the kerygmatic speeches attributed to Peter in Acts (1, 16–22; 2, 14–36; 3, 12–26; 4, 8–12). Such evidence, though valuable, is not conclusive for Petrine authorship since other Christians of the first century familiar with the church's teachings could have been responsible for these formulations. For those who believe Peter wrote the epistle, it must be dated before 64–67 A.D., the period within which his execution under Nero took place. Those who regard it as a pseudonymous work date it at 90–95 A.D. It is generally conceded that its place of composition was Rome—the *Babylon* referred to in 5, 13.

Unlike the Epistle of James, this letter presents the moral exhortation which is its dominant feature in close relationship to Christian doctrine: the Trinity of persons in God (1, 2f.12; 4, 14); the redemptive value of Jesus' death and resurrection (1, 3; 3, 21f); the sinfulness of man (1, 18; 2, 24), whom God destined to be holy (1, 15f). Some scholars are of the opinion that 1 Peter 1, 3—2, 10 is taken substantially from an early Christian baptismal liturgy. Whether this view is correct or not, the passages in question are among the clearest expositions on the meaning of Christian baptism to be found in the New Testament.

THE SECOND EPISTLE OF PETER

EARLY CHRISTIAN tradition was not so impressed by the claim of Petrine authorship of this epistle (1, 1.14.16ff; 3, 1.15f) as to concede its authenticity without question. Both Origen (185–254) and St. Jerome (342–420) found it debatable. In the early fifth century the epistle was accepted into the canon of the Scriptures.

The chief reason for concluding that 2 Peter was not composed by the chief of the apostles is its discussion of the parousia (3, 1–13). The main purpose of the epistle was to meet the difficulty caused in many minds by the non-fulfillment of the expectation of Christ's second coming. This difficulty could not have arisen in the lifetime of Peter, who died between the years 64 and 67 A.D. Only after the destruction of Jerusalem, in 70 A.D., did Christians begin slowly to realize that the parousia was reserved for a date in the more remote future. The epistle was written at a time when Christian teaching was placing less emphasis on the proximity of the parousia, and therefore not while Peter was still living. Scholars add other arguments against Petrine authorship from the epistle's vocabulary and theology, and from its clear relationship to Jude—without, however, removing all doubt on the question.

It is not unreasonable to conclude that 2 Peter was written by an unknown author who followed the pseudonymous convention of the time in order to attract readers to his work. The date of composition is conjectural. Some think that the author was close enough to the tradition of Petrine teaching to assume the important name Peter, but it is probable that he was a third- or fourth-generation Christian who wrote in the period between 100 and 125. The letter is addressed to Christians generally (1, 1), without giving any indication of its place of composition.

The epistle is well composed, leading gradually to its discussion of the parousia. It reminds its readers of the divine authenticity of Christ's teaching (1, 3f), continues reflections on Christian conduct (1, 5–15), then returns to the exalted dignity of Jesus by incorporating in the text the apostolic witness to his transfiguration (1, 16ff). It takes up the question of the interpretation of Scripture by pointing out that it is possible to misunderstand the sacred writings (1, 19—2, 1) and that divine punishment will be visited upon false teachers (2, 2–22). It explains that the parousia is the doctrine of Jesus and of the apostles and is therefore an eventual certainty (3, 1–13); at the same time it warns that the meaning of St. Paul's writing on this question should not be distorted (3, 14–18).

THE FIRST EPISTLE OF JOHN

EARLY CHRISTIAN tradition attributed this letter to John the apostle. Subsequently, the majority of scholars have concluded, from its resemblance to the fourth gospel in style, vocabulary, and ideas, that one author actually was responsible for both works. These resemblances are not so compelling as absolutely to exclude the possibility of separate authors, as some critics have shown. But it is very probable that the person who composed the fourth gospel also wrote 1 John. On the identity of this author, see the Introduction to the gospel itself.

The opening of the epistle does not state to whom it is addressed, but the data indicate that it was written to specific Christian communities some of whose members were advocating false doctrines (2, 18f.26; 3, 7). These errors are here recognized and rejected (4, 4); although their advocates have left the community (2, 19), the threat posed by them remains (3, 11). They have refused to acknowledge that Jesus is the Christ (2, 22) the Son of God (2, 23) who came into the world as true man (4, 2). They are difficult people to deal with, claiming special knowledge of God but disregarding the divine commandments (2, 4), particularly the commandment of love of neighbor (4, 8), and refusing to accept faith in Christ as the source of sanctification (1, 6; 2, 6.9). Thus they are denying the redemptive value of Jesus' death (5, 6). Scholars generally agree that the group so stigmatized had adopted some form of Gnosticism, but as yet it has not been identified with any specific body of heretical teaching.

The epistle is of particular value for its declaration of the humanity and divinity of Christ as apostolic teaching (1, 1–4), and for its development of the intrinsic connection between Christian moral conduct and Christian doctrine. Although the author recognizes that Christian doctrine presents intangible mysteries of faith about Christ, he insists that the concrete Christian life brings to light the deeper realities of the gospel. The epistle is generally held to date at the same time as the fourth gospel, c 90–100 A.D.

THE SECOND EPISTLE OF JOHN

THE SECOND and Third Epistles of John are of the same length (probably determined by the practical consideration of the writing space on one piece of papyrus). Each is in the usual letter format, and treats a specific problem. In each, the writer calls himself "the elder"; and their common authorship is further evidenced internally by similarities in style and wording, especially in the introductions and conclusions. The mention in each of an impending visit by the elder to the respective community (2 Jn 12; 3 Jn 14) has led to the suggestion that they were written about the same time and perhaps carried by the same messenger to the two localities, both on the elder's proposed route of travel. The traditionally assigned place and date of composition, Ephesus in the 90's, are plausible.

The identity of the elder is a problem. Certainly, more than age is implied in the use of the title. If the man was simply one of the group of elders or presbyters who were officials in Christian churches by the latter part of the first century (Jas 5, 14; 1 Pt 5, 1; 1 Tm 5, 17), the absence of a proper name that would distinguish him from the other elders is curious. Seemingly, the title "elder" was also applicable to an apostle (1 Pt 1, 5); and it was certainly applicable to the disciple of an apostle, as we learn from Papias and Irenaeus. It is doubtful that the elder who wrote 3 John was an apostle, for he admits that the leader of the community involved in the letter ignores his authority. One can scarcely believe that a member of the Christian community, even a leader, could resist an apostle, especially at this time toward the close of the century, when the Twelve were venerated as the foundation of the church (Rv 21, 14).

On the other hand, the elder is important enough to exercise a certain authority over communities other than his own, to teach authoritatively and brand others as heretical, to send out missionary preachers, etc. The most probable supposition is that the elder was the disciple of an apostle, with a claim to some of the apostolic prestige and authority—a claim not, however, accepted by all. The traditional association with John, son of Zebedee, may mean that the elder was one of John's prominent disciples. Whether or not he is the same disciple who was the fourth evangelist is disputed; see the Introduction to the Gospel according to John.

The Second Epistle is addressed to "a Lady who is elect and to her children." Since the contents of the letter are scarcely appropriate to an individual, scholars assume that the elder was using an accepted literary device by personifying a Christian community as a woman.

Love and truth are the great themes of the letter. The elder encourages the Christians of this community to let their Christianity show forth in their daily lives in two ways: first, by truly adhering to the great commandment of mutual love; and second, by adhering to the truth about Jesus. There is critical need for this admonition because heretical missionaries are about to descend upon the community. The heresy in question is apparently the one referred to in 1 Jn 4, 2—a denial of the reality of the incarnation of Jesus. The elder urgently insists that no hospitality be shown to these false teachers lest they use the opportunity to infiltrate the community.

THE THIRD EPISTLE OF JOHN

GENERAL questions concerning format and authorship are adverted to in the Introduction to 2 John. The main purpose of the letter is to secure hospitality and support for missionaries approved by the elder and perhaps sent out by him. Although the missionaries preach to the pagans, it is possible also that they embody the elder's influence and doctrinal authority over communities. Perhaps this is why Diotrephes, the ambitious leader of the community who rejects the elder's authority refuses to receive the missionaries and tries to force others within the community to follow the same policy. The exact position of Diotrephes himself is not clear; for example, is he a monarchical bishop, as we might conceive the office nowadays, or one of the elders who by force of personality has taken over leadership?

To gain his purpose despite Diotrephes' opposition, the elder writes to Gaius, seemingly a man of position and wealth within the community. The elder praises Gaius' past hospitality, emphasizing that this attitude represents the true exercise of Christianity—"walking in the path of truth." He urges Gaius to continue to extend hospitality and to help outfit the missionaries for further travels. He recommends Demetrius to Gaius, perhaps for the double reason that Demetrius is the head of the missionary band and yet is unknown to Gaius. The elder also mentions a forthcoming visit of his own. This visit, during which he will also rebuke Diotrephes, may be meant to assure Gaius of support if Diotrephes seeks to expel Gaius from the church for granting the hospitality the elder requests. Despite its brevity and the inadequacy of its details, 3 John furnishes an extremely important insight into the problem of authority and influence in Christianity at the end of the first century.

THE EPISTLE OF JUDE

THE EPISTLE purports to have been written by *Jude, a servant of Jesus Christ and brother of James* (see Introduction to James). Since this claimant is not identified as one of the Twelve, he is presumably not Jude the apostle (Lk 6, 16), but that relative of Jesus who doubted him during the ministry (Mk 6, 3). Nearly all scholars agree on this point of identification. However, some hold that the epistle itself cannot be dated early enough to make the superscription anything but pseudonymous. They instance the allusion to the apostles as men of a past time (v 17; cf v 3), and assert, in addition, that the characterization of the false teachers (v 18) and the use of a Greek translation of 1 Henoch (14f) point to the date of approximately 100 A.D.

These arguments, however, should be viewed with caution. Though the allusion to the apostles cited above does indicate that the author of Jude was thinking of a second-generation Christian community, the reference point need not have been the end of that generation; it could equally well have been its beginning, therefore not long after 70 A.D. Moreover, the author of Jude might have so described false teachers about 80 A.D., and might also have had access to a Greek translation of 1 Henoch. The date of about 80 A.D. for the epistle remains entirely possible. For this reason many other scholars accept Jude, the relative of Jesus and brother of James of Jerusalem, as its author. Nothing is known of this Jude's history, nor does his epistle provide information on the location of the Christians to whom it is addressed. Since he invokes the name of James by way of introducing himself, he seems not to have been very well known among the Christians to whom he wrote.

The epistle warns its recipients against the false brethren who have infiltrated their community (v 4). These malignants are to be identified by their exaggerated doctrine of Christian freedom, for they encourage sensuality (v 4) and reject authority (v 8). The community must be alert to this threat in its midst, mindful of the divine judgments against those who fail to live according to faith or to Christian standards of conduct (5ff. 11; 14ff). An important feature of the brief Epistle of Jude is its rich doctrinal content. Many of the principal teachings of the faith are found here: the Blessed Trinity (20f); the pre-existence of Christ and redemption through him (4f); good and bad angels and the punishment of the latter (v 6); judgment and divine retribution (4.6.13.21.23f). On the foundation of faith, supported by prayer, the Christian is preserved in the love of God, and awaits a merciful judgment and eternal life (20f). This common faith delivered to the saints is the criterion of right belief (v 3). What is contrary to it is *destined for condemnation* because it turns the grace of God into wantonness and denies Jesus Christ, the *only Master and Lord* (v 4).

Scholars agree that the author of 2 Peter drew upon the Epistle of Jude.

THE BOOK OF REVELATION

THE BOOK OF REVELATION, or the Apocalypse, is the last book of the Bible, and perhaps the least read. It is also one of the most difficult to understand because it abounds in unfamiliar and extravagant symbolism, which at best appears unusual to the modern reader. Symbolic language, however, is one of the chief characteristics of apocalyptic literature, of which this book is an outstanding example. Such literature enjoyed wide popularity in both Jewish and Christian circles from 200 B.C. to 200 A.D.

This book contains the account of visions in symbolic and allegorical language borrowed in part from the Old Testament, especially Ezekiel, Zechariah, and the apocalyptic Book of Daniel. Whether these visions were real experiences of the author or simply literary conventions employed by him is an open question, the solution of which in no way adds to, or detracts from, the divine inspiration of the book.

Symbolic descriptions are not to be taken as literal descriptions, nor is the symbolism capable of being pictured realistically. One would find it both difficult and repulsive to visualize a lamb with seven horns and seven eyes; yet Christ our Lord is described in precisely such words (5, 6). The author used these images to suggest Christ's universal power (seven horns) and knowledge (seven eyes). Another significant feature of apocalyptic writing is the use of symbolic colors (1, 13–16; 3, 18; 4, 4; 6, 1–8; 17, 4; 19, 8) and numbers (*four* signifies the world; *six*, imperfection; *seven*, totality or perfection; *twelve*, Israel's tribes or the Apostles; *thousand*, immensity). Finally, the vindictive language in the book (6, 9f; 18, 1— 19, 4) is also to be understood symbolically, and not literally. The cries for vengeance that sound so harsh on the lips of Christian martyrs are in fact literary devices the author employed to evoke in the reader and hearer a feeling of horror for apostasy and rebellion, which will be severely punished by God.

The Book of Revelation cannot be adequately comprehended except against the historical background which occasioned its writing. Like the Book of Daniel and other apocalypses, it was composed as resistance literature to meet a crisis. The book itself suggests that the crisis was ruthless persecution of the early Church by the Roman authorities; the harlot Babylon symbolizes pagan Rome, the city on seven hills (17, 9). The book is, then, an exhortation and admonition to the Christian to stand firm in the faith and to avoid compromise with paganism, despite the threat of adversity and martyrdom; he is to await patiently the fulfillment of God's mighty promises. The triumph of God in the world of men remains a mystery, to be accepted in faith and longed for in hope. It is a triumph that unfolded in the history of Jesus of Nazareth, and continues to unfold in the history of the individual Christian who follows the way of the cross, even, if necessary, to a martyr's death.

Though the perspective is eschatological—ultimate salvation and victory are said to take place at the end of the present age when Christ will come in glory at the Parousia—the book presents the decisive struggle of Christ and his followers against Satan and his cohorts as already over. Christ's overwhelming defeat of the kingdom of Satan has ushered in the everlasting reign of God (11, 15; 12, 10). Even the forces of evil unwittingly carry out the divine plan (17, 17), for God is the sovereign Lord of history.

The Book of Revelation had its origin in a time of crisis, but it remains valid for Christians of all time. In the face of evils from within and without, the Christian can confidently trust in God's promise to be with the Church forever.

The author of the book calls himself John (1, 1.4.9; 22, 8), who because of his Christian faith had been exiled to the rocky island of Patmos. Although he never claims to be the apostle of the same name, many of the early Church Fathers so identified him. This identification is not altogether certain. Vocabulary, grammar and style make it doubtful that the book could have been put into its present form by the person(s) responsible for the fourth gospel. Nevertheless, there are definite linguistic and theological affinities between the two books. The tone of the letters to the seven churches (1, 4—3, 22) is indicative of the great authority the writer enjoyed over the Christian communities in Asia. It is quite likely, therefore, that he was at least a disciple of the apostle John, who also lived in that part of the world. The date of composition is probably near the end of the reign of Domitian (81–96 A.D.), a fierce persecutor of the Christians.

The principal divisions of the Book of Revelation are the following:

   I: Prologue (1, 1–3)
  II: Letters to the Churches of Asia (1, 4—3, 22)
 III: Preparation for the Day of the Lord (4, 1—16, 21)
 IV: Punishment of Babylon (17, 1—19, 10)
  V: Destruction of Pagan Nations (19, 11—20, 15)
 VI: New Creation (21, 1—22, 5)
VII: Epilogue (22, 6–21)

A Prayer

TO BE RECITED BEFORE READING
THE SACRED SCRIPTURES

Come, Holy Spirit, fill the hearts of your faithful and enkindle in them the fire of your love.

A partial indulgence is granted for the recitation of this prayer.

[ENCHIRIDION INDULGENTIARUM, No. 62]

A partial indulgence is granted to the faithful who use Sacred Scripture for spiritual reading with the veneration due the word of God. A plenary indulgence is granted if the reading continues for at least one-half hour.

[ENCHIRIDION INDULGENTIARUM, No. 50]

The
OLD TESTAMENT

Genesis

THE PRIMEVAL HISTORY

First Story of Creation

IN the beginning, when God created the heavens and the earth, 2 the earth was a formless wasteland, and darkness covered the abyss, while a mighty wind swept over the waters. 3 Then God said, "Let there be light," and there was light. 4 God saw how good the light was. God then separated the light from the darkness. 5 God called the light "day," and the darkness he called "night." Thus evening came, and morning followed—the first day.

6 Then God said, "Let there be a dome in the middle of the waters, to separate one body of water from the other." And so it happened: 7 God made the dome, and it separated the water above the dome from the water below it. 8 God called the dome "the sky." Evening came, and morning followed—the second day.

9 Then God said, "Let the water under the sky be gathered into a single basin, so that the dry land may appear." And so it happened: the water under the sky was gathered into its basin, and the dry land appeared. 10 God called the dry land "the earth," and the basin of the water he called "the sea." God saw how good it was. 11 Then God said, "Let the earth bring forth vegetation: every kind of plant that bears seed and every kind of fruit tree on earth that bears fruit with its seed in it." And so it happened: 12 the earth brought forth every kind of plant that bears seed and every kind of fruit tree on earth that bears fruit with its seed in it. God saw how good it was. 13 Evening came, and morning followed—the third day.

14 Then God said: "Let there be lights in the dome of the sky, to separate day from night. Let them mark the fixed times, the days and the years, 15 and serve as luminaries in the dome of the sky, to shed light upon the earth." And so it happened: 16 God made the two great lights, the greater one to govern the day, and the lesser one to govern the night; and he made the stars. 17 God set them in the dome of the sky, to shed light upon the earth, 18 to govern the day and the night, and to separate the light from the darkness. God saw how good it was. 19 Evening came, and morning followed—the fourth day.

20 Then God said, "Let the water teem with an abundance of living creatures, and on the earth let birds fly beneath the dome of the sky." And so it happened: 21 God created the great sea monsters and all kinds of swimming creatures with which the water teems, and all kinds of winged birds. God saw how good it was, 22 and God blessed them, saying, "Be

1, 1—2, 4a: This section introduces the whole Pentateuch. It shows how God brought an orderly universe out of primordial chaos.

1, 2: *The abyss:* the primordial ocean according to the ancient Semitic cosmogony. After God's creative activity, part of this vast body forms the salt-water seas (vv 9f); part of it is the fresh water under the earth (Ps 33, 7; Ez 31, 4), which wells forth on the earth as springs and fountains (Gn 7, 11; 8, 2; Prv 3, 20). Part of it, "the upper water" (Ps 148, 4; Dn 3, 60), is held up by the dome of the sky (Gn 1, 6f), from which rain descends on the earth (Gn 7, 11; 2 Kgs 7, 2.19; Ps 104, 13). *A mighty wind:* literally, "a wind of God," or "a spirit of God"; cf Gn 8, 1.

1, 5: In ancient Israel a day was considered to begin at sunset. According to the highly artificial literary structure of Gn 1, 1—2, 4a, God's creative activity is divided into six days to teach the sacredness of the sabbath rest on the seventh day in the Israelite religion (2, 2f).

1

fertile, multiply, and fill the water of the seas; and let the birds multiply on the earth." 23 Evening came, and morning followed—the fifth day.

24 Then God said, "Let the earth bring forth all kinds of living creatures: cattle, creeping things, and wild animals of all kinds." And so it happened. 25 God made all kinds of wild animals, all kinds of cattle, and all kinds of creeping things of the earth. God saw how good it was. 26 Then God said: "Let us make man in our image, after our likeness. Let them have dominion over the fish of the sea, the birds of the air, and the cattle, and over all the wild animals and all the creatures that crawl on the ground."

27 God created man in his image;
    in the divine image he created
        him;
    male and female he created
        them.

28 God blessed them, saying: "Be fertile and multiply; fill the earth and subdue it. Have dominion over the fish of the sea, the birds of the air, and all the living things that move on the earth." 29 God also said: "See, I give you every seed-bearing plant all over the earth and every tree that has seed-bearing fruit on it to be your food; 30 and to all the animals of the land, all the birds of the air, and all the living creatures that crawl on the ground, I give all the green plants for food." And so it happened. 31 God looked at everything he had made, and he found it very good. Evening came, and morning followed —the sixth day.

2 Thus the heavens and the earth and all their array were completed. 2 Since on the seventh day God was finished with the work he had been doing, he rested on the seventh day from all the work he had undertaken. 3 So God blessed the seventh day and made it holy, because on it he rested from all the work he had done in creation.

4 Such is the story of the heavens and the earth at their creation.

Second Story of Creation

At the time when the LORD God made the earth and the heavens— 5 while as yet there was no field shrub on earth and no grass of the field had sprouted, for the LORD God had sent no rain upon the earth and there was no man to till the soil, 6 but a stream was welling up out of the earth and was watering all the surface of the ground— 7 the LORD God formed man out of the clay of the ground and blew into his nostrils the breath of life, and so man became a living being.

8 Then the LORD God planted a garden in Eden, in the east, and he placed there the man whom he had formed. 9 Out of the ground the LORD God made various trees grow that were delightful to look at and good for food, with the tree of life in the middle of the garden and the tree of the knowledge of good and bad.

10 A river rises in Eden to water the garden; beyond there it divides and becomes four branches. 11 The name of the first is the Pishon; it is the one that winds through the whole land of Havilah, where there is gold. 12 The gold of that land is excellent; bdellium and lapis lazuli are also there. 13 The name of the second river is the Gihon; it is the one that winds all through the land of Cush. 14 The name of the third river is the Tigris; it is the one that flows east of Asshur. The fourth river is the Euphrates.

15 The LORD God then took the man and settled him in the garden of Eden, to cultivate and care for it. 16 The LORD God gave man this order: "You are free to eat from any of the trees of the garden 17 except the tree of the knowledge of good and bad. From that tree you shall not eat; the moment you eat from it you are surely doomed to die."

18 The LORD God said: "It is not good for the man to be alone. I will make a suitable partner for him." 19 So the LORD God formed out of the ground various wild animals and various birds of the air, and he brought them to the man to see what he would call them; whatever the man called each of them would be its name. 20 The man gave names to all the cattle, all the birds of the air, and all the wild animals; but none proved to be the suitable partner for the man.

21 So the LORD God cast a deep sleep on the man, and while he was asleep, he took out one of his ribs and closed up its place with flesh. 22 The LORD God then built up into a woman the rib that he had taken from the man. When he brought her to the man, 23 the man said:

"This one, at last, is bone of my
        bones
    and flesh of my flesh;
This one shall be called 'woman,'
    for out of 'her man' this one
        has been taken."

24 That is why a man leaves his father and mother and clings to his wife, and the two of them become one body.

25 The man and his wife were both naked, yet they felt no shame.

The Fall of Man

3 Now the serpent was the most cunning of all the animals that the LORD God had made. The serpent asked the woman, "Did God really tell you not to eat from any of the trees in the garden?" 2 The woman answered the serpent: "We may eat of the fruit of the trees in the garden; 3 it is only about the fruit of the tree

---

1, 26: Man is here presented as the climax of God's creative activity; he resembles God primarily because of the dominion God gives him over the rest of creation.

2, 4b–25: This section is chiefly concerned with the creation of man. It is much older than the narrative of 1, 1—2, 4a. Here God is depicted as creating man before the rest of his creatures, which are made for man's sake.

2, 7: God is portrayed as a potter molding man's body out of clay. There is a play on words in Hebrew between *adam* ("man") and *adama* ("ground"). *Being:* literally "soul."

2, 8: *Eden:* used here as the name of a region in southern Mesopotamia; the term is derived from the Sumerian word *eden,* "fertile plain." A similar-sounding Hebrew word means "delight"; the *garden in Eden* could therefore be understood as the "garden of delight," so that, through the Greek version, it is now known also as "paradise," literally, a "pleasure park."

2, 10–14: *Rises:* in flood to overflow its banks. *Beyond there:* as one travels upstream. *Branches:* literally, "heads," i.e., upper courses. Eden is near the head of the Persian Gulf, where the Tigris and the

Euphrates join with two other streams to form a single river. *The land of Cush* here and in 10, 8, is not Ethiopia (Nubia) as elsewhere, but the region of the Kassites, east of Mesopotamia.

2, 23: There is a play on the similar-sounding Hebrew words *ishsha* ("woman") and *ishah* ("her man, her husband").

2, 24: *One body:* literally "one flesh"; classical Hebrew has no specific word for "body." The sacred writer stresses the fact that conjugal union is willed by God.

in the middle of the garden that God said, 'You shall not eat it or even touch it, lest you die.'" 4 But the serpent said to the woman: "You certainly will not die! 5 No, God knows well that the moment you eat of it you will be like gods who know what is good and what is bad." 6 The woman saw that the tree was good for food, pleasing to the eyes, and desirable for gaining wisdom. So she took some of its fruit and ate it; and she also gave some to her husband, who was with her, and he ate it. 7 Then the eyes of both of them were opened, and they realized that they were naked; so they sewed fig leaves together and made loincloths for themselves.

8 When they heard the sound of the LORD God moving about in the garden at the breezy time of the day, the man and his wife hid themselves from the LORD God among the trees of the garden. 9 The LORD God then called to the man and asked him, "Where are you?" 10 He answered, "I heard you in the garden; but I was afraid, because I was naked, so I hid myself." 11 Then he asked, "Who told you that you were naked? You have eaten, then, from the tree of which I had forbidden you to eat!" 12 The man replied, "The woman whom you put here with me—she gave me fruit from the tree, and so I ate it." 13 The LORD God then asked the woman, "Why did you do such a thing?" The woman answered, "The serpent tricked me into it, so I ate it."

14 Then the LORD God said to the serpent:

"Because you have done this, you
    shall be banned
  from all the animals
  and from all the wild creatures;
On your belly shall you crawl,
  and dirt shall you eat
  all the days of your life.

15 I will put enmity between you
    and the woman,
  and between your offspring
    and hers;
He will strike at your head,
  while you strike at his heel."

16 To the woman he said:

"I will intensify the pangs of your
    childbearing;
  in pain shall you bring forth
    children.
Yet your urge shall be for your
    husband,
  and he shall be your master."

17 To the man he said: "Because you listened to your wife and ate from the tree of which I had forbidden you to eat,

"Cursed be the ground because of
    you!
In toil shall you eat its yield
  all the days of your life.

18 Thorns and thistles shall it bring
    forth to you,
  as you eat of the plants of the
    field.

19 By the sweat of your face
  shall you get bread to eat,
Until you return to the ground,
  from which you were taken;
For you are dirt,
  and to dirt you shall return."

20 The man called his wife Eve, because she became the mother of all the living. 21 For the man and his wife the LORD God made leather garments, with which he clothed them. 22 Then the LORD God said: "See! The man has become like one of us, knowing what is good and what is bad! Therefore, he must not be allowed to put out his hand to take fruit from the tree of life also, and thus eat of it and live forever." 23 The LORD God therefore banished him from the garden of Eden, to till the ground from which he had been taken. 24 When he expelled the man, he settled him east of the garden of Eden; and he stationed the cherubim and the fiery revolving sword, to guard the way to the tree of life.

Cain and Abel

4 The man had relations with his wife Eve, and she conceived and bore Cain, saying, "I have produced a man with the help of the LORD." 2 Next she bore his brother Abel. Abel became a keeper of flocks, and Cain a tiller of the soil. 3 In the course of time Cain brought an offering to the LORD from the fruit of the soil, 4 while Abel, for his part, brought one of the best firstlings of his flock. The LORD looked with favor on Abel and his offering, 5 but on Cain and his offering he did not. Cain greatly resented this and was crestfallen. 6 So the LORD said to Cain: "Why are you so resentful and crestfallen? 7 If you do well, you can hold up your head; but if not, sin is a demon lurking at the door: his urge is toward you, yet you can be his master."

8 Cain said to his brother Abel, "Let us go out in the field." When they were in the field, Cain attacked his brother Abel and killed him. 9 Then the LORD asked Cain, "Where is your brother Abel?" He answered, "I do not know. Am I my brother's keeper?" 10 The LORD then said: "What have you done! Listen: your brother's blood cries out to me from the soil! 11 Therefore you shall be banned from the soil that opened its mouth to receive your brother's blood from your hand. 12 If you till the soil, it shall no longer give you its produce. You shall become a restless wanderer on the earth." 13 Cain said to the LORD: "My punishment is too great to bear. 14 Since you have now banished me from the soil, and I must avoid your presence

---

3, 5: *Like gods who know:* or "like God who knows."

3, 8: *The breezy time of the day:* literally "the wind of the day." On most days in Palestine a cooling breeze blows from the sea shortly before sunset.

3, 15: *He will strike . . . at his heel:* since the antecedent for *he* and *his* is the collective noun *offspring*, i.e., all the descendants of the woman, a more exact rendering of the sacred writer's words would be, "They will strike . . . at their heels." However, later theology saw in this passage more

than unending hostility between snakes and men. The serpent was regarded as the devil (Wis 2, 24; Jn 8, 44; Rv 12, 9; 20, 2), whose eventual defeat seems implied in the contrast between *head* and *heel*. Because "the Son of God appeared that he might destroy the works of the devil" (1 Jn 3, 8), the passage can be understood as the first promise of a Redeemer for fallen mankind. The woman's offspring then is primarily Jesus Christ.

3, 20: This verse seems to be out of place; it would fit better after v 24. The Hebrew name *hawwa*

("Eve") is related to the Hebrew word *hay* ("living").

3, 24: The above rendering is based on the ancient Greek version; that of the current Hebrew is, When he expelled the man, he settled, east of the garden of Eden; the cherubim. . . .

4, 1: The Hebrew name *qayin* ("Cain") and the term *qaniti* ("I have produced") present another play on words.

4, 7: *Demon lurking:* in Hebrew, *robes*, literally "croucher," is used here, like the similar Akkadian term *rabisu*, to designate a certain kind of evil spirit.

and become a restless wanderer on the earth, anyone may kill me at sight." 15 "Not so!" the LORD said to him. "If anyone kills Cain, Cain shall be avenged sevenfold." So the LORD put a mark on Cain, lest anyone should kill him at sight. 16 Cain then left the LORD's presence and settled in the land of Nod, east of Eden.

Descendants of Cain and Seth

17 Cain had relations with his wife, and she conceived and bore Enoch. Cain also became the founder of a city, which he named after his son Enoch. 18 To Enoch was born Irad, and Irad became the father of Mehujael; Mehujael became the father of Methusael, and Methusael became the father of Lamech. 19 Lamech took two wives; the name of the first was Adah, and the name of the second Zillah. 20 Adah gave birth to Jabal, the ancestor of all who dwell in tents and keep cattle. 21 His brother's name was Jubal; he was the ancestor of all who play the lyre and the pipe. 22 Zillah on her part, gave birth to Tubalcain, the ancestor of all who forge instruments of bronze and iron. The sister of Tubalcain was Naamah.

23 Lamech said to his wives:

"Adah and Zillah, hear my voice;
    wives of Lamech, listen to my
        utterance:
I have killed a man for wounding
    me,
    a boy for bruising me.
24 If Cain is avenged sevenfold,
    then Lamech seventy-seven-
        fold."

25 Adam again had relations with his wife, and she gave birth to a son whom she called Seth. "God has granted me more offspring in place of Abel," she said, "because Cain

slew him." 26 To Seth, in turn, a son was born, and he named him Enosh.

At that time men began to invoke the LORD by name.

Generations: Adam to Noah

5 This is the record of the descendants of Adam. When God created man, he made him in the likeness of God; 2 he created them male and female. When they were created, he blessed them and named them "man."

3 Adam was one hundred and thirty years old when he begot a son in his likeness, after his image; and he named him Seth. 4 Adam lived eight hundred years after the birth of Seth, and he had other sons and daughters. 5 The whole lifetime of Adam was nine hundred and thirty years; then he died.

6 When Seth was one hundred and five years old, he became the father of Enosh. 7 Seth lived eight hundred and seven years after the birth of Enosh, and he had other sons and daughters. 8 The whole lifetime of Seth was nine hundred and twelve years; then he died.

9 When Enosh was ninety years old, he became the father of Kenan. 10 Enosh lived eight hundred and fifteen years after the birth of Kenan, and he had other sons and daughters. 11 The whole lifetime of Enosh was nine hundred and five years; then he died.

12 When Kenan was seventy years old, he became the father of Mahalalel. 13 Kenan lived eight hundred and forty years after the birth of Mahalalel, and he had other sons and daughters. 14 The whole lifetime of Kenan was nine hundred and ten years; then he died.

15 When Mahalalel was sixty-five years old, he became the father of

Jared. 16 Mahalalel lived eight hundred and thirty years after the birth of Jared, and he had other sons and daughters. 17 The whole lifetime of Mahalalel was eight hundred and ninety-five years; then he died.

18 When Jared was one hundred and sixty-two years old, he became the father of Enoch. 19 Jared lived eight hundred years after the birth of Enoch, and he had other sons and daughters. 20 The whole lifetime of Jared was nine hundred and sixty-two years; then he died.

21 When Enoch was sixty-five years old, he became the father of Methuselah. 22 Enoch lived three hundred years after the birth of Methuselah, and he had other sons and daughters. 23 The whole lifetime of Enoch was three hundred and sixty-five years. 24 Then Enoch walked with God, and he was no longer here, for God took him.

25 When Methuselah was one hundred and eighty-seven years old, he became the father of Lamech. 26 Methuselah lived seven hundred and eighty-two years after the birth of Lamech, and he had other sons and daughters. 27 The whole lifetime of Methuselah was nine hundred and sixty-nine years; then he died.

28 When Lamech was one hundred and eighty-two years old, he begot a son 29 and named him Noah, saying, "Out of the very ground that the LORD has put under a curse, this one shall bring us relief from our work and the toil of our hands." 30 Lamech lived five hundred and ninety-five years after the birth of Noah, and he had other sons and daughters. 31 The whole lifetime of Lamech was seven hundred and seventy-seven years; then he died.

32 When Noah was five hundred years old, he became the father of Shem, Ham, and Japheth.

4, 15: *A mark:* probably a tattoo. The use of tattooing for tribal marks has always been common among the nomads of the Near Eastern deserts.

4, 16: *The land of Nod:* not a definite geographic region. The term merely means "the land of nomads."

4, 17–22: In vv 12–16 Cain was presented as the archetype of nomadic peoples. The sacred author in this section follows another ancient tradition that makes Cain the prototype of sedentary peoples with higher material culture.

4, 25f: *Has granted:* Hebrew *shat,* a wordplay on the name *shet* ("Seth"). *Enosh:* in Hebrew, a synonym of *adam* ("man"). *At that time . . . name:* men began to call God by his personal name, Yahweh, rendered as "the LORD" in this version of the Bible. The

ancient, so-called Yahwist, source used here employs the name Yahweh long before the time of Moses. Another ancient source, the Elohist (from its use of the term *Elohim,* "God," instead of *Yahweh,* "Lord," for the pre-Mosaic period), makes Moses the first to use Yahweh as the proper name of Israel's God, previously known by other names as well; cf Ex 3, 13ff.

5, 1–32: Although this chapter, with its highly schematic form, belongs to the relatively late "Priestly document," it is based on very ancient traditions. Together with 11, 10–26, its primary purpose is to bridge the genealogical gap between Adam and Abraham. Adam's line is traced through Seth, but several names in the series are the same as, or similar to, certain names in Cain's line (4, 17ff).

The long lifespans attributed to these ten antediluvian patriarchs have a symbolic rather than a historical value. Babylonian tradition also recorded ten kings with fantastically high ages who reigned successively before the flood.

5, 24: In place of the usual formula, *Then he died,* the change to *Enoch walked with God* clearly implies that he did not die, but like Elijah (2 Kgs 2, 11f) was taken alive to God's abode.

5, 29: There is a similarity in sound between the Hebrew word *noah,* "Noah," and the verbal phrase *yenahamenu,* "he will bring us relief"; this latter refers both to the curse put on the soil because of the fall of man (3, 17ff) and to Noah's success in agriculture, especially in raising grapes for wine (9, 20f).

Origin of the Nephilim

6 When men began to multiply on earth and daughters were born to them, 2 the sons of heaven saw how beautiful the daughters of man were, and so they took for their wives as many of them as they chose. 3 Then the LORD said: "My spirit shall not remain in man forever, since he is but flesh. His days shall comprise one hundred and twenty years."

4 At that time the Nephilim appeared on earth (as well as later), after the sons of heaven had intercourse with the daughters of man, who bore them sons. They were the heroes of old, the men of renown.

Warning of the Flood

5 When the LORD saw how great was man's wickedness on earth, and how no desire that his heart conceived was ever anything but evil, 6 he regretted that he had made man on the earth, and his heart was grieved.

7 So the LORD said: "I will wipe out from the earth the men whom I have created, and not only the men, but also the beasts and the creeping things and the birds of the air, for I am sorry that I made them." 8 But Noah found favor with the LORD.

9 These are the descendants of Noah. Noah, a good man and blameless in that age, 10 for he walked with God, begot three sons: Shem, Ham, and Japheth.

11 In the eyes of God the earth was corrupt and full of lawlessness. 12 When God saw how corrupt the earth had become, since all mortals led depraved lives on earth, 13 he said to Noah: "I have decided to put an end to all mortals on earth; the earth is full of lawlessness because of them. So I will destroy them and all life on earth.

Preparation for the Flood

14 "Make yourself an ark of gopherwood, put various compartments in it, and cover it inside and out with pitch. 15 This is how you shall build it: the length of the ark shall be three hundred cubits, its width fifty cubits, and its height thirty cubits. 16 Make an opening for daylight in the ark, and finish the ark a cubit above it. Put an entrance in the side of the ark, which you shall make with bottom, second and third decks. 17 I, on my part, am about to bring the flood [waters] on the earth, to destroy everywhere all creatures in which there is the breath of life; everything on earth shall perish. 18 But with you I will establish my covenant; you and your sons, your wife, and your sons' wives, shall go into the ark. 19 Of all other living creatures you shall bring two into the ark, one male and one female, that you may keep them alive with you. 20 Of all kinds of birds, of all kinds of beasts, and of all kinds of creeping things, two of each shall come into the ark with you, to stay alive. 21 Moreover, you are to provide yourself with all the food that is to be eaten, and store it away, that it may serve as provisions for you and for them." 22 This Noah did; he carried out all the commands that God gave him.

7 Then the LORD said to Noah: "Go into the ark, you and all your household, for you alone in this age have I found to be truly just. 2 Of every clean animal, take with you seven pairs, a male and its mate; and of the unclean animals, one pair, a male and its mate; 3 likewise, of every clean bird of the air, seven pairs, a male and a female, and of all the unclean birds, one pair, a male and a female. Thus you will keep their issue alive all over the earth. 4 Seven days from now I will bring rain down on the earth for forty days and forty nights, and so I will wipe out from the surface of the earth every moving creature that I have made." 5 Noah did just as the LORD had commanded him.

The Great Flood

6 Noah was six hundred years old when the flood water came upon the earth. 7 Together with his sons, his wife, and his sons' wives, Noah went into the ark because of the waters of the flood. 8 Of the clean animals and the unclean, of the birds, and of everything that creeps on the ground, 9 [two by two,] male and female entered the ark with Noah, just as the LORD had commanded him. 10 As soon as the seven days were over, the waters of the flood came upon the earth.

11 In the six hundredth year of Noah's life, in the second month, on the seventeenth day of the month: it was on that day that

> All the fountains of the great abyss
> 　burst forth,
> 　and the floodgates of the sky
> 　were opened.

12 For forty days and forty nights heavy rain poured down on the earth.

6, 1–4: This is apparently a fragment of an old legend that had borrowed much from ancient mythology. The sacred author incorporates it here, not only in order to account for the prehistoric giants of Palestine, whom the Israelites called the *Nephilim*, but also to introduce the story of the flood with a moral orientation—the constantly increasing wickedness of mankind.

6, 2: *The sons of heaven:* literally "the sons of the gods" or "the sons of God," i.e., the celestial beings of mythology.

6, 3: *My spirit:* the breath of life referred to in 2, 7. *His days . . . years:* probably the time God would still let men live on earth before destroying them with the flood, rather than the maximum span of life God would allot to individual men in the future.

6, 4: *As well as later:* According to Nm 13, 33, when the Israelites invaded Palestine and found there the tall aboriginal Anakim, they likened them to *the Nephilim;* cf Dt 2, 10f. Perhaps the huge megalithic structures in Palestine were thought to

have been built by a race of giants, whose superhuman strength was attributed to semi-divine origin. *The heroes of old:* the legendary worthies of ancient mythology.

6, 5—8, 22: The story of the great flood here recorded is a composite narrative based on two separate sources interwoven into an intricate patchwork. To the Yahwist source, with some later editorial additions, are usually assigned 6, 5-8; 7, 1–5.7–10.12.16b.17b.22–23; 8, 2b–3a.6–12.13b.20–22. The other sections come from the "Priestly document." The combination of the two sources produced certain duplications (e.g., 6, 13–22 of the Yahwist source, beside 7, 1–5 of the Priestly source); also certain inconsistencies, such as the number of the various animals taken into the ark (6, 19f; 7, 14f of the Priestly source, beside 7, 2f of the Yahwist source), and the timetable of the flood (8, 3–5.13f of the Priestly source, beside 7, 4.10.12.17b; 8, 6.10.12 of the Yahwist source). Both biblical sources go back ultimately to an ancient Mesopotamian

story of a great flood, preserved in the eleventh tablet of the Gilgamesh Epic. The latter account, in some respects remarkably similar to the biblical account, is in others very different from it.

6, 14: *Gopherwood:* an unidentified wood not mentioned elsewhere; *gopher* is merely the Hebrew word for it.

6, 15: The dimensions of Noah's ark were approximately 440 × 73 × 44 feet, a foot and a half to the cubit. The ark of the Babylonian flood story was an exact cube, 120 cubits in length, width and height.

6, 16: *Opening for daylight:* a conjectural rendering of the Hebrew word *sohar,* occurring only here. The reference is probably to an open space on all sides near the top of the ark to admit light and air. The ark also had a window or hatch, which could be opened and closed (8, 6).

7, 11: *Abyss:* the subterranean ocean; see note on 1, 2.

13 On the precise day named, Noah and his sons Shem, Ham, and Japheth, and Noah's wife, and the three wives of Noah's sons had entered the ark, 14 together with every kind of wild beast, every kind of domestic animal, every kind of creeping thing of the earth, and every kind of bird. 15 Pairs of all creatures in which there was the breath of life entered the ark with Noah. 16 Those that entered were male and female, and of all species they came, as God had commanded Noah. Then the LORD shut him in.

17 The flood continued upon the earth for forty days. As the waters increased, they lifted the ark, so that it rose above the earth. 18 The swelling waters increased greatly, but the ark floated on the surface of the waters. 19 Higher and higher above the earth rose the waters, until all the highest mountains everywhere were submerged, 20 the crest rising fifteen cubits higher than the submerged mountains. 21 All creatures that stirred on earth perished: birds, cattle, wild animals, and all that swarmed on the earth, as well as all mankind. 22 Everything on dry land with the faintest breath of life in its nostrils died out. 23 The LORD wiped out every living thing on earth: man and cattle, the creeping things and the birds of the air; all were wiped out from the earth. Only Noah and those with him in the ark were left.

24 The waters maintained their crest over the earth for one hundred and fifty days. 8 1 And then God remembered Noah and all the animals, wild and tame, that were with him in the ark. So God made a wind sweep over the earth, and the waters began to subside. 2 The fountains of the abyss and the floodgates of the sky were closed, and the downpour from the sky was held back. 3 Gradually the waters receded from the earth. At the end of one hundred and fifty days,

the waters had so diminished 4 that, in the seventh month, on the seventeenth day of the month, the ark came to rest on the mountains of Ararat. 5 The waters continued to diminish until the tenth month, and on the first day of the tenth month the tops of the mountains appeared.

6 At the end of forty days Noah opened the hatch he had made in the ark, 7 and he sent out a raven, to see if the waters had lessened on the earth. It flew back and forth until the waters dried off from the earth. 8 Then he sent out a dove, to see if the waters had lessened on the earth 9 But the dove could find no place to alight and perch, and it returned to him in the ark, for there was water all over the earth. Putting out his hand, he caught the dove and drew it back to him inside the ark. 10 He waited seven days more and again sent the dove out from the ark. 11 In the evening the dove came back to him, and there in its bill was a plucked-off olive leaf! So Noah knew that the waters had lessened on the earth. 12 He waited still another seven days and then released the dove once more; and this time it did not come back.

13 In the six hundred and first year of Noah's life, in the first month, on the first day of the month, the water began to dry up on the earth. Noah then removed the covering of the ark and saw that the surface of the ground was drying up. 14 In the second month, on the twenty-seventh day of the month, the earth was dry.

15 Then God said to Noah: 16 "Go out of the ark, together with your wife and your sons and your sons' wives. 17 Bring out with you every living thing that is with you— all bodily creatures, be they birds or animals or creeping things of the earth—and let them abound on the earth, breeding and multiplying on it." 18 So Noah came out, together with his wife and his sons and his sons' wives; 19 and all the animals,

wild and tame, all the birds, and all the creeping creatures of the earth left the ark, one kind after another.

20 Then Noah built an altar to the LORD, and choosing from every clean animal and every clean bird, he offered holocausts on the altar. 21 When the LORD smelled the sweet odor, he said to himself: "Never again will I doom the earth because of man, since the desires of man's heart are evil from the start; nor will I ever again strike down all living beings, as I have done.

22 As long as the earth lasts,
　　seedtime and harvest,
　　cold and heat,
　Summer and winter,
　　and day and night
　　shall not cease."

Covenant with Noah

9 God blessed Noah and his sons and said to them: "Be fertile and multiply and fill the earth. 2 Dread fear of you shall come upon all the animals of the earth and all the birds of the air, upon all the creatures that move about on the ground and all the fishes of the sea; into your power they are delivered. 3 Every creature that is alive shall be yours to eat; I give them all to you as I did the green plants. 4 Only flesh with its lifeblood still in it you shall not eat. 5 For your own lifeblood, too, I will demand an accounting: from every animal I will demand it, and from man in regard to his fellow man I will demand an accounting for human life.

6 If anyone sheds the blood of man,
　　by man shall his blood be shed;
　For in the image of God
　　has man been made.

7 Be fertile, then, and multiply; abound on earth and subdue it."

8 God said to Noah and to his sons with him: 9 "See, I am now establishing my covenant with you and your descendants after you 10 and

---

8, 4: *Ararat:* ancient Urartu, north of the Mesopotamian plain, part of modern Armenia.

8, 6: In the original Yahwist source, from which this verse is taken, the forty days refer to the full period of the flood itself (cf 7, 4.17); in the present context, however, they seem to refer to a period following the date just given in v 5 from the Priestly source.

8, 21: *From the start:* literally "from his youth." It is uncertain whether this means from the beginning of the human race or from the early years of the individual.

9, 3: Antediluvian creatures, including man, are depicted as vegetarians (1, 29f), becoming carnivorous only after the flood.

9, 4: Because a living being dies when it loses most

of its blood, the ancients regarded blood as the seat of life, and therefore as sacred. Although in itself the prohibition against eating meat with blood in it is comparable to the ritual laws of the Mosaic code, the Jews considered it binding on all men, because it was given by God to Noah, the new ancestor of all mankind; therefore the early Christian Church retained it for a time (Acts 15, 20.29).

with every living creature that was with you: all the birds, and the various tame and wild animals that were with you and came out of the ark. 11 I will establish my covenant with you, that never again shall all bodily creatures be destroyed by the waters of a flood; there shall not be another flood to devastate the earth." 12 God added: "This is the sign that I am giving for all ages to come, of the covenant between me and you and every living creature with you: 13 I set my bow in the clouds to serve as a sign of the covenant between me and the earth. 14 When I bring clouds over the earth, and the bow appears in the clouds, 15 I will recall the covenant I have made between me and you and all living beings, so that the waters shall never again become a flood to destroy all mortal beings. 16 As the bow appears in the clouds, I will see it and recall the everlasting covenant that I have established between God and all living beings—all mortal creatures that are on earth." 17 God told Noah: "This is the sign of the covenant I have established between me and all mortal creatures that are on earth."

Noah and His Sons

18 The sons of Noah who came out of the ark were Shem, Ham, and Japheth. (Ham was the father of Canaan.) 19 These three were the sons of Noah, and from them the whole earth was peopled.

20 Now Noah, a man of the soil, was the first to plant a vineyard. 21 When he drank some of the wine, he became drunk and lay naked inside his tent. 22 Ham, the father of Canaan, saw his father's nakedness, and he told his two brothers outside about it. 23 Shem and Japheth, however, took a robe, and holding it on their backs, they walked backward and covered their father's nakedness; since their faces were turned the other way, they did not see their father's nakedness. 24 When Noah woke up from his drunkenness and learned what his youngest son had done to him, 25 he said:

"Cursed be Canaan!
The lowest of slaves
shall he be to his brothers."

26 He also said:
"Blessed be the LORD, the God of Shem!
Let Canaan be his slave.

27 May God expand Japheth,
so that he dwells among the tents of Shem;
and let Canaan be his slave."

28 Noah lived three hundred and fifty years after the flood. 29 The whole lifetime of Noah was nine hundred and fifty years; then he died.

Table of the Nations

10 These are the descendants of Noah's sons, Shem, Ham, and Japheth, to whom sons were born after the flood.

2 The descendants of Japheth:
Gomer, Magog, Madai, Javan, Tubal, Meshech, and Tiras.
3 The descendants of Gomer:
Ashkenaz, Riphath, and Togarmah.
4 The descendants of Javan:
Elishah, Tarshish, the Kittim, and the Rodanim.

5 These are the descendants of Japheth, and from them sprang the maritime nations, in their respective lands—each with its own language—by their clans within their nations.

6 The descendants of Ham:
Cush, Mizraim, Put, and Canaan.
7 The descendants of Cush:
Seba, Havilah, Sabtah, Raamah, and Sabteca.
The descendants of Raamah:
Sheba and Dedan.

8 Cush became the father of Nimrod, who was the first potentate on earth. 9 He was a mighty hunter by the grace of the LORD; hence the saying, "Like Nimrod, a mighty hunter by the grace of the LORD." 10 The chief cities of his kingdom were Babylon, Erech, and Accad, all of them in the land of Shinar. 11 From that land he went forth to Asshur, where he built Nineveh, Rehoboth-Ir, and Calah, 12 as well as Resen, between Nineveh and Calah, the latter being the principal city.

13 Mizraim became the father of the Ludim, the Anamim, the Lehabim, the Naphtuhim, 14 the Pathrusim, the Casluhim, and the Caphtorim from whom the Philistines sprang.

15 Canaan became the father of Sidon, his first-born, and of Heth; 16 also of the Jebusites, the Amorites, the Girgashites, 17 the Hivites, the Arkites, the Sinites, 18 the Arvadites, the Zemarites, and the Hamathites. Afterward, the clans of the Canaanites spread out, 19 so that the Canaanite borders extended from

---

9, 18–27: This story seems to be a composite of two earlier accounts; in the one, Ham was guilty, whereas in the other, it was Canaan. One purpose of the story is to justify the Israelites' enslavement of the Canaanites because of certain indecent sexual practices in the Canaanite religion. Obviously the story offers no justification for enslaving African Negroes, even though Canaan is presented as a "son" of Ham because the land of Canaan belonged to Hamitic Egypt at the time of the Israelite invasion.
9, 26: *Blessed ... Shem:* Perhaps the text read originally, "Blessed of the LORD be Shem," which would be expected in the context.
9, 27: In the Hebrew text there is a play on the words *yapt* ("expand") and *yepet* ("Japheth").
10, 1–32: This chapter presents a remarkably good classification of the various peoples known to the ancient Israelites; it is theologically important as stressing the basic family unity of all men on earth. The relationship between the various peoples is based partly on linguistic, partly on geographic, and partly on political grounds, *according to their . . . languages, . . . lands and nations* (v 31). In general,

the descendants of Japheth (vv 2–5) are the peoples of the Indo-European languages to the north and west of Mesopotamia and Syria; *the descendants of Ham* (vv 6–20) are the Hamitic-speaking peoples of northern Africa; and *the descendants of Shem* (vv 21–31) are the Semitic-speaking peoples of Mesopotamia, Syria and Arabia. But there are many exceptions to this rule; the Semitic-speaking peoples of Canaan, for instance, are considered descendants of Ham, because at the time they were subject to Hamitic Egypt (vv 6.15–19). This chapter is a composite from the Yahwist source (vv 8–19.21.24–30) of about the ninth century B.C., and the Priestly source (vv 1–7.20.22f.31f) of a few centuries later. That is why certain tribes of Arabia are listed under both Ham (v 7) and Shem (vv 26ff).
10, 2: *Gomer:* the Cimmerians; *Madai:* the Medes; *Javan:* the Greeks.
10, 3: *Ashkenaz:* the Scythians.
10, 4: *Elishah:* Cyprus; *the Kittim:* certain inhabitants of Cyprus; *the Rodanim:* the inhabitants of Rhodes.
10, 6: *Cush:* Biblical Ethiopia, modern Nubia;

Mizraim: Egypt; *Put:* either Punt in East Africa or Libya.
10, 8: *Cush:* here, the Kassites; see note on 2, 10–14. *Nimrod:* probably Tukulti-Ninurta I (thirteenth century B.C.), the first Assyrian conqueror of Babylonia and a famous city-builder at home.
10, 10: *Shinar:* ancient Sumer in southern Mesopotamia, mentioned also in 11, 2; 14, 1.
10, 11: *Asshur:* Assyria. *Rehoboth-Ir:* literally "wide-streets city," was probably not the name of another city, but an epithet of Nineveh; cf Jon 3, 3.
10, 12: *Calah:* Assyrian Kalhu, the capital of Assyria in the ninth century B.C.
10, 14: *The Pathrusim:* the people of upper (southern) Egypt; cf Is 11, 11; Jer 44, 1; Ez 29, 14; 30, 14. *Caphtorim:* Crete; for Caphtor as the place of origin of the Philistines, cf Dt 2, 23; Am 9, 7; Jer 47, 4.
10, 15: *Heth:* the biblical Hittites; see note on Gn 23, 3.
10, 19: *Lasha:* the reading of this name is uncertain; perhaps it should be "Bela"; cf 14, 2.

Sidon all the way to Gerar, near Gaza, and all the way to Sodom, Gomorrah, Admah, and Zeboiim, near Lasha.

20 These are the descendants of Ham, according to their clans and languages, by their lands and nations.

21 To Shem also, Japheth's oldest brother and the ancestor of all the children of Eber, sons were born.

22 The descendants of Shem:
　　Elam, Asshur, Arpachshad,
　　　Lud, and Aram.
23 The descendants of Aram:
　　Uz, Hul, Gether, and Mash.

24 Arpachshad became the father of Shelah, and Shelah became the father of Eber. 25 To Eber two sons were born: the name of the first was Peleg, for in his time the world was divided; and the name of his brother was Joktan.

26 Joktan became the father of Almodad, Sheleph, Hazarmaveth, Jerah, 27 Hadoram, Uzal, Diklah, 28 Obal, Abimael, Sheba, 29 Ophir, Havilah, and Jobab. All these were descendants of Joktan. 30 Their settlements extended all the way to Sephar, the eastern hill country.

31 These are the descendants of Shem, according to their clans and languages, by their lands and nations.

32 These are the groupings of Noah's sons, according to their origins and by their nations. From these the other nations of the earth branched out after the flood.

The Tower of Babel

11 The whole world spoke the same language, using the same words. 2 While men were migrating in the east, they came upon a valley in the land of Shinar and settled there.

3 They said to one another. "Come, let us mold bricks and harden them with fire." They used bricks for stone, and bitumen for mortar. 4 Then they said, "Come, let us build ourselves a city and a tower with its top in the sky and so make a name for ourselves; otherwise we shall be scattered all over the earth."

5 The LORD came down to see the city and the tower that the men had built. 6 Then the LORD said: "If now, while they are one people, all speaking the same language, they have started to do this, nothing will later stop them from doing whatever they presume to do. 7 Let us then go down and there confuse their language, so that one will not understand what another says." 8 Thus the LORD scattered them from there all over the earth, and they stopped building the city. 9 That is why it was called Babel, because there the LORD confused the speech of all the world. It was from that place that he scattered them all over the earth.

The Line from Shem to Abraham

10 This is the record of the descendants of Shem. When Shem was one hundred years old, he became the father of Arpachshad, two years after the flood. 11 Shem lived five hundred years after the birth of Arpachshad, and he had other sons and daughters.

12 When Arpachshad was thirty-five years old, he became the father of Shelah. 13 Arpachshad lived four hundred and three years after the birth of Shelah, and he had other sons and daughters.

14 When Shelah was thirty years old, he became the father of Eber. 15 Shelah lived four hundred and three years after the birth of Eber, and he had other sons and daughters.

16 When Eber was thirty-four years old, he became the father of Peleg. 17 Eber lived four hundred and thirty years after the birth of Peleg, and he had other sons and daughters.

18 When Peleg was thirty years old, he became the father of Reu. 19 Peleg lived two hundred and nine years after the birth of Reu, and he had other sons and daughters.

20 When Reu was thirty-two years old, he became the father of Serug. 21 Reu lived two hundred and seven years after the birth of Serug, and he had other sons and daughters.

22 When Serug was thirty years old, he became the father of Nahor. 23 Serug lived two hundred years after the birth of Nahor, and he had other sons and daughters.

24 When Nahor was twenty-nine years old, he became the father of Terah. 25 Nahor lived one hundred and nineteen years after the birth of Terah, and he had other sons and daughters.

26 When Terah was seventy years old, he became the father of Abram, Nahor, and Haran.

THE PATRIARCH ABRAHAM

Terah

27 This is the record of the descendants of Terah. Terah became the father of Abram, Nahor, and Haran, and Haran became the father of Lot. 28 Haran died before his father Terah, in his native land, in Ur of the Chaldeans. 29 Abram and Nahor took wives; the name of Abram's wife was Sarai, and the name of Nahor's wife was Milcah, daughter of Haran, the father of Milcah and Iscah. 30 Sarai was barren; she had no child.

31 Terah took his son Abram, his

10, 25: In the Hebrew text there is a play on the name *Peleg* and the word *niplega*, "was divided."

11, 1–9: This story, based on traditions about the temple towers or ziggurats of Babylonia, is used by the sacred writer primarily to illustrate man's increasing wickedness, shown here in his presumptuous effort to create an urban culture apart from God. The secondary motive in the story is to present an imaginative origin of the diversity of languages among the various peoples inhabiting the earth, as well as an artificial explanation of the name "Babylon."

11, 2: *Shinar:* see note on 10, 10.

11, 4: *Tower with its top in the sky:* a direct reference to the chief ziggurat of Babylon, the *E-sag-ila,* signifying "the house that raises high its head." Babylonian ziggurats were the earliest skyscrapers.

11, 9: *Babel:* the Hebrew form of the name "Babylon"; the native name, *Bab-ili,* means "gate of the gods." The Hebrew word *balil,* "he confused," has a similar sound. Apparently the name referred originally only to a certain part of the city, the district near the gate that led to the temple area.

11, 10–26: This section is a continuation of the genealogical record given in 5, 1–32; see note there. Although the ages of the patriarchs in this list are much lower than those of the antediluvian patriarchs, they are still artificial and devoid of historical value. The ages given here are from the current Hebrew text; the Samaritan and Greek texts have divergent sets of numbers in most cases.

11, 12: The Greek text has a certain Kenan

(cf 5, 9f) between Arpachshad and Shelah. This text is followed in Lk 3, 36.

11, 16: *Eber:* the eponymous ancestor of the Hebrews, "descendants of Eber" (10, 21.24–30 see note on 14, 13.

11, 28: *Ur of the Chaldeans:* Ur was an extremely ancient city of the Sumerians (later, of the Babylonians) in southern Mesopotamia. The Greek text has "the land of the Chaldeans." In either case, the term *Chaldeans* is an anachronism, because the Chaldeans were not known to history until approximately a thousand years after Abraham's time.

11, 31: The Samaritan and Greek texts include Nahor and his wife in Terah's migration to Haran. Although this is probably due to scribal harmonization, Nahor's family actually did migrate to Haran; cf. 24, 10; 27, 43.

grandson Lot, son of Haran, and his daughter-in-law Sarai, the wife of his son Abram, and brought them out of Ur of the Chaldeans, to go to the land of Canaan. But when they reached Haran, they settled there. 32 The lifetime of Terah was two hundred and five years; then Terah died in Haran.

Abram's Call and Migration

12 The LORD said to Abram: "Go forth from the land of your kinsfolk and from your father's house to a land that I will show you.

2 "I will make of you a great nation, and I will bless you;
I will make your name great, so that you will be a blessing.
3 I will bless those who bless you and curse those who curse you.
All the communities of the earth shall find blessing in you."

4 Abram went as the LORD directed him, and Lot went with him. Abram was seventy-five years old when he left Haran. 5 Abram took his wife Sarai, his brother's son Lot, all the possessions that they had accumulated, and the persons they had acquired in Haran, and they set out for the land of Canaan. When they came to the land of Canaan, 6 Abram passed through the land as far as the sacred place at Shechem, by the terebinth of Moreh. (The Canaanites were then in the land.)

7 The LORD appeared to Abram and said, "To your descendants I will give this land." So Abram built an altar there to the LORD who had appeared to him. 8 From there he moved on to the hill country east of Bethel, pitching his tent with Bethel to the west and Ai to the east. He built an altar there to the LORD and invoked the LORD by name. 9 Then Abram journeyed on by stages to the Negeb.

Abram and Sarai in Egypt

10 There was famine in the land; so Abram went down to Egypt to sojourn there, since the famine in the land was severe. 11 When he was about to enter Egypt, he said to his wife Sarai: "I know well how beautiful a woman you are. 12 When the Egyptians see you, they will say, 'She is his wife'; then they will kill me, but let you live. 13 Please say, therefore, that you are my sister, so that it may go well with me on your account and my life may be spared for your sake." 14 When Abram came to Egypt, the Egyptians saw how beautiful the woman was; and when Pharaoh's courtiers saw her, 15 they praised her to Pharaoh. So she was taken into Pharaoh's palace. 16 On her account it went very well with Abram, and he received flocks and herds, male and female slaves, male and female asses, and camels.

17 But the LORD struck Pharaoh and his household with severe plagues because of Abram's wife Sarai. 18 Then Pharaoh summoned Abram and said to him: "How could you do this to me! Why didn't you tell me she was your wife? 19 Why did you say, 'She is my sister,' so that I took her for my wife? Here, then, is your wife. Take her and be gone!" 20 Then Pharaoh gave men orders concerning him, and they sent him on his way, with his wife and all that belonged to him.

Abram and Lot Part

13 From Egypt Abram went up to the Negeb with his wife and all that belonged to him, and Lot accompanied him. 2 Now Abram was very rich in livestock, silver, and gold. 3 From the Negeb he traveled by stages toward Bethel, to the place between Bethel and Ai where his tent had formerly stood, 4 the site where he had first built the altar; and there he invoked the LORD by name.

5 Lot, who went with Abram, also had flocks and herds and tents, 6 so that the land could not support them if they stayed together; their possessions were so great that they could not dwell together. 7 There were quarrels between the herdsmen of Abram's livestock and those of Lot's. (At this time the Canaanites and the Perizzites were occupying the land.)

8 So Abram said to Lot: "Let there be no strife between you and me, or between your herdsmen and mine, for we are kinsmen. 9 Is not the whole land at your disposal? Please separate from me. If you prefer the left, I will go to the right; if you prefer the right, I will go to the left." 10 Lot looked about and saw how well watered the whole Jordan Plain was as far as Zoar, like the LORD's own garden, or like Egypt. (This was before the LORD had destroyed Sodom and Gomorrah.) 11 Lot, therefore, chose for himself the whole Jordan Plain and set out eastward. Thus they separated from each other; 12 Abram stayed in the land of Canaan, while Lot settled among the cities of the Plain, pitching his tents near Sodom. 13 Now the inhabitants of Sodom were very wicked in the sins they committed against the LORD.

14 After Lot had left, the LORD said to Abram: "Look about you, and from where you are, gaze to the north and south, east and west; 15 all the land that you see I will give to you and your descendants forever. 16 I will make your descendants like the dust of the earth; if anyone could count the dust of the earth, your descendants too might be counted. 17 Set forth and walk about in the land, through its length and breadth, for to you I will give it." 18 Abram moved his tents and went on to settle

11, 32: Since Terah was seventy years old when his son Abraham was born (v 26), and Abraham was seventy-five when he left Haran (12, 4), Terah lived in Haran for sixty years after Abraham's departure. According to the tradition in the Samaritan text, Terah died when he was one hundred and forty-five years old, therefore, in the same year in which Abraham left Haran. This is the tradition followed in St. Stephen's speech: Abraham left Haran "after his father's death" (Acts 7, 4).

12, 3: *Shall find blessing in you:* the sense of the Hebrew expression is probably reflexive, "shall bless themselves through you" (i.e., in giving a blessing they shall say, "May you be as blessed as Abraham"),

rather than passive, "shall be blessed in you." Since the term is understood in a passive sense in the New Testament (Acts 3, 25; Gal. 3, 8), it is rendered here by a neutral expression that admits of both meanings. So also in the blessings given by God to Isaac (26, 4) and Jacob (28, 14).

12, 5: *Persons:* slaves and retainers that formed the social aggregate under the leadership of Abraham; cf 14, 14.

12, 9: *The Negeb:* the semidesert land of southern Palestine.

12, 13: *You are my sister:* although Abraham's deceit may not be fully defensible, his statement was at least a half-truth; Sarah was indeed his relative,

called "a sister" in Hebrew; cf 20, 12. Moreover, the ancient traditions on which this story and the parallel ones in 20, 1-18 and 26, 6-11 are based, probably come from the Hurrian custom of wife-sister marriage. Among the Hurrians, with whom Abraham's clan lived in close contact at Haran, a man could adopt his wife as his sister and thus give her higher status.

12, 16: *Camels:* domesticated camels probably did not come into common use in the ancient Near East until the end of the second millennium B.C. Thus the mention of camels at the time of the patriarchs (24, 11-64; 30, 43; 31, 17.34; 32, 8.16; 37, 25) is seemingly an anachronism.

near the terebinth of Mamre, which is at Hebron. There he built an altar to the LORD.

The Four Kings

14 In the days of . . . , Amraphel king of Shinar, Arioch king of Ellasar, Chedorlaomer king of Elam, and Tidal king of Goiim 2 made war on Bera king of Sodom, Birsha king of Gomorrah, Shinab king of Admah, Shemeber king of Zeboiim, and the king of Bela (that is, Zoar). 3 All the latter kings joined forces in the Valley of Siddim (that is, the Salt Sea). 4 For twelve years they had been subject to Chedorlaomer, but in the thirteenth year they rebelled. 5 In the fourteenth year Chedorlaomer and the kings allied with him came and defeated the Rephaim in Ashteroth-karnaim, the Zuzim in Ham, the Emim in Shaveh-kiriathaim, 6 and the Horites in the hill country of Seir, as far as El-paran, close by the wilderness. 7 They then turned back and came to Enmishpat (that is, Kadesh), and they subdued the whole country both of the Amalekites and of the Amorites who dwelt in Hazazon-tamar. 8 Thereupon the king of Sodom, the king of Gomorrah, the king of Admah, the king of Zeboiim, and the king of Bela (that is, Zoar) marched out, and in the Valley of Siddim they went into battle against them: 9 against Chedorlaomer king of Elam, Tidal king of Goiim, Amraphel king of Shinar, and Arioch king of Ellasar —four kings against five. 10 Now the Valley of Siddim was full of bitumen pits; and as the kings of Sodom and Gomorrah fled, they fell into these, while the rest fled to the mountains. 11 The victors seized all the possessions and food supplies of Sodom and Gomorrah and then went their way, 12 taking with them Abram's nephew Lot, who had been living in Sodom, as well as his possessions.

13 A fugitive came and brought the news to Abram the Hebrew, who was camping at the terebinth of Mamre the Amorite, a kinsman of Eshcol and Aner; these were in league with Abram. 14 When Abram heard that his nephew had been captured, he mustered three hundred and eighteen of his retainers, born in his house, and went in pursuit as far as Dan. 15 He and his party deployed against them at night, defeated them, and pursued them as far as Hobah, which is north of Damascus. 16 He recovered all the possessions, besides bringing back his kinsman Lot and his possessions, along with the women and the other captives.

17 When Abram returned from his victory over Chedorlaomer and the kings who were allied with him, the king of Sodom went out to greet him in the Valley of Shaveh (that is, the King's Valley).

18 Melchizedek, king of Salem, brought out bread and wine, and being a priest of God Most High, he blessed Abram with these words:

19 "Blessed be Abram by God Most High,
    the creator of heaven and earth;
20 And blessed be God Most High,
    who delivered your foes into your hand."

Then Abram gave him a tenth of everything.

21 The king of Sodom said to Abram, "Give me the people; the goods you may keep." 22 But Abram replied to the king of Sodom: "I have sworn to the LORD, God Most High, the creator of heaven and earth, 23 that I would not take so much as a thread or a sandal strap from anything that is yours, lest you should say, 'I made Abram rich.' 24 Nothing for me except what my servants have used up and the share that is due to the men who joined me —Aner, Eshcol and Mamre; let them take their share."

The Covenant with Abram

15 Some time after these events, this word of the LORD came to Abram in a vision:

"Fear not, Abram!
  I am your shield;
  I will make your reward very great."

2 But Abram said, "O Lord GOD, what good will your gifts be, if I keep on being childless and have as my heir the steward of my house, Eliezer?" 3 Abram continued, "See, you have given me no offspring, and so one of my servants will be my heir." 4 Then the word of the LORD came to him: "No, that one shall not be your heir; your own issue shall be your heir." 5 He took him outside and said: "Look up at the sky and count the stars, if you can. Just so," he added, "shall your descendants be." 6 Abram put his faith in the LORD, who credited it to him as an act of righteousness.

7 He then said to him, "I am the LORD who brought you from Ur of the Chaldeans to give you this land as a possession." 8 "O Lord GOD," he asked, "how am I to know that I shall possess it?" 9 He answered him, "Bring me a three-year-old heifer, a three-year-old she-goat, a three-year-old ram, a turtledove, and a young pigeon." 10 He brought him all these, split them in two, and placed each half opposite the other; but the birds he did not cut up. 11 Birds of prey swooped down on the carcasses, but Abram stayed with

---

14, 1: *In the days of . . . :* the personal name by which the event is dated has not been preserved.

14, 3: *The Salt Sea:* now known as the Dead Sea.

14, 5f: The five kings came from north to south through the land east of the Jordan.

14, 13: *Abram the Hebrew:* elsewhere in the Old Testament, until the last pre-Christian centuries, the term "Hebrew" is used only by non-Israelites, or by Israelites in speaking to foreigners, since it evidently had a disparaging connotation—something like "immigrant." The account in this chapter may, therefore, have been taken originally from a non-Israelite source, in which Abraham, a warlike sheik of Palestine, appears as a truly historical figure of profane history.

14, 18: *Salem:* traditionally identified with Jerusalem (Ps 76, 3), but the Hebrew text is not certain; instead of the present *melek shalem* ("king of Salem"), the original may have been *melek shelomo* ("a king allied to him"). In Heb 7, 2, "king of Salem" is interpreted as "king of peace" (*shalom*).

14, 19: *God Most High:* in Hebrew, *el-elyon.* In Canaanite texts, each element may occur separately as the name of a specific deity, or they may be applied together to a single deity, as is done here by the Canaanite priest Melchizedek. For the Israelites, *el* became a poetic synonym for *elohim* ("God"); *elyon* ("Most High") became one of the titles of their God Yahweh.

14, 20: *Abram gave him:* literally "he gave him";

but *Abram* is to be understood as the subject of the sentence, for the tithes were the tenth part assigned to priests; cf Heb 7, 4–10.

14, 22: Abraham uses the name of the Canaanite god *el-elyon* ("God the Most High") in apposition to the name of his God, *yahweh* ("the LORD").

15, 6: Abraham's *faith* in God's promises was regarded as *an act of righteousness,* i.e., as expressing the "right" attitude of man toward God. In turn, God credited this to Abraham, i.e., gave him title to the fulfillment of God's promises. St. Paul (Rom 4, 1–25; Gal 3, 6–9) makes Abraham's faith a model for that of Christians.

15, 9: *Three-year-old:* ritually mature.

them. 12 As the sun was about to set, a trance fell upon Abram, and a deep, terrifying darkness enveloped him.

13 Then the LORD said to Abram: "Know for certain that your descendants shall be aliens in a land not their own, where they shall be enslaved and oppressed for four hundred years. 14 But I will bring judgment on the nation they must serve, and in the end they will depart with great wealth. 15 You, however, shall join your forefathers in peace; you shall be buried at a contented old age. 16 In the fourth time-span the others shall come back here; the wickedness of the Amorites will not have reached its full measure until then."

17 When the sun had set and it was dark, there appeared a smoking brazier and a flaming torch, which passed between those pieces. 18 It was on that occasion that the LORD made a covenant with Abram, saying: "To your descendants I give this land, from the Wadi of Egypt to the Great River [the Euphrates], 19 the land of the Kenites, the Kenizzites, the Kadmonites, 20 the Hittites, the Perizzites, the Rephaim, 21 the Amorites, the Canaanites, the Girgashites, and the Jebusites."

Birth of Ishmael

16 Abram's wife Sarai had borne him no children. She had, however, an Egyptian maidservant named Hagar. 2 Sarai said to Abram: "The LORD has kept me from bearing children. Have intercourse, then, with my maid; perhaps I shall have sons through her." Abram heeded Sarai's request. 3 Thus, after Abram had lived ten years in the land of Canaan, his wife Sarai took her maid, Hagar the Egyptian, and gave her to her husband Abram to be his concubine. 4 He had inter-

course with her, and she became pregnant. When she became aware of her pregnancy, she looked on her mistress with disdain. 5 So Sarai said to Abram: "You are responsible for this outrage against me. I myself gave my maid to your embrace; but ever since she became aware of her pregnancy, she has been looking on me with disdain. May the LORD decide between you and me!" 6 Abram told Sarai: "Your maid is in your power. Do to her whatever you please." Sarai then abused her so much that Hagar ran away from her.

7 The LORD's messenger found her by a spring in the wilderness, the spring on the road to Shur, 8 and he asked, "Hagar, maid of Sarai, where have you come from and where are you going?" She answered, "I am running away from my mistress, Sarai." 9 But the LORD's messenger told her: "Go back to your mistress and submit to her abusive treatment. 10 I will make your descendants so numerous," added the LORD's messenger, "that they will be too many to count. 11 Besides," the LORD's messenger said to her:

"You are now pregnant and shall
    bear a son;
  you shall name him Ishmael,
For the LORD has heard you,
    God has answered you.
12 He shall be a wild ass of a man,
    his hand against everyone,
  and everyone's hand against
    him;
In opposition to all his kin
    shall he encamp."

13 To the LORD who spoke to her she gave a name, saying, "You are the God of Vision"; she meant, "Have I really seen God and remained alive after my vision?" 14 That is why the well is called Beer-lahai-roi. It is between Kadesh and Bered.

15 Hagar bore Abram a son, and Abram named the son whom Hagar bore him Ishmael. 16 Abram was eighty-six years old when Hagar bore him Ishmael.

Covenant of Circumcision

17 When Abram was ninety-nine years old, the LORD appeared to him and said: "I am God the Almighty. Walk in my presence and be blameless. 2 Between you and me I will establish my covenant, and I will multiply you exceedingly."

3 When Abram prostrated himself, God continued to speak to him: 4 "My covenant with you is this: you are to become the father of a host of nations. 5 No longer shall you be called Abram; your name shall be Abraham, for I am making you the father of a host of nations. 6 I will render you exceedingly fertile; I will make nations of you; kings shall stem from you. 7 I will maintain my covenant with you and your descendants after you throughout the ages as an everlasting pact, to be your God and the God of your descendants after you. 8 I will give to you and to your descendants after you the land in which you are now staying, the whole land of Canaan, as a permanent possession; and I will be their God."

9 God also said to Abraham: "On your part, you and your descendants after you must keep my covenant throughout the ages. 10 This is my covenant with you and your descendants after you that you must keep: every male among you shall be circumcised. 11 Circumcise the flesh of your foreskin, and that shall be the mark of the covenant between you and me. 12 Throughout the ages, every male among you, when he is eight days old, shall be circumcised, including houseborn slaves and those acquired with money from any

---

15, 16: *Time-span:* the Hebrew term *dor* is commonly rendered as "generation," but it may signify a period of varying length. Neither this passage nor the statement about the four hundred years has any value for determining how long the Israelites were in Egypt.

15, 17: *Brazier:* literally "oven"; a portable one is meant here. The smoke and fire represent God's presence. Although the text does not mention it, Abraham no doubt also walked between the split carcasses. For the meaning of this strange ceremony, see note on Jer 38, 18ff.

15, 18: *Made a covenant:* literally "cut a cove-

nant"; the expression derives from the ceremony of cutting the animals in two.

16, 1–6: Sarah's actions are all in keeping with the laws of the time, as known from ancient extra-biblical sources.

16, 7: *The Lord's messenger:* a manifestation of God in human form; therefore in v 13 the messenger is identified with the Lord himself.

16, 11: *Ishmael:* in Hebrew the name means "God has heard."

16, 13: *The God of Vision:* in Hebrew, *el-roi;* hence the name of the spring. *Remained alive:* for the ancient notion that a person died on seeing God,

cf 32, 31; Ex 20, 19; Dt 4, 33; Jgs 13, 22.

16, 14: *Beer-lahai-roi:* probably "the well of living sight," i.e., the well where one can see (God) and yet live.

17, 1: *The Almighty:* traditional but incorrect rendering of the divine title *shaddai*, of uncertain meaning.

17, 5: *Abram* and *Abraham* are merely two forms of the same name, both meaning, "the father is exalted"; another variant form is Abiram (Nm 16, 1; 1 Kgs 16, 34). The additional *-ha-* in the form Abraham is explained by folk etymology as coming from *ab-hamon goyim,* "father of a host of nations."

foreigner who is not of your blood. 13 Yes, both the houseborn slaves and those acquired with money must be circumcised. Thus my covenant shall be in your flesh as an everlasting pact. 14 If a male is uncircumcised, that is, if the flesh of his foreskin has not been cut away, such a one shall be cut off from his people; he has broken my covenant."

15 God further said to Abraham: "As for your wife Sarai, do not call her Sarai; her name shall be Sarah. 16 I will bless her, and I will give you a son by her. Him also will I bless; he shall give rise to nations, and rulers of peoples shall issue from him." 17 Abraham prostrated himself and laughed as he said to himself, "Can a child be born to a man who is a hundred years old? Or can Sarah give birth at ninety?" 18 Then Abraham said to God, "Let but Ishmael live on by your favor!" 19 God replied: "Nevertheless, your wife Sarah is to bear you a son, and you shall call him Isaac. I will maintain my covenant with him as an everlasting pact, to be his God and the God of his descendants after him. 20 As for Ishmael, I am heeding you: I hereby bless him. I will make him fertile and will multiply him exceedingly. He shall become the father of twelve chieftains, and I will make of him a great nation. 21 But my covenant I will maintain with Isaac, whom Sarah shall bear to you by this time next year." 22 When he had finished speaking with him, God departed from Abraham.

23 Then Abraham took his son Ishmael and all his slaves, whether born in his house or acquired with his money—every male among the members of Abraham's household—and he circumcised the flesh of their foreskins on that same day, as God had told him to do. 24 Abraham was ninety-nine years old when the flesh of his foreskin was circumcised, 25 and his son Ishmael was thirteen years old when the flesh of his foreskin was circumcised. 26 Thus, on that same day Abraham and his son Ishmael were circumcised; 27 and all the male members of his household, including the slaves born in his house or acquired with his money from foreigners, were circumcised with him.

Abraham's Visitors

18 The LORD appeared to Abraham by the terebinth of Mamre, as he sat in the entrance of his tent, while the day was growing hot. 2 Looking up, he saw three men standing nearby. When he saw them, he ran from the entrance of the tent to greet them; and bowing to the ground, 3 he said: "Sir, if I may ask you this favor, please do not go on past your servant. 4 Let some water be brought, that you may bathe your feet, and then rest yourselves under the tree. 5 Now that you have come this close to your servant, let me bring you a little food, that you may refresh yourselves; and afterward you may go on your way." "Very well," they replied, "do as you have said."

6 Abraham hastened into the tent and told Sarah, "Quick, three seahs of fine flour! Knead it and make rolls." 7 He ran to the herd, picked out a tender, choice steer, and gave it to a servant, who quickly prepared it. 8 Then he got some curds and milk, as well as the steer that had been prepared, and set these before them; and he waited on them under the tree while they ate.

9 "Where is your wife Sarah?" they asked him. "There in the tent," he replied. 10 One of them said, "I will surely return to you about this time next year, and Sarah will then have a son." Sarah was listening at the entrance of the tent, just behind him. 11 Now Abraham and Sarah were old, advanced in years, and Sarah had stopped having her womanly periods. 12 So Sarah laughed to herself and said, "Now that I am so withered and my husband is so old, am I still to have sexual pleasure?" 13 But the LORD said to Abraham: "Why did Sarah laugh and say, 'Shall I really bear a child, old as I am?' 14 Is anything too marvelous for the LORD to do? At the appointed time, about this time next year, I will return to you, and Sarah will have a son." 15 Because she was afraid, Sarah dissembled, saying, "I didn't laugh." But he said, "Yes you did."

Abraham Intercedes for Sodom

16 The men set out from there and looked down toward Sodom; Abraham was walking with them, to see them on their way. 17 The LORD reflected: "Shall I hide from Abraham what I am about to do, 18 now that he is to become a great and populous nation, and all the nations of the earth are to find blessing in him? 19 Indeed, I have singled him out that he may direct his sons and his posterity to keep the way of the LORD by doing what is right and just, so that the LORD may carry into effect for Abraham the promises he made about him." 20 Then the LORD said: "The outcry against Sodom and Gomorrah is so great, and their sin so grave, 21 that I must go down and see whether or not their actions fully correspond to the cry against them that comes to me. I mean to find out."

22 While the two men walked on farther toward Sodom, the LORD remained standing before Abraham. 23 Then Abraham drew nearer to him and said: "Will you sweep away the innocent with the guilty? 24 Suppose there were fifty innocent people in the city; would you wipe out the place, rather than spare it for the sake of the fifty innocent people within it? 25 Far be it from you to do such a thing, to make the innocent

---

17, 15: *Sarai* and *Sarah* are variant forms of the same name, both meaning "princess."

17, 17: *Laughed: yishaq,* which is the Hebrew form of the name "Isaac"; other similar explanations of the name are given in 18, 12, and 21, 6.

18, 3: Abraham addresses the leader of the group, whom he does not yet recognize as Yahweh; in the next two verses he speaks to all *three men.* The other two are later (19, 1) identified as messengers.

18, 6: *Three seahs:* one ephah, about half a bushel.

18, 8: *Curds:* a type of soft cheese or yoghurt.

18, 10: *One of them:* i.e., the Lord. Abraham now realizes this for the first time when he hears the prediction of a miraculous birth. *About this time next year:* literally "when the time becomes alive," i.e., at the time when birth is due after the period of gestation; the conception is understood as taking place soon after the prediction.

18, 12: *Sarah laughed:* see note on 17, 17.

18, 20: Israelite tradition was unanimous in ascribing the destruction of Sodom and Gomorrah to the wickedness of these cities, but tradition varied in regard to the nature of this wickedness. According to the present account of the Yahwist, the sin of Sodom was homosexuality (19, 4f), which is therefore also known as sodomy; but according to Isaiah (1, 9f; 3, 9), it was a lack of social justice; Ezekiel (16, 46–51) described it as a disregard for the poor, whereas Jeremiah (23, 14) saw it as general immorality.

die with the guilty, so that the innocent and the guilty would be treated alike! Should not the judge of all the world act with justice?" 26 The LORD replied, "If I find fifty innocent people in the city of Sodom, I will spare the whole place for their sake." 27 Abraham spoke up again: "See how I am presuming to speak to my Lord, though I am but dust and ashes! 28 What if there are five less than fifty innocent people? Will you destroy the whole city because of those five?" "I will not destroy it," he answered, "if I find forty-five there." 29 But Abraham persisted, saying, "What if only forty are found there?" He replied, "I will forbear doing it for the sake of the forty." 30 Then he said, "Let not my Lord grow impatient if I go on. What if only thirty are found there?" He replied, "I will forbear doing it if I can find but thirty there." 31 Still he went on, "Since I have thus dared to speak to my Lord, what if there are no more than twenty?" "I will not destroy it," he answered, "for the sake of the twenty." 32 But he still persisted: "Please, let not my Lord grow angry if I speak up this last time. What if there are at least ten there?" "For the sake of those ten," he replied, "I will not destroy it."

33 The LORD departed as soon as he had finished speaking with Abraham, and Abraham returned home.

Destruction of Sodom and Gomorrah

19 The two angels reached Sodom in the evening, as Lot was sitting at the gate of Sodom. When Lot saw them, he got up to greet them; and bowing down with his face to the ground, 2 he said, "Please, gentlemen, come aside into your servant's house for the night, and bathe your feet; you can get up early to continue your journey." But they replied, "No, we shall pass the night in the town square."

3 He urged them so strongly, however, that they turned aside to his place and entered his house. He prepared a meal for them, baking cakes without leaven, and they dined.

4 Before they went to bed, all the townsmen of Sodom, both young and old—all the people to the last man—closed in on the house. 5 They called to Lot and said to him, "Where are the men who came to your house tonight? Bring them out to us that we may have intimacies with them." 6 Lot went out to meet them at the entrance. When he had shut the door behind him, 7 he said, "I beg you, my brothers, not to do this wicked thing. 8 I have two daughters who have never had intercourse with men. Let me bring them out to you, and you may do to them as you please. But don't do anything to these men, for you know they have come under the shelter of my roof." 9 They replied, "Stand back! This fellow," they sneered, "came here as an immigrant, and now he dares to give orders! We'll treat you worse than them!" With that, they pressed hard against Lot, moving in closer to break down the door. 10 But his guests put out their hands, pulled Lot inside with them, and closed the door; 11 at the same time they struck the men at the entrance of the house, one and all, with such a blinding light that they were utterly unable to reach the doorway.

12 Then the angels said to Lot: "Who else belongs to you here? Your sons [sons-in-law] and your daughters and all who belong to you in the city—take them away from it! 13 We are about to destroy this place, for the outcry reaching the LORD against those in the city is so great that he has sent us to destroy it." 14 So Lot went out and spoke to his sons-in-law, who had contracted marriage with his daughters. "Get up and leave this place," he

told them; "the LORD is about to destroy the city." But his sons-in-law thought he was joking.

15 As dawn was breaking, the angels urged Lot on, saying, "On your way! Take with you your wife and your two daughters who are here, or you will be swept away in the punishment of the city." 16 When he hesitated, the men, by the LORD's mercy, seized his hand and the hands of his wife and his two daughters and led them to safety outside the city. 17 As soon as they had been brought outside, he was told: "Flee for your life! Don't look back or stop anywhere on the Plain. Get off to the hills at once, or you will be swept away." 18 "Oh, no, my lord!" replied Lot. 19 "You have already thought enough of your servant to do me the great kindness of intervening to save my life. But I cannot flee to the hills to keep the disaster from overtaking me, and so I shall die. 20 Look, this town ahead is near enough to escape to. It's only a small place. Let me flee there—it's a small place, isn't it?—that my life may be saved." 21 "Well, then," he replied, "I will also grant you the favor you now ask. I will not overthrow the town you speak of. 22 Hurry, escape there! I cannot do anything until you arrive there." That is why the town is called Zoar.

23 The sun was just rising over the earth as Lot arrived in Zoar; 24 at the same time the LORD rained down sulphurous fire upon Sodom and Gomorrah [from the LORD out of heaven]. 25 He overthrew those cities and the whole Plain, together with the inhabitants of the cities and the produce of the soil. 26 But Lot's wife looked back, and she was turned into a pillar of salt.

27 Early the next morning Abraham went to the place where he had stood in the LORD's presence. 28 As he looked down toward Sodom and Gomorrah and the whole region of

---

19, 2: *Gentlemen:* Lot does not yet know that the distinguished-looking men are God's messengers; cf 18, 3.

19, 11: *Blinding light:* a preternatural flash that temporarily dazed the wicked men and revealed to Lot the true nature of his guests.

19, 12: Since Lot apparently had no *sons,* a glossator interpreted the term to mean *sons-in-law.*

19, 14: It is uncertain whether Lot's *sons-in-law* were fully married to his daughters or only "engaged"

to them (Israelite "engagement" was the first part of the marriage ceremony), or even whether the daughters involved were the same as, or different from, the two daughters who were still in their father's house.

19, 20: *A small place:* the Hebrew word *misar* literally "a little thing," has the same root consonants as the name of the town *Zoar* in v 22.

19, 25: *Overthrew:* The consistent use of this term, literally "turned upside down," to describe the

destruction of the Cities of the Plain seems to imply that their upheaval (v 29) was caused primarily by an earthquake; this would naturally be accompanied by a disastrous fire, especially in a region containing bitumen (14, 10) and its accompanying gases.

19, 28f: From the height east of Hebron, Abraham could easily see the region at the southern end of the Dead Sea, where the *Cities of the Plain* were probably located.

the Plain, he saw dense smoke over the land rising like fumes from a furnace.

29 Thus it came to pass: when God destroyed the Cities of the Plain, he was mindful of Abraham by sending Lot away from the upheaval by which God overthrew the cities where Lot had been living.

Moabites and Ammonites

30 Since Lot was afraid to stay in Zoar, he and his two daughters went up from Zoar and settled in the hill country, where he lived with his two daughters in a cave. 31 The older one said to the younger: "Our father is getting old, and there is not a man on earth to unite with us as was the custom everywhere. 32 Come, let us ply our father with wine and then lie with him, that we may have offspring by our father." 33 So that night they plied their father with wine, and the older one went in and lay with her father; but he was not aware of her lying down or her getting up. 34 Next day the older one said to the younger: "Last night it was I who lay with my father. Let us ply him with wine again tonight, and then you go in and lie with him, that we may both have offspring by our father." 35 So that night, too, they plied their father with wine, and then the younger one went in and lay with him; but again he was not aware of her lying down or her getting up.

36 Thus both of Lot's daughters became pregnant by their father. 37 The older one gave birth to a son whom she named Moab, saying, "From my father." He is the ancestor of the Moabites of today. 38 The younger one, too, gave birth to a son, and she named him Ammon, saying, "The son of my kin." He is the ancestor of the Ammonites of today.

Abraham at Gerar

20 Abraham journeyed on to the region of the Negeb, where he settled between Kadesh and Shur. While he stayed in Gerar, 2 he said of his wife Sarah, "She is my sister." So Abimelech, king of Gerar, sent and took Sarah. 3 But God came to Abimelech in a dream one night and said to him, "You are about to die because of the woman you have taken, for she has a husband." 4 Abimelech, who had not approached her, said: "O Lord, would you slay a man even though he is innocent? 5 He himself told me, 'She is my sister,' and she herself also stated, 'He is my brother.' I did it in good faith and with clean hands." 6 God answered him in the dream: "Yes, I know you did it in good faith. In fact, it was I who kept you from sinning against me; that is why I did not let you touch her. 7 Therefore, return the man's wife—as a spokesman he will intercede for you—that your life may be saved. If you do not return her, you can be sure that you and all who are yours will certainly die."

8 Early the next morning Abimelech called all his court officials and informed them of everything that had happened, and the men were horrified. 9 Then Abimelech summoned Abraham and said to him: "How could you do this to us! What wrong did I do to you that you should have brought such monstrous guilt on me and my kingdom? You have treated me in an intolerable way. 10 What were you afraid of," he asked him, "that you should have done such a thing?" 11 "I was afraid," answered Abraham, "because I thought there would surely be no fear of God in this place, and so they would kill me on account of my wife. 12 Besides, she is in truth my sister, but only my father's daughter, not my mother's; and so she became my wife. 13 When God sent me wandering from my father's house, I asked her: 'Would you do me this favor? In whatever place we come to, say that I am your brother.'"

14 Then Abimelech took flocks and herds and male and female slaves and gave them to Abraham; and after he restored his wife Sarah to him, 15 he said, "Here, my land lies at your disposal; settle wherever you please." 16 To Sarah he said: "See, I have given your brother a thousand shekels of silver. Let that serve you as a vindication before all who are with you; your honor has been preserved with everyone." 17 Abraham then interceded with God, and God restored health to Abimelech, that is, to his wife and his maidservants, so that they could bear children; 18 for God had tightly closed every womb in Abimelech's household on account of Abraham's wife Sarah.

Birth of Isaac

21 The LORD took note of Sarah as he had said he would; he did for her as he had promised. 2 Sarah became pregnant and bore Abraham a son in his old age, at the set time that God had stated. 3 Abraham gave the name Isaac to this son of his whom Sarah bore him. 4 When his son Isaac was eight days old, Abraham circumcised him, as God had commanded. 5 Abraham was a hundred years old when his son Isaac was born to him. 6 Sarah then said, "God has given me cause to laugh, and all who hear of it will laugh with me. 7 Who would have told Abraham," she added, "that Sarah would nurse children! Yet I have borne him a son in his old age." 8 Isaac grew, and on the day of the child's weaning, Abraham held a great feast.

9 Sarah noticed the son whom Hagar the Egyptian had borne to Abraham playing with her son Isaac; 10 so she demanded of Abraham: "Drive out that slave and her son! No son of that slave is going to share the inheritance with my son Isaac!" 11 Abraham was greatly distressed, especially on ac-

---

19, 30–38: This Israelite tale about the origin of Israel's neighbors east of the Jordan and the Dead Sea was told partly to ridicule these racially related but rival nations and partly to give folk etymologies from their names.

19, 37: From my father: in Hebrew, meabi, similar in sound to the name "Moab."

19, 38: The son of my kin: in Hebrew, ben-ammi, similar in sound to the name "Ammonites."

20, 1–18: This story from the Elohist source (see note on 4, 25) combines elements found in the two very similar but distinct stories of the Yahwist source, in 12, 10–20 and 26, 6–11.

20, 7: Spokesman: the Hebrew term nabi used here is regularly translated as "prophet," but it simply means "one who speaks on behalf of another," whether the latter is God, as in almost all cases, or another man, as in Ex 4, 16.

20, 16: A thousand shekels of silver: not a gift distinct from that of the animals and the slaves (v 14), but the monetary value of these.

21, 9–19: This story of Hagar's expulsion, in the Elohist source, is in general a duplicate of the one from the Yahwist source in 16, 5–14; but the two stories differ greatly in detail.

count of his son Ishmael. 12 But God said to Abraham: "Do not be distressed about the boy or about your slave woman. Heed the demands of Sarah, no matter what she is asking of you; for it is through Isaac that descendants shall bear your name. 13 As for the son of the slave woman, I will make a great nation of him also, since he too is your offspring."

14 Early the next morning Abraham got some bread and a skin of water and gave them to Hagar. Then, placing the child on her back, he sent her away. As she roamed aimlessly in the wilderness of Beer-sheba, 15 the water in the skin was used up. So she put the child down under a shrub, 16 and then went and sat down opposite him, about a bowshot away; for she said to herself, "Let me not watch the child die." As she sat opposite him, he began to cry. 17 God heard the boy's cry, and God's messenger called to Hagar from heaven: "What is the matter, Hagar? Don't be afraid; God has heard the boy's cry in this plight of his. 18 Arise, lift up the boy and hold him by the hand; for I will make of him a great nation." 19 Then God opened her eyes, and she saw a well of water. She went and filled the skin with water, and then let the boy drink.

20 God was with the boy as he grew up. He lived in the wilderness and became an expert bowman, 21 with his home in the wilderness of Paran. His mother got a wife for him from the land of Egypt.

The Pact at Beer-sheba

22 About that time Abimelech, accompanied by Phicol, the commander of his army, said to Abraham: "God is with you in everything you do. 23 Therefore, swear to me

by God at this place that you will not deal falsely with me or with my progeny and posterity, but will act as loyally toward me and the land in which you stay as I have acted toward you." 24 To this Abraham replied, "I so swear."

25 Abraham, however, reproached Abimelech about a well that Abimelech's men had seized by force. 26 "I have no idea who did that," Abimelech replied. "In fact, you never told me about it, nor did I ever hear of it until now."

27 Then Abraham took sheep and cattle and gave them to Abimelech and the two made a pact. 28 Abraham also set apart seven ewe lambs of the flock, 29 and Abimelech asked him, "What is the purpose of these seven ewe lambs that you have set apart?" 30 Abraham answered, "The seven ewe lambs you shall accept from me that thus I may have your acknowledgment that the well was dug by me." 31 This is why the place is called Beer-sheba; the two took an oath there. 32 When they had thus made the pact in Beer-sheba, Abimelech, along with Phicol, the commander of his army, left and returned to the land of the Philistines.

33 Abraham planted a tamarisk at Beer-sheba, and there he invoked by name the LORD, God the Eternal. 34 Abraham resided in the land of the Philistines for many years.

The Testing of Abraham

22 Some time after these events, God put Abraham to the test. He called to him, "Abraham!" "Ready!" he replied. 2 Then God said: "Take your son Isaac, your only one, whom you love, and go to the land of Moriah. There you shall offer him up as a holocaust on a height that I will point out to you."

3 Early the next morning Abraham saddled his donkey, took with him his son Isaac, and two of his servants as well, and with the wood that he had cut for the holocaust, set out for the place of which God had told him.

4 On the third day Abraham got sight of the place from afar. 5 Then he said to his servants: "Both of you stay here with the donkey, while the boy and I go on over yonder. We will worship and then come back to you." 6 Thereupon Abraham took the wood for the holocaust and laid it on his son Isaac's shoulders, while he himself carried the fire and the knife. 7 As the two walked on together, Isaac spoke to his father Abraham. "Father!" he said. "Yes, son," he replied. Isaac continued, "Here are the fire and the wood, but where is the sheep for the holocaust?" 8 "Son," Abraham answered, "God himself will provide the sheep for the holocaust." Then the two continued going forward.

9 When they came to the place of which God had told him, Abraham built an altar there and arranged the wood on it. Next he tied up his son Isaac, and put him on top of the wood on the altar. 10 Then he reached out and took the knife to slaughter his son. 11 But the LORD's messenger called to him from heaven, "Abraham, Abraham!" "Yes, Lord," he answered. 12 "Do not lay your hand on the boy," said the messenger. "Do not do the least thing to him. I know now how devoted you are to God, since you did not withhold from me your own beloved son." 13 As Abraham looked about, he spied a ram caught by its horns in the thicket. So he went and took the ram and offered it up as a holocaust in place of his son. 14 Abraham named the site Yahweh-

---

21, 14: *Placing the child on her back:* the phrase is translated from an emended form of the Hebrew text. In the current faulty Hebrew text, Abraham put the bread and the waterskin on Hagar's back, while her son apparently walked beside her. This reading seems to be a scribal attempt at harmonizing the present passage with the data of the Priestly source, in which Ishmael would have been at least fourteen years old when Isaac was born; compare 16, 16 with 21, 5; cf 17, 25. But in the present Elohist story Ishmael is obviously a little boy, not much older than Isaac; cf 15.18.
21, 22: Here and in v 32 the Greek text has "... Abimelech, accompanied by Ahuzzath, his

councilor, and Phicol ..."; but this is probably a secondary harmonization with 26, 26. Abimelech took Phicol with him in order to intimidate Abraham by a show of strength.
21, 23: *This place:* Beer-sheba (v 31). Abimelech had come from Gerar (20, 2) about thirty miles west of Beer-sheba.
21, 31: *Beer-sheba:* the Hebrew name really means, "the well of the seven," i.e., the place where there are seven wells, alluded to in the episode of the *seven ewe lambs*, vv 28ff; but it can also be interpreted to mean "the well of the oath."
21, 33: *God the Eternal:* in Hebrew, *el olam*, perhaps the name of the deity of the pre-Israelite sanc-

tuary at Beer-sheba, but used by Abraham merely as a title of Yahweh; cf Is 40, 28.
22, 1: *God put Abraham to the test:* to prove the firmness of Abraham's faith in God's promise that through Isaac all the nations of the earth would find blessing; cf 18, 10.18; 21, 12.
22, 2: *Only one:* uniquely precious, especially loved; therefore the same term is rendered in vv 12.17 as "beloved."
22, 14: *Yahweh-yireh:* a Hebrew expression meaning "the Lord will see"; the reference is to the words in v 8, "God himself will see to it."

yireh; hence people now say, "On the mountain the LORD will see."

15 Again the LORD's messenger called to Abraham from heaven 16 and said: "I swear by myself, declares the LORD, that because you acted as you did in not withholding from me your beloved son, 17 I will bless you abundantly and make your descendants as countless as the stars of the sky and the sands of the seashore; your descendants shall take possession of the gates of their enemies, 18 and in your descendants all the nations of the earth shall find blessing—all this because you obeyed my command."

19 Abraham then returned to his servants, and they set out together for Beer-sheba, where Abraham made his home.

Nahor's Descendants

20 Some time afterward, the news came to Abraham: "Milcah too has borne sons, to your brother Nahor: 21 Uz, his first-born, his brother Buz, Kemuel (the father of Aram), 22 Chesed, Hazo, Pildash, Jidlaph, and Bethuel." 23 Bethuel became the father of Rebekah. These eight Milcah bore to Abraham's brother Nahor. 24 His concubine, whose name was Reumah, also bore children: Tebah, Gaham, Tahash, and Maacah.

Purchase of a Burial Place

23 The span of Sarah's life was one hundred and twenty-seven years. 2 She died in Kiriath-arba (that is, Hebron) in the land of Canaan, and Abraham performed the customary mourning rites for her. 3 Then he left the side of his dead one and addressed the Hittites: 4 "Although I am a resident alien among you, sell me from your holdings a piece of property for a burial ground, that I may bury my dead wife." 5 The Hittites answered Abraham: "Please, sir, 6 listen to us! You are an elect of God among us. Bury your dead in the choicest of our burial sites. None of us would deny you his burial ground for the burial of your dead." 7 Abraham, however, began to bow low before the local citizens, the Hittites, 8 while he appealed to them: "If you will allow me room for burial of my dead, listen to me! Intercede for me with Ephron, son of Zohar, asking him 9 to sell me the cave of Machpelah that he owns; it is at the edge of his field. Let him sell it to me in your presence, at its full price, for a burial place."

10 Now Ephron was present with the Hittites. So Ephron the Hittite replied to Abraham in the hearing of the Hittites who sat on his town council: 11 "Please, sir, listen to me! I give you both the field and the cave in it; in the presence of my kinsmen I make this gift. Bury your dead!" 12 But Abraham, after bowing low before the local citizens, addressed Ephron in the hearing of these men: 13 "Ah, if only you would please listen to me! I will pay you the price of the field. Accept it from me, that I may bury my dead there." 14 Ephron replied to Abraham, "Please, 15 sir, listen to me! A piece of land worth four hundred shekels of silver—what is that between you and me, as long as you can bury your dead?" 16 Abraham accepted Ephron's terms; he weighed out to him the silver that Ephron had stipulated in the hearing of the Hittites, four hundred shekels of silver at the current market value.

17 Thus Ephron's field in Machpelah, facing Mamre, together with its cave and all the trees anywhere within its limits, was conveyed 18 to Abraham by purchase in the presence of all the Hittites who sat on Ephron's town council. 19 After this transaction, Abraham buried his wife Sarah in the cave of the field of Machpelah, facing Mamre (that is, Hebron) in the land of Canaan. 20 Thus the field with its cave was transferred from the Hittites to Abraham as a burial place.

Isaac and Rebekah

24 Abraham had now reached a ripe old age, and the LORD had blessed him in every way. 2 Abraham said to the senior servant of his household, who had charge of all his possessions: "Put your hand under my thigh, 3 and I will make you swear by the LORD, the God of heaven and the God of earth, that you will not procure a wife for my son from the daughters of the Canaanites among whom I live, 4 but that you will go to my own land and to my kindred to get a wife for my son Isaac." 5 The servant asked him: "What if the woman is unwilling to follow me to this land? Should I then take your son back to the land from which you migrated?" 6 "Never take my son back there for any reason," Abraham told him. 7 "The LORD, the God of heaven, who took me from my father's house and the land of my kin, and who confirmed by oath the promise he then made to me, 'I will give this land to your descendants'— he will send his messenger before you, and you will obtain a wife for my son there. 8 If the woman is unwilling to follow you, you will be released from this oath. But never take my son back there!" 9 So the servant put his hand under the thigh of his master Abraham and swore to him in this undertaking.

10 The servant then took ten of

22, 20–24: A list of Aramean tribes who lived to the east and northeast of Israel, twelve in number, like the twelve tribes of Israel (35, 23) and the twelve tribes of Ishmael (25, 12–16).

23, 3: *The Hittites:* a non-Semitic people in Canaan; their relationship to the well-known Hittites of Asia Minor is uncertain.

23, 4: *A resident alien:* literally "a sojourner and a settler," i.e., a long-term resident alien. Such a one would normally not have the right to own property. The importance of Abraham's purchase of the field in Machpelah, which is worded in technical legal terms, lies in the fact that it gave his descendants their first, though small, land rights in the country that God had promised the patriarch they would one day inherit as their own. Abraham therefore insists on purchasing the field and not receiving it as a gift.

23, 10: *Who sat on his town council:* probable meaning of the literal translation, "who came in at the gate of his city"; so also in v 18.

23, 15: *Four hundred shekels:* probably an exorbitant sum; Jeremiah (32, 9) paid only seventeen shekels for his field in Anathoth, though the Babylonian invasion no doubt helped to reduce the price.

23, 16: *The current market value:* the standard weight called a shekel varied according to time and place.

24, 2: *Put your hand under my thigh:* the symbolism of this act was apparently connected with the Hebrew concept of children issuing from their father's "thigh" (46, 26; Ex 1, 5). Perhaps the man who took such an oath was thought to bring the curse of sterility on himself if he did not fulfill his sworn promise. Jacob made Joseph swear in the same way (Gn 47, 29). In both these instances, the oath was taken to carry out the last request of a man upon his death.

24, 10: *Nahor:* it is uncertain whether this is to be understood as the name of Abraham's brother (11, 27), Rebekah's grandfather (24, 25), or the city of the same name (as known from the Mari documents): *Aram Naharaim*, situated near Haran (11, 31) in northern Mesopotamia.

his master's camels, and bearing all kinds of gifts from his master, he made his way to the city of Nahor in Aram Naharaim. 11 Near evening, at the time when women go out to draw water, he made the camels kneel by the well outside the city. 12 Then he prayed: "LORD, God of my master Abraham, let it turn out favorably for me today and thus deal graciously with my master Abraham. 13 While I stand here at the spring and the daughters of the townsmen are coming out to draw water, 14 if I say to a girl, 'please lower your jug, that I may drink,' and she answers, 'Take a drink, and let me give water to your camels, too,' let her be the one whom you have decided upon for your servant Isaac. In this way I shall know that you have dealt graciously with my master."

15 He had scarcely finished these words when Rebekah (who was born to Bethuel, son of Milcah, the wife of Abraham's brother Nahor) came out with a jug on her shoulder. 16 The girl was very beautiful, a virgin, untouched by man. She went down to the spring and filled her jug. As she came up, 17 the servant ran toward her and said, "Please give me a sip of water from your jug." 18 "Take a drink, sir," she replied, and quickly lowering the jug onto her hand, she gave him a drink. 19 When she had let him drink his fill, she said, "I will draw water for your camels, too, until they have drunk their fill." 20 With that, she quickly emptied her jug into the drinking trough and ran back to the well to draw more water, until she had drawn enough for all the camels. 21 The man watched her the whole time, silently waiting to learn whether or not the LORD had made his errand successful. 22 When the camels had finished drinking, the man took out a gold ring weighing half a shekel, which he fastened on her nose, and two gold bracelets weighing ten shekels, which he put on her wrists. 23 Then he asked her: "Whose daughter are you? Tell me, please. And is there room in your father's

house for us to spend the night?" 24 She answered: "I am the daughter of Bethuel the son of Milcah, whom she bore to Nahor. 25 There is plenty of straw and fodder at our place," she added, "and room to spend the night." 26 The man then bowed down in worship to the LORD, 27 saying: "Blessed be the LORD, the God of my master Abraham, who has not let his constant kindness toward my master fail. As for myself also, the LORD has led me straight to the house of my master's brother."

28 Then the girl ran off and told her mother's household about it. 29 Now Rebekah had a brother named Laban. 30 As soon as he saw the ring and the bracelets on his sister Rebekah and heard her words about what the man had said to her, Laban rushed outside to the man at the spring. When he reached him, he was still standing by the camels at the spring. 31 So he said to him: "Come, blessed of the LORD! Why are you staying outside when I have made the house ready for you, as well as a place for the camels?" 32 The man then went inside; and while the camels were being unloaded and provided with straw and fodder, water was brought to bathe his feet and the feet of the men who were with him. 33 But when the table was set for him, he said, "I will not eat until I have told my tale." "Do so," they replied.

34 "I am Abraham's servant," he began. 35 "The LORD has blessed my master so abundantly that he has become a wealthy man; he has given him flocks and herds, silver and gold, male and female slaves, and camels and asses. 36 My master's wife Sarah bore a son to my master in her old age, and he has given him everything he owns. 37 My master put me under oath, saying: 'You shall not procure a wife for my son among the daughters of the Canaanites in whose land I live; 38 instead, you shall go to my father's house, to my own relatives, to get a wife for my son.' 39 When I asked my master, 'What if the woman will not follow me?,' 40 he replied: 'The LORD, in whose presence I have always walked, will send his messenger with you and make your

errand successful, and so you will get a wife for my son from my own kindred of my father's house. 41 Then you shall be released from my ban. If you visit my kindred and they refuse you, then, too, you shall be released from my ban.'

42 "When I came to the spring today, I prayed: 'LORD, God of my master Abraham, may it be your will to make successful the errand I am engaged on! 43 While I stand here at the spring, if I say to a young woman who comes out to draw water, Please give me a little water from your jug, 44 and she answers, Not only may you have a drink, but I will give water to your camels, too—let her be the woman whom the LORD has decided upon for my master's son.'

45 "I had scarcely finished saying this prayer to myself when Rebekah came out with a jug on her shoulder. After she went down to the spring and drew water, I said to her, 'Please let me have a drink.' 46 She quickly lowered the jug she was carrying and said, 'Take a drink, and let me bring water for your camels, too.' So I drank, and she watered the camels also. 47 When I asked her, 'Whose daughter are you?' she answered, 'The daughter of Bethuel, son of Nahor, borne to Nahor by Milcah.' So I put the ring on her nose and the bracelets on her wrists. 48 Then I bowed down in worship to the LORD, blessing the LORD, the God of my master Abraham, who had led me on the right road to obtain the daughter of my master's kinsman for his son. 49 If, therefore, you have in mind to show true loyalty to my master, let me know; but if not, let me know that, too. I can then proceed accordingly."

50 Laban and his household said in reply: "This thing comes from the LORD; we can say nothing to you either for or against it. 51 Here is Rebekah, ready for you; take her with you, that she may become the wife of your master's son, as the LORD has said." 52 When Abraham's servant heard their answer, he bowed to the ground before the LORD. 53 Then he brought out objects of silver and gold and articles of clothing and presented them to

---

24, 12: *Let it turn out favorably for me:* let me have a favorable omen; cf end of v 14.

Rebekah; he also gave costly presents to her brother and mother. 54 After he and the men with him had eaten and drunk, they spent the night there.

When they were up the next morning, he said, "Give me leave to return to my master." 55 Her brother and mother replied, "Let the girl stay with us a short while, say ten days; after that she may go." 56 But he said to them, "Do not detain me, now that the LORD has made my errand successful; let me go back to my master." 57 They answered, "Let us call the girl and see what she herself has to say about it." 58 So they called Rebekah and asked her, "Do you wish to go with this man?" She answered, "I do." 59 At this they allowed their sister Rebekah and her nurse to take leave, along with Abraham's servant and his men. 60 Invoking a blessing on Rebekah, they said:

"Sister, may you grow
    into thousands of myriads;
And may your descendants
    gain possession
    of the gates of their
    enemies!"

61 Then Rebekah and her maids started out; they mounted their camels and followed the man. So the servant took Rebekah and went on his way.

62 Meanwhile Isaac had gone from Beer-lahai-roi and was living in the region of the Negeb. 63 One day toward evening he went out . . . in the field, and as he looked around, he noticed that camels were approaching. 64 Rebekah, too, was looking about, and when she saw him, she alighted from her camel 65 and asked the servant, "Who is the man out there, walking through the fields toward us?" "That is my master," replied the servant. Then she covered herself with her veil.

66 The servant recounted to Isaac all the things he had done. Then Isaac took Rebekah into his tent; 67 he married her, and thus she became his wife. In his love for her Isaac found solace after the death of his mother Sarah.

Abraham's Sons by Keturah

25 Abraham married another wife, whose name was Keturah. 2 She bore him Zimran, Jokshan, Medan, Midian, Ishbak, and Shuah. 3 Jokshan became the father of Sheba and Dedan. The descendants of Dedan were the Asshurim, the Letushim, and the Leummim. 4 The descendants of Midian were Ephah, Epher, Hanoch, Abida, and Eldaah. All of these were descendants of Keturah.

5 Abraham deeded everything that he owned to his son Isaac. 6 To his sons by concubinage, however, he made grants while he was still living, as he sent them away eastward, to the land of Kedem, away from his son Isaac.

Death of Abraham

7 The whole span of Abraham's life was one hundred and seventy-five years. 8 Then he breathed his last, dying at a ripe old age, grown old after a full life; and he was taken to his kinsmen. 9 His sons Isaac and Ishmael buried him in the cave of Machpelah, in the field of Ephron, son of Zohar the Hittite, which faces Mamre, 10 the field that Abraham had bought from the Hittites; there he was buried next to his wife Sarah. 11 After the death of Abraham, God blessed his son Isaac, who made his home near Beer-lahai-roi.

Descendants of Ishmael

12 These are the descendants of Abraham's son Ishmael, whom Hagar the Egyptian, Sarah's slave, bore to Abraham. 13 These are the names of Ishmael's sons, listed in the order of their birth: Nebaioth

(Ishmael's first-born), Kedar, Adbeel, Mibsam, 14 Mishma, Dumah, Massa, 15 Hadad, Tema, Jetur, Naphish, and Kedemah. 16 These are the sons of Ishmael, their names by their villages and encampments; twelve chieftains of as many tribal groups.

17 The span of Ishmael's life was one hundred and thirty-seven years. After he had breathed his last and died, he was taken to his kinsmen. 18 The Ishmaelites ranged from Havilah-by-Shur, which is on the border of Egypt, all the way to Asshur; and each of them pitched camp in opposition to his various kinsmen.

THE PATRIARCHS ISAAC AND JACOB

Birth of Esau and Jacob

19 This is the family history of Isaac, son of Abraham; Abraham had begotten Isaac. 20 Isaac was forty years old when he married Rebekah, the daughter of Bethuel the Aramean of Paddan-aram and the sister of Laban the Aramean. 21 Isaac entreated the LORD on behalf of his wife, since she was sterile. The LORD heard his entreaty, and Rebekah became pregnant. 22 But the children in her womb jostled each other so much that she exclaimed, "If this is to be so, what good will it do me!" She went to consult the LORD, 23 and he answered her:

"Two nations are in your womb,
    two peoples are quarreling
    while still within you;
But one shall surpass the other,
    and the older shall serve the
    younger."

24 When the time of her delivery came, there were twins in her womb. 25 The first to emerge was reddish, and his whole body was like a hairy mantle; so they named him Esau. 26 His brother came out next, gripping Esau's heel; so they named

---

24, 63: *He went out:* the meaning of the Hebrew term that follows this is obscure.

25, 1–11: Though mentioned here, Abraham's marriage to a concubine, or wife of secondary rank, and his death are not to be understood as happening chronologically after the events narrated in the preceding chapter.

25, 6: *The land of Kedem:* or "the country of the East," the region inhabited by the Kedemites or Easterners (29, 1; Jgs 6, 3.33; Jb 1, 3; Is 11, 14). The names mentioned in vv 2ff, as far as they can be

identified, are those of tribes in the Arabian desert.

25, 18: *Pitched camp:* literally "fell"; the same Hebrew verb is used in Jgs 7, 12 in regard to the hostile encampment of Bedouin tribes. The present passage shows the fulfillment of the prediction contained in Gn 16, 12.

25, 25: *Reddish:* in Hebrew, *admoni*, a reference to Edom, another name for Esau (v 30; 36, 1). Edom, however, was really the name of the country south of Moab where the descendants of Esau lived. It was called the "red" country because of its reddish

sandstone. *Hairy:* in Hebrew, *sear*, a reference to Seir, another name for Edom (36, 8). One might expect the text to say, "So they named him Seir"; but Esau (*esaw*) also means "hairy."

25, 26: *Esau's heel:* the Hebrew is *baaqeb esaw*, a reference to the name Jacob; cf 27, 36. Probably, however, the name Jacob has no true etymological connection with the Hebrew word for "heel" (*aqeb*) but is instead a shortened form of some such name as *yaaqob-el* ("may God protect").

him Jacob. Isaac was sixty years old when they were born.

27 As the boys grew up, Esau became a skillful hunter, a man who lived in the open; whereas Jacob was a simple man, who kept to his tents. 28 Isaac preferred Esau, because he was fond of game; but Rebekah preferred Jacob. 29 Once, when Jacob was cooking a stew, Esau came in from the open, famished. 30 He said to Jacob, "Let me gulp down some of that red stuff; I'm starving." (That is why he was called Edom.) 31 But Jacob replied, "First give me your birthright in exchange for it." 32 "Look," said Esau, "I'm on the point of dying. What good will any birthright do me?" 33 But Jacob insisted, "Swear to me first!" So he sold Jacob his birthright under oath. 34 Jacob then gave him some bread and the lentil stew; and Esau ate, drank, got up, and went his way. Esau cared little for his birthright.

Isaac and Abimelech

26 There was a famine in the land (distinct from the earlier one that had occurred in the days of Abraham), and Isaac went down to Abimelech, king of Philistines in Gerar. 2 The LORD appeared to him and said: "Do not go down to Egypt, but continue to camp wherever in this land I tell you. 3 Stay in this land, and I will be with you and bless you; for to you and your descendants I will give all these lands, in fulfillment of the oath that I swore to your father Abraham. 4 I will make your descendants as numerous as the stars in the sky and give them all these lands, and in your descendants all the nations of the earth shall find blessing— 5 this because Abraham obeyed me, keeping my mandate (my commandments, my ordinances, and my instructions)."

6 So Isaac settled in Gerar. 7 When the men of the place asked questions about his wife, he answered, "She is my sister." He was afraid, if he called her his wife, the men of the place would kill him on account of Rebekah, since she was very beautiful. 8 But when he had been there for a long time, Abimelech, king of the Philistines, happened to look out of a window and was surprised to see Isaac fondling his wife Rebekah. 9 He called for Isaac and said: "She must certainly be your wife! How could you have said, 'She is my sister'?" Isaac replied, "I thought I might lose my life on her account." 10 "How could you do this to us!" exclaimed Abimelech. "It would have taken very little for one of the men to lie with your wife, and you would have thus brought guilt upon us!" 11 Abimelech therefore gave this warning to all his men: "Anyone who molests this man or his wife shall forthwith be put to death."

12 Isaac sowed a crop in that region and reaped a hundred-fold the same year. Since the LORD blessed him, 13 he became richer and richer all the time, until he was very wealthy indeed. 14 He acquired such flocks and herds, and so many work animals, that the Philistines became envious of him. 15 (The Philistines had stopped up and filled with dirt all the wells that his father's servants had dug back in the days of his father Abraham.) 16 So Abimelech said to Isaac, "Go away from us; you have become far too numerous for us." 17 Isaac left there and made the Wadi Gerar his regular campsite. 18 (Isaac reopened the wells which his father's servants had dug back in the days of his father Abraham and which the Philistines had stopped up after Abraham's death; he gave them the same names that his father had given them.) 19 But when Isaac's servants dug in the wadi and reached spring water in their well, 20 the shepherds of Gerar quarreled with Isaac's servants, saying, "The water belongs to us!" So the well was called Esek, because they had challenged him there. 21 Then they dug another well, and they quarreled over that one too; so it was called Sitnah. 22 When he had moved on from there, he dug still another well; but over this one they did not quarrel. It was called Rehoboth, because he said, "The LORD has now given us ample room, and we shall flourish in the land."

23 From there Isaac went up to Beer-sheba. 24 The same night the LORD appeared to him and said: "I am the God of your father Abraham. You have no need to fear, since I am with you. I will bless you and multiply your descendants for the sake of my servant Abraham." 25 So he built an altar there and invoked the LORD by name. After he had pitched his tent there, his servants began to dig a well nearby.

26 Abimelech had meanwhile come to him from Gerar, accompanied by Ahuzzath, his councilor, and Phicol, the general of his army. 27 Isaac asked them, "Why have you come to me, seeing that you hate me and have driven me away from you?" 28 They answered: "We are convinced that the LORD is with you, so we propose that there be a sworn agreement between our two sides— between you and us. Let us make a pact with you: 29 you shall not act unkindly toward us, just as we have not molested you, but have always acted kindly toward you and have let you depart in peace. Henceforth, 'The LORD's blessing be upon you!'" 30 Isaac then made a feast for them, and they ate and drank. 31 Early the next morning they exchanged oaths. Then Isaac bade them farewell, and they departed from him in peace.

32 That same day Isaac's servants came and brought him news about the well they had been digging; they told him, "We have reached water!" 33 He called it Shibah; hence the

---

25, 30: *Red stuff:* in Hebrew, *adom;* another play on the word "Edom," the "red" land.

25, 31: *Birthright:* the privilege that entitled the first-born son to a position of honor in the family and to a double share in the possessions inherited from the father.

26, 6–11: The Yahwist's version of the wife-sister episode at Gerar; the Elohist's version (20, 1–18) is connected with Abraham and Sarah.

26, 12–33: The Yahwist's version of the story about the wells at Beer-sheba; again, the Elohist's version (21, 22f) is connected with Abraham. A redactor joined the two accounts by means of the parenthetical verses 15 and 18.

26, 20: *Esek:* "challenge."

26, 21: *Sitnah:* "opposition"; one might expect

the text to be continued by some such words as "because they were in opposition there."

26, 33: *Shibah:* "seven," for the sake of a closer assonance with Beer-sheba; but the present version of the story says nothing about there being seven wells there as implied in 21, 28–31. The Greek version understood the Hebrew text more logically as *shebua,* "oath," in keeping with the present story.

name of the city, Beer-sheba, to this day.

34 When Esau was forty years old, he married Judith, daughter of Beeri the Hittite, and Basemath, daughter of Elon the Hivite. 35 But they became a cause of embitterment to Isaac and Rebekah.

Jacob's Deception

27 When Isaac was so old that his eyesight had failed him, he called his older son Esau and said to him, "Son!" "Yes, father!" he replied. 2 Isaac then said, "As you can see, I am so old that I may now die at any time. 3 Take your gear, therefore—your quiver and bow—and go out into the country to hunt some game for me. 4 With your catch prepare an appetizing dish for me, such as I like, and bring it to me to eat, so that I may give you my special blessing before I die."

5 Rebekah had been listening while Isaac was speaking to his son Esau. So when Esau went out into the country to hunt some game for his father, 6 Rebekah said to her son Jacob, "Listen! I overheard your father tell your brother Esau, 7 'Bring me some game and with it prepare an appetizing dish for me to eat, that I may give you my blessing with the LORD's approval before I die.' 8 Now, son, listen carefully to what I tell you. 9 Go to the flock and get me two choice kids. With these I will prepare an appetizing dish for your father, such as he likes. 10 Then bring it to your father to eat, that he may bless you before he dies." 11 "But my brother Esau is a hairy man," said Jacob to his mother Rebekah, "and I am smooth-skinned! 12 Suppose my father feels me? He will think I am making sport of him, and I shall bring on myself a curse instead of a blessing." 13 His mother, however, replied: "Let any curse against you, son, fall on me! Just do as I say. Go and get me the kids."

14 So Jacob went and got them and brought them to his mother; and with them she prepared an appetizing dish, such as his father liked. 15 Rebekah then took the best clothes of her older son Esau that she had in the house, and gave them to her younger son Jacob to wear; 16 and with the skins of the kids she covered up his hands and the hairless parts of his neck. 17 Then she handed her son Jacob the appetizing dish and the bread she had prepared.

18 Bringing them to his father, Jacob said, "Father!" "Yes?" replied Isaac. "Which of my sons are you?" 19 Jacob answered his father: "I am Esau, your first-born. I did as you told me. Please sit up and eat some of my game, so that you may give me your special blessing." 20 But Isaac asked, "How did you succeed so quickly, son?" He answered, "The LORD, your God, let things turn out well with me." 21 Isaac then said to Jacob, "Come closer, son, that I may feel you, to learn whether you really are my son Esau or not." 22 So Jacob moved up closer to his father. When Isaac felt him, he said, "Although the voice is Jacob's, the hands are Esau's." 23 (He failed to identify him because his hands were hairy, like those of his brother Esau; so in the end he gave him his blessing.) 24 Again he asked him, "Are you really my son Esau?" "Certainly," he replied. 25 Then Isaac said, "Serve me your game, son, that I may eat of it and then give you my blessing." Jacob served it to him, and Isaac ate; he brought him wine, and he drank. 26 Finally his father Isaac said to him, "Come closer, son, and kiss me." 27 As Jacob went up and kissed him, Isaac smelled the fragrance of his clothes. With that, he blessed him, saying,

"Ah, the fragrance of my son
　　is like the fragrance of a field
　　that the LORD has blessed!

28 "May God give to you
　　of the dew of the heavens
And of the fertility of the earth
　　abundance of grain and wine.

29 "Let peoples serve you,
　　and nations pay you homage;
Be master of your brothers,
　　and may your mother's sons
　　　bow down to you.
Cursed be those who curse you,
　　and blessed be those who
　　　bless you."

30 Jacob had scarcely left his father, just after Isaac had finished blessing him, when his brother Esau came back from his hunt. 31 Then he too prepared an appetizing dish with his game, and bringing it to his father, he said, "Please, father, eat some of your son's game, that you may then give me your special blessing." 32 "Who are you?" his father Isaac asked him. "I am Esau," he replied, "your first-born son." 33 With that, Isaac was seized with a fit of uncontrollable trembling. "Who was it, then," he asked, "that hunted game and brought it to me? I finished eating it just before you came, and I blessed him. Now he must remain blessed!" 34 On hearing his father's words, Esau burst into loud, bitter sobbing. "Father, bless me too!" he begged. 35 When Isaac explained, "Your brother came here by a ruse and carried off your blessing," 36 Esau exclaimed, "He has been well named Jacob! He has now supplanted me twice! First he took away my birthright, and now he has taken away my blessing." Then he pleaded, "Haven't you saved a blessing for me?" 37 Isaac replied: "I have already appointed him your master, and I have assigned to him all his kinsmen as his slaves; besides, I have enriched him with grain and wine. What then can I do for you, son?" 38 But Esau urged his father, "Have you only one blessing, father? Bless me too!" Isaac, however, made no reply; and Esau wept aloud. 39

26, 34f: These verses from the Priestly source, which have no logical connection with the preceding stories, serve as an introduction to the following section on Esau's loss of his birthright by suggesting a motivation for this in Isaac's and Rebekah's dislike for Esau's Canaanite wives.

27, 1–45: What Jacob did in deceiving his father and thereby cheating Esau out of Isaac's deathbed blessing is condemned as blameworthy, not only by

Hosea (12, 4) and Jeremiah (9, 3), but also, indirectly, by the Yahwist narrator of the present story, who makes the reader sympathize with Esau as the innocent victim of a cruel plot, and shows that Jacob and his mother, the instigator of the plot, paid for it by a lifelong separation from each other. The story was told because it was part of the mystery of God's ways in salvation history—his use of weak, sinful men to achieve his own ultimate purpose.

27, 4: My special blessing: "the blessing of my soul." The same expression is used also in vv 19.25.31. In the context it must mean something like a solemn deathbed blessing, believed to be especially efficacious.

27, 36: He has now supplanted me: in Hebrew, wayyaqebeni, a wordplay on the name Jacob, yaaqob; see Jer 9, 3 and note, as well as Gn 25, 26. There is also a play between the Hebrew words bekora ("birthright") and beraka ("blessing").

Finally Isaac spoke again and said to him:

"Ah, far from the fertile earth
 shall be your dwelling;
 far from the dew of the
  heavens above!

40 "By your sword you shall live,
 and your brother you shall
  serve;
But when you become restive,
 you shall throw off his yoke
  from your neck."

41 Esau bore Jacob a grudge because of the blessing his father had given him. He said to himself, "When the time of mourning for my father comes, I will kill my brother Jacob." 42 When Rebekah got news of what her older son Esau had in mind, she called her younger son Jacob and said to him: "Listen! Your brother Esau intends to settle accounts with you by killing you. 43 Therefore, son, do what I tell you: flee at once to my brother Laban in Haran, 44 and stay with him a while until your brother's fury subsides 45 [until your brother's anger against you subsides] and he forgets what you did to him. Then I will send for you and bring you back. Must I lose both of you in a single day?"

Jacob Sent to Laban

46 Rebekah said to Isaac: "I am disgusted with life because of the Hittite women. If Jacob also should marry a Hittite woman, a native of the land, like these women, what 28 good would life be to me?" 1 Isaac therefore called Jacob, greeted him with a blessing, and charged him: "You shall not marry a Canaanite woman! 2 Go now to Paddan-aram, to the home of your mother's father Bethuel, and there choose a wife for yourself from among the daughters of your uncle Laban. 3 May God Almighty bless you and make you fertile, multiply you that you may become an assembly of peoples. 4 May he extend to you and your descendants the blessing he gave to Abraham, so that you may gain possession of the land where you are staying, which he assigned to Abraham." 5 Then Isaac sent Jacob on his way; he went to Paddan-aram, to Laban, son of Bethuel the Aramean, and brother of Rebekah, the mother of Jacob and Esau.

6 Esau noted that Isaac had blessed Jacob when he sent him to Paddan-aram to get himself a wife there, charging him, as he gave him his blessing, not to marry a Canaanite woman, 7 and that Jacob had obeyed his father and mother and gone to Paddan-aram. 8 Esau realized how displeasing the Canaanite women were to his father Isaac, 9 so he went to Ishmael, and in addition to the wives he had, married Mahalath, the daughter of Abraham's son Ishmael and sister of Nebaioth.

Jacob's Dream at Bethel

10 Jacob departed from Beer-sheba and proceeded toward Haran. 11 When he came upon a certain shrine, as the sun had already set, he stopped there for the night. Taking one of the stones at the shrine, he put it under his head and lay down to sleep at that spot. 12 Then he had a dream: a stairway rested on the ground, with its top reaching to the heavens; and God's messengers were going up and down on it. 13 And there was the LORD standing beside him and saying:

"I, the LORD, am the God of your forefather Abraham and the God of Isaac; the land on which you are lying I will give to you and your descendants. 14 These shall be as plentiful as the dust of the earth, and through them you shall spread out east and west, north and south. In you and your descendants all the nations of the earth shall find blessing. 15 Know that I am with you; I will protect you wherever you go, and bring you back to this land. I will never leave you until I have done what I promised you."

16 When Jacob awoke from his sleep, he exclaimed, "Truly, the LORD is in this spot, although I did not know it!" 17 In solemn wonder he cried out: "How awesome is this shrine! This is nothing else but an abode of God, and that is the gateway to heaven!" 18 Early the next morning Jacob took the stone that he had put under his head, set it up as a memorial stone, and poured oil on top of it. 19 He called that site Bethel, whereas the former name of the town had been Luz.

20 Jacob then made this vow: "If God remains with me, to protect me on this journey I am making and to give me enough bread to eat and clothing to wear, 21 and I come back safe to my father's house, the LORD shall be my God. 22 This stone that I have set up as a memorial stone shall be God's abode. Of everything you give me, I will faithfully return a tenth part to you."

Arrival in Haran

29 After Jacob resumed his journey, he came to the land of the Easterners. 2 Looking about, he saw a well in the open country, with three droves of sheep huddled near it, for droves were watered from that well. A large stone covered the mouth of the well. 3 Only when all the shepherds were assembled there could they roll the stone away from the mouth of the well and

---

27, 46–48, 9: This section, which is from the Priestly source and a direct sequel of 26, 34f, presents a different, though not contradictory, reason for Jacob's going to Paddan-aram: namely, to preserve racial purity among the chosen people. The account of Esau's marriages is given for the purpose of explaining the racial mixture of the Edomites, who were descended in part from tribes related to Israel, in part from older peoples in Edom called Hittites, Horites or Hivites, and in part from the Ishmaelite (Arabian) tribes who later invaded the region.
28, 11: Shrine: literally "place," often used specifically of a sacred site. Here the place was

Bethel (v 19), a sacred site as early as the time of Abraham (12, 8).
 28, 12: Stairway: in Hebrew, sullam, traditionally but inaccurately translated as "ladder." The corresponding verb, salal, means "to heap up" something, such as dirt for a highway or ramp. The imagery in Jacob's dream is derived from the Babylonian ziggurat or temple tower, "with its top in the sky" (11, 4), and with brick steps leading up to a small temple at the top.
 28, 17: This: the stone Jacob used as a headrest; cf v 22. That: the stairway Jacob saw in his dream.
 28, 18: Memorial stone: in Hebrew, masseba, a

stone which might vary in shape and size, set upright and usually intended for some religious purpose. Since the custom of erecting such "sacred pillars" in Palestine went back to its pre-Israelite period, their pagan associations were often retained; therefore, later Israelite religion forbade their erection (Lv 26, 1; Dt 16, 22) and ordered the destruction of those that were associated with paganism (Ex 34, 31; Dt 12, 3).
 28, 19: Bethel: i.e., "house of God"; the reference is to the abode of God in v 17.
 29, 1: Easterners: see note on 25, 6.

water the flocks. Then they would put the stone back again over the mouth of the well.

4 Jacob said to them, "Friends, where are you from?" "We are from Haran," they replied. 5 Then he asked them, "Do you know Laban, son of Nahor?" "We do," they answered. 6 He inquired further, "Is he well?" "He is," they answered; "and here comes his daughter Rachel with his flock." 7 Then he said: "There is still much daylight left; it is hardly the time to bring the animals home. Why don't you water the flocks now, and then continue pasturing them?" 8 "We cannot," they replied, "until all the shepherds are here to roll the stone away from the mouth of the well; only then can we water the flocks."

9 While he was still talking with them, Rachel arrived with her father's sheep; she was the one who tended them. 10 As soon as Jacob saw Rachel, the daughter of his uncle Laban, with the sheep of his uncle Laban, he went up, rolled the stone away from the mouth of the well, and watered his uncle's sheep. 11 Then Jacob kissed Rachel and burst into tears. 12 He told her that he was her father's relative, Rebekah's son, and she ran to tell her father. 13 When Laban heard the news about his sister's son Jacob, he hurried out to meet him. After embracing and kissing him, he brought him to his house. Jacob then recounted to Laban all that had happened, 14 and Laban said to him, "You are indeed my flesh and blood."

Marriage to Leah and Rachel

After Jacob had stayed with him a full month, 15 Laban said to him: "Should you serve me for nothing just because you are a relative of mine? Tell me what your wages should be." 16 Now Laban had two daughters; the older was called Leah, the younger Rachel. 17 Leah had lovely eyes, but Rachel was well formed and beautiful. 18 Since Jacob had fallen in love with Rachel, he answered Laban, "I will serve you seven years for your younger daughter Rachel." 19 Laban replied, "I prefer to give her to you rather than to an outsider. Stay with me." 20 So Jacob served seven years for Rachel, yet they seemed to him but a few days because of his love for her.

21 Then Jacob said to Laban, "Give me my wife, that I may consummate my marriage with her, for my term is now completed." 22 So Laban invited all the local inhabitants and gave a feast. 23 At nightfall he took his daughter Leah and brought her to Jacob, and Jacob consummated the marriage with her. 24 (Laban assigned his slave girl Zilpah to his daughter Leah as her maidservant.) 25 In the morning Jacob was amazed: it was Leah! So he cried out to Laban: "How could you do this to me! Was it not for Rachel that I served you? Why did you dupe me?" 26 "It is not the custom in our country," Laban replied, "to marry off a younger daughter before an older one. 27 Finish the bridal week for this one, and then I will give you the other too, in return for another seven years of service with me."

28 Jacob agreed. He finished the bridal week for Leah, and then Laban gave him his daughter Rachel in marriage. 29 (Laban assigned his slave girl Bilhah to his daughter Rachel as her maidservant.) 30 Jacob then consummated his marriage with Rachel also, and he loved her more than Leah. Thus he re-mained in Laban's service another seven years.

Jacob's Children

31 When the LORD saw that Leah was unloved, he made her fruitful, while Rachel remained barren. 32 Leah conceived and bore a son, and she named him Reuben; for she said, "It means, 'The LORD saw my misery; now my husband will love me.'" 33 She conceived again and bore a son, and said, "It means, 'The LORD heard that I was unloved,' and therefore he has given me this one also"; so she named him Simeon. 34 Again she conceived and bore a son, and she said, "Now at last my husband will become attached to me, since I have now borne him three sons"; that is why she named him Levi. 35 Once more she conceived and bore a son, and she said, "This time I will give grateful praise to the LORD"; therefore she named him Judah. Then she stopped bearing children.

30 When Rachel saw that she failed to bear children to Jacob, she became envious of her sister. She said to Jacob, "Give me children or I shall die!" 2 In anger Jacob retorted, "Can I take the place of God, who has denied you the fruit of the womb?" 3 She replied, "Here is my maid-servant Bilhah. Have intercourse with her, and let her give birth on my knees, so that I too may have offspring, at least through her." 4 So she gave him her maidservant Bilhah as a consort, and Jacob had intercourse with her. 5 When Bilhah conceived and bore a son, 6 Rachel said, "God has vindicated me; indeed he has heeded my plea and given me a son." Therefore she named him Dan. 7 Rachel's maid-

---

29, 11: *Burst into tears:* literally "raised his voice and wept," i.e., for joy.

29, 14: *Flesh* and *blood:* literally "bone and flesh," i.e., a close relative; on the Hebrew idiom, see 2, 23.

29, 17: *Lovely eyes:* the adjective modifying *eyes* is often translated as "weak," but "lovely" is the more probable word.

29, 18: Jacob offers to render service (Jos 15, 16f; 1 Sm 17, 25; 18, 17) in lieu of the customary bridal price (Ex 22, 16f; Dt 22, 29).

29, 25: *Jacob was amazed:* he had not recognized Leah because a bride was veiled when she was brought to her bridegroom; cf 24, 65.

29, 27: *The bridal week:* an ancient wedding lasted for seven days of festivities; cf Jgs 14, 12.

29, 32: *Reuben:* the literal meaning of the Hebrew name is "look, a son!" But in this case, as also with the names of all the other sons of Jacob, a symbolic rather than an etymological interpretation of the name is given, because the name and the persons were regarded as closely interrelated. The symbolic interpretation of Reuben's name, according to the Yahwist source, is based on the similar-sounding *raa beonyi,* "he saw my mistery." In the Elohist source, the name is explained by the similar-sounding *yeehabani,* "he will love me."

29, 33: *Simeon:* in popular etymology, related to *shama,* "he heard."

29, 34: *Levi:* related to *yillaweh,* "he will become attached."

29, 35: *Judah:* related to *odeh,* "I will give grateful praise."

30, 3: *On my knees:* in the ancient Near East, a father would take a newborn child in his lap to signify that he acknowledged it as his own; Rachel uses this ceremony in order to adopt the child and establish her legal rights to it.

30, 4: *Consort:* The Hebrew word normally means "wife," but here it refers to a wife of secondary rank, who did not have the full legal rights of an ordinary wife.

30, 6: *Dan:* explained by the term *dannanni,* "he has vindicated me."

servant Bilhah conceived again and bore a second son, 8 and Rachel said, "I engaged in a fateful struggle with my sister, and I prevailed." So she named him Naphtali.

9 When Leah saw that she had ceased to bear children, she gave her maidservant Zilpah to Jacob as a consort. 10 So Jacob had intercourse with Zilpah, and she conceived and bore a son. 11 Leah then said, "What good luck!" So she named him Gad. 12 Then Leah's maidservant Zilpah bore a second son to Jacob; 13 and Leah said, "What good fortune!"—meaning, "Women call me fortunate." So she named him Asher.

14 One day, during the wheat harvest, when Reuben was out in the field, he came upon some mandrakes which he brought home to his mother Leah. Rachel asked Leah, "Please let me have some of your son's mandrakes." 15 Leah replied, "Was it not enough for you to take away my husband, that you must now take my son's mandrakes too?" "Very well, then!" Rachel answered. "In exchange for your son's mandrakes, Jacob may lie with you tonight." 16 That evening, when Jacob came home from the fields, Leah went out to meet him. "You are now to come in with me," she told him, "because I have paid for you with my son's mandrakes." So that night he slept with her, 17 and God heard her prayer; she conceived and bore a fifth son to Jacob. 18 Leah then said, "God has given me my reward for having let my husband have my maidservant"; so she named him Issachar. 19 Leah conceived again and bore a sixth son to Jacob; 20 and she said, "God has brought me a precious gift. This time my husband will offer me presents, now that I have borne him six sons"; so she named him Zebulun. 21 Finally, she gave birth to a daughter, and she named her Dinah.

22 Then God remembered Rachel; he heard her prayer and made her fruitful. 23 She conceived and bore a son, and she said, "God has removed my disgrace." 24 So she named him Joseph, meaning, "May the LORD add another son to this one for me!"

Jacob Outwits Laban

25 After Rachel gave birth to Joseph, Jacob said to Laban: "Give me leave to go to my homeland. 26 Let me have my wives, for whom I served you, and my children, too, that I may depart. You know very well the service that I have rendered you." 27 Laban answered him: "If you will please. . . .

"I have learned through divination that it is because of you that God has blessed me. 28 So," he continued, "state what wages you want from me, and I will pay them." 29 Jacob replied: "You know what work I did for you and how well your livestock fared under my care; 30 the little you had before I came has grown into very much, since the LORD's blessings came upon you in my company. Therefore I should now do something for my own household as well." 31 "What should I pay you?" Laban asked. Jacob answered: "You do not have to pay me anything outright. I will again pasture and tend your flock, if you do this one thing for me: 32 go through your whole flock today and remove from it every dark animal among the sheep and every spotted or speckled one among the goats. Only such animals shall be my wages. 33 In the future, whenever you check on these wages of mine, let my honesty testify against me: any animal in my possession that is not a speckled or spotted goat, or a dark sheep, got there by theft!" 34 "Very well," agreed Laban. "Let it be as you say."

35 That same day Laban removed the streaked and spotted he-goats and all the speckled and spotted she-goats, all those with some white on them, as well as the fully dark-colored sheep; these he left . . . in charge of his sons. 36 Then he put a three days' journey between himself and Jacob, while Jacob continued to pasture the rest of Laban's flock.

37 Jacob, however, got some fresh shoots of poplar, almond and plane trees, and he made white stripes in them by peeling off the bark down to the white core of the shoots. 38 The rods that he had thus peeled he then set upright in the watering troughs, so that they would be in front of the animals that drank from the troughs. When the animals were in heat as they came to drink, 39 the goats mated by the rods, and so they brought forth streaked, speckled and spotted kids. 40 The sheep, on the other hand, Jacob kept apart, and he set these animals to face the streaked or fully dark-colored animals of Laban. Thus he produced special flocks of his own, which he did not put with Laban's flock. 41 Moreover, whenever the hardier animals were in heat, Jacob would set the rods in the troughs in full view of these animals, so that they mated by the rods; 42 but with the weaker animals he would not put the rods there. So the feeble animals would go to Laban, but the sturdy ones to Jacob. 43 Thus the man grew increasingly prosperous, and he came to own, not only large flocks, but also male and female servants and camels and asses.

30, 8: *Naphtali:* explained by the phrase *"naptule lohim niptali,"* literally, "in a divine wrestling match I have wrestled," perhaps implying the concept of an ordeal; hence the above rendering, *I engaged in a fateful struggle.*

30, 11: *Gad:* explained by the Hebrew term *begad,* literally "in luck," i.e., *what good luck!*

30, 13: *Asher:* explained by the term *beoshri,* literally "in my good fortune," i.e., *what good fortune* and by the term *ishsheruni* "they call me fortunate."

30, 14: *Mandrakes:* an herb whose root was anciently thought to promote conception. The Hebrew word for mandrakes, *dudaim,* has erotic connotations, since it sounds like the words *daddayim* ("breasts") and *dodim* ("sexual pleasure").

30, 18: *Issachar:* explained by the terms *sekari,* "my reward," and in v 16, *sakor sekartika,* literally "I have hired you," i.e., *I have paid for you.*

30, 20: *Zebulun:* related to the Akkadian word *zubullum,* "bridegroom's gift," is explained by the terms *zebadani . . . zebed tob,* "he has brought me a precious gift," and *yizbeleni,* "he will offer me presents."

30, 24: *Joseph:* explained by the words *yosep,* "may he add," and in v 23, *asap,* "he has removed."

30, 32: *Dark . . . sheep . . . spotted or speckled goats:* In the Near East the normal color of sheep is light gray, whereas that of goats is uniform dark brown or black. Ordinarily, therefore, Jacob would have received but few animals.

30, 35: By giving the abnormally colored animals to his sons, Laban not only deprived Jacob of his first small wages, but he also designed to prevent in his way the future breeding of such animals in the part of his flock entrusted to Jacob.

30, 39–42: Jacob's stratagem was based on the widespread notion among simple people that visual stimuli can have prenatal effects on the offspring of breeding animals. Thus, the rods on which Jacob had whittled stripes or bands or chevron marks were thought to cause the female goats that looked at them to bear kids with lighter-colored marks on their dark hair, while the gray ewes were thought to bear lambs with dark marks on them simply by visual crossbreeding with the dark goats.

Flight from Laban

31 Jacob learned that Laban's sons were saying, "Jacob has taken everything that belonged to our father, and he has accumulated all this wealth of his by using our father's property." 2 Jacob perceived, too, that Laban's attitude toward him was not what it had previously been. 3 Then the LORD said to Jacob, "Return to the land of your fathers, where you were born, and I will be with you."

4 So Jacob sent for Rachel and Leah to meet him where he was in the field with his flock. 5 There he said to them: "I have noticed that your father's attitude toward me is not as it was in the past; but the God of my father has been with me. 6 You well know what effort I put into serving your father; 7 yet your father cheated me and changed my wages time after time. God, however, did not let him do me any harm. 8 Whenever your father said, 'The speckled animals shall be your wages,' the entire flock would bear speckled young; whenever he said, 'The streaked animals shall be your wages,' the entire flock would bear streaked young. 9 Thus God reclaimed your father's livestock and gave it to me. 10 Once, in the breeding season, I had a dream in which I saw mating he-goats that were streaked, speckled and mottled. 11 In the dream God's messenger called to me, 'Jacob!' 'Here!' I replied. 12 Then he said: 'Note well. All the he-goats in the flock, as they mate, are streaked, speckled and mottled, for I have seen all the things that Laban has been doing to you. 13 I am the God who appeared to you in Bethel, where you anointed a memorial stone and made a vow to me. Up, then! Leave this land and return to the land of your birth.'"

14 Rachel and Leah answered him: "Have we still an heir's portion in our father's house? 15 Are we not regarded by him as outsiders? He not only sold us; he has even used up the money that he got for us! 16 All the wealth that God reclaimed from our father really belongs to us and our children. Therefore, do just as God has told you." 17 Jacob proceeded to put his children and wives on camels, 18 and he drove off with all his livestock and all the property he had acquired in Paddan-aram, to go to his father Isaac in the land of Canaan.

19 Now Laban had gone away to shear his sheep, and Rachel had meanwhile appropriated her father's household idols. 20 Jacob had hoodwinked Laban the Aramean by not telling him of his intended flight. 21 Thus he made his escape with all that he had. Once he was across the Euphrates, he headed for the highlands of Gilead.

22 On the third day, word came to Laban that Jacob had fled. 23 Taking his kinsmen with him, he pursued him for seven days until he caught up with him in the hill country of Gilead. 24 But that night God appeared to Laban the Aramean in a dream and warned him, "Take care not to threaten Jacob with any harm!"

Jacob and Laban in Gilead

25 When Laban overtook Jacob, Jacob's tents were pitched in the highlands; Laban also pitched his tents there, on Mount Gilead. 26 "What do you mean," Laban demanded of Jacob, "by hoodwinking me and carrying off my daughters like war captives? 27 Why did you dupe me by stealing away secretly? You should have told me, and I would have sent you off with merry singing to the sound of tambourines and harps. 28 You did not even allow me a parting kiss to my daughters and grandchildren! What you have now done is a senseless thing. 29 I have it in my power to harm all of you; but last night the God of your father said to me, 'Take care not to threaten Jacob with any harm!' 30 Granted that you had to leave because you were desperately homesick for your father's house, why did you steal my gods?" 31 "I was frightened," Jacob replied to Laban, "at the thought that you might take your daughters away from me by force. 32 But as for your gods, the one you find them with shall not remain alive! If, with my kinsmen looking on, you identify anything here as belonging to you, take it." Jacob, of course, had no idea that Rachel had stolen the idols.

33 Laban then went in and searched Jacob's tent and Leah's tent, as well as the tents of the two maidservants; but he did not find the idols. Leaving Leah's tent, he went into Rachel's. 34 Now Rachel had taken the idols, put them inside a camel cushion, and seated herself upon them. When Laban had rummaged through the rest of her tent without finding them, 35 Rachel said to her father, "Let not my lord feel offended that I cannot rise in your presence; a woman's period is upon me." So, despite his search, he did not find his idols.

36 Jacob, now enraged, upbraided Laban. "What crime or offense have I committed," he demanded, "that you should hound me so fiercely? 37 Now that you have ransacked all my things, have you found a single object taken from your belongings? If so, produce it here before your kinsmen and mine, and let them decide between us two.

38 "In the twenty years that I was under you, no ewe or she-goat of yours ever miscarried, and I have never feasted on a ram of your flock. 39 I never brought you an animal torn by wild beasts; I made good the loss myself. You held me responsible for anything stolen by day or night.

31, 8–12: This Elohist account of the miraculous increase in Jacob's flock differs somewhat from the Yahwist account given in 30, 32–42.

31, 15: *Outsiders:* literally "foreign women"; they lacked the favored legal status of native women. *Used up:* literally "eaten, consumed"; the bridal price that a man received for giving his daughter in marriage was legally reserved as her inalienable dowry.

31, 19: *Household idols:* in Hebrew, *teraphim,* figurines used in divination (Ez 21, 26; Zec 10, 2). Laban calls them his "gods" (v 30).

31, 20: *Hoodwinked:* literally "stolen the heart of," i.e., lulled the mind of. *Aramean:* The earliest extra-biblical references to the Arameans date from several centuries after the time of Jacob; to call Laban an *Aramean* and to have him speak Aramaic (v 47) would seem to be an anachronism.

31, 23: *For seven days:* literally "a way of seven days," a general term to designate a long distance; it would have taken a camel caravan many more days to travel from Haran to Gilead, the region east of the northern half of the Jordan.

31, 26: *War captives:* literally "women captured by the sword"; the women of a conquered people were treated as part of the victor's booty; cf 1 Sm 30, 2; 2 Kgs 5, 2.

31, 39: Laban's actions were contrary to the customs of the ancient Near East, as recorded in the Code of Hammurabi: "If in a sheepfold an act of god has occurred, or a lion has made a kill, the shepherd shall clear himself before the deity, and the owner of the fold must accept the loss" (par. 266); cf Ex 22, 12.

40 How often the scorching heat ravaged me by day, and the frost by night, while sleep fled from my eyes! 41 Of the twenty years that I have now spent in your household, I slaved fourteen years for your two daughters and six years for your flock, while you changed my wages time after time. 42 If my ancestral God, the God of Abraham and the Awesome One of Isaac, had not been on my side, you would now have sent me away empty-handed. But God saw my plight and the fruits of my toil, and last night he gave judgment."

43 Laban replied to Jacob: "The women are mine, their children are mine, and the flocks are mine; everything you see belongs to me. But since these women are my daughters, I will now do something for them and for the children they have borne. 44 Come, then, we will make a pact, you and I; the LORD shall be a witness between us."

45 Then Jacob took a stone and set it up as a memorial stone. 46 Jacob said to his kinsmen, "Gather some stones." So they got some stones and made a mound; and they had a meal there at the mound. 47 Laban called it Jegar-sahadutha, but Jacob named it Galeed. 48 "This mound," said Laban, "shall be a witness from now on between you and me." That is why it was named Galeed— 49 and also Mizpah, for he said: "May the LORD keep watch between you and me when we are out of each other's sight. 50 If you mistreat my daughters, or take other wives besides my daughters, remember that even though no one else is about, God will be witness between you and me."

51 Laban said further to Jacob: "Here is this mound, and here is the memorial stone that I have set up between you and me. 52 This mound shall be witness, and this memorial stone shall be witness, that, with hostile intent, neither may I pass beyond this mound into your territory, nor may you pass beyond it into mine. 53 May the God of Abraham and the god of Nahor [their ancestral deities] maintain justice between us!" Jacob took the oath by the Awesome One of Isaac. 54 He then offered a sacrifice on the mountain and invited his kinsmen to share in the meal. When they had eaten, they passed the night on the mountain.

32 Early the next morning, Laban kissed his grandchildren and his daughters goodbye; then he set out on his journey back home, 2 while Jacob continued on his own way. Then God's messengers encountered Jacob. 3 When he saw them he said, "This is God's encampment." So he named that place Mahanaim.

Embassy to Esau

4 Jacob sent messengers ahead to his brother Esau in the land of Seir, the country of Edom, 5 with this message: "Thus shall you say to my lord Esau: 'Your servant Jacob speaks as follows: I have been staying with Laban and have been detained there until now. 6 I own cattle, asses and sheep, as well as male and female servants. I am sending my lord this information in the hope of gaining your favor.'" 7 When the messengers returned to Jacob, they said, "We reached your brother Esau. He is now coming to meet you, accompanied by four hundred men."

8 Jacob was very much frightened. In his anxiety, he divided the people who were with him, as well as his flocks, herds and camels, into two camps. 9 "If Esau should attack and overwhelm one camp," he reasoned, "the remaining camp may still survive." 10 Then he prayed: "O God of my father Abraham and God of my father Isaac! You told me, O LORD, 'Go back to the land of your birth, and I will be good to you.' 11 I am unworthy of all the acts of kindness that you have loyally performed for your servant: although I crossed the Jordan here with nothing but my staff, I have now grown into two companies. 12 Save me, I pray, from the hand of my brother Esau! Otherwise I fear that when he comes he will strike me down and slay the mothers and children. 13 You yourself said, 'I will be very good to you, and I will make your descendants like the sands of the sea, which are too numerous to count.'"

14 After passing the night there, Jacob selected from what he had with him the following presents for his brother Esau: 15 two hundred she-goats and twenty he-goats; two hundred ewes and twenty rams; 16 thirty milch camels and their young; forty cows and ten bulls; twenty she-asses and ten he-asses. 17 He put these animals in charge of his servants, in separate droves, and he told the servants, "Go on ahead of me, but keep a space between one drove and the next." 18 To the servant in the lead he gave this instruction: "When my brother Esau meets you, he may ask you, 'Whose man are you? Where are you going? To whom do these animals ahead of you belong?' 19 Then you shall answer, 'They belong to your brother Jacob, but they have been sent as a gift to my lord Esau; and Jacob himself is right behind us.'" 20 He gave similar instructions to the second servant and the third and to all the others who followed behind the droves, namely: "Thus and thus shall you say to Esau, when you reach him; 21 be sure to add, 'Your servant Jacob is right behind us.'" For Jacob reasoned, "If I first appease him with gifts that precede me, then later, when I face him, perhaps he will forgive me." 22 So the gifts went on ahead of him, while he stayed that night in the camp.

Struggle with the Angel

23 In the course of that night, however, Jacob arose, took his two wives, with the two maidservants and his eleven children, and crossed the ford of the Jabbok. 24 After he had taken them across the stream and

---

31, 43–54: In this account of the treaty between Laban and Jacob, the Yahwist and Elohist sources are closely interwoven. The *mound* or cairn of stones comes from the Yahwist source, the *memorial stone* or stele from the Elohist.

31, 47: *Jegar-sahadutha:* an Aramaic term mean-

ing "mound of witness." *Galeed:* in Hebrew, *galed,* with the same meaning; also offers an explanation of the regional name Gilead.

31, 49: *Mizpah:* a town in Gilead; cf. Jgs 10,17; 11, 11.34; Hos 5, 1. The Hebrew name *mispa* ("lookout") is allied to *yisep yhwh* ("may the Lord

keep watch"), and also echoes the word *masseba* ("memorial pillar").

32, 3: *Mahanaim:* a town in Gilead (Jos 13, 26.30; 21, 38; 2 Sm 2, 8; etc.). The Hebrew name means "two camps." There are other allusions to the name in vv 8.11.

had brought over all his possessions, 25 Jacob was left there alone. Then some man wrestled with him until the break of dawn. 26 When the man saw that he could not prevail over him, he struck Jacob's hip at its socket, so that the hip socket was wrenched as they wrestled. 27 The man then said, "Let me go, for it is daybreak." But Jacob said, "I will not let you go until you bless me." 28 "What is your name?" the man asked. He answered, "Jacob." 29 Then the man said, "You shall no longer be spoken of as Jacob, but as Israel, because you have contended with divine and human beings and have prevailed." 30 Jacob then asked him, "Do tell me your name, please." He answered, "Why should you want to know my name?" With that, he bade him farewell. 31 Jacob named the place Peniel, "Because I have seen God face to face," he said, "yet my life has been spared."

32 At sunrise, as he left Penuel, Jacob limped along because of his hip. 33 That is why, to this day, the Israelites do not eat the sciatic muscle that is on the hip socket, inasmuch as Jacob's hip socket was struck at the sciatic muscle.

Jacob and Esau Meet

33 Jacob looked up and saw Esau coming, accompanied by four hundred men. So he divided his children among Leah, Rachel and the two maidservants, 2 putting the maids and their children first, Leah and her children next, and Rachel and Joseph last. 3 He himself went on ahead of them, bowing to the ground seven times, until he reached his brother. 4 Esau ran to meet him, embraced him, and flinging himself on his neck, kissed him as he wept.

5 When Esau looked about, he saw the women and children. "Who

are these with you?" he asked. Jacob answered, "They are the children whom God has graciously bestowed on your servant." 6 Then the maidservants and their children came forward and bowed low; 7 next, Leah and her children came forward and bowed low; lastly, Rachel and her children came forward and bowed low. 8 Then Esau asked, "What did you intend with all those droves that I encountered?" Jacob answered, "It was to gain my lord's favor." 9 "I have plenty," replied Esau; "you should keep what is yours, brother." 10 "No, I beg you!" said Jacob. "If you will do me the favor, please accept this gift from me, since to come into your presence is for me like coming into the presence of God, now that you have received me so kindly. 11 Do accept the present I have brought you; God has been generous toward me, and I have an abundance." Since he so urged him, Esau accepted.

12 Then Esau said, "Let us break camp and be on our way; I will travel alongside you." 13 But Jacob replied: "As my lord can see, the children are frail. Besides, I am encumbered with the flocks and herds, which now have sucklings; if overdriven for a single day, the whole flock will die. 14 Let my lord, then, go on ahead of me, while I proceed more slowly at the pace of the livestock before me and at the pace of my children, until I join my lord in Seir." 15 Esau replied, "Let me at least put at your disposal some of the men who are with me." But Jacob said, "For what reason? Please indulge me in this, my lord." 16 So on the same day that Esau began his journey back to Seir, 17 Jacob journeyed to Succoth. There he built a home for himself and made booths for his livestock. That is why the place was called Succoth.

18 Having thus come from Paddan-aram, Jacob arrived safely at the city of Shechem, which is in the land of Canaan, and he encamped in sight of the city. 19 The plot of ground on which he had pitched his tent he bought for a hundred pieces of bullion from the descendants of Hamor, the founder of Shechem. 20 He set up a memorial stone there and invoked "El, the God of Israel."

The Rape of Dinah

34 Dinah, the daughter whom Leah had borne to Jacob, went out to visit some of the women of the land. 2 When Shechem, son of Hamor the Hivite, who was chief of the region, saw her, he seized her and lay with her by force. 3 Since he was strongly attracted to Dinah, daughter of Jacob, indeed was really in love with the girl, he endeavored to win her affection. 4 Shechem also asked his father Hamor, "Get me this girl for a wife."

5 Meanwhile, Jacob heard that Shechem had defiled his daughter Dinah; but since his sons were out in the fields with his livestock, he held his peace until they came home. 6 Now Hamor, the father of Shechem, went out to discuss the matter with Jacob, 7 just as Jacob's sons were coming in from the fields. When they heard the news, the men were shocked and seethed with indignation. What Shechem had done was an outrage in Israel; such a thing could not be tolerated.

8 Hamor appealed to them, saying: "My son Shechem has his heart set on your daughter. Please give her to him in marriage. 9 Intermarry with us; give your daughters to us, and take our daughters for yourselves. 10 Thus you can live among us. The land is open before you; you can settle and move about freely in it, and acquire landed property here." 11 Then Shechem,

32, 25: *Some man:* a messenger of the Lord in human form, as is clear from vv 29ff.

32, 29: *Israel:* the first part of the Hebrew name *Yisrael* is given a popular explanation in the word *sarita*, "you contended"; the second part is the first syllable of *elohim*, "divine beings." The present incident, with a similar allusion to the name Israel, is referred to in Hos 12, 5, where the mysterious wrestler is explicitly called an angel.

32, 31: *Peniel:* a variant of the word Penuel (v 32) the name of a town on the north bank of the Jabbok in Gilead (Jgs 8, 8f.17; 1 Kgs 12, 25). The name is

explained as meaning "the face of God," *peni-el. Yet my life has been spared:* see note on 16, 13.

33, 17: *Succoth:* an important town near the confluence of the Jabbok and the Jordan (Jos 13, 27; Jgs 8, 5–16; 1 Kgs 7, 46). *Booths:* in Hebrew, *sukkot,* of the same sound as the name of the town.

33, 19: *Pieces of bullion:* in Hebrew, *kesita,* a monetary unit of which the value is now unknown. *Descendants of Hamor:* Hamorites, "the men of Hamor"; cf Jgs 9, 28. Hamor was regarded as the eponymous ancestor of the pre-Israelite inhabitants of Shechem.

34, 1–31: Behind the story of the rape of Dinah and the revenge of Jacob's sons on the men of the city of Shechem there probably lies a dimly recollected historical event connected with an armed conflict between the earliest Israelite tribes invading central Canaan and the Hurrian inhabitants of the Shechem region.

34, 2: *Hivite:* the Greek text has "Horite"; the terms were apparently used indiscriminately to designate the Hurrian or other non-Semitic elements in Palestine.

too, appealed to Dinah's father and brothers: "Do me this favor, and I will pay whatever you demand of me. 12 No matter how high you set the bridal price, I will pay you whatever you ask; only give me the maiden in marriage."

Revenge of Jacob's Sons

13 Jacob's sons replied to Shechem and his father Hamor with guile, speaking as they did because their sister Dinah had been defiled. 14 "We could not do such a thing," they said, "as to give our sister to an uncircumcised man; that would be a disgrace for us. 15 We will agree with you only on this condition, that you become like us by having every male among you circumcised. 16 Then we will give you our daughters and take yours in marriage; we will settle among you and become one kindred people with you. 17 But if you do not comply with our terms regarding circumcision, we will take our daughter and go away."

18 Their proposal seemed fair to Hamor and his son Shechem. 19 The young man lost no time in acting in the matter, since he was deeply in love with Jacob's daughter. Moreover he was more highly respected than anyone else in his clan. 20 So Hamor and his son Shechem went to their town council and thus presented the matter to their fellow townsmen: 21 "These men are friendly toward us. Let them settle in the land and move about in it freely; there is ample room in the country for them. We can marry their daughters and give our daughters to them in marriage. 22 But the men will agree to live with us and form one kindred people with us only on this condition, that every male among us be circumcised as they themselves are. 23 Would not the livestock they have acquired—all their animals —then be ours? Let us, therefore, give in to them, so that they may settle among us."

24 All the able-bodied men of the town agreed with Hamor and his son Shechem, and all the males, including every able-bodied man in the community, were circumcised. 25 On the third day, while they were still in pain, Dinah's full brothers Simeon and Levi, two of Jacob's sons, took their swords, advanced against the city without any trouble, and massacred all the males. 26 After they had put Hamor and his son Shechem to the sword, they took Dinah from Shechem's house and left. 27 Then the other sons of Jacob followed up the slaughter and sacked the city in reprisal for their sister Dinah's defilement. 28 They seized their flocks, herds and asses, whatever was in the city and in the country around. 29 They carried off all their wealth, their women, and their children, and took for loot whatever was in the houses.

30 Jacob said to Simeon and Levi: "You have brought trouble upon me by making me loathsome to the inhabitants of the land, the Canaanites and the Perizzites. I have so few men that, if these people unite against me and attack me, I and my family will be wiped out." 31 But they retorted, "Should our sister have been treated like a harlot?"

Bethel Revisited

35 God said to Jacob: "Go up now to Bethel. Settle there and build an altar there to the God who appeared to you while you were fleeing from your brother Esau." 2 So Jacob told his family and all the others who were with him: "Get rid of the foreign gods that you have among you; then purify yourselves and put on fresh cloths. 3 We are now to go up to Bethel, and I will build an altar there to the God who answered me in my hour of distress and who has been with me wherever I have gone." 4 They therefore handed over to Jacob all the foreign gods in their possession and also the rings they had in their ears. 5 Then, as they set out, a terror from God fell upon the towns round about, so that no one pursued the sons of Jacob.

6 Thus Jacob and all the people who were with him arrived in Luz [that is, Bethel] in the land of Canaan. 7 There he built an altar and named the place Bethel, for it was there that God had revealed himself to him when he was fleeing from his brother.

8 Death came to Rebekah's nurse Deborah; she was buried under the oak below Bethel, and so it was called Allon-bacuth.

9 On Jacob's arrival from Paddan-aram, God appeared to him again and blessed him. 10 God said to him:

> "You whose name is Jacob
> shall no longer be called Jacob,
> but Israel shall be your name."

Thus he was named Israel. 11 God also said to him:

> "I am God Almighty;
> be fruitful and multiply.
> A nation, indeed an assembly of nations,
> shall stem from you,
> and kings shall issue from your loins.

12 The land I once gave
> to Abraham and Isaac
> I now give to you;
> And to your descendants after you
> will I give this land."

13 Then God departed from him. 14 On the site where God had spoken with him, Jacob set up a memorial stone, and upon it he made a libation and poured out oil. 15 Jacob named the site Bethel, because God had spoken with him there.

Jacob's Family

16 Then they departed from Bethel; but while they still had some distance to go on the way to Ephrath, Rachel began to be in labor and to suffer great distress. 17 When her pangs were most severe, her midwife said to her, "Have no fear!

34, 24: *Every able-bodied man in the community:* literally "all those who go out at the gate of the city," apparently meaning the men who go out to war. By temporarily crippling them through circumcision, Jacob's sons deprived the city of its defenders.

35, 2: *Foreign gods:* pagan images, including household idols (see note on 31, 19), that Jacob's people brought with them from Paddan-aram.
· 35, 4: *Rings:* Earrings were often worn as amulets connected with pagan magic.

35, 8: This verse may have stood originally in some other context. Rebekah's nurse is spoken of without a name in 24, 59. *Allon-bacuth:* the Hebrew name means "oak of weeping."

This time, too, you have a son." 18 With her last breath—for she was at the point of death—she called him Ben-oni; his father, however, named him Benjamin. 19 Thus Rachel died; and she was buried on the road to Ephrath [that is, Bethlehem]. 20 Jacob set up a memorial stone on her grave, and the same monument marks Rachel's grave to this day.

21 Israel moved on and pitched his tent beyond Migdaleder. 22 While Israel was encamped in that region, Reuben went and lay with Bilhah, his father's concubine. When Israel heard of it, he was greatly offended.

The sons of Jacob were now twelve. 23 The sons of Leah: Reuben, Jacob's first-born, Simeon, Levi, Judah, Issachar, and Zebulun; 24 the sons of Rachel: Joseph and Benjamin; 25 the sons of Rachel's maid Bilhah: Dan and Naphtali; 26 the sons of Leah's maid Zilpah: Gad and Asher. These are the sons of Jacob who were born to him in Paddan-aram.

27 Jacob went home to his father Isaac at Mamre, in Kiriath-arba [that is, Hebron], where Abraham and Isaac had stayed. 28 The lifetime of Isaac was one hundred and eighty years; then he breathed his last. 29 After a full life, he died as an old man and was taken to his kinsmen. His sons Esau and Jacob buried him.

Edomite Lists

36 These are the descendants of Esau [that is, Edom]. 2 Esau took his wives from among the Canaanite women: Adah, daughter of Elon the Hittite; Oholibamah, granddaughter through Anah of Zibeon the Hivite; 3 and Basemath, daughter of Ishmael and sister of Nebaioth. 4 Adah bore Eliphaz to Esau; Basemath bore Reuel;

5 and Oholibamah bore Jeush, Jalam and Korah. These are the sons of Esau who were born to him in the land of Canaan.

6 Esau took his wives, his sons, his daughters, and all the members of his household, as well as his livestock comprising various animals and all the property he had acquired in the land of Canaan, and went to the land of Seir, out of the way of his brother Jacob. 7 Their possessions had become too great for them to dwell together, and the land in which they were staying could not support them because of their livestock. 8 So Esau settled in the highlands of Seir. [Esau is Edom.] 9 These are the descendants of Esau, ancestor of the Edomites, in the highlands of Seir.

10 These are the names of Esau's sons: Eliphaz, son of Esau's wife Adah; and Reuel, son of Esau's wife Basemath. 11 The sons of Eliphaz were Teman, Omar, Zepho, Gatam, and Kenaz. 12 (Esau's son Eliphaz had a concubine Timna, and she bore Amalek to Eliphaz.) These are the descendants of Esau's wife Adah. 13 The sons of Reuel were Nahath, Zerah, Shammah, and Mizzah. These are the descendants of Esau's wife Basemath. 14 The descendants of Esau's wife Oholibamah—granddaughter through Anah of Zibeon—whom she bore to Esau were Jeush, Jalam, and Korah.

15 The following are the clans of Esau's descendants. The descendants of Eliphaz, Esau's first-born: the clans of Teman, Omar, Zepho, Kenaz, 16 Korah, Gatam, and Amalek. These are the clans of Eliphaz in the land of Edom; they are descended from Adah. 17 The descendants of Esau's son Reuel: the clans of Nahath, Zerah, Shammah, and Mizzah. These are the clans of Reuel in the land of Edom; they are descended from Esau's wife

Basemath. 18 The descendants of Esau's wife Oholibamah: the clans of Jeush, Jalam, and Korah. These are the clans of Esau's wife Oholibamah, daughter of Anah. 19 Such are the descendants of Esau [that is, Edom] according to their clans.

20 The following are the descendants of Seir the Horite, the original settlers in the land: Lotan, Shobal, Zibeon, Anah, 21 Dishon, Ezer, and Dishan; they are the Horite clans descended from Seir, in the land of Edom. 22 Lotan's descendants were Hori and Hemam, and Lotan's sister was Timna. 23 Shobal's descendants were Alvan, Mahanath, Ebal, Shepho, and Onam. 24 Zibeon's descendants were Aiah and Anah. (He is the Anah who found water in the desert while he was pasturing the asses of his father Zibeon.) 25 The descendants of Anah were Dishon and Oholibamah, daughter of Anah. 26 The descendants of Dishon were Hemdan, Eshban, Ithran, and Cheran. 27 The descendants of Ezer were Bilhan, Zaavan, and Akan. 28 The descendants of Dishan were Uz and Aran. 29 These are the Horite clans: the clans of Lotan, Shobal, Zibeon, Anah, 30 Dishon, Ezer, and Dishan; they were the clans of the Horites, clan by clan, in the land of Seir.

31 The following are the kings who reigned in the land of Edom before any king reigned over the Israelites. 32 Bela, son of Beor, became king in Edom; the name of his city was Dinhabah. 33 When Bela died, Jobab, son of Zerah, from Bozrah, succeeded him as king. 34 When Jobab died, Husham, from the land of the Temanites, succeeded him as king. He defeated the Midianites in the country of Moab; the name of his city was Avith. 35 When Husham died, Hadad, son of Bedad, succeeded him as king. 36

35, 18: *Ben-oni*: either "son of my vigor" or, more likely in the context, "son of affliction." *Benjamin*: "son of the right hand." This may be interpreted to signify a son who is his father's help and support, but more likely its original meaning was "southerner." In the Hebrew idiom, the south lies to one's right hand, and Benjamin was the southernmost of the Rachel tribes.

35, 19: *Bethlehem*: the gloss comes from a later tradition that identified the site with Bethlehem, also called Ephrath or Ephratha (Jos 15, 59; Ru 4, 11;

Mi 5, 1). But Rachel's grave was actually near Ramah (Jer 31, 15), a few miles north of Jerusalem, in the territory of Benjamin (1 Sm 10, 2).

35, 24ff: Benjamin is here said to have been born in *Paddan-aram*, either because all twelve sons of Jacob are considered as a unit, or because the Priestly source, from which vv 23–29 are taken, follows a tradition different from that of the Elohistic source found in vv 16–20.

36, 2–14: The names of Esau's wives and of their fathers given here differ considerably from their

names cited from other old sources in 26, 34 and 28, 9. *Zibeon the Hivite*: in v 20 he is called a *Horite*; see note on 34, 2.

36, 20: *Seir the Horite*: according to Dt 2, 12, the highlands of Seir were inhabited by Horites before they were occupied by the Edomites.

36, 31: *Before any king reigned over the Israelites*: obviously this statement was written after the time of Saul, Israel's first king.

When Hadad died, Samlah, from Masrekah, succeeded him as king. 37 When Samlah died, Shaul, from Rehoboth-on-the-River, succeeded him as king. 38 When Shaul died, Baal-hanan, son of Achbor, succeeded him as king. 39 When Baal-hanan died, Hadar succeeded him as king; the name of his city was Pau. (His wife's name was Mehetabel; she was the daughter of Matred, son of Mezahab.)

40 The following are the names of the clans of Esau individually according to their subdivisions and localities: the clans of Timna, Alvah, Jetheth, 41 Oholibamah, Elah, Pinon, 42 Kenaz, Teman, Mibzar, 43 Magdiel, and Iram. These are the clans of the Edomites, according to their settlements in their territorial holdings. [Esau was the father of the Edomites.]

JOSEPH AND HIS BROTHERS

Joseph Sold into Egypt

37 Jacob settled in the land where his father had stayed, the land of Canaan. 2 This is his family history. When Joseph was seventeen years old, he was tending the flocks with his brothers; he was an assistant to the sons of his father's wives Bilhah and Zilpah, and he brought his father bad reports about them.

3 Israel loved Joseph best of all his sons, for he was the child of his old age; and he had made him a long tunic. 4 When his brothers saw that their father loved him best of all his sons, they hated him so much that they would not even greet him.

5 Once Joseph had a dream, which he told to his brothers: 6 "Listen to this dream I had. 7 There we were, binding sheaves in the field, when suddenly my sheaf rose to an upright position, and your sheaves formed a ring around my sheaf and bowed down to it." 8 "Are you really going to make yourself king over us?" his brothers asked him. "Or impose your rule on us?" So

they hated him all the more because of his talk about his dreams.

9 Then he had another dream, and this one, too, he told to his brothers. "I had another dream," he said; "this time, the sun and the moon and eleven stars were bowing down to me." 10 When he also told it to his father, his father reproved him. "What is the meaning of this dream of yours?" he asked. "Can it be that I and your mother and your brothers are to come and bow to the ground before you?" 11 So his brothers were wrought up against him but his father pondered the matter.

12 One day, when his brothers had gone to pasture their father's flocks at Shechem, 13 Israel said to Joseph, "Your brothers, you know, are tending our flocks at Shechem. Get ready; I will send you to them." "I am ready," Joseph answered. 14 "Go then," he replied; "see if all is well with your brothers and the flocks, and bring back word." So he sent him off from the valley of Hebron. When Joseph reached Shechem, 15 a man met him as he was wandering about in the fields. "What are you looking for?" the man asked him. 16 "I am looking for my brothers," he answered. "Could you please tell me where they are tending the flocks?" 17 The man told him, "They have moved on from here; in fact, I heard them say, 'Let us go on to Dothan.'" So Joseph went after his brothers and caught up with them in Dothan. 18 They noticed him from a distance, and before he came up to them, they plotted to kill him. 19 They said to one another: "Here comes that master dreamer! 20 Come on, let us kill him and throw him into one of the cisterns here; we could say that a wild beast devoured him. We shall then see what comes of his dreams."

21 When Reuben heard this, he tried to save him from their hands, saying: "We must not take his life. 22 Instead of shedding blood," he continued, "just throw him into that

cistern there in the desert; but don't kill him outright." His purpose was to rescue him from their hands and restore him to his father. 23 So when Joseph came up to them, they stripped him of the long tunic he had on; 24 then they took him and threw him into the cistern, which was empty and dry.

25 They then sat down to their meal. Looking up, they saw a caravan of Ishmaelites coming from Gilead, their camels laden with gum, balm, and resin to be taken down to Egypt. 26 Judah said to his brothers: "What is to be gained by killing our brother and concealing his blood? 27 Rather, let us sell him to these Ishmaelites, instead of doing away with him ourselves. After all, he is our brother, our own flesh." His brothers agreed. 28 They sold Joseph to the Ishmaelites for twenty pieces of silver.

Some Midianite traders passed by, and they pulled Joseph up out of the cistern and took him to Egypt. 29 When Reuben went back to the cistern and saw that Joseph was not in it, he tore his clothes, 30 and returning to his brothers, he exclaimed: "The boy is gone! And I— where can I turn?" 31 They took Joseph's tunic, and after slaughtering a goat, dipped the tunic in its blood. 32 Then they sent someone to bring the long tunic to their father, with the message: "We found this. See whether it is your son's tunic or not." 33 He recognized it and exclaimed: "My son's tunic! A wild beast has devoured him! Joseph has been torn to pieces!" 34 Then Jacob rent his clothes, put sackcloth on his loins, and mourned his son many days. 35 Though his sons and daughters tried to console him, he refused all consolation, saying, "No, I will go down mourning to my son in the nether world." Thus did his father lament him.

36 The Midianites, meanwhile, sold Joseph in Egypt to Potiphar, a courtier of Pharaoh and his chief steward.

37, 21–36: The chapter thus far is from the Yahwist source, as are also vv 25–28a. But vv 21–24 and 28b–36 are from the Elohist source. In the latter, Reuben tries to rescue Joseph, who is taken in Reuben's absence by certain Midianites; in the Yahwist source, it is Judah who saves Joseph's life

by having him sold to certain Ishmaelites. Although the two variant forms in which the story was handed down in early oral tradition differ in these minor points, they agree on the essential fact that Joseph was brought as a slave into Egypt because of the jealousy of his brothers.

37, 28: *They sold Joseph . . . silver:* in the Hebrew text, these words occur between *out of the cistern* and *and (they) took him to Egypt* at the end of the verse.

Judah and Tamar

38 About that time Judah parted from his brothers and pitched his tent near a certain Adullamite named Hirah. 2 There he met the daughter of a Canaanite named Shua, married her, and had relations with her. 3 She conceived and bore a son, whom she named Er. 4 Again she conceived and bore a son, whom she named Onan. 5 Then she bore still another son, whom she named Shelah. They were in Chezib when he was born.

6 Judah got a wife named Tamar for his first-born, Er. 7 But Er, Judah's first-born, greatly offended the LORD; so the LORD took his life. 8 Then Judah said to Onan, "Unite with your brother's widow, in fulfillment of your duty as brother-in-law, and thus preserve your brother's line." 9 Onan, however, knew that the descendants would not be counted as his; so whenever he had relations with his brother's widow, he wasted his seed on the ground, to avoid contributing offspring for his brother. 10 What he did greatly offended the LORD, and the LORD took his life too. 11 Thereupon Judah said to his daughter-in-law Tamar, "Stay as a widow in your father's house until my son Shelah grows up"—for he feared that Shelah also might die like his brothers. So Tamar went to live in her father's house.

12 Years passed, and Judah's wife, the daughter of Shua, died. After Judah completed the period of mourning, he went up to Timnah for the shearing of his sheep, in company with his friend Hirah the Adullamite. 13 When Tamar was told that her father-in-law was on his way up to Timnah to shear his sheep, 14 she took off her widow's garb, veiled her face by covering herself with a shawl, and sat down at the entrance to Enaim, which is on the way to Timnah; for she was aware that, although Shelah was now grown up, she had not been given to him in marriage. 15 When Judah saw her, he mistook her for a harlot, since she had covered her face. 16 So he went over to her at the roadside, and not realizing that she was his daughter-in-law, he said, "Come, let me have intercourse with you." She replied, "What will you pay me for letting you have intercourse with me?" 17 He answered, "I will send you a kid from the flock." "Very well," she said, "provided you leave a pledge until you send it." 18 Judah asked, "What pledge am I to give to you?" She answered, "Your seal and cord, and the staff you carry." So he gave them to her and had intercourse with her, and she conceived by him. 19 When she went away, she took off her shawl and put on her widow's garb again.

20 Judah sent the kid by his friend the Adullamite to recover the pledge from the woman; but he could not find her. 21 So he asked the men of the place, "Where is the temple prostitute, the one by the roadside in Enaim?" But they answered, "There has never been a temple prostitute here." 22 He went back to Judah and told him, "I could not find her; and besides, the men of the place said there was no temple prostitute there." 23 "Let her keep the things," Judah replied; "otherwise we shall become a laughingstock. After all, I did send her the kid, even though you were unable to find her."

24 About three months later, Judah was told that his daughter-in-law Tamar had played the harlot and was then with child from her harlotry. "Bring her out," cried Judah; "she shall be burned." 25 But as they were bringing her out, she sent word to her father-in-law, "It is by the man to whom these things belong that I am with child. Please verify," she added, "whose seal and cord and whose staff these are." 26 Judah recognized them and said, "She is more in the right than I am, since I did not give her to my son Shelah." But he had no further relations with her.

27 When the time for her delivery came, she was found to have twins in her womb. 28 While she was giving birth, one infant put out his hand; and the midwife, taking a crimson thread, tied it on his hand, to note that this one came out first. 29 But as he withdrew his hand, his brother came out; and she said, "What a breach you have made for yourself!" So he was called Perez. 30 Afterward his brother came out; he was called Zerah.

Joseph's Temptation

39 When Joseph was taken down to Egypt, a certain Egyptian (Potiphar, a courtier of Pharaoh and his chief steward) bought him from the Ishmaelites who had brought him there. 2 But since the LORD was with him, Joseph got on very well and was assigned to the household of his Egyptian master. 3 When his master saw that the LORD was with him and brought him success in whatever he did, 4 he took a liking to Joseph and made him his personal attendant; he put him in charge of his household and entrusted to him all his possessions. 5 From the

---

38, 1–30: This chapter, from the Yahwist source, has nothing to do with the Joseph story in which Judah is still living with his father and brothers. The sacred author inserted this independent account from the life of Judah at this place to mark the long lapse of time during which Joseph's family knew nothing of his life in Egypt. This is apparently a personalized history of the early days of the tribe of Judah, which interbred with several Canaanite clans, though some of these soon became extinct.

38, 5: *Chezib:* a variant form of Achzib (Jos 15, 44; Mi 1, 14), a town in the Judean Shephelah.

38, 8: *Preserve your brother's line:* literally "raise up seed for your brother." The ancient Israelites regarded as very important their law of levirate, or "brother-in-law" marriage; see notes on Dt 25, 5; Ru 2, 20. In the present story, it is primarily Onan's

violation of this law, rather than the means he used to circumvent it, that brought on him God's displeasure (vv 9f).

38, 18: *Seal and cord:* the cylinder seal, through which a hole was bored lengthwise so that it could be worn from the neck by a cord, was a distinctive means of identification. Apparently a man's staff was also marked with his name (Nm 17, 16f) or other sign of identification.

38, 21: *Temple prostitute:* the Hebrew term *qedesha,* literally "consecrated woman," designates a woman who had ritual intercourse with men in pagan fertility rites; cf Dt 23, 18; Hos 4, 14, where the same Hebrew word is used. Hirah the Adullamite uses a word that refers to a higher social class than that designated by the term *zona,* common "harlot," used in vv 15.24.

38, 29: *He was called Perez:* the Hebrew word means "breach."

38, 30: *He was called Zerah:* a name connected here by popular etymology with a Hebrew verb for the red light of dawn, alluding apparently to the crimson thread.

39, 1: (*Potiphar . . . chief steward*): These words in the text serve to harmonize ch 39 from the Yahwist source with 37, 36 and 40, 1–23 from the Elohist. In the former, the Ishmaelites who bought Joseph from his brothers (37, 28) sold him to the unnamed "Egyptian master" of ch 39. In the latter, the Midianites who kidnaped Joseph (37, 28; 40, 15) sold him to Potiphar, Pharaoh's chief steward (37, 36), whose house was used as a royal prison (40, 2f).

moment that he put him in charge of his household and all his possessions, the LORD blessed the Egyptian's house for Joseph's sake; in fact, the LORD's blessing was on everything he owned, both inside the house and out. 6 Having left everything he owned in Joseph's charge, he gave no thought, with Joseph there, to anything but the food he ate.

Now Joseph was strikingly handsome in countenance and body. 7 After a time, his master's wife began to look fondly at him and said, "Lie with me." 8 But he refused. "As long as I am here," he told her, "my master does not concern himself with anything in the house, but has entrusted to me all he owns. 9 He wields no more authority in this house than I do, and he has withheld from me nothing but yourself, since you are his wife. How, then, could I commit so great a wrong and thus stand condemned before God?" 10 Although she tried to entice him day after day, he would not agree to lie beside her, or even stay near her.

11 One such day, when Joseph came into the house to do his work, and none of the household servants were then in the house, 12 she laid hold of him by his cloak, saying, "Lie with me!" But leaving the cloak in her hand, he got away from her and ran outside. 13 When she saw that he had left his cloak in her hand as he fled outside, 14 she screamed for her household servants and told them, "Look! my husband has brought in a Hebrew slave to make sport of us! He came in here to lie with me, but I cried out as loud as I could. 15 When he heard me scream for help, he left his cloak beside me and ran away outside."

16 She kept the cloak with her until his master came home. 17 Then she told him the same story: "The Hebrew slave whom you brought here broke in on me, to make sport of me. 18 But when I screamed for help, he left his cloak beside me and fled outside." 19 As soon as the master heard his wife's story about how his slave had treated her, he became enraged. 20 He

seized Joseph and threw him into the jail where the royal prisoners were confined.

But even while he was in prison, 21 the LORD remained with Joseph; he showed him kindness by making the chief jailer well-disposed toward him. 22 The chief jailer put Joseph in charge of all the prisoners in the jail, and everything that had to be done there was done under his management. 23 The chief jailer did not concern himself with anything at all that was in Joseph's charge, since the LORD was with him and brought success to all he did.

The Dreams Interpreted

40 Some time afterward, the royal cupbearer and baker gave offense to their lord, the king of Egypt. 2 Pharaoh was angry with his two courtiers, the chief cupbearer and the chief baker, 3 and he put them in custody in the house of the chief steward (the same jail where Joseph was confined). 4 The chief steward assigned Joseph to them, and he became their attendant.

After they had been in custody for some time, 5 the cupbearer and the baker of the king of Egypt who were confined in the jail both had dreams on the same hight, each dream with its own meaning. 6 When Joseph came to them in the morning, he noticed that they looked disturbed. 7 So he asked Pharaoh's courtiers who were with him in custody in his master's house, "Why do you look so sad today?" 8 They answered him, "We have had dreams, but there is no one to interpret them for us." Joseph said to them, "Surely, interpretations come from God. Please tell the dreams to me."

9 Then the chief cupbearer told Joseph his dream. "In my dream," he said, "I saw a vine in front of me, 10 and on the vine were three branches. It had barely budded when its blossoms came out, and its clusters ripened into grapes. Pharaoh's cup was in my hand; 11 so I took the grapes, pressed them out into his cup, and put it in Pharaoh's hand." 12 Joseph said to him: "This is what

it means. The three branches are three days; 13 within three days Pharaoh will lift up your head and restore you to your post. You will be handing Pharaoh his cup as you formerly used to do when you were his cupbearer. 14 So if you will still remember, when all is well with you, that I was here with you, please do me the favor of mentioning me to Pharaoh, to get me out of this place. 15 The truth is that I was kidnaped from the land of the Hebrews, and here I have not done anything for which I should have been put into a dungeon."

16 When the chief baker saw that Joseph had given this favorable interpretation, he said to him: "I too had a dream. In it I had three wicker baskets on my head; 17 in the top one were all kinds of bakery products for Pharaoh, but the birds were pecking at them out of the basket on my head." 18 Joseph said to him in reply: "This is what it means. The three baskets are three days; 19 within three days Pharaoh will lift up your head and have you impaled on a stake, and the birds will be pecking the flesh from your body."

20 And in fact, on the third day, which was Pharaoh's birthday, when he gave a banquet to all his staff, with his courtiers around him, he lifted up the heads of the chief cupbearer and chief baker. 21 He restored the chief cupbearer to his office, so that he again handed the cup to Pharaoh; 22 but the chief baker he impaled—just as Joseph had told them in his interpretation. 23 Yet the chief cupbearer gave no thought to Joseph; he had forgotten him.

Pharaoh's Dream

41 After a lapse of two years, Pharaoh had a dream. He saw himself standing by the Nile, 2 when up out of the Nile came seven cows, handsome and fat; they grazed in the reed grass. 3 Behind them seven other cows, ugly and gaunt, came up out of the Nile; and standing on the bank of the Nile beside the others, 4 the ugly, gaunt cows ate

40, 13: *Lift up your head:* signifying "pardon you." In v 19 "to lift up the head" means "to be- head"; and finally, in v 20, the same expression means "to review the case (of someone)." Joseph couches his interpretation of the dreams in equivocal terms.

up the seven handsome, fat cows. Then Pharaoh woke up.

5 He fell asleep again and had another dream. He saw seven ears of grain, fat and healthy, growing on a single stalk. 6 Behind them sprouted seven ears of grain, thin and blasted by the east wind; 7 and the seven thin ears swallowed up the seven fat, healthy ears. Then Pharaoh woke up, to find it was only a dream.

8 Next morning his spirit was agitated. So he summoned all the magicians and sages of Egypt and recounted his dreams to them; but no one could interpret his dreams for him. 9 Then the chief cupbearer spoke up and said to Pharaoh: "On this occasion I am reminded of my negligence. 10 Once, when Pharaoh was angry, he put me and the chief baker in custody in the house of the chief steward. 11 Later, we both had dreams on the same night, and each of our dreams had its own meaning. 12 There with us was a Hebrew youth, a slave of the chief steward; and when we told him our dreams, he interpreted them for us and explained for each of us the meaning of his dream. 13 And it turned out just as he had told us: I was restored to my post, but the other man was impaled."

14 Pharaoh therefore had Joseph summoned, and they hurriedly brought him from the dungeon. After he shaved and changed his clothes, he came into Pharaoh's presence. 15 Pharaoh then said to him: "I had certain dreams that no one can interpret. But I hear it said of you that the moment you are told a dream you can interpret it." 16 "It is not I," Joseph replied to Pharaoh, "but God who will give Pharaoh the right answer."

17 Then Pharaoh said to Joseph: "In my dream, I was standing on the bank of the Nile, 18 when up from the Nile came seven cows, fat and well-formed; they grazed in the reed grass. 19 Behind them came seven

other cows, scrawny, most ill-formed and gaunt. Never have I seen such ugly specimens as these in all the land of Egypt! 20 The gaunt, ugly cows ate up the first seven fat cows. 21 But when they had consumed them, no one could tell that they had done so, because they looked as ugly as before. Then I woke up. 22 In another dream I saw seven ears of grain, fat and healthy, growing on a single stalk. 23 Behind them sprouted seven ears of grain, shriveled and thin and blasted by the east wind; 24 and the seven thin ears swallowed up the seven healthy ears. I have spoken to the magicians, but none of them can give me an explanation."

25 Joseph said to Pharaoh: "Both of Pharaoh's dreams have the same meaning. God has thus foretold to Pharaoh what he is about to do. 26 The seven healthy cows are seven years, and the seven healthy ears are seven years—the same in each dream. 27 So also, the seven thin, ugly cows that came up after them are seven years, as are the seven thin, windblasted ears; they are seven years of famine. 28 It is just as I told Pharaoh: God has revealed to Pharaoh what he is about to do. 29 Seven years of great abundance are now coming throughout the land of Egypt; 30 but these will be followed by seven years of famine, when all the abundance in the land of Egypt will be forgotten. 31 When the famine has ravaged the land, no trace of the abundance will be found in the land because of the famine that follows it—so utterly severe will that famine be. 32 That Pharaoh had the same dream twice means that the matter has been reaffirmed by God and that God will soon bring it about.

33 "Therefore, let Pharaoh seek out a wise and discerning man and put him in charge of the land of Egypt. 34 Pharaoh should also take action to appoint overseers, so as to regiment the land during the seven years of abundance. 35 They

should husband all the food of the coming good years, collecting the grain under Pharaoh's authority, to be stored in the towns for food. 36 This food will serve as a reserve for the country against the seven years of famine that are to follow in the land of Egypt, so that the land may not perish in the famine."

37 This advice pleased Pharaoh and all his officials. 38 "Could we find another like him," Pharaoh asked his officials, "a man so endowed with the spirit of God?" 39 So Pharaoh said to Joseph: "Since God has made all this known to you, no one can be as wise and discerning as you are. 40 You shall be in charge of my palace, and all my people shall dart at your command. Only in respect to the throne shall I outrank you. 41 Herewith," Pharaoh told Joseph, "I place you in charge of the whole land of Egypt." 42 With that, Pharaoh took off his signet ring and put it on Joseph's finger. He had him dressed in robes of fine linen and put a gold chain about his neck. 43 He then had him ride in the chariot of his vizier, and they shouted "Abrek!" before him.

Thus was Joseph installed over the whole land of Egypt. 44 "I, Pharaoh, proclaim," he told Joseph, "that without your approval no one shall move hand or foot in all the land of Egypt." 45 Pharaoh also bestowed the name of Zaphenath-paneah on Joseph, and he gave him in marriage Asenath, the daughter of Potiphera, priest of Heliopolis. 46 Joseph was thirty years old when he entered the service of Pharaoh, king of Egypt.

After Joseph left Pharaoh's presence, he traveled throughout the land of Egypt. 47 During the seven years of plenty, when the land produced abundant crops, 48 he husbanded all the food of these years of plenty that the land of Egypt was enjoying and stored it in the towns, placing in each town the crops of the

---

41, 42: *Signet ring:* a finger ring in which was set a stamp seal, different from the cylinder seal such as Judah wore; see note on 38, 18. This is an authentic detail. By receiving Pharaoh's signet ring, Joseph was made vizier of Egypt (v 43); the vizier was known as "seal-bearer of the king of Lower Egypt." Another authentic detail is the *gold chain,* a symbol of

high office in ancient Egypt.

41, 43: *Abrek:* apparently a cry of homage, though the word's derivation and actual meaning are uncertain.

41, 45: *Zaphenath-paneah:* a Hebrew transcription of an Egyptian name meaning "the god speaks and he (the new-born child) lives." *Asenath:* means "be-

longing to (the Egyptian goddess) Neith." *Potiphera:* means "he whom Ra (the Egyptian god) gave"; a shorter form of the same name was borne by Joseph's master (37, 36). *Heliopolis:* in Hebrew, *On,* a city seven miles northeast of modern Cairo, site of the chief temple of the sun god; it is mentioned also in v 50; 46, 20; Ez 30, 17.

fields around it. 49 Joseph garnered grain in quantities like the sands of the sea, so vast that at last he stopped measuring it, for it was beyond measure.

50 Before the famine years set in, Joseph became the father of two sons, borne to him by Asenath, daughter of Potiphera, priest of Heliopolis. 51 He named his first-born Manasseh, meaning, "God has made me forget entirely the sufferings I endured at the hands of my family"; 52 and the second he named Ephraim, meaning, "God has made me fruitful in the land of my affliction."

53 When the seven years of abundance enjoyed by the land of Egypt came to an end, 54 the seven years of famine set in, just as Joseph had predicted. Although there was famine in all the other countries, food was available throughout the land of Egypt. 55 When hunger came to be felt throughout the land of Egypt and the people cried to Pharaoh for bread, Pharaoh directed all the Egyptians to go to Joseph and do whatever he told them. 56 When the famine had spread throughout the land, Joseph opened all the cities that had grain and rationed it to the Egyptians, since the famine had gripped the land of Egypt. 57 In fact, all the world came to Joseph to obtain rations of grain, for famine had gripped the whole world.

The Brothers' First Journey to Egypt

42 When Jacob learned that grain rations were available in Egypt, he said to his sons: "Why do you keep gaping at one another? 2 I hear," he went on, "that rations of grain are available in Egypt. Go down there and buy some for us, that we may stay alive rather than die of hunger." 3 So ten of Joseph's brothers went down to buy an emergency supply of grain from Egypt. 4 It was only Joseph's full brother Benjamin that Jacob did not send with the rest, for he thought some disaster might befall him. 5 Thus, since there was famine in the land of Canaan also, the sons of Israel were among those who came to procure rations.

6 It was Joseph, as governor of the country, who dispensed the rations to all the people. When Joseph's brothers came and knelt down before him with their faces to the ground, 7 he recognized them as soon as he saw them. But he concealed his own identity from them and spoke sternly to them. "Where do you come from?" he asked them. They answered, "From the land of Canaan, to procure food."

8 When Joseph recognized his brothers, although they did not recognize him, 9 he was reminded of the dreams he had about them. He said to them: "You are spies. You have come to see the nakedness of the land." 10 "No, my lord," they replied. "On the contrary, your servants have come to procure food. 11 All of us are sons of the same man. We are honest men; your servants have never been spies." 12 But he answered them: "Not so! You have come to see the nakedness of the land." 13 "We your servants," they said, "were twelve brothers, sons of a certain man in Canaan; but the youngest one is at present with our father, and the other one is gone." 14 "It is just as I said," Joseph persisted; "you are spies. 15 This is how you shall be tested: unless your youngest brother comes here, I swear by the life of Pharaoh that you shall not leave here. 16 So send one of your number to get your brother, while the rest of you stay here under arrest. Thus shall your words be tested for their truth; if they are untrue, as Pharaoh lives, you are spies!" 17 With that, he locked them up in the guardhouse for three days.

18 On the third day Joseph said to them: "Do this, and you shall live; for I am a God-fearing man. 19 If you have been honest, only one of your brothers need be confined in this prison, while the rest of you may go and take home provisions for your starving families. 20 But you must come back to me with our youngest brother. Your words will thus be verified, and you will not die." To this they agreed. 21 To one another, however, they said: "Alas, we are being punished because of our brother. We saw the anguish of his heart when he pleaded with us, yet we paid no heed; that is why this anguish has now come upon us." 22 "Didn't I tell you," broke in Reuben, "not to do wrong to the boy? But you wouldn't listen! Now comes the reckoning for his blood." 23 They did not know, of course, that Joseph understood what they said, since he spoke with them through an interpreter. 24 But turning away from them, he wept. When he was able to speak to them again, he had Simeon taken from them and bound before their eyes. 25 Then Joseph gave orders to have their containers filled with grain, their money replaced in each one's sack, and provisions given them for their journey. After this had been done for them, 26 they loaded their donkeys with the rations and departed.

27 At the night encampment, when one of them opened his bag to give his donkey some fodder, he was surprised to see his money in the mouth of his bag. 28 "My money has been returned!" he cried out to his brothers. "Here it is in my bag!" At that their hearts sank. Trembling, they asked one another, "What is this that God has done to us?"

29 When they got back to their father Jacob in the land of Canaan, they told him all that had happened to them. 30 "The man who is lord of the country," they said, "spoke to us sternly and put us in custody as if we were spying on the land. But we said to him: 31 'We are honest men: we have never been spies. 32 There were twelve of us brothers, sons of the same father; but one is gone, and the youngest one is at present with our father in the land of Canaan.' 33 Then the man who is lord of the country said to us: 'This is how I shall know if you are honest men: leave one of your brothers with

---

41, 51: *Manasseh:* allusion to this name is in the Hebrew expression, *nishshani,* "he made me forget."

41, 52: *Ephraim:* related to the Hebrew expression *hiphrani,* "(God) has made me fruitful."

42, 9.12: *The nakedness of the land:* the military weakness of the land, like human nakedness, should not be seen by strangers.

42, 27–28: These two verses are from the Yahwist

source, whereas the rest of the chapter is from the Elohist source, in which the men find the money in their sacks (not "bags"—a different Hebrew word) only when they arrive home (v 35); cf. 43, 21.

me, while the rest of you go home with rations for your starving families. 34 When you come back to me with your youngest brother, and I know that you are honest men and not spies, I will restore your brother to you, and you may move about freely in the land.'"

35 When they were emptying their sacks, there in each one's sack was his moneybag! At the sight of their moneybags, they and their father were dismayed. 36 Their father Jacob said to them: "Must you make me childless? Joseph is gone, and Simeon is gone, and now you would take away Benjamin! Why must such things always happen to me?" 37 Then Reuben told his father: "Put him in my care, and I will bring him back to you. You may kill my own two sons if I do not return him to you." 38 But Jacob replied: "My son shall not go down with you. Now that his full brother is dead, he is the only one left. If some disaster should befall him on the journey you must make, you would send my white head down to the nether world in grief."

The Second Journey to Egypt

43 Now the famine in the land grew more severe. 2 So when they had used up all the rations they had brought from Egypt, their father said to them, "Go back and procure us a little more food." 3 But Judah replied: "The man strictly warned us, 'You shall not appear in my presence unless your brother is with you.' 4 If you are willing to let our brother go with us, we will go down to procure food for you. 5 But if you are not willing, we will not go down, because the man told us, 'You shall not appear in my presence unless your brother is with you.'" Israel demanded, 6 "Why did you bring this trouble on me by telling the man that you had another brother?" 7 They answered: "The man kept asking about ourselves and our family: 'Is your father still living? Do you have another brother?' We had to answer his questions. How could we

know that he would say, 'Bring your brother down here'?"

8 Then Judah urged his father Israel: "Let the boy go with me, that we may be off and on our way if you and we and our children are to keep from starving to death. 9 I myself will stand surety for him. You can hold me responsible for him. If I fail to bring him back, to set him in your presence, you can hold it against me forever. 10 Had we not dillydallied, we could have been there and back twice by now!"

11 Their father Israel then told them: "If it must be so, then do this: Put some of the land's best products in your baggage and take them down to the man as gifts: some balm and honey, gum and resin, and pistachios and almonds. 12 Also take extra money along, for you must return the amount that was put back in the mouths of your bags; it may have been a mistake. 13 Take your brother, too, and be off on your way back to the man. 14 May God Almighty dispose the man to be merciful toward you, so that he may let your other brother go, as well as Benjamin. As for me, if I am to suffer bereavement, I shall suffer it."

15 So the men got the gifts, took double the amount of money with them, and, accompanied by Benjamin, were off on their way down to Egypt to present themselves to Joseph. 16 When Joseph saw Benjamin with them, he told his head steward, "Take these men into the house, and have an animal slaughtered and prepared, for they are to dine with me at noon." 17 Doing as Joseph had ordered, the steward conducted the men to Joseph's house. 18 But on being led to his house, they became apprehensive. "It must be," they thought, "on account of the money put back in our bags the first time, that we are taken inside; they want to use it as a pretext to attack us and take our donkeys and seize us as slaves." 19 So they went up to Joseph's head steward and talked to him at the entrance of the house. 20 "If you please, sir," they said, "we came down here once

before to procure food. 21 But when we arrived at a night's encampment and opened our bags, there was each man's money in the mouth of his bag—our money in the full amount! We have now brought it back. 22 We have brought other money to procure food with. We do not know who put the first money in our bags." 23 "Be at ease," he replied; "you have no need to fear. Your God and the God of your father must have put treasures in your bags for you. As for your money, I received it." With that, he led Simeon out to them.

24 The steward then brought the men inside Joseph's house. He gave them water to bathe their feet, and got fodder for their donkeys. 25 Then they set out their gifts to await Joseph's arrival at noon, for they had heard that they were to dine there. 26 When Joseph came home, they presented him with the gifts they had brought inside, while they bowed down before him to the ground. 27 After inquiring how they were, he asked them, "And how is your aged father, of whom you spoke? Is he still in good health?" 28 "Your servant our father is thriving and still in good health," they said, as they bowed respectfully. 29 When Joseph's eye fell on his full brother Benjamin, he asked, "Is this your youngest brother, of whom you told me?" Then he said to him, "May God be gracious to you, my boy!" 30 With that, Joseph had to hurry out, for he was so overcome with affection for his brother that he was on the verge of tears. He went into a private room and wept there.

31 After washing his face, he reappeared and, now in control of himself, gave the order, "Serve the meal." 32 It was served separately to him, to the brothers, and to the Egyptians who partook of his board. (Egyptians may not eat with Hebrews; that is abhorrent to them.) 33 When they were seated by his directions according to their age, from the oldest to the youngest, they looked at one another in amazement; 34 and as portions were brought to them from

Joseph's table, Benjamin's portion was five times as large as anyone else's. So they drank freely and made merry with him.

Final Test

44 Then Joseph gave his head steward these instructions: "Fill the men's bags with as much food as they can carry, and put each man's money in the mouth of his bag. 2 In the mouth of the youngest one's bag put also my silver goblet, together with the money for his rations." 3 The steward carried out Joseph's instructions. At daybreak the men and their donkeys were sent off. 4 They had not gone far out of the city when Joseph said to his head steward: "Go at once after the men! When you overtake them, say to them, 'Why did you repay good with evil? Why did you steal the silver goblet from me? 5 It is the very one from which my master drinks and which he uses for divination. What you have done is wrong.'"

6 When the steward overtook them and repeated these words to them, they remonstrated with him: 7 "How can my lord say such things? Far be it from your servants to do such a thing! 8 We even brought back to you from the land of Canaan the money that we found in the mouths of our bags. Why, then, would we steal silver or gold from your master's house? 9 If any of your servants is found to have the goblet, he shall die, and as for the rest of us, we shall become my lord's slaves." 10 But he replied, "Even though it ought to be as you propose, only the one who is found to have it shall become my slave, and the rest of you shall be exonerated." 11 Then each of them eagerly lowered his bag to the ground and opened it; 12 and when a search was made, starting with the oldest and ending with the youngest, the goblet turned up in Benjamin's bag. 13 At this, they tore their clothes. Then, when each man had reloaded his donkey, they returned to the city.

14 As Judah and his brothers re-entered Joseph's house, he was still there; so they flung themselves on the ground before him. 15 "How could you do such a thing?" Joseph asked them. "You should have known that such a man as I could discover by divination what happened." 16 Judah replied: "What can we say to my lord? How can we plead or how try to prove our innocence? God has uncovered your servants' guilt. Here we are, then, the slaves of my lord—the rest of us no less than the one in whose possession the goblet was found." 17 "Far be it from me to act thus!" said Joseph. "Only the one in whose possession the goblet was found shall become my slave; the rest of you may go back safe and sound to your father."

18 Judah then stepped up to him and said: "I beg you, my lord, let your servant speak earnestly to my lord, and do not become angry with your servant, for you are the equal of Pharaoh. 19 My lord asked your servants, 'Have you a father, or another brother?' 20 So we said to my lord, 'We have an aged father, and a young brother, the child of his old age. This one's full brother is dead, and since he is the only one by that mother who is left, his father dotes on him.' 21 Then you told your servants, 'Bring him down to me that my eyes may look on him.' 22 We replied to my lord, 'The boy cannot leave his father; his father would die if he were to leave him.' 23 But you told your servants, 'Unless your youngest brother comes back with you, you shall not come into my presence again.' 24 When we returned to your servant our father, we reported to him the words of my lord. 25 "Later, our father told us to come back and buy some food for the family. 26 So we reminded him, 'We cannot go down there; only if our youngest brother is with us can we go, for we may not see the man if our youngest brother is not with us.' 27 Then your servant our father said to us, 'As you know, my wife bore me

two sons. 28 One of them, however, disappeared, and I had to conclude that he must have been torn to pieces by wild beasts; I have not seen him since. 29 If you now take this one away from me too, and some disaster befalls him, you will send my white head down to the nether world in grief.'

30 "If then the boy is not with us when I go back to your servant my father, whose very life is bound up with his, he will die as soon as he sees that the boy is missing; 31 and your servants will thus send the white head of our father down to the nether world in grief. 32 Besides, I, your servant, got the boy from his father by going surety for him, saying, 'If I fail to bring him back to you, father, you can hold it against me forever.' 33 Let me, your servant, therefore, remain in place of the boy as the slave of my lord, and let the boy go back with his brothers. 34 How could I go back to my father if the boy were not with me? I could not bear to see the anguish that would overcome my father."

The Truth Revealed

45 Joseph could no longer control himself in the presence of all his attendants, so he cried out, "Have everyone withdraw from me!" Thus no one else was about when he made himself known to his brothers. 2 But his sobs were so loud that the Egyptians heard him, and so the news reached Pharaoh's palace. 3 "I am Joseph," he said to his brothers. "Is my father still in good health?" But his brothers could give him no answer, so dumbfounded were they at him.

4 "Come closer to me," he told his brothers. When they had done so, he said: "I am your brother Joseph, whom you once sold into Egypt. 5 But now do not be distressed, and do not reproach yourselves for having sold me here. It was really for the sake of saving lives that God sent me here ahead of you. 6 For two years now the famine has been in the land,

---

44, 1f: Replacement of the money in the men's bags is probably a redactional addition here, taken from the Yahwist account of the first visit. It is only the goblet in Benjamin's bag, not any replaced money, that plays a part in the rest of the chapter.

44, 5: *Divination:* seeking omens through liquids

poured into a cup or bowl was a common practice in the ancient Near East; cf v 15. Even though divination was frowned on in later Israel (Lv 19, 31), it is in this place an authentic touch which the sacred author does not hesitate to ascribe to Joseph, the wisest man in Egypt.

44, 16: *Guilt:* in trying to do away with Joseph when he was young.

44, 19: *My lord . . . your servants:* such frequently repeated expressions in Judah's speech show the formal court style used by a subject in speaking to a high official.

and for five more years tillage will yield no harvest. 7 God, therefore, sent me on ahead of you to ensure for you a remnant on earth and to save your lives in an extraordinary deliverance. 8 So it was not really you but God who had me come here; and he has made of me a father to Pharaoh, lord of all his household, and ruler over the whole land of Egypt.

9 "Hurry back, then, to my father and tell him: 'Thus says your son Joseph: God has made me lord of all Egypt; come to me without delay. 10 You will settle in the region of Goshen, where you will be near me— you and your children and grandchildren, your flocks and herds, and everything that you own. 11 Since five years of famine still lie ahead, I will provide for you there, so that you and your family and all that are yours may not suffer want.' 12 Surely, you can see for yourselves, and Benjamin can see for himself, that it is I, Joseph, who am speaking to you. 13 Tell my father all about my high position in Egypt and what you have seen. But hurry and bring my father down here." 14 Thereupon he flung himself on the neck of his brother Benjamin and wept, and Benjamin wept in his arms. 15 Joseph then kissed all his brothers, crying over each of them; and only then were his brothers able to talk with him.

16 When the news reached Pharaoh's palace that Joseph's brothers had come, Pharaoh and his courtiers were pleased. 17 So Pharaoh told Joseph: "Say to your brothers: 'This is what you shall do: Load up your animals and go without delay to the land of Canaan. 18 There get your father and your families, and then come back here to me; I will assign you the best land in Egypt, where you will live off the fat of the land.' 19 Instruct them further: 'Do this. Take wagons from the land of Egypt for your children and your wives and to transport your father on your way back here. 20 Do not be concerned about your belongings, for the best in the whole land of Egypt shall be yours.'"

21 The sons of Israel acted accordingly. Joseph gave them the wagons, as Pharaoh had ordered, and he supplied them with provisions for the journey. 22 He also gave to each of them fresh clothing, but to Benjamin he gave three hundred shekels of silver and five sets of garments. 23 Moreover, what he sent to his father was ten jackasses loaded with the finest products of Egypt and ten jennies loaded with grain and bread and other provisions for his journey. 24 As he sent his brothers on their way, he told them, "Let there be no recriminations on the way."

25 So they left Egypt and made their way to their father Jacob in the land of Canaan. 26 When they told him, "Joseph is still alive—in fact, it is he who is ruler of all the land of Egypt," he was dumbfounded; he could not believe them. 27 But when they recounted to him all that Joseph had told them, and when he saw the wagons that Joseph had sent for his transport, the spirit of their father Jacob revived. 28 "It is enough," said Israel. "My son Joseph is still alive! I must go and see him before I die."

Migration to Egypt

46 Israel set out with all that was his. When he arrived at Beersheba, he offered sacrifices to the God of his father Isaac. 2 There God, speaking to Israel in a vision by night, called, "Jacob! Jacob!" "Here I am," he answered. 3 Then he said: "I am God, the God of your father. Do not be afraid to go down to Egypt, for there I will make you a great nation. 4 Not only will I go down to Egypt with you; I will also bring you back here, after Joseph has closed your eyes."

5 So Jacob departed from Beersheba, and the sons of Israel put their father and their wives and children on the wagons that Pharaoh had sent for his transport. 6 They took with them their livestock and the possessions they had acquired in the land of Canaan. Thus Jacob and all his descendants migrated to Egypt. 7 His sons and his grandsons, his daughters and his granddaughters— all his descendants—he took with him to Egypt.

8 These are the names of the Israelites, Jacob and his descendants, who migrated to Egypt.

Reuben, Jacob's first-born, 9 and the sons of Reuben: Hanoch, Pallu, Hezron, and Carmi. 10 The sons of Simeon: Nemuel, Jamin, Ohad, Jachin, Zohar, and Shaul, son of a Canaanite woman. 11 The sons of Levi: Gershon, Kohath, and Merari. 12 The sons of Judah: Er, Onan, Shelah, Perez, and Zerah—but Er and Onan had died in the land of Canaan; and the sons of Perez were Hezron and Hamul. 13 The sons of Issachar: Tola, Puah, Jashub, and Shimron. 14 The sons of Zebulun: Sered, Elon, and Jahleel. 15 These were the sons whom Leah bore to Jacob in Paddan-aram, along with his daughter Dinah—thirty-three persons in all, male and female.

16 The sons of Gad: Zephon, Haggi, Shuni, Ezbon, Eri, Arod, and Areli. 17 The sons of Asher: Imnah, Ishvah, Ishvi, and Beriah, with their sister Serah; and the sons of Beriah: Heber and Malchiel. 18 These were the descendants of Zilpah, whom Laban had given to his daughter Leah; these she bore to Jacob—sixteen persons in all.

19 The sons of Jacob's wife Rachel: Joseph and Benjamin. 20 In the land of Egypt Joseph became the father of Manasseh and Ephraim, whom Asenath, daughter of Potiphera, priest of Heliopolis, bore to him. 21 The sons of Benjamin: Bela, Becher, Ashbel, Gera, Naaman, Ahiram, Shupham, Hupham, and Ard. 22 These were the sons whom Rachel bore to Jacob—fourteen persons in all.

45, 8: *Father to Pharaoh:* a term applied to a vizier in ancient Egypt.

45, 9–15: In these verses, as in 46, 31—47, 5a, all from the Yahwist source, Joseph in his own name invites his father and brothers to come to Egypt. Only after their arrival is Pharaoh informed of the fact. On the other hand, in 45, 16–20, from the Elohist source, it is Pharaoh himself who invites Joseph's kinsmen to migrate to his domain.

45, 10: *The region of Goshen:* modern Wadi Tumilat in the eastern part of the Nile delta.

46, 3: *I am God:* more precisely according to the Hebrew text, "I am El." "El" is here a divine name, not the common noun "god."

46, 9–27: This genealogical list has here been inserted by a redactor who bases it on the clan lists (Nm 26, 5–50) at the time of Moses. Therefore it includes some of Jacob's grandchildren, who would hardly have been born when Joseph was still a relatively young man. The number *fourteen* (v 22) is based on a garbled version of the genealogical list.

23 The sons of Dan: Hushim. 24 The sons of Naphtali: Jahzeel, Guni, Jezer, and Shillem. 25 These were the sons of Bilhah, whom Laban had given to his daughter Rachel; these she bore to Jacob—seven persons in all.

26 Jacob's people who migrated to Egypt—his direct descendants, not counting the wives of Jacob's sons—numbered sixty-six persons in all. 27 Together with Joseph's sons who were born to him in Egypt—two persons—all the people comprising Jacob's family who had come to Egypt amounted to seventy persons in all.

28 Israel had sent Judah ahead to Joseph, so that he might meet him in Goshen. On his arrival in the region of Goshen, 29 Joseph hitched the horses to his chariot and rode to meet his father Israel in Goshen. As soon as he saw him, he flung himself on his neck and wept a long time in his arms. 30 And Israel said to Joseph, "At last I can die, now that I have seen for myself that Joseph is still alive."

31 Joseph then said to his brothers and his father's household: "I will go and inform Pharaoh, telling him: 'My brothers and my father's household, whose home is in the land of Canaan, have come to me. 32 The men are shepherds, having long been keepers of livestock; and they have brought with them their flocks and herds, as well as everything else they own.' 33 So when Pharaoh summons you and asks what your occupation is, you must answer, 34 'We your servants, like our ancestors, have been keepers of livestock from the beginning until now,' in order that you may stay in the region of Goshen, since all shepherds are abhorrent to the Egyptians."

Settlement in Goshen

47 Joseph went and told Pharaoh, "My father and my brothers have come from the land of Canaan, with their flocks and herds and everything else they own; and they are now in the region of Goshen."

2 He then presented to Pharaoh five of his brothers whom he had selected from their full number. 3 When Pharaoh asked them what their occupation was, they answered, "We your servants, like our ancestors, are shepherds. 4 We have come," they continued, "in order to stay in this country, for there is no pasture for your servants' flocks in the land of Canaan, so severe has the famine been there. Please, therefore, let your servants settle in the region of Goshen." 5 Pharaoh said to Joseph, "They may settle in the region of Goshen; and if you know any of them to be qualified, you may put them in charge of my own livestock."

Thus, when Jacob and his sons came to Joseph in Egypt, and Pharaoh, king of Egypt, heard about it, Pharaoh said to Joseph, "Now that your father and brothers have come to you, 6 the land of Egypt is at your disposal; settle your father and brothers in the pick of the land." 7 Then Joseph brought his father Jacob and presented him to Pharaoh. After Jacob had paid his respects to Pharaoh, 8 Pharaoh asked him, "How many years have you lived?" 9 Jacob replied: "The years I have lived as a wayfarer amount to a hundred and thirty. Few and hard have been these years of my life, and they do not compare with the years my ancestors lived as wayfarers." 10 Then Jacob bade Pharaoh farewell and withdrew from his presence.

11 As Pharaoh had ordered, Joseph settled his father and brothers and gave them holdings in Egypt on the pick of the land, in the region of Rameses. 12 And Joseph sustained his father and brothers and his father's whole household, down to the youngest, with food.

Joseph's Land Policy

13 Since there was no food in any country because of the extreme severity of the famine, and the lands of Egypt and Canaan were languishing from hunger, 14 Joseph gathered in, as payment for the rations that were being dispensed, all the money that was to be found in Egypt and Canaan, and he put it in Pharaoh's palace. 15 When all the money in Egypt and Canaan was spent, all the Egyptians came to Joseph, pleading, "Give us food or we shall perish under your eyes; for our money is gone." 16 "Since your money is gone," replied Joseph, "give me your livestock, and I will sell you bread in return for your livestock." 17 So they brought their livestock to Joseph, and he sold them food in return for their horses, their flocks of sheep and herds of cattle, and their donkeys. Thus he got them through that year with bread in exchange for all their livestock. 18 When that year ended, they came to him in the following one and said: "We cannot hide from my lord that, with our money spent and our livestock made over to my lord, there is nothing left to put at my lord's disposal except our bodies and our farm land. 19 Why should we and our land perish before your very eyes? Take us and our land in exchange for food, and we will become Pharaoh's slaves and our land his property; only give us seed, that we may survive and not perish, and that our land may not turn into a waste."

20 Thus Joseph acquired all the farm land of Egypt for Pharaoh, since with the famine too much for them to bear, every Egyptian sold his field; so the land passed over to Pharaoh, 21 and the people were reduced to slavery, from one end of Egypt's territory to the other. 22 Only the priests' lands Joseph did not take over. Since the priests had a fixed allowance from Pharaoh and lived off the allowance Pharaoh had granted them, they did not have to sell their land.

23 Joseph told the people: "Now that I have acquired you and your land for Pharaoh, here is your seed for sowing the land. 24 But when the harvest is in, you must give a fifth of it to Pharaoh, while you keep four-fifths as seed for your fields and as food for yourselves and your families [and as food for your

---

46, 27: *Seventy persons:* either to be understood as a round number, or arrived at by including Jacob and Joseph with the preceding persons, who add up to sixty-eight.

47, 9: *Wayfarer . . . wayfarers:* man is merely a sojourner on earth; cf Ps 39, 13.

47, 11: *The region of Rameses:* same as the region of Goshen; see note on 45, 10. The name Rameses, however, is an anachronism, since this royal name did not come into use before the end of the fourteenth century B.C., long after the time of Joseph.

children].'' 25 ''You have saved our lives!'' they answered. ''We are grateful to my lord that we can be Pharaoh's slaves.'' 26 Thus Joseph made it a law for the land in Egypt, which is still in force, that a fifth of its produce should go to Pharaoh. Only the land of the priests did not pass over to Pharaoh.

Jacob Blesses Ephraim and Manasseh

27 Thus Israel settled in the land of Egypt, in the region of Goshen. There they acquired property, were fertile, and increased greatly. 28 Jacob lived in the land of Egypt for seventeen years; the span of his life came to a hundred and forty-seven years. 29 When the time approached for Israel to die, he called his son Joseph and said to him: ''If you really wish to please me, put your hand under my thigh as a sign of your constant loyalty to me; do not let me be buried in Egypt. 30 When I lie down with my ancestors, have me taken out of Egypt and buried in their burial place.'' 31 ''I will do as you say,'' he replied. But his father demanded, ''Swear it to me!'' So Joseph swore to him. Then Israel bowed at the head of the bed.

48 Some time afterward, Joseph was informed, ''Your father is failing.'' So he took along with him his two sons, Manasseh and Ephraim. 2 When Jacob was told, ''Your son Joseph has come to you,'' he rallied his strength and sat up in bed.

3 Jacob then said to Joseph: ''God Almighty appeared to me at Luz in the land of Canaan, and blessing me, 4 he said, 'I will make you fertile and numerous and raise you into an assembly of tribes, and I will give this land to your descendants after you as a permanent possession.' 5 Your two sons, therefore, who were born to you in the land of Egypt before I joined you here, shall be mine; Ephraim and Manasseh shall be mine as much as Reuben and Simeon are

mine. 6 Progeny born to you after them shall remain yours; but their heritage shall be recorded in the names of their two brothers. 7 I do this because, when I was returning from Paddan, your mother Rachel died, to my sorrow, during the journey in Canaan, while we were still a short distance from Ephrath; and I buried her there on the way to Ephrath [that is, Bethlehem].''

8 When Israel saw Joseph's sons, he asked, ''Who are these?'' 9 ''They are my sons,'' Joseph answered his father, ''whom God has given me here.'' ''Bring them to me,'' said his father, ''that I may bless them.'' 10 (Now Israel's eyes were dim from age, and he could not see well.) When Joseph brought his sons close to him, he kissed and embraced them. 11 Then Israel said to Joseph, ''I never expected to see your face again, and now God has allowed me to see your descendants as well!''

12 Joseph removed them from his father's knees and bowed down before him with his face to the ground. 13 Then Joseph took the two, Ephraim with his right hand, to Israel's left, and Manasseh with his left hand, to Israel's right, and led them to him. 14 But Israel, crossing his hands, put out his right hand and laid it on the head of Ephraim, although he was the younger, and his left hand on the head of Manasseh, although he was the first-born. 15 Then he blessed them with these words:

''May the God in whose ways
　my fathers Abraham and
　　Isaac walked,
The God who has been my
　shepherd
　　from my birth to this day,
16 The Angel who has delivered
　me from all harm,
　　bless these boys
That in them my name be
　recalled,
　and the names of my fathers
　　Abraham and Isaac,

And they may become teeming
　multitudes
　　upon the earth!''

17 When Joseph saw that his father had laid his right hand on Ephraim's head, this seemed wrong to him; so he took hold of his father's hand, to remove it from Ephraim's head to Manasseh's, 18 saying, ''That is not right, father; the other one is the first-born; lay your right hand on his head!'' 19 But his father resisted. ''I know it, son,'' he said, ''I know. That one too shall become a tribe, and he too shall be great. Nevertheless, his younger brother shall surpass him, and his descendants shall become a multitude of nations.'' 20 So when he blessed them that day and said, ''By you shall the people of Israel pronounce blessings; may they say, 'God make you like Ephraim and Manasseh,''' he placed Ephraim before Manasseh.

21 Then Israel said to Joseph: ''I am about to die. But God will be with you and will restore you to the land of your fathers. 22 As for me, I give to you, as to the one above his brothers, Shechem, which I captured from the Amorites with my sword and bow.''

Jacob's Testament

49 Jacob called his sons and said: ''Gather around, that I may tell you what is to happen to you in days to come.

2 ''Assemble and listen, sons of
　Jacob,
　listen to Israel, your father.

3 ''You, Reuben, my first-born,
　my strength and the first
　　fruit of my manhood,
　excelling in rank and
　　excelling in power!

4 Unruly as water, you shall no
　longer excel,
　for you climbed into your
　　father's bed
　and defiled my couch to my
　　sorrow.

47, 31: *Israel bowed at the head of the bed:* meaning perhaps that he gave a nod of assent and appreciation as he lay on his bed. By reading with different vowels the Hebrew word for ''bed,'' the Greek version translated it as ''staff,'' and understood the phrase to mean that he bowed in worship, leaning on the top of his staff; it is thus quoted in Heb 11, 21.
48, 3: *Luz:* an older name of Bethel (28, 19).

48, 7: Since her early death prevented Rachel from bearing more than two sons, Jacob feels justified in treating her two grandsons as if they were her own offspring.
48, 22: Both the meaning of the Hebrew and the historical reference in this verse are obscure. By taking the Hebrew word for Shechem as a common noun meaning shoulder or mountain slope, some

translators render the verse, ''I give you one portion more than your brothers, which I captured. . . .'' The reference may be to the capture of Shechem by the sons of Jacob (34, 24–29). Shechem lay near the border separating the tribal territory of Manasseh from that of Ephraim (Jos 16, 4–9; 17, 1f.7).

5 "Simeon and Levi, brothers indeed,
    weapons of violence are their knives.
6 Let not my soul enter their council,
    or my spirit be joined with their company;
For in their fury they slew men,
    in their willfulness they maimed oxen.
7 Cursed be their fury so fierce,
    and their rage so cruel!
I will scatter them in Jacob,
    disperse them thoughout Israel.

8 "You, Judah, shall your brothers praise
    —your hand on the neck of your enemies;
    the sons of your father shall bow down to you.
9 Judah, like a lion's whelp,
    you have grown up on prey, my son.
He crouches like a lion recumbent,
    the king of beasts—who would dare rouse him?
10 The scepter shall never depart from Judah,
    or the mace from between his legs,
While tribute is brought to him,
    and he receives the peoples' homage.
11 He tethers his donkey to the vine,
    his purebred ass to the choicest stem.
In wine he washes his garments,
    his robe in the blood of grapes.
12 His eyes are darker than wine,
    and his teeth are whiter than milk.

13 "Zebulun shall dwell by the seashore
    [This means a shore for ships],
    and his flank shall be based on Sidon.

14 "Issachar is a rawboned ass,
    crouching between the saddlebags.
15 When he saw how good a settled life was,
    and how pleasant the country,
He bent his shoulder to the burden.
    and became a toiling serf.

16 "Dan shall achieve justice for his kindred
    like any other tribe of Israel.
17 Let Dan be a serpent by the roadside,
    a horned viper by the path,
That bites the horse's heel,
    so that the rider tumbles backward.

18 "[I long for your deliverance, O LORD!]

19 "Gad shall be raided by raiders,
    but he shall raid at their heels.

20 "Asher's produce is rich,
    and he shall furnish dainties for kings.

21 "Naphtali is a hind let loose
    which brings forth lovely fawns.

22 "Joseph is a wild colt,
    a wild colt by a spring,
    a wild ass on a hillside.
23 Harrying and attacking,
    the archers opposed him;
24 But each one's bow remained stiff,
    as their arms were unsteady,
By the power of the Mighty One of Jacob,
    because of the Shepherd, the Rock of Israel,
25 The God of your father, who helps you,
    God Almighty, who blesses you,
With the blessings of the heavens above,
    the blessings of the abyss that crouches below,

The blessings of breasts and womb,
26   the blessings of fresh grain and blossoms,
The blessings of the everlasting mountains,
    the delights of the eternal hills.
May they rest on the head of Joseph,
    on the brow of the prince among his brothers.

27 "Benjamin is a ravenous wolf;
    mornings he devours the prey,
    and evenings he distributes the spoils."

Farewell and Death

28 All these are the twelve tribes of Israel, and this is what their father said about them, as he bade them farewell and gave to each of them an appropriate message. 29 Then he gave them this charge: "Since I am about to be taken to my kindred, bury me with my fathers in the cave that lies in the field of Ephron the Hittite, 30 the cave in the field of Machpelah, facing on Mamre, in the land of Canaan, the field that Abraham bought from Ephron the Hittite for a burial ground. 31 There Abraham and his wife Sarah are buried, and so are Isaac and his wife Rebekah, and there, too, I buried Leah 32 —the field and the cave in it that had been purchased from the Hittites."

33 When Jacob had finished giving these instructions to his sons, he drew his feet into the bed, breathed his last, and was taken to his kindred.

Jacob's Funeral

50 Joseph threw himself on his father's face and wept over him as he kissed him. 2 Then he ordered the physicians in his service to embalm his father. 3 When they embalmed Israel, they spent forty days at it, for that is the full period of

---

49, 5: *Knives:* if this is the meaning of the obscure Hebrew word here, the reference may be to the knives used in circumcising the men of Shechem (34, 24; cf Jos 5, 2).

49, 10: *While tribute is brought to him:* this translation is based on a slight change in the Hebrew text, which, as it stands, would seem to mean, "until he comes to Shiloh." A somewhat different reading of the Hebrew text would be, "until he comes to whom it

belongs." This last has been traditionally understood in a Messianic sense. In any case, the passage foretells the supremacy of the tribe of Judah, which found its fulfillment in the Davidic dynasty and ultimately in the Messianic Son of David, Jesus Christ.

49, 11: *In wine ... the blood of grapes:* Judah's clothes are poetically pictured as soaked with grape juice from trampling in the wine press, the rich vintage of his land; cf Is 63, 2.

49, 16: In Hebrew the verb for *achieve justice* is from the same root as the name *Dan.*

49, 19: In Hebrew there is a certain assonance between the name *Gad* and the words for "raided," "raiders" and "raid."

49, 25f: A very similar description of the agricultural riches of the tribal land of Joseph is given in Dt 33, 13–16.

embalming; and the Egyptians mourned him for seventy days. 4 When that period of mourning was over, Joseph spoke to Pharaoh's courtiers. "Please do me this favor," he said, "and convey to Pharaoh this request of mine. 5 Since my father, at the point of death, made me promise on oath to bury him in the tomb that he had prepared for himself in the land of Canaan, may I go up there to bury my father and then come back?" 6 Pharaoh replied, "Go and bury your father, as he made you promise on oath."

7 So Joseph left to bury his father; and with him went all of Pharaoh's officials who were senior members of his court and all the other dignitaries of Egypt, 8 as well as Joseph's whole household, his brothers, and his father's household; only their children and their flocks and herds were left in the region of Goshen. 9 Chariots, too, and charioteers went up with him; it was a very large retinue.

10 When they arrived at Goren-ha-atad, which is beyond the Jordan, they held there a very great and solemn memorial service; and Joseph observed seven days of mourning for his father. 11 When the Canaanites who inhabited the land saw the mourning at Goren-ha-atad, they said, "This is a solemn funeral the Egyptians are having." That is why the place was named Abel-mizraim. It is beyond the Jordan.

12 Thus Jacob's sons did for him as he had instructed them. 13 They carried him to the land of Canaan and buried him in the cave in the field of Machpelah, facing on Mamre, the field that Abraham had bought for a burial ground from Ephron the Hittite.

14 After Joseph had buried his father he returned to Egypt, together with his brothers and all who had gone up with him for the burial of his father.

Plea for Forgiveness

15 Now that their father was dead, Joseph's brothers became fearful and thought, "Suppose Joseph has been nursing a grudge against us and now plans to pay us back in full for all the wrong we did him!" 16 So they approached Joseph and said: "Before your father died, he gave us these instructions: 17 'You shall say to Joseph, Jacob begs you to forgive the criminal wrongdoing of your brothers, who treated you so cruelly.' Please, therefore, forgive the crime that we, the servants of your father's God, committed." When they spoke these words to him, Joseph broke into tears. 18 Then his brothers proceeded to fling themselves down before him and said, "Let us be your slaves!" 19 But Joseph replied to them: "Have no fear. Can I take the place of God? 20 Even though you meant harm to me, God meant it for good, to achieve his present end, the survival of many people. 21 Therefore have no fear. I will provide for you and for your children." By thus speaking kindly to them, he reassured them.

22 Joseph remained in Egypt, together with his father's family. He lived a hundred and ten years. 23 He saw Ephraim's children to the third generation, and the children of Manasseh's son Machir were also born on Joseph's knees.

Death of Joseph

24 Joseph said to his brothers: "I am about to die. God will surely take care of you and lead you out of this land to the land that he promised on oath to Abraham, Isaac and Jacob." 25 Then, putting the sons of Israel under oath, he continued, "When God thus takes care of you, you must bring my bones up with you from this place." 26 Joseph died at the age of a hundred and ten. He was embalmed and laid to rest in a coffin in Egypt.

50, 10f: *Goren-ha-atad:* "Threshing Floor of the Brambles." *Abel-mizraim:* although the name really means "watercourse of the Egyptians," it is understood here, by a play on the first part of the term, to mean "mourning of the Egyptians." The site has not been identified through either reading of the name. But it is difficult to see why the mourning rites should have been held in the land *beyond the Jordan* when the burial was at Hebron. Perhaps an earlier form of the story placed the mourning rites beyond the Wadi of Egypt, the traditional boundary between Canaan and Egypt (Nm 34, 5; Jos 15, 4.47).

Exodus

THE ISRAELITES IN EGYPT

Jacob's Descendants in Egypt

THESE are the names of the sons of Israel who, accompanied by their households, migrated with Jacob into Egypt: 2 Reuben, Simeon, Levi and Judah; 3 Issachar, Zebulun and Benjamin; 4 Dan and Naphtali, Gad and Asher. 5 The total number of direct descendants of Jacob was seventy. Joseph was already in Egypt.

6 Now Joseph and all his brothers and that whole generation died. 7 But the Israelites were fruitful and prolific. They became so numerous and strong that the land was filled with them.

The Oppression

8 Then a new king, who knew nothing of Joseph, came to power in Egypt. 9 He said to his subjects, "Look how numerous and powerful the Israelite people are growing, more so than we ourselves! 10 Come, let us deal shrewdly with them to stop their increase; otherwise, in time of war they too may join our enemies to fight against us, and so leave our country." 11 Accordingly, taskmasters were set over the Israelites to oppress them with forced labor. Thus they had to build for Pharaoh the supply cities of Pithom and Raamses. 12 Yet the more they were oppressed, the more they multiplied and spread. The Egyptians, then, dreaded the Israelites 13 and reduced them to cruel slavery 14 making life bitter for them with hard work in mortar and brick and all kinds of field work—the whole cruel fate of slaves.

Command to the Midwives

15 The king of Egypt told the Hebrew midwives, one of whom was called Shiphrah and the other Puah, 16 "When you act as midwives for the Hebrew women and see them giving birth, if it is a boy, kill him; but if it is a girl, she may live." 17 The midwives, however, feared God; they did not do as the king of Egypt had ordered them, but let the boys live. 18 So the king summoned the midwives and asked them, "Why have you acted thus, allowing the boys to live?" 19 The midwives answered Pharaoh, "The Hebrew women are not like the Egyptian women. They are robust and give birth before the midwife arrives." 20 Therefore God dealt well with the midwives. The people, too, increased and grew strong. 21 And because the midwives feared God, he built up families for them. 22 Pharaoh then commanded all his subjects, "Throw into the river every boy that is born to the Hebrews, but you may let all the girls live."

Birth and Adoption of Moses

2 Now a certain man of the house of Levi married a Levite woman, 2 who conceived and bore a son.

1, 1: *Sons of Israel:* here literally the first-generation sons of Jacob. Cf v 5. However, beginning with 1, 7 the same Hebrew phrase refers to the more remote descendants of Jacob; hence, from there on, it is ordinarily rendered as "the Israelites." *Households:* the family in its fullest sense, including wives, children and servants.

1, 2: The sons of Jacob are listed here according to the respective mothers. Cf Gn 29, 31; 30, 20; 35, 16–26.

1, 5: *Direct descendants:* literally, persons coming from the loins of Jacob; hence, wives and servants are here excluded. Cf Gn 46, 26.

1, 8: *Who knew nothing of Joseph:* this king ignored the services that Joseph had rendered to Egypt.

1, 11: *Pharaoh:* not a personal name, but a title common to all the kings of Egypt.

1, 14: *Mortar:* either the wet clay with which the bricks were made, as in Na 3, 14, or the cement used between the bricks in building, as in Gn 11, 3.

1, 16: *And see them giving birth:* the Hebrew text is uncertain.

1, 22: *The river:* the Nile, which was "the" river for the Egyptians.

Seeing that he was a goodly child, she hid him for three months. 3 When she could hide him no longer, she took a papyrus basket, daubed it with bitumen and pitch, and putting the child in it, placed it among the reeds on the river bank. 4 His sister stationed herself at a distance to find out what would happen to him.

5 Pharaoh's daughter came down to the river to bathe, while her maids walked along the river bank. Noticing the basket among the reeds, she sent her handmaid to fetch it. 6 On opening it, she looked, and lo, there was a baby boy, crying! She was moved with pity for him and said, "It is one of the Hebrews' children." 7 Then his sister asked Pharaoh's daughter, "Shall I go and call one of the Hebrew women to nurse the child for you?" 8 "Yes, do so," she answered. So the maiden went and called the child's own mother. 9 Pharaoh's daughter said to her, "Take this child and nurse it for me, and I will repay you." The woman therefore took the child and nursed it. 10 When the child grew, she brought him to Pharaoh's daughter, who adopted him as her son and called him Moses; for she said, "I drew him out of the water."

Moses' Flight to Midian

11 On one occasion, after Moses had grown up, when he visited his kinsmen and witnessed their forced labor, he saw an Egyptian striking a Hebrew, one of his own kinsmen. 12 Looking about and seeing no one, he slew the Egyptian and hid him in the sand. 13 The next day he went out again, and now two Hebrews were fighting! So he asked the culprit, "Why are you striking your fellow Hebrew?" 14 But he replied, "Who has appointed you ruler and judge over us? Are you thinking of killing me as you killed the Egyptian?" Then Moses became afraid and thought, "The affair must certainly be known."

15 Pharaoh, too, heard of the affair and sought to put him to death. But Moses fled from him and stayed in the land of Midian. As he was seated there by a well, 16 seven daughters of a priest of Midian came to draw water and fill the troughs to water their father's flock. 17 But some shepherds came and drove them away. Then Moses got up and defended them and watered their flock. 18 When they returned to their father Reuel, he said to them, "How is it you have returned so soon today?" 19 They answered, "An Egyptian saved us from the interference of the shepherds. He even drew water for us and watered the flock!" 20 "Where is the man?" he asked his daughters. "Why did you leave him there? Invite him to have something to eat." 21 Moses agreed to live with him, and the man gave him his daughter Zipporah in marriage. 22 She bore him a son, whom he named Gershom; for he said, "I am a stranger in a foreign land."

The Burning Bush

23 A long time passed, during which the king of Egypt died. Still the Israelites groaned and cried out because of their slavery. As their cry for release went up to God, 24 he heard their groaning and was mindful of his covenant with Abraham, Isaac and Jacob. 25 He saw the Israelites and knew. . . .

3 Meanwhile Moses was tending the flock of his father-in-law Jethro, the priest of Midian. Leading the flock across the desert, he came to Horeb, the mountain of God. 2 There an angel of the LORD appeared to him in fire flaming out of a bush. As he looked on, he was surprised to see that the bush, though on fire, was not consumed. 3 So Moses decided, "I must go over to look at this remarkable sight, and see why the bush is not burned."

The Call of Moses

4 When the LORD saw him coming over to look at it more closely, God called out to him from the bush, "Moses! Moses!" He answered, "Here I am." 5 God said, "Come no nearer! Remove the sandals from your feet, for the place where you stand is holy ground. 6 I am the God of your father," he continued, "the God of Abraham, the God of Isaac, the God of Jacob." Moses hid his face, for he was afraid to look at God. 7 But the LORD said, "I have witnessed the affliction of my people in Egypt and have heard their cry of complaint against their slave drivers, so I know well what they are suffering. 8 Therefore I have come down to rescue them from the hands of the Egyptians and lead them out of that land into a good and spacious land, a land flowing with milk and honey, the country of the Canaanites, Hittites, Amorites, Perizzites, Hivites and Jebusites. 9 So indeed the cry of the Israelites has reached me, and I have truly noted that the Egyptians are oppressing them. 10 Come, now! I will send you to Pharaoh to lead my people, the Israelites, out of Egypt."

2, 3: *Basket:* literally, "chest" or "ark"; the same Hebrew word is used in Gn 6, 14 for Noe's ark. Here, however, the chest was made of papyrus stalks.

2, 10: *When the child grew:* probably when he was weaned or a little later. *Moses:* in hebrew, *Mosheh;* the Hebrew word for "draw out" in *mashah.* This explanation of the name is not intended as a scientific etymology but as a play on words. The name is probably derived from an Egyptian word for "has been born," referring the birth to a god thought to be its sponsor.

2, 11: *After Moses had grown up:* Acts 7, 23 indicates that this was after an interval of nearly forty years. Cf Ex 7, 7. *Striking:* probably in the sense of "flogging"; according to some, "slaying."

2, 18: *Reuel:* he was also called Jethro. Cf 3, 1; 4, 18; 18, 1.

2, 19: *An Egyptian:* Moses was probably wearing Egyptian dress, or spoke Egyptian to Reuel's daughters.

2, 22: *Gershom:* the name is explained as if it came from the Hebrew word *ger,* "stranger," joined *to* the Hebrew word *sham,* "there." Some Greek and Latin manuscripts add here a passage taken from 18, 4.

3, 1: *The mountain of God:* probably given this designation because of the divine apparitions which took place there, such as on this occasion and when the Israelites were there after the departure from Egypt.

3, 2: *An angel of the Lord:* the visual form under which God appeared and spoke to men is referred to

indifferently in some Old Testament texts either as God's angel or as God Himself. Cf Gn 16, 7.13; Ex 14, 19.24f; Nm 22, 22–35; Jgs 6, 11–18.

3, 6: The appearance of God caused fear of death, since it was believed that no one could see God and live; cf Gn 32, 30. *The God of Abraham . . . Jacob:* cited by Christ in proof of the resurrection since the patriarchs, long dead, live on in God who is the God of the living. Cf Mt 22, 32; Mk 12, 26; Lk 20, 37.

3, 8: *I have come down:* a figure of speech signifying an extraordinary divine intervention in human affairs. Cf Gn 11, 5.7. *Flowing with milk and honey:* an expression denoting agricultural prosperity, which seems to have been proverbial in its application to Palestine. Cf 13, 5; Nm 13, 27; Jos 5, 6; Jer 11, 5; 32, 22; Ez 20, 6.15.

11 But Moses said to God, "Who am I that I should go to Pharaoh and lead the Israelites out of Egypt?" 12 He answered, "I will be with you; and this shall be your proof that it is I who have sent you: when you bring my people out of Egypt, you will worship God on this very mountain." 13 "But," said Moses to God, "when I go to the Israelites and say to them, 'The God of your fathers has sent me to you,' if they ask me, 'What is his name?' what am I to tell them?" 14 God replied, "I am who am." Then he added, "This is what you shall tell the Israelites: I AM sent me to you."

15 God spoke further to Moses, "Thus shall you say to the Israelites: The LORD, the God of your fathers, the God of Abraham, the God of Isaac, the God of Jacob, has sent me to you.

"This is my name forever;
　　this is my title for all
　　　generations.

16 "Go and assemble the elders of the Israelites, and tell them: The LORD, the God of your fathers, the God of Abraham, Isaac and Jacob, has appeared to me and said: I am concerned about you and about the way you are being treated in Egypt; 17 so I have decided to lead you up out of the misery of Egypt into the land of the Canaanites, Hittites, Amorites, Perizzites, Hivites and Jebusites, a land flowing with milk and honey. 18 "Thus they will heed your message. Then you and the elders of Israel shall go to the king of Egypt and say to him: The LORD, the God of the Hebrews, has sent us word. Permit us, then, to go a three days' journey in the desert, that we may offer sacrifice to the LORD, our God. 19 "Yet I know that the king of Egypt will not allow you to go unless he is forced. 20 I will stretch out my hand, therefore, and smite Egypt by doing all kinds of wondrous deeds there. After that he will send you away. 21 I will even make the Egyptians so well-disposed toward this people that, when you leave, you will not go empty-handed. 22 Every woman shall ask her neighbor and her house guest for silver and gold articles and for clothing to put on your sons and daughters. Thus you will despoil the Egyptians."

Confirmation of Moses' Mission

4 "But," objected Moses, "suppose they will not believe me, nor listen to my plea? For they may say, 'The LORD did not appear to you.'" 2 The LORD therefore asked him, "What is that in your hand?" "A staff," he answered. 3 The LORD then said, "Throw it on the ground." When he threw it on the ground it was changed into a serpent, and Moses shied away from it. 4 "Now, put out your hand," the LORD said to him, "and take hold of its tail." So he put out his hand and laid hold of it, and it became a staff in his hand. 5 "This will take place so that they may believe," he continued, "that the LORD, the God of their fathers, the God of Abraham, the God of Isaac, the God of Jacob, did appear to you."

6 Again the LORD said to him, "Put your hand in your bosom." He put it in his bosom, and when he withdrew it, to his surprise his hand was leprous, like snow. 7 The LORD then said, "Now, put your hand back in your bosom." Moses put his hand back in his bosom, and when he withdrew it, to his surprise it was again like the rest of his body. 8 "If they will not believe you, nor heed the message of the first sign, they should believe the message of the second. 9 And if they will not believe even these two signs, nor heed your plea, take some water from the river and pour it on the dry land. The water you take from the river will become blood on the dry land."

Aaron's Office as Assistant

10 Moses, however, said to the LORD, "If you please, Lord, I have never been eloquent, neither in the past, nor recently, nor now that you have spoken to your servant; but I am slow of speech and tongue." 11 The LORD said to him, "Who gives one man speech and makes another deaf and dumb? Or who gives sight to one and makes another blind? Is it not I, the LORD? 12 Go, then! It is I who will assist you in speaking and will teach you what you are to say." 13 Yet he insisted, "If you please, Lord, send someone else!" 14 Then the LORD became angry with Moses and said, "Have you not your brother, Aaron the Levite? I know that he is an eloquent speaker. Besides, he is now on his way to meet you. 15 When he sees you, his heart will be glad. You are to speak to him, then, and put the words in his mouth. I will assist both you and him in speaking and will teach the two of you what you are to do. He shall speak to the people for you: 16 he shall be your spokesman, and you shall be as God to him. 17 Take this staff in your hand; with it you are to perform the signs."

Moses' Return to Egypt

18 After this Moses returned to his father-in-law Jethro and said to him, "Let me go back, please, to my kinsmen in Egypt, to see whether they are still living." Jethro replied, "Go in peace." 19 In Midian the LORD said to Moses, "Go back to Egypt, for all the men who sought your life are dead." 20 So Moses took his wife and his sons, and started

---

3, 11: *Who am I*: besides naturally shrinking from such a tremendous undertaking, Moses realized that, as a fugitive from Pharaoh, he could hardly hope to carry out a mission to him. Perhaps he also recalled that on one occasion even his own kinsmen questioned his authority. Cf 2, 14.

3, 14: *I am who am*: apparently this utterance is the source of the word *Yahweh*, the proper personal name of the God of Israel. It is commonly explained in reference to God as the absolute and necessary Being. It may be understood of God as the Source of all created beings. Out of reverence for this name, the term *Adonai*, "my Lord," was later used as a sub-

stitute. The word LORD in the present version represents this traditional usage. The word "Jehovah" arose from a false reading of this name as it is written in the current Hebrew text.

3, 16: *Elders*: the Israelite leaders, who were usually older men. They were representatives of the people.

3, 22: *Articles*: probably jewelry. *Despoil*: this was permissible, that the Israelites might compensate themselves for their many years of servitude; besides, the Egyptians would give these things willingly. Cf 12, 33–36.

4, 13: *Send someone else*: literally, "Send by means of him whom you will send," that is, "Send whom you will."

4, 16: *Spokesman*: literally, "mouth"; Aaron was to serve as a mouthpiece for Moses, as a prophet does for God; hence the relation between Moses and Aaron is compared to that between God and his prophet. Cf 7, 1.

4, 17: *This staff*: probably the same as that of vv 2ff; but some understand it here of a new staff now given by God to Moses.

4, 18: Moses did not tell his father-in-law his main reason for returning to Egypt, but this secondary motive which he offered was also true.

back to the land of Egypt, with them riding the ass. The staff of God he carried with him. 21 The Lord said to him, "On your return to Egypt, see that you perform before Pharaoh all the wonders I have put in your power. I will make him obstinate, however, so that he will not let the people go. 22 So you shall say to Pharaoh: Thus says the Lord: Israel is my son, my first-born. 23 Hence I tell you: Let my son go, that he may serve me. If you refuse to let him go, I warn you, I will kill your son, your first-born."

24 On the journey, at a place where they spent the night, the Lord came upon Moses and would have killed him. 25 But Zipporah took a piece of flint and cut off her son's foreskin and, touching his person, she said, "You are a spouse of blood to me." 26 Then God let Moses go. At that time she said, "A spouse of blood," in regard to the circumcision.

27 The Lord said to Aaron, "Go into the desert to meet Moses." So he went, and when they met at the mountain of God, Aaron kissed him. 28 Moses informed him of all the Lord had said in sending him, and of the various signs he had enjoined upon him. 29 Then Moses and Aaron went and assembled all the elders of the Israelites. 30 Aaron told them everything the Lord had said to Moses, and he performed the signs before the people: 31 The people believed, and when they heard that the Lord was concerned about them and had seen their affliction, they bowed down in worship.

Pharaoh's Obduracy

5 After that, Moses and Aaron went to Pharaoh and said, "Thus says the Lord, the God of Israel: Let my people go, that they may celebrate a feast to me in the desert." 2 Pharaoh answered, "Who is the Lord, that I should heed his plea to let Israel go? I do not know the Lord; even if I did, I would not let Israel go." 3 They replied, "The

God of the Hebrews has sent us word. Let us go a three days' journey in the desert, that we may offer sacrifice to the Lord, our God; otherwise he will punish us with pestilence or the sword."

4 The king of Egypt answered them, "What do you mean, Moses and Aaron, by taking the people away from their work? Off to your labor! 5 Look how numerous the people of the land are already," continued Pharaoh, "and yet you would give them rest from their labor!"

6 That very day Pharaoh gave the taskmasters and foremen of the people this order: 7 "You shall no longer supply the people with straw for their brickmaking as you have previously done. Let them go and gather straw themselves! 8 Yet you shall levy upon them the same quota of bricks as they have previously made. Do not reduce it. They are lazy; that is why they are crying, 'Let us go to offer sacrifice to our God.' 9 Increase the work for the men, so that they keep their mind on it and pay no attention to lying words."

10 So the taskmasters and foremen of the people went out and told them, "Thus says Pharaoh: I will not provide you with straw. 11 Go and gather the straw yourselves, wherever you can find it. Yet there must not be the slightest reduction in your work." 12 The people, then, scattered throughout the land of Egypt to gather stubble for straw, 13 while the taskmasters kept driving them on, saying, "Finish your work, the same daily amount as when your straw was supplied."

Complaint of the Foremen

14 The foremen of the Israelites, whom the taskmasters of Pharaoh had placed over them, were beaten, and were asked, "Why have you not completed your prescribed amount of bricks yesterday and today, as before?"

15 Then the Israelite foremen came and made this appeal to Pharaoh: "Why do you treat your servants in

this manner? 16 No straw is supplied to your servants, and still we are told to make bricks. Look how your servants are beaten! It is you who are at fault." 17 Pharaoh answered, "It is just because you are lazy that you keep saying, 'Let us go and offer sacrifice to the Lord.' 18 Off to work, then! Straw shall not be provided for you, but you must still deliver your quota of bricks."

19 The Israelite foremen knew they were in a sorry plight, having been told not to reduce the daily amount of bricks. 20 When, therefore, they left Pharaoh and came upon Moses and Aaron, who were waiting to meet them, 21 they said to them, "The Lord look upon you and judge! You have brought us into bad odor with Pharaoh and his servants and have put a sword in their hands to slay us."

Renewal of God's Promise

22 Moses again had recourse to the Lord and said, "Lord, why do you treat this people so badly? And why did you send me on such a mission? 23 Ever since I went to Pharaoh to speak in your name, he has maltreated this people of yours, and you have done nothing to rescue them." 6 1 Then the Lord answered Moses, "Now you shall see what I will do to Pharaoh. Forced by my mighty hand, he will send them away; compelled by my outstretched arm, he will drive them from his land."

2 God also said to Moses, "I am the Lord. 3 As God the Almighty I appeared to Abraham, Isaac and Jacob, but my name, Lord, I did not make known to them. 4 I also established my covenant with them, to give them the land of Canaan, the land in which they were living as aliens. 5 And now that I have heard the groaning of the Israelites, whom the Egyptians are treating as slaves, I am mindful of my covenant. 6 Therefore, say to the Israelites: I am the Lord. I will free you from the forced labor of the Egyptians and

---

4, 21: *Make him obstinate:* literally, "harden his heart." God permitted Pharaoh to be stubborn in his opposition to the departure of the Israelites. Cf Rom 9, 17f.

4, 24ff: Apparently God was angry with Moses for

having failed to keep the divine command given to Abraham in Gn 17, 10ff. Moses' life is spared when his wife circumcises their son.

5, 6: *The taskmasters and foremen:* the former were higher officials and probably Egyptians; the

latter were lower officials, chosen from the Israelites themselves. Cf v 14.

5, 7: Straw was mixed with the clay to give the sun-dried bricks greater consistency.

will deliver you from their slavery. I will rescue you by my outstretched arm and with mighty acts of judgment. 7 I will take you as my own people, and you shall have me as your God. You will know that I, the LORD, am your God when I free you from the labor of the Egyptians 8 and bring you into the land which I swore to give to Abraham, Isaac and Jacob. I will give it to you as your own possession—I, the LORD!" 9 But when Moses told this to the Israelites, they would not listen to him because of their dejection and hard slavery.

10 Then the LORD said to Moses, 11 "Go and tell Pharaoh, king of Egypt, to let the Israelites leave his land." 12 But Moses protested to the LORD, "If the Israelites would not listen to me, how can it be that Pharaoh will listen to me, poor speaker that I am!" 13 Still, the LORD, to bring the Israelites out of Egypt, spoke to Moses and Aaron and gave them his orders regarding both the Israelites and Pharaoh, king of Egypt.

Genealogy of Moses and Aaron

14 These are the heads of the ancestral houses. The sons of Reuben, the first-born of Israel, were Hanoch, Pallu, Hezron and Carmi; these are the clans of Reuben. 15 The sons of Simeon were Jemuel, Jamin, Ohad, Jachin, Zohar and Shaul, who was the son of a Canaanite woman; these are the clans of Simeon. 16 The names of the sons of Levi, in their genealogical order, are Gershon, Kohath and Merari. Levi lived one hundred and thirty-seven years.

17 The sons of Gershon, as heads of clans, were Libni and Shimei. 18 The sons of Kohath were Amram, Izhar, Hebron and Uzziel. Kohath lived one hundred and thirty-three years. 19 The sons of Merari were Mahli and Mushi. These are the clans of Levi in their genealogical order.

20 Amram married his aunt Jochebed, who bore him Aaron, Moses and Miriam. Amram lived one hundred and thirty-seven years. 21 The sons of Izhar were Korah, Nepheg and Zichri. 22 The sons of Uzziel were Mishael, Elzaphan and Sithri. 23 Aaron married Amminadab's daughter, Elisheba, the sister of Nahshon; she bore him Nadab, Abihu, Eleazar and Ithamar. 24 The sons of Korah were Assir, Elkanah and Abiasaph. These are the clans of the Korahites. 25 Aaron's son, Eleazar, married one of Putiel's daughters, who bore him Phinehas. These are the heads of the ancestral clans of the Levites. 26 This is the Aaron and this the Moses to whom the LORD said, "Lead the Israelites from the land of Egypt, company by company." 27 These are the ones who spoke to Pharaoh, king of Egypt, to bring the Israelites out of Egypt—the same Moses and Aaron.

Moses and Aaron before Pharaoh

28 On the day the LORD spoke to Moses in Egypt 29 he said, "I am the LORD. Repeat to Pharaoh, king of Egypt, all that I tell you." 30 But Moses protested to the LORD, "Since I am a poor speaker, how can it be that Pharaoh will listen to me?" 7 1 The LORD answered him, "See! I have made you as God to Pharaoh, and Aaron your brother shall act as your prophet. 2 You shall tell him all that I command you. In turn, your brother Aaron shall tell Pharaoh to let the Israelites leave his land. 3 Yet I will make Pharaoh so obstinate that, despite the many signs and wonders that I will work in the land of Egypt, 4 he will not listen to you. Therefore I will lay my hand on Egypt and by great acts of Judgment I will bring the hosts of my people, the Israelites, out of the land of Egypt, 5 so that the Egyptians may learn that I am the LORD, as I stretch out my hand against Egypt and lead the Israelites out of their midst."

6 Moses and Aaron did as the LORD had commanded them. 7

Moses was eighty years old and Aaron eighty-three when they spoke to Pharaoh.

The Staff Turned into a Snake

8 The LORD told Moses and Aaron, 9 "If Pharaoh demands that you work a sign or wonder, you shall say to Aaron: Take your staff and throw it down before Pharaoh, and it will be changed into a snake." 10 Then Moses and Aaron went to Pharaoh and did as the LORD had commanded. Aaron threw his staff down before Pharaoh and his servants, and it was changed into a snake. 11 Pharaoh, in turn, summoned wise men and sorcerers, and they also, the magicians of Egypt, did likewise by their magic arts. 12 Each one threw down his staff, and it was changed into a snake. But Aaron's staff swallowed their staffs. 13 Pharaoh, however, was obstinate and would not listen to them, just as the LORD had foretold.

First Plague: Water Turned into Blood

14 Then the LORD said to Moses, "Pharaoh is obdurate in refusing to let the people go. 15 Tomorrow morning, when he sets out for the water, go and present yourself by the river bank, holding in your hand the staff that turned into a serpent. 16 Say to him: The LORD, the God of the Hebrews, sent me to you with the message: Let my people go to worship me in the desert. But as yet you have not listened. 17 The LORD now says: This is how you shall know that I am the LORD. I will strike the water of the river with the staff I hold, and it shall be changed into blood. 18 The fish in the river shall die, and the river itself shall become so polluted that the Egyptians will be unable to drink its water."

19 The LORD then said to Moses, "Say to Aaron: Take your staff and stretch out your hand over the waters of Egypt—their streams and canals and pools, all their supplies of water —that they may become blood.

6, 14: The purpose of the genealogy here is to give the line from which Moses and Aaron sprang. Reuben and Simeon are first mentioned because, as older brothers of Levi, their names occur before his in the genealogy.

6, 20: *His aunt:* more exactly, "his father's sister."

Later on such a marriage was forbidden. Cf Lv 18, 12. Hence, the Greek and Latin versions render here, "his cousin."

7, 1: Just as God had his prophets to speak to men in his name, so Moses had Aaron as his "prophet" to speak to Pharaoh. Cf 4, 16.

7, 14: Most of the ten plagues of Egypt seem to be similar to certain natural phenomena of that country; but they are represented as supernatural at least in their greater intensity and in their occurring exactly according to Moses' commands.

Throughout the land of Egypt there shall be blood, even in the wooden pails and stone jars."

20 Moses and Aaron did as the LORD had commanded. Aaron raised his staff and struck the waters of the river in full view of Pharaoh and his servants, and all the water of the river was changed into blood. 21 The fish in the river died, and the river itself became so polluted that the Egyptians could not drink its water. There was blood throughout the land of Egypt. 22 But the Egyptian magicians did the same by their magic arts. So Pharaoh remained obstinate and would not listen to Moses and Aaron, just as the LORD had foretold. 23 He turned away and went into his house, with no concern even for this. 24 All the Egyptians had to dig in the neighborhood of the river for drinking water, since they could not drink the river water.

Second Plague: the Frogs

25 Seven days passed after the LORD had struck the river. 26 Then the LORD said to Moses, "Go to Pharaoh and tell him: Thus says the LORD: Let my people go to worship me. 27 If you refuse to let them go, I warn you, I will send a plague of frogs over all your territory. 28 The river will teem with frogs. They will come up into your palace and into your bedroom and onto your bed, into the houses of your servants, too, and your subjects, even into your ovens and your kneading bowls. 29 The frogs will swarm all over you and your subjects and your servants."

8 The LORD then told Moses, "Say to Aaron: Stretch out your hand and your staff over the streams and canals and pools, to make frogs overrun the land of Egypt." 2 Aaron stretched out his hand over the waters of Egypt, and the frogs came up and covered the land of Egypt. 3 But the magicians did the same by their magic arts. They, too, made frogs overrun the land of Egypt.

4 Then Pharaoh summoned Moses and Aaron and said, "Pray the LORD to remove the frogs from me and my subjects, and I will let the people go to offer sacrifice to the LORD." 5 Moses answered Pharaoh, "Do me the favor of appointing the time when I am to pray for you and your servants and your subjects, that the frogs may be taken away from you and your houses and be left only in the river." 6 "Tomorrow," said Pharaoh. Then Moses replied, "It shall be as you have said, so that you may learn that there is none like the LORD, our God. 7 The frogs shall leave you and your houses, your servants and your subjects; only in the river shall they be left."

8 After Moses and Aaron left Pharaoh's presence, Moses implored the LORD to fulfill the promise he had made to Pharaoh about the frogs; 9 and the LORD did as Moses had asked. The frogs in the houses and courtyards and fields died off. 10 Heaps and heaps of them were gathered up, and there was a stench in the land. 11 But when Pharaoh saw that there was a respite, he became obdurate and would not listen to them, just as the LORD had foretold.

Third Plague: the Gnats

12 Thereupon the LORD said to Moses, "Tell Aaron to stretch out his staff and strike the dust of the earth, that it may be turned into gnats throughout the land of Egypt." 13 They did so. Aaron stretched out his hand, and with his staff he struck the dust of the earth, and gnats came upon man and beast. The dust of the earth was turned into gnats throughout the land of Egypt. 14 Though the magicians tried to bring forth gnats by their magic arts, they could not do so. As the gnats infested man and beast, 15 the magicians said to Pharaoh, "This is the finger of God." Yet Pharaoh remained obstinate and would not listen to them, just as the LORD had foretold.

Fourth Plague: the Flies

16 Again the LORD told Moses, "Early tomorrow morning present yourself to Pharaoh when he goes forth to the water, and say to him: Thus says the LORD: Let my people go to worship me. 17 If you will not let my people go, I warn you, I will loose swarms of flies upon you and your servants and your subjects and your houses. The houses of the Egyptians and the very ground on which they stand shall be filled with swarms of flies. 18 But on that day I will make an exception of the land of Goshen: there shall be no flies where my people dwell, that you may know that I am the LORD in the midst of the earth. 19 I will make this distinction between my people and your people. This sign shall take place tomorrow." 20 This the LORD did. Thick swarms of flies entered the house of Pharaoh and the houses of his servants; throughout Egypt the land was infested with flies.

21 Then Pharaoh summoned Moses and Aaron and said to them, "Go and offer sacrifice to your God in this land." 22 But Moses replied, "It is not right to do so, for the sacrifices we offer to the LORD, our God, are an abomination to the Egyptians. If before their very eyes we offer sacrifices which are an abomination to them, will not the Egyptians stone us? 23 We must go a three days' journey in the desert to offer sacrifice to the LORD, our God, as he commands us." 24 "Well, then," said Pharaoh, "I will let you go to offer sacrifice to the LORD, your God, in the desert, provided that you do not go too far away and that you pray for me." 25 Moses answered, "As soon as I leave your presence I will pray to the LORD that the flies may depart tomorrow from Pharaoh and his servants and his subjects. Pharaoh, however, must not play false again by refusing to let the people go to offer sacrifice to the LORD." 26 When Moses left Pharaoh's presence, he prayed to the LORD; 27 and the LORD did as Moses had asked. He removed the flies from Pharaoh and his servants and subjects. Not one remained. 28 But once more Pharaoh became

---

7, 26—8, 28: This is 8, 1–32 in the verse enumeration of the Vulgate.

8, 9: *Courtyards:* some render "farmhouses."

8, 12.17: *Gnats, flies:* it is uncertain what species of troublesome insects are here meant.

8, 15: *The finger of God:* understood by the magicians as the *staff* mentioned in 8, 13. Cf Lk 11, 20.

8, 22: The Egyptians would fiercely resent the sacrifice of any animal they considered sacred. Certain animals were worshiped in Egypt, at least as the symbols of various deities.

obdurate and would not let the people go.

Fifth Plague: the Pestilence

9 Then the LORD said to Moses, "Go to Pharaoh and tell him: Thus says the LORD, the God of the Hebrews: Let my people go to worship me. 2 If you refuse to let them go and persist in holding them, 3 I warn you, the LORD will afflict all your livestock in the field—your horses, asses, camels, herds and flocks —with a very severe pestilence. 4 But the LORD will distinguish between the livestock of Israel and that of Egypt, so that none belonging to the Israelites will die." 5 And setting a definite time, the LORD added, "Tomorrow the LORD shall do this in the land." 6 And on the next day the LORD did so. All the livestock of the Egyptians died, but not one beast belonging to the Israelites. 7 But though Pharaoh's messengers informed him that not even one beast belonging to the Israelites had died, he still remained obdurate and would not let the people go.

Sixth Plague: the Boils

8 Then the LORD said to Moses and Aaron, "Take a double handful of soot from a furnace, and in the presence of Pharaoh let Moses scatter it toward the sky. 9 It will then turn into fine dust over the whole land of Egypt and cause festering boils on man and beast throughout the land."

10 So they took soot from a furnace and stood in the presence of Pharaoh. Moses scattered it toward the sky, and it caused festering boils on man and beast. 11 The magicians could not stand in Moses' presence, for there were boils on the magicians no less than on the rest of the Egyptians. 12 But the LORD made Pharaoh obstinate, and he would not listen to them, just as the LORD had foretold to Moses.

Seventh Plague: the Hail

13 Then the LORD told Moses, "Early tomorrow morning present yourself to Pharaoh and say to him:

Thus says the LORD, the God of the Hebrews: Let my people go to worship me, 14 or this time I will hurl all my blows upon you and your servants and your subjects, that you may know that there is none like me anywhere on earth. 15 For by now I would have stretched out my hand and struck you and your subjects with such pestilence as would wipe you from the earth. 16 But this is why I have spared you: to show you my power and to make my name resound throughout the earth! 17 Will you still block the way for my people by refusing to let them go? 18 I warn you, then, tomorrow at this hour I will rain down such fierce hail as there has never been in Egypt from the day the nation was founded up to the present. 19 Therefore, order all your livestock and whatever else you have in the open fields to be brought to a place of safety. Whatever man or beast remains in the fields and is not brought to shelter shall die when the hail comes upon them." 20 Some of Pharaoh's servants feared the warning of the LORD and hurried their servants and livestock off to shelter. 21 Others, however, did not take the warning of the LORD to heart and left their servants and livestock in the fields.

22 The LORD then said to Moses, "Stretch out your hand toward the sky, that hail may fall upon the entire land of Egypt, on man and beast and every growing thing in the land of Egypt." 23 When Moses stretched out his staff toward the sky, the LORD sent forth hail and peals of thunder. Lightning flashed toward the earth, and the LORD rained down hail upon the land of Egypt; 24 and lightning constantly flashed through the hail, such fierce hail as had never been seen in the land since Egypt became a nation. 25 It struck down every man and beast that was in the open throughout the land of Egypt; it beat down every growing thing and splintered every tree in the fields. 26 Only in the land of Goshen, where the Israelites dwelt, was there no hail.

27 Then Pharaoh summoned Moses and Aaron and said to them, "I have sinned again! The LORD is just; it is I and my subjects who are

at fault. 28 Pray to the LORD, for we have had enough of God's thunder and hail. Then I will let you go; you need stay no longer." 29 Moses replied, "As soon as I leave the city I will extend my hands to the LORD; the thunder will cease, and there will be no more hail. Thus you shall learn that the earth is the LORD's. 30 But you and your servants, I know, do not yet fear the LORD God."

31 Now the flax and the barley were ruined, because the barley was in ear and the flax in bud. 32 But the wheat and the spelt were not ruined, for they grow later.

33 When Moses had left Pharaoh's presence and had gone out of the city, he extended his hands to the LORD. Then the thunder and the hail ceased, and the rain no longer poured down upon the earth. 34 But Pharaoh, seeing that the rain and hail and thunder had ceased, sinned again: he with his servants became obdurate, 35 and in his obstinacy he would not let the Israelites go, as the LORD had foretold through Moses.

Eighth Plague: the Locusts

10 Then the LORD said to Moses, "Go to Pharaoh, for I have made him and his servants obdurate in order that I may perform these signs of mine among them 2 and that you may recount to your son and grandson how ruthlessly I dealt with the Egyptians and what signs I wrought among them, so that you may know that I am the LORD."

3 So Moses and Aaron went to Pharaoh and told him, "Thus says the LORD, the God of the Hebrews: How long will you refuse to submit to me? Let my people go to worship me. 4 If you refuse to let my people go, I warn you, tomorrow I will bring locusts into your country. 5 They shall cover the ground, so that the ground itself will not be visible. They shall eat up the remnant you saved unhurt from the hail, as well as all the foliage that has since sprouted in your fields. 6 They shall fill your houses and the houses of your servants and of all the Egyptians; such a sight your fathers or grandfathers have not seen from the day they first

---

9, 16: *To show you:* some ancient versions read, "to show through you." Cf Rom 9, 17.

settled on this soil up to the present day." With that he turned and left Pharaoh.

7 But Pharaoh's servants said to him, "How long must he be a menace to us? Let the men go to worship the LORD, their God. Do you not yet realize that Egypt is being destroyed?" 8 So Moses and Aaron were brought back to Pharaoh, who said to them, "You may go and worship the LORD, your God. But how many of you will go?" 9 "Young and old must go with us," Moses answered, "our sons and daughters as well as our flocks and herds must accompany us. That is what a feast of the LORD means to us." 10 "The LORD help you," Pharaoh replied, "if I ever let your little ones go with you! Clearly, you have some evil in mind. 11 No, no! Just you men can go and worship the LORD. After all, that is what you want." With that they were driven from Pharaoh's presence.

12 The LORD then said to Moses, "Stretch out your hand over the land of Egypt, that locusts may swarm over it and eat up all the vegetation and whatever the hail has left." 13 So Moses stretched out his staff over the land all that day and all that night. At dawn the east wind brought the locusts. 14 They swarmed over the whole land of Egypt and settled down on every part of it. Never before had there been such a fierce swarm of locusts, nor will there ever be. 15 They covered the surface of the whole land, till it was black with them. They ate up all the vegetation in the land and the fruit of whatever trees the hail had spared. Nothing green was left on any tree or plant throughout the land of Egypt.

16 Hastily Pharaoh summoned Moses and Aaron and said, "I have sinned against the LORD, your God, and against you. 17 But now, do forgive me my sin once more, and pray the LORD, your God, to take at least this deadly pest from me." 18

When Moses left the presence of Pharaoh, he prayed to the LORD, 19 and the LORD changed the wind to a very strong west wind, which took up the locusts and hurled them into the Red Sea. But though not a single locust remained within the confines of Egypt, 20 the LORD made Pharaoh obstinate, and he would not let the Israelites go.

Ninth Plague: the Darkness

21 Then the LORD said to Moses, "Stretch out your hand toward the sky, that over the land of Egypt there may be such intense darkness that one can feel it." 22 So Moses stretched out his hand toward the sky, and there was dense darkness throughout the land of Egypt for three days. 23 Men could not see one another, nor could they move from where they were, for three days. But all the Israelites had light where they dwelt.

24 Pharaoh then summoned Moses and Aaron and said, "Go and worship the LORD. Your little ones, too, may go with you. But your flocks and herds must remain." 25 Moses replied, "You must also grant us sacrifices and holocausts to offer up to the LORD, our God. 26 Hence, our livestock also must go with us. Not an animal must be left behind. Some of them we must sacrifice to the LORD, our God, but we ourselves shall not know which ones we must sacrifice to him until we arrive at the place itself." 27 But the LORD made Pharaoh obstinate, and he would not let them go. 28 "Leave my presence," Pharaoh said to him, "and see to it that you do not appear before me again! The day you appear before me you shall die!" 29 Moses replied, "Well said! I will never appear before you again."

Tenth Plague: the Death of the First-born

11 Then the LORD told Moses, "One more plague will I bring

upon Pharaoh and upon Egypt. After that he will let you depart. In fact, he will not merely let you go; he will drive you not away. 2 Instruct your people that every man is to ask his neighbor, and every woman her neighbor, for silver and gold articles and for clothing." 3 The LORD indeed made the Egyptians well-disposed toward the people; Moses himself was very highly regarded by Pharaoh's servants and the people in the land of Egypt.

4 Moses then said, "Thus says the LORD: At midnight I will go forth through Egypt. 5 Every first-born in this land shall die, from the first-born of Pharaoh on the throne to the first-born of the slave-girl at the handmill, as well as all the first-born of the animals. 6 Then there shall be loud wailing throughout the land of Egypt, such as has never been, nor will ever be again. 7 But among the Israelites and their animals not even a dog shall growl, so that you may know how the LORD distinguishes between the Egyptians and the Israelites. 8 All these servants of yours shall then come down to me, and prostrate before me, they shall beg me, 'Leave us, you and all your followers!' Only then will I depart." With that he left Pharaoh's presence in hot anger.

9 The LORD said to Moses, "Pharaoh refuses to listen to you that my wonders may be multiplied in the land of Egypt." 10 Thus, although Moses and Aaron performed these various wonders in Pharaoh's presence, the LORD made Pharaoh obstinate, and he would not let the Israelites leave his land.

The Passover Ritual Prescribed

12 The LORD said to Moses and Aaron in the land of Egypt, 2 "This month shall stand at the head of your calendar; you shall reckon it the first month of the year. 3 Tell the whole community of Israel: On the tenth of this month every one of

10, 10: *The Lord help you ...:* literally, "May the LORD be with you in the same way as I let you ...": a sarcastic blessing intended as a curse.

10, 11: Pharaoh realized that if the men alone went they would have to return to their families. He suspected that the Hebrews had no intention of returning.

10, 13: *East wind:* coming across the desert from

Arabia, the strong east wind brings Egypt the burning sirocco and, at times, locusts. Cf 14, 21.

10, 19: *The Red Sea:* according to the traditional translation, but the Hebrew is literally, "the Reed Sea"; hence the Red Sea of Exodus was probably a body of shallow water somewhat to the north of the present deep Red Sea.

10, 21: *Darkness:* at times a storm from the

south, called the *khamsin*, blackens the sky of Egypt with sand from the Sahara; the dust in the air is then so thick that the darkness can, in a sense, "be felt."

12, 2: *This month:* Abib, the month of "ripe grain." Cf 13, 4; 23, 15; 34, 18; Dt 16, 1. It occurred near the vernal equinox, March–April. Later it was known by the Babylonian name of Nisan. Cf Neh 2, 1; Est 3, 7.

your families must procure for itself a lamb, one apiece for each household. 4 If a family is too small for a whole lamb, it shall join the nearest household in procuring one and shall share in the lamb in proportion to the number of persons who partake of it. 5 The lamb must be a year-old male and without blemish. You may take it from either the sheep or the goats. 6 You shall keep it until the fourteenth day of this month, and then, with the whole assembly of Israel present, it shall be slaughtered during the evening twilight. 7 They shall take some of its blood and apply it to the two doorposts and the lintel of every house in which they partake of the lamb. 8 That same night they shall eat its roasted flesh with unleavened bread and bitter herbs. 9 It shall not be eaten raw or boiled, but roasted whole, with its head and shanks and inner organs. 10 None of it must be kept beyond the next morning; whatever is left over in the morning shall be burned up.

11 "This is how you are to eat it: with your loins girt, sandals on your feet and your staff in hand, you shall eat like those who are in flight. It is the Passover of the LORD. 12 For on this same night I will go through Egypt, striking down every first-born of the land, both man and beast, and executing judgment on all the gods of Egypt—I, the LORD! 13 But the blood will mark the houses where you are. Seeing the blood, I will pass over you; thus, when I strike the land of Egypt, no destructive blow will come upon you.

14 "This day shall be a memorial feast for you, which all your generations shall celebrate with pilgrimage to the LORD, as a perpetual institution. 15 For seven days you must eat unleavened bread. From the very first day you shall have your houses clear of all leaven. Whoever eats leavened bread from the first day to the seventh shall be cut off from Israel. 16 On the first day you shall hold a sacred assembly, and likewise on the seventh. On these days you shall not do any sort of work, except

to prepare the food that everyone needs.

17 "Keep, then, this custom of the unleavened bread. Since it was on this very day that I brought your ranks out of the land of Egypt, you must celebrate this day throughout your generations as a perpetual institution. 18 From the evening of the fourteenth day of the first month until the evening of the twenty-first day of this month you shall eat unleavened bread. 19 For seven days no leaven may be found in your houses. Anyone, be he a resident alien or a native, who eats leavened food shall be cut off from the community of Israel. 20 Nothing leavened may you eat; wherever you dwell you may eat only unleavened bread."

Promulgation of the Passover

21 Moses called all the elders of Israel and said to them, "Go and procure lambs for your families, and slaughter them as Passover victims. 22 Then take a bunch of hyssop, and dipping it in the blood that is in the basin, sprinkle the lintel and the two doorposts with this blood. But none of you shall go outdoors until morning. 23 For the LORD will go by, striking down the Egyptians. Seeing the blood on the lintel and the two doorposts, the LORD will pass over that door and not let the destroyer come into your houses to strike you down.

24 "You shall observe this as a perpetual ordinance for yourselves and your descendants. 25 Thus, you must also observe this rite when you have entered the land which the LORD will give you as he promised. 26 When your children ask you, 'What does this rite of yours mean?' 27 you shall reply, 'This is the Passover sacrifice of the LORD, who passed over the houses of the Israelites in Egypt; when he struck down the Egyptians, he spared our houses.'"

Then the people bowed down in worship, 28 and the Israelites went and did as the LORD had commanded Moses and Aaron.

Death of the First-born

29 At midnight the LORD slew every first-born in the land of Egypt, from the first-born of Pharaoh on the throne to the first-born of the prisoner in the dungeon, as well as all the first-born of the animals. 30 Pharaoh arose in the night, he and all his servants and all the Egyptians; and there was loud wailing throughout Egypt, for there was not a house without its dead.

Permission to Depart

31 During the night Pharaoh summoned Moses and Aaron and said, "Leave my people at once, you and the Israelites with you! Go and worship the LORD as you said. 32 Take your flocks, too, and your herds, as you demanded, and begone; and you will be doing me a favor."

33 The Egyptians likewise urged the people on, to hasten their departure from the land; they thought that otherwise they would all die. 34 The people, therefore, took their dough before it was leavened, in their kneading bowls wrapped in their cloaks on their shoulders. 35 The Israelites did as Moses had commanded: they asked the Egyptians for articles of silver and gold and for clothing. 36 The LORD indeed had made the Egyptians so well-disposed toward the people that they let them have whatever they asked for. Thus did they despoil the Egyptians.

THE EXODUS FROM EGYPT AND THE JOURNEY TO SINAI

Departure from Egypt

37 The Israelites set out from Rameses for Succoth, about six hundred thousand men on foot, not counting the children. 38 A crowd of mixed ancestry also went up with them, besides their livestock, very numerous flocks and herds. 39 Since the dough they had brought out of Egypt was not leavened, they baked it into unleavened loaves. They had been rushed out of Egypt and had no opportunity even to prepare food for the journey.

12, 4: *Share in the lamb:* probably, in the expenses of its purchase. Some explain, "reckon for the lamb the number of persons required to eat it." Cf 12, 10.
12, 11: *Passover:* in Hebrew, *pesach,* in Aramaic,

pascha. In the following verses the same root is used in the verb "to pass over." The word may be originally Egyptian, *pesach,* "the blow," i.e., the final plague which destroyed the Egyptian first-born.

12, 22: *Hyssop:* a plant with many woody branchlets that made a convenient sprinkler.
12, 38: *Mixed ancestry:* half-Hebrew and half-Egyptian. Cf Nm 11, 4; Lv 24, 10f.

40 The time the Israelites had stayed in Egypt was four hundred and thirty years. 41 At the end of four hundred and thirty years, all the hosts of the LORD left the land of Egypt on this very date. 42 This was a night of vigil for the LORD, as he led them out of the land of Egypt; so on this same night all the Israelites must keep a vigil for the LORD throughout their generations.

Passover Regulations

43 The LORD said to Moses and Aaron, "These are the regulations for the Passover. No foreigner may partake of it. 44 However, any slave who has been bought for money may partake of it, provided you have first circumcised him. 45 But no transient alien or hired servant may partake of it. 46 It must be eaten in one and the same house; you may not take any of its flesh outside the house. You shall not break any of its bones. 47 The whole community of Israel must keep this feast. 48 If any aliens living among you wish to celebrate the Passover of the LORD, all the males among them must first be circumcised, and then they may join in its observance just like the natives. But no man who is uncircumcised may partake of it. 49 The law shall be the same for the resident alien as for the native."

50 All the Israelites did just as the LORD had commanded Moses and Aaron. 51 On that same day the LORD brought the Israelites out of Egypt company by company.

Consecration of First-born

13 The LORD spoke to Moses and said, 2 "Consecrate to me every first-born that opens the womb among the Israelites, both of man and beast, for it belongs to me."

3 Moses said to the people, "Remember this day on which you came out of Egypt, that place of slavery. It was with a strong hand that the LORD brought you away. Nothing

made with leaven must be eaten. 4 This day of your departure is in the month of Abib. 5 Therefore, it is in this month that you must celebrate this rite, after the LORD, your God, has brought you into the land of the Canaanites, Hittites, Amorites, Hivites and Jebusites, which he swore to your fathers he would give you, a land flowing with milk and honey. 6 For seven days you shall eat unleavened bread, and the seventh day shall also be a festival to the LORD. 7 Only unleavened bread may be eaten during the seven days; no leaven and nothing leavened may be found in all your territory. 8 On this day you shall explain to your son, 'This is because of what the LORD did for me when I came out of Egypt.' 9 It shall be as a sign on your hand and as a reminder on your forehead; thus the law of the LORD will ever be on your lips, because with a strong hand the LORD brought you out of Egypt. 10 Therefore, you shall keep this prescribed rite at its appointed time from year to year.

11 "When the LORD, your God, has brought you into the land of the Canaanites, which he swore to you and your fathers he would give you, 12 you shall dedicate to the LORD every son that opens the womb; and all the male firstlings of your animals shall belong to the LORD. 13 Every first-born of an ass you shall redeem with a sheep. If you do not redeem it, you shall break its neck. Every first-born son you must redeem. 14 If your son should ask you later on, 'What does this mean?' you shall tell him, 'With a strong hand the LORD brought us out of Egypt, that place of slavery. 15 When Pharaoh stubbornly refused to let us go, the LORD killed every first-born in the land of Egypt, every first-born of man and of beast. That is why I sacrifice to the LORD everything of the male sex that opens the womb, and why I redeem every first-born of my sons.' 16 Let this, then, be as a sign on your hand and as a pendant on your forehead:

with a strong hand the LORD brought us out of Egypt."

Toward the Red Sea

17 Now, when Pharaoh let the people go, God did not lead them by way of the Philistines' land, though this was the nearest; for he thought, should the people see that they would have to fight, they might change their minds and return to Egypt. 18 Instead, he rerouted them toward the Red Sea by way of the desert road. In battle array the Israelites marched out of Egypt. 19 Moses also took Joseph's bones along, for Joseph had made the Israelites swear solemnly that, when God should come to them, they would carry his bones away with them.

20 Setting out from Succoth, they camped at Etham near the edge of the desert.

21 The LORD preceded them, in the daytime by means of a column of cloud to show them the way, and at night by means of a column of fire to give them light. Thus they could travel both day and night. 22 Neither the column of cloud by day nor the column of fire by night ever left its place in front of the people.

14 Then the LORD said to Moses, 2 "Tell the Israelites to turn about and camp before Pi-hahiroth, between Migdol and the sea. You shall camp in front of Baal-zephon, just opposite, by the sea. 3 Pharaoh will then say, 'The Israelites are wandering about aimlessly in the land. The desert has closed in on them.' 4 Thus will I make Pharaoh so obstinate that he will pursue them. Then I will receive glory through Pharaoh and all his army, and the Egyptians will know that I am the LORD."

This the Israelites did. 5 When it was reported to the king of Egypt that the people had fled, Pharaoh and his servants changed their minds about them. "What have we done!"

12, 40: *In Egypt:* according to some ancient sources, "in Canaan and Egypt," thus reckoning from the time of Abraham. Cf Gal 3, 17.

12, 46: *You shall not break any of its bones:* the application of these words to our Lord on the cross shows that the Paschal lamb was a prophetic type of Christ, immolated to free men from the bondage of

sin. Cf also 1 Cor 5, 7; 1 Pt 1, 19.

13, 17: *By way of the Philistines' land:* the most direct route from Egypt to Palestine, along the shore of the Mediterranean.

13, 21: *A column of cloud . . . a column of fire:* probably one and the same preternatural phenomenon, a central nucleus of fire surrounded by

smoke; only at night was its luminous nature visible. Cf 40, 38.

14, 2: These places have not been definitively identified. Even the relative position of *Pi-hahiroth* and *Baal-zephon* is not clear; perhaps the former was on the west shore of the sea, where the Israelites were, and the latter on the opposite shore.

they exclaimed. "Why, we have released Israel from our service!" 6 So Pharaoh made his chariots ready and mustered his soldiers— 7 six hundred first-class chariots and all the other chariots of Egypt, with warriors on them all. 8 So obstinate had the LORD made Pharaoh that he pursued the Israelites even while they were marching away in triumph. 9 The Egyptians, then, pursued them; Pharaoh's whole army, his horses, chariots and charioteers, caught up with them as they lay encamped by the sea, at Pi-hahiroth, in front of Baal-zephon.

Crossing of the Red Sea

10 Pharaoh was already near when the Israelites looked up and saw that the Egyptians were on the march in pursuit of them. In great fright they cried out to the LORD. 11 And they complained to Moses, "Were there no burial places in Egypt that you had to bring us out here to die in the desert? Why did you do this to us? Why did you bring us out of Egypt? 12 Did we not tell you this in Egypt, when we said, 'Leave us alone. Let us serve the Egyptians'? Far better for us to be the slaves of the Egyptians than to die in the desert." 13 But Moses answered the people, "Fear not! Stand your ground, and you will see the victory the LORD will win for you today. These Egyptians whom you see today you will never see again. 14 The LORD himself will fight for you; you have only to keep still."

15 Then the LORD said to Moses, "Why are you crying out to me? Tell the Israelites to go forward. 16 And you, lift up your staff and, with hand outstretched over the sea, split the sea in two, that the Israelites may pass through it on dry land. 17 But I will make the Egyptians so obstinate that they will go in after them. Then I will receive glory through Pharaoh and all his army, his chariots and charioteers. 18 The Egyptians shall know that I am the LORD, when I receive glory through Pharaoh and his chariots and charioteers."

19 The angel of God, who had been leading Israel's camp, now moved and went around behind them. The column of cloud also, leaving the front, took up its place behind them, 20 so that it came between the camp of the Egyptians and that of Israel. But the cloud now became dark, and thus the night passed without the rival camps coming any closer together all night long. 21 Then Moses stretched out his hand over the sea, and the LORD swept the sea with a strong east wind throughout the night and so turned it into dry land. When the water was thus divided, 22 the Israelites marched into the midst of the sea on dry land, with the water like a wall to their right and to their left.

Destruction of the Egyptians

23 The Egyptians followed in pursuit; all Pharaoh's horses and chariots and charioteers went after them right into the midst of the sea. 24 In the night watch just before dawn the LORD cast through the column of the fiery cloud upon the Egyptian force a glance that threw it into a panic; 25 and he so clogged their chariot wheels that they could hardly drive. With that the Egyptians sounded the retreat before Israel, because the LORD was fighting for them against the Egyptians.

26 Then the LORD told Moses, "Stretch out your hand over the sea, that the water may flow back upon the Egyptians, upon their chariots and their charioteers." 27 So Moses stretched out his hand over the sea, and at dawn the sea flowed back to its normal depth. The Egyptians were fleeing head on toward the sea, when the LORD hurled them into its midst. 28 As the water flowed back, it covered the chariots and the charioteers of Pharaoh's whole army which had followed the Israelites into the sea. Not a single one of them escaped, 29 But the Israelites had marched on dry land through the midst of the sea, with the water like a wall to their right and to their left. 30 Thus the LORD saved Israel on that day from the power of the Egyptians. When Israel saw the Egyptians lying dead on the seashore 31 and beheld the great power that the LORD had shown against the Egyptians, they feared the LORD and believed in him and in his servant Moses.

15 Then Moses and the Israelites sang this song to the LORD:

I will sing to the LORD, for he is
  gloriously triumphant;
  horse and chariot he has cast
  into the sea.
2 My strength and my courage is
  the LORD,
  and he has been my savior.
He is my God, I praise him;
  the God of my father, I extol
  him.

3 The LORD is a warrior,
  LORD is his name!
4 Pharaoh's chariots and army he
  hurled into the sea;
  the elite of his officers were
  submerged in the Red Sea.
5 The flood waters covered them,
  they sank into the depths like
  a stone.

6 Your right hand, O LORD,
  magnificent in power,
  your right hand, O LORD, has
  shattered the enemy.
7 In your great majesty you overthrew your adversaries;
  you loosed your wrath to
  consume them like stubble.
8 At a breath of your anger the
  waters piled up,
  the flowing waters stood like a
  mound,
  the flood waters congealed in
  the midst of the sea.

9 The enemy boasted, "I will
  pursue and overtake them;
  I will divide the spoils and
  have my fill of them;
  I will draw my sword; my
  hand shall despoil them!"
10 When your wind blew, the sea
  covered them;
  like lead they sank in the
  mighty waters.

11 Who is like to you among the
  gods, O LORD?

14, 20: *The cloud now became dark:* the light which it ordinarily cast at night would now have been a help to the Egyptians; its present obscurity serves as a shield for the Israelites. However, the reading of the original text here is not quite certain.

15, 1–21: This canticle (used in Christian liturgy) celebrates God's saving power, miraculously delivering his people from their enemies, and leading them to the victorious conquest of the Promised Land.

Who is like to you, magnificent
in holiness?
O terrible in renown, worker of
wonders,

12 when you stretched out your
right hand, the earth
swallowed them!

13 In your mercy you led the
people you redeemed;
in your strength you guided
them to your holy dwelling.

14 The nations heard and quaked;
anguish gripped the dwellers
in Philistia.

15 Then were the princes of Edom
dismayed;
trembling seized the chieftains
of Moab;
All the dwellers in Canaan
melted away;

16 terror and dread fell upon
them.
By the might of your arm they
were frozen like stone,
while your people, O LORD,
passed over,
while the people you had
made your own passed over.

17 And you brought them in and
planted them on the
mountain of your
inheritance—
the place where you made
your seat, O LORD,
the sanctuary, O Lord, which
your hands established.

18 The LORD shall reign forever
and ever.

19 They sang thus because Pharaoh's horses and chariots and charioteers had gone into the sea, and the LORD made the waters of the sea flow back upon them, though the Israelites had marched on dry land through the midst of the sea. 20 The prophetess Miriam, Aaron's sister, took a tambourine in her hand, while all the women went out after her with tambourines, dancing; 21 and she led them in the refrain:

Sing to the LORD, for he is
gloriously triumphant;
horse and chariot he has cast
into the sea.

At Marah and Elim

22 Then Moses led Israel forward from the Red Sea, and they marched out to the desert of Shur. After traveling for three days through the desert without finding water, 23 they arrived at Marah, where they could not drink the water, because it was too bitter. Hence this place was called Marah. 24 As the people grumbled against Moses, saying, "What are we to drink?" 25 he appealed to the LORD, who pointed out to him a certain piece of wood. When he threw this into the water, the water became fresh.

It was here that the LORD, in making rules and regulations for them, put them to the test. 26 "If •you really listen to the voice of the LORD, your God," he told them, "and do what is right in his eyes: if you heed his commandments and keep all his precepts, I will not afflict you with any of the diseases with which I afflicted the Egyptians; for I, the LORD, am your healer."

27 Then they came to Elim, where there were twelve springs of water and seventy palm trees, and they camped there near the water.

The Desert of Sin

16 Having set out from Elim, the whole Israelite community came into the desert of Sin, which is between Elim and Sinai, on the fifteenth day of the second month after their departure from the land of Egypt. 2 Here in the desert the whole Israelite community grumbled against Moses and Aaron. 3 The Israelites said to them, "Would that we had died at the LORD's hand in the land of Egypt, as we sat by our fleshpots and ate our fill of bread! But you had to lead us into this desert to make the whole community die of famine!"

The Quail and Manna

4 Then the LORD said to Moses, "I will now rain down bread from heaven for you. Each day the people are to go out and gather their daily portion; thus will I test them, to see whether they follow my instructions or not. 5 On the sixth day, however, when they prepare what they bring in, let it be twice as much as they gather on the other days." 6 So Moses and Aaron told all the Israelites, "At evening you will know that it was the LORD who brought you out of the land of Egypt; 7 and in the morning you will see the glory of the LORD, as he heeds your grumbling against him. But what are we that you should grumble against us? 8 When the LORD gives you flesh to eat in the evening," continued Moses, "and in the morning your fill of bread, as he heeds the grumbling you utter against him, what then are we? Your grumbling is not against us, but against the LORD."

9 Then Moses said to Aaron, "Tell the whole Israelite community: Present yourselves before the LORD, for he has heard your grumbling." 10 When Aaron announced this to the whole Israelite community, they turned toward the desert, and lo, the glory of the LORD appeared in the cloud! 11 The Lord spoke to Moses and said, 12 "I have heard the grumbling of the Israelites. Tell them: In the evening twilight you shall eat flesh, and in the morning you shall have your fill of bread, so that you may know that I, the LORD, am your God."

13 In the evening quail came up and covered the camp. In the morning a dew lay all about the camp, 14 and when the dew evaporated, there on the surface of the desert were fine flakes like hoarfrost on the ground. 15 On seeing it, the Israelites asked one another, "What is this?" for they did not know what it was. But Moses told them, "This is

15, 21: *She led them:* Miriam's refrain re-echoes the first verse of this song and was probably sung as an antiphon after each verse.

16, 1: *On the fifteenth day of the second month:* just one full month after their departure from Egypt. Cf 12, 2.51; Nm 33, 3f. They encamped in the desert of Sin on a Friday; the murmuring (vv 2f) occurred on the sabbath, the arrival of the quail (v 13) the evening before Sunday, followed by six mornings (vv 14–27) of collecting manna before the next sabbath.

16, 4: *Bread from heaven:* as a gift from God, the manna is said to come down from the sky. Cf Ps 78, 25; Wis 16, 20. Perhaps it was similar to a natural substance that is still found in small quantities on the Sinai peninsula, but here it is, at least in part, clearly miraculous. Our Lord referred to the manna as a type of the Blessed Eucharist. Cf Jn 6, 32.49–52.

16, 15: *What is this:* the original *man hu* is thus rendered by the ancient versions, which understood the phrase as a popular etymology of the Hebrew word *man*, "manna"; some render, "This is manna."

the bread which the LORD has given you to eat.

Regulations Regarding the Manna

16 "Now, this is what the LORD has commanded. So gather it that everyone has enough to eat, an omer for each person, as many of you as there are, each man providing for those of his own tent." 17 The Israelites did so. Some gathered a large and some a small amount. 18 But when they measured it out by the omer, he who had gathered a large amount did not have too much, and he who had gathered a small amount did not have too little. They so gathered that everyone had enough to eat. 19 Moses also told them, "Let no one keep any of it over until tomorrow morning." 20 But they would not listen to him. When some kept a part of it over until the following morning, it became wormy and rotten. Therefore Moses was displeased with them.

21 Morning after morning they gathered it, till each had enough to eat; but when the sun grew hot, the manna melted away. 22 On the sixth day they gathered twice as much food, two omers for each person. When all the leaders of the community came and reported this to Moses, 23 he told them, "That is what the LORD prescribed. Tomorrow is a day of complete rest, the sabbath, sacred to the LORD. You may either bake or boil the manna, as you please; but whatever is left put away and keep for the morrow." 24 When they put it away for the morrow, as Moses commanded, it did not become rotten or wormy. 25 Moses then said, "Eat it today, for today is the sabbath of the LORD. On this day you will not find any of it on the ground. 26 On the other six days you can gather it, but on the seventh day, the sabbath, none of it will be there." 27 Still, on the seventh day some of the people went out to gather it, although they did not find any. 28 Then the LORD said to Moses, "How long will you refuse to keep my commandments and laws? 29 Take note! The LORD has given you the sabbath. That is why on the sixth day he gives you food for two days. On the seventh day everyone is to stay home and no one is to go out." 30 After that the people rested on the seventh day.

31 The Israelites called this food manna. It was like coriander seed, but white, and it tasted like wafers made with honey.

32 Moses said, "This is what the LORD has commanded. Keep an omerful of manna for your descendants, that they may see what food I gave you to eat in the desert when I brought you out of the land of Egypt." 33 Moses then told Aaron, "Take an urn and put an omer of manna in it. Then place it before the LORD in safekeeping for your descendants." 34 So Aaron placed it in front of the commandments for safekeeping, as the LORD had commanded Moses.

35 The Israelites ate this manna for forty years, until they came to settled land; they ate manna until they reached the borders of Canaan. 36 [An omer is one tenth of an ephah.]

Water from the Rock

17 From the desert of Sin the whole Israelite community journeyed by stages, as the LORD directed, and encamped at Rephidim.

Here there was no water for the people to drink. 2 They quarreled, therefore, with Moses and said, "Give us water to drink." Moses replied, "Why do you quarrel with me? Why do you put the LORD to a test?" 3 Here, then, in their thirst for water, the people grumbled against Moses, saying, "Why did you ever make us leave Egypt? Was it just to have us die here of thirst with our children and our livestock?" 4 So Moses cried out to the LORD, "What shall I do with this people? A little more and they will stone me!" 5 The LORD answered Moses, "Go over there in front of the people, along with some of the elders of Israel, holding in your hand, as you go, the staff with which you struck the river. 6 I will be standing there in front of you on the rock in Horeb. Strike the rock, and the water will flow from it for the people to drink." This Moses did, in the presence of the elders of Israel. 7 The place was called Massah and Meribah, because the Israelites quarreled there and tested the LORD, saying, "Is the LORD in our midst or not?"

Battle with Amalek

8 At Rephidim, Amalek came and waged war against Israel. 9 Moses, therefore, said to Joshua, "Pick out certain men, and tomorrow go out and engage Amalek in battle. I will be standing on top of the hill with the staff of God in my hand." 10 So Joshua did as Moses told him: he engaged Amalek in battle after Moses had climbed to the top of the hill with Aaron and Hur. 11 As long as Moses kept his hands raised up, Israel had the better of the fight, but when he let his hands rest, Amalek had the better of the fight. 12 Moses' hands, however, grew tired; so they put a rock in place for him to sit on. Meanwhile Aaron and Hur supported his hands, one on one side and one on the other, so that his hands remained steady till sunset. 13 And Joshua mowed down Amalek and his people with the edge of the sword.

14 Then the LORD said to Moses, "Write this down in a document as something to be remembered, and recite it in the ears of Joshua: I will completely blot out the memory of Amalek from under the heavens." 15 Moses also built an altar there, which he called Yahweh-nissi; 16 for he said, "The LORD takes in hand his banner; the LORD will war against Amalek through the centuries."

16, 18: St. Paul cites this passage as an example of equitable sharing. Cf 2 Cor 8, 15.

16, 31: *Coriander seed:* small, round, aromatic seeds of bright brown color; the comparison, therefore, refers merely to the size and shape, not to the taste or color of the manna.

16, 33: *Urn:* according to the Greek translation, which is followed in Heb 9, 4, this was a golden vessel.

16, 34: *The commandments:* the two tablets of the ten commandments, which were kept in the ark. Cf 25, 16.21f.

17, 7: *Massah ... Meribah:* Hebrew words meaning respectively, "the (place of the) test," and, "the (place of the) quarreling."

17, 8: *Amalek:* the Amalekites were an aboriginal people of southern Palestine and the Sinai peninsula. Cf Nm 24, 20.

17, 15: *Yahweh-nissi:* meaning, "the LORD is my banner."

Meeting with Jethro

18 Now Moses' father-in-law Jethro, the priest of Midian, heard of all that God had done for Moses and for his people Israel: how the LORD had brought Israel out of Egypt. 2 So his father-in-law Jethro took along Zipporah, Moses' wife, whom Moses had sent back to him, 3 and her two sons. One of these was called Gershom; for he said, "I am a stranger in a foreign land." 4 The other was called Eliezer; for he said, "My father's God is my helper; he has rescued me from Pharaoh's sword." 5 Together with Moses' wife and sons, then, his father-in-law Jethro came to him in the desert where he was encamped near the mountain of God, 6 and he sent word to Moses, "I, Jethro, your father-in-law, am coming to you, along with your wife and her two sons."

7 Moses went out to meet his father-in-law, bowed down before him, and kissed him. Having greeted each other, they went into the tent. 8 Moses then told his father-in-law of all that the LORD had done to Pharaoh and the Egyptians for the sake of Israel, and of all the hardships they had had to endure on their journey, and how the LORD had come to their rescue. 9 Jethro rejoiced over all the goodness that the LORD had shown Israel in rescuing them from the hands of the Egyptians. 10 "Blessed be the LORD," he said, "who has rescued his people from the hands of Pharaoh and the Egyptians. 11 Now I know that the LORD is a deity great beyond any other; for he took occasion of their being dealt with insolently to deliver the people from the power of the Egyptians." 12 Then Jethro, the father-in-law of Moses, brought a holocaust and other sacrifices to God, and Aaron came with all the elders of Israel to participate with Moses' father-in-law in the meal before God.

Appointment of Minor Judges

13 The next day Moses sat in judgment for the people, who waited about him from morning until evening. 14 When his father-in-law saw all that he was doing for the people, he inquired, "What sort of thing is this that you are doing for the people? Why do you sit alone while all the people have to stand about you from morning till evening?" 15 Moses answered his father-in-law, "The people come to me to consult God. 16 Whenever they have a disagreement, they come to me to have me settle the matter between them and make known to them God's decisions and regulations."

17 "You are not acting wisely," his father-in-law replied. 18 "You will surely wear yourself out, and not only yourself but also these people with you. The task is too heavy for you; you cannot do it alone. 19 Now, listen to me, and I will give you some advice, that God may be with you. Act as the people's representative before God, bringing to him whatever they have to say. 20 Enlighten them in regard to the decisions and regulations, showing them how they are to live and what they are to do. 21 But you should also look among all the people for able and God-fearing men, trustworthy men who hate dishonest gain, and set them as officers over groups of thousands, of hundreds, of fifties, and of tens. 22 Let these men render decisions for the people in all ordinary cases. More important cases they should refer to you, but all the lesser cases they can settle themselves. Thus, your burden will be lightened, since they will bear it with you. 23 If you do this, when God gives you orders you will be able to stand the strain, and all these people will go home satisfied."

24 Moses followed the advice of his father-in-law and did all that he had suggested. 25 He picked out able men from all Israel and put them in charge of the people as officers over groups of thousands, of hundreds, of fifties, and of tens. 26 They rendered decisions for the people in all ordinary cases. The more difficult cases they referred to Moses, but all the lesser cases they settled themselves. 27 Then Moses bade farewell to his father-in-law, who went off to his own country.

THE COVENANT AT MOUNT SINAI

Arrival at Sinai

19 In the third month after their departure from the land of Egypt, on its first day, the Israelites came to the desert of Sinai. 2 After the journey from Rephidim to the desert of Sinai, they pitched camp.

While Israel was encamped here in front of the mountain, 3 Moses went up the mountain to God. Then the LORD called to him and said, "Thus shall you say to the house of Jacob; tell the Israelites: 4 You have seen for yourselves how I treated the Egyptians and how I bore you up on eagle wings and brought you here to myself. 5 Therefore, if you hearken to my voice and keep my covenant, you shall be my special possession, dearer to me than all other people, though all the earth is mine. 6 You shall be to me a kingdom of priests, a holy nation. That is what you must tell the Israelites." 7 So Moses went and summoned the elders of the people. When he set before them all that the LORD had ordered him to tell them, 8 the people all answered together, "Everything the LORD has said, we will do." Then Moses brought back to the LORD the response of the people.

9 The LORD also told him, "I am coming to you in a dense cloud, so that when the people hear me speaking with you, they may always have faith in you also." When Moses, then, had reported to the LORD the response of the people, 10 the LORD added, "Go to the people and have them sanctify themselves today and tomorrow. Make them wash their garments 11 and be ready for the third day; for on the third day the LORD will come down on Mount Sinai before the eyes of all the people. 12 Set limits for the people all around the mountain, and tell them: Take care not to go up the mountain, or even to touch its base. If anyone

---

19, 6: *Kingdom of priests:* inasmuch as the whole Israelite nation was consecrated to God in a special way, it formed a race of royal priests who participated in the liturgical sacrifices, even though the actual offering of the sacrifices was the exclusive prerogative of the Aaronic priesthood. The same condition exists in the New Dispensation as regards the whole Christian people and the Christian priesthood in the strict sense. Cf Is 61, 6; 1 Pt 2, 5.9.

touches the mountain he must be put to death. 13 No hand shall touch him; he must be stoned to death or killed with arrows. Such a one, man or beast, must not be allowed to live. Only when the ram's horn resounds may they go up to the mountain." 14 Then Moses came down from the mountain to the people and had them sanctify themselves and wash their garments. 15 He warned them, "Be ready for the third day. Have no intercourse with any woman."

The Great Theophany

16 On the morning of the third day there were peals of thunder and lightning, and a heavy cloud over the mountain, and a very loud trumpet blast, so that all the people in the camp trembled. 17 But Moses led the people out of the camp to meet God, and they stationed themselves at the foot of the mountain. 18 Mount Sinai was all wrapped in smoke, for the LORD came down upon it in fire. The smoke rose from it as though from a furnace, and the whole mountain trembled violently. 19 The trumpet blast grew louder and louder, while Moses was speaking and God answering him with thunder.
20 When the LORD came down to the top of Mount Sinai, he summoned Moses to the top of the mountain, and Moses went up to him. 21 Then the LORD told Moses, "Go down and warn the people not to break through toward the LORD in order to see him; otherwise many of them will be struck down. 22 The priests, too, who approach the LORD must sanctify themselves; else he will vent his anger upon them." 23 Moses said to the LORD, "The people cannot go up to Mount Sinai, for you yourself warned us to set limits around the mountain to make it sacred." 24 The LORD repeated, "Go down now! Then come up again along with Aaron. But the priests and the people must not break through to come up to the LORD; else he will vent his anger upon them." 25 So

Moses went down to the people and told them this.

The Ten Commandments

20 Then God delivered all these commandments:
2 "I, the LORD, am your God, who brought you out of the land of Egypt, that place of slavery. 3 You shall not have other gods besides me. 4 You shall not carve idols for yourselves in the shape of anything in the sky above or on the earth below or in the waters beneath the earth; 5 you shall not bow down before them or worship them. For I, the LORD, your God, am a jealous God, inflicting punishment for their fathers' wickedness on the children of those who hate me, down to the third and fourth generation; 6 but bestowing mercy down to the thousandth generation, on the children of those who love me and keep my commandments.
7 "You shall not take the name of the LORD, your God, in vain. For the LORD will not leave unpunished him who takes his name in vain.
8 "Remember to keep holy the sabbath day. 9 Six days you may labor and do all your work, 10 but the seventh day is the sabbath of the LORD, your God. No work may be done then either by you, or your son or daughter, or your male or female slave, or your beast, or by the alien who lives with you. 11 In six days the LORD made the heavens and the earth, the sea and all that is in them; but on the seventh day he rested. That is why the LORD has blessed the sabbath day and made it holy.
12 "Honor your father and your mother, that you may have a long life in the land which the LORD, your God, is giving you.
13 "You shall not kill.
14 "You shall not commit adultery.
15 "You shall not steal.
16 "You shall not bear false witness against your neighbor.
17 "You shall not covet your neighbor's house. You shall not covet

your neighbor's wife, nor his male or female slave, nor his ox or ass, nor anything else that belongs to him."

The Fear of God

18 When the people witnessed the thunder and lightning, the trumpet blast and the mountain smoking, they all feared and trembled. So they took up a position much farther away 19 and said to Moses, "You speak to us, and we will listen; but let not God speak to us, or we shall die." 20 Moses answered the people, "Do not be afraid, for God has come to you only to test you and put his fear upon you, lest you should sin." 21 Still the people remained at a distance, while Moses approached the cloud where God was.
22 The LORD told Moses, "Thus shall you speak to the Israelites: You have seen for yourselves that I have spoken to you from heaven. 23 Do not make anything to rank with me; neither gods of silver nor gods of gold shall you make for yourselves.
24 "An altar of earth you shall make for me, and upon it you shall sacrifice your holocausts and peace offerings, your sheep and your oxen. In whatever place I choose for the remembrance of my name I will come to you and bless you. 25 If you make an altar of stone for me, do not build it of cut stone, for by putting a tool to it you desecrate it. 26 You shall not go up by steps to my altar, on which you must not be indecently uncovered.

Laws Regarding Slaves

21 "These are the rules you shall lay before them. 2 When you purchase a Hebrew slave, he is to serve you for six years, but in the seventh year he shall be given his freedom without cost. 3 If he comes with a wife, his wife shall leave with him. 4 But if his master gives him a wife and she bears him sons or daughters, the woman and her children shall remain the master's property and the man shall leave alone. 5 If, however, the slave

---

20, 1–17: The precise division of these precepts into "ten commandments" is somewhat uncertain. Traditionally among Catholics vv 1–6 are considered as only one commandment, and v 17 as two. Cf Dt 5, 6–21.
20, 5: *Jealous:* demanding exclusive allegiance,

such as a wife must have for her husband.
20, 24: *I choose for the remembrance of my name:* literally, "where I make my name to be remembered": at the sacred site where God wishes to be worshiped and his name revered.
21, 1: *Rules:* judicial precedents to be used in

settling questions of law and custom. This introductory phrase serves as the title of the following collection of civil and religious laws (chapters 21–23) which is called in 24, 7, *the book of the covenant.*

declares, 'I am devoted to my master and my wife and children; I will not go free,' 6 his master shall bring him to God and there, at the door or doorpost, he shall pierce his ear with an awl, thus keeping him as his slave forever.

7 When a man sells his daughter as a slave, she shall not go free as male slaves do. 8 But if her master, who had destined her for himself, dislikes her, he shall let her be redeemed. He has no right to sell her to a foreigner, since he has broken faith with her. 9 If he destines her for his son, he shall treat her like a daughter. 10 If he takes another wife, he shall not withhold her food, her clothing, or her conjugal rights. 11 If he does not grant her these three things, she shall be given her freedom absolutely, without cost to her.

Personal Injury

12 "Whoever strikes a man a mortal blow must be put to death. 13 He, however, who did not hunt a man down, but caused his death by an act of God, may flee to a place which I will set apart for this purpose. 14 But when a man kills another after maliciously scheming to do so, you must take him even from my altar and put him to death. 15 Whoever strikes his father or mother shall be put to death.

16 "A kidnaper, whether he sells his victim or still has him when caught, shall be put to death.

17 "Whoever curses his father or mother shall be put to death.

18 "When men quarrel and one strikes the other with a stone or with his fist, not mortally, but enough to put him in bed, 19 the one who struck the blow shall be acquitted, provided the other can get up and walk around with the help of his staff. Still, he must compensate him for his enforced idleness and provide for his complete cure.

20 "When a man strikes his male or female slave with a rod so hard that the slave dies under his hand, he shall be punished. 21 If, however, the slave survives for a day or two, he is not to be punished, since the slave is his own property.

22 "When men have a fight and hurt a pregnant woman, so that she suffers a miscarriage, but no further injury, the guilty one shall be fined as much as the woman's husband demands of him, and he shall pay in the presence of the judges. 23 But if injury ensues, you shall give life for life, 24 eye for eye, tooth for tooth, hand for hand, foot for foot, 25 burn for burn, wound for wound, stripe for stripe.

26 "When a man strikes his male or female slave in the eye and destroys the use of the eye, he shall let the slave go free in compensation for the eye. 27 If he knocks out a tooth of his male or female slave, he shall let the slave go free in compensation for the tooth.

28 "When an ox gores a man or a woman to death, the ox must be stoned; its flesh may not be eaten. The owner of the ox, however, shall go unpunished. 29 But if an ox was previously in the habit of goring people and its owner, though warned, would not keep it in; should it then kill a man or a woman, not only must the ox be stoned, but its owner also must be put to death. 30 If, however, a fine is imposed on him, he must pay in ransom for his life whatever amount is imposed on him. 31 This law applies if it is a boy or a girl that the ox gores. 32 But if it is a male or a female slave that it gores, he must pay the owner of the slave thirty shekels of silver, and the ox must be stoned.

Property Damage

33 "When a man uncovers or digs a cistern and does not cover it over again, should an ox or an ass

fall into it, 34 the owner of the cistern must make good by restoring the value of the animal to its owner; the dead animal, however, he may keep.

35 "When one man's ox hurts another's ox so badly that it dies, they shall sell the live ox and divide this money as well as the dead animal equally between them. 36 But if it was known that the ox was previously in the habit of goring and its owner would not keep it in, he must make full restitution, an ox for an ox; but the dead animal he may keep.

37 "When a man steals an ox or a sheep and slaughters or sells it, he shall restore five oxen for the one ox, and four sheep for the one sheep.

22 1 [If a thief is caught in the act of housebreaking and beaten to death, there is no bloodguilt involved. 2 But if after sunrise he is thus beaten, there is bloodguilt.] He must make full restitution. If he has nothing, he shall be sold to pay for his theft. 3 If what he stole is found alive in his possession, be it an ox, an ass or a sheep, he shall restore two animals for each one stolen.

4 "When a man is burning over a field or a vineyard, if he lets the fire spread so that it burns in another's field, he must make restitution with the best produce of his own field or vineyard. 5 If the fire spreads further, and catches on to thorn bushes, so that shocked grain or standing grain or the field itself is burned up, the one who started the fire must make full restitution.

Trusts and Loans

6 "When a man gives money or any article to another for safekeeping and it is stolen from the latter's house, the thief, if caught, must make twofold restitution. 7 If the thief is not caught, the owner of the house shall be brought to God, to swear

---

21, 6: *To God:* to the sanctuary; or perhaps the phrase is to be rendered, "to the gods," in the sense of "to the judges." Cf Ps 82, 1. Since the expression "to have an open ear" meant "to obey," a pierced ear lobe was an ancient symbol of obedience. Cf Ps 40, 7.

21, 8: *Destined her:* intended her as a wife of second rank.

21, 23ff: This section is known as the *lex talionis*, the law of tit for tat. The purpose of this law was not

merely the enforcement of rigorous justice, but also the prevention of greater penalties than would be just. Christ refers to this passage when he exhorts Christians to cede their lawful rights for the sake of charity. Cf Mt 5, 38ff.

21, 37—22, 30: In the Vulgate, 22, 1–31.

22, 1f: *If a thief is caught:* this seems to be a fragment of what was once a longer law on housebreaking, which has been inserted here into the middle of a law on stealing animals. At night the householder

would be justified in killing a burglar outright, but not so in the daytime, when the burglar could more easily be caught alive. *He must make full restitution:* this stood originally immediately after 21, 37.

22, 4: The Greek and Latin versions understood this verse as a prohibition against allowing one's cattle to graze in the field of another.

22, 7: *Brought to God:* see note on 21, 6. Cf also 22, 10.

that he himself did not lay hands on his neighbor's property. 8 In every question of dishonest appropriation, whether it be about an ox, or an ass, or a sheep, or a garment, or anything else that has disappeared, where another claims that the thing is his, both parties shall present their case before God; the one whom God convicts must make twofold restitution to the other.

9 "When a man gives an ass, or an ox, or a sheep, or any other animal to another for safekeeping, if it dies, or is maimed or snatched away, without anyone witnessing the fact, 10 the custodian shall swear by the LORD that he did not lay hands on his neighbor's property; the owner must accept the oath, and no restitution is to be made. 11 But if the custodian is really guilty of theft, he must make restitution to the owner. 12 If it has been killed by a wild beast, let him bring it as evidence, and he need not make restitution for the mangled animal.

13 "When a man borrows an animal from his neighbor, if it is maimed or dies while the owner is not present, the man must make restitution. 14 But if the owner is present, he need not make restitution. If it was hired, this was covered by the price of its hire.

Social Laws

15 "When a man seduces a virgin who is not betrothed, and lies with her, he shall pay her marriage price and marry her. 16 If her father refuses to give her to him, he must still pay him the customary marriage price for virgins.

17 "You shall not let a sorceress live.

18 "Anyone who lies with an animal shall be put to death.

19 "Whoever sacrifices to any god, except to the LORD alone, shall be doomed.

20 "You shall not molest or oppress an alien, for you were once aliens yourselves in the land of Egypt. 21 You shall not wrong any

widow or orphan. 22 If ever you wrong them and they cry out to me, I will surely hear their cry. 23 My wrath will flare up, and I will kill you with the sword; then your own wives will be widows, and your children orphans.

24 "If you lend money to one of your poor neighbors among my people, you shall not act like an extortioner toward him by demanding interest from him. 25 If you take your neighbor's cloak as a pledge, you shall return it to him before sunset; 26 for this cloak of his is the only covering he has for his body. What else has he to sleep in? If he cries out to me, I will hear him; for I am compassionate.

27 "You shall not revile God, nor curse a prince of your people.

28 "You shall not delay the offering of your harvest and your press. You shall give me the first-born of your sons. 29 You must do the same with your oxen and your sheep; for seven days the firstling may stay with its mother, but on the eighth day you must give it to me.

30 "You shall be men sacred to me. Flesh torn to pieces in the field you shall not eat; throw it to the dogs.

23 "You shall not repeat a false report. Do not join the wicked in putting your hand, as an unjust witness, upon anyone. 2 Neither shall you allege the example of the many as an excuse for doing wrong, nor shall you, when testifying in a lawsuit, side with the many in perverting justice. 3 You shall not favor a poor man in his lawsuit.

4 "When you come upon your enemy's ox or ass going astray, see to it that it is returned to him. 5 When you notice the ass of one who hates you lying prostrate under its burden, by no means desert him; help him, rather, to raise it up.

6 "You shall not deny one of your needy fellow men his rights in his lawsuit. 7 You shall keep away from anything dishonest. The innocent and the just you shall not put to death, nor shall you acquit the guilty.

8 Never take a bribe, for a bribe blinds even the most clear-sighted and twists the words even of the just. 9 You shall not oppress an alien; you well know how it feels to be an alien, since you were once aliens yourselves in the land of Egypt.

Religious Laws

10 "For six years you may sow your land and gather in its produce. 11 But the seventh year you shall let the land lie untilled and unharvested, that the poor among you may eat of it and the beasts of the field may eat what the poor leave. So also shall you do in regard to your vineyard and your olive grove.

12 "For six days you may do your work, but on the seventh day you must rest, that your ox and your ass may also have rest, and that the son of your maidservant and the alien may be refreshed. 13 Give heed to all that I have told you.

"Never mention the name of any other god; it shall not be heard from your lips.

14 "Three times a year you shall celebrate a pilgrim feast to me. 15 You shall keep the feast of Unleavened Bread. As I have commanded you, you must eat unleavened bread for seven days at the prescribed time in the month of Abib, for it was then that you came out of Egypt. No one shall appear before me empty-handed. 16 You shall also keep the feast of the grain harvest with the first of the crop that you have sown in the field; and finally, the feast at the fruit harvest at the end of the year, when you gather in the produce from the fields. 17 Thrice a year shall all your men appear before the Lord GOD.

18 "You shall not offer the blood of my sacrifice with leavened bread; nor shall the fat of my feast be kept overnight till the next day. 19 The choicest first fruits of your soil you shall bring to the house of the LORD, your God.

"You shall not boil a kid in its mother's milk.

22, 16: *The customary marriage price for virgins:* fifty shekels according to Dt 22, 29.

22, 27: *God:* or perhaps "the gods," in the sense of "the judges," as the parallel with *a prince of your people* suggests.

23, 14: These three feasts are elsewhere called the Passover, Pentecost and Booths. Cf 34, 18–26; Lv 23; Dt 16.

23, 15: *Appear before me:* the original expression was "see my face"; so also in several other places,

as 23, 17; 34, 23f; Dt 16, 16; 31, 11.

23, 19: *Boil a kid in its mother's milk:* this was part of a Canaanite ritual; hence it is forbidden here as a pagan ceremony.

Reward of Fidelity

20 "See, I am sending an angel before you, to guard you on the way and bring you to the place I have prepared. 21 Be attentive to him and heed his voice. Do not rebel against him, for he will not forgive your sin. My authority resides in him. 22 If you heed his voice and carry out all I tell you, I will be an enemy to your enemies and a foe to your foes.

23 "My angel will go before you and bring you to the Amorites, Hittites, Perizzites, Canaanites, Hivites and Jebusites; and I will wipe them out. 24 Therefore, you shall not bow down in worship before their gods, nor shall you make anything like them; rather, you must demolish them and smash their sacred pillars. 25 The LORD, your God, you shall worship; then I will bless your food and drink, and I will remove all sickness from your midst; 26 no woman in your land will be barren or miscarry; and I will give you a full span of life.

27 "I will have the fear of me precede you, so that I will throw into panic every nation you reach. I will make all your enemies turn from you in flight, 28 and ahead of you I will send hornets to drive the Hivites, Canaanites and Hittites out of your way. 29 But not in one year will I drive them all out before you; else the land will become so desolate that the wild beasts will multiply against you. 30 Instead, I will drive them out little by little before you, until you have grown numerous enough to take possession of the land. 31 I will set your boundaries from the Red Sea to the sea of the Philistines, and from the desert to the River; all who dwell in this land I will hand over to you to be driven out of your way. 32 You shall not make a covenant with them or their gods. 33 They must not abide in your land, lest they make you sin against me by ensnaring you into worshiping their gods."

Ratification of the Covenant

24 Moses himself was told, "Come up to the LORD, you and Aaron, with Nadab, Abihu, and seventy of the elders of Israel. You shall all worship at some distance, 2 but Moses alone is to come close to the LORD; the others shall not come too near, and the people shall not come up at all with Moses."

3 When Moses came to the people and related all the words and ordinances of the LORD, they all answered with one voice, "We will do everything that the LORD has told us." 4 Moses then wrote down all the words of the LORD and, rising early the next day, he erected at the foot of the mountain an altar and twelve pillars for the twelve tribes of Israel. 5 Then, having sent certain young men of the Israelites to offer holocausts and sacrifice young bulls as peace offerings to the LORD, 6 Moses took half of the blood and put it in large bowls; the other half he splashed on the altar. 7 Taking the book of the covenant, he read it aloud to the people, who answered, "All that the LORD has said, we will heed and do." 8 Then he took the blood and sprinkled it on the people, saying, "This is the blood of the covenant which the LORD has made with you in accordance with all these words of his."

9 Moses then went up with Aaron, Nadab, Abihu, and seventy elders of Israel, 10 and they beheld the God of Israel. Under his feet there appeared to be sapphire tilework, as clear as the sky itself. 11 Yet he did not smite these chosen Israelites. After gazing on God, they could still eat and drink.

Moses on the Mountain

12 The LORD said to Moses, "Come up to me on the mountain and, while you are there, I will give you the stone tablets on which I have written the commandments intended for their instruction." 13 So Moses set out with Joshua, his aide, and went up to the mountain of God. 14 The elders, however, had been told by him, "Wait here for us until we return to you. Aaron and Hur are staying with you. If anyone has a complaint, let him refer the matter to them." 15 After Moses had gone up, a cloud covered the mountain. 16 The glory of the LORD settled upon Mount Sinai. The cloud covered it for six days, and on the seventh day he called to Moses from the midst of the cloud. 17 To the Israelites the glory of the LORD was seen as a consuming fire on the mountaintop. 18 But Moses passed into the midst of the cloud as he went up on the mountain; and there he stayed for forty days and forty nights.

THE DWELLING AND ITS FURNISHINGS

Collection of Materials

25 This is what the LORD then said to Moses: 2 "Tell the Israelites to take up a collection for me. From every man you shall accept the contribution that his heart prompts him to give me. 3 These are the contributions you shall accept from them: gold, silver and bronze; 4 violet, purple and scarlet yarn; fine linen and goat hair; 5 rams' skins dyed red, and tahash skins; acacia wood; 6 oil for the light; spices for the anointing oil and for the fragrant incense; 7 onyx stones and other gems for mounting on the ephod and the breastpiece.

8 "They shall make a sanctuary for me, that I may dwell in their midst. 9 This Dwelling and all its furnishings you shall make exactly according to the pattern that I will now show you.

23, 21: *My authority resides in him:* literally, "My name is within him."

23, 24: *Make anything like them:* some render, "act according to their conduct." *Sacred pillars:* objects of religious veneration at Canaanite sanctuaries.

23, 28: *Hornets:* some understand this figuratively of various troublesome afflictions; others translate the Hebrew word as "leprosy." Cf Dt 7, 20; Jos 24, 12; Wis 12, 8.

23, 31: *The sea of the Philistines:* the Mediterranean. *The River:* the Euphrates. Only in the time of David and Solomon did the territory of Israel come near to reaching such distant borders.

24, 4: *Pillars:* stone shafts or slabs, erected as symbols of the fact that each of the twelve tribes had entered into this covenant with God; not idolatrous as in 23, 24, although the same Hebrew word is used in both passages. See note on Gn 28, 18.

24, 11: *After gazing on God:* the ancients thought that the sight of God would bring instantaneous death. Cf 33, 20; Gn 16, 13; 32, 31; Jgs 6, 22f; 13, 22. *Eat and drink:* partake of the sacrificial meal.

25, 5: *Tahash:* perhaps the name of a marine animal, such as the dugong or the porpoise. The Greek and Latin versions took it for the color hyacinth.

Plan of the Ark

10 "You shall make an ark of acacia wood, two and a half cubits long, one and a half cubits wide, and one and a half cubits high. 11 Plate it inside and outside with pure gold, and put a molding of gold around the top of it. 12 Cast four gold rings and fasten them on the four supports of the ark, two rings on one side and two on the opposite side. 13 Then make poles of acacia wood and plate them with gold. 14 These poles you are to put through the rings on the sides of the ark, for carrying it; 15 they must remain in the rings of the ark and never be withdrawn. 16 In the ark you are to put the commandments which I will give you.

17 "You shall then make a propitiatory of pure gold, two cubits and a half long, and one and a half cubits wide. 18 Make two cherubim of beaten gold for the two ends of the propitiatory, 19 fastening them so that one cherub springs direct from each end. 20 The cherubim shall have their wings spread out above, covering the propitiatory with them; they shall be turned toward each other, but with their faces looking toward the propitiatory. 21 This propitiatory you shall then place on top of the ark. In the ark itself you are to put the commandments which I will give you. 22 There I will meet you and there, from above the propitiatory, between the two cherubim on the ark of the commandments, I will tell you all the commands that I wish you to give the Israelites.

The Table

23 "You shall also make a table of acacia wood, two cubits long, a cubit wide, and a cubit and a half high. 24 Plate it with pure gold and make a molding of gold around it. 25 Surround it with a frame, a handbreadth high, with a molding of gold around the frame. 26 You shall also make four rings of gold for it and fasten them at the four corners, one at each leg, 27 on two opposite sides of the frame as holders for the poles to carry the table. 28 These poles for carrying the table you shall make of acacia wood and plate with gold. 29 Of pure gold you shall make its plates and cups, as well as its pitchers and bowls for pouring libations. 30 On the table you shall always keep showbread set before me.

The Lampstand

31 "You shall make a lampstand of pure beaten gold—its shaft and branches—with its cups and knobs and petals springing directly from it. 32 Six branches are to extend from the sides of the lampstand, three branches on one side, and three on the other. 33 On one branch there are to be three cups, shaped like almond blossoms, each with its knob and petals; on the opposite branch there are to be three cups, shaped like almond blossoms, each with its knob and petals; and so for the six branches that extend from the lampstand. 34 On the shaft there are to be four cups, shaped like almond blossoms, with their knobs and petals, 35 including a knob below each of the three pairs of branches that extend from the lampstand. 36 Their knobs and branches shall so spring from it that the whole will form but a single piece of pure beaten gold. 37 You shall then make seven lamps for it and so set up the lamps that they shed their light on the space in front of the lampstand. 38 These, as well as the trimming shears and trays, must be of pure gold. 39 Use a talent of pure gold for the lampstand and all its appurtenances. 40 See that you make them according to the pattern shown you on the mountain.

The Tent Cloth

26 "The Dwelling itself you shall make out of sheets woven of fine linen twined and of violet, purple and scarlet yarn, with cherubim embroidered on them. 2 The length of each shall be twenty-eight cubits, and the width four cubits; all the sheets shall be of the same size. 3 Five of the sheets are to be sewed together, edge to edge; and the same for the other five. 4 Make loops of violet yarn along the edge of the end sheet in one set, and the same along the edge of the end sheet in the other set. 5 There are to be fifty loops along the edge of the end sheet in the first set, and fifty loops along the edge of the corresponding sheet in the second set, and so placed that the loops are directly opposite each other. 6 Then make fifty clasps of gold, with which to join the two sets of sheets, so that the Dwelling forms one whole.

7 "Also make sheets woven of goat hair, to be used as a tent covering over the Dwelling. 8 Eleven such sheets are to be made; the length of each shall be thirty cubits, and the width four cubits: all eleven sheets shall be of the same size. 9 Sew five of the sheets, edge to edge, into one set, and the other six sheets into another set. Use the sixth sheet double at the front of the tent. 10 Make fifty loops along the edge of the end sheet in one set, and fifty loops along the edge of the end sheet in the second set. 11 Also make

---

25, 17: *Propitiatory:* this traditional rendering of the Hebrew term, which may mean merely "cover," is derived from its connection with the ceremony of the Day of Atonement whereby God was rendered "propitious." Cf Lv 16, 14ff.

25, 18ff: *Cherubim:* probably in the form of human-headed winged lions. The cherubim over the ark formed the throne for the invisible LORD. Cf Ps 80, 2. For a more detailed description of the somewhat different cherubim in the temple of Solomon, see 1 Kgs 6, 23–28; 2 Chr 3, 10–13.

25, 25: *A frame:* probably placed near the bottom of the legs to keep them steady. The golden table of Herod's temple is pictured thus on the Arch of Titus.

25, 29f: The *plates* held the showbread, that is, the

holy bread which was placed upon the table every sabbath as an offering to God, and was later eaten by the priests. The *cups* held the incense which was strewn upon the bread. Cf Lv 24, 5–9. The libation wine was poured from the *pitchers* into the *bowls*. All these vessels were kept on the golden table.

25, 33: In keeping with the arrangement of the ornaments on the shaft, the three sets of ornaments on each branch were probably so placed that one was at the top and the other two equally spaced along the length of the branch. *Knob:* the cup-shaped seed capsule at the base of a flower.

25, 34f: Of the four ornaments on the shaft, one was at the top and one was below each of the three sets of side branches.

25, 37: The lamps were probably shaped like small

boats, with the wick at one end; the end with the wick was turned toward the front of the lampstand.

25, 38: *Trays:* small receptacles for the burnt-out wicks.

26, 1: *Sheets:* strips of tapestry, woven of white linen, the colored threads being used for the cherubim which were embroidered on them. These sheets were stretched across the top of the Dwelling to form a roof, their free ends hanging down inside the boards which formed walls.

26, 7: *Tent covering:* the cloth made of sheets of goat hair to cover the Dwelling.

26, 9: Half the width of the end strip was folded back at the front of the Dwelling, thus leaving another half-strip to hang down at the rear. Cf v 12.

fifty bronze clasps and put them into the loops, to join the tent into one whole. 12 There will be an extra half sheet of tent covering, which shall be allowed to hang down over the rear of the Dwelling. 13 Likewise, the sheets of the tent will have an extra cubit's length to be left hanging down on either side of the Dwelling to protect it. 14 Over the tent itself you shall make a covering of rams' skins dyed red, and above that, a covering of tahash skins.

The Wooden Walls

15 "You shall make boards of acacia wood as walls for the Dwelling. 16 The length of each board is to be ten cubits, and its width one and a half cubits. 17 Each board shall have two arms that shall serve to fasten the boards in line. In this way all the boards of the Dwelling are to be made. 18 Set up the boards of the Dwelling as follows: twenty boards on the south side, 19 with forty silver pedestals under the twenty boards, so that there are two pedestals under each board, at its two arms; 20 twenty boards on the other side of the Dwelling, the north side, 21 with their forty silver pedestals, two under each board; 22 six boards for the rear of the Dwelling, to the west; 23 and two boards for the corners at the rear of the Dwelling. 24 These two shall be double at the bottom, and likewise double at the top, to the first ring. That is how both boards in the corners are to be made. 25 Thus, there shall be in the rear eight boards, with their sixteen silver pedestals, two pedestals under each board. 26 Also make bars of acacia wood: five for the boards on one side of the Dwelling, 27 five for those on the other side, and five for those at the rear, toward the west. 28 The center bar, at the middle of the boards, shall reach across from end to end. 29 Plate the boards with gold, and make gold rings on them as holders for the bars, which are also to be plated with gold.

30 You shall erect the Dwelling according to the pattern shown you on the mountain.

The Veils

31 "You shall have a veil woven of violet, purple and scarlet yarn, and of fine linen twined, with cherubim embroidered on it. 32 It is to be hung on four gold-plated columns of acacia wood, which shall have hooks of gold and shall rest on four silver pedestals. 33 Hang the veil from clasps. The ark of the commandments you shall bring inside, behind this veil which divides the holy place from the holy of holies. 34 Set the propitiatory on the ark of the commandments in the holy of holies.

35 "Outside the veil you shall place the table and the lampstand, the latter on the south side of the Dwelling, opposite the table, which is to be put on the north side. 36 For the entrance of the tent make a variegated curtain of violet, purple and scarlet yarn and of fine linen twined. 37 Make five columns of acacia wood for this curtain; have them plated with gold, with their hooks of gold; and cast five bronze pedestals for them.

The Altar of Holocausts

27 "You shall make an altar of acacia wood, on a square, five cubits long and five cubits wide; it shall be three cubits high. 2 At the four corners there are to be horns, so made that they spring directly from the altar. You shall then plate it with bronze. 3 Make pots for removing the ashes, as well as shovels, basins, forks and fire pans, all of which shall be of bronze. 4 Make a grating of bronze network for it; this to have four bronze rings, one at each of its four corners. 5 Put it down around the altar, on the ground. This network is to be half as high as the altar. 6 You shall also make poles of acacia wood for the altar, and plate them with bronze. 7 These poles are to be put through the rings, so that they

are on either side of the altar when it is carried. 8 Make the altar itself in the form of a hollow box, just as it was shown you on the mountain.

Court of the Dwelling

9 "You shall also make a court for the Dwelling. On the south side the court shall have hangings a hundred cubits long, woven of fine linen twined, 10 with twenty columns and twenty pedestals of bronze; the hooks and bands on the columns shall be of silver. 11 On the north side there shall be similar hangings, a hundred cubits long, with twenty columns and twenty pedestals of bronze; the hooks and bands on the columns shall be of silver. 12 On the west side, across the width of the court, there shall be hangings, fifty cubits long, with ten columns and ten pedestals. 13 The width of the court on the east side shall be fifty cubits. 14 On one side there shall be hangings to the extent of fifteen cubits, with three columns and three pedestals; 15 on the other side there shall be hangings to the extent of fifteen cubits, with three columns and three pedestals.

16 "At the entrance of the court there shall be a variegated curtain, twenty cubits long, woven of violet, purple and scarlet yarn and of fine linen twined. It shall have four columns and four pedestals.

17 "All the columns around the court shall have bands and hooks of silver, and pedestals of bronze. 18 The enclosure of the court is to be one hundred cubits long, fifty cubits wide, and five cubits high. Fine linen twined must be used, and the pedestals must be of bronze. 19 All the fittings of the Dwelling, whatever be their use, as well as all its tent pegs and all the tent pegs of the court, must be of bronze.

Oil for the Lamps

20 "You shall order the Israelites to bring you clear oil of crushed olives, to be used for the light, so that you may keep lamps burning

---

26, 17: *Arms:* literally, "hands." According to some, they served as "tongue and groove" to mortise the boards together; according to others, they were pegs at the bottom of the boards and fitted into sockets in the pedestals.

26, 32: *Hooks:* probably placed near the tops of the columns, to hold the rope from which the veils and curtains hung.

26, 36: *Variegated:* without definite designs such as the cherubim on the inner veil.

27, 4: *Grating:* it is not clear whether this was flush with the altar or at some small distance from it; in the latter case the space between the altar and the grating would be filled with stones and serve as a platform around the altar, which would otherwise be too high for the priest to reach conveniently.

27, 8: *Hollow:* probably filled with earth or stones when in use. Cf 20, 24f.

regularly. 21 From evening to morning Aaron and his sons shall maintain them before the LORD in the meeting tent, outside the veil which hangs in front of the commandments. This shall be a perpetual ordinance for the Israelites throughout their generations.

The Priestly Vestments

28 "From among the Israelites have your brother Aaron, together with his sons Nadab, Abihu, Eleazar and Ithamar, brought to you, that they may be my priests. 2 For the glorious adornment of your brother Aaron you shall have sacred vestments made. 3 Therefore, to the various expert workmen whom I have endowed with skill, you shall give instructions to make such vestments for Aaron as will set him apart for his sacred service as my priest. 4 These are the vestments they shall make: a breastpiece, an ephod, a robe, a brocaded tunic, a miter and a sash. In making these sacred vestments which your brother Aaron and his sons are to wear in serving as my priests, 5 they shall use gold, violet, purple and scarlet yarn and fine linen.

The Ephod and Breastpiece

6 "The ephod they shall make of gold thread and of violet, purple and scarlet yarn, embroidered on cloth of fine linen twined. 7 It shall have a pair of shoulder straps joined to its two upper ends. 8 The embroidered belt on the ephod shall extend out from it and, like it, be made on gold thread, of violet, purple and scarlet yarn, and of fine linen twined.

9 "Get two onyx stones and engrave on them the names of the sons of Israel: 10 six of their names on one stone, and the other six on the other stone, in the order of their birth. 11 As a gem-cutter engraves a seal, so shall you have the two stones

engraved with the names of the sons of Israel and then mounted in gold filigree work. 12 Set these two stones on the shoulder straps of the ephod as memorial stones of the sons of Israel. Thus Aaron shall bear their names on his shoulders as a reminder before the LORD. 13 Make filigree rosettes of gold, 14 as well as two chains of pure gold, twisted like cords, and fasten the cordlike chains to the filigree rosettes.

15 "The breastpiece of decision you shall also have made, embroidered like the ephod with gold thread and violet, purple and scarlet yarn on cloth of fine linen twined. 16 It is to be square when folded double, a span high and a span wide. 17 On it you shall mount four rows of precious stones: in the first row, a carnelian, a topaz and an emerald; 18 in the second row, a garnet, a sapphire and a beryl; 19 in the third row, a jacinth, an agate and an amethyst; 20 in the fourth row, a chrysolite, an onyx and a jasper. These stones are to be mounted in gold filigree work, 21 twelve of them to match the names of the sons of Israel, each stone engraved like a seal with the name of one of the twelve tribes.

22 "When the chains of pure gold, twisted like cords, have been made for the breastpiece, 23 you shall then make two rings of gold for it and fasten them to the two upper ends of the breastpiece. 24 The gold cords are then to be fastened to the two rings at the upper ends of the breastpiece, 25 the other two ends of the cords being fastened in front to the two filigree rosettes which are attached to the shoulder straps of the ephod. 26 Make two other rings of gold and put them on the two lower ends of the breastpiece, on its edge that faces the ephod. 27 Then make two more rings of gold and fasten them to the bottom of the shoulder straps next to where they join the

ephod in front, just above its embroidered belt. 28 Violet ribbons shall bind the rings of the breastpiece to the rings of the ephod, so that the breastpiece will stay right above the embroidered belt of the ephod and not swing loose from it.

29 "Whenever Aaron enters the sanctuary, he will thus bear the names of the sons of Israel on the breastpiece of decision over his heart as a constant reminder before the LORD. 30 In this breastpiece of decision you shall put the Urim and Thummim, that they may be over Aaron's heart whenever he enters the presence of the LORD. Thus he shall always bear the decisions for the Israelites over his heart in the LORD's presence.

Other Vestments

31 "The robe of the ephod you shall make entirely of violet material. 32 It shall have an opening for the head in the center, and around this opening there shall be a selvage, woven as at the opening of a shirt, to keep it from being torn. 33 All around the hem at the bottom you shall make pomegranates, woven of violet, purple and scarlet yarn and fine linen twined, with gold bells between them; 34 first a gold bell, then a pomegranate, and thus alternating all around the hem of the robe. 35 Aaron shall wear it when ministering, that its tinkling may be heard as he enters and leaves the LORD's presence in the sanctuary; else he will die.

36 "You shall also make a plate of pure gold and engrave on it, as on a seal engraving, "Sacred to the LORD." 37 This plate is to be tied over the miter with a violet ribbon in such a way that it rests on the front of the miter, 38 over Aaron's forehead. Since Aaron bears whatever guilt the Israelites may incur in consecrating any of their sacred gifts, this plate must always be over his forehead, so that they may find favor with the LORD.

28, 6: *Ephod:* this Hebrew word is retained in the translation because it is the technical term for a peculiar piece of the priestly vestments, the exact nature of which is uncertain. It seems to have been a sort of apron that hung from the shoulders of the priest by *shoulder straps* (v 7) and was tied around his waist by the loose ends of the attached belt (v 8).

28, 15–30: *Breastpiece:* in shape like a modern

altar burse, it was a pocketlike receptacle for holding the *Urim* and *Thummim* (v 30), and formed an integral part of the ephod, to which it was attached by an elaborate system of rings and chains. Both the ephod and its breastpiece were made of brocaded linen.

28, 17–20: The translation of the Hebrew names of some of these gems is quite conjectural.

28, 30: *Urim and Thummim:* both the meaning of these Hebrew words and the exact nature of the objects so designated are uncertain. They were apparently lots of some kind which were drawn or cast by the priest to ascertain God's decision in doubtful matters. Hence, the burse in which they were kept was called "the breastpiece of decision."

39 "The tunic of fine linen shall be brocaded. The miter shall be made of fine linen. The sash shall be of variegated work.

40 "Likewise, for the glorious adornment of Aaron's sons you shall have tunics and sashes and turbans made. 41 With these you shall clothe your brother Aaron and his sons. Anoint and ordain them, consecrating them as my priests. 42 You must also make linen drawers for them, to cover their naked flesh from their lions to their thighs. 43 Aaron and his sons shall wear them whenever they go into the meeting tent or approach the altar to minister in the sanctuary, lest they incur guilt and die. This shall be a perpetual ordinance for him and for his descendants.

Consecration of the Priests

29 "This is the rite you shall perform in consecrating them as my priests. Procure a young bull and two unblemished rams. 2 With fine wheat flour make unleavened cakes mixed with oil, and unleavened wafers spread with oil, 3 and put them in a basket. Take the basket of them along with the bullock and the two rams. 4 Aaron and his sons you shall also bring to the entrance of the meeting tent, and there wash them with water. 5 Take the vestments and clothe Aaron with the tunic, the robe of the ephod, the ephod itself, and the breastpiece, fastening the embroidered belt of the ephod around him. 6 Put the miter on his head, the sacred diadem on the miter. 7 Then take the anointing oil and anoint him with it, pouring it on his head. 8 Bring forward his sons also and clothe them with the tunics, 9 gird them with the sashes, and tie the turbans on them. Thus shall the priesthood be theirs by perpetual law, and thus shall you ordain Aaron and his sons.

Ordination Sacrifices

10 "Now bring forward the bullock in front of the meeting tent.

There Aaron and his sons shall lay their hands on its head. 11 Then slaughter the bullock before the LORD, at the entrance of the meeting tent. 12 Take some of its blood and with your finger put it on the horns of the altar. All the rest of the blood you shall pour out at the base of the altar. 13 All the fat that covers its inner organs, as well as the lobe of its liver and its two kidneys, together with the fat that is on them, you shall take and burn on the altar. 14 But the flesh and hide and offal of the bullock you must burn up outside the camp, since this is a sin offering.

15 "Then take one of the rams, and after Aaron and his sons have laid their hands on its head, 16 slaughter it. The blood you shall take and splash on all the sides of the altar. 17 Cut the ram into pieces; its inner organs and shanks you shall first wash, and then put them with the pieces and with the head. 18 The entire ram shall then be burned on the altar, since it is a holocaust, a sweet-smelling oblation to the LORD.

19 "After this take the other ram, and when Aaron and his sons have laid their hands on its head, 20 slaughter it. Some of its blood you shall take and put on the tip of Aaron's right ear and on the tips of his sons' right ears and on the thumbs of their right hands and the great toes of their right feet. Splash the rest of the blood on all the sides of the altar. 21 Then take some of the blood that is on the altar, together with some of the anointing oil, and sprinkle this on Aaron and his vestments, as well as on his sons and their vestments, that his sons and their vestments may be sacred.

22 "Now, from this ram you shall take its fat: its fatty tail, the fat that covers its inner organs, the lobe of its liver, its two kidneys with the fat that is on them, and its right thigh, since this is the ordination ram; 23 then, out of the basket of unleavened food that you have set

before the LORD, you shall take one of the loaves of bread, one of the cakes made with oil, and one of the wafers. 24 All these things you shall put into the hands of Aaron and his sons, so that they may wave them as a wave offering before the LORD. 25 After you have received them back from their hands, you shall burn them on top of the holocaust on the altar as a sweet-smelling oblation to the LORD. 26 Finally, take the breast of Aaron's ordination ram and wave it as a wave offering before the LORD; this is to be your own portion.

27 "Thus shall you set aside the breast of whatever wave offering is waved, as well as the thigh of whatever raised offering is raised up, whether this be the ordination ram or anything else belonging to Aaron or to his sons. 28 Such things are due to Aaron and his sons from the Israelites by a perpetual ordinance as a contribution. From their peace offering, too, the Israelites shall make a contribution, their contribution to the LORD.

29 "The sacred vestments of Aaron shall be passed down to his descendants, that in them they may be anointed and ordained. 30 The descendant who succeeds him as priest and who is to enter the meeting tent to minister in the sanctuary shall be clothed with them for seven days.

31 "You shall take the flesh of the ordination ram and boil it in a holy place. 32 At the entrance of the meeting tent Aaron and his sons shall eat the flesh of the ram and the bread that is in the basket. 33 They themselves are to eat of these things by which atonement was made at their ordination and consecration; but no layman may eat of them, since they are sacred. 34 If some of the flesh of the ordination sacrifice or some of the bread remains over on the next day, this remnant must be burned up; it is not to be eaten, since it is sacred. 35 Carry out all these orders in regard to Aaron and

---

28, 41: *Ordain them:* literally, "fill their hands," a technical expression used solely for the installation of priests. The phrase probably originated in the custom of placing in the priests' hands the instruments or other symbols of the sacerdotal office.

29, 22: *Fatty tail:* the thick layer of fat surround-

ing the tails of sheep and rams bred in Palestine even today. It is regarded as a choice food. Cf Lv 3, 9.

29, 24–26: *Wave offering:* the portions of a peace offering, breast and right thigh, which the officiating priest moved to and fro (waved) in the presence of

the LORD. They were reserved for Aaron and his sons.

29, 27–30: These verses are a parenthetical interruption of the ordination ritual; v 31 belongs logically immediately after v 26.

his sons just as I have given them to you.

"Seven days you shall spend in ordaining them, 36 sacrificing a bullock each day as a sin offering, to make atonement. Thus also shall you purge the altar in making atonement for it; you shall anoint it in order to consecrate it. 37 Seven days you shall spend in making atonement for the altar and in consecrating it. Then the altar will be most sacred, and whatever touches it will become sacred.

38 "Now, this is what you shall offer on the altar: two yearling lambs as the sacrifice established for each day; 39 one lamb in the morning and the other lamb at the evening twilight. 40 With the first lamb there shall be a tenth of an ephah of fine flour mixed with a fourth of a hin of oil of crushed olives and, as its libation, a fourth of a hin of wine. 41 The other lamb you shall offer at the evening twilight, with the same cereal offering and libation as in the morning. You shall offer this as a sweet-smelling oblation to the LORD. 42 Throughout your generations this established holocaust shall be offered before the LORD at the entrance of the meeting tent, where I will meet you and speak to you.

43 "There, at the altar, I will meet the Israelites; hence, it will be made sacred by my glory. 44 Thus I will consecrate the meeting tent and the altar, just as I also consecrate Aaron and his sons to be my priests. 45 I will dwell in the midst of the Israelites and will be their God. 46 They shall know that I, the LORD, am their God who brought them out of the land of Egypt, so that I, the LORD, their God, might dwell among them.

Altar of Incense

30 "For burning incense you shall make an altar of acacia wood, 2 with a square surface, a cubit long, a cubit wide, and two cubits high, with horns that spring directly from it. 3 Its grate on top, its walls on all four sides, and its horns you shall

plate with pure gold. Put a gold molding around it. 4 Underneath the molding you shall put gold rings, two on one side and two on the opposite side, as holders for the poles used in carrying it. 5 Make the poles, too, of acacia wood and plate them with gold. 6 This altar you are to place in front of the veil that hangs before the ark of the commandments where I will meet you.

7 "On it Aaron shall burn fragrant incense. Morning after morning, when he prepares the lamps, 8 and again in the evening twilight, when he lights the lamps, he shall burn incense. Throughout your generations this shall be the established incense offering before the LORD. 9 On this altar you shall not offer up any profane incense, or any holocaust or cereal offering; nor shall you pour out a libation upon it. 10 Once a year Aaron shall perform the atonement rite on its horns. Throughout your generations this atonement is to be made once a year with the blood of the atoning sin offering. This altar is most sacred to the LORD."

Census Tax

11 The LORD also said to Moses, 12 "When you take a census of the Israelites who are to be registered, each one, as he is enrolled, shall give the LORD a forfeit for his life, so that no plague may come upon them for being registered. 13 Everyone who enters the registered group must pay a half-shekel, according to the standard of the sanctuary shekel, twenty gerahs to the shekel. This payment of a half-shekel is a contribution to the LORD. 14 Everyone of twenty years or more who enters the registered group must give this contribution to the LORD. 15 The rich need not give more, nor shall the poor give less, than a half-shekel in this contribution to the LORD to pay the forfeit for their lives. 16 When you receive this forfeit money from the Israelites, you shall donate it to the service of the meeting tent, that there it may be the Israelites' reminder

before the LORD, of the forfeit paid for their lives."

The Laver

17 The LORD said to Moses, 18 "For ablutions you shall make a bronze laver with a bronze base. Place it between the meeting tent and the altar, and put water in it. 19 Aaron and his sons shall use it in washing their hands and feet. 20 When they are about to enter the meeting tent, they must wash with water, lest they die. Likewise when they approach the altar in their ministry, to offer an oblation to the LORD, 21 they must wash their hands and feet, lest they die. This shall be a perpetual ordinance for him and his descendants throughout their generations."

The Anointing Oil

22 The LORD said to Moses, 23 "Take the finest spices: five hundred shekels of free-flowing myrrh; half that amount, that is, two hundred and fifty shekels, of fragrant cinnamon; two hundred and fifty shekels of fragrant cane; 24 five hundred shekels of cassia— all according to the standard of the sanctuary shekel; together with a hin of olive oil; 25 and blend them into sacred anointing oil, perfumed ointment expertly prepared. 26 With this sacred anointing oil you shall anoint the meeting tent and the ark of the commandments, 27 the table and all its appurtenances, the lampstand and its appurtenances, the altar of incense · 28 and the altar of holocausts with all its appurtenances, and the laver with its base. 29 When you have consecrated them, they shall be most sacred; whatever touches them shall be sacred. 30 Aaron and his sons you shall also anoint and consecrate as my priests. 31 To the Israelites you shall say: As sacred anointing oil this shall belong to me throughout your generations. 32 It may not be used in any ordinary anointing of the body, nor may you make any other oil of a like mixture. It is sacred, and shall be treated as sacred by

---

29 36f: *Purge the altar:* the construction of an altar by profane hands rendered it impure. The

anointing and consecration of the altar purified it and made it sacred.

29 38–42: A parenthesis inserted into the rubrics for consecrating the altar; v 43 belongs directly after v 37.

you. 33 Whoever prepares a perfume like this, or whoever puts any of this on a layman, shall be cut off from his kinsmen."

The Incense

34 The LORD told Moses, "Take these aromatic substances: storax and onycha and galbanum, these and pure frankincense in equal parts; 35 and blend them into incense. This fragrant powder, expertly prepared, is to be salted and so kept pure and sacred. 36 Grind some of it into fine dust and put this before the commandments in the meeting tent where I will meet you. This incense shall be treated as most sacred by you. 37 You may not make incense of a like mixture for yourselves; you must treat it as sacred to the LORD. 38 Whoever makes an incense like this for his own enjoyment of its fragrance, shall be cut off from his kinsmen."

Choice of Artisans

31 The LORD said to Moses, 2 "See, I have chosen Bezalel, son of Uri, son of Hur, of the tribe of Judah, 3 and I have filled him with a divine spirit of skill and understanding and knowledge in every craft: 4 in the production of embroidery, in making things of gold, silver or bronze, 5 in cutting and mounting precious stones, in carving wood, and in every other craft. 6 As his assistant I have appointed Oholiab, son of Ahisamach, of the tribe of Dan. I have also endowed all the experts with the necessary skill to make all the things I have ordered you to make: 7 the meeting tent, the ark of the commandments with the propitiatory on top of it, all the furnishings of the tent, 8 the table with its appurtenances, the pure gold lampstand with all its appurtenances, the altar of incense, 9 the altar of holocausts with all its appurtenances, the laver with its base, 10 the service cloths, the sacred vestments for Aaron the priest, the vestments for his sons in their ministry, 11 the anointing oil, and the fragrant incense for the sanctu-

ary. All these things they shall make just as I have commanded you."

Sabbath Laws

12 The LORD said to Moses, 13 "You must also tell the Israelites: Take care to keep my sabbaths, for that is to be the token between you and me throughout the generations, to show that it is I, the LORD, who make you holy. 14 Therefore, you must keep the sabbath as something sacred. Whoever desecrates it shall be put to death. If anyone does work on that day, he must be rooted out of his people. 15 Six days there are for doing work, but the seventh day is the sabbath of complete rest, sacred to the LORD. Anyone who does work on the sabbath day shall be put to death. 16 So shall the Israelites observe the sabbath, keeping it throughout their generations as a perpetual covenant. 17 Between me and the Israelites it is to be an everlasting token; for in six days the LORD made the heavens and the earth, but on the seventh day he rested at his ease."

18 When the LORD had finished speaking to Moses on Mount Sinai, he gave him the two tablets of the commandments, the stone tablets inscribed by God's own finger.

The Golden Calf

32 When the people became aware of Moses' delay in coming down from the mountain, they gathered around Aaron and said to him, "Come, make us a god who will be our leader; as for the man Moses who brought us out of the land of Egypt, we do not know what has happened to him." 2 Aaron replied, "Have your wives and sons and daughters take off the golden earrings they are wearing, and bring them to me." 3 So all the people took off their earrings and brought them to Aaron, 4 who accepted their offering, and fashioning this gold with a graving tool, made a molten calf. Then they cried out, "This is your God, O Israel, who brought you out of the land of Egypt." 5 On seeing this, Aaron built an altar before the calf and proclaimed, "Tomorrow is a

feast of the LORD." 6 Early the next day the people offered holocausts and brought peace offerings. Then they sat down to eat and drink, and rose up to revel.

7 With that, the LORD said to Moses, "Go down at once to your people, who you brought out of the land of Egypt, for they have become depraved. 8 They have soon turned aside from the way I pointed out to them, making for themselves a molten calf and worshiping it, sacrificing to it and crying out, 'This is your God, O Israel, who brought you out of the land of Egypt!' 9 I see how stiff-necked this people is," continued the LORD to Moses. 10 "Let me alone, then, that my wrath may blaze up against them to consume them. Then I will make of you a great nation."

11 But Moses implored the LORD, his God, saying, "Why, O LORD, should your wrath blaze up against your own people, whom you brought out of the land of Egypt with such great power and with so strong a hand? 12 Why should the Egyptians say, 'With evil intent he brought them out, that he might kill them in the mountains and exterminate them from the face of the earth'? Let your blazing wrath die down; relent in punishing your people. 13 Remember your servants Abraham, Isaac and Israel, and how you swore to them by your own self, saying, 'I will make your descendants as numerous as the stars in the sky; and all this land that I promised, I will give your descendants as their perpetual heritage.'" 14 So the LORD relented in the punishment he had threatened to inflict on his people.

15 Moses then turned and came down the mountain with the two tablets of the commandments in his hands, tablets that were written on both sides, front and back; 16 tablets that were made by God, having inscriptions on them that were engraved by God himself. 17 Now, when Joshua heard the noise of the people shouting, he said to Moses, "That sounds like a battle in the camp." 18 But Moses answered,

---

31, 10: *The service cloths:* so the Greek. They were perhaps the colored cloths mentioned in Nm 4, 4–15.
32, 5: *The calf . . . a feast of the Lord:* from this

it is clear that the golden calf was intended as an image, not of a false god, but of the LORD himself, his strength being symbolized by the strength of a

young bull. The Israelites, however, had been forbidden to represent the LORD under any visible form. Cf 20, 4.

"It does not sound like cries of victory, nor does it sound like cries of defeat; the sounds that I hear are cries of revelry." 19 As he drew near the camp, he saw the calf and the dancing. With that, Moses' wrath flared up, so that he threw the tablets down and broke them on the base of the mountain. 20 Taking the calf they had made, he fused it in the fire and then ground it down to powder, which he scattered on the water and made the Israelites drink.

21 Moses asked Aaron, "What did this people ever do to you that you should lead them into so grave a sin?" Aaron replied, "Let not my lord be angry. 22 You know well enough how prone the people are to evil. 23 They said to me, 'Make us a god to be our leader; as for the man Moses who brought us out of the land of Egypt, we do not know what has happened to him.' 24 So I told them, 'Let anyone who has gold jewelry take it off.' They gave it to me, and I threw it into the fire, and this calf came out."

25 When Moses realized that, to the scornful joy of their foes, Aaron had let the people run wild, 26 he stood at the gate of the camp and cried, "Whoever is for the LORD, let him come to me!" All the Levites then rallied to him, 27 and he told them, "Thus says the LORD, the God of Israel: Put your sword on your hip, every one of you! Now go up and down the camp, from gate to gate, and slay your own kinsmen, your friends and neighbors!" 28 The Levites carried out the command of Moses, and that day there fell about three thousand of the people. 29 Then Moses said, "Today you have been dedicated to the LORD, for you were against your own sons and kinsmen, to bring a blessing upon yourselves this day."

The Atonement

30 On the next day Moses said to the people, "You have committed a grave sin. I will go up to the LORD,

then; perhaps I may be able to make atonement for your sin." 31 So Moses went back to the LORD and said, "Ah, this people has indeed committed a grave sin in making a god of gold for themselves! 32 If you would only forgive their sin! If you will not, then strike me out of the book that you have written." 33 The LORD answered, "Him only who has sinned against me will I strike out of my book. 34 Now, go and lead the people whither I have told you. My angel will go before you. When it is time for me to punish, I will punish them for their sin."

35 Thus the LORD smote the people for having had Aaron make the calf for them.

33 The LORD told Moses, "You and the people whom you have brought up from the land of Egypt, are to go up from here to the land which I swore to Abraham, Isaac and Jacob I would give to their descendants. 2 Driving out the Canaanites, Amorites, Hittites, Perizzites, Hivites and Jebusites, I will send an angel before you 3 to the land flowing with milk and honey. But I myself will not go up in your company, because you are a stiff-necked people; otherwise I might exterminate you on the way." 4 When the people heard this bad news, they went into mourning, and no one wore his ornaments.

5 The LORD said to Moses, "Tell the Israelites: You are a stiff-necked people. Were I to go up in your company even for a moment, I would exterminate you. Take off your ornaments, therefore; I will then see what I am to do with you." 6 So, from Mount Horeb onward, the Israelites laid aside their ornaments.

Moses' Intimacy with God

7 The tent, which was called the meeting tent, Moses used to pitch at some distance away, outside the camp. Anyone who wished to consult the LORD would go to this meeting

tent outside the camp. 8 Whenever Moses went out to the tent, the people would all rise and stand at the entrace of their own tents, watching Moses until he entered the tent. 9 As Moses entered the tent, the column of cloud would come down and stand at its entrance while the LORD spoke with Moses. 10 On seeing the column of cloud stand at the entrance of the tent, all the people would rise and worship at the entrance of their own tents. 11 The LORD used to speak to Moses face to face, as one man speaks to another. Moses would then return to the camp, but his young assistant, Joshua, son of Nun, would not move out of the tent.

12 Moses said to the LORD, "You, indeed, are telling me to lead this people on; but you have not let me know whom you will send with me. Yet you have said, 'You are my intimate friend,' and also, 'You have found favor with me.' 13 Now, if I have found favor with you, do let me know your ways so that, in knowing you, I may continue to find favor with you. Then, too, this nation is, after all, your own people." 14 "I myself," the LORD answered, "will go along, to give you rest." 15 Moses replied, "If you are not going yourself, do not make us go up from here. 16 For how can it be known that I, your people and I, have found favor with you, except by your going with us? Then we, your people and I will be singled out from every other people on the earth." 17 The LORD said to Moses, "This request, too, which you have just made, I will carry out, because you have found favor with me and you are my intimate friend."

18 Then Moses said, "Do let me see your glory!" 19 He answered, "I will make all my beauty pass before you, and in your presence I will pronouce my name, 'LORD'; I who show favors to whom I will, I who grant mercy to whom I will. 20 But my face you cannot see, for no man

---

32, 20: *The water:* the stream that flowed down Mount Sinai. Cf Dt 9, 21.

32, 27: *Slay your own kinsmen . . . :* those who were especially guilty of the idolatry.

32, 29: *Dedicated to the Lord:* because of their zeal for the true worship of the Lord, the Levites were chosen to be special ministers of the ritual

service. However, the meaning of the Hebrew here is somewhat disputed.

32, 32: *The book that you have written:* the list of God's intimate friends. In a similar sense St. Paul wished to be anathema from Christ for the sake of his brethren. Cf Rom 9, 3.

33, 7–11: *The meeting tent* is mentioned here by

anticipation; its actual construction is described in the following chapters.

33, 14: *I myself:* literally, "my face," that is, "my presence." *To give you rest:* in the Promised Land; some understand, "to put your mind at rest"; others, by a slight emendation in the text, render, "to lead you."

sees me and still lives. 21 Here," continued the LORD, "is a place near me where you shall station yourself on the rock. 22 When my glory passes I will set you in the hollow of the rock and will cover you with my hand until I have passed by. 23 Then I will remove my hand, so that you may see my back; but my face is not to be seen."

Renewal of the Tablets

34 The LORD said to Moses, "Cut two stone tablets like the former, that I may write on them the commandments which were on the former tablets that you broke. 2 Get ready for tomorrow morning, when you are to go up Mount Sinai and there present yourself to me on the top of the mountain. 3 No one shall come up with you, and no one is even to be seen on any part of the mountain; even the flocks and the herds are not to go grazing toward this mountain." 4 Moses then cut two stone tablets like the former, and early the next morning he went up Mount Sinai as the LORD had commanded him, taking along the two stone tablets.

5 Having come down in a cloud, the LORD stood with him there and proclaimed his name, "LORD." 6 Thus the LORD passed before him and cried out, "The LORD, the LORD, a merciful and gracious God, slow to anger and rich in kindness and fidelity, 7 continuing his kindness for a thousand generations, and forgiving wickedness and crime and sin; yet not declaring the guilty guiltless, but punishing children and grandchildren to the third and fourth generation for their fathers' wickedness!" 8 Moses at once bowed down to the ground in worship. 9 Then he said, "If I find favor with you, O Lord, do come along in our company. This is indeed a stiff-necked people; yet pardon our wickedness and sins, and receive us as your own."

Religious Laws

10 "Here, then," said the LORD, "is the covenant I will make. Before the eyes of all your people I will work such marvels as have never been wrought in any nation anywhere on earth, so that this people among whom you live may see how awe-inspiring are the deeds which I, the LORD, will do at your side. 11 But you, on your part, must keep the commandments I am giving you today.

"I will drive out before you the Amorites, Canaanites, Hittites, Perizzites, Hivites and Jebusites. 12 Take care, therefore, not to make a covenant with these inhabitants of the land that you are to enter; else they will become a snare among you. 13 Tear down their altars; smash their sacred pillars, and cut down their sacred poles. 14 You shall not worship any other god, for the LORD is 'the Jealous One'; a jealous God is he. 15 Do not make a covenant with the inhabitants of that land; else, when they render their wanton worship to their gods and sacrifice to them, one of them may invite you and you may partake of his sacrifice. 16 Neither shall you take their daughters as wives for your sons; otherwise, when their daughters render their wanton worship to their gods, they will make your sons do the same.

17 "You shall not make for yourselves molten gods.

18 "You shall keep the feast of Unleavened Bread. For seven days at the prescribed time in the month of Abib you are to eat unleavened bread, as I commanded you; for in the month of Abib you came out of Egypt.

19 "To me belongs every first-born male that opens the womb among all your livestock, whether in the herd or in the flock. 20 The firstling of an ass you shall redeem with one of the flock; if you do not redeem it, you must break its neck.

The first-born among your sons you shall redeem.

"No one shall appear before me empty-handed.

21 "For six days you may work, but on the seventh day you shall rest; on that day you must rest even during the seasons of plowing and harvesting.

22 "You shall keep the feast of Weeks with the first of the wheat harvest; likewise, the feast at the fruit harvest at the close of the year. 23 Three times a year all your men shall appear before the Lord, the LORD God of Israel. 24 Since I will drive out the nations before you to give you a large territory, there will be no one to covet your land when you go up three times a year to appear before the LORD, your God.

25 "You shall not offer me the blood of sacrifice with leavened bread, nor shall the sacrifice of the Passover feast be kept overnight for the next day.

26 "The choicest first fruits of your soil you shall bring to the house of the LORD, your God.

"You shall not boil a kid in its mother's milk."

Radiance of Moses' Face

27 Then the LORD said to Moses, "Write down these words, for in accordance with them I have made a covenant with you and with Israel." 28 So Moses stayed there with the LORD for forty days and forty nights, without eating any food or drinking any water, and he wrote on the tablets the words of the covenant, the ten commandments.

29 As Moses came down from Mount Sinai with the two tablets of the commandments in his hands, he did not know that the skin of his face had become radiant while he conversed with the LORD. 30 When Aaron, then, and the other Israelites saw Moses and noticed how radiant the skin of his face had become, they were afraid to come near him. 31 Only after Moses called to them

---

33, 23: *You may see my back:* man can see God's glory as reflected in creation, but his "face," that is, God as he is in himself, mortal man cannot behold. Cf 1 Cor 13, 12.
34, 13: *Sacred poles:* "Ashera" was the name of a Canaanite goddess. In her honor wooden poles

(asherot) were erected, just as stone pillars (massebot) were erected in honor of the god Baal. Both were placed near the altar in a Canaanite shrine.
34, 14: *The Lord is "the Jealous One":* see note on 20, 5. Some, by a slight emendation, render, "The LORD is jealous for his name." Cf Ez 39, 25.

34, 22: *Feast of Weeks:* the festival of thanksgiving for the harvest, celebrated seven weeks or fifty days after the beginning of the harvest. It was also called Pentecost (fiftieth) and coincided with the giving of the law on Mount Sinai, fifty days after the offering of the first fruits (Lv 23, 10f; Dt 16, 9).

did Aaron and all the rulers of the community come back to him. Moses then spoke to them. 32 Later on, all the Israelites came up to him, and he enjoined on them all that the LORD had told him on Mount Sinai. 33 When he finished speaking with them, he put a veil over his face. 34 Whenever Moses entered the presence of the LORD to converse with him, he removed the veil until he came out again. On coming out, he would tell the Israelites all that had been commanded. 35 Then the Israelites would see that the skin of Moses' face was radiant; so he would again put the veil over his face until he went in to converse with the LORD.

Sabbath Regulations

35 Moses assembled the whole Israelite community and said to them, "This is what the LORD has commanded to be done. 2 On six days work may be done, but the seventh day shall be sacred to you as the sabbath of complete rest to the LORD. Anyone who does work on that day shall be put to death. 3 You shall not even light a fire in any of your dwellings on the sabbath day."

Collection of Materials

4 Moses told the whole Israelite community, "This is what the LORD has commanded: 5 Take up among you a collection for the LORD. Everyone, as his heart prompts him, shall bring a contribution to the LORD, gold, silver and bronze; 6 violet, purple and scarlet yarn; fine linen and goat hair; 7 rams' skins dyed red, and tahash skins; acacia wood; 8 oil for the light; spices for the anointing oil and for the fragrant incense; 9 onyx stones and other gems for mounting on the ephod and on the breastpiece.

Call for Artisans

10 "Let every expert among you come and make all that the LORD has commanded: the Dwelling, 11 with its tent, its covering, its clasps, its boards, its bars, its columns and its pedestals; 12 the ark, with its poles, the propitiatory, and the curtain veil; 13 the table, with its poles and all its appurtenances, and the showbread; 14 the lampstand, with its appurtenances, the lamps, and the oil for the light; 15 the altar of incense, with its poles; the anointing oil, and the fragrant incense; the entrance curtain for the entrance of the Dwelling; 16 the altar of holocausts, with its bronze grating, its poles, and all its appurtenances; the laver, with its base; 17 the hangings of the court, with their columns and pedestals; the curtain for the entrance of the court; 18 tent pegs for the Dwelling and for the court, with their ropes; 19 the service cloths for use in the sanctuary; the sacred vestments for Aaron, the priest, and the vestments worn by his sons in their ministry."

The Contribution

20 When the whole Israelite community left Moses' presence, 21 everyone, as his heart suggested and his spirit prompted, brought a contribution to the LORD for the construction of the meeting tent, for all its services, and for the sacred vestments. 22 Both the men and the women, all as their heart prompted them, brought brooches, earrings, rings, necklaces and various other gold articles. Everyone who could presented an offering of gold to the LORD. 23 Everyone who happened to have violet, purple or scarlet yarn, fine linen or goat hair, rams' skins dyed red or tahash skins, brought them. 24 Whoever could make a contribution of silver or bronze offered it to the LORD; and everyone who happened to have acacia wood for any part of the work, brought it. 25 All the women who were expert spinners brought hand-spun violet, purple and scarlet yarn and fine linen thread. 26 All the women who possessed the skill, spun goat hair. 27 The princes brought onyx stones and other gems for mounting on the ephod and on the breastpiece; 28 as well as spices, and oil for the light, anointing oil, and fragrant incense. 29 Every Israelite man and woman brought to the LORD such voluntary offerings as they thought best, for the various kinds of work which the LORD had commanded Moses to have done.

The Artisans

30 Moses said to the Israelites, "See, the LORD has chosen Bezalel, son of Uri, son of Hur, of the tribe of Judah, 31 and has filled him with a divine spirit of skill and understanding and knowledge in every craft: 32 in the production of embroidery, in making things of gold, silver or bronze, 33 in cutting and mounting precious stones, in carving wood, and in every other craft. 34 He has also given both him and Oholiab, son of Ahisamach, of the tribe of Dan, the ability to teach others. 35 He has endowed them will skill to execute all types of work: engraving, embroidering, the making of variegated cloth of violet, purple and scarlet yarn and fine linen thread, weaving, and all other arts and crafts.

36 "Bezalel, therefore, will set to work with Oholiab and with all the experts whom the LORD has endowed with skill and understanding in knowing how to execute all the work for the service of the sanctuary, just as the LORD has commanded."

2 Moses then called Bezalel and Oholiab and all the other experts whom the LORD had endowed with skill, men whose hearts moved them to come and take part in the work. 3 They received from Moses all the contributions which the Israelites had brought for establishing the service of the sanctuary. Still, morning after morning the people continued to bring their voluntary offerings to Moses. 4 Thereupon the experts who were executing the various kinds of work for the sanctuary, all left the work they were doing, 5 and told Moses, "The people are bringing much more than is needed to carry out the work which the LORD has commanded us to do." 6 Moses, therefore, ordered a proclamation to be made throughout the camp: "Let neither man nor woman

---

34, 33: *He put a veil over his face:* St. Paul sees in this a symbol of the failure of the Jews to recognize Jesus as the promised Messiah: the true spiritual meaning of the writings of Moses and the prophets is still veiled from the unbelieving Jews. Cf 2 Cor 3, 7–18.

make any more contributions for the sanctuary." So the people stopped bringing their offerings; 7 there was already enough at hand, in fact, more than enough, to complete the work to be done.

The Tent Cloth and Coverings

8 The various experts who were executing the work, made the Dwelling with its ten sheets woven of fine linen twined, having cherubim embroidered on them with violet, purple and scarlet yarn. 9 The length of each sheet was twenty-eight cubits, and the width four cubits; all the sheets were of the same size. 10 Five of the sheets were sewed together, edge to edge; and the same for the other five. 11 Loops of violet yarn were made along the edge of the end sheet in the first set, and the same along the edge of the end sheet in the second set. 12 Fifty loops were thus put on one inner sheet, and fifty loops on the inner sheet in the other set, with the loops directly opposite each other. 13 Then fifty clasps of gold were made, with which the sheets were joined so that the Dwelling formed one whole.

14 Sheets of goat hair were also woven as a tent over the Dwelling. Eleven such sheets were made. 15 The length of each sheet was thirty cubits and the width four cubits; all eleven sheets were of the same size. 16 Five of these sheets were sewed edge to edge into one set; and the other six sheets into another set. 17 Fifty loops were made along the edge of the end sheet in one set, and fifty loops along the edge of the corresponding sheet in the other set. 18 Fifty bronze clasps were made with which the tent was joined so that it formed one whole. 19 A covering for the tent was made of rams' skins dyed red, and above that, a covering of tahash skins.

The Boards

20 Boards of acacia wood were made as walls for the Dwelling. 21 The length of each board was ten cubits, and the width one and a half cubits. 22 Each board had two arms, fastening them in line. In this way all the boards of the Dwelling were made. 23 They were set up as

follows: twenty boards on the south side, 24 with forty silver pedestals under the twenty boards, so that there were two pedestals under each board, at its two arms; 25 twenty boards on the other side of the Dwelling, the north side, 26 with their forty silver pedestals, two under each board; 27 six boards at the rear of the Dwelling, to the west; 28 and two boards at the corners in the rear of the Dwelling. 29 These were double at the bottom, and likewise double at the top, to the first ring. That is how both boards in the corners were made. 30 Thus, there were in the rear eight boards, with their sixteen silver pedestals, two pedestals under each board. 31 Bars of acacia wood were also made, five for the boards on one side of the Dwelling, 32 five for those on the other side, and five for those at the rear, to the west. 33 The center bar, at the middle of the boards, was made to reach across from end to end. 34 The boards were plated with gold, and gold rings were made on them as holders for the bars, which were also plated with gold.

The Veil

35 The veil was woven of violet, purple and scarlet yarn, and of fine linen twined, with cherubim embroidered on it. 36 Four gold-plated columns of acacia wood, with gold hooks, were made for it, and four silver pedestals were cast for them.

37 The curtain for the entrance of the tent was made of violet, purple and scarlet yarn, and of fine linen twined, woven in a variegated manner. 38 Its five columns, with their hooks as well as their capitals and bands, were plated with gold; their five pedestals were of bronze.

The Ark

37 Bezalel made the ark of acacia wood, two and a half cubits long, one and a half cubits wide, and one and a half cubits high. 2 The inside and outside were plated with gold, and a molding of gold was put around it. 3 Four gold rings were cast and put on its four supports, two rings for one side and two for the opposite side. 4 Poles of acacia

wood were made and plated with gold; 5 these were put through the rings on the sides of the ark, for carrying it.

6 The propitiatory was made of pure gold, two and a half cubits long and one and a half cubits wide. 7 Two cherubim of beaten gold were made for the two ends of the propitiatory, 8 one cherub fastened at one end, the other at the other end, springing directly from the propitiatory at its two ends. 9 The cherubim had their wings spread out above, covering the propitiatory with them. They were turned toward each other, but with their faces looking toward the propitiatory.

The Table

10 The table was made of acacia wood, two cubits long, one cubit wide, and one and a half cubits high. 11 It was plated with pure gold, and a molding of gold was put around it. 12 A frame a handbreadth high was also put around it, with a molding of gold around the frame. 13 Four rings of gold were cast for it and fastened, one at each of the four corners. 14 The rings were alongside the frame as holders for the poles to carry the table. 15 These poles were made of acacia wood and plated with gold. 16 The vessels that were set on the table, its plates and cups, as well as its pitchers and bowls for puring libations, were of pure gold.

The Lampstand

17 The lampstand was made of pure beaten gold—its shaft and branches as well as its cups and knobs and petals springing directly from it. 18 Six branches extended from its sides, three branches on one side and three on the other. 19 On one branch there were three cups, shaped like almond blossoms, each with its knob and petals; on the opposite branch there were three cups, shaped like almond blossoms, each with its knob and petals; and so for the six branches that extended from the lampstand. 20 On the shaft there were four cups, shaped like almond blossoms, with their knobs and petals, 21 including a knob below each of the three pairs

of branches that extended from the lampstand. 22 The knobs and branches sprang so directly from it that the whole formed but a single piece of pure beaten gold. 23 Its seven lamps, as well as its trimming shears and trays, were made of pure gold. 24 A talent of pure gold was used for the lampstand and its various appurtenances.

The Altar of Incense

25 The altar of incense was made of acacia wood, on a square, a cubit long, a cubit wide, and two cubits high, having horns that sprang directly from it. 26 Its grate on top, its walls on all four sides, and its horns were plated with pure gold; and a molding of gold was put around it. 27 Underneath the molding gold rings were placed, two on one side and two on the opposite side, as holders for the poles to carry it. 28 The poles, too, were made of acacia wood and plated with gold.

29 The sacred anointing oil and the fragrant incense were prepared in their pure form by a perfumer.

The Altar of Holocausts

38 The altar of holocausts was made of acacia wood, on a square, five cubits long and five cubits wide; its height was three cubits. 2 At the four corners horns were made that sprang directly from the altar. The whole was plated with bronze. 3 All the utensils of the altar, the pots, shovels, basins, forks and fire pans, were likewise made of bronze. 4 A grating of bronze network was made for the altar and placed round it, on the ground, half as high as the altar itself. 5 Four rings were cast for the four corners of the bronze grating, as holders for the poles, 6 which were made of acacia wood and plated with bronze. 7 The poles were put through the rings on the sides of the altar for carrying it. The altar was made in the form of a hollow box.

8 The bronze laver, with its bronze base, was made from the mirrors of the women who served at the entrance of the meeting tent.

38, 8: The reflecting surface of ancient mirrors was usually of polished bronze. *The women who served:* cf 1 Sm 2, 22.

The Court

9 The court was made as follows. On the south side of the court there were hangings, woven of fine linen twined, a hundred cubits long, 10 with twenty columns and twenty pedestals of bronze, the hooks and bands of the columns being of silver. 11 On the north side there were similar hangings, one hundred cubits long, with twenty columns and twenty pedestals of bronze, the hooks and bands of the columns being of silver. 12 On the west side there were hangings, fifty cubits long, with ten columns and ten pedestals, the hooks and bands of the columns being of silver. 13 On the east side the court was fifty cubits long. 14 Toward one side there were hangings to the extent of fifteen cubits, with three columns and three pedestals; 15 toward the other side, beyond the entrance of the court, there were likewise hangings to the extent of fifteen cubits, with three columns and three pedestals. 16 The hangings on all sides of the court were woven of fine linen twined. 17 The pedestals of the columns were of bronze, while the hooks and bands of the columns were of silver; the capitals were silver-plated, and all the columns of the court were banded with silver.

18 At the entrance of the court there was a variegated curtain, woven of violet, purple and scarlet yarn and of fine linen twined, twenty cubits long and five cubits wide, in keeping with the hangings of the court. 19 There were four columns and four pedestals of bronze for it, while their hooks were of silver. 20 All the tent pegs for the Dwelling and for the court around it were of bronze.

Amount of Metal Used

21 The following is an account of the various amounts used on the Dwelling, the Dwelling of the commandments, drawn up at the command of Moses by the Levites under the direction of Ithamar, son of Aaron the priest. 22 However, it was Bezalel, son of Uri, son of Hur, of the tribe of Judah, who made all that the LORD commanded Moses,

23 and he was assisted by Oholiab, son of Ahisamach, of the tribe of Dan, who was an engraver, an embroiderer, and a weaver of variegated cloth of violet, purple and scarlet yarn and of fine linen.

24 All the gold used in the entire construction of the sanctuary, having previously been given as an offering, amounted to twenty-nine talents and seven hundred ånd thirty shekels, according to the standard of the sanctuary shekel. 25 The amount of the silver received from the community was one hundred talents and one thousand seven hundred and seventy-five shekels, according to the standard of the sanctuary shekel; 26 one bekah apiece, that is, a half-shekel apiece, according to the standard of the sanctuary shekel, was received from every man of twenty years or more who entered the registered group; the number of these was six hundred and three thousand five hundred and fifty men. 27 One hundred talents of silver were used for casting the pedestals of the sanctuary and the pedestals of the veil, one talent for each pedestal, or one hundred talents for the one hundred pedestals. 28 The remaining one thousand seven hundred and seventy-five shekels were used for making the hooks on the columns, for plating the capitals, and for banding them with silver. 29 The bronze, given as an offering, amounted to seventy talents and two thousand four hundred shekels. 30 With this were made the pedestals at the entrance of the meeting tent, the bronze altar with its bronze gratings and all the appurtenances of the altar, 31 the pedestals around the court, the pedestals at the entrance of the court, and all the tent pegs for the Dwelling and for the court around it.

The Vestments

39 With violet, purple and scarlet yarn were woven the service cloths for use in the sanctuary, as well as the sacred vestments for Aaron, as the LORD had commanded Moses.

2 The ephod was woven of gold thread and of violet, purple and scarlet yarn and of fine linen twined. 3 Gold was first hammered into

gold leaf and then cut up into threads, which were woven with the violet, purple and scarlet yarn into an embroidered pattern on the fine linen. 4 Shoulder straps were made for it and joined to its two upper ends. 5 The embroidered belt on the ephod extended out from it, and like it, was made of gold thread, of violet, purple and scarlet yarn, and of fine linen twined, as the LORD had commanded Moses. 6 The onyx stones were prepared and mounted in gold filigree work; they were engraved like seal engravings with the names of the sons of Israel. 7 These stones were set on the shoulder straps of the ephod as memorial stones of the sons of Israel, just as the LORD had commanded Moses.

8 The breastpiece was embroidered like the ephod, with gold thread and violet, purple and scarlet yarn on cloth of fine linen twined. 9 It was square and folded double, a span high and a span wide in its folded form. 10 Four rows of precious stones were mounted on it: in the first row a carnelian, a topaz and an emerald; 11 in the second row, a garnet, a sapphire and a beryl; 12 in the third row a jacinth, an agate and an amethyst; 13 in the fourth row a chrysolite, an onyx and a jasper. They were mounted in gold filigree work. 14 These stones were twelve, to match the names of the sons of Israel, and each stone was engraved like a seal with the name of one of the twelve tribes.

15 Chains of pure gold, twisted like cords, were made for the breastpiece, 16 together with two gold filigree rosettes and two gold rings. The two rings were fastened to the two upper ends of the breastpiece. 17 The two gold chains were then fastened to the two rings at the ends of the breastpiece. 18 The other two ends of the two chains were fastened in front to the two filigree rosettes, which were attached to the shoulder straps of the ephod. 19 Two other gold rings were made and put on the two lower ends of the breastpiece, on the edge facing the ephod. 20 Two more gold rings

were made and fastened to the bottom of the two shoulder straps next to where they joined the ephod in front, just above its embroidered belt. 21 Violet ribbons bound the rings of the breastpiece to the rings of the ephod, so that the breastpiece stayed right above the embroidered belt of the ephod and did not swing loose from it. All this was just as the LORD had commanded Moses.

The Other Vestments

22 The robe of the ephod was woven entirely of violet yarn, 23 with an opening in its center like the opening of a shirt, with selvage around the opening to keep it from being torn. 24 At the hem of the robe pomegranates were made of violet, purple and scarlet yarn and of fine linen twined; 25 bells of pure gold were also made and put between the pomegranates all around the hem of the robe: 26 first a bell, then a pomegranate, and thus alternating all around the hem of the robe which was to be worn in performing the ministry—all this, just as the LORD had commanded Moses.

27 For Aaron and his sons there were also woven tunics of fine linen; 28 the miter of fine linen; the ornate turbans of fine linen; drawers of linen [of fine linen twined]; 29 and sashes of variegated work made of fine linen twined and of violet, purple and scarlet yarn, as the LORD had commanded Moses. 30 The plate of the sacred diadem was made of pure gold and inscribed, as on a seal engraving: "Sacred to the LORD." 31 It was tied over the miter with a violet ribbon, as the LORD had commanded Moses.

Presentation of the Work to Moses

32 Thus the entire work of the Dwelling of the meeting tent was completed. The Israelites did the work just as the LORD had commanded Moses. 33 They then brought to Moses the Dwelling, the tent with all its appurtenances, the clasps, the boards, the bars, the columns, the pedestals, 34 the covering of rams' skins dyed red, the covering of tahash skins, the curtain veil; 35 the ark of the commandments with

its poles, the propitiatory, 36 the table with all its appurtenances and the showbread, 37 the pure gold lampstand with its lamps set up on it and with all its appurtenances, the oil for the light, 38 the golden altar, the anointing oil, the fragrant incense; the curtain for the entrance of the tent, 39 the altar of bronze with its bronze grating, its poles and all its appurtenances, the laver with its base, 40 the hangings of the court with their columns and pedestals, the curtain for the entrance of the court with its ropes and tent pegs, all the equipment for the service of the Dwelling of the meeting tent; 41 the service cloths for use in the sanctuary, the sacred vestments for Aaron the priest, and the vestments to be worn by his sons in their ministry. 42 The Israelites had carried out all the work just as the LORD had commanded Moses. 43 So when Moses saw that all the work was done just as the LORD had commanded, he blessed them.

Erection of the Dwelling

40 Then the LORD said to Moses, 2 "On the first day of the first month you shall erect the Dwelling of the meeting tent. 3 Put the ark of the commandments in it, and screen off the ark with the veil. 4 Bring in the table and set it. Then bring in the lampstand and set up the lamps on it. 5 Put the golden altar of incense in front of the ark of the commandments, and hang the curtain at the entrance of the Dwelling. 6 Put the altar of holocausts in front of the entrance of the Dwelling of the meeting tent. 7 Place the laver between the meeting tent and the altar, and put water in it. 8 Set up the court round about, and put the curtain at the entrance of the court.

9 "Take the anointing oil and anoint the Dwelling and everything in it, consecrating it and all its furnishings, so that it will be sacred. 10 Anoint the altar of holocausts and all its appurtenances, consecrating it, so that it will be most sacred. 11 Likewise, anoint the laver with its base, and thus consecrate it.

12 "Then bring Aaron and his sons to the entrance of the meeting tent, and there wash them with water.

40, 2: *On the first day of the first month:* almost a year after the departure of the Israelites from Egypt. Cf v 17.

13 Clothe Aaron with the sacred vestments and anoint him, thus consecrating him as my priest. 14 Bring forward his sons also, and clothe them with the tunics. 15 As you have anointed their father, anoint them also as my priests. Thus, by being anointed, shall they receive a perpetual priesthood throughout all future generations."

16 Moses did exactly as the LORD had commanded him. 17 On the first day of the first month of the second year the Dwelling was erected. 18 It was Moses who erected the Dwelling. He placed its pedestals, set up its boards, put in it bars, and set up its columns. 19 He spread the tent over the Dwelling and put the covering on top of the tent, as the LORD had commanded him. 20 He took the commandments and put them in the ark; he placed poles alongside the ark and set the propitiatory upon it. 21 He brought the ark into the Dwelling and hung the curtain veil, thus screening off the ark of the commandments, as the LORD

had commanded him. 22 He put the table in the meeting tent, on the north side of the Dwelling, outside the veil, 23 and arranged the bread on it before the LORD, as the LORD had commanded him. 24 He placed the lampstand in the meeting tent, opposite the table, on the south side of the Dwelling, 25 and he set up the lamps before the LORD, as the LORD had commanded him. 26 He placed the golden altar in the meeting tent, in front of the veil, 27 and on it he burned fragrant incense, as the LORD had commanded him. 28 He hung the curtain at the entrance of the Dwelling. 29 He put the altar of holocausts in front of the entrance of the Dwelling of the meeting tent, and offered holocausts and cereal offerings on it, as the LORD had commanded him. 30 He placed the laver between the meeting tent and the altar, and put water in it for washing. 31 Moses and Aaron and his sons used to wash their hands and feet there, 32 for they washed themselves whenever they went into the

meeting tent or approached the altar, as the LORD had commanded Moses. 33 Finally, he set up the court around the Dwelling and the altar and hung the curtain at the entrance of the court. Thus Moses finished all the work.

God's Presence in the Dwelling

34 Then the cloud covered the meeting tent, and the glory of the LORD filled the Dwelling. 35 Moses could not enter the meeting tent, because the cloud settled down upon it and the glory of the LORD filled the Dwelling. 36 Whenever the cloud rose from the Dwelling, the Israelites would set out on their journey. 37 But if the cloud did not lift, they would not go forward; only when it lifted did they go forward. 38 In the daytime the cloud of the LORD was seen over the Dwelling; whereas at night, fire was seen in the cloud by the whole house of Israel in all the stages of their journey.

Leviticus

RITUAL OF SACRIFICES

Holocausts

THE LORD called Moses, and from the meeting tent gave him this message: 2 "Speak to the Israelites and tell them: When any one of you wishes to bring an animal offering to the LORD, such an offering must be from the herd or from the flock. 3 "If his holocaust offering is from the herd, it must be a male without blemish. To find favor with the LORD, he shall bring it to the entrance of the meeting tent 4 and there lay his hand on the head of the holocaust, so that it may be acceptable to make atonement for him. 5 He shall then slaughter the bull before the LORD, but Aaron's sons, the priests, shall offer up its blood by splashing it on the sides of the altar which is at the entrance of the meeting tent. 6 Then he shall skin the holocaust and cut it up into pieces. 7 After Aaron's sons, the priests, have put some burning embers on the altar and laid some wood on them, 8 they shall lay the pieces of meat, together with the head and the suet, on top of the wood and embers on the altar. 9 The inner organs and the shanks, however, the offerer shall first wash with water. The priest shall then burn the whole offering on the altar as a holocaust, a sweet-smelling oblation to the LORD.

10 "If his holocaust offering is from the flock, that is, a sheep or a goat, he must bring a male without blemish. 11 This he shall slaughter before the LORD at the north side of the altar. Then Aaron's sons, the priests, shall splash its blood on the sides of the altar. 12 When the offerer has cut it up into pieces, the priest shall lay these, together with the head and suet, on top of the wood and the fire on the altar. 13 The inner organs and the shanks, however, the offerer shall first wash with water. The priest shall offer them up and then burn the whole offering on the altar as a holocaust, a sweet-smelling oblation to the LORD.

14 "If he offers a bird as a holocaust to the LORD, he shall choose a turtledove or a pigeon as his offering. 15 Having brought it to the altar where it is to be burned, the priest shall snap its head loose and squeeze out its blood against the side of the altar. 16 Its crop and feathers shall be removed and thrown on the ash heap at the east side of the altar. 17 Then, having split the bird down the middle without separating the halves, the priest shall burn it on the altar, over the wood on the fire, as a holocaust, a sweet-smelling oblation to the LORD.

Cereal Offerings

2 "When anyone wishes to bring a cereal offering to the LORD, his offering must consist of fine flour. He shall pour oil on it and put frankincense over it. 2 When he has brought it to Aaron's sons, the priests, one of them shall take a handful of this fine flour and oil, together with all the frankincense, and this he shall burn on the altar as a token

---

1, 2: *From the herd or from the flock:* the only animals which could be used as sacrificial victims were either of the bovine class (bulls, cows and calves) or the ovine class (sheep and lambs, goats and kids). Excluded, therefore, were not only all wild animals, but also such "unclean" domestic animals as the camel and the ass. See note on 11, 1ff.

1, 3: *Holocaust:* from the Greek word meaning "wholly burned," this is the technical term for the special type of sacrifice in which an entire animal except its hide was consumed in the fire on the altar. The primary purpose of this complete gift was to render glory and praise to God.

2, 2: *Token offering:* literally, "reminder." Instead of burning the whole cereal offering, they burned only this part of it on the altar; it thus corresponded to the fat of the peace offering. See note on 3, 1.

offering, a sweet-smelling oblation to the LORD. 3 The rest of the cereal offering belongs to Aaron and his sons. It is a most sacred oblation to the LORD.

4 "When the cereal offering you present is baked in an oven, it must be in the form of unleavened cakes made of fine flour mixed with oil, or of unleavened wafers spread with oil. 5 If you present a cereal offering that is fried on a griddle, it must be of fine flour mixed with oil and unleavened. 6 Such a cereal offering must be broken into pieces, and oil must be poured over it. 7 If you present a cereal offering that is prepared in a pot, it must be of fine flour, deep-fried in oil. 8 A cereal offering that is made in any of these ways you shall bring to the LORD, offering it to the priest, who shall take it to the altar. 9 Its token offering the priest shall then lift from the cereal offering and burn on the altar as a sweet-smelling oblation to the LORD. 10 The rest of the cereal offering belongs to Aaron and his sons. It is a most sacred oblation to the LORD.

11 "Every cereal offering that you present to the LORD shall be unleavened, for you shall not burn any leaven or honey as an oblation to the LORD. 12 Such you may indeed present to the LORD in the offering of first fruits, but they are not to be placed on the altar for a pleasing odor. 13 However, every cereal offering that you present to the LORD shall be seasoned with salt. Do not let the salt of the covenant of your God be lacking from your cereal offering. On every offering you shall offer salt.

14 "If you present a cereal offering of first fruits to the LORD, you shall offer it in the form of fresh grits of new ears of grain, roasted by fire. 15 On this cereal offering you shall put oil and frankincense. 16 For its token offering the priest shall then burn some of the grits and oil, to-

gether with all the frankincense, as an oblation to the LORD.

Peace Offerings

3 "If someone in presenting a peace offering makes his offering from the herd, he may offer before the LORD either a male or a female animal, but it must be without blemish. 2 He shall lay his hand on the head of his offering, and then slaughter it at the entrance of the meeting tent; but Aaron's sons, the priests, shall splash its blood on the sides of the altar. 3 From the peace offering he shall offer as an oblation to the LORD the fatty membrane over the inner organs, and all the fat that adheres to them, 4 as well as the two kidneys, with the fat on them near the loins, and the lobe of the liver, which he shall sever above the kidneys. 5 All this Aaron's sons shall then burn on the altar with the holocaust, on the wood over the fire, as a sweet-smelling oblation to the LORD.

6 "If the peace offering he presents to the LORD is from the flock, he may offer either a male or a female animal, but it must be without blemish. 7 If he presents a lamb as his offering, he shall bring it before the LORD, 8 and after laying his hand on the head of his offering, he shall slaughter it before the meeting tent; but Aaron's sons shall splash its blood on the sides of the altar. 9 As an oblation to the LORD he shall present the fat of the peace offering: the whole fatty tail, which he must sever close to the spine, the fatty membrane over the inner organs, and all the fat that adheres to them, 10 as well as the two kidneys, with the fat on them near the loins, and the lobe of the liver, which he must sever above the kidneys. 11 All this the priest shall burn on the altar as the food of the LORD's oblation.

12 "If he presents a goat, he shall bring it before the LORD, 13 and

after laying his hand on its head, he shall slaughter it before the meeting tent; but Aaron's sons shall splash its blood on the sides of the altar. 14 From it he shall offer as an oblation to the LORD the fatty membrane over the inner organs, and all the fat that adheres to them, 15 as well as the two kidneys, with the fat on them near the loins, and the lobe of the liver, ·which he must sever above the kidneys. 16 All this the priest shall burn on the altar as the food of the sweet-smelling oblation. All the fat belongs to the LORD. 17 This shall be a perpetual ordinance for your descendants wherever they may dwell. You shall not partake of any fat or any blood."

Sin Offerings: For Priests

4 The LORD said to Moses, 2 "Tell the Israelites: When a person inadvertently commits a sin against some command of the LORD by doing one of the forbidden things, 3 if it is the anointed priest who thus sins and thereby makes the people also become guilty, he shall present to the LORD a young, unblemished bull as a sin offering for the sin he committed. 4 Bringing the bullock to the entrance of the meeting tent, before the LORD, he shall lay his hand on its head and slaughter it before the LORD. 5 The anointed priest shall then take some of the bullock's blood and bring it into the meeting tent, 6 where, dipping his finger in the blood, he shall sprinkle it seven times before the LORD, toward the veil of the sanctuary. 7 The priest shall also put some of the blood on the horns of the altar of fragrant incense which is before the LORD in the meeting tent. The rest of the bullock's blood he shall pour out at the base of the altar of holocausts which is at the entrance of the meeting tent. 8 From the sin-offering bullock he shall remove all the fat: the fatty membrane over the inner

---

2, 13: *The salt of the covenant of your God:* the partaking in common of salt by those seated together at table was an ancient symbol of friendship and alliance. Cf Mk 9, 49 and Col 4, 6; and see note on Nm 18, 19.

3, 1: *Peace offering:* thus the ancient versions have rendered the Hebrew word, which perhaps means more exactly, "fulfillment sacrifice," offered up in fulfillment of a vow. Cf Prv 7, 14. Its characteristic

feature was the sacred banquet at which the offerer and his guests partook of the meat of the sacrificed animal. Cf 7, 11–21.

3, 4: *The lobe of the liver:* some render, "the fatty covering of the liver."

3, 9: *The whole fatty tail:* see note on Ex 29, 22.

3, 17: *Any fat:* only the fat mentioned in vv 9f.14f is meant; other fat could be eaten by the Israelites.

4, 2: *A sin:* not necessarily a moral fault; included

are all the cases of ritual uncleanness which people necessarily incurred in certain unavoidable circumstances.

4, 3: *The anointed priest:* his violation of the ceremonial law brought a sort of collective guilt on all the people whom he represented before God. *Sin offering:* more exactly, "sacrifice for remitting sin"; sin is here understood as explained above.

organs, and all the fat that adheres to them, 9 as well as the two kidneys, with the fat on them near the loins, and the lobe of the liver, which he must sever above the kidneys. 10 This is the same as is removed from the ox of the peace offering; and the priest shall burn it on the altar of holocausts. 11 The hide of the bullock and all its flesh, with its head, legs, inner organs and offal, 12 in short, the whole bullock, shall be brought outside the camp to a clean place where the ashes are deposited and there be burned up in a wood fire. At the place of the ash heap, there it must be burned.

For the Community

13 "If the whole community of Israel inadvertently and without even being aware of it does something that the LORD has forbidden and thus makes itself guilty, 14 should it later on become known that the sin was committed, the community shall present a young bull as a sin offering. They shall bring it before the meeting tent, 15 and here, before the LORD, the elders of the community shall lay their hands on the bullock's head. When the bullock has been slaughtered before the LORD, 16 the anointed priest shall bring some of its blood into the meeting tent, 17 and dipping his finger in the blood, he shall sprinkle it seven times before the LORD, toward the veil. 18 He shall also put some of the blood on the horns of the altar of fragrant incense which is before the LORD in the meeting tent. The rest of the blood he shall pour out at the base of the altar of holocausts which is at the entrance of the meeting tent. 19 All of its fat he shall take from it and burn on the altar, 20 doing with this bullock just as he did with the other sin-offering bullock. Thus the priest shall make atonement for them, and they will be forgiven. 21 This bullock must also be brought outside the camp and burned, just as has been prescribed for the other one. This is the sin offering for the community.

For the Princes

22 "Should a prince commit a sin inadvertently by doing one of the things which are forbidden by some commandment of the LORD, his God, and thus become guilty, 23 if later on he learns of the sin he committed, he shall bring as his offering an unblemished male goat. 24 Having laid his hands on its head, he shall slaughter the goat as a sin offering before the LORD, in the place where the holocausts are slaughtered. 25 The priest shall then take some of the blood of the sin offering on his finger and put it on the horns of the altar of holocausts. The rest of the blood he shall pour out at the base of this altar. 26 All of the fat he shall burn on the altar like the fat of the peace offering. Thus the priest shall make atonement for the prince's sin, and it will be forgiven.

For Private Persons

27 "If a private person commits a sin inadvertently by doing one of the things which are forbidden by the commandments of the LORD, and thus becomes guilty, 28 should he later on learn of the sin he committed, he shall bring an unblemished she-goat as the offering for his sin. 29 Having laid his hand on the head of the sin offering, he shall slaughter it at the place of the holocausts. 30 The priest shall then take some of its blood on his finger and put it on the horns of the altar of holocausts. The rest of the blood he shall pour out at the base of the altar. 31 All the fat shall be removed, just as the fat is removed from the peace offering, and the priest shall burn it on the altar for an odor pleasing to the LORD. Thus the priest shall make atonement for him, and he will be forgiven.
32 "If, however, for his sin offering he presents a lamb, he shall bring an unblemished female. 33 Having laid his hand on its head, he shall slaughter this sin offering in the place where the holocausts are slaughtered. 34 The priest shall then take some of the blood of the sin offering on his finger and put it on the horns of the altar of holocausts. The rest of the blood he shall pour out at the base of the altar. 35 All the fat shall be removed, just as the fat is removed from the peace-offering lamb, and the priest shall burn it on the altar with the other oblations of the LORD. Thus the

priest shall make atonement for the man's sin, and it will be forgiven.

For Special Cases

5 "If any person refuses to give the information which, as a witness of something he has seen or learned, he has been adjured to give, and thus commits a sin and has guilt to bear; 2 or if someone, without being aware of it, touches any unclean thing, as the carcass of an unclean wild animal, or that of an unclean domestic animal, or that of an unclean swarming creature, and thus becomes unclean and guilty; 3 or if someone, without being aware of it, touches some human uncleanness, whatever kind of uncleanness this may be, and then recognizes his guilt; 4 or if someone, without being aware of it, rashly utters an oath to do good or evil, such as men are accustomed to utter rashly, and then recognizes that he is guilty of such an oath; 5 then whoever is guilty in any of these cases shall confess the sin he has incurred, 6 and as his sin offering for the sin he has committed he shall bring to the LORD a female animal from the flock, a ewe lamb or a she-goat. The priest shall then make atonement for his sin.
7 "If, however, he cannot afford an animal of the flock, he shall bring to the LORD as the sin offering for his sin two turtledoves or two pigeons, one for a sin offering and the other for a holocaust. 8 He shall bring them to the priest, who shall offer the one for the sin offering first. Snapping its head loose at the neck, yet without breaking it off completely, 9 he shall sprinkle some of the blood of the sin offering against the side of the altar. The rest of the blood shall be squeezed out against the base of the altar. Such is the offering for sin. 10 The other bird shall be offered as a holocaust in the usual way. Thus the priest shall make atonement for the sin the man committed, and it will be forgiven.
11 "If he is unable to afford even two turtledoves or two pigeons, he shall present as a sin offering for his sin one tenth of an ephah of fine flour. He shall not put oil or frankincense on it, because it is a sin offering. 12 When he has brought it to the

priest, the latter shall take a handful of this flour as a token offering, and this he shall burn as a sin offering on the altar with the other oblations of the LORD. 13 Thus the priest shall make atonement for the sin that the man committed in any of the above cases, and it will be forgiven. The rest of the flour, like the cereal offerings, shall belong to the priest."

Guilt Offerings

14 The LORD said to Moses, 15 "If someone commits a sin by inadvertently cheating in the LORD's sacred dues, he shall bring to the LORD as his guilt offering an unblemished ram from the flock, valued at two silver shekels according to the standard of the sanctuary shekel. 16 He shall also restore what he has sinfully withheld from the sanctuary, adding to it a fifth of its value. This is to be given to the priest, who shall then make atonement for him with the guilt-offering ram, and he will be forgiven. 17 "If someone, without being aware of it, commits such a sin by doing one of the things which are forbidden by some commandment of the LORD, that he incurs guilt for which he must answer, 18 he shall bring as a guilt offering to the priest an unblemished ram of the flock of the established value. The priest shall then make atonement for the fault which was unwittingly committed, and it will be forgiven. 19 Such is the offering for guilt; the penalty of the guilt must be paid to the LORD."

20 The LORD said to Moses, 21 "If someone commits a sin of dishonesty against the LORD by denying his neighbor a deposit or a pledge or a stolen article, or by otherwise retaining his neighbor's goods unjustly, 22 or if, having found a lost article, he denies the fact and swears falsely about it with any of the sinful oaths that men make in such cases, 23 he shall therefore, since he has incurred guilt by his sin, restore the thing that was stolen or unjustly retained by him or the deposit left with him or the lost article he found 24 or whatever else he swore falsely about; on the day of his guilt offering he shall make full restitution of the thing itself, and in addition, give the owner one fifth of its value. 25 As his guilt offering he shall bring to the LORD an unblemished ram of the flock of the established value. When he has presented this as his guilt offering to the priest, 26 the latter shall make atonement for him before the LORD, and he will be forgiven whatever guilt he may have incurred."

The Daily Holocaust

6 The LORD said to Moses, 2 "Give Aaron and his sons the following command: This is the ritual for holocausts. The holocaust is to remain on the hearth of the altar all night until the next morning, and the fire is to be kept burning on the altar. 3 The priest, clothed in his linen robe and wearing linen drawers on his body, shall take away the ashes to which the fire has reduced the holocaust on the altar, and lay them at the side of the altar. 4 Then, having taken off these garments and put on other garments, he shall carry the ashes to a clean place outside the camp. 5 The fire on the altar is to be kept burning; it must not go out. Every morning the priest shall put firewood on it. On this he shall lay out the holocaust and burn the fat of the peace offerings. 6 The fire is to be kept burning continuously on the altar; it must not go out.

Daily Cereal Offering

7 "This is the ritual of the cereal offering. One of Aaron's sons shall first present it before the LORD, in front of the altar. 8 Then he shall take from it a handful of its fine flour and oil, together with all the frankincense that is on it, and this he shall burn on the altar as its token offering, a sweet-smelling oblation to the LORD. 9 The rest of it Aaron and his sons may eat; but it must be eaten in the form of unleavened cakes and in a sacred place: in the court of the meeting tent they shall eat it. 10 It shall not be baked with leaven. I have given it to them as their portion from the oblations of the LORD; it is most sacred, like the sin offering and the guilt offering. 11 All the male descendants of Aaron may partake of it as their rightful share in the oblations of the LORD perpetually throughout your generations. Whatever touches the oblations becomes sacred."

12 The LORD said to Moses, 13 "This is the offering that Aaron and his sons shall present to the LORD [on the day he is anointed]: one tenth of an ephah of fine flour for the established cereal offering, half in the morning and half in the evening. 14 It shall be well kneaded and fried in oil on a griddle when you bring it in. Having broken the offering into pieces, you shall present it as a sweet-smelling oblation to the LORD. 15 Aaron's descendant who succeeds him as the anointed priest shall do likewise. This is a perpetual ordinance: for the LORD the whole offering shall be burned. 16 Every cereal offering of a priest shall be a whole burnt offering; it may not be eaten."

Sin Offerings

17 The LORD said to Moses, 18 "Tell Aaron and his sons: This is the ritual for sin offerings. At the place where holocausts are slaughtered, there also, before the LORD, shall the sin offering be slaughtered. It is most sacred. 19 The priest who presents the sin offering may partake of it; but it must be eaten in a sacred place, in the court of the meeting tent. 20 Whatever touches its flesh shall become sacred. If any of its blood is spilled on a garment, the stained part must be washed in a sacred place. 21 A clay vessel in

---

5, 15: *Cheating:* not offering the full amount in tithes, first fruits, etc. *Guilt offering:* its characteristic was a certain additional penalty imposed as reparation for the injustice involved in the fault which was atoned for by this sacrifice. However, in certain passages, e.g., 14, 12f; Nm 6, 12; Ezr 10, 19, the term "guilt offering" is used for more important cases of "sin offerings" where no apparent injustice is involved.

5, 17: *Without being aware of it:* the case naturally presupposes that later on the offender learns of his mistake. Cf 4, 13f.

6, 2: *Ritual:* literally, "law, instruction." Here, and in the following paragraphs, are given additional prescriptions for various kinds of sacrifices which were, in part, treated of in the preceding chapters.

6, 12–16: This is another law about the daily or

"established" cereal offering. It differs in some respects from the preceding law (vv 7–11) and also from the law in Ex 29, 38–42. Hence, the words *on the day he is anointed* were probably added by some later scribe in order to avoid the difficulty of harmonizing this law with the other two laws on the same matter.

which it has been cooked shall thereafter be broken; if it is cooked in a bronze vessel, this shall be scoured afterward and rinsed with water. 22 All the males of the priestly line may partake of the sin offering, since it is most sacred. 23 But no one may partake of any sin offering of which some blood has been brought into the meeting tent to make atonement in the sanctuary; such an offering must be burned up in the fire.

Guilt Offerings

7 "This is the ritual for guilt offerings, which are most sacred. 2 At the place where the holocausts are slaughtered, there also shall the guilt offering be slaughtered. Its blood shall be splashed on the sides of the altar. 3 All of its fat shall be taken from it and offered up: the fatty tail, the fatty membrane over the inner organs, 4 as well as the two kidneys with the fat on them near the loins, and the lobe of the liver, which must be severed above the kidneys. 5 All this the priest shall burn on the altar as an oblation to the LORD. This is the guilt offering. 6 All the males of the priestly line may partake of it; but it must be eaten in a sacred place, since it is most sacred.

7 "Because the sin offering and the guilt offering are alike, both having the same ritual, the guilt offering likewise belongs to the priest who makes atonement with it. 8 Similarly, the priest who offers a holocaust for someone may keep for himself the hide of the holocaust that he has offered. 9 Also, every cereal offering that is baked in an oven or deep-fried in a pot or fried on a griddle shall belong to the priest who offers it, 10 whereas all cereal offerings that are offered up dry or mixed with oil shall belong to all of Aaron's sons without distinction.

Peace Offerings

11 "This is the ritual for the peace offerings that are presented to the LORD. 12 When anyone makes a peace offering in thanksgiving, together with his thanksgiving sacrifice he shall offer unleavened cakes mixed with oil, unleavened wafers spread with oil, and cakes made of fine flour mixed with oil and well kneaded. 13 His offering shall also include loaves of leavened bread along with the victim of his peace offering for thanksgiving. 14 From each of his offerings he shall present one portion as a contribution to the LORD; this shall belong to the priest who splashes the blood of the peace offering.

15 "The flesh of the thanksgiving sacrifice shall be eaten on the day it is offered; none of it may be kept till the next day. 16 However, if the sacrifice is a votive or a free-will offering, it should indeed be eaten on the day the sacrifice is offered, but what is left over may be eaten on the next day. 17 Should any flesh from the sacrifice be left over on the third day, it must be burned up in the fire. 18 If, therefore, any of the flesh of the peace offering is eaten on the third day, it shall not win favor for him nor shall it be reckoned to his credit; rather, it shall be considered as refuse, and anyone who eats of it shall have his guilt to bear. 19 Should the flesh touch anything unclean, it may not be eaten, but shall be burned up in the fire.

"All who are clean may partake of this flesh. 20 If, however, someone while in a state of uncleanness eats any of the flesh of a peace offering belonging to the LORD, that person shall be cut off from his people. 21 Likewise, if someone touches anything unclean, whether the uncleanness be of human or of animal origin or from some loathsome crawling creature, and then eats of a peace offering belonging to the LORD, that person, too, shall be cut off from his people."

Prohibition against Blood and Fat

22 The LORD said to Moses, 23 "Tell the Israelites: You shall not eat the fat of any ox or sheep or goat. 24 Although the fat of an animal that has died a natural death or has been killed by wild beasts may be put to any other use, you may not eat it. 25 If anyone eats the fat of an animal from which an oblation is made to the LORD, such a one shall be cut off from his people. 26 Wherever you dwell, you shall not partake of any blood, be it of bird or of animal. 27 Every person who partakes of any blood shall be cut off from his people."

The Portions for Priests

28 The LORD said to Moses, 29 "Tell the Israelites: He who presents a peace offering to the LORD shall bring a part of it as his special offering to him, 30 carrying in with his own hands the oblations to the LORD. The fat is to be brought in, together with the breast, which is to be waved as a wave offering before the LORD. 31 The priest shall burn the fat on the altar, but the breast belongs to Aaron and his sons. 32 Moreover, from your peace offering you shall give to the priest the right leg as a raised offering. 33 The descendant of Aaron who offers up the blood and fat of the peace offering shall have the right leg as his portion, 34 for from the peace offerings of the Israelites I have taken the breast that is waved and the leg that is raised up, and I have given them to Aaron, the priest, and to his sons by a perpetual ordinance as a contribution from the Israelites."

35 This is the priestly share from the oblations of the LORD, allotted to Aaron and his sons on the day he called them to be the priests of the LORD; 36 on the day he anointed them the LORD ordered the Israelites to give them this share by a perpetual ordinance throughout their generations.

37 This is the ritual for holocausts, cereal offerings, sin offerings, guilt offerings, [ordination offerings] and peace offerings, 38 which the LORD enjoined on Moses at Mount Sinai at the time when he commanded the Israelites in the wilderness of Sinai to bring their offerings to the LORD.

7, 13: *Leavened bread:* these loaves were not burned on the altar (cf 2, 11), but were eaten at the "communion" meal which followed the sacrifice. See note on 3, 1.

7, 23: *The fat:* only the particular portions specified in 3, 9f.14f are meant. *Ox or sheep or goat:* such animals as could be sacrificed; the fat of other clean animals could be eaten.

7, 30–34: *A wave offering ... a raised offering:* these ceremonies are described in Ex 29, 24–28. The Hebrew word for "raised offering" is also rendered, in certain contexts, as "contribution."

7, 35: *The priestly share:* literally, "the anointed part."

CEREMONY OF ORDINATION

Ordination of Aaron and His Sons

8 The LORD said to Moses, 2 "Take Aaron and his sons, together with the vestments, the anointing oil, the bullock for a sin offering, the two rams, and the basket of unleavened food. 3 Then assemble the whole community at the entrance of the meeting tent." 4 And Moses did as the LORD had commanded. When the community had assembled at the entrance of the meeting tent, 5 Moses told them what the LORD had ordered to be done. 6 Bringing forward Aaron and his sons, he first washed them with water. 7 Then he put the tunic on Aaron, girded him with the sash, clothed him with the robe, placed the ephod on him, and girded him with the embroidered belt of the ephod, fastening it around him. 8 He then set the breastpiece on him, with the Urim and Thummim in it, 9 and put the miter on his head, attaching the gold plate, the sacred diadem, over the front of the miter, at his forehead, as the LORD had commanded him to do.

10 Taking the anointing oil, Moses anointed and consecrated the Dwelling, with all that was in it. 11 Then he sprinkled some of this oil seven times on the altar, and anointed the altar, with all its appurtenances, and the laver, with its base, thus consecrating them. 12 He also poured some of the anointing oil on Aaron's head, thus consecrating him. 13 Moses likewise brought forward Aaron's sons, clothed them with tunics, girded them with sashes, and put turbans on them, as the LORD had commanded him to do.

Ordination Sacrifices

14 When he had brought forward the bullock for a sin offering, Aaron and his sons laid their hands on its head. 15 Then Moses slaughtered it, and taking some of its blood, with his finger he put it on the horns around the altar, thus purifying the altar. He also made atonement for the altar by pouring out the blood at its base when he consecrated it. 16 Taking all the fat that was over the inner organs, as well as the lobe of the liver and the two kidneys with their fat, Moses burned them on the altar. 17 The bullock, however, with its hide and flesh and offal he burned in the fire outside the camp, as the LORD had commanded him to do.

18 He next brought forward the holocaust ram, and Aaron and his sons laid their hands on its head. 19 When he had slaughtered it, Moses splashed its blood on all sides of the altar. 20 After cutting up the ram into pieces, he burned the head, the cut-up pieces and the suet; 21 then, having washed the inner organs and the shanks with water, he also burned these remaining parts of the ram on the altar as a holocaust, a sweet-smelling oblation to the LORD, as the LORD had commanded him to do.

22 Then he brought forward the second ram, the ordination ram, and Aaron and his sons laid their hands on its head. 23 When he had slaughtered it, Moses took some of its blood and put it on the tip of Aaron's right ear, on the thumb of his right hand, and on the big toe of his right foot. 24 Moses had the sons of Aaron also come forward, and he put some of the blood on the tips of their right ears, on the thumbs of their right hands, and on the big toes of their right feet. The rest of the blood he splashed on the sides of the altar. 25 He then took the fat: the fatty tail and all the fat over the inner organs, the lobe of the liver and the two kidneys with their fat, and likewise the right leg; 26 from the basket of unleavened food that was set before the LORD he took one unleavened cake, one loaf of bread made with oil, and one wafer; these he placed on top of the portions of fat and the right leg. 27 He then put all these things into the hands of Aaron and his sons, whom he had wave them as a wave offering before the LORD. 28 When he had received them back, Moses burned them with the holocaust on the altar as the ordination offering, a sweet-smelling oblation to the LORD. 29 He then took the breast and waved it as a wave offering before the LORD; this was Moses' own portion of the ordination ram. All this was in keeping with the LORD's command to Moses. 30 Taking some of the anointing oil and some of the blood that was on the altar, Moses sprinkled with it Aaron and his vestments, as well as his sons and their vestments, thus consecrating both Aaron and his vestments and his sons and their vestments.

31 Finally, Moses said to Aaron and his sons, "Boil the flesh at the entrance of the meeting tent, and there eat it with the bread that is in the basket of the ordination offering, in keeping with the command I have received: 'Aaron and his sons shall eat of it.' 32 What is left over of the flesh and the bread you shall burn up in the fire. 33 Moreover, you are not to depart from the entrance of the meeting tent for seven days, until the days of your ordination are completed; for your ordination is to last for seven days. 34 The LORD has commanded that what has been done today be done to make atonement for you. 35 Hence you must remain at the entrance of the meeting tent day and night for seven days, carrying out the prescriptions of the LORD; otherwise you shall die; for this is the command I have received." 36 So Aaron and his sons did all that the LORD had commanded through Moses.

Octave of the Ordination

9 On the eighth day Moses summoned Aaron and his sons, together with the elders of Israel, 2 and said to Aaron, "Take a calf for a sin offering and a ram for a holocaust, both without blemish, and offer them before the LORD. 3 Tell the elders of Israel, too: Take a he-goat for a sin offering, a calf and a lamb, both unblemished yearlings,

8, 1—9, 21: Though presented in the form of a narrative, this description of Aaron's ordination was intended to serve as a guide for all future ordinations.
8, 2: *The vestments, etc.:* already described in Ex 28–29.

8, 8: *The Urim and Thummim:* see note on Ex 28, 30.
8, 34: The sense is not quite clear. Either the verse gives merely the reason why God ordered this ceremony, or it contains God's command that the same ceremony be used in all future ordinations, or it decrees a repetition of the entire ceremony on each of the seven days. At least a sin offering for atonement was made on each of these days. Cf Ex 29, 29–36.

for a holocaust, 4 and an ox and a ram for a peace offering, to sacrifice them before the LORD, along with a cereal offering mixed with oil; for today the LORD will reveal himself to you." 5 So they brought what Moses had ordered. When the whole community had come forward and stood before the LORD, 6 Moses said, "This is what the LORD orders you to do, that the glory of the LORD may be revealed to you. 7 Come up to the altar," Moses then told Aaron, "and offer your sin offering and your holocaust in atonement for yourself and for your family; then present the offering of the people in atonement for them, as the LORD has commanded."

8 Going up to the altar, Aaron first slaughtered the calf that was his own sin offering. 9 When his sons presented the blood to him, he dipped his finger in the blood and put it on the horns of the altar. The rest of the blood he poured out at the base of the altar. 10 He then burned on the altar the fat, the kidneys and the lobe of the liver that were taken from the sin offering, as the LORD had commanded Moses; 11 but the flesh and the hide he burned up in the fire outside the camp. 12 Then Aaron slaughtered his holocaust. When his sons brought him the blood, he splashed it on all sides of the altar. 13 They then brought him the pieces and the head of the holocaust, and he burned them on the altar. 14 Having washed the inner organs and the shanks, he burned these also with the holocaust on the altar.

15 Thereupon he had the people's offering brought up. Taking the goat that was for the people's sin offering, he slaughtered it and offered it up for sin as before. 16 Then he brought forward the holocaust, other than the morning holocaust, and offered it in the usual manner. 17 He then presented the cereal offering; taking a handful of it, he burned it on the altar. 18 Finally he slaughtered the ox and the ram, the peace offering of the people. When his sons

brought him the blood, Aaron splashed it on all sides of the altar. 19 The portions of fat from the ox and from the ram, the fatty tail, the fatty membrane over the inner organs, the two kidneys, with the fat that is on them, and the lobe of the liver, 20 he placed on top of the breasts and burned them on the altar, 21 having first waved the breasts and the right legs as a wave offering before the LORD, in keeping with the LORD's command to Moses.

Revelation of the Lord's Glory

22 Aaron then raised his hands over the people and blessed them. When he came down from offering the sin offering and holocaust and peace offering, 23 Moses and Aaron went into the meeting tent. On coming out they again blessed the people. Then the glory of the LORD was revealed to all the people. 24 Fire came forth from the LORD's presence and consumed the holocaust and the remnants of the fat on the altar. Seeing this, all the people cried out and fell prostrate.

Nadab and Abihu

10 During this time Aaron's sons Nadab and Abihu took their censers and, strewing incense on the fire they had put in them, they offered up before the LORD profane fire, such as he had not authorized. 2 Fire therefore came forth from the LORD's presence and consumed them, so that they died in his presence. 3 Moses then said to Aaron, "This is as the LORD said:

Through those who approach me
    I will manifest my sacredness;
In the sight of all the people I
    will reveal my glory."

But Aaron said nothing. 4 Then Moses summoned Mishael and Elzaphan, the sons of Aaron's uncle Uzziel, with the order, "Come, remove your kinsmen from the sanctuary and carry them to a place outside the camp." 5 So they went

in and took them, in their tunics, outside the camp, as Moses had commanded.

Conduct of the Priests

6 Moses said to Aaron and his sons Eleazar and Ithamar, "Do not bare your heads or tear your garments, lest you bring not only death on yourselves but God's wrath also on the whole community. Your kinsmen, the rest of the house of Israel, shall mourn for those whom the LORD's fire has smitten; 7 but do not you go beyond the entry of the meeting tent, else you shall die; for the anointing oil of the LORD is upon you." So they did as Moses told them.

8 The LORD said to Aaron, 9 "When you are to go to the meeting tent, you and your sons are forbidden under pain of death, by a perpetual ordinance throughout your generations, to drink any wine or strong drink. 10 You must be able to distinguish between what is sacred and what is profane, between what is clean and what is unclean; 11 you must teach the Israelites all the laws that the LORD has given them through Moses."

The Eating of the Priestly Portions

12 Moses said to Aaron and his surviving sons, Eleazar and Ithamar, "Take the cereal offering left over from the oblations of the LORD, and eat it beside the altar in the form of unleavened cakes. Since it is most sacred, 13 you must eat it in a sacred place. This is your due from the oblations of the LORD, and that of your sons; such is the command I have received. 14 With your sons and daughters you shall also eat the breast of the wave offering and the leg of the raised offering, in a clean place; for these have been assigned to you and your children as your due from the peace offerings of the Israelites. 15 The leg of the raised offering and the breast of the wave offering shall first be brought in with the oblations, the fatty portions, that

---

10, 1: *Nadab and Abihu:* the older sons of Aaron. Cf Ex 6, 23f.

10, 2: *Fire:* perhaps after the manner of lightning.

10, 3: *I will manifest my sacredness:* the presence of God is so sacred that it strikes dead those who

approach him without the proper holiness. Cf Nm 20, 13; Ez 28, 22.

10, 5: *In their tunics:* they were buried just as they were, with no shroud or funeral solemnities.

10, 6: *Bare your heads:* go without the customary head covering, as a sign of mourning. Some inter-

preters, however, understand it as the cutting off of one's hair, which ordinarily all the Israelites, men as well as women, let grow long. Cf Is 15, 2; Jer 7, 29. Still others understand the verb to mean "to let one's hair hang loose and wild." Cf 13, 45; 21, 10, where the same phrase is used.

are to be waved as a wave offering before the LORD. Then they shall belong to you and your children by a perpetual ordinance, as the LORD has commanded."

16 When Moses inquired about the goat of the sin offering, he discovered that it had all been burned. So he was angry with the surviving sons of Aaron, Eleazar and Ithamar, and said, 17 "Why did you not eat the sin offering in the sacred place, since it is most sacred? It has been given to you that you might bear the guilt of the community and make atonement for them before the LORD. 18 If its blood was not brought into the inmost part of the sanctuary, you should certainly have eaten the offering in the sanctuary, in keeping with the command I had received." 19 Aaron answered Moses, "Even though they presented their sin offering and holocaust before the LORD today, yet this misfortune has befallen me. Had I then eaten of the sin offering today, would it have been pleasing to the LORD?" 20 On hearing this, Moses was satisfied.

LEGAL PURITY

Clean and Unclean Food

11 The LORD said to Moses and Aaron, 2 "Speak to the Israelites and tell them: Of all land animals these are the ones you may eat: 3 any animal that has hoofs you may eat, provided it is cloven-footed and chews the cud. 4 But you shall not eat any of the following that only chew the cud or only have hoofs: the camel, which indeed chews the cud, but does not have hoofs and is therefore unclean for you; 5 the rock badger, which indeed chews the cud, but does not have hoofs and is therefore unclean for you; 6 the hare, which indeed chews the cud, but does not have hoofs and is

therefore unclean for you; 7 and the pig, which does indeed have hoofs and is clovenfooted, but does not chew the cud and is therefore unclean for you. 8 Their flesh you shall not eat, and their dead bodies you shall not touch; they are unclean for you.

9 "Of the various creatures that live in the water, you may eat the following: whatever in the seas or in river waters has both fins and scales you may eat. 10 But of the various creatures that crawl or swim in the water, whether in the sea or in the rivers, all those that lack either fins or scales are loathsome for you, 11 and you shall treat them as loathsome. Their flesh you shall not eat, and their dead bodies you shall loathe. 12 Every water creature that lacks fins or scales is loathsome for you.

13 "Of the birds, these you shall loathe and, as loathsome, they shall not be eaten: the eagle, the vulture, the osprey, 14 the kite, the various species of falcons, 15 the various species of crows, 16 the ostrich, the nightjar, the gull, the various species of hawks, 17 the owl, the cormorant, the screech owl, 18 the barn owl, the desert owl, the buzzard, 19 the stork, the various species of herons, the hoopoe, and the bat.

20 "The various winged insects that walk on all fours are loathsome for you. 21 But of the various winged insects that walk on all fours you may eat those that have jointed legs for leaping on the ground; 22 hence of these you may eat the following: the various kinds of locusts, the various kinds of grasshoppers, the various kinds of katydids, and the various kinds of crickets. 23 All other winged insects that have four legs are loathsome for you.

24 "Such is the uncleanness that

you contract, that everyone who touches their dead bodies shall be unclean until evening, 25 and everyone who picks up any part of their dead bodies shall wash his garments and be unclean until evening. 26 All hoofed animals that are not cloven-footed or do not chew the cud are unclean for you; everyone who touches them becomes unclean. 27 Of the various quadrupeds, all those that walk on paws are unclean for you; everyóne who touches their dead bodies shall be unclean until evening, 28 and everyone who picks up their dead bodies shall wash his garments and be unclean until evening. Such is their uncleanness for you.

29 "Of the creatures that swarm on the ground, the following are unclean for you: the rat, the mouse, the various kinds of lizards, 30 the gecko, the chameleon, the agama, the skink, and the mole. 31 Among the various swarming creatures, these are unclean for you. Everyone who touches them when they are dead shall be unclean until evening. 32 Everything on which one of them falls when dead becomes unclean. Any such article that men use, whether it be an article of wood, cloth, leather or goat hair, must be put in water and remain unclean until evening, when it again becomes clean. 33 Should any of these creatures fall into a clay vessel, everything in it becomes unclean, and the vessel itself you must break. 34 Any solid food that was in contact with water, and any liquid that men drink, in any such vessel become unclean. 35 Any object on which one of their dead bodies falls, becomes unclean; if it is an oven or a jar-stand, this must be broken to pieces; they are unclean and shall be treated as unclean by you. 36 However, a spring or a cistern for collecting water remains clean; but

---

10, 16–19: *Eleazar and Ithamar* burned the entire goat of the sin offering (9, 15) instead of eating it in a sacred place (6, 19) to bear the guilt of the community. Aaron defends this action of his sons against Moses' displeasure by implying that they did not have sufficient sanctity to eat the flesh of the victim and thus perform the expiation of the people. They themselves still labored under the blow of the divine anger which struck their brothers Nadab and Abihu.

11, 1ff: These distinctions between edible and inedible meats were probably based on traditional ideas of hygiene, but they are here given a moral, religious basis: the inedible varieties are classified

as "unclean" to remind the Israelites that they are to be a pure and holy people, dedicated to the LORD.

11, 5f: According to modern zoology, *the rock badger* (hyrax Syriacus) is classified as an ungulate, and *the hare* as a rodent; neither is a ruminant. They appear to chew their food as the true ruminants do, and it is upon this appearance that the classification in the text is based.

11, 13–19.30: The identification of the various Hebrew names for these birds and reptiles is in many cases uncertain.

11, 19: *The bat:* actually a mammal, but listed here with the birds because of its wings.

11, 22: The Hebrew distinguishes four classes of edible locust-like insects, but the difference between them is quite uncertain. Cf Mt 3, 4.

11, 24–28: This paragraph sharpens the prohibition against unclean animals: not only is their meat unfit for food, but contact with their dead bodies makes a person ritually unclean.

11, 26: *All hoofed animals that are not cloven-footed:* such as the horse and the ass.

11, 27: *All those that walk on paws:* such as dogs and cats.

11, 36: *Whoever touches the dead body:* to remove the dead insect from the water supply.

whoever touches the dead body becomes unclean. 37 Any sort of cultivated grain remains clean even though one of their dead bodies falls on it; 38 but if the grain has become moistened, it becomes unclean when one of these falls on it.

39 "When one of the animals that you could otherwise eat, dies of itself, anyone who touches its dead body shall be unclean until evening; 40 and anyone who eats of its dead body shall wash his garments and be unclean until evening; so also, anyone who removes its dead body shall wash his garments and be unclean until evening.

41 "All the creatures that swarm on the ground are loathsome and shall not be eaten. 42 Whether it crawls on its belly, goes on all fours, or has many legs, you shall eat no swarming creature: they are loathsome. 43 Do not make yourselves loathsome or unclean with any swarming creature through being contaminated by them. 44 For I, the LORD, am your God; and you shall make and keep yourselves holy, because I am holy. You shall not make yourselves unclean, then, by any swarming creature that crawls on the ground. 45 Since I, the LORD, brought you up from the land of Egypt that I might be your God, you shall be holy, because I am holy.

46 "This is the law for animals and birds and for all the creatures that move about in the water or swarm on the ground, 47 that you may distinguish between the clean and the unclean, between creatures that may be eaten and those that may not be eaten."

Uncleanness of Childbirth

12 The LORD said to Moses, 2 "Tell the Israelites: When a woman has conceived and gives birth to a boy, she shall be unclean for seven days, with the same uncleanness as at her menstrual period. 3 On the eighth day, the flesh of the boy's foreskin shall be circumcised, 4 and then she shall spend thirty-three days more in becoming purified of her blood; she shall not touch anything sacred nor enter the sanctuary till the days of her purification are fulfilled. 5 If she gives birth to a girl, for fourteen days she shall be as unclean as at her menstruation, after which she shall spend sixty-six days in becoming purified of her blood.

6 "When the days of her purification for a son or for a daughter are fulfilled, she shall bring to the priest at the entrance of the meeting tent a yearling lamb for a holocaust and a pigeon or a turtledove for a sin offering. 7 The priest shall offer them up before the LORD to make atonement for her, and thus she will be clean again after her flow of blood. Such is the law for the woman who gives birth to a boy or a girl child. 8 If, however, she cannot afford a lamb, she may take two turtledoves or two pigeons, the one for a holocaust and the other for a sin offering. The priest shall make atonement for her, and thus she will again be clean."

Leprosy

13 The LORD said to Moses and Aaron, 2 "If someone has on his skin a scab or pustule or blotch which appears to be the sore of leprosy, he shall be brought to Aaron, the priest, or to one of the priests among his descendants, 3 who shall examine the sore on his skin. If the hair on the sore has turned white and the sore itself shows that it has penetrated below the skin, it is indeed the sore of leprosy; the priest, on seeing this, shall declare the man unclean. 4 If, however, the blotch on the skin is white, but does not seem to have penetrated below the skin, nor has the hair turned white, the priest shall quarantine the stricken man for seven days. 5 On the seventh day the priest shall again examine him. If he judges that the sore has remained unchanged and has not spread on the skin, the priest shall quarantine him for another seven days, 6 and once more examine him on the seventh day. If the sore is now dying out and has not spread on the skin, the priest shall declare the man clean; it was merely eczema. The man shall wash his garments and so become clean. 7 But if, after he has shown himself to the priest to be declared clean, the eczema spreads at all on his skin, he shall once more show himself to the priest. 8 Should the priest, on examining it, find that the eczema has indeed spread on the skin, he shall declare the man unclean; it is leprosy.

9 "When someone is stricken with leprosy, he shall be brought to the priest. 10 Should the priest, on examining him, find that there is a white scab on the skin which has turned the hair white and that there is raw flesh in it, 11 it is skin leprosy that has long developed. The priest shall declare the man unclean without first quarantining him, since he is certainly unclean. 12 If leprosy breaks out on the skin and, as far as the priest can see, covers all the skin of the stricken man from head to foot, 13 should the priest then, on examining him, find that the leprosy does cover his whole body, he shall declare the stricken man clean; since it has all turned white, the man is clean. 14 But as soon as raw flesh appears on him, he is unclean; 15 on observing the raw flesh, the priest shall declare him unclean, because raw flesh is unclean; it is leprosy. 16 If, however, the raw flesh again turns white, he shall return to the priest; 17 should the latter, on examining him, find that the sore has indeed turned white, he shall declare the stricken man clean, and thus he will be clean.

18 "If a man who had a boil on

12, 2f: The uncleanness of the woman was more serious during the first period, the seven days after the birth of a boy or the fourteen days after the birth of a girl; only during this period would the rules given in 15, 19–24 apply.

12, 8: Forty days after the birth of Jesus, his Virgin Mother made this offering of the poor (Lk 2, 22.24); since the holocaust was offered in

thanksgiving for the birth of the child, this was most fittingly offered by Mary. However, because of her miraculous delivery, she was not really obliged to make the sin offering of purification.

13, 2ff: Various kinds of skin blemishes are treated here which were not contagious but simply disqualified their subjects from association with others, especially in public worship, until they were declared

ritually clean. The Hebrew term used does not refer to Hansen's disease, currently called leprosy.

13, 12ff: If leprosy breaks out on the skin: the symptoms described here point to a form of skin disease which is merely on the surface and therefore easily cured.

his skin which later healed, 19 should now in the place of the boil have a white scab or a pink blotch, he shall show himself to the priest. 20 If the latter, on examination, sees that it is deeper than the skin and that the hair has turned white, he shall declare the man unclean; it is the sore of leprosy that has broken out in the boil. 21 But if the priest, on examining him, finds that there is no white hair in it and that it is not deeper than the skin and is already dying out, the priest shall quarantine him for seven days. 22 If it has then spread on the skin, the priest shall declare him unclean; the man is stricken. 23 But if the blotch remains in its place without spreading, it is merely the scar of the boil; the priest shall therefore declare him clean.

24 "If a man had a burn on his skin, and the proud flesh of the burn now becomes a pink or a white blotch, 25 the priest shall examine it. If the hair has turned white on the blotch and this seems to have penetrated below the skin, it is leprosy that has broken out in the burn; the priest shall therefore declare him unclean and stricken with leprosy. 26 But if the priest, on examining it, finds that there is no white hair on the blotch and that this is not deeper than the skin and is already dying out, the priest shall quarantine him for seven days. 27 Should the priest, when examining it on the seventh day, find that it has spread at all on the skin, he shall declare the man unclean and stricken with leprosy. 28 But if the blotch remains in its place without spreading on the skin and is already dying out, it is merely the scab of the burn; the priest shall therefore declare the man clean, since it is only the scar of the burn.

29 "When a man or a woman has a sore on the head or cheek, 30 should the priest, on examining it, find that the sore has penetrated below the skin and that there is fine yellow hair on it, the priest shall declare the person unclean, for this is scall, a leprous disease of the head or cheek. 31 But if the priest, on examining the scall sore, finds that

it has not penetrated below the skin, though the hair on it may not be black, the priest shall quarantine the person with scall sore for seven days, 32 and on the seventh day again examine the sore. If the scall has not spread and has no yellow hair on it and does not seem to have penetrated below the skin, 33 the man shall shave himself, but not on the diseased spot. Then the priest shall quarantine him for another seven days. 34 If the priest, when examining the scall on the seventh day, finds that it has not spread on the skin and that it has not penetrated below the skin, he shall declare the man clean; the latter shall wash his garments, and thus he will be clean. 35 But if the scall spreads at all on his skin after he has been declared clean, 36 the priest shall again examine it. If the scall has indeed spread on the skin, he need not look for yellow hair; the man is surely unclean. 37 If, however, he judges that the scall has remained in its place and that black hair has grown on it, the disease has been healed; the man is clean, and the priest shall declare him clean.

38 "When the skin of a man or a woman is spotted with white blotches 39 the priest shall make an examination. If the blotches on the skin are white and already dying out, it is only tetter that has broken out on the skin, and the person therefore is clean.

40 "When a man loses the hair of his head, he is not unclean merely because of his bald crown. 41 So too, if he loses the hair on the front of his head, he is not unclean merely because of his bald forehead. 42 But when there is a pink sore on his bald crown or bald forehead, it is leprosy that is breaking out there. 43 The priest shall examine him; and if the scab on the sore of the bald spot has the same pink appearance as that of skin leprosy of the fleshy part of the body, 44 the man is leprous and unclean, and the priest shall declare him unclean by reason of the sore on his head.

45 "The one who bears the sore of leprosy shall keep his garments

rent and his head bare, and shall muffle his beard; he shall cry out, 'Unclean, unclean!' 46 As long as the sore is on him he shall declare himself unclean, since he is in fact unclean. He shall dwell apart, making his abode outside the camp.

Leprosy of Clothes

47 "When a leprous infection is on a garment of wool or of linen, 48 or on woven or knitted material of linen or wool, or on a hide or anything made of leather, 49 if the infection on the garment or hide, or on the woven or knitted material, or on any leather article is greenish or reddish, the thing is indeed infected with leprosy and must be shown to the priest. 50 Having examined the infection, the priest shall quarantine the infected article for seven days.

51 "On the seventh day the priest shall again examine the infection. If it has spread on the garment, or on the woven or knitted material, or on the leather, whatever be its use, the infection is malignant leprosy, and the article is unclean. 52 He shall therefore burn up the garment, or the woven or knitted material of wool or linen, or the leather article, whatever it may be, which is infected; since it has malignant leprosy, it must be destroyed by fire. 53 But if the priest, on examining the infection, finds that it has not spread on the garment, or on the woven or knitted material, or on the leather article. 54 he shall give orders to have the infected article washed and then quarantined for another seven days.

55 "Then the priest shall again examine the infected article after it has been washed. If the infection has not changed its appearance, even though it may not have spread, the article is unclean and shall be destroyed by fire. 56 But if the priest, on examining the infection, finds that it is dying out after the washing, he shall tear the infected part out of the garment, or the leather, or the woven or knitted material. 57 If, however, the infection again appears on the garment, or on the woven or knitted material, or on the leather article,

---

13, 30: *Scall:* a scabby or scaly eruption of the scalp. According to some, "ringworm."

13, 39: *Tetter:* vitiligo, a harmless form of skin disease.

13, 47: *A leprous infection:* some mold or fungus growth resembling human leprosy.

it is still virulent and the thing infected shall be destroyed by fire. 58 But if, after the washing, the infection has left the garment, or the woven or knitted material, or the leather article, the thing shall be washed a second time, and thus it will be clean. 59 This is the law for leprous infection on a garment of wool or linen, or on woven or knitted material, or on any leather article, to determine whether it is clean or unclean."

Purification after Leprosy

14 The LORD said to Moses, 2 "This is the law for the victim of leprosy at the time of his purification. He shall be brought to the priest, 3 who is to go outside the camp to examine him. If the priest finds that the sore of leprosy has healed in the leper, 4 he shall order the man who is to be purified, to get two live, clean birds, as well as some cedar wood, scarlet yarn, and hyssop. 5 The priest shall then order him to slay one of the birds over an earthen vessel with spring water in it. 6 Taking the living bird with the cedar wood, the scarlet yarn and the hyssop the priest shall dip them all in the blood of the bird that was slain over the spring water, 7 and then sprinkle seven times the man to be purified from his leprosy. When he has thus purified him, he shall let the living bird fly away over the countryside. 8 The man being purified shall then wash his garments and shave off all his hair and bathe in water; only when he is thus made clean may he come inside the camp; but he shall still remain outside his tent for seven days. 9 On the seventh day he shall again shave off all the hair of his head, his beard, his eyebrows, and any other hair he may have, and also wash his garments and bathe his body in water; and so he will be clean.

Purification Sacrifices

10 "On the eighth day he shall take two unblemished male lambs, one unblemished yearling ewe lamb, three tenths of an ephah of fine flour mixed with oil for a cereal offering, and one log of oil. 11 The priest who performs the purification ceremony shall place the man who is being purified, as well as all these offerings, before the LORD at the entrance of the meeting tent. 12 Taking one of the male lambs, the priest shall present it as a guilt offering, along with the log of oil, waving them as a wave offering before the LORD. 13 (This lamb he shall slaughter in the sacred place where the sin offering and the holocaust are slaughtered; because, like the sin offering, the guilt offering belongs to the priest and is most sacred.) 14 Then the priest shall take some of the blood of the guilt offering and put it on the tip of the man's right ear, the thumb of his right hand, and the big toe of his right foot. 15 The priest shall also take the log of oil and pour some of it into the palm of his own left hand; 16 then, dipping his right forefinger in it, he shall sprinkle it seven times before the LORD. 17 Of the oil left in his hand the priest shall put some on the tip of the man's right ear, the thumb of his right hand, and the big toe of his right foot, over the blood of the guilt offering. 18 The rest of the oil in his hand the priest shall put on the head of the man being purified. Thus shall the priest make atonement for him before the LORD. 19 Only after he has offered the sin offering in atonement for the man's uncleanness shall the priest slaughter the holocaust 20 and offer it, together with the cereal offering, on the altar before the LORD. When the priest has thus made atonement for him, the man will be clean.

Poor Leper's Sacrifice

21 "If a man is poor and cannot afford so much, he shall take one male lamb for a guilt offering, to be used as a wave offering in atonement for himself, one tenth of an ephah of fine flour mixed with oil for a cereal offering, a log of oil, 22 and two turtledoves or pigeons, which he can more easily afford, the one as a sin offering and the other as a holocaust. 23 On the eighth day of his purification he shall bring them to the priest, at the entrance of the meeting tent before the LORD. 24 Taking the guilt-offering lamb, along with the log of oil, the priest shall wave them as a wave offering before the LORD. 25 When he has slaughtered the guilt-offering lamb, he shall take some of its blood, and put it on the tip of the right ear of the man being purified, on the thumb of his right hand, and on the big toe of his right foot. 26 The priest shall then pour some of the oil into the palm of his own left hand 27 and with his right forefinger sprinkle it seven times before the LORD. 28 Some of the oil in his hand the priest shall also put on the tip of the man's right ear, the thumb of his right hand, and the big toe of his right foot, over the blood of the guilt offering. 29 The rest of the oil in his hand the priest shall put on the man's head. Thus shall he make atonement for him before the LORD. 30 Then, of the turtledoves or pigeons, such as the man can afford, 31 the priest shall offer up one as a sin offering and the other as a holocaust, along with the cereal offering. Thus shall the priest make atonement before the LORD for the man who is to be purified. 32 This is the law for one afflicted with leprosy who has insufficient means for his purification."

Leprosy of Houses

33 The LORD said to Moses and Aaron, 34 "When you come into the land of Canaan, which I am giving you to possess, if I put a leprous infection on any house of the land you occupy, 35 the owner of the house shall come and report to the priest, 'It looks to me as if my house were infected.' 36 The priest shall then order the house to be cleared out before he goes in to examine the infection, lest everything in the house become unclean. Only after this is he to go in to examine the house. 37 If the priest, on examining it, finds that the infection

---

14, 4: *Scarlet yarn:* probably used for tying the hyssop sprig to the cedar branchlet.
14, 5: *Spring water:* literally, "living water,"
taken from some source of running water, not from a cistern.
14, 22: *Two turtledoves:* substitutes for the two
additional lambs, similar to the offering of a poor woman after childbirth. Cf 12, 8.

on the walls of the house consists of greenish or reddish depressions which seem to go deeper than the surface of the wall, 38 he shall close the door of the house behind him and quarantine the house for seven days. 39 On the seventh day the priest shall return to examine the house again. If he finds that the infection has spread on the walls, 40 he shall order the infected stones to be pulled out and cast in an unclean place outside the city. 41 The whole inside of the house shall then be scraped, and the mortar that has been scraped off shall be dumped in an unclean place outside the city. 42 Then new stones shall be brought and put in the place of the old stones, and new mortar shall be made and plastered on the house.

43 If the infection breaks out once more after the stones have been pulled out and the house has been scraped and replastered, 44 the priest shall come again; and if he finds that the infection has spread in the house, it is corrosive leprosy, and the house is unclean. 45 It shall be pulled down, and all its stones, beams and mortar shall be hauled away to an unclean place outside the city. 46 Whoever enters a house while it is quarantined shall be unclean until evening. 47 Whoever sleeps or eats in such a house shall also wash his garments. 48 If the priest finds, when he comes to examine the house, that the infection has in fact not spread after the plastering, he shall declare the house clean, since the infection has been healed. 49 To purify the house, he shall take two birds, as well as cedar wood, scarlet yarn, and hyssop. 50 One of the birds he shall slay over an earthen vessel with spring water in it. 51 Then, taking the cedar wood, the hyssop and the scarlet yarn, together with the living bird, he shall dip them all in the blood of the slain bird and the spring water, and sprinkle the house seven times. 52 Thus shall he purify the house with the bird's blood and the spring water, along with the living bird, the cedar wood, the hyssop, and the

scarlet yarn. 53 He shall then let the living bird fly away over the countryside outside the city. When he has thus made atonement for it, the house will be clean.

54 "This is the law for every kind of human leprosy and scall, 55 for leprosy of garments and houses, 56 as well as for scabs, pustules and blotches, 57 so that it may be manifest when there is a state of uncleanness and when a state of cleanness. This is the law for leprosy.

Personal Uncleanness

15 The LORD said to Moses and Aaron, 2 "Speak to the Israelites and tell them: Every man who is afflicted with a chronic flow from his private parts is thereby unclean. 3 Such is his uncleanness from this flow that it makes no difference whether the flow drains off or is blocked up; his uncleanness remains. 4 Any bed on which the man afflicted with the flow lies, is unclean, and any piece of furniture on which he sits, is unclean. 5 Anyone who touches his bed shall wash his garments, bathe in water, and be unclean until evening. 6 Whoever sits on a piece of furniture on which the afflicted man was sitting, shall wash his garments, bathe in water, and be unclean until evening. 7 Whoever touches the body of the afflicted man shall wash his garments, bathe in water, and be unclean until evening. 8 If the afflicted man spits on a clean man, the latter shall wash his garments, bathe in water, and be unclean until evening. 9 Any saddle on which the afflicted man rides, is unclean. 10 Whoever touches anything that was under him shall be unclean until evening; whoever lifts up any such thing shall wash his garments, bathe in water, and be unclean until evening. 11 Anyone whom the afflicted man touches with unrinsed hands shall wash his garments, bathe in water, and be unclean until evening. 12 Earthenware touched by the afflicted man shall be broken; and every wooden article shall be rinsed with water.

13 "When a man who has been afflicted with a flow becomes free of his affliction, he shall wait seven

days for his purification. Then he shall wash his garments and bathe his body in fresh water, and so he will be clean. 14 On the eighth day he shall take two turtledoves or two pigeons, and going before the LORD, to the entrance of the meeting tent, he shall give them to the priest, 15 who shall offer them up, the one as a sin offering and the other as a holocaust. Thus shall the priest make atonement before the LORD for the man's flow.

16 "When a man has an emission of seed, he shall bathe his whole body in water and be unclean until evening. 17 Any piece of cloth or leather with seed on it shall be washed with water and be unclean until evening.

18 "If a man lies carnally with a woman, they shall both bathe in water and be unclean until evening.

19 "When a woman has her menstrual flow, she shall be in a state of impurity for seven days. Anyone who touches her shall be unclean until evening. 20 Anything on which she lies or sits during her impurity shall be unclean. 21 Anyone who touches her bed shall wash his garments, bathe in water, and be unclean until evening. 22 Whoever touches any article of furniture on which she was sitting, shall wash his garments, bathe in water, and be unclean until evening. 23 But if she is on the bed or on the seat when he touches it, he shall be unclean until evening. 24 If a man dares to lie with her, he contracts her impurity and shall be unclean for seven days; every bed on which he then lies also becomes unclean.

25 "When a woman is afflicted with a flow of blood for several days outside her menstrual period, or when her flow continues beyond the ordinary period, as long as she suffers this unclean flow she shall be unclean, just as during her menstrual period. 26 Any bed on which she lies during such a flow becomes unclean, as it would during her menstruation, and any article of furniture on which she sits becomes unclean just as during her menstruation. 27 Anyone who touches them becomes unclean; he shall wash his garments, bathe in water, and be unclean until evening.

28 "If she becomes freed from her affliction, she shall wait seven days, and only then is she to be purified. 29 On the eighth day she shall take two turtledoves or two pigeons and bring them to the priest at the entrance of the meeting tent. 30 The priest shall offer up one of them as a sin offering and the other as a holocaust. Thus shall the priest make atonement before the LORD for her unclean flow.

31 "You shall warn the Israelites of their uncleanness, lest by defiling my Dwelling, which is in their midst, their uncleanness be the cause of their death.

32 "This is the law for the man who is afflicted with a chronic flow, or who has an emission of seed, and thereby becomes unclean; 33 as well as for the woman who has her menstrual period, or who is afflicted with a chronic flow; the law for male and female; and also for the man who lies with an unclean woman."

The Day of Atonement

16 After the death of Aaron's two sons, who died when they approached the LORD's presence, the LORD spoke to Moses 2 and said to him, "Tell your brother Aaron that he is not to come whenever he pleases into the sanctuary, inside the veil, in front of the propitiatory on the ark; otherwise, when I reveal myself in a cloud above the propitiatory, he will die. 3 Only in this way may Aaron enter the sanctuary. He shall bring a young bullock for a sin offering and a ram for a holocaust. 4 He shall wear the sacred linen tunic, with the linen drawers next his flesh, gird himself with the linen sash and put on the linen miter. But since these vestments are sacred, he shall not put them on until he has first bathed his body in water. 5 From the Israelite community he shall receive two male goats for a sin offering and one ram for a holocaust.

6 "Aaron shall bring in the bullock, his sin offering to atone for himself and for his household. 7 Taking the two male goats and setting them before the LORD at the entrance of the meeting tent, 8 he shall cast lots to determine which one is for the LORD and which for Azazel.

9 The goat that is determined by lot for the LORD, Aaron shall bring in and offer up as a sin offering. 10 But the goat determined by lot for Azazel he shall set alive before the LORD, so that with it he may make atonement by sending it off to Azazel in the desert.

11 "Thus shall Aaron offer up the bullock, his sin offering, to atone for himself and for his family. When he has slaughtered it, 12 he shall take a censer full of glowing embers from the altar before the LORD, as well as a double handful of finely ground fragrant incense, and bringing them inside the veil, 13 there before the LORD he shall put incense on the fire, so that a cloud of incense may cover the propitiatory over the commandments; else he will die. 14 Taking some of the bullock's blood, he shall sprinkle it with his finger on the fore part of the propitiatory and likewise sprinkle some of the blood with his finger seven times in front of the propitiatory.

15 "Then he shall slaughter the people's sin-offering goat, and bringing its blood inside the veil, he shall do with it as he did with the bullock's blood, sprinkling it on the propitiatory and before it. 16 Thus he shall make atonement for the sanctuary because of all the sinful defilements and faults of the Israelites. He shall do the same for the meeting tent, which is set up among them in the midst of their uncleanness. 17 No one else may be in the meeting tent from the time he enters the sanctuary to make atonement until he departs. When he has made atonement for himself and his household, as well as for the whole Israelite community, 18 he shall come out to the altar before the LORD and make atonement for it also.

Taking some of the bullock's and the goat's blood, he shall put it on the horns around the altar, 19 and with his finger sprinkle some of the blood on it seven times. Thus he shall render it clean and holy, purged of the defilements of the Israelites.

The Scapegoat

20 "When he has completed the atonement rite for the sanctuary, the meeting tent and the altar, Aaron shall bring forward the live goat. 21 Laying both hands on its head, he shall confess over it all the sinful faults and transgressions of the Israelites, and so put them on the goat's head. He shall then have it led into the desert by an attendant. 22 Since the goat is to carry off their iniquities to an isolated region, it must be sent away into the desert.

23 "After Aaron has again gone into the meeting tent, he shall strip off and leave in the sanctuary the linen vestments he had put on when he entered there. 24 After bathing his body with water in a sacred place, he shall put on his vestments, and then come out and offer his own and the people's holocaust, in atonement for himself and for the people, 25 and also burn the fat of the sin offering on the altar.

26 "The man who has led away the goat for Azazel shall wash his garments and bathe his body in water; only then may he enter the camp. 27 The sin-offering bullock and goat whose blood was brought into the sanctuary to make atonement, shall be taken outside the camp, where their hides and flesh and offal shall be burned up in the fire. 28 The one who burns them shall wash his garments and bathe his body in water; only then may he enter the camp.

The Fast

29 "This shall be an everlasting ordinance for you: on the tenth day of the seventh month every one of you, whether a native or a resident

---

16, 2: *The sanctuary, inside the veil:* the innermost part of the sanctuary, known as "the holy of holies." Cf Ex 26, 33f. Here the high priest was allowed to enter only once a year, on *Yom Kippur,* the Day of Atonement. In Heb 9, 3–12 this ceremony is applied to Christ's single act of Redemption, whereby he won for us an everlasting atonement. *Propitiatory:* see note on Ex 25, 17.

16, 8: *Azazel:* perhaps a name for Satan, used only in this chapter. The ancient versions translated this word as "the escaping goat," whence the English word "scapegoat."

16, 13: *Else he will die:* the smoke is to conceal the resplendent majesty of God, the sight of which would strike any man dead.

16, 23: This verse is best read after v 25. According

to later Jewish practice the high priest again went into the holy of holies to remove the censer.

16, 29: *Mortify himself:* literally, "afflict his soul"; traditionally understood by the Jews as signifying abstinence from all food. This is the only fast day prescribed in the Mosaic law.

alien, shall mortify himself and shall do no work. 30 Since on this day atonement is made for you to make you clean, so that you may be cleansed of all your sins before the LORD, 31 by everlasting ordinance it shall be a most solemn sabbath for you, on which you must mortify yourselves.

32 "This atonement is to be made by the priest who has been anointed and ordained to the priesthood in succession to his father. He shall wear the linen garments, the sacred vestments, 33 and make atonement for the sacred sanctuary, the meeting tent and the altar, as well as for the priests and all the people of the community. 34 This, then, shall be an everlasting ordinance for you: once a year atonement shall be made for all the sins of the Israelites."

Thus was it done, as the LORD had commanded Moses.

LEGAL HOLINESS

Sacredness of Blood

17 The LORD said to Moses, 2 "Speak to Aaron and his sons, as well as to all the Israelites, and tell them: This is what the LORD has commanded. 3 Any Israelite who slaughters an ox or a sheep or a goat, whether in the camp or outside of it, 4 without first bringing it to the entrance of the meeting tent to present it as an offering to the LORD in front of his Dwelling, shall be judged guilty of bloodshed; and for this, such a man shall be cut off from among his people. 5 Therefore, such sacrifices as they used to offer up in the open field the Israelites shall henceforth offer to the LORD, bringing them to the priest at the entrance of the meeting tent and sacrificing them there as peace offerings to the LORD, 6 The priest shall splash the blood on the altar of the LORD at the entrance of the meeting tent and there burn the fat for an odor pleasing to the LORD. 7

No longer shall they offer their sacrifices to the satyrs to whom they used to render their wanton worship. This shall be an everlasting ordinance for them and their descendants.

8 "Tell them, therefore: Anyone, whether of the house of Israel or of the aliens residing among them, who offers a holocaust or sacrifice 9 without bringing it to the entrance of the meeting tent to offer it to the LORD, shall be cut off from his kinsmen. 10 And if anyone, whether of the house of Israel or of the aliens residing among them, partakes of any blood, I will set myself against that one who partakes of blood and will cut him off from among his people. 11 Since the life of a living body is in its blood, I have made you put it on the altar, so that atonement may thereby be made for your own lives, because it is the blood, as the seat of life, that makes atonement. 12 That is why I have told the Israelites: No one among you, not even a resident alien, may partake of blood.

13 "Anyone hunting, whether of the Israelites or of the aliens residing among them, who catches an animal or a bird that may be eaten, shall pour out its blood and cover it with earth. 14 Since the life of every living body is its blood, I have told the Israelites: You shall not partake of the blood of any meat. Since the life of every living body is its blood, anyone who partakes of it shall be cut off.

15 "Everyone, whether a native or an alien, who eats of an animal that died of itself or was killed by a wild beast, shall wash his garments, bathe in water, and be unclean until evening, and then he will be clean. 16 If he does not wash or does not bathe his body, he shall have the guilt to bear."

The Sanctity of Sex

18 The LORD said to Moses, 2 "Speak to the Israelites and

tell them: I, the LORD, am your God. 3 You shall not do as they do in the land of Egypt, where you once lived, nor shall you do as they do in the land of Canaan, where I am bringing you; do not conform to their customs. 4 My decrees you shall carry out, and my statutes you shall take care to follow. I, the LORD, am your God. 5 Keep, then, my statutes and decrees, for the man who carries them out will find life through them. I am the LORD.

6 "None of you shall approach a close relative to have sexual intercourse with her. I am the LORD. 7 You shall not disgrace your father by having intercourse with your mother. Besides, since she is your own mother, you shall not have intercourse with her. 8 You shall not have intercourse with your father's wife, for that would be a disgrace to your father. 9 You shall not have intercourse with your sister, your father's daughter or your mother's daughter, whether she was born in your own household or born elsewhere. 10 You shall not have intercourse with your son's daughter or with your daughter's daughter, for that would be a disgrace to your own family. 11 You shall not have intercourse with the daughter whom your father's wife bore to him, since she, too, is your sister. 12 You shall not have intercourse with your father's sister, since she is your father's relative. 13 You shall not have intercourse with your mother's sister, since she is your mother's relative. 14 You shall not disgrace your father's brother by being intimate with his wife, since she, too, is your aunt. 15 You shall not have intercourse with your daughter-in-law; she is your son's wife, and therefore you shall not disgrace her. 16 You shall not have intercourse with your brother's wife, for that would be a disgrace to your brother. 17 You shall not have intercourse with a woman and also with her

---

17, 3ff: The ancients considered blood the seat and sign of life, and therefore something sacred, even in animals. Cf Gn 9, 4f. Hence, even the ordinary butchering of an animal for meat was looked upon as having a sacrificial character, so that it should be performed at the sanctuary. This law, however, could not be carried out without great difficulty when the Israelites were scattered throughout Palestine, and so was modified in Dt 12, 20ff.

17, 11: *That atonement may thereby be made for your own lives:* hence, the sacrifice of an animal was a symbolic act which substituted the victim's life for the life of the offerer, who thus acknowledged that he deserved God's punishment for his sins. This idea of sacrifice is applied in Heb 9–10 to the death of Christ, inasmuch as "without the shedding of blood there is no forgiveness" (Heb 9, 22).

18, 6–18: These laws are formulated as directed to

the male Israelites only, but naturally the same norms of consanguinity and affinity would apply to the women as well. Marriage, as well as casual intercourse, is here forbidden between men and women of the specified degrees of relationship.

18, 16: *With your brother's wife:* it was the violation of this law which aroused the wrath of John the Baptist against Herod Antipas. Cf Mk 6, 18. An exception to this law is made in Dt 25, 5.

daughter, nor shall you marry and have intercourse with her son's daughter or her daughter's daughter; this would be shameful, because they are related to her. 18 While your wife is still living you shall not marry her sister as her rival; for thus you would disgrace your first wife.

19 "You shall not approach a woman to have intercourse with her while she is unclean from menstruation. 20 You shall not have carnal relations with your neighbor's wife, defiling yourself with her. 21 You shall not offer any of your offspring to be immolated to Molech, thus profaning the name of your God. I am the LORD. 22 You shall not lie with a male as with a woman; such a thing is an abomination. 23 You shall not have carnal relations with an animal, defiling yourself with it; nor shall a woman set herself in front of an animal to mate with it; such things are abhorrent.

24 "Do not defile yourselves by any of these things by which the nations whom I am driving out of your way have defiled themselves. 25 Because their land has become defiled, I am punishing it for its wickedness, by making it vomit out its inhabitants. 26 You, however, whether natives or resident aliens, must keep my statutes and decrees forbidding all such abominations 27 by which the previous inhabitants defiled the land; 28 otherwise the land will vomit you out also for having defiled it, just as it vomited out the nations before you. 29 Everyone who does any of these abominations shall be cut off from among his people. 30 Heed my charge, then, not to defile yourselves by observing the abominable customs that have been observed before you. I, the LORD, am your God."

Various Rules of Conduct

19 The LORD said to Moses, 2 "Speak to the whole Israelite community and tell them: Be holy,

for I, the LORD, your God, am holy. 3 Revere your mother and father, and keep my sabbaths. I, the LORD, am your God.

4 "Do not turn aside to idols, nor make molten gods for yourselves. I, the LORD, am your God.

5 "When you sacrifice your peace offering to the LORD, if you wish it to be acceptable, 6 it must be eaten on the very day of your sacrifice or on the following day. Whatever is left over until the third day shall be burned up in the fire. 7 If any of it is eaten on the third day, the sacrifice will be unacceptable as refuse; 8 whoever eats of it then shall pay the penalty for having profaned what is sacred to the LORD. Such a one shall be cut off from his people.

9 "When you reap the harvest of your land, you shall not be so thorough that you reap the field to its very edge, nor shall you glean the stray ears of grain. 10 Likewise, you shall not pick your vineyard bare, nor gather up the grapes that have fallen. These things you shall leave for the poor and the alien. I, the LORD, am your God.

11 "You shall not steal. You shall not lie or speak falsely to one another. 12 You shall not swear falsely by my name, thus profaning the name of your God. I am the LORD.

13 "You shall not defraud or rob your neighbor. You shall not withhold overnight the wages of your day laborer. 14 You shall not curse the deaf, or put a stumbling block in front of the blind, but you shall fear your God. I am the LORD.

15 "You shall not act dishonestly in rendering judgment. Show neither partiality to the weak nor deference to the mighty, but judge your fellow men justly. 16 You shall not go about spreading slander among your kinsmen; nor shall you stand by idly when your neighbor's life is at stake. I am the LORD.

17 "You shall not bear hatred for your brother in your heart. Though

you may have to reprove your fellow man, do not incur sin because of him. 18 Take no revenge and cherish no grudge against your fellow countrymen. You shall love your neighbor as yourself. I am the LORD.

19 "Keep my statutes: do not breed any of your domestic animals with others of a different species; do not sow a field of yours with two different kinds of seed; and do not put on a garment woven with two different kinds of thread.

20 "If a man has carnal relations with a female slave who has already been living with another man but has not yet been redeemed or given her freedom, they shall be punished but not put to death, because she is not free. 21 The man, moreover, shall bring to the entrance of the meeting tent a ram as his guilt offering to the LORD. 22 With this ram the priest shall make atonement before the LORD for the sin he has committed, and it will be forgiven him.

23 "When you come into the land and plant any fruit tree there, first look upon its fruit as if it were uncircumcised. For three years, while its fruit remains uncircumcised, it may not be eaten. 24 In the fourth year, however, all of its fruit shall be sacred to the LORD as a thanksgiving feast to him. 25 Not until the fifth year may you eat its fruit. Thus it will continue its yield for you. I, the LORD, am your God.

26 "Do not eat meat with the blood still in it. Do not practice divination or soothsaying. 27 Do not clip your hair at the temples, nor trim the edges of your beard. 28 Do not lacerate your bodies for the dead, and do not tattoo yourselves. I am the LORD.

29 "You shall not degrade your daughter by making a prostitute of her; else the land will become corrupt and full of lewdness. 30 Keep my sabbaths, and reverence my sanctuary. I am the LORD.

31 "Do not go to mediums or

18, 21: *Immolated to Molech:* the reference is to the Canaanite custom of sacrificing children to the god Molech. The little victims were first slain and then cremated. Cf Ez 16, 20ff; 20, 26.31; 23, 37.

19, 18: *You shall love your neighbor as yourself:* cited by our Lord as the second of the two most

important commandments of God. Cf Mt 22, 39; Mk 12, 31. Although in the present context the word "neighbor" is restricted to "fellow countrymen," in Lk 10, 29–37 Christ extends its meaning to embrace all men, even enemies. Cf also Mt 5, 43ff.

19, 20ff: This law seems out of its proper context here; perhaps it stood originally after 20, 12. *Female*

slave . . . given her freedom: reference is to the case treated of in Ex 21, 7–11.

19, 23ff: *Uncircumcised:* by analogy with a new-born boy, the newly planted tree was considered impure until "circumcised" by offering to the LORD all the fruit it bore in the fourth year.

19, 27: See note on 21, 5.

consult fortune tellers, for you will be defiled by them. I, the LORD, am your God.

32 "Stand up in the presence of the aged, and show respect for the old; thus shall you fear your God. I am the LORD.

33 "When an alien resides with you in your land, do not molest him. 34 You shall treat the alien who resides with you no differently than the natives born among you; have the same love for him as for yourself; for you too were once aliens in the land of Egypt. I, the LORD, am your God.

35 "Do not act dishonestly in using measures of length or weight or capacity. 36 You shall have a true scale and true weights, an honest ephah and an honest hin. I, the LORD, am your God, who brought you out of the land of Egypt. 37 Be careful, then, to observe all my statutes and decrees. I am the LORD."

Penalties for Various Sins

20 The LORD said to Moses, 2 "Tell the Israelites: Anyone, whether an Israelite or an alien residing in Israel, who gives any of his offspring to Molech shall be put to death. Let his fellow citizens stone him. 3 I myself will turn against such a man and cut him off from the body of his people; for in giving his offspring to Molech, he has defiled my sanctuary and profaned my holy name. 4 Even if his fellow citizens connive at such a man's crime of giving his offspring to Molech, and fail to put him to death, 5 I myself will set my face against that man and his family and will cut off from their people both him and all who join him in his wanton worship of Molech. 6 Should anyone turn to mediums and fortunetellers and follow their wanton ways, I will turn against such a one and cut him off from his people. 7 Sanctify yourselves, then, and be holy; for I, the LORD, your God, am holy. 8 Be careful, therefore,

to observe what I, the LORD, who make you holy, have prescribed.

9 "Anyone who curses his father or mother shall be put to death; since he has cursed his father or mother, he has forfeited his life. 10 If a man commits adultery with his neighbor's wife, both the adulterer and the adulteress shall be put to death. 11 If a man disgraces his father by lying with his father's wife, both the man and his stepmother shall be put to death; they have forfeited their lives. 12 If a man lies with his daughter-in-law, both of them shall be put to death; since they have committed an abhorrent deed, they have forfeited their lives. 13 If a man lies with a male as with a woman, both of them shall be put to death for their abominable deed; they have forfeited their lives. 14 If a man marries a woman and her mother also, the man and the two women as well shall be burned to death for their shameful conduct, so that such shamefulness may not be found among you. 15 If a man has carnal relations with an animal, the man shall be put to death, and the animal shall be slain. 16 If a woman goes up to any animal to mate with it, the woman and the animal shall be slain; let them both be put to death; their lives are forfeit. 17 If a man consummates marriage with his sister or his half-sister, they shall be publicly cut off from their people for this shameful deed; the man shall pay the penalty of having had intercourse with his own sister. 18 If a man lies in sexual intercourse with a woman during her menstrual period, both of them shall be cut off from their people, because they have laid bare the flowing fountain of her blood. 19 You shall not have intercourse with your mother's sister or your father's sister; whoever does so shall pay the penalty of incest. 20 If a man disgraces his uncle by having intercourse with his uncle's wife, the man and his aunt shall pay the penalty by dying childless. 21 If a man marries his brother's wife and thus disgraces his brother, they

shall be childless because of this incest.

22 "Be careful to observe all my statutes and all my decrees; otherwise the land where I am bringing you to dwell will vomit you out. 23 Do not conform, therefore, to the customs of the nations whom I am driving out of your way, because all these things that they have done have filled me with disgust for them. 24 But to you I have said: Their land shall be your possession, a land flowing with milk and honey. I am giving it to you as your own, I, the LORD, your God, who have set you apart from the other nations. 25 You, too, must set apart, then, the clean animals from the unclean, and the clean birds from the unclean, so that you may not be contaminated with the uncleanness of any beast or bird or of any swarming creature in the land that I have set apart for you. 26 To me, therefore, you shall be sacred; for I, the LORD, am sacred, I, who have set you apart from the other nations to be my own.

27 "A man or a woman who acts as a medium or fortuneteller shall be put to death by stoning; they have no one but themselves to blame for their death."

Sanctity of the Priesthood

21 The LORD said to Moses, "Speak to Aaron's sons, the priests, and tell them: None of you shall make himself unclean for any dead person among his people, 2 except for his nearest relatives, his mother or father, his son or daughter, his brother 3 or his maiden sister, who is of his own family while she remains unmarried; for these he may make himself unclean. 4 But for a sister who has married out of his family he shall not make himself unclean; this would be a profanation.

5 "The priests shall not make bare the crown of the head, nor shave the edges of the beard, nor lacerate the body. 6 To their God they shall be sacred, and not profane his name; since they offer up the obla-

<hr>

20, 27: This verse is best read immediately after v 6.

21, 1: *Unclean for any dead person:* by preparing the corpse for burial. Cf Nm 6, 6; 19, 11–19.

21, 5: Such mourning customs of the Canaanites were forbidden to all the Israelites, but especially to the priests. Cf 19, 27f.

21, 6: *Sacred:* the same Hebrew word has both

the active meaning of "holy," that is, keeping oneself free from profane impurities, and the passive meaning of "sacred," that is, set apart from what is profane and therefore with religious reverence.

tions of the LORD, the food of their God, they must be holy.

7 "A priest shall not marry a woman who has been a prostitute or has lost her honor, nor a woman who has been divorced by her husband; for the priest is sacred to his God. 8 Honor him as sacred who offers up the food of your God; treat him as sacred, because I, the LORD, who have consecrated him, am sacred.

9 "A priest's daughter who loses her honor by committing fornication and thereby dishonors her father also, shall be burned to death.

10 "The most exalted of. the priests, upon whose head the anointing oil has been poured and who has been ordained to wear the special vestments, shall not bare his head or rend his garments, 11 nor shall he go near any dead person. Not even for his father or mother may he thus become unclean 12 or leave the sanctuary; otherwise he will profane the sanctuary of his God, for with the anointing oil upon him, he is dedicated to his God, to me, the LORD.

13 "The priest shall marry a virgin. 14 Not a widow or a woman who has been divorced or a woman who has lost her honor as a prostitute, but a virgin, taken from his own people, shall he marry; 15 otherwise he will have base offspring among his people. I, the LORD, have made him sacred."

Irregularities

16 The LORD said to Moses, 17 "Speak to Aaron and tell him: None of your descendants, of whatever generation, who has any defect shall come forward to offer up the food of his God. 18 Therefore, he who has any of the following defects may not come forward: he who is blind, or lame, or who has any disfigurement or malformation, 19 or a crippled foot or hand, 20 or who is humpbacked or weakly or wall-eyed, or who is afflicted with eczema, ringworm or hernia. 21 No descendant of Aaron the priest who has any such defect may draw near to offer up the oblations of the LORD;

on account of his defect he may not draw near to offer up the food of his God. 22 He may, however, partake of the food of his God: of what is most sacred as well as of what is sacred. 23 Only, he may not approach the veil nor go up to the altar on account of his defect; he shall not profane these things that are sacred to me, for it is I, the LORD, who make them sacred."

24 Moses, therefore, told this to Aaron and his sons and to all the Israelites.

Sacrificial Banquets

22 The LORD said to Moses, 2 "Tell Aaron and his sons to respect the sacred offerings which the Israelites consecrate to me; else they will profane my holy name. I am the LORD.

3 "Tell them. If any one of you, or of your descendants in any future generation, dares, while he is in a state of uncleanness, to draw near the sacred offerings which the Israelites consecrate to the LORD, such a one shall be cut off from my presence. I am the LORD.

4 "No descendant of Aaron who is stricken with leprosy, or who suffers from a flow, may eat of these sacred offerings, unless he again becomes clean. Moreover, if anyone touches a person who has become unclean by contact with a corpse, or if anyone has had an emission of seed, 5 or if anyone touches any swarming creature or any man whose uncleanness, of whatever kind it may be, is contagious, 6 the one who touches such as these shall be unclean until evening and may not eat of the sacred portions until he has first bathed his body in water; 7 then, when the sun sets, he again becomes clean. Only then may he eat of the sacred offerings, which are his food. 8 He shall not make himself unclean by eating of any animal that has died of itself or has been killed by wild beasts. I am the LORD.

9 "They shall keep my charge and not do wrong in this matter; else they will die for their profanation. I am the LORD who have consecrated them.

10 "Neither a lay person nor a priest's tenant or hired servant may eat of any sacred offering. 11 But a

slave whom a priest acquires by purchase or who is born in his house may eat of his food. 12 A priest's daughter who is married to a layman may not eat of the sacred contributions. 13 But if a priest's daughter is widowed or divorced and, having no children, returns to her father's house, she may then eat of her father's food as in her youth. No layman, however, may eat of it. 14 If such a one eats of a sacred offering through inadvertence, he shall make restitution to the priest for the sacred offering, with an increment of one fifth of the amount. 15 The sacred offerings which the Israelites contribute to the LORD the priests shall not allow to be profaned 16 nor in the eating of the sacred offering shall they bring down guilt that must be punished; it is I, the LORD, who make them sacred."

Unacceptable Victims

17 The LORD said to Moses, 18 "Speak to Aaron and his sons and to all the Israelites, and tell them: When anyone of the house of Israel, or any alien residing in Israel, who wishes to offer a sacrifice, brings a holocaust as a votive offering or as a free-will offering to the LORD, 19 if it is to be acceptable, the ox or sheep or goat that he offers must be an unblemished male. 20 You shall not offer one that has any defect, for such a one would not be acceptable for you. 21 When anyone presents a peace offering to the LORD from the herd or the flock in fulfillment of a vow, or as a free-will offering, if it is to find acceptance, it must be unblemished; it shall not have any defect. 22 One that is blind or crippled or maimed, or one that has a running sore or mange or ringworm, you shall not offer to the LORD; do not put such an animal on the altar as an oblation to the LORD. 23 An ox or a sheep that is in any way ill-proportioned or stunted you may indeed present as a free-will offering, but it will not be acceptable as a votive offering. 24 One that has its testicles bruised or crushed or torn out or cut off you shall not offer to the LORD. You shall neither do this in your own land 25 nor receive from a foreigner any such animals to offer

---

21, 10: *Bare his head:* see note on 10, 6.

up as the food of your God; since they are deformed or defective, they will not be acceptable for you."

26 The LORD said to Moses, 27 "When an ox or a lamb or a goat is born, it shall remain with its mother for seven days; only from the eighth day onward will it be acceptable, to be offered as an oblation to the LORD. 28 You shall not slaughter an ox or a sheep on one and the same day with its young. 29 Whenever you offer a thanksgiving sacrifice to the LORD, so offer it that it may be acceptable for you; 30 it must, therefore, be eaten on the same day; none of it shall be left over until the next day. I am the LORD.

31 "Be careful to observe the commandments which I, the LORD, give you, 32 and do not profane my holy name; in the midst of the Israelites I, the LORD, must be held as sacred. It is I who made you sacred 33 and led you out of the land of Egypt, that I, the LORD, might be your God."

Holy Days

23 The LORD said to Moses, 2 "Speak to the Israelites and tell them: The following are the festivals of the LORD, my feast days, which you shall celebrate with a sacred assembly.

3 "For six days work may be done; but the seventh day is the sabbath rest, a day for sacred assembly, on which you shall do no work. The sabbath shall belong to the LORD wherever you dwell.

Passover

4 "These, then, are the festivals of the LORD which you shall celebrate at their proper time with a sacred assembly. 5 The Passover of the LORD falls on the fourteenth day of the first month, at the evening twilight. 6 The fifteenth day of this month is the LORD's feast of Unleavened Bread. For seven days you shall eat unleavened bread. 7 On

the first of these days you shall hold a sacred assembly and do no sort of work. 8 On each of the seven days you shall offer an oblation to the LORD. Then on the seventh day you shall again hold a sacred assembly and do no sort of work."

9 The LORD said to Moses, 10 "Speak to the Israelites and tell them: When you come into the land which I am giving you, and reap your harvest, you shall bring a sheaf of the first fruits of your harvest to the priest, 11 who shall wave the sheaf before the LORD that it may be acceptable for you. On the day after the sabbath the priest shall do this. 12 On this day, when your sheaf is waved, you shall offer to the LORD for a holocaust an unblemished yearling lamb. 13 Its cereal offering shall be two tenths of an ephah of fine flour mixed with oil, as a sweet-smelling oblation to the LORD; and its libation shall be a fourth of a hin of wine. 14 Until this day, when you bring your God this offering, you shall not eat any bread or roasted grain or fresh kernels. This shall be a perpetual statute for you and your descendants wherever you dwell.

Pentecost

15 "Beginning with the day after the sabbath, the day on which you bring the wave-offering sheaf, you shall count seven full weeks, 16 and then on the day after the seventh week, the fiftieth day, you shall present the new cereal offering to the LORD. 17 For the wave offering of your first fruits to the LORD, you shall bring with you from wherever you live two loaves of bread made of two tenths of an ephah of fine flour and baked with leaven. 18 Besides the bread, you shall offer to the LORD a holocaust of seven unblemished yearling lambs, one young bull, and two rams, along with their cereal offering and libations, as a sweet-smelling oblation to the LORD. 19 One male goat shall be sacrificed as a sin offering, and two yearling

lambs as a peace offering. 20 The priest shall wave the bread of the first fruits and the two lambs as a wave offering before the LORD; these shall be sacred to the LORD and belong to the priest. 21 On this same day you shall by proclamation have a sacred assembly, and no sort of work may be done. This shall be a perpetual statute for you and your descendants wherever you dwell.

22 "When you reap the harvest of your land, you shall not be so thorough that you reap the field to its very edge, nor shall you glean the stray ears of your grain. These things you shall leave for the poor and the alien. I, the LORD, am your God."

New Year's Day

23 The LORD said to Moses, 24 "Tell the Israelites: On the first day of the seventh month you shall keep a sabbath rest, with a sacred assembly and with the trumpet blasts as a reminder; 25 you shall then do no sort of work, and you shall offer an oblation to the LORD."

The Day of Atonement

26 The LORD said to Moses, 27 "The tenth of this seventh month is the Day of Atonement, when you shall hold a sacred assembly and mortify yourselves and offer an oblation to the LORD. 28 On this day you shall not do any work, because it is the Day of Atonement, when atonement is made for you before the LORD, your God. 29 Anyone who does not mortify himself on this day shall be cut off from his people; 30 and if anyone does any work on this day, I will remove him from the midst of his people. 31 This is a perpetual statute for you and your descendants wherever you dwell: you shall do no work, 32 but shall keep a sabbath of complete rest and mortify yourselves. Beginning on the evening of the ninth of the month, you shall keep this sabbath of yours from evening to evening."

23, 11: *The sabbath:* according to the Jewish tradition this was the feast day itself, the fifteenth of Nisan, which was a special day of rest. Cf v 7. However, some understand here the Saturday of the Passover week, cf Jn 19, 31, or even the Saturday following it.

23, 14: *Any bread:* made from the new grain. The harvest had first to be sanctified for man's use by this offering to God.
23, 16: *The fiftieth:* from the Greek word for this we have the name "Pentecost." Cf 2 Mc 12, 31; Acts 2, 1. It was also called "the feast of the Seven

Weeks," or simply "the feast of Weeks" (Nm 28, 26; Dt 16, 10; Tb 2, 1). *The new cereal offering:* of flour made from the new grain. Pentecost was the thanksgiving feast at the end of the grain harvest, which began after Passover. Later tradition made it a commemoration of the giving of the law at Sinai.

The Feast of Booths

33 The LORD said to Moses, 34 "Tell the Israelites: The fifteenth day of this seventh month is the LORD's feast of Booths, which shall continue for seven days. 35 On the first day there shall be a sacred assembly, and you shall do no sort of work. 36 For seven days you shall offer an oblation to the LORD, and on the eighth day you shall again hold a sacred assembly and offer an oblation to the LORD. On that solemn closing you shall do no sort of work.

37 "These, therefore, are the festivals of the LORD on which you shall proclaim a sacred assembly, and offer as an oblation to the LORD holocausts and cereal offerings, sacrifices and libations, as prescribed for each day, 38 in addition to those of the LORD's sabbaths, your donations, your various votive offerings and the freewill offerings that you present to the LORD.

39 "On the fifteenth day, then, of the seventh month, when you have gathered in the produce of the land, you shall celebrate a pilgrim feast of the LORD for a whole week. The first and the eighth day shall be days of complete rest. 40 On the first day you shall gather foliage from majestic trees, branches of palms and boughs of myrtles and of valley poplars, and then for a week you shall make merry before the LORD, your God. 41 By perpetual statute for you and your descendants you shall keep this pilgrim feast of the LORD for one whole week in the seventh month of the year. 42 During this week every native Israelite among you shall dwell in booths, 43 that your descendants may realize that, when I led the Israelites out of the land of Egypt, I made them dwell in booths. I, the LORD, am your God."

44 Thus did Moses announce to the Israelites the festivals of the LORD.

The Sanctuary Light

24 The LORD said to Moses, 2 "Order the Israelites to bring you clear oil of crushed olives for the light, so that you may keep lamps burning regularly. 3 In the meeting tent, outside the veil that hangs in front of the commandments, Aaron shall set up the lamps to burn before the LORD regularly, from evening till morning. Thus, by a perpetual statute for you and your descendants, 4 the lamps shall be set up on the pure gold lampstand, to burn regularly before the LORD.

The Showbread

5 "You shall take fine flour and bake it into twelve cakes, using two tenths of an ephah of flour for each cake. 6 These you shall place in two piles, six in each pile, on the pure gold table before the LORD. 7 On each pile put some pure frankincense, which shall serve as an oblation to the LORD, a token offering for the bread. 8 Regularly on each sabbath day this bread shall be set out afresh before the LORD, offered on the part of the Israelites by an everlasting agreement. 9 It shall belong to Aaron and his sons, who must eat it in a sacred place, since, as something most sacred among the various oblations to the LORD, it is his by perpetual right."

Punishment of Blasphemy

10 Among the Israelites there was a man born of an Israelite mother (Shelomith, daughter of Dibri, of the tribe of Dan) and an Egyptian father. 11 This man quarreled publicly with another Israelite and cursed and blasphemed the LORD's name. So the people brought him to Moses, 12 who kept him in custody till a decision from the LORD should settle the case for them. 13 The LORD then said to Moses, 14 "Take the blasphemer outside the camp, and when all who heard him have laid their hands on his head, let the whole community stone him. 15 Tell the Israelites: Anyone who curses his God shall bear the penalty of his sin; 16 whoever blasphemes the name of the LORD shall be put to death. The whole community shall stone him; alien and native alike must be put to death for blaspheming the LORD's name.

17 "Whoever takes the life of any human being shall be put to death; 18 whoever takes the life of an animal shall make restitution of another animal. A life for a life! 19 Anyone who inflicts an injury on his neighbor shall receive the same in return. 20 Limb for limb, eye for eye, tooth for tooth! The same injury that a man gives another shall be inflicted on him in return. 21 Whoever slays an animal shall make restitution, but whoever slays a man shall be put to death. 22 You shall have but one rule, for alien and native alike. I, the LORD, am your God."

23 When Moses told this to the Israelites, they took the blasphemer outside the camp and stoned him; they carried out the command that the LORD had given Moses.

The Sabbatical Year

25 The LORD said to Moses on Mount Sinai, 2 "Speak to the Israelites and tell them: When you enter the land that I am giving you, let the land, too, keep a sabbath for the LORD. 3 For six years you may sow your field, and for six years prune your vineyard, gathering in their produce. 4 But during the seventh year the land shall have a complete rest, a sabbath for the LORD, when you may neither sow your field nor prune your vineyard. 5 The aftergrowth of your harvest you shall not reap, nor shall you pick the grapes of your untrimmed vines in this year of sabbath rest for the land. 6 While the land has its sabbath, all its produce will be food equally for you yourself and for your male and female slaves, for your hired help and the tenants who live

---

23, 34: *Feast of Booths:* the joyful observance of the vintage and fruit harvest. Cf Dt 16, 13. During the seven days of the feast the Israelites camped in booths of branches erected on the roofs of their houses or in the streets in commemoration of their wanderings in the desert, where they dwelt in booths.

23, 40: *Foliage:* literally, "fruit," but here probably used in the general sense of "produce, growth." These branches were used for constructing the "booths" or huts in which the people lived during the feast. Cf Neh 8, 15. However, from about the time of Christ on, the Jews have understood this of "fruit" in the strict sense; hence, branches of lemons and oranges were carried with the other branches in joyous procession.

25, 5ff: As long as the produce of the sabbatical year remains on the field, it remains available to everyone; cf v 12. In Ex 23, 10f the poor and the wild beasts that have no other source of nourishment are alone mentioned.

with you, 7 and likewise for your livestock and for the wild animals on your land.

The Jubilee Year

8 "Seven weeks of years shall you count—seven times seven years—so that the seven cycles amount to forty-nine years. 9 Then, on the tenth day of the seventh month let the trumpet resound; on this, the Day of Atonement, the trumpet blast shall re-echo throughout your land. 10 This fiftieth year you shall make sacred by proclaiming liberty in the land for all its inhabitants. It shall be a jubilee for you, when every one of you shall return to his own property, every one to his own family estate. 11 In this fiftieth year, your year of jubilee, you shall not sow, nor shall you reap the aftergrowth or pick the grapes from the untrimmed vines. 12 Since this is the jubilee, which shall be sacred for you, you may not eat of its produce, except as taken directly from the field.

13 "In this year of jubilee, then, every one of you shall return to his own property. 14 Therefore, when you sell any land to your neighbor or buy any from him, do not deal unfairly. 15 On the basis of the number of years since the last jubilee shall you purchase the land from him; and so also, on the basis of the number of years for crops, shall he sell it to you. 16 When the years are many, the price shall be so much the more; when the years are few, the price shall be so much the less. For it is really the number of crops that he sells you. 17 Do not deal unfairly, then; but stand in fear of your God. I, the LORD, am your God.

18 "Observe my precepts and be careful to keep my regulations, for then you will dwell securely in the land. 19 The land will yield its fruit and you will have food in abundance, so that you may live there without worry. 20 Therefore, do not say, 'What shall we eat in the seventh year, if we do not then sow or reap our crop?' 21 I will bestow such blessings on you in the sixth year that there will then be crop

enough for three years. 22 When you sow in the eighth year, you will continue to eat from the old crop; and even into the ninth year, when the crop comes in, you will still have the old to eat from.

Redemption of Property

23 "The land shall not be sold in perpetuity; for the land is mine, and you are but aliens who have become my tenants. 24 Therefore, in every part of the country that you occupy, you must permit the land to be redeemed. 25 When one of your countrymen is reduced to poverty and has to sell some of his property, his closest relative, who has the right to redeem it, may go and buy back what his kinsman has sold. 26 If, however, the man has no relative to redeem his land, but later on acquires sufficient means to buy it back in his own name, 27 he shall make a deduction from the price in proportion to the number of years since the sale, and then pay back the balance to the one to whom he sold it, so that he may thus regain his own property. 28 But if he does not acquire sufficient means to buy back his land, what he has sold shall remain in the possession of the purchaser until the jubilee, when it must be released and returned to its original owner.

29 "When someone sells a dwelling in a walled town, he has the right to buy it back during the time of one full year from its sale. 30 But if such a house in a walled town has not been redeemed at the end of a full year, it shall belong in perpetuity to the purchaser and his descendants; nor shall it be released in the jubilee. 31 However, houses in villages that are not encircled by walls shall be considered as belonging to the surrounding farm land; they may be redeemed at any time, and in the jubilee they must be released.

32 "In levitical cities the Levites shall always have the right to redeem the town houses that are their property. 33 Any town house of the Levites in their cities that had been sold and not redeemed, shall be re-

leased in the jubilee; for the town houses of the Levites are their hereditary property in the midst of the Israelites. 34 Moreover, the pasture land belonging to their cities shall not be sold at all; it must always remain their hereditary property.

35 "When one of your fellow countrymen is reduced to poverty and is unable to hold out beside you, extend to him the privileges of an alien or a tenant, so that he may continue to live with you. 36 Do not exact interest from your countryman either in money or in kind, but out of fear of God let him live with you. 37 You are to lend him neither money at interest nor food at a profit. 38 I, the LORD, am your God, who brought you out of the land of Egypt to give you the land of Canaan and to be your God.

39 "When, then, your countryman becomes so impoverished beside you that he sells you his services, do not make him work as a slave. 40 Rather, let him be like a hired servant or like your tenant, working with you until the jubilee year, 41 when he, together with his children, shall be released from your service and return to his kindred and to the property of his ancestors. 42 Since those whom I brought out of the land of Egypt are servants of mine, they shall not be sold as slaves to any man. 43 Do not lord it over them harshly, but stand in fear of your God.

44 "Slaves, male and female, you may indeed possess, provided you buy them from among the neighboring nations. 45 You may also buy them from among the aliens who reside with you and from their children who are born and reared in your land. Such slaves you may own as chattels, 46 and leave to your sons as their hereditary property, making them perpetual slaves. But you shall not lord it harshly over any of the Israelites, your kinsmen.

47 "When one of your countrymen is reduced to such poverty that he sells himself to a wealthy alien who has a permanent or a temporary residence among you, or to one of the descendants of an immigrant family,

---

25, 10: *Fiftieth year:* to arrive at this number, the preceding year of jubilee is included in the count, and therefore this is more exactly the forty-ninth year,

the seventh sabbatical year. *Liberty:* Israelite slaves were set free (v 50) and landed property was returned to its original owner (v 13): two important laws for

preserving the social and economic equilibrium. *Jubilee:* derived from the Hebrew word *yobel,* "ram's horn," which was blown on this occasion.

48 even after he has thus sold his services he still has the right of redemption; he may be redeemed by one of his own brothers, 49 or by his uncle or cousin, or by some other relative or fellow clansman; or, if he acquires the means, he may redeem himself. 50 With his purchaser he shall compute the years from the sale to the jubilee, distributing the sale price over these years as though he had been hired as a day laborer. 51 The more such years there are, the more of the sale price he shall pay back as ransom; 52 the fewer years there are left before the jubilee year, the more he has to his credit; in proportion to his years of service shall he pay his ransom. 53 The alien shall treat him as a servant hired on an annual basis, and he shall not lord it over him harshly under your very eyes. 54 If he is not thus redeemed, he shall nevertheless be released, together with his children, in the jubilee year. 55 For to me the Israelites belong as servants; they are servants of mine, because I brought them out of the land of Egypt, I, the LORD, your God.

The Reward of Obedience

26 "Do not make false gods for yourselves. You shall not erect an idol or a sacred pillar for yourselves, nor shall you set up a stone figure for worship in your land; for I, the LORD, am your God. 2 Keep my sabbaths, and reverence my sanctuary. I am the LORD.

3 "If you live in accordance with my precepts and are careful to observe my commandments, 4 I will give you rain in due season, so that the land will bear its crops, and the trees their fruit; 5 your threshing will last till vintage time, and your vintage till the time for sowing, and you will have food to eat in abundance, so that you may dwell securely in your land. 6 I will establish peace in the land, that you may lie down to rest without anxiety. I will rid the country of ravenous beasts, and keep the sword of war from sweeping across your land. 7 You

will rout your enemies and lay them low with your sword. 8 Five of you will put a hundred of your foes to flight, and a hundred of you will chase ten thousand of them, till they are cut down by your sword. 9 I will look with favor upon you, and make you fruitful and numerous, as I carry out my covenant with you. 10 So much of the old crops will you have stored up for food that you will have to discard them to make room for the new. 11 I will set my Dwelling among you, and will not disdain you. 12 Ever present in your midst, I will be your God, and you will be my people; 13 for it is I, the LORD, your God, who brought you out of the land of the Egyptians and freed you from their slavery, breaking the yoke they had laid upon you and letting you walk erect.

Punishment of Disobedience

14 "But if you do not heed me and do not keep all these commandments, 15 if you reject my precepts and spurn my decrees, refusing to obey all my commandments and breaking my covenant, 16 then I, in turn, will give you your deserts. I will punish you with terrible woes—with wasting and fever to dim the eyes and sap the life. You will sow your seed in vain, for your enemies will consume the crop. 17 I will turn against you, till you are beaten down before your enemies and lorded over by your foes. You will take to flight though no one pursues you.

18 "If even after this you do not obey me, I will increase the chastisement for your sins sevenfold, 19 to break your haughty confidence. I will make the sky above you as hard as iron, and your soil as hard as bronze, 20 so that your strength will be spent in vain; your land will bear no crops, and its trees no fruit.

21 "If then you become defiant in your unwillingness to obey me, I will multiply my blows another sevenfold, as your sins deserve. 22 I will unleash the wild beasts against you, to rob you of your children and wipe out your livestock, till your pop-

ulation dwindles away and your roads become deserted.

23 "If, with all this, you still refuse to be chastened by me and continue to defy me, 24 I, too, will defy you and will smite you for your sins seven times harder than before. 25 I will make the sword, the avenger of my covenant, sweep over you. Though you then huddle together in your walled cities, I will send in pestilence among you, till you are forced to surrender to the enemy. 26 And as I cut off your supply of bread, ten women will need but one oven for baking all the bread they dole out to you in rations—not enough food to still your hunger.

27 "If, despite all this, you still persist in disobeying and defying me, 28 I, also, will meet you with fiery defiance and will chastise you with sevenfold fiercer punishment for your sins, 29 till you begin to eat the flesh of your own sons and daughters. 30 I will demolish your high places, overthrow your incense stands, and cast your corpses on those of your idols. In my abhorrence of you, 31 I will lay waste your cities and devastate your sanctuaries, refusing to accept your sweet-smelling offerings. 32 So devastated will I leave the land that your very enemies who come to live there will stand aghast at the sight of it. 33 You yourselves I will scatter among the nations at the point of my drawn sword, leaving your countryside desolate and your cities deserted. 34 Then shall the land retrieve its lost sabbaths during all the time it lies waste, while you are in the land of your enemies; then shall the land have rest and make up for its sabbaths 35 during all the time that it lies desolate, enjoying the rest that you would not let it have on the sabbaths when you lived there.

36 "Those of you who survive in the lands of their enemies I will make so fainthearted that, if leaves rustle behind them, they will flee headlong, as if from the sword, though no one pursues them; 37 stumbling over one another as if to escape a weapon, while no one is after them—so help-

---

26, 3–45: Since God's covenant was with the Israelite nation as a whole, these promises and threats are made primarily to the entire community. The rewards and punishments are of a temporal

nature because the community as such exists only here on earth, not in the hereafter.
26, 29: *Eat the flesh of your own sons and daughters:* extreme famine in cities under siege often forced

their inhabitants to such dire means of subsistence. Cf Dt 28, 53; Jer 19, 9; Ez 5, 10; 2 Kgs 6, 28f.

less will you be to take a stand against your foes! 38 You will be lost among the Gentiles, swallowed up in your enemies' country. 39 Those of you who survive in the lands of their enemies will waste away for their own and their fathers' guilt.

40 "Thus they will have to confess that they and their fathers were guilty of having rebelled against me and of having defied me, 41 so that I, too, had to defy them and bring them into their enemies' land. Then, when their uncircumcised hearts are humbled and they make amends for their guilt, 42 I will remember my covenant with Jacob, my covenant with Isaac, and my covenant with Abraham; and of the land, too, I will be mindful. 43 But the land must first be rid of them, that in its desolation it may make up its lost sabbaths, and that they, too, may make good the debt of their guilt for having spurned my precepts and abhorred my statutes. 44 Yet even so, even while they are in their enemies' land, I will not reject or spurn them, lest, by wiping them out, I make void my covenant with them; for I, the Lord, am their God. 45 I will remember them because of the covenant I made with their forefathers, whom I brought out of the land of Egypt under the very eyes of the Gentiles, that I, the Lord, might be their God."

46 These are the precepts, decrees and laws which the Lord had Moses promulgate on Mount Sinai in the pact between himself and the Israelites.

REDEMPTION OF OFFERINGS

Redemption of Votive Offerings

27 The Lord said to Moses, 2 "Speak to the Israelites and tell them: When anyone fulfills a vow of offering one or more persons to the Lord, who are to be ransomed at a fixed sum of money, 3 for persons between the ages of twenty and sixty, the fixed sum, in sanctuary shekels, shall be fifty silver shekels

for a man, 4 and thirty shekels for a woman; 5 for persons between the ages of five and twenty, the fixed sum shall be twenty shekels for a youth, and ten for a maiden; 6 for persons between the ages of one month and five years, the fixed sum shall be five silver shekels for a boy, and three for a girl; 7 for persons of sixty or more, the fixed sum shall be fifteen shekels for a man, and ten for a woman. 8 However, if the one who took the vow is too poor to meet the fixed sum, the person must be set before the priest, who shall determine the sum for his ransom in keeping with the means of the one who made the vow.

9 "If the offering vowed to the Lord is an animal that may be sacrificed, every such animal, when vowed to the Lord, becomes sacred. 10 The offerer shall not present a substitute for it by exchanging either a better for a worse one or a worse for a better one. If he attempts to offer one animal in place of another, both the original and its substitute shall be treated as sacred. 11 If the animal vowed to the Lord is unclean and therefore unfit for sacrifice, it must be set before the priest, 12 who shall determine its value in keeping with its good or bad qualities, and the value set by the priest shall stand. 13 If the offerer wishes to redeem the animal, he shall pay one fifth more than this valuation.

14 "When someone dedicates his house as sacred to the Lord, the priest shall determine its value in keeping with its good or bad points, and the value set by the priest shall stand. 15 If the one who dedicated his house wishes to redeem it, he shall pay one fifth more than the price thus established, and then it will again be his.

16 "If the object which someone dedicates to the Lord is a piece of his hereditary land, its valuation shall be made according to the amount of seed required to sow it, the acreage sown with a homer of barley seed being valued at fifty silver shekels.

17 If the dedication of a field is made at the beginning of a jubilee period, the full valuation shall hold; 18 but if it is some time after this, the priest shall estimate its money value according to the number of years left until the next jubilee year, with a corresponding rebate on the valuation. 19 If the one who dedicated his field wishes to redeem it, he shall pay one fifth more than the price thus established, and so reclaim it. 20 If, instead of redeeming such a field, he sells it to someone else, it may no longer be redeemed; 21 but at the jubilee it shall be released as sacred to the Lord; like a field that is doomed, it shall become priestly property.

22 "If the field that some man dedicates to the Lord is one he had purchased and not a part of his hereditary property, 23 the priest shall compute its value in proportion to the number of years until the next jubilee, and on the same day the price thus established shall be given as sacred to the Lord; 24 at the jubilee, however, the field shall revert to the hereditary owner of this land from whom it had been purchased.

25 "Every valuation shall be made according to the standard of the sanctuary shekel. There are twenty gerahs to the shekel.

Offerings Not To Be Redeemed

26 "Note that a first-born animal, which as such already belongs to the Lord, may not be dedicated by vow to him. If it is an ox or a sheep, it shall be ceded to the Lord; 27 but if it is an unclean animal, it may be redeemed by paying one fifth more than its fixed value. If it is not redeemed, it shall be sold at its fixed value.

. 28 "Note, also, that any one of his possessions which a man vows as doomed to the Lord, whether it is a human being or an animal or a hereditary field, shall be neither sold nor ransomed; everything that is thus doomed becomes most sacred to the

---

26, 46: The Book of Leviticus seems originally to have ended here; the following chapter is an appendix.

27, 12: *Determine its value:* fix the price at which the animal may be sold to someone else. Only the original owner must pay the twenty percent tax, as a

penalty for buying back what he had vowed to God. So also for houses and fields that are vowed to the Lord, as treated of in the following verses. The money from the sale or from the redemption of such vowed property naturally goes to the sanctuary.

27, 27: *An unclean animal:* such as the first-born

of an ass, which was unfit for sacrifice. According to Ex 13, 13; 34, 20, a first-born ass was to be redeemed by offering a sheep in its stead, or was to have its neck broken. The present law is probably a later modification of the earlier one.

LORD. 29 All human beings that are doomed lose the right to be redeemed; they must be put to death.

30 "All tithes of the land, whether in grain from the fields or in fruit from the trees, belong to the LORD, as sacred to him. 31 If someone wishes to buy back any of his tithes, he shall pay one fifth more than their value. 32 The tithes of the herd and the flock shall be determined by ceding to the LORD as sacred every tenth animal as they are counted by the herdsman's rod. 33 It shall not matter whether good ones or bad ones are thus chosen, and no exchange may be made. If any exchange is attempted, both the original animal and its substitute shall be treated as sacred, without the right of being bought back."

34 These are the commandments which the LORD gave Moses on Mount Sinai for the Israelites.

27, 29: *All human beings that are doomed:* according to some interpreters, this signifies the idolatrous Canaanites, who were doomed to destruction by divine authority; according to others, this drastic law was enacted for the purpose of discouraging private persons from rashly vowing their slaves or other dependents as offerings to God. Cf Ex 22, 19; Dt 13, 13–19.

Numbers

The Census

IN the year following that of the Israelites' departure from the land of Egypt, on the first day of the second month, the LORD said to Moses in the meeting tent in the desert of Sinai: 2 "Take a census of the whole community of the Israelites, by clans and ancestral houses, registering each male individually. 3 You and Aaron shall enroll in companies all the men in Israel of twenty years or more who are fit for military service.

Moses' Assistants

4 "To assist you there shall be a man from each tribe, the head of his ancestral house. 5 These are the names of those who are to assist you:

from Reuben: Elizur, son of Shedeur;

6 from Simeon: Shelumiel, son of Zurishaddai;

7 from Judah: Nahshon, son of Amminadab;

8 from Issachar: Nethanel, son of Zuar;

9 from Zebulun: Eliab, son of Helon;

10 from Ephraim: Elishama, son of Ammihud, and

from Manasseh: Gamaliel, son of Pedahzur, for the descendants of Joseph;

11 from Benjamin: Abidan, son of Gideoni;

12 from Dan: Ahiezer, son of Ammishaddai;

13 from Asher: Pagiel, son of Ochran;

14 from Gad: Eliasaph, son of Reuel;

15 from Naphtali: Ahira, son of Enan."

16 These were councilors of the community, princes of their ancestral tribes, chiefs of the troops of Israel. 17 So Moses and Aaron took these men who had been designated, 18 and assembled the whole community on the first day of the second month. Every man of twenty years or more then declared his name and lineage according to clan and ancestral house, 19 as the LORD had commanded Moses.

Count of the Twelve Tribes

This is their census as taken in the desert of Sinai. 20 Of the descendants of Reuben, the first-born of Israel, registered by lineage in clans and ancestral houses: when all the males of twenty years or more who were fit for military service were polled, 21 forty-six thousand five hundred were enrolled in the tribe of Reuben.

22 Of the descendants of Simeon, registered by lineage in clans and ancestral houses: when all the males of twenty years or more who were fit for military service were polled, 23 fifty-nine thousand three hundred were enrolled in the tribe of Simeon.

24 Of the descendants of Gad, registered by lineage in clans and ancestral houses: when all the males of twenty years or more who were fit for military service were polled, 25 forty-five thousand six hundred and fifty were enrolled in the tribe of Gad.

26 Of the descendants of Judah, registered by lineage in clans and ancestral houses: when all the males of twenty years or more who were fit for military service were polled, 27 seventy-four thousand six hun-

---

1, 2: All Israel was divided into tribes, each tribe into clans, and each clan into ancestral houses.

1, 16: *Troops:* literally "thousands"; this division of the Israelites, with its subdivisions of "hundreds,

fifties and tens," was primarily for military and judicial purposes. Cf Ex 18, 21; 2 Sm 18, 1.

dred were enrolled in the tribe of Judah.

28 Of the descendants of Issachar, registered by lineage in clans and ancestral houses: when all the males of twenty years or more who were fit for military service were polled, 29 fifty-four thousand four hundred were enrolled in the tribe of Issachar.

30 Of the descendants of Zebulun, registered by lineage in clans and ancestral houses: when all the males of twenty years or more who were fit for military service were polled, 31 fifty-seven thousand four hundred were enrolled in the tribe of Zebulun.

32 Of the descendants of Joseph—

Of the descendants of Ephraim, registered by lineage in clans and ancestral houses: when all the males of twenty years or more who were fit for military service were polled, 33 forty thousand five hundred were enrolled in the tribe of Ephraim.

34 Of the descendants of Manasseh, registered by lineage in clans and ancestral houses: when all the males of twenty years or more who were fit for military service were polled, 35 thirty-two thousand two hundred were enrolled in the tribe of Manasseh.

36 Of the descendants of Benjamin, registered by lineage in clans and ancestral houses: when all the males of twenty years or more who were fit for military service were polled, 37 thirty-five thousand four hundred were enrolled in the tribe of Benjamin.

38 Of the descendants of Dan, registered by lineage in clans and ancestral houses: when all the males of twenty years or more who were fit for military service were polled, 39 sixty-two thousand seven hundred were enrolled in the tribe of Dan.

40 Of the descendants of Asher, registered by lineage in clans and ancestral houses: when all the males of twenty years or more who were fit for military service were polled,

41 forty-one thousand five hundred were enrolled in the tribe of Asher.

42 Of the descendants of Naphtali, registered by lineage in clans and ancestral houses: when all the males of twenty years or more who were fit for military service were polled, 43 fifty-three thousand four hundred were enrolled in the tribe of Naphtali.

44 It was these who were registered, each according to his ancestral house, in the census taken by Moses and Aaron and the twelve princes of Israel. 45 The total number of the Israelites of twenty years or more who were fit for military service, registered by ancestral houses, 46 was six hundred and three thousand, five hundred and fifty.

Levites Omitted in the Census

47 The Levites, however, were not registered by ancestral tribe with the others. 48 For the LORD had told Moses, 49 "The tribe of Levi alone you shall not enroll nor include in the census along with the other Israelites. 50 You are to give the Levites charge of the Dwelling of the commandments with all its equipment and all that belongs to it. It is they who shall carry the Dwelling with all its equipment and who shall be its ministers. They shall therefore camp around the Dwelling. 51 When the Dwelling is to move on, the Levites shall take it down; when the Dwelling is to be pitched, it is the Levites who shall set it up. Any layman who comes near it shall be put to death. 52 While the other Israelites shall camp by companies, each in his own division of the camp, 53 the Levites shall camp around the Dwelling of the commandments. Otherwise God's wrath will strike the Israelite community. The Levites, then, shall have charge of the Dwelling of the commandments." 54 All this the Israelites fulfilled as the LORD had commanded Moses.

Arrangement of the Tribes

2 The LORD said to Moses and Aaron: 2 "The Israelites shall camp, each in his own division, under

the ensigns of their ancestral houses. They shall camp around the meeting tent, but at some distance from it.

3 "Encamped on the east side, toward the sunrise, shall be the divisional camp of Judah, arranged in companies. [The prince of the Judahites was Nahshon, son of Amminidab, 4 and his soldiers amounted in the census to seventy-four thousand six hundred.] 5 With Judah shall camp the tribe of Issachar [Their prince was Nethanel, son of Zuar, 6 and his soldiers amounted in the census to fifty-four thousand four hundred.] 7 and the tribe of Zebulun. [Their prince was Eliab, son of Helon, 8 and his soldiers amounted in the census to fifty-seven thousand four hundred. 9 The total number of those registered by companies in the camp of Judah was one hundred and eighty-six thousand four hundred.] These shall be first on the march.

10 "On the south side shall be the divisional camp of Reuben, arranged in companies. [Their prince was Elizur, son of Shedeur, 11 and his soldiers amounted in the census to forty-six thousand five hundred.] 12 Beside them shall camp the tribe of Simeon [Their prince was Shelumiel, son of Zurishaddai, 13 and his soldiers amounted in the census to fifty-nine thousand three hundred.] 14 and next the tribe of Gad. [Their prince was Eliasaph, son of Reuel, 15 and his soldiers amounted in the census to forty-five thousand six hundred and fifty. 16 The total number of those registered by companies in the camp of Reuben was one hundred and fifty-one thousand four hundred and fifty.] These shall be second on the march.

17 "Then the meeting tent and the camp of the Levites shall set out in the middle of the line. As in camp, so also on the march, every man shall be in his proper place, with his own division.

18 "On the west side shall be the divisional camp of Ephraim, arranged in companies. [Their prince was Elishama, son of Ammihud, 19 and his soldiers amounted in the

1, 47: The Levites were not enrolled in this census, which was principally for military purposes, but a separate census was made of them. Cf 3, 15f. 39. 2, 3–31: A similar arrangement of the tribes around the central sanctuary in the ideal Israelite state is given in Ez 48.

census to forty thousand five hundred.] 20 Beside them shall camp the tribe of Manasseh [Their prince was Gamaliel, son of Pedahzur, 21 and his soldiers amounted in the census to thirty-two thousand two hundred.] 22 and the tribe of Benjamin. [Their prince was Abidan, son of Gideoni, 23 and his soldiers amounted in the census to thirty-five thousand four hundred. 24 The total number of those registered by companies in the camp of Ephraim was one hundred and eight thousand one hundred.] These shall be third on the march.

25 "On the north side shall be the divisional camp of Dan, arranged in companies. [Their prince was Ahiezer, son of Ammishaddai, 26 and his soldiers amounted in the census to sixty-two thousand seven hundred.] 27 Beside them shall camp the tribe of Asher [Their prince was Pagiel, son of Ochran 28 and his soldiers amounted in the census to forty-one thousand five hundred.] 29 and next the tribe of Naphtali. [Their prince was Ahira, son of Enan, 30 and his soldiers amounted in the census to fifty-three thousand four hundred. 31 The total number of those registered by companies in the camp of Dan was one hundred and fifty-seven thousand six hundred.] These shall be the last of the divisions on the march."

32 This was the census of the Israelites taken by ancestral houses. The total number of those registered by companies in the camps was six hundred and three thousand five hundred and fifty. 33 The Levites, however, were not registered with the other Israelites, for so the LORD had commanded Moses. 34 The Israelites did just as the LORD had commanded Moses; both in camp and on the march they were in their own divisions, every man according to his clan and his ancestral house.

The Sons of Aaron

3 The following were the descendants of Aaron and Moses at the time that the LORD spoke to Moses on Mount Sinai. 2 The sons of Aaron were Nadab his first-born, Abihu, Eleazar, and Ithamar. 3 These are the names of the sons of Aaron, the anointed priests who were ordained to exercise the priesthood. 4 But when Nadab and Abihu offered profane fire before the LORD in the desert of Sinai, they met death in the presence of the LORD, and left no sons. Thereafter only Eleazar and Ithamar performed the priestly functions under the direction of their father Aaron.

Levites in Place of the First-born

5 Now the LORD said to Moses: 6 "Summon the tribe of Levi and present them to Aaron the priest, as his assistants. 7 They shall discharge his obligations and those of the whole community before the meeting tent by serving at the Dwelling. 8 They shall have custody of all the furnishings of the meeting tent and discharge the duties of the Israelites in the service of the Dwelling. 9 You shall give the Levites to Aaron and his sons; they have been set aside from among the Israelites as dedicated to me. 10 But only Aaron and his descendants shall you appoint to have charge of the priestly functions. Any layman who comes near shall be put to death."

11 The LORD said to Moses, 12 "It is I who have chosen the Levites from the Israelites in place of every first-born that opens the womb among the Israelites. The Levites, therefore, are mine, 13 because every first-born is mine. When I slew all the first-born in the land of Egypt, I made all the first-born in Israel sacred to me, both of man and of beast. They belong to me; I am the LORD."

Census of the Levites

14 The LORD said to Moses in the desert of Sinai, 15 "Take a census of the Levites by ancestral houses and clans, registering every male of a month or more." 16 Moses, therefore, took their census in accordance with the command the LORD had given him.

17 The sons of Levi were named Gershon, Kohath and Merari. 18 The descendants of Gershon, by clans, were named Libni and Shimei. 19 The descendants of Kohath, by clans, were Amram, Izhar, Hebron and Uzziel. 20 The descendants of Merari, by clans, were Mahli and Mushi. These were the clans of the Levites by ancestral houses.

Duties of the Levitical Clans

21 To Gershon belonged the clan of the Libnites and the clan of the Shimeites; these were the clans of the Gershonites. 22 When all their males of a month or more were registered, they numbered seven thousand five hundred. 23 The clans of the Gershonites camped behind the Dwelling, to the west. 24 The prince of their ancestral house was Eliasaph, son of Lael. 25 At the meeting tent they had charge of whatever pertained to the Dwelling, the tent and its covering, the curtain at the entrance of the meeting tent, 26 the hangings of the court, the curtain at the entrance of the court enclosing both the Dwelling and the altar, and the ropes.

27 To Kohath belonged the clans of the Amramites, the Izharites, the Hebronites, and the Uzzielites; these were the clans of the Kohathites. 28 When all their males of a month or more were registered, they numbered eight thousand three hundred. They had charge of the sanctuary. 29 The clans of the Kohathites camped at the south side of the Dwelling. 30 The prince of their ancestral house was Elizaphan, son of Uzziel. 31 They had charge of whatever pertained to the ark, the table, the lampstand, the altars, the utensils with which the ministry of the sanctuary was exercised, and the veil. 32 The chief prince of the Levites, however, was Eleazar, son of Aaron the priest; he was supervisor over those who had charge of the sanctuary.

33 To Merari belonged the clans of the Mahlites and the Mushites; these were the clans of Merari.

3, 25f: The Gershonites had two wagons for transporting these things; cf 7, 7. For a description of *the Dwelling*, see Ex 26, 1–6; *the tent*, Ex 26, 7–13; *its covering*, Ex 26, 14; *the curtain at the entrance*, Ex 26, 36; *the hangings of the court*, Ex 27, 9–15; *the curtain at the entrance of the court*, Ex 27, 16; *the ropes* of the Dwelling, Ex 35, 18.

3, 31: The Kohathites had to carry these sacred objects on their shoulders; cf 7, 9. For a description of *the ark*, see Ex 25, 10–22; *the table*, Ex 25, 23–30; *the lampstand*, Ex 25, 31–40; *the altars*, Ex 27, 1–8; 30, 1–10.

34 When all their males of a month or more were registered, they numbered six thousand two hundred. 35 The prince of the ancestral house of the clans of Merari was Zuriel, son of Abihail. They camped at the north side of the Dwelling. 36 The Merarites were charged with the care of whatever pertained to the boards of the Dwelling, its bars, columns, pedestals, and all its fittings, 37 as well as the columns of the surrounding court with their pedestals, pegs and ropes.

38 East of the Dwelling, that is, in front of the meeting tent, toward the sunrise, were camped Moses and Aaron and the latter's sons. They discharged the obligations of the sanctuary for the Israelites. Any layman who came near was to be put to death.

39 The total number of male Levites a month old or more whom Moses had registered by clans in keeping with the LORD's command, was twenty-two thousand.

Census and Ransom of First-born

40 The LORD then said to Moses, "Take a census of all the first-born males of the Israelites a month old or more, and compute their total number. 41 Then assign the Levites to me, the LORD, in place of all the first-born of the Israelites, as well as their cattle in place of all the first-born among the cattle of the Israelites." 42 So Moses took a census of all the first-born of the Israelites, as the LORD had commanded him. 43 When all the first-born males of a month or more were registered, they numbered twenty-two thousand two hundred and seventy-three.

44 The LORD said to Moses: 45 "Take the Levites in place of all the first-born of the Israelites, and the Levites' cattle in place of their cattle, that the Levites may belong to me. I am the LORD. 46 As ransom for the two hundred and seventy-three first-born of the Israelites who outnumber the Levites, 47 you

shall take five shekels for each individual, according to the standard of the sanctuary shekel, twenty gerahs to the shekel. 48 Give this silver to Aaron and his sons as ransom for the extra number." 49 So Moses took the silver as ransom from those who were left when the rest had been redeemed by the Levites. 50 From the first-born of the Israelites he received in silver one thousand three hundred and sixty-five shekels according to the sanctuary standard. 51 He then gave this ransom silver to Aaron and his sons, as the LORD had commanded him.

Duties Further Defined

4 The LORD said to Moses and Aaron: 2 "Among the Levites take a total of the Kohathites, by clans and ancestral houses, all the men of the Kohathites 3 between thirty and fifty years of age; these are to undertake obligatory tasks in the meeting tent.

4 "The service of the Kohathites in the meeting tent concerns the most sacred objects. 5 In breaking camp, Aaron and his sons shall go in and take down the screening curtain and cover the ark of the commandments with it. 6 Over these they shall put a cover of tahash skin, and on top of this spread an all-violet cloth. They shall then put the poles in place. 7 On the table of the Presence they shall spread a violet cloth and put on it the plates and cups, as well as the bowls and pitchers for libations; the established bread offering shall remain on the table. 8 Over these they shall spread a scarlet cloth and cover all this with tahash skin. They shall then put the poles in place. 9 They shall use a violet cloth to cover the lampstand with its lamps, trimming shears, and trays, as well as the various containers of oil from which it is supplied. 10 The lampstand with all its utensils they shall then enclose in a covering of tahash skin, and place on a litter. 11 Over the golden altar they shall spread a

violet cloth, and cover this also with a covering of tahash skin. They shall then put the poles in place. 12 Taking the utensils of the sanctuary service, they shall wrap them all in violet cloth and cover them with tahash skin. They shall then place them on a litter. 13 After cleansing the altar of its ashes, they shall spread a purple cloth over it. 14 On this they shall put all the utensils with which it is served: the fire pans, forks, shovels, basins, and all the utensils of the altar. They shall then spread a covering of tahash skin over this, and put the poles in place.

15 "Only after Aaron and his sons have finished covering the sacred objects and all their utensils on breaking camp, shall the Kohathites enter to carry them. But they shall not touch the sacred objects; if they do they will die. These, then, are the objects in the meeting tent that the Kohathites shall carry.

16 "Eleazar, son of Aaron the priest, shall be in charge of the oil for the light, the fragrant incense, the established cereal offering, and the anointing oil. He shall be in charge of the whole Dwelling with all the sacred objects and utensils that are in it."

17 The LORD said to Moses and Aaron: 18 "Do not let the group of Kohathite clans perish from the body of the Levites. 19 That they may live and not die when they approach the most sacred objects, this is what you shall do for them: Aaron and his sons shall go in and assign to each of them his task and what he must carry; 20 but the Kohathites shall not go in to look upon the sacred objects, even for an instant; if they do, they will die."

21 The LORD said to Moses, 22 "Take a total among the Gershonites also, by ancestral houses and clans, 23 of all the men between thirty and fifty years of age; these are to undertake obligatory tasks in the meeting tent. 24 This is the task of the clans of the Gershonites, what

---

3, 36f: The Merarites had four wagons for transporting this heavy material; cf 7, 8. For a description of *the boards, bars, etc., of the Dwelling,* see Ex 26, 15–30; *the columns, pedestals, etc., of the court,* Ex 27, 9–19.

4, 3: *Thirty:* at a later period the Levites began to serve when they were twenty-five (8, 24) or even only

twenty years old (1 Chr 23, 24.27; 2 Chr 31, 17; Ezr 3, 8; but cf 1 Chr 23, 3).

4, 5: *The screening curtain:* the veil between the inner and the outer rooms of the sanctuary. Cf Ex 26, 31–33.

4, 11: *The golden altar:* the altar of incense. Cf Ex 30, 1–6.

4, 13: *The altar:* the bronze altar of holocausts. Cf Ex 27, 1–8.

4, 14: *Forks:* used in turning over the sacrificed animal on the fire of the altar. *Basins:* to receive the sacrificial blood; cf Zec 9, 15.

they must do and what they must carry: 25 they shall carry the sheets of the Dwelling, the meeting tent with its covering and the outer wrapping of tahash skin, the curtain at the entrance of the meeting tent, 26 the hangings of the court, the curtain at the entrance of the court that encloses both the Dwelling and the altar, together with their ropes and all other objects necessary in their use. Whatever is to be done with these things shall be their task. 27 The service of the Gershonites shall be entirely under the direction of Aaron and his sons, with regard to what they must do and what they must carry; you shall make each man of them responsible for what he is to carry. 28 This, then, is the task of the Gershonites in the meeting tent; and they shall be under the supervision of Ithamar, son of Aaron the priest.

29 "Among the Merarites, too, you shall enroll by clans and ancestral houses 30 all their men between thirty and fifty years of age; these are to undertake obligatory tasks in the meeting tent. 31 This is what they shall be responsible for carrying, all the years of their service in the meeting tent: the boards of the Dwelling with its bars, columns and pedestals, 32 and the columns of the surrounding court with their pedestals, pegs and ropes. You shall designate for each man of them all the objects connected with his service, which he shall be responsible for carrying. 33 This, then, is the task of the clans of the Merarites during all their service in the meeting tent under the supervision of Ithamar, son of Aaron the priest."

Number of Adult Levites

34 So Moses and Aaron and the princes of the community made a registration among the Kohathites, by clans and ancestral houses, 35 of all the men between thirty and fifty years of age. These were to undertake obligatory tasks in the meeting tent; 36 as registered by clans, they numbered two thousand seven hundred and fifty. 37 Such was the census of all the men of the Kohathite clans who were to serve in the meeting tent, which Moses took, together with Aaron, as the LORD bade him.

38 The registration was then made among the Gershonites, by clans and ancestral houses, 39 of all the men between thirty and fifty years of age. These were to undertake obligatory tasks in the meeting tent; 40 as registered by clans and ancestral houses, they numbered two thousand six hundred and thirty. 41 Such was the census of all the men of the Gershonite clans who were to serve in the meeting tent, which Moses took, together with Aaron, at the LORD's bidding.

42 Then the registration was made among the Merarites, by clans and ancestral houses, 43 of all the men from thirty up to fifty years of age. These were to undertake obligatory tasks in the meeting tent; 44 as registered by clans, they numbered three thousand two hundred. 45 Such was the census of the men of the Merarite clans which Moses took, together with Aaron, as the LORD bade him.

46 Therefore, when Moses and Aaron and the Israelite princes had completed the registration among the Levites, by clans and ancestral houses, 47 of all the men between thirty and fifty years of age who were to undertake tasks of service or transport of the meeting tent, 48 the total number registered was eight thousand five hundred and eighty. 49 According to the LORD's bidding to Moses, they gave them their individual assignments for service and for transport; so the LORD had commanded Moses.

The Unclean Expelled

5 The LORD said to Moses: 2 "Order the Israelites to expel from camp every leper, and everyone suffering from a discharge, and everyone who has become unclean by contact with a corpse. 3 Male and female alike, you shall compel them to go out of the camp; they are not to defile the camp in which I dwell." 4 The Israelites obeyed the command that the LORD had given Moses; they expelled them from the camp.

Unjust Possession

5 The LORD said to Moses. 6 "Tell the Israelites: If a man (or woman) commits a fault against his fellow man and wrongs him, thus breaking faith with the LORD, 7 he shall confess the wrong he has done, restore his ill-gotten goods in full, and in addition give one fifth of their value to the one he has wronged. 8 However, if the latter has no next of kin to whom restoration of the ill-gotten goods can be made, the goods to be restored shall be the LORD's and shall fall to the priest; this is apart from the atonement ram with which the priest makes amends for the guilty man. 9 Likewise, every sacred contribution that the Israelites are bound to make shall fall to the priest. 10 Each Israelite man may dispose of his own sacred contributions; they become the property of the priest to whom he gives them."

Ordeal for a Suspected Adulteress

11 The Lord said to Moses, 12 "Speak to the Israelites and tell them: If a man's wife goes astray and becomes unfaithful to him 13 by having intercourse with another man, though her husband has not sufficient evidence of the fact, so that her impurity remains unproved for lack of a witness who might have caught her in the act; 14 or if a man is overcome by a feeling of jealousy that makes him suspect his wife, whether she was actually impure or not: 15 he shall bring his wife to the priest and shall take along as offering for her a tenth of an ephah of barley meal. However, he shall not pour oil on it nor put frankincense over it, since it is a

---

5, 2: For the laws regarding victims of leprosy, see Lv 13–14; those *suffering from a discharge*, Lv 15; the *unclean by contact with a corpse*, 19, 11–22; Lv 21, 1–4.

5, 5–10: The basic law on unjust possession is given in Lv 5, 14–26. The new item here concerns the case where the injured party has died and left no heirs, in which case the restitution must be made to the priest.

5, 8: *Next of kin:* literally "redeemer," a technical term denoting the nearest relative, upon whom devolved the obligation of "redeeming" the family property, in order to keep it within the family. Cf Lv 25, 25; Ru 4, 1–6.

cereal offering of jealousy, a cereal offering for an appeal in a question of guilt.

16 "The priest shall first have the woman come forward and stand before the LORD. 17 In an earthen vessel he shall meanwhile put some holy water, as well as some dust that he has taken from the floor of the Dwelling. 18 Then, as the woman stands before the LORD, the priest shall uncover her head and place in her hands the cereal offering of her appeal, that is, the cereal offering of jealousy, while he himself shall hold the bitter water that brings a curse. 19 Then he shall adjure the woman, saying to her, 'If no other man has had intercourse with you, and you have not gone astray by impurity while under the authority of your husband, be immune to the curse brought by this bitter water. 20 But if you have gone astray while under the authority of your husband and have acted impurely by letting a man other than your husband have intercourse with you' 21 —so shall the priest adjure the woman with this oath of imprecation—'may the LORD make you an example of malediction and imprecation among your people by causing your thighs to waste away and your belly to swell! 22 May this water, then, that brings a curse, enter your body to make your belly swell and your thighs waste away!' And the woman shall say, 'Amen, amen!' 23 The priest shall put these imprecations in writing and shall then wash them off into the bitter water, 24 which he is to have the woman drink, so that it may go into her with all its bitter curse. 25 But first he shall take the cereal offering of jealousy from the woman's hand, and having waved this offering before the LORD, shall put it near the altar, 26 where he shall take a handful of the cereal offering as its token offering and burn it on the altar. Only then shall he have the

woman drink the water. 27 Once she has done so, if she has been impure and unfaithful to her husband, this bitter water that brings a curse will go into her, and her belly will swell and her thighs will waste away, so that she will become an example of imprecation among her people. 28 If, however, the woman has not defiled herself, but is still pure, she will be immune and will still be able to bear children.

29 "This, then, is the law for jealousy: When a woman goes astray while under the authority of her husband and acts impurely, 30 or when such a feeling of jealousy comes over a man that he becomes suspicious of his wife, he shall have her stand before the LORD, and the priest shall apply this law in full to her. 31 The man shall be free from guilt, but the woman shall bear such guilt as she may have."

Laws concerning Nazirites

6 The LORD said to Moses: 2 "Speak to the Israelites and tell them: When a man (or a woman) solemnly takes the nazirite vow to dedicate himself to the LORD, 3 he shall abstain from wine and strong drink; he may neither drink wine vinegar, other vinegar, or any kind of grape juice, nor eat either fresh or dried grapes. 4 As long as he is a nazirite he shall not eat anything of the produce of the vine; not even unripe grapes or grapeskins. 5 While he is under the nazirite vow, no razor shall touch his hair. Until the period of his dedication to the LORD is over, he shall be sacred, and shall let the hair of his head grow freely. 6 As long as he is dedicated to the LORD, he shall not enter where a dead person is. 7 Not even for his father or mother, his sister or brother, should they die, may he become unclean, since his head bears his dedication to God. 8 As long

as he is a nazirite he is sacred to the LORD.

9 "If someone dies very suddenly in his presence, so that his dedicated head becomes unclean, he shall shave his head on the day of his purification, that is, on the seventh day. 10 On the eighth day he shall bring two turtledoves or two pigeons to the priest at the entrance of the meeting tent. 11 The priest shall offer up the one as a sin offering and the other as a holocaust, thus making atonement for him for the sin he has committed by reason of the dead person. On the same day he shall re-consecrate his head 12 and begin anew the period of his dedication to the LORD as a nazirite, bringing a yearling lamb as a guilt offering. The previous period is not valid, because his dedicated head became unclean.

13 "This is the ritual for the nazirite: On the day he completes the period of his dedication he shall go to the entrance of the meeting tent, 14 bringing as his offering to the LORD one unblemished yearling lamb for a holocaust, one unblemished yearling ewe lamb for a sin offering, one unblemished ram as a peace offering, along with their cereal offerings and libations, 15 and a basket of unleavened cakes of fine flour mixed with oil and of un-leavened wafers spread with oil. 16 The priest shall present them before the LORD, and shall offer up the sin offering and the holocaust for him. 17 He shall then offer up the ram as a peace offering to the LORD, with its cereal offering and libation, and the basket of unleavened cakes. 18 Then at the entrance of the meeting tent the nazirite shall shave his dedicated head, collect the hair, and put it in the fire that is under the peace offering. 19 After the nazi-rite has shaved off his dedicated hair, the priest shall take a boiled shoulder of the ram, as well as one unleavened cake and one unleavened wafer from

---

5, 17: *Holy water:* water from the laver that stood in the court of the Dwelling.

5, 18: *Appeal:* by which she invokes the Lord and refers her case to his decision.

5, 21: *An example of malediction and imprecation:* the woman's name would be used in curses and oaths to invoke a similar misfortune on another person or on oneself. Cf Is 65, 15; Jer 29, 22.

5, 22: *Amen:* a Hebrew word meaning, "certainly, truly," used to give assent to a statement, a curse, a

blessing, a prayer, or the like; in this sense of "so be it," the Christian liturgy also uses it after prayers and blessings.

5, 31: *Free from guilt:* by fulfilling his obligation of obtaining a decision in the matter.

6, 1ff: *Nazirite:* from the Hebrew word *nazir,* meaning "set apart as sacred, dedicated, vowed." The nazirite vow could be either for a limited period or for life. Those bound by this vow had to abstain from all the products of the grapevine, from cutting

or shaving their hair, and from contact with a corpse. They were regarded as men of God like the prophets; cf Am 2, 11f. Examples of lifelong nazirites were Samson (Jgs 13, 4f.7; 16, 17), Samuel (1 Sm 1, 11), and John the Baptist (Lk 1, 15). At the time of Christ the practice of taking the nazirite vow for a limited period seems to have been quite common, even among the early Christians; cf Acts 18, 18; 21, 23f.26.

the basket, and shall place them in the hands of the nazirite. 20 The priest shall then wave them as a wave offering before the LORD. They become sacred and shall belong to the priest, along with the breast of the wave offering and the leg of the raised offering. Only after this may the nazirite drink wine.

21 "This, then, is the law for the nazirite; this is the offering to the LORD which is included in his vow of dedication apart from anything else which his means may allow. Thus shall he carry out the law of his dedication in keeping with the vow he has taken."

The Priestly Blessing

22 The LORD said to Moses: 23 "Speak to Aaron and his sons and tell them: This is how you shall bless the Israelites. Say to them:

24 The LORD bless you and keep you!
25 The LORD let his face shine upon you, and be gracious to you!
26 The LORD look upon you kindly and give you peace!

27 So shall they invoke my name upon the Israelites, and I will bless them."

Offerings of Princes

7 Now, when Moses had completed the erection of the Dwelling and had anointed and consecrated it with all its equipment (as well as the altar with all its equipment), 2 an offering was made by the princes of Israel, who were heads of ancestral houses; the same princes of the tribes who supervised the census. 3 The offering they brought before the LORD consisted of six baggage wagons and twelve oxen, that is, a wagon for every two princes, and an ox for every prince. These they presented as their offering before the Dwelling.

4 The LORD then said to Moses, 5 "Accept their offering, that these things may be put to use in the service of the meeting tent. Assign them to the Levites, to each group in proportion to the duties." 6 So

Moses accepted the wagons and oxen, and assigned them to the Levites. 7 He gave two wagons and four oxen to the Gershonites in proportion to their duties, 8 and four wagons and eight oxen to the Merarites in proportion to their duties, under the supervision of Ithamar, son of Aaron the priest. 9 He gave none to the Kohathites, because they had to carry on their shoulders the sacred objects which were their charge.

10 For the dedication of the altar also, the princes brought offerings before the altar on the day it was anointed. 11 But the LORD said to Moses, "Let one prince a day present his offering for the dedication of the altar."

12 The one who presented his offering on the first day was Nahshon, son of Amminadab, prince of the tribe of Judah. 13 His offering consisted of one silver plate weighing a hundred and thirty shekels according to the sanctuary standard and one silver basin weighing seventy shekels, both filled with fine flour mixed with oil for a cereal offering; 14 one gold cup of ten shekels' weight filled with incense; 15 one young bull, one ram, and one yearling lamb for a holocaust; 16 one goat for a sin offering; 17 and two oxen, five rams, five goats, and five yearling lambs for a peace offering. This was the offering of Nahshon, son of Amminadab.

18 On the second day Nethanel, son of Zuar, prince of Issachar, made his offering. 19 He presented as his offering one silver plate weighing a hundred and thirty shekels according to the sanctuary standard and one silver basin weighing seventy shekels, both filled with fine flour mixed with oil for a cereal offering; 20 one gold cup of ten shekels' weight filled with incense; 21 one young bull, one ram, and one yearling lamb for a holocaust; 22 one goat for a sin offering; 23 and two oxen, five rams, five goats, and five yearling lambs for a peace offering. This was the offering of Nethanel, son of Zuar.

24 On the third day it was the turn of Eliab, son of Helon, prince of the Zebulunites. 25 His offering consisted of one silver plate weighing a hundred and thirty shekels according to the sanctuary standard and one silver basin weighing seventy shekels, both filled with fine flour mixed with oil for a cereal offering; 26 one gold cup of ten shekels' weight filled with incense; 27 one young bull, one ram, and one yearling lamb for a holocaust; 28 one goat for a sin offering; 29 and two oxen, five rams, five goats, and five yearling lambs for a peace offering. This was the offering of Eliab, son of Helon.

30 On the fourth day it was the turn of Elizur, son of Shedeur, prince of the Reubenites. 31 His offering consisted of one silver plate weighing a hundred and thirty shekels according to the sanctuary standard and one silver basin weighing seventy shekels, both filled with fine flour mixed with oil for a cereal offering; 32 one gold cup of ten shekels' weight filled with incense; 33 one young bull, one ram, and one yearling lamb for a holocaust; 34 one goat for a sin offering; 35 and two oxen, five rams, five goats, and five yearling lambs for a peace offering. This was the offering of Elizur, son of Shedur.

36 On the fifth day it was the turn of Shelumiel, son of Zurishaddai, prince of the Simeonites. 37 His offering consisted of one silver plate weighing a hundred and thirty shekels according to the sanctuary standard and one silver basin weighing seventy shekels, both filled with fine flour mixed with oil for a cereal offering; 38 one gold cup of ten shekels' weight filled with incense; 39 one young bull, one ram, and one yearling lamb for a holocaust; 40 one goat for a sin offering; 41 and two oxen, five rams, five goats, and five yearling lambs for a peace offering. This was the offering of Shelumiel, son of Zurishaddai.

42 On the sixth day it was the turn of Eliasaph, son of Reuel, prince of the Gadites. 43 His offering con-

---

6, 25: *Let his face shine:* a Hebrew idiom for "smile."

6, 26: *Peace:* the Hebrew word includes the idea of "prosperity, happiness."

7, 12–88: The repetitious account of the same

offerings brought by each of the twelve tribal princes and the summary of them are characteristic of an official registration.

sisted of one silver plate weighing a hundred and thirty shekels according to the sanctuary standard and one silver basin weighing seventy shekels, both filled with fine flour mixed with oil for a cereal offering; 44 one gold cup of ten shekels' weight filled with incense; 45 one young bull, one ram, and one yearling lamb for a holocaust; 46 one goat for a sin offering; 47 and two oxen, five rams, five goats, and five yearling lambs for a peace offering. This was the offering of Eliasaph, son of Reuel.

48 On the seventh day it was the turn of Elishama, son of Ammihud, prince of the Ephraimites. 49 His offering consisted of one silver plate weighing a hundred and thirty shekels according to the sanctuary standard and one silver basin weighing seventy shekels, both filled with fine flour mixed with oil for a cereal offering; 50 one gold cup of ten shekels' weight filled with incense; 51 one young bull, one ram, and one yearling lamb for a holocaust; 52 one goat for a sin offering; 53 and two oxen, five rams, five goats, and five yearling lambs for a peace offering. This was the offering of Elishama, son of Ammihud.

54 On the eighth day it was the turn of Gamaliel, son of Pedahzur, prince of the Manassehites. 55 His offering consisted of one silver plate weighing a hundred and thirty shekels according to the sanctuary standard, one silver basin weighing seventy shekels, both filled with fine flour mixed with oil for a cereal offering; 56 one gold cup of ten shekels' weight filled with incense; 57 one young bull, one ram, and one yearling lamb for a holocaust; 58 one goat for a sin offering; 59 and two oxen, five rams, five goats, and five yearling lambs for a peace offering. This was the offering of Gamaliel, son of Pedahzur.

60 On the ninth day it was the turn of Abidan, son of Gideoni, prince of the Benjaminites. 61 His offering consisted of one silver plate weighing a hundred and thirty shekels according to the sanctuary standard and one silver basin weigh-

ing seventy shekels, both filled with fine flour mixed with oil for a cereal offering; 62 one gold cup of ten shekels' weight filled with incense; 63 one young bull, one ram, and one yearling lamb for a holocaust; 64 one goat for a sin offering; 65 and two oxen, five rams, five goats, and five yearling lambs for a peace offering. This was the offering of Abidan, son of Gideoni.

66 On the tenth day it was the turn of Ahiezer, son of Ammishaddai, prince of the Danites. 67 His offering consisted of one silver plate weighing a hundred and thirty shekels according to the sanctuary standard and one silver basin weighing seventy shekels, both filled with fine flour mixed with oil for a cereal offering; 68 one gold cup of ten shekels' weight filled with incense; 69 one young bull, one ram, and one yearling lamb for a holocaust; 70 one goat for a sin offering; 71 and two oxen, five rams, five goats, and five yearling lambs for a peace offering. This was the offering of Ahiezer, son of Ammishaddai.

72 On the eleventh day it was the turn of Pagiel, son of Ochran, prince of the Asherites. 73 His offering consisted of one silver plate weighing one hundred and thirty shekels according to the sanctuary standard and one silver basin weighing seventy shekels, both filled with fine flour mixed with oil for a cereal offering; 74 one gold cup of ten shekels' weight filled with incense; 75 one young bull, one ram, and one yearling lamb for a holocaust; 76 one goat for a sin offering; 77 and two oxen, five rams, five goats, and five yearling lambs for a peace offering. This was the offering of Pagiel, son of Ochran.

78 On the twelfth day it was the turn of Ahira, son of Enan, prince of the Naphtalites. 79 His offering consisted of one silver plate weighing a hundred and thirty shekels according to the sanctuary standard and one silver basin weighing seventy shekels, both filled with fine flour mixed with oil for a cereal offering; 80 one gold cup of ten shekels' weight filled with incense; 81 one young bull,

one ram, and one yearling lamb for a holocaust; 82 one goat for a sin offering; 83 and two oxen, five rams, five goats, and five yearling lambs for a peace offering. This was the offering of Ahira, son of Enan.

84 These were the offerings for the dedication of the altar, given by the princes of Israel on the occasion of its anointing: twelve silver plates, twelve silver basins, and twelve gold cups. 85 Each silver plate weighed a hundred and thirty shekels, and each silver basin seventy, so that all the silver of these vessels amounted to two thousand four hundred shekels, according to the sanctuary standard. 86 The twelve gold cups that were filled with incense weighed ten shekels apiece, according to the sanctuary standard, so that all the gold of the cups amounted to one hundred and twenty shekels. 87 The animals for the holocausts were, in all, twelve young bulls, twelve rams, and twelve yearling lambs, with their cereal offerings; those for the sin offerings were twelve goats. 88 The animals for the peace offerings were, in all, twenty-four oxen, sixty rams, sixty goats, and sixty yearling lambs. These, then, were the offerings for the dedication of the altar after it was anointed.

The Voice

89 When Moses entered the meeting tent to speak with him, he heard the voice addressing him from above the propitiatory on the ark of the commandments, from between the two cherubim; and it spoke to him. . . .

The Lamps Set Up

8 The LORD spoke to Moses, and said, 2 "Give Aaron this command: When you set up the seven lamps, have them throw their light toward the front of the lampstand." 3 Aaron did so, setting up the lamps to face toward the front of the lampstand, just as the LORD had commanded Moses. 4 The lampstand was made of beaten gold in both its shaft and its branches, according to the pattern which the LORD had shown Moses.

Purification of the Levites

5 The LORD said to Moses: 6 "Take the Levites from among the Israelites and purify them. 7 This is what you shall do to them to purify them. Sprinkle them with the water of remission; then have them shave their whole bodies and wash their clothes, and so purify themselves. 8 They shall take a young bull, along with its cereal offering of fine flour mixed with oil; you shall take another young bull for a sin offering. 9 Then have the Levites come forward in front of the meeting tent, where you shall assemble also the whole community of the Israelites. 10 While the Levites are present before the LORD, the Israelites shall lay their hands upon them. 11 Let Aaron then offer the Levites before the LORD as a wave offering from the Israelites, thus devoting them to the service of the LORD. 12 The Levites in turn shall lay their hands on the heads of the bullocks, which shall then be immolated, the one as a sin offering and the other as a holocaust to the LORD, in atonement for the Levites. 13 Thus, then, shall you have the Levites stand before Aaron and his sons, to be offered as a wave offering to the LORD; 14 and thus shall you set aside the Levites from the rest of the Israelites, that they may be mine.

15 "Only then shall the Levites enter upon their service in the meeting tent. You shall purify them and offer them as a wave offering; 16 because they, among the Israelites, are strictly dedicated to me; I have taken them for myself in place of every first-born that opens the womb among the Israelites. 17 Indeed, all the first-born among the Israelites, both of man and of beast, belong to me; I consecrated them to myself on the day I slew all the first-born in the land of Egypt. 18 But in place of all the first-born Israelites I have taken the Levites; 19 and I have given these dedicated Israelites to Aaron and his sons to discharge the duties of the Israelites in the meeting tent and to make atonement for them, so that no plague may strike among the Israelites should they come near the sanctuary."

20 Thus, then, did Moses and Aaron and the whole community of the Israelites deal with the Levites, carrying out exactly the command which the LORD had given Moses concerning them. 21 When the Levites had cleansed themselves of sin and washed their clothes, Aaron offered them as a wave offering before the LORD, and made atonement for them to purify them. 22 Only then did they enter upon their service in the meeting tent under the supervision of Aaron and his sons. The command which the LORD had given Moses concerning the Levites was carried out.

Age Limits for Levitical Service

23 The LORD said to Moses: 24 "This is the rule for the Levites. Each from his twenty-fifth year onward shall perform the required service in the meeting tent. 25 When he is fifty years old, he shall retire from the required service and work no longer. 26 His service with his fellow Levites shall consist in sharing their responsibilities in the meeting tent, but he shall not do the work. This, then, is how you are to regulate the duties of the Levites."

Second Passover

9 In the first month of the year following their departure from the land of Egypt, the LORD said to Moses in the desert of Sinai, 2 "Tell the Israelites to celebrate the Passover at the prescribed time. 3 The evening twilight of the fourteenth day of this month is the prescribed time when you shall celebrate it, observing all its rules and regulations." 4 Moses, therefore, told the Israelites to celebrate the Passover. 5 And they did so, celebrating the Passover in the desert of Sinai during the evening twilight of the fourteenth day of the first month, just as the LORD had commanded Moses.

6 There were some, however, who were unclean because of a human corpse and so could not keep the Passover that day. These men came up to Moses and Aaron that same day 7 and said, "Although we are unclean because of a corpse, why should we be deprived of presenting the LORD's offering at its proper time along with the other Israelites?" Moses answered them, 8 "Wait until I learn what the LORD will command in your regard."

9 The LORD then said to Moses: 10 "Speak to the Israelites and say: If any one of you or of your descendants is unclean because of a corpse, or if he is absent on a journey, he may still keep the LORD's Passover. 11 But he shall keep it in the second month, during the evening twilight of the fourteenth day of that month, eating it with unleavened bread and bitter herbs, 12 and not leaving any of it over till morning, nor breaking any of its bones, but observing all the rules of the Passover. 13 However, anyone who is clean and not away on a journey, who yet fails to keep the Passover, shall be cut off from his people, because he did not present the LORD's offering at the prescribed time. That man shall bear the consequences of his sin.

14 "If an alien who lives among you wishes to keep the LORD's Passover, he too shall observe the rules and regulations for the Passover. You shall have the same law for the resident alien as for the native of the land."

The Fiery Cloud

15 On the day when the Dwelling was erected, the cloud covered the Dwelling, the tent of the commandments; but from evening until morning it took on the appearance of fire over the Dwelling. 16 It was always so: during the day the Dwelling was covered by the cloud, which at night had the appearance of fire. 17 Whenever the cloud rose from the tent, the Israelites would break

---

8, 6: *Purify them:* in the language of the Pentateuch only the priests were "consecrated," that is, made sacred or set aside for the Lord, in an elaborate ceremony described in Ex 29; Lv 8. The Levites were merely "purified," that is, made ritually clean for their special work.

8, 7: *Water of remission:* literally, "water of sin," that is, for the remission of sin.

8, 21: *Cleansed themselves of sin:* by having the "water of remission" sprinkled on them as prescribed in v 7.

9, 14: *An alien:* this passage presupposes that he is already circumcised as prescribed in Ex 12, 48.

9, 15: *The cloud:* already mentioned at the departure from Egypt; cf Ex 13, 21f.

camp; wherever the cloud came to rest, they would pitch camp. 18 At the bidding of the LORD the Israelites moved on, and at his bidding they encamped. As long as the cloud stayed over the Dwelling, they remained in camp.

19 Even when the cloud tarried many days over the Dwelling, the Israelites obeyed the LORD and would not move on; 20 yet sometimes the cloud was over the Dwelling only for a few days. It was at the bidding of the LORD that they stayed in camp, and it was at his bidding that they departed. 21 Sometimes the cloud remained there only from evening until morning; and when it rose in the morning, they would depart. Or if the cloud lifted during the day, or even at night, they would then set out. 22 Whether the cloud tarried over the Dwelling for two days or for a month or longer, the Israelites remained in camp and did not depart; but when it lifted, they moved on. 23 Thus, it was always at the bidding of the LORD that they encamped, and at his bidding that they set out; ever heeding the charge of the LORD, as he had bidden them through Moses.

The Silver Trumpets

10 The LORD said to Moses: 2 "Make two trumpets of beaten silver, which you shall use in assembling the community and in breaking camp. 3 When both are blown, the whole community shall gather round you at the entrance of the meeting tent; 4 but when one of them is blown, only the princes, the chiefs of the troops of Israel, shall gather round you. 5 When you sound the first alarm, those encamped on the east side shall set out; 6 when you sound the second alarm, those encamped on the south side shall set out; when you sound the third alarm, those encamped on the west side shall set out; when you sound the fourth alarm, those encamped on the north side shall set out. Thus shall the alarm be sounded for them to depart. 7 But in calling forth an assembly you are to blow an ordinary blast, without sounding the alarm.

8 "It is the sons of Aaron, the priests, who shall blow the trumpets; and the use of them is prescribed by perpetual statute for you and your descendants. 9 When in your own land you go to war against an enemy that is attacking you, you shall sound the alarm on the trumpets, and the LORD, your God, will remember you and save you from your foes. 10 On your days of celebration, your festivals, and your new-moon feasts, you shall blow the trumpets over your holocausts and your peace offerings; this will serve as a reminder of you before your God. I, the LORD, am your God."

FROM SINAI TO THE PLAINS OF MOAB

Departure from Sinai

11 In the second year, on the twentieth day of the second month, the cloud rose from the Dwelling of the commandments. 12 The Israelites moved on from the desert of Sinai by stages, until the cloud came to rest in the desert of Paran. 13 The first time that they broke camp at the bidding of the LORD through Moses, 14 the camp of the Judahites, under its own standard and arranged in companies, was the first to set out. Nahshon, son of Amminadab, was over their host, 15 and Nethanel, son of Zuar, over the host of the tribe of Issachar, 16 and Eliab, son of Helon, over the host of the tribe of Zebulun. 17 Then, after the Dwelling was dismantled, the clans of Gershon and Merari set out, carrying the Dwelling. 18 The camp of the Reubenites, under its own standard and arranged in companies, was the next to set out, with Elizur, son of Shedeur, over their host, 19 and Shelumiel, son of Zurishaddai, over the host of the tribe of Simeon, 20 and Eliasaph, son of Reuel, over the host of the tribe of Gad. 21 The clan of Kohath then set out, carrying the sacred objects for the Dwelling, which was to be erected before their arrival. 22 The camp of the Ephraimites next set out, under its own standard and arranged in companies, with Elishama, son of Ammihud, over their host, 23 and Gamaliel, son of Pedahzur, over the host of the tribe of Manasseh, 24 and Abidan, son of Gideoni, over the host of the tribe of Benjamin. 25 Finally, as rear guard for all the camps, the camp of the Danites set out, under its own standard and arranged in companies, with Ahiezer, son of Ammishaddai, over their host, 26 and Pagiel, son of Ochran, over the host of the tribe of Asher, 27 and Ahira, son of Enan, over the host of the tribe of Naphtali. 28 This was the order of departure for the Israelites, company by company.

Hobab as Guide

As they were setting out, 29 Moses said to his brother-in-law Hobab, son of Reuel the Midianite, "We are setting out for the place which the LORD has promised to give us. Come with us, and we will be generous toward you, for the LORD has promised prosperity to Israel." 30 But he answered, "No, I will not come. I am going instead to my own country and to my own kindred." 31 Moses said, "Please, do not leave us; you know where we can camp in the desert, and you will serve as eyes for us. 32 If you come with us, we will share with you the prosperity the LORD will bestow on us."

Into the Desert

33 They moved on from the mountain of the LORD, a three days' journey, and the ark of the covenant of the LORD which was to seek out their resting place went the three days' journey with them. 34 And when they set out from camp, the cloud of the LORD was over them by day.

35 Whenever the ark set out, Moses would say,

"Arise, O LORD, that your enemies
    may be scattered, and those
    who hate you may flee before
    you."

10, 10: *Days of celebration:* special holidays, such as the occasion of a victory. *Festivals:* the great annual feasts of the Passover, Pentecost and Booths

described in Lv 23; Nm 28—29.
10, 30ff: Hobab wished to be coaxed before granting the favor. From Jgs 1, 16 it seems probable

that he did accede to Moses' request.
10, 33: *The mountain of the Lord:* Sinai (Horeb), elsewhere always called "the mountain of God."

36 And when it came to rest, he would say,

> "Return, O LORD, you who ride upon the clouds, to the troops of Israel."

Discontent of the People

11 Now the people complained in the hearing of the LORD; and when he heard it his wrath flared up so that the fire of the LORD burned among them and consumed the outskirts of the camp. 2 But when the people cried out to Moses, he prayed to the LORD and the fire died out. 3 Hence that place was called Taberah, because there the fire of the LORD burned among them.

4 The foreign elements among them were so greedy for meat that even the Israelites lamented again, "Would that we had meat for food! 5 We remember the fish we used to eat without cost in Egypt, and the cucumbers, the melons, the leeks, the onions, and the garlic. 6 But now we are famished; we see nothing before us but this manna."

7 Manna was like coriander seed and had the appearance of bdellium. 8 When they had gone about and gathered it up, the people would grind it between millstones or pound it in a mortar, then cook it in a pot and make it into loaves, which tasted like cakes made with oil. 9 At night, when the dew fell upon the camp, the manna also fell.

10 When Moses heard the people, family after family, crying at the entrance of their tents, so that the LORD became very angry, he was grieved. 11 "Why do you treat your servant so badly?" Moses asked the LORD. "Why are you so displeased with me that you burden me with all this people? 12 Was it I who conceived all this people? or was it I who gave them birth, that you tell me to carry them at my bosom, like a foster father carrying an infant, to the land you have promised under oath to their fathers? 13 Where can I get meat to give to all this people? For they are crying to me, 'Give us meat for our food.' 14 I cannot carry all this people by myself, for they are too heavy for me. 15 If this is the way you will deal with me, then please do me the favor of killing me at once, so that I need no longer face this distress."

The Seventy Elders

16 Then the LORD said to Moses, "Assemble for me seventy of the elders of Israel, men you know for true elders and authorities among the people, and bring them to the meeting tent. When they are in place beside you, 17 I will come down and speak with you there. I will also take some of the spirit that is on you and will bestow it on them, that they may share the burden of the people with you. You will then not have to bear it by yourself.

18 "To the people, however, you shall say: Sanctify yourselves for tomorrow, when you shall have meat to eat. For in the hearing of the LORD you have cried, 'Would that we had meat for food! Oh, how well off we were in Egypt!' Therefore the LORD will give you meat for food, 19 and you will eat it, not for one day, or two days, or five, or ten, or twenty days, 20 but for a whole month—until it comes out of your very nostrils and becomes loathsome to you. For you have spurned the LORD who is in your midst, and in his presence you have wailed, 'Why did we ever leave Egypt?'"

21 But Moses said, "The people around me include six hundred thousand soldiers; yet you say, 'I will give them meat to eat for a whole month.' 22 Can enough sheep and cattle be slaughtered for them? If all the fish of the sea were caught for them, would they have enough?" 23 The LORD answered Moses, "Is this beyond the LORD's reach? You shall see now whether or not what I have promised you takes place."

The Spirit on the Elders

24 So Moses went out and told the people what the LORD had said. Gathering seventy elders of the people, he had them stand around the tent. 25 The LORD then came down in the cloud and spoke to him. Taking some of the spirit that was on Moses, he bestowed it on the seventy elders; and as the spirit came to rest on them, they prophesied.

26 Now two men, one named Eldad and the other Medad, were not in the gathering but had been left in the camp. They too had been on the list, but had not gone out to the tent; yet the spirit came to rest on them also, and they prophesied in the camp. 27 So, when a young man quickly told Moses, "Eldad and Medad are prophesying in the camp," 28 Joshua, son of Nun, who from his youth had been Moses' aide, said, "Moses, my lord, stop them." 29 But Moses answered him, "Are you jealous for my sake? Would that all the people of the LORD were prophets! Would that the LORD might bestow his spirit on them all!" 30 Then Moses retired to the camp, along with the elders of Israel.

The Quail

31 There arose a wind sent by the LORD, that drove in quail from the sea and brought them down over the camp site at a height of two cubits from the ground for the distance of a day's journey all around the camp. 32 All that day, all night, and all the next day the people gathered in the quail. Even the one who got the least gathered ten homers of them. Then they spread them out all around the camp. 33 But while the meat was still between their teeth, before it could be consumed, the LORD's wrath flared up against the people, and he struck them with a very great plague. 34 So that place was named Kibroth-hattaavah, because it was there that the greedy people were buried.

11, 3: *Taberah* means "the burning."
11, 7: *Coriander seed:* see note on Ex 16, 31. *Bdellium:* a transparent, amber-colored gum resin, which is also mentioned in Gn 2, 12.
11, 25: *They prophesied:* in the sense, not of foretelling the future, but of speaking in enraptured enthusiasm. Such manifestations of mystic exaltation occurred in the early days of Hebrew prophecy (1 Sm 10, 10ff; 19, 20ff) and in the first years of the Church (Acts 2, 6–11.17; 19, 6; 1 Cor 12—14).

11, 31: *At a height of two cubits from the ground:* exhausted by the storm, the quail could take but short, low flights, so that they were easily captured. To give food to the hungry people, God may have used the natural phenomenon of the annual migration of quail across the Sinai Peninsula. In the spring large flocks of these birds cross the Gulf of Aqabah flying toward the west; in the fall they fly back eastward from the Mediterranean. *The sea* mentioned here probably refers to the former body of water.
11, 32: *They spread them out:* to cure by drying.
11, 34: *Kibroth-hattaavah* means "graves of greed."

35 From Kibroth-hattaavah the people set out for Hazeroth.

Jealousy of Aaron and Miriam

12 While they were in Hazeroth, 1 Miriam and Aaron spoke against Moses on the pretext of the marriage he had contracted with a Cushite woman. 2 They complained, "Is it through Moses alone that the LORD speaks? Does he not speak through us also?" And the LORD heard this. 3 Now, Moses himself was by far the meekest man on the face of the earth. 4 So at once the LORD said to Moses and Aaron and Miriam, "Come out, you three, to the meeting tent." And the three of them went. 5 Then the LORD came down in the column of cloud, and standing at the entrance of the tent, called Aaron and Miriam. When both came forward, 6 he said, "Now listen to the words of the LORD:

Should there be a prophet among you, in visions will I reveal myself to him, in dreams will I speak to him;

7 Not so with my servant Moses! Throughout my house he bears my trust:

8 face to face I speak to him, plainly and not in riddles. The presence of the LORD he beholds.

Why, then, did you not fear to speak against my servant Moses?"

Miriam's Leprosy

9 So angry was the LORD against them that when he departed, 10 and the cloud withdrew from the tent, there was Miriam, a snow-white leper! When Aaron turned and saw her a leper, 11 "Ah, my lord!" he said to Moses, "please do not charge us with the sin that we have foolishly committed! 12 Let her not thus be like the stillborn babe that comes forth from its mother's womb with its flesh half consumed." 13 Then Moses cried to the LORD, "Please, not this! Pray, heal her!" 14 But the LORD answered Moses, "Suppose her father had spit in her face, would she not hide in shame for seven days? Let her be confined outside the camp for seven days; only then may she be brought back." 15 So Miriam was confined outside the camp for seven days, and the people did not start out again until she was brought back.

16 After that the people set out from Hazeroth and encamped in the desert of Paran.

The Twelve Scouts

13 The LORD said to Moses, 2 "Send men to reconnoiter the land of Canaan, which I am giving the Israelites. You shall send one man from each ancestral tribe, all of them princes." 3 So Moses dispatched them from the desert of Paran, as the LORD has ordered. All of them were leaders among the Israelites; 4 by name they were:

Shammua, son of Zaccur, of the tribe of Reuben;

5 Shaphat, son of Hori, of the tribe of Simeon;

6 Caleb, son of Jephunneh, of the tribe of Judah;

7 Igal [son of Joseph], of the tribe of Issachar;

10 Gaddiel, son of Sodi, of the tribe of Zebulun;

11 Gaddi, son of Susi, of the tribe of Manasseh, for the Josephites, with

8 Hoshea, son of Nun, of the tribe of Ephraim;

9 Palti, son of Raphu, of the tribe of Benjamin;

12 Ammiel, son of Gemalli, of the tribe of Dan;

13 Sethur, son of Michael, of the tribe of Asher;

14 Nahbi, son of Vophsi, of the tribe of Naphtali;

15 Geuel, son of Machi, of the tribe of Gad.

16 These are the names of the men whom Moses sent out to reconnoiter the land. But Hoshea, son of Nun, Moses called Joshua.

17 In sending them to reconnoiter the land of Canaan, Moses said to them, "Go up here in the Negeb, up into the highlands, 18 and see what kind of land it is. Are the people living there strong or weak, few or many? 19 Is the country in which they live good or bad? Are the towns in which they dwell open or fortified? 20 Is the soil fertile or barren, wooded or clear? And do your best to get some of the fruit of the land." It was then the season for early grapes.

21 So they went up and reconnoitered the land from the desert of Zin as far as where Rehob adjoins Labo of Hamath. 22 Going up by way of the Negeb, they reached Hebron, where Ahiman, Sheshai and Talmai, descendants of the Anakim, were living. [Hebron had been built seven years before Zoan in Egypt.] 23 They also reached the Wadi Eshcol, where they cut down a branch with a single cluster of grapes on it, which two of them carried on a pole, as well as some pomegranates and figs. 24 It was because of the cluster the Israelites cut there that they called the place Wadi Eshcol.

Their Return

25 After reconnoitering the land for forty days they returned, 26 met Moses and Aaron and the whole community of the Israelites in the desert of Paran at Kadesh, made a report to them all, and showed them the fruit of the country. 27 They told Moses: "We went into the land to which you sent us. It does indeed

---

12, 1: *Cushite woman:* apparently Zipporah, the Midianitess, is meant; cf Ex 2, 21. Perhaps the term is used here merely in the sense of "despised foreigner."

12, 2: The real reason for Miriam's quarrel with her brother Moses was her jealousy of his superior position; his *Cushite* wife served only as an occasion for the dispute. Aaron merely followed his sister in her rebellion; hence she alone was punished.

12, 10: *A snow-white leper:* afflicted with "white leprosy," a skin disease that generally is not serious or of long duration. Cf Lv 13, 3–6.

13, 16: *Joshua:* in Hebrew, "Jehoshua," which was later modified to "Jeshua," the Hebrew pronunciation of the name "Jesus." Hoshea and Joshua are variants of one original name meaning "the LORD saves." Cf Mt 1, 21.

13, 21: *The desert of Zin:* north of Paran and southwest of the Dead Sea. It is quite distinct from "the desert of Sin" near the border of Egypt (Ex 16, 1; 17, 1; Nm 33, 11). *Labo of Hamath:* a town near Riblah (Jer 39, 5f) at the southern border of *Hamath,* an independent kingdom in southern Syria. David's conquests extended as far as Hamath (2 Sm 8, 9ff), and Labo thus formed the northern

border of the ideal extent of Israel's possessions (34, 7ff; Ez 47, 15; 48, 1). Some commentators think that this verse is a later addition to the text; cf Dt 1, 24

13, 22.28: *Anakim:* an aboriginal race in southern Palestine, largely absorbed by the Canaanites before the Israelite invasion. Either because of their tall stature or because of the massive stone structures left by them the Israelites regarded them as giants.

13, 23: *Eshcol* means "cluster."

flow with milk and honey, and here is its fruit. 28 However, the people who are living in the land are fierce, and the towns are fortified and very strong. Besides, we saw descendants of the Anakim there. 29 Amalekites live in the region of the Negeb; Hittites, Jebusites and Amorites dwell in the highlands, and Canaanites along the seacoast and the banks of the Jordan."

30 Caleb, however, to quiet the people toward Moses, said, "We ought to go up and seize the land, for we can certainly do so." 31 But the men who had gone up with him said, "We cannot attack these people; they are too strong for us." 32 So they spread discouraging reports among the Israelites about the land they had scouted, saying, "The land that we explored is a country that consumes its inhabitants. And all the people we saw there are huge men, 33 veritable giants [the Anakim were a race of giants]; we felt like mere grasshoppers, and so we must have seemed to them."

Threats of Revolt

14 At this, the whole community broke out with loud cries, and even in the night the people wailed. 2 All the Israelites grumbled against Moses and Aaron, the whole community saying to them, "Would that we had died in the land of Egypt, or that here in the desert we were dead! 3 Why is the LORD bringing us into this land only to have us fall by the sword? Our wives and little ones will be taken as booty. Would it not be better for us to return to Egypt?" 4 So they said to one another, "Let us appoint a leader and go back to Egypt."

5 But Moses and Aaron fell prostrate before the whole assembled community of the Israelites; 6 while Joshua, son of Nun, and Caleb, son of Jephunneh, who had been in the party that scouted the land, tore their garments 7 and said to the whole community of the Israelites, "The country which we went through and explored is a fine, rich land 8 If the

LORD is pleased with us, he will bring us in and give us that land, a land flowing with milk and honey. 9 But do not rebel against the LORD! You need not be afraid of the people of that land; they are but food for us! Their defense has left them, but the LORD is with us. Therefore, do not be afraid of them." 10 In answer, the whole community threatened to stone them.

The Lord's Sentence

But then the glory of the LORD appeared at the meeting tent to all the Israelites. 11 And the LORD said to Moses, "How long will this people spurn me? How long will they refuse to believe in me, despite all the signs I have performed among them? 12 I will strike them with pestilence and wipe them out. Then I will make of you a nation greater and mightier than they."

13 But Moses said to the LORD: "Are the Egyptians to hear of this? For by your power you brought out this people from among them. 14 And are they to tell of it to the inhabitants of this land? It has been heard that you, O LORD, are in the midst of this people; you, LORD, who plainly reveal yourself! Your cloud stands over them, and you go before them by day in a column of cloud and by night in a column of fire. 15 If now you slay this whole people, the nations who have heard such reports of you will say, 16 'The LORD was not able to bring this people into the land he swore to give them; that is why he slaughtered them in the desert.' 17 Now then, let the power of my Lord be displayed in its greatness, even as you have said, 18 'The LORD is slow to anger and rich in kindness, forgiving wickedness and crime; yet not declaring the guilty guiltless, but punishing children to the third and fourth generation for their fathers' wickedness.' 19 Pardon, then, the wickedness of this people in keeping with your great kindness, even as you have forgiven them from Egypt until now."

20 The LORD answered: "I pardon them as you have asked. 21 Yet, by my life and the LORD's glory that fills the whole earth, 22 of all the men who have seen my glory and the signs I worked in Egypt and in the desert, and who nevertheless have put me to the test ten times already and have failed to heed my voice, 23 not one shall see the land which I promised on oath to their fathers. None of these who have spurned me shall see it. 24 But because my servant Caleb has a different spirit and follows me unreservedly, I will bring him into the land where he has just been, and his descendants shall possess it. 25 But now, since the Amalekites and Canaanites are living in the valleys, turn away tomorrow and set out in the desert on the Red Sea road."

26 The LORD also said to Moses and Aaron: 27 "How long will this wicked community grumble against me? I have heard the grumblings of the Israelites against me. 28 Tell them: By my life, says the LORD, I will do to you just what I have heard you say. 29 Here in the desert shall your dead bodies fall. Of all your men of twenty years or more, registered in the census, who grumbled against me, 30 not one shall enter the land where I solemnly swore to settle you, except Caleb, son of Jephunneh, and Joshua, son of Nun. 31 Your little ones, however, who you said would be taken as booty, I will bring in, and they shall appreciate the land you spurned. 32 But as for you, your bodies shall fall here in the desert, 33 here where your children must wander for forty years, suffering for your faithlessness, till the last of you lies dead in the desert. 34 Forty days you spent in scouting the land; forty years shall you suffer for your crimes: one year for each day. Thus you will realize what it means to oppose me. 35 I, the LORD, have sworn to do this to all this wicked community that conspired against me: here in the desert they shall die to the last man."

36 And so it happened to the men whom Moses had sent to reconnoiter

---

13, 33: *Giants:* in Hebrew, "nephilim." Cf Gn 6, 4.
14, 9: *They are but food for us:* that is, "we can easily consume and destroy them." This is the answer to the pessimistic report that this land "consumes its inhabitants" (13, 32).

14, 25: *The valleys:* the low-lying plains in the Negeb and along the seacoast and in the Jordan depression, as well as the higher valleys in the mountains farther north: cf 14, 45.
14, 28f: God punished the malcontents by giving

them their wish; cf v 2. Their lack of faith and of confidence in God is cited in 1 Cor 10, 10, and Heb 3, 12–18, as a warning for Christians.

the land and who on returning had set the whole community grumbling against him by spreading discouraging reports about the land; 37 these men who had given out the bad report about the land were struck down by the LORD and died. 38 Of all the men who had gone to reconnoiter the land, only Joshua, son of Nun, and Caleb, son of Jephunneh, survived.

Unsuccessful Invasion

39 When Moses repeated these words to all the Israelites, the people felt great remorse. 40 Early the next morning they started up into the foothills, saying, "Here we are, ready to go up to the place that the LORD spoke of: for we were indeed doing wrong." 41 But Moses said, "Why are you again disobeying the LORD's orders? This cannot succeed. 42 Do not go up, because the LORD is not in your midst; if you go, you will be beaten down before your enemies. 43 For there the Amalekites and Canaanites face you, and you will fall by the sword. You have turned back from following the LORD; therefore the LORD will not be with you."

44 Yet they dared to go up into the foothills, even though neither the ark of the covenant of the LORD nor Moses left the camp. 45 And the Amalekites and Canaanites who dwelt in that hill country came down and defeated them, beating them back as far as Hormah.

Secondary Offerings

15 The LORD said to Moses, 2 "Give the Israelites these instructions: When you have entered the land that I will give you for your homesteads, 3 if you make to the LORD a sweet-smelling oblation from the herd or from the flock, in holocaust, in fulfillment of a vow, or as a freewill offering, or for one of your festivals, 4 whoever does so shall also present to the LORD a cereal offering consisting of a tenth of an ephah of fine flour mixed with a fourth of a hin of oil, 5 as well as a libation of a fourth of a hin of wine, with each lamb sacrificed in holocaust or otherwise. 6 With each sacrifice of a ram you shall present a cereal offering of two tenths of an ephah of fine flour mixed with a third of a hin of oil, 7 and a libation of a third of a hin of wine, thus making a sweet-smelling offering to the LORD. 8 When you sacrifice an ox as a holocaust, or in fulfillment of a vow, or as a peace offering to the LORD, 9 with it you shall present a cereal offering of three tenths of an ephah of fine flour mixed with half a hin of oil, 10 and a libation of half a hin of wine, as a sweet-smelling oblation to the LORD. 11 The same is to be done for each ox, ram, lamb or goat. 12 Whatever the number you offer, do the same for each of them.

13 "All the native-born shall make these offerings in the same way, whenever they present a sweet-smelling oblation to the LORD. 14 Likewise, in any future generation, any alien residing with you permanently or for a time, who presents a sweet-smelling oblation to the LORD, shall do as you do. 15 There is but one rule for you and for the resident alien, a perpetual rule for all your descendants. Before the LORD you and the alien are alike, 16 with the same law and the same application of it for the alien residing among you as for yourselves."

17 The LORD said to Moses, 18 "Speak to the Israelites and tell them: When you enter the land into which I will bring you 19 and begin to eat of the food of that land, you shall offer the LORD a contribution 20 consisting of a cake of your first batch of dough. You shall offer it just as you offer a contribution from the threshing floor. 21 Throughout your generations you shall give a contribution to the LORD from your first batch of dough.

Sin Offerings

22 "When through inadvertence you fail to carry out any of these commandments which the LORD gives to Moses, 23 and through Moses to you, from the time the LORD first issues the commandment down through your generations: 24 if the community itself unwittingly becomes guilty of the fault of inadvertence, the whole community shall offer the holocaust of one young bull as a sweet-smelling oblation pleasing to the LORD, along with its prescribed cereal offering and libation, as well as one he-goat as a sin offering. 25 Then the priest shall make atonement for the whole Israelite community; thus they will be forgiven the inadvertence for which they have brought their holocaust as an oblation to the LORD. 26 Not only the whole Israelite community, but also the aliens residing among you, shall be forgiven, since the fault of inadvertence affects all the people.

27 "However, if it is an individual who sins inadvertently, he shall bring a yearling she-goat as a sin offering, 28 and the priest shall make atonement before the LORD for him who sinned inadvertently; when atonement has been made for him, he will be forgiven. 29 You shall have but one law for him who sins inadvertently, whether he be a native Israelite or an alien residing with you.

30 "But anyone who sins defiantly, whether he be a native or an alien, insults the LORD, and shall be cut off from among his people. 31 Since he has despised the word of the LORD and has broken his commandment, he must be cut off. He has only himself to blame."

The Sabbath-breaker

32 While the Israelites were in the desert, a man was discovered gathering wood on the sabbath day. 33 Those who caught him at it brought him to Moses and Aaron and the whole assembly. 34 But they kept him in custody, for there was no clear decision as to what should be done with him. 35 Then the LORD said to Moses, "This man shall be put to death; let the whole community stone him outside the camp."

14, 45: *Hormah:* one of the Canaanite royal cities in southern Judea (Jos 12, 14), known at this time as "Zephath"; the origin of the later name is told in 21, 3; Jgs 1, 17.

15, 2–16: These laws on sacrifice are complementary to those of Lv 1—3. Since the food of the Israelites consisted not only of meat but also of bread, oil and wine, so, besides the animal oblations, they offered flour, wine and oil in sacrifice to the Lord.

15, 20: *Dough:* some render, "barley grits." This word is used elsewhere only in Ez 44, 30 and Neh 10, 33; a related Hebrew word is used in Lv 2, 14.

15, 22ff: Although no moral guilt is incurred by an inadvertent violation of God's commandments, the sanctity of the law can require even some reparation for such violations.

15, 34: *No clear decision:* they already knew that a willful violation of the sabbath was a capital offense, but they did not yet know how the death penalty was to be inflicted.

36 So the whole community led him outside the camp and stoned him to death, as the LORD had commanded Moses.

Tassels on the Cloak

37 The LORD said to Moses, 38 "Speak to the Israelites and tell them that they and their descendants must put tassels on the corners of their garments, fastening each corner tassel with a violet cord. 39 When you use these tassels, let the sight of them remind you to keep all the commandments of the LORD, without going wantonly astray after the desires of your hearts and eyes. 40 Thus you will remember to keep all my commandments and be holy to your God. 41 I, the LORD, am your God who, as God, brought you out of Egypt that I, the LORD, may be your God."

Rebellion of Korah

16 Korah, son of Izhar, son of Kohath, son of Levi, [and Dathan and Abiram, sons of Eliab, son of Pallu, son of Reuben] took 2 two hundred and fifty Israelites who were leaders in the community, members of the council and men of note. They stood before Moses, 3 and held an assembly against Moses and Aaron, to whom they said, "Enough from you! The whole community, all of them, are holy; the LORD is in their midst. Why then should you set yourselves over the LORD's congregation?"

4 When Moses heard this, he fell prostrate. 5 Then he said to Korah and to all his band, "May the LORD make known tomorrow morning who belongs to him and who is the holy one and whom he will have draw near to him! Whom he chooses, he will have draw near him. 6 Do this: take your censers [Korah and all his band] 7 and put fire in them and place incense in them before the LORD tomorrow. He whom the LORD

then chooses is the holy one. Enough from you Levites!"

8 Moses also said to Korah, "Listen to me, you Levites! 9 Is it too little for you that the God of Israel has singled you out from the community of Israel, to have you draw near him for the service of the LORD's Dwelling and to stand before the community to minister for them? 10 He has allowed you and your kinsmen, the descendants of Levi, to approach him, and yet you now seek the priesthood too. 11 It is therefore against the LORD that you and all your band are conspiring. For what has Aaron done that you should grumble against him?"

Rebellion of Dathan and Abiram

12 Moses summoned Dathan and Abiram, sons of Eliab, but they answered, "We will not go. 13 Are you not satisfied with having led us here away from a land flowing with milk and honey, to make us perish in the desert, that you must now lord it over us? 14 Far from bringing us to a land flowing with milk and honey, or giving us fields and vineyards for our inheritance, will you also gouge out our eyes? No, we will not go."

15 Then Moses became very angry and said to the LORD, "Pay no heed to their offering. I have never taken a single ass from them, nor have I wronged any one of them."

Korah

16 Moses said to Korah, "You and all your band shall appear before the LORD tomorrow—you and they and Aaron too. 17 Then each of your two hundred and fifty followers shall take his own censer, put incense in it, and offer it to the LORD; and you and Aaron, each with his own censer, shall do the same." 18 So they all took their censers, and laying incense on the fire they had put in them, they took their stand by the

entrance of the meeting tent along with Moses and Aaron. 19 Then, when Korah had assembled all his band against them at the entrance of the meeting tent, the glory of the LORD appeared to the entire community, 20 and the LORD said to Moses and Aaron, 21 "Stand apart from this band, that I may consume them at once." 22 But they fell prostrate and cried out, "O God, God of the spirits of all mankind, will one man's sin make you angry with the whole community?" 23 The LORD answered Moses, 24 "Speak to the community and tell them: Withdraw from the space around the Dwelling" [of Korah, Dathan and Abiram].

Punishment of Dathan and Abiram

25 Moses, followed by the elders of Israel, arose and went to Dathan and Abiram. 26 Then he warned the community, "Keep away from the tents of these wicked men and do not touch anything that is theirs: otherwise you too will be swept away because of all their sins." 27 When Dathan and Abiram had come out and were standing at the entrances of their tents with their wives and sons and little ones, 28 Moses said, "This is how you shall know it was the LORD who sent me to do all I have done, and that it was not I who planned it: 29 if these men die an ordinary death, merely suffering the fate common to all mankind, then it was not the LORD who sent me. 30 But if the LORD does something entirely new, and the ground opens its mouth and swallows them alive down into the nether world, with all belonging to them, then you will know that these men have defied the LORD." 31 No sooner had he finished saying all this than the ground beneath them split open, 32 and the earth opened its mouth and swallowed them and their families [and all of Korah's men] and all their

---

15, 38: *Tassels:* at the time of Christ these tassels were worn by all pious Jews, including our Lord (Mt 9, 20f; Mk 6, 56); the Pharisees wore very large ones in ostentation of their zeal for the law (Mt 23, 5).

16, 1ff: The evidence seems to show that there were two distinct rebellions: one of Korah and his band (27, 3) and the other of Dathan and Abiram (Dt 11, 6); cf Ps 106. The present account combines both events into one narrative; but even here it is rather easy to separate the two, once certain proper

names (vv 1.6.24.32.35) have been identified as glosses. The rebellion of the Reubenites, Dathan and Abiram, was of a political nature, against Moses alone as the civil leader; these rebels were punished by being swallowed alive in an earthquake. The rebellion of Korah was of a religious nature, against the religious leadership of both Moses and Aaron; about two hundred and fifty malcontents joined Korah's *band;* they were punished by fire. The parts of the present section which refer to the rebellion of

Dathan and Abiram are vv 12–15 and vv 25–34 of chapter 16; the rest of chapter 16 and all of chapter 17 concern the rebellion of Korah.

16, 12: *We will not go:* to appear before Moses' tribunal.

16, 14: *Gouge out our eyes:* blind us to the real state of affairs.

16, 25: Since Dathan and Abiram had refused to go to Moses (vv 12ff), he, with the elders as witnesses, was obliged to go to their tent.

possessions. 33 They went down alive to the nether world with all belonging to them; the earth closed over them, and they perished from the community. 34 But all the Israelites near them fled at their shrieks, saying, "The earth might swallow us too!"

Punishment of Korah

35 So they withdrew from the space around the Dwelling [of Korah, Dathan and Abiram]. And fire from the LORD came forth which consumed the two hundred and fifty men who were offering the incense.

17 The LORD said to Moses, 2 "Tell Eleazar, son of Aaron the priest, to remove the censers from the embers; and scatter the fire some distance away, 3 for these sinners have consecrated the censers at the cost of their lives. Have them hammered into plates to cover the altar, because in being presented before the LORD they have become sacred. In this way they shall serve as a sign to the Israelites." 4 So Eleazar the priest had the bronze censers of those burned during the offering hammered into a covering for the altar, 5 in keeping with the orders which the LORD had given him through Moses. This cover was to be a reminder to the Israelites that no layman, no one who was not a descendant of Aaron, should approach the altar to offer incense before the LORD, lest he meet the fate of Korah and his band.

6 The next day the whole Israelite community grumbled against Moses and Aaron, saying, "It is you who have slain the LORD's people." 7 But while the community was deliberating against them, Moses and Aaron turned toward the meeting tent, and the cloud now covered it and the glory of the LORD appeared. 8 Then Moses and Aaron came to the front of the meeting tent, 9 and the LORD said to Moses and Aaron,

10 "Depart from this community, that I may consume them at once." But they fell prostrate. 11 Then Moses said to Aaron, "Take your censer, put fire from the altar in it, lay incense on it, and bring it quickly to the community to make atonement for them; for wrath has come forth from the LORD and the blow is falling." 12 Obeying the orders of Moses, Aaron took his censer and ran in among the community, where the blow was already falling on the people. Then, as he offered the incense and made atonement for the people, 13 standing there between the living and the dead, the scourge was checked. 14 Yet fourteen thousand seven hundred died from the scourge, in addition to those who died because of Korah. 15 When the scourge had been checked, Aaron returned to Moses at the entrance of the meeting tent.

Aaron's Staff

16 The LORD now said to Moses, 17 "Speak to the Israelites and get one staff from them for each ancestral house, twelve staffs in all, one from each of their tribal princes. Mark each man's name on his staff; 18 and mark Aaron's name on Levi's staff, for the head of Levi's ancestral house shall also have a staff. 19 Then lay them down in the meeting tent, in front of the commandments, where I meet you. 20 There the staff of the man of my choice shall sprout. Thus will I suppress from my presence the Israelites' grumbling against you."

21 So Moses spoke to the Israelites, and their princes gave him staffs, twelve in all, one from each tribal prince; and Aaron's staff was with them. 22 Then Moses laid the staffs down before the LORD in the tent of the commandments. 23 The next day, when Moses entered the tent, Aaron's staff, representing the house of Levi, had sprouted and put

forth not only shoots, but blossoms as well, and even bore ripe almonds! 24 Moses thereupon brought out all the staffs from the LORD's presence to the Israelites. After each prince identified his own staff and took it, 25 the LORD said to Moses, "Put back Aaron's staff in front of the commandments, to be kept there as a warning to the rebellious, so that their grumbling may cease before me; if it does not, they will die." 26 And Moses did as the LORD had commanded him.

Charge of the Sacred Things

27 Then the Israelites cried out to Moses, "We are perishing; we are lost, we are all lost! 28 Every time anyone approaches the Dwelling of the LORD, he dies! Are we to perish to the last man?"

18 The LORD said to Aaron, "You and your sons as well as the other members of your ancestral house shall be responsible for the sanctuary; but the responsibility of the priesthood shall rest on you and your sons alone. 2 Bring with you also your other kinsmen of the tribe of Levi, your ancestral tribe, as your associates and assistants, while you and your sons are in front of the tent of the commandments. 3 They shall look after your persons and the whole tent; however, they shall not come near the sacred vessels or the altar, lest both they and you died. 4 As your associates they shall have charge of all the work connected with the meeting tent. But no layman shall come near you. 5 You shall have charge of the sanctuary and of the altar, that wrath may not fall again upon the Israelites.

6 "Remember, it is I who have taken your kinsmen, the Levites, from the body of the Israelites; they are a gift to you, dedicated to the LORD for the service of the meeting

---

16, 35: This verse continues v 24; the first sentence is transposed from v 27.

17, 3: Whatever was brought into intimate contact with something sacred shared in its sacredness. See note on 19, 20.

17, 17: The staff was not merely an article of practical use, but also a symbol of authority [cf Gn 49, 10; Nm 24, 17; Jer 48, 17. Hence, the staff of a leader of a tribe was considered the emblem of his tribe; in fact, certain Hebrew words for "staff" also mean "tribe." Perhaps for this reason, to avoid

confusion, the author here uses the term "ancestral house" instead of the ordinary word for "tribe."

17, 18: Levi's staff: it is not clear whether this is considered as one of the twelve mentioned in the preceding verse, or as a thirteenth staff. Sometimes Levi is reckoned as one of the twelve tribes (e.g., Dt 27, 12f), but more often the number twelve is arrived at by counting the two sub-tribes of Joseph, i.e., Ephraim and Manasseh, as distinct tribes. In this passage also it seems probable that the tribe of Levi is considered apart from the other twelve.

17, 27f: Logically these two verses belong immediately after 16, 35.

18, 1ff: This law, which kept unqualified persons from contact with sacred things, is the answer to the Israelites' cry in 17, 28. It is followed by other laws concerning priests and Levites.

18, 2: Associates: in Hebrew this word alludes to the popular etymology of the name "Levi." Cf Gn 29, 34.

18, 4: Layman: here, "one who is not a Levite"; in v 7, "one who is not a priest."

tent. 7 But only you and your sons are to have charge of performing the priestly functions in whatever concerns the altar and the room within the veil. I give you the priesthood as a gift. Any layman who draws near shall be put to death."

The Priests' Share of the Sacrifices

8 The LORD said to Aaron, "I myself have given you charge of the contributions made to me in the various sacred offerings of the Israelites; by perpetual ordinance I have assigned them to you and to your sons as your priestly share. 9 You shall have the right to share in the oblations that are most sacred, in whatever they offer me as cereal offerings or sin offerings or guilt offerings; these shares shall accrue to you and to your sons. 10 In eating them you shall treat them as most sacred; every male among you may partake of them. As sacred, they belong to you.

11 "You shall also have what is removed from the gift in every wave offering of the Israelites; by perpetual ordinance I have assigned it to you and to your sons and daughters. All in your family who are clean may partake of it. 12 I have also assigned to you all the best of the new oil and of the new wine and grain that they give to the LORD as their first fruits; 13 and likewise, of whatever grows on their land, the first products that they bring in to the LORD shall be yours; all of your family who are clean may partake of them. 14 Whatever is doomed in Israel shall be yours. 15 Every living thing that opens the womb, whether of man or of beast, such as are to be offered to the LORD, shall be yours; but you must let the first-born of man, as well as of unclean animals, be redeemed. 16 The ransom for a boy is to be paid when he is a month old; it is fixed at five silver shekels according to the sanctuary standard, twenty gerahs to the shekel. 17 But the first-born of cattle, sheep or goats shall not be redeemed; they are sacred. Their blood you must splash on the altar and their fat you must burn as a sweet-smelling oblation to the LORD. 18 Their meat, however, shall be yours, just as the breast and the right leg of the wave offering belong to you. 19 By perpetual ordinance I have assigned to you and to your sons and daughters all the contributions from the sacred gifts which the Israelites make to the LORD; this is an inviolable covenant to last forever before the LORD, for you and for your descendants." 20 Then the LORD said to Aaron, "You shall not have any heritage in the land of the Israelites nor hold any portion among them; I will be your portion and your heritage among them.

Tithes Due the Levites

21 "To the Levites, however, I hereby assign all tithes in Israel as their heritage in recompense for the service they perform in the meeting tent. 22 The Israelites may no longer approach the meeting tent; else they will incur guilt deserving death. 23 Only the Levites are to perform the service of the meeting tent, and they alone shall be held responsible; this is a perpetual ordinance for all your generations. The Levites, therefore, shall not have any heritage among the Israelites, 24 for I have assigned to them as their heritage the tithes which the Israelites give as a contribution to the LORD. That is why I have ordered that they are not to have any heritage among the Israelites."

Tithes Paid by the Levites

25 The LORD said to Moses, 26 "Give the Levites these instructions: When you receive from the Israelites the tithes I have assigned you from them as your heritage, you are to make a contribution from them to the LORD, a tithe of the tithes; 27 and your contribution will be credited to you as if it were grain from the threshing floor or new wine from the press. 28 Thus you too shall make a contribution from all the tithes you receive from the Israelites, handing over to Aaron the priest the part to be contributed to the LORD. 29 From all the gifts that you receive, and from the best parts, you are to consecrate to the LORD your own full contribution.

30 "Tell them also: Once you have made your contribution from the best part, the rest of the tithes will be credited to you Levites as if it were produce of the threshing floor or of the wine press. 31 Your families, as well as you, may eat them anywhere, since they are your recompense for service at the meeting tent. 32 You will incur no guilt so long as you make a contribution of the best part. Do not profane the sacred gifts of the Israelites and so bring death on yourselves."

Ashes of the Red Heifer

19 The LORD said to Moses and Aaron: 2 "This is the regulation which the law of the LORD prescribes. Tell the Israelites to procure for you a red heifer that is free from every blemish and defect and on which no yoke has ever been laid. 3 This is to be given to Eleazar the priest, to be led outside the camp and slaughtered in his presence. 4 Eleazar the priest shall take some of its blood on his finger and sprinkle it seven times toward the front of the meeting tent. 5 Then the heifer shall be burned in his sight, with its hide and flesh, its blood and offal; 6 and the priest shall take

---

18, 7: *Veil:* the outer veil, or "curtain," is probably meant.

18, 8ff: Two classes of offerings are here distinguished: the *most sacred* offering, which only the male members of the priestly families could eat (vv 8ff), and the other offerings, which even the women of the priestly families could eat (vv 11–19).

18, 11: *Wave offering:* this included the breast and right leg (v 18), the shoulder of the peace offering (Lv 7, 30–34), and portions of the nazirite sacrifice (Nm 6, 19f).

18, 14: *Doomed:* in Hebrew, *berem,* which means here "set aside from profane use and made sacred to the Lord." Cf Lv 27, 21.28.

18, 19: *An inviolable covenant:* literally, "a covenant of salt." Cf 2 Chr 13, 5. The reference may perhaps be to the preservative power of salt (cf Mt 5, 13); but more likely the phrase refers to the custom of partaking of the same salt in common to render a contract unbreakable. See note on Lv 2, 13.

18, 20: The priests and Levites were forbidden to own hereditary land such as the other Israelites possessed; therefore in the allotment of the land they were not to receive any portion of it. Certain cities, however, were assigned to them for their residence; cf 35, 1–8.

19, 3: *Outside the camp:* several Fathers of the Church saw in this a prefiguring of the sacrificial death of Christ outside the walls of Jerusalem; cf Jn 19, 20; Heb 13, 12; in the purifying water, into which the ashes of the red heifer were put, they saw a type of the water of Baptism.

19, 4: *Toward the front of the meeting tent:* since the tabernacle faced the east (Ex 26, 15–30), the killing of the heifer took place east of the camp; in later times it was done on the Mount of Olives, east of the Temple.

some cedar wood, hyssop and scarlet yarn and throw them into the fire in which the heifer is being burned. 7 The priest shall then wash his garments and bathe his body in water. He remains unclean until the evening and only afterward may he return to the camp. 8 Likewise, he who burned the heifer shall wash his garments, bathe his body in water, and be unclean until evening. 9 Finally, a man who is clean shall gather up the ashes of the heifer and deposit them in a clean place outside the camp. There they are to be kept for preparing lustral water for the Israelite community. The heifer is a sin offering. 10 He who has gathered up the ashes of the heifer shall also wash his garments and be unclean until evening. This is a perpetual ordinance, both for the Israelites and for the aliens residing among them.

Use of the Ashes

11 "Whoever touches the dead body of any human being shall be unclean for seven days; 12 he shall purify himself with the water on the third and on the seventh day, and then he will be clean again. But if he fails to purify himself on the third and on the seventh day, he will not become clean. 13 Everyone who fails to purify himself after touching the body of any deceased person, defiles the Dwelling of the LORD and shall be cut off from Israel. Since the lustral water has not been splashed over him, he remains unclean: his uncleanness still clings to him.

14 "This is the law: When a man dies in a tent, everyone who enters the tent, as well as everyone already in it, shall be unclean for seven days; 15 likewise, every vessel that is open, or with its lid unfastened, shall be unclean. 16 Moreover, everyone who in the open country touches a dead person, whether he was slain by the sword or died naturally, or who touches a human bone or a grave, shall be unclean for seven days. 17

For anyone who is thus unclean, ashes from the sin offering shall be put in a vessel, and spring water shall be poured on them. 18 Then a man who is clean shall take some hyssop, dip it in this water, and sprinkle it on the tent and on all the vessels and persons that were in it, or on him who touched a bone, a slain person or other dead body, or a grave. 19 The clean man shall sprinkle the unclean on the third and on the seventh day; thus purified on the seventh day, he shall wash his garments and bathe his body in water, and in the evening he will be clean again. 20 Any unclean man who fails to have himself purified shall be cut off from the community, because he defiles the sanctuary of the LORD. As long as the lustral water has not been splashed over him, he remains unclean. 21 This shall be a perpetual ordinance for you.

"One who sprinkles the lustral water shall wash his garments, and anyone who comes in contact with this water shall be unclean until evening. 22 Moreover, whatever the unclean person touches becomes unclean itself, and anyone who touches it becomes unclean until evening."

Death of Miriam

20 The whole Israelite community arrived in the desert of Zin in the first month, and the people settled at Kadesh. It was here that Miriam died, and here that she was buried.

Water Famine at Kadesh

2 As the community had no water, they held a council against Moses and Aaron. 3 The people contended with Moses, exclaiming, "Would that we too had perished with our kinsmen in the LORD's presence! 4 Why have you brought the LORD's community into this desert where we and our livestock are dying? 5 Why did you lead us out

of Egypt, only to bring us to this wretched place which has neither grain nor figs nor vines nor pomegranates? Here there is not even water to drink!" 6 But Moses and Aaron went away from the assembly to the entrance of the meeting tent, where they fell prostrate.

Sin of Moses and Aaron

Then the glory of the LORD appeared to them, 7 and the LORD said to Moses, 8 "Take the staff and assemble the community, you and your brother Aaron, and in their presence order the rock to yield its waters. From the rock you shall bring forth water for the community and their livestock to drink." 9 So Moses took the staff from its place before the LORD, as he was ordered. 10 He and Aaron assembled the community in front of the rock, where he said to them, "Listen to me, you rebels! Are we to bring water for you out of this rock?" 11 Then, raising his hand, Moses struck the rock twice with his staff, and water gushed out in abundance for the community and their livestock to drink. 12 But the LORD said to Moses and Aaron, "Because you were not faithful to me in showing forth my sanctity before the Israelites, you shall not lead this community into the land I will give them."

13 These are the waters of Meribah, where the Israelites contended against the LORD, and where he revealed his sanctity among them.

Edom's Refusal

14 From Kadesh Moses sent men to the king of Edom with the message: "Your brother Israel has this to say: You know of all the hardships that have befallen us, 15 how our fathers went down to Egypt, where we stayed a long time, how the Egyptians maltreated us and our fathers, 16 and how, when we cried to the LORD, he heard our cry and sent an angel who led us out of

19, 17ff: "If . . . the sprinkled ashes of a heifer sanctify the unclean unto the cleansing of the flesh, how much more will the blood of Christ . . . cleanse your conscience from dead works?" (Heb 9, 13f).
19, 20: Ritual uncleanness is, as it were, contagious, so also sacredness; see note on 17, 3.
20, 1: The first month: we would expect the mention also of the day and of the year (after the exodus) when this took place; cf similar dates in 1, 1; 10, 11;

33, 38; Dt 1, 3. Here the full date seems to have been lost. Probably the Israelites arrived in Kadesh in the third year after the exodus. Cf Dt 1, 46. The desert of Zin: a barren region with a few good oases, southwest of the Dead Sea. See note on 13, 21.
20, 11: Twice: perhaps because he had not sufficient faith to work the miracle with the first blow. Cf v 12.
20, 12f: The sin of Moses and Aaron consisted in

doubting God's mercy toward the ever-rebellious people. In showing forth my sanctity: God's sacred power and glory: an allusion to the name of the place, Kadesh, which means "sanctified, sacred." Meribah means "contention." Cf Ex 17, 7.
20, 14: Your brother Israel: the Edomites were descended from Esau, the brother of Jacob. Their country, to the southeast of the Dead Sea, was also known as Seir; cf Gn 25, 24ff; 36, 1.8f.

Egypt. Now here we are at the town of Kadesh at the edge of your territory. 17 Kindly let us pass through your country. We will not cross any fields or vineyards, nor drink any well water, but we will go straight along the royal road without turning to the right or to the left, until we have passed through your territory."

18 But Edom answered him, "You shall not pass through here; if you do, I will advance against you with the sword." 19 The Israelites insisted, "We want only to go up along the highway. If we or our livestock drink any of your water, we will pay for it. Surely there is no harm in merely letting us march through." 20 But Edom still said, "No, you shall not pass through," and advanced against them with a large and heavily armed force. 21 Therefore, since Edom refused to let them pass through their territory, Israel detoured around them.

Death of Aaron

22 Setting out from Kadesh, the whole Israelite community came to Mount Hor. 23 There at Mount Hor, on the border of the land of Edom, the LORD said to Moses and Aaron, 24 "Aaron is about to be taken to his people; he shall not enter the land I am giving to the Israelites, because you both rebelled against my commandment at the waters of Meribah. 25 Take Aaron and his son Eleazar and bring them up on Mount Hor. 26 Then strip Aaron of his garments and put them on his son Eleazar; for there Aaron shall be taken in death."

27 Moses did as the LORD commanded. When they had climbed Mount Hor in view of the whole community, 28 Moses stripped Aaron of his garments and put them on his son Eleazar. Then Aaron died there on top of the mountain. When Moses and Eleazar came down from the mountain, 29 all the community understood that Aaron had passed away; and for thirty days the whole house of Israel mourned him.

Victory over Arad

21 When the Canaanite king of Arad, who lived in the Negeb, heard that the Israelites were coming along the way of Atharim, he engaged them in battle and took some of them captive. 2 Israel then made this vow to the LORD: "If you deliver this people into my hand, I will doom their cities." 3 Later, when the LORD heeded Israel's prayer and delivered up the Canaanites, they doomed them and their cities. Hence that place was named Hormah.

The Bronze Serpent

4 From Mount Hor they set out on the Red Sea road, to by-pass the land of Edom. But with their patience worn out by the journey, 5 the people complained against God and Moses, "Why have you brought us up from Egypt to die in this desert, where there is no food or water? We are disgusted with this wretched food!"

6 In punishment the LORD sent among the people saraph serpents, which bit the people so that many of them died. 7 Then the people came to Moses and said, "We have sinned in complaining against the LORD and you. Pray the LORD to take the serpents from us." So Moses prayed for the people, 8 and the LORD said to Moses, "Make a saraph and mount it on a pole, and if anyone who has been bitten looks at it, he will recover." 9 Moses accordingly made a bronze serpent and mounted it on a pole, and whenever anyone who had been bitten by a serpent looked at the bronze serpent, he recovered.

Journey around Moab

10 The Israelites moved on and encamped in Oboth. 11 Setting out from Oboth, they encamped in Iyeabarim in the desert fronting Moab on the east. 12 Setting out from there, they encamped in the Wadi Zered. 13 Setting out from there, they encamped on the other side of the Arnon, in the desert that extends from the territory of the Amorites; for the Arnon forms Moab's boundary with the Amorites. 14 Hence it is said in the "Book of the Wars of the LORD":

"Waheb in Suphah and the wadies,
15   Arnon and the wadi gorges
That reach back toward the site of Ar
and slant to the border of Moab."

16 From there they went to Beer, where there was the well of which the LORD said to Moses, "Bring the people together, and I will give them water." 17 Then it was that Israel sang this song:

"Spring up, O well!—so sing to it—
18 The well that the princes sank, that the nobles of the people dug, with their scepters and their staffs."

From Beer they went to Mattanah, 19 from Mattanah to Nahaliel, from Nahaliel to Bamoth, 20 from Bamoth to the cleft in the plateau of Moab at the headland of Pisgah that overlooks Jeshimon.

20, 17: *The royal road:* an important highway, running north and south along the plateau east of the Dead Sea. In ancient times it was much used by caravans and armies; later it was improved by the Romans, and large stretches of it are still clearly recognizable.

20, 22: *Mount Hor:* not definitively identified, but probably to be sought in the vicinity of Kadesh. According to Dt 10, 6, Aaron died at Moserah (cf "Moseroth" in Nm 33, 30f), which is apparently the name of the region in which Mount Hor is situated.

21, 1–3: The account of this episode seems to be a later insertion here, for 21, 4, belongs logically immediately after 20, 29. Perhaps this is the same event as that mentioned in Jgs 1, 16f.

21, 3: *Hormah:* related to the Hebrew word *herem*, meaning "doomed." See notes on 14, 45; 18, 14.

21, 5: *This wretched food:* apparently the manna is meant.

21, 6: *Saraph:* the Hebrew name for a certain species of venomous snakes; the word probably signifies "the fiery one," these snakes being so called from the burning effect of their poisonous bite.

21, 8: *If anyone who has been bitten looks at it, he will recover:* "and as Moses lifted up the serpent in the desert, even so must the Son of Man be lifted up, that those who believe in him may not perish, but may have life everlasting" (Jn 3, 14f).

21, 9: King Hezekiah, in his efforts to abolish idolatry, "smashed the bronze serpent which Moses had made" (2 Kgs 18, 4).

21, 11: *Iyeabarim* probably means "the ruins in the Abarim (Mountains)." See note on 27, 12.

21, 14: *The "Book of the Wars of the Lord":* an ancient collection of Israelite songs, now lost. *Waheb in Suphah:* since neither place is mentioned elsewhere, it is quite uncertain whether these dubious Hebrew words are even to be considered as place names; some Hebrew words apparently lost must have preceded this phrase.

21, 16: *Beer* means a well.

21, 20: *Jeshimon:* "the wasteland"; in 1 Sm 23, 19.24, and 26, 1.3, this is the desert of Judah, on the western side of the Dead Sea, but here and in Nm 23, 28, it seems to refer to the southern end of the Jordan valley where Beth-jeshimoth was situated.

Victory over Sihon

21 Now Israel sent men to Sihon, king of the Amorites, with the message, 22 "Let us pass through your country. We will not turn aside into any field or vineyard, nor will we drink any well water, but we will go straight along the royal road until we have passed through your territory." 23 Sihon, however, would not let Israel pass through his territory, but mustered all his forces and advanced into the desert against Israel. When he reached Jahaz, he engaged Israel in battle. 24 But Israel defeated him at the point of the sword, and took possession of his land from the Arnon to the Jabbok and as far as the country of the Ammonites, whose boundary was at Jazer. 25 Israel seized all the towns here and settled in these towns of the Amorites, in Heshbon and all its dependencies. 26 Now Heshbon was the capital of Sihon, king of the Amorites, who had fought against the former king of Moab and had seized all his land from Jazer to the Arnon. 27 That is why the poets say:

"Come to Heshbon, let it be
        rebuilt,
    let Sihon's capital be firmly
        constructed.
28 For fire went forth from
        Heshbon
    and a blaze from the city of
        Sihon;
It consumed the cities of Moab
    and swallowed up the high
        places of the Arnon.
29 Woe to you, O Moab!
    You are ruined, O people of
        Chemosh!
He let his sons become fugitives
    and his daughters be taken
        captive
    by the Amorite king Sihon.
30 Their plowland is ruined from
        Heshbon to Dibon;
    Ar is laid waste; fires blaze
        as far as Medeba."

31 When Israel had settled in the land of the Amorites, 32 Moses sent spies to Jazer; Israel then captured it with its dependencies and dispossessed the Amorites who were there.

Victory over Og

33 Then they turned and went up along the road to Bashan. But Og, king of Bashan, advanced against them with all his people to give battle at Edrei. 34 The LORD, however, said to Moses, "Do not be afraid of him; for into your hand I will deliver him with all his people and his land. Do to him as you did to Sihon, king of the Amorites, who lived in Heshbon." 35 So they struck him down with his sons and all his people, until not a survivor was left to him, and they took possession of his land.

22 Then the Israelites moved on and encamped in the plains of Moab on the other side of the Jericho stretch of the Jordan.

ON THE PLAINS OF MOAB

Balaam Summoned

2 Now Balak, son of Zippor, saw all that Israel did to the Amorites. 3 Indeed, Moab feared the Israelites greatly because of their numbers, and detested them. 4 So Moab said to the elders of Midian, "Soon this horde will devour all the country around us as an ox devours the grass of the field." And Balak, Zippor's son, who was king of Moab at that time, 5 sent messengers to Balaam, son of Beor, at Pethor on the Euphrates, in the land of the Amawites, summoning him with these words, "A people has come here from Egypt who now cover the face of the earth and are settling down opposite us! 6 Please come and curse this people for us; they are stronger than we are. We may then be able to defeat them and drive them out of the country. For I know that whoever you bless is blessed and whoever you curse is cursed." 7 Then the elders of Moab and of Midian left with the divination fee in hand and went to Balaam. When they had given him Balak's message, 8 he said to them in reply, "Stay here overnight, and I will give you whatever answer the LORD gives me." So the princes of Moab lodged with Balaam.

9 Then God came to Balaam and said, "Who are these men visiting you?" 10 Balaam answered God, "Balak, son of Zippor, king of Moab, sent me the message: 11 'This people that came here from Egypt now cover the face of the earth. Please come and lay a curse on them for us; we may then be able to give them battle and drive them out.'" 12 But God said to Balaam, "Do not go with them and do not curse this people, for they are blessed." 13 The next morning Balaam arose and told the princes of Balak, "Go back to your own country, for the LORD has refused to let me go with you." 14 So the princes of Moab went back to Balak with the report, "Balaam refused to come with us."

Second Appeal to Balaam

15 Balak again sent princes, who were more numerous and more distinguished than the others. 16 On coming to Balaam they told him, "This is what Balak, son of Zippor, has to say: Please do not refuse to come to me. 17 I will reward you very handsomely and will do anything you ask of me. Please come and lay a curse on this people for me." 18 But Balaam replied to Balak's officials, "Even if Balak gave me his house full of silver and gold, I could not do anything, small or great, contrary to the command of the LORD, my God. 19 But, you too shall stay here overnight, till I learn what else the LORD may tell me."

20 That night God came to Balaam and said to him, "If these men have come to summon you, you may go with them; yet only on the condition that you do exactly as I tell you." 21 So the next morning when Balaam arose, he saddled his ass, and went off with the princes of Moab.

21, 29: *Chemosh:* the chief god of the Moabites, and mentioned as such in the famous inscription of Mesha, king of Moab, who was the contemporary of the dynasty of Omri in Israel. Cf 1 Kgs 11, 7.33; 2 Kgs 23, 13; Jer 48, 7.13.

22, 1: *The plains of Moab:* the lowlands to the northeast of the Dead Sea, between the Jordan and the foothills below Mount Nebo. Here the Israelites remained until they crossed the Jordan, as told in Jos 1–4. *Jericho* lay to the west of the Jordan.

22, 6: *Curse this people for us:* Balak believed that if Balaam forecast an evil omen for Israel, this evil would come to pass, as if by magic. Balaam was a soothsayer or foreteller; cf Jos 13, 22.

The Talking Ass

22 But now the anger of God flared up at him for going, and the angel of the LORD stationed himself on the road to hinder him as he was riding along on his ass, accompanied by two of his servants. 23 When the ass saw the angel of the LORD standing on the road with sword drawn, she turned off the road and went into the field, and Balaam had to beat her to bring her back on the road. 24 Then the angel of the LORD took his stand in a narrow lane between vineyards with a stone wall on each side. 25 When the ass saw the angel of the LORD there, she shrank against the wall; and since she squeezed Balaam's leg against it, he beat her again. 26 The angel of the LORD then went ahead, and stopped next in a passage so narrow that there was no room to move either to the right or to the left. 27 When the ass saw the angel of the LORD there, she cowered under Balaam. So, in anger, he again beat the ass with his stick.

28 But now the LORD opened the mouth of the ass, and she asked Balaam, "What have I done to you that you should beat me these three times?" 29 "You have acted so willfully against me," said Balaam to the ass, "that if I but had a sword at hand, I would kill you here and now." 30 But the ass said to Balaam, "Am I not your own beast, and have you not always ridden upon me until now? Have I been in the habit of treating you this way before?" "No," replied Balaam.

31 Then the LORD removed the veil from Balaam's eyes, so that he too saw the angel of the LORD standing on the road with sword drawn; and he fell on his knees and bowed to the ground. 32 But the angel of the LORD said to him, "Why have you beaten your ass these three times? It is I who have come armed to hinder you because this rash journey of yours is directly opposed

to me. 33 When the ass saw me, she turned away from me these three times. If she had not turned away from me, I would have killed you; her I would have spared." 34 Then Balaam said to the angel of the LORD, "I have sinned. Yet I did not know that you stood against me to oppose my journey. Since it has displeased you, I will go back home." 35 But the angel of the LORD said to Balaam, "Go with the men; but you may say only what I tell you." So Balaam went on with the princes of Balak.

36 When Balak heard that Balaam was coming, he went out to meet him at the boundary city Ir-Moab on the Arnon at the end of the Moabite territory. 37 And he said to Balaam, "I sent an urgent summons to you! Why did you not come to me? Did you think I could not reward you?" 38 Balaam answered him, "Well, I have come to you after all. But what power have I to say anything? I can speak only what God puts in my mouth." 39 Then Balaam went with Balak, and they came to Kiriath-huzoth. 40 Here Balak slaughtered oxen and sheep, and sent portions to Balaam and to the princes who were with him.

The First Oracle

41 The next morning Balak took Balaam up on Bamoth-baal, and from there he saw some of the clans. 23 1 Then Balaam said to Balak, "Build me seven altars, and prepare seven bullocks and seven rams for me here." 2 So he did as Balaam had ordered, offering a bullock and a ram on each altar. And Balak said to him, "I have erected the seven altars, and have offered a bullock and a ram on each." 3 Balaam then said to him, "Stand here by your holocaust while I go over there. Perhaps the LORD will meet me, and then I will tell you whatever he lets me see." He went out on the barren height, 4 and God met him. 5 When he had put

an utterance in Balaam's mouth, the LORD said to him, "Go back to Balak, and speak accordingly." 6 So he went back to Balak, who was still standing by his holocaust together with all the princes of Moab. 7 Then Balaam gave voice to his oracle:

From Aram has Balak brought
 me here,
 Moab's king, from the
 Eastern Mountains:
"Come and lay a curse for me
 on Jacob,
 come and denounce Israel."
8 How can I curse whom God has
 not cursed?
 How denounce whom the
 LORD has not denounced?
9 For from the top of the crags I
 see him,
 from the heights I behold him.
Here is a people that lives apart
 and does not reckon itself
 among the nations.
10 Who has ever counted the dust
 of Jacob,
 or numbered Israel's wind-
 borne particles?
May I die the death of the just,
 may my descendants be as
 many as theirs!

11 "What have you done to me?" cried Balak to Balaam. "It was to curse my foes that I brought you here; instead, you have even blessed them." 12 Balaam replied, "Is it not what the LORD puts in my mouth that I must repeat with care?"

The Second Oracle

13 Then Balak said to him, "Please come with me to another place from which you can see only some and not all of them, and from there curse them for me." 14 So he brought him to the lookout field on the top of Pisgah, where he built seven altars and offered a bullock and a ram on each of them. 15 Balaam then said to Balak, "Stand here by your holocaust, while I seek a meeting over there." 16 Then the LORD met

---

22, 22: *The anger of God flared up:* not merely because Balaam was going to Balak, for he had God's permission for the journey (v 20), but perhaps because he was tempted by avarice to curse Israel against God's command. "They have followed the way of Balaam, son of Bosor, who loved the wages of wrongdoing" (2 Pt 2, 15); "and have rushed on thoughtlessly into the error of Balaam for the sake of gain" (Jude 11). Cf v 32 and compare Ex 4, 18–26.

23, 7: *Aram:* the ancient name of the region later known as Syria. *The Eastern Mountains:* the low ranges in the Syrian desert near the Euphrates and Balaam's town of Pethor; cf 22, 5.

23, 9: *A people that lives apart:* Israel, as the chosen people of God, occupied a unique place among the nations, from which they kept themselves aloof.

23, 10: *The dust of Jacob . . . Israel's wind-borne particles:* the Israelites will be as numerous as dust in a

desert sandstorm. *May I . . . as many as theirs:* a formula by which Balaam swears he is speaking the truth; he sees the reward of virtue in having numerous descendants.

23, 13: *To another place:* Balak thought that if Balaam would view Israel from a different site, he could forecast a different kind of omen.

Balaam, and having put an utterance in his mouth, he said to him, "Go back to Balak, and speak accordingly." 17 So he went back to Balak, who was still standing by his holocaust together with the princes of Moab. When Balak asked him, "What did the LORD say?" 18 Balaam gave voice to his oracle:

Be aroused, O Balak, and
　　hearken;
　　give ear to my testimony,
　　O son of Zippor!
19 God is not man that he should
　　speak falsely,
　　nor human, that he should
　　change his mind.
　　Is he one to speak and not act,
　　to decree and not fulfill?
20 It is a blessing I have been
　　given to pronounce;
　　a blessing which I cannot
　　restrain.
21 Misfortune is not observed in
　　Jacob,
　　nor misery seen in Israel.
　　The LORD, his God, is with him;
　　with him is the triumph of
　　his King.
22 It is God who brought him out
　　of Egypt,
　　a wild bull of towering might.
23 No, there is no sorcery against
　　Jacob,
　　nor omen against Israel.
　　It shall yet be said of Jacob,
　　and of Israel, "Behold what
　　God has wrought!"
24 Here is a people that springs up
　　like a lioness,
　　and stalks forth like a lion;
　　It rests not till it has devoured its
　　prey
　　and has drunk the blood of the
　　slain.

25 "Even though you cannot curse them," said Balak to Balaam, "at least do not bless them." 26 But Balaam answered Balak, "Did I not warn you that I must do all that the LORD tells me?"

The Third Oracle
27 Then Balak said to Balaam,

"Come, let me bring you to another place; perhaps God will approve of your cursing them for me from there." 28 So he took Balaam to the top of Peor, that overlooks Jeshimon. 29 Balaam then said to him, "Here build me seven altars; and here prepare for me seven bullocks and seven rams." 30 And Balak did as Balaam had ordered, offering a bullock and a ram on each

24 altar. 1 Balaam, however, perceiving that the LORD was pleased to bless Israel, did not go aside as before to seek omens, but turned his gaze toward the desert. 2 When he raised his eyes and saw Israel encamped, tribe by tribe, the spirit of God came upon him, 3 and he gave voice to his oracle:

The utterance of Balaam, son
　　of Beor,
　　the utterance of the man whose
　　eye is true,
4 The utterance of one who hears
　　what God says,
　　and knows what the Most High
　　knows,
　　Of one who sees what the
　　Almighty sees,
　　enraptured, and with eyes
　　unveiled:
5 How goodly are your tents,
　　O Jacob;
　　your encampments, O Israel!
6 They are like gardens beside a
　　stream,
　　like the cedars planted by the
　　LORD.
7 His wells shall yield free-flowing
　　waters,
　　he shall have the sea within
　　reach;
　　His king shall rise higher than . . .
　　and his royalty shall be exalted.
8 It is God who brought him out
　　of Egypt,
　　a wild bull of towering might.
　　He shall devour the nations like
　　grass,
　　their bones he shall strip bare.
9 He lies crouching like a lion,
　　or like a lioness; who shall
　　arouse him?

Blessed is he who blesses you,
　　and cursed is he who curses
　　you!

10 Balak beat his palms together in a blaze of anger at Balaam and said to him, "It was to curse my foes that I summoned you here; yet three times now you have even blessed them instead! 11 Be off at once, then, to your home. I promised to reward you richly, but the LORD has withheld the reward from you!" 12 Balaam replied to Balak, "Did I not warn the very messengers whom you sent to me, 13 'Even if Balak gave me his house full of silver and gold, I could not of my own accord do anything, good or evil, contrary to the command of the LORD'? Whatever the LORD says I must repeat.

The Fourth Oracle
14 "But now that I am about to go to my own people, let me first warn you what this people will do to your people in the days to come." 15 Then Balaam gave voice to his oracle:

The utterance of Balaam, son of
　　Beor,
　　the utterance of the man whose
　　eye is true,
16 The utterance of one who hears
　　what God says,
　　and knows what the Most High
　　knows,
　　Of one who sees what the
　　Almighty sees,
　　enraptured and with eyes
　　unveiled.
17 I see him, though not now;
　　I behold him, though not near:
　　A star shall advance from Jacob,
　　and a staff shall rise from Israel.
　　That shall smite the brows of
　　Moab,
　　and the skulls of all the
　　Shuthites,
18 Till Edom is dispossessed,
　　and no fugitive is left in Seir.
　　Israel shall do valiantly,
19　　and Jacob shall overcome his
　　foes.

23, 21: *Misfortune . . . misery:* Balaam admits that he is unable to predict any evils for Israel.
23, 22: *A wild bull of towering might:* the reference is to Israel, rather than to God.
24, 10: *Balak beat his palms:* a sign of disclaiming

any responsibility for paying the promised reward.
24, 17: *A star . . . a staff:* many of the Fathers have understood this as a Messianic prophecy, although it is not referred to anywhere in the New Testament; in this sense the *star* is Christ himself, just as he is the

staff from Israel; cf Is 11, 1. But it is doubtful whether this passage is to be connected with the "star of the Magi" in Mt 2, 1-12. *The Shuthites:* mentioned in other documents of this period as nomads on the borders of Palestine.

20 Upon seeking Amalek, Balaam gave voice to his oracle:

First of the peoples was Amalek,
but his end is to perish forever.

21 Upon seeing the Kenites, he gave voice to his oracle:

Your abode is enduring, O smith,
and your nest is set on a cliff;
22 Yet destined for burning—
even as I watch—are your
inhabitants.

23 Upon seeing . . . he gave voice to his oracle:

Alas, who shall survive of
Ishmael,
24 to deliver his people from the
hands of the Kittim?
When they have conquered
Asshur and conquered Eber,
He too shall perish forever.

25 Then Balaam set out on his journey home; and Balak also went his way.

Worship of Baal of Peor

25 While Israel was living at Shittim, the people degraded themselves by having illicit relations with the Moabite women. 2 These then invited the people to the sacrifices of their god, and the people ate of the sacrifices and worshiped their god. 3 When Israel thus submitted to the rites of Baal of Peor, the LORD's anger flared up against Israel, 4 and he said to Moses, "Gather all the leaders of the people, and hold a public execution of the guilty ones before the LORD, that his blazing wrath may be turned away from Israel." 5 So Moses told the Israelite judges, "Each of you shall kill those of his men who have submitted to the rites of Baal of Peor."

Zeal of Phinehas

6 Yet a certain Israelite came and brought in a Midianite woman to his clansmen in the view of Moses and of the whole Israelite community, while they were weeping at the entrance of the meeting tent. 7 When Phinehas, son of Eleazar, son of Aaron the priest, saw this, he left the assembly, and taking a lance in hand, 8 followed the Israelite into his retreat where he pierced the pair of them, the Israelite and the woman. Thus the slaughter of Israelites was checked; 9 but only after twenty-four thousand had died.

10 Then the LORD said to Moses, 11 "Phinehas, son of Eleazar, son of Aaron the priest, has turned my anger from the Israelites by his zeal for my honor among them; that is why I did not put an end to the Israelites for the offense to my honor. 12 Announce, therefore, that I hereby give him my pledge of friendship, 13 which shall be for him and for his descendants after him the pledge of an everlasting priesthood, because he was zealous on behalf of his God and thus made amends for the Israelites."

14 The Israelite slain with the Midianite woman was Zimri, son of Salu, prince of an ancestral house of the Simeonites. 15 The slain Midianite woman was Cozbi, daughter of Zur, who was head of a clan, an ancestral house, in Midian.

Vengeance on the Midianites

16 The LORD then said to Moses, 17 "Treat the Midianites as enemies and crush them, 18 for they have been your enemies by their wily dealings with you as regards Peor and as regards their kinswoman Cozbi, the daughter of a Midianite

prince, who was killed at the time of the slaughter because of Peor."

The Second Census

26 19 After the slaughter 1 the LORD said to Moses and Eleazar, son of Aaron the priest, 2 "Take a census, by ancestral houses, throughout the community of the Israelites of all those of twenty years or more who are fit for military service in Israel." 3 So on the plains of Moab along the Jericho stretch of the Jordan, Moses and the priest Eleazar registered 4 those of twenty years or more, as the LORD had commanded Moses.

The Israelites who came out of the land of Egypt were as follows:

5 Of Reuben, the first-born of Israel, the Reubenites by clans were: through Hanoch the clan of the Hanochites, through Pallu the clan of the Palluites, 6 through Hezron the clan of the Hezronites, through Carmi the clan of the Carmites. 7 These were the clans of the Reubenites, of whom forty-three thousand seven hundred and thirty men were registered.

8 From Pallu descended Eliab, 9 and the descendants of Eliab were Dathan and Abiram—the same Dathan and Abiram, councilors of the community, who revolted against Moses and Aaron [like Korah's band when it rebelled against the LORD]. 10 The earth opened its mouth and swallowed them as a warning [Korah too and the band that died when the fire consumed two hundred and fifty men. 11 The descendants of Korah, however, did not die out].

12 The Simeonites by clans were: through Nemuel the clan of the Nemuelites, through Jamin the clan of the Jaminites, through Jachin the clan of the Jachinites, 13 through

---

24, 20: *First:* literally "the beginning." Amalek was an aboriginal people in Palestine and therefore considered as of great antiquity. There is a deliberate contrast here between the words *first* and *end.*

24, 21: *The Kenites* lived in high strongholds in the mountains of southern Palestine and the Sinai Peninsula, and were skilled in working the various metals found in their territory. Their name is connected, at least by popular etymology, with the Hebrew word for "smith"; of similar sound is the Hebrew word for "nest"—hence the play on words in the present passage.

24, 23f: The translation of this short oracle is based on a reconstructed text and is rather uncertain. *Ishmael:* the survival of Ishmael is indicated in Gn 17, 20; 21, 13.18.

25, 1: *Shittim:* the full name was Abel-shittim, a locality at the foot of the mountains in the northeastern corner of *the plains of Moab* (33, 49). *Illicit relations:* perhaps as part of the licentious worship of Baal of Peor.

25, 4: *Hold a public execution:* the same phrase occurs in 2 Sm 21, 6–14, where the context shows that at least a part of the penalty consisted in being denied honorable burial. In both passages, dismemberment as a punishment for the breaking of covenant pledges is a current understanding of the phrase.

25, 6: *Midianite woman:* at this time the Midianites were leagued with the Moabites in opposing Israel; cf 22, 4.7. Balaam had induced both the Midianites (31, 16) and the Moabites (Ap 2, 14) to lure the Israelites to the obscene rites of Baal of Peor. *They*

were weeping: on account of the plague that had struck them; cf v 8.

25, 11: *For my honor:* by taking vengeance on those who had made Baal of Peor a rival of the Lord.

25, 14f: The nobility of the slain couple is mentioned in order to stress the courage of Phinehas in punishing them. The zeal of Phinehas became proverbial; cf Ps 106, 30; Sir 45, 23; 1 Mc 2, 26.54.

25, 16ff: The account of the execution of this command is given in Nm 31, 1–18.

26, 12: *Nemuel:* so also in Gn 46, 10; 1 Chr 4, 24. In Ex 6, 15, the same man is called "Jemuel"; it is uncertain which form is correct.

Sohar the clan of the Soharites, through Shaul the clan of the Shaulites. 14 These were the clans of the Simeonites, of whom twenty-two thousand two hundred men were registered.

15 The Gadites by clans were: through Zephon the clan of the Zephonites, through Haggi the clan of the Haggites, through Shuni the clan of the Shunites, 16 through Ozni the clan of the Oznites, through Eri the clan of the Erites, 17 through Arod the clan of the Arodites, through Areli the clan of the Arelites. 18 These were the clans of the Gadites, of whom forty thousand five hundred men were registered.

19 The sons of Judah who died in the land of Canaan were Er and Onan. 20 The Judahites by clans were: through Shelah the clan of the Shelahites, through Perez the clan of the Perezites, through Zerah the clan of the Zerahites. 21 The Perezites were: through Hezron the clan of the Hezronites, through Hamul the clan of the Hamulites. 22 These were the clans of Judah, of whom seventy-six thousand five hundred men were registered.

23 The Issacharites by clans were: through Tola the clan of the Tolaites, through Puvah the clan of the Puvahites, 24 through Jashub the clan of the Jashubites, through Shimron the clan of the Shimronites. 25 These were the clans of Issachar, of whom sixty-four thousand three hundred men were registered.

26 The Zebulunites by clans were: through Sered the clan of the Seredites, through Elon the clan of the Elonites, through Jahleel the clan of the Jahleelites. 27 These were the clans of the Zebulunites, of whom sixty thousand five hundred men were registered.

28 The sons of Joseph were Manasseh and Ephraim. 29 The Manassehites by clans were: through Machir the clan of the Machirites, through Gilead, a descendant of Machir, the clan of the Gileadites. 30 The Gileadites were: through Abiezer the clan of the Abiezerites,

through Helek the clan of the Helekites, 31 through Asriel the clan of the Asrielites, through Shechem the clan of the Shechemites, 32 through Shemida the clan of the Shemidaites, through Hepher the clan of the Hepherites. 33 Zelophehad, son of Hepher, had no sons, but only daughters, whose names were Mahlah, Noah, Hoglah, Milcah and Tirzah. 34 These were the clans of Manasseh, of whom fifty-two thousand seven hundred men were registered.

35 The Ephraimites by clans were: through Shuthelah the clan of the Shuthelahites, through Becher the clan of the Becherites, through Tahan the clan of the Tahanites. 36 The Shuthelahites were: through Eran the clan of the Eranites. 37 These were the clans of the Ephraimites, of whom thirty-two thousand five hundred men were registered.

These were the descendants of Joseph by clans.

38 The Benjaminites by clans were through Bela the clan of the Belaites, through Ashbel the clan of the Ashbelites, through Ahiram the clan of the Ahiramites, 39 through Shupham the clan of the Shuphamites, through Hupham the clan of the Huphamites. 40 The descendants of Bela were Arad and Naaman: through Arad the clan of the Aradites, through Naaman the clan of the Naamanites. 41 These were the Benjaminites by clans, of whom forty-five thousand six hundred men were registered.

42 The Danites by clans were: through Shuham the clan of the Shuhamites. These were the clans of Dan, 43 of whom sixty-four thousand four hundred men were registered.

44 The Asherites by clans were: through Imnah the clan of the Imnites, through Ishvi the clan of the Ishvites, through Beriah the clan of the Beriites, 45 through Heber the clan of the Heberites, through Malchiel the clan of the Malchielites. 46 The name of Asher's daughter was Serah. 47 These were the clans of Asher, of whom fifty-three thou-

sand four hundred men were registered.

48 The Naphtalites by clans were: through Jahzeel the clan of the Jahzeelites, through Guni the clan of the Gunites, 49 through Jezer the clan of the Jezerites, through Shillem the clan of the Shillemites. 50 These were the clans of Naphtali, of whom forty-five thousand four hundred men were registered.

51 These six hundred and one thousand seven hundred and thirty were the Israelites who were registered.

Allotment of the Land

52 The LORD said to Moses, 53 "Among these groups the land shall be divided as their heritage in keeping with the number of individuals in each group. 54 To a large group you shall assign a large heritage, to a small group a small heritage, each group receiving its heritage in proportion to the number of men registered in it. 55 But the land shall be divided by lot, as the heritage of the various ancestral tribes. 56 As the lot falls shall each group, large or small, be assigned its heritage."

Census of the Levites

57 The Levites registered by clans were: through Gershon the clan of the Gershonites, through Kohath the clan of the Kohathites, through Merari the clan of the Merarites. 58 These also were clans of Levi: the clan of the Libnites, the clan of the Hebronites, the clan of the Mahlites, the clan of the Mushites, the clan of the Korahites.

Among the descendants of Kohath was Amram, 59 whose wife was named Jochebed. She also was of the tribe of Levi, born to the tribe in Egypt. To Amram she bore Aaron and Moses and their sister Miriam. 60 To Aaron were born Nadab and Abihu, Eleazar and Ithamar. 61 But Nadab and Abihu died when they offered profane fire before the LORD.

62 The total number of male Levites one month or more of age, who were registered, was twenty-three

---

26, 52-56: The division of Canaan among the various tribes and clans and families was determined partly by the size of each group and partly by lot.

Perhaps the lots determined the respective locality of each tribal land and the section reserved for each clan, while the relative size of the allotted locality and section

depended on the numerical strength of each group. The Hebrews considered the outcome of the drawing of lots as an expression of God's will; cf Acts 1, 23-26.

thousand. They were not registered with the other Israelites, however, for no heritage was given them among the Israelites. 63 These, then, were the men registered by Moses and the priest Eleazar in the census of the Israelites taken on the plains of Moab along the Jericho stretch of the Jordan. 64 Among them there was not a man of those who had been registered by Moses and the priest Aaron in the census of the Israelites taken in the desert of Sinai. 65 For the LORD had told them that they would surely die in the desert, and not one of them was left except Caleb, son of Jephunneh, and Joshua, son of Nun.

Zelophehad's Daughters

27 Zelophehad, son of Hepher, son of Gilead, son of Machir, son of Manasseh, son of Joseph, had daughters named Mahlah, Noah, Hoglah, Milcah and Tirzah. They came forward, 2 and standing in the presence of Moses, the priest Eleazar, the princes, and the whole community at the entrance of the meeting tent, said: 3 "Our father died in the desert. Although he did not join those who banded together against the LORD [in Korah's band], he died for his own sin without leaving any sons. 4 But why should our father's name be withdrawn from his clan merely because he had no son? Let us, therefore, have property among our father's kinsmen."

Laws concerning Heiresses

5 When Moses laid their case before the LORD, 6 the LORD said to him, 7 "The plea of Zelophehad's daughters is just; you shall give them hereditary property among their father's kinsmen, letting their father's heritage pass on to them. 8 Therefore, tell the Israelites: If a man dies without leaving a son, you

shall let his heritage pass on to his daughter; 9 if he has no daughter, you shall give his heritage to his brothers; 10 if he has no brothers, you shall give his heritage to his father's brothers; 11 if his father had no brothers, you shall give his heritage to his nearest relative in his clan, who shall then take possession of it." This is the legal norm for the Israelites, as the LORD commanded Moses.

Joshua to Succeed Moses

12 The LORD said to Moses, "Go up here into the Abarim Mountains and view the land that I am giving to the Israelites. 13 When you have viewed it, you too shall be taken to your people, as was your brother Aaron, 14 because in the rebellion of the community in the desert of Zin you both rebelled against my order to manifest my sanctity to them by means of the water." [This is the water of Meribah of Kadesh in the desert of Zin.] 15 Then Moses said to the LORD, 16 "May the LORD, the God of the spirits of all mankind, set over the community a man 17 who shall act as their leader in all things, to guide them in all their actions; that the LORD's community may not be like sheep without a shepherd." 18 And the LORD replied to Moses, "Take Joshua, son of Nun, a man of spirit, and lay your hand upon him. 19 Have him stand in the presence of the priest Eleazar and of the whole community, and commission him before their eyes. 20 Invest him with some of your own dignity, that the whole Israelite community may obey him. 21 He shall present himself to the priest Eleazar, to have him seek out for him the decisions of the Urim in the LORD's presence; and as he directs, Joshua, all the Israelites with him, and the com-

munity as a whole shall perform all their actions." 22 Moses did as the LORD had commanded him. Taking Joshua and having him stand in the presence of the priest Eleazar and of the whole community, 23 he laid his hands on him and gave him his commission, as the LORD had directed through Moses.

General Sacrifices

28 The LORD said to Moses, 2 "Give the Israelites this commandment: At the times I have appointed, you shall be careful to present to me the food offerings that are offered to me as sweet-smelling oblations.

Each Morning and Evening

3 "You shall tell them therefore: This is the oblation which you shall offer to the LORD: two unblemished yearling lambs each day as the established holocaust, 4 offering one lamb in the morning and the other during the evening twilight, 5 each with a cereal offering of one tenth of an ephah of fine flour mixed with a fourth of a hin of oil of crushed olives. 6 This is the established holocaust that was offered at Mount Sinai as a sweet-smelling oblation to the LORD. 7 And as the libation for the first lamb, you shall pour out to the LORD in the sanctuary a fourth of a hin of wine. 8 The other lamb, to be offered during the evening twilight, you shall offer with the same cereal offering and the same libation as in the morning, as a sweet-smelling oblation to the LORD.

On the Sabbath

9 "On the sabbath day you shall offer two unblemished yearling lambs with their cereal offering, two tenths of an ephah of fine flour mixed with oil, and with their libations. 10

27, 3: *He did not join . . . against the Lord:* had he done so, he and his heirs could have rightly been deprived of the privilege of receiving a portion in the Promised Land.

27, 5-11: The purpose of this law, as also that of the related laws in Nm 36, 2-10 (heiresses to marry within the same tribe), Dt 25, 5-10 (levirate marriage), and Lv 25, 10 (return of property in the jubilee year), was to keep the landed property within the proper domain of each tribe.

27, 12: *The Abarim Mountains:* the range on the eastern side of the Dead Sea.

27, 16: *The God of the spirits of all mankind:* the

sense is either that God knows the character and abilities of all men and therefore knows best whom to appoint (cf Acts 1, 24), or, more probably, that God is Master of life and death and therefore can call Moses from this world whenever he wishes; cf the same phrase in Nm 16, 22, where "spirit" evidently means "the life principle."

27, 18: *A man of spirit:* literally, "a man in whom there is spirit": one who has the qualities of a good leader—courage, prudence, and strength of will. Cf Gn 41, 38; Dt 34, 9.

27, 31: *The Urim:* certain sacred objects which the Hebrew priests employed to ascertain the divine will,

probably by obtaining a positive or negative answer to a given question. The full expression was "the Urim and Thummim"; cf Ex 28, 30; Lv 8, 8; Dt 33, 8; Ezr 2, 63; Neh 7, 65. Joshua was ordinarily not to receive direct revelations from God as Moses had received them.

28, 3: *The established holocaust:* "the *tamid* holocaust," the technical term for the daily sacrifice.

28, 5: *Oil of crushed olives:* this oil, made in a mortar, was purer and more expensive than oil extracted in the olive press.

28, 7: *In the sanctuary:* according to Sir 50, 15, it was at the base of the altar.

Each sabbath there shall be the sabbath holocaust in addition to the established holocaust and its libation.

At the New Moon Feast

11 "On the first of each month you shall offer as a holocaust to the LORD two bullocks, one ram, and seven unblemished yearling lambs, 12 with three tenths of an ephah of fine flour mixed with oil as the cereal offering for each bullock, two tenths of an ephah of fine flour mixed with oil as the cereal offering for the ram, 13 and one tenth of an ephah of fine flour mixed with oil as the cereal offering for each lamb, that the holocaust may be a sweet-smelling oblation to the LORD. 14 Their libations shall be half a hin of wine for each bullock, a third of a hin for the ram, and a fourth of a hin for each lamb. This is the new moon holocaust for every new moon of the year. 15 Moreover, one goat shall be sacrificed as a sin offering to the LORD. These are to be offered in addition to the established holocaust and its libation.

At the Passover

16 "On the fourteenth day of the first month falls the Passover of the LORD, 17 and the fifteenth day of this month is the pilgrimage feast. For seven days unleavened bread is to be eaten. 18 On the first of these days you shall hold a sacred assembly, and do no sort of work. 19 As an oblation you shall offer a holocaust to the LORD, which shall consist of two bullocks, one ram, and seven yearling lambs that you are sure are unblemished, 20 with their cereal offerings of fine flour mixed with oil; offering three tenths of an ephah for each bullock, two tenths for the ram, 21 and one tenth for each of the seven lambs; 22 and offer one goat as a sin offering in atonement for yourselves.

23 These offerings you shall make in addition to the established morning holocaust: 24 you shall make exactly the same offerings each day for seven days as food offerings, in addition to the established holocaust with its libation, for a sweet-smelling oblation to the LORD. 25 On the seventh day you shall hold a sacred assembly, and do no sort of work.

At Pentecost

26 "On the day of first fruits, on your feast of Weeks, when you present to the LORD the new cereal offering, you shall hold a sacred assembly, and do no sort of work. 27 You shall offer as a sweet-smelling holocaust to the LORD two bullocks, one ram, and seven yearling lambs that you are sure are unblemished, 28 with their cereal offerings of fine flour mixed with oil; offering three tenths of an ephah for each bullock, two tenths for the ram, 29 and one tenth for each of the seven lambs. 30 Moreover, one goat shall be offered as a sin offering in atonement for yourselves. 31 You shall make these offerings, together with their libations, in addition to the established holocaust with its cereal offering.

On New Year's Day

29 "On the first day of the seventh month you shall hold a sacred assembly, and do no sort of work; it shall be a day on which you sound the trumpet. 2 You shall offer as a sweet-smelling holocaust to the LORD one bullock, one ram, and seven unblemished yearling lambs, 3 with their cereal offerings of fine flour mixed with oil; offering three tenths of an ephah for the bullock, two tenths for the ram, 4 and one tenth for each of the seven lambs. 5 Moreover, one goat shall be offered as a sin offering in atonement for yourselves. 6 These are to be offered in addition to the

ordinary new moon holocaust with its cereal offering, and in addition to the established holocaust with its cereal offering, together with the libations prescribed for them, as a sweet-smelling oblation to the LORD.

On the Day of Atonement

7 "On the tenth day of this seventh month you shall hold a sacred assembly, and mortify yourselves, and do no sort of work. 8 You shall offer as a sweet-smelling holocaust to the LORD one bullock, one ram, and seven yearling lambs that you are sure are unblemished, 9 with their cereal offerings of fine flour mixed with oil; offering three tenths of an ephah for the bullock, two tenths for the ram, 10 and one tenth for each of the seven lambs. 11 Moreover, one goat shall be sacrificed as a sin offering. These are to be offered in addition to the atonement sin offering, the established holocaust with its cereal offering, and their libations.

On the Feast of Booths

12 "On the fifteenth day of the seventh month you shall hold a sacred assembly, and do no sort of work; then, for seven days following, you shall celebrate a pilgrimage feast to the LORD. 13 You shall offer as a sweet-smelling holocaust to the LORD thirteen bullocks, two rams, and fourteen yearling lambs that are unblemished, 14 with their cereal offerings of fine flour mixed with oil; offering three tenths of an ephah for each of the thirteen bullocks, two tenths for each of the two rams, 15 and one tenth for each of the fourteen lambs. 16 Moreover, one goat shall be sacrificed as a sin offering. These are to be offered in addition to the established holocaust with its cereal offering and libation.

17 "On the second day you shall offer twelve bullocks, two rams, and fourteen unblemished yearling lambs,

---

28, 11: *On the first of each month:* literally, "at the new moons"; beginning on the evening when the crescent of the new moon first appeared.

28, 16: *On the fourteenth day:* toward evening at the end of this day; cf Ex 12, 6.18.

28, 26: *The day of first fruits:* a unique term for this feast, which is usually called "the feast of Weeks"; it was celebrated as a thanksgiving for the wheat harvest seven weeks after the barley harvest (Passover). In the time of Christ it was commonly

known by the Greek word "Pentecost," that is, "fiftieth" (day after the Passover); see note on Lv 23, 16.

29, 1: *The first day of the seventh month* (about September–October) is now the Jewish New Year's Day. In the older calendar the year began with the first of Nisan (March–April); cf Ex 12, 2.

29, 7: *The tenth day of this seventh month:* the Day of Atonement. *Mortify yourselves:* literally, "afflict your souls," that is, with fasting.

29, 11: *The atonement sin offering:* the bullock prescribed in Lv 16, 11f.

29, 12: This feast of Booths celebrating the vintage harvest was the most popular of all and therefore had the most elaborate ritual. See note on Lv 23, 34.

29, 13: *Thirteen bullocks:* the number of bullocks sacrificed before the octave day was seventy, arranged on a descending scale so that the number on the seventh day was the sacred number seven.

18 with their cereal offerings and libations as prescribed for the bullocks, rams and lambs in proportion to their number, 19 as well as one goat for a sin offering, besides the established holocaust with its cereal offering and libation.

20 "On the third day you shall offer eleven bullocks, two rams, and fourteen unblemished yearling lambs, 21 with their cereal offerings and libations as prescribed for the bullocks, rams and lambs in proportion to their number, 22 as well as one goat for a sin offering, besides the established holocaust with its cereal offering and libation.

23 "On the fourth day you shall offer ten bullocks, two rams, and fourteen unblemished yearling lambs, 24 with their cereal offerings and libations as prescribed for the bullocks, rams and lambs in proportion to their number, 25 as well as one goat for a sin offering, besides the established holocaust with its cereal offering and libation.

26 "On the fifth day you shall offer nine bullocks, two rams, and fourteen unblemished yearling lambs, 27 with their cereal offerings and libations as prescribed for the bullocks, rams and lambs in proportion to their number, 28 as well as one goat for a sin offering, besides the established holocaust with its cereal offering and libation.

29 "On the sixth day you shall offer eight bullocks, two rams, and fourteen unblemished yearling lambs, 30 with their cereal offerings and libations as prescribed for the bullocks, rams and lambs in proportion to their number, 31 as well as one goat for a sin offering, besides the established holocaust with its cereal offering and libation.

32 "On the seventh day you shall offer seven bullocks, two rams, and fourteen unblemished yearling lambs, 33 with their cereal offerings and libations as prescribed for the bullocks, rams and lambs in proportion to their number, 34 as well as one goat for a sin offering, besides the

established holocaust with its cereal offering and libation.

35 "On the eighth day you shall hold a solemn meeting, and do no sort of work. 36 You shall offer up in holocaust as a sweet-smelling oblation to the LORD one bullock, one ram, and seven unblemished yearling lambs, 37 with their cereal offerings and libations as prescribed for the bullocks, rams and lambs in proportion to their number, 38 as well as one goat for a sin offering, besides the established holocaust with its cereal offering and libation.

39 "These are the offerings you shall make to the LORD on your festivals, besides whatever holocausts, cereal offerings, libations, and peace offerings you present as your votive or freewill offerings."

30 Moses then gave the Israelites these instructions, just as the LORD had ordered him.

Validity and Annulment of Vows

2 Moses said to the heads of the Israelite tribes, "This is what the LORD has commanded: 3 When a man makes a vow to the LORD or binds himself under oath to a pledge of abstinence, he shall not violate his word, but must fulfill exactly the promise he has uttered.

4 "When a woman, while still a maiden in her father's house, makes a vow to the LORD, or binds herself to a pledge, 5 if her father learns of her vow or the pledge to which she bound herself and says nothing to her about it, then any vow or any pledge she has made remains valid. 6 But if on the day he learns of it her father expresses to her his disapproval, then any vow or any pledge she has made becomes null and void; and the LORD releases her from it, since her father has expressed to her his disapproval.

7 "If she marries while under a vow or under a rash pledge to which she bound herself, 8 and her husband learns of it, yet says nothing to her that day about it, then the vow

or pledge she had made remains valid. 9 But if on the day he learns of it her husband expresses to her his disapproval, he thereby annuls the vow she had made or the rash pledge to which she had bound herself, and the LORD releases her from it. 10 The vow of a widow or of a divorced woman, or any pledge to which such a woman binds herself, is valid.

11 "If it is in her husband's house that she makes a vow or binds herself under oath to a pledge, 12 and her husband learns of it yet says nothing to express to her his disapproval, then any vow or any pledge she has made remains valid. 13 But if on the day he learns of them her husband annuls them, then whatever she has expressly promised in her vow or in her pledge becomes null and void; since her husband has annulled them, the LORD releases her from them.

14 "Any vow or any pledge that she makes under oath to mortify herself, her husband can either allow to remain valid or render null and void. 15 But if her husband, day after day, says nothing at all to her about them, he thereby allows as valid any vow or any pledge she has made; he has allowed them to remain valid, because on the day he learned of them he said nothing to her about them. 16 If, however, he countermands them some time after he first learned of them, he is responsible for her guilt."

17 These are the statutes which the LORD prescribed through Moses concerning the relationship between a husband and his wife, as well as between a father and his daughter while she is still a maiden in her father's house.

Extermination of the Midianites

31 The LORD said to Moses, 2 "Avenge the Israelites on the Midianites, and then you shall be taken to your people." 3 So Moses told the people, "Select men from your midst and arm them for war,

---

29, 35: *A solemn meeting:* the Hebrew word is the technical term for the closing celebration of the three major feasts of the Passover, Pentecost and Booths, or of other special feasts that lasted for a week. Cf Lv 23, 36; Dt 16, 8; 2 Chr 7, 9; Neh 8, 18.

30, 3: *A vow . . . a pledge:* here the former signifies

the doing of some positive good deed, in particular the offering of some sacrifice; the latter signifies the abstaining from some otherwise licit action or pleasure; cf v 14.

30, 11: *In her husband's house:* after her marriage. This contrasts with the case given in vv 7ff.

30, 16: *He countermands them:* he prevents their fulfillment. Since he has first allowed the vows to remain valid, he can no longer annul them.

31, 1ff: The narrative of Israel's relations with Midian, which was interrupted after 25, 18, is now resumed.

to attack the Midianites and execute the LORD's vengeance on them. 4 From each of the tribes of Israel you shall send a band of one thousand men to war." 5 From the clans of Israel, therefore, a thousand men of each tribe were levied, so that there were twelve thousand men armed for war. 6 Moses sent them out on the campaign, a thousand from each tribe, with Phinehas, son of Eleazar, the priest for the campaign, who had with him the sacred vessels and the trumpets for sounding the alarm. 7 They waged war against the Midianites, as the LORD had commanded Moses, and killed every male among them. 8 Besides those slain in battle, they killed the five Midianite kings: Evi, Rekem, Zur, Hur and Reba; and they also executed Balaam, son of Beor, with the sword. 9 But the Israelites kept the women of the Midianites with their little ones as captives, and all their herds and flocks and wealth as spoil, 10 while they set on fire all the towns where they had settled and all their encampments. 11 Then they took all the booty, with the people and beasts they had captured, and brought the captives, together with the spoils and booty, 12 to Moses and the priest Eleazar and to the Israelite community at their camp on the plains of Moab, along the Jericho stretch of the Jordan.

Treatment of the Captives

13 When Moses and the priest Eleazar, with all the princes of the community, went outside the camp to meet them, 14 Moses became angry with the officers of the army, the clan and company commanders, who were returning from combat. 15 "So you have spared all the women!" he exclaimed. 16 "Why, they are the very ones who on Balaam's advice prompted the unfaithfulness of the Israelites toward the LORD in the Peor affair, which began the slaughter of the LORD's community. 17 Slay, therefore, every male child and every woman who has had intercourse with a man. 18 But you may spare and keep for yourselves all girls who had no intercourse with a man.

Purification after Combat

19 "Moreover, you shall stay outside the camp for seven days, and those of you who have slain anyone or touched anyone slain in battle shall purify yourselves on the third and on the seventh day. This applies both to you and to your captives. 20 You shall also purify every article of cloth, leather, goat's hair, or wood."

21 Eleazar the priest told the soldiers who had returned from combat: "This is what the law, as prescribed by the LORD to Moses, ordains: 22 Whatever can stand fire, such as gold, silver, bronze, iron, tin and lead, 23 you shall put into the fire, that it may become clean; however, it must also be purified with lustral water. But whatever cannot stand fire you shall put into the water. 24 On the seventh day you shall wash your clothes, and then you will again be clean. After that you may enter the camp."

Division of the Booty

25 The LORD said to Moses: 26 "With the help of the priest Eleazar and of the heads of the ancestral houses, count up all the human captives and the beasts that have been taken; 27 then divide them evenly, giving half to those who took active part in the war by going out to combat, and half to the rest of the community. 28 You shall levy a tax for the LORD on the warriors who went out to combat: one out of every five hundred persons, oxen, asses and sheep 29 in their half of the spoil you shall turn over to the priest Eleazar as a contribution to the LORD. 30 From the Israelites' half you shall take one out of every fifty persons, and the same from the different beasts, oxen, asses and sheep, and give them to the Levites, who have charge of the LORD's Dwelling." 31 So Moses and the priest Eleazar did this, as the LORD had commanded Moses.

Amount of Booty

32 This booty, what was left of the loot which the soldiers had taken, amounted to six hundred and seventy-five thousand sheep, 33 seventy-two thousand oxen, 34 sixty-one thousand asses, 35 and thirty-two thousand girls who were still virgins.

36 The half that fell to those who had gone out to combat was: three hundred and thirty-seven thousand five hundred sheep, 37 of which six hundred and seventy-five fell as tax to the LORD; 38 thirty-six thousand oxen, of which seventy-two fell as tax to the LORD; 39 thirty thousand five hundred asses, of which sixty-one fell as tax to the LORD; 40 and sixteen thousand persons, of whom thirty-two fell as tax to the LORD. 41 The taxes contributed to the LORD, Moses gave to the priest Eleazar, as the LORD had commanded him.

42 The half for the other Israelites, which fell to the community when Moses had taken it from the soldiers, was: 43 three hundred and thirty-seven thousand five hundred sheep, 44 thirty-six thousand oxen, 45 thirty thousand five hundred asses, 46 and sixteen thousand persons. 47 From this, the Israelites' share, Moses, as the LORD had ordered, took one out of every fifty, both of persons and of beasts, and gave them to the Levites, who had charge of the LORD's Dwelling.

Gifts of the Officers

48 Then the officers who had been clan and company commanders of the army came up to Moses 49 and said to him, "Your servants have counted up the soldiers under our command, and not one is missing. 50 So, to make atonement for ourselves before the LORD, each of us will bring as an offering to the LORD some gold article he has picked up,

---

31, 8: *The five Midianite kings:* they are called "Midianite princes, Sihon's vassals" in Jos 13, 21.

31, 17: There are later references to Midian in Jgs 6–8; 1 Kgs 11, 18; Is 60, 6. The present raid was only against those Midianites who were dwelling at this time near the encampment of the Israelites.

31, 23: *Lustral water:* water mixed with the ashes of the red heifer as prescribed in Nm 19, 9.

31, 27: *Divide them evenly:* for a similar division of the booty into two equal parts, between those who engaged in the fray and those who stayed with the baggage, cf 1 Sm 30, 24. But note that here the tax

on the booty of the noncombatants is ten times as much as that on the soldier's booty.

31, 50: The precise nature and use of some of these articles of gold is not certain.

such as an anklet, a bracelet, a ring, an earring, or a necklace." 51 Moses and the priest Eleazar accepted this gold from them, all of it in well-wrought articles. 52 The gold that they gave as a contribution to the LORD amounted in all to sixteen thousand seven hundred and fifty shekels. This was from the clan and company commanders; 53 what the common soldiers had looted each one kept for himself. 54 Moses, then, and the priest Eleazar accepted the gold from the clan and company commanders, and put it in the meeting tent as a memorial for the Israelites before the LORD.

Request of Gad and Reuben

32 Now the Reubenites and Gadites had a very large number of livestock. Noticing that the land of Jazer and of Gilead was grazing country, 2 they came to Moses and the priest Eleazar and to the princes of the community and said, 3 "The region of Ataroth, Dibon, Jazer, Nimrah, Heshbon, Elealeh, Sebam, Nebo and Baal-meon, 4 which the LORD has laid low before the community of Israel, is grazing country. Now, since your servants have livestock," 5 they continued, "if we find favor with you, let this land be given to your servants as their property. Do not make us cross the Jordan."

Moses' Rebuke

6 But Moses answered the Gadites and Reubenites: "Are your kinsmen, then, to engage in war, while you remain here? 7 Why do you wish to discourage the Israelites from crossing to the land the LORD has given them? 8 That is just what your fathers did when I sent them from Kadesh-barnea to reconnoiter the land. 9 They went up to the Wadi Eshcol and reconnoitered the land, then so discouraged the Israelites that they would not enter the land the LORD had given them. 10 At that time the wrath of the LORD

flared up, and he swore, 11 'Because they have not followed me unreservedly, none of these men of twenty years or more who have come up from Egypt shall ever see this country I promised under oath to Abraham and Isaac and Jacob, 12 except the Kenizzite Caleb, son of Jephunneh, and Joshua, son of Nun, who have followed the LORD unreservedly.' 13 So in his anger with the Israelites the LORD made them wander in the desert forty years, until the whole generation that had done evil in the sight of the LORD had died out. 14 And now here you are, a brood of sinners, rising up in your fathers' place to add still more to the LORD's blazing wrath against the Israelites. 15 If you turn away from following him, he will make them stay still longer in the desert, and so you will bring about the ruin of this whole nation."

Counter Proposal

16 But they were insistent with him: "We wish only to build sheepfolds here for our flocks, and towns for our families; 17 but we ourselves will march as troops in the van of the Israelites, until we have led them to their destination. Meanwhile our families can remain here in the fortified towns, safe from attack by the natives. 18 We will not return to our homes until every one of the Israelites has taken possession of his heritage, 19 and will not claim any heritage with them once we cross the Jordan, so long as we receive a heritage for ourselves on this eastern side of the Jordan."

Agreement Reached

20 Moses said to them in reply: "If you keep your word to march as troops in the LORD's vanguard 21 and to cross the Jordan in full force before the LORD until he has driven his enemies out of his way 22 and the land is subdued before him, then

you may return here, quit of every obligation to the LORD and to Israel, and this region shall be your possession before the LORD. 23 But if you do not do this, you will sin against the LORD, and you can be sure that you will not escape the consequences of your sin. 24 Build the towns, then, for your families, and the folds for your flocks, but also fulfill your express promise."

25 The Gadites and Reubenites answered Moses, "Your servants will do as you command, my lord. 26 While our wives and children, our herds and other livestock remain in the towns of Gilead, 27 all your servants will go across as armed troops to battle before the LORD, just as your lordship says."

28 Moses, therefore, gave this order in their regard to the priest Eleazar, to Joshua, son of Nun, and to the heads of the ancestral tribes of the Israelites: 29 "If all the Gadites and Reubenites cross the Jordan with you as combat troops before the LORD, you shall give them Gilead as their property when the land has been subdued before you. 30 But if they will not go across with you as combat troops before the LORD, you shall bring their wives and children and livestock across before you into Canaan, and they shall have their property with you in the land of Canaan."

31 To this the Gadites and Rubenites replied, "We will do what the LORD has commanded us, your servants. 32 We ourselves will go across into the land of Canaan as troops before the LORD, but we will retain our hereditary property on this side of the Jordan." 33 So Moses gave them [the Gadites and Reubenites, as well as half the tribe of Manasseh, son of Joseph, the kingdom of Sihon, king of the Amorites, and the kingdom of Og, king of Bashan,] the land with its towns and the districts that surrounded them.

32, 1: *Gilead:* the name of the western part of the plateau east of the Jordan, sometimes signifying the whole region from the Yarmuk to the Jordan, sometimes only the northern part of this region, and sometimes, as here, only its southern part. *Jazer* lay to the east of southern Gilead.

32, 3: The places named in this verse, as well as the additional ones given in vv 34–38, were all in the former kingdom of Sihon, that is, in the region

between the Jabbok and the Arnon. Cf 21, 23f; Jos 13, 19–21.24–27.

32, 12: *Kenizzite:* a member of the clan of Kenaz, which, according to Gn 36, 11.15.42, was Edomitic; hence, although Caleb belonged to the tribe of Judah (Nm 13, 6; 34, 19), he must have had Edomite blood in his veins; cf also Jos 14, 6.14.

32, 20ff: Since the ark of the Lord was borne into

battle with the Israelite army, the vanguard was said to march *before the Lord.*

32, 33: The preceding is concerned solely with the two tribes of Gad and Reuben and with the land of the former kingdom of Sihon; hence it seems probable that the sudden reference here to the half-tribe of Manasseh and to their territory in Bashan, the former kingdom of Og, is a later addition to the text.

34 The Gadites rebuilt the fortified towns of Dibon, Ataroth, Aroer, 35 Atroth-shophan, Jazer, Jogbehah, 36 Beth-nimrah and Beth-haran, and they built sheepfolds. 37 The Reubenites rebuilt Heshbon, Elealeh, Kiriathaim, 38 Nebo, Baal-meon [names to be changed!], and Sibmah. These towns, which they rebuilt, they called by their old names.

Other Conquests

39 The descendants of Machir, son of Manasseh, invaded Gilead and captured it, driving out the Amorites who were there. 40 [Moses gave Gilead to Machir, son of Manasseh, and he settled there.] 41 Jair, a Manassehite clan, campaigned against the tent villages, captured them and called them Havvoth-jair. 42 Nobah also campaigned against Kenath, captured it with its dependencies and called it Nobah after his own name.

Stages on the Journey

33 The following are the stages by which the Israelites journeyed up by companies from the land of Egypt under the guidance of Moses and Aaron. 2 By the LORD's command Moses recorded the starting places of the various stages. The starting places of the successive stages were:

3 They set out from Rameses in the first month,
   on the fifteenth day of the first month.
On the Passover morrow the Israelites went forth
   in triumph, in view of all Egypt,
4 While the Egyptians buried their first-born
   all of whom the LORD had struck down;
   on their gods, too, the LORD executed judgments.

From Egypt to Sinai

5 Setting out from Rameses, the Israelites camped at Succoth. 6 Setting out from Succoth, they camped at Etham near the edge of the desert. 7 Setting out from Etham, they turned back to Pi-hahiroth, which is opposite Baal-zephon, and they camped opposite Migdol. 8 Setting out from Pi-hahiroth, they crossed over through the sea into the desert, and after a three days' journey in the desert of Etham, they camped at Maran. 9 Setting out from Maran, they came to Elim, where there were twelve springs of water and seventy palm trees, and they camped there. 10 Setting out from Elim, they camped beside the Red Sea. 11 Setting out from the Red Sea, they camped in the desert of Sin. 12 Setting out from the desert of Sin, they camped at Dophkah, 13 Setting out from Dophkah, they camped at Alush. 14 Setting out from Alush, they camped at Rephidim, where there was no water for the people to drink. 15 Setting out from Rephidim, they camped in the desert of Sinai.

From Sinai to Kadesh

16 Setting out from the desert of Sinai, they camped at Kibroth-hattaavah. 17 Setting out from Kibroth-hattaavah, they camped at Hazeroth. 18 Setting out from Hazeroth, they camped at Rithmah. 19 Setting out from Rithmah, they camped at Rimmon-perez. 20 Setting out from Rimmon-perez, they camped at Libnah. 21 Setting out from Libnah, they camped at Rissah. 22 Setting out from Rissah, they camped at Kehelathah. 23 Setting out from Kehelathah, they camped at Mount Shepher. 24 Setting out from Mount Shepher, they camped at Haradah. 25 Setting out from Haradah, they camped

at Makheloth. 26 Setting out from Makheloth, they camped at Tahath. 27 Setting out from Tahath, they camped at Terah. 28 Setting out from Terah, they camped at Mithkah. 29 Setting out from Mithkah, they camped at Hashmonah. 30 Setting out from Hashmonah,—

From Mount Hor to Ezion-geber

They camped at Moseroth. 31 Setting out from Moseroth, they camped at Bene-jaakan. 32 Setting out from Bene-jaakan, they camped at Mount Gidgad. 33 Setting out from Mount Gidgad, they camped at Jotbathah. 34 Setting out from Jotbathah, they camped at Abronah. 35 Setting out from Abronah, they camped at Ezion-geber. 36 Setting out from Ezion-geber,—

From Kadesh to Mount Hor

They camped in the desert of Zin, at Kadesh. 37 Setting out from Kadesh, they camped at Mount Hor on the border of the land of Edom. 38 [Aaron the priest ascended Mount Hor at the LORD's command, and there he died in the fortieth year from the departure of the Israelites from the land of Egypt, on the first day of the fifth month. 39 Aaron was a hundred and twenty-three years old when he died on Mount Hor. 40 Now, when the Canaanite king of Arad, who lived in the Negeb in the land of Canaan, heard that the Israelites were coming . . . .] 41 Setting out from Mount Hor,—

From Ezion-geber to the Plains of Moab

They camped at Zalmonah. 42 Setting out from Zalmonah, they camped at Punon. 43 Setting out from Punon, they camped at Oboth. 44 Setting out from Oboth, they camped at Iye-abarim on the border of Moab. 45 Setting out from Iye-abarim, they camped at Dibon-gad.

32, 38: The phrase in brackets is a gloss, warning the reader either to change the order of the preceding names, or, more probably, to read some other word, such as *bosheth*, "shame," for *Baal. They called by their old names:* literally, "they called by their names"; however, some understand the current Hebrew text to mean, "they called by new names."

33, 1ff: This list of camping sites was drawn up by Moses, as v 2 expressly states. However, in its present form it probably includes some glosses. Moreover, a comparison with the more detailed accounts of the journey as given elsewhere shows that this list is not

complete. It records just forty camping sites, not counting the starting place, Rameses, and the terminus, the plains of Moab. This number, which corresponds exactly to the forty years of wandering in the desert, is probably a schematic device. Besides, it seems that in its present form the order of some of these names has been disturbed. Several names listed here are not recorded elsewhere.

33, 3f: These two verses were probably borrowed from some ancient song celebrating the exodus from Egypt.

33, 30–36: Moseroth is mentioned in Dt 10, 6

(in the form of "Moserah"), as the place where Aaron died. It must therefore have been close to Mount Hor; cf Nm 20, 22ff. It seems very probable that the section vv 36b–41a stood originally immediately after v 30a.

33, 40: The verse begins the same account of the victory over Arad as is given in 21, 1ff, where it also follows the account of Aaron's death.

33, 41b–49: It seems that this section stood originally immediately after v 36a.

46 Setting out from Dibon-gad, they camped at Almon-diblathaim. 47 Setting out from Almon-diblathaim, they camped in the Abarim Mountains opposite Nebo. 48 Setting out from the Abarim Mountains, they camped on the plains of Moab along the Jericho stretch of the Jordan. 49 Their camp along the Jordan on the plains of Moab extended from Beth-jeshimoth to Abel-shittim.

Conquest and Division of Canaan

50 The LORD spoke to Moses on the plains of Moab beside the Jericho stretch of the Jordan and said to him: 51 "Tell the Israelites: When you go across the Jordan into the land of Canaan, 52 drive out all the inhabitants of the land before you: destroy all their stone figures and molten images, and demolish all their high places.

53 "You shall take possession of the land and settle in it, for I have given you the land as your property. 54 You shall apportion the land among yourselves by lot, clan by clan, assigning a large heritage to a large group and a small heritage to a small group. Wherever anyone's lot falls, there shall his property be within the heritage of his ancestral tribe.

55 "But if you do not drive out the inhabitants of the land before you, those whom you allow to remain will become as barbs in your eyes and thorns in your sides, and they will harass you in the country where you live, 56 and I will treat you as I had intended to treat them."

The Boundaries

34 The LORD said to Moses, 2 "Give the Israelites this order: When you enter the land of Canaan, this is the territory that shall fall to you as your heritage—the land of Canaan with its boundaries:

3 "Your southern boundary shall be at the desert of Zin along the border of Edom; on the east it shall begin at the end of the Salt Sea, 4 and turning south of the Akrabbim Pass, it shall cross Zin, and extend south of Kadesh-barnea to Hazaraddar; thence it shall cross to Azmon, 5 and turning from Azmon to the Wadi of Egypt, shall terminate at the Sea.

6 "For your western boundary you shall have the Great Sea with its coast; this shall be your western boundary.

7 "The following shall be your boundary on the north: from the Great Sea you shall draw a line to Mount Hor, 8 and shall continue it from Mount Hor to Labo in the land of Hamath, with the boundary extending through Zedad. 9 Thence the boundary shall reach to Ziphron and terminate at Hazar-enan. This shall be your northern boundary.

10 "For your eastern boundary you shall draw a line from Hazarenan to Shepham. 11 From Shepham the boundary shall go down to Ar-Baal, east of Ain, and descending further, shall strike the ridge on the east side of the Sea of Chinnereth; 12 thence the boundary shall continue along the Jordan and terminate with the Salt Sea.

"This is the land that shall be yours, with the boundaries that surround it."

13 Moses also gave this order to the Israelites: "This is the land, to be apportioned among you by lot, which the LORD has commanded to be given to the nine and one half tribes. 14 For all the ancestral houses of the tribe of Reuben, and the ancestral houses of the tribe of Gad, as well as half of the tribe of Manasseh, have already received their heritage; 15 these two and one half tribes have received their heritage on the eastern side of the Jericho stretch of the Jordan, toward the sunrise."

Supervisors of the Allotment

16 The LORD said to Moses, 17 "These are the names of the men who shall apportion the land among you: Eleazar the priest, and Joshua, son of Nun, 18 and one prince from each of the tribes whom you shall designate for this task. 19 These shall be as follows:

from the tribe of Judah: Caleb, son of Jephunneh,
20 from the tribe of Simeon: Samuel, son of Ammihud;
21 from the tribe of Benjamin: Elidad, son of Chislon;
22 from the tribe of Dan: Bukki, son of Jogli,
23 from the tribe of Manasseh: Hanniel, son of Ephod; and
24 from the tribe of Ephraim: Kemuel, son of Shiphtan, for the descendants of Joseph;
25 from the tribe of Zebulun: Elizaphan, son of Parnach;
26 from the tribe of Issachar: Paltiel, son of Azzan;
27 from the tribe of Asher: Ahihud, son of Shelomi;
28 from the tribe of Naphtali: Pedahel, son of Ammihud."

29 These are they whom the LORD commanded to assign the Israelites their heritage in the land of Canaan.

Cities for the Levites

35 The LORD gave these instructions to Moses on the plains of Moab beside the Jericho stretch of the Jordan: 2 "Tell the Israelites that out of their hereditary property they shall give the Levites cities for homes, as well as pasture lands around the cities. 3 The cities shall serve them to dwell in, and the pasture lands shall serve their herds and flocks and other animals. 4 The pasture lands of the cities to be assigned the Levites shall extend a thousand cubits from the city walls in each direction. 5 Thus you shall measure out two thousand cubits outside the city along each side— east, south, west and north—with the city lying in the center. This shall serve them as the pasture lands of their cities.

6 "Now these are the cities you shall give to the Levites: the six cities of asylum which you must establish as places where a homicide can take refuge, and in addition forty-two other cities 7 —a total of forty-eight cities with their pasture lands to be assigned the Levites. 8 In assigning the cities from the

---

34, 6: *The Great Sea:* the Mediterranean.
34, 7f: *Mount Hor:* different from the one where Aaron died; cf Nm 20, 22; 33, 37f.

35, 8: This provision was hardly observed in the actual assignment of the Levitical cities as narrated in Jos 21.

property of the Israelites, take more from a larger group and fewer from a smaller one, so that each group will cede cities to the Levites in proportion to its own heritage."

Cities of Asylum

9 The LORD said to Moses, 10 "Tell the Israelites: When you go across the Jordan into the land of Canaan, 11 select for yourselves cities to serve as cities of asylum, where a homicide who has killed someone unintentionally may take refuge. 12 These cities shall serve you as places of asylum from the avenger of blood, so that a homicide shall not be put to death unless he is first tried before the community. 13 Six cities of asylum shall you assign: 14 three beyond the Jordan, and three in the land of Canaan. 15 These six cities of asylum shall serve not only the Israelites but all the resident or transient aliens among them, so that anyone who has killed another unintentionally may take refuge there.

Murder and Manslaughter

16 "If a man strikes another with an iron instrument and causes his death, he is a murderer and shall be put to death. 17 If a man strikes another with a death-dealing stone in his hand and causes his death, he is a murderer and shall be put to death. 18 If a man strikes another with a death-dealing club in his hand and causes his death, he is a murderer and shall be put to death. 19 The avenger of blood may execute the murderer, putting him to death on sight.

20 "If a man pushes another out of hatred, or after lying in wait for him throws something at him, and causes his death, 21 or if he strikes another out of enmity and causes his death, he shall be put to death as a murderer. The avenger of blood may execute the murderer on sight.

22 "However, if a man pushes another accidentally and not out of enmity, or if without lying in wait

for him he throws some object at him, 23 or without seeing him throws a death-dealing stone which strikes him and causes his death, although he was not his enemy nor seeking to harm him: 24 then the community, deciding the case between the slayer and the avenger of blood in accordance with these norms, 25 shall free the homicide from the avenger of blood and shall remand him to the city of asylum where he took refuge; and he shall stay there until the death of the high priest who has been anointed with sacred oil. 26 If the homicide of his own accord leaves the bounds of the city of asylum where he has taken refuge, 27 and the avenger of blood finds him beyond these bounds and kills him, the avenger incurs no bloodguilt; 28 the homicide was bound to stay in his city of asylum until the death of the high priest. Only after the death of the high priest may the homicide return to his own district.

29 "These shall be norms for you and all your descendants, wherever you live, for rendering judgment.

Witnesses

30 "Whenever someone kills another, the evidence of witnesses is required for the execution of the murderer. The evidence of a single witness is not sufficient for putting a person to death.

No Indemnity

31 "You shall not accept indemnity in place of the life of a murderer who deserves the death penalty; he must be put to death. 32 Nor shall you accept indemnity to allow a refugee to leave his city of asylum and again dwell elsewhere in the land before the death of the high priest. 33 You shall not desecrate the land where you live. Since bloodshed desecrates the land, the land can have no atonement for the blood shed on it except through the blood of him who shed it. 34 Do not

defile the land in which you live and in the midst of which I dwell; for I am the LORD who dwells in the midst of the Israelites."

Property of Heiresses

36 The heads of the ancestral houses in the clan of descendants of Gilead, son of Machir, son of Manasseh—one of the Josephite clans—came up and laid this plea before Moses and the priest Eleazar and before the princes who were the heads of the ancestral houses of the other Israelites. 2 They said: "The LORD commanded you, my lord, to apportion the land by lot among the Israelites; and you, my lord, were also commanded by the LORD to give the heritage of our kinsman Zelophehad to his daughters. 3 But if they marry into one of the other Israelite tribes, their heritage will be withdrawn from our ancestral heritage and will be added to that of the tribe into which they marry; thus the heritage that fell to us by lot will be diminished. 4 When the Israelites celebrate the jubilee year, the heritage of these women will be permanently added to that of the tribe into which they marry and will be withdrawn from that of our ancestral tribe."

5 So Moses gave this regulation to the Israelites according to the instructions of the LORD: "The tribe of the Josephites are right in what they say. 6 This is what the LORD commands with regard to the daughters of Zelophehad: They may marry anyone they please, provided they marry into a clan of their ancestral tribe, 7 so that no heritage of the Israelites will pass from one tribe to another, but all the Israelites will retain their own ancestral heritage. 8 Therefore, every daughter who inherits property in any of the Israelite tribes shall marry someone belonging to a clan of her own ancestral tribe, in order that all the Israelites may remain in possession of their own ancestral heritage. 9 Thus, no heritage can pass from one

---

35, 12: *The avenger of blood:* one of the close relatives of the slain (2 Sm 14, 7) who, as executor of public justice, had the right and duty to take the life of the murderer; cf Dt 19, 6.12; Jos 20, 3.5.9.

35, 16–25: Here, as also in Dt 19, 1–13, there is a

casuistic development of the original law as stated in Ex 21, 12ff.

36, 4: Before the jubilee year various circumstances, such as divorce, could make such property revert to its original tribal owners; but in the jubilee

year it became irrevocably attached to its new owners.

36, 5–9: This is a supplement to the law given in 27, 5–11.

tribe to another, but all the Israelite tribes will retain their own ancestral heritage."

10 The daughters of Zelophehad obeyed the command which the LORD had given to Moses. 11 Mahlah, Tirzah, Hoglah, Milcah and Noah, Zelophehad's daughters, married relatives on their father's side 12 within the clans of the descendants of Manasseh, son of Joseph; hence their heritage remained in the tribe of their father's clan.

Conclusion

13 These are the commandments and decisions which the LORD prescribed for the Israelites through Moses, on the plains of Moab beside the Jericho stretch of the Jordan.

Deuteronomy

HISTORICAL REVIEW AND EXHORTATION

Introduction

THESE are the words which Moses spoke to all Israel beyond the Jordan [in the desert, in the Arabah, opposite Suph, between Paran and Tophel, Laban, Hazeroth and Dizahab; 2 it is a journey of eleven days from Horeb to Kadesh-barnea by way of the highlands of Seir].

3 In the fortieth year, on the first day of the eleventh month, Moses spoke to the Israelites all the commands that the LORD had given him in their regard. 4 After he had defeated Sihon, king of the Amorites, who lived in Heshbon, and Og, king of Bashan, who lived in Ashtaroth and in Edrei, 5 Moses began to explain the law in the land of Moab beyond the Jordan, as follows:

Departure from Horeb

6 "The LORD, our God, said to us at Horeb, 'You have stayed long enough at this mountain. 7 Leave here and go to the hill country of the Amorites and to all the surrounding regions, the land of the Canaanites in the Arabah, the mountains, the foothills, the Negeb and the seacoast; to Lebanon, and as far as the Great River [the Euphrates]. 8 I have given that land over to you. Go now and occupy the land I swore to your fathers, Abraham, Isaac and Jacob, I would give to them and to their descendants.'

Appointment of Elders

9 "At that time I said to you, 'Alone, I am unable to carry you. 10 The LORD, your God, has so multiplied you that you are now as numerous as the stars in the sky. 11 May the LORD, the God of your fathers, increase you a thousand times over, and bless you as he promised! 12 But how can I alone bear the crushing burden that you are, along with your bickering? 13 Choose wise, intelligent and experienced men from each of your tribes, that I may appoint them as your leaders.' 14 You answered me, 'We agree to do as you have proposed.' 15 So I took outstanding men of your tribes, wise and experienced, and made them your leaders as officials over thousands, over hundreds, over fifties and over tens, and other tribal officers. 16 I charged your judges at that time, 'Listen to complaints among your kinsmen, and administer true justice to both parties even if one of them

is an alien. 17 In rendering judgment, do not consider who a person is; give ear to the lowly and to the great alike, fearing no man, for judgment is God's. Refer to me any case that is too hard for you and I will hear it.' 18 Thereupon I gave you all the commands you were to fulfill.

The Twelve Scouts

19 "Then, in obedience to the command of the LORD, our God, we set out from Horeb and journeyed through the whole desert, vast and fearful as you have seen, in the direction of the hill country of the Amorites. We had reached Kadesh-barnea 20 when I said to you, 'You have come to the hill country of the Amorites, which the LORD, our God, is giving us. 21 The LORD, your God, has given this land over to you. Go up and occupy it, as the LORD, the God of your fathers, commands you. Do not fear or lose heart.' 22 Then all of you came up to me and said, 'Let us

1, 1: The local setting of all these discourses is *in the land of Moab beyond the Jordan* (cf v 5), also known as *the plains of Moab* (Nm 36, 13).
1, 7: The Amorites and the Canaanites formed the

principal part of the pre-Israelite population of Palestine. *The foothills:* the hills on the western slope of the Judean mountain range. *The Arabah:* the valley of the Jordan and the depression south of the

Dead Sea. *The Negeb:* the arid land in southern Palestine.
1, 9: *Carry you:* cf v 31.

send men ahead to reconnoiter the land for us and report to us on the road we must follow and the cities we must take.' 23 Agreeing with the proposal, I chose twelve men from your number, one from each tribe. 24 They set out into the hill country as far as the Wadi Eshcol, and explored it. 25 Then, taking along some of the fruit of the land, they brought it down to us and reported, 'The land which the LORD, our God, gives us is good.'

Threats of Revolt

26 "But you refused to go up, and after defying the command of the LORD, your God, 27 you set to murmuring in your tents, 'Out of hatred for us the LORD has brought us up out of the land of Egypt, to deliver us into the hands of the Amorites and destroy us. 28 What shall we meet with up there? Our kinsmen have made us fainthearted by reporting that the people are stronger and taller than we, and their cities are large and fortified to the sky; besides, they saw the Anakim there.'

29 "But I said to you, 'Have no dread or fear of them. 30 The LORD, your God, who goes before you, will himself fight for you, just as he took your part before your very eyes in Egypt, 31 as well as in the desert, where you saw how the LORD, your God, carried you, as a man carries his child, all along your journey until you arrived at this place.' 32 Despite this you would not trust the LORD, your God, 33 who journeys before you to find you a resting place—by day in the cloud, and by night in the fire, to show the way you must go. 34 When the LORD heard your words, he was angry; 35 and he swore, 'Not one man of this evil generation shall look upon the good land I swore to give to your fathers, 36 except Caleb, son of Jephunneh; he shall see it. For to him and to his sons I will give the land he trod upon, because he has followed the LORD unreservedly.'

37 "The LORD was angered against

me also on your account, and said, 'Not even you shall enter there, 38 but your aide Joshua, son of Nun, shall enter. Encourage him, for he is to give Israel its heritage. 39 Your little ones, who you said would become booty, and your children, who as yet do not know good from bad—they shall enter; to them I will give it, and they shall occupy it. 40 But as for yourselves: turn about and proceed into the desert on the Red Sea road.'

Unsuccessful Invasion

41 "In reply you said to me, 'We have sinned against the LORD. We will go up ourselves and fight, just as the LORD, our God, commanded us.' And each of you girded on his weapons, making light of going up into the hill country. 42 But the LORD said to me, 'Warn them: Do not go up and fight, lest you be beaten down before your enemies, for I will not be in your midst.' 43 I gave you this warning but you would not listen. In defiance of the LORD's command you arrogantly marched off into the hill country. 44 Then the Amorites living there came out against you and, like bees, chased you, cutting you down in Seir as far as Hormah. 45 On your return you wept before the LORD, but he did not listen to your cry or give ear to you. 46 That is why you had to stay as long as you did at Kadesh.

Northward along Edom

2 "When we did turn and proceed into the desert on the Red Sea road, as the LORD had commanded me, we circled around the highlands of Seir for a long time. 2 Finally the LORD said to me, 3 'You have wandered round these highlands long enough; turn and go north. Give this order to the people: 4 You are now about to pass through the territory of your kinsmen, the descendants of Esau, who live in Seir. Though they are afraid of you, be very careful 5 not to come in conflict with them, for I will not give you so much as a foot of their land, since I have already given Esau possession

of the highlands of Seir. 6 You shall purchase from them with silver the food you eat and the well water you drink. 7 The LORD, your God, has blessed you in all your undertakings; he has been concerned about your journey through this vast desert. It is now forty years that he has been with you, and you have never been in want.'

Along Moab

8 "Then we left behind us the Arabah route, Elath, Ezion-geber, and Seir, where our kinsmen, the descendants of Esau, live; and we went on toward the desert of Moab. 9 And the LORD said to me, 'Do not show hostility to the Moabites or engage them in battle, for I will not give you possession of any of their land, since I have given Ar to the descendants of Lot as their own. 10 [Formerly the Emim lived there, a people strong and numerous and tall like the Anakim; 11 like them they were considered Rephaim. It was the Moabites who called them Emim. 12 In Seir, however, the former inhabitants were the Horites; the descendants of Esau dispossessed them, clearing them out of the way and taking their place, just as the Israelites have done in the land of their heritage which the LORD has given them.] 13 Get ready, then, to cross the Wadi Zered.' So we crossed it. 14 Thirty-eight years had elapsed between our departure from Kadesh-barnea and that crossing; in the meantime the whole generation of soldiers had perished from the camp, as the LORD had sworn they should. 15 For it was the LORD's hand that was against them, till he wiped them out of the camp completely.

Along Ammon

16 "When at length death had put an end to all the soldiers among the people, 17 the LORD said to me, 18 'You are now about to leave Ar and the territory of Moab behind. 19 As you come opposite the Ammonites, do not show hostility or come in conflict with them,

---

1, 27: *In your tents:* among yourselves.

1, 36: *Except Caleb:* Joshua also was allowed to enter, but he is not referred to here because special mention is made of him in v 38 as the successor of Moses.

for I will not give you possession of any land of the Ammonites, since I have given it to the descendants of Lot as their own. 20 [This also was considered a country of the Rephaim from its former inhabitants, whom the Ammonites called Zamzummim, 21 a people strong and numerous and tall like the Anakim. But these, too, the LORD cleared out of the way for the Ammonites, who ousted them and took their place. 22 He had done the same for the descendants of Esau, who dwell in Seir, by clearing the Horites out of their way, so that the descendants of Esau have taken their place down to the present. 23 So also the Caphtorim, migrating from Caphtor, cleared away the Avvim, who once dwelt in villages as far as Gaza, and took their place.]

Defeat of Sihon

24 "'Advance now across the Wadi Arnon. I now deliver into your hands Sihon, the Amorite king of Heshbon, and his land. Begin the occupation; engage him in battle. 25 This day I will begin to put a fear and dread of you into every nation under the heavens, so that at the mention of your name they will quake and tremble before you.' 26 "So I sent messengers from the desert of Kedemoth to Sihon, king of Heshbon, with this offer of peace: 27 'Let me pass through your country by the highway; I will go along it without turning aside to the right or to the left. 28 For the food I eat which you will supply, and for the water you give me to drink, you shall be paid in silver. Only let me march through, 29 as the descendants of Esau who dwell in Seir and the Moabites who dwell in Ar have done, until I cross the Jordan into the land which the LORD, our God, is about to give us.' 30 But Sihon, king of Heshbon, refused to let us pass through his land, because the LORD, your God, made him stubborn in mind and obstinate in heart that he might deliver him up to you, as indeed he has now done.

31 "Then the LORD said to me, 'Now that I have already begun to hand over to you Sihon and his land, begin the actual occupation.' 32 So Sihon and all his people advanced against us to join battle at Jahaz; 33 but since the LORD, our God, had delivered him to us, we defeated him and his sons and all his people. 34 At that time we seized all his cities and doomed them all, with their men, women and children; we left no survivor. 35 Our only booty was the livestock and the loot of the captured cities. 36 From Aroer on the edge of the Wadi Arnon and from the city in the wadi itself, as far as Gilead, no city was too well fortified for us to whom the LORD had delivered them up. 37 However, in obedience to the command of the LORD, our God, you did not encroach upon any of the Ammonite land, neither the region bordering on the Wadi Jabbok, nor the cities of the highlands.

Defeat of Og

3 "Then we turned and proceeded toward Bashan. But Og, king of Bashan, advanced against us with all his people to give battle at Edrei. 2 The LORD, however, said to me, 'Do not be afraid of him, for I have delivered him into your hand with all his people and his land. Do to him as you did to Sihon, king of the Amorites, who lived in Heshbon.' 3 And thus the LORD, our God, delivered into our hands Og, king of Bashan, with all his people. We defeated him so completely that we left him no survivor. 4 At that time we captured all his cities, none of them eluding our grasp, the whole region of Argob, the kingdom of Og in Bashan: sixty cities in all, 5 to say nothing of the great number of unwalled towns. All the cities were fortified with high walls and gates and bars. 6 As we had done to Sihon, king of Heshbon, so also here we doomed all the cities, with their men, women and children; 7 but all the livestock and the loot of each city we took as booty for ourselves.

8 "And so at that time we took from the two kings of the Amorites beyond the Jordan the territory from the Wadi Arnon to Mount Hermon 9 [which is called Sirion by the Sidonians and Senir by the Amorites], 10 comprising all the cities of the plateau and all Gilead and all the cities of the kingdom of Og in Bashan including Salecah and Edrei. 11 [Og, king of Bashan, was the last remaining survivor of the Rephaim. He had a bed of iron, nine regular cubits long and four wide, which is still preserved in Rabbah of the Ammonities.]

Allotment of the Conquered Lands

12 "When we occupied the land at that time, I gave Reuben and Gad the territory from Aroer, on the edge of the Wadi Arnon, halfway up into the highlands of Gilead, with the cities therein. 13 The rest of Gilead and all of Bashan, the kingdom of Og, the whole Argob region, I gave to the half-tribe of Manasseh. [All this region of Bashan was once called a land of the Rephaim. 14 Jair, a Manassehite clan, took all the region of Argob as far as the border of the Geshurites and Maacathites, and called it after his own name Bashan Havvothjair, the name it bears today.] 15 To Machir I gave Gilead, 16 and to Reuben and Gad the territory from Gilead to the Wadi Arnon—including the wadi bed and its banks—and to the Wadi Jabbok, which is the border of the Ammonities, 17 as well as the Arabah with the Jordan and its eastern banks from Chinnereth to the Salt Sea of the Arabah, under the slopes of Pisgah.

18 "At that time I charged them as follows: 'The LORD, your God, has given you this land as your own. But all you troops equipped for battle must cross over in the vanguard of your brother Israelites. 19 Only your wives and children, as well as your livestock, of which I know you have a large number, shall remain behind in the towns I have given you, 20 until the

---

2, 23: *The Caphtorim:* members of one of the groups of sea peoples who invaded the coast of Egypt and the southern part of Palestine about 1200 B.C. *Caphtor:* the ancient name of the island of Crete. Cf Am 9, 7.

2, 34: *Doomed:* see notes on Nm 18, 14; 21, 3.

3, 11: *Bed of iron:* some translate, "a sarcophagus of basalt."

3, 18: *I charged them:* the words which follow were spoken to the men of Reuben and Gad (cf Nm 32).

LORD has settled your kinsmen as well, and they too possess the land which the LORD, your God, will give them on the other side of the Jordan. Then you may all return to the possessions I have given you.'

21 "It was then that I instructed Joshua, 'Your eyes have seen all that the LORD, your God, has done to both these kings; so, too, will the LORD do to all the kingdoms which you will encounter over there. 22 Fear them not, for the LORD, your God, will fight for you.'

Refusal to Moses

23 "And it was then that I besought the LORD, 24 'O Lord GOD, you have begun to show to your servant your greatness and might. For what god in heaven or on earth can perform deeds as mighty as yours? 25 Ah, let me cross over and see this good land beyond the Jordan, this fine hill country, and the Lebanon!' 26 But the LORD was angry with me on your account and would not hear me. 'Enough!' the LORD said to me. 'Speak to me no more of this. 27 Go up to the top of Pisgah and look out to the west, and to the north, and to the south, and to the east. Look well, for you shall not cross this Jordan. 28 Commission Joshua, and encourage and strengthen him, for he shall cross at the head of this people and shall put them in possession of the land you are to see.' 29 This was while we were in the ravine opposite Beth-peor.

Advantages of Fidelity

4 "Now, Israel, hear the statutes and decrees which I am teaching you to observe, that you may live, and may enter in and take possession of the land which the LORD, the God of your fathers, is giving you. 2 In your observance of the commandments of the LORD, your God, which I enjoin upon you, you shall not add to what I command you nor subtract from it. 3 You have seen with your own eyes what the LORD

did at Baal-peor: the LORD, your God, destroyed from your midst everyone that followed the Baal of Peor; 4 but you, who clung to the LORD, your God, are all alive today. 5 Therefore, I teach you the statutes and decrees as the LORD, my God, has commanded me, that you may observe them in the land you are entering to occupy. 6 Observe them carefully, for thus will you give evidence of your widsom and intelligence to the nations, who will hear of all these statutes and say, 'This great nation is truly a wise and intelligent people.' 7 For what great nation is there that has gods so close to it as the LORD, our God, is to us whenever we call upon him? 8 Or what great nation has statutes and decrees that are as just as this whole law which I am setting before you today?

Revelation at Horeb

9 "However, take care and be earnestly on your guard not to forget the things which your own eyes have seen, nor let them slip from your memory as long as you live, but teach them to your children and to your children's children: 10 There was the day on which you stood before the LORD, your God, at Horeb, and he said to me, 'Assemble the people for me; I will have them hear my words, that they may learn to fear me as long as they live in the land and may so teach their children.' 11 You came near and stood at the foot of the mountain, which blazed to the very sky with fire and was enveloped in a dense black cloud. 12 Then the LORD spoke to you from the midst of the fire. You heard the sound of the words, but saw no form; there was only a voice. 13 He proclaimed to you his covenant, which he commanded you to keep: the ten commandments, which he wrote on two tablets of stone. 14 The LORD charged me at that time to teach you the statutes and decrees which you are to observe over in the land you will occupy.

Danger of Idolatry

15 "You saw no form at all on the day the LORD spoke to you at Horeb from the midst of the fire. Be strictly on your guard, therefore, 16 not to degrade yourselves by fashioning an idol to represent any figure, whether it be the form of a man or of a woman, 17 of any animal on the earth or of any bird that flies in the sky, 18 of anything that crawls on the ground or of any fish in the waters under the earth. 19 And when you look up to the heavens and behold the sun or the moon or any star among the heavenly hosts, do not be led astray into adoring them and serving them. These the LORD, your God, has let fall to the lot of all other nations under the heavens; 20 but you he has taken and led out of that iron foundry, Egypt, that you might be his very own people, as you are today. 21 Since the LORD was angered against me on your account and swore that I should not cross the Jordan nor enter the good land which he is giving you as a heritage, 22 I myself shall die in this country without crossing the Jordan; but you will cross over and take possession of that good land. 23 Take heed, therefore, lest, forgetting the covenant which the LORD, your God, has made with you, you fashion for yourselves against his command an idol in any form whatsoever. 24 For the LORD, your God, is a consuming fire, a jealous God.

God's Fidelity

25 "When you have children and grandchildren, and have grown old in the land, should you then degrade yourselves by fashioning an idol in any form and by this evil done in his sight provoke the LORD, your God, 26 I call heaven and earth this day to witness against you, that you shall all quickly perish from the land which you will occupy when you cross the Jordan. You shall not live in it for any length of time but shall be promptly wiped out. 27 The

---

4, 10: Beginning here and continuing on for several verses (at least to the end of v 14) is the "reminiscence," the account of the things that the Israelites should recall and teach their children.

4, 20: Egypt is called an *iron foundry*, or furnace for smelting iron, because God allowed the Israelites to be afflicted there for the sake of their spiritual purification; the same expression for Egypt occurs

also in 1 Kgs 8, 51; Jer 11, 4; compare the expression, "the furnace of affliction," in Is 48, 10.

4, 25: *Grown old:* Israel will lose the freshness of its youthful fervor.

LORD will scatter you among the nations, and there shall remain but a handful of you among the nations to which the LORD will lead you. 28 There you shall serve gods fashioned by the hands of man out of wood and stone, gods which can neither see nor hear, neither eat nor smell. 29 Yet there too you shall seek the LORD, your God; and you shall indeed find him when you search after him with your whole heart and your whole soul. 30 In your distress, when all these things shall have come upon you, you shall finally return to the LORD, your God, and heed his voice. 31 Since the LORD, your God, is a merciful God, he will not abandon and destroy you, nor forget the covenant which under oath he made with your fathers.

Proofs of God's Love

32 "Ask now of the days of old, before your time, ever since God created man upon the earth; ask from one end of the sky to the other: Did anything so great ever happen before? Was it ever heard of? 33 Did a people ever hear the voice of God speaking from the midst of fire, as you did, and live? 34 Or did any god venture to go and take a nation for himself from the midst of another nation, by testings, by signs and wonders, by war, with his strong hand and outstretched arm, and by great terrors, all of which the LORD, your God, did for you in Egypt before your very eyes? 35 All this you were allowed to see that you might know the LORD is God and there is no other. 36 Out of the heavens he let you hear his voice to discipline you; on earth he let you see his great fire, and you heard him speaking out of the fire. 37 For love of your fathers he chose their descendants and personally led you out of Egypt by his great power, 38 driving out of your way nations greater and mightier than you, so as to bring you in and to make their land your heritage, as it is today. 39 This is why you must

now know, and fix in your heart, that the LORD is God in the heavens above and on earth below, and that there is no other. 40 You must keep his statutes and commandments which I enjoin on you today, that you and your children after you may prosper, and that you may have long life on the land which the LORD, your God, is giving you forever."

Cities of Refuge

41 Then Moses set apart three cities in the region east of the Jordan, 42 that a homicide might take refuge there if he unwittingly killed his neighbor to whom he had previously borne no malice, and that he might save his life by fleeing to one of these cities: 43 Bezer in the desert, in the region of the plateau, for the Reubenites; Ramoth in Gilead for the Gadites; and Golan in Bashan for the Manassehites.

GOD AND HIS COVENANT

Introduction

44 This is the law which Moses set before the Israelites. 45 These are the ordinances, statutes and decrees which he proclaimed to them when they had come out of Egypt 46 and were beyond the Jordan in the ravine opposite Beth-peor, in the land of Sihon, king of the Amorites, who dwelt in Heshbon and whom Moses and the Israelites defeated after coming out of Egypt. 47 They occupied his land and the land of Og, king of Bashan, as well— the land of these two kings of the Amorites in the region east of the Jordan: 48 from Aroer on the edge of the Wadi Arnon to Mount Sion (that is Hermon) 49 and all the Arabah east of the Jordan, as far as the Arabah Sea under the slopes of Pisgah.

The Covenant at Horeb

5 Moses summoned all Israel and said to them, "Hear, O Israel, the statutes and decrees which I proclaim in your hearing this day,

that you may learn them and take care to observe them. 2 The LORD, our God, made a covenant with us at Horeb; 3 not with our fathers did he make this covenant, but with us, all of us who are alive here this day. 4 The LORD spoke with you face to face on the mountain from the midst of the fire. 5 Since you were afraid of the fire and would not go up the mountain, I stood between the LORD and you at that time, to announce to you these words of the LORD:

The Decalogue

6 'I, the LORD, am your God, who brought you out of the land of Egypt, that place of slavery. 7 You shall not have other gods besides me. 8 You shall not carve idols for yourselves in the shape of anything in the sky above or on the earth below or in the waters beneath the earth; 9 you shall not bow down before them or worship them. For I, the LORD, your God, am a jealous God, inflicting punishments for their fathers' wickedness on the children of those who hate me, down to the third and fourth generation 10 but bestowing mercy, down to the thousandth generation, on the children of those who love me and keep my commandments.

11 'You shall not take the name of the LORD, your God, in vain. For the LORD will not leave unpunished him who takes his name in vain.

12 'Take care to keep holy the sabbath day as the LORD, your God, commanded you. 13 Six days you may labor and do all your work; 14 but the seventh day is the sabbath of the LORD, your God. No work may be done then, whether by you, or your son or daughter, or your male or female slave, or your ox or ass or any of your beasts, or the alien who lives with you. Your male and female slave should rest as you do. 15 For remember that you too were once slaves in Egypt, and the LORD, your God, brought

---

4, 34: *Testings:* the demonstrations of God's power as in the ten great plagues of Egypt; cf 7, 19; 29, 2.

4, 48: *Sion:* another name for Mount Hermon,

besides those mentioned in 3, 9.

5, 9f: God does not punish us for another's sins, but because of the solidarity of human society, the good or evil deeds of one generation may make their

effects felt even in later generations. Yet note how God's mercy allows the good effects of virtue to last much longer than the bad effects of vice: a thousand generations compared to three or four.

you from there with his strong hand and outstretched arm. That is why the LORD, your God, has commanded you to observe the sabbath day.

16 'Honor your father and your mother, as the LORD, your God, has commanded you, that you may have a long life and prosperity in the land which the LORD, your God, is giving you.

17 'You shall not kill.

18 'You shall not commit adultery.

19 'You shall not steal.

20 'You shall not bear dishonest witness against your neighbor.

21 'You shall not covet your neighbor's wife.

'You shall not desire your neighbor's house or field, nor his male or female slave, nor his ox or ass, nor anything that belongs to him.'

Moses as Mediator

22 "These words, and nothing more, the LORD spoke with a loud voice to your entire assembly on the mountain from the midst of the fire and the dense cloud. He wrote them upon two tablets of stone and gave them to me. 23 But when you heard the voice from the midst of the darkness, while the mountain was ablaze with fire, you came to me in the person of all your tribal heads and elders, 24 and said, 'The LORD, our God, has indeed let us see his glory and his majesty! We have heard his voice from the midst of the fire and have found out today that a man can still live after God has spoken with him. 25 But why should we die now? Surely this great fire will consume us. If we hear the voice of the LORD, our God, any more, we shall die. 26 For what mortal has heard, as we have, the voice of the living God speaking from the midst of fire, and survived? 27 Go closer, you, and hear all that the LORD, our God, will say, and then tell us what the LORD,

our God, tells you; we will listen and obey.'

28 "The LORD heard your words as you were speaking to me and said to me, 'I have heard the words these people have spoken to you, which are all well said. 29 Would that they might always be of such a mind, to fear me and to keep all my commandments! Then they and their descendants would prosper forever. 30 Go, tell them to return to their tents. 31 Then you wait here near me and I will give you all the commandments, the statutes and decrees you must teach them, that they may observe them in the land which I am giving them to possess.'

32 "Be careful, therefore, to do as the LORD, your God, has commanded you, not turning aside to the right or to the left, 33 but following exactly the way prescribed for you by the LORD, your God, that you may live and prosper, and may have long life in the land which you are to occupy.

6 "These then are the commandments, the statutes and decrees which the LORD, your God, has ordered that you be taught to observe in the land into which you are crossing for conquest, 2 so that you and your son and your grandson may fear the LORD, your God, and keep, throughout the days of your lives, all his statutes and commandments which I enjoin on you, and thus have long life. 3 Hear then, Israel, and be careful to observe them, that you may grow and prosper the more, in keeping with the promise of the LORD, the God of your fathers, to give you a land flowing with milk and honey.

The Great Commandment

4 "Hear, O Israel! The LORD is our God, the LORD alone! 5 Therefore, you shall love the LORD, your God, with all your heart, and with all your soul, and with all your strength. 6 Take to heart these

words which I enjoin on you today. 7 Drill them into your children. Speak of them at home and abroad, whether you are busy or at rest. 8 Bind them at your wrist as a sign and let them be as a pendant on your forehead. 9 Write them on the doorposts of your houses and on your gates.

Fidelity in Prosperity

10 "When the LORD, your God, brings you into the land which he swore to your fathers. Abraham, Isaac and Jacob, that he would give you, a land with fine, large cities that you did not build, 11 with houses full of goods of all sorts that you did not garner, with cisterns that you did not dig, with vineyards and olive groves that you did not plant; and when, therefore, you eat your fill, 12 take care not to forget the LORD, who brought you out of the land of Egypt, that place of slavery. 13 The LORD, your God, shall you fear; him shall you serve, and by his name shall you swear. 14 You shall not follow other gods, such as those of the surrounding nations, 15 lest the wrath of the LORD, your God, flare up against you and he destroy you from the face of the land; for the LORD, your God, who is in your midst, is a jealous God.

16 "You shall not put the LORD, your God, to the test, as you did at Massah. 17 But keep the commandments of the LORD, your God, and the ordinances and statutes he has enjoined on you. 18 Do what is right and good in the sight of the LORD, that you may, according to his word, prosper, and may enter in and possess the good land which the LORD promised on oath to your fathers, 19 thrusting all your enemies out of your way.

Instruction to Children

20 "Later on, when your son asks you what these ordinances, statutes and decrees mean which the LORD, our God, has enjoined on

---

6, 4f: This passage contains the basic principle of the whole Mosaic law, the keynote of the Book of Deuteronomy; since the Lord alone is God, we must love him with an undivided heart. Christ cited these words as "the greatest and the first commandment,"

embracing in itself the whole law of God (Mt 22, 37f and parallels).

6, 8: *Bind them . . . as a sign:* these injunctions were probably meant merely in a figurative sense; cf Ex 13, 9.16. However, the later Jews understood them literally, and tied on their wrists and foreheads

"phylacteries," boxes containing strips of parchment on which these words were inscribed; cf Mt 23, 5.

6, 13: *Him shall you serve:* here, to "serve" God means especially to "worship" him; in this sense it is quoted by our Lord (Mt 4, 10) as an argument against worshiping the devil.

you, 21 you shall say to your son, 'We were once slaves of Pharaoh in Egypt, but the LORD brought us out of Egypt with his strong hand 22 and wrought before our eyes signs and wonders, great and dire, against Egypt and against Pharaoh and his whole house. 23 He brought us from there to lead us into the land he promised on oath to our fathers, and to give it to us. 24 Therefore, the LORD commanded us to observe all these statutes in fear of the LORD, our God, that we may always have as prosperous and happy a life as we have today; 25 and our justice before the LORD, our God, is to consist in carefully observing all these commandments he has enjoined on us.'

Destruction of Pagans

7 "When the LORD, your God, brings you into the land which you are to enter and occupy, and dislodges great nations before you— the Hittites, Girgashites, Amorites, Canaanites, Perizzites, Hivites and Jebusites: seven nations more numerous and powerful than you— 2 and when the LORD, your God, delivers them up to you and you defeat them, you shall doom them. Make no covenant with them and show them no mercy. 3 You shall not intermarry with them, neither giving your daughters to their sons nor taking their daughters for your sons. 4 For they would turn your sons from following me to serving other gods, and then the wrath of the LORD would flare up against you and quickly destroy you.

5 "But this is how you must deal with them: Tear down their altars, smash their sacred pillars, chop down their sacred poles, and destroy their idols by fire. 6 For you are a people sacred to the LORD, your God; he has chosen you from all the nations on the face of the earth to be a people peculiarly his own. 7 It was not because you are the largest of all nations that the LORD set his heart on you and chose you, for you are really the smallest of all nations. 8 It was because the LORD

loved you and because of his fidelity to the oath he had sworn to your fathers, that he brought you out with his strong hand from the place of slavery, and ransomed you from the hand of Pharaoh, king of Egypt. 9 Understand, then, that the LORD, your God, is God indeed, the faithful God who keeps his merciful covenant down to the thousandth generation toward those who love him and keep his commandments, 10 but who repays with destruction the person who hates him; he does not dally with such a one, but makes him personally pay for it. 11 You shall therefore carefully observe the commandments, the statutes and the decrees which I enjoin on you today.

Blessings of Obedience

12 "As your reward for heeding these decrees and observing them carefully, the LORD, your God, will keep with you the merciful covenant which he promised on oath to your fathers. 13 He will love and bless and multiply you; he will bless the fruit of your womb and the produce of your soil, your grain and wine and oil, the issue of your herds and the young of your flocks, in the land which he swore to your fathers he would give you. 14 You will be blessed above all peoples; no man or woman among you shall be childless nor shall your livestock be barren. 15 The LORD will remove all sickness from you; he will not afflict you with any of the malignant diseases that you know from Egypt, but will leave them with all your enemies.

16 "You shall consume all the nations which the LORD, your God, will deliver up to you. You are not to look on them with pity, lest you be ensnared into serving their gods. 17 Perhaps you will say to yourselves, 'These nations are greater than we. How can we dispossess them?' 18 But do not be afraid of them. Rather, call to mind what the LORD, your God, did to Pharaoh and to all Egypt: 19 the great testings which your own eyes have seen, the signs and wonders, his

strong hand and outstretched arm with which the LORD, your God, brought you out. The same also will he do to all the nations of whom you are now afraid. 20 Moreover, the LORD, your God, will send hornets among them, until the survivors who have hidden from you are destroyed. 21 Therefore, do not be terrified by them, for the LORD, your God, who is in your midst, is a great and awesome God. 22 He will dislodge these nations before you little by little. You cannot exterminate them all at once, lest the wild beasts become too numerous for you. 23 The LORD, your God, will deliver them up to you and will rout them utterly until they are annihilated. 24 He will deliver their kings into your hand, that you may make their names perish from under the heavens. No man will be able to stand up against you, till you have put an end to them. 25 The images of their gods you shall destroy by fire. Do not covet the silver or gold on them, nor take it for yourselves, lest you be ensnared by it; for it is an abomination to the LORD, your God. 26 You shall not bring any abominable thing into your house, lest you be doomed with it; loathe and abhor it utterly as a thing that is doomed.

God's Care

8 "Be careful to observe all the commandments I enjoin on you today, that you may live and increase, and may enter in and possess the land which the LORD promised on oath to your fathers. 2 Remember how for forty years now the LORD, your God, has directed all your journeying in the desert, so as to test you by affliction and find out whether or not it was your intention to keep his commandments. 3 He therefore let you be afflicted with hunger, and then fed you with manna, a food unknown to you and your fathers, in order to show you that not by bread alone does man live, but by every word that comes forth from the mouth of the LORD. 4 The clothing did not fall from

---

7, 5: *Sacred pillars ... poles:* see note on Ex 34, 13.

8, 3: *Not by bread alone, etc.:* quoted by our Lord in Mt 4, 4. The sense is: God takes care of those who

love him even when natural means seem to fail them.

you in tatters, nor did your feet swell these forty years. 5 So you must realize that the LORD, your God, disciplines you even as a man disciplines his son.

Danger of Prosperity

6 "Therefore, keep the commandments of the LORD, your God, by walking in his ways and fearing him. 7 For the LORD, your God, is bringing you into a good country, a land with streams of water, with springs and fountains welling up in the hills and valleys, 8 a land of wheat and barley, of vines and fig trees and pomegranates, of olive trees and of honey, 9 a land where you can eat bread without stint and where you will lack nothing, a land whose stones contain iron and in whose hills you can mine copper. 10 But when you have eaten your fill, you must bless the LORD, your God, for the good country he has given you. 11 Be careful not to forget the LORD, your God, by neglecting his commandments and decrees and statutes which I enjoin on you today: 12 lest, when you have eaten your fill, and have built fine houses and lived in them, 13 and have increased your herds and flocks, your silver and gold, and all your property, 14 you then become haughty of heart and unmindful of the LORD, your God, who brought you out of the land of Egypt, that place of slavery; 15 who guided you through the vast and terrible desert with its saraph serpents and scorpions, its parched and waterless ground; who brought forth water for you from the flinty rock 16 and fed you in the desert with manna, a food unknown to your fathers, that he might afflict you and test you, but also make you prosperous in the end. 17 Otherwise, you might say to yourselves, 'It is my own power and the strength of my own hand that has obtained for me this wealth.' 18 Remember then, it is the LORD, your God, who gives you the power to acquire wealth, by fulfilling, as he has now done, the covenant which he swore to your fathers. 19 But if you forget the LORD, your God, and follow other gods, serving

and worshiping them, I forewarn you this day that you will perish utterly. 20 Like the nations which the LORD destroys before you, so shall you too perish for not heeding the voice of the LORD, your God.

Unmerited Success

9 "Hear, O Israel! You are now about to cross the Jordan to enter in and dispossess nations greater and stronger than yourselves, having large cities fortified to the sky, 2 the Anakim, a people great and tall. You know of them and have heard it said of them, 'Who can stand up against the Anakim?' 3 Understand, then, today that it is the LORD, your God, who will cross over before you as a consuming fire; he it is who will reduce them to nothing and subdue them before you, so that you can drive them out and destroy them quickly, as the LORD promised you. 4 After the LORD, your God, has thrust them out of your way, do not say to yourselves, 'It is because of my merits that the LORD has brought me in to possess this land'; for it is really because of the wickedness of these nations that the LORD is driving them out before you. 5 No, it is not because of your merits or the integrity of your heart that you are going in to take possession of their land; but the LORD, your God, is driving these nations out before you on account of their wickedness and in order to keep the promise which he made on oath to your fathers, Abraham, Isaac and Jacob. 6 Understand this, therefore: it is not because of your merits that the LORD, your God, is giving you this good land to possess, for you are a stiff-necked people.

The Golden Calf

7 "Bear in mind and do not forget how you angered the LORD, your God, in the desert. From the day you left the land of Egypt until you arrived in this place, you have been rebellious toward the LORD. 8 At Horeb you so provoked the LORD that he was angry enough to destroy you, 9 when I had gone up the mountain to receive the stone tablets of the covenant which the LORD made with you. Meanwhile I stayed

on the mountain forty days and forty nights without eating or drinking, 10 till the LORD gave me the two tablets of stone inscribed, by God's own finger, with a copy of all the words that the LORD spoke to you on the mountain from the midst of the fire on the day of the assembly. 11 Then, at the end of the forty days and forty nights, when the LORD had given me the two stone tablets of the covenant, 12 he said to me, 'Go down from here now, quickly, for your people whom you have brought out of Egypt have become depraved; they have already turned aside from the way I pointed out to them and have made for themselves a molten idol. 13 I have seen now how stiff-necked this people is,' the LORD said to me. 14 'Let me be, that I may destroy them and blot out their name from under the heavens. I will then make of you a nation mightier and greater than they.'

15 "When I had come down again from the blazing, fiery mountain, with the two tablets of the covenant in both my hands, 16 I saw how you had sinned against the LORD, your God: you had already turned aside from the way which the LORD had pointed out to you by making for yourselves a molten calf! 17 Raising the two tablets with both hands I threw them from me and broke them before your eyes. 18 Then, as before, I lay prostrate before the LORD for forty days and forty nights without eating or drinking, because of all the sin you had committed in the sight of the LORD and the evil you had done to provoke him. 19 For I dreaded the fierce anger of the LORD against you: his wrath would destroy you. Yet once again the LORD listened to me. 20 With Aaron, too, the LORD was deeply angry, and would have killed him had I not prayed for him also at that time. 21 Then, taking the calf, the sinful object you had made, and fusing it with fire, I ground it down to powder as fine as dust, which I threw into the wadi that went down the mountainside. 22 "At Taberah, at Massah, and at Kibroth-hattaavah likewise, you provoked the LORD to anger. 23

And when he sent you up from Kadesh-barnea to take possession of the land he was giving you, you rebelled against this command of the LORD, your God, and would not trust or obey him. 24 Ever since I have known you, you have been rebels against the LORD.

25 "Those forty days, then, and forty nights, I lay prostrate before the LORD, because he had threatened to destroy you. 26 This was my prayer to him: O Lord GOD, destroy not your people, the heritage which your majesty has ransomed and brought out of Egypt with your strong hand. 27 Remember your servants, Abraham, Isaac and Jacob. Look not upon the stubbornness of this people nor upon their wickedness and sin, 28 lest the people from whose land you have brought us say, 'The LORD was not able to bring them into the land he promised them'; or 'Out of hatred for them, he brought them out to slay them in the desert.' 29 They are, after all, your people and your heritage, whom you have brought out by your great power and with your outstretched arm.

10 "At that time the LORD said to me, 'Cut two tablets of stone like the former; then come up the mountain to me. Also make an ark of wood. 2 I will write upon the tablets the commandments that were on the former tablets that you broke, and you shall place them in the ark.' 3 So I made an ark of acacia wood, and cut two tablets of stone like the former, and went up the mountain carrying the two tablets. 4 The LORD then wrote on them, as he had written before, the ten commandments which he spoke to you on the mountain from the midst of the fire on the day of the assembly. After the LORD had given them to me, 5 I turned and came down the mountain, and placed the tablets in the ark I had made. There they have remained, in keeping with the command the LORD gave me. 6 [The Israelites set out from

Beeroth Bene-jaakan for Moserah, where Aaron died and was buried, his son Eleazar succeeding him in the priestly office. 7 From there they set out for Gudgodah, and from Gudgodah for Jotbathah, a region where there is water in the wadies.] 8 "At that time the LORD set apart the tribe of Levi to carry the ark of the covenant of the LORD, to be in attendance before the LORD and minister to him, and to give blessings in his name, as they have done to this day. 9 For this reason, Levi has no share in the heritage with his brothers; the LORD himself is his heritage, as the LORD, your God, has told him.

10 "After I had spent these other forty days and forty nights on the mountain, and the LORD had once again heard me and decided not to destroy you, 11 he said to me, 'Go now and set out at the head of your people, that they may enter in and occupy the land which I swore to their fathers I would give them.'

The Lord's Majesty

12 "And now, Israel, what does the LORD, your God, ask of you but to fear the LORD, your God, and follow his ways exactly, to love and serve the LORD, your God, with all your heart and all your soul, 13 to keep the commandments and statutes of the LORD which I enjoin on you today for your own good? 14 Think! The heavens, even the highest heavens, belong to the LORD, your God, as well as the earth and everything on it. 15 Yet in his love for your fathers the LORD was so attached to them as to choose you, their descendants, in preference to all other peoples, as indeed he has now done. 16 Circumcise your hearts, therefore, and be no longer stiff-necked. 17 For the LORD, your God, is the God of gods, the LORD of lords, the great God, mighty and awesome, who has no favorites, accepts no bribes; 18 who executes justice for the orphan and the widow, and befriends the alien, feeding and clothing him. 19 So you too must befriend the alien, for you were once

aliens yourselves in the land of Egypt. 20 The LORD, your God, shall you fear, and him shall you serve; hold fast to him and swear by his name. 21 He is your glory, he, your God, who has done for you those great and terrible things which your own eyes have seen. 22 Your ancestors went down to Egypt seventy strong, and now the LORD, your God, has made you as numerous as the stars of the sky.

The Wonders of the Lord

11 "Love the LORD, your God, therefore, and always heed his charge: his statutes, decrees and commandments. 2 It is not your children, who have not known it from experience, but you yourselves who must now understand the discipline of the LORD, your God; his majesty, his strong hand and outstretched arm; 3 the signs and deeds he wrought among the Egyptians, on Pharaoh, king of Egypt, and on all his land; 4 what he did to the Egyptian army and to their horses and chariots, engulfing them in the water of the Red Sea as they pursued you, and bringing ruin upon them even to this day; 5 what he did for you in the desert until you arrived in this place; 6 and what he did to the Reubenites Dathan and Abiram, sons of Eliab, when the ground opened its mouth and swallowed them up out of the midst of Israel, with their families and tents and every living thing that belonged to them. 7 With your own eyes you have seen all these great deeds that the LORD has done. 8 Keep all the commandments, then, which I enjoin on you today, that you may be strong enough to enter in and take possession of the land into which you are crossing, 9 and that you may have long life on the land which the LORD swore to your fathers he would give to them and their descendants, a land flowing with milk and honey.

The Gift of Rain

10 "For the land which you are to enter and occupy is not like the land

---

10, 14: *Even the highest heavens:* literally, "and the heavens of the heavens"; compare the phrase, "the third heaven," in 2 Cor 12, 2.

10, 16: *Circumcise your hearts:* cf 30, 6; Jer 4, 4; Rom 2, 29. The "uncircumcised heart" (Lv 26, 41; Jer 9, 25; Ez 44, 7.9) is closed and unreceptive to

divine grace and guidance, just as "uncircumcised ears" (Jer 6, 10) are closed to sound, and "uncircumcised lips" (Ex 6, 12.30) do not open well in speech.

of Egypt from which you have come, where you would sow your seed and then water it by hand, as in a vegetable garden. 11 No, the land into which you are crossing for conquest is a land of hills and valleys that drinks in rain from the heavens, 12 a land which the LORD, your God, looks after; his eyes are upon it continually from the beginning of the year to the end. 13 If, then, you truly heed my commandments which I enjoin on you today, loving and serving the LORD, your God, with all your heart and all your soul, 14 I will give the seasonal rain to your land, the early rain and the late rain, that you may have your grain, wine and oil to gather in; 15 and I will bring forth grass in your fields for your animals. Thus you may eat your fill. 16 But be careful lest your heart be so lured away that you serve other gods and worship them. 17 For then the wrath of the LORD will flare up against you and he will close up the heavens, so that no rain will fall, and the soil will not yield its crops, and you will soon perish from the good land he is giving you.

Reward of Fidelity

18 "Therefore, take these words of mine into your heart and soul. Bind them at your wrist as a sign, and let them be a pendant on your forehead. 19 Teach them to your children, speaking of them at home and abroad, whether you are busy or at rest. 20 And write them on the doorposts of your houses and on your gates, 21 so that, as long as the heavens are above the earth, you and your children may live on in the land which the LORD swore to your fathers he would give them.

22 "For if you are careful to observe all these commandments I enjoin on you, loving the LORD, your God, and following his ways exactly, and holding fast to him, 23 the LORD will drive all these nations

out of your way, and you will dispossess nations greater and mightier than yourselves. 24 Every place where you set foot shall be yours: from the desert and from Lebanon, from the Euphrates River to the Western Sea, shall be your territory. 25 None shall stand up against you; the LORD, your God, will spread the fear and dread of you through any land where you set foot, as he promised you.

A Blessing and a Curse

26 "I set before you here, this day, a blessing and a curse: 27 a blessing for obeying the commandments of the LORD, your God, which I enjoin on you today; 28 a curse if you do not obey the commandments of the LORD, your God, but turn aside from the way I ordain for you today, to follow other gods, whom you have not known. 29 When the LORD, your God, brings you into the land which you are to enter and occupy, then you shall pronounce the blessing on Mount Gerizim, the curse on Mount Ebal. 30 [Are they not beyond the Jordan, on the other side of the western road in the country of the Canaanites who live in the Arabah, opposite the Gilgal beside the terebinth of Moreh?] 31 For you are about to cross the Jordan to enter and occupy the land which the LORD, your God, is giving you. When, therefore, you take possession of it and settle there, 32 be careful to observe all the statutes and decrees that I set before you today.

EXPOSITION OF THE LAW

One Sanctuary

12 "These are the statutes and decrees which you must be careful to observe in the land which the LORD, the God of your fathers, has given you to occupy, as long as you live on its soil. 2 Destroy without fail every place on the high mountains, on the hills, and under

every leafy tree where the nations you are to dispossess worship their gods. 3 Tear down their altars, smash their sacred pillars, destroy by fire their sacred poles, and shatter the idols of their gods, that you may stamp out the remembrance of them in any such place.

4 "That is not how you are to worship the LORD, your God. 5 Instead, you shall resort to the place which the LORD, your God, chooses out of all your tribes and designates as his dwelling 6 and there you shall bring your holocausts and sacrifices, your tithes and personal contributions, your votive and freewill offerings, and the firstlings of your herds and flocks. 7 There, too, before the LORD, your God, you and your families shall eat and make merry over all your undertakings, because the LORD, your God, has blessed you. 8 You shall not do as we are now doing; here, everyone does what seems right to himself, 9 since you have not yet reached your resting place, the heritage which the LORD, your God, will give you. 10 But after you have crossed the Jordan and dwell in the land which the LORD, your God, is giving you as a heritage, when he has given you rest from all your enemies round about and you live there in security, 11 then to the place which the LORD, your God, chooses as the dwelling place for his name you shall bring all the offerings I command you: your holocausts and sacrifices, your tithes and personal contributions, and every special offering you have vowed to the LORD. 12 You shall make merry before the LORD, your God, with your sons and daughters, your male and female slaves, as well as with the Levite who belongs to your community but has no share of his own in your heritage. 13 Take care not to offer up your holocausts in any place you fancy, 14 but offer them up in the place which the LORD chooses from among your tribes; there you shall make whatever offerings I enjoin upon you.

11,13ff: As often in the Prophets, the discourse passes into the words of God himself. Cf 7, 4; 17, 3; 28, 20; 29, 4f.

11,14: *The early rain:* the rains which begin in October or November and continue intermittently

throughout the winter. *The late rain:* the heavy showers of March and April. In Palestine the crops are sown in the autumn and reaped in the spring.

11, 24: *The Western Sea:* the Mediterranean.

11, 29: *You shall pronounce the blessing . . . the*

curse: for the full ceremony, see chapters 27 and 28. *Gerizim . . . Ebal:* adjacent mountains in Samaria with a deep ravine between them. Their summits command an excellent view of the entire country.

Profane and Sacred Meals

15 "However, in any of your communities you may slaughter and eat to your heart's desire as much meat as the LORD, your God, has blessed you with; and the unclean as well as the clean may eat it, as they do the gazelle or the deer. 16 Only, you shall not partake of the blood, but must pour it out on the ground like water. 17 Moreover, you shall not, in your own communities, partake of your tithe of grain or wine or oil, of the first-born of your herd or flock, of any offering you have vowed, of your freewill offerings, or of your personal contributions. 18 These you must eat before the LORD, your God, in the place he chooses, along with your son and daughter, your male and female slave, and the Levite who belongs to your community; and there, before the LORD, you shall make merry over all your undertakings. 19 Take care, also, that you do not neglect the Levite as long as you live in the land.

20 "After the LORD, your God, has enlarged your territory, as he promised you, when you wish meat for food, you may eat it at will, to your heart's desire; 21 and if the place which the LORD, your God, chooses for the abode of his name is too far, you may slaughter in the manner I have told you any of your herd or flock that the LORD has given you, and eat it to your heart's desire in your own community. 22 You may eat it as you would the gazelle or the deer: the unclean and the clean eating it alike. 23 But make sure that you do not partake of the blood; for blood is life, and you shall not consume this seat of life with the flesh. 24 Do not partake of the blood, therefore, but pour it out on the ground like water. 25 Abstain from it, that you and your children after you may prosper for doing what is right in the sight of the LORD. 26 However, any sacred gifts or votive offering that you may have, you shall bring with you to the place which the LORD chooses, 27 and there you

must offer both the flesh and the blood of your holocausts on the altar of the LORD, your God; of your other sacrifices the blood indeed must be poured out against the altar of the LORD, your God, but their flesh may be eaten. 28 Be careful to heed all these commandments I enjoin on you, that you and your descendants may always prosper for doing what is good and right in the sight of the LORD, your God.

Pagan Rites

29 "When the LORD, your God, removes the nations from your way as you advance to dispossess them, be on your guard! Otherwise, once they have been wiped out before you and you have replaced them and are settled in their land, 30 you will be lured into following them. Do not inquire regarding their gods, 'How did these nations worship their gods? I, too, would do the same.' 31 You shall not thus worship the LORD, your God, because they offered to their gods every abomination that the LORD detests, even burning their sons and daughters to their gods.

Penalties for Idolatry

13 "Every command that I enjoin on you, you shall be careful to observe, neither adding to it nor subtracting from it.

2 "If there arises among you a prophet or a dreamer who promises you a sign or wonder, 3 urging you to follow other gods, whom you have not known, and to serve them: even though the sign or wonder he has foretold you comes to pass, 4 pay no attention to the words of that prophet or that dreamer; for the LORD, your God, is testing you to learn whether you really love him with all your heart and with all your soul. 5 The LORD, your God, shall you follow, and him shall you fear; his commandment shall you observe, and his voice shall you heed, serving him and holding fast to him alone. 6 But that prophet or that dreamer shall be put to

death, because, in order to lead you astray from the way which the LORD, your God, has directed you to take, he has preached apostasy from the LORD, your God, who brought you out of the land of Egypt and ransomed you from that place of slavery. Thus shall you purge the evil from your midst.

7 "If your own full brother, or your son or daughter, or your beloved wife or your intimate friend, entices you secretly to serve other gods, whom you and your fathers have not known, 8 gods of any other nation, near at hand or far away, from one end of the earth to the other: 9 do not yield to him or listen to him, nor look with pity upon him, to spare or shield him, 10 but kill him. Your hand shall be the first raised to slay him; the rest of the people shall join in with you. 11 You shall stone him to death, because he sought to lead you astray from the LORD, your God, who brought you out of the land of Egypt, that place of slavery. 12 And all Israel, hearing of it, shall fear and never again do such evil as this in your midst.

13 "If, in any of the cities which the LORD, your God, gives you to dwell in, you hear it said 14 that certain scoundrels have sprung up among you and have led astray the inhabitants of their city to serve other gods whom you have not known, 15 you must inquire carefully into the matter and investigate it thoroughly. If you find that it is true and an established fact that this abomination has been committed in your midst, 16 you shall put the inhabitants of that city to the sword, dooming the city and all life that is in it, even its cattle, to the sword. 17 Having heaped up all its spoils in the middle of its square, you shall burn the city with all its spoils as a whole burnt offering to the LORD, your God. Let it be a heap of ruins forever, never to be rebuilt. 18 You shall not retain anything that is doomed, that the blazing wrath of the LORD may die down and he may show you mercy and in his

---

12, 20: *Meat for food:* as on special feasts. Meat was not eaten every day in Israel, even by the wealthy.

13, 2.4.6: *Dreamer:* a false prophet who pretended to have received revelations from God in his dreams; cf Jer 23, 25–32; Zec 10, 2. But dreams could

also be a channel of true prophecy (Nm 12, 6; Jl 3, 1) and of genuine revelations (Gn 20, 3.6; 31, 10.24; 37, 5.9; Mt 1, 20; 2.12f.19; etc.).

mercy for you may multiply you as he promised your fathers on oath; 19 because you have heeded the voice of the LORD, your God, keeping all his commandments which I enjoin on you today, doing what is right in his sight.

Pagan Mourning Rites

14 "You are children of the LORD, your God. You shall not gash yourselves nor shave the hair above your foreheads for the dead. 2 For you are a people sacred to the LORD, your God, who has chosen you from all the nations on the face of the earth to be a people peculiarly his own.

Clean and Unclean Animals

3 "You shall not eat any abominable thing. 4 These are the animals you may eat: the ox, the sheep, the goat, 5 the red deer, the gazelle, the roe deer, the ibex, the addax, the oryx, and the mountain sheep. 6 Any animal that has hoofs you may eat, provided it is cloven-footed and chews the cud. 7 But you shall not eat any of the following that only chew the cud or only have cloven hoofs: the camel, the hare and the rock badger, which indeed chew the cud, but do not have hoofs and are therefore unclean for you; 8 and the pig, which indeed has hoofs and is cloven-footed, but does not chew the cud and is therefore unclean for you. Their flesh you shall not eat, and their dead bodies you shall not touch.

9 "Of the various creatures that live in the water, whatever has both fins and scales you may eat, 10 but all those that lack either fins or scales you shall not eat; they are unclean for you.

11 "You may eat all clean birds. 12 But you shall not eat any of the following: the eagle, the vulture, the osprey, 13 the various kites and falcons, 14 all the various species of crows, 15 the ostrich, the night-jar, the gull, the various species of hawks, 16 the owl, the screech owl, the ibis, 17 the desert owl, the buzzard, the cormorant, 18 the stork, the various species of herons, the hoopoe, and the bat. 19 All winged insects, too, are unclean for you and shall not be eaten. 20 But you may eat any clean winged creatures.

21 "You must not eat any animal that had died of itself, for you are a people sacred to the LORD, your God. But you may give it to an alien who belongs to your community, and he may eat it, or you may sell it to a foreigner.

"You shall not boil a kid in its mother's milk.

Tithes

22 "Each year you shall tithe all the produce that grows in the field you have sown; 23 then in the place which the LORD, your God, chooses as the dwelling place of his name you shall eat in his presence your tithe of the grain, wine and oil, as well as the firstlings of your herd and flock, that you may learn always to fear the LORD, your God. 24 If, however, the journey is too much for you and you are not able to bring your tithe, because the place which the LORD, your God, chooses for the abode of his name is too far for you, considering how the LORD has blessed you, 25 you may exchange the tithe for money and, with the purse of money in hand, go to the place which the LORD, your God, chooses. 26 You may then exchange the money for whatever you desire, oxen or sheep, wine or strong drink, or anything else you would enjoy, and there before the LORD, your God, you shall partake of it and make merry with your family.

27 But do not neglect the Levite who belongs to your community, for he has no share in the heritage with you.

28 "At the end of every third year you shall bring out all the tithes of your produce for that year and deposit them in community stores, 29 that the Levite who has no share in the heritage with you, and also the alien, the orphan and the widow who belong to your community, may come and eat their fill; so that the LORD, your God, may bless you in all that you undertake.

Debts and the Poor

15 "At the end of every seven-year period you shall have a relaxation of debts, 2 which shall be observed as follows. Every creditor shall relax his claim on what he has loaned his neighbor; he must not press his neighbor, his kinsman, because a relaxation in honor of the LORD has been proclaimed. 3 You may press a foreigner, but you shall relax the claim on your kinsman for what is yours. Nay, more! 4 since the LORD, your God, will bless you abundantly in the land he will give you to occupy as your heritage, there should be no one of you in need. 5 If you but heed the voice of the LORD, your God, and carefully observe all these commandments which I enjoin on you today, 6 you will lend to many nations, and borrow from none; you will rule over many nations, and none will rule over you, since the LORD, your God, will bless you as he promised. 7 If one of your kinsmen in any community is in need in the land which the LORD, your God, is giving you, you shall not harden your heart nor close your hand to him in his need. 8 Instead, you shall open your hand to him and freely lend him enough to meet his need. 9 Be on your guard lest, entertaining the mean thought that the seventh year, the year of relaxation, is near, you grudge help to your needy kinsman and give him nothing; else he will cry to the LORD against you and you will be held guilty. 10 When you give to him, give freely and not with ill will; for the LORD, your God, will bless you

14, 5: The gazelle, the addax, the oryx: species of antelopes. The ibex: a species of wild goat.
14, 19f: The apparent contradiction is to be resolved in the light of Lv 11, 20–23: the unclean winged insects are those that walk on the ground; the clean winged creatures are those that leap on the ground, such as certain species of locusts.

14, 21: Boil a kid in its mother's milk: see note on Ex 23, 19.
14, 24: Considering how the Lord has blessed you: should the Israelite farmer be blessed with an abundant harvest, a tenth of this would be too much to transport for a great distance.
15, 1: At the end of every seven-year period: in

every seventh, or sabbatical, year. Cf v 9; 31, 10; and compare Jer 34, 14 with Dt 15, 12. A relaxation of debts: it is uncertain whether a full cancellation of debts is meant, or merely a suspension of payment on them or on their interest among the Israelites. Cf Ex 23, 11 where the same Hebrew root is used of a field that is "let lie fallow" in the sabbatical year.

for this in all your works and undertakings. 11 The needy will never be lacking in the land; that is why I command you to open your hand to your poor and needy kinsman in your country.

Hebrew Slaves

12 "If your kinsman, a Hebrew man or woman, sells himself to you, he is to serve you for six years, but in the seventh year you shall dismiss him from your service, a free man. 13 When you do so, you shall not send him away empty-handed, 14 but shall weight him down with gifts from your flock and threshing floor and wine press, in proportion to the blessing the LORD, your God, has bestowed on you. 15 For remember that you too were once slaves in the land of Egypt, and the LORD, your God, ransomed you. That is why I am giving you this command today. 16 If, however, he tells you that he does not wish to leave you, because he is devoted to you and your household, since he fares well with you, 17 you shall take an awl and thrust it through his ear into the door, and he shall then be your slave forever. Your female slave, also, you shall treat in the same way. 18 You must not be reluctant to let your slave go free, since the service he has given you for six years was worth twice a hired man's salary; then also the LORD, your God, will bless you in everything you do.

Firstlings

19 "You shall consecrate to the LORD, your God, all the male firstlings of your herd and of your flock. You shall not work the firstlings of your cattle, nor shear the firstlings of your flock. 20 Year after year you and your family shall eat them before the LORD, your God, in the place he chooses. 21 If, however, a firstling is lame or blind or has any other serious defect, you shall not sacrifice it to the LORD, your God, 22 but in your own communities you may eat it, the unclean and the clean eating it

alike, as you would a gazelle or a deer. 23 Only, you shall not partake of its blood, which must be poured out on the ground like water.

Feast of the Passover

16 "Observe the month of Abib by keeping the Passover of the LORD, your God, since it was in the month of Abib that he brought you by night out of Egypt. 2 You shall offer the Passover sacrifice from your flock or your herd to the LORD, your God, in the place which he chooses as the dwelling place of his name. 3 You shall not eat leavened bread with it. For seven days you shall eat with it only unleavened bread, the bread of affliction, that you may remember as long as you live the day of your departure from the land of Egypt; for in frightened haste you left the land of Egypt. 4 Nothing leavened may be found in all your territory for seven days, and none of the meat which you sacrificed on the evening of the first day shall be kept overnight for the next day.

5 "You may not sacrifice the Passover in any of the communities which the LORD, your God, gives you; 6 only at the place which he chooses as the dwelling place of his name, and in the evening at sunset, on the anniversary of your departure from Egypt, shall you sacrifice the Passover. 7 You shall cook and eat it at the place the LORD, your God, chooses; then in the morning you may return to your tents. 8 For six days you shall eat unleavened bread, and on the seventh there shall be a solemn meeting in honor of the LORD, your God; on that day you shall not do any sort of work.

Feast of Weeks

9 "You shall count off seven weeks, computing them from the day when the sickle is first put to the standing grain. 10 You shall then keep the feast of Weeks in honor of the LORD, your God, and the measure of your own freewill offering shall be in proportion to the blessing the

LORD, your God, has bestowed on you. 11 In the place which the LORD, your God, chooses as the dwelling place of his name, you shall make merry in his presence together with your son and daughter, your male and female slave, and the Levite who belongs to your community, as well as the alien, the orphan and the widow among you. 12 Remember that you too were once slaves in Egypt, and carry out these statutes carefully.

Feast of Booths

13 "You shall celebrate the feast of Booths for seven days, when you have gathered in the produce from your threshing floor and wine press. 14 You shall make merry at your feast, together with your son and daughter, your male and female slave, and also the Levite, the alien, the orphan and the widow who belong to your community. 15 For seven days you shall celebrate this pilgrim feast in honor of the LORD, your God, in the place which he chooses; since the LORD, your God, has blessed you in all your crops and in all your undertakings, you shall do nought but make merry.

16 "Three times a year, then, every male among you shall appear before the LORD, your God, in the place which he chooses: at the feast of Unleavened Bread, at the feast of Weeks, and at the feast of Booths. No one shall appear before the LORD empty-handed, 17 but each of you with as much as he can give, in proportion to the blessings which the LORD, your God, has bestowed on you.

Judges

18 "You shall appoint judges and officials throughout your tribes to administer true justice for the people in all the communities which the LORD, your God, is giving you. 19 You shall not distort justice; you must be impartial. You shall not take a bribe; for a bribe blinds the eyes even of the wise and twists the words even of the just. 20 Justice

---

15, 11: *The needy will never be lacking:* compare the words of Christ, "The poor you have always with you" (Mt 26, 11).
15, 17: *His ear:* Cf Ex 21, 6 and the note there.

16, 1: *Abib:* "ear of grain, ripe grain," the name of the month in which the barley harvest fell, corresponding to our March and April; at a later period this month received the Babylonian name of "Nisan."

16, 10: *Feast of Weeks:* later known more commonly as "Pentecost."
16, 13: See note on Lv 23, 34.

and justice alone shall be your aim, that you may have life and may possess the land which the LORD, your God, is giving you.

Pagan Worship

21 "You shall not plant a sacred pole of any kind of wood beside the altar of the LORD, your God, which you will build; 22 nor shall you erect a sacred pillar, such as the LORD, your God, detests.

17 "You shall not sacrifice to the LORD, your God, from the herd or from the flock an animal with any serious defect; that would be an abomination to the LORD, your God.

2 "If there is found among you, in any one of the communities which the LORD, your God, gives you, a man or a woman who does evil in the sight of the LORD, your God, and transgresses his covenant, 3 by serving other gods, or by worshiping the sun or the moon or any of the host of the sky, against my command; 4 and if, on being informed of it, you find by careful investigation that it is true and an established fact that this abomination has been committed in Israel: 5 you shall bring the man (or woman) who has done the evil deed out to your city gates and stone him to death. 6 The testimony of two or three witnesses is required for putting a person to death; no one shall be put to death on the testimony of only one witness. 7 At the execution, the witnesses are to be the first to raise their hands against him; afterward all the people are to join in. Thus shall you purge the evil from your midst.

Judges

8 "If in your own community there is a case at issue which proves too complicated for you to decide, in a matter of bloodshed or of civil rights or of personal injury, you shall then go up to the place which the LORD, your God, chooses, 9 to the levitical priests or to the judge who is in office at that time. They shall study the case and then hand down to you their decision. 10 According to this decision that they give you in the place which the LORD chooses, you shall act, being careful to do exactly as they direct. 11 You shall carry out the directions they give you and the verdict they pronounce for you, without turning aside to the right or to the left from the decision they hand down to you. 12 Any man who has the insolence to refuse to listen to the priest who officiates there in the ministry of the LORD, your God, or to the judge, shall die. Thus shall you purge the evil from your midst. 13 And all the people, on hearing of it, shall fear, and never again be so insolent.

The King

14 "When you have come into the land which the LORD, your God, is giving you, and have occupied it and settled in it, should you then decide to have a king over you like all the surrounding nations, 15 you shall set that man over you as your king whom the LORD, your God, chooses. He whom you set over you as king must be your kinsman; a foreigner, who is no kin of yours, you may not set over you. 16 But he shall not have a great number of horses; nor shall he make his people go back again to Egypt to acquire them, against the LORD's warning that you must never go back that way again. 17 Neither shall he have a great number of wives, lest his heart be estranged, nor shall he accumulate a vast amount of silver and gold. 18 When he is enthroned in his kingdom, he shall have a copy of this law made from the scroll that is in the custody of the levitical priests. 19 He shall keep it with him and read it all the days of his life that he may learn to fear the LORD, his God, and to heed and fulfill all the words of this law and these statutes. 20 Let him not become estranged from his countrymen through pride, nor turn aside to the right or to the left from these commandments. Then he and his descendants will enjoy a long reign in Israel.

Priests

18 "The whole priestly tribe of Levi shall have no share in the heritage with Israel; they shall live on the oblations of the LORD and the portions due to him. 2 Levi shall have no heritage among his brothers; the LORD himself is his heritage, as he has told him. 3 The priests shall have a right to the following things from the people: from those who are offering a sacrifice, whether the victim is from the herd or from the flock, the priest shall receive the shoulder, the jowls and the stomach. 4 You shall also give him the first fruits of your grain and wine and oil, as well as the first fruits of the shearing of your flock; 5 for the LORD, your God, has chosen him and his sons out of all your tribes to be always in attendance to minister in the name of the LORD.

6 "When a Levite goes from one of your communities anywhere in Israel in which he ordinarily resides, to visit, as his heart may desire, the place which the LORD chooses, 7 he may minister there in the name of the LORD, his God, like all his fellow Levites who are in attendance there before the LORD. 8 He shall then receive the same portions to eat as the rest, along with his monetary offerings and heirlooms.

Prophets

9 "When you come into the land which the LORD, your God, is giving you, you shall not learn to imitate the abominations of the peoples

---

16, 21—17,7: This section seems to be out of its proper place, since it interrupts the natural sequence of the laws for the judges (16, 18–20 and 17, 8–13). It probably belongs to the similar section, 12–29—14, 2.

16, 21f: *Sacred pole . . . sacred pillar:* see note on Ex 34, 13.

17, 5: *Out to your city gates:* outside the gates in

an unclean place; cf Lv 24, 14; Nm 15, 36; Acts 7, 58; Heb 13, 12.

17, 12: *The priest:* the high priest; *the judge:* a layman. The former presided over the court in cases which directly concerned religion, the latter in cases of a more secular nature; cf 2 Chr 19, 8–11.

17, 16: *Horses:* chariotry for war. *The Lord's warning:* the same warning is also referred to in

28, 68, although it is not mentioned explicitly elsewhere in the Pentateuch. We know from other sources that Egypt used to export war horses to Palestine. The danger envisioned here is that some king might make Israel a vassal of Egypt for the sake of such military aid.

there. 10 Let there not be found among you anyone who immolates his son or daughter in the fire, nor a fortuneteller, soothsayer, charmer, diviner, 11 or caster of spells, nor one who consults ghosts and spirits or seeks oracles from the dead. 12 Anyone who does such things is an abomination to the LORD, and because of such abominations the LORD, your God, is driving these nations out of your way. 13 You, however, must be altogether sincere toward the LORD, your God. 14 Though these nations whom you are to dispossess listen to their soothsayers and fortunetellers, the LORD, your God, will not permit you to do so.

15 "A prophet like me will the LORD, your God, raise up for you from among your own kinsmen; to him you shall listen. 16 This is exactly what you requested of the LORD, your God, at Horeb on the day of the assembly, when you said, 'Let us not again hear the voice of the LORD, our God, nor see this great fire any more, lest we die.' 17 And the LORD said to me, 'This was well said. 18 I will raise up for them a prophet like you from among their kinsmen, and will put my words into his mouth; he shall tell them all that I command him. 19 If any man will not listen to my words which he speaks in my name, I myself will make him answer for it. 20 But if a prophet presumes to speak in my name an oracle that I have not commanded him to speak, or speaks in the name of other gods, he shall die.'

21 "If you say to yourselves, 'How can we recognize an oracle which the LORD has spoken?', 22 know that, even though a prophet speaks in the name of the LORD, if his oracle is not fulfilled or verified, it is an oracle which the LORD did not speak. The prophet has spoken it presumptuously, and you shall have no fear of him.

Cities of Refuge

19 "When the LORD, your God, removes the nations whose land he is giving you, and you have taken their place and are settled in their cities and houses, 2 you shall set apart three cities in the land which the LORD, your God, is giving you to occupy. 3 You shall thereby divide into three regions the land which the LORD, your God, will give you as a heritage, and so arrange the routes that every homicide will be able to find a refuge.

4 "It is in the following case that a homicide may take refuge in such a place to save his life: when someone unwittingly kills his neighbor to whom he had previously borne no malice. 5 For example, if he goes with his neighbor to a forest to cut wood, and as he swings his ax to fell a tree, its head flies off the handle and hits his neighbor a mortal blow, he may take refuge in one of these cities to save his life. 6 Should the distance be too great, the avenger of blood may in the heat of his anger pursue the homicide and overtake him and strike him dead, even though he does not merit death since he had previously borne the slain man no malice. 7 That is why I order you to set apart three cities.

8 "But if the LORD, your God, enlarges your territory, as he swore to your fathers, and gives you all the land he promised your fathers he would give 9 in the event that you carefully observe all these commandments which I enjoin on you today, loving the LORD, your God, and ever walking in his ways: then add three cities to these three. 10 Thus, in the land which the LORD, your God, is giving you as a heritage, innocent blood will not be shed and you will not become guilty of bloodshed.

11 "However, if someone lies in wait for his neighbor out of hatred for him, and rising up against him,

strikes him mortally, and then takes refuge in one of these cities, 12 the elders of his own city shall send for him and have him taken from there, and shall hand him over to be slain by the avenger of blood. 13 Do not look on him with pity, but purge from Israel the stain of shedding innocent blood, that you may prosper.

Removal of Landmarks

14 "You shall not move your neighbor's landmarks erected by your forefathers in the heritage you receive in the land which the LORD, your God, is giving you to occupy.

False Witnesses

15 "One witness alone shall not take the stand against a man in regard to any crime or any offense of which he may be guilty; a judicial fact shall be established only on the testimony of two or three witnesses.

16 "If an unjust witness takes the stand against a man to accuse him of a defection from the law, 17 the two parties in the dispute shall appear before the LORD in the presence of the priests or judges in office at that time; 18 and if after a thorough investigation the judges find that the witness is a false witness and has accused his kinsman falsely, 19 you shall do to him as he planned to do to his kinsman. Thus shall you purge the evil from your midst. 20 The rest, on hearing of it, shall fear, and never again do a thing so evil among you. 21 Do not look on such a man with pity. Life for life, eye for eye, tooth for tooth, hand for hand, and foot for foot!

Courage in War

20 "When you go out to war against your enemies and you see horses and chariots and an army greater than your own, do not be afraid of them, for the LORD, your God, who brought you up from the land of Egypt, will be with you.

18, 10f: *Immolates his son or daughter in the fire:* to Molech. See note on Lv 18, 21. Such human sacrifices are classed here with other pagan superstitions because they were believed to possess magical powers for averting a calamity; cf 2 Kgs 3, 27. Three other forms of superstition are listed here: augury (by a *fortune-teller, a soothsayer* or a *diviner*); black magic (by a *charmer ... or caster of spells*); and necromancy (by *one who consults ghosts and spirits*

or seeks oracles from the dead).

18, 15: *A prophet like me:* from the context (opposition to the pagan soothsayers) it seems that Moses is referring in general to all the true prophets who were to succeed him. But since Christ is the Great Prophet in whom the prophetic office finds its fulfillment and completion, this passage was understood in a special Messianic sense both by the Jews (Jn 6, 14; 7, 40) and by the Apostles (Acts 3, 22; 7, 37).

19, 2: *Set apart three cities:* the Israelites were to have at least six cities of refuge, three in the land east of the Jordan and three in the land of Canaan west of the Jordan (Nm 35, 9–34); but since the three cities east of the Jordan had now been appointed (Dt 4, 41–43), reference is made here only to the three west of the Jordan. The execution of this command is narrated in Jos 20.

19, 6: *The avenger of blood:* see note on Nm 35, 12.

2 "When you are about to go into battle, the priest shall come forward and say to the soldiers: 3 'Hear, O Israel! Today you are going into battle against your enemies. Be not weakhearted or afraid; be neither alarmed nor frightened by them. 4 For it is the LORD, your God, who goes with you to fight for you against your enemies and give you victory.

5 "Then the officials shall say to the soldiers, 'Is there anyone who has built a new house and not yet had the housewarming? Let him return home, lest he die in battle and another dedicate it. 6 Is there anyone who has planted a vineyard and never yet enjoyed its fruits? Let him return home, lest he die in battle and another enjoy its fruits in his stead. 7 Is there anyone who has betrothed a woman and not yet taken her as his wife? Let him return home, lest he die in battle and another take her to wife.' 8 In fine, the officials shall say to the soldiers, 'Is there anyone who is afraid and weakhearted? Let him return home, lest he make his fellows as fainthearted as himself.'

9 "When the officials have finished speaking to the soldiers, military officers shall be appointed over the army.

Cities of the Enemy

10 "When you march up to attack a city, first offer it terms of peace. 11 If it agrees to your terms of peace and opens its gates to you, all the people to be found in it shall serve you in forced labor. 12 But if it refuses to make peace with you and instead offers you battle, lay siege to it, 13 and when the LORD, your God, delivers it into your hand, put every male in it to the sword; 14 but the women and children and livestock and all else in it that is worth plundering you may take as your booty, and you may use this plunder of your enemies which the LORD, your God, has given you.

15 "That is how you shall deal with any city at a considerable distance from you, which does not belong to the peoples of this land. 16 But in the cities of those nations which the LORD, your God, is giving you as your heritage, you shall not leave a single soul alive. 17 You must doom them all—the Hittites, Amorites, Canaanites, Perizzites, Hivites and Jebusites—as the LORD, your God, has commanded you, 18 lest they teach you to make any such abominable offerings as they make to their gods, and you thus sin against the LORD, your God.

Trees of a Besieged City

19 "When you are at war with a city and have to lay siege to it for a long time before you capture it, you shall not destroy its trees by putting an ax to them. You may eat their fruit, but you must not cut down the trees. After all, are the trees of the field men, that they should be included in your siege? 20 However, those trees which you know are not fruit trees you may destroy, cutting them down to build siegeworks with which to reduce the city that is resisting you.

Expiation of Untraced Murder

21 "If the corpse of a slain man is found lying in the open on the land which the LORD, your God, is giving you to occupy, and it is not known who killed him, 2 your elders and judges shall go out and measure the distances to the cities that are in the neighborhood of the corpse. 3 When it is established which city is nearest the corpse, the elders of that city shall take a heifer that has never been put to work as a draft animal under a yoke, 4 and bringing it down to a wadi with an everflowing stream at a place that has not been plowed or sown, they shall cut the heifer's throat there in the wadi. 5 The priests, the descendants of Levi, shall also be present, for the LORD, your God, has chosen

them to minister to him and to give blessings in his name, and every case of dispute or violence must be settled by their decision. 6 Then all the elders of that city nearest the corpse shall wash their hands over the heifer whose throat was cut in the wadi, 7 and shall declare, 'Our hands did not shed this blood, and our eyes did not see the deed. 8 Absolve, O LORD, your people Israel, whom you have ransomed, and let not the guilt of shedding innocent blood remain in the midst of your people Israel.' Thus they shall be absolved from the guilt of bloodshed, 9 and you shall purge from your midst the guilt of innocent blood, that you may prosper for doing what is right in the sight of the LORD.

Marriage with a Female Captive

10 "When you go out to war against your enemies and the LORD, your God, delivers them into your hand, so that you take captives, 11 if you see a comely woman among the captives and become so enamored of her that you wish to have her as wife, 12 you may take her home to your house. But before she may live there, she must shave her head and pare her nails, 13 and lay aside her captive's garb. After she has mourned her father and mother for a full month, you may have relations with her, and you shall be her husband and she shall be your wife. 14 However, if later on you lose your liking for her, you shall give her her freedom, if she wishes it; but you shall not sell her or enslave her, since she was married to you under compulsion.

Rights of the First-born

15 "If a man with two wives loves one and dislikes the other; and if both bear him sons, but the first-born is of her whom he dislikes: 16 when he comes to bequeath his property to his sons, he may not consider as his first-born the son of the wife he loves, in preference to his true

---

21, 1-9: This paragraph is best read immediately after 19, 21. The *slain man* may not necessarily have been murdered; he may have been killed by a wild beast. But the blood of the slain cries out to God from the soil where it was shed; cf Gn 4, 10. Therefore a religious ceremony of propitiation is here prescribed in order to avert God's anger on the community.

21, 4: *They shall cut the heifer's throat there in the wadi:* its blood is to be carried away by the stream, signifying thereby the removal of the human blood from the soil. This is not a sacrifice but a symbolic action; the priests are present merely as official witnesses.

21, 6: *Wash their hands:* a symbolic gesture in protestation of one's own innocence when human

blood is unjustly shed; cf Mt 27, 24.

21, 7: *This blood:* the blood of the slain man as symbolized by the heifer's blood.

21, 12f: *Shave her head . . .:* these symbolic actions are meant to signify the purification of the woman from her pagan defilement or perhaps the end of her period of mourning for her previous husband.

first-born, the son of the wife whom he dislikes. 17 On the contrary, he shall recognize as his first-born the son of her whom he dislikes, giving him a double share of whatever he happens to own, since he is the first fruits of his manhood, and to him belong the rights of the first-born.

The Incorrigible Son

18 "If a man has a stubborn and unruly son who will not listen to his father or mother, and will not obey them even though they chastise him, 19 his father and mother shall have him apprehended and brought out to the elders at the gate of his home city, 20 where they shall say to those city elders, 'This son of ours is a stubborn and unruly fellow who will not listen to us; he is a glutton and a drunkard.' 21 Then all his fellow citizens shall stone him to death. Thus shall you purge the evil from your midst, and all Israel, on hearing of it, shall fear.

Corpse of a Criminal

22 "If a man guilty of a capital offense is put to death and his corpse hung on a tree, 23 it shall not remain on the tree overnight. You shall bury it the same day; otherwise, since God's curse rests on him who hangs on a tree, you will defile the land which the LORD, your God, is giving you as an inheritance.

Care for Lost Animals

22 "You shall not see your kinsman's ox or sheep driven astray without showing concern about it; see to it that it is returned to your kinsman. 2 If this kinsman does not live near you, or you do not know who he may be, take it to your own place and keep it with you until he claims it; then give it back to him. 3 You shall do the same with his ass, or his garment, or anything else which your kinsman loses and you happen to find; you may not be unconcerned about them. 4 You shall not see your kinsman's ass or ox foundering on the road without showing concern about it; see to it that you help him lift it up.

Various Precepts

5 "A woman shall not wear an article proper to a man, nor shall a man put on a woman's dress; for anyone who does such things is an abomination to the LORD, your God.

6 "If, while walking along, you chance upon a bird's nest with young birds or eggs in it, in any tree or on the ground, and the mother bird is sitting on them, you shall not take away the mother bird along with her brood; 7 you shall let her go, although you may take her brood away. It is thus that you shall have prosperity and a long life.

8 "When you build a new house, put a parapet around the roof; otherwise, if someone falls off, you will bring bloodguilt upon your house.

9 "You shall not sow your vineyard with two different kinds of seed; if you do, its produce shall become forfeit, both the crop you have sown and the yield of the vineyard. 10 You shall not plow with an ox and an ass harnessed together. 11 You shall not wear cloth of two different kinds of thread, wool and linen, woven together.

12 "You shall put twisted cords on the four corners of the cloak that you wrap around you."

Crimes against Marriage

13 "If a man, after marrying a woman and having relations with her, comes to dislike her, 14 and makes monstrous charges against her and defames her by saying, 'I married this woman, but when I first had relations with her I did not find her a virgin,' 15 the father and mother of the girl shall take the evidence of her virginity and bring it to the elders at the city gate. 16 There the father of the girl shall say to the elders, 'I gave my daughter to this man in marriage, but he has come to dislike her, 17 and now brings monstrous charges against her, saying: I did not find your daughter a virgin. But here is the evidence of my daughter's virginity!' And they shall spread out the cloth before the elders of the city. 18 Then these city elders shall take the man and chastise him, 19 besides fining him one hundred silver shekels, which they shall give to the girl's father, because the man defamed a virgin in Israel. Moreover, she shall remain his wife, and he may not divorce her as long as he lives.

20 "But if this charge is true, and evidence of the girl's virginity is not found, 21 they shall bring the girl to the entrance of her father's house and there her townsmen shall stone her to death, because she committed a crime against Israel by her unchasteness in her father's house. Thus shall you purge the evil from your midst.

22 "If a man is discovered having relations with a woman who is married to another, both the man and the woman with whom he has had relations shall die. Thus shall you purge the evil from your midst.

23 "If within the city a man comes upon a maiden who is betrothed, and has relations with her, 24 you shall bring them both out to the gate of the city and there stone them to death: the girl because she did not cry out for help though she was in the city, and the man because he violated his neighbor's wife. Thus shall you purge the evil from your midst.

25 "If, however, it is in the open fields that a man comes upon such a betrothed maiden, seizes her and

---

21, 19: *The gate:* in the city walls. This open space served as the forum for the administration of justice. Cf 22, 15; 25, 7; Ru 4, 1f.11; Is 29, 21; Am 5, 10.12. 15.

21, 22: *Hung on a tree:* some understand, "impaled on a stake." In any case the hanging or impaling was not the means used to execute the criminal; he was first put to death by the ordinary means, stoning, and his corpse was then exposed on high as a salutary warning for others. Cf Jos 8, 29; 10, 26;

1 Sm 31, 10; 2 Sm 21, 9.

21, 23: *God's curse rests on him who hangs on a tree:* St. Paul quotes these words in Gal 3, 13, where he applies them to the crucified Savior, who "redeemed us from the curse of the law, becoming a curse for us."

22, 9: *Become forfeit:* to the sanctuary; cf Lv 19, 19; Jos 6, 19.

22, 12: *Twisted cords:* referred to as "tassels" on "violet cords" in Nm 15, 38. See note there.

22, 15: *The evidence of her virginity:* the bridal garment or sheet stained with a little blood from the first nuptial relations.

22, 18: *Chastise him:* flog him, as prescribed in 25, 1–3.

22, 23: *A maiden who is betrothed:* a girl who is married but not yet brought to her husband's home and whose marriage is therefore still unconsummated.

has relations with her, the man alone shall die. 26 You shall do nothing to the maiden, since she is not guilty of a capital offense. This case is like that of a man who rises up against his neighbor and murders him: 27 it was in the open fields that he came upon her, and though the betrothed maiden may have cried out for help, there was no one to come to her aid.

28 "If a man comes upon a maiden that is not betrothed, takes her and has relations with her, and their deed is discovered, 29 the man who had relations with her shall pay the girl's father fifty silver shekels and take her as his wife, because he has deflowered her. Moreover, he may not divorce her as long as he lives.

23 "A man shall not marry his father's wife, nor shall he dishonor his father's bed.

Membership in the Community

2 "No one whose testicles have been crushed or whose penis has been cut off may be admitted into the community of the LORD. 3 No child of an incestuous union may be admitted into the community of the LORD nor any descendant of his even to the tenth generation. 4 No Ammonite or Moabite may ever be admitted into the community of the LORD, nor any descendants of theirs even to the tenth generation, 5 because they would not succor you with food and water on your journey after you left Egypt, and because Moab hired Balaam, son of Beor, from Pethor in Aram-Naharaim, to curse you; 6 though the LORD, your God, would not listen to Balaam and turned his curse into a blessing for you, because he loves you. 7 Never promote their peace and prosperity as long as you live. 8 But do not abhor the Edomite, since he is your brother, nor the Egyptian, since you were an alien in his country. 9 Children born to them may in the third generation be admitted into the community of the LORD.

Cleanliness in Camp

10 "When you are in camp during an expedition against your enemies, you shall keep yourselves from everything offensive. 11 If one of you becomes unclean because of a nocturnal emission, he shall go outside the camp, and not return until, 12 toward evening, he has bathed in water; then, when the sun has set, he may come back into the camp. 13 Outside the camp you shall have a place set aside to be used as a latrine. 4 You shall also keep a trowel in your equipment and with it, when you go outside to ease nature, you shall first dig a hole and afterward cover up your excrement. 15 Since the LORD, your God, journeys along within your camp to defend you and to put your enemies at your mercy, your camp must be holy; otherwise, if he sees anything indecent in your midst, he will leave your company.

Various Precepts

16 "You shall not hand over to his master a slave who has taken refuge from him with you. 17 Let him live with you wherever he chooses, in any one of your communities that pleases him. Do not molest him.

18 "There shall be no temple harlot among the Israelite women, nor a temple prostitute among the Israelite men. 19 You shall not offer a harlot's fee or a dog's price as any kind of votive offering in the house of the LORD, your God; both these things are an abomination to the LORD, your God.

20 "You shall not demand interest from your countrymen on a loan of money or of food or of anything else on which interest is usually demanded. 21 You may demand interest from a foreigner, but not from your countryman, so that the LORD, your God, may bless you in all your undertakings on the land you are to enter and occupy.

22 "When you make a vow to the LORD, your God, you shall not delay in fulfilling it; otherwise you will be held guilty, for the LORD, your God, is strict in requiring it of you. 23 Should you refrain from making a vow, you will not be held guilty. 24 But you must keep your solemn word and fulfill the votive offering you have freely promised to the LORD.

25 "When you go through your neighbor's vineyard, you may eat as many of his grapes as you wish, but do not put them in your basket. 26 When you go through your neighbor's grainfield, you may pluck some of the ears with your hand, but do not put a sickle to your neighbor's grain.

Marriage Laws

24 "When a man, after marrying a woman and having relations with her, is later displeased with her because he finds in her something indecent, and therefore he writes out a bill of divorce and hands it to her, thus dismissing her from his house: 2 if on leaving his house she goes and becomes the wife of another man, 3 and the second husband, too, comes to dislike her and dismisses her from his house by handing her a written bill of divorce; or if this second man who has married her, dies; 4 then her former husband, who dismissed her, may not again take her as his wife after she has become defiled. That would be an abomination before the LORD, and you shall not bring such guilt upon the land which the LORD, your God, is giving you as a heritage.

5 "When a man is newly wed, he

23, 1: *Father's wife:* stepmother. *Dishonor:* cf 27, 20.

23, 17: *In any one of your communities:* from this it would seem that the slave in question is a fugitive from a foreign country.

23, 18f: The pagans believed that they could enter into special relationship with their gods and goddesses by having sexual relations with the pagan priests and priestesses who prostituted themselves for this purpose. The money paid for this was considered a sort of votive offering made to the pagan sanctuary. Such abominations were naturally forbidden in Israel. *A dog's price:* the money paid to the pagan priest for his indecent service.

24, 1-4: This law is directly concerned only with forbidding divorced couples to remarry each other, and indirectly with checking hasty divorces, by demanding sufficient cause and certain legal formalities. Divorce itself is taken for granted and tolerated as an existing custom whose evils this law seeks to lessen. Cf 22, 19.29; Mal 2, 14ff. Christ gave the authentic interpretation of this law: "Moses, by reason of the hardness of your heart, permitted you to put away your wives; but it was not so from the beginning" (Mt 19, 8f).

24, 1: *Something indecent:* a rather indefinite phrase, meaning perhaps "immodest conduct." At the time of Christ the rabbis differed in opinion concerning the sufficient grounds for divorce; cf Mt 19, 3.

need not go out on a military expedition, nor shall any public duty be imposed on him. He shall be exempt for one year for the sake of his family, to bring joy to the wife he has married.

Justice, Equity and Charity

6 "No one shall take a hand mill or even its upper stone as a pledge for debt, for he would be taking the debtor's sustenance as a pledge.

7 "If any man is caught kidnaping a fellow Israelite in order to enslave him and sell him, the kidnaper shall be put to death. Thus shall you purge the evil from you midst.

8 "In an attack of leprosy you shall be careful to observe exactly and to carry out all the directions of the levitical priests. Take care to act in accordance with the instructions I have given them. 9 Remember what the LORD, your God, did to Miriam on the journey after you left Egypt.

10 "When you make a loan of any kind to your neighbor, you shall not enter his house to receive a pledge from him, 11 but shall wait outside until the man to whom you are making the loan brings his pledge outside to you. 12 If he is a poor man, you shall not sleep in the mantle he gives as a pledge, 13 but shall return it to him at sunset that he himself may sleep in it. Then he will bless you, and it will be a good deed of yours before the LORD, your God.

14 "You shall not defraud a poor and needy hired servant, whether he be one of your own countrymen or one of the aliens who live in your communities. 15 You shall pay him each day's wages before sundown on the day itself, since he is poor and looks forward to them. Otherwise he will cry to the LORD against you, and you will be held guilty.

16 "Fathers shall not be put to death for their children, nor children for their fathers; only for his own guilt shall a man be put to death.

17 "You shall not violate the rights of the alien or of the orphan, nor take the clothing of a widow as a pledge. 18 For, remember, you were once slaves in Egypt, and the LORD, your God, ransomed you from there; that is why I command you to observe this rule.

19 "When you reap the harvest in your field and overlook a sheaf there, you shall not go back to get it; let it be for the alien, the orphan or the widow, that the LORD, your God, may bless you in all your undertakings. 20 When you knock down the fruit of your olive trees, you shall not go over the branches a second time; let what remains be for the alien, the orphan and the widow. 21 When you pick your grapes, you shall not go over the vineyard a second time; let what remains be for the alien, the orphan, and the widow. 22 For remember that you were once slaves in Egypt; that is why I command you to observe this rule.

25 "When men have a dispute and bring it to court, and a decision is handed down to them acquitting the innocent party and condemning the guilty party, 2 if the latter deserves stripes, the judge shall have him lie down and in his presence receive the number of stripes his guilt deserves. 3 Forty stripes may be given him, but no more; lest, if he were beaten with more stripes than these, your kinsman should be looked upon as disgraced because of the severity of the beating.

4 "You shall not muzzle an ox when it is treading out grain.

Levirate Marriage

5 "When brothers live together and one of them dies without a son, the widow of the deceased shall not marry anyone outside the family; but her husband's brother shall go to her and perform the duty of a brother-in-law by marrying her. 6 The first-born son she bears shall continue the line of the deceased brother, that his name may not be blotted out from Israel. 7 If, however, a man does not care to marry his brother's wife, she shall go up to the elders at the gate and declare, 'My brother-in-law does not intend to perform his duty toward me and refuses to perpetuate his brother's name in Israel.' 8 Thereupon the elders of his city shall summon him and admonish him. If he persists in saying, 'I am not willing to marry her,' 9 his sister-in-law, in the presence of the elders, shall go up to him and strip his sandal from his foot and spit in his face, saying publicly, 'This is how one should be treated who will not build up his brother's family!' 10 And his lineage shall be spoken of in Israel as 'the family of the man stripped of his sandal.'

Various Precepts

11 "When two men are fighting and the wife of one intervenes to save her husband from the blows of his opponent, if she stretches out her hand and seizes the latter by his private parts, 12 you shall chop off her hand without pity.

13 "You shall not keep two differing weights in your bag, 14 one large and the other small; nor shall you keep two different measures in your house, one large and the other small. 15 But use a true and just weight, and a true and just measure, that you may have a long life on the land which the LORD, your God, is giving you. 16 Everyone who is dishonest in any of these matters is an abomination to the LORD, your God.

17 "Bear in mind what Amalek did to you on the journey after you

---

24, 6: Since the Israelites ground their grain into flour only in sufficient quantity for their current need, to deprive a debtor of his hand mill was virtually equivalent to condemning him to starve to death.

24, 10f: The debtor had the right to select the pledge that the creditor demanded as a guarantee for his loan.

25, 3: *Forty stripes:* a relatively mild punishment in ancient times. Later Jewish practice limited the number to thirty-nine; cf 2 Cor 11, 24.

25, 4: St. Paul argues from this verse that a laborer has the right to live on the fruits of his labor; cf

1 Cor 9, 9; 1 Tm 5, 18.

25, 5: *When brothers live together:* when relatives of the same clan, though married, hold their property in common. It was only in this case that the present law was to be observed, since one of its purposes was to keep the property of the deceased within the same clan. Such a marriage of a widow with her brother-in-law is known as a "levirate" marriage from the Latin word *levir*, meaning "a husband's brother."

25, 9f: The penalty decreed for a man who refuses to comply with this law of family loyalty is public disgrace (the widow is to *spit in his face*) and the curse

of poverty; sandals were proverbially a man's cheapest possession (cf Am 2, 6; 8, 6), and therefore "a man without sandals" was the poorest of the poor. Some commentators, however, connect this symbolic act with the ceremony mentioned in Ru 4, 7f.

25, 17-19: This attack on Israel by Amalek is not mentioned elsewhere in the Old Testament, although it probably was connected with the battle mentioned in Ex 17, 8. A campaign against Amalek was carried out by Saul; cf 1 Sm 15.

left Egypt, 18 how without fear of any god he harassed you along the way, weak and weary as you were, and cut off at the rear all those who lagged behind. 19 Therefore, when the LORD, your God, gives you rest from all your enemies round about in the land which he is giving you to occupy as your heritage, you shall blot out the memory of Amalek from under the heavens. Do not forget!

Thanksgiving for the Harvest

26 "When you have come into the land which the LORD, your God, is giving you as a heritage, and have occupied it and settled in it, 2 you shall take some first fruits of the various products of the soil which you harvest from the land which the LORD, your God, gives you, and putting them in a basket, you shall go to the place which the LORD, your God, chooses for the dwelling place of his name. 3 There you shall go to the priest in office at that time and say to him, 'Today I acknowledge to the LORD, my God, that I have indeed come into the land which he swore to our fathers he would give us.' 4 The priest shall then receive the basket from you and shall set it in front of the altar of the LORD, your God. 5 Then you shall declare before the LORD, your God, 'My father was a wandering Aramean who went down to Egypt with a small household and lived there as an alien. But there he became a nation great, strong and numerous. 6 When the Egyptians maltreated and oppressed us, imposing hard labor upon us, 7 we cried to the LORD, the God of our fathers, and he heard our cry and saw our affliction, our toil and our oppression. 8 He brought us out of Egypt with his strong hand and outstretched arm, with terrifying power, with signs and wonders; 9 and bringing us into this country, he gave us this land flowing with milk and honey. 10 Therefore, I have now brought you the first fruits of the products of the soil which you, O

LORD, have given me.' And having set them before the LORD, your God, you shall bow down in his presence. 11 Then you and your family, together with the Levite and the aliens who live among you, shall make merry over all these good things which the LORD, your God, has given you.

Prayer with the Tithes

12 "When you have finished setting aside all the tithes of your produce in the third year, the year of the tithes, and you have given them to the Levite, the alien, the orphan and the widow, that they may eat their fill in your own community, 13 you shall declare before the LORD, your God, 'I have purged my house of the sacred portion and I have given it to the Levite, the alien, the orphan and the widow, just as you have commanded me. In this I have not broken or forgotten any of your commandments: 14 I have not eaten any of the tithe as a mourner; I have not brought any of it out as one unclean; I have not offered any of it to the dead. I have thus hearkened to the voice of the LORD, my God, doing just as you have commanded me. 15 Look down, then, from heaven, your holy abode, and bless your people Israel and the soil you have given us in the land flowing with milk and honey which you promised on oath to our fathers.'

The Covenant

16 "This day the LORD, your God, commands you to observe these statutes and decrees. Be careful, then, to observe them with all your heart and with all your soul. 17 Today you are making this agreement with the LORD: he is to be your God and you are to walk in his ways and observe his statutes, commandments and decrees, and to hearken to his voice. 18 And today the LORD is making this agreement with you: you are to be a people peculiarly his own, as he promised you; and provided you keep all

his commandments, 19 he will then raise you high in praise and renown and glory above all other nations he has made, and you will be a people sacred to the LORD, your God, as he promised."

FINAL WORDS OF MOSES

Ceremonies

27 Then Moses, with the elders of Israel, gave the people this order: "Keep all these commandments which I enjoin on you today. 2 On the day you cross the Jordan into the land which the LORD, your God, is giving you, set up some large stones and coat them with plaster. 3 Also write on them, at the time you cross, all the words of this law, that you may thus enter into the land flowing with milk and honey, which the LORD, your God, and the God of your fathers, is giving you as he promised you. 4 When, moreover, you have crossed the Jordan, besides setting up on Mount Ebal these stones concerning which I command you today, and coating them with plaster, 5 you shall also build to the LORD, your God, an altar made of stones that no iron tool has touched. 6 You shall make this altar of the LORD, your God, with undressed stones, and shall offer on it holocausts to the LORD, your God. 7 You shall also sacrifice peace offerings and eat them there, making merry before the LORD, your God. 8 On the stones you shall inscribe all the words of this law very clearly."

9 Moses, with the levitical priests, then said to all Israel: "Be silent, O Israel, and listen! This day you have become the people of the LORD, your God. 10 You shall therefore hearken to the voice of the LORD, your God, and keep his commandments and statutes which I enjoin on you today."

11 That same day Moses gave the people this order: 12 "When you cross the Jordan, Simeon, Levi, Judah, Issachar, Joseph and Benjamin shall stand on Mount Gerizim to

26, 5: *Aramean:* either in reference to the origin of the patriarchs from Aram Naharaim (cf Gn 24, 10; 25, 20; 28, 5; 31, 20.24), or merely in the sense of "nomad," in the same way as "Arab" was later used;

cf Jer 3, 2.
26, 12: *And you have given them to the Levite, . . .:* as prescribed in 14, 28f.
26, 14: These are allusions to pagan religious

practices.
27, 8: *On the stones:* cf vv 3f; not the stones of the altar.

pronounce blessings over the people, 13 while Reuben, Gad, Asher, Zebulun, Dan and Naphtali shall stand on Mount Ebal to pronounce curses.

The Twelve Curses

14 "The Levites shall proclaim aloud to all the men of Israel: 15 'Cursed be the man who makes a carved or molten idol—an abomination to the LORD, the product of a craftsman's hands—and sets it up in secret!' And all the people shall answer, 'Amen!'

16 'Cursed be he who dishonors his father or his mother!' And all the people shall answer, 'Amen!'

17 'Cursed be he who moves his neighbor's landmarks!' And all the people shall answer, 'Amen!'

18 'Cursed be he who misleads a blind man on his way!' And all the people shall answer, 'Amen!'

19 'Cursed be he who violates the rights of the alien, the orphan or the widow!' And all the people shall answer, 'Amen!'

20 'Cursed be he who has relations with his father's wife, for he dishonors his father's bed!' And all the people shall answer, 'Amen!'

21 'Cursed be he who has relations with any animal!' And all the people shall answer, 'Amen!'

22 'Cursed be he who has relations with his sister or his half-sister!' And all the people shall answer, 'Amen!'

23 'Cursed be he who has relations with his mother-in-law!' And all the people shall answer, 'Amen!'

24 'Cursed be he who slays his neighbor in secret!' And all the people shall answer, 'Amen!'

25 'Cursed be he who accepts payment for slaying an innocent man!' And all the people shall answer, 'Amen!'

26 'Cursed be he who fails to fulfill any of the provisions of this law!' And all the people shall answer 'Amen!'

Blessings for Obedience

28 "Thus, then, shall it be: if you continue to heed the voice of the LORD, your God, and are careful to observe all his commandments which I enjoin on you today, the LORD, your God, will raise you high above all the nations of the earth. 2 When you hearken to the voice of the LORD, your God, all these blessings will come upon you and overwhelm you:

3 "May you be blessed in the city, and blessed in the country!

4 "Blessed be the fruit of your womb,
the produce of your soil and the offspring of your livestock,
the issue of your herds and the young of your flocks!
5 "Blessed be your grain bin and your kneading bowl!

6 "May you be blessed in your coming in,
and blessed in your going out!

Victory and Prosperity

7 "The LORD will beat down before you the enemies that rise up against you; though they come out against you from but one direction, they will flee before you in seven. 8 The LORD will affirm his blessing upon you, on your barns and on all your undertakings, blessing you in the land that the LORD, your God, gives you. 9 Provided that you keep the commandments of the LORD, your God, and walk in his ways, he will establish you as a people sacred to himself, as he swore to you; 10 so that, when all the nations of the earth see you bearing the name of the LORD, they will stand in awe of you. 11 The LORD will increase in more than goodly measure the fruit of your womb, the offspring of your livestock, and the produce of your soil, in the land which he swore to your fathers he would give you. 12 The LORD will open up for you his rich treasure house of the heavens, to give your land rain in due season, blessing all your undertakings, so that you will lend to many nations and borrow from none. 13 The LORD will make

you the head, not the tail, and you will always mount higher and not decline as long as you obey the commandments of the LORD, your God, which I order you today to observe carefully; 14 not turning aside to the right or to the left from any of the commandments which I now give you, in order to follow other gods and serve them.

Curses for Disobedience

15 "But if you do not hearken to the voice of the LORD, your God, and are not careful to observe all his commandments which I enjoin on you today, all these curses shall come upon you and overwhelm you:

16 "May you be cursed in the city, and cursed in the country!

17 "Cursed be your grain bin and your kneading bowl!
18 "Cursed be the fruit of your womb,
the produce of your soil and the offspring of your livestock,
the issue of your herds and the young of your flocks!

19 "May you be cursed in your coming in
and cursed in your going out!

Sickness and Defeat

20 "The LORD will put a curse on you, defeat and frustration in every enterprise you undertake, until you are speedily destroyed and perish for the evil you have done in forsaking me. 21 The LORD will bring a pestilence upon you that will persist until he has exterminated you from the land you are entering to occupy. 22 The LORD will strike you with wasting and fever, with scorching, fiery drought, with blight and searing wind, that will plague you until you perish. 23 The sky over your heads will be like bronze and the earth under your feet like iron. 24 For rain the LORD will give your land powdery dust, which will come down upon you from the sky until you are destroyed. 25 The LORD will let

---

27, 15–26: *Amen:* see note on Nm 5, 22.

28, 1–69: This chapter would read better immediately after chapter 26.

28, 6: *In your coming in . . . in your going out:* at the beginning and end of every action, or in all actions in general.

28, 7.25: *From but one direction . . . in seven:* in one compact mass, contrasted with many scattered groups.

28, 10: *You bearing the name of the Lord:* literally, "The LORD's name is called over you," an expression signifying ownership and protection. Cf 2 Sm 12, 28;

1 Kgs 8, 43; Is 4, 1; 63, 19; Jer 7, 10f; 14, 9; 15, 16; 25, 29; Am 9, 12.

28, 13: *The head, not the tail:* in the honorable position as leader. Cf Is 9, 14; 19, 15.

you be beaten down before your enemies; though you advance against them from one direction, you will flee before them in seven, so that you will become a terrifying example to all the kingdoms of the earth. 26 Your carcasses will become food for all the birds of the air and for the beasts of the field, with no one to frighten them off. 27 The LORD will strike you with Egyptian boils and with tumors, eczema and the itch, until you cannot be cured. 28 And the LORD will strike you with madness, blindness and panic, 29 so that even at midday you will grope like a blind man in the dark, unable to find your way.

Despoilment

"You will be oppressed and robbed continually, with no one to come to your aid. 30 Though you betroth a wife, another man will have her. Though you build a house, you will not live in it. Though you plant a vineyard, you will not enjoy its fruits. 31 Your ox will be slaughtered before your eyes, and you will not eat of its flesh. Your ass will be stolen in your presence, but you will not recover it. Your flocks will be given to your enemies, with no one to come to your aid. 32 Your sons and daughters will be given to a foreign nation while you look on and grieve for them in constant helplessness. 33 A people whom you do not know will consume the fruit of your soil and of all your labor, and you will be oppressed and crushed at all times without surcease, 34 until you are driven mad by what your eyes must look upon. 35 The LORD will strike you with malignant boils of which you cannot be cured, on your knees and legs, and from the soles of your feet to the crown of your head.

Exile

36 "The LORD will bring you, and your king whom you have set over you, to a nation which you and your fathers have not known, and there you will serve strange gods of wood and stone, 37 and will call forth amazement, reproach and barbed scorn from all the nations to which the LORD will lead you.

Fruitless Labors

38 "Though you spend much seed on your field, you will harvest but little, for the locusts will devour the crop. 39 Though you plant and cultivate vineyards, you will not drink or store up the wine, for the grubs will eat the vines clean. 40 Though you have olive trees throughout your country, you will have no oil for ointment, for your olives will drop off unripe. 41 Though you beget sons and daughters, they will not remain with you, but will go into captivity. 42 Buzzing insects will infest all your trees and the crops of your soil. 43 The alien residing among you will rise higher and higher above you, while you sink lower and lower. 44 He will lend to you, not you to him. He will become the head, you the tail.

45 "All these curses will come upon you, pursuing you and over-whelming you, until you are destroyed because you would not hearken to the voice of the LORD, your God, nor keep the commandments and statutes he gave you. 46 They will light on you and your descendants as a sign and a wonder for all time. 47 Since you would not serve the LORD, your God, with joy and gratitude for abundance of every kind, 48 therefore in hunger and thirst, in nakedness and utter poverty, you will serve the enemies whom the LORD will send against you. He will put an iron yoke on your neck, until he destroys you.

Invasion and Siege

49 "The LORD will raise up against you a nation from afar, from the end of the earth, that swoops down like an eagle, a nation whose tongue you do not understand, 50 a nation of stern visage, that shows neither respect for the aged nor pity for the young. 51 They will consume the offspring of your livestock and the produce of your soil, until you are destroyed; they will leave you no grain or wine or oil, no issue of your herds or young of your flocks, until they have brought about your ruin. 52 They will besiege you in each of your communities, until the great, unscalable walls you trust in come tumbling down all over your land. They will so besiege you in every community throughout the land which the LORD, your God, has given you, 53 that in the distress of the siege to which your enemy subjects you, you will eat the fruit of your womb, the flesh of your own sons and daughters whom the LORD, your God, has given you. 54 The most refined and fastidious man among you will begrudge his brother and his beloved wife and his surviving children 55 any share in the flesh of his children that he himself is using for food when nothing else is left him in the straits of the siege to which your enemy will subject you in all your communities. 56 The most refined and delicate woman among you, so delicate and refined that she would not venture to set the sole of her foot on the ground, will begrudge her beloved husband and her son and daughter 57 the afterbirth that issues from her womb and the infant she brings forth when she secretly uses them for food for want of anything else, in the straits of the siege to which your enemy will subject you in your communities.

Plagues

58 "If you are not careful to observe every word of the law which is written in this book, and to revere the glorious and awesome name of the LORD, your God, 59 he will smite you and your descendants with severe and constant blows, malignant and lasting maladies. 60 He will again afflict you with all the diseases of Egypt which you dread, and they will persist among you. 61 Should there be any kind of sickness or calamity not mentioned in this book of the law, that too the LORD will bring upon you until you are destroyed. 62 Of you who were numerous as the stars in the sky, only a few will be left, because you would not hearken to the voice of the LORD, your God.

28, 35: This verse is best read with v 27.
28, 46: *A sign and a wonder:* an ominous example, attracting attention; cf 29, 21–28.
28, 60: *He will again afflict you with all the diseases of Egypt:* such as the Lord had promised to remove from his people; cf 7, 15.

Exile

63 "Just as the LORD once took delight in making you grow and prosper, so will he now take delight in ruining and destroying you, and you will be plucked out of the land you are now entering to occupy. 64 The LORD will scatter you among all the nations from one end of the earth to the other, and there you will serve strange gods of wood and stone, such as you and your fathers have not known. 65 Among these nations you will find no repose, not a foot of ground to stand upon, for there the LORD will give you an anguished heart and wasted eyes and a dismayed spirit. 66 You will live in constant suspense and stand in dread both day and night, never sure of your existence. 67 In the morning you will say, 'Would that it were evening!' and in the evening you will say, 'Would that it were morning!' for the dread that your heart must feel and the sight that your eyes must see. 68 The LORD will send you back in galleys to Egypt, to the region I told you that you were never to see again; and there you will offer yourselves for sale to your enemies as male and female slaves, but there will be no buyer."

69 These are the words of the covenant which the LORD ordered Moses to make with the Israelites in the land of Moab, in addition to the covenant which he made with them at Horeb.

Past Favors Recalled

29 Moses summoned all Israel and said to them, "You have seen all that the LORD did in the land of Egypt before your very eyes to Pharaoh and all his servants and to all his land; 2 the great testings your own eyes have seen, and those great signs and wonders. 3 But not even at the present day has the LORD yet given you a mind to understand, or eyes to see, or ears to hear. 4 'I led you for forty years in the desert.

Your clothes did not fall from you in tatters nor your sandals from your feet; 5 bread was not your food, nor wine or beer your drink. Thus you should know that I, the LORD, am your God.' 6 When we came to this place, Sihon, king of Heshbon, and Og, king of Bashan, came out to engage us in battle, but we defeated them 7 and took over their land, which we then gave as a heritage to the Reubenites, Gadites, and half the tribe of Manasseh. 8 Keep the terms of this covenant, therefore, and fullfil them, that you may succeed in whatever you do.

All Israel Bound to the Covenant

9 "You are all now standing before the LORD, your God—your chiefs and judges, your elders and officials, and all of the men of Israel, 10 together with your wives and children and the aliens who live in your camp, down to those who hew wood and draw water for you 11 —that you may enter into the covenant of the LORD, your God, which he concluded with you today under this sanction of a curse; 12 so that he may now establish you as his people and he may be your God, as he promised you and as he swore to your fathers Abraham, Isaac and Jacob. 13 But it is not with you alone that I am making this covenant, under this sanction of a curse; 14 it is just as much with those who are not here among us today as it is with those of us who are now here present before the LORD, our God.

Warning against Idolatry

15 "You know in what surroundings we lived in the land of Egypt and what we passed by in the nations we traversed, 16 and you saw the loathsome idols of wood and stone, of gold and silver, that they possess. 17 Let there be, then, no man or woman, no clan or tribe among you who would now turn away their hearts from the LORD, our God, to go and serve these pagan gods!

Let there be no root that would bear such poison and wormwood among you! 18 If any such person, upon hearing the words of this curse, should beguile himself into thinking that he can safely persist in his stubbornness of heart, as though to sweep away both the watered soil and the parched ground, 19 the LORD will never consent to pardon him. Instead, the LORD's wrath and jealousy will flare up against that man, and every curse mentioned in this book will alight on him. The LORD will blot out his name from under the heavens 20 and will single him out from all the tribes of Israel for doom, in keeping with all the curses of the covenant inscribed in this book of the law.

Punishment for Infidelity

21 "Future generations, your own descendants who will rise up after you, as well as the foreigners who will come here from far-off lands, when they see the calamities of this land and the ills with which the LORD has smitten it 22 —and its soil being nothing but sulpher and salt, a burnt-out waste, unsown and unfruitful, without a blade of grass, destroyed like Sodom and Gomorrah, Admah and Zeboiim, which the LORD overthrew in his furious wrath 23 —they and all the nations will ask, 'Why has the LORD dealt thus with this land? Why this fierce outburst of wrath?' 24 And the answer will be, 'Because they forsook the covenant which the LORD, the God of their fathers, had made with them when he brought them out of the land of Egypt, 25 and they went and served other gods and adored them, gods whom they did not know and whom he had not let fall to their lot: 26 that is why the LORD was angry with this land and brought on it all the imprecations listed in this book; 27 in his furious wrath and tremendous anger the LORD uprooted them from their soil and cast them out into a strange land, where they are

---

28, 65: *Wasted eyes:* worn out and disappointed in their longing gaze.

28, 68: *In galleys:* in the ships of the Phoenician slave traders (Ez 27, 13; Jl 4, 6; Am 1, 9), who also dealt with Egypt (Is 23, 3).

29, 3: *Eyes to see . . . ears to hear:* with inner,

spiritual discernment. Cf Mt 13, 43.

29, 11: *Sanction of a curse:* the present pact binds under penalty of the curses mentioned in this book. Cf v 20.

29, 14: *Not here among us:* this includes their descendants.

29, 18: *To sweep away both the watered soil and the parched ground:* apparently a proverb signifying that such an unfaithful Israelite will cause God to punish the good with the wicked, to root out the good plants growing in irrigated soil, together with the worthless plants growing in the dry ground.

today.' 28 [Both what is still hidden and what has already been revealed concern us and our descendants forever, that we may carry out all the words of this law.]

Mercy for the Repentant

30 "When all these things which I have set before you, the blessings and the curses, are fulfilled in you, and from among whatever nations the LORD, your God, may have dispersed you, you ponder them in your heart: 2 then, provided that you and your children return to the LORD, your God, and heed his voice with all your heart and all your soul, just as I now command you, 3 the LORD, your God, will change your lot; and taking pity on you, he will again gather you from all the nations wherein he has scattered you. 4 Though you may have been driven to the farthest corner of the world, even from there will the LORD, your God, gather you; even from there will he bring you back. 5 The LORD, your God, will then bring you into the land which your fathers once occupied, that you too may occupy it, and he will make you more prosperous and numerous than your fathers. 6 The LORD, your God, will circumcise your hearts and the hearts of your descendants, that you may love the LORD, your God, with all your heart and all your soul, and so may live. 7 But all those curses the LORD, your God, will assign to your enemies and the foes who persecuted you. 8 You, however, must again heed the LORD's voice and carry out all his commandments which I now enjoin on you. 9 Then the LORD, your God, will increase in more than goodly measure the returns from all your labors, the fruit of your womb, the offspring of your livestock, and the produce of your soil; for the LORD, your God, will again take delight in your prosperity, even as he took delight in your fathers', 10 if only you heed the voice of the LORD, your God, and keep his commandments and statutes that are written in this book of the law, when you return to the LORD, your God, with all your heart and all your soul.

God's Command Clear

11 "For this command which I enjoin on you today is not too mysterious and remote for you. 12 It is not up in the sky, that you should say, 'Who will go up in the sky to get it for us and tell us of it, that we may carry it out?' 13 Nor is it across the sea, that you should say, 'Who will cross the sea to get it for us and tell us of it, that we may carry it out?' 14 No, it is something very near to you, already in your mouths and in your hearts: you have only to carry it out.

The Choice before Israel

15 "Here, then, I have today set before you life and prosperity, death and doom. 16 If you obey the commandments of the LORD, your God, which I enjoin on you today, loving him, and walking in his ways, and keeping his commandments, statutes and decrees, you will live and grow numerous, and the LORD, your God, will bless you in the land you are entering to occupy. 17 If, however, you turn away your hearts and will not listen, but are led astray and adore and serve other gods, 18 I tell you now that you will certainly perish; you will not have a long life on the land which you are crossing the Jordan to enter and occupy. 19 I call heaven and earth today to witness against you: I have set before you life and death, the blessing and the curse. Choose life, then, that you and your descendants may live, 20 by loving the LORD, your God, heeding his voice, and holding fast to him. For that will mean life for you, a long life for you to live on the land which the LORD swore he would give to your fathers Abraham, Isaac and Jacob."

The Lord's Leadership

31 When Moses had finished speaking these words to all Israel, 2 he said to them, "I am now one hundred and twenty years old and am no longer able to move about freely; besides, the LORD has told me that I shall not cross this Jordan. 3 It is the LORD, your God, who will cross before you; he will destroy these nations before you, that you may supplant them. [It is Joshua who will cross before you, as the LORD promised.] 4 The LORD will deal with them just as he dealt with Sihon and Og, the kings of the Amorites whom he destroyed, and with their country. 5 When, therefore, the LORD delivers them up to you, you must deal with them exactly as I have ordered you. 6 Be brave and steadfast; have no fear or dread of them, for it is the LORD, your God, who marches with you; he will never fail you or forsake you."

Call of Joshua

7 Then Moses summoned Joshua and in the presence of all Israel said to him, "Be brave and steadfast, for you must bring this people into the land which the LORD swore to their fathers he would give them; you must put them in possession of their heritage. 8 It is the LORD who marches before you; he will be with you and will never fail you or forsake you. So do not fear or be dismayed."

The Reading of the Law

9 When Moses had written down this law, he entrusted it to the levitical priests who carry the ark of the covenant of the LORD, and to all the elders of Israel, 10 giving them this order: "On the feast of Booths, at the prescribed time in the year of relaxation which comes at the end of every seven-year period, 11 when all Israel goes to appear before the LORD, your God, in the place which he chooses, you shall read this law aloud in the presence of all Israel.

29, 28: *What is still hidden:* the events of the future. *What has already been revealed:* God's law and the punishments in store for those who break it. Leave the future to God; our business is to keep his law.

30, 6: *Circumcise your hearts:* see note on 10, 16.

30, 11–14: God has revealed his will so clearly that ignorance of his law can be no excuse. St. Paul in Rom 10, 6–10, applies these words to the ease with which we can come to faith and salvation in Christ.

30, 14: *In your mouths:* that you may readily talk about it; cf 6, 7; 11, 19. *And in your hearts:* that you may easily remember it; cf 6, 6; 11, 18.

31, 10: *The year of relaxation:* cf 15, 1ff and the note there.

31, 11ff: Reading the law not only instructed the people but also consoled them by the assurance of the divine goodness.

12 Assemble the people—men, women and children, as well as the aliens who live in your communities—that they may hear it and learn it, and so fear the LORD, your God, and carefully observe all the words of this law. 13 Their children also, who do not know it yet, must hear it and learn it, that they too may fear the LORD, your God, as long as you live on the land which you will cross the Jordan to occupy.''

Commission of Joshua

14 The LORD said to Moses, "The time is now approaching for you to die. Summon Joshua, and present yourselves at the meeting tent that I may give him his commission." So Moses and Joshua went and presented themselves at the meeting tent. 15 And the LORD appeared at the tent in a column of cloud, which stood still at the entrance of the tent.

A Command to Moses

16 The LORD said to Moses, "Soon you will be at rest with your fathers, and then this people will take to rendering wanton worship to the strange gods among whom they will live in the land they are about to enter. They will forsake me and break the covenant which I have made with them. 17 At that time my anger will flare up against them; I will forsake them and hide my face from them, so that they will become a prey to be devoured, and many evils and troubles will befall them. At that time they will indeed say, 'Is it not because our God is not among us that these evils have befallen us?' 18 Yet I will be hiding my face from them at that time only because of all the evil they have done in turning to other gods. 19 Write out this song, then, for yourselves. Teach it to the Israelites and have them recite it, so that this song may be a witness for me against the Israelites. 20 For when I have brought them into the land flowing with milk and honey which I promised on oath to their fathers, and they have eaten their fill and grown fat, if they turn to

other gods and serve them, despising me and breaking my covenant; 21 then, when many evils and troubles befall them, this song, which their descendants will not have forgotten to recite, will bear witness against them. For I know what they are inclined to do even at the present time, before I have brought them into the land which I promised on oath to their fathers." 22 So Moses wrote this song that same day, and he taught it to the Israelites.

Commission of Joshua

23 Then the LORD commissioned Joshua, son of Nun, and said to him, "Be brave and steadfast, for it is you who must bring the Israelites into the land which I promised them on oath. I myself will be with you."

The Law Placed in the Ark

24 When Moses had finished writing out on a scroll the words of the law in their entirety, 25 he gave the Levites who carry the ark of the covenant of the LORD this order: 26 "Take this scroll of the law and put it beside the ark of the covenant of the LORD, your God, that there it may be a witness against you. 27 For I already know how rebellious and stiff-necked you will be. Why, even now, while I am alive and among you, you have been rebels against the LORD! How much more, then, after I am dead! 28 Therefore, assemble all your tribal elders and your officials before me, that I may speak these words for them to hear, and so may call heaven and earth to witness against them. 29 For I know that after my death you are sure to become corrupt and to turn aside from the way along which I directed you, so that evil will befall you in some future age because you have done evil in the LORD's sight, and provoked him by your deeds."

The Song of Moses

30 Then Moses recited the words of this song from beginning to end, for the whole assembly of Israel to hear:

A

32 Give ear, O heavens, while I
     speak;
  let the earth hearken to the
     words of my mouth!
2 May my instruction soak in like
     the rain,
  and my discourse permeate
     like the dew,
  Like a downpour upon the grass,
     like a shower upon the crops:

3 For I will sing the LORD's
     renown.
  Oh, procaim the greatness of
     our God!
4 The Rock—how faultless are his
     deeds,
  how right all his ways!
  A faithful God, without deceit,
     how just and upright he is!

5 Yet basely has he been treated
     by his degenerate children,
  a perverse and crooked race!
6 Is the LORD to be thus repaid by
     you,
  O stupid and foolish people?
  Is he not your father who
     created you?
  Has he not made you and
     established you?

7 Think back on the days of old,
     reflect on the years of age upon
     age.
  Ask your father and he will
     inform you,
  ask your elders and they will
     tell you:

8 When the Most High assigned
     the nations their heritage,
  when he parceled out the
     descendants of Adam,
  He set up the boundaries of the
     peoples
  after the number of the sons of
     God;
9 While the LORD's own portion
     was Jacob,
  His hereditary share was
     Israel.

10 He found them in a wilderness,
     a wasteland of howling
     desert.

31, 14f.23: V 23 is best read immediately after v 15; perhaps the original order was vv 7–8.14–15.23.

32, 1–43: In the style of the great prophets, the speaker is often God himself. The whole song is a poetic sermon, having for its theme God's benefits to

Israel (vv 1–14) and Israel's ingratitude and idolatry in turning to the gods of the pagans, which sins will be punished by the pagans themselves (vv 15–29); in turn, the foolish pride of the pagans will be punished, and the Lord's honor will be vindicated (vv 30–43).

32, 8: The sons of God: the angels; cf Jb 1, 6; 2, 1; 38, 7; Ps 89, 7f. Here the various nations are portrayed as having their respective guardian angels. Cf Dn 10, 20f; 12, 1.

He shielded them and cared for
    them,
    guarding them as the apple of
      his eye.

11 As an eagle incites its nestlings
    forth
    by hovering over its brood,
So he spread his wings to receive
    them
    and bore them up on his
      pinions.

12 The LORD alone was their leader,
    no strange god was with him.

13 He had them ride triumphant
    over the summits of the land
    and live off the products of its
      fields,
Giving them honey to suck from
    its rocks
    and olive oil from its hard,
      stony ground;

14 Butter from its cows and milk
    from its sheep,
    with the fat of its lambs and
      rams;
Its Bashan bulls and its goats,
    with the cream of its finest
      wheat;
    and the foaming blood of its
      grapes you drank.

B

15 [So Jacob ate his fill,]
    the darling grew fat and frisky;
    you became fat and gross and
      gorged.
They spurned the God who made
    them
    and scorned their saving Rock.

16 They provoked him with strange
    gods
    and angered him with
      abominable idols.

17 They offered sacrifice to demons,
    to "no-gods,"
    to gods whom they had not
      known before,
To newcomers just arrived,
    of whom their fathers had
      never stood in awe.

18 You were unmindful of the Rock
    that begot you,
    You forgot the God who gave
      you birth.

19 When the LORD saw this, he
    was filled with loathing
    and anger toward his sons and
      daughters.

20 "I will hide my face from them,"
    he said,
    "and see what will then become
      of them.
What a fickle race they are,
    sons with no loyalty in them!

21 "Since they have provoked me
    with their 'no-god'
    and angered me with their
      vain idols,
I will provoke them with a
    'no-people';
    with a foolish nation I will
      anger them.

22 "For by my wrath a fire is
    enkindled
    that shall rage to the depths
      of the nether world,
Consuming the earth with its
    yield,
    and licking with flames the
      roots of the mountains.

23 I will spend on them woe upon woe
    and exhaust all my arrows
      against them:

24 "Emaciating hunger and
    consuming fever
    and bitter pestilence,
And the teeth of wild beasts I
    will send among them,
    with the venom of reptiles
      gliding in the dust.

25 "Snatched away by the sword in
    the street
    and by sheer terror at home
Shall be the youth and the
    maiden alike,
    the nursing babe as well as
      the hoary old man.

26 "I would have said, 'I will make
    an end of them
    and blot out their name from
      men's memories,'

27 Had I not feared the insolence
    of their enemies,
    feared that these foes would
      mistakenly boast,
'Our own hand won the victory;
    the LORD had nothing to do
      with it.'"

28 For they are a people devoid of
    reason,
    having no understanding.

29 If they had insight they would
    realize what happened,
    they would understand their
      future and say,

C

30 "How could one man rout a
    thousand,
    or two men put ten thousand
      to flight,
Unless it was because their Rock
    sold them
    and the LORD delivered them
      up?"

31 Indeed, their "rock" is not like
    our Rock,
    and our foes are under
      condemnation.

32 They are a branch of Sodom's
    vinestock,
    from the vineyards of
      Gomorrah.
Poisonous are their grapes
    and bitter their clusters.

33 Their wine is the venom of
    dragons
    and the cruel poison of cobras.

34 "Is not this preserved in my
    treasury,
    sealed up in my storehouse,

35 Against the day of vengeance
    and requital,
    against the time they lose their
      footing?"
Close at hand is the day of their
    disaster,
    and their doom is rushing
      upon them!

36 Surely, the LORD shall do justice
    for his people;
    on his servants he shall have
      pity.
When he sees their strength
    failing,
    and their protected and
      unprotected alike
      disappearing,

37 He will say, "Where are their
    gods
    whom they relied on as their
      'rock'?

32, 13: *The Land:* Canaan.
32, 14: *Bashan:* a fertile grazing land east of the Jordan, famous for its strong cattle. Cf Ps 22, 13; Ez 39, 18; Am 4, 1.

32, 15: *The darling:* a probable meaning of the Hebrew word *yeshurun,* a term of endearment for "Israel." Cf 33, 5.26; Is 44, 2.
32, 28–35: The reference is to the pagan nations, not to Israel.

32, 36: *Their protected and unprotected:* the meaning of the Hebrew is uncertain; according to some, the idea is "slaves and freemen."

38 Let those who ate the fat of
      your sacrifices
  and drank the wine of your
      libations
  Rise up now and help you!
  Let them be your protection!

39 "Learn then that I, I alone, am
      God,
  and there is no god besides me.
  It is I who bring both death and
      life,
  I who inflict wounds and heal
      them,
  and from my hand there is no
      rescue.

40 "To the heavens I raise my hand
      and swear:
  As surely as I live forever,
41 I will sharpen my flashing
      sword,
  and my hand shall lay hold of
      my quiver.

  "With vengeance I will repay my
      foes
  and requite those who hate me.
42 I will make my arrows drunk
      with blood,
  and my sword shall gorge
      itself with flesh—
  With the blood of the slain and
      the captured,
  Flesh from the heads of the
      enemy leaders."

43 Exult with him, you heavens,
      glorify him, all you angels of
      God;
  For he avenges the blood of his
      servants
  and purges his people's land.

  44 So Moses, together with Joshua
son of Nun, went and recited all the
words of this song for the people to
hear.

Final Appeal

  45 When Moses had finished speaking all these words to all Israel, 46
he said, "Take to heart all the
warning which I have now given you
and which you must impress on your
children, that you may carry out
carefully every word of this law.
47 For this is no trivial matter for
you; rather, it means your very life,
since it is by this means that you are
to enjoy a long life on the land which
you will cross the Jordan to occupy."

Moses to View Canaan

  48 On that very day the LORD said
to Moses, 49 "Go up on Mount
Nebo, here in the Abarim Mountains
[it is in the land of Moab facing
Jericho], and view the land of Canaan,
which I am giving to the Israelites as
their possession. 50 Then you shall
die on the mountain you have climbed
and shall be taken to your people,
just as your brother Aaron died on
Mount Hor and there was taken to
his people; 51 because both of you
broke faith with me among the
Israelites at the waters of Meribath-
kadesh in the desert of Zin by failing
to manifest my sanctity among the
Israelites. 52 You may indeed view
the land at a distance, but you shall
not enter that land which I am giving
to the Israelites."

Blessing upon the Tribes

33 This is the blessing which
      Moses, the man of God,
pronounced upon the Israelites before he died. 2 He said:

  "The LORD came from Sinai
      and dawned on his people
          from Seir;
  He shone forth from Mount
      Paran
  and advanced from
      Meribath-kadesh,
  While at his right hand a fire
      blazed forth
  and his wrath devastated the
      nations.
3 But all his holy ones were in his
      hand;
  they followed at his feet
  and he bore them up on his
      pinions.

4 A law he gave to us;
  he made the community of
      Jacob his domain,
5   and he became king of his
      darling,
  When the chiefs of the people
      assembled
  and the tribes of Israel came
      together.

6 "May Reuben live and not die
      out,
  but let his men be few."

7 The following is for Judah. He
said:
  "The LORD hears the cry of
      Judah;
  you will bring him to his
      people.
  His own hands defend his cause
  and you will be his help against
      his foes."

8 Of Levi he said:
  "To Levi belong your Thummim,
  to the man of your favor your
      Urim;
  For you put him to the test at
      Massah
  and you contended with him
      at the waters of Meribah.
9 He said of his father, 'I regard
      him not';
  his brothers he would not
      acknowledge,
  and his own children he refused
      to recognize.
  Thus the Levites keep your
      words,
  and your covenant they
      uphold.
10 They promulgate your decisions
      to Jacob
  and your law to Israel
  They bring the smoke of
      sacrifice to your nostrils,
  and burnt offerings to your
      altar.
11 Bless, O LORD, his possessions
  and accept the ministry of his
      hands.
  Break the backs of his adversaries
  and of his foes, that they may
      not rise."

33, 2–5.26–29: These verses seem to form an
independent hymn describing, in the form of a
theophany, the conquest of Canaan. The first section
of this hymn (vv 2–5) serves here as an introduction to
the various "blessings"; the second section (vv 26–29),
as their conclusion.
  33, 3: *His holy ones were in his hand:* the Israelites
were protected by the Lord.

33, 5.26: *The darling:* see note on 32, 15.
33, 6: In keeping with the other blessings, probably this verse was once introduced by the phrase,
"Of Reuben he said." It is to be noted that there is no
blessing here for Simeon.
  33, 7: *Bring him to his people:* this probably refers
to the isolated position of the tribe of Judah during
the conquest of the Promised Land (cf Jgs 1, 17–19);

according to some commentators the reference is to
the divided kingdom.
  33, 8: *Thummim . . . Urim:* see note on Ex 28, 30.
  33, 9: The reference is probably to the Levites'
slaughter of their brethren after the affair of the golden
calf in the desert; cf Ex 32, 27–29.

12 Of Benjamin he said:
"Benjamin is the beloved of the
    LORD,
  who shelters him all the day,
  while he abides securely at his
    breast."

13 Of Joseph he said:
"Blessed by the LORD is his land
  with the best of the skies
    above
  and of the abyss crouching
    beneath;
14 With the best of the produce of
    the year,
  and the choicest sheaves of the
    months;
15 With the finest gifts of the
    age-old mountains
  and the best from the timeless
    hills;
16 With the best of the earth and
    its fullness,
  and the favor of him who
    dwells in the bush.
  These shall come upon the head
    of Joseph
  and upon the brow of the
    prince among his brothers,
17 The majestic bull, his father's
    first-born,
  whose horns are those of the
    wild ox
  With which to gore the nations
    even those at the ends of the
    earth."
  [These are the myriads of
    Ephraim,
  and these the thousands of
    Manasseh.]

18 Of Zebulun he said:
"Rejoice, O Zebulun, in your
    pursuits,
  and you, Issachar, in your
    tents!
19 You who invite the tribes to the
    mountains
  where feasts are duly held,
  Because you suck up the
    abundance of the seas
  and the hidden treasures of the
    sand."

20 Of Gad he said:
"Blessed be he who has made
    Gad so vast!
  He lies there like a lion
  that has seized the arm and
    head of the prey.
21 He saw that the best should be
    his
  when the princely portion
    was assigned,
  while the heads of the people
    were gathered.
  He carried out the justice of the
    LORD
  and his decrees respecting
    Israel."

22 Of Dan he said:
"Dan is a lion's whelp,
  that springs fourth from
    Bashan!"

23 Of Naphtali he said:
"Naphtali is enriched with
    favors
  and filled with the blessings of
    the LORD;
  The lake and south of it are
    his possession!"

24 Of Asher he said:
"More blessed than the other
    sons be Asher!
  May he be the favorite among
    his brothers,
  as the oil of his olive trees
    runs over his feet!
25 May your bolts be of iron and
    bronze;
  may your strength endure
    through all your days!"

26 "There is no god like the God
    of the darling,
  who rides the heavens in his
    power,
  and rides the skies in his
    majesty;
27 He spread out the primeval tent;
  he extended the ancient
    canopy.
  He drove the enemy out of your
    way
  and the Amorite he destroyed.

28 Israel has dwelt securely,
  and the fountain of Jacob has
    been undisturbed
  In a land of grain and wine,
  where the heavens drip with
    dew.
29 How fortunate you are, O
    Israel!
  Where else is a nation
    victorious in the LORD?
  The LORD is your saving shield,
  and his sword is your glory.
  Your enemies fawn upon you,
  as you stride upon their
    heights."

Death and Burial of Moses

34 Then Moses went up from the plains of Moab to Mount Nebo, the headland of Pisgah which faces Jericho, and the LORD showed him all the land—Gilead, and as far as Dan, 2 all Naphtali, the land of Ephraim and Manasseh, all the land of Judah as far as the Western Sea, 3 the Negeb, the circuit of the Jordan with the lowlands at Jericho, city of palms, and as far as Zoar. 4 The LORD then said to him, "This is the land which I swore to Abraham, Isaac and Jacob that I would give to their descendants. I have let you feast your eyes upon it, but you shall not cross over." 5 So there, in the land of Moab, Moses, the servant of the LORD, died as the LORD had said; 6 and he was buried in the ravine opposite Beth-poer in the land of Moab, but to this day no one knows the place of his burial. 7 Moses was one hundred and twenty years old when he died, yet his eyes were undimmed and his vigor unabated. 8 For thirty days the Israelites wept for Moses in the plains of Moab, till they had completed the period of grief and mourning for Moses.

9 Now Joshua, son of Nun, was filled with the spirit of wisdom, since Moses had laid his hands upon him; and so the Israelites gave him their

---

33, 16: *Him who dwells in the bush:* a title given to the Lord because of his appearance to Moses in the burning bush; cf Ex 3.

33, 19: *The abundance of the seas:* perhaps the wealth that comes from sea-borne trade or from fishing. *The hidden treasures of the sand:* possibly an allusion to the valuable purple dye extracted from certain marine shells found on the coast of northern Palestine.

33, 21: *The princely portion:* Moses gave the tribe of Gad their land on the east of the Jordan only on condition that they would help the other tribes conquer the land west of the river; cf Nm 32; Jos 22.

33, 22: The sense is, "May he leap up like a lion of Bashan"; the heavily wooded hills of Bashan were notorious for their lions, but the tribe of Dan was not settled in this region.

33, 23: *The lake:* The Lake of Gennesaret on which the land of this tribe bordered.

33, 24: The land of the tribe of Asher was covered with olive groves.

obedience, thus carrying out the LORD's command to Moses.

10 Since then no prophet has arisen in Israel like Moses, whom the LORD knew face to face. 11 He had no equal in all the signs and wonders the LORD sent him to perform in the land of Egypt against Pharaoh and all his servants and against all his land, 12 and for the might and the terrifying power that Moses exhibited in the sight of all Israel.

Joshua

CONQUEST OF CANAAN

Divine Promise of Assistance

AFTER Moses, the servant of the LORD, had died, the LORD said to Moses' aide Joshua, son of Nun: 2 "My servant Moses is dead. So prepare to cross the Jordan here, with all the people into the land I will give the Israelites. 3 As I promised Moses, I will deliver to you every place where you set foot. 4 Your domain is to be all the land of the Hittites, from the desert and from Lebanon east to the great river Euphrates and west to the Great Sea. 5 No one can withstand you while you live. I will be with you as I was with Moses: I will not leave you nor forsake you. 6 Be firm and steadfast, so that you may give this people possession of the land which I swore to their fathers I would give them. 7 Above all, be firm and steadfast, taking care to observe the entire law which my servant Moses enjoined on you. Do not swerve from it either to the right or to the left, that you may succeed wherever you go. 8 Keep this book of the law on your lips. Recite it by day and by night, that you may observe carefully all that is written in it; then you will successfully attain your goal. 9 I command you: be firm and steadfast! Do not fear nor be dismayed, for the LORD, your God, is with you wherever you go."

10 So Joshua commanded the officers of the people: 11 "Go through the camp and instruct the people, 'Prepare your provisions, for three days from now you shall cross the Jordan here, to march in and take possession of the land which the LORD, your God, is giving you.'"

The Transjordan Tribes

12 Joshua reminded the Reubenites, the Gadites, and the half-tribe of Manasseh: 13 "Remember what Moses, the servant of the LORD, commanded you when he said, 'The LORD, your God, will permit you to settle in this land.' 14 Your wives, your children, and your livestock shall remain in the land Moses gave you here beyond the Jordan. But all the warriors among you must cross over armed ahead of your kinsmen and you must help them 15 until the LORD has settled your kinsmen, and they like you possess the land which the LORD, your God, is giving them. Afterward you may return and occupy your own land, which Moses, the servant of the LORD, has given you east of the Jordan." 16 "We will do all you have commanded us," they answered Joshua, "and we will go wherever you send us. We will obey you as completely as we obeyed Moses. 17 But may the LORD, your God, be with you as he was with Moses. 18 If anyone rebels against your orders and does not obey every command you give him, he shall be put to death. But be firm and steadfast."

Spies Saved by Rahab

2 Then Joshua, son of Nun, secretly sent out two spies from Shittim, saying, "Go, reconnoiter the land and Jericho." When the two reached Jericho, they went into the house of a harlot named Rahab, where they lodged. 2 But a report was brought to the king of Jericho that some Israelites had come there that night to spy out the land. 3 So the king of Jericho sent Rahab the order,

---

1, 4: The ideal frontiers are given: in the south *the desert* of Sinai, in the north the *Lebanon* range, in the east the *Euphrates*, and in the west *the Great Sea*, the Mediterranean.

2, 1: *Harlot:* this is the regular equivalent of the Hebrew word, but perhaps it is used here of Rahab in the broader sense of a woman who kept a public house. Joshua's spies hoped to remain undetected at such an inn.

"Put out the visitors who have entered your house, for they have come to spy out the entire land." 4 The woman had taken the two men and hidden them, so she said, "True, the men you speak of came to me, but I did not know where they came from. 5 At dark, when it was time for the gate to be shut, they left, and I do not know where they went. You will have to pursue them immediately to overtake them." 6 Now, she had led them to the roof, and hidden them among her stalks of flax spread out there. 7 But the pursuers set out along the way to the fords of the Jordan, and once they had left, the gate was shut.

8 Before the spies fell asleep, Rahab came to them on the roof 9 and said: "I know that the LORD has given you the land, that a dread of you has come upon us, and that all the inhabitants of the land are overcome with fear of you. 10 For we have heard how the LORD dried up the waters of the Red Sea before you when you came out of Egypt, and how you dealt with Sihon and Og, the two kings of the Amorites beyond the Jordan, whom you doomed to destruction. 11 At these reports, we are disheartened; everyone is discouraged because of you, since the LORD, your God, is God in heaven above and on earth below. 12 Now then, swear to me by the LORD that, since I am showing kindness to you, you in turn will show kindness to my family; and give me an unmistakable token 13 that you are to spare my father and mother, brothers and sisters, and all their kin, and save us from death." 14 "We pledge our lives for yours," the men answered her. "If you do not betray this errand of ours, we will be faithful in showing kindness to you when the LORD gives us the land."

15 Then she let them down through the window with a rope; for she lived in a house built into the city wall. 16 "Go up into the hill country," she suggested to them, "that your pursuers may not find you. Hide there for three days, until they return; then you may proceed on your way." 17 The men answered her, "This is how we will fulfill the oath you made us take: 18 When we come into the land, tie this scarlet cord in the window through which you are letting us down; and gather your father and mother, your brothers and all your family into your house. 19 Should any of them pass outside the doors of your house, he will be responsible for his own death, and we shall be guiltless. But we shall be responsible if anyone in the house with you is harmed. 20 If, however, you betray this errand of ours, we shall be quit of the oath you have made us take." 21 "Let it be as you say," she replied, and bade them farewell. When they were gone, she tied the scarlet cord in the window.

22 They went up into the hills, where they stayed three days until their pursuers, who had sought them all along the road without finding them, returned. 23 Then the two came back down from the hills, crossed the Jordan to Joshua, son of Nun, and reported all that had befallen them. 24 They assured Joshua, "The LORD has delivered all this land into our power, indeed, all the inhabitants of the land are ovecome with fear of us."

Preparations for Crossing the Jordan

3 Early the next morning, Joshua moved with all the Israelites from Shittim to the Jordan, where they lodged before crossing over. 2 Three days later the officers went through the camp 3 and issued these instructions to the people: "When you see the ark of the covenant of the LORD, your God, which the levitical priests will carry, you must also break camp and follow it, 4 that you may know the way to take, for you have not gone over this road before. But let there be a space of two thousand cubits between you and the ark. Do not come nearer to it." 5 Joshua also said to the people, "Sanctify yourselves, for tomorrow the LORD will perform wonders among you." 6 And he directed the priests to take up the ark of the covenant and go on ahead of the people; and they did so.

7 Then the LORD said to Joshua, "Today I will begin to exalt you in the sight of all Israel, that they may know I am with you, as I was with Moses. 8 Now command the priests carrying the ark of the covenant to come to a halt in the Jordan when they reach the edge of the waters."

9 So Joshua said to the Israelites, "Come here and listen to the words of the LORD, your God." 10 He continued: "This is how you will know that there is a living God in your midst, who at your approach will dispossess the Canaanites, Hittites, Hivites, Perizzites, Girgashites, Amorites and Jebusites. 11 The ark of the covenant of the Lord of the whole earth will precede you into the Jordan. 12 [Now choose twelve men, one from each of the tribes of Israel.] 13 When the soles of the feet of the priests carrying the ark of the LORD, the Lord of the whole earth, touch the water of the Jordan, it will cease to flow; for the water flowing down from upstream will halt in a solid bank."

The Crossing Begun

14 The people struck their tents to cross the Jordan, with the priests carrying the ark of the covenant ahead of them. 15 No sooner had these priestly bearers of the ark waded into the waters at the edge of the Jordan, which overflows all its banks during the entire season of the harvest, 16 than the waters flowing from upstream halted, backing up in

---

2, 6: *Stalks of flax spread out:* to dry in the sun, after they had been soaked in water, according to the ancient process of preparing flax for linen-making. In the Near East the flax harvest occurs near the time of the feast of the Passover (4, 19; 5, 10); cf Ex 9, 31.

2, 8–11: Rahab's faith and good works are praised in the New Testament; cf Heb 11, 31; Jas 2, 25.

2, 15: *A house built into the city wall:* such houses, which used the city wall for their own inner walls, have been found at ancient sites. The upper story of

Rahab's house was evidently higher than the city wall. It was through the window of such a house that St. Paul escaped from Damascus; cf Acts 9, 25; 2 Cor 11, 33.

3, 15: *Season of the harvest:* toward the end of March and the beginning of April, when the grain and other crops that grew during the rainy season of winter were reaped. The crossing took place "on the tenth day of the first month" of the Hebrew year, which began with the first new moon after the spring

equinox; cf 4, 19. At this time of the year the Jordan would be swollen as a result of the winter rains and the melting snow of Mount Hermon.

3, 16: The sudden damming of the river could have been caused by a landslide, as has happened on other occasions. The miraculous character of this event would not thereby be removed because God, who foretold it (3, 13), also caused it to take place at precisely the right moment (3, 15), whether or not he used natural forces to accomplish his will.

a solid mass for a very great distance indeed, from Adam, a city in the direction of Zarethan; while those flowing downstream toward the Salt Sea of the Arabah disappeared entirely. Thus the people crossed over opposite Jericho. 17 While all Israel crossed over on dry ground, the priests carrying the ark of the covenant of the LORD remained motionless on dry ground in the bed of the Jordan until the whole nation had completed the passage.

Memorial Stones

4 After the entire nation had crossed the Jordan, the LORD said to Joshua, 2 "Choose twelve men from the people, one from each tribe, 3 and instruct them to take up twelve stones from this spot in the bed of the Jordan where the priests have been standing motionless. Carry them over with you, and place them where you are to stay tonight."

4 Summoning the twelve men whom he had selected from among the Israelites, one from each tribe, 5 Joshua said to them: "Go to the bed of the Jordan in front of the ark of the LORD, your God; lift to your shoulders one stone apiece, so that they will equal in number the tribes of the Israelites. 6 In the future, these are to be a sign among you. When your children ask you what these stones mean to you, 7 you shall answer them, 'The waters of the Jordan ceased to flow before the ark of the covenant of the LORD when it crossed the Jordan.' Thus these stones are to serve as a perpetual memorial to the Israelites." 8 The twelve Israelites did as Joshua had commanded: they took up as many stones from the bed of the Jordan as there were tribes of the Israelites, and carried them along to the camp site, where they placed them, according to the LORD's direction. 9 Joshua also had twelve stones set up in the bed of the Jordan on the spot where the priests stood who were carrying the ark of the covenant. They are there to this day.

10 The priests carrying the ark remained in the bed of the Jordan until everything had been done that the LORD had commanded Joshua to tell the people. The people crossed over quickly, 11 and when all had reached the other side, the ark of the LORD, borne by the priests, also crossed to its place in front of them. 12 The Reubenites, Gadites, and half-tribe of Manasseh, armed, marched in the vanguard of the Israelites, as Moses had ordered. 13 About forty thousand troops equipped for battle passed over before the LORD to the plains of Jericho.

14 That day the LORD exalted Joshua in the sight of all Israel, and thenceforth during his whole life they respected him as they had respected Moses.

15 Then the LORD said to Joshua, 16 "Command the priests carrying the ark of the commandments to come up from the Jordan." 17 Joshua did so, 18 and when the priests carrying the ark of the covenant of the LORD had come up from the bed of the Jordan, as the soles of their feet regained the dry ground, the waters of the Jordan resumed their course and as before overflowed all its banks.

19 The people came up from the Jordan on the tenth day of the first month, and camped in Gilgal on the eastern limits of Jericho. 20 At Gilgal Joshua set up the twelve stones which had been taken from the Jordan, 21 saying to the Israelites, "In the future, when the children among you ask their fathers what these stones mean, 22 you shall inform them, 'Israel crossed the Jordan here on dry ground.' 23 For the LORD, your God, dried up the waters of the Jordan in front of you until you crossed over, just as the LORD, your God, had done at the Red Sea, which he dried up in front of us until we crossed over; 24 in order that all the peoples of the earth may learn that the hand of the LORD is mighty, and that you may fear the LORD, your God, forever."

Rites at Gilgal

5 When the kings of the Amorites to the west of the Jordan and all the kings of the Canaanites by the sea heard that the LORD had dried up the waters of the Jordan before the Israelites until they crossed over, they were disheartened and lost courage at their approach.

2 On this occasion the LORD said to Joshua, "Make flint knives and circumcise the Israelite nation for the second time." 3 So Joshua made flint knives and circumcised the Israelites at Gibeath-haaraloth, 4 under the circumstances: Of all the people who came out of Egypt, every man of military age had died in the desert during the journey after they left Egypt. 5 Though all the men who came out were circumcised, none of those born in the desert during the journey after the departure from Egypt were circumcised. 6 Now the Israelites had wandered forty years in the desert, until all the warriors among the people that came forth from Egypt died off because they had not obeyed the command of the LORD. For the LORD swore that he would not let them see the land flowing with milk and honey which he had promised their fathers he would give us. 7 It was the children whom he raised up in their stead whom Joshua circumcised, for these were yet with foreskins, not having been circumcised on the journey. 8 When the rite had been performed, the whole nation remained in camp where they were, until they recovered. 9 Then the LORD said to Joshua, "Today I have removed the reproach of Egypt from you." Therefore the place is called Gilgal to the present day.

10 While the Israelites were encamped at Gilgal on the plains of Jericho, they celebrated the Passover on the evening of the fourteenth of the month. 11 On the day after the Passover they ate of the produce of the land in the form of unleavened cakes and parched grain. On that

---

4, 10–18: After the digression about the two sets of memorial stones, the author resumes the narrative by briefly repeating the story of the crossing, which he had already told in 3, 14–17.

5, 3: *Gibeath-haaraloth:* "Hill of the Foreskins."

5, 9: *The place is called Gilgal:* by popular etymology, because of the similarity of sound with the Hebrew word *gallōthi,* "I have removed." Gilgal probably means "(the place of) the circle of standing stones." Cf 4, 4–8.

5, 10: *The month:* the first month of the year, later called Nisan; see note of 3, 15. The crossing of the Jordan occurred, therefore, about the same time of the year as did the equally miraculous crossing of the Red Sea; cf Ex 12–14.

same day 12 after the Passover on which they ate of the produce of the land, the manna ceased. No longer was there manna for the Israelites, who that year ate of the yield of the land of Canaan.

Siege at Jericho

13 While Joshua was near Jericho, he raised his eyes and saw one who stood facing him, drawn sword in hand. Joshua went up to him and asked, "Are you one of us or of our enemies?" 14 He replied, "Neither, I am the captain of the host of the LORD and I have just arrived." Then Joshua fell prostrate to the ground in worship, and said to him, "What has my lord to say to his servant?" 15 The captain of the host of the LORD replied to Joshua, "Remove your sandals from your feet, for the place on which you are standing is holy." And Joshua obeyed.

6 Now Jericho was in a state of siege because of the presence of the Israelites, so that no one left or entered. 2 And to Joshua the LORD said, "I have delivered Jericho and its king into your power. 3 Have all the soldiers circle the city, marching once around it. Do this for six days, 4 with seven priests carrying ram's horns ahead of the ark. On the seventh day march around the city seven times, and have the priests blow the horns. 5 When they give a long blast on the ram's horns and you hear that signal, all the people shall shout aloud. The wall of the city will collapse, and they will be able to make a frontal attack."

6 Summoning the priests, Joshua, son of Nun, then ordered them to take up the ark of the covenant with seven of the priests carrying ram's horns in front of the ark of the LORD. 7 And he ordered the people to proceed in a circle around the city, with the picked troops marching ahead of the ark of the LORD. 8 At this order

they proceeded, with the seven priests who carried the ram's horns before the LORD blowing their horns, and the ark of the covenant of the LORD following them. 9 In front of the priests with the horns marched the picked troops; the rear guard followed the ark, and the blowing of horns was kept up continually as they marched. 10 But the people had been commanded by Joshua not to shout or make any noise or outcry until he gave the word: only then were they to shout. 11 So he had the ark of the LORD circle the city, going once around it, after which they returned to camp for the night.

12 Early the next morning, Joshua had the priests take up the ark of the LORD. 13 The seven priests bearing the ram's horns marched in front of the ark of the LORD, blowing their horns. Ahead of these marched the picked troops, while the rear guard followed the ark of the LORD, and the blowing of horns was kept up continually. 14 On this second day they again marched around the city once before returning to camp; and for six days in all they did the same.

15 On the seventh day, beginning at daybreak, they marched around the city seven times in the same manner; on that day only did they march around the city seven times. 16 The seventh time around, the priests blew the horns and Joshua said to the people, "Now shout, for the LORD has given you the city 17 and everything in it. It is under the LORD's ban. Only the harlot Rahab and all who are in the house with her are to be spared, because she hid the messengers we sent. 18 But be careful not to take, in your greed, anything that is under the ban; else you will bring upon the camp of Israel this ban and the misery of it. 19 All silver and gold, and the articles of bronze or iron, are sacred to the LORD. They shall be put in the treasury of the LORD."

The Fall of Jericho

20 As the horns blew, the people began to shout. When they heard the signal horn, they raised a tremendous shout. The wall collapsed, and the people stormed the city in a frontal attack and took it. 21 They observed the ban by putting to the sword all living creatures in the city: men and women, young and old, as well as oxen, sheep and asses.

22 Joshua directed the two men who had spied out the land, "Go into the harlot's house and bring out the woman with all her kin, as you swore to her you would do." 23 The spies entered and brought out Rahab, with her father, mother, brothers, and all her kin. Her entire family they led forth and placed them outside the camp of Israel. 24 The city itself they burned with all that was in it, except the silver, gold, and articles of bronze and iron, which were placed in the treasury of the house of the LORD. 25 Because Rahab the harlot had hidden the messengers whom Joshua had sent to reconnoiter Jericho, Joshua spared her with her family and all her kin, who continue in the midst of Israel to this day.

26 On that occasion Joshua imposed the oath. Cursed before the LORD be the man who attempts to rebuild this city, Jericho. He shall lose his first-born when he lays its foundation, and he shall lose his youngest son when he sets up its gates. 27 Thus the LORD was with Joshua so that his fame spread throughout the land.

Defeat at Ali

7 But the Israelites violated the ban; Achan, son of Carmi, son of Zerah, son of Zara of the tribe of Judah, took goods that were under the ban, and the anger of the LORD flared up against the Israelites.

2 Joshua next sent men from

5, 13—6, 26: The account of the siege of Jericho embraces: (1) The command of the Lord, through his angel to, Joshua (5, 13—6, 5); (2) Joshua's instructions to the Israelites, with a brief summary of how these orders were carried out (6, 6-11); (3) a description of the action on each of the first six days (6, 12-14); (4) the events on the seventh day (6, 15-26).

6, 18: *That is under the ban:* that is doomed to

destruction; see notes on Lv 27, 29; Nm 18, 14; 21, 3.

6, 20: *The wall collapsed:* by the miraculous intervention of God. The blowing of the horns and the shouting of the people were a customary feature of ancient warfare, here intended by God as a test of the people's obedience and of their faith in his promise; cf Heb 11, 30.

6, 25: From Mt 1, 5, we learn that Rahab married Salmon of the tribe of Judah and thus became the

great-great-grandmother of David, Christ's ancestor; cf Ru 4, 18–22.

6, 26: *He shall lose his first-born . . . its gates:* this curse was fulfilled when Hiel rebuilt Jericho as a fortified city during the reign of Ahab, king of Israel; cf 1 Kgs 16, 34. Till then Jericho was merely an unwalled village; cf Jos 18, 12.21; Jgs 3, 13; 2 Sm 10, 5.

Jericho to Ai, which is near Bethel on its eastern side, with instructions to go up and reconnoiter the land. When they had explored Ai, 3 they returned to Joshua and advised, "Do not send all the people up; if only about two or three thousand go up, they can overcome Ai. The enemy there are few; you need not call for an effort from all the people." 4 About three thousand of the people made the attack, but they were defeated by those at Ai, 5 who killed some thirty-six of them. They pressed them back across the clearing in front of the city gate till they broke ranks, and defeated them finally on the descent, so that the confidence of the people melted away like water.

6 Joshua, together with the elders of Israel, rent his garments and lay prostrate before the ark of the LORD until evening, and they threw dust on their heads. 7 "Alas, O Lord GOD," Joshua prayed, "why did you ever allow this people to pass over the Jordan, delivering us into the power of the Amorites, that they might destroy us? Would that we had been content to dwell on the other side of the Jordan. 8 Pray, Lord, what can I say, now that Israel has turned its back to its enemies? 9 When the Canaanites and the other inhabitants of the land hear of it, they will close in around us and efface our name from the earth. What will you do for your great name?"

10 The LORD replied to Joshua: "Stand up. Why are you lying prostrate? 11 Israel has sinned: they have violated the covenant which I enjoined on them. They have stealthily taken goods subject to the ban, and have deceitfully put them in their baggage. 12 If the Israelites cannot stand up to their enemies, but must turn their back to them, it is because they are under the ban. I will not remain with you unless you remove from among you whoever has incurred the ban. 13 Rise, sanctify the people. Tell them to sanctify themselves before tomorrow, for the LORD, the God of Israel, says: You are under the ban, O Israel. You cannot stand up to your enemies until you remove from among you whoever has incurred the ban. 14 In the morning you must present yourselves by tribes. The tribe which the LORD designates shall come forward by clans; the clan which the LORD designates shall come forward by families; the family which the LORD designates shall come forward one by one. 15 He who is designated as having incurred the ban shall be destroyed by fire, with all that is his, because he has violated the covenant of the LORD and has committed a shameful crime in Israel."

Achan's Guilt and Punishment

16 Early the next morning Joshua had Israel come forward by tribes, and the tribe of Judah was designated. 17 Then he had the clans of Judah come forward, and the clan of Zerah was designated. He had the clan of Zerah come forward by families, and Zabdi was designated. 18 Finally he had that family come forward one by one, and Achan, son of Carmi, son of Zabdi, son of Zerah of the tribe of Judah, was designated. Joshua said to Achan, 19 "My son, give to the LORD, the God of Israel, glory and honor by telling me what you have done; do not hide it from me." 20 Achan answered Joshua, "I have indeed sinned against the LORD, the God of Israel. This is what I have done: 21 Among the spoils, I saw a beautiful Babylonian mantle, two hundred shekels of silver, and a bar of gold fifty shekels in weight; in my greed I took them. They are now hidden in the ground inside my tent, with the silver underneath." 22 The messengers whom Joshua sent hastened to the tent and found them hidden there, with the silver underneath. 23 They took them from the tent, brought them to Joshua and all the Israelites, and spread them out before the LORD.

24 Then Joshua and all Israel took Achan, son of Zerah, with the silver, the mantle, and the bar of gold, and with his sons and daughters, his ox, his ass and his sheep, his tent, and all his possessions, and led them off to the Valley of Achor. 25 Joshua said, "The LORD bring upon you today the misery with which you have afflicted us!" And all Israel stoned him to death 26 and piled a great heap of stones over him, which remains to the present day. Then the anger of the LORD relented. That is why the place is called the Valley of Achor to this day.

Capture of Ai

8 The LORD then said to Joshua, "Do not be afraid or dismayed. Take all the army with you and prepare to attack Ai. I have delivered the king of Ai into your power, with his people, city, and land. 2 Do to Ai and its king what you did to Jericho and its king; except that you may take its spoil and livestock as booty. Set an ambush behind the city." 3 So Joshua and all the soldiers prepared to attack Ai. Picking out thirty thousand warriors, Joshua sent them off by night 4 with these orders: "See that you ambush the city from the rear, at no great distance; then all of you be on the watch. 5 The rest of the people and I will come up to the city, and when they make a sortie against us as they did the last time, we will flee from them. 6 They will keep coming out after us until we have drawn them away from the city, for they will think we are fleeing from them as we did the last time. When this occurs, 7 rise from ambush and take possession of the city, which the LORD, your God, will deliver into your power. 8 When you have taken the city, set it afire in obedience to the LORD's command. These are my orders to you." 9 Then Joshua sent them away. They went to the place of ambush, taking up their position to the west of Ai, towards Bethel. Joshua, however, spent that night in the plain.

7, 16ff: *Was designated:* probably by means of the Urim and Thummim; cf 1 Sm 14, 38–42. See note on Ex 28, 30.
7, 26: *Achor:* "misery, affliction." The reference is to the saying of Joshua in v 25, with an allusion also to the similar-sounding name of Achan.
8, 3: *Thirty thousand warriors:* this figure of the Hebrew text, which seems extremely high, may be due to a copyist's error; some manuscripts of the Septuagint have "three thousand," which is the number of the whole army in the first, unsuccessful attack (7, 4); the variant reading in v 12 mentions "five thousand."

10 Early the next morning Joshua mustered the army and went up to Ai at its head, with the elders of Israel. 11 When all the troops he led were drawn up in position before the city, they pitched camp north of Ai, on the other side of the ravine. 12 [He took about five thousand men and set them in ambush between Bethel and Ai, west of the city.] 13 Thus the people took up their stations, with the main body north of the city and the ambush west of it, and Joshua waited overnight among his troops. 14 The king of Ai saw this, and he and all his army came out very early in the morning to engage Israel in battle at the descent toward the Arabah, not knowing that there was an ambush behind the city. 15 Joshua and the main body of the Israelites fled in seeming defeat toward the desert, 16 till the last of the soldiers in the city had been called out to pursue them. 17 Since they were drawn away from the city, with every man engaged in this pursuit of Joshua and the Israelites, not a soldier remain in Ai [or Bethel], and the city was open and unprotected.

18 Then the LORD directed Joshua, "Stretch out the javelin in your hand toward Ai, for I will deliver it into your power." Joshua stretched out the javelin in his hand toward the city, 19 and as soon as he did so, the men in ambush rose from their post, rushed in, captured the city, and immediately set it on fire. 20 By the time the men of Ai looked back, the smoke from the city was already sky-high. Escape in any direction was impossible, because the Israelites retreating toward the desert now turned on their pursuers; 21 for when Joshua and the main body of Israelites saw that the city had been taken from ambush and was going up in smoke, they struck back at the men of Ai. 22 Since those in the city came out to intercept them, the men of Ai were hemmed in by Israelites on either side, who cut them down without any fugitives or survivors 23 except the king, whom they took alive and brought to Joshua.

24 All the inhabitants of Ai who had pursued the Israelites into the desert were slain by the sword there in the open, down to the last man. Then all Israel returned and put to the sword those inside the city. 25 There fell that day a total of twelve thousand men and women, the entire population of Ai. 26 Joshua kept the javelin in his hand stretched out until he had fulfilled the doom on all the inhabitants of Ai. 27 However, the Israelites took for themselves as booty the livestock and the spoil of that city, according to the command of the LORD issued to Joshua. 28 Then Joshua destroyed the place by fire, reducing it to an everlasting mound of ruins, as it remains today. 29 He had the king of Ai hanged on a tree until evening; then at sunset Joshua ordered the body removed from the tree and cast at the entrance of the city gate, where a great heap of stones was piled up over it, which remains to the present day.

Altar on Mount Ebal

30 Later Joshua built an altar to the LORD, the God of Israel, on Mount Ebal, 31 of unhewn stones on which no iron tool had been used, in keeping with the command to the Israelites of Moses, the servant of the LORD, as recorded in the book of the law. On this altar they offered holocausts and peace offerings to the LORD. 32 There, in the presence of the Israelites, Joshua inscribed upon the stones a copy of the law written by Moses. 33 And all Israel, stranger and native alike, with their elders, officers and judges, stood on either side of the ark facing the levitical priests who were carrying the ark of the covenant of the LORD. Half of them were facing Mount Gerizim and half Mount Ebal, thus carrying out the instructions of Moses, the servant of the LORD, for the blessing of the people of Israel on this first occasion. 34 Then were read aloud all the words of the law, the blessings and the curses, exactly as written in the book of the law. 35 Every single word that Moses had commanded, Joshua read aloud to the entire community, including the women and children, and the strangers who had accompanied Israel.

Confederacy against Israel

9 When the news reached the kings west of the Jordan, in the mountain regions and in the foothills, and all along the coast of the Great Sea as far as Lebanon: Hittites, Amorites, Canaanites, Perizzites, Hivites and Jebusites, 2 they all formed an alliance to launch a common attack against Joshua and Israel.

The Gibeonite Deception

3 On learning what Joshua had done to Jericho and Ai, the inhabitants of Gibeon 4 put into effect a device of their own. They chose provisions for a journey, making use of old sacks for their asses, and old wine-skins, torn and mended. 5 They wore old, patched sandals and shabby garments; and all the bread they took was dry and crumbly. 6 Thus they journeyed to Joshua in the camp at Gilgal, where they said to him and to the men of Israel, "We have come from a distant land to propose that you make an alliance with us." 7 But the men of Israel replied to the Hivites, "You may be living in land that is ours. How, then, can we make an alliance with you?" 8 But they answered Joshua, "We are your servants." Then Joshua asked them, "Who are you? Where do you come from?" 9 They answered him, "Your servants have come from a far-off land, because of the fame of the LORD, your God. For we have heard reports of all that he did in Egypt 10 and all that he did to the two kings of the Amorites beyond the Jordan, Sihon, king of Heshbon, and Og, king of Bashan, who lived in Ashtaroth. 11 So our elders and all the inhabitants of our country said to us, 'Take along provisions for the journey and go to meet them. Say to them: We are your servants; we propose that you make an alliance with us.' 12 This bread of ours was still warm when we brought it from home as provisions the day we left to come to you, but now it is dry and crumbled. 13

8, 30–35: These ceremonies were prescribed in Dt 11, 29 and 27, 2–26. See notes on those passages.
9, 7: The Hivites: apparently the Gibeonites belonged to this larger ethnic group (cf also 11, 19), although in 2 Sm 21, 2 they are classed as Amorites; both groups are listed among the seven nations in Canaan whom the Israelites were to exterminate; cf Dt 7, 1f.

Here are our wineskins, which were new when we filled them, but now they are torn. Look at our garments and sandals, which are worn out from the very long journey." 14 Then the Israelite princes partook of their provisions, without seeking the advice of the LORD. 15 So Joshua made an alliance with them and entered into an agreement to spare them, which the princes of the community sealed with an oath.

Gibeonites Made Vassals

16 Three days after the agreement was entered into, the Israelites learned that these people were from nearby, and would be living in Israel. 17 The third day on the road, the Israelites came to their cities of Gibeon, Chephirah, Beeroth and Kiriath-jearim. 18 but did not attack them, because the princes of the community had sworn to them by the LORD, the God of Israel. When the entire community grumbled against the princes, 19 these all remonstrated with the people, "We have sworn to them by the LORD, the God of Israel, and so we cannot harm them. 20 Let us therefore spare their lives and so deal with them that we shall not be punished for the oath we have sworn to them." 21 Thus the princes recommended that they be let live, as hewers of wood and drawers of water for the entire community; and the community did as the princes advised them.

22 Joshua summoned the Gibeonites and said to them, "Why did you lie to us and say that you lived at a great distance from us, when you will be living in our very midst? 23 For this are you accursed: every one of you shall always be a slave [hewers of wood and drawers of water] for the house of my God." 24 They answered Joshua, "Your servants were fully informed of how the LORD, your God, commanded his servant Moses that you be given the entire land and that all its inhabitants be destroyed

before you. Since, therefore, at your advance, we were in great fear for our lives, we acted as we did. 25 And now that we are in your power, do with us what you think fit and right." 26 Joshua did what he had decided: while he saved them from being killed by the Israelites, 27 at the same time he made them, as they still are, hewers of wood and drawers of water for the community and for the altar of the LORD, in the place of the LORD's choice.

The Siege of Gibeon

10 Now Adonizedek, king of Jerusalem, heard that, in the capture and destruction of Ai, Joshua had done to that city and its king as he had done to Jericho and its king. He heard also that the inhabitants of Gibeon had made their peace with Israel, remaining among them, 2 and that there was great fear abroad, because Gibeon was large enough for a royal city, larger even than the city of Ai, and all its men were brave. 3 So Adonizedek, king of Jerusalem, sent for Hoham, king of Hebron, Piram, king of Jarmuth, Japhia, king of Lachish, and Debir, king of Eglon, 4 to come to his aid for an attack on Gibeon, since it had concluded peace with Joshua and the Israelites. 5 The five Amorite kings of Jerusalem, Hebron, Jarmuth, Lachish and Eglon, united all their forces and marched against Gibeon, where they took up siege positions. 6 Thereupon, the men of Gibeon sent an appeal to Joshua in his camp at Gilgal: "Do not abandon your servants. Come up here quickly and save us. Help us, because all the Amorite kings of the mountain country have joined forces against us."

Joshua's Victory

7 So Joshua marched up from Gilgal with his picked troops and the rest of his soldiers. 8 Meanwhile the LORD said to Joshua, "Do not

fear them, for I have delivered them into your power. Not one of them will be able to withstand you." 9 And when Joshua made his surprise attack upon them after an all-night march from Gilgal, 10 the LORD threw them into disorder before him. The Israelites inflicted a great slaughter on them at Gibeon and pursued them down the Beth-horon slope, harassing them as far as Azekah and Makkedah.

11 While they fled before Israel along the descent from Beth-horon, the LORD hurled great stones from the sky above them all the way to Azekah, killing many. More died from these hailstones than the Israelites slew with the sword. 12 On this day, when the LORD delivered up the Amorites to the Israelites,

Joshua prayed to the LORD,
  and said in the presence of
    Israel:
Stand still, O sun, at Gibeon,
  O moon, in the valley of
    Aijalon!
13 And the sun stood still,
  and the moon stayed,
    while the nation took
      vengeance on its foes.

Is this not recorded in the Book of Jashar? The sun halted in the middle of the sky; not for a whole day did it resume its swift course. 14 Never before or since was there a day like this, when the LORD obeyed the voice of a man; for the LORD fought for Israel. 15 [Then Joshua and all Israel returned to the camp at Gilgal.]

Execution of Amorite Kings

16 Meanwhile the five kings who had fled, hid in a cave at Makkedah. 17 When Joshua was told that the five kings had been discovered hiding in a cave at Makkedah, he said, 18 "Roll large stones to the mouth of the cave and post men over it to guard them. 19 But do not remain there yourselves. Pursue your enemies, and

---

9, 21: *Hewers of wood and drawers of water:* proverbial terms for the lowest social class in the Israelite community; cf Dt 29, 10f.

9, 26f: Later on, Saul violated the immunity of the Gibeonites, but David vindicated it; cf 2 Sm 21, 1–9.

10, 5: *Hebron . . . Eglon:* these four cities were to the south and southwest of Jerusalem.

10, 11: *Great stones from the sky:* the hailstones

mentioned in the next sentence.

10, 13: *Is this not recorded:* the reference is to the preceding, poetic passage. Evidently the *Book of Jashar*, like the *Book of the Wars of the Lord* (Nm 21, 14), recounted in epic style the exploits of Israel's early heroes. *The sun halted:* though it is widely supposed that this passage describes in popular language and according to external appearances a

miraculous lengthening of the day, it is equally probable that Joshua's prayer was rather for an abrupt obscuration of the sun, which would impede his enemies in their flight homeward and also prevent them from rallying their forces; this request would have been answered by the hailstorm (cf Sir 46, 5) and by a darkness relieved only twenty-four hours later, well into the next day.

harry them in the rear. Do not allow them to escape to their cities, for the LORD, your God, has delivered them into your power."

20 Once Joshua and the Israelites had finally inflicted the last blows in this very great slaughter, and the survivors had escaped from them into the fortified cities, 21 all the army returned safely to Joshua and the camp at Makkedah, no man uttering a sound against the Israelites. 22 Then Joshua said, "Open the mouth of the cave and bring out those five kings to me." 23 Obediently, they brought out to him from the cave the five kings, of Jerusalem, Hebron, Jarmuth, Lachish and Eglon. 24 When they had done so, Joshua summond all the men of Israel and said to the commanders of the soldiers who had marched with him, "Come forward and put your feet on the necks of these kings." They came forward and put their feet upon their necks. 25 Then Joshua said to them, "Do not be afraid or dismayed, be firm and steadfast. This is what the LORD will do to all the enemies against whom you fight." 26 Thereupon Joshua struck and killed them, and hanged them on five trees, where they remained hanging until evening. 27 At sunset they were removed from the trees at the command of Joshua and cast into the cave where they had hidden; over the mouth of the cave large stones were placed, which remain until this very day.

Conquest of Southern Canaan

28 Makkedah, too, Joshua captured and put to the sword at that time. He fulfilled the doom on the city, on its king, and on every person in it, leaving no survivors. Thus he did to the king of Makkedah what he had done to the king of Jericho. 29 Joshua then passed on with all Israel from Makkedah to Libnah, which he attacked. 30 Libnah also, with its king, the LORD delivered into the power of Israel. He put it to the

sword with every person there, leaving no survivors. Thus he did to its king what he had done to the king of Jericho. 31 Joshua next passed on with all Israel from Libnah to Lachish, where they set up a camp during the attack. 32 The LORD delivered Lachish into the power of Israel, so that on the second day Joshua captured it and put it to the sword with every person in it, just as he had done to Libnah. 33 At that time Horam, king of Gezer, came up to help Lachish, but Joshua defeated him and his people, leaving him no survivors. 34 From Lachish, Joshua passed on with all Israel to Eglon; encamping near it, they attacked it 35 and captured it the same day, putting it to the sword. He fulfilled the doom that day on every person in it, just as he had done at Lachish. 36 From Eglon, Joshua went up with all Israel to Hebron, which they attacked 37 and captured. They put it to the sword with its king, all its towns, and every person there, leaving no survivors, just as Joshua had done to Eglon. He fulfilled the doom on it and on every person there. 38 Then Joshua and all Israel turned back to Debir and attacked it, 39 capturing it with its king and all its towns. They put them to the sword and fulfilled the doom on every person there, leaving no survivors. Thus was done to Debir and its king what had been done to Hebron, as well as to Libnah and its king.

40 Joshua conquered the entire country; the mountain regions, the Negeb, the foothills, and the mountain slopes, with all their kings. He left no survivors, but fulfilled the doom on all who lived there, just as the LORD, the God of Israel, had commanded. 41 Joshua conquered from Kadeshbarnea to Gaza, and all the land of Goshen to Gibeon. 42 All these kings and their lands Joshua captured in a single campaign, for the LORD, the God of Israel, fought for Israel. 43 Thereupon Joshua with all Israel returned to the camp at Gilgal.

Northern Confederacy

11 When Jabin, king of Hazor, learned of this, he sent a message to Jobab, king of Madon, to the king of Shimron, to the king of Achshaph, 2 and to the northern kings in the mountain regions and in the Arabah near Chinnereth, in the foothills, and in Naphath-dor to the west. 3 These were Canaanites to the east and west, Amorites, Hittites, Perizzites and Jebusites in the mountain regions, and Hivites at the foot of Hermon in the land of Mizpeh. 4 They came out with all their troops, an army numerous as the sands on the seashore, and with a multitude of horses and chariots. 5 All these kings joined forces and marched to the waters of Merom, where they encamped together to fight against Israel.

6 The LORD said to Joshua, "Do not fear them, for by this time tomorrow I will stretch them slain before Israel. You must hamstring their horses and burn their chariots." 7 Joshua with his whole army came upon them at the waters of Merom in a surprise attack. 8 The LORD delivered them into the power of the Israelites, who defeated them and pursued them to Greater Sidon, to Misrephoth-maim, and eastward to the valley of Mizpeh. They struck them all down, leaving no survivors. 9 Joshua did to them as the LORD had commanded: he hamstrung their horses and burned their chariots.

Conquest of Northern Canaan

10 At that time Joshua, turning back, captured Hazor and slew its king with the sword; for Hazor formerly was the chief of all those kingdoms. 11 He also fulfilled the doom by putting every person there to the sword, till none was left alive. Hazor itself he burned. 12 Joshua thus captured all those kings with their cities and put them to the sword, fulfilling the doom on them, as Moses, the servant of the LORD, had commanded. 13 However, Israel did

---

10, 41: *Goshen:* a town and its surrounding district at the southern end of the Judean mountains (cf 11, 16; 15, 51); not to be confused with the *land of Goshen* in northeastern Egypt (Gn 45, 10), although in the current Hebrew Bible both names are spelled the same.

11, 1ff: *Hazor, Madon, Shimron,* and *Chinnereth:* cities and their surrounding districts in eastern Galilee. *Achshaph* and *Naphath-dor:* southwest of Galilee. *The mountain regions:* in central and northern Galilee.

11, 5: *The waters of Merom:* a stream in central Galilee that flows southeast to water the fertile Arabah, or plain of Chinnereth on the western shore of the Lake of Gennesaret.

not destroy by fire any of the cities built on raised sites, except Hazor, which Joshua burned. 14 The Israelites took all the spoil and livestock of these cities as their booty; but the people they put to the sword, until they had exterminated the last of them, leaving none alive. 15 As the Lord had commanded his servant Moses, so Moses commanded Joshua, and Joshua acted accordingly. He left nothing undone that the Lord had commanded Moses should be done.

Survey of the Conquest

16 So Joshua captured all this land: the mountain regions, the entire Negeb, all the land of Goshen, the foothills, the Arabah, as well as the mountain regions and foothills of Israel, 17 from Mount Halak that rises toward Seir as far as Baal-gad in the Lebanon valley at the foot of Mount Hermon. All their kings he captured and put to death. 18 Joshua waged war against all these kings for a long time. 19 With the exception of the Hivites who lived in Gibeon, no city made peace with the Israelites; all were taken in battle. 20 For it was the design of the Lord to encourage them to wage war against Israel, that they might be doomed to destruction and thus receive no mercy, but be exterminated, as the Lord had commanded Moses.
21 At that time Joshua penetrated the mountain regions and exterminated the Anakim in Hebron, Debir, Anab, the entire mountain region of Judah, and the entire mountain region of Israel. Joshua fulfilled the doom on them and on their cities, 22 so that no Anakim were left in the land of the Israelites. However, some survived in Gaza, in Gath, and in Ashdod. 23 Thus Joshua captured the whole country, just as the Lord had foretold to Moses. Joshua gave it to Israel as their heritage, apportioning it among the tribes. And the land enjoyed peace.

Lists of Conquered Kings

12 The kings of the land east of the Jordan, from the River Arnon to Mount Hermon, including all the eastern section of the Arabah, whom the Israelites conquered and whose lands they occupied, were: 2 First, Sihon, king of the Amorites, who lived in Heshbon. His domain extended from Aroer, which is on the bank of the Wadi Arnon, to include the wadi itself, and the land northward through half of Gilead to the Wadi Jabbok, 3 as well as the Arabah from the eastern side of the Sea of Chinnereth, as far south as the eastern side of the Salt Sea of the Arabah in the direction of Beth-jeshimoth, to a point under the slopes of Pisgah. 4 Secondly, Og, king of Bashan, a survivor of the Rephaim, who lived at Ashtaroth and Edrei. 5 He ruled over Mount Hermon, Salecah, and all Bashan as far as the boundary of the Geshurites and Maacathites, and over half of Gilead as far as the territory of Sihon, king of Heshbon. 6 After Moses, the servant of the Lord, and the Israelites conquered them, he assigned their land to the Reubenites, the Gadites, and the half-tribe of Manasseh, as their property.
7 This is a list of the kings whom Joshua and the Israelites conquered west of the Jordan and whose land, from Baal-gad in the Lebanon valley to Mount Halak which rises toward Seir, Joshua apportioned to the tribes of Israel. 8 It included the mountain regions and foothills, the Arabah, the slopes, the desert, and the Negeb, belonging to the Hittites, Amorites, Canaanites, Perizzites, Hivites and Jebusites. 9 They were the kings of Jericho, Ai (which is near Bethel), 10 Jerusalem, Hebron, 11 Jarmuth, Lachish, 12 Eglon, Gezer, 13 Debir, Geder, 14 Hormah, Arad, 15 Libnah, Adullam, 16 Makkedah, Bethel, 17 Tappuah, Hepher, 18 Aphek, Lasharon, 19 Madon, Hazor, 20 Shimron, Achshaph, 21 Taanach, Megiddo, 22 Kedesh, Jokneam (at Carmel), 23 and Dor (in Naphath-dor), the foreign king at Gilgal, 24 and the king of Tirzah: thirty-one kings in all.

DIVISION OF THE LAND

Division of Land Commanded

13 When Joshua was old and advanced in years, the Lord said to him: "Though now you are old and advanced in years, a very large part of the land still remains to be conquered. 2 This additional land includes all Geshur and all the districts of the Philistines 3 (from the stream adjoining Egypt to the boundary of Ekron in the north is reckoned Canaanite territory, though held by the five lords of the Philistines in Gaza, Ashdod, Ashkelon, Gath and Ekron); also where the Avvim are in the south; 4 all the land of the Canaanites from Mearah of the Sidonians to Aphek, and the boundaries of the Amorites; 5 and the Gebalite territory; and all the Lebanon on the east, from Baal-gad at the foot of Mount Hermon to Labo in the land of Hamath. 6 At the advance of the Israelites I will drive out all the Sidonian inhabitants of the mountain regions between Lebanon and Misrephoth-maim; at least include these areas in the division of the Israelite heritage, just as I have commanded you. 7 Now, therefore, apportion among the nine tribes and the half-tribe of Manasseh the land which is to be their heritage."

The Eastern Tribes

8 Now the other half of the tribe of Manasseh as well as the Reubenites and Gadites, had received their heritage which Moses, the servant of the Lord, had given them east of the Jordan: 9 from Aroer on the bank of the Wadi Arnon and the city in the wadi itself, through the tableland of Medeba and Dibon, 10 with the rest of the cities of Sihon,

---

11, 21ff: Most of the land assigned to the tribe of Judah was not conquered by it till the early period of the Judges. See note on Jgs 1, 1–36.
11, 23: *The land enjoyed peace:* of a limited and temporary nature. Many of the individual tribes had still to fight against the remaining Canaanites; cf 15, 13–17; 17, 12f. This verse forms the conclusion to the

first part of the book. Cf note on 12, 1–24.
12, 1–24: This chapter, inserted between the two principal parts of the book (chapters 1–11 and 13–21), resembles the lists of conquered cities which are inscribed on monuments of the Egyptian and Assyrian monarchs. Perhaps it was copied here from some such public Israelite record.

13, 2: *Geshur:* not to be confused with the large Aramaean district of the same name in Bashan (vv 11–13; Dt 3, 14); here it is a region to the south of the Philistine country, since vv 2–5 list the unconquered lands along the coast from south to north; cf also 1 Sm 27, 8.

king of the Amorites, who reigned in Heshbon, to the boundary of the Ammonites; 11 also Gilead and the territory of the Geshurites and Maacathites, all Mount Hermon, and all Bashan as far as Salecah, 12 the entire kingdom in Bashan of Og, a survivor of the Rephaim, who reigned at Ashtaroth and Edrei. Though Moses conquered and occupied these territories, 13 the Israelites did not dislodge the Geshurites and Maacathites, so that Geshur and Maacath survive in the midst of Israel to this day. 14 However, to the tribe of Levi Moses assigned no heritage since, as the LORD had promised them, the LORD, the God of Israel, is their heritage.

Reuben

15 What Moses gave to the Reubenite clans: 16 Their territory reached from Aroer, on the bank of the Wadi Arnon, and the city in the wadi itself, through the tableland about Medeba, 17 to include Heshbon and all its towns which are on the tableland, Dibon, Bamoth-baal, Beth-baal-meon, 18 Jahaz, Kedemoth, Mephaath, 19 Kiriathaim, Sibmah, Zereth-shahar on the knoll within the valley, 20 Beth-peor, the slopes of Pisgah, Beth-jeshimoth, 21 and the other cities of the tableland and, generally, of the kingdom of Sihon. This Amorite king, who reigned in Heshbon, Moses had killed, with his vassals, the princes of Midian, who were settled in the land: Evi, Rekem, Zur, Hur and Reba; 22 and among their slain followers the Israelites put to the sword also the soothsayer Balaam, son of Beor. 23 The boundary of the Reubenites was the bank of the Jordan. These cities and their villages were the heritage of the clans of the Reubenites.

Gad

24 What Moses gave to the Gadite clans: 25 Their territory included Jazer, all the cities of Gilead, and half the land of the Ammonites as far as Aroer, toward Rabbah 26 (that is, from Heshbon to Ramath-mizpeh and Betonim, and from Mahanaim to the boundary of Lodebar); 27 and in the Jordan valley: Beth-haram, Beth-nimrah, Succoth, Zaphon, the other part of the kingdom of Sihon, king of Heshbon, with the bank of the Jordan to the southeastern tip of the Sea of Chinnereth. 28 These cities and their villages were the heritage of the clans of the Gadites.

Manasseh

29 What Moses gave to the clans of the half-tribe of Manasseh: 30 Their territory included Mahanaim, all of Bashan, the entire kingdom of Og, king of Bashan, and all the villages of Jair, which are sixty cities in Bashan. 31 Half of Gilead, with Ashtaroth and Edrei, once the royal cities of Og in Bashan, fell to the descendants of Machir, son of Manasseh, for half the clans descended from Machir.

32 These are the portions which Moses gave when he was in the plains of Moab, beyond the Jordan east of Jericho. 33 However, Moses gave no heritage to the tribe of Levi, since the LORD himself, the God of Israel, is their heritage, as he promised.

The Western Tribes

14 Here follows the portions which the Israelites received in the land of Canaan. Eleazar the priest, Joshua, son of Nun, and the heads of families in the tribes of the Israelites determined 2 their heritage by lot, in accordance with the instructions the LORD had given through Moses concerning the remaining nine and a half tribes. 3 For to two and a half tribes Moses had already given a heritage beyond the Jordan; and though the Levites were given no heritage among the tribes, 4 the descendants of Joseph formed two tribes, Manasseh and Ephraim. The Levites themselves received no share of the land except cities to live in, with their pasture lands for the cattle and flocks.

5 Thus, in apportioning the land, did the Israelites carry out the instructions of the LORD to Moses.

Caleb's Portion

6 When the Judahites came up to Joshua in Gilgal, the Kenizzite Caleb, son of Jephunneh, said to him: "You know what the LORD said to the man of God, Moses, about you and me in Kadesh-barnea. 7 I was forty years old when the servant of the LORD, Moses, sent me from Kadesh-barnea to reconnoiter the land; and I brought back to him a conscientious report. 8 My fellow scouts who went up with me discouraged the people, but I was completely loyal to the LORD, my God. 9 On that occasion Moses swore this oath, 'The land where you have set foot shall become your heritage and that of your descendants forever, because you have been completely loyal to the LORD, my God.' 10 Now, as he promised, the LORD has preserved me while Israel was journeying through the desert, for the forty-five years since the LORD spoke thus to Moses; and although I am now eight-five years old, 11 I am still as strong today as I was the day Moses sent me forth, with no less vigor whether for war or for ordinary tasks. 12 Give me, therefore, this mountain region which the LORD promised me that day, as you yourself heard. True, the Anakim are there, with large fortified cities, but if the LORD is with me I shall be able to drive them out, as the LORD promised." 13 Joshua blessed Caleb, son of Jephunneh, and gave him Hebron as his heritage. 14 Therefore Hebron remains the heritage of the Kenizzite Caleb, son of Jephunneh, to the present day, because he was completely loyal to the LORD, the God of Israel. 15 Hebron was formerly called Kiriath-arba, for Arba, the greatest among the Anakim. And the land enjoyed peace.

Boundaries of Judah

15 The lot for the clans of the Judahite tribe fell in the extreme south toward the boundary of Edom, the desert of Zin in the Negeb. 2 The boundary there ran from the bay that forms the southern end of the Salt Sea, 3 southward below the pass of Akrabbim, across through Zin, up to a point south of Kadesh-barnea, across to Hezron, and up to Addar; from there, looping around Karka, 4 it crossed to Azmon and then joined the Wadi of Egypt before coming out at the sea. [This is your southern boundary.]

5 The eastern boundary was the Salt Sea as far as the mouth of the Jordan.

6 The northern boundary climbed from the bay where the Jordan meets the sea, up to Beth-hoglah, and ran north of Beth-arabah, up to Eben-Bohan-ben-Reuben. 7 Thence it climbed to Debir, north of the vale of Achor, in the direction of the Gilgal that faces the pass of Adummim, on the south side of the wadi; from there it crossed to the waters of En-shemesh and emerged at En-rogel. 8 Climbing again to the Valley of Ben-hinnom on the southern flank of the Jebusites [that is, Jerusalem], the boundary rose to the top of the mountain at the northern end of the Valley of Rephaim, which bounds the Valley of Hinnom on the west. 9 From the top of the mountain it ran to the fountain of waters of Neph-toah, extended to the cities of Mount Ephron, and continued to Baalah, or Kiriath-jearim. 10 From Baalah the boundary curved westward to Mount Seir and passed north of the ridge of Mount Jearim (that is, Chesalon); thence it descended to Beth-shemesh, and ran across to Timnah. 11 It then extended along the northern flank of Ekron, continued through Shikkeron, and across to Mount Baalah, thence to include Jabneel, before it came out at the sea. 12 The western boundary was the Great Sea and its coast. This was the complete boundary of the clans of the Judahites.

Conquest by Caleb

13 As the LORD had commanded, Joshua gave Caleb, son of Jephun-neh, a portion among the Judahites, namely, Kiriath-arba (Arba was the father of Anak), that is, Hebron. 14 And Caleb drove out from there the three Anakim, the descendants of Anak: Sheshia, Ahiman and Talmai. 15 From there he marched up against the inhabitants of Debir, which was formerly called Kiriath-sepher. 16 Caleb said, "I will give my daughter Achsah in marriage to the one who attacks Kiriath-sepher and captures it." 17 Othniel, son of Caleb's brother Kenaz, captured it, and so Caleb gave him his daughter Achsah in marriage. 18 On the day of her marriage to Othniel, she induced him to ask her father for some land. Then, as she alighted from the ass, Caleb asked her, "What is troubling you?" 19 She answered, "Give me an additional gift! Since you have assigned to me land in the Negeb, give me also pools of water." So he gave her the upper and the lower pools.

Cities of Judah

20 This is the heritage of the clans of the tribe of Judahites: 21 The cities of the tribe of the Judahites in the extreme southern district toward Edom were: Kabzeel, Eder, Jagur, 22 Kinah, Dimonah, Adadah, 23 Kedesh, Hazor and Ithnan; 24 Ziph, Telem, Bealoth, 25 Hazor-hadattah, and Kerioth-hezron (that is, Hazor); 26 Amam, Shema, Mo-ladah, 27 Hazar-gaddah, Heshmon, Beth-pelet, 28 Hazar, shual, Beer-sheba and Biziothiah; 29 Baalah, Iim, Ezem, 30 Eltolad, Chesil, Hor-mah, 31 Ziklag, Madmannah, San-sannah, 32 Lebaoth, Shilhim and En-rimmon; a total of twenty-nine cities with their villages.

33 In the foothills: Eshtaol, Zorah, Ashnah, 34 Zanoah, Engannim, Tappuah, Enam, 35 Jarmuth, Adul-lam, Socoh, Azekah, 36 Shaaraim, Adithaim, Gederah, and Gederoth-aim; fourteen cities and their villages. 37 Zenan, Hadashah, Migdalgad, 38 Dilean, Mizpeh, Joktheel, 39 Lachish, Bozkath, Eglon 40 Cab-bon, Lahmam, Chitlish, 41 Geder-oth, Beth-dagon, Naamah and Makkedah; sixteen cities and their villages. 42 Libnah, Ether, Ashan, 43 Iphtah, Ashnah, Nezib, 44 Kei-lah, Achzib and Maresha; nine cities and their villages. 45 Ekron and its towns and villages; 46 from Ekron to the sea, all the towns that lie alongside Ashdod, and their villages; 47 Ashdod and its towns and villages; Gaza and its towns and villages; as far as the Wadi of Egypt and the coast of the Great Sea.

48 In the mountain regions: Sha-mir, Jattir, Socoh, 49 Dannah, Kiri-ath-sannah (that is, Debir), 50 Anab, Eshtemoh, Anim, 51 Gosh-en, Holon and Giloh; eleven cities and their villages. 52 Arab, Du-mah, Eshan, 53 Janim, Beth-tap-puah, Aphekah, 54 Humtah, Kiriath-arba (that is, Hebron), and Zior; nine cities and their villages. 55 Maon, Carmel, Ziph, Juttah, 56 Jezreel, Jokdeam, Zanoah, 57 Kain, Gibbeah, Timnah; ten cities and their villages. 58 Halhul, Beth-zur, Gedor, 59 Maarath, Beth-anoth and Eltekon; six cities and their villages. Tekoa, Ephrathah (that is, Bethlehem), Peor, Etam, Kulom, Tatam, Zores, Karim, Gal-lim, Bether and Manoko; eleven cities and their villages. 60 Kiriath-baal (that is, Kiriath-jearim) and Rabbah; two cities and their villages.

61 In the desert: Beth-arabah, Middin, Secacah, 62 Nibshan, Ir-hamelah and En-gedi; six cities and their villages. 63 [But the Jebusites who lived in Jerusalem the Judahites could not drive out; so the Jebusites dwell in Jerusalem beside the Juda-hites to the present day.]

The Joseph Tribes

16 The lot that fell to the Josephites extended from the Jordan at Jericho to the waters of Jericho east of the desert; then the boundary went up from Jericho to the heights at Bethel. 2 Leaving Bethel for Luz, it crossed the ridge to the border of the Archites at Ataroth, 3 and descended westward to the border of the Japhletites, to that of the Lower Beth-horon, and to Gezer, ending thence at the sea.

15, 8: *The Valley of Ben-hinnom:* the southern limit of Jerusalem. *Ben-hinnom* means "son of Hinnom." The place was also called *Valley of Hinnom,* in Hebrew *gê-hinnom,* whence the word "Gehenna" is derived.

15, 17-19: The story of Othniel is told again in Jgs 1, 13-15; cf also Jgs 3, 9-11.

15, 20-62: This elaborate list of the cities of Judah was probably taken from a document made originally for administrative purposes; the cities are divided into four provincial districts, some of which have further subdivisions. For similar lists of the cities of Judah, cf 19, 2-7; 1 Chr 4, 28-32; Neh 11, 25-30. This list has suffered in transmission, so that the totals given in vv 32 and 36 are not exact, and some of the names are probably misspelled; many of the cities cannot be identified.

15, 33: *In the foothills:* see note on Dt 1, 7.

15, 61: *In the desert:* in the Jordan rift near the Dead Sea.

16, 1—17, 18: The boundaries and cities of Judah, the most important tribe, having been given, the land of the next most important group, the two Josephite tribes of Ephraim and Manasseh, is now described, though it was separated from Judah by the territories of Benjamin (18, 11-20) and Dan (19, 40-48).

16, 1-3: This line formed the southern boundary of Ephraim and the northern boundaries of Benjamin and of Dan.

Ephraim

4 Within the heritage of Manasseh and Ephraim, sons of Joseph, 5 the dividing line for the heritage of the clans of the Ephraimites ran from east of Ataroth-addar to Upper Beth-horon 6 and thence to the sea. From Michmethah on the north, their boundary curved eastward around Taanath-shiloh, and continued east of it to Janoah; 7 from there it descended to Ataroth and Naarah, and skirting Jericho, it ended at the Jordan. 8 From Tappuah the boundary ran westward to the Wadi Kanah and ended at the sea. This was the heritage of the clans of the Ephraimites, 9 including the villages that belonged to each city set aside for the Ephraimites within the territory of the Manassehites. 10 But they did not drive out the Canaanites living in Gezer, who live on within Ephraim to the present day, though they have been impressed as laborers.

Manasseh

17 Now as for the lot that fell to the tribe of Manasseh as the first-born of Joseph: since his eldest son, Machir, the father of Gilead, was a warrior, who had already obtained Gilead and Bashan, 2 the allotment was now made to the other descendants of Manasseh, the clans of Abiezer, Helek, Asriel, Shechem, Hepher and Shemida, the other male children of Manasseh, son of Joseph.

3 Furthermore, Zelophehad, son of Hepher, son of Gilead, son of Machir, son of Manasseh, had had no sons, but only daughters, whose names were Mahlah, Noah, Hoglah, Milcah, and Tirzah. 4 These presented themselves to Eleazar the priest, to Joshua, son of Nun, and to the princes, saying, "The Lord commanded Moses to give us a heritage among our kinsmen." So in obedience to the command of the Lord a heritage was given to each of them among their father's kinsmen. 5 Thus ten shares fell to Manasseh apart from the land of Gilead and Bashan beyond the Jordan, 6 since these female descendants of Manasseh received each a portion among his sons. The land of Gilead fell to the rest of the Manassehites.

7 Manasseh bordered on Asher. From Michmethath near Shechem, another boundary ran southward to include the natives of En-Tappuah, 8 because the district of Tappuah belonged to Manasseh, although Tappuah itself was an Ephraimite city on the border of Manasseh. 9 This same boundary continued down to the Wadi Kanah. The cities that belonged to Ephraim from among the cities in Manasseh were those to the south of that wadi; thus the territory of Manasseh ran north of the wadi and ended at the sea. 10 The land on the south belonged to Ephraim and that on the north to Manasseh; with the sea as their common boundary, they reached Asher on the north and Issachar on the east.

11 Moreover, in Issachar and in Asher Manasseh was awarded Beth-shean and its towns, Ibleam and its towns, Dor and its towns and the natives there, Endor and its towns and natives, Taanach and its towns and natives, and Megiddo and its towns and natives [the third is Naphath-dor]. 12 Since the Manassehites could not conquer these cities, the Canaanites persisted in this region. 13 When the Israelites grew stronger they impressed the Canaanites as laborers, but they did not drive them out.

Protest of Joseph Tribes

14 The descendants of Joseph said to Joshua, "Why have you given us only one lot and one share as our heritage? Our people are too many, because of the extent to which the Lord has blessed us." 15 Joshua answered them, "If you are too many, go up to the forest and clear out a place for yourselves there in the land of the Perizzites and Rephaim, since the mountain regions of Ephraim are so narrow." 16 For the Josephites said, "Our mountain regions are not enough for us; on the other hand, the Canaanites living in the valley region all have iron chariots, in particular those in Beth-shean and its towns, and those in the valley of Jezreel." 17 Joshua therefore said to Ephraim and Manasseh, the house of Joseph, "You are a numerous people and very strong. You shall have not merely one share, 18 for the mountain region which is now forest shall be yours when you clear it. Its adjacent land shall also be yours if, despite their strength and iron chariots, you drive out the Canaanites."

18 After they had subdued the land, the whole community of the Israelites assembled at Shiloh, where they set up the meeting tent.

The Seven Remaining Portions

2 Seven tribes among the Israelites had not yet received their heritage. 3 Joshua therefore said to the Israelites, "How much longer will you put off taking steps to possess the land which the Lord, the God of your fathers, has given you? 4 Choose three men from each of your tribes; I will commission them to begin a survey of the land, which they shall describe for purposes of inheritance. When they return to me 5 you shall divide it into seven parts. Judah is to retain its territory in the south, and the house of Joseph its territory in the north. 6 You shall bring here to me the description of the land in seven sections. I will then cast lots for you here before the Lord, our God. 7 For the Levites have no share among you, because the priesthood of the Lord is their heritage; while Gad, Reuben, and the half-tribe of Manasseh have already received the heritage east of the Jordan which Moses, the servant of the Lord, gave them."

8 When those who were to map out the land were ready for the journey, Joshua instructed them to survey the land, prepare a description of it, and return to him; then he would cast lots for them there before the Lord in Shiloh. 9 So they went through the land, listed its cities

---

16, 5: *The dividing lines:* separating Ephraim from Manasseh. Ephraim's northern border (v 5) is given in an east-to-west direction; its eastern border (v 6f) in a north-to-south direction.

17, 7: *Manasseh bordered on Asher:* only at the extreme northwestern section of Manasseh's territory. The boundary given in the following sentences (vv 7–10) is a more detailed description of the one

already mentioned in 16, 5ff, as separating Manasseh from Ephraim.

in writing in seven sections, and returned to Joshua in the camp at Shiloh. 10 Joshua then divided up the land for the Israelites into their separate shares, casting lots for them before the LORD in Shiloh.

Benjamin

11 One lot fell to the clans of the tribe of Benjaminites. The territory allotted them lay between the descendants of Judah and those of Joseph. 12 Their northern boundary began at the Jordan and went over the northern flank of Jericho, up westward into the mountains, till it reached the desert of Beth-aven. 13 From there it crossed over to the southern flank of Luz (that is, Bethel). Then it ran down to Ataroth-addar, on the mountaintop south of Lower Beth-horon. 14 For the western border, the boundary line swung south from the mountaintop opposite Beth-horon till it reached Kiriath-baal (that is, Kiriath-jearim), which city belonged to the Judahites. This was the western boundary. 15 The southern boundary began at the limits of Kiriath-jearim and projected to the spring at Nephtoah. 16 It went down to the edge of the mountain on the north of the Valley of Rephaim, where it faces the Valley of Ben-hinnom; and continuing down the Valley of Hinnom along the southern flank of the Jebusites, reached En-rogel. 17 Inclining to the north, it extended to En-shemesh, and thence to Geliloth, opposite the pass of Adummim. Then it dropped to Eben-Bohan-ben-Reuben, 18 across the northern flank of the Arabah overlook, down into the Arabah. 19 From there the boundary continued across the northern flank of Beth-hoglah and extended to the northern tip of the Salt Sea, at the southern end of the Jordan. 20 This was the southern boundary. The Jordan bounded it on the east. This

was how the heritage of the clans of the Benjaminites was bounded on all sides.

21 Now the cities belonging to the clans of the tribe of the Benjaminites were: Jericho, Beth-hoglah, Emek-keziz, 22 Beth-arabah, Zemaraim, Bethel, 23 Avvim, Parah, Ophrah, 24 Chephar-ammoni, Ophni and Geba; twelve cities and their villages. 25 Also Gibeon, Ramah, Beeroth, 26 Mizpeh, Chephirah, Mozah, 27 Rekem, Irpeel, Taralah, 28 Zela, Haeleph, the Jebusite city (that is, Jerusalem), Gibeah and Kiriath; fourteen cities and their villages. This was the heritage of the clans of Benjaminites.

Simeon

19 The second lot fell to Simeon. The heritage of the clans of the tribe of Simeonites lay within that of the Judahites. 2 For their heritage they received Beer-sheba, Shema, Moladah, 3 Hazar-shual, Balah, Ezem, 4 Eltolad, Bethul, Hormah, 5 Ziklag, Bethmar-caboth, Hazar-susah, 6 Beth-lebaoth and Sharuhen; thirteen cities and their villages. Also En-rimmon, Ether and Ashan; 7 four cities and their villages, 8 besides all the villages around these cities as far as Baalath-beer (that is, Ramoth-negeb). This was the heritage of the clans of the tribe of the Simeonites. 9 This heritage of the Simeonites was within the confines of the Judahites; for since the portion of the latter was too large for them, the Simeonites obtained their heritage within it.

Zebulun

10 The third lot fell to the clans of the Zebulunites. The limit of their heritage was at Sarid. 11 Their boundary went up west ... and through Mareal, reaching Dabbesheth and the wadi that is near Jokneam. 12 From Sarid eastward it ran to the

district of Chisloth-tabor, on to Daberath, and up to Japhia. 13 From there it continued eastward to Gath-hepher and to Eth-kazin, extended to Rimmon, and turned to Neah. 14 Skirting north of Hannathon, the boundary ended at the valley of Iphtahel. 15 Thus, with Kattath, Nathalal, Shimron, Idalah and Bethlehem, there were twelve cities and their villages 16 to comprise the heritage of the clans of the Zebulunites.

Issachar

17 The fourth lot fell to Issachar. The territory of the clans of the Issacharites 18 included Jezreel, Chesulloth, Shunem, 19 Hapharaim, Shion, Anaharath, 20 Rabbith, Kishion, Ebez, 21 Remeth, En-gannim, En-haddah and Beth-pazzez. 22 The boundary reached Tabor, Shahazumah and Beth-shemesh, ending at the Jordan. These sixteen cities and their villages 23 were the heritage of the clans of the Issacharites.

Asher

24 The fifth lot fell to the clans of the tribe of the Asherites. 25 Their territory included Helkath, Hali, Beten, Achshaph, 26 Allammelech, Amad and Mishal, and reached Carmel on the west, and Shihor-libnath. 27 In the other direction, it ran eastward of Beth-dagon, reached Zebulun and the valley of Iphtahel; then north of Beth-emek and Neiel, it extended to Cabul, 28 Mishal, Abdon, Rehob, Hammon and Kanah, near Greater Sidon. 29 Then the boundary turned back to Ramah and to the fortress city of Tyre; thence it cut back to Hosah and ended at the sea. Thus, with Mahalab, Achzib, 30 Ummah, Acco, Aphek and Rehob, there were twenty-two cities and their villages 31 to comprise the heritage of the clans of the tribe of the Asherites.

18, 12–20: Benjamin's *northern boundary* (vv 12f) corresponded to part of the southern boundary of Ephraim (16, 1f). Their *western border* (v 14) was the eastern border of Dan (cf 19, 40–47). Their *southern boundary* (vv 15–19) corresponded to part of the northern boundary of Judah (15, 6–9).
19, 10–16: Zebulun's territory was in the central section of the Plain of Esdraelon and of southern Galilee; it was bounded on the south by Manasseh, on the southeast by Issachar, on the northeast and

north by Naphtali, and on the west by Asher. The site of the later city of Nazareth was within its borders. *Bethlehem* of Zebulun was, of course, distinct from the city of the same name in Judah. *Twelve cities:* apparently seven of the names are missing from v 15, unless some of the places mentioned in vv 12–14 are to be included in the number.
19, 17–23: Issachar's land was on the eastern watershed of the Plain of Esdraelon, but also included the southeastern end of the Galilean mountains. It

was surrounded by Manasseh on the south and east, by Naphtali on the north, and by Zebulun on the west. *Jezreel* (v 18) dominated the plain to which it gave its name, the later form of which was Esdraelon.
19, 24–31: Asher inherited the western slope of the Galilean hills as far as the sea, with Manasseh to the south, Zebulun and Naphtali to the east, and Phoenicia to the north.

Naphtali

32 The sixth lot fell to the Naphtalites. The boundary of the clans of the Naphtalites 33 extended from Heleph, from the oak at Zaanannim to Lakkum, including Adaminekeb and Jabneel, and ended at the Jordan. 34 In the opposite direction, westerly, it ran through Aznoth-tabor and from there extended to Hukkok; it touched Zebulum on the south, Asher on the west, and the Jordan on the east. 35 The fortified cities were Ziddim, Zer, Hammath, Rakkath, Chinnereth, 36 Adamah, Ramah, Hazor, 37 Kedesh, Edrei, Enhazor, 38 Yiron, Migdal-el, Horem, Beth-anath and Beth-shemesh; nineteen cities and their villages, 39 to comprise the heritage of the clans of the tribe of the Naphtalites.

Dan

40 The seventh lot fell to the clans of the tribe of Danites. 41 Their heritage was the territory of Zorah, Eshtaol, Ir-shemesh, 42 Shaalabbin, Aijalon, Ithlah, 43 Elon, Timnah, Ekron, 44 Eltekoh, Gibbethon, Baalath, 45 Jehud, Bene-berak, Gath-rimmon, 46 Me-jarkon and Rakkon, with the coast at Joppa. 47 But the territory of the Danites was too small for them; so the Danites marched up and attacked Leshem, which they captured and put to the sword. Once they had taken possession of Leshem, they renamed the settlement after their ancestor Dan. 48 These cities and their villages were the heritage of the clans of the tribes of the Danites.

Joshua's City

49 When the last of them had received the portions of the land they were to inherit, the Israelites assigned a heritage in their midst to Joshua, son of Nun. 50 In obedience to the command of the LORD, they gave him the city which he requested, Timnah-serah in the mountain region of Ephraim. He rebuilt the city and made it his home.

51 These are the final portions into which Eleazar the priest, Joshua, son of Nun, and the heads of families in the tribes of the Israelites divided the land by lot in the presence of the LORD, at the door of the meeting tent in Shiloh.

Cities of Asylum

20 The LORD said to Joshua: 2 "Tell the Israelites to designate the cities of which I spoke to them through Moses, 3 to which one guilty of accidental and unintended homicide may flee for asylum from the avenger of blood. 4 To one of these cities the killer shall flee, and standing at the entrance of the city gate, he shall plead his case before the elders, who must receive him and assign him a place in which to live among them. 5 Though the avenger of blood pursues him, they are not to deliver up the homicide who slew his fellow man unintentionally and not out of previous hatred. 6 Once he has stood judgment before the community, he shall live on in that city till the death of the high priest who is in office at the time. Then the killer may go back home to his own city from which he fled."

List of Cities

7 So they set apart Kedesh in Galilee in the mountain region of Naphtali, Shechem in the mountain region of Ephraim, and Kiriath-arba (that is, Hebron) in the mountain region of Judah. 8 And beyond the Jordan east of Jericho they designated Bezer on the open tableland in the tribe of Reuben, Ramoth in Gilead in the tribe of Gad, and Golan in Bashan in the tribe of Manasseh. 9 These were the designated cities to which any Israelite or stranger living among them who had killed a person accidentally might flee to escape death at the hand of the avenger of blood, until he could appear before the community.

Levitical Cities

21 The heads of the Levite families came up to Eleazar the priest, to Joshua, son of Nun, and to the heads of families of the other tribes of the Israelites 2 at Shiloh in the land of Canaan, and said to them, "The LORD commanded, through Moses, that cities be given us to dwell in, with pasture lands for our livestock." 3 Out of their own heritage, in obedience to this command of the LORD, the Israelites gave the Levites the following cities with their pasture lands.

4 When the first lot among the Levites fell to the clans of the Kohathites, the descendants of Aaron the priest obtained thirteen cities by lot from the tribes of Judah, Simeon and Benjamin. 5 The rest of the Kohathites obtained ten cities by lot from the clans of the tribe of Ephraim, from the tribe of Dan, and from the half-tribe of Manasseh. 6 The Gershonites obtained thirteen cities by lot from the clans of the tribe of Issachar, from the tribe of Asher, from the tribe of Naphtali, and from the half-tribe of Manasseh. 7 The clans of the Merarites obtained twelve cities from the tribes of Reuben, Gad and Zebulun. 8 These cities with their pasture lands the Israelites allotted to the Levites in obedience to the LORD's command through Moses.

Cities of the Priests

9 From the tribes of the Judahites and Simeonites they designated the following cities, 10 and assigned them to the descendants of Aaron in the Kohathite clan of the Levites, since the first lot fell to them: 11 first, Kiriath-arba (Arba was the father of Anak), that is, Hebron, in the mountain region of Judah, with the adjacent pasture lands, 12 although the open country and villages belonging to the city had been given to Caleb, son of Jephunneh, as his property. 13 Thus to the descend-

---

19, 32–39: Naphtali received eastern Galilee; Asher was to the west and Zebulun and Issachar were to the south, while the upper Jordan and Mount Hermon formed the eastern border. Part of the tribe of Dan later on occupied the northern extremity of Naphtali's lands, at the sources of the Jordan (v 47).

19, 40–46: The original territory of Dan was a small enclave between Judah, Benjamin, Ephraim and the Philistines.

19, 47: *Leshem:* called *Laish* in Jgs 18, where the story of the migration of the Danites is told at greater length.

20, 1–9: The laws concerning the cities of refuge are given in Nm 35, 9–28; Dt 19, 1–13; see notes on Nm 35, 16–25; Dt 19, 2.

21, 1: The order to establish special cities for the

Levites is given in Nm 35, 1–8. The forty-eight cities listed here were hardly the exclusive possession of the Levites; at least the more important of them, such as Hebron, Shechem and Ramoth in Gilead, were certainly peopled for the most part by the tribe in whose territory they were situated. But in all these cities the Levites had special property rights which they did not possess in other cities; cf Lv 25, 32ff.

ants of Aaron the priest were given the city of asylum for homicides at Hebron, with its pasture lands; also, Libnah with its pasture lands, 14 Jattir with its pasture lands, Eshtemoa with its pasture lands, 15 Holon with its pasture lands, Debir with its pasture lands, 16 Ashan with its pasture lands, Juttah with its pasture lands, and Beth-shemesh with its pasture lands; nine cities from the two tribes mentioned. 17 From the tribe of Benjamin they obtained the four cities of Gibeon with its pasture lands, Geba with its pasture lands, 18 Anathoth with its pasture lands, and Almon with its pasture lands. 19 These cities which with their pasture lands belonged to the priestly descendants of Aaron, were thirteen in all.

Cities of the Other Kohathites

20 The rest of the Kohathite clans among the Levites obtained by lot, from the tribe of Ephraim, four cities. 21 They were assigned, with its pasture lands, the city of asylum for homicides at Shechem in the mountain region of Ephraim; also Gezer with its pasture lands, 22 Kibzaim with its pasture lands, and Bethhoron with its pasture lands. 23 From the tribe of Dan they obtained the four cities of Elteke with its pasture lands, Gibbethon with its pasture lands, 24 Aijalon with its pasture lands, and Gath-rimmon with its pasture lands; 25 and from the half-tribe of Manasseh the two cities of Taanach with its pasture lands and Ibleam with its pasture lands. 26 These cities which with their pasture lands belonged to the rest of the Kohathite clans were ten in all.

Cities of the Gershonites

27 The Gershonite clan of the Levites received from the half-tribe of Manasseh two cities: the city of asylum for homicides at Golan, with its pasture lands; and also Bethashtaroth with its pasture lands. 28 From the tribe of Issachar they obtained the four cities of Kishion with its pasture lands, Daberath with its pasture lands, 29 Jarmuth with its pasture lands, and En-gannim with its pasture lands; from the tribe

of Asher, 30 the four cities of Mischal with its pasture lands, Abdon with its pasture lands, 31 Helkath with its pasture lands, and Rehob with its pasture lands; 32 and from the tribe of Naphtali, three cities; the city of asylum for homicides at Kedesh in Galilee, with its pasture lands; also Hammath with its pasture lands, and Rakkath with its pasture lands. 33 These cities which with their pasture lands belonged to the Gershonite clans were thirteen in all.

Cities of the Merarites

34 The Merarite clans, the last of the Levites, received from the tribe of Zebulun the four cities of Jokneam with its pasture lands, Kartah with its pasture lands, 35 Rimmon with its pasture lands, and Nahalal with its pasture lands; 36 also across the Jordan, from the tribe of Reuben, four cities: the city of asylum for homicides at Bezer with its pasture lands, Jahaz with its pasture lands, 37 Kedemoth with its pasture lands, and Mephaath with its pasture lands; 38 and from the tribe of Gad a total of four cities: the city of asylum for homicides at Ramoth in Gilead with its pasture lands, also Mahanaim with its pasture lands, 39 Heshbon with its pasture lands, and Jazer with its pasture lands. 40 The cities which were allotted to the Merarite clans, the last of the Levites, were therefore twelve in all.

41 Thus the total number of cities within the territory of the Israelites which, with their pasture lands, belonged to the Levites, was forty-eight. 42 With each and every one of these cities went the pasture lands round about it.

43 And so the LORD gave Israel all the land he had sworn to their fathers he would give them. Once they had conquered and occupied it, 44 the LORD gave them peace on every side, just as he had promised their fathers. Not one of their enemies could withstand them; the LORD brought all their enemies under their power. 45 Not a single promise that the LORD made to the house of Israel was broken; every one was fulfilled.

RETURN OF THE TRANSJORDAN TRIBES AND JOSHUA'S FAREWELL

The Eastern Tribes Dismissed

22 At that time Joshua summoned the Reubenites, the Gadites, and the half-tribe of Manasseh 2 and said to them: "You have done all that Moses, the servant of the LORD, commanded you, and have obeyed every command I gave you. 3 For many years now you have not once abandoned your kinsmen, but have faithfully carried out the commands of the LORD, your God. 4 Since, therefore, the LORD, your God, has settled your kinsmen as he promised them, you may now return to your tents beyond the Jordan; to your own land, which Moses, the servant of the LORD, gave you. 5 But be very careful to observe the precept and law which Moses, the servant of the LORD, enjoined upon you: love the LORD, your God; follow him faithfully; keep his commandments; remain loyal to him; and serve him with your whole heart and soul." 6 Joshua then blessed them and sent them away to their own tents.

7 (For, to half the tribe of Manasseh Moses had assigned land in Bashan; and to the other half Joshua had given a portion along with their kinsmen west of the Jordan.) What Joshua said to them when he sent them off to their tents with his blessing was, 8 "Now that you are returning to your own tents with great wealth, with very numerous livestock, with silver, gold, bronze and iron, and with a very large supply of clothing, divide these spoils of your enemies with your kinsmen there." 9 So the Reubenites, the Gadites, and the half-tribe of Manasseh left the other Israelites at Shiloh in the land of Canaan and returned to the land of Gilead, their own property, which they had received according to the LORD's command through Moses.

The Altar beside the Jordan

10 When the Reubenites, the Gadites, and the half-tribe of Manasseh came to the region of the Jordan in the land of Canaan, they built there at the Jordan a conspicuously large

altar. 11 The other Israeilites heard the report that the Reubenites, the Gadites, and the half-tribe of Manasseh had built an altar in the region of the Jordan facing the land of Canaan, across from them, 12 and therefore they assembled their whole community at Shiloh to declare war on them.

Accusation of the Western Tribes

13 First, however, they sent to the Reubenites, the Gadites, and the half-tribe of Manasseh in the land of Gilead an embassy consisting of Phinehas, son of Eleazar the priest, 14 and ten princes, one from every tribe of Israel, each one being both prince and military leader of his ancestral house. 15 When these came to the Reubenites, the Gadites, and the half-tribe of Manasseh in the land of Gilead, they said to them: 16 "The whole community of the LORD sends this message: What act of treachery is this you have committed against the God of Israel? You have seceded from the LORD this day, and rebelled against him by building an altar of your own! 17 For the sin of Peor, a plague came upon the community of the LORD. 18 We are still not free of that; must you now add to it? You are rebelling against the LORD today and by to-morrow he will be angry with the whole community of Israel! 19 If you consider the land you now possess unclean, cross over to the land the LORD possesses, where the Dwelling of the LORD stands, and share that with us. But do not rebel against the LORD, nor involve us in rebellion, by building an altar of your own in addition to the altar of the LORD, our God. 20 When Achan, son of Zerah, violated the ban, did not wrath fall upon the entire community of Israel? Though he was but a single man, he did not perish alone for his guilt!"

Reply of the Eastern Tribes

21 The Reubenites, the Gadites, and the half-tribe of Manasseh replied to the military leaders of the Israelites: "The LORD is the God of gods. 22 The LORD, the God of gods, knows and Israel shall know. If now we have acted out of rebellion or treachery against the LORD, our God, 23 and if we have built an altar of our own to secede from the LORD, or to offer holocausts, grain offerings or peace offerings upon it, the LORD himself will exact the penalty, 24 We did it rather out of our anxious concern lest in the future your children should say to our children: 'What have you to do with the LORD, the God of Israel? 25 For the LORD has placed the Jordan as a boundary between you and us. You descendants of Reuben and Gad have no share in the LORD.' Thus your children would prevent ours from revering the LORD. 26 So we decided to guard our interests by building this altar of our own: not for holocausts or for sacrifices, 27 but as evidence for you on behalf of ourselves and our descendants, that we have the right to worship the LORD in his presence with our holocausts, sacrifices, and peace offerings. Now in the future your children cannot say to our children, 'You have no share in the LORD.' 28 Our thought was, that if in the future they should speak thus to us or to our descendants, we could answer: 'Look at the model of the altar of the LORD which our fathers made, not for holocausts or for sacrifices, but to witness between you and us.' 29 Far be it from us to rebel against the LORD or to secede now from the LORD by building an altar for holocaust, grain offering, or sacrifice in addition to the altar of the LORD, our God, which stands before his Dwelling."

30 When Phinehas the priest and the princes of the community, the military leaders of the Israelites, heard what the Reubenites, the Gadites and the Manassehites had to say, they were satisfied, 31 Phinehas, son of Eleazar the priest, said to the Reubenites, the Gadites and the Manassehites, "Now we know that the LORD is with us. Since you have not committed this act of treachery against the LORD, you have kept the Israelites free from punishment by the LORD."

32 Phinehas, son of Eleazar the priest, and the princes returned from the Reubenites and the Gadites in the land of Gilead to the Israelites in the land of Canaan, and reported the matter to them. 33 The report satisfied the Israelites, who blessed God and decided against declaring war on the Reubenites and Gadites or ravaging the land they occupied.

34 The Reubenites and the Gadites gave the altar its name as a witness among them that the LORD is God.

Joshua's Final Plea

23 Many years later, after the LORD had given the Israelites rest from all their enemies round about them and when Joshua was old and advanced in years, 2 he summoned all Israel (including their elders, leaders, judges and officers) and said to them: "I am old and advanced in years. 3 You have seen all that the LORD, your God, has done for you against all these nations; for it has been the LORD, your God, himself who fought for you. 4 Bear in mind that I have apportioned among your tribes as their heritage the nations that survive [as well as those I destroyed] between the Jordan and the Great Sea in the west. 5 The LORD, your God, will drive them out and dislodge them

---

22, 11: *In the region of the Jordan facing the land of Canaan:* on the eastern side of the Jordan valley. The river itself formed the boundary between these eastern tribes and the rest of the tribes who lived in what was formerly Canaan—though the term *Canaan* could also be used of both sides of the Jordan valley (cf v 10). The Transjordan tribes naturally built their altar in their own territory.

22, 12: *To declare war on them:* the western Israel-ites considered this altar, which seemed to violate the customary unity of the sanctuary (cf Lv 17, 1–9;

Dt 12, 4–14), as a sign of secession and dangerous to national unity. The motives for the war were political as well as religious.

22, 19: *Unclean:* not sanctified by the Dwelling of the Lord.

22, 20: *Achan . . . did not perish alone:* his guilt caused the failure of the first attack on Ai (7, 4–23); this fact is adduced as an argument for the solidarity and mutual responsibility of all the Israelites.

22, 22: *The Lord, the God of gods:* the Hebrew, which cannot be adequately rendered in English here,

adds to the divine name Yahweh ("the LORD") two synonymous words for "God," *el* and *elohim.* The repetition of these three sacred words adds force to the protestations of fidelity and innocence.

22, 28: *To witness:* far from being destined to form a rival sanctuary, the *model of the altar* was intended by the eastern tribes solely as a means of teaching their children to be faithful to the one true sanctuary beyond the Jordan.

22, 34: The name of this altar was the Hebrew word for "witness," *ced.*

at your approach, so that you will take possession of their land as the LORD, your God, promised you. 6 Therefore strive hard to observe and carry out all that is written in the book of the law of Moses, not straying from it in any way, 7 or mingling with these nations while they survive among you. You must not invoke their gods, or swear by them, or serve them, or worship them, 8 but you must remain loyal to the LORD, your God, as you have been to this day. 9 At your approach the LORD has driven out large and strong nations, and to this day no one has withstood you. 10 One of you puts to flight a thousand, because it is the LORD, your God, himself who fights for you, as he promised you. 11 Take great care, however, to love the LORD, your God. 12 For if you ever abandon him and ally yourselves with the remnant of these nations while they survive among you, by intermarrying and intermingling with them, 13 know for certain that the LORD, your God, will no longer drive these nations out of your way. Instead they will be a snare and a trap for you, a scourge for your sides and thorns for your eyes, until you perish from this good land which the LORD, your God, has given you.

14 "Today, as you see, I am going the way of all men. So now acknowledge with your whole heart and soul that not one of all the promises the LORD, your God, made to you has remained unfulfilled. Every promise has been fulfilled for you, with not one single exception. 15 But just as every promise the LORD, your God, made to you has been fulfilled for you, so will he fulfill every threat, even so far as to exterminate you from this good land which the LORD, your God, has given you. 16 If you transgress the covenant of the LORD, your God, which he enjoined on you, serve other gods and worship them, the anger of the LORD will flare up against you and you will quickly perish from the good land which he has given you."

Reminder of the Divine Goodness

24 Joshua gathered together all the tribes of Israel at Shechem, summoning their elders, their leaders, their judges and their officers. When they stood in ranks before God, 2 Joshua addressed all the people: "Thus says the LORD, the God of Israel: In times past your fathers, down to Terah, father of Abraham and Nahor, dwelt beyond the River and served other gods. 3 But I brought your father Abraham from the region beyond the River and led him through the entire land of Canaan. I made his descendants numerous, and gave him Isaac. 4 To Isaac I gave Jacob and Esau. To Esau I assigned the mountain region of Seir in which to settle, while Jacob and his children went down to Egypt.

5 "Then I sent Moses and Aaron, and smote Egypt with the prodigies which I wrought in her midst. 6 Afterward I led you out of Egypt, and when you reached the sea, the Egyptians pursued your fathers to the Red Sea with chariots and horsemen. 7 Because they cried out to the LORD, he put darkness between your people and the Egyptians, upon whom he brought the sea so that it engulfed them. After you witnessed what I did to Egypt, and dwelt a long time in the desert, 8 I brought you into the land of the Amorites who lived east of the Jordan. They fought against you, but I delivered them into your power. You took possession of their land, and I destroyed them [the two kings of the Amorites] before you. 9 Then Balak, son of Zippor, king of Moab, prepared to war against Israel. He summoned Balaam son of Beor, to curse you; 10 but I would not listen to Balaam. On the contrary, he had to bless you and I saved you from him. 11 Once you crossed the Jordan and came to Jericho, the men of Jericho fought against you, but I delivered them also into your power. 12 And I sent the hornets ahead of you which drove them [the Amorites, Perizzites, Ca-

naanites, Hittites, Girgashites, Hivites and Jebusites] out of your way; it was not your sword or your bow.

13 "I gave you a land which you had not tilled and cities which you had not built, to dwell in; you have eaten of vineyards and olive groves which you did not plant.

14 "Now, therefore, fear the LORD and serve him completely and sincerely. Cast out the gods your fathers served beyond the River and in Egypt, and serve the LORD. 15 If it does not please you to serve the LORD, decide today whom you will serve, the gods your fathers served beyond the River or the gods of the Amorites in whose country you are dwelling. As for me and my household, we will serve the LORD."

Renewal of the Covenant

16 But the people answered, "Far be it from us to forsake the LORD for the service of other gods. 17 For it was the LORD, our God, who brought us and our fathers up out of the land of Egypt, out of a state of slavery. He performed those great miracles before our very eyes and protected us along our entire journey and among all the peoples through whom we passed. 18 At our approach the LORD drove out [all the peoples, including] the Amorites who dwelt in the land. Therefore we also will serve the LORD, for he is our God."

19 Joshua in turn said to the people, "You may not be able to serve the LORD, for he is a holy God; he is a jealous God who will not forgive your transgressions or your sins. 20 If, after the good he has done for you, you forsake the LORD and serve strange gods, he will do evil to you and destroy you."

21 But the people answered Joshua, "We will still serve the LORD." 22 Joshua therefore said to the people, "You are your own witnesses that you have chosen to serve the LORD." They replied, "We are, indeed!" 23 "Now, therefore, put away the strange gods that are

---

23, 14: *Going the way of all men:* drawing near to death, the inevitable goal of all; cf 1 Kgs 2, 1f.

23, 15: *Every threat:* mentioned especially in Dt 28, 15–68.

24, 2: *Beyond the River:* east of the Euphrates;

cf Gn 11, 28–31.

24, 12: *The hornets:* see note on Ex 23, 28.

24, 15: *The gods your fathers served:* Abraham's ancestors were polytheists.

24, 19: *You may not be able:* fidelity to God's

service is not easy, and therefore those who take such solemn obligations on themselves must be ever vigilant against human weakness.

among you and turn your hearts to the LORD, the God of Israel." 24 Then the people promised Joshua, "We will serve the LORD, our God, and obey his voice."

25 So Joshua made a covenant with the people that day and made statutes and ordinances for them at Shechem, 26 which he recorded in the book of the law of God. Then he took a large stone and set it up there under the oak that was in the sanctuary of the LORD. 27 And Joshua said to all the people, "This stone shall be our witness, for it has heard all the words which the LORD spoke to us. It shall be a witness against you, should you wish to deny your God." 28 Then Joshua dismissed the people, each to his own heritage.

Death of Joshua

29 After these events, Joshua, son of Nun, servant of the LORD, died at the age of a hundred and ten. 30 He was buried within the limits of his heritage at Timnath-serah in the mountain region of Ephraim north of Mount Gaash. 31 Israel served the LORD during the entire lifetime of Joshua and that of the elders who outlived Joshua and knew all that the LORD had done for Israel. 32 The bones of Joseph, which the Israelites had brought up from Egypt, were buried in Shechem in the plot of ground Jacob had bought from the sons of Hamor, father of Shechem, for a hundred pieces of money. This was a heritage of the descendants of Joseph. 33 When Eleazar, son of Aaron, also died, he was buried on the hill which had been given to his son Phinehas in the mountain region of Ephraim.

24, 32: *The bones of Joseph:* the mummified body of Joseph (Gn 50, 25f), which the Israelites took with them as they left Egypt (Ex 13, 19), was fittingly buried at the ancient city of Shechem, near the border between the two Josephite tribes of Ephraim and Manasseh.

Judges

PALESTINE AFTER THE DEATH OF JOSHUA

Pagan Survivors in Palestine

AFTER the death of Joshua the Israelites consulted the LORD, asking, "Who shall be first among us to attack the Canaanites and to do battle with them?" 2 The LORD answered, "Judah shall attack: I have delivered the land into his power." 3 Judah then said to his brother Simeon, "Come up with me into the territory allotted to me, and let us engage the Canaanites in battle. I will likewise accompany you into the territory allotted to you." So Simeon went with him.

4 When the forces of Judah attacked, the LORD delivered the Canaanites and Perizzites into their power, and they slew ten thousand of them in Bezek. 5 It was in Bezek that they came upon Adonibezek and fought against him. When they defeated the Canaanites and Perizzites, 6 Adonibezek fled. They set out in pursuit, and when they caught him, cut off his thumbs and his big toes. 7 At this Adonibezek said, "Seventy kings, with their thumbs and big toes cut off, used to pick up scraps under my table. As I have done, so has God repaid me." He was brought to Jerusalem, and there he died. 8 [The Judahites fought against Jerusalem and captured it, putting it to the sword; then they destroyed the city by fire.]

9 Afterward the Judahites went down to fight against the Canaanites who lived in the mountain region, in the Negeb, and in the foothills. 10 Judah also marched against the Canaanites who dwelt in Hebron, which was formerly called Kiriath-arba, and defeated Sheshai, Ahiman and Talmai. 11 From there they marched against the inhabitants of Debir, which was formerly called Kiriath-sepher. 12 And Caleb said, "I will give my daughter Achsah in marriage to the one who attacks Kiriath-sepher and captures it." 13 Othniel, son of Caleb's younger brother Kenaz, captured it; so Caleb gave him his daughter Achsah in marriage. 14 On the day of her marriage to Othniel she induced him to ask her father for some land. Then, as she alighted from the ass, Caleb asked her, "What is troubling you?"

15 "Give me an additional gift," she answered. "Since you have assigned land in the Negeb to me, give me also pools of water." So Caleb gave her the upper and the lower pool. 16 The descendants of the Kenite, Moses' father-in-law, came up with the Judahites from the city of palms to the desert at Arad [which is in the Negeb]. But they later left and settled among the Amalekites.

17 Judah then went with his brother Simeon, and they defeated the Canaanites who dwelt in Zephath. After having doomed the city to destruction, they renamed it Hormah. 18 Judah, however, did not occupy Gaza with its territory, Ashkelon with its territory, or Ekron with its territory. 19 Since the LORD was with Judah, he gained possession of the mountain region. Yet he could not dislodge those who lived on the plain, because they had iron chariots. 20 As Moses had commanded,

---

1, 1–36: This chapter summarizes events most of which occurred shortly after the death of Joshua. Perhaps because they were planned and inaugurated by him, they are also attributed to him in the last half of the preceding book (Jos 14—22).

1, 16: *Moses' father-in-law:* Reuel; cf Nm 10, 29–32 and note. *City of palms:* Jericho (cf Dt 34, 3) or a town in the Negeb.

Hebron was given to Caleb, who then drove from it the three sons of Anak.

21 The Benjaminites did not dislodge the Jebusites who dwelt in Jerusalem, with the result that the Jebusites live in Jerusalem beside the Benjaminites to the present day.

22 The house of Joseph, too, marched up against Bethel, and the LORD was with them. 23 The house of Joseph had a reconnaissance made of Bethel, which formerly was called Luz. 24 The scouts saw a man coming out of the city and said to him, "Show us a way into the city, and we will spare you." 25 He showed them a way into the city, which they then put to the sword; but they let the man and his whole clan go free. 26 He then went to the land of the Hittites, where he built a city and called it Luz, as it is still called.

27 Manasseh did not take possession of Beth-shean with its towns or of Taanach with its towns. Neither did he dislodge the inhabitants of Dor and its towns, those of Ibleam and its towns, or those of Megiddo and its towns. The Canaanites kept their hold in this district. 28 When the Israelites grew stronger, they impressed the Canaanites as laborers, but did not drive them out. 29 Similarly, the Ephraimites did not drive out the Canaanites living in Gezer, and so the Canaanites live in Gezer in their midst.

30 Zebulun did not dislodge the inhabitants of Kitron or those of Nahalol; the Canaanites live among them, but have become forced laborers.

31 Nor did Asher drive out the inhabitants of Acco or those of Sidon, or take possession of Mahaleb, Achzib, Helbib, Aphik or Rehob. 32 The Asherites live among the Canaanite natives of the land, whom they have not dislodged.

33 Naphtali did not drive out the inhabitants of Beth-shemesh or those of Beth-anath, and so they live among the Canaanite natives of the land. However, the inhabitants of Beth-

shemesh and Beth-anath have become forced laborers for them.

34 The Amorites hemmed in the Danites in the mountain region, not permitting them to go down into the plain. 35 The Amorites had a firm hold in Har-heres, Aijalon and Shaalbim, but as the house of Joseph gained the upper hand, they were impressed as laborers.

36 The territory of the Amorites extended from the Akrabbim pass to Sela and beyond.

Infidelities of the Israelites

2 An angel of the LORD went up from Gilgal to Bochim and said, "It was I who brought you up from Egypt and led you into the land which I promised on oath to your fathers. I said that I would never break my covenant with you, 2 but that you were not to make a pact with the inhabitants of this land, and you were to pull down their altars. Yet you have not obeyed me. What did you mean by this? 3 For now I tell you, I will not clear them out of your way; they shall oppose you and their gods shall become a snare for you."

4 When the angel of the LORD had made these threats to all the Israelites, the people wept aloud; 5 and so that place came to be called Bochim. They offered sacrifice there to the LORD.

6 When Joshua dismissed the people, each Israelite went to take possession of his own hereditary land. 7 The people served the LORD during the entire lifetime of Joshua, and of those elders who outlived Joshua and who had seen all the great work which the LORD had done for Israel. 8 Joshua, son of Nun, the servant of the LORD, was a hundred and ten years old when he died; 9 and they buried him within the borders of his heritage at Timnath-heres in the mountain region of Ephraim north of Mount Gaash.

10 But once the rest of that generation were gathered to their fathers, and a later generation arose

that did not know the LORD, or what he had done for Israel, 11 the Israelites offended the LORD by serving the Baals. 12 Abandoning the LORD, the God of their fathers, who had led them out of the land of Egypt, they followed the other gods of the various nations around them, and by their worship of these gods provoked the LORD.

13 Because they had thus abandoned him and served Baal and the Ashtaroth, 14 the anger of the LORD flared up against Israel, and he delivered them over to plunderers who despoiled them. He allowed them to fall into the power of their enemies round about whom they were no longer able to withstand. 15 Whatever they undertook, the LORD turned into disaster for them, as in his warning he had sworn he would do, till they were in great distress. 16 Even when the LORD raised up judges to deliver them from the power of their despoilers, 17 they did not listen to their judges, but abandoned themselves to the worship of other gods. They were quick to stray from the way their fathers had taken, and did not follow their example of obedience to the commandments of the LORD. 18 Whenever the LORD raised up judges for them, he would be with the judge and save them from the power of their enemies as long as the judge lived; it was thus the LORD took pity on their distressful cries of affliction under their oppressors. 19 But when the judge died, they would relapse and do worse than their fathers, following other gods in service and worship, relinquishing none of their evil practices or stubborn conduct.

20 In his anger toward Israel the LORD said, "Inasmuch as this nation has violated my covenant which I enjoined on their fathers, and has disobeyed me, 21 I for my part will not clear away for them any more of the nations which Joshua left when he died." 22 Through these nations the Israelites were to be made to prove whether or not they would keep

---

1, 21: According to Jos 18, 16, Jerusalem was assigned to the tribe of Benjamin. But it was not actually taken from the Jebusites until David captured it (2 Sm 5, 6–9) and made it his capital, outside the tribal organization.

2, 5: *Bochim:* the Hebrew word for "weepers."
2, 11: *Baals:* the chief god of the Canaanites and the Phoenicians was called "Baal," a word meaning "lord." He was honored by various titles, hence the plural form here, equivalent to "the pagan gods."

2, 13: *Ashtaroth:* the Canaanite Phoenician goddess of love and fertility was Astarte. The plural form used here refers to her various titles and images and is equivalent to "goddesses."

to the way of the Lord and continue in it as their fathers had done; 23 therefore the Lord allowed them to remain instead of expelling them immediately, or delivering them into the power of Israel.

3 The following are the nations which the Lord allowed to remain, so that through them he might try all those Israelites who had no experience of the battles with Canaan 2 [just to instruct, by training them in battle, those generations only of the Israelites who would not have had that previous experience]: 3 the five lords of the Philistines; and all the Canaanites, the Sidonians, and the Hivites who dwell in the mountain region of Lebanon between Baal-hermon and the entrance to Hamath. 4 These served to put Israel to the test, to determine whether they would obey the commandments the Lord had enjoined on their fathers through Moses. 5 Besides, the Israelites were living among the Canaanites, Hittites, Amorites, Perizzites, Hivites and Jebusites. 6 In fact, they took their daughters in marriage, and gave their own daughters to their sons in marriage, and served their gods.

STORIES OF THE JUDGES

Othniel

7 Because the Israelites had offended the Lord by forgetting the Lord, their God, and serving the Baals and the Asherahs, 8 the anger of the Lord flared up against them, and he allowed them to fall into the power of Cushan-rishathaim, king of Aram Naharaim, whom they served for eight years. 9 But when the Israelites cried out to the Lord, he raised up for them a savior, Othniel, son of Caleb's younger brother Kenaz, who rescued them. 10 The spirit of the Lord came upon him, and he judged Israel. When he went out to war, the Lord delivered Cushan-rishathaim, king of Aram, into his power, so that he made him subject. 11 The land then was at rest for forty years, until Othniel, son of Kenaz died.

Ehud

12 Again the Israelites offended the Lord, who because of this offence strengthened Eglon, king of Moab, against Israel. 13 In alliance with the Ammonites and Amalekites, he attacked and defeated Israel, taking possession of the city of palms. 14 The Israelites then served Eglon, king of Moab, for eighteen years.

15 But when the Israelites cried out to the Lord, he raised up for them a savior, the Benjaminite Ehud, son of Gera, who was left-handed. It was by him that the Israelites sent their tribute to Eglon, king of Moab. 16 Ehud made himself a two-edged dagger a foot long, and wore it under his clothes over his right thigh. 17 He presented the tribute to Eglon, king of Moab, who was very fat, 18 and after the presentation went off with the tribute bearers. 19 He returned, however, from where the idols are, near Gilgal, and said, "I have a private message for you, O king." And the king said, "Silence!" Then when all his attendants had left his presence, 20 and Ehud went in to him where he sat alone in his cool upper room, Ehud said, "I have a message from God for you." So the king rose from his chair, 21 and then Ehud with his left hand drew the dagger from his right thigh, and thrust it into Eglon's belly. 22 The hilt also went in after the blade, and the fat closed over the blade because he did not withdraw the dagger from his body.

23 Then Ehud went out into the hall, shutting the doors of the upper room on him and locking them. 24 When Ehud had left and the servants came, they saw that the doors of the upper room were locked, and thought, "He must be easing himself in the cool chamber." 25 They waited until they finally grew suspicious. Since he did not open the doors of the upper room, they took the key and opened them. There on the floor, dead, lay their lord!

26 During their delay Ehud made good his escape and, passing the idols, took refuge in Seirah. 27 On his arrival he sounded the horn in the mountain region of Ephraim, and the Israelites went down from the mountains with him as their leader. 28 "Follow me," he said to them, "for the Lord has delivered your enemies the Moabites into your power." So they followed him down and seized the fords of the Jordan leading to Moab, permitting no one to cross, 29 On that occasion they slew about ten thousand Moabites, all of them strong and valiant men. Not a man escaped. 30 Thus was Moab brought under the power of Israel at that time; and the land had rest for eighty years.

Shamgar

31 After him there was Shamgar, son of Anath, who slew six hundred Philistines with an oxgoad. He, too, rescued Israel.

Deborah and Barak

4 After Ehud's death, however, the Israelites again offended the Lord. 2 So the Lord allowed them to fall into the power of the Canaanite king, Jabin, who reigned in Hazor. The general of his army was Sisera, who dwelt in Harosheth-ha-goiim. 3 But the Israelites cried out to the Lord; for with his nine hundred iron chariots he sorely oppressed the Israelites for twenty years.

4 At this time the prophetess Deborah, wife of Lappidoth, was judging Israel. 5 She used to sit under Deborah's palm tree, situated between Ramah and Bethel in the mountain region of Ephraim, and there the Israelites came up to her for judgment. 6 She sent and summoned Barak, son of Abinoam, from Kedesh of Naphtali. "This is what the Lord, the God of Israel, commands," she said to him; "go, march on Mount Tabor, and take with you ten thousand Naphtalites and Zebulunites. 7 I will lead Sisera, the general of Jabin's army, out to you at the Wadi Kishon, together with his chariots and troops, and will deliver them into your power."

3, 3: *The Philistines:* non-Semitic invaders who gave their name to all Palestine, although they occupied only its southwestern plains. Their confederation embraced the five leading cities of Gaza, Ashkelon, Ashdod, Gath and Ekron.
3, 7: *Asherahs:* elsewhere rendered "sacred poles."

See note on Ex 34, 13; and on Dt 7, 5. Here the word seems to mean "goddesses."

8 But Barak answered her, "If you come with me, I will go; if you do not come with me, I will not go." 9 "I will certainly go with you," she replied, "but you shall not gain the glory in the expedition on which you are setting out, for the LORD will have Sisera fall into the power of a woman," So Deborah joined Barak and journeyed with him to Kedesh.

10 Barak summoned Zebulun and Naphtali to Kedesh, and ten thousand men followed him. Deborah also went up with him. 11 Now the Kenite Heber had detached himself from his own people, the descendants of Hobab, Moses' brother-in-law, and had pitched his tent by the terebinth of Zaanannim, which was near Kedesh.

12 It was reported to Sisera that Barak, son of Abinoam, had gone up to Mount Tabor, 13 So Sisera assembled from Harosheth-ha-goiim at the Wadi Kishon all nine hundred of his iron chariots and all his forces. 14 Deborah then said to Barak, "Be off, for this is the day on which the LORD has delivered Sisera into your power. The LORD marches before you." So Barak went down Mount Tabor, followed by his ten thousand men. 15 And the LORD put Sisera and all his chariots and all his forces to rout before Barak. Sisera himself dismounted from his chariot and fled on foot. 16 Barak, however, pursued the chariots and the army as far as Harosheth-ha-goiim. The entire army of Sisera fell beneath the sword, not even one man surviving.

17 Sisera, in the meantime, had fled on foot to the tent of Jael, wife of the Kenite Heber, since Jabin, king of Hazor, and the family of the Kenite Heber were at peace with one another. 18 Jael went out to meet Sisera and said to him, "Come in, my lord, come in with me; do not be afraid." So he went into her tent, and she covered him with a rug. 19 He said to her, "Please give me a little water to drink. I am thirsty." But she opened a jug

of milk for him to drink, and then covered him over. 20 "Stand at the entrance of the tent," he said to her. "If anyone comes and asks, 'Is there someone here?' say, 'No!'" 21 Instead Jael, wife of Heber, got a tent peg and took a mallet in her hand. While Sisera was sound asleep, she stealthily approached him and drove the peg through his temple down into the ground, so that he perished in death. 22 Then when Barak came in pursuit of Sisera, Jael went out to meet him and said to him, "Come, I will show you the man you seek." So he went in with her, and there lay Sisera dead, with the tent peg through his temple.

23 Thus on that day God humbled the Canaanite king, Jabin, before the Israelites; 24 their power weighed ever heavier upon him, till at length they destroyed the Canaanite king, Jabin.

Canticle of Deborah

5 On that day Deborah [and Barak, son of Abinoam,] sang this song:

2 Of chiefs who took the lead in Israel,
of noble deeds by the people who bless the LORD,
3 Hear, O kings! Give ear, O princes!
I to the LORD will sing my song,
my hymn to the LORD, the God of Israel.

4 O LORD, when you went out from Seir,
when you marched from the land of Edom,
The earth quaked and the heavens were shaken,
while the clouds sent down showers.
5 Mountains trembled
in the presence of the LORD,
the One of Sinai,
in the presence of the LORD,
the God of Israel.

6 In the days of Shamgar, son of Anath,
in the days of slavery caravans ceased:
Those who traveled the roads went by roundabout paths.
7 Gone was freedom beyond the walls.
gone indeed from Israel.

When I, Deborah, rose,
when I rose, a mother in Israel,
8 New gods were their choice;
then the war was at their gates.
Not a shield could be seen, not a lance,
among forty thousand in Israel!

9 My heart is with the leaders of Israel,
nobles of the people who bless the LORD;
10 They who ride on white asses,
seated on saddlecloths as they go their way;
11 Sing of them to the strains of the harpers at the wells,
where men recount the just deeds of the LORD,
his just deeds that brought freedom to Israel.

12 Awake, awake, Deborah!
awake, awake, strike up a song.
Strength! arise, Barak,
make despoilers your spoil, son of Abinoam.
13 Then down came the fugitives with the mighty,
the people of the LORD came down for me as warriors.

14 From Ephraim, princes were in the valley;
behind you was Benjamin, among your troops.
From Machir came down commanders,
from Zebulun wielders of the marshal's staff.

4, 11: Most of the Kenites occupied a district in the southern part of Judah (1, 16). A group of them, however, had detached themselves and settled in lower Galilee.
4, 17–22: It is to be noted that the sacred author merely records the fact of the murder of Sisera. We must not construe this as approval of Jael's action.
5, 2–31: This canticle is an excellent example of

early Hebrew poetry, even though some of its verses are now obscure.
5, 8: *New gods:* pagan deities; cf Dt 32, 16–18. God punished the idolatry of the Israelites by leaving them relatively unarmed before the attacks of their enemies, who had better weapons, made of iron; cf 1 Sm 13, 19–22.
5, 14–22: Praise for the tribes which formed the

Israelite league against Sisera: Ephraim, Benjamin, Manasseh (represented by Machir), Zebulun, Issachar, and Naphtali (led by Barak). The tribes of Reuben, Gad (Gilead), Dan, and Asher are chided for their lack of co-operation. The more distant tribes of Judah and Simeon are not mentioned.

15 With Deborah were the princes
   of Issachar;
   Barak, too, was in the valley,
   his course unchecked.

Among the clans of Reuben
   great were the searchings of
   heart.
16 Why do you stay beside your
   hearths
   listening to the lowing of the
   herds?
Among the clans of Reuben
   great were the searchings of
   heart!
17 Gilead, beyond the Jordan,
   rests;
   why does Dan spend his time
   in ships?
Asher, who dwells along the
   shore,
   is resting in his coves.
18 Zebulun is the people defying
   death;
   Naphtali, too, on the open
   heights!
19 The kings came and fought;
   then they fought, those kings
   of Canaan,
At Taanach by the waters of
   Megiddo;
   no silver booty did they take.
20 From the heavens the stars, too,
   fought;
   from their courses they fought
   against Sisera.
21 The Wadi Kishon swept them
   away;
   a wadi . . ., the Kishon.
22 Then the hoofs of the horses
   pounded,
   with the dashing, dashing of
   his steeds.
23 "Curse Meroz," says the LORD,
   "hurl a curse at its inhabitants!
For they came not to my help,
   as warriors to the help of the
   LORD."
24 Blessed among women be Jael,
   blessed among tent-dwelling
   women.
25 He asked for water, she gave him
   milk;
   in a princely bowl she offered
   curds.

26 With her left hand she reached
   for the peg,
   with her right, for the
   workman's mallet.

She hammered Sisera, crushed
   his head;
   she smashed, stove in his
   temple.
27 At her feet he sank down, fell,
   lay still;
   down at her feet he sank and
   fell;
   where he sank down, there he
   fell, slain.
28 From the window peered down
   and wailed
   the mother of Sisera, from the
   lattice:
"Why is his chariot so long in
   coming?
   why are the hoofbeats of his
   chariots delayed?"
29 The wisest of her princesses
   answers her,
   and she, too, keeps answering
   herself:
30 "They must be dividing the spoil
   they took:
   there must be a damsel or two
   for each man,
Spoils of dyed cloth as Sisera's
   spoil,
   an ornate shawl or two for me
   in the spoil."
31 May all your enemies perish
   thus, O LORD!
   but your friends be as the sun
   rising in its might!

And the land was at rest for forty
years.

The Call of Gideon

6 The Israelites offended the LORD,
who therefore delivered them
into the power of Midian for seven
years, 2 so that Midian held Israel
subject. For fear of Midian the
Israelites established the fire signals
on the mountains, the caves for
refuge, and the strongholds. 3 And
it used to be that when the Israelites
had completed their sowing, Midian,
Amalek and the Kedemites would

come up, 4 encamp opposite them,
and destroy the produce of the land
as far as the outskirts of Gaza, leaving no sustenance in Israel, nor sheep,
oxen or asses. 5 For they would
come up with their livestock, and
their tents would become as numerous as locusts; and neither they
nor their camels could be numbered,
when they came into the land to lay
it waste. 6 Thus was Israel reduced
to misery by Midian, and so the
Israelites cried out to the LORD.

7 When Israel cried out to the
LORD because of Midian, 8 he sent
a prophet to the Israelites who said
to them, "The LORD, the God of
Israel, says: I led you up from Egypt;
I brought you out of the place of
slavery. 9 I rescued you from the
power of Egypt and of all your other
oppressors. I drove them out before
you and gave you their land. 10
And I said to you: I, the LORD, am
your God; you shall not venerate the
gods of the Amorites in whose land
you are dwelling. But you did not
obey me."

11 Then the angel of the LORD
came and sat under the terebinth in
Ophrah that belonged to Joash the
Abiezrite. While his son Gideon was
beating out wheat in the wine press to
save it from the Midianites, 12 the
angel of the LORD appeared to him
and said, "The LORD is with you, O
champion!" 13 "My lord," Gideon
said to him, "If the LORD is with us,
why has all this happened to us?
Where are his wondrous deeds of
which our fathers told us when they
said, 'Did not the LORD bring us up
from Egypt?' For now the LORD has
abandoned us and has delivered us
into the power of Midian." 14 The
LORD turned to him and said, "Go
with the strength you have and save
Israel from the power of Midian. It is
I who send you." 15 But he answered him, "Please, my lord, how
can I save Israel? My family is the
meanest in Manasseh, and I am the
most insignificant in my father's
house." 16 "I shall be with you,"
the LORD said to him, "and you will
cut down Midian to the last man."
17 He answered him, "If I find favor

5, 20f: It would seem that nature aided the Hebrews
in some way. Perhaps the torrential rains swelled the

waters of Kishon, which then overwhelmed the
Canaanites.

5, 23: *Meroz*: an unknown locality in which
Hebrews probably resided, since its inhabitants are
cursed for their failure to proffer aid.

with you, give me a sign that you are speaking with me. 18 Do not depart from here, I pray you, until I come back to you and bring out my offering and set it before you." He answered, "I will await your return."

19 So Gideon went off and prepared a kid and an ephah of flour in the form of unleavened cakes. Putting the meat in a basket and the broth in a pot, he brought them out to him under the terebinth and presented them. 20 The angel of God said to him, "Take the meat and unleavened cakes and lay them on this rock; then pour out the broth." When he had done so, 21 the angel of the LORD stretched out the tip of the staff he held, and touched the meat and unleavened cakes. Thereupon a fire came up from the rock which consumed the meat and unleavened cakes, and the angel of the LORD disappeared from sight. 22 Gideon, now aware that it had been the angel of the LORD, said, "Alas, Lord GOD, that I have seen the angel of the LORD face to face!" 23 The LORD answered him, "Be calm, do not fear. You shall not die." 24 So Gideon built there an altar to the LORD and called it Yahweh-shalom. To this day it is still in Ophrah of the Abiezrites.

25 That same night the LORD said to him, "Take the seven-year-old spare bullock and destroy your father's altar to Baal and cut down the sacred pole that is by it. 26 You shall build, instead, the proper kind of altar to the LORD, your God, on top of this stronghold. Then take the spare bullock and offer it as a holocaust on the wood from the sacred pole you have cut down." 27 So Gideon took ten of his servants and did as the LORD had commanded him. But through fear of his family and of the townspeople, he would not do it by day, but did it at night. 28 Early the next morning the townspeople found that the altar of Baal had been destroyed, the sacred pole near it cut down, and the spare bullock offered on the altar that was built. 29 They asked one another, "Who did this?"

Their inquiry led them to the conclusion that Gideon, son of Joash, had done it. 30 So the townspeople said to Joash, "Bring out your son that he may die, for he has destroyed the altar of Baal and has cut down the sacred pole that was near it." 31 But Joash replied to all who were standing around him, "Do you intend to act in Baal's stead, or be his champion? If anyone acts for him, he shall be put to death by morning. If he whose altar has been destroyed is a god, let him act for himself!" 32 So on that day Gideon was called Jerubbaal, because of the words, "Let Baal take action against him, since he destroyed his altar."

33 Then all Midian and Amalek and the Kedemites mustered and crossed over into the valley of Jezreel, where they encamped. 34 The spirit of the LORD enveloped Gideon; he blew the horn that summoned Abiezer to follow him. 35 He sent messengers, too, throughout Manasseh, which also obeyed his summons; through Asher, Zebulun and Naphtali, likewise, he sent messengers and these tribes advanced to meet the others. 36 Gideon said to God, "If indeed you are going to save Israel through me, as you promised, 37 I am putting this woolen fleece on the threshing floor. If dew comes on the fleece alone, while all the ground is dry, I shall know that you will save Israel through me, as you promised." 38 That is what took place. Early the next morning he wrung the dew from the fleece, squeezing out of it a bowlful of water. 39 Gideon then said to God, "Do not be angry with me if I speak once more. Let me make just one more test with the fleece. Let the fleece alone be dry, but let there be dew on all the ground." 40 That night God did so; the fleece alone was dry, but there was dew on all the ground.

Defeat of Midian

7 Early the next morning Jerubbaal (that is, Gideon) encamped by En-harod with all his soldiers. The camp of Midian was in the valley north of Gibeath-hammoreh. 2 The LORD said to Gideon, "You have too many soldiers with you for me to deliver Midian into their power, lest Israel vaunt itself against me and say, 'My own power brought me the victory.' 3 Now proclaim to all the soldiers, 'If anyone is afraid or fearful, let him leave.'" When Gideon put them to this test on the mountain, twenty-two thousand of the soldiers left, but ten thousand remained. 4 The LORD said to Gideon, "There are still too many soldiers. Lead them down to the water and I will test them for you there. If I tell you that a certain man is to go with you, he must go with you. But no one is to go if I tell you he must not." 5 When Gideon led the soldiers down to the water, the LORD said to him, "You shall set to one side everyone who laps up the water as a dog does with its tongue; to the other, everyone who kneels down to drink." 6 Those who lapped up the water raised to their mouths by hand numbered three hundred, but all the rest of the soldiers knelt down to drink the water. 7 The LORD said to Gideon, "By means of the three hundred who lapped up the water I will save you and will deliver Midian into your power. So let all the other soldiers go home." 8 Their horns, and such supplies as the soldiers had with them, were taken up, and Gideon ordered the rest of the Israelites to their tents, but kept the three hundred men. Now the camp of Midian was beneath him in the valley.

9 That night the LORD said to Gideon, "Go, descend on the camp, for I have delivered it up to you. 10 If you are afraid to attack, go down to the camp with your aid Purah. 11 When you hear what they are saying, you will have the courage to descend on the camp." So he went down with his aid Purah to the outposts of the camp. 12 The Midianites, Amalekites, and all the Kedemites lay in the valley, as numerous as locusts. Nor could their camels be counted, for these were as many as the sands on

---

6, 24: *Yahweh-shalom:* Hebrew for "the LORD is peace," a reference to the LORD's words, "Be calm," literally, "Peace be to you!"

6, 25: *The sacred pole:* see note on Ex 34, 13.

6, 32: *Jerubbaal:* similar in sound to the Hebrew words meaning, "Let Baal take action."

7, 5: The LORD desired not numerous but reliable soldiers. Those who drank from their hands were

alert, standing ready to resist attack, whereas the others were careless and undependable. The cowardly soldiers had already been dismissed (v 3); cf Dt 20, 8.

the seashore. 13 When Gideon arrived, one man was telling another about a dream. "I had a dream," he said, "that a round loaf of barley bread was rolling into the camp of Midian. It came to our tent and struck it, and as it fell it turned the tent upside down." 14 "This can only be the sword of the Israelite Gideon, son of Joash," the other replied. "God has delivered Midian and all the camp into his power." 15 When Gideon heard the description and explanation of the dream, he prostrated himself. Then returning to the camp of Israel, he said, "Arise, for the LORD has delivered the camp of Midian into your power."

16 He divided the three hundred men into three companies, and provided them all with horns and with empty jars and torches inside the jars. 17 "Watch me and follow my lead," he told them. "I shall go to the edge of the camp, and as I do, you must do also. 18 When I and those with me blow horns, you too must blow horns all around the camp and cry out, 'For the LORD and for Gideon!'" 19 So Gideon and the hundred men who were with him came to the edge of the camp at the beginning of the middle watch, just after the posting of the guards. They blew the horns and broke the jars they were holding. 20 All three companies blew horns and broke their jars. They held the torches in their left hands, and in their right the horns they were blowing, and cried out, "A sword for the LORD and Gideon!" 21 They all remained standing in place around the camp, while the whole camp fell to running and shouting and fleeing. 22 But the three hundred men kept blowing the horns, and throughout the camp the LORD set the sword of one against another. The army fled as far as Beth-shittah in the direction of Zarethan, near the border of Abel-meholah at Tabbath.

23 The Israelites were called to arms from Naphtali, from Asher, and from all Manasseh, and they pursued Midian. 24 Gideon also sent messengers throughout the mountain region of Ephraim to say, "Go down to confront Midian, and seize the water courses against them as far as Beth-barah, as well as the Jordan." So all the Ephraimites were called to arms, and they seized the water courses as far as Beth-barah, and the Jordan as well. 25 They captured the two princes of Midian, Oreb and Zeeb, killing Oreb at the rock of Oreb and Zeeb at the wine press of Zeeb. Then they pursued Midian and carried the heads of Oreb and Zeeb to Gideon beyond the Jordan.

8 But the Ephraimites said to him, "What have you done to us, not calling us when you went to fight against Midian!" And they quarreled bitterly with him. 2 "What have I accomplished now in comparison with you?" he answered them. "Is not the gleaning of Ephraim better than the vintage of Abiezer? 3 Into your power God delivered the princes of Midian, Oreb and Zeeb. What have I been able to do in comparison with you?" When he said this, their anger against him subsided.

4 When Gideon reached the Jordan and crossed it with his three hundred men, they were exhausted and famished. 5 So he said to the men of Succoth, "Will you give my followers some loaves of bread? They are exhausted, and I am pursuing Zebah and Zalmunna, kings of Midian." 6 But the princes of Succoth replied, "Are the hands of Zebah and Zalmunna already in your possession, that we should give food to your army?" 7 Gideon said, "Very well; when the LORD has delivered Zebah and Zalmunna into my power, I will grind your flesh in with the thorns and briers of the desert." 8 He went up from there to Penuel and made the same request of them, but the men of Penuel answered him as had the men of Succoth. 9 So to the men of Penuel, too, he said, "When I return in triumph, I will demolish this tower."

10 Now Zebah and Zalmunna were in Karkor with their force of about fifteen thousand men; these were all who were left of the whole Kedemite army, a hundred and twenty thousand swordsmen having fallen. 11 Gideon went up by the route of the nomads east of Nobah and Jogbehah, and attacked the camp when it felt secure. 12 Zebah and Zalmunna fled. He pursued them and took the two kings of Midian, Zebah and Zalmunna, captive, throwing the entire army into panic.

13 Then Gideon, son of Joash, returned from battle by the pass of Heres. 14 He captured a young man of Succoth, who upon being questioned listed for him the seventy-seven princes and elders of Succoth. 15 So he went to the men of Succoth and said, "Here are Zebah and Zalmunna, with whom you taunted me, 'Are the hands of Zebah and Zalmunna already in your possession, that we should give food to your weary followers?'" 16 He took the elders of the city, and thorns and briers of the desert, and ground these men of Succoth into them. 17 He also demolished the tower of Penuel and slew the men of the city.

18 Then he said to Zebah and Zalmunna, "Where now are the men you killed at Tabor?" "They all resembled you," they replied. "They appeared to be princes." 19 "They were my brothers, my mother's sons," he said. "As the LORD lives, if you had spared their lives, I should not kill you." 20 Then he said to his first-born, Jether, "Go, kill them." Since Jether was still a boy, he was afraid and did not draw his sword. 21 Zebah and Zalmunna said, "Come, kill us yourself, for a man's strength is like the man." So Gideon stepped forward and killed Zebah and Zalmunna. He also took the crescents that were on the necks of their camels.

22 The Israelites then said to Gideon, "Rule over us—you, your son, and your son's son—for you rescued us from the power of Midian." 23 But Gideon answered

---

7, 13: The barley loaf represents the agricultural Hebrews while the tent refers to the nomadic Midianites. The overthrow of the tent indicates the victory of the Hebrews over their Midianite oppressors.

7, 19: *At the beginning of the middle watch:* about two hours before midnight. The ancient Hebrews divided the night into four watches of about four hours each. At the beginning of a watch the sentinels were changed.

8, 6: *Are the hands . . . in your possession . . .?:* i.e., can you already boast of victory? The hands as well as the heads of slain enemies were cut off and counted as trophies; cf 2 Sm 4, 8; 2 Kgs 10, 7f; and the Ugaritic Anath Epic, V AB, II 10ff.

181

them, "I will not rule over you, nor shall my son rule over you. The LORD must rule over you."

24 Gideon went on to say, "I should like to make a request of you. Will each of you give me a ring from his booty?" (For being Ishmaelites, the enemy had gold rings.) 25 "We will gladly give them," they replied, and spread out a cloak into which everyone threw a ring from his booty. 26 The gold rings that he requested weighed seventeen hundred gold shekels, in addition to the crescents and pendants, the purple garments worn by the kings of Midian, and the trappings that were on the necks of their camels. 27 Gideon made an ephod out of the gold and placed it in his city Ophrah. However, all Israel paid idolatrous homage to it there, and caused the ruin of Gideon and his family.

28 Thus was Midian brought into subjection by the Israelites; no longer did they hold their heads high. And the land had rest for forty years, during the lifetime of Gideon.

Gideon's Son Abimelech

29 Then Jerubbaal, son of Joash, went back home to stay. 30 Now Gideon had seventy sons, his direct descendants, for he had many wives. 31 His concubine who lived in Shechem also bore him a son, whom he named Abimelech. 32 At a good old age Gideon, son of Joash died, and was buried in the tomb of his father Joash in Ophrah of the Abiezrites. 33 But after Gideon was dead, the Israelites again abandoned themselves to the Baals, making Baal of Berith their god 34 and forgetting the LORD, their God, who had delivered them from the power of their enemies all around them. 35 Nor were they grateful to the family of Jerubbaal [Gideon] for all the good he had done for Israel.

9 Abimelech, son of Jerubbaal, went to his mother's kinsmen in Shechem, and said to them and to the whole clan to which his mother's family belonged, 2 "Put this question to all the citizens of Shechem: 'Which is better for you: that seventy men, or all Jerubbaal's sons, rule over you, or that one man rule over you? You must remember that I am your own flesh and bone.'" 3 When his mother's kin repeated these words to them on his behalf, all the citizens of Shechem sympathized with Abimelech, thinking, "He is our kinsman." 4 They also gave him seventy silver shekels from the temple of Baal of Berith, with which Abimelech hired shiftless men and ruffians as his followers. 5 He then went to his ancestral house in Ophrah, and slew his brothers, the seventy sons of Jerubbaal, on one stone. Only the youngest son of Jerubbaal, Jotham, escaped, for he was hidden. 6 Then all the citizens of Shechem and all Beth-millo came together and proceeded to make Abimelech king by the terebinth at the memorial pillar in Shechem.

7 When this was reported to him, Jotham went to the top of Mount Gerizim, and standing there, cried out to them in a loud voice: "Hear me, citizens of Shechem, that God may then hear you! 8 Once the trees went to anoint a king over themselves. So they said to the olive tree, 'Reign over us.' 9 But the olive tree answered them, 'Must I give up my rich oil, whereby men and gods are honored, and go to wave over the trees?' 10 Then the trees said to the fig tree, 'Come; you reign over us!' 11 But the fig tree answered them, 'Must I give up my sweetness and my good fruit, and go to wave over the trees?' 12 Then the trees said to the vine, 'Come you, and reign over us.' 13 But the vine answered them, 'Must I give up my wine that cheers gods and men, and go to wave over the trees?' 14 Then all the trees said to the buckthorn, 'Come; you reign over us!' 15 But the buckthorn replied to the trees, 'If you wish to anoint me king over you in good faith, come and take refuge in my shadow. Otherwise, let fire come from the buckthorn and devour the cedars of Lebanon.'

16 "Now then, if you have acted in good faith and honorably in appointing Abimelech your king, if you have dealt well with Jerubbaal and with his family, and if you have treated him as he deserved 17 —for my father fought for you at the risk of his life when he saved you from the power of Midian; 18 but you have risen against his family this day and have killed his seventy sons upon one stone, and have made Abimelech, the son of his handmaid, king over the citizens of Shechem, because he is your kinsman— 19 if, then, you have acted in good faith and with honor toward Jerubbaal and his family this day, rejoice in Abimelech and may he in turn rejoice in you. 20 But if not, let fire come forth from Abimelech to devour the citizens of Shechem and Beth-millo, and let fire come forth from the citizens and from Beth-millo to devour Abimelech." 21 Then Jotham went in flight to Beer, where he remained for fear of his brother Abimelech.

22 When Abimelech had ruled Israel for three years, 23 God put bad feelings between Abimelech and the citizens of Shechem, who rebelled against Abimelech. 24 This was to repay the violence done to the seventy sons of Jerubbaal and to avenge their blood upon their brother Abimelech, who killed them, and upon the citizens of Shechem, who encouraged him to kill his brothers. 25 The citizens of Shechem then set men in ambush for him on the mountaintops, and these robbed all who passed them on the road. But it was reported to Abimelech.

26 Now Gaal, son of Ebed, came over to Shechem with his kinsmen. The citizens of Shechem put their trust in him, 27 and went out into the fields, harvested their grapes and trod them out. Then they held a

8, 24: *Ishmaelites:* here as in Gn 37, 25–28, the designation is not ethnic; it refers rather to their status as nomads.

8, 31: *Concubine:* see note on Gn 22, 24.

8, 33: *Baal of Berith:* one of the titles of Baal as worshiped by the Canaanites of Shechem, meaning "the lord of the covenant."

9, 9: *Whereby men and gods are honored:* oil was used in the worship both of the true God and of false gods; it was prescribed in the worship of Yahweh (Lv 2, 1.6.15; 24, 2). It was also used to consecrate prophets, priests and kings (Ex 30, 25.30; 1 Sm 10, 1; 16, 13).

9, 13: *Cheers gods:* wine was used in the libations

both of the Temple of Jerusalem and of pagan temples.

9, 16: Just as the noble trees refused the honor of royalty and were made subject to a mean plant, so did Abimelech of less noble birth than the seventy sons of Gideon now tyrannize over the people.

festival and went to the temple of their god, where they ate and drank and cursed Abimelech. 28 Gaal, son of Ebed, said, "Who is Abimelech? And why should we of Shechem serve him? Were not the son of Jerubbaal and his lieutenant Zebul once subject to the men of Hamor, father of Shechem? Why should we serve him? 29 Would that this people were entrusted to my command! I would depose Abimelech. I would say to Abimelech, 'Get a larger army and come out!'"

30 At the news of what Gaal, son of Ebed, had said, Zebul, the ruler of the city, was angry 31 and sent messengers to Abimelech in Arumah with the information: "Gaal, son of Ebed, and his kinsmen have come to Shechem and are stirring up the city against you. 32 Now rouse yourself; set an ambush tonight in the fields, you and the men who are with you. 33 Promptly at sunrise tomorrow morning, make a raid on the city. When he and his followers come out against you, deal with him as best you can."

34 During the night Abimelech advanced with all his soldiers and set up an ambush for Shechem in four companies. 35 Gaal, son of Ebed, went out and stood at the entrance of the city gate. When Abimelech and his soldiers rose from their place of ambush, 36 Gaal saw them and said to Zebul, "There are men coming down from the hilltops!" But Zebul answered him, "You see the shadow of the hills as men." 37 But Gaal went on to say, "Men are coming down from the region of Tabbur-Haares, and one company is coming by way of Elon-Meonenim." 38 Zebul said to him, "Where now is the boast you uttered, 'Who is Abimelech that we should serve him?' Are these not the men for whom you expressed contempt? Go out now and fight with them." 39 So Gaal went out at the head of the citizens of Shechem and fought against Abimelech. 40 But Abimelech routed him, and he fled before him; and many fell slain right up to the entrance of the gate. 41 Abimelech

returned to Arumah, but Zebul drove Gaal and his kinsmen from Shechem, which they had occupied.

42 The next day, when the people were taking the field, it was reported to Abimelech, 43 who divided the men he had into three companies, and set up an ambush in the fields. He watched till he saw the people leave the city, and then rose against them for the attack. 44 Abimelech and the company with him dashed in and stood by the entrance of the city gate, while the other two companies rushed upon all who were in the field and attacked them. 45 That entire day Abimelech fought against the city, and captured it. He then killed its inhabitants and demolished the city, sowing the site with salt.

46 When they heard of this, all the citizens of Migdal-shechem went into the crypt of the temple of El-berith. 47 It was reported to Abimelech that all the citizens of Migdal-shechem were gathered together. 48 So he went up Mount Zalmon with all his soldiers, took his axe in his hand, and cut down some brushwood. This he lifted to his shoulder, then said to the men with him, "Hurry! Do just as you have seen me do." 49 So all the men likewise cut down brushwood, and following Abimelech, placed it against the crypt. Then they set the crypt on fire over their heads, so that every one of the citizens of Migdal-shechem, about a thousand men and women, perished.

50 Abimelech proceeded to Thebez, which he invested and captured. 51 Now there was a strong tower in the middle of the city, and all the men and women, in a word all the citizens of the city, fled there, shutting themselves in and going up to the roof of the tower. 52 Abimelech came up to the tower and fought against it, advancing to the very entrance of the tower to set it on fire. 53 But a certain woman cast the upper part of a millstone down on Abimelech's head, and it fractured his skull. 54 He immediately called his armor-bearer and said to him, "Draw your sword and dispatch me, lest they say of me that a woman

killed me." So his attendant ran him through and he died. 55 When the Israelites saw that Abimelech was dead, they all left for their homes.

56 Thus did God requite the evil Abimelech had done to his father in killing his seventy brothers. 57 God also brought all their wickedness home to the Shechemites, for the curse of Jotham, son of Jerubbaal, overtook them.

Tola

10 After Abimelech there rose to save Israel the Issacharite Tola, son of Puah, son of Dodo, a resident of Shamir in the mountain region of Ephraim. 2 When he had judged Israel twenty-three years, he died and was buried in Shamir.

Jair

3 Jair the Gileadite came after him and judged Israel twenty-two years. 4 He had thirty sons who rode on thirty saddle-asses and possessed thirty cities in the land of Gilead; these are called Havvoth-jair to the present day. 5 Jair died and was buried in Kamon.

Oppression by the Ammonites

6 The Israelites again offended the LORD, serving the Baals and Ashtaroth, the gods of Aram, the gods of Sidon, the gods of Moab, the gods of the Ammonites, and the gods of the Philistines. Since they had abandoned the LORD and would not serve him, 7 the LORD became angry with Israel and allowed them to fall into the power of [the Philistines and] the Ammonites. 8 For eighteen years they afflicted and oppressed the Israelites in Bashan, and all the Israelites in the Amorite land beyond the Jordan in Gilead. 9 The Ammonites also crossed the Jordan to fight against Judah, Benjamin, and the house of Ephraim, so that Israel was in great distress.

10 Then the Israelites cried out to the LORD, "We have sinned against you; we have forsaken our God and have served the Baals." 11 The LORD answered the Israelites: "Did

---

9, 45: *Sowing the site with salt:* a severe measure, which was a symbol of desolation, and even more, since it actually rendered the ground barren and useless.

10, 4: *Saddle-asses:* a sign of rank and wealth; cf 5, 10; 12, 14.

not the Egyptians, the Amorites, the Ammonites, the Philistines, 12 the Sidonians, the Amalekites, and the Midianites oppress you? Yet when you cried out to me, and I saved you from their grasp, 13 you still forsook me and worshipped other gods. Therefore I will save you no more. 14 Go and cry out to the gods you have chosen; let them save you now that you are in distress." 15 But the Israelites said to the LORD, "We have sinned. Do to us whatever you please. Only save us this day." 16 And they cast out the foreign gods from their midst and served the LORD, so that he grieved over the misery of Israel.

17 The Ammonites had gathered for war and encamped in Gilead, while the Israelites assembled and encamped in Mizpah. 18 And among the people the princes of Gilead said to one another, "The one who begins the war against the Ammonites shall be leader of all the inhabitants of Gilead."

Jephthah

11 There was a chieftain, the Gileadite Jephthah, born to Gilead of a harlot. 2 Gilead's wife had also borne him sons, and on growing up the sons of the wife had driven Jephthah away, saying to him, "You shall inherit nothing in our family, for you are the son of another woman." 3 So Jephthah had fled from his brothers and had taken up residence in the land of Tob. A rabble had joined company with him, and went out with him on raids.

4 Some time later, the Ammonites warred on Israel. 5 When this occurred the elders of Gilead went to bring Jephthah from the land of Tob. 6 "Come," they said to Jephthah, "be our commander that we may be able to fight the Ammonites." 7 "Are you not the ones who hated me and drove me from my father's house?" Jephthah replied to the elders of Gilead. "Why do you come to me now, when you are in distress?" 8 The elders of Gilead said to Jeph-

thah, "In any case, we have now come back to you; if you go with us to fight against the Ammonites, you shall be the leader of all of us who dwell in Gilead." 9 Jephthah answered the elders of Gilead, "If you bring me back to fight against the Ammonites and the LORD delivers them up to me, I shall be your leader." 10 The elders of Gilead said to Jephthah, "The LORD is witness between us that we will do as you say."

11 So Jephthah went with the elders of Gilead, and the people made him their leader and commander. In Mizpah, Jephthah settled all his affairs before the LORD. 12 Then he sent messengers to the king of the Ammonites to say, "What have you against me that you come to fight with me in my land?" 13 He answered the messengers of Jephthah, "Israel took away my land from the Arnon to the Jabbok and the Jordan when they came up from Egypt. Now restore the same peaceably."

14 Again Jephthah sent messengers to the king of the Ammonites, 15 saying to him, "This is what Jephthah says: Israel did not take the land of Moab or the land of the Ammonites. 16 For when they came up from Egypt, Israel went through the desert to the Red Sea and came to Kadesh. 17 Israel then sent messengers to the king of Edom saying, 'Let me pass through your land.' But the king of Edom did not give consent. They also sent to the king of Moab, but he too was unwilling. So Israel remained in Kadesh. 18 Then they went through the desert, and by-passing the land of Edom and the land of Moab, went east of the land of Moab and encamped across the Arnon. Thus they did not go through the territory of Moab, for the Arnon is the boundary of Moab. 19 Then Israel sent messengers to Sihon, king of the Amorites, king of Heshbon. Israel said to him, 'Let me pass through your land to my own place.' 20 But Sihon refused to let Israel pass through his

territory. On the contrary, he gathered all his soldiers, who encamped at Jahaz and fought Israel. 21 But the LORD, the God of Israel, delivered Sihon and all his men into the power of Israel, who defeated them and occupied all the land of the Amorites dwelling in that region, 22 the whole territory from the Arnon to the Jabbok, from the desert to the Jordan. 23 If now the LORD, the God of Israel, has cleared the Amorites out of the way of his people, are you to dislodge Israel? 24 Should you not possess that which your god Chemosh gave you to possess, and should we not possess all that the LORD, our God, has cleared out for us? 25 Again, are you any better than Balak, son of Zippor, king of Moab? Did he ever quarrel with Israel, or did he war against them 26 when Israel occupied Heshbon and its villages, Aroer and its villages, and all the cities on the banks of the Arnon? Three hundred years have passed; why did you not recover them during that time? 27 I have not sinned against you, but you wrong me by warring against me. Let the LORD, who is judge, decide this day between the Israelites and the Ammonites!" 28 But the king of the Ammonites paid no heed to the message Jephthah sent him.

Jephthah's Vow

29 The spirit of the LORD came upon Jephthah. He passed through Gilead and Manasseh, and through Mizpah-Gilead as well, and from there he went on to the Ammonites. 30 Jephthah made a vow to the LORD. "If you deliver the Ammonites into my power," he said, 31 "whoever comes out of the doors of my house to meet me when I return in triumph from the Ammonites shall belong to the LORD. I shall offer him up as a holocaust."

32 Jephthah then went on to the Ammonites to fight against them, and the LORD delivered them into his power, 33 so that he inflicted a severe defeat on them, from Aroer to

11, 24: *Chemosh:* the chief god of the Moabites— not of the Ammonites, whose leading deity was called Molech or Milcom; cf Nm 21, 29; 1 Kgs 11, 7; 2 Kgs 23, 13. The error is probably due to an ancient copyist. Jephthah argues from the viewpoint of his

adversaries, the Ammonites, that they were entitled to all the land they had conquered with the aid of their god. It does not necessarily follow that Jephthah himself believed in the actual existence of this pagan god.

11, 30–40: The text clearly implies that Jephthah vowed a human sacrifice, according to the custom of his pagan neighbors; cf 2 Kgs 3, 27. The inspired author merely records the fact; he does not approve of the action.

the approach of Minnith (twenty cities in all) and as far as Abel-keramin. Thus were the Ammonites brought into subjection by the Israelites. 34 When Jephthah returned to his house in Mizpah, it was his daughter who came forth, playing the tambourines and dancing. She was an only child: he had neither son nor daughter besides her. 35 When he saw her, he rent his garments and said, "Alas, daughter, you have struck me down and brought calamity upon me. For I have made a vow to the LORD and I cannot retract." 36 "Father," she replied, "you have made a vow to the LORD. Do with me as you have vowed, because the LORD has wrought vengeance for you on your enemies the Ammonites." 37 Then she said to her father, "Let me have this favor. Spare me for two months, that I may go off down the mountains to mourn my virginity with my companions." 38 "Go," he replied, and sent her away for two months. So she departed with her companions and mourned her virginity on the mountains. 39 At the end of the two months she returned to her father, who did to her as he had vowed. She had not been intimate with man. It then became a custom in Israel 40 for Israelite women to go yearly to mourn the daughter of Jephthah the Gileadite for four days of the year.

The Shibboleth Incident

12 The men of Ephraim gathered together and crossed over to Zaphon. They said to Jephthah, "Why do you go on to fight with the Ammonites without calling us to go with you? We will burn your house over you." 2 Jephthah answered them, "My soldiers and I were engaged in a critical contest with the Ammonites. I summoned you, but you did not rescue me from their power. 3 When I saw that you would not effect a rescue, I took my life in my own hand and went on to the Ammonites, and the LORD delivered them into my power. Why,

then, do you come up against me this day to fight with me?"

4 Then Jephthah called together all the men of Gilead and fought against Ephraim, whom they defeated; for the Ephraimites had said, "You of Gilead are Ephraimite fugitives in territory belonging to Ephraim and Manasseh." 5 The Gileadites took the fords of the Jordan toward Ephraim. When any of the fleeing Ephraimites said, "Let me pass," the men of Gilead would say to him, "Are you an Ephraimite?" If he answered, "No!" 6 they would ask him to say "Shibboleth." If he said "Sibboleth," not being able to give the proper pronunciation, they would seize him and kill him at the fords of the Jordan. Thus forty-two thousand Ephraimites fell at that time.

7 After having judged Israel for six years, Jephthah the Gileadite died and was buried in his city in Gilead.

Ibzan

8 After him Ibzan of Bethlehem judged Israel. 9 He had thirty sons. He also had thirty daughters married outside the family, and he brought in as wives for his sons thirty young women from outside the family. After having judged Israel for seven years, 10 Ibzan died and was buried in Bethlehem.

Elon

11 After him the Zebulunite Elon judged Israel. When he had judged Israel for ten years, 12 the Zebulunite Elon died and was buried in Elon in the land of Zebulun.

Abdon

13 After him the Pirathonite Abdon, son of Hillel, judged Israel. 14 He had forty sons and thirty grandsons who rode on seventy saddle-asses. After having judged Israel for eight years, 15 the Pirathonite Abdon, son of Hillel, died and was buried in Pirathon in the land of

Ephraim on the mountain of the Amalekites.

The Birth of Samson

13 The Israelites again offended the LORD, who therefore delivered them into the power of the Philistines for forty years.

2 There was a certain man from Zorah, of the clan of the Danites, whose name was Manoah. His wife was barren and had borne no children. 3 An angel of the LORD appeared to the woman and said to her, "Though you are barren and have had no children, yet you will conceive and bear a son. 4 Now, then, be careful to take no wine or strong drink and to eat nothing unclean. 5 As for the son you will conceive and bear, no razor shall touch his head, for this boy is to be consecrated to God from the womb. It is he who will begin the deliverance of Israel from the power of the Philistines."

6 The woman went and told her husband, "A man of God came to me; he had the appearance of an angel of God, terrible indeed. I did not ask him where he came from, nor did he tell me his name. 7 But he said to me, 'You will be with child and will bear a son. So take neither wine nor strong drink, and eat nothing unclean. For the boy shall be consecrated to God from the womb, until the day of his death.'" 8 Manoah then prayed to the LORD. "O Lord, I beseech you," he said, "may the man of God whom you sent, return to us to teach us what to do for the boy who will be born."

9 God heard the prayer of Manoah, and the angel of God came again to the woman as she was sitting in the field. Since her husband Manoah was not with her, 10 the woman ran in haste and told her husband. "The man who came to me the other day has appeared to me," she said to him; 11 so Manoah got up and followed his wife. When he reached the man, he said to him, "Are you the one who spoke to my wife?" "Yes," he answered. 12 Then

---

11, 37: *Mourn my virginity:* to bear children was woman's greatest pride; to be childless was regarded as a great misfortune. Hence Jephthah's daughter asks permission to mourn the fact that she will be put to death before she can bear children.

12, 6: *Shibboleth:* "an ear of grain." But this

Hebrew word can also mean "flood water" as in Ps 69, 3.16. Apparently the Gileadites engaged the Ephraimites in conversation about the "flood water" of the Jordan. Differences in enunciating the initial sibilant of the Hebrew word betrayed different tribal affinities.

13, 5: *Consecrated:* in Hebrew, *nazir.* Samson therefore was for life to be under the nazirite vow, which obliged him to abstain from drinking wine or having his hair cut; cf Nm 6, 2–8.

Manoah asked, "Now, when that which you say comes true, what are we expected to do for the boy?" 13 The angel of the LORD answered Manoah, "Your wife is to abstain from all the things of which I spoke to her. 14 She must not eat anything that comes from the vine, nor take wine or strong drink, nor eat anything unclean. Let her observe all that I have commanded her." 15 Then Manoah said to the angel of the LORD, "Can we persuade you to stay, while we prepare a kid for you?" 16 But the angel of the LORD answered Manoah, "Although you press me, I will not partake of your food. But if you will, you may offer a holocaust to the LORD." Not knowing that it was the angel of the LORD, 17 Manoah said to him, "What is your name, that we may honor you when your words come true?" 18 The angel of the LORD answered him, "Why do you ask my name, which is mysterious?" 19 Then Manoah took the kid with a cereal offering and offered it on the rock to the LORD, whose works are mysteries. While Manoah and his wife were looking on, 20 as the flame rose to the sky from the altar, the angel of the LORD ascended in the flame of the altar. When Manoah and his wife saw this, they fell prostrate to the ground; 21 but the angel of the LORD was seen no more by Manoah and his wife. Then Manoah, realizing that it was the angel of the LORD, 22 said to his wife, "We will certainly die, for we have seen God." 23 But his wife pointed out to him, "If the LORD had meant to kill us, he would not have accepted a holocaust and cereal offering from our hands! Nor would he have let us see all this just now, or hear what we have heard."

24 The woman bore a son and named him Samson. The boy grew up and the LORD blessed him; 25 the spirit of the LORD first stirred him in Mahaneh-dan, which is between Zorah and Eshtaol.

Marriage of Samson

14 Samson went down to Timnah and saw there one of the Philistine women. 2 On his return he told his father and mother, "There is a Philistine woman I saw in Timnah who I wish you to get as a wife for me." 3 His father and mother said to him. "Can you find no wife among your kinsfolk or among all our people, that you must go and take a wife from the uncircumcised Philistines?" But Samson answered his father, "Get her for me, for she pleases me." 4 Now his father and mother did not know that this had been brought about by the LORD, who was providing an opportunity against the Philistines; for at that time they had dominion over Israel.

5 So Samson went down to Timnah with his father and mother. When they had come to the vineyards of Timnah, a young lion came roaring to meet him. 6 But the spirit of the LORD came upon Samson, and although he had no weapons, he tore the lion in pieces as one tears a kid. 7 However, on the journey to speak for the woman, he did not mention to his father or mother what he had done. 8 Later, when he returned to marry the woman who pleased him, he stepped aside to look at the remains of the lion and found a swarm of bees and honey in the lion's carcass. 9 So he scooped the honey out into his palms and ate it as he went along. When he came to his father and mother, he gave them some to eat, without telling them that he had scooped the honey from the lion's carcass.

10 His father also went down to the woman, and Samson gave a banquet there, since it was customary for the young men to do this. 11 When they met him, they brought thirty men to be his companions. 12 Samson said to them, "Let me propose a riddle to you. If within the seven days of the feast you solve it for me successfully, I will give you thirty

linen tunics and thirty sets of garments. 13 But if you cannot answer it for me, you must give me thirty tunics and thirty sets of garments." "Propose your riddle," they responded; "we will listen to it." 14 So he said to them,

"Out of the eater came forth food,
    and out of the strong came
        forth sweetness."

After three days' failure to answer the riddle, 15 they said on the fourth day to Samson's wife, "Coax your husband to answer the riddle for us, or we will burn you and your family. Did you invite us here to reduce us to poverty?" 16 At Samson's side, his wife wept and said, "You must hate me; you do not love me, for you have proposed a riddle to my countrymen, but have not told me the answer." He said to her, "If I have not told it even to my father or my mother, must I tell it to you?" 17 But she wept beside him during the seven days the feast lasted. On the seventh day, since she importuned him, he told her the answer, and she explained the riddle to her countrymen.

18 On the seventh day, before the sun set, the men of the city said to him,

"What is sweeter than honey,
    and what is stronger than a
        lion?"

He replied to them,

"If you had not plowed with my
        heifer,
    you would not have solved my
        riddle."

19 The spirit of the LORD came upon him, and he went down to Ashkelon, where he killed thirty of their men and despoiled them; he gave their garments to those who had answered the riddle. Then he went off to his own family in anger, 20 and Samson's wife was married to the one who had been best man at his wedding.

13, 18: *Mysterious:* incomprehensible, above human understanding. Hence, the angel speaks in the name of the LORD himself, to whom Manoah at once offers a sacrifice.

14, 1–3: Marriages were arranged by the parents of the bridegroom as well as of the bride; cf Gn 24, 2–8; 34, 3–6. The Mosaic law specified only seven

pagan nations, not including the Philistines, in the prohibition against mixed marriages; cf Dt 7, 1–4. But national and religious sentiment was against any marriage with a non-Israelite; cf Gn 28, 1f; 1 Kgs 11, 1–10.

14, 5ff: Although Samson was accompanied by his parents on the journey to Timnah, v 7 implies that he

was not near them when *he tore the lion in pieces.*

14, 11: *Companions:* known at a later period as "the friends of the bridegroom" (1 Mc 9, 39; Mk 2, 19), the best man and his fellows. Here they are Philistines (v 16), appointed by the family of the bride, who would also have several bridesmaids; cf Mt 25, 1–13.

Samson Defeats the Philistines

15 After some time, in the season of the wheat harvest, Samson visited his wife, bringing a kid. But when he said, "Let me be with my wife in private," her father would not let him enter, 2 saying, "I thought it certain you wished to repudiate her; so I gave her to your best man. Her younger sister is more beautiful than she; you may have her instead." 3 Samson said to them, "This time the Philistines cannot blame me if I harm them." 4 So Samson left and caught three hundred foxes. Turning them tail to tail, he tied between each pair of tails one of the torches he had at hand. 5 He then kindled the torches and set the foxes loose in the standing grain of the Philistines, thus burning both the shocks and the standing grain, and the vineyards and olive orchards as well.

6 When the Philistines asked who had done this, they were told, "Samson, the son-in-law of the Timnite, because his wife was taken and given to his best man." So the Philistines went up and destroyed her and her family by fire. 7 Samson said to them, "If this is how you act, I will not stop until I have taken revenge on you." 8 And with repeated blows, he inflicted a great slaughter on them. Then he went down and remained in a cavern of the cliff of Etam.

9 The Philistines went up and, from a camp in Judah, deployed against Lehi. 10 When the men of Judah asked, "Why have you come up against us?" they answered, "To take Samson prisoner; to do to him as he has done to us." 11 Three thousand men of Judah went down to the cavern in the cliff of Etam and said to Samson, "Do you not know that the Philistines are our rulers? Why, then have you done this to us?" He answered them, "As they have done to me, so have I done to them." 12 They said to him, "We have come to take you prisoner, to deliver you over to the Philistines." Samson said to them, "Swear to me that you will not kill me yourselves." 13 "No," they replied, "we will certainly not

kill you but will only bind you and deliver you over to them." So they bound him with two new ropes and brought him up from the cliff. 14 When he reached Lehi, and the Philistines came shouting to meet him, the spirit of the LORD came upon him: the ropes around his arms became as flax that is consumed by fire and his bonds melted away from his hands. 15 Near him was the fresh jawbone of an ass; he reached out, grasped it, and with it killed a thousand men. 16 Then Samson said,

"With the jawbone of an ass
I have piled them in a heap;
With the jawbone of an ass
I have slain a thousand men."

17 As he finished speaking he threw the jawbone from him; and so that place was named Ramath-lehi. 18 Being very thirsty, he cried to the LORD and said, "You have granted this great victory by the hand of your servant. Must I now die of thirst or fall into the hands of the uncircumcised?" 19 Then God split the cavity in Lehi, and water issued from it, which Samson drank till his spirit returned and he revived. Hence that spring in Lehi is called En-hakkore to this day.

20 Samson judged Israel for twenty years in the days of the Philistines.

16 Once Samson went to Gaza, where he saw a harlot and visited her. 2 Informed that Samson had come there, the men of Gaza surrounded him with an ambush at the city gate all night long. And all the night they waited, saying, "Tomorrow morning we will kill him." 3 Samson rested there until midnight. Then he rose, seized the doors of the city gate and the two gateposts, and tore them loose, bar and all. He hoisted them on his shoulders and carried them to the top of the ridge opposite Hebron.

Samson and Delilah

4 After that he fell in love with a woman in the Wadi Sorek whose name was Delilah. 5 The lords of the Philistines came to her and said, "Beguile him and find out the secret of his great strength, and how we may

overcome and bind him so as to keep him helpless. We will each give you eleven hundred shekels of silver."

6 So Delilah said to Samson, "Tell me the secret of your great strength and how you may be bound so as to be kept helpless." 7 "If they bind me with seven fresh bowstrings which have not dried," Samson answered her, "I shall be as weak as any other man." 8 So the lords of the Philistines brought her seven fresh bowstrings which had not dried, and she bound him with them. 9 She had men lying in wait in the chamber and so she said to him, "The Philistines are upon you, Samson!" But he snapped the strings as a thread of tow is severed by a whiff of flame; and the secret of his strength remained unknown.

10 Delilah said to Samson, "You have mocked me and told me lies. Now tell me how you may be bound." 11 "If they bind me tight with new ropes, with which no work has been done," he answered her, "I shall be as weak as any other man." 12 So Delilah took new ropes and bound him with them. Then she said to him, "The Philistines are upon you, Samson!" For there were men lying in wait in the chamber. But he snapped them off his arms like thread.

13 Delilah said to Samson again, "Up to now you have mocked me and told me lies. Tell me how you may be bound." He said to her, "If you weave my seven locks of hair into the web and fasten them with the pin, I shall be as weak as any other man." 14 So while he slept, Delilah wove his seven locks of hair into the web, and fastened them in with the pin. Then she said, "The Philistines are upon you, Samson!" Awakening from his sleep, he pulled out both the weaver's pin and the web.

15 Then she said to him, "How can you say that you love me when you do not confide in me? Three times already you have mocked me, and not told me the secret of your great strength!" 16 She importuned him continually and vexed him with her complaints till he was deathly weary of them. 17 So he took her completely into his confidence and told her, "No razor has touched my head, for I have been consecrated to God

15, 17: *Ramath-lehi:* "heights of the jawbone."
15, 19: *En-hakkore:* "the spring of him who cries out," an allusion to Samson's cry in v. 18.

from my mother's womb. If I am shaved, my strength will leave me, and I shall be as weak as any other man." 18 When Delilah saw that he had taken her completely into her confidence, she summoned the lords of the Philistines, saying, "Come up this time, for he has opened his heart to me." So the lords of the Philistines came and brought up the money with them. 19 She had him sleep on her lap, and called for a man who shaved off his seven locks of hair. Then she began to mistreat him, for his strength had left him. 20 When she said, "The Philistines are upon you, Samson!", and he woke from his sleep, he thought he could make good his escape as he had done time and again, for he did not realize that the LORD had left him. 21 But the Philistines seized him and gouged out his eyes. Then they brought him down to Gaza and bound him with bronze fetters, and he was put to grinding in the prison. 22 But the hair of his head began to grow as soon as it was shaved off.

The Death of Samson

23 The lords of the Philistines assembled to offer a great sacrifice to their god Dagon and to make merry. They said,

"Our god has delivered into our
　　power
Samson our enemy."

25 When their spirits were high, they said, "Call Samson that he may amuse us." So they called Samson from the prison, and he played the buffoon before them. 24 When the people saw him, they praised their god. For they said,

"Our god has delivered into our
　　power
our enemy, the ravager of our
　　land,
the one who has multipled our
　　slain."

Then they stationed him between the columns. 26 Samson said to the attendant who was holding his

hand, "Put me where I may touch the columns that support the temple and may rest against them." 27 The temple was full of men and women: all the lords of the Philistines were there, and from the roof about three thousand men and women looked on as Samson provided amusement. 28 Samson cried out to the LORD and said, "O Lord GOD, remember me! Strengthen me, O God, this last time that for my two eyes I may avenge myself once and for all on the Philistines." 29 Samson grasped the two middle columns on which the temple rested and braced himself against them, one at his right hand, the other at his left. 30 And Samson said, "Let me die with the Philistines!" He pushed hard, and the temple fell upon the lords and all the people who were in it. Those he killed at his death were more than those he had killed during his lifetime.

31 All his family and kinsmen went down and bore him up for burial in the grave of his father Manoah between Zorah and Eshtaol. He had judged Israel for twenty years.

THE TRIBES OF DAN AND BENJAMIN IN THE DAYS OF THE JUDGES

Micah and the Levite

17 There was a man in the mountain region of Ephraim whose name was Micah. 2 He said to his mother, "The eleven hundred shekels of silver over which you pronounced a curse in my hearing when they were taken from you, are in my possession. It was I who took them; so now I will restore them to you." 3 When he restored the eleven hundred shekels of silver to his mother, she took two hundred of them and gave them to the silversmith, who made of them a carved idol overlaid with silver. 4 Then his mother said, "May the LORD bless my son! I have consecrated the silver to the LORD as my gift in favor of my son, by making a carved idol overlaid with silver." It remained in the house of Micah. 5

Thus the layman Micah had a sanctuary. He also made an ephod and household idols, and consecrated one of his sons, who became his priest. 6 In those days there was no king in Israel; everyone did what he thought best.

7 There was a young Levite who had resided within the tribe of Judah at Bethlehem of Judah. 8 From that city he set out to find another place of residence. On his journey he came to the house of Micah in the mountain region of Ephraim. 9 Micah said to him, "Where do you come from?" He answered him, "I am a Levite from Bethlehem in Judah, and am on my way to find some other place of residence." 10 "Stay with me," Micah said to him. "Be father and priest to me, and I will give you ten silver shekels a year, a set of garments, and your food." 11 So the young Levite decided to stay with the man, to whom he became as one of his own sons. 12 Micah consecrated the young Levite, who became his priest, remaining in his house. 13 Therefore Micah said, "Now I know that the LORD will prosper me, since the Levite has become my priest."

Migration of the Danites

18 At that time there was no king in Israel. Moreover the tribe of Danites were in search of a district to dwell in, for up to that time they had received no heritage among the tribes of Israel.

2 So the Danites sent from their clan a detail of five valiant men of Zorah and Eshtaol, to reconnoiter the land and scout it. With their instructions to go and scout the land, they traveled as far as the house of Micah in the mountain region of Ephraim, where they passed the night. 3 Near the house of Micah, they recognized the voice of the young Levite and turned in that direction. "Who brought you here and what are you doing here?" they asked him. "What is your interest here?" 4 "This is how Micah treats

---

16, 23: Dagon was originally a Mesopotamian deity, whom the Philistines came to worship as their own god of grain.

17, 3: *Idol:* an image, not of a pagan god, but of the LORD. The Mosaic law forbade the making of an image even of the true God.

17, 12f: According to Nm 18, 1–7 only those Levites who were descended from Aaron could be consecrated as priests.

18, 1: The tribe of Dan had been assigned a territory with definite limits in central Palestine. However they were unable to gain possession of the

better portion of their land (1, 34). So they now seek territory elsewhere in Palestine.

18, 3: *Recognized the voice:* perhaps they noticed the peculiar pronunciation of his south Hebrew dialect.

me," he replied to them. "He pays me a salary and I am his priest." 5 They said to him, "Consult God, that we may know whether the undertaking we are engaged in will succeed." 6 The priest said to them, "Go and prosper: the LORD is favorable to the undertaking you are engaged in."

7 So the five men went on and came to Laish. They saw that the people dwelling there lived securely after the manner of the Sidonians, quiet and trusting, with no lack of any natural resources. They were distant from the Sidonians and had no contact with other people. 8 When the five returned to their kinsmen in Zorah and Eshtaol and were asked for a report, 9 they replied, "Come, let us attack them, for we have seen the land and it is very good. Are you going to hesitate? Do not be slothful about beginning your expedition to possess the land. 10 Those against whom you go are a trusting people, and the land is ample. God has indeed given it into your power: a place where no natural resource is lacking."

11 So six hundred men of the clan of the Danites, fully armed with weapons of war, set out from where they were in Zorah and Eshtaol, 12 and camped in Judah, up near Kiriath-jearim; hence to this day the place, which lies west of Kiriath-jearim, is called Mahaneh-dan.

13 From there they went on to the mountain region of Ephraim and came to the house of Micah. 14 The five men who had gone to reconnoiter the land of Laish said to their kinsmen, "Do you know that in these houses there are an ephod, household idols, and a carved idol overlaid with silver? Now decide what you must do!" 15 So turning in that direction, they went to the house of the young Levite at the home of Micah and greeted him. 16 The six hundred men girt with weapons of war, who were Danites, stood by the entrance of the gate, and the priest stood there also. 17 Meanwhile the five men who had gone to reconnoiter the land went up and entered the house of Micah. 18 When they had gone in and taken the ephod, the household idols, and the carved idol overlaid with silver, the priest said to them, "What are you doing?" 19 They said to him, "Be still: put your hand over your mouth. Come with us and be our father and priest. Is it better for you to be priest for the family of one man or to be priest for a tribe and a clan in Israel?" 20 The priest, agreeing, took the ephod, household idols, and carved idol and went off in the midst of the band. 21 As they turned to depart, they placed their little ones, their livestock, and their goods at the head of the column.

22 The Danites had already gone some distance, when those in the houses near that of Micah took up arms and overtook them. 23 They called to the Danites, who turned about and said to Micah, "What do you want, that you have taken up arms?" 24 "You have taken my god, which I made, and have gone off with my priest as well," he answered. "What is left for me? How, then, can you ask me what I want?" 25 The Danites said to him, "Let us hear no further sound from you, lest fierce men fall upon you and you and your family lose your lives." 26 The Danites then went on their way, and Micah, seeing that they were stronger than he, returned home.

27 Having taken what Micah had made, and the priest he had had, they attacked Laish, a quiet and trusting people; they put them to the sword and destroyed their city by fire. 28 No one came to their aid, since the city was far from Sidon and they had no contact with other people. The Danites then rebuilt the city, which was in the valley that belongs to Beth-rehob, and lived there. 29 They named it Dan after their ancestor Dan, son of Israel. However, the name of the city was formerly Laish. 30 The Danites set up the carved idol for themselves, and Jonathan, son of Gershom, son of Moses, and his descendants were priests for the tribe of the Danites until the time of the captivity of the land. 31 They maintained the carved idol Micah had made as long as the house of God was in Shiloh.

The Levite from Ephraim

19 At that time, when there was no king in Israel, there was a Levite residing in remote parts of the mountain region of Ephraim who had taken for himself a concubine from Bethlehem of Judah. 2 His concubine was unfaithful to him and left him for her father's house in Bethlehem of Judah, where she stayed for some four months. 3 Her husband then set out with his servant and a pair of asses, and went after her to forgive her and take her back. She brought him into her father's house, and on seeing him, the girl's father joyfully made him welcome. 4 He was detained by the girl's father, and so he spent three days with this father-in-law of his, eating and drinking and passing the night there. 5 On the fourth day they rose early in the morning and he prepared to go. But the girl's father said to his son-in-law, "Fortify yourself with a little food; you can go later on." 6 So they stayed and the two men ate and drank together. Then the girl's father said to the husband, "Why not decide to spend the night here and enjoy yourself?" 7 The man still made a move to go, but when the father-in-law pressed him he went back and spent the night there.

8 On the fifth morning he rose early to depart, but the girl's father said, "Fortify yourself and tarry until the afternoon." When he and his father-in-law had eaten, 9 and the husband was ready to go with his concubine and servant, the girl's father said to him, "It is already growing dusk. Stay for the night. See, the day is coming to an end. Spend the night here and enjoy yourself. Early tomorrow you can start your journey home." 10 The man, however, refused to stay another night; he and his concubine set out with a pair of saddled asses, and traveled till they came opposite Jebus, which is Jerusalem. 11 Since they were near Jebus with the day far gone, the servant said to his master, "Come, let

---

18, 30: *Until . . . land:* about the year 734 B.C., when the Assyrian emperor Tiglathpileser III subjected northern Palestine.

19, 5–9: Such importuning of guests to prolong their stay at the home of their host is characteristic of Oriental hospitality.

us turn off to this city of the Jebusites and spend the night in it." 12 But his master said to him, "We will not turn off to a city of foreigners, who are not Israelites, but will go on to Gibeah. 13 Come," he said to his servant, "let us make for some other place, either Gibeah or Ramah, to spend the night." 14 So they continued on their way till the sun set on them when they were abreast of Gibeah of Benjamin.

15 There they turned off to enter Gibeah for the night. The man waited in the public square of the city he had entered, but no one offered them the shelter of his home for the night. 16 In the evening, however, an old man came from his work in the field; he was from the mountain region of Ephraim, though he lived among the Benjaminite townspeople of Gibeah. 17 When he noticed the traveler in the public square of the city, the old man asked where he was going, and whence he had come. 18 He said to him, "We are traveling from Bethlehem of Judah far up into the mountain region of Ephraim, where I belong. I have been to Bethlehem of Judah and am now going back home; but no one has offered us the shelter of his house. 19 We have straw and fodder for our asses, and bread and wine for the woman and myself and for our servant; there is nothing else we need." 20 "You are welcome," the old man said to him, "but let me provide for all your needs, and do not spend the night in the public square." 21 So he led them to his house and provided fodder for the asses. Then they washed their feet, and ate and drank.

The Outrage at Gibeah

22 While they were enjoying themselves, the men of the city, who were corrupt, surrounded the house and beat on the door. They said to the old man whose house it was, "Bring out your guest, that we may abuse him." 23 The owner of the house went out

to them and said, "No, my brothers; do not be so wicked. Since this man is my guest, do not commit this crime. 24 Rather let me bring out my maiden daughter or his concubine. Ravish them, or do whatever you want with them; but against the man you must not commit this wanton crime." 25 When the men would not listen to his host, the husband seized his concubine and thrust her outside to them. They had relations with her and abused her all night until the following dawn, when they let her go. 26 Then at daybreak the woman came and collapsed at the entrance of the house in which her husband was a guest, where she lay until the morning. 27 When her husband rose that day and opened the door of the house to start out again on his journey, there lay the woman, his concubine, at the entrance of the house with her hands on the threshold. 28 He said to her, "Come, let us go"; but there was no answer. So the man placed her on an ass and started out again for home.

29 On reaching home, he took a knife to the body of his concubine, cut her into twelve pieces, and sent them throughout the territory of Israel. 30 Everyone who saw this said, "Nothing like this has been done or seen from the day the Israelites came up from the land of Egypt to this day. Take note of it, and state what you propose to do."

Assembly of Israelites

20 So all the Israelites came out as one man: from Dan to Beer-sheba, and from the land of Gilead, the community was gathered to the LORD at Mizpah. 2 The leaders of all the people and all the tribesmen of Israel, four hundred thousand foot soldiers who were swordsmen, presented themselves in the assembly of the people of God. 3 Meanwhile, the Benjaminites heard that the Israelites had gone up to Mizpah. The Israelites asked to be

told how the crime had taken place, 4 and the Levite, the husband of the murdered woman, testified: "My concubine and I went into Gibeah of Benjamin for the night. 5 But the citizens of Gibeah rose up against me by night and surrounded the house in which I was. Me they attempted to kill, and my concubine they abused so that she died. 6 So I took my concubine and cut her up and sent her through every part of the territory of Israel, because of the monstrous crime they had committed in Israel. 7 Now that you are all here, O Israelites, state what you propose to do." 8 All the people rose as one man to say, "None of us is to leave for his tent or return to his home. 9 Now as for Gibeah, this is what we will do: We will proceed against it by lot, 10 taking from all the tribes of Israel ten men for every hundred, a hundred for every thousand, a thousand for every ten thousand, and procuring supplies for the soldiers who will go to deal fully and suitably with Gibeah of Benjamin for the crime it committed in Israel."

11 When, therefore, all the men of Israel, without exception were leagued together against the city, 12 the tribes of Israel sent men throughout the tribe of Benjamin to say, "What is this evil which has occurred among you? 13 Now give up these corrupt men of Gibeah, that we may put them to death and thus purge the evil from Israel." But the Benjaminites refused to accede to the demand of their brothers, the Israelites. 14 Instead, the Benjaminites assembled from their other cities to Gibeah, to do battle with the Israelites. 15 The number of the Benjaminite swordsmen from the other cities on that occasion was twenty-six thousand, in addition to the inhabitants of Gibeah. 16 Included in this total were seven hundred picked men who were left-handed, every one of them able to sling a stone at a hair without missing. 17 Meanwhile the other Israelites

---

19, 15: Private hospitality was the customary means of providing comfort for travelers where public facilities were so rare.

19, 22: *Who were corrupt:* literally "sons of Belial," indicating extreme perversion; cf Gn 19, 4-8. This crime and its punishment made the name *Gibeah* proverbial as a place of shameful wickedness; cf Hos 9, 9; 10, 9.

19, 29: A drastic means for arousing the tribes to avenge the unheard of crime of the Benjaminites.

20, 1: *From Dan to Beer-sheba:* from north to south. *The land of Gilead:* all the territory east of the Jordan.

20, 7: The Israelites were asked to decide at once what action to take concerning this crime; cf 2 Sm 16, 20. The Levite undoubtedly addressed the tribal heads

who would speak in behalf of the multitude.

20, 12: Before the crime at Gibeah was punished, the Benjaminites were invited to join their brethren, the Israelites, in punishing the crime. Since they failed to respond, special messengers were sent asking them to deliver up the guilty ones. They replied by gathering their forces for combat.

who, without Benjamin, mustered four hundred thousand swordsmen ready for battle, 18 moved on to Bethel and consulted God. When the Israelites asked who should go first in the attack on the Benjaminites, the LORD said, "Judah shall go first." 19 The next day the Israelites advanced on Gibeah with their forces.

War with Benjamin

20 On the day the Israelites drew up in battle array at Gibeah for the combat with Benjamin, 21 the Benjaminites came out of the city and felled twenty-two thousand men of Israel. 23 Then the Israelites went up and wept before the LORD until evening. "Shall I again engage my brother Benjamin in battle?" they asked the LORD; and the LORD answered that they should. 22 But though the Israelite soldiers took courage and again drew up for combat in the same place as on the previous day, 24 when they met the Benjaminites for the second time, 25 once again the Benjaminites who came out of Gibeah against them felled eighteen thousand Israelites, all of them swordsmen. 26 So the entire Israelite army went up to Bethel, where they wept and remained fasting before the LORD until evening of that day, besides offering holocausts and peace offerings before the LORD. 27 When the Israelites consulted the LORD (for the ark of the covenant of God was there in those days, 28 and Phinehas, son of Eleazar, son of Aaron, was ministering to him in those days), and asked, "Shall I go out again to battle with Benjamin, my brother, or shall I desist?" the LORD said, "Attack! for tomorrow I will deliver him into your power." 29 So Israel set men in ambush around Gibeah.

30 The Israelites went up against the Benjaminites for the third time and formed their line of battle at Gibeah as on other occasions. 31 The Benjaminites went out to meet them, and in the beginning they killed off about thirty of the Israelite soldiers in the open field, just as on the other occasions. 32 Therefore the Benjaminites thought, "We are defeating them as before"; not realizing that disaster was about to overtake them. The Israelites, however, had planned the flight so as to draw them away from the city onto the highways. They were drawn away from the city onto the highways, of which the one led to Bethel, the other to Gibeon. 33 And then all the men of Israel rose from their places. They re-formed their ranks at Baal-tamar, and the Israelites in ambush rushed from their place west of Gibeah, 34 ten thousand picked men from all Israel, and advanced against the city itself. In a fierce battle, 35 the LORD defeated Benjamin before Israel; and on that day the Israelites killed twenty-five thousand one hundred men of Benjamin, all of them swordsmen.

36 To the Benjaminites it had looked as though the enemy were defeated, for the men of Israel gave ground to Benjamin, trusting in the ambush they had set at Gibeah. 37 But then the men in ambush made a sudden dash into Gibeah, overran it, and put the whole city to the sword. 38 Now, the other Israelites had agreed with the men in ambush on a smoke signal they were to send up from the city. 39 And though the men of Benjamin had begun by killing off some thirty of the men of Israel, under the impression that they were defeating them as surely as in the earlier fighting, the Israelites wheeled about to resist 40 as the smoke of the signal column began to rise up from the city. It was when Benjamin looked back and saw the whole city in flames against the sky 41 that the men of Israel wheeled about. Therefore the men of Benjamin were thrown into confusion, for they realized the disaster that had overtaken them. 42 They retreated before the men of Israel in the direction of the desert, with the fight being pressed against them. In their very midst, meanwhile, those who had been in the city were spreading destruction. 43 The men of Benjamin had been surrounded, and were now pursued to a point east of Gibeah, 44 while eighteen thousand of them fell, warriors to a man. 45 The rest turned and fled through the desert to the rock Rimmon. But on the highways the Israelites picked off five thousand men among them, and chasing them up to Gidom, killed another two thousand of them there. 46 Those of Benjamin who fell on that day were in all twenty-five thousand swordsmen, warriors to a man. 47 But six hundred others who turned and fled through the desert reached the rock Rimmon, where they remained for four months.

48 The men of Israel withdrew through the territory of the Benjaminites, putting to the sword the inhabitants of the cities, the livestock, and all they chanced upon. Moreover they destroyed by fire all the cities they came upon.

Wives for the Survivors

21 Now the men of Israel had sworn at Mizpah that none of them would give his daughter in marriage to anyone from Benjamin. 2 So the people went to Bethel and remained there before God until evening, raising their voices in bitter lament. 3 They said, "LORD, God of Israel, why has it come to pass in Israel that today one tribe of Israel should be lacking?" 4 Early the next day the people built an altar there and offered holocausts and peace offerings. 5 Then the Israelites asked, "Are there any among all the tribes of Israel who did not come up to the LORD for the assembly?" For they had taken a solemn oath that anyone who did not go up to the LORD at Mizpah should be put to death without fail.

6 The Israelites were disconsolate over their brother Benjamin and said, "Today one of the tribes of Israel has been cut off. 7 What can we do about wives for the survivors, since

---

20, 18: *Judah shall go first:* the same response as in 1, 1f, but without the assurance of immediate success. Only after the Israelites were punished at the hands of the Benjaminites for their own grossness, and had performed penance, did they succeed in punishing the latter for their part in the crime of rape and murder, by gaining the victory over them.

20, 29-46: This stratagem proved more useful to the Israelites than force, as in the siege of Ai (Jos 8, 3-21). In the parallel accounts the first (vv 29-35) is a summary of the second (vv 36-46).

21, 1-3: The anger of the Israelites led them to destroy their brethren, the Benjaminites. Having realized their goal, however, they were soon filled with dismay, and sought to restore the tribe they had all but exterminated.

21, 6-9: This account is summarized in the parallel passage in vv 2-5.

we have sworn by the LORD not to give them any of our daughters in marriage?" 8 And when they asked whether anyone among the tribes of Israel had not come up to the LORD in Mizpah, they found that none of the men of Jabesh-gilead had come to the encampment for the assembly. 9 A roll call of the army established that none of the inhabitants of that city were present. 10 The community, therefore, sent twelve thousand warriors with orders to go to Jabesh-gilead and put those who lived there to the sword, including the women and children. 11 They were told to include under the ban all males and every woman who was not still a virgin. 12 Finding among the inhabitants of Jabesh-gilead four hundred young virgins, who had had no relations with men, they brought them to the camp at Shiloh in the land of Canaan. 13 Then the whole community sent a message to the Benjaminites at the rock Rimmon,

offering them peace. 14 When Benjamin returned at that time, they gave them as wives the women of Jabesh-gilead whom they had spared; but these proved to be not enough for them.

15 The people were still disconsolate over Benjamin because the LORD had made a breach among the tribes of Israel. 16 And the elders of the community said, "What shall we do for wives for the survivors? For every woman in Benjamin has been put to death." 17 They said, "Those of Benjamin who survive must have heirs, else one of the Israelite tribes will be wiped out. 18 Yet we cannot give them any of our daughters in marriage, because the Israelites have sworn, 'Cursed be he who gives a woman to Benjamin!'" 19 Then they thought of the yearly feast of the LORD at Shiloh, north of Bethel, east of the highway that goes up from Bethel to Shechem, and south of Lebonah. 20 And they

instructed the Benjaminites, "Go and lie in wait in the vineyards. 21 When you see the girls of Shiloh come out to do their dancing, leave the vineyards and each of you seize one of the girls of Shiloh for a wife, and go to the land of Benjamin. 22 When their fathers or their brothers come to complain to us, we shall say to them. 'Release them to us as a kindness, since we did not take a woman apiece in the war. Had you yourselves given them these wives, you would now be guilty.'"

23 The Benjaminites did this; they carried off a wife for each of them from their raid on the dancers, and went back to their own territory, where they rebuilt and occupied the cities. 24 Also at that time the Israelites dispersed; each of them left for his own heritage in his own clan and tribe.

25 In those days there was no king in Israel; everyone did what he thought best.

21, 11: *Under the ban:* see note on Nm 21, 3.

21, 15: *Had made a breach:* what is here attributed to God was in reality the free and deliberate act of the Israelites and happened only by the permissive will of

God. The ancients attributed to the first primary cause what is more directly due to secondary causes.

21, 18: Regardless of the serious consequences of their vow, the Israelites considered themselves

obliged to fulfill it; cf 11, 31.35f.39.

21, 25: Cf 17, 6; 18, 1; 19, 1. The verse gives the reason why the lawlessness of the period of judges, and the events described herein, were possible.

Ruth

Naomi in Moab

ONCE in the time of the judges there was a famine in the land; so a man from Bethlehem of Judah departed with his wife and two sons to reside on the plateau of Moab. 2 The man was named Elimelech, his wife Naomi, and his sons Mahlon and Chilion; they were Ephrathites from Bethlehem of Judah. Some time after their arrival on the Moabite plateau, 3 Elimelech, the husband of Naomi, died, and she was left with her two sons, 4 who married Moabite women, one named Orpah, the other Ruth. When they had lived there about ten years, 5 both Mahlon and Chilion died also, and the woman was left with neither her two sons nor her husband. 6 She then made ready to go back from the plateau of Moab because word reached her there that the LORD had visited his people and given them food.

7 She and her two daughters-in-law left the place where they had been living. Then as they were on the road back to the land of Judah, 8 Naomi said to her two daughters-in-law, "Go back, each of you, to your mother's house! May the LORD be kind to you as you were to the departed and to me! 9 May the LORD grant each of you a husband and a home in which you will find rest." She kissed them good-by, but they wept with loud sobs, 10 and told her they would return with her to her people. 11 "Go back, my daughters!" said Naomi. "Why should you come with me? Have I other sons in my womb who may become your husbands? 12 Go back, my daughters! Go, for I am too old to marry again. And even if I could offer any hopes, or if tonight I had a husband or had borne sons, 13 would you then wait and deprive yourselves of husbands until those sons grew up? No, my daughters! my lot is too bitter for you, because the LORD has extended his hand against me." 14 Again they sobbed aloud and wept; and Orpah kissed her mother-in-law good-by, but Ruth stayed with her.

15 "See now!" she said, "your sister-in-law has gone back to her people and her god. Go back after your sister-in-law!" 16 But Ruth said, "Do not ask me to abandon or forsake you! for wherever you go I will go, wherever you lodge I will lodge, your people shall be my people, and your God my God. 17 Wherever you die I will die, and there be buried. May the LORD do so and so to me, and more besides, if aught but death separates me from you!" 18 Naomi then ceased to urge her, for she saw she was determined to go with her.

The Return to Bethlehem

19 So they went on together till they reached Bethlehem. On their arrival there, the whole city was astir over them, and the women asked, "Can this be Naomi?" 20 But she said to them, "Do not call me Naomi. Call me Mara, for the Almighty has made it very bitter for me. 21 I went away with an abundance, but the LORD has brought me back destitute. Why should you call me

---

1, 1f: *In the time of the judges:* three generations before the end of the period of judges; cf 4, 21f. *Bethlehem of Judah:* to distinguish it from the town of the same name in the tribe of Zebulun (Jos 19, 15). *Ephrathites from Bethlehem:* belonging to a Judean clan which settled in Bethlehem; cf 1 Sm 17, 12; 1 Chr 2, 50f; 4, 4.

1, 8: *Mother's house:* the women's part of the dwelling; cf Jgs 4, 17; Sg 3, 4.

1, 11: *Have I other sons ... husbands?* Naomi insisted that her daughters-in-law remain in their own country only for the sake of posterity. If she had had other sons, the levirate law would have obliged them to marry the widows of her deceased sons to perpetuate the names of the deceased; cf Gn 38, 8; Dt 25, 5f.

1, 16f: An example of heroic fidelity and piety. Ruth's decision, confirmed with an oath, to adhere to her mother-in-law impelled her to abandon her country and its pagan worship.

1, 20f: *Naomi:* "amiable" or "pleasant," suggesting God's favor toward her. *The Almighty has brought evil upon me:* the ancients regarded adversity as a punishment from God for personal sin, as if good and evil were always repaid in a temporal and material manner.

Naomi, since the LORD has pronounced against me and the Almighty has brought evil upon me?" 22 Thus it was that Naomi returned with the Moabite daughter-in-law, Ruth, who accompanied her back from the plateau of Moab. They arrived in Bethlehem at the beginning of the barley harvest.

The Meeting

2 Naomi had a prominent kinsman named Boaz, of the clan of her husband Elimelech. 2 Ruth the Moabite said to Naomi, "Let me go and glean ears of grain in the field of anyone who will allow me that favor." Naomi said to her, "Go, my daughter," 3 and she went. The field she entered to glean after the harvesters happened to be the section belonging to Boaz of the clan of Elimelech. 4 Boaz himself came from Bethlehem and said to the harvesters, "The LORD be with you!" and they replied, "The LORD bless you!" 5 Boaz asked the overseer of his harvesters, "Whose girl is this?" 6 The overseer of the harvesters answered, "She is the Moabite girl who returned from the plateau of Moab with Naomi. 7 She asked leave to gather the gleanings into sheaves after the harvesters; and ever since she came this morning she has remained here until now, with scarcely a moment's rest."

8 Boaz said to Ruth, "Listen, my daughter! Do not go to glean in anyone else's field; you are not to leave here. Stay here with my women servants. 9 Watch to see which field is to be harvested, and follow them; I have commanded the young men to do you no harm. When you are thirsty, you may go and drink from the vessels the young men have filled." 10 Casting herself prostrate upon the ground, she said to him, "Why should I, a foreigner, be favored with your notice?" 11 Boaz answered her: "I have had a complete account of what you have done for your mother-in-law after your

husband's death; you have left your father and your mother and the land of your birth, and have come to a people whom you did not know previously. 12 May the LORD reward what you have done! May you receive a full reward from the LORD, the God of Israel, under whose wings you have come for refuge." 13 She said, "May I prove worthy of your kindness, my lord: you have comforted me, your servant, with your consoling words; would indeed that I were a servant of yours!" 14 At mealtime Boaz said to her, "Come here and have some food; dip your bread in the sauce." Then as she sat near the reapers, he handed her some roasted grain and she ate her fill and had some left over. 15 She rose to glean, and Boaz instructed his servants to let her glean among the sheaves themselves without scolding her, 16 and even to let drop some handfuls and leave them for her to glean without being rebuked.

17 She gleaned in the field until evening, and when she beat out what she had gleaned it came to about an ephah of barley, 18 which she took into the city and showed to her mother-in-law. Next she brought out and gave her what she had left over from lunch. 19 So her mother-in-law said to her. "Where did you glean today? Where did you go to work? May he who took notice of you be blessed!" Then she told her mother-in-law with whom she had worked. "The man at whose place I worked today is named Boaz," she said. 20 "May he be blessed by the LORD, who is ever merciful to the living and to the dead," Naomi exclaimed to her daughter-in-law; and she continued, "He is a relative of ours, one of our next of kin." 21 "He even told me," added Ruth the Moabite, "that I should stay with his servants until they complete his entire harvest." 22 "You would do well, my dear," Naomi rejoined, "to go out with his servants; for in some-

one else's field you might be insulted." 23 So she stayed gleaning with the servants of Boaz until the end of the barley and wheat harvests.

Ruth Again Presents Herself

When she was back with her 3 mother-in-law, 1 Naomi said to her, "My daughter, I must seek a home for you that will please you. 2 Now is not Boaz, with whose servants you were, a relative of ours? This evening he will be winnowing barley at the threshing floor. 3 So bathe and anoint yourself; then put on your best attire and go down to the threshing floor. Do not make yourself known to the man before he has finished eating and drinking. 4 But when he lies down, take note of the place where he does so. Then go, uncover a place at his feet, and lie down. He will tell you what to do." 5 "I will do whatever you advise," Ruth replied. 6 So she went down to the threshing floor and did just as her mother-in-law had instructed her.

7 Boaz ate and drank to his heart's content. Then when he went and lay down at the edge of the sheaves, she stole up, uncovered a place at his feet, and lay down. 8 In the middle of the night, however, the man gave a start and turned around to find a woman lying at his feet. 9 He asked, "Who are you!" And she replied, "I am your servant Ruth. Spread the corner of your cloak over me, for you are my next of kin." 10 He said, "May the LORD bless you, my daughter! You have been even more loyal now than before in not going after the young men, whether poor or rich. 11 So be assured, daughter, I will do for you whatever you say; all my townspeople know you for a worthy woman. 12 Now, though indeed I am closely related to you, you have another relative still closer. 13 Stay as you are for tonight, and tomorrow, if he wishes to claim you,

---

1, 22: *Barley harvest:* early April. This circumstance favored the events of the narrative that follow.

2, 2: *Let me go and glean . . . grain:* even the poor, the widow, the stranger, and the orphan had a right to glean at harvest time; cf Lv 19, 9f; 23, 22; Dt 24, 19–22.

2, 4: *The Lord be with you:* courtesy and religious feeling characterize the salutations of the Hebrews. This greeting is used in the Christian liturgy.

2, 20: *One of our next of kin:* literally "our redeemer," a near relative of the same clan who had the right and duty to restore the land which an impoverished kinsman had alienated (Lv 25, 25–28), and to marry the widow of a relative who had died without male offspring so as to raise up posterity to his name (Dt 25, 5–10).

3, 4: *Uncover a place at his feet, . . .:* confident of the virtue of Ruth and Boaz, Naomi advises this

unusual expedient to her daughter-in-law for the purpose of introducing her claim.

3, 9: *Spread the corner of your cloak over me:* be my protector by marrying me according to the duty of a near kinsman; cf Dt 25, 5; Ez 16, 8.

3, 12: *Relative still closer:* who had a prior right and duty to marry Ruth.

good! let him do so. But if he does not wish to claim you, as the LORD lives, I will claim you myself. Lie there until morning." 14 So she lay at his feet until morning but rose before men could recognize one another. Boaz said, "Let it not be known that this woman came to the threshing floor." 15 Then he said to her, "Take off your cloak and hold it out." When she did so, he poured out six measures of barley, helped her lift the bundle, and left for the city.

16 Ruth went home to her mother-in-law, who asked, "How have you fared, my daughter?" So she told her all the man had done for her, 17 and concluded, "He gave me these six measures of barley because he did not wish me to come back to my mother-in-law empty-handed!" 18 Naomi then said, "Wait here, my daughter, until you learn what happens, for the man will not rest, but will settle the matter today."

Boaz Marries Ruth

4 Boaz went and took a seat at the gate; and when he saw the closer relative of whom he had spoken come along, he called to him by name, "Come and sit beside me!" And he did so. 2 Then Boaz picked out ten of the elders of the city and asked them to sit nearby. When they had done this, 3 he said to the near relative: "Naomi, who has come back from the Moabite plateau, is putting up for sale the piece of land that belonged to our kinsman Elimelech.

4 So I thought I would inform you, bidding you before those here present, including the elders of my people, to put in your claim for it if you wish to acquire it as next of kin. But if you do not wish to claim it, tell me so, that I may be guided accordingly, for no one has a prior claim to yours, and mine is next." He answered, "I will put in my claim."

5 Boaz continued, "Once you acquire the field from Naomi, you must take also Ruth the Moabite, the widow of the late heir, and raise up a family for the departed on his estate." 6 The near relative replied, "I cannot exercise my claim lest I depreciate my own estate. Put in a claim yourself in my stead, for I cannot exercise my claim." 7 Now it used to be the custom in Israel that, to make binding a contract of redemption or exchange, one party would take off his sandal and give it to the other. This was the form of attestation in Israel. 8 So the near relative, in saying to Boaz, "Acquire it for yourself," drew off his sandal. 9 Boaz then said to the elders and to all the people, "You are witnesses today that I have acquired from Naomi all the holdings of Elimelech, Chilion and Mahlon. 10 I also take Ruth the Moabite, the widow of Mahlon, as my wife, in order to raise up a family for her late husband on his estate, so that the name of the departed may not perish among his kinsmen and fellow citizens. Do you witness this today?" 11 All those at the gate, including the elders, said, "We do so.

May the LORD make this wife come into your house like Rachel and Leah, who between them built up the house of Israel. May you do well in Ephrathah and win fame in Bethlehem. 12 With the offspring the LORD will give you from this girl, may your house become like the house of Perez, whom Tamar bore to Judah."

13 Boaz took Ruth. When they came together as man and wife, the LORD enabled her to conceive and she bore a son. 14 Then the women said to Naomi, "Blessed is the LORD who has not failed to provide you today with an heir! May he become famous in Israel! 15 He will be your comfort and the support of your old age for his mother is the daughter-in-law who loves you. She is worth more to you than seven sons!" 16 Naomi took the child, placed him on her lap, and became his nurse. 17 And the neighbor women gave him his name, at the news that a grandson had been born to Naomi. They called him Obed. He was the father of Jesse, the father of David.

18 These are the descendants of Perez: Perez was the father of Hezron, 19 Hezron was the father of Ram, Ram was the father of Amminadab, 20 Amminadab was the father of Nahshon, Nahshon was the father of Salmon, 21 Salmon was the father of Boaz, Boaz was the father of Obed, 22 Obed was the father of Jesse, and Jesse became the father of David.

4, 1: *Took a seat at the gate:* i.e., of the city, where business affairs were settled.

4, 2: *Ten of the elders:* to serve as judges in legal matters as well as witnesses of the settlement of business affairs; cf Dt 25, 7–9.

4, 4: Poverty had obliged Naomi to sell the land of her deceased husband. The law permitted the nearest kinsman to redeem the land and thus preserve the family patrimony; cf Lv 25, 25.

4, 5f: The heir of Elimelech's field had died without children (1, 5). The nearest of kin could now redeem the land but he must also take Ruth, *the widow of the late heir,* to wife to perpetuate the family of the deceased; cf Dt 25, 5f. The first male child of such a marriage would be the legal son of Mahlon and grandson of Elimelech.

4, 7: *Take off his sandal . . . :* by this act the near relative renounced his legal right, both to the field of Elimelech and to the marriage with Ruth. The custom mentioned in Dt 25, 6 is somewhat different.

4, 12: *Perez, whom Tamar bore to Judah:* the right which Judah unwittingly satisfied for his daughter-in-law Tamar (Gn 38), Boaz willingly rendered to Ruth.

4, 16: *Placed him on her lap:* took him as her own; cf Gn 30, 3; 48, 12; Nm 11, 12.

4, 17: *The father of Jesse, the father of David:* indicating the place of Obed, Jesse and David in the line of Judah and the ancestry of Christ, the Messiah; cf Mt 1, 5f.

THE FIRST BOOK OF

Samuel

THE LAST JUDGES—ELI AND SAMUEL

Elkanah and His Family at Shiloh

THERE was a certain man from Ramathaim, Elkanah by name, a Zuphite from the hill country of Ephraim. He was the son of Jeroham, son of Elihu, son of Tohu, son of Zuph, an Ephraimite. 2 He had two wives, one named Hannah, the other Peninnah; Peninnah had children, but Hannah was childless. 3 This man regularly went on pilgrimage from his city to worship the LORD of hosts and to sacrifice to him at Shiloh, where the two sons of Eli, Hophni and Phinehas, were ministering as priests of the LORD. 4 When the day came for Elkanah to offer sacrifice, he used to give a portion each to his wife Peninnah and to all her sons and daughters, 5 but a double portion to Hannah because he loved her, though the LORD had made her barren. 6 Her rival, to upset her, turned it into a constant reproach to her that the LORD had left her barren. 7 This went on year after year; each time they made their pilgrimage to the sanctuary of the LORD, Peninnah would approach her, and Hannah would weep and refuse to eat. 8 Her husband Elkanah used to ask her: "Hannah, why do you weep, and why do you refuse to eat? Why do you grieve? Am I not more to you than ten sons?"

Hannah's Prayer

9 Hannah rose after one such meal at Shiloh, and presented herself before the LORD; at the time, Eli the priest was sitting on a chair near the doorpost of the LORD's temple. 10 In her bitterness she prayed to the LORD, weeping copiously, 11 and she made a vow, promising: "O LORD of hosts, if you look with pity on the misery of your handmaid, if you remember me and do not forget me, if you give your handmaid a male child, I will give him to the LORD for as long as he lives; neither wine nor liquor shall he drink, and no razor shall ever touch his head." 12 As she remained long at prayer before the LORD, Eli watched her mouth, 13 for Hannah was praying silently; though her lips were moving, her voice could not be heard. Eli, thinking her drunk, 14 said to her, "How long will you make a drunken show of yourself? Sober up from

your wine!" 15 "It isn't that, my lord," Hannah answered. "I am an unhappy woman. I have had neither wine nor liquor; I was only pouring out my troubles to the LORD. 16 Do not think your handmaid a ne'er-do-well; my prayer has been prompted by my deep sorrow and misery." 17 Eli said, "Go in peace, and may the God of Israel grant you what you have asked of him." 18 She replied, "Think kindly of your maidservant," and left. She went to her quarters, ate and drank with her husband, and no longer appeared downcast. 19 Early the next morning they worshiped before the LORD, and then returned to their home in Ramah.

Hannah Bears a Son

When Elkanah had relations with his wife Hannah, the LORD remembered her. 20 She conceived, and at the end of her term bore a son whom she called Samuel, since she had asked the LORD for him. 21 The

---

1, 11: *Give him to the Lord:* some ancient texts call Samuel a *nazir* in this context; see note on Nm 6, 1ff.

1, 20: *Since she had asked:* this explanation would be more directly appropriate for the name Saul, which means "asked"; Samuel means "name of God."

next time her husband Elkanah was going up with the rest of his household to offer the customary sacrifice to the LORD and to fulfill his vows, 22 Hannah did not go, explaining to her husband, "Once the child is weaned, I will take him to appear before the LORD and to remain there forever; I will offer him as a perpetual nazirite." 23 Her husband Elkanah answered her: "Do what you think best; wait until you have weaned him. Only, may the LORD bring your resolve to fulfilment!" And so she remained at home and nursed her son until she had weaned him.

Samuel is Offered to God

24 Once he was weaned, she brought him up with her, along with a three-year-old bull, an ephah of flour, and a skin of wine, and presented him at the temple of the LORD in Shiloh. 25 After the boy's father had sacrificed the young bull, Hannah, his mother, approached Eli 26 and said: "Pardon, my lord! As you live, my lord, I am the woman who stood near you here, praying to the LORD. 27 I prayed for this child, and the LORD granted my request. 28 Now I, in turn, give him to the LORD; as long as he lives, he shall be dedicated to the LORD." She left him

2 there; 1 and as she worshiped the LORD, she said:

"My heart exults in the LORD, my
   horn is exalted in my God.
I have swallowed up my enemies;
   I rejoice in my victory.
2 There is no Holy One like the
   LORD;
   there is no Rock like our God.

3 "Speak boastfully no longer,
   nor let arrogance issue from
      your mouths.
For an all-knowing God is the
   LORD,
   a God who judges deeds.
4 The bows of the mighty are
      broken,
   while the tottering gird on
      strength.

5 The well-fed hire themselves out
      for bread,
   while the hungry batten on
      spoil.
The barren wife bears seven sons,
   while the mother of many
      languishes.

6 "The LORD puts to death and
   gives life;
   he casts down to the nether
      world;
   he raises up again.
7 The LORD makes poor and makes
   rich,
   he humbles, he also exalts.
8 He raises the needy from the dust;
   from the ash heap he lifts up the
      poor,
To seat them with nobles
   and make a glorious throne
      their heritage.
He gives to the vower his vow,
   and blesses the sleep of the just.

"For the pillars of the earth are
   the LORD's,
   and he has set the world upon
      them.
9 He will guard the footsteps of his
   faithful ones,
   but the wicked shall perish in
      the darkness.
For not by strength does man
      prevail;
10   the LORD's foes shall be
      shattered.
The Most High in heaven
      thunders;
   the LORD judges the ends of the
      earth,
Now may he give strength to his
   king,
   and exalt the horn of his
      anointed!"

11 When Elkanah returned home to Ramah, the child remained in the service of the LORD under the priest Eli.

Wickedness of Eli's Sons

12 Now the sons of Eli were wicked; they had respect neither for the LORD 13 nor for the priests'

duties toward the people. When someone offered a sacrifice, the priest's servant would come with a three-pronged fork, while the meat was still boiling, 14 and would thrust it into the basin, kettle, caldron, or pot. Whatever the fork brought up, the priest would keep. That is how all the Israelites were treated who came to the sanctuary at Shiloh. 15 In fact, even before the fat was burned, the priest's servant would come and say to the man offering the sacrifice, "Give me some meat to roast for the priest. He will not accept boiled meat from you, only raw meat." 16 And if the man protested to him, "Let the fat be burned first as is the custom, then take whatever you wish," he would reply, "No, give it to me now, or else I will take it by force." 17 Thus the young men sinned grievously in the presence of the LORD; they treated the offerings to the LORD with disdain.

The Lord Rewards Hannah

18 Meanwhile the boy Samuel, girt with a linen apron, was serving in the presence of the LORD. 19 His mother used to make a little garment for him, which she would bring him each time she went up with her husband to offer the customary sacrifice. 20 And Eli would bless Elkanah and his wife, as they were leaving for home. He would say, "May the LORD repay you with children from this woman for the gift she has made to the LORD!" 21 The LORD favored Hannah so that she conceived and gave birth to three more sons and two daughters, while young Samuel grew up in the service of the LORD.

Eli's Futile Rebuke

22 When Eli was very old, he heard repeatedly how his sons were treating all Israel [and that they were having relations with the women serving at the entry of the meeting tent]. 23 So he said to them: "Why are you doing such things? 24 No, my sons, you must not do these things!

1, 24: *An ephah:* a little more than a bushel.
2, 1-10: A hymn attributed to Hannah, the mother of Samuel, as her thanksgiving to God because she has borne a son despite her previous sterility. She praises God as the helper of the weak (1f), who casts down the mighty and raises up the lowly (3ff), and who alone is the source of true strength (8ff); the hymn ends with a prayer for the king (v 10). This

canticle has several points of resemblance with our Lady's *Magnificat.*
2, 1: *Horn:* the symbol of strength; cf Pss 18, 3; 75, 5; 89, 18: 112, 9.
2, 3: *Speak . . . mouths:* addressed to the *enemies* mentioned in v 1.
2, 18: *Linen apron:* called in Hebrew "ephod," but not the same as the high priest's ephod (Ex 28,

6-14) or the ephod used in divination (v 28). Samuel wore a simple apron such as was worn by the priests (22, 18), and on one occasion also by David (2 Sm 6, 14).
2, 22: The bracketed words, which recall Ex 38, 8, are a gloss in the received text; they are lacking in the oldest Greek translation, and in a Hebrew manuscript from Qumran.

It is not a good report that I hear the people of the LORD spreading about you. 25 If a man sins against another man, one can intercede for him with the LORD; but if a man sins against the LORD, who can intercede for him?" But they disregarded their father's warning, since the LORD had decided on their death. 26 Meanwhile, young Samuel was growing in stature and in worth in the estimation of the LORD and of men.

Doom of Eli's House

27 A man of God came to Eli and said to him: "This is what the LORD says: 'I went so far as to reveal myself to your father's family when they were in Egypt as slaves to the house of Pharaoh. 28 I chose them out of all the tribes of Israel to be my priests, to go up to my altar, to burn incense, and to wear the ephod before me; and I assigned all the oblations of the Israelites to your father's family. 29 Why do you keep a greedy eye on my sacrifices and on the offerings which I have prescribed? And why do you honor your sons in preference to me, fattening yourselves with the choicest part of every offering of my people Israel?' 30 This, therefore, is the oracle of the LORD, the God of Israel: 'I said in the past that your family and your father's family should minister in my presence forever. But now,' the LORD declares, 'away with this! for I will honor those who honor me, but those who spurn me shall be accursed. 31 Yes, the time is coming when I will break your strength and the strength of your father's family, so that no man in your family shall reach old age. 32 You shall witness as a disappointed rival all the benefits enjoyed by Israel, but there shall never be an old man in your family. 33 I will permit some of your family to remain at my altar, to wear out their eyes in consuming greed; but the rest of the men of your family shall die by the sword. 34 You shall have a sign in what will happen to your two

sons, Hophni and Phinehas: both shall die on the same day. 35 I will choose a faithful priest who shall do what I have in heart and mind. I will establish a lasting house for him which shall function in the presence of my anointed forever. 36 Then whoever is left of your family will come to grovel before him for a piece of silver or a loaf of bread, and will say: Appoint me, I beg you, to a priestly function, that I may have a morsel of bread to eat.'"

Revelation to Samuel

3 During the time young Samuel was minister to the Lord under Eli, a revelation of the LORD was uncommon and vision infrequent. 2 One day Eli was asleep in his usual place. His eyes had lately grown so weak that he could not see. 3 The lamp of God was not yet extinguished, and Samuel was sleeping in the temple of the LORD where the ark of God was. 4 The LORD called to Samuel, who answered, "Here I am." 5 He ran to Eli and said, "Here I am. You called me." "I did not call you," Eli said. "Go back to sleep." So he went back to sleep. 6 Again the LORD called Samuel, who rose and went to Eli. "Here I am," he said. "You called me." But he answered, "I did not call you, my son. Go back to sleep." 7 At that time Samuel was not familiar with the LORD, because the LORD had not revealed anything to him as yet. 8 The LORD called Samuel again, for the third time. Getting up and going to Eli, he said, "Here I am. You called me." Then Eli understood that the LORD was calling the youth. 9 So he said to Samuel, "Go to sleep, and if you are called, reply, 'Speak, LORD, for your servant is listening.'" When Samuel went to sleep in his place, 10 the LORD came and revealed his presence, calling out as before, "Samuel, Samuel!" Samuel answered, Speak, for your servant is listening." 11 The LORD said to Samuel: "I am about to do something in Israel that

will cause the ears of everyone who hears it to ring. 12 On that day I will carry out in full against Eli everything I threatened against his family. 13 I announce to him that I am condemning his family once and for all, because of this crime: though he knew his sons were blaspheming God, he did not reprove them. 14 Therefore, I swear to the family of Eli that no sacrifice or offering will ever expiate its crime." 15 Samuel then slept until morning, when he got up early and opened the doors of the temple of the LORD. He feared to tell Eli the vision, 16 but Eli called to him, "Samuel, my son!" He replied, "Here I am." 17 Then Eli asked, "What did he say to you? Hide nothing from me! May God do thus and so to you if you hide a single thing he told you." 18 So Samuel told him everything, and held nothing back. Eli answered "He is the LORD. He will do what he judges best."

Samuel Acknowledged as Prophet

19 Samuel grew up, and the LORD was with him, not permitting any word of his to be without effect. 20 Thus all Israel from Dan to Beersheba came to know that Samuel was an accredited prophet of the LORD. 21 The LORD continued to appear at Shiloh; he manifested himself to 4 Shiloh through his word, 1 and Samuel spoke to all Israel.

Defeat of the Israelites

At that time, the Philistines gathered for an attack on Israel. Israel went out to engage them in battle and camped at Ebenezer, while the Philistines camped at Aphek. 2 The Philistines then drew up in battle formation against Israel. After a fierce struggle Israel was defeated by the Philistines, who slew about four thousand men on the battlefield. 3 When the troops retired to the camp, the elders of Israel said, "Why has the LORD permitted us to be defeated today by the Philistines? Let us fetch

---

2, 27–36: These verses propose the punishment of Eli from a point of view contemporary with the reform of Josiah (2 Kgs 23, 9; cf v 36); they hint at the events recorded in 22, 18–23 and 1 Kgs 2, 27. The older story of this divine warning is that in 3, 11–14.

2, 28: *Ephod:* a portable container, presumably of

cloth, for the lots used in ritual consultation of God during the days of the Judges (Jgs 17, 5; 18, 14–15) and down into the time of David (14, 3ff; 23, 6ff; 30, 7f). The ephod of the high priest described in Ex 28, 6ff becomes a garment upon which a *breast-piece of decision* symbolizes, but no longer serves for, such consultation. The Exodus text codifies a later

form of the tradition.

3, 1: *Uncommon:* prophetic communications from God were almost unknown.

3, 17: *May God do thus and so to you:* the Biblical writers avoid repeating for us the specific terms of a curse as the speaker would have uttered it.

the ark of the LORD from Shiloh that it may go into battle among us and save us from the grasp of our enemies."

Loss of the Ark

4 So the people sent to Shiloh and brought from there the ark of the LORD of hosts, who is enthroned upon the cherubim. The two sons of Eli, Hophni and Phinehas, were with the ark of God. 5 When the ark of the LORD arrived in the camp, all Israel shouted so loudly that the earth resounded. 6 The Philistines, hearing the noise of shouting, asked, "What can this loud shouting in the camp of the Hebrews mean?" On learning that the ark of the LORD had come into the camp, 7 the Philistines were frightened. They said, "Gods have come to their camp." They said also, "Woe to us! This has never happened before. 8 Woe to us! Who can deliver us from the power of these mighty gods? These are the gods that struck the Egyptians with various plagues and with pestilence. 9 Take courage and be manly, Philistines; otherwise you will become slaves to the Hebrews, as they were your slaves. So fight manfully!" 10 The Philistines fought and Israel was defeated; every man fled to his own tent. It was a disastrous defeat, in which Israel lost thirty thousand foot soldiers. 11 The ark of God was captured, and Eli's two sons, Hophni and Phinehas, were among the dead.

Death of Eli

12 A Benjaminite fled from the battlefield and reached Shiloh that same day, with his clothes torn and his head covered with dirt. 13 When he arrived, Eli was sitting in his chair beside the gate, watching the road, for he was troubled at heart about the ark of God. The man, however, went into the city to divulge his news, which put the whole city in an uproar. 14 Hearing the outcry of the men standing near him, Eli inquired, "What does this commotion mean?" 15 (Eli was ninety-eight years old, and his eyes would not focus, so that he could not see.) 16 The man quickly came up to Eli and said, "It is I who have come from the battlefield; I fled from there today." He asked, "What happened, my son?" 17 And the messenger answered: "Israel fled from the Philistines; in fact, the troops suffered heavy losses. Your two sons, Hophni and Phinehas, are among the dead, and the ark of God has been captured." 18 At this mention of the ark of God, Eli fell backward from his chair into the gateway; since he was an old man and heavy, he died of a broken neck. He had judged Israel for forty years.

19 His daughter-in-law, the wife of Phinehas, was with child and at the point of giving birth. When she heard the news concerning the capture of the ark and the deaths of her father-in-law and her husband, she was seized with the pangs of labor, and gave birth. 20 She was about to die when the women standing around her said to her, "Never fear! You have given birth to a son." Yet she neither answered nor paid any attention. 21 [She named the child Ichabod, saying, "Gone is the glory from Israel," with reference to the capture of the ark of God and to her father-in-law and her husband.] 22 She said, "Gone is the glory from Israel," because the ark of God had been captured.

The Ark in the Temple of Dagon

5 The Philistines, having captured the ark of God, transferred it from Ebenezer to Ashdod. 2 They took the ark of God, and brought it into the temple of Dagon, placing it beside Dagon. 3 When the people of Ashdod rose early the next morning, Dagon was lying prone on the ground before the ark of the LORD. So they picked Dagon up and replaced him. 4 But the next morning early, when they arose, Dagon lay prone on the ground before the ark of the LORD, his head and hands broken off and lying on the threshold, his trunk alone intact. 5 For this reason, neither the priests of Dagon nor any others who enter the temple of Dagon tread on the threshold of Dagon in Ashdod to this very day; they always step over it.

The Ark is Carried About

6 Now the LORD dealt severely with the people of Ashdod. He ravaged and afflicted the city and its vicinity with hemorrhoids; he brought upon the city a great and deadly plague of mice that swarmed in their ships and overran their fields. 7 On seeing how matters stood, the men of Ashdod decided, "The ark of the God of Israel must not remain with us, for he is handling us and our god Dagon severely." 8 So they summoned all the Philistine lords and inquired of them, "What shall we do with the ark of the God of Israel?" The men of Gath replied, "Let them move the ark of the God of Israel on to us." 9 So they moved the ark of the God of Israel to Gath! But after it had been brought there, the LORD threw the city into utter turmoil: he afflicted its inhabitants, young and old, and hemorrhoids broke out on them. 10 The ark of God was next sent to Ekron; but as it entered that city, the people there cried out, "Why have they brought the ark of the God of Israel here to kill us and our kindred?" 11 Then they, too, sent a summons to all the Philistine lords and pleaded: "Send away the ark of the God of Israel. Let it return to its own place, that it may not kill us and our kindred." A deadly panic had seized the whole city, since the hand of God had been very heavy upon it. 12 Those who escaped death were afflicted with hemorrhoids, and the outcry from the city went up to the heavens.

The Ark to be Returned

6 The ark of the LORD had been in the land of the Philistines seven months 2 when they summoned priests and fortune-tellers to ask,

4, 4: *Enthroned upon the cherubim:* this title of the Lord seems to have originated in the sanctuary at Shiloh; it represents the divine Majesty as seated upon a throne on which he can be borne through the heaven by winged creatures somewhat as in the visions of Ez 1 and 10.
4, 8: *These mighty gods:* The Philistines, who were polytheists, are represented as supposing the Israelites honored several gods.
5, 6: *Hemorrhoids . . . mice:* a double calamity fell upon them—a plague of mice or rats, and a severe epidemic of pestilential tumors, probably the bubonic plague.

"What shall we do with the ark of the LORD? Tell us what we should send back with it." 3 They replied: "If you intend to send away the ark of the God of Israel, you must not send it alone, but must, by all means, make amends to him through a guilt offering. Then you will be healed, and will learn why he continues to afflict you." 4 When asked further, "What guilt offering should be our amends to him?", they replied:

"Five golden hemorrhoids and five golden mice to correspond to the number of Philistine lords, since the same plague has struck all of you and your lords. 5 Therefore, make images of the hemorrhoids and of the mice that are infesting your land and give them as a tribute to the God of Israel. Perhaps then he will cease to afflict you, your gods, and your land. 6 Why should you become stubborn, as the Egyptians and Pharaoh were stubborn? Was it not after he had dealt ruthlessly with them that the Israelites were released and departed? 7 So now set to work and make a new cart. Then take two milch cows that have not borne the yoke; hitch them to the cart, but drive their calves indoors away from them. 8 You shall next take the ark of the LORD and place it on the cart, putting in a box beside it the golden articles that you are offering, as amends for your guilt. Start it on its way, and let it go. 9 Then watch! if it goes up to Beth-shemesh along the route to his own territory, he has brought this great calamity upon us; if not, we will know it was not he who struck us, but that an accident happened to us."

The Ark in Beth-shemesh

10 They acted upon this advice. Taking two milch cows, they hitched them to the cart but shut up their calves indoors. 11 Then they placed the ark of the LORD on the cart, along with the box containing the golden mice and the images of the hemorrhoids. 12 The cows went straight for the route to Beth-shemesh and continued along this road, mooing as they went, without turning right or left. The Philistine lords followed them as far as the border of Beth-shemesh. 13 The people of Beth-shemesh were harvesting the wheat in the valley. When they looked up and spied the ark, they greeted it with rejoicing. 14 The cart came to the field of Joshua the Beth-shemite and stopped there. At a large stone in the field, the wood of the cart was split up and the cows were offered as a holocaust to the LORD. 15 The Levites, meanwhile, had taken down the ark of God, and the box beside it, in which the golden articles were, and had placed them on the great stone. The men of Beth-shemesh also offered other holocausts and sacrifices to the LORD that day. 16 After witnessing this, the five Philistine lords returned to Ekron the same day.

Guilt Offering

17 The golden hemorrhoids the Philistines sent back as a guilt offering to the LORD were as follows: one for Ashdod, one for Gaza, one for Ashkelon, one for Gath, and one for Ekron. 18 The golden mice, however, corresponded to the number of all the cities of the Philistines belonging to the five lords, including fortified cities and open villages. The large stone on which the ark of the LORD was placed is still in the field of Joshua the Beth-shemite at the present time.

Penalty for Irreverence

19 The descendants of Jeconiah did not join in the celebration with the inhabitants of Beth-shemesh when they greeted the ark of the LORD, and seventy of them were struck down. The people went into mourning at this great calamity with which the LORD had afflicted them. 20 The men of Beth-shemesh asked, "Who can stand in the presence of this Holy One? To whom shall he go from us?" 21 They then sent messengers to the inhabitants of Kiriath-jearim, saying, "The Philistines have returned the ark of the LORD; come down and get it."

7 1 So the inhabitants of Kiriath-jearim came for the ark of the LORD and brought it into the house of Abinadab on the hill, appointing his son Eleazar as guardian of the ark of the LORD.

Religious Reform

2 From the day the ark came to rest in Kiriath-jearim a long time—twenty years—elapsed, and the whole Israelite population turned to the LORD. 3 Samuel said to them: "If you wish with your whole heart to return to the LORD, put away your foreign gods and your Ashtaroth, devote yourselves to the LORD, and worship him alone. Then he will deliver you from the power of the Philistines." 4 So the Israelites put away their Baals and Ashtaroth, and worshiped the LORD alone. 5 Samuel then gave orders, "Gather all Israel to Mizpah, that I may pray to the LORD for you." 6 When they were gathered at Mizpah, they drew water and poured it out on the ground before the LORD, and they fasted that day, confessing, "We have sinned against the LORD." It was at Mizpah that Samuel began to judge the Israelites.

Rout of the Philistines

7 When the Philistines heard that the Israelites had gathered at Mizpah, their lords went up against Israel. Hearing this, the Israelites became afraid of the Philistines 8 and said to Samuel, "Implore the LORD our God unceasingly for us, to save us from the clutches of the Philistines." 9 Samuel therefore took an unweaned lamb and offered it entire as a holocaust to the LORD. He implored the LORD for Israel, and the LORD heard him. 10 While Samuel was offering the holocaust, the Philistines advanced to join battle with Israel. That day, however, the LORD thundered loudly against the Philistines, and threw them into such confusion that they were defeated by Israel. 11 Thereupon the Israelites sallied forth from Mizpah and pursued the Philistines, harrying them down beyond Beth-car. 12 Samuel then took a stone

---

6, 3: *A guilt offering:* a propitiatory offering customary after unwitting transgression of the ordinances of God regarding holy things or property rights;

cf Lv 6, 1ff.
7, 6: *Poured it out on the ground:* for the symbolism, cf 2 Sm 14, 14.

7, 12: *Ebenezer:* or *eben ha-ezer,* means "stone of help."

and placed it between Mizpah and Jeshanah; he named it Ebenezer, explaining, "To this point the LORD helped us." 13 Thus were the Philistines subdued, never again to enter the territory of Israel, for the LORD was severe with them as long as Samuel lived. 14 The cities from Ekron to Gath which the Philistines had taken from Israel were restored to them. Israel also freed the territory of these cities from the dominion of the Philistines. Moreover there was peace between Israel and the Amorites.

15 Samuel judged Israel as long as he lived. 16 He made a yearly journey, passing through Bethel, Gilgal and Mizpah and judging Israel at each of these sanctuaries. 17 Then he used to return to Ramah, for that was his home. There, too, he judged Israel and built an altar to the LORD.

ESTABLISHMENT OF THE MONARCHY IN ISRAEL

Request for a King

8 In his old age Samuel appointed his sons judges over Israel. 2 His first-born was named Joel, his second son, Abijah; they judged at Beer-sheba. 3 His sons did not follow his example but sought illicit gain and accepted bribes, perverting justice. 4 Therefore all the elders of Israel came in a body to Samuel at Ramah 5 and said to him, "Now that you are old, and your sons do not follow your example, appoint a king over us, as other nations have, to judge us."

God Grants the Request

6 Samuel was displeased when they asked for a king to judge them. He prayed to the LORD, however, 7 who said in answer: "Grant the people's every request. It is not you they reject, they are rejecting me as their king. 8 As they have treated me constantly from the day I brought them up from Egypt to this day,

deserting me and worshiping strange gods, so do they treat you too. 9 Now grant their request; but at the same time, warn them solemnly and inform them of the rights of the king who will rule them."

The Rights of a King

10 Samuel delivered the message of the LORD in full to those who were asking him for a king. 11 He told them: "The rights of the king who will rule you will be as follows: He will take your sons and assign them to his chariots and horses, and they will run before his chariot. 12 He will also appoint from among them his commanders of groups of a thousand and of a hundred soldiers. He will set them to do his plowing and his harvesting, and to make his implements of war and the equipment of his chariots. 13 He will use your daughters as ointment-makers, as cooks, and as bakers. 14 He will take the best of your fields, vineyards, and olive groves, and give them to his officials. 15 He will tithe your crops and your vineyards, and give the revenue to his eunuchs and his slaves. 16 He will take your male and female servants, as well as your best oxen and your asses, and use them to do his work. 17 He will tithe your flocks and you yourselves will become his slaves. 18 When this takes place, you will complain against the king whom you have chosen, but on that day the LORD will not answer you."

Persistent Demand

19 The people, however, refused to listen to Samuel's warning and said, "Not so! There must be a king over us. 20 We too must be like other nations, with a king to rule us and to lead us in warfare and fight our battles." 21 When Samuel had listened to all the people had to say, he repeated it to the LORD, 22 who then said to him, "Grant their request and appoint a king to rule them." Samuel thereupon said to the

men of Israel, "Each of you go to his own city."

9 There was a stalwart man from Benjamin named Kish, who was the son of Abiel, son of Zeror, son of Becorath, son of Aphiah, a Benjaminite. 2 He had a son named Saul, who was a handsome young man. There was no other Israelite handsomer than Saul; he stood head and shoulders above the people.

The Lost Asses

3 Now the asses of Saul's father, Kish, had wandered off. Kish said to his son Saul, "Take one of the servants with you and go out and hunt for the asses." 4 Accordingly they went through the hill country of Ephraim, and through the land of Shalishah. Not finding them there, they continued through the land of Shaalim without success. They also went through the land of Benjamin, but they failed to find the animals. 5 When they came to the land of Zuph, Saul said to the servant who was with him, "Come, let us turn back, lest my father forget about the asses and become anxious about us." 6 The servant replied, "Listen! There is a man of God in this city, a man held in high esteem; all that he says is sure to come true. Let us go there now! Perhaps he can tell us how to accomplish our errand." 7 But Saul said to his servant, "If we go, what can we offer the man? There is no bread in our bags, and we have no present to give the man of God. What have we?" 8 Again the servant answered Saul, "I have a quarter of a silver shekel. If I give that to the man of God, he will tell us our way." 10 Saul then said to his servant, "Well said! Come on, let us go!" And they went to the city where the man of God lived.

Quest for Samuel's Aid

11 As they were going up the ascent to the city, they met some girls coming out to draw water and inquired of them, "Is the seer in town?" 9 (In former times in Israel, anyone

8, 1: From this chapter on, the First Book of Samuel gives us two and sometimes three viewpoints on most of the events with which it is concerned, such as the appointment of Saul as king, the reasons for his downfall, his relationship with David, even the circumstances of Saul's death (1 Sm 31; 2 Sm 1).

The choice of Saul as king is seen, in ch 8, followed by 10, 17–24 and ch 12, as motivated by the people's defection from the proper service of God; this later editorial approach incorporates not only narratives with which it is consistent, but also early traditions (9, 1–10.16; ch 11) which portray the events and their

motivation quite differently.
9, 8: A quarter of a silver shekel: about a tenth of an ounce of silver.
9, 9: This verse is a later explanation of the term seer, first used in the text in 9, 11.

who went to consult God used to say, "Come, let us go to the seer." For he who is now called prophet was formerly called seer.) 12 The girls answered, "Yes, there—straight ahead. Hurry now; just today he came to the city, because the people have a sacrifice today on the high place. 13 When you enter the city, you may reach him before he goes up to the high place to eat. The people will not eat until he arrives; only after he blesses the sacrifice will the invited guests eat. Go up immediately, for you should find him right now."

Samuel's Revelation about Saul

14 So they went up to the city. As they entered it, Samuel was coming toward them on his way to the high place. 15 The day before Saul's arrival, the LORD had given Samuel the revelation: 16 "At this time tomorrow I will send you a man from the land of Benjamin whom you are to anoint as commander of my people Israel. He shall save my people from the clutches of the Philistines, for I have witnessed their misery and accepted their cry for help." 17 When Samuel caught sight of Saul, the LORD assured him, "This is the man of whom I told you; he is to govern my people."

18 Saul met Samuel in the gateway and said, "Please tell me where the seer lives." 19 Samuel answered Saul: "I am the seer. Go up ahead of me to the high place and eat with me today. In the morning, before dismissing you, I will tell you whatever you wish. 20 As for the asses you lost three days ago, do not worry about them, for they have been found. Whom does Israel desire ardently if not you and your father's family?" 21 Saul replied: "Am I not a Benjaminite, of one of the smallest tribes of Israel, and is not my clan the least among the clans of the tribe of Benjamin? Why say such things to me?"

22 Samuel then took Saul and his servant and brought them to the room, where he placed them at the head of the guests, of whom there were about thirty. 23 He said to the cook, "Bring the portion I gave you and told you to put aside." 24 So the cook took up the leg and what went with it, and placed it before Saul. Samuel said: "This is a reserved portion that has been set before you. Eat, for it was kept for you until your arrival; I explained that I was inviting some guests." Thus Saul dined with Samuel that day. 25 When they came down from the high place into the city, a mattress was spread for Saul on the roof 26 and he slept there.

Saul's Anointing

At daybreak Samuel called to Saul on the roof, "Get up, and I will start you on your journey." Saul rose, and he and Samuel went outside the city together. 27 As they were approaching the edge of the town, Samuel said to Saul, "Tell the servant to go on ahead of us, but stay here yourself for the moment, that I may give you a message from God."

10 1 Then, from a flask he had with him Samuel poured oil on Saul's head; he also kissed him, saying: "The LORD anoints you commander over his heritage. You are to govern the LORD's people Israel, and to save them from the grasp of their enemies round about.

"This will be the sign for you that the LORD has anointed you commander over his heritage: 2 When you leave me today, you will meet two men near Rachel's tomb at Zelzah in the territory of Benjamin, who will say to you, 'The asses you went to look for have been found. Your father is no longer worried about the asses, but is anxious about you and says, What shall I do about my son?' 3 Farther on, when you arrive at the terebinth of Tabor, you will be met by three men going up to God at Bethel; one will be bringing three kids, another three loaves of bread, and the third a skin of wine. 4 They will greet you and offer you two wave offerings of bread, which you will take from them. 5 After that you will come to Gibeath-elohim, where there is a garrison of the Philistines. As you enter that city, you will meet a band of prophets, in a prophetic state, coming down from the high place preceded by lyres, tambourines, flutes and harps. 6 The spirit of the LORD will rush upon you, and you will join them in their prophetic state and will be changed into another man. 7 When you see these signs fulfilled, do whatever you judge feasible, because God is with you. 8 Now go down ahead of me to Gilgal, for I shall come down to you, to offer holocausts and to sacrifice peace offerings. Wait seven days until I come to you: I shall then tell you what you must do."

Fulfillment of the Signs

9 As Saul turned to leave Samuel, God gave him another heart. That very day all these signs came to pass. . . . 10 When they were going from there to Gibeah, a band of prophets met him, and the spirit of God rushed upon him, so that he joined them in their prophetic state. 11 When all who had known him previously saw him in a prophetic state among the prophets, they said to one another, "What has happened to the son of Kish? Is Saul also among the prophets?" 12 And someone from that district added, "And who is their father?" Thus the proverb arose, "Is Saul also among the prophets?" 13 When he came out of the prophetic state, he went home.

9, 12: *On the high place:* the local sanctuary on the top of a hill, where the sacrifice was offered and the sacrificial meal eaten.

9, 24: *And what went with it:* a slight change would give "and the fatty tail" as perhaps the original reading. Sheep in the Near East are exceptionally fat-tailed, and such a portion would be thought a special delicacy by the Hebrews. However, the ritual legislation as we know it (Lv 3, 9) would require that the fat tail be burned on the altar. If this general rule was later than the time of Samuel, the present text may have been retouched so as not to seem to contravene it. A Qumran text has "the festive (leg)" here.

10, 2: Here, as in Jer 31, 15, Rachel's tomb is placed north of Jerusalem. Later tradition understood Gn 35, 19f in the sense given by Mt 2, 16ff, and placed the tomb at Bethlehem, farther south.

10, 5: *A garrison of the Philistines:* the Hebrew word for "garrison" has been explained alternatively to mean a pillar erected to mark the Philistine occupation, or an inspector or officer for the collection of taxes. *In a prophetic state:* in an ecstatic condition due to strong feelings of religious enthusiasm induced by a communal observance, possibly accompanied by music and dancing.

10, 8: By inserting this verse, with its *seven days,* an editor has prepared for one narrative of the rejection of Saul (13, 8–15) in the very context of Saul's anointing.

10, 10: The story has here been abridged by omitting the fulfillment of the first two signs given by Samuel (10, 2ff).

Silence about the Kingship

14 Saul's uncle inquired of him and his servant, "Where have you been?" Saul replied, "To look for the asses. When we could not find them, we went to Samuel." 15 Then Saul's uncle said, "Tell me, then, what Samuel said to you." 16 Saul said to his uncle, "He assured us that the asses had been found." But he mentioned nothing to him of what Samuel had said about the kingship.

Saul Chosen King by Lot

17 Samuel called the people together to the LORD at Mizpah 18 and addressed the Israelites: "Thus says the LORD, the God of Israel, 'It was I who brought Israel up from Egypt and delivered you from the power of the Egyptians and from the power of all the kingdoms that oppressed you.' 19 But today you have rejected your God, who delivers you from all your evils and calamities, by saying to him. 'Not so, but you must appoint a king over us.' Now, therefore, take your stand before the LORD according to tribes and families." 20 So Samuel had all the tribes of Israel come forward, and the tribe of Benjamin was chosen. 21 Next he had the tribe of Benjamin come forward in clans, and the clan of Matri was chosen, and finally Saul, son of Kish, was chosen. But they looked for him in vain. 22 Again they consulted the LORD, "Has he come here?" The LORD answered, "He is hiding among the baggage." 23 They ran to bring him from there; and when he stood among the people, he was head and shoulders above all the crowd. 24 Samuel said to all the people, "Do you see the man whom the LORD has chosen? There is none like him among all the people!" Then all the people shouted, "Long live the king!"

25 Samuel next explained to the people the law of royalty and wrote it in a book, which he placed in the presence of the LORD. This done, Samuel dismissed the people, each to his own place. 26 Saul also went home to Gibeah, accompanied by warriors whose hearts the LORD had touched. 27 But certain worthless men said, "How can this fellow save us?" They despised him and brought him no present.

Defeat of the Ammonites

11 About a month later, Nahash the Ammonite went up and laid siege to Jabesh-gilead. All the men of Jabesh begged Nahash, "Make a treaty with us, and we will be your subjects." 2 But Nahash the Ammonite replied, "This is my condition for a treaty with you: I must gouge out every man's right eye, that I may thus bring ignominy on all Israel." 3 The elders of Jabesh said to him: "Give us seven days to send messengers throughout the territory of Israel. If no one rescues us, we will surrender to you." 4 When the messengers arrived at Gibeah of Saul, they related the news to the people, all of whom wept aloud.

5 Just then Saul came in from the field, behind his oxen. "Why are the people weeping?" he asked. The message of the inhabitants of Jabesh was repeated to him. 6 As he listened to this report, the spirit of God rushed upon him and he became very angry. 7 Taking a yoke of oxen, he cut them into pieces, which he sent throughout the territory of Israel by couriers with the message, "If anyone does not come out to follow Saul [and Samuel], the same as this will be done to his oxen!" In dread of the LORD, the people turned out to a man. 8 When he reviewed them in Bezek, there were three hundred thousand Israelites and seventy thousand Judahites.

9 To the messengers who had come he said, "Tell the inhabitants of Jabesh-gilead that tomorrow, while the sun is hot, they will be rescued." The messengers came and reported this to the inhabitants of Jabesh, who were jubilant, 10 and said to Nahash, "Tomorrow we will surrender to you, and you may do whatever you please with us." 11 On the appointed day, Saul arranged his troops in three companies and invaded the camp during the dawn watch. They slaughtered Ammonites until the heat of the day; by then the survivors were so scattered that no two were left together.

Saul Accepted as King

12 The people then said to Samuel: "Who questioned whether Saul should rule over us? Hand over the men and we will put them to death." 13 But Saul broke in to say, "No man is to be put to death this day, for today the LORD has saved Israel." 14 Samuel said to the people, "Come, let us go to Gilgal to inaugurate the kingdom there." 15 So all the people went to Gilgal, where, in the presence of the LORD, they made Saul king. They also sacrificed peace offerings there before the LORD, and Saul and all the Israelites celebrated the occasion with great joy.

Samuel's Integrity

12 Samuel addressed all Israel: "I have granted your request in every respect," he said. "I have set a king over you 2 and now the king is your leader. As for me, I am old and gray, and have sons among you. I have lived with you from my youth to the present day. 3 Here I stand! Answer me in the presence of the LORD and of his anointed. Whose ox have I taken? Whose ass have I taken? Whom have I cheated? Whom have I oppressed? From whom have I accepted à bribe and overlooked his guilt? I will make restitution to you." 4 They replied, "You have neither cheated us, nor oppressed us, nor accepted anything from anyone." 5 So he said to them, "The LORD is witness against you this day, and his anointed as well, that you have found nothing in my possession." "He is witness," they agreed.

Samuel Upbraids the People

6 Continuing, Samuel said to the people: "The LORD is witness, who

---

10, 25: *The law of royalty:* the charter defining the rights of the king.

11, 1: *About a month later:* there is ancient evidence for a longer introduction to this campaign. The time indication here may refer to its earlier stages rather than to the events of ch 10.

11, 12–14: With these verses, an editor has harmonized the account of the acknowledgment of Saul as king at Mizpah (10, 17–24) with the public acclamation at Gilgal (11, 15) after the defeat of the Ammonites (11, 1–11). The Greek text of 11, 15 reads "and Samuel anointed Saul as king," instead of *they made Saul king.*

appointed Moses and Aaron, and who brought your fathers up from the land of Egypt. 7 Now, therefore, take your stand, and I shall arraign you before the LORD, and shall recount for you all the acts of mercy the LORD has done for you and your fathers. 8 When Jacob and his sons went to Egypt and the Egyptians oppressed them, your fathers appealed to the LORD, who sent Moses and Aaron to bring them out of Egypt, and he gave them this place to live in. 9 But they forgot the LORD their God; and he allowed them to fall into the clutches of Sisera, the captain of the army of Jabin, king of Hazor, into the grasp of the Philistines, and into the grip of the king of Moab, who made war against them. 10 Each time they appealed to the LORD and said, 'We have sinned in forsaking the LORD and worshiping Baals and Ashtaroth; but deliver us now from the power of our enemies, and we will worship you.' 11 Accordingly, the LORD sent Jerubbaal, Barak, Jephthah, and Samson; he delivered you from the power of your enemies on every side, so that you were able to live in security. 12 Yet, when you saw Nahash, king of the Ammonites, advancing against you, you said to me, 'Not so, but a king must rule us,' even though the LORD your God is your king.

Warnings for People and King

13 "Now you have the king you want, a king the LORD has given you. 14 If you fear the LORD and worship him, if you are obedient to him and do not rebel against the LORD's command, if both you and the king who rules you follow the LORD your God —well and good. 15 But if you do not obey the LORD and if you rebel against his command, the LORD will deal severely with you and your king, and destroy you. 16 Now then, stand ready to witness the great marvel the LORD is about to accomplish before your eyes. 17 Are we not in the harvest time for wheat? Yet I

shall call to the LORD, and he will send thunder and rain. Thus you will see and understand how greatly the LORD is displeased that you have asked for a king." 18 Samuel then called to the LORD, and the LORD sent thunder and rain that day.

Assistance Promised

As a result, all the people dreaded the LORD and Samuel. 19 They said to Samuel, "Pray to the LORD your God for us, your servants, that we may not die for having added to all our other sins the evil of asking for a king." 20 "Do not fear," Samuel answered them. "It is true you have committed all this evil; still, you must not turn from the LORD, but must worship him with your whole heart. 21 Do not turn to meaningless idols which can neither profit nor save; they are nothing. 22 For the sake of his own great name the LORD will not abandon his people, since the LORD himself chose to make you his people. 23 As for me, far be it from me to sin against the LORD by ceasing to pray for you and to teach you the good and right way. 24 But you must fear the LORD and worship him faithfully with your whole heart; keep in mind the great things he has done among you. 25 If instead you continue to do evil, both you and your king shall perish."

13 [Saul was ... years old when he became king and he reigned ... (two) years over Israel.]

Saul Offers Sacrifice

2 Saul chose three thousand men of Israel, of whom two thousand remained with him in Michmash and in the hill country of Bethel, and one thousand were with Jonathan in Gibeah of Benjamin. He sent the rest of the people back to their tents. 3 Now Jonathan overcame the Philistine garrison which was in Gibeah, and the Philistines got word of it.

Then Saul sounded the horn throughout the land, with a proclamation, "Let the Hebrews hear!" 4 Thus all Israel learned that Saul had overcome the garrison of the Philistines and that Israel had brought disgrace upon the Philistines; and the soldiers were called up to Saul in Gilgal. 5 The Philistines also assembled for battle, with three thousand chariots, six thousand horsemen, and foot soldiers as numerous as the sands of the seashore. Moving up against Israel, they encamped in Michmash, east of Beth-aven. 6 Some Israelites, aware of the danger and of the difficult situation, hid themselves in caves, in thickets, among rocks, in caverns, and in cisterns, 7 and other Hebrews passed over the Jordan into the land of Gad and Gilead. Saul, however, held out at Gilgal, although all his followers were seized with fear.

8 He waited seven days—the time Samuel had determined. When Samuel did not arrive at Gilgal, the men began to slip away from Saul. 9 He then said, "Bring me the holocaust and offerings," and he offered up the holocaust.

King Saul Reproved

10 He had just finished this offering when Samuel arrived. Saul went out to greet him, 11 and Samuel asked him, "What have you done?" Saul replied: "When I saw that the men were slipping away from me, since you had not come by the specified time, and with the Philistines assembled at Michmash, 12 I said to myself, 'Now the Philistines will come down against me at Gilgal, and I have not yet sought the LORD's blessing.' So in my anxiety I offered up the holocaust." 13 Samuel's response was: "You have been foolish! Had you kept the command the LORD your God gave you, the LORD would now establish your kingdom in Israel as lasting; 14 but as things are, your kingdom shall not endure. The LORD has sought out a man after his own heart and has appointed him

13, 1: A formula like that of 2 Sm 5, 4 was introduced here at some time; but the age of Saul when he became king remains a blank, and the two years assigned for his reign in the received text cannot be correct. Tradition (Acts 13, 21) offers the round number, "forty years."

13, 3–4: The Philistine garrison: see note on 10, 5. Let the Hebrews hear: a different reading of these verses, based on the Greek, would yield: "And the Philistines heard that the Hebrews (or: the slaves) had revolted. Saul in the meantime sounded the trumpet

throughout all the land (v 4), and all Israel heard that Saul. . . ."
13, 7–15: These verses, like 10, 8, anticipate the rejection of Saul; a different occasion and motivation for this are given in ch 15, resumed in 28, 17f.

commander of his people, because you broke the LORD's command."

Philistine Invasion

15 Then Samuel set out from Gilgal and went his own way; but the rest of the people went up after Saul to meet the soldiers, going from Gilgal to Gibeah of Benjamin. Saul then numbered the soldiers he had with him, who were about six hundred. 16 Saul, his son Jonathan, and the soldiers they had with them were now occupying Geba of Benjamin, and the Philistines were encamped at Michmash. 17 Meanwhile, raiders left the camp of the Philistines in three bands. One band took the Ophrah road toward the district of Shual; 18 another turned in the direction of Beth-horon; and the third took the road for Geba that overlooks the Valley of the Hyenas toward the desert.

Disarmament of Israel

19 Not a single smith was to be found in the whole land of Israel, for the Philistines had said, "Otherwise the Hebrews will make swords or spears." 20 All Israel, therefore, had to go down to the Philistines to sharpen their plowshares, mattocks, axes, and sickles. 21 The price for the plowshares and mattocks was two-thirds of a shekel, and a third of a shekel for sharpening the axes and for setting the ox-goads. 22 And so on the day of battle neither sword nor spear could be found in the possession of any of the soldiers with Saul or Jonathan. Only Saul and his son Jonathan had them.

Jonathan's Exploit

23 An outpost of the Philistines had pushed forward to the pass of Michmash. 1 One day Jonathan, son of Saul, said to his armor-bearer, "Come let us go over to the Philistine outpost on the other side." But he did not inform his father. 2 (Saul's command post was under the pomegranate tree near the threshing floor on the outskirts of Geba; those with him numbered

14

about six hundred men. 3 Ahijah, son of Ahitub, brother of Ichabod, who was the son of Phinehas, son of Eli, the priest of the LORD at Shiloh was wearing the ephod.) Nor did the soldiers know that Jonathan had gone. 4 Flanking the ravine through which Jonathan intended to get over to the Philistine outpost there was a rocky crag on each side, one called Bozez, the other Seneh. 5 One crag was to the north, toward Michmash, the other to the south, toward Geba. 6 Jonathan said to his armor-bearer: "Come, let us go over to that outpost of the uncircumcised. Perhaps the LORD will help us, because it is no more difficult for the LORD to grant victory through a few than through many." 7 His armor-bearer replied, "Do whatever you are inclined to do; I will match your resolve." 8 Jonathan continued: "We shall go over to those men and show ourselves to them. 9 If they say to us, 'Stay there until we can come to you,' we shall stop where we are; we shall not go up to them. 10 But if they say, 'Come up to us,' we shall go up, because the LORD has delivered them into our grasp. That will be our sign." 11 Accordingly, the two of them appeared before the outpost of the Philistines, who said, "Look, some Hebrews are coming out of the holes where they have been hiding." 12 The men of the outpost called to Jonathan and his armor-bearer. "Come up here," they said, "and we will teach you a lesson." So Jonathan said to his armor-bearer, "Climb up after me, for the LORD has delivered them into the grasp of Israel." 13 Jonathan clambered up with his armor-bearer behind him; as the Philistines turned to flee him, he cut them down, and his armor-bearer followed him and finished them off. 14 In this first exploit Jonathan and his armor-bearer slew about twenty men within half a furlong. 15 Then panic spread to the army and to the countryside, and all the soldiers, including the outpost and the raiding parties, were terror-stricken. The earth also shook, so that the panic was beyond human endurance.

Rout of the Philistines

16 The lookouts of Saul in Geba of Benjamin saw that the enemy camp had scattered and were running about in all directions. 17 Saul said to those around him, "Count the troops and find out if any of us are missing." When they had investigated, they found Jonathan and his armor-bearer missing. 18 Saul then said to Ahijah, "Bring the ephod here." (Ahijah was wearing the ephod in front of the Israelites at that time.) 19 While Saul was speaking to the priest, the tumult in the Philistine camp kept increasing. So he said to the priest, "Withdraw your hand." 20 And Saul and all his men shouted and rushed into the fight, where the Philistines, wholly confused, were thrusting swords at one another. 21 In addition, the Hebrews who had previously sided with the Philistines and had gone up with them to the camp, turned to join the Israelites under Saul and Jonathan. 22 Likewise, all the Israelites who were hiding in the hill country of Ephraim, on hearing that the Philistines were fleeing, pursued them in the rout. 23 Thus the LORD saved Israel that day.

Saul's Oath

The battle continued past Beth-horon; 24 the whole people, about ten thousand combatants, were with Saul, and there was scattered fighting in every town in the hill country of Ephraim. And Saul swore a very rash oath that day, putting the people under this ban: "Cursed be the man who takes food before evening, before I am able to avenge myself on my enemies." So none of the people tasted food. 25 Indeed, there was a honeycomb lying on the ground, 26 and when the soldiers came to the comb the swarm had left it; yet no one would raise a hand to his mouth from it, because the people feared the oath.

Violation of the Oath

27 Jonathan, who had not heard that his father had put the people

---

14, 18: *Ephod:* to be used in consulting God; see note on v 41, and that on 2, 28 above.

14, 23: *Past Beth-horon:* this is a textual correction

influenced by 14, 18; the received Hebrew text refers to Bethel (Beth-aven), but the effect of the victory would seem to have been that the main ridge of

mountains in the territories of Benjamin and Ephraim was cleared of Philistines.

under oath, thrust out the end of the staff he was holding and dipped it into the honey. Then he raised it to his mouth and his eyes lit up. 28 At this one of the soldiers spoke up: "Your father put the people under a strict oath, saying, 'Cursed be the man who takes food this day!' As a result the people are weak." 29 Jonathan replied: "My father brings trouble to the land. Look how bright my eyes are from this small taste of honey I have had. 30 What is more, if the people had eaten freely today of their enemy's booty when they came across it, would not the slaughter of the Philistines by now have been the greater for it?"

Use of Flesh with Blood Forbidden

31 After the Philistines were routed that day from Michmash to Aijalon, the people were completely exhausted. 32 So they pounced upon the spoil and took sheep, oxen and calves, slaughtering them on the ground and eating the flesh with blood. 33 Informed that the people were sinning against the LORD by eating the flesh with blood, Saul said "You have broken faith. Roll a large stone here for me." 34 He continued: "Mingle with the people and tell each of them to bring his ox or his sheep to me. Slaughter it here and then eat, but you must not sin against the LORD by eating the flesh with blood." So everyone brought to the LORD whatever ox he had seized, and they slaughtered them there; 35 and Saul built an altar to the LORD— this was the first time he built an altar to the LORD.

Jonathan in Danger of Death

36 Then Saul said, "Let us go down in pursuit of the Philistines by night, to plunder among them until daybreak and to kill them all off." They replied, "Do what you think best." But the priest said, "Let us consult God." 37 So Saul inquired of God: "Shall I go down in pursuit of the Philistines? Will you deliver them into the power of Israel?" But he received no answer on this occasion. 38 Saul then said, "Come here, all officers of the army. We must investigate and find out how this sin was committed today. 39 As the LORD lives who has given victory to Israel, even if my son Jonathan has committed it, he shall surely die!" But none of the people answered him. 40 So he said to all Israel, "Stand on one side, and I and my son Jonathan will stand on the other." The people responded, "Do what you think best." 41 And Saul said to the LORD, the God of Israel: "Why did you not answer your servant this time? If the blame for this resides in me or my son Jonathan, LORD, God of Israel, respond with Urim; but if this guilt is in your people Israel, respond with Thummim." Jonathan and Saul were designated, and the people went free. 42 Saul then said, "Cast lots between me and my son Jonathan." And Jonathan was designated. 43 Saul said to Jonathan, "Tell me what you have done." Jonathan replied, "I only tasted a little honey from the end of the staff I was holding. Am I to die for this?" 44 Saul said, "May God do thus and so to me if you do not indeed die, Jonathan!"

Rescue of Jonathan

45 But the army said to Saul: "Is Jonathan to die, though it was he who brought Israel this great victory? This must not be! As the LORD lives, not a single hair of his head shall fall to the ground, for God was with him in what he did today!" Thus the soldiers were able to rescue Jonathan from death. 46 After that Saul gave up the pursuit of the Philistines, who returned to their own territory.

Wars and Victories

47 After taking over the kingship of Israel, Saul waged war on all their surrounding enemies—Moab, the Ammonites, Aram, Beth-rehob, the king of Zobah, and the Philistines.

Wherever he turned, he was successful 48 and fought bravely. He defeated Amalek and delivered Israel from the hands of those who were plundering them.

Saul's Family

49 The sons of Saul were Jonathan, Ishvi, and Malchishua; his two daughters were named, the elder, Merob, and the younger, Michal. 50 Saul's wife, who was named Ahinoam, was the daughter of Ahimaaz. The name of his general was Abner, son of Saul's uncle, Ner; 51 Kish, Saul's father, and Ner, Abner's father, were sons of Abiel.

52 An unremitting war was waged against the Philistines during Saul's lifetime. When Saul saw any strong or brave man, he took him into his service.

15 Samuel said to Saul: "It was I the LORD sent to anoint you king over his people Israel. Now, therefore, listen to the message of the LORD. 2 This is what the LORD of hosts has to say: 'I will punish what Amalek did to Israel when he barred his way as he was coming up from Egypt. 3 Go, now, attack Amalek, and deal with him and all that he has under the ban. Do not spare him, but kill men and women, children and infants, oxen and sheep, camels and asses.'"

Disobedience of Saul

4 Saul alerted the soldiers, and at Telaim reviewed two hundred thousand foot soldiers and ten thousand men of Judah. 5 Saul went to the city of Amalek, and after setting an ambush in the wadi, 6 warned the Kenites: "Come! Leave Amalek and withdraw, that I may not have to destroy you with them, for you were kind to the Israelites when they came up from Egypt." After the Kenites left, 7 Saul routed Amalek from Havilah to the approaches of Shur, on the frontier of Egypt. 8 He took Agag, king of Amalek, alive, but on

---

14, 41: The Urim and Thummim, or sacred lots, were a device for ascertaining the will of God; they ceased to be used after the time of David. The material and the shape of these objects, and the manner in which they were used, are unknown. They gave a "yes" or "no" answer to specific questions.

14, 45: Rescue: the Hebrew word used is that for

the "redemption" of the first-born (Ex 13, 13ff).

14, 49: Ishvi: known also as Ishbaal, in 2 Sm 2, 8 and elsewhere. The name may once have read "Ishyo" here.

15, 3: Under the ban: in such wars of extermination, all things (men, cities, beasts, etc.) were to be blotted out; nothing could be reserved for private use. The interpretation of God's will here attributed

to Samuel is in keeping with the abhorrent practices of blood revenge prevalent among pastoral, seminomadic peoples such as the Hebrews had recently been. The slaughter of the innocent has never been in conformity with the will of God.

15, 4: The numbers here are not realistic; compare 14, 24 above.

the rest of the people he put into effect the ban of destruction by the sword. 9 He and his troops spared Agag and the best of the fat sheep and oxen, and the lambs. They refused to carry out the doom on anything that was worthwhile, dooming only what was worthless and of no account.

Saul is Reproved

10 Then the LORD spoke to Samuel: 11 "I regret having made Saul king, for he turned from me and has not kept my command." At this Samuel grew angry and cried out to the LORD all night. 12 Early in the morning he went to meet Saul, but was informed that Saul had gone to Carmel, where he erected a trophy in his own honor, and that on his return he had passed on and gone down to Gilgal. 13 When Samuel came to him, Saul greeted him: "The LORD bless you! I have kept the command of the LORD." 14 But Samuel asked, "What, then, is the meaning of this bleating of sheep that comes to my ears, and the lowing of oxen that I hear?" 15 Saul replied: "They were brought from Amalek. The men spared the best sheep and oxen to sacrifice to the LORD, your God; but we have carried out the ban on the rest." 16 Samuel said to Saul: "Stop! Let me tell you what the LORD said to me last night." "Speak!" he replied. 17 Samuel then said: "Though little in your own esteem, are you not leader of the tribes of Israel? The LORD anointed you king of Israel 18 and sent you on a mission, saying, 'Go and put the sinful Amalekites under a ban of destruction. Fight against them until you have exterminated them.' 19 Why then have you disobeyed the LORD? You have pounced on the spoil, thus displeasing the LORD." 20 Saul answered Samuel: "I did indeed obey the LORD and fulfill the mission on which the LORD sent me. I have brought back Agag, and I have destroyed Amalek under the ban. 21 But from the spoil the men took sheep and oxen, the best of what had been banned, to sacrifice to the LORD their God in Gilgal."
22 But Samuel said:

"Does the LORD so delight in holocausts and sacrifices as in obedience to the command of the LORD? Obedience is better than sacrifice, and submission than the fat of rams.
23 For a sin like divination is rebellion, and presumption is the crime of idolatry. Because you have rejected the command of the LORD, he, too, has rejected you as ruler."

Saul Asks Forgiveness

24 Saul replied to Samuel: "I have sinned, for I have disobeyed the command of the LORD and your instructions. In my fear of the people, I did what they said. 25 Now forgive my sin, and return with me, that I may worship the LORD." 26 But Samuel said to Saul, "I will not return with you, because you rejected the command of the LORD and the LORD rejects you as king of Israel." 27 As Samuel turned to go, Saul seized a loose end of his mantle, and it tore off. 28 So Samuel said to him: "The LORD has torn the kingdom of Israel from you this day, and has given it to a neighbor of yours, who is better than you. 29 The Glory of Israel neither retracts nor repents, for he is not man that he should repent." 30 But he answered: "I have sinned, yet honor me now before the elders of my people and before Israel. Return with me that I may worship the LORD your God." 31 And so Samuel returned with him, and Saul worshiped the LORD.

Agag is Cut Down

32 Afterward Samuel commanded, "Bring Agag, king of Amalek, to me." Agag came to him struggling and saying, "So it is bitter death!" 33 And Samuel said,

"As your sword has made women childless, so shall your mother be childless among women."

Then he cut Agag down before the LORD in Gilgal.
34 Samuel departed for Ramah, while Saul went up to his home in Gibeah of Saul. 35 Never again, as long as he lived, did Samuel see Saul. Yet he grieved over Saul, because the LORD regretted having made him king of Israel.

Samuel Sent to Bethlehem

16 The LORD said to Samuel: "How long will you grieve for Saul, whom I have rejected as king of Israel? Fill your horn with oil, and be on your way. I am sending you to Jesse of Bethlehem, for I have chosen my king from among his sons." 2 But Samuel replied: "How can I go? Saul will hear of it and kill me." To this the LORD answered: "Take a heifer along and say, 'I have come to sacrifice to the LORD.' 3 Invite Jesse to the sacrifice, and I myself will tell you what to do; you are to anoint for me the one I point out to you."
4 Samuel did as the LORD had commanded him. When he entered Bethlehem, the elders of the city came trembling to meet him and inquired, "Is your visit peaceful, O seer?" 5 He replied: "Yes! I have come to sacrifice to the LORD. So cleanse yourselves and join me today for the banquet." He also had Jesse and his sons cleanse themselves and invited them to the sacrifice. 6 As they came, he looked at Eliab and thought, "Surely the LORD's anointed is here before him." 7 But the LORD said to Samuel: "Do not judge from his appearance or from his lofty stature, because I have rejected him. Not as man sees does God see, because man sees the appearance but the LORD looks into the heart." 8 Then Jesse called Abinadab and presented him before Samuel, who said, "The LORD has not chosen him." 9 Next Jesse presented Shammah, but Samuel

---

15, 11: *I regret:* God manifests "regret" when, offended by men, he takes away his benefits, graces and favors. It is not God, but men, who change, to their own detriment.

15, 22: Samuel is disapproving, not of sacrifices in general, but of merely external sacrifices offered in defiance of God's commandment and without heartfelt obedience.

16, 1: The anointing here prepared for is unknown to David's brother Eliab in the next chapter (17, 28), and David is twice anointed after Saul's death (2 Sm 2, 4; 5, 3).

said, "The LORD has not chosen this one either." 10 In the same way Jesse presented seven sons before Samuel, but Samuel said to Jesse, "The LORD has not chosen any one of these." 11 Then Samuel asked Jesse, "Are these all the sons you have?" Jesse replied, "There is still the youngest, who is tending the sheep." Samuel said to Jesse, "Send for him; we will not begin the sacrificial banquet until he arrives here." 12 Jesse sent and had the young man brought to them. He was ruddy, a youth handsome to behold and making a splendid appearance. The LORD said, "There—anoint him, for this is he!" 13 Then Samuel, with the horn of oil in hand, anointed him in the midst of his brothers; and from that day on, the spirit of the LORD rushed upon David. When Samuel took his leave, he went to Ramah.

Saul's Spirit of Melancholy

14 The spirit of the LORD had departed from Saul, and he was tormented by an evil spirit sent by the LORD. 15 So the servants of Saul said to him: "Please! An evil spirit from God is tormenting you. 16 If your lordship will order it, we, your servants here in attendance on you will look for a man skilled in playing the harp. When the evil spirit from God comes over you, he will play and you will feel better." 17 Saul then told his servants, "Find me a skillful harpist and bring him to me." 18 A servant spoke up to say: "I have observed that one of the sons of Jesse of Bethlehem is a skillful harpist. He is also a stalwart soldier, besides being an able speaker, and handsome. Moreover, the LORD is with him."

David made Armor-bearer

19 Accordingly, Saul dispatched messengers to ask Jesse to send him his son David, who was with the flock. 20 Then Jesse took five loaves of bread, a skin of wine, and a kid,

and sent them to Saul by his son David. 21 Thus David came to Saul and entered his service. Saul became very fond of him, made him his armor-bearer, 22 and sent Jesse the message, "Allow David to remain in my service, for he meets with my approval." 23 Whenever the spirit from God seized Saul, David would take the harp and play, and Saul would be relieved and feel better, for the evil spirit would leave him.

The Challenge of Goliath

17 The Philistines rallied their forces for battle at Socoh in Judah and camped between Socoh and Azekah at Ephes-dammim. 2 Saul and the Israelites also gathered and camped in the Vale of the Terebinth drawing up their battle line to meet the Philistines. 3 The Philistines were stationed on one hill and the Israelites on an opposite hill, with a valley between them.

4 A champion named Goliath of Gath came out from the Philistine camp; he was six and a half feet tall. 5 He had a bronze helmet on his head and wore a bronze corselet of scale armor weighing five thousand shekels, 6 and bronze greaves, and had a bronze scimitar slung from a baldric. 7 The shaft of his javelin was like a weaver's heddlebar, and its iron head weighed six hundred shekels. His shield-bearer went before him. 8 He stood and shouted to the ranks of Israel: "Why come out in battle formation? I am a Philistine, and you are Saul's servants. Choose one of your men, and have him come down to me. 9 If he beats me in combat and kills me, we will be your vassals; but if I beat him and kill him, you shall be our vassals and serve us." 10 The Philistine continued: "I defy the ranks of Israel today. Give me a man and let us fight together." 11 Saul and all the men of Israel, when they heard this challenge of the Philistine, were dismayed and terror-stricken.

David Comes to the Camp

12 [David was the son of an Ephrathite named Jesse, who was from Bethlehem in Judah. He had eight sons, and in the days of Saul was old and well on in years. 13 The three oldest sons of Jesse had followed Saul to war; these three sons who had gone off to war were named, the first-born Eliab, the second son Abinadab, and the third Shammah. 14 David was the youngest. While the three oldest had joined Saul, 15 David would go and come from Saul to tend his father's sheep at Bethlehem.

16 [Meanwhile the Philistine came forward and took his stand morning and evening for forty days.

17 [Now Jesse said to his son David: "Take this ephah of roasted grain and these ten loaves for your brothers, and bring them quickly to your brothers in the camp. 18 Also take these ten cheeses for the field officer. Greet your brothers and bring home some token from them. 19 Saul, and they, and all Israel are fighting against the Philistines in the Vale of the Terebinth." 20 Early the next morning, having left the flock with a shepherd, David set out on his errand, as Jesse had commanded him. He reached the barricade of the camp just as the army, on their way to the battleground, were shouting their battle cry. 21 The Israelites and the Philistines drew up opposite each other in battle array. 22 David entrusted what he had brought to the keeper of the baggage and hastened to the battle line, where he greeted his brothers. 23 While he was talking with them, the Philistine champion, by name Goliath of Gath, came up from the ranks of the Philistines and spoke as before, and David listened. 24 When the Israelites saw the man, they all retreated before him, very much afraid. 25 The Israelites had been saying: "Do you see this man coming up? He

---

16, 14: *An evil spirit sent by the Lord:* the Lord permitted Saul to be tormented with violent fits of rage.

16, 18: Of the two traditions which describe the coming of David into Saul's service, the oldest Greek translation retains only the one comprised in 16, 14–23; 17, 1–11.32–54. This effort at consistency is not in accord with the character of the rest of the

book; see note on 8, 1. Though square brackets are used in this edition to indicate the passages lacking in the oldest translation, this is meant only to help the reader follow one account at a time. Both are equally a part of the inspired text, as are also the various amplifications and retouchings of the narrative given within brackets in chs 18 and 19.

17, 6: *Scimitar:* the Hebrew word for this is rather

rare, and the nature of the weapon was in doubt until recent years. It is not the same as the *sword* of v 5.

17, 7: *Six hundred shekels:* over 15 pounds.

17, 12–31: An alternative account of how David came to undertake the combat with the Philistine is here inserted; it is continued in 17, 55—18, 6. See note on 16, 18.

comes up to insult Israel. If anyone should kill him, the king would give him great wealth, and his daughter as well, and would grant exemption to his father's family in Israel." 26 David now said to the men standing by: "What will be done for the man who kills this Philistine and frees Israel of the disgrace? Who is this uncircumcised Philistine in any case, that he should insult the armies of the living God?" 27 They repeated the same words to him and said, "That is how the man who kills him will be rewarded." 28 When Eliab, his oldest brother, heard him speaking with the men, he grew angry with David and said: "Why did you come down? With whom have you left those sheep in the desert meanwhile? I know your arrogance and your evil intent. You came down to enjoy the battle!" 29 David replied, "What have I done now?—I was only talking." 30 Yet he turned from him to another and asked the same question; and everyone gave him the same answer as before. 31 The words that David had spoken were overheard and reported to Saul, who sent for him.]

David Fights Goliath

32 Then David spoke to Saul: "Let your majesty not lose courage. I am at your service to go and fight the Philistine." 33 But Saul answered David, "You cannot go up against this Philistine and fight with him, for you are only a youth, while he has been a warrior from his youth." 34 Then David told Saul: "Your servant used to tend his father's sheep, and whenever a lion or bear came to carry off a sheep from the flock, 35 I would go after it and attack it and rescue the prey from its mouth. If it attacked me, I would seize it by the jaw, strike it, and kill it. 36 Your servant has killed both a lion and a bear, and this uncircumcised Philistine will be as one of them, because he has insulted the armies of the living God."

37 David continued: "The LORD, who delivered me from the claws of the lion and the bear, will also keep

me safe from the clutches of this Philistine." Saul answered David, "Go! the LORD will be with you."

Preparation for the Encounter

38 Then Saul clothed David in his own tunic, putting a bronze helmet on his head and arming him with a coat of mail, 39 David also girded himself with Saul's sword over the tunic. He walked with difficulty, however, since he had never tried armor before. He said to Saul, "I cannot go in these, because I have never tried them before." So he took them off. 40 Then, staff in hand, David selected five smooth stones from the wadi and put them in the pocket of his shepherd's bag. With his sling also ready to hand, he approached the Philistine.

David's Victory

41 With his shield-bearer marching before him, the Philistine also advanced closer and closer to David. 42 When he had sized David up, and seen that he was youthful, and ruddy, and handsome in appearance, he held him in contempt. 43 The Philistine said to David, "Am I a dog that you come against me with a staff?" Then the Philistine cursed David by his gods 44 and said to him, "Come here to me, and I will leave your flesh for the birds of the air and the beasts of the field." 45 David answered him:

"You come against me with sword and spear and scimitar, but I come against you in the name of the LORD of hosts, the God of the armies of Israel that you have insulted. 46 Today the LORD shall deliver you into my hand; I will strike you down and cut off your head. This very day I will leave your corpse and the corpses of the Philistine army for the birds of the air and the beasts of the field; thus the whole land shall learn that Israel has a God. 47 All this multitude, too, shall learn that it is not by sword or spear that the LORD saves. For the battle is the LORD's, and he shall deliver you into our hands.

48 The Philistine then moved to meet David at close quarters, while David ran quickly toward the battle line in the direction of the Philistine.

49 David put his hand into the bag and took out a stone, hurled it with the sling, and struck the Philistine on the forehead. The stone embedded itself in his brow, and he fell prostrate on the ground 50 [Thus David overcame the Philistine with sling and stone; he struck the Philistine mortally, and did it without a sword.] 51 Then David ran and stood over him; with the Philistine's own sword [which he drew from its sheath] he dispatched him and cut off his head.

Flight of the Philistines

When they saw that their hero was dead, the Philistines took to flight. 52 Then the men of Israel and Judah, with loud shouts went in pursuit of the Philistines to the approaches of Gath and to the gates of Ekron, and Philistines fell wounded along the road from Sha-araim as far as Gath and Ekron. 53 On their return from the pursuit of the Philistines, the Israelites looted their camp. 54 David took the head of the Philistine and brought it to Jerusalem; but he kept Goliath's armor in his own tent.

David Presented to Saul

55 [When Saul saw David go out to meet the Philistine, he asked his general Abner, "Abner, whose son is that youth?" Abner replied, "As truly as your majesty is alive, I have no idea." 56 And the king said, "Find out whose son the lad is." 57 So when David returned from slaying the Philistine, Abner took him and presented him to Saul. David was still holding the Philistine's head. 58 Saul then asked him, "Whose son are you, young man?" David replied, "I am the son of your servant Jesse of Bethlehem."

David and Jonathan

18 [By the time David finished speaking with Saul, Jonathan had become as fond of David as if his life depended on him; he loved him as he loved himself. 2 Saul laid claim to David that day and did not allow him to return to his father's house. 3 And Jonathan entered into a bond with David, because he loved him as himself. 4 Jonathan divested himself of the mantle he was

---

17, 54: At the time supposed by this narrative, Jerusalem was still Jebusite, and David had no military tent of his own; the verse is a later gloss.

wearing and gave it to David, along with his military dress, and his sword, his bow and his belt. 5 David then carried out successfully every mission on which Saul sent him. So Saul put him in charge of his soldiers, and this was agreeable to the whole army, even to Saul's own officers.]

Saul's Jealousy

6 At the approach of Saul and David (on David's return after slaying the Philistine), women came out from each of the cities of Israel to meet King Saul, singing and dancing, with tambourines, joyful songs, and sistrums. 7 The women played and sang:

"Saul has slain his thousands,
and David his ten thousands."

8 Saul was very angry and resentful of the song, for he thought: "They give David ten thousands, but only thousands to me. All that remains for him is the kingship." 9 [And from that day on, Saul was jealous of David.

10 [The next day an evil spirit from God came over Saul, and he raged in his house. David was in attendance, playing the harp as at other times, while Saul was holding his spear. 11 Saul poised the spear, thinking to nail David to the wall, but twice David escaped him.] 12 Saul then began to fear David, [because the LORD was with him, but had departed from Saul himself.] 13 Accordingly, Saul removed him from his presence on their military expeditions, 14 and prospered in all his enterprises, for the LORD was with him. 15 Seeing how successful he was, Saul conceived a fear of David; 16 on the other hand, all Israel and Judah loved him, since he led them on their expeditions.

17 [Saul said to David, "There is my older daughter, Merob, whom I will give you in marriage if you become my champion and fight the battles of the LORD." Saul had in mind, "I shall not touch him; let the Philistines strike him." 18 But David answered Saul: "Who am I? And who are my kin or my father's clan in Israel that I should become the king's son-in-law?" 19 However, when it was time for Saul's daughter Merob to be given to David, she was given in marriage to Adriel the Meholathite instead.]

20 Now Saul's daughter Michal loved David, and it was reported to Saul, who was pleased at this, 21 for he thought, "I will offer her to him to become a snare for him, so that the Philistines may strike him." [Thus for the second time Saul said to David, "You shall become my son-in-law today."] 22 Saul then ordered his servants to speak to David privately and to say: "The king is fond of you, and all his officers love you. You should become the king's son-in-law." 23 But when Saul's servants mentioned this to David, he said: "Do you think it easy to become the king's son-in-law? I am poor and insignificant." 24 When his servants reported to him the nature of David's answer, 25 Saul commanded them to say this to David: "The king desires no other price for the bride than the foreskins of one hundred Philistines, that he may thus take vengeance on his enemies." Saul intended in this way to bring about David's death through the Philistines. 26 When the servants reported this offer to David, he was pleased with the prospect of becoming the king's son-in-law. [Before the year was up,] 27 David made preparations and sallied forth with his men and slew two hundred Philistines. He brought back their foreskins and counted them out before the king, that he might thus become the king's son-in-law. So Saul gave him his daughter Michal in marriage. 28 Saul thus came to recognize that the LORD was with David; besides, his own daughter Michal loved David. 29 Therefore Saul feared David all the more [and was his enemy ever after].

30 [The Philistine chiefs continued to make forays, but each time they took to the field, David was more successful against them than any other of Saul's officers, and as a result acquired great fame.]

Persecution of David

19 Saul discussed his intention of killing David with his son Jonathan and with all his servants. But Saul's son Jonathan, who was very fond of David, 2 told him: "My father Saul is trying to kill you. Therefore, please be on your guard tomorrow morning; get out of sight and remain in hiding. 3 I, however, will go out and stand beside my father in the countryside where you are, and will speak to him about you. If I learn anything, I will let you know."

4 Jonathan then spoke well of David to his father Saul, saying to him: "Let not your majesty sin against his servant David, for he has committed no offense against you, but has helped you very much by his deeds. 5 When he took his life in his hands and slew the Philistine, and the LORD brought about a great victory for all Israel through him, you were glad to see it. Why, then, should you become guilty of shedding innocent blood by killing David without cause?" 6 Saul heeded Jonathan's plea and swore, "As the LORD lives, he shall not be killed." 7 So Jonathan summoned David and repeated the whole conversation to him. Jonathan then brought David to Saul, and David served him as before.

8 When war broke out again, David went out to fight against the Philistines and inflicted a great defeat upon them, putting them to flight. 9 Then an evil spirit from the LORD came upon Saul as he was sitting in his house with spear in hand and David was playing the harp nearby. 10 Saul tried to nail David to the wall with the spear, but David eluded Saul, so that the spear struck only the wall, and David got away safe.

11 The same night, Saul sent messengers to David's house to guard it, that he might kill him in the morning. David's wife Michal informed him, "Unless you save yourself tonight, tomorrow you will be killed." 12 Then Michal let David down through a window, and he made his escape in safety. 13 Michal took the household idol and laid it in the bed, putting a net of goat's hair at its head and covering it with a spread. 14 When Saul sent messengers to arrest David, she said, "He is sick."

19, 11: This story in all probability originally followed 18, 29, placing the episode of David's escape on the night of his marriage with Michal.

15 Saul, however, sent the messengers back to see David and commanded them, "Bring him up to me in the bed, that I may kill him." 16 But when the messengers entered, they found the household idol in the bed, with the net of goat's hair at its head. 17 Saul therefore asked Michal: "Why did you play this trick on me? You have helped my enemy to get away!" Michal answered Saul: "He threatened me, 'Let me go or I will kill you.'"

David and Samuel in Ramah

18 Thus David got safely away; he went to Samuel in Ramah, informing him of all that Saul had done to him. Then he and Samuel went to stay in the sheds. 19 When Saul was told that David was in the sheds near Ramah, 20 he sent messengers to arrest David. But when they saw the band of prophets, presided over by Samuel, in a prophetic frenzy, they too fell into the prophetic state. 21 Informed of this, Saul sent other messengers, who also fell into the prophetic state. For the third time Saul sent messengers, but they too fell into the prophetic state.

Saul among the Prophets

22 Saul then went to Ramah himself. Arriving at the cistern of the threshing floor on the bare hilltop, he inquired, "Where are Samuel and David?", and was told, "At the sheds near Ramah." 23 As he set out from the hilltop toward the sheds, the spirit of God came upon him also, and he continued on in a prophetic condition until he reached the spot. 24 At the sheds near Ramah he, too, stripped himself of his garments and he, too, remained in the prophetic state in the presence of Samuel; all that day and night he lay naked. That is why they say, "Is Saul also among the prophets?"

David Consults with Jonathan

20 David fled from the sheds near Ramah, and went to Jonathan. "What have I done?" he asked him. "What crime or what offense does your father hold against me that he seeks my life?" 2 Jonathan answered him: "Heaven forbid that you should die! My father does nothing, great or small, without disclosing it to me. Why, then, should my father conceal this from me? This cannot be so!" 3 But David replied: "Your father is well aware that I am favored with your friendship, so he has decided, 'Jonathan must not know of this lest he be grieved.' Nevertheless, as the LORD lives and as you live, there is but a step between me and death." 4 Jonathan then said to David, "I will do whatever you wish." 5 David answered: "Tomorrow is the new moon, when I should in fact dine with the king. Let me go and hide in the open country until evening. 6 If it turns out that your father misses me, say, 'David urged me to let him go on short notice to his city Bethlehem, because his whole clan is holding its seasonal sacrifice there.' 7 If he says, 'Very well,' your servant is safe. But if he becomes quite angry, you can be sure he has planned some harm. 8 Do this kindness for your servant because of the LORD's bond between us, into which you brought me: if I am guilty, kill me yourself! Why should you give me up to your father?" 9 But Jonathan answered: "Not I! If ever I find out that my father is determined to inflict injury upon you, I will certainly let you know." 10 David then asked Jonathan, "Who will tell me if your father gives you a harsh answer?"

Mutual Agreement

11 [Jonathan replied to David, "Come, let us go out into the field." When they were out in the open country together, 12 Jonathan said to David: "As the LORD, the God of Israel, lives, I will sound out my father about this time tomorrow. Whether he is well disposed toward David or not, I will send you the information. 13 Should it please my father to bring any injury upon you, may the LORD do thus and so to Jonathan if I do not apprise you of it and send you on your way in peace. May the LORD be with you even as he was with my father. 14 Only this: if I am still alive, may you show me the kindness of the LORD. But if I die, 15 never withdraw your kindness from my house. And when the LORD exterminates all the enemies of David from the surface of the earth 16 the name of Jonathan must never be allowed by the family of David to die out from among you, or the LORD will make you answer for it." 17 And in his love for David, Jonathan renewed his oath to him, because he loved him as his very self.]

18 Jonathan then said to him: "Tomorrow is the new moon; and you will be missed, since your place will be vacant. 19 On the following day you will be missed all the more. Go to the spot where you hid on the other occasion and wait near the mound there. 20 On the third day of the month I will shoot arrows, as though aiming at a target. 21 I will then send my attendant to go and recover the arrows. If in fact I say to him, 'Look, the arrow is this side of you; pick it up,' come, for you are safe. As the LORD lives, there will be nothing to fear. 22 But if I say to the boy, 'Look, the arrow is beyond you,' go, for the LORD sends you away. 23 However, in the matter which you and I have discussed, the LORD shall be between you and me forever." 24 So David hid in the open country.

On the day of the new moon, when the king sat at table to dine, 25 taking his usual place against the wall, Jonathan sat facing him, while Abner sat at the king's side, and David's place was vacant. 26 Saul, however, said nothing that day, for he thought, "He must have become unclean by accident, and not yet have been cleansed." 27 On the next day, the second day of the month, David's place was vacant. Saul inquired of his son Jonathan, "Why has the son of Jesse not come to table yesterday or today?" 28 Jonathan answered Saul: "David urgently asked me to let him go to his city, Bethlehem. 29 'Please let me go,' he begged, 'for we are to have a clan sacrifice in our city, and my brothers insist on my presence. Now, therefore, if you think well of me, give me leave to visit my brothers.' That is why he has not come to the king's table." 30 But Saul was

---

20, 26: The meal on the first day of the month would have religious overtones, and a ritual impurity (Lv 15, 16; Dt 23, 10ff) would bar David from sharing in it.

extremely angry with Jonathan and said to him: "Son of a rebellious woman, do I not know that, to your own shame and to the disclosure of your mother's shame, you are the companion of Jesse's son? 31 Why, as long as the son of Jesse lives upon the earth, you cannot make good your claim to the kingship! So send for him, and bring him to me, for he is doomed." 32 But Jonathan asked his father Saul: "Why should he die? What has he done?" 33 At this Saul brandished his spear to strike him, and thus Jonathan learned that his father was resolved to kill David. 34 Jonathan sprang up from the table in great anger and took no food that second day of the month, for he was grieved on David's account, since his father had railed against him.

Jonathan's Farewell

35 The next morning Jonathan went out into the field with a little boy for his appointment with David. 36 There he said to the boy, "Run and fetch the arrow." And as the boy ran, he shot an arrow beyond him in the direction of the city. 37 When the boy made for the spot where Jonathan had shot the arrow, Jonathan called after him, "The arrow is farther on!" 38 Again he called to his lad, "Hurry, be quick, don't delay!" Jonathan's boy picked up the arrow and brought it to his master. 39 The boy knew nothing; only Jonathan and David knew what was meant. 40 Then Jonathan gave his weapons to this boy of his and said to him, "Go, take them to the city." 41 When the boy had left, David rose from beside the mound and prostrated himself on the ground three times before Jonathan in homage. They kissed each other and wept aloud together. 42 At length Jonathan said to David, "Go in peace in keeping with what we two have sworn by the name of the LORD: 'The LORD shall be between you and me, and between your posterity and mine forever.'" 1 Then David departed on his way, while Jonathan went back into the city.

The Holy Bread

2 David went to Ahimelech, the priest of Nob, who came trembling to meet him and asked, "Why are you alone? Is there no one with you?" 3 David answered the priest: "The king gave me a commission and told me to let no one know anything about the business on which he sent me or the commission he gave me. For that reason I have arranged a meeting place with my men. 4 Now what have you on hand? Give me five loaves, or whatever you can find." 5 But the priest replied to David, "I have no ordinary bread on hand, only holy bread; if the men have abstained from women, you may eat some of that." 6 David answered the priest: "We have indeed been segregated from women as on previous occasions. Whenever I go on a journey, all the young men are consecrated—even for a secular journey. All the more so today, when they are consecrated at arms!" 7 So the priest gave him holy bread, for no other bread was on hand except the showbread which had been removed from the LORD's presence and replaced by fresh bread when it was taken away. 8 One of Saul's servants was there that day, detained before the LORD; his name was Doeg the Edomite, and he was Saul's chief henchman.

The Sword of Goliath

9 David then asked Ahimelech: "Do you have a spear or a sword on hand? I brought along neither my sword nor my weapons, because the king's business was urgent." 10 The priest replied: "The sword of Goliath the Philistine, whom you killed in the Vale of the Terebinth, is here [wrapped in a mantle] behind an ephod. If you wish to take that, take it; there is no sword here except that one." David said: "There is none to match it, Give it to me!"

David a Fugitive

11 That same day David took to flight from Saul, going to Achish, king of Gath. 12 But the servants of Achish said, "Is this not David, the king of the land? During their dances do they not sing,

'Saul has slain his thousands,
but David his ten thousands'?"

13 David took note of these remarks and became very much afraid of Achish, king of Gath. 14 So, as they watched, he feigned insanity and acted like a madman in their hands, drumming on the doors of the gate and drooling onto his beard. 15 Finally Achish said to his servants: "You see the man is mad. Why did you bring him to me? 16 Do I not have enough madmen, that you bring in this one to carry on in my presence? Should this fellow come into my house?"

22 David left Gath and escaped to the cave of Adullam. When his brothers and the rest of his family heard about it, they came down to him there. 2 He was joined by all those who were in difficulties or in debt, or who were embittered, and he became their leader. About four hundred men were with him.

3 From there David went to Mizpeh of Moab and said to the king of Moab, "Let my father and mother stay with you, until I learn what God will do for me." 4 He left them with the king of Moab, and they stayed with him as long as David remained in the refuge.

5 But the prophet Gad said to David: "Do not remain in the refuge. Leave, and go to the land of Judah." And so David left and went to the forest of Hereth.

Doeg Betrays Ahimelech

6 Now Saul heard that David and his men had been located. At the time he was sitting in Gibeah under a tamarisk tree on the high place, holding his spear, while all his servants were standing by. 7 So he said to them: "Listen, men of Benjamin! Will the son of Jesse give all of you fields and vineyards? Will he make each of you an officer over a thousand or a hundred men, 8 that you have all conspired against me

21, 5f: *From women:* the high priest, willing to distribute the holy bread to David and his men, requires that they be free from ritual uncleanness, associated in Old Testament times (Lv 15, 18) with the marriage act. David's answer supposes the discipline of a military campaign under the conditions of "holy war" (Dt 23, 10).

22, 4–5: *Refuge:* seemingly connected with the cave complex spoken of in v 1.

and no one tells me that my son has made an agreement with the son of Jesse? None of you shows sympathy for me or discloses to me that my son has stirred up my servant to be an enemy against me, as is the case today." 9 Then Doeg the Edomite, who was standing with the officers of Saul, spoke up: "I saw the son of Jesse come to Ahimelech, son of Ahitub, in Nob. 10 He consulted the LORD for him and gave him supplies, and the sword of Goliath the Philistine as well."

Slaughter of the Priests

11 At this the king sent a summons to Ahimelech the priest, son of Ahitub, and to all his family who were priests in Nob; and they all came to the king. 12 Then Saul said, "Listen, son of Ahitub!" He replied, "Yes, my lord." 13 Saul asked him, "Why did you conspire against me with the son of Jesse by giving him food and a sword and by consulting God for him, that he might rebel against me and become my enemy, as is the case today?" 14 Ahimelech answered the king: "And who among all your servants is as loyal as David, the king's son-in-law, captain of your bodyguard, and honored in your own house? 15 Is this the first time I have consulted God for him? No indeed! Let not the king accuse his servant or anyone in my family of such a thing. Your servant knows nothing at all, great or small, about the whole matter." 16 But the king said, "You shall die, Ahimelech, with all your family." 17 The king then commanded his henchmen standing by: "Make the rounds and kill the priests of the LORD, for they assisted David. They knew he was a fugitive and yet failed to inform me." But the king's servants refused to lift a hand to strike the priests of the LORD. 18 The king therefore commanded Doeg, "You make the rounds and kill the priests!" So Doeg the Edomite went from one to the next and killed the priests himself, slaying on that day eighty-five who wore the linen ephod. 19 Saul also put the priestly city of Nob to the sword, including men and women, children and infants, and oxen, asses and sheep.

Abiathar Escapes

20 One son of Ahimelech, son of Ahitub, named Abiathar, escaped and fled to David. 21 When Abiathar told David that Saul had slain the priests of the LORD, 22 David said to him: "I knew that day, when Doeg the Edomite was there, that he would surely tell Saul. I am responsible for the death of all your family. 23 Stay with me. Fear nothing; he that seeks your life must seek my life also. You are under my protection."

Keilah Liberated

23 David received information that the Philistines were attacking Keilah and plundering the threshing floors. 2 So he consulted the LORD, inquiring, "Shall I go and defeat these Philistines?" The LORD answered, "Go, for you will defeat the Philistines and rescue Keilah." 3 But David's men said to him: "We are afraid here in Judah. How much more so if we go to Keilah against the forces of the Philistines!" 4 Again David consulted the LORD, who answered, "Go down to Keilah, for I will deliver the Philistines into your power." 5 David then went with his men to Keilah and fought with the Philistines. He drove off their cattle and inflicted a severe defeat on them, and thus rescued the inhabitants of Keilah.

6 Abiathar, son of Ahimelech, who had fled to David, went down with David to Keilah, taking the ephod with him.

Flight from Keilah

7 When Saul was told that David had entered Keilah, he said: "God has put him in my grip. Now he has shut himself in, for he has entered a city with gates and bars." 8 Saul then called all the people to war, in order to go down to Keilah and besiege David and his men. 9 When David found out that Saul was planning to harm him, he said to the priest Abiathar, "Bring forward the ephod." 10 David then said: "O LORD God of Israel, your servant has heard a report that Saul plans to come to Keilah, to destroy the city on my account. 11 Will they hand me over? And now: will Saul come

down as your servant has heard? O LORD God of Israel, tell your servant." The LORD answered, "He will come down." 12 David then asked, "Will the citizens of Keilah deliver me and my men into the grasp of Saul?" And the LORD answered, "Yes." 13 So David and his men, about six hundred in number, left Keilah and wandered from place to place. When Saul was informed that David had escaped from Keilah, he abandoned the expedition.

David and Jonathan in Horesh

14 David now lived in the refuges in the desert, or in the barren hill country near Ziph. Though Saul sought him continually, the LORD did not deliver David into his grasp. 15 David was apprehensive because Saul had come out to seek his life; but while he was at Horesh in the barrens near Ziph, 16 Saul's son, Jonathan, came down there to David and strengthened his resolve in the LORD. 17 He said to him: "Have no fear, my father Saul shall not lay a hand to you. You shall be king of Israel and I shall be second to you. Even my father Saul knows this." 18 They made a joint agreement before the LORD in Horesh, where David remained, while Jonathan returned to his home.

Treachery of the Ziphites

19 Some of the Ziphites went up to Saul in Gibeah and said, "David is hiding among us, now in the refuges, and again at Horesh, or on the hill of Hachilah, south of the wasteland. 20 Therefore, whenever the king wishes to come down, let him do so. It will be our task to deliver him into the king's grasp." 21 Saul replied: "The LORD bless you for your sympathy toward me. 22 Go now and make sure once more! Take note of the place where he sets foot" (for he thought, perhaps they are playing some trick on me), 23 "Look around and learn in which of all the various hiding places he is holding out. Then come back to me with sure information, and I will go with you. If he is in the region, I will search him out among all the families of Judah." 24 So they went off to Ziph ahead of Saul. At this

time David and his men were in the desert below Maon, in the Arabah south of the wasteland.

Escape from Saul

25 When Saul and his men came looking for him, David got word of it and went down to the gorge in the desert below Maon. Saul heard of this and pursued David into the desert below Maon. 26 As Saul moved along one rim of the gorge, David and his men took to the other. David was in anxious flight to escape Saul, and Saul and his men were attempting to outflank David and his men in order to capture them, 27 when a messenger came to Saul, saying, "Come quickly, because the Philistines have invaded the land." 28 Saul interrupted his pursuit of David and went to meet the Philistines. This is how that place came to be called the Gorge of Divisions.

David Spares Saul

24 David then went up from there and stayed in the refuges behind Engedi. 2 And when Saul returned from the pursuit of the Philistines, he was told that David was in the desert near Engedi. 3 So Saul took three thousand picked men from all Israel and went in search of David and his men in the direction of the wild goat crags. 4 When he came to the sheepfolds along the way, he found a cave, which he entered to ease nature. David and his men were occupying the inmost recesses of the cave.

5 David's servants said to him, "This is the day of which the LORD said to you, 'I will deliver your enemy into your grasp; do with him as you see fit.'" So David moved up and stealthily cut off an end of Saul's mantle. 6 Afterward, however, David regretted that he had cut off an end of Saul's mantle. 7 He said to his men, "The LORD forbid that I should do such a thing to my master, the LORD's anointed, as to lay a hand on him, for he is the LORD's anointed." 8 With these words David restrained his men and would not permit them to attack Saul. Saul then left the cave and went on his way. 9 David also stepped out of the cave, calling to Saul "My

lord the king!" When Saul looked back, David bowed to the ground in homage 10 and asked Saul:

"Why do you listen to those who say, 'David is trying to harm you'? 11 You see for yourself today that the LORD just now delivered you into my grasp in the cave. I had some thought of killing you, but I took pity on you instead. I decided, 'I will not raise a hand against my lord, for he is the LORD's anointed and a father to me.' 12 Look here at this end of your mantle which I hold. Since I cut off an end of your mantle and did not kill you, see and be convinced that I plan no harm and no rebellion. I have done you no wrong, though you are hunting me down to take my life. 13 The LORD will judge between me and you, and the LORD will exact justice from you in my case. I shall not touch you. 14 The old proverb says, 'From the wicked comes forth wickedness.' So I will take no action against you. 15 Against whom are you on campaign, O king of Israel? Whom are you pursuing? A dead dog, or a single flea! 16 The LORD will be the judge; he will decide between me and you. May he see this, and take my part, and grant me justice beyond your reach!"

Saul's Remorse

17 When David finished saying these things to Saul, Saul answered, "Is that your voice, my son David?" And he wept aloud. 18 Saul then said to David: "You are in the right rather than I; you have treated me generously, while I have done you harm. 19 Great is the generosity you showed me today, when the LORD delivered me into your grasp and you did not kill me. 20 For if a man meets his enemy, does he send him away unharmed? May the LORD reward you generously for what you have done this day. 21 And now, since I know that you shall surely be king and that sovereignty over Israel shall come into your possession, 22 swear to me by the LORD that you will not destroy my descendants and that you will not blot out my name and family." 23 David gave Saul his oath and Saul returned home, while David and his men went up to the refuge.

Death of Samuel

25 Samuel died, and all Israel gathered to mourn him; they buried him at his home in Ramah.

Nabal and Abigail

Then David went down to the desert of Maon. 2 There was a man of Maon who had property in Carmel; he was very wealthy, owning three thousand sheep and a thousand goats. At this time he was present for the shearing of his flock in Carmel. 3 The man was named Nabal, his wife, Abigail. The woman was intelligent and attractive, but Nabal himself, a Calebite, was harsh and ungenerous in his behavior. 4 When David heard in the desert that Nabal was shearing his flock, 5 he sent ten young men, instructing them: "Go up to Carmel. Pay Nabal a visit and greet him in my name. 6 Say to him, 'Peace be with you, my brother, and with your family, and with all who belong to you. 7 I have just heard that shearers are with you. Now, when your shepherds were with us, we did them no injury, neither did they miss anything all the while they were in Carmel. 8 Ask your servants and they will tell you so. Look kindly on these young men, since we come at a festival time. Please give your servants and your son David whatever you can manage.'"

9 When David's young men arrived, they delivered this message fully to Nabal in David's name, and then waited. 10 But Nabal answered the servants of David: "Who is David? Who is the son of Jesse? Nowadays there are many servants who run away from their masters. 11 Must I take my bread, my wine, my meat that I have slaughtered for my own shearers, and give them to men who come from I know not where?" 12 So David's young men retraced their steps and on their return reported to him all that had been said. 13 Thereupon David said to his men, "Let everyone gird on his sword." And so everyone, David included, girded on his sword. About four hundred men went up after David, while two hundred remained with the baggage.

14 But Nabal's wife Abigail was

informed of this by one of the servants, who said: "David sent messengers from the desert to greet our master, but he flew at them screaming. 15 Yet these men were very good to us. We were done no injury, neither did we miss anything all the while we were living among them during our stay in the open country. 16 For us they were like a rampart night and day the whole time we were pasturing the sheep near them. 17 Now, see what you can do, for you must realize that otherwise evil is in store for our master and for his whole family. He is so mean that no one can talk to him." 18 Abigail quickly got together two hundred loaves, two skins of wine, five dressed sheep, five seahs of roasted grain, a hundred cakes of pressed raisins, and two hundred cakes of pressed figs, and loaded them on asses. 19 She then said to her servants, "Go on ahead; I will follow you." But she did not tell her husband Nabal.

20 As she came down through a mountain defile riding on an ass, David and his men were also coming down from the opposite direction. When she met them, 21 David had just been saying: "Indeed, it was in vain that I guarded all this man's possessions in the desert, so that he missed nothing. He has repaid good with evil. 22 May God do thus and so to David, if by morning I leave a single male alive among all those who belong to him." 23 As soon as Abigail saw David, she dismounted quickly from the ass and, falling prostrate on the ground before David, did him homage. 24 As she fell at his feet she said:

"My lord, let the blame be mine. Please let your handmaid speak to you, and listen to the words of your handmaid. 25 Let not my lord pay attention to that worthless man Nabal, for he is just like his name. Fool is his name, and he acts the fool. I, your handmaid, did not see the young men whom my lord sent. 26 Now, therefore, my lord, as the LORD lives, and as you live, it is the LORD who has kept you from shed-

ding blood and from avenging yourself personally. May your enemies and those who seek to harm my lord become as Nabal! 27 Accept this present, then, which your maidservant has brought for my lord, and let it be given to the young men who follow my lord. 28 Please forgive the transgression of your handmaid, for the LORD shall certainly establish a lasting dynasty for my lord, because your lordship is fighting the battles of the LORD, and there is no evil to be found in you your whole life long. 29 If anyone rises to pursue you and to seek your life, may the life of my lord be bound in the bundle of the living in the care of the LORD your God; but may he hurl out the lives of your enemies as from the hollow of a sling. 30 And when the LORD carries out for my lord the promise of success he has made concerning you, and appoints you as commander over Israel, 31 you shall not have this as a qualm or burden on your conscience, my lord, for having shed innocent blood or for having avenged yourself personally. When the LORD confers this benefit on your lordship, remember your handmaid."

32 David said to Abigail: "Blessed be the LORD, the God of Israel, who sent you to meet me today. 33 Blessed be your good judgment and blessed be you yourself, who this day have prevented me from shedding blood and from avenging myself personally. 34 Otherwise, as the LORD, the God of Israel, lives, who has restrained me from harming you, if you had not come so promptly to meet me, by dawn Nabal would not have had a single man or boy left alive." 35 David then took from her what she had brought him and said to her: 'Go up to your home in peace! See, I have granted your request as a personal favor."

Nabal's Death

36 When Abigail came to Nabal, there was a drinking party in his house like that of a king, and Nabal was merry because he was very

drunk. So she told him nothing at all before daybreak the next morning. 37 But then, when Nabal had become sober, his wife told him what had happened. At this his courage died within him, and he became like a stone. 38 About ten days later the LORD struck him and he died. 39 On hearing that Nabal was dead, David said: "Blessed be the LORD, who has requited the insult I received at the hand of Nabal, and who restrained his servant from doing evil, but has punished Nabal for his own evil deeds."

David Marries Abigail and Ahinoam

David then sent a proposal of marriage to Abigail. 40 When David's servants came to Abigail in Carmel, they said to her, "David has sent us to you that he may take you as his wife." 41 Rising and bowing to the ground, she answered, "Your handmaid would become a slave to wash the feet of my lord's servants." 42 She got up immediately, mounted an ass, and followed David's messengers, with her five maids following in attendance upon her. She became his wife, 43 and David also married Ahinoam of Jezreel. Thus both of them were his wives; but Saul gave David's wife Michal, Saul's own daughter, to Palti, son of Laish, who was from Gallim.

Saul's Life Again Spared

26 Men from Ziph came to Saul in Gibeah, reporting that David was hiding on the hill of Hachilah at the edge of the wasteland. 2 So Saul went off down to the desert of Ziph with three thousand picked men of Israel, to search for David in the desert of Ziph. 3 Saul camped beside the road on the hill of Hachilah, at the edge of the wasteland. David, who was living in the desert, saw that Saul had come into the desert after him 4 and sent out scouts, who confirmed Saul's arrival. 5 David himself then went to the place where Saul was encamped and examined the spot where Saul and

---

25, 25: *Fool is his name:* Nabal in Hebrew means "a fool."

25, 26: Abigail anticipates that some misfortune will shortly overtake Nabal, as in fact it does (vv 37–38).

25, 29: *The bundle of the living:* the figure is perhaps taken from the practice of tying up valuables in a kerchief or bag for safekeeping. Abigail desires that David enjoy permanent peace and security, but

that his enemies be subject to constant agitation and humiliation like a stone whirled about, cast out of the sling, and thereafter disregarded.

Abner, son of Ner, the general, had their sleeping quarters. Saul's were within the barricade, and all his soldiers were camped around him. 6 David asked Ahimelech the Hittite, and Abishai, son of Zeruiah and brother of Joab, "Who will go down into the camp with me to Saul?" Abishai replied, "I will." 7 So David and Abishai went among Saul's soldiers by night and found Saul lying asleep within the barricade, with his spear thrust into the ground at his head and Abner and his men sleeping around him.

8 Abishai whispered to David: "God has delivered your enemy into your grasp this day. Let me nail him to the ground with one thrust of the spear; I will not need a second thrust!" 9 But David said to Abishai, "Do not harm him, for who can lay hands on the LORD's anointed and remain unpunished? 10 As the LORD lives," David continued, "it must be the LORD himself who will strike him, whether the time comes for him to die, or he goes out and perishes in battle. 11 But the LORD forbid that I touch his anointed! Now take the spear which is at his head and the water jug, and let us be on our way." 12 So David took the spear and the water jug from their place at Saul's head, and they got away without anyone's seeing or knowing or awakening. All remained asleep, because the LORD had put them into a deep slumber.

David Taunts Abner

13 Going across to an opposite slope, David stood on a remote hilltop at a great distance from Abner, son of Ner, and the troops. 14 He then shouted, "Will you not answer, Abner?" And Abner answered, "Who is it that calls me?" 15 David said to Abner: "Are you not a man whose like does not exist in Israel? Why, then, have you not guarded your lord the king when one of his subjects went to kill the king, your lord? 16 This is no creditable service you have performed. As the LORD lives, you people deserve death because you have not guarded your lord, the

LORD's anointed. Go, look: where are the king's spear and the water jug that was at his head?"

Saul Admits His Guilt

17 Saul recognized David's voice and asked, "Is that your voice, my son David?" David answered, "Yes, my lord the king." 18 He continued: "Why does my lord pursue his servant? What have I done? What evil do I plan? 19 Please, now, let my lord the king listen to the words of his servant. If the LORD has incited you against me, let an offering appease him; but if men, may they be cursed before the LORD, because they have exiled me so that this day I have no share in the LORD's inheritance, but am told: 'Go, serve other gods!' 20 Do not let my blood flow to the ground far from the presence of the LORD. For the king of Israel has come out to seek a single flea as if he were hunting partridge in the mountains." 21 Then Saul said: "I have done wrong, Come back, my son David, I will not harm you again, because you have held my life precious today. Indeed, I have been a fool and have made a serious mistake." 22 But David answered: "Here is the king's spear. Let an attendant come over to get it. 23 The LORD will reward each man for his justice and faithfulness. Today, though the LORD delivered you into my grasp, I would not harm the LORD's anointed. 24 As I valued your life highly today, so may the LORD value my life highly and deliver me from all difficulties." 25 Then Saul said to David: "Blessed are you, my son David! You shall certainly succeed in whatever you undertake." David went his way, and Saul returned to his home.

Refuge among Philistines

27 But David said to himself: "I shall perish some day at the hand of Saul. I have no choice but to escape to the land of the Philistines; then Saul will give up his continual search for me throughout the land of Israel, and I shall be out of his reach." 2 Accordingly, David de-

parted with his six hundred men and went over to Achish, son of Maoch, king of Gath. 3 David and his men lived in Gath with Achish; each one had his family, and David had his two wives, Ahinoam from Jezreel and Abigail, the widow of Nabal from Carmel. 4 When Saul was told that David had fled to Gath, he no longer searched for him.

In Ziklag

5 David said to Achish: "If I meet with your approval, let me have a place to live in one of the country towns. Why should your servant live with you in the royal city?" 6 That same day Achish gave him Ziklag, which has, therefore, belonged to the kings of Judah up to the present time. 7 In all, David lived a year and four months in the country of the Philistines.

Raids on Israel's Foes

8 David and his men went up and made raids on the Geshurites, Girzites, and Amalekites—peoples living in the land between Telam, on the approach to Shur, and the land of Egypt. 9 In attacking the land David would not leave a man or woman alive, but would carry off sheep, oxen, asses, camels, and clothes. On his return he brought these to Achish, 10 who asked, "Whom did you raid this time?" And David answered, "The Negeb of Judah," or "The Negeb of Jerahmeel," or "The Negeb of the Kenites." 11 But David would not leave a man or woman alive to be brought to Gath, fearing that they would betray him by saying, "This is what David did." This was his custom as long as he lived in the country of the Philistines. 12 And Achish trusted David, thinking, "He must certainly be detested by his people Israel. I shall have him as my vassal forever."

28 In those days the Philistines mustered their military forces to fight against Israel. So Achish said to David, "You realize, of course, that you and your men must go out on campaign with me to Jezreel." 2

26, 19: *The Lord's inheritance:* the land of Israel (Dt 32, 8f), under the Lord's special protection, where he could be freely worshiped.

27, 6: *Has ... belonged to the kings of Judah:* as a personal holding, outside the system of tribal lands; Jerusalem, when taken by David, had

a similar status (2 Sm 5, 7–9).

David answered Achish, "Good! Now you shall learn what your servant can do." Then Achish said to David, "I shall appoint you my permanent bodyguard."

3 Now Samuel had died, and after being mourned by all Israel, was buried in his city, Ramah. Meanwhile Saul had driven mediums and fortune-tellers out of the land.

Saul in Dismay

4 The Philistine levies advanced to Shunem and encamped. Saul, too, mustered all Israel; they camped on Giboa. 5 When Saul saw the camp of the Philistines, he was dismayed and lost heart completely. 6 He therefore consulted the LORD; but the LORD gave no answer, whether in dreams or by the Urim or through prophets. 7 Then Saul said to his servants, "Find me a woman who is a medium, to whom I can go to seek counsel through her." His servants answered him, "There is a woman in Endor who is a medium."

The Witch of Endor

8 So he disguised himself, putting on other clothes, and set out with two companions. They came to the woman by night, and Saul said to her, "Tell my fortune through a ghost; conjure up for me the one I ask you to." 9 But the woman answered him, "You are surely aware of what Saul has done, in driving the mediums and fortunetellers out of the land. Why, then, are you laying snares for my life, to have me killed?" 10 But Saul swore to her by the LORD, "As the LORD lives, you shall incur no blame for this." 11 Then the woman asked him, "Whom do you want me to conjure up?" and he answered, "Samuel."

Samuel Appears

12 When the woman saw Samuel, she shrieked at the top of her voice and said to Saul, "Why have you deceived me? You are Saul!" 13 But the king said to her, "Have no fear. What do you see?" The woman answered Saul, "I see a preternatural

being rising from the earth." 14 "What does he look like?" asked Saul. And she replied, "It is an old man who is rising, clothed in a mantle." Saul knew that it was Samuel, and so he bowed face to the ground in homage.

Saul's Doom

15 Samuel then said to Saul, "Why do you disturb me by conjuring me up?" Saul replied: "I am in great straits, for the Philistines are waging war against me and God has abandoned me. Since he no longer answers me through prophets or in dreams, I have called you to tell me what I should do." 16 To this Samuel said: "But why do you ask me, if the LORD has abandoned you and is with your neighbor? 17 The LORD has done to you what he foretold through me: he has torn the kingdom from your grasp and has given it to your neighbor David. 18 "Because you disobeyed the LORD's directive and would not carry out his fierce anger against Amalek, the LORD has done this to you today. 19 Moreover, the LORD will deliver Israel, and you as well, into the clutches of the Philistines. By tomorrow you and your sons will be with me, and the LORD will have delivered the army of Israel into the hands of the Philistines."

Saul's Despair

20 Immediately Saul fell full length on the ground, for he was badly shaken by Samuel's message. Moreover, he had no bodily strength left, since he had eaten nothing all that day and night. 21 Then the woman came to Saul, and seeing that he was quite terror-stricken, said to him: "Remember, your maidservant obeyed you: I took my life in my hands and fulfilled the request you made of me. 22 Now you, in turn, please listen to your maidservant. Let me set something before you to eat, so that you may have strength when you go on your way." 23 But he refused, saying, "I will not eat." However, when his servants joined

the woman in urging him, he listened to their entreaties, got up from the ground, and sat on a couch. 24 The woman had a stall-fed calf in the house, which she now quickly slaughtered. Then taking flour, she kneaded it and baked unleavened bread. 25 She set the meal before Saul and his servants, and they ate. Then they stood up and left the same night.

David's Aid Rejected

29 Now the Philistines had mustered all their forces in Aphek, and the Israelites were encamped at the spring of Harod near Jezreel. 2 As the Philistine lords were marching their groups of a hundred and a thousand, David and his men were marching in the rear guard with Achish. 3 The Philistine chiefs asked, "What are those Hebrews doing here?" And Achish answered them: "Why, that is David, the officer of Saul, king of Israel. He has been with me now for a year or two, and I have no fault to find with him from the day he came over to me until the present." 4 But the Philistine chiefs were angered at this and said to him: "Send that man back! Let him return to the place you picked out for him. He must not go down into battle with us, lest during the battle he become our enemy. For how else can he win back his master's favor, if not with the heads of these men of ours? 5 Is this not the David of whom they sing during their dances,

'Saul has slain his thousands,
but David his ten thousands'?"

6 So Achish summoned David and said to him: "As the LORD lives, you are honest, and I should be pleased to have you active with me in the camp, for I have found nothing wrong with you from the day of your arrival to this day. But you are not welcome to the lords. 7 Withdraw peaceably, now, and do nothing that might displease the Philistine lords." 8 But David said to Achish: "What have I done? Or what have you against your servant from the first day

---

28, 12: Human beings cannot communicate at will with the souls of the dead. God may, however, permit a departed soul to appear to the living and even to disclose things unknown to them. Saul's own prohibition of necromancy and divination (v 3) was in keeping with the consistent teaching of the Old Testament. If we are to credit the reality of the apparition to Saul, it was due, not to the summons of the witch, but to God's will; the woman merely furnished the occasion.

I have been with you to this day, that I cannot go to fight against the enemies of my lord the king?" 9 "You know," Achish answered David, "that you are acceptable to me. But the Philistine chiefs have determined you are not to go up with us to battle. 10 So the first thing tomorrow, you and your lord's servants who came with you, go to the place I picked out for you. Do not decide to take umbrage at this; you are as acceptable to me as an angel of God. But make an early morning start, as soon as it grows light, and be on your way." 11 So David and his men left early in the morning to return to the land of the Philistines. The Philistines, however, went on up to Jezreel.

Ziklag in Ruins

30 Before David and his men reached Ziklag on the third day, the Amalekites had raided the Negeb and Ziklag, had stormed the city, and had set it on fire. 2 They had taken captive the women and all who were in the city, young and old, killing no one; they had carried them off when they left. 3 David and his men arrived at the city to find it burned to the ground and their wives, sons and daughters taken captive. 4 Then David and those who were with him wept aloud until they could weep no more. 5 David's two wives, Ahinoam of Jezreel and Abigail, the widow of Nabal from Carmel, had also been carried off with the rest. 6 Now David found himself in great difficulty, for the men spoke of stoning him, so bitter were they over the fate of their sons and daughters. But with renewed trust in the LORD his God, 7 David said to Abiathar, the priest, son of Ahimelech, "Bring me the ephod!" When Abiathar brought him the ephod, 8 David inquired of the LORD, "Shall I pursue these raiders? Can I overtake them?" The LORD answered him, "Go in pursuit, for you shall surely overtake them and effect a rescue."

Raid of the Amalekites

9 So David went off with his six hundred men and came as far as the Wadi Besor, where those who were to remain behind halted. 10 David continued the pursuit with four hundred men, but two hundred were too exhausted to cross the Wadi Besor and remained behind. 11 An Egyptian was found in the open country and brought to David. He was provided with food, which he ate, and given water to drink; 12 a cake of pressed figs and two cakes of pressed raisins were also offered to him. When he had eaten, he revived; he had not taken food nor drunk water for three days and three nights. 13 Then David asked him, "To whom do you belong, and where do you come from?" He replied: "I am an Egyptian, the slave of an Amalekite. My master abandoned me because I fell sick three days ago today. 14 We raided the Negeb of the Cherethites, the territory of Judah, and the Negeb of Caleb; and we set Ziklag on fire." 15 David then asked him, "Will you lead me down to this raiding party?" He answered, "Swear to me by God that you will not kill me or deliver me to my master, and I will lead you to the raiding party." 16 He did lead them, and there were the Amalekites scattered all over the ground, eating, drinking, and in a festive mood because of all the rich booty they had taken from the land of the Philistines and from the land of Judah.

The Booty Recovered

17 From dawn to sundown David attacked them, putting them under the ban so that none escaped except four hundred young men, who mounted their camels and fled. 18 David recovered everything the Amalekites had taken, and rescued his two wives. 19 Nothing was missing, small or great, booty or sons or daughters, of all that the Amalekites had taken. David brought back everything. 20 Moreover, David took all the sheep and oxen, and as they drove these before him, they shouted, "This is David's spoil!"

Division of the Spoils

21 When David came to the two hundred men who had been too exhausted to follow him, and whom he had left behind at the Wadi Besor, they came out to meet David and the men with him. On nearing them David greeted them. 22 But all the stingy and worthless men among those who had accompanied David spoke up to say, "Since they did not accompany us, we will not give them anything from the booty, except to each man his wife and children. Let them take those along and be on their way." 23 But David said: "You must not do this, my brothers, after what the LORD has given us. He has protected us and delivered into our grip the band that came against us. 24 Who could agree with this proposal of yours? Rather, the share of the one who goes down to battle and that of the one who remains with the baggage shall be the same; they shall share alike." 25 And from that day forward he made it a law and a custom in Israel, as it still is today.

David's Gifts to Judah

26 When David came to Ziklag, he sent part of the spoil to the elders of Judah, city by city, saying, "This is a gift to you from the spoil of the enemies of the LORD": 27 to those in Bethel, to those in Ramoth-negeb, to those in Jattir, 28 to those in Aroer, to those in Siphmoth, to those in Eshtemoa, 29 to those in Racal, to those in the Jerahmeelite cities, to those in the Kenite cities, 30 to those in Hormah, to those in Borashan, to those in Athach, 31 to those in Hebron, and to all the places frequented by David and his men.

Death of Saul and His Sons

31 As they pressed their attack on Israel, with the Israelites fleeing before them and falling mortally wounded on Mount Gilboa, 2 the Philistines pursued Saul and his sons closely, and slew Jonathan, Abinadab, and Malchishua, sons of Saul. 3 The battle raged around Saul, and the archers hit him; he was pierced through the abdomen. 4 Then Saul said to his armor-bearer, "Draw your sword and run me through, lest these uncircumcised come and make sport of me." But his armor-bearer, badly

frightened, refused to do it. So Saul took his own sword and fell upon it. 5 When the armor-bearer saw that Saul was dead, he too fell upon his sword and died with him. 6 Thus Saul, his three sons, and his armor-bearer died together on that same day.

7 When the Israelites on the slope of the valley and those along the Jordan saw that the men of Israel had fled and that Saul and his sons were dead, they too abandoned their cities

and fled. Then the Philistines came and lived in those cities.

8 The day after the battle the Philistines came to strip the slain, and found Saul and his three sons lying on Mount Gilboa. 9 They cut off Saul's head and stripped him of his armor, and then sent the good news throughout the land of the Philistines to their idols and to the people. 10 They put his armor in the temple of Astarte, but impaled his body on the wall of Beth-shan.

Burial of Saul

11 When the inhabitants of Jabesh-gilead heard what the Philistines had done to Saul, 12 all their warriors set out, and after marching through-out the night, removed the bodies of Saul and his sons from the wall of Beth-shan, and brought them to Jabesh, where they cremated them. 13 Then they took their bones and buried them under the tamarisk tree in Jabesh, and fasted for seven days.

31, 5: This report of the suicidal act of Saul is presented as a part of his downfall, to be judged accordingly.

31, 12: *Cremated them:* cremation was not nor- mally practiced in Israel, though it was known in the country from pre-Israelite times.

THE SECOND BOOK OF

Samuel

Report of Saul's Death

AFTER the death of Saul, David returned from his defeat of the Amalekites and spent two days in Ziklag. 2 On the third day a man came from Saul's camp, with his clothes torn and dirt on his head. Going to David, he fell to the ground in homage. 3 David asked him, "Where do you come from?" He replied, "I have escaped from the Israelite camp." 4 "Tell me what happened," David bade him. He answered that the soldiers had fled the battle and that many of them had fallen and were dead, among them Saul and his son Jonathan. 5 Then David said to the youth who was reporting to him, "How do you know that Saul and his son Jonathan are dead?" 6 The youthful informant replied: "It was by chance that I found myself on Mount Gilboa and saw Saul leaning on his spear, with chariots and horsemen closing in on him. 7 He turned around and, seeing me, called me to him. When I said, 'Here I am,' 8 he asked me, 'Who are you?' and I replied, 'An Amalekite.' 9 Then he said to me, 'Stand up to me, please, and finish me off, for I am in great suffering, yet fully alive.' 10 So I stood up to him and dispatched him, for I knew that he could not survive his wound. I removed the crown from his head and the armlet from his arm and brought them here to my lord."

11 David seized his garments and rent them, and all the men who were with him did likewise. 12 They mourned and wept and fasted until evening for Saul and his son Jonathan, and for the soldiers of the LORD of the clans of Israel, because they had fallen by the sword. 13 Then David said to the young man who had brought him the information, "Where are you from?" He replied, "I am the son of an Amalekite immigrant." 14 David said to him, "How is it that you were not afraid to put forth your hand to desecrate the LORD's anointed?" 15 David then called one of the attendants and said to him, "Come, strike him down"; and the youth struck him a mortal blow. 16 Meanwhile David said to him, "You are responsible for your own death, for you testified against yourself when you said, 'I dispatched the LORD's anointed.'"

Elegy for Saul and Jonathan

17 Then David chanted this elegy for Saul and his son Jonathan, 18 which is recorded in the Book of Jashar to be taught to the Judahites. He sang:

19 "Alas! the glory of Israel, Saul,
    slain upon your heights;
    how can the warriors have
      fallen!

20 "Tell it not in Gath,
    herald it not in the streets of
      Ashkelon,
Lest the Philistine maidens
      rejoice,
    lest the daughters of the
      strangers exult!
21 Mountains of Gilboa,
    may there be neither dew nor
      rain upon you,
    nor upsurgings of the deeps!
Upon you lie begrimed the
      warriors' shields,
    the shield of Saul, no longer
      anointed with oil.

1, 21: *Upsurgings of the deep:* this reading attempts to recover from an unintelligible Hebrew phrase the poetic parallel to dew and rain. The sense would be a wish that the mountain should have neither moisture from above nor water from springs or wells.

22 "From the blood of the slain,
    from the bodies of the valiant,
The bow of Jonathan did not turn
    back,
    or the sword of Saul return
    unstained.
23 Saul and Jonathan, beloved and
    cherished,
    separated neither in life nor in
    death,
    swifter than eagles, stronger
    than lions!
24 Women of Israel, weep over Saul,
    who clothed you in scarlet and
    in finery,
    who decked your attire with
    ornaments of gold.
25 "How can the warriors have
    fallen—
    in the thick of the battle,
    slain upon your heights!
26 "I grieve for you, Jonathan my
    brother!
    most dear have you been to me;
    More precious have I held love for
    you
    than love for women.
27 "How can the warriors have
    fallen,
    the weapons of war have
    perished!"

David Anointed King

2 After this David inquired of the
LORD, "Shall I go up into one of
the cities of Judah?" The LORD
replied to him," Yes." Then David
asked, "Where shall I go?" He
replied, "To Hebron." 2 So David
went up there accompanied by his
two wives, Ahinoam of Jezreel and
Abigail, the widow of Nabal of Carmel. 3 David also brought up his
men with their families, and they
dwelt in the cities near Hebron. 4
Then the men of Judah came there
and anointed David king of the
Judahites.

A report reached David that the
men of Jabesh-gilead had buried
Saul. 5 So David sent messengers
to the men of Jabesh-gilead and said
to them: "May you be blessed by the
LORD for having done this kindness
to your lord Saul in burying him. 6

And now may the LORD be kind and
faithful to you. I, too, will be generous to you for having done this. 7
Take courage, therefore, and prove
yourselves valiant men, for though
your lord Saul is dead, the Judahites
have anointed me their king."

THE REIGN OF DAVID

Ishbaal King of Israel

8 Abner, son of Ner, Saul's general, took Ishbaal, son of Saul, and
brought him over to Mahanaim, 9
where he made him king over
Gilead, the Ashurites, Jezreel, Ephraim, Benjamin, and the rest of
Israel. 10 Ishbaal, son of Saul,
was forty years old when he became
king over Israel, and he reigned for
two years. The Judahites alone followed David. 11 In all, David spent
seven years and six months in Hebron
as king of the Judahites.

Combat near Gibeon

12 Now Abner, son of Ner, and
the servants of Ishbaal, Saul's son,
left Mahanaim for Gibeon. 13
Joab, son of Zeruiah, and David's
servants also set out and met them at
the pool of Gibeon. And they sat
down, one group on one side of the
pool and the other on the opposite
side. 14 Then Abner said to Joab,
"Let the young men rise and perform
for us." Joab replied, "All right!"
15 So they rose and were counted off:
twelve of the Benjaminites of Ishbaal,
son of Saul, and twelve of David's
servants. 16 Then each one grasped
his opponent's head and thrust his
sword into his opponent's side, and
all fell down together. And so that
place, which is in Gibeon, was named
the Field of the Sides.

Death of Asahel

17 After a very fierce battle that
day, Abner and the men of Israel
were defeated by David's servants.
18 The three sons of Zeruiah were
there—Joab, Abishai, and Asahel.
Asahel, who was as fleet of foot as a
gazelle in the open field, 19 set out
after Abner, turning neither right nor
left in his pursuit. 20 Abner turned
around and said, "Is that you,
Asahel?" He replied, "Yes." 21

Abner said to him, "Turn right or
left; seize one of the young men and
take what you can strip from him."
But Asahel would not desist from his
pursuit. 22 Once more Abner said
to Asahel: "Stop pursuing me! Why
must I strike you to the ground?
How could I face your brother
Joab?" 23 Still he refused to stop.
So Abner struck him in the abdomen
with the heel of his javelin, and the
weapon protruded from his back.He
fell there and died on the spot. And
all who came to the place where
Asahel had fallen and died, came to a
halt. 24 Joab and Abishai, however, continued the pursuit of Abner.
The sun had gone down when they
came to the hill of Ammah which lies
east of the valley toward the desert
near Geba.

Truce between Joab and Abner

25 Here the Benjaminites rallied
around Abner, forming a single
group, and made a stand on the hilltop. 26 Then Abner called to Joab
and said: "Must the sword destroy to
the utmost? Do you not know that
afterward there will be bitterness?
How much longer will you refrain
from ordering the people to stop the
pursuit of their brothers?" 27 Joab
replied, "As God lives, if you had not
spoken, the soldiers would not have
been withdrawn from the pursuit of
their brothers until morning." 28
Joab then sounded the horn, and all
the soldiers came to a halt, pursuing
Israel no farther and fighting no more.

29 Abner and his men marched all
night long through the Arabah,
crossed the Jordan, marched all
through the morning, and came to
Mahanaim, 30 Joab, after inter-
rupting the pursuit of Abner, assembled all the men. Besides Asahel,
nineteen other servants of David were
missing. 31 But David's servants
had fatally wounded three hundred
and sixty men of Benjamin, followers
of Abner. 32 They took up Asahel
and buried him in his father's tomb
in Bethlehem. Joab and his men made
an all-night march, and dawn found

3 them in Hebron. 1 There followed a long war between the
house of Saul and that of David, in
which David grew stronger, but the
house of Saul weaker.

2, 16: The nature of this gruesome game is not
clear, and the place name is variously given in the
older texts.

Sons Born in Hebron

2 Sons were born to David in Hebron: his firstborn, Amnon, of Ahinoam from Jezreel; 3 the second, Chileab, of Abigail the widow of Nabal of Carmel; the third, Absalom, son of Maacah the daughter of Talmai, king of Geshur; 4 the fourth, Adonijah, son of Haggith; the fifth, Shephatiah, son of Abital; 5 and the sixth, Ithream, of David's wife Eglah. These were born to David in Hebron.

Ishbaal and Abner quarrel

6 During the war between the house of Saul and that of David, Abner was gaining power in the house of Saul. 7 Now Saul had had a concubine, Rizpah, the daughter of Aiah. And Ishbaal, son of Saul, said to Abner, "Why have you been intimate with my father's concubine?" 8 Enraged at the words of Ishbaal, Abner said, "Am I a dog's head in Judah? At present I am doing a kindness to the house of your father Saul, to his brothers and his friends, by keeping you out of David's clutches; yet this day you charge me with a crime involving a woman! 9 May God do thus and so to Abner if I do not carry out for David what the LORD swore to him—10 that is, take away the kingdom from the house of Saul and establish the throne of David over Israel and over Judah from Dan to Beer-sheba." 11 In his fear of Abner, Ishbaal was no longer able to say a word to him.

Abner and David Reconciled

12 Then Abner sent messengers to David in Telam, where he was at the moment, to say, "Make an agreement with me, and I will aid you by bringing all Israel over to you." 13 He replied, "Very well, I will make an agreement with you. But one thing I require of you. You must not appear before me unless you bring back Michal, Saul's daughter, when you come to present yourself to me." 14 At the same time David sent messengers to Ishbaal, son of Saul, to say, "Give me my wife Michal, whom I espoused by paying a hundred Philistine foreskins." 15 Ishbaal sent for her and took her away from her husband Paltiel, son of Laish, 16 who followed her weeping as far as Bahurim. But Abner said to him, "Go back!" And he turned back.

17 Abner then said in discussion with the elders of Israel: "For a long time you have been seeking David as your king. 18 Now take action, for the LORD has said of David, 'By my servant David I will save my people Israel from the grasp of the Philistines and from the grasp of all their enemies.'" 19 Abner also spoke personally to Benjamin, and then went to make his own report to David in Hebron concerning all that would be agreeable to Israel and to the whole house of Benjamin. 20 When Abner, accompanied by twenty men, came to David in Hebron, David prepared a feast for Abner and for the men who were with him. 21 Then Abner said to David, "I will now go to assemble all Israel for my lord the king, that they may make an agreement with you; you will then be king over all whom you wish to rule." So David bade Abner farewell, and he went away in peace.

Death of Abner

22 Just then David's servants and Joab were coming in from an expedition, bringing much plunder with them. Abner, having been dismissed by David, was no longer with him in Hebron but had gone his way in peace. 23 When Joab and the whole force he had with him arrived, he was informed, "Abner, son of Ner, came to David; he has been sent on his way in peace." 24 So Joab went to the king and said: "What have you done? Abner came to you. Why did you let him go peacefully on his way? 25 Are you not aware that Abner came to deceive you and to learn the ins and outs of all that you are doing?" 26 Joab then left David, and without David's knowledge sent messengers after Abner, who brought him back from the cistern of Sirah. 27 When Abner returned to Hebron, Joab took him aside within the city gate as though to speak with him privately. There he stabbed him in the abdomen, and he died in revenge for the killing of Joab's brother Asahel. 28 Later David heard of it and said: "Before the LORD, I and my king-dom are forever innocent. 29 May the full responsibility for the death of Abner, son of Ner, be laid to Joab and to all his family. May the men of Joab's family never be without one suffering from a discharge, or a leper, or one unmanly, one falling by the sword, or one in need of bread!" 30 [Joab and his brother Abishai had lain in wait for Abner because he killed their brother Asahel in battle at Gibeon.]

David Mourns Abner

31 Then David said to Joab and to all the people who were with him, "Rend your garments, gird yourselves with sackcloth, and mourn over Abner." King David himself followed the bier. 32 When they had buried Abner in Hebron, the king wept aloud at the grave of Abner, and the people also wept. 33 And the king sang this elegy over Abner:

"Would Abner have died like a fool?
34 Your hands were not bound with chains,
nor your feet placed in fetters;
as men fall before the wicked, you fell."

And all the people continued to weep for him. 35 Then they went to console David with food while it was still day. But David swore, "May God do thus and so to me if I eat bread or anything else before sunset." 36 All the people noted this with approval, just as they were pleased with everything that the king did. 37 So on that day all the people and all Israel came to know that the king had no part in the killing of Abner, son of Ner. 38 The king then said to his servants: "You must recognize that a great general has fallen today in Israel. 39 Although I am the anointed king, I am weak this day, and these men, the sons of Zeruiah, are too ruthless for me. May the LORD requite the evildoer in accordance with his evil deed."

Death of Ishbaal

4 When Ishbaal, son of Saul, heard that Abner had died in Hebron, he ceased to resist and all Israel was alarmed. 2 Ishbaal, son of Saul, had two company leaders named

Baanah and Rechab, sons of Rimmon the Beerothite, of the tribe of Benjamin. [Beeroth, too, was ascribed to Benjamin: 3 the Beerothites fled to Gittaim, where they have been resident aliens to this day. 4 Jonathan, son of Saul, had a son named Meribbaal with crippled feet. He was five years old when the news about Saul and Jonathan came from Jezreel, and his nurse took him up and fled. But in their hasty flight, he fell and became lame.] 5 The sons of Rimmon the Beerothite, Rechab and Baanah, came into the house of Ishbaal during the heat of the day, while he was taking his siesta. 6 The portress of the house had dozed off while sifting wheat, and was asleep. So Rechab and his brother Baanah slipped past 7 and entered the house while Ishbaal was lying asleep in his bedroom. They struck and killed him, and cut off his head. Then, taking the head, they traveled on the Arabah road all night long.

The Murder Avenged

8 They brought the head of Ishbaal to David in Hebron and said to the king: "This is the head of Ishbaal, son of your enemy Saul, who sought your life. Thus has the LORD this day avenged my lord the king on Saul and his posterity." 9 But David replied to Rechab and his brother Baanah, sons of Rimmon the Beerothite: "As the LORD lives, who rescued me from all difficulty, 10 in Ziklag I seized and put to death the man who informed me of Saul's death, thinking himself the bearer of good news for which I ought to give him a reward. 11 How much more now, when wicked men have slain an innocent man in bed at home, must I hold you responsible for his death and destroy you from the earth!" 12 So at a command from David, the young men killed them and cut off their hands and feet, hanging them up near the pool in Hebron. But he took the head of Ishbaal and buried it in Abner's grave in Hebron.

David King of Israel

5 All the tribes of Israel came to David in Hebron and said: "Here we are, your bone and your flesh. 2 In days past, when Saul was our king, it was you who led the Israelites out and brought them back. And the LORD said to you, 'You shall shepherd my people Israel and shall be commander of Israel.'" 3 When all the elders of Israel came to David in Hebron, King David made an agreement with them there before the LORD, and they anointed him king of Israel. 4 David was thirty years old when he became king, and he reigned for forty years: 5 seven years and six months in Hebron over Judah, and thirty-three years in Jerusalem over all Israel and Judah.

Capture of Zion

6 Then the king and his men set out for Jerusalem against the Jebusites who inhabited the region. David was told, "You cannot enter here: the blind and the lame will drive you away!" which was their way of saying, "David cannot enter here." 7 But David did take the stronghold of Zion, which is the City of David. 8 On that day David said: "All who wish to attack the Jebusites must strike at them through the water shaft. The lame and the blind shall be the personal enemies of David." That is why it is said, "The blind and the lame shall not enter the palace."

9 David then dwelt in the stronghold, which was called the City of David; he built up the area from Millo to the palace. 10 David grew steadily more powerful, for the LORD of hosts was with him. 11 Hiram, king of Tyre, sent ambassadors to David; he furnished cedar wood, as well as carpenters and masons, who built a palace for David. 12 And David knew that the LORD had established him as king of Israel and had exalted his rule for the sake of his people Israel.

David's Family in Jerusalem

13 David took more concubines and wives in Jerusalem after he had come from Hebron, and more sons and daughters were born to him in Jerusalem. 14 These are the names of those who were born to him in Jerusalem: Shammua, Shobab, Nathan, Solomon, 15 Ibhar, Elishua, Nepheg, Japhia, 16 Elishama, Baaliada, and Eliphelet.

Rout of the Philistines

17 When the Philistines heard that David had been anointed king of Israel, they all took the field in search of him. On hearing this, David went down to the refuge. 18 The Philistines came and overran the valley of Rephaim. 19 David inquired of the LORD, "Shall I attack the Philistines—will you deliver them into my grip?" The LORD replied to David, "Attack, for I will surely deliver the Philistines into your grip." 20 David then went to Baal-perazim, where he defeated them. He said, "The LORD has scattered my enemies before me like waters that have broken free." That is why the place is called Baal-perazim. 21 They abandoned their gods there, and David and his men carried them away. 22 But the Philistines came up again and overran the valley of Rephaim. 23 So David inquired of the LORD, who replied: "You must not attack frontally, but circle their rear and meet them before the mastic trees. 24 When you hear a sound of marching in the tops of the mastic trees, act decisively, for the LORD will have gone forth before you to attack the camp of the Philistines." 25 David obeyed the LORD's command and routed the Philistines from Gibeon as far as Gezer.

The Ark Brought to Jerusalem

6 David again assembled all the picked men of Israel, thirty thousand in number. 2 Then David and all the people who were with him

---

4, 4: Saul's grandson Meribbaal is the subject of chapter 9 below. The text of this verse may owe its present place to the fact that pre-Christian copies of the Books of Samuel tended to confuse his name with that of his uncle Ishbaal, Saul's son and successor, a principal figure in chapters 2–4.

5, 6–12: David's most important military exploit, the taking of Jerusalem, is here presented before his

battles with the Philistines, vv 17–25, which were earlier in time. The sense of vv 6 and 8 is in doubt.

5, 17: *Refuge:* probably near Adullam (1 Sm 22, 1–5).

5, 18–25: The successive defeats of the Philistines in the *valley of Rephaim* southwest of Jerusalem had the effect of blocking their access to the mountain ridge near *Gibeon*, and confining them to their

holdings on the coast and in the foothills beyond Gezer to the west and south.

5, 20: *Baal-perazim:* means approximately "the lord of scatterings."

5, 24: *Sound of marching:* the wind in the treetops suggestive of the Lord's footsteps.

set out for Baala of Judah to bring up from there the ark of God, which bears the name of the LORD of hosts enthroned above the cherubim. 3 The ark of God was placed on a new cart and taken away from the house of Abinadab on the hill. Uzzah and Ahio, sons of Abinadab, guided the cart, 4 with Ahio walking before it, 5 while David and all the Israelites made merry before the LORD with all their strength, with singing and with citharas, harps, tambourines, sistrums and cymbals.

6 When they came to the threshing floor of Nodan, Uzzah reached out his hand to the ark of God and steadied it, for the oxen were making it tip. 7 But the LORD was angry with Uzzah; God struck him on that spot, and he died there before God. 8 David was disturbed because the LORD had vented his anger on Uzzah. (The place has been called Perezuzzah down to the present day.) 9 David feared the LORD that day and said, "How can the ark of the LORD come to me?" 10 So David would not have the ark of the LORD brought to him in the City of David but diverted it to the house of Obed-edom the Gittite.

11 The ark of the LORD remained in the house of Obed-edom the Gittite for three months, and the LORD blessed Obed-edom and his whole house. 12 When it was reported to King David that the LORD had blessed the family of Obed-edom and all that belonged to him, David went to bring up the ark of God from the house of Obed-edom into the City of David amid festivities. 13 As soon as the bearers of the ark of the LORD had advanced six steps, he sacrificed an ox and a fatling. 14 Then David, girt with a linen apron, came dancing before the LORD with abandon, 15 as he and all the Israelites were bringing up the ark of the LORD with shouts of joy and to the sound of the horn. 16 As the ark of the LORD was entering the City of David, Saul's daughter Michal looked down through the window and saw King

David leaping and dancing before the LORD, and she despised him in her heart. 17 The ark of the LORD was brought in and set in its place within the tent David had pitched for it. Then David offered holocausts and peace offerings before the LORD. 18 When he finished making these offerings, he blessed the people in the name of the LORD of hosts. 19 He then distributed among all the people, to each man and each woman in the entire multitude of Israel, a loaf of bread, a cut of roast meat, and a raisin cake. With this, all the people left for their homes.

20 When David returned to bless his own family, Saul's daughter Michal came out to meet him and said, "How the king of Israel has honored himself today, exposing himself to the view of the slave girls of his followers, as a commoner might do!" 21 But David replied to Michal: "I was dancing before the LORD. As the LORD lives, who preferred me to your father and his whole family when he appointed me commander of the LORD's people, Israel, not only will I make merry before the LORD, 22 but I will demean myself even more. I will be lowly in your esteem, but in the esteem of the slave girls you spoke of I will be honored." 23 And so Saul's daughter Michal was childless to the day of her death.

David's Concern for the Ark

7 When King David was settled in his palace, and the LORD had given him rest from his enemies on every side, 2 he said to Nathan the prophet, "Here I am living in a house of cedar, while the ark of God dwells in a tent?" 3 Nathan answered the king, "Go, do whatever you have in mind, for the LORD is with you." 4 But that night the LORD spoke to Nathan and said: 5 "Go, tell my servant David, 'Thus says the LORD: Should you build me a house to dwell in? 6 I have not dwelt in a house from the day on which I led the Israelites out of Egypt

to the present, but I have been going about in a tent under cloth. 7 In all my wanderings everywhere among the Israelites, did I ever utter a word to any one of the judges whom I charged to tend my people Israel, to ask: Why have you not built me a house of cedar?'

The Lord's Promises

8 "Now then, speak thus to my servant David, 'The LORD of hosts has this to say: It was I who took you from the pasture and from the care of the flock to be commander of my people Israel. 9 I have been with you wherever you went, and I have destroyed all your enemies before you. And I will make you famous like the great ones of the earth. 10 I will fix a place for my people Israel; I will plant them so that they may dwell in their place without further disturbance. Neither shall the wicked continue to afflict them as they did of old, 11 since the time I first appointed judges over my people Israel. I will give you rest from all your enemies. The LORD also reveals to you that he will establish a house for you. 12 And when your time comes and you rest with your ancestors, I will raise up your heir after you, sprung from your loins, and I will make his kingdom firm. 13 It is he who shall build a house for my name. And I will make his royal throne firm forever. 14 I will be a father to him, and he shall be a son to me. And if he does wrong, I will correct him with the rod of men and with human chastisements; 15 but I will not withdraw my favor from him as I withdrew it from your predecessor Saul, whom I removed from my presence. 16 Your house and your kingdom shall endure forever before me; your throne shall stand firm forever.'"

17 Nathan reported all these words and this entire vision to David.

King David's Prayer

18 Then King David went in and sat before the LORD and said, "Who

---

7, 8–16: The prophecy to David contained in these verses is cited again, in poetic form, in Ps 89, 20–38, and alluded to in Ps 132. The promise regarding the people of Israel, vv 10–11, is a part of the promise to David at least as old as the composition of this chapter of Samuel, where it is anticipated in vv 6–7, and alluded to in David's thanksgiving, vv 23–24; it applies to the people an expression used of David in Ps 89, 23.

The prophecy to David is the basis for Jewish expectation of a messiah, son of David, which Jesus Christ fulfilled in a transcendent way; cf Acts 2, 30; Heb 1, 5.

am I, Lord God, and who are the members of my house, that you have brought me to this point? 19 Yet even this you see as too little, Lord God; you have also spoken of the house of your servant for a long time to come: this too you have shown to man, Lord God! 20 What more can David say to you? You know your servant, Lord God! 21 For your servant's sake and as you have had at heart, you have brought about this entire magnificent disclosure to your servant. 22 And so—

"Great are you, Lord God! There is none like you and there is no God but you, just as we have heard it told. 23 What other nation on earth is there like your people Israel, which God has led, redeeming it as his people; so that you have made yourself renowned by doing this magnificent deed, and by doing awe-inspiring things as you cleared nations and their gods out of the way of your people, which you redeemed for yourself from Egypt? 24 You have established for yourself your people Israel as yours forever, and you, Lord, have become their God. 25 And now, Lord God, confirm for all the time the prophecy you have made concerning your servant and his house, and do as you have promised. 26 Your name will be forever great, when men say, 'The Lord of hosts is God of Israel,' and the house of your servant David stands firm before you. 27 It is you Lord of hosts, God of Israel, who said in a revelation to your servant, 'I will build a house for you.' Therefore your servant now finds the courage to make this prayer to you. 28 And now, Lord God, you are God and your words are truth; you have made this generous promise to your servant. 29 Do, then, bless the house of your servant that it may be before you forever; for you, Lord God, have promised, and by your blessing the house of your servant shall be blessed forever."

Summary of David's Wars

8 After this David attacked the Philistines and conquered them, wresting . . . from the Philistines. 2 He also defeated Moab and then measured them with a line, making them lie down on the ground. He told off two lengths of line for execution, and a full length to be spared. Thus the Moabites became tributary to David. 3 Next David defeated Hadadezer, son of Rehob, king of Zobah, when he went to reestablish his dominion at the Euphrates River. 4 David captured from him one thousand seven hundred horsemen and twenty thousand foot soldiers. And he hamstrung all the chariot horses, preserving only enough for a hundred chariots. 5 When the Arameans of Damascus came to the aid of Hadadezer, king of Zobah, David slew twenty-two thousand of them. 6 David then placed garrisons in Aram of Damascus, and the Arameans became subjects, tributary to David. The Lord brought David victory in all his undertakings. 7 David also took away the golden shields used by Hadadezer's servants and brought them to Jerusalem. [These Shishak, king of Egypt, took away when he came to Jerusalem in the days of Rehoboam, son of Solomon.] 8 From Tebah and Berothai, towns of Hadadezer, King David removed a very large quantity of bronze. 9 When Toi, king of Hamath, heard that David had defeated all the forces of Hadadezer, 10 he sent his son Hadoram to King David to greet him and to congratulate him for his victory over Hadadezer in battle, because Toi had been in many battles with Hadadezer. Hadoram also brought with him articles of silver, gold, and bronze. 11 These, too, King David consecrated to the Lord, together with the silver and gold he had taken from every nation he had conquered: 12 from Edom and Moab, from the Ammonites,

from the Philistines, from the Amalekites, and from the plunder of Hadadezer, son of Rehob, king of Zobah.

13 On his return, David became famous for having slain eighteen thousand Edomites in the Salt Valley; 14 after which he placed garrisons in Edom. Thus all the Edomites became David's subjects, and the Lord brought David victory in all his undertakings.

David's Officials

15 David reigned over all Israel, judging and administering justice to all his people. 16 Joab, son of Zeruiah, was in command of the army. Jehoshaphat, son of Ahilud, was chancellor. 17 Zadok, son of Ahitub, and Ahimelech, son of Abiathar, were priests. Shawsha was scribe. 18 Benaiah, son of Jehoiada, was in command of the Cherethites and Pelethites. And David's sons were priests.

David and Meribbaal

9 David asked, "Is there any survivor of Saul's house to whom I may show kindness for the sake of Jonathan?" 2 Now there was a servant of the family of Saul named Ziba. He was summoned to David, and the king asked him, "Are you Ziba?" He replied, "Your servant." 3 Then the king inquired, "Is there any survivor of Saul's house to whom I may show God's kindness?" Ziba answered the king, "There is still Jonathan's son, whose feet are crippled." 4 The king said to him, "Where is he?" and Ziba answered, "He is in the house of Machir, son of Ammiel, in Lodebar." 5 So King David sent for him and had him brought from the house of Machir, son of Ammiel, in Lodebar. 6 When Meribbaal, son of Jonathan, son of Saul, came to David, he fell prostrate in homage. David said, "Meribbaal," and he answered,

---

7, 19: *This too you have shown to man:* the text as transmitted has, rather, "and this is instruction for (or: the law of) mankind." The author of Chronicles (1 Chr 17, 17) saw approximately the same phrase, which he endeavored to fit into the context in a quite different sense. The above is conjectural; cf Dt 5, 24.

8, 1: *Wresting . . .:* the Hebrew text here gives "the

bridle of the cubit"; 1 Chr 18, 1 understood "Gath and its dependent villages"; others implausibly read "dominion of the capital city."

8, 2: *Two lengths . . . a full length:* usually taken to mean that two-thirds of them were executed; but it could mean that two-thirds were spared, if the line was used full length in their case but doubled on itself

to make "two lines" for those to be put to death.

8, 13: *On his return:* possibly to Jerusalem, after the revolt of Absalom, a circumstance which this catalogue of victories would avoid mentioning. 1 Chr 18, 13 attributes the defeat of the Edomites to Abishai.

"Your servant," 7 "Fear not," David said to him, "I will surely be kind to you for the sake of your father Jonathan. I will restore to you all the lands of your grandfather Saul, and you shall always eat at my table." 8 Bowing low, he answered, "What is your servant that you should pay attention to a dead dog like me?" 9 The king then called Ziba, Saul's attendant, and said to him: "I am giving your lord's son all that belonged to Saul and to all his family. 10 You and your sons and servants must till the land for him. You shall bring in the produce, which shall be food for your lord's family to eat. But Meribbaal, your lord's son, shall always eat at my table." Ziba, who had fifteen sons and twenty servants, 11 said to the king, "Your servant shall do just as my lord the king has commanded him." And so Meribbaal ate at David's table like one of the king's sons. 12 Meribbaal had a young son whose name was Mica; and all the tenants of Ziba's family worked for Meribbaal. 13 But Meribbaal lived in Jerusalem, because he always ate at the king's table. He was lame in both feet.

Insult of the Ammonites

10 Some time later the king of the Ammonites died, and his son Hanun succeeded him as king. 2 David thought, "I will be kind to Hanun, son of Nahash, as his father was kind to me." So David sent his servants with condolences to Hanun for the loss of his father. But when David's servants entered the country of the Ammonites, 3 the Ammonite princes said to their lord Hanun: "Do you think that David is honoring your father by sending men with condolences? Is it not rather to explore the city, to spy on it, and to overthrow it, that David has sent his messengers to you?" 4 Hanun, therefore, seized David's servants and, after shaving off half their beards and cutting away the lower halves of their garments at the buttocks, sent them away. 5 When he was told of it, King David sent out

word to them, since the men were quite ashamed. "Stay in Jericho until your beards grow," he said, "and then come back."

Ammonites Defeated

6 In view of the offense they had given to David, the Ammonites sent for and hired twenty thousand Aramean foot soldiers from Bethrehob and Zobah, as well as the king of Maacah with one thousand men, and twelve thousand men from Tob. 7 On learning this, David sent out Joab with the entire levy of trained soldiers. 8 The Ammonites came out and drew up in battle formation at the entrance of their city gate, while the Arameans of Zobah and Rehob and the men of Tob and Maacab remained apart in the open country. 9 When Joab saw the battle lines drawn up against him, both front and rear, he made a selection from all the picked troops of Israel and arrayed them against the Arameans. 10 He placed the rest of the soldiers under the command of his brother Abishai, who arrayed them against the Ammonites. 11 Joab said, "If the Arameans are stronger than I, you shall help me. But if the Ammonites are stronger than you, I will come to help you. 12 Be brave; let us prove our valor for the sake of our people and the cities of our God; the LORD will do what he judges best." 13 When Joab and the soldiers who were with him approached the Arameans for battle, they fled before him. 14 The Ammonites, seeing that the Arameans had fled, also fled from Abishai and withdrew into the city. Joab then ceased his attack on the Ammonites and returned to Jerusalem.

Arameans Defeated

15 Then the Arameans responded to their defeat by Israel with a full mustering of troops; 16 Hadadezer sent for and enlisted Arameans from beyond the Euphrates. They came to Helam, with Shobach, general of Hadadezer's army, at their head. 17 On receiving this news, David as-

sembled all Israel, crossed the Jordan, and went to Helam. The Arameans drew up in formation against David and fought with him. 18 But the Arameans gave way before Israel, and David's men killed seven hundred charioteers and forty thousand of the Aramean foot soldiers. Shobach, general of the army, was struck down and died on the field. 19 All of Hadadezer's vassal kings, in view of their defeat by Israel, then made peace with the Israelites and became their subjects. And the Arameans were afraid to give further aid to the Ammonites.

David's Sin

11 At the turn of the year, when kings go out on campaign, David sent out Joab along with his officers and the army of Israel, and they ravaged the Ammonites and besieged Rabbah. David, however, remained in Jerusalem. 2 One evening David rose from his siesta and strolled about on the roof of the palace. From the roof he saw a woman bathing, who was very beautiful. 3 David had inquiries made about the woman and was told, "She is Bathsheba, daughter of Eliam, and wife of [Joab's armorbearer] Uriah the Hittite." 4 Then David sent messengers and took her. When she came to him, he had relations with her, at a time when she was just purified after her monthly period. She then returned to her house. 5 But the woman had conceived, and sent the information to David, "I am with child."

6 David therefore sent a message to Joab, "Send me Uriah the Hittite." So Joab sent Uriah to David. 7 When he came, David questioned him about Joab, the soldiers, and how the war was going, and Uriah answered that all was well. 8 David then said to Uriah, "Go down to your house and bathe your feet." Uriah left the palace, and a portion was sent out after him from the king's table. 9 But Uriah slept at the entrance of the royal palace with the other officers of his lord, and

---

10, 1: *Some time later:* early in the reign of David, since Hanun's father had been ruling in Ammon at the beginning of Saul's reign (1 Sm 11) and Solomon was as yet unborn (2 Sm 11, 1; 12, 24).

10, 6–9: A Hebrew text from Qumran (4Q Sam^a) comes closer in these verses to what is given in 1 Chr 19, 6–9. The scene of the conflict is more likely Rabbath-Ammon, with Josephus (Ant., vii, 123),

than Madeba, as in Chr; compare ch 11.
11, 1: *At the turn of the year:* in the spring.

did not go down to his own house. 10 David was told that Uriah had not gone home. So he said to Uriah, "Have you not come from a journey? Why, then, did you not go down to your house?" 11 Uriah answered David, "The ark and Israel and Judah are lodged in tents, and my lord Joab and your majesty's servants are encamped in the open field. Can I go home to eat and to drink and to sleep with my wife? As the LORD lives and as you live, I will do no such thing." 12 Then David said to Uriah, "Stay here today also, I shall dismiss you tomorrow." So Uriah remained in Jerusalem that day. On the day following, 13 David summoned him, and he ate and drank with David, who made him drunk. But in the evening he went out to sleep on his bed among his lord's servants, and did not go down to his home. 14 The next morning David wrote a letter to Joab which he sent by Uriah. 15 In it he directed: "Place Uriah up front, where the fighting is fierce. Then pull back and leave him to be struck down dead." 16 So while Joab was besieging the city, he assigned Uriah to a place where he knew the defenders were strong. 17 When the men of the city made a sortie against Joab, some officers of David's army fell, and among them Uriah the Hittite died.

18 Then Joab sent David a report of all the details of the battle, 19 instructing the messenger, "When you have finished giving the king all the details of the battle, 20 the king may become angry and say to you: 'Why did you go near the city to fight? Did you not know that they would shoot from the wall above? 21 Who killed Abimelech, son of Jerubbaal? Was it not a woman who threw a millstone down on him from the wall above, so that he died in Thebez? Why did you go near the wall?' Then you in turn shall say, 'Your servant Uriah the Hittite is also dead.'" 22 The messenger set out, and on his arrival he relayed to David all the details as Joab had instructed him. 23 He told David:

"The men had us at a disadvantage and came out into the open against us, but we pushed them back to the entrance of the city gate. 24 Then the archers shot at your servants from the wall above, and some of the king's servants died, among them your servant Uriah." 25 David said to the messenger: "This is what you shall convey to Joab: 'Do not be chagrined at this, for the sword devours now here and now there. Strengthen your attack on the city and destroy it.' Encourage him."

26 When the wife of Uriah heard that her husband had died, she mourned her lord. 27 But once the mourning was over, David sent for her and brought her into his house. She became his wife and bore him a son. But the LORD was displeased with what David had done.

Nathan's Parable

12 The LORD sent Nathan to David, and when he came to him, he said: "Judge this case for me! In a certain town there were two men, one rich, the other poor. 2 The rich man had flocks and herds in great numbers. 3 But the poor man had nothing at all except one little ewe lamb that he had bought. He nourished her, and she grew up with him and his children. She shared the little food he had and drank from his cup and slept in his bosom. She was like a daughter to him. 4 Now, the rich man received a visitor, but he would not take from his own flocks, and herds to prepare a meal for the wayfarer who had come to him. Instead he took the poor man's ewe lamb and made a meal of it for his visitor." 5 David grew very angry with that man and said to Nathan: "As the LORD lives, the man who has done this merits death! 6 He shall restore the ewe lamb fourfold because he has done this and has had no pity."

David's Punishment

7 Then Nathan said to David: "You are the man! Thus says the

LORD God of Israel: 'I anointed you king of Israel. I rescued you from the hand of Saul, 8 I gave you your lord's house and your lord's wives for your own. I gave you the house of Israel and of Judah. And if this were not enough, I could count up for you still more. 9 Why have you spurned the LORD and done evil in his sight? You have cut down Uriah the Hittite with the sword; you took his wife as your own, and him you killed with the sword of the Ammonites. 10 Now, therefore, the sword shall never depart from your house, because you have despised me and have taken the wife of Uriah to be your wife.' 11 Thus says the LORD: 'I will bring evil upon you out of your own house. I will take your wives while you live to see it, and will give them to your neighbor. He shall lie with your wives in broad daylight. 12 You have done this deed in secret, but I will bring it about in the presence of all Israel, and with the sun looking down.'"

David's Repentance

13 Then David said to Nathan, "I have sinned against the LORD." Nathan answered David: "The LORD on his part has forgiven your sin: you shall not die. 14 But since you have utterly spurned the LORD by this deed, the child born to you must surely die." 15 Then Nathan returned to his house.

The LORD struck the child that the wife of Uriah had borne to David, and it became desperately ill. 16 David besought God for the child. He kept a fast, retiring for the night to lie on the ground clothed in sackcloth. 17 The elders of his house stood beside him urging him to rise from the ground; but he would not, nor would he take food with them. 18 On the seventh day, the child died. David's servants, however, were afraid to tell him that the child was dead, for they said: "When the child was alive, we spoke to him, but he would not listen to what we said. How can we tell him the child is dead? He may do some harm!"

11, 22: After this verse, the Greek text, which is here the older form, has David, angry with Joab, repeat exactly the questions Joab had foreseen in

vv 20f. In v 24 of our oldest Greek text, the messenger specifies that about eighteen men were killed.

12, 1–4: This utterance of Nathan is in regular lines

in Hebrew, resembling English blank verse.

19 But David noticed his servants whispering among themselves and realized that the child was dead. He asked his servants, "Is the child dead?" They replied, "Yes, he is." 20 Rising from the ground, David washed and anointed himself, and changed his clothes. Then he went to the house of the LORD and worshiped. He returned to his own house, where at his request food was set before him, and he ate. 21 His servants said to him: "What is this you are doing? While the child was living, you fasted and wept and kept vigil; now that the child is dead, you rise and take food." 22 He replied: "While the child was living, I fasted and wept, thinking, 'Perhaps the LORD will grant me the child's life.' 23 But now he is dead. Why should I fast? Can I bring him back again? I shall go to him, but he will not return to me."

24 Then David comforted his wife Bathsheba. He went and slept with her; and she conceived and bore him a son, who was named Solomon. The LORD loved 25 him and sent the prophet Nathan to name him Jedidiah, on behalf of the LORD.

Ammonite War Ends

26 Joab fought against Rabbah of the Ammonites and captured this royal city. 27 He sent messengers to David with the word: "I have fought against Rabbah and have taken the water-city. 28 Therefore, assemble the rest of the soldiers, join the siege against the city and capture it, lest it be I that capture the city and it be credited to me." 29 So David assembled the rest of the soldiers and went to Rabbah. When he had fought against it and captured it, 30 he took the crown from Milcom's head. It weighed a talent, of gold and precious stones; it was placed on David's head. He brought out immense booty from the city, 31 and also led away the inhabitants, whom he assigned to work with saws, iron picks, and iron axes, or put to work at the brick-mold. This is what he did to all the Ammonite cities. David and all the soldiers then returned to Jerusalem.

The Crime of Amnon

13 Some time later the following incident occurred. David's son Absalom had a beautiful sister named Tamar, and David's son Amnon loved her. 2 He was in such straits over his sister Tamar that he became sick; since she was a virgin, Amnon thought it impossible to carry out his designs toward her. 3 Now Amnon had a friend named Jonadab, son of David's brother Shimeah, who was very clever. 4 He asked him, "Prince, why are you so dejected morning after morning? Why not tell me?" So Amnon said to him, "I am in love with Tamar, my brother Absalom's sister." 5 Then Jonadab replied, "Lie down on your bed and pretend to be sick. When your father comes to visit you, say to him, 'Please let my sister Tamar come and encourage me to take food. If she prepares something appetizing in my presence, for me to see, I will eat it from her hand.'" 6 So Amnon lay down and pretended to be sick. When the king came to visit him, Amnon said to the king, "Please let my sister Tamar come and prepare some fried cakes before my eyes, that I may take nourishment from her hand."

7 David then sent home a message to Tamar, "Please go to the house of your brother Amnon and prepare some nourishment for him." 8 Tamar went to the house of her brother Amnon, who was in bed. Taking dough and kneading it, she twisted it into cakes before his eyes and fried the cakes. 9 Then she took the pan and set out the cakes before him. But Amnon would not eat; he said, "Have everyone leave me." When they had all left him, 10 Amnon said to Tamar, "Bring the nourishment into the bedroom, that I may have it from your hand." So Tamar picked up the cakes she had prepared and brought them to her brother Amnon in the bedroom. 11 But when she brought them to him to eat, he seized her and said to her, "Come! Lie with me, my sister!" 12 But she answered him, "No, my brother! Do not shame me! That is

an intolerable crime in Israel. Do not commit this insensate deed. 13 Where would I take my shame? And you would be a discredited man in Israel. So please, speak to the king; he will not keep me from you."

14 Not heeding her plea, he overpowered her; he shamed her and had relations with her. 15 Then Amnon conceived an intense hatred for her, which far surpassed the love he had had for her. "Get up and leave," he said to her. 16 She replied, "No, brother, because to drive me out would be far worse than the first injury you have done me." He would not listen to her, 17 but called the youth who was his attendant and said, "Put her outside, away from me, and bar the door after her." 18 Now she had on a long tunic, for that is how maiden princesses dressed in olden days. When his attendant put her out and barred the door after her, 19 Tamar put ashes on her head and tore the long tunic in which she was clothed. Then, putting her hands to her head, she went away crying loudly. 20 Her brother Absalom said to her: "Has your brother Amnon been with you? Be still now, my sister; he is your brother. Do not take this affair to heart." But Tamar remained grief-stricken and forlorn in the house of her brother Absalom. 21 King David, who got word of the whole affair, became very angry. He did not, however, spark the resentment of his son Amnon, whom he favored because he was his first-born. 22 Absalom, moreover, said nothing at all to Amnon, although he hated him for having shamed his sister Tamar.

Absalom's Plot

23 After a period of two years, Absalom had shearers in Baal-hazor near Ephraim, and he invited all the princes. 24 Absalom went to the king and said: "Your servant is having shearers. Please, your majesty, come with all your retainers to your servant." 25 But the king said to Absalom, "No, my son, all of us should not go lest we be a burden to you." And though Absalom urged

---

12, 30: *Weighed a talent:* since this would be more than 75 pounds, some commentators picture the

idol's crown as displaying a single precious stone of large size, which David took to wear: but the text

does not say this.

him, he refused to go and began to bid him goodbye. 26 Absalom then said, "If you will not come yourself, please let my brother Amnon come to us." The king asked him, "Why should he go to you?" 27 At Absalom's urging, however, he sent Amnon and all the other princes with him. Absalom prepared a banquet fit for royalty. 28 But he had instructed his servants: "Now watch! When Amnon is merry with wine and I say to you, 'Kill Amnon,' put him to death. Do not be afraid, for it is I who order you to do it. Be resolute and act manfully."

Death of Amnon

29 When the servants did to Amnon as Absalom had commanded, all the other princes rose, mounted their mules, and fled. 30 While they were still on the road, a report reached David that Absalom had killed all the princes and that not one of them had survived. 31 The king stood up, rent his garments, and then lay on the ground. All his servants standing by him also rent their garments. 32 But Jonadab, son of David's brother Shimeah, spoke up: "Let not my lord think that all the young princes have been killed! Amnon alone is dead, for Absalom was determined on this ever since Amnon shamed his sister Tamar. 33 So let not my lord the king put faith in the report that all the princes are dead. Amnon alone is dead." 34 Meanwhile, Absalom had taken flight. Then the servant on watch looked about and saw a large group coming down the slope from the direction of Bahurim. He came in and reported this, telling the king that he had seen some men coming down the mountainside from the direction of Bahurim. 35 So Jonadab said to the king: "There! The princes have come. It is as your servant said." 36 No sooner had he finished speaking than the princes came in, weeping aloud. The king, too, and all his servants wept very bitterly. 37 But Absalom, who had taken flight, went to Talmai, son of Ammihud, king of Geshur, 38 and stayed in Geshur for three years.

Efforts for Absalom's Return

39 The king continued during all that time to mourn over his son; but his longing reached out for Absalom as he became reconciled to the death **14** of Amnon. 1 When Joab, son of Zeruiah, observed how the king felt toward Absalom, 2 he sent to Tekoa and brought from there a gifted woman, to whom he said: "Pretend to be in mourning. Put on mourning apparel and do not anoint yourself with oil, that you may appear to be a woman who has been long in mourning for a departed one. 3 Then go to the king and speak to him in this manner." And Joab instructed her what to say.

4 So the woman of Tekoa went to the king and fell prostrate to the ground in homage, saying, "Help, your majesty!" 5 The king said to her, "What do you want?" She replied: "Alas, I am a widow; my husband is dead. 6 Your servant had two sons, who quarreled in the field. There being no one to part them, one of them struck his brother and killed him. 7 Then the whole clan confronted your servant and demanded: 'Give up the one who killed his brother. We must put him to death for the life of his brother whom he has slain; we must extinguish the heir also.' Thus they will quench my remaining hope and leave my husband neither name nor posterity upon the earth." 8 The king then said to the woman: "Go home. I will issue a command on your behalf." 9 The woman of Tekoa answered him, "Let me and my family be to blame, my lord king, you and your throne are innocent." 10 Then the king said, "If anyone says a word to you, have him brought to me, and he shall not touch you again." 11 But she went on to say, "Please, your majesty, keep in mind the LORD your God, that the avenger of blood may not go too far in destruction and that my son may not be done away with." He replied, "As the LORD lives, not a hair of your son shall fall to the ground."

12 The woman continued, "Please let your servant say still another word to my lord the king." He replied, "Speak." 13 So the woman said: "Why, then, do you think of this same kind of thing against the people of God? In pronouncing as he has, the king shows himself guilty, for not bringing back his own banished son. 14 We must indeed die; we are then like water that is poured out on the ground and cannot be gathered up. Yet, though God does not bring back life he does take thought how not to banish anyone from him. 15 And now, if I have presumed to speak of this matter to your majesty, it is because the people have given me cause to fear. And so your servant thought: 'Let me speak to the king. Perhaps he will grant the petition of his maidservant. 16 For the king must surely consent to free his servant from the grasp of one who would seek to destroy me and my son as well from God's inheritance.'" 17 And the woman concluded: "Let the word of my lord the king provide a resting place; indeed, my lord the king is like an angel of God, evaluating good and bad. The LORD your God be with you."

18 The king answered the woman, "Now do not conceal from me anything I may ask you!" The woman said, "Let my lord the king speak." 19 So the king asked, "Is Joab involved with you in all this?" And the woman answered: "As you live, my lord the king, it is just as your majesty has said, and not otherwise. It was your servant Joab who instructed me and told your servant all these things she was to say. 20 Your servant Joab did this to come at the issue in a roundabout way. But my lord is as wise as an angel of God, so that he knows all things on earth."

Absalom's Return

21 Then the king said to Joab: "I hereby grant this request. Go, therefore, and bring back young

---

14, 7: *Hope:* literally, "glowing coal." The image is similar to that of the lighted lamp, e.g., Ps 89, 17, to keep alive the ancestral name.

14, 14: *How not to banish:* a possible allusion to the religious institution of cities of refuge for involuntary murderers; see Nm 35, 9–15.

14, 17: *A resting place:* cf Ps 95, 11; Heb 3, 7—4, 11. The reference here is to a return home for Absalom to Israel.

Absalom." 22 Falling prostrate to the ground in homage and blessing the king, Joab said, "This day I know that I am in good favor with you, my lord the king, since the king has granted the request of his servant." 23 Joab then went off to Geshur and brought Absalom to Jerusalem. 24 But the king said, "Let him go to his own house; he shall not appear before me." So Absalom went off to his house and did not appear before the king.

25 In all Israel there was not a man who could so be praised for his beauty as Absalom, who was without blemish from the sole of his foot to the crown of his head. 26 When he shaved his head—which he used to do at the end of every year, because his hair became too heavy for him— the hair weighed two hundred shekels according to the royal standard. 27 Absalom had three sons born to him, besides a daughter named Tamar who was a beautiful woman.

Absalom Is Pardoned

28 Absalom lived in Jerusalem for two years without appearing before the king. 29 Then he summoned Joab to send him to the king, but Joab would not come to him. Although he summoned him a second time, Joab refused to come. 30 He therefore instructed his servants: "You see Joab's field that borders mine, on which he has barley. Go, set it on fire." And so Absalom's servants set the field on fire. Joab's farmhands came to him with torn garments and reported to him what had been done. 31 At this, Joab went to Absalom in his house and asked him, "Why have your servants set my field on fire?" 32 Absalom answered Joab: "I was summoning you to come here, that I may send you to the king to say: 'Why did I come back from Geshur? I would be better off if I were still there! Now, let me appear before the king. If I am guilty, let him put me to death.'" 33 Joab went to the king and reported this. The king then called Absalom, who came to him and in homage fell on his face to the ground before the king. Then the king kissed him.

Absalom's Plot

15 After this Absalom provided himself with chariots, horses, and fifty henchmen. 2 Moreover, Absalom used to rise early and stand alongside the road leading to the gate. If someone had a lawsuit to be decided by the king, Absalom would call to him and say, "From what city are you?" And when he replied, "Your servant is of such and such a tribe of Israel," 3 Absalom would say to him, "Your suit is good and just, but there is no one to hear you in the king's name." 4 And he would continue: "If only I could be appointed judge in the land! Then everyone who has a lawsuit to be decided might come to me and I would render him justice." 5 Whenever a man approached him to show homage, he would extend his hand, hold him, and kiss him. 6 By behaving in this way toward all the Israelites who came to the king for judgment, Absalom was stealing away the loyalties of the men of Israel.

Conspiracy in Hebron

7 After a period of four years, Absalom said to the king: "Allow me to go to Hebron and fulfill a vow I made to the LORD. 8 For while living in Geshur in Aram, your servant made this vow: 'If the LORD ever brings me back to Jerusalem, I will worship him in Hebron.'" 9 The king wished him a safe journey, and he went off to Hebron. 10 Then Absalom sent spies throughout the tribes of Israel to say, "When you hear the sound of the horn, declare Absalom king in Hebron." 11 Two hundred men had accompanied Absalom from Jerusalem. They had been invited and went in good faith, knowing nothing of the plan. 12 Absalom also sent to Ahithophel the Gilonite, David's counselor, an invitation to come from his town, Giloh, for the sacrifices he was about to offer. So the conspiracy gained strength, and the people with Absalom increased in numbers.

David Flees Jerusalem

13 An informant came to David with the report, "The Israelites have transferred their loyalty to Absalom." 14 At this, David said to all his servants who were with him in Jerusalem: "Up! Let us take flight, or none of us will escape from Absalom. Leave quickly, lest he hurry and overtake us, then visit disaster upon us and put the city to the sword." 15 The king's officers answered him, "Your servants are ready, whatever our lord the king chooses to do." 16 Then the king set out, accompanied by his entire household, except for ten concubines whom he left behind to take care of the palace. 17 As the king left the city, with all his officers accompanying him, they halted opposite the ascent of the Mount of Olives, at a distance, 18 while the whole army marched past him.

David and Ittai

As all the Cherethites and Pelethites, and the six hundred men of Gath who had accompanied him from that city, were passing in review before the king, 19 he said to Ittai the Giettite: "Why should you also go with us? Go back and stay with the king, for you are a foreigner and you, too, are an exile from your own country. 20 You came only yesterday, and shall I have you wander about with us today, wherever I have to go? Return and take your brothers with you, and may the LORD be kind and faithful to you." 21 But Ittai answered the king, "As the LORD lives, and as my lord the king lives, your servant shall be wherever my lord the king may be, whether for death or for life." 22 So the king said to Ittai, "Go, then, march on." And Ittai the Gittite, with all his men and all the dependents that were with him, marched on. 23 Everyone in the countryside wept aloud as the last of the soldiers went by, and the king crossed the Kidron Valley with all the soldiers moving on ahead of him by way of the Mount of Olives, toward the desert.

David and the Priests

24 Zadok, too [with all the Levite bearers of the ark of the covenant of God], and Abiathar brought the ark of God to a halt until the soldiers had marched out of the city. 25 Then

the king said to Zadok: "Take the ark of God back to the city. If I find favor with the LORD, he will bring me back and permit me to see it and its lodging. 26 But if he should say, 'I am not pleased with you,' I am ready; let him do to me as he sees fit." 27 The king also said to the priest Zadok: "See to it that you and Abiathar return to the city in peace, and both your sons with you, your own son Ahimaaz, and Abiathar's son Jonathan. 28 Remember, I shall be waiting at the fords near the desert until I receive information from you." 29 So Zadok and Abiathar took the ark of God back to Jerusalem and remained there.

30 As David went up the Mount of Olives, he wept without ceasing. His head was covered, and he was walking barefoot. All those who were with him also had their heads covered and were weeping as they went. 31 When David was informed that Ahithophel was among the conspirators with Absalom, he said, "O LORD, turn the counsel of Ahithophel to folly!"

David and Hushai

32 When David reached the top, where men used to worship God, Hushai the Archite was there to meet him, with rent garments and dirt upon his head. 33 David said to him: "If you come with me, you will be a burden to me. 34 But if you return to the city and say to Absalom, 'Let me be your servant, O king; I was formerly your father's servant but now I will be yours,' you will undo for me the counsel of Ahithophel. 35 You will have the priests Zadok and Abiathar there with you. If you hear anything from the royal palace, you shall report it to the priests Zadok and Abiathar, 36 who have there with them both Zadok's son Ahimaaz and Abiathar's son Jonathan. Through them you shall send on to me whatever you hear." 37 So David's friend Hushai went into the city of Jerusalem as Absalom was about to enter it.

16, 8: *Bloodshed . . . Saul:* refers to the episode recounted in 21, 1–14.

David and Ziba

16 David had gone a little beyond the top when Ziba, the servant of Meribbaal, met him with saddled asses laden with two hundred loaves of bread, an ephah of cakes of pressed raisins, an ephah of summer fruits, and a skin of wine. 2 The king said to Ziba, "What do you plan to do with these?" Ziba replied: "The asses are for the king's household to ride on. The bread and summer fruits are for your servants to eat, and the wine for those to drink who are weary in the desert." 3 Then the king said, "And where is your lord's son?" Ziba answered the king, "He is staying in Jerusalem, for he said, 'Now the Israelites will restore to me my father's kingdom.'" 4 The king therefore said to Ziba, "So! Everything Meribbaal had is yours." Then Ziba said: "I pay you homage, my lord the king. May I find favor with you!"

David and Shimei

5 As David was approaching Bahurim, a man named Shimei, the son of Gera of the same clan as Saul's family, was coming out of the place, cursing as he came. 6 He threw stones at David and at all the king's officers, even though all the soldiers, including the royal guard, were on David's right and on his left. 7 Shimei was saying as he cursed: "Away, away, you murderous and wicked man! 8 The LORD has requited you for all the bloodshed in the family of Saul, in whose stead you became king, and the LORD has given over the kingdom to your son Absalom. And now you suffer ruin because you are a murderer." 9 Abishai, son of Zeruiah, said to the king: "Why should this dead dog curse my lord the king? Let me go over, please, and lop off his head." 10 But the king replied: "What business is it of mine or of yours, sons of Zeruiah, that he curses? Suppose the LORD has told him to curse David; who then will dare to say, 'Why are you doing this?'" 11 Then the king said to Abishai and to all his servants: "If my own son, who came forth from my loins, is seeking my life, how much more

might this Benjaminite do so! Let him alone and let him curse, for the LORD has told him to. 12 Perhaps the LORD will look upon my affliction and make it up to me with benefits for the curses he is uttering this day." 13 David and his men continued on the road, while Shimei kept abreast of them on the hillside, all the while cursing and throwing stones and dirt as he went. 14 The king and all the soldiers with him arrived at the Jordan tired out, and stopped there for a rest.

Absalom's Counselors

15 In the meantime Absalom, accompanied by Ahithophel, entered Jerusalem with all the Israelites. 16 When David's friend Hushai the Archite came to Absalom, he said to him: "Long live the king! Long live the king!" 17 But Absalom asked Hushai: "Is this your devotion to your friend? Why did you not go with your friend?" 18 Hushai replied to Absalom: "On the contrary, I am his whom the LORD and all this people and all Israel have chosen, and with him I will stay. 19 Furthermore, as I was in attendance upon your father, so will I be before you. Whom should I serve, if not his son?" 20 Then Absalom said to Ahithophel, "Offer your counsel on what we should do." 21 Ahithophel replied to Absalom: "Have relations with your father's concubines, whom he left behind to take care of the palace. When all Israel hears how odious you have made yourself to your father, all your partisans will take courage." 22 So a tent was pitched on the roof for Absalom, and he visited his father's concubines in view of all Israel.

Counsel of Ahithophel

23 Now the counsel given by Ahithophel at that time was as though one had sought divine revelation. Such was all his counsel both to David and to Absalom. **17** 1 Ahithophel went on to say to Absalom: "Please let me choose twelve thousand men, and be off in pursuit of David tonight. 2 If I come upon him when he is weary and discouraged, I shall cause him panic.

When all the people with him flee, I shall strike down the king alone. 3 Then I can bring back the rest of the people to you, as a bride returns to her husband. It is the death of only one man you are seeking; then all the people will be at peace." 4 This plan was agreeable to Absalom and to all the elders of Israel.

Counsel of Hushai

5 Then Absalom said, "Now call Hushai the Archite also; let us hear what he too has to say." 6 When Hushai came to Absalom, Absalom said to him: "This is what Ahithophel proposed. Shall we follow his proposal? If not, speak up." 7 Hushai replied to Absalom, "This time Ahithophel has not given good counsel." 8 And he went on to say: "You know that your father and his men are warriors, and that they are as fierce as a bear in the wild robbed of her cubs. Moreover, since your father is skilled in warfare, he will not spend the night with the people. 9 Even now he lies hidden in one of the caves or in some other place. And if some of our soldiers should fall at the first attack, whoever hears of it will say, 'Absalom's followers have been slaughtered.' 10 Then even the brave man with the heart of a lion will lose courage. For all Israel knows that your father is a warrior and that those who are with him are brave.

11 "This is what I counsel: Let all Israel from Dan to Beer-sheba, who are as numerous as the sands by the sea, be called up for combat; and go with them yourself. 12 We can then attack him wherever we find him, settling down upon him as dew alights on the ground. None shall survive—neither he nor any of his followers. 13 And if he retires into a city, all Israel shall bring ropes to that city and we can drag it into the gorge, so that not even a pebble of it can be found." 14 Then Absalom and all the Israelites pronounced the counsel of Hushai the Archite better than that of Ahithophel. For the LORD had decided to undo Ahithophel's good counsel, in order thus to bring Absalom to ruin.

David Told of the Plan

15 Then Hushai said to the priests Zadok and Abiathar: "This is the counsel Ahithophel gave Absalom and the elders of Israel, and this is what I counseled. 16 So send a warning to David immediately, not to spend the night at the fords near the desert, but to cross over without fail. Otherwise the king and all the people with him will be destroyed." 17 Now Jonathan and Ahimaaz were staying at En-rogel, since they could not risk being seen entering the city. A maidservant was to come with information for them, and they in turn were to go and report to King David. 18 But an attendant saw them and informed Absalom. They sped on their way and reached the house of a man in Bahurim who had a cistern in his courtyard. They let themselves down into this, 19 and the housewife took the cover and spread it over the cistern, strewing ground grain on the cover so that nothing could be noticed. 20 When Absalom's servants came to the woman at the house, they asked, "Where are Ahimaaz and Jonathan?" The woman replied, "They went by a short while ago toward the water." They searched, but found no one, and so returned to Jerusalem. 21 As soon as they left, Ahimaaz and Jonathan came up out of the cistern and went on to inform King David. They said to him: "Leave! Cross the water at once, for Ahithophel has given the following counsel in regard to you." 22 So David and all his people moved on and crossed the Jordan. By daybreak, there was no one left who had not crossed.

23 When Ahithophel saw that his counsel was not acted upon, he saddled his ass and departed, going to his home in his own city. Then, having left orders concerning his family, he hanged himself. And so he died and was buried in his father's tomb.

24 Now David had gone to Mahanaim when Absalom crossed the Jordan accompanied by all the Israelites. 25 Absalom had put Amasa in command of the army in Joab's place. Amasa was the son of an Ishmaelite named Ithra, who had married Abigail, daughter of Jesse and sister of Joab's mother Zeruiah. 26 Israel and Absalom encamped in the territory of Gilead.

27 When David came to Mahanaim, Shobi, son of Nahash from Rabbah of the Ammonites, Machir, son of Ammiel from Lodebar, and Barzillai, the Gileadite from Rogelim, 28 brought couches, coverlets, basins and earthenware, as well as wheat, barley, flour, roasted grain, beans, lentils, 29 honey, butter and cheese from the flocks and herds, for David and those who were with him to eat; for they said, "The people have been hungry and tired and thirsty in the desert."

Preparation for Battle

18 After mustering the troops he had with him, David placed officers in command of groups of a thousand and groups of a hundred. 2 David then put a third part of the soldiers under Joab's command, a third under command of Abishai, son of Zeruiah and brother of Joab, and a third under command of Ittai the Gittite. The king then said to the soldiers, "I intend to go out with you myself." 3 But they replied: "You must not come out with us. For if we should flee, we shall not count; even if half of us should die, we shall not count. You are equal to ten thousand of us. Therefore it is better that we have you to help us from the city." 4 So the king said to them, "I will do what you think best"; and he stood by the gate as all the soldiers marched out in units of a hundred and of a thousand. 5 But the king gave this command to Joab, Abishai and Ittai: "Be gentle with young Absalom for my sake." All the soldiers heard the king instruct the various leaders with regard to Absalom.

Defeat of Absalom

6 David's army then took the field against Israel, and a battle was fought in the forest near Mahanaim. 7 The forces of Israel were defeated by David's servants, and the casualties there that day were heavy—twenty thousand men. 8 The battle spread out over that entire region,

and the thickets consumed more combatants that day than did the sword.

Death of Absalom

9 Absalom unexpectedly came up against David's servants. He was mounted on a mule, and, as the mule passed under the branches of a large terebinth, his hair caught fast in the tree. He hung between heaven and earth while the mule he had been riding ran off. 10 Someone saw this and reported to Joab that he had seen Absalom hanging from a terebinth. 11 Joab said to his informant: "If you saw him, why did you not strike him to the ground on the spot? Then it would have been my duty to give you fifty pieces of silver and a belt." 12 But the man replied to Joab: "Even if I already held a thousand pieces of silver in my two hands, I would not harm the king's son, for the king charged you and Abishai and Ittai in our hearing to protect the youth Absalom for his sake. 13 Had I been disloyal and killed him, the whole matter would have come to the attention of the king, and you would stand aloof." 14 Joab replied, "I will not waste time with you in this way." And taking three pikes in hand, he thrust for the heart of Absalom, still hanging from the tree alive. 15 Next, ten of Joab's young armor-bearers closed in on Absalom, and killed him with further blows. 16 Joab then sounded the horn, and the soldiers turned back from the pursuit of the Israelites, because Joab called on them to halt. 17 Absalom was taken up and cast into a deep pit in the forest, and a very large mound of stones was erected over him. And all the Israelites fled to their own tents. 18 During his lifetime Absalom had taken a pillar and erected it for himself in the King's Valley, for he said, "I have no son to perpetuate my name." The pillar which he named for himself is called Yad-abshalom to the present day.

David Told of Absalom's Death

19 Then Ahimaaz, son of Zadok, said, "Let me run to take the good news to the king that the LORD has set him free from the grasp of his enemies." 20 But Joab said to him: "You are not the man to bring the news today. On some other day you may take the good news, but today you would not be bringing good news, for in fact the king's son is dead." 21 Then Joab said to a Cushite, "Go, tell the king what you have seen." The Cushite bowed to Joab and sped away. 22 But Ahimaaz, son of Zadok, said to Joab again, "Come what may, permit me also to run after the Cushite." Joab replied: "Why do you want to run, my son? You will receive no reward." 23 But he insisted, "Come what may, I want to run." Joab said to him, "Very well." Ahimaaz sped off by way of the Jordan plain and outran the Cushite.

24 Now David was sitting between the two gates, and a lookout mounted to the roof of the gate above the city wall, where he looked about and saw a man running all alone. 25 The lookout shouted to inform the king, who said, "If he is alone, he has good news to report." As he kept coming nearer, 26 the lookout spied another runner. From his place atop the gate he cried out, "There is another man running by himself." And the king responded, "He, too, is bringing good news." 27 Then the lookout said, "I notice that the first one runs like Ahimaaz, son of Zadok." The king replied, "He is a good man; he comes with good news." 28 Then Ahimaaz called out and greeted the king. With face to the ground he paid homage to the king and said, "Blessed be the LORD your God, who has delivered up the men who rebelled against my lord the king." 29 But the king asked, "Is the youth Absalom safe?" And Ahimaaz replied, "I saw a great disturbance when the king's servant Joab sent your servant on, but I do not know what it was." 30 The king said, "Step aside and remain in attendance here." So he stepped aside and remained there. 31 When the Cushite came in, he said, "Let my lord the king receive the good news that this day the LORD has taken your part, freeing you from the grasp of all who rebelled against you." 32 But the king asked the Cushite, "Is

young Absalom safe?" The Cushite replied, "May the enemies of my lord the king and all who rebel against you with evil intent be as that young man!"

19 The king was shaken, and went up to the room over the city gate to weep. He said as he wept, "My son Absalom! My son, my son Absalom! If only I had died instead of you, Absalom, my son, my son!"

Joab Reproves David

2 Joab was told that the king was weeping and mourning for Absalom; 3 and that day's victory was turned into mourning for the whole army when they heard that the king was grieving for his son. 4 The soldiers stole into the city that day like men shamed by flight in battle. 5 Meanwhile the king covered his face and cried out in a loud voice, "My son Absalom! Absalom! My son, my son!" 6 Then Joab went to his residence and said: "Though they saved your life and your sons' and daughters' lives, also the lives of your wives and those of your concubines, you have put all your servants to shame today 7 by loving those who hate you and hating those who love you. For you have shown today that officers and servants mean nothing to you. Indeed I am now certain that if Absalom were alive today and all of us dead, you would think that more suitable. 8 Now then, get up! Go out and speak kindly to your servants. I swear by the LORD that if you do not go out, not a single man will remain with you overnight, and this will be a far greater disaster for you than any that has afflicted you from your youth until now." 9 So the king stepped out and sat at the gate. When the people were informed that the king was sitting at the gate, they came into his presence.

The Reconciliation

Now the Israelites had fled to their separate tents, 10 but throughout the tribes of Israel all the people were arguing among themselves, saying to one another: "The king delivered us from the clutches of our enemies, and it was he who rescued us from the grip of the Philistines. But now he has fled from the country before Absalom, 11 and Absalom, whom we anointed over us, died in battle. Why, then, should you remain silent about restoring the king to his palace?" When the talk of all Israel reached the king, 12 David sent word to the priests Zadok and Abiathar: "Say to the elders of Judah: 'Why should you be last to restore the king to his palace? 13 You are my brothers, you are my bone and flesh. Why should you be last to restore the king?' 14 Also say to Amasa: 'Are you not my bone and flesh? May God do thus and so to me, if you do not become my general permanently in place of Joab.'" 15 He won over all the Judahites as one man, and so they summoned the king to return, with all his servants.

David and Shimei

16 When the king, on his return, reached the Jordan, Judah had come to Gilgal to meet him and to escort him across the Jordan. 17 Shimei, son of Gera, the Benjaminite from Bahurim, hurried down with the Judahites to meet King David, 18 accompanied by a thousand men from Benjamin. Ziba, too, the servant of the house of Saul, accompanied by his fifteen sons and twenty servants, hastened to the Jordan before the king. 19 They crossed over the ford to bring the king's household over and to do whatever he wished. When Shimei, son of Gera, crossed the Jordan, he fell down before the king 20 and said to him: "May my lord not hold me guilty, and may he not remember and take to heart the wrong that your servant did the day my lord the king left Jerusalem. 21 For your servant knows that he has done wrong. Yet realize that I have been the first of the whole house of Joseph to come down today to meet my lord the king." 22 But Abishai, son of Zeruiah, countered: "Shimei must be put to death for this. He cursed the LORD's anointed." 23 David replied: "What has come between you and me, sons of Zeruiah, that you would create enmity for me this day? Should anyone die today in Israel? Am I not aware that today I am king of Israel?" 24 Then the king said to Shimei, "You shall not die." And the king gave him his oath.

David and Meribbaal

25 Meribbaal, son of Saul, also went down to meet the king. He had not washed his feet nor trimmed his mustache nor washed his clothes from the day the king left until he returned safely. 26 When he came from Jerusalem to meet the king, the king asked him, "Why did you not go with me, Meribbaal?" 27 He replied: "My lord the king, my servant betrayed me. For your servant, who is lame, said to him, 'Saddle the ass for me, that I may ride on it and go with the king.' 28 But he slandered your servant before my lord the king. But my lord the king is like an angel of God. Do what you judge best. 29 For though my father's entire house deserved only death from my lord the king, yet you placed your servant among the guests at your table. What right do I still have to make further appeal to the king?" 30 But the king said to him: "Why do you go on talking? I say, 'You and Ziba shall divide the property.'" 31 Meribbaal answered the king, "Indeed let him have it all, now that my lord the king has returned safely to his palace."

David and Barzillai

32 Barzillai the Gileadite also came down from Rogelim and escorted the king to the Jordan for his crossing, taking leave of him there. 33 It was Barzillai, a very old man of eighty and very wealthy besides, who had provisioned the king during his stay in Mahanaim. 34 The king said to Barzillai, "Cross over with me, and I will provide for your old age as my guest in Jerusalem." 35 But Barzillai answered the king: "How much longer have I to live, that I should go up to Jerusalem with the king? 36 I am now eighty years old. Can I distinguish between good and bad? Can your servant taste what he eats and drinks, or still appreciate the voices of singers and songstresses? Why should your servant be any further burden to my lord the king? 37 In escorting the king across the Jordan, your servant is doing little enough! Why should the king give me this reward? 38 Please let your servant go back to die in his own city by the tomb of his father and mother. Here is your servant Chimham. Let him cross over with my lord the king. Do for him whatever you will." 39 Then the king said to him, "Chimham shall come over with me, and I will do for him as you would wish. And anything else you would like me to do for you, I will do." 40 Then all the people crossed over the Jordan, but the king remained; he kissed Barzillai and bade him Godspeed as he returned to his own district. 41 Finally the king crossed over to Gilgal, accompanied by Chimham.

Israel and Judah Quarrel

All the people of Judah and half of the people of Israel had escorted the king across. 42 But all these Israelites began coming to the king and saying, "Why did our brothers the Judahites steal you away and escort the king and his household across the Jordan, along with all David's men?" 43 All the Judahites replied to the men of Israel: "Because the king is our relative. Why are you angry over this affair? Have we had anything to eat at the king's expense? Or have portions from his table been given to us?" 44 The Israelites answered the Judahites: "We have ten shares in the king. Also, we are the firstborn rather than you. Why do you slight us? Were we not first to speak of restoring the king?" Then the Judahites in turn spoke even more fiercely than the Israelites.

Sheba's Rebellion

20 Now a rebellious individual from Benjamin named Sheba, the son of Bichri, happened to be there. He sounded the horn and cried out,

"We have no portion in David,
nor any share in the son of Jesse.
Every man to his tent, O Israel!"

2 So all the Israelites left David for Sheba, son of Bichri. But from the Jordan to Jerusalem the Judahites remained loyal to their king. 3 When King David came to his palace in Jerusalem, he took the ten concubines whom he had left behind to take care of the palace and placed them in confinement. He provided for them, but had no further relations with them. And so they remained in confinement to the day of their death, lifelong widows.

Amasa's Death

4 Then the king said to Amasa: "Summon the Judahites for me within three days. Then present yourself here." 5 Accordingly Amasa set out to summon Judah, but delayed beyond the time set for him by David. 6 Then David said to Abishai: "Sheba, son of Bichri, may now do us more harm than Absalom did. Take your lord's servants and pursue him, lest he find fortified cities and take shelter while we look on." 7 So Joab and the Cherethites and Pelethites and all the warriors marched out behind Abishai from Jerusalem to campaign in pursuit of Sheba, son of Bichri. 8 They were at the great stone in Gibeon when Amasa met them. Now Joab had a belt over his tunic, from which was slung, in its sheath near his thigh, a sword that could be drawn with a downward movement. 9 And Joab asked Amasa, "How are you, my brother?" With his right hand Joab held Amasa's beard as if to kiss him. 10 And since Amasa was not on his guard against the sword in Joab's other hand, Joab stabbed him in the abdomen with it, so that his entrails burst forth to the ground, and he died without receiving a second thrust. Then Joab and his brother Abishai pursued Sheba, son of Bichri. 11 One of Joab's attendants stood by Amasa and said, "Let him who favors Joab and is for David follow Joab." 12 Amasa lay covered with blood in the middle of the highroad, and the man noticed that all the soldiers were stopping. So he removed Amasa from the road to the field and placed a garment over him, because all who came up to him were stopping. 13 When he had been removed from the road, everyone went on after Joab in pursuit of Sheba, son of Bichri.

Joab Pursues Sheba

14 Sheba passed through all the tribes of Israel to Abel Beth-maacah. Then all the Bichrites assembled and they too entered the city after him. 15 So David's servants came and besieged him in Abel Beth-maacah. They threw up a mound against the city, and all the soldiers who were with Joab began battering the wall to throw it down. 16 Then a wise woman from the city stood on the outworks and called out, "Listen, listen! Tell Joab to come here, that I may speak with him." 17 When Joab had come near her, the woman said, "Are you Joab?" And he replied, "Yes." She said to him, "Listen to what your maidservant has to say." He replied, "I am listening." 18 Then she went on to say: "There is an ancient saying, 'Let them ask if they will in Abel 19 or in Dan whether loyalty is finished or ended in Israel.' You are seeking to beat down a city that is a mother in Israel. Why do you wish to destroy the inheritance of the LORD?" 20 Joab answered, "Not at all, not at all! I do not wish to destroy or to ruin anything. 21 That is not the case at all. A man named Sheba, son of Bichri, from the hill country of Ephraim has rebelled against King David. Surrender him alone, and I will withdraw from the city." Then the woman said to Joab, "His head shall be thrown to you across the wall." 22 She went to all the people with her advice, and they cut off the head of Sheba, son of Bichri, and threw it out to Joab. He then sounded the horn, and they scattered from the city to their own tents, while Joab returned to Jerusalem to the king.

David's Officials

23 Joab was in command of the whole army of Israel. Benaiah, son of Jehoiada, was in command of the Cherethites and Pelethites. 24 Adoram was in charge of the forced labor. Jehoshaphat, son of Ahilud, was the chancellor. 25 Shawsha was the scribe. Zadok and Abiathar were priests. 26 Ira the Jairite was also David's priest.

APPENDIXES

Gibeonite Vengeance

21 During David's reign there was a famine for three successive years. David had recourse to the LORD, who said, "There is bloodguilt on Saul and his family because he put the Gibeonites to death." 2 So the king called the Gibeonites and spoke to them. (Now the Gibeonites were not Israelites, but survivors of the Amorites; and although the Israelites had given them their oath, Saul had attempted to kill them off in his zeal for the men of Israel and Judah.) 3 David said to the Gibeonites, "What must I do for you and how must I make atonement, that you may bless the inheritance of the LORD?" 4 The Gibeonites answered him, "We have no claim against Saul and his house for silver or gold, nor is it our place to put any man to death in Israel." Then he said, "I will do for you whatever you propose." 5 They said to the king, "As for the man who was exterminating us and who intended to destroy us that we might have no place in all the territory of Israel, 6 let seven men from among his descendants be given to us, that we may dismember them before the LORD in Gibeon, on the LORD's mountain." The king replied, "I will give them up." 7 The king, however, spared Meribbaal, son of Jonathan, son of Saul, because of the LORD's oath that formed a bond between David and Saul's son Jonathan. 8 But the king took Armoni and Meribbaal, the two sons that Aiah's daughter Rizpah had borne to Saul, and the five sons of Saul's daughter Merob that she had borne to Adriel, son of Barzillai the Meholathite, 9 and surrendered them to the Gibeonites. They then dismembered them on the mountain before the LORD. The seven fell at the one time; they were put to death during the first days of the harvest

20, 8: The text of this verse is quite uncertain.
20, 18f: The proverbial expression here has been poorly transmitted, and its sense is doubtful.

—that is, at the beginning of the barley harvest.

10 Then Rizpah, Aiah's daughter, took sackcloth and spread it out for herself on the rock from the beginning of the harvest until rain came down on them from the sky, fending off the birds of the sky from settling on them by day, and the wild animals by night. 11 When David was informed of what Rizpah, Aiah's daughter, the concubine of Saul, had done, 12 he went and obtained the bones of Saul and of his son Jonathan from the citizens of Jabesh-gilead, who had carried them off secretly from the public square of Bethshan, where the Philistines had hanged them at the time they killed Saul on Gilboa. 13 When he had brought up from there the bones of Saul and of his son Jonathan, the bones of those who had been dismembered were also gathered up. 14 Then the bones of Saul and of his son Jonathan were buried in the tomb of his father Kish at Zela in the territory of Benjamin. After all that the king commanded had been carried out, God granted relief to the land.

Exploits in Philistine Wars

15 There was another battle between the Philistines and Israel. David went down with his servants and fought the Philistines, but David grew tired. 16 Dadu, one of the Rephaim, whose bronze spear weighed three hundred shekels, was about to take him captive. Dadu was girt with a new sword and planned to kill David, 17 but Abishai, son of Zeruiah, came to his assistance and struck and killed the Philistine. Then David's men swore to him, "You must not go out to battle with us again, lest you quench the lamp of Israel."

18 After this there was another battle with the Philistines in Gob.

On that occasion Sibbecai, from Husha, killed Saph, one of the Rephaim. 19 There was another battle with the Philistines in Gob, in which Elhanan, son of Jair from Bethlehem, killed Goliath of Gath, who had a spear with a shaft like a weaver's heddle-bar. 20 There was another battle at Gath in which there was a man of large stature with six fingers on each hand and six toes on each foot—twenty-four in all. He too was one of the Rephaim. 21 And when he insulted Israel, Jonathan, son of David's brother Shimei, killed him. 22 These four were Rephaim in Gath, and they fell at the hands of David and his servants.

Song of Thanksgiving

22 David sang the words of this song to the LORD when the LORD had rescued him from the grasp of all his enemies and from the hand of Saul. 2 This is what he sang:

A

I

"O LORD, my rock, my fortress,
    my deliverer,
3   my God, my rock of refuge!
My shield, the horn of my
        salvation,
    my stronghold, my refuge,
    my savior, from violence you
        keep me safe.
4 'Praised be the LORD,' I exclaim,
    and I am safe from my enemies.

II

5 "The breakers of death surged
        round about me,
    the floods of perdition
        overwhelmed me;
6 The cords of the nether world
        enmeshed me,
    the snares of death overtook
        me.

7 In my distress I called upon the
        LORD
    and cried out to my God;
From his temple he heard my
        voice,
    and my cry reached his ears.

III

8 "The earth swayed and quaked;
    the foundations of the heavens
        trembled
    and shook when his wrath
        flared up.
9 Smoke rose from his nostrils,
    and a devouring fire from his
        mouth;
    he kindled coals into flame.
10 He inclined the heavens and
        came down,
    with dark clouds under his feet.
11 He mounted a cherub and flew,
    borne on the wings of the wind.
12 He made darkness the shelter
        about him,
    with spattering rain and
        thickening clouds.
13 From the brightness of his
        presence
    coals were kindled to flame.

14 "The LORD thundered from
        heaven;
    the Most High gave forth his
        voice.
15 He sent forth arrows to put them
        to flight;
    he flashed lightning and routed
        them.
16 Then the wellsprings of the sea
        appeared,
    the foundations of the earth
        were laid bare,
At the rebuke of the LORD,
    at the blast of the wind of his
        wrath.

17 "He reached out from on high
        and grasped me;
    he drew me out of the deep
        waters.

22, 1–51. This song of thanksgiving is also given, with a few small variants, in Ps 18. In both places it is attributed to David. Two main sections can be distinguished. In the first part, after an introductory stanza of praise to God (2–4), David describes the peril he was in (5–7), and then poetically depicts, under the form of a theophany, God's intervention in his behalf (8–20), concluding with an acknowledgment of God's justice (21–31). In the second part, God is praised for having prepared the psalmist for war (32–35), given him victory over his enemies

(36–39), whom he put to flight (40–43), and bestowed on him dominion over many peoples (44–46). The entire song ends with a paean of grateful praise (47–51).
22, 3: *The horn of my salvation:* my strong savior. The horn, the dreadful weapon of an enraged bull, was a symbol of strength; cf Lk 1, 69.
22, 5f: These verses are to be understood figuratively.
22, 7: *His temple:* his heavenly abode.
22, 8ff: God's intervention is graphically portrayed

under the figures of an earthquake (vv 8.16) and a thunderstorm (vv 9–15); cf Jgs 5, 4f; Pss 29; 97, 2–6; Hb 3.
22, 11: *He mounted a cherub:* since God makes the winds his messengers, or "angels" (Ps 104, 4), he is spoken of poetically as riding on the clouds, or on the angelic creatures called "cherubim." His earthly throne, above the ark of the covenant was likewise associated with two winged cherubim: cf Ex 37, 7ff. In both senses the Lord is enthroned upon the cherubim; cf Pss 79 2; 99, 1.

18 He rescued me from my mighty
       enemy,
     from my foes, who were too
       powerful for me.
19 They attacked me on my day of
       calamity,
     but the LORD came to my
       support.
20 He set me free in the open,
     and rescued me, because he
       loves me.

                    IV

21 "The LORD rewarded me
       according to my justice;
     according to the cleanness of
       my hands he requited me.
22 For I kept the ways of the LORD
     and was not disloyal to my
       God.
23 For his ordinances were all
       present to me,
     and his statutes I put not from
       me;
24 But I was wholehearted toward
       him,
     and I was on my guard against
       guilt.
25 And the LORD requited me
       according to my justice,
     according to my innocence in
       his sight.

26 "Toward the faithful you are
       faithful;
     toward the wholehearted you
       are wholehearted;
27 Toward the sincere you are
       sincere;
     but toward the crooked you
       are astute.
28 You save lowly people,
     though on the lofty your eyes
       look down.
29 You are my lamp, O LORD!
     O my God, you brighten the
       darkness about me.
30 For with your aid I run against
       an armed band,
     and by the help of my God I
       leap over a wall.
31 God's way is unerring;
     the promise of the LORD is
       fire-tried;
     he is a shield to all who take
       refuge in him."

                    B

                    I

32 "For who is God except the
       LORD?
     Who is a rock save our God?
33 The God who girded me with
       strength
     and kept my way unerring;
34 Who made my feet swift as those
       of hinds
     and set me on the heights;
35 Who trained my hands for war
     till my arms could bend a bow
       of brass.

                    II

36 "You have given me your saving
       shield,
     and your help has made me
       great.
37 You made room for my steps;
     unwavering was my stride.
38 I pursued my enemies and
       destroyed them,
     nor did I turn again till I made
       an end of them.
39 I smote them and they did not
       rise;
     they fell beneath my feet.

                    III

40 "You girded me with strength
       for war;
     you subdued my adversaries
       beneath me.
41 My enemies you put to flight
       before me
     and those who hated me I
       destroyed.
42 They cried for help—but no one
       saved them;
     to the LORD—but he answered
       them not.
43 I ground them fine as the dust of
       the earth;
     like the mud in the streets I
       trampled them down.

                    IV

44 "You rescued me from the strife
       of my people;
     you made me head over
       nations.
     A people I had not known
       became my slaves;

45   as soon as they heard me,
       they obeyed.
46 The foreigners fawned and
       cringed before me;
     they staggered forth from their
       fortresses."

                    C

47 "The LORD live! And blessed be
       my Rock!
     Extolled be my God, rock of
       my salvation.
48 O God, who granted me
       vengeance,
     who made peoples subject to
       me
49   and helped me escape from
       my enemies,
     Above my adversaries you exalt
       me
     and from the violent man you
       rescue me.
50 Therefore will I proclaim you,
       O LORD, among the nations,
     and I will sing praise to your
       name,
51 You who gave great victories to
       your king
     and showed kindness to your
       anointed,
     to David and his posterity
       forever."

The Last Words of David

23 These are the last words of
       David:

"The utterance of David, son of
       Jesse;
     the utterance of the man God
       raised up, .
     Anointed of the God of Jacob,
       favorite of the Mighty One of
       Israel.
2 The spirit of the LORD spoke
       through me;
     his word was on my tongue.
3 The God of Israel spoke;
     of me the Rock of Israel said,
     'He that rules over men in justice,
       that rules in the fear of God,
4 Is like the morning light at
       sunrise
     on a cloudless morning,
     making the greensward sparkle
       after rain.'

22, 26f: Men are treated by God in the same way
they treat him and their fellow men.
  22, 29: *My lamp:* a figure of life and happiness;

cf 1 Kgs 11, 36.
  22, 34: *The heights:* a natural stronghold safe from
attack; cf Ps 62, 3; Hb 3, 19.

23, 1–7: The text of this short composition in the
spirit of the wisdom writers (Prv 30, 1–6) is difficult
in places; it views David's career in retrospect.

5 Is not my house firm before God?
 He has made an eternal
  covenant with me,
 set forth in detail and secured.
Will he not bring to fruition
 all my salvation and my every
  desire?
6 But the wicked are all like thorns
  to be cast away;
 they cannot be taken up by
  hand.
7 He who wishes to touch them
 must arm himself with iron and
  the shaft of a spear,
 and they must be consumed by
  fire."

David's Warriors

8 These are the names of David's warriors. Ishbaal, son of Hachamoni, was the first of the Three. It was he who brandished his battle-ax over eight hundred slain in a single encounter. 9 Next to him, among the Three warriors, was Eleazar, son of Dodo the Ahohite. He was with David at Ephes-dammim when the Philistines assembled there for battle. The Israelites had retreated, 10 but he stood his ground and fought the Philistines until his hand grew tired and became cramped, holding fast to the sword. The LORD brought about a great victory on that day; the soldiers turned back after Eleazar, but only to strip the slain. 11 Next to him was Shammah, son of Agee the Hararite. The Philistines had assembled at Lehi, where there was a plot of land full of lentils. When the soldiers fled from the Philistines, 12 he took his stand in the middle of the plot and defended it. He slew the Philistines, and the LORD brought about a great victory. Such were the deeds of the Three warriors.

13 During the harvest three of the Thirty went down to David in the cave of Adullam, while a Philistine clan was encamped in the Vale of Rephaim. 14 At that time David was in the refuge, and there was a garrison of Philistines in Bethlehem. 15 Now David had a strong craving and said, "Oh, that someone would give me a drink of water from the cistern that is by the gate of Bethlehem!" 16 So the Three warriors broke through the Philistine camp and drew water from the cistern that is by the gate of Bethlehem. But when they brought it to David he refused to drink it, and instead poured it out to the LORD, 17 saying: "The LORD forbid that I do this! Can I drink the blood of these men who went at the risk of their lives?" So he refused to drink it.

18 Abishai, brother of Joab, son of Zeruiah, was at the head of the Thirty. It was he who brandished his spear over three hundred slain. He was listed among the Thirty 19 and commanded greater respect than the Thirty, becoming their leader. However, he did not attain to the Three.

20 Benaiah, son of Jehoiada, a stalwart from Kabzeel, was a man of great achievements. It was he who slew the two lions in Moab. He also went down and killed the lion in the cistern at the time of the snow. 21 It was he, too, who slew an Egyptian of large stature. Although the Egyptian was armed with a spear, he went against him with a club and wrested the spear from the Egyptian's hand, then killed him with his own spear. 22 Such were the deeds performed by Benaiah, son of Jehoiada. He was listed among the Thirty warriors 23 and commanded greater respect than the Thirty. However, he did not attain to the Three. David put him in command of his bodyguard. 24 Asahel, brother of Joab. . . .

Among the Thirty were: Elhanan, son of Dodo, from Bethlehem; 25 Shammah from En-harod; Elika from En-harod; 26 Helez from Beth-pelet; Ira, son of Ikkesh, from Tekoa; 27 Abiezer from Anathoth; Sibbecai from Hushah; 28 Zalmon from Ahoh; Maharai from Netophah; 29 Heled, son of Baanah, from Netophah; Ittai, son of Ribai, from Gibeah of the Benjaminites; 30 Benaiah from Pirathon; Hiddai from Nahale-gaash; 31 Abibaal from Beth-arabah; Azmaveth from Bahurim; 32 Eliahba from Shaalbon; Jashen the Gunite; Jonathan, 33 son of Shammah the Hararite; Ahiam, son of Sharar the Hararite; 34 Eliphelet, son of Ahasbai, from Beth-maacah; Eliam, son of Ahithophel, from Gilo; 35 Hezrai from Carmel; Paarai the Arbite; 36 Igal, son of Nathan, from Zobah; Bani the Gadite; 37 Zelek the Ammonite; Naharai from Beeroth, armorbearer of Joab, son of Zeruiah; 38 Ira from Jattir; Gareb from Jattir; 39 Uriah the Hittite—thirty-seven in all.

Census of the People

24 The LORD's anger against Israel flared again, and he incited David against the Israelites by prompting him to number Israel and Judah. 2 Accordingly the king said to Joab and the leaders of the army who were with him, "Tour all the tribes in Israel from Dan to Beer-sheba and register the people, that I may know their number." 3 But Joab said to the king: "May the LORD your God increase the number of people a hundredfold for your royal majesty to see it with his own eyes. But why does it please my lord the king to order a thing of this kind?" 4 The king, however, overruled Joab and the leaders of the army, so they left the king's presence in order to register the people of Israel. 5 Crossing the Jordan, they began near Aroer, south of the city in the wadi, and went in the direction of Gad, toward Jazer. 6 They continued on to Gilead and to the district below Mount Hermon. Then they proceeded to Dan; from there they turned toward Sidon, 7 going to the fortress of Tyre and to all the cities of the Hivites and Canaanites, and ending up at Beer-sheba in the Negeb of Judah. 8 Thus they toured the whole country, reaching Jerusalem again after nine months and twenty days. 9 Joab then reported to the king the number

---

23, 8ff: There are thirty-seven warriors in all mentioned in this list. First there are the Three warriors most noted for single-handed exploits (vv 8–12). Then comes the story of a daring adventure by three unnamed members of the larger group (vv 13–17). Next come the commanders of the king's bodyguard, Abishai (vv 18–19) and Benaiah (vv 20–23), with whom must be counted Asahel (v 24) and Joab (vv 18.24.37), and finally the group of the Thirty (vv 24–39).

23, 24: A more complete notice about Asahel, who died early in his career (2 Sm 2, 16–23), is to be presumed lost at this point. Elhanan is the first of the Thirty.

24, 1ff: This story was probably joined at one time to 21, 1–14.

of people registered. In Israel, eight hundred thousand men fit for military service; in Judah, five hundred thousand.

The Pestilence

10 Afterward, however, David regretted having numbered the people, and said to the LORD: "I have sinned grievously in what I have done. But now, LORD, forgive the guilt of your servant, for I have been very foolish." 11 When David rose in the morning, the LORD had spoken to the prophet Gad, David's seer, saying: 12 "Go and say to David, 'This is what the LORD says: I offer you three alternatives; choose one of them, and I will inflict it on you.'" 13 Gad then went to David to inform him. He asked: "Do you want a three years' famine to come upon your land, or to flee from your enemy three months while he pursues you, or to have a three days' pestilence in your land? Now consider and decide what I must reply to him who sent me." 14 David answered Gad: "I am in very serious difficulty. Let us fall by the hand of God, for he is most merciful; but let me not fall by the hand of man." 15 Thus David chose the pestilence. Now it was the time of the wheat harvest when the plague broke out among the people. [The LORD then sent a pestilence over Israel from morning until the time appointed, and seventy thousand of the people from Dan to Beer-sheba died.] 16 But when the angel stretched forth his hand toward Jerusalem to destroy it, the LORD regretted the calamity and said to the angel causing the destruction among the people, "Enough now! Stay your hand." The angel of the LORD was then standing at the threshing floor of Araunah the Jebusite. 17 When David saw the angel who was striking the people, he said to the LORD: "It is I who have sinned; it is I, the shepherd, who have done wrong. But these are sheep; what have they done? Punish me and my kindred."

Sacrifice of Atonement

18 On the same day Gad went to David and said to him, "Go up and build an altar to the LORD on the threshing floor of Araunah the Jebusite." 19 Following Gad's bidding, David went up as the LORD had commanded. 20 Now Araunah looked down and noticed the king and his servants coming toward him while he was threshing wheat. So he went out and paid homage to the king, with face to the ground. 21 Then Araunah asked, "Why does my lord the king come to his servant?" David replied, "To buy the threshing floor from you, to build an altar to the LORD, that the plague may be checked among the people." 22 But Araunah said to David: "Let my lord the king take and offer up whatever he may wish. Here are oxen for holocausts, and threshing sledges and the yokes of the oxen for wood. 23 All this does Araunah give to the king." Araunah then said to the king, "May the LORD your God accept your offering." 24 The king, however, replied to Araunah, "No, I must pay you for it, for I cannot offer to the LORD my God holocausts that cost nothing." So David bought the threshing floor and the oxen for fifty silver shekels. 25 Then David built an altar there to the LORD, and offered holocausts and peace offerings. The LORD granted relief to the country, and the plague was checked in Israel.

24, 10: The narrative supposes that since the people belonged to the Lord rather than to the king, only the Lord should know their exact number.

24, 17: Before this verse a Qumran manuscript (4Q Sam^a) gives the fuller text of 1 Chr 21, 16, an alternative to the words *When David saw the angel who was striking the people.*

Kings

REIGN OF SOLOMON

WHEN King David was old and advanced in years, though they spread covers over him he could not keep warm. 2 His servants therefore said to him, "Let a young virgin be sought to attend you, lord king, and to nurse you. If she sleeps with your royal majesty, you will be kept warm." 3 So they sought for a beautiful girl throughout the territory of Israel, and found Abishag the Shunamite, whom they brought to the king. 4 The maiden, who was very beautiful, nursed the king and cared for him, but the king did not have relations with her.

Ambition of Adonijah

5 Adonijah, son of Haggith, began to display his ambition to be king. He acquired chariots, drivers, and fifty henchmen. 6 Yet his father never rebuked him or asked why he was doing this. Adonijah was also very handsome, and next in age to Absalom by the same mother. 7 He conferred with Joab, son of Zeruiah, and with Abiathar the priest, and they supported him. 8 However, Zadok the priest, Benaiah, son of Jehoiada, Nathan the prophet, and Shimei and his companions, the pick of David's army, did not side with Adonijah. 9 When he slaughtered sheep, oxen, and fatlings at the stone Zoheleth, near En-rogel, Adonijah invited all his brothers, the king's sons, and all the royal officials of Judah. 10 But he did not invite the prophet Nathan, or Benaiah, or the pick of the army, or his brother Solomon.

Solomon Proclaimed King

11 Then Nathan said to Bathsheba, Solomon's mother: "Have you not heard that Adonijah, son of Haggith, has become king without the knowledge of our lord David? 12 Come now, let me advise you so that you may save your life and that of your son Solomon. 13 Go, visit King David, and say to him, 'Did you not, lord king, swear to your handmaid: Your son Solomon shall be king after me and shall sit upon my throne? Why, then, has Adonijah become king?' 14 And while you are still there speaking to the king, I will come in after you and confirm what you have said."

15 So Bathsheba visited the king in his room, while Abishag the Shunamite was attending him because of his advanced age. 16 Bathsheba bowed in homage to the king, who said to her, "What do you wish?" 17 She answered him: "My lord, you swore to me your handmaid by the LORD, your God, that my son Solomon should reign after you and sit upon your throne. 18 But now Adonijah has become king, and you, my lord king, do not know it. 19 He has slaughtered oxen, fatlings, and sheep in great numbers; he has invited all the king's sons, Abiathar the priest, and Joab, the general of the army, but not your servant Solomon. 20 Now, my lord king, all Israel is waiting for you to make known to them who is to sit on the throne after your royal majesty. 21 If this is not done, when my lord the king sleeps with

---

1, 9: *En-rogel:* the modern Job's Well southeast of Jerusalem. It marked the ancient boundary between the tribes of Benjamin and Judah (Jos 15, 7; 18, 16).

Here David's men sought information about Absalom's revolt (2 Sm 17, 17).
1, 20: At this time, neither law nor the right of

primogeniture, but the will of the ruling monarch, determined succession to the throne.

his fathers, I and my son Solomon will be considered criminals."

22 While she was still speaking to the king, the prophet Nathan came in. 23 When he had been announced, the prophet entered the king's presence and, bowing to the floor, did him homage. 24 Then Nathan said: "Have you decided, my lord king, that Adonijah is to reign after you and sit on your throne? 25 He went down today and slaughtered oxen, fatlings, and sheep in great numbers; he invited all the king's sons, the commanders of the army, and Abiathar the priest, and they are eating and drinking in his company and saying, 'Long live King Adonijah!' 26 But me, your servant, he did not invite; nor Zadok the priest, nor Benaiah, son of Jehoiada, nor your servant Solomon. 27 Was this done by my royal master's order without my being told who was to succeed to your majesty's kingly throne?"

28 King David answered, "Call Bathsheba here." When she reentered the king's presence and stood before him, 29 the king swore, "As the LORD lives, who has delivered me from all distress, 30 this very day I will fulfill the oath I swore to you by the LORD, the God of Israel, that your son Solomon should reign after me and should sit upon my throne in my place." 31 Bowing to the floor in homage to the king, Bathsheba said, "May my lord, King David, live forever!" 32 Then King David summoned Zadok the priest, Nathan the prophet, and Benaiah, son of Jehoiada. When they had entered the king's presence, 33 he said to them: "Take with you the royal attendants. Mount my son Solomon upon my own mule and escort him down to Gihon. 34 There Zadok the priest and Nathan the prophet are to anoint him king of Israel, and you shall blow the horn and cry, 'Long live King Solomon!' 35 When you come back in his train, he is to go in and sit upon my throne and reign in my

place. I designate him ruler of Israel and of Judah." 36 In answer to the king, Benaiah, son of Jehoiada, said: "So be it! May the LORD, the God of my lord the king, so decree! 37 As the LORD has been with your royal majesty, so may he be with Solomon, and exalt his throne even more than that of my lord, King David!"

38 So Zadok the priest, Nathan the prophet, Benaiah, son of Jehoiada, and the Cherethites and Pelethites went down, and mounting Solomon on King David's mule, escorted him to Gihon. 39 Then Zadok the priest took the horn of oil from the tent and anointed Solomon. They blew the horn and all the people shouted, "Long live King Solomon!" 40 Then all the people went up after him, playing flutes and rejoicing so much as to split open the earth with their shouting.

41 Adonijah and all the guests who were with him heard it, just as they ended their banquet. When Joab heard the sound of the horn, he asked, "What does this uproar in the city mean?" 42 As he was speaking, Jonathan, son of Abiathar the priest, arrived. "Come," said Adonijah, "you are a man of worth and must bring good news." 43 "On the contrary!" Jonathan answered him. "Our lord, King David, has made Solomon king. 44 The king sent with him Zadok the priest, Nathan the prophet, Benaiah, son of Jehoiada, and the Cherethites and Pelethites, and they mounted him upon the king's own mule. 45 Zadok the priest and Nathan the prophet anointed him king at Gihon, and they went up from there rejoicing, so that the city is in an uproar. That is the noise you heard. 46 Besides, Solomon took his seat on the royal throne, 47 and the king's servants went in and paid their respects to our lord, King David, saying, 'May God make Solomon more famous than you and exalt his throne more than your own!' And the king in his bed worshiped God,

48 and this is what he said: 'Blessed be the LORD, the God of Israel, who has this day seated one of my sons upon my throne, so that I see it with my own eyes.'"

49 All the guests of Adonijah left in terror, each going his own way. 50 Adonijah, in fear of Solomon, also left; he went and seized the horns of the altar. 51 It was reported to Solomon that Adonijah, in his fear of King Solomon, had seized the horns of the altar and said, "Let King Solomon first swear that he will not kill me, his servant, with the sword." 52 Solomon answered, "If he proves himself worthy, not a hair shall fall from his head. But if he is found guilty of crime, he shall die." 53 King Solomon sent to have him brought down from the altar, and he came and paid homage to the king. Solomon then said to him, "Go to your home."

David's Last Instructions and Death

2 When the time of David's death drew near, he gave these instructions to his son Solomon: 2 "I am going the way of all mankind. Take courage and be a man. 3 Keep the mandate of the LORD, your God, following his ways and observing his statutes, commands, ordinances, and decrees as they are written in the law of Moses, that you may succeed in whatever you do, wherever you turn, 4 and the LORD may fulfill the promise he made on my behalf when he said, 'If your sons so conduct themselves that they remain faithful to me with their whole heart and with their whole soul, you shall always have someone of your line on the throne of Israel.' 5 You yourself know what Joab, son of Zeruiah, did to me when he slew the two generals of Israel's armies, Abner, son of Ner, and Amasa, son of Jether. He took revenge for the blood of war in a time of peace, and put blood shed without provocation on the belt about my waist and the sandal

---

1, 38: *Cherethites and Pelethites:* mercenaries in David's bodyguard. They became part of his retinue after he defeated the Philistines and established himself in Jerusalem; cf 2 Sm 8, 18; 15, 18; 20, 23.

1, 50: *Horns of the altar:* the protuberances on each of the four corners of the altar were surrounded

with a special degree of holiness (Ex 27, 2; 29, 12), and constituted a place of asylum for transgressors of the law (Ex 21, 13f; 1 Kgs 2, 28).

2, 1–6.8–9: Solomon is expected to remove from his father's family the imputation of blood guilt brought upon it by Joab in the unwarranted killings

of Abner (2 Sm 3, 27–29) and Amasa (2 Sm 19, 9–10); and likewise to punish Shimei for his curse, the effects of which David had pledged himself not to avenge in person (2 Sm 19, 21–23). The standards of morality presumed in these verses are far from the Christian ones.

on my foot. 6 Act with the wisdom you possess; you must not allow him to go down to the grave in peaceful old age.

7 "But be kind to the sons of Barzillai the Gileadite, and have them eat at your table. For they received me kindly when I was fleeing your brother Absalom.

8 "You also have with you Shimei, son of Gera, the Benjaminite of Bahurim, who cursed me balefully when I was going to Mahanaim. Because he came down to meet me at the Jordan, I swore to him by the LORD that I would not put him to the sword. 9 But you must not let him go unpunished. You are a prudent man and will know how to deal with him to send down his hoary head in blood to the grave."

10 David rested with his ancestors and was buried in the City of David. 11 The length of David's reign over Israel was forty years: he reigned seven years in Hebron and thirty-three years in Jerusalem.

The Kingdom Made Secure

12 When Solomon was seated on the throne of his father David, with his sovereignty firmly established, 13 Adonijah, son of Haggith, went to Bathsheba, the mother of Solomon. "Do you come as a friend?" she asked. "Yes," he answered, 14 and added, "I have something to say to you." She replied, "Say it." 15 So he said: "You know that the kingdom was mine, and all Israel expected me to be king. But the kingdom escaped me and became my brother's, for the LORD gave it to him. 16 But now there is one favor I would ask of you. Do not refuse me." And she said, "Speak on." 17 He said, "Please ask King Solomon, who will not refuse you, to give me Abishag the Shunamite for my wife." 18 "Very well," replied Bathsheba, "I will speak to the king for you."

19 So Bathsheba went to King Solomon to speak to him for Adonijah, and the king stood up to meet her and paid her homage. Then he sat down upon his throne, and a throne was provided for the king's mother, who sat at his right. 20 "There is one small favor I would ask of you," she said. "Do not refuse me." "Ask it, my mother," the king said to her, "for I will not refuse you." 21 So she said, "Let Abishag the Shunamite be given to your brother Adonijah for his wife." 22 "And why do you ask Abishag the Shunamite for Adonijah?" King Solomon answered his mother. "Ask the kingdom for him as well, for he is my elder brother and has with him Abiathar the priest and Joab, son of Zeruiah." 23 And King Solomon swore by the LORD: "May God do thus and so to me, and more besides, if Adonijah has not proposed this at the cost of his life. 24 And now, as the LORD lives, who has seated me firmly on the throne of my father David and made of me a dynasty as he promised, this day shall Adonijah be put to death." 25 Then King Solomon sent Benaiah, son of Jehoiada, who struck him dead.

26 The king said to Abiathar the priest: "Go to your land in Anathoth. Though you deserve to die, I will not put you to death this time, because you carried the ark of the Lord GOD before my father David and shared in all the hardships my father endured." 27 So Solomon deposed Abiathar from his office of priest of the LORD, thus fulfilling the prophecy which the LORD had made in Shiloh about the house of Eli.

28 When the news came to Joab, who had sided with Adonijah, though not with Absalom, he fled to the tent of the LORD and seized the horns of the altar. 29 King Solomon was told that Joab had fled to the tent of the LORD and was at the altar. He sent Benaiah, son of Jehoiada, with the order, "Go, strike him down." 30 Benaiah went to the tent of the LORD and said to him, "The king says, 'Come out.'" But he answered, "No! I will die here." Benaiah reported to the king, "This is what Joab said to me in reply." 31 The king answered him:

"Do as he has said. Strike him down and bury him, and you will remove from me and from my family the blood which Joab shed without provocation. 32 The LORD will hold him responsible for his own blood, because he struck down two men better and more just than himself, and slew them with the sword without my father David's knowledge: Abner, son of Ner, general of Israel's army, and Amasa, son of Jether, general of Judah's army. 33 Joab and his descendants shall be responsible forever for their blood. But there shall be the peace of the LORD forever for David, and his descendants, and his house, and his throne." 34 Benaiah, son of Jehoiada, went back, struck him down and killed him; he was buried in his house in the desert. 35 The king appointed Benaiah, son of Jehoiada, over the army in his place, and put Zadok the priest in place of Abiathar.

36 Then the king summoned Shimei and said to him: "Build yourself a house in Jerusalem and live there. Do not go anywhere else. 37 For if you leave, and cross the Kidron Valley, be certain you shall die without fail. You shall be responsible for your own blood." 38 Shimei answered the king: "I accept. Your servant will do just as the king's majesty has said." So Shimei stayed in Jerusalem for a long time. 39 But three years later, two of Shimei's servants ran away to Achish, son of Maacah, king of Gath, and Shimei was informed that his servants were in Gath. 40 So Shimei rose, saddled his ass, and went to Achish in Gath in search of his servants, whom he brought back. 41 When Solomon was informed that Shimei had gone from Jerusalem to Gath, and had returned, 42 the king summoned Shimei and said to him: "Did I not have you swear by the LORD to your clear understanding of my warning that, if you left and went anywhere else, you should die without fail? And you answered, 'I accept and obey.' 43 Why, then, have you not kept the oath of the LORD and the command that I gave you?"

2, 17.22–25: *Abishag* had been the concubine of King David (1, 4). His successor, Solomon, inherited his father's harem. When Adonijah requested Abishag as his wife, he was subtly undermining the security of Solomon's throne and exposing himself to the suspicion of insurrection that would cost him his life; cf 2 Sm 3, 6–11; 16, 22.

44 And the king said to Shimei: "You know in your heart the evil that you did to my father David. Now the LORD requites you for your own wickedness. 45 But King Solomon shall be blessed, and David's throne shall endure before the LORD forever." 46 The king then gave the order to Benaiah, son of Jehoiada, who struck him dead as he left.

Wisdom of Solomon

3 With the royal power firmly in his grasp, Solomon allied himself by marriage with Pharaoh, king of Egypt. The daughter of Pharaoh, whom he married, he brought to the City of David, until he should finish building his palace, and the temple of the LORD, and the wall around Jerusalem.

2 However, the people were sacrificing on the high places, for up to that time no temple had been built to the name of the LORD. 3 Solomon loved the LORD, and obeyed the statutes of his father David; yet he offered sacrifice and burned incense on the high places.

4 The king went to Gibeon to sacrifice there, because that was the most renowned high place. Upon its altar Solomon offered a thousand holocausts. 5 In Gibeon the LORD appeared to Solomon in a dream at night. God said, "Ask something of me and I will give it to you." 6 Solomon answered: "You have shown great favor to your servant, my father David, because he behaved faithfully toward you, with justice and an upright heart; and you have continued this great favor toward him, even today, seating a son of his on his throne. 7 O LORD, my God, you have made me, your servant, king to succeed my father David; but I am a mere youth, not knowing at all how to act. 8 I serve you in the midst of the people whom you have chosen, a people so vast that it cannot be numbered or counted. 9 Give your servant, therefore, an understanding heart to judge your people and to distinguish right from wrong. For who is able to govern this vast people of yours?"

10 The LORD was pleased that Solomon made this request. 11 So God said to him: "Because you have asked for this—not for a long life for yourself, nor for riches, nor for the life of your enemies, but for understanding so that you may know what is right— 12 I do as you requested. I give you a heart so wise and understanding that there has never been anyone like you up to now, and after you there will come no one to equal you. 13 In addition, I give you what you have not asked for, such riches and glory that among kings there is not your like. 14 And if you follow me by keeping my statutes and commandments, as your father David did, I will give you a long life."

15 When Solomon awoke from his dream, he went to Jerusalem, stood before the ark of the covenant of the LORD, offered holocausts and peace offerings, and gave a banquet for all his servants.

Solomon's Judgment

16 Later, two harlots came to the king and stood before him. 17 One woman said: "By your leave, my lord, this woman and I live in the same house, and I gave birth in the house while she was present. 18 On the third day after I gave birth, this woman also gave birth. We were alone in the house; there was no one there but us two. 19 This woman's son died during the night; she smothered him by lying on him. 20 Later that night she got up and took my son from my side, as I, your handmaid, was sleeping. Then she laid him in her bosom, after she had laid her dead child in my bosom. 21 I rose in the morning to nurse my child, and I found him dead. But when I examined him in the morning light, I saw it was not the son whom I had borne."

22 The other woman answered, "It is not so! The living one is my son, the dead one is yours." But the first kept saying, "No, the dead one is your child, the living one is mine!" Thus they argued before the king.

23 Then the king said: "One woman claims, 'This, the living one, is my child, and the dead one is yours.' The other answers, 'No! The

dead one is your child; the living one is mine.'" 24 The king continued, "Get me a sword." When they brought the sword before him, 25 he said, "Cut the living child in two, and give half to one woman and half to the other." 26 The woman whose son it was, in the anguish she felt for it, said to the king, "Please, my lord, give her the living child— please do not kill it!" The other, however, said, "It shall be neither mine nor yours. Divide it!" 27 The king then answered, "Give the first one the living child! By no means kill it, for she is the mother."

28 When all Israel heard the judgment the king had given, they were in awe of him, because they saw that the king had in him the wisdom of God for giving judgment.

Chief Officers of the Kingdom

4 Solomon was king over all Israel 2 and these were the officials he had in his service:

Azariah, son of Zadok, priest;
3 Elihoreph and Ahijah, sons of Shisha, scribes;
Jehoshaphat, son of Ahilud, chancellor;
4 [Benaiah, son of Jehoiada, commander of the army;
Zadok and Abiathar, priests;]
5 Azariah, son of Nathan, chief of the commissaries;
Zabud, son of Nathan, companion to the king;
6 Ahishar, major-domo of the palace; and
Adoniram, son of Abda, superintendent of the forced labor.

Solomon's Royal State

7 Solomon had twelve commissaries for all Israel who supplied food for the king and his household, each having to provide for one month in the year. 8 Their names were:

the son of Hur in the hill country of Ephraim;
9 the son of Deker in Makaz, Shaalbim, Beth-shemesh, Elon and Beth-hanan;
10 the son of Hesed in Arubboth, as well as in Socoh and the whole region of Hepher;

4, 7-19: The administration of the kingdom thus initiated by Solomon continued in its main features for the duration of the monarchy in Israel and Judah.

11 the son of Abinadab, who was married to Solomon's daughter Taphath, in all the Naphath-dor;

12 Baana, son of Ahilud, in Taanach and Megiddo, and beyond Jokmeam, and in all Beth-shean, and in the country around Zarethan below Jezreel from Beth-shean to Abel-me-holah;

13 the son of Geber in Ramoth-gilead, having charge of the villages of Jair, son of Manas-seh, in Gilead; and of the district of Argob in Bashan—sixty large walled cities with gates barred with bronze;

14 Ahinadab, son of Iddo, in Maha-naim;

15 Ahimaaz, who was married to Basemath, another daughter of Solomon, in Naphtali;

16 Baana, son of Hushai, in Asher and along the rocky coast;

17 Jehoshaphat, son of Paruah, in Issachar;

18 Shimei, son of Ela, in Benjamin;

19 Geber, son of Uri, in the land of Gilead, the land of Sihon, king of the Amorites, and of Og, king of Bashan.

There was one prefect besides, in the king's own land.

5 7 These commissaries, one for each month, provided food for King Solomon and for all the guests at the royal table. They left nothing un-provided. 8 For the chariot horses and draft animals also, each brought his quota of barley and straw to the required place.

(4) 20 Judah and Israel were as numerous as the sands by the sea; they ate and drank and made merry. (5) 1 Solomon ruled over all the kingdoms from the River to the land of the Philistines, down to the border of Egypt; they paid Solomon tribute and were his vassals as long as he lived.

2 Solomon's supplies for each day were thirty kors of fine flour, sixty kors of meal, 3 ten fatted oxen, twenty pasture-fed oxen, and a hundred sheep, not counting harts, gazelles, roebucks, and fatted fowl.

4 He ruled over all the land west of the Euphrates, from Tiphsah to Gaza, and over all its kings, and he had peace on all his borders round about. 5 Thus Judah and Israel lived in security, every man under his vine or under his fig tree from Dan to Beer-sheba, as long as Solomon lived.

6 Solomon had four thousand stalls for his twelve thousand chariot horses.

9 Moreover, God gave Solomon wisdom and exceptional understand-ing and knowledge, as vast as the sand on the seashore. 10 Solomon surpassed all the Cedemites and all the Egyptians in wisdom. 11 He was wiser than all other men—than Ethan the Ezrahite, or Heman, Chalcol, and Darda, the musicians —and his fame spread throughout the neighboring nations. 12 Solo-mon also uttered three thousand proverbs, and his songs numbered a thousand and five. 13 He discussed plants, from the cedar on Lebanon to the hyssop growing out of the wall, and he spoke about beasts, birds, reptiles, and fishes. 14 Men came to hear Solomon's wisdom from all nations, sent by all the kings of the earth who had heard of his wisdom.

Preparations for the Temple

15 When Hiram, king of Tyre, heard that Solomon had been anointed king in place of his father, he sent an embassy to him; for Hiram had always been David's friend. 16 Solomon sent back this message to Hiram: 17 "You know that my father David, because of the enemies surrounding him on all sides, could not build a temple in honor of the LORD, his God, until such a time as the LORD should put these enemies under the soles of his feet. 18 But now the LORD, my God, has given me peace on all sides. There is no enemy or threat of danger. 19 So I propose to build a temple in honor of the LORD, my God, as the LORD predicted to my father David when he said: 'It is your son whom I will put upon your

throne in your place who shall build the temple in my honor.' 20 Give orders, then, to have cedars from the Lebanon cut down for me. My servants shall accompany yours, since you know that there is no one among us who is skilled in cutting timber like the Sidonians, and I will pay you whatever you say for your servants' salary."

21 When he had heard the words of Solomon, Hiram was pleased and said, "Blessed be the LORD this day, who has given David a wise son to rule this numerous people." 22 Hiram then sent word to Solomon, "I agree to the proposal you sent me, and I will provide all the cedars and fir trees you wish. 23 My servants shall bring them down from the Lebanon to the sea, and I will arrange them into rafts in the sea and bring them wherever you say. There I will break up the rafts, and you shall take the lumber. You, for your part, shall furnish the provisions I desire for my household."

24 So Hiram continued to provide Solomon with all the cedars and fir trees he wished; 25 while Solomon every year gave Hiram twenty thou-sand kors of wheat to provide for his household, and twenty thousand measures of pure oil. 26 The LORD, moreover, gave Solomon wisdom as he promised him, and there was peace between Hiram and Solomon, since they were parties to a treaty.

27 King Solomon conscripted thirty thousand workmen from all Israel. 28 He sent them to the Lebanon each month in relays of ten thousand, so that they spent one month in the Lebanon and two months at home. Adoniram was in charge of the draft. 29 Solomon had seventy thousand carriers and eighty thousand stonecutters in the mountain, 30 in addition to three thousand three hundred overseers, answerable to Solomon's prefects for the work, directing the people en-gaged in the work. 31 By order of the king, fine, large blocks were quarried to give the temple a foundation of hewn stone. 32 Sol-omon's and Hiram's builders, along with the Gebalites, hewed them out,

---

4, 19: *One prefect . . . in the king's own land:* the royal territory of Judah had its own peculiar adminis-tration different from that of the twelve districts which had to supply the king and his household with a month's provisions of food each year (v 7).

and prepared the wood and stones for building the temple.

Building of the Temple

6 In the four hundred and eightieth year from the departure of the Israelites from the land of Eygpt, in the fourth year of Solomon's reign over Israel, in the month of Ziv, which is the second month, the construction of the temple of the LORD was begun.

2 The temple which King Solomon built for the LORD was sixty cubits long, twenty wide, and twenty-five high. 3 The porch in front of the temple was twenty cubits from side to side, along the width of the nave, and ten cubits deep in front of the temple. 4 Splayed windows with trellises were made for the temple, 5 and adjoining the wall of the temple, which enclosed the nave and the sanctuary, an annex of several stories was built. 6 Its lowest story was five cubits wide, the middle one six cubits wide, the third seven cubits wide, because there were offsets along the outside of the temple so that the beams would not be fastened into the walls of the temple. 7 (The temple was built of stone dressed at the quarry, so that no hammer, axe, or iron tool was to be heard in the temple during its construction.) 8 The entrance to the lowest floor of the annex was at the right side of the temple, and stairs with intermediate landings led up to the middle story and from the middle story to the third. 9 When the temple was built to its full height, it was roofed in with rafters and boards of cedar. 10 The annex, with its lowest story five cubits high, was built all along the outside of the temple, to which it was joined by cedar beams.

11 This word of the LORD came to Solomon: 12 "As to this temple you are building—if you observe my statutes, carry out my ordinances, keep and obey all my com-

mands, I will fulfill toward you the promise I made to your father David. 13 I will dwell in the midst of the Israelites and will not forsake my people Israel."

14 When Solomon finished building the temple, 15 its walls were lined from floor to ceiling beams with cedar paneling, and its floor was laid with fir planking. 16 At the rear of the temple a space of twenty cubits was set off by cedar partitions from the floor to the rafters, enclosing the sanctuary, the holy of holies. 17 The nave, or part of the temple in front of the sanctuary, was forty cubits long. 18 The cedar in the interior of the temple was carved in the form of gourds and open flowers; all was of cedar, and no stone was to be seen.

19 In the innermost part of the temple was located the sanctuary to house the ark of the LORD's covenant, 20 twenty cubits long, twenty wide, and twenty high. 21 Solomon overlaid the interior of the temple with pure gold. He made in front of the sanctuary a cedar altar, overlaid it with gold, and looped it with golden chains. 22 The entire temple was overlaid with gold so that it was completely covered with it; the whole altar before the sanctuary was also overlaid with gold. 23 In the sanctuary were two cherubim, each ten cubits high, made of olive wood. 24 Each wing of a cherub measured five cubits so that the space from wing tip to wing tip of each was ten cubits. 25 The cherubim were identical in size and shape, 26 and each was exactly ten cubits high. 27 The cherubim were placed in the inmost part of the temple, with their wings spread wide, so that one wing of each cherub touched a side wall while the other wing, pointing toward the middle of the room, touched the corresponding wing of the second cherub. 28 The cherubim, too, were overlaid with gold.

29 The walls on all sides of both

the inner and the outer rooms had carved figures of cherubim, palm trees, and open flowers. 30 The floor of both the inner and the outer rooms was overlaid with gold. 31 At the entrance of the sanctuary, doors of olive wood were made; the doorframes had beveled posts. 32 The two doors were of olive wood, with carved figures of cherubim, palm trees, and open flowers. The doors were overlaid with gold, which was also molded to the cherubim and the palm trees. 33 The same was done at the entrance to the nave, where the doorposts of olive wood were rectangular. 34 The two doors were of fir wood; each door was banded by a metal strap, front and back, 35 and had carved cherubim, palm trees, and open flowers, over which gold was evenly applied.

36 The inner court was walled off by means of three courses of hewn stones and one course of cedar beams.

37 The foundations of the LORD's temple were laid in the month of Ziv 38 in the fourth year, and it was completed in all particulars, exactly according to plan, in the month of Bul, the eighth month, in the eleventh year. Thus it took Solomon seven years to build it.

Building of the Palace

7 His own palace Solomon completed after thirteen years of construction. 2 He built the hall called the Forest of Lebanon one hundred cubits long, fifty wide, and thirty high; it was supported by four rows of cedar columns, with cedar capitals upon the columns. 3 Moreover, it had a ceiling of cedar above the beams resting on the columns; these beams numbered forty-five, fifteen to a row. 4 There were three window frames at either end, with windows in strict alignment. 5 The posts of all the doorways were rectangular, and the doorways faced each other, three at either end.

6, 1: *Construction of the temple of the Lord* is here paralleled in importance with the founding of the nation after the departure from Egypt. In both, God is the central figure, who chose Israel as his people, and now chooses the place where his temple should be built (Dt 12, 4–18.26). The year is given in a round number, 480, which corresponds to twelve generations. The *fourth year of Solomon's reign*: c. 968 B.C.
6, 11ff: *The word of the Lord . . . my people*

Israel: the oracle, which came as a climax at the completion of the work, was an expression of God's acceptance and approval. Nevertheless the fulfillment of God's promises to David and his royal descendants will depend on their observance of his ordinances and commands.
6, 19: *The innermost part of the temple:* the sanctuary or holy of holies reserved exclusively for the Lord. Here through his presence he dwelt as on a

throne between the cherubim above the ark of the covenant (23–28; 2 Chr 3, 10–13). See note on Ex 25, 18ff.
6, 20: *Twenty (cubits) high:* it is usually supposed that the holy of holies was of this height because it had a raised floor, five cubits above the floor level of the nave, rather than a dropped ceiling. The building was twenty-five cubits high (v 2) according to the reading here followed.

6 The porch of the columned hall he made fifty cubits long and thirty wide. The porch extended the width of the columned hall, and there was a canopy in front. 7 He also built the vestibule of the throne where he gave judgment—that is, the tribunal; it was paneled with cedar from floor to ceiling beams. 8 His living quarters were in another court, set in deeper than the tribunal and of the same construction. A palace like this tribunal was built for Pharaoh's daughter, whom Solomon had married.

9 All these buildings were of fine stones, hewn to size and trimmed front and back with a saw, from the foundation to the bonding course. 10 (The foundation was made of fine, large blocks, some ten cubits and some eight cubits. 11 Above were fine stones hewn to size, and cedar wood.) 12 The great court was enclosed by three courses of hewn stones and a bonding course of cedar beams. So also were the inner court of the temple of the LORD and the temple porch.

Furnishing of the Temple

13 King Solomon had Hiram brought from Tyre. 14 He was a bronze worker, the son of a widow from the tribe of Naphtali; his father had been from Tyre. He was endowed with skill, understanding, and knowledge of how to produce any work in bronze. He came to King Solomon and did all his metal work.

15 Two hollow bronze columns were cast, each eighteen cubits high and twelve cubits in circumference; their metal was of four fingers' thickness. 16 There were also two capitals cast in bronze, to place on top of the columns, each of them five cubits high. 17 Two pieces of network with a chainlike mesh were made to cover the (nodes of the) capitals on top of the columns, one for each capital. 18 Four hundred pomegranates were also cast; two hundred of them in a double row encircled the piece of network on each of the two capitals. 19 The capitals on top of the columns were finished wholly in a lotus pattern 20 above the level of the nodes and their enveloping network. 21 The columns were then erected adjacent to the porch of the temple, one to the right, called Jachin, and the other to the left, called Boaz. 22 Thus the work on the columns was completed.

23 The sea was then cast; it was made with a circular rim, and measured ten cubits across, five in height, and thirty in circumference. 24 Under the brim, gourds encircled it, ten to the cubit all the way around; the gourds were in two rows and were cast in one mold with the sea. 25 This rested on twelve oxen, three facing north, three facing west, three facing south, and three facing east, with their haunches all toward the center, where the sea was set upon them. 26 It was a handbreadth thick, and its brim resembled that of a cup, being lily-shaped. Its capacity was two thousand measures.

27 Ten stands were also made of bronze, each four cubits long, four wide, and three high. 28 When these stands were constructed, panels were set within the framework. 29 On the panels between the frames there were lions, oxen, and cherubim; and on the frames likewise, above and below the lions and oxen, there were wreaths in relief.

30 Each stand had four bronze wheels and bronze axles. 32 The four wheels were below the paneling, and the axle-trees of the wheels and the stand were of one piece. Each wheel was a cubit and a half high. 33 The wheels were constructed like chariot wheels; their axles, fellies, spokes, and hubs were all cast.

The four legs of each stand had cast braces, which were under the basin; they had wreaths on each side. 34 These four braces, extending to the corners of each stand, were of one piece with the stand.

35 On top of the stand there was a raised collar half a cubit high, with supports and panels which were of one piece with the top of the stand. 31 This was surmounted by a crown one cubit high within which was a rounded opening to provide a receptacle a cubit and a half in depth. There was carved work at the opening, on panels that were angular, not curved. 36 On the surfaces of the supports and on the panels, wherever there was a clear space, cherubim, lions, and palm trees were carved, as well as wreaths all around. 37 This was how the ten stands were made, all of the same casting, the same size, the same shape. 38 Ten bronze basins were then made, each four cubits in diameter with a capacity of forty measures, one basin for the top of each of the ten stands. 39 The stands were placed, five on the south side of the temple and five on the north. The sea was placed off to the southeast from the south side of the temple.

40 When Hiram made the pots, shovels, and bowls, he therewith completed all his work for King Solomon in the temple of the LORD: 41 two columns, two nodes for the capitals on top of the columns, two pieces of network covering the nodes for the capitals on top of the columns, 42 four hundred pomegranates in double rows on both pieces of network that covered the two nodes of the capitals where they met the columns, 43 ten stands, ten basins on the stands, 44 one sea, twelve oxen supporting the sea, 45 pots, shovels, and bowls. All these articles which Hiram made for King Solomon in the temple of the LORD were of burnished bronze. 46 The king had them cast in the neighborhood of the Jordan, in the clayey ground between Succoth and Zarethan. 47 Solomon did not weigh all the articles because they were so numerous; the weight of the bronze, therefore, was not determined.

48 Solomon had all the articles made for the interior of the temple of the LORD: the golden altar; the golden table on which the showbread lay; 49 the lampstands of pure gold, five to the right and five to the left before the sanctuary, with their flowers, lamps, and tongs of gold; 50 basins, snuffers, bowls, cups, and fire pans of pure gold; and hinges of gold for the doors of the inner room,

---

7, 15–21: The *two hollow bronze columns*, Jachin and Boaz (2 Chr 3, 17), stood free to the right and left of the temple porch. The names are related to

God's power (*Boaz*) founding (*Jachin*) the temple and his people.

7, 23–26: *The sea ... rested on twelve oxen:* this

was a large circular tank containing about twelve thousand gallons of water.

or holy of holies, and for the doors of the outer room, the nave.

51 When all the work undertaken by King Solomon in the temple of the LORD was completed, he brought in the dedicated offerings of his father David, putting the silver, gold, and other articles in the treasuries of the temple of the LORD.

Dedication of the Temple

8 At the order of Solomon, the elders of Israel and all the leaders of the tribes, the princes in the ancestral houses of the Israelites, came to King Solomon in Jerusalem, to bring up the ark of the LORD's convenant from the City of David [which is Zion]. 2 All the men of Israel assembled before King Solomon during the festival in the month of Ethanim (the seventh month). 3 When all the elders of Israel had arrived, the priests took up the ark; 4 they carried the ark of the LORD and the meeting tent with all the sacred vessels that were in the tent. (The priests and Levites carried them.)

5 King Solomon and the entire community of Israel present for the occasion sacrificed before the ark sheep and oxen too many to number or count. 6 The priests brought the ark of the covenant of the LORD to its place beneath the wings of the cherubim in the sanctuary, the holy of holies of the temple. 7 The cherubim had their wings spread out over the place of the ark, sheltering the ark and its poles from above. 8 The poles were so long that their ends could be seen from that part of the holy place adjoining the sanctuary; however, they could not be seen beyond. (They have remained there to this day.) 9 There was nothing in the ark but the two stone tablets which Moses had put there at Horeb, when the LORD made a covenant with the Israelites at their departure from the land of Egypt.

10 When the priests left the holy place, the cloud filled the temple of the LORD 11 so that the priests could no longer minister because of the cloud, since the LORD's glory had filled the temple of the LORD. 12 Then Solomon said, "The LORD intends to dwell in the dark cloud; 13 I have truly built you a princely house, a dwelling where you may abide forever."

14 The king turned and greeted the whole community of Israel as they stood. 15 He said to them: "Blessed be the LORD, the God of Israel, who with his own mouth made a promise to my father David and by his hand has brought it to fulfillment. It was he who said, 16 'Since the day I brought my people Israel out of Egypt, I have not chosen a city out of any tribe of Israel for the building of a temple to my honor; but I choose David to rule my people Israel.' 17 When my father David wished to build a temple to the honor of the LORD, the God of Israel, 18 the LORD said to him, 'In wishing to build a temple to my honor, you do well. 19 It will not be you, however, who will build the temple; but the son who will spring from you, he shall build the temple to my honor.' 20 And now the LORD has fulfilled the promise that he made: I have succeeded my father David and sit on the throne of Israel, as the LORD foretold, and I have built this temple to honor the LORD, the God of Israel. 21 I have provided in it a place for the ark in which is the covenant of the LORD, which he made with our fathers when he brought them out of the land of Egypt."

Solomon's Prayer

22 Solomon stood before the altar of the LORD in the presence of the whole community of Israel, and stretching forth his hands toward heaven, 23 he said, "LORD, God of Israel, there is no God like you in heaven above or on earth below; you keep your covenant of kindness with your servants who are faithful to you with their whole heart. 24 You have kept the promise you made to my father David, your servant. You who spoke that promise, have this day, by your own power, brought it to fulfillment. 25 Now, therefore, LORD, God of Israel, keep the further promise you made to my father David, your servant, saying, 'You shall always have someone from your line to sit before me on the throne of Israel, provided only that your descendants look to their conduct so that they live in my presence, as you have lived in my presence.' 26 Now, LORD, God of Israel, may this promise which you made to my father David, your servant, be confirmed.

27 "Can it indeed be that God dwells among men on earth? If the heavens and the highest heavens cannot contain you, how much less this temple which I have built! 28 Look kindly on the prayer and petition of your servant, O LORD, my God, and listen to the cry of supplication which I, your servant, utter before you this day. 29 May your eyes watch night and day over this temple, the place where you have decreed you shall be honored; may you heed the prayer which I, your servant, offer in this place. 30 Listen to the petitions of your servant and of your people Israel which they offer in this place. Listen from your heavenly dwelling and grant pardon.

31 "If a man sins against his neighbor and is required to take an oath sanctioned by a curse, when he comes and takes the oath before your altar in this temple, 32 listen in heaven; take action and pass judgment on your servants. Condemn the wicked and punish him for his conduct, but acquit the just and establish his innocence.

33 "If your people Israel sin against you and are defeated by an enemy, and if then they return to you, praise your name, pray to you, and entreat you in this temple, 34 listen in heaven and forgive the sin of your people Israel, and bring them back to the land you gave their fathers.

35 "If the sky is closed, so that there is no rain, because they have sinned against you and you afflict

---

8, 6–9: The transfer of the ark of the covenant into the newly constructed temple building, and the oracle of God's acceptance (9, 3–9), and his act of possession (8, 10–13), constituted the temple's solemn dedication, and made of it the abiding dwelling of God among his

people for which David had hoped (2 Sm 6, 12–15; 7, 1–3). The concurrence of the feast of Booths marks an appropriate transition of God's dwelling among nomadic tribes to his permanent abode among a settled people.

8, 33–34.46–53: These references to deportation of Israelites to *a hostile land* are an expansion of Solomon's prayer dating from the Babylonian exile four centuries later.

them, and if then they repent of their sin, and pray, and praise your name in this place, 36 listen in heaven and forgive the sin of your servant and of your people Israel, teaching them the right way to live and sending rain upon this land of yours which you have given to your people as their heritage.

37 "If there is famine in the land or pestilence; or if blight comes, or mildew, or a locust swarm, or devouring insects; if an enemy of your people besieges them in one of their cities; whatever plague or sickness there may be, 38 if then any one [of your entire people Israel] has remorse of conscience and offers some prayer or petition, stretching out his hands toward this temple, 39 listen from your heavenly dwelling place and forgive. You who alone know the hearts of all men, render to each one of them according to his conduct; knowing their hearts, so treat them 40 that they may fear you as long as they live on the land you gave our fathers.

41 "To the foreigner, likewise, who is not of your people Israel, but comes from a distant land to honor you 42 (since men will learn of your great name and your mighty hand and your outstretched arm), when he comes and prays toward this temple, 43 listen from your heavenly dwelling. Do all that the foreigner asks of you, that all the peoples of the earth may know your name, may fear you as do your people Israel, and may acknowledge that this temple which I have built is dedicated to your honor.

44 "Whatever the direction in which you may send your people forth to war against their enemies, if they pray to you, O LORD, toward the city you have chosen and the temple I have built in your honor, 45 listen in heaven to their prayer and petition, and defend their cause.

46 "When they sin against you (for there is no man who does not sin), and in your anger against them you deliver them to the enemy, so that their captors deport them to a hostile land, far or near, 47 may they repent in the land of their captivity and be converted. If then they entreat you in the land of their captors and say, 'We have sinned and done wrong; we have been wicked'; 48 if with their whole heart and soul they turn back to you in the land of the enemies who took them captive, pray to you toward the land you gave their fathers, the city you have chosen, and the temple I have built in your honor, 49 listen from your heavenly dwelling. 50 Forgive your people their sins and all the offenses they have committed against you, and grant them mercy before their captors, so that these will be merciful to them. 51 For they are your people and your inheritance, whom you brought out of Egypt, from the midst of an iron furnace.

52 "Thus may your eyes be open to the petition of your servant and to the petition of your people Israel. Hear them whenever they call upon you, 53 because you have set them apart among all the peoples of the earth for your inheritance, as you declared through your servant Moses when you brought our fathers out of Egypt, O Lord GOD."

54 When Solomon finished offering this entire prayer of petition to the LORD, he rose from before the altar of the LORD, where he had been kneeling with his hands outstretched toward heaven. 55 He stood and blessed the whole community of Israel, saying in a loud voice: 56 "Blessed be the LORD who has given rest to his people Israel, just as he promised. Not a single word has gone unfulfilled of the entire generous promise he made through his servant Moses. 57 May the LORD, our God, be with us as he was with our fathers and may he not forsake us nor cast us off. 58 May he draw our hearts to himself, that we may follow him in everything and keep the commands, statutes, and ordinances which he enjoined on our fathers. 59 May this prayer I have offered to the LORD, our God, be present to him day and night, that he may uphold the cause of his servant and of his people Israel as each day requires, 60 that all the peoples of the earth may know the LORD is God and there is no other. 61 You must be wholly devoted to the LORD, our God, observing his statutes and keeping his commandments, as on this day."

62 The king and all Israel with him offered sacrifices before the LORD. 63 Solomon offered as peace offerings to the LORD twenty-two thousand oxen and one hundred twenty thousand sheep. Thus the king and all the Israelites dedicated the temple of the LORD. 64 On that day the king consecrated the middle of the court facing the temple of the LORD; he offered there the holocausts, the cereal offerings, and the fat of the peace offerings, because the bronze altar before the LORD was too small to hold these offerings.

65 On this occasion Solomon and all the Israelites, who had assembled in large numbers from Labo of Hamath to the Wadi of Egypt, celebrated the festival before the LORD, our God, for seven days. 66 On the eighth day he dismissed the people, who bade the king farewell and went to their homes, rejoicing and happy over all the blessings the LORD had given to his servant David and to his people Israel.

Promise and Warning to Solomon

9 After Solomon finished building the temple of the LORD, the royal palace, and everything else that he had planned, 2 the LORD appeared to him a second time, as he had appeared to him in Gibeon. 3 The LORD said to him: "I have heard the prayer of petition which you offered in my presence. I have consecrated this temple which you have built; I confer my name upon it forever, and my eyes and my heart shall be there always. 4 As for you, if you live in my presence as your father David lived, sincerely and uprightly, doing just as I have commanded you, keeping my statutes and decrees, 5 I will establish your throne of sovereignty over Israel forever, as I promised your father David when I said, 'You shall always have someone from your line on the throne of Israel.' 6 But if you and your descendants ever withdraw from me, fail to keep the commandments and statutes which I set before you, and proceed to venerate and worship strange gods, 7 I will cut off Israel from the land I gave them and repu-

diate the temple I have consecrated to my honor. Israel shall become a proverb and a byword among all nations, 8 and this temple shall become a heap of ruins. Every passerby shall catch his breath in amazement, and ask, 'Why has the LORD done this to the land and to this temple?' 9 Men will answer: 'They forsook the LORD, their God, who brought their fathers out of the land of Egypt; they adopted strange gods which they worshiped and served. That is why the LORD has brought down upon them all this evil.'"

Other Acts of the King

10 After the twenty years during which Solomon built the two houses, the temple of the LORD and the palace of the king 11 —Hiram, king of Tyre, supplying Solomon with all the cedar wood, fir wood, and gold he wished—King Solomon gave Hiram twenty cities in the land of Galilee. 12 Hiram left Tyre to see the cities Solomon had given him, but was not satisfied with them. 13 So he said, "What are these cities you have given me, my brother?" And he called them the land of Cabul, as they are called to this day. 14 Hiram, however, had sent King Solomon one hundred and twenty talents of gold.

15 This is an account of the forced labor which King Solomon levied in order to build the temple of the LORD, his palace, Millo, the wall of Jerusalem, Hazor, Megiddo, Gezer 16 (Pharaoh, king of Egypt, had come up and taken Gezer and, after destroying it by fire and slaying all the Canaanites living in the city, had given it as dowry to his daughter, Solomon's wife; 17 Solomon then rebuilt Gezer), Lower Beth-horon, 18 Baalath, Tamar in the desert of Judah, 19 all his cities for supplies, cities for chariots and for horses, and whatever else Solomon decided should be built in Jerusalem, in Lebanon, and in the entire land under his dominion. 20 All the non-Israel-ite people who remained in the land, descendants of the Amorites, Hittites, Perizzites, Hivites, and Jebusites 21 whose doom the Israelites had been unable to accomplish, Solomon conscripted as forced laborers, as they are to this day. 22 But Solomon enslaved none of the Israelites, for they were his fighting force, his ministers, commanders, adjutants, chariot officers, and charioteers. 23 The supervisors of Solomon's works who policed the people engaged in the work numbered five hundred and fifty.

24 As soon as Pharaoh's daughter went from the City of David to her palace, which he had built for her, Solomon built Millo.

25 Three times a year Solomon used to offer holocausts and peace offerings on the altar which he had built to the LORD, and to burn incense before the LORD; and he kept the temple in repair.

26 King Solomon also built a fleet at Ezion-geber, which is near Elath on the shore of the Red Sea in the land of Edom. 27 In this fleet Hiram placed his own expert seamen with the servants of Solomon. 28 They went to Ophir, and brought back four hundred and twenty talents of gold to King Solomon.

Visit of the Queen of Sheba

10 The queen of Sheba, having heard of Solomon's fame, came to test him with subtle questions. 2 She arrived in Jerusalem with a very numerous retinue, and with camels bearing spices, a large amount of gold, and precious stones. She came to Solomon and questioned him on every subject in which she was interested. 3 King Solomon explained everything she asked about, and there remained nothing hidden from him that he could not explain to her.

4 When the queen of Sheba witnessed Solomon's great wisdom, the palace he had built, 5 the food at his table, the seating of his ministers, the attendance and garb of his waiters, his banquet service, and the holocausts he offered in the temple of the LORD, she was breathless. 6 "The report I heard in my country about your deeds and your wisdom is true," she told the king. 7 "Though I did not believe the report until I came and saw with my own eyes, I have discovered that they were not telling me the half. Your wisdom and prosperity surpass the report I heard. 8 Happy are your men, happy these servants of yours, who stand before you always and listen to your wisdom. 9 Blessed be the LORD, your God, whom it has pleased to place you on the throne of Israel. In his enduring love for Israel, the LORD has made you king to carry out judgment and justice." 10 Then she gave the king one hundred and twenty gold talents, a very large quantity of spices, and precious stones. Never again did anyone bring such an abundance of spices as the queen of Sheba gave to King Solomon.

11 Hiram's fleet, which used to bring gold from Ophir, also brought from there a large quantity of cabinet wood and precious stones. 12 With the wood the king made supports for the temple of the LORD and for the palace of the king, and harps and lyres for the chanters. No more such wood was brought or seen to the present day.

13 King Solomon gave the queen of Sheba everything she desired and asked for, besides such presents as were given her from Solomon's royal bounty. Then she returned with her servants to her own country.

Solomon's Wealth

14 The gold that Solomon received every year weighed six hundred and sixty-six gold talents, 15 in addition to what came from the Tarshish fleet, from the traffic of merchants, and from all the kings of Arabia and the governors of the country. 16 Moreover, King Solomon made two hundred shields of beaten gold (six hundred gold shekels went into each shield) 17 and three hundred

9, 14: One hundred and twenty talents of gold: approximately three million six hundred thousand dollars.
9, 15: Millo: probably means a filling, and may refer to an artificial earthwork or platform of stamped ground south of the temple area. It was begun by

David (2 Sm 5, 9); cf 9, 24; 11, 27.
9, 26: Ezion-geber . . . Edom: the first mention of maritime commerce in the Israelite kingdom (to which the land of Edom was subject after its conquest by King David; cf 2 Sm 8, 14).
10, 1: Queen of Sheba: women rulers among the

Arabs are recorded in eighth-century-B.C. Assyrian inscriptions. Sheba was for centuries the leading principality in what is now the Yemen.
10, 11f: Cabinet: an unknown wood, probably fragrant.

bucklers of beaten gold (three minas of gold went into each buckler); and he put them in the hall of the Forest of Lebanon. 18 The king also had a large ivory throne made, and overlaid it with refined gold. 19 The throne had six steps, a back with a round top, and an arm on each side of the seat. Next to each arm stood a lion; 20 and twelve other lions stood on the steps, two to a step, one on either side of each step. Nothing like this was produced in any other kingdom. 21 In addition, all King Solomon's drinking vessels were of gold, and all the utensils in the hall of the Forest of Lebanon were of pure gold. There was no silver, for in Solomon's time it was considered worthless. 22 The king had a fleet of Tarshish ships at sea with Hiram's fleet. Once every three years the fleet of Tarshish ships would come with a cargo of gold, silver, ivory, apes, and monkeys. 23 Thus King Solomon surpassed in riches and wisdom all the kings of the earth. 24 And the whole world sought audience with Solomon, to hear from him the wisdom which God had put in his heart. 25 Each one brought his yearly tribute: silver or gold articles, garments, weapons, spices, horses and mules.

26 Solomon collected chariots and drivers; he had one thousand four hundred chariots and twelve thousand drivers; these he allocated among the chariot cities and to the king's service in Jerusalem. 27 The king made silver as common in Jerusalem as stones, and cedars as numerous as the sycamores of the foothills. 28 Solomon's horses were imported from Cilicia, where the king's agents purchased them. 29 A chariot imported from Egypt cost six hundred shekels, a horse one hundred and fifty shekels; they were exported at these rates to all the Hittite and Aramean kings.

The Sins of Solomon

11 King Solomon loved many foreign women besides the daughter of Pharaoh (Moabites, Ammonites, Edomites, Sidonians, and Hittites), 2 from nations with which the LORD had forbidden the Israelites to inter-marry, "because," he said, "they will turn your hearts to their gods." But Solomon fell in love with them. 3 He had seven hundred wives of princely rank and three hundred concubines, and his wives turned his heart.

4 When Solomon was old his wives had turned his heart to strange gods, and his heart was not entirely with the LORD, his God, as the heart of his father David had been. 5 By adoring Astarte, the goddess of the Sidonians, and Milcom, the idol of the Ammonites, 6 Solomon did evil in the sight of the LORD; he did not follow him unreservedly as his father David had done. 7 Solomon then built a high place to Chemosh, the idol of Moab, and to Molech, the idol of the Ammonites, on the hill opposite Jerusalem. 8 He did the same for all his foreign wives who burned incense and sacrificed to their gods. 9 The LORD, therefore, became angry with Solomon, because his heart was turned away from the LORD, the God of Israel, who had appeared to him twice 10 (for though the LORD had forbidden him this very act of following strange gods, Solomon had not obeyed him).

11 So the LORD said to Solomon: "Since this is what you want, and you have not kept my covenant and my statutes which I enjoined on you, I will deprive you of the kingdom and give it to your servant. 12 I will not do this during your lifetime, however, for the sake of your father David; it is your son whom I will deprive. 13 Nor will I take away the whole kingdom. I will leave your son one tribe for the sake of my servant David and of Jerusalem, which I have chosen."

14 The LORD then raised up an adversary to Solomon: Hadad the Edomite, who was of the royal line in Edom. 15 Earlier, when David had conquered Edom, Joab, the general of the army, while going to bury the slain, put to death every male in Edom. 16 Joab and all Israel remained there six months until they had killed off every male in Edom. 17 Meanwhile, Hadad, who was only a boy, fled toward Egypt with some Edomite servants of his father. 18 They left Midian and passing through Paran, where they picked up additional men, they went into Egypt to Pharoah, king of Egypt, who gave Hadad a house, appointed him rations, and assigned him land.

19 Hadad won great favor with Pharaoh, so that he gave him in marriage the sister of Queen Tahpenes, his own wife. 20 Tahpenes' sister bore Hadad a son, Genubath. After his weaning, the queen kept him in Pharaoh's palace, where he then lived with Pharaoh's own sons. 21 When Hadad in Egypt heard that David rested with his ancestors and that Joab, the general of the army, was dead, he said to Pharaoh, 22 "Give me leave to return to my own country." Pharaoh said to him, "What do you lack with me, that you are seeking to return to your own country?" "Nothing," he said, "but please let me go!"

23 God raised up against Solomon another adversary, in Rezon, the son of Eliada, who had fled from his lord, Hadadezer, king of Zobah, 24 when David defeated them with slaughter. Rezon gathered men about him and became leader of a band, went to Damascus, settled there, and became king in Damascus. 25 He was an enemy of Israel as long as Solomon lived; this added to the harm done by Hadad, who made a rift in Israel by becoming king over Edom.

26 Solomon's servant Jeroboam, son of Nebat, an Ephraimite from Zeredah with a widowed mother, Zeruah, also rebelled against the king. 27 This is why he rebelled. King Solomon was building Millo, closing up the breach of his father's

---

10, 22: *Tarshish ships:* large, strong vessels for long voyages. *Tarshish* was the ancient Tartessus, a Phoenician colony in southern Spain, the name of which denotes a center for smelting metallic ore.

11, 1–3.7: The glorious rise of Solomon, his piety and wisdom, administrative skill and wealth, the extension of his kingdom, his prestige among neighboring rulers, his reign of peace, above all his friendship with God—these are now eclipsed by his sins of intermarriage with great numbers of pagan wives and the consequent forbidden worship of their gods (Ex 34, 11–16; Dt 7, 1–5). His construction of temples in their honor merited the punishment of loss of a united kingdom to his posterity, and the opposition of

adversaries to himself (vv 14.23–37). Hadad the Edomite rebelled against Solomon at the beginning of his reign (v 25). Rezon of Syria established a new kingdom in Damascus; Jeroboam of Israel constituted the greatest threat because of his revolt from within. This threefold threat culminated in the breakup of Solomon's kingdom.

City of David. 28 Jeroboam was a man of means, and when Solomon saw that he was also an industrious young man, he put him in charge of the entire labor force of the house of Joseph. 29 At that time Jeroboam left Jerusalem, and the prophet Ahijah the Shilonite met him on the road. The two were alone in the area, and the prophet was wearing a new cloak. 30 Ahijah took off his new cloak, tore it into twelve pieces, 31 and said to Jeroboam:

"Take ten pieces for yourself; the LORD, the God of Israel, says: 'I will tear away the kingdom from Solomon's grasp and will give you ten of the tribes. 32 One tribe shall remain to him for the sake of David my servant, and of Jerusalem, the city I have chosen out of all the tribes of Israel. 33 The ten I will give you because he has forsaken me and has worshiped Astarte, goddess of the Sidonians, Chemosh, god of Moab, and Milcom, god of the Ammonites; he has not followed my ways or done what is pleasing to me according to my statutes and my decrees, as his father David did. 34 Yet I will not take any of the kingdom from Solomon himself, but will keep him a prince as long as he lives for the sake of my servant David, whom I chose, who kept my commandments and statutes. 35 But I will take the kingdom from his son and will give it to you—that is, the ten tribes. 36 I will give his son one tribe, that my servant David may always have a lamp before me in Jerusalem, the city in which I choose to be honored. 37 I will take you; you shall reign over all that you desire and shall become king of Israel. 38 If, then, you heed all that I command you, follow my ways, and please me by keeping my statutes and my commandments like my servant David, I will be with you. I will establish for you, as I did for David, a lasting dynasty; I will give Israel to you. 39 I will punish David's line for this, but not forever.'"

40 When Solomon tried to have Jeroboam killed for his rebellion, he escaped to King Shishak, in Egypt, where he remained until Solomon's death.

41 The rest of the acts of Solomon, with all his deeds and his wisdom, are recorded in the book of the chronicles of Solomon. 42 The time that Solomon reigned in Jerusalem over all Israel was forty years. 43 Solomon rested with his ancestors; he was buried in his father's City of David, and his son Rehoboam succeeded him as king.

JUDAH AND ISRAEL TO THE TIME OF AHAB

Secession of Israel

12 Rehoboam went to Shechem, where all Israel had come to proclaim him king. 3 They said to Rehoboam: 4 "Your father put on us a heavy yoke. If you now lighten the harsh service and the heavy yoke your father imposed on us, we will serve you." 5 "Come back to me in three days," he answered them. When the people had departed, 6 King Rehoboam consulted the elders who had been in his father's service while he was alive, and asked, "What answer do you advise me to give this people?" 7 They replied, "If today you will be the servant of this people and submit to them, giving them a favorable answer, they will be your servants forever." 8 But he ignored the advice the elders had given him, and consulted the young men who had grown up with him and were in his service. 9 He said to them, "What answer do you advise me to give this people, who have asked me to lighten the yoke my father imposed on them?" 10 The young men who had grown up with him replied, "This is what you must say to this people who have asked you to lighten the yoke your father put on them: 'My little finger is thicker than my father's body. 11 Whereas my father put a heavy yoke on you, I will make it heavier. My father beat you with whips, but I will beat you with scorpions.'"

12 On the third day all Israel came back to King Rehoboam, as he had instructed them to do. 13 Ignoring the advice the elders had given him, the king gave the people a harsh answer. 14 He said to them, as the young men had advised: "My father put on you a heavy yoke, but I will make it heavier. My father beat you with whips, but I will beat you with scorpions." 15 The king did not listen to the people, for the LORD brought this about to fulfill the prophecy he had uttered to Jeroboam, son of Nebat, through Ahijah the Shilonite.

16 When all Israel saw that the king did not listen to them, the people answered the king:

"What share have we in David?
We have no heritage in the son of
    Jesse.
To your tents, O Israel!
Now look to your own house,
    David."

So Israel went off to their tents, 17 but Rehoboam reigned over the Israelites who lived in the cities of Judah. 18 King Rehoboam then sent out Adoram, superintendent of the forced labor, but all Israel stoned him to death. Rehoboam managed to mount his chariot to flee to Jerusalem, 19 and Israel went into rebellion against David's house to this day. 2 Jeroboam, son of Nebat, who was still in Egypt, where he had fled from King Solomon, returned from Egypt as soon as he learned this. 20 When all Israel heard that Jeroboam had returned, they summoned him to an assembly and made him king over all Israel. None remained loyal to David's house except the tribe of Judah alone.

21 On his arrival in Jerusalem, Rehoboam gathered together all the house of Judah and the tribe of Benjamin—one hundred eighty thousand seasoned warriors—to fight against the house of Israel, to restore the kingdom to Rehoboam, son of Solomon. 22 However, the LORD spoke to Shemaiah, a man of God: 23 "Say to Rehoboam, son of

---

12, 1: *Shechem:* chief city of the northern tribes, where a covenant of fidelity had previously been made between the Lord and his people and a stone of witness had been erected in memory of the event

(Jos 24, 25ff).
12, 16: *What share have we in David:* even in David's time the northern tribes seemed ready to withdraw from Judah (2 Sm 20, 1). The unreasonable

attitude of Rehoboam toward them intensified the discontent caused by the oppression of Solomon (v 4) and thus precipitated the establishment of a rival monarchy (v 20).

Solomon, king of Judah, and to the house of Judah and to Benjamin, and to the rest of the people: 24 'Thus says the LORD: You must not march out to fight against your brother Israelites. Let every man return home, for I have brought this about.'" They accepted this message of the LORD and gave up the expedition accordingly.

25 Jeroboam built up Shechem in the hill country of Ephraim and lived there. Then he left it and built up Penuel.

Religious Rebellion

26 Jeroboam thought to himself: "The kingdom will return to David's house. 27 If now this people go up to offer sacrifices in the temple of the LORD in Jerusalem, the hearts of this people will return to their master, Rehoboam, king of Judah, and they will kill me." 28 After taking counsel, the king made two calves of gold and said to the people: "You have been going up to Jerusalem long enough. Here is your God, O Israel, who brought you up from the land of Egypt." 29 And he put one in Bethel, the other in Dan. 30 This led to sin, because the people frequented these calves in Bethel and in Dan. 31 He also built temples on the high places and made priests from among the people who were not Levites. 32 Jeroboam established a feast in the eighth month on the fifteenth day of the month to duplicate in Bethel the pilgrimage feast of Judah, with sacrifices to the calves he had made; and he stationed in Bethel priests of the high places he had built.

Message of the Prophet from Judah

33 Jeroboam ascended the altar he built in Bethel on the fifteenth day of the eighth month, the month in which he arbitrarily chose to establish a feast for the Israelites; he was going **13** to offer sacrifice. 1 A man of God came from Judah to Bethel by the word of the LORD, while

Jeroboam was standing at the altar to offer sacrifice. 2 He cried out against the altar the word of the LORD: "O altar, altar, the LORD says, 'A child shall be born to the house of David, Josiah by name, who shall slaughter upon you the priests of the high places who offer sacrifice upon you, and he shall burn human bones upon you.'" 3 He gave a sign that same day and said: "This is the sign that the LORD has spoken: The altar shall break up and the ashes on it shall be strewn about."

4 When King Jeroboam heard what the man of God was crying out against the altar, he stretched forth his hand from the altar and said, "Seize him!" But the hand he stretched forth against him withered, so that he could not draw it back. 5 Moreover, the altar broke up and the ashes from it were strewn about—the sign the man of God had given as the word of the LORD. 6 Then the king appealed to the man of God. "Entreat the LORD, your God," he said, "and intercede for me that I may be able to withdraw my hand." So the man of God entreated the LORD, and the king recovered the normal use of his hand. 7 "Come home with me for some refreshment," the king invited the man of God, "and I will give you a present." 8 "If you gave me half your kingdom," the man of God said to the king, "I would not go with you, nor eat bread or drink water in this place. 9 For I was instructed by the word of the LORD not to eat bread or drink water and not to return by the way I came." 10 So he departed by another road and did not go back the way he had come to Bethel.

11 There was an old prophet living in the city, whose sons came and told him all that the man of God had done that day in Bethel. When they repeated to their father the words he had spoken to the king, 12 the father asked them, "Which way did he go?" And his sons pointed out to him the road taken by the man of God who had come from Judah. 13

Then he said to his sons, "Saddle the ass for me." 14 When they had saddled it, he mounted and followed the man of God, who he found seated under a terebinth. When he asked him, "Are you the man of God who came from Judah?" he answered, "Yes." 15 Then he said, "Come home with me and have some bread." 16 "I cannot go back with you, and I cannot eat bread or drink water with you in this place," he answered, 17 "for I was told by the word of the LORD neither to eat bread nor drink water here, and not to go back the way I came." 18 but he said to him, "I, too, am a prophet like you, and an angel told me in the word of the LORD to bring you back with me to my house and to have you eat bread and drink water." He was lying to him, however.

19 So he went back with him, and ate bread and drank water in his house. 20 But while they were sitting at table, the LORD spoke to the prophet who had brought him back, 21 and he cried out to the man of God who had come from Judah: "The LORD says, 'Because you rebelled against the command of the LORD and did not keep the command which the LORD, your God, gave you, 22 but returned and ate bread and drank water in the place where he told you to do neither, your corpse shall not be brought to the grave of your ancestors.'"

23 After he had eaten bread and drunk water, the ass was saddled for him, and he again 24 set out. But a lion met him on the road, and killed him. His corpse lay sprawled on the road, and the ass remained standing by it, and so did the lion. 25 Some passers-by saw the body lying in the road, with the lion standing beside it, and carried the news to the city where the old prophet lived. 26 On hearing it, the prophet who had brought him back from his journey said: "It is the man of God who rebelled against the command of the LORD. He has delivered him to a lion, which mangled and killed him, as the LORD

12, 26–32: *Jeroboam* feared reunification of the divided kingdom through worship in the single temple in Jerusalem. To prevent this he encouraged shrines on the high places, and appointed false priests to supplement those of levitical descent. The golden

bullocks he installed in two of his sanctuaries, though probably intended as bearers of the invisible Divine Majesty, quickly became occasions for idolatry. Thus Jeroboam caused Israel to sin, and sealed his doom and that of his royal house (13, 34; 14, 7–14).

12, 29: *Bethel* and *Dan*: at the southern and northern boundaries of the separate kingdom of Israel, where sanctuaries had existed in the past (Gn 12, 8; 13, 3; 18, 10–22; 25, 1–16; Jgs 18, 1–31).

predicted to him." 27 Then he said to his sons, "Saddle the ass for me." When they had saddled it, 28 he went off and found the body lying in the road with the ass and the lion standing beside it. The lion had not eaten the body nor had it harmed the ass. 29 The prophet lifted up the body of the man of God and put it on the ass, and brought it back to the city to mourn over it and to bury it. 30 He laid the man's body in his own grave, and they mourned over it: "Alas, my brother!" 31 After he had buried him, he said to his sons, "When I die, bury me in the grave where the man of God is buried. Lay my remains beside his. 32 For the word of the LORD which he proclaimed against the altar in Bethel and against all the shrines on the high places in the cities of Samaria shall certainly come to pass."

33 Jeroboam did not give up his evil ways after this event, but again made priests for the high places from among the common people. Whoever desired it was consecrated and became a priest of the high places. 34 This was a sin on the part of the house of Jeroboam for which it was to be cut off and destroyed from the earth.

Death of Abijah

14 At that time Abijah, son of Jeroboam, took sick. 2 So Jeroboam said to his wife, "Get ready and disguise yourself so that none will recognize you as Jeroboam's wife. Then go to Shiloh, where you will find the prophet Ahijah. It was he who predicted my reign over this people. 3 Take along ten loaves, some cakes, and a jar of preserves, and go to him. He will tell you what will happen to the child." 4 The wife of Jeroboam obeyed. She made the journey to Shiloh and entered the house of Ahijah who could not see because age had dimmed his sight.

5 The LORD had said to Ahijah: "Jeroboam's wife is coming to consult you about her son, for he is sick. This is what you must tell her. When she comes, she will be in disguise."

6 So Ahijah, hearing the sound of her footsteps as she entered the door, said, "Come in, wife of Jeroboam. Why are you in disguise? I have been commissioned to give you bitter news. 7 Go, tell Jeroboam, 'This is what the LORD, the God of Israel, says: I exalted you from among the people and made you ruler of my people Israel. 8 I deprived the house of David of the kingdom and gave it to you. Yet you have not been like my servant David, who kept my commandments and followed me with his whole heart, doing only what pleased me. 9 You have done worse than all who preceded you: you have gone and made for yourself strange gods and molten images to provoke me; but me you have cast behind your back. 10 Therefore, I am bringing evil upon the house of Jeroboam: I will cut off every male in Jeroboam's line, whether slave or freeman in Israel, and will burn up the house of Jeroboam completely, as though dung were being burned. 11 When one of Jeroboam's line dies in the city, dogs will devour him; when one of them dies in the field, he will be devoured by the birds of the sky. For the LORD has spoken!' 12 So leave; go home! As you step inside the city, the child will die, 13 and all Israel will mourn him and bury him, for he alone of Jeroboam's line will be laid in the grave, since in him alone of Jeroboam's house has something pleasing to the LORD, the God of Israel, been found. 14 Today, at this very moment, the LORD will raise up for himself a king of Israel who will destroy the house of Jeroboam. 15 The LORD will stroke Israel like a reed tossed about in the water and will pluck out Israel from this good land which he gave their fathers, scattering them beyond the River, because they made sacred poles for themselves and thus provoked the LORD. 16 He will give up Israel because of the sins Jeroboam has committed and caused Israel to commit."

17 So Jeroboam's wife started back; when she reached Tirzah and crossed the threshold of her house, the child died. 18 He was buried with all Israel mourning him, as the LORD had prophesied through his servant the prophet Ahijah.

19 The rest of the acts of Jeroboam, with his warfare and his reign, are recorded in the book of the chronicles of the kings of Israel. 20 The length of Jeroboam's reign was twenty-two years. He rested with his ancestors, and his son Nadab succeeded him as king.

Reign of Rehoboam

21 Rehoboam, son of Solomon, reigned in Judah. He was forty-one years old when he became king, and he reigned seventeen years in Jerusalem, the city in which, out of all the tribes of Israel, the LORD chose to be honored. His mother was the Ammonite named Naamah.

22 Judah did evil in the sight of the LORD, and by their sins angered him even more than their fathers had done. 23 They, too, built for themselves high places, pillars, and sacred poles, upon every hill and under every green tree. 24 There were also cult prostitutes in the land. Judah imitated all the abominable practices of the nations whom the LORD had cleared out of the Israelites' way.

25 In the fifth year of King Rehoboam, Shishak, king of Egypt, attacked Jerusalem. 26 He took everything, including the treasures of the temple of the LORD and those of the royal palace, as well as all the gold shields made under Solomon. 27 To replace them, King Rehoboam had bronze shields made, which he entrusted to the officers of the guard on duty at the entrance of the royal palace. 28 Whenever the king visited the temple of the LORD, those on duty would carry the shields, and then return them to the guardroom.

29 The rest of the acts of Rehoboam, with all that he did, are recorded in the book of the chronicles of the kings of Judah. 30 There was constant warfare between Rehoboam and Jeroboam. 31 Rehoboam rested with his ancestors; he was buried

---

14, 25: *In the fifth year . . . Shishak, king of Egypt, attacked Jerusalem:* c. 926 B.C. According to 2 Chr 12, 1–12, the repentance of King Rehoboam and of the princes of Israel after the warning of the prophet

Shemaiah diverted the actual attack on Jerusalem. Shishak, however, *carried off the treasures of the temple of the Lord and of the king's palace* (2 Chr 12, 9). A bas-relief of this Pharaoh in the temple of

Amon at Karnak commemorates his conquest of some hundred and fifty Palestinian and Trans-Jordanian cities and towns.

with them in the City of David. His mother was the Ammonite named Naamah. His son Abijam succeeded him as king.

Reign of Abijam

15 In the eighteenth year of King Jeroboam, son of Nebat, Abijam became king of Judah; 2 he reigned three years in Jerusalem. His mother's name was Maacah, daughter of Abishalom. 3 He imitated all the sins his father had committed before him, and his heart was not entirely with the LORD, his God, like the heart of his grandfather David. 4 Yet for David's sake the LORD, his God, gave him a lamp in Jerusalem, raising up his son after him and permitting Jerusalem to endure; 5 because David had pleased the LORD and did not disobey any of his commands as long as he lived, except in the case of Uriah the Hittite.

7 The rest of Abijam's acts, with all that he did, are written in the book of the chronicles of the kings of Judah. 6 There was war between Abijam and Jeroboam. 8 Abijam rested with his ancestors; he was buried in the City of David, and his son Asa succeeded him as king.

Reign of Asa

9 In the twentieth year of Jeroboam, king of Israel, Asa, king of Judah, began to reign; 10 he reigned forty-one years in Jerusalem. His grandmother's name was Maacah, daughter of Abishalom. 11 Asa pleased the LORD like his forefather David, 12 banishing the temple prostitutes from the land and removing all the idols his father had made. 13 He also deposed his grandmother Maacah from her position as queen mother, because she had made an outrageous object for Asherah. Asa cut down this object and burned it in the Kidron Valley. 14 The high places did not disappear; yet Asa's heart was entirely with the LORD as long as he lived. 15 He brought into the temple of the LORD his father's and his own votive

offerings of silver, gold, and various utensils.

16 There was war between Asa and Baasha, king of Israel, as long as they both reigned. 17 Baasha, king of Israel, attacked Judah and fortified Ramah to prevent communication with Asa, king of Judah. 18 Asa then took all the silver and gold remaining in the treasuries of the temple of the LORD and of the royal palace. Entrusting them to his ministers, King Asa sent them to Ben-hadad, son of Tabrimmon, son of Hezion, king of Aram, resident in Damascus. He said: 19 "There is a treaty between you and me, as there was between your father and my father. I am sending you a present of silver and gold. Go, break your treaty with Baasha, king of Israel, that he may withdraw from me." 20 Ben-hadad agreed with King Asa and sent the leaders of his troops against the cities of Israel. They attacked Ijon, Dan, Abel-beth-maacah, and all Chinnereth, besides all the land of Naphtali. 21 When Baasha heard of it, he left off fortifying Ramah, and stayed in Tirzah. 22 Then King Asa summoned all Judah without exception, and they carried away the stones and beams with which Baasha was fortifying Ramah. With them King Asa built Geba of Benjamin and Mizpeh.

23 The rest of the acts of Asa, with all his valor and accomplishments, and the cities he built, are written in the book of the chronicles of the kings of Judah. In his old age, Asa had an infirmity in his feet. 24 He rested with his ancestors; he was buried in his forefather's City of David, and his son Jehoshaphat succeeded him as king.

Reign of Nadab

25 In the second year of Asa, king of Judah, Nadab, son of Jeroboam, became king of Israel; he reigned over Israel two years. 26 He did evil in the LORD's sight, imitating his father's conduct and the sin which he had caused Israel to commit. 27 Baasha, son of Ahijah, of the house of Issachar, plotted against him and struck him down at Gibbethon of the Philistines, which Nadab and all Israel were besieging. 28 Baasha

killed him in the third year of Asa, king of Judah, and reigned in his stead. 29 Once he was king, he killed off the entire house of Jeroboam, not leaving a single soul to Jeroboam but destroying him utterly, according to the warning which the LORD had pronounced through his servant, Ahijah the Shilonite, 30 because of the sins Jeroboam committed and caused Israel to commit, by which he provoked the LORD, the God of Israel, to anger.

31 The rest of the acts of Nadab, with all that he did, are written in the book of the chronicles of the kings of Israel. 32 [There was war between Asa and Baasha, king of Israel, as long as they lived.]

Reign of Baasha

33 In the third year of Asa, king of Judah, Baasha, son of Ahijah, began his twenty-four-year reign over Israel in Tirzah. 34 He did evil in the LORD's sight, imitating the conduct of Jeroboam and the sin he had caused Israel to commit.

16 The LORD spoke against Baasha to Jehu, son of Hanani, and said: 2 "Inasmuch as I lifted you up from the dust and made you ruler of my people Israel, but you have imitated the conduct of Jeroboam and have caused my people Israel to sin, provoking me to anger by their sins, 3 I will destroy you, Baasha, and your house; 4 I will make your house like that of Jeroboam, son of Nebat. If anyone of Baasha's line dies in the city, dogs shall devour him; if he dies in the field, he shall be devoured by the birds of the sky."

5 The rest of the acts of Baasha, with all his valor and accomplishments, are written in the book of the chronicles of the kings of Israel. 6 Baasha rested with his ancestors; he was buried in Tirzah, and his son Elah succeeded him as king. 7 [Through the prophet Jehu, son of Hanani, the LORD had threatened Baasha and his house, because of all the evil Baasha did in the sight of the LORD, provoking him to anger by his evil deeds, so that he became like the house of Jeroboam; and because he killed Nadab.]

15, 18: *Ben-hadad . . . king of Aram:* Ben-hadad I, third successor of Rezon, who had thrown off the yoke of the Israelites during the reign of Solomon and become king of Aram (11, 23f).

Reign of Elah

8 In the twenty-sixth year of Asa, king of Judah, Elah, son of Baasha, began his two-year reign over Israel in Tirzah. 9 His servant Zimri, commander of half his chariots, plotted against him. As he was in Tirzah, drinking to excess in the house of Azra, superintendent of his palace in Tirzah, 10 Zimri entered; he struck and killed him in the twenty-seventh year of Asa, king of Judah, and reigned in his place. 11 Once he was seated on the royal throne, he killed off the whole house of Baasha, not sparing a single male relative or friend of his. 12 Zimri destroyed the entire house of Baasha, as the LORD had prophesied to Baasha through the prophet Jehu, 13 because of all the sins which Baasha and his son Elah committed and caused Israel to commit, provoking the LORD, the God of Israel, to anger by their idols.

14 The rest of the acts of Elah, with all that he did, are written in the book of the chronicles of the kings of Israel.

Reign of Zimri

15 In the twenty-seventh year of Asa, king of Judah, Zimri reigned seven days in Tirzah. The army was besieging Gibbethon of the Philistines 16 when they heard that Zimri had formed a conspiracy and had killed the king. So that day in the camp all Israel proclaimed Omri, general of the army, king of Israel. 17 Omri marched up from Gibbethon, accompanied by all Israel, and laid siege to Tirzah. 18 When Zimri saw the city was captured, he entered the citadel of the royal palace and burned down the palace over him. He died 19 because of the sins he had committed, doing evil in the sight of the LORD by imitating the sinful conduct of Jeroboam, thus causing Israel to sin.

20 The rest of the acts of Zimri, with the conspiracy he carried out, are written in the book of the chronicles of the kings of Israel.

21 At that time the people of Israel were divided, half following Tibni, son of Ginath, to make him king, and half for Omri. 22 The partisans of Omri prevailed over those of Tibni, son of Ginath. Tibni died and Omri became king.

Reign of Omri

23 In the thirty-first year of Asa, king of Judah, Omri became king; he reigned over Israel twelve years, the first six of them in Tirzah. 24 He then bought the hill of Samaria from Shemer for two silver talents and built upon the hill, naming the city he built Samaria after Shemer, the former owner. 25 But Omri did evil in the LORD's sight beyond any of his predecessors. 26 He closely imitated the sinful conduct of Jeroboam, son of Nebat, causing Israel to sin and to provoke the LORD, the God of Israel, to anger by their idols.

27 The rest of the acts of Omri, with all his valor and accomplishments, are written in the book of the chronicles of the kings of Israel. 28 Omri rested with his ancestors, he was buried in Samaria, and his son Ahab succeeded him as king.

Reign of Ahab

29 In the thirty-eighth year of Asa, king of Judah, Ahab, son of Omri, became king of Israel; he reigned over Israel in Samaria for twenty-two years. 30 Ahab, son of Omri, did evil in the sight of the LORD more than any of his predecessors. 31 It was not enough for him to imitate the sins of Jeroboam, son of Nebat. He even married Jezebel, daughter of Ethbaal, king of the Sidonians, and went over to the veneration and worship of Baal. 32 Ahab erected an altar to Baal in the temple of Baal which he built in Samaria, 33 and also made a sacred pole. He did more to anger the LORD, the God of Israel, than any of the kings of Israel before him.

34 During his reign, Hiel from Bethel rebuilt Jericho. He lost his first-born son, Abiram, when he laid the foundation, and his youngest son, Segub, when he set up the gates, as the LORD had foretold through Joshua, son of Nun.

STORIES OF THE PROPHETS

Drought Predicted by Elijah

17 Elijah the Tishbite, from Tishbe in Gilead, said to Ahab: "As the LORD, the God of Israel, lives, whom I serve, during these years there shall be no dew or rain except at my word." 2 The LORD then said to Elijah: 3 "Leave here, go east and hide in the Wadi Cherith, east of the Jordan. 4 You shall drink of the stream, and I have commanded ravens to feed you there." 5 So he left and did as the LORD had commanded. He went and remained by the Wadi Cherith, east of the Jordan. 6 Ravens brought him bread and meat in the morning, and bread and meat in the evening, and he drank from the stream.

Elijah and the Widow

7 After some time, however, the brook ran dry, because no rain had fallen in the land. 8 So the LORD said to him: 9 "Move on to Zarephath of Sidon and stay there. I have designated a widow there to provide for you." 10 He left and went to Zarephath. As he arrived at the entrance of the city, a widow was gathering sticks there; he called out to her, "Please bring me a small cupful of water to drink." 11 She left to get it, and he called out after her, "Please bring along a bit of bread." 12 "As the LORD, your God, lives," she answered, "I have nothing baked; there is only a handful of flour in my jar and a little oil in my jug. Just now I was collecting a couple of sticks to go in and prepare something for myself and my son; when we have eaten it, we shall die." 13 "Do not be afraid," Elijah said to her. "Go and do as you propose. But first make me a little cake and bring it to me. Then you can prepare something for yourself and your son. 14 For the LORD, the God of Israel, says, 'The jar of flour shall not go empty, nor

17, 1: *Elijah the Tishbite:* one of the most important figures in Old Testament history. As his name indicates ("Yahweh is my God"), Elijah was the successful leader in the struggle to preserve the knowledge and worship of Yahweh against the encroaching worship of Baal introduced into Israel by Jezebel, the Tyrian wife of Ahab. The Elijah cycle of narratives includes, besides the above struggle, miracle stories, denunciations of kings, and a preparation for the prophet's role as eschatological forerunner of the "great day of the Lord"; cf Mal 3, 23–24; Mt 17; 10–13; Lk 1, 17.

the jug of oil run dry, until the day when the LORD sends rain upon the earth.'" 15 She left and did as Elijah had said. She was able to eat for a year, and he and her son as well; 16 the jar of flour did not go empty, nor the jug of oil run dry, as the LORD had foretold through Elijah.

17 Some time later the son of the mistress of the house fell sick, and his sickness grew more severe until he stopped breathing. 18 So she said to Elijah, "Why have you done this to me, O man of God? Have you come to me to call attention to my guilt and to kill my son?" 19 "Give me your son," Elijah said to her. Taking him from her lap, he carried him to the upper room where he was staying, and laid him on his own bed. 20 He called out to the LORD: "O LORD, my God, will you afflict even the widow with whom I am staying by killing her son?" 21 Then he stretched himself out upon the child three times and called out to the LORD: "O LORD, my God, let the life breath return to the body of this child." 22 The LORD heard the prayer of Elijah; the life breath returned to the child's body and he revived. 23 Taking the child, Elijah brought him down into the house from the upper room and gave him to his mother. "See!" Elijah said to her, "your son is alive." 24 "Now indeed I know that you are a man of God," the woman replied to Elijah. "The word of the LORD comes truly from your mouth."

Elijah and the Prophets of Baal

18 Long afterward, in the third year, the LORD spoke to Elijah. "Go, present yourself to Ahab," he said, "that I may send rain upon the earth." 2 So Elijah went to present himself to Ahab.

3 Now the famine in Samaria was bitter, 4 and Ahab had summoned Obadiah, his vizier, who was a zealous follower of the LORD. When Jezebel was murdering the prophets of the LORD, Obadiah took a hundred prophets, hid them away fifty each in two caves, and supplied them with food and drink. 5 Ahab said to Obadiah, "Come, let us go through the land to all sources of

water and to all the streams. We may find grass and save the horses and mules, so that we shall not have to slaughter any of the beasts." 6 Dividing the land to explore between them, Ahab went one way by himself, Obadiah another way by himself.

7 As Obadiah was on his way, Elijah met him. Recognizing him, Obadiah fell prostrate and asked, "Is it you, my lord Elijah?" 8 "Yes," he answered. "Go tell your master, 'Elijah is here!'" 9 But Obadiah said, "What sin have I committed, that you are handing me over to Ahab to have me killed? 10 As the LORD, your God, lives, there is no nation or kingdom where my master has not sent in search of you. When they replied, 'He is not here,' he made each kingdom and nation swear they could not find you. 11 And now you say, 'Go tell your master: Elijah is here!' 12 After I leave you, the spirit of the LORD will carry you to some place I do not know, and when I go to inform Ahab and he does not find you, he will kill me. Your servant has revered the LORD from his youth. 13 Have you not been told, my lord, what I did when Jezebel was murdering the prophets of the LORD—that I hid a hundred of the prophets of the LORD, fifty each in two caves, and supplied them with food and drink? 14 And now you say, 'Go tell your master: Elijah is here!' He will kill me!" 15 Elijah answered, "As the LORD of hosts lives, whom I serve, I will present myself to him today."

16 So Obadiah went to meet Ahab and informed him. Ahab came to meet Elijah, 17 and when he saw Elijah, said to him, "Is it you, you disturber of Israel?" 18 "It is not I who disturb Israel," he answered, "but you and your family, by forsaking the commands of the LORD and following the Baals. 19 Now summon all Israel to me on Mount Carmel, as well as the four hundred and fifty prophets of Baal and the four hundred prophets of Asherah who eat at Jezebel's table." 20 So Ahab sent to all the Israelites and had the prophets assemble on Mount Carmel.

21 Elijah appealed to all the people and said, "How long will you

straddle the issue? If the LORD is God, follow him; if Baal, follow him." The people, however, did not answer him. 22 So Elijah said to the people, "I am the only surviving prophet of the LORD, and there are four hundred and fifty prophets of Baal. 23 Give us two young bulls. Let them choose one, cut it into pieces, and place it on the wood, but start no fire. I shall prepare the other and place it on the wood, but shall start no fire. 24 You shall call on your gods, and I will call on the LORD. The God who answers with fire is God." All the people answered, "Agreed!"

25 Elijah then said to the prophets of Baal, "Choose one young bull and prepare it first, for there are more of you. Call upon your gods, but do not start the fire." 26 Taking the young bull that was turned over to them, they prepared it and called on Baal from morning to noon, saying, "Answer us, Baal!" But there was no sound, and no one answering. And they hopped around the altar they had prepared. 27 When it was noon, Elijah taunted them: "Call louder, for he is a god and may be meditating, or may have retired, or may be on a journey. Perhaps he is asleep and must be awakened." 28 They called out louder and slashed themselves with swords and spears, as was their custom, until blood gushed over them. 29 Noon passed and they remained in a prophetic state until the time for offering sacrifice. But there was not a sound: no one answered, and no one was listening.

30 Then Elijah said to all the people, "Come here to me." When they had done so, he repaired the altar of the LORD which had been destroyed. 31 He took twelve stones, for the number of tribes of the sons of Jacob, to whom the LORD had said, "Your name shall be Israel." 32 He built an altar in honor of the LORD with the stones, and made a trench around the altar large enough for two seahs of grain. 33 When he had arranged the wood, he cut up the young bull and laid it on the wood. 34 "Fill four jars with water," he said, "and pour it over the holocaust and over the wood." "Do it again,"

he said, and they did it again. "Do it a third time," he said, and they did it a third time. 35 The water flowed around the altar, and the trench was filled with the water.

36 At the time for offering sacrifice, the prophet Elijah came forward and said, "LORD, God of Abraham, Isaac, and Israel, let it be known this day that you are God in Israel and that I am your servant and have done all these things by your command. 37 Answer me, LORD! Answer me, that this people may know that you, LORD, are God and that you have brought them back to their senses." 38 The LORD's fire came down and consumed the holocaust, wood, stones, and dust, and it lapped up the water in the trench. 39 Seeing this, all the people fell prostrate and said, "The LORD is God! The LORD is God!" 40 Then Elijah said to them, "Seize the prophets of Baal. Let none of them escape!" They were seized, and Elijah had them brought down to the brook Kishon and there he slit their throats.

41 Elijah then said to Ahab, "Go up, eat and drink, for there is the sound of a heavy rain." 42 So Ahab went up to eat and drink, while Elijah climbed to the top of Carmel, crouched down to the earth, and put his head between his knees. 43 "Climb up and look out to sea," he directed his servant, who went up and looked, but reported, "There is nothing," Seven times he said, "Go, look again!" 44 And the seventh time the youth reported, "There is a cloud as small as a man's hand rising from the sea." Elijah said, "Go and say to Ahab, 'Harness up and leave the mountain before the rain stops you.'" 45 In a trice, the sky grew dark with clouds and wind, and a heavy rain fell. Ahab mounted his chariot and made for Jezreel. 46 But the hand of the LORD was on Elijah, who girded up his clothing and ran before Ahab as far as the approaches to Jezreel.

Flight to Horeb

19 Ahab told Jezebel all that Elijah had done—that he had put all the prophets to the sword. 2 Jezebel then sent a messenger to Elijah and said, "May the gods do thus and so to me if by this time tomorrow I have not done with your life what was done to each of them." 3 Elijah was afraid and fled for his life, going to Beer-sheba of Judah. He left his servant there 4 and went a day's journey into the desert, until he came to a broom tree and sat beneath it. He prayed for death: "This is enough, O LORD! Take my life, for I am no better than my fathers." 5 He lay down and fell asleep under the broom tree, but then an angel touched him and ordered him to get up and eat. 6 He looked and there at his head was a hearth cake and a jug of water. After he ate and drank, he lay down again, 7 but the angel of the LORD came back a second time, touched him, and ordered, "Get up and eat, else the journey will be too long for you!" 8 He got up, ate and drank; then strengthened by that food, he walked forty days and forty nights to the mountain of God, Horeb.

9 There he came to a cave, where he took shelter. But the word of the LORD came to him, "Why are you here, Elijah?" 10 He answered: "I have been most zealous for the LORD, the God of hosts, but the Israelites have forsaken your covenant, torn down your altars, and put your prophets to the sword. I alone am left, and they seek to take my life." 11 Then the LORD said, "Go outside and stand on the mountain before the LORD; the LORD will be passing by." A strong and heavy wind was rending the mountains and crushing rocks before the LORD—but the LORD was not in the wind. After the wind there was an earthquake—but the LORD was not in the earthquake. 12 After the earthquake there was fire—but the

LORD was not in the fire. After the fire there was a tiny whispering sound. 13 When he heard this, Elijah hid his face in his cloak and went and stood at the entrance of the cave. A voice said to him, "Elijah, why are you here?" 14 He replied, "I have been most zealous for the LORD, the God of hosts. But the Israelites have forsaken your covenant, torn down your altars, and put your prophets to the sword. I alone am left, and they seek to take my life." 15 "Go, take the road back to the desert near Damascus," the LORD said to him. "When you arrive, you shall anoint Hazael as king of Aram. 16 Then you shall anoint Jehu, son of Nimshi, as king of Israel, and Elisha, son of Shaphat of Abel-meholah, as prophet to succeed you. 17 If anyone escapes the sword of Hazael, Jehu will kill him. If he escapes the sword of Jehu, Elisha will kill him. Yet I will leave seven thousand men in Israel— 18 all those who have not knelt to Baal or kissed him."

Call of Elisha

19 Elijah set out, and came upon Elisha, son of Shaphat, as he was plowing with twelve yoke of oxen; he was following the twelfth. Elijah went over to him and threw his cloak over him. 20 Elisha left the oxen, ran after Elijah, and said, "Please, let me kiss my father and mother goodbye, and I will follow you." "Go back!" Elijah answered. "Have I done anything to you?" 21 Elisha left him and, taking the yoke of oxen, slaughtered them; he used the plowing equipment for fuel to boil their flesh, and gave it to his people to eat. Then he left and followed Elijah as his attendant.

Ahab's Victories over Ben-hadad

20 Ben-hadad, king of Aram, gathered all his forces, and accompanied by thirty-two kings with horses and chariotry, proceeded to invest and attack Samaria. 2 He

---

19, 11ff: Compare these divine manifestations to Elijah with those to Moses (Ex 19, 1–23; 33, 21ff; 34, 5) on the same Mount Horeb (Sinai) (Dt 4, 10–15). Though various phenomena, such as wind, storms, earthquakes, fire (Ex 19, 18f), herald the divine presence, they do not constitute the presence itself which, like the *tiny whispering sound*, is imperceptible and bespeaks the spirituality of God. It was fitting that Elijah, whose mission it was to re-establish the

covenant and restore the pure faith, should have returned to Horeb where the covenant was revealed to Moses and through him to the Israelite people (Ex 3, 1–4.17; 33, 18–34, 9). Moses and Elijah appeared with Christ at the time of his transfiguration (Mt 17, 1–9; Mk 9, 1–7; Lk 9, 28–36).

19, 15–17: Elijah himself carried out only the third of the commissions entrusted to him (vv 19–21); Elisha was deputed to perform the first in person

(2 Kgs 8, 7–19), and the second through one of his followers (2 Kgs 9, 1–10).

19, 19–21: Elijah's act of throwing his mantle over the shoulders of Elisha expressed the divine call to share the prophetic mission. Elisha's prompt response through destruction of his plow and oxen is an example of total obedience and detachment from his former manner of living in order to promote the glory of God.

sent couriers to Ahab, king of Israel, within the city, 3 and said to him, "This is Ben-hadad's message: 'Your silver and gold are mine, and your wives and your promising sons are mine.'" 4 The king of Israel answered, "As you say, my lord king, I and all I have are yours." 5 But the couriers came again and said, "This is Ben-hadad's message: 'I sent you word to give me your silver and gold, your wives and your sons. 6 Now, however, at this time tomorrow I will send my servants to you, and they shall ransack your house and the houses of your servants. They shall seize and take away whatever they consider valuable.'"

7 The king of Israel then summoned all the elders of the land and said: "Understand clearly that this man wants to ruin us. When he sent to me for my wives and sons, my silver and my gold, I did not refuse him." 8 All the elders and all the people said to him, "Do not listen. Do not give in." 9 Accordingly he directed the couriers of Ben-hadad, "Say to my lord the king, 'I will do all that you demanded of your servant the first time. But this I cannot do.'" The couriers left and reported this. 10 Ben-hadad then sent him the message, "May the gods do thus and so to me if there is enough dust in Samaria to make handfuls for all my followers." 11 The king of Israel replied, "Tell him, 'It is not for the man who is buckling his armor to boast as though he were taking it off.'" 12 Ben-hadad was drinking in the pavilions with the kings when he heard this reply. "Prepare the assault," he commanded his servants; and they made ready to storm the city.

13 Then a prophet came up to Ahab, king of Israel, and said: "The LORD says, 'Do you see all this huge army? When I deliver it up to you today, you will know that I am the LORD.'" 14 But Ahab asked, "Through whom will it be delivered up?" He answered, "The LORD says, 'Through the retainers of the governors of the provinces.'" Then Ahab asked, "Who is to attack?" He replied, "You are." 15 So Ahab

called up the retainers of the governors of the provinces, two hundred thirty-two of them. Behind them he mustered all the Israelite soldiery, who numbered seven thousand. 16 They marched out at noon, while Ben-hadad was drinking heavily in the pavilion with the thirty-two kings who were his allies. 17 When the retainers of the governors of the provinces marched out first, Ben-hadad received word that some men had marched out of Samaria. 18 He answered, "Whether they have come out for peace or for war, in any case take them alive." 19 But when these had come out of the city—the soldiers of the governors of the provinces with the army following them —20 each of them struck down his man. The Arameans fled with Israel pursuing them, while Ben-hadad, king of Aram, escaped on a chariot steed. 21 The king of Israel went out, took the horses and chariots, and inflicted a severe defeat on Aram.

22 Then the prophet went up to the king of Israel and said to him: "Go, regroup your forces. Mark well what you do, for at the beginning of the year the king of Aram will attack you." 23 On the other hand, the servants of the king of Aram said to him: "Their gods are gods of mountains. That is why they defeated us. But if we fight them on level ground, we shall be sure to defeat them. 24 This is what you must do: Take the kings from their posts and put prefects in their places. 25 Mobilize an army as large as the army that has deserted you, horse for horse, chariot for chariot. Let us fight them on level ground, and we shall surely defeat them." He took their advice and did this.

26 At the beginning of the year, Ben-hadad mobilized Aram and went up to Aphek to fight against Israel. 27 The Israelites, too, were called to arms and supplied with provisions; then they went out to engage the foe. The Israelites, encamped opposite them, seemed like a couple of small flocks of goats, while Aram covered the countryside. 28 A man of God came up and said to the king of Israel: "The LORD says, 'Because Aram has said the LORD is a god of mountains, not a god of plains, I will

deliver up to you all this large army, that you may know I am the LORD.'" 29 They were encamped opposite each other for seven days. On the seventh day battle was joined, and the Israelites struck down one hundred thousand foot soldiers of Aram in one day. 30 The survivors, twenty-seven thousand of them, fled into the city of Aphek, and there the wall collapsed. Ben-hadad, too, fled, and took refuge within the city, in an inside room.

31 His servants said to him: "We have heard that the kings of the land of Israel are merciful kings. Allow us, therefore, to garb ourselves in sackcloth, with cords around our heads, and go out to the king of Israel. Perhaps he will spare your life." 32 So they dressed in sackcloth girded at the waist, and wearing cords around their heads, they went to the king of Israel. "Your servant Ben-hadad pleads for his life," they said. "Is he still alive?" the king asked. "He is my brother." 33 Hearing this as a good omen, the men quickly took him at his word and said, "Ben-hadad is your brother." He answered, "Go and get him." When Ben-hadad came out to him, the king had him mount his chariot. 34 Ben-hadad said to him, "I will restore the cities which my father took from your father, and you may make yourself bazaars in Damascus, as my father did in Samaria." "On these terms," Ahab replied, "I will set you free." So he made an agreement with him and then set him free.

35 One of the guild prophets was prompted by the LORD to say to his companion, "Strike me." But he refused to strike him. 36 Then he said to him, "Since you did not obey the voice of the LORD, a lion will kill you when you leave me." When they parted company, a lion came upon him and killed him. 37 The prophet met another man and said, "Strike me." The man struck him a blow and wounded him. 38 The prophet went on and waited for the king on the road, having disguised himself with a bandage over his eyes. 39 As the king was passing, he called out to the king and said: "Your servant went into the thick of the battle, and suddenly someone turned

20, 22: *At the beginning of the year:* in the spring.

and brought me a man and said, 'Guard this man. If he is missing, you shall have to pay for his life with your life or pay out a talent of silver.' 40 But while your servant was looking here and there, the man disappeared." The king of Israel said to him. "That is your sentence. You have decided it yourself." 41 He immediately removed the bandage from his eyes, and the king of Israel recognized him as one of the prophets. 42 He said to him: "The LORD says, 'Because you have set free the man I doomed to destruction, your life shall pay for his life, your people for his people.'" 43 Disturbed and angry, the king of Israel went off homeward and entered Samaria.

Seizure of Naboth's Vineyard

21 Some time after this, as Naboth the Jezreelite had a vineyard in Jezreel next to the palace of Ahab, king of Samaria, 2 Ahab said to Naboth, "Give me your vineyard to be my vegetable garden, since it is close by, next to my house. I will give you a better vineyard in exchange, or, if you prefer, I will give you its value in money." 3 "The LORD forbid," Naboth answered him, "that I should give you my ancestral heritage." 4 Ahab went home disturbed and angry at the answer Naboth the Jezreelite had made to him: "I will not give you my ancestral heritage." Lying down on his bed, he turned away from food and would not eat.

5 His wife Jezebel came to him and said to him, "Why are you so angry that you will not eat?" 6 He answered her, "Because I spoke to Naboth the Jezreelite and said to him, 'Sell me your vineyard, or, if you prefer, I will give you a vineyard in exchange.' But he refused to let me have his vineyard." 7 "A fine ruler over Israel you are indeed!" his wife Jezebel said to him. "Get up. Eat and be cheerful. I will obtain the vineyard of Naboth the Jezreelite for you."

8 So she wrote letters in Ahab's name and, having sealed them with his seal, sent them to the elders and to the nobles who lived in the same city with Naboth. 9 This is what she wrote in the letters: "Proclaim a fast and set Naboth at the head of the people. 10 Next, get two scoundrels to face him and accuse him of having cursed God and king. Then take him out and stone him to death." 11 His fellow citizens—the elders and the nobles who dwelt in his city —did as Jezebel had ordered them in writing, through the letters she had sent them. 12 They proclaimed a fast and placed Naboth at the head of the people. 13 Two scoundrels came in and confronted him with the accusation, "Naboth has cursed God and king." And they led him out of the city and stoned him to death. 14 Then they sent the information to Jezebel that Naboth had been stoned to death.

15 When Jezebel learned that Naboth had been stoned to death, she said to Ahab, "Go on, take possession of the vineyard of Naboth the Jezreelite which he refused to sell you, because Naboth is not alive, but dead." 16 On hearing that Naboth was dead, Ahab started off on his way down to the vineyard of Naboth the Jezreelite, to take possession of it.

17 But the LORD said to Elijah the Tishbite: 18 "Start down to meet Ahab, king of Israel, who rules in Samaria. He will be in the vineyard of Naboth, of which he has come to take possession. 19 This is what you shall tell him, 'The LORD says: After murdering, do you also take possession? For this, the LORD says: In the place where the dogs licked up the blood of Naboth, the dogs shall lick up your blood, too.'" 20 "Have you found me out, my enemy?" Ahab said to Elijah. "Yes," he answered. "Because you have given yourself up to doing evil in the LORD's sight, 21 I am bringing evil upon you: I will destroy you and will cut off every male in Ahab's line, whether slave or freeman, in Israel. 22 I will make your house like that of Jeroboam, son of Nebat, and like

that of Baasha, son of Ahijah, because of how you have provoked me by leading Israel into sin." 23 (Against Jezebel, too, the LORD declared. "The dogs shall devour Jezebel in the district of Jezreel.") 24 "When one of Ahab's line dies in the city, dogs will devour him; when one of them dies in the field, the birds of the sky will devour him." 25 Indeed, no one gave himself up to the doing of evil in the sight of the LORD as did Ahab, urged on by his wife Jezebel. 26 He became completely abominable by following idols, just as the Amorites had done, whom the LORD drove out before the Israelites.

27 When Ahab heard these words, he tore his garments and put on sackcloth over his bare flesh. He fasted, slept in the sackcloth, and went about subdued. 28 Then the LORD said to Elijah the Tishbite, 29 "Have you seen that Ahab has humbled himself before me? Since he has humbled himself before me, I will not bring the evil in his time. I will bring the evil upon his house during the reign of his son."

Campaign against Ramoth-gilead

22 Three years passed without war between Aram and Israel. 2 In the third year, however, King Jehoshaphat of Judah came down to the king of Israel, 3 who said to his servants, "Do you not know that Ramoth-gilead is ours and we are doing nothing to take it from the king of Aram?" 4 He asked Jehoshaphat, "Will you come with me to fight against Ramoth-gilead?" Jehoshaphat answered the king of Israel, "You and I are as one, and your people and my people, your horses and my horses as well." 5 Jehoshaphat also said to the king of Israel, "Seek the word of the LORD at once."

6 The king of Israel gathered together the prophets, about four hundred of them, and asked, "Shall I go to attack Ramoth-gilead or shall I refrain?" "Go up," they answered.

21, 19: The response of Ahab to this divine judgment is described in v 27, and the consequences are given in vv 28–29, and in 2 Kgs 9, 21–26.

21, 20–26: In these verses the Judean editor of the Books of Kings substitutes, for the message of Elijah prepared for in v 19, a sweeping and definitive

judgment against the whole family of Ahab in the same terms as were used against the families of Jeroboam I (14, 9–11) and Baasha (16, 2–4). This judgment is the fruit of later theological reflection; it is not occasioned directly by the crime against Naboth, but by the idolatry of Ahab and Jezebel. The judgment on Jezebel

herself (v 23) may have been uttered by Elijah during the Naboth episode; it finds its fulfillment in 2 Kgs 9, 36–37. Still another theological explanation for the death of Ahab is given by the North Israelite writer of 20, 35–42 above.

"The Lord will deliver it over to the king." 7 But Jehoshaphat said, "Is there no other prophet of the LORD here whom we may consult?" 8 The king of Israel answered, "There is one other through whom we might consult the LORD, Micaiah, son of Imlah; but I hate him because he prophesies not good but evil about me." Jehoshaphat said, "Let not your majesty speak of evil against you."

9 So the king of Israel called an official and said to him, "Get Micaiah, son of Imlah, at once." 10 The king of Israel and King Jehoshaphat of Judah were seated, each on his throne, clothed in their robes of state on a threshing floor at the entrance of the gate of Samaria, and all the prophets were prophesying before them. 11 Zedekiah, son of Chenaanah, made himself horns of iron and said, "The LORD says, 'With these you shall gore Aram until you have destroyed them.'" 12 The other prophets prophesied in a similar vein, saying: "Go up to Ramoth-gilead; you shall succeed. The LORD will deliver it over to the king."

13 The messenger who had gone to call Micaiah said to him, "Look now, the prophets are unanimously predicting good for the king. Let your word be the same as any of theirs; predict good." 14 "As the LORD lives," Micaiah answered, "I shall say whatever the LORD tells me."

15 When he came to the king, the king said to him, "Micaiah, shall we go to fight against Ramoth-gilead, or shall we refrain?" "Go up," he answered, "you shall succeed! The LORD will deliver it over to the king." 16 But the king answered him, "How many times must I adjure you to tell me nothing but the truth in the name of the LORD?" 17 So Micaiah said:

"I see all Israel
scattered on the mountains,
like sheep without a shepherd,
and the LORD saying, 'These have
no master!
Let each of them go back home in
peace.'"

18 The king of Israel said to Jehoshaphat, "Did I not tell you he prophesies not good but evil about me?" 19 Micaiah continued: "Therefore hear the word of the LORD: I saw the LORD seated on his throne, with the whole host of heaven standing by to his right and to his left. 20 The LORD asked, 'Who will deceive Ahab, so that he will go up and fall at Ramoth-gilead?' And one said this, another that, 21 until one of the spirits came forth and presented himself to the LORD, saying, 'I will deceive him.' The LORD asked, 'How?' 22 He answered, 'I will go forth and become a lying spirit in the mouths of all his prophets.' The LORD replied, 'You shall succeed in deceiving him. Go forth and do this.' 23 So now, the LORD has put a lying spirit in the mouths of all these prophets of yours, but the LORD himself has decreed evil against you."

24 Thereupon Zedekiah, son of Chenaanah, came up and slapped Micaiah on the cheek, saying, "Has the spirit of the LORD, then, left me to speak with you?" 25 "You shall find out," Micaiah replied, "on that day when you retreat into an inside room to hide." 26 The king of Israel then said, "Seize Micaiah and take him back to Amon, prefect of the city, and to Joash, the king's son, 27 and say, 'This is the king's order: Put this man in prison and feed him scanty rations of bread and water until I return in safety.'" 28 But Micaiah said, "If ever you return in safety, the LORD has not spoken through me."

29 The king of Israel and King Jehoshaphat of Judah went up to Ramoth-gilead, 30 and the king of Israel said to Jehoshaphat, "I will disguise myself and go into battle, but you put on your own clothes." So the king of Israel disguised himself and entered the fray. 31 In the meantime the king of Aram had given his thirty-two chariot commanders the order, "Do not fight with anyone at all except the king of Israel." 32 When the chariot commanders saw Jehoshaphat, they cried

out, "That must be the king of Israel!" and shifted to fight him. But Jehoshaphat shouted his battle cry, 33 and the chariot commanders, aware that he was not the king of Israel, gave up pursuit of him. 34 Someone, however, drew his bow at random, and hit the king of Israel between the joints of his breastplate. He ordered his charioteer, "Rein about and take me out of the ranks, for I am disabled." 35 The battle grew fierce during the day, and the king, who was propped up in his chariot facing the Arameans, died in the evening. The blood from his wound flowed to the bottom of the chariot. 36 At sunset a cry went through the army, "Every man to his city, every man to his land, 37 for the king is dead!" So they went to Samaria, where they buried the king. 38 When the chariot was washed at the pool of Samaria, the dogs licked up his blood and harlots bathed there, as the LORD had prophesied.

39 The rest of the acts of Ahab, with all that he did, including the ivory palace and all the cities he built, are recorded in the book of the chronicles of the kings of Israel. 40 Ahab rested with his ancestors, and his son Ahaziah succeeded him as king.

Reign of Jehoshaphat

41 Jehoshaphat, son of Asa, began to reign over Judah in the fourth year of Ahab, king of Israel. 42 Jehoshaphat was thirty-five years old when he began to reign, and he reigned twenty-five years in Jerusalem. His mother's name was Azubah, daughter of Shilhi. 43 He followed all the ways of his father Asa unswervingly, doing what was right in the LORD's sight. 44 Nevertheless, the high places did not disappear, and the people continued to sacrifice and to burn incense on the high places. 45 Jehoshaphat also made peace with the king of Israel. 46 The rest of the acts of Jehoshaphat, with his prowess, what he did

---

22, 19–23: The prophet Micaiah uses as a last resort to deter Ahab from his foolhardy design of fighting against Ramoth-gilead the literary device of describing false prophets as messengers of a lying spirit which God, after holding counsel with his angels, permits to deceive them.

22, 28: A note in the Hebrew text after this verse attributes to Micaiah ben Imlah the first words of the book of a different Micaiah, the minor prophet of Moresheth.

and how he fought, are recorded in the book of the chronicles of the kings of Judah.

47 He removed from the land the rest of the cult prostitutes who had remained in the reign of his father Asa. 48 There was no king in Edom, but an appointed regent. 49 Jehoshaphat made Tarshish ships to go to Ophir for gold; but in fact the ships did not go, because they were wrecked at Ezion-geber. 50 Then Ahaziah, son of Ahab, said to Jehoshaphat, "Let my servants accompany your servants in the ships." But Jehoshaphat would not agree. 51 Jehoshaphat rested with his ancestors; he was buried in his forefathers' City of David. His son Jehoram succeeded him as king.

Reign of Ahaziah

52 Ahaziah, son of Ahab, began to reign over Israel in Samaria in the seventeenth year of Jehoshaphat, king of Judah; he reigned two years over Israel. 53 He did evil in the sight of the LORD, behaving like his father, his mother, and Jeroboam, son of Nebat, who caused Israel to sin. 54 He served and worshiped Baal, thus provoking the LORD, the God of Israel, just as his father had done.

22, 52: *Seventeenth year:* so the present Hebrew text. More consistent with 2 Kgs 1, 17 would be a date in the twenty-fourth year of Jehoshaphat for Ahab's death; see note on 2 Kgs 3, 1.

THE SECOND BOOK OF

Kings

THE KINGDOMS OF ISRAEL AND JUDAH

Ahaziah Consults Baalzebub

AFTER Ahab's death, Moab rebelled against Israel. 2 Ahaziah had fallen through the lattice of his roof terrace at Samaria and had been injured. So he sent out messengers with the instructions: "Go and inquire of Baalzebub, the god of Ekron, whether I shall recover from this injury."

3 Meanwhile, the angel of the LORD said to Elijah the Tishbite: "Go, intercept the messengers of Samaria's king, and ask them, 'Is it because there is no God in Israel that you are going to inquire of Baalzebub, the god of Ekron?' 4 For this, the LORD says: 'You shall not leave the bed upon which you lie; instead, you shall die.'" And with that, Elijah departed. 5 The messengers then returned to Ahaziah, who asked them, "Why have you returned?" 6 "A man came up to us," they answered, "who said to us, 'Go back to the king who sent you and tell him: The LORD says, Is it because there is no God in Israel that you are

sending to inquire of Baalzebub, the god of Ekron? For this you shall not leave the bed upon which you lie; instead, you shall die.'" 7 The king asked them, "What was the man like who came up to you and said these things to you?" 8 "Wearing a hairy garment," they replied, "with a leather girdle about his loins." "It is Elijah the Tishbite!" he exclaimed.

Death of Two Captains

9 Then the king sent a captain with his company of fifty men after Elijah. The prophet was seated on a hilltop when he found him. "Man of God," he ordered, "the king commands you to come down." 10 "If I am a man of God," Elijah answered the captain, "may fire come

down from heaven and consume you and your fifty men." And fire came down from heaven and consumed him and his fifty men. 11 Ahaziah sent another captain with his company of fifty men after Elijah. "Man of God," he called out to Elijah, "the king commands you to come down immediately." 12 "If I am a man of God," Elijah answered him, "may fire come down from heaven and consume you and your fifty men." And divine fire came down from heaven, consuming him and his fifty men.

Death of the King

13 Again, for the third time, Ahaziah sent a captain with his company of fifty men. When the third captain arrived, he fell to his

---

1, 2: *Baalzebub:* in this form, "Baal of flies." The name in the Hebrew text is a derisive alteration of Baalzebul, "Prince Baal." The best New Testament evidence supports the latter form in Mt 10, 25; Lk 11, 15. Later associations with Aramaic *beeldebaba*, "enemy," gave the ancient name its connotation of "devil."

1, 8: *Hairy garment:* a sign of ascetical and prophetic calling, imitated by John the Baptist; see Mt 3, 4; Mk 1, 6.
1, 12: *Divine fire:* literally, "fire of God," which in Hebrew sounds quite like *man of God.* The play on words is the basis for Elijah's alleged retort. This story was told among the people to enhance the

dignity of the prophet and to reflect the power of God whom he served. The mercy which God extends even to the wicked is described in Wis 11, 17—12, 22, and the prophet Elijah was well aware of it (1 Kgs 21, 28f).

knees before Elijah, pleading with him. "Man of God," he implored him, "let my life and the lives of these fifty men, your servants, count for something in your sight! 14 Already fire has come down from heaven, consuming two captains with their companies of fifty men. But now, let my life mean something to you!" 15 Then the angel of the LORD said to Elijah, "Go down with him; you need not be afraid of him."

16 So Elijah left and went down with him and stated to the king: "Thus says the LORD: 'Because you sent messengers to inquire of Baalzebub, the god of Ekron, you shall not leave the bed upon which you lie; instead you shall die.'"

17 Ahaziah died in fulfillment of the prophecy of the LORD spoken by Elijah. Since he had no son, his brother Joram succeeded him as king, in the second year of Jehoram, son of Jehoshaphat, king of Judah. 18 The rest of the acts of Ahaziah are recorded in the book of chronicles of the kings of Israel.

Elijah and Elisha

2 When the LORD was about to take Elijah up to heaven in a whirlwind, he and Elisha were on their way from Gilgal. 2 "Stay here, please," Elijah said to Elisha. "The LORD has sent me on to Bethel." "As the LORD lives, and as you yourself live," Elisha replied, "I will not leave you." So they went down to Bethel, 3 where the guild prophets went out to Elisha and asked him, "Do you know that the LORD will take your master from over you today?" "Yes, I know it," he replied. "Keep still."

4 Then Elijah said to him, "Stay here, please, Elisha, for the LORD has sent me on to Jericho." "As the LORD lives, and as you yourself live," Elisha replied, "I will not leave you."

5 They went on to Jericho, where the guild prophets approached Elisha and asked him, "Do you know that the LORD will take your master from over you today?" "Yes, I know it," he replied. "Keep still."

6 Elijah said to Elisha, "Please stay here; the LORD has sent me on to the Jordan." "As the LORD lives, and as you yourself live," Elisha replied, "I will not leave you." And so the two went on together. 7 Fifty of the guild prophets followed, and when the two stopped at the Jordan, stood facing them at a distance. 8 Elijah took his mantle, rolled it up and struck the water, which divided, and both crossed over on dry ground.

Elisha succeeds Elijah

9 When they had crossed over, Elijah said to Elisha, "Ask for whatever I may do for you, before I am taken from you." Elisha answered, "May I receive a double portion of your spirit." 10 "You have asked something that is not easy," he replied. "Still, if you see me taken up from you, your wish will be granted; otherwise not." 11 As they walked on conversing, a flaming chariot and flaming horses came between them, and Elijah went up to heaven in a whirlwind. 12 When Elisha saw it happen he cried out, "My father! my father! Israel's chariots and drivers!" But when he could no longer see him, Elisha gripped his own garment and tore it in two.

13 Then he picked up Elijah's mantle which had fallen from him, and went back and stood at the bank of the Jordan. 14 Wielding the mantle which had fallen from Elijah, he struck the water in his turn and said, "Where is the LORD, the God of Elijah?" When Elisha struck the water it divided and he crossed over.

15 The guild prophets in Jericho, who were on the other side, saw him and said, "The spirit of Elijah rests on Elisha." They went to meet him, bowing to the ground before him. 16 "Among your servants are fifty brave men," they said. "Let them go in search of your master. Perhaps the spirit of the LORD has carried him away to some mountain or some valley." "Do not send them," he answered. 17 However, they kept urging him, until he was embarrassed and said, "Send them." So they sent the fifty men, who searched for three days without finding him. 18 When they returned to Elisha in Jericho, where he was staying, he said to them, "Did I not tell you not to go?"

Healing of the Water

19 Once the inhabitants of the city complained to Elisha, "The site of the city is fine indeed, as my lord can see, but the water is bad and the land unfruitful." 20 "Bring me a new bowl," Elisha said, "and put salt into it." When they had brought it to him, 21 he went out to the spring and threw salt into it, saying, "Thus says the LORD, 'I have purified this water. Never again shall death or miscarriage spring from it.'" 22 And the water has stayed pure even to this day, just as Elisha prophesied.

The Prophet's Curse

23 From there Elisha went up to Bethel. While he was on the way, some small boys came out of the city and jeered at him. "Go up, baldhead," they shouted, "go up, baldhead!" 24 The prophet turned and saw them, and he cursed them in the name of the LORD. Then two she-bears came out of the woods and tore forty-two of the children to pieces.

25 From there he went to Mount Carmel, and thence he returned to Samaria.

1, 17: *Joram:* in the Second Book of Kings the name Joram (*yoram*), alternately Jehoram (*yehoram*), appears in numerous passages to designate both the king of Judah, son and successor of Jehoshaphat (848–841 B.C.), and the contemporary king of Israel, son of Ahab (852–841 B.C.). For the convenience of the reader in distinguishing these two kings, the longer form, Jehoram, is used to designate the king of Judah and the shorter form, Joram, to designate the king of Israel. See note on 3, 1.

2, 1: *Gilgal:* commonly identified with Jiljulieh,

about seven miles north of Bethel, and different from the Gilgal in Dt 11, 30 near Shechem, and that in Jos 4 and 5, passim, near Jericho.

2, 9: *Double portion of your spirit:* as the firstborn son inherited a double portion of his father's property (Dt 21, 17), so Elisha asks to inherit from Elijah his spirit of prophecy in the degree befitting his principal disciple. In Nm 11, 17.25, God bestows some of the spirit of Moses on others.

2, 12: *My father:* a religious title accorded prophetic leaders; cf 6, 21; 8, 9. *Israel's chariots and*

drivers: Elijah was worth more than a whole army in defending Israel and the true religion. King Joash of Israel uses the same phrase of Elisha himself (13, 14).

2, 23f: This story, like the one about Elijah and the captains (ch. 1), is preserved for us in Scripture to convey a popular understanding of the dignity of the prophet. Told in popular vein, it becomes a caricature, in which neither Elisha nor the bears behave in character. See note on 1, 12 and the contrasting narrative in ch. 4.

Campaign of Joram against Moab

3 Joram, son of Ahab, became king of Israel in Samaria [in the eighteenth year of Jehoshaphat, king of Judah, and he reigned for twelve years]. 2 He did evil in the LORD's sight, though not as much as his father and mother. He did away with the pillar of Baal, which his father had made, 3 but he still clung to the sin to which Jeroboam, son of Nebat, had lured Israel; this he did not give up.

4 Now Mesha, king of Moab, who raised sheep, used to pay the king of Israel as tribute a hundred thousand lambs and the wool of a hundred thousand rams. 5 But when Ahab died, the king of Moab had rebelled against the king of Israel. 6 Joram as king mustered all Israel, and when he set out on a campaign from Samaria, 7 he sent the king of Judah the message: "The king of Moab is in rebellion against me. Will you join me in battle against Moab?" "I will," he replied. "You and I shall be as one, your people and mine, and your horses and mine as well." 8 They discussed the route for their attack, and settled upon the route through the desert of Edom.

9 So the king of Israel set out, accompanied by the king of Judah and the king of Edom. After their roundabout journey of seven days the water gave out for the army and for the animals with them. 10 "Alas!" exclaimed the king of Israel. "The LORD has called together these three kings to put them in the grasp of Moab." 11 But the king of Judah asked, "Is there no prophet of the LORD here through whom we may inquire of the LORD?" One of the officers of the king of Israel replied, "Elisha, son of Shaphat, who poured water on the hands of Elijah, is here." 12 "He has the word of the LORD," the king of Judah agreed. So the kings of Israel, Judah, and Edom went down to Elisha. 13 What do you want with me?" Elisha asked the king of Israel. "Go to the prophets of your father and to the prophets of your mother." "No," the king of Israel replied. "The LORD has called these three kings together to put them in the grasp of Moab." 14 Then Elisha said, "As the LORD of hosts lives, whom I serve, were it not that I respect the king of Judah, I should neither look at you nor notice you at all. 15 Now get me a minstrel."

When the minstrel played, the power of the LORD came upon Elisha 16 and he announced: "Thus says the LORD, 'Provide many catch basins in this wadi.' 17 For the LORD says, 'Though you will see neither wind nor rain, yet this wadi will be filled with water for you, your livestock, and your pack animals to drink.' 18 And since the LORD does not consider this enough, he will also deliver Moab into your grasp. 19 You shall destroy every fortified city, fell every fruit tree, stop up all the springs, and ruin every fertile field with stones."

20 In the morning, at the time of the sacrifice, water came from the direction of Edom and filled the land. 21 Meanwhile, all Moab heard that the kings had come to give them battle; every man capable of bearing arms was called up and stationed at the border. 22 Early that morning, when the sun shone on the water, the Moabites saw the water at a distance as red as blood. 23 "This is blood!" they exclaimed. "The kings have fought among themselves and killed one another. Quick! To the spoils, Moabites!" 24 But when they reached the camp of Israel, the Israelites rose up and attacked the Moabites, who fled from them. They ranged through the countryside striking down the Moabites, and 25 destroying the cities; each of them cast stones onto every fertile field till they had loaded it down; all the springs they stopped up and every useful tree they felled. Finally only Kir-hareseth was left behind its stone walls, and the slingers had surrounded it and were attacking it. 26 When he saw that he was losing the battle, the king of Moab took seven hundred swordsmen to break through to the king of Aram, but he failed. 27 So he took his firstborn, his heir apparent, and offered him as a holocaust upon the wall. The wrath against Israel was so great that they gave up the siege and returned to their own land.

The Widow's Oil

4 A certain woman, the widow of one of the guild prophets, complained to Elisha: "My husband, your servant, is dead. You know that he was a God-fearing man, yet now his creditor has come to take my two children as his slaves." 2 "How can I help you?" Elisha answered her. "Tell me what you have in the house." "This servant of yours has nothing in the house but a jug of oil," she replied. 3 "Go out," he said, "borrow vessels from all your neighbors—as many empty vessels as you can. 4 Then come back and close the door on yourself and your children; pour the oil into all the vessels, and as each is filled, set it aside." 5 She went and did so, closing the door on herself and her children. As they handed her the vessels, she would pour in oil. 6 When all the vessels were filled, she said to her son, "Bring me another vessel." "There is none left," he

---

3, 1: The sequence of the reigns between Ahab and Jehu of Israel may be reconstructed as follows: Jehoshaphat of Judah outlived Ahab by a short time, so that Ahaziah of Israel was his contemporary. Jehoram of Judah succeeded his father Jehoshaphat while Ahaziah of Israel was still alive. Jehoram (Joram) of Israel became king, following his brother Ahaziah, in the second year of Jehoram of Judah (2 Kgs 1, 17); this is one datum on which the earliest Greek evidence and the standard Hebrew text are in agreement.

The two Jehorams were contemporary for much of their reigns; Jehoram of Judah was succeeded by Ahaziah something more than a year before Jehu

did away with the rulers of both kingdoms (2 Kgs 9, 1–29).

The Moabite campaign of 2 Kgs 3, 4–27 is thus best placed under the two Kings Jehoram, before the Edomite rebellion mentioned in 2 Kgs 8, 20. In the received Hebrew text, Jehoshaphat has been made the Judahite protagonist in the campaign against Moab as a tribute to his piety; this assimilates the story of 2 Kgs 3 to that of 1 Kgs 22, but creates difficulties in the chronology which the extant data leave partly unresolved. An older practice for stories of the Israelite kings was to leave them and their fellow kings without identification by name; cf 2 Kgs 6, 8–7, 20. The name of Jehoshaphat has been omitted from a number of

places in 2 Kgs 3–8, in this translation; cf 1 Kgs 22, 51.

3, 22: Red as blood: possibly caused by the red sandstone of the Wadi Zered (Dt 2, 13), south of Moab.

3, 25: Kir-hareseth: modern Kerak, east of the Dead Sea; cf Is 16, 7.11; Jer 48, 31.36.

3, 27: The wrath against Israel: probably the wrath of Chemosh, the Moabite god to whom the child was offered. He was feared by the Israelites who lost heart on foreign soil.

4, 1: His creditor . . . slaves: Hebrew law permitted the selling of wife and children as chattels for debt; cf Ex 21, 7; Am 2, 6; 8, 6; Is 50.

answered her. And then the oil stopped. 7 She went and told the man of God, who said, "Go and sell the oil to pay off your creditor; with what remains, you and your children can live."

Elisha and the Shunammite

8 One day Elisha came to Shunem, where there was a woman of influence, who urged him to dine with her. Afterward, whenever he passed by, he used to stop there to dine. 9 So she said to her husband, "I know that he is a holy man of God. Since he visits us often, 10 let us arrange a little room on the roof and furnish it for him with a bed, table, chair, and lamp, so that when he comes to us he can stay there." 11 Sometime later Elisha arrived and stayed in the room overnight. 12 Then he said to his servant Gehazi, "Call this Shunammite woman." He did so, and when she stood before Elisha, 13 he told Gehazi, "Say to her, 'You have lavished all this care on us; what can we do for you? Can we say a good word for you to the king or to the commander of the army?'" She replied, "I am living among my own people." 14 Later Elisha asked, "Can something be done for her?" "Yes!" Gehazi answered. "She has no son, and her husband is getting on in years." 15 "Call her," said Elisha. When she had been called, and stood at the door, 16 Elisha promised, "This time next year you will be fondling a baby son." "Please, my lord," she protested, "you are a man of God; do not deceive your servant." 17 Yet the woman conceived, and by the same time the following year she had given birth to a son, as Elisha promised.

18 The day came when the child was old enough to go out to his father among the reapers. 19 "My head hurts!" he complained to his father. "Carry him to his mother," the father said to a servant. 20 The servant picked him up and carried him to his mother; he stayed with her until noon, when he died in her lap. 21 The mother took him upstairs and laid him on the bed of the man of God. Closing the door on him, she went out 22 and called to her husband, "Let me have a servant and a donkey. I must go quickly to the man of God, and I will be back." 23 "Why are you going to him today?" he asked. "It is neither the new moon nor the sabbath." But she bade him good-bye, 24 and when the donkey was saddled, said to her servant: "Lead on! Do not stop my donkey unless I tell you to." 25 She kept going till she reached the man of God on Mount Carmel. When he spied her at a distance, the man of God said to his servant Gehazi: "There is the Shunammite! 26 Hurry to meet her, and ask if all is well with her, with her husband, and with the boy." "Greetings," she replied. 27 But when she reached the man of God on the mountain, she clasped his feet. Gehazi came near to push her away, but the man of God said: "Let her alone, she is in bitter anguish; the LORD hid it from me and did not let me know." 28 "Did I ask my lord for a son?" she cried out. "Did I not beg you not to deceive me?" "Gird your loins," 29 Elisha said to Gehazi, "take my staff with you and be off; if you meet anyone, do not greet him, and if anyone greets you, do not answer. Lay my staff upon the boy." 30 But the boy's mother cried out: "As the LORD lives and as you yourself live, I will not release you." So he started to go back with her.

31 Meanwhile, Gehazi had gone on ahead and had laid the staff upon the boy, but there was no sound or sign of life. He returned to meet Elisha and informed him that the boy had not awakened. 32 When Elisha reached the house, he found the boy lying dead. 33 He went in, closed the door on them both, and prayed to the LORD. 34 Then he lay upon the child on the bed, placing his mouth upon the child's mouth, his eyes upon the eyes, and his hands upon the hands. As Elisha stretched himself over the child, the body became warm. 35 He arose, paced up and down the room, and then once more lay down upon the boy, who now sneezed seven times and opened his eyes. 36 Elisha summoned Gehazi and said, "Call the Shunammite." She came at his call, and Elisha said to her, "Take your son." 37 She came in and fell at his feet in gratitude; then she took her son and left the room.

The Poisoned Stew

38 When Elisha returned to Gilgal, there was a famine in the land. Once, when the guild prophets were seated before him, he said to his servant, "Put the large pot on, and make some vegetable stew for the guild prophets." 39 Someone went out into the field to gather herbs and found a wild vine, from which he picked a clothful of wild gourds. On his return he cut them up into the pot of vegetable stew without anybody's knowing it. 40 The stew was poured out for the men to eat, but when they began to eat it, they exclaimed, "Man of God, there is poison in the pot!" And they could not eat it. 41 "Bring some meal," Elisha said. He threw it into the pot and said, "Serve it to the people to eat." And there was no longer anything harmful in the pot.

Multiplication of Loaves

42 A man came from Baal-shalishah bringing the man of God twenty barley loaves made from the firstfruits, and fresh grain in the ear. "Give it to the people to eat," Elisha said. 43 But his servant objected, "How can I set this before a hundred men?" "Give it to the people to eat," Elisha insisted. "For thus says the LORD, 'They shall eat and there shall be some left over.'" 44 And when they had eaten, there was some left over, as the LORD had said.

Cure of Naaman

5 Naaman, the army commander of the king of Aram, was highly esteemed and respected by his master, for through him the LORD had brought victory to Aram. But valiant as he was, the man was a leper. 2 Now the Arameans had captured from the land of Israel in a raid a

---

4, 26: *Greetings:* the conventional answer to Gehazi's question, which tells him nothing.
4, 29: *Does not greet him:* the profuse exchange of compliments among Orientals meeting and greeting one another consumed time. Urgency necessitated their omission, as our Lord counseled his disciples (Lk 10, 4).

little girl, who became the servant of Naaman's wife. 3 "If only my master would present himself to the prophet in Samaria," she said to her mistress, "he would cure him of his leprosy." 4 Naaman went and told his lord just what the slave girl from the land of Israel had said. 5 "Go," said the king of Aram. "I will send along a letter to the king of Israel." So Naaman set out, taking along ten silver talents, six thousand gold pieces, and ten festal garments. 6 To the king of Israel he brought the letter, which read: "With this letter I am sending my servant Naaman to you, that you may cure him of his leprosy."

7 When he read the letter, the king of Israel tore his garments and exclaimed: "Am I a god with power over life and death, that this man should send someone to me to be cured of leprosy? Take note! You can see he is only looking for a quarrel with me!" 8 When Elisha, the man of God, heard that the king of Israel had torn his garments, he sent word to the king: "Why have you torn your garments? Let him come to me and find out that there is a prophet in Israel."

9 Naaman came with his horses and chariots and stopped at the door of Elisha's house. 10 The prophet sent him the message: "Go and wash seven times in the Jordan, and your flesh will heal, and you will be clean." 11 But Naaman went away angry, saying, "I thought that he would surely come out and stand there to invoke the LORD his God, and would move his hand over the spot, and thus cure the leprosy. 12 Are not the rivers of Damascus, the Abana and the Pharpar, better than all the waters of Israel? Could I not wash in them and be cleansed?" With this, he turned about in anger and left.

13 But his servants came up and reasoned with him. "My father," they said, "if the prophet had told you to to something extraordinary, would you not have done it? All the more now, since he said to you. 'Wash and be clean,' should you do as he said."

14 So Naaman went down and plunged into the Jordan seven times at the word of the man of God. His flesh became again like the flesh of a little child, and he was clean.

15 He returned with his whole retinue to the man of God. On his arrival he stood before him and said, "Now I know that there is no God in all the earth, except in Israel. Please accept a gift from your servant."

16 "As the LORD lives whom I serve, I will not take it," Elisha replied; and despite Naaman's urging, he still refused. 17 Naaman said: "If you will not accept, please let me, your servant, have two mule-loads of earth, for I will no longer offer holocaust or sacrifice to any other god except to the LORD. 18 But I trust the LORD will forgive your servant this: when my master enters the temple of Rimmon to worship there, then I, too, as his adjutant, must bow down in the temple of Rimmon. May the LORD forgive your servant this." 19 "Go in peace," Elisha said to him.

Naaman had gone some distance 20 when Gehazi, the servant of Elisha, the man of God, thought to himself: "My master was too easy with this Aramean Naaman, not accepting what he brought. As the LORD lives, I will run after him and get something out of him." 21 So Gehazi hurried after Naaman. Aware that someone was running after him, Naaman alighted from his chariot to wait for him. "Is everything all right?" he asked. 22 "Yes," Gehazi replied, "but my master sent me to say. 'Two young men have just come to me, guild prophets from the hill country of Ephraim. Please give them a talent of silver and two festal garments.'" 23 "Please take two talents," Naaman said, and pressed them upon him. He tied up these silver talents in bags and gave them, with the two festal garments, to two of his servants, who carried them before Gehazi. 24 When they reached the hill, Gehazi took what they had, carried it into the house, and sent the men on their way.

25 He went in and stood before Elisha his master, who asked him, "Where have you been, Gehazi?" He answered, "Your servant has not gone anywhere." 26 But Elisha said to him: "Was I not present in spirit when the man alighted from his chariot to wait for you? Is this a time to take money or to take garments, olive orchards or vineyards, sheep or cattle, male or female servants? 27 The leprosy of Naaman shall cling to you and your descendants forever." And Gehazi left Elisha, a leper white as snow.

Recovery of the Lost Ax

6 The guild prophets once said to Elisha: "There is not enough room for us to continue to live here with you. 2 Let us go to the Jordan, where by getting one beam apiece we can build ourselves a place to live." "Go," Elisha said. 3 "Please agree to accompany your servants," one of them requested. "Yes, I will come," he replied.

4 So he went with them, and when they arrived at the Jordan they began to fell trees. 5 While one of them was felling a tree trunk, the iron ax-head slipped into the water. "O master," he cried out, "it was borrowed!" 6 "Where did it fall?" asked the man of God. When he pointed out the spot, Elisha cut off a stick, threw it into the water, and brought the iron to the surface. 7 "Pick it up," he said. And the man reached down and grasped it.

Aramean Ambush

8 When the king of Aram was waging war on Israel, he would make plans with his servants to attack a particular place. 9 But the man of God would send word to the king of Israel, "Be careful! Do not pass by this place, for Aram will attack there." 10 So the king of Israel would send word to the place which the man of God had indicated, and alert it; then they would be on guard. This happened several times.

11 Greatly disturbed over this, the king of Aram called together his

5, 12: *Wash in them and be cleansed:* typical of the ambiguity in ritual healing or cleanliness. The muddy waters of the Jordan are no match hygienically for the mountain spring waters of Damascus; ritually, it is

the other way around.
5, 17: *Two mule-loads of earth:* Israelite earth on which to erect in Aram an altar to the God of Israel.
5, 19: *Go in peace:* Elisha understands and ap-

proves the situation of Naaman who, though a proselyte as regards belief in and worship of the God of Israel, is required by his office to assist his master, the king, worshiping in the pagan temple of Rimmon.

officers. "Will you not tell me," he asked them, "who among us is for the king of Israel?" 12 "No one, my lord king," answered one of the officers. "The Israelite prophet Elisha can tell the king of Israel the very words you speak in your bedroom." 13 "Go, find out where he is," he said, "so that I may take him captive."

Blinded Aramean Soldiers

Informed that Elisha was in Dothan, 14 he sent there a strong force with horses and chariots. They arrived by night and surrounded the city. 15 Early the next morning, when the attendant of the man of God arose and went out, he saw the force with its horses and chariots surrounding the city. "Alas!" he said to Elisha. "What shall we do, my lord?" 16 "Do not be afraid," Elisha answered. "Our side outnumbers theirs." 17 Then he prayed, "O LORD, open his eyes, that he may see." And the LORD opened the eyes of the servant, so that he saw the mountainside filled with horses and fiery chariots around Elisha.

18 When the Arameans came down to get him, Elisha prayed to the LORD, "Strike this people blind, I pray you." And in answer to the prophet's prayer the LORD struck them blind. 19 Then Elisha said to them: "This is the wrong road, and this is the wrong city. Follow me! I will take you to the man you want." And he led them to Samaria. 20 When they entered Samaria, Elisha prayed, "O LORD, open their eyes that they may see." The LORD opened their eyes, and they saw that they were inside Samaria. 21 When the king of Israel saw them, he asked, "Shall I kill them, my father?" 22 "You must not kill them," replied Elisha. "Do you slay those whom you have taken captive with your sword or bow? Serve them bread and water. Let them eat and drink, and then go back to their master." 23 The king spread a great feast for them. When they had eaten and drunk he sent them away, and they went back to their master. No more

Aramean raiders came into the land of Israel.

Siege of Samaria

24 After this, Ben-hadad, king of Aram, mustered his whole army and laid siege to Samaria. 25 Because of the siege the famine in Samaria was so severe that an ass's head sold for eighty pieces of silver, and a fourth of a kab of wild onion for five pieces of silver.

26 One day, as the king of Israel was walking on the city wall, a woman cried out to him, "Help, my lord king!" 27 "No," he replied, "the LORD help you! Where could I find help for you: from the threshing floor or the winepress?" 28 Then the king asked her, "What is your trouble?" She replied: "This woman said to me, 'Give up your son that we may eat him today; then tomorrow we will eat my son.' 29 So we boiled my son and ate him. The next day I said to her, 'Now give up your son that we may eat him.' But she hid her son." 30 When the king heard the woman's words, he tore his garments. And as he was walking on the wall, the people saw that he was wearing sackcloth underneath, next to his skin. 31 "May God do thus and so to me," the king exclaimed, "if the head of Elisha, son of Shaphat, stays on him today!" 32 Meanwhile, Elisha was sitting in his house in conference with the elders. The king had sent a man ahead before he himself should come to him. Elisha had said to the elders: "Do you know that this son of a murderer is sending someone to cut off my head? When the messenger comes, see that you close the door and hold it fast against him. His master's footsteps are echoing behind him." 33 While Elisha was still speaking, the king came down to him and said, "This evil is from the LORD. Why should I trust in the LORD any longer?"

7 Elisha said: "Hear the word of the LORD! Thus says the LORD, 'At this time tomorrow a seah of fine flour will sell for a shekel, and two

seahs of barley for a shekel, in the market of Samaria.'" 2 But the adjutant on whose arm the king leaned, answered the man of God, "Even if the LORD were to make windows in heaven, how could this happen?" "You shall see it with your own eyes," Elisha said, "but you shall not eat of it."

The Lepers at the Gate

3 At the city gate were four lepers who were deliberating, "Why should we sit here until we die? 4 If we decide to go into the city, we shall die there, for there is famine in the city. If we remain here, we shall die too. Come, let us desert to the camp of the Arameans. If they spare us, we live; if they kill us, we die." 5 At twilight they left for the Arameans; but when they reached the edge of the camp, no one was there. 6 The LORD had caused the army of the Arameans to hear the sound of chariots and horses, the din of a large army, and they had reasoned among themselves, "The king of Israel has hired the kings of the Hittites and the kings of the borderlands to fight us." 7 Then in the twilight they fled, abandoning their tents, their horses, and their asses, the whole camp just as it was, and fleeing for their lives.

8 After the lepers reached the edge of the camp, they went first into one tent, ate and drank, and took silver, gold, and clothing from it, and went out and hid them. Back they came into another tent, took things from it, and again went out and hid them. 9 Then they said to one another: "We are not doing right. This is a day of good news, and we are keeping silent. If we wait until morning breaks, we shall be blamed. Come, let us go and inform the palace."

10 They came and summoned the city gatekeepers. "We went to the camp of the Arameans," they said, "but no one was there—not a human voice, only the horses and asses tethered, and the tents just as they were left." 11 The gatekeepers announced this and it was reported

6, 22: *With your sword or bow:* since the king would not slay prisoners who had surrendered to his power, much less should he slay prisoners captured by God's

power. By oriental custom they became guests within Samaria's walls.
7, 1: *Market:* literally "gate," the principal place

of trading in ancient walled cities in time of peace.
7, 6: *Kings of the borderlands:* from Musur in Anatolia rather than Egypt.

within the palace. 12 Though it was night, the king got up; he said to his servants: "Let me tell you what the Arameans have done to us. Knowing that we are in famine, they have left their camp to hide in the field, hoping to take us alive and enter our city when we leave it." 13 One of his servants, however, suggested: "Since those who are left in the city are no better off than all the throng that has perished, let some of us take five of the abandoned horses and send scouts to investigate."

End of the Siege

14 They took two chariots, and horses, and the king sent them to reconnoiter the Aramean army. "Go and find out," he ordered. 15 They followed the Arameans as far as the Jordan, and the whole route was strewn with garments and other objects that the Arameans had thrown away in their haste. The messengers returned and told the king. 16 The people went out and plundered the camp of the Arameans; and then a seah of fine flour sold for a shekel and two seahs of barley for a shekel, as the LORD had said. 17 The king put in charge of the gate the officer who was his adjutant; but the people trampled him to death at the gate, just as the man of God had predicted when the king visited him. 18 Thus was fulfilled the prophecy of the man of God to the king, "Two seahs of barley will sell for a shekel, and one seah of fine flour for a shekel at this time tomorrow at the gate of Samaria." 19 The adjutant had answered the man of God, "Even if the LORD were to make windows in heaven, how could this happen?" And Elisha had replied, "You shall see it with your own eyes, but you shall not eat of it." 20 And that is what happened to him, for the people trampled him to death at the gate.

Prediction of Famine

8 Elisha once said to the woman whose son he had restored to life: "Get ready! Leave with your family and settle wherever you can, because the LORD has decreed a seven-year famine which is coming upon the land." 2 The woman got ready and did as the man of God said, setting out with her family and settling in the land of the Philistines for seven years. 3 At the end of the seven years, the woman returned from the land of the Philistines and went out to the king to claim her house and her field. 4 The king was talking with Gehazi, the servant of the man of God. "Tell me," he said, "all the great things that Elisha has done." 5 Just as he was relating to the king how his master had restored a dead person to life, the very woman whose son Elisha had restored to life came to the king to claim her house and field. "My lord king," Gehazi said, "this is the woman, and this is that son of hers whom Elisha restored to life." 6 The king questioned the woman, and she told him her story. With that the king placed an official at her disposal, saying, "Restore all her property to her, with all that the field produced from the day she left the land until now."

Death of Ben-hadad Foretold

7 Elisha came to Damascus at a time when Ben-hadad, king of Aram, lay sick. When he was told that the man of God had come there, 8 the king said to Hazael, "Take a gift with you and go call on the man of God. Have him consult the LORD as to whether I shall recover from this sickness." 9 Hazael went to visit him, carrying a present, and with forty camel loads of the best goods of Damascus. On his arrival, he stood before the prophet and said, "Your son Ben-hadad, king of Aram, has sent me to ask you whether he will recover from his sickness." 10 "Go and tell him," Elisha answered, "that he will surely recover. However, the LORD has showed me that he will in fact die." 11 Then he stared him down until Hazael became ill at ease. The man of God wept, 12 and Hazael asked, "Why are you weeping, my lord?" Elisha replied, "Because I know the evil that you will inflict upon the Israelites. You will burn their fortresses, you will slay their youth with the sword, you will dash their little children to pieces, you will rip open their pregnant women." 13 Hazael exclaimed, "How can a dog like me, your servant, do anything so important?" "The LORD has showed you to me as king over Aram," replied Elisha. 14 Hazael left Elisha and returned to his master. "What did Elisha tell you?" asked Ben-hadad. "He told me that you would surely recover," replied Hazael. 15 The next day, however, Hazael took a cloth, dipped it in water, and spread it over the king's face, so that he died. And Hazael reigned in his stead.

Reign of Jehoram of Judah

16 In the fifth year of Joram, son of Arab, king of Israel, Jehoram, son of Jehoshaphat, king of Judah, became king. 17 He was thirty-two years old when he began to reign, and he reigned eight years in Jerusalem. 18 He conducted himself like the kings of Israel of the line of Ahab, since the sister of Ahab was his wife; and he did evil in the LORD's sight. 19 Even so, the LORD was unwilling to destroy Judah, because of his servant David. For he had promised David that he would leave him a lamp in the LORD's presence for all time. 20 During Jehoram's reign, Edom revolted against the sovereignty of Judah and chose a king of its own. 21 Thereupon Jehoram with all his chariots crossed over to Zair. He arose by night and broke through the Edomites when they had surrounded him and the commanders of his chariots. Then his army fled homeward. 22 To this day Edom has been in revolt against the rule of Judah. Libnah also revolted at that time. 23 The rest of the acts of Jehoram, with all that he did, are recorded in the book of the chronicles of the kings of Judah. 24 Jehoram rested with his ancestors and was buried with them in the City

---

8, 6: *An official:* literally "eunuch," and perhaps actually so in this instance.

8, 13: *A dog . . . your servant:* Hazael feigns humility (1 Sm 24, 14; 2 Sm 9, 8), without attending to the crimes he would commit after usurping the royal power as the prophet predicts. *Anything so important:* literally "a great deed" for a patriotic Syrian.

8, 16: *Jehoram* of Judah succeeded his father Jehoshaphat during the reign of Ahaziah of Israel. See note on 3, 1.

of David. His son Ahaziah succeeded him as king.

Accession of Ahaziah

25 Ahaziah, son of Jehoram, king of Judah, became king in the twelfth year of Joram, son of Ahab, king of Israel. 26 He was twenty-two years old when he began his reign, and he reigned one year in Jerusalem. His mother's name was Athaliah; she was the daughter of Omri, king of Israel. 27 He conducted himself like the house of Ahab, doing evil in the LORD's sight as they did, since he was related to them by marriage. 28 He joined Joram, son of Ahab, in battle against Hazael, king of Aram, at Ramoth-gilead, where the Arameans wounded Joram. 29 King Joram returned to Jezreel to be healed of the wounds which the Arameans had inflicted on him at Ramah in his battle against Hazael, king of Aram. Then Ahaziah, son of Jehoram, king of Judah, went down to Jezreel to visit him there in his illness.

Anointing of Jehu

9 The prophet Elisha called one of the guild prophets and said to him: "Gird your loins, take this flask of oil with you, and go to Ramoth-gilead. 2 When you get there, look for Jehu, son of Jehoshaphat, son of Nimshi. Enter and take him away from his companions into an inner chamber. 3 From the flask you have, pour oil on his head, and say, 'Thus says the LORD: I anoint you king over Israel.' Then open the door and flee without delay." 4 The young man (the guild prophet) went to Ramoth-gilead. 5 When he arrived, the commanders of the army were in session. "I have a message for you, commander," he said. "For which one of us?" asked Jehu. "For you, commander," he answered. 6 Jehu got up and went into the house. Then the young man poured the oil on his head and said, "Thus says the LORD, the God of Israel: 'I anoint you king over the people of the LORD, over Israel. 7 You shall

destroy the house of Ahab your master; thus will I avenge the blood of my servants the prophets, and the blood of all the other servants of the LORD shed by Jezebel, 8 and by all the rest of the family of Ahab. I will cut off every male in Ahab's line, whether slave or freeman in Israel. 9 I will deal with the house of Ahab as I dealt with the house of Jeroboam, son of Nebat, and with the house of Baasha, son of Ahijah. 10 Dogs shall devour Jezebel at the confines of Jezreel, so that no one can bury her.'" Then he opened the door and fled.

11 When Jehu rejoined his master's servants, they asked him, "Is all well? Why did that madman come to you?" "You know that kind of man and his talk," he replied. 12 But they said, "Not at all! Come, tell us." So he told them what the young man had said to him, and finally, "Thus says the LORD: 'I anoint you king over Israel.'" 13 At once each took his garment, spread it under Jehu on the bare steps, blew the trumpet, and cried out, "Jehu is king!"

14 Thus Jehu, son of Jehoshaphat, son of Nimshi, formed a conspiracy against Joram. Joram, with all Israel, had been besieging Ramoth-gilead against Hazael, king of Aram, 15 but had returned to Jezreel to be healed of the wounds the Arameans had inflicted on him in the battle against Hazael, king of Aram.

Murder of Joram

"If you are truly with me," Jehu said, "see that no one escapes from the city to report in Jezreel." 16 Then Jehu mounted his chariot and drove to Jezreel, where Joram lay ill and Ahaziah, king of Judah, had come to visit him.

17 The watchman standing on the tower in Jezreel saw the troop of Jehu coming and reported, "I see chariots." "Get a driver," Joram said, "and send him to meet them and to ask whether all is well." 18 So a driver went out to meet him and said "The king asks whether all is well." "What does it matter to you how things are?" Jehu said. "Get behind

me." The watchman reported to the king, "The messenger has reached them, but is not returning."

19 Joram sent a second driver, who went to them and said, "The king asks whether all is well." "What does it matter to you how things are?" Jehu replied. "Get behind me."

20 The watchman reported, "The messenger has reached them, but is not returning. The driving is like that of Jehu, son of Nimshi, in its fury." 21 "Prepare my chariot," said Joram. When they had done so, Joram, king of Israel, and Ahaziah, king of Judah, set out, each in his own chariot, to meet Jehu. They reached him near the field of Naboth the Jezreelite. 22 When Joram recognized Jehu, he asked, "Is all well, Jehu?" "How can all be well," Jehu replied, "as long as the many fornications and witchcrafts of your mother Jezebel continue?" 23 Joram reigned about and fled, crying to Ahaziah, "Treason, Ahaziah!" 24 But Jehu drew his bow and shot Joram between the shoulders, so that the arrow went through his heart and he collapsed in his chariot. 25 Then Jehu said to his adjutant Bidkar, "Take him and throw him into the field of Naboth the Jezreelite. For I remember that when we were driving teams behind his father Ahab, the LORD delivered this oracle against him: 26 'As surely as I saw yesterday the blood of Naboth and the blood of his sons,' says the LORD, 'I will repay you for it in that very plot of ground, says the LORD.' So now take him into this plot of ground, in keeping with the word of the LORD."

Death of Ahaziah

27 Seeing what was happening, Ahaziah, king of Judah, fled toward Beth-haggan. Jehu pursued him, shouting, "Kill him too!" And they pierced him as he rode through the pass of Gur near Ibleam. He continued his flight as far as Megiddo and died there. 28 His servants brought him in a chariot to Jerusalem and buried him in the tomb of his ancestors in the City of David.

8, 25: *Twelfth year of Joram:* i.e., of Israel, who probably reigned only eight years.
9, 7–10: The editors of the Books of Kings have here added to the prophet's message the same type of

indictment and sanctions against *the family of Ahab* as were invoked against the dynasties of *Jeroboam* (1 Kgs 14, 10f), *Baasha* (1 Kgs 16, 3f), and *Ahab* on a previous occasion (1 Kgs 21, 21–24).

9, 22: *Fornications and witchcrafts:* the worship of foreign gods.

29 Ahaziah had become king of Judah in the eleventh year of Joram, son of Ahab.

Death of Jezebel

30 When Jezebel learned that Jehu had arrived in Jezreel, she shadowed her eyes, adorned her hair, and looked down from her window. 31 As Jehu came through the gate, she cried out, "Is all well, Zimri, murderer of your master?" 32 Jehu looked up to the window and shouted, "Who is on my side? Anyone?" At this, two or three eunuchs looked down toward him. 33 "Throw her down," he ordered. They threw her down, and some of her blood spurted against the wall and against the horses. Jehu rode in over her body 34 and, after eating and drinking, he said: "Attend to that accursed woman and bury her; after all, she was a king's daughter." 35 But when they went to bury her, they found nothing of her but the skull, the feet, and the hands. 36 They returned to Jehu, and when they told him, he said, "This is the sentence which the LORD pronounced through his servant Elijah the Tishbite: 'In the confines of Jezreel dogs shall eat the flesh of Jezebel. 37 The corpse of Jezebel shall be like dung in the field in the confines of Jezreel, so that no one can say: This was Jezebel.'"

Killing of Ahab's Descendants

10 Ahab had seventy descendants in Samaria. Jehu prepared letters and sent them to the city rulers, to the elders, and to the guardians of Ahab's descendants in Samaria. 2 "Since your master's sons are with you," he wrote, "and you have the chariots, the horses, a fortified city, and the weapons, when this letter reaches you 3 decide which is the best and the fittest of your master's offspring, place him on his father's throne, and fight for your master's house." 4 They were overcome with fright and said, "If two kings could not withstand him, how can we?" 5 So the vizier and the ruler of the city, along with the elders and the guardians, sent this message to Jehu: "We are your servants, and we will do everything you

tell us. We will proclaim no one king; do whatever you think best." 6 So Jehu wrote them a second letter: "If you are on my side and will obey me, count the heads of your master's sons and come to me in Jezreel at this time tomorrow." [The seventy princes were in the care of prominent men of the city, who were rearing them.]

7 When the letter arrived, they took the princes and slew all seventy of them, put their heads in baskets, and sent them to Jehu in Jezreel. 8 "They have brought the heads of the princes," a messenger came in and told him. "Pile them in two heaps at the entrance of the city until morning," he ordered. 9 Going out in the morning, he stopped and said to all the people: "You are not responsible, and although I conspired against my lord and slew him, yet who killed all these? 10 Know that not a single word which the LORD has spoken against the house of Ahab shall go unfulfilled. The LORD has accomplished all that he foretold through his servant Elijah." 11 Thereupon Jehu slew all who were left of the family of Ahab in Jezreel, as well as all his powerful supporters, intimates, and priests, leaving him no survivor.

Ahaziah's Kinsmen

12 Then he set out for Samaria, and at Beth-eked-haroim on the way, 13 he came across kinsmen of Ahaziah, king of Judah. "Who are you?" he asked. "We are kinsmen of Ahaziah," they replied. "We are going down to visit the princes and the family of the queen mother." 14 "Take them alive," Jehu ordered. They were taken alive, forty-two in number, then slain at the pit of Beth-eked. Not one of them was spared.

Jehu in Samaria

15 When he had left there, Jehu met Jehonadab, son of Rechab, on the road. He greeted him and asked, "Are you sincerely disposed toward me, as I am toward you?" "Yes," replied Jehonadab. "If you are," continued Jehu, "give me your hand." Jehonadab gave him his hand, and Jehu drew him up into his chariot. 16 "Come with me," he said, "and

see my zeal for the LORD." And he took him along in his own chariot.

17 When he arrived in Samaria, Jehu slew all who remained there of Ahab's line, doing away with them completely and thus fulfilling the prophecy which the LORD had spoken to Elijah.

Baal's Temple Destroyed

18 Jehu gathered all the people together and said to them: "Ahab served Baal to some extent, but Jehu will serve him yet more. 19 Now summon for me all Baal's prophets, all his worshipers, and all his priests. See that no one is absent, for I have a great sacrifice for Baal. Whoever is absent shall not live." This Jehu did as a ruse, so that he might destroy the worshipers of Baal. 20 Jehu said further, "Proclaim a solemn assembly in honor of Baal." They did so, 21 and Jehu sent word of it throughout the land of Israel. All the worshipers of Baal without exception came into the temple of Baal, which was filled to capacity. 22 Then Jehu said to the custodian of the wardrobe, "Bring out the garments for all the worshipers of Baal." When he had brought out the garments for them, 23 Jehu, with Jehonadab, son of Rechab, entered the temple of Baal and said to the worshipers of Baal, "Search and be sure that there is no worshiper of the LORD here with you, but only worshipers of Baal." 24 Then they proceeded to offer sacrifices and holocausts. Now Jehu had stationed eighty men outside with this warning, "If one of you lets anyone escape of those whom I shall deliver into your hands, he shall pay life for life." 25 As soon as he finished offering the holocaust, Jehu said to the guards and officers, "Go in and slay them. Let no one escape." So the guards and officers put them to the sword and cast them out. Afterward they went into the inner shrine of the temple of Baal, 26 took out the stele of Baal, and burned the shrine. 27 Then they smashed the stele of Baal, tore down the building, and turned it into a latrine, as it remains today.

28 Thus Jehu rooted out the worship of Baal from Israel. 29 However, he did not desist from the sins

which Jeroboam, son of Nebat, had caused Israel to commit, as regards the golden calves at Bethel and at Dan. 30 The LORD said to Jehu, "Because you have done well what I deem right, and have treated the house of Ahab as I desire, your sons to the fourth generation shall sit upon the throne of Israel." 31 But Jehu was not careful to observe wholeheartedly the law of the LORD, the God of Israel, since he did not desist from the sins which Jeroboam caused Israel to commit.

32 At that time the LORD began to dismember Israel. Hazael defeated the Israelites throughout their territory 33 east of the Jordan (all the land of Gilead, of the Gadites, Reubenites and Manassehites), from Aroer on the river Arnon up through Gilead and Bashan.

34 The rest of the acts of Jehu, his valor and all his accomplishments, are written in the book of the chronicles of the kings of Israel. 35 Jehu rested with his ancestors and was buried in Samaria. His son Jehoahaz succeeded him as king. 36 The length of Jehu's reign over Israel in Samaria was twenty-eight years.

Rule of Athaliah

11 When Athaliah, the mother of Ahaziah, saw that her son was dead, she began to kill off the whole royal family. 2 But Jehosheba, daughter of King Jehoram and sister of Ahaziah, took Joash, his son, and spirited him away, along with his nurse, from the bedroom where the princes were about to be slain. She concealed him from Athaliah, and so he did not die. 3 For six years he remained hidden in the temple of the LORD, while Athaliah ruled the land.

4 But in the seventh year, Jehoiada summoned the captains of the Carians and of the guards. He had them come to him in the temple of the LORD, exacted from them a sworn commitment, and then showed them the king's son. 5 He gave them these orders: "This is what you must do: the third of you who come on duty on the sabbath shall guard the king's

palace; 6 another third shall be at the gate Sur; and the last third shall be at the gate behind the guards. 7 The two of your divisions who are going off duty that week shall keep guard over the temple of the LORD for the king. 8 You shall surround the king, each with drawn weapons, and if anyone tries to approach the cordon, kill him; stay with the king, whatever he may do."

9 The captains did just as Jehoiada the priest commanded. Each one with his men, both those going on duty for the sabbath and those going off duty that week, came to Jehoiada the priest. 10 He gave the captains King David's spears and shields, which were in the temple of the LORD. 11 And the guards, with drawn weapons, lined up from the southern to the northern limit of the enclosure, surrounding the altar and the temple on the king's behalf. 12 Then Jehoiada led out the king's son and put the crown and the insignia upon him. They proclaimed him king and anointed him, clapping their hands and shouting, "Long live the king!"

13 Athaliah heard the noise made by the people, and appeared before them in the temple of the LORD. 14 When she saw the king standing by the pillar, as was the custom, and the captains and trumpeters near him, with all the people of the land rejoicing and blowing trumpets, she tore her garments and cried out, "Treason, treason!" 15 Then Jehoiada the priest instructed the captains in command of the force: "Bring her outside through the ranks. If anyone follows her," he added, "let him die by the sword." He had given orders that she should not be slain in the temple of the LORD. 16 She was led out forcibly to the horse gate of the royal palace, where she was put to death.

17 Then Jehoiada made a covenant between the LORD as one party and the king and the people as the other, by which they would be the LORD's people; and another covenant, between the king and the people. 18 Thereupon all the people of the land went to the temple of Baal and demolished it. They shattered its altars and images completely, and

slew Mattan, the priest of Baal, before the altars. After appointing a detachment for the temple of the LORD, Jehoiada 19 with the captains, the Carians, the guards, and all the people of the land, led the king down from the temple of the LORD through the guards' gate to the palace, where Joash took his seat on the royal throne. 20 All the people of the land rejoiced and the city was quiet, now that Athaliah had been slain with the sword at the royal palace.

Reign of Joash

12 Joash was seven years old when he became king. 2 Joash began to reign in the seventh year of Jehu, and he reigned forty years in Jerusalem. His mother, who was named Zibiah, was from Beer-sheba. 3 Joash did what was pleasing to the LORD as long as he lived, because the priest Jehoiada guided him. 4 Still, the high places did not disappear; the people continued to sacrifice and to burn incense there.

5 For the priests Joash made this rule: "All the funds for sacred purposes that are brought to the temple of the LORD—the census tax, personal redemption money, and whatever funds are freely brought to the temple of the LORD— 6 the priests may take for themselves, each from his own clients. However, they must make whatever repairs on the temple may prove necessary." 7 Nevertheless, as late as the twenty-third year of the reign of King Joash, the priests had not made needed repairs on the temple. 8 Accordingly, King Joash summoned the priest Jehoiada and the other priests. "Why do you not repair the temple?" he asked them. "You must no longer take funds from your clients, but you shall turn them over for the repairs." 9 So the priests agreed that they would neither take funds from the people nor make the repairs on the temple.

10 The priest Jehoiada then took a chest, bored a hole in its lid, and set it beside the stele, on the right as one entered the temple of the LORD. The priests who guarded the entry would put into it all the funds that were brought to the temple of the LORD.

11, 2: *Jehosheba* was the wife of Jehoida, the high priest; cf 2 Chr 22, 11.
11, 14: *By the pillar:* see note on 2 Chr 23, 13.

11 When they noticed that there was a large amount of silver in the chest, the royal scribe [and the priest] would come up, and they would melt down all the funds that were in the temple of the LORD, and weigh them. 12 The amount thus realized they turned over to the master workmen in the temple of the LORD. They in turn would give it to the carpenters and builders working in the temple of the LORD, 13 and to the lumbermen and stone cutters, and for the purchase of the wood and hewn stone used in repairing the breaches, and for any other expenses that were necessary to repair the temple. 14 None of the funds brought to the temple of the LORD were used there to make silver cups, snuffers, basins, trumpets, or any gold or silver article 15 Instead, they were given to the workmen, and with them they repaired the temple of the LORD. 16 Moreover, no reckoning was asked of the men who were provided with the funds to give to the workmen, because they held positions of trust. 17 The funds from guilt-offerings and from sin-offerings, however, were not brought to the temple of the LORD; they belonged to the priests.

18 Then King Hazael of Aram mounted a siege against Gath. When he had taken it, Hazael decided to go on to attack Jerusalem. 19 But King Jehoash of Judah took all the dedicated offerings presented by his forebears, Jehoshaphat, Jehoram, and Ahaziah, kings of Judah, as well as his own, and all the gold there was in the treasuries of the temple and the palace, and sent them to King Hazael of Aram, who then led his forces away from Jerusalem. 20 The rest of the acts of Joash, with all that he did, are recorded in the book of the chronicles of the kings of Judah. 21 Certain of his officials entered into a plot against him and killed him at Beth-millo. 22 Jozacar, son of Shimeath, and Jehozabad, son of Shomer, were the officials who killed him. He was buried in his forefathers' City of David, and his son Amaziah succeeded him as king.

Reign of Jehoahaz of Israel

13 In the twenty-third year of Joash, son of Ahaziah, king of Judah, Jehoahaz, son of Jehu, began his seventeen-year reign over Israel in Samaria. 2 He did evil in the LORD's sight, conducting himself like Jeroboam, son of Nebat, and not renouncing the sin he had caused Israel to commit. 3 The LORD was angry with Israel and for a long time left them in the power of Hazael, king of Aram, and of Ben-hadad, son of Hazael. 4 Then Jehoahaz entreated the LORD, who heard him, since he saw the oppression to which the king of Aram had subjected Israel. 5 So the LORD gave Israel a savior, and the Israelites, freed from the power of Aram, dwelt in their own homes as formerly. 6 Nevertheless, they did not desist from the sins which the house of Jeroboam had caused Israel to commit, but persisted in them. The sacred pole also remained standing in Samaria. 7 No soldiers were left to Jehoahaz, except fifty horsemen with ten chariots and ten thousand foot soldiers, since the king of Aram had destroyed them and trampled them like dust. 8 The rest of the acts of Jehoahaz, with all his valor and accomplishments, are recorded in the book of the chronicles of the kings of Israel. 9 Jehoahaz rested with his ancestors and was buried in Samaria. His son Joash succeeded him as king.

Reign of Joash of Israel

10 In the thirty-seventh year of Joash, king of Judah, Jehoash, son of Jehoahaz, began his sixteen-year reign over Israel in Samaria. 11 He did evil in the sight of the LORD; he did not desist from any of the sins which Jeroboam, son of Nebat, had caused Israel to commit, but persisted in them. 12 [The rest of the acts of Joash, the valor with which he fought against Amaziah, king of Judah, and all his accomplishments, are recorded in the book of the chronicles of the kings of Israel. 13 Joash rested with his ancestors, and Jeroboam occupied the throne. Joash

was buried with the kings of Israel in Samaria.]

14 When Elisha was suffering from the sickness of which he was to die, King Joash of Israel went down to visit him. "My father, my father!" he exclaimed, weeping over him. "Israel's chariots and horsemen!" 15 "Take a bow and some arrows," Elisha said to him. When he had done so, 16 Elisha said to the king of Israel, "Put your hand on the bow." As the king held the bow, Elisha placed his hands over the king's hands 17 and said, "Open the window toward the east." He opened it. Elisha said, "Shoot," and he shot. The prophet exclaimed, "The LORD's arrow of victory! The arrow of victory over Aram! You will completely conquer Aram at Aphec." 18 Then he said to the king of Israel, "Take the arrows," which he did. Elisha said to him, "Strike the ground!" He struck the ground three times and stopped. 19 Angry with him, the man of God said: "You should have struck five or six times; you would have defeated Aram completely. Now, you will defeat Aram only three times."

20 Elisha died and was buried. At the time, bands of Moabites used to raid the land each year. 21 Once some people were burying a man, when suddenly they spied such a raiding band. So they cast the dead man into the grave of Elisha, and everyone went off. But when the man came in contact with the bones of Elisha, he came back to life and rose to his feet.

22 King Hazael of Aram oppressed Israel during the entire reign of Jehoahaz. 23 But the LORD was merciful with Israel and looked on them with compassion because of his covenant with Abraham, Isaac, and Jacob. He was unwilling to destroy them or to cast them out from his presence. 24 So when King Hazael of Aram died and his son Ben-hadad succeeded him as king, 25 Joash, son of Jehoahaz, took back from Ben-hadad, son of Hazael, the cities

---

13, 5: *A savior:* by this language, typical of the Book of Judges (3, 9. 15), Jeroboam II of Israel is meant; cf 14, 27.

13, 6: *Sacred pole:* see note on Ex 34, 13.

13, 12f: The conclusion to the reign of Joash is given again in 14, 15f, where it is more appropriate.

13, 14: *My father, my father:* the king expresses here the same sentiments as those with which Elisha

addressed Elijah.

13, 16–19: Symbolic acts similar to these are seen in Ex 17, 8ff; Jos 8, 18ff; Ez 4, 1ff.

which Hazael had taken in battle from his father Jehoahaz. Joash defeated Ben-hadad three times, and thus recovered the cities of Israel.

Amaziah of Judah

14 In the second year of Joash, son of Jehoahaz, king of Israel, Amaziah, son of Joash, king of Judah, began to reign. 2 He was twenty-five years old when he became king, and he reigned twenty-nine years in Jerusalem. His mother, who name was Jehoaddin, was from Jerusalem. 3 He pleased the LORD, yet not like his forefather David, since he did just as his father Joash had done. 4 Thus the high places did not disappear, but the people continued to sacrifice and to burn incense on them. 5 When Amaziah had the kingdom firmly in hand, he slew the officials who had murdered the king, his father. 6 But the children of the murderers he did not put to death, obeying the LORD's command written in the book of the law of Moses, "Fathers shall not be put to death for their children, nor shall children be put to death for their fathers; each one shall die for his own sin."

7 Amaziah slew ten thousand Edomites in the Salt Valley, and took Sela in battle. He renamed it Joktheel, the name it has to this day.

8 Then Amaziah sent messengers to Jehoash, son of Jehoahaz, son of Jehu, king of Israel, with this challenge. "Come, let us meet face to face." 9 King Jehoash of Israel sent this reply to the king of Judah: "The thistle of Lebanon sent word to the cedar of Lebanon, 'Give your daughter to my son in marriage,' but an animal of Lebanon passed by and trampled the thistle underfoot. 10 You have indeed conquered Edom, and you have become ambitious. Enjoy your glory, but stay at home! Why involve yourself and Judah with you in misfortune and failure?"

11 But Amaziah would not listen. King Jehoash of Israel then advanced, and he and King Amaziah of Judah met in battle at Beth-shemesh of Judah. 12 Judah was defeated by Israel, and all the Judean soldiery fled homeward. 13 King Jehoash of Israel captured Amaziah, son of Jehoash, son of Ahaziah, king of Judah, at Beth-shemesh. He went on to Jerusalem where he tore down four hundred cubits of the city wall, from the Gate of Ephraim to the Corner Gate. 14 He took all the gold and silver and all the utensils there were in the temple of the LORD and in the treasuries of the palace, and hostages as well. Then he returned to Samaria. 15 The rest of the acts of Jehoash, his valor, and how he fought Amaziah, king of Judah, are recorded in the book of the chronicles of the kings of Israel. 16 Jehoash rested with his ancestors; he was buried in Samaria with the kings of Israel. His son Jeroboam succeeded him as king.

17 Amaziah, son of Joash, king of Judah, survived Jehoash, son of Jehoahaz, king of Israel, by fifteen years. 18 The rest of the acts of Amaziah are written in the book of the chronicles of the kings of Judah. 19 When a conspiracy was formed against him in Jerusalem, he fled to Lachish. But he was pursued to Lachish and killed there. 20 He was brought back on horses and buried with his ancestors in the City of David in Jerusalem. 21 Thereupon all the people of Judah took the sixteen-year-old Azariah and proclaimed him king to succeed his father Amaziah. 22 It was Azariah who rebuilt Elath and restored it to Judah, after King Amaziah rested with his ancestors.

Jeroboam II of Israel

23 In the fifteenth year of Amaziah, son of Joash, king of Judah, Jeroboam, son of Joash, king of Israel, began his forty-one-year reign in Samaria. 24 He did evil in the sight of the LORD; he did not desist from any of the sins which Jeroboam, son of Nebat, had caused Israel to commit. 25 He restored the boundaries of Israel from Labo-of-Hamath to the sea of the Arabah, just as the LORD, the God of Israel, had prophesied through his servant, the prophet Jonah, son of Amittai, from Gath-hepher. 26 For the LORD saw the very bitter affliction of Israel, where there was neither slave nor freeman, no one at all to help Israel. 27 Since the LORD had not determined to blot out the name of Israel from under the heavens, he saved them through Jeroboam, son of Joash. 28 The rest of the acts of Jeroboam, his valor and all his accomplishments, how he fought with Damascus and turned back Hamath from Israel, are recorded in the book of the chronicles of the kings of Israel. 29 Jeroboam rested with his ancestors, the kings of Israel, and his son Zechariah succeeded him as king.

Azariah of Judah

15 Azariah, son of Amaziah, king of Judah, became king in the twenty-seventh year of Jeroboam, king of Israel. 2 He was sixteen years old when he began to reign and he reigned fifty-two years in Jerusalem. His mother, whose name was Jecholiah, was from Jerusalem. 3 He pleased the LORD just as his father Amaziah had done. 4 Yet the high places did not disappear; the people continued to sacrifice and to burn incense on them. 5 The LORD afflicted the king, and he was a leper to the day of his death. He lived in a house apart, while Jotham, the king's son, was vizier and regent for the people of the land. 6 The rest of the acts of Azariah, and all his accomplishments, are recorded in the book of the chronicles of the kings of Judah. 7 Azariah rested with his ancestors, and was buried with them in the City of David. His son Jotham succeeded him as king.

Zechariah of Israel

8 In the thirty-eighth year of Azariah, king of Judah, Zechariah, son of Jeroboam, was king of Israel in Samaria for six months. 9 He did evil in the sight of the LORD as his

---

14, 1f: *In the second year . . . twenty-nine years in Jerusalem:* the reigns of the kings of Judah between Athaliah and Ahaz are assigned too many years in all to correspond to the reigns in Israel from Jehu to the fall of Samaria. It seems probable that Amaziah was murdered as soon as his son Azariah was old enough to rule, and that Amaziah's reign was nearer nineteen than twenty-nine years. The correlation, in 15, 1, of the beginning of Azariah's reign with the 27th year of Jeroboam II can hardly be correct; and the sixteen-year reign of Joatham of Judah (15, 33) consisted for the most part of a regency during the illness of his father (15, 5).

14, 17: See note on 14, 1f.

14, 21: *Azariah:* also called Uzziah in many texts.

14, 25: *Sea of the Arabah:* the Dead Sea. *Jonah:* see note on Jon 1, 1.

15, 1: *Twenty-seventh year:* see note on 14, 1f.

fathers had done, and did not desist from the sins which Jeroboam, son of Nebat, had caused Israel to commit. 10 Shallum, son of Jabesh, conspired against Zechariah, attacked and killed him at Ibleam, and reigned in his place. 11 The rest of the acts of Zechariah are recorded in the book of the chronicles of the kings of Israel. 12 Thus the LORD's promise to Jehu. "Your descendants to the fourth generation shall sit upon the throne of Israel," was fulfilled.

Shallum of Israel

13 Shallum, son of Jabesh, became king in the thirty-ninth year of Uzziah, king of Judah; he reigned one month in Samaria. 14 Menahem, son of Gadi, came up from Tirzah to Samaria, where he attacked and killed Shallum, son of Jabesh, and reigned in his place. 15 The rest of the acts of Shallum, and the fact of his conspiracy, are recorded in the book of the chronicles of the kings of Israel. 16 At that time, Menahem punished Tappuah, all the inhabitants of the town and of its whole district, because on his way from Tirzah they did not let him in. He punished them even to ripping open all the pregnant women.

Menahem of Israel

17 In the thirty-ninth year of Azariah, king of Judah, Menahem, son of Gadi, began his ten-year reign over Samaria. 18 He did evil in the sight of the LORD, not desisting from the sins which Jeroboam, son of Nebat, had caused Israel to commit. During his reign, 19 Pul, king of Assyria, invaded the land, and Menahem gave him a thousand talents of silver to have his assistance in strengthening his hold on the kingdom. 20 Menahem secured the money to give to the king of Assyria by exacting it from all the men of substance in the country, fifty silver shekels from each. The king of Assyria did not remain in the country but withdrew. 21 The rest of the acts of Menahem, and all his accomplishments, are recorded in the

book of the chronicles of the kings of Israel. 22 Menahem rested with his ancestors, and his son Pekahiah succeeded him as king.

Pekahiah of Israel

23 In the fiftieth year of Azariah, king of Judah, Pekahiah, son of Menahem, began his two-year reign over Israel in Samaria. 24 He did evil in the sight of the LORD, not desisting from the sins which Jeroboam, son of Nebat, had caused Israel to commit. 25 His adjutant Pekah, son of Remaliah, who had with him fifty men from Gilead, conspired against him, killed him within the palace stronghold in Samaria, and reigned in his place. 26 The rest of the acts of Pekahiah, and all his accomplishments, are recorded in the book of the chronicles of the kings of Israel.

Pekah of Israel

27 In the fifty-second year of Azariah, king of Judah, Pekah, son of Remaliah, began his twenty-year reign over Israel in Samaria. 28 He did evil in the sight of the LORD, not desisting from the sins which Jeroboam, son of Nebat, had caused Israel to commit. 29 During the reign of Pekah, king of Israel, Tiglath-pileser, king of Assyria, came and took Ijon, Abel-beth-maacah, Janoah, Kedesh, Hazor, all the territory of Naphtali, Gilead, and Galilee, deporting the inhabitants to Assyria. 30 Hoshea, son of Elah, conspired against Pekah, son of Remaliah; he attacked and killed him, and reigned in his place [in the twentieth year of Jotham, son of Uzziah]. 31 The rest of the acts of Pekah, and all his accomplishments, are recorded in the book of the chronicles of the kings of Israel.

Jotham of Judah

32 In the second year of Pekah, son of Remaliah, king of Israel, Jotham, son of Uzziah, king of Judah, began to reign. 33 He was twenty-five years old when he became king, and he reigned sixteen years in

Jerusalem. His mother's name was Jerusha, daughter of Zadok. 34 He pleased the LORD, just as his father Uzziah had done. 35 Nevertheless the high places did not disappear and the people continued to sacrifice and to burn incense on them. It was he who built the Upper Gate of the temple of the LORD. 36 The rest of the acts of Jotham, and all his accomplishments, are recorded in the book of the chronicles of the kings of Judah. 37 It was at that time that the LORD first loosed Rezin, king of Aram, and Pekah, son of Remaliah, against Judah. 38 Jotham rested with his ancestors and was buried with them in his forefather's City of David. His son Ahaz succeeded him as king.

Ahaz of Judah

16 In the seventeenth year of Pekah, son of Remaliah, Ahaz, son of Jotham, king of Judah, began to reign. 2 Ahaz was twenty years old when he became king, and he reigned sixteen years in Jerusalem. He did not please the LORD, his God, like his forefather David, 3 but conducted himself like the kings of Israel, and even immolated his son by fire, in accordance with the abominable practice of the nations whom the LORD had cleared out of the way of the Israelites. 4 Further, he sacrificed and burned incense on the high places, on hills, and under every leafy tree.

5 Then Rezin, king of Aram, and Pekah, son of Remaliah, king of Israel, came up to Jerusalem to attack it. Although they besieged Ahaz, they were unable to conquer him. 6 At the same time the king of Edom recovered Elath for Edom, driving the Judeans out of it. The Edomites then entered Elath, which they have occupied until the present. 7 Meanwhile, Ahaz sent messengers to Tiglath-pileser, king of Assyria, with the plea: "I am your servant and your son. Come up and rescue me from the clutches of the king of Aram and the king of Israel, who are attacking me."

15, 19: *Pul:* The Babylonian throne name of the Assyrian Tiglath-pileser III; cf 15, 29.
15, 27: The twenty years here ascribed to *Pekah* are an impossibility; the calculation which made his

reign, of five years at most, appear so long may have been based on the attempt to give Jotham of Judah a full sixteen-year reign independently of his regency. See 16, 1 and the note on 14, 1f.

15, 35: *The Upper Gate:* also the Gate of Benjamin; cf Jer 20, 2; Ez 9, 2.

8 Ahaz took the silver and gold that were in the temple of the LORD and in the palace treasuries and sent them as a present to the king of Assyria, 9 who listened to him and moved against Damascus, which he captured. He deported its inhabitants to Kir and put Rezin to death.

10 King Ahaz went to Damascus to meet Tiglath-pileser, king of Assyria. When he saw the altar in Damascus, King Ahaz sent to Uriah the priest a model of the altar and a detailed design of its construction. 11 Uriah the priest built an altar according to the plans which King Ahaz sent him from Damascus, and had it completed by the time the king returned home. 12 On his arrival from Damascus, the king inspected this altar, then went up to it and offered sacrifice on it, 13 burning his holocaust and cereal-offering, pouring out his libation, and sprinkling the blood of his peace-offerings on the altar. 14 The bronze altar that stood before the LORD he brought from the front of the temple —that is, from the space between the new altar and the temple of the LORD—and set it on the north side of his altar. 15 "Upon the large altar." King Ahaz commanded Uriah the priest, "burn the morning holocaust and the evening cereal-offering, the royal holocaust and cereal-offering, as well as the holocausts, cereal-offerings, and libations of the people. You must also sprinkle on it all the blood of holocausts and sacrifices. But the old bronze altar shall be mine for consultation." 16 Uriah the priest did just as King Ahaz had commanded. 17 King Ahaz detached the frames from the bases and removed the lavers from them; he also took down the bronze sea from the bronze oxen that supported it, and set it on a stone pavement. 18 In deference to the king of Assyria he removed from the temple of the LORD the emplacement which had been built in the temple for a throne,

and the outer entrance for the king. 19 The rest of the acts of Ahaz are recorded in the book of the chronicles of the kings of Judah. 20 Ahaz rested with his ancestors and was buried with them in the City of David. His son Hezekiah succeeded him as king.

Hoshea of Israel

17 In the twelfth year of Ahaz, king of Judah, Hoshea, son of Elah, began his nine-year reign over Israel in Samaria. 2 He did evil in the sight of the LORD, yet not to the extent of the kings of Israel before him. 3 Shalmaneser, king of Assyria, advanced against him, and Hoshea became his vassal and paid him tribute. 4 But the king of Assyria found Hoshea guilty of conspiracy for sending envoys to the king of Egypt at Sais, and for failure to pay the annual tribute to his Assyrian overlord. 5 For this, the king of Assyria arrested and imprisoned Hoshea; he then occupied the whole land and attacked Samaria, which he besieged for three years. 6 In the ninth year of Hoshea, the king of Assyria took Samaria, and deported the Israelites to Assyria, settling them in Halah, at the Habor, a river of Gozan, and in the cities of the Medes.

7 This came about because the Israelites sinned against the LORD, their God, who had brought them up from the land of Egypt, from under the domination of Pharaoh, king of Egypt, and because they venerated other gods. 8 They followed the rites of the nations whom the LORD had cleared out of the way of the Israelites [and the kings of Israel whom they set up]. 9 They adopted unlawful practices toward the LORD, their God. They built high places in all their settlements, the watchtowers as well as the walled cities. 10 They set up pillars and sacred poles for themselves on every high hill and under every leafy tree. 11 There,

on all the high places, they burned incense like the nations whom the LORD had sent into exile at their coming. They did evil things that provoked the LORD, 12 and served idols, although the LORD had told them, "You must not do this."

13 And though the LORD warned Israel and Judah by every prophet and seer, "Give up your evil ways and keep my commandments and statutes, in accordance with the entire law which I enjoined on your fathers and which I sent you by my servants the prophets," 14 they did not listen, but were as stiff-necked as their fathers, who had not believed in the LORD, their God. 15 They rejected his statutes, the covenant which he had made with their fathers, and the warnings which he had given them. The vanity they pursued, they themselves became: they followed the surrounding nations whom the LORD had commanded them not to imitate. 16 They disregarded all the commandments of the LORD, their God, and made for themselves two molten calves; they also made a sacred pole and worshiped all the host of heaven, and served Baal. 17 They immolated their sons and daughters by fire, practiced fortune-telling and divination, and sold themselves into evildoing in the LORD's sight, provoking him 18 till, in his great anger against Israel, the LORD put them away out of his sight. Only the tribe of Judah was left.

19 Even the people of Judah, however, did not keep the commandments of the LORD, their God, but followed the rites practiced by Israel. 20 So the LORD rejected the whole race of Israel. He afflicted them and delivered them over to plunderers, finally casting them out from before him. 21 When he tore Israel away from the house of David, they made Jeroboam, son of Nebat, king; he drove the Israelites away from the LORD, causing them to commit a

---

16,9: Firmly dated events bearing on chapters 16 through 20 are: the fall of Damascus (16, 9) in 732 B.C., the fall of Samaria (18, 9–11) in 721 B.C., and Sennacherib's invasion of Judah (18, 3) in 701 B.C., which is equated both in Kgs and in Is 36, 1 with the 14th year of Hezekiah. These data make it necessary to credit Ahaz with at least a twenty-year reign, between 735 and c. 715 B.C., and to exclude the correlations between Hoshea of Israel and Hezekiah

in chapter 18.
If the 14th-year correspondence for 701 B.C. is given up, other arrangements are possible. The alleged ages of Jotham (15, 33), Ahaz (16, 2), and Hezekiah (18, 2) at their successive accessions to the throne do not argue for an early date for Hezekiah; but one or more of these may be artificial. Azariah (15, 1–7; Is 6, 1) was still on the throne of Judah in 743 B.C.
16, 15: For consultation: perhaps the introduction

into Judah of the Babylonian practice of omen sacrifices; cf Ez 21, 16.
16, 18: Emplacement . . . for a throne, and the outer entrance for the king: signs of sovereignty for the Hebrew kings.
17, 3: Shalmaneser: son and successor of Tiglath-pileser.
17, 6: The king of Assyria: Shalmaneser's successor and usurper, Sargon II.

great sin. 22 The Israelites imitated Jeroboam in all the sins he committed, nor would they desist from them. 23 Finally, the LORD put Israel away out of his sight as he had foretold through all his servants, the prophets; and Israel went into exile from their native soil to Assyria, an exile lasting to the present.

24 The king of Assyria brought people from Babylon, Cuthah, Avva, Hamath, and Sepharvaim, and settled them in the cities of Samaria in place of the Israelites. They took possession of Samaria and dwelt in its cities. 25 When they first settled there, they did not venerate the LORD, so he sent lions among them that killed some of their number. 26 A report reached the king of Assyria: "The nations whom you deported and settled in the cities of Samaria do not know how to worship the God of the land, and he has sent lions among them that are killing them, since they do not know how to worship the God of the land." 27 The king of Assyria gave the order, "Send back one of the priests whom I deported, to go there and settle, to teach them how to worship the God of the land." 28 So one of the priests who had been deported from Samaria returned and settled in Bethel, and taught them how to venerate the LORD.

29 But these peoples began to make their own gods in the various cities in which they were living; in the shrines on the high places which the Samaritans had made, each people set up gods. 30 Thus the Babylonians made Marduk and his consort; the men of Cuth made Nergal; the men of Hamath made Ashima; 31 the men of Avva made Nibhaz and Tartak; and the men of Sepharvaim immolated their children by fire to their city gods, King Hadad and his consort Anath. 32 They also venerated the LORD, choosing from their number priests for the high places, who officiated for them in the shrines on the high places. 33 But, while venerating the LORD, they served their own gods, following the worship of

the nations from among whom they had been deported.

34 To this day they worship according to their ancient rites. [They did not venerate the LORD nor observe the statutes and regulations, the law and commandments, which the LORD enjoined on the descendants of Jacob, whom he had named Israel. 35 When he made a covenant with them, he commanded them: "You must not venerate other gods, nor worship them, nor serve them, nor offer sacrifice to them. 36 The LORD, who brought you up from the land of Egypt with great power and outstretched arm: him shall you venerate, him shall you worship, and to him shall you sacrifice. 37 You must be careful to observe forever the statutes and regulations, the law and commandment, which he wrote for you, and you must not venerate other gods. 38 The covenant which I made with you, you must not forget; you must not venerate other gods. 39 But the LORD, your God, you must venerate; it is he who will deliver you from the power of all your enemies." 40 They did not listen, however, but continued in their earlier manner.] 41 Thus these nations venerated the LORD, but also served their idols. And their sons and grandsons, to this day, are doing as their fathers did.

THE KINGDOM OF JUDAH AFTER 721 B.C.

Hezekiah

18 In the third year of Hoshea, son of Elah, king of Israel, Hezekiah, son of Ahaz, king of Judah, began to reign. 2 He was twenty-five years old when he became king, and he reigned twenty-nine years in Jerusalem. His mother's name was Abi, daughter of Zechariah. 3 He pleased the LORD, just as his forefather David had done. 4 It was he who removed the high places, shattered the pillars, and cut down the sacred poles. He smashed the bronze serpent called Nehushtan which Moses had made, because up

to that time the Israelites were burning incense to it. 5 He put his trust in the LORD, the God of Israel; and neither before him nor after him was there anyone like him among all the kings of Judah. 6 Loyal to the LORD, Hezekiah never turned away from him, but observed the commandments which the LORD had given Moses. 7 The LORD was with him, and he prospered in all that he set out to do. He rebelled against the king of Assyria and did not serve him. 8 He also subjugated the watchtowers and walled cities of the Philistines, all the way to Gaza and its territory.

9 In the fourth year of King Hezekiah, which was the seventh year of Hoshea, son of Elah, king of Israel, Shalmaneser, king of Assyria, attacked Samaria, laid siege to it, 10 and after three years captured it. In the sixth year of Hezekiah, the ninth year of Hoshea, king of Israel, Samaria was taken. 11 The king of Assyria then deported the Israelites to Assyria and settled them in Halah, at the Habor, a river of Gozan, and in the cities of the Medes. 12 This came about because they had not heeded the warning of the LORD, their God, but violated his covenant, not heeding and not fulfilling the commandments of Moses, the servant of the LORD.

Invasion of Sennacherib

13 In the fourteenth year of King Hezekiah, Sennacherib, king of Assyria, went on an expedition against all the fortified cities of Judah and captured them. 14 Hezekiah, king of Judah, sent this message to the king of Assyria at Lachish: "I have done wrong. Leave me, and I will pay whatever tribute you impose on me." The king of Assyria exacted three hundred talents of silver and thirty talents of gold from Hezekiah, king of Judah. 15 Hezekiah paid him all the funds there were in the temple of the LORD and in the palace treasuries. 16 He broke up the door panels and the uprights of the temple of the LORD which he himself had ordered

17, 34–40: *They did not ... earlier manner:* this passage is an adaptation of language denouncing the Israelites to make it applicable to the later Samaritan sect of postexilic times. The original bearing of the

discourse [13–15] can be seen by reading it between 22 and 23. Cf also 18, 12.
18, 9: See note on 16, 9.
18, 13: *Sennacherib* succeeded Sargon II as king of

Assyria. His Judean campaign was waged in 701 B.C. See note on 16, 9.
18, 13—20, 11: Duplication of Is 36, 1—38, 8.21.22.

to be overlaid with gold, and gave the gold to the king of Assyria.

17 The king of Assyria sent the general, the lord chamberlain, and the commander from Lachish with a great army to King Hezekiah at Jerusalem. They went up, and on their arrival in Jerusalem, stopped at the conduit of the upper pool on the highway of the fuller's field. 18 They called for the king, who sent out to them Eliakim, son of Hilkiah, the master of the palace; Shebnah the scribe; and the herald Joah, son of Asaph. 19 The commander said to them, "Tell Hezekiah, 'Thus says the great king, the king of Assyria: On what do you base this confidence of yours? 20 Do you think mere words substitute for strategy and might in war? On whom, then, do you rely, that you rebel against me? 21 This Egypt, the staff on which you rely, is in fact a broken reed which pierces the hand of anyone who leans on it. That is what Pharaoh, king of Egypt, is to all who rely on him. 22 But if you say to me, We rely on the LORD, our God, is not he the one whose high places and altars Hezekiah has removed, commanding Judah and Jerusalem to worship before this altar in Jerusalem?'

23 "Now, make a wager with my lord, the king of Assyria: I will give you two thousand horses if you can put riders on them. 24 How then can you repulse even one of the least servants of my lord, relying as you do on Egypt for chariots and horsemen? 25 Was it without the LORD's will that I have come up to destroy this place? The LORD said to me, 'Go up and destroy that land!'"

26 Then Eliakim, son of Hilkiah, and Shebnah and Joah said to the commander: "Please speak to your servants in Aramaic; we understand it. Do not speak to us in Judean within earshot of the people who are on the wall."

27 But the commander replied: "Was it to your master and to you that my lord sent me to speak these words? Was it not rather to the men sitting on the wall, who, with you, will have to eat their own excrement and drink their urine?" 28 Then the commander stepped forward and cried out in a loud voice in Judean, "Listen to the words of the great king, the king of Assyria. 29 Thus says the king: 'Do not let Hezekiah deceive you, since he cannot deliver you out of my hand. 30 Let not Hezekiah induce you to rely on the LORD, saying, The LORD will surely save us; this city will not be handed over to the king of Assyria. 31 Do not listen to Hezekiah, for the king of Assyria says: Make peace with me and surrender! Then each of you will eat of his own vine and of his own fig-tree, and drink the water of his own cistern, 32 until I come to take you to a land like your own, a land of grain and wine, of bread and orchards, of olives, oil and fruit syrup. Choose life, not death. Do not listen to Hezekiah when he would seduce you by saying, The LORD will rescue us. 33 Has any of the gods of the nations ever rescued his land from the hand of the king of Assyria? 34 Where are the gods of Hamath and Arpad? Where are the gods of Sepharvaim, Hena, and Avva? Where are the gods of the land of Samaria? 35 Which of the gods for all these lands ever rescued his land from my hand? Will the LORD then rescue Jerusalem from my hand?'" 36 But the people remained silent and did not answer him one word, for the king had ordered them not to answer him.

37 Then the master of the palace, Eliakim, son of Hilkiah, Shebnah the scribe, and the herald Joah, son of Asaph, came to Hezekiah with their garments torn, and reported to him what the commander had said.

Hezekiah and Isaiah

19 When King Hezekiah heard this, he tore his garments, wrapped himself in sackcloth, and went into the temple of the LORD. 2 He sent Eliakim, the master of the palace, Shebnah the scribe, and the elders of the priests, wrapped in sackcloth, to tell the prophet Isaiah, son of Amoz, 3 "Thus says Hezekiah: 'This is a day of distress, of rebuke, and of disgrace. Children are at the point of birth, but there is no strength to bring them forth. 4 Perhaps the LORD, your God, will hear all the words of the commander, whom his master, the king of Assyria, sent to taunt the living God, and will rebuke him for the words which the LORD, your God, has heard. So send up a prayer for the remnant that is here.'"

5 When the servants of King Hezekiah had come to Isaiah, 6 he said to them, "Tell this to your master: 'Thus says the LORD: Do not be frightened by the words you have heard, with which the servants of the king of Assyria have blasphemed me. 7 I am about to put in him such a spirit that, when he hears a certain report, he will return to his own land, and there I will cause him to fall by the sword.'"

8 When the commander, on his return, heard that the king of Assyria had withdrawn from Lachish, he found him besieging Libnah. 9 The king of Assyria heard a report that Tirhakah, king of Ethiopia, had come out to fight against him. Again he sent envoys to Hezekiah with this message: 10 "Thus shall you say to Hezekiah, king of Judah: 'Do not let your God on whom you rely deceive you by saying that Jerusalem will not be handed over to the king of Assyria. 11 You have heard what the kings of Assyria have done to all other countries: they doomed them! Will you, then, be saved? 12 Did the gods of the nations destroyed save them? Gozan, Haran, Rezeph, or the Edenites in Telassar? 13 Where are the king of Hamath, the king of Arpad, or the kings of the cities Sepharvaim, Hena and Avva?'"

14 Hezekiah took the letter from the hand of the messengers and read it; then he went up to the temple of the LORD, and spreading it out before him, 15 he prayed in the LORD's presence: "O LORD, God of Israel, enthroned upon the cherubim! You alone are God over all the kingdoms of the earth. You have made the heavens and the earth. 16 Incline your ear, O LORD, and listen! Open

---

18, 17: *General, the lord chamberlain . . . commander:* the text lists three major functionaries by their Assyrian titles, of which only the first, more nearly "lord lieutenant," is military in origin; the *com-* *mander* was technically the king's chief butler.
19, 3: See note on Is 37, 3.

your eyes, O LORD, and see! Hear the words of Sennacherib which he sent to taunt the living God. 17 Truly, O LORD, the kings of Assyria have laid waste the nations and their lands, 18 and cast their gods into the fire; they destroyed them because they were not gods, but the work of human hands, wood and stone. 19 Therefore, O LORD, our God, save us from the power of this man, that all the kingdoms of the earth may know that you alone, O LORD, are God."

Punishment of Sennacherib

20 Then Isaiah, son of Amoz, sent this message to Hezekiah: "Thus says the LORD, the God of Israel, in answer to your prayer for help against Sennacherib, king of Assyria: I have listened! 21 This is the word the LORD has spoken concerning him:

"'She despises you, laughs you to scorn,
    the virgin daughter Zion!
Behind you she wags her head,
    daughter Jerusalem.
22 Whom have you insulted and blasphemed,
    against whom have you raised your voice
And lifted up your eyes on high?
    Against the Holy One of Israel!
23 Through your servants you have insulted the Lord.
    You said: With my many chariots
I climbed the mountain heights,
    the recesses of Lebanon;
I cut down its lofty cedars,
    its choice cypresses;
I reached the remotest heights,
    its forest park.
24 I dug wells and drank water in foreign lands;
    I dried up with the soles of my feet
    all the rivers of Egypt.

25 "'Have you not heard?
    Long ago I prepared it,
From days of old I planned it.
    Now I have brought it to pass:
That you should reduce fortified cities
    into heaps of ruins,

26 While their inhabitants, shorn of power,
    are dismayed and ashamed,
Becoming like the plants of the field,
    like the green growth,
    like the scorched grass on the housetops.
27 I am aware whether you stand or sit;
    I know whether you come or go,
28 and also your rage against me.
Because of your rage against me
    and your fury which has reached my ears,
I will put my hook in your nose
    and my bit in your mouth,
    and make you return the way you came.

29 "'This shall be a sign for you:
    this year you shall eat the aftergrowth,
    next year, what grows of itself;
But in the third year, sow and reap,
    plant vineyards and eat their fruit!
30 The remaining survivors of the house of Judah
    shall again strike root below
    and bear fruit above.
31 For out of Jerusalem shall come a remnant,
    and from Mount Zion, survivors.
    The zeal of the LORD of hosts shall do this.'

32 "Therefore, thus says the LORD concerning the king of Assyria: 'He shall not reach this city, nor shoot an arrow at it, nor come before it with a shield, nor cast up siegeworks against it. 33 He shall return by the same way he came, without entering the city, says the LORD. 34 I will shield and save this city for my own sake, and for the sake of my servant David.'"

35 That night the angel of the LORD went forth and struck down one hundred and eight-five thousand men in the Assyrian camp. Early the next morning, there they were, all the corpses of the dead. 36 So Sennacherib, the king of Assyria, broke camp, and went back home to Nineveh. 37 When he was worshiping in the temple of his god Nisroch, his sons Adrammelech and Sharezer slew him with the sword and fled into the land of Ararat. His son Esarhaddon reigned in his stead.

Hezekiah's Illness

20 In those days, when Hezekiah was mortally ill, the prophet Isaiah, son of Amoz, came and said to him: "Thus says the LORD: 'Put your house in order, for you are about to die; you shall not recover.'" 2 He turned his face to the wall and prayed to the LORD: 3 "O LORD, remember how faithfully and wholeheartedly I conducted myself in your presence, doing what was pleasing to you!" And Hezekiah wept bitterly.

4 Before Isaiah had left the central courtyard, the word of the LORD came to him: 5 "Go back and tell Hezekiah, the leader of my people: 'Thus says the LORD, the God of your forefather David: I have heard your prayer and seen your tears. I will heal you. In three days you shall go up to the LORD's temple; 6 I will add fifteen years to your life. I will rescue you and this city from the hand of the king of Assyria; I will be a shield to this city for my own sake, and for the sake of my servant David.'"

7 Isaiah then ordered a poultice of figs to be brought and applied to the boil, that he might recover. 8 Then Hezekiah asked Isaiah, "What is the sign that the LORD will heal me and that I shall go up to the temple of the LORD on the third day?" 9 Isaiah replied, "This will be the sign for you from the LORD that he will do what he has promised: Shall the shadow go forward or back ten steps?" 10 "It is easy for the shadow to advance ten steps," Hezekiah answered. "Rather, let it go back ten steps." 11 So the prophet Isaiah invoked the LORD, who made the shadow retreat the ten steps it had descended on the staircase to the terrace of Ahaz.

12 At that time, when Merodach-baladan, son of Baladan, king of Babylon, heard that Hezekiah had been ill, he sent letters and gifts to him. 13 Hezekiah was pleased at this, and therefore showed the messengers his whole treasury, his silver, gold, spices and fine oil, his armory, and all that was in his storerooms;

19, 21–31: vv 21–28 are addressed to Sennacherib, vv 29–31 to Judah.
20, 12–19: Duplication of Is 39, 1–8.

there was nothing in his house or in all his realm that Hezekiah did not show them.

14 Then Isaiah the prophet came to King Hezekiah and asked him: "What did these men say to you? Where did they come from?" "They came from a distant land, from Babylon," replied Hezekiah. 15 "What did they see in your house?" the prophet asked. "They saw everything in my house," answered Hezekiah. "There is nothing in my storerooms that I did not show them."

16 Then Isaiah said to Hezekiah: "Hear the word of the LORD: 17 The time is coming when all that is in your house, and everything that your fathers have stored up until this day, shall be carried off to Babylon; nothing shall be left, says the LORD. 18 Some of your own bodily descendants shall be taken and made servants in the palace of the king of Babylon."

19 Hezekiah replied to Isaiah, "The word of the LORD which you have spoken is favorable." For he thought, "There will be peace and security in my lifetime."

20 The rest of the acts of Hezekiah, all his valor, and his construction of the pool and conduit by which water was brought into the city, are written in the book of the chronicles of the kings of Judah. 21 Hezekiah rested with his ancestors and his son Manasseh succeeded him as king.

Reign of Manasseh

21 Manasseh was twelve years old when he began to reign, and he reigned fifty-five years in Jerusalem. His mother's name was Hephzibah. 2 He did evil in the sight of the LORD, following the abominable practices of the nations whom the LORD had cleared out of the way of the Israelites. 3 He rebuilt the high places which his father Hezekiah had destroyed. He erected altars to Baal, and also set up a sacred pole, as Ahab, king of Israel, had done. He worshiped and served the whole host of heaven. 4 He built altars in the temple of the LORD,

about which the LORD had said, "I will establish my name in Jerusalem"— 5 altars for the whole host of heaven, in the two courts of the temple.

6 He immolated his son by fire. He practiced soothsaying and divination, and reintroduced the consulting of ghosts and spirits. He did much evil in the LORD's sight and provoked him to anger.

7 The Asherah idol he had made, he set up in the temple, of which the LORD had said to David and to his son Solomon: "In this temple and in Jerusalem, which I have chosen out of all the tribes of Israel, I shall place my name forever. 8 I will not in future allow Israel to be driven off the land I gave their fathers, provided that they are careful to observe all I have commanded them, the entire law which my servant Moses enjoined upon them." 9 But they did not listen, and Manasseh misled them into doing even greater evil than the nations whom the LORD had destroyed at the coming of the Israelites.

10 Then the LORD spoke through his servants the prophets: 11 "Because Manasseh, king of Judah, has practiced these abominations and has done greater evil than all that was done by the Amorites before him, and has led Judah into sin by his idols, 12 therefore thus says the LORD, the God of Israel: 'I will bring such evil on Jerusalem and Judah that, whenever anyone hears of it, his ears shall ring. 13 I will measure Jerusalem with the same cord as I did Samaria, and with the plummet I used for the house of Ahab. I will wipe Jerusalem clean as one wipes a dish, wiping it inside and out. 14 I will cast off the survivors of my inheritance and deliver them into enemy hands, to become a prey and a booty for all their enemies, 15 because they have done evil in my sight and provoked me from the day their fathers came forth from Egypt until today.'"

16 In addition to the sin which he caused Judah to commit, Manasseh did evil in the sight of the LORD, shedding so much innocent blood as

to fill the length and breadth of Jerusalem. 17 The rest of the acts of Manasseh, the sin he committed and all that he did, are written in the book of the chronicles of the kings of Judah. 18 Manasseh rested with his ancestors and was buried in his palace garden, the garden of Uzza. His son Amon succeeded him as king.

Reign of Amon

19 Amon was twenty-two years old when he began to reign, and he reigned two years in Jerusalem. His mother's name was Meshullemeth, daughter of Haruz of Jotbah. 20 He did evil in the sight of the LORD, as his father Manasseh had done. 21 He followed exactly the path his father had trod, serving and worshiping the idols his father had served. 22 He abandoned the LORD, the God of his fathers, and did not follow the path of the LORD. 23 Subjects of Amon conspired against him and slew the king in his palace, 24 but the people of the land then slew all who had conspired against King Amon, and proclaimed his son Josiah king in his stead. 25 The rest of the acts that Amon did are written in the book of the chronicles of the kings of Judah. 26 He was buried in his own grave in the garden of Uzza, and his son Josiah succeeded him as King.

Reign of Josiah

22 Josiah was eight years old when he began to reign, and he reigned thirty-one years in Jerusalem. His mother's name was Jedidah, daughter of Adaiah of Bozkath. 2 He pleased the LORD and conducted himself unswervingly just as his ancestor David had done.

3 In his eighteenth year, King Josiah sent the scribe Shaphan, son of Azaliah, son of Meshullam, to the temple of the LORD with orders to 4 go to the high priest Hilkiah and have him smelt down the precious metals that had been donated to the temple of the LORD, which the doorkeepers had collected from the

---

20, 20: *Pool and conduit:* Hezekiah's tunnel; cf 2 Chr 32, 30.

22, 3: *Shaphan:* head of a prominent family in the reign of Josiah, secretary to the king, bearer and reader of the newfound book of the law (3–13; 2 Chr 34, 8f.15–20). He and his sons favored the reform of King Josiah and supported the prophet Jeremiah; cf Jer 26, 24.

people. 5 They were to be consigned to the master workmen in the temple of the LORD, who should then pay them out to the carpenters, builders, and lumbermen making repairs on the temple, 6 and for the purchase of wood and hewn stone for the temple repairs. 7 No reckoning was asked of them regarding the funds consigned to them, because they held positions of trust.

The Book of the Law

8 The high priest Hilkiah informed the scribe Shaphan, "I have found the book of the law in the temple of the LORD." Hilkiah gave the book to Shaphan, who read it. 9 Then the scribe Shaphan went to the king and reported, "Your servants have smelted down the metals available in the temple and have consigned them to the master workmen in the temple of the LORD." 10 The scribe Shaphan also informed the king that the priest Hilkiah had given him a book, and then read it aloud to the king. 11 When the king had heard the contents of the book of the law, he tore his garments 12 and issued this command to Hilkiah the priest, Ahikam, son of Shaphan, Achbor, son of Micaiah, the scribe Shaphan, and the king's servant Asaiah: 13 "Go, consult the LORD for me, for the people, for all Judah, about the stipulations of this book that has been found, for the anger of the LORD has been set furiously ablaze against us, because our fathers did not obey the stipulations of this book, nor fulfill our written obligations."

14 So Hilkiah the priest, Ahikam, Achbor, Shaphan, and Asaiah betook themselves to the Second Quarter in Jerusalem, where the prophetess Huldah resided. She was the wife of Shallum, son of Tikvah, son of Harhas, keeper of the wardrobe. When they had spoken to her, 15 she said to them, "Thus says the LORD, the God of Israel: 'Say to the man who sent you to me, 16 Thus says the LORD: I will bring upon

this place and upon its inhabitants all the evil that is threatened in the book which the king of Judah has read. 17 Because they have forsaken me and have burned incense to other gods, provoking me by everything to which they turn their hands, my anger is ablaze against this place and it cannot be extinguished.'

18 "But to the king of Judah who sent you to consult the LORD, give this response: 'Thus says the LORD, the God of Israel: As for the threats you have heard, 19 because you were heartsick and have humbled yourself before the LORD when you heard my threats that this place and its inhabitants would become a desolation and a curse; because you tore your garments and wept before me; I in turn have listened, says the LORD. 20 I will therefore gather you to your ancestors; you shall go to your grave in peace, and your eyes shall not see all the evil I will bring upon this place.'" This they reported to the king.

23 The king then had all the elders of Judah and of Jerusalem summoned together before him. 2 The king went up to the temple of the LORD with all the men of Judah and all the inhabitants of Jerusalem: priests, prophets, and all the people, small and great. He had the entire contents of the book of the covenant that had been found in the temple of the LORD, read out to them. 3 Standing by the column, the king made a covenant before the LORD that they would follow him and observe his ordinances, statutes and decrees with their whole hearts and souls, thus reviving the terms of the covenant which were written in this book. And all the people stood as participants in the covenant.

4 Then the king commanded the high priest Hilkiah, his vicar, and the doorkeepers to remove from the temple of the LORD all the objects that had been made for Baal, Asherah, and the whole host of heaven. He had these burned outside Jeru-

salem on the slopes of the Kidron and their ashes carried to Bethel. 5 He also put an end to the pseudo-priests whom the kings of Judah had appointed to burn incense on the high places in the cities of Judah and in the vicinity of Jerusalem, as well as those who burned incense to Baal, to the sun, moon, and signs of the Zodiac, and to the whole host of heaven. 6 From the temple of the LORD he also removed the sacred pole, to the Kidron Valley, outside Jerusalem; there he had it burned and beaten to dust, which was then scattered over the common graveyard. 7 He tore down the apartments of the cult prostitutes which were in the temple of the LORD, and in which the women wove garments for the Asherah.

8 He brought in all the priests from the cities of Judah, and then defiled, from Geba to Beer-sheba, the high places where they had offered incense. He also tore down the high place of the satyrs, which was at the entrance of the Gate of Joshua, governor of the city, to the left as one enters the city gate. 9 The priests of the high places could not function at the altar of the LORD in Jerusalem; but they, along with their relatives, ate the unleavened bread.

10 The king also defiled Topheth in the Valley of Benhinnom, so that there would no longer be any immolation of sons or daughters by fire in honor of Molech. 11 He did away with the horses which the kings of Judah had dedicated to the sun; these were at the entrance of the temple of the LORD, near the chamber of Nathan-melech the eunuch, which was in the large building. The chariots of the sun he destroyed by fire. 12 He also demolished the altars made by the kings of Judah on the roof (the roof terrace of Ahaz), and the altars made by Manasseh in the two courts of the temple of the LORD. He pulverized them and threw the dust into the Kidron Valley. 13 The king defiled the high places east of Jerusalem, south of the Mount of Mis-

23, 7: *Cult prostitutes:* of both sexes; cf 1 Kgs 14, 24.

23, 10: *Topheth . . . by fire:* condemned by Deuteronomic law and denounced by Jeremiah (Dt 12, 31; Jer 7, 29ff; Jer 19).

23, 11: *Large building:* to the west of the temple area (1 Chr 26, 18), named in the Hebrew by an Egyptian name for a similar construction.

23, 13: *Mount of Misconduct:* a paranomasia on "Mount of Olives" (in Hebrew *Maschit/mishcheh*) as

suggested by the Targum. Cf Vulgate, "Mount of Offense." *Horror . . . idol:* in all three phrases here the Hebrew uses a pejorative designation meaning "abomination."

conduct, which Solomon, king of Israel, had built in honor of Astarte, the Sidonian horror, of Chemosh, the Moabite horror, and of Milcom, the idol of the Ammonites. 14 He broke to pieces the pillars, cut down the sacred poles, and filled the places where they had been with human bones. 15 Likewise the altar which was at Bethel, the high place built by Jeroboam, son of Nebat, who caused Israel to sin—this same altar and high place he tore down, breaking up the stones and grinding them to powder, and burning the Asherah.

16 When Josiah turned and saw the graves there on the mountainside, he ordered the bones taken from the graves and burned on the altar, and thus defiled it in fulfillment of the word of the LORD which the man of God had proclaimed as Jeroboam was standing by the altar on the feast day. When the king looked up and saw the grave of the man of God who had proclaimed these words, 17 he asked, "What is that tombstone I see?" The men of the city replied, "It is the grave of the man of God who came from Judah and predicted the very things you have done to the altar of Bethel." 18 "Let his be," he said, "let no one move his bones." So they left his bones undisturbed together with the bones of the prophet who had come from Samaria.

19 Josiah also removed all the shrines on the high places near the cities of Samaria which the kings of Israel had erected, thereby provoking the LORD; he did the very same to them as he had done in Bethel. 20 He slaughtered upon the altars all the priests of the high places that were at the shrines, and burned human bones upon them. Then he returned to Jerusalem.

21 The king issued a command to all the people to observe the Passover of the LORD, their God, as it was prescribed in that book of the covenant. 22 No Passover such as this had been observed during the period when the judges ruled Israel, or during the entire period of the kings of Israel and the kings of Judah, 23

until the eighteenth year of King Josiah, when this Passover of the LORD was kept in Jerusalem.

24 Further, Josiah did away with the consultation of ghosts and spirits, with the household gods, idols, and all the other horrors to be seen in the land of Judah and in Jerusalem, so that he might carry out the stipulations of the law written in the book that the priest Hilkiah had found in the temple of the LORD.

25 Before him there had been no king who turned to the LORD as he did, with his whole heart, his whole soul, and his whole strength, in accord with the entire law of Moses; nor could any after him compare with him.

26 Yet, because of all the provocations that Manasseh had given, the LORD did not desist from his fiercely burning anger against Judah. 27 The LORD said: "Even Judah will I put out of my sight as I did Israel. I will reject this city, Jerusalem, which I chose, and the temple of which I said, 'There shall my name be.'"

28 The rest of the acts of Josiah, with all that he did, are written in the book of the chronicles of the kings of Judah. 29 In his time Pharaoh Neco, king of Egypt, went up toward the river Euphrates to the king of Assyria. King Josiah set out to confront him, but was slain at Megiddo at the first encounter. 30 His servants brought his body on a chariot from Megiddo to Jerusalem, where they buried him in his own grave. Then the people of the land took Jehoahaz, son of Josiah, anointed him, and proclaimed him king to succeed his father.

Reign of Jehoahaz

31 Jehoahaz was twenty-three years old when he began to reign, and he reigned three months in Jerusalem. His mother, whose name was Hamutal, daughter of Jeremiah, was from Libnah. 32 He did evil in the sight of the LORD, just as his forebears had done. 33 Pharaoh Neco took him prisoner at Riblah in

the land of Hamath, thus ending his reign in Jerusalem. He imposed a fine upon the land of a hundred talents of silver and a talent of gold. 34 Pharaoh Neco then appointed Eliakim, son of Josiah, king in place of his father Josiah; he changed his name to Jehoiakim. Jehoahaz he took away with him to Egypt, where he died. 35 Jehoiakim gave the silver and gold to Pharaoh, but taxed the land to raise the amount Pharaoh demanded. He exacted the silver and gold from the people of the land, from each proportionately, to pay Pharaoh Neco.

Reign of Jehoiakim

36 Jehoiakim was twenty-five years old when he began to reign, and he reigned eleven years in Jerusalem. His mother's name was Zebidah, daughter of Pedaiah, from Rumah. 37 He did evil in the sight of the LORD, just as his forebears had done.

24 During his reign Nebuchadnezzar, king of Babylon moved against him, and Jehoiakim became his vassal for three years. Then Jehoiakim turned and rebelled against him. 2 The LORD loosed against him bands of Chaldeans, Arameans, Moabites, and Ammonites; he loosed them against Judah to destroy it, as the LORD had threatened through his servants the prophets. 3 This befell Judah because the LORD had stated that he would inexorably put them out of his sight for the sins Manasseh had committed in all that he did; 4 and especially because of the innocent blood he shed, with which he filled Jerusalem, the LORD would not forgive.

5 The rest of the acts of Jehoiakim, with all that he did, are written in the book of the chronicles of the kings of Judah. 6 Jehoiakim rested with his ancestors, and his son Jehoiachin succeeded him as king. 7 The king of Egypt did not again leave his own land, for the king of Babylon had taken all that belonged to the king of Egypt from the Wadi of Egypt to the Euphrates River.

23, 18: *From Samaria:* more narrowly, from Bethel; cf 1 Kgs 13, 31f.

23, 24: *Household gods, idols:* teraphim. See note

on Gn 31, 19.

23, 30.35: *People of the land:* in this period, the phrase referred to "landed gentry"; in later times it

meant "the poor." Cf 24, 14.

23, 33: *A talent of gold:* Some manuscripts of the Greek and Syriac texts have "ten talents."

Reign of Jehoiachin

8 Jehoiachin was eighteen years old when he began to reign, and he reigned three months in Jerusalem. His mother's name was Nehushta, daughter of Elnathan of Jerusalem. 9 He did evil in the sight of the LORD, just as his forebears had done.

10 At that time the officials of Nebuchadnezzar, king of Babylon, attacked Jerusalem, and the city came under siege. 11 Nebuchadnezzar, king of Babylon, himself arrived at the city while his servants were besieging it. 12 Then Jehoiachin, king of Judah, together with his mother, his ministers, officers, and functionaries, surrendered to the king of Babylon, who, in the eighth year of his reign, took him captive. 13 He carried off all the treasures of the temple of the LORD and those of the palace, and broke up all the gold utensils that Solomon, king of Israel, had provided in the temple of the LORD, as the LORD had foretold. 14 He deported all Jerusalem; all the officers and men of the army, ten thousand in number, and all the craftsmen and smiths. None were left among the people of the land except the poor. 15 He deported Jehoiachin to Babylon, and also led captive from Jerusalem to Babylon the king's mother and wives, his functionaries, and the chief men of the land. 16 The king of Babylon also led captive to Babylon all seven thousand men of the army, and a thousand craftsmen and smiths, all of them trained soldiers. 17 In place of Jehoiachin, the king of Babylon appointed his uncle Mattaniah king, and changed his name to Zedekiah.

Reign of Zedekiah

18 Zedekiah was twenty-one years old when he became king, and he reigned eleven years in Jerusalem. His mother's name was Hamutal, daughter of Jeremiah of Libnah. 19 He also did evil in the sight of the LORD, just as Jehoiakim had done. 20 The LORD's anger befell Jerusalem and Judah till he cast them out from

his presence. Thus Zedekiah rebelled against the king of Babylon.

25 In the tenth month of the ninth year of Zedekiah's reign, on the tenth day of the month, Nebuchadnezzar, king of Babylon, and his whole army advanced against Jerusalem, encamped around it, and built siege walls on every side. 2 The siege of the city continued until the eleventh year of Zedekiah. 3 On the ninth day of the fourth month, when famine had gripped the city, and the people had no more bread, 4 the city walls were breached. Then the king and all the soldiers left the city by night through the gate between the two walls which was near the king's garden. Since the Chaldeans had the city surrounded, they went in the direction of the Arabah. 5 But the Chaldean army pursued the king and overtook him in the desert near Jericho, abandoned by his whole army.

6 The king was therefore arrested and brought to Riblah to the king of Babylon, who pronounced sentence on him. 7 He had Zedekiah's sons slain before his eyes. Then he blinded Zedekiah, bound him with fetters, and had him brought to Babylon.

8 On the seventh day of the fifth month (this was in the nineteenth year of Nebuchadnezzar, king of Babylon), Nebuzaradan, captain of the bodyguard, came to Jerusalem as the representative of the king of Babylon. 9 He burned the house of the LORD, the palace of the king, and all the houses of Jerusalem; every large building was destroyed by fire. 10 Then the Chaldean troops who were with the captain of the guard tore down the walls that surrounded Jerusalem.

11 Then Nebuzaradan, captain of the guard, led into exile the last of the people remaining in the city, and those who had deserted to the king of Babylon, and the last of the artisans. 12 But some of the country's poor, Nebuzaradan, captain of the guard, left behind as vinedressers and farmers.

13 The bronze pillars that be-

longed to the house of the LORD, and the wheeled carts and the bronze sea in the house of the LORD, the Chaldeans broke into pieces; they carried away the bronze to Babylon. 14 They took also the pots, the shovels, the snuffers, the bowls, the pans and all the bronze vessels used for service. 15 The fire-holders and the bowls which were of gold or silver the captain of the guard also carried off. 16 The weight in bronze of the two pillars, the bronze sea, and the wheeled carts, all of them furnishings which Solomon had made for the house of the LORD, was never calculated. 17 Each of the pillars was eighteen cubits high; a bronze capital five cubits high surmounted each pillar, and a network with pomegranates encircled the capital, all of bronze; and so for the other pillar, as regards the network.

18 The captain of the guard also took Seraiah the high priest, Zephaniah the second priest, and the three keepers of the entry. 19 And from the city he took one courtier, a commander of soldiers, five men in the personal service of the king who were still in the city, the scribe of the army commander, who mustered the people of the land, and sixty of the common people still remaining in the city. 20 The captain of the guard, Nebuzaradan, arrested these and brought them to the king of Babylon at Riblah; 21 the king had them struck down and put to death in Riblah, in the land of Hamath. Thus was Judah exiled from her land.

Governorship of Gedaliah

22 As for the people whom he had allowed to remain in the land of Judah, Nebuchadnezzar, king of Babylon, appointed as their governor Gedaliah, son of Ahikam, son of Shaphan. 23 Hearing that the king of Babylon had appointed Gedaliah governor, all the army commanders with their men came to him at Mizpah: Ishmael, son of Nethaniah, Johanan, son of Kareah, Seraiah, son of Tanhumeth the Netophathite, and Jaazaniah, from Beth-maacah. 24 Gedaliah gave the commanders and

24, 8: *He reigned three months:* in the year 597 B.C. 25, 1-30: This chapter parallels Jer 39 and 52; see notes to those parts of Jeremiah. 25, 11: *Those who had deserted:* perhaps on the advice of Jeremiah; cf Jer 38, 2f.

their men his oath. "Do not be afraid of the Chaldean officials," he said to them. "Remain in the country and serve the king of Babylon, and all will be well with you."

25 But in the seventh month Ishmael, son of Nethaniah, son of Elishama, of royal descent, came with ten men, attacked Gedaliah and killed him, along with the Jews and Chaldeans who were in Mizpah with him. 26 Then all the people, great and small, left with the army commanders and went to Egypt for fear of the Chaldeans.

Release of Jehoiachin

27 In the thirty-seventh year of the exile of Jehoiachin, king of Judah, on the twenty-seventh day of the twelfth month, Evilmerodach, king of Babylon, in the inaugural year of his own reign, raised up Jehoiachin, king of Judah, from prison. 28 He spoke kindly to him and gave him a throne higher than that of the other kings who were with him in Babylon. 29 Jehoiachin took off his prison garb and ate at the king's table as long as he lived. 30 The allowance granted him by the king was a perpetual allowance, in fixed daily amounts, for as long as he lived.

THE FIRST BOOK OF THE

GENEALOGICAL TABLES

From Adam to Abraham

ADAM, Seth, Enosh, 2 Kenan, Mahalalel, Jared, 3 Enoch, Methuselah, Lamech, 4 Noah, Shem, Ham, and Japheth. 5 The descendants of Japheth were Gomer, Magog, Madai, Javan, Tubal, Meshech, and Tiras. 6 The descendants of Gomer were Ashkenaz, Riphath, and Togarmah. 7 The descendants of Javan were Elishah, Tarshish, the Kittim, and the Rodanim.

8 The descendants of Ham were Cush, Mizraim, Put, and Canaan. 9 The descendants of Cush were Seba, Havilah, Sabta, Raama, and Sabteca. The descendants of Raama were Sheba and Dedan. 10 Cush became the father of Nimrod, who was the first to be a conqueror on the earth. 11 Mizraim became the father of the Ludim, Anamim, Lehabim, Naphtuhim, 12 Pathrusim, Casluhim, and Caphtorim, from whom the Philistines sprang. 13 Canaan became the father of Sidon, his first-born, and Heth, 14 and the Jebusite, the Amorite, the Girgashite, 15 the Hivite, the Akite, the Sinite, 16 the Arvadite, the Zemarite, and the Hamathite.

17 The descendants of Shem were Elam, Asshur, Arpachshad, Lud, and Aram. The descendants of Aram were Uz, Hul, Gether, and Mash. 18 Arpachshad became the father of Shelah, and Shelah became the father of Eber. 19 Two sons were born to Eber; the first was named Peleg (for in his time the world was divided), and his brother was Joktan. 20 Joktan became the father of Almodad, Sheleph, Hazarmaveth, Jerah, 21 Hadoram, Uzal, Diklah, 22 Ebal, Abimael, Sheba, 23 Ophir, Havilah, and Jobab; all these were the sons of Joktan.

24 Shem, Arpachshad, Shelah, 25 Eber, Peleg, Reu, 26 Serug, Nahor, Terah, 27 Abram, who was Abraham.

From Abraham to Jacob

28 The sons of Abraham were Isaac and Ishmael. 29 These were their descendants:

Nebaioth, the first-born of Ishmael, then Kedar, Abdeel, Mibsam, 30 Mishma, Dumah, Massa, Hadad, Tema, 31 Jetur, Naphish, and Kedemah. These were the descendants of Ishmael.

32 The descendants of Keturah, Abraham's concubine: she bore Zimran, Jokshan, Medan, Midian, Ishbak, and Shuah. The sons of Jokshan were Sheba and Dedan. 33 The descendants of Midian were Ephah, Epher, Hanoch, Abida, and Eldaah. All these were the descendants of Keturah.

34 Abraham became the father of Isaac. The sons of Isaac were Esau and Israel.

35 The sons of Esau were Eliphaz, Reuel, Jeush, Jalam, and Korah. 36 The sons of Eliphaz were Teman, Omar, Zephi, Gatam, Kenaz, [Timna,] and Amalek. 37 The sons of Reuel were Nahath, Zerah, Shammah, and Mizzah.

1, 1–9, 34: The Chronicler set as his task the retelling, from his particular viewpoint, of the story of God's people from the beginning to his own day. Since his primary interest was the history of David and the Davidic dynasty of Judah, he presents through mere genealogical lists a summary of what preceded the reign of Saul, David's predecessor in the kingdom. The sources for these genealogies are mostly the canonical Hebrew Scriptures that were already in their present form in his time. The cross references in this book indicate in each case the scriptural sources used.

38 The descendants of Seir were Lotan, Shobal, Zibeon, Anah, Dishon, Ezer, and Dishan. 39 The sons of Lotan were Hori and Homam; Timna was the sister of Lotan. 40 The sons of Shobal were Alian, Manahath, Ebal, Shephi, and Onam. The sons of Zibeon were Aiah and Anah. 41 The sons of Anah: Dishon. The sons of Dishon were Hemdan. Eshban, Ithran, and Cheran. 42 The sons of Esher were Bilhan, Zaavan, and Jaakan. The sons of Dishan were Uz and Aran.

43 The kings who reigned in the land of Edom before they had Israelite kings were the following: Bela, son of Beor, the name of whose city was Dinhabah. 44 When Bela died, Jobab, son of Zerah, from Bozrah, succeeded him. 45 When Jobab died, Husham, from the land of the Temanites, succeeded him. 46 Husham died and Hadad, son of Bedad, succeeded him. He overthrew the Midianites on the Moabite plateau, and the name of his city was Avith. 47 Hadad died and Samlah of Masrekah succeeded him. 48 Samlah died and Shaul from Rehoboth-han-nahar succeeded him. 49 When Shaul died, Baalhanan, son of Achbor, succeeded him. 50 Baalhanan died and Hadad succeeded him. The name of his city was Pai, and his wife's name was Mehetabel. She was the daughter of Matred, who was the daughter of Mezahab. 51 After Hadad died. . . .

These were the chiefs of Edom: the chiefs of Timna, Aliah, Jetheth, 52 Oholibamah, Elah, Pinon, 53 Kenaz, Teman, Mibzar, 54 Magdiel, and Iram were the chiefs of Edom.

2 These were the sons of Israel: Reuben, Simeon, Levi, Judah, Issachar, Zebulun, 2 Dan, Joseph, Benjamin, Naphtali, Gad, and Asher.

Judah

3 The sons of Judah were: Er, Onan, and Shelah; these three were born to him of Bathshua, a Canaanite woman. But Judah's first-born, Er, was wicked in the sight of the LORD, so he killed him. 4 Judah's daughter-in-law Tamar bore him Perez and Zerah, so that he had five sons in all.

5 The sons of Perez were Hezron and Hamul. 6 The sons of Zerah were Zimri, Ethan, Heman, Calcol, and Darda—five in all. 7 The sons of Zimri: Carmi. The sons of Carmi: Achar, who brought trouble upon Israel by violating the ban. 8 The sons of Ethan: Azariah. 9 The sons born to Hezron were Jerahmeel, Ram, and Chelubai.

10 Ram became the father of Amminadab, and Amminadab became the father of Nahshon, a prince of the Judahites. 11 Nahshon became the father of Salmah. Salmah became the father of Boaz. 12 Boaz became the father of Obed. Obed became the father of Jesse. 13 Jesse became the father of Eliab, his first-born, of Abinadab, the second son, Shimea, the third, 14 Nethanel, the fourth, Raddai, the fifth, 15 Ozem, the sixth, and David, the seventh. 16 Their sisters were Zeruiah and Abigail. Zeruiah had three sons: Abishai, Joab, and Asahel. 17 Abigail bore Amasa, whose father was Jether the Ishmaelite.

18 By his wife Azubah, Caleb, son of Hezron, became the father of a daughter, Jerioth. Her sons were Jesher, Shobab, and Ardon. 19 When Azubah died, Caleb married Ephrath, who bore him Hur. 20 Hur became the father of Uri, and Uri became the father of Bezalel. 21 Then Hezron had relations with the daughter of Machir, the father of Gilead, having married her when he was sixty years old. She bore him Segub. 22 Segub became the father of Jair, who possessed twenty-three cities in the land of Gilead. 23 Geshur and Aram took from them the villages of Jair, that is, Kenath and its towns, sixty cities in all, which belonged to the sons of Machir, the father of Gilead. 24 After the death of Hezron, Caleb had relations with Ephrathah, the widow of his father Hezron, and she bore him Ashhur, the father of Tekoa.

25 The sons of Jerahmeel, the first-born of Hezron, were Ram, the first-born, then Bunah, Oren, and Ozem, his brothers. 26 Jerahmeel also had another wife, Atarah by name, who was the mother of Onam. 27 The sons of Ram, the first-born of Jerahmeel, were Maaz, Jamin, and Eker. 28 The sons of Onam were Shammai and Jada. The sons of Shammai were Nadab and Abishur. 29 Abishur's wife, who was named Abihail, bore him Ahban and Molid. 30 The sons of Nadab were Seled and Appaim. 31 Seled died without sons. The sons of Appaim: Ishi. The sons of Ishi: Sheshan. The sons of Sheshan: Ahlai. 32 The sons of Jada, the brother of Shammai, were Jether and Jonathan. Jether died without sons. 33 The sons of Jonathan were Peleth and Zaza. These were the descendants of Jerahmeel. 34 Sheshan, who had no sons, only daughters, had an Egyptian slave named Jarha. 35 Sheshan gave his daughter in marriage to his slave Jarha, and she bore him Attai. 36 Attai became the father of Nathan. Nathan became the father of Zabad. 37 Zabad became the father of Ephlal. Ephlal became the father of Obed. 38 Obed became the father of Jehu. Jehu became the father of Azariah. 39 Azariah became the father of Helez. Helez became the father of Eleasah. 40 Eleasah became the father of Sismai. Sismai became the father of Shallum. 41 Shallum became the father of Jekamiah. Jekamiah became the father of Elishama.

42 The descendants of Caleb, the brother of Jerahmeel: [Mesha] his first-born, who was the father of Ziph. Then the sons of Mareshah, who was the father of Hebron. 43 The sons of Hebron were Korah, Tappuah, Rekem, and Shema. 44 Shema became the father of

---

1, 38: *Seir*: another name for *Esau* (v 35) or *Edom* (v 43).

2, 3—4, 23: For two reasons, the Chronicler places the genealogy of the tribe of Judah before that of the other tribes, giving it also a greater length than the others: because of his interest in David and because in the Chronicler's time the people of God were almost exclusively Jews. Both David and the Jews were of the tribe of Judah.

2, 9: *Chelubai*: a variant form of the name *Caleb* (vv 18.42), distinct from *Chelub* of 4, 11.

2, 10—17: Immediate ancestors of David. A similar list is given in Ru 4, 19—22; each list, independent of the other, derives from a common source.

2, 18—24: Descendants of Caleb. In 4, 15, as is often the case in the Pentateuch (Nm 13, 6; 14, 6.30; 26, 65;

etc.), Caleb is called *son of Jephunneh*. Here he is called *son of Hezron*, perhaps because the Calebites were reckoned as part of the clan of the Hezronites.

2, 25—41: The Jerahmeelites were a clan in the Negeb of Judah.

2, 42—49: Another list, dating from preexilic times, of the Calebites, a clan that inhabited the south of Judah.

Raham, who was the father of Jorkeam. Rekem became the father of Shammai. 45 The son of Shammai: Maon, who was the father of Beth-zur. 46 Ephah, Caleb's concubine, bore Haran, Moza, and Gazez. Haran became the father of Gazez. 47 The sons of Jahdai were Regem, Jotham, Geshan, Pelet, Ephah, and Shaaph. 48 Maacha, Caleb's concubine, bore Sheber and Tirhanah. 49 She also bore Shaaph the father of Madmannah, Sheva, the father of Machbenah, and the father of Gibea. Achsah was Caleb's daughter.

50 These were the descendants of Caleb, sons of Hur, the first-born of Ephrathah: Shobal, the father of Kiriath-jearim, 51 Salma, the father of Bethlehem, and Hareph, the father of Bethgader. 52 The sons of Shobal, the father of Kiriarh-jearim, were Reaiah, half the Manahathites, 53 and the clans of Kiriath-jearim: the Ithrites, the Puthites, the Shumathites, and the Mishraites. From these the people of Zorah and the Eshtaolites derived. 54 The descendants of Salma were Bethlehem, the Netophathites, Atroth-beth-Joab, half the Manahathites, and the Zorites. 55 The clans of the Sopherim dwelling in Jabez were the Tirathites, the Shimeathites, and the Sucathites. They were the Kenites, who came from Hammath of the ancestor of the Rechabites.

3 The following were the sons of David who were born to him in Hebron: the first-born, Amnon, by Ahinoam of Jezreel; the second, Daniel, by Abigail of Carmel; 2 the third, Absalom, son of Maacah, who was the daughter of Talmai, king of Geshur; the fourth, Adonijah, son of Haggith; 3 the fifth, Shephatiah, by Abital; the sixth, Ithream, by his wife Eglah. 4 Six in all were born to him in Hebron, where he reigned seven years and six months. Then he

reigned thirty-three years in Jerusalem, 5 where the following were born to him: Shimea, Shobab, Nathan, Solomon—four by Bathsheba, the daughter of Ammiel; 6 Ibhar, Elishua, Eliphelet, 7 Nogah, Nepheg, Japhia, 8 Elishama, Eliada, and Eliphelet—nine. 9 All these were sons of David, in addition to other sons by concubines; and Tamar was their sister.

10 The son of Solomon was Rehoboam, whose son was Abijah, whose son was Asa, whose son was Jehoshaphat, 11 whose son was Joram, whose son was Ahaziah, whose son was Joash, 12 whose son was Amaziah, whose son was Azariah, whose son was Jotham, 13 whose son was Ahaz, whose son was Hezekiah, whose son was Manasseh, 14 whose son was Amon, whose son was Josiah. 15 The sons of Josiah were: the first-born, Johanan; the second, Jehoiakim; the third, Zedekiah; the fourth, Shallum. 16 The sons of Jehoiakim were: Jeconiah, his son; Zedekiah, his son.

17 The sons of Jeconiah the captive were: Shealtiel, 18 Malchiram, Pedaiah, Shenazzar, Jekamiah, Shama, and Nedabiah. 19 The sons of Pedaiah were Zerubbabel and Shimei. The sons of Zerubbabel were Meshullam and Hananiah; 20 Shelomith was their sister. The sons of Meshullam were Hashubah, Ohel, Berechiah, Hasadiah, Jushab-hesed—five. 21 The sons of Hananiah were Pelatiah, Jeshaiah, Rephaiah, Arnan, Obadiah, and Shecaniah. 22 The sons of Shecaniah were Shemiah, Hattush, Igal, Bariah, Neariah, Shaphat—six. 23 The sons of Neariah were Elioenai, Hizkiah, and Azrikam—three. 24 The sons of Elioenai were Hodaviah, Eliashib, Pelaiah, Akkub, Johanan, Delaiah, and Anani—seven.

4 The descendants of Judah were: Perez, Hezron, Carmi, Hur, and

Shobal. 2 Reaiah, the son of Shobal, became the father of Jahath, and Jahath became the father of Ahumai and Lahad. These were the clans of the Zorathites.

3 These were the descendants of Hareph, the father of Etam: Jezreel, Ishma, and Idbash; their sister was named Hazzelelponi. 4 Penuel was the father of Gedor, and Ezer the father of Hushah. These were the descendants of Hur, the first-born of Ephrathah, the father of Bethlehem.

5 Ashhur, the father of Tekoa, had two wives, Helah and Naarah. 6 Naarah bore him Ahuzzam, Hepher, the Temenites and the Ahashtarites. These were the descendants of Naarah. 7 The sons of Helah were Zereth, Izhar, Ethnan, and Koz. 8 Koz became the father of Anub and Zobebah, as well as of the clans of Aharhel, son of Harum. 9 Jabez was the most distinguished of the brothers. His mother had named him Jabez, saying, "I bore him with pain." 10 Jabez prayed to the God of Israel: "Oh, that you may truly bless me and extend my boundaries! Help me and make me free of misfortune, without pain!" And God granted his prayer.

11 Chelub, the brother of Shuhah, became the father of Mehir, who was the father of Eshton. 12 Eshton became the father of Bethrapha, Paseah, and Tehinnah, the father of the city of Nahash. These were the men of Recah.

13 The sons of Kenaz were Othniel and Seraiah. The sons of Othniel were Hathath and Meonothai; 14 Meonothai became the father of Ophrah. Seraiah became the father of Joab, the father of Geharashim, so called because they were craftsmen. 15 The sons of Caleb, son of Jephunneh, were Ir, Elah, and Naam. The sons of Elah were . . . and Kenaz.

16 The sons of Jehallelel were Ziph, Ziphah, Tiria, and Asarel. 17 The sons of Ezrah were Jether, Mered, Epher, and Jalon. Jether became the father of Miriam, Shammai,

---

2, 50–55: The Hurites, a clan dwelling to the south and west of Jerusalem and related to the Calebites.
3, 1–9: David's sons.
3, 1: *Daniel:* called *Chileab* in 2 Sm 3, 3.
3, 5: *Shimea:* called *Shammua* in 2 Sm 5, 14. *Ammiel:* called *Eliam* in 2 Sm 11, 3.
3, 10–16: The kings of Judah from Solomon to the destruction of Jerusalem by the Babylonians.
3, 15: *Shallum:* the same as Jehoahaz, Josiah's successor; cf Jer 22, 11.

3, 17–24: The descendants of King *Jechoniah* up to the time of the Chronicler. If twenty-five years are allowed to each generation, the ten generations between *Jechoniah* and *Anani* (the last name on the list) would bring the birth of the latter to about 405 B.C.—an important date in establishing the approximate date of the Chronicler.
3, 18: *Shenazzar:* presumably the same as *Sheshbazzar* of Ezr 1, 8.11; 5, 14ff, the prince of Judah who was the first Jewish governor of Judah after the exile.

Both forms of the name probably go back to the Babylonian name Sin-ab-ussar signifying, "O [god] Sin, protect [our] father!"
3, 19: *Zerubbabel:* here called the son of *Pedaiah,* though elsewhere (Hg 1, 12.14; 2, 2.23; Ezr 3, 2; 5, 2; Neh 12, 1) called *son of Shealtiel.* The latter term may merely mean that Zerubbabel succeeded Shealtiel as head of the house of David.
4, 1–43: The southern tribes.

and Ishbah, the father of Eshtemoa. [. . . . .] 18 His (Mered's) Egyptian wife bore Jered, the father of Gedor, Heber, the father of Soco, and Jekuthiel, the father of Zanoah. These were the sons of Bithiah, the daughter of Pharaoh, whom Mered married. 19 The sons of his Jewish wife, the sister of Naham, the father of Keilah, were Shimon the Garmite and Ishi the Maacathite. 20 The sons of Shimon were Amnon, Rinnah Benhanan, and Tilon. The son of Ishi was Zoheth and the son of Zoheth.... 21 The descendants of Shelah, son of Judah, were: Er, the father of Lecah; Laadah, the father of Mareshah; the clans of the linen weavers' guild in Bethashbea; 22 Jokim; the men of Cozeba; and Joash and Saraph, who held property in Moab, but returned to Bethlehem. [These are events of old.] 23 They were potters and inhabitants of Netaim and Gederah, where they lived in the king's service.

Simeon

24 The sons of Simeon were Nemuel, Jamin, Jachin, Zerah, and Shaul, 25 whose son was Shallum, whose son was Mibsam, whose son was Mishma. 26 The descendants of Mishma were his son Hammuel, whose son was Zaccur, whose son was Shimei. 27 Shimei had sixteen sons and six daughters. His brothers, however, did not have many sons, and as a result all their clans did not equal the number of the Judahites. 28 They dwelt in Beersheba, Moladah, Hazar-shual, 29 Billah, Ezem, Tolad, 30 Bethuel, Hormah, Ziklag, 31 Beth-marcaboth, Hazarsusim, Bethbiri, and Shaaraim. Until David came to reign, these were their cities 32 and their villages. Etam, also, and Ain, Rimmon, Tochen, and Ashan—five cities, 33 together with all their outlying villages as far as Baal. Here is where they dwelt, and so it was inscribed of them in their family records. 34 Meshobab, Jamlech, Joshah, son of Amaziah, 35 Joel, Jehu, son of Joshibiah, son of Seraiah, son of Asiel, 36 Elioenai, Jaakobath, Je-

shohaiah, Asaiah, Adiel, Jesimiel, Benaiah, 37 Ziza, son of Shiphi, son of Allon, son of Jedaiah, son of Shimri, son of Shemaiah— 38 these just named were princes in their clans, and their ancestral houses spread out to such an extent 39 that they went to the approaches of Gedor, east of the valley, seeking pasture for their flocks. 40 They found abundant and good pastures, and the land was spacious, quiet, and peaceful. 41 They who have just been listed by name set out during the reign of Hezekiah, king of Judah, and attacked the tents of Ham (for Hamites dwelt there formerly) and also the Meunites who were there. They pronounced against them the ban that is still in force and dwelt in their place because they found pasture there for their flocks. 42 Five hundred of them (the Simeonites) went to Mount Seir under the leadership of Pelatiah, Neariah, Rephaiah, and Uzziel, sons of Ishi. 43 They attacked the surviving Amalekites who had escaped, and have resided there to the present day.

Reuben

5 The sons of Reuben, the first-born of Israel. (He was indeed the first-born, but because he disgraced the couch of his father his birthright was given to the sons of Joseph, son of Israel, so that he is not listed in the family records according to birthright. 2 Judah, in fact, became powerful among his brothers, so that the ruler came from him. though the birthright had been Joseph's.) 3 The sons of Reuben, the first-born of Israel, were Hanoch, Pallu, Hezron, and Carmi. 4 His son was Joel, whose son was Shemaiah, whose son was Gog, whose son was Shimei, 5 whose son was Micah whose son was Reaiah, whose son was Baal, 6 whose son was Beerah, whom Tiglath-pileser, the king of Assyria, took into exile; he was a prince of the Reubenites. 7 His brothers who belonged to his clans, when they were listed in the family records according to their descendants, were: Jeiel, the chief, and Zechariah, 8 and Bela, son of Azaz, son of Shema, son of Joel. The

Reubenites lived in Aroer and as far as Nebo and Baal-meon; 9 toward the east they dwelt as far as the desert which extends from the Euphrates River, for they had much livestock in the land of Gilead. 10 During the reign of Saul they waged war with the Hagrites, and when they had defeated them they occupied their tents throughout the region east of Gilead.

Gad

11 The Gadites lived alongside them in the land of Bashan as far as Salecah. 12 Joel was chief, Shapham was second in command, and Janai was judge in Bashan. 13 Their brothers, corresponding to their ancestral houses, were: Michael, Meshullam, Sheba, Jorai, Jacan, Zia, and Eber—seven. 14 These were the sons of Abihail, son of Huri, son of Jaroah, son of Gilead, son of Michael, son of Jeshishai, son of Jahdo, son of Buz. 15 Ahi, son of Abdiel, son of Guni, was the head of their ancestral houses. 16 They dwelt in Gilead, in Bashan and its towns, and in all the pasture lands of Sirion to the borders. 17 All were listed in the family records in the time of Jotham, king of Judah, and of Jeroboam, king of Israel.

18 The Reubenites, Gadites, and half-tribe of Manasseh were warriors, men who bore shield and sword and who drew the bow, trained in warfare—forty-four thousand seven hundred and sixty men fit for military service. 19 When they waged war against the Hagrites and against Jetur, Naphish, and Nodab, 20 they received help so that they mastered the Hagrites and all who were with them. For during the battle they called on God, and he heard them because they had put their trust in him. 21 Along with one hundred thousand men they also captured their livestock: fifty thousand camels, two hundred fifty thousand sheep, and two thousand asses. 22 Many had fallen in battle, for victory is from God; and they took over their dwelling place until the time of the exile.

East Manasseh

23 The numerous members of the half-tribe of Manasseh lived in the

---

4, 39: *Gedor:* in the Greek, Gerar, no doubt correct.
5, 1–26: The Transjordan tribes.

land of Bashan as far as Baal-hermon, Senir, and Mount Hermon. 24 The following were the heads of their ancestral houses: Epher, Ishi, Eliel, Azriel, Jeremiah, Hodaviah, and Jahdiel—men who were warriors, famous men, and heads over their ancestral houses.

25 However, they offended the God of their fathers by lusting after the gods of the natives of the land, whom God had cleared out of their way. 26 Therefore the God of Israel incited against them the anger of Pul, king of Assyria, and of Tiglath-pileser, king of Assyria, who deported the Reubenites, the Gadites, and the half-tribe of Manasseh and brought them to Halah, Habor, and Hara, and to the river Gozan, where they have remained to this day.

Levi

27 The sons of Levi were Gershon, Kohath, and Merari. 28 The sons of Kohath were Amram, Izhar, Hebron, and Uzziel. 29 The children of Amram were Aaron, Moses, and Miriam. The sons of Aaron were Nadab, Abihu, Eleazar, and Ithamar. 30 Eleazar became the father of Phinehas. Phinehas became the father of Abishua. 31 Abishua became the father of Bukki. Bukki became the father of Uzzi. 32 Uzzi became the father of Zerahiah. Zerahiah became the father of Meraioth. 33 Meraioth became the father of Amariah. Amariah became the father of Ahitub. 34 Ahitub became the father of Zadok. Zadok became the father of Ahimaaz. 35 Ahimaaz became the father of Azariah. Azariah became the father of Johanan. 36 Johanan became the father of Azariah, who served as a priest in the temple Solomon built in Jerusalem. 37 Azariah became the father of Ahitub. 38 Ahitub became the father of Zadok. Zadok became the father of Shallum. 39 Shallum became the father of Hilkiah. Hilkiah became the father of Azariah. 40 Azariah became the father of Seraiah. Seraiah

became the father of Jehozadak. 41 Jehozadak was one of those who went into the exile which the LORD inflicted on Judah and Jerusalem through Nebuchadnezzar.

6 The sons of Levi were Gershon, Kohath, and Merari. 2 The sons of Gershon were named Libni and Shimei. 3 The sons of Kohath were Amram, Izhar, Hebron, and Uzziel. 4 The sons of Merari were Mahli and Mushi.

The following were the clans of Levi, distributed according to their ancestors: 5 of Gershon: his son Libni, whose son was Jahath, whose son was Zimmah, 6 whose son was Joah, whose son was Iddo, whose son was Zerah, whose son was Jetherai.

7 The descendants of Kohath were: his son Amminadab, whose son was Korah, whose son was Assir, 8 whose son was Elkanah, whose son was Ebiasaph, whose son was Assir, 9 whose son was Tahath, whose son was Uriel, whose son was Uzziah, whose son was Shaul. 10 The sons of Elkanah were Amasai and Ahimoth, 11 whose son was Elkanah, whose son was Zophai, whose son was Nahath, 12 whose son was Eliab, whose son was Jeroham, whose son was Elkanah whose son was Samuel. 13 The sons of Samuel were Joel, the first-born, and Abijah, the second.

14 The descendants of Merari were Mahli, whose son was Libni, whose son was Shimei, whose son was Uzzah, 15 whose son was Shimea, whose son was Haggiah, whose son was Asaiah.

16 The following were entrusted by David with the choir services in the LORD's house from the time when the ark had obtained a permanent resting place. 17 They served as singers before the Dwelling of the meeting tent until Solomon built temple of the LORD in Jerusalem, and they performed their services in an order prescribed for them. 18 Those who so performed are the following, together with their descendants.

Among the Kohathites: Heman, the chanter, son of Joel, son of Samuel, 19 son of Elkanah, son of Jeroham, son of Eliel, son of Toah, 20 son of Zuth, son of Elkanah, son of Manath, son of Amasi, 21 son of Elkanah, son of Joel, son of Azariah, son of Zaphaniah, 22 son of Tahath son of Assir, son of Ebiasaph, son of Korah, 23 son of Izhar, son of Kohath, son of Levi, son of Israel.

24 His brother Asaph stood at his right hand. Asaph was the son of Berechiah, son of Shimea, 25 son of Michael, son of Baaseiah, son of Malchijah, 26 son of Ethni, son of Zerah, son of Adaiah, 27 son of Ethan, son of Zimmah, son of Shimei, 28 son of Jahath, son of Gershon, son of Levi.

29 Their brothers, the Merarites, stood at the left: Ethan, son of Kishi, son of Abdi, son of Malluch, 30 son of Hashabiah, son of Amaziah, son of Hilkiah, 31 son of Amzi, son of Bani, son of Shemer, 32 son of Mahli, son of Mushi, son of Merari, son of Levi.

33 Their brother Levites were appointed to all the other services of the Dwelling of the house of God. 34 However, it was Aaron and his descendants who burnt the offerings on the altar of holocausts and on the altar of incense; they alone had charge of the holy of holies and of making atonement for Israel, as Moses, the servant of God, had ordained.

35 These were the descendants of Aaron: his son Eleazar, whose son was Phinehas, whose son was Abishua, 36 whose son was Bukki, whose son was Uzzi, whose son was Zerahiah, 37 whose son was Meraioth, whose son was Amariah, whose son was Ahitub, 38 whose son was Zadok, whose son was Ahimaaz.

39 The following were their dwelling places to which their encampment was limited. To the descendants of Aaron who belonged to the clan of the Kohathites, since the first lot fell to them, 40 was assigned Hebron with its adjacent pasture lands in the

---

5, 26: *Pul:* the name which the Assyrian king *Tiglath-pileser* III (745–727 B.C.) took as king of Babylon.
5, 27—6, 66: The tribe of Levi. The list gives special prominence to Levi's son *Kohath*, from whom were descended both the Aaronite priests (5, 28–41) and the leading group of temple singers (6, 18–23).

5, 30–41: The line of preexilic priests, The list seems to be confused in vv 36ff, which repeat the names, mostly in inverse order, that occur in vv 34ff. A similar but shorter list is given, with variations, in Ezr 7, 1–5.
6, 16–32: The origin of the *choir services* performed by the levitical families in the postexilic temple at the

time of the Chronicler is here attributed to David, somewhat as all the laws in the Pentateuch are attributed to Moses.
6, 39–66: Regarding the nature of the rights of Levites in the cities assigned to them, see note on Jos 21, 1.

land of Judah, 41 although the open country and the villages belonging to the city had been given to Caleb, the son of Jephunneh. 42 There were assigned to the descendants of Aaron: Hebron, a city of asylum, Libnah with its pasture lands, Jattir with its pasture lands, Eshtemoa with its pasture lands, 43 Holon with its pasture lands, Debir with its pasture lands, 44 Ashan with its pasture lands, Jetta with its pasture lands, and Beth-shemesh with its pasture lands. 45 Also from the tribe of Benjamin: Gibeon with its pasture lands, Geba with its pasture lands, Almon with it pasture lands, Anathoth with its pasture lands. In all they had thirteen cities with their pasture lands. 49 The Israelites assigned these cities with their pasture lands to the Levites, 50 designating them by name and assigning them by lot from the tribes of the Judahites, Simeonites, and Benjaminites.

46 The other Kohathites obtained ten cities by lot for their clans from the tribe of Ephraim, from the tribe of Dan, and from the half-tribe of Manasseh. 47 The clans of the Gershonites obtained thirteen cities from the tribes of Issachar, Asher, and Naphtali, and from the half-tribe of Manasseh in Bashan. 48 The clans of the Merarites obtained twelve cities by lot from the tribes of Reuben, Gad, and Zebulun.

51 The clans of the Kohathites obtained cities by lot from the tribe of Ephraim. 52 They were assigned Shechem in the mountain region of Ephraim, a city of asylum, with its pasture lands, Gezer with its pasture lands, 53 Kibzaim with its pasture lands, and Beth-horon with its pasture lands. 54 From the tribe of Dan: Elteke with its pasture lands, Gibbethon with its pasture lands, Aijalon with its pasture lands, and Gath-rimmon with its pasture lands. 55 From the half-tribe of Manasseh: Taanach with its pasture lands and Ibleam with its pasture lands. These belonged to the rest of the Kohathite clan.

56 The clans of the Gershonites received from the half-tribe of Manasseh: Golan in Bashan with its pas-

ture lands and Ashtaroth with its pasture lands. 57 From the tribe of Issachar: Kedesh with its pasture lands, Daberath with its pasture lands 58 Ramoth with its pasture lands, and Engannim with its pasture lands. 59 From the tribe of Asher: Mashal with its pasture lands, Abdon with its pasture lands, 60 Hilkath with its pasture lands, and Rehob with its pasture lands. 61 From the tribe of Naphtali: Kedesh in Galilee with its pasture lands, Hammon with its pasture lands, and Kiriathaim with its pasture-lands.

62 The rest of the Merarites received from the tribe of Zebulun: Jokneam with its pasture lands, Kartah with its pasture lands, Rimmon with its pasture lands, and Tabor with its pasture lands. 63 Across the Jordan at Jericho [that is, east of the Jordan] they received from the tribe of Reuben: Bezer in the desert with its pasture lands, Jahzah with its pasture lands, 64 Kedemoth with its pasture lands, and Mephaath with its pasture lands. 65 From the tribe of Gad: Ramoth in Gilead with its pasture lands, Mahanaim with its pasture lands, 66 Heshbon with its pasture lands, and Jazer with its pasture lands.

Issachar

7 The sons of Issachar were Tola, Puah, Jashub, and Shimron: four. 2 The sons of Tola were Uzzi, Rephaiah, Jeriel, Jahmai, Ibsam, and Shemuel, warrior heads of the ancestral houses of Tola. Their kindred numbered twenty-two thousand six hundred in the time of David. 3 The sons of Uzzi: Izarahiah. The sons of Izarahiah were Michael, Obadiah, Joel, and Isshiah. All five of these were chiefs. 4 Their kindred, by ancestral houses, numbered thirty-six thousand men in organized military troops, since they had more wives and sons 5 than their fellow tribesmen. In all the clans of Issachar there was a total of eighty-seven thousand warriors in their family records.

Benjamin

6 The sons of Benjamin were Bela, Becher, and Jediael—three. 7 The sons of Bela were Ezbon, Uzzi, Uzziel Jerimoth, and Iri—five. They were

the heads of their ancestral houses and warriors. Their family records listed twenty-two thousand and thirty four. 8 The sons of Becher were Zemirah, Joash, Eliezer, Elioenai, Omri, Jeremoth, Abijah, Anathoth, and Alemeth—all these were the sons of Becher. 9 Their family records listed twenty thousand two hundred of their kindred who were heads of their ancestral houses and warriors. 10 The sons of Jediael: Bilhan. The sons of Bilhan were Jeush, Benjamin, Ehud, Chenaanah, Zethan, Tarshish, and Ahishahar. 11 All these were descendants of Jediael, heads of ancestral houses and warriors. They numbered seventeen thousand two hundred men fit for military service . . . Shupham and Hupham.

Dan, Naphtali and Manasseh

12 The sons of Dan: Hushim. 13 The sons of Naphtali were Jahziel, Guni, Jezer, and Shallum. These were descendants of Bilhah. 14 The sons of Manasseh, whom his Aramean concubine bore: she bore Machir, the father of Gilead. 15 Machir took a wife whose name was Maacah; his sister's name was Molecheth. Manasseh's second son was named Zelophehad, but to Zelophehad only daughters were born. 16 Maacah, Machir's wife, bore a son whom she named Peresh. He had a brother named Sheresh, whose sons were Ulam and Rakem. 17 The sons of Ulam: Bedan. These were the descendants of Gilead, the son of Machir, the son of Manasseh. 18 His sister Molecheth bore Ishbod, Abiezer, and Mahlah. 19 The sons of Shemida were Ahian, Shechem, Likhi, and Aniam.

Ephraim

20 The sons of Ephraim: Shuthelah, whose son was Bered, whose son was Tahath, whose son was Eleadah, whose son was Tahath, 21 whose son was Zabad. Ephraim's son Shuthelah, and Ezer and Elead, who were born in the land, were slain by the inhabitants of Gath because they had gone down to take away their livestock. 22 Their father Ephraim mourned for a long time, but after his kinsmen had come and comforted him, 23 he visited his wife, who

7, 1–40: The northern tribes.

conceived and bore him a son whom he named Beriah, since evil had befallen his house. 24 He had a daughter, Sheerah, who built lower and upper Beth-horon and Uzzensheerah. 25 Zabad's son was Rephah, whose son was Resheph, whose son was Telah, whose son was Tahan, 26 whose son was Ladan, whose son was Ammihud, whose son was Elishama, 27 whose son was Nun, whose son was Joshua.

28 Their property and their dwellings were in Bethel and its towns, Naraan to the east, Gezer and its towns to the west, and also Shechem and its towns as far as Ayyah and its towns. 29 Manasseh, however, had possession of Beth-shean and its towns, Taanach and its towns, Megiddo and its towns, and Dor and its towns. In these dwelt the descendants of Joseph, the son of Israel.

Asher

30 The sons of Asher were Imnah, Iishvah, Ishvi, and Beriah; their sister was Serah. 31 Beriah's sons were Heber and Malchiel, who was the father of Birzaith. 32 Heber became the father of Japhlet, Shomer, Hotham, and their sister Shua. 33 The sons of Japhlet were Pasach, Bimhal, and Ashvath; these were the sons of Japhlet. 34 The sons of Shomer were Ahi, Rohgah, Jehubbah and Aram. 35 The sons of his brother Hotham were Zophah, Imna, Shelesh, and Amal. 36 The sons of Zophah were Suah, Harnepher, Shual, Beri, Imrah, 37 Bezer, Hod, Shamma, Shilshah, Ithran, and Beera 38 The sons of Jether were Jephunneh, Pispa, and Ara. 39 The sons of Ulla were Arah, Hanniel, and Rizia. 40 All these were descendants of Asher, heads of ancestral houses, distinguished men, warriors, and chiefs among princes. Their family records numbered twenty-six thousand men fit for military service.

Benjamin

8 Benjamin became the father of Bela, his first-born, Ashbel, the second son, Aharah, the third, 2 Nohah, the fourth, and Rapha, the fifth. 3 The sons of Bela were Addar and Gera, the father of Ehud. 4 The sons of Ehud were Abishua, Naaman, Ahoah, 5 Gera, Shephuphan, and Huram. 6 These were the sons of Ehud, family heads over those who dwelt in Geba and were deported to Manahath, 7 Also Naaman, Ahijah, and Gera. The last, who led them into exile, became the father of Uzza and Ahihud. 8 Shaharaim became a father on the Moabite plateau after he had put away his wives Hushim and Baara. 9 By his wife Hodesh he became the father of Jobab, Zibia, Mesha, Malcam, 10 Jeuz, Sachia, and Mirmah. These were his sons, family heads. 11 By Hushim he became the father of Abitub and Elpaal. 12 The sons of Elpaal were Eber, Misham, Shemed, who built Ono and Lod with its nearby towns, 13 Beriah and Shema. They were family heads of those who dwelt in Aijalon, and they put the inhabitants of Gath to flight. 14 Their brethren were Elpaal, Shashak, and Jeremoth. 15 Zebadiah, Arad, Eder, 16 Michael, Ishpah, and Joah were the sons of Beriah. 17 Zebadiah, Meshullam, Hizki, Heber, 18 Ishmerai, Izliah, and Jobab were the sons of Elpaal. 19 Jakim, Zichri, Zabdi, 20 Elienai, Zillethai, Eliel, 21 Adaiah, Beraiah, and Shimrath were the sons of Shimei. 22 Ishpan, Eber, Eliel, 23 Abdon, Zichri, Hanan, 24 Hananiah, Elam, Anthothijah, 25 Iphdeiah, and Penuel were the sons of Shashak. 26 Shamsherai, Shehariah Athaliah, 27 Jaareshiah, Elijah, Zichri were the sons of Jeroham. 28 These were the family heads over their kindred, chiefs who dwelt in Jerusalem.

29 In Gibeon dwelt Jeiel, the founder of Gibeon, whose wife's name was Maacah; 30 also his first-born son, Abdon, and Zur, Kish, Baal, Ner, Nadab, 31 Gedor, Ahio, Zecher, and Mikloth. 32 Mikloth became the father of Shimeah. These, too, dwelt with their relatives in Jerusalem, opposite their fellow tribesmen. 33 Ner became the father of Kish, and Kish became the father of Saul. Saul became the father of Jonathan, Malchishua, Abinadab, and Eshbaal. 34 The son of Jonathan was Meribbaal, and Meribbaal became the father of Micah. 35 The sons of Micah were Pithon, Melech, Tarea, and Ahaz. 36 Ahaz became the father of Jehoaddah, and Jehoaddah, became the father of Alemeth, Azmaveth, and Zimri. Zimri became the father of Moza. 37 Moza became the father of Binea, whose son was Raphah, whose son was Eleasah, whose son was Azel. 38 Azel had six sons, whose names were Azrikam, his first-born, Ishmael, Sheariah, Azariah, Obadiah, and Hanan; all these were the sons of Azel. 39 The sons of Eshek, his brother, were Ulam, his first-born, Jeush, the second son, and Eliphelet, the third. 40 The sons of Ulam were combat archers, and many were their sons and grandsons: one hundred and fifty. All these were the descendants of Benjamin.

9 Thus all Israel was inscribed in its family records which are recorded in the book of the kings of Israel.

Now Judah had been carried into captivity to Babylon because of its rebellion. 2 The first to settle again in their cities and dwell there were certain lay Israelites, the priests, the Levites, and the temple slaves.

Jerusalemites

3 In Jerusalem lived Judahites and Benjaminites; also Ephraimites and Manassehites. 4 Among the Judahites was Uthai, son of Ammihud, son of Omri, son of Imri, son of Bani, one of the descendants of Perez, son of Judah. 5 Among the Shelanites were Asaiah, the first-born, and his sons. 6 Among the Zeraites were Jeuel and six hundred and ninety of their brethren. 7 Among the Benjaminites were Sallu, son of Meshullam, son of Hodaviah, son of Hassenuah; 8 Ibneiah, son of Jeroham; Elah, son of Uzzi, son of Michri; Meshullam, son of Shephatiah, son of Reuel, son of Ibnijah. 9 Their kindred of various families were nine

---

8, 1–40: A second, variant list of the Benjaminites, with special prominence given to Saul's family (vv 33–40).

9, 2–34: The inhabitants of Jerusalem after the exile. A similar list, with many variants in the names, is given in Neh 11, 3–24.

hundred and fifty-six. All those named were heads of their ancestral houses.

10 Among the priests were Jedaiah; Jehoiarib; Jachin; 11 Azariah, son of Hilkiah, son of Meshullam, son of Zadok, son of Meraioth, son of Ahitub, the ruler of the house of God; 12 Adaiah, son of Jeroham, son of Pashhur, son of Malchijah; Maasai, son of Adiel, son of Jahzerah, son of Meshullam, son of Meshillemith, son of Immer. 13 Their brethren, heads of their ancestral houses, were one thousand seven hundred and sixty, valiant for the work of the service of the house of God.

14 Among the Levites were Shemaiah, son of Hasshub, son of Azrikam, son of Hashabiah, one of the descendants of Merari; 15 Bakbakkar; Heresh; Galal; Mattaniah, son of Mica, son of Zichri, a descendant of Asaph; 16 Obadiah, son of Shemaiah, son of Galal, a descendant of Jeduthun; and Berechiah, son of Asa, son of Elkanah, whose family lived in the villages of the Netophathites.

17 The gatekeepers were Shallum, Akkub, Talmon, Ahiman, and their brethren; Shallum was the chief. 18 Previously they had stood guard at the king's gate on the east side; now they became gatekeepers for the encampments of the Levites. 19 Shallum, son of Kore, son of Ebiasaph, a descendant of Korah, and his brethren of the same ancestral house of the Korahites had as their assigned task the guarding of the threshold of the tent, just as their fathers had guarded the entrance to the encampment of the LORD. 20 Phinehas, son of Eleazar, had been their chief in times past—the LORD be with him! 21 Zechariah, son of Meshelemiah, guarded the gate of the meeting tent. 22 In all, those who were chosen for gatekeepers at the threshold were two hundred and twelve. They were inscribed in the family records of their villages. David and Samuel the seer had established them in their position of trust. 23 Thus they and their sons kept guard over the gates of the house of the LORD, the house which was then a tent. 24 The gatekeepers were stationed at the four sides, to

the east, the west, the north, and the south. 25 Their kinsmen who lived in their own villages took turns in assisting them for seven-day periods, 26 while the four chief gatekeepers were on constant duty. These were the Levites who also had charge of the chambers and treasures of the house of God. 27 At night they lodged about the house of God, for it was in their charge and they had the duty of opening it each morning.

28 Some of them had charge of the liturgical equipment, tallying it as it was brought in and taken out. 29 Others were appointed to take care of the utensils and all the sacred vessels, as well as the fine flour, the wine, the oil, the frankincense, and the spices. 30 It was the sons of priests, however, who mixed the spiced ointments. 31 Mattithiah, one of the Levites, the first-born of Shallum the Koreite, was entrusted with preparing the cakes. 32 Benaiah the Kohathite, one of their brethren, was in charge of setting out the showbread each sabbath.

33 These were the chanters and the gatekeepers, family heads over the Levites. They stayed in the chambers when free of duty, for day and night they had to be ready for service. 34 These were the levitical family heads over their kindred, chiefs who dwelt in Jerusalem.

THE HISTORY OF DAVID

Genealogy of Saul

35 In Gibeon dwelt Jeiel, the founder of Gibeon, whose wife's name was Maacah. 36 His first-born son was Abdon; then came Zur, Kish, Baal, Ner, Nadab, 37 Gedor, Ahio, Zechariah, and Mikloth. 38 Mikloth became the father of Shimean. These, too, with their brethren, dwelt opposite their brethren in Jerusalem. 39 Ner became the father of Kish, and Kish became the father of Saul. Saul became the father of Jonathan, Malchishua, Abinadab, and Eshbaal. 40 The son of Jonathan was Meribbaal, and Meribbaal became the father of Micah. 41 The sons of Micah were Pithon, Melech, Tahrea, and Ahaz. 42 Ahaz became the father of Jehoaddah, and

Jehoaddah became the father of Alemeth, Azmaveth, and Zimri. Zimri became the father of Moza. 43 Moza became the father of Binea, whose son was Rephaiah, whose son was Eleasah, whose son was Azel. 44 Azel had six sons, whose names were Azrikam, his first-born, Ishmael, Sheariah, Azariah, Obadiah, and Hanan; these were the sons of Azel.

His Death and Burial

10 Now the Philistines were at war with Israel; the Israelites fled before the Philistines, and a number of them fell, slain on Mount Gilboa. 2 The Philistines pressed hard after Saul and his sons. When the Philistines had killed Jonathan, Abinadab, and Malchishua, sons of Saul, 3 the whole fury of the battle descended upon Saul. Then the archers found him, and wounded him with their arrows.

4 Saul said to his armor-bearer, "Draw your sword and thrust me through with it, that these uncircumcised may not come and maltreat me." But the armor-bearer, in great fear, refused. So Saul took his own sword and fell on it; 5 and seeing him dead, the armor-bearer also fell on his sword and died. 6 Thus, with Saul and his three sons, his whole house died at one time. 7 When all the Israelites who were in the valley saw that Saul and his sons had died in the rout, they left their cities and fled; thereupon the Philistines came and occupied them.

8 On the following day, when the Philistines came to strip the slain, they found Saul and his three sons where they had fallen on Mount Gilboa. 9 They stripped him, cut off his head, and took his armor; these they sent throughout the land of the Philistines to convey the good news to their idols and their people. 10 His armor they put in the house of their gods, but his skull they impaled on the temple of Dagon.

11 When all the inhabitants of Jabesh-gilead had heard what the Philistines had done to Saul, 12 its warriors rose to a man, recovered the bodies of Saul and his sons, and brought them to Jabesh. They buried their bones under the oak of Jabesh, and fasted seven days.

13 Thus Saul died because of his rebellion against the LORD in disobeying his command, and also because he had sought the counsel of a necromancer, 14 and had not rather inquired of the LORD. Therefore the LORD slew him, and transferred his kingdom to David, the son of Jesse.

David is Made King

11 Then all Israel gathered about David in Hebron, and they said: "Surely, we are of the same bone and flesh as you. 2 Even formerly, when Saul was still the king, it was you who led Israel in all its battles. And now the LORD your God, has said to you, 'You shall shepherd my people Israel and be ruler over them.'" 3 Then all the elders of Israel came to the king at Hebron, and there David made a covenant with them in the presence of the LORD; and they anointed him king over Israel, in accordance with the word of the LORD as revealed through Samuel.

Jerusalem Captured

4 Then David and all Israel went to Jerusalem, that is, Jebus, where the natives of the land were called Jebusites. 5 The inhabitants of Jebus said to David, "You shall not enter here." David nevertheless captured the fortress of Zion, which is the City of David. 6 David said, "Whoever strikes the Jebusites first shall be made the chief commander." Joab, the son of Zeruiah, was the first to go up; and so he became chief. 7 David took up his residence in the fortress, which thenceforth was called the City of David. 8 He rebuilt the city on all sides, from the Millo all the way around, while Joab restored the rest of the city. 9 David became more and more powerful, for the LORD of hosts was with him.

David's Warriors

10 These were David's chief warriors who, together with all Israel, supported him in his reign in order to make him a true king, even as the LORD had commanded concerning Israel. 11 Here is the list of David's warriors:

Ishbaal, the son of Hachamoni, chief of the Three. He brandished his spear against three hundred, whom he slew in a single encounter. 12 Next to him Eleazar, the son of Dodo the Ahohite, one of the Three warriors. 13 He was with David at Pasdammim, where the Philistines had massed for battle. The plowland was fully planted with barley, but its defenders were retreating before the Philistines. 14 He made a stand on the sown ground, kept it safe, and cut down the Philistines. Thus the LORD brought about a great victory.

15 Three of the Thirty chiefs went down to the rock, to David, who was in the cave of Adullam while the Philistines were encamped in the valley of Rephaim. 16 David was then in the stronghold, and a Philistine garrison was at Bethlehem. 17 David expressed a desire: "Oh, that someone would give me a drink from the cistern that is by the gate at Bethlehem!" 18 Thereupon the Three broke through the encampment of the Philistines, drew water from the cistern by the gate at Bethlehem, and carried it back to David. But David refused to drink it. Instead, he poured it out as a libation to the LORD, 19 saying, "God forbid that I should do such a thing! Could I drink the blood of these men who risked their lives?" For at the risk of their lives they had brought it; and so he refused to drink it. Such deeds as these the Three warriors performed.

20 Abishai, the brother of Joab. He was the chief of the Thirty; he brandished his spear against three hundred, and slew them. Thus he had a reputation like that of the Three. 21 He was twice as famous as any of the Thirty and became their commander, but he did not attain to the Three.

22 Benaiah, son of Jehoiada, a valiant man of mighty deeds, from Kabzeel. He killed the two sons of Ariel of Moab, and also, on a snowy day, he went down and killed the lion in the cistern. 23 He likewise slew the Egyptian, a huge man five cubits tall. The Egyptian carried a spear that was like a weaver's heddle-bar, but he came against him with a staff, wrested the spear from the Egyptian's hand, and killed him with his own spear. 24 Such deeds as these of Benaiah, the son of Jehoiada, gave him a reputation like that of the Three. 25 He was more famous than any of the Thirty, but he did not attain to the Three. David put him in charge of his bodyguard.

26 Also these warriors: Asahel, the brother of Joab; Elhanan, son of Dodo, from Bethlehem; 27 Shammoth, from En-harod; Helez, from Palti; 28 Ira, son of Ikkesh, from Tekoa; Abiezer, from Anathoth; 29 Sibbecai, from Husha; Ilai, from Ahoh; 30 Maharia, from Netophah; Heled, son of Baanah, from Netophah; 31 Ithai, son of Ribai, from Gibeah of Benjamin; Benaiah, from Pirathon; 32 Hurai, from the valley of Gaash; Abiel, from Betharabah; 33 Azmaveth, from Bahurim; Eliahba, from Shaalbon; 34 Jashen the Gunite; Jonathan, son of Shagee, from En-harod; 35 Ahiam, son of Sacher, from En-harod; Elipheleth, son of 36 Ahasabi, from Bethmaacah; Ahijah, from Gilo; 37 Hezro, from Carmel; Naarai, the son of Ezbai; 38 Joel, brother of Nathan, from Rehob, the Gadite; 39 Zelek the Ammonite; Naharai, from Beeroth, the armor-bearer of Joab, son of Zeruiah; 40 Ira, from Jattir; Gareb, from Jattir; 41 Uriah the Hittite; Zabad, son of Ahlai, 42 and, in addition to the Thirty, Adina, son of Shiza, the Reubenite, chief of the tribe of Reuben; 43 Hanan, from Beth-maacah; Joshaphat the Mithnite; 44 Uzzia, from Ashterath; Shama and Jeiel, sons of Hotham, from Aroer; 45 Jediael, son of Shimri, and Joha, his brother, the Tizite; 46 Eliel the Mahavite; Jeribai and Joshaviah, sons of Elnaam; Ithmah from Moab; 47 Eliel, Obed, and Jaasiel the Mezobian.

10, 13f: The Chronicler's comment on why Saul met his tragic end: he had disobeyed the Lord's command given through the prophet Samuel (1 Sm 15, 3–9), and had sought counsel of a necromancer (1 Sm 28, 6–19), contrary to the Mosaic law against necromancy (Dt 18, 10f).

11, 11f: The Three: the Chronicler names only two of them: Ishbaal and Eleazar. According to 2 Sm 23,

8–12, the Three were Ishbaal, Eleazar, and Shammah.

11, 20: The Thirty: listed by name in vv 26–47. The list given in 2 Sm 23, 8–39 often differs in names and spellings; for the numbers, see the note there.

David's Early Followers

12 The following men came to David in Ziklag while he was still under banishment from Saul, son of Kish; they, too, were among the warriors who helped him in his battles. 2 They were archers who could use either the right or the left hand, both in slinging stones and in shooting arrows with the bow. They were some of Saul's kinsmen, from Benjamin. 3 Ahiezer was their chief, along with Joash, both sons of Shemaah of Gibeah; also Jeziel and Pelet, sons of Azmaveth; Beracah; Jehu, from Anathoth; 4 Ishmaiah the Gibeonite, a warrior on the level of the Thirty, and in addition to their number; 5 Jeremiah; Jahaziel; Johanan: Jozabad from Gederah; 6 Eluzai; Jerimoth; Bealiah; Shemariah; Shephatiah the Haruphite; 7 Elkanah, Isshiah, Azarel, Joezer, and Ishbaal, who were Korahites; 8 Joelah, finally, and Zebadiah, sons of Jeroham, from Gedor.

9 Some of the Gadites also went over to David when he was at the stronghold in the wilderness. They were valiant warriors, experienced soldiers equipped with shield and spear, who bore themselves like lions, and were as swift as the gazelles on the mountains. 10 Ezer was their chief, Obadiah was second, Eliab third, 11 Mishmannah fourth, Jeremiah fifth, 12 Attai sixth, Eliel seventh, 13 Johanan eighth, Elzabad ninth, 14 Jerenmiah tenth, and Machbannai eleventh. 15 These Gadites were army commanders, the lesser placed over hundreds and the greater over thousands. 16 It was they who crossed over the Jordan when it was overflowing both its banks in the first month, and dispersed all who were in the valleys to the east and the west.

17 Some Benjaminites and Judahites also came to Davd at the stronghold 18 David went out to meet them and addressed them in these words: "If you come peacefully, to help me, I am of a mind to have you join me. But if you have come to betray me to my enemies though my hands have done no wrong, may the God of our fathers see and punish you."

19 Then spirit enveloped Amasai, the chief of the Thirty, who spoke:

"We are yours, O David,
  we are with you, O son of Jesse.
Peace, peace to you,
  and peace to him who helps you;
  your God it is who helps you."

So David received them and placed them among the leaders of his troops.

20 Men from Manasseh also deserted to David when he came with the Philistines to battle against Saul. However, he did not help the Philistines, for their lords took counsel and sent him home, saying, "At the cost of our heads he will desert to his master Saul." 21 As he was returning to Zilkag, therefore, these deserted to him from Manasseh: Adnah, Jozabad, Jediael, Michael, Jozabad, Elihu, and Zillethai, chiefs of thousands of Manasseh. 22 They helped David by taking charge of his troops, for they were all warriors and became commanders of his army. 23 And from day to day men kept coming to David's help until there was a vast encampment, like an encampment of angels.

The Assembly at Hebron

24 This is a muster of the detachments of armed troops that came to David at Hebron to transfer to him Saul's kingdom, as the LORD had ordained. 25 Judahites bearing shields and spears: six thousand eight hundred armed troops. 26 Of the Simeonites, warriors fit for battle: seven thousand one hundred. 27 Of the Levites: four thousand six hundred, 28 along with Jehoiada, leader of the line of Aaron, with another three thousand seven hundred, 29 and Zadok, a young warrior, with twenty-two princes of his father's house. 30 Of the Benjaminites, the brethren of Saul: three thousand—until this time, most of them had held their allegiance to the house of Saul. 31 Of the Ephraimites: twenty thousand eight hundred warriors, men renowned in their ancestral houses. 32 Of the half-tribe of Manasseh: eighteen thousand designated by name to come and make David king. 33 Of the Issacharites, their chiefs who were endowed with an understanding of the times and who knew what Israel had to do: two hundred chiefs, together with all their brethren under their command. 34 From Zebulun, men fit for military service, set in battle array with every kind of weapon for war: fifty thousand men rallying with a single purpose. 35 From Naphtali: one thousand captains, and with them, armed with shield and lance, thirty-seven thousand men. 36 Of the Danites, set in battle array: twenty-eight thousand six hundred. 37 From Asher, fit for military service and set in battle array: forty thousand. 38 From the other side of the Jordan, of the Reubenites, Gadites and the half-tribe of Manasseh, men equipped with every kind of weapon of war: one hundred and twenty thousand.

39 All these soldiers, drawn up in battle order, came to Hebron with the resolute intention of making David king over all Israel. The rest of Israel was likewise of one mind to make David king. 40 They remained with David for three days, feasting and drinking, for their brethren had prepared for them. 41 Moreover, their neighbors from as far as Issachar, Zebulun, and Naphtali came bringing food on asses, camels, mules, and oxen—provisions in great quantity of meal, presesd figs, raisins, wine, oil, oxen, and sheep. For their was rejoicing in Israel.

Transfer of the Ark

13 After David had taken counsel with his commanders of thousands and of hundreds, that is to say, with every one of his leaders, 2 he said to the whole assembly of Israel: "If it seems good to you, and is so decreed by the LORD our God, let us summon the rest of our brethren from all the districts of Israel, and also

---

12, 25–38: The Chronicler fills out the pageantry of joyous occasions in keeping with his much later appreciation of the significance of the event in the history of God's people: the numbers in attendance at David's crowning in Hebron (cf 2 Sm 5, 1ff) are recounted in the same spirit of enthusiasm which in v 23 compares David's band of desert freebooters to a numerous encampment of angels.

the priests and the Levites from their cities with pasture lands, that they may join us; 3 and let us bring the ark of our God here among us, for in the days of Saul we did not visit it." 4 And the whole assembly agreed to do this, for the idea was pleasing to all the people.

5 Then David assembled all Israel, from Shibor of Egypt to Labo of Hamath, to bring the ark of God from Kiriath-jearim. 6 David and all Israel went up to Baalah, that is, to Kiriath-jearim, of Judah, to bring back the ark of God, which was known by the name "LORD enthroned upon the cherubim." 7 They transported the ark of God on a new cart from the house of Abinadab; Uzzah and Ahio were guiding the cart, 8 while David and all Israel danced before God with great enthusiasm, amid songs and music on lyres, harps, tambourines, cymbals, and trumpets.

9 As they reached the threshing floor of Chidon, Uzzah stretched out his hand to steady the ark, for the oxen were upsetting it. 10 Then the LORD became angry with Uzzah and struck him; he died there in God's presence, because he had laid his hand on the ark. 11 David was disturbed because the LORD's anger had broken out against Uzzah. Therefore that place has been called Perez-uzza even to this day.

12 David was now afraid of God, and he said, "How can I bring the ark of God with me?" 13 Therefore he did not take the ark back with him to the City of David, but he took it instead to the house of Obed-edom the Gittite. 14 The ark of God remained in the house of Obed-edom with his family for three months, and the LORD blessed Obed-edom's household and all that he possessed.

David in Jerusalem

14 Hiram, king of Tyre, sent envoys to David along with masons and carpenters, and cedar wood to build him a house. 2 David now understood that the LORD had truly confirmed him as king over Israel, for his kingdom was greatly exalted for the sake of his people

Israel. 3 David took other wives in Jerusalem and became the father of more sons and daughters. 4 These are the names of those who were born to him in Jerusalem: Shammua, Shobab, Nathan, Solomon, 5 Ibhar, Elishua, Elpelet, 6 Nogah, Nepheg, Japhia, 7 Elishama, Beeliada, and Eliphelet.

The Philistine Wars

8 When the Philistines had heard that David was anointed king over all Israel, they went up in unison to seek him out. But when David heard of this, he marched out against them. 9 Meanwhile the Philistines had come and raided the valley of Rephaim. 10 David inquired of God, "Shall I advance against the Philistines, and will you deliver them into my power?" The LORD answered him "Advance, for I will deliver them into your power." 11 They advanced, therefore, to Baal-perazim, and David defeated them there. Then David said, "God has used me to break through my enemies just as water breaks through a dam." Therefore that place was called Baal-perazim. 12 The Philistines had left their gods there, and David ordered them to be burnt.

13 Once again the Philistines raided the valley, 14 and again David inquired of God. But God answered him: "Do not try to pursue them, but go around them and come upon them from the direction of the mastic trees. 15 When you hear the sound of marching in the tops of the mastic trees, then go forth to battle, for God has already gone before you to strike the army of the Philistines." 16 David did as God commanded him, and they routed the Philistine army from Gibeon to Gezer.

17 Thus David's fame was spread abroad through every land, and the LORD made all the nations fear him.

The Ark Brought to Jerusalem

15 David built houses for himself in the City of David and prepared a place for the ark of God, pitching a tent for it there. 2 At that time he said, "No one may carry

the ark of God except the Levites, for the LORD chose them to carry the ark of the LORD and to minister to him forever." 3 Then David assembled all Israel in Jerusalem to bring the ark of the LORD to the place which he had prepared for it. 4 David also called together the sons of Aaron and the Levites: 5 of the sons of Kohath, Uriel, their chief, and one hundred and twenty of his brethren; 6 of the sons of Merari, Asaiah, their chief, and two hundred and twenty of his brethren; 7 of the sons of Gershon, Joel, their chief, and one hundred and thirty of his brethren; 8 of the sons of Elizaphan, Shemaiah, their chief, and two hundred of his brethren; 9 of the sons of Hebron, Eliel, their chief, and eighty of his brethren; 10 of the sons of Uzziel, Amminadab, their chief, and one hundred and twelve of his brethren.

11 David summoned the priests Zadok and Abiathar, and the Levites Uriel, Asaiah, Joel, Shemaiah, Eliel, and Amminadab, 12 and said to them: "You, the heads of the levitical families, must sanctify yourselves along with your brethren and bring the ark of the LORD, the God of Israel, to the place which I have prepared for it. 13 Because you were not with us the first time, the wrath of the LORD our God burst upon us, for we did not seek him aright." 14 Accordingly, the priests and the Levites sanctified themselves to bring the ark of the LORD, the God of Israel. 15 The Levites bore the ark of God on their shoulders with poles, as Moses had ordained according to the word of the LORD.

16 David commanded the chiefs of the Levites to appoint their brethren as chanters, to play on musical instruments, harps, lyres, and cymbals, to make a loud sound of rejoicing. 17 Therefore the Levites appointed Heman, son of Joel, and, among his brethren, Asaph, son of Berechiah, and among the sons of Merari, their brethren, Ethan, son of Kushaiah; 18 and, together with these, their brethren of the second rank: the gatekeepers Zechariah,

---

13, 5: *Shihor of Egypt:* the eastern branch of the Nile delta. *Labo of Hamath:* in southern Syria.

13, 9: *Chidon:* in 2 Sm 6, 6, *Nodan.*
13, 11: *Perez-uzza:* a Hebrew term meaning "the

breaking out against Uzza."

Uzziel, Shemiramoth, Jehiel, Unni, Eliab, Benaiah, Maaseiah, Mattithiah, Eliphelehu, Mikneiah, Obed-edom, and Jeiel. 19 The chanters, Heman, Asaph, and Ethan, sounded brass cymbals. 20 Zechariah, Uzziel, She-miramoth, Jehiel, Unni, Eliab, Maaseiah, and Benaiah played on harps set to "Alamoth." 21 But Mattithiah, Eliphelehu, Mikneiah, Obed-edom, and Jeiel led the chant on lyres set to the "eighth." 22 Che-naniah was the chief of the Levites in the chanting; he directed the chant-ing, for he was skillful. 23 Bere-chiah and Elkanah were gatekeepers before the ark. 24 The priests, Shebaniah, Joshaphat, Nethanel, Amasai, Zechariah, Benaiah, and Eliezer, sounded the trumpets before the ark of God. Obed-edom and Jeiel were also gatekeepers before the ark.

25 Thus David, the elders of Israel and the commanders of thousands went to bring up the ark of the cove-nant of the LORD with joy from the house of Obed-edom. 26 While the Levites, with God's help, were bear-ing the ark of the covenant of the LORD, seven bulls and seven rams were sacrificed. 27 David was clothed in a robe of fine linen, as were all the Levites who carried the ark, the singers, and Chenaniah, the leader of the chant; David was also wearing a linen ephod. 28 Thus all Israel brought back the ark of the covenant of the LORD with joyful shouting, to the sound of horns, trumpets, and cymbals, and the music of harps and lyres. 29 But as the ark of the covenant of the LORD was entering the City of David, Michal, daughter of Saul, looked down from her window, and when she saw King David leaping and dancing, she despised him in her heart.

16 They brought in the ark of God and set it within the tent which David had pitched for it. Then they offered up holocausts and peace offerings to God. 2 When David had finished offering up the holo-causts and peace offerings, he blessed the people in the name of the LORD, 3 and distributed to every Israelite,

to every man and every woman, a loaf of bread, a piece of meat, and a raisin cake.

The Ministering Levites

4 He now appointed certain Le-vites to minister before the ark of the LORD, to celebrate, thank, and praise the LORD the God of Israel. 5 Asaph was their chief, and second to him were Zechariah, Uzziel, Shemi-ramoth, Jehiel, Mattithiah, Eliab, Benaiah, Obed-edom, and Jeiel. These were to play on harps and lyres, while Asaph was to sound the cymbals, 6 and the priests Benaiah and Jahaziel were to be the regular trumpeters before the ark of the covenant of God.

7 Then, on that same day, David appointed Asaph and his brethren to sing for the first time these praises of the LORD:

8 Give thanks to the LORD, invoke his name;
    make known among the nations his deeds.
9 Sing to him, sing his praise,
    proclaim all his wondrous deeds.
10 Glory in his holy name;
    rejoice, O hearts that seek the LORD!
11 Look to the LORD in his strength;
    seek to serve him constantly.
12 Recall the wondrous deeds that he has wrought,
    his portents, and the judgments he has uttered,
13 You descendants of Israel, his servants,
    sons of Jacob, his chosen ones!
14 He, the LORD, is our God;
    throughout the earth his judgments prevail.
15 He remembers forever his covenant
    which he made binding for a thousand generations—
16 Which he entered into with Abraham
    and by his oath to Isaac;
17 Which he established for Jacob by statute,
    for Israel as an everlasting covenant,

18 Saying, "To you will I give the land of Canaan
    as your allotted inheritance."
19 When they were few in number,
    a handful, and strangers there,
20 Wandering from nation to nation,
    from one kingdom to another people,
21 He let no one oppress them,
    and for their sake he rebuked kings:
22 "Touch not my anointed,
    and to my prophets do no harm."
23 Sing to the LORD, all the earth,
    announce his salvation, day after day
24 Tell his glory among the nations;
    among all his peoples, his wondrous deeds.
25 For great is the LORD and highly to be praised;
    and awesome is he, beyond all gods.
26 For all the gods of the nations are things of nought,
    but the LORD made the heavens.
27 Splendor and majesty go before him;
    praise and joy are in his holy place.
28 Give to the LORD, you families of nations,
    give to the LORD glory and praise;
29 give to the LORD the glory due his name!
    Bring gifts, and enter his presence;
    worship the LORD in holy attire.
30 Tremble before him, all the earth;
    he has made the world firm, not to be moved.
31 Let the heavens be glad and the earth rejoice;
    let them say among the nations: The LORD is king.
32 Let the sea and what fills it resound;
    let the plains rejoice and all that is in them!

15, 20: *Alamoth*: a musical term (literally, "young women") of uncertain meaning, occurring also in Ps 46, 1, where it is rendered as *virgins*. Perhaps it may

mean something like "soprano," whereas the term "eighth" (Hebrew *sheminith*, v 21) may then mean "bass"; cf Pss 6, 1; 12, 1.

16, 8–36: A hymn composed of parts, with textual variants, from several Psalms: vv 8–22 = Ps 105, 1–15; vv 23–33 = Ps 96, 1–13; vv 34–36 = Ps 106, 1.47f.

33 Then shall all the trees of the
forest exult
before the LORD, for he comes:
he comes to rule the earth.

34 Give thanks to the LORD, for he
is good,
for his kindness endures
forever;
35 And say, "Save us, O God, our
savior,
gather us and deliver us from
the nations,
That we may give thanks to your
holy name
and glory in praising you."

36 Blessed be the LORD, the God of
Israel, through all
eternity!
Let all the people say, Amen!
Alleluia.

37 Then David left Asaph and his
brethren there before the ark of the
covenant of the LORD to minister
before the ark regularly according to
the daily ritual; 38 he also left
there Obed-edom and sixty-eight of
his brethren; including Obed-edom,
son of Jeduthun, and Hosah, to be
gatekeepers.
39 But the priest Zadok and his
priestly brethren he left before the
Dwelling of the LORD on the high
place at Gibeon, 40 to offer holocausts to the LORD on the altar of
holocausts regularly, morning and
evening, and to do all that is written
in the law of the LORD which he has
decreed for Israel. 41 With them
were Heman and Jeduthun and the
others who were chosen and designated by name to give thanks to the
LORD, "because his kindness endures
forever," 42 with trumpets and
cymbals for accompaniment, and
instruments for the sacred chant. The
sons of Jeduthun kept the gate.
43 Then all the people departed,
each to his own home, and David
returned to bless his household.

The Oracle of Nathan

17 After David had taken up
residence in his house, he said
to Nathan the prophet, "See, I am
living in a house of cedar, but the ark
of the covenant of the LORD dwells
under tentcloth." 2 Nathan replied

to David, "Do, therefore, whatever
you desire, for God is with you."
3 But that same night the word of
God came to Nathan: 4 "Go and
tell my servant David, Thus says the
LORD: It is not you who are to build
a house for me to dwell in. 5 For I
have never dwelt in a house, from the
time when I led Israel onward, even
to this day, but I have been lodging
in tent or pavilion 6 as long as I
have wandered about with all of
Israel. Did I ever say a word to any
of the judges of Israel whom I commanded to guide my people, such as,
'Why have you not built me a house
of cedar?' 7 Therefore, tell my
servant David, Thus says the LORD
of hosts: I took you from the pasture,
from following the sheep, that you
might become ruler over my people
Israel. 8 I was with you wherever
you went, and I cut down all your
enemies before you. I will make your
name great like that of the greatest
on the earth. 9 I will assign a place
for my people Israel and I will plant
them in it to dwell there henceforth
undisturbed: nor shall wicked men
ever again oppress them, as they did
at first, 10 and during all the time
when I appointed judges over my
people Israel. And I will subdue all
your enemies. Moreover, I declare to
you that I, the LORD, will build you a
house; 11 so that when your days
have been completed and you must
join your fathers, I will raise up your
offspring after you who will be one of
your own sons, and I will establish
his kingdom. 12 He it is who shall
build me a house, and I will establish
his throne forever. 13 I will be a
father to him, and he shall be a son
to me, and I will not withdraw my
favor from him as I withdrew it from
him who precede you; 14 but I will
maintain him in my house and in my
kingdom forever, and his throne
shall be firmly established forever."
15 All these words and this whole
vision Nathan related exactly to
David.

David's Thanksgiving

16 Then David came in and sat in
the LORD's presence, saying: "Who
am I, O LORD God, and what are my
family, that you should have brought
me as far as I have come? 17 And

yet, even this you now consider too
little, O God! For you have made a
promise regarding your servant's
family reaching into the distant
future, and you have looked on me as
henceforth the most notable of men,
O LORD God. 18 What more can
David say to you? You know your
servant. 19 O LORD, for your servant's sake and in keeping with your
purpose, you have done this great
thing. 20 O LORD, there is no one
like you and there is no God but you,
just as we have always understood.
21 "Is there, like your people
Israel, whom you redeemed from
Egypt, another nation on earth whom
a god went to redeem as his people?
You have won for yourself a name
for great and awesome deeds by
driving out the nations before your
people. 22 You made your people
Israel your own forever, and you, O
LORD, became their God. 23 Therefore, O LORD, may the promise that
you have uttered concerning your
servant and his house remain firm
forever. 24 Bring about what you
have promised, that your renown as
LORD of hosts, God of Israel, may be
great and abide forever, while the
house of David, your servant, is
established in your presence.
25 "Because you, O my God, have
revealed to your servant that you will
build him a house, your servant has
made bold to pray before you.
26 Since you, O LORD, are truly God
and have promised this good thing to
your servant, 27 and since you
have deigned to bless the house of
your servant, so that it will remain
forever—since it is you, O LORD, who
blessed it, it is blessed forever.

David's Victories

18 After this, David defeated the
Philistines and subdued them;
he took Gath and its towns away
from the control of the Philistines.
2 He also defeated Moab, and the
Moabites became his subjects, paying
tribute.
3 David then defeated Hadadezer,
king of Zobah toward Hamath, when
the latter was on his way to set up his
victory stele at the river Euphrates.
4 David took from him twenty
thousand foot soldiers, one thousand

chariots, and seven thousand horsemen. Of the chariot horses, David hamstrung all but one hundred. 5 The Arameans of Damascus came up to the aid of Hadadezer, king of Zobah, but David also slew twenty-two thousand of their men. 6 Then David set up garrisons in the Damascus region of Aram, and the Arameans became his subjects, paying tribute. Thus the LORD made David victorious in all his campaigns.

7 David took the golden shields that were carried by Hadadezer's attendants and brought them to Jerusalem. 8 He likewise took away from Tibhath and Cun, cities of Hadadezer, large quantities of bronze which Solomon later used to make the bronze sea and the pillars and the vessels of bronze.

9 When Tou, king of Hamath, heard that David had defeated the entire army of Hadadezer, king of Zobah, 10 he sent his son Hadoram to wish King David well and to congratulate him on having waged a victorious war against Hadadezer; for Hadadezer had been at war with Tou. He also sent David gold, silver, and bronze utensils of every sort. 11 These also King David consecrated to the LORD along with all the silver and gold that he had taken from the nations: from Edom, Moab, the Ammonites, the Philistines, and Amalek. 12 Abishai, the son of Zeruiah, also slew eighteen thousand Edomites in the valley of Salt. 13 He set up garrisons in Edom, and all the Edomites became David's subjects. Thus the LORD made David victorious in all his campaigns.

David's Officials

14 David reigned over all Israel and dispensed justice and right to all his people. 15 Joab, son of Zeruiah was in command of the army; Jehoshaphat, son of Ahilud, was herald; 16 Zadok, son of Ahitub, and Ahimelech, son of Abiathar, were priests; Shavsha was scribe; 17 Benaiah, son of Jehoiada, was in command of

the Cherethites and the Pelethites; and David's sons were the chief assistants to the king.

Campaigns against Ammon

19 Afterward Nahash, king of the Ammonites, died and his son succeeded him as king. 2 David said, "I will show kindness to Hanun, the son of Nahash, for his father treated me with kindness." Therefore he sent envoys to him to comfort him over the death of his father. But when David's servants had entered the land of the Ammonites to comfort Hanun, 3 the Ammonite princes said to Hanun, "Do you think David is doing this—sending you consolers—to honor your father? Have not his servants rather come to you to explore the land, spying it out for its overthrow?" 4 Thereupon Hanun seized David's servants and had them shaved and their garments cut off half-way at the hips. Then he sent them away. 5 When David was informed of what had happened to his men, he sent messengers to meet them, for the men had been greatly disgraced. "Remain at Jericho," the king told them, "until your beards have grown again; and then you may come back here."

6 When the Ammonites realized that they had put themselves in bad odor with David, Hanun and the Ammonites sent a thousand talents of silver to hire chariots and horsemen from Aram-naharaim, from Aram-maacah, and from Zibah. 7 They hired thirty-two thousand chariots along with the king of Maacah and his army, who came and encamped before Medeba. The Ammonites also assembled from their cities and came out for war. 8 When David heard of this, he sent Joab and his whole army of warriors against them. 9 The Ammonites marched out and lined up for battle at the gate of the city, while the kings who had come to their help remained apart in the open field. 10 When Joab saw that there was a battle line both in front and behind

him, he chose some of the best fighters among the Israelites and set them in array against the Arameans; 11 the rest of the army, which he placed under the command of his brother Abishai, then lined up to oppose the Ammonites. 12 And he said: "If the Arameans prove too strong for me, you must come to my help; and if the Ammonites prove too strong for you, I will save you. 13 Hold steadfast and let us show ourselves courageous for the sake of our people and the cities of our God; then may the LORD do what seems best to him." 14 Joab therefore advanced with his men to engage the Arameans in battle but they fled before him. 15 And when the Ammonites saw that the Arameans had fled, they also took to flight before his brother Abishai, and reentered the city. Joab then returned to Jerusalem.

16 Seeing themselves vanquished by Israel, the Arameans sent messengers to bring out the Arameans from the other side of the River, with Shophach, the general of Hadadezer's army at their head. 17 When this was reported to David, he gathered all Israel together, crossed the Jordan, and met them. With the army of David drawn up to fight the Arameans, they gave battle. 18 But the Arameans fled before Israel, and David slew seven thousand of their chariot fighters and forty thousand of their foot soldiers; he also killed Shophach, the general of the army. 19 When the vassals of Hadadezer saw themselves vanquished by Israel, they made peace with David and became his subjects. After this, the Arameans refused to come to the aid of the Ammonites.

20 At the beginning of the following year, the time when kings go to war, Joab led the army out in force, laid waste the land of the Ammonites, and went on to besiege Rabbah, while David himself remained in Jerusalem. When Joab had attacked Rabbah and destroyed it, 2 David took the crown of Milcom

---

18, 16: *Zadok . . . and Ahimelech, son of Abiathar, were priests:* as in the Chronicler's source, 2 Sm 8, 17. But according to 2 Sm 15, 24.29.35; 17, 15; 19, 11; 20, 25, and even 1 Chr 15, 11, it was Abiathar who shared the priestly office with Zadok, and he remained in this office even during the early years of Solomon's

reign (1 Kgs 2, 26; 4, 4). Moreover, according to 1 Sm 22, 20; 23, 6; 30, 7, Ahimelech was the father, not the son, of Abiathar. If the text *Ahimelech, son of Abiathar* is not due to a scribal change, one must assume that Abiathar had a son who was named after his grandfather and who shared the priestly office with his

father during the last years of David's reign.
18, 17: *David's sons were the chief assistants to the king:* in the parallel passage, 2 Sm 8, 18, which was the Chronicler's source, *David's sons were priests.* The change is characteristic of the Chronicler, for whom only Aaron's descendants could be priests.

from the idol's head. It was found to weigh a talent of gold; and it contained precious stones, which David wore on his own head. He also brought out a great amount of booty from the city. 3 He deported the people of the city and set them to work with saws, iron picks, and axes. Thus David dealt with all the cities of the Ammonites. Then he and his whole army returned to Jerusalem.

Victories over the Philistines

4 Afterward there was another battle with the Philistines, at Gezer. At that time, Sibbecai the Hushathite slew Sippai, one of the descendants of the Raphaim, and the Philistines were subdued. 5 Once again there was war with the Philistines, and Elhanan, the son of Jair, slew Lahmi, the brother of Goliath of Gath, whose spear shaft was like a weaver's heddle-bar.

6 In still another battle, at Gath, they encountered a giant, also a descendant of the Raphaim, who had six fingers to each hand and six toes to each foot; twenty-four in all. 7 He defied Israel, and Jonathan, the son of Shimea, David's brother, slew him. 8 These were the descendants of the Raphaim of Gath who died at the hands of David and his servants.

David's Census; the Plague

21 A satan rose up against Israel, and he enticed David into taking a census of Israel. 2 David therefore said to Joab and to the other generals of the army, "Go, find out the number of the Israelites from Beer-sheba to Dan, and report back to me that I may know their number." 3 But Joab replied: "May the LORD increase his people a hundredfold! My lord king, are not all of them my lord's subjects? Why does my lord seek to do this thing? Why will he bring guilt upon Israel?" 4 However, the king's command prevailed over Joab, who departed and tra-

versed all of Israel, and then returned to Jerusalem. 5 Joab reported the result of the census to David: of men capable of wielding a sword, there were in all Israel one million one hundred thousand, and in Judah four hundred and seventy thousand. 6 Levi and Benjamin, however, he did not include in the census, for the king's command was repugnant to Joab. 7 This command displeased God, who began to punish Israel. 8 Then David said to God, "I have sinned greatly in doing this thing. Take away your servant's guilt, for I have acted very foolishly."

9 Then the LORD spoke to Gad, David's seer, in these words: 10 "Go, tell David: Thus says the LORD: I offer you three alternatives; choose one of them, and I will inflict it on you." 11 Accordingly, Gad went to David and said to him; "Thus says the LORD: Decide now— 12 will it be three years of famine; or three months of fleeing your enemies, with the sword of your foes ever at your back; or three days of the LORD's own sword, a pestilence in the land, with the LORD's destroying angel in every part of Israel? Therefore choose: What answer am I to give him who sent me?" 13 Then David said to Gad: "I am in dire straits. But I prefer to fall into the hand of the LORD, whose mercy is very great, than into the hands of men."

14 Therefore the LORD sent pestilence upon Israel, and seventy thousand men of Israel died. 15 God also sent an angel to destroy Jerusalem; but as he was on the point of destroying it, the LORD saw and decided against the calamity, and said to the destroying angel, "Enough now! Stay your hand!"

Ornan's Threshing Floor

The angel of the LORD was then standing by the threshing floor of Ornan the Jebusite. 16 When David raised his eyes, he saw the angel of the LORD standing between earth and

heaven, with a naked sword in his hand stretched out against Jerusalem. David and the elders, clothed in sackcloth, prostrated themselves face to the ground, 17 and David prayed to God: "Was it not I who ordered the census of the people? I am the one who sinned, I did this wicked thing. But these sheep, what have they done? O LORD, my God, strike me and my father's family, but do not afflict your people with this plague!"

18 Then the angel of the LORD commanded Gad to tell David to go up and erect an altar to the LORD on the threshing floor of Ornan the Jebusite. 19 David went up at Gad's command, given in the name of the LORD. 20 While Ornan was threshing wheat, he turned around and saw the king, and his four sons who were with him, without recognizing them. 21 But as David came on toward him, he looked up and saw that it was David. Then he left the threshing floor and bowed down before David, his face to the ground. 22 David said to Ornan: "Sell me the ground of this threshing floor, that I may build on it an altar to the LORD. Sell it to me at its full price, that the plague may be stayed from the people." 23 But Ornan said to David: "Take it as your own, and let my lord the king do what seems best to him. See, I also give you the oxen for the holocausts, the threshing sledges for the wood, and the wheat for the cereal offering. I give it all to you." 24 But King David replied to Ornan: "No! I will buy it from you properly, at its full price. I will not take what is yours for the LORD, nor offer up holocausts that cost me nothing." 25 So David paid Ornan six hundred shekels of gold for the place.

Altar of Holocausts

26 David then built an altar there to the LORD, and offered up holocausts and peace offerings. When he

---

20, 5: *Elhanan ... slew Lahmi, the brother of Goliath:* the Chronicler thus solves the difficulty of the apparent contradiction between 1 Sm 17, 49ff (David killed Goliath) and 2 Sm 21, 19 (*Elhanan killed Goliath*).

21, 1: *A satan:* in the parallel passage of 2 Sm 24, 1, *the Lord's anger*. The change in the term reflects the changed theological outlook of postexilic Israel, when

evil could no longer be attributed directly to God. At an earlier period the Hebrew word *satan* ("adversary," or, especially in a court of law, "accuser"), when not used of men, designated an angel who accused men before God (Jb 1, 6–12; 2, 1–7; Zec 3, 1f). Here, as in later Judaism (Wis 2, 24) and in the New Testament, *satan*, or the "devil" (from the Greek translation of the word), designates an evil spirit who tempts

men to wrongdoing.

21, 25: *Six hundred shekels of gold:* about 10,000 dollars. According to 2 Sm 24, 24, David paid 50 shekels of silver, about 20 dollars, for Ornan's threshing floor; but for the Chronicler the site of the temple was much more precious than that.

called upon the LORD, he answered him by sending down fire from the heaven upon the altar of holocausts. 27 Then the LORD gave orders to the angel to return his sword to its sheath.

28 Once David saw that the LORD had heard him on the threshing floor of Ornan the Jebusite, he continued to offer sacrifices there. 29 The Dwelling of the LORD, which Moses had built in the desert, and the altar of holocausts were at that time on the high place at Gibeon. 30 But David could not go there to worship God, for he was fearful of the sword of the angel of the LORD. 22 1 Therefore David said, "This is the house of the LORD God, and this is the altar of holocausts for Israel."

Material for the Temple

2 David then ordered that all the aliens who lived in the land of Israel be brought together, and he appointed stonecutters to hew out stone blocks for building the house of God. 3 He also laid up large stores of iron to make nails for the doors of the gates, and clamps, together with so much bronze that it could not be weighed, 4 and cedar trees without number. The Sidonians and Tyrians brought great stores of cedar logs to David, 5 who said: "My son Solomon is young and immature; but the house that is to be built for the LORD must be made so magnificent that it will be renowned and glorious in all countries. Therefore I will make preparations for it." Thus before his death David laid up materials in abundance.

Charge to Solomon

6 Then he called for his son Solomon and commanded him to build a house for the LORD, the God of Israel. 7 David said to Solomon: "My son it was my purpose to build a house myself for the honor of the LORD, my God. 8 But this word of the LORD came to me: 'You have shed much blood, and you have waged great wars. You may not build a

house in my honor, because you have shed too much blood upon the earth in my sight. 9 However, a son is to be born to you. He will be a peaceful man, and I will give him rest from all his enemies on every side. For Solomon shall be his name, and in his time I will bestow peace and tranquillity on Israel. 10 It is he who shall build a house in my honor; he shall be a son to me, and I will be a father to him, and I will establish the throne of his kingship over Israel forever.' 11 Now, my son, the LORD be with you, and may you succeed in building the house of the LORD your God, as he has said you shall. 12 May the LORD give you prudence and discernment when he brings you to rule over Israel, so that you keep the law of the LORD, your God. 13 Only then shall you succeed, if you are careful to observe the precepts and decrees which the LORD gave Moses for Israel. Be brave and steadfast; do not fear or lose heart. 14 See, with great effort I have laid up for the house of the LORD a hundred thousand talents of gold, a million talents of silver, and bronze and iron in such great quantities that they cannot be weighed. I have also stored up wood and stones to which you must add. 15 Moreover, you have available an unlimited supply of workmen, stonecutters, masons, carpenters, and every kind of craftsman 16 skilled in gold, silver, bronze, and iron. Set to work, therefore, and the LORD be with you!"

Charge to the Leaders

17 David also commanded all of Israel's leaders to help his son Solomon: 18 "Is not the LORD your God with you? Has he not given you rest on every side? Indeed, he has delivered the occupants of the land into my power, and the land is subdued before the LORD and his people. 19 Therefore, devote your hearts and souls to seeking the LORD your God. Proceed to build the sanctuary of the LORD God, that the ark of the

covenant of the LORD and God's sacred vessels may be brought into the house built in honor of the LORD."

The Levitical Classes

23 When David had grown old and was near the end of his days, he made his son Solomon king over Israel. 2 He then gathered together all the leaders of Israel, together with the priests and the Levites.

3 The Levites thirty years old and above were counted, and their total number was found to be thirty-eight thousand men. 4 Of these, twenty-four thousand were to direct the service of the house of the LORD, six thousand were to be officials and judges, 5 four thousand were to be gatekeepers, and four thousand were to praise the LORD with the instruments which David had devised for praise. 6 David divided them into classes according to the sons of Levi: Gershon, Kohath, and Merari.

7 To the Gershonites belonged Ladan and Shimei. 8 The sons of Ladan: Jehiel the chief, then Zetham and Joel; three in all. 9 The sons of Shimei were Shelomoth, Haziel, and Haran; three. These were the heads of the families of Ladan. 10 The sons of Shimei were Jahath, Zizah, Jeush, and Beriah; these were the sons of Shimei, four in all. 11 Jahath was the chief and Zizah was second to him; but Jeush and Beriah had not may sons, and therefore they were classed as a single family, fulfilling a single office.

12 The sons of Kohath: Amram, Izhar, Hebron and Uzziel; four in all. 13 The sons of Amram were Aaron and Moses. Aaron was set apart to be consecrated as most holy, he and his sons forever, to offer sacrifice before the LORD, to minister to him, and to bless his name forever. 14 As for Moses, however, the man of God, his sons were counted as part of the tribe of Levi. 15 The sons of Moses were Gershom and Eliezer. 16 The sons of Gershom:

22, 2ff: According to 1 Kgs 5, 15–32, it was Solomon who made the material preparations for building the temple, even though David had wished to do so (1 Kgs 5, 17ff). The Chronicler, however, sought to have David, who was Israel's ideal king, more closely connected with Israel's most sacred sanctuary, the temple of Jerusalem.

22, 9: The Hebrew word for peace, *shalom*, is

reflected in the name Solomon, in Hebrew, *Shelomo*. A contrast is drawn here between Solomon, the *peaceful man*, and David, who *waged great wars* (v 8). David was prevented from building the temple, not only because all his time was taken up in waging war (1 Kgs 5, 17), but also because he *shed much blood* (v 8), and in the eyes of the Chronicler this made him ritually unfit for the task.

22, 14: *A hundred thousand talents of gold:* about 3,775 tons of gold. *A million talents of silver:* about 37,750 tons of silver. The fantastically exaggerated figures are intended merely to stress the inestimable value of the temple as the center of Israelite worship. More modest figures are given in 1 Kgs 9, 14.28; 10, 10.14.

Shubael the chief. 17 The sons of Eliezer were Rehabiah the chief—Eliezer had no other sons, but the sons of Rahabiah were very numerous. 18 The sons of Izhar: Shelomith the chief. 19 The sons of Hebron: Jeriah, the chief, Amariah, the second, Jahaziel, the third, and Jekameam, the fourth. 20 The sons of Uzziel: Micah, the chief, and Isshiah, the second.

21 The sons of Merari: Mahli and Mushi. The sons of Mahli: Eleazar and Kish. 22 Eleazar died leaving no sons, only daughters; the sons of Kish, their kinsmen, married them. 23 The sons of Mushi: Mahli, Eder, and Jeremoth; three in all.

24 These were the sons of Levi according to their ancestral houses, the family heads as they were enrolled one by one according to their names. They performed the work of the service of the house of the LORD from twenty years of age upwards, 27 for David's final orders were to enlist the Levites from the time they were twenty years old.

25 David said: "The LORD, the God of Israel, has given rest to his people, and has taken up his dwelling in Jerusalem. 26 Henceforth the Levites need not carry the Dwelling or any of its furnishings or equipment. 28 Rather, their duty shall be to assist the sons of Aaron in the service of the house of the LORD, having charge of the courts, the chambers, and the preservation of everything holy: they shall take part in the service of the house of God. 29 They shall also have charge of the showbread, of the fine flour for the cereal offering, of the wafers of unleavened bread, and of the baking and mixing, and of all measures of quantity and size. 30 They must be present every morning to offer thanks and to praise the LORD, and likewise in the evening; 31 and at every offering of holocausts to the LORD on sabbaths, new moons, and feast days, in such numbers as are prescribed, they must always be present before the LORD. 32 They shall observe what is prescribed for them concerning the

meeting tent, the sanctuary, and the sons of Aaron, their brethren, in the service of the house of the LORD."

The Priestly Classes

24 The descendants of Aaron also were divided into classes. The sons of Aaron were Nadab, Abihu, Eleazar, and Ithamar. 2 Nadab and Abihu died before their father, leaving no sons; therefore only Eleazar and Ithamar served as priests. 3 David, with Zadok, a descendant of Eleazar, and Ahimelech, a descendant of Ithamar, assigned the functions for the priestly service. 4 But since the descendants of Eleazar were found to be more numerous than those of Ithamar, the former were divided into sixteen groups, and the latter into eight groups, each under its family head. 5 Their functions were assigned impartially by lot, for there were officers of the holy place, and officers of the divine presence, descended both from Eleazar and from Ithamar, 6 The scribe Shemaiah, son of Nethanel, a Levite, made a record of it in the presence of the king, and of the leaders, of Zadok the priest, and of Ahimelech, son of Abiathar, and of the heads of the ancestral houses of the priests and of the Levites, listing two successive family groups from Eleazar before each one from Ithamar.

7 The first lot fell to Jehoiarib, the second to Jedaiah, 8 the third to Harim, the fourth to Seorim, 9 the fifth to Malchijah, the sixth to Mijamin, 10 the seventh to Hakkoz the eighth to Abijah, 11 the ninth to Jeshua, the tenth to Shecaniah 12 the eleventh to Eliashib, the twelfth to Jakim, 13 the thirteenth to Huppah, the fourteenth to Ishbaal, 14 the fifteenth to Bilgah, the sixteenth to Immer, 15 the seventeenth to Hezir, the eighteenth to Happizzez, 16 the nineteenth to Pethahiah, the twentieth to Jehezkel, 17 the twenty-first to Jachin, the twenty-second to Gamul, 18 the twenty-third to Delaiah, the twenty-fourth to Maaziah. 19 This was

the appointed order of their service when they functioned in the house of the LORD in keeping with the precepts given them by Aaron, their father, as the LORD, the God of Israel, had commanded him.

Other Levites

20 Of the remaining Levites, there were Shubael, of the descendants of Amram, and Jehdeiah, of the descendants of Shubael; 21 Isshiah, the chief, of the descendants of Rehabiah; 22 Shelomith of the Izharites, and Jahath of the descendants of Shelomith. 23 The descendants of Hebron were Jeriah, the chief, Amariah, the second, Jahaziel, the third, Jekameam, the fourth. 24 The descendants of Uzziel were Micah; Shamir, of the descendants of Micah; 25 Isshiah, the brother of Micah; and Zechariah, a descendant of Isshiah. 26 The descendants of Merari were Mahli, Mushi, and the descendants of his son Uzziah. 27 The descendants of Merari through his son Uzziah: Shoham, Zaccur, and Ibri. 28 Descendants of Mahli were Eleazar, who had no sons, 29 and Jerahmeel, of the descendants of Kish. 30 The descendants of Mushi were Mahli, Eder, and Jerimoth.

These were the descendants of the Levites according to their ancestral houses. 31 They too, in the same manner as their relatives, the descendants of Aaron, cast lots in the presence of King David, Zadok, Ahimelech, and the heads of the priestly and levitical families; the more important family did so in the same way as the less important one.

The Singers

25 David and the leaders of the liturgical cult set apart for service the descendants of Asaph, Heman, and Jeduthun, as singers of inspired songs to the accompaniment of lyres and harps and cymbals.

This is the list of those who performed this service: 2 Of the sons of Asaph: Zaccur, Joseph, Nethaniah, and Asharelah, sons of Asaph, under

---

24, 6: *Ahimelech, son of Abiathar:* see note on 18, 16.
25, 2-31: This list of twenty-four classes of temple singers balances the list of the twenty-four classes of

priests (24, 4-19). The last nine names in 25, 4, which seem to form a special group, appear to have been originally fragments or *incipits* of hymns. With some slight changes in the vocalization, the names would

mean: "Have mercy on me, O LORD," "Have mercy on me," "You are my God," "I magnify," "I extol the help of . . . ," "Sitting in adversity," "I have fulfilled," "He made abundant," and "Visions."

the direction of Asaph, who sang inspired songs under the guidance of the king. 3 Of Jeduthun, these sons of Jeduthun: Gedaliah, Zeri, Jeshaiah Shimei, Hashabiah, and Mattithiah; six, under the direction of their father Jeduthun, who sang inspired songs to the accompaniment of a lyre, to give thanks and praise to the LORD. 4 Of Heman, these sons of Heman: Buttiah, Mattaniah, Uzziel, Shubael, and Jerimoth; Hananiah, Hanani, Eliathah, Giddalti, Romamti-ezer, Joshbekashah, Mallothi, Hothir, and Mahazioth. 5 All these were the sons of Heman, the king's seer in divine matters; to enhance his prestige, God gave Heman fourteen sons and three daughters. 6 All these, whether of Asaph, Jeduthun, or Heman, were under their fathers' direction in the singing in the house of the LORD to the accompaniment of cymbals, harps and lyres, serving in the house of God, under the guidance of the king. 7 Their number, together with that of their brethren who were trained in singing to the LORD, all of them skilled men, was two hundred and eighty-eight. 8 They cast lots for their functions equally, young and old, master and pupil alike.

9 The first lot fell to Asaph, the family of Joseph; he and his sons and his brethren were twelve. Gedaliah was the second; he and his brethren and his sons were twelve. 10 The third was Zaccur, his sons, and his brethren: twelve. 11 The fourth fell to Izri, his sons, and his brethren: twelve. 12 The fifth was Nethaniah, his sons, and his brethren: twelve. 13 The sixth was Bukkiah, his sons, and his brethren: twelve. 14 The seventh was Jesarelah, his sons, and his brethren: twelve. 15 The eighth was Jeshaiah, his sons and his brethren: twelve. 16 The ninth was Mattaniah, his sons, and his brethren: twelve. 17 The tenth was Shimei, his sons and his brethren: twelve. 18 The eleventh was Uzziel, his sons, and his brethren: twelve. 19 The twelfth fell to Hashabiah, his sons, and his brethren: twelve. 20 The thirteenth was Shubael, his sons, and his brethren:

twelve. 21 The fourteenth was Mattithiah, his sons, and his brethren: twelve. 22 The fifteenth fell to Jeremoth, his sons, and his brethren: twelve. 23 The sixteenth fell to Hananiah, his sons, and his brethren: twelve. 24 The seventeenth fell to Joshbekashah, his sons, and his brethren: twelve. 25 The eighteenth fell to Hanani, his sons, and his brethren: twelve. 26 The nineteenth fell to Mallothi, his sons, and his brethren: twelve. 27 The twentieth fell to Eliathah, his sons, and his brethren: twelve. 28 The twenty-first fell to Hothir, his sons, and his brethren: twelve. 29 The twenty-second fell to Giddalti, his sons, and his brethren: twelve. 30 The twenty-third fell to Mahazioth, his sons, and his brethren: twelve. 31 The twenty-fourth fell to Romamti-ezer, his sons, and his brethren: twelve.

Classes of Gatekeepers

26 As for the classes of gatekeepers. Of the Korahites was Meshelemiah, the son of Kore, one of the sons of Abiasaph. 2 Meshelemiah's sons: Zechariah, the first-born, Jediael, the second son, Zebadiah, the third, Jathniel, the fourth, 3 Elam, the fifth, Jehohanan, the sixth, Eliehoenai, the seventh. 4 Obed-edom's sons: Shemaiah, the first-born, Jehozabad, a second son, Joah, the third, Sachar, the fourth, Nethanel, the fifth, 5 Ammiel, the sixth, Issachar, the seventh, Peullethai, the eighth, for God blessed him. 6 To his son Shemaiah were born sons who ruled over their family, for they are warriors. 7 The sons of Shemaiah were Othni, Rephael, Obed, and Elzabad; also his brethren who were men of might, Elihu and Semachiah. 8 All these were of the sons of Obed-edom, who together with their sons and their brethren, were mighty men, fit for the service. Of Obed-edom, sixty-two. 9 Of Meshelemiah, eighteen sons and brethren, mighty men.

10 Hosah, a descendant of Merari, had these sons: Shimri, the chief (for though he was not the first-born, his father made him chief), 11 Hilkiah, the second son, Tebaliah, the third, Zechariah, the fourth. All the sons and brethren of Hosah were thirteen.

12 To these classes of gatekeepers, under their chief men, were assigned watches in the service of the house of the LORD, for each group in the same way. 13 They cast lots for each gate the small and the large families alike. 14 When the lot was cast for the eastside, it fell to Meshelemiah. Then they cast lots for his son Zechariah, a prudent counselor, and the north side fell to his lot. 15 To Obed-edom fell the south side, and to his sons the storehouse. 16 To Hosah fell the west side with the Shallecheth gate at the ascending highway. For each family, watches were established. 17 On the east, six watched each day, on the north, four each day, on the south, four each day, and at the storehouse they were two and two; 18 as for the large building on the west, there were four at the highway and two at the large building. 19 These were the classes of the gatekeepers, descendants of Kore and Merari.

Treasurers

20 Their brother Levites superintended the stores for the house of God and the stores of votive offerings. 21 Among the descendants of Ladan the Gershonite, the family heads were descendants of Jehiel: the descendants of Jehiel, 22 Zetham and his brother Joel, who superintended the treasures of the house of the LORD. 23 From the Amramites, Izharites, Hebronites, and Uzzielites, 24 Shubael, son of Gershon, son of Moses, was chief superintendent over the treasures. 25 His associate pertained to Eliezer, whose son was Rehabiah, whose son was Jeshaiah, whose son was Joram, whose son was Zichri, whose son was Shelomith. 26 This Shelomith and his brethren superintended all the stores of the votive offerings dedicated by King David, the heads of the families, the commanders of thousands and of hundreds, and the commanders of the army, 27 from the booty they had taken in the wars, for the enhancement of the house of the LORD. 28 Also whatever Samuel the seer, Saul, son of Kish, Abner son of Ner, Joab, son of Zeruiah, and all others had consecrated, was under the charge of Shelomith and his brethren.

26, 18: *The large building* (in the Hebrew text *Parbar*): see note on 2 Kgs 23, 11.

Magistrates

29 Among the Izharites, Chenaniah and his sons were in charge of Israel's civil affairs as officials and judges. 30 Among the Hebronites, Hashabiah and his brethren, one thousand seven hundred police officers, had the administration of Israel on the western side of the Jordan in all the work of the LORD and in the service of the king. 31 Among the Hebronites, Jerijah was their chief according to their family records. In the fortieth year of David's reign search was made, and there were found among them outstanding officers at Jazer of Gilead. 32 His brethren were also police officers, two thousand seven hundred heads of families. King David appointed them to the administration of the Reubenites, the Gadites, and the half-tribe of Manasseh in everything pertaining to God and to the king.

Army Commanders

27 This is the list of the Israelite family heads, commanders of thousands and of hundreds, and other officers who served the king in all that pertained to the divisions, of twenty-four thousand men each, that came and went month by month throughout the year.

2 Over the first division for the first month was Ishbaal, son of Zabdiel, and in his division were twenty-four thousand men; 3 a descendant of Perez, he was chief over all the commanders of the army for the first month. 4 Over the division of the second month was Eleazar, son of Dodo, from Ahoh, and in his division were twenty-four thousand men. 5 The third army commander chief for the third month, was Benaiah, son of Jehoiada the priest, and in his division were twenty-four thousand men. 6 This Benaiah was a warrior among the Thirty and over the Thirty. His son Ammizabad was over his division. 7 Fourth, for the fourth month, was Asahel, brother of Joab, and after him his son

Zebadiah, and in his division were twenty-four thousand men. 8 Fifth, for the fifth month, was the commander Shamhuth, a descendant of Zerah, and in his division were twenty-four thousand men. 9 Sixth, for the sixth month, was Ira, son of Ikkesh, from Tekoa, and in his division were twenty-four thousand men. 10 Seventh, for the seventh month, was Hellez, from Beth-phelet, of the sons of Ephraim, and in his division were twenty-four thousand men. 11 Eighth, for the eighth month, was Sibbecai the Hushathite, a descendant of Zerah, and in his division were twenty-four thousand men. 12 Ninth, for the ninth month, was Abiezer from Anathoth, of Benjamin, and in his division were twenty-four thousand men. 13 Tenth, for the tenth month, was Maharai from Netophah, a descendant of Zerah, and in his division were twenty-four thousand men. 14 Eleventh, for the eleventh month, was Benaiah the Pirathonite, of Ephraim, and in his division were twenty-four thousand men. 15 Twelfth, for the twelfth month, was Heldai the Netophathite, of the family of Othniel, and in his division were twenty-four thousand men.

Tribal Heads

16 Over the tribes of Israel, for the Reubenites the leader was Eliezer, son of Zichri; for the Simeonites, Shephatiah, son of Maacah; 17 for Levi, Hashabiah, son of Kemuel; for Aaron, Zadok; 18 for Judah, Eliab, one of David's brothers; for Issachar, Omri, son of Michael; 19 for Zebulun, Ishmaiah, son of Obadiah; 20 for Naphtali, Jeremoth, son of Azriel; for the sons of Ephraim, Hoshea, son of Azaziah; for the half-tribe of Manasseh, Joel, son of Pedaiah; 21 for the half-tribe of Manasseh in Gilead, Iddo, son of Zechariah; for Benjamin, Jaasiel, son of Abner; 22 for Dan, Azarel, son of Jeroham. These were the commanders of the tribes of Israel.

23 David did not count those who

were twenty years of age or younger, for the LORD had promised to multiply Israel like the stars of the heavens. 24 Joab, son of Zeruiah, began to take the census, but he did not complete it, for because of it wrath fell upon Israel. Therefore the number did not enter into the book of chronicles of King David.

Overseers

25 Over the treasures of the king was Azmaveth, the son of Adiel. Over the stores in the country, the cities, the villages, and the towers was Jonathan, son of Uzziah. 26 Over the farm workers who tilled the soil was Ezri, son of Chelub. 27 Over the vineyards was Shimei from Ramah, and over their produce for the wine cellars was Zabdi the Shiphmite. 28 Over the olive trees and sycamores of the foothills was Baalhanan the Gederite, and over the stores of oil was Josah. 29 Over the cattle that grazed in Sharon was Shitrai the Sharonite, and over the cattle in the valleys was Shaphat, the son of Adlai; 30 over the camels was Obil the Ishmaelite; over the she-asses was Jehdeiah the Meronothite; 31 and over the flocks was Jaziz the Hagrite. All these were the overseers of King David's possessions.

David's Court

32 Jonathan, David's uncle and a man of intelligence, was counselor and scribe; he and Jehiel, the son of Hachmoni, were tutors of the king's sons. 33 Ahithophel was also the king's counselor, and Hushai the Archite was the king's confidant. 34 After Ahithophel came Jehoiada, the son of Benaiah, and Abiathar. The commander of the king's army was Joab.

The Assembly at Jerusalem

28 David assembled at Jerusalem all the leaders of Israel, the heads of the tribes, the commanders of the divisions who were in the

---

27, 1–15: This list of army commanders is similar to, but distinct from, the list of David's warriors as given in 11, 10–47. The schematic enumeration of the soldiers as presented here is, no doubt, artificial and grossly exaggerated ($12 \times 24,000 = 288,000$ men!),

unless the Hebrew word (*eleph*) for *thousand* is understood as designating a military unit of much smaller size; see note on 12, 25–38.

27, 34: *After Ahithophel:* after his suicide (2 Sm 17, 23). Jehoiada then succeeded him as the king's

counselor. *Abiathar:* the priest. The Chronicler does not mention his office because he regards only the Zadokites as legitimate high priests.

service of the king, the commanders of thousands and of hundreds, the overseers of all the king's estates and possessions, and his sons, together with the courtiers, the warriors, and every important man. 2 King David rose to his feet and said: "Hear me, my brethren and my people. It was my purpose to build a house of repose myself for the ark of the covenant of the LORD, the footstool for the feet of our God; and I was preparing to build it. 3 But God said to me, 'You may not build a house in my honor, for you are a man who fought wars and shed blood.' 4 However, the LORD, the God of Israel, chose me from all my father's family to be king over Israel forever. For he chose Judah as leader, then one family of Judah, that of my father; and finally, among all the sons of my father, it pleased him to make me king over all Israel. 5 And of all my sons— for the LORD has given me many sons —he has chosen my son Solomon to sit on the LORD's royal throne over Israel. 6 For he said to me: 'It is your son Solomon who shall build my house and my courts, for I have chosen him for my son, and I will be a father to him. 7 I will establish his kingdom forever, if he perseveres in keeping my commandments and decrees as he keeps them now.' 8 Therefore, in the presence of all Israel, the assembly of the LORD, and in the hearing of our God, I exhort you to keep and to carry out all the commandments of the LORD, your God, that you may continue to possess this good land and afterward leave it as an inheritance to your children forever.

9 "As for you, Solomon, my son, know the God of your father and serve him with a perfect heart and a willing soul, for the LORD searches all hearts and understands all the mind's thoughts. If you seek him, he will let himself be found by you; but if you abandon him, he will cast you off forever. 10 See, then! The LORD has chosen you to build a house as his sanctuary. Take courage and set to work."

Temple Plans Given to Solomon

11 Then David gave to his son Solomon the pattern of the portico and of the building itself, with its storerooms, its upper rooms and inner chambers, and the room with the propitiatory. 12 He provided also the pattern for all else that he had in mind by way of courts for the house of the LORD, with the surrounding compartments for the stores for the house of God and the stores of the votive offerings, 13 as well as for the divisions of the priests and Levites, for all the work of the service of the house of the LORD, and for all liturgical vessels of the house of the LORD. 14 He specified the weight of gold to be used in the golden vessels for the various services and the weight of silver to be used in the silver vessels for the various services; 15 likewise for the golden lampstands and their lamps he specified the weight of gold for each lampstand and its lamps, and for the silver lampstands he specified the weight of silver for each lampstand and its lamps, depending on the use to which each lampstand was to be put. 16 He specified the weight of gold for each table to hold the showbread, and the silver for the silver tables; the pure gold to be used for the forks and pitchers; 17 the amount of gold for each golden bowl and the silver for each silver bowl; 18 the refined gold, and its weight, to be used for the altar of incense; and, finally, gold for what would suggest a chariot throne: the cherubim that spread their wings and covered the ark of the covenant of the LORD. 19 He had successfully committed to writing the exact specifications of the pattern, because the hand of the LORD was upon him.

20 Then David said to his son Solomon: "Be firm and steadfast; go to work without fear or discouragement, for the LORD God, my God, is with you. He will not fail you or abandon you before you have completed all the work for the service of the house of the LORD. 21 The

classes of the priests and Levites are ready for all the service of the house of God; they will help you in all your work with all those who are eager to show their skill in every kind of craftsmanship. Also the leaders and all the people will do everything that you command."

Offerings for the Temple

29 King David then said to the whole assembly: "My son Solomon whom alone God has chosen, is still young and immature; the work, however, is great, for this castle is not intended for man, but for the LORD God. 2 For this reason I have stored up for the house of my God, as far as I was able, gold for what will be made of gold, silver for what will be made of silver, bronze for what will be made of bronze, iron for what will be made of iron, wood for what will be made of wood, onyx stones and settings for them, carnelian and mosaic stones, every other kind of precious stone, and great quantities of marble. 3 But now, because of the delight I take in the house of my God, in addition to all that I have stored up for the holy house, I give to the house of my God my personal fortune in gold and silver: 4 three thousand talents of Ophir gold, and seven thousand talents of refined silver, for overlaying the walls of the rooms, 5 for the various utensils to be made of gold and silver, and for every work that is to be done by artisans. Now, who else is willing to contribute generously this day to the LORD?"

6 Then the heads of the families, the leaders of the tribes of Israel, the commanders of thousands and of hundreds, and the overseers of the king's affairs came forward willingly 7 and contributed for the service of the house of God five thousand talents and ten thousand darics of gold, ten thousand talents of silver, eighteen thousand talents of bronze, and one hundred thousand talents of iron. 8 Those who had precious stones gave them into the keeping of Jehiel the Gershonite for the treasury

---

28, 2: *The ark . . . , the footstool . . . of our God:* the Lord, who was invisibly enthroned upon the cherubim that were associated with the ark of the covenant at Shiloh and later in the Jerusalem temple,

had the ark as his footstool; cf Pss 99, 5; 132, 7. The *propitiatory* (28, 11) and the *chariot throne* (28, 18) reflect the different circumstances of the postexilic community, for whom only the place of the ark was a

focal point of worship, though the ark itself was no longer present.

28, 18: *Chariot throne:* probably suggested by Ez 1, 4–24; 10, 1–22.

of the house of the LORD. 9 The people rejoiced over these free-will offerings, which had been contributed to the LORD wholeheartedly. King David also rejoiced greatly.

David's Prayer

10 Then David blessed the LORD in the presence of the whole assembly, praying in these words:

"Blessed may you be, O LORD,
    God of Israel our father,
    from eternity to eternity.

11 "Yours, O LORD, are grandeur
        and power,
    majesty, splendor, and glory.

For all in heaven and on earth
        is yours;
    yours, O LORD, is the
        sovereignty;
    you are exalted as head over
        all.

12 "Riches and honor are from
        you,
    and you have dominion over
        all.
In your hand are power and
        might;
    it is yours to give grandeur
        and strength to all.
13 Therefore, our God, we give
        you thanks
    and we praise the majesty of
        your name."

14 "But who am I, and who are

29, 22: *For a second time:* the first time is referred to in 23, 1. Here there is a solemn public ratification of David's earlier appointment of Solomon as his successor.

my people, that we should have the means to contribute so freely? For everything is from you, and we only give you what we have received from you. 15 For we stand before you as aliens: we are only your guests, like all our fathers. Our life on earth is like a shadow that does not abide. 16 O LORD our God, all this wealth that we have brought together to build you a house in honor of your holy name comes from you and is entirely yours. 17 I know, O my God, that you put hearts to the test and that you take pleasure in uprightness. With a sincere heart I have willingly given all these things, and now with joy I have seen your people here present also giving to you generously. 18 O LORD, God of our fathers Abraham, Isaac, and Israel, keep such thoughts in the hearts and minds of your people forever, and direct their hearts toward you. 19 Give to my son Solomon a wholehearted desire to keep your commandments, precepts, and statutes, that he may carry out all these plans and build the castle for which I have made preparation."

20 Then David besought the whole assembly, "Now bless the LORD your God!" And the whole assembly blessed the LORD, the God of their fathers, bowing down and prostrating themselves before the LORD and before the king. 21 On the following day they offered sacrifices and holocausts to the LORD, a thousand bulls, a thousand rams, and a thousand lambs, together with their libations and many other sacrifices for all

Israel; 22 and on that day they ate and drank in the LORD's presence with great rejoicing.

Solomon Anointed

Then for a second time they proclaimed David's son Solomon king, and they anointed him as the LORD's prince, and Zadok as priest. 23 Thereafter Solomon sat on the throne of the LORD as king in place of his father David; he prospered, and all Israel obeyed him. 24 All the leaders and warriors, and also all the other sons of King David, swore allegiance to King Solomon. 25 And the LORD exalted Solomon greatly in the eyes of all Israel, giving him a glorious reign such as had not been enjoyed by any king over Israel before him.

Death of David

26 Thus David, the son of Jesse, had reigned over all Israel. 27 The time that he reigned over Israel was forty years: in Hebron he reigned seven years, and in Jerusalem thirty-three. 28 He died at a ripe old age, rich in years and wealth and glory, and his son Solomon succeeded him as king.

29 Now the deeds of King David, first and last, can be found written in the history of Samuel the seer, the history of Nathan the prophet, and the history of Gad the seer, 30 together with the particulars of his reign and valor, and of the events that affected him and all Israel and all the kingdoms of the surrounding lands.

THE SECOND BOOK OF THE

Chronicles

THE REIGN OF SOLOMON

Solomon at Gibeon

SOLOMON, son of David, strengthened his hold on the kingdom, for the LORD, his God, was with him, constantly making him more renowned. 2 He sent a summons to all Israel, to the commanders of thousands and of hundreds, the judges, the princes of all Israel, and the family heads; 3 and, accompanied by the whole assembly, he went to the high place at Gibeon, because the meeting tent of God, made in the desert by Moses, the LORD's servant, was there. 4 (The Ark of God, however, David had brought up from Kiriath-jearim to Jerusalem, where he had provided a place and pitched a tent for it.) 5 The bronze altar made by Bezalel, son of Uri, son of Hur, he put in front of the LORD's Dwelling on the high place. There Solomon and the assembly consulted the LORD, 6 and Solomon offered sacrifice in the LORD's presence on the bronze altar at the meeting tent; he offered a thousand holocausts upon it.

7 That night God appeared to Solomon and said to him, "Make a request of me, and I will grant it to you." 8 Solomon answered God: "You have shown great favor to my father David, and you have allowed me to succeed him as king. 9 Now, LORD God, may your promise to my father David be fulfilled, for you have made me king over a people as numerous as the dust of the earth. 10 Give me therefore, wisdom and knowledge to lead this people, for otherwise who could rule this great people of yours?" 11 God then replied to Solomon: "Since this has been your wish and you have not asked for riches, treasures and glory, nor for the life of those who hate you, nor even for a long life for yourself, but have asked for wisdom and knowledge in order to rule my people over whom I made you king, 12 wisdom and knowledge are given you; but I will also give you riches, treasures and glory, such as kings before you never had, nor will those have them who come after you."

Solomon's Wealth

13 Solomon returned to Jerusalem from the high place at Gibeon, from the meeting tent, and became king over Israel. 14 He gathered together chariots and drivers, so that he had one thousand four hundred chariots and twelve thousand drivers he could station in the chariot cities and with the king in Jerusalem. 15 The king made silver and gold as common in Jerusalem as stones, while cedars became as numerous as the sycamores of the foothills. 16 Solomon also imported horses from Egypt and Cilicia. The king's agents would acquire them by purchase from Cilicia, 17 and would then bring up chariots from Egypt and

---

1, 5: *The bronze altar . . . the* LORD's *Dwelling:* the Chronicler justifies Solomon's worship at the high place of Gibeon. He pictures *the* LORD's *dwelling,* i.e., the Mosaic meeting tent, and *the bronze altar* made at Moses' command (Ex 31, 1–9) as still at Gibeon after David had removed the ark of the covenant from there to a new tent in Jerusalem (1 Chr 15, 1.25; 16, 1). The altar made by Bezalel is described as being of acacia wood plated with bronze (Ex 27, 1f). Solomon later made an all-bronze altar for the temple in Jerusalem (2 Chr 4, 1).

1, 16f: *Egypt . . . Cilicia:* it seems likely that the horses came from Cilicia and the chariots from Egypt. Some read the source of these data in 1 Kgs 10, 28f as containing the name (Musur) of a mountain district north of Cilicia, rather than of Egypt; but the author of Chronicles surely understood *Egypt;* cf 9, 28.

export them at six hundred silver shekels, with the horses going for a hundred and fifty shekels. At these rates they served as middlemen for all the Hittite and Aramean kings.

Preparations for the Temple

18 Solomon gave orders for the building of a house to honor the LORD and also of a house for his own **2** royal estate. 1 He conscripted seventy thousand men to carry stone and eighty thousand to cut the stone in the mountains, and over these he placed three thousand six hundred overseers. 2 Moreover, Solomon sent this message to Huram, king of Tyre: "As you dealt with my father David, sending him cedars to build a house for his dwelling, so deal with me. 3 I intend to build a house for the honor of the LORD, my God, and to consecrate it to him, for the burning of fragrant incense in his presence, for the perpetual display of the showbread, for holocausts morning and evening, and for the sabbaths, new moons, and festivals of the LORD, our God: such is Israel's perpetual obligation. 4 And the house I intend to build must be large, for our God is greater than all other gods. 5 Yet who is really able to build him a house, since the heavens and even the highest heavens cannot contain him? And who am I that I should build him a house, unless it be to offer incense in his presence? 6 Now, send me men skilled at work in gold, silver, bronze and iron, in purple, crimson, and violet fabrics, and who know how to do engraved work, to join the craftsmen who are with me in Judah and Jerusalem, whom my father appointed. 7 Also send me boards of cedar, cypress and cabinet wood from Lebanon, for I realize that your servants know how to cut the wood of the Lebanon. My servants will labor with yours 8 in order to prepare for me a great quantity of wood, since the house I intend to build must be lofty and wonderful.

9 I will furnish as food for your servants, the hewers who cut the wood, twenty thousand kors of wheat twenty thousand kors of barley, twenty thousand measures of wine, and twenty thousand measures of oil."

10 Huram, king of Tyre, wrote an answer which he sent to Solomon: "Because the LORD loves his people, he has placed you over them as king." 11 He added: "Blessed be the LORD, the God of Israel, who made heaven and earth, for having given King David a wise son of intelligence and understanding, who will build a house for the LORD and also a house for his royal estate. 12 I am now sending you a craftsman of great skill, Huram-abi, 13 son of a Danite woman and of a father from Tyre; he knows how to work with gold, silver, bronze and iron, with stone and wood, with purple, violet, fine linen and crimson, and also how to do all kinds of engraved work and to devise every type of artistic work that may be given him and your craftsmen and the craftsmen of my lord David your father. 14 And now, let my lord send to his servants the wheat, barley, oil and wine which he has promised. 15 For our part, we will cut trees on Lebanon, as many as you need, and float them down to you at the port of Joppe, whence you may take them up to Jerusalem."

16 Thereupon Solomon took a census of all the alien men who were in the land of Israel (following the census David his father had taken of them), who were found to number one hundred fifty-three thousand six hundred. 17 Of these he made seventy thousand carriers and eighty thousand cutters in the mountains, and three thousand six hundred overseers to keep the people working.

Building of the Temple

3 Then Solomon began to build the house of the LORD in Jerusa-lem on Mount Moriah, which had been pointed out to his father David, on the spot which David had selected, the threshing-floor of Ornan the Jebusite. 2 He began to build in the second month of the fourth year of his reign. 3 These were the specifications laid down by Solomon for building the house of God: the length was sixty cubits according to the old measure, and the width was twenty cubits; 4 the porch which lay before the nave along the width of the house was also twenty cubits, and it was twenty cubits high. He overlaid its interior with pure gold. 5 The nave he overlaid with cypress wood which he covered with fine gold, embossing on it palms and chains. 6 He also decorated the building with precious stones. 7 The house, its beams and thresholds, as well as its walls and its doors, he overlaid with gold, and he engraved cherubim upon the walls. (The gold was from Parvaim.) 8 He also made the room of the holy of holies. Its length corresponded to the width of the house, twenty cubits, and its width was also twenty cubits. He overlaid it with fine gold to the amount of six hundred talents. 9 The weight of the nails was fifty gold shekels. The upper chambers he likewise covered with gold.

10 For the room of the holy of holies he made two cherubim of carved workmanship, which were then overlaid with gold. 11 The wings of the cherubim spanned twenty cubits: 12 one wing of each cherub, five cubits in length, extended to a wall of the building, while the other wing, also five cubits in length, touched the corresponding wing of the second cherub. 13 The combined wingspread of the two cherubim was thus twenty cubits. They stood upon their own feet, facing toward the nave. 14 He made the veil of violet, purple, crimson and fine linen, and had cherubim embroidered upon it.

2, 13: *A Danite women:* a widow of the tribe of Naphtali (1 Kgs 7, 14). The Danites had settled in the northern section of Naphtali territory (Jgs 18, 27ff). Bezalel's fellow craftsman was of the tribe of Dan (Ex 31, 6).

3, 1: *Mount Moriah:* the *height* in *the land of Moriah* (Gn 22, 2). This is the only place in the Bible where the temple mount is identified with the site where Abraham was to sacrifice Isaac.

3, 4: *The porch . . . twenty cubits high:* this measurement, not given in the Books of Kings, is here based on a variant Greek text that may be a later revision. The received Hebrew text says, "one hundred and twenty cubits high." The height of the two freestanding columns adjacent to the porch (1 Kgs 7, 15–16) is nearly doubled by the Chronicler (3, 15).

3, 14: *The veil:* at the entrance of the holy of holies, as also in the Mosaic meeting tent (Ex 26, 31f). Solomon's temple had doors at this place (1 Kgs 6, 31). Apparently there was a veil here in the temple of the Chronicler's time as there also was in Herod's temple (Mt 27, 51; Mk 15, 38; Lk 23, 45).

15 In front of the building he set two columns thirty-five cubits high; the capital topping each was of five cubits. 16 He worked out chains in the form of a collar with which he encircled the capitals of the columns, and he made a hundred pomegranates which he set on the chains. 17 He set up the columns to correspond with the nave, one for the right side and the other for the left, and he called the one to the right Jachin and the one to the left Boaz.

4 Then he made a bronze altar twenty cubits long, twenty cubits wide and ten cubits high. 2 He also made the molten sea. It was perfectly round, ten cubits in diameter, five in depth, and thirty in circumference; 3 below the rim a ring of figures of oxen encircled the sea, ten to the cubit, all the way around; there were two rows of these cast in the same mold with the sea. 4 It rested on twelve oxen, three facing north, three west, three south, and three east, with their haunches all toward the center; the sea rested on their backs. 5 It was a handbreadth thick, and its brim was made like that of a cup, being lily-shaped. It had a capacity of three thousand measures.

6 Then he made ten basins for washing, placing five of them to the right and five to the left. Here were cleansed the victims for the holocausts; but the sea was for the priests to wash in.

7 He made the lampstands of gold, ten of them as was prescribed, and placed them in the nave, five to the right and five to the left. 8 He made ten tables and had them set in the nave, five to the right and five to the left; and he made a hundred golden bowls. 9 He made the court of the priests and the great courtyard and the gates of the courtyard; the gates he overlaid with bronze. 10 The sea was placed off to the southeast from the right side of the temple. 11 Huram also made the pots, the shovels and the bowls. Huram thus

completed the work he had to do for King Solomon in the house of God: 12 two columns, two nodes for the capitals topping these two columns; also four hundred pomegranates for the two networks, 13 with two rows of pomegranates to each network, to cover the two nodes of the capitals topping the columns. 14 He made the stands, and the basins on the stands; 15 one sea, and the twelve oxen under it; 16 likewise the pots, the shovels and the forks. Huram-abi made all these articles for King Solomon from polished bronze for the house of the LORD. 17 The king had them cast in the Jordan region, in the clayey ground between Succoth and Zeredah. 18 Solomon made all these vessels, so many in number that the weight of the bronze was not ascertained.

19 Solomon had all these articles made for the house of God: the golden altar, the tables on which the showbread lay, 20 the lampstands and their lamps of pure gold which were to burn according to prescription before the sanctuary, 21 flowers, lamps and gold tongs [this was the purest gold], 22 snuffers, bowls, cups and firepans of pure gold. As for the entry to the house, its inner doors to the holy of holies, as well as the doors to the nave, were of gold.

Dedication of the Temple

5 When all the work undertaken by Solomon for the temple of the LORD had been completed, he brought in the dedicated offerings of his father David, putting the silver, the gold and all the other articles in the treasuries of the house of God. 2 At Solomon's order the elders of Israel and all the leaders of the tribes, the princes of the Israelite ancestral houses, came to Jerusalem to bring up the ark of the LORD's covenant from the City of David (which is Zion). 3 All the men of Israel assembled before the king during the festival of the seventh month. 4

When all the elders of Israel had arrived, the Levites took up the ark, 5 and they carried the ark and the meeting tent with all the sacred vessels that were in the tent; it was the levitical priests who carried them.

6 King Solomon and the entire community of Israel gathered about him before the ark were sacrificing sheep and oxen so numerous that they could not be counted or numbered. 7 The priests brought the ark of the covenant of the LORD to its place beneath the wings of the cherubim in the sanctuary, the holy of holies of the temple. 8 The cherubim had their wings spread out over the place of the ark, sheltering the ark and its poles from above. 9 The poles were long enough so that their ends could be seen from that part of the holy place nearest the sanctuary; however, they could not be seen beyond. The ark has remained there to this day. 10 There was nothing in it but the two tablets which Moses put there on Horeb, the tablets of the covenant which the LORD made with the Israelites at their departure from Egypt.

11 When the priests came out of the holy place (all the priests who were present had purified themselves without reference to the rotation of their various classes), 12 the Levites who were singers, all who belonged to Asaph, Heman, Jeduthun, and their sons and brothers, clothed in fine linen, with cymbals, harps and lyres, stood east of the altar, and with them a hundred and twenty priests blowing trumpets.

13 When the trumpeters and singers were heard as a single voice praising and giving thanks to the LORD, and when they raised the sound of the trumpets, cymbals and other musical instruments to "give thanks to the LORD, for he is good, for his mercy endures forever," the building of the LORD's temple was filled with a cloud. 14 The priests could not continue to minister because of the cloud, since the LORD's glory filled the house of God.

4, 3: *Oxen:* in 1 Kgs 7, 24 this double row of ornaments is described as being gourds. The text of Kings available to the Chronicler may have been faulty on this point as the words are similar in sound. In 4, 16 the *forks* correspond in a similar way to *bowls* in the text of 1 Kings (7, 40).

4, 5: *Three thousand measures:* according to 1 Kgs 7, 26, *two thousand measures.*

5, 4: *The Levites:* The parallel passage in 1 Kgs 8, 3 has *the priests;* but see 2 Chr 5, 5, where the Deuteronomic term *levitical priests* is used, as also in 23, 18; 30, 27.

5, 9: *The ark has remained there to this day:* the Chronicler must have copied this from his source (1 Kgs 8, 8) without reflecting that the ark was lost in the Babylonian destruction of Jerusalem; cf 2 Mc 2, 4–8.

6 Then Solomon said: "The LORD intends to dwell in the dark cloud. 2 I have truly built you a princely house and dwelling, where you may abide forever." 3 Turning about, the king greeted the whole community of Israel as they stood. 4 He said: "Blessed be the LORD, the God of Israel, who with his own mouth made a promise to my father David and by his own hands brought it to fulfillment. He said: 5 'Since the day that I brought my people out of the land of Egypt, I have not chosen any city among all the tribes of Israel for the building of a temple to my honor, nor have I chosen any man to be commander of my people Israel; 6 but now I choose Jerusalem, where I shall be honored, and I choose David to rule my people Israel.' 7 My father David wished to build a temple to the honor of the LORD, the God of Israel, 8 but the LORD said to him: 'In wishing to build a temple to my honor, you do well. 9 However, you shall not build the temple; rather, your son, whom you will beget shall build the temple to my honor.'

10 "Now the LORD has fulfilled the promise that he made. I have succeeded my father David and have taken my seat on the throne of Israel, as the LORD foretold, and I have built the temple to the honor of the LORD, the God of Israel. 11 And I have placed there the ark, in which abides the covenant of the LORD which he made with the Israelites."

Solomon's Prayer

12 Solomon then took his place before the altar of the LORD in the presence of the whole community of Israel and stretched forth his hands. 13 He had made a bronze platform five cubits long, five cubits wide, and three cubits high, which he had placed in the middle of the courtyard. Having ascended it, Solomon knelt in the presence of the whole of Israel and stretched forth his hands toward heaven. 14 Thus he prayed: "LORD, God of Israel, there is no god like you in heaven or on earth; you keep your covenant and show kindness to your servants who are wholeheartedly faithful to you. 15 You have kept the promise you made to my father David your servant. With your own mouth you spoke it, and by your own hand you have brought it to fulfillment this day. 16 Now, therefore, LORD, God of Israel, keep the further promise you made to my father David, your servant, when you said, 'You shall always have someone from your line to sit before me on the throne of Israel, provided only that your descendants look to their conduct so as always to live according to my law, even as you have lived in my presence.' 17 Now, LORD, God of Israel, may this promise which you have made to your servant David be confirmed.

18 "Can it indeed be that God dwells with mankind on earth? If the heavens and the highest heavens cannot contain you, how much less this temple which I have built! 19 Look kindly on the prayer and petition of your servant, O LORD, my God, and listen to the cry of supplication your servant makes before you. 20 May your eyes watch day and night over this temple, the place where you have decreed you shall be honored; may you heed the prayer which I your servant offer toward this place. 21 Listen to the petitions of your servant and of your people Israel which they direct toward this place. Listen from your heavenly dwelling, and when you have heard, pardon.

22 "When any man sins against his neighbor and is required to take an oath of execration against himself, and when he comes for the oath before your altar in this temple, 23 listen from heaven: take action and pass judgment on your servants, requiting the wicked man and holding him responsible for his conduct, but absolving the innocent and rewarding him according to his virtue. 24 When your people Israel have sinned against you and are defeated by the enemy, but afterward they return and praise your name, and they pray for you and entreat you in this temple, 25 listen from heaven and forgive the sin of your people Israel, and bring them back to the land which you gave them and their fathers. 26 When the sky is closed so that there is no rain, because they have sinned against you, but then they pray toward this place and praise your name, and they withdraw from sin because you afflict them, 27 listen in heaven and forgive the sin of your servants and of your people Israel. But teach them the right way to live, and send rain upon your land which you gave your people as their heritage. 28 When there is famine in the land, when there is pestilence, or blight, or mildew, or locusts, or caterpillars; when their enemies besiege them at any of their gates; whenever there is a plague or sickness of any kind; 29 when any Israelite of all your people offers a prayer or petition of any kind, and in awareness of his affliction and pain, stretches out his hands toward this temple, 30 listen from your heavenly dwelling place, and forgive. Knowing his heart, render to everyone according to his conduct, for you alone know the hearts of men. 31 So may they fear you and walk in your ways as long as they live on the land you gave our fathers.

32 "For the foreigner, too, who is not of your people Israel, when he comes from a distant land to honor your great name, your mighty power, and your outstretched arm, when they come in prayer to this temple, 33 listen from your heavenly dwelling place, and do whatever the foreigner entreats you, that all the peoples of the earth may know your name, fearing you as do your people Israel, and knowing that this house which I have built is dedicated to your honor.

34 "When your people go forth to war against their enemies, wherever you send them, and pray to you in the direction of this city and of the house I have built to your honor, 35 listen from heaven to their prayer and petition, and defend their cause. 36 When they sin against you (for there is no man who does not sin), and in your anger against them you deliver them to the enemy, so that their

---

6, 13: This verse is not found in the Chronicler's source; cf 1 Kgs 8, 22f. He has Solomon praying on a

bronze platform ... in the middle of the courtyard because at the time of the Chronicler only the priests

prayed before the altar.

captors deport them to another land, far or near, 37 when they repent in the land where they are captive and are converted, when they entreat you in the land of their captivity and say, 'We have sinned and done wrong; we have been wicked,' 38 and with their whole heart and with their whole soul they turn back to you in the land of those who hold them captive, when they pray in the direction of their land which you gave their fathers, and of the city you have chosen, and of the house which I have built to your honor, 39 listen from your heavenly dwelling place, hear their prayer and petitions, and uphold their cause. Forgive your people who have sinned against you. 40 My God, may your eyes be open and your ears attentive to the prayer of this place. 41 And now,

"Advance, LORD God, to your
    resting place,
  you and the ark of your
    majesty.
May your priests, LORD God,
    be clothed with salvation,
  may your faithful ones
    rejoice in good things.
42 LORD God, reject not the plea
    of your anointed,
  remember the devotion of
    David your servant."

7 When Solomon had ended his prayer, fire came down from heaven and consumed the holocaust and the sacrifices, and the glory of the LORD filled the house. 2 But the priests could not enter the house of the LORD, for the glory of the LORD had filled the house of the LORD. 3 All the Israelites looked on while the fire came down and the glory of the LORD was upon the house, and they fell down upon the pavement with their faces to the earth and adored, praising the LORD, "for he is good, for his mercy endures forever." 4 The king and all the people were offering sacrifices before the LORD. 5 King Solomon offered as sacrifice

twenty-two thousand oxen, and one hundred twenty thousand sheep.

End of the Dedication

6 Thus the king and all the people dedicated the house of God. The priests were standing at their stations, as were the Levites, with the musical instruments of the LORD which King David had made for "praising the LORD, for his mercy endures forever," when David used them to accompany the hymns. Across from them the priests blew the trumpets and all Israel stood.

7 Then Solomon consecrated the middle part of the court which lay before the house of the LORD; there he offered the holocausts and the fat of the peace offerings, since the bronze altar which Solomon had made could not hold the holocausts, the cereal offerings and the fat.

8 On this occasion Solomon and with him all Israel who had assembled in very large numbers from Labo of Hamath to the Wadi of Egypt, celebrated the festival for seven days. 9 On the eighth day they held a special meeting, for they had celebrated the dedication of the altar for seven days and the feast for seven days. 10 On the twenty-third day of the seventh month he sent the people back to their tents, rejoicing and glad at heart at the good things the LORD had done for David, for Solomon, and for his people Israel. 11 Solomon completed the house of the LORD and the royal palace; he successfully accomplished everything he had planned to do in regard to the house of the LORD and his own house.

God's Promise to Solomon

12 The LORD appeared to Solomon during the night and said to him: "I have heard your prayer, and I have chosen this place for my house of sacrifice. 13 If I close heaven so that there is no rain, if I command the locust to devour the land, if I send pestilence among my people, 14

and if my people, upon whom my name has been pronounced, humble themselves and pray, and seek my presence and turn from their evil ways, I will hear them from heaven and pardon their sins and revive their land. 15 Now my eyes shall be open and my ears attentive to the prayer of this place. 16 And now I have chosen and consecrated this house that my name may be there forever; my eyes and my heart also shall be there always.

17 "As for you, if you live in my presence as your father David did, doing all that I have commanded you and keeping my statutes and ordinances, 18 I will establish your royal throne as I covenanted with your father David when I said, 'There shall never be lacking someone of yours as ruler in Israel.' 19 But if you turn away and forsake my statutes and commands which I placed before you, if you proceed to venerate and worship strange gods, 20 then I will uproot the people from the land I gave them; I will cast from my sight this house which I have consecrated to my honor, and I will make it a proverb and a byword among all peoples. 21 This temple which is so exalted—everyone passing by it will be amazed and ask: 'Why has the LORD done this to this land and to this house?' 22 And men will answer: 'They forsook the LORD, the God of their fathers, who brought them out of the land of Egypt, and they adopted strange gods and worshiped them and served them. That is why he has brought down upon them all this evil.' "

Public Works

8 After the twenty years during which Solomon built the house of the LORD and his own house, 2 he built up the cities which Huram had given him, and settled Israelites there. 3 Then Solomon went to Hamath of Zoba and conquered it. 4 He built Tadmor in the desert region and all

---

7, 9f: *The feast:* of Booths, celebrated on the fifteenth day of the seventh month and followed by a solemn octave lasting through the twenty-second day (Lv 23, 33–36; Nm 29, 12–35); the people are therefore sent home on the twenty-third day (v 10). The festival (v 8) for *the dedication of the altar* and of the temple lasted for seven days before the feast of Booths,

from the seventh to the fourteenth day. According to 1 Kgs 8, 65f, the people are dismissed at the end of these seven days.

8, 2: *The cities which Huram had given him:* according to 1 Kgs 9, 10–14, Solomon had ceded the cities as payment for the timber and gold received from Tyre. But since Huram was dissatisfied, he may have

returned the cities to Solomon.

8, 4: *Tadmor:* later known as Palmyra, an important caravan city in the Syrian desert. The parallel passage in 1 Kgs 9, 18 has *Tamar,* in southern Judah; cf Ez 47, 19; 48, 28. But Solomon may well have fortified Tadmor against the Arameans.

the supply cities, which he built in Hamath. 5 He built Upper Beth-horon and Lower Beth-horon, fortified cities with walls, gates and bars; 6 also Baalath, all the supply cities belonging to Solomon, and all the cities for the chariots, the cities for the horsemen, and whatever else Solomon decided should be built in Jerusalem, in the Lebanon, and in the entire land under his dominion. 7 All the people that remained of the Hittites, Amorites, Perizzites, Hivites, and Jebusites, who were not of Israel — 8 that is, their descendants remaining in the land, whom the Israelites had not destroyed—Solomon subjected to forced labor, as they continue to this day. 9 But Solomon did not enslave the Israelites for his works. They became soldiers, commanders of his warriors, and commanders of his chariots and his horsemen. 10 They were also King Solomon's two hundred and fifty overseers who had charge of the people.

Solomon's Piety

11 Solomon brought the daughter of Pharaoh up from the City of David to the palace which he had built for her, for he said, "No wife of mine shall dwell in the house of David, king of Israel, for the places where the ark of the LORD has come are holy." 12 In those times Solomon offered holocausts to the LORD upon the altar of the LORD which he had built in front of the porch, 13 as was required day by day according to the command of Moses, and in particular on the sabbaths, at the new moons, and on the fixed festivals three times a year: on the feast of the Unleavened Bread, the feast of Weeks and the feast of Booths.

14 And according to the ordinance of his father David he appointed the various classes of the priests for their service, and the Levites according to their functions of praise and ministry alongside the priests, as the daily duty required. The gatekeepers of the various classes stood guard at each gate, since such was the command of David, the man of God. 15 There was no deviation from the king's command in any respect relating to the priests and Levites or

the treasuries. 16 All of Solomon's work was carried out successfully from the day the foundation of the house of the LORD was laid until the house of the LORD has been completed in every detail.

Glories of the Court

17 In those times Solomon went to Ezion-geber and to Elath on the seashore of the land of Edom. 18 Huram, through his servants, sent him ships and crewmen acquainted with the sea, who accompanied Solomon's servants to Ophir and brought back from there four hundred and fifty talents of gold to King Solomon.

9 When the queen of Sheba heard of Solomon's fame, she came to Jerusalem to test him with subtle questions, accompanied by a very numerous retinue and by camels bearing spices, much gold, and precious stones. She came to Solomon and questioned him on every subject in which she was interested. 2 Solomon explained to her everything she asked about, and there remained nothing hidden from Solomon that he could not explain to her.

3 When the queen of Sheba witnessed Solomon's wisdom, the palace he had built, 4 the food at his table, the seating of his ministers, the attendance of his servants and their dress, his cupbearers and their dress, and the holocausts he offered in the house of the LORD, it took her breath away. 5 "The account I heard in my country about your deeds and your wisdom is true," she told the king. 6 "Yet I did not believe the report until I came and saw with my own eyes. I have discovered that they did not tell me the half of your great wisdom; you have surpassed the stories I heard. 7 Happy are your men, happy these servants of yours, who stand before you always and listen to your wisdom. 8 Blessed be the LORD, your God, who has been so pleased with you as to place you on his throne as king for the LORD, your God. Because your God has so loved Israel as to will to make it last forever, he has appointed you over them as king to administer right and justice." 9

Then she gave the king one hundred and twenty gold talents and a very large quantity of spices, as well as precious stones. There was no other spice like that which the queen of Sheba gave to King Solomon.

10 The servants of Huram and of Solomon who brought gold from Ophir also brought cabinet wood and precious stones. 11 With the cabinet wood the king made stairs for the temple of the LORD and the palace of the king; also lyres and harps for the chanters. The like of these had not been seen before in the land of Judah.

12 King Solomon gave the queen of Sheba everything she desired and asked him for, more than she had brought to the king. Then she returned to her own country with her servants.

13 The gold that Solomon received each year weighed six hundred and sixty-six gold talents, 14 in addition to what was collected from travelers and what the merchants brought. All the kings of Arabia also, and the governors of the country, brought gold and silver to Solomon.

15 Moreover, King Solomon made two hundred large shields of beaten gold, six hundred shekels of beaten gold going into each shield, 16 and three hundred bucklers of beaten gold, three hundred shekels of gold going into each buckler; these the king put in the hall of the Forest of Lebanon.

17 King Solomon also made a large ivory throne which he overlaid with fine gold. 18 The throne had six steps; a footstool of gold was fastened to it, and there was an arm on each side of the seat, with two lions standing beside the arms. 19 Twelve other lions also stood there, one on either side of each step. Nothing like this had ever been produced in any other kingdom. 20 Furthermore, all of King Solomon's drinking vessels were of gold, and all the utensils in the hall of the Forest of Lebanon were of pure gold; silver was not considered of value in Solomon's time. 21 For the king had ships that went to Tarshish with the servants of Huram. Once every three years the fleet of Tarshish would return with a cargo of gold and silver, ivory, apes and monkeys.

22 Thus King Solomon surpassed all the other kings of the earth in riches as well as in wisdom.

23 All the kings of the earth sought audience with Solomon, to hear from him the wisdom which God had put in his heart. 24 Year in and year out, each one would bring his tribute—silver and gold articles, garments, weapons, spices, horses and mules. 25 Solomon also had four thousand stalls of horses, chariots, and twelve thousand horsemen, which he assigned to the chariot cities and to the king in Jerusalem. 26 He was ruler over all the kings from the River to the land of the Philistines and down to the border of Egypt. 27 The king made silver as common in Jerusalem as stones, while cedars became as numerous as the sycamores of the foothills. 28 Horses were imported for Solomon from Egypt and from all the lands.

The Death of Solomon

29 The rest of the acts of Solomon, first and last, are written, as is well known, in the acts of Nathan the prophet, in the prophecy of Ahijah the Shilonite, and in the visions of Iddo the seer which concern Jeroboam, son of Nebat. 30 Solomon reigned in Jerusalem over all Israel for forty years. 31 He rested with his ancestors; he was buried in his father's City of David, and his son Rehoboam succeeded him as king.

THE MONARCHY BEFORE HEZEKIAH

Division of the Kingdom

10 Rehoboam went to Shechem, for all Israel had come to Shechem to proclaim him king. 2 When Jeroboam, son of Nebat, heard of this in Egypt where he had fled from King Solomon, he returned from Egypt. 3 Jeroboam was summoned to the assembly, and he and all Israel said to Rehoboam: 4 "Your father laid a heavy yoke upon us. If you now lighten the harsh service and the heavy yoke that your father imposed on us, we will serve you." 5 "In three days," he answered them, "come back to me."

When the people had departed, 6 King Rehoboam consulted the elders who had been in the service of his father during Solomon's lifetime, asking, "What answer do you advise me to give this people?" 7 They replied, "If you will deal kindly with this people and give in to them, acceding to their request, they will be your servants forever." 8 But he ignored the advice the elders had given him and consulted the young men who had grown up with him and were in his service. 9 He said to them, "What answer do you advise me to give this people, who have asked me to lighten the yoke my father imposed on them?" 10 The young men who had grown up with him replied: "This is the answer you should give to this people who have said to you, 'Your father laid a heavy yoke upon us, but do you lighten our yoke'; this you should say to them: 'My little finger is thicker than my father's body. 11 Whereas my father put a heavy yoke on you, I will make it heavier! My father beat you with whips, but I will beat you with scorpions!'"

12 On the third day, Jeroboam and all the people came back to King Rehoboam as he had instructed them to do. 13 Ignoring the advice the elders had given him, the king gave them a harsh answer, 14 speaking to them according to the advice of the young men: "My father laid a heavy yoke on you, but I will make it heavier. My father beat you with whips, but I will beat you with scorpions." 15 The king would not listen to the people, for this turn of events was divinely ordained to fulfill the prophecy the LORD had uttered to Jeroboam, the son of Nebat, through Ahijah the Shilonite.

16 When all Israel saw that the king would not listen to them, the people answered the king,

"What share have we in David?
We have no heritage in the
     son of Jesse.
Everyone to your tents, O Israel!
Now look to your own house,
     David!"

So all Israel went off to their tents. 17 Rehoboam, therefore, reigned over only those Israelites who lived in the cities of Judah. 18 King Rehoboam then sent out Hadoram, who was superintendent of the forced labor force, but the Israelites stoned him to death. Rehoboam himself managed to mount his chariot and flee to Jerusalem. 19 Thus Israel has been in rebellion against David's house to this day.

11 On his arrival in Jerusalem Rehoboam gathered together the house of Judah and Benjamin, a hundred and eighty thousand warriors, to have them fight against Israel and restore the kingdom to him. 2 However, the word of the LORD came to Shemaiah, a man of God: 3 "Say to Rehoboam, son of Solomon, king of Judah, and to all the Israelites in Judah and Benjamin: 4 'Thus says the LORD: You must not march out to fight against your brothers. Let every man return home, for what has occurred I have brought about.'" They obeyed this message of the LORD and gave up the expedition against Jeroboam.

Rehoboam's Works

5 Rehoboam took up residence in Jerusalem and built fortified cities in Judah. 6 He built up Bethlehem, Etam, Tekoa, 7 Beth-zur, Soco, Adullam, 8 Gath, Mareshah, Ziph, 9 Adoraim, Lachish, Azekah, 10 Zorah, Aijalon, and Hebron; these were fortified cities in Judah and Benjamin. 11 Then he strengthened the fortifications and put commanders in them, with supplies of food, oil and wine. 12 In every city were shields and spears, and he made them very strong. Thus Judah and Benjamin remained his.

Refugees from the North

13 Now the priests and Levites throughout Israel presented themselves to him from all parts of their land, 14 for the Levites left their assigned pasture lands and their holdings and came to Judah and Jerusalem, because Jeroboam and

---

9, 28: See note on 1, 16f.
10, 1: *All Israel:* as in the original source (1 Kgs 12, 1), the northern tribes, distinct from Judah and Ben-

jamin. Contrast the Chronicler's own terms, *those Israelites who lived in the cities of Judah* (v 17), and *all the Israelites* [literally, all Israel] *in Judah and*

Benjamin (11, 3).
11, 5–12: These verses, though not found in 1 Kgs, are apparently based on a reliable, ancient source.

his sons repudiated them as priests of the LORD. 15 In their place, he himself appointed priests for the high places and satyrs and calves he had made. 16 After them, all those of the Israelite tribes who firmly desired to seek the LORD, the God of Israel, came to Jerusalem to sacrifice to the LORD, the God of their fathers. 17 Thus they strengthened the kingdom of Judah and made Rehoboam, son of Solomon, prevail for three years; for they walked in the way of David and Solomon three years.

Rehoboam's Family

18 Rehoboam took to himself as wife Mahalath, daughter of Jerimoth, son of David and of Abihail, daughter of Eliab, son of Jesse. 19 She bore him sons: Jehush, Shemariah and Zaham. 20 After her, he married Maacah, daughter of Absalom, who bore him Abijah, Attai, Ziza and Shelomith. 21 Rehoboam loved Maacah, daughter of Absalom, more than all his other wives and concubines; he had taken eighteen wives and sixty concubines, and he fathered twenty-eight sons and sixty daughters. 22 Rehoboam constituted Abijah, son of Maacah, commander among his brothers, for he intended to make him king. 23 He acted prudently, distributing various of his sons throughout all the districts of Judah and Benjamin, in all the fortified cities; and he furnished them with copious provisions and sought an abundance of wives for them.

His Apostasy

12 After Rehoboam had consolidated his rule and had become powerful, he abandoned the law of the LORD, he and all Israel with him. 2 Thus it happened that in the fifth year of King Rehoboam, Shishak, king of Egypt, attacked Jerusalem, for they had been unfaithful to the LORD. 3 He came up with twelve hundred chariots and sixty thousand horsemen, and there was no counting the army that came with him from Egypt—Libyans, Sukkites and Ethiopians. 4 They

captured the fortified cities of Judah and came as far as Jerusalem. 5 Then Shemaiah the prophet came to Rehoboam and the commanders of Judah who had gathered at Jerusalem because of Shishak, and said to them: "Thus says the LORD: 'You have abandoned me, and therefore I have abandoned you to the power of Shishak.'"

6 However, the commanders of Israel and the king humbled themselves saying, "The LORD is just." 7 When the LORD saw that they had humbled themselves, the word of the LORD came to Shemaiah: "Because they have humbled themselves, I will not destroy them; I will give them some deliverance, and my wrath shall not be poured out upon Jerusalem through Shishak. 8 But they shall be his servants, that they may know what it is to serve me and what it is to serve earthly kingdoms." 9 Therefore Shishak, king of Egypt, attacked Jerusalem and carried off the treasures of the temple of the LORD and of the king's palace. He took everything, including the gold bucklers that Solomon had made. 10 (To replace them, King Rehoboam made bronze bucklers, which he entrusted to the officers of the guard on duty at the entrance of the royal palace. 11 Whenever the king visited the temple of the LORD, the troops would come bearing them, and then they would return them to the guardroom.) 12 Because he had humbled himself, the anger of the LORD turned from him so that it did not destroy him completely; and in Judah, moreover, good deeds were found.

13 King Rehoboam consolidated his power in Jerusalem and continued to rule; he was forty-one years old when he became king, and he reigned seventeen years in Jerusalem, the city in which, out of all the tribes of Israel, the LORD chose to be honored. Rehoboam's mother was named Naamah, an Ammonite. 14 He did evil, for he had not truly resolved to seek the LORD. 15 The acts of Rehoboam, first and last, are written, as is well known, in the history of

Shemaiah the prophet and of Iddo the seer [his family record]. There was war continually between Rehoboam and Jeroboam. 16 Rehoboam rested with his ancestors; he was buried in the City of David. His son Abijah succeeded him as king.

War between Abijah and Jeroboam

13 In the eighteenth year of King Jeroboam, Abijah became king of Judah; 2 he reigned three years in Jerusalem. His mother was named Michaiah, daughter of Uriel of Gibeah. There was war between Abijah and Jeroboam.

3 Abijah joined battle with a force of four hundred thousand picked warriors, while Jeroboam lined up against him in battle with eight hundred thousand picked and valiant warriors. 4 Abijah stood on Mount Zemaraim, which is in the highlands of Ephraim, and said: "Listen to me, Jeroboam and all Israel! 5 Do you not know that the LORD, the God of Israel, has given the kingdom of Israel to David forever, to him and to his sons, by a covenant made in salt? 6 Yet Jeroboam, son of Nebat, the servant of Solomon, son of David has stood up and rebelled against his lord! 7 Worthless men, scoundrels, joined him and overcame Rehoboam, son of Solomon, when Rehoboam was young and unthinking, and no match for them. 8 But now, do you think you are a match for the kingdom of the LORD commanded by the sons of David, simply because you are a huge multitude and have with you the golden calves which Jeroboam made you for gods?

9 "Have you not expelled the priests of the LORD, the sons of Aaron, and the Levites, and made for yourselves priests like the peoples of foreign lands? Everyone who comes to consecrate himself with a young bull and seven rams becomes a priest of no-gods. 10 But as for us, the LORD is our God, and we have not forsaken him. The priests ministering to the LORD are sons of Aaron, and the Levites also have their

12, 3: *Sukkites:* foreign mercenaries in the Egyptian army.

13, 4–12: This is a free composition of the Chronicler to show that his was a religious, rather than a political, war.

offices. 11 They burn holocausts to the LORD and fragrant incense morning after morning and evening after evening; they display the showbread on the pure table, and the lamps of the golden lampstand burn evening after evening; for we observe our duties to the LORD, our God, but you have abandoned him. 12 See, God is with us, at our head, and his priests are here with trumpets to sound the attack against you. Do not battle against the LORD, the God of your fathers, O Israelites, for you will not succeed!"

13 But Jeroboam had an ambush go around them to come at them from the rear; so that while his army faced Judah, his ambush lay behind them. 14 When Judah turned and saw that they had to battle on both fronts, they cried out to the LORD and the priests sounded the trumpets. 15 Then the men of Judah shouted; and when they did so, God defeated Jeroboam and all Israel before Abijah and Judah. 16 The Israelites fled before Judah, and God delivered them into their hands. 17 Abijah and his people inflicted a severe defeat upon them; five hundred thousand picked men of Israel fell slain. 18 The Israelites were subdued on that occasion and the Judahites were victorious because they relied on the LORD, the God of their fathers. 19 Abijah pursued Jeroboam and took cities from him: Bethel and its dependencies Jeshanah and its dependencies, and Ephron and its dependencies. 20 Jeroboam did not regain power during the time of Abijah; the LORD struck him down and he died, 21 while Abijah continued to grow stronger. He took to himself fourteen wives and fathered twenty-two sons and sixteen daughters.

Death of Abijah

22 The rest of Abijah's acts, his deeds and his words, are written in the midrash of the prophet Iddo. 23 Abijah rested with his ancestors; they buried him in the City of David. His son Asa succeeded him as king.

During his time, ten years of peace began in the land.

Asa the Reformer

14 Asa did what was good and pleasing to the LORD, his God, 2 removing the heathen altars and the high places, breaking to pieces the sacred pillars, and cutting down the sacred poles. 3 He commanded Judah to seek the LORD, the God of their fathers, and to observe the law and its commands. 4 He removed the high places and incense stands from all the cities of Judah, and under him the kingdom had peace. 5 He built fortified cities in Judah, for the land had peace and no war was waged against him during these years, because the LORD had given him peace. 6 He said to Judah: "Let us build these cities and surround them with walls, towers, gates and bars. The land is still ours, for we have sought the LORD, our God; we sought him, and he has given us rest on every side." So they built and prospered.

The Ethiopian Invasion

7 Asa had an army of three hundred thousand shield- and lance-bearers from Judah, and two hundred and eighty thousand from Benjamin who carried bucklers and were archers, all of them valiant warriors. 8 Zerah the Ethiopian moved against them with a force of one million men and three hundred chariots, and he came as far as Mareshah. 9 Asa went out to meet him and set himself in battle array in the valley of Zephathah, near Mareshah. 10 Asa called upon the LORD, his God, praying: "O LORD, there is none like you to help the powerless against the strong. Help us, O LORD, our God, for we rely on you, and in your name we have come against this multitude. You are the LORD, our God; let no man prevail against you." 11 And so the LORD defeated the Ethiopians before Asa and Judah, and they fled. 12 Asa and those with him pursued them as far as Gerar, and the Ethiopians fell until there were no sur-

vivors, for they were crushed before the LORD and his army, which carried away enormous spoils. 13 Then the Judahites conquered all the cities around Gerar, for the fear of the LORD was upon them; they despoiled all the cities, for there was much booty in them. 14 They attacked also the tents of the cattle-herders and carried off a great number of sheep and camels. Then they returned to Jerusalem.

Cult Reform

15 Upon Azariah, son of Oded, came the spirit of God. 2 He went forth to meet Asa and said to him: "Hear me, Asa and all Judah and Benjamin! The LORD is with you when you are with him, and if you seek him he will be present to you; but if you abandon him, he will abandon you. 3 For a long time Israel had no true God, no priest-teacher and no law, 4 but when in their distress they turned to the LORD, the God of Israel, and sought him, he was present to them. 5 In that former time there was no peace for anyone to go or come, but there were many terrors upon the inhabitants of the lands. 6 Nation crushed nation and city crushed city, for God destroyed them by every kind of adversity. 7 But as for you, be strong and do not relax, for your work shall be rewarded."

8 When Asa heard these words and the prophecy [Oded the prophet], he was encouraged to remove the detestable idols from the whole land of Judah and Benjamin and from the cities he had taken in the highlands of Ephraim, and to restore the altar of the LORD which was before the vestibule of the LORD. 9 Then he convened all Judah and Benjamin, together with those of Ephraim, Manasseh and Simeon who sojourned with them; for many had fled to him from Israel when they saw that the LORD, his God was with him. 10 They gathered at Jerusalem in the third month of the fifteenth year of Asa's reign, 11 and sacrificed to the LORD at that time seven hundred

---

14, 7–14: An Ethiopian invasion of Judah is mentioned only in 1 Chronicles. This account may be a legend contrived to show how the pious King Asa was rewarded through divine assistance. There may, however, have been an incursion of nomads from the

Negeb at this time; cf vv 13f.

15, 10ff : With this description of a covenant ceremony in the *third month* of a year beginning in the spring, the Chronicler lays a foundation for celebrating the ancient feast of Pentecost (Weeks) as the time

for a solemn renewal of the people's covenant with God on Mount Sinai; see Ex 19, 1ff; Lv 23, 16 and the note there. This is also the background for Pentecost as the "birthday of the Church."

oxen and seven thousand sheep of the booty they had brought. 12 They entered into a covenant to seek the LORD, the God of their fathers, with all their heart and soul; 13 and everyone who would not seek the LORD, the God of Israel, was to be put to death, whether small or great, whether man or woman. 14 They swore to the LORD with a loud voice, with shouting and with trumpets and horns. 15 All Judah rejoiced over the oath, for they had sworn with their whole heart and sought him with complete desire, so that he was present to them. And the LORD gave them rest on every side.

16 Maacah, the mother of King Asa, he deposed as queen mother because she had made an outrageous object for Asherah; Asa cut this down, smashed it, and burnt it in the Kidron Valley. 17 Although the high places did not disappear from Israel, yet Asa's heart was undivided as long as he lived. 18 He brought into the house of God his father's votive offerings and his own: silver, gold, and various utensils. 19 There was no war until the thirty-fifth year of Asa's reign.

Asa's Infidelity

16 In the thirty-sixth year of Asa's reign Baasha, king of Israel, attacked Judah and fortified Ramah to prevent any communication with Asa, king of Judah. 2 Asa then brought out silver and gold from the treasuries of the temple of the LORD and of the royal palace and sent them to Ben-hadad, king of Aram, who lived in Damascus, with this message: 3 "There is a treaty between you and me, as there was between your father and my father. See, I am sending you silver and gold. Go break your treaty with Baasha, king of Israel, that he may withdraw from me." 4 Ben-hadad agreed to King Asa's request and sent the leaders of his troops against the cities of Israel. They attacked Ijon, Dan, Abel-maim, and all the store cities of Naphtali. 5 When Baasha heard of it, he left off fortifying Ramah; he stopped his

work. 6 Then King Asa commandeered all Judah to carry away the stone and wood with which Baasha had been fortifying Ramah and with them he fortified Geba and Mizpah.

7 At that time Hanani the seer came to Asa, king of Judah, and said to him: "Because you relied on the king of Aram and did not rely on the LORD, your God, the army of the king of Aram has escaped your hand. 8 Were not the Ethiopians and Libyans a vast army, with great numbers of chariots and drivers? And yet, because you relied on the LORD, he delivered them into your power. 9 The eyes of the LORD roam over the whole earth, to encourage those who are devoted to him wholeheartedly. You have acted foolishly in this matter, for from now on you will have wars." 10 But Asa became angry with the seer and imprisoned him in the stocks, so greatly was he enraged at him over this. Asa also oppressed some of his people at this time.

11 Now the acts of Asa, first and last, can be found recorded in the book of kings of Judah and Israel. 12 In the thirty-ninth year of his reign, Asa contracted a serious disease in his feet. But even in his sickness he did not see the LORD, but only the physicians. 13 Asa rested with his ancestors; he died in the forty-first year of his reign. 14 They buried him in the tomb he had hewn for himself in the City of David, having laid him upon a couch which was filled with spices and various kinds of aromatics compounded into an ointment. They also burned a very great funeral pyre for him.

Zeal of Jehoshaphat for the Law

17 His son Jehoshaphat succeeded him as king and strengthened his hold against Israel. 2 He placed armed forces in all the fortified cities of Judah and in the cities of Ephraim which his father Asa had taken. 3 The LORD was with Jehoshaphat, for he walked in the ways his father had pursued in the beginning, and he did not consult the Baals. 4 Rather he sought the God of his

father and observed his commands, and not the practices of Israel. 5 As a result, the LORD made his kingdom secure, and all Judah gave Jehoshaphat gifts, so that he enjoyed great wealth and glory. 6 Thus he was encouraged to follow the LORD's ways, and again he removed the high places and the sacred poles from Judah.

7 In the third year of his reign he sent his leading men, Ben-hail, Obadiah, Zechariah, Nethanel and Micaiah, to teach in the cities of Judah. 8 With them he sent the Levites Shemaiah, Nethaniah, Zebadiah, Asahel, Shemiramoth, Jehonathan, Adonijah and Tobijah, together with the priests Elishama and Jehoram. 9 They taught in Judah, having with them the book containing the law of the LORD; they traveled through all the cities of Judah and taught among the people.

His Power

10 Now the fear of the LORD was upon all the kingdoms of the countries surrounding Judah, so that they did not war against Jehoshaphat. 11 Some of the Philistines brought Jehoshaphat gifts and a tribute of silver; and the Arabs also brought him a flock of seven thousand seven hundred rams and seven thousand seven hundred he-goats.

12 Jehoshaphat grew steadily greater. He built strongholds and store cities in Judah. 13 He carried out many works in the cities of Judah, and he had soldiers, valiant warriors, in Jerusalem. 14 This was their mustering according to their ancestral houses. Of Judah, the commanders of thousands: Adnah the commander, and with him three hundred thousand valiant warriors. 15 Next to him, Jehohanan the commander, and with him two hundred eighty thousand. 16 Next to him, Amasiah, son of Zichri, who offered himself to the LORD, and with him two hundred thousand valiant warriors. From Benjamin: 17 Eliada, a valiant warrior, and with him two hundred thousand armed with bow and buckler. 18 Next to him, Jozabad, and with him one hundred and

---

16, 7: *The king of Aram ... escaped:* according to the Lucianic recension, "the king of Israel escaped": this may well be the original reading; Asa was friendly with Aram.

17, 3: *The Lord was with Jehoshaphat:* along with Hezekiah and Josiah, Jehoshaphat was one of the

Chronicler's favorite kings.

eighty thousand equipped for war. 19 These were at the service of the king; in addition were those whom the king had placed in the fortified cities throughout all Judah.

Alliance with Israel

18 Jehoshaphat therefore had wealth and glory in abundance but he became related to Ahab by marriage. 2 After some years he went down to Ahab at Samaria; Ahab offered numerous sheep and oxen for him and the people with him, and persuaded him to go up against Ramoth-gilead. 3 Ahab, king of Israel, asked Jehoshaphat, king of Judah, "Will you come with me to Ramoth-gilead?" "You and I are as one," was his answer; "your people and my people as well. We will be with you in the battle." 4 But Jehoshaphat also said to the king of Israel, "Seek the word of the LORD at once."

The Prophets

5 The king of Israel gathered his prophets, four hundred in number, and asked them, "Shall we go to attack Ramoth-gilead, or shall I refrain?" "Go up," they answered. "God will deliver it over to the king." 6 But Jehoshaphat said, "Is there no other prophet of the LORD here whom we may consult?" 7 The king of Israel answered Jehoshaphat, "There is still another through whom we may consult the LORD, but I hate him, for he prophesies not good but always evil about me. That is Micaiah, son of Imlah." Jehoshaphat said, "Let not your Majesty speak of evil against you." 8 So the king of Israel called an official, to whom he said, "Get Micaiah, son of Imlah, at once." 9 The king of Israel and King Jehoshaphat of Judah were seated each on his throne, clothed in their robes of state on a threshing floor at the entrance of the gate of Samaria, and all the prophets were prophesying before them.

10 Zedekiah, son of Chenaanah, made iron horns for himself and said: "The LORD says, 'With these you shall gore Aram until you have des-troyed them.' " 11 The other prophets prophesied in the same vein, saying: "Go up to Ramoth-gilead. You shall succeed; the LORD will deliver it over to the king." 12 The messenger who had gone to call Micaiah said to him: "Look now, the prophets unanimously predict good for the king. Let your word, like each of theirs, predict good." 13 "As the LORD lives," Micaiah answered, "I will say what my God tells me."

14 When he came to the king, the king said to him, "Micaiah, shall we go to fight against Ramoth-gilead, or shall I refrain?" "Go up," he answered, "and succeed; they will be delivered into your power." 15 But the king said to him, "How many times must I adjure you to tell me nothing but the truth in the name of the LORD?" 16 Then Micaiah answered:

"I see all Israel
scattered on the mountains,
like sheep without a shepherd,
and the LORD saying, 'These
    have no master!
Let each of them go back home
    in peace.' "

17 The king of Israel said to Jehoshaphat, "Did I not tell you that he prophesies no good about me, but only evil?" 18 But Micaiah continued:

"Therefore hear the word of the LORD: I saw the LORD seated on his throne, with the whole host of heaven standing by to his right and to his left. 19 The LORD asked, 'Who will deceive Ahab, king of Israel, so that he will go up and fall at Ramoth-gilead?' And one said this, another that, 20 until a spirit came forward and presented himself to the LORD, saying, 'I will deceive him.' The LORD asked, 'How?' 21 He answered, 'I will go forth and become a lying spirit in the mouths of all his prophets.' The LORD agreed: 'You shall succeed in deceiving him. Go forth and do this.' 22 So now the LORD has put a lying spirit in the mouths of these your prophets, but the LORD himself has decreed evil against you."

23 Thereupon Zedekiah, son of Chenaanah, came up and slapped Micaiah on the cheek, saying, "Which way did the spirit of the LORD go when he left me to speak to you?" 24 "You shall find out," Micaiah replied, "on that day when you enter an innermost chamber to hide." 25 The king of Israel then said: "Seize Micaiah and take him back to Amon, prefect of the city, and to Joash the king's son, 26 and say, 'This is the king's order: Put this man in prison and feed him scanty rations of bread and water until I return in safety!'" 27 But Micaiah said, "If ever you return in safety, the LORD has not spoken through me." And he said, "Hear, O peoples, all of you!"

Ahab's Death

28 The king of Israel and King Jehoshaphat of Judah went up to Ramoth-gilead 29 and the king of Israel said to Jehoshaphat, "I will go into battle disguised, but you put on your own clothes." So the king of Israel disguised himself and they entered the fray. 30 Meanwhile, the king of Aram had given his chariot commanders the order, "Fight with no one, small or great, except the king of Israel." 31 When the commanders saw Jehoshaphat, they exclaimed, "That must be the king of Israel!" and shifted to fight him. But Jehoshaphat cried out and the LORD helped him; God induced them to leave him. 32 The chariot commanders became aware that he was not the king of Israel and gave up their pursuit of him. 33 Someone, however, drew his bow at random and hit the king of Israel between the joints of his breastplate. He ordered his charioteer, "Rein about and take me out of the ranks, for I am disabled." 34 The battle grew fierce during the day, and the king of Israel braced himself up on his chariot facing the Arameans until evening. He died as the sun was setting.

Jehoshaphat Rebuked

19 King Jehoshaphat of Judah returned in safety to his house in Jerusalem. 2 Jehu the seer son of Hanani, met King Jehoshaphat

18, 12–22: See note on 1 Kgs 22, 19–23.
18, 27: *"Hear, O peoples, all of you!,"* this quotation which appears in some texts of 1 Kgs 22, 28, ascribes to the prophet Micaiah ben Imlah the opening words of the prophetic utterance of Micah of Moresheth (Mi 1, 2), a century later.

19, 2: *Jehu the seer, son of Hanani:* hardly the same seer as Jehu, son of Hanani, who prophesied against Baasha almost fifty years earlier (1 Kgs 16, 1).

and said to him: "Should you help the wicked and love those who hate the LORD? For this reason, wrath is upon you from the LORD. 3 Yet some good things are to be found in you, since you have removed the sacred poles from the land and have been determined to seek God."

Judges Appointed

4 Jehoshaphat dwelt in Jerusalem; but he went out again among the people from Beer-sheba to the highlands of Ephraim and brought them back to the LORD, the God of their fathers. 5 He appointed judges in the land, in all the fortified cities of Judah, city by city, 6 and he said to them: "Take care what you do, for you are judging, not on behalf of man, but on behalf of the LORD; he judges with you. 7 And now, let the fear of the LORD be upon you. Act carefully, for with the LORD, our God, there is no injustice, no partiality, no bribe-taking." 8 In Jerusalem also, Jehoshaphat appointed some Levites and priests and some of the family heads of Israel to judge in the name of the LORD and to settle quarrels among the inhabitants of Jerusalem. 9 He gave them this command: "You shall act faithfully and wholeheartedly in the fear of the LORD. 10 And in every dispute that your brethren living in their cities bring to you, whether it concerns bloodguilt or questions of law, command, statutes, or judgments, warn them lest they become guilty before the LORD and his wrath come upon you and your brethren. Do that and you shall be guiltless. 11 See now, Amariah is high priest over you in everything that pertains to the LORD, and Zebadiah, son of Ishmael, is leader of the house of Judah in all that pertains to the king; and the Levites will be your officials. Act firmly, and the LORD will be with the good."

Invasion from Edom

20 After this the Moabites, the Ammonites, and with them some Meunites came to fight against Jehoshaphat. 2 The message was brought to Jehoshaphat: "A great multitude is coming against you from across the sea, from Edom; they are already in Hazazon-tamar" (which is En-gedi). 3 Jehoshaphat was frightened, and he hastened to consult the LORD. He proclaimed a fast for all Judah. 4 Then Judah gathered to seek help from the LORD; from every one of the cities of Judah they came to seek the LORD.

Prayer of Jehoshaphat

5 Jehoshaphat stood up in the assembly of Judah and Jerusalem in the house of the LORD before the new court, 6 and he said: "LORD, God of our fathers, are you not the God in heaven, and do you not rule over all the kingdoms of the nations? In your hand is power and might, and no one can withstand you. 7 Was it not you, our God, who drove out the inhabitants of this land before your people Israel and gave it forever to the descendants of Abraham, your friend? 8 They have dwelt in it and they built in it a sanctuary to your honor, saying, 9 'When evil comes upon us, the sword of judgment, or pestilence, or famine, we will stand before this house and before you, for your name is in this house, and we will cry out to you in our affliction, and you will hear and save!' 10 And now, see the Ammonites, Moabites, and those of Mount Seir whom you did not allow Israel to invade when they came from the land of Egypt, but instead they passed them by and did not destroy them. 11 See how they are now repaying us by coming to drive us out of the possession you have given us. 12 O our God, will you not pass judgment on them? We are powerless before this vast multitude that comes against us. We are at a loss what to do, hence our eyes are turned toward you."

Victory Prophesied

13 All Judah was standing before the LORD, with their little ones, their wives and their young sons. 14 And the spirit of the LORD came upon Jahaziel, son of Zechariah, son of Benaiah, son of Jeiel, son of Mattaniah, a Levite of the clan of Asaph, in the midst of the assembly, 15 and he said: "Listen, all of Judah, inhabitants of Jerusalem, and King Jehoshaphat! The LORD says to you: 'Do not fear or lose heart at the sight of this vast multitude, for the battle is not yours but God's. 16 Go down against them tomorrow. You will see them coming up by the ascent of Ziz, and you will come upon them at the end of the wadi which opens on the wilderness of Jeruel. 17 You will not have to fight in this encounter. Take your places, stand firm, and see how the LORD will be with you to deliver you, Judah and Jerusalem. Do not fear or lose heart. Tomorrow go out to meet them, and the LORD will be with you.'" 18 Then Jehoshaphat knelt down with his face to the ground, and all Judah and the inhabitants of Jerusalem fell down before the LORD in worship. 19 Levites from among the Kohathites and Korahites rose to sing the praises of the LORD, the God of Israel, in a resounding chorus.

The Invaders Destroyed

20 In the early morning they hastened out to the wilderness of Tekoa. As they were going out, Jehoshaphat halted and said: "Listen to me, Judah and inhabitants of Jerusalem! Trust in the LORD, your God, and you will be found firm. Trust in his prophets and you will succeed." 21 After consulting with the people, he appointed some to sing to the LORD and some to praise the holy Appearance as it went forth at the head of the army. They sang: "Give thanks to the LORD, for his mercy endures forever." 22 At the moment they began their jubilant hymn, the LORD laid an ambush against the Ammonites, Moabites, and those of Mount Seir who were coming against Judah, so that they were vanquished. 23 For the Ammonites and Moabites set upon the

---

20, 1–30: Although the account here seems to be a free composition of the Chronicler, there is probably a basis in fact for it; there could well have been a raid of nomads against Judah in the reign of Jehoshaphat, similar to Zerah's attack on Asa (14, 8–14). The story may also, in some way, be connected with the campaign of Israel and Judah against Moab through the territory of Edom (2 Kgs 3, 4–27).

20, 21: *Holy Appearance:* the Lord, who is with the Israelite army (v 17), manifests himself (the same language is in Ps 29, 2) in bringing Israel the victory (Ex 14, 14.24).

inhabitants of Mount Seir and completely exterminated them. And when they had finished with the inhabitants of Seir, they began to destroy each other.

24 When Judah came to the watchtower of the desert and looked toward the throng, they saw only corpses fallen on the ground, with no survivors. 25 Jehoshaphat and his people came to take plunder, and they found an abundance of cattle and personal property, garments and precious vessels. They took so much that they were unable to carry it all; they were three days taking the spoil, so great was it. 26 On the fourth day they held an assembly in the Valley of Beracah—for there they blessed the LORD; therefore that place has ever since been called the Valley of Beracah. 27 Then all the men of Judah and Jerusalem, with Jehoshaphat at their head, turned back toward Jerusalem celebrating the joyful victory the LORD had given them over their enemies. 28 They came to Jerusalem, to the house of the LORD, with harps, lyres and trumpets. 29 And the fear of God came upon all the kingdoms of the surrounding lands when they heard how the LORD had fought against the enemies of Israel. 30 Thereafter Jehoshaphat's kingdom enjoyed peace, for his God gave him rest on every side.

Jehoshaphat's Other Deeds

31 Thus Jehoshaphat reigned over Judah. He was thirty-five years old when he became king, and he reigned twenty-five years in Jerusalem. His mother was named Azubah, daughter of Shilhi. 32 He followed the path of his father Asa unswervingly, doing what was right in the LORD's sight. 33 But the high places were not removed nor as yet had the people fixed their hearts on the God of their fathers. 34 The rest of the acts of Jehoshaphat, first and last, can be found written in the chronicle of Jehu, son of Hanani, which is inserted in the

book of the kings of Israel. 35 After this, King Jehoshaphat of Judah allied himself with King Ahaziah of Israel, who did evil. 36 He joined with him in building ships to sail to Tarshish; the fleet was built at Ezion-geber. 37 But Eliezer, son of Dodavahu from Mareshah, prophesied against Jehoshaphat, saying, "Because you have joined with Ahaziah, the LORD will shatter your work." And the ships were wrecked and were unable to sail to Tarshish.

21 Jehoshaphat rested with his ancestors; he was buried with them in the City of David. Jehoram, his son, succeeded him as king. 2 His brothers, sons of Jehoshaphat, were Azariah, Jehiel, Zechariah, Azariah, Michael and Shephatiah; all these were sons of King Jehoshaphat of Judah. 3 Their father gave them numerous gifts of silver, gold and precious objects, together with fortified cities in Judah, but the kingship he gave to Jehoram because he was the first-born.

Evil Deeds of Jehoram

4 When Jehoram had come into his father's kingdom and had consolidated his power he put to the sword all his brothers and also some of the princes of Israel. 5 Jehoram was thirty-two years old when he became king, and he reigned eight years in Jerusalem. 6 He conducted himself like the kings of Israel of the line of Ahab, because one of Ahab's daughters was his wife. He did evil in the sight of the LORD, 7 but the LORD would not destroy the house of David because of the covenant he had made with David and because of his promise to give him and his sons a lamp for all time.

8 During his time Edom revolted against the sovereignty of Judah; they chose a king of their own. 9 Thereupon Jehoram crossed over with his officers and all the chariots he had. He arose by night and broke through the Edomites when they surrounded him and the commanders

of his chariots. 10 However, Edom has continued in revolt against the sovereignty of Judah down to the present time. Libhah also revolted at that time against Jehoram's sovereignty because he had forsaken the LORD, the God of his fathers. 11 He also set up high places in the mountains of Judah; he led the inhabitants of Jerusalem into idolatry and seduced Judah.

Retribution

12 He received a letter from the prophet Elijah with this message: "Thus says the LORD, the God of your ancestor David: 'Because you have not followed the path of your father Jehoshaphat, nor of Asa, king of Judah, 13 but instead have walked in the way of the kings of Israel and have led Judah and the inhabitants of Jerusalem into idolatry, as did the house of Ahab, and also because you have murdered your brothers of your father's house who were better than you, 14 the LORD will strike your people, your children, your wives, and all that is yours with a great plague; 15 and you shall have severe pains from a disease in your bowels, while your bowels issue forth because of the disease, day after day.'"

16 Then the LORD stirred up against Jehoram the animosity of the Philistines and of the Arabs who bordered on the Ethiopians. 17 They came up against Judah, invaded it, and carried away all the wealth found in the king's palace, along with his sons and his wives; there was left to him only one son, Jehoahaz, his youngest. 18 After these events, the LORD afflicted him with an incurable disease of the bowels. 19 As time went on until a period of two years had elapsed, his bowels issued forth because of the disease and he died in great pain. His people did not make a pyre for him like that of his fathers. 20 He was thirty-two years old when he became king, and he reigned eight years in Jerusalem. He departed

---

20, 26: *Beracah:* the Hebrew word for "blessing."
21, 6: *One of Ahab's daughters:* Athaliah. In 22, 2 (and its source, 2 Kgs 8, 26) she is called Omri's daughter; but this should probably be understood in

the sense of granddaughter.
21, 12: *Elijah:* the only mention by the Chronicler of this prophet of the northern kingdom of Israel. It is doubtful that Elijah was still living in the reign of

Jehoram of Judah; in any case, the attribution of the letter to him is most likely an imaginative filling out of the narration.

unloved and was buried in the City of David, but not in the tombs of the kings.

Ahaziah

22 Then the inhabitants of Jerusalem made Ahaziah, his youngest son, king in his stead, since all the older sons had come into the fort with the Arabs. Thus Ahaziah, son of Jehoram reigned as king of Judah. 2 He was twenty-two years old when he became king, and he reigned one year in Jerusalem. His mother was named Athaliah, daughter of Omri. 3 He, too, followed the ways of the house of Ahab, because his mother counseled him to act sinfully. 4 To his own destruction, he did evil in the sight of the LORD, as did the house of Ahab, since they were his counselors after the death of his father.

5 He was also following their counsel when he accompanied Jehoram, son of Ahab, king of Israel, to battle against Hazael, king of Aram, at Ramoth-gilead. There Jehoram was wounded by the Arameans. 6 He returned to Jezreel to be healed of the wounds he had received at Rama in his battle against Hazael, king of Aram. Because of this illness, Ahaziah son of Jehoram, king of Judah, went down to visit Jehoram, son of Ahab, in Jezreel. 7 Now it was willed by God for Ahaziah's downfall that he should join Jehoram, for after his arrival he rode out with Jehoram to Jehu, son of Nimshi, whom the LORD had anointed to cut down the house of Ahab. 8 While Jehu was executing judgment on the house of Ahab, he also encountered the princes of Judah and the nephews of Ahaziah who were his attendants, and he slew them. 9 Then he looked for Ahaziah himself. They caught him where he was hiding in Samaria and brought him to Jehu, who put him to death. They buried him, for they said, "He was the grandson of Jehoshaphat, who sought the LORD with his whole heart." There remained in Ahaziah's house no one powerful enough to wield the kingship.

Usurpation of Athaliah

10 When Athaliah, mother of Ahaziah, learned that her son was dead, she proceeded to kill off all the royal offspring of the house of Judah. 11 But Jehosheba, a royal princess, secretly took Ahaziah's son Joash from among the king's sons who were about to be slain, and put him and his nurse in a bedroom. In this way Jehosheba, who was the daughter of King Jehoram, a sister of Ahaziah, and wife of Jehoiada the priest, hid the child from Athaliah's sight, so that she did not put him to death. 12 For six years he remained hidden with them in the house of God, while Athaliah ruled over the land.

Athaliah Overthrown

23 In the seventh year, Jehoiada took courage and entered a conspiracy with certain captains: Azariah, son of Jeroham; Ishmael, son of Jehohanan; Azariah, son of Obed; Masseiah, son of Adaiah; and Elishaphat, son of Zichri. 2 They journeyed about Judah, gathering the Levites from all the cities of Judah and also the heads of the Israelite families. When they had come to Jerusalem, 3 the whole assembly made a covenant with the king in the house of God. Jehoiada said to them: "Here is the king's son who must reign, as the LORD promised concerning the sons of David. 4 This is what you must do: a third of your number, both priests and Levites, who came in on the sabbath must guard the thresholds, 5 another third must be at the king's palace, and the final third at the Foundation Gate, when all the people will be in the courts of the LORD's temple. 6 Let no one enter the LORD's house except the priests and those Levites who are ministering. They may enter because they are holy; but all the other people must observe the prescriptions of the LORD. 7 The Levites shall surround the king on all sides, each with his weapon drawn. Whoever tries to

enter the house must be slain. Stay with the king wherever he goes."

8 The Levites and all Judah did just as Jehoiada the priest commanded. Each brought his men, those who were to come in on the sabbath as well as those who were to depart on the sabbath, since Jehoiada the priest had not dismissed any of the divisions. 9 Jehoiada the priest gave the captains the spears, shields and bucklers of King David which were in the house of God. 10 He stationed all the people, each with a spear in hand, from the southern to the northern extremity of the enclosure, around the altar and the temple on the king's behalf. 11 Then they brought out the king's son, set the crown and the insignia upon him, and made him king. Jehoiada and his sons anointed him, and they cried, "Long live the king!"

12 When Athaliah heard the din of the people running and acclaiming the king, she went to the people in the temple of the LORD. 13 She looked and there was the king standing beside his pillar at the entrance, the officers and the trumpeters around him, and all the people of the land rejoicing and blowing trumpets, while the singers with their musical instruments were leading the acclaim. Athaliah tore her garments and cried out, "Treason! treason!" 14 Then Jehoiada the priest sent out the captains who were in command of the army; he said to them: "Take her outside through the ranks, and if anyone tries to follow her, let him die by the sword. For," the priest continued, "you must not put her to death in the LORD's temple." 15 So they seized her, and when she arrived at the entrance to the Horse Gate of the palace, they put her to death there.

16 Then Jehoiada made a covenant between himself and all the people and the king, that they should be the LORD's people. 17 And all the people went to the temple of Baal and tore it down. They smashed its altars and images, and they slew Mattan, the priest of Baal, before the altars. 18 Then Jehoiada gave the

---

22, 9: This account of the death of Ahaziah of Judah is not derived from 2 Kgs 9, 27f, with which it is at variance.

23, 13: *Beside his pillar:* the king had a special

place in the eastern gateway of the temple court that contained the altar of holocausts. He occupied this place on feasts and sabbaths at the time of the statutory offerings, or when he made freewill offerings of his

own; cf 2 Kgs 11, 4 and also Ez 46, 1–8 for a later reflection of this.

charge of the LORD's temple into the hands of the levitical priests, to whom David had assigned turns in the temple for offering the holocausts of the LORD, as is written in the law of Moses, with rejoicing and song, as David had provided. 19 Moreover, he stationed guards at the gates of the LORD's temple, so that no one unclean in any respect might enter. 20 Then he took the captains, the nobles, the rulers among the people, and all the people of the land, and led the king out of the LORD's house. When they had come within the upper gate of the king's house they seated the king upon the royal throne. 21 All the people of the land rejoiced and the city was quiet, now that Athaliah had been put to death by the sword.

The Temple Restored

24 Joash was seven years old when he became king, and he reigned forty years in Jerusalem. His mother, named Zibiah, was from Beer-sheba. 2 Joash did what was pleasing to the LORD as long as Jehoiada the priest lived. 3 Jehoiada provided him with two wives, and he became the father of sons and daughters.

4 After some time, Joash decided to restore the LORD's temple. 5 He called together the priests and Levites and said to them: "Go out to all the cities of Judah and collect money from all Israel that you may repair the house of your God over the years. You must hasten this affair." But the Levites did not hasten. 6 Then the king summoned Jehoiada, who was in charge, and said to him: "Why have you not required the Levites to bring in from Judah and Jerusalem the tax levied by Moses, the servant of the LORD, and by the assembly of Israel, for the tent of the testimony?" 7 For the wicked Athaliah and her sons had damaged the house of God and had even turned over to the Baals the dedicated resources of the LORD's temple.

8 At the king's command, therefore, they made a chest, which they put outside the gate of the LORD's temple.

9 They had it proclaimed throughout Judah and Jerusalem that the tax which Moses, the servant of God, had imposed on Israel in the desert should be brought to the LORD. 10 All the princes and the people rejoiced; they brought what was asked and cast it into the chest until it was filled. 11 Whenever the chest was brought to the royal officials by the Levites and they saw that it contained much money, the royal scribe and an overseer for the high priest came, emptied the chest, then took it back and returned it to its place. This they did day after day until they had collected a large sum of money. 12 Then the king and Jehoiada gave it to the workmen in charge of the labor on the LORD's temple, who hired masons and carpenters to restore the temple, and also iron- and bronze-smiths to repair it. 13 The workmen labored and the task of restoration progressed under their hands. They restored the house of God according to its original form, and reinforced it. 14 After they had finished, they brought the rest of the money to the king and to Jehoiada, who had it made into utensils for the LORD's temple, utensils for the service and the holocausts, and basins and other gold and silver utensils. They offered holocausts in the LORD's temple continually throughout the lifetime of Jehoiada. 15 Jehoiada lived to a ripe old age; he was a hundred and thirty years old when he died. 16 He was buried in the City of David with the kings, because he had done good in Israel, in particular with respect to God and his temple.

Apostasy of King Joash

17 After the death of Jehoiada, the princes of Judah came and paid homage to the king, and the king then listened to them. 18 They forsook the temple of the LORD, the God of their fathers, and began to serve the sacred poles and the idols; and because of this crime of theirs, wrath came upon Judah and Jerusalem. 19 Although prophets were sent to convert them to the LORD, the people would not listen to their warnings.

20 Then the spirit of God possessed Zechariah, son of Jehoiada the priest. He took his stand above the people and said to them: "God says, 'Why are you transgressing the LORD's commands, so that you cannot prosper? Because you have abandoned the LORD, he has abandoned you.'" 21 But they conspired against him, and at the king's order they stoned him to death in the court of the LORD's temple. 22 Thus King Joash was unmindful of the devotion shown him by Jehoiada, Zechariah's father, and slew his son. And as he was dying, he said, "May the LORD see and avenge."

Retribution

23 At the turn of the year a force of Arameans came up against Joash. They invaded Judah and Jerusalem, did away with all the princes of the people, and sent all their spoil to the king of Damascus. 24 Though the Aramean force came with few men, the LORD surrendered a very large force into their power, because Judah had abandoned the LORD, the God of their fathers. So punishment was meted out to Joash. 25 After the Arameans had departed from him, leaving him in grievous suffering, his servants conspired against him because of the murder of the son of Jehoiada the priest. They killed him on his sickbed. He was buried in the City of David, but not in the tombs of the kings. 26 These conspired against him: Zabad, son of Shimeath from Ammon, and Jehozabad, son of Shimrith from Moab. 27 Of his sons, and the great tribute imposed on him, and of his rebuilding of the house of God, there is a written account in the midrash of the book of the kings. His son Amaziah succeeded him as king.

Campaign In Edom

25 Amaziah was twenty-five years old when he became king, and he reigned twenty-nine years in Jerusalem. His mother, named Jehoaddan, was from Jerusalem. 2 He did what was pleasing in the sight of the LORD, though not wholeheartedly.

24, 5: *Collect money:* according to 2 Kgs 12, 5, the people themselves brought the money to the temple; consisted, at least in part, of voluntary contributions.

At the time of the Chronicler (see Neh 10, 32) there was a fixed head tax for the upkeep of the temple (2 Chr 34, 9), based on Ex 30, 12–16. This was still in

force in New Testament times (Mt 17, 24f).

3 After he had strengthened his hold on the kingdom, he slew those of his servants who had killed the king, his father; 4 but he did not put their children to death, for he acted according to what is written in the law, in the Book of Moses, as the LORD commanded: "Fathers shall not be put to death for their children, nor children for their fathers; but only for his own guilt shall a man be put to death."

5 Amaziah mustered Judah and placed them, out of all Judah and Benjamin according to their ancestral houses, under leaders of thousands and of hundreds. When he had counted those of twenty years and over, he found them to be three hundred thousand picked men fit for war, capable of handling lance and shield. 6 He also hired a hundred thousand valiant warriors from Israel for a hundred talents of silver. 7 But a man of God came to him and said: "O king, let not the army of Israel go with you, for the LORD is not with Israel, with any Ephraimite. 8 Instead, go on your own, strongly prepared for the conflict; otherwise the LORD will defeat you in the face of the enemy. It is God who has the power to reinforce or to defeat." 9 Amaziah answered the man of God, "But what is to be done about the hundred talents that I paid for the troops of Israel?" The man of God replied, "The LORD can give you much more than that." 10 Amaziah then disbanded the troops that had come to him from Ephraim, and sent them home. They however, became furiously angry with Judah, and returned home blazing with resentment.

11 Amaziah now assumed command of his army. They proceeded to the Valley of Salt, and there they killed ten thousand men of Seir. 12 The Judahites also brought back another ten thousand alive, whom they led to the summit of the Rock and then cast down, so that they were all crushed. 13 Meanwhile, the mercenaries whom Amaziah had dismissed from battle service with

him raided the cities of Judah from Samaria to Beth-horon. They killed three thousand of the inhabitants and took away much booty.

Infidelity of Amaziah

14 When Amaziah returned from his conquest of the Edomites he brought back with him the gods of the people of Seir, which he set up as his own gods; he bowed down before them and offered sacrifice to them. 15 Then the anger of the LORD blazed out against Amaziah, and he sent a prophet to him who said: "Why have you had recourse to this people's gods that could not save their own people from your hand?" 16 While he was still speaking, however, the king said to him: "Have you been made the king's counselor? Be silent! Why should it be necessary to kill you?" Therefore the prophet desisted. "I know, however," he said, "that God has let you take counsel to your own destruction, because you have done this thing and have refused to hear my counsel."

Retribution

17 Having taken counsel, King Amaziah of Judah sent messengers to Joash, son of Jehoahaz, son of Jehu, the king of Israel, saying, "Come let us meet each other face to face." 18 King Joash of Israel sent this reply to King Amaziah of Judah: "The thistle of the Lebanon sent a message to the cedar of the Lebanon, saying, 'Give your daughter to my son for his wife.' But the wild beasts of the Lebanon passed by and trampled the thistle down. 19 You are thinking, 'See, I have beaten Edom!', and thus ambition makes you proud. Remain at home. Why involve yourself, and Judah with you, in misfortune and failure?" 20 But Amaziah would not listen, for God had determined to hand them over because they had had recourse to the gods of Edom.

21 Therefore King Joash of Israel advanced and he and King Amaziah met in battle at Beth-shemesh of

Judah. 22 There Judah was defeated by Israel, and all the Judean soldiers fled homeward. 23 King Joash of Israel captured Amaziah, king of Judah, son of Joash, son of Jehoahaz, at Beth-shemesh and brought him to Jerusalem. Then he tore down the wall of Jerusalem from the Ephraim Gate to the Corner Gate, a distance of four hundred cubits. 24 He took away all the gold and silver and all the vessels he found in the house of God with Obed-edom, together with the treasures of the palace, and hostages as well. Then he returned to Samaria.

25 Amaziah, son of Joash, king of Judah, survived Joash, son of Jehoahaz, king of Israel, by fifteen years. 26 The rest of the acts of Amaziah, first and last, can be found written, as is well known, in the book of the kings of Judah and Israel. 27 Now from the time that Amaziah ceased to follow the LORD, a conspiracy was formed against him in Jerusalem; hence he fled to Lachish. But they pursued him to Lachish and put him to death there. 28 They brought him back on horses and buried him with his ancestors in the City of Judah.

The Works of Uzziah

26 All the people of Judah chose Uzziah, though he was but sixteen years of age, and proclaimed him king to succeed his father Amaziah. 2 He rebuilt Elath and restored it to Judah; this was after King Amaziah had gone to rest with his ancestors. 3 Uzziah was sixteen years old when he became king, and he reigned fifty-two years in Jerusalem. His mother, named Jecoliah, was from Jerusalem. 4 He pleased the LORD, just as his father Amaziah had done.

5 He was prepared to seek God as long as Zechariah lived, who taught him to fear God; and as long as he sought the LORD, God made him prosper 6 He went out and fought the Philistines and razed the walls of Gath, Jebneh and Ashdod [and built cities in the district of

---

25, 24: *With Obed-edom:* possibly a reference to the priest of an Edomite false worship (cf v 14), if not to a levitical family of gatekeepers; cf 1 Chr 15, 18; 26, 12–15.

25, 28: *The City of Judah:* in the parallel passage of 2 Kgs 14, 20, *the City of David.* The Chronicler is referring, by this term, to the capital of Judah, Jerusalem.

26, 5: *Zechariah:* this person, not otherwise identified, is referred to in language suggesting a pious layman rather than a priest or prophet; cf 29, 1.

Ashdod and in Philistia]. 7 God helped him against the Philistines, against the Arabs who dwelt in Gurbaal, and against the Meunites. 8 The Ammonites paid tribute to Uzziah and his fame spread as far as Egypt, for he grew stronger and stronger. 9 Moreover, Uzziah built towers in Jerusalem at the Corner Gate, at the Valley Gate, and at the Angle, and he fortified them. 10 He built towers in the desert and dug numerous cisterns, for he had many cattle. He had plowmen in the foothills and the plains, and vinedressers in the highlands and the garden land. He was a lover of the soil.

11 Uzziah also had a standing army of fit soldiers divided into bands according to the number in which they were mustered by Jeiel the scribe and Maaseiah the recorder, under the command of Hananiah, one of the king's officials. 12 The entire number of family heads over these valiant warriors was two thousand six hundred, 13 and at their disposal was a mighty army of three hundred seven thousand five hundred fighting men of great valor to help the king against his enemies. 14 Uzziah provided for them—for the entire army —bucklers, lances, helmets, breastplates, bows and slingstones. 15 He also built machines in Jerusalem, devices contrived to stand on the towers and at the angles of the walls to shoot arrows and cast large stones. His fame spread far and wide, and his power was ascribed to the marvelous help he had received.

Pride and Fall

16 But after he had become strong, he became proud of his own destruction and broke faith with the LORD, his God. He entered the temple of the LORD to make an offering on the altar of incense. 17 But Azariah the priest, and with him eighty other priests of the LORD, courageous men, followed him. 18 They opposed King Uzziah, saying to him: "It is not for you, Uzziah, to burn incense to the LORD, but for the priests, the sons of Aaron, who have been consecrated for this purpose. Leave the sanctuary, for you have broken faith and no longer have a part in the

glory that comes from the LORD God. 19 Uzziah, who was holding a censer for burning the incense, became angry, but at the moment he showed his anger to the priests, while they were looking at him in the house of the LORD beside the altar of incense, leprosy broke out on his forehead. 20 Azariah the chief priest and all the other priests examined him, and when they saw that his forehead was leprous, they expelled him from the temple. He himself fled willingly, for the LORD had afflicted him. 21 King Uzziah remained a leper to the day of his death. As a leper he dwelt in a segregated house, for he was excluded from the house of the LORD. Therefore his son Jotham was regent of the palace and ruled the people of the land.

22 The prophet Isaiah, son of Amos, wrote the rest of the acts of Uzziah, first and last 23 Uzziah rested with his ancestors; he was buried with them in the field adjoining the royal cemetery, for they said, "He was a leper." His son Jotham succeeded him as king.

Jotham

27 Jotham was twenty-five years old when he became king, and he reigned sixteen years in Jerusalem. His mother was named Jerusa, daughter of Zadok. 2 He pleased the LORD just as his father Uzziah had done, though he did not enter the temple of the LORD; the people, however, continued to act sinfully.

3 He built the upper gate of the LORD's house and had much construction done on the wall of Ophel. 4 Moreover, he built cities in the hill country of Judah, and in the forest land he set up fortresses and towers. 5 He fought with the king of the Ammonites and conquered them. That year the Ammonites paid him one hundred talents of silver, together with ten thousand kors of wheat and ten thousand of barley. They brought the same to him also in the second and in the third year. 6 Thus Jotham continued to grow strong because he lived resolutely in the presence of the LORD, his God. 7 The rest of the acts of Jotham, his wars and his activities, can be found written in the book of the kings of

Israel and Judah. 8 He was twenty-five years old when he became king and he reigned sixteen years in Jerusalem. 9 Jotham rested with his ancestors and was buried in the City of David, and his son Ahaz succeeded him as king.

REFORMS OF HEZEKIAH AND JOSIAH

Impiety of Ahaz

28 Ahaz was twenty years old when he became king, and he reigned sixteen years in Jerusalem. He did not please the LORD as his forefather David had done, 2 but conducted himself like the kings of Israel and even made molten idols of the Baals. 3 Moreover, he offered sacrifice in the Valley of Ben-hinnom, and immolated his sons by fire according to the abominable practice of the nations which the LORD had cleared out before the Israelites. 4 He offered sacrifice and incense on the high places, on hills, and under every leafy tree.

Retribution

5 Therefore the LORD, his God, delivered him into the power of the king of Aram. The Arameans defeated him and carried away captive a large number of his people, whom they brought to Damascus. He was also delivered into the power of the king of Israel, who defeated him with great slaughter. 6 For Pekah, son of Remaliah, slew one hundred and twenty thousand of Judah in a single day, all of them valiant men, because they had abandoned the LORD, the God of their fathers. 7 Zichri, an Ephraimite warrior, killed Maaseiah, the king's son, and Azrikam, the master of the palace, and also Elkanah, who was second to the king. 8 The Israelites took away as captives two hundred thousand of their brethren's wives, sons and daughters; they also took from them much plunder, which they brought to Samaria.

The Prophecy of Oded

9 In Samaria there was a prophet of the LORD by the name of Oded. He went out to meet the army returning to Samaria and said to them:

"It was because the LORD, the God of your fathers, was angry with Judah that he delivered them into your hands. You, however, have slaughtered them with a fury that has reached up to heaven. 10 And now you are planning to make the children of Judah and Jerusalem your slaves and bondwomen. Are not you yourselves, therefore, guilty of a crime against the LORD, your God? 11 Now listen to me: send back the captives you have carried off from among your brethren, for the burning anger of the LORD is upon you."

12 At this, some of the Ephraimite leaders, Azariah, son of Johanan, Berechiah, son of Meshillemoth, Jehizkiah, son of Shallum, and Amasa, son of Hadlai, themselves stood up in opposition to those who had returned from the war. 13 They said to them: "Do not bring the captives here, for what you propose will make us guilty before the LORD and increase our sins and our guilt. Our guilt is already great, and there is a burning anger upon Israel." 14 Therefore the soldiers left their captives and the plunder before the princes and the whole assembly. 15 Then the men just named proceeded to help the captives. All of them who were naked they clothed from the booty; they clothed them, put sandals on their feet, gave them food and drink, anointed them and all who were weak they set on asses. They brought them to Jericho, the city of palms, to their brethren. Then they returned to Samaria.

Further Sins of Ahaz

16 At that time King Ahaz sent an appeal for help to the kings of Assyria. 17 The Edomites had returned, attacked Judah, and carried off captives. 18 The Philistines too had raided the cities of the foothills and the Negeb of Judah; they captured Beth-shemesh, Aijalon, Gederoth, Soco and its dependencies, Timnah and its dependencies, and Gimzo and its dependencies, and occupied them. 19 For the LORD

had brought Judah low because of Ahaz, king of Israel, who let Judah go its own way and proved utterly faithless to the LORD. 20 Tilgath-pilneser, king of Assyria, did indeed come to him, but to oppress him rather than to help him. 21 Though Ahaz plundered the LORD's house and the houses of the king and the princes to make payment to the king of Assyria, it availed him nothing.

22 While he was already in distress, the same King Ahaz became even more unfaithful to the LORD. 23 He sacrificed to the gods of Damascus who had defeated him, saying, "Since it was the gods of the kings of Aram who helped them, I will sacrifice to them that they may help me also." However, they only caused further disaster to him and to all Israel. 24 Ahaz gathered up the utensils of God's house and broke them in pieces. He closed the doors of the LORD's house and had altars made for himself in every corner of Jerusalem. 25 In every city throughout Judah he set up high places to offer sacrifice to other gods. Thus he angered the LORD, the God of his fathers.

26 The rest of his deeds and his activities, first and last, can be found written in the book of the kings of Judah and Israel. 27 Ahaz rested with his ancestors and was buried in Jerusalem—in the city, for they did not bring him to the tombs of the kings of Israel. His son Hezekiah succeeded him as king.

Reforms of Hezekiah

29 Hezekiah was twenty-five years old when he became king, and he reigned twenty-nine years in Jerusalem. His mother was named Abia, daughter of Zechariah. 2 He pleased the LORD just as his forefather David had done. 3 It was he who, in the first month of the first year of his reign, opened the doors of the LORD's house and repaired them. 4 He summoned the priests and Levites, gathered them in the open space to the east 5 and said to them: "Listen to me, you Levites! Sanctify yourselves now and sanctify the house of the

LORD, the God of your fathers, and clean out the filth from the sanctuary. 6 Our fathers acted faithlessly and did evil in the eyes of the LORD our God. They abandoned him, turned away their faces from the LORD's dwelling, and turned their backs on him. 7 They also closed the doors of the vestibule, extinguished the lamps, and refused to burn incense and offer holocausts in the sanctuary to the honor of the God of Israel. 8 Therefore the anger of the LORD has come upon Judah and Jerusalem; he has made them an object of terror, astonishment and mockery, as you see with your own eyes. 9 For our fathers, as you know, fell by the sword, and our sons, our daughters and our wives have been taken captive because of this. 10 Now, I intend to make a covenant with the LORD, the God of Israel, that his burning anger may withdraw from us. 11 My sons, be not negligent any longer, for it is you whom the LORD has chosen to stand before him, to minister to him, to be his ministers and to offer incense."

12 Then the Levites arose: Mahath, son of Amasai, and Joel, son of Azariah, descendants of the Kohathites; of the sons of Merari: Kish, son of Abdi, and Azariah, son of Jehallel; of the Gershonites: Joah, son of Zimmah, and Eden, son of Joah; 13 of the sons of Elizaphan: Shimri and Jeuel; of the sons of Asaph: Zechariah and Mattaniah; 14 of the sons of Heman: Jehuel and Shimei; of the sons of Jeduthun: Shemiah and Uzziel. 15 They gathered their brethren together and sanctified themselves; then they came as the king had ordered, to cleanse the LORD's house in keeping with his words.

16 The priests entered the interior of the LORD's house to cleanse it; and whatever they found in the LORD's temple that was unclean they brought out to the court of the LORD's house, where the Levites took it from them and carried it out to the Kidron Valley. 17 They began the work of consecration on the first day of the first month, and on the eighth day of the month they arrived at the vestibule of the LORD; they

---

28, 19: *Ahaz, king of Israel:* in the period of the divided kingdom the term *king of Israel* would elsewhere mean "king of the Northern Kingdom of Israel."

consecrated the LORD's house during eight days, and on the sixteenth day of the first month, they had finished. 18 Then they went inside to King Hezekiah and said: "We have cleansed the entire house of the LORD, the altar of holocausts with all its utensils, and the table for the showbread with all its utensils. 19 All the articles which King Ahaz during his reign had thrown away because of his apostasy, we have restored and consecrated, and they are now before the LORD's altar."

The Rite of Expiation

20 Then King Hezekiah hastened to convoke the princes of the city and went up to the LORD's house. 21 Seven bulls, seven rams, seven lambs and seven he-goats were brought for a sin offering for the kingdom, for the sanctuary, and for Judah, and he ordered the sons of Aaron, the priests, to offer them on the altar of the LORD. 22 They slaughtered the bulls, and the priests collected the blood and cast it on the altar. Then they slaughtered the rams and cast the blood on the altar; then they slaughtered the lambs and cast the blood on the altar. 23 Then the he-goats for the sin offering were led before the king and the assembly, who laid their hands upon them. 24 The priests then slaughtered them and offered their blood on the altar to atone for the sin of all Israel; for "The holocaust and the sin offering," the king had said, "is for all Israel."

25 He stationed the Levites in the LORD's house with cymbals, harps and lyres according to the prescriptions of David, of Gad the king's seer, and of Nathan the prophet; for the prescriptions were from the LORD through his prophets. 26 The Levites were stationed with the instruments of David, and the priests with the trumpets. 27 Then Hezekiah ordered the holocaust to be sacrificed on the altar, and in the same instant that the holocaust began, they also began the song of the LORD, to the accompaniment of the trumpets and the instruments of David, king of Israel. 28 The entire assembly prostrated itself, and

they continued to sing the song and to sound the trumpets until the holocaust had been completed. 29 As the holocaust was completed, the king and all who were with him knelt and prostrated themselves. 30 King Hezekiah and the princes then commanded the Levites to sing the praises of the LORD in the words of David and of Asaph the seer. They sang praises till their joy was full, then fell down and prostrated themselves.

31 Hezekiah now spoke out this command: "You have undertaken a work for the LORD. Approach, and bring forward the sacrifices and thank offerings for the house of the LORD." Then the assembly brought forward the sacrifices and thank offerings and all the holocausts which were free-will offerings. 32 The number of holocausts that the assembly brought forward was seventy oxen, one hundred rams, and two hundred lambs: all of these as a holocaust to the LORD. 33 As consecrated gifts there were six hundred oxen and three thousand sheep. 34 Since the priests were too few in number to be able to skin all the victims for the holocausts, their brethren the Levites assisted them until the task was completed and the priests had sanctified themselves; the Levites, in fact, were more willing than the priests to sanctify themselves. 35 Also, the holocausts were many, along with the fat of the peace offerings and the libations for the holocausts. Thus the service of the house of the LORD was reestablished. 36 Hezekiah and all the people rejoiced over what God had reestablished for the people, and at how suddenly this had been done.

Invitation to the Passover

30 Hezekiah sent a message to all Israel and Judah, and even wrote letters to Ephraim and Manasseh saying that they should come to the house of the LORD in Jerusalem to celebrate the Passover in honor of the LORD, the God of Israel. 2 The king, his princes, and the entire assembly in Jerusalem had agreed to celebrate the Passover during the second

month, 3 for they could not celebrate it at the time of the restoration: the priests had not sanctified themselves in sufficient numbers, and the people were not gathered at Jerusalem. 4 When this proposal had been approved by the king and the entire assembly, 5 they issued a decree to be proclaimed throughout all Israel from Beer-sheba to Dan, that everyone should come to Jerusalem to celebrate the Passover in honor of the LORD, the God of Israel; for not many had kept it in the manner prescribed. 6 Accordingly the couriers, with the letters written by the king and his princes, traversed all Israel and Judah, and at the king's command they said, "Israelites, return to the LORD, the God of Abraham, Isaac and Israel, that he may return to you, the remnant left from the hands of the Assyrian kings. 7 Be not like your fathers and your brethren who proved faithless to the LORD, the God of their fathers, so that he delivered them over to desolation, as you yourselves now see. 8 Be not obstinate, as your fathers were; extend your hands to the LORD and come to his sanctuary that he has consecrated forever, and serve the LORD, your God, that he may turn away his burning anger from you. 9 For when you return to the LORD, your brethren and your children will find mercy with their captors and return to this land; for merciful and compassionate is the LORD, your God, and he will not turn away his face from you if you return to him."

10 So the couriers passed from city to city in the land of Ephraim and Manasseh and as far as Zebulun, but they were derided and scoffed at. 11 Nevertheless, some from Asher, Manasseh and Zebulun humbled themselves and came to Jerusalem. 12 In Judah, however, the power of God brought it about that the people were of one mind to carry out the command of the king and the princes in accordance with the word of the LORD. 13 Thus many people gathered in Jerusalem to celebrate the feast of Unleavened Bread in the second month; it was a very great assembly.

The Passover Celebrated

14 They proceeded to take down the altars that were in Jerusalem; also they removed all the altars of incense and cast them into the Kidron Valley. 15 They slaughtered the Passover on the fourteenth day of the second month. The priests and Levites, touched with shame, sanctified themselves and brought holocausts into the house of the LORD. 16 They stood in the places prescribed for them according to the law of Moses, the man of God. The priests sprinkled the blood given them by the Levites; 17 for many in the assembly had not sanctified themselves, and the Levites were in charge of slaughtering the Passover victims for all who were unclean and therefore could not consecrate them to the LORD. 18 The greater part of the people, in fact, chiefly from Ephraim, Manasseh, Issachar and Zebulun, had not cleansed themselves. Nevertheless they ate the Passover, contrary to the prescription; for Hezekiah prayed for them, saying, "May the LORD, who is good, grant pardon to 19 everyone who has resolved to seek God, the LORD, the God of his fathers, though he be not clean as holiness requires." 20 The LORD heard Hezekiah and spared the people. 21 Thus the Israelites who were in Jerusalem celebrated the feast of Unleavened Bread with great rejoicing for seven days, and the Levites and the priests sang the praises of the LORD day after day with all their strength. 22 Hezekiah spoke encouragingly to all the Levites who had shown themselves well skilled in the service of the LORD. And when they had completed the seven days of festival, slaying peace offerings and singing praises to the LORD, the God of their fathers, 23 the whole assembly agreed to celebrate another seven days. With joy, therefore, they continued the festivity seven days longer. 24 King Hezekiah of Judah had contributed a thousand bulls and seven thousand sheep to the assembly, and the princes had contributed to the assembly a thousand bulls and ten thousand sheep. The priests sanctified themselves in great numbers, 25 and the whole assembly of Judah rejoiced, together with the priests and Levites and the rest of the assembly that had come from Israel, as well as the sojourners from the land of Israel and those that lived in Judah. 26 There was great rejoicing in Jerusalem, for since the days of Solomon, son of David, king of Israel, there had not been the like in the city. 27 Then the levitical priests rose and blessed the people; their voice was heard and their prayer reached heaven, God's holy dwelling.

Liturgical Reform

31 After all this was over, those Israelites who had been present went forth to the cities of Judah and smashed the sacred pillars, cut down the sacred poles, and tore down the high places and altars throughout Judah, Benjamin, Ephraim and Manasseh, until all were destroyed. Then the Israelites returned to their various cities, each to his own possession.

2 Hezekiah reestablished the classes of the priests and the Levites according to their former classification, assigning to each priest and Levite his proper service whether in regard to holocausts or peace offerings, thanksgiving or praise, or ministering in the gates of the encampment of the LORD. 3 From his own wealth the king allotted a portion for holocausts, those of morning and evening and those on sabbaths, new moons and festivals, as prescribed in the law of the LORD. 4 He also commanded the people living in Jerusalem to provide the support of the priests and Levites, that they might devote themselves entirely to the law of the LORD.

5 As soon as the order was promulgated, the Israelites brought, in great quantities, the best of their grain, wine, oil and honey, and all the produce of the fields; they gave a generous tithe of everything. 6 Israelites and Judahites living in other cities of Judah also brought in tithes of oxen, sheep, and things that had been consecrated to the LORD, their God; these they brought in and set out in heaps. 7 It was in the third month that they began to establish these heaps, and they completed them in the seventh month. 8 When Hezekiah and the princes had come and seen the heaps, they blessed the LORD and his people Israel. 9 Then Hezekiah questioned the priests and the Levites concerning the heaps, 10 and the priest Azariah, head of the house of Zadok, answered him, "Since they began to bring the offerings to the house of the LORD, we have eaten to the full and have had much left over, for the LORD has blessed his people. This great supply is what was left over."

11 Hezekiah then gave orders that chambers be constructed in the house of the LORD. When this had been done, 12 the offerings, tithes and consecrated things were deposited there in safekeeping. The overseer of these things was Conaniah the Levite, and his brother Shimei was second in charge. 13 Jehiel, Azaziah, Nahath, Asahel, Jerimoth, Jozabad, Eliel, Ismachiah, Mahath and Benaiah were supervisors subject to Conaniah and his brother Shimei by appointment of King Hezekiah and of Azariah, the prefect of the house of God. 14 Kore, the son of Imnah, a Levite and the keeper of the eastern gate, was in charge of the free-will gifts made to God; he distributed the offerings made to the LORD and the most holy of the consecrated things. 15 Under him in the priestly cities were Eden, Miniamin, Jeshua, Shemaiah, Amariah and Shecaniah, who faithfully made the distribution to their brethren, great and small alike, according to their classes.

16 There was also a register by ancestral houses of males thirty years of age and over, for all priests who were eligible to enter the house of the LORD according to the daily rule to fulfill their service in the order of their classes. 17 The priests were inscribed in their family records according to their ancestral houses, and the Levites of twenty years and over according to their

---

31, 7: *Third month . . . seventh month:* between the feast of Pentecost and that of Booths, an interval without rain in Palestine, at the end of which the problem of storage (v 11) would become more urgent.

various offices and classes. 18 A distribution was also made to all who were inscribed in the family records, for their little ones, wives, sons and daughters—thus for the entire assembly, since they were to sanctify themselves by sharing faithfully in the consecrated things. 19 The sons of Aaron, the priests who lived on the lands attached to their cities, had in every city men designated by name to distribute portions to every male among the priests and to every Levite listed in the family records.

20 This Hezekiah did in all Judah. He did what was good, upright and faithful before the LORD, his God. 21 Everything that he undertook, for the service of the house of God or for the law and the commandments, was to do the will of his God. He did this wholeheartedly, and he prospered.

Invasion of Sennacherib

32 But after he had proved his fidelity by such deeds, Sennacherib, king of Assyria, came. He invaded Judah, besieged the fortified cities, and proposed to take them by storm. 2 When Hezekiah saw that Sennacherib was coming with the intention of attacking Jerusalem, 3 he decided in counsel with his princes and warriors to stop the waters of the springs outside the city. When they had pledged him their support, 4 a large crowd was gathered which stopped all the springs and also the running stream in the valley nearby. For they said, "Why should the kings of Assyria come and find an abundance of water?" 5 He then looked to his defenses: he rebuilt the wall where it was broken down, raised towers upon it, and built another wall outside. He strengthened the Millo of the City of David and had a great number of spears and shields prepared. 6 Then he appointed army commanders over the people. He gathered them together in his presence in the open space at the gate of the city and encouraged them with these words: 7 "Be brave and steadfast; do not be afraid or dismayed because of the king of Assyria and all the throng that is coming with him, for there is more with us than with him. 8 For he has only an arm of flesh, but we have the LORD, our God, to help us and to fight our battles." And the people took confidence from the words of King Hezekiah of Judah.

Threat of Sennacherib

9 After this, while Sennacherib, king of Assyria, himself remained at Lachish with all his forces, he sent his officials to Jerusalem with this message for King Hezekiah of Judah, and all the Judahites who were in Jerusalem: 10 "King Sennacherib of Assyria has this to say: On what are you relying, while you remain under siege in Jerusalem? 11 Has not Hezekiah deceived you, delivering you over to a death of famine and thirst, by his claim that 'the LORD, our God, will save us from the grasp of the king of Assyria'? 12 Has not this same Hezekiah removed his high places and altars and commanded Judah and Jerusalem, 'You shall prostrate yourselves before one altar only, and on it alone you shall offer incense'? 13 Do you not know what my fathers and I have done to all the peoples of other lands? Were the gods of the nations in those lands able to save their lands from my hand? 14 Who among all the gods of those nations which my fathers put under the ban was able to save his people from my hand? Will your god, then, be able to save you from my hand? 15 Let not Hezekiah mislead you further and deceive you in any such way. Do not believe him! Since no other god of any other nation or kingdom has been able to save his people from my hand or the hands of my fathers, how much the less shall your god save you from my hand!"

16 His officials said still more against the LORD God and against his servant Hezekiah, 17 for he had written letters to deride the LORD, the God of Israel, speaking of him in these terms: "As the gods of the nations in other lands have not saved their people from my hand, neither shall Hezekiah's god save his people from my hand." 18 In a loud voice they shouted in the Judean language to the people of Jerusalem who were on the wall, to frighten and terrify them so that they might capture their city. 19 They spoke of the God of Israel as though he were one of the gods of the other peoples of the earth, a work of human hands. 20 But because of this, King Hezekiah and the prophet Isaiah, son of Amos, prayed and called out to heaven.

Defeat of Sennacherib

21 Then the LORD sent an angel, who destroyed every valiant warrior, leader and commander in the camp of the Assyrian king, so that he had to return shamefaced to his own country. And when he entered the temple of his god, some of his own offspring struck him down there with the sword. 22 Thus the LORD saved Hezekiah and the inhabitants of Jerusalem from the hand of Sennacherib, king of Assyria, as from every other power; he gave them rest on every side. 23 Many brought gifts for the LORD to Jerusalem and costly objects for King Hezekiah of Judah, who thereafter was exalted in the eyes of all the nations.

Hezekiah's Other Deeds

24 In those days Hezekiah became mortally ill. He prayed to the LORD, who answered him by giving him a sign. 25 Hezekiah, however, did not then discharge his debt of gratitude, for he had become proud. Therefore anger descended upon him and upon Judah and Jerusalem. 26 But then Hezekiah humbled himself for his pride—both he and the inhabitants of Jerusalem; and therefore the LORD did not vent his anger on them during the time of Hezekiah.

27 Hezekiah possessed very great wealth and glory. He had treasuries made for his silver, gold, precious stones, spices, jewels, and other precious things of all kinds; 28 also storehouses for the harvest of grain, for wine and oil, and barns for the various kinds of cattle and for the flocks. 29 He built cities for himself, and he acquired sheep and oxen in great numbers, for God gave him very great riches. 30 This same Hezekiah stopped the upper outflow

of water from Gihon and led it underground westward to the City of David. Hezekiah prospered in all his undertakings. 31 Nevertheless, in respect to the ambassadors [princes] sent to him from Babylon to investigate the sign that had occurred in the land, God forsook him to test him, that he might know all that was in his heart.

32 The rest of Hezekiah's acts, including his pious works, can be found written in the Vision of the Prophet Isaiah, son of Amos, and in the book of the kings of Judah and Israel. 33 Hezekiah rested with his ancestors; he was buried at the approach to the tombs of the descendants of David. All Judah and the inhabitants of Jerusalem paid him honor at his death. His son Manasseh succeeded him as king.

Impiety of Manasseh

33 Manasseh was twelve years old when he became king, and he reigned fifty-five years in Jerusalem. 2 He did evil in the sight of the LORD, following the abominable practices of the nations whom the LORD had cleared out of the way of the Israelites. 3 He rebuilt the high places which his father Hezekiah had torn down, erected altars for the Baals, made sacred poles, and prostrated himself before the whole host of heaven and worshiped them. 4 He even built altars in the temple of the LORD, of which the LORD had said, "In Jerusalem shall my name be forever": 5 he built altars to the whole host of heaven in the two courts of the LORD's house. 6 It was he, too, who immolated his sons in the Valley of Benhinnom. He practiced augury, divination and magic, and appointed necromancers and diviners of spirits, so that he provoked the LORD with the great evil that he did in his sight. 7 He placed an idol that he had carved

in the house of God, of which God had said to David and his son Solomon: "In this house and in Jerusalem which I have chosen from all the tribes of Israel I shall place my name forever. 8 I will not again allow Israel's feet to leave the land which I assigned to your fathers, provided they are careful to observe all that I commanded them, keeping the whole law and the statutes and the ordinances given by Moses." 9 Manasseh misled Judah and the inhabitants of Jerusalem into doing even greater evil than the nations which the LORD had destroyed at the coming of the Israelites. 10 The LORD spoke to Manasseh and his people, but they paid no attention.

His Conversion

11 Therefore the LORD brought against them the army commanders of the Assyrian king; they took Manasseh with hooks, shackled him with chains, and transported him to Babylon. 12 In this distress, he began to appease the LORD, his God. He humbled himself abjectly before the God of his fathers 13 and prayed to him. The LORD let himself be won over: he heard his prayer and restored him to his kingdom in Jerusalem. Then Manasseh understood that the LORD is indeed God.

14 Afterward he built an outer wall for the City of David to the west of Gihon in the valley, extending to the Fish Gate and encircling Ophel; he built it very high. He stationed army officers in all the fortified cities of Judah. 15 He removed the foreign gods and the idol from the LORD's house and all the altars he had built on the mount of the LORD's house and in Jerusalem, and he cast them outside the city. 16 He restored the altar of the LORD, and sacrificed on it peace offerings and thank offerings, and commanded Judah to serve the LORD, the God of Israel. 17 Though the people

continued to sacrifice on the high places, they now did so to the LORD, their God.

18 The rest of the acts of Manasseh, his prayer to his God, and the words of the seers who spoke to him in the name of the LORD, the God of Israel, can be found written in the chronicles of the kings of Israel. 19 His prayer and how his supplication was heard, all his sins and his infidelity, the sites where he built high places and erected sacred poles and carved images before he humbled himself, all can be found written down in the history of his seers. 20 Manasseh rested with his ancestors and was buried in his own palace. His son Amon succeeded him as king.

Amon

21 Amon was twenty-two years old when he became king, and he reigned two years in Jerusalem. 22 He did evil in the sight of the LORD, just as his father Manasseh had done. Amon offered sacrifice to all the idols which his father Manasseh had made, and worshiped them. 23 Moreover, he did not humble himself before the LORD as his father Manasseh had done; on the contrary, Amon only increased his guilt. 24 His servants conspired against him and put him to death in his own house. 25 But the people of the land slew all those who had conspired against King Amon, and then they, the people of the land, made his son Josiah king in his stead.

Reforms of Josiah

34 Josiah was eight years old when he became king, and he reigned thirty-one years in Jerusalem. 2 He pleased the LORD, following the path of his ancestor David. 3 In the eighth year of his reign, while he was still a youth, he began to seek after the God of his forefather David, and in his twelfth year he

---

32, 33: *The approach to the tombs:* literally, "the ascent of the tombs," which may mean "the upper section of the tombs," their most prominent and honored place.

33, 11: There is no evidence elsewhere for an imprisonment of King Manasseh in Babylon. However, according to the Assyrian inscriptions, he paid tribute to the Assyrian kings Esarhaddon (680–669 B.C.) and Asshurbanipal (668–627 B.C.). He may

well have been obliged to go to Nineveh to take the oath of allegiance as vassal to the king of Assyria.

33, 13: *And prayed to him:* these words led an unknown writer to compose the apocryphal "Prayer of Manasseh," which is added as an appendix to many editions of the Vulgate Bible and is used in the public prayers of the Church.

34, 3: *In his twelfth year:* c. 628 B.C., the year after Asshurbanipal's death, when Judah could free itself

from Assyrian domination. From 2 Kgs 22, 1—23, 25 alone, one might think that Josiah's reform began only after the discovery of the book of the law in the temple, in the eighteenth year of his reign. But the Chronicler is no doubt right in placing the beginning of the reform at an earlier period. The very repair of the temple, which led to the finding of the book of the law, must have been occasioned by a cultic reform.

began to purge Judah and Jerusalem of the high places, the sacred poles and the carved and molten images. 4 In his presence, the altars of the Baals were destroyed; the incense stands erected above them were torn down; the sacred poles and the carved and molten images were shattered and beaten into dust, which was strewn over the tombs of those who had sacrificed to them; 5 and the bones of the priests he burned upon their altars. Thus he purged Judah and Jerusalem. 6 He did likewise in the cities of Manasseh, Ephraim, Simeon, and in the ruined villages of the surrounding country as far as Naphtali; 7 he destroyed the altars, broke up the sacred poles and carved images and beat them into dust, and tore down the incense stands throughout the land of Israel. Then he returned to Jerusalem.

The Temple Restored

8 In the eighteenth year of his reign, in order to cleanse the temple as well as the land, he sent Shaphan, son of Azaliah, Maaseiah, the ruler of the city, and Joah, son of Joahaz, the chamberlain, to restore the house of the LORD, his God. 9 They came to Hilkiah the high priest and turned over the money brought to the house of God which the Levites, the guardians of the threshold, had collected from Manasseh, Ephraim, and all the remnant of Israel, as well as from all of Judah, Benjamin, and the inhabitants of Jerusalem. 10 They turned it over to the master workmen in the house of the LORD, and these in turn used it to pay the workmen in the LORD's house who were restoring and repairing the temple. 11 They also gave it to the carpenters and the masons to buy hewn stone and timber for the tie beams and rafters of the buildings which the kings of Judah had allowed to fall into ruin. 12 The men worked faithfully at their task; their overseers were Jahath and Obadiah, Levites of the line of Merari, and Zechariah and Meshullam, of the Kohathites, who directed them. All those Levites who were skillful with

musical instruments 13 were in charge of the men who carried the burdens, and they directed all the workers in every kind of labor. Some of the other Levites were scribes, officials and gatekeepers.

The Finding of the Law

14 When they brought out the money that had been deposited in the house of the LORD, Hilkiah the priest found the book of the law of the LORD given through Moses. 15 He reported this to Shaphan the scribe, saying, "I have found the book of the law in the house of the LORD." Hilkiah gave the book to Shaphan, 16 who brought it to the king at the same time that he was making his report to him. He said, "Your servants are doing everything that has been entrusted to them; 17 they have turned into bullion the metals deposited in the LORD's house and have handed it over to the overseers and the workmen." 18 Then Shaphan the scribe announced to the king, "Hilkiah the priest has given me a book." And Shaphan read from it before the king.

19 When the king heard the words of the law, he tore his garments 20 and issued this command to Hilkiah, to Ahikam, son of Shaphan, to Abdon, son of Michah, to Shaphan the scribe, and to Asaiah, the king's servant: 21 "On behalf of myself and those who are left in Israel and Judah, go, consult the LORD concerning the words of the book that has been found. For the anger of the LORD has been set furiously ablaze against us, since our fathers have not kept the word of the LORD and have not done all that is written in this book." 22 Then Hilkiah and the other men from the king went to the prophetess Huldah, the wife of Shallum, son of Tokhath, son of Hasrah, the guardian of the wardrobe; she dwelt in Jerusalem, in the new quarter. They spoke to her as they had been instructed, 23 and she said to them: "Thus says the LORD, the God of Israel: 'Tell the one who sent you to me, 24 The LORD says: I am prepared to bring evil upon this place and upon its

inhabitants, all the curses written in the book that has been read before the king of Judah. 25 Because they have abandoned me and have offered incense to other gods, provoking me by every deed that they have performed, my anger is ablaze against this place and cannot be extinguished.'

26 "But to the king of Judah who sent you to consult the LORD, give this response: 'Thus says the LORD, the God of Israel, concerning the threats you have heard: 27 Because you were heartsick and have humbled yourself before God on hearing his words spoken against this place and its inhabitants; because you have humbled yourself before me, have torn your garments, and have wept before me, I in turn have listened—so declares the LORD 28 I will gather you to your ancestors and you shall be taken to your grave in peace. Your eyes shall not see all the evil I will bring upon this place and upon its inhabitants.'"

They brought back this message to the king.

Renewal of the Covenant

29 The king now convened all the elders of Judah and Jerusalem. 30 He went up to the house of the LORD with all the men of Judah and the inhabitants of Jerusalem, the priests, the Levites, and all the people, great and small; and he had read aloud to them the entire text of the book of the covenant that had been found in the house of the LORD. 31 Standing at his post, the king made a covenant before the LORD to follow the LORD and to keep his commandments, decrees, and statutes with his whole heart and soul, thus observing the terms of the covenant written in this book. 32 He thereby committed all who were of Jerusalem and Benjamin, and the inhabitants of Jerusalem conformed themselves to the covenant of God, the God of their fathers. 33 Josiah removed every abominable thing from all the territory belonging to the Israelites, and he obliged all who were in Israel to serve the LORD, their God. During his lifetime they did not desert the LORD, the God of their fathers.

34, 31: *Standing at his post:* see note on 23, 13.

The Passover

35 Josiah celebrated in Jerusalem a Passover to honor the LORD; the Passover sacrifice was slaughtered on the fourteenth day of the first month. 2 He reappointed the priests to their duties and encouraged them in the service of the LORD's house. 3 He said to the Levites who were to instruct all Israel, and who were consecrated to the LORD: "Put the holy ark in the house built by Solomon, son of David, king of Israel. It shall no longer be a burden on your shoulders. Serve now the LORD, your God, and his people Israel. 4 Prepare yourselves in your ancestral houses and your classes according to the prescriptions of King David of Israel and his son Solomon. 5 Stand in the sanctuary according to the divisions of the ancestral houses of your brethren, the common people, so that the distribution of the Levites and the families may be the same. 6 Slay the Passover sacrifice, sanctify yourselves, and be at the disposition of your brethren, that all may be carried out according to the word of the LORD given through Moses."

7 Josiah contributed to the common people a flock of lambs and kids, thirty thousand in number, each to serve as a Passover victim for any who were present, and also three thousand oxen; these were from the king's property. 8 His princes also gave a free-will gift to the people, the priests and the Levites. Hilkiah, Zechariah and Jehiel, prefects of the house of God, gave to the priests two thousand six hundred Passover victims together with three hundred oxen. 9 Conaniah and his brothers Shemaiah, Nethanel, Hashabiah, Jehiel and Jozabad, the rulers of the Levites, contributed to the Levites five thousand Passover victims, together with five hundred oxen.

10 When the service had been arranged, the priests took their places, as did the Levites in their classes according to the king's command. 11 The Passover sacrifice was slaughtered, whereupon the priests sprinkled some of the blood and the Levites proceeded to the skinning. 12 They separated what was destined for the holocaust and gave it to various groups of the ancestral houses of the common people to offer to the LORD, as is prescribed in the book of Moses. They did the same with the oxen. 13 They cooked the Passover on the fire as prescribed, and also cooked the sacred meals in pots, caldrons and pans, then brought them quickly to all the common people. 14 Afterward they prepared the Passover for themselves and for the priests. Indeed the priests, the sons of Aaron, were busy offering holocausts and the fatty portions until night; therefore the Levites prepared for themselves and for the priests, the sons of Aaron. 15 The singers, the sons of Asaph, were at their posts as prescribed by David: Asaph, Heman and Jeduthun, the king's seer. The gatekeepers were at every gate; there was no need for them to leave their stations, for their brethren, the Levites, prepared for them. 16 Thus the entire service of the LORD was arranged that day so that the Passover could be celebrated and the holocausts offered on the altar of the LORD, as King Josiah had commanded. 17 The Israelites who were present on that occasion kept the Passover and the feast of the Unleavened Bread for seven days. 18 No such Passover had been observed in Israel since the time of the prophet Samuel, nor had any king of Israel kept a Passover like that of Josiah, the priests and Levites, all of Judah and Israel that were present, and the inhabitants of Jerusalem. 19 It was in the eighteenth year of Josiah's reign that this Passover was observed.

Josiah's Reign Ends

20 After Josiah had done all this to restore the temple, Neco, king of Egypt, came up to fight at Carchemish on the Euphrates, and Josiah went out to intercept him. 21 Neco sent messengers to him, saying: "What quarrel is between us, king of Judah? I have not come against you this day, for my war is with another kingdom, and God has told me to hasten. Do not interfere with God who is with me, as otherwise he will destroy you." 22 But Josiah would not withdraw from him, for he had sought a pretext for fighting with him. Therefore he would not listen to the words of Neco that came from the mouth of God, but went out to fight in the plain of Magiddo. 23 Then the archers shot King Josiah, who said to his servants, "Take me away, for I am seriously wounded." 24 His servants removed him from his own chariot, placed him in another he had in reserve, and brought him to Jerusalem, where he died. He was buried in the tombs of his ancestors, and all Judah and Jerusalem mourned him. 25 Jeremiah also composed a lamentation over Josiah, which is recited to this day by all the male and female singers in their lamentations over Josiah. These have been made obligatory for Israel, and can be found written in the Lamentations.

26 The rest of the chronicle of Josiah, his pious deeds in regard to what is written in the law of the LORD, and his acts, first and last, can be found written in the book of the kings of Israel and Judah.

36 The people of the land took Jehoahaz, son of Josiah, and made him king in Jerusalem in his father's stead.

END OF THE KINGDOM

Jehoahaz

2 Jehoahaz was twenty-three years old when he became king, and he reigned three months in Jerusalem. 3 The king of Egypt deposed him in Jerusalem and fined the land one hundred talents of silver and a talent of gold. 4 Then the king of Egypt made his brother Eliakim king over Judah and Jerusalem, and changed his name to Jehoiakim. Neco took his brother Jehoahaz away and brought him to Egypt.

35, 25: The reference to a *lamentation over Josiah* composed by Jeremiah is not found either in 2 Kgs or Jer; but see note on Zec 12, 11. *Their lamentations:* probably a reference to the canonical Book of Lamentations.

Jehoiakim

5 Jehoiakim was twenty-five years old when he became king, and he reigned eleven years in Jerusalem. He did evil in the sight of the LORD, his God. 6 Nebuchadnezzar, king of Babylon, came up against him and bound him with chains to take him to Babylon. 7 Nebuchadnezzar also carried away to Babylon some of the vessels of the house of the LORD and put them in his palace in Babylon. 8 The rest of the acts of Jehoiakim, the abominable things that he did, and what therefore happened to him, can be found written in the book of the kings of Israel and Judah. His son Jehoiachin succeeded him as king.

Jehoiachin

9 Jehoiachin was eighteen years old when he became king, and he reigned three months [and ten days] in Jerusalem. He did evil in the sight of the LORD. 10 At the turn of the year, King Nebuchadnezzar sent for him and had him brought to Babylon, along with precious vessels from the temple of the LORD. He made his brother Zedekiah king over Judah and Jerusalem.

Zedekiah

11 Zedekiah was twenty-one years old when he became king, and he reigned eleven years in Jerusalem. 12 He did evil in the sight of the LORD, his God, and he did not humble himself before the prophet Jeremiah, who spoke the word of the LORD. 13 He also rebelled against King Nebuchadnezzar, who had made him swear by God. He became stiff-necked and hardened his heart rather than return to the LORD, the God of Israel. 14 Likewise all the princes of Judah, the priests and the people added infidelity to infidelity practicing all the abominations of the nations and polluting the LORD's temple which he had consecrated in Jerusalem.

Dissolution of Judah

15 Early and often did the LORD, the God of their fathers, send his messengers to them, for he had compassion on his people and his dwelling place. 16 But they mocked the messengers of God, despised his warnings, and scoffed at his prophets, until the anger of the LORD against his people was so inflamed that there was no remedy. 17 Then he brought up against them the king of the Chaldeans, who slew their young men in their own sanctuary building, sparing neither young man nor maiden, neither the aged nor the decrepit; he delivered all of them over into his grip. 18 All the utensils of the house of God, the large and the small, and the treasures of the LORD's house and of the king and his princes, all these he brought to Babylon. 19 They burnt the house of God, tore down the walls of Jerusalem, set all its palaces afire, and destroyed all its precious objects. 20 Those who escaped the sword he carried captive to Babylon, where they became his and his son's servants until the kingdom of the Persians came to power. 21 All this was to fulfill the word of the LORD spoken by Jeremiah: "Until the land has retrieved its lost sabbaths, during all the time it lies waste it shall have rest while seventy years are fulfilled."

Decree of Cyrus

22 In the first year of Cyrus, king of Persia, in order to fulfill the word of the LORD spoken by Jeremiah, the LORD inspired King Cyrus of Persia to issue this proclamation throughout his kingdom, both by word of mouth and in writing: 23 "Thus says Cyrus, king of Persia: 'All the kingdoms of the earth the LORD, the God of heaven, has given to me, and he has also charged me to build him a house in Jerusalem, which is in Judah. Whoever, therefore, among you belongs to any part of his people, let him go up, and may his God be with him!'"

36, 6: *Nebuchadnezzar . . . bound him with chains to take him to Babylon:* the Chronicler does not say that Jehoiakim was actually taken to Babylon. According to 2 Kgs 24, 1–6, Jehoiakim revolted after being Nebuchadnezzar's vassal for three years; he died in Jerusalem before the Babylonian king could reach the city. However, Dn 1, 1f, apparently based on 2 Chr 36, 6f, speaks of Jehoiakim's deportation to Babylon.

36, 10: *His brother Zedekiah:* Zedekiah was actually the brother of Jehoiakim and the uncle of *Jehoiachin* (2 Kgs 24, 17; Jer 37, 1), though scarcely older than his nephew (2 Kgs 24, 8.18; 2 Chr 36, 9.11).

36, 22f: The words of these verses are identical with those of Ezr 1, 1–3a. Originally Ezra-Nehemiah formed the last part of the single work of the Chronicler, of which 1 and 2 Chronicles formed the first part. But when Ezra-Nehemiah was regarded as a natural sequence to the Books of Samuel and of Kings, it was separated from 1 and 2 Chronicles and placed before them. Thus, 1 and 2 Chronicles became the last part of the Hebrew Bible. To prevent this work from ending on a note of doom, Ezr 1, 1–3a was repeated as 2 Chr 36, 22f.

Ezra

THE RETURN FROM EXILE

The Decree of Cyrus

IN the first year of Cyrus, king of Persia, in order to fulfill the word of the LORD spoken by Jeremiah, the LORD inspired King Cyrus of Persia to issue this proclamation throughout his kingdom, both by word of mouth and in writing: 2 "Thus says Cyrus, king of Persia: 'All the kingdoms of the earth the LORD, the God of heaven, has given to me, and he has also charged me to build him a house in Jerusalem, which is in Judah. 3 Whoever, therefore, among you belongs to any part of his people, let him go up, and may his God be with him! 4 Let everyone who has survived, in whatever place he may have dwelt, be assisted by the people of that place with silver, gold, goods, and cattle, together with free-will offerings for the house of God in Jerusalem.'"

5 Then the family heads of Judah and Benjamin and the priests and Levites—everyone, that is, whom God had inspired to do so—prepared to go up to build the house of the LORD in Jerusalem. 6 All their neighbors gave them help in every way, with silver, gold, goods, and cattle, and with many precious gifts besides all their free-will offerings. 7 King Cyrus, too, had the utensils of the house of the LORD brought forth which Nebuchadnezzar had taken away from Jerusalem and placed in the house of his god. 8 Cyrus, king of Persia, had them brought forth by the treasurer Mithredath, and counted out to Sheshbazzar, the prince of Judah. 9 This was the inventory: sacks of goldware, thirty; sacks of silverware, one thousand and twenty-nine; 10 golden bowls, thirty; silver bowls, four hundred and ten; other ware, one thousand pieces. 11 Total of the gold- and silver-ware: five thousand four hundred pieces. All these Sheshbazzar took with him when the exiles were brought back from Babylon to Jerusalem.

Census of the Province

2 These are the inhabitants of the province who returned from the captivity of the exiles, whom Nebuchadnezzar, king of Babylon, had carried away to Babylon, and who came back to Jerusalem and Judah, each man in his own city 2 (those who returned with Zerubbabel, Jeshua, Nehemiah, Seraiah, Reelaiah, Mordecai, Bilshan, Mispereth, Bigvai, Rehum, and Baanah):

The census of the men of Israel: 3 sons of Parosh, two thousand one hundred and seventy-two; 4 sons of Shephatiah, three hundred and seventy-two; 5 sons of Arah, seven hundred and seventy-five; 6 sons of Pahath-moab, who were sons of Jeshua and Joab, two thousand eight hundred and twelve; 7 sons of Elam, one thousand two hundred and fifty-four; 8 sons of Zattu, nine hundred and forty-five; 9 sons of Zaccai, seven hundred and sixty; 10 sons of Bani, six hundred and forty-two; 11 sons of Bebai, six hundred and twenty-three; 12 sons of Azgad, one thousand two hundred and twenty-two; 13 sons of Ad-

---

1, 1: *In the first year of Cyrus:* as sovereign over the world empire which began with his conquest of Babylon; that is, 538 B.C.

1, 8: *Sheshbazzar:* very probably the fourth son of Jehoiachin, king of Judah, taken captive to Babylon in 598 B.C., listed in 1 Chr 3,18 as Senneser; if so, he was the uncle of Zerubbabel (3, 2ff); see note on 1 Chr 3, 18.

1, 11: *Total . . . five thousand four hundred pieces:* either this figure or the figures given for one or more of the items listed (vv 9f) have been corrupted in the transmission of the text.

2, 1–67: As it now stands, this list is an expanded form of the lists of returned captives from the sixth century B.C.; see Neh 7, 6–72, where it reappears.

onikam, six hundred and sixty-six; 14 sons of Bigvai, two thousand and fifty-six; 15 sons of Adin, four hundred and fifty-four; 16 sons of Ater, who were sons of Hezekiah, ninety-eight; 17 sons of Bezai, three hundred and twenty-three; 18 sons of Jorah, one hundred and twelve; 19 sons of Hashum, two hundred and twenty-three; 20 sons of Gibeon, ninety-five; 21 sons of Bethlehem, one hundred and twenty-three; 22 men of Netophah, fifty-six; 23 men of Anathoth, one hundred and twenty-eight; 24 men of Beth-azmaveth, forty-two; 25 men of Kiriath-jearim, Chephirah, and Beeroth, seven hundred and forty-three; 26 men of Ramah and Geba, six hundred and twenty-one; 27 men of Michmas, one hundred and twenty-two; 28 men of Bethel and Ai, two hundred and twenty-three; 29 sons of Nebo, fifty-two; 30 sons of Magbish, one hundred and fifty-six; 31 sons of the other Elam, one thousand two hundred and fifty-four; 32 sons of Harim, three hundred and twenty; 33 sons of Lod, Hadid, and Ono, seven hundred and twenty-five; 34 sons of Jericho, three hundred and forty-five; 35 sons of Senaah, three thousand six hundred and thirty.

36 The priests: sons of Jedaiah, who were of the house of Jeshua, nine hundred and seventy-three; 37 sons of Immer, one thousand and fifty-two; 38 sons of Pashhur, one thousand two hundred and forty-seven; 39 sons of Harim, one thousand and seventeen.

40 The Levites: sons of Jeshua, Kadmiel, Binnui, and Hodaviah, seventy-four.

41 The singers: sons of Asaph, one hundred and twenty-eight.

42 The gatekeepers: sons of Shallum, sons of Ater, sons of Talmon, sons of Akkub, sons of Hatita, sons of Shobai, one hundred and thirty-nine in all.

43 The temple slaves: sons of Ziha, sons of Hasupha, sons of Tabbaoth, 44 sons of Keros, sons of Siaha, sons of Padon, 45 sons of Lebanah, sons of Hagabah, sons of Akkub, 46 sons of Hagab, sons of Shamlai, sons of Hanan, 47 sons of Giddel, sons of Gahar, sons of Reaiah, 48 sons of Rezin, sons of Nekoda, sons of Gazzam, 49 sons of Uzza, sons of Paseah, sons of Besai, 50 sons of Asnah, sons of the Meunites, sons of the Nephusites, 51 sons of Bakbuk, sons of Hakupha, sons of Harhur, 52 sons of Bazluth, sons of Mehida, sons of Harsha, 53 sons of Barkos, sons of Sisera, sons of Temah, 54 sons of Neziah, sons of Hatipha.

55 Descendants of the slaves of Solomon: sons of Sotai, sons of Hassophereth, sons of Peruda, 56 sons of Jaalah, sons of Darkon, sons of Giddel, 57 sons of Shephatiah, sons of Hattil, sons of Pochereth-hazzebaim, sons of Ami. 58 The total of the temple slaves and the descendants of the slaves of Solomon was three hundred and ninety-two.

59 The following who returned from Tel-melah, Tel-harsha, Cherub, Addan, and Immer were unable to prove that their ancestral houses and their descent were Israelite: 60 sons of Delaiah, sons of Tobiah, sons of Nekoda, six hundred and fifty-two. 61 Also, of the priests: sons of Habaiah, sons of Hakkoz, sons of Barzillai (he had married one of the daughters of Barzillai the Gileadite and became known by his name). 62 These men searched their family records, but their names could not be found written there; hence they were degraded from the priesthood, 63 and His Excellency ordered them not to partake of the most holy foods until there should be a priest bearing the Urim and Thummim.

64 The entire assembly taken together came to forty-two thousand three hundred and sixty, 65 not counting their male and female slaves, who were seven thousand three hundred and thirty-seven. They also had two hundred male and female singers. 66 Their horses were seven hundred and thirty-six, their mules two hundred and forty-five, 67 their camels four hundred and thirty-five, their asses six thousand seven hundred and twenty.

68 When they arrived at the house of the LORD in Jerusalem, some of the family heads made free-will offerings for the house of God, to rebuild it in its place. 69 According to their means they contributed to the treasury for the temple service: sixty-one thousand drachmas of gold, five thousand minas of silver, and one hundred garments for the priests. 70 The priests, the Levites, and some of the common people took up residence in Jerusalem; but the singers, the gatekeepers, and the temple slaves dwelt in their cities. Thus all the Israelites dwelt in their cities.

Restoration of the Altar

3 Now when the seventh month came, after the Israelites had settled in their cities, the people gathered at Jerusalem as one man. 2 Then Jeshua, son of Jozadak, together with his brethren the priests, and Zerubbabel, son of Shealtiel, together with his brethren, set about rebuilding the altar of the God of Israel in order to offer on it the holocausts prescribed in the law of Moses, the man of God. 3 Despite their fear of the peoples of the land, they replaced the altar on its foundations and offered holocausts to the LORD on it, both morning and evening. 4 They also kept the feast of Booths in the manner prescribed, and they offered the daily holocausts in the proper number required for each day. 5 Thereafter they offered the established holocaust, the sacrifices prescribed for the new moons and all the festivals sacred to the LORD, and those which anyone might offer as a free-will gift to the LORD. 6 From the first day of the seventh month they

---

2, 63: *His excellency*: the deputy of the Persian government; from the context, he was one of the Jewish exile leaders. Nehemiah as governor receives the same title (Neh 8, 9; 10, 2). *Urim and Thummim*: see note on Ex 28, 30.

3, 1f: *The seventh month*: Tishri (September-October), apparently of 538 B.C.; cf 1, 1; 4, 5. In this case, it was Sheshbazzar who erected the first altar, since he began the work on the foundations of the temple in Jerusalem; cf 5, 16. It was in the second year of Darius I, i.e., in 520 B.C., that *Jeshua* and *Zerubbabel* resumed the work on the temple that had been temporarily interrupted (4, 24—5, 1; Hg 1, 1; 2, 1). The Chronicler or a later editor of the text here attributes to them the beginning of the work which, in reality, they merely completed. *Shealtiel*: the eldest son of King Jehoiachin of Judah and the brother of Sheshbazzar (1 Chr 3, 18f); Zerubbabel was therefore the grandson of Jehoiachin; see note on 1, 8.

began to offer holocausts to the LORD, though the foundation of the temple of the LORD had not yet been laid.

Founding of the Temple

7 Then they hired stonecutters and carpenters, and sent food and drink and oil to the Sidonians and Tyrians that they might ship cedar trees from the Lebanon to the port of Joppa, as Cyrus, king of Persia, had authorized. 8 In the year after their coming to the house of God in Jerusalem, in the second month, Zerubbabel, son of Shealtiel, and Jeshua, son of Jozadak, together with the rest of their brethren, the priests and Levites and all who had come from the captivity to Jerusalem, began by appointing the Levites twenty years of age and over to supervise the work on the house of the LORD. 9 Jeshua and his sons and brethren, with Kadmiel and Binnui, son of Henadad, and their sons and their brethren, the Levites, stood as one man to supervise those who were engaged in the work on the house of God. 10 When the builders had laid the foundation of the LORD's temple, the vested priests with the trumpets and the Levites, sons of Asaph, were stationed there with the cymbals to praise the LORD in the manner laid down by David, king of Israel. 11 They alternated in songs of praise and thanksgiving to the LORD, "for he is good, for his kindness to Israel endures forever"; and all the people raised a great shout of joy, praising the LORD because the foundation of the LORD's house had been laid. 12 Many of the priests, Levites, and family heads, the old men who had seen the former house, cried out in sorrow as they watched the foundation of the present house being laid. Many others, however, lifted up their voices in shouts of joy, 13 and no one could distinguish the sound of the joyful shouting from the sound of those who were weeping; for

the people raised a mighty clamor which was heard afar off.

Samaritan Interference

4 When the enemies of Judah and Benjamin heard that the exiles were building a temple for the LORD, the God of Israel, 2 they approached Zerubbabel and the family heads and said to them, "Let us build with you, for we seek your God just as you do, and we have sacrificed to him since the days of Esarhaddon, king of Assyria, who had us brought here." 3 But Zerubbabel, Jeshua, and the rest of the family heads of Israel answered them, "It is not your responsibility to build with us a house for our God, but we alone must build it for the LORD, the God of Israel, as King Cyrus of Persia has commanded us." 4 Thereupon the people of the land set out to intimidate and dishearten the people of Judah so as to keep them from building. 5 They also suborned counselors to work against them and thwart their plans during the remaining years of Cyrus, king of Persia, and until the reign of Darius, king of Persia.

Later Hostility

6 Also at the beginning of the reign of Ahashuerus they prepared a written accusation against the inhabitants of Judah and Jerusalem. 7 Again, in the time of Artaxerxes, Mithredath wrote in concert with Tabeel and the rest of his fellow officials to Artaxerxes, king of Persia. The document was written in Aramaic and was accompanied by a translation. [Aramaic:] 8 Then Rehum, the governor, and Shimshai, the scribe, wrote the following letter against Jerusalem to King Artaxerxes: 9 "Rehum, the governor, Shimshai, the scribe, and their fellow judges, officials, and agents from among the Persian, Urukian, Babylonian, Susian (that is Elamite), 10 and the other peoples whom the great and illustrious Assurbanipal transported and settled

in the city of Samaria and elsewhere in the province West-of-Euphrates, as follows. . . ." 11 This is a copy of the letter that they sent to him:

"To King Artaxerxes, your servants, the men of West-of-Euphrates, as follows: 12 Let it be known to the king that the Jews who came up from you to us have arrived at Jerusalem and are now rebuilding this rebellious and evil city. They are raising up its walls, and the foundations have already been laid. 13 Now let it be known to the king that if this city is rebuilt and its walls are raised up again, they will no longer pay taxes, tributes, or tolls; thus it can only result in harm to the throne. 14 Now, since we partake of the salt of the palace, we ought not simply to look on while the king is being dishonored. Therefore we have sent this message to inform you, O king, 15 so that inquiry may be made in the historical records of your fathers. In the historical records you can discover and verify that this city is a rebellious city which has proved fatal to kings and provinces, and that sedition has been fostered there since ancient times. For that reason this city was destroyed. 16 We inform you, O king, that if this city is rebuilt and its walls are raised up again, by that very fact you will no longer own any part of West-of-Euphrates."

17 The king sent this answer: "To Rehum, the governor, Shimshai, the scribe, and their fellow officials living in Samaria and elsewhere in the province West-of-Euphrates, greetings and the following: 18 The communication which you sent us has been read plainly in my presence. 19 When at my command inquiry was made, it was verified that from ancient times this city has risen up against kings and that rebellion and sedition have been fostered there. 20 Powerful kings were once in Jerusalem who ruled over all West-of-Euphrates, and taxes, tributes, and tolls were

---

4, 5: *Darius:* Darius I (521–485 B.C.). The temple-building narrative continues in 4, 24. In between (4, 6–23) is a series of notes about the opposition to the returned exiles voiced at the Persian court in the early fifth century B.C., after the temple had been reestablished.

4, 7: *Aramaic:* this word in the original text seems to be a note indicating a change of language from Hebrew to Aramaic, which in fact takes place here. The Aramaic section ends with 6,18, but again in 7, 12–26 a royal letter is cited in Aramaic.
4, 8–23: The central question here is the rebuilding

of the fortification walls of Jerusalem, not the building of the temple. The interruption of work on the city wall some time before 445 B.C. was the occasion for the coming of Nehemiah to Palestine (Neh 1, 1–4; 2, 1–5). *Artaxerxes:* Artaxerxes I (464–423 B.C.).

paid to them. 21 Give orders, therefore, that will stop the work of these men. This city may not be rebuilt until a further decree has been issued by me. 22 Take care that you do not neglect this matter, lest the evil grow to the detriment of the throne." 23 As soon as a copy of King Artaxerxes' letter had been read before Rehum, the governor, Shimshai, the scribe, and their fellow officials, they went in all haste to the Jews in Jerusalem and stopped their work by force of arms.

Rebuilding of the Temple

24 Thus it was that the work on the house of God in Jerusalem was halted. This inaction lasted until the second year of the reign of **5** Darius, king of Persia. 1 Then the prophets Haggai and Zechariah, son of Iddo, began to prophesy to the Jews in Judah and Jerusalem in the name of the God of Israel. 2 Thereupon Zerubbabel, son of Shealtiel, and Jeshua, son of Jozadak, began again to build the house of God in Jerusalem, with the prophets of God giving them support. 3 At that time there came to them Tattenai, governor of West-of-Euphrates, and Shethar-bozenai, and their fellow officials, who asked of them: "Who issued the decree for you to build this house and raise this edifice? 4 What are the names of the men who are building this structure?" 5 But their God watched over the elders of the Jews so that they were not hindered, until a report could go to Darius and then a written order be sent back concerning this matter.

6 A copy of the letter sent to King Darius by Tattenai, governor of West-of-Euphrates, and Shethar-bozenai, and their fellow officials from West-of-Euphrates; 7 they sent him a report in which was written the following:

"To King Darius, all good wishes! 8 Let it be known to the king that we have visited the province of Judah and the house of the great God: it is being rebuilt of cut stone and the walls are being reinforced with timber; the work is being carried on diligently and is making good progress under their hands. 9 We then questioned the elders, addressing to them the following words: 'Who issued the decree for you to build this house and raise this edifice?' 10 We also asked them their names, to report them to you in a list of the men who are their leaders. 11 This was their answer to us: 'We are the servants of the God of heaven and earth, and we are rebuilding the house built here long years ago, which a great king of Israel built and finished. 12 But because our fathers provoked the wrath of the God of heaven, he delivered them into the power of the Chaldean, Nebuchadnezzar, king of Babylon, who destroyed this house and led the people captive to Babylon. 13 However, in the first year of Cyrus, king of Babylon, King Cyrus issued a decree for the rebuilding of this house of God. 14 Moreover, the gold and silver utensils of the house of God which Nebuchadnezzar had taken from the temple in Jerusalem and carried off to the temple in Babylon, King Cyrus ordered to be removed from the temple in Babylon and consigned to a certain Sheshbazzar, whom he named governor. 15 And he commanded him: Take these utensils and deposit them in the temple of Jerusalem, and let the house of God be rebuilt on its former site. 16 Then this same Sheshbazzar came and laid the foundations of the house of God in Jerusalem. Since that time the building has been going on, and it is not yet completed.' 17 Now, if it please the king, let a search be made in the royal archives of Babylon to discover whether a decree really was issued by King Cyrus for the rebuilding of this house of God in Jerusalem. And may the king's pleasure in this matter be communicated to us."

The Decree of Darius

6 Thereupon King Darius issued an order to search the archives in which the Babylonian records were stored away; 2 and in Ecbatana, the stronghold in the province of Media, a scroll was found containing the following text: "Memorandum. 3 In the first year of King Cyrus, King Cyrus issued a decree: The house of God in Jerusalem. The house is to be rebuilt as a place for offering sacrifices and bringing burnt offerings. Its height is to be sixty cubits and its width sixty cubits. 4 It shall have three courses of cut stone for each one of timber. The costs are to be borne by the royal palace. 5 Also, the gold and silver utensils of the house of God which Nebuchadnezzar took from the temple of Jerusalem and brought to Babylon are to be sent back: to be returned to their place in the temple of Jerusalem and deposited in the house of God.

6 "Now, therefore, Tattenai, governor of West-of-Euphrates, and Shethar-bozenai, and you, their fellow officials in West-of-Euphrates, do not interfere in that place. 7 Let the governor and the elders of the Jews continue the work on that house of God; they are to rebuild it on its former site. 8 I also issue this decree concerning your dealing with these elders of the Jews in the rebuilding of that house of God: From the royal revenue, the taxes of West-of-Euphrates, let these men be repaid for their expenses, in full and without delay. 9 Whatever else is required—young bulls, rams, and lambs for holocausts to the God of heaven, wheat, salt, wine, and oil, according to the requirements of the priests who are in Jerusalem— is to be delivered to them day by day without fail, 10 that they may continue to offer sacrifices of pleasing odor to the God of heaven and pray for the life of the king and his sons. 11 I also issue this decree: If any man violates this edict, a beam is to be taken from his house, and he is to be lifted up and impaled on it; and his house is to be reduced to rubble for this offense. 12 And may the God who causes his name to dwell there overthrow every king or people who may undertake to alter this or to destroy this house of God

---

4, 24: *The second year . . . of Darius:* that is, 520 B.C.; it marks the beginning of the successful restoration of the temple, which was accomplished within the five years following (5, 1—16, 8).
   5, 1: *The prophets Haggai and Zechariah:* two of the Minor Prophets, whose books record their role in the encouragement of this work.

in Jerusalem. I, Darius, have issued this decree; let it be carefully executed."

13 Then Tattenai, the governor of West-of-Euphrates, and Shethar-bozenai, and their fellow officials carried out fully the instructions King Darius had sent them. 14 The elders of the Jews continued to make progress in the building, supported by the message of the prophets, Haggai and Zechariah, son of Iddo. They finished the building according to the command of the God of Israel and the decrees of Cyrus and Darius [and of Artaxerxes, king of Persia]. 15 They completed this house on the third day of the month Adar, in the sixth year of the reign of King Darius. 16 The Israelites—priests, Levites, and the other returned exiles—celebrated the dedication of this house of God with joy. 17 For the dedication of this house of God, they offered one hundred bulls, two hundred rams, and four hundred lambs, together with twelve he-goats as a sin-offering for all Israel, in keeping with the number of the tribes of Israel. 18 Finally they set up the priests in their classes and the Levites in their divisions for the service of God in Jerusalem, as is prescribed in the book of Moses.

The Passover

19 The exiles kept the Passover on the fourteenth day of the first month. 20 The Levites, every one of whom had purified himself for the occasion, sacrificed the Passover for the rest of the exiles, for their brethren the priests, and for themselves. 21 The Israelites who had returned from the exile partook of it together with all those who had separated themselves from the uncleanness of the peoples of the land to join them in seeking the LORD, the God of Israel. 22 They joyfully kept the feast of Unleavened Bread for seven days, for the LORD had filled them with joy by making the king of Assyria favorable to them, so that he gave

them help in their work on the house of God, the God of Israel.

THE DEEDS OF EZRA

Ezra the Scribe

7 After these events, during the reign of Artaxerxes, king of Persia, Ezra, son of Seraiah, son of Azariah, son of Hilkiah 2 son of Shallum, son of Zadok, son of Ahitub, 3 son of Amariah, son of Azariah, son of Meraioth, 4 son of Zerahiah, son of Uzzi, son of Bukki 5 son of Abishua, son of Phinehas, son of Eleazar, son of the high priest Aaron— 6 this Ezra came up from Babylon. He was a scribe, well-versed in the law of Moses which was given by the LORD, the God of Israel. Because the hand of the LORD, his God, was upon him, the king granted him all that he requested.

7 Some of the Israelites and some priests, Levites, singers, gatekeepers, and temple slaves also came up to Jerusalem in the seventh year of King Artaxerxes 8 Ezra came to Jerusalem in the fifth month of that seventh year of the king. 9 On the first day of the first month he resolved on the journey up from Babylon, and on the first day of the fifth month he arrived at Jerusalem, for the favoring hand of his God was upon him. 10 Ezra had set his heart on the study and practice of the law of the LORD and on teaching statutes and ordinances in Israel.

The Decree of Artaxerxes

11 This is a copy of the rescript which King Artaxerxes gave to Ezra the priest-scribe, the scribe of the text of the LORD's commandments and statutes for Israel:

12 "Artaxerxes, king of kings, to Ezra the priest, scribe of the law of the God of heaven (then, after greetings): 13 I have issued this decree, that anyone in my kingdom belonging to the people of Israel, its priests or Levites, who is minded to go up to

Jerusalem with you, may do so. 14 You are the envoy from the king and his seven counselors to supervise Judah and Jerusalem in respect of the law of your God which is in your possession, 15 and to bring with you the silver and gold which the king and his counselors have freely contributed to the God of Israel, whose dwelling is in Jerusalem, 16 as well as all the silver and gold which you may receive throughout the province of Babylon, together with the free-will offerings which the people and priests freely contribute for the house of their God in Jerusalem. 17 You must take care, therefore, to use this money to buy bulls, rams, lambs, and the cereal offerings and libations proper to these, and to offer them on the altar of the house of your God in Jerusalem. 18 You and your brethren may do whatever seems best to you with the remainder of the silver and gold, conformably to the will of your God. 19 The utensils consigned to you for the service of the house of your God you are to deposit before the God of Jerusalem. 20 Whatever else you may be required to supply for the needs of the house of your God, you may draw from the royal treasury. 21 I, Artaxerxes the king, issue this decree to all the treasurers of West-of-Euphrates: Whatever Ezra the priest, scribe of the law of the God of heaven, requests of you, dispense to him accurately, 22 within these limits: silver, one hundred talents; wheat, one hundred kors; wine, one hundred baths; oil, one hundred baths; salt, without limit. 23 Let everything that is ordered by the God of heaven be carried out exactly for the house of the God of heaven, that wrath may not come upon the realm of the king and his sons. 24 We also inform you that it is not permitted to impose taxes, tributes, or tolls on any priest, Levite, singer, gatekeeper, temple slave, or any other servant of that house of God.

6, 22: *Assyria:* used here in a broad sense for the Persian Empire.

7, 1-8: The date of Ezra's journey to Palestine is not known with certainty. The *seventh year* of King Artaxerxes I would be 458 B.C., and the present order

of the text suggests that date. The narratives of Ezra and Nehemiah make it seem to many, however, that the arrival of Nehemiah in 445 B.C. should precede that of Ezra. If so, Ezra may be thought to have come in 398 B.C., the seventh year of King

Artaxerxes II. Others argue for the thirty-seventh year of Artaxerxes I, that is, 428 B.C.; this would suppose that the date given in the text has suffered in transmission.

25 "As for you, Ezra, in accordance with the wisdom of your God which is in your possession, appoint magistrates and judges to administer justice to all the people in West-of-Euphrates, to all, that is, who know the laws of your God. 26 Instruct those who do not know these laws. Whoever does not obey the law of your God and the law of the king, let strict judgment be executed upon him, whether death, or corporal punishment, or a fine on his goods, or imprisonment."

Ezra and His Companions

27 Blessed be the LORD, the God of our fathers, who thus disposed the mind of the king to glorify the house of the LORD in Jerusalem, 28 and who let me find favor with the king, with his counselors, and with all the most influential royal officials. I therefore took courage and, with the hand of the LORD, my God, upon me, I gathered together Israelite family heads to make the return journey with me.

8 This is the list of the family heads who returned with me from Babylon during the reign of King Artaxerxes:

2 Of the sons of Phinehas, Gershon; of the sons of Ithamar, Daniel; of the sons of David, Hattush, 3 son of Shecaniah; of the sons of Parosh, Zechariah, and with him one hundred and fifty males were enrolled; 4 of the sons of Pahathmoab, Eliehoenai, son of Zerahiah, and with him two hundred males; 5 of the sons of Zattu, Shecaniah, son of Jahaziel, and with him three hundred males; 6 of the sons of Adin, Ebed, son of Jonathan and with him fifty males; 7 of the sons of Elam, Jeshaiah, son of Athaliah, and with him seventy males; 8 of the sons of Shephatiah, Zebadiah, son of Michael, and with him eighty males; 9 of the sons of Joab, Obadiah, son of Jehiel, and with him two hundred and eighteen males; 10 of the sons of Bani, Shelomith, son of Josiphiah, and with him one hundred and sixty males; 11 of the sons of Bebai, Zechariah, son of Bebai, and with him twenty-eight males; 12 of the sons of Azgad, Johanan, son of Hakkatan, and with him one hundred and ten males; 13 of the sons of Adonikam, younger sons, whose names were Eliphelet, Jeiel, and Shemaiah, and with them sixty males; 14 of the sons of Bigvai, Uthai, son of Zakkur, and with him seventy males.

The Journey to Jerusalem

15 I had them assemble by the river that flows toward Ahava, where we made camp for three days. There I perceived that both laymen and priests were present, but I could not discover a single Levite. 16 Therefore I sent Eliezer, Ariel, Shemaiah, Jarib, Elnathan, Nathan, Zechariah, and Meshullam, wise leaders, 17 with a command for Iddo, the leader in the place Casiphia, instructing them what to say to Iddo and his brethren, and to the temple slaves in Casiphia, in order to procure for us ministers for the house of our God. 18 They sent to us—for the favoring hand of our God was upon us—a well-instructed man, one of the sons of Mahli, son of Levi, son of Israel, namely Sherebiah, with his sons and brethren, eighteen men. 19 They also sent us Hashabiah, and with him Jeshaiah, sons of Merari, and their brethren and their sons, twenty men. 20 Of the temple slaves (those whom David and the princes appointed to serve the Levites) there were two hundred and twenty. All these men were enrolled by name.

21 Then I proclaimed a fast, there by the river of Ahava, that we might humble ourselves before our God to petition from him a safe journey for ourselves, our children, and all our possessions. 22 For I would have been ashamed to ask the king for troops and horsemen to protect us against enemies along the way, since we had said to the king, "The favoring hand of our God is upon all who seek him, but his mighty wrath is against all who forsake him." 23 So we fasted, and prayed to our God for this, and our petition was granted. 24 Next I selected twelve of the priestly leaders along with Sherebiah, Hashabiah, and ten of their brethren, 25 and I weighed out before them the silver and the gold and the utensils offered for the house of our God by the king, his counselors, his officials, and all the Israelites of that region. 26 I consigned it to them in these amounts: silver, six hundred and fifty talents; silver utensils, one hundred; gold, one hundred talents; 27 twenty golden bowls valued at a thousand darics; two vases of excellent polished bronze, as precious as gold. 28 I addressed them in these words: "You are consecrated to the LORD, and the utensils are also consecrated; the silver and the gold are a free-will offering to the LORD, the God of your fathers. 29 Keep good watch over them till you weigh them out in Jerusalem in the presence of the chief priests and Levites and the family leaders of Israel, in the chambers of the house of the LORD." 30 The priests and the Levites then took over the silver, the gold, and the utensils that had been weighed out, to bring them to Jerusalem, to the house of our God.

31 We set out for Jerusalem from the river of Ahava on the twelfth day of the first month. The hand of our God remained upon us, and he protected us from enemies and bandits along the way. 32 Thus we arrived in Jerusalem, where we first rested for three days. 33 On the fourth day, the silver, the gold, and the utensils were weighed out in the house of our God and consigned to the priest Meremoth, son of Uriah, who was assisted by Eleazar, son of Phinehas; they were assisted by the Levites Jozabad, son of Jeshua, and Noadiah, son of Binnui. 34 Everything was in order as to number and weight, and the total weight was registered. At that same time, 35 those who had returned from the captivity, the exiles, offered

---

7, 25: *The wisdom of your God:* the Mosaic law; cf vv 6, 14.

8, 15: *Ahava:* a town at an unidentified site in Babylonia. The river that flowed toward it was probably a branch or canal of the Euphrates.

as holocausts to the God of Israel twelve bulls for all Israel, ninety-six rams, seventy-seven lambs, and twelve goats as sin-offerings: all these as a holocaust to the LORD. 36 Finally, the orders of the king were presented to the king's satraps and to the governors in West-of-Euphrates, who gave their support to the people and to the house of God.

Denunciation of Mixed Marriages

9 When these matters had been concluded, the leaders approached me with this report: "Neither the Israelite laymen nor the priests nor the Levites have kept themselves aloof from the peoples of the land and their abominations [Canaanites, Hittites, Perizzites, Jebusites, Ammonites, Moabites, Egyptians, and Amorites]; 2 for they have taken some of their daughters as wives for themselves and their sons, and thus they have desecrated the holy race with the peoples of the land. Furthermore, the leaders and rulers have taken a leading part in this apostasy!"

Ezra's Exhortation

3 When I had heard this thing, I tore my cloak and my mantle, plucked hair from my head and beard, and sat there stupefied. 4 Around me gathered all who were in dread of the sentence of the God of Israel on this apostasy of the exiles, while I remained motionless until the evening sacrifice. 5 Then, at the time of the evening sacrifice, I rose in my wretchedness, and with cloak and mantle torn I fell on my knees, stretching out my hands to the LORD my God.

6 I said: "My God, I am too ashamed and confounded to raise my face to you, O my God for our wicked deeds are heaped up above our heads and our guilt reaches up to heaven. 7 From the time of our fathers even to this day great has

been our guilt, and for our wicked deeds we have been delivered over, we and our kings and our priests, to the will of the kings of foreign lands, to the sword, to captivity, to pillage, and to disgrace, as is the case today.

8 "And now, but a short time ago, mercy came to us from the LORD our God, who left us a remnant and gave us a stake in his holy place; thus our God has brightened our eyes and given us relief in our servitude. 9 For slaves we are, but in our servitude our God has not abandoned us; rather, he has turned the good will of the kings of Persia toward us. Thus he has given us new life to raise again the house of our God and restore its ruins, and has granted us a fence in Judah and Jerusalem. 10 But now, O our God, what can we say after all this? For we have abandoned your commandments, 11 which you gave through your servants the prophets: the land which you are entering to take as your possession is a land unclean with the filth of the peoples of the land, with the abominations with which they have filled it from one end to the other in their uncleanness. 12 Do not, then, give your daughters to their sons in marriage, and do not take their daughters for your sons. Never promote their peace and prosperity; thus you will grow strong, enjoy the produce of the land, and leave it as an inheritance to your children forever.

13 "After all that has come upon us for our evil deeds and our great guilt—though you, our God, have made less of our sinfulness than it deserved and have allowed us to survive as we do— 14 shall we again violate your commandments by intermarrying with these abominable peoples? Would you not become so angered with us as to destroy us without remnant or survivor? 15 O LORD, God of Israel, you are just; yet we have been spared, the remnant we are today. Here we are

before you in our sins. Because of all this, we can no longer stand in your presence."

The People's Response

10 While Ezra prayed and acknowledged their guilt, weeping and prostrate before the house of God, a very large assembly of Israelites gathered about him, men, women, and children; and the people wept profusely. 2 Then Shecaniah, the son of Jehiel, one of the sons of Elam, made this appeal to Ezra: "We have indeed betrayed our God by taking as wives foreign women of the peoples of the land. Yet even now there remains a hope for Israel. 3 Let us therefore enter into a covenant before our God to dismiss all our foreign wives and the children born of them, in keeping with what you, my lord, advise, and those who fear the commandments of our God. Let the law be observed! 4 Rise, then, for this is your duty! We will stand by you, so have courage and take action!" 5 Ezra rose to his feet and demanded an oath from the chiefs of the priests, from the Levites and from all Israel that they would do as had been proposed; and they swore it. 6 Then Ezra retired from his place before the house of God and entered the chamber of Johanan, son of Eliashib, where he spent the night neither eating food nor drinking water, for he was in mourning over the betrayal by the exiles. 7 A proclamation was made throughout Judah and Jerusalem that all the exiles should gather together in Jerusalem, 8 and that whoever failed to appear within three days would, according to the judgment of the leaders and elders, suffer the confiscation of all his possessions, and himself be excluded from the assembly of the exiles.

9 All the men of Judah and Benjamin gathered together in Jerusalem within the three-day period: it was in the ninth month, on the

---

8, 36: The story of Ezra's mission is seemingly continued from this point by Neh 7, 72b—8, 18, which may be read before Ezr 9, 1.

9, 7: After this verse, the next part of the prayer attributed to Ezra is perhaps to be found in Neh 9, 6-37, which may be read as leading up to Ezr 9, 8-15.

10, 6: *Johanan, son of Eliashib:* actually, the grandson of Eliashib; the father of Johanan was Eliashib's son Joiada (Neh 12, 10f.22). Since Eliashib was high priest at the time of Nehemiah (Neh 3, 1.20f; 13, 4.7) and Johanan, if not yet high priest, was at least old enough to have his own separate quarters (*chamber*) in the temple at the time of Ezra, it is practically

certain that Nehemiah's activity in Jerusalem must have preceded that of Ezra.

10, 9: *Ninth month:* Chislev (November-December), during the "early rains" in Palestine. Since the assembly took place *in the open . . . all the people . . . were trembling . . . because it was raining.*

twentieth day of the month. All the people, standing in the open place before the house of God, were trembling both over the matter at hand and because it was raining. 10 Then Ezra, the priest, stood up and said to them: "Your unfaithfulness in taking foreign women as wives has added to Israel's guilt. 11 But now, give praise to the LORD, the God of your fathers, and do his will: separate yourselves from the peoples of the land and from these foreign women." 12 In answer, the whole assembly cried out with a loud voice: "Yes, it is our duty to do as you say! 13 But the people are numerous and it is the rainy season, so that we cannot remain out-of-doors; besides, this is not a task that can be performed in a single day or even two, for those of us who have sinned in this regard are many. 14 Let our leaders represent the whole assembly; then let all those in our cities who have taken foreign women for wives appear at appointed times, accompanied by the elders and magistrates of each city in question, till we have turned away from us our God's burning anger over this affair." 15 Only Jonathan, son of Asahel, and Jahzeiah, son of Tikvah, were against this proposal, with Meshullam and Shabbethai the Levite supporting them.

The Guilty

16 The exiles did as agreed. Ezra appointed as his assistants men who were family heads, one for each family, all of them designated by name. They held sessions to examine the matter, beginning with the first day of the tenth month. 17 By the first day of the first month they had passed judgment on all the men who had taken foreign women for wives. 18 Among the priests, the following were found to have taken foreign women for wives: Of the sons of Jeshua, son of Jozadak, and his brethren: Maaseiah, Eliezer, Jarib, and Gedaliah. 19 They pledged themselves to dismiss their wives, and as a guilt-offering for their guilt they gave a ram from the flock. 20 Of the sons of Immer: Hanani and Zebadiah; 21 of the sons of Harim: Maaseiah, Elijah, Shemaiah, Jehiel, and Uzziah; 22 of the sons of Pashhur: Elioenai, Maaseiah, Ishmael, Nethanel, Jozabad, and Elasah.

23 Of the Levites: Jozabad, Shimei, Kelaiah (also called Kelita), Pethahiah, Judah, and Eliezer.

24 Of the singers: Eliashib and Zakkur; of the gatekeepers: Shallum, Telem, and Uri.

25 Among the other Israelites: Of the sons of Parosh: Ramiah, Izziah, Malchijah, Mijamin, Eleazar, Malchijah, and Benaiah; 26 of the sons of Elam: Mattaniah, Zechariah, Jehiel, Abdi, Jeremoth, and Elijah; 27 of the sons of Zattu: Elioenai, Eliashib, Mattaniah, Jeremoth, Zabad, and Aziza; 28 of the sons of Bebai: Jehohanan, Hananiah, Zabbai, and Athlai; 29 of the sons of Bani: Meshullam, Malluch, Adaiah, Jashub, Sheal, and Jeremoth; 30 of the sons of Pahath-moab: Adna, Chelal, Benaiah, Maaseiah, Mattaniah, Bezalel, Binnui, and Manasseh; 31 of the sons of Harim: Eliezer, Isshijah, Malchijah, Shemaiah, Shimeon, 32 Benjamin, Malluch, Shemariah; 33 of the sons of Hashum: Mattenai, Mattattah, Zabad, Eliphelet, Jeremai, Manasseh, Shimei; 34 of the sons of Begui: Maadai, Amram, Uel, 35 Benaiah, Bedeiah, Cheluhi, 36 Vaniah, Meremoth, Eliashib, 37 Mattaniah, Mattenai, and Jaasu; 38 of the sons of Binnui: Shimei, 39 Shelemiah, Nathan, and Adaiah; 40 of the sons of Zachai: Shashai, Sharai, 41 Azarel, Shelemiah, Shemariah, 42 Shallum, Amariah, Joseph; 43 of the sons of Nebo: Jeiel, Mattithiah, Zabad, Zebina, Jaddai, Joel, Benaiah.

44 All these had taken foreign wives; but they sent them away, both the women and their children.

10, 16f: The work of the committee lasted three months, from *the first day of the tenth month*, Tebet (December-January), to *the first day of the first month*, Nisan (March-April), of the following Jewish year.

10, 44: The account of the problem of mixed marriages at the time of Ezra is continued in Neh 9, 1–5; this may be read immediately after Ezr 10, 44, though the date given in Neh 9, 1 fits more precisely after Ezr 10, 15; cf Hg 2, 10–14.

Nehemiah

THE DEEDS OF NEHEMIAH

Nehemiah's Vocation

THE words of Nehemiah, the son of Hacaliah.

In the month Chislev of the twentieth year, I was in the citadel of Susa 2 when Hanani, one of my brothers, came with other men from Judah. I asked them about the Jews, the remnant preserved after the captivity, and about Jerusalem, 3 and they answered me: "The survivors of the captivity there in the province are in great distress and under reproach. Also, the wall of Jerusalem lies breached, and its gates have been gutted with fire." 4 When I heard this report, I began to weep and continued mourning for several days; I fasted and prayed before the God of heaven. 5 I prayed: "O LORD, God of heaven, great and awesome God, you who preserve your covenant of mercy toward these who love you and keep your commandments, 6 may your ear be attentive, and your eyes open, to heed the prayer which I, your servant, now offer in your presence day and night for your servants the Israelites, confessing the sins which we of Israel have committed against you, I and my father's house included. 7 Grievously have we offended you, not keeping the commandments, the statutes, and the ordinances which you committed to your servant Moses. 8 But remember, I pray, the promise which you gave through Moses, your servant, when you said: 'Should you prove faithless, I will scatter you among the nations; 9 but should you return to me and carefully keep my commandments, even though your outcasts have been driven to the farthest corner of the world, I will gather them from there, and bring them back to the place which I have chosen as the dwelling place for my name.' 10 They are your servants, your people, whom you freed by your great might and your strong hand. 11 O Lord, may your ear be attentive to my prayer and that of all your willing servants who revere your name. Grant success to your servant this day, and let him find favor with this man"—for I was cupbearer to the king.

Appointment by the King

2 In the month Nisan of the twentieth year of King Artaxerxes, when the wine was in my charge, I took some and offered it to the king. As I had never before been sad in his presence, 2 the king asked me, "Why do you look sad? If you are not sick, you must be sad at heart." Though I was seized with great fear, 3 I answered the king: "May the king live forever! How could I not look sad when the city where my ancestors are buried lies in ruins, and its gates have been eaten out by fire?" 4 The king asked me, "What is it, then, that you wish?" I prayed to the God of heaven 5 and then answered the king: "If it please the king, and if your servant is deserving of your favor, send me to Judah, to the city of my ancestors' graves, to rebuild it." 6 Then the king, and the queen seated beside him, asked me how long my journey would take and when I would return. I set a date that was acceptable to him, and the king agreed that I might go.

7 I asked the king further: "If it

1, 1: The first mission of Nehemiah, from the *twentieth year* of Artaxerxes I, lasted from the spring (2, 1) of 445 B.C. until 433 B.C. (5, 14). It is recounted in Neh 1, 1—6, 15; 12, 27-43; 6, 16—7, 5;

11, 1-21, which may be read in that order.
1, 11: *Cupbearer to the king:* an important official in the royal household. Because Nehemiah could appear in the queen's presence (2, 6), it is commonly

presumed that he was a eunuch; but this is not necessarily so.

please the king, let letters be given to me for the governors of West-of-Euphrates, that they may afford me safe-conduct till I arrive in Judah; 8 also a letter for Asaph, the keeper of the royal park, that he may give me wood for timbering the gates of the temple-citadel and for the city wall and the house that I shall occupy." The king granted my requests, for the favoring hand of my God was upon me. 9 Thus I proceeded to the governors of West-of-Euphrates and presented the king's letters to them. The king also sent with me army officers and cavalry.

10 When Sunballat the Horonite and Tobiah the Ammonite slave had heard of this, they were very much displeased that someone had come to seek the welfare of the Israelites.

Circuit of the City

11 When I had arrived in Jerusalem, I first rested there for three days. 12 Then I set out by night with only a few other men (for I had not told anyone what my God had inspired me to do for Jerusalem) and with no other animals but my own mount. 13 I rode out at night by the Valley Gate, passed by the Dragon Spring, and came to the Dung Gate, observing how the walls of Jerusalem lay in ruins and its gates had been eaten out by fire. 14 Then I passed over to the Spring Gate and to the King's Pool. Since there was no room here for my mount to pass with me astride, 15 I continued on foot up the wadi by night, inspecting the wall all the while till I once more reached the Valley Gate, by which I went back in. 16 The magistrates knew nothing of where I had gone or what I was doing, for as yet I had disclosed nothing to the Jews, neither to the

priests, nor to the nobles, nor to the magistrates, nor to the others who would be concerned about the matter.

Rebuilding Jerusalem's Walls

17 Afterward I said to them: "You see the evil plight in which we stand: how Jerusalem lies in ruins and its gates have been gutted by fire. Come, let us rebuild the wall of Jerusalem, so that we may no longer be an object of derision!" 18 Then I explained to them how the favoring hand of my God had rested upon me, and what the king had said to me. They replied, "Let us be up and building!" And they undertook the good work with vigor. 19 On hearing of this, Sanballat the Horonite, Tobiah the Ammonite slave, and Geshem the Arab mocked us and ridiculed us. "What is this that you are about?" they asked. "Are you rebelling against the king?" 20 My answer to them was this: "It is the God of heaven who will grant us success. We, his servants, shall set about the rebuilding; but for you there is to be neither share nor claim nor memorial in Jerusalem."

List of Workers

3 Eliashib the high priest and his priestly brethren took up the task of rebuilding the Sheep Gate. They timbered it and set up its doors, its bolts, and its bars, then continued the rebuilding to the Tower of Hananel. 2 At their side the men of Jericho were rebuilding and next to them was Zaccur, son of Imri. 3 The Fish Gate was rebuilt by the sons of Hassenaah; they timbered it and set up its doors, its bolts, and its bars. 4 At their

side Meremoth, son of Uriah, son of Hakkoz, carried out the work of repair; next to him was Meshullam, son of Berechiah, son of Meshezabel; and next to him was Zadok, son of Baana. 5 Next to him the Tekoites carried out the work of repair; however, some of their outstanding men would not submit to the labor asked by their lords. 6 The New City Gate was repaired by Joiada, son of Paseah; and Meshullam, son of Besodeiah; they timbered it and set up its doors, its bolts, and its bars. 7 At their side were Melatiah the Gibeonite, Jadon the Meronothite, and the men of Gibeon and of Mizpah, who were under the jurisdiction of the governor of West-of-Euphrates. 8 Next to them the work of repair was carried out by Uzziel, son of Harhaiah, a member of the goldsmiths' guild, and at his side was Hananiah, one of the perfumers' guild. They restored Jerusalem as far as the wall of the public square. 9 Next to them the work of repair was carried out by Rephaiah, son of Hur, leader of half the district of Jerusalem, 10 and at his side was Jedaiah, son of Harumaph, who repaired opposite his own house. Next to him Hattush, son of Hashabneiah, carried out the work of repair. 11 The adjoining sector, as far as the Oven Tower, was repaired by Malchijah, son of Harim, and Hasshub, of Pahath-moab. 12 At their side the work of repair was carried out by Shallum, son of Hallohesh, leader of half the district of Jerusalem, by himself and his daughters. 13 The Valley Gate was repaired by Hanun and the inhabitants of Zanoah; they rebuilt it and set up its doors, its bolts, and its bars. They also repaired a thousand cubits of the wall up to the Dung

2, 10: *Sanballat the Horonite:* the governor of the province of Samaria (3, 33f), apparently a native of one of the Beth-horons. A letter from the Jews living at Elephantine in southern Egypt, dated 408-407 B.C., mentions "Delayah and Shelemyah, the sons of Sanballat, the governor of Samaria." Although his own name was Babylonian—*Sin-uballit,* i.e., "Sin (the moon god) has given life"—his two sons had names referring to Yahweh. *Tobiah, the Ammonite slave:* the governor of the province of Ammon in Trans-jordan. His honorary title, "servant" (in Hebrew, *ebed*), i.e., of the king, could also be understood as *slave,* and Nehemiah no doubt meant it in this derogatory sense. The Tobiads remained a powerful family even in Maccabean times (2 Mc 3, 11). Sanballat and Tobiah, together with Geshem the

Arab (2, 19; 6, 1f), who was probably in charge of Edom and the regions to the south and southeast of Judah, opposed the rebuilding of Jerusalem's walls on political grounds; the city was the capital of a rival province.

2, 13ff: Nehemiah left Jerusalem by *the Valley Gate* near the northwestern end of the old City of David and went south down the Tyropoean Valley toward *the Dragon Spring* (or the En-rogel of Jos 15, 7; 18, 16; 2 Sm 17, 17; 1 Kgs 1, 9, now known as Job's Well) at the juncture of the Valley of Hinnom and the Kidron Valley; he then turned north at *the Dung Gate* (or *the Potsherd Gate* of Jer 19, 2) at the southern end of the city and proceeded up *the wadi,* that is, the Kidron Valley, passing *the Spring Gate* (at the Spring of Gihon) and *the King's Pool* (unidenti-

fied); finally he turned west and then south to his starting point.

2, 20: *Neither share nor claim nor memorial:* although Sanballat and Tobiah were Yahwist, Nehemiah would not let them participate in any of the rights of the religious community in Jerusalem.

3, 1-32: The construction work on the gates and walls of the city is described in counterclockwise direction, beginning and ending at *the Sheep Gate* (to the north of the temple). The exact sites of many of the topographical points mentioned are uncertain.

3, 8: *Wall of the public square:* that is, the section of wall bounding the place of assembly outside the Gate of Ephraim, or New City Gate; cf 3, 6; 8, 16.

Gate. 14 The Dung Gate was repaired by Malchijah, son of Rechab, leader of the district of Beth-haccherem; he rebuilt it and set up its doors, its bolts, and its bars. 15 The Spring Gate was repaired by Shallum, son of Colhozeh, leader of the district of Mizpah; he rebuilt it, roofed it over, and set up its doors, its bolts, and its bars. He also repaired the wall of the Aqueduct Pool near the king's garden as far as the steps that lead down from the City of David. 16 After him, the work of repair was carried out by Nehemiah, son of Azbuk, leader of half the district of Beth-zur, to a place opposite the tombs of David, as far as the artificial pool and the barracks.

17 After him, the Levites carried out the work of repair: Rehum, son of Bani. Next to him, for his own district, was Hashabiah, leader of half the district of Keilah. 18 After him, their brethren carried out the work of repair: Binnui, son of Henadad, leader of half the district of Keilah; 19 next to him Ezer, son of Jeshua, leader of Mizpah, who repaired the adjoining sector, the Corner, opposite the ascent to the arsenal. 20 After him, Baruch, son of Zabbai, repaired the adjoining sector from the Corner to the entrance of the house of Eliashib, the high priest. 21 After him, Meremoth, son of Uriah, son of Hakkoz, repaired the adjoining sector from the entrace of Eliashib's house to the end of the house. 22 After him, the work of repair was carried out by the priests, men of the surrounding country. 23 After them, Benjamin and Hasshub carried out the repair in front of their houses; after them, Azariah, son of Maaseiah, son of Ananiah, made the repairs alongside his house. 24 After him, Binnui, son of Henadad, repaired the adjoining sector from the house of Azariah to the Corner [that is, to the Angle]. 25 After him, Palal, son of Uzai, carried out the work of repair opposite the Corner and the tower projecting from the Upper Palace at the quarters of the guard. After him, Pedaiah, son of Parosh, carried out the work of repair 26 to a point opposite the Water Gate on the east, and the projecting tower.

27 After him, the Tekoites repaired the adjoining sector opposite the great projecting tower, to the wall of Ophel [the temple slaves were dwelling on Ophel]. 28 Above the Horse Gate the priests carried out the work of repair, each before his own house. 29 After them Zadok, son of Immer, carried out the repair before his house, and after him the repair was carried out by Shemaiah, son of Shecaniah, keeper of the East Gate. 30 After him, Hananiah, son of Shelemiah, and Hanun, the sixth son of Zalaph, repaired the adjoining sector; after them, Meshullam, son of Berechiah, repaired the place opposite his own lodging. 31 After him, Malchijah, a member of the goldsmiths' guild, carried out the work of repair as far as the quarters of the temple slaves and the merchants, before the Gate of Inspection and as far as the upper chamber of the Angle. 32 Between the upper chamber of the Angle and the Sheep Gate, the goldsmiths and the merchants carried out the work of repair.

Opposition from Judah's Foes

33 When Sanballat heard that we were rebuilding the wall, it roused his anger and he became very much incensed. He ridiculed the Jews, 34 saying in the presence of his brethren and the troops of Samaria: "What are these miserable Jews trying to do? Will they complete their restoration in a single day? Will they recover these stones, burnt as they are, from the heaps of dust?" 35 Tobiah the Ammonite was beside him, and he said: "It is a rubble heap they are building. Any fox that attacked it would breach their wall of stones!" 36 Take note, O our God, how we were mocked! Turn back their derision upon their own heads and let them be carried away to a land of captivity! 37 Hide not their crime and let not their sin be blotted out in your sight, for they insulted the builders to their face! 38 We, however, continued to build the wall, which was soon filled in and completed up to half its height. The people worked with a will.

When Sanballat, Tobiah, the Arabs, the Ammonites, and the Ashdodites heard that the restoration of the walls of Jerusalem was progressing—for the gaps were beginning to be closed up—they became extremely angry. 2 Thereupon they all plotted together to come and fight against Jerusalem and thus to throw us into confusion. 3 We prayed to our God and posted a watch against them day and night for fear of what they might do. 4 Meanwhile the Judahites were saying:

"Slackened is the bearers'
      strength,
   there is no end to the rubbish;
Never shall we be able
   the wall to rebuild."

5 Our enemies thought, "Before they are aware of it or see us, we shall come into their midst, kill them, and put an end to the work." 6 When the Jews who lived near them had come to us from one place after another, and had told us ten times over that they were about to attack us, 7 I stationed guards down below, behind the wall, near the exposed points, assigning them by family groups with their swords, their spears, and their bows. 8 I made an inspection, then addressed these words to the nobles, the magistrates, and the rest of the people: "Have no fear of them! Keep in mind the Lord, who is great and to be feared, and fight for your brethren, your sons and daughters, your wives and your homes." 9 When our enemies became aware that we had been warned and that God had upset their plan, we all went back, each to his own task at the wall.

10 From that time on, however, only half my able men took a hand in the work, while the other half, armed with spears, bucklers, bows, and breastplates, stood guard behind the whole house of Judah 11 as they rebuilt the wall. The load carriers, too, were armed; each did his work with one hand and held a weapon with the other. 12 Every builder, while he worked, had his sword girt at his side. Also, a

trumpeter stood beside me, 13 for I had said to the nobles, the magistrates, and the rest of the people: "Our work is scattered and extensive, and we are widely separated from one another along the wall; 14 wherever you hear the trumpet sound, join us there; our God will fight with us." 15 Thus we went on with the work, half of the men with spears at the ready, from daybreak till the stars came out.

16 At the same time I told the people to spend the nights inside Jerusalem, each man with his own attendant, so that they might serve as a guard by night and a working force by day. 17 Neither I, nor my kinsmen, nor any of my attendants, nor any of the bodyguard that accompanied me took off his clothes; everyone kept his weapon at his right hand.

Antisocial Conduct

5 Then there rose a great outcry of the common people and their wives against certain of their fellow Jews. 2 Some said: "We are forced to pawn our sons and daughters in order to get grain to eat that we may live." 3 Others said: "We are forced to pawn our fields, our vineyards, and our houses, that we may have grain during the famine." 4 Still others said: "To pay the king's tax we have borrowed money on our fields and our vineyards. 5 And though these are our own kinsmen and our children are as good as theirs, we have had to reduce our sons and daughters to slavery, and violence has been done to some of our daughters! Yet we can do nothing about it, for our fields and our vineyards belong to others."

Nehemiah's Action

6 I was extremely angry when I heard the reasons they had for complaint. 7 After some deliberation, I called the nobles and magistrates to account, saying to them, "You are exacting interest from your own kinsmen!" I then rebuked them

severely, 8 saying to them: "As far as we were able, we bought back our fellow Jews who had been sold to Gentiles; you, however, are selling your own brothers, to have them bought back by us." They remained silent, for they could find no answer. 9 I continued: "What you are doing is not good. Should you not walk in the fear of our God, and put an end to the derision of our Gentile enemies? 10 I myself, my kinsmen, and my attendants have lent the people money and grain without charge. Let us put an end to this usury! 11 I ask that you return to them this very day their fields, their vineyards, their olive groves, and their houses, together with the interest on the money, the grain, the wine, and the oil that you have lent them." 12 They answered: "We will return everything and exact nothing further from them. We will do just what you ask." Then I called for the priests and had them administer an oath to these men that they would do as they had promised. 13 I also shook out the folds of my garment, saying, "Thus may God shake from his home and his fortune every man who fails to keep this promise, and may he thus be shaken out and emptied!" And the whole assembly answered, "Amen," and praised the Lord. Then the people did as they had promised.

Nehemiah's Lack of Self-interest

14 Moreover, from the time that King Artaxerxes appointed me governor in the land of Judah, from his twentieth to this thirty-second year —during these twelve years neither I nor my brethren lived from the governor's allowance. 15 The earlier governors, my predecessors, had laid a heavy burden on the people, taking from them each day forty silver shekels for their food; then too, their men oppressed the people. But I, because I feared God, did not act thus. 16 Moreover, though I had acquired no land of my own, I did my part in this work on the wall, and all my men were gathered there for the work. 17 Though I set my table for a hundred and

fifty persons, Jews and magistrates, as well as those who came to us from the nations round about, 18 and though the daily preparations were made at my expense—one beef, six choice muttons, poultry—besides all kinds of wine in abundance every ten days, despite this I did not claim the governor's allowance, for the labor lay heavy upon this people. 19 Keep in mind, O my God, in my favor all that I did for this people.

Plots against Nehemiah

6 When it had been reported to Sanballat, Tobiah, Geshem the Arab, and our other enemies that I had rebuilt the wall and that there was no breach left in it (though up to that time I had not yet set up the doors in the gates), 2 Sanballat and Geshem sent me this message: "Come, let us hold council together at Caphirim in the plain of Ono." They were planning to do me harm. 3 However, I sent messengers to them with this reply: "I am engaged in a great enterprise and am unable to come down; why should the work stop, while I leave it to come down to you?" 4 Four times they sent me this same proposal, and each time I gave the same reply. 5 Then, the fifth time, Sanballat sent me the same message by one of his servants, who bore an unsealed letter 6 containing this text: 6 "Among the nations it has been reported—Geshem is witness to this—that you and the Jews are planning a rebellion; that for this reason you are rebuilding the wall; and that you are to be their king"—and so on. 7 "Also, that you have set up prophets in Jerusalem to proclaim you king of Judah. Now, since matters like these must reach the ear of the king, come, let us hold council together." 8 I sent him this answer: "Nothing of what you report has taken place; rather, it is the invention of your own mind." 9 They were all trying to frighten us, thinking, "Their hands will slacken in the work, and it will never be completed." But instead, I now redoubled my efforts.

10 I went to the house of Shemaiah, son of Delaiah, son of Mehatabel,

---

5,7: *You are exacting interest from your own kinsmen!:* contrary to the Mosaic law (Dt 23, 20).

who was unable to go about, and he said:

"Let us meet in the house of God,
    inside the temple building;
    let us lock the doors of the
        temple.
For men are coming to kill you;
    by night they are coming to
        kill you."

11 My answer was: "A man like me take flight? Can a man like me enter the temple to save his life? I will not go!" 12 For on consideration it was plain to me that God had not sent him; rather, because Tobiah and Sanballat had bribed him, he voiced this prophecy concerning me 13 that I might act on it out of fear and commit this sin. Then they would have had a shameful story with which to discredit me. 14 Keep in mind Tobiah and Sanballat, O my God, because of these things they did; keep in mind as well Noadiah the prophetess and the other prophets who were trying to frighten me.

Conclusion of the Work

15 The wall was finished on the twenty-fifth day of Elul; it had taken fifty-two days. 16 When all our enemies had heard of this, and all the nations round about had taken note of it, our enemies lost much face in the eyes of the nations, for they knew that it was with our God's help that this work had been completed. 17 At that same time, however, many letters were going to Tobiah from the nobles of Judah, and Tobiah's letters were reaching them, 18 for many in Judah were in league with him, since he was the son-in-law of Shecaniah, son of Arah, and his son Jehohanan had married the daughter of Meshullam, son of Berechiah. 19 Thus they would praise his good deeds in my presence and relate to him whatever I said; and Tobiah sent letters trying to frighten me.

7 When the wall had been rebuilt, I had the doors set up, and the gatekeepers [and the singers and the Levites] were put in charge of them. 2 Over Jerusalem I placed Hanani, my brother, and Hananiah, the commander of the citadel, who was a more trustworthy and God-fearing man than most. 3 I said to them: "The gates of Jerusalem are not to be opened until the sun is hot, and while the sun is still shining they shall shut and bar the doors. Appoint as watchmen the inhabitants of Jerusalem, some at their watch posts, and others before their own houses."

Census of the Province

4 Now the city was quite wide and spacious, but its population was small, and none of the houses had been rebuilt. 5 When my God had put it into my mind to gather together the nobles, the magistrates, and the common people, and to examine their family records, I came upon the family list of those who had returned in the earliest period. There I found the following written:

6 These are the inhabitants of the province who returned from the captivity of the exiles whom Nebuchadnezzar, king of Babylon, had carried away, and who came back to Jerusalem and Judah, each man to his own city 7 (those who returned with Zerubbabel, Jeshua, Nehemiah, Azariah, Raamiah, Nahamani, Mordecai, Bilshan, Mispereth, Bigvai, Nehum, and Baanah).

8 The census of the men of Israel: sons of Parosh, two thousand one hundred and seventy-two; 9 sons of Shephatiah, three hundred and seventy-two; 10 sons of Arah, six hundred and fifty-two; 11 sons of Pahath-moab who were sons of Jeshua and Joab, two thousand eight hundred and eighteen; 12 sons of Elam, one thousand two hundred and fifty-four; 13 sons of Zattu, eight hundred and forty-five; 14 sons of Zaccai, seven hundred and sixty; 15 sons of Binnui, six hundred and forty-eight; 16 sons of Bebai, six hundred and twenty-eight; 17 sons of Azgad, two thousand three hundred and twenty-two; 18 sons of Adonikam, six hundred and sixty-seven; 19 sons of Bigvai, two thousand and sixty-seven; 20 sons of Adin, six hundred and fifty-five; 21 sons of Ater who were sons of Hezekiah, ninety-eight; 22 sons of Hashum, three hundred and twenty-eight; 23 sons of Bezai, three hundred and twenty-four; 24 sons of Hariph, one hundred and twelve; 25 sons of Gibeon, ninety-five; 26 men of Bethlehem and Netophah, one hundred and eighty-eight; 27 men of Anathoth, one hundred and twenty-eight; 28 men of Beth-azmaveth, forty-two; 29 men of Kiriath-jearim, Chephirah, and Beeroth, seven hundred and forty-three; 30 men of Ramah and Geba, six hundred and twenty-one; 31 men of Michmas, one hundred and twenty-two; 32 men of Bethel and Ai, one hundred and twenty-three; 33 men of Nebo, fifty-two; 34 sons of another Elam, one thousand two hundred and fifty-four; 35 sons of Harim, three hundred and twenty; 36 sons of Jericho, three hundred and forty-five; 37 sons of Lod, Hadid, and Ono, seven hundred and twenty-one; 38 sons of Senaah, three thousand nine hundred and thirty. 39 The priests: sons of Jedaiah who were of the house of Jeshua, nine hundred and seventy-three; 40 sons of Immer, one thousand and fifty-two; 41 sons of Pashhur, one thousand two hundred and forty-seven; 42 sons of Harim, one thousand and seventeen.

43 The Levites: sons of Jeshua, Kadmiel, Binnui, Hodeviah, seventy-four.

44 The singers: sons of Asaph, one hundred and forty-eight. 45 The gatekeepers: sons of Shallum, sons of Ater, sons of Talmon, sons of Akkub, sons of Hatita, sons of Shobai, one hundred and thirty-eight.

46 The temple slaves: sons of Ziha, sons of Hasupha, sons of Tabbaoth, 47 sons of Keros, sons of Sia, sons of Padon, 48 sons of Lebana, sons of Hagaba, sons of Shalmai, 49 sons of Hanan, sons of Giddel, sons of Gahar, 50 sons

---

6, 15: *Elul:* the sixth month (August–September). *Fifty-two days:* according to Josephus (*Antiquities* XI, v 8), the rebuilding of the walls of Jerusalem by

Nehemiah took two years and four months, which seems more probable.

6, 17ff These verses should be read immediately after v 14.

7, 6–72a: See note on Ezr 2, 1–67.

of Reaiah, sons of Rezin, sons of Nekoda, 51 sons of Gazzam, sons of Uzza, sons of Paseah, 52 sons of Besai, sons of the Meunites, sons of the Nephusites, 53 sons of Bakbuk, sons of Hakupha, sons of Harhur, 54 sons of Bazlith, sons of Mehida, sons of Harsha, 55 sons of Barkos, sons of Sisera, sons of Temah, 56 sons of Neziah, sons of Hatipha.

57 Descendants of the slaves of Solomon: sons of Sotai, sons of Sophereth, sons of Perida, 58 sons of Jaala, sons of Darkon, sons of Giddel, 59 sons of Shephatiah, sons of Hattil, sons of Pochereth-hazze-baim, sons of Amon. 60 The total of the temple slaves and the de-scendants of the slaves of Solomon was three hundred and ninety-two.

61 The following who returned from Tel-melah, Telharsha, Cherub, Addon, and Immer were unable to prove that their ancestral houses and their descent were Israelite: 62 sons of Delaiah, sons of Tobiah, sons of Nekoda, six hundred and forty-two. 63 Also, of the priests: sons of Hobaiah, sons of Hakkoz, sons of Barzillai (he had married one of the daughters of Barzillai the Gileadite and became known by his name). 64 These men searched their family records, but their names could not be found written there; hence they were degraded from the priest-hood, 65 and His Excellency ord-ered them not to partake of the most holy foods until there should be a priest bearing the Urim and Thum-mim. 66 The entire assembly taken together came to forty-two thousand three hundred and sixty, 67 not counting their male and female slaves, who were seven thousand three hundred and thirty-seven. They also had two hundred male and female singers. Their horses were seven hundred and thirty-six, their mules two hundred and forty-five, 68 their camels four hundred and thirty-five, their asses six thousand seven hundred and twenty.

69 Certain of the family heads contributed to the service. His Excellency put into the treasury one thousand drachmas of gold, fifty basins, thirty garments for priests, and five hundred minas of silver. 70 Some of the family heads contributed to the treasury for the temple service: twenty thousand drachmas of gold and two thousand two hundred minas of silver. 71 The contributions of the rest of the people amounted to twenty thousand drachmas of gold, two thousand minas of silver, and sixty-seven garments for priests. 72 The priests, the Levites, the gatekeepers, the singers, the temple slaves, and all Israel took up residence in their cities.

PROMULGATION OF THE LAW

Ezra Reads the Law

8 Now when the seventh month came, the whole people gathered as one man in the open space before the Water Gate, and they called upon Ezra the scribe to bring forth the book of the law of Moses which the LORD prescribed for Israel. 2 On the first day of the seventh month, therefore, Ezra the priest brought the law before the assembly, which consisted of men, women, and those children old enough to understand. 3 Standing at one end of the open place that was before the Water Gate, he read out of the book from daybreak till midday, in the presence of the men, the women and those children old enough to understand; and all the people lis-tened attentively to the book of the law. 4 Ezra the scribe stood on a wooden platform that had been made for the occasion; at his right side stood Mattithiah, Shema, Anaiah, Uriah, Hilkiah, and Maaseiah, and on his left Pedaiah, Mishael, Malchi-jah, Hashum, Hashbaddanah, Zech-ariah, Meshullam. 5 Ezra opened the scroll so that all the people might see it (for he was standing higher up than any of the people); and, as he opened it, all the people rose. 6 Ezra blessed the LORD, the great God, and all the people, their hands raised high, answered, "Amen, amen!" Then they bowed down and

prostrated themselves before the LORD, their faces to the ground. 7 [The Levites Jeshua, Bani, Shere-biah, Jamin, Akkub, Shabbethai, Hodiah, Maaseiah, Kelita, Azariah, Jozabad, Hanan, and Pelaiah ex-plained the law to the people, who remained in their places.] 8 Ezra read plainly from the book of the law of God, interpreting it so that all could understand what was read. 9 Then [Nehemiah, that is, His Excellency, and] Ezra the priest-scribe [and the Levites who were in-structing the people] said to all the people: "Today is holy to the LORD your God. Do not be sad, and do not weep"—for all the people were weeping as they heard the words of the law. 10 He said further: "Go, eat rich foods and drink sweet drinks, and allot portions to those who had nothing prepared; for today is holy to our Lord. Do not be saddened this day, for rejoicing in the LORD must be your strength!" 11 [And the Levites quieted all the people, saying, "Hush, for today is holy, and you must not be saddened."] 12 Then all the people went to eat and drink, to distribute portions, and to celebrate with great joy, for they understood the words that had been expounded to them.

The Feast of Booths

13 On the second day, the family heads of the whole people and also the priests and the Levites gathered around Ezra the scribe and examined the words of the law more closely. 14 They found it written in the law prescribed by the LORD through Moses that the Israelites must dwell in booths during the feast of the seventh month; 15 and that they should have this proclamation made throughout their cities and in Jeru-salem: "Go out into the hill country and bring in branches of olive trees, oleasters, myrtle, palm, and other leafy trees, to make booths, as the law prescribes." 16 The people went out and brought in branches with which they made booths for themselves, on the roofs of their houses, in their courtyards, in the

---

7, 65.69: *His excellency:* see note on Ezr 2, 63.
7, 72b–8, 18: to be read after Ezr 8, 36. The gloss mentioning *Nehemiah* in v 9 was inserted in this

Ezra section after the dislocation of several parts of Ezra-Nehemiah had occurred. There is no clear evidence of a simultaneous presence of Nehemiah

and Ezra in Jerusalem; Neh 12, 26 and 12, 36 are also scribal glosses.

courts of the house of God, and in the open spaces of the Water Gate and the Gate of Ephraim. 17 Thus the entire assembly of the returned exiles made booths and dwelt in them. Now the Israelites had done nothing of this sort from the days of Jeshua, son of Nun, until this occasion; therefore there was very great joy. 18 Ezra read from the book of the law of God day after day, from the first day to the last. They kept the feast for seven days, and the solemn assembly on the eighth day, as was required.

Confession of the People

9 On the twenty-fourth day of this month, the Israelites gathered together fasting and in sackcloth, their heads covered with dust. 2 Those of Israelite descent separated themselves from all who were of foreign extraction, then stood forward and confessed their sins and the guilty deeds of their fathers. 3 When they had taken their places, they read from the book of the law of the LORD their God, for a fourth part of the day, and during another fourth part they made their confession and prostrated themselves before the LORD their God. 4 Standing on the platform of the Levites were Jeshua, Binnui, Kadmiel, Shebaniah, Bunni, Sherebiah, Bani, and Chenani, who cried out to the LORD their God, with a loud voice. 5 The Levites Jeshua, Kadmiel, Bani, Hashabneiah, Sherebiah, Hodiah, Shebaniah, and Pethahiah said,

"Arise, bless the LORD, your God,
from eternity to eternity!"

The Israelites answered with the blessing,

"Blessed is your glorious name,
and exalted above all blessing
and praise."

6 Then Ezra said: "It is you, O LORD, you are the only one; you made the heavens, the highest heavens and all their host, the earth and all that is upon it, the seas and all that is in them. To all of them you give life,

and the heavenly hosts bow down before you.

7 "You, O LORD, are the God who chose Abram, who brought him out from Ur of the Chaldees, and named him Abraham. 8 When you had found his heart faithful in your sight, you made the covenant with him to give to him and his posterity the land of the Canaanites, Hittites, Amorites, Perizzites, Jebusites, and Girgashites. These promises of yours you fulfilled, for you are just.

9 "You saw the affliction of our
fathers in Egypt,
you heard their cry by the Red
Sea;
10 You worked signs and wonders
against Pharaoh,
against all his servants and the
people of his land,
Because you knew of their
insolence toward them;
thus you made for yourself a
name even to this day.
11 The sea you divided before them,
on dry ground they passed
through the midst of the sea;
Their pursuers you hurled into
the depths,
like a stone into the mighty
waters.
12 With a column of cloud you led
them by day,
and by night with a column of
fire,
To light the way of their journey,
the way in which they must
travel.
13 On Mount Sinai you came down,
you spoke with them from
heaven;
You gave them just ordinances,
firm laws,
good statutes, and
commandments;
14 Your holy sabbath you made
known to them,
commandments, statutes, and
law you prescribed for
them,
by the hand of Moses your
servant.
15 Food from heaven you gave
them in their hunger,
water from a rock you sent
them in their thirst.

You bade them enter and occupy
the land
which you had sworn with
upraised hand to give them.

16 "But they, our fathers, proved to be insolent; they held their necks stiff and would not obey your commandments. 17 They refused to obey and no longer remembered the miracles you had worked for them. They stiffened their necks and turned their heads to return to their slavery in Egypt. But you are a God of pardons, gracious and compassionate, slow to anger and rich in mercy; you did not forsake them. 18 Though they made for themselves a molten calf, and proclaimed, 'Here is your God who brought you up out of Egypt,' and were guilty of great effronteries, 19 yet in your great mercy you did not forsake them in the desert. The column of cloud did not cease to lead them by day on their journey, nor did the column of fire by night cease to light for them the way by which they were to travel.

20 "Your good spirit you bestowed on them, to give them understanding; your manna you did not withhold from their mouths, and you gave them water in their thirst. 21 Forty years in the desert you sustained them: they did not want; their garments did not become worn, and their feet did not become swollen. 22 You gave them kingdoms and peoples, which you divided up among them as border lands. They possessed the land of Sihon, king of Heshbon, and the land of Og, king of Bashan.

23 "You made their children as numerous as the stars of the heavens, and you brought them into the land which you had commanded their fathers to enter and possess. 24 The sons went in to take possession of the land, and you humbled before them the Canaanite inhabitants of the land and delivered them over into their power, their kings as well as the peoples of the land, to do with them as they would. 25 They captured fortified cities and fertile land; they took possession of houses filled with all good things, cisterns already dug,

---

9, 1–5: This is a continuation of the account concerning the problem of mixed marriages at the time of Ezra; it should be read immediately after Ezr 10, 44.
9, 6–37: The prayer of Ezra which began in Ezr 9, 6f is here continued; see note on Ezr 9, 7.

344

vineyards, olive groves, and fruit trees in abundance. They could eat and have their fill, fatten and feast themselves on your immense good gifts.

26 "But they were contemptuous and rebellious: they cast your law behind their backs, they slew your prophets who bore witness against them in order to bring them back to you, and they were guilty of great effronteries. 27 Therefore you delivered them into the power of their enemies, who oppressed them. But in the time of their oppression they would cry out to you, and you would hear them from heaven, and according to your great mercy give them saviors to deliver them from the power of their enemies.

28 "As soon as they had relief, they would go back to doing evil in your sight. Then again you abandoned them to the power of their enemies, who crushed them. Then they cried out to you, and you heard them from heaven and delivered them according to your mercy, many times over. 29 You bore witness against them, in order to bring them back to your law. But they were insolent and would not obey your commandments; they sinned against your ordinances, from which men draw life when they practice them. They turned stubborn backs, stiffened their necks, and would not obey. 30 You were patient with them for many years, bearing witness against them through your spirit, by means of your prophets; still they would not listen. Thus you delivered them over into the power of the peoples of the lands. 31 Yet in your great mercy you did not completely destroy them and you did not forsake them, for you are a kind and merciful God.

32 "Now, therefore, O our God, great, mighty, and awesome God, you who in your mercy preserve the covenant, take into account all the disasters that have befallen us, our kings, our princes, our priests, our prophets, our fathers, and your entire people, from the time of the kings of Assyria until this day!

33 In all that has come upon us you have been just, for you kept faith while we have done evil. 34 Yes, our kings, our princes, our priests, and our fathers have not kept your law; they paid no attention to your commandments and the obligations of which you reminded them. 35 While they were yet in their kingdom, in the midst of the many good things that you had given them and in the wide and fertile land that you had spread out before them, they did not serve you nor did they turn away from their evil deeds. 36 But, see, we today are slaves; and as for the land which you gave our fathers that they might eat its fruits and good things—see, we have become slaves upon it! 37 Its rich produce goes to the kings whom you have set over us because of our sins, who rule over our bodies and our cattle as they please. We are in great distress!"

Agreement of the People

10 In view of all this, we are entering into a firm pact, which we are putting into writing. On the sealed document appear the names of our princes, our Levites, and our priests.

2 On the sealed document: His Excellency Nehemiah, son of Hacaliah, and Zedekiah.

3 Seraiah, Azariah, Jeremiah, 4 Pashhur, Amariah, Malchijah, 5 Hattush, Shebaniah, Malluch, 6 Harim, Meremoth, Obadiah, 7 Daniel Ginnethon, Baruch, 8 Meshullam, Abijah, Mijamin, 9 Maaziah, Bilgai, Shemaiah: these are the priests.

10 The Levites: Jeshua, son of Azaniah; Binnui, of the sons of Henadad; 11 Kadmiel; and their brethren Shebaniah, Hodiah, Kelita, Pelaiah, Hanan, 12 Mica, Rehob, Hashabiah, 13 Zaccur, Sherebiah, Shebaniah, 14 Hodiah, Bani, Beninu.

15 The leaders of the people: Parosh, Pahath-moab, Elam, Zattu, Bani, 16 Bunni, Azgad, Bebai, 17 Adonijah, Bigvai, Adin, 18 Ater, Hezekiah, Azzur, 19 Hodiah, Hashum, Bezai, 20 Hariph, Anathoth, Nebai, 21 Magpiash, Meshullam, Hezir, 22 Meshezabel, Zadok, Jaddua, 23 Pelatiah, Hanan, Anaiah,

24 Hoshea, Hananiah, Hasshub, 25 Hallohesh, Pilha, Shobek, 26 Rehum, Hashabnah, Maaseiah, 27 Ahiah, Hanan, Anan, 28 Malluch, Harim, Baanah.

Provisions of the Pact

29 The rest of the people, priests, Levites, gatekeepers, singers, temple slaves, and all others who have separated themselves from the peoples of the lands in favor of the law of God, with their wives, their sons, their daughters, all who are of the age of discretion, 30 join with their brethren who are their princes, and with the sanction of a curse take this oath to follow the law of God which was given through Moses, the servant of God, and to observe carefully all the commandments of the LORD, our Lord, his ordinances and his statutes.

31 Agreed, that we will not marry our daughters to the peoples of the land, and that we will not take their daughters for our sons.

32 When the peoples of the land bring in merchandise or any kind of grain for sale on the sabbath day, we will not buy from them on the sabbath or on any other holyday. We will forgo the seventh year, as well as every kind of debt.

33 We impose these commandments on ourselves: to give a third of a shekel each year for the service of the house of our God, 34 for the showbread, for the daily cereal offering, for the daily holocaust, for the sabbaths, new moons, and festivals, for the holy offerings, for sin offerings to make atonement for Israel, and for every service of the house of our God. 35 We, priests, Levites, and people, have determined by lot concerning the procurement of wood: it is to be brought to the house of our God by each of our family houses at stated times each year, to be burnt on the altar of the LORD, our God, as the law prescribes. 36 We have agreed to bring each year to the house of the LORD the first fruits of our fields and of our fruit trees, of whatever kind; 37 also, as is prescribed in the law, to bring to the house of our God, to the priests who serve in the house of our God, the first-born of our children and our animals, including the

---

10, 1–40: This section belongs to the Nehemiah narrative rather than to that of Ezra. It is best read after Neh 13, 31. *In view of all this:* considering the situation described in Neh 13, 4–31.

first-born of our flocks and herds. 38 The first batch of our dough, and our offerings of the fruit of every tree, of wine and of oil, we will bring to the priests, to the chambers of the house of our God. The tithe of our fields we will bring to the Levites; they, the Levites, shall take the tithe in all the cities of our service. 39 An Aaronite priest shall be with the Levites when they take the tithe, and the Levites shall bring the tithe of the tithes to the house of our God, to the chambers of the treasury. 40 For to these chambers the Israelites and Levites bring the offerings of grain, wine, and oil; there also are housed the utensils of the sanctuary, and the ministering priests, the gatekeepers, and the singers. We will not neglect the house of our God.

Repeopling of Jerusalem

11 The leaders of the people took up residence in Jerusalem, and the rest of the people cast lots to bring one man in ten to reside in Jerusalem, the holy city, while the other nine would remain in the other cities. 2 The people applauded all those men who willingly agreed to take up residence in Jerusalem.

The Residents of Jerusalem

3 These are the heads of the province who took up residence in Jerusalem. (In the cities of Judah dwelt lay Israelites, priests, Levites, temple slaves, and the descendants of the slaves of Solomon, each man on the property he owned in his own city.)
4 In Jerusalem dwelt both Judahites and Benjaminites. Of the Judahites: Athaiah, son of Uzziah, son of Zechariah, son of Amariah, son of Shephatiah, son of Mehallalel, of the sons of Perez; 5 Maaseiah, son of Baruch, son of Colhozeh, son of Hazaiah, son of Adaiah, son of Joiarib, son of Zechariah, a son of the Shelanites. 6 The total of the sons of Perez who dwelt in Jerusalem was four hundred and sixty-eight valiant men.
7 These were the Benjaminites:

Sallu, son of Meshullam, son of Joed, son of Pedaiah, son of Kolaiah, son of Maaseiah, son of Ithiel, son of Jeshaiah, 8 and his brethren, warriors, nine hundred and twenty-eight in number. 9 Joel, son of Zichri, was their commander, and Judah, son of Hassenuah, was second in charge of the city.
10 Among the priests were: Jedaiah; Joiarib; Jachin; 11 Seraiah, son of Hilkiah, son of Meshullam, son of Zadok, son of Meraioth, son of Ahitub, the ruler of the house of God, 12 and their brethren who carried out the temple service, eight hundred and twenty-two; Adaiah, son of Jeroham, son of Pelaliah, son of Amzi, son of Zechariah, son of Pashhur, son of Malchijah, 13 and his brethren, family heads, two hundred and forty-two; and Amasai, son of Azarel, son of Ahzai, son of Meshillemoth, son of Immer, 14 and his brethren, warriors, one hundred and twenty-eight. Their commander was Zabdiel, son of Haggadol.
15 Among the Levites were Shemaiah, son of Hasshub, son of Azrikam, son of Hashabiah, son of Bunni; 16 Shabbethai and Jozabad, levitical chiefs who were placed over the external affairs of the house of God; 17 Mattaniah, son of Micah, son of Zabdi, son of Asaph, director of the psalms, who led the thanksgiving at prayer; Bakbukiah, second in rank among his brethren; and Abda, son of Shammua, son of Galal, son of Jeduthun. 18 The total of the Levites in the holy city was two hundred and eighty-four.
19 The gatekeepers were Akkub, Talmon, and their brethren, who kept watch over the gates; one hundred and seventy-two in number.
20 The rest of Israel, including priests and Levites, were in all the other cities of Judah, each man in his inheritance.
21 The temple slaves lived on Ophel. Ziha and Gishpa were in charge of the temple slaves.
22 The prefect of the Levites in Jerusalem was Uzzi, son of Bani, son of Hashabiah, son of Mattaniah, son of Micah; he was one of the sons of

Asaph, the singers appointed to the service of the house of God— 23 for they had been appointed by royal decree, and there was a fixed schedule for the singers assigning them their daily duties.
24 Pethahiah, son of Meshezabel, a descendant of Zerah, son of Judah, was royal deputy in all affairs that concerned the people.

The Other Cities

25 As concerns their villages in the country: Judahites lived in Kiriath-arba and its dependencies, in Dibon and its dependencies, in Jekabzeel and its villages, 26 in Jeshua, Moladah, Beth-pelet, 27 in Hazarshual, in Beer-sheba and its dependencies, 28 in Ziklag, in Meconah and its dependencies, 29 in Enrimmon, Zorah, Jarmuth, 30 Zanoah, Adullam, and their villages, Lachish and its countryside, Azekah and its dependencies. They were settled from Beer-sheba to Ge-hinnom.
31 Benjaminites were in Geba, Michmash, Aija, Bethel and its dependencies, 32 Anathoth, Nob, Ananiah, 33 Hazor, Ramah, Gittaim, 34 Hadid, Zeboim, Neballat, 35 Lod, Ono, and the Valley of the Artisans.
36 Some sections of the Levites from Judah settled in Benjamin.

Priests and Levites under Zerubbabel

12 The following are the priests and Levites who returned with Zerubbabel, son of Shealtiel, and Jeshua: Seraiah, Jeremiah, Ezra, 2 Amariah, Malluch, Hattush, 3 Shecaniah, Rehum, Meremoth, 4 Iddo, Ginnethon, Abijah, 5 Mijamin, Maadiah, Bilgah, 6 Shemaiah and Joiarib, Jedaiah, 7 Sallu, Amok, Hilkiah, Jedaiah. These were the priestly heads and their brethren in the days of Jeshua.
8 The Levites were Jeshua, Binnui, Kadmiel, Sherebiah, Judah, Mattaniah, the last-mentioned, together with his brethren, was in charge of the hymns, 9 while Bakbukiah and

---

11, 1–19: This list of the family heads who lived in Jerusalem at the time of Nehemiah is best read after 7, 72a. It is basically the same as that given in 1 Chr 9, 2–17, but there are many differences between the two lists.

Unno and their brethren ministered opposite them by turns.

High Priests

10 Jeshua became the father of Joiakim, Joiakim became the father of Eliashib, and Eliashib became the father of Joiada, 11 Joiada become the father of Johanan, and Johanan became the father of Jaddua.

Priests and Levites under Joiakim

12 In the days of Joiakim these were the priestly family heads: for Seraiah, Meraiah; for Jeremiah, Hananiah; 13 for Ezra, Meshullam; for Amariah, Jehohanan; 14 for Malluchi, Jonathan; for Shebaniah, Joseph; 15 for Harim, Adna; for Meremoth, Helkai; 16 for Iddo, Zechariah; for Ginnethon, Meshullam; 17 for Abijah, Zichri; for Miamin, ... ; for Maadiah, Piltai; 18 for Bilgah, Shammua; for Shemaiah, Jehonathan; 19 and for Joiarib, Mattenai; for Jedaiah, Uzzi; 20 for Sallu, Kallai; for Amok, Eber; 21 for Hilkiah, Hashabiah; for Jedaiah, Nethanel.

22 In the time of Eliashib, Joiada, Johanan, and Jaddua, the family heads of the priests were written down in the Book of Chronicles, up until the reign of Darius the Persian. 23 The sons of Levi: the family heads were written down in the Book of Chronicles, up until the time of Johanan, the son of Eliashib. 24 The heads of the Levites were Hashabiah, Sherebiah, Jeshua, Binnui, Kadmiel. Their brethren who stood opposite them to sing praises and thanksgiving in fulfillment of the command of David, the man of God, one section opposite the other, 25 were Mattaniah, Bakbukiah, Obadiah.

Meshullam, Talmon, and Akkub were gatekeepers. They kept watch over the storerooms at the gates.

26 All these lived in the time of Joiakim, son of Jeshua, son of Jozadak [and in the time of Nehemiah the governor and of Ezra the priest-scribe].

Dedication of the City Wall

27 At the dedication of the wall of Jerusalem, the Levites were sought out wherever they lived and were brought to Jerusalem to celebrate a joyful dedication with thanksgiving hymns and the music of cymbals, harps, and lyres. 28 The levitical singers gathered together from the region about Jerusalem, from the villages of the Netophathites, 29 from Beth-gilgal, and from the plains of Geba and Azmaveth (for the singers had built themselves settlements about Jerusalem). 30 The priests and Levites first purified themselves, then they purified the people, the gates, and the wall.

31 I had the princes of Judah mount the wall, and I arranged two great choirs. The first of these proceeded to the right, along the top of the wall, in the direction of the Dung Gate, 32 followed by Hoshaiah and half the princes of Judah, 33 along with Azariah, Ezra, Meshullam, 34 Judah, Benjamin, Shemaiah, and Jeremiah, 35 priests with trumpets, and also Zechariah, son of Jonathan, son of Shemaiah, son of Mattaniah, son of Micaiah, son of Zaccur, son of Asaph, 36 and his brethren Shemaiah, Azarel, Milalai, Gilalai, Maai, Nethanel, Judah, and Hanani, with the musical instruments of David, the man of God. [Ezra the scribe was at their head.] 37 At the Spring Gate they went straight up by the steps of the city of David and continued along the top of the wall above the house of David until they came to the Water Gate on the east.

38 The second choir proceeded to the left, followed by myself and the other half of the princes of the people,

along the top of the wall past the Oven Tower as far as the Broad Wall, then past the Ephraim Gate 39 [the New City Gate], the Fish Gate, the Tower of Hananel, and the Hundred Tower, as far as the Sheep Gate [and they came to halt at the Prison Gate].

40 The two choirs took up a position in the house of God; I, too, who had with me half the magistrates, 41 the priests Eliakim, Maaseiah, Minjamin, Micaiah, Elioenai, Zechariah, Hananiah, with the trumpets, 42 and Maaseiah, Shemaiah, Eleazar, Uzzi, Jehohanan, Malchijah, Elam, and Ezer. The singers were heard under the leadership of Jezrahiah. 43 Great sacrifices were offered on that day, and there was rejoicing over the great feast of the Lord in which they shared. The women and the children joined in, and the rejoicing at Jerusalem could be heard from afar off.

Offerings for Priests and Levites

44 At that time men were appointed over the chambers set aside for stores, offerings, first fruits and tithes; in them they were to collect from the fields of the various cities the portions legally assigned to the priests and Levites. For Judah rejoiced in its appointed priests and Levites 45 who carried out the ministry of their God and the ministry of purification (as did the singers and the gatekeepers) in accordance with the prescriptions of David and of Solomon, his son. 46 For the heads of the families of the singers and the hymns of praise and thanksgiving to God came down from the days of David and Asaph in times of old. 47 Thus all Israel, in the days of Zerubbabel [and in the days of Nehemiah], gave the singers and the gatekeepers their portions, according to their daily needs. They made their consecrated offering to the Levites, and the Levites made theirs to the sons of Aaron.

12, 10f: *Jeshua,* the high priest when Zerubbabel was governor, i.e., the last decades of the sixth century B.C. (Hg 1, 1.12.14; 2, 2.4). He was the grandfather of *Eliashib,* the high priest at least in the early period of Nehemiah's governorship, i.e., 445–433 B.C. (Ezr 10, 6; Neh 3, 1.20f; 13, 4.7). Eliashib, in turn, was the grandfather of *Johanan,* a grown man, if not yet a high priest, at the time of Ezra, i.e., c. 400 B.C. (Ezr 10, 6; and note). According to Josephus (*Antiquities* XI, v), whose testimony here is doubtful, *Jaddua,* son of

Johanan, died as an old man about the time that Alexander the Great died, i.e., 323 B.C. If this list of the postexilic high priests, at least as far as Johanan, comes, as seems probable (cf v 23), from the Chronicler himself and not from a later scribe, it is of prime importance for dating the Chronicler's work in the first decades of the fourth century B.C.

12, 27–43: *The dedication of the wall of Jerusalem* took place, no doubt, soon after the restoration of the wall and its gates had been completed. Therefore, this

section is best read after 6, 15.

12, 44–47: This account of the provisions made for the temple services is apparently a composition of the Chronicler. *At that time:* a mere connective: no particular time is meant, but the account fits best after that of the restoration of the temple (Ezr 6, 13–18) in the days of Zerubbabel (v 47). The gloss mentioning Nehemiah is not in the ancient Greek version.

Separation from Aliens

13 At that time, when there was reading from the book of Moses in the hearing of the people, it was found written there that "no Ammonite or Moabite may ever be admitted into the assembly of God; 2 for they would not succor the Israelites with food and water, but they hired Balaam to curse them, though our God turned the curse into a blessing." 3 When they had heard the law, they separated from Israel every foreign element.

Reform in the Temple

4 Before this, the priest Eliashib, who had been placed in charge of the chambers of the house of our God and who was an associate of Tobiah, 5 had set aside for the latter's use a large chamber in which had been previously stored the cereal offerings, incense and utensils, the tithes in grain, wine, and oil allotted to the Levites, singers, and gatekeepers, and the offerings due the priests. 6 During all this time I had not been in Jerusalem, for in the thirty-second year of Artaxerxes, king of Babylon, I had gone back to the king. After due time, however, I asked leave of the king 7 and returned to Jerusalem, where I discovered the evil thing that Eliashib had done for Tobiah, in setting aside for him a chamber in the courts of the house of God. 8 This displeased me very much, and I had all of Tobiah's household goods thrown outside the chamber. 9 Then I gave orders to purify the chambers, and I had them replace there the utensils of the house of God, the cereal offerings, and the incense.

10 I learned, too, that the portions due the Levites were no longer being given, so that the Levites and the singers who should have been carrying out the services had deserted each man to his own field. 11 I took the magistrates to task, demanding, "Why is the house of God abandoned?" Then I brought the Levites together and had them resume their stations. 12 All Judah once more brought in the tithes of grain, wine, and oil to the storerooms; 13 and in charge of the storerooms I appointed the priest Shelemiah, Zadok the scribe, and Pedaiah, one of the Levites together with Hanan, son of Zaccur, son of Mattaniah, as their assistant; for these men were held to be trustworthy. It was their duty to make the distribution to their brethren. 14 Remember this to my credit, O my God! Let not the devotion which I showed for the house of my God and its services be forgotten!

Sabbath Observance

15 In those days I perceived that men in Judah were treading the winepresses on the sabbath; that they were bringing in the sheaves of grain, loading them on their asses, together with wine, grapes, figs, and every other kind of burden, and bringing them to Jerusalem on the sabbath day. I warned them to sell none of these victuals. 16 In Jerusalem itself the Tyrians who were resident there were importing fish and every other kind of merchandise and selling it to the Judahites on the sabbath. 17 I took the nobles of Judah to task, demanding of them: "What is this evil thing you are doing, profaning the sabbath day? 18 Did not your fathers act in this same way, with the result that our God brought all this evil upon us and upon this city? Would you add to the wrath against Israel by once more profaning the sabbath?"

19 When the shadows were falling on the gates of Jerusalem before the sabbath, I ordered the doors to be closed and forbade them to be reopened till after the sabbath. I posted some of my own men at the gates so that no burden might enter on the sabbath day. 20 The merchants and sellers of various kinds of merchandise spent the night once or twice outside Jerusalem, 21 but then I warned them, saying to them: "Why do you spend the night alongside the wall? If you keep this up, I will lay hands on you!" From that time on they did not return on the sabbath. 22 Then I ordered the Levites to purify themselves and to go and watch the gates, so that the sabbath day might be kept holy. This, too, remember in my favor, O my God, and have mercy on me in accordance with your great mercy!

Mixed Marriages

23 Also in those days I saw Jews who had married Ashdodite, Ammonite, or Moabite wives. 24 Of their children, half spoke Ashdodite, and none of them knew how to speak Jewish; and so it was in regard to the languages of the various other peoples. 25 I took them to task and cursed them; I had some of them beaten and their hair pulled out; and I adjured them by God: "You shall not marry your daughters to their sons nor take any of their daughters for your sons or for yourselves! 26 Did not Solomon, the king of Israel, sin because of them? Though among the many nations there was no king like him, and though he was beloved of his God and God had made him king over all Israel, yet even he was made to sin by foreign women. 27 Must it also be heard of you that you have done this same great evil, betraying our God by marrying foreign women?"

28 One of the sons of Joiada, son of Eliashib the high priest, was the son-in-law of Sanballat the Horonite! I drove him from my presence. 29 Remember against them, O my God, how they defiled the priesthood and the covenant of the priesthood and the Levites!

30 Thus I cleansed them of all foreign contamination. I established the various functions for the priests and Levites so that each had his appointed task. 31 I also provided for the procurement of wood at stated times and for the first fruits. Remember this in my favor, O my God!

13, 1ff: These verses were composed by the Chronicler to serve as an introduction to the reforms that Nehemiah instituted during his second mission in Jerusalem (vv 4–31). The part of *the book of Moses* read to the people is freely quoted here from Dt 23, 3–6.

13, 4–31: This is part of the "Memoirs of Nehemiah"; it is continued in 10, 1–40.
13, 6: *After due time:* It is not known when Nehemiah returned to Jerusalem or how long his second period of activity there lasted, but it probably ended before Ezra came to Palestine; see note on Ezr 7, 1–8.
13, 24: *Ashdodite:* the language spoken at Ashdod, more likely an Aramaic rather than a Philistine dialect. *Jewish:* Hebrew as spoken in postexilic Judah.

Tobit

THIS book tells the story of Tobit, son of Tobiel, son of Hananiel, son of Aduel, son of Gabael of the family of Asiel, of the tribe of Naphtali, 2 who during the reign of Shalmaneser, king of Assyria, was taken captive from Thisbe, which is south of Kedesh Naphtali in upper Galilee, above and to the west of Asser, north of Phogor.

TOBIT'S ORDEALS

His Virtue

3 I, Tobit have walked all the days of my life on the paths of truth and righteousness. I performed many charitable works for my kinsmen and my people have been deported with me to Nineveh, in Assyria. 4 When I lived as a young man in my own country, Israel, the entire tribe of my forefather Naphtali had broken away from the house of David and from Jerusalem. This city had been singled out of all Israel's tribes, so that they all might offer sacrifice in the place where the temple, God's dwelling, had been built and consecrated for all generations to come. 5 All my kinsmen, like the rest of the tribe of my forefather Naphtali, used to offer sacrifice on all the mountains of Galilee as well as to the young bull which Jeroboam, king of Israel, had made in Dan.

6 I, for my part, would often make the pilgrimage alone to Jerusalem for the festivals, as is prescribed for all Israel by perpetual decree. Bringing with me the first fruits of the field and the firstlings of the flock, together with a tenth of my income and the first shearings of the sheep, I would hasten to Jerusalem 7 and present them to the priests, Aaron's sons, at the altar. To the Levites who were doing service in Jerusalem I would give the tithe of grain, wine, olive oil, pomegranates, figs, and other fruits. And except for sabbatical years, I used to give a second tithe in money, which each year I would go and disburse in Jerusalem. 8 The third tithe I gave to orphans and widows, and to converts who were living with the Israelites. Every third year I would bring them this offering, and we ate it in keeping with the decree of the Mosaic law and the commands of Deborah, the mother of my father Tobiel; for when my father died, he left me an orphan.

9 When I reached manhood, I married Anna, a woman of our own lineage. By her I had a son whom I named Tobiah. 10 Now, after I had been deported to Nineveh, all my brothers and relatives ate the food of heathens, 11 but I refrained from eating that kind of food. 12 Because of this wholehearted service of God, 13 the Most High granted me favor and status with Shalmaneser, so that I became purchasing agent for all his needs. 14 Every now and then until his death I would go to Media to buy goods for him. I also deposited several pouches containing a great sum of money with my

---

1, 1: *Tobit:* in the fragments of the book found at Qumran, is given as *Tôbi*, an abbreviated form of *Tôbiyāh* (v 9; Ezr 2, 60) or of *Tôbiyāhû* (2 Chr 17, 8), a name which means "Yahweh is good." *Tobiel,* "God is good"; *Hananiel,* "God is merciful." The book abounds in theophoric names.

1, 2: *Shalmaneser* (V) (727–722 B.C.): began the siege of Samaria; the inhabitants of the northern kingdom were taken into captivity by his successor, Sargon II (722–705). *Thisbe* and *Phogor:* towns of Galilee

that have not been identified; Thisbe in Gilead was perhaps the birthplace of Elijah. *Kedesh:* cf Jos 20, 7. *Asser:* Hazor (Jos 11, 1).

1, 5: Jeroboam established sanctuaries in Dan and Bethel so that the people would no longer go to Jerusalem for the festivals. The gold statues of bulls which he placed in the sanctuaries were considered the throne of Yahweh; but the people soon came to worship the images themselves. Jeroboam also encouraged the high places or hilltop shrines (1 Kgs 12, 26–33).

1, 6ff: *Perpetual decree:* Dt 12, 11.13–14. Refusing to worship at Jeroboam's shrines, the faithful Tobit continued to bring his offerings to Jerusalem; see 2 Chr 11, 16. For the various tithes, cf Nm 18, 20–32; 2 Chr 31, 4–6; Dt 14, 22–29; 26, 12f.

1, 14: *A great sum of money:* literally, "ten silver talents," about ten thousand dollars. *Rages:* modern Rai, about five miles southeast of Teheran. *Media:* the northwestern part of modern Iran.

kinsman Gabael, son of Gabri, who lived at Rages, in Media. 15 But when Shalmaneser died and his son Sennacherib succeeded him as king, the roads to Media became unsafe, so I could no longer go there.

Courage in Burying the Dead

16 During Shalmaneser's reign I performed many charitable works for my kinsmen and my people. 17 I would give my bread to the hungry and my clothing to the naked. If I saw one of my people who had died and been thrown outside the walls of Nineveh, I would bury him. 18 I also buried anyone whom Sennacherib slew when he returned as a fugitive from Judea during the days of judgment decreed against him by the heavenly King because of the blasphemies he had uttered. In his rage he killed many Israelites, but I used to take their bodies by stealth and bury them; so when Sennacherib looked for them, he could not find them. 19 But a certain citizen of Nineveh informed the king that it was I who buried the dead. When I found out that the king knew all about me and wanted to put me to death, I went into hiding; then in my fear I took flight. 20 Afterward, all my property was confiscated; I was left with nothing. All that I had was taken to the king's palace, except for my wife Anna and my son Tobiah. 21 But less than forty days later the king was assassinated by two of his sons, who then escaped into the mountains of Ararat. His son Esarhaddon, who succeeded him as king, placed Ahiqar, my brother Anael's son, in charge of all the accounts of his kingdom, so that he took control over the entire administration. 22 Then Ahiqar interceded on my behalf, and I was able to return to Nineveh. For under Sennacherib, king of Assyria, Ahiqar had been

chief cup-bearer, keeper of the seal, administrator, and treasurer; and Esarhaddon reappointed him. He was a close relative—in fact, my nephew.

2 Thus under King Esarhaddon I returned to my home, and my wife Anna and my son Tobiah were restored to me. Then on the festival of Pentecost, the feast of Weeks, a fine dinner was prepared for me, and I reclined to eat. 2 The table was set for me, and when many different dishes were placed before me, I said to my son Tobiah: "My son, go out and try to find a poor man from among our kinsmen exiled here in Nineveh. If he is a sincere worshiper of God, bring him back with you, so that he can share this meal with me. Indeed, son, I shall wait for you to come back."

3 Tobiah went out to look for some poor kinsman of ours. When he returned he exclaimed, "Father!" I said to him, "What is it, son?" He answered, "Father, one of our people has been murdered! His body lies in the market place where he was just strangled!" 4 I sprang to my feet, leaving the dinner untouched; and I carried the dead man from the street and put him in one of the rooms, so that I might bury him after sunset. 5 Returning to my own quarters, I washed myself and ate my food in sorrow. 6 I was reminded of the oracle pronounced by the prophet Amos against Bethel:

"Your festivals shall be turned
    into mourning,
And all your songs into
    lamentation."

7 And I wept. Then at sunset I went out, dug a grave, and buried him. 8 The neighbors mocked me, saying to one another: "Will this man never learn! Once before he was hunted down for execution because

of this very thing; yet now that he has escaped, here he is again burying the dead!"

Tobit's Blindness

9 That same night I bathed, and went to sleep next to the wall of my courtyard. Because of the heat I left my face uncovered. 10 I did not know there were birds perched on the wall above me, till their warm droppings settled in my eyes, causing cataracts. I went to see some doctors for a cure, but the more they anointed my eyes with various salves, the worse the cataracts became, until I could see no more. For four years I was deprived of eyesight, and all my kinsmen were grieved at my condition. Ahiqar, however, took care of me for two years, until he left for Elymais.

11 At that time my wife Anna worked for hire at weaving cloth, the kind of work women do. 12 When she sent back the goods to their owners, they would pay her. Late in winter she finished the cloth and sent it back to the owners. They paid her the full salary, and also gave her a young goat for the table. 13 On entering my house the goat began to bleat. I called to my wife and said: "Where did this goat come from? Perhaps it was stolen! Give it back to its owners; we have no right to eat stolen food!" 14 But she said to me, "It was given to me as a bonus over and above my wages." Yet I would not believe her, and told her to give it back to its owners. I became very angry with her over this. So she retorted: "Where are your charitable deeds now? Where are your virtuous acts? See! Your true character is finally showing itself!"

3 Grief-stricken in spirit, I groaned and wept aloud. Then with sobs I began to pray:

1, 15: *Sennacherib* (705–681 B.C.): the son of Sargon (722–705 B.C.); neither was descended from Shalmaneser. Inconsistencies such as this point to the fact that the book of Tobit is a religious novel (see Introduction; also notes on 5, 6 and 14, 15).

1, 17–18: Tobit risked his own life to bury the dead. Deprivation of burial was viewed with horror by the Jews. Cf 4, 3–4; 6, 15; 14, 12–13.

1, 21: *Esarhaddon:* 681–669 B.C. *Ahiqar:* a hero of ancient folklore, known for his outstanding wisdom. The *Story* (or *Wisdom*) *of Ahiqar* was very popular in antiquity and is extant in many different forms:

Aramaic, Syriac, Armenian, Arabic (*Arabian Nights*), Greek (*Aesop's Fables*), Slavonic, Ethiopic, and Romanian. The sacred author makes Tobit the uncle of the famous Ahiqar in order to enhance Tobit's own prestige. See note on 14, 10.

2, 1: *The feast of Weeks:* also called by its Greek name *Pentecost*, was celebrated fifty days after the Passover. Cf Lv 23, 15–21; Dt 16, 9–12.

2, 2: Almsgiving and charity to the poor are important virtues taught by the book (4, 7–11.16f; 14, 10f).

2, 5: *I washed myself:* because of ritual defilement

from touching a corpse (Nm 19, 11–13).

2, 10: *Cataracts:* literally, "white scales, or films." *Elymais:* the Greek name of ancient Elam, a district northeast of the head of the Persian Gulf.

2, 12: *Late in winter:* literally "seventh of Dystros," the Macedonian month which corresponds to the Jewish month of Shebat (January-February). *For the table:* literally, "for the hearth"; the gift had probably been made in view of some springtime festival like the Jewish Purim.

2, 14: Anna's sharp rebuke calls to mind the words of Job's wife (Jb 2, 9).

Tobit's Prayer for Death

2 "You are righteous, O Lord,
   and all your deeds are just;
All your ways are mercy and
      truth;
   you are the judge of the world.

3 And now, O Lord, may you be
      mindful of me,
   and look with favor upon me.
Punish me not for my sins,
   nor for my inadvertent
      offenses,
   nor for those of my fathers,

"They have sinned against you,
4   and disobeyed your
         commandments.
So you handed us over to
      plundering, exile, and death,
   till we were an object lesson, a
         byword, a reproach
   in all the nations among
      whom you scattered us.

5 "Yes, your judgments are many
      and true
   in dealing with me as my sins
   and those of my fathers
      deserve.
For we have not kept your
      commandments,
   nor have we trodden the paths
      of truth before you.

6 "So now, deal with me as you
      please,
   and command my life breath
      to be taken from me,
   that I may go from the face of
      the earth into dust.
It is better for me to die than to
      live,
   because I have heard insulting
      calumnies,
   and I am overwhelmed with
      grief.

"Lord, command me to be
      delivered from such anguish;
   let me go to the everlasting
      abode;
   Lord, refuse me not.

For it is better for me to die
   than to endure so much misery
      in life,
   and to hear these insults!"

SARAH'S PLIGHT

Sarah Falsely Accused

7 On the same day, at Ecbatana in
Media, it so happened that Raguel's
daughter Sarah also had to listen to
abuse, from one of her father's maids.
8 For she had been married to seven
husbands, but the wicked demon
Asmodeus killed them off before they
could have intercourse with her, as it
is prescribed for wives. So the maid
said to her: "You are the one who
strangles your husbands! Look at
you! You have already been married
seven times, but you have had no joy
with any one of your husbands. 9
Why do you beat us? Because your
husbands are dead? Then why not
join them! May we never see a son or
daughter of yours!"

10 That day she was deeply grieved
in spirit. She went in tears to an upstairs room in her father's house with
the intention of hanging herself. But
she reconsidered, saying to herself:
"No! People would level this insult
against my father: 'You had only one
beloved daughter, but she hanged
herself because of ill fortune!' And
thus would I cause my father in his
old age to go down to the nether
world laden with sorrow. It is far
better for me not to hang myself, but
to beg the Lord to have me die, so
that I need no longer live to hear such
insults."

11 At that time, then, she spread
out her hands, and facing the window
poured out this prayer:

Sarah's Prayer for Death

"Blessed are you, O Lord,
   merciful God!
Forever blessed and honored
   is your holy name;
   may all your works forever
      bless you.

12 And now, O Lord, to you I turn
      my face
   and raise my eyes.
13 Bid me to depart from the earth,
   never again to hear such insults.

14 "You know, O Master, that I am
      innocent
   of any impure act with a man,
15 And that I have never defiled my
      own name
   or my father's name in the
      land of my exile.

"I am my father's only daughter,
   and he has no other child to
      make his heir,
Nor does he have a close
      kinsman or other relative
   whom I might bide my time to
      marry.
I have already lost seven
      husbands;
   why then should I live any
      longer?
But if it please you, Lord, not to
      slay me,
   look favorably upon me and
      have pity on me:
   never again let me hear these
      insults!"

An Answer to Prayer

16 At that very time, the prayer of
these two suppliants was heard in the
glorious presence of Almighty God.
17 So Raphael was sent to heal them
both: to remove the cataracts from
Tobit's eyes, so that he might again
see God's sunlight; and to marry
Raguel's daughter Sarah to Tobit's
son Tobiah, and then drive the
wicked demon Asmodeus from her.
For Tobiah had the right to claim her
before any other who might wish to
marry her.

In the very moment that Tobit returned from the courtyard to his
house, Raguel's daughter Sarah came
downstairs from her room.

3, 6: *It is better for me to die than to live:* in his distress Tobit uses the words of the petulant Jonah (Jon
4, 3.8), who wished to die because God did not destroy
the hated Ninevites. In similar circumstances, Moses
(Nm 11, 15), Elijah (1 Kgs 19, 4), and Job (Jb 7, 15)
also prayed for death. *Everlasting abode:* a reference
to Sheol, the dismal abode of the dead from which no
one returns (Jb 7, 9–10; 14, 12; Is 26, 14). The revelation of a blessed immortality had not yet been made.
See note on 4, 6.

3, 7: From here on, the story is told in the third
person. V 7 relates one of the several marvelous co-
incidences which the storyteller uses to heighten
interest; see also vv 16.17; 4, 1; 5, 4. *Ecbatana:* Hama-
dan in modern Iran; this was the capital of ancient
Media. *Raguel:* "friend of God."

3, 8: *Asmodeus:* in Persian *aeshma daeva*, "demon
of wrath," adopted into Aramaic with the sense of
"the Destroyer." He will be subdued (8, 3) by Raphael
(v 17), "God heals."

3, 11: *Facing the window:* that is, looking toward
Jerusalem; cf Dn 6, 11.
Blessed are you and "Blessed be God" are traditional openings of Jewish prayers (8, 5.15; 11, 14; 13,
1).

3, 17: *Tobiah had the right:* according to the
patriarchal custom of marriage within the family
group. Tobiah was Sarah's closest eligible relative
(6, 12). Cf 4, 12–13; Gn 24.

TOBIAH'S JOURNEY AND MARRIAGE TO SARAH

A Father's Instruction

4 That same day Tobit remembered the money he had deposited with Gabael at Rages in Media, 2 and he thought, "Now that I have asked for death, why should I not call my son Tobiah and let him know about this money before I die?" 3 So he called his son Tobiah; and when he came, he said to him: "My son, when I die, give me a decent burial. Honor your mother, and do not abandon her as long as she lives. Do whatever pleases her, and do not grieve her spirit in any way. 4 Remember, my son, that she went through many trials for your sake while you were in her womb. And when she dies, bury her in the same grave with me.

5 "Through all your days, my son, keep the Lord in mind, and suppress every desire to sin or to break his commandments. Perform good works all the days of your life, and do not tread the paths of wrongdoing. 6 For if you are steadfast in your service, your good works will bring success, not only to you, but also to all those who live uprightly.

7 "Give alms from your possessions. Do not turn your face away from any of the poor, and God's face will not be turned away from you. 8 Son, give alms in proportion to what you own. If you have great wealth, give alms out of your abundance; if you have but little, distribute even some of that. But do not hesitate to give alms; 9 you will be storing up a goodly treasure for yourself against the day of adversity. 10 Almsgiving frees one from death, and keeps one from going into the dark abode. 11 Alms are a worthy offering in the sight of the Most High for all who give them.

12 "Be on your guard, son, against every form of immorality, and above all, marry a woman of the lineage of your forefathers. Do not marry a stranger who is not of your father's tribe, because we are sons of the prophets. My boy, keep in mind Noah, Abraham, Isaac, and Jacob, our fathers from of old: all of them took wives from among their own kinsmen and were blessed in their children. Remember that their posterity shall inherit the land. 13 Therefore, my son, love your kinsmen. Do not be so proudhearted toward your kinsmen, the sons and daughters of your people, as to refuse to take a wife for yourself from among them. For in such arrogance there is ruin and great disorder. Likewise, in worthlessness there is decay and dire poverty, for worthlessness is the mother of famine.

14 "Do not keep with you overnight the wages of any man who works for you, but pay him immediately. If you thus behave as God's servant, you will receive your reward. Keep a close watch on yourself, my son, in everything you do, and discipline yourself in all your conduct. 15 Do to no one what you yourself dislike. Do not drink wine till you become drunk, nor let drunkenness accompany you on your way.

16 "Give to the hungry some of your bread, and to the naked some of your clothing. Whatever you have left over, give away as alms; and do not begrudge the alms you give. 17 Be lavish with your bread and wine at the burial of the virtuous, but do not share them with sinners.

18 "Seek counsel from every wise man, and do not think lightly of any advice that can be useful. 19 At all times bless the Lord God, and ask him to make all your paths straight and to grant success to all your endeavors and plans. For no pagan nation possesses good counsel, but the Lord himself gives all good things. If the Lord chooses, he raises a man up; but if he should decide otherwise, he casts him down to the deepest recesses of the nether world. So now, my son, keep in mind my commandments, and never let them be erased from your heart.

20 "And now, son, I wish to inform you that I have deposited a great sum of money with Gabri's son Gabael at Rages in Media. 21 Do not be discouraged, my child, because of our poverty. You will be a rich man if you fear God, avoid all sin, and do what is right before the Lord your God."

The Angel Raphael

5 Then Tobiah replied to his father Tobit: "Everything that you have commanded me, father, I will do. 2 But how shall I be able to obtain the money from him, since he does not know me nor do I know him? What can I show him to make him recognize me and trust me, so that he will give me the money? I do not even know which roads to take for the journey into Media!" 3 Tobit answered his son Tobiah: "We exchanged signatures on a document written in duplicate; I divided it into two parts, and each of us kept one; his copy I put with the money. Think of it, twenty years have already passed since I deposited that money! So now, my son, find yourself a trustworthy man who will make the journey with you. We will, of course, give him a salary when you return; but get back that money from Gabael."

4 Tobiah went to look for someone acquainted with the roads who would travel with him to Media. As soon as he went out, he found the angel Raphael standing before him, though he did not know that this was an angel of God. 5 Tobiah said to him, "Who are you, young man?" He replied, "I am an Israelite, one of

---

4, 3–19: A collection of maxims which parallel those in the wisdom literature, especially Prv and Sir (see Introduction): duties toward parents (3–4); cf also 14, 13; perseverance in virtue and avoidance of evil (5–6.14b); necessity and value of almsgiving and charity (7–11.16–17); marriage to a kinsman (12–13a); industry (13b); prompt payment of wages (14a); the golden rule (15a); temperance (15b); docility (18); prayer (19).

4, 6: Before the revelation of retribution for all men in the afterlife—a doctrine taught in the Book of Wisdom—Old Testament man believed that virtue guaranteed earthly prosperity, and sin earthly disaster (cf Dt 28).

4, 17: Tobit counsels his son either to give alms in honor of the dead, or, more probably, to give the "bread of consolation" to the family of the deceased. Cf Jer 16, 7; Ez 24, 17.

4, 19: Prayer is the foundation of a moral life.

5, 3: *Document:* in Greek *cheirographon*. In the Middle Ages, notably in England, a deed and its duplicate were written on one piece of parchment, with the Latin word *chirographum* inscribed across the top of the sheet or between the two copies of the text. The document was then cut in two in either a straight or a wavy line, the parts being given to the persons concerned. Perhaps this procedure derived from the present verse of Tobit. Duplicate documents, usually one open and the other sealed, are well known from the ancient Near East.

5, 4: *He did not know:* The theme of an angel in disguise occurs frequently in folklore as well as in the Old Testament (Gn 18; cf Heb 13, 2).

your kinsmen. I have come here to work." Tobiah said, "Do you know the way to Media?" 6 The other replied: "Yes, I have been there many times. I know the place well and I know all the routes. I have often traveled to Media; I used to stay with our kinsman Gabael, who lives at Rages in Media. It is a good two day's travel from Ecbatana to Rages, for Rages is situated at the mountains, Ecbatana out on the plateau." 7 Tobiah said to him, "Wait for me, young man, till I go back and tell my father; for I need you to make the journey with me. I will, of course, pay you." 8 Raphael replied, "Very well, I will wait for you; but do not be long."

9 Tobiah went back to tell his father Tobit what had happened. He said to him, "I have just found a man who is one of our own Israelite kinsmen!" Tobit said, "Call the man, so that I may find out what family and tribe he comes from, and whether he is trustworthy enough to travel with you, son." Tobiah went out to summon the man, saying, "Young man, my father would like to see you."

10 When Raphael entered the house, Tobit greeted him first. Raphael said, "Hearty greetings to you!" Tobit replied: "What joy is left for me any more? Here I am, a blind man who cannot see God's sunlight, but must remain in darkness, like the dead who no longer see the light! Though alive, I am among the dead. I can hear a man's voice, but I cannot see him." Raphael said, "Take courage! God has healing in store for you; so take courage!" Tobit then said: "My son Tobiah wants to go to Media. Can you go with him to show him the way? I will of course pay you, brother." Raphael answered: "Yes, I can go with him, for I know all the routes. I have often traveled to Media and crossed all its plains and mountains; so I know every road well." 11 Tobit asked,

"Brother, tell me, please, what family and tribe are you from?" 12 Raphael said: "Why? Do you need a tribe and a family? Or are you looking for a hired man to travel with your son?" Tobit replied, "I wish to know truthfully whose son you are, brother, and what your name is."

13 Raphael answered, "I am Azariah, son of Hananiah the elder, one of your own kinsmen." 14 Tobit exclaimed: "Welcome! God save you, brother! Do not be provoked with me, brother, for wanting to learn the truth about your family. So it turns out that you are a kinsman, and from a noble and good line! I knew Hananiah and Nathaniah, the two sons of Shemaiah the elder; with me they used to make the pilgrimage to Jerusalem, where we would worship together. No, they did not stray from the right path; your kinsmen are good men. You are certainly of good lineage, and welcome!"

15 Then he added: "For each day you are away I will give you the normal wages, plus expenses for you and for my son. If you go with my son, 16 I will even add a bonus to your wages!" Raphael replied: "I will go with him; have no fear. In good health we shall leave you, and in good health we shall return to you, for the way is safe." 17 Tobit said, "God bless you, brother." Then he called his son and said to him: "My son, prepare whatever you need for the journey, and set out with your kinsman. May God in heaven protect you on the way and bring you back to me safe and sound; and may his angel accompany you for safety, my son."

Before setting out on his journey, Tobiah kissed his father and mother. Tobit said to him, "Have a safe journey." 18 But his mother began to weep. She said to Tobit: "Why have you decided to send my child away? Is he not the staff to which we cling, ever there with us in all that we

do? 19 I hope more money is not your chief concern! Rather let it be a ransom for our son! 20 What the Lord has given us to live on is certainly enough for us." 21 Tobit reassured her: "Have no such thought. Our son will leave in good health and come back to us in good health. Your own eyes will see the day when he returns to you safe and sound. 22 So, no such thought; do not worry about them, my love. For a good angel will go with him, his journey will be successful, and he will return unharmed." 1 Then

6

she stopped weeping.

Journey to Rages

2 When the boy left home, accompanied by the angel, the dog followed Tobiah out of the house and went with them. The travelers walked till nightfall, and made camp beside the Tigris River. 3 Now when the boy went down to wash his feet in the river, a large fish suddenly leaped out of the water and tried to swallow his foot. He shouted in alarm. 4 But the angel said to him, "Take hold of the fish and don't let it get away!" The boy seized the fish and hauled it up on the shore. 5 The angel then told him: "Cut the fish open and take out its gall, heart, and liver, and keep them with you; but throw away the entrails. Its gall, heart, and liver make useful medicines." 6 After the lad had cut the fish open, he put aside the gall, heart, and liver. Then he broiled and ate part of the fish; the rest he salted and kept for the journey.

Raphael's Instructions

7 Afterward they traveled on together till they were near Media. The boy asked the angel this question: "Brother Azariah, what medicinal value is there in the fish's heart, liver, and gall?" 8 He answered: "As regards the fish's heart and liver, if you burn them so that the smoke surrounds a man or a woman who is

---

5, 6: *It is a good two days' travel from Ecbatana to Rages:* Alexander's army took eleven days in forced marches to cover this distance, about 180 miles. The author is merely using popular impressions about faraway places; he is not teaching geography. (See notes on 1, 15; 3, 7 and Introduction.)

5, 10: *Hearty greetings* and *what joy* form a word-play on the Greek verb *chairein,* "to greet" and "to

be joyful."

5, 13–14: *Azariah,* "Yahweh helps"; *Hananiah,* "Yahweh is merciful"; *Nathaniah,* "Yahweh gives"; *Shemaiah,* "Yahweh hears."

5, 15: *The normal wages:* literally, "a drachma," about seventeen cents, a day's wage for a working man.

5, 22: *My love:* literally, "sister," a term of endearment applied to one's wife; cf 7, 11.15; 8, 4.21;

10, 6.13; Sg 4, 9.10.12; 5, 1f.

A good angel: a reference to the guardian angel, though Tobit does not know, of course, that Raphael himself, disguised as Azariah, is the good angel in this case.

6, 5: *Its gall . . . medicines:* belief in the healing power of these organs was common among even the physicians of antiquity.

afflicted by a demon or evil spirit, the affliction will leave him completely, and no demons will ever return to him again. 9 And as for the gall, if you rub it on the eyes of a man who has cataracts, blowing into his eyes right on the cataracts, his sight will be restored."

10 When they had entered Media and were getting close to Ecbatana, 11 Raphael said to the boy, "Brother Tobiah!" He answered, "Yes, what is it?" Raphael continued: "Tonight we must stay with Raguel, who is a relative of yours. He has a daughter named Sarah, 12 but no other child. Since you are Sarah's closest relative, you before all other men have the right to marry her. Also, her father's estate is rightfully yours to inherit. Now the girl is sensible, courageous, and very beautiful; and her father loves her dearly." 13 He continued: "Since you have the right to marry her, listen to me, brother. Tonight I will ask the girl's father to let us have her as your bride. When we return from Rages, we will hold the wedding feast for her. I know that Raguel cannot keep her from you or let her become engaged to another man; that would be a capital crime according to the decree in the Book of Moses, and he knows that it is your right, before all other men, to marry his daughter. So heed my words, brother; tonight we must speak for the girl, so that we may have her engaged to you. And when we return from Rages, we will take her and bring her back with us to your house."

14 Tobiah objected, however: "Brother Azariah, I have heard that this woman has already been married seven times, and that her husbands died in their bridal chambers. On the very night they approached her, they dropped dead. And I have heard it said that it was a demon who killed them. 15 So now I too am afraid of this demon. Because he loves her, he does not harm her; but he does slay any man who wishes to come close to her. I am my father's only child. If I should die, I would bring my father and mother down to their grave in sorrow over me. And they have no other son to bury them!"

16 Raphael said to him: "Do you not remember your father's orders? He commanded you to marry a woman from your own family. So now listen to me, brother; do not give another thought to this demon, but marry Sarah. I know that tonight you shall have her for your wife! 17 When you go into the bridal chamber, take the fish's liver and heart, and place them on the embers for the incense. 18 As soon as the demon smells the odor they give off, he will flee and never again show himself near her. Then when you are about to have intercourse with her, both of you first rise up to pray. Beg the Lord of heaven to show you mercy and grant you deliverance. But do not be afraid, for she was set apart for you before the world existed. You will save her, and she will go with you. And I suppose that you will have children by her, who will take the place of brothers for you. So do not worry."

When Tobiah heard Raphael say that she was his kinswoman, of his own family's lineage, he fell deeply in love with her, and his heart became set on her.

At the House of Raguel

7 When they entered Ecbatana, Tobiah said, "Brother Azariah, lead me straight to our kinsman Raguel." So he brought him to the house of Raguel, whom they found seated by his courtyard gate. They greeted him first. He said to them, "Greetings to you too, brothers! Good health to you, and welcome!" When he brought them into his home, 2 he said to his wife Edna, "This young man looks just like my kinsman Tobit!" 3 So Edna asked them, "Who are you, brothers?" They answered, "We are of the exiles from Naphtali at Nineveh." 4 She said, "Do you know our kinsman Tobit?" They answered, "Indeed we do!" She asked, "Is he well?" 5 They answered, "Yes, he is alive and well." Then Tobiah exclaimed, "He is my father!" 6 Raguel sprang up and kissed him, shedding tears of joy. 7 But when he heard that Tobit had lost his eyesight, he was grieved and wept aloud. He said to Tobiah: "My child, God bless you! You are the son of a noble and good father. But what a terrible misfortune that such a righteous and charitable man should be afflicted with blindness!" He continued to weep in the arms of his kinsman Tobiah. 8 His wife Edna also wept for Tobit; and even their daughter Sarah began to weep.

Marriage of Tobiah and Sarah

9 Afterward, Raguel slaughtered a ram from the flock and gave them a cordial reception. When they had bathed and reclined to eat, Tobiah said to Raphael, "Brother Azariah, ask Raguel to let me marry my kinswoman Sarah." 10 Raguel overheard the words; so he said to the boy: "Eat and drink and be merry tonight, for no man is more entitled to marry my daughter Sarah than you, brother. Besides, not even I have the right to give her to anyone but you, because you are my closest relative. But I will explain the situation to you very frankly. 11 I have given her in marriage to seven men, all of whom were kinsmen of ours, and all died on the very night they approached her. But now, son, eat and drink. I am sure the Lord will look after you both." Tobiah answered, "I will eat or drink nothing until you set aside what belongs to me."

Raguel said to him: "I will do it. She is yours according to the decree of the Book of Moses. Your marriage to her has been decided in heaven! Take your kinswoman; from now on you are her love, and she is your beloved. She is yours today and ever after. And tonight, son, may the Lord of heaven prosper you both. May he grant you mercy and peace." 12 Then Raguel called his daughter Sarah, and she came to him. He took her by the hand and gave her to Tobiah with the words: "Take her according to the law. According to the decree written in the Book of

---

6, 13: *Raguel ... Book of Moses:* Nm 36, 6-8 prescribed marriage within the ancestral tribe, but no death penalty is mentioned.

6, 18: *Rise up to pray:* prayer is needed to drive out the demon.

Moses she is your wife. Take her and bring her back safely to your father. And may the God of heaven grant both of you peace and prosperity." 13 He then called her mother and told her to bring a scroll, so that he might draw up a marriage contract stating that he gave Sarah to Tobiah as his wife according to the decree of the Mosaic law. Her mother brought the scroll, and he drew up the contract, to which they affixed their seals.

14 Afterward they began to eat and drink. 15 Later Raguel called his wife Edna and said, "My love, prepare the other bedroom and bring the girl there." 16 She went and made the bed in the room, as she was told, and brought the girl there. After she had cried over her, she wiped away the tears and said: 17 "Be brave, my daughter. May the Lord of heaven grant you joy in place of your grief. Courage, my daughter." Then she left.

Expulsion of the Demon

8 When they had finished eating and drinking, the girl's parents wanted to retire. They brought the young man out of the dining room and led him into the bedroom. 2 At this point Tobiah, mindful of Raphael's instructions, took the fish's liver and heart from the bag which he had with him, and placed them on the embers for the incense. 3 The demon, repelled by the odor of the fish, fled into Upper Egypt; Raphael pursued him there and bound him hand and foot. Then Raphael returned immediately.

4 When the girl's parents left the bedroom and closed the door behind them, Tobiah arose from bed and said to his wife, "My love, get up. Let us pray and beg our Lord to have mercy on us and to grant us deliverance." 5 She got up, and they started to pray and beg that deliverance might be theirs. He began with these words:

"Blessed are you, O God of our fathers;
praised be your name forever and ever.
Let the heavens and all your creation
praise you forever.
6 You made Adam and you gave him his wife Eve
to be his help and support;
and from these two the human race descended.
You said, 'It is not good for the man to be alone;
let us make him a partner like himself.'
7 Now, Lord, you know that I take this wife of mine
not because of lust,
but for a noble purpose.
Call down your mercy on me and on her,
and allow us to live together to a happy old age."

8 They said together, "Amen, amen," 9 and went to bed for the night.

But Raguel got up and summoned his servants. With him they went out to dig a grave, 10 for he said, "I must do this, because if Tobiah should die, we would be subjected to ridicule and insult." 11 When they had finished digging the grave, Raguel went back into the house and called his wife, 12 saying, "Send one of the maids in to see whether Tobiah is alive or dead, so that if necessary we may bury him without anyone's knowing about it." 13 She sent the maid, who lit a lamp, opened the bedroom door, went in, and found them sound asleep together. 14 The maid went out and told the girl's parents that Tobiah was alive, and that there was nothing wrong. 15 Then Raguel praised the God of heaven in these words:

"Blessed are you, O God, with every holy and pure blessing!
Let all your chosen ones praise you;
let them bless you forever!
16 Blessed are you, who have made me glad;
what I feared did not happen.
Rather you have dealt with us according to your great mercy.
17 Blessed are you, for you were merciful
toward two only children.
Grant them, Master, mercy and deliverance,
and bring their lives to fulfillment
with happiness and mercy."

18 Then he told his servants to fill in the grave before dawn.

Wedding Feast

19 He asked his wife to bake many loaves of bread; he himself went out to the herd and picked out two steers and four rams which he ordered to be slaughtered. So the servants began to prepare the feast. 20 He summoned Tobiah and made an oath in his presence, saying: "For fourteen days you shall not stir from here, but shall remain here eating and drinking with me; and you shall bring joy to my daughter's sorrowing spirit. 21 Take, to begin with, half of whatever I own when you go back in good health to your father; the other half will be yours when I and my wife die. Be of good cheer, my son! I am your father, and Edna is your mother; and we belong to you and to your beloved now and forever. So be happy, son!"

The Money Recovered

9 Then Tobiah called Raphael and said to him: 2 "Brother Azariah, take along with you four servants and two camels and travel to Rages. Go to Gabael's house and give him this bond. Get the money and then bring him along with you to the wedding celebration. 4 For you know that my father is counting the days. If I should delay my return by a single day, I would cause him intense grief. 3 You witnessed the oath that Raguel has sworn; I cannot violate his oath." 5 So Raphael, together with the four servants and

---

8, 2f: The manner of coping with demonic influences among the ancients seems quaint to us. However, the fish here is part of the story, and not a recipe for exorcism. It is clear that the author places primary emphasis on the value of prayer to God

(6, 18; 8, 4–8), on the role of the angel as God's agent, and on the pious dispositions of Tobiah.

8, 3: Into Upper Egypt: to the desert there. The desert was considered the dwelling place of demons. Cf Is 13, 21; 34, 14; Mt 4, 1; 12, 43.

8, 20: For fourteen days: because of the happy, and unexpected, turn of events, Raguel doubles the time of the wedding feast. When Tobiah returns home, the usual seven-day feast is held (11, 18). Cf Jgs 14, 12.

two camels, traveled to Rages in Media, where they stayed at Gabael's house. Raphael gave Gabael his bond and told him about Tobit's son Tobiah, and that he had married and was inviting him to the wedding celebration. Gabael promptly checked over the sealed moneybags, and they placed them on the camels.

6 The following morning they got an early start and traveled to the wedding celebration. When they entered Raguel's house, they found Tobiah reclining at table. He sprang up and greeted Gabael, who wept and blessed him, exclaiming: "O noble and good child, son of a noble and good, upright and charitable man, may the Lord grant heavenly blessing to you and to your wife, and to your wife's father and mother. Blessed be God, because I have seen the very image of my cousin Tobit!"

TOBIAH'S RETURN: CURE OF TOBIT'S BLINDNESS

Anxiety of the Parents

10 Meanwhile, day by day, Tobit was keeping track of the time Tobiah would need to go and to return. When the number of days was reached and his son did not appear, 2 he said, "I wonder what has happened. Perhaps he has been detained there; or perhaps Gabael is dead, and there is no one to give him the money." 3 And he began to worry. 4 His wife Anna said, "My son has perished and is no longer among the living!" And she began to weep aloud and to wail over her son: 5 "Alas, my child, light of my eyes, that I let you make this journey!" 6 But Tobit kept telling her: "Hush, do not think about it, my love; he is safe! Probably they have to take care of some unexpected business there. The man who is traveling with him is trustworthy, and is one of our own kinsmen. So do not worry over him, my love. He will be here soon." 7 But she retorted, "Stop it, and do not lie to me! My child has perished!" She would go out and keep watch all day at the road her son had taken, and she ate nothing. At sunset she would go back home to wail and cry the whole night through, getting no sleep at all.

Departure from Ecbatana

Now at the end of the fourteen-day wedding celebration which Raguel had sworn to hold for his daughter, Tobiah went to him and said: "Please let me go, for I know that my father and mother do not believe they will ever see me again. So I beg you, father, let me go back to my father. I have already told you how I left him." 8 Raguel said to Tobiah: "Stay, my child, stay with me. I am sending messengers to your father Tobit, and they will give him news of you." 9 But Tobiah insisted, "No, I beg you to let me go back to my father."

10 Raguel then promptly handed over to Tobiah Sarah his wife, together with half of all his property: male and female slaves, oxen and sheep, asses and camels, clothing, money, and household goods. 11 Bidding them farewell, he let them go. He embraced Tobiah and said to him: "Goodbye, my son. Have a safe journey. May the Lord of heaven grant prosperity to you and to your wife Sarah. And may I see children of yours before I die!" 12 Then he kissed his daughter Sarah and said to her: "My daughter, honor your father-in-law and your mother-in-law, because from now on they are as much your parents as the ones who brought you into the world. Go in peace, my daughter; let me hear good reports about you as long as I live." Finally he said good-bye to them and sent them away.

13 Then Edna said to Tobiah: "My child and beloved kinsman, may the Lord bring you back safely, and may I live long enough to see children of you and of my daughter Sarah before I die. Before the Lord, I entrust my daughter to your care. Never cause her grief at any time in your life. Go in peace, my child. From now on I am your mother, and Sarah is your beloved. May all of us be prosperous all the days of our lives." She kissed them both and sent them away in peace.

14 When Tobiah left Raguel, he was full of happiness and joy, and he blessed the Lord of heaven and earth, the King of all, for making his journey so successful. Finally he said

good-bye to Raguel and his wife Edna, and added, "May I honor you all the days of my life!"

Homeward Journey

11 Then they left and began their return journey. When they were near Kaserin, just before Nineveh, 2 Raphael said: "You know how we left your father. 3 Let us hurry on ahead of your wife to prepare the house while the rest of the party are still on the way." 4 So they both went on ahead and Raphael said to Tobiah, "Have the gall in your hand!" And the dog ran along behind them.

5 Meanwhile, Anna sat watching the road by which her son was to come. 6 When she saw him coming, she exclaimed to his father, "Tobit, your son is coming, and the man who traveled with him!"

7 Raphael said to Tobiah before he reached his father: "I am certain that his eyes will be opened. 8 Smear the fish gall on them. This medicine will make the cataracts shrink and peel off from his eyes; then your father will again be able to see the light of day."

Sight Restored

9 Then Anna ran up to her son, threw her arms around him, and said to him, "Now that I have seen you again, son, I am ready to die!" And she sobbed aloud. 10 Tobit got up and stumbled out through the courtyard gate. Tobiah went up to him 11 with the fish gall in his hand, and holding him firmly, blew into his eyes. "Courage, father," he said. 12 Next he smeared the medicine on his eyes, 13 and it made them smart. Then, beginning at the corners of Tobit's eyes, Tobiah used both hands to peel off the cataracts. When Tobit saw his son, he threw his arms around him 14 and wept. He exclaimed, "I can see you, son, the light of my eyes!" Then he said:

"Blessed be God,
   and praised be his great name,
   and blessed be all his holy
     angels.
May his holy name be praised
   throughout all the ages,

15 Because it was he who scourged
   me,
     and it is he who has had mercy
       on me.
   Behold, I now see my son
     Tobiah!"

Then Tobit went back in, rejoicing and praising God with full voice. Tobiah told his father that his journey had been a success; that he had brought back the money; and that he had married Raguel's daughter Sarah, who would arrive shortly, for she was approaching the gate of Nineveh.

16 Rejoicing and praising God, Tobit went out to the gate of Nineveh to meet his daughter-in-law. When the people of Nineveh saw him walking along briskly, with no one leading him by the hand, they were amazed. 17 Before them all Tobit proclaimed how God had mercifully restored sight to his eyes. When Tobit reached Sarah, the wife of his son Tobiah, he greeted her: "Welcome, my daughter! Blessed be your God for bringing you to us, daughter! Blessed are your father and your mother. Blessed is my son Tobiah, and blessed are you, daughter! Welcome to your home with blessing and joy. Come in, daughter!" That day there was joy for all the Jews who lived in Nineveh. 18 Ahiqar and his nephew Nadab also came to rejoice with Tobit. They celebrated Tobiah's wedding feast for seven happy days, and he received many gifts.

RAPHAEL REVEALS HIS IDENTITY

Raphael's Wages

12 When the wedding celebration came to an end, Tobit called his son Tobiah and said to him, "Son, see to it that you give what is due to the man who made the journey with you; give him a bonus too." 2 Tobiah said: "Father, how much shall I pay him? It would not hurt me at all to give him half of all the wealth he brought back with me. 3 He led me back safe and sound; he cured my wife; he brought the money back with me; and he cured you. How much of a bonus should I give him?" 4 Tobit answered, "It is only fair, son, that he should receive half of all that he brought back." 5 So Tobiah called Raphael and said, "Take as your wages half of all that you have brought back, and go in peace."

Exhortation

6 Raphael called the two men aside privately and said to them: "Thank God! Give him the praise and the glory. Before all the living, acknowledge the many good things he has done for you, by blessing and extolling his name in song. Before all men, honor and proclaim God's deeds, and do not be slack in praising him. 7 A king's secret it is prudent to keep, but the works of God are to be declared and made known. Praise them with due honor. Do good, and evil will not find its way to you. 8 Prayer and fasting are good, but better than either is almsgiving accompanied by righteousness. A little with righteousness is better than abundance with wickedness. It is better to give alms than to store up gold; 9 for almsgiving saves one from death and expiates every sin. Those who regularly give alms shall enjoy a full life; 10 but those habitually guilty of sin are their own worst enemies.

Raphael's Identity

11 "I will now tell you the whole truth; I will conceal nothing at all from you. I have already said to you, 'A king's secret it is prudent to keep, but the works of God are to be made known with due honor.' 12 I can now tell you that when you, Tobit, and Sarah prayed, it was I who presented and read the record of your prayer before the Glory of the Lord; and I did the same thing when you used to bury the dead. 13 When you did not hesitate to get up and leave your dinner in order to go and bury the dead, 14 I was sent to put you to the test. At the same time, however, God commissioned me to heal you and your daughter-in-law Sarah. 15 I am Raphael, one of the seven angels who enter and serve before the Glory of the Lord."

16 Stricken with fear, the two men fell to the ground. 17 But Raphael said to them: "No need to fear; you are safe. Thank God now and forever. 18 As for me, when I came to you it was not out of any favor on my part, but because it was God's will. So continue to thank him every day; praise him with song. 19 Even though you watched me eat and drink, I did not really do so; what you were seeing was a vision. 20 So now get up from the ground and praise God. Behold, I am about to ascend to him who sent me; write down all these things that have happened to you." 21 When Raphael ascended, they rose to their feet and could no longer see him. 22 They kept thanking God and singing his praises; and they continued to acknowledge these marvelous deeds which he had done when the angel of God appeared to them.

TOBIT'S SONG OF PRAISE

13 Then Tobit composed this joyful prayer:

Blessed be God who lives forever,
   because his kingdom lasts for
     all ages.
2 For he scourges and then has
     mercy;
   he casts down to the depths of
     the nether world,
   and he brings up from the great
     abyss.
No one can escape his hand.

12, 1–5: Tobit and his son generously agree to give Azariah far more than the wages agreed upon in 5, 15–16.

12, 6–10: In the fashion of a wisdom teacher, Raphael gives the two men a short exhortation similar to the one Tobit gave his son in 4, 3–19.

12, 6f: The Jews considered the duty of praising God their most esteemed privilege. Without praise of God, life was meaningless. Cf Is 38, 16–20.

12, 8: Prayer ... fasting ... almsgiving ... righteous-

ness: these, together with the proper attitude toward wealth, are treated in great detail by Christ our LORD in the Sermon on the Mount (Mt 6).

12, 12.15: Raphael is one of the seven specially designated intercessors who present man's prayers to God. Angelology was developing in this period. The names of two other angels are given in the Bible: Gabriel (Dn 8, 16; 9, 21; Lk 1, 19.26) and Michael (Dn 10, 13.21; 12, 1; Jude 9; Rv 12, 7).

12, 14: I was sent ... test: God often sends trials

to purify his faithful servants further. Cf Jb 1—2.

13, 1–18: Tobit's hymn of praise (cf Ex 15, 1–18; Jdt 16, 1–17) is divided into two parts. The first part (vv 1–8) is a song of praise that echoes themes from the hymns and psalms of the kingdom; the second (vv 9–18) is addressed to Jerusalem in the style of the prophets who spoke of a new and ideal Jerusalem (Is 60); cf Rv 21.

3 Praise him, you Israelites, before
   the Gentiles,
   for though he has scattered you
      among them,
4 he has shown you his greatness
   even there.
   Exalt him before every living
      being,
   because he is the Lord our
      God,
   our Father and God forever.

5 He scourged you for your
      iniquities,
   but will again have mercy on
      you all.
   He will gather you from all the
      Gentiles
   among whom you have been
      scattered.

6 When you turn back to him with
      all your heart,
   to do what is right before him,
   Then he will turn back to you,
   and no longer hide his face
      from you.

   So now consider what he has done
      for you,
   and praise him with full voice.
   Bless the Lord of righteousness,
   and exalt the King of the ages.

   In the land of my exile I praise
      him,
   and show his power and majesty
      to a sinful nation.
   "Turn back, you sinners! do the
      right before him:
   perhaps he may look with favor
      upon you
   and show you mercy.

7 "As for me, I exalt my God,
   and my spirit rejoices in the
      King of heaven.
8 Let all men speak of his majesty,
   and sing his praises in
      Jerusalem."

9 O Jerusalem, holy city,
   he scourged you for the works
      of your hands,
   but will again pity the children
      of the righteous.
10 Praise the Lord for his goodness,
   and bless the King of the ages,
   so that his tent may be rebuilt
      in you with joy.

   May he gladden within you all
      who were captives;
   all who were ravaged may he
      cherish within you
   for all generations to come.

11 A bright light will shine to all
      parts of the earth;
   many nations shall come to you
      from afar,
   And the inhabitants of all the
      limits of the earth,
   drawn to you by the name of
      the Lord God,
   Bearing in their hands their gifts
      for the King of heaven.
   Every generation shall give joyful
      praise in you,
   and shall call you the chosen
      one,
   through all ages forever.

12 Accursed are all who speak a
      harsh word against you;
   accursed are all who destroy
      you
   and pull down your walls,
   And all who overthrow your
      towers
   and set fire to your homes;
   but forever blessed are all those
      who build you up.

13 Go, then, rejoice over the children
      of the righteous,
   who shall all be gathered
      together
   and shall bless the Lord of the
      ages.
14 Happy are those who love you,
   and happy those who rejoice in
      your prosperity.

   Happy are all the men who shall
      grieve over you,
   over all your chastisements,
   For they shall rejoice in you
   as they behold all your joy
      forever.

15 My spirit blesses the Lord, the
      great King;
16   Jerusalem shall be rebuilt as his
      home forever.
   Happy for me if a remnant of my
      offspring survive
   to see your glory and to praise
      the King of heaven!

   The gates of Jerusalem shall be
      built with sapphire and
      emerald,
   and all your walls with precious
      stones.
   The towers of Jerusalem shall be
      built with gold,
   and their battlements with pure
      gold.
17 The streets of Jerusalem shall be
      paved
   with rubies and stones of
      Ophir;
18 The gates of Jerusalem shall sing
      hymns of gladness,
   and all her houses shall cry out,
      "Alleluia!

   "Blessed be God who has raised
      you up!
   may he be blessed for all ages!"
   For in you they shall praise his
      holy name forever.

EPILOGUE

Parting Advice

14 Tobit died peacefully at the
age of a hundred and twelve,
and received an honorable burial in
Nineveh.   2 He was sixty-two years
old when he lost his eyesight, and
after he recovered it he lived in
prosperity, giving alms and continually blessing God and praising
the divine Majesty.

3 Just before he died, he called his
son Tobiah and Tobiah's seven sons,
and gave him this command: "Son,
take your children 4 and flee into
Media, for I believe God's word
which was spoken by Nahum against
Nineveh. It shall all happen, and
shall overtake Assyria and Nineveh;
indeed, whatever was said by Israel's
prophets, whom God commissioned,
shall occur. Not one of all the oracles
shall remain unfulfilled, but everything shall take place in the time
appointed for it. So it will be safer in
Media than in Assyria or Babylon.
For I know and believe that whatever
God has spoken will be accomplished.
It shall happen, and not a single word
of the prophecies shall prove false.

"As for our kinsmen who dwell in
Israel, they shall all be scattered and

13, 9: *Works of your hands:* idols.
14, 4f: *Nahum:* one of the minor prophets, whose
book contains oracles of doom against Nineveh. Here,
in keeping with the period to which he assigns his

story, the sacred author makes Tobit speak as if the
punishment of Nineveh, the destruction of Jerusalem
(587 B.C.), the exile from Judah and the return, would
all take place in the future. The technique of using

the facts of past history as seemingly future predic-
tions, is a frequent device of apocalyptic writers. *The
Good Land:* a favorite name for the promised land.
Cf Dt 1, 35; 3, 25; 4, 21.22.

led away into exile from the Good Land. The entire country of Israel shall become desolate; even Samaria and Jerusalem shall become desolate! God's temple there shall be burnt to the ground and shall be desolate for a while. 5 But God will again have mercy on them and bring them back to the land of Israel. They shall rebuild the temple, but it will not be like the first one, until the era when the appointed times shall be completed. Afterward all of them shall return from their exile, and they shall rebuild Jerusalem with splendor. In her the temple of God shall also be rebuilt; yes, it will be rebuilt for all generations to come, just as the prophets of Israel said of her. 6 All the nations of the world shall be converted and shall offer God true worship; all shall abandon their idols which have deceitfully led them into error, 7 and shall bless the God of the ages in righteousness. Because all the Israelites who are to be saved in those days will truly be mindful of God, they shall be gathered together and go to Jerusalem; in security shall they dwell forever in the land of Abraham, which will be given over to them. Those who sincerely love God

shall rejoice, but those who become guilty of sin shall completely disappear from the land. 9 "Now, children, I give you this command: serve God faithfully and do what is right before him; you must tell your children to do what is upright and to give alms, to be mindful of God and at all times to bless his name sincerely and with all their strength.

8 "Now, as for you, my son, depart from Nineveh; do not remain here. 10 The day you bury your mother next to me, do not even stay overnight with the confines of the city. For I see that people here shamelessly commit all sorts of wickedness and treachery. Think, my son, of all that Nadab did to Ahiqar, the very one who brought him up: Ahiqar went down alive into the earth! Yet God made Nadab's disgraceful crime rebound against him. Ahiqar came out again into the light, but Nadab went into the everlasting darkness, for he had tried to kill Ahiqar. Because Ahiqar had given alms to me, he escaped from the deadly trap Nadab had set for him. But Nadab himself fell into the deadly trap, and it destroyed him. 11 So, my children, note well what

almsgiving does, and also what wickedness does—it kills! But now my spirit is about to leave me."

Death of Tobit and Tobiah

They placed him on his bed and he died; and he received an honorable burial. 12 When Tobiah's mother died, he buried her next to his father. He then departed with his wife and children for Media, where he settled in Ecbatana with his father-in-law Raguel. 13 He took respectful care of his aging father-in-law and mother-in-law; and he buried them at Ecbatana in Media. Then he inherited Raguel's estate as well as that of his father Tobit. 14 He died at the venerable age of a hundred and seventeen. 15 But before he died, he heard of the destruction of Nineveh and saw its effects. He witnessed the exile of the city's inhabitants when Cyaxares, king of Media, led them captive into Media. Tobiah praised God for all that he had done against the citizens of Nineveh and Assyria. Before dying he rejoiced over Nineveh's destruction, and he blessed the Lord God forever and ever. Amen.

14, 5: *Until the era . . . completed:* a reference to the advent of Messianic times, in which a new, more perfect temple was to be expected. Cf Heb 9, 1–14.

14, 6: Conversion of the Gentiles is also to come in the Messianic era.

14, 10: *Nadab:* In the *Story of Ahiqar*, the hero Ahiqar, chancellor under the Assyrian kings Sen-

nacherib and Esarhaddon, adopts his nephew Nadab and prepares him to become his successor. But Nadab treacherously plots to have his uncle put to death. Ahiqar hides in a friend's house, and is finally vindicated (*came out again into the light*) when Nadab's scheme is discovered. Thereupon Nadab is thrown into a dungeon where he dies (*went into*

everlasting darkness). It was Ahiqar's almsgiving that delivered him from death; see note on 2, 2.

14, 15: *Cyaxares:* Nabopolassar, king of Babylon, and Cyaxares conquered and destroyed Nineveh in 612 B.C.; see note on 1, 15.

Judith

PERIL OF THE JEWS

War Against the Medes

T was the twelfth year of the reign of Nebuchadnezzar, king of the Assyrians in the great city of Nineveh. At that time Arphaxad ruled over the Medes in Ecbatana. 2 Around this city he built a wall of blocks of stone, each three cubits in height and six in length. He made the wall seventy cubits high and fifty thick. 3 At the gates he raised towers of a hundred cubits, with a thickness of sixty cubits at the base. 4 The gateway he built to a height of seventy cubits, with an opening forty cubits wide for the passage of his chariot forces and the marshaling of his infantry. 5 Then King Nebuchadnezzar waged war against King Arphaxad in the vast plain, in the district of Ragae. 6 To him there rallied all the inhabitants of the mountain region, all who dwelt along the Euphrates, the Tigris, and the Hydaspes, and King Arioch of the Elamites, in the plain. Thus many nations came together to resist the people of Cheleoud.

Ultimatum to the West

7 Now Nebuchadnezzar, king of the Assyrians, sent messengers to all the inhabitants of Persia, and to all those who dwelt in the West; to the inhabitants of Cilicia and Damascus, Lebanon and Anti-Lebanon, to all who dwelt along the seacoast, 8 to the peoples of Carmel, Gilead, Upper Galilee, and the vast plain of Esdraelon, 9 to all those in Samaria and its cities, and west of the Jordan as far as Jerusalem, Bethany, Chelous, Kadesh, and the River of Egypt; to Tahpanhes, Raamses, all the land of Goshen, 10 Tanis, Memphis and beyond, and to all the inhabitants of Egypt as far as the borders of Ethiopia.

11 But the inhabitants of all that land disregarded the summons of Nebuchadnezzar, king of the Assyrians, and would not go with him to the war. They were not afraid of him but regarded him as a lone individual opposed to them, and turned away his envoys empty-handed, in disgrace. 12 Then Nebuchadnezzar fell into a violent rage against all that land, and swore by his throne and his kingdom that he would avenge himself on all the territories of Cilicia and Damascus and Syria, and also destroy with his sword all the inhabitants of Moab, Ammon, the whole of Judea, and those living anywhere in Egypt as far as the borders of the two seas.

Defeat of Arphaxad

13 In the seventeenth year he proceeded with his army against King Arphaxad, and was victorious in his campaign. He routed the whole force of Arphaxad, his entire cavalry and all his chariots, 14 and took possession of his cities. He pressed on to Ecbatana and took its towers, sacked its market places, and turned its glory into shame. 15 Arphaxad himself he overtook in the mountains of Ragae, ran him through with spears, and utterly destroyed him. 16 Then he returned home with all his numerous, motley horde of warriors; and there he and his army relaxed and feasted for a hundred and twenty days.

Council of War against the West

2 In the eighteenth year, on the twenty-second day of the first month, there was a discussion in the

---

1, 6: *Cheleoud:* probably the Chaldeans are meant.
1, 12: *The two seas:* the ancient rulers in Meso-potamia often designated the limits of their realm as extending from the Upper Sea (the Mediterranean) to the Lower Sea (the Persian Gulf).

palace of Nebuchadnezzar, king of the Assyrians, about taking revenge on the whole world, as he had threatened. 2 He summoned all his ministers and nobles, laid before them his secret plan, and urged the total destruction of those countries. 3 They decided to do away with all those who had refused to comply with the order he had issued.

4 When he had completed his plan, Nebuchadnezzar, king of the Assyrians, summoned Holofernes, general in chief of his forces, second to himself in command, and said to him:

5 "Thus says the great king, the lord of all the earth: Go forth from my presence, take with you men of proven valor, a hundred and twenty thousand infantry and twelve thousand cavalry, 6 and proceed against all the land of the West, because they did not comply with the order I issued. 7 Tell them to have earth and water ready, for I will come against them in my wrath; I will cover all the land with the feet of my soldiers, to whom I will deliver them as spoils. 8 Their slain shall fill their ravines and wadies, the swelling torrent shall be choked with their dead; 9 and I will deport them as exiles to the very ends of the earth.

10 "You go before me and take possession of all their territories for me. If they surrender to you, guard them for me till the day of their punishment. 11 As for those who resist, show them no quarter, but deliver them up to slaughter and plunder in each country you occupy. 12 For as I live, and by the strength of my kingdom, what I have spoken I will accomplish by my power. 13 Do not disobey a single one of the orders of your lord; fulfill them exactly as I have commanded you, and do it without delay."

Campaign of Holofernes

14 So Holofernes left the presence of his lord, and summoned all the princes, and the generals and officers of the Assyrian army. 15 He mustered a hundred and twenty thousand picked troops, as his lord had commanded, and twelve thousand mounted archers, 16 and grouped them into a complete combat force. 17 He took along a very large number of camels, asses, and mules for their baggage; innumerable sheep, cattle, and goats for their food supply; 18 abundant provisions for each man, and much gold and silver from the royal palace.

19 Then he and his whole army proceeded on their expedition in advance of King Nebuchadnezzar, to cover all the western region with their chariots and cavalry and regular infantry. 20 A huge, irregular force, too many to count, like locusts or the dust of the earth, went along with them.

21 After a three-day march from Nineveh, they reached the plain of Bectileth, and from Bectileth they next encamped near the mountains to the north of Upper Cilicia. 22 From there Holofernes took his whole force, the infantry, cavalry, and chariots, and marched into the mountain region. 23 He devastated Put and Lud, and plundered all the Rassisites and the Ishmaelites on the border of the desert toward the south of Chaldea. 24 Then, following the Euphrates, he went through Mesopotamia, and battered down every fortified city along the Wadi Abron, until he reached the sea. 25 He seized the territory of Cilicia, and cut down everyone who resisted him. Then he proceeded to the southern borders of Japheth, toward Arabia. 26 He surrounded all the Midianites, burned their tents, and plundered their sheepfolds. 27 Descending to the plain of Damascus at the time of the wheat harvest, he set fire to all their fields, destroyed their flocks and herds, despoiled their cities, devastated their plains, and put all their youths to the sword.

28 The fear and dread of him fell upon all the inhabitants of the coastland, upon those in Sidon and Tyre, and those who dwelt in Sur and Ocina, and the inhabitants of Jamnia. Those in Azotus and Ascalon also feared him greatly.

Submission of the West

3 They therefore sent messengers to him to sue for peace in these words: 2 "We, the servants of Nebuchadnezzar the great king, lie prostrate before you; do with us as you will. 3 Our dwellings and all our wheat fields, our flocks and herds, and all our encampments are at your disposal; make use of them as you please. 4 Our cities and their inhabitants are also at your service; come and deal with them as you see fit."

5 After the spokesmen had reached Holofernes and given him this message, 6 he went down with his army to the seacoast, and stationed garrisons in the fortified cities; from them he impressed picked troops as auxiliaries. 7 The people of these cities and all the inhabitants of the countryside received him with garlands and dancing to the sound of timbrels. 8 Nevertheless, he devastated their whole territory and cut down their sacred groves, for he had been commissioned to destroy all the gods of the earth, so that every nation might worship Nebuchadnezzar alone, and every people and tribe invoke him as a god. 9 At length Holofernes reached Esdraelon in the neighborhood of Dothan, the approach to the main ridge of the Judean mountains; 10 he set up his camp between Geba and Scythopolis, and stayed there a whole month to refurbish all the equipment of his army.

Israelite Defense

4 When the Israelites who dwelt in Judea heard of all that Holofernes, commander in chief of Nebuchadnezzar, king of the Assyrians, had done to the nations, and how he

---

2, 7: *Earth and water:* in the Persian period, the offering of these to a conqueror was a symbolic gesture of unconditional surrender.

2, 12: *As I live:* in the Old Testament, an oath proper to divinity; cf Dt 32, 40. Nebuchadnezzar is making himself equal to God; see 6, 2. *By my power:* literally "by my hand." The hand of Nebuchadnezzar

raised in opposition to God and to his people is the occasion for Judith's intervention *by a woman's hand;* cf 9, 9f; Is 10, 5–14.

2, 23: *Put and Lud:* the same as the "Put and Lud" mentioned in Ez 30, 5 as allies of Egypt, and in Ez 27, 10 as supplying mercenary soldiers to Tyre. Here they seem inserted to embellish the narrative with as-

sonance and prophetic associations rather than to indicate definite localities.

3, 10: *Geba:* perhaps originally "Gelboe," the mountain range near the eastern end of which lay *Scythopolis,* the Greek name for ancient Beth-shean (Jos 17, 11).

had despoiled all their temples and destroyed them, 2 they were in extreme dread of him, and greatly alarmed for Jerusalem and the temple of the Lord, their God. 3 Now, they had lately returned from exile, and only recently had all the people of Judea been gathered together, and the vessels, the altar, and the temple been purified from profanation. 4 So they sent word to the whole region of Samaria, to Kona, Beth-horon, Belmain, and Jericho, to Choba and Aesora, and to the valley of Salem. 5 The people there posted guards on all the summits of the high mountains, fortified their villages, and since their fields had recently been harvested, stored up provisions in preparation for war.

6 Joakim, who was high priest in Jerusalem in those days, wrote to the inhabitants of Bethulia [and Betomesthaim], which is on the way to Esdraelon, facing the plain near Dothan, 7 and instructed them to keep firm hold of the mountain passes, since these offered access to Judea. It would be easy to ward off the attacking forces, as the defile was only wide enough for two abreast. 8 The Israelites carried out the orders given them by Joakim, the high priest, and the senate of the whole people of Israel, which met in Jerusalem.

Prayer and Penance

9 All the men of Israel cried to God with great fervor and did penance— 10 they, along with their wives, and children, and domestic animals. All their resident aliens, hired laborers, and slaves also girded themselves with sackcloth. 11 And all the Israelite men, women, and children who lived in Jerusalem prostrated themselves in front of the temple building, with ashes strewn on their heads, displaying their sackcloth covering before the Lord. 12 The altar, too, they draped in sackcloth; and with one accord they

cried out fervently to the God of Israel not to allow their children to be seized, their wives to be taken captive, the cities of their inheritance to be ruined, or the sanctuary to be profaned and mocked for the nations to gloat over.

13 The Lord heard their cry and had regard for their distress. For the people observed a fast of many days' duration throughout Judea, and before the sanctuary of the Lord Almighty in Jerusalem. 14 The high priest Joakim, and all the priests in attendance on the Lord who served his altar, were also girded with sackcloth as they offered the daily holocaust, the votive offerings, and the free-will offerings of the people. 15 With ashes upon their turbans, they cried to the Lord with all their strength to look with favor on the whole house of Israel.

Council against the Israelites

5 It was reported to Holofernes, commander in chief of the Assyrian army, that the Israelites were ready for battle, and had blocked the mountain passes, fortified the summits of all the higher peaks, and placed roadblocks in the plains. 2 In great anger he summoned all the rulers of the Moabites, the generals of the Ammonites, and all the satraps of the seacoast 3 and said to them: "Now tell me, you Canaanites, what sort of people is this that dwells in the mountains? Which cities do they inhabit? How large is their army? In what does their power and strength consist? Who has set himself up as their king and the leader of their army? 4 Why have they refused to come out to meet me along with all the other inhabitants of the West?"

Achior's Speech

5 Then Achior, the leader of all the Ammonites, said to him: "My lord, hear this account from your servant; I will tell you the truth about this

people that lives near you [that inhabits this mountain region]; no lie shall escape your servant's lips.

6 "These people are descendants of the Chaldeans. 7 They formerly dwelt in Mesopotamia, for they did not wish to follow the gods of their forefathers who were born in the land of the Chaldeans. 8 Since they abandoned the way of their ancestors, and acknowledged with divine worship the God of heaven, their forefathers expelled them from the presence of their gods. So they fled to Mesopotamia and dwelt there a long time. 9 Their God bade them leave their abode and proceed to the land of Canaan. Here they settled, and grew very rich in gold, silver, and a great abundance of livestock. 10 Later, when famine had gripped the whole land of Canaan, they went down into Egypt. They stayed there as long as they found sustenance, and grew into such a great multitude that the number of their race could not be counted. 11 The king of Egypt, however, rose up against them, shrewdly forced them to labor at brickmaking, oppressed and enslaved them. 12 But they cried to their God, and he struck the land of Egypt with plagues for which there was no remedy. When the Egyptians expelled them, 13 God dried up the Red Sea before them, 14 and led them along the route to Sinai and Kadesh-barnea. First they drove out all the inhabitants of the desert; 15 then they settled in the land of the Amorites, destroyed all the Heshbonites by main force, crossed the Jordan, and took possession of the whole mountain region. 16 They expelled the Canaanites, the Perizzites, the Jebusites, the Shechemites, and all the Gergesites; and they lived in these mountains a long time.

17 "As long as the Israelites did not sin in the sight of their God, they prospered, for their God, who hates wickedness, was with them. 18 But when they deviated from the way he

---

4, 3: *Returned from exile . . . profanation:* these allusions are variously attributed—to the Persian period (538–323 B.C.), or even to a condition in the days of Antiochus Epiphanes (175–164 B.C.).

4, 6: *Joakim, who was high priest:* see Bar 1, 7 and the footnote on Bar 1, 8f; this name for a high priest cannot be used in dating the events in Jdt.

4, 8: The organization of the Jewish nation as

subject to a *high priest* and a *senate*, or council of elders, was proper to the Greek period (after 323 B.C.), and is reflected in the coinage of John Hyrcancus (135–104 B.C.).

4, 10: *Domestic animals:* see note on Jon 3, 8.

4, 11: *Prostrated themselves in front of the temple building:* for a parallel to this ceremony of entreaty, see Jl 1, 13f; 2, 15ff, and the note on Jl 2, 17.

5, 6–9: Achior outlines the early history of the Hebrews, whose forefather, Abraham, first lived in Ur of the *Chaldeans* (Gn 11, 28) and then migrated to Haran (Gn 11, 31) in Aram Naharaim (Gn 24, 10), which was called *Mesopotamia* by the Greeks. The *gods of their forefathers* were the pagan deities worshiped by Abraham's relatives (Jos 24, 2).

prescribed for them, they were ground down steadily, more and more, by frequent wars, and finally taken as captives into foreign lands. The temple of their God was razed to the ground, and their cities were occupied by their enemies. 19 But now that they have returned to their God, they have come back from the Dispersion wherein they were scattered, and have repossessed Jerusalem, where their sanctuary is, and have settled again in the mountain region which was unoccupied.

20 "So now, my lord and master, if these people are at fault, and are sinning against their God, and if we verify this offense of theirs, then we shall be able to go up and conquer them. 21 But if they are not a guilty nation, then your lordship should keep his distance; otherwise their Lord and God will shield them, and we shall become the laughing-stock of the whole world."

22 Now when Achior had concluded his recommendation, all the people standing round about the tent murmured; and the officers of Holofernes and all the inhabitants of the seacoast and of Moab alike said he should be cut to pieces. 23 "We are not afraid of the Israelites," they said, "for they are a powerless people, incapable of a strong defense. 24 Let us therefore attack them; your great army, Lord Holofernes, will swallow them up."

Holofernes' Answer

6 When the noise of the crowd surrounding the council had subsided, Holofernes, commander in chief of the Assyrian army, said to Achior, in the presence of the whole throng of coastland peoples, of the Moabites, and of the Ammonite mercenaries: 2 "Who are you, Achior, to prophesy among us as you have done today, and to tell us not to fight against the Israelites because their God protects them? What god is there beside Nebuchadnezzar? He will send his force and destroy them from the face of the earth. 3 Their God will not save them; but we, the servants of Nebuchadnezzar, will

strike them down as one man, for they will be unable to withstand the force of our cavalry. 4 We will overwhelm them with it, and the mountains shall be drunk with their blood, and their plains filled with their corpses. Not a trace of them shall survive our attack: they shall utterly perish, says King Nebuchadnezzar, lord of all the earth; for he has spoken, and his words shall not remain unfulfilled. 5 As for you, Achior, you Ammonite mercenary, for saying these things in a moment of perversity you shall not see my face after today, until I have taken revenge on this race of people from Egypt. 6 Then at my return, the sword of my army or the spear of my servants will pierce your sides, and you shall fall among their slain. 7 My servants will now conduct you to the mountain region, and leave you at one of the towns along the ascent. 8 You shall not die till you are destroyed together with them. 9 If you still cherish the hope that they will not be taken, then there is no need for you to be downcast. I have spoken, and my words shall not prove false in any respect."

Achior in Bethulia

10 Then Holofernes ordered the servants who were standing by in his tent to seize Achior, conduct him to Bethulia, and hand him over to the Israelites. 11 So the servants took him in custody and brought him out of the camp into the plain. From there they led him into the mountain region till they reached the springs below Bethulia. 12 When the men of the city saw them, they seized their weapons and ran out of the city to the crest of the ridge; and all the slingers blocked the ascent of Holofernes' servants by hurling stones upon them. 13 So they took cover below the mountain, where they bound Achior and left him lying at the foot of the mountain; then they returned to their lord.

14 The Israelites came down to him from their city, loosed him, and brought him into Bethulia. They haled him before the rulers of the

city, 15 who in those days were Uzziah, son of Micah of the tribe of Simeon, Chabris, son of Gothoniel, and Charmis, son of Melchiel. 16 They then convened all the elders of the city; and all their young men, as well as the women, gathered in haste at the place of assembly. They placed Achior in the center of the throng, and Uzziah questioned him about what had happened. 17 He replied by giving them an account of what was said in the council of Holofernes, and of all his own words among the Assyrian officers, and of all the boasting threats of Holofernes against the house of Israel.

18 At this the people fell prostrate and worshiped God; and they cried out: 19 "Lord, God of heaven, behold their arrogance! Have pity on the lowliness of our people, and look with favor this day on those who are consecrated to you." 20 Then they reassured Achior and praised him highly. 21 Uzziah brought him from the assembly to his home, where he gave a banquet for the elders. That whole night they called upon the God of Israel for help.

Siege of Bethulia

7 The following day Holofernes ordered his whole army, and all the allied troops that had come to his support, to move against Bethulia, seize the mountain passes, and engage the Israelites in battle. 2 That same day all their fighting men went into action. Their forces numbered a hundred and seventy thousand infantry and twelve thousand horsemen, not counting the baggage train or the men who accompanied it on foot—a very great army. 3 They encamped at the spring in the valley near Bethulia, and spread out in breadth toward Dothan as far as Balbaim, and in length from Bethulia to Cyamon, which faces Esdraelon.

4 When the Israelites saw how many there were, they said to one another in great dismay: "Soon they will devour the whole country. Neither the high mountains nor the valleys and hills can support the mass

---

6, 19: The Latin Vulgate (6, 15) has a longer form of this prayer: "Lord, God of heaven and earth, behold their arrogance; regard our lowliness and look

with favor on your holy ones; show that you do not abandon those who trust in you, but that you humble

those who trust in themselves and glory in their own strength."

of them," 5 Yet they all seized their weapons, lighted fires on their bastions, and kept watch throughout the night.

6 On the second day Holofernes led out all his cavalry in the sight of the Israelites who were in Bethulia. 7 He reconnoitered the approaches to their city and located their sources of water; these he seized, stationing armed detachments around them, while he himself returned to his troops.

8 All the commanders of the Edomites and all the leaders of the Ammonites, together with the generals of the seacoast, came to Holofernes and said: 9 "Sir, listen to what we have to say, that there may be no losses among your troops. 10 These Israelites do not rely on their spears, but on the height of the mountains where they dwell; it is not easy to reach the summit of their mountains. 11 Therefore, sir, do not attack them in regular formation; thus not a single one of your troops will fall. 12 Stay in your camp, and spare all your soldiers. Have some of your servants keep control of the source of water that flows out at the base of the mountain, 13 for that is where the inhabitants of Bethulia get their water. Then thirst will begin to carry them off, and they will surrender their city. Meanwhile, we and our men will go up to the summits of the nearby mountains, and encamp there to guard against anyone's leaving the city. 14 They and their wives and children will languish with hunger, and even before the sword strikes them thay will be laid low in the streets of their city. 15 Thus you will render them dire punishment for their rebellion and their refusal to meet you peacefully."

16 Their words pleased Holofernes and all his ministers, and he ordered their proposal to be carried out. 17 Thereupon the Moabites moved camp, together with five thousand Assyrians. They encamped in the valley, and held the water supply and the springs of the Israelites. 18 The Edomites and the Ammonites went up and encamped in the mountain region opposite Dothan; and they sent some of their men to the south and to the east opposite Egrebel, near Chusi, which is on Wadi Mochmur. The rest of the Assyrian army was encamped in the plain, covering the whole countryside. Their enormous store of tents and equipment was spread out in profusion everywhere.

19 The Israelites cried to the Lord, their God, for they were disheartened, since all their enemies had them surrounded, and there was no way of slipping through their lines. 20 The whole Assyrian camp, infantry, chariots, and cavalry, kept them thus surrounded for thirty-four days. All the reservoirs of water failed the inhabitants of Bethulia, 21 and the cisterns ran dry, so that on no day did they have enough to drink, but their drinking water was rationed. 22 Their children fainted away, and the women and youths were consumed with thirst and were collapsing in the streets and gateways of the city, with no strength left in them.

23 All the people, therefore, including youths, women, and children, went in a crowd to Uzziah and the rulers of the city. They set up a great clamor and said before the elders: 24 "God judge between you and us! You have done us grave injustice in not making peace with the Assyrians. 25 There is no help for us now! Instead, God has sold us into their power by laying us prostrate before them in thirst and utter exhaustion. 26 Therefore, summon them and deliver the whole city as booty to the troops of Holofernes and to all his forces; 27 we would be better off to become their prey. We should indeed be made slaves, but at least we should live, and not have to behold our little ones dying before our eyes and our wives and children breathing out their souls. 28 We adjure you by heaven and earth, and by our God, the Lord of our forefathers, who is punishing us for our sins and those of our forefathers, to do as we have proposed, this very day."

29 All in the assembly with one accord broke into shrill wailing and loud cries to the Lord their God. 30 But Uzziah said to them, "Courage, my brothers! Let us wait five days more for the Lord our God, to show his mercy toward us; he will not utterly forsake us. 31 But if those days pass without help coming to us, I will do as you say." 32 Then he dispersed the men to their posts, and they returned to the walls and towers of the city; the women and children he sent to their homes. Throughout the city they were in great misery.

DELIVERANCE OF THE JEWS

Judith

8 Now in those days Judith, daughter of Merari, son of Joseph, son of Oziel, son of Elkiah, son of Ananias, son of Gideon, son of Raphain, son of Ahitob, son of Elijah, son of Hilkiah, son of Eliab, son of Nathanael, son of Salamiel, son of Sarasadai, son of Simeon, son of Israel, heard of this. 2 Her husband, Manasseh, of her own tribe and clan, had died at the time of the barley harvest. 3 While he was in the field supervising those who bound the sheaves, he suffered sunstroke; and he died of this illness in Bethulia, his native city. He was buried with his forefathers in the field between Dothan and Balamon. 4 The widowed Judith remained three years and four months at home, 5 where she set up a tent for herself on the roof of her house. She put sackcloth about her loins and wore widow's weeds. 6 She fasted all the days of her widowhood, except sabbath eves and sabbaths, new moon eves and new moons, feastdays and holidays of the house of Israel. 7 She was beautifully formed and lovely to behold. Her husband, Manasseh left, had her gold and silver, servants and maids, livestock and fields, which she was maintaining. 8 No one had a bad word to say about her, for she was a very God-fearing woman.

7, 5: *Lighted fires on their bastions:* to serve as signals for alerting the neighboring towns. Reference to fire signals in time of siege is made in the Lachish ostraca at the beginning of the sixth century B.C.

Kept watch throughout the night: to prevent a surprise attack.

8, 1: *Salamiel, son of Sarasadai:* head of the tribe of *Simeon* during the wanderings of the Israelites in the desert (Nm 1, 6).

8, 5: *A tent:* erected by Judith on the roof of her house (v 5); it was here that the elders came to confer with her (v 11).

Her Words to the Elders

9 When Judith, therefore, heard of the harsh words which the people, discouraged by their lack of water had spoken against their ruler, and of all that Uzziah had said to them in reply, swearing that he would hand over the city to the Assyrians at the end of five days, 10 she sent the maid who was in charge of all her things to ask Uzziah, Chabris, and Charmis, the elders of the city, to visit her. 11 When they came, she said to them: "Listen to me, you rulers of the people of Bethulia. What you said to the people today is not proper. When you promised to hand over the city to our enemies at the end of five days unless within that time the Lord comes to our aid, you interposed between God and yourselves this oath which you took. 12 Who are you, then, that you should have put God to the test this day, setting yourselves in the place of God in human affairs? 13 It is the Lord Almighty for whom you are laying down conditions; will you never understand anything? 14 You cannot plumb the depths of the human heart or grasp the workings of the human mind; how then can you fathom God, who has made all these things, discern his mind, and understand his plan?

"No, my brothers, do not anger the Lord our God. 15 For if he does not wish to come to our aid within the five days, he has it equally within his power to protect us at such time as he pleases, or to destroy us in the face of our enemies. 16 It is not for you to make the Lord our God give surety for his plans.

"God is not man that he should be moved by threats, nor human, that he may be given an ultimatum.

17 "So while we wait for the salvation that comes from him, let us call upon him to help us, and he will hear our cry if it is his good pleasure. 18 For there has not risen among us in recent generations, nor does there exist today, any tribe, or clan or town or city of ours that worships gods made by hands, as happened in former days. 19 It was for such conduct that our forefathers were handed over to the sword and to pillage, and fell with great destruction before our enemies. 20 But since we acknowledge no other god but the Lord, we hope that he will not disdain us or any of our people. 21 If we are taken, all Judea will fall, our sanctuary will be plundered, and God will make us pay for its profanation with our life's blood. 22 For the slaughter of our kinsmen, for the taking of exiles from the land, and for the devastation of our inheritance, he will lay the guilt on our heads. Wherever we shall be enslaved among the nations, we shall be a mockery and a reproach in the eyes of our masters. 23 Our enslavement will not be turned to our benefit, but the Lord our God, will maintain it to our disgrace.

24 "Therefore, my brothers, let us set an example for our kinsmen. Their lives depend on us, and the defense of the sanctuary, the temple, and the altar rests with us. 25 Besides all this, we should be grateful to the Lord our God, for putting us to the test, as he did our forefathers. 26 Recall how he dealt with Abraham, and how he tried Isaac, and all that happened to Jacob in Syrian Mesopotamia while he was tending the flocks of Laban, his mother's brother. 27 Not for vengeance did the Lord put them in the crucible to try their hearts, nor has he done so with us. It is by way of admonition that he chastises those who are close to him."

Uzziah's Response

28 Then Uzziah said to her: "All that you have said was spoken with good sense, and no one can gainsay your words. 29 Not today only is your wisdom made evident, but from your earliest years all the people have recognized your prudence, which corresponds to the worthy dispositions of your heart. 30 The people, however, were so tortured with thirst that they forced us to speak to them as we did, and to bind ourselves by an oath that we cannot break. 31 But now, God-fearing woman that you are, pray for us that the Lord may send rain to fill up our cisterns, lest we be weakened still further."

32 Then Judith said to them: "Listen to me! I will do something that will go down from generation to generation among the descendants of our race. 33 Stand at the gate tonight to let me pass through with my maid; and within the days you have specified before you will surrender the city to our enemies, the Lord will rescue Israel by my hand. 34 You must not inquire into what I am doing, for I will not tell you until my plan has been accomplished." 35 Uzziah and the rulers said to her, "Go in peace, and may the Lord God go before you to take vengeance upon our enemies!" 36 Then they withdrew from the tent and returned to their posts.

The Prayer of Judith

9 Judith threw herself down prostrate, with ashes strewn upon her head, and wearing nothing over her sackcloth. While the incense was being offered in the temple of God in Jerusalem that evening, Judith prayed to the Lord with a loud voice: 2 "Lord, God of my forefather Simeon! You put a sword into his hand to take revenge upon the foreigners who had immodestly loosened the maiden's girdle, shamefully exposed her thighs, and disgracefully violated her body. This they did, though you forbade it. 3 Therefore you had their rulers slaughtered; and you covered with their blood the bed in which they lay deceived, the same bed that had felt the shame of their own deceiving. You smote the slaves together with their princes, and the princes together with their servants. 4 Their wives you handed over to plunder, and their daughters to captivity; and all the spoils you divided among your favored sons, who burned with zeal for you, and in their abhorrence

9, 2: *The Maiden:* Dinah, Jacob's daughter, who was violated by Shechem, the Hivite (Gn 34, 2).

9, 3: Because Shechem had deceived and violated Dinah, her brothers, Simeon and Levi, tricked Shechem and the men of his city into being circumcised, and then slew them while they were confined to bed from the circumcision; cf Gn 34, 13–29.

of the defilement of their kinswoman, called on you for help.

5 "O God, my God, hear me also, a widow. It is you who were the author of those events and of what preceded and followed them. The present, also, and the future you have planned. 6 Whatever you devise comes into being; the things you decide on come forward and say, 'Here we are!' All your ways are in readiness, and your judgment is made with foreknowledge.

7 "Here are the Assyrians, a vast force priding themselves on horse and rider, boasting of the power of their infantry, trusting in shield and spear, bow and sling. They do not know that

8 "'You, the Lord, crush warfare; Lord is your name.'

"Shatter their strength in your might, and crush their force in your wrath; for they have resolved to profane your sanctuary, to defile the tent where your glorious name resides, and to overthrow with iron the horns of your altar. 9 See their pride, and send forth your wrath upon their heads. Give me, a widow, the strong hand to execute my plan. 10 With the guile of my lips, smite the slave together with the ruler, the ruler together with his servant; crush their pride by the hand of a woman. 11 "Your strength is not in numbers, nor does your power depend upon stalwart men; but you are the God of the lowly, the helper of the oppressed, the supporter of the weak, the protector of the forsaken, the savior of those without hope.

12 "Please, please, God of my forefather, God of the heritage of Israel, Lord of heaven and earth, Creator of the waters, King of all you have created, hear my prayer! 13 Let my guileful speech bring wound and wale on those who have planned dire things against your covenant, your holy temple, Mount Zion, and the homes your children have inherited. 14 Let your whole nation and all the tribes know clearly that you are the God of all power

and might and that there is no other who protects the people of Israel but you alone."

Judith's Departure

10 As soon as Judith had thus concluded, and ceased her invocation to the God of Israel, 2 she rose from the ground. She called her maid and they went down into the house, which she used only on sabbaths and feast days. 3 She took off the sackcloth she had on, laid aside the garments of her widowhood washed her body with water, and anointed it with rich ointment. She arranged her hair and bound it with a fillet, and put on the festive attire she had worn while her husband, Manasseh, was living. 4 She chose sandals for her feet, and put on her anklets, bracelets, rings, earrings, and all her other jewelry. Thus she made herself very beautiful, to captivate the eyes of all the men who should see her.

5 She gave her maid a leather flask of wine and a cruse of oil. She filled a bag with roasted grain, fig cakes, bread and cheese; all these provisions she wrapped up and gave to the maid to carry.

6 Then they went out to the gate of the city of Bethulia and found Uzziah and the elders of the city, Chabri and Charmis, standing there. 7 When these men saw Judith transformed in looks and differently dressed, they were very much astounded at her beauty and said to her, 8 "May the God of our fathers bring you to favor, and make your undertaking a success, for the glory of the Israelites and the exaltation of Jerusalem."

Judith bowed down to God. Then she said to them, 9 "Order the gate of the city opened for me, that I may go to carry out the business we discussed." So they ordered the youths to open the gate for her as she requested. 10 When they did so, Judith and her maid went out. The men of the city kept her in view as she went down the mountain and crossed the valley; then they lost sight of her.

Judith Captured

11 As Judith and her maid walked directly across the valley, they encountered the Assyrian outpost. 12 The men took her in custody and asked her, "To what people do you belong? Where do you come from, and where are you going?" She replied: "I am a daughter of the Hebrews, and I am fleeing from them, because they are about to be delivered up to you as prey. 13 I have come to see Holofernes, the general in chief of your forces, to give him a trustworthy report; I will show him the route by which he can ascend and take possession of the whole mountain district without a single one of his men suffering injury or loss of life."

14 When the men heard her words and gazed upon her face, which appeared wondrously beautiful to them, they said to her, 15 "By coming down thus promptly to see our master, you have saved your life. Now go to his tent; some of our men will accompany you to present you to him. 16 When you stand before him, have no fear in your heart; give him the report you speak of, and he will treat you well." 17 So they detailed a hundred of their men as an escort for her and her maid, and these conducted them to the tent of Holofernes.

18 When the news of her arrival spread among the tents, a crowd gathered in the camp. They came and stood around her as she waited outside the tent of Holofernes, while he was being informed about her. 19 They marveled at her beauty, regarding the Israelites with wonder because of her, and they said to one another, "Who can despise this people that has such women among them? It is not wise to leave one man of them alive, for if any were to be spared they could beguile the whole world."

Judith Meets Holofernes

20 The guard of Holofernes and all his servants came out and ushered her into the tent.

10, 12f: The deceitful means used by Judith against Holofernes, here and in 11, 5–19, are to be judged in the light of the moral concepts of Old Testament times; cf Gn 27, 1–25; 34, 13–29; 37, 32ff; Jos 2, 1–7; Jgs 4, 17–22.

21 Now Holofernes was reclining on his bed under a canopy with a netting of crimson and gold, emeralds and other precious stones. 22 When they announced her to him, he came out to the antechamber, preceded by silver lamps; 23 and when Holofernes and his servants beheld Judith, they all marveled at the beauty of her face. She threw herself down prostrate before him, but his servants raised her up.

11 Then Holofernes said to her: "Take courage, lady; have no fear in your heart! Never have I harmed anyone who chose to serve Nebuchadnezzar, king of all the earth. 2 Nor would I have raised my spear against your people who dwell in the mountain region, had they not despised me and brought this upon themselves. 3 But now tell me why you fled from them and came to us. In any case, you have come to safety. Take courage! Your life is spared tonight and for the future. 4 No one at all will harm you. Rather you will be well treated, as are all the servants of my lord, King Nebuchadnezzar."

5 Judith answered him: "Listen to the words of your servant, and let your handmaid speak in your presence! I will tell no lie to my lord this night, 6 and if you follow out the words of your handmaid, God will give you complete success, and my lord will not fail in any of his undertakings. 7 By the life of Nebuchadnezzar, king of all the earth, and by the power of him who has sent you to set all creatures aright! not only do men serve him through you; but even the wild beasts and the cattle and the birds of the air, because of your strength, will live for Nebuchadnezzar and his whole house. 8 Indeed, we have heard of your wisdom and sagacity, and all the world is aware that throughout the kingdom you alone are competent, rich in experience, and distinguished in military strategy.

9 "As for Achoir's speech in your council, we have heard of it. When the men of Bethulia spared him, he told them all he had said to you. 10 So then, my lord and master, do not disregard his word, but bear it in mind, for it is true. For our people are not punished, nor does the sword prevail against them, except when they sin against their God. 11 But now their guilt has caught up with them, by which they bring the wrath of their God upon them whenever they do wrong; so that my lord will not be repulsed and fail, but death will overtake them. 12 Since their food gave out and all their water ran low, they decided to kill their animals, and determined to consume all the things which God in his laws forbade them to eat. 13 They decreed that they would use up the first fruits of grain and the tithes of wine and oil which they had sanctified and reserved for the priests who minister in the presence of our God in Jerusalem: things which no layman should even touch with his hands. 14 They have sent messengers to Jerusalem to bring back with them authorization from the council of the elders; for the inhabitants there have also done these things. 15 On the very day when the response reaches them and they act upon it, they will be handed over to you for destruction.

16 "As soon as I, your handmaid, learned all this, I fled from them. God has sent me to perform with you such deeds that people throughout the world will be astonished on hearing of them. 17 Your handmaid is, indeed, a God-fearing woman, serving the God of heaven night and day. Now I will remain with you, my lord; but each night your handmaid will go out to the ravine and pray to God. He will tell me when the Israelites have committed their crimes. 18 Then I will come and let you know, so that you may go out with your whole force, and not one of them will be able to withstand you. 19 I will lead you through Judea, till you come to Jerusalem, and there I will set up your judgment seat. You will drive them like sheep that have no shepherd, and not even a dog will growl at you. This was told me, and announced to me in advance, and I in turn have been sent to tell you."

20 Her words pleased Holofernes and all his servants; they marveled at her wisdom and exclaimed, 21 "No other woman from one end of the world to the other looks so beautiful and speaks so wisely!" 22 Then Holofernes said to her: "God has done well in sending you ahead of your people, to bring victory to our arms, and destruction to those who have despised my lord. 23 You are fair to behold, and your words are well spoken. If you do as you have said, your God will be my God; you shall dwell in the palace of King Nebuchadnezzar, and shall be renowned throughout the earth."

Judith's Conduct

12 Then he ordered them to lead her into the room where his silverware was kept, and bade them set a table for her with his own delicacies to eat and his own wine to drink. 2 But Judith said, "I will not partake of them, lest it be an occasion of sin; but I shall be amply supplied from the things I brought with me." 3 Holofernes asked her: "But if your provisions give out, where shall we get more of the same to provide for you? None of your people are with us." 4 Judith answered him, "As surely as you, my lord, live, your handmaid will not use up her supplies till the Lord accomplishes by my hand what he has determined."

5 Then the servants of Holofernes led her into the tent, where she slept till midnight. In the night watch just before dawn, she rose 6 and sent this message to Holofernes, "Give orders, my lord, to let your handmaid go out for prayer." 7 So Holofernes ordered his bodyguard not to hinder her. Thus she stayed in the camp three days. Each night she went out to the ravine of Bethulia, where she washed herself at the spring of the camp. 8 After bathing, she besought the Lord, the God of Israel to direct her way for the triumph of his people. 9 Then she returned purified to the tent, and remained there until her food was brought to her toward evening.

Holofernes' Banquet

10 On the fourth day Holofernes gave a banquet for his servants alone, to which he did not invite any of the

---

12, 10: *Banquet for his servants alone . . . officers:* Holofernes invited the officials of his household, but not the officers of his army, who were needed for military duty.

officers. 11 And he said to Bagoas, the eunuch in charge of his household: "Go and persuade this Hebrew woman in your care to come and to eat and drink with us. 12 It would be a disgrace for us to have such a woman with us without enjoying her company. If we do not entice her, she will laugh us to scorn."

13 So Bagoas left the presence of Holofernes, and came to Judith and said, "So fair a maiden should not be reluctant to come to my lord to be honored by him, to enjoy drinking wine with us, and to be like one of the Assyrian women who live in the palace of Nebuchadnezzar." 14 She replied, "Who am I to refuse my lord? Whatever is pleasing to him I will promptly do. This will be a joy for me till the day of my death."

15 Thereupon she proceeded to put on her festive garments and all her feminine adornments. Meanwhile her maid went ahead and spread out on the ground for her in front of Holofernes the fleece Bagoas had furnished for her daily use in reclining at her dinner. 16 Then Judith came in and reclined on it. The heart of Holofernes was in rapture over her, and his spirit was shaken. He was burning with the desire to possess her, for he had been biding his time to seduce her from the day he saw her. 17 Holofernes said to her, "Drink and be merry with us!" 18 Judith replied, "I will gladly drink, my lord, for at no time since I was born have I ever enjoyed life as much as I do today." 19 She then took the things her maid had prepared, and ate and drank in his presence. Holofernes, charmed by her, drank a great quantity of wine, more than he had ever drunk on one single day in his life.

13 When it grew late, his servants quickly withdrew. Bagoas closed the tent from the outside and excluded the attendants from their master's presence. They went off to their beds, for they were all tired from the prolonged banquet. 2 Judith was left alone in the tent with Holofernes, who lay prostrate on his bed, for he was sodden with wine. 3 She had ordered her maid to stand outside the bedroom and wait, as on the

other days, for her to come out; she said she would be going out for her prayer. To Bagoas she had said this also.

Beheading of Holofernes

4 When all had departed, and no one, small or great, was left in the bedroom, Judith stood by Holofernes' bed and said within herself: "O Lord, God of all might, in this hour look graciously on my undertaking for the exaltation of Jerusalem; 5 now is the time for aiding your heritage and for carrying out my design to shatter the enemies who have risen against us." 6 She went to the bedpost near the head of Holofernes, and taking his sword from it, 7 drew close to the bed, grasped the hair of his head, and said, "Strengthen me this day, O God of Israel!" 8 Then with all her might she struck him twice in the neck and cut off his head. 9 She rolled his body off the bed and took the canopy from its supports. Soon afterward, she came out and handed over the head of Holofernes to her maid, 10 who put it into her food pouch; and the two went off together as they were accustomed to do for prayer.

The Return to Bethulia

They passed through the camp, and skirting the ravine, reached Bethulia on the mountain. As they approached its gates, 11 Judith shouted to the guards from a distance: "Open! Open the gate! God, our God, is with us. Once more he has made manifest his strength in Israel and his power against our enemies; he has done it this very day." 12 When the citizens heard her voice, they quickly descended to their city gate and summoned the city elders. 13 All the people, from the least to the greatest, hurriedly assembled, for her return seemed unbelievable. They opened the gate and welcomed the two women. They made a fire for light; and when they gathered around the two, 14 Judith urged them with a loud voice: "Praise God, praise him! Praise God, who has not withdrawn his mercy from the house of Israel, but has shattered our enemies by my hand this very night."

15 Then she took the head out of the pouch, showed it to them, and said: "Here is the head of Holofernes, general in charge of the Assyrian army, and here is the canopy under which he lay in his drunkenness. The Lord struck him down by the hand of a woman. 16 As the Lord lives, who has protected me in the path I have followed, I swear that it was my face that seduced Holofernes to his ruin, and that he did not sin with me to my defilement or disgrace."

17 All the people were greatly astonished. They bowed down and worshiped God, saying with one accord, "Blessed are you, our God, who today have brought to nought the enemies of your people." 18 Then Uzziah said to her: "Blessed are you, daughter, by the Most High God, above all the women on earth; and blessed be the Lord God, the creator of heaven and earth, who guided your blow at the head of the chief of our enemies. 19 Your deed of hope will never be forgotten by those who tell of the might of God. 20 May God make this redound to your everlasting honor, rewarding you with blessings, because you risked your life when your people were being oppressed, and you averted our disaster, walking uprightly before our God." And all the people answered, "Amen! Amen!"

Judith's Counsel

14 Then Judith said to them: "Listen to me, my brothers. Take this head and hang it on the parapet of your wall. 2 At daybreak, when the sun rises on the earth, let each of you seize his weapons, and let all the able-bodied men rush out of the city under command of a captain, as if about to go down into the plain against the advance guard of the Assyrians, but without going down. 3 They will seize their armor and hurry to their camp to awaken the generals of the Assyrian army. When they run to the tent of Holofernes and do not find him, panic will seize them, and they will flee before you. 4 Then you and all the other inhabitants of the whole territory of Israel will pursue them and strike them down in their tracks. 5 But before doing this, summon for me Achior the Ammonite, that he may see and recognize the one who despised the house of Israel and sent him here to meet his death.''

Achior Summoned

6 So they called Achior from the house of Uzziah. When he came and saw the head of Holofernes in the hand of one of the men in the assembly of the people, he fell forward in a faint. 7 Then, after they lifted him up, he threw himself at the feet of Judith in homage, saying: ''Blessed are you in every tent of Judah; and, in every foreign nation, all who hear of you will be struck with terror. 8 But now, tell me all that you did during these days.'' So Judith told him, in the presence of the people, all that she had been doing from the day she left till the time she began speaking to them. 9 When she finished her account, the people cheered loudly, and their city resounded with shouts of joy. 10 Now Achior, seeing all that the God of Israel had done, believed firmly in him. He had the flesh of his foreskin circumcised, and he has been united with the house of Israel to the present day.

VICTORY

Consternation in the Camp

11 At daybreak they hung the head of Holofernes on the wall. Then all the Israelite men took up their arms and went to the slopes of the mountain. 12 When the Assyrians saw them, they notified their captains; these in turn went to the generals and division leaders and all their other commanders. 13 They came to the tent of Holofernes and said to the one in charge of all his things, ''Waken our master, for the slaves have dared come down to give us battle, to their utter destruction.'' 14 Bagoas went in, and knocked at the entry of the tent, presuming that he was sleeping with Judith. 15 As no one answered, he parted the curtains, entered the bedroom, and found him lying on the floor, a head-

less corpse. 16 He broke into a loud clamor of weeping, groaning, and howling, and rent his garments. 17 Then he entered the tent where Judith had her quarters; and, not finding her, he rushed out to the troops and cried: 18 ''The slaves have duped us! A single Hebrew woman has brought disgrace on the house of King Nebuchadnezzar. Here is Holofernes headless on the ground!''

19 When the commanders of the Assyrian army heard these words, they rent their tunics and were seized with consternation. Loud screaming and howling arose in the **15** camp. 1. On hearing what had happened, those still in their tents were amazed, 2 and overcome with fear and trembling. No one kept ranks any longer; they scattered in all directions, and fled along every road, both through the valley and in the mountain. 3 Those also who were stationed in the mountain district around Bethulia took to flight. Then all the Israelite warriors overwhelmed them.

Pursuit

4 Uzziah sent messengers to Betomasthaim, to Choba and Kona, and to the whole country of Israel to report what had happened, that all might fall upon the enemy and destroy them. 5 On hearing this, all the Israelites, with one accord, attacked them and cut them down as far as Choba. Even those from Jerusalem and the rest of the mountain region took part in this, for they too had been notified of the happenings in the camp of their enemies. The Gileadites and the Galileans struck the enemy's flanks with great slaughter, even beyound Damascus and its territory. 6 The remaining inhabitants of Bethulia swept down on the camp of the Assyrians, plundered it, and acquired great riches. 7 The Israelites who returned from the slaughter took possession of what was left, till the towns and villages in the mountains and on the plain were crammed with the enormous quantity of booty they had seized.

8 The high priest Joakim and the elders of the Israelites who dwelt in Jerusalem, came to see for themselves the good things that the Lord had done for Israel, and to meet and congratulate Judith. 9 When they had visited her, all with one accord blessed her, saying:

''You are the glory of Jerusalem
　　the surpassing joy of Israel;
　You are the splendid boast
　　of our people.
10 With your own hand you have
　　done all this;
　You have done good to Israel,
　　and God is pleased with
　　what you have wrought.
May you be blessed by the
　　Lord Almighty
　forever and ever!''

And all the people answered, ''Amen!''

11 For thirty days the whole populace plundered the camp, giving Judith the tent of Holofernes, with all his silver, his couches, his dishes, and all his furniture, which she accepted. She harnessed her mules, hitched her wagons to them and loaded these things on them. 12 All the women of Israel gathered to see her; and they blessed her and performed a dance in her honor. She took branches in her hands and distributed them to the women around her, 13 and she and the other women crowned themselves with garlands of olive leaves. At the head of all the people, she led the women in the dance, while the men of Israel followed in their armor, wearing garlands and singing hymns.

Hymn of Praise

14 Judith led all Israel in this song of thanksgiving, and the people swelled this hymn of praise:

16 ''Strike up the instruments,
　　a song to my God with
　　　timbrels,
　chant to the Lord with
　　cymbals;
　Sing to him a new song,
　　exalt and acclaim his name.

14, 6-10: In recognizing the head of Holofernes, whom he had known personally, Achior was so overcome with the evidence of the Lord's power exerted through a woman that he believed in the God of Israel.

15, 9: *You are the glory of Jerusalem, the surpassing*

joy of Israel; you are the splendid boast of our people: These words are used in the liturgy of the Church in regard to the Blessed Virgin Mary.

2 For the Lord is God; he
　　crushes warfare,
　and sets his encampment
　　among his people;
　he snatched me from the
　　hands of my persecutors.

3 "The Assyrian came from the
　　mountains of the north,
　with the myriads of his forces
　　he came;
　Their numbers blocked the
　　torrents,
　their horses covered the hills.
4 He threatened to burn my land,
　　put my youths to the sword,
　Dash my babes to the ground,
　　make my children a prey,
　and seize my virgins as spoil.

5 "But the Lord Almighty
　　thwarted them,
　by a woman's hand he
　　confounded them.
6 Not by youths was their mighty
　　one struck down,
　nor did titans bring him low,
　　nor huge giants attack him;
　But Judith, the daughter of
　　Merari,
　by the beauty of her
　　countenance disabled him.
7 She took off her widow's garb
　　to raise up the afflicted in
　　Israel.
　She anointed her face with
　　fragrant oil;
8 　with a fillet she fastened her
　　tresses,
　and put on a linen robe to
　　beguile him.
9 Her sandals caught his eyes,
　　and her beauty captivated his
　　mind.
　The sword cut through his
　　neck.

10 "The Persians were dismayed
　　at her daring,
　the Medes appalled at her
　　boldness.
11 When my lowly ones shouted,
　　they were terrified;
　when my weaklings cried out,
　　they trembled;
　at the sound of their war cry,
　　they took to flight.
12 Sons of slave girls pierced them
　　through;
　the supposed sons of rebel
　　mothers cut them down;
　they perished before the ranks
　　of my Lord.

13 "A new hymn I will sing to my
　　God.
　O Lord, great are you and
　　glorious,
　wonderful in power and
　　unsurpassable.
14 Let your every creature serve
　　you;
　for you spoke, and they were
　　made,
　You sent forth your spirit, and
　　they were created;
　no one can resist your word.
15 The mountains to their bases,
　　and the seas, are shaken;
　the rocks, like wax, melt
　　before your glance.

　"But to those who fear you,
　　you are very merciful.

16 Though the sweet odor of every
　　sacrifice is a trifle,
　and the fat of all holocausts
　　but little in your sight,
　one who fears the Lord is
　　forever great.

17 "Woe to the nations that rise
　　against my people!
　the Lord Almighty will
　　requite them;

in the day of judgment he
　　will punish them:
He will send fire and worms
　　into their flesh,
　and they shall burn and suffer
　　forever."

Thanksgiving

18 The people then went to Jerusalem to worship God; when they were purified, they offered their holocausts, free-will offerings, and gifts. 19 Judith dedicated, as a votive offering to God, all the things of Holofernes that the people had given her, as well as the canopy that she herself had taken from his bedroom. 20 For three months the people continued their celebration in Jerusalem before the sanctuary, and Judith remained with them.

Judith's Renown

21 When those days were over, each one returned to his inheritance. Judith went back to Bethulia and remained on her estate. For the rest of her life she was renowned throughout the land. 22 Many wished to marry her, but she gave herself to no man all the days of her life from the time of the death and burial of her husband, Manasseh. 23 She lived to be very old in the house of her husband, reaching the advanced age of a hundred and five. She died in Bethulia, where they buried her in the tomb of her husband, Manasseh; 24 and the house of Israel mourned her for seven days. Before she died, she distributed her goods to the relatives of her husband, Manasseh, and to her own relatives; and to the maid she gave her freedom.

25 During the life of Judith and for a long time after her death, no one again disturbed the Israelites.

16, 17: *Fire and worms in their flesh:* see footnote on Is 66, 24.
16, 25: The Vulgate adds: "The feast of this victory was adopted by the Hebrews into the calendar of their holy days, and has been celebrated by the Jews from that time to the present." However, there is no other evidence of such a festivity; and it is the ancient feast of Passover to which the narrative is especially suited.

Esther

PROLOGUE

Dream of Mordecai

IN the second year of the reign of the great King Ahasuerus, on the first day of Nisan, Mordecai, son of Jair, son of Shimei, son of Kish, of the tribe of Benjamin, had a dream. 2 He was a Jew residing in the city of Susa, a prominent man who served at the king's court, 3 and one of the captives whom Nebuchadnezzar, king of Babylon, had taken from Jerusalem with Jeconiah, king of Judah.

4 This was his dream. There was noise and tumult, thunder and earthquake—confusion upon the earth. 5 Two great dragons came on, both poised for combat. They uttered a mighty cry, 6 and at their cry every nation prepared for war, to fight against the race of the just. 7 It was a dark and gloomy day. Tribulation and distress, evil and great confusion, lay upon the earth. 8 The whole race of the just were dismayed with fear of the evils to come upon them, and were at the point of destruction. 9 Then they cried out to God, and as they cried, there appeared to come forth a great river, a flood of water from a little spring.

10 The light of the sun broke forth; the lowly were exalted and they devoured the nobles.

11 Having seen this dream and what God intended to do, Mordecai awoke. He kept it in mind, and tried in every way, until night, to understand its meaning.

The Plot Discovered

12 Mordecai lodged at the court with Bagathan and Thares, two eunuchs of the king who were court guards. 13 He overheard them plotting, investigated their plans, and discovered that they were preparing to lay hands on King Ahasuerus. So he informed the king about them, 14 and the king had the two eunuchs questioned and, upon their confession, put to death. 15 Then the king had these things recorded; Mordecai, too, put them into writing. 16 The king also appointed Mordecai to serve at the court, and rewarded him for his actions.

17 Haman, however, son of Hammedatha the Agagite who was in high honor with the king, sought to harm Mordecai and his people because of the two eunuchs of the king.

ELEVATION OF ESTHER

The Banquet of Ahasuerus

1 During the reign of Ahasuerus— this was the Ahasuerus who ruled over a hundred and twenty-seven provinces from India to Ethiopia— 2 while he was occupying the royal throne in the stronghold of Susa, 3 in the third year of his reign, he

---

A, 1: *King Ahasuerus:* Xerxes I (486–465 B.C.). *Mordecai:* a Babylonian name, after the god Marduk. The genealogy of Mordecai is designed to reflect opposition to Israel's enemy, as narrated in 1 Sm 15, 7ff, where Saul (whose father's name was *Kish of the Tribe of Benjamin*) conquered Agag the Amalekite; in A, 17 Haman is said to be the son of an Agagite. Further emphasis on the Benjaminite-Agagite opposition can be seen in *Shimei*, the Benjaminite who reviled David (2 Sm 16, 5ff). Jair appears to be the minor Judge, a Transjordanian Manassehite (Jgs 10,

3). The chronology of the book would make Mordecai well over one hundred years old, since he was deported with Jehoiachin about 598 B.C., cf 2, 5f.

A, 4: The interpretation of this dream is given in F, 1–6.

A, 16: *Rewarded him:* this reward comes only later; see the sequence of events from the Hebrew text of Esther at 2, 22f, and 6, 3 below.

A, 17: *Haman . . . the Agagite:* opposed Mordecai the Benjaminite, by whom, however, he was overcome (7, 9f), just as King Agag, the Amalekite, was con-

quered by King Saul, ancestor of Mordecai (1 Sm 15, 7ff).

1, 1: *From India to Ethiopia:* from western India to Upper Egypt, the greatest extent of the Persian Empire achieved under Darius the Great, father of Ahasuerus.

1, 2: *Susa* ancient capital of Elam (Gn 14, 1); under the Achamenid kings, one of the two capitals of the Persian Empire. The other was Persepolis, the summer palace of the kings.

presided over a feast for all his officers and ministers: the Persian and Median aristocracy, the nobles, and the governors of the provinces. 4 For as many as a hundred and eighty days, he displayed the glorious riches of his kingdom and the resplendent wealth of his royal estate.

5 At the end of this time the king gave a feast of seven days in the garden court of the royal palace for all the people, great and small, who were in the stronghold of Susa. 6 There were white cotton draperies and violet hangings, held by cords of crimson byssus from silver rings on marble pillars. Gold and silver couches were on the pavement, which was of porphyry, marble, mother-of-pearl, and colored stones. 7 Liquor was served in a variety of golden cups, and the royal wine flowed freely, as befitted the king's munificence. 8 By ordinance of the king the drinking was unstinted, for he had instructed all the stewards of his household to comply with the good pleasure of everyone.

9 Queen Vashti also gave a feast for the women inside the royal palace of King Ahasuerus.

Deposal of Vashti

10 On the seventh day, when the king was merry with wine, he instructed Mehuman, Biztha, Harbona, Bigtha, Abagtha, Zethar, and Carkas, the seven eunuchs who attended King Ahasuerus, 11 to bring Queen Vashti into his presence wearing the royal crown, that he might display her beauty to the populace and the officials, for she was lovely to behold. 12 But Queen Vashti refused to come at the royal order issued through the eunuchs. At this the king's wrath flared up, and he burned with fury. 13 He conferred with the wise men versed in the law, because the king's business was conducted in general consultation with lawyers and jurists. 14 He summoned Carshena, Shethar, Admatha, Tarshish, Meres, Marsena and Memucan, the seven Persian and

Median officials who were in the king's personal service and held first rank in the realm, 15 and asked them, "What is to be done by law with Queen Vashti for disobeying the order of the King Ahasuerus issued through the eunuchs?"

16 In the presence of the king and of the officials, Memucan answered: "Queen Vashti has not wronged the king alone, but all the officials and the populace throughout the provinces of King Ahasuerus. 17 For the queen's conduct will become known to all the women, and they will look with disdain upon their husbands when it is reported, 'King Ahasuerus commanded that Queen Vashti be ushered into his presence, but she would not come.' 18 This very day the Persian and Median ladies who hear of the queen's conduct will rebel against all the royal officials, with corresponding distain and rancor. 19 If it please the king, let an irrevocable royal decree be issued by him and inscribed among the laws of the Persians and Medes, forbidding Vashti to come into the presence of King Ahasuerus and authorizing the king to give her royal dignity to one more worthy than she. 20 Thus, when the decree which the king will issue is published throughout his realm, vast as it is, all wives will honor their husbands, from the greatest to the least."

21 This proposal found acceptance with the king and the officials, and the king acted on the advice of Memucan. 22 He sent letters to all the royal provinces, to each province in its own script and to each people in its own language, to the effect that every man should be lord in his own home.

Esther Made Queen

2 After this, when King Ahasuerus' wrath had cooled, he thought over what Vashti had done and what had been decreed against her. 2 Then the king's personal attendants suggested: "Let beautiful young virgins be sought for the king. 3

Let the king appoint commissaries in all the provinces of his realm to bring together all beautiful young virgins to the harem in the stronghold of Susa. Under the care of the royal eunuch Hegai, custodian of the women, let cosmetics be given them. 4 Then the girl who pleases the king shall reign in the place of Vashti." This suggestion pleased the king, and he acted accordingly.

5 There was in the stronghold of Susa a certain Jew named Mordecai, son of Jair, son of Shimei, son of Kish, a Benjaminite, 6 who had been exiled from Jerusalem with the captives taken with Jeconiah, king of Judah, whom Nebuchadnezzar, king of Babylon, had deported. 7 He was foster father to Hadassah, that is, Esther, his cousin; for she had lost both father and mother. The girl was beautifully formed and lovely to behold. On the death of her father and mother, Mordecai had taken her as his own daughter.

8 When the king's order and decree had been obeyed and many maidens brought together to the stronghold of Susa under the care of Hegai, Esther also was brought in to the royal palace under the care of Hegai, custodian of the women. 9 The girl pleased him and won his favor. So he promptly furnished her with cosmetics and provisions. Then picking out seven maids for her from the royal palace, he transferred both her and her maids to the best place in the harem. 10 Esther did not reveal her nationality or family, for Mordecai had commanded her not to do so. 11 Day by day Mordecai would walk about in front of the court of the harem, to learn how Esther was faring and what was to become of her.

12 Each girl went in turn to visit King Ahasuerus after the twelve months' preparation decreed for the women. Of this period of beautifying treatment, six months were spent with oil of myrrh, and the other six months with perfumes and cosmetics. 13 Then, when the girl was to visit

1, 9: *Queen Vashti:* Herodotus (*Histories* 7, 61) relates that the wife of Ahasuerus was Amestris.
1, 19: *Irrevocable royal decree:* The historian Siculus indicates that such a concept of *irrevocable* laws existed in the time of Darius III (335–331 B.C.), the last of the Persian kings; cf 8, 8.

1, 22: *To each province . . . script and to each people . . . language:* many languages were spoken in the Persian Empire, the principal ones being Persian, Elamite, Babylonian, Aramaic, Phoenician, Egyptian, and Greek. Each of them had its own script.
2, 7: *Hadassah* (the feminine form of *hadas,*

myrtle), was the name by which this woman would be known among her Jewish compatriots. *Esther* is a variant of the name of the Babylonian goddess Ishtar.

the king, she was allowed to take with her from the harem to the royal palace whatever she chose. 14 She would go in the evening and return in the morning to a second harem under the care of the royal eunuch Shaashgaz, custodian of the concubines. She could not return to the king unless he was pleased with her and had her summoned by name.

15 As for Esther, daughter of Abihail and adopted daughter of his nephew Mordecai, when her turn came to visit the king, she did not ask for anything but what the royal eunuch Hegai, custodian of the women, suggested. Yet she won the admiration of all who saw her. 16 Esther was led to King Ahasuerus in his palace in the tenth month, Tebeth, in the seventh year of his reign. 17 The king loved Esther more than all the other women, and of all the virgins she won his favor and benevolence. So he placed the royal diadem on her head and made her queen in place of Vashti 18 Then the king gave a great feast in honor of Esther to all his officials and ministers, granting a holiday to the provinces and bestowing gifts with royal bounty.

The Plot Discovered

19 [To resume: From the time the virgins had been brought together, and while Mordecai was passing his time at the king's gate, 20 Esther had not revealed her family or nationality, because Mordecai had told her not to; and Esther continued to follow Mordecai's instructions, just as she had when she was being brought up by him. 21 And during the time that Mordecai spent at the king's gate, Bagathan and Thares, two of the royal eunuchs who guarded the entrance, had plotted in anger to lay hands on King Ahasuerus. 22 When the plot became known to Mordecai, he told Queen Esther, who in turn informed the king for Mordecai. 23 The matter was investigated and verified, and both of

them were hanged on a gibbet. This was written in the annals for the king's use.]

HAMAN'S PLOT AGAINST THE JEWS

Mordecai Refuses To Honor Haman

3 After these events King Ahasuerus raised Haman, son of Hammedatha the Agagite, to high rank, seating him above all his fellow officials. 2 All the king's servants who were at the royal gate would kneel and bow down to Haman, for that is what the king had ordered in his regard. Mordecai, however, would not kneel and bow down. 3 The king's servants who were at the royal gate said to Mordecai, "Why do you disobey the king's order?" 4 When they had reminded him day after day and he would not listen to them, they informed Haman, to see whether Mordecai's explanation was acceptable, since he had told them that he was a Jew.

Haman's Reprisal

5 When Haman observed that Mordecai would not kneel and bow down to him, he was filled with anger. 6 Moreover, he thought it was not enough to lay hands on Mordecai alone. Since they had told Haman of Mordecai's nationality, he sought to destroy all the Jews, Mordecai's people, throughout the realm of King Ahasuerus. 7 In the first month, Nisan, in the twelfth year of King Ahasuerus, the *pur*, or lot, was cast in Haman's presence to determine the day and the month for the destruction of Mordecai's people on a single day, and the lot fell on the thirteenth day of the twelfth month, Adar.

Decree against the Jews

8 Then Haman said to King Ahasuerus: "Dispersed among the nations throughout the provinces of your kingdom there is a certain

people living apart, with laws differing from those of every other people. They do not obey the laws of the king, and so it is not proper for the king to tolerate them. 9 If it please the king, let a decree be issued to destroy them; and I will deliver to the procurators ten thousand silver talents for deposit in the royal treasury." 10 The king took the signet ring from his hand and gave it to Haman, son of Hammedatha the Agagite, the enemy of the Jews. 11 "The silver you may keep." the king said to Haman, "but as for this people, do with them whatever you please."

12 So the royal scribes were summoned; and on the thirteenth day of the first month they wrote, at the dictation of Haman, an order to the royal satraps, the governors of every province, and the officials of every people, to each province in its own script and to each people in its own language. It was written in the name of King Ahasuerus and sealed with the royal signet ring. 13 Letters were sent by couriers to all the royal provinces, that all the Jews, young and old, including women and children, should be killed, destroyed wiped out in one day, the thirteenth day of the twelfth month, Adar, and that their goods should be seized as spoil.

B This is a copy of the letter: "The great King Ahasuerus writes to the satraps of the hundred and twenty-seven provinces from India to Ethiopia, and the governors subordinate to them, as follows: 2 When I came to rule many peoples and to hold sway over the whole world, I determined not to be carried away with the sense of power, but always to deal fairly and with clemency; to provide for my subjects a life of complete tranquillity; and by making my government humane and effective as far as the borders, to restore the peace desired by all men. 3 When I consulted my counselors as to how this might be

---

2, 18: *A holiday:* or perhaps, "a remission of taxes."
2, 19–23: This is a resumption, in a slightly different form, of the story already told in A, 12–15.
2, 21: *Mordecai . . . at the king's gate:* to exercise watchful care for Esther. Some understand this to mean that Mordecai was stationed at the gate to render royal service; cf A, 2.

2, 23: *Hanged on a gibbet:* impaled, perhaps, after the Babylonian manner.
3, 2: *Mordecai would not kneel and bow down:* in order not to render to man the homage which he regarded as belonging to God alone; cf C, 5ff.
3, 7: *Pur:* a Babylonian word which the Hebrew translates as *goral,* "lot." This word is preserved in the

text because its plural, *purim,* became the name of the feast of Purim commemorating the deliverance of the Jews; cf 9, 24.26.
3, 10: *Signet ring:* a ring containing a seal which was impressed on documents to authenticate them. By giving this ring to Haman, the king bestowed on him the power to authenticate royal decrees.

accomplished, Haman, who excels among us in wisdom, who is outstanding for constant devotion and steadfast loyalty, and who has gained the second rank in the kingdom, 4 brought it to our attention that, mixed in with all the races throughout the world, there is one people of bad will, which by its laws is opposed to every other people and continually disregards the decrees of kings, so that the unity of empire blamelessly designed by us cannot be established.

5 "Having noted, therefore, that this most singular people is continually at variance with all men, lives by divergent and alien laws, is inimical to our interests, and commits the worst crimes, so that stability of government cannot be obtained, 6 we hearby decree that all those who are indicated to you in the letters of Haman, who is in charge of the administration and is a second father to us, shall, together with their wives and children, be utterly destroyed by the swords of their enemies, without any pity or mercy, on the fourteenth day of the twelfth month, Adar, of the current year; 7 so that when these people, who present ill will is of long standing, have gone down into the nether world by a violent death on a single day, they may at last leave our affairs stable and undisturbed for the future."

(3) 14 A copy of the decree to be promulgated as law in every province was published to all the peoples, that they might be prepared for that day. 15 The couriers set out in haste at the king's command; meanwhile the decree was promulgated in the stronghold of Susa. The king and Haman then sat down to feast, but the city of Susa was thrown into confusion.

Esther's Aid Sought by Mordecai

4 When Mordecai learned all that was happening, he tore his garments, put on sackcloth and ashes, and walked through the city crying out loudly and bitterly, 2 till he came before the royal gate, which no one clothed in sackcloth might enter. 3 (Likewise in each of the provinces, wherever the king's legal enactment reached, the Jews went into deep mourning, with fasting, weeping, and lament; they all slept on sackcloth and ashes.)

4 Queen Esther's maids and eunuchs came and told her. Overwhelmed with anguish, she sent garments for Mordecai to put on, so that he might take off his sackcloth; but he refused. 5 Esther then summoned Hathach, one of the king's eunuchs whom he had placed at her service, and commanded him to find out what this action of Mordecai meant and the reason for it. 6 So Hathach went out to Mordecai in the public square in front of the royal gate, 7 and Mordecai told him all that had happened, as well as the exact amount of silver Haman had promised to pay to the royal treasury for the slaughter of the Jews. 8 He also gave him a copy of the written decree for their destruction which had been promulgated in Susa, to show and explain to Esther. He was to instruct her to go to the king; she was to plead and intercede with him in behalf of her people. (B) 8 "Remember the days of your lowly estate," Mordecai had him say, "when you were brought up in my charge; for Haman, who is second to the king, has asked for our death. 9 Invoke the Lord and speak to the king for us; save us from death."

(4) 9 Hathach returned to Esther and told her what Mordecai had said. 10 Then Esther replied to Hathach and gave him this message for Mordecai: 11 "All the servants of the king and the people of his provinces know that any man or woman who goes to the king in the inner court without being summoned, suffers the automatic penalty of death, unless the king extends to him the golden scepter, thus sparing his life. Now as for me, I have not been summoned to the king for thirty days."

12 When Esther's words were reported to Mordecai, 13 he had this reply brought to her: "Do not imagine that because you are in the king's palace, you alone of all the Jews will escape. 14 Even if you now remain silent, relief and deliverance will come to the Jews from another source; but you and your father's house will perish. Who knows but that it was for a time like this that you obtained the royal dignity?"

15 Esther sent back to Mordecai the response: 16 "Go and assemble all the Jews who are in Susa; fast on my behalf, all of you, not eating or drinking, night or day, for three days. I and my maids will also fast in the same way. Thus prepared, I will go to the king, contrary to the law. If I perish, I perish!"

Prayer of Mordecai

C Mordecai went away and did exactly as Esther had commanded. Recalling all that the Lord had done, he prayed to him 2 and said: "O Lord God, almighty King, all things are in your power, and there is no one to oppose you in your will to save Israel. 3 You made heaven and earth and every wonderful thing under the heavens. 4 You are Lord of all, and there is no one who can resist you, Lord. 5 You know all things. You know, O Lord, that it was not out of insolence or pride or desire for fame that I acted thus in not bowing down to the proud Haman.

6 Gladly would I have kissed the soles of his feet for the salvation of Israel. 7 But I acted as I did so as not to place the honor of man above that of God. I will not bow down to anyone but you, my Lord. It is not out of pride that I am acting thus. 8 And now, Lord God, King, God of Abraham, spare your people, for our enemies plan our ruin and are bent upon destroying the inheritance that was yours from the beginning. 9 Do not spurn your portion, which you redeemed for yourself out of Egypt. 10 Hear my prayer; have pity on your inheritance and turn our sorrow into joy: thus we shall live to sing praise to your name, O Lord. Do not silence those who praise you."

B, 6: *Fourteenth day:* the Hebrew text, as in 2, 13 above, and the Greek text here translated do not agree on the day of the month specified by the king; a two-day celebration is decreed in chapter 9, and the 13th, 14th and 15th of Adar are all mentioned; see 9, 15.18.

4, 14: *From another source:* very probably Mordecai refers to divine aid; the Greek additions (C) are explicit about this.

11 All Israel, too, cried out with all their strength, for death was staring them in the face.

Prayer of Esther

12 Queen Esther, seized with mortal anguish, likewise had recourse to the Lord. 13 Taking off her splendid garments, she put on garments of distress and mourning. In place of her precious ointments she covered her head with dirt and ashes. She afflicted her body severely; all her festive adornments were put aside, and her hair was wholly disheveled.

14 Then she prayed to the Lord, the God of Israel, saying: "My Lord, our King, you alone are God. Help me, who am alone and have no help but you, 15 for I am taking my life in my hand. 16 As a child I was wont to hear from the people of the land of my forefathers that you, O Lord, chose Israel from among all peoples, and our fathers from among all their ancestors, as a lasting heritage, and that you fulfilled all your promises to them. 17 But now we have sinned in your sight, and you have delivered us into the hands of our enemies, 18 because we worshiped their gods. You are just, O Lord. 19 But now they are not satisfied with our bitter servitude, but have undertaken 20 to do away with the decree you have pronounced, and to destroy your heritage; to close the mouths of those who praise you, and to extinguish the glory of your temple and your altar; 21 to open the mouths of the heathen to acclaim their false gods, and to extol an earthly king forever.

22 "O Lord, do not relinquish your scepter to those that are nought. Let them not gloat over our ruin, but turn their own counsel against them and make an example of our chief enemy. 23 Be mindful of us, O Lord. Manifest yourself in the time of our distress and give me courage, King of Gods and Ruler of every power. 24 Put in my mouth persuasive words in the presence of the lion, and turn his heart to hatred for our enemy, so that he and those who

are in league with him may perish. 25 Save us by your power, and help me, who am alone and have no one but you, O Lord.

"You know all things. 26 You know that I hate the glory of the pagans, and abhor the bed of the uncircumcised or of any foreigner. 27 You know that I am under constraint, that I abhor the sign of grandeur which rests on my head when I appear in public; abhor it like a polluted rag, and do not wear it in private. 28 I, your handmaid, have never eaten at the table of Haman, nor have I graced the banquet of the king or drunk the wine of libations. 29 From the day I was brought here till now, your handmaid has had no joy except in you, O Lord, God of Abraham. 30 O God, more powerful than all, hear the voice of those in despair. Save us from the power of the wicked, and deliver me from my fear."

Esther is Received by the King

D On the third day, putting an end to her prayers, she took off her penitential garments and arrayed herself in her royal attire. 2 In making her state appearance, after invoking the all-seeing God and savior, she took with her two maids; 3 on the one she leaned gently for support, 4 while the other followed her, bearing her train. 5 She glowed with the perfection of her beauty and her countenance was as joyous as it was lovely, though her heart was shrunk with fear. 6 She passed through all the portals till she stood face to face with the king, who was seated on his royal throne, clothed in full robes of state, and covered with gold and precious stones, so that he inspired great awe. 7 As he looked up, his features ablaze with the height of majestic anger, the queen staggered, changed color, and leaned weakly against the head of the maid in front of her. 8 But God changed the king's anger to gentleness. In great anxiety he sprang from his throne, held her in his arms until she recovered, and comforted her with reassuring words. 9 "What is it, Esther?" he said to her. "I am your brother. Take courage! 10 You shall not die because of this

general decree of ours. 11 Come near!" Raising the golden scepter, 12 he touched her neck with it, embraced her, and said, "Speak to me."

13 She replied: "I saw you, my lord, as an angel of God, and my heart was troubled with fear of your majesty. 14 For you are awesome, my lord, though your glance is full of kindness." 15 As she said this, she fainted. 16 The king became troubled and all his attendants tried to revive her.

5 [Now on the third day, Esther put on her royal garments and stood in the inner courtyard, looking toward the royal palace, while the king was seated on his royal throne in the audience chamber, facing the palace doorway. 2 He saw Queen Esther standing in the courtyard, and made her welcome by extending toward her the golden staff which he held. She came up to him, and touched the top of the staff.]

3 Then the king said to her, "What is it, Queen Esther? What is your request? Even if it is half of my kingdom, it shall be granted you." 4 "If it please your majesty," Esther replied, "come today with Haman to a banquet I have prepared." 5 And the king ordered, "Have Haman make haste to fulfill the wish of Esther."

First Banquet of Esther

So the king went with Haman to the banquet Esther had prepared. 6 During the drinking of the wine, the king said to Esther, "Whatever you ask for shall be granted, and whatever request you make shall be honored, even if it be half my kingdom." 7 Esther replied: "This is my petition and request: 8 if I have found favor with the king and if it pleases your majesty to grant my petition and honor my request, come with Haman tomorrow to a banquet which I shall prepare for you; and then I will do as you ask."

Haman's Plot against Mordecai

9 That day Haman left happy and in good spirits. But when he saw that Mordecai at the royal gate did not

---

C, 28: *Wine of libations:* offered in sacrifice to the gods.

5, 1f: The Hebrew text here translated is a short form of the account already given in Greek.

rise and showed no fear of him, he was filled with anger toward him. 10 Haman restrained himself, however, and went home, where he summoned his friends and his wife Zeresh. 11 He recounted the greatness of his riches, the large number of his sons, and just how the king had promoted him and placed him above the officials and royal servants. 12 "Moreover," Haman added, "Queen Esther invited no one but me to the banquet with the king; again tomorrow I am to be her guest, with the king. 13 Yet none of this satisfies me as long as I continue to see the Jew Mordecai sitting at the royal gate." 14 His wife Zeresh and all his friends said to him, "Have a gibbet set up, fifty cubits in height, and in the morning ask the king to have Mordecai hanged on it. Then go to the banquet with the king in good cheer." This suggestion pleased Haman, and he had the gibbet erected.

VINDICATION OF THE JEWS

Mordecai's Reward from the King

6 That night the king, unable to sleep, asked that the chronicle of notable events be brought in. While this was being read to him, 2 the passage occurred in which Mordecai reported Bagathan and Teresh, two of the royal eunuchs who guarded the entrance, for seeking to lay hands on King Ahasuerus. 3 The king asked, "What was done to reward and honor Mordecai for this?" The king's attendants replied, "Nothing was done for him."

4 "Who is in the court?" the king asked. Now Haman had entered the outer court of the king's palace to suggest to the king that Mordecai should be hanged on the gibbet he had raised for him. 5 The king's servants answered him, "Haman is waiting in the court." "Let him come in," the king said. 6 When Haman entered, the king said to him, "What should be done for the man whom the king wishes to reward?" Now Haman thought to himself, "Whom would the king more probably wish to reward than me?" 7 So he replied to the king: "For the man whom the king wishes to reward 8 there should be brought the royal robe which the king wore and the horse on which the king rode when the royal crown was placed on his head. 9 The robe and the horse should be consigned to one of the noblest of the king's officials, who must clothe the man the king wishes to reward, have him ride on the horse in the public square of the city, and cry out before him, 'This is what is done for the man whom the king wishes to reward!'" 10 Then the king said to Haman: "Hurry! Take the robe and horse as you have proposed, and do this for the Jew Mordecai, who is sitting at the royal gate. Do not omit anything you proposed." 11 So Haman took the robe and horse, clothed Mordecai, had him ride in the public square of the city, and cried out before him, "This is what is done for the man whom the king wishes to reward!"

12 Mordecai then returned to the royal gate, while Haman hurried home, his head covered in grief. 13 When he told his wife Zeresh and all his friends everything that had happened to him, his advisers and his wife Zeresh said to him, "If Mordecai, before whom you are beginning to decline, is of the Jewish race, you will not prevail against him, but will surely be defeated by him."

Esther's Second Banquet

14 While they were speaking with him, the king's eunuchs arrived and hurried Haman off to the banquet 7 Esther had prepared. 1 So the king and Haman went to the banquet with Queen Esther. 2 Again, on this second day, during the drinking of the wine, the king said to Esther, "Whatever you ask, Queen Esther, shall be granted you. Whatever request you make shall be honored, even for half the kingdom." 3 Queen Esther replied: "If I have found favor with you, O king, and if it pleases your majesty, I ask that my life be spared, and I beg that you spare the lives of my people. 4 For my people and I have been delivered to destruction, slaughter and extinction. If we were to be sold into slavery I would remain silent, but as it is, the enemy will be unable to compensate for the harm done to the king." 5 "Who and where," said King Ahasuerus to Queen Esther, "is the man who has dared to do this?" 6 Esther replied, "The enemy oppressing us is this wicked Haman." At this, Haman was seized with dread of the king and queen.

7 The king left the banquet in anger and went into the garden of the palace, but Haman stayed to beg Queen Esther for his life, since he saw that the king had decided on his doom. 8 When the king returned from the garden of the palace to the banquet hall, Haman had thrown himself on the couch on which Esther was reclining; and the king exclaimed, "Will he also violate the queen while she is with me in my own house!" Scarcely had the king spoken when the face of Haman was covered over.

Punishment of Haman

9 Harbona, one of the eunuchs attended the king, said, "At the house of Haman stands a gibbet fifty cubits high. Haman prepared it for Mordecai, who gave the report that benefited the king." The king answered, "Hang him on it." 10 So they hanged Haman on the gibbet which he had made ready for Mordecai, and the anger of the king abated.

8 That day King Ahasuerus gave the house of Haman, enemy of the Jews, to Queen Esther; and Mordecai was admitted to the king's presence, for Esther had revealed his relationship to her. 2 The king removed his signet ring from Haman, and transferred it into the keeping of Mordecai; and Esther put Mordecai in charge of the house of Haman.

The Second Royal Decree

3 In another audience with the king, Esther fell at his feet and tearfully implored him to revoke the harm done by Haman the Agagite, and the plan he had devised against the Jews. 4 The king stretched forth the golden scepter to Esther. So she rose and, standing in his presence, 5 said: "If it pleases your majesty and seems proper to you, and if I have found favor with you and you love me, let a document be issued to

revoke the letters which that schemer Haman, son of Hammedatha the Agagite, wrote for the destruction of the Jews in all the royal provinces. 6 For how can I witness the evil that is to befall my people, and how can I behold the destruction of my race?"

7 King Ahasuerus then said to Queen Esther and to the Jew Mordecai: "Now that I have given Esther the house of Haman, and they have hanged him on the gibbet because he attacked the Jews, 8 you in turn may write in the king's name what you see fit concerning the Jews and seal the letter with the royal signet ring." For whatever is written in the name of the king and sealed with the royal signet ring cannot be revoked.

9 At that time, on the twenty-third day of the third month, Sivan, the royal scribes were summoned. Exactly as Mordecai dictated, they wrote to the Jews and to the satraps, governors and officials of the hundred and twenty-seven provinces from India to Ethiopia: to each province in its own script and to each people in its own language, and to the Jews in their own script and language. 10 These letters, which he wrote in the name of King Ahasuerus and sealed with the royal signet ring, he sent by mounted couriers riding thoroughbred royal steeds. 11 In these letters the king authorized the Jews in each and every city to group together and defend their lives, and to kill, destroy, wipe out, along with their wives and children, every armed group of any nation or province which should attack them, and to seize their goods as spoil 12 throughout the provinces of King Ahasuerus, on a single day, the thirteenth of the twelfth month, Adar.

E The following is a copy of the letter:

"King Ahasuerus the Great to the governors of the provinces in the hundred and twenty-seven satrapies from India to Ethiopia, and to those responsible for our interests: Greetings!

2 "Many have become the more ambitious the more they were showered with honors through the bountiful generosity of their patrons. 3 Not only do they seek to do harm to our subjects; incapable of bearing such greatness, they even begin plotting against their own benefactors. 4 Not only do they drive out gratitude from among men; with the arrogant boastfulness of those to whom goodness has no meaning, they suppose they will escape the vindictive judgment of the all-seeing God.

5 "Often, too, the fair speech of friends entrusted with the administration of affairs has induced many placed in authority to become accomplices in the shedding of innocent blood, and has involved them in irreparable calamities 6 by deceiving with malicious slander the sincere good will of rulers. 7 This can be verified in the ancient stories that have been handed down to us, but more fully when one considers the wicked deeds perpetrated in your midst by the pestilential influence of those undeserving of authority. 8 We must provide for the future, so as to render the kingdom undisturbed and peaceful for all men, 9 taking advantage of changing conditions and deciding always with equitable treatment matters coming to our attention.

10 "For instance, Haman, son of Hammedatha, a Macedonian, certainly not of Persian blood, and very different from us in generosity, was hospitably received by us. 11 He so far enjoyed the good will which we have toward all peoples that he was proclaimed 'father of the king,' before whom everyone was to bow down; he attained the rank second to the royal throne. 12 But, unequal to this dignity, he strove to deprive us of kingdom and of life; 13 and by weaving intricate webs of deceit, he demanded the destruction of Mordecai, our savior and constant benefactor, and of Esther, our blameless royal consort, together with their

whole race. 14 For by such measures he hoped to catch us defenseless and to transfer the rule of the Persians to the Macedonians. 15 But we find that the Jews, who were doomed to extinction by this archcriminal, are not evildoers, but rather are governed by very just laws 16 and are the children of the Most High, the living God of majesty, who has maintained the kingdom in a flourishing condition for us and for our forebears.

17 "You will do well, then, to ignore the letter sent by Haman, son of Hammedatha, 18 for he who composed it has been hanged, together with his entire household, before the gates of Susa. Thus swiftly has God, who governs all, brought just punishment upon him.

19 "You shall exhibit a copy of this letter publicly in every place, to certify that the Jews may follow their own laws, 20 and that you may help them on the day set for their ruin, the thirteenth day of the twelfth month, Adar, to defend themselves against those who attack them. 21 For God, the ruler of all, has turned that day for them from one of destruction of the chosen race into one of joy. 22 Therefore, you too must celebrate this memorable day among your designated feasts with all rejoicing, 23 so that both now and in the future it may be, for us and for loyal Persians, a celebration of victory, and for those who plot against us a reminder of destruction.

24 "Every city and province, without exception, that does not observe this decree shall be ruthlessly destroyed with fire and sword, so that it will be left not merely untrodden by men, but even shunned by wild beasts and birds forever."

8 13 A copy of the letter to be promulgated as law in each and every province was published among all the peoples, so that the Jews might be prepared on that day to avenge themselves on their enemies.

8, 8: *Whatever is written . . . cannot be revoked:* the king cannot directly grant Esther's request (v 5) to revoke the precious decree against the Jews because of the irrevocable character of the laws of the Medes and Persians (1, 19; Dn 6, 9); but he empowers Esther to issue a new decree in his name which renders the earlier decree without effect; cf 3, 12f.

E, 10: *Macedonian:* a redactor of the book in the Hellenistic period used the designation *Macedonian,* here and in v 14, to express, after Macedonia's conquest of Persia, the most odious kind of man that a Persian ruler could be supposed to think of; the Hebrew text, for a similar reason, called Haman an Agagite. See note on A, 17.

8, 13: *Avenge themselves on their enemies:* partly in self-defense (E, 20), and partly to express the fact that the extreme cruelty designed against the Jews by their enemies now recoiled upon the latter as a punishment. Cf 9, 1f.

14 Couriers mounted on royal steeds sped forth in haste at the king's order, and the decree was promulgated in the stronghold of Susa.

15 Mordecai left the king's presence clothed in a royal robe of violet and of white cotton, with a large crown of gold and a cloak of crimson byssus. The city of Susa shouted with joy, 16 and there was splendor and merriment for the Jews, exultation and triumph. 17 In each and every province and in each and every city, wherever the king's order arrived, there was merriment and exultation, banqueting and feasting for the Jews. And many of the peoples of the land embraced Judaism, for they were seized with a fear of the Jews.

Victory of the Jews

9 When the day arrived on which the order decreed by the king was to be carried out, the thirteenth day of the twelfth month, Adar, on which the enemies of the Jews had expected to become masters of them, the situation was reversed: the Jews became masters of their enemies. 2 The Jews mustered in their cities throughout the provinces of King Ahasuerus to attack those who sought to do them harm, and no one could withstand them, but all peoples were seized with a fear of them. 3 Moreover, all the officials of the provinces, the satraps, governors, and royal procurators supported the Jews from fear of Mordecai; 4 for Mordecai was powerful in the royal palace, and the report was spreading through all the provinces that he was continually growing in power.

5 The Jews struck down all their enemies with the sword, killing and destroying them; they did to their enemies as they pleased. 6 In the stronghold of Susa, the Jews killed and destroyed five hundred men. 7 They also killed Parshandatha, Dalphon, Aspatha, 8 Porathai, Adalia, Aridatha, 9 Parmashta, Arisai, Aridai, and Vaizatha, 10 the ten sons

of Haman, son of Hammedatha, the foe of the Jews. However, they did not engage in plundering.

11 On the same day, when the number of those killed in the stronghold of Susa was reported to the king, 12 he said to Queen Esther: "In the stronghold of Susa the Jews have killed and destroyed five hundred men, as well as the ten sons of Haman. What must they have done in the other royal provinces! You shall again be granted whatever you ask, and whatever you request shall be honored." 13 So Esther said, "If it pleases your majesty, let the Jews in Susa be permitted again tomorrow to act according to today's decree, and let the ten sons of Haman be hanged on gibbets." 14 The king then gave an order to this effect, and the decree was published in Susa. So the ten sons of Haman were hanged, 15 and the Jews in Susa mustered again on the fourteenth of the month of Adar and killed three hundred men in Susa. However, they did not engage in plundering.

16 The other Jews, who dwelt in the royal provinces, also mustered and defended themselves, and obtained rest from their enemies. They killed seventy-five thousand of their foes, without engaging in plunder, 17 on the thirteenth day of the month of Adar. On the fourteenth of the month they rested, and made it a day of feasting and rejoicing. 18 (The Jews in Susa, however, mustered on the thirteenth and fourteenth of the month. But on the fifteenth they rested, and made it a day of feasting and rejoicing.) 19 That is why the rural Jews, who dwell in villages, celebrate the fourteenth of the month of Adar as a day of rejoicing and feasting, a holiday on which they send gifts of food to one another.

The Feast of Purim

20 Mordecai recorded these events and sent letters to all the Jews, both near and far, in all the provinces of

King Ahasuerus. 21 He ordered them to celebrate every year both the fourteenth and the fifteenth of the month of Adar 22 as the days on which the Jews obtained rest from their enemies and as the month which was turned for them from sorrow into joy, from mourning into festivity. They were to observe these days with feasting and gladness, sending food to one another and gifts to the poor. 23 The Jews took upon themselves for the future this observance which they instituted at the written direction of Mordecai.

24 Haman, son of Hammedatha the Agagite, the foe of all the Jews, had planned to destroy them and had cast the *pur*, or lot, for the time of their defeat and destruction. 25 Yet when Esther entered the royal presence, the king ordered in writing that the wicked plan Haman had devised against the Jews should instead be turned against Haman and that he and his sons should be hanged on gibbets. 26 And so these days have been named Purim after the word *pur*.

Thus, because of all that was contained in this letter, and because of what they had witnessed and experienced in this affair, 27 the Jews established and took upon themselves, their descendants, and all who should join them, the inviolable obligation of celebrating these two days every year in the manner prescribed by this letter, and at the time appointed. 28 These days were to be commemorated and kept in every generation, by every clan, in every province, and in every city. These days of Purim were never to fall into disuse among the Jews, nor into oblivion among their descendants.

29 Queen Esther, daughter of Abihail and of Mordecai the Jew, wrote to confirm with full authority this second letter about Purim, 30 when Mordecai sent documents concerning peace and security to all the Jews in the hundred and twenty-seven provinces of Ahasuerus' king-

---

9, 10: *They did not engage in plundering:* in contrast to the Israelites who fought Agag (1 Sm 15, 9); cf also vv 15f.

9, 15: This second slaughter explains the two dates (13th and 14th) of the Purim celebration by Jews in Susa (v 18).

9, 16: *Seventy-five thousand:* according to the Greek text this number was fifteen thousand.

9, 29: *Queen Esther, daughter of Abihail and of Mordecai:* the natural offspring of Abihail and adopt-

ed daughter of Mordecai; cf 2, 15. *This second letter:* for the burden of this letter see 9, 20ff. It was endorsed by Queen Esther. The first letter, written in the king's name is referred to in 8, 9.

dom.   31 Thus were established, for their appointed time, these days of Purim which Mordecai the Jew and Queen Esther had designated for the Jews, just as they had previously enjoined upon themselves and upon their race the duty of fasting and supplication.   32 The command of Esther confirmed these prescriptions for Purim and was recorded in the book.

10 King Ahasuerus laid tribute on the land and on the islands of the sea.   2 All the acts of his power and valor, as well as a detailed account of the greatness of Mordecai, whom the king promoted, are recorded in the chronicles of the kings of Media and Persia.   3 The Jew Mordecai was next in rank to King Ahasuerus, in high standing among the Jews, and was regarded with favor by his many brethren, as the promoter of his people's welfare and the herald of peace for his whole race.

EPILOGUE

Mordecai's Dream Fulfilled

F Then Mordecai said: "This is the work of God.   2 I recall the dream I had about these very things, and not a single detail has been left unfulfilled—   3 the tiny spring that grew into a river, the light of the sun, the many waters. The river is Esther, whom the king married and made queen.   4 The two dragons are myself and Haman.   5 The nations are those who assembled to destroy the name of the Jews,   6 but my people is Israel, who cried to God and was saved.

"The LORD saved his people and delivered us from all these evils. God worked signs and great wonders, such as have not occurred among the nations.   7 For this purpose he arranged two lots: one for the people of God, the second for all the other nations.   8 These two lots were fulfilled in the hour, the time, and the day of judgment before God and among all the nations.   9 God remembered his people and rendered justice to his inheritance.

10 "Gathering together with joy and happiness before God, they shall celebrate these days on the fourteenth and fifteenth of the month Adar throughout all future generations of his people Israel."

9, 31: *Fasting and supplication:* as the Jews had previously undertaken the duty of fasting and supplication to prevent the impending disaster, they now observe days of festival to commemorate their deliverance—in both cases (cf 4, 3.15f) at the request of Mordecai and Esther.

F, 7: *Two lots:* in this passage of the Greek text, which gives a more religious interpretation of the feast, the *two lots* are drawn by God to determine respectively, the destiny of Israel and that of the nations. In 3, 7 above, translated from the Hebrew text, the feast is called *Purim* because of the lots which Aman cast to determine the day for the extinction of the Jews.

THE FIRST BOOK OF

Maccabees

INTRODUCTION: HELLENISM IN ASIA MINOR

Conquests and Death of Alexander

AFTER Alexander the Macedonian, Philip's son, who came from the land of Kittim, had defeated Darius, king of the Persians and Medes, he became king in his place, having first ruled in Greece. 2 He fought many campaigns, captured fortresses, and put kings to death. 3 He advanced to the ends of the earth, gathering plunder from many nations; the earth fell silent before him, and his heart became proud and arrogant. 4 He collected a very strong army and conquered provinces, nations, and rulers, and they became his tributaries. 5 But after all this he took to his bed, realizing that he was going to die. 6 He therefore summoned his officers, the nobles, who had been brought up with him from his youth, to divide his kingdom among them while he was still alive. 7 Alexander had reigned twelve years when he died.

8 So his officers took over his kingdom, each in his own territory, 9 and after his death they all put on royal crowns, and so did their sons after them for many years, causing much distress over the earth.

THE MACCABEAN REVOLT

Pact between Jews and Gentiles

10 There sprang from these a sinful offshoot, Antiochus Epiphanes, son of King Antiochus, once a hostage at Rome. He became king in the year one hundred and thirty-seven of the kingdom of the Greeks.

11 In those days there appeared in Israel men who were breakers of the law, and they seduced many people, saying: "Let us go and make an alliance with the Gentiles all around us; since we separated from them, many evils have come upon us." 12 The proposal was agreeable; 13 some from among the people promptly went to the king, and he authorized them to introduce the way of living of the Gentiles. 14 Thereupon they built a gymnasium in Jerusalem according to the Gentile custom. 15 They covered over the mark of their circumcision and abandoned the holy covenant; they allied themselves with the Gentiles and sold themselves to wrongdoing.

Egyptian Campaign of Antiochus

16 When his kingdom seemed secure, Antiochus proposed to become king of Egypt, so as to rule over

---

1, 1: *Land of Kittim:* Greece. The name referred originally to inhabitants of Kiti, capital of the isle of Cyprus, then to any Cypriots (Is 23, 1; Jer 2, 10), later to Greeks in general, and finally even to Romans. See note on Dn 11, 30. *Darius:* Darius III, Codoman (336–331 B.C.).

1, 7: *Twelve years:* 336–323 B.C.

1, 10: *The year one hundred and thirty-seven:* Antiochus IV seized the throne in September,

175 B.C. Dates are given in this book according to the Seleucid era, which however was reckoned in two different ways. Antiochians considered this date to be October, 312 B.C. (Syrian calendar), while Babylonians and Jewish priests accepted April, 311 B.C. as the commencement of the era (temple calendar). The author of 1 Mc dates political events by the Syrian calendar but religious events by the temple calendar. Accordingly, the civil New Year occurred variously

in September or October, the religious New Year in March or April.

1, 14: *Gymnasium:* symbol and center of athletic and intellectual life, it was the chief instrument of Hellenistic propaganda. Jewish youth were attracted by sports and encouraged to join youth clubs. They received training in military skills and in the duties of citizens. Through participation in the intellectual life, many were gradually won over to paganism.

both kingdoms. 17 He invaded Egypt with a strong force, with chariots and elephants, and with a large fleet, 18 to make war on Ptolemy, king of Egypt. Ptolemy was frightened at his presence and fled, leaving many casualties. 19 The fortified cities in the land of Egypt were captured, and Antiochus plundered the land of Egypt.

Persecution of the Jews

20 After Antiochus had defeated Egypt in the year one hundred and forty-three, he returned and went up to Israel and to Jerusalem with a strong force. 21 He insolently invaded the sanctuary and took away the golden altar, the lampstand for the light with all its fixtures, 22 the offering table, the cups and the bowls, the golden censers, the curtain, the crowns, and the golden ornament on the façade of the temple. He stripped off everything, 23 and took away the gold and silver and the precious vessels; he also took all the hidden treasures he could find. 24 Taking all this, he went back to his own country, after he had spoken with great arrogance and shed much blood.

25 And there was great mourning
    for Israel, in every place
    where they dwelt,
26 and the rulers and the elders
    groaned.
Virgins and young men
    languished,
and the beauty of the women
    was disfigured.
27 Every bridegroom took up
    lamentation,
she who sat in the bridal
    chamber mourned,
28 And the land was shaken on
    account of its inhabitants,
and all the house of Jacob was
    covered with shame.

29 Two years later, the king sent the Mysian commander to the cities of Judah, and he came to Jerusalem with a strong force. 30 He spoke to them deceitfully in peaceful terms, and won their trust. Then he attacked the city suddenly, in a great onslaught, and destroyed many of the people in Israel. 31 He plundered the city and set fire to it, 32 demolished its houses and its surrounding walls, took captive the women and children, and seized the cattle. 33 Then they built up the City of David with a high, massive wall and strong towers, and it became their citadel. 34 There they installed a sinful race, perverse men, who fortified themselves inside it, 35 storing up weapons and provisions, and depositing there the plunder they had collected from Jerusalem. And they became a great threat.

36 The citadel became an ambush
        against the sanctuary,
    and a wicked adversary to Israel
        at all times.
37 And they shed innocent blood
        around the sanctuary;
    they defiled the sanctuary.
38 Because of them the inhabitants of
        Jerusalem fled away,
    and she became the abode of
        strangers.
    She became a stranger to her own
        offspring,
    and her children forsook her.
39 Her sanctuary was as desolate as
        a wilderness;
    her feasts were turned into
        mourning,
    Her sabbaths to shame,
        her honor to contempt.
40 Her dishonor was as great as her
        glory had been,
    and her exaltation was turned
        into mourning.

Prohibitions against Religion

41 Then the king wrote to his whole kingdom that all should be one people, 42 each abandoning his particular customs. All the Gentiles conformed to the command of the king, 43 and many Israelites were in favor of his religion; they sacrificed to idols and profaned the sabbath.

44 The king sent messengers with letters to Jerusalem and to the cities of Judah, ordering them to follow customs foreign to their land; 45 to prohibit holocausts, sacrifices, and libations in the sanctuary, to profane the sabbaths and feast days, 46 to desecrate the sanctuary and the sacred ministers, to build pagan altars and temples and shrines, 47 to sacrifice swine and unclean animals, 48 to leave their sons uncircumcised, and to let themselves be defiled with every kind of impurity and abomination, 49 so that they might forget the law and change all their observances. 50 Whoever refused to act according to the command of the king should be put to death.

51 Such were the orders he published throughout his kingdom. He appointed inspectors over all the people, and he ordered the cities of Judah to offer sacrifices, each city in turn. 52 Many of the people, those who abandoned the law, joined them and committed evil in the land. 53 Israel was driven into hiding, wherever places of refuge could be found.

54 On the fifteenth day of the month Chislev, in the year one hundred and forty-five, the king erected the horrible abomination upon the altar of holocausts, and in the surrounding cities of Judah they built pagan altars. 55 They also burnt incense at the doors of houses and in the streets. 56 Any scrolls of the law which they found they tore up and burnt. 57 Whoever was found with a scroll of the covenant, and whoever observed the law, was condemned to death by royal decree. 58 So they used their power against Israel, against those who were caught, each month, in the cities. 59 On the twenty-fifth day of each month they sacrificed on the altar erected over the altar of holocausts. 60 Women who had had their children circumcised

---

1, 17: *Elephants:* an important part of Seleucid armament. About 300 B.C. Seleucus I, founder of the dynasty, procured five hundred of them from India; cf 6, 34–37.

1, 20: *Defeated Egypt in the year one hundred and forty-three:* 169 B.C. No mention is made in 1 Mc of the second expedition to Egypt a year later, described in 2 Mc 5, 1.11. Dn 11, 25.29 records both.

1, 33: *City of David:* not Mount Zion on the eastern hill of Jerusalem, which David captured from the Jebusites (2 Sm 5, 7), but a new fortress built on the western hill and overlooking the temple and its courts on Mount Zion. It was occupied for twenty-six years by the Syro-Macedonian garrison, together with apostate Jews, and was a continual threat to the temple and the Jewish people (v 36); cf 13, 49ff.

1, 54: *Fifteenth day of the month Chislev, in the year one hundred and forty-five:* December 6, 167 B.C.

Horrible abomination: in the original Hebrew, a contemptuous pun on the title "Lord of heaven" given to the god Zeus Olympios, to whom an image or perhaps an altar was erected *upon the altar of holocausts* in the temple of Jerusalem; cf Dn 9, 27; 11, 31.

1, 56f: *Scrolls of the law:* one or more of the first five books of the Old Testament.

were put to death, in keeping with the decree, 61 with the babies hung from their necks; their families also and those who had circumcised them were killed. 62 But many in Israel were determined and resolved in their hearts not to eat anything unclean; 63 they preferred to die rather than to be defiled with unclean food or to profane the holy covenant; and they did die. Terrible affliction was upon Israel.

Mattathias and His Sons

2 In those days Mattathias, son of John, son of Simeon, a priest of the family of Joarib, left Jerusalem and settled in Modein. 2 He had five sons: John, who was called Gaddi; 3 Simon, who was called Thassi; 4 Judas, who was called Maccabeus; 5 Eleazar, who was called Avaran; and Jonathan, who was called Apphus. 6 When he saw the sacrileges that were being committed in Judah and in Jerusalem, 7 he said: "Woe is me! Why was I born to see the ruin of my people and the ruin of the holy city, and to sit idle while it is given into the hands of enemies, and the sanctuary into the hands of strangers?

8 "Her temple has become like a
    man disgraced,
9   her glorious ornaments have
    been carried off as spoils,
  Her infants have been murdered
    in her streets,
  her young men by the sword of
    the enemy.
10 What nation has not taken its
    share of her realm,
  and laid its hand on her
    possessions?
11 All her adornment has been taken
    away.
  From being free, she has
    become a slave.
12 We see our sanctuary and our
    beauty
  and our glory laid waste,
  And the Gentiles have defiled
    them!
13 Why are we still alive?"

14 Then Mattathias and his sons tore their garments, put on sackcloth, and mourned bitterly.

Pagan Worship Refused

15 The officers of the king in charge of enforcing the apostasy came to the city of Modein to organize the sacrifices. 16 Many of Israel joined them, but Mattathias and his sons gathered in a group apart. 17 Then the officers of the king addressed Mattathias: "You are a leader, an honorable and great man in this city, supported by sons and kinsmen. 18 Come now, be the first to obey the king's command, as all the Gentiles and the men of Judah and those who are left in Jerusalem have done. Then you and your sons shall be numbered among the King's Friends, and shall be enriched with silver and gold and many gifts." 19 But Mattathias answered in a loud voice: "Although all the Gentiles in the king's realm obey him, so that each forsakes the religion of his fathers and consents to the king's orders, 20 yet I and my sons and my kinsmen will keep to the covenant of our fathers. 21 God forbid that we should forsake the law and the commandments. 22 We will not obey the words of the king nor depart from our religion in the slightest degree."

23 As he finished saying these words, a certain Jew came forward in the sight of all to offer sacrifice on the altar in Modein according to the king's order. 24 When Mattathias saw him, he was filled with zeal; his heart was moved and his just fury was aroused; he sprang forward and killed him upon the altar. 25 At the same time, he also killed the messenger of the king who was forcing them to sacrifice, and he tore down the altar. 26 Thus he showed his zeal for the law, just as Phinehas did with Zimri, son of Salu.

27 Then Mattathias went through the city shouting, "Let everyone who is zealous for the law and who stands by the covenant follow after me!"

28 Thereupon he fled to the mountains with his sons, leaving behind in the city all their possessions. 29 Many who sought to live according to righteousness and religious custom went out into the desert to settle there, 30 they and their sons, their wives and their cattle, because misfortunes pressed so hard on them.

31 It was reported to the officers and soldiers of the king who were in the City of David, in Jerusalem, that certain men who had flouted the king's order had gone out to the hiding places in the desert. 32 Many hurried out after them, and having caught up with them, camped opposite and prepared to attack them on the sabbath. 33 "Enough of this!" the pursuers said to them. "Come out and obey the king's command, and your lives will be spared." 34 But they replied, "We will not come out, nor will we obey the king's command to profane the sabbath." 35 Then the enemy attacked them at once; 36 but they did not retaliate; they neither threw stones, nor blocked up their own hiding places. 37 They said, "Let us all die without reproach; heaven and earth are our witnesses that you destroy us unjustly." 38 So the officers and soldiers attacked them on the sabbath, and they died with their wives, their children and their cattle, to the number of a thousand persons.

39 When Mattathias and his friends heard of it, they mourned deeply for them. 40 "If we all do as our kinsmen have done," they said to one another, "and do not fight against the Gentiles for our lives and our traditions, they will soon destroy us from the earth." 41 On that day they came to this decision: "Let us fight against anyone who attacks us on the sabbath, so that we may not all die as our kinsmen died in the hiding places."

42 Then they were joined by a group of Hasideans, valiant Israelites, all of them devout followers of the law. 43 And all those who were fleeing from the disaster joined

---

2, 1: *Modein:* a village twenty miles northwest of Jerusalem.

2, 18: *The King's Friends:* a regular order of nobility at Hellenistic courts. The various grades are frequently mentioned in this book: Friends, Chief Friends, Kinsmen.

2, 29: *The desert:* the sparsely inhabited mountain country southward from Jerusalem and west of the Dead Sea. It was an arid region with some perennial springs and a fair amount of rain in winter.

2, 42: *Hasideans:* in Hebrew *hasidim,* "pious ones," a religious group devoted to the strict observance of

the law. They were the forerunners of both the Pharisees and the Essenes. They first supported the Maccabean movement, but subsequently opposed it, regarding it as too political.

them and supported them. 44 They gathered an army and struck down sinners in their anger and lawbreakers in their wrath, and the survivors fled to the Gentiles for safety. 45 Mattathias and his friends went about and tore down the pagan altars; 46 they also enforced circumcision for any uncircumcised boys whom they found in the territory of Israel. 47 They put to flight the arrogant, and the work prospered in their hands. 48 They saved the law from the hands of the Gentiles and of the kings and did not let the sinner triumph.

Death of Mattathias

49 When the time came for Mattathias to die, he said to his sons: "Arrogance and scorn have now grown strong; it is a time of disaster and violent anger. 50 Therefore, my sons, be zealous for the law and give your lives for the covenant of our fathers.

51 "Remember the deeds that our
     fathers did in their times,
     and you shall win great glory
          and an everlasting name.
52 Was not Abraham found faithful
          in trial,
     and it was reputed to him as
          uprightness?
53 Joseph, when in distress, kept the
          commandment,
     and he became master of Egypt.
54 Phinehas our father, for his
          burning zeal,
     received the covenant of an
          everlasting priesthood.
55 Joshua, for executing his
          commission,
     became a judge in Israel.
56 Caleb, for bearing witness before
          the assembly,
     received an inheritance in the
          land.
57 David, for his piety,
     received as a heritage a throne
          of everlasting royalty.
58 Elijah, for his burning zeal for the
          law,
     was taken up to heaven.
59 Hananiah, Azariah and Mishael,
          for their faith,
     were saved from the fire.

60 Daniel, for his innocence,
     was delivered from the jaws of
          lions.
61 And so, consider this from
          generation to generation,
     that none who hope in him shall
          fail in strength.
62 Do not fear the words of a sinful
          man,
     for his glory ends in corruption
          and worms.
63 Today he is exalted, and
     tomorrow he is not to be
          found,
     before he has returned to his
          dust,
     and his schemes have perished.
64 Children! be courageous and
     strong in keeping the law,
     for by it you shall be glorified.

65 "Here is your brother Simeon who I know is a wise man; listen to him always, and he will be a father to you. 66 And Judas Maccabeus, a warrior from his youth, shall be the leader of your army and direct the war against the nations. 67 You shall also gather about you all who observe the law, and you shall avenge the wrongs of your people. 68 Pay back the Gentiles what they deserve, and observe the precepts of the law."

69 Then he blessed them, and he was united with his fathers. 70 He died in the year one hundred and forty-six, and was buried in the tombs of his fathers in Modein, and all Israel mourned him greatly.

LEADERSHIP OF JUDAS MACCABEUS

Defeat of Apollonius and Seron

3 Then his son Judas, who was called Maccabeus, took his place. 2 All his brothers and all who had joined his father supported him, and they carried on Israel's war joyfully.

3 He spread abroad the glory of his
          people,
     and put on his breastplate like
          a giant.
     He armed himself with weapons
          of war;
     he planned battles and
     protected the camp with his
          sword.

4 In his actions he was like a lion,
     like a young lion roaring for
          prey.
5 He pursued the wicked, hunting
          them out,
     and those who troubled his
          people he destroyed by fire.
6 The lawbreakers were cowed by
          fear of him,
     and all evildoers were dismayed.
     By his hand redemption was
          happily achieved,
7   and he afflicted many kings;
     He made Jacob glad by his deeds,
     and his memory is blessed
          forever.
8 He went about the cities of
          Judah
     destroying the impious there.
     He turned away wrath from Israel
9 and was renowned to the ends
          of the earth;
     he gathered together those who
          were perishing.

10 Then Apollonius gathered the Gentiles, together with a large army from Samaria, to fight against Israel. 11 When Judas learned of it, he went out to meet him and defeated and killed him. Many fell wounded, and the rest fled. 12 Their possessions were seized and the sword of Apollonius was taken by Judas, who fought with it the rest of his life.

13 But Seron, commander of the Syrian army, heard that Judas had gathered many about him, an assembly of faithful men ready for war. 14 So he said, "I will make a name for myself and win glory in the kingdom by defeating Judas and his followers, who have despised the king's command." 15 And again a large company of renegades advanced with him to help him take revenge on the Israelites. 16 When he reached the ascent of Beth-horon, Judas went out to meet him with a few men. 17 But when they saw the army coming against them, they said to Judas: "How can we, few as we are, fight such a mighty host as this? Besides, we are weak today from fasting." 18 But Judas said: "It is easy for many to be overcome by a few; in the sight of Heaven there is no difference between deliverance by

---

2, 70: *In the year one hundred and forty-six:* 166 B.C.
3, 10: *Apollonius:* the Mysian commander men-

tioned in 1, 29 and in 2 Mc 5, 24.
3, 16: *Beth-horon:* the famous pass leading up from the coastal plain to the Judean hill country.

Here Joshua won an important battle (Jos 10, 10f), and in A.D. 66 a Roman force under Cestius was trapped and massacred.

many or by few; 19 for victory in war does not depend upon the size of the army, but on strength that comes from Heaven. 20 With great presumption and lawlessness they come against us to destroy us and our wives and children and to despoil us; 21 but we are fighting for our lives and our laws. 22 He himself will crush them before us; so do not be afraid of them." 23 When he finished speaking, he rushed suddenly upon Seron and his army, who were crushed before him. 24 He pursued Seron down the descent of Beth-horon into the plain. About eight hundred of their men fell, and the rest fled to the country of the Philistines. 25 Then Judas and his brothers began to be feared, and dread fell upon the Gentiles about them. 26 His fame reached the king, and all the Gentiles talked about the battles of Judas.

Regency of Lysias

27 When Antiochus heard about these events, he was angry; so he ordered a muster of all the forces of his kingdom, a very strong army. 28 He opened his treasure chests, gave his soldiers a year's pay, and commanded them to be prepared for anything. 29 He then found that this exhausted the money in his treasury; moreover the income from the province was small, because of the dissension and distress he had brought upon the land by abolishing the laws which had been in effect from of old. 30 He feared that, as had happened more than once, he would not have enough for his expenses and for the gifts that he had previously given with a more liberal hand than the preceding kings. 31 Greatly perplexed, he decided to go to Persia and levy tribute on those provinces, and so raise a large sum of money. 32 He left Lysias, a nobleman of royal blood, in charge of the king's affairs from the Euphrates River to the frontier of Egypt, 33 and com-

missioned him to take care of his son Antiochus until his own return. 34 He entrusted to him half of the army, and the elephants, and gave him instructions concerning everything he wanted done. As for the inhabitants of Judea and Jerusalem, 35 Lysias was to send an army against them to crush and destroy the power of Israel and the remnant of Jerusalem and efface their memory from the land. 36 He was to settle foreigners in all their territory and distribute their land by lot.

37 The king took the remaining half of the army and set out from Antioch, his capital, in the year one hundred and forty-seven; he crossed the Euphrates River and advanced inland.

The Victories of Judas

38 Lysias chose Ptolemy, son of Dorymenes, and Nicanor and Gorgias, capable men among the King's Friends, 39 and with them he sent forty thousand men and seven thousand cavalry to invade the land of Judah and ravage it according to the king's orders. 40 Setting out with all their forces, they came and pitched their camp near Emmaus in the plain. 41 When the merchants of the country heard of their fame, they came to the camp, bringing fetters and a large sum of silver and gold, to buy the Israelites as slaves. A force from Idumea and from Philistia joined with them.

42 Judas and his brothers saw that the situation had become critical now that armies were encamped within their territory; they knew of the orders which the king had given to destroy and utterly wipe out the people. 43 So they said to one another, "Let us restore our people from their ruined estate, and fight for our people and our sanctuary!"

44 The assembly gathered together to prepare for battle and to pray and implore mercy and compassion.

45 Jerusalem was uninhabited, like a desert;
　　not one of her children
　　　entered or came out.
The sanctuary was trampled on,
　　and foreigners were in the citadel;
　　it was a habitation of Gentiles.
Joy had disappeared from Jacob,
　　and the flute and the harp were silent.

46 Thus they assembled and went to Mizpah near Jerusalem, because there was formerly at Mizpah a place of prayer for Israel. 47 That day they fasted and wore sackcloth; they sprinkled ashes on their heads and tore their clothes. 48 They unrolled the scroll of the law, to learn about the things for which the Gentiles consulted the images of their idols. 49 They brought with them the priestly vestments, the first fruits, and the tithes; and they brought forward the nazirites who had completed the time of their vows. 50 And they cried aloud to Heaven: "What shall we do with these men, and where shall we take them? 51 For your sanctuary has been trampled on and profaned, and your priests are in mourning and humiliation. 52 Now the Gentiles are gathered together against us to destroy us. You know what they plot against us. 53 How shall we be able to resist them unless you help us?" 54 Then they blew the trumpets and cried out loudly.

55 After this Judas appointed officers among the people, over thousands, over hundreds, over fifties, and over tens. 56 He proclaimed that those who were building houses, or were just married, or were planting vineyards, and those who were afraid, could each return to his home, according to the law. 57 Then the army moved off, and they camped to the south of Emmaus. 58 Judas said: "Arm yourselves and be brave: in the morning be ready to

---

3, 22: *He himself:* out of reverence for God, the author of 1 Mc prefers to use this and other expressions, such as "Heaven," instead of the divine name. Cf 1 Mc 3, 50.

3, 24: *About eight hundred:* the figures given in this book for strength of armies and number of casualties are not to be taken literally. In accordance with biblical usage, they indicate rather the importance of the battle described or the greatness of the victory.

3, 37: This expedition, in the spring of 165 B.C., resulted in failure; cf ch 6.

3, 38: *Nicanor:* the leader of another attack against the Jews four years later. He was finally killed by Judas; cf 7, 26-46.

3, 40: *Emmaus:* probably not the village mentioned in Lk 24, 13, but a settlement about twenty miles west of Jerusalem at the edge of the hill country.

3, 46: *. . . Mizpah a place of prayer for Israel:* a

holy place established of old eight miles north and slightly west of Jerusalem. It was here that Samuel began to judge the Israelites (1 Sm 7, 5-11; 10, 17).

3, 48: *To learn . . . idols:* favorable omens for the coming battle. A contrast is intended between the idol worship of the pagans and the consultation of the word of God by the Jews; cf 2 Mc 8, 23.

3, 49: *Nazirites:* see note on Nm 6, 1ff.

fight these Gentiles who have assembled against us to destroy us and our sanctuary. 59 It is better for us to die in battle than to witness the ruin of our nation and our sanctuary. Whatever Heaven wills, he will do."

4 Now Gorgias took five thousand infantry and a thousand picked calvary, and this detachment set out at night 2 in order to attack the camp of the Jews and take them by surprise. Some men from the citadel were their guides. 3 Judas heard of it, and himself set out with his soldiers to attack the king's army at Emmaus, 4 while the latter's forces were still scattered away from the camp. 5 During the night Gorgias came into the camp of Judas, and found no one there; so he began to hunt for them in the mountains, saying, "They are fleeing from us."

6 But at daybreak Judas appeared in the plain with three thousand men, who lacked such armor and swords as they would have wished. 7 They saw the army of the Gentiles, strong and breastplated, flanked with cavalry, and made up of expert soldiers. 8 Judas said to the men with him: "Do not be afraid of their numbers or dread their attack. 9 Remember how our fathers were saved in the Red Sea, when Pharaoh pursued them with an army. 10 So now let us cry to Heaven in the hope that he will favor us, remember his covenant with our fathers, and destroy this army before us today. 11 All the Gentiles shall know that there is One who redeems and delivers Israel."

12 When the foreigners looked up and saw them marching toward them, 13 they came out of their camp for battle, and the men with Judas blew the trumpet. 14 The battle was joined and the Gentiles were defeated and fled toward the plain. 15 Their whole rearguard fell by the sword, and they were pursued as far as Gazara and the plains of Judea, to Azotus and Jamnia. About three thousand of their men fell.

16 When Judas and the army returned from the pursuit, 17 he said to the people: "Do not be greedy for the plunder, for there is a fight ahead of us, 18 and Gorgias and his army are near us on the mountain. But now stand firm against our enemies and overthrow them. Afterward you can freely take the plunder."

19 As Judas was finishing this speech, a detachment appeared, looking down from the mountain. 20 They saw that their army had been put to flight and their camp was being burned. The smoke that could be seen indicated what had happened. 21 When they realized this, they were terrified; and when they also saw the army of Judas in the plain ready to attack, 22 they all fled to Philistine territory.

23 Then Judas went back to plunder the camp, and his men collected much gold and silver, violet and crimson cloth, and great treasure. 24 As they returned, they were singing hymns and glorifying Heaven, "for he is good, for his mercy endures forever." 25 Thus Israel had a great deliverance that day.

Victory over Lysias

26 But those of the foreigners who had escaped went and told Lysias all that had occurred. 27 When he heard it he was disturbed and discouraged, because things in Israel had not turned out as he intended and as the king had ordered. 28 So the following year he gathered together sixty thousand picked men and five thousand cavalry, to subdue them. 29 They came into Idumea and camped at Beth-zur, and Judas met them with ten thousand men. 30 Seeing that the army was strong, he prayed thus:

"Blessed are you, O Savior of Israel, who broke the rush of the mighty one by the hand of your servant David and delivered the camp of the Philistines into the hand of Jonathan, the son of Saul, and his armor-bearer. 31 Give this army

into the hands of your people Israel; make them ashamed of their troops and their cavalry. 32 Strike them with fear, weaken the boldness of their strength, and let them tremble at their own destruction. 33 Strike them down by the sword of those who love you, that all who know your name may hymn your praise."

34 Then they engaged in battle, and about five thousand of Lysias' men fell in hand-to-hand fighting. 35 When Lysias saw his ranks beginning to give way, and the increased boldness of Judas, whose men were ready either to live or to die bravely, he withdrew to Antioch and began to recruit mercenaries so as to return to Judea with greater numbers.

Purification of the Temple

36 Then Judas and his brothers said, "Now that our enemies have been crushed, let us go up to purify the sanctuary and rededicate it." 37 So the whole army assembled, and went up to Mount Zion. 38 They found the sanctuary desolate, the altar desecrated, the gates burnt, weeds growing in the courts as in a forest or on some mountain, and the priests' chambers demolished. 39 Then they tore their clothes and made great lamentation; they sprinkled their heads with ashes 40 and fell with their faces to the ground. And when the signal was given with trumpets, they cried out to Heaven.

41 Judas appointed men to attack those in the citadel, while he purified the sanctuary. 42 He chose blameless priests, devoted to the law; 43 these purified the sanctuary and carried away the stones of the Abomination to an unclean place. 44 They deliberated what ought to be done with the altar of holocausts that had been desecrated. 45 The happy thought came to them to tear it down, lest it be a lasting shame to them that the Gentiles had defiled it; so they tore down the altar. 46 They stored the stones in a suitable place on the temple hill, until a prophet should

---

4, 15: *Gazara: Gezer* of the Hebrew Bible, five miles northwest of Emmaus; *Azotus*, Hebrew *Ashdod*, lay to the southwest; and *Jamnia*, Hebrew *Jabneel* (Jos 15, 11) or *Jabneh* (2 Chr 26, 6), to the west of Gazara.
4, 22: *Philistine territory:* the coastal cities of southern Palestine, traditionally hostile to Jerusalem.

Jamnia in particular was an important base for the Seleucid power.
4, 29: *Beth-zur:* an important frontier city in the mountain area, fifteen miles south of Jerusalem. Its inhabitants were sympathetic to the Maccabees and refused to receive Lysias.
4, 35: According to 2 Mc 11, 13–15, peace negotia-

tions followed between Lysias and Judas.
4, 36: *The sanctuary:* the whole temple area with its walls, courts and outbuildings, to be distinguished from the temple proper, the oblong edifice with porch, main room and inner shrine.

come and decide what to do with them. 47 Then they took uncut stones, according to the law, and built a new altar like the former one. 48 They also repaired the sanctuary and the interior of the temple and purified the courts. 49 They made new sacred vessels and brought the lampstand, the altar of incense, and the table into the temple. 50 Then they burned incense on the altar and lighted the lamps on the lampstand, and these illuminated the temple. 51 They also put loaves on the table and hung up the curtains. Thus they finished all the work they had undertaken.

52 Early in the morning on the twenty-fifth day of the ninth month, that is, the month of Chislev, in the year one hundred and forty-eight, 53 they arose and offered sacrifice according to the law on the new altar of holocausts that they had made. 54 On the anniversary of the day on which the Gentiles had defiled it, on that very day it was reconsecrated with songs, harps, flutes, and cymbals. 55 All the people prostrated themselves and adored and praised Heaven, who had given them success.

56 For eight days they celebrated the dedication of the altar and joyfully offered holocausts and sacrifices of deliverance and praise. 57 They ornamented the façade of the temple with gold crowns and shields; they repaired the gates and the priests' chambers and furnished them with doors. 58 There was great joy among the people now that the disgrace of the Gentiles was removed. 59 Then Judas and his brothers and the entire congregation of Israel decreed that the days of the dedication of the altar should be osberved with joy and gladness on the anniversary every year for eight days, from the twenty-fifth day of the month Chislev.

60 At that time they built high walls and strong towers around Mount Zion, to prevent the Gentiles from coming and trampling over it as they had done before. 61 Judas also placed a garrison there to protect it, and likewise fortified Beth-zur, that the people might have a stronghold facing Idumea.

Punishment of Hostile Acts

5 When the Gentiles round about heard that the altar had been rebuilt and the sanctuary consecrated as before, they were very angry. 2 So they decided to destroy the descendants of Jacob who were among them, and they began to massacre and persecute the people. 3 Then Judas attacked the sons of Esau at Akrabattene in Idumea, because they were blockading Israel; he defeated them heavily, overcame and despoiled them. 4 He also remembered the malice of the sons of Baean, who had become a snare and a stumblingblock to the people by ambushing them along the roads. 5 He forced them to take refuge in towers, which he beseiged; he vowed their annihilation and burned down the towers along with all the persons in them. 6 Then he crossed over to the Ammonites, where he found a strong army and a large body of people with Timothy as their leader. 7 He fought many battles with them, routed them, and struck them down. 8 After seizing Jazer and its villages, he returned to Judea.

Liberation of Galilean Jews

9 The Gentiles in Gilead assembled to attack and destroy the Israelites who were in their territory; these then fled to the stronghold of Dathema. 10 They sent a letter to Judas and his brothers saying: "The Gentiles around us have combined against us to destroy us, 11 and they are preparing to come and seize this stronghold to which we have fled. Timothy is the leader of their army. 12 Come at once and rescue us from them, for many of us have fallen. 13 All our kinsmen who were among the Tobiads have been killed; the Gentiles have carried away their wives and children and their goods, and they have slain there about a thousand men."

14 While they were reading this letter, suddenly other messengers, in torn clothes, arrived from Galilee to deliver a similar message: 15 that the inhabitants of Ptolemais, Tyre, and Sidon, and the whole of Gentile Galilee had joined forces to destroy them. 16 When Judas and the people heard this, a great assembly convened to consider what they should do for their unfortunate kinsmen who were being attacked by enemies.

17 Judas said to his brother Simon: "Choose men for yourself, and go, rescue your kinsmen in Galilee; I and my brother Jonathan will go to Gilead." 18 In Judea he left Joseph, son of Zechariah, and Azariah, leader of the people, with the rest of the army to guard it. 19 "Take charge of these people," he commanded them, "but do not fight against the Gentiles until we return." 20 Three thousand men were allotted to Simon, to go into Galilee, and eight thousand men to Judas, for Gilead.

21 Simon went into Galilee and fought many battles with the Gentiles. They were crushed before him, 22 and he pursued them to the very gate of Ptolemais. About three thousand men of the Gentiles fell, and he gathered their spoils. 23 He took with him the Jews who were in Galilee and in Arbatta, with their wives and children and all that they had, and brought them to Judea with great rejoicing.

Rescue in Gilead

24 Judas Maccabeus and his brother Jonathan crossed the Jordan and marched for three days through the desert. 25 There they met some Nabateans, who received them

4, 52: *Twenty-fifth day of the ninth month . . . in the year one hundred and forty-eight:* December 14, 164 B.C.
4, 59: *Days of the dedication . . . Chislev:* institution of the feast of Hannukah, also called the feast of Dedication (Jn 10, 22). Josephus Flavius calls it the feast of Lights.
5, 1: The events of this chapter occurred within the year 163 B.C.
5, 3: *Akrabattene:* a district southwest of the

Dead Sea.
5, 4: *Sons of Baean:* 2 Mc 10, 15–23 calls them simply Idumeans.
5, 6ff: This summary anticipates the order of events and would fit better between vv 36 and 37. It corresponds to 2 Mc 12, 17–23. The action was probably a reprisal for the massacre referred to in v 13. Timothy was the Seleucid governor of Trans-Jordan. *Jazer:* a town on the road from the Jordan to Amman.

5, 15: *Ptolemais:* Hebrew *Acco* (Jgs 1, 31), modern Acre, on the coast north of Haifa.
5, 25: *Nabateans:* an Arab people who acquired wealth and power as caravan merchants in the final two centuries B.C. They settled down, established Petra as their capital, and for a time controlled all of Trans-Jordan, even as far as Damascus. It was from a Nabatean governor that St. Paul escaped about A.D. 38 (2 Cor 11, 32f).

peacefully and told them all that had happened to the Jews in Gilead: 26 "Many of them have been imprisoned in Bozrah, in Bosor near Alema, in Chaspho, Maked, and Carnaim"—all of these are large, fortified cities—27 "and some have been imprisoned in other cities of Gilead. Tomorrow their enemies plan to attack the strongholds and to seize and destroy all these people in one day."

28 Thereupon Judas suddenly changed direction with his army, marched across the desert to Bozrah, and captured the city. He slaughtered all the male population, took all their possessions, and set fire to the city. 29 He led his army from that place by night, and they marched toward the stronghold of Dathema. 30 When morning came, they looked ahead and saw a countless multitude of people, with ladders and devices for capturing the stronghold, and beginning to attack the people within. 31 When Judas perceived that the struggle had begun and that the noise of the battle was resounding to heaven with trumpet blasts and loud shouting, 32 he said to the men of his army, "Fight for our kinsmen today."

33 He came up behind them with three columns blowing their trumpets and shouting in prayer. 34 When the army of Timothy realized that it was Maccabeus, they fell back before him, and he inflicted on them a crushing defeat. About eight thousand of their men fell that day. 35 Then he turned toward Alema and attacked and captured it; he killed all the male population, plundered the place, and burned it down. 36 From there he moved on and took Chaspho, Maked, Bosor, and the other cities of Gilead.

37 After these events Timothy assembled another army and camped opposite Raphon, on the other side of the stream. 38 Judas sent men to spy on the camp, and they reported to him: "All the Gentiles around us have rallied to him, making a very large force; 39 they have also hired Arabs to help them, and have camped beyond the stream, ready to attack

you." So Judas went forward to attack them.

40 As Judas and his army were approaching the running stream, Timothy said to the officers of his army: "If he crosses over to us first, we shall not be able to resist him; he will certainly defeat us. 41 But if he is afraid and camps on the other side of the river, we will cross over to him and defeat him."

42 But when Judas reached the running stream, he stationed the officers of the people beside the stream and gave them this order: "Do not allow any man to pitch a tent; all must go into battle." 43 He was the first to cross to the attack, with all the people behind him, and the Gentiles were crushed before them; they threw away their arms and fled to the temple enclosure at Carnaim. 44 The Jews captured that city and burnt the enclosure with all who were in it. So Carnaim was subdued, and Judas met with no more resistance.

45 Then he assembled all the Israelites, great and small, who were in Gilead, with their wives and children and their goods, a great crowd of people, to go into the land of Judah. 46 When they reached Ephron, a large and strongly fortified city along the way, they found it impossible to encircle it on either the right or the left; they would have to march right through it. 47 But the men in the city shut them out and blocked up the gates with stones. 48 Then Judas sent them this peaceful message: "We wish to cross your territory in order to reach our own; no one will harm you; we will only march through." But they would not open to him.

49 So Judas ordered a proclamation to be made in the camp that everyone make an attack from the place where he was. 50 When the men of the army took up their positions, he assaulted the city all that day and night, and it was delivered to him. 51 He slaughtered every male, razed and plundered the city, and passed through it over the slain.

52 Then they crossed the Jordan

to the great plain in front of Bethshan; 53 and Judas kept rounding up the stragglers and encouraging the people the whole way, until he reached the land of Judah. 54 They ascended Mount Zion in joy and gladness, and offered holocausts, because not one of them had fallen; they had returned in safety.

Joseph and Azariah Defeated

55 During the time that Judas and Jonathan were in the land of Gilead, and Simon his brother was in Galilee opposite Ptolemais, 56 Joseph, son of Zechariah, and Azariah, the leaders of the army, heard about the brave deeds and the fighting that they were doing. 57 They said, "Let us also make a name for ourselves by going out and fighting against the Gentiles around us."

58 They gave orders to the men of their army who were with them, and marched toward Jamnia. 59 But Gorgias and his men came out of the city to meet them in battle. 60 Joseph and Azariah were beaten, and were pursued to the frontiers of Judea, and about two thousand Israelites fell that day. 61 It was a bad defeat for the people, because they had not obeyed Judas and his brothers, thinking that they would do brave deeds. 62 But they did not belong to the family of those men to whom it was granted to achieve Israel's salvation. 63 The valiant Judas and his brothers were greatly renowned in all Israel and among all the Gentiles, wherever their name was heard; 64 and men gathered about them and praised them.

65 Then Judas and his brothers went out and attacked the sons of Esau in the country toward the south; he took Hebron and its villages, and he destroyed its strongholds and burned the towers around it. 66 He then set out for the land of the Philistines and passed through Marisa. 67 At that time some priests fell in battle who had gone out rashly to fight in their desire to distinguish themselves. 68 Judas then turned toward Azotus in the land of the Philistines. He destroyed their altars

---

5, 46: *Ephron:* a city in Trans-Jordan opposite Bethshan, about five miles east of the Jordan River.

Situated on a height, it dominated the valleys of the two tributaries of the Jordan.

5, 65: *Sons of Esau:* Idumeans.

and burned the statues of their gods; and after plundering their cities he returned to the land of Judah.

Defeat and Death of Antiochus IV

6 As King Antiochus was traversing the inland provinces, he heard that in Persia there was a city called Elymais, famous for its wealth in silver and gold, 2 and that its temple was very rich, containing gold helmets, breastplates, and weapons left there by Alexander, son of Philip, king of Macedon, the first king of the Greeks. 3 He went therefore and tried to capture and pillage the city. But he could not do so, because his plan became known to the people of the city 4 who rose up in battle against him. So he retreated and in great dismay withdrew from there to return to Babylon.

5 While he was in Persia, a messenger brought him news that the armies sent into the land of Judah had been put to flight; 6 that Lysias had gone at first with a strong army and been driven back by the Israelites; that they had grown strong by reason of the arms, men, and abundant possessions taken from the armies they had destroyed; 7 that they had pulled down the Abomination which he had built upon the altar in Jerusalem; and that they had surrounded with high walls both the sanctuary, as it had been before, and his city of Beth-zur.

8 When the king heard this news, he was struck with fear and very much shaken. Sick with grief because his designs had failed, he took to his bed. 9 There he remained many days, overwhelmed with sorrow, for he knew he was going to die. 10 So he called in all his Friends and said to them: "Sleep has departed from my eyes, for my heart is sinking with anxiety. 11 I said to myself: 'Into what tribulation have I come, and in what floods of sorrow am I now! 12 Yet I was kindly and beloved in my rule.' But I now recall the evils I did in Jerusalem, when I carried away all the vessels of gold and silver that were in it, and for no cause gave orders that the inhabitants of Judah be destroyed. 13 I know that this is why these evils have overtaken me; and now I am dying, in bitter grief, in a foreign land."

14 Then he summoned Philip, one of his Friends, and put him in charge of his whole kingdom. 15 He gave him his crown, his robe, and his signet ring, so that he might guide the king's son Antiochus and bring him up to be king. 16 King Antiochus died in Persia in the year one hundred and forty-nine.

The Citadel Besieged

17 When Lysias learned that the king was dead, he set up the king's son Antiochus, whom he had reared as a child, to be king in his place; and he gave him the title Eupator.

18 The men in the citadel were hemming in Israel around the sanctuary, continually trying to harm them and to strengthen the Gentiles. 19 But Judas planned to destroy them, and called all the people together to besiege them. 20 So in the year one hundred and fifty they assembled and stormed the citadel, for which purpose he constructed catapults and other devices. 21 Some of the besieged escaped, joined by impious Israelites; 22 they went to the king and said:

"How long will you fail to do justice and avenge our kinsmen? 23 We agreed to serve your father and to follow his orders and obey his edicts. 24 And for this the sons of our people have become our enemies; they have put to death as many of us as they could find and have plundered our estates. 25 They have acted aggressively not only against us, but throughout their whole territory. 26 Look! They have now besieged the citadel in Jerusalem in order to capture it, and they have fortified the sanctuary and Beth-zur. 27 Unless you quickly forestall them, they will do even worse things than these, and you will not be able to stop them."

Campaign against Judas

28 When the king heard this he was angry, and he called together all his Friends, the officers of his army, and the commanders of the cavalry. 29 Mercenary forces also came to him from other kingdoms and from the islands of the seas. 30 His army numbered a hundred thousand footsoldiers, twenty thousand cavalry, and thirty-two elephants trained for war. 31 They passed through Idumea and camped before Beth-zur. For many days they attacked it; they constructed siege-devices, but the besieged made a sortie and burned these, and they fought bravely.

32 Then Judas marched away from the citadel and moved his camp to Beth-zechariah, on the way to the king's camp. 33 The king, rising before dawn, moved his force hastily along the road to Beth-zechariah; and the armies prepared for battle, while the trumpets sounded. 34 They showed the elephants, the juice of grapes and mulberries to provoke them to fight. 35 The beasts were distributed along the phalanxes, each elephant having assigned to it a thousand men in coats of mail, with bronze helmets, and five hundred picked cavalry. 36 These anticipated the beast wherever it was; and wherever it moved, they moved too and never left it. 37 A strong wooden tower covering each elephant, and fastened to it by a harness, held, besides the Indian mahout, three soldiers who fought from it. 38 The remaining cavalry were stationed on one or the other of the two flanks of the army, to harass the enemy and to be protected from the phalanxes. 39 When the sun shone on the gold and bronze shields, the mountains gleamed with their brightness and blazed like flaming torches. 40 Part of the king's army extended over the heights, while some were on low ground, but they marched forward steadily and in good order. 41 All who heard the noise of their numbers, the tramp of their marching,

---

6, 1: *Elymais:* the mountainous region of Elam, north of the Persian Gulf. This section continues the story from 3, 37 and pertains to events preceding those in 4, 37ff.

6, 16: *The year one hundred and forty-nine:* September 22, 164, to October 9, 163 B.C. A Baby-

Ionian list of the Seleucid kings indicates that Antiochus died in November or early December of 164.

6, 17: *The king's son Antiochus:* Antiochus V Eupator, then about nine years old. He was in Antioch, still in the charge of Lysias, who proceeded

to govern and wage wars in his name. Both were put to death two years later, when Demetrius, brother of Antiochus IV, arrived to claim the kingship: cf 7, 1ff.

6, 20: *The year one hundred and fifty:* October, 163, to September, 162 B.C.

and the clashing of the arms, trembled; for the army was very great and strong.

42 Judas with his army advanced to fight, and six hundred men of the king's army fell. 43 Eleazar, son of Avaran, saw one of the beasts bigger than any of the others and covered with royal armor, and he thought the king must be on it. 44 So he gave up his life to save his people and win an everlasting name for himself. 45 He dashed up to it in the middle of the phalanx, killing men right and left, so that they fell back from him on both sides. 46 He ran right under the elephant and stabbed it in the belly, killing it. The beast fell to the ground on top of him, and he died there.

47 When the Jews saw the strength of the royal army and the ardor of its forces, they retreated from them. 48 A part of the king's army went up to Jerusalem to attack them, and the king established camps in Judea and at Mount Zion. 49 He made peace with the men of Beth-zur, and they evacuated the city, because they had no food there to enable them to stand a siege, for that was a sabbath year in the land. 50 The king took Beth-zur and stationed a garrison there to hold it. 51 For many days he besieged the sanctuary, setting up artillery and machines, fire-throwers, catapults and mechanical bows for shooting arrows and slingstones. 52 The Jews countered by setting up machines of their own, and kept up the fight a long time. 53 But there were no provisions in the storerooms, because it was the seventh year, and the tide-over provisions had been eaten up by those who had been rescued from the Gentiles and brought to Judea. 54 Few men remained in the sanctuary; the rest scattered, each to his own home, for the famine was too much for them.

Peace Treaty

55 Lysias heard that Philip, whom King Antiochus, before his death,

had appointed to train his son Antiochus to be king, 56 had returned from Persia and Media with the army that accompanied the king, and that he was seeking to take over the government. 57 So he hastily resolved to withdraw. He said to the king, the leaders of the army, and the soldiers: "We are growing weaker every day, our provisions are scanty, the place we are besieging is strong, and it is our duty to take care of the affairs of the kingdom. 58 Therefore let us now come to terms with these men, and make peace with them and all their nation. 59 Let us grant them freedom to live according to their own laws as formerly; it was on account of their laws, which we abolished, that they became angry and did all these things."

60 The proposal found favor with the king and the leaders; he sent peace terms to the Jews, and they accepted. 61 So the king and the leaders swore an oath to them, and on these terms they evacuated the fortification. 62 But when the king entered Mount Zion and saw how the place was fortified, he broke the oath he had sworn and gave orders for the encircling wall to be destroyed. 63 Then he departed in haste and returned to Antioch, where he found Philip in possession of the city. He fought against him and took the city by force.

Expedition of Bacchides and Alcimus

7 In the year one hundred and fifty-one, Demetrius, son of Seleucus, set out from Rome, arrived with a few men in a city on the seacoast, and began to rule there. 2 As he was preparing to enter the royal palace of his ancestors, the soldiers seized Antiochus and Lysias to bring them to him. 3 When he was informed of this, he said, "Do not show me their faces." 4 So the soldiers killed them, and Demetrius sat on the royal throne.

5 Then all the lawless and impious men of Israel came to him. They were led by Alcimus, who desired to be high priest. 6 They made this accusation to the king against the people: "Judas and his brothers have destroyed all your friends and have driven us out of our country. 7 So now, send a man whom you trust to go and see all the havoc Judas has done to us and to the king's land, and let him punish them and all their supports."

8 Then the king chose Bacchides, one of the King's Friends, governor of West-of-Euphrates, a great man in the kingdom, and faithful to the king. 9 He sent him and the impious Alcimus, to whom he granted the high priesthood, with orders to take revenge on the Israelites. 10 They set out and, on arriving in the land of Judah with a great army, sent messengers who spoke deceitfully to Judas and his brothers in peaceful terms. 11 But these paid no attention to their words, seeing that they had come with a great army. 12 A group of scribes, however, gathered about Alcimus and Bacchides to ask for a just agreement. 13 The Hasideans were the first among the Israelites to seek peace with them, 14 for they said, "A priest of the line of Aaron has come with the army, and he will not do us any wrong." 15 He spoke with them peacefully and swore to them, "We will not try to injure you or your friends." 16 So they trusted him. But he arrested sixty of them and killed them in one day, according to the text of Scripture:

17 "The flesh of your saints they have strewn,
      and their blood they have shed
         round about Jerusalem,
      and there was no one to bury
         them."

18 Then fear and dread of them came upon all people, who said: "There is no truth or justice among them; they

---

6, 49: *A sabbath year in the land:* when sowing and reaping were prohibited (Ex 23, 10f; Lv 25, 2–7). The year without a harvest (autumn of 164 to autumn of 163) was followed by a food shortage.

7, 1ff: *The year one hundred and fifty-one:* the spring of 161 B.C. *Demetrius,* son of Seleucus, was the lawful heir to the kingdom; but when only nine

years old, he was taken as a hostage at Rome in place of his uncle, who ruled as Antiochus IV Epiphanes. At the age of twenty-five Demetrius fled secretly from Rome and, with the support of the Syrians, overcame his rival Antiochus V and put him to death. *The royal palace:* at Antioch.

7, 5f: *Alcimus:* a renegade Jew hostile to the

Maccabees, who became high priest after the death of Menelaus (2 Mc 14, 3). He received confirmation in his office from the new King Demetrius (v 9), and brought malicious charges against *Judas and his brothers* and the people (v 6). He wrought more evils on the Israelites than the Gentiles had done (v 23).

violated the agreement and the oath that they swore."

19 Bacchides withdrew from Jerusalem and pitched his camp in Bethzaith. He had many of the men arrested who deserted to him, throwing them into the great pit. 20 He handed the province over to Alcimus, leaving troops to help him, while he himself returned to the king.

21 Alcimus spared no pains to maintain his high priesthood, 22 and all those who were disturbing their people gathered about him. They took possession of the land of Judah and caused great distress in Israel. 23 When Judas saw all the evils that Alcimus and his men were bringing upon the Israelites, more then even the Gentiles had done, 24 he went about all the borders of Judea and took revenge on the men who had deserted, preventing them from going out into the country. 25 But when Alcimus saw that Judas and his followers were gaining strength and realized that he could not oppose them, he returned to the king and accused them of grave crimes.

Defeat of Nicanor

26 Then the king sent Nicanor, one of his famous officers, who was a bitter enemy of Israel, with orders to destroy the people. 27 Nicanor came to Jerusalem with a large force and deceitfully sent to Judas and his brothers this peaceable message: 28 "Let there be no fight between me and you. I will come with a few men to meet you peaceably."

29 So he came to Judas, and they greeted one another peaceably. But Judas' enemies were prepared to seize him. 30 When he became aware that Nicanor had come to him with treachery in mind, Judas was afraid and would not meet him

again. 31 When Nicanor saw that his plan had been discovered, he went out to fight Judas near Capharsalama. 32 About five hundred men of Nicanor's army fell; the rest fled to the City of David.

33 After this, Nicanor went up to Mount Zion. Some of the priests from the sanctuary and some of the elders of the people came out to greet him peaceably and to show him the holocaust that was being offered for the king. 34 But he mocked and ridiculed them, defiled them, and spoke disdainfully. 35 In a rage he swore: "If Judas and his army are not delivered to me at once, when I return victorious I will burn this temple down." He went away in great anger. 36 The priests, however, went in and stood before the altar and the sanctuary. They wept and said: 37 "You have chosen this house to bear your name, to be a house of prayer and petition for your people. 38 Take revenge on this man and his army, and let them fall by the sword. Remember their blasphemies, and do not let them continue."

39 Nicanor left Jerusalem and pitched his camp at Beth-horon, where the Syrian army joined him. 40 But Judas camped in Adasa with three thousand men. Here Judas uttered this prayer: 41 "When they who were sent by the king blasphemed, your angel went out and killed a hundred and eighty-five thousand of them. 42 In the same way, crush this army before us today, and let the rest know that Nicanor spoke wickedly against your sanctuary; judge him according to his wickedness."

43 The armies met in battle on the thirteenth day of the month Adar. Nicanor's army was crushed, and he

himself was the first to fall in the battle. 44 When his army saw that Nicanor was dead, they threw down their arms and fled. 45 The Jews pursued them a day's journey, from Adasa to near Gazara, blowing the trumpets behind them as signals. 46 From all the surrounding villages of Judea people came out and closed in on them. They hemmed them in, and all the enemies fell by the sword; not a single one escaped.

47 Then the Jews collected the spoils and the booty; they cut off Nicanor's head and his right arm, which he had lifted up so arrogantly. These they brought to Jerusalem and displayed there. 48 The people rejoiced greatly, and observed that day as a great festival. 49 They decreed that it should be observed every year on the thirteenth of Adar. 50 And for a short time the land of Judah was quiet.

Treaty with the Romans

8 Judas had heard of the reputation of the Romans. They were valiant fighters and acted amiably to all who took their side. They established a friendly alliance with all who applied to them. 2 He was also told of their battles and the brave deeds that they had performed against the Gauls, conquering them and forcing them to pay tribute. 3 They had gotten possession of the silver and gold mines in Spain, 4 and by planning and persistence had conquered the whole country, although it was very remote from their own. They had crushed the kings who had come against them from the far corners of the earth and had inflicted on them severe defeat, and the rest paid tribute to them every year. 5 Philip and Perseus, king of the Macedonians, and the others

---

7, 19: *Beth-zaith:* about three miles north of Beth-zur and twelve miles south of Jerusalem.

7, 27: *Nicanor . . . deceitfully sent to Judas:* A more favorable picture of Nicanor, as an honest man who became a personal friend of Judas, is given in 2 Mc 14, 17–25. Their friendship was broken by the intrigues of Alcimus (2 Mc 14, 26–30).

7, 31: *Caphar-salama:* a village seven miles north-northwest of Jerusalem, on the road leading to Beth-horon.

7, 34: *Defiled them:* spitting on the priests caused them to become legally defiled.

7, 40: *Adasa:* a village southeast of Caphar-salama.

7, 49: *The thirteenth of Adar:* March 27, 160 B.C. This day in the Jewish calendar was called the "Day of Nicanor" (2 Mc 15, 36), but it was not long celebrated by the Jews.

7, 50: *A short time:* about one month following the death of Nicanor. After that began the attack of Bacchides resulting in the death of Judas (9, 1–18).

8, 1: This chapter contains the account of the embassy which Judas sent to Rome, probably before the death of Nicanor, to conclude a treaty of alliance between Rome and the Jewish nation. Without precise chronology, the pertinent data are gathered into a unified theme.

The image of the Roman Republic greatly impressed the smaller Eastern peoples seeking support against their overlords (1–16), because of the Roman success in war (2–11) and effective aid to their allies (12–13). Numerous interventions by Rome in the politics of the Near East bear witness to its power and prestige in the second century B.C. Cf 1 Mc 1, 10; 7, 2; 12, 3; 15, 15–24; 2 Mc 11, 34. With the Roman

control of Palestine in 63 B.C., the Republic and later the Empire became heartily detested. The eulogy of Rome in this chapter is one of the reasons why 1 Maccabees was not preserved by the Palestinian Jews of the century that followed.

8, 2: *Gauls:* probably the Celts of northern Italy and southern France, subdued by the Romans in 222 B.C., and again in 200–191 B.C.; but perhaps also those in Asia Minor (the Galatians), whom the Romans defeated in 189 B.C.

8, 5: *Philip:* Philip V of Macedonia, defeated by a Graeco-Roman alliance at Cynoscephalae in 197 B.C. *Perseus,* his son, was defeated at Pydna in 168 B.C., and died a prisoner. With this, the kingdom of Macedonia came to an end.

who opposed them in battle had been overwhelmed and subjugated. 6 Antiochus the Great, king of Asia, who had fought against them with a hundred and twenty elephants and with cavalry and chariots and a very great army, had been defeated by them. 7 They had taken him alive and obliged him and the kings who succeeded him to pay a heavy tribute, to give hostages and a section of 8 Lycia, Mysia, and Lydia from among their best provinces. The Romans took these from him and gave them to King Eumenes. 9 When the men of Greece had planned to come and destroy them, 10 the Romans discovered it, and sent against the Greeks a single general who made war on them. Many were wounded and fell, and the Romans took their wives and children captive. They plundered them, took possession of their land, tore down their strongholds and reduced them to slavery even to this day. 11 All the other kingdoms and islands that had ever opposed them they destroyed and enslaved; 12 with their friends, however, and those who relied on them, they maintained friendship. They had conquered kings both far and near, and all who heard of their fame were afraid of them. 13 In truth, those whom they desired to help to a kingdom became kings, and those whom they wished to depose they deposed; and they were greatly exalted. 14 Yet with all this, none of them put on a crown or wore purple as a display of grandeur. 15 They had made for themselves a senate house, and every day three hundred and twenty men took counsel, deliberating on all that concerned the people and their well-being. 16 They entrusted their government to one man every year, to rule over their entire country, and

they all obeyed that one, and there was no envy or jealousy among them.

17 So Judas chose Eupolemus, son of John, son of Accos, and Jason, son of Eleazar, and sent them to Rome to establish an alliance of friendship with them. 18 He did this to get rid of the yoke, for it was obvious that the kingdom of the Greeks was subjecting Israel to slavery. 19 After making a very long journey to Rome, the envoys entered the senate and spoke as follows: 20 "Judas, called Maccabeus, and his brothers, with the Jewish people, have sent us to you to make a peaceful alliance with you, and to enroll ourselves among your allies and friends." 21 The proposal pleased the Romans, 22 and this is a copy of the reply they inscribed on bronze tablets and sent to Jerusalem, to remain there with the Jews as a record of peace and alliance:

23 "May it be well with the Romans and the Jewish nation at sea and on land forever; may sword and enemy be far from them. 24 But if war is first made on Rome, or any of its allies in any of their dominions, 25 the Jewish nation will help them wholeheartedly, as the occasion shall demand; 26 and to those who wage war they shall not give nor provide grain, arms, money, or ships; this is Rome's decision. They shall fulfill their obligations without receiving any recompense. 27 In the same way, if war is made first on the Jewish nation, the Romans will help them willingly, as the occasion shall demand, 28 and to those who are attacking them there shall not be given grain, arms, money, or ships; this is Rome's decision. They shall fulfill their obligations without deception. 29 On these terms the Romans have made an agreement with

the Jewish people. 30 But if both parties hereafter decide to add or take away anything, they shall do as they choose, and whatever they shall add or take away shall be valid.

31 "Moreover, concerning the wrongs that King Demetrius has done to them, we have written to him thus: 'Why have you made your yoke heavy upon our friends and allies the Jews? 32 If they complain about you again, we will do them justice and make war on you by land and sea.'"

Invasion of Judah

9 When Demetrius heard that Nicanor and his army had fallen in battle, he again sent Bacchides and Alcimus into the land of Judah, along with the right wing of his army. 2 They took the road to Galilee, and camping opposite the ascent at Arbela, they captured it and killed many people. 3 In the first month of the year one hundred and fifty-two, they encamped against Jerusalem. 4 Then they set out for Berea with twenty thousand men and two thousand cavalry. 5 Judas, with three thousand picked men, had camped at Elasa. 6 When his men saw the great number of the troops, they were very much afraid, and many slipped away from the camp, until only eight hundred men remained.

7 As Judas saw that his army was melting away just when the battle was imminent, he was panic-striken, because he had no time to gather them together. 8 But in spite of his discouragement, he said to those who remained: "Let us go forward to meet our enemies; perhaps we can put up a good fight against them." 9 They tried to dissuade him, saying: "We certainly cannot. Let us save our lives now, and come back with our kinsmen, and then fight against them.

8, 6: *Antiochus:* Antiochus III, greatest of the Seleucid kings. He was defeated at Magnesia in 190 B.C. By the Treaty of Apamea in 189, he was obliged to pay Rome a crushing indemnity of 15,000 talents. It was the weakening of Antiochene power and the growing military and economic influence of Rome that led Antiochus IV to adopt the policy of political, religious and cultural unification of Syria and Palestine.

8, 8: *Lycia, Mysia:* regions in western Asia Minor. These names are restored here by conjectural emendation; the Greek text has "India, Media," most likely through scribal error. *Eumenes:* Eumenes II (197–158), king of Pergamum, an ally of Rome who benefited greatly from Antiochus' losses.

8, 9f: The revolt of the Achaean League, inserted here, occurred in 146 B.C., after Judas' time. It was crushed by the Roman consul Lucius Mummius and marked the end of Greek independence. The author regards all Greeks as the enemies of God.

8, 16: *They entrusted their government to one man:* actually the Roman Republic always had two consuls as joint heads of the government. Presumably, a single one dealt with embassies and answered letters, hence the impression the Jews received; cf 15, 16.

8, 22: *The reply . . . on bronze tablets and sent to Jerusalem:* The decree of the Senate would be inscribed on bronze and kept in the Roman Capitol, with only a copy in letter form sent to Jerusalem. The translation of the decree into Hebrew and then

into Greek, as found here in 1 Mc, may have occasioned this error.

9, 2: *They took the road . . . Arbela, they captured it:* This passage is restored, in part, by conjectural emendation. The present Greek text could be translated, "They took the road to Gilgal, and camping opposite Mesaloth at Arbela, they captured it." But Arbela (modern Khirbet Irbid) was in Galilee—on a high hill overlooking the western shore of the Sea of Galilee. Gilgal, on the contrary, was in the Jordan valley near Jericho. "Mesaloth" is probably a corrupt form of a Hebrew word meaning "steps, ascent."

9, 3: *The first month of the year one hundred and fifty-two:* April/May 160 B.C., by the temple calendar.

Now we are too few." 10 But Judas said: "Far be it from me to do such a thing as to flee from them! If our time has come, let us die bravely for our kinsmen and not leave a stain upon our glory!"

Death of Judas

11 Then the army of Bacchides moved out of camp and took its position for combat. The cavalry were divided into two squadrons, and the slingers and the archers came on ahead of the army, and all the valiant men were in the front line. 12 Bacchides was on the right wing. Flanked by the two squadrons, the phalanx attacked as they blew their trumpets. Those who were on Judas' side also blew their trumpets. 13 The earth shook with the noise of the armies, and the battle raged from morning until evening. 14 Seeing that Bacchides was on the right, with the main force of his army, Judas, with all the most stout-hearted rallying to him, 15 drove back the right wing and pursued them as far as the mountain slopes. 16 But when the men on the left wing saw that the right wing was driven back, they turned and followed Judas and his men, taking them in the rear. 17 The battle was fought desperately, and many on both sides fell wounded. 18 Then Judas fell, and the rest fled.

19 Jonathan and Simon took their brother Judas and buried him in the tomb of their fathers at Modein. 20 All Israel bewailed him in great grief. They mourned for him many days, and they said, 21 "How the mighty one has fallen, the savior of Israel!" 22 The other acts of Judas, his battles, the brave deeds he performed, and his greatness have not been recorded; but they were very many.

LEADERSHIP OF JONATHAN

Bacchides and Jonathan

23 After the death of Judas, the transgressors of the law raised their heads in every part of Israel, and all kinds of evildoers appeared. 24 In those days there was a very great famine, and the country deserted to them. 25 Bacchides chose impious men and made them masters of the country. 26 These sought out and hunted down the friends of Judas and brought them to Bacchides, who punished and derided them. 27 There had not been such great distress in Israel since the time prophets ceased to appear among the people.

28 Then all the friends of Judas came together and said to Jonathan: 29 "Since your brother Judas died, there has been no one like him to oppose our enemies, Bacchides and those who are hostile to our nation. 30 Now therefore we have chosen you today to be our ruler and leader in his place, and to fight our battle." 31 From that moment Jonathan accepted the leadership, and took the place of Judas his brother.

32 When Bacchides learned of it, he sought to kill him. 33 But Jonathan and his brother Simon and all the men with him discovered this, and they fled to the desert of Tekoa and camped by the waters of the pool of Asphar.

35 Jonathan sent his brother as leader of the convoy to ask permission of his friends, the Nabateans, to deposit with them their great quantity of baggage. 36 But the sons of Jambri from Medaba made a raid and seized and carried off John and everything he had. 37 After this, word was brought to Jonathan and his brother Simon: "The sons of Jambri are celebrating a great wedding, and with a large escort they are bringing the bride, the daughter of one of the great princes of Canaan, from Nadabath." 38 Remembering the blood of John their brother, they went up and hid themselves under cover of the mountain. 39 They watched, and suddenly saw a noisy crowd with baggage; the bridegroom and his friends and kinsmen had come out to meet the bride's party with tambourines and musicians and much equipment. 40 The Jews rose up against them from their ambush and killed them. Many fell wounded, and after the survivors fled toward the mountain, all their spoils were taken. 41 Thus the wedding was turned into mourning, and the sound of music into lamentation. 42 Having taken their revenge for the blood of their brother, the Jews returned to the marshes of the Jordan.

43 When Bacchides heard of it, he came on the sabbath to the banks of the Jordan with a large force. 44 Then Jonathan said to his companions, "Let us get up now and fight for our lives, for today is not like yesterday and the day before. 45 The battle is before us, and behind us are the waters of the Jordan on one side, marsh and thickets on the other, and there is no way of escape. 46 Cry out now to Heaven for deliverance from our enemies." 47 When they joined battle, Jonathan raised his arm to strike Bacchides, but Bacchides backed away from him. 48 Jonathan and his men jumped into the Jordan and swam across to the other side, but the enemy did not pursue them across the Jordan. 49 A thousand men on Bacchides' side fell that day.

50 On returning to Jerusalem, Bacchides built strongholds in Judea: the Jericho fortress, as well as Emmaus, Beth-horon, Bethel, Timnath, Pharathon, and Tephon, with high walls and gates and bars. 51 In each he put a garrison to oppose Israel. 52 He fortified the city of Beth-zur, Gazara and the citadel, and put soldiers in them and stores of provisions. 53 He took as hostages the sons of the leaders of the country and put them in custody in the citadel at Jerusalem.

54 In the year one hundred and fifty-three, in the second month, Alcimus ordered the wall of the inner court of the sanctuary to be torn down, thus destroying the work of the prophets. But he only began to tear it down. 55 Just at that time he had a stroke, and his work was interrupted; his mouth was closed and

---

9, 15: *As far as the mountain slopes:* conjectural emendation. The Greek text has "as far as Mount Azotus"; this is most unlikely. Apparently the Greek translator mistook the Hebrew word *ashdôt,* "slopes," for *aôdôd,* "Azotus."

9, 33: *Tekoa:* home of the prophet Amos in the wild country above the Dead Sea, southeast of Jerusalem.

9, 36: *Medaba:* northeast of the Dead Sea.

9, 45: Jonathan's force was apparently trapped in one of the many oxbows of the lower Jordan. Bacchides had crossed and caught them still on the east bank.

9, 50: These sites constitute a ring on the edges of the province of Judea.

9, 54: *In the year . . . second month:* May, 159 B.C.

he was paralyzed, so that he could no longer utter a word to give orders concerning his house. 56 Finally he died in great agony. 57 Seeing that Alcimus was dead, Bacchides returned to the king, and the land of Judah was quiet for two years.

58 Then all the transgressors of the law held a council and said: "Jonathan and his companions are living in peace and security. Now then, let us have Bacchides return, and he 59 will capture all of them in a single night." So they went and took counsel with him. 60 When Bacchides was setting out with a large force, he sent letters secretly to all his allies in Judea, telling them to seize Jonathan and his companions. They were not able to do this, however, because their plot became known. 61 In fact, Jonathan's men seized about fifty of the men of the country who were ringleaders in the mischief and put them to death. 62 Then Jonathan and Simon and their companions withdrew to Bethbasi in the desert; they rebuilt and strengthened its fortifications that had been demolished. 63 When Bacchides learned of this, he gathered together his whole force and sent word to those who were in Judea. 64 He came and pitched his camp before Bethbasi, and constructing siege-machines, he fought against it for many days.

65 Leaving his brother Simon in the city, Jonathan, accompanied by a small group of men, went out into the field. 66 He struck down Odomera and his kinsmen and the sons of Phasiron in their encampment; these men had set out to go up to the siege with their forces. 67 Simon and his men then sallied forth from the city and set fire to the machines. 68 They fought against Bacchides, and he was beaten. This caused him great distress. Because the enterprise he had planned came to nought, 69 he was angry with the lawless men who had advised him to invade the province. He killed many of them and resolved to return to his own country.

70 Jonathan learned of this and sent ambassadors to make peace with him and to obtain the release of the prisoners. 71 He agreed to do as Jonathan had asked. He swore an oath to him that he would never try to injure him for the rest of his life; 72 and he released the prisoners he had previously taken from the land of Judah. He returned to his own country and never came into their territory again.

73 Then the sword ceased in Israel. Jonathan settled in Michmash; he began to judge the people, and he destroyed the impious in Israel.

Revolt of Alexander

10 In the year one hundred and sixty, Alexander, who was called Epiphanes, son of Antiochus, came up and took Ptolemais. He was accepted and began to reign there. 2 When King Demetrius heard of it, he mustered a very large army and marched out to engage him in combat. 3 Demetrius sent a letter to Jonathan written in peaceful terms, to pay him honor; 4 for he said: "Let us be the first to make peace with him, before he makes peace with Alexander against us, 5 since he will remember all the wrongs we have done to him, his brothers, and his nation."

6 So Demetrius authorized him to gather an army and procure arms as his ally; and he ordered that the hostages in the citadel be released to him. 7 Accordingly Jonathan went up to Jerusalem and read the letter to all the people. The men in the citadel 8 were struck with fear when they heard that the king had given him authority to gather an army. 9 They released the hostages to Jonathan, and he gave them back to their parents. 10 Thereafter Jonathan dwelt in Jerusalem, and began to build and restore the city. 11 He ordered the workmen to build the walls and encircle Mount Zion with square stones for its fortification, which they did. 12 The for-

eigners in the strongholds that Bacchides had built, took flight; 13 each one of them left his place and returned to his own country. 14 Only in Beth-zur did some remain of those who had abandoned the law and the commandments, for they used it as a place of refuge.

Jonathan Supports Alexander

15 King Alexander heard of the promises that Demetrius had made to Jonathan; he was also told of the battles and valiant deeds of Jonathan and his brothers and the troubles that they had endured. 16 He said, "Shall we ever find another man like him? Let us now make him our friend and ally." 17 So he sent Jonathan a letter written in these terms: 18 "King Alexander sends greetings to his brother Jonathan. 19 We have heard of you, that you are a mighty warrior and worthy to be our friend. 20 We have therefore appointed you today to be high priest of your nation; you are to be called the King's Friend, and you are to look after our interests and preserve amity with us." He also sent him a purple robe and a crown of gold.

21 Jonathan put on the sacred vestments in the seventh month of the year one hundred and sixty at the feast of Booths, and he gathered an army and procured many arms. 22 When Demetrius heard of these things, he was distressed and said: 23 "Why have we allowed Alexander to get ahead of us by gaining the friendship of the Jews and thus strengthening himself? 24 I too will write them conciliatory words and offer dignities and gifts, so that they may be an aid to me."

25 So he sent them this message: "King Demetrius sends greetings to the Jewish nation. 26 We have heard how you have kept the treaty with us and continued in our friendship and not gone over to our enemies, and we are glad. 27 Continue, therefore, to keep faith with us, and

---

9, 62: *Bethbasi:* two miles east of Bethlehem and six miles north of Tekoa.

9, 73: *Began to judge:* exercise the governing authority as in the book of Judges. With Jerusalem and the garrison towns (v 50) firmly in Seleucid hands, Jonathan's freedom of action was greatly restricted. *Michmash,* southeast of Bethel, famous for the exploit of the former Jonathan, son of Saul; cf 1 Sm 14.

10, 1: *The year one hundred and sixty:* 152 B.C. *Alexander . . . Antiochus:* Alexander Balas claimed to be a son of Antiochus IV. He had the backing of the Romans, who had never forgiven Demetrius for becoming king without their permission. The latter meanwhile had become unpopular with his own people as well as with the Jews.

10, 21: *Jonathan . . . feast of Booths:* Jonathan

began to discharge the office of high priest October 23–30, 152 B.C. For seven years after the death of Alcimus there had been no high priest in Jerusalem. It was taken for granted that the king, though a Gentile, had the power to appoint one. The Maccabees, though a priestly family, were not of the line of Zadok, and some in Israel regarded Jonathan's tenure as a usurpation.

we will reward you with favors in return for what you do in our behalf. 28 We will grant you many exemptions and will bestow gifts on you.

29 "I now free you, as I also exempt all the Jews, from the tribute, the salt tax, and the crown levies. 30 Instead of collecting the third of the grain and the half of the fruit of the trees that should be my share, I renounce the right from this day forward: Neither now nor in the future will I collect them from the land of Judah or from the three districts annexed from Samaria. 31 Let Jerusalem and her territory, her tithes and her tolls, be sacred and free from tax. 32 I also yield my authority over the citadel in Jerusalem, and I transfer it to the high priest, that he may put in it such men as he shall choose to guard it. 33 Every one of the Jews who has been carried into captivity from the land of Judah into any part of my kingdom I set at liberty without ransom; and let all their taxes, even those on their cattle, be canceled. 34 Let all feast days, sabbaths, new moon festivals, appointed days, and the three days that precede each feast day, and the three days that follow, be days of immunity and exemption for every Jew in my kingdom. 35 Let no man have authority to exact payment from them or to molest any of them in any matter.

36 "Let thirty thousand Jews be enrolled in the king's army and allowances be given them, as is due to all the king's soldiers. 37 Let some of them be stationed in the king's principal strongholds, and of these let some be given positions of trust in the affairs of the kingdom. Let their superiors and their rulers be taken from among them, and let them follow their own laws, as the king has commanded in the land of Judah.

38 "Let the three districts that have been added to Judea from the province of Samaria be incorporated with Judea so that they may be under one man and obey no other authority than the high priest. 39 Ptolemais and its confines I give as a present to the sanctuary in Jerusalem for the necessary expenses of the sanctuary. 40 I make a yearly personal grant of fifteen thousand silver shekels out of the royal revenues, from appropriate places. 41 All the additional funds that the officials did not hand over as they had done in the first years, shall henceforth be handed over for the services of the temple. 42 Moreover, the dues of five thousand silver shekels that used to be taken from the revenue of the sanctuary every year shall be canceled, since these funds belong to the priests who perform the services. 43 Whoever takes refuge in the temple of Jerusalem or in any of its precincts, because of money he owes the king, or because of any other debt, shall be released, together with all the goods he possesses in my kingdom. 44 The cost of rebuilding and restoring the structures of the sanctuary shall be covered out of the royal revenue. 45 Likewise the cost of building the walls of Jerusalem and fortifying it all around, and of building walls in Judea, shall be donated from the royal revenue."

46 When Jonathan and the people heard these words, they neither believed nor accepted them, for they remembered the great evil that Demetrius had done in Israel, and how sorely he had afflicted them. 47 They therefore decided in favor of Alexander, for he had been the first to address them peaceably, and they remained his allies for the rest of his life.

48 King Alexander gathered together a large army and encamped opposite Demetrius. 49 The two kings joined battle, and when the army of Demetrius fled, Alexander pursued him, and overpowered his soldiers. 50 He pressed the battle hard until sunset, and Demetrius fell that day.

Treaty of Ptolemy and Alexander

51 Alexander sent ambassadors to Ptolemy, king of Egypt, with this message: 52 "Now that I have returned to my realm, taken my seat on the throne of my fathers, and established my rule by crushing Demetrius and gaining control of my country— 53 for I engaged him in battle, defeated him and his army, and recovered the royal throne— 54 let us now establish friendship with each other. Give me your daughter for my wife; and as your son-in-law, I will give to you and to her gifts worthy of you."

55 King Ptolemy answered in these words: "Happy the day on which you returned to the land of your fathers and took your seat on their royal throne! 56 I will do for you what you have written; but meet me in Ptolemais, so that we may see each other, and I will become your father-in-law as you have proposed."

57 So Ptolemy with his daughter Cleopatra set out from Egypt and came to Ptolemais in the year one hundred and sixty-two. 58 There King Alexander met him, and Ptolemy gave him his daughter Cleopatra in marriage. Their wedding was celebrated at Ptolemais with great spendor according to the custom of kings.

59 King Alexander also wrote to Jonathan to come and meet him. 60 So he went with pomp to Ptolemais, where he met the two kings and gave them and their friends silver and gold and many gifts and thus won their favor. 61 Some pestilent Israelites, transgressors of the law, united against him to accuse him, but the king paid no heed to them. 62 He ordered Jonathan to be divested of his ordinary garments and to be clothed in royal purple; and so it was done. 63 The king also had him seated at his side. He said to his magistrates: "Go with him to the center of the city and make a proclamation that no one is to bring charges against him on any grounds or be troublesome to him in any way."

64 When his accusers saw the honor paid to him in the proclamation, and the purple with which he was clothed, they all fled. 65 The king also honored him by numbering him among his Chief Friends and

---

10, 30: *The three districts annexed from Samaria:* mentioned by name in 11, 34. The present Greek text, by a scribal error, has added "and Galilee" after

"Samaria."

10, 57: *Cleopatra:* Cleopatra Thea, then about fifteen years old. She later married Demetrius II,

and later still, his brother Antiochus VII. *The year one hundred and sixty-two:* 151/150 B.C.

made him military commander and governor of the province. 66 So Jonathan returned in peace and happiness to Jerusalem.

Victory over Apollonius

67 In the year one hundred and sixty-five, Demetrius, son of Demetrius, came from Crete to the land of his fathers. 68 When King Alexander heard of it he was greatly troubled, and returned to Antioch. 69 Demetrius appointed Apollonius governor of Coelesyria. Having gathered a large army, Apollonius pitched his camp at Jamnia. From there he sent this message to Jonathan the high priest:

70 "You are the only one who resists us. I am laughed at and put to shame on your account. Why are you displaying power against us in the mountains? 71 If you have confidence in your forces, come down now to us in the plain, and let us test each other's strength there; the city forces are on my side. 72 Inquire and learn who I am and who the others are who are helping me. Men say that you cannot make a stand against us because your fathers were twice put to flight in their own land. 73 Now you too will be unable to withstand our cavalry and such a force as this in the plain, where there is not a stone or a pebble or a place to flee."

74 When Jonathan heard the message of Apollonius, he was roused. Choosing ten thousand men, he set out from Jerusalem, and Simon his brother joined him to help him. 75 He pitched camp near Joppa, but the men in the city shut him out because Apollonius had a garrison there. When the Jews besieged it, 76 the men of the city became afraid and opened the gates, and so Jonathan took possession of Joppa.

77 When Apollonius heard of it, he drew up three thousand horsemen and an innumerable infantry. He marched on Azotus as though he were going on through the country, but at the same time he advanced into the plain, because he had such a large

number of horsemen to rely on. 78 Jonathan followed him to Azotus, and they engaged in battle. 79 Apollonius, however, had left a thousand cavalry in hiding behind them. 80 When Jonathan discovered that there was an ambush behind him, his army was surrounded. From morning until evening they showered his men with arrows. 81 But his men held their ground, as Jonathan had commanded, whereas the enemy's horses became tired out. 82 When the horsemen were exhausted, Simon attacked the phalanx, overwhelmed it and put it to flight. 83 The horsemen too were scattered over the plain. The enemy fled to Azotus and entered Beth-dagon, the temple of their idol, to save themselves. 84 But Jonathan burned and plundered Azotus with its neighboring towns, and destroyed by fire both the temple of Dagon and the men who had taken refuge in it. 85 Those who fell by the sword, together with those who were burned alive, came to about eight thousand men. 86 Then Jonathan left there and pitched his camp at Ashkalon, and the people of that city came out to meet him with great pomp. 87 He and his men then returned to Jerusalem, laden with much booty. 88 When King Alexander heard of these events, he accorded new honors to Jonathan. 89 He sent him a gold buckle, such as is usually given to King's Kinsmen; he also gave him Ekron and all its territory as a possession.

Alliance of Demetrius and Ptolemy

11 The king of Egypt gathered his forces, as numerous as the sands of the seashore, and many ships; and he sought by deceit to take Alexander's kingdom and add it to his own. 2 He entered Syria with peaceful words, and the people in the cities opened their gates to welcome him, as King Alexander had ordered them to do, since Ptolemy was his

father-in-law. 3 But when Ptolemy entered the cities, he stationed garrison troops in each one. 4 When he reached Azotus, he was shown the temple of Dagon destroyed by fire, Azotus and its suburbs demolished, corpses lying about, and the charred bodies of those burned by Jonathan in the war and stacked up along his route. 5 To prejudice the king against Jonathan, he was told what the latter had done; but the king said nothing. 6 Jonathan met the king with pomp at Joppa, and they greeted each other and spent the night there. 7 Jonathan accompanied the king as far as the river called Eleutherus and then returned to Jerusalem.

8 Plotting evil against Alexander, King Ptolemy took possession of the cities along the seacoast as far as Seleucia-by-the-Sea. 9 He sent ambassadors to King Demetrius, saying: "Come, let us make a pact with each other; I will give you my daughter whom Alexander has married, and you shall reign over your father's kingdom. 10 I regret that I gave him my daughter, for he has sought to kill me." 11 His real reason for accusing Alexander, however, was that he coveted Alexander's kingdom. 12 After taking his daughter away and giving her to Demetrius, Ptolemy broke with Alexander; their enmity became open. 13 Then Ptolemy entered Antioch and assumed the crown of Asia; he thus wore two crowns on his head, that of Egypt and that of Asia.

Deaths of Alexander and Ptolemy

14 King Alexander was in Cilicia at that time, because the people of that region had revolted. 15 When Alexander heard the news, he came to challenge Ptolemy in battle. Ptolemy marched out and met him with a strong force and put him to flight. 16 Alexander fled to Arabia to seek protection. King Ptolemy's triumph was complete 17 when the Arab Zabdiel cut off Alexander's head and sent it to Ptolemy. 18 But

---

10, 67: *The year one hundred and sixty-five:* 147 B.C. *Demetrius:* Demetrius II Nicator.

10, 76: *Joppa:* about forty miles northwest of Jerusalem. For the first time the Maccabees took possession of a seaport; nominally it was on behalf of King Alexander.

10, 89: *Kinsmen:* a class higher than Chief Friends.

11, 7: *Eleutherus:* modern Nahr el-Kebir, the northern border of modern Lebanon; in the second century B.C. the northern limit of Coelesyria.

11, 8: *Seleucia-by-the-Sea:* at the mouth of the Orontes, the port city of Antioch.

11, 10: *I regret ... to kill me:* according to Josephus, Ammonius, a friend of Alexander, had tried to assassinate Ptolemy, and the latter claimed that Alexander was the instigator, thus calumniating him to gain his kingdom (v 11).

three days later King Ptolemy himself died, and his men in the fortified cities were killed by the inhabitants of the strongholds. 19 Thus Demetrius became king in the year one hundred and sixty-seven.

Pact with Demetrius

20 At that time Jonathan gathered together the men of Judea to attack the citadel in Jerusalem, and they set up many machines against it. 21 Some transgressors of the law, enemies of their own nation, went to the king and informed him that Jonathan was besieging the citadel. 22 When Demetrius heard this, he was furious, and set out immediately for Ptolemais. He wrote to Jonathan to discontinue the siege and to meet him for a conference at Ptolemais as soon as possible.

23 On hearing this, Jonathan ordered the siege to continue. He selected some elders and priests of Israel and exposed himself to danger 24 by going to the king at Ptolemais. He brought with him silver, gold apparel, and many other presents, and found favor with the king. 25 Although some impious men of his own nation brought charges against him, 26 the king treated him just as his predecessors had done and showed him great honor in the presence of all his Friends. 27 He confirmed him in the high priesthood and in all the honors he had previously held, and had him enrolled among his Chief Friends.

28 Jonathan asked the king to exempt Judea and the three districts of Samaria from tribute, promising him in return three hundred talents. 29 The king agreed and wrote the following letter to Jonathan about all these matters:

30 "King Demetrius sends greetings to his brother Jonathan and to the Jewish nation. 31 We are sending you, for your information, a copy of the letter that we wrote to Lasthenes our kinsman concerning you.

32 'King Demetrius sends greetings to his father Lasthenes. 33 Because of the good will they show us, we have decided to bestow benefits on the Jewish nation, who are our friends and who observe their obligations to us. 34 Therefore we confirm their possession, not only of the territory of Judea, but also of the three districts of Aphairema, Lydda, and Ramathaim. These districts, together with all their dependencies, were transferred from Samaria to Judea in favor of all those who offer sacrifices for us in Jerusalem instead of paying the royal taxes that formerly the king received from them each year from the produce of the soil and the fruit of the trees. 35 From this day on we grant them release from payment of all other things that would henceforth be due to us, that is, of tithes and tribute and of the tax on the salt pans and the crown tax. 36 Henceforth none of these provisions shall ever be revoked. 37 Be sure, therefore, to have a copy of these instructions made and given to Jonathan, that it may be displayed in a conspicuous place on the holy hill.'"

The Intrigue of Trypho

38 When King Demetrius saw that the land was peaceful under his rule and that he had no opposition, he dismissed his entire army, every man to his home, except the foreign troops which he had hired from the islands of the nations. So all the soldiers who had served under his predecessors hated him. 39 When a certain Trypho, who had previously belonged to Alexander's party, saw that all the troops were grumbling at Demetrius, he went to Imalkue the Arab, who was bringing up Alexander's young son Antiochus. 40 Trypho kept urging Imalkue to hand over the boy to him, that he might make him king in his father's place. During his stay there of many days, he told him of all that Demetrius had done and of the hatred that his soldiers had for him.

Jonathan Aids Demetrius

41 Meanwhile Jonathan sent the request to King Demetrius to withdraw his troops from the citadel of Jerusalem and from the other strongholds, for they were constantly hostile to Israel. 42 Demetrius, in turn, sent this work to Jonathan: "I will not only do this for you and your nation, but I will greatly honor you and your nation when I find the opportunity. 43 Do me the favor, therefore, of sending men to fight for me, because all my troops have revolted."

44 So Jonathan sent three thousand good fighting men to him at Antioch. When they came to the king, he was delighted over their arrival, 45 for the populace, one hundred and twenty thousand strong, had massed in the center of the city in an attempt to kill him. 46 But he took refuge in the palace, while the populace gained control of the main streets and began to fight. 47 So the king called the Jews to his aid. They all rallied around him and spread out through the city. On that day they killed about a hundred thousand men in the city, 48 which, at the same time, they set on fire and plundered on a large scale. Thus they saved the king's life. 49 When the populace saw that the Jews held the city at their mercy, they lost courage and cried out to the king in supplication, 50 "Give us your terms and let the Jews stop attacking us and our city." So they threw down their arms and made peace. 51 The Jews thus gained glory in the eyes of the king and all his subjects, and they became renowned throughout his kingdom. Finally they returned to Jerusalem with much spoil.

52 But when King Demetrius was sure of his royal throne, and the land was peaceful under his rule, 53 he broke all his promises and became estranged from Jonathan. Instead of rewarding Jonathan for all the favors

---

11, 19: *The year one hundred and sixty-seven:* 146/145 B.C. The two deaths (vv 17–18) occurred in the summer of 145 B.C.

11, 30: *Brother:* this title and *father* in v 32 are honorific titles used by the Kinsmen.

11, 31: *Lasthenes:* leader of the mercenary troops who had come with Demetrius from Crete. He was

now the young king's chief minister and was apparently responsible for the disastrous policy (v 38) of disbanding the national army.

11, 34: *Aphairema:* the Ophrah of Jos 18, 23; 1 Sm 23, 6; the Ephron of 2 Chr 13, 19; and the Ephraim of Jn 11, 54—modern et-Taiyibeh, five miles northeast of Bethel. *Lydda:* the Lod of the postexilic

Jews (Ez 2, 33; Neh 11, 35) and the hometown of Aeneas, who was cured by Peter (Acts 9, 32ff). It is ten miles southeast of Joppa. *Ramathaim:* the Ramathaim-zophim of 1 Sm 1, 1, and the Arimathea of Mt 27, 57—modern Rentis, nine miles northeast of Lydda.

he had received from him, he caused him much trouble.

Alliance with Trypho

54 After this, Trypho returned and brought with him the young boy Antiochus, who became king and wore the royal crown. 55 All the soldiers whom Demetrius had discharged rallied around Antiochus and fought against Demetrius, who was routed and fled. 56 Trypho captured the elephants and occupied Antioch. 57 Then young Antiochus wrote to Jonathan: "I confirm you in the high priesthood and appoint you ruler over the four districts and 58 wish you to be one of the King's Friends." He also sent him gold dishes and a dinner service, gave him the right to drink from gold cups, to dress in royal purple, and to wear a gold buckle. 59 Likewise, he made Jonathan's brother Simon governor of the region from the Ladder of Tyre to the frontier of Egypt.

60 Jonathan set out and traveled through West-of-Euphrates and its cities, and all the forces of Syria espoused his cause as allies. When he arrived at Ashkalon, the citizens welcomed him with pomp. 61 But when he set out for Gaza, the people of Gaza locked their gates against him. So he besieged it and burned and plundered its suburbs. 62 Then the people of Gaza appealed to him for mercy, and he granted them peace. He took the sons of their chief men as hostages and sent them to Jerusalem. He then traveled on through the province as far as Damascus.

War with Demetrius

63 Jonathan heard that the generals of Demetrius had come with a strong force to Kadesh in Galilee, intending to remove him from office. 64 So he went to meet them, leaving his brother Simon in the province. 65 Simon besieged Beth-zur, attacked it for many days, and blockaded the inhabitants. 66 When they

sued for peace, he granted it to them. He expelled them from the city, took possession of it, and put a garrison there.

67 Meanwhile, Jonathan and his army pitched their camp near the waters of Gennesaret, and at daybreak they went to the plain of Hazor. 68 There, in front of him on the plain, was the army of the foreigners. This army attacked him in the open, having first detached an ambush against him in the mountains. 69 Then the men in ambush rose out of their places and joined in the battle. 70 All of Jonathan's men fled; no one stayed except the army commanders Mattathias, son of Absalom, and Judas, son of Chalphi. 71 Jonathan tore his clothes, threw earth on his head, and prayed. 72 Then he went back to the combat and so overwhelmed the enemy that they took to flight. 73 Those of his men who were running away saw it and returned to him; and with him they pursued the enemy as far as their camp in Kadesh, where they pitched their own camp. 74 Three thousand of the foreign troops fell on that day. Then Jonathan returned to Jerusalem.

Alliances with Rome and Sparta

12 When Jonathan saw that the times favored him, he sent selected men to Rome to confirm and renew his friendship with the Romans. 2 He also sent letters to Sparta and other places for the same purpose.

3 After reaching Rome, the men entered the senate chamber and said, "The high priest Jonathan and the Jewish people have sent us to renew the earlier friendship and alliance between you and them." 4 The Romans gave them letters addressed to the authorities in the various places, requesting them to provide the envoys with safe conduct to the land of Judah.

5 This is a copy of the letter that Jonathan wrote to the Spartans: 6

"Jonathan the high priest, the senate of the nation, the priests, and the rest of the Jewish people send greetings to their brothers the Spartans. 7 Long ago a letter was sent to the high priest Onias from Arius, who then reigned over you, stating that you are our brothers, as the attached copy shows. 8 Onias welcomed the envoy with honor and received the letter, which clearly referred to alliance and friendship. 9 Though we have no need of these things, since we have for our encouragement the sacred books that are in our possession, 10 we have ventured to send word to you for the renewal of brotherhood and friendship, so as not to become strangers to you altogether; a long time has passed since your mission to us. 11 We, on our part, have never ceased to remember you in the sacrifices and prayers that we offer on our feasts and other appropriate days, as it is right and proper to remember brothers. 12 We likewise rejoice in your renown. 13 But many hardships and wars have beset us, and the kings around us have attacked us. 14 We did not wish to be troublesome to you and to the rest of our allies and friends in these wars; 15 with the help of Heaven for our support, we have been saved from our enemies, and they have been humbled. 16 So we have chosen Numenius, son of Antiochus, and Antipater, son of Jason, and we have sent them to the Romans to renew our former friendship and alliance with them. 17 We have also ordered them to come to you and greet you, and to deliver to you our letter about the renewal of our brotherhood. 18 Therefore kindly send us an answer on this matter."

19 This is a copy of the letter that was sent to Onias: 20 "Arius, king of the Spartans, sends greetings to Onias the high priest. 21 A document has been found stating that the Spartans and the Jews are brothers; both nations descended from Abraham. 22 Now that we have learned this, kindly write to us about your

---

11, 59: *Ladder of Tyre:* modern Rās en-Nāqūrah, on the border between Lebanon and Israel, where the mountains reach the sea, so that the coastal road must ascend in a series of steps.

11, 60: *West-of-Euphrates:* refers here to the territory of Palestine and Coelesyria, but not Upper Syria;

cf 3, 32; 7, 8.

11, 67: *Plain of Hazor:* the site of the ancient Canaanite city (Jos 11, 10), ten miles north of the Lake of Gennesaret.

12, 7: *Onias:* Onias I, high priest from 323–300 or 290 B.C. *Arius:* Arius I, king from 309 to 265 B.C. The

letter was sent *long ago,* i.e., a century and a half before.

12, 9: *The sacred books . . . in our possession:* a reference to "the law, the prophets and other books," as mentioned in the Prologue to Sirach (v 1), after 132 B.C.

welfare. 23 We, on our part, are informing you that your cattle and your possessions are ours, and ours are yours. We have, therefore, given orders that you should be told of this."

Demetrius Repelled

24 Jonathan heard that the generals of Demetrius had returned to attack him with a stronger army than before. 25 He set out from Jerusalem and went into the country of Hamath to meet them, giving them no time to enter his province. 26 The spies he had sent into their camp came back and reported that the enemy had made ready to attack the Jews that very night. 27 Therefore, when the sun set, Jonathan ordered his men to be on guard and to remain armed, ready for combat, throughout the night. He also set outposts all around the camp. 28 When the enemy heard that Jonathan and his men were ready for battle, their hearts sank with fear and dread. They lighted fires and then withdrew. 29 But because Jonathan and his men were watching the lights burning, they did not know what had happened until morning. 30 Then Jonathan pursued them, but he could not overtake them, for they had crossed the river Eleutherus. 31 So Jonathan turned aside against the Arabs who are called Zabadeans, overwhelming and plundering them. 32 Then he marched on to Damascus and traversed that whole region.

33 Simon also set out and went as far as Ashkalon and its neighboring strongholds. He then turned to Joppa and occupied it, 34 for he heard that its men had intended to hand over this stronghold to the supporters of Demetrius. He left a garrison there to guard it.

35 When Jonathan returned, he assembled the elders of the people, and with them he made plans for building strongholds in Judea, 36 for making the walls of Jerusalem still higher, and for erecting a high barrier between the citadel and the city, that would isolate the citadel and so prevent its garrison from commerce with the city. 37 The people therefore worked together on building up the city, for part of the east wall above the ravine had collapsed. The quarter called Chaphenatha was also repaired. 38 Simon likewise built up Adida in the Shephelah, and strengthened its fortifications by providing them with gates and bars.

Capture of Jonathan

39 Trypho was determined to become king of Asia, assume the crown, and do away with King Antiochus. 40 But he was afraid that Jonathan would not permit him, but would fight against him. Looking for a way to seize and kill him, he set out and reached Beth-shan. 41 Jonathan marched out against him with forty thousand picked fighting men and came to Beth-shan. 42 But when Trypho saw that Jonathan had arrived with a large army, he was afraid to offer him violence. 43 Instead, he received him with honor, introduced him to all his friends, and gave him presents. He also ordered his friends and soldiers to obey him as they would himself. 44 Then he said to Jonathan: "Why have you put all your soldiers to so much trouble when we are not at war? 45 Pick out a few men to stay with you, send the rest back home, and then come with me to Ptolemais. I will hand it over to you together with other strongholds and their garrisons, as well as the officials, then I will leave and go home. That is why I came here."

46 Jonathan believed him and did as he said. He dismissed his troops, and they returned to the land of Judah. 47 But he kept with him three thousand men, of whom he sent two thousand to Galilee while one thousand accompanied him. 48 Then as soon as Jonathan had entered Ptolemais, the men of the city closed the gates and seized him; all who had entered with him, they killed with the sword.

49 Trypho sent soldiers and cavalry to Galilee and the Great Plain to destroy all Jonathan's men. 50 These, upon learning that Jonathan had been captured and his companions killed, encouraged one another and went out in compact body ready to fight. 51 As their pursuers saw that they were ready to fight for their lives, they turned back. 52 Thus all these men of Jonathan came safely into the land of Judah. They mourned over Jonathan and his men, and were in great fear, and all Israel fell into deep mourning.

53 All the nations round about sought to destroy them. They said, "Now that they have no leader to help them, let us make war on them and wipe out their memory from among men."

SIMON, HIGH PRIEST AND ETHNARCH

Simon, Leader of the Jews

13 When Simon heard that Trypho was gathering a large army to invade and ravage the land of Judah, 2 and saw that the people were in dread and terror, he went up to Jerusalem. 3 There he assembled the people and exhorted them in these words: "You know what I, my brothers, and my father's house have done for the laws and the sanctuary; what battles and disasters we have been through. 4 It was for the sake of these, for the sake of Israel, that all my brothers have perished, and I alone am left. 5 Far be it from me, then, to save my own life in any time of distress, for I am not better than my brothers. 6 Rather will I avenge my nation and the sanctuary, as well as your wives and children, for all the nations out of hatred have united to destroy us."

7 As the people heard these words, their spirit was rekindled. 8 They shouted in reply: "You are our leader in place of your brothers Judas and Jonathan. 9 Fight our battles, and we will do everything that you tell us." 10 So Simon mustered all the men able to fight, and quickly completing the walls of Jerusalem, fortified it on every side. 11 He sent Jonathan, son of Absalom, to Joppa with a large force; Jonathan drove out the occupants and remained there.

12, 25: *Country of Hamath:* the Seleucid territory of Upper Syria northeast of Coelesyria and separated from it by the Eleutherus River. The latter territory was under the command of Jonathan (11, 59f).

12, 49: *The Great Plain:* of Beth-shan (v 41), where Jonathan's disbanded troops remained.

Deceit and Treachery of Trypho

12 Then Trypho moved from Ptolemais with a large army to invade the land of Judah, bringing Jonathan with him as a prisoner. 13 But Simon pitched his camp at Adida, facing the plain. 14 When Trypho learned that Simon had succeeded his brother Jonathan, and that he intended to fight him, he sent envoys to him with this message: 15 "We have detained your brother Jonathan on account of the money that he owed the royal treasury in connection with the offices that he held. 16 Therefore, if you send us a hundred talents of silver, and two of his sons as hostages to guarantee that when he is set free he will not revolt against us, we will release him."

17 Although Simon knew that they were speaking deceitfully to him, he gave orders to get the money and the boys, for fear of provoking much hostility among the people, who might say 18 that Jonathan perished because Simon would not send Trypho the money and the boys. 19 So he sent the boys and the hundred talents; but Trypho broke his promise and would not let Jonathan go. 20 Next he began to invade and ravage the country. His troops went around by the road that leads to Adora, but Simon and his army moved along opposite him everywhere he went. 21 The men in the citadel sent messengers to Trypho, urging him to come to them by way of the desert, and to send them provisions. 22 Although Trypho got all his cavalry ready to go, there was a heavy fall of snow that night, and he could not go. So he left for Gilead. 23 When he was approaching Baskama, he had Jonathan killed and buried there. 24 Then Trypho returned to his own country.

Jonathan's Tomb

25 Simon sent for the remains of his brother Jonathan, and buried him in Modein, the city of his fathers. 26 All Israel bewailed him with solemn lamentation, mourning over him for many days. 27 Then Simon erected over the tomb of his father and his brothers a monument of stones, polished front and back, and raised high enough to be seen at a distance. 28 He set up seven pyramids facing one another for his father and his mother and his four brothers. 29 For the pyramids he devised a setting of big columns, on which he carved suits of armor as a perpetual memorial and next to the armor he placed carved ships, which could be seen by all who sailed the sea. 30 This tomb which he built at Modein is there to the present day.

Pact between Simon and Demetrius

31 Trypho dealt treacherously with the young King Antiochus. He killed him 32 and assumed the kingship in his place, putting on the crown of Asia. Thus he brought much evil on the land. 33 Simon, on his part, built up the strongholds of Judea, strengthening their fortifications with high towers, thick walls, and gates with bars, and he stored up provisions in the fortresses. 34 Simon also sent chosen men to King Demetrius with the request that he grant the land a release from taxation, for all that Trypho did was to plunder the land. 35 In reply, King Demetrius sent him the following letter:

36 "King Demetrius sends greetings to Simon the high priest, the friend of kings, and to the elders and the Jewish people. 37 We have received the gold crown and the palm branch that you sent. We are willing to be on most peaceful terms with you and to write to our official to grant you release from tribute. 38 Whatever we have guaranteed to you remains in force, and the strongholds that you have built shall remain yours. 39 We remit any oversights and defaults incurred up to now, as well as the crown tax that you owe. Any other tax that may have been collected in Jerusalem shall no longer be collected there. 40 If any of you are qualified for enrollment in our service, let them be enrolled. Let there be peace between us."

41 Thus in the year one hundred and seventy, the yoke of the Gentiles was removed from Israel, 42 and the people began to write in their records and contracts, "In the first year of Simon, high priest, governor, and leader of the Jews."

Capture of Gazara and the Citadel

43 In those days Simon besieged Gazara and surrounded it with troops. He made a siege machine, pushed it up against the city, and attacked and captured one of the towers. 44 The men who had been on the siege machine jumped down into the city and caused a great tumult there. 45 The men of the city, joined by their wives and children, went up on the wall, with their garments rent, and cried out in loud voices, begging Simon to grant them peace. 46 "Do not treat us according to our evil deeds," they said, "but according to your mercy."

47 So Simon came to terms with them and did not destroy them. He made them leave the city, however, and he purified the houses in which there were idols. Then he entered the city with hymns and songs of praise. 48 After removing from it everything that was impure, he settled there men who observed the law. He improved its fortifications and built himself a residence.

49 The men in the citadel in Jerusalem were prevented from going out into the country and back for the purchase of food; they suffered greatly from hunger, and many of them died of starvation. 50 They finally cried out to Simon for peace, and he gave them peace. He expelled them from the citadel and cleansed it of impurities. 51 On the twenty-third day of the second month, in the year one hundred and seventy-one, the Jews entered the citadel with shouts of jubilation, waving of palm branches, the music of harps and cymbals and lyres, and the singing of hymns and canticles, because a great

---

13, 20f: The invaders made a wide flanking movement to invade Judea from the south. *Adora* was a few miles southwest of Beth-zur. They would avoid Beth-zur itself and other strongholds of the Maccabees by following the *way of the desert.*

13, 23: *Baskama:* northeast of the Sea of Galilee.

13, 41: *The year one hundred and seventy:* March, 142, to April, 141 B.C., by the temple calendar.

13, 43: *Gazara:* a key position in the Shephelah, fortified by Bacchides in 160 B.C., cf 9, 52.

13, 51: *The twenty-third day of the second month:* June 3, 141 B.C.

enemy of Israel had been destroyed.
52 Simon decreed that this day should
be celebrated every year with rejoicing. He also strengthened the
fortifications of the temple hill alongside the citadel, and he and his companions dwelt there. 53 Seeing that
his son John was now a grown man,
Simon made him commander of all
his soldiers, with his residence in
Gazara.

Capture of Demetrius

14 In the year one hundred and
seventy-two, King Demetrius
assembled his army and marched into
Media to obtain help so that he could
fight Trypho. 2 When Arsaces, king
of Persia and Media, heard that
Demetrius had invaded his territory,
he sent one of his generals to take
him alive. 3 The general went forth
and defeated the army of Demetrius;
he captured him and brought him to
Arsaces, who put him in prison.

Glory of Simon

4 The land was at rest all the days of
Simon,
who sought the good of his
nation.
His people were delighted with his
power
and his magnificence
throughout his reign.
5 As his crowning glory he
captured the port of Joppa
and made it a gateway to the
isles of the sea.
6 He enlarged the borders of his
nation
and gained control of the
country.
7 He took many enemies prisoners
of war
and made himself master of
Gazara, Beth-zur, and the
citadel.
He cleansed the citadel of its
impurities,
there was no one to withstand
him.
8 The people cultivated their land
in peace;

the land yielded its produce
and the trees of the field their
fruit.
9 Old men sat in the squares,
all talking about the good
times,
while the young men wore the
glorious apparel of war.
10 He supplied the cities with food
and equipped them with means
of defense,
till his glorious name reached
the ends of the earth.
11 He brought peace to the land,
and Israel was filled with
happiness.
12 Every man sat under his vine and
his fig tree,
with no one to disturb him.
13 No one was left to attack them in
their land;
the kings in those days were
crushed.
14 He strengthened all the lowly
among his people
and was zealous for the law;
he suppressed all the lawless
and the wicked.
15 He made the temple splendid
and enriched its equipment.

Alliance with Rome and Sparta

16 When people heard in Rome
and even in Sparta that Jonathan had
died, they were deeply grieved. 17
But when the Romans heard that his
brother Simon had been made high
priest in his place and was master of
the country and the cities, 18 they
sent him inscribed tablets of bronze
to renew with him the friendship and
alliance that they had established
with his brothers Judas and Jonathan. 19 These were read before the
assembly in Jerusalem.
20 This is a copy of the letter that
the Spartans sent: "The rulers and
the citizens of Sparta send greetings
to Simon the high priest, the elders,
the priests, and the rest of the Jewish
people, our brothers. 21 The envoys
you sent to our people have informed us of your glory and fame,
and we were happy that they came.
22 In accordance with what they said

we have recorded the following in the
public decrees: Since Numenius, son
of Antiochus, and Antipater, son of
Jason, envoys of the Jews, have come
to us to renew their friendship with
us, 23 the people have voted to
receive the men with honor, and to
deposit a copy of their words in the
public archives, so that the people of
Sparta may have a record of them.
A copy of this decree has been made
for Simon the high priest."
24 After this, Simon sent Numenius to Rome with a great gold shield
weighing a thousand minas, to confirm the alliance with the Romans.

Decree of Honor

25 When the people heard of these
things, they said, "How can we thank
Simon and his sons? 26 He and his
brothers and his father's house have
stood firm and repulsed Israel's
enemies. They have thus preserved its
liberty." So they made an inscription
on bronze tablets, which they affixed
to pillars on Mount Zion. 27 The
following is a copy of the inscription:

"On the eighteenth day of Elul, in
the year one hundred and seventy-
two, that is, the third year under
Simon the high priest in Asaramel,
28 in a great assembly of priests,
people, rulers of the nation, and
elders of the country, the following
proclamation was made:
29 "'Since there have often been
wars in our country, Simon, son of the
priest Mattathias, descendant of
Joarib, and his brothers have put
themselves in danger and resisted the
enemies of their nation, so that their
sanctuary and law might be maintained, and they have thus brought
great glory to their nation. 30
After Jonathan had rallied his nation
and become their high priest, he was
gathered to his kinsmen. 31 When
the enemies of the Jews sought to
invade and devastate their country
and to lay hands on their temple, 32
Simon rose up and fought for his
nation, spending large sums of his
own money to equip the men of his

13, 53: *John:* John Hyrcanus, who was to succeed his father as ruler and high priest; cf 16, 23f.
14, 1: *The year one hundred and seventy-two:* 141–140 B.C. The expedition began most probably in the spring of 140.
14, 2: *Arsaces:* Arsaces VI, also called Mithridates

I, the Parthian king (171–138 B.C.). Parthians had overrun Persia and now held Babylonia, both of which had hitherto belonged to the Seleucid empire. The Greeks and Macedonians in these countries had appealed to Demetrius for help.
14, 16: The embassy to Rome and Sparta was sent

soon after Simon's accession to power, and the replies were received before Demetrius' expedition (vv 1–3)—probably in 142 B.C.
14, 27: *Eighteenth day of Elul:* September 13, 140 B.C. *Asaramel:* a Hebrew name meaning "court of the people of God."

nation's armed forces and giving them their pay. 33 He fortified the cities of Judea, especially the frontier city of Beth-zur, where he stationed a garrison of Jewish soldiers, and where previously the enemy's arms had been stored. 34 He also fortified Joppa by the sea and Gazara on the border of Azotus, a place previously occupied by the enemy; these cities he re-settled with Jews, and furnished them with all that was necessary for their restoration. 35 When the Jewish people saw Simon's loyalty and the glory he planned to bring to his nation, they made him their leader and high priest because of all he had accomplished and the loyalty and justice he had shown his nation. In every way he sought to exalt his people.

36 "'In his time and under his guidance they succeeded in driving the Gentiles out of their country, especially those in the City of David in Jerusalem, who had built for them-selves a citadel from which they used to sally forth to defile the environs of the temple and inflict grave injury on its purity. 37 In this citadel he stationed Jewish soldiers, and he strengthened its fortifications for the defense of the land and the city, while he also raised the wall of Jerusalem to a greater height. 38 Consequently, King Demetrius confirmed him in the high priesthood, 39 made him one of his Friends, and conferred the highest honors on him. 40 He had indeed heard that the Romans had addressed the Jews as friends, allies, and brothers and that they had received Simon's envoys with honor.

41 "'The Jewish people and their priest have, therefore, made the following decisions. Simon shall be their permanent leader and high priest until a true prophet arises. 42 He shall act as governor general over them, and shall have charge of the temple, to make regulations con-cerning its functions and concerning the country, its weapons and strong-holds; 43 he shall be obeyed by all. All contracts made in the country

shall be dated by his name. He shall have the right to wear royal purple and gold ornaments. 44 It shall not be lawful for any of the people or priests to nullify any of these deci-sions, or to contradict the orders given by him, or to convene an assembly in the country without his consent, to be clothed in royal purple or wear an official gold brooch. 45 Whoever acts otherwise or violates any of these prescriptions shall be liable to punishment.

46 "'All the people approved of granting Simon the right to act in accord with these decisions, 47 and Simon accepted and agreed to act as high priest, governor general, and ethnarch of the Jewish people and priests and to exercise supreme authority over all.'"

48 It was decreed that this inscrip-tion should be engraved on bronze tablets, to be set up in a conspicuous place in the precincts of the temple, 49 and that copies of it should be deposited in the treasury, where they would be available to Simon and his sons.

Letter of Antiochus

15 Antiochus, son of King Deme-trius, sent a letter from the islands of the sea to Simon, the priest and ethnarch of the Jews, and to all the nation, 2 which read as follows:

"King Antiochus sends greetings to Simon, the priest and ethnarch, and to the Jewish nation. 3 Whereas certain villains have gained control of the kingdom of my ancestors, I intend to reclaim it, that I may restore it to its former state. I have recruited a large number of merce-nary troops and equipped warships 4 to make a landing in my country and take revenge on those who have ruined it and laid waste many cities in my realm.

5 Now, therefore, I confirm to you all the tax exemptions that the kings before me granted you and whatever other privileges they conferred on you. 6 I authorize you to coin your

own money, as legal tender in your country. 7 Jerusalem and its temple shall be free. All the weapons you have prepared and all the strong-holds you have built and now occupy shall remain in your possession. 8 All debts, present or future, due to the royal treasury shall be canceled for you, now and for all time. 9 When we recover our kingdom, we will greatly honor you and your na-tion and the temple, so that your glory will be manifest in all the earth."

10 In the year one hundred and seventy-four, Antiochus invaded the land of his ancestors, and all the troops rallied to him, so that few were left with Trypho. 11 Pursued by Antiochus, Trypho fled to Dor, by the sea, 12 realizing what a mass of troubles had come upon him now that his soldiers had deserted him. 13 Antiochus encamped before Dor with a hundred and twenty thousand infantry and eight thousand horse-men. 14 While he invested the city, his ships closed in along the coast, so that he blockaded it by land and sea and let no one go in or out.

Roman Alliance Renewed

15 Meanwhile, Numenius and his companions left Rome with letters such as this addressed to various kings and countries:

16 "Lucius, Consul of the Romans, sends greetings to King Ptolemy. 17 Certain envoys of the Jews, our friends and allies, have come to us to renew their earlier alliance of friend-ship. They had been sent by Simon the high priest and the Jewish people, 18 and they brought with them a gold shield worth a thousand minas. 19 Therefore we have decided to write to various kings and countries, that they are not to harm them, or wage war against them or their cities or their country, and are not to assist those who fight against them. 20 We have also decided to accept the shield from them. 21 If, then, any troublemakers from their country take refuge with you, hand them over

---

14, 47: *Ethnarch:* a subaltern ruler over a racial group whose office needed confirmation by a higher authority within the empire.

15, 1: *Antiochus:* Antiochus VII Sidetes, son of Demetrius I, and younger brother of Demetrius II, now a prisoner of the Parthians. At the age of twenty

he set out from the island of Rhodes to take his brother's place and drive out the usurper Trypho.

15, 10: *The year one hundred and seventy-four:* 138 B.C.

15, 11: *Dor, by the sea:* a fortress on the Palestinian coast, fifteen miles south of Carmel.

15, 16: *Lucius:* Perhaps Lucius Caecilius Metellus, consul in 142 B.C., or Lucius Calpurnicus Piso, consul in 140–139 B.C. This document pertains to Simon's first years as leader.

to Simon the high priest, so that he may punish them according to their law."

22 The consul sent similar letters to Kings Demetrius, Attalus, Ariarthes and Arsaces; 23 to all the countries—Sampsames, Sparta, Delos, Myndos, Sicyon, Caria, Samos, Pamphylia, Lycia, Halicarnassus, Rhodes, Phaselis, Cos, Side, Aradus, Gortyna, Cnidus, Cyprus, and Cyrene. 24 A copy of the letter was also sent to Simon the high priest.

Hostility of Antiochus

25 When King Antiochus was encamped before Dor, he assaulted it continuously both with troops and with the siege machines he had made. He blockaded Trypho by preventing anyone from going in or out. 26 Simon sent to Antiochus' support two thousand elite troops, together with gold and silver and much equipment. 27 But he refused to accept the aid; in fact, he broke all the agreements he had previously made with Simon and became hostile toward him.

28 He sent Athenobius, one of his Friends, to confer with Simon and say: "You are occupying Joppa and Gazara and the citadel of Jerusalem; these are cities of my kingdom. 29 You have laid waste their territories, done great harm to the land, and taken possession of many districts in my realm. 30 Therefore, give up the cities you have seized and the tribute money of the districts outside the territory of Judea of which you have taken possession; 31 or instead, pay me five hundred talents of silver for the devastation you have caused and five hundred talents more for the tribute money of the cities. If you do not do this, we will come and make war on you."

32 So Athenobius, the king's Friend, came to Jerusalem, and on seeing the splendor of Simon's court, the gold and silver plate on the sideboard, and the rest of his rich display, he was amazed. When he gave him the king's message, 33 Simon said to him in reply:

"We have not seized any foreign land; what we took is not the property of others, but our ancestral heritage which for a time had been unjustly held by our enemies. 34 Now that we have the opportunity, we are holding on to the heritage of our ancestors. 35 As for Joppa and Gazara, which you demand, the men of these cities were doing great harm to our people and laying waste our country; however, we are willing to pay you a hundred talents for these cities."

36 Athenobius made no reply, but returned to the king in anger. When he told him of Simon's words, of his splendor, and of all he had seen, the king fell into a violent rage.

Victory over Cendebeus

37 Trypho had gotten aboard a ship and escaped to Orthosia. 38 Then the king appointed Cendebeus commander-in-chief of the sea-coast, and gave him infantry and cavalry forces. 39 He ordered him to move his troops against Judea and to fortify Kedron and strengthen its gates, so that he could launch attacks against the Jewish people. Meanwhile, the king went in pursuit of Trypho. 40 When Cendebeus came to Jamnia, he began to harass the people and to make incursions into Judea, where he took people captive or massacred them. 41 As the king ordered, he fortified Kedron and stationed horsemen and infantry there, so that they could go out and patrol the roads of Judea.

16 John then went up from Gazara and told his father Simon what Cendebeus was doing, 2 Simon called his two oldest sons, Judas and John, and said to them: "I and my brothers and my father's house have fought the battles of Israel from our youth until today, and many times we succeeded in saving Israel. 3 I have now grown old, but you, by the mercy of Heaven, have come to man's estate. Take my place and my

brother's, and go out and fight for our nation; and may the help of Heaven be with you!"

4 John then mustered in the land twenty thousand warriors and horsemen. Setting out against Cendebeus, they spent the night at Modein, 5 rose early, and marched into the plain. There, facing them, was an immense army of foot soldiers and horsemen, and between the two armies was a stream. 6 John and his men took their position against the enemy. Seeing that his men were afraid to cross the stream, John crossed first. When his men saw this, they crossed over after him. 7 Then he divided his infantry into two corps and put his cavalry between them, for the enemy's horsemen were very numerous. 8 They blew the trumpets, and Cendebeus and his army were put to flight; many of them fell wounded, and the rest fled toward the stronghold. 9 It was then that John's brother Judas fell wounded; but John pursued them until Cendebeus reached Kedron, which he had fortified. 10 Some took refuge in the towers on the plain of Azotus, but John set fire to these, and about two thousand of the enemy perished. He then returned to Judea in peace.

Murder of Simon and His Sons

11 Ptolemy, son of Abubus, had been appointed governor of the plain of Jericho, and he had much silver and gold, 12 being the son-in-law of the high priest. 13 But he became ambitious and sought to get control of the country. So he made treacherous plans to do away with Simon and his sons. 14 As Simon was inspecting the cities of the country and providing for their needs, he and his sons Mattathias and Judas went down to Jericho in the year one hundred and seventy-seven, in the eleventh month (that is, the month Shebat). 15 The son of Abubus gave them a deceitful welcome in the little stronghold called Dok which he had built. While serving them a sumptuous banquet,

---

15, 22: *Attalus:* Attalus II of Pergamum, reigned 159–138 B.C. *Ariarthes:* Ariarthes V of Cappadocia, reigned 162–130 B.C. *Arsaces:* see note on 14, 2.

15, 37: *Orthosia:* a port between Tripoli and the

Eleutherus River.

15, 39: *Kedron:* a few miles southeast of Jamnia and facing the fortress of Gazara held by John Hyrcanus.

16, 14: *In the year one hundred and seventy-seven,*

in the eleventh month: January–February, 134 B C., by the temple calendar.

16, 15: *Dok:* a fortress built on a cliff three miles northwest of Jericho, near modern Ain Duq.

he had his men hidden there. 16 Then, when Simon and his sons had drunk freely, Ptolemy and his men sprang up, weapons in hand, rushed upon Simon in the banquet hall, and killed him, his two sons, and some of his servants. 17 By this vicious act of treason he repaid good with evil.

18 Then Ptolemy wrote an account of this and sent it to the king asking that troops be sent to help him and that the country be turned over to him. 19 He sent other men to Gazara to do away with John. To the army officers he sent letters inviting them to come to him so that he might present them with silver, gold, and gifts. 20 He also sent others to seize Jerusalem and the mount of the temple. 21 But someone ran ahead and brought word to John at Gazara that his father and his brothers had perished, and that Ptolemy had sent men to kill him also. 22 On hearing this, John was utterly astounded. When the men came to kill him, he had them arrested and put to death, for he knew what they meant to do.

23 Now the rest of the history of John, his wars and the brave deeds he performed, his rebuilding of the walls, and his other achievements— 24 these things are recorded in the chronicle of his pontificate, from the time that he succeeded his father as high priest.

16, 23f: John Hyrcanus was ruler and high priest from 134 B.C. till his death in 104 B.C. These verses suggest that the book was written, or at least completed, only after he died.

THE SECOND BOOK OF

Maccabees

LETTERS TO THE JEWS IN EGYPT

First Letter 124 B.C.

THE Jews in Jerusalem and in the land of Judea send greetings to their brethren the Jews in Egypt and wish them true peace! 2 May God bless you and remember his covenant with his faithful servants, Abraham, Isaac and Jacob. 3 May he give to all of you a heart to worship him and to do his will readily and generously. 4 May he open your heart to his law and his commandments and grant you peace. 5 May he hear your prayers, and be reconciled to you, and never forsake you in time of adversity. 6 Even now we are praying for you here.

7 In the reign of Demetrius, the year one hundred and sixty-nine, we Jews wrote to you during the trouble and violence that overtook us in those years after Jason and his followers had revolted against the holy land and the kingdom, 8 setting fire to the gatehouse and shedding innocent blood. But we prayed to the Lord, and our prayer was heard; we offered sacrifices and fine flour; we lighted the lamps and set out the loaves of bread. 9 We are now reminding you to celebrate the feast of Booths in the month of Chislev. 10 Dated in the year one hundred and eighty-eight.

Festival Letter 164 B.C.

The people of Jerusalem and Judea, the senate, and Judas send greetings and good wishes to Aristobulus, counselor of King Ptolemy and member of the family of the anointed priests, and to the Jews in Egypt. 11 Since we have been saved by God from grave dangers, we give him great thanks for having fought on our side against the king; 12 it was he who drove out those who fought against the holy city. 13 When their leader arrived in Persia with his seemingly irresistible army, they were cut to pieces in the temple of the goddess Nanea through a deceitful stratagem employed by Nanea's priests. 14 On the pretext of marrying the goddess, Antiochus with his Friends had come to the place to get its great treasures by way of dowry. 15 When the priests of the Nanaeon had displayed the treasures, Antiochus with a few attendants came to the temple precincts. As soon as he entered the temple, the priests locked the doors. 16 Then they opened a hidden trap-door in the ceiling, hurled stones at the leader and his companions and

---

1, 7: *Demetrius:* Demetrius II, king of Syria (145–139, 129–125 B.C.). *The year one hundred and sixty-nine* of the Seleucid era, 143 B.C. Regarding the dates in 1 and 2 Mc, see note on 1 Mc 1, 10. On the troubles caused by *Jason* and his revolt against *the kingdom,* i.e. the rule of the legitimate high priest, see 4, 7–22.

1, 8: *Our prayer was heard:* in the ultimate victory of the Maccabees.

1, 9: *Feast of Booths in the month of Chislev:* really the feast of the Dedication of the temple (10, 1–8),

celebrated on the twenty-fifth of Chislev (Nov.–Dec.). Its solemnity resembles that of the true feast of Booths (Lv 23, 33–43), celebrated on the fifteenth of Tishri (Sept.–Oct.); cf 1, 18.

1, 10: 124 B.C. The date pertains to the preceding, not the following letter.

1, 10: *King Ptolemy:* Ptolemy VI Philometor, ruler of Egypt from 180 to 145 B.C., he is mentioned also in 1 Mc 1, 18; 10, 51–59.

1, 11f: *The king:* Antiochus IV of Syria, the bitter persecutor of the Jews, who, as *leader* of the Syrian

army that invaded Persia, perished there in 164 B.C.

1, 13: *Nanea:* an oriental goddess comparable to Artemis of the Greeks.

1, 14–17: A different account of the death of Antiochus IV is given in 9, 1–29, and another variant account in 1 Mc 6, 1–16. The writer of this letter had probably heard a distorted rumor of the king's death. This fact and other indications show that the letter was written very soon after Antiochus IV died, hence in 164 B.C.

struck them down. They dismembered the bodies, cut off their heads and tossed them to the people outside. 17 Forever blessed be our God, who has thus punished the wicked!

18 We shall be celebrating the purification of the temple on the twenty-fifth day of the month Chislev, so we thought it right to inform you, that you too may celebrate the feast of Booths and of the fire that appeared when Nehemiah, the rebuilder of the temple and the altar, offered sacrifices. 19 When our fathers were being exiled to Persia, devout priests of the time took some of the fire from the altar and hid it secretly in the hollow of a dry cistern, making sure that the place would be unknown to anyone. 20 Many years later, when it so pleased God, Nehemiah, commissioned by the king of Persia, sent the descendants of the priests who had hidden the fire to look for it. 21 When they informed us that they could not find any fire, but only muddy water, he ordered them to scoop some out and bring it. After the material for the sacrifices had been prepared, Nehemiah ordered the priests to sprinkle with the water the wood and what lay on it. 22 When this was done and in time the sun, which had been clouded over, began to shine, a great fire blazed up, so that everyone marveled. 23 While the sacrifice was being burned, the priests recited a prayer, and all present joined in with them, Jonathan leading and the rest responding with Nehemiah.

24 The prayer was as follows: "Lord, Lord God, creator of all things, awesome and strong, just and merciful, the only king and benefactor, 25 who alone are gracious, just, almighty, and eternal, Israel's savior from all evil, who chose our forefathers and sanctified them: 26 accept this sacrifice on behalf of all your people Israel and guard and sanctify your heritage. 27 Gather together our scattered people, free those who

are the slaves of the Gentiles, look kindly on those who are despised and detested, and let the Gentiles know that you are our God. 28 Punish those who tyrannize over us and arrogantly mistreat us. 29 Plant your people in your holy place, as Moses promised."

30 Then the priests began to sing hymns. 31 After the sacrifice was burned, Nehemiah ordered the rest of the liquid to be poured upon large stones. 32 As soon as this was done, a flame blazed up, but its light was lost in the brilliance cast from a light on the altar. 33 When the event became known and the king of the Persians was told that, in the very place where the exiled priests had hidden the fire, a liquid was found with which Nehemiah and his people had burned the sacrifices, 34 the king, after verifying the fact, fenced the place off and declared it sacred. 35 To those on whom the king wished to bestow favors he distributed the large revenues he received there. 36 Nehemiah and his companions called the liquid nephthar, meaning purification, but most people name it naphtha.

2 You will find in the records, not only that Jeremiah the prophet ordered the deportees to take some of the aforementioned fire with them, 2 but also that the prophet, in giving them the law, admonished them not to forget the commandments of the Lord or be led astray in their thoughts, when seeing the gold and silver idols and their ornaments. 3 With other similar words he urged them not to let the law depart from their hearts. 4 The same document also tells how the prophet, following a divine revelation, ordered that the tent and the ark should accompany him and how he went off to the mountain which Moses climbed to see God's inheritance. 5 When Jeremiah arrived there, he found a room in a cave in which he put the tent, the ark, and

the altar of incense; then he blocked up the entrance. 6 Some of those who followed him came up intending to mark the path, but they could not find it. 7 When Jeremiah heard of this, he reproved them: "The place is to remain unknown until God gathers his people together again and shows them mercy. 8 Then the Lord will disclose these things, and the glory of the Lord will be seen in the cloud, just as it appeared in the time of Moses and when Solomon prayed that the Place might be gloriously sanctified."

9 It is also related how Solomon in his wisdom offered a sacrifice at the dedication and the completion of the temple. 10 Just as Moses prayed to the Lord and fire descended from the sky and consumed the sacrifices, so Solomon also prayed and fire came down and burned up the holocausts. 11 Moses had said, "Because it had not been eaten, the sin offering was burned up." 12 Solomon also celebrated the feast in the same way for eight days.

13 Besides these things, it is also told in the records and in Nehemiah's Memoirs how he collected the books about the kings, the writings of the prophets and of David, and the royal letters about sacred offerings. 14 In like manner Judas also collected for us the books that had been scattered because of the war, and we now have them in our possession. 15 If you need them, send messengers to get them for you.

16 As we are about to celebrate the feast of the purification of the temple, we are writing to you requesting you also to please celebrate the feast. 17 It is God who has saved all his people and has restored to all of them their heritage, the kingdom, the priesthood, and the sacred rites, 18 as he promised through the law. We trust in God, that he will soon have mercy on us and gather us together from everywhere under the heavens to his holy Place, for he has rescued

1, 18–36: This purely legendary account of Nehemiah's miraculous fire is incorporated in the letter because of its connection with the temple and its rededication.
1, 18: *Nehemiah, the rebuilder of the temple:* he rebuilt the walls of Jerusalem, but the temple had been rebuilt by Zerubbabel almost a century before.
1, 19: *Persia:* actually Babylonia, which later

became part of the Persian Empire.
1, 36: By a play on words, the Greek term *naphtha* (petroleum) is assimilated to some Semitic word, perhaps *nephthar,* meaning "loosened."
2, 1–8: This legendary account of how Jeremiah hid the sacred tent (which was not mentioned after the time of Solomon!), the ark, and the altar is given for the purpose of explaining why the postexilic

temple was the legitimate place of worship even without these sacred objects.
2, 4: *The mountain:* Nebo; cf Dt 34, 1.
2, 8: *The Place:* the temple of Jerusalem.
2, 11: The statement attributed here to Moses seems to be based on Lv 10, 16–20.
2, 13: *Nehemiah's Memoirs:* a lost apocryphal work.

us from great perils and has purified his Place.

19 This is the story of Judas Maccabeus and his brothers, of the purification of the great temple, the dedication of the altar, 20 the campaigns against Antiochus Epiphanes and his son Eupator, 21 and of the heavenly manifestations accorded to the heroes who fought bravely for Judaism, so that, few as they were, they seized the whole land, put to flight the barbarian hordes, 22 regained possession of the world-famous temple, liberated the city, and reestablished the laws that were in danger of being abolished, while the Lord favored them with all his generous assistance. 23 All this, which Jason of Cyrene set forth in detail in five volumes, we will try to condense into a single book.

Purpose and Method

24 In view of the flood of statistics, and the difficulties encountered by those who wish to plunge into historical narratives where the material is abundant, 25 we have aimed to please those who prefer simple reading, as well as to make it easy for the studious who wish to commit things to memory, and to be helpful to all. 26 For us who have taken upon ourselves the labor of making this digest, the task, far from being easy, is one of sweat and of sleepless nights, 27 just as the preparation of a festive banquet is no light matter for one who thus seeks to give enjoyment to others. Similarly, to win the gratitude of many we will gladly endure these inconveniences, 28 while we leave the responsibility for exact details to the original author, and confine our efforts to giving only a summary outline. 29 As the architect of a new house must give his attention to the whole structure, while the man who undertakes the decoration and the frescoes has only

to concern himself with what is needed for ornamentation, so I think it is with us. 30 To enter into questions and examine them thoroughly from all sides is the task of the professional historian; 31 but the man who is making an adaptation should be allowed to aim at brevity of expression and to omit detailed treatment of the matter. 32 Here, then, we shall begin our account without further ado; it would be nonsense to write a long preface to a story and then abbreviate the story itself.

HELIODORUS' ATTEMPT TO PROFANE THE TEMPLE

Treachery of Simon

3 While the holy city lived in perfect peace and the laws were strictly observed because of the piety of the high priest Onias and his hatred of evil, 2 the kings themselves honored the Place and glorified the temple with the most magnificent gifts. 3 Thus Seleucus, king of Asia, defrayed from his own revenues all the expenses necessary for the sacrificial services. 4 But a certain Simon, of the priestly course of Bilgah, who had been appointed superintendent of the temple, had a quarrel with the high priest about the supervision of the city market. 5 Since he could not prevail against Onias, he went to Apollonius of Tarsus, who at that time was governor of Coelesyria and Phoenicia, 6 and reported to him that the treasury in Jerusalem was so full of untold riches that the total sum of money was incalculable and out of all proportion to the cost of the sacrifices, and that it would be possible to bring it all under the control of the king.

Mission of Heliodorus

7 When Apollonius had an audience with the king, he informed him about the riches that had been reported to him. The king chose his minister Heliodorus and sent him with instructions to expropriate the

aforesaid wealth. 8 So Heliodorus immediately set out on his journey, ostensibly to visit the cities of Coelesyria and Phoenicia, but in reality to carry out the king's purpose. 9 When he arrived in Jerusalem and had been graciously received by the high priest of the city, he told him about the information that had been given, and explained the reason for his presence, and he asked if these things were really true. 10 The high priest explained that part of the money was a care fund for widows and orphans, 11 and a part was the property of Hyrcanus, son of Tobias, a man who occupied a very high position. Contrary to the calumnies of the impious Simon, the total amounted to four hundred talents of silver and two hundred of gold. 12 He added that it was utterly unthinkable to defraud those who had placed their trust in the sanctity of the Place and in the sacred inviolability of a temple venerated all over the world. 13 But because of the order he had from the king, Heliodorus said that in any case the money must be confiscated for the royal treasury. 14 So on the day he had set he went in to take an inventory of the funds.

Anguish of the Faithful

There was a great distress throughout the city. 15 Priests prostrated themselves in their priestly robes before the altar, and loudly begged him in heaven who had given the law about deposits to keep the deposits safe for those who had made them. 16 Whoever saw the appearance of the high priest was pierced to the heart, for the changed color of his face manifested the anguish of his soul. 17 The terror and bodily trembling that had come over the man clearly showed those who saw him the pain that lodged in his heart. 18 People rushed out of their houses in crowds to make public supplication, because the Place was in danger of being profaned. 19 Women,

---

2, 20: For the account of *the campaigns against Antiochus* IV *Epiphanes*, see 4, 7—10, 9: and for the account of those against *his son* Antiochus V *Eupator*, see 10, 10—13, 26.

3, 1—40: This legendary episode about Heliodorus is recounted here for the purpose of stressing the inviolability of the temple of Jerusalem; its later

profanation was allowed by God because of the people's sins; cf 5, 17f.

3, 1: *The high priest Onias*: Onias III, who was high priest from 196 to 175 B.C., and died in 171 B.C. He was the son of Simon, whose praises are sung in Sir 50, 1–21.

3, 3: *Seleucus*: Seleucus IV Philopator, who reigned

from 187 to 175 B.C.

3, 4: *Bilgah*: a priestly family mentioned in Neh 12, 5.18.

3, 11: *Son of Tobias*: a member of the Tobiad family of Transjordan (Neh 2, 10; 6, 17ff; 13, 4–8). Hyrcanus' father was Joseph, whose mother was the sister of the high priest Onias II.

girded with sackcloth below their breasts, filled the streets; maidens secluded indoors ran together, some to the gates, some to the walls, others peered through the windows, 20 all of them with hands raised toward heaven, making supplication. 21 It was pitiful to see the populace variously prostrated in prayer and the high priest full of dread and anguish.

Divine Intervention

22 While they were imploring the almighty Lord to keep the deposits safe and secure for those who had placed them in trust, 23 Heliodorus went on with his plan. 24 But just as he was approaching the treasury with his bodyguards, the Lord of spirits who holds all power manifested himself in so striking a way that those who had been bold enough to follow Heliodorus were panic-stricken at God's power and fainted away in terror. 25 There appeared to them a richly caparisoned horse, mounted by a dreadful rider. Charging furiously, the horse attacked Heliodorus with its front hoofs. The rider was seen to be wearing golden armor. 26 Then two other young men, remarkably strong, strikingly beautiful, and splendidly attired, appeared before him. Standing on each side of him, they flogged him unceasingly until they had given him innumerable blows. 27 Suddenly he fell to the ground, enveloped in great darkness. Men picked him up on a stretcher. 28 The man who a moment before had entered that treasury with a great retinue and his whole bodyguard was carried away helpless, having clearly experienced the sovereign power of God. 29 While he lay speechless and deprived of all hope of aid, due to an act of God's power, 30 the Jews praised the Lord who had marvelously glorified his holy Place; and the temple, charged so shortly before with fear and commotion, was filled with joy and gladness, now that the almighty Lord had manifested himself.

31 Soon some of the companions of Heliodorus begged Onias to invoke the Most High, praying that the life of the man who was about to expire might be spared. 32 Fearing that the king might think that Heliodorus had suffered some foul play at the hands of the Jews, the high priest offered a sacrifice for the man's recovery. 33 While the high priest was offering the sacrifice of atonement, the same young men in the same clothing again appeared and stood before Heliodorus. "Be very grateful to the high priest Onias," they told him. "It is for his sake that the Lord has spared your life. 34 Since you have been scourged by Heaven, proclaim to all men the majesty of God's power." When they had said this, they disappeared.

Testimony of Heliodorus

35 After Heliodorus had offered a sacrifice to the Lord and made most solemn vows to him who had spared his life, he bade Onias farewell, and returned with his soldiers to the king. 36 Before all men he gave witness to the deeds of the most high God that he had seen with his own eyes. 37 When the king asked Heliodorus who would be a suitable man to be sent to Jerusalem next, he answered: 38 "If you have an enemy or a plotter against the government, send him there, and you will receive him back well-flogged, if indeed he survives at all; for there is certainly some special divine power about the Place. 39 He who has his dwelling in heaven watches over that Place and protects it, and he strikes down and destroys those who come to harm it." 40 This was how the matter concerning Heliodorus and the preservation of the treasury turned out.

PROFANATION AND PERSECUTION

Onias Appeals to the King

4 The Simon mentioned above as the informer about the funds against his own country, made false accusation that it was Onias who threatened Heliodorus and instigated the whole miserable affair. 2 He dared to brand as a plotter against the government the man who was a benefactor of the city, a protector of his compatriots, and a zealous defender of the laws. 3 When Simon's hostility reached such a point that murders were being committed by one of his henchmen, 4 Onias saw that the opposition was serious and that Apollonius, son of Menestheus, the governor of Coelesyria and Phoenicia, was abetting Simon's wickedness. 5 So he had recourse to the king, not as an accuser of his countrymen, but as a man looking to the general and particular good of all the people. 6 He saw that, unless the king intervened, it would be impossible to have a peaceful government, and that Simon would not desist from his folly.

Jews Led by Jason to Apostatize

7 But Seleucus died, and when Antiochus surnamed Epiphanes succeeded him on the throne, Onias' brother Jason obtained the high priesthood by corrupt means: 8 in an interview, he promised the king three hundred and sixty talents of silver, as well as eighty talents from another source of income. 9 Besides this he agreed to pay a hundred and fifty more, if he were given authority to establish a gymnasium and a youth club for it and to enroll men in Jerusalem as Antiochians.

10 When Jason received the king's approval and came into office, he immediately initiated his countrymen into the Greek way of life. 11 He set aside the royal concessions granted to the Jews through the mediation of John, father of Eupolemus (that Eupolemus who would later go on an embassy to the Romans to establish a treaty of friendship with them); he abrogated the lawful institutions and introduced customs contrary to the law. 12 He quickly established a gymnasium at the very foot of the

4, 7: *Seleucus died:* he was murdered by Heliodorus. *Antiochus Epiphanes* was his younger brother. Onias' brother showed his love for *the Greek way of life* (v 10) by changing his Hebrew name Joshua, or Jesus, to the Greek name *Jason.*
4, 9: *Youth club:* an educational institution in which young men were trained both in Greek intellectual culture and in physical fitness. *Antiochians:*

honorary citizens of Antioch, a Hellenistic city of the Seleucid Kingdom that had a corporation of such Antiochians, who enjoyed certain political and commercial privileges.
4, 11: *Eupolemus:* one of the two envoys sent to Rome by Judas Maccabeus (1 Mc 8, 17).
4, 12: Since the *gymnasium*, where the youth exercised naked (Greek *gymnos*), lay in the Tyropoeon

Valley to the east of the citadel, it was directly next to the temple on its eastern side. *The Greek hat:* a widebrimmed hat, traditional headgear of Hermes, the patron god of athletic contests; it formed part of the distinctive costume of the members of the "youth club."

acropolis, where he induced the noblest young men to wear the Greek hat. 13 The craze for Hellenism and foreign customs reached such a pitch, through the outrageous wickedness of the ungodly pseudo-high-priest Jason, 14 that the priests no longer cared about the service of the altar. Disdaining the temple and neglecting the sacrifices, they hastened, at the signal for the discus-throwing, to take part in the unlawful exercises on the athletic field. 15 They despised what their ancestors had regarded as honors, while they highly prized what the Greeks esteemed as glory. 16 Precisely because of this, they found themselves in serious trouble: the very people whose manner of life they emulated, and whom they desired to imitate in everything, became their enemies and oppressors. 17 It is no light matter to flout the laws of God, as the following period will show.

18 When the quinquennial games were held at Tyre in the presence of the king, 19 the vile Jason sent envoys as representatives of the Antiochians of Jerusalem, to bring there three hundred silver drachmas for the sacrifice to Hercules. But the bearers themselves decided that the money should not be spent on a sacrifice, as that was not right, but should be used for some other purpose. 20 So the contribution destined by the sender for the sacrifice to Hercules was in fact applied, by those who brought it, to the construction of triremes.

21 When Apollonius, son of Menestheus, was sent to Egypt for the coronation of King Philometor, Antiochus learned that the king was opposed to his policies; so he took measures for his own security. 22 After going to Joppa, he proceeded to Jerusalem. There he was received with great pomp by Jason and the people of the city, who escorted him with torchlights and acclamations; following this, he led his army into Phoenicia.

Menelaus Supplants Jason

23 Three years later Jason sent Menelaus, brother of the aforementioned Simon, to deliver the money to the king, and to obtain decisions on some important matters. 24 When he had been introduced to the king, he flattered him with such an air of authority that he secured the high priesthood for himself, outbidding Jason by three hundred talents of silver. 25 He returned with the royal commission, but with nothing that made him worthy of the high priesthood; he had the temper of a cruel tyrant and the rage of a wild beast. 26 Then Jason, who had cheated his own brother and now saw himself cheated by another man, was driven out as a fugitive to the country of the Ammonites.

27 Although Menelaus had obtained the office, he did not make any payments of the money he had promised to the king, 28 in spite of the demand of Sostratus, the commandant of the citadel, whose duty it was to collect the taxes. For this reason, both were summoned before the king. 29 Menelaus left his brother Lysimachus as his substitute in the high priesthood, while Sostratus left Crates, commander of the Cypriots, as his substitute.

Murder of Onias

30 While these things were taking place, the people of Tarsus and Mallus rose in revolt, because their cities had been given as a gift to Antiochis, the king's mistress. 31 The king, therefore, went off in haste to settle the affair, leaving Andronicus, one of his nobles, as his deputy. 32 Then Menelaus, thinking this a good opportunity, stole some gold vessels from the temple and presented them to Andronicus; he had already sold some other vessels in Tyre and in the neighboring cities. 33 When Onias had clear evidence of the facts, he made a public protest, after withdrawing to the inviolable sanctuary at Daphne, near Antioch.

34 Thereupon Menelaus approached Andronicus privately and asked him to lay hands on Onias. So Andronicus went to Onias, and by treacherously reassuring him through sworn pledges with right hands joined, persuaded him, in spite of his supicions, to leave the sanctuary. Then, without any regard for justice, he immediately put him to death.

35 As a result, not only the Jews, but many people of other nations as well, were indignant and angry over the unjust murder of the man. 36 When the king returned from the region of Cilicia, the Jews of the city, together with the Greeks who detested the crime, went to see him about the murder of Onias. 37 Antiochus was deeply grieved and full of pity; he wept as he recalled the prudence and noble conduct of the deceased. 38 Inflamed with anger, he immediately stripped Andronicus of his purple robe, tore off his other garments, and had him led through the whole city to the very place where he had committed the outrage against Onias; and there he put the murderer to death. Thus the LORD rendered him the punishment he deserved.

Riot against Lysimachus

39 Many sacrilegious thefts had been committed by Lysimachus in the city with the connivance of Menelaus. When word was spread that a large number of gold vessels had been stolen, the people assembled in protest against Lysimachus. 40 As the crowds, now thoroughly enraged, began to riot, Lysimachus launched an unjustified attack against them with about three thousand armed men under the leadership of Auranus, a man as advanced in folly as he was in years. 41 Reacting against Lysimachus' attack, the people picked up stones or pieces of wood or handfuls of the ashes lying there and threw them in wild confusion at Lysimachus and his men. 42 As a result, they wounded many of them and even killed a few, while they put all the

---

4, 20: *Triremes:* war vessels with three banks of oars.
4, 21: *Philometor:* Ptolemy VI, king of Egypt, c. 172 to c. 145 B.C.

4, 23: *Menelaus:* Jewish high priest from c. 172 to his execution in 162 B.C. (13, 3–8).
4 30: *Mallus:* a city of Cilicia (v 36) in southeastern Asia Minor, about thirty miles east of *Tarsus.*

4, 36: *The city:* Antioch. But some understand the Greek to mean "each city."
4, 39: *The city:* Jerusalem. *Menelaus* was still in Syria.

rest to flight. The sacrilegious thief himself they slew near the treasury.

43 Charges about this affair were brought against Menelaus. 44 When the king came to Tyre, three men sent by the senate presented to him the justice of their cause. 45 But Menelaus, seeing himself on the losing side, promised Ptolemy, son of Dorymenes, a substantial sum of money if he would win the king over. 46 So Ptolemy retired with the king under a colonnade, as if to get some fresh air, and persuaded him to change his mind. 47 Menelaus, who was the cause of all the trouble, the king acquitted of the charges, while he condemned to death those poor men who would have been declared innocent even if they had pleaded their case before Scythians. 48 Thus, those who had prosecuted the case for the city, for the people, and for the sacred vessels, quickly suffered unjust punishment. 49 For this reason, even some Tyrians were indignant over the crime and provided sumptuously for their burial. 50 But Menelaus, thanks to the covetousness of the men in power, remained in office, where he grew in wickedness and became the chief plotter against his fellow citizens.

Sedition and Death of Jason

5 About this time Antiochus sent his second expedition into Egypt. 2 It then happened that all over the city, for nearly forty days, there appeared horsemen charging in mid-air, clad in garments interwoven with gold—companies fully armed with lances 3 and drawn swords; squadrons of cavalry in battle array, charges and countercharges on this side and that, with brandished shields and bristling spears, flights of arrows and flashes of gold ornaments, together with armor of every sort. 4 Therefore all prayed that this vision might be a good omen.

5 But when a false rumour circulated that Antiochus was dead,

Jason gathered fully a thousand men and suddenly attacked the city. As the defenders on the walls were forced back and the city was finally being taken, Menelaus took refuge in the citadel. 6 Jason then slaughtered his fellow citizens without mercy, not realizing that triumph over one's own kindred was the greatest failure, but imagining that he was winning a victory over his enemies, not his fellow countrymen. 7 Even so, he did not gain control of the government, but in the end received only disgrace for his treachery, and once again took refuge in the country of the Ammonites. 8 At length he met a miserable end. Called to account before Aretas, king of the Arabs, he fled from city to city, hunted by all men, hated as a transgressor of the laws, abhorred as the butcher of his country and his countrymen. After being driven into Egypt, 9 he crossed the sea to the Spartans, among whom he hoped to find protection because of his relations with them. There he who had exiled so many from their country perished in exile; 10 and he who had cast out so many to be unburied went unmourned himself with no funeral of any kind or any place in the tomb of his ancestors.

The City Ravaged

11 When these happenings were reported to the king, he thought that Judea was in revolt. Raging like a wild animal, he set out from Egypt and took Jerusalem by storm. 12 He ordered his soldiers to cut down without mercy those whom they met and to slay those who took refuge in their houses. 13 There was a massacre of young and old, a killing of women and children, a slaughter of virgins and infants. 14 In the space of three days, eighty thousand were lost, forty thousand meeting a violent death, and the same number being sold into slavery. 15 Not satisfied with this, the king dared to enter the holiest temple in the world; Menelaus,

that traitor both to the laws and to his country, served as guide. 16 He laid his impure hands on the sacred vessels and gathered up with profane hands the votive offerings made by other kings for the advancement, the glory, and the honor of the Place. 17 Puffed up in spirit, Antiochus did not realize that it was because of the sins of the city's inhabitants that the Lord was angry for a little while and hence disregarded the holy Place. 18 If they had not become entangled in so many sins, this man, like Heliodorus, who was sent by King Seleucus to inspect the treasury, would have been flogged and turned back from his presumptuous action as soon as he approached. 19 The Lord, however, had not chosen the people for the sake of the Place, but the Place for the sake of the people. 20 Therefore, the Place itself, having shared in the people's misfortunes, afterward participated in their good fortune; and what the Almighty had forsaken in his anger was restored in all its glory, once the great Sovereign became reconciled.

21 Antiochus carried off eighteen hundred talents from the temple, and hurried back to Antioch. In his arrogance he planned to make the land navigable and the sea passable on foot, so carried away was he with pride. 22 But he left governors to harass the nation: at Jerusalem, Philip, a Phrygian by birth, and in character more cruel than the man who appointed him; 23 at Mount Gerizim, Andronicus; and besides these, Menelaus, who lorded it over his fellow citizens worse than the others did. Out of hatred for the Jewish citizens, 24 the king sent Apollonius, commander of the Mysians, at the head of an army of twenty-two thousand men, with orders to kill all the grown men and sell the women and young men into slavery. 25 When this man arrived in Jerusalem, he pretended to be peacefully disposed and waited until

---

4,44: *The senate:* the council of Jewish elders at Jerusalem; cf 1 Mc 12, 6.

5,1: *Second expedition:* the first invasion of Egypt by Antiochus in 169 B.C. (1 Mc 1, 16–20) is not mentioned in 2 Mc, unless the coming of the Syrian army to Palestine (2 Mc 4, 21f) is regarded as the first invasion. The author of 2 Mc apparently combines the first pillage of Jerusalem in 169 B.C. after Antiochus' first invasion of Egypt (1 Mc 1, 20–28; cf 2 Mc

5, 5ff) with the second pillage of the city two years later (167 B.C.), following the king's second invasion of Egypt in 168 B.C. (1 Mc 1, 29–35; cf 2 Mc 5, 24ff).

5, 5: *Jason:* brother of Onias III, was claimant of the high priesthood (4, 7–10). Later he was supplanted by Menelaus who drove him into Transjordan (4, 26).

5, 8: *Aretas:* King Aretas I of the Nabateans; cf 1 Mc 5, 25.

5, 19: Man is more important than even the most sacred institutions; cf Mk 2, 27.

5, 22: *Philip, a Phrygian by birth:* the Philip of 6, 11 and 8, 8, but probably not the same as Philip the regent of 9, 29 and 1 Mc 6, 14.

5, 23: *Mount Gerizim:* the sacred mountain of the Samaritans at Shechem; cf 6, 2.

5, 24: *Apollonius:* the *Mysian commander* of 1 Mc 1, 29; mentioned also in 2 Mc 3, 5; 4, 4.

the holy day of the sabbath; then, finding the Jews refraining from work, he ordered his men to parade fully armed. 26 All those who came out to watch, he massacred, and running through the city with armed men, he cut down a large number of people.

27 But Judas Maccabeus and about nine others withdrew to the wilderness, where he and his companions lived like wild animals in the hills, continuing to eat what grew wild to avoid sharing the defilement.

The Temple Desecrated

6 Not long after this the king sent an Athenian senator to force the Jews to abandon the customs of their ancestors and live no longer by the laws of God; 2 also to profane the temple in Jerusalem and dedicate it to Olympian Zeus, and that on Mount Gerizim to Zeus the Hospitable, as the inhabitants of the place requested. 3 This intensified the evil in an intolerable and utterly disgusting way. 4 The Gentiles filled the temple with debauchery and revelry; they amused themselves with prostitutes and had intercourse with women even in the sacred court. They also brought into the temple things that were forbidden, 5 so that the altar was covered with abominable offerings prohibited by the laws.

Abolition of the Law

6 A man could not keep the sabbath or celebrate the traditional feasts, nor even admit that he was a Jew. 7 Moreover, at the monthly celebration of the king's birthday the Jews had, from bitter necessity, to partake of the sacrifices, and when the festival of Dionysus was celebrated, they were compelled to march in his procession, wearing wreaths of ivy. 8 At the suggestion of the citizens of Ptolemais, a decree was issued ordering the neighboring Greek cities to act in the same way against the Jews: oblige them to partake of the sacrifices, 9 and put to death those

who would not consent to adopt the customs of the Greeks. It was obvious, therefore, that disaster impended. 10 Thus, two women who were arrested for having circumcised their children were publicly paraded about the city with their babies hanging at their breasts and then thrown down from the top of the city wall. 11 Others, who had assembled in nearby caves to observe the sabbath in secret, were betrayed to Philip and all burned to death. In their respect for the holiness of that day, they had scruples about defending themselves.

Purpose of Divine Judgment

12 Now I beg those who read this book not to be disheartened by these misfortunes, but to consider that these chastisements were meant not for the ruin but for the correction of our nation. 13 It is, in fact, a sign of great kindness to punish sinners promptly instead of letting them go for long. 14 Thus, in dealing with other nations, the Lord patiently waits until they reach the full measure of their sins before he punishes them; but with us he has decided to deal differently, 15 in order that he may not have to punish us more severely later, when our sins have reached their fullness. 16 He never withdraws his mercy from us. Although he disciplines us with misfortunes, he does not abandon his own people. 17 Let these words suffice for recalling this truth. Without further ado we must go on with our story.

Martyrdom of Eleazar

18 Eleazar, one of the foremost scribes, a man of advanced age and noble appearance, was being forced to open his mouth to eat pork. 19 But preferring a glorious death to a life of defilement, he spat out the meat, and went forward of his own accord to the instrument of torture, 20 as men ought to do who have the courage to reject the food which it is unlawful to taste even for love of life. 21 Those in charge of that unlawful ritual meal took the man aside

privately, because of their long acquaintance with him, and urged him to bring meat of his own providing, such as he could legitimately eat, and to pretend to be eating some of the meat of the sacrifice prescribed by the king; 22 in this way he would escape the death penalty, and be treated kindly because of their old friendship with him. 23 But he made up his mind in a noble manner, worthy of his years, the dignity of his advanced age, the merited distinction of his gray hair, and of the admirable life he had lived from childhood; and so he declared that above all he would be loyal to the holy laws given by God.

He told them to send him at once to the abode of the dead, explaining: 24 "At our age it would be unbecoming to make such a pretense; many young men would think the ninety-year-old Eleazar had gone over to an alien religion. 25 Should I thus dissimulate for the sake of a brief moment of life, they would be led astray by me, while I would bring shame and dishonor on my old age. 26 Even if, for the time being, I avoid the punishment of men, I shall never, whether alive or dead, escape the hands of the Almighty. 27 Therefore, by manfully giving up my life now, I will prove myself worthy of my old age, 28 and I will leave to the young a noble example of how to die willingly and generously for the revered and holy laws."

He spoke thus, and went immediately to the instrument of torture. 29 Those who shortly before had been kindly disposed, now became hostile toward him because what he had said seemed to them utter madness. 30 When he was about to die under the blows, he groaned and said, "The Lord in his holy knowledge knows full well that, although I could have escaped death, I am not only enduring terrible pain in my body from this scourging, but also suffering it with joy in my soul because of my devotion to him." 31 This is how he died, leaving in his

---

6, 2: *Olympian Zeus:* equated with the Syrian Baal Shamen ("the lord of the heavens"), a term which the Jews rendered as "Shiqqus shomem," *horrible abomination* (Dn 9, 27; 11, 31; 12, 11; 1 Mc 1, 54).

6, 4: *Amused themselves with prostitutes:* as in the

fertility cults of the ancient Near East; see notes on Bar 6, 10.42f.

6, 7: *Dionysus:* called also Bacchus, the god of the grape harvest and of wine; *ivy* was one of his symbols.

6, 18—7, 42: The stories of Eleazar and of the mother and her seven sons, among the earliest models

of "martyrology," were understandably popular among the Christians of the early centuries. Written originally to encourage God's people in times of persecution, they add gruesome details to the record of tortures, and place long speeches in the mouths of the martyrs.

death a model of courage and an unforgettable example of virtue not only
for the young but for the whole
nation.

Martyrdom of a Mother and Her Sons

7 It also happened that seven brothers with their mother were arrested and tortured with whips and scourges by the king, to force them to eat pork in violation of God's law. 2 One of the brothers, speaking for the others, said: "What do you expect to achieve by questioning us? We are ready to die rather than transgress the laws of our ancestors." 3 At that the king, in a fury, gave orders to have pans and caldrons heated. 4 While they were being quickly heated, he commanded his executioners to cut out the tongue of the one who had spoken for the others, to scalp him and cut off his hands and feet, while the rest of his brothers and his mother looked on. 5 When he was completely maimed but still breathing, the king ordered them to carry him to the fire and fry him. As a cloud of smoke spread from the pan, the brothers and their mother encouraged one another to die bravely, saying such words as these: 6 "The Lord God is looking on, and he truly has compassion on us, as Moses declared in his canticle, when he protested openly with the words, 'And he will have pity on his servants.'"

7 When the first brother had died in this manner, they brought the second to be made sport of. After tearing off the skin and hair of his head, they asked him, "Will you eat the pork rather than have your body tortured limb by limb?" 8 Answering in the language of his forefathers, he said, "Never!" So he too in turn suffered the same tortures as the first. 9 At the point of death he said: "You accursed fiend, you are depriving us of this present life, but the King of the world will raise us up to live again forever. It is for his laws that we are dying."

10 After him the third suffered their cruel sport. He put out his

tongue at once when told to do so, and bravely held out his hands, 11 as he spoke these noble words: "It was from Heaven that I received these; for the sake of his laws I disdain them; from him I hope to receive them again." 12 Even the king and his attendants marveled at the young man's courage, because he regarded his sufferings as nothing.

13 After he had died, they tortured and maltreated the fourth brother in the same way. 14 When he was near death, he said, "It is my choice to die at the hands of men with the God-given hope of being restored to life by him; but for you, there will be no resurrection to life."

15 They next brought forward the fifth brother and maltreated him. Looking at the king, 16 he said: "Since you have power among men, mortal though you are, do what you please. But do not think that our nation is forsaken by God. 17 Only wait, and you will see how his great power will torment you and your descendants."

18 After him they brought the sixth brother. When he was about to die, he said: "Have no vain illusions. We suffer these things on our own account, because we have sinned against our God; that is why such astonishing things have happened to us. 19 Do not think, then, that you will go unpunished for having dared to fight against God."

20 Most admirable and worthy of everlasting remembrance was the mother, who saw her seven sons perish in a single day, yet bore it courageously because of her hope in the Lord. 21 Filled with a noble spirit that stirred her womanly heart with manly courage, she exhorted each of them in the language of their forefathers with these words: 22 "I do not know how you came into existence in my womb; it was not I who gave you the breath of life, nor was it I who set in order the elements of which each of you is composed. 23 Therefore, since it is the Creator of the universe who shapes each man's beginning, as he brings about the origin of everything, he, in

his mercy, will give you back both breath and life, because you now disregard yourselves for the sake of his law."

24 Antiochus, suspecting insult in her words, thought he was being ridiculed. As the youngest brother was still alive, the king appealed to him, not with mere words, but with promises on oath, to make him rich and happy if he would abandon his ancestral customs: he would make him his Friend and entrust him with high office. 25 When the youth paid no attention to him at all, the king appealed to the mother, urging her to advise her boy to save his life. 26 After he had urged her for a long time, she went through the motions of persuading her son. 27 In derision of the cruel tyrant, she leaned over close to her son and said in their native language: "Son, have pity on me, who carried you in my womb for nine months, nursed you for three years, brought you up, educated and supported you to your present age. 28 I beg you, child, to look at the heavens and the earth and see all that is in them; then you will know that God did not make them out of existing things; and in the same way the human race came into existence. 29 Do not be afraid of this executioner, but be worthy of your brothers and accept death, so that in the time of mercy I may receive you again with them."

30 She had scarcely finished speaking when the youth said: "What are you waiting for? I will not obey the king's command. I obey the command of the law given to our forefathers through Moses. 31 But you, who have contrived every kind of affliction for the Hebrews, will not escape the hands of God. 32 We, indeed, are suffering because of our sins. 33 Though our living Lord treats us harshly for a little while to correct us with chastisements, he will again be reconciled with his servants. 34 But you, wretch, vilest of all men! do not, in your insolence, concern yourself with unfounded hopes, as you raise your hand against the children of Heaven. 35 You have

---

7, 9: *The King of the world will raise us up:* here, and in vv 11.14.23.29.36, belief in the future resurrection of the body, at least for the just, is clearly stated; cf also

12, 44; 14, 46; Dn 12, 2.

7, 28: *God did not make them out of existing things:* that is, God made all things solely by his omnipotent

will and his creative word; cf Heb 11, 3.

not yet escaped the judgment of the almighty and all-seeing God. 36 My brothers, after enduring brief pain, have drunk of never-failing life, under God's covenant, but you, by the judgment of God, shall receive just punishments for your arrogance. 37 Like my brothers, I offer up my body and my life for our ancestral laws, imploring God to show mercy soon to our nation, and by afflictions and blows to make you confess that he alone is God. 38 Through me and my brothers, may there be an end to the wrath of the Almighty that has justly fallen on our whole nation." 39 At that, the king became enraged and treated him even worse than the others, since he bitterly resented the boy's contempt. 40 Thus he too died undefiled, putting all his trust in the Lord. 41 The mother was last to die, after her sons.

42 Enough has been said about the sacrificial meals and the excessive cruelties.

VICTORIES OF JUDAS AND PURIFICATION OF THE TEMPLE

Judas Maccabeus

8 Judas Maccabeus and his companions entered the villages secretly, summoned their kinsmen, and by also enlisting others who remained faithful to Judaism, assembled about six thousand men. 2 They implored the Lord to look kindly upon his people, who were being oppressed on all sides, to have pity on the temple, which was profaned by godless men; 3 to have mercy on the city, which was being destroyed and about to be leveled to the ground; to hearken to the blood that cried out to him; 4 to remember the criminal slaughter of innocent children and the blasphemies uttered against his name; and to manifest his hatred of evil. 5 Once Maccabeus got his men organized, the Gentiles could not withstand him, for the Lord's wrath had now changed to mercy. 6 Coming unexpectedly upon towns and villages, he would

set them on fire. He captured strategic positions, and put to flight a large number of the enemy. 7 He preferred the nights as being especially helpful for such attacks. Soon the fame of his valor spread everywhere.

First Victory over Nicanor

8 When Philip saw that Judas was gaining ground little by little and that his successful advances were becoming more frequent, he wrote to Ptolemy, governor of Coelesyria and Phoenicia, to come to the aid of the king's government. 9 Ptolemy promptly selected Nicanor, son of Patroclus, one of the Chief Friends, and sent him at the head of at least twenty thousand armed men of various nations to wipe out the entire Jewish race. With him he associated Gorgias, a professional military commander, well-versed in the art of war. 10 Nicanor planned to raise the two thousand talents of tribute owed by the king to the Romans by selling captured Jews into slavery. 11 So he immediately sent word to the coastal cities, inviting them to buy Jewish slaves and promising to deliver ninety slaves for a talent—little did he dream of the punishment that was to fall upon him from the Almighty.

12 When Judas learned of Nicanor's advance and informed his companions about the approach of the army, 13 the cowardly and those who lacked faith in God's justice deserted and got away. 14 But the others sold everything they had left, and at the same time besought the Lord to deliver those whom the ungodly Nicanor had sold before even meeting them. 15 They begged the Lord to do this, if not for their sake, at least for the sake of the covenants made with their forefathers, and because they themselves bore his holy, glorious name. 16 Maccabeus assembled his men, six thousand strong, and exhorted them not be panic-stricken before the enemy, nor to fear the large number of the Gentiles attacking them unjustly, but to fight courageously, 17 keeping before

their eyes the lawless outrage perpetrated by the Gentiles against the holy Place and the affliction of the humiliated city, as well as the subversion of their ancestral way of life. 18 "They trust in weapons and acts of daring," he said, "but we trust in almighty God, who can by a mere nod destroy not only those who attack us, but the whole world." 19 He went on to tell them of the times when help had been given their ancestors: both the time of Sennacherib, when a hundred and eighty-five thousand of his men were destroyed, 20 and the time of the battle in Babylonia against the Galatians, when only eight thousand Jews fought along with four thousand Macedonians; yet when the Macedonians were hard pressed, the eight thousand routed one hundred and twenty thousand and took a great quantity of booty, because of the help they received from Heaven. 21 With such words he encouraged them and made them ready to die for their laws and their country.

Then Judas divided his army into four, 22 placing his brothers, Simon, Joseph, and Jonathan, each over a division, assigning to each fifteen hundred men. 23 (There was also Eleazar.) After reading to them from the holy book and giving them the watchword, "The Help of God," he himself took charge of the first division and joined in battle with Nicanor. 24 With the Almighty as their ally, they killed more than nine thousand of the enemy, wounded and disabled the greater part of Nicanor's army, and put all of them to flight. 25 They also seized the money of those who had come to buy them as slaves. When they had pursued the enemy for some time, 26 they were obliged to return by reason of the late hour. It was the day before the sabbath, and for that reason they could not continue the pursuit. 27 They collected the enemy's arms and stripped them of their spoils, and then observed the sabbath with fervent praise and thanks to the Lord who kept them safe for that day on

---

8, 8–29.34ff: This account of the campaign of Nicanor and Gorgias against Judas is paralleled, with certain differences, in 1 Mc 3, 38—4, 24.
8, 22: *Joseph:* called John in 1 Mc 2, 2; 9, 36.38;

this paragraph interrupts the story of Nicanor's defeat, which is resumed in v 34. The purpose of the author apparently is to group together the defeats suffered by the Syrians on various occasions. Battles

against Timothy are recounted in 1 Mc 5, 37–44 and 2 Mc 12, 10–25; against Bacchides, in 1 Mc 7, 8–20.

which he let descend on them the first dew of his mercy. 28 After the sabbath, they gave a share of the booty to the persecuted and to widows and orphans; the rest they divided among themselves and their children. 29 When this was done, they made supplication in common, imploring the merciful Lord to be completely reconciled with his servants.

Timothy and Bacchides Defeated

30 They also challenged the forces of Timothy and Bacchides, killed more than twenty thousand of them, and captured some very high fortresses. They divided the enormous plunder, allotting half to themselves and the rest to the persecuted, to orphans, widows, and the aged. 31 They collected the enemies' weapons and carefully stored them in suitable places; the rest of the spoils they carried to Jerusalem. 32 They also killed the commander of Timothy's forces, a most wicked man, who had done great harm to the Jews. 33 While celebrating the victory in their ancestral city, they burned both those who had set fire to the sacred gates and Callisthenes, who had taken refuge in a little house; so he received the reward his wicked deeds deserved.

Humiliation of Nicanor

34 The accursed Nicanor, who had brought the thousand slave dealers to buy the Jews, 35 after being humbled through the Lord's help by those whom he had thought of no account, laid aside his fine clothes and fled alone across country like a runaway slave, until he reached Antioch. He was eminently successful in destroying his own army. 36 So he who had promised to provide tribute for the Romans by the capture of the people of Jerusalem testified that the Jews had a champion, and that they were invulnerable for the very reason that they followed the laws laid down by him.

Punishment and Death of Antiochus

9 About that time Antiochus retreated in disgrace from the region of Persia. 2 He had entered the city called Persepolis and attempted to rob the temple and gain control of the city. Thereupon the people had swift recourse to arms, and Antiochus' men were routed, so that in the end Antiochus was put to flight by the natives and forced to beat a shameful retreat. 3 On his arrival in Ecbatana, he learned what had happened to Nicanor and to Timothy's forces. 4 Overcome with anger, he planned to make the Jews suffer for the injury done by those who had put him to flight. Therefore he ordered his charioteer to drive without stopping until he finished the journey.

Yet the condemnation of Heaven rode with him, since he said in his arrogance, "I will make Jerusalem the common graveyard of the Jews as soon as I arrive there." 5 So the all-seeing Lord, the God of Israel, struck him down with an unseen but incurable blow; for scarcely had he uttered those words when he was seized with excruciating pains in his bowels and sharp internal torment, 6 a fit punishment for him who had tortured the bowels of others with many barbarous torments. 7 Far from giving up his insolence, he was all the more filled with arrogance. Breathing fire in his rage against the Jews, he gave orders to drive even faster. As a result he hurtled from the dashing chariot, and every part of his body was racked by the violent fall. 8 Thus he who previously, in his superhuman presumption, thought he could command the waves of the sea, and imagined he could weigh the mountaintops in his scales, was now thrown to the ground and had to be carried on a litter, clearly manifesting to all the power of God. 9 The body of this impious man swarmed with worms, and while he was still alive in hideous torments, his flesh rotted off, so that the entire army was sickened by the stench of his corruption. 10 Shortly before, he had thought that he could reach the stars of heaven, and now, no one could endure to transport the man because of this intolerable stench.

11 At last, broken in spirit, he began to give up his excessive arrogance, and to gain some understanding, under the scourge of God, for he was racked with pain unceasingly. 12 When he could no longer bear his own stench, he said, "It is right to be subject to God, and not to think one's mortal self divine." 13 Then this vile man vowed to the Lord, who would no longer have mercy on him, 14 that he would set free the holy city, toward which he had been hurrying with the intention of leveling it to the ground and making it a common graveyard; 15 he would put on perfect equality with the Athenians all the Jews, whom he had judged not even worthy of burial, but fit only to be thrown out with their children to be eaten by vultures and wild animals; 16 he would adorn with the finest offerings the holy temple which he had previously despoiled; he would restore all the sacred vessels many times over; and would provide from his own revenues the expenses required for the sacrifices. 17 Besides all this, he would become a Jew himself and visit every inhabited place to proclaim there the power of God. 18 But since God's punishment had justly come upon him, his sufferings were not lessened, so he lost hope for himself and wrote the following letter to the Jews in the form of a supplication. It read thus:

19 "To my esteemed Jewish citizens, Antiochus, their king and general, sends hearty greetings and best wishes for their health and happiness. 20 If you and your children are well and your affairs are going as you wish, I thank God very much, for my hopes are in heaven. 21 Now that I am ill, I recall with affection the esteem and good will

---

9, 1-28: In order to keep together the various accounts of God's punishment of the persecutors of his people, the author places here the stories of Antiochus' illness and death (in actuality the king died only after the purification of the temple; cf 1 Mc 4, 36-59; 6, 1-16; 2 Mc 10, 1-8); of Judas' campaigns

in Idumea and Transjordan; cf 1 Mc 5, 1-51; 2 Mc 10, 14-38; and of the first expedition of Lysias (1 Mc 4, 26-35; 2 Mc 11, 1-15).

9, 19-27: Despite the statement in v 18, this letter is not really a *supplication*. It is rather a notification to all the king's subjects of the appointment of his son

as his successor and a request that they be loyal to the new king. Apparently the same letter, which has every appearance of being authentic, was sent to the various peoples throughout the kingdom, with only a few words of address changed for each group.

you bear me. On returning from the regions of Persia, I fell victim to a troublesome illness; so I thought it necessary to form plans for the general welfare of all. 22 Actually, I do not despair about my health, since I have great hopes of recovering from my illness. 23 Nevertheless, I know that my father, whenever he went on campaigns in the hinterland, would name his successor, 24 so that, if anything unexpected happened or any unwelcome news came, the people throughout the realm would know to whom the government had been entrusted, and so not be disturbed. 25 I am also bearing in mind that the neighboring rulers, especially those on the borders of our kingdom, are on the watch for opportunities and waiting to see what will happen. I have therefore appointed as king my son Antiochus, whom I have often before entrusted and commended to most of you, when I made hurried visits to the outlying provinces. I have written to him the letter copied below. 26 Therefore I beg and entreat each of you to remember the general and individual benefits you have received, and to continue to show good will toward me and my son. 27 I am confident that, following my policy, he will treat you with mildness and kindness in his relations with you."

28 So this murderer and blasphemer, after extreme sufferings, such as he had inflicted on others, died a miserable death in the mountains of a foreign land. 29 His foster brother Philip brought the body home; but fearing Antiochus' son, he later withdrew into Egypt, to Ptolemy Philometor.

Purification of Temple and City

10 When Maccabeus and his companions, under the Lord's leadership, had recovered the temple and the city, 2 they destroyed the altars erected by the Gentiles in the market-place and the sacred enclosures. 3 After purifying the temple, they made a new altar. Then, with fire struck from flint, they offered sacrifice for the first time in two years, burned incense, and lighted lamps. They also set out the showbread. 4 When they had done this, they prostrated themselves and begged the Lord that they might never again fall into such misfortunes, and that if they should sin at any time, he might chastise them with moderation and not hand them over to blasphemous and barbarous Gentiles. 5 On the anniversary of the day on which the temple had been profaned by the Gentiles, that is, the twenty-fifth of the same month Chislev, the purification of the temple took place. 6 The Jews celebrated joyfully for eight days as on the feast of Booths, remembering how, a little while before, they had spent the feast of Booths living like wild animals in caves on the mountains. 7 Carrying rods entwined with leaves, green branches and palms, they sang hymns of grateful praise to him who had brought about the purification of his own Place. 8 By public edict and decree they prescribed that the whole Jewish nation should celebrate these days every year.

RENEWED PERSECUTION

Death of Ptolemy

9 Such was the end of Antiochus surnamed Epiphanes. 10 Now we shall relate what happened under Antiochus Eupator, the son of that godless man, and shall give a summary of the chief evils caused by the wars. 11 When Eupator succeeded to the kingdom, he put a certain Lysias in charge of the government as commander-in-chief of Coelesyria and Phoenicia. 12 Ptolemy, surnamed Macron, had taken the lead in treating the Jews fairly because of the previous injustice that had been done them, and he endeavored to have peaceful relations with them. 13 As a result, he was accused before Eupator by the King's Friends. In fact, on all sides he heard himself called traitor for having abandoned Cyprus, which Philometor had entrusted to him, and for having gone over to Antiochus Epiphanes. Since he could not command the respect due to his high office, he ended his life by taking poison.

Victory over the Idumeans

14 When Gorgias became governor of the region, he employed foreign troops and used every opportunity to attack the Jews. 15 At the same time the Idumeans, who held some important strongholds, were harassing the Jews; they welcomed fugitives from Jerusalem and endeavored to continue the war. 16 Maccabeus and his companions, after public prayers asking God to be their ally, moved quickly against the strongholds of the Idumeans. 17 Attacking vigorously, they gained control of the places, drove back all who manned the walls, and cut down those who opposed them, killing as many as twenty thousand men. 18 When at least nine thousand took refuge in two very strong towers, containing everything necessary to sustain a siege, 19 Maccabeus left Simon and Joseph, along with Zacchaeus and his men, in sufficient numbers to besiege them, while he himself went off to places where he was more urgently needed. 20 But some of the men in Simon's force who were money lovers let themselves be bribed by some of the men in the towers; on receiving seventy thousand drachmas, they allowed a number of them to escape. 21 When Maccabeus was told what had happened, he assembled the rulers of the people and accused those men of having sold their kinsmen for money by setting their enemies free to fight against them. 22 So he put them to death as traitors, and without delay captured the two towers. 23 As he was successful at arms in all his undertakings, he destroyed more than twenty thousand men in the two strongholds.

Victory over Timothy

24 Timothy, who had previously been defeated by the Jews, gathered

---

9, 25: *The letter copied below:* not included in the text of 2 Mc.

10, 3: *Two years:* three years according to 1 Mc 1, 54 and 4, 52.

10, 12: *Ptolemy Macron:* son of Dorymenes (4, 45), was formerly hostile to the Jews (6, 8).

10, 14–23: Probably the same campaign of Judas

against the Idumeans that is mentioned in 1 Mc 5, 1–3.

10, 24: *Timothy . . . previously . . . defeated by the Jews:* as recounted in 8, 30ff.

a tremendous force of foreign troops and collected a large number of cavalry from Asia; then he appeared in Judea, ready to conquer it by force. 25 At his approach, Maccabeus and his men made supplication to God, sprinkling earth upon their heads and girding their loins in sackcloth. 26 Lying prostrate at the foot of the altar, they begged him to be gracious to them, and to be an enemy to their enemies, and a foe to their foes, as the law declares. 27 After the prayer, they took up their arms and advanced a considerable distance from the city, halting when they were close to the enemy. 28 As soon as dawn broke, the armies joined battle, the one having as pledge of success and victory not only their valor but also their reliance on the Lord, and the other taking fury as their leader in the fight. 29 In the midst of the fierce battle, there appeared to the enemy from the heavens five majestic men riding on golden-bridled horses, who led the Jews on. 30 They surrounded Maccabeus, and shielding him with their own armor, kept him from being wounded. They shot arrows and hurled thunderbolts at the enemy, who were bewildered and blinded, thrown into confusion and routed. 31 Twenty-five hundred of their foot soldiers and six hundred of their horsemen were slain. 32 Timothy, however, fled to a well-fortified stronghold called Gazara, where Chaereas was in command. 33 For four days Maccabeus and his men eagerly besieged the fortress. 34 Those inside, relying on the strength of the place, kept repeating outrageous blasphemies and uttering abominable words. 35 When the fifth day dawned, twenty young men in the army of Maccabeus, angered over such blasphemies, bravely stormed the wall and with savage fury cut down everyone they encountered. 36 Others who climbed up the same way swung around on the defenders, taking the besieged in the rear; they put the towers to the

torch, spread the fire and burned the blasphemers alive. Still others broke down the gates and let in the rest of the troops, who took possession of the city. 37 Timothy had hidden in a cistern, but they killed him, along with his brother Chaereas, and Apollophanes. 38 On completing these exploits, they blessed, with hymns of grateful praise, the Lord who shows great kindness to Israel and grants them victory.

Defeat of Lysias

11 Very soon afterward, Lysias, guardian and Kinsman of the king and head of the government, being greatly displeased at what had happened, 2 mustered about eighty thousand infantry and all his cavalry and marched against the Jews. His plan was to make Jerusalem a Greek settlement; 3 to levy tribute on the temple, as he did on the sanctuaries of the other nations; and to put the high priesthood up for sale every year. 4 He did not take God's power into account at all, but felt exultant confidence in his myriads of foot soldiers, his thousands of horsemen, and his eighty elephants. 5 So he invaded Judea, and when he reached Beth-zur, a fortified place about twenty miles from Jerusalem, launched a strong attack against it. 6 When Maccabeus and his men learned that Lysias was besieging the strongholds, they and all the people begged the Lord with lamentations and tears to send a good angel to save Israel. 7 Maccabeus himself was the first to take up arms, and he exhorted the others to join him in risking their lives to help their kinsmen. Then they resolutely set out together. 8 Suddenly, while they were still near Jerusalem, a horseman appeared at their head, clothed in white garments and brandishing gold weapons. 9 Then all of them together thanked God for his mercy, and their hearts were filled with such courage that they were ready to assault not only men, but the most savage beasts, yes, even walls of iron.

10 Now that the Lord had shown his mercy toward them, they advanced in battle order with the aid of their heavenly ally. 11 Hurling themselves upon the enemy like lions, they laid low eleven thousand foot soldiers and sixteen hundred horsemen, and put all the rest to flight. 12 Most of those who got away were wounded and stripped of their arms, while Lysias himself escaped only by shameful flight.

Peace with the Syrians

13 But Lysias was not a stupid man. He reflected on the defeat he had suffered, and came to realize that the Hebrews were invincible because the mighty God was their ally. 14 He therefore sent a message persuading them to settle everything on just terms, and promising to persuade the king also, and to induce him to become their friend. 15 Maccabeus, solicitous for the common good, agreed to all that Lysias proposed; and the king, on his part, granted in behalf of the Jews all the written requests of Maccabeus to Lysias.

Official Letters

16 These are the terms of the letter which Lysias wrote to the Jews: "Lysias sends greetings to the Jewish people. 17 John and Absalom, your envoys, have presented your signed communication and asked about the matters contained in it. 18 Whatever had to be referred to the king I called to his attention, and the things that were acceptable he has granted. 19 If you maintain your loyalty to the government, I will endeavor to further your interests in the future. 20 On the details of these matters I have authorized my representatives, as well as your envoys, to confer with you. 21 Farewell." The year one hundred and forty-eight, the twenty-fourth of Dioscorinthius. 22 The king's letter read thus: "King Antiochus sends greetings to his brother Lysias. 23 Now that our father has taken his place

among the gods, we wish the subjects of our kingdom to be undisturbed in conducting their own affairs. 24 We understand that the Jews do not agree with our father's policy concerning Greek customs but prefer their own way of life. They are petitioning us to let them retain their own customs. 25 Since we desire that this people too should be undisturbed, our decision is that their temple be restored to them and that they live in keeping with the customs of their ancestors. 26 Accordingly, please send them messengers to give them our assurances of friendship, so that, when they learn of our decision, they may have nothing to worry about but may contentedly go about their own business."

27 The king's letter to the people was as follows: "King Antiochus sends greetings to the Jewish senate and to the rest of the Jews. 28 If you are well, it is what we desire. We too are in good health. 29 Menelaus has told us of your wish to return home and attend to your own affairs. 30 Therefore, those who return by the thirtieth of Xanthicus will have our assurance of full permission 31 to observe their dietary laws and other laws, just as before, and none of the Jews shall be molested in any way for faults committed through ignorance. 32 I have also sent Menelaus to reassure you. 33 Farewell." In the year one hundred and forty-eight, the fifteenth of Xanthicus.

34 The Romans also sent them a letter as follows: "Quintus Memmius and Titus Manius, legates of the Romans, send greetings to the Jewish people. 35 Whatever Lysias, kinsman of the king, has granted you, we also approve. 36 But the matters on which he passed judgment should be submitted to the king. As soon as you have considered them, send someone to us with your decisions so that we may present them to your advantage, for we are on our way to Antioch. 37 Make haste, then, to send us those who can inform us of your intentions.

38 Farewell." In the year one hundred and forty-eight, the fifteenth of Xanthicus.

Persecution Renewed

12 After these agreements were made, Lysias returned to the king, and the Jews went about their farming. 2 But some of the local governors, Timothy and Apollonius, son of Gennaeus, as also Hieronymus and Demophon, to say nothing of Nicanor, the commander of the Cyprians, would not allow them to live in peace.

3 Some people of Joppa also committed this outrage: they invited the Jews who lived among them, together with their wives and children, to embark on boats which they had provided. There was no hint of enmity toward them; 4 this was done by public vote of the city. When the Jews, not suspecting treachery and wishing to live on friendly terms, accepted the invitation, the people of Joppa took them out to sea and drowned at least two hundred of them.

Activity of Judas

5 As soon as Judas heard of the barbarous deed perpetrated against his countrymen, he summoned his men; 6 and after calling upon God, the just judge, he marched against the murderers of his kinsmen. In a night attack he set the harbor on fire, burnt the boats, and put to the sword those who had taken refuge there. 7 When the gates of the town were shut, he withdrew, intending to come back later and wipe out the entire population of Joppa.

8 On hearing that the men of Jamnia planned to give like treatment to the Jews who lived among them, 9 he attacked the Jamnian populace by night, setting fire to the harbor and the fleet, so that the glow of the flames was visible as far as Jerusalem, thirty miles away.

10 When the Jews had gone about a mile from there in the campaign

against Timothy, they were attacked by Arabs numbering at least five thousand foot soldiers, and five hundred horsemen. 11 After a hard fight, Judas and his companions, with God's help, were victorious. The defeated nomads begged Judas to make friends with them and promised to supply the Jews with cattle and to help them in every other way. 12 Realizing that they could indeed be useful in many respects, Judas agreed to make peace with them. After the pledge of friendship had been exchanged, the Arabs withdrew to their tents.

13 He also attacked a certain city called Caspin, fortified with earthworks and ramparts and inhabited by a mixed population of Gentiles. 14 Relying on the strength of their walls and their supply of provisions, the besieged treated Judas and his men with contempt, insulting them and even uttering blasphemies and profanity. 15 But Judas and his men invoked the aid of the great Sovereign of the world, who, in the day of Joshua, overthrew Jericho without battering-ram or siege machine; then they furiously stormed the ramparts. 16 Capturing the city by the will of God, they inflicted such indescribable slaughter on it that the adjacent pool, which was about a quarter of a mile wide, seemed to be filled with the blood that flowed into it.

17 When they had gone on some ninety miles, they reached Charax, where there were certain Jews known as Toubiani. 18 But they did not find Timothy in that region, for he had already departed from there without having done anything except to leave behind in one place a very strong garrison. 19 But Dositheus and Sosipater, two of Maccabeus' captains, marched out and destroyed the force of more than ten thousand men that Timothy had left in the stronghold. 20 Meanwhile, Maccabeus divided his army into cohorts, with a commander over each cohort, and went in pursuit of Timothy, who had a force of a hundred and twenty

11, 33: The date, which is the same as the date of the Romans' letter (v 38), cannot be correct. The king's letter must be connected with the peace treaty of the year 149 of the Seleucid era, i.e., 163 B.C. Perhaps the mention of the month of Xanthicus in the body of the letter (v 30) caused the date of the

Romans' letter to be transferred to this one.
11, 38: The date is March 12, 164 B.C.
12, 2: Apollonius, son of Gennaeus: not the Apollonius who was the son of Menestheus (4, 21). Nicanor: probably distinct from the Nicanor of 14, 2.
12, 10: From there: not from the aforesaid Jamnia

(vv 8f) or Joppa (vv 3–7), but from a place in Transjordan; vv 10–26 parallel the account given in 1 Mc 5, 9–13.24–54 of Judas' campaign in northern Transjordan.
12, 17: Certain Jews known as Toubiani: because they lived "in the land of Tob" (1 Mc 5, 13).

thousand foot soldiers and twenty-five hundred horsemen. 21 When Timothy learned of the approach of Judas, he sent on ahead of him the women and children, as well as the baggage, to a place called Karnion, which was hard to besiege and even hard to reach because of the difficult terrain of that region. 22 But when Judas' first cohort appeared, the enemy was overwhelmed with fear and terror at the manifestation of the All-seeing. Scattering in every direction, they rushed away in such headlong flight that in many cases they wounded one another, pierced by the swords of their own men. 23 Judas pressed the pursuit vigorously, putting the sinners to the sword and destroying as many as thirty thousand men.

24 Timothy himself fell into the hands of the men under Dositheus and Sosipater; but with great cunning, he asked them to spare his life and let him go, because he had in his power the parents and relatives of many of them, and could make these suffer. 25 When he had fully confirmed his solemn pledge to restore them unharmed, they let him go for the sake of saving their brethren.

Further Successes

26 Judas then marched to Karnion and the shrine of Atargatis, where he killed twenty-five thousand people. 27 After the defeat and destruction of these, he moved his army to Ephron, a fortified city inhabited by people of many nationalities. Robust young men took up their posts in defense of the walls, from which they fought valiantly; inside were large supplies of machines and missiles. 28 But the Jews, invoking the Sovereign who forcibly shatters the might of his enemies, got possession of the city and slaughtered twenty-five thousand of the people in it. 29 Then they set out from there and hastened on to Scythopolis, seventy-five miles from Jerusalem. 30 But when the Jews who lived there testified to the good will shown by the Scythopolitans and to their kind treatment even in times of adversity, 31 Judas and his men thanked them and exhorted them to be well disposed to their race in the future also. Finally they arrived in Jerusalem, shortly before the feast of Weeks.

32 After this feast called Pentecost, they lost no time in marching against Gorgias, governor of Idumea, 33 who opposed them with three thousand foot soldiers and four hundred horsemen. 34 In the ensuing battle, a few of the Jews were slain. 35 A man called Dositheus, a powerful horseman and one of Bacenor's men, caught hold of Gorgias, grasped his military cloak and dragged him along by main strength, intending to capture the vile wretch alive, when a Thracian horseman attacked Dositheus and cut off his arm at the shoulder. Then Gorgias fled to Marisa. 36 After Esdris and his men had been fighting for a long time and were weary, Judas called upon the Lord to show himself their ally and leader in the battle. 37 Then, raising a battle cry in his ancestral language, and with songs, he charged Gorgias' men when they were not expecting it and put them to flight.

Expiation for the Dead

38 Judas rallied his army and went to the city of Adullam. As the week was ending, they purified themselves according to custom and kept the sabbath there. 39 On the following day, since the task had now become urgent, Judas and his men went to gather up the bodies of the slain and bury them with their kinsmen in their ancestral tombs. 40 But under the tunic of each of the dead they found amulets sacred to the idols of Jamnia, which the law forbids the Jews to wear. So it was clear to all that this was why these men had been slain. 41 They all therefore praised the ways of the Lord, the just judge who brings to light the things that are hidden. 42 Turning to supplication, they prayed that the sinful deed might be fully blotted out. The noble Judas warned the soldiers to keep themselves free from sin, for they had seen with their own eyes what had happened because of the sin of those who had fallen. 43 He then took up a collection among all his soldiers, amounting to two thousand silver drachmas, which he sent to Jerusalem to provide for an expiatory sacrifice. In doing this he acted in a very excellent and noble way, inasmuch as he had the resurrection of the dead in view; 44 for if he were not expecting the fallen to rise again, it would have been useless and foolish to pray for them in death. 45 But if he did this with a view to the splendid reward that awaits those who had gone to rest in godliness, it was a holy and pious thought. 46 Thus he made atonement for the dead that they might be freed from this sin.

The Syrians Invade Judea

13 In the year one hundred and forty-nine, Judas and his men learned that Antiochus Eupator was invading Judea with a large force, 2 and that with him was Lysias, his guardian, who was in charge of the government. They led a Greek army of one hundred and ten thousand foot soldiers, fifty-three hundred horsemen, twenty-two elephants, and three hundred chariots armed with scythes.

Death of Menelaus

3 Menelaus also joined them, and with great duplicity kept urging Antiochus on, not for the welfare of his country, but in the hope of being established in office. 4 But the King of kings aroused the anger of Antiochus against the scoundrel. When the king was shown by Lysias that Menelaus was to blame for all the trouble, he ordered him to be taken to Beroea and executed there

---

12, 26: *Atargatis:* a Syrian goddess, represented by the body of a fish.

12, 29: *Scythopolis:* the Greek name of the city of Beth-shan; cf 1 Mc 5, 52.

12, 35: *One of Bacenor's men:* certain ancient witnesses to the text have "one of the Toubiani"; cf v 17.

12, 42-46: This is the earliest statement of the doctrine that prayers (v 42) and sacrifices (v 43) for the dead are efficacious. The statement is made here, however, only for the purpose of proving that Judas believed in the resurrection of the just (7, 9.14.23. 36). That is, he believed that expiation could be made for certain sins of otherwise good men—soldiers who had given their lives for God's cause. Thus, they could share in the resurrection. His belief was similar to, but not quite the same as, the Catholic doctrine of purgatory.

13, 1: *In the year one hundred and forty-nine:* 163–162 B.C.

13, 2: *They led:* the Greek means literally "Each (of them) led," but it is unlikely that the author meant the already immense numbers to be doubled; the numbers are similar to those in 1 Mc 6, 30.

13, 4: *Beroea:* the Greek name of Aleppo.

in the customary local method. 5 There is at that place a tower seventy-five feet high, full of ashes, with a circular rim sloping down steeply on all sides towards the ashes. 6 A man guilty of sacrilege or notorious for certain other crimes is brought up there and then hurled down to destruction. 7 In such a manner was Menelaus, the transgressor of the law, fated to die; he was deprived even of decent burial. 8 It was altogether just that he who had committed so many sins against the altar with its pure fire and ashes should meet his death in ashes.

Skirmish near Modein

9 The king was advancing, his mind full of savage plans for inflicting on the Jews worse things than those they suffered in his father's time. 10 When Judas learned of this, he urged the people to call upon the Lord night and day, to help them now, if ever, 11 when they were about to be deprived of their law, their country, and their holy temple; and not to allow this nation, which had just begun to revive, to be subjected again to blasphemous Gentiles. 12 When they had all joined in doing this, and had implored the merciful Lord continuously with weeping and fasting and prostrations for three days, Judas encouraged them and told them to stand ready. 13 After a private meeting with the elders, he decided that, before the king's army could invade Judea and take possession of the city, the Jews should march out and settle the matter with God's help. 14 Leaving the outcome to the Creator of the world, and exhorting his followers to fight nobly to death for the laws, the temple, the city, the country, and the government, he pitched his camp near Modein. 15 Giving his men the battle cry "God's Victory," he made a night attack on the king's pavilion with a picked force of the bravest young men and killed about two thousand in the camp. They also slew the lead elephant and its rider.

16 Finally they withdrew in triumph, having filled the camp with terror and confusion. 17 Day was just breaking when this was accomplished with the help and protection of the Lord.

Treaty with Antiochus V

18 The king, having had a taste of the Jews' daring, tried to take their positions by a stratagem. 19 So he marched against Beth-zur, a strong fortress of the Jews; but he was driven back, checked, and defeated. 20 Judas then sent supplies to the men inside, 21 but Rhodocus, of the Jewish army, betrayed military secrets to the enemy. He was found out, arrested, and imprisoned. 22 The king made a second attempt by negotiating with the men of Beth-zur. After giving them his pledge and receiving theirs, he withdrew 23 and attacked Judas and his men. But he was defeated. Next he heard that Philip, who was left in charge of the government in Antioch, had rebelled. Dismayed, he parleyed with the Jews, submitted to their terms, and swore to observe their rights. Having come to this agreement, he offered a sacrifice, and honored the temple with a generous donation. 24 He approved of Maccabeus and left him as military and civil governor of the territory from Ptolemais to the region of the Gerrenes. 25 When he came to Ptolemais, the people of that city were angered by the peace treaty; in fact they were so indignant that they wanted to annul its provisions. 26 But Lysias took the platform, defended the treaty as well as he could and won them over by persuasion. After calming them and gaining their good will, he returned to Antioch.

That is how the king's attack and withdrawal went.

Antagonism of Alcimus

14 Three years later, Judas and his men learned that Demetrius, son of Seleucus, had sailed into the port of Tripolis with a powerful army and a fleet, 2 and that he had

occupied the country, after doing away with Antiochus and his guardian Lysias.

3 A certain Alcimus, a former high priest, who had willfully incurred defilement at the time of the revolt, realized that there was no way for him to salvage his position and regain access to the holy altar. 4 So he went to King Demetrius in the year one hundred and fifty-one and presented him with a gold crown and a palm branch, as well as some of the customary olive branches from the temple. On that occasion he kept quiet. 5 But he found an opportunity to further his mad scheme when he was invited to the council by Demetrius and questioned about the dispositions and intentions of the Jews. He replied: 6 "Those Jews called Hasideans, led by Judas Maccabeus, are warmongers, who stir up sedition and keep the kingdom from enjoying peace and quiet. 7 For this reason, now that I am deprived of my ancestral dignity, that is to say, the high priesthood, I have come here— 8 first, out of my genuine concern for the king's interests, and secondly, out of consideration for my own countrymen, since our entire nation is suffering great affliction from the unreasonable conduct of the people just mentioned. 9 When you have informed yourself in detail on these matters, O king, act in the interest of our country and its hardpressed people with the same gracious consideration that you show toward all. 10 As long as Judas is around, it is impossible for the state to enjoy peace." 11 When he had said this, the other Friends who were hostile to Judas quickly added fuel to Demetrius' indignation.

Dealings with Nicanor

12 The king immediately chose Nicanor, who had been in command of the elephants, and appointed him governor of Judea. He sent him off 13 with orders to put Judas to death, to disperse his followers, and to set up Alcimus as high priest of the

---

13, 5: *Ashes:* probably smoldering ashes; the *tower* resembles the ancient Persian fire towers.
13, 15: *Slew:* literally "stabbed"; the deed was done by Eleazar (1 Mc 6, 43–46).
13, 16: *They withdrew in triumph:* according to 1 Mc 6, 47 they fled.

13, 21: *Military secret:* probably about the lack of provisions in the besieged city; cf 1 Mc 6, 49.
13, 24: The Greek text is uncertain and may be rendered: "He approved of Maccabeus, then left Hegemonides as governor of the territory...."

Gerrenes: probably the inhabitants of Gerat, southeast of Gaza.
14, 1: *Three years later:* actually, *Demetrius* (I Soter), *son of Seleucus* (IV), landed at *Tripolis* in the year 151 of the Seleucid era (v 4), i.e., 162–161 B.C.; cf 1 Mc 7, 1–7.

great temple.   14 The Gentiles from Judea, who would have banished Judas, came flocking to Nicanor, thinking that the misfortunes and calamities of the Jews would mean prosperity for themselves.   15 When the Jews heard of Nicanor's coming, and that the Gentiles were rallying to him, they sprinkled themselves with earth and prayed to him who established his people forever, and who always comes to the aid of his heritage.   16 At their leader's command, they set out at once and came upon the enemy at the village of Adasa.   17 Judas' brother Simon had engaged Nicanor, but because of the sudden appearance of the enemy suffered a slight repulse.   18 However, when Nicanor heard of the valor of Judas and his men, and the great courage with which they fought for their country, he shrank from deciding the issue by bloodshed.   19 So he sent Posidonius, Theodotus and Mattathias to arrange an agreement.   20 After a long discussion of the terms, each leader communicated them to his troops; and when general agreement was expressed, they assented to the treaty.   21 A day was set on which the leaders would meet by themselves. From each side a chariot came forward and thrones were set in place.   22 Judas had posted armed men in readiness at suitable points for fear that the enemy might suddenly carry out some treacherous plan. But the conference was held in the proper way.   23 Nicanor stayed on in Jerusalem, where he did nothing out of place. He got rid of the throngs of ordinary people who gathered around him; 24 but he always kept Judas in his company, for he had a cordial affection for the man.   25 He urged him to marry and have children; so Judas married, settled down, and shared the common life.

Threats against Judas

26 When Alcimus saw their friendship for each other, he took the treaty that had been made, went to Demetrius, and said that Nicanor was plotting against the state, and that he

had appointed Judas, the conspirator against the kingdom, to be his successor.   27 Stirred up by the villain's calumnies, the king became enraged. He wrote to Nicanor, stating that he was displeased with the treaty, and ordering him to send Maccabeus as a prisoner to Antioch without delay.   28 When this message reached Nicanor he was dismayed, for he hated to break his agreement with a man who had done no wrong.   29 However, there was no way of opposing the king, so he watched for an opportunity to carry out this order by a stratagem.   30 But Maccabeus noticed that Nicanor was becoming cool in his dealings with him, and acting with unaccustomed rudeness when they met; he concluded that this coldness betokened no good. So he gathered together a large number of his men, and went into hiding from Nicanor.

31 When Nicanor realized that he had been disgracefully outwitted by the man, he went to the great and holy temple, at a time when the priests were offering the customary sacrifices, and ordered them to surrender Judas.   32 As they declared under oath that they did not know where the wanted man was, 33 he raised his right hand toward the temple and swore this oath: "If you do not hand Judas over to me as prisoner, I will level this shrine of God to the ground; I will tear down the altar, and erect here a splendid temple to Dionysus."   34 With these words he went away. The priests stretched out their hands toward heaven, calling upon the unfailing defender of our nation in these words: 35. "Lord of all, though you are in need of nothing, you have approved of a temple for your dwelling place among us.   36 Therefore, O holy One, Lord of all holiness, preserve forever undefiled this house, which has been so recently purified."

The Story of Razis

37 A certain Razis, one of the elders of Jerusalem, was denounced to Nicanor as a patriot. A man highly regarded, he was called a father of the

Jews because of his love for them. 38 In the early days of the revolt, he had been convicted of Judaism, and had risked body and life in his ardent zeal for it.   39 Nicanor, to show his detestation of the Jews, sent more than five hundred soldiers to arrest him.   40 He thought that by arresting such a man he would deal the Jews a hard blow.   41 But when these troops, on the point of capturing the tower, were forcing the outer gate and calling for fire to set the door ablaze, Razis, now caught on all sides, turned his sword against himself,   42 preferring to die nobly rather than fall into the hands of vile men and suffer outrages unworthy of his noble birth.   43 In the excitement of the struggle he failed to strike exactly. So while the troops rushed in through the doors, he gallantly ran up to the top of the wall and with manly courage threw himself down into the crowd.   44 But as they quickly drew back and left an opening, he fell into the middle of the empty space.   45 Still breathing, and inflamed with anger, he got up and ran through the crowd, with blood gushing from his frightful wounds. 46 Then, standing on a steep rock, as he lost the last of his blood, he tore out his entrails and flung them with both hands into the crowd, calling upon the Lord of life and of spirit to give these back to him again. Such was the manner of his death.

Nicanor's Blasphemy

15 When Nicanor learned that Judas and his companions were in the territory of Samaria, he decided to attack them in all safety on the day of rest.   2 The Jews who were forced to follow him pleaded, "Do not massacre them in that way, like a savage barbarian, but show respect for the day which the All-seeing has exalted with holiness above all other days."   3 At this the thrice-sinful wretch asked if there was a ruler in heaven who prescribed the keeping of the sabbath day.   4 When they replied that there was indeed such a ruler in heaven, the living Lord himself, who commanded the

---

14, 14: *Who would have banished Judas:* the meaning of the Greek is uncertain; some render it: "who

had fled before Judas."
14, 37-46: The story of *Razis* belongs to the

"martyrology" class of literature; it is similar to the stories in 6, 18—7, 42.

observance of the sabbath day, 5 he said, "I, on my part, am ruler on earth and my orders are that you take up arms and carry out the king's business." Nevertheless he did not succeed in carrying out his cruel plan.

Fresh Hope

6 In his utter boastfulness and arrogance Nicanor had determined to erect a public monument of victory over Judas and his men. 7 But Maccabeus remained confident, fully convinced that he would receive help from the Lord. 8 He urged his men not to fear the enemy, but mindful of the help they had received from Heaven in the past, to expect that now, too, victory would be given them by the Almighty. 9 By encouraging them with words from the law and the prophets, and by reminding them of the battles they had already won, he filled them with fresh enthusiasm. 10 Having stirred up their courage, he gave his orders and pointed out at the same time the perfidy of the Gentiles and their violation of oaths. 11 When he had armed each of them, not so much with the safety of shield and spear as with the encouragement of noble words, he cheered them all by relating a dream, a kind of vision, worthy of belief.

12 What he saw was this: Onias, the former high priest, a good and virtuous man, modest in appearance, gentle in manners, distinguished in speech, and trained from childhood in every virtuous practice, was praying with outstretched arms for the whole Jewish community. 13 Then in the same way another man appeared, distinguished by his white hair and dignity, and with an air about him of extraordinary, majestic authority. 14 Onias then said of him, "This is God's prophet Jeremiah, who loves his brethren and fervently prays for his people and their holy city." 15 Stretching out his right hand, Jeremiah presented a gold sword to Judas. As he gave it to him he said, 16 "Accept this holy sword as a gift from God; with it you shall crush your adversaries."

Defeat and Death of Nicanor

17 Encouraged by Judas' noble words, which had power to instill valor and stir young hearts to courage, the Jews determined not to delay, but to charge gallantly and decide the issue by hand-to-hand combat with the utmost courage, since their city and its temple with the sacred vessels were in danger. 18 They were not so much concerned about their wives and children or their brothers and kinsmen; their first and foremost fear was for the consecrated sanctuary. 19 Those who remained in the city suffered a like agony, anxious as they were about the battle in the open country.

20 Everyone now awaited the decisive moment. The enemy were already drawing near with their troops drawn up in battle line, their elephants placed in strategic positions, and their cavalry stationed on the flanks. 21 Maccabeus, contemplating the hosts before him, their elaborate equipment, and the fierceness of their elephants, stretched out his hands toward heaven and called upon the Lord who works miracles; for he knew that it is not through arms but through the Lord's decision that victory is won by those who deserve it. 22 He prayed to him thus: "You, O Lord, sent your angel in the days of King Hezekiah of Judea, and he slew a hundred and eighty-five thousand men of Sennacherib's army. 23 Sovereign of the heavens, send a good angel now to spread fear and dread before us. 24 By the might of your arm may those be struck down who have blasphemously come against your holy people!" With this he ended his prayer.

25 Nicanor and his men advanced to the sound of trumpets and battle songs. 26 But Judas and his men met the army with supplication and prayers. 27 Fighting with their hands and praying to God with their hearts, they laid low at least thirty-five thousand, and rejoiced greatly over this manifestation of God's power. 28 When the battle was over and they were joyfully departing, they discovered Nicanor lying there in all his armor; 29 so they raised tumultuous shouts in their native tongue in praise of the divine Sovereign.

30 Then Judas, who was ever in body and soul the chief defender of his fellow citizens, and had maintained from youth his affection for his countrymen, ordered Nicanor's head and whole right arm to be cut off and taken to Jerusalem. 31 When he arrived there, he assembled his countrymen, stationed the priests before the altar, and sent for those in the citadel. 32 He showed them the vile Nicanor's head and the wretched blasphemer's arm that had been boastfully stretched out against the holy dwelling of the Almighty. 33 He cut out the tongue of the godless Nicanor, saying he would feed it piecemeal to the birds and would hang up the other wages of his folly opposite the temple. 34 At this, everyone looked toward heaven and praised the Lord who manifests his divine power, saying, "Blessed be he who has kept his own Place undefiled!"

35 Judas hung up Nicanor's head on the wall of the citadel, a clear and evident proof to all of the Lord's help. 36 By public vote it was unanimously decreed never to let this day pass unobserved, but to celebrate it on the thirteenth day of the twelfth month, called Adar in Aramaic, the eve of Mordecai's Day.

EPILOGUE

Author's Apology

37 Since Nicanor's doings ended in this way, with the city remaining in possession of the Hebrews from that time on, I will bring my own

---

15, 6: *Public monument of victory:* a heap of stones covered with the arms and armor of the fallen enemy.

15, 9: *The law and the prophets:* the first of the three parts of the Hebrew Scriptures, called *the sacred books* (1 Mc 12, 9).

15, 12: *Onias, the former high priest:* Onias III

(3, 1–40). Evidently the author believed that the departed just were in some way alive even before the resurrection.

15, 14: *Jeremiah:* regarded by the postexilic Jews as one of the greatest figures in their history; cf 2, 1; Mt 16, 14. *Who . . . prays for his people:* a clear belief in the intercession of the saints.

15, 31: *Those in the citadel:* presumably Jewish soldiers; actually, the citadel was still in the possession of the Syrians.

15, 36: *Mordecai's Day:* the feast of Purim, celebrated on the fourteenth and fifteenth days of Adar (Est 9, 17–22).

story to an end here too. 38 If it is well written and to the point, that is what I wanted; if it is poorly done and mediocre, that is the best I could do. 39 Just as it is harmful to drink wine alone or water alone, whereas mixing wine with water makes a more pleasant drink that increases delight, so a skillfully composed story delights the ears of those who read the work. Let this, then, be the end.

PROLOGUE

Job's Wealth and Piety

IN the land of Uz there was a blameless and upright man named Job, who feared God and avoided evil. 2 Seven sons and three daughters were born to him; 3 and he had seven thousand sheep, three thousand camels, five hundred yoke of oxen, five hundred she-asses, and a great number of work animals, so that he was greater than any of the men of the East. 4 His sons used to take turns giving feasts, sending invitations to their three sisters to eat and drink with them. 5 And when each feast had run its course, Job would send for them and sanctify them, rising early and offering holocausts for every one of them. For Job said, "It may be that my sons have sinned and blasphemed God in their hearts." This Job did habitually.

6 One day, when the sons of God came to present themselves before the LORD, Satan also came among them. 7 And the LORD said to Satan, "Whence do you come?" Then Satan answered the LORD and said. "From roaming the earth and patrolling it." 8 And the LORD said to Satan, "Have you noticed my servant Job, and that there is no one on earth like him, blameless and upright, fearing God and avoiding evil?"

9 But Satan answered the LORD and said, "Is it for nothing that Job is God-fearing? 10 Have you not surrounded him and his family and all that he has with your protection? You have blessed the work of his hands, and his livestock are spread over the land. 11 But now put forth your hand and touch anything that he has, and surely he will blaspheme you to your face." 12 And the LORD said to Satan, "Behold, all that he has is in your power; only do not lay a hand upon his person." So Satan went forth from the presence of the LORD.

The First Trial

13 And so one day, while his sons and his daughters were eating and drinking wine in the house of their eldest brother, 14 a messenger came to Job and said. "The oxen were plowing and the asses grazing beside them, 15 and the Sabeans carried them off in a raid. They put the herdsmen to the sword, and I alone have escaped to tell you." 16 While he was yet speaking, another came and said, "Lightning has fallen from heaven and struck the sheep and their shepherds and consumed them: and I alone have escaped to tell you." 17 While he was yet speaking, another came and said, "The Chaldeans formed three columns, seized the camels, carried them off, and put those tending them to the sword, and I alone have escaped to tell you." 18 While he was yet speaking, another came and said, "Your sons and daughters were eating and drinking wine in the house of their eldest brother, 19 when suddenly a great wind came across the desert and smote the four corners of the house. It fell upon the young people and they are dead; and I alone have escaped to tell you." 20 Then Job began to tear his cloak and cut

---

1, 1: *Uz:* somewhere in Edom or Arabia. *Job:* a not uncommon name in ancient Semitic circles, its original meaning was "enemy."
1, 2f: The numbers mentioned here indicate Job's

great wealth and happiness, external proof of God's friendship.
1, 3: *Men of the East:* that is, east of Palestine.

1, 6: *Sons of God:* angels. *Satan:* literally, "adversary."
1, 15: *Sabeans:* from southern Arabia.
1, 16: *Lightning:* literally, "God's fire."

off his hair. He cast himself prostrate upon the ground,   21 and said,

"Naked I came forth from my
   mother's womb,
   and naked shall I go back
      again.
The LORD gave and the LORD
   has taken away;
   blessed be the name of the
      LORD!"

22 In all this Job did not sin, nor did he say anything disrespectful of God.

The Second Trial

2 Once again the sons of God came to present themselves before the LORD, and Satan also came with them.   2 And the LORD said to Satan, "Whence do you come?" And Satan answered the LORD and said, "From roaming the earth and patrolling it."   3 And the LORD said to Satan, "Have you noticed my servant Job, and that there is no one on earth like him, faultless and upright, fearing God and avoiding evil? He still holds fast to his innocence although you incited me against him to ruin him without cause."   4 And Satan answered the LORD and said, "Skin for skin! All that a man has he will give for his life.   5 But now put forth your hand and touch his bone and his flesh, and surely he will blaspheme you to your face."   6 And the LORD said to Satan, "He is in your power; only spare his life."   7 So Satan went forth from the presence of the LORD and smote Job with severe boils from the soles of his feet to the crown of his head.   8 And he took a potsherd to scrape himself, as he sat among the ashes.   9 Then his wife said to him, "Are you still holding to your innocence? Curse God and die."   10 But he said to her, "Are even you going to speak as senseless women do? We accept good things from God; and should we not accept evil?" Through all this, Job said nothing sinful.

Job's Three Friends

11 Now when three of Job's friends heard of all the misfortune that had come upon him, they set out each one from his own place: Eliphaz from Teman, Bildad from Shuh, and Zophar from Naamath. They met and journeyed together to give him sympathy and comfort.   12 But when, at a distance, they lifted up their eyes and did not recognize him, they began to weep aloud; they tore their cloaks and threw dust upon their heads.   13 Then they sat down upon the ground with him seven days and seven nights, but none of them spoke a word to him; for they saw how great was his suffering.

FIRST CYCLE OF SPEECHES

Job's Plaint

3 After this, Job opened his mouth and cursed his day.   2 Job spoke out and said:

3 Perish the day on which I was
      born,
   the night when they said,
      "The child is a boy!"
4 May that day be darkness:
   let not God above call for it,
   nor light shine upon it!
5 May darkness and gloom claim
      it,
   clouds settle upon it,
   the blackness of night affright
      it!
6 May obscurity seize that day;
   let it not occur among the
      days of the year,
   nor enter into the count of
      the months!

7 May that night be barren;
   let no joyful outcry greet it!
8 Let them curse it who curse
      the sea,
   the appointed disturbers of
      Leviathan!

9 May the stars of its twilight
      be darkened;
   may it look for daylight,
      but have none,
   nor gaze on the eyes of
      the dawn,
10 Because it kept not shut the
      doors of the womb
   to shield my eyes from
      trouble!

11 Why did I not perish at birth,
   come forth from the womb
      and expire?
16 Or why was I not buried away
      like an untimely birth,
   like babies that have never
      seen the light?
12 Wherefore did the knees receive
      me?
   or why did I suck at the
      breasts?

13 For then I should have lain
      down and been tranquil;
   had I slept, I should then
      have been at rest
14 With kings and counsellors
      of the earth
   who built where now there
      are ruins
15 Or with princes who had gold
      and filled their houses
      with silver.

17 There the wicked cease from
      troubling,
   there the weary are at rest.
18 There the captives are at ease
      together,
   and hear not the voice of the
      slave driver.
19 Small and great are there
      the same,
   and the servant is free from
      his master.

20 Why is light given to the toilers,
   and life to the bitter in spirit?
21 They wait for death and it
      comes not;
   they search for it rather than
      for hidden treasures,

1, 21: *Go back again:* to the earth; cf Gn 2, 7; Sir 40, 1.

2, 4: *Skin for skin:* an expression which, as applied to Job, means that he has borne his suffering patiently thus far only because he seeks to avoid greater suffering and to receive greater favors from God.

2, 9: *Curse God and die:* you have nothing to hope for from God and therefore nothing to live for.

2, 11: The names of Job's friends suggest Edomite origin. The Edomites (Ab 8f) and more specifically

the Temanites (Jer 49, 7) enjoyed a reputation for wisdom.

3, 8: *Leviathan:* in 40, 25, the crocodile; here the reference is probably to a mythological sea monster symbolizing primeval chaos. Cf 9, 13; 26, 13; Pss 74, 13f; 104, 26; Is 27, 1.

3, 16: This verse has been placed between vv 11 and 12 where it probably stood originally. There is reason to believe that here, as well as in several other places in Job, the original order of the poetic lines was acci-

dentally disturbed in the early transmission of the text; so in chapters 12–15; 19–21; 24–31; 34; 36; 38–42. The verse numbers given in such cases are always those of the current Hebrew text, though the arrangement may differ. The footnotes will advise the reader of the difficulties and provide him with further indications for following the process of thought in the book.

3, 17: *There:* in death.

22 Rejoice in it exultingly,
   and are glad when they reach
      the grave:
23 Men whose path is hidden
      from them,
   and whom God has hemmed
      in!

24 For sighing comes more
      readily to me than food,
   and my groans well forth
      like water.
25 For what I fear overtakes me,
   and what I shrink from
      comes upon me.
26 I have no peace nor ease;
   I have no rest, for trouble
      comes!

Eliphaz's First Speech

4 Then spoke Eliphaz the Temanite,
  who said:

2 If someone attempts a word
      with you, will you mind?
   For how can anyone refrain
      from speaking?
3 Behold, you have instructed
      many,
   and have made firm their
      feeble hands.
4 Your words have upheld the
      stumbler;
   you have strengthened his
      faltering knees.
5 But now that it comes to you,
      you are impatient;
   when it touches yourself,
      you are dismayed.
6 Is not your piety a source
      of confidence,
   and your integrity of life
      your hope?

7 Reflect now, what innocent
      person perishes?
   Since when are the upright
      destroyed?
8 As I see it, those who plow for
      mischief
   and sow trouble, reap the
      same.
9 By the breath of God they
      perish,
   and by the blast of his wrath
      they are consumed.

10 Though the lion roars, though
      the king of beasts cries out,
   yet the teeth of the young
      lions are broken;
11 The old lion perishes for lack
      of prey,
   and the cubs of the lioness
      are scattered.

12 For a word was stealthily
      brought to me,
   and my ear caught a whisper
      of it.
13 In my thoughts during visions
      of the night,
   when deep sleep falls on men,
14 Fear came upon me, and
      shuddering,
   that terrified me to the bones.
15 Then a spirit passed before me,
   and the hair of my flesh
      stood up.
16 It paused, but its likeness I
      could not discern;
   a figure was before my eyes,
   and I heard a still voice:

17 "Can a man be righteous as
      against God?
   Can a mortal be blameless
      against his Maker?
18 Lo, he puts no trust in his
      servants,
   and with his angels he can
      find fault.
19 How much more with those that
      dwell in houses of clay,
   whose foundation is in the
      dust,
   who are crushed more easily
      than the moth!
20 Morning or evening they may
      be shattered;
   with no heed paid to it, they
      perish forever.
21 The pegs of their tent are
      plucked up;
   they die without knowing
      wisdom."

5 Call now! Will anyone respond
      to you?
   To which of the holy ones
      will you appeal?
2 Nay, impatience kills the fool
   and indignation slays the
      simpleton.

3 I have seen a fool spreading
      his roots,
   but his household suddenly
      decayed.
4 His children shall be far from
      safety;
   they shall be crushed at the
      gate without a rescuer.
5 What they have reaped the
      hungry shall eat up;
   [or God shall take it away
      by blight;]
   and the thirsty shall swallow
      their substance.
6 For mischief comes not out of
      the earth,
   nor does trouble spring out
      of the ground;
7 But man himself begets mischief,
   as sparks fly upward.

8 In your place, I would appeal
      to God,
   and to God I would state
      my plea.
10 He gives rain upon the earth
   and sends water upon the
      fields;
11 He sets up on high the lowly,
   and those who mourn he
      exalts to safety.
12 He frustrates the plans of the
      cunning,
   so that their hands achieve
      no success;
13 He catches the wise in their
      own ruses,
   and the designs of the crafty
      are routed.

14 They meet with darkness in
      the daytime,
   and at noonday they grope as
      though it were night.
15 But the poor from the edge of
      the sword
   and from the hand of the
      mighty, he saves.
16 Thus the unfortunate have hope
   and iniquity closes her mouth.

17 Happy is the man whom God
      reproves!
   The Almighty's chastening do
      not reject.
18 For he wounds, but he binds up;
   he smites, but his hands give
      healing.

4, 10: *The lion:* used figuratively here for the violent
rapacious sinner who cannot prevail against God.
4, 12–21: A dramatic presentation of the idea of
man's nothingness in contrast to God's greatness.
   5, 4: *At the gate:* of the city, where justice was administered.
5, 7: *Sparks:* in Hebrew, "sons of resheph," which
the ancient versions took as the name of a bird.
5, 9: omitted here; it is a duplicate of 9, 10.

19 Out of six troubles he will
      deliver you,
      and at the seventh no evil
      shall touch you.
20 In famine he will deliver you
      from death,
      and in war from the threat
      of the sword;
21 From the scourge of the tongue
      you shall be hidden,
      and shall not fear
      approaching ruin.

22 At destruction and want you
      shall laugh;
      and the beast of the earth
      you need not dread.
23 You shall be in league with the
      stones of the field,
      and the wild beasts shall be
      at peace with you.
24 And you shall know that your
      tent is secure;
      taking stock of your
      household, you shall miss
      nothing.
25 You shall know that your
      descendants are many,
      and your offspring as the
      grass of the earth.
26 You shall approach the grave
      in full vigor,
      as a shock of grain comes in
      at its season.
27 Lo, this we have searched out;
      so it is!
      This we have heard, and you
      should know.

Job's First Reply

6 Then Job answered and said:

2   Ah, could my anguish but be
      measured
      and my calamity laid with it
      in the scales,
3 They should outweigh the sands
      of the sea!
      Because of this I speak
      without restraint.
4 For the arrows of the Almighty
      pierce me,
      and my spirits drink in their
      poison;
      the terrors of God are arrayed
      against me.

5 Does the wild ass bray when
      he has grass?
      Does the oxen low over his
      fodder?
6 Can a thing insipid be eaten
      without salt?
      Is there flavor in the white
      of an egg?
7 I refuse to touch them;
      they are loathsome food to me.

8 Oh, that I might have my
      request,
      and that God would grant
      what I long for:
9 Even that God would decide
      to crush me,
      that he would put forth his
      hand and cut me off!
10 Then I should still have
      consolation
      and could exult through
      unremitting pain,
      because I have not
      transgressed the commands
      of the Holy One.
11 What strength have I that I
      should endure?
      and what is my limit that I
      should be patient?
12 Have I the strength of stones?
      or is my flesh of bronze?
13 Have I no helper,
      and has advice deserted me?
14 A friend owes kindness to one
      in despair,
      though he have forsaken the
      fear of the Almighty.

15 My brethren are undependable
      as a brook,
      as watercourses that run dry
      in the wadies;
16 Though they may be black
      with ice,
      and with snow heaped upon
      them,
17 Yet once they flow, they cease
      to be;
      in the heat, they disappear
      from their place.
18 Caravans turn aside from
      their routes;
      they go into the desert
      and perish.

19 The caravans of Tema search,
      the companies of Sheba
      have hopes;
20 They are disappointed, though
      they were confident;
      they come there and are
      frustrated.
21 It is thus that you have now
      become for me;
      you see a terrifying thing and
      are afraid.
22 Have I asked you to give me
      anything,
      to offer a gift for me from
      your possessions,
23 Or to deliver me from the
      enemy,
      or to redeem me from
      oppressors?
24 Teach me, and I will be silent;
      prove to me wherein I have
      erred.
25 How agreeable are honest words;
      yet how unconvincing is your
      argument!
26 Do you consider your words
      as proof,
      but the sayings of a desperate
      man as wind?
27 You would even cast lots for
      the orphan,
      and would barter away your
      friend!

28 Come, now, give me your
      attention;
      surely I will not lie to your
      face.
29 Think it over; let there be no
      injustice.
      Think it over; I still am right.
30 Is there insincerity on my tongue,
      or cannot my taste discern
      falsehood?

7 Is not man's life on earth a
      drudgery?
      Are not his days those of a
      hireling?
2 He is a slave who longs for
      the shade,
      a hireling who waits for
      his wages.
3 So I have been assigned months
      of misery,
      and troubled nights have been
      told off for me.

5, 19: *Six . . . the seventh:* proverbial expression for any large number; cf Prv 24, 16; Lk 17, 4.
6, 5f: Job would not complain if his life were as pleasant to him as fodder to a hungry animal; but his life is as disagreeable as insipid food. *White of an egg:* thus the obscure Hebrew has been understood in Jewish tradition; some render it "mallow juice."

6, 19: *Tema:* in northwest Arabia. *Sheba:* see note on 1, 15.
7, 1: *Drudgery:* taken by some to refer to military service; cf also 14, 14.

4 If in bed I say, "When shall I
arise?"
then the night drags on;
I am filled with restlessness
until the dawn.
5 My flesh is clothed with worms
and scabs;
my skin cracks and festers;
6 My days are swifter than a
weaver's shuttle;
they come to an end without
hope.
7 Remember that my life is like
the wind;
I shall not see happiness
again.
8 The eye that now sees me shall
no more behold me;
as you look at me I shall be
gone.
9 As a cloud dissolves and
vanishes,
so he that goes down to the
nether world shall come up
no more.
10 He shall not again return to
his house;
his place shall know him no
more.

11 My own utterance I will not
restrain;
I will speak in the anguish
of my spirit;
I will complain in the
bitterness of my soul.
12 Am I the sea, or a monster
of the deep,
that you place a watch over me?
Why have you set me up as an
object of attack;
or why should I be a target
for you?
13 When I say, "My bed shall
comfort me,
my couch shall ease my
complaint."
14 Then you affright me with
dreams
and with visions terrify me,
15 So that I should prefer choking
and death rather than my
pains.
16 I waste away: I cannot live
forever;
let me alone, for my days are
but a breath.

17 What is man, that you make
much of him,
or pay him any heed?
18 You observe him with each new day
and try him at every moment!
19 How long will it be before you
look away from me,
and let me alone long enough
to swallow my spittle?
20 Though I have sinned, what can
I do to you,
O watcher of men?
21 Why do you not pardon my
offense,
or take away my guilt?
For soon I shall lie down in the
dust;
and should you seek me I
shall then be gone.

Bildad's First Speech

8 Bildad the Shuhite spoke out and
said:

2 How long will you utter such
things?
The words from your mouth
are like a mighty wind!
3 Does God pervert judgment,
and does the Almighty distort
justice?
4 If your children have sinned
against him
and he has left them in the
grip of their guilt,
5 Still, if you yourself have
recourse to God
and make supplication to the
Almighty,
6 Should you be blameless and
upright,
surely now he will awake
for you
and restore your rightful
domain;
7 Your former state will be of
little moment,
for in time to come you will
flourish indeed.
8 If you inquire of the former
generations,
and give heed to the
experience of the fathers
9 (As we are but of yesterday
and have no knowledge,
because our days on earth
are but a shadow),

10 Will they not teach you and
tell you
and utter their words of
understanding?
11 Can the papyrus grow up
without mire?
Can the reed grass flourish
without water?
12 While it is yet green and uncut,
it withers quicker than any
grass.
13 So is the end of everyone who
forgets God,
and so shall the hope of the
godless man perish.

14 His confidence is but a
gossamer thread
and his trust is a spider's web.
15 He shall rely upon his family,
but it shall not last;
he shall cling to it, but it
shall not endure.
16 He is full of sap before sunrise,
and beyond his garden his
shoots go forth;
17 About a heap of stones are his
roots entwined;
among the rocks he takes hold.
18 Yet if one tears him from his
place,
it will disown him: "I have
never seen you!"
19 There he lies rotting beside
the road,
and out of the soil another
sprouts.

20 Behold, God will not cast away
the upright;
neither will he take the hand
of the wicked.
21 Once more will he fill your
mouth with laughter,
and your lips with rejoicing.
22 They that hate you shall be
clothed with shame,
and the tent of the wicked
shall be no more.

Job's Second Reply

9 Then Job answered and said:

2 I know well that it is so;
but how can a man be
justified before God?

7, 12: An allusion in poetic imagery to primeval chaos as a monstrous ocean vanquished by God at the world's creation.

7, 12–21: Job now speaks, not to his friends, but to God.

8, 11ff: As marsh plants need water, so man needs

God. These verses are taken by some as a quotation from the teaching of the forefathers; cf v 10.

3 Should one wish to contend
    with him,
  he could not answer him once
    in a thousand times.
4 God is wise in heart and mighty
    in strength;
  who has withstood him and
    remained unscathed?

5 He removes the mountains
    before they know it;
  he overturns them in his
    anger.
6 He shakes the earth out of its
    place,
  and the pillars beneath it
    tremble.
7 He commands the sun, and it
    rises not;
  he seals up the stars.
8 He alone stretches out the
    heavens
  and treads upon the crests
    of the sea.
9 He made the Bear and Orion,
    the Pleiades and the
    constellations of the south;
10 He does great things past
    finding out,
  marvelous things beyond
    reckoning.
11 Should he come near me,
    I see him not;
  should he pass by, I am not
    aware of him;
12 Should he seize me forcibly,
    who can say him nay?
  Who can say to him, "What
    are you doing?"
13 He is God and he does not
    relent;
  the helpers of Rahab bow
    beneath him.
14 How much less shall I give him
    any answer,
  or choose out arguments
    against him!
15 Even though I were right, I
    could not answer him,
  but should rather beg for
    what was due me.
16 If I appealed to him and he
    answered my call,
  I could not believe that he
    would hearken to my words;

17 With a tempest he might
    overwhelm me,
  and multiply my wounds
    without cause;
18 He need not suffer me to draw
    breath,
  but might fill me with bitter
    griefs.

19 If it be a question of strength,
    he is mighty;
  and if of judgment, who will
    call him to account?
20 Though I were right, my own
    mouth might condemn me;
  were I innocent, he might
    put me in the wrong.
21 Though I am innocent, I myself
    cannot know it;
  I despise my life.

22 It is all one! therefore I say:
  Both the innocent and the
    wicked he destroys.
23 When the scourge slays suddenly,
  he laughs at the despair of
    the innocent.
24 The earth is given into the
    hands of the wicked;
  he covers the faces of its
    judges.
  If it is not he, who then is it?

25 My days are swifter than a
    runner,
  they flee away; they see no
    happiness;
26 They shoot by like skiffs of reed,
  like an eagle swooping upon
    its prey.
27 If I say: I will forget my
    complaining,
  I will lay aside my sadness and
    be of good cheer,
28 Then I am in dread of all my
    pains;
  I know that you will not hold
    me innocent.

29 If I must be accounted guilty,
  why then should I strive
    in vain?
30 If I should wash myself with
    snow
  and cleanse my hands with lye,
31 Yet you would plunge me in
    the ditch,
  so that my garments would
    abhor me.

32 For he is not a man like myself,
    that I should answer him,
  that we should come together
    in judgment.
33 Would that there were an
    arbiter between us,
  who could lay his hand upon
    us both
34   and withdraw his rod from me.
  Would that his terrors did not
    frighten me;
35   that I might speak without
    being afraid of him.
  Since this is not the case with me.

10 I loathe my life.

  I will give myself up to
    complaint;
  I will speak from the
    bitterness of my soul.
2 I will say to God: Do not put
    me in the wrong!
  Let me know why you
    oppose me.

3 Is it a pleasure for you to
    oppress,
  to spurn the work of your
    hands,
  and smile on the plan of the
    wicked?
4 Have you eyes of flesh?
  Do you see as man sees?
5 Are your days as the days of a
    mortal,
  and are your years as a man's
    lifetime,
6 That you seek for guilt in me
  and search after my sins,
7 Even though you know that I
    am not wicked,
  and that none can deliver me
    out of your hand?

8 Your hands have formed me and
    fashioned me;
  will you then turn and destroy
    me?
9 Oh, remember that you
    fashioned me from clay!
  Will you then bring me down
    to dust again?
10 Did you not pour me out as
    milk,
  and thicken me like cheese?
11 With skin and flesh you
    clothed me,
  with bones and sinews knit
    me together.

9, 13: *Rahab:* cf 26, 12. See note on Ps 89, 11.
9, 28–31: *You:* refers to God.

12 Grace and favor you granted me,
and your providence has
preserved my spirit.

13 Yet these things you have
hidden in your heart;
I know that they are your
purpose:

14 If I should sin, you would keep
a watch against me,
and from my guilt you would
not absolve me.

15 If I should be wicked, alas
for me!
if righteous, I dare not hold
up my head,
filled with ignominy and
sodden with affliction!

16 Should it lift up, you hunt me
like a lion:
repeatedly you show your
wondrous power against
me.

17 You renew your attack upon me
and multiply your harassment
of me;
in waves your troops come
against me.

18 Why then did you bring me
forth from the womb?
I should have died and no
eye have seen me.

19 I should be as though I had
never lived;
I should have been taken
from the womb to the
grave.

20 Are not the days of my life few?
Let me alone, that I may
recover a little

21 Before I go whence I shall not
return,
to the land of darkness and
of gloom,

22 The black, disordered land
where darkness is the only
light.

Zophar's First Speech

11 And Zophar the Naamathite
spoke out and said:

2 Should not the man of many
words be answered,
or must the garrulous man
necessarily be right?

3 Shall your babblings keep men
silent,
and shall you deride and no
one give rebuke?

4 Shall you say: "My teaching
is pure,
and I am clean in your sight"?

5 But oh, that God would speak,
and open his lips against you,

6 And tell you that the secrets of
wisdom
are twice as effective:
So you might learn that God
will make you answer for
your guilt.

7 Can you penetrate the designs
of God?
Dare you vie with the
perfection of the Almighty?

8 It is higher than the heavens;
what can you do?
It is deeper than the nether
world; what can you know?

9 It is longer than the earth in
measure,
and broader than the sea.

10 If he seize and imprison
or call to judgment, who then
can say him nay?

11 For he knows the worthlessness
of men
and sees iniquity; will he then
ignore it?

12 Will empty man then gain
understanding,
and the wild jackass be made
docile?

13 If you set your heart aright
and stretch out your hands
toward him,

14 If you remove all iniquity from
your conduct,
and let not injustice dwell in
your tent,

15 Surely then you may lift up
your face in innocence;
you may stand firm and
unafraid.

16 For then you shall forget your
misery,
or recall it like waters that
have ebbed away.

17 Then your life shall be
brighter than the noonday;
its gloom shall become as the
morning,

18 And you shall be secure,
because there is hope;

you shall look round you and
lie down in safety,

19 and you shall take your rest
with none to disturb.

Many shall entreat your favor,

20 but the wicked, looking on,
shall be consumed with
envy.
Escape shall be cut off from
them,
they shall wait to expire.

Job's Third Reply

12 Then Job replied and said:

2 No doubt you are the intelligent
folk,
and with you wisdom shall die!

3 But I have intelligence as well
as you;
for who does not know such
things as these?

4 I have become the sport of my
neighbors:
"The one whom God answers
when he calls upon him,
the just, the perfect man," is
a laughingstock;

5 The undisturbed esteem my
downfall a disgrace
such as awaits unsteady feet;

6 Yet the tents of the robbers are
prosperous,
and those who provoke God
are secure.

7 But now ask the beasts to teach
you,
and the birds of the air to
tell you;

8 Or the reptiles on earth to
instruct you,
and the fish of the sea to
inform you.

9 Which of all these does not know
that the hand of God has
done this?

10 In his hand is the soul of every
living thing,
and the life breath of all
mankind.

11 Does not the ear judge words
as the mouth tastes food?

12 So with old age is wisdom,
and with length of days
understanding.

13 With him are wisdom and might;
his are counsel and
understanding.

12, 4f: The Hebrew is somewhat obscure, but the
general sense is that the wicked mock at the pious
when the latter appear to be abandoned by God; cf Ps
22, 7ff; Mt 27. 39–43.

14 If he breaks a thing down, there
    is no rebuilding;
  if he imprisons a man, there
    is no release.
15 He holds back the waters and
    there is drought;
  he sends them forth and they
    overwhelm the land.
18 He loosens the bonds imposed
    by kings
  and leaves but a waistcloth to
    bind the king's own loins.
21 He breaks down the barriers
    of the streams
19   and lets their never-failing
    waters flow away.

16 With him are strength and
    prudence;
  the misled and the misleaders
    are his.
17 He sends counselors away
    barefoot,
  and of judges he makes fools.
20 He silences the trusted adviser,
  and takes discretion from the
    aged.
22 The recesses of the darkness he
    discloses,
  and brings the gloom forth
    to the light.
23 He makes nations great and he
    destroys them;
  he spreads peoples abroad and
    he abandons them.
24 He takes understanding from
    the leaders of the land,
25   till they grope in the darkness
    without light;
  he makes them stagger like
    drunken men.

13 Lo, all this my eye has seen;
    my ear has heard and
    perceived it.
2 What you know, I also know;
  I fall not short of you.
3 But I would speak with the
    Almighty;
  I wish to reason with God.
4 You are glossing over
    falsehoods
  and offering vain remedies,
    every one of you!
5 Oh, that you would be
    altogether silent!
  This for you would be wisdom.

6 Hear now the rebuke I shall
    utter
  and listen to the reproof from
    my lips.
7 Is it for God you speak
    falsehood?
  Is it for him you utter deceit?
8 Is it for him you show partiality?
  Do you play advocate on
    behalf of God?
9 Will it be well when he shall
    search you out?
  Would you impose on him as
    one does on man?

10 He will openly rebuke you
  if even in secret you show
    partiality.
11 Surely will his majesty affright
    you
  and the dread of him fall
    upon you.

12 Your reminders are ashy maxims,
  your fabrications are mounds
    of clay.
13 Be silent, let me alone! that I
    may speak
  and give vent to my feelings.
14 I will carry my flesh between
    my teeth,
  and take my life in my hand.
15 Slay me though he might, I will
    wait for him;
  I will defend my conduct
    before him.
16 And this shall be my salvation,
  that no impious man can
    come into his presence.

17 Pay careful heed to my speech,
  and give my statement a
    hearing.
18 Behold, I have prepared my case
  I know that I am in the right.
19 If anyone can make a case
    against me,
  then I shall be silent and die.
20 These things only do not use
    against me,
  then from your presence I
    need not hide:
21 Withdraw your hand far from
    me.
  and let not the terror of you
    frighten me.

22 Then call me, and I will respond;
  or let me speak first, and
    answer me.
23 What are my faults and my
    sins?
  My misdeeds and my sins
    make known to me!
24 Why do you hide your face
  and consider me your enemy?
25 Will you harass a wind-driven
    leaf,
  or pursue a withered straw?
26 For you draw up bitter
    indictments against me,
  and punish in me the faults
    of my youth.
27 You put my feet in the stocks;
  you watch all my paths
  and trace out all my footsteps.

14 Man born of woman
    is short-lived and full of
    trouble,
2 Like a flower that springs up
    and fades,
  swift as a shadow that does
    not abide.
3 Upon such a one will you cast
    your eyes
  so as to bring him into
    judgment before you,
(13) 28 Though he wears out like
    a leather bottle,
  like a garment that the moth
    has consumed?

(14) 4 Can a man be found who is
    clean of defilement?
5   There is none, however short
    his days.
  You know the number of his
    months;
  you have fixed the limit
    which he cannot pass.
6 Look away from him and let
    him be,
  while like a hireling, he
    completes his day.

7 For a tree there is hope,
  if it be cut down, that it will
    sprout again
  and that its tender shoots will
    not cease.

12, 18: *Waistcloth . . . loins:* he reduces kings to the condition of slaves, who wear only a cloth wrapped about the waist.
13, 14: The second half of the verse is a common biblical expression for risking one's life; cf Jgs 12, 3; 1 Sm 19, 5; 28, 21; Ps 119, 109; the first half of the verse must have a similar meaning. Job is so confident of his innocence that he is willing to risk his life by going to judgment with God.
13,20: From here to the end of chapter 14, Job pleads his case, addressing God rather than his three friends.

8 Even though its root grow old
   in the earth,
     and its stump die in the dust,
9 Yet at the first whiff of water
   it may flourish again
     and put forth branches like
     a young plant.

10 But when a man dies, all vigor
    leaves him;
    when man expires, where then
    is he?
11 As when the waters of a lake
    fail,
    or a stream grows dry and
    parches,
12 So men lie down and rise not
    again.
    Till the heavens are no more,
    they shall not awake,
    nor be roused out of their
    sleep.

13 Oh, that you would hide me in
    the nether world
    and keep me sheltered till
    your wrath is past;
    would fix a time for me, and
    then remember me!
14 When a man has died, were he
    to live again,
    all the days of my drudgery
    I would wait,
    until my relief should come.
15 You would call, and I would
    answer you;
    you would esteem the work
    of your hands.

16 Surely then you would count
    my steps,
    and not keep watch for sin
    in me.
17 My misdeeds would be sealed
    up in a pouch,
    and you would cover over
    my guilt.
18 But as a mountain falls at last
    and its rock is moved from
    its place,
19 As waters wear away the stones
    and floods wash away the soil
    of the land,
    so you destroy the hope of
    man.
20 You prevail once for all against
    him and he passes on;
    with changed appearance you
    send him away.

14, 17: *Sealed up in a pouch:* hidden away and
forgotten.

21 If his sons are honored, he is
    not aware of it;
    if they are in disgrace, he
    does not know about them.
22 Only his own flesh pains him,
    and his soul grieves for him.

SECOND CYCLE OF SPEECHES

Second Speech of Eliphaz

15 Then Eliphaz the Temanite
    spoke and said:

2 Should a wise man answer with
    airy opinions,
    or puff himself up with wind?
3 Should he argue in speech
    which does not avail,
    and in words which are no
    profit?
4 You in fact do away with piety,
    and you lessen devotion
    toward God,
5 Because your wickedness
    instructs your mouth,
    and you choose to speak
    like the crafty.
6 Your own mouth condemns
    you, not I;
    your own lips refute you.

7 Are you indeed the first-born
    of mankind,
    or were you brought forth
    before the hills?
8 Are you privy to the counsels
    of God,
    and do you restrict wisdom
    to yourself?
9 What do you know that we do
    not know?
    What intelligence have you
    which we have not?
10 There are gray-haired old men
    among us
    more advanced in years than
    your father.
11 Are the consolations of God
    not enough for you,
    and speech that deals gently
    with you?

12 Why do your notions carry
    you away,
    and why do your eyes blink,
13 So that you turn your anger
    against God
    and let such words escape
    your mouth!

14 What is a man that he should
    be blameless,
    one born of woman that he
    should be righteous?
15 If in his holy ones God places
    no confidence,
    and if the heavens are not
    clean in his sight,
16 How much less so is the
    abominable, the corrupt:
    man, who drinks in iniquity
    like water!

17 I will show you, if you listen
    to me;
    what I have seen I will tell—
18 What wise men relate
    and have not contradicted
    since the days of their
    fathers,
19 To whom alone the land was given,
    when no foreigner moved
    among them.

20 The wicked man is in torment
    all his days,
    and limited years are in store
    for the tyrant;
21 The sound of terrors is in
    his ears;
    when all is prosperous, the
    spoiler comes upon him.
22 He despairs of escaping the
    darkness,
    and looks ever for the sword;
23 A wanderer, food for the
    vultures,
    he knows that his destruction
    is imminent.
24 By day the darkness fills him
    with dread;
    distress and anguish
    overpower him.

25 Because he has stretched out
    his hand against God
    and bade defiance to the
    Almighty,
26 One shall rush sternly upon him
    with the stout bosses of
    his shield,
    like a king prepared for the
    charge.
27 Because he has blinded himself
    with his crassness,
    padding his loins with fat,
28 He shall dwell in ruinous cities,
    in houses that are deserted,
    That are crumbling into clay
29   with no shadow to lengthen
    over the ground.

He shall not be rich, and his
　　possessions shall not endure;
31 for vain shall be his
　　bartering.
30 A flame shall wither him up in
　　his early growth,
　　and with the wind his
　　blossoms shall disappear.
32 His stalk shall wither before
　　its time,
　　and his branches shall be
　　green no more.
33 He shall be like a vine that
　　sheds its grapes unripened,
　　and like an olive tree casting
　　off its bloom.
34 For the breed of the impious
　　shall be sterile,
　　and fire shall consume the
　　tents of extortioners.

35 They conceive malice and bring
　　forth emptiness;
　　they give birth to failure.

Job's Fourth Reply

16 Then Job answered and said:

2 I have heard this sort of thing
　　many times.
　　Wearisome comforters are
　　you all!
3 Is there no end to windy words?
　　Or what sickness have you
　　that you speak on?
4 I also could talk as you do.
　　were you in my place.
　　I could declaim over you,
　　or wag my head at you;
5 I could strengthen you with talk,
　　or shake my head with silent
　　lips.
6 If I speak, this pain I have will
　　not be checked;
　　if I leave off, it will not
　　depart from me.

7 But now that I am exhausted
　　and stunned,
　　all my company has closed
　　in on me.
8 As a witness there rises up
　　my traducer, speaking openly
　　against me;
9 I am the prey his wrath assails,
　　he gnashes his teeth against
　　me.

My enemies lord it over me;
10 their mouths are agape to
　　bite me.
They smite me on the cheek
　　insultingly;
　　they are all enlisted against me.
11 God has given me over to the
　　impious;
　　into the clutches of the
　　wicked he has cast me.
12 I was in peace, but he
　　dislodged me;
　　he seized me by the neck and
　　dashed me to pieces.

He has set me up for a target;
13 his arrows strike me from
　　all directions,
He pierces my sides without
　　mercy,
　　he pours out my gall upon
　　the ground.
14 He pierces me with thrust upon
　　thrust;
　　he attacks me like a warrior.
15 I have fastened sackcloth over
　　my skin,
　　and have laid my brow in the
　　dust.
16 My face is inflamed with
　　weeping
　　and there is darkness over
　　my eyes,
17 Although my hands are free
　　from violence,
　　and my prayer is sincere.

18 O earth, cover not my blood,
　　nor let my outcry come to
　　rest!
19 Even now, behold, my witness
　　is in heaven,
　　and my spokesman is on high.
20 My friends it is who wrong me;
　　before God my eyes drop
　　tears,
21 That he may do justice for a
　　mortal in his presence
　　and decide between a man
　　and his neighbor.
22 For my years are numbered now,
　　and I am on a journey from
　　which I shall not return.

17 My spirit is broken, my
　　lamp of life extinguished;
　　my burial is at hand.

2 I am indeed mocked,
　　and, as their provocation
　　mounts, my eyes grow dim.

3 Grant me one to offer you a
　　pledge on my behalf:
　　who is there that will give
　　surety for me?
4 You darken their minds to
　　knowledge;
　　therefore they do not
　　understand.
5 My lot is described as evil,
6 and I am made a byword of
　　the people;
　　their object lesson I have
　　become.
7 My eye has grown blind with
　　anguish,
　　and all my frame is
　　shrunken to shadow.
8 Upright men are astonished
　　at this,
　　and the innocent aroused
　　against the wicked.
9 Yet the righteous shall hold to
　　his way,
　　and he who has clean hands
　　increase in strength.

10 But turn now, and come on again;
　　for I shall not find a wise
　　man among you!
11 My days are passed away,
　　my plans are at an end,
　　the cherished purposes of my
　　heart.
12 Such men change the night
　　into day;
　　where there is darkness they
　　talk of approaching light.
13 If I look for the nether world
　　as my dwelling,
　　if I spread my couch in the
　　darkness,
14 If I must call corruption "my
　　father,"
　　and the maggot "my mother"
　　and "my sister,"
15 Where then is my hope?
　　and my prosperity, who shall
　　see?
16 Will they descend with me into
　　the nether world?
　　Shall we go down together
　　into the dust?

15, 35: *They gave birth to failure:* their wicked plans
yield nothing but futile results. Cf Ps 7, 15; Is 59, 4.
　16, 18: As the blood of those who were unjustly

slain cries to heaven for vengeance (Gn 4, 10; Ez 24
6–9), so Job's sufferings demand redress.

16, 19: *Witness:* refers either to God or, more
probably, to Job's prayer.
　17, 3: Addressed to God; v 10 to Job's friends,

Bildad's Second Speech

18 Then Bildad the Shuhite replied and said:

2 When will you put an end
    to words?
  Reflect, and then we can
    have discussion.
3 Why are we accounted like
    the beasts,
  their equals in your sight?
4 You who tear yourself in your
    anger,
  shall the earth be neglected
    on your account
  [or the rock be moved out of
    its place]?

5 Truly, the light of the wicked
    is extinguished;
  no flame brightens his hearth.
6 The light is darkened in his
    tent;
  in spite of him, his lamp goes
    out.
7 His vigorous steps are hemmed
    in,
  and his own counsel casts
    him down.

8 For he rushes headlong into a
    net,
  and he wanders into a pitfall.
9 A trap seizes him by the heel,
  and a snare lays hold of him.
10 A noose for him is hid on the
    ground,
  and the toils for him on the
    way.

11 On every side terrors affright
    him;
  they harry him at each step.
12 Disaster is ready at his side,
13   the first-born of death
    consumes his limbs.
14 Fiery destruction lodges in his
    tent,
  and marches him off to the
    king of terrors.

  He is plucked from the security
    of his tent,
15   over his abode brimstone is
    scattered.

16 Below, his roots dry up,
  and above, his branches
    wither.
17 His memory perishes from the
    land,
  and he has no name on the
    earth.
18 He is driven from light into
    darkness,
  and banished out of the world.
19 He has neither son nor grandson
    among his people,
  nor any survivor where once
    he dwelt.
20 They who come after shall be
    appalled at his fate;
  they who went before are
    struck with horror.

21 So is it then with the dwelling
    of the impious man,
  and such is the place of him
    who knows not God!

Job's Fifth Reply

19 Then Job answered and said:

2 How long will you vex my soul,
  grind me down with words?
3 These ten times you have
    reviled me,
  have assailed me without
    shame!
4 Be it indeed that I am at fault
  and that my fault remains
    with me,
5 Even so, if you would vaunt
    yourselves against me
  and cast up to me my
    reproach,
6 Know then that God has dealt
    unfairly with me,
  and compassed me round
    with his net.

7 If I cry out "Injustice!" I am
    not heard.
  I cry for help, but there is no
    redress.
8 He has barred my way and I
    cannot pass;
  he has veiled my path in
    darkness;

9 He has stripped me of my
    glory,
  and taken the diadem from
    my brow.
10 He breaks me down on every
    side, and I am gone;
  my hope he has uprooted like
    a tree.
11 His wrath he has kindled
    against me;
  he counts me among his
    enemies.
12 His troops advance as one man;
  they build up their road to
    attack me,
  and they encamp around my
    tent.

13 My brethren have withdrawn
    from me,
  and my friends are wholly
    estranged.
14 My kinsfolk and companions
    neglect me,
  and my guests have forgotten
    me.
15 Even my handmaids treat me as
    a stranger;
  I am an alien in their sight.
16 I call my servant, but he gives
    no answer,
  though in my speech I plead
    with him.
17 My breath is abhorred by my
    wife;
  I am loathsome to the men of
    my family.
18 The young children, too,
    despise me;
  when I appear, they speak
    against me.
19 All my intimate friends hold
    me in horror;
  those whom I loved have
    turned against me!
20 My bones cleave to my skin,
  and I have escaped with my
    flesh between my teeth.
21 Pity me, pity me, O you my
    friends,
  for the hand of God has
    struck me!
22 Why do you hound me as
    though you were divine,
  and insatiably prey upon me?

18, 4: Job himself is portrayed as having the heedless rage of wild beasts, despite which God does not forsake the usual course of Divine Providence.
18, 13: *First-born of death:* that is, disease, plague.
18, 14: *The king of terrors:* of the nether world,

death; however, the Hebrew is obscure.
19, 20: *With my flesh between my teeth:* meaning perhaps that Job has been reduced to such an extremity that he scarcely has thin lips over his teeth.

But the current Hebrew text of this line is probably corrupt.
19, 22: *Divine:* possessing God's attributes of judgment and authority to punish.

23 Oh, would that my words were
   written down!
   Would that they were
   inscribed in a record:
24 That with an iron chisel and
   with lead
   they were cut in the rock
   forever!
25 But as for me, I know that my
   Vindicator lives,
   and that he will at last stand
   forth upon the dust;
27 Whom I myself shall see:
   my own eyes, not another's,
   shall behold him,
26 And from my flesh I shall see
   God;
   my inmost being is
   consumed with longing.

28 But you who say, "How shall
   we persecute him,
   seeing that the root of the
   matter is found in him?"
29 Be afraid of the sword for
   yourselves,
   for these crimes deserve the
   sword;
   that you may know that there
   is a judgment.

Zophar's Second Speech

20 Then Zophar the Naamathite
   spoke and said:

3 A rebuke which puts me to
   shame I hear,
2   and because of this I am
   disturbed.
   So now my thoughts provide
   me with an answer,
   and from my understanding a
   spirit gives me a reply.

4 Do you not know this from
   olden time,
   since man was placed upon
   the earth,
5 That the triumph of the wicked
   is short
   and the joy of the impious
   but for a moment?
6 Though his pride mount up to
   the heavens
   and his head reach to the
   clouds,

7 Yet he perishes forever like the
   fuel of his fire,
   and the onlookers say,
   "Where is he?"
8 Like a dream he takes flight and
   is not found again;
   he fades away like a vision of
   the night.
9 The eye which saw him does so
   no more;
   nor shall his dwelling again
   behold him.
11 Though his frame is full of
   youthful vigor,
   this shall lie with him in the
   dust.
12 Though wickedness is sweet in
   his mouth,
   and he hides it under his
   tongue,
13 Though he retains it and will
   not let it go
   but keeps it still within his
   mouth,
14 Yet in his stomach the food
   shall turn;
   it shall be venom of asps
   inside him.
15 The riches he swallowed he
   shall disgorge;
   God shall compel his belly to
   disown them.
16 The poison of asps he shall
   drink in;
   the viper's fangs shall slay
   him.
17 He shall see no streams of oil,
   no torrents of honey or milk.
18 Restoring his gains, he shall not
   enjoy them;
   though his wealth increases,
   he shall not rejoice.
19 Because he has oppressed the
   poor,
   and stolen a patrimony he had
   not built up,
21 Therefore his prosperity shall
   not endure,
10   and his hands shall yield up
   his riches.
20 Though he has known no quiet
   in his greed,
   his treasures shall not save
   him.

22 When he abounds to
   overflowing, he shall be
   brought into straits,
   and nought shall be left of
   his goods.
23 God shall send against him the
   fury of his wrath
   and rain down his missiles of
   war upon him.
24 Should he escape the iron
   weapon,
   the bow of bronze shall
   pierce him through;
25 The dart shall come out of his
   back;
   terrors shall fall upon him.
26 Complete darkness is in store
   for him;
   the fire which shall consume
   him needs not to be fanned.
27 The heavens shall reveal his
   guilt,
   and the earth shall rise up
   against him.
28 The flood shall sweep away his
   house
   with the waters that run off
   in the day of God's anger.

29 This is the portion of a wicked
   man,
   and the heritage appointed
   him by God.

Job's Sixth Reply

21 Then Job said in reply:

2 At least listen to my words,
   and let that be the consolation
   you offer.
3 Bear with me while I speak;
   and after I have spoken, you
   can mock!
4 Is my complaint toward man?
   And why should I not be
   impatient?
5 Look at me and be astonished,
   put your hands over your
   mouths.
6 When I think of it, I am
   dismayed,
   and horror takes hold on my
   flesh.

19, 23f: Job regards what he is about to say as so
important that he wishes it recorded in a permanent
manner.
19, 25.27: The meaning of this passage is obscure
because the original text has been poorly preserved

and the ancient versions do not agree among themselves. It is certain that Job expresses his belief in a
future vindication by God (called here in the Hebrew
"Goel"), but the time and manner of this vindication
are undefined. In the Vulgate Job is made to indicate

a belief in physical resurrection after death, but the
Hebrew and the other ancient versions are less specific.
20, 17: *Oil:* olive oil, one of the main agricultural
products of Palestine, a land proverbially rich in
honey and *milk*.

7 Why do the wicked survive,
   grow old, become mighty in
      power?
8 Their progeny is secure in their
      sight;
   they see before them their
      kinsfolk and their offspring.
9 Their homes are safe and
      without fear,
   nor is the scourge of God
      upon them.
10 Their bulls gender without fail;
   their cows calve and do not
      miscarry.
11 These folks have infants
      numerous as lambs,
   and their children dance.
12 They sing to the timbrel and
      harp,
   and make merry to the sound
      of the flute.

13 They live out their days in
      prosperity,
   and tranquilly go down to the
      nether world.
14 Yet they say to God, "Depart
      from us,
   for we have no wish to learn
      your ways!
15 What is the Almighty that we
      should serve him?
   And what gain shall we have
      if we pray to him?"
16 If their happiness is not in
      their own hands
   and if the counsel of the
      wicked is repulsive to God,
17 How often is the lamp of the
      wicked put out?
   How often does destruction
      come upon them,
   the portion he allots in his
      anger?

18 Let them be like straw before
      the wind,
   and like chaff which the storm
      snatches away!
19 May God not store up the
      man's misery for his
      children;
   let him requite the man
      himself so that he feels it,
20 Let his own eyes see the
      calamity,
   and the wrath of the Almighty
      let him drink!

21 For what interest has he in his
      family after him,
   when the number of his
      months is finished?
23 One dies in his full vigor,
   wholly at ease and content;
24 His figure is full and
      nourished,
   and his bones are rich in
      marrow.
25 Another dies in bitterness of
      soul,
   having never tasted happiness.
26 Alike they lie down in the dust,
   and worms cover them both.

27 Behold, I know your thoughts,
   and the arguments you
      rehearse against me.
28 For you say, "Where is the
      house of the magnate,
   and where the dwelling place
      of the wicked?"
29 Have you not asked the
      wayfarers
   and do you not recognize
      their monuments?

30 Nay, the evil man is spared
      calamity when it comes;
32   and on the day he is carried
         to the grave
31 Who will charge him with his
      conduct to his face,
   and for what he has done
      who will repay him?
33 Sweet to him are the clods of
      the valley,
   and over him the funeral
      mound keeps watch,
   While all the line of mankind
      follows him,
   and the countless others who
      have gone before.
34 How then can you offer me vain
      comfort,
   while in your answers perfidy
      remains?

THIRD CYCLE OF SPEECHES

Eliphaz's Third Speech

22 Then Eliphaz the Temanite
      answered and said:

2 Can a man be profitable to
      God?
   Though to himself a wise
      man be profitable!

(21) 22 Can anyone teach God
         knowledge,
   seeing that he judges those on
      high?
(22) 3 Is it of advantage to the
         Almighty if you are just?
   Or is it a gain to him if you
      make your ways perfect?
4 Is it because of your piety that
      he reproves you—
   that he enters with you into
      judgment?
5 Is not your wickedness manifold?
   Are not your iniquities
      endless?

6 You have unjustly kept your
      kinsmen's goods in pawn,
   left them stripped naked of
      their clothing.
7 To the thirsty you have given
      no water to drink,
   and from the hungry you
      have withheld bread;
8 As if the land belonged to the
      man of might,
   and only the privileged were
      to dwell in it.
9 You have sent widows away
      empty-handed,
   and the resources of orphans
      you have destroyed.
10 Therefore snares are round
      about you,
   and a sudden terror causes
      you dismay,
11 Or darkness, in which you
      cannot see;
   a deluge of waters covers you.

12 Does not God, in the heights
      of the heavens,
   behold the stars, high though
      they are?
13 Yet you say, "What does God
      know?
   Can he judge through the
      thick darkness?
14 Clouds hide him so that he
      cannot see;
   he walks upon the vault of
      the heavens!"

15 Do you indeed keep to the
      ancient way
   trodden by worthless men,

21, 22: *Those on high:* the angels.
22, 6ff: This criticism of Job by Eliphaz is alto-

gether untrue, but it is made to dramatize the latter's
argument that God always acts justly when he

causes someone to suffer. V 8 is misplaced.

16 Who were snatched away
    before their time;
    whose foundations a flood
    swept away?
17 These men said to God,
    "Depart from us!"
    and, "What can the Almighty
    do to us?"
18 [Yet he had filled their houses
    with good things!
    But far be from me the mind
    of the impious!]
19 The just look on and are
    gladdened,
    and the innocent deride
    them:
20 "Truly these have been
    destroyed where they stood,
    and such as were left, fire has
    consumed!"

21 Come to terms with him to be
    at peace.
    In this shall good come to
    you:
22 Receive instruction from his
    mouth,
    and lay up his words in your
    heart.
23 If you return to the Almighty,
    you will be restored;
    if you put iniquity far from
    your tent,
24 And treat raw gold like dust,
    and the fine gold of Ophir as
    pebbles from the brook,
25 Then the Almighty himself shall
    be your gold
    and your sparkling silver.

26 For then you shall delight in the
    Almighty
    and you shall lift up your
    face toward God.
27 You shall entreat him and he
    will hear you,
    and your vows you shall fulfill.
28 When you make a decision, it
    shall succeed for you,
    and upon your ways the light
    shall shine.
29 For he brings down the pride
    of the haughty,
    but the man of humble mien
    he saves.

30 God delivers him who is
    innocent;
    you shall be delivered through
    cleanness of hands.

Job's Seventh Reply

23 Again Job answered and said:

2 Though I know my complaint
    is bitter,
    his hand is heavy upon me in
    my groanings.
3 Oh, that today I might find
    him,
    that I might come to his
    judgment seat!
4 I would set out my cause
    before him,
    and fill my mouth with
    arguments;
5 I would learn the words with
    which he would answer,
    and understand what he
    would reply to me.
6 Even should he contend against
    me with his great power,
    yet, would that he himself
    might heed me!
7 There the upright man might
    reason with him,
    I should once and for all
    preserve my rights.

8 But if I go to the east, he is not
    there;
    or to the west, I cannot
    perceive him;
9 Where the north enfolds him, I
    behold him not;
    by the south he is veiled, and
    I see him not.
10 Yet he knows my way;
    if he proved me, I should
    come forth as gold.
11 My foot has always walked in
    his steps;
    his way I have kept and have
    not turned aside.

12 From the commands of his
    lips I have not departed;
    the words of his mouth I
    have treasured in my heart.
13 But he has decided, and who
    can say him nay?
    What he desires, that he does.

14 For he will carry out what is
    appointed for me;
    and many such things may
    yet be in his mind.
15 Therefore am I dismayed before
    him;
    when I take thought, I fear
    him.
16 Indeed God has made my
    courage fail;
    the Almighty has put me in
    dismay.
17 Yes, would that I had
    vanished in darkness,
    and that thick gloom were
    before me to conceal me.

24 Why are not times set by the
    Almighty,
    and why do his friends not
    see his days?
2 The wicked remove landmarks;
    they steal away herds and
    pasture them.
3 The asses of orphans they drive
    away;
    they take the widow's ox for
    a pledge.

4 They force the needy off the
    road;
    all the poor of the land are
    driven into hiding.
5 Like wild asses in the desert,
    these go forth
    to their task of seeking food;
    The steppe provides food for
    the young among them;
6   they harvest at night in the
    untilled land.
7 They pass the night naked,
    without clothing,
    for they have no covering
    against the cold;
8 They are drenched with the rain
    of the mountains,
    and for want of shelter they
    cling to the rock.
11 Between the rows they press out
    the oil;
    they glean in the vineyard of
    the wicked.
    They tread the wine presses, yet
    suffer thirst,
10   and famished are those who
    carry the sheaves.

22, 18: A gloss, taken partly from 21, 16.
22, 24: *Ophir:* cf note to Ps 45, 10.

24, 1: Why does not God favor his friends by the
speedy punishment of his enemies? (The text and
order of verses in this chapter are not certain; note
the omission of v 9 which duplicates words of vv 2–4.)

12 From the dust the dying groan,
　　and the souls of the wounded
　　　cry out
　　[yet God does not treat it as
　　　unseemly].

13 There are those who are rebels
　　against the light;
　　they know not its ways;
　　they abide not in its paths.
14 When there is no light the
　　murderer rises,
　　to kill the poor and needy.
15 The eye of the adulterer watches
　　for the twilight;
　　he says, "No eye will see me."
　In the night the thief roams
　　about,
　　and he puts a mask over his
　　　face;
16 　in the dark he breaks into
　　　houses.
　By day they shut themselves in;
　　none of them know the light,
17 　for daylight they regard as
　　darkness.

* * *

18 Their portion in the land is
　　accursed,
20 　and wickedness is splintered
　　like wood.
19.21 . . . .
22 To him who rises without
　　assurance of his life
23 　he gives safety and support.
　He sustains the mighty by his
　　strength,
　　and his eyes are on their
　　　ways.
24 They are exalted for a while,
　　and then they are gone;
　they are laid low and, like all
　　others, are gathered up;
　like ears of grain they shrivel.

* * *

25 If this be not so, who will
　　confute me,

and reduce my argument to
　nought?

Bildad's Third Speech

25 Then Bildad the Shuhite
　answered and said:

2 Dominion and awesomeness are
　　his
　who brings about harmony
　　in his heavens.
3 Is there any numbering of his
　　troops?
　Yet to which of them does
　　not his light extend?
4 How can a man be just in
　　God's sight,
　or how can any woman's
　　child be innocent?
5 Behold, even the moon is not
　　bright
　and the stars are not clear in
　　his sight.
6 How much less man, who is but
　　a maggot,
　the son of man, who is only
　　a worm?

Job's Reply

26 Then Job spoke again and
　said:

2 What help you give to the
　　powerless,
　what strength to the feeble
　　arm!
3 How you counsel, as though he
　　had no wisdom;
　how profuse is the advice
　　you offer!
4 With whose help have you
　　uttered those words,
　and whose is the breath that
　　comes forth from you?
5 The shades beneath writhe in
　　terror,
　the waters, and their
　　inhabitants.
6 Naked before him is the nether
　　world,
　and Abaddon has no covering.

7 He stretches out the North
　　over empty space,
　and suspends the earth over
　　nothing at all;
8 He binds up the waters in his
　　clouds,
　yet the cloud is not rent by
　　their weight;
9 He holds back the appearance
　　of the full moon
　by spreading his clouds before
　　it.

10 He has marked out a circle on
　　the surface of the deep
　as the boundary of light and
　　darkness.
11 The pillars of the heavens
　　tremble
　and are stunned at his
　　thunderous rebuke;
12 By his power he stirs up the
　　sea,
　and by his might he crushes
　　Rahab;
13 With his angry breath he
　　scatters the waters,

27 22 and he hurls the lightning
　　against them relentlessly;
　His hand pierces the fugitive
　　dragon
　as from his hand it strives to
　　flee.

(26) 14 Lo, these are but the
　　outlines of his ways,
　and how faint is the word we
　　hear!

Job's Reply

(27) 11 I will teach you the manner
　　of God's dealings,
　and the way of the Almighty
　　I will not conceal.
2 As God lives, who withholds
　　my deserts,
　the Almighty, who has made
　　bitter my soul,

24, 17: The asterisks which follow this verse mark
off a passage (vv 18–24) which cannot be ascribed to
Job with certainty. Vv 17–24 are in general poorly
preserved; and much of vv 18–21 has not been
translated because these verses are obscure. St.
Jerome renders them as follows: (18) "He is light
upon the face of the water, cursed be his portion on
the earth; let him not walk by the way of vineyards.
(19) Let him pass from the snow waters to excessive
heat, and his sin even to hell. (20) Let mercy forget
him; may worms be his sweetness; let him be remembered no more, but be broken in pieces as an
unfruitful tree. (21) For he has fed the barren that
bears not, and to the widow he has done no good."

25, 3: *His troops:* the heavenly hosts, the stars or
the angels. *His light:* compare the wording in 24, 13:
those who are rebels against the light.
26, 1–14: Probably to be read as Job's reply to
Bildad's short speech. Some, however, would make it
the reply to Zophar (27, 13–21); it would thus lead
up to the poem of ch 28.
26, 5: *Shades:* the dead in Sheol, the nether world;
cf Pss 6, 6; 88, 11.
26, 6: *Nether world:* cf note to Ps 6, 6. *Abaddon:*
Hebrew for "(place of) destruction," a synonym for
nether world; cf 28, 22; Rv 9, 11.
26, 7: *The North:* used here as a synonym for the
firmament, the heavens; cf Is 14, 13.

26, 10: *Circle:* the horizon of the ocean which
serves as the boundary for the activity of light and
darkness.
26, 12: *Rahab:* cf 9, 13; see note on Ps 89, 11.
27, 22: *The fugitive dragon:* the same term occurs
in Is 27, 1 in apposition to Leviathan; see note on
3, 8.
27, 2–12: This is probably to be read as
Job's reply to Zophar's speech of 27, 13–21. In the
current Hebrew text the heading for this chapter
(27, 1 here omitted) is identical with 29, 1; we
should expect rather such a heading as in 21, 1; 23, 1;
26, 1.

3 So long as I still have life in me
   and the breath of God is in
   my nostrils,
4 My lips shall not speak
   falsehood,
   nor my tongue utter deceit!
5 Far be it from me to account
   you right;
   till I die I will not renounce
   my innocence.
6 My justice I maintain and I will
   not relinquish it;
   my heart does not reproach
   me for any of my days.
7 Let my enemy be as the wicked
   and my adversary as the
   unjust!

8 For what can the impious man
   expect when he is cut off,
   when God requires his life?
9 Will God then attend to his cry
   when calamity comes upon
   him?
10 Will he then delight in the
   Almighty
   and call upon him constantly?
12 Behold, you yourselves have all
   seen it;
   why then do you spend
   yourselves in idle words!

* * *

13 This is the portion of a
   wicked man from God,
   the inheritance an oppressor
   receives from the Almighty:
14 Though his children be many,
   the sword is their destiny.
   His offspring shall not be
   filled with bread.
15 His survivors, when they die,
   shall have no burial,
   and their widows shall not be
   mourned.

16 Though he heap up silver like
   dust
   and store away mounds of
   clothing,
17 What he has stored the just
   man shall wear,
   and the innocent shall divide
   the silver.

18 He builds his house as of
   cobwebs,
   or like a booth put up by the
   vine-keeper.
19 He lies down a rich man, one
   last time;
   he opens his eyes and nothing
   remains to him.
20 Terrors rush upon him by day;
   at night the tempest carries
   him off.
21 The storm wind seizes him and
   he disappears;
   it sweeps him out of his place.

* * *

The Inaccessibility of Wisdom

28 There is indeed a mine for
   silver,
   and a place for gold which
   men refine.
2 Iron is taken from the earth,
   and copper is melted out of
   stone.
4 ....
5 The earth, though out of it
   comes forth bread,
   is in fiery upheaval
   underneath.
6 Its stones are the source of
   sapphires,
   and there is gold in its dust.

12 But whence can wisdom be
   obtained,
   and where is the place of
   understanding?
13 Man knows nothing to equal it,
   nor is it to be had in the land
   of the living.
15 Solid gold cannot purchase it,
   nor can its price be paid with
   silver.
16 It cannot be bought with gold of
   Ophir,
   with the precious onyx or the
   sapphire.
17 Gold or crystal cannot equal it,
   nor can golden vessels reach
   its worth.
18 Neither coral nor jasper should
   be thought of;

19 it surpasses pearls and
   Arabian topaz.
20 Whence, then, comes wisdom,
   and where is the place of
   understanding?
21 It is hid from the eyes of any
   beast;
   from the birds of the air it is
   concealed.
7 The path to it no bird of prey
   knows,
   nor has the hawk's eye seen
   that path.
8 The proud beasts have not
   trodden it,
   nor has the lion gone that
   way.
14 The abyss declares, "It is not
   in me";
   and the sea says, "I have it
   not."
22 Abaddon and Death say,
   "Only by rumor have we
   heard of it."
23 God knows the way to it;
   it is he who is familiar with
   its place.
24 For he beholds the ends of the
   earth
   and sees all that is under the
   heavens.
3 He has set a boundary for the
   darkness;
   to the farthest confines he
   penetrates.
9 He sets his hand to the flinty
   rock,
   and overturns the mountains
   at their foundations.
10 He splits channels in the rocks;
   his eyes behold all that is
   precious.
11 He probes the wellsprings of the
   streams,
   and brings hidden things to
   light.
25 He has weighed out the wind,
   and fixed the scope of the
   waters;
26 When he made rules for the
   rain
   and a path for the
   thunderbolts,

27, 13–21: This is probably to be read as Zophar's
third speech. The asterisks are present to indicate it
is not likely that the sacred writer intended these
words to be ascribed to Job.
   27, 21: The Hebrew has two more verses: v 22
(read above with 26, 13); and v 23, a variant form of
v 21.
   28, 1–28: Note the changed order of verses;

v 4 is uncertain.
   This chapter contains a beautifully vivid description
of that Wisdom which is beyond the attainment of
creatures; known only to God, it is reflected in the
order and majesty of his creation. Man, however, can,
in a way, participate in this Wisdom by fearing the
LORD and avoiding evil. Scholars are not agreed
regarding the authorship of this poem, though it is

altogether worthy of the author of the Book of Job.
Used here as a counterpoise to ch 3 at the beginning
of the dialogue, it may have been first conceived as an
independent poem.
   28, 16: *Ophir:* cf note to Ps 45, 10.
   28, 22: *Abaddon:* cf note to 26, 6.

27 Then he saw wisdom and
      appraised it,
   gave it its setting, knew it
      through and through.
28 And to man he said:
   Behold, the fear of the LORD
      is wisdom;
   and avoiding evil is under-
      standing.

JOB'S FINAL SUMMARY OF HIS CAUSE

29 Job took up his theme anew
   and said:

2 Oh, that I were as in the
      months past!
   as in the days when God
      watched over me,
3 While he kept his lamp shining
      above my head,
   and by his light I walked
      through darkness;
4 As I was in my flourishing days,
   when God sheltered my tent;

5 When the Almighty was yet
      with me,
   and my children were round
      about me;
6 When my footsteps were
      bathed in milk,
   and the rock flowed with
      streams of oil;
7 When I went forth to the gate
      of the city
   and set up my seat in the
      square—

8 Then the young men saw me
      and withdrew,
   while the elders rose up and
      stood;
9 The chief men refrained from
      speaking
   and covered their mouths
      with their hands;
10 The voice of the princes was
      silenced,
   and their tongues stuck to the
      roofs of their mouths.

21 For me they listened and
      waited;
   they were silent for my
      counsel.

22 Once I spoke, they said no
      more,
   but received my
      pronouncement drop by
      drop.
23 They waited for me as for the
      rain;
   they drank in my words like
      the spring rains.

24 When I smiled on them they
      were reassured;
25   mourners took comfort from
      my cheerful glance.
   I chose out their way and
      presided;
   I took a king's place in the
      armed forces.
11 Whoever heard of me blessed
      me;
   those who saw me
      commended me.

12 For I rescued the poor who
      cried out for help,
   the orphans, and the
      unassisted;
13 The blessing of those in
      extremity came upon me,
   and the heart of the widow I
      made joyful.
14 I wore my honesty like a
      garment;
   justice was my robe and my
      turban.

15 I was eyes to the blind,
   and feet to the lame was I;
16 I was a father to the needy;
   the rights of the stranger I
      studied,
17 And I broke the jaws of the
      wicked man;
   from his teeth I forced the
      prey.

18 Then I said: "In my own nest I
      shall grow old;
   I shall multiply years like the
      phoenix.
19 My root is spread out to the
      waters;
   the dew rests by night on
      my branches.
20 My glory is fresh within me,
   and my brow is renewed in
      my hand!"

30 But now they hold me in
      derision
   who are younger in years
      than I;
   Whose fathers I should have
      disdained
   to rank with the dogs of my
      flock.
2 Such strength as they had, to
      me meant nought;
   they were utterly destitute.

3 In want and hunger was their
      lot,
   they who fled to the parched
      wastelands:
4 They plucked saltwort and
      shrubs;
   the roots of the broom plant
      were their food.
5 They were banished from
      among men,
   with an outcry like that
      against a thief—

6 To dwell on the slopes of the
      wadies,
   in caves of sand and stone;
7 Among the bushes they raised
      their raucous cry;
   under the nettles they huddled
      together.
8 Irresponsible, nameless men,
   they were driven out of the
      land.

9 Yet now they sing of me in
      mockery;
   I am become a byword
      among them.
10 They abhor me, they stand
      aloof from me,
   they do not hesitate to spit
      in my face!
11 Indeed, they have loosed their
      bonds; they lord it over
      me,
   and have thrown off restraint
      in my presence.

12 To subvert my paths they rise
      up;
   they build their approaches
      for my ruin.
13 To destroy me, they attack with
      none to stay them;

29, 6: Hyperbole to express abundance; see note
on 20, 17.
  29, 18: *Phoenix:* a legendary bird which, after
several centuries of life, consumed itself in fire, then
rose from its ashes in youthful freshness. This mean-

ing, originally intended in the Greek, later came to
mean "palm tree." Some render the Hebrew as
"sand."
  30, 4: *Saltwort:* found in salt marshes and very
sour to the taste; eaten by the extremely poor as a

cooked vegetable. *Broom plant:* the juniper or
brushwood; cf Ps 120, 4; a figure of bitterness and
poverty, because of its bitter-tasting roots which are
practically inedible.

14 as through a wide breach
        they advance.
    Amid the uproar they come on
        in waves;
15 over me rolls the terror.

    My dignity is borne off on the
        wind,
        and my welfare vanishes like
        a cloud.
18 One with great power lays hold
        of my clothing;
        by the collar of my tunic he
        seizes me:
19 He has cast me into the mire;
        I am leveled with the dust
        and ashes.

20 I cry to you, but you do not
        answer me;
        you stand off and look at
        me,
2! Then you turn upon me without
        mercy
        and with your strong hand
        you buffet me.
22 You raise me up and drive me
        before the wind;
        I am tossed about by the
        tempest.

23 Indeed I know you will turn
        me back in death
        to the destined place of
        everyone alive.
24 Yet should not a hand be held
        out
        to help a wretched man in his
        calamity?
25 Or have I not wept for the
        hardships of others;
        was not my soul grieved for
        the destitute?
26 Yet when I looked for good,
        then evil came;
        when I expected light, then
        came darkness.

16 My soul ebbs away from me;
27   days of affliction have
        overtaken me.
17 My frame takes no rest by
        night;
        my inward parts seethe and
        will not be stilled.
28 I go about in gloom, without
        the sun;
        I rise up in public to voice
        my grief.

29 I have become the brother of
        jackals,
        companion to the ostrich.
30 My blackened skin falls away
        from me;
        the heat scorches my very
        frame.
31 My harp is turned to mourning,
        and my reed pipe to sounds
        of weeping.

31

2   But what is man's lot from
        God above,
        his inheritance from the
        Almighty on high?
3   Is it not calamity for the
        unrighteous,
        and woe for evildoers?
4   Does he not see my ways,
        and number all my steps?
6   Let God weigh me in the scales
        of justice;
        thus will he know my
        innocence!

5   If I have walked in falsehood
        and my foot has hastened to
        deceit;
7   If my steps have turned out of
        the way,
        and my heart has followed
        my eyes,
        or any stain clings to my
        hands,
8   Then may I sow, but another
        eat of it,
        or may my planting be rooted
        up!

38 If my land has cried out
        against me
        till its very furrows
        complained;
39 If I have eaten its produce
        without payment
        and grieved the hearts of its
        tenants;
40 Then let the thistles grow
        instead of wheat
        and noxious weeds instead of
        barley!

1   If I have made an agreement
        with my eyes
        and entertained any thoughts
        against a maiden;

9   If my heart has been enticed
        toward a woman,
        and I have lain in wait at my
        neighbor's door;
10 Then may my wife grind for
        another,
        and may others cohabit with
        her!

11 For that would be heinous,
        a crime to be condemned;
12 A fire that should burn down
        to the abyss
        till it consumed all my
        possessions to the roots.

13 Had I refused justice to my
        manservant
        or to my maid, when they
        had a claim against me,
14 What then should I do when
        God rose up;
        what could I answer when he
        demanded an account?
15 Did not he who made me in the
        womb make him?
        Did not the same One fashion
        us before our birth?

16 If I have denied anything to the
        poor,
        or allowed the eyes of the
        widow to languish
17 While I ate my portion alone,
        with no share in it for the
        fatherless,
18 Though like a father God has
        reared me from my youth,
        guiding me even from my
        mother's womb—
19 If I have seen a wanderer
        without clothing,
        or a poor man without
        covering,
20 Whose limbs have not blessed
        me
        when warmed with the fleece
        of my sheep;
21 If I have raised my hand
        against the innocent
        because I saw that I had
        supporters at the gate—
22 Then may my arm fall from the
        shoulder,
        my forearm be broken at the
        elbow!

30, 18–23: Job here refers to God's stern treatment
of him.
    31, 5–34: Job's final protestation of his innocence.

31, 1.9: Note the gradation: avoidance of sinful
glances and thoughts against a maiden; desire for
another's wife.

31, 21: *Gate:* cf notes on Jb 5, 4; Ru 4, 1.

23 For the dread of God will be
     upon me,
     and his majesty will
     overpower me.

24 Had I put my trust in gold
     or called fine gold my security;
25 Or had I rejoiced that my
     wealth was great,
     or that my hand had acquired
     abundance—

26 Had I looked upon the sun as
     it shone,
     or the moon in the splendor
     of its progress,
27 And had my heart been secretly
     enticed
     to waft them a kiss with my
     hand;
28 This too would be a crime for
     condemnation,
     for I should have denied God
     above.

29 Had I rejoiced at the destruction
     of my enemy
     or exulted when evil fell
     upon him,
30 Even though I had not suffered
     my mouth to sin
     by uttering a curse against
     his life—

31 Had not the men of my tent
     exclaimed,
     "Who has not been fed with
     his meat!"
32 Because no stranger lodged in
     the street,
     but I opened my door to
     wayfarers—

33 Had I, out of human weakness,
     hidden my sins
     and buried my guilt in my
     bosom
34 Because I feared the noisy
     multitude
     and the scorn of the tribes
     terrified me—
     then I should have remained
     silent, and not come out of
     doors!

35 Oh, that I had one to hear my
     case,
     and that my accuser would
     write out his indictment!
36 Surely, I should wear it on my
     shoulder
     or put it on me like a
     diadem;
37 Of all my steps I should give
     him an account;
     like a prince I should present
     myself before him.

This is my final plea; let the
Almighty answer me!

The words of Job are ended.

ELIHU'S SPEECHES

32 Then the three men ceased to
answer Job, because he was
righteous in his own eyes. 2 But
the anger of Elihu, son of Barachel
the Buzite, of the family of Ram,
was kindled. He was angry with Job
for considering himself rather than
God to be in the right. 3 He was
angry also with the three friends
because they had not found a good
answer and had not condemned
Job. 4 But since these men were
older than he, Elihu bided his time
before addressing Job. 5 When,
however, Elihu saw that there was no
reply in the mouths of the three
men, his wrath was inflamed. 6 So
Elihu, son of Barachel the Buzite,
spoke out and said:

I am young and you are very
     old;
     therefore I held back and was
     afraid
     to declare to you my
     knowledge.
7 Days should speak, I thought,
     and many years teach
     wisdom!
8 But it is a spirit in man,
     the breath of the Almighty,
     that gives him
     understanding.

9 It is not those of many days
     who are wise,
     nor the aged who understand
     the right.
10 Therefore I say, hearken to me;
     let me too set forth my
     knowledge!

11 Behold, I have waited for your
     discourses,
     and have given ear to your
     arguments.
12 Yes, I followed you attentively
     as you searched out what to
     say;
     And behold, there is none who
     has convicted Job,
     not one of you who could
     refute his statements.
13 Yet do not say, "We have met
     wisdom.
     God may vanquish him but
     not man!"
14 For had he addressed his words
     to me,
     I should not then have
     answered him as you have
     done.

15 They are dismayed, they make
     no more reply;
     words fail them.
16 Must I wait? Now that they
     speak no more,
     and have ceased to make
     reply,
17 I too will speak my part;
     I also will show my
     knowledge!

18 For I am full of matters to
     utter;
     the spirit within me compels
     me.
19 Like a new wineskin with wine
     under pressure,
     my bosom is ready to burst.
20 Let me speak and obtain
     relief;
     let me open my lips, and
     make reply.
21 I would not be partial to
     anyone,
     nor give flattering titles to any.

31, 26ff: Job never sinned by worshiping the sun
or the moon; *waft them a kiss:* an act of idolatrous
worship.
31, 31: The members of his household will testify
to his hospitality.
31, 33f: Job's present protest is made, not in spite
of hidden sins which he had been unwilling to disclose, but out of genuine innocence.
31, 36: *On my shoulder:* i.e., boldly, proudly.

31, 37: *Like a prince:* not as a frightened criminal.
Final plea: literally, "tau," the last letter of the
Hebrew alphabet; in the current Hebrew text this
line is in v 35, while the following one ends v 40.
32, 2: *Elihu* means "My God is he." This speaker
was from Buz, which, according to Jer 25, 23, was
near Tema and Dedan. A young man, he impetuously
and impatiently upbraids Job for his boldness toward God, and the three friends for not successfully

answering Job. He undertakes to defend God's
absolute justice and to explain more clearly why
there is suffering. While fundamentally his position is
the same as that of the three friends, he does locate
more definitely, though not perfectly, the place of
suffering in the divine plan.
32, 13: *Met wisdom:* in Job's arguments.

22 For I know nought of flattery;
　　if I did, my Maker would
　　　soon take me away.

33

Therefore, O Job, hear my
　　discourse,
　and hearken to all my words.
2 Behold, now I open my mouth;
　　my tongue and my voice
　　　form words.
3 I will state directly what is in
　　my mind,
　　my lips shall utter knowledge
　　　sincerely;
4 For the spirit of God has made
　　me,
　the breath of the Almighty
　　keeps me alive.

5 If you are able, refute me;
　　draw up your arguments and
　　　stand forth.
6 Behold I, like yourself, have
　　been taken
　from the same clay by God.
7 Therefore no fear of me should
　　dismay you,
　nor should my presence weigh
　　heavily upon you.

8 But you have said in my
　　hearing,
　as I listened to the sound of
　　your words:
9 "I am clean and without
　　transgression;
　I am innocent; there is no
　　guilt in me.
10 Yet he invents pretexts against
　　me
　and reckons me as his enemy.
11 He puts my feet in the stocks;
　　he watches all my ways!"

12 In this you are not just, let me
　　tell you;
　for God is greater than man.
13 Why, then, do you make
　　complaint against him
　that he gives no account of
　　his doings?
14 For God does speak, perhaps
　　once,
　or even twice, though one
　　perceive it not.

15 In a dream, in a vision of the
　　night,
　[when deep sleep falls upon
　　men]
　　as they slumber in their beds,
16 It is then he opens the ears of
　　men
　and as a warning to them,
　　terrifies them;
17 By turning man from evil
　　and keeping pride away from
　　him,
18 He withholds his soul from the
　　pit
　and his life from passing to
　　the grave.

19 Or a man is chastened on his
　　bed by pain
　and unceasing suffering within
　　his frame,
20 So that to his appetite food
　　becomes repulsive,
　and his senses reject the
　　choicest nourishment.
21 His flesh is wasted so that it
　　cannot be seen,
　and his bones, once invisible,
　　appear;
22 His soul draws near to the pit,
　　his life to the place of the
　　　dead.

23 If then there be for him an
　　angel,
　one out of a thousand, a
　　mediator,
　To show him what is right for
　　him
　and bring the man back to
　　justice,
24 He will take pity on him and
　　say,
　"Deliver him from going
　　down to the pit;
　I have found him a ransom."

25 Then his flesh shall become soft
　　as a boy's;
　he shall be again as in the
　　days of his youth.
26 He shall pray and God will
　　favor him;
　he shall see God's face with
　　rejoicing.
27 He shall sing before men and
　　say,
　"I sinned and did wrong,
　yet he has not punished me
　　accordingly.

28 He delivered my soul from
　　passing to the pit,
　and I behold the light of life."
29 Lo, all these things God does,
　　twice, or thrice, for a man,
30 Bringing back his soul from the
　　pit
　to the light, in the land of the
　　living.
31 Be attentive, O Job; listen to me!
　　Be silent and I will speak.
32 If you have aught to say,
　　then answer me.
　Speak out! I should like to
　　see you justified.
33 If not, then do you listen to me;
　　be silent while I teach you
　　　wisdom.

34

Then Elihu continued and
　said:

2 Hear, O wise men, my discourse,
　　and you that have knowledge,
　　　hear me!
3 For the ear tests words,
　　as the taste does food.
4 Let us discern for ourselves
　　what is right;
　let us learn between us
　　what is good.
5 For Job has said, "I am
　　innocent,
　but God has taken what is
　　my due.
6 Notwithstanding my right I am
　　set at nought;
　in my wound the arrow
　　rankles, sinless though I
　　　am."

7 What man is like Job?
　　He drinks in blasphemies
　　　like water,
8 Keeps company with evildoers
　　and goes along with wicked
　　　men,
9 When he says, "It profits a man
　　nought
　that he is pleasing to God."

10 Therefore, men of understanding,
　　hearken to me:
　far be it from God to do
　　wickedness;
　far from the Almighty to do
　　wrong!
11 Rather, he requites men for
　　their conduct,
　and brings home to a man his
　　way of life.

33, 23: *Angel:* one of the thousands who stand
between God and man as intermediaries, reminding
man of his duties and giving God an account of their
fulfillment.

12 Surely, God cannot act
        wickedly,
    the Almighty cannot violate
        justice.
13 Who gave him government
        over the earth,
    or who set all the land
        in its place?
14 If he were to take back his
        spirit to himself,
    withdraw to himself his
        breath,
15 All flesh would perish together,
    and man would return to
        the dust.

16 Now, do you, O Job, hear this!
    Hearken to the words I speak!
17 Can an enemy of justice indeed
        be in control,
    or will you condemn the
        supreme Just One,
18 Who says to a king, "You
        are worthless!"
    and to nobles, "You are
        wicked!"
19 Who neither favors the person
        of princes,
    nor respects the rich more
        than the poor?
    For they are all the work of
        his hands:
20 in a moment they die, even
        at midnight.
    He brings on nobles, and takes
        them away,
    removing the powerful
        without lifting a hand;
21 For his eyes are upon the ways
        of man,
    and he beholds all his steps.

22 There is no darkness so dense
    that evildoers can hide in it.
25 Therefore he discerns their
        works;
    he turns at night and
        crushes them.
23 For he forewarns no man of
        his time
    to come before God in
        judgment.
24 Without a trial he breaks the
        mighty,
    and sets others in their stead,

27 Because they turned away from
        him
    and heeded none of his ways,
28 But caused the cries of the poor
        to reach him,
    so that he heard the plea
        of the afflicted.
29 If he remains tranquil, who then
        can condemn?
    If he hides his face, who then
        can behold him?
30 . . . .
31 When anyone says to God,
    "I was misguided; I will offend
        no more.
32 Teach me wherein I have sinned;
    if I have done wrong, I will
        do so no more,"
33 Would you then say that God
        must punish,
    since you reject what he is
        doing?
    It is you who must choose,
        not I;
    speak, therefore, what you
        know.

34 Men of understanding will say
        to me,
    every wise man who hears
        my views:
35 "Job speaks without intelligence,
    and his words are without
        sense."
36 Let Job be tried to the limit,
    and since his answers are
        those of the impious;
37 For he is adding rebellion to
        his sin
    by brushing off our arguments
    and addressing many words
        to God.

35 Then Elihu proceeded and
        said:

2 Do you think it right to say,
    "I am just rather than God?"
3 To say, "What does it profit me;
    what advantage have I more
        than if I had sinned?"
4 I have words for a reply to you
    and your three companions
        as well.

5 Look up to the skies and behold;
    regard the heavens high
        above you.
6 If you sin, what injury do you
        do to God?
    Even if your offenses are
        many, how do you hurt him?
7 If you are righteous, what do
        you give him,
    or what does he receive from
        your hand?
8 Your wickedness can affect only
        a man like yourself;
    and your justice only a fellow
        human being.

9 In great oppression men cry out;
    they call for help because of
        the power of the mighty,
10 Saying, "Where is God, my
        Maker,
    who has given visions in the
        night,
11 Taught us rather than the beasts
        of the earth,
    and made us wise rather than
        the birds of the heavens?"
12 Though thus they cry out,
    he answers not
    against the pride of the wicked.

13 But it is idle to say God does
        not hear
    or that the Almighty does not
        take notice.
14 Even though you say that you
        see him not,
    the case is before him; with
        trembling you should wait
        upon him.
15 But now that you have done
        otherwise, God's anger
        punishes,
    nor does he show concern
        that a man will die.
16 Yet Job to no purpose opens
        his mouth,
    and without knowledge
        multiplies words.

36 Elihu proceeded further and
        said:

2 Wait yet a little and I will
        instruct you,
    for there are still words to be
        said on God's behalf.

34, 26.29f: The extant Hebrew text of these verses
contains several added phrases which either represent
duplication or are very obscure.

35, 4: *A reply to you:* Elihu refers to Job's state-

ment that the innocent suffer as much as the wicked,
and especially to Eliphaz's words in 22, 2f.

35, 14f: The text here is uncertain. It seems to
indicate that Job should have realized God's in-

difference is only apparent, and that, because he has
not done so, God will punish him.

3 I will bring my knowledge
    from afar,
    and to my Maker I will
    accord the right.
4 For indeed, my theme cannot
    fail me:
    the one perfect in knowledge
    I set before you.

5 Behold, God rejects the
    obstinate in heart;
    he preserves not the life of
    the wicked.
6 He withholds not the just
    man's rights,
    but grants vindication to
    the oppressed,
7 And with kings upon thrones
    he sets them, exalted forever.

8 Or if they are bound with fetters
    and held fast with bonds of
    affliction,
9 Then he makes known to them
    what they have done
    and their sins of boastful
    pride.
10 He opens their ears to correction
    and exhorts them to turn
    back from evil.

11 If they obey and serve him,
    they spend their days in
    prosperity,
    their years in happiness.
12 But if they obey not, they perish;
    they die for lack of knowledge.

13 The impious in heart lay up
    anger for themselves;
    they cry not for help when
    he enchains them;
14 Therefore they expire in youth,
    and perish among the
    reprobate.
15 But he saves the unfortunate
    through their affliction,
    and instructs them through
    distress.
16–20 . . . .
21 Take heed, turn not to evil;
    for you have preferred
    carousal to affliction.

22 Behold, God is sublime in his
    power.
    What teacher is there like
    him?
23 Who prescribes for him his
    conduct,
    or who can say, "You have
    done wrong"?
24 Remember, you should extol
    his work,
    which men have praised
    in song.
25 All men contemplate it;
    man beholds it from afar.

26 Lo, God is great beyond our
    knowledge;
    the number of his years is
    past searching out.
27 He holds in check the
    waterdrops
    that filter in rain through
    his mists,
28 Till the skies run with them
    and the showers rain down
    on mankind.
31 For by these he nourishes the
    nations,
    and gives them food in
    abundance.

29.30 Lo! he spreads the clouds
    in layers
    as the carpeting of his tent.
32 In his hands he holds the
    lightning,
    and he commands it to strike
    the mark.
33 His thunder speaks for him
    and incites the fury of the
    storm.

37 At this my heart trembles
    and leaps out of its place,
2 To hear his angry voice
    as it rumbles forth from his
    mouth!
3 Everywhere under the heavens
    he sends it,
    with his lightning, to the
    ends of the earth.

4 Again his voice roars—
    the majestic sound of his
    thunder.

5 He does great things beyond
    our knowing;
    wonders past our searching
    out.
6 For he says to the snow, "Fall
    to the earth";
    likewise to his heavy,
    drenching rain.
7 He shuts up all mankind indoors;
8   the wild beasts take to cover
    and remain quietly in their
    dens.

9 Out of its chamber comes forth
    the tempest;
    from the north winds, the cold.
10 With his breath God brings
    the frost,
    and the broad waters become
    congealed.
11 With hail, also, the clouds are
    laden,
    as they scatter their flashes
    of light.
12 He it is who changes their
    rounds, according to his
    plans,
    in their task upon the surface
    of the earth,
13   whether for punishment or
    mercy, as he commands.

14 Hearken to this, O Job!
    Stand and consider the
    wondrous works of God!
15 Do you know how God lays his
    commands upon them,
    and makes the light shine
    forth from his clouds?
16 Do you know how the clouds
    are banked,
    the wondrous work of him
    who is perfect in knowledge?
17 You, whom the streams of
    water fail
    when a calm from the south
    comes over the land,

36, 5–21: Perhaps this section should be read between vv 6 and 7 of chapter 34.
36, 12: *Knowledge:* practical wisdom in serving
God, which they lack because they refused it when
warned (cf v 10).
36, 14: *Reprobate:* cf Dt 23, 18f.
36, 16–20: The Hebrew text here is in disorder. The
Vulgate has: "(16) Therefore he will give you most
ample salvation from the narrow mouth which has no
foundation beneath it; but the repose of your table

will be filled with fatness. (17) Your case has been
judged as that of the wicked; case and judgment you
will receive. (18) Let no wrath, then, overcome you,
that you oppress anyone; nor let numerous gifts mislead you. (19) Lay down your greatness without tribulation, and all who are mighty in strength. (20) Do not
draw out the night, that people may go in place of
them."
36, 31: *These:* refers to *the showers* of v 28, if the
verse order indicated above is correct.

36, 29f: Because of the uncertainty of the text, no
translation of these verses has received unanimous
approval from exegetes.
37, 2: *Voice:* the thunder.
37, 9: *Chamber:* where it was popularly believed
storms were kept enclosed.
37, 12: *Their rounds:* of rain (36, 27), of *clouds*
(36, 29f), of *lightning* and *thunder* (36, 32f), of *snow*
(37, 6), of *winds* (37, 9).

18 Do you spread out with him
        the firmament of the skies,
    hard as a brazen mirror?
19 Teach us then what we shall
        say to him;
    we cannot, for the darkness,
        make our plea.
20 Will he be told about it when
        I speak,
    or when a man says he is
        being destroyed?
21 Nay, rather, it is as the light
        which men see not
    while it is obscured among
        the clouds,
    till the wind comes by and
        sweeps the clouds away.

22 From the North the splendor
        comes,
    surrounding God's awesome
        majesty!
23 The Almighty! we cannot
        discover him,
    pre-eminent in power and
        judgment;
    his great justice owes no one
        an accounting.
24 Therefore men revere him,
    though none can see him,
    however wise their hearts.

THE LORD'S SPEECH

38 Then the LORD addressed Job
    out of the storm and said:

2 Who is this that obscures divine
        plans
    with words of ignorance?
3 Gird up your loins now, like a
        man;
    I will question you, and you
        tell me the answers!

4 Where were you when I founded
        the earth?
    Tell me, if you have
        understanding.
5 Who determined its size;
        do you know?
    Who stretched out the
        measuring line for it?

6 Into what were its pedestals
        sunk,
    and who laid the cornerstone,
7 While the morning stars sang in
        chorus
    and all the sons of God
        shouted for joy.

8 And who shut within doors
        the sea,
    when it burst forth from the
        womb;
9 When I made the clouds its
        garment
    and thick darkness its
        swaddling bands?
10 When I set limits for it
    and fastened the bar of its
        door,
11 And said: Thus far shall you
        come but no farther,
    and here shall your proud
        waves be stilled!

12 Have you ever in your lifetime
        commanded the morning
    and shown the dawn its place
13 For taking hold of the ends
        of the earth,
    till the wicked are shaken
        from its surface?
14 The earth is changed as is clay
        by the seal,
    and dyed as though it were
        a garment;
15 But from the wicked the light
        is withheld,
    and the arm of pride is
        shattered.

16 Have you entered into the
        sources of the sea,
    or walked in the depths
        of the abyss?
17 Have the gates of death been
        shown to you,
    or have you seen the gates
        of darkness?
18 Have you comprehended the
        breadth of the earth?
    Tell me, if you know all:

19 Which is the way to the
        dwelling place of light,
    and where is the abode of
        darkness,
20 That you may take them to
        their boundaries
    and set them on their
        homeward paths?
21 You know, because you were
        born before them,
    and the number of your years
        is great!

22 Have you entered the storehouse
        of the snow,
    and seen the treasury of the
        hail
23 Which I have reserved for times
        of stress,
    for the days of war and of
        battle?
24 Which way to the parting of
        the winds,
    whence the east wind spreads
        over the earth?

25 Who has laid out a channel
        for the downpour
    and for the thunderstorm
        a path
26 To bring rain to no man's land,
    the unpeopled wilderness;
27 To enrich the waste and desolate
        ground
    till the desert blooms with
        verdure?

28 Has the rain a father;
    or who has begotten the
        drops of dew?
29 Out of whose womb comes the
        ice,
    and who gives the hoarfrost
        its birth in the skies,
30 When the waters lie covered as
        though with stone
    that holds captive the surface
        of the deep?

31 Have you fitted a curb to the
        Pleiades,
    or loosened the bonds of
        Orion?

37, 18: *The firmament ... mirror:* the ancients thought of the sky as a ceiling above which were the "upper waters" (cf Gn 1, 6f; 7, 11); when this ceiling became as hard as metal, the usual rain failed to fall on the earth (cf Lv 26, 19; Dt 28, 23).

37, 20: Will an angel bring this to God's attention?

37, 21: Even though God seems not to know our circumstances, he does know them, just as surely as the sun shines, unseen by man, behind the clouds.

37, 22: Now the storms of doubt and ignorance

disappear, and *from the North*, used here as a symbol for God's mysterious abode, comes the *splendor* of the manifestation of God's majestic ways.

38, 1: Now the LORD enters the debate and addresses two discourses (38—39 and 40—41) to Job, in which he speaks of his wisdom and power, which are altogether beyond the capacity of Job, who therefore should never dare to demand a reason for the divine actions. *Out of the storm:* frequently the background of the appearances of the LORD in the Old Testament; cf Pss 18; 50; Na 1, 3; Hb 3.

38, 3: *Gird up your loins:* prepare for combat—figuratively, be ready to defend yourself in debate.

38, 7: *Sons of God:* angels; cf 1, 6.

38, 21: Divine irony.

38, 22f: *Hail ... of war:* thus God used a hailstorm to rout Joshua's foes in the battle of Gibeon; cf Jos 10, 11; Sir 46, 5.

38, 31f: *Pleiades ... Orion ... Bear:* cf 9, 9. *Mazzaroth:* It is uncertain what astronomical group is meant by this Hebrew word; perhaps a southern constellation (cf 9, 9).

32 Can you bring forth the
Mazzaroth in their season,
or guide the Bear with its
train?
33 Do you know the ordinances
of the heavens;
can you put into effect their
plan on the earth?

34 Can you raise your voice
among the clouds,
or veil yourself in the waters
of the storm?
35 Can you send forth the
lightnings on their way,
or will they say to you,
"Here we are"?
37 Who counts the clouds in his
wisdom?
Or who tilts the water jars
of heaven
38 So that the dust of earth is
fused into a mass
and its clods made solid?

39 Do you hunt the prey for the
lioness
or appease the hunger of
her cubs,
40 While they crouch in their dens,
or lie in wait in the thicket?
36 Who puts wisdom in the heart,
and gives the cock its
understanding?
41 Who provides nourishment for
the ravens
when their young ones cry
out to God,
and they rove abroad
without food?

39 Do you know about the
birth of the mountain goats,
watch for the birth pangs
of the hinds,
2 Number the months that they
must fulfill,
and fix the time of their
bringing forth?
3 They crouch down and bear
their young;
they deliver their progeny
in the desert.
4 When their offspring thrive
and grow,
they leave and do not return.

5 Who has given the wild ass
his freedom,
and who has loosed him
from bonds?
6 I have made the wilderness
his home
and the salt flats his dwelling.
7 He scoffs at the uproar of the
city.
and hears no shouts of a
driver.
8 He ranges the mountains for
pasture,
and seeks out every patch
of green.

9 Will the wild ox consent to
serve you,
and to pass the nights by
your manger?
10 Will a rope bind him in the
furrow,
and will he harrow the
valleys after you?
11 Will you trust him for his
great strength
and leave to him the fruits
of your toil?
12 Can you rely on him to thresh
out your grain
and gather in the yield of
your threshing floor?

13 The wings of the ostrich beat idly;
her plumage is lacking in
pinions.
14 When she leaves her eggs on
the ground
and deposits them in the sand,
15 Unmindful that a foot may
crush them,
that the wild beasts may
trample them,
16 She cruelly disowns her young
and ruthlessly makes nought
of her brood;
17 For God has withheld wisdom
from her
and has given her no share
in understanding
18 Yet in her swiftness of foot
she makes sport of the horse
and his rider.

19 Do you give the horse his
strength,
and endow his neck with
splendor?

20 Do you make the steed to quiver
while his thunderous
snorting spreads terror?
21 He jubilantly paws the plain
and rushes in his might
against the weapons.
22 He laughs at fear and cannot
be deterred;
he turns not back from the
sword.
23 Around him rattles the quiver,
flashes the spear and the
javelin.
24 Frenzied and trembling he
devours the ground;
he holds not back at the
sound of the trumpet,
25 but at each blast he cries
"Aha!"
Even from afar he scents the
battle,
the roar of the chiefs and the
shouting.

26 Is it by your discernment that
the hawk soars,
that he spreads his wings
toward the south?
27 Does the eagle fly up at your
command
to build his nest aloft?
28 On the cliff he dwells and
spends the night,
on a spur of the cliff or the
fortress.
29 From thence he watches for his
prey;
his eyes behold it afar off.
30 His young ones greedily drink
the blood;
where the slain are, there is he.

40 The LORD then said to Job:

2 Will we have arguing with the
Almighty by the critic?
Let him who would correct
God give answer!

3 Then Job answered the LORD and
said:

4 Behold, I am of little account;
what can I answer you?
I put my hand over my
mouth.

38, 34: *Veil yourself . . . storm:* wrap yourself in a cloud, as God comes in a theophany; cf Ps 18, 12.
38, 35: *Here we are:* at your service.
38, 36: *Understanding:* the reflection of divine

Wisdom discernible in the created animal instincts of the *cock.*
39, 13: *The wings of the ostrich* cannot raise her from the ground, but they help her to run swiftly.

39, 14ff: It was popularly believed that, because the ostrich laid her eggs on the sand, she was thereby cruelly abandoning them; cf Lam 4, 3.
39, 19–25: The famous description of a war horse.

5 Though I have spoken once, I
     will not do so again;
   though twice, I will do so no
     more.

6 Then the LORD addressed Job out
of the storm and said:

7 Gird up your loins now, like
     a man.
   I will question you, and you
     tell me the answers!
8 Would you refuse to
     acknowledge my right?
   Would you condemn me that
     you may be justified?

9 Have you an arm like that of
     God,
   or can you thunder in a voice
     like his?
10 Adorn yourself with grandeur
     and majesty,
   and array yourself with glory
     and splendor.
11 Let loose the fury of your wrath;
12   tear down the wicked and
     shatter them.
   Bring down the haughty with a
     glance;
13   bury them in the dust together;
   in the hidden world imprison
     them.
14 Then will I too acknowledge
   that your own right hand can
     save you.

15 See, beside you I made
     Behemoth,
   that feeds on grass like an ox.
16 Behold the strength in his loins,
   and his vigor in the sinews of
     his belly.
17 He carries his tail like a cedar;
   the sinews of his thighs are
     like cables.
18 His bones are like tubes of
     bronze;
   his frame is like iron rods.
19 He came at the beginning of
     God's ways,
   and was made the taskmaster
     of his fellows;
20 For the produce of the
     mountains is brought to him,
   and of all wild animals he
     makes sport.

21 Under the lotus trees he lies,
   in coverts of the reedy swamp.
22 The lotus trees cover him with
     their shade;
   all about him are the poplars
     on the bank.
23 If the river grows violent, he is
     not disturbed;
   he is tranquil though the
     torrent surges about his
     mouth.
24 Who can capture him by his eyes
   or pierce his nose with a trap?

25 Can you lead about Leviathan
     with a hook,
   or curb his tongue with a bit?
26 Can you put a rope into his
     nose,
   or pierce through his cheek
     with a gaff?
27 Will he then plead with you,
     time after time,
   or address you with tender
     words?
28 Will he make an agreement
     with you
   that you may have him as a
     slave forever?
29 Can you play with him, as with
     a bird?
   Can you put him in leash for
     your maidens?
30 Will the traders bargain for him?
   Will the merchants divide
     him up?

31 Can you fill his hide with barbs,
   or his head with fish spears?
32 Once you but lay a hand upon
     him,
   no need to recall any other
     conflict!

41
   2 Is he not relentless when
     aroused;
   who then dares stand before
     him?
1 Whoever might vainly hope to do
     so
   need only see him to be
     overthrown.
3 Who has assailed him and come
     off safe—
   Who under all the heavens?

4 I need hardly mention his limbs,
   his strength, and the fitness of
     his armor.
5 Who can strip off his outer
     garment,
   or penetrate his double
     corselet?
6 Who can force open the doors
     of his mouth,
   close to his terrible teeth?
7 Rows of scales are on his back,
   tightly sealed together;
8 They are fitted each so close to
     the next
   that no space intervenes;
9 So joined to one another
   that they hold fast and cannot
     be parted.

10 When he sneezes, light flashes
     forth;
   his eyes are like those of the
     dawn.
11 Out of his mouth go forth
     firebrands;
   sparks of fire leap forth.
12 From his nostrils issues steam,
   as from a seething pot or bowl.
13 His breath sets coals afire;
   a flame pours from his mouth.
14 Strength abides in his neck,
   and terror leaps before him.
15.16 His heart is hard as stone;
   his flesh, as the lower
     millstone.
17 When he rises up, the mighty
     are afraid;
   the waves of the sea fall back.
18 Should the sword reach him,
     it will not avail;
   nor will the spear, nor the dart,
     nor the javelin.
19 He regards iron as straw,
   and bronze as rotten wood.
20 The arrow will not put him to
     flight;
   slingstones used against him
     are but straws.
21 Clubs he esteems as splinters;
   and he laughs at the crash of
     the spear.

22 His belly is sharp as pottery
     fragments;
   he spreads like a threshing
     sledge upon the mire.

40, 15: *Behemoth:* the hippopotamus.
40, 24: *Eyes . . . nose:* the only exposed parts of the submerged beast.
40, 25: *Leviathan* here is the crocodile. But cf 3, 8.

40, 30: *Merchants:* literally, "Canaanites," whose reputation for trading was so widespread that their name came to be used for merchants; cf Prv 31, 24. The meaning of this verse is that the crocodile is too

---

powerful a creature to be sold like common fish.
41, 2: *Before him:* some read, "before me," i.e., God; also in v 3.
41, 17: The text here is uncertain.

23 He makes the depths boil like a
   pot;
   the sea he churns like perfume
   in a kettle.
24 Behind him he leaves a shining
   path;
   you would think the deep had
   the hoary head of age.
25 Upon the earth there is not his
   like,
   intrepid he was made.
26 All, however lofty, fear him;
   he is king over all proud
   beasts.

42 Then Job answered the LORD
   and said:

2 I know that you can do all
   things,
   and that no purpose of yours
   can be hindered.
3 I have dealt with great things
   that I do not understand;
   things too wonderful for me,
   which I cannot know.
5 I had heard of you by word of
   mouth,
   but now my eye has seen you.

6 Therefore I disown what I have
   said,
   and repent in dust and ashes.

EPILOGUE

Job's Restoration

7 And it came to pass after the
LORD had spoken these words to Job,
that the LORD said to Eliphaz the
Temanite, "I am angry with you and
with your two friends; for you have
not spoken rightly concerning me, as
has my servant Job. 8 Now, therefore, take seven bullocks and seven
rams, and go to my servant Job, and
offer up a holocaust for yourselves;
and let my servant Job pray for you;
for his prayer I will accept, not to
punish you severely. For you have
not spoken rightly concerning me, as
has my servant Job." 9 Then Eliphaz the Temanite, and Bildad the
Shuhite, and Zophar the Naamathite,
went and did as the LORD had commanded them. And the LORD accepted the intercession of Job.

10 Also, the LORD restored the
prosperity of Job, after he had

prayed for his friends; the LORD even
gave to Job twice as much as he had
before. 11 Then all his brethren
and sisters came to him, and all his
former acquaintances, and they dined
with him in his house. They condoled
with him and comforted him for all
the evil which the LORD had brought
upon him; and each one gave him a
piece of money and a gold ring.

12 Thus the LORD blessed the
latter days of Job more than his
earlier ones. For he had fourteen
thousand sheep, six thousand camels,
a thousand yoke of oxen, and a thousand she-asses. 13 And he had
seven sons and three daughters,
14 of whom he called the first
Jemimah, the second Keziah, and
the third Keren-happuch. 15 In all
the land no other women were as
beautiful as the daughters of Job;
and their father gave them an inheritance among their brethren.
16 After this, Job lived a hundred
and forty years; and he saw his
children, his grandchildren, and even
his great-grandchildren. 17 Then
Job died, old and full of years.

42, 2–6: In the current Hebrew text, this final
utterance of Job is interrupted by words ascribed to
God (vv 3f) which are in large part a duplication of
38, 2f.
   42, 7: The three friends of Job (Elihu is ignored in
the Epilogue) are criticized by the LORD because they
had (even though in good faith) leveled false charges
against him.
   42, 8: Job becomes the intercessor for his friends,

as were other great Old Testament characters, e.g.,
Abraham and Moses, and as our Lord would be,
whom he prefigured. *Seven:* a symbolic number.
   42, 11: *A piece of money:* the term is the same as
that used in Gn 33, 19; Jos 24, 32. *Gold ring:* for the
nose or ear.
   42, 14: Job's daughters had names symbolic of
their charms: *Jemimah,* dove; *Keziah,* precious perfume (cf Ps 45, 9); *Keren-happuch,* cosmetic jar—more

precisely, a container for a black powder that was used
like modern mascara.
   42, 15: Ordinarily daughters did not inherit
property unless there were no sons; cf Nm 27,
1–11.
   42, 16: As his other rewards were *twice as much as
he had before* (v 10), so Job's *hundred and forty years*
were double the expected span of human life; cf Ps
90, 10.

THE Psalms

THE FIRST BOOK—*Psalms 1–41*

PSALM 1

True Happiness

HAPPY the man who follows not the counsel of the wicked Nor walks in the way of sinners, nor sits in the company of the insolent, 2 But delights in the law of the LORD and meditates on his law day and night. 3 He is like a tree planted near running water, That

yields its fruit in due season,
    and whose leaves never fade.
    [Whatever he does, prospers.]

II

4 Not so the wicked, not so;
    they are like chaff which the
    wind drives away.
5 Therefore in judgment the
    wicked shall not stand,
    nor shall sinners, in the
    assembly of the just.
6 For the LORD watches over the
    way of the just,
    but the way of the wicked
    vanishes.

PSALM 2

*The Universal Reign of the
Messiah*

I

1 Why do the nations rage
    and the peoples utter folly?

2 The kings of the earth rise up,
    and the princes conspire
    together
    against the LORD and against
    his anointed:
3 "Let us break their fetters
    and cast their bonds from us!"

II

4 He who is throned in heaven
    laughs;
    the LORD derides them.
5 Then in anger he speaks to them;
    he terrifies them in his wrath:
6 "I myself have set up my king
    on Zion, my holy mountain."

III

7 I will proclaim the decree of the
    LORD:
    The LORD said to me, "You
    are my son;
    this day I have begotten you.

8 Ask of me and I will give you
    the nations for an inheritance
    and the ends of the earth for
    your possession.
9 You shall rule them with an
    iron rod;
    you shall shatter them like an
    earthen dish."

IV

10 And now, O kings, give heed;
    take warning you rulers of the
    earth.
11 Serve the LORD with fear, and
    rejoice before him;
    with trembling 12 pay homage
    to him,
    Lest he be angry and you perish
    from the way,
    when his anger blazes
    suddenly.
    Happy are all who take
    refuge in him!

Ps 1: A preface to the whole Book of Psalms; it outlines the lot of the good and of the wicked.
1, 1: *The way:* a common biblical term for "manner of living" or moral conduct.
Ps 2: A Messianic psalm, i.e., it refers to the Messiah, Christ. The psalmist depicts the revolt of the nations against God and his anointed Son (1–3),

God's answer (4–6), the Messianic decree (7–9), and the warning given to the rebels (10–12).
2, 2: *Anointed:* in Hebrew, *Mashiah* (whence the word "Messiah"), which the Greek translated as *Christos.* Among the Hebrews both the kings (Jgs 9, 8; 1 Sm 9, 16; 16, 12f) and the high priests (Lv 8, 12;

Nm 3, 3) received the power of their office by being anointed with oil.
2, 11f: *And rejoice before him; with trembling pay homage to him:* a shorter reading, "pay homage to him with trembling," may have been the original. *Pay homage:* literally, "kiss his feet."

PSALM 3

Trust in God in Time of Danger

1 A psalm of David, when he fled from his son Absalom.

I

2 O Lord, how many are my
    adversaries!
    Many rise up against me!
3 Many are saying of me,
    "There is no salvation for
    him in God."
4 But you, O Lord, are my shield;
    my glory, you lift up my
    head!

II

5 When I call out to the Lord,
    he answers me from his holy
    mountain.
6 When I lie down in sleep,
    I awake again, for the Lord
    sustains me.
7 I fear not the myriads of people
    arrayed against me on every
    side.

III

8 Rise up, O Lord!
    Save me, my God!
For you strike all my enemies
    on the cheek;
    the teeth of the wicked you
    break.
9 Salvation is the Lord's!
    Upon your people be your
    blessing!

PSALM 4

Joyful Confidence in God

1 For the leader; with stringed instruments. A psalm of David.

I

2 When I call, answer me, O my
    just God,
    you who relieve me when I
    am in distress;
    Have pity on me, and hear my
    prayer!

II

3 Men of rank, how long will you
    be dull of heart?
    Why do you love what is vain
    and seek after falsehood?
4 Know that the Lord does
    wonders for his faithful
    one;
    the Lord will hear me when
    I call upon him.
5 Tremble, and sin not;
    reflect, upon your beds, in
    silence.
6 Offer just sacrifices,
    and trust in the Lord.

III

7 Many say, "Oh, that we might
    see better times!"
    O Lord, let the light of your
    countenance shine upon us!
8 You put gladness in my heart,
    more than when grain and
    wine abound.
9 As soon as I lie down, I fall
    peacefully asleep,
    for you alone, O Lord,
    bring security to my dwelling.

PSALM 5

Prayer for Divine Help

1 For the leader; with wind instruments. A psalm of David.

I

2 Hearken to my words, O Lord,
    attend to my sighing.
3 Heed my call for help,
    my king and my God!
To you I pray,   4 O Lord;
    at dawn you hear my voice;
    at dawn I bring my plea
    expectantly before you.

II

5 For you, O God, delight not in
    wickedness;
    no evil man remains with you;

6 the arrogant may not stand
    in your sight.
You hate all evildoers;
7 you destroy all who speak
    falsehood;
The bloodthirsty and the
    deceitful
    the Lord abhors.

III

8 But I, because of your abundant
    kindness,
    will enter your house;
I will worship at your holy
    temple
    in fear of you,   9 O Lord;
Because of my enemies, guide
    me in your justice;
    make straight your way before
    me.

IV

10 For in their mouth there is no
    sincerity;
    their heart teems with
    treacheries.
Their throat is an open grave;
    they flatter with their tongue.
11 Punish them, O God;
    let them fall by their own
    devices;
For their many sins, cast them
    out
    because they have rebelled
    against you.

V

12 But let all who take refuge in
    you
    be glad and exult forever.
Protect them, that you may be
    the joy
    of those who love your name.
13 For you, O Lord, bless the just
    man;
    you surround him with the
    shield of your good will.

Ps 3: The psalmist, surrounded by enemies, implores God's help (2–4), arouses himself to trust in God (5–7), and prays for himself and the people (8f).

Ps 4: The psalmist begs God's aid (2), admonishes the incredulous worldlings to put their trust in God (3–6), and reaffirms his own confidence in Him (7–9).

4, 1: *For the leader:* very many of the psalms have this phrase prefixed to them. It probably signifies that they were copied from a collection which once belonged "to the choirmaster." Cf 1 Chr 15, 21.

4, 5: An admonition not to utter rash words against the Lord, even in distress or affliction; the right conduct, after silent acceptance of trials, is proposed in v 6. *Tremble:* the Hebrew verb means, "to be deeply moved" with any emotion; in the present context, "with fear or dismay." The Greek understood it as, "to be moved with anger," and thus it is quoted in Eph 4, 26.

Ps 5: At dawn the psalmist calls upon God (2–4), who hates sinners (5–7); trusting in divine guidance for himself (8f), he asks God to punish the wicked (10f) and protect the just (12f).

5, 9: The Greek reads, "Make straight the way before you."

5, 10: *An open grave:* while they feign words of friendship, their hidden thoughts, the words in *their throat,* i.e., in their heart, are murderous, ready to swallow up men to death. Cf Jer 5, 16.

PSALM 6

Prayer in Time of Distress

1 For the leader; with stringed instruments, "upon the eighth." A psalm of David.

I

2 O LORD, reprove me not in
        your anger,
    nor chastise me in your wrath.
3 Have pity on me, O LORD, for I
        am languishing;
    heal me, O LORD, for my
        body is in terror;
4 My soul, too, is utterly terrified;
    but you, O LORD, how
        long . . . ?

II

5 Return, O LORD, save my life;
    rescue me because of your
        kindness,
6 For among the dead no one
        remembers you;
    in the nether world who gives
        you thanks?

III

7 I am wearied by sighing;
    every night I flood my bed
        with weeping;
    I drench my couch with my
        tears.
8 My eyes are dimmed with
        sorrow;
    they have aged because of all
        my foes.

IV

9 Depart from me, all evildoers,
    for the LORD has heard the
        sound of my weeping;
10 The LORD has heard my plea;
    the LORD has accepted my
        prayer.
11 All my enemies shall be put to
        shame in utter terror;
    they shall fall back in sudden
        shame.

PSALM 7

An Appeal to the Divine Judge

1 A plaintive song of David, which he sang
to the LORD because of Cush the Benjaminite.

I

2 O LORD, my God, in you I take
        refuge;
    save me from all my pursuers
        and rescue me,
3 Lest I become like the lion's
        prey,
    to be torn to pieces, with no
        one to rescue me.

II

4 O LORD, my God, if I am at
        fault in this,
    if there is guilt on my hands,
5 If I have repaid my friend with
        evil,
    I who spared those who without
        cause were my foes—
6 Let the enemy pursue and
        overtake me;
    let him trample my life to the
        ground,
    and lay my glory in the dust.

III

7 Rise, up O LORD, in your anger;
    rise against the fury of my
        foes;
    wake to the judgment you
        have decreed.
8 Let the assembly of the peoples
        surround you;
    above them on high be
        enthroned.
9 [The LORD judges the nations.]
    Do me justice, O LORD, because
        I am just,
    and because of the innocence
        that is mine.
10 Let the malice of the wicked
        come to an end,
    but sustain the just,
    O searcher of heart and soul,
        O just God.

IV

11 A shield before me is God,
    who saves the upright of
        heart;
12 A just judge is God,
    a God who punishes day by
        day.
13 Unless they be converted, God
        will sharpen his sword;
    he will bend and aim his bow,
14 Prepare his deadly weapons
        against them,
    and use fiery darts for arrows.

V

15 He who conceived iniquity and
        was pregnant with mischief,
    brings forth failure.
16 He has opened a hole, he has
        dug it deep,
    but he falls into the pit which
        he has made.
17 His mischief shall recoil upon
        his own head;
    upon the crown of his head
        his violence shall rebound.
18 I will give thanks to the LORD
        for his justice,
    and sing praise to the name of
        the LORD Most High.

PSALM 8

The Majesty of God and the Dignity of Man

1 For the leader; "upon the gittith."
    A psalm of David.

I

2 O LORD, our Lord,
    how glorious is your name
        over all the earth!
    You have exalted your
        majesty above the heavens.
3 Out of the mouths of babes and
        sucklings
    you have fashioned praise
        because of your foes,
    to silence the hostile and the
        vengeful.

Ps 6: The first of the Penitential Psalms. In his affliction the psalmist begs God for mercy (2–4); praying to be saved from death (5f), he describes his misery (7f); then, certain of being heard, he rejects all fellowship with sinners (9–11).

6, 4: *How long:* an elliptical exclamation for, "How long will it be before you answer my prayer?" Cf Ps 13, 2ff.

6, 6: The ancient concept of the abode of the dead (*the nether world,* in Hebrew, *Sheol*) supposed no activity or lofty emotion among the deceased, who were pictured as surrounded by the darkness of oblivion. The Hebrews shared in this common idea almost to the time of Christ, when God revealed a clearer notion of the hereafter. Cf Wis 3.

Ps 7: Slandered by his enemies, the psalmist prays for help against them (2f), as he swears that he is innocent (4–6) and calls upon God, the just judge of the world, to defend him (7–10); confident of God's justice (11–14), he foretells the punishment of his calumniators (15–17), and promises a thanksgiving sacrifice (18).

7, 4: *At fault in this:* in these accusations made against the psalmist.

7, 5: *I who spared:* cf David's generous treatment of Saul (1 Sm 24, 11; 26, 9).

Ps 8: After contrasting man's finite nature with God's infinite majesty (2–5), the psalmist extols the dignity and power to which God has raised man (6–10).

4 When I behold your heavens,
   the work of your fingers.
   the moon and stars which you
   set in place—
5 What is man that you should be
   mindful of him,
   or the son of man that you
   should care for him?

II

6 You have made him little less
   than the angels,
   and crowned him with glory
   and honor.
7 You have given him rule over
   the works of your hands,
   putting all things under his feet:
8 All sheep and oxen,
   yes, and the beasts of the field,
9 The birds of the air, the fishes
   of the sea,
   and whatever swims the paths
   of the seas.
10 O Lord, our Lord,
   how glorious is your name
   over all the earth!

PSALM 9

Thanksgiving for the Overthrow of Hostile Nations

1 For the leader; according to *Muth labben.* A psalm of David.

I

2 I will give thanks to you, O
   Lord, with all my heart;
   I will declare all your
   wondrous deeds.
3 I will be glad and exult in you;
   I will sing praise to your name,
   Most High,
4 Because my enemies are turned
   back,
   overthrown and destroyed
   before you.

II

5 For you upheld my right and
   my cause,
   seated on your throne,
   judging justly.

6 You rebuked the nations and
   destroyed the wicked;
   their name you blotted out
   forever and ever.
7 The enemies are ruined
   completely forever;
   the remembrance of the cities
   you uprooted has perished.

III

8 But the Lord sits enthroned
   forever;
   he has set up his throne for
   judgment.
9 He judges the world with justice;
   he governs the peoples with
   equity.
10 The Lord is a stronghold for
   the oppressed,
   a stronghold in times of
   distress.
11 They trust in you who cherish
   your name,
   for you forsake not those who
   seek you, O Lord.

IV

12 Sing praise to the Lord
   enthroned in Zion;
   proclaim among the nations
   his deeds;
13 For the avenger of blood has
   remembered;
   he has not forgotten the cry
   of the afflicted.

V

14 Have pity on me, O Lord; see
   how I am afflicted by my
   foes,
   you who have raised me up
   from the gates of death,
15 That I may declare all your praises
   and, in the gates of the
   daughter of Zion, rejoice
   in your salvation.

VI

16 The nations are sunk in the pit
   they have made;
   in the snare they set, their
   foot is caught;

17 In passing sentence, the Lord is
   manifest;
   the wicked are trapped by the
   work of their own hands.

VII

18 To the nether world the wicked
   shall turn back,
   all the nations that forget God.
19 For the needy shall not always
   be forgotten,
   nor shall the hope of the
   afflicted forever perish.
20 Rise, O Lord, let not man
   prevail;
   let the nations be judged in
   your presence.
21 Strike them with terror, O Lord;
   let the nations know that they
   are but men.

PSALM 10

Prayer for Help against Oppressors

I

1 Why, O Lord, do you stand
   aloof?
   Why hide in times of distress?
2 Proudly the wicked harass the
   afflicted,
   who are caught in the devices
   the wicked have contrived.

II

3 For the wicked man glories in
   his greed,
   and the covetous blasphemes,
   sets the Lord at nought.
4 The wicked man boasts, "He
   will not avenge it";
   "There is no God," sums up
   his thoughts.
5 His ways are secure at all times;
   your judgments are far from
   his mind;
   all his foes he scorns.
6 He says in his heart, "I shall not
   be disturbed;
   from age to age I shall be
   without misfortune."

8, 6: *The angels:* in Hebrew, *elohim,* which is the ordinary word for "God" or "the gods"; hence, some translate, "a little less than godlike." Cf Pss 45, 7; 58, 2; 82, 1; 97, 7. But the ancient versions generally understood the term as referring to the heavenly spirits. Cf Ps 138, 1. In Heb 2, 9 this passage is shown to be eminently fulfilled in the God-man Jesus Christ. Cf 1 Cor 15, 27 also, where St. Paul applies to Christ the words, *putting all things under his feet.*

8, 10: The verse with which this psalm begins is repeated as a refrain at the end.

Ps 9: The Vulgate consists of two parts (A and B), each of which forms a separate psalm (Pss 9 and 10) in the current Hebrew text. In favor of the original unity of this psalm is its acrostic character, now partially lost in the poorly preserved text: the first letter of each stanza (of two couplets apiece) originally followed the order of the Hebrew alphabet consecutively throughout both halves of the psalm. Those who consider the two halves as separate psalms point to their somewhat diverse subject matter, the prayer in the first being mainly against the enemies of Israel,

that in the second mainly against the wicked within Israel. However, as in all the alphabetic psalms, there is not much logical sequence between the verses.

9, 15: *The daughter of Zion:* or, "daughter Zion"; Hebrew idiom for the "city of Zion."

9, 17: God's honor and glory are vindicated when he judges and punishes the wicked.

10, 5: *Are far from his mind:* the current Hebrew text may be read, "are lofty beyond him,"

7 His mouth is full of cursing,
        guile and deceit;
    under his tongue are mischief
        and iniquity.
8 He lurks in ambush near the
        villages;
    in hiding he murders the
        innocent;
    his eyes spy upon the
        unfortunate.
9 He waits in secret like a lion in
        his lair;
    he lies in wait to catch the
        afflicted;
    he catches the afflicted and
        drags them off in his net.
10 He stoops and lies prone
        till by his violence fall the
        unfortunate.
11 He says in his heart, "God has
        forgotten;
    he hides his face, he never
        sees."

III

12 Rise, O Lord! O God, lift up
        your hand!
    Forget not the afflicted!
13 Why should the wicked man
        despise God,
    saying in his heart, "He will
        not avenge it"?
14 You do see, for you behold
        misery and sorrow,
    taking them in your hands.
    On you the unfortunate man
        depends;
    of the fatherless you are the
        helper.
15 Break the strength of the wicked
    and of the evildoer;
    punish their wickedness; let
        them not survive.

IV

16 The Lord is king forever and
        ever;
    the nations have perished out
        of his land.
17 The desire of the afflicted you
        hear, O Lord;
    strengthening their hearts, you
        pay heed

18 To the defense of the fatherless
        and the oppressed,
    that man, who is of earth,
        may terrify no more.

PSALM 11

Unshaken Confidence in God

1 For the leader. Of David.

I

In the Lord I take refuge; how
        can you say to me,
    "Flee to the mountain like a
        bird!
2 For see the wicked bend the bow;
    they place the arrow on the
        the string
    to shoot in the dark at the
        upright of heart.
3 When the pillars are overthrown,
    what can the just man do?"

II

4 The Lord is in his holy temple;
    the Lord's throne is in
        heaven.
    His eyes behold,
    his searching glance is on
        mankind.
5 The Lord searches the just and
        the wicked;
    the lover of violence he hates.
6 He rains upon the wicked fiery
        coals and brimstone;
    a burning blast is their
        allotted cup.
7 For the Lord is just, he loves
        just deeds;
    the upright shall see his face.

PSALM 12

Prayer against Evil Tongues

1 For the leader; "upon the eighth."
    A psalm of David.

I

2 Help, O Lord! for no one now
        is dutiful;
    faithfulness has vanished from
        among men.
3 Everyone speaks falsehood to
        his neighbor;
    with smooth lips they speak,
        and double heart.

II

4 May the Lord destroy all
        smooth lips,
    every boastful tongue,
5 Those who say, "We are heroes
        with our tongues;
    our lips are our own; who is
        lord over us?"

III

6 "Because they rob the afflicted,
        and the needy sigh,
    now will I arise," says the
        Lord;
    "I will grant safety to him
        who longs for it."

IV

7 The promises of the Lord are
        sure,
    like tried silver, freed from
        dross, sevenfold refined.
8 You, O Lord, will keep us
    and preserve us always from
        this generation,
9 While about us the wicked strut
    and in high place are the
        basest of men.

PSALM 13

Prayer of One in Sorrow

1 For the leader. A psalm of David.

I

2 How long, O Lord? Will you
        utterly forget me?
    How long will you hide your
        face from me?
3 How long shall I harbor sorrow
        in my soul,
    grief in my heart day after
        day?
    How long will my enemy
        triumph over me?
4   Look, answer me, O Lord,
        my God!

II

    Give light to my eyes that I may
        not sleep in death
5   lest my enemy say, "I have
        overcome him";

Ps 11: While fainthearted friends advise flight in
the present peril (1–3), the psalmist reaffirms his confidence in the all-knowing Lord who gives just retribution to both the good and the wicked (4–7).

11, 3: *The pillars:* usually understood as "the
foundations of public order." Cf Ps 82, 5.

11, 6: *Allotted cup:* the cup which God gives man
to drink is a common biblical figure for the destiny he
assigns them. Cf Pss 16, 5; 23, 5; 75, 9; Mt 20, 22;
26, 39; Rv 14, 10.

Ps 12: The psalmist prays for help against deceit
(2f) and pride (4f) of the wicked; God's promises (6)

fill him with confidence (7–9).

12, 6–9: The Hebrew text is obscure in part, and
the versions differ; the above translation follows the
revised Latin Psalter.

Ps 13: Oppressed by his foes, the psalmist laments
his desolation (2–4a) and prays for God's help (4b–6).

Lest my foes rejoice at my
downfall
6   though I trusted in your
kindness.
Let my heart rejoice in your
salvation;
let me sing to the LORD, "He
has been good to me."

PSALM 14

A Lament over Widespread Corruption

1 For the leader. Of David.

I

The fool says in his heart,
"There is no God."
Such are corrupt; they do
abominable deeds;
there is not one who does good.
2 The LORD looks down from
heaven upon the children
of men,
to see if there be one who is
wise and seeks God.
3 All alike have gone astray; they
have become perverse;
there is not one who does
good, not even one.

II

4 Will all these evildoers never learn,
they who eat up my people
just as they eat bread?
They have not called upon the
LORD;
5   then they shall be in great fear,
for God is with the just
generation.
6 You would confound the plans
of the afflicted,
but the LORD is his refuge.

III

7 Oh, that out of Zion would
come the salvation of Israel!
When the LORD restores the
well-being of his people,
than shall Jacob exult and
Israel be glad.

PSALM 15

The Guest of God

1 A psalm of David.

I

O LORD, who shall sojourn in
your tent?
Who shall dwell on your
holy mountain?

II

2 He who walks blamelessly and
does justice;
who thinks the truth in his
heart
3   and slanders not with his
tongue;
Who harms not his fellow man,
nor takes up a reproach
against his neighbor;
4 By whom the reprobate is
despised,
while he honors those who
fear the LORD;
Who, though it be to his loss,
changes not his pledged
word;
5   who lends not his money at
usury
and accepts no bribe against
the innocent.

III

He who does these things
shall never be disturbed.

PSALM 16

God the Supreme Good

1 A *miktam* of David.

I

Keep me. O God, for in you
I take refuge;
2 I say to the LORD, "My Lord
are you.
Apart from you I have no
god."

3 How wonderfully has he made
me cherish
the holy ones who are in
his land!
4 They multiply their sorrows
who court other gods.
Blood libations to them I will
not pour out,
nor will I take their names
upon my lips.
5 O LORD, my allotted portion
and my cup,
you it is who hold fast my lot.
6 For me the measuring lines have
fallen on pleasant sites;
fair to me indeed is my
inheritance.

II

7 I bless the LORD who counsels me;
even in the night my heart
exhorts me.
8 I set the LORD ever before me;
with him at my right hand I
shall not be disturbed.
9 Therefore my heart is glad and
my soul rejoices,
my body, too, abides in
confidence;
10 Because you will not abandon
my soul to the nether world,
nor will you suffer your
faithful one to undergo
corruption.
11 You will show me the path to
life,
fullness of joys in your
presence,
the delights at your right
hand forever.

PSALM 17

Prayer against Persecutors

1 A prayer of David.

I

Hear, O LORD, a just suit;
attend to my outcry;
hearken to my prayer from
lips without deceit.

Ps 14: Bewailing the widespread corruption of the godless (1–3), the psalmist foretells their punishment (4–6), as he prays for his people (7). This psalm is repeated in almost identical form as Ps 53.

14, 3: Here many Greek and Latin texts insert the Old Testament quotations which were first combined in Rom 3, 13–18.

Ps 15: Lists the moral qualities which he should possess who would enter the Lord's sanctuary worthily; the social virtues of justice and charity are especially emphasized.

Ps 16: Pledging his loyalty to God, the psalmist proclaims his hostility toward the idolators and his

friendship toward the faithful in Israel (1–6); therefore he is aware of the constant presence of God, who will keep him in this blessed union by granting him bodily resurrection and everlasting life (7–11).

16, 4: *Take their names:* the pious Israelite not only refrained from praying to false gods and from swearing by them; he would not even mention their names. Cf Hos 2, 18.

16, 5: In the worship of the true God the psalmist finds his best inheritance.

16, 10: *To undergo corruption:* some commentators render this: "to see the grave," understanding this to mean that God will not let the psalmist die in the

present circumstances. But the Hebrew word *shahath* means not only "the pit," "the grave," but also "corruption." In the latter sense the ancient Greek version rendered this passage, and it was thus quoted by St. Peter (Acts 2, 25–32) and St. Paul (Acts 13, 35–37), both of whom interpret this as referring to Christ's Resurrection.

Ps 17: Certain of his innocence, the psalmist appeals to God's just judgment (1–5), imploring his help against the enemies (6–9) who persecute him (10–12); these worldlings shall be punished, whereas the psalmist shall enjoy God's presence hereafter (13–15).

2 From you let my judgment
    come;
    your eyes behold what is
        right.
3 Though you test my heart,
    searching it in the night,
    though you try me with fire,
    you shall find no malice
        in me.
4 My mouth has not transgressed
    after the manner of man;
    according to the words of
        your lips I have kept the
        ways of the law.
5 My steps have been steadfast
    in your paths,
    my feet have not faltered.

II

6 I call upon you, for you will
    answer me, O God;
    incline your ear to me; hear
        my word.
7 Show your wondrous kindness,
    O savior of those who flee
    from their foes to refuge at
        your right hand.
8 Keep me as the apple of your
        eye;
    hide me in the shadow of
        your wings
9 from the wicked who use
    violence against me.

III

    My ravenous enemies beset me;
10   they shut up their cruel hearts,
        their mouths speak proudly.
11 Their steps even now surround
        me;
    crouching to the ground, they
        fix their gaze,
12 Like lions hungry for prey,
    like young lions lurking in
        hiding.

IV

13 Rise, O LORD, confront them
    cast them down;
    rescue me by your sword
    from the wicked,

14 by your hand, O LORD, from
        mortal men;
    From mortal men whose portion
        in life is in this world,
    where with your treasures you
        fill their bellies.
    Their sons are enriched
    and bequeath their abundance
        to their little ones.
15 But I in justice shall behold
    your face;
    on waking, I shall be content
    in your presence.

PSALM 18

Thanksgiving for Help and Victory

1 For the leader. Of David, the servant of the
LORD, who sang to the LORD the words of this
song when the LORD had rescued him from the
grasp of all his enemies and from the hand of
Saul.

A

I

2 I love you, O LORD, my strength,
3   O LORD, my rock, my
        fortress, my deliverer.
    My God, my rock of refuge,
        my shield, the horn of my
        salvation, my stronghold!
4 Praised be the LORD, I exclaim,
    and I am safe from my
        enemies.

II

5 The breakers of death surged
        round about me,
    the destroying floods
        overwhelmed me;
6 The cords of the nether world
    enmeshed me,
    the snares of death overtook
        me.
7 In my distress I called upon the
        LORD
    and cried out to my God;
    From his temple he heard my
        voice,
    and my cry to him reached
        his ears.

III

8 The earth swayed and quaked;
    the foundations of the
        mountains trembled
    and shook when his wrath
        flared up.
9 Smoke rose from his nostrils,
    and a devouring fire from
        his mouth
    that kindled coals into flame.
10 And he inclined the heavens
    and came down,
    with dark clouds under his feet.
11 He mounted a cherub and flew,
    borne on the wings of the
        wind.
12 And he made darkness the
        cloak about him;
    dark, misty rain-clouds his
        wrap.
13 From the brightness of his
        presence
    coals were kindled to flame.
14 And the LORD thundered from
        heaven,
    the Most High gave forth
        his voice;
15 He sent forth his arrows to put
        them to flight,
    with frequent lightnings he
        routed them.
16 Then the bed of the sea
        appeared,
    and the foundations of the
        world were laid bare,
    At the rebuke of the LORD,
    at the blast of the wind of his
        wrath.
17 He reached out from on high
        and grasped me;
    he drew me out of the deep
        waters.
18 He rescued me from my mighty
        enemy
    and from my foes, who were
        too powerful for me.
19 They attacked me in the day
    of my calamity,
    but the LORD came to my
        support.

17, 15: *On waking:* to a new life after death.
Death is often compared to sleep. Cf Ps 76, 6; Dn 12,
2.

Ps 18: This psalm of thanksgiving is also given,
with a few small variants, in 2 Sm 22. In both places
it is attributed to David. Two main sections can be
distinguished. In the first part, after an introductory
stanza of praise to God (2–4), the royal psalmist describes the peril he was in (5–7), and then poetically
depicts, under the form of a theophany, God's intervention in his behalf (8–20), concluding with an
acknowledgment of God's justice (21–31). In the

second part, God is praised for having prepared the
psalmist for war (32–35), given him victory over his
enemies (36–39), whom he put to flight (40–43), and
bestowed on him dominion over many peoples (44–
46). The whole psalm ends with a paean of grateful
praise (47–51).
18, 3: *The horn of my salvation:* my strong savior.
The horn, the dreadful weapon of an enraged bull,
was a symbol of strength. Cf Lk 1, 69.
18, 5f: These verses are to be understood figuratively.
18, 7: *His temple:* His heavenly abode.

18, 8ff: God's intervention is graphically portrayed
under the figures of an earthquake (8, 16), and a
thunderstorm (9–15). Cf Jgs 5, 4f; Pss 29; 97, 2–6;
Hb 3.
18, 11: *He mounted a cherub:* since God makes the
winds his *messengers,* or "angels" (Ps 104, 4), he is
also spoken of poetically as riding the storm clouds,
or on the angelic creatures called *cherubim.* His earthly
throne on the ark of the covenant was likewise formed
by two winged *cherubim.* Cf Ex 37, 7–9. In both senses
the Lord is enthroned upon the cherubim. Cf Pss 80,
2; 99, 1.

20 He set me free in the open,
     and rescued me, because he
        loves me.

IV

21 The Lord rewarded me
     according to my justice;
     according to the cleanness of
        my hands he requited me;
22 For I kept the ways of the Lord
     and was not disloyal to my
        God;
23 For his ordinances were all
        present to me,
     and his statutes I put not from
        me,
24 But I was wholehearted toward
        him,
     and I was on my guard
        against guilt.
25 And the Lord requited me
     according to my justice,
     according to the cleanness of
        my hands in his sight.
26 Toward the faithful you are
        faithful,
     toward the wholehearted you
        are wholehearted,
27 Toward the sincere you are
        sincere,
     but toward the crooked you
        are astute;
28 For lowly people you save
     but haughty eyes you bring low;
29 You indeed, O Lord, give light
        to my lamp;
     O my God, you brighten the
        darkness about me;
30 For with your aid I run against
        an armed band,
     and by the help of God I leap
        over a wall.
31 God's way is unerring,
     the promise of the Lord is
        fire-tried;
     he is a shield to all who take
        refuge in him.

B

I

32 For who is God except the
        Lord?
     Who is a rock, save our God?

33 The God who girded me with
        strength
     and kept my way unerring;
34 Who made my feet swift as those
        of hinds
     and set me on the heights;
35 Who trained my hands for war
     and my arms to bend a bow
        of brass.

II

36 You have given me your
        saving shield;
     your right hand has upheld
        me,
     and you have stooped to
        make me great.
37 You made room for my steps;
     unwavering was my stride.
38 I pursued my enemies and
        overtook them,
     nor did I turn again till I
        made an end of them.
39 I smote them and they could
        not rise;
     they fell beneath my feet.

III

40 And you girded me with
        strength for war;
     you subdued my adversaries
        beneath me.
41 My enemies you put to flight
        before me,
     and those who hated me you
        destroyed.
42 They cried for help—but no one
        saved them;
     to the Lord—but he
        answered them not.
43 I ground them fine as the dust
        before the wind;
     like the mud in the streets I
        trampled them down.

IV

44 You rescued me from the
        strife of the people;
     you made me head over
        nations;
     A people I had not known
        became my slaves;

45   as soon as they heard me
        they obeyed.
     The foreigners fawned and
        cringed before me;
46   as they staggered forth from
        their fortresses.

C

47 The Lord live! And blessed be
        my Rock!
     Extolled be God my savior.
48 O God, who granted me
        vengeance,
     who made peoples subject to
        me
49   and preserved me from my
        enemies,
     Truly above my adversaries you
        exalt me
     and from the violent man you
        have rescued me.
50 Therefore will I proclaim you,
        O Lord, among the nations,
     and I will sing praise to your
        name,
51 You who gave great victories
        to your king
     and showed kindness to your
        anointed,
     to David and his posterity
        forever.

PSALM 19

God's Glory in the Heavens and in the Law

1 For the leader. A psalm of David.

A

I

2 The heavens declare the glory
        of God.
     and the firmament proclaims
        his handiwork.
3 Day pours out the word to day,
     and night to night imparts
        knowledge;
4 Not a word nor a discourse
     whose voice is not heard;

18, 26f: Men are treated by God in the same way they treat him and their fellow men.
18, 29: *Light to my lamp:* a figure of life and happiness. Cf 1 Kgs 11, 36.
18, 34: *The heights:* a natural stronghold, safe from attack. Cf Ps 61, 3; Hb 3, 19.
Ps 19 consists of two distinct parts, perhaps origin-

ally two independent psalms. The first section presents the heavenly firmament, especially the sun, as singing the glories of the Creator (2-7). In the second section the psalmist praises God's moral law (8-11) and prays for grace to keep it (12-15).
19, 3: *Day pours out the word:* as if under divine inspiration, each day proclaims to the next the message

of God's grandeur.
19, 4: *Not a word:* this message is so clear that the hearts and minds of all men cannot help but hear it. However, some commentators interpret the passage to mean, "Although no physical sound is heard, yet the heavens have a language of their own that is understood throughout the world."

5 Through all the earth their
        voice resounds,
    and to the ends of the world,
        their message.

II

He has pitched a tent there for
    the sun,
6   which comes forth like the
        groom from his bridal
        chamber
    and, like a giant, joyfully runs
        its course.
7 At one end of the heavens it
        comes forth,
    and its course is to their other
        end;
    nothing escapes its heat.

B

I

8 The law of the LORD is perfect,
        refreshing of the soul;
    The decree of the LORD is
        trustworthy,
        giving wisdom to the simple.
9 The precepts of the LORD are
        right,
        rejoicing the heart;
    The command of the LORD is
        clear,
        enlightening the eye;
10 The fear of the LORD is pure,
        enduring forever;
    The ordinances of the LORD are
        true,
        all of them just;
11 They are more precious than
        gold,
        than a heap of purest gold;
    Sweeter also than syrup
        or honey from the comb.

II

12 Though your servant is careful
        of them,
        very diligent in keeping them,
13 Yet who can detect failings?
        Cleanse me of my unknown
        faults!
14 From wanton sin especially,
        restrain your servant;
    let it not rule over me.

Then shall I be blameless and
        innocent
    of serious sin.
15 Let the words of my mouth and
        the thought of my heart
    find favor before you,
    O LORD, my rock and my
        redeemer.

PSALM 20

*Prayer for the King in Time of
War*

1 For the leader. A psalm of David.

I

2 The LORD answer you in time of
        distress;
    the name of the God of Jacob
        defend you!
3 May he send you help from the
        sanctuary,
    from Zion may he sustain you.
4 May he remember all your
        offerings
    and graciously accept your
        holocaust.
5 May he grant you what is in
        your heart
    and fulfill your every plan.
6 May we shout for joy at your
        victory
    and raise the standards in the
        name of our God.
    The LORD grant all your
        requests!

II

7 Now I know that the LORD has
        given victory to his
        anointed,
    that he has answered him
        from his holy heaven
    with the strength of his
        victorious right hand.
8 Some are strong in chariots;
        some, in horses;
    but we are strong in the name
        of the LORD, our God.
9 Though they bow down and fall,
        yet we stand erect and firm.
10 O LORD, grant victory to the
        king,
    and answer us when we call
        upon you.

PSALM 21

*Thanksgiving and Prayers for
the King*

1 For the leader. A psalm of David.

I

2 O LORD, in your strength the
        king is glad;
    in your victory how greatly
        he rejoices!
3 You have granted him his
        heart's desire;
    you refused not the wish of
        his lips.
4 For you welcomed him with
        goodly blessings,
    you placed on his head a
        crown of pure gold.
5 He asked life of you: you gave
        him
    length of days forever and ever.
6 Great is his glory in your
        victory;
    majesty and splendor you
        conferred upon him.
7 For you made him a blessing
        forever;
    you gladdened him with the
        joy of your presence.
8 For the king trusts in the LORD,
    and through the kindness of
        the Most High he stands
        unshaken.

II

9 May your hand reach all your
        enemies,
    may your right hand reach
        your foes!
10 Make them burn as though in a
        fiery furnace,
        when you appear.
    May the LORD consume them
        in his anger;
    let fire devour them.
11 Destroy their fruit from the
        earth
    and their posterity from
        among men.
12 Though they intend evil against
        you,
        devising plots, they cannot
        succeed,

19, 5: *Through all the earth:* these two lines are
applied in Rom 10, 18 to the preachers of the Gospel.
There: in the heavens, below the horizon.
    19, 6: *A giant:* literally, "a powerful man"; used
also in the sense of "a champion," "a hero," and here
perhaps, "an athlete."
    19, 8–10: Six synonyms are used for the same idea,

divine law. Cf Ps 119.
    Pss 20 and 21 are complementary, having a similar
structure. The former sung before the battle, expresses
good wishes for the king (2–6), with assurance of
victory (7–9). The latter, sung after the battle, thanks
God for the victory (2–8) and again invokes God's
blessing on the king (9–13). Both psalms end with a

refrain sung by the people.
    20, 8: The pious place their trust, not in material
means, but in the help of God whom they invoke. Cf
1 Sm 17, 45; Is 31, 1; 36, 9.
    21, 9ff: These words are addressed to the king.

13 For you shall put them to
     flight;
   you shall aim your shafts
     against them.
14 Be extolled, O LORD, in your
     strength!
   We will sing, chant the
     praise of your might.

PSALM 22

Passion and Triumph of the Messiah

1 For the leader; according to "The hind of
   the dawn." A psalm of David.

A

I

2 My God, my God, why have
     you forsaken me,
   far from my prayer, from the
     words of my cry?
3 O my God, I cry out by day,
     and you answer not;
   by night, and there is no
     relief for me.
4 Yet you are enthroned in the
     holy place,
   O glory of Israel!
5 In you our fathers trusted;
   they trusted, and you
     delivered them.
6 To you they cried, and they
     escaped;
   in you they trusted, and they
     were not put to shame.

7 But I am a worm, not a man;
   the scorn of men, despised by
     the people.
8 All who see me scoff at me;
   they mock me with parted lips,
   they wag their heads:

9 "He relied on the LORD, let him
     deliver him,
   let him rescue him, if he loves
     him."
10 You have been my guide since
      I was first formed,
   my security at my mother's
     breast.
11 To you I was committed at birth,
   From my mother's womb you
     are my God.

12 Be not far from me, for I am in
     distress;
   be near, for I have no one to
     help me.   (II)
13 Many bullocks surround me;
   the strong bulls of bashan
     encircle me.
14 They open their mouths against
     me
   like ravening and roaring lions.

15 I am like water poured out;
   all my bones are racked.
   My heart has become like wax
   melting away within my
     bosom.
16 My throat is dried up like baked
     clay,
   my tongue cleaves to my jaws;
   to the dust of death you have
     brought me down.

17 Indeed, many dogs surround me,
   a pack of evildoers closes in
     upon me;
   They have pierced my hands
     and my feet;
18 I can count all my bones.
   They look on and gloat over me;
19   they divide my garments
     among them,
   and for my vesture they cast
     lots.

III

20 But you, O LORD, be not far
     from me;
   O my help, hasten to aid me.
21 Rescue my soul from the
     sword,
   my loneliness from the grip
     of the dog.
22 Save me from the lion's mouth;
   from the horns of the wild
     bulls, my wretched life.

B

I

23 I will proclaim your name to my
     brethren;
   in the midst of the assembly I
     will praise you:
24 "You who fear the LORD,
     praise him;
   all you descendants of Jacob,
     give glory to him;
   revere him, all you
     descendants of Israel!
25 For he has not spurned nor
     disdained
   the wretched man in his
     misery,
   Nor did he turn his face away
     from him,
   but when he cried out to him,
     he heard him."
26 So by your gift will I utter
     praise in the vast assembly;
   I will fulfill my vows before
     those who fear him.
27 The lowly shall eat their fill;
   they who seek the LORD
     shall praise him:
   "May your hearts be ever
     merry!"

Ps 22 is one of the most important of the Messianic
psalms. Our Lord himself on the cross repeated its
first line, and several other verses are directly quoted,
or at least alluded to, in the New Testament as pertaining to his Passion. Of no other person is this
touching description of spiritual and physical suffering so eminently true as it is of Jesus Christ. Hence,
the entire psalm has been traditionally interpreted in
the Catholic Church as referring to him. The psalmist,
therefore, speaks in Christ's name when in the first
section (2–22) he describes the Messiah's derelic-
tion (2–6), opprobrium (7–9) and physical sufferings (13–
19), together with his unshaken confidence in the
heavenly Father (10–12.20–22); and in the second
part, the fruits of his redemption; the grateful praise
of the redeemed (23–27), the conversion of the Gentiles
(28–30d), and the glory of God and his beloved son
(30e–32).

22, 2: *Far from my prayer:* when he prays, God
seems too distant to hear his cry.

22, 3: *There is no relief for me:* the Hebrew phrase
here is obscure; the revised Latin Psalter renders it,

"You heed me not."

22, 8: *Parted lips:* a sign of scorn. *They wag their
heads:* another gesture of derision; it was indulged in
by Christ's enemies on Calvary.

22, 9: These words were spoken, in unwitting fulfillment of the prophecy, by the Jews at our Lord's
crucifixion. Cf Mt 27, 42. *If he loves him:* the natural
sense seems to be, "If God loves the sufferer"; but
some understand it as, "Since he (the sufferer) has
loved him (the LORD)."

22, 10: *My Guide:* so in the revised Latin Psalter,
but the meaning of the Hebrew is uncertain.

22, 11: *To you I was committed:* literally, "upon
you I was thrown." Some see in this a reference to the
ancient custom of placing a newborn baby upon its
father's lap, so that he might acknowledge its paternity.
But more probably the meaning is simply, "I was
given to your care."

22, 13: *Bashan:* a fertile grazing land east of the
Jordan, famous for its strong cattle. Cf Dt 32, 14;
Ez 39, 18; Am 4, 1. The various beasts mentioned here
are, of course, to be understood figuratively, as sig-

nifying cruel persecutors.

22, 17: *They have pierced my hands:* so in the
ancient versions. The current Hebrew text reads,
"Like the lion my hands," which hardly makes good
sense. This passage finds its complete fulfillment in
the nailing of Christ's hands and feet to the cross.

22, 19: Explicitly cited in Jn 19, 24 as a prophecy
fulfilled in the dividing of our Lord's garments by the
soldiers on calvary.

22, 21: *My loneliness:* his desolate soul. Cf Ps 35,
17.

22, 23: The transition from deepest sorrow to the
great joy of the Risen Savior. The language of vv 23–
27 is based on the custom whereby a person who
offered a thanksgiving sacrifice in the temple would
recount to his fellow worshippers the favor received
from God and then invite them to share in his sacrificial banquet.

22, 27: *May your hearts be ever merry:* addressed to
the lowly. Cf Ps 69, 33.

II

28 All the ends of the earth
    shall remember and turn to
        the LORD;
    All the families of the nations
    shall bow down before him.
29 For dominion is the LORD's,
    and he rules the nations.
30 To him alone shall bow down
    all who sleep in the earth;
    Before him shall bend
    all who go down into the dust.
                              (III)
    And to him my soul shall live;
31 my descendants shall serve
        him.
    Let the coming generation be
        told of the LORD
32 that they may proclaim to a
        people yet to be born
    the justice he has shown.

PSALM 23

The Lord, Shepherd and Host
1 A psalm of David.

I

The LORD is my shepherd;
    I shall not want.
2   In verdant pastures he gives
        me repose;
    Beside restful waters he leads me;
3   he refreshes my soul.
    He guides me in right paths
        for his name's sake.
4 Even though I walk in the dark
        valley
    I fear no evil; for you are
        at my side
    With your rod and your staff
        that give me courage.

II

5 You spread the table before me
    in the sight of my foes;
    You anoint my head with oil;
        my cup overflows.

6 Only goodness and kindness
        follow me
    all the days of my life;
    And I shall dwell in the house
        of the LORD
    for years to come.

PSALM 24

The Lord's Solemn Entry into Zion
1 A psalm of David.

I

The LORD's are the earth and
        its fullness;
    the world and those who
        dwell in it.
2 For he founded it upon the
        seas
    and established it upon the
        rivers.

II

3 Who can ascend the mountain
        of the LORD?
    or who may stand in his holy
        place?
4 He whose hands are sinless,
        whose heart is clean.
    who desires not what is vain,
    nor swears deceitfully to his
        neighbor.
5 He shall receive a blessing from
        the LORD,
    a reward from God his savior.
6 Such is the race that seeks for
        him,
    that seeks the face of the God
        of Jacob.

III

7 Lift up, O gates, your lintels;
    reach up, you ancient portals,
    that the king of glory may
        come in!
8 Who is this king of glory?
    The LORD, strong and mighty,
    the LORD, mighty in battle.

9 Lift up, O gates, your lintels;
    reach up, you ancient portals,
    that the king of glory may
        come in!
10 Who is this king of glory?
    The LORD of hosts; he is the
        king of glory.

PSALM 25

Prayer for Guidance and Help
1 Of David.

I

To you I lift up my soul,
    O LORD,   2 my God.
In you I trust; let me not be put
        to shame,
    let not my enemies exult over
        me.
3 No one who waits for you shall
        be put to shame;
    those shall be put to shame
    who heedlessly break faith.

4 Your ways, O LORD, make
        known to me;
    teach me your paths,
5 Guide me in your truth and
        teach me,
    for you are God my savior,
    and for you I wait all the day.
6 Remember that your compassion,
        O LORD,
    and your kindness are from
        of old.
7 The sins of my youth and my
        frailties remember not;
    in your kindness remember me
    because of your goodness,
        O LORD.

II

8 Good and upright is the LORD;
    thus he shows sinners the way.
9 He guides the humble to justice,
    he teaches the humble his way.
10 All the paths of the LORD are
        kindness and constancy
    toward those who keep his
        covenant and his decrees.

22, 30f: The Hebrew text is poorly preserved here. The translation given above follows the revised Latin Psalter in restoring the text to accord with the ancient versions.
Ps 23: God's loving care for his devoted servant is here portrayed under the figures of a shepherd's solicitude for his sheep (1-4) and a host's generosity toward his guest (5f).
23, 1: The idea of God as the Good Shepherd of his flock is common in both the Old and the New Testament. Cf especially Jn 10, 11-18.
23, 4: *Your rod and your staff:* to guide and defend the sheep.
23, 5: *Oil:* a perfumed ointment, used especially at banquets. Cf Mt 26, 7; Lk 7, 37.46; Jn 12, 3.

Ps 24: After a strophe in praise of God's universal dominion (1f), the psalm lays down the moral requirements for assisting at divine worship (3-6), and then gives the words which were sung when the ark, representing God's presence, was carried to Zion or into the temple (7-10). From the dialogue structure it seems probable that this psalm was composed for liturgical use, to be sung by alternating choirs. Cf 2 Sm 6, 12ff.
24, 2: According to the ancient notion of the world, the earth was regarded as a flat disc resting on a vast underground sea, "the deep." Cf Ps 33, 7.
24, 3-6: Ps 15 is similar in structure and content: a question, an answer giving the conditions, and a conclusion.

24, 7.9: *Your lintels:* literally, "your heads." The doorway is pictured as too low for the great God to enter. The *gates* and *portals* are either those of the temple or of the *ancient* citadel of the Jebusites.
Ps 25: An alphabetic psalm. Cf Ps 9. The thoughts are rather loosely connected, but the first part (1-7) is principally a prayer for guidance and pardon; the second (8-15), a meditation on God's goodness toward the just; the third (16-22), a prayer for protection and consolation.
25, 5: *And for you I wait all the day:* perhaps the third line of v 7 should be inserted immediately after these words. Elsewhere in this psalm there are two lines apiece for each letter of the Hebrew alphabet.

11 For your name's sake, O Lord,
    you will pardon my guilt,
        great as it is.

12 When a man fears the Lord,
    he shows him the way he
        should choose.
13 He abides in prosperity,
    and his descendants inherit
        the land.
14 The friendship of the Lord is
        with those who fear him,
    and his covenant, for their
        instruction.
15 My eyes are ever toward the
        Lord,
    for he will free my feet from
        the snare.

III

16 Look toward me, and have pity
        on me,
    for I am alone and afflicted.
17 Relieve the troubles of my heart,
    and bring me out of my
        distress.
18 Put an end to my affliction
        and my suffering,
    and take away all my sins.
19 Behold, my enemies are many,
    and they hate me violently.
20 Preserve my life, and rescue me;
    let me not be put to shame,
        for I take refuge in you.
21 Let integrity and uprightness
        preserve me,
    because I wait for you, O
        Lord.

22 Redeem Israel, O God,
    from all its distress!

PSALM 26

Prayer of an Innocent Man
1 Of David.

I

Do me justice, O Lord! for I
    have walked in integrity,
    and in the Lord I trust
        without wavering.

2 Search me, O Lord, and try me;
    test my soul and my heart.

II

3 For your kindness is before
        my eyes,
    and I walk in your truth.
4 I stay not with worthless men,
    nor do I consort with
        hypocrites.
5 I hate the assembly of evildoers,
    and with the wicked I will not
        stay.
6 I wash my hands in innocence,
    and I go round your altar,
        O Lord,
7 Giving voice to my thanks,
    and recounting all your
        wondrous deeds.
8 O Lord, I love the house in
        which you dwell,
    the tenting-place of your
        glory.

III

9 Gather not my soul with those
        of sinners,
    nor with men of blood my life.
10 On their hands are crimes,
    and their right hands are full
        of bribes.
11 But I walk in integrity;
    redeem me, and have pity
        on me.
12 My foot stands on level ground;
    in the assemblies I will bless
        the Lord.

PSALM 27

Trust in God
1 Of David.

A

I

The Lord is my light and my
    salvation;
    whom should I fear?
The Lord is my life's refuge;
    of whom should I be afraid?

2 When evildoers come at me
        to devour my flesh,
    My foes and my enemies
        themselves stumble and fall.
3 Though an army encamp
        against me
    my heart will not fear;
    Though war be waged upon me,
        even then will I trust.

II

4 One thing I ask of the Lord;
        this I seek:
    To dwell in the house of the
        Lord
    all the days of my life,
    That I may gaze upon the
        loveliness of the Lord
    and contemplate his temple.
5 For he will hide me in his abode
        in the day of trouble;
    He will conceal me in the
        shelter of his tent,
    he will set me high upon a
        rock.
6 Even now my head is held high
        above my enemies on every
        side.
    And I will offer in his tent
        sacrifices with shouts of
        gladness;
    I will sing and chant praise to
        the Lord.

B

I

7 Hear, O Lord, the sound of my
        call;
    have pity on me, and answer
        me.
8 Of you my heart speaks; you
        my glance seeks;
    your presence, O Lord, I seek.
9 Hide not your face from me;
    do not in anger repel your
        servant.
    You are my helper: cast me
        not off;
    forsake me not, O God my
        savior.

25, 18f: The wording and the order of these verses are not wholly free from doubt.

25, 22: This final verse is an addition to the original psalm.

Ps 26: Protesting his innocence (1f), the psalmist enumerates his virtues (3–8), that God may not condemn him with the wicked (9–12).

26, 6: *I wash my hands:* although the washing of hands was a liturgical act (Ex 30, 19.21; 40, 31), here it is probably to be understood figuratively, as in Is 1, 16. The words from here to the end of the psalm were

long recited at Mass, at the "Lavabo" or washing of hands. Cf Ps 73, 13.

26, 12: *On level ground:* in safety, where there is no danger of tripping or falling; here used figuratively. Some join the two lines of this verse to read. "When my feet stand on level ground, . . . I will bless the Lord." *In the assemblies:* in the temple, where the psalmist will offer a service of thanksgiving.

Ps 27: Asserting his boundless confidence that God will rescue him (1–3), the psalmist longs for the shelter of the temple where, united with the Lord, he

will be safe from his enemies (4–6). The second half seems originally to have been an independent psalm. Here the psalmist prays that he may not be abandoned by God (7–10), asks for guidance and protection (11f), and ends on a note of confidence (13f).

27, 2: *To devour my flesh:* to destroy me completely. Cf Ps 14, 4; Mi 3, 3.

27, 4: *Contemplate his temple:* the meaning of the Hebrew is not quite certain. Some render it as, "visit his temple at dawn."

10 Though my father and mother
        forsake me,
    yet will the LORD receive me.

                    II

11 Show me, O LORD, your way,
        and lead me on a level path,
    because of my adversaries.
12 Give me not up to the wishes
        of my foes;
    for false witnesses have risen
        up against me,
    and such as breathe out
        violence.
13 I believe that I shall see the
        bounty of the LORD
    in the land of the living.
14 Wait for the LORD with courage;
    be stouthearted and wait for
        the LORD.

                PSALM 28

        Petition and Thanksgiving
                1 Of David.

                    I

    To you, O LORD, I call;
        O my Rock, be not deaf to me,
    Lest, if you heed me not,
        I become one of those going
            down into the pit.
2 Hear the sound of my pleading,
        when I cry to you,
    lifting up my hands toward
        your holy shrine.
3 Drag me not away with the
        wicked,
    with those who do wrong,
    Who speak civilly to their
        neighbors
        though evil is in their hearts.
4 Repay them for their deeds,
        for the evil of their doings.
    For the work of their hands
        repay them;
    give them their deserts.

5 Because they consider not
        the deeds of the LORD nor the
        work of his hands,
    may he tear them down and
        not build them up.

                    II

6 Blessed be the LORD,
        for he has heard the sound
            of my pleading;
7 the LORD is my strength and
        my shield.
    In him my heart trusts, and I
        find help;
    then my heart exults, and
        with my song I give him
            thanks.

                    III

8 The LORD is the strength of his
        people,
    the saving refuge of his
        anointed.
9 Save your people, and bless your
        inheritance;
    feed them, and carry them
        forever!

                PSALM 29

        God's Majesty in the Storm
                1 A psalm of David.

                    I

    Give to the LORD, you sons of
        God,
        give to the LORD glory and
            praise,
2 Give to the LORD the glory due
        his name;
    adore the LORD in holy attire.

                    II

3 The voice of the LORD is over
        the waters,
    the God of glory thunders,
    the LORD, over vast waters.

4 The voice of the LORD is mighty;
    the voice of the LORD is
        majestic.
5 The voice of the LORD breaks
        the cedars,
    the LORD breaks the cedars
        of Lebanon.
6 He makes Lebanon leap like a
        calf
    and Sirion like a young bull.
7 The voice of the LORD strikes
        fiery flames;
8 the voice of the LORD shakes
        the desert,
    the LORD shakes the
        wilderness of Kadesh.
9 The voice of the LORD twists the
        oaks and strips the forests,
    and in his temple all say
        "Glory!"

                    III

10 The LORD is enthroned above
        the flood;
    the LORD is enthroned as king
        forever.
11 May the LORD give strength to
        his people;
    may the LORD bless his people
        with peace!

                PSALM 30

        *Thanksgiving for Deliverance
                from Death*
1 A psalm. A song for the dedication of the
        temple. Of David.

2 I will extol you, O LORD, for
        you drew me clear
    and did not let my enemies
        rejoice over me.

                    A

3 O LORD, my God,
    I cried out to you and you
        healed me.

27, 11: *A level path:* see note on Ps 26, 12.
    27, 13: *In the land of the living:* the meaning is,
"While I am still living here on earth." But these
words may also be used in an accommodated sense, as
the Church uses them in the Office of the Dead, to
mean, "In heaven, where there is true life."
    Ps 28 consists of a prayer asking that the psalmist
may not be punished with the wicked (1–5), followed
by anticipated thanksgiving to God for having heard
him (6f), and ending with an intercession for the king
and the nation (8f).
    28, 2: *Your holy shrine:* the innermost part of the
temple, the holy of holies, containing the ark of the
Lord.
    28, 4f: Since the wicked have no care for God, he
will have no care for them.
    Ps 29: After an invocation to praise the Lord (1f),
this striking psalm describes a magnificent theophany,

the revelation of God's majesty in a tremendous
thunderstorm (3–10), and ends with a prayer for the
people (11).
    29, 1: *Sons of God:* although this phrase regularly
refers to the angels, as in Jb 1, 6; 2, 1: 38, 7, here it
may be understood of "godly, virtuous men"; in Ps 96,
7ff, a very similar invocation is addressed to the
families of nations. Cf Ps 89, 7.
    29, 3: *The voice of the Lord:* the thunder and the
thunderbolt, the sound of which is here attributed
directly to God.
    29, 6: *He makes Lebanon leap:* the mountains are
pictured as trembling with fear; perhaps an earthquake is meant. Cf Ps 114, 4.6f. *Sirion:* the Phoenician
name for Mount Hermon. Cf Dt 3, 9. Several expressions in this psalm are also found in the Canaanite
texts written in the fifteenth century B.C. at Ugarit, in
in the north of Phoenicia.

29, 8: *The wilderness of Kadesh:* formerly identified
with the oasis of Kadesh in the northern part of the
Sinai peninsula. Cf Nm 20, 1. More probably, however, it was north of Palestine, for it is also mentioned
in one of the Ugaritic texts, and in the present context
seems to be in the neighborhood of Lebanon and
Hermon.
    Ps 30: The psalmist, after announcing his theme
(2), thanks God for having restored him to health
when sickness was about to bring him to the grave
(3–6). He then gives the details of what had occurred:
confident of robust health, he was suddenly stricken
with some disease (7f), but he cried to the Lord for
help (9–11), and his prayer was heard (12f).
    30, 1: *For the dedication of the temple:* a later
adaptation of this psalm.

4 O Lord, you brought me up
    from the nether world;
    you preserved me from among
    those going down into
    the pit.
5 Sing praise to the Lord, you his
    faithful ones,
    and give thanks to his holy
    name.
6 For his anger lasts but a
    moment;
    a lifetime, his good will.
    At nightfall, weeping enters in,
    but with the dawn, rejoicing.

B

I

7 Once, in my security, I said,
    "I shall never be disturbed."
8 O Lord, in your good will you
    had endowed me with
    majesty and strength:
    but when you hid your face
    I was terrified.

II

9 To you, O Lord, I cried out;
    with the Lord I pleaded;
10 "What gain would there be
    from my lifeblood,
    from my going down into
    the grave?
    Would dust give you thanks
    or proclaim your faithfulness?
11 Hear, O Lord, and have pity on
    me;
    O Lord, be my helper."

III

12 You changed my mourning
    into dancing;
    you took off my sackcloth
    and clothed me with
    gladness,
13 That my soul might sing praise
    to you without ceasing;
    O Lord, my God, forever will
    I give you thanks.

PSALM 31

Prayer in Distress and Thanksgiving for Escape

1 For the leader. A psalm of David.

I

2 In you, O Lord, I take refuge;
    let me never be put to shame.
    In your justice rescue me,
3   incline your ear to me,
    make haste to deliver me!
    Be my rock of refuge,
    a stronghold to give me
    safety.
4 You are my rock and my
    fortress;
    for your name's sake you will
    lead and guide me.
5 You will free me from the snare
    they set for me,
    for you are my refuge.
6 Into your hands I commend my
    spirit;
    you will redeem me, O Lord,
    O faithful God.
7 You hate those who worship
    vain idols,
    but my trust is in the Lord.
8 I will rejoice and be glad of
    your kindness,
    when you have seen my
    affliction
    and watched over me in my
    distress,
9 Not shutting me up in the grip
    of the enemy
    but enabling me to move
    about at large.

II

10 Have pity on me, O Lord,
    for I am in distress;
    with sorrow my eye is
    consumed; my soul also,
    and my body.
11 For my life is spent with grief
    and my years with sighing;
    My strength has failed
    through affliction,
    and my bones are consumed.

12 For all my foes I am an object
    of reproach,
    a laughingstock of my
    neighbors, and a dread
    to my friends;
    they who see me abroad flee
    from me.
13 I am forgotten like the
    unremembered dead;
    I am like a dish that is broken.
14 I hear the whispers of the
    crowd, that frighten me
    from every side,
    as they consult together
    against me, plotting to
    take my life.
15 But my trust is in you, O Lord;
    I say, "You are my God."
16 In your hands is my destiny;
    rescue me
    from the clutches of my
    enemies and my persecutors.
17 Let your face shine upon your
    servant;
    save me in your kindness.
18 O Lord, let me not be put to
    shame, for I call upon you;
    let the wicked be put to
    shame; let them be reduced
    to silence in the nether world.
19 Let dumbness strike their lying
    lips
    that speak insolence against
    the just in pride and scorn.

III

20 How great is the goodness,
    O Lord,
    which you have in store for
    those who fear you,
    And which, toward those who
    take refuge in you,
    you show in the sight of men.
21 You hide them in the shelter of
    your presence
    from the plottings of men;
    You screen them within your
    abode
    from the strife of tongues.
22 Blessed be the Lord whose
    wondrous kindness
    he has shown me in a fortified
    city.

30, 10: See note on Ps 6, 6.
30, 12: *Sackcloth:* worn in times of mourning and penance. Cf 2 Sm 3, 31; 1 Kgs 21, 27; Pss 35, 13; 69, 12.
Ps 31: In the first two sections (2–19) the psalmist describes in pathetic words his extreme misery and affliction, while with unshaken confidence in God's goodness he prays for heavenly aid. The third section (20–25) is a typical hymn of thanksgiving. If it was

originally joined to the preceding verses and not an independent psalm, it must be considered as an anticipated acknowledgment of favors the psalmist hopes to receive.
31, 6: *Into your hands I commend my spirit:* our Lord made these words his own as he died on the cross. Cf Lk 23, 46. Hence the whole psalm may be fittingly considered as an expression of Christ's feelings of anguish, joined with filial confidence in his heavenly

Father, during his bitter passion.
31, 13: *Like a dish that is broken:* a common comparison for something ruined and useless. Cf Is 30, 14; Jer 19, 11; 22, 28.
31, 14: *That frighten me from every side:* literally, "terror from round about." This phrase occurs several times also in Jeremiah. Cf Jer 6, 25; 20, 3.10; 46, 5; 49, 29. There are certain other marks of similarity between this psalm and the writings of that prophet.

23 Once I said in my anguish,
  "I am cut off from your sight";
  Yet you heard the sound of my
    pleading
    when I cried out to you.
24 Love the LORD, all you his
    faithful ones!
  The LORD keeps those who
    are constant,
  but more than requites those
    who act proudly.
25 Take courage and be
    stouthearted,
  all you who hope in the LORD.

PSALM 32

Remission of Sin

1 Of David. A *maskil*.

I

Happy is he whose fault is
    taken away,
  whose sin is covered.
2 Happy is the man to whom the
    LORD imputes not guilt,
  in whose spirit there is no
    guile.

II

3 As long as I would not speak,
    my bones wasted away
  with my groaning all the day,
4 For day and night your hand
    was heavy upon me;
  my strength was dried up as
    by the heat of summer.
5 Then I acknowledged my sin
    to you,
  my guilt I covered not,
  I said, "I confess my faults to
    the LORD,"
  and you took away the guilt
    of my sin.
6 For this shall every faithful man
    pray to you
  in time of stress.
  Though deep waters overflow,
    they shall not reach him.

7 You are my shelter; from
    distress you will preserve
    me;
  with glad cries of freedom
    you will ring me round.

III

8 I will instruct you and show
    you the way you should
    walk;
  I will counsel you, keeping my
    eye upon you.
9 Be not senseless like horses or
    mules:
  with bit and bridle their
    temper must be curbed,
  else they will not come near
    you.

IV

10 Many are the sorrows of the
    wicked,
  but kindness surrounds him
    who trusts in the LORD.
11 Be glad in the LORD and rejoice,
    you just;
  exult, all you upright of heart.

PSALM 33

*Praise of the Lord's Power and
Providence*

I

1 Exult, you just, in the LORD;
  praise from the upright is
    fitting.
2 Give thanks to the LORD on the
    harp;
  with the ten-stringed lyre
    chant his praises.
3 Sing to him a new song;
  pluck the strings skillfully,
    with shouts of gladness.
4 For upright is the word of the
    LORD,
  and all his works are
    trustworthy.
5 He loves justice and right;
  of the kindness of the LORD
    the earth is full.

II

6 By the word of the LORD the
    heavens were made;
  by the breath of his mouth
    all their host.
7 He gathers the waters of the
    sea as in a flask;
  in cellars he confines the deep.

III

8 Let all the earth fear the LORD;
  let all who dwell in the world
    revere him.
9 For he spoke, and it was made;
  he commanded, and it stood
    forth.
10 The LORD brings to nought the
    plans of nations;
  he foils the designs of peoples.
11 But the plan of the LORD
    stands forever;
  the design of his heart,
    through all generations.
12 Happy the nation whose God
    is the LORD,
  the people he has chosen for
    his own inheritance.

IV

13 From heaven the LORD looks
    down;
  he sees all mankind.
14 From his fixed throne he
    beholds
  all who dwell on the earth,
15 He who fashioned the heart of
    each,
  he who knows all their works.

V

16 A king is not saved by a
    mighty army,
  nor is a warrior delivered by
    great strength.
17 Useless is the horse for safety;
  great though its strength,
    it cannot provide escape.
18 But see, the eyes of the LORD are
    upon those who fear him,
  upon those who hope for his
    kindness,

Ps 32: The second of the Penitential Psalms, and a favorite of St. Augustine's. The psalmist describes the blessedness of having one's sins forgiven by God (1f), as well as his own spiritual consolation when he confessed his sins (3–7); he then exhorts others to be submissive to God's will (8f), and to confide with joy in his goodness (10f).
32, 2: *No guile:* no hypocrisy in acknowledging his sins.
32, 3: *I would not speak:* I refused at first to confess my sins.
32, 5: St. Augustine's comment is that, even before the sin is acknowledged by the penitent's lips, God hears the cry of his heart. Pardon at once follows sincere contrition. Cf 2 Sm 12, 13.
32, 9: The Hebrew text of this verse is obscure, and is variously interpreted.
Ps 33: A hymn of praise in which the just are invited to chant the glories of God (1–3), because he is ever faithful to his promises (4f), the all-powerful Creator (6f), and the wise and mighty Ruler of the world (8–12), who sees and knows all things (13–15) and who alone is the source of victory and salvation (16–19). The hymn concludes with an expression of confidence in God's goodness (20–22).
33, 6: *All their host:* by a common figure, the countless stars of the sky are viewed as a vast army. Cf Neh 9, 6; Is 40, 26; 45, 12; Jer 33, 22.
33, 7: The ancients marveled at the power which kept the mighty seas from overwhelming the dry land. According to pagan mythology, this was achieved by a fierce battle in which the heavenly gods triumphed over the gods of the deep. For the Lord, however, this is as simple as putting water into a bottle; he can store away the immense subterranean ocean as easily as a man stores wine in his cellar.

19 To deliver them from death
　　and preserve them in spite
　　　of famine.

VI

20 Our soul waits for the LORD,
　　who is our help and our shield,
21 For in him our hearts rejoice;
　　in his holy name we trust.
22 May your kindness, O LORD,
　　be upon us
　　who have put our hope in you.

PSALM 34

Praise of God, the Protector of
the Just

1 Of David, when he feigned madness before
　Abimelech, who forced him to depart.

I

2 I will bless the LORD at all
　　times;
　　his praise shall be ever in my
　　　mouth.
3 Let my soul glory in the LORD;
　　the lowly will hear me and be
　　　glad.
4 Glorify the LORD with me,
　　let us together extol his
　　　name.

II

5 I sought the LORD, and he
　　answered me
　　and delivered me from all
　　　my fears.
6 Look to him that you may be
　　radiant with joy,
　　and your faces may not blush
　　　with shame.
7 When the afflicted man called
　　out, the LORD heard,
　　and from all his distress he
　　　saved him.
8 The angel of the LORD encamps
　　around those who fear him,
　　and delivers them.
9 Taste and see how good the
　　LORD is;
　　happy is the man who takes
　　　refuge in him.

10 Fear the LORD, you his holy
　　ones,
　　for nought is lacking to those
　　　who fear him.
11 The great grow poor and
　　hungry;
　　but those who seek the LORD
　　　want for no good thing.

III

12 Come, children, hear me;
　　I will teach you the fear of the
　　　LORD.
13 Which of you desires life,
　　and takes delight in
　　　prosperous days?
14 Keep your tongue from evil
　　and your lips from speaking
　　　guile;
15 Turn from evil, and do good;
　　seek peace, and follow after
　　　it.
16 The LORD has eyes for the just,
　　and ears for their cry.
17 The LORD confronts the
　　evildoers,
　　to destroy remembrance of
　　　them from the earth.
18 When the just cry out, the LORD
　　hears them,
　　and from all their distress he
　　　rescues them.
19 The LORD is close to the
　　brokenhearted;
　　and those who are crushed in
　　　spirit he saves.
20 Many are the troubles of the
　　just man,
　　but out of them all the LORD
　　　delivers him;
21 He watches over all his bones;
　　not one of them shall be
　　　broken.
22 Vice slays the wicked,
　　and the enemies of the just
　　　pay for their guilt.
23 But the LORD redeems the lives
　　of his servants;
　　no one incurs guilt who takes
　　　refuge in him.

PSALM 35

Prayer for Help against Unjust
Enemies

1 Of David.

I

Fight, O LORD, against those
　　who fight me;
　　war against those who make
　　　war upon me.
2 Take up the shield and buckler,
　　and rise up in my defense.
3 Brandish the lance, and block
　　the way
　　in the face of my pursuers;
Say to my soul,
　　"I am your salvation."
4 Let those be put to shame and
　　disgraced
　　who seek my life;
Let those be turned back and
　　confounded
　　who plot evil against me.
5 Let them be like chaff before
　　the wind,
　　with the angel of the LORD
　　　driving them on.
6 Let their way be dark and
　　slippery,
　　with the angel of the LORD
　　　pursuing them.

II

7 For without cause they set
　　their snare for me,
　　without cause they dug a pit
　　　against my life.
8 Let ruin come upon them
　　unawares,
　　and let the snare they have set
　　　catch them;
　　into the pit they have dug let
　　　them fall.
9 But I will rejoice in the LORD,
　　I will be joyful because of his
　　　salvation.
10 All my being shall say,
　　"O LORD, who is like you,
　　The rescuer of the afflicted man
　　　from those too strong for him,
　　of the afflicted and the needy
　　　from their despoilers?"

Ps 34: An alphabetic psalm having no apparent connection with the events mentioned in v 1. After an exhortation to glorify the Lord (2–4), the psalmist sings his grateful praise to God for having rescued him from danger (5–11), and concludes with an admonition to fear the Lord and keep his commandments (12–23).

34, 1: It was at the court of the Philistine King Achish that David feigned insanity after he had departed from the priest Abimelech. Some early scribe appears to have confused these two names here.

34, 7: *When the afflicted man called out, the Lord heard:* some render the passage, "Here is an afflicted man who called out, and the LORD heard him." The psalmist himself would then be this *afflicted man.*

34, 9: *Taste and see:* figurative language for, "know by experience."

34, 12: *Children:* in Hebrew wisdom literature a rabbi or teacher customarily addresses his disciples in this way.

Ps 35: Calling upon God to defend him (1–6), the psalmist describes the wickedness (7–12) and ingratitude (13–16) of his enemies, and then reiterates his plea for divine assistance (17–28).

35, 1–3: The martial language is purely figurative; the psalmist's enemies are not actually armed against him, but rather are those who have falsely accused him of serious crimes. Cf vv 11.21.

11 Unjust witnesses have risen up;
       things I knew not of, they lay
       to my charge.
12 They have repaid me evil for
       good,
       bringing bereavement to my
       soul.

III

13 But I, when they were ill, put on
       sackcloth;
       I afflicted myself with fasting
       and poured forth prayers
       within my bosom.
14 As though it were a friend of
       mine, or a brother, I went
       about;
       like one bewailing a mother,
       I was bowed down in
       mourning.
15 Yet when I stumbled they were
       glad and gathered together;
       they gathered together
       striking me unawares.
   They tore at me without ceasing;
16   they put me to the test; they
       mocked me,
       gnashing their teeth at me.

IV

17 O Lord, how long will you
       look on?
       Save me from the roaring
       beasts; from the lions,
       my only life.
18 I will give you thanks in the
       vast assembly,
       in the mighty throng I will
       praise you.
19 Let not my unprovoked enemies
       rejoice over me;
       let not my undeserved foes
       wink knowingly.
20 For civil words they speak not,
       but against the peaceful in the
       land
       they fashion treacherous
       speech.
21 And they open wide their
       mouths against me,
       saying, "Aha, aha! We saw
       him with our own eyes!"

22 You, O Lord, have seen; be not
       silent;
       Lord, be not far from me!
23 Awake, and be vigilant in my
       defense;
       in my cause, my God and my
       Lord.
24 Do me justice, because you
       are just, O Lord;
       my God, let them not rejoice
       over me.
25 Let them not say in their hearts,
       "Aha! This is what we
       wanted!"
       Let them not say, "We have
       swallowed him up!"

26 Let all be put to shame and
       confounded
       who are glad at my
       misfortune.
       Let those be clothed with shame
       and disgrace
       who glory over me.
27 But let those shout for joy and
       be glad
       who favor my just cause;
   And may they ever say, "The
       Lord be glorified;
       he wills the prosperity of his
       servant!"
28 Then my tongue shall recount
       your justice,
       your praise, all the day.

PSALM 36

Human Wickedness and
Divine Providence

1 For the leader. Of David, the servant of
the Lord.

I

2 Sin speaks to the wicked man
       in his heart;
       there is no dread of God
       before his eyes,
3 For he beguiles himself with the
       thought
       that his guilt will not be found
       out or hated.

4 The words of his mouth are
       empty and false;
       he has ceased to understand
       how to do good.
5 He plans wickedness in his bed;
       he sets out on a way that is
       not good, with no
       repugnance for evil.

II

6 O Lord, your kindness reaches
       to heaven;
       your faithfulness, to the
       clouds.
7 Your justice is like the
       mountains of God;
       your judgments, like the
       mighty deep;
       man and beast you save,
       O Lord.
8 How precious is your kindness,
       O God!
       The children of men take
       refuge in the shadow of
       your wings.
9 They have their fill of the prime
       gifts of your house;
       from your delightful stream
       you give them to drink.
10 For with you is the fountain
       of life,
       and in your light we see light.

III

11 Keep up your kindness toward
       your friends,
       your just defense of the
       upright of heart.
12 Let not the foot of the proud
       overtake me
       nor the land of the wicked
       disquiet me.
13 See how the evildoers have
       fallen;
       they are thrust down and
       cannot rise.

35, 13.15–17: In several places the Hebrew text of
these verses is obscure and their translation somewhat
uncertain.
   35, 13: *And poured forth prayers within my bosom:*
literally, "my prayers returned upon my bosom."
Some take this to mean that he prayed with deeply
bowed head so that his voice reverberated against his
chest; but more probably it refers to the saying of
silent prayers which remained within his heart.
   35, 19: *Unprovoked . . . undeserved:* he has never

given them a just reason for hating and persecuting
him.
   Ps 36: The thought of man's wickedness, which
leads him to forget or ignore the just punishments due
to his sins (2–5), is here contrasted with God's loving
care for mankind (6–10). Hence, the psalmist prays to
be delivered from wicked men (11–13).
   36, 2: *Speaks:* the Hebrew word used here is used
elsewhere only of the Lord speaking to his inspired
prophets. Hence the sense here is, "It is the sinfulness

in man's heart that inspires, or instigates, him to
wickedness."
   36, 3: *Hated:* punished by God.
   36, 7: *Like the mountains of God:* as immense as the
loftiest mountains.
   36, 10: *In your light we see light:* light is the symbol
of goodness and happiness; hence, "Through your
goodness we enjoy true happiness."

PSALM 37

*The Fate of Sinners and the
Reward of the Just*

1 Of David.

Be not vexed over evildoers,
  nor jealous of those who do
    wrong;
2 For like grass they quickly
    wither,
  and like green herbs they wilt.

3 Trust in the LORD and do
    good,
  that you may dwell in the
    land and enjoy security.
4 Take delight in the LORD,
  and he will grant you your
    heart's requests.

5 Commit to the LORD your way;
  trust in him, and he will act.
6 He will make justice dawn for
    you like the light;
  bright as the noonday shall
    be your vindication.

7 Leave it to the LORD,
  and wait for him;
  Be not vexed at the successful
    path
  of the man who does
    malicious deeds.

8 Give up your anger, and forsake
    wrath;
  be not vexed, it will only
    harm you.
9 For evildoers shall be cut off,
  but those who wait for the
    LORD shall possess the land.

10 Yet a little while, and the
    wicked man shall be no
      more;
  though you mark his place he
    will not be there.
11 But the meek shall possess the
    land,
  they shall delight in abounding
    peace.

12 The wicked man plots against
    the just
  and gnashes his teeth at them;
13 But the LORD laughs at him,
  for he sees that his day is
    coming.

14 A sword the wicked draw; they
    bend their bow
  to bring down the afflicted
    and the poor,
  to slaughter those whose path
    is right.
15 But their swords shall pierce
    their own hearts,
  and their bows shall be
    broken.

16 Better is the scanty store of the
    just
  than the great wealth of the
    wicked,
17 For the power of the wicked
    shall be broken,
  but the LORD supports the
    just.

18 The LORD watches over the lives
    of the wholehearted;
  their inheritance lasts forever.
19 They are not put to shame in an
    evil time;
  in days of famine they have
    plenty.

20 But the wicked perish,
  and the enemies of the LORD,
    like the beauty of the
      meadows,
  vanish; like smoke they
    vanish.

21 The wicked man borrows and
    does not repay;
  the just man is kindly and
    gives,
22 But those whom he blesses shall
    possess the land,
  while those he curses shall be
    cut off.

23 By the LORD are the steps of a
    man made firm,
  and he approves his way.
24 Though he fall, he does not lie
    prostrate,
  for the hand of the LORD
    sustains him.

25 Neither in my youth, nor now
    that I am old,
  have I seen a just man
    forsaken
  nor his descendants begging
    bread.

26 All the day he is kindly and
    lends,
  and his descendants shall be
    blessed.

27 Turn from evil and do good,
  that you may abide forever;
28 For the LORD loves what is
    right,
  and forsakes not his faithful
    ones.

  Criminals are destroyed,
  and the posterity of the
    wicked is cut off.
29 The just shall possess the land
  and dwell in it forever.

30 The mouth of the just man tells
    of wisdom
  and his tongue utters what is
    right.
31 The law of his God is in his
    heart,
  and his steps do not falter.

32 The wicked man spies on the
    just,
  and seeks to slay him.
33 The LORD will not leave him in
    his power
  nor let him be condemned
    when he is on trial.

34 Wait for the LORD,
  and keep his way;
  He will promote you to
    ownership of the land;
  when the wicked are
    destroyed, you shall look
      on.

35 I saw a wicked man, fierce,
  and stalwart as a flourishing,
    age-old tree.
36 Yet as I passed by, lo! he was
    no more;
  I sought him, but he could
    not be found.

37 Watch the wholehearted man,
  and mark the upright;
  for there is a future for the
    man of peace.
38 Sinners shall all alike be
    destroyed;
  the future of the wicked shall
    be cut off.

Ps 37 treats of the problem of evil: why the wicked seem to prosper while the good suffer. The answer of the psalmist is that this seeming injustice is short-lived. God will reward the good and punish the wicked even here on earth. Since this is an alphabetic psalm,

these thoughts are repeated without much logical sequence throughout the whole psalm.
37, 3.9.11.22.29.34: *The land:* the Promised Land, Palestine, which however is a type or figure of heaven. Cf Heb 11, 9f.13–16. Therefore, when our Lord in the

Beatitudes (Mt 5, 4) quoted v 11 of this psalm, he meant it in the sense of, "The meek shall possess the kingdom of heaven."
37, 37f: *A future for the man of peace . . . the future of the wicked:* in his own life and offspring.

39 The salvation of the just is from
    the Lord;
    he is their refuge in time of
      distress.
40 And the Lord helps them and
    delivers them;
    he delivers them from the
      wicked and saves them,
    because they take refuge in him.

PSALM 38

Prayer of an Afflicted Sinner

1 A psalm of David. For remembrance.

I

2 O Lord, in your anger punish
    me not,
    in your wrath chastise me not;
3 For your arrows have sunk deep
    in me,
    and your hand has come
      down upon me.
4 There is no health in my flesh
    because of your indignation;
    there is no wholeness in my
      bones because of my sin,
5 For my iniquities have
    overwhelmed me;
    they are like a heavy burden,
      beyond my strength.

II

6 Noisome and festering are my
    sores
    because of my folly,
7 I am stooped and bowed down
    profoundly;
    all the day I go in mourning,
8 For my loins are filled with
    burning pains;
    there is no health in my flesh.
9 I am numbed and severely
    crushed;
    I roar with anguish of heart.

10 O Lord, all my desire is before
    you;
    from you my groaning is not
      hid.
11 My heart throbs; my strength
    forsakes me;
    the very light of my eyes has
      failed me.

12 My friends and my
    companions stand back
    because of my affliction;
    my neighbors stand afar off.
13 Men lay snares for me seeking
    my life;
    they look to my misfortune,
    they speak of ruin,
    treachery they talk of all the
      day.

III

14 But I am like a deaf man,
    hearing not,
    like a dumb man who opens
      not his mouth.
15 I am become like a man who
    neither hears
    nor has in his mouth a retort.
16 Because for you, O Lord, I wait;
    you, O Lord my God, will
      answer
17 When I say, "Let them not be
    glad on my account
    who, when my foot slips,
      glory over me."

IV

18 For I am very near to falling,
    and my grief is with me
      always.
19 Indeed, I acknowledge my guilt;
    I grieve over my sin.
20 But my undeserved enemies are
    strong;
    many are my foes without
      cause.
21 Those who repay evil for good
    harass me for pursuing good.
22 Forsake me not, O Lord;
    my God, be not far from me!
23 Make haste to help me,
    O Lord my salvation!

PSALM 39

The Brevity and Vanity of Life

1 For the leader, for Jeduthun.
    A psalm of David.

I

2 I said, "I will watch my ways,
    so as not to sin with my
      tongue;
    I will set a curb on my
      mouth."

While the wicked man was
    before me
3 I kept dumb and silent;
    I refrained from rash speech.
But my grief was stirred up;
4   hot grew my heart within me;
    in my thoughts, a fire blazed
      forth.
I spoke out with my tongue:

II

5 Let me know, O Lord, my end
    and what is the number of my
      days,
    that I may learn how frail
      I am.
6 A short span you have made my
    days,
    and my life is nought before
      you;
    only a breath is any human
      existence.
7 A phantom only, man goes his
    ways;
    like vapor only are his
      restless pursuits;
    he heaps up stores, and knows
      not who will use them.

III

8 And now, for what do I wait,
    O Lord?
    in you is my hope.
9 From all my sins deliver me;
    a fool's taunt let me not
      suffer.

IV

10 I was speechless and opened not
    my mouth,
    because it was your doing;
11 Take away your scourge from me;
    at the blow of your hand I
      wasted away.
12 With rebukes for guilt you
    chasten man;
    you dissolve like a cobweb all
      that is dear to him;
    only a breath is any man.
13 Hear my prayer, O Lord;
    to my cry give ear;
    to my weeping be not deaf!
    For I am but a wayfarer before
      you,
    a pilgrim like all my fathers.

Ps 38: The third of the Penitential Psalms. Acknowledging that his sickness is a punishment for his sins (2–5), the psalmist describes his misery (6–13), which he is patiently bearing with trust in God (14–17) whose pardon and help he implores (18–23).

38, 1: *For remembrance:* or, "For the memorial sacrifice." Cf Lv 2, 2.9.16; 5, 12; Is 66, 3.
38, 21: *Harass:* the Hebrew expression, from which the word "Satan" is derived, signifies either "to harass" or "to slander." Cf Ps 109, 4.

Ps 39: Although he had resolved not to complain (2–4), the psalmist, like Ecclesiastes, laments the brevity and vanity of life (5–1); yet his hope is in the Lord (8f), to whom he prays for pardon and health (10–14).

14 Turn your gaze from me, that I
      may find respite
   ere I depart and be no more.

PSALM 40

Gratitude and Prayer for Help

1 For the leader. A psalm of David.

A

I

2 I have waited, waited for the
      LORD,
   and he stooped toward me
      and heard my cry.
3 He drew me out of the pit of
      destruction,
   out of the mud of the swamp;
   He set my feet upon a crag;
      he made firm my steps.
4 And he put a new song into my
      mouth,
   a hymn to our God.
   Many shall look on in awe
      and trust in the LORD.

II

5 Happy is the man who makes
      the LORD his trust;
   who turns not to idolatry
      or to those who stray after
      falsehood.
6 How numerous have you made,
      O LORD, my God, your
      wondrous deeds!
   And in your plans for us
      there is none to equal you;
   Should I wish to declare or to
      tell them,
   they would be too many to
      recount.

III

7 Sacrifice or oblation you wished
      not,
   but ears open to obedience
      you gave me.

   Holocausts or sin-offerings you
      sought not;
8   then said I, "Behold I come;
   in the written scroll it is
      prescribed for me,
9 To do your will, O my God, is
      my delight,
   and your law is within my
      heart!"
10 I announced your justice in the
      vast assembly;
   I did not restrain my lips, as
      you, O LORD, know.
11 Your justice I kept not hid
      within my heart;
   your faithfulness and your
      salvation I have spoken of;
   I have made no secret of your
      kindness and your truth
      in the vast assembly.

B

I

12 Withhold not, O LORD, your
      compassion from me;
   may your kindness and your
      truth ever preserve me.
13 For all about me are evils
      beyond reckoning;
   my sins so overcome me that
      I cannot see;
   They are more numerous than
      the hairs of my head,
      and my heart fails me.

II

14 Deign, O LORD, to rescue me;
   O LORD, make haste to help
      me.
15 Let all be put to shame and
      confusion
   who seek to snatch away my
      life.
   Let them be turned back in
      disgrace
   who desire my ruin.

16 Let them be dismayed in their
      shame
   who say to me, "Aha, aha!"
17 But may all who seek you
      exult and be glad in you,
   And may those who love your
      salvation
   say ever, "The LORD be
      glorified."
18 Though I am afflicted and poor,
      yet the LORD thinks of me.
   You are my help and my
      deliverer;
   O my God, hold not back!

PSALM 41

Thanksgiving after Sickness

1 For the leader. A psalm of David.

I

2 Happy is he who has regard for
      the lowly and the poor;
   in the day of misfortune the
      LORD will deliver him.
3 The LORD will keep and preserve
      him;
   he will make him happy on
      the earth,
   and not give him over to the
      will of his enemies.
4 The LORD will help him on his
      sickbed,
   he will take away all his
      ailment when he is ill.

II

5 Once I said, "O LORD, have pity
      on me;
   heal me, though I have sinned
      against you.
6 My enemies say the worst of me:
   'When will he die and his
      name perish?'
7 When one comes to see me, he
      speaks without sincerity;
   his heart stores up malice;
   when he leaves he gives voice
      to it outside.

39, 14: *And be no more:* here on earth. The psalmist naturally shared the common belief in a certain kind of life in the nether world after death. Job also complained in a similar strain of the brevity of life and the finality of death, while asserting at the same time his faith in a future life. Cf Jb 3, 13–19.
   Ps 40 consists of two distinct parts, probably once independent psalms. In the first section (2–11) the psalmist thanks God for having rescued him from the danger of death (2–4), and praises the Lord for his goodness toward all who trust in him (5f); to do God's will is the best sacrifice, he says (7–9), as he offers up this hymn of thanksgiving among the worshippers in

the temple (10f). The second section (12–18), which is the same as Ps 70, is a typical supplication of one afflicted and persecuted.
   40, 4: *A new song:* the hymn of thanksgiving in vv 5–11. Many hymns of praise and thanksgiving are thus described because they represent a complete change from the attitude of lamentation.
   40, 7–9: Obedience is better than sacrifice. Cf 1 Sm 15, 22; Is 1, 10–20; Mi 6, 6–8. In Heb 10, 5–7 this passage, according to the somewhat different form of the ancient Greek version, is quoted and most fittingly applied to Christ, whose sacrifice of perfect obedience

immeasurably surpasses the liturgical sacrifices of the old law.
   Ps 41: After speaking in general terms about the merciful man obtaining God's mercy (2–4), the psalmist recounts how he had once prayed for that mercy when, in his sickness, he was reviled and persecuted even by his friends (5–11); therefore he now acknowledges with gratitude that God has heard his prayer (12–13).
   41, 3: In the form of a prayer, "May the Lord keep," etc., this verse is employed in the liturgy of the Church as an invocation for the pope.

8 All my foes whisper together
    against me;
  against me they imagine the
    worst:
9 'A malignant disease fills his
    frame';
  and 'Now that he lies ill, he
    will not rise again.'
10 Even my friend who had my
    trust
   and partook of my bread, has
    raised his heel against me.

                                (III)

11 But you, O LORD, have pity on
    me, and raise me up,
   that I may repay them."
12 That you love me I know by
    this,
   that my enemy does not
    triumph over me,
13 But because of my integrity
    you sustain me
   and let me stand before you
    forever.

          * * *

14 Blessed be the LORD, the God
    of Israel,
   from all eternity and forever.
   Amen. Amen.

THE SECOND BOOK
Psalms 42–72

PSALM 42

Desire for God and His Temple

1 For the leader. A *maskil* of the sons
  of Korah.

          I

2 As the hind longs for the
    running waters,
  so my soul longs for you,
    O God.

---

3 Athirst is my soul for God,
    the living God.
  When shall I go and behold
    the face of God?
4 My tears are my food day and
    night,
  as they say to me day after
    day, "Where is your God?"
5 Those times I recall,
  now that I pour out my soul
    within me,
  When I went with the throng
    and led them in procession to
    the house of God,
  Amid loud cries of joy and
    thanksgiving,
  with the multitude keeping
    festival.
6 Why are you so downcast,
    O my soul?
  Why do you sigh within me?
  Hope in God! For I shall
    again be thanking him,
  in the presence of my
    savior and my God.

          II

7 Within me my soul is
    downcast;
  so will I remember you
  From the Land of the Jordan
    and of Hermon,
    from Mount Mizar.
8 Deep calls unto deep
  and in the roar of your
    cataracts;
  All your breakers and your
    billows
    pass over me.
9 By day the LORD bestows his
    grace,
  and at night I have his song,
  a prayer to my living God.
10 I sing to God, my rock:
  "Why do you forget me?
  Why must I go about in
    mourning,
  with the enemy oppressing
    me?"

---

11 It crushes my bones that my
    foes mock me,
  as they say to me day after
    day, "Where is your God?"
12 Why are you so downcast, O
    my soul?
  Why do you sigh within me?
  Hope in God! For I shall
    again be thanking him,
  in the presence of my savior
    and my God.

PSALM 43

          III

1 Do me justice, O God, and
    fight my fight
  against a faithless people;
  from the deceitful and impious
    man rescue me.
2 For you, O God, are my
    strength.
  Why do you keep me so far
    away?
  Why must I go about in
    mourning,
  with the enemy oppressing
    me?
3 Send forth your light and your
    fidelity;
  they shall lead me on
  And bring me to your holy
    mountain,
  to your dwelling place.
4 Then will I go in to the altar of
    God,
  the God of my gladness and
    joy;
  Then will I give you thanks
    upon the harp,
  O God, my God!
5 Why are you so downcast,
    O my soul?
  Why do you sigh within me?
  Hope in God! For I shall
    again be thanking him,
  in the presence of my savior
    and my God.

41, 10: These words were cited by our Lord at the Last Supper in regard to Judas, the perfect fulfillment of this type of treacherous friend. Cf Jn 13, 18.

41, 14: Doxology closing the First Book of the Psalter. It is not part of the psalm to which it is appended.

Pss 42–43 represent respectively two thirds and one third of what was originally a single psalm. Each of the three parts ends in an identical refrain (42, 6.12; 43, 5). The psalmist is in exile north of Palestine, far from Jerusalem. Homesick for the solemn services of the temple, he keeps up his courage by an ardent hope and an unshaken trust in God. The high lyrical style

of this psalm makes it one of the finest poems in the Bible.

42, 2: *O God:* in the Second Book of the Psalms the proper name of God, *Yahweh*, "The LORD," was changed in almost all places by some early scribe to read, *Elohim,* "God." Thus we have the strange phrase "O God, my God," instead of the original, "O LORD, my God," e.g., in Ps 43, 4.

42, 3: *Go and behold the face of God:* a Hebrew idiom meaning, "Visit the temple." Cf Ex 23, 17.

42, 4: *Where is your God?:* God gives no evidence of coming to his aid.

42, 7: *The land of the Jordan:* the region at the sources of the Jordan, at the foot of Mount Hermon.

Mount Mizar: probably means, "the small mountain," presumably one of Hermon's foothills.

42, 8: *Deep calls unto deep:* the re-echoing roar of stormy waters. The figure of affliction as a raging sea is common. Cf Pss 18, 5; 69, 2ff.15f; Jn 2, 3–6. Here, however, the thought may also have been suggested by the cataracts of the upper Jordan.

42, 9: *My living God:* literally "the God of my life"; hence some understand it as, "the God who gives me life." Perhaps Ps 42, 3 also was originally, "the God of my life." Cf Ps 43, 4.

43, 4: *To the altar of God:* because of these words the Church used Ps 43 at the beginning of Holy Mass.

PSALM 44

Israel's Past Glory and Present Need

1 For the leader. A *maskil* for the sons of Korah.

I

2 O God, our ears have heard,
  our fathers have declared to us,
The deeds you did in their days,
  in days of old;
3 How with your own hand you
    rooted out the nations and
    planted them;
  you smashed the peoples, but
    for them you made room.
4 For not with their own sword
    did they conquer the land,
  nor did their own arm make
    them victorious,
  But it was your arm and your
    right hand
  and the light of your
    countenance, in your love
    for them.
5 You are my king and my God,
    who bestowed victories on
    Jacob.
6 Our foes through you we struck
    down;
  through your name we
    trampled down our
    adversaries.
7 For not in my bow did I trust,
    nor did my sword save me;
8 But you saved us from our foes,
    and those who hated us you
    put to shame.
9 In God we gloried day by day;
    your name we praised always.

II

10 Yet now you have cast us off
    and put us in disgrace,
    and you go not forth with our
    armies.
11 You have let us be driven back
    by our foes;
  those who hated us plundered
    us at will,

12 You marked us out as sheep to
    be slaughtered;
  among the nations you
    scattered us.
13 You sold your people for no
    great price;
  you made no profit from the
    sale of them.
14 You made us the reproach of
    our neighbors,
  the mockery and the scorn of
    those around us.
15 You made us a byword among
    the nations,
  a laughingstock among the
    peoples.
16 All the day my disgrace is
    before me,
  and shame covers my face
17 At the voice of him who mocks
    and blasphemes,
  and in the presence of the
    enemy and the avenger.

III

18 All this has come upon us,
    though we have not
    forgotten you,
  nor have we been disloyal to
    your covenant;
19 Our hearts have not shrunk
    back.
  nor our steps turned aside
    from your path,
20 Though you thrust us down into
    a place of misery
  and covered us with
    darkness.
21 If we had forgotten the name of
    our God
  and stretched out our hands
    to a strange God,
22 Would not God have discovered
    this?
  For he knows the secrets of
    the heart.
23 Yet for your sake we are being
    slain all the day;
  we are looked upon as sheep
    to be slaughtered.

IV

24 Awake! Why are you asleep,
    O Lord?
  Arise! Cast us not off forever!
25 Why do you hide your face,
    forgetting our woe and our
    oppression?
26 For our souls are bowed down
    to the dust,
  our bodies are pressed to the
    earth.
27 Arise, help us!
  Redeem us for your kindness'
    sake.

PSALM 45

Nuptial Ode for the Messianic King

1 For the leader; according to "Lilies." A *maskil* of the sons of Korah. A love song.

I

2 My heart overflows with a goodly
    theme;
  as I sing my ode to the king,
  my tongue is as nimble as the
    pen of a skillful scribe.

II

3 Fairer in beauty are you than
    the sons of men;
  grace is poured out upon
    your lips;
  thus God has blessed you
    forever.
4 Gird your sword upon your
    thigh, O mighty one!
  In your splendor and your
    majesty ride on triumphant
5 In the cause of truth and for the
    sake of justice;
  and may your right hand
    show you wondrous deeds.
6 Your arrows are sharp; peoples
    are subject to you;
  the king's enemies lose heart.
7 Your throne, O God, stands
    forever and ever;
  a tempered rod is your royal
    scepter.

Ps 44: A supplication of the community, reminding God of his past favors to Israel (2–9) in contrast to the present sad state of affairs, when the nation suffers from military defeat (10–17) and seems abandoned by him (18–23); therefore the people cry out to him to come to their aid (24–27). The historical circumstances of the psalm cannot be determined with certainty. The occasion may have been the invasion of the Assyrians under Sennacherib at the time of King Hezekiah (2 Kgs 18–19) or the calamities which followed on the defeat of King Josiah and the invasion of the Babylonians (2 Kgs 23, 29—25, 26), or the time of national degradation during the Persian period, the fifth to the

fourth century B.C. But there are no compelling reasons to put this psalm as late as the Maccabean times.

Ps 45: After a dedicatory prologue (2), the psalmist sings the praises of the royal bridegroom (3–10) and his bride (11f); he then describes the wedding procession (13–16) and wishes the king illustrious offspring (17f). The occasion of this epithalamium may have been the marriage of some prince of the Davidic dynasty, perhaps Solomon, with a foreign princess who was apparently from Tyre. But Catholic tradition, in keeping with the inspired interpretation given in Heb 1, 8f, has always understood this psalm as referring

at least in a typical sense, to Christ and his bride, the Church. Cf Eph 5, 25ff.

45, 3: *Fairer . . . than the sons of men:* i.e., than other men; or, "Fairest among the sons of men."

45, 7: *Your throne, O God:* the Hebrew king was called *Elohim*, "God," not in the polytheistic sense common among the ancient pagans, but as meaning "godlike," or, "taking the place of God." Cf Pss 58, 2; 82, 1.6. Of Christ alone can this passage be understood in its full literal sense. Some, however, amend the text to read, "Your throne is the throne of God." Cf 1 Chr 29, 23, where Solomon's throne is referred to as "the throne of the Lord."

8 You love justice and hate
    wickedness;
    therefore God, your God, has
        anointed you
    with the oil of gladness above
        your fellow kings.
9 With myrrh and aloes and cassia
        your robes are fragrant;
    from ivory palaces string
        music brings you joy.
10 The daughters of kings come to
        meet you;
    the queen takes her place at
        your right hand in gold of
        Ophir.

III

11 Hear, O daughter, and see;
        turn your ear,
    forget your people and your
        father's house.
12 So shall the king desire your
        beauty;
    for he is your lord, and you
        must worship him.
13 And the city of Tyre is here
        with gifts;
    the rich among the people
        seek your favor.
14 All glorious is the king's
        daughter as she enters;
    her raiment is threaded with
        spun gold.
15 In embroidered apparel she is
        borne in to the king;
    behind her the virgins of her
        train are brought to you.
16 They are borne in with gladness
        and joy;
    they enter the palace of the king.

IV

17 The place of your fathers your
        sons shall have;
    you shall make them princes
        through all the land.
18 I will make your name
        memorable through all
        generations;
    therefore shall nations praise
        you forever and ever.

PSALM 46

God the Refuge of Israel

1 For the leader. A song of the sons of
Korah; according to "Virgins."

I

2 God is our refuge and our
        strength,
    an ever-present help in distress.
3 Therefore we fear not, though
        the earth be shaken
    and mountains plunge into
        the depths of the sea;
4 Though its waters rage and
        foam
    and the mountains quake at
        its surging.
    The LORD of hosts is with
        us;
    our stronghold is the
        God of Jacob.

II

5 There is a stream whose runlets
        gladden the city of God,
    the holy dwelling of the Most
        High.
6 God is in its midst; it shall not
        be disturbed;
    God will help it at the break
        of dawn.
7 Though nations are in turmoil,
        kingdoms totter,
    his voice resounds, the earth
        melts away,
8   The LORD of hosts is with
        us;
    our stronghold is the
        God of Jacob.

III

9 Come! behold the deeds of the
        LORD,
    the astounding things he has
        wrought on earth:
10 He has stopped wars to the end
        of the earth:
    the bow he breaks; he splinters
        the spears;
    he burns the shields with fire.

11 Desist! and confess that I am
        God,
    exalted among the nations,
        exalted upon the earth.
12   The LORD of hosts is with
        us;
    our stronghold is the
        God of Jacob.

PSALM 47

The Lord the King of all Nations

1 For the leader. A psalm of the sons
of Korah.

I

2 All you peoples, clap your
        hands,
    shout to God with cries of
        gladness,
3 For the LORD, the Most High,
        the awesome,
    is the great king over all the
        earth.
4 He brings peoples under us;
    nations under our feet.
5 He chooses for us our
        inheritance,
    the glory of Jacob, whom he
        loves.

II

6 God mounts his throne amid
        shouts of joy;
    the LORD, amid trumpet
        blasts.
7 Sing praise to God, sing praise;
    sing praise to our king, sing
        praise.

III

8 For king of all the earth is God;
    sing hymns of praise.
9 God reigns over the nations,
    God sits upon his holy throne.
10 The princes of the peoples are
        gathered together
    with the people of the God of
        Abraham.
    For God's are the guardians of
        the earth;
    he is supreme.

45, 10: *Ophir:* a region on the coast of southern Arabia or eastern Africa, famous for its gold. Cf 1 Kgs 9, 28; 10, 11.22; Jb 22, 24.

45, 12: *Worship him:* pay him homage and be submissive to him.

45, 13: *Your favor:* in the current Hebrew text this is read as addressed to the bride, but it should probably be understood as referring to the king. The *you* in v 15 certainly signifies the king.

Ps 46: A hymn of victory whose dominant note is the refrain, *The Lord of hosts is with us.* The first strophe (2–4) sings of Israel's unshaken trust in the Lord; the second (5–8), of God's protection over Zion; the third (9–12), of his victory over war itself.

46, 3f: Figurative language for social and political upheavals.

46, 5: *There is a stream:* merely a symbol of divine favors. Jerusalem is not situated on a river, and its natural water supply is very meager.

Ps 47: A hymn calling on all the nations of the earth to acknowledge the God of Israel as the only true God (2–5); when the Lord manifests himself as King of all (6f), the whole earth will proclaim his dominion (8–10). This prophecy finds its fulfillment only in the universal kingship of Christ.

47, 10: *With the people of the God of Abraham:* perhaps, with the ancient versions, to be read simply, "With the God of Abraham." By *the princes of the peoples* and *the guardians of the earth* are probably meant the angelic spirits who watch over the various nations. Cf Dt 32, 8–9; Dn 10 13.

PSALM 48

Thanksgiving for Jerusalem's Deliverance

1 A psalm of the sons of Korah; a song.

I

2 Great is the LORD and wholly
   to be praised
   in the city of our God.
His holy mountain, 3 fairest of
   heights,
   is the joy of all the earth;
Mount Zion, "the recesses of the
   North,"
   is the city of the great King.
4 God is with her castles;
   renowned is he as a stronghold.

II

5 For lo! the kings assemble,
   they come on together;
6 They also see, and at once are
   stunned,
   terrified, routed;
7 Quaking seizes them there;
   anguish like a woman's in
   labor,
8 As though a wind from the east
   were shattering ships of
   Tarshish.

III

9 As we had heard, so have we
   seen
   in the city of the LORD of
   hosts,
In the city of our God;
   God makes it firm forever.
10 O God, we ponder your kindness
   within your temple.
11 As your name, O God, so also
   your praise
   reaches to the ends of the
   earth.
Of justice your right hand is full;
12   let Mount Zion be glad,
   Let the cities of Judah rejoice,
   because of your judgments.

IV

13 Go about Zion, make the
   round;
   count her towers.
14 Consider her ramparts,
   examine her castles,
That you may tell a future
   generation
15   that such is God,
Our God forever and ever;
   he will guide us.

PSALM 49

The Vanity of Worldly Riches

1 For the leader. A psalm of the sons
   of Korah.

2 Hear this, all you peoples;
   hearken, all who dwell in the
   world,
3 Of lowly birth or high degree,
   rich and poor alike.
4 My mouth shall speak wisdom;
   prudence shall be the utterance
   of my heart.
5 My ear is intent upon a proverb;
   I will set forth my riddle to
   the music of the harp.

I

6 Why should I fear in evil days
   when my wicked ensnarers
   ring me round?
7 They trust in their wealth;
   the abundance of their riches
   is their boast.
8 Yet in no way can a man
   redeem himself,
   or pay his own ransom to
   God;
9 Too high is the price to redeem
   one's life; he would never
   have enough
10   to remain alive always and
   not see destruction.
11 For he can see that wise men
   die,
   and likewsie the senseless and
   the stupid pass away,
   leaving to others their wealth.

12 Tombs are their homes forever,
   their dwellings through all
   generations,
   though they have called
   lands by their names.
13   Thus man, for all his splendor,
   does not abide;
   he resembles the beasts that
   perish.

II

14 This is the way of those whose
   trust is folly,
   the end of those contented
   with their lot.
15 Like sheep they are herded into
   the nether world;
   death is their shepherd, and
   the upright rule over them.
Quickly their form is consumed;
   the nether world is their
   palace.
16 But God will redeem me
   from the power of the nether
   world by receiving me.

III

17 Fear not when a man grows
   rich,
   when the wealth of his house
   becomes great,
18 For when he dies, he shall take
   none of it;
   his wealth shall not follow
   him down.
19 Though in his lifetime he counted
   himself blessed,
   "They will praise you for
   doing well for yourself,"
20 He shall join the circle of his
   forebears
   who shall never more see
   light.
21 Man, for all his splendor, if he
   have not prudence,
   resembles the beasts that
   perish.

Ps 48: A hymn of thanksgiving, sung in the temple after Jerusalem had successfully withstood an attack launched by a league of hostile kings. It is uncertain which of the many attacks on Jerusalem is referred to here. This magnificent paean of triumph first praises God as Israel's true bulwark (2–4); then, briefly recounting how the enemies' attack was repulsed (5–8), the psalmist proclaims the Lord as the author of this great victory (9–12); finally, the people are invited to gaze with wonder on the strong fortifications of the city (13–15).
48, 3: "The recesses of the North": in Palestine and Syria, a traditional name for the earthly abode of God.

Cf Is 14, 13.
48, 8: Ships of Tarshish: large ocean-going vessels, named after the distant land or port of Tarshish, probably ancient Tartessus in southern Spain, although other identifications have been proposed. Cf Is 2, 16; 60, 9; Jon 1, 3. Here the phrase is merely part of the figure and does not imply that the hostile kings came by boat.
48, 9: As we had heard of the wonders that God did in the days of our forefathers, so we have seen similar wonders now with our own eyes.
48, 15: He will guide us: "through the ages" should perhaps be added, with some ancient sources.

Ps 49: A sapiential psalm, treating of the problem as to why the wicked prosper. Here the answer is that wealth cannot save anyone from death, but for the good there is the hope of blessedness after death. Cf Pss 37; 73. After inviting all to listen to his wise words (2–5), the psalmist teaches that we should not envy the unjust rich, who must all die and leave their wealth behind (6–13.17–21); they shall be brought to nought, but God will save the just (14–16).
49, 5: My riddle: this enigma, the problem of evil.
49, 8f: No man is rich enough to buy God off in order to save himself from death.

PSALM 50

The Acceptable Sacrifice
1 A psalm of Asaph.

I

God the LORD has spoken and
    summoned the earth,
    from the rising of the sun to
      its setting.
2 From Zion, perfect in beauty,
    God shines forth.
3 May our God come and not be
    deaf to us!
    Before him is a devouring fire;
    around him is a raging
      storm.
4 He summons the heavens from
    above,
    and the earth, to the trial of
      his people:
5 "Gather my faithful ones before
    me,
    those who have made a
      covenant with me by
      sacrifice."
6 And the heavens proclaim his
    justice;
    for God himself is the judge.

II

7 "Hear, my people, and I will
    speak;
    Israel, I will testify against
      you;
    God, your God, am I.
8 Not for your sacrifices do I
    rebuke you
    for your holocausts are
      before me always.
9 I take from your house no
    bullock,
    no goats out of your fold.
10 For mine are all the animals of
    the forests,
    beasts by the thousand on my
      mountains.
11 I know all the birds of the air,
    and whatever stirs in the
      plains, belongs to me.

12 If I were hungry, I should not
    tell you,
    for mine are the world and its
      fullness.
13 Do I eat the flesh of strong bulls,
    or is the blood of goats my
      drink?
14 Offer to God praise as your
    sacrifice
    and fulfill your vows to the
      Most High;
15 Then call upon me in time of
    distress;
    I will rescue you, and you
      shall glorify me."

III

16 But to the wicked man God says:
    "Why do you recite my
      statutes,
    and profess my covenant with
      your mouth,
17 Though you hate discipline
    and cast my words behind
      you?
18 When you see a thief, you keep
    pace with him,
    and with adulterers you throw
      in your lot.
19 To your mouth you give free
    rein for evil,
    you harness your tongue
      to deceit.
20 You sit speaking against your
    brother;
    against your mother's son
      you spread rumors.
21 When you do these things, shall
    I be deaf to it?
    Or do you think that I am
      like yourself?
    I will correct you by drawing
      them up before your eyes.

IV

22 "Consider this, you who forget
    God,
    lest I rend you and there be
      no one to rescue you.

23 He that offers praise as a
    sacrifice glorifies me;
    and to him that goes the right
      way I will show the salvation
      of God."

PSALM 51

The Miserere: Prayer of
Repentance
1 For the leader. A psalm of David, 2 when
Nathan the prophet came to him after his sin
with Bathsheba.

A

3 Have mercy on me, O God, in
    your goodness;
    in the greatness of your
      compassion wipe out my
      offense.
4 Thoroughly wash me from my
    guilt
    and of my sin cleanse me.

B

I

5 For I acknowledge my offense,
    and my sin is before me
      always:
6 "Against you only have I sinned,
    and done what is evil in your
      sight"—
    That you may be justified in
      your sentence,
    vindicated when you condemn.
7 Indeed, in guilt was I born,
    and in sin my mother
      conceived me;
8 Behold, you are pleased with
    sincerity of heart,
    and in my inmost being you
      teach me wisdom.

II

9 Cleanse me of sin with hyssop,
    that I may be purified;
    wash me, and I shall be
      whiter than snow.

Ps 50: Like the prophets of old, the psalmist shows the worthlessness of external worship when it is divorced from true morality. God calls a solemn assembly (1–6), in which he tells his people he does not need their liturgical sacrifices but wants of them the true sacrifice of prayer (7–15); he then rebukes the hypocritical sinner (16–21), for without true worship, joined with true morality, there can be no salvation (22f).

50, 1: *God the Lord:* the Hebrew text has two synonyms for *God (El* and *Elohim)* before the word *Yahweh (the Lord).* A translation cannot adequately render this.

50, 21: *That I am like yourself:* perhaps the original was, "that I, the LORD, am like yourself."

Ps 51: The fourth and most famous of the Penitential Psalms. The psalmist begs pardon for his sins (3f), which he sincerely confesses (5–8); he prays to be restored to grace and purity (9–14); in return, he will make God's mercy known to others and will offer him the sacrifice of a contrite heart (15–19). An added strophe asks for the restoration of Jerusalem (20f).

51, 6: *Against you only have I sinned:* although sin may also be an injustice against a fellow man, yet the very essence of sin consists in its being an offense against God. *That you may be justified:* this refers to v 5 and gives the reason why the psalmist confesses his sins: when men see God punishing him, they will know that he is receiving his deserts.

51, 7: The penitent offers the fact of his innate sinfulness partly as a mitigating circumstance and partly as a humble acknowledgment of his profound corruption. Catholic tradition sees in this passage a foreshadowing of the basic Christian doctrine of original sin, which was not clearly revealed before the time of Christ. Cf Rom 5, 12–19; Eph 2, 3.

51, 9: *Hyssop:* a small bush whose many woody twigs made a natural sprinkler. It was prescribed in the Mosaic law as an instrument for scattering sacrificial blood or lustral water on persons to be ritually cleansed. Cf Ex 12, 22; Lv 14, 4; Nm 19, 18. These ceremonies were mere symbols of purification; here the psalmist prays that God may effectively "un-sin" him, as the Hebrew literally means.

10 Let me hear the sounds of joy
     and gladness;
     the bones you have crushed
     shall rejoice.
11 Turn away your face from my
     sins,
     and blot out all my guilt.

III

12 A clean heart create for me,
     O God,
     and a steadfast spirit renew
     within me.
13 Cast me not out from your
     presence,
     and your holy spirit take not
     from me.
14 Give me back the joy of your
     salvation,
     and a willing spirit sustain in
     me.

IV

15 I will teach transgressors your
     ways,
     and sinners shall return to you.
16 Free me from blood guilt, O God,
     my saving God;
     then my tongue shall revel in
     your justice.
17 O Lord, open my lips,
     and my mouth shall proclaim
     your praise.
18 For you are not pleased with
     sacrifices;
     should I offer a holocaust,
     you would not accept it.
19 My sacrifice, O God, is a
     contrite spirit;
     a heart contrite and humbled,
     O God, you will not
     spurn.

C

20 Be bountiful, O LORD, to Zion
     in your kindness
     by rebuilding the walls of
     Jerusalem;

21 Then shall you be pleased with
     due sacrifices,
     burnt offerings and holocausts;
     then shall they offer up
     bullocks on your altar.

PSALM 52

The Deceitful Tongue

1 For the leader. A *maskil* of David,   2 when
Doeg the Edomite went and told Saul, "David
went to the house of Ahimelech."

I

3 Why do you glory in evil,
     you champion of infamy?
   All the day   4 you plot harm;
     your tongue is like a sharpened
     razor, you practiced
     deceiver!
5 You love evil rather than good,
     falsehood rather than honest
     speech.
6 You love all that means ruin,
     you of the deceitful tongue!

II

7 God himself shall demolish
     you;
     forever he shall break you;
   He shall pluck you from your
     tent,
     and uproot you from the land
     of the living.

III

8 The just shall look on with awe;
     then they shall laugh at him:
9 "This is the man who made not
     God the source of his
     strength,
   But put his trust in his great
     wealth,
     and his strength in harmful
     plots."
10 But I, like a green olive tree
     in the house of God,
   Trust in the kindness of God
     forever and ever.

11 I will thank you always for what
     you have done,
     and proclaim the goodness of
     your name
     before your faithful ones.

PSALM 53

Lament over Widespread Corruption

1 For the leader; according to *Mahalath*.
     A *maskil* of David.

I

2 The fool says in his heart,
     "There is no God."
   Such are corrupt; they do
     abominable deeds;
     there is not one who does
     good.
3 God looks down from heaven
     upon the children of men
   to see if there be one who is
     wise and seeks God.
4 All alike have gone astray; they
     have become perverse;
     there is not one who does
     good, not even one.

II

5 Will all these evildoers never
     learn,
     they who eat up my people
     just as they eat bread,
     who call not upon God?
6 There they were in great fear,
     where no fear was,
   For God has scattered the
     bones of your besiegers;
     they are put to shame,
     because God has rejected
     them.

III

7 Oh, that out of Zion would
     come the salvation of
     Israel!
   When God restores the well-
     being of his people,
     then shall Jacob exult and
     Israel be glad.

51, 16: *Blood guilt:* the guilt of murder. This is in
keeping with the traditional ascription of the psalm
to David. Cf 2 Sm 11, 6f; 12, 9.

51, 18: *Not pleased with sacrifices:* the mere offering of the ritual sacrifice apart from good dispositions
is not acceptable to God. Cf Ps 50. Others explain
that the Mosaic law prescribes no sacrifice to expiate
sins of adultery and murder, such as David was guilty
of.

51, 20f: These two verses were added to the psalm
some time after the destruction of Jerusalem by the
Babylonians.
Ps 52: The psalmist inveighs against his deceitful
enemy (3–6), foretelling the divine punishment in
store for him (7) when God avenges the just (8–11).
52, 10: The just will flourish as unshaken in the
house of God as a green olive tree which is well rooted
in the soil. The words do not imply that olive trees

grew in the courts of the temple. Cf Pss 92, 14;
128, 3.
Ps 53: With a few slight differences this is the same
as Ps 14.
53, 6: *God has scattered the bones of your besiegers:*
a reference, perhaps to the annihilation of Sennacherib's army before the walls of Jerusalem. Cf 2 Kgs
19, 35.

PSALM 54

Confident Prayer in Great Peril

1 For the leader with stringed instruments. A *maskil* of David, 2 when the Ziphites went and said to Saul, "David is hiding among us."

I

3 O God, by your name save me,
　　and by your might defend my
　　　cause.
4 O God, hear my prayer;
　　hearken to the words of my
　　　mouth.
5 For haughty men have risen up
　　against me,
　　and fierce men seek my life;
　　they set not God before their
　　　eyes.

II

6 Behold, God is my helper;
　　the Lord sustains my life.
7 Turn back the evil upon my
　　foes;
　　in your faithfulness destroy
　　　them.
8 Freely will I offer you
　　sacrifice;
　　I will praise your name, O
　　　LORD, for its goodness,
9 Because from all distress you
　　have rescued me,
　　and my eyes look down upon
　　　my enemies.

PSALM 55

Complaint against Enemies and a Disloyal Companion

1 For the leader; with stringed instruments. A *maskil* of David.

I

2 Hearken, O God, to my prayer;
　　turn not away from my
　　　pleading;
3 give heed to me, and answer
　　me.
　　I rock with grief, and am
　　　troubled
4 at the voice of the enemy and
　　the clamor of the wicked.

For they bring down evil upon
　　me,
　　and with fury they persecute
　　　me.
5 My heart quakes within me;
　　the terror of death has fallen
　　　upon me.
6 Fear and trembling come upon
　　me,
　　and horror overwhelms me,
7 And I say, "Had I but wings
　　like a dove,
　　I would fly away and be at
　　　rest.
8 Far away I would flee;
　　I would lodge in the
　　　wilderness.
9 I would hasten to find shelter
　　from the violent storm and the
　　　tempest."

II

10 Engulf them, O Lord; divide
　　their counsels,
　　for in the city I see violence
　　　and strife;
11 day and night they prowl
　　about upon its walls.
　　Evil and mischief are in its
　　　midst;
12 [treachery is in its midst;]
　　oppression and fraud never
　　　depart from its streets.
13 If an enemy had reviled me,
　　I could have borne it;
　　If he who hates me had vaunted
　　　himself against me,
　　I might have hidden from him.
14 But you, my other self,
　　my companion and my
　　　bosom friend!
15 You, whose comradeship I
　　enjoyed;
　　at whose side I walked in
　　　procession in the house of
　　　God!

III

16 Let death surprise them;
　　let them go down alive to the
　　　nether world,
　　for evil is in their dwellings,
　　in their very midst.

17 But I will call upon God,
　　and the LORD will save me.
18 In the evening, and at dawn,
　　and at noon,
　　I will grieve and moan,
　　and he will hear my voice.
19 He will give me freedom and
　　peace
　　from those who war against
　　　me,
　　for many there are who
　　　oppose me.
20 God will hear me and will
　　humble them
　　from his eternal throne;
　　For improvement is not in them,
　　nor do they fear God.
21 Each one lays hands on his
　　associates,
　　and violates his pact.
22 Softer than butter is his speech,
　　but war is in his heart;
　　His words are smoother than oil,
　　but they are drawn swords.
23 Cast your care upon the LORD,
　　and he will support you;
　　never will he permit the just
　　　man to be disturbed.
24 And you, O God, will bring
　　them down
　　into the pit of destruction;
　　Men of blood and deceit shall
　　not live out half their days.
　　But I trust in you, O LORD.

PSALM 56

Trust in God, the Helper in Need

1 For the leader; according to *Jonath ... rehokim.* A *miktam* of David, when the Philistines held him in Gath.

I

2 Have pity on me, O God, for
　　men trample upon me;
　　all the day they press their
　　　attack against me.
3 My adversaries trample upon
　　me all the day;
　　yes, many fight against me.
　　O Most High, 4 when I begin
　　to fear,
　　in you will I trust.

Ps 54: The psalmist implores God's assistance against foes that seek his life (3–5) and, confident of this aid, promises a sacrifice of thanksgiving (6–9).

54, 3: *By your name:* through the power of the Lord. God's name is his nature as revealed by man; hence this term is frequently used as practically synonymous with God himself, his majesty, power, etc.

Ps 55: Vividly describing his fear and his longing to flee (2–9), the psalmist bewails the disorders about

him, especially the treachery of a former friend (10–15); full of confidence in God, he prays for the overthrow of the wicked and his own deliverance (16–24).

55, 10: *Divide their counsels:* some see here an allusion to the story of the tower of Babel. Cf Gn 11, 1–9.

55, 12: *Treachery is in its midst:* apparently this is merely a variant reading of the preceding line.

55, 16: *Go down alive to the nether world:* die a sudden death. Perhaps there is an allusion here to the death of Korah and his fellow rebels. Cf Nm 16, 31ff.

Ps 56: The psalmist prays for help against his enemies (2–4) and bewails their machinations (6–10) in a twice-repeated refrain (5.11) he expresses his confidence in God, to whom he vows a thanksgiving sacrifice (13).

5   In God, in whose promise I
        glory,
        in God I trust without
            fear;
        what can flesh do against
            me?

II

6   All the day they molest me in my
        efforts;
        their every thought is of evil
            against me.
7   They gather together in hiding,
        they watch my steps.
        As they have waited for my life,
8   because of their wickedness
        keep them in view:
        in your wrath bring down the
            peoples, O God.
9   My wanderings you have
        counted;
        my tears are stored in your
            flask;
        are they not recorded in your
            book?
10 Then do my enemies turn back,
        when I call upon you;
        now I know that God is
            with me.
11   In God, in whose promise I
            glory,
12   in God I trust without
            fear;
        what can flesh do against
            me?

III

13 I am bound, O God, by vows
        to you;
        your thank offerings I will
            fulfill.
14 For you have rescued me from
        death,
        my feet, too, from
            stumbling;
        that I may walk before God in
            the light of the living.

PSALM 57

Confident Prayer for Deliverance

1 For the leader. (Do not destroy!) A *miktam*
of David, when he fled away from Saul into the
cave.

I

2 Have pity on me, O God; have
        pity on me,
    for in you I take refuge.
    In the shadow of your wings I
        take refuge,
    till harm pass by.
3 I call to God the Most High,
    to God, my benefactor.
4 May he send from heaven and
        save me;
    may he make those a reproach
        who trample upon me;
    may God send his kindness
        and his faithfulness.
5 I lie prostrate in the midst of
        lions
    which devour men;
    Their teeth are spears and
        arrows,
    their tongue is a sharp sword.
6   Be exalted above the
        heavens, O God;
    above all the earth be
        your glory!

II

7 They have prepared a net for
        my feet;
    they have bowed me down;
    They have dug a pit before me,
    but they fall into it.
8 My heart is steadfast, O God;
    my heart is steadfast;
    I will sing and chant praise.
9 Awake, O my soul; awake, lyre
        and harp!
    I will wake the dawn.
10 I will give thanks to you among
        the peoples, O Lord.
    I will chant your praise
        among the nations,
11 For your kindness towers to the
        heavens,

---

and your faithfulness to the
    skies.
12 Be exalted above the
        heavens, O God;
    above all the earth be
        your glory!

PSALM 58

Against Unjust Judges

1 For the leader. (Do not destroy!)
    A *miktam* of David.

I

2 Do you indeed like gods
        pronounce justice
    and judge fairly, you men of
        rank?
3 Nay, you willingly commit
        crimes;
    on earth you look to the
        fruits of extortion.
4 From the womb the wicked are
        perverted;
    astray from birth have the
        liars gone.
5 Theirs is poison like a serpent's,
    like that of a stubborn snake
        that stops its ears,
6 That it may not hear the voice
        of enchanters
    casting cunning spells.

II

7 O God, smash their teeth in
        their mouths;
    the jaw-teeth of the lions,
        break, O LORD!
8 Let them vanish like water
        flowing off;
    when they draw the bow, let
        their arrows be headless
            shafts.
9 Let them dissolve like a melting
        snail,
    like an untimely birth that
        never sees the sun.
10 Unexpectedly, like a thorn-bush,
    or like thistles, let the
        whirlwind carry them away.

56, 9: *My tears are stored in your flask:* a quaint
figure to express that God knows the psalmist's weeping and will requite it, for he is carefully collecting all
his tears in a bottle.

Ps 57: Each of the two equal strophes contains a
prayer for help, accompanied by joyful trust in God
(2–5.7–11), and each strophe ends with the same refrain to God's glory (6.12).

57, 1: *Do not destroy:* here and in the next two
psalms, as well as in Ps 75, this is probably a mere
annotation by some early scribe who wished to keep
his copy from being discarded,

57, 8–12: With a few small variations these verses

appear again at the beginning of Ps 108.

57, 9: *I will wake the dawn:* by a bold figure of
speech the psalmist imagines that the sound he makes
at night with his singing and music will arouse a new
day to life.

Ps 58: The psalmist rebukes certain unjust judges
(2–6), and invokes God's punishment upon them (7–
12).

58, 2: *Like gods:* literally, "O Gods!" Here, as also
in Ps 82, judges are called "gods" in the sense of
"possessing godlike power," or of "taking God's
place in pronouncing judgment." See note on Ps 45, 7.

58, 5f: Two figures derived from snake life are here

skillfully combined: the harm done by these wicked
judges is as deadly as a serpent's venom, and these
men are as unresponsive to God's teaching as certain
stubborn snakes are to the music of the snake charmer.

58, 9: *Like a melting snail:* the Hebrew is not entirely certain, but if the text is correct, it would seem
that the ancients thought a snail "melted" or gradually
wasted away to nothing—an idea derived, perhaps,
from the sight of the trail of slime a snail leaves behind
as it moves along and from the fact that dead snails
are soon but empty shells.

58, 10: The Hebrew text of this verse is obscure and
is variously reconstructed.

11 The just man shall be glad when
    he sees vengeance;
    he shall bathe his feet in the
    blood of the wicked.
12 And men shall say, "Truly there
    is a reward for the just;
    truly there is a God who is
    judge on earth!"

PSALM 59

Against Bloodthirsty Enemies

1 For the leader. (Do not destroy!) A *miktam*
of David when Saul sent men to watch his house
and put him to death.

I

2 Rescue me from my enemies, O
    my God;
    from my adversaries defend me.
3 Rescue me from evildoers;
    from bloodthirsty men save me.
4 For behold, they lie in wait for
    my life;
    mighty men come together
    against me.
    Not for any offense or sin of
    mine, O LORD;
5   for no guilt of mine they hurry
    to take up arms.
    Rouse yourself to see it, and
    aid me,
6   for you are the LORD of hosts,
    the God of Israel.
    Arise; punish all the nations;
    have no pity on any worthless
    traitors.

7   Each evening they return,
       they snarl like dogs
       and prowl about the city.
8 Though they bay with their
    mouths,
    and blasphemies are on their
    lips—
    "Who is there to listen?"—
9 You, O LORD, laugh at them;
    you deride all the nations.
10   O my strength! for you I
       watch;
       for you, O God, are my
       stronghold,
11   my gracious God!

II

May God come to my aid;
    may he show me the fall of
    my foes.
12 O God, slay them, lest they
    beguile my people;
    shake them by your power,
    and bring them down,
    O Lord our shield!
13 By the sin of their mouths and
    the word of their lips
    let them be caught in their
    arrogance,
    for the lies they have told
    under oath.
14 Consume them in wrath;
    consume, till they are no
    more;
    that men may know that God
    is the ruler of Jacob,
    yes, to the ends of the earth.

15   Each evening they return,
       they snarl like dogs
       and prowl about the city;
16 They wander about as
    scavengers;
    if they are not filled, they howl.
17 But I will sing of your strength
    and revel at dawn in your
    kindness;
    You have been my stronghold,
    my refuge in the day of
    distress.
18   O my strength! your praise
       will I sing;
       for you, O God, are my
       stronghold,
       my gracious God!

PSALM 60

Prayer after Defeat in Battle

1 For the leader; according to "The Lily of
. . ." A *miktam* of David (for teaching)
2 when he fought against Aram-naharaim and
Aram-zobah; and Joab, coming back, killed
twelve thousand Edomites in the "valley of
salt."

I

3 O God, you have rejected us and
    broken our defenses;

you have been angry; rally us!
4 You have rocked the country
    and split it open;
    repair the cracks in it, for it is
    tottering.
5 You have made your people
    feel hardships;
    you have given us stupefying
    wine.
6 You have raised for those who
    fear you a banner
    to which they may flee out of
    bowshot
7 That your loved ones may
    escape;
    help us by your right hand,
    and answer us!

II

8 God promised in his sanctuary:
    "Exultantly I will apportion
    Shechem,
    and measure off the valley of
    Succoth.
9 Mine is Gilead, and mine
    Manasseh;
    Ephraim in the helmet for my
    head; Judah, my scepter;
10 Moab shall serve as my
    washbowl;
    upon Edom I will set my shoe;
    I will triumph over Philistia."

III

11 Who will bring me into the
    fortified city?
    Who will lead me into Edom?
12 Have not you, O God, rejected
    us,
    so that you go not forth, O
    God, with our armies?
13 Give us aid against the foe,
    for worthless is the help of
    men.
14 Under God we shall do valiantly;
    it is he who will tread down
    our foes.

58, 11: *He shall bathe his feet in the blood:* by the
figure of hyperbole, victorious soldiers may be said to
wade through the blood of the vanquished. Cf Ps 68,
24; Is 63, 1–6.

Ps 59: In each of the two similar strophes (2–6.11b–
14) the psalmist beseeches God to defend him against
his wicked enemies. In the two similar refrains (7–
11a.15–18) he compares the wicked to ravenous dogs.

59, 8: *Who is there to listen?:* this is their blasphemy,
that they say, "God does not even hear of our
wickedness."

Ps 60: Bewailing a military disaster, the psalmist

first thanks God for having saved at least part of the
army (3–7); then, recalling God's promise to sub-
jugate the neighboring nations (8–10), he puts his
trust in the Lord's strong assistance (11–14).

60, 7–14: These verses occur again as the second
half of Ps 108.

60, 8: *I will apportion . . . and measure off:* God will
claim these places as his own. *The valley of Succoth:*
probably the lower stretch of the Jabbok valley. Cf
Gn 32, 23; 33, 17.

60, 9: *Judah, my scepter:* An allusion to the Blessing
of Jacob. Cf Gn 49, 10.

60, 10: *Moab shall serve as my washbowl:* the Moabites shall perform menial service for Israel; possibly
there is also an allusion to the "basin" of the Dead
Sea, which formed the western border of Moab. *Upon
Edom I will set my shoe:* God will use Edom as his
footstool; thus the ancient kings treated their conquered enemies. Cf Ps 110, 1. Some render, "Upon
Edom I will throw my shoe, and understand this
casting of a shoe on conquered territory as a sign of
possession.

60, 11: *The fortified city:* perhaps Bozrah, the impregnable capital of Edom. Cf Is 34, 6; 36, 1; Am 1, 12.

PSALM 61

Prayer of the King in Exile

1 For the leader; with stringed instruments. Of David.

I

2 Hear, O God, my cry;
  listen to my prayer!
3 From the earth's end I call to
  you
  as my heart grows faint.
  You will set me high upon a
  rock; you will give me rest,
4 for you are my refuge,
  a tower of strength against the
  enemy.
5 Oh, that I might lodge in your
  tent forever,
  take refuge in the shelter of
  your wings!

II

6 You indeed, O God, have
  accepted my vows;
  you granted me the heritage of
  those who fear your name.
7 Add to the days of the king's
  life;
  let his years be many
  generations;
8 Let him sit enthroned before
  God forever,
  bid kindness and faithfulness
  preserve him.
9 So will I sing the praises of your
  name forever,
  fulfilling my vows day by day.

PSALM 62

Trust in God Alone

1 For the leader; 'al Jeduthun. A psalm of David.

I

2 Only in God is my soul at
  rest;
  from him comes my
  salvation.
3 He only is my rock and my
  salvation,
  my stronghold; I shall not
  be disturbed at all.

4 How long will you set upon a
  man and all together beat
  him down
  as though he were a sagging
  fence, a battered wall?
5 Truly from my place on high
  they plan to dislodge me;
  they delight in lies;
  They bless with their mouths,
  but inwardly they curse.

II

6 Only in God be at rest, my
  soul,
  for from him comes my
  hope.
7 He only is my rock and my
  salvation,
  my stronghold; I shall not
  be disturbed.
8 With God is my safety and my
  glory,
  he is the rock of my strength;
  my refuge is in God.
9 Trust in him at all times, O my
  people!
  Pour out your hearts before
  him;
  God is our refuge!

III

10 Only a breath are mortal men;
  an illusion are men of rank;
  In a balance they prove lighter,
  all together, than a breath.
11 Trust not in extortion; in
  plunder take no empty
  pride;
  though wealth abound, set
  not your heart upon it.
12 One thing God said; these two
  things which I heard:
13 that power belongs to God,
  and yours, O Lord, is
  kindness;
  and that you render to
  everyone according to his
  deeds.

PSALM 63

Ardent Longing for God

1 A psalm of David, when he was in the wilderness of Judah.

I

2 O God, you are my God whom I
  seek;
  for you my flesh pines and my
  soul thirsts
  like the earth, parched, lifeless
  and without water.
3 Thus have I gazed toward you
  in the sanctuary
  to see your power and your
  glory,
4 For your kindness is a greater
  good than life;
  my lips shall glorify you.

II

5 Thus will I bless you while I
  live;
  lifting up my hands, I will call
  upon your name.
6 As with the riches of a banquet
  shall my soul be satisfied,
  and with exultant lips my
  mouth shall praise you.
7 I will remember you upon my
  couch,
  and through the night-watches
  I will meditate on you:
8 That you are my help,
  and in the shadow of your
  wings I shout for joy.
9 My soul clings fast to you;
  your right hand upholds me.

III

10 But they shall be destroyed who
  seek my life,
  they shall go into the depths
  of the earth;
11 They shall be delivered over to
  the sword,
  and shall be the prey of
  jackals.
12 The king, however, shall rejoice
  in God;
  everyone who swears by him
  shall glory,
  but the mouths of those who
  speak falsely shall be
  stopped.

Ps 61: Far away from Jerusalem, the Psalmist longs for God's help and the shelter of his abode (2–5); confident of being heard, he prays for the king (6–9). This may be interpreted as a prayer of David when he had to flee from Jerusalem during the rebellion of Absalom. Cf 2 Sm 15–19.

Ps 62: The keynote of trust in God is struck in the twice repeated refrain (2f.6f); though attacked by his enemies (4f), the psalmist asserts his unshaken confidence in the Lord (8f), for true strength comes not from earthly power but from God's grace (10–13).

62, 5: My place on high: a place of safety such as a fortress set on a cliff.

62, 12: One thing . . . two things: such use of progressive numbers is a device of Hebrew poetry. Cf Am 1, 3; Prv 6, 16–19; 30, 15.18.21.

Ps 63: Homesick for God's sanctuary (2–4), the psalmist holds fast to the Lord in spirit (5–9), confident that his enemies will be destroyed while the king and his loyal followers will triumph (10–12).

63, 11: The prey of the jackals: their dead bodies shall be devoured by wild animals. Lack of proper burial was dreaded by the ancients.

PSALM 64

Treacherous Conspirators Punished by God

1 For the leader. A psalm of David.

I

2 Hear, O God, my voice in my
　　lament;
　　from the dread enemy
　　　preserve my life.
3 Shelter me against the council of
　　malefactors,
　　against the tumult of evildoers,
4 Who sharpen their tongues like
　　swords,
　　who aim like arrows their
　　　bitter words,
5 Shooting from ambush at the
　　innocent man,
　　suddenly shooting at him
　　　without fear.
6 They resolve on their wicked plan;
　　they conspire to set snares,
　　saying, "Who will see us?"
7 They devised a wicked scheme,
　　and conceal the scheme they
　　　have devised;
　　deep are the thoughts of each
　　　heart.

II

8 But God shoots his arrows at them;
　　suddenly they are struck.
9 He brings them down by their
　　own tongues;
　　all who see them nod their heads.
10 And all men fear and proclaim
　　the work of God,
　　and ponder what he has done.
11 The just man is glad in the LORD
　　and takes refuge in him;
　　in him glory all the upright of
　　　heart.

PSALM 65

Thanksgiving for God's Blessings

1 For the leader. A psalm of David. A song.

I

2 To you we owe our hymn of
　　praise,

O God, in Zion;
　To you must vows be fulfilled,
　　you who hear prayers.
3 To you all flesh must come
4 　because of wicked deeds.
　We are overcome by our sins;
　　it is you who pardon them.
5 Happy the man you choose,
　　and bring
　　to dwell in your courts.
　May we be filled with the good
　　things of your house,
　　the holy things of your temple!

II

6 With awe-inspiring deeds of
　　justice you answer us,
　O God our savior,
　The hope of all the ends of the
　　earth
　and of the distant seas.
7 You set the mountains in place
　　by your power,
　　you who are girt with might;
8 You still the roaring of the seas,
　　the roaring of their waves and
　　the tumult of the peoples.
9 And the dwellers at the earth's
　　ends are in fear at your
　　marvels;
　　the farthest east and west you
　　make resound with joy.

III

10 You have visited the land and
　　watered it;
　　greatly have you enriched it.
　God's watercourses are filled;
　　you have prepared the grain.
11 Thus have you prepared the
　　land: drenching its furrows,
　　breaking up its clods,
　Softening it with showers,
　　blessing its yield.
12 You have crowned the year
　　with your bounty,
　　and your paths overflow with
　　a rich harvest;
13 The untilled meadows overflow
　　with it,
　　and rejoicing clothes the hills.

14 The fields are garmented with
　　flocks
　　and the valleys blanketed with
　　grain.
　They shout and sing for joy.

PSALM 66

Praise for God, Israel's Deliverer

1 For the leader. A psalm; a song.

Shout joyfully to God, all you
　　on earth,
2 　sing praise to the glory of his
　　name;
　　proclaim his glorious praise.
3 Say to God, "How tremendous
　　are your deeds!
　　for your great strength your
　　enemies fawn upon you.
4 Let all on earth worship and
　　sing praise to you,
　　sing praise to your name!"

I

5 Come and see the works of God,
　　his tremendous deeds among
　　men.
6 He has changed the sea into dry
　　land;
　　through the river they passed
　　on foot;
　　therefore let us rejoice in him.
7 He rules by his might forever;
　　his eyes watch the nations;
　　rebels may not exalt
　　themselves.
8 Bless our God, you peoples,
　　loudly sound his praise;
9 He has given life to our souls,
　　and has not let our feet slip.
10 For you have tested us, O God!
　　You have tried us as silver is
　　tried by fire;
11 You have brought us into a
　　snare;
　　and laid a heavy burden on
　　our backs.
12 You let men ride over our heads;
　　we went through fire and
　　water,
　　but you have led us out to
　　refreshment.

Ps 64: The psalmist prays for God's help against
deceitful foes who secretly plot against him (2–7); God
will repay them with exemplary punishment (8–11).
64, 9: Nod their heads: a gesture of derision. Cf
Pss 22, 8; 44, 15; 109, 25.
Ps 65: A hymn of thanksgiving, sung by the community for a bountiful harvest. Humbly acknowledging that they are unworthy of God's favors (2–5), the
people praise him for his power over all the earth (6–
9), and thank him for the rains which produced such

abundant crops (10–14).
65, 2: Vows: the Israelites were accustomed to
promise sacrifices in the temple if their prayers were
heard.
65, 3: To you all flesh must come: all men must have
recourse to God's mercy.
65, 12: Your paths overflow with a rich harvest:
literally, "Your wagon-wheel tracks drip with oil."
Ps 66: There are two distinct parts here, which perhaps originally were two independent psalms. The first

part (1–12) is a hymn of the community praising
God's omnipotence as revealed throughout history,
especially at the Exodus (5–7), and now in the recent
restoration of the nation from some calamity (8–12).
The second part (13–20) is the thanksgiving hymn of
an individual fulfilling his vows in the temple (13–15)
and recounting how the Lord had heard his prayer
(16–20).
66, 3: Fawn upon you: pay an unwilling tribute of
praise. Cf Pss 18, 45; 81, 16.

II

13 I will bring holocausts to your
    house;
    to you I will fulfill the vows
14 Which my lips uttered
    and my words promised in my
    distress.
15 Holocausts of fatlings I will
    offer you,
    with burnt offerings of rams;
    I will sacrifice oxen and goats.
16 Hear now, all you who fear God,
    while I declare
    what he has done for me.
17 When I appealed to him in words,
    praise was on the tip of my
    tongue.
18 Were I to cherish wickedness in
    my heart,
    the Lord would not hear;
19 But God has heard;
    he has hearkened to the sound
    of my prayer.
20 Blessed be God who refused me
    not
    my prayer or his kindness!

PSALM 67

Harvest Prayer that All Men May Worship God

1 For the leader; with stringed instruments.
  A psalm; a song.

I

2 May God have pity on us and
    bless us;
    may he let his face shine upon
    us.
3 So may your way be known
    upon earth;
    among all nations, your
    salvation.
4   May the peoples praise you,
      O God;
      may all the peoples praise
      you!

II

5 May the nations be glad and
    exult
    because you rule the peoples
    in equity;
    the nations on the earth you
    guide.
6   May the peoples praise you,
      O God;
      may all the peoples praise
      you!

III

7 The earth has yielded its fruits;
    God, our God has blessed us.
8 May God bless us,
    and may all the ends of the
    earth fear him!

PSALM 68

God's Triumphal Procession

1 For the leader. A psalm of David; a song.

I

2 God arises; his enemies are
    scattered,
    and those who hate him flee
    before him.
3 As smoke is driven away, so
    are they driven;
    as wax melts before the fire,
    so the wicked perish before
    God.
4 But the just rejoice and exult
    before God;
    they are glad and rejoice.

II

5 Sing to God, chant praise to his
    name,
    extol him who rides upon the
    clouds,
    Whose name is the LORD;
    exult before him.

6 The father of orphans and the
    defender of widows
    is God in his holy dwelling.
7 God gives a home to the
    forsaken;
    he leads forth prisoners to
    prosperity;
    only rebels remain in the
    parched land.

III

8 O God, when you went forth at
    the head of your people,
    when you marched through
    the wilderness,
9 The earth quaked; it rained from
    heaven at the presence of God,
    at the presence of God, the
    God of Israel, the One of
    Sinai.
10 A bountiful rain you showered
    down, O God, upon your
    inheritance;
    you restored the land when it
    languished;
11 Your flock settled in it;
    in your goodness, O God, you
    provided it for the needy.

IV

12 The Lord gives the word;
    women bear the glad tidings,
    a vast army:
13 "Kings and their hosts are
    fleeing, fleeing,
    and the household shall divide
    the spoils.
14 Though you rested among the
    sheepfolds,
    the wings of the dove shone
    with silver,
    and her pinions with a golden
    hue.
15 While the Almighty dispersed
    the kings there,
    snow fell on Zalmon."

66, 17: *Praise was on the tip of my tongue:* literally, "praise was under my tongue." Even while the psalmist was praying aloud for help, he was already thanking God silently for having heard his prayer.

Ps 67: The refrain (4.6 and perhaps originally after 8) calls on all the nations of the earth to praise the Lord, because he blesses Israel (2f), governs all peoples wisely (5), and bestows an abundant harvest (7). Israel's hope of seeing the Lord acknowledged as the only God by all the nations was based on, and found its sole fulfillment in, the promise of the Messiah. Cf Gn 12, 2f.

67, 2: These words are similar to the priestly blessing of Nm 6, 22–27.

67, 4.6: *Praise:* the Hebrew means more exactly, "give grateful praise"; hence, according to the context, it is often translated, "give thanks."

Ps 68: One of the most magnificent, but at the same time, one of the most difficult hymns of the

Psalter. In several places the Hebrew text is poorly preserved. It was written to be sung as the ark of the covenant was carried in solemn procession into the temple. Beginning with the ancient war cry of Israel, which was used when the ark was carried into battle (2), the opening strophe proclaims the defeat of the wicked and the triumph of the just (3f). After general praise of God's goodness (5–7), the Lord's victorious march from Egypt to Sinai (8–11) and the conquest of the Promised Land (12–15) are briefly and poetically recounted; reference is then made to God's choice of Zion for his dwelling (16–19), as well as to his victories (20–24); finally, with a description of the present procession serving as an interlude (25–28), God is implored to spread his mighty rule (29–32) until all the earth sings his glory (33–36).

68, 2: What is here stated as a fact is given in the form of a prayer in Nm 10, 35.

68, 5: *Extol him who rides upon the clouds:* the

meaning of the Hebrew is not entirely certain. The revised Latin Psalter has, "Lay a road for him who rides through the desert." However, the expression "The Rider of the Clouds" as a divine epithet is very ancient, since it occurs in Canaanite literature even before the time of Moses, and it is not uncommon in the Old Testament. Cf Dt 33, 26; Pss 18, 10ff; 68, 34; Is 19, 1; Hb 3, 8.

68, 12: The Israelite women took an active part in celebrating a victory. Cf Ex 15, 20; 1 Sm 18. 6f.

68, 14f: The Hebrew text of these verses is very obscure. The translation given above follows the revised Latin Psalter. *The Dove:* perhaps a figure of the victorious army of Israel. Cf Ps 74, 19. *Snow fell:* either literally, or figuratively of the fallen enemy lying as thick as snowflakes on the battlefield. *Zalmon:* probably a mountain in the Hauran or in Bashan, The historical event referred to is uncertain. Cf Nm 21, 33ff; Dt 3, 1–10.

V

16 High the mountains of Bashan;
   rugged the mountains of
   Bashan.
17 Why look you jealously, you
   rugged mountains,
   at the mountain God has
   chosen for his throne,
   where the LORD himself will
   dwell forever?
18 The chariots of God are myriad,
   thousands on thousands;
   the LORD advances from
   Sinai to the sanctuary.
19 You have ascended on high,
   taken captives,
   received men as gifts—
   even rebels; the LORD God
   enters his dwelling.

VI

20 Blessed day by day be the
   LORD,
   who bears our burdens; God,
   who is our salvation.
21 God is a saving God for us;
   the LORD, my Lord, controls
   the passageways of death.
22 Surely God crushes the heads of
   his enemies,
   the hairy crowns of those who
   stalk about in their guilt.
23 The Lord said: "I will fetch
   them back from Bashan;
   I will fetch them back from
   the depths of the sea,
24 So that you will bathe your
   feet in blood;
   the tongues of your dogs will
   have their share of your
   enemies."

VII

25 They view your progress, O God,
   the progress of my God, my
   King, into the sanctuary;
26 The singers lead, the minstrels
   follow,
   in their midst the maidens
   play on timbrels.

27 In your choirs bless God;
   bless the Lord, you of
   Israel's wellspring!
28 There is Benjamin, the youngest,
   leading them;
   the princes of Judah in a body,
   the princes of Zebulun, the
   princes of Naphtali.

VIII

29 Show forth, O God, your
   power,
   the power, O God, with which
   you took our part;
30 For your temple in Jerusalem
   let the kings bring you gifts.
31 Rebuke the wild beast of the
   reeds,
   the herd of strong bulls and
   the bullocks, the nations.
   Let them prostrate themselves
   with bars of silver;
   scatter the peoples who
   delight in war.
32 Let nobles come from Egypt;
   let Ethiopia extend its hands
   to God.

IX

33 You kingdoms of the earth, sing
   to God,
   chant praise to the Lord
34   who rides on the heights of
   the ancient heavens.
   Behold, his voice resounds, the
   voice of power:
35 "Confess the power of God!"
   Over Israel is his majesty;
   his power is in the skies.
36 Awesome in his sanctuary is
   God, the God of Israel;
   he gives power and strength to
   his people.
   Blessed be God!

PSALM 69

A Cry of Anguish in Great Distress

1 For the leader; according to "Lilies."
  Of David.

I

2 Save me, O God,
   for the waters threaten my life;
3 I am sunk in the abysmal
   swamp
   where there is no foothold;
   I have reached the watery
   depths;
   the flood overwhelms me.
4 I am wearied with calling,
   my throat is parched;
   My eyes have failed
   with looking for my God.
5 Those outnumber the hairs of
   my head
   who hate me without cause.
   Too many for my strength
   are they who wrongfully are
   my enemies.
   Must I restore what I did not
   steal?

II

6 O God, you know my folly,
   and my faults are not hid
   from you.
7 Let not those who wait for you
   be put to shame through me,
   O Lord, GOD of hosts.
   Let not those who seek you
   blush for me,
   O God of Israel,
8 Since for your sake I bear
   insult,
   and shame covers my face.
9 I have become an outcast to my
   brothers,
   a stranger to my mother's
   sons,
10 Because zeal for your house
   consumes me,
   and the insults of those who
   blaspheme you fall upon me.
11 I humbled myself with fasting,
   and this was made a reproach
   to me.
12 I made sackcloth my garment,
   and I became a byword for
   them.

68, 17: *The mountain God has chosen:* Mount Zion.
68, 19: *Ascended on high:* to the divine throne, either on Zion or in heaven. *Received men as gifts:* St. Paul quotes this somewhat freely according to the Greek version as, "He gave gifts to men," and then applies it to Christ bestowing his charismatic graces on the Church after his ascension into heaven. Cf Eph 4, 8.
68, 31: *The wild beast of the reeds:* most probably Egypt. Cf Ez 29, 2ff. *Bars of silver:* tribute from the foreign nations brought to Zion.
68, 34: *Who rides:* see note on v 5.
Ps 69: A lamentation similar to Ps 22. The psalmist

describes his extreme misery (2–5) and unmerited disgrace (6–13), imploring God to vindicate him (14–22) and punish his enemies (23–29); in return he will offer God a sacrifice of praise (30–35). As in Ps 51, two verses were added at the end foretelling the restoration of Israel from exile in Babylon (36f). Since several passages are quoted in the New Testament in reference to Christ, Catholic tradition has always considered this psalm as at least indirectly Messianic.
69, 2: *The waters:* a common metaphor for affliction. Cf Pss 18, 5: 42, 8; 88, 8.
69, 5: *Who hate me without cause:* according to our

Lord's own statement these words are fully verified in the hatred his enemies bore him. Cf Jn 15, 25.
69, 6: *My folly, and my faults:* the psalmist is guilty he admits, of certain sins, but not of the grave crimes his enemies charge him with. This verse cannot be interpreted in a Messianic sense except in so far as Christ took upon himself the sins of the world.
69, 10: *Zeal for your house consumes me:* eminently fulfilled in Christ's cleansing of the temple. Cf Jn 2, 17. *The insults of those who blaspheme you fall upon me:* cited by St. Paul as an example of our Lord's unselfishness. Cf Rom 15, 3.

13 They who sit at the gate gossip
       about me,
   and drunkards make me the
       butt of their songs.

III

14 But I pray to you, O LORD,
       for the time of your favor,
       O God!
   In your great kindness answer
       me
   with your constant help.
15 Rescue me out of the mire; may
       I not sink!
   may I be rescued from my
       foes,
   and from the watery depths.
16 Let not the flood-waters
       overwhelm me,
   nor the abyss swallow me up,
   nor the pit close its mouth
       over me.
17 Answer me, O LORD, for
       bounteous is your kindness;
   in your great mercy turn
       toward me.
18 Hide not your face from your
       servant;
   in my distress, make haste to
       answer me.
19 Come and ransom my life;
   as an answer for my enemies,
       redeem me.
20 You know my reproach, my
       shame and my ignominy;
   before you are all my foes.
21 Insult has broken my heart, and
       I am weak,
   I looked for sympathy, but
       there was none;
   for comforters, and I found
       none.
22 Rather they put gall in my food,
   and in my thirst they gave me
       vinegar to drink.

IV

23 Let their own table be a snare
       before them,
   and a net for their friends.
24 Let their eyes grow dim so that
       they cannot see,
   and keep their backs always
       feeble.

25 Pour out your wrath upon them;
   let the fury of your anger
       overtake them.
26 Let their encampment become
       desolate;
   in their tents let there be no
       one to dwell.
27 For they kept after him whom
       you smote,
   and added to the pain of him
       you wounded.
28 Heap guilt upon their guilt,
   and let them not attain to
       your reward.
29 May they be erased from the
       book of the living,
   and not be recorded with the
       just!

V

30 But I am afflicted and in pain;
   let your saving help, O God,
       protect me.
31 I will praise the name of God in
       song,
   and I will glorify him with
       thanksgiving;
32 This will please the LORD more
       than oxen
   or bullocks with horns and
       divided hooves:
33 "See, you lowly ones, and be
       glad;
   you who seek God, may your
       hearts be merry!
34 For the LORD hears the poor,
   and his own who are in bonds
       he spurns not.
35 Let the heavens and the earth
       praise him,
   the seas and whatever moves
       in them!"

36 For God will save Zion
   and rebuild the cities of Judah.
   They shall dwell in the land and
       own it,
37   and the descendants of his
           servants shall inherit it,
   and those who love his name
       shall inhabit it.

PSALM 70

Prayer for Divine Help

1 For the leader; of David. For remembrance.

2 Deign, O God, to rescue me:
   O LORD, make haste to help
       me.
3 Let them be put to shame and
       confounded
   who seek my life.
   Let them be turned back in
       disgrace
   who desire my ruin.
4 Let them retire in their shame
   who say to me, "Aha, aha!"
5 But may all who seek you
   exult and be glad in you,
   And may those who love your
       salvation
   say ever, "God be glorified!"
6 But I am afflicted and poor;
   O God, hasten to me!
   You are my help and my
       deliverer;
   O LORD, hold not back!

PSALM 71

Humble Prayer in Time of Old Age

I

1 In you, O LORD, I take refuge;
   let me never be put to shame.
2 In your justice rescue me, and
       deliver me;
   incline your ear to me, and
       save me.
3 Be my rock of refuge,
   a stronghold to give me
       safety,
   for you are my rock and my
       fortress.
4 O my God, rescue me from the
       land of the wicked,
   from the grasp of the criminal
       and the violent.
5 For you are my hope, O Lord;
   my trust, O GOD, from my
       youth.
6 On you I depend from birth;
   from my mother's womb you
       are my strength;
   constant has been my hope in
       you.

69, 22: A prophecy fulfilled in the bitter drink
given to Christ on the cross. Cf Jn 19, 28. *Gall:* the
Hebrew word probably signifies the juice of some
bitter and poisonous plant.

69, 23: *Table:* a mere tablecloth spread upon the
ground, on which one might trip.

69, 26: Applied to Judas in Acts 1, 20.
Ps 70: Almost identical with Ps 40, 14–18.
Ps 71: The aged psalmist who has always put his
trust in the Lord, implores his aid (1–7) now that he
is afflicted and persecuted (9–13); each of these two
sections ends with the promise of grateful praise

(8.14–16); almost all of the third section (17–24) likewise describes the same confident expectation of being
heard by God.

71, 6: *My strength:* the exact meaning of the Hebrew is uncertain. The revised Latin Psalter still retains "my protector" of the older Latin version.

7 A portent am I to many,
    but you are my strong refuge!
8 My mouth shall be filled with
    your praise,
    with your glory day by day.

II

9 Cast me not off in my old age;
    as my strength fails, forsake
    me not,
10 For my enemies speak against
    me,
    and they who keep watch
    against my life take counsel
    together.
11 They say, "God has forsaken
    him;
    pursue and seize him,
    for there is no one to rescue
    him."
12 O God, be not far from me;
    my God, make haste to help
    me.
13 Let them be put to shame and
    consumed who attack my
    life;
    let them be wrapped in
    ignominy and disgrace who
    seek to harm me.
14 But I will always hope
    and praise you ever more and
    more.
15 My mouth shall declare your
    justice,
    day by day your salvation,
    though I know not their
    extent.
16 I will treat of the mighty works
    of the Lord;
    O GOD, I will tell of your
    singular justice.

III

17 O God, you have taught me
    from my youth,
    and till the present I proclaim
    your wondrous deeds;
18 And now that I am old and
    gray,
    O God, forsake me not

Till I proclaim your strength
    to every generation that is to
    come.
19 Your power and your justice,
    O God, reach to heaven.
    You have done great things;
    O God, who is like you?
20 Though you have made me feel
    many bitter afflictions,
    you will again revive me;
    from the depths of the earth
    you will once more raise me.

21 Renew your benefits toward me,
    and comfort me over and
    over.
22 So will I give you thanks with
    music on the lyre,
    for your faithfulness, O my
    God!
    I will sing your praises with the
    harp,
    O Holy One of Israel!
23 My lips shall shout for joy
    as I sing your praises;
    My soul also, which you have
    redeemed,
24   and my tongue day by day
    shall discourse on your
    justice
    How shamed and how disgraced
    are those who sought to harm
    me!

PSALM 72

The Kingdom of the Messiah
1 Of Solomon.

I

O God, with your judgment
    endow the king,
    and with your justice, the
    king's son;
2 He shall govern your people
    with justice
    and your afflicted ones with
    judgment.
3 The mountains shall yield peace
    for the people,
    and the hills justice.

4 He shall defend the afflicted
    among the people,
    save the children of the poor,
    and crush the oppressor.

II

5 May he endure as long as the
    sun,
    and like the moon through all
    generations.
6 He shall be like rain coming
    down on the meadow,
    like showers watering the earth.
7 Justice shall flower in his days,
    and profound peace, till the
    moon be no more.

III

8 May he rule from sea to sea,
    and from the River to the
    ends of the earth.
9 His foes shall bow before him,
    and his enemies shall lick the
    dust.
10 The kings of Tarshish and the
    Isles shall offer gifts;
    the kings of Arabia and Seba
    shall bring tribute.
11 All kings shall pay him homage,
    all nations shall serve him.

IV

12 For he shall rescue the poor
    man when he cries out,
    and the afflicted when he has
    no one to help him.
13 He shall have pity for the lowly
    and the poor;
    the lives of the poor he shall
    save.
14 From fraud and violence he
    shall redeem them,
    and precious shall their blood
    be in his sight.

V

15 May he live to be given the gold
    of Arabia,
    and to be prayed for
    continually;
    day by day shall they bless him.

71, 7: *A portent:* many marvel that the psalmist is so afflicted, looking on him as cursed by God. Cf Dt 28, 46. Some commentators, however, understand this as, "Many marvel at my invincible confidence in God and at the great graces he bestows on me."

71, 15: *Though I know not their extent:* the psalmist admits that God's acts of kindness toward him are more numerous than he himself realizes.

Ps 72: A song of good wishes for the king, perhaps composed originally for the coronation ceremonies of one of David's successors. But some of the expressions cannot be understood of any earthly monarch except

as pure hyperbole. They find their complete fulfillment only in Christ. Hence the traditional interpretation rightly treats the psalm as Messianic, at least in a typical sense. The earthly king is here a type or figure of Christ the King. The Hebrew verbs seem to vary between the future and the jussive. Some commentators render them all in the future. The thoughts here expressed concern the king's just rule (1–4), his long and glorious reign (5–7), his universal dominion (8–11), his defense of the poor and oppressed (12–14), and the prosperity of his kingdom (15–17).

72, 1: *The king . . . the king's son:* the same indivi-

dual is meant; his father was also a king.

72, 2: *With judgment:* he shall procure their rights for them.

72, 8: Indicates the boundaries of the civilized world at that time: from the Mediterranean Sea to the Persian Gulf (the "Eastern Sea"), and from the Euphrates (*the River*) to the islands and land of southwestern Europe, then considered *the ends of the earth.*

72, 10: *Tarshish and the Isles:* the far west. Cf Ps 48, 8. *Arabia and Seba:* the far south, Cf 1 Kgs 10, 1.

16 May there be an abundance of
    grain upon the earth;
  on the tops of the mountains
    the crops shall rustle like
    Lebanon;
  the city dwellers shall flourish
    like the verdure of the
    fields.
17 May his name be blessed
    forever;
  as long as the sun his name
    shall remain.
  In him shall all the tribes of the
    earth be blessed;
  all the nations shall proclaim
    his happiness.

* * *

18 Blessed be the LORD, the God of
    Israel,
  who alone does wondrous
    deeds.
19 And blessed forever be his
    glorious name;
  may the whole earth be filled
    with his glory.
  Amen. Amen.

20 The prayers of David the son of
    Jesse are ended.

THE THIRD BOOK
Psalms 73–89

PSALM 73

The False Happiness of the Wicked

1 A psalm of Asaph.

  How good God is to the
    upright;
  the LORD, to those who are
    clean of heart!
2 But, as for me, I almost lost my
    balance;
  my feet all but slipped,

3 Because I was envious of the
    arrogant
  when I saw them prosper
    though they were wicked.

I

4 For they are in no pain;
  their bodies are sound and
    sleek;
5 They are free from the burdens
    of mortals,
  and are not afflicted like the
    rest of men.
6 So pride adorns them as a
    necklace;
  as a robe violence enwraps
    them.
7 Out of their crassness comes
    iniquity;
  their fancies overflow their
    hearts.
8 They scoff and speak evil;
  outrage from on high they
    threaten.
9 They set their mouthings in
    place of heaven,
  and their pronouncements
    roam the earth:
10 "So he brings his people to
    such a pass
  that they have not even
    water!"
11 And they say, "How does God
    know?"
  And, "Is there any knowledge
    in the Most High?"
12 Such, then, are the wicked;
  always carefree, while they
    increase in wealth.

II

13 Is it but in vain I have kept my
    heart clean
  and washed my hands as an
    innocent man?
14 For I suffer affliction day after
    day
  and chastisement with each
    new dawn.

15 Had I thought, "I will speak as
    they do,"
  I had been false to the
    fellowship of your children.
16 Though I tried to understand this
  it seemed to me too difficult,
17 Till I entered the sanctuary of
    God
  and considered their final
    destiny.

III

18 You set them, indeed, on a
    slippery road;
  you hurl them down to ruin.
19 How suddenly they are made
    desolate!
  They are completely wasted
    away amid horrors.
20 As though they were the dream
    of one who had awakened,
    O Lord,
  so will you, when you arise, set
    at nought these phantoms.
21 Because my heart was embittered
  and my soul was pierced,
22 I was stupid and understood not;
  I was like a brute beast in
    your presence.

IV

23 Yet with you I shall always be;
  you have hold of my right
    hand;
24 With your counsel you guide me,
  and in the end you will
    receive me in glory.
25 Whom else have I in heaven?
  And when I am with you, the
    earth delights me not.
26 Though my flesh and my heart
    waste away,
  God is the rock of my
    heart and my portion
    forever.
27 For indeed, they who withdraw
    from you perish;
  you destroy everyone who is
    unfaithful to you.

72, 17: *In him ... be blessed:* either, "Because of him all men shall receive God's blessings," or, "All men shall use his name in giving a blessing, saying, 'May you be as blessed as this king.'" Cf Gn 48, 20.
72, 18f: The doxology at the end of the second Book of the psalms: a later edition. Cf 41, 14.
72, 20: This note shows that Ps 72 once constituted the end of a certain collection of Davidic psalms. It does not exclude the possibility of some other Davidic psalms being incorporated in the following collections.
Ps 73: Like Pss 37 and 49, this sapiential psalm is concerned with the problem of why the wicked seem to prosper. After showing how dangerous the thought of such apparent injustice may be (1–3), the psalmist

sets forth the difficulty in clear terms by describing the earthly happiness of the wicked who blaspheme God with seeming impunity (4–12), whereas the good apparently suffer in vain (13–16); the only solution, as he has learned from God himself, lies in the hereafter (17), where the fortunes of the prosperous sinner will suddenly be reversed (18–22) while the good will enjoy God's presence forever (23–28).
73, 9: *They set their mouthings in place of heaven:* literally, "They set their mouths in heaven," which seems to mean, "They speak as if they were God." The revised Latin Psalter renders it, "They attack heaven with their mouths."
73, 10: This verse is defective in the current Hebrew

text. The translation given above understands it as one of the blasphemies uttered by the wicked, ridiculing God's justice. The revised Latin Psalter understands it as said by the psalmist himself, "So my people turn to them, and they suck up water in abundance."
73, 17: *I entered the sanctuary of God:* in spirit the psalmist penetrated God's heavenly sanctuary.
73, 20: *When you arise:* in judgment. The Lord seems to act as if he were asleep. Cf Ps 78, 65. The Temporary injustice will prove to be but a bad dream.
73, 21f: The psalmist reverts to the time when he was scandalized by the prosperity of the wicked.

28 But for me, to be near God is
my good;
to make the Lord GOD my
refuge.
I shall declare all your works
in the gates of the daughter of
Zion.

PSALM 74

Prayer in Time of National Calamity

1 A *maskil* of Asaph.

I

Why, O God, have you cast us
off forever?
Why does your anger smolder
against the sheep of your
pasture?
2 Remember your flock which
you built up of old,
the tribe you redeemed as
your inheritance,
Mount Zion, where you took
up your abode.
3 Turn your steps toward the
utter ruins;
toward all the damage the
enemy has done in the
sanctuary.
4 Your foes roar triumphantly in
your shrine;
they have set up their tokens
of victory.
5 They are like men coming up
with axes to a clump of
trees;
6 and now with chisel and
hammer they hack at all its
paneling.
7 They set your sanctuary on fire;
the place where your name
abides they have razed and
profaned.
8 They said in their hearts, "Let
us destroy them;
burn all the shrines of God in
the land."

9 Deeds on our behalf we do not
see; there is no prophet now,
and no one of us knows how
long. . . .
10 How long, O God, shall the foe
blaspheme?
Shall the enemy revile your
name forever?
11 Why draw back your hand
and keep your right hand idle
beneath your cloak?

II

12 Yet, O God, my king from of
old,
you doer of saving deeds on
earth,
13 You stirred up the sea by your
might;
you smashed the heads of the
dragons in the waters.
14 You crushed the heads of
Leviathan,
and made food of him for the
dolphins.
15 You released the springs and
torrents;
you brought dry land out of
the primeval waters.
16 Yours is the day, and yours the
night;
you fashioned the moon and
the sun.
17 You fixed all the limits of the
land;
summer and winter you made.

18 Remember how the enemy has
blasphemed you, O LORD,
and how a stupid people has
reviled your name.
19 Give not to the vulture the life
of your dove;
be not forever unmindful of
the lives of your afflicted
ones.
20 Look to your covenant,
for the hiding places in the
land and the plains are full
of violence.

21 May the humble not retire in
confusion;
may the afflicted and the
poor praise your name.
22 Arise, O God; defend your
cause;
remember how the fool
blasphemes you day after
day.
23 Be not unmindful of the voice of
your foes;
the uproar of those who
rebel against you is
unceasing.

PSALM 75

God the Just Judge of the Wicked

1 For the leader. (Do not destroy!)
A psalm of Asaph; a song.

I

2 We give you thanks, O God, we
give thanks,
and we invoke your name; we
declare your wondrous
deeds.

II

3 "When I seize the appointed
time,
I will judge with equity.
4 Though the earth and all who
dwell in it quake,
I have set firm its pillars.
5 I say to the boastful: Boast not;
and to the wicked: Lift not up
your horns."

6 Lift not up your horns against
the Most High;
speak not haughtily against
the Rock.
7 For neither from the east nor
from the west,
neither from the desert nor
from the mountains—
8 But God is the judge;
one he brings low; another he
lifts up.

Ps 74: A lamentation over the destruction of the temple. The event referred to is probably the taking of Jerusalem by the Babylonians in 587 B.C. The psalmist graphically describes the frightful havoc and desolation in the temple as he implores God to be mindful of his people (1–11); then, recalling the glorious deeds the Lord has done of old (12–17), he humbly reminds God that his own honor is at stake in the fate of his chosen people (18–32).

74, 1: *Forever:* this word seems to imply that the disaster is already of long duration.

74, 5: The Hebrew text of this verse is rather obscure.

74, 9: *Deeds on our behalf:* literally, "our signs,"

which probably means, "signs done for us," wonderful exploits such as God performed for the Israelites during the Exodus. *There is no prophet now:* Jeremiah and Ezekiel may have been dead, or at least may not have been in Jerusalem. There is no need, because of these words, to fix the date of this psalm as late as Maccabean times. Cf Lam 2, 9.

74, 13–17: These verses were probably borrowed from some much older hymn. The imagery used here to describe God's creative power at the beginning of the world may have been taken over in part from the ancient Canaanite literature. *The dragons . . . Leviathan:* mythological monsters. Cf Is 27, 1. Here they are the personification of the watery chaos at the begin-

ning of creation. Cf Ps 89, 11.
74, 19: *The vulture:* the ferocious foes. *Your dove:* Israel. Cf Ps 68, 14.

Ps 75: After an introductory verse of praise sung by the community (2), the word of the Lord is heard, foretelling the condemnation of the proud (3–5); the psalmist then repeats and develops the same thought (6–9), praising God for this victory over the sinners (10f).

75, 5f.11: *Horns:* the symbol of power. See note on Ps 18, 3.

75, 7: The sentence is intentionally left incomplete; for the sense, add, "does justice come." *The desert:* the south. *The mountains:* the north.

9 For a cup is in the LORD's hand,
full of spiced and foaming wine,
And he pours out from it; even
to the dregs they shall
drain it;
all the wicked of the earth
shall drink.

III

10 But as for me, I will exult
forever;
I will sing praise to the God
of Jacob.
11 And I will break off the horns
of all the wicked;
the horns of the just shall be
lifted up.

PSALM 76

*Thanksgiving for the Overthrow
of Israel's Foes*

1 For the leader; a psalm with stringed
instruments. A song of Asaph.

I

2 God is renowned in Judah,
in Israel great is his name.
3 In Salem is his abode;
his dwelling is in Zion.
4 There he shattered the flashing
shafts of the bow,
shield and sword, and
weapons of war.

II

5 Resplendent you came, O
powerful One,
from the everlasting mountains.
6 Despoiled are the stouthearted;
they sleep their sleep;
the hands of all the mighty
ones have failed.
7 At your rebuke, O God of Jacob,
chariots and steeds lay stilled.

III

8 You are terrible; and who can
withstand you
for the fury of your anger?

9 From heaven you made your
intervention heard;
the earth feared and was
silent
10 When God arose for judgment,
to save all the afflicted of the
earth.

IV

11 For wrathful Edom shall glorify
you,
and the survivors of Hamath
shall keep your festivals.
12 Make vows to the LORD, your
God, and fulfill them;
let all round about him bring
gifts to the terrible Lord
13 Who checks the pride of princes,
who is terrible to the kings of
the earth.

PSALM 77

*Lament and Comfort in Time of
Distress*

1 For the leader; 'al Jeduthun.
A psalm of Asaph.

I

2 Aloud to God I cry;
aloud to God, to hear me;
3 on the day of my distress I
seek the Lord.
By night my hands are stretched
out without flagging;
my soul refuses comfort.
4 When I remember God, I moan;
when I ponder, my spirit grows
faint.
5 You keep my eyes watchful;
I am troubled and cannot
speak.
6 I consider the days of old;
the years long past   7 I
remember.
In the night I meditate in my
heart;
I ponder, and my spirit
broods:

8 "Will the LORD reject forever
and nevermore be favorable?
9 Will his kindness utterly cease,
his promise fail for all
generations?
10 Has God forgotten pity?
Does he in anger withhold his
compassion?"
11 And I say, "This is my sorrow,
that the right hand of the
Most High is changed."
12 I remember the deeds of the
LORD;
yes, I remember your wonders
of old.
13 And I meditate on your works;
your exploits I ponder.

II

14 O God, your way is holy;
what great god is there like
our God?
15 You are the God who works
wonders;
among the peoples you have
made known your power.
16 With your strong arm you
redeemed your people,
the sons of Jacob and
Joseph.
17 The waters saw you, O God;
the waters saw you and
shuddered;
the very depths were troubled;
18 The clouds poured down water;
the skies gave forth their
voice;
your arrows also sped abroad.
19 Your thunder resounded in the
whirlwind;
your lightning illumined the
world;
the earth quivered and quaked.
20 Through the sea was your way,
and your path through the
deep waters,
though your footsteps were
not seen.

75,9: *A cup:* see note on Ps 11,6. Here it is "the cup of God's wrath," the punishment he inflicts on sinners. Cf Is 51,17; Jer 25,15–29; 49,12; Ez 23,31ff. *Spiced:* literally, "a mixed drink"; spices or drugs were put into wine to make it more intoxicating. Cf Is 5,22; Prv 9,2.5.

Ps 76: A hymn of triumph in which Jerusalem's victory is attributed primarily to God (2–4) He has overwhelmed the enemy (5–7) and avenged the oppressed (8–10); to him, therefore, sacrifices of thanksgiving are due (11–13).

76,3: *Salem:* Jerusalem. Perhaps on account of its allusion to the Hebrew word for peace, this ancient form of the city's name was chosen here. Cf

Gn 14,18; Heb 7,1f.
76,5: *From the everlasting mountains:* from the temple on Mount Zion, the "ancient," age-old fortress of the Jebusites. Cf Ps 24,7.9.
76,6: *Their sleep:* of death.
76,11: *Edom . . . Hamath:* the words are not certain. The reference would be to Israel's pagan neighbors south and north. The current Hebrew text may perhaps be rendered, "For the wrath of man must be turned to your praise, and the survivors of fury shall keep your festivals."
76,13: *Checks the pride:* or perhaps, "Cuts short the courage"; literally, "Shortens (or cuts off) the spirit." The Syriac version renders this as, "Humbles

the pride"; the Greek version as, "Cuts off the life."
Ps 77: The first section (2–13) is a lamentation in which the psalmist bewails, probably not his own misfortune, but rather the seeming abandonment of his nation by God; the second section (14–21) is in the tones of a typical hymn of praise, which the psalmist perhaps borrowed from an older hymn, in order to contrast the present situation with God's glorious deeds in the past, particularly in the Exodus.
77,11: *The right hand of the Most High:* God's strong guidance and protection. Cf Pss 17,7; 18,36; Is 41,10.

21 You led your people like a
flock
under the care of Moses and
Aaron.

PSALM 78

*God's Goodness despite Israel's
Ingratitude*

1 A *maskil* of Asaph.

Hearken, my people, to my
teaching;
incline your ears to the words
of my mouth.
2 I will open my mouth in a
parable,
I will utter mysteries from of
old.
3 What we have heard and know,
and what our fathers have
declared to us,
4 We will not hide from their
sons;
we will declare to the
generation to come
The glorious deeds of the LORD
and his strength
and the wonders that he
wrought.
5 He set it up as a decree in
Jacob,
and established it as a law in
Israel,
That what he commanded our
fathers
they should make known to
their sons;
6 So that the generation to come
might know,
their sons yet to be born,
That they too may rise and
declare to their sons
7 that they should put their
hope in God,
And not forget the deeds of God
but keep his commands,
8 And not be like their fathers,
a generation wayward and
rebellious,

A generation that kept not its
heart steadfast
nor its spirit faithful toward
God.

I

9 The sons of Ephraim, ordered
ranks of bowmen,
retreated in the day of battle.
10 They kept not the covenant with
God;
according to his law they
would not walk;
11 And they forgot his deeds,
the wonders he had shown
them.
12 Before their fathers he did
wondrous things,
in the land of Egypt, in the
plain of Zoan.
13 He cleft the sea and brought
them through,
and he made the waters stand
as in a mound.
14 He led them with a cloud by day,
and all night with a glow of
fire.
15 He cleft the rocks in the desert
and gave them water in
copious floods.
16 He made streams flow from the
crag
and brought the waters forth
in rivers.

II

17 But they sinned yet more
against him,
rebelling against the Most
High in the wasteland,
18 And they tempted God in their
hearts
by demanding the food they
craved.
19 Yes, they spoke against God,
saying,
"Can God spread a table in
the desert?
20 For when he struck the rock,
waters gushed forth,
and the streams overflowed;

Can he also give bread
and provide meat for his
people?"
21 Then the LORD heard and was
enraged;
and fire blazed up against
Jacob,
and anger rose against Israel,
22 Because they believed not God
nor trusted in his help.
23 Yet he commanded the skies
above
and the doors of heaven he
opened;
24 He rained manna upon them for
food
and gave them heavenly bread.
25 The bread of the mighty was
eaten by men;
even a surfeit of provisions he
sent them.
26 He stirred up the east wind in
the heavens,
and by his power brought on
the south wind.
27 And he rained meat upon them
like dust,
and, like the sand of the sea,
winged fowl,
28 Which fell in the midst of their
camp
round about their tents.
29 So they ate and were wholly
surfeited;
he had brought them what
they craved.
30 They had not given over their
craving,
and their food was still in
their mouths,
31 When the anger of God rose
against them
and slew their best men,
and laid low the young men
of Israel.

III

32 Yet for all this they sinned still
more
and believed not in his
wonders.

Ps 78: A didactic psalm, drawing salutary lessons from Israel's history. Cf Pss 106; 107. After an elaborate introduction on the importance of handing down the tradition of God's dealings with his people (1–8), the psalmist teaches that the Northern Kingdom of Israel became disloyal to God (9–11), just as did their forefathers for whom God had worked wonders in the Exodus (12–16) and in the journey through the wilderness (17–31); these ancestors were punished for giving mere lip service to God (32–39) although they had witnessed his power in the plagues of Egypt (40–51) and in the journey to the Promised Land (52–55); so also God rejected their descendants, the Israelites of the Northern Kingdom (56–64) and chose Judah and the house of David (65–72).

78, 2: This verse is applied by St. Matthew to our Lord's teaching in parables (Mt 13, 35). *A parable*: the Hebrew word *mashal* signifies properly, "a comparison," then any saying in which some deeper meaning lies, to be understood by means of the hidden comparison; here the entire psalm is a *mashal*. *Mysteries from of old*: the meanings which the

psalmist sees hidden in the ancient history of his ancestors.
78, 9: *Ephraim*: the most important of the northern tribes of Israel; hence here, as often, the Northern Kingdom in general.
78, 12.43: *Zoan*: a city in the delta of the Nile, the capital of Egypt at the time of the Exodus.
78, 25: *The mighty*: the angels, according to the Greek version and Wis 16, 20. Cf Ps 103, 20.

33 Therefore he quickly ended
their days
and their years with sudden
destruction.
34 While he slew them they sought
him
and inquired after God again,
35 Remembering that God was
their rock
and the Most High God, their
redeemer.
36 But they flattered him with their
mouths
and lied to him with their
tongues,
37 Though their hearts were not
steadfast toward him,
nor were they faithful to his
covenant.
38 Yet he, being merciful, forgave
their sin
and destroyed them not;
Often he turned back his anger
and let none of his wrath be
roused.
39 He remembered that they were
flesh,
a passing breath that returns
not.

IV

40 How often they rebelled against
him in the desert
and grieved him in the
wilderness!
41 Again and again they tempted God
and provoked the Holy One
of Israel.
42 They remembered not his hand
nor the day he delivered them
from the foe,
43 When he wrought his signs in
Egypt
and his marvels in the plain
of Zoan,
44 And changed into blood their
streams—
their running water, so that
they could not drink;
45 He sent among them flies that
devoured them
and frogs that destroyed them.
46 He gave their harvest to the
caterpillar,
the fruits of their toil to the
locust.

47 He killed their vines with hail
and their sycamores with frost.
48 He gave over to the hail their
beasts
and their flocks to the lightning.
49 He loosed against them his
fierce anger,
wrath and fury and strife,
a detachment of messengers of
doom.
50 When he measured the course of
his anger
he spared them not from death,
and delivered their beasts to
the plague.
51 He smote every first-born in
Egypt,
the first fruits of manhood in
the tents of Ham;
52 But his people he led forth like
sheep
and guided them like a herd
in the desert.
53 He led them on secure and
unafraid,
while he covered their enemies
with the sea.
54 And he brought them to his
holy land,
to the mountains his right
hand had won.
55 And he drove out nations before
them;
he distributed their
inheritance by lot,
and settled the tribes of
Israel in their tents.

V

56 But they tempted and rebelled
against God the Most High,
and kept not his decrees.
57 They turned back and were
faithless like their fathers;
they recoiled like a treacherous
bow.
58 They angered him with their
high places
and with their idols roused
his jealousy.
59 God heard and was enraged
and utterly rejected Israel.
60 And he forsook the tabernacle
in Shiloh,
the tent where he dwelt
among men.

61 And he surrendered his strength
into captivity,
his glory into the hands of the
foe.
62 He abandoned his people to the
sword
and was enraged against his
inheritance.
63 Fire consumed their young men,
and their maidens were not
betrothed.
64 Their priests fell by the sword,
and their widows sang no
dirges.

VI

65 Then the Lord awoke, as wakes
from sleep
a champion overcome with
wine;
66 And he put his foes to flight
and cast them into everlasting
disgrace.
67 And he rejected the tent of
Joseph,
and the tribe of Ephraim he
chose not;
68 But he chose the tribe of Judah,
Mount Zion which he loved.
69 And he built his shrine like
heaven,
like the earth which he founded
forever.
70 And he chose David, his
servant,
and took him from the
sheepfolds;
71 From following the ewes he
brought him
to shepherd Jacob, his people,
and Israel, his inheritance.
72 And he tended them with a
sincere heart,
and with skillful hands he
guided them.

PSALM 79

The Destruction of Jerusalem
and its Temple

1 A psalm of Asaph.

I

O God, the nations have come
into your inheritance;

78, 50: *Measured:* with his eye, surveyed.
78, 66: *He put his foes to flight:* literally, "He struck
his foes back," or, "in the back"; some commentators
see in this an allusion to 1 Sm 5, 6.9.
Ps 79: A lamentation of the people over the havoc

wrought by the enemy in Jerusalem. The situation
may well have been the capture of the city by the
Babylonians in 587 B.C. Cf Ps 74. Here the people
bewail the destruction and slaughter in the city (1–4),
and pray God to avenge them and pardon their sins

(5–8) for the sake of his own honor and glory (9f);
if he frees the captive Jews and punishes their
enemies, they will offer him eternal thanks (11–13).

they have defiled your holy
　　temple,
they have laid Jerusalem in
　　ruins.
2 They have given the corpses of
　　your servants
　　as food to the birds of heaven,
　　the flesh of your faithful ones
　　to the beasts of the earth.
3 They have poured out their
　　blood like water
　　round about Jerusalem,
　　and there is no one to bury
　　them.
4 We have become the reproach of
　　our neighbors,
　　the scorn and derision of those
　　around us.

II

5 O Lord, how long? Will you be
　　angry forever?
　　Will your jealousy burn like
　　fire?
6 Pour out your wrath upon the
　　nations that acknowledge
　　you not,
　　upon the kingdoms that call
　　not upon your name;
7 For they have devoured Jacob
　　and laid waste his dwelling.
8 Remember not against us the
　　iniquities of the past;
　　may your compassion quickly
　　come to us,
　　for we are brought very low.

III

9 Help us, O God our savior,
　　because of the glory of your
　　name;
　　Deliver us and pardon our sins
　　for your name's sake.
10 Why should the nations say,
　　"Where is their God?"
　　Let it be known among the
　　nations in our sight
　　that you avenge the shedding
　　of your servants' blood.

IV

11 Let the prisoners' sighing come
　　before you;
　　with your great power free
　　those doomed to death.
12 And repay our neighbors
　　sevenfold into their bosoms
　　the disgrace they have
　　inflicted on you, O Lord.
13 Then we, your people and the
　　sheep of your pasture,
　　will give thanks to you
　　forever;
　　through all generations we
　　will declare your praise.

PSALM 80

Prayer for the Restoration of the Lord's Vineyard

1 For the leader; according to "Lilies."
　Eduth. A psalm of Asaph.

I

2 O shepherd of Israel, hearken,
　　O guide of the flock of Joseph!
　From your throne upon the
　　cherubim, shine forth
3 　before Ephraim, Benjamin and
　　Manasseh.
　Rouse your power,
　　-and come to save us.
4 　　O Lord of hosts, restore us;
　　　if your face shine upon us,
　　　then we shall be safe.

II

5 O Lord of hosts, how long will
　　you burn with anger
　　while your people pray?
6 You have fed them with the
　　bread of tears
　　and given them tears to drink
　　in ample measure.
7 You have left us to be fought
　　over by our neighbors,
　　and our enemies mock us.
8 　　O Lord of hosts, restore us;
　　　if your face shine upon us,
　　　then we shall be safe.

III

9 A vine from Egypt you trans-
　　planted;
　　you drove away the nations
　　and planted it.
10 You cleared the ground for it,
　　and it took root and filled the
　　land.
11 The mountains were hidden in
　　its shadow;
　　by its branches, the cedars of
　　God.
12 It put forth its foliage to the
　　Sea,
　　its shoots as far as the River.

IV

13 Why have you broken down its
　　walls,
　　so that every passer-by
　　plucks its fruit,
14 The boar from the forest lays it
　　waste,
　　and the beasts of the field feed
　　upon it?
15 Once again, O Lord of hosts,
　　look down from heaven, and
　　see;
　　Take care of this vine,
16 　and protect what your right
　　hand has planted
　　[the son of man whom you
　　yourself made strong].

V

17 Let those who would burn it
　　with fire or cut it down
　　perish before you at your
　　rebuke.
18 May your help be with the man
　　of your right hand,
　　with the son of man whom
　　you yourself made strong.
19 Then we will no more withdraw
　　from you;
　　give us new life, and we will
　　call upon your name.
20 　O Lord of hosts, restore us;
　　　if your face shine upon us,
　　　then we shall be safe.

79, 2f: *The flesh . . . to bury them:* these four lines are quoted somewhat freely in 1 Mc 7, 17 as describing the treacherous slaughter of sixty Pious Jews in Jerusalem during the Maccabean wars. But this does not prove that the psalm was written at such a late period.

79, 12: *Into their bosoms:* the ample folds at the front of full-length garments were used in accepting gifts or rewards of grain. Cf Lk 6, 38. The same figure is used here for full (sevenfold) punishment.

Ps 80: The Lord's help is besought for Israel,
especially for the northern tribes (2f), for they are sorely oppressed by their enemies (5–7); they were once God's well-tended vine (9–12), but now this vineyard is devastated (13–16); therefore his saving help is implored (17–19). The refrain after the first, second and fifth stanzas (4.8.20) perhaps stood originally after the third and fourth stanzas also.

80, 4: *If your face shine upon us:* if God brighten their lives with his gracious smile.

80, 9: *A vine:* a frequent metaphor for Israel. Cf Is 5, 1–7; 27, 2f; Jer 2, 21; Hos 10, 1; Mt 21, 33.

80, 11: *The cedars of God:* the giant cedars of Lebanon, considered as especially planted by God. Cf Nm 24, 6.

80, 12: *The Sea:* the Mediterranean. *The River:* the Euphrates. Cf Ps 72, 8.

80, 16: *The son of man:* this line is presumably an accidental duplication of the similar line in v 18.

80, 17: *Let those who would burn it:* this line, as here translated, is a reconstruction; but the two halves of the Hebrew line do not properly belong together.

PSALM 81

*Festive Song with an Admonition
to Fidelity*

1 For the leader; "upon the *gittith*."
Of Asaph.

A

2 Sing joyfully to God our
    strength;
    acclaim the God of Jacob.
3 Take up a melody, and sound
    the timbrel,
    the pleasant harp and the lyre.
4 Blow the trumpet at the new
    moon,
    at the full moon, on our
    solemn feast;
5 For it is a statute in Israel,
    an ordinance of the God of
    Jacob,
6 Who made it a decree for
    Joseph
    when he came forth from the
    land of Egypt.

B

I

An unfamiliar speech I hear:
7 "I relieved his shoulders of
    the burden;
    his hands were freed from the
    basket.
8 In distress you called, and I
    rescued you;
    Unseen, I answered you in
    thunder;
    I tested you at the waters of
    Meribah.
9 Hear, my people, and I will
    admonish you;
    O Israel, will you not hear me?
10 There shall be no strange god
    among you
    nor shall you worship any
    alien god.

11 I, the Lord, am your God
    who led you forth from the
    land of Egypt;
    open wide your mouth, and I
    will fill it.

II

12 "But my people heard not my
    voice,
    and Israel obeyed me not;
13 So I gave them up to the
    hardness of their hearts;
    they walked according to their
    own counsels.
14 If only my people would hear me,
    and Israel walk in my ways,
15 Quickly would I humble their
    enemies;
    against their foes I would
    turn my hand.
16 Those who hated the Lord would
    seek to flatter me,
    but their fate would endure
    forever,
17 While Israel I would feed with
    the best of wheat,
    and with honey from the rock
    I would fill them."

PSALM 82

Judgment against Wicked Judges

1 A psalm of Asaph.

God arises in the divine assembly;
    he judges in the midst of the
    gods.

I

2 "How long will you judge
    unjustly
    and favor the cause of the
    wicked?
3 Defend the lowly and the
    fatherless;
    render justice to the afflicted
    and the destitute.

4 Rescue the lowly and the poor;
    from the hand of the wicked
    deliver them.

II

5 "They know not, neither do they
    understand;
    they go about in darkness;
    all the foundations of the
    earth are shaken.
6 I said: You are gods,
    all of you sons of the Most
    High;
7 Yet like men you shall die,
    and fall like any prince."
8 Rise, O God; judge the earth,
    for yours are all the nations.

PSALM 83

Prayer against a Hostile Alliance

1 A song; a psalm of Asaph.

I

2 O God, do not remain unmoved;
    be not silent, O God, and be
    not still!
3 For behold, your enemies raise
    a tumult,
    and they who hate you lift up
    their heads.
4 Against your people they plot
    craftily;
    they conspire against those
    whom you protect.
5 They say, "Come, let us destroy
    their nation;
    let the name of Israel be
    remembered no more!"

6 Yes, they consult together with
    one mind,
    and against you they are
    allied:

Ps 81: Two distinct sections. The first section (2–6a) is a short song sung on the feast of Booths. The second section (6b–17) is a divine oracle in which the Lord reminds the people that it was he who led them out of Egypt and commanded them at that time to worship no other God but him (7–11); he has punished them for their disobedience, but will now give them victory and prosperity if they obey him (12–17).

81, 4: *Blow the trumpet:* to assemble the people for the feast. This custom was observed on various feasts, but it was especially prescribed for the first day of each month, that is, for the feast of *the new moon*, and in particular for the first day of the seventh month, during which month the feast of Booths, a very *solemn feast*, was celebrated on the fifteenth day, *the full moon*, Cf Lv 23, 24.34–43; Nm 10, 10; 29, 1.12.

81, 6: *An unfamiliar speech I hear:* these words are uttered by a prophet who then continues to speak in God's name.

81, 7: A reference to the liberation of Israel from slavery in Egypt. *The basket:* for carrying clay to make bricks. Cf Ex 1, 14.

81, 11: *Open wide your mouth, and I will fill it:* God tells the people that, no matter how great their desires, he will fulfill them.

81, 17: *Honey . . . rock:* extreme abundance. Cf Jl 4, 18.

Ps 82: The psalmist presents God himself (1) rebuking the unjust judges (2–4) and passing sentences on them (5–7). A short prayer for universal justice concludes the psalm (8). Cf Is 3, 13ff for a similar judgment scene.

82, 1: *The gods:* human judges, who are "godlike" in their prerogative of establishing justice on earth. Cf Ps 58, 2.

82, 5: *The foundations of the Earth:* the very basis of law and order. Cf Ps 11, 3.

82, 6: *I said, You are gods:* our Lord's own comment on these words is, "He called them gods to whom the word of God was addressed." Cf Jn 10, 34.

82, 7: *Like men:* like the rest of men.

82, 8: This verse can be fittingly understood as addressed to Christ, to whom all judgment has been given. Cf Jn 5, 22.

Ps 83: The psalmist prays for divine aid against a powerful league of hostile nations (2–5), which he enumerates (6–9), asking God to overcome them as he did Israel's enemies of old (10–13), and to destroy them completely (14–19).

7 The tents of Edom and the
    Ishmaelites,
    Moab and the people of
        Hagar,
8 Gebal and Ammon and Amalek,
    Philistia with the inhabitants
        of Tyre;
9 The Assyrians, too, are leagued
        with them;
    they are the forces of the sons
        of Lot.

II

10 Deal with them as with Midian;
    as with Sisera and Jabin at
        the torrent Kishon,
11 Who perished at Endor;
    they became dung on the
        ground.
12 Make their nobles like Oreb and
        Zeeb;
    all their chiefs like Zebah and
        Zalmunna,
13 Who said, "Let us take for
        ourselves
    the dwelling place of God."

14 O my God, make them like
    leaves in a whirlwind,
    like chaff before the wind.
15 As a fire raging in a forest,
    as a flame setting the
        mountains ablaze,
16 So pursue them with your
        tempest
    and rout them with your
        storm.
17 Darken their faces with disgrace,
    that men may seek your name,
        O LORD.
18 Let them be shamed and put to
        rout forever;
    let them be confounded and
        perish,
19 Knowing that you alone are the
        LORD,
    the Most High over all the
        earth.

PSALM 84

Desire for the Sanctuary

1 For the leader; "upon the *gittith.*"
A psalm of the sons of Korah.

I

2 How lovely is your dwelling place,
    O LORD of hosts!
3 My soul yearns and pines
    for the courts of the LORD.
My heart and my flesh
    cry out for the living God.
4 Even the sparrow finds a home,
    and the swallow a nest
    in which she puts her young—
Your altars, O LORD of hosts,
    my king and my God!

II

5 Happy they who dwell in your
        house!
    continually they praise you.
6 Happy the men whose strength
        you are!
    their hearts are set upon the
        pilgrimage:
7 When they pass through the
        valley of the mastic trees
    they make a spring of it;
    the early rain clothes it with
        generous growth.
8 They go from strength to
        strength;
    they shall see the God of
        gods in Zion.

III

9 O LORD of hosts, hear my
        prayer;
    hearken, O God of Jacob!
10 O God, behold our shield,
    and look upon the face of
        your anointed.
11 I had rather one day in your
        courts
    than a thousand elsewhere;
I had rather lie at the threshold
    of the house of my God
    than dwell in the tents of the
        wicked.

12 For a sun and a shield is the
    LORD God;
    grace and glory he bestows;
The LORD withholds no good
        thing
    from those who walk in
        sincerity.
13 O LORD of hosts,
    happy the men who trust in
        you!

PSALM 85

Prayer for Complete Restoration

1 For the leader. A psalm of the sons of
Korah.

I

2 You have favored, O LORD,
    your land;
    you have restored the well-
        being of Jacob.
3 You have forgiven the guilt of
    your people;
    you have covered all their sins.
4 You have withdrawn all your
    wrath;
    you have revoked your
        burning anger.

II

5 Restore us, O God our savior,
    and abandon your displeasure
        against us.
6 Will you be ever angry with us,
    prolonging your anger to all
        generations?
7 Will you not instead give us life;
    and shall not your people
        rejoice in you?
8 Show us, O LORD, your kindness,
    and grant us your salvation.

III

9 I will hear what God proclaims;
    the LORD—for he proclaims
        peace
To his people, and to his
        faithful ones,
    and to those who put in him
        their hope.

83, 7ff: Apart from *the Assyrians*, all the nations
listed here were neighbors of Israel. *The people of
Hagar:* a seminomadic tribe of the desert regions
east of *Ammon* and *Moab;* cf 1 Chr 5, 10.19f. *Gebal*
was a mountain region south of the Dead Sea. History
knows of no occasion when all these peoples were
leagued together against Israel. Perhaps their names
are used here poetically as figures of the hostile
Gentiles in general.
83, 10ff: For the historical events here referred to,
see Jgs 4–8.
Ps 84: Although similar in style and general content
to Pss 42–43, this seems to be one of the "Pilgrim

Songs" sung on the journeys to the temple for the
annual feasts. The psalmist expresses his ardent
longing to visit the house of the Lord (2–4), describing
the happiness of those who dwell there at all times or
who at least have the privilege of going there as
pilgrims (5–8); hence he prays that this privilege may
be his (9–13).
84, 4: Since in God's providence even "the birds
of the air have nests" (Mt 8, 20), all the more will the
Lord welcome his pious pilgrims to the shelter of
his sanctuary and the refuge of his altars.
84, 6ff: The Hebrew text of these two verses is
obscure in several places.

84, 10: *Our shield:* the king. Cf Ps 89, 19.
Ps 85: After thanking God for the blessings so
far received (2–4), the people beseech him to remove
the hardships which they still suffer (5–8); then a
prophet tells them of the coming happiness which
the Lord has revealed to him (9–14). The situation
suggests the conditions in Judea during the early
post-exilic period, fifth century B.C.; the thoughts are
likewise similar to those expressed by the post-exilic
prophets. Cf Hg 1, 5–11; 2, 6–9; Mal 3, 13–21.
85, 9: The prophet listens to God's revelation.
Cf Hb 2, 1.

10 Near indeed is his salvation to
    those who fear him,
      glory dwelling in our land.
11 Kindness and truth shall meet;
    justice and peace shall kiss.
12 Truth shall spring out of the earth,
    and justice shall look down
      from heaven.
13 The LORD himself will give his
    benefits;
      our land shall yield its
      increase.
14 Justice shall walk before him,
    and salvation, along the way
      of his steps.

PSALM 86

Prayer in Time of Distress
1 A prayer of David.

I

Incline your ear, O LORD;
    answer me,
      for I am afflicted and poor.
2 Keep my life, for I am devoted
    to you;
      save your servant who trusts
      in you.
3 You are my God; have pity on
    me, O Lord,
      for to you I call all the day.
4 Gladden the soul of your servant,
    for to you, O Lord, I lift up
      my soul;
5 For you, O Lord, are good and
    forgiving,
      abounding in kindness to all
      who call upon you.
6 Hearken, O LORD, to my prayer
    and attend to the sound of my
      pleading.
7 In the day of my distress I call
    upon you,
      for you will answer me.

II

8 There is none like you among
    the gods, O Lord,
      and there are no works like
      yours.

9 All the nations you have made
    shall come
    and worship you, O Lord,
    and glorify your name.
10 For you are great, and you do
    wondrous deeds;
      you alone are God.

III

11 Teach me, O LORD, your way
    that I may walk in your truth;
    direct my heart that it may
      fear your name.
12 I will give thanks to you, O
    LORD my God,
    with all my heart,
    and I will glorify your name
      forever.
13 Great has been your kindness
    toward me;
    you have rescued me from the
      depths of the nether world.
14 O God, the haughty have risen
    up against me,
    and the company of fierce men
      seeks my life,
    nor do they set you before
      their eyes.
15 But you, O Lord, are a God
    merciful and gracious,
    slow to anger, abounding in
      kindness and fidelity.
16 Turn toward me, and have pity
    on me;
    give your strength to your
      servant,
    and save the son of your
      handmaid.
17 Grant me a proof of your favor,
    that my enemies may see, to
      their confusion,
    that you, O LORD, have
      helped and comforted me.

PSALM 87

Zion the Home of All Nations
1 A psalm of the sons of Korah. A song.

His foundation upon the holy
    mountains

2   the LORD loves:
    The gates of Zion,
      more than any dwelling of
      Jacob.
3 Glorious things are said of you,
    O city of God!
4 I tell of Egypt and Babylon
    among those that know the
      LORD;
    Of Philistia, Tyre, Ethiopia:
    "This man was born there."
5 And of Zion they shall say:
    "One and all were born in her;
    And he who has established her
      is the Most High LORD."
6 They shall note, when the
    peoples are enrolled:
    "This man was born there."
7 And all shall sing, in their
    festive dance:
    "My home is within you."

PSALM 88

Lament and Prayer in Affliction
1 A song; a psalm of the sons of Korah. For the leader; according to *Mahalath*. For singing; a *maskil* of Heman the Ezrahite.

I

2 O Lord, my God, by day I cry
    out;
    at night I clamor in your
      presence.
3 Let my prayer come before you;
    incline your ear to my call for
      help,
4 For my soul is surfeited with
    troubles
    and my life draws near to the
      nether world.
5 I am numbered with those who
    go down into the pit;
    I am a man without strength.
6 My couch is among the dead,
    like the slain who lie in the
      grave,
    Whom you remember no longer
    and who are cut off from your
      care.

85, 10: *Glory:* the glory of the Lord which departed from Jerusalem when the temple was destroyed. Cf Ez 11, 23. Now it returns to the Holy Land. Cf Hg 2, 9.

85, 11–14: The social virtues are here poetically personified as courtiers of the returning king.

Ps 86: A supplication for help (1–7.11–17), divided in the middle by a short hymn of praise (8–10). Several of the verses occur in similar form in various other psalms, and they are here joined together with no close logical sequence.

86, 8: *The gods:* those whom the pagans call "gods." In v 10 the psalmist clearly denies their

reality. Cf Ex 15, 11; Dt 4, 7. Some translate the word *elohim* here not as "gods" but as "angels."

Ps 87: A song of Zion, extolling the holy city as the spiritual home of all the nations of the earth.

87, 2: *The gates:* the city itself, a common Hebrew idiom.

87, 4: *Egypt:* literally, "Rahab," the name of an ocean monster; here used poetically for Egypt. Cf Ps 89, 11; Is 30, 7.

87, 5: *Of Zion they shall say:* most manuscripts of the Greek version read, 'Mother Zion,' they shall say." St. Paul is probably alluding to this reading

when in Gal 4, 26 he speaks of "Jerusalem which is our mother."

Ps 88: The supplication of a desolate man in mortal illness. The psalmist complains that God seems to have abandoned him (2–9); he reminds the Lord that, if he dies, he can no longer praise him (10–13), and bitterly bewails his misery (14–19).

88, 6: *My couch:* the meaning of the Hebrew is uncertain. *Who lies in the grave:* Hebrew thought would lead us to expect, "who are deprived of any grave," and this may have been the original reading. Cf Ps 63, 11.

7 You have plunged me into the
  bottom of the pit,
  into the dark abyss.
8 Upon me your wrath lies heavy,
  and with all your billows you
  overwhelm me.
9 You have taken my friends
  away from me;
  you have made me an
  abomination to them;
  I am imprisoned, and I cannot
  escape.

II

10 My eyes have grown dim through
  affliction;
  daily I call upon you, O Lord;
  to you I stretch out my hands.
11 Will you work wonders for the
  dead?
  Will the shades arise to give
  you thanks?
12 Do they declare your kindness
  in the grave,
  your faithfulness among those
  who have perished?
13 Are your wonders made known
  in the darkness,
  or your justice in the land of
  oblivion?

III

14 But I, O Lord, cry out to you;
  with my morning prayer I
  wait upon you.
15 Why, O Lord, do you reject me?
  why hide from me your face?
16 I am afflicted and in agony
  from my youth;
  I am dazed with the burden of
  your dread.
17 Your furies have swept over me;
  your terrors have cut me off.
18 They encompass me like water
  all the day;
  on all sides they close in upon
  me.
19 Companion and neighbor you
  have taken away from me;
  my only friend is darkness.

PSALM 89

*Prayer for the Fulfillment of
God's Promises to David*

1 A *maskil* of Ethan the Ezrahite.

I

2 The favors of the Lord I will
  sing forever;
  through all generations my
  mouth shall proclaim your
  faithfulness.
3 For you have said, "My kindness
  is established forever";
  in heaven you have confirmed
  your faithfulness:
4 "I have made a covenant with
  my chosen one,
  I have sworn to David my
  servant:
5 Forever will I confirm your
  posterity
  and establish your throne for
  all generations."

II

6 The heavens proclaim your
  wonders, O Lord,
  and your faithfulness, in the
  assembly of the holy ones.
7 For who in the skies can rank
  with the Lord?
  Who is like the Lord among
  the sons of God?
8 God is terrible in the council of
  the holy ones;
  he is great and awesome
  beyond all round about him.
9 O Lord, God of hosts, who is
  like you?
  Mighty are you, O Lord, and
  your faithfulness surrounds
  you.
10 You rule over the surging of the
  sea;
  you still the swelling of its
  waves.
11 You have crushed Rahab with a
  mortal blow;
  with your strong arm you
  have scattered your enemies.

12 Yours are the heavens, and
  yours is the earth;
  the world and its fullness you
  have founded;
13 North and south you created;
  Tabor and Hermon rejoice at
  your name.
14 Yours is a mighty arm;
  strong is your hand, exalted
  your right hand.
15 Justice and judgment are the
  foundation of your throne;
  kindness and truth go before
  you.
16 Happy the people who know the
  joyful shout;
  in the light of your
  countenance, O Lord, they
  walk.
17 At your name they rejoice all the
  day,
  and through your justice they
  are exalted.
18 For you are the splendor of
  their strength,
  and by your favor our horn is
  exalted.
19 For to the Lord belongs our
  shield,
  and to the Holy One of
  Israel, our king.

III

20 Once you spoke in a vision,
  and to your faithful ones you
  said:
  "On a champion I have placed a
  crown;
  over the people I have set a
  youth.
21 I have found David, my servant;
  with my holy oil I have
  anointed him,
22 That my hand may be always
  with him,
  and that my arm may make
  him strong.
23 "No enemy shall deceive him,
  nor shall the wicked afflict him.

88, 11ff: See note on Ps 6, 6.
Ps 89: An exilic or post-exilic psalm, but composed in part from older sources. Having announced his theme—God's covenant with David—(2-5), the psalmist first sings the praise of the Lord in phrases reminiscent of much older hymns (6-19). The divine promises to David, as narrated in 2 Sm 7, 8-16, are then retold here at considerable length (20-38), in order to contrast these with the present sad state of affairs (39-46), when God seems to have forgotten his promises (47-52).
89, 2: *The favors of the Lord:* the promise of an

everlasting dynasty which God made to David through the prophet Nathan. Cf v 50.
89, 6, 8: *The holy ones:* the heavenly spirits, called the *sons of God* in v 7.
89, 11: *Rahab:* a mythological sea monster whose name is used in the Bible merely as a poetical personification of the primeval chaos of Gn 1, 2.6f. Here it is a symbol of God's dominion over the sea and over all rebellious creatures. Cf Jb 9, 13; 26, 12; Ps 74, 13f; Is 51, 9.
89, 13: *North and south:* in Hebrew, *saphon* and *yamin*, which some retain here as proper nouns, the

names of mountains sacred to the ancients, in order to have a better parallelism with the two mountains *Tabor and Hermon*, in the second half of the verse. "Saphon" is indeed mentioned elswhere in a similar sense. Cf Ps 48, 3; Is 14, 13. However, no "Mount Yamin" is known; perhaps it may be taken here as a synonym for Sinai.
89, 16: *The joyful shout:* one of the characteristic features of Israelite public worship of God.
89, 18.25: *Horn:* a symbol of strength. See note on Ps 18, 3.
89, 20: *Your faithful ones:* Nathan and David.

24 But I will crush his foes before
    him
    and those who hate him I will
    smite.
25 My faithfulness and my kindness
    shall be with him,
    and through my name shall
    his horn be exalted.
26 I will set his hand upon the sea,
    his right hand upon the rivers.

27 "He shall say of me, 'You are my
    father,
    my God, the rock, my savior.'
28 And I will make him the
    first-born,
    highest of the kings of the
    earth.
29 Forever I will maintain my
    kindness toward him,
    and my covenant with him
    stands firm.
30 I will make his posterity endure
    forever
    and his throne as the days of
    heaven.

31 "If his sons forsake my law
    and walk not according to my
    ordinances,
32 If they violate my statutes
    and keep not my commands,
33 I will punish their crime with a
    rod
    and their guilt with stripes.
34 Yet my kindness I will not take
    from him,
    nor will I belie my faithfulness.

35 "I will not violate my covenant;
    the promise of my lips I will
    not alter.
36 Once, by my holiness, have I
    sworn;
    I will not be false to David.
37 His posterity shall continue
    forever,
    and his throne shall be like
    the sun before me;

38 Like the moon, which remains
    forever—
    a faithful witness in the sky."

IV

39 Yet you have rejected and
    spurned
    and been enraged at your
    anointed.
40 You have renounced the covenant
    with your servant,
    and defiled his crown in the
    dust.
41 You have broken down all his
    walls;
    you have laid his strongholds
    in ruins.
42 All who pass by the way have
    plundered him;
    he is made the reproach of his
    neighbors.

43 You have exalted the right hands
    of his foes,
    you have gladdened all his
    enemies.
44 You have turned back his
    sharp sword
    and have not sustained him
    in battle.
45 You have deprived him of his
    luster
    and hurled his throne to the
    ground.
46 You have shortened the days of
    his youth;
    you have covered him with
    shame.

V

47 How long, O LORD? Will you
    hide yourself forever?
    Will your wrath burn like fire?
48 Remember how short my life is;
    how frail you created all the
    children of men!
49 What man shall live, and not see
    death,
    but deliver himself from the
    power of the nether world?

50 Where are your ancient favors,
    O Lord,
    which you pledged to David by
    your faithfulness?
51 Remember, O Lord, the insults
    to your servants:
    I bear in my bosom all the
    accusations of the nations
52 With which your enemies have
    reviled, O LORD,
    with which they have reviled
    your anointed on his way!

* * *

53 Blessed be the LORD forever.
    Amen, and amen!

THE FOURTH BOOK
Psalms 90–106

PSALM 90

God's Eternity and Man's Frailty

1 A prayer of Moses, the man of God.

I

O Lord, you have been our
    refuge
    through all generations.
2 Before the mountains were
    begotten
    and the earth and the world
    were brought forth,
    from everlasting to everlasting
    you are God.
3 You turn man back to dust,
    saying, "Return, O children of
    men."
4 For a thousand years in your
    sight
    are as yesterday, now that it is
    past,
    or as a watch of the night.
5 You make an end of them in
    their sleep;
    the next morning they are like
    the changing grass,
6 Which at dawn springs up anew,
    but by evening wilts and fades.

89, 26: *The sea:* the Mediterranean to the west.
The rivers: the Euphrates and its tributaries to the
east.
  89, 30: *As the days of heaven:* as steadfast as the
sun in the sky. Cf Ps 72, 5.17 and vv 37f of this
psalm.
  89, 31–38: Note that God's promises are in part
provisional and in part absolute. In as much as
David's descendants failed to carry out the conditions
of the covenant, God did not fulfill his promises to
them. But as absolute promises they find complete
fulfillment in the Son of God who is also the Son of
David.

89, 45: The Hebrew text of this verse is somewhat
obscure.
  89, 53: The doxology at the end of the Third
Book of the Psalms; it is not a part of the preceding
psalm.
  Ps 90: A meditation on the brevity and misery of
life. The psalmist contrasts God's eternity with man's
short span of life on earth (1–6), and sees in suffering
and death the punishment for sin (7–11); he prays
God to grant him some respite of happiness before
death (12–17).
  90, 3: *Saying, "Return . . .":* one word of God is
enough to reduce man to the dust from which he

was created. There is an allusion here to the sentence
passed on Adam after the fall. Cf Gn 2, 7; 3, 19.
  90, 4: *A watch of the night:* the Hebrews divided
the night into three sentry periods or "watches."
Cf Jgs 7, 19.
  90, 5: The Hebrew text is obscure and variously
translated. The revised Latin Psalter renders it,
"You make an end of them; they become like sleep
at dawn."
  90, 6: The transitory nature of grass under the
scorching sun of the Orient was proverbial. Cf Pss
103, 15f; 129, 6; Is 40, 6ff.

II

7 Truly we are consumed by your
      anger,
    and by your wrath we are put
      to rout.
8 You have kept our iniquities
      before you,
    our hidden sins in the light of
      your scrutiny.
9 All our days have passed away
      in your indignation;
    we have spent our years like a
      sigh.
10 Seventy is the sum of our years,
      or eighty, if we are strong,
    And most of them are fruitless
      toil,
    for they pass quickly and we
      drift away.
11 Who knows the fury of your
      anger
    or your indignation toward
      those who should fear you?

III

12 Teach us to number our days
      aright,
    that we may gain wisdom of
      heart.
13 Return, O LORD! How long?
    Have pity on your servants!
14 Fill us at daybreak with your
      kindness,
    that we may shout for joy and
      gladness all our days.
15 Make us glad, for the days when
      you afflicted us,
    for the years when we saw
      evil.
16 Let your work be seen by your
      servants
    and your glory by their
      children;
17 And may the gracious care of
      the LORD our God be ours;
    prosper the work of our hands
      for us!
    [Prosper the work of our
      hands!]

PSALM 91

Security under God's Protection

I

1 You who dwell in the shelter of
      the Most High,
    who abide in the shadow of the
      Almighty,
2 Say to the LORD, "My refuge
      and my fortress,
    my God, in whom I trust."
3 For he will rescue you from the
      snare of the fowler,
    from the destroying pestilence.
4 With his pinions he will cover
      you,
    and under his wings you shall
      take refuge;
    his faithfulness is a buckler
      and a shield.
5 You shall not fear the terror of
      the night
    nor the arrow that flies by day;
6 Not the pestilence that roams in
      darkness
    nor the devastating plague at
      noon.
7 Though a thousand fall at your
      side,
    ten thousand at your right
      side,
    near you it shall not come.
8 Rather with your eyes shall you
      behold
    and see the requital of the
      wicked,
9 Because you have the LORD for
      your refuge;
    you have made the Most
      High your stronghold.
10 No evil shall befall you,
    nor shall affliction come near
      your tent,
11 For to his angels he has given
      command about you,
    that they guard you in all
      your ways.
12 Upon their hands they shall
      bear you up,
    lest you dash your foot against
      a stone.

13 You shall tread upon the asp
      and the viper;
    you shall trample down the
      lion and the dragon.

II

14 Because he clings to me, I will
      deliver him;
    I will set him on high because
      he acknowledges my name.
15 He shall call upon me, and I
      will answer him;
    I will be with him in distress;
    I will deliver him and glorify
      him;
16   with length of days I will
      gratify him
    and will show him my
      salvation.

PSALM 92

*Praise of God's Just Government
of Mankind*

1 A psalm; a song for the Sabbath day.

I

2 It is good to give thanks to the
      LORD,
    to sing praise to your name,
      Most High,
3 To proclaim your kindness at
      dawn
    and your faithfulness through-
      out the night,
4 With ten-stringed instrument and
      lyre,
    with melody upon the harp.
5 For you make me glad, O LORD,
      by your deeds;
    at the works of your hands I
      rejoice.

II

6 How great are your works, O
      LORD!
    How very deep are your
      thoughts!
7 A senseless man knows not,
    nor does a fool understand
      this.

90, 15: *For the days when:* either, "as a recompense for the days when," or, "for as many days
as."
    90, 17: *Prosper the work of our hands:* the second
occurrence of these words is probably accidental
repetition.
    Ps 91: By means of various metaphors the psalmist
indicates the benefits of trusting in God (1–13); in

the epilogue God himself speaks, confirming the
psalmist's words (14–16).
    91, 8: *Rather with your eyes:* the pious man will
be a spectator of these plagues and afflictions without
being struck himself.
    91, 11f: These words were quoted by Satan when
he tempted Christ to presumption against God's
providence. This promise would not be true if we

should put ourselves unnecessarily into danger. *His
angels:* the doctrine of guardian angels is common
in the Old Testament. Cf Gn 24, 7; Ex 23, 20; Ps
34, 8.
    Ps 92: A hymn extolling God's just deeds (2–5);
the wicked fail to understand them (6–9), but they
will receive their due punishment (10–12), whereas
the just will be rewarded with blessedness (13–16).

8 Though the wicked flourish like
grass
and all evildoers thrive,
9 They are destined for eternal
destruction;
while you, O LORD, are the
Most High forever.

III

10 For behold, your enemies, O
LORD,
for behold, your enemies shall
perish;
all evildoers shall be scattered.
11 You have exalted my horn like
the wild bull's;
you have anointed me with
rich oil.
12 And my eye has looked down
upon my foes,
and my ears heard of the fall
of my wicked adversaries.

IV

13 The just man shall flourish like
the palm tree,
like a cedar of Lebanon shall
he grow.
14 They that are planted in the
house of the LORD
shall flourish in the courts of
our God.
15 They shall bear fruit even in old
age;
vigorous and sturdy shall they
be,
16 Declaring how just is the LORD,
my rock, in whom there is no
wrong.

PSALM 93

The Glory of the Lord's Kingdom

1 The LORD is king, in splendor
robed;
robed is the LORD and girt
about with strength;
And he has made the world firm,
not to be moved.

2 Your throne stands firm from of
old;
from everlasting you are, O
LORD.
3 The floods lift up, O LORD,
the floods lift up their voice;
the floods lift up their tumult.
4 More powerful than the roar of
many waters,
more powerful than the
breakers of the sea —
powerful on high is the LORD.

5 Your decrees are worthy of
trust indeed:
holiness befits your house,
O LORD, for length of days.

PSALM 94

A Warning to Israel's Oppressors

A

I

1 God of vengeance, LORD,
God of vengeance, show
yourself.
2 Rise up, judge of the earth;
render their deserts to the
proud.
3 How long, O LORD, shall the
wicked,
how long shall the wicked
glory,
4 Mouthing insolent speeches,
boasting, all the evildoers?

II

5 Your people, O LORD, they
trample down,
your inheritance they afflict.
6 Widow and stranger they slay,
the fatherless they murder,
7 And they say, "The LORD sees
not;
the God of Jacob perceives
not."

III

8 Understand, you senseless ones
among the people;
and, you fools, when will you
be wise?
9 Shall he who shaped the ear not
hear?
or he who formed the eye not
see?
10 Shall he who instructs nations
not chastise,
he who teaches men
knowledge?
11 The LORD knows the thoughts of
men,
and that they are vain.

B

I

12 Happy the man whom you
instruct, O LORD,
whom by your law you teach,
13 Giving him rest from evil days,
till the pit be dug for the
wicked.
14 For the LORD will not cast off
his people,
nor abandon his inheritance;
15 But judgment shall again be
with justice,
and all the upright of heart
shall follow it.

II

16 Who will rise up for me against
the wicked?
Who will stand by me against
the evildoers?
17 Were not the LORD my help,
I would soon dwell in the
silent grave.
18 When I say, "My foot is slipping,"
your kindness, O LORD,
sustains me;
19 When cares abound within me,
your comfort gladdens my
soul.

92, 11: *My horn like the wild bull's:* see note on Ps
18, 3. The horns of the wild bull, the *bos primigenius*,
were especially formidable. Cf Ps 22, 22; Dt 33,
17.

92, 14: *Planted:* the pious are so steadfast in their
attendance in the temple that they can figuratively be
said to be rooted there. These words do not imply that
cedars and palm trees actually grew in the temple.
Cf Pss 52, 10; 128, 3.

Ps 93: A hymn in praise of the eternal kingship of
the Lord (1f), who triumphs over the stormy forces

of rebellion (3f); hence he is always to be obeyed and
worshiped (5).

93, 1: *Is king:* literally, "has become king." This
is the cry with which the people acclaimed a new king
at his coronation. Therefore this psalm as well as
Pss 96, 97 and 99 can be understood as enthronement
psalms of the Messiah celebrating the inauguration
of his reign.

93, 3: The raging storm is here a figure of chaos
and rebellion.

Ps 94: A fervent prayer to God together with an

indictment of wicked tyrants and unjust judges.
Calling down divine vengeance upon these (1–14), as
he sets forth their crimes and blasphemies (5–7), the
psalmist directly rebukes them for their folly (8–11);
then in a calmer tone he speaks of the blessedness of
justice and fidelity to God's law (12–15). Confident of
the Lord's assistance (16–19), he affirms his unwavering faith in the triumph of righteousness
(20–23).

94, 15: The decisions of the judges will again be
just.

III

20 How could the tribunal of
wickedness be leagued with
you,
which creates burdens in the
guise of law?
21 Though they attack the life of
the just
and condemn innocent blood,
22 Yet the LORD is my stronghold,
and my God the rock of my
refuge.
23 And he will requite them for
their evildoing,
and for their wickedness he
will destroy them;
the LORD, our God, will
destroy them.

PSALM 95

A Call to Praise and Obedience

I

1 Come, let us sing joyfully to the
LORD;
let us acclaim the Rock of our
salvation.
2 Let us greet him with
thanksgiving;
let us joyfully sing psalms to
him.
3 For the LORD is a great God,
and a great king above all
gods;
4 In his hands are the depths of
the earth,
and the tops of the mountains
are his.
5 His is the sea, for he has made it,
and the dry land, which his
hands have formed.

II

6 Come, let us bow down in
worship;
let us kneel before the LORD
who made us.
7 For he is our God,
and we are the people he
shepherds, the flocks he
guides.

III

Oh, that today you would hear
his voice:
8 "Harden not your hearts as at
Meribah,
as in the day of Massah in the
desert,
9 Where your fathers tempted me;
they tested me though they
had seen my works.
10 Forty years I loathed that
generation,
and I said: They are a people
of erring heart,
and they know not my ways.
11 Therefore I swore in my anger:
They shall not enter into my
rest."

PSALM 96

*The Glories of the Lord, the King
of the Universe*

I

1 Sing to the LORD a new song;
sing to the LORD, all you
lands.
2 Sing to the LORD; bless his
name;
announce his salvation, day
after day.
3 Tell his glory among the nations;
among all peoples, his
wondrous deeds.

II

4 For great is the LORD and highly
to be praised;
awesome is he, beyond all
gods.
5 For all the gods of the nations
are things of nought,
but the LORD made the
heavens.
6 Splendor and majesty go before
him;
praise and grandeur are in his
sanctuary.

III

7 Give to the LORD, you families
of nations,
give to the LORD glory and
praise;
8 give to the LORD the glory due
his name!
Bring gifts, and enter his courts;
9 worship the LORD in holy
attire.
Tremble before him, all the
earth;
10 say among the nations: The
LORD is king.
He has made the world firm, not
to be moved;
he governs the peoples with
equity.

IV

11 Let the heavens be glad and the
earth rejoice;
let the sea and what fills it
resound;
12 let the plains be joyful and all
that is in them!
Then shall all the trees of the
forest exult
13 before the LORD, for he comes;
for he comes to rule the earth.
He shall rule the world with
justice
and the peoples with his
constancy.

PSALM 97

*The Divine King, the Just Judge
of All*

I

1 The LORD is king; let the earth
rejoice;
let the many isles be glad.
2 Clouds and darkness are round
about him,
justice and judgment are the
foundation of his throne.
3 Fire goes before him
and consumes his foes round
about.

Ps 95: The *Venite Exultemus*, the psalm which daily opens the Divine Office of the Church. Twice the psalmist invites the people to praise and worship the Lord (1f.6), for he is king of all his creatures (3–5) and shepherd of his flock (7a–b). In the last strophe the psalmist, speaking in God's name, warns the people to be more faithful to him than were their forefathers in the journey to the Promised Land (7c–11).

95, 8: *Meribah:* literally, "contention"; the place where the Israelites quarreled with the Lord. *Massah:* the place of "testing," where they put him to the trial. Cf Ex 17, 7; Nm 20, 13.
95, 11: *My rest:* in Heb 4 this is applied to the eternal rest of heaven; here it refers directly to the Promised Land.
Ps 96: A hymn inviting all mankind to praise the glories of the Lord (1–3), for he alone is God (4–6);

to the just king of all men belongs adoration (7–10), even inanimate creation should praise him (11ff). This psalm somewhat altered occurs in 1 Chr 16; 23–33.
Ps 97: The first stanza of this hymn is a theophany portraying the coming of the Lord as judge (1–6); Israel rejoices to behold the overthrow of paganism (7–9) and the rewarding of the true worshipers of God (10–12).

4 His lightnings illumine the
    world;
    the earth sees and trembles.
5 The mountains melt like wax
    before the LORD,
    before the LORD of all the
    earth.
6 The heavens proclaim his justice,
    and all peoples see his glory.

II

7 All who worship graven things
    are put to shame,
    who glory in the things of
    nought;
    all gods are prostrate before
    him.
8 Zion hears and is glad,
    and the cities of Judah rejoice
    because of your judgments, O
    LORD.
9 Because you, O LORD, are the
    Most High over all the
    earth,
    exalted far above all gods.

10 The LORD loves those that hate
    evil;
    he guards the lives of his
    faithful ones;
    from the hand of the wicked
    he delivers them.
11 Light dawns for the just;
    and gladness, for the upright
    of heart.
12 Be glad in the LORD, you just,
    and give thanks to his holy
    name.

PSALM 98

*The Lord, the Victorious King
and Just Judge*

1 A psalm.

I

Sing to the LORD a new song,
    for he has done wondrous
    deeds;
His right hand has won victory
    for him,
    his holy arm.
2 The LORD has made his
    salvation known:

    in the sight of the nations he
    has revealed his justice.
3 He has remembered his kindness
    and his faithfulness
    toward the house of Israel.
All the ends of the earth have
    seen
    the salvation by our God.

II

4 Sing joyfully to the LORD, all
    you lands;
    break into song; sing praise.
5 Sing praise to the LORD with the
    harp,
    with the harp and melodious
    song.
6 With trumpets and the sound of
    the horn
    sing joyfully before the King,
    the LORD.

III

7 Let the sea and what fills it
    resound,
    the world and those who
    dwell in it;
8 Let the rivers clap their hands,
    the mountains shout with them
    for joy
9 Before the LORD, for he comes,
    for he comes to rule the
    earth;
He will rule the world with
    justice
    and the peoples with equity.

PSALM 99

The Lord the Holy King

I

1 The LORD is king; the peoples
    tremble;
    he is throned upon the
    cherubim; the earth quakes.
2 The LORD in Zion is great,
    he is high above all the
    peoples.

3 Let them praise your great and
    awesome name;
    holy is he!

II

4 The King in his might loves
    justice;
    you have established equity;
    justice and judgment in Jacob
    you have wrought.
5   Extol the LORD, our God,
    and worship at his
    footstool;
    holy is he!

III

6 Moses and Aaron were among
    his priests,
    and Samuel, among those who
    called upon his name;
    they called upon the LORD,
    and he answered them.
7 From the pillar of cloud he
    spoke to them;
    they heard his decrees and the
    law he gave them.
8 O LORD, our God, you answered
    them;
    a forgiving God you were to
    them,
    though requiting their misdeeds.
9   Extol the LORD, our God,
    and worship at his holy
    mountain;
    for holy is the LORD, our
    God.

PSALM 100

Processional Hymn

1 A psalm of thanksgiving.

Sing joyfully to the LORD, all
    you lands;
2   serve the LORD with gladness;
    come before him with joyful
    song.
3 Know that the LORD is God;
    he made us, his we are;
    his people, the flock he tends.
4 Enter his gates with thanksgiving,
    his courts with praise;
    Give thanks to him; bless his

97, 7: *All gods:* some render, with the Greek, "All
the angels." Cf Heb 1, 6.
  Ps 98: A hymn of praise, very similar to Ps 96,
extolling the Lord for the victory he has given to
Israel (1–3); all the nations of the earth and even
inanimate creation should welcome the just Savior
with joy (4–9).
  98, 1: *His right hand . . . his holy arm:* concrete
expressions of God's infinite power.

Ps 99: Another hymn in praise of the Lord as
king, but here with special emphasis on his holiness.
Each of the three strophes ends in a varying refrain
(3b.5.9). The people extol the Lord's majesty (1–3a)
and just rule (4), as well as his dealings with their
great leaders of old (6–8).
  99, 1: *The cherubim:* the figures of angels with
outspread wings on the ark of the covenant. Cf Ex
25, 22; 1 Sm 4, 4; 2 Sm 6, 2; Ps 80, 2.

99, 5: *His footstool:* the ark itself. Cf 1 Chr 28,
2; Ps 132, 7.
  Ps 100: A short hymn, sung at the solemn entry
into the temple, probably in connection with the
offering up of a thanksgiving sacrifice.
  100, 3: Although the people call on all the nations
of the earth to join them in their hymn, they are
concious of being the chosen people of the one true
God.

name, 5 for he is good:
the LORD, whose kindness
  endures forever,
and his faithfulness, to all
  generations.

PSALM 101

Norm of Life for Rulers

1 A psalm of David.

Of kindness and judgment I will
  sing;
to you, O LORD, I will sing
  praise.
2 I will persevere in the way of
  integrity;
when will you come to me?

I will walk in the integrity of my
  heart,
within my house;
3 I will not set before my eyes
  any base thing.
I hate him who does perversely;
he shall not remain with me.
4 A crooked heart shall be far from
  me;
evil I will not know.

5 Whoever slanders his neighbor
  in secret,
him will I destroy.
The man of haughty eyes
  and puffed-up heart
I will not endure.
6 My eyes are upon the faithful of
  the land,
that they may dwell with me.
He who walks in the way of
  integrity
shall be in my service.
7 He shall not dwell within my
  house
who practices deceit.
He who speaks falsehood
  shall not stand
before my eyes.
8 Each morning I will destroy
  all the wicked of the land,
And uproot from the city of the
  LORD
  all evildoers.

PSALM 102

Prayer in Time of Distress

1 The prayer of an afflicted one when he is faint
and pours out his anguish before the LORD.

I

2 O LORD, hear my prayer,
  and let my cry come to you.
3 Hide not your face from me
  in the day of my distress.
Incline your ear to me;
  in the day when I call,
  answer me speedily.
4 For my days vanish like smoke,
  and my bones burn like fire.
5 Withered and dried up like grass
  is my heart;
I forget to eat my bread.
6 Because of my insistent sighing
  I am reduced to skin and bone.
7 I am like a desert owl;
  I have become like an owl
  among the ruins.
8 I am sleepless, and I moan;
  I am like a sparrow alone on
  the housetop.
9 All the day my enemies revile me;
  in their rage against me they
  make a curse of me.
10 For I eat ashes like bread
  and mingle my drink with
  tears,
11 Because of your fury and your
  wrath;
for you lifted me up only to
  cast me down.
12 My days are like a lengthening
  shadow,
and I wither like grass.

II

13 But you, O LORD, abide
  forever,
and your name through all
  generations.
14 You will arise and have mercy
  on Zion,
for it is time to pity her,
for the appointed time has
  come.

15 For her stones are dear to your
  servants,
and her dust moves them to
  pity.
16 And the nations shall revere
  your name, O LORD,
and all the kings of the earth
  your glory,
17 When the LORD has rebuilt
  Zion
and appeared in his glory;
18 When he has regarded the
  prayer of the destitute,
and not despised their prayer.

19 Let this be written for the
  generation to come,
and let his future creatures
  praise the LORD:
20 "The LORD looked down from
  his holy height,
from heaven he beheld the
  earth,
21 To hear the groaning of the
  prisoners,
to release those doomed to
  die"—
22 That the name of the LORD may
  be declared in Zion;
and his praise, in Jerusalem,
23 When the peoples gather
  together,
and the kingdoms, to serve
  the LORD.

III

24 He has broken down my strength
  in the way;
he has cut short my days.
25   I say: O my God,
Take me not hence in the midst
  of my days;
through all generations your
  years endure.
26 Of old you established the
  earth,
and the heavens are the work
  of your hands.
27 They shall perish, but you
  remain

Ps 101: After an introductory strophe setting forth
his theme (1–2b), the psalmist pronounces several
good resolutions concerning the exercise of his
authority, both in his own conduct (2c–4) and in his
suppression of evil in others (5–8).
  101, 2: *When will you come to me?*: as a reward
for his virtue, the psalmist desires union with God.
With a slight emendation of the Hebrew text some
render, "I will attend to the affairs of the wholehearted man whenever he comes to me."
  101, 8: *Each morning*: the normal time for administering justice. Cf 2 Sm 15, 2; Jer 21, 12.

Ps 102: A composite psalm of three distinct parts.
In the first section (2–12), the psalmist prays as a man
who is very ill and abandoned by all; in the second,
he prays for the restoration of Zion (13–18) and for
her exiled children (19–23); the third section is a
meditation on the brevity of human life compared to
God's unchanging eternity (24–29). The psalm in its
present form is perhaps a compilation made from
parts of older psalms. This is the fifth of the Penitential
Psalms.
  102, 7: *A desert owl*: what exact species of birds
the Hebrew words signify is uncertain, but evidently

the solitary life of these birds as well as their desolate
surroundings forms the point of comparison. Cf
v 8b.
  102, 9: *They make a curse of me*: the enemies of
the psalmist use his name when they curse, saying to
others, "May you be as miserable as this man."
  102, 12: *A lengthening shadow*: life's day draws to
a close.
  102, 25: *In the midst of my days*: when the normal
span of life is but half completed. Cf Is 38, 10;
Jer 17, 11.

though all of them grow old
      like a garment.
Like clothing you change them,
      and they are changed,
28   but you are the same, and
      your years have no end.
29 The children of your servants
      shall abide,
   and their posterity shall
      continue in your presence.

PSALM 103

Praise of Divine Goodness
1 Of David.

I

Bless the LORD, O my soul;
   and all my being, bless his
      holy name.
2 Bless the LORD, O my soul,
   and forget not all his benefits;
3 He pardons all your iniquities,
   he heals all your ills.
4 He redeems your life from
      destruction,
   he crowns you with kindness
      and compassion,
5 He fills your lifetime with good;
   your youth is renewed like the
      eagle's.

II

6 The LORD secures justice
   and the rights of all the
      oppressed.
7 He has made known his ways to
      Moses,
   and his deeds to the children
      of Israel.
8 Merciful and gracious is the
      LORD,
   slow to anger and abounding
      in kindness.
9 He will not always chide,
   nor does he keep his wrath
      forever.
10 Not according to our sins does
      he deal with us,

nor does he requite us
   according to our crimes.

III

11 For as the heavens are high
      above the earth,
   so surpassing is his kindness
      toward those who fear him.
12 As far as the east is from the
      west,
   so far has he put our
      transgressions from us.
13 As a father has compassion on
      his children,
   so the LORD has compassion
      on those who fear him,
14 For he knows how we are
      formed;
   he remembers that we are
      dust.
15 Man's days are like those of
      grass;
   like a flower of the field he
      blooms;
16 The wind sweeps over him and
      he is gone,
   and his place knows him no
      more.
17 But the kindness of the LORD is
      from eternity
   to eternity toward those who
      fear him,
   And his justice toward children's
      children
18   among those who keep his
      covenant
   and remember to fulfill his
      precepts.

IV

19 The LORD has established his
      throne in heaven,
   and his kingdom rules over
      all.
20 Bless the LORD, all you his
      angels,
   you mighty in strength, who
      do his bidding,
   obeying his spoken word.

21 Bless the LORD, all you his hosts,
   his ministers, who do his will.
22 Bless the LORD, all his works,
   everywhere in his domain.
   Bless the LORD, O my soul!

PSALM 104

Praise of God the Creator

I

1 Bless the LORD, O my soul!
   O LORD, my God, you are
      great indeed!
   You are clothed with majesty
      and glory,
2   robed in light as with a cloak.
   You have spread out the heavens
      like a tent-cloth;
3   you have constructed your
      palace upon the waters.
   You make the clouds your
      chariot;
   you travel on the wings of the
      wind.
4 You make the winds your
      messengers,
   and flaming fire your
      ministers.

II

5 You fixed the earth upon its
      foundation,
   not to be moved forever;
6 With the ocean, as with a
      garment, you covered it;
   above the mountains the
      waters stood.
7 At your rebuke they fled,
   at the sound of your thunder
      they took to flight;
8 As the mountains rose, they
      went down the valleys
   to the place you had fixed for
      them.
9 You set a limit they may not
      pass,
   nor shall they cover the
      earth again.

Ps 103: A hymn of thanksgiving, remarkable for its tender piety, in praise of the LORD's generosity to the psalmist himself (1–5) as well as to his nation (6–10). God's mercy is so great because he knows man's frailty (11–18); therefore the psalmist calls upon the heavenly spirits and all creation to join him in his hymn of graceful praise (19–22).

103, 5: *Your youth is renewed like the eagle's:* because of its long life—sometimes covering the span of a hundred years—the eagle was a symbol of perennial youth and vigor. Cf Is 40, 31. It is doubtful whether there is any allusion here to the fabled phoenix.

Ps 104: A magnificent hymn praising God's creative wisdom and power. Filled with wonder at the glorious works of the Creator, the psalmist

depicts in vivid colors the marvels of the atmosphere and sky (1–4); of the dry land and the ocean (5–9); of the streams and fields that give drink and food to man and beast and bird (10–18); of the sun and moon, with the activities of day and night (19–23); and of the manifold life in the mighty sea (24–26). Acknowledging that it is the Lord who governs and sustains all his creatures (27–30), the psalmist proclaims his omnipotence and sanctity (31–35).

104, 2: *Light:* created on the first day. In general the psalmist follows the order of creation as given in Gn 1.

104, 3: *Your palace upon the waters:* God's heavenly dwelling above the upper waters of the sky. Cf Gn 1, 6f; Ps 29, 9f.

104, 4: *Flaming fire:* lightning. In Heb 1, 7 this verse is cited as an argument for the superiority of Christ over the angels: if God uses mere wind and lightning as his messengers and ministers, then the ministering spirits in heaven whom God also uses as his messengers must be immeasurably lower than the eternal Son of God. In Greek the argument is more striking because the word *pneuma* means both "wind" and "spirit," while the word *angelos* means both "messenger" and "angel."

104, 5: The ancients compared the earth to a large building set upon firm foundations.

104, 6–9: According to Gn 1, 9f the whole earth was once covered with water; by elevating a part of the earth, God made the dry land appear.

III

10 You send forth springs into
    the watercourses
    that wind among the
    mountains,
11 And give drink to every beast of
    the field,
    till the wild asses quench
    their thirst.
12 Beside them the birds of heaven
    dwell;
    from among the branches they
    send forth their song.
13 You water the mountains from
    your palace;
    the earth is replete with the
    fruit of your works.
14 You raise grass for the cattle,
    and vegetation for men's use,
    Producing bread from the earth,
15   and wine to gladden men's
    hearts,
    So that their faces gleam with
    oil,
    and bread fortifies the hearts
    of men.
16 Well watered are the trees of
    the LORD,
    the cedars of Lebanon, which
    he planted;
17 In them the birds build their
    nests;
    fir trees are the home of the
    stork.
18 The high mountains are for
    wild goats;
    the cliffs are a refuge for
    rock-badgers.

IV

19 You made the moon to mark
    the seasons;
    the sun knows the hour of its
    setting.
20 You bring darkness, and it is
    night;
    then all the beasts of the
    forest roam about;
21 Young lions roar for the prey
    and seek their food from God.

22 When the sun rises, they
    withdraw
    and couch in their dens.
23 Man goes forth to his work
    and to his tillage till the
    evening.

V

24 How manifold are your works,
    O LORD!
    In wisdom you have wrought
    them all—
    the earth is full of your
    creatures;
25 The sea also, great and wide,
    in which are schools without
    number
    of living things both small
    and great,
26 And where ships move about
    with Leviathan, which you
    formed to make sport of it.

VI

27 They all look to you
    to give them food in due time.
28 When you give it to them, they
    gather it;
    when you open your hand,
    they are filled with good
    things.
29 If you hide your face, they are
    dismayed;
    if you take away their breath,
    they perish
    and return to their dust.
30 When you send forth your
    spirit, they are created,
    and you renew the face of the
    earth.

VII

31 May the glory of the LORD
    endure forever;
    may the LORD be glad in his
    works!
32 He who looks upon the earth,
    and it trembles;
    who touches the mountains,
    and they smoke!

33 I will sing to the LORD all my
    life;
    I will sing praise to my God
    while I live.
34 Pleasing to him be my theme;
    I will be glad in the LORD.
35 May sinners cease from the
    earth,
    and may the wicked be no
    more.
    Bless the LORD, O my soul!
    Alleluia.

PSALM 105

God's Fidelity to His Promise

I

1 Give thanks to the LORD, invoke
    his name;
    make known among the
    nations his deeds.
2 Sing to him, sing his praise,
    proclaim all his wondrous
    deeds.
3 Glory in his holy name;
    rejoice, O hearts that seek the
    LORD!
4 Look to the LORD in his
    strength;
    seek to serve him constantly.
5 Recall the wondrous deeds that
    he has wrought,
    his portents, and the
    judgments he has uttered,
6 You descendants of Abraham,
    his servants,
    sons of Jacob, his chosen
    ones!

7 He, the LORD, is our God;
    throughout the earth his
    judgments prevail.   (II)
8 He remembers forever his
    covenant
    which he made binding for a
    thousand generations—
9 Which he entered into with
    Abraham
    and by his oath to Isaac;

104, 13: God is pictured as sending down the rain
from the reservoir of the upper waters referred to in
v 3. Cf Gn 7, 11; Jb 38, 22; Sir 43, 14.

104, 18: *Rock-badgers:* the *hyrax syriacus,* a
small harelike, ungulate mammal. Cf Lv 11, 5; Dt 14,
7; Prv 30, 26.

104, 26: *Ships:* some emend the Hebrew text to
read, "sea dragons," for the sake of the parallelism
with *Leviathan.* The latter was the name of a mythological sea monster personifying primeval chaos. Cf
Ps 74, 14; Is 27, 1. However, in Jb 40, 25 it stands for

the crocodile, and here it may well signify the dolphin
or some other large marine creature.

104, 27: *They all:* all the creatures, man included,
mentioned in vv 10–26.

104, 30: *Your spirit:* the "breath" or spirit of God
is the divine creative power, the source of all life in
nature. Cf Gn 1, 2; 2, 7. So also the Holy Spirit of
God is the source of all supernatural life. Hence, this
verse is applied by the Church to the Third Person of
the Blessed Trinity.

104, 31: *Glad in his works:* Cf Gn 1, 31, "God
saw that all he had made was very good."

Ps 105: A hymn in praise of God's goodness as
shown in Israel's history. Cf Pss 78; 106; 136. After
the introductory invocation (1–7), the psalmist
recounts the Lord's promise to the patriarchs (8–11),
their early wanderings in Canaan (12–15), the story
of Joseph (16–22) and of the Israelites in Egypt
(23–27), the Egyptian plagues (28–38), the journey
through the desert (39–43), and the occupation of the
Promised Land (44f).

10 Which he established for Jacob
       by statute,
   for Israel as an everlasting
       covenant,
11 Saying, "To you will I give the
       land of Canaan
   as your allotted inheritance."

III

12 When they were few in number,
       a handful, and strangers
       there,
13 Wandering from nation to nation
       and from one kingdom to
       another people,
14 He let no man oppress them,
       and for their sake he rebuked
       kings:
15 "Touch not my anointed,
       and to my prophets do no
       harm."

IV

16 When he called down a famine
       on the land
   and ruined the crop that
       sustained them,
17 He sent a man before them,
       Joseph, sold as a slave;
18 They had weighed him down
       with fetters,
   and he was bound with chains,
19 Till his prediction came to pass
   and the word of the LORD
       proved him true.
20 The king sent and released him,
   the ruler of the peoples set
       him free.
21 He made him lord of his house
       and ruler of all his possessions,
22 That he might train his princes
       to be like him
   and teach his elders wisdom.

V

23 Then Israel came to Egypt,
       and Jacob sojourned in the
       land of Ham.
24 He greatly increased his people
       and made them stronger than
       their foes,   (VI)

25 Whose hearts he changed, so
       that they hated his people,
   and dealt deceitfully with his
       servants.
26 He sent Moses his servant;
       Aaron, whom he had chosen.
27 They wrought his signs among
       them,
   and wonders in the land of
       Ham.

VII

28 He sent the darkness; it grew
       dark,
   but they rebelled against his
       words.
29 He turned their waters into blood
       and killed their fish.
30 Their land swarmed with frogs,
       even in the chambers of their
       kings.
31 He spoke, and there came
       swarms of flies;
   gnats, throughout all their
       borders.
32 For rain he gave them hail,
       with flashing fires throughout
       their land.
33 He struck down their vines and
       their fig trees
   and shattered the trees
       throughout their borders.
34 He spoke, and there came
       locusts
   and grasshoppers without
       number;
35 And they devoured every plant
       throughout the land;
   they devoured the fruit of their
       soil.
36 Then he struck every first-born
       throughout their land,
   the first fruits of all their
       manhood.
37 And he led them forth laden
       with silver and gold,
   with not a weakling among
       their tribes.
38 Egypt rejoiced at their going,
       for the dread of them had
       fallen upon it.

VIII

39 He spread a cloud to cover them
   and fire to give them light by
       night.
40 They asked, and he brought
       them quail,
   and with bread from heaven
       he satisfied them.
41 He cleft the rock, and the water
       gushed forth;
   it flowed through the dry
       lands like a stream,
42 For he remembered his holy
       word
   to his servant Abraham.
43 And he led forth his people
       with joy;
   with shouts of joy, his
       chosen ones.

IX

44 And he gave them the lands of
       the nations,
   and they took what the peoples
       had toiled for,
45 That they might keep his
       statutes
   and observe his laws.
       Alleluia.

PSALM 106

Israel's Confession of Sin

1 Alleluia.

A

Give thanks to the LORD, for he
       is good,
   for his kindness endures
       forever.
2 Who can tell the mighty deeds
       of the LORD,
   or proclaim all his praises?
3 Happy are they who observe
       what is right,
   who do always what is just.
4 Remember me, O LORD, as you
       favor your people;
   visit me with your saving help,

105, 14: *Kings:* Pharaoh, and Abimelech of
Gerar. Cf Gn 12, 17; 20, 6f.
   105, 15: *My anointed . . . my prophets:* the patriarchs, Abraham, Isaac and Jacob, who were in a certain
sense "anointed," that is, consecrated to God, and
were the recipients of his revelations.
   105, 16b: Literally, "And broke every staff of
bread."
   105, 23.27: *The land of Ham:* a synonym for
Egypt. Cf Gn 10, 6, where Mizraim is the Hebrew
name for Egypt.

105, 28–38: Here, as also in Ps 78, 43–51, the
plagues of Egypt are retold with some poetic license,
so that the order of the plagues is not quite the same
as in Ex 7, 14—12, 30.
   Ps 106: Like the preceding psalm, this hymn
reviews Israel's history, but here the salient thought is
the rebellious spirit of the chosen people despite
God's goodness to them. After an introductory
prayer for God's mercy on himself and on his nation
(1–5), the psalmist recounts the lack of faith shown by
the Israelites at the Exodus (6–12), their craving for

meat in the desert (13–15), the rebellions of Korah,
Dathan and Abiram (16–18), the worship of the golden
calf at Sinai (19–23), the cowardice and foolhardiness
of the Israelites at their first contact with the Canaanites (24–27), their paganism at Peor (28–31), their
causing Moses to sin at Meribah (32f), and their
mingling with the Canaanites (34–39); confessing that
it was their wickedness which made God punish
them with repeated calamities and defeats (40–46),
the psalmist prays for the return and restoration of
scattered Israel (47).

5 That I may see the prosperity
    of your chosen ones,
    rejoice in the joy of your
      people,
    and glory with your
      inheritance.

B

I

6 We have sinned, we and our
    fathers;
    we have committed crimes;
    we have done wrong.
7 Our fathers in Egypt
    consider not your wonders;
    They remembered not your
      abundant kindness,
    but rebelled against the Most
      High at the Red Sea.
8 Yet he saved them for his
    name's sake,
    to make known his power.
9 He rebuked the Red Sea, and it
    was dried up,
    and he led them through the
      deep as though a desert.
10 He saved them from hostile
    hands
    and freed them from the hands
      of the enemy.
11 The waters covered their foes;
    not one of them was left.
12 Then they believed his words
    and sang his praises.

II

13 But soon they forgot his works;
    they waited not for his
      counsel.
14 They gave way to craving in the
    desert
    and tempted God in the
      wilderness.
15 He gave them what they asked
    but sent a wasting disease
      against them.

III

16 They envied Moses in the camp,
    and Aaron, the holy one of
      the LORD.
17 The earth opened and swallowed
    up Dathan,
    and covered the faction of
      Abiram.

18 Fire broke out against their
    faction;
    a flame consumed the
      wicked.

IV

19 They made a calf in Horeb
    and adored a molten image;
20 They exchanged their glory
    for the image of a grass-eating
      bullock.
21 They forgot the God who had
    saved them,
    who had done great deeds in
      Egypt,
22 Wondrous deeds in the land of
    Ham,
    terrible things at the Red Sea.
23 Then he spoke of exterminating
    them,
    but Moses, his chosen one,
    Withstood him in the breach
    to turn back his destructive
      wrath.

V

24 Yet they despised the desirable
    land;
    they believed not his word.
25 They murmured in their tents,
    and obeyed not the voice of
      the LORD.
26 Then with raised hand he
    swore against them
    to let them perish in the
      desert,
27 To scatter their descendants
    among the nations,
    and to disperse them over
      the lands.

VI

28 And they submitted to the rites
    of Baal of Peor
    and ate the sacrifices of dead
      gods.
29 They provoked him by their
    deeds,
    and a plague attacked them.
30 Then Phinehas stood forth in
    judgment
    and the plague was checked;
31 And it was imputed to him for
    merit
    through all generations forever.

VII

32 They angered him at the
    waters of Meribah,

and Moses fared ill on their
    account,
33 For they embittered his spirit,
    and the rash utterance passed
      his lips.

VIII

34 They did not exterminate the
    peoples,
    as the LORD had commanded
      them,
35 But mingled with the nations
    and learned their works.
36 They served their idols,
    which became a snare for
      them.
37 They sacrificed their sons
    and their daughters to
      demons,
38 And they shed innocent blood,
    the blood of their sons and
      their daughters,
    Whom they sacrificed to the
      idols of Canaan,
    desecrating the land with
      bloodshed;
39 They became defiled by their
    works,
    and wanton in their crimes.

C

40 And the LORD grew angry with
    his people,
    and abhorred his inheritance;
41 He gave them over into the
    hands of the nations,
    and their foes ruled over them.
42 Their enemies oppressed them,
    and they were humbled under
      their power.
43 Many times did he rescue them,
    but they embittered him with
      their counsels
    and were brought low by their
      guilt.
44 Yet he had regard for their
    affliction
    when he heard their cry;
45 And for their sake he was
    mindful of his covenant
    and relented, in his abundant
      kindness,
46 And he won for them compassion
    from all who held them
      captive.

47 Save us, O LORD, our God,
    and gather us from among the
      nations,

106, 32: *Moses fared ill:* refers to the fact that he
was not allowed to enter the Promised Land. Cf Nm
20, 12.

502

That we may give thanks to
  your holy name
  and glory in praising you.

* * *

48 Blessed be the LORD, the God of
  Israel, through all eternity!
  Let all the people say,
  Amen!   Alleluia.

THE FIFTH BOOK
Psalms 107–150

PSALM 107

God the Savior of Men in Distress

1 "Give thanks to the LORD, for
  he is good,
  for his kindness endures
  forever!"
2 Thus let the redeemed of the
  LORD say,
  those whom he has redeemed
  from the hand of the foe
3 And gathered from the lands,
  from the east and the west,
  from the north and the
  south.

A
I

4 They went astray in the desert
  wilderness;
  the way to an inhabited city
  they did not find.
5 Hungry and thirsty,
  their life was wasting away
  within them.
6   They cried to the LORD in
    their distress;
    from their straits he
    rescued them.
7 And he led them by a direct
  way
  to reach an inhabited city.
8   Let them give thanks to the
    LORD for his kindness
    and his wondrous deeds
    to the children of men,

9 Because he satisfied the longing
  soul
  and filled the hungry soul
  with good things.

II

10 They dwelt in darkness and
  gloom,
  bondsmen in want and in
  chains,
11 Because they had rebelled against
  the words of God
  and scorned the counsel of
  the Most High.
12 And he humbled their hearts
  with trouble;
  when they stumbled, there
  was no one to help them.
13   They cried to the LORD in
    their distress;
    from their straits he
    rescued them.
14 And he led them forth from
  darkness and gloom
  and broke their bonds
  asunder.
15   Let them give thanks to the
    LORD for his kindness
    and his wondrous deeds to
    the children of men,
16 Because he shattered the gates
  of brass
  and burst the bars of iron.

III

17 Stricken because of their wicked
  ways
  and afflicted because of their
  sins,
18 They loathed all manner of food,
  so that they were near the
  gates of death.
19   They cried to the LORD in
    their distress;
    from their straits he
    rescued them.
20 He sent forth his word to heal
  them
  and to snatch them from
  destruction.
21   Let them give thanks to the
    LORD for his kindness
    and his wondrous deeds to
    the children of men.

22 Let them make thank offerings
  and declare his works with
  shouts of joy.

IV

23 They who sailed the sea in ships,
  trading on the deep waters,
24 These saw the works of the
  LORD
  and his wonders in the abyss.
25 His command raised up a
  storm wind
  which tossed its waves on high.
26 They mounted up to heaven;
  they sank to the depths;
  their hearts melted away in
  their plight.
27 They reeled and staggered like
  drunken men,
  and all their skill was
  swallowed up.
28   They cried to the LORD in
    their distress;
    from their straits he
    rescued them.
29 He hushed the storm to a gentle
  breeze,
  and the billows of the sea
  were stilled;
30 They rejoiced that they were
  calmed,
  and he brought them to their
  desired haven.
31   Let them give thanks to the
    LORD for his kindness
    and his wondrous deeds to
    the children of men.
32 Let them extol him in the
  assembly of the people
  and praise him in the council
  of the elders.

B

33 He changed rivers into desert,
  water springs into thirsty
  ground,
34 Fruitful land into salt marsh,
  because of the wickedness of
  its inhabitants.
35 He changed the desert into
  pools of water,
  waterless land into water
  springs,

106, 48: The doxology at the end of the Fourth
Book of the Psalms; a later addition.
  Ps 107: Besides the prologue (1–3), in which the
people thank the Lord for their return from exile,
this psalm consists of two parts. In the first (4–32),
where each of the four stanzas has the same divided
refrain, God is praised as the helper and rescuer of
wanderers lost in the wilderness (4–9), of the imprisoned (10–16), of the sick (17–22), and of storm-
tossed seafarers (23–32). The second part (33–43)
describes how God's beneficent providence changed
deserts into fertile fields (33–35) where the needy
found prosperity (36–38); and how, when bad rulers
brought hard times upon them, God restored the
fortunes of the poor (39–41). All this, therefore,
should be recognized as coming from him (42f).
  107, 1: A standard cry of praise in the liturgy of
the temple, and frequently cited in the Bible. Cf 1
Chr 16, 34; Pss 118, 1; 136, 1; Jer 33, 11; Dn 3, 89;
1 Mc 4, 24.

36 And there he settled the hungry,
       and they built a city to dwell
       in.
37 They sowed fields and planted
       vineyards,
   And they obtained a fruitful
       yield.
38 He blessed them, and they
       became very many;
   nor did he suffer their cattle
       to decrease.
39 And they dwindled and were
       brought low
   through oppression, affliction
       and sorrow.
40 But he who pours out contempt
       upon princes,
   and sends them astray through
       a trackless waste,
41 Lifted up the needy out of
       misery
   and made the families
       numerous like flocks.
42 The upright see this and
       rejoice,
   and all wickedness closes its
       mouth.
43 Who is wise enough to observe
       these things
   and to understand the favors
       of the LORD?

PSALM 108

Prayer for Victory

1 A song; a psalm of David.

I

2 My heart is steadfast, O God;
       my heart is steadfast;
   I will sing and chant praise.
3 Awake, O my soul; awake, lyre
       and harp;
   I will wake the dawn.
4 I will give thanks to you among
       the peoples, O LORD;
   I will chant your praise
       among the nations,
5 For your kindness towers to the
       heavens,
   and your faithfulness to the
       skies.

6 Be exalted above the heavens, O
       God;
   over all the earth be your
       glory!
7 That your loved ones may
       escape,
   help us by your right hand,
       and answer us.

II

8 God promised in his sanctuary:
   "Exultantly I will apportion
       Shechem,
   and measure off the valley of
       Succoth;
9 Mine is Gilead, and mine
       Manasseh,
   Ephraim is the helmet for my
       head; Judah, my scepter;
10 Moab shall serve as my
       washbowl;
   upon Edom I will set my
       shoe;
   I will triumph over Philistia."
11 Who will bring me into the
       fortified city?
   Who will lead me into Edom?
12 Have not you, O God, rejected
       us,
   So that you go not forth, O
       God, with our armies?
13 Give us aid against the foe,
   for worthless is the help of
       men.
14 Under God we shall do
       valiantly;
   it is he who will tread down
       our foes.

PSALM 109

Prayer against a Slanderous Enemy

1 For the leader. A psalm of David.

I

O God, whom I praise, be not
       silent,
2   for they have opened wicked
       and treacherous mouths
       against me.
   They have spoken to me with
       lying tongues,

3 and with words of hatred they
       have encompassed me
   and attacked me without
       cause.
4 In return for my love they
       slandered me,
   but I prayed.
5 They repaid me evil for good
   and hatred for my love.

II

6 Raise up a wicked man against
       him,
   and let the accuser stand at
       his right hand.
7 When he is judged, let him go
       forth condemned,
   and may his plea be in vain.
8 May his days be few;
   may another take his office.
9 May his children be fatherless,
   and his wife a widow.
10 May his children be roaming
       vagrants and beggars;
   may they be cast out of the
       ruins of their homes.
11 May the usurer ensnare all his
       belongings,
   and strangers plunder the
       fruit of his labors.
12 May there be no one to do him
       a kindness,
   nor anyone to pity his
       orphans.
13 May his posterity meet with
       destruction;
   in the next generation may
       their name be blotted out.
14 May the guilt of his fathers be
       remembered by the LORD;
   let not his mother's sin be
       blotted out.
15 May they be continually before
       the LORD,
   till he banish the memory of
       these parents from the
       earth,
16 Because he remembered not to
       show kindness,
   but persecuted the wretched
       and poor
   and the brokenhearted, to do
       them to death.

107, 36–41: Although his words seem to refer to
God's providence in general, the psalmist probably
has in mind the settlement and development of the
Promised Land (36ff), the hard times caused by the
Assyrian and Babylonian invasions (39), the humiliation and exile of the last kings of Judah (40), and the
restoration of Zion after the exile (41).
   Ps 108: A compilation of parts from two other
psalms: 2–6 are the same as Ps 57, 8–12; 7–14 are the

same as Ps 60, 7–14.
   Ps 109: The first and the third sections are prayers
of supplication from one who is cursed and calum-
niated by numerous enemies (1–5.20–31). The middle
section is a series of strong curses against a certain
individual (6–19). Whether the imprecations of this
section were uttered by the psalmist himself against
one of his foes, or by these foes against him, is a
disputed question; the answer depends principally on

the interpretation of v 20. See note on this verse.
   109, 6: the accuser: the Hebrew word is satan.
Cf Zec 3, 1, where Satan stands at the right hand of
the high priest to bring accusations against him
before the Lord. But here a human accuser is meant,
unless the phrase, a wicked man, is rendered, "the
wicked one," that is, the devil.

17 He loved cursing; may it come
      upon him;
   he took no delight in blessing;
      may it be far from him.
18 And may he be clothed with
      cursing as with a robe;
   may it penetrate into his
      entrails like water
   and like oil into his bones;
19 May it be for him like a
      garment which covers him,
   like a girdle which is always
      about him.

III

20 May this be the recompense
      from the LORD upon my
      accusers
   and upon those who speak
      evil against me.
21 But do you, O God, my LORD,
      deal kindly with me for
      your name's sake;
   in your generous kindness
      rescue me;
22 For I am wretched and poor,
      and my heart is pierced
      within me.
23 Like a lengthening shadow I
      pass away;
   I am swept away like the
      locust.
24 My knees totter from my
      fasting,
   and my flesh is wasted of its
      substance.
25 And I am become a mockery to
      them;
   when they see me, they shake
      their heads.
26 Help me, O LORD, my God;
   save me, in your kindness,

27 And let them know that this is
      your hand;
   that you, O LORD, have done
      this.
28 Let them curse, but do you
      bless;
   may my adversaries be put to
      shame,
   but let your servant rejoice.
29 Let my accusers be clothed with
      disgrace
   and let them wear shame like
      a mantle.
30 I will speak my thanks
      earnestly to the LORD,
   and in the midst of the throng
      I will praise him,
31 For he stood at the right hand
      of the poor man,
   to save him from those who
      would condemn him.

PSALM 110

*The Messiah: King, Priest and
Conqueror*

1 A psalm of David.

I

The LORD said to my LORD:
   "Sit at my right hand
   till I make your enemies your
      footstool."
2 The scepter of your power the
      LORD will stretch forth from
      Zion:
   "Rule in the midst of your
      enemies.
3 Yours is princely power in the
      day of your birth in holy
      splendor;

before the daystar, like the
   dew, I have begotten you."

II

4 The LORD has sworn, and he
      will not repent:
   "You are a priest forever,
      according to the order of
      Melchizedek."

III

5 The LORD is at your right hand;
   he will crush kings on the day
      of his wrath.
6 He will do judgment on the
      nations, heaping up corpses;
   he will crush heads over the
      wide earth.
7 From the brook by the wayside
      he will drink;
   therefore will he lift up his
      head.

PSALM 111

Praise of God for His Goodness

1 Alleluia.

I will give thanks to the LORD
   with all my heart
   in the company and assembly
      of the just.
2 Great are the works of the LORD,
   exquisite in all their delights.
3 Majesty and glory are his work,
   and his justice endures forever.
4 He has won renown for his
      wondrous deeds;
   gracious and merciful is the
      LORD.

109, 20: *Recompense:* the Hebrew word means either "work done" or "wages for work done." The above translation takes it in the latter sense. Accordingly, the preceding dire curses may be understood either as directly spoken by the psalmist against his chief enemy, or as spoken first by his enemies against him and then willed by him to recoil on them. The other possible translation would be, "This is the work of those who would bring harm upon me from the Lord." In this case the only imprecations of the psalmist himself would be those in v 29, which are comparatively mild.

109, 23: *Swept away:* a strong wind sometimes ends a plague of locusts by blowing them out into the sea. Cf Ex 10, 19; Jl 2, 20. Some render, "Shaken off," and understand this of the custom of knocking locusts off the plants in order to kill them on the ground.

109, 27: *This:* both the misery suffered and the deliverance expected from the Lord.

109, 28: *Let them curse:* this gives some probability to the view that the imprecations in vv 6–19 were uttered by the enemies of the psalmist.

Ps 110: One of the most important of the Messianic psalms. Following the teaching of our Lord and the

Apostles, Catholic tradition has constantly and unanimously interpreted this psalm as referring to Christ. However, in some verses the Hebrew text is obscure and the interpretation uncertain. Here are set forth the dignity of the Messiah as the king appointed by God (1–3), as the royal priest (4), and as victor over his foes (5–7).

110, 1: *The Lord said to my Lord:* literally, "The oracle of the LORD (*Yahweh*) for my Lord." *My Lord:* a Hebrew phrase of polite address, equivalent to "you," and used when a subject addresses his superior. Cf 1 Sm 25, 25ff; 2 Sm 1, 10. The force of our Lord's argument from this passage is as follows: David was universally recognized as the author of this psalm, which was acknowledged by all as referring to the Messiah; but the psalmist addresses the Messiah here as his superior; therefore the Messiah must be David's superior and not merely his "son" or descendant. Cf Mt 22, 41–45 and parallels. *At my right hand:* the place of honor next to the royal throne. Cf 1 Kgs 2, 19. *Your footstool:* in ancient times vanquished enemies had to suffer the victor's putting their feet on their prostrate bodies as a sign of their submission.

110, 3: The current Hebrew text is obscure and

seems corrupt. The translation here follows the reading of the revised Latin Psalter, which is based on the ancient versions. *Before the daystar:* when the sun has not yet been created, that is, from all eternity. *Like the dew:* in a secret, mysterious manner.

110, 4: *According to the order of Melchizedek:* in the same way as Melchizedek was a priest. There are three main points of resemblance between Melchizedek, the prophetic type, and Christ who fulfilled this prophecy: both are kings as well as priests, both offer bread and wine to God, and both have their priesthood directly from God and not through Aaron, since neither belongs to the tribe of Levi. Cf Gn 14, 18; Heb 7.

110, 7: Figurative language of uncertain significance. The sense, according to some, is: The Messianic king will bow down in humility to drink of the waters of divine assistance, and then go on to new victories. Cf Is 8, 6; Jer 2, 13.17f.

Ps 111: An alphabetic hymn in praise of God's law and of his merciful deeds for Israel. As is customary in such psalms, the thoughts here are rather loosely strung together.

111, 1: *In the company and assembly of the just:* in the temple. Cf Ps 149, 1.

5 He has given food to those who
    fear him;
    he will forever be mindful of
    his covenant.
6 He has made known to his
    people the power of his
    works,
    giving them the inheritance of
    the nations.
7 The works of his hands are
    faithful and just;
    sure are all his precepts,
8 Reliable forever and ever,
    wrought in truth and equity.
9 He has sent deliverance to his
    people;
    he has ratified his covenant
    forever;
    holy and awesome is his name.
10 The fear of the LORD is the
    beginning of wisdom;
    prudent are all who live by it.
    His praise endures forever.

PSALM 112

The Blessings of the Just Man
1 Alleluia.

Happy the man who fears the
    LORD,
    who greatly delights in his
    commands.
2 His posterity shall be mighty
    upon the earth;
    the upright generation shall
    be blessed.
3 Wealth and riches shall be in
    his house;
    his generosity shall endure
    forever.
4 He dawns through the darkness,
    a light for the upright;
    he is gracious and merciful
    and just.
5 Well for the man who is gracious
    and lends,
    who conducts his affairs with
    justice;

6 He shall never be moved;
    the just man shall be in
    everlasting remembrance.
7 An evil report he shall not fear;
    his heart is firm, trusting in
    the LORD.
8 His heart is steadfast; he shall
    not fear
    till he looks down upon his
    foes.
9 Lavishly he gives to the poor;
    his generosity shall endure
    forever;
    his horn shall be exalted in
    glory.
10 The wicked man shall see it and
    be vexed;
    he shall gnash his teeth and
    pine away;
    the desire of the wicked shall
    perish.

PSALM 113

Praise of the Lord for his Care of the Lowly
1 Alleluia.

I

Praise, you servants of the
    LORD,
    praise the name of the LORD.
2 Blessed be the name of the LORD
    both now and forever.
3 From the rising to the setting of
    the sun
    is the name of the LORD to be
    praised.

II

4 High above all nations is the
    LORD;
    above the heavens is his glory.
5 Who is like the LORD, our God,
    who is enthroned on high
6   and looks upon the heavens
    and the earth below?

III

7 He raises up the lowly from the
    dust;
    from the dunghill he lifts up
    the poor
8 To seat them with princes,
    with the princes of his own
    people.
9 He establishes in her home the
    barren wife
    as the joyful mother of
    children.

PSALM 114

The Lord's Wonders at the Exodus
1 Alleluia.

When Israel came forth from
    Egypt,
    the house of Jacob from a
    people of alien tongue,
2 Judah became his sanctuary,
    Israel his domain.

3 The sea beheld and fled;
    Jordan turned back.
4 The mountains skipped like
    rams,
    the hills like the lambs of the
    flock.

5 Why is it, O sea, that you flee?
    O Jordan, that you turn back?
6 You mountains, that you skip
    like rams?
    You hills, like the lambs of the
    flock?

7 Before the face of the Lord,
    tremble, O earth,
    before the face of the God of
    Jacob,
8 Who turned the rock into pools
    of water,
    the flint into flowing springs.

111, 5: *Food to those who fear him:* the manna in the desert. In the liturgy of the Church these words are applied to the Blessed Eucharist, of which the manna was the type or figure. Cf Jn 6, 31ff.49ff.

111, 10: *The fear of the Lord:* reverence for God; the Hebrew term for "religion."

Ps 112: An alphabetic psalm of didactic character, lauding the virtues of the God-fearing man. In style and diction this is very similar to the preceding psalm; both may well have had the same author.

112, 3: *Generosity:* the original meaning of the Hebrew word is "justice," but in a later period of the language it also acquired the meaning of "liberality, almsgiving." Cf Sir 3, 30; 7, 10; also Mt 6, 1.

112, 4: Some interpret this verse as said of God.

Cf Ps 111, 4b. But more probably the subject of this sentence is the same as the subject of all the preceding and following sentences, that is, the just man. He acts in the same way as God does.

112, 9: *His horn:* his power, dignity and authority. Cf note on Ps 18, 3.

Ps 113: A hymn praying that God may be glorified at all times and in all places (1–3), because he who is supreme over all (4–6) stoops down to raise up the lowly and the barren (7–9).

113, 1: *Servants of the Lord:* devout worshipers; in particular, the Levites. Cf Pss 134, 1; 135, 1; Dn 3, 85.

113, 3: *From the rising to the setting of the sun:* either temporally, "from morning to evening," or

spatially, "from the east to the west." Cf Mal 1, 11.

113, 9: Because of the importance in Israel of large families, the barren wife was considered disgraced and cursed by God. Cf Gn 16, 4f; 1 Sm 1, 5f.11; 2, 5; Lk 1, 25.

Ps 114: A song commemorating Israel's deliverance from Egypt. When the Lord chose Israel as his own special people (1f), marvelous things took place in nature (3f) of which he was the cause (5–8). In the Greek and Latin versions, this song is joined to the following one to form a single psalm, but originally they were probably distinct.

114, 4: A poetic description of the earthquake that took place when God appeared on Mount Sinai. Cf Ex 19, 16f.

PSALM 115

The Greatness and Goodness of the True God

I

1 Not to us, O LORD, not to us
  but to your name give glory
  because of your kindness,
  because of your truth.
2 Why should the pagans say,
  "Where is their God?"
3 Our God is in heaven;
  whatever he wills, he does.

II

4 Their idols are silver and gold,
  the handiwork of men.
5 They have mouths but speak not;
  they have eyes but see not;
6 They have ears but hear not;
  they have noses but smell not;
7 They have hands but feel not;
  they have feet but walk not;
  they utter no sound from their
  throat.
8 Their makers shall be like them,
  everyone that trusts in them.

III

9 The house of Israel trusts in the
  LORD;
  he is their help and their
  shield.
10 The house of Aaron trusts in the
  LORD;
  he is their help and their
  shield.
11 Those who fear the LORD trust
  in the LORD;
  he is their help and their
  shield.
12 The LORD remembers us and
  will bless us:
  he will bless the house of
  Israel;
  he will bless the house of
  Aaron;

13 He will bless those who fear the
  LORD,
  both the small and the great.
14 May the LORD bless you more
  and more,
  both you and your children.
15 May you be blessed by the
  LORD,
  who made heaven and earth.
16 Heaven is the heaven of the
  LORD,
  but the earth he has given to
  the children of men.
17 It is not the dead who praise the
  LORD,
  nor those who go down into
  silence;
18 But we bless the LORD,
  both now and forever.

PSALM 116

Thanksgiving to God for Help in Need

A

1 Alleluia.

I

I love the LORD because he has
  heard
  my voice in supplication,
2 Because he has inclined his ear
  to me
  the day I called.
3 The cords of death encompassed
  me;
  the snares of the nether world
  seized upon me;
  I fell into distress and sorrow,
4 And I called upon the name of
  the LORD,
  "O LORD, save my life!"

II

5 Gracious is the LORD and just;
  yes, our God is merciful.

6 The LORD keeps the little ones;
  I was brought low, and he
  saved me.
7 Return, O my soul, to your
  tranquillity,
  for the LORD has been good
  to you.
8 For he has freed my soul from
  death,
  my eyes from tears, my feet
  from stumbling.
9 I shall walk before the LORD
  in the lands of the living.

B

10 I believed, even when I said,
  "I am greatly afflicted";
11 I said in my alarm,
  "No man is dependable."

12 How shall I make a return to
  the LORD
  for all the good he has done
  for me?
13 The cup of salvation I will take
  up,
  and I will call upon the name
  of the LORD;
14 My vows to the LORD I will pay
  in the presence of all his
  people.
15 Precious in the eyes of the LORD
  is the death of his faithful
  ones.

16 O LORD, I am your servant;
  I am your servant, the son of
  your handmaid;
  you have loosed my bonds.
17 To you will I offer sacrifice of
  thanksgiving,
  and I will call upon the name
  of the LORD.
18 My vows to the LORD I will pay
  in the presence of all his
  people,

Ps 115: A song in praise of the living God (1–3) and in derision of the lifeless idols of the pagans (4–8). To this are added a brief "liturgy," consisting of a litany in which the various classes of the people express their confidence in God (9–11); a blessing given by the priests (12–15); and a short hymn of praise (16–18). In Ps 135, 15–18 a very similar song in mockery of the pagan gods occurs, and there also it is followed by a similar litany and hymn (vv 19ff).

115, 2: *Where is their God?*: implying that God does not help them.

115, 9ff: *The house of Israel . . . the house of Aaron . . . those who fear the Lord:* the laity of Israelite birth, the priests, and the converts to Judaism. Cf Pss 118, 2ff; 135, 19f. In the New Testament likewise, the phrase, "those who fear the Lord," is

used for the proselytes or converts to Judaism. Cf Acts 10, 2.22.35; 13, 16.26.

115, 17: See note on Ps 6, 6.

Pss 116: The Greek and Latin versions divide this psalm into two parts: Ps 144 (vv 1–9), Ps 115 (vv 10–19). This is a hymn of thanksgiving sung in the temple by an individual who, when mortally ill, had been cured by the Lord. Recalling how he prayed when he was at death's door (1–4), the psalmist now praises God for having heard his prayer (5–9). Referring again to his former period of need (10f), he offers up his sacrifice and hymn of grateful praise (12–19).

116, 3: Death is pictured as a trapper catching his prey. Cf Ps 18, 6.

116, 10: *I believed*: the psalmist did not doubt that

God would be faithful to his promise of help.

116, 13: *The cup of salvation*: the libation of wine poured out in gratitude for having been saved. Cf Ex 25, 29; Nm 15, 1–10. This verse was very appropriately chosen as the prayer which the priest said before drinking the Precious Blood at Holy Mass.

116, 15: Humanly speaking, the Lord looks upon the death of his faithful servants and the consequent loss of their praise as too costly for him to allow. The sentiment of the psalmist is naturally connected with his ideas of the nether world. Cf Ps 6, 6. In the liturgy this verse was used, after the reading of the Martyrology at Prime, in an applied sense: in the eyes of God the death of his holy martyrs is as precious as gold which has been proved in a furnace. Cf Wis 3, 4–7.

19 In the courts of the house of the
    LORD,
    in your midst, O Jerusalem.

PSALM 117

Doxology of All the Nations

1 Alleluia.

Praise the LORD, all you nations;
    glorify him, all you peoples!
2 For steadfast is his kindness
    toward us,
    and the fidelity of the LORD
    endures forever.

PSALM 118

*Hymn of Thanksgiving to the
Savior of Israel*

1 Alleluia.

A

Give thanks to the LORD, for he
    is good,
    for his mercy endures forever.
2 Let the house of Israel say,
    "His mercy endures forever."
3 Let the house of Aaron say,
    "His mercy endures forever."
4 Let those who fear the LORD say,
    "His mercy endures forever."

B

I

5 In my straits I called upon the
    LORD;
    the LORD answered me and
    set me free.
6 The LORD is with me; I fear not;
    what can man do against me?
7 The LORD is with me to help me,
    and I shall look down upon
    my foes.

8 It is better to take refuge in the
    LORD
    than to trust in man.
9 It is better to take refuge in the
    LORD
    than to trust in princes.

II

10 All the nations encompassed me;
    in the name of the LORD I
    crushed them.
11 They encompassed me on every
    side;
    in the name of the LORD I
    crushed them.
12 They encompassed me like bees,
    they flared up like fire among
    thorns;
    in the name of the LORD I
    crushed them.
13 I was hard pressed and was
    falling,
    but the LORD helped me.
14 My strength and my courage is
    the LORD,
    and he has been my savior.

III

15 The joyful shout of victory
    in the tents of the just:
    "The right hand of the LORD has
    struck with power:
16 the right hand of the LORD is
    exalted;
    the right hand of the LORD has
    struck with power."
17 I shall not die, but live,
    and declare the works of the
    LORD.
18 Though the LORD has indeed
    chastised me,
    yet he has not delivered me to
    death.

C

I

19 Open to me the gates of justice;
    I will enter them and give
    thanks to the LORD.

20 This gate is the LORD's;
    the just shall enter it.

21 I will give thanks to you, for you
    have answered me
    and have been my savior.

22 The stone which the builders
    rejected
    has become the cornerstone.
23 By the LORD has this been done;
    it is wonderful in our eyes.

24 This is the day the LORD has
    made;
    let us be glad and rejoice in it.
25 O LORD, grant salvation!
    O LORD, grant prosperity!

II

26 Blessed is he who comes in the
    name of the LORD;
    we bless you from the house
    of the LORD.
27 The LORD is God, and he has
    given us light.
    Join in procession with leafy
    boughs
    up to the horns of the altar.

28 You are my God, and I give
    thanks to you;
    O my God, I extol you.
29 Give thanks to the LORD, for he
    is good;
    for his kindness endures
    forever.

Ps 117: The shortest of all the psalms; a brief hymn of praise calling on all mankind to glorify the Lord for his kindness and fidelity to his promises. This invitation to all the nations finds its fulfillment in Christ's universal kingdom. Cf Rom 15, 11.

Ps 118: A dramatic "liturgy" of thanksgiving. After an invocation in the form of a litany (1–4), the psalmist, who very likely is speaking here in the name of the whole community, describes how the nation confidently implored the Lord's help (5–9) when hostile peoples threatened its life (10–14); in vivid words he recounts how God came to the rescue (15–18). Then follows a dialogue between the priests at the temple gates and the psalmist as he enters to offer the thanksgiving sacrifice (19–25); finally the priests impart their blessing (26f), and the psalmist

sings his hymn of grateful praise (28f).

118, 2ff: See note on Ps 115, 9ff.

118, 5–18: Although many of the phrases in this section resemble those used in the supplications of individuals, other phrases make it probable that the psalmist is speaking here in the name of the whole nation. The occasion may have been such as described in Neh 12, 27–43.

118, 19–29: In this dramatic dialogue the words of the representative of the people seem to be limited to vv 19.21ff.28f. Probably vv 20.24–27 are spoken by the priests.

118, 22: *The stone which the builders rejected:* directly, Israel, which the empire-builders thought unworthy of a place in their worldly plans. But Israel is here a type of Christ, in whom this prophecy has

been most eminently fulfilled; hence these words are often cited in the New Testament as referring to our Lord's rejection by the Jews.

118, 25: *Grant salvation:* the Hebrew for this cry, as far as English letters can represent it, is "Hosanna." This word and the words in the next line were used as a welcome to Christ when he entered the temple on Psalm Sunday. Cf Mk 11, 10f.

118, 26: The sense is, "May he who now comes into the temple be blessed by having the LORD's name invoked upon him."

118, 27: *The horns of the altar:* the four corners of the altar of holocausts. Cf Ex 27, 2; 38, 2; Lv 4, 25.30.34.

PSALM 119

Praise of God's Law

Aleph

1 Happy are they whose way is
    blameless,
    who walk in the law of the
    LORD.
2 Happy are they who observe his
    decrees,
    who seek him with all their
    heart,
3 And do no wrong,
    but walk in his ways.
4 You have commanded that your
    precepts
    be diligently kept.
5 Oh, that I might be firm in the
    ways
    of keeping your statutes!
6 Then should I not be put to shame
    when I beheld all your
    commands.
7 I will give you thanks with an
    upright heart,
    when I have learned your just
    ordinances.
8 I will keep your statutes;
    do not utterly forsake me.

Beth

9 How shall a young man be
    faultless in his way?
    By keeping to your words.
10 With all my heart I seek you;
    let me not stray from your
    commands.
11 Within my heart I treasure your
    promise,
    that I may not sin against you.
12 Blessed are you, O LORD;
    teach me your statutes.
13 With my lips I declare
    all the ordinances of your
    mouth.
14 In the way of your decrees I
    rejoice,
    as much as in all riches.
15 I will meditate on your precepts
    and consider your ways.
16 In your statutes I will delight;
    I will not forget your words.

Gimel

17 Be good to your servant; that I
    may live
    and keep your words.
18 Open my eyes that I may
    consider
    the wonders of your law.
19 I am a wayfarer of earth;
    hide not your commands
    from me.
20 My soul is consumed with
    longing
    for your ordinances at all
    times.
21 You rebuke the accursed proud,
    who turn away from your
    commands.
22 Take away from me reproach
    and contempt,
    for I observe your decrees.
23 Though princes meet and talk
    against me,
    your servant meditates on
    your statutes.
24 Yes, your decrees are my
    delight;
    they are my counselors.

Daleth

25 I lie prostrate in the dust;
    give me life according to your
    word.
26 I declared my ways, and you
    answered me;
    teach me your statutes.
27 Make me understand the way of
    your precepts,
    and I will meditate on your
    wondrous deeds.
28 My soul weeps for sorrow;
    strengthen me according to
    your words.
29 Remove from me the way of
    falsehood,
    and favor me with your law.
30 The way of truth I have chosen;
    I have set your ordinances
    before me.
31 I cling to your decrees;
    O LORD, let me not be put to
    shame.

32 I will run the way of your
    commands
    when you give me a docile
    heart.

He

33 Instruct me, O LORD, in the way
    of your statutes,
    that I may exactly observe
    them.
34 Give me discernment, that I may
    observe your law
    and keep it with all my heart.
35 Lead me in the path of your
    commands,
    for in it I delight.
36 Incline my heart to your decrees
    and not to gain.
37 Turn away my eyes from seeing
    what is vain;
    by your way give me life.
38 Fulfill for your servant
    your promise to those who
    fear you.
39 Turn away from me the reproach
    which I dread,
    for your ordinances are good.
40 Behold, I long for your precepts;
    in your justice give me life.

Waw

41 Let your kindness come to me,
    O LORD,
    your salvation according to
    your promise.
42 So shall I have an answer for
    those who reproach me,
    for I trust in your words.
43 Take not the word of truth
    from my mouth,
    for in your ordinances is my
    hope.
44 And I will keep your law
    continually,
    forever and ever.
45 And I will walk at liberty,
    because I seek your precepts.
46 I will speak of your decrees
    before kings
    without being ashamed.
47 And I will delight in your
    commands,
    which I love.

Ps 119: An alphabetic psalm of didactic nature; in the form of prayer it inculcates the excellence of keeping the divinely revealed law. Some of the strophes show a certain logical development of thought, but on the whole there is merely a constant repetition of the main theme with numerous disconnected variations of it. The external form is based on an elaborately constructed scheme. The psalmist chose eight synonyms—law, statutes, commands,

ordinances, decrees, precepts, words and promise—and in his strophes of eight verses apiece planned perhaps to use a different synonym in each verse. In the present form of the text, however, this plan is not perfectly carried out, nor is it certain whether these departures are due to mistakes of later copyists or to the original author himself. This psalm is the longest by far of any in the Psalter. Each of the eight verses of the first strophe begins with the first letter of the

Hebrew alphabet, each verse of the second strophe with the second letter, and so on for all the twenty-two letters. Hence, the whole consists of 176 verses.
    119, 19: *A wayfarer of earth:* the psalmist realizes that he has but a short life here below. Cf Ps 39, 13. Some render, "I am a stranger in the land"; the desire of the psalmist would then be that he might learn all the laws and customs of the land that God has chosen for his people.

48 And I will lift up my hands to
    your commands
    and meditate on your statutes.

Zayin

49 Remember your word to your
    servant
    since you have given me hope.
50 My comfort in my affliction is
    that your promise gives me
    life.
51 Though the proud scoff bitterly
    at me,
    I turn not away from your
    law.
52 I remember your ordinances of
    old, O Lord,
    and I am comforted.
53 Indignation seizes me because of
    the wicked
    who forsake your law.
54 Your statutes are the theme of
    my song
    in the place of my exile.
55 By night I remember your name,
    O Lord,
    and I will keep your law.
56 This I have had,
    that I have observed your
    precepts.

Heth

57 I have said, O Lord, that my
    part
    is to keep your words.
58 I entreat you with all my heart,
    have pity on me according to
    your promise.
59 I considered my ways
    and turned my feet to your
    decrees.
60 I was prompt and did not
    hesitate
    in keeping your commands.
61 Though the snares of the wicked
    are twined about me
    your law I have not forgotten.
62 At midnight I rise to give you
    thanks
    because of your just
    ordinances.
63 I am the companion of all who
    fear you
    and keep your precepts.

64 Of your kindness, O Lord, the
    earth is full;
    teach me your statutes.

Teth

65 You have done good to your
    servant,
    O Lord, according to your
    word.
66 Teach me wisdom and
    knowledge,
    for in your commands I trust.
67 Before I was afflicted I went
    astray,
    but now I hold to your promise.
68 You are good and bountiful;
    teach me your statutes.
69 Though the proud forge lies
    against me,
    with all my heart I will
    observe your precepts.
70 Their heart has become gross
    and fat;
    as for me, your law is my
    delight.
71 It is good for me that I have
    been afflicted,
    that I may learn your statutes.
72 The law of your mouth is to me
    more precious
    than thousands of gold and
    silver pieces.

Yodh

73 Your hands have made me and
    fashioned me;
    give me discernment that I
    may learn your commands.
74 Those who fear you shall see
    me and be glad,
    because I hope in your word.
75 I know, O Lord, that your
    ordinances are just,
    and in your faithfulness you
    have afflicted me.
76 Let your kindness comfort me
    according to your promise to
    your servants.
77 Let your compassion come to
    me that I may live,
    for your law is my delight.
78 Let the proud be put to shame
    for oppressing me unjustly;
    I will meditate on your
    precepts.

79 Let those turn to me who fear
    you
    and acknowledge your
    decrees.
80 Let my heart be perfect in your
    statutes,
    that I be not put to shame.

Kaph

81 My soul pines for your salvation;
    I hope in your word.
82 My eyes strain after your
    promise;
    when will you comfort me?
83 Though I am shriveled like a
    leathern flask in the smoke,
    I have not forgotten your
    statutes.
84 How many are the days of your
    servant?
    When will you do judgment
    on my persecutors?
85 The proud have dug pits for me;
    this is against your law.
86 All your commands are
    steadfast;
    they persecute me wrongfully;
    help me!
87 They have all but put an end to
    me on the earth,
    but I have not forsaken your
    precepts.
88 In your kindness give me life,
    that I may keep the decrees
    of your mouth.

Lamedh

89 Your word, O Lord, endures
    forever;
    it is firm as the heavens.
90 Through all generations your
    truth endures;
    you have established the earth,
    and it stands firm.
91 According to your ordinances
    they still stand firm:
    all things serve you.
92 Had not your law been my
    delight,
    I should have perished in my
    affliction.
93 Never will I forget your precepts,
    for through them you give
    me life.

119, 48: *I will lift up my hands:* an ancient and
natural gesture of supplication. Some render, "I
will put my hand to (the task of keeping) your
commands."
119, 70: *Their heart has become gross and fat:* a

Hebrew idiom for, "Their mind has become dull and
insensitive." But it may also be understood to signify
a "cruel heart." Cf Ps 17, 10.
119, 83: *A leathern flask:* tanned hides were used
for holding water or wine; such containers, if kept in

the dry heat near the fireplace, gradually became
brittle and useless.
119, 85: *This is against your law:* or perhaps the
sense may be, "that is, to make me act against your
law."

94 I am yours; save me,
   for I have sought your
      precepts.
95 Sinners wait to destroy me,
   but I pay heed to your decrees.
96 I see that all fulfillment has its
      limits;
   broad indeed is your
      command.

Mem

97 How I love your law, O LORD!
   It is my meditation all the day.
98 Your command has made me
      wiser than my enemies,
   for it is ever with me.
99 I have more understanding than
      all my teachers
   when your decrees are my
      meditation.
100 I have more discernment than
      the elders,
   because I observe your
      precepts.
101 From every evil way I withhold
      my feet,
   that I may keep your words.
102 From your ordinances I turn
      not away,
   for you have instructed me.
103 How sweet to my palate are
      your promises,
   sweeter than honey to my
      mouth!
104 Through your precepts I gain
      discernment;
   therefore I hate every false
      way.

Nun

105 A lamp to my feet is your word,
   a light to my path.
106 I resolve and swear
   to keep your just ordinances.
107 I am very much afflicted;
   O LORD, give me life
      according to your word.
108 Accept, O LORD, the free
      homage of my mouth,
   and teach me your decrees.
109 Though constantly I take my
      life in my hands,
   yet I forget not your law.
110 The wicked have laid a snare
      for me,
   but from your precepts I
      have not strayed.

111 Your decrees are my
      inheritance forever;
   the joy of my heart they are.
112 I intend in my heart to fulfill
      your statutes
   always, to the letter.

Samekh

113 I hate men of divided heart,
   but I love your law.
114 You are my refuge and my
      shield;
   in your word I hope.
115 Depart from me, you
      wrongdoers,
   and I will observe the
      commands of my God.
116 Sustain me as you have
      promised, that I may live;
   disappoint me not in my
      hope.
117 Help me, that I may be safe
   and ever delight in your
      statutes.
118 You despise all who stray from
      your statutes,
   for their deceitfulness is in
      vain.
119 You account all the wicked of
      the earth as dross;
   therefore I love your decrees.
120 My flesh shudders with dread
      of you,
   and I fear your ordinances.

Ayin

121 I have fulfilled just ordinances;
   leave me not to my
      oppressors.
122 But surety for the welfare of
      your servant;
   let not the proud oppress me.
123 My eyes strain after your
      salvation
   and your just promise.
124 Deal with your servant
      according to your kindness,
   and teach me your statutes.
125 I am your servant; give me
      discernment
   that I may know your
      decrees.
126 It is time for the LORD to act:
   they have broken your law.
127 For I love your command
   more than gold, however fine.

128 For in all your precepts I go
      forward;
   every false way I hate.

Peh

129 Wonderful are your decrees;
   therefore I observe them.
130 The revelation of your words
      sheds light,
   giving understanding to the
      simple.
131 I gasp with open mouth
   in my yearning for your
      commands.
132 Turn to me in pity
   as you turn to those who
      love your name.
133 Steady my footsteps according
      to your promise,
   and let no iniquity rule over
      me.
134 Redeem me from the oppression
      of men,
   that I may keep your precepts.
135 Let your countenance shine
      upon your servant,
   and teach me your statutes.
136 My eyes shed streams of tears
   because your law has not
      been kept.

Sadhe

137 You are just, O LORD,
   and your ordinance is right.
138 You have pronounced your
      decrees in justice
   and in perfect faithfulness.
139 My zeal consumes me,
   because my foes forget your
      words.
140 Your promise is very sure,
   and your servant loves it.
141 I am mean and contemptible,
   but your precepts I have not
      forgotten.
142 Your justice is everlasting
      justice,
   and your law is permanent.
143 Though distress and anguish
      have come upon me,
   your commands are my
      delight.
144 Your decrees are forever just;
   give me discernment that I
      may live.

119, 109f: The psalmist's life is always threatened by the wicked who persecute him for keeping God's law.
119, 113: *Men of divided heart:* those who hesitate between fidelity and infidelity to God. Cf 1 Kgs 18, 21.
119, 135: *Let your countenance shine:* the psalmist asks God to smile on him with favor. Cf Nm 6, 25; Pss 67, 2; 80, 4.
119, 140: *Very sure:* literally, "fire-tried," said of purified metals that are genuine and reliable. Cf Ps 12, 7.

Qoph

145 I call out with all my heart;
     answer me, O LORD;
     I will observe your statutes.
146 I call upon you; save me,
     and I will keep your decrees.
147 Before dawn I come and cry
     out;
     I hope in your words.
148 My eyes greet the night
     watches
     in meditation on your
     promise.
149 Hear my voice according to
     your kindness, O LORD;
     according to your ordinance
     give me life.
150 I am attacked by malicious
     persecutors
     who are far from your law.
151 You, O LORD, are near,
     and all your commands are
     permanent.
152 Of old I know from your
     decrees,
     that you have established
     them forever.

Resh

153 Behold my affliction, and rescue
     me,
     for I have not forgotten
     your law.
154 Plead my cause, and redeem
     me;
     for the sake of your promise
     give me life.
155 Far from sinners is salvation,
     because you seek not your
     statutes.
156 Your compassion is great, O
     LORD;
     according to your ordinances
     give me life.
157 Though my persecutors and my
     foes are many,
     I turn not away from your
     decrees.

158 I beheld the apostates with
     loathing,
     because they kept not to your
     promise.
159 See how I love your precepts,
     O LORD;
     in your kindness give me life.
160 Permanence is your word's
     chief trait;
     each of your just ordinances
     is everlasting.

Shin

161 Princes persecute me without
     cause
     but my heart stands in awe
     of your word.
162 I rejoice at your promise,
     as one who has found rich
     spoil.
163 Falsehood I hate and abhor;
     your law I love.
164 Seven times a day I praise you
     for your just ordinances.
165 Those who love your law have
     great peace,
     and for them there is no
     stumbling block.
166 I wait for your salvation, O
     LORD,
     and your commands I fulfill.
167 I keep your decrees
     and love them deeply.
168 I keep your precepts and your
     decrees,
     for all my ways are before
     you.

Taw

169 Let my cry come before you,
     O LORD;
     in keeping with your word,
     give me discernment.
170 Let my supplication reach you;
     rescue me according to your
     promise.
171 My lips pour forth your praise,
     because you teach me your
     statutes.

172 May my tongue sing of your
     promise,
     for all your commands are
     just.
173 Let your hand be ready to
     help me,
     for I have chosen your
     precepts.
174 I long for your salvation, O
     LORD,
     and your law is my delight.
175 Let my soul live to praise you,
     and may your ordinances
     help me.
176 I have gone astray [like a lost
     sheep]; seek your servant,
     because your commands I
     do not forget.

PSALM 120

*A Complaint against Treacherous
     Tongues*

1 A song of ascents.

I

In my distress I called to the
     LORD,
     and he answered me.
2 O LORD, deliver me from lying
     lip,
     from treacherous tongue.

II

3 What will he inflict on you, with
     more besides,
     O treacherous tongue?
4 Sharp arrows of a warrior
     with fiery coals of brushwood.

III

5 Woe is me that I sojourn in
     Meshech,
     that I dwell amid the tents of
     Kedar!
6 All too long have I dwelt
     with those who hate peace.
7 When I speak of peace,
     they are ready for war.

119, 148: *The night watches:* even at the time when people are usually asleep, the psalmist meditates on God's word. Cf v 62 and Ps 77, 3.5.

119, 164: *Seven times:* a Hebrew idiom for "many times." Cf Gn 4, 24; Ps 12, 7; Prv 24, 16; Mt 18, 21f; Lk 17, 4.

Ps 120: The psalmist implores God's help against his deceitful foe (1f); he asks the Lord to punish this enemy (3f) as he bewails his long exile among hostile strangers (5–7).

120, 1: *A song of ascents:* this title also occurs in each of the next fourteen psalms. The most probable explanation is that these fifteen psalms form a little collection of "Pilgrim Psalms," that is, songs which

were sung by the pilgrims when they "went up" to Jerusalem for the great annual feasts. Cf Ex 23, 17; Dt 16, 16; 1 Kgs 12, 28; Mt 20, 17; Lk 2, 41f. Less probable explanations are that these psalms were sung by the returning exiles when they "went up" to Jerusalem from Babylon (Ezr 7, 9), or that they were sung by the Levites on the fifteen steps by which they ascended from the Court of the Women to the Court of the Israelites in the temple. Hence, these psalms are also known as the "Gradual Psalms," or "Psalms of the Steps."

120, 3: *With more besides:* the common formula of a curse in Hebrew was, "May the LORD do such and such evils to you (the evils being specified), and

add still more to them." Cf 1 Sm 3, 17; 14, 44; 25, 22. Here the psalmist is at a loss for a suitable malediction.

120, 4: The punishment which the psalmist finally decides to wish on his enemy is that the latter may be shot in battle or overwhelmed with glowing charcoal. *Brushwood:* more exactly, the broom plant; charcoal made of this wood burns with an intense heat.

120, 5: *Meshech:* an ancient people dwelling in northeastern Asia Minor. Cf Gn 10, 2. *Kedar:* a tribe of the north Arabian desert. Cf Gn 25, 13. Probably these names are used here merely in a metaphorical sense for barbarians in general.

PSALM 121

The Lord our Guardian

1 A song of ascents.

I

I lift up my eyes toward the
   mountains;
   whence shall help come to me?
2 My help is from the LORD,
   who made heaven and earth.

II

3 May he not suffer your foot to
   slip;
   may he slumber not who
   guards you:
4 Indeed he neither slumbers nor
   sleeps,
   the guardian of Israel.

III

5 The LORD is your guardian; the
   LORD is your shade;
   he is beside you at your right
   hand.
6 The sun shall not harm you by
   day,
   nor the moon by night.

IV

7 The LORD will guard you from
   all evil;
   he will guard your life.
8 The LORD will guard your
   coming and your going,
   both now and forever.

PSALM 122

The Pilgrim's Greetings to Jerusalem

1 A song of ascents. Of David.

I

I rejoiced because they said to me,
   "We will go up to the house of
   the LORD."
2 And now we have set foot
   within your gates, O
   Jerusalem—

3 Jerusalem, built as a city
   with compact unity.

II

4 To it the tribes go up,
   the tribes of the LORD,
   According to the decree for
   Israel,
   to give thanks to the name of
   the LORD.
5 In it are set up judgment seats,
   seats for the house of David.

III

6 Pray for the peace of Jerusalem!
   May those who love you
   prosper!
7 May peace be within your walls,
   prosperity in your buildings.
8 Because of my relatives and
   friends
   I will say, "Peace be within
   you!"
9 Because of the house of the
   LORD, our God,
   I will pray for your good.

PSALM 123

Israel's Prayer in Persecution

1 A song of ascents.

I

To you I lift up my eyes
   who are enthroned in heaven.
2 Behold, as the eyes of servants
   are on the hands of their
   masters,
   As the eyes of a maid
   are on the hands of her
   mistress,
   So are our eyes on the LORD,
   our God,
   till he have pity on us.

II

3 Have pity on us, O LORD, have
   pity on us,
   for we are more than sated
   with contempt;

4 Our souls are more than sated
   with the mockery of the
   arrogant,
   with the contempt of the
   proud.

PSALM 124

The Lord the Rescuer of His People

1 A song of ascents. Of David.

I

Had not the LORD been with us,
   let Israel say,
2 had not the LORD been with
   us—
When men rose up against us,
3 then would they have
   swallowed us alive.
When their fury was inflamed
   against us,
4 then would the waters have
   overwhelmed us;
The torrent would have swept
   over us;
5 over us then would have
   swept
   the raging waters.

II

6 Blessed be the LORD, who did
   not leave us
   a prey to their teeth.
7 We were rescued like a bird
   from the fowler's snare;
Broken was the snare,
   and we were freed.
8 Our help is in the name of the
   LORD,
   who made heaven and earth.

PSALM 125

The Lord the Protector of Israel

1 A song of ascents.

I

They who trust in the LORD are
   like Mount Zion,
   which is immovable; which
   forever stands.

Ps 121: Since he himself is full of confidence in the Lord's help (1f), the psalmist also reassures his companion of God's protection (3–8).

121, 1: *The mountain:* the ridge on which Mount Zion with its temple was situated. Cf Pss 87, 1; 125, 2.

121, 6: The harm caused by sunstroke was known to the ancients. Cf 2 Kgs 4, 18ff. The Orientals even today think that the moon also may have harmful effects. Some amend the Hebrew text to read, "Nor the cold by night." Cf Gn 31, 40.

121, 8: *Your coming and your going:* by a common idiom, the Hebrew uses the expression "to come in and to go out" to signify all ordinary human activity.

Cf Dt 28, 6; 31, 2; Jos 14, 11; 2 Sm 3, 25.

Ps 122: A song of Zion. Full of joy at his arrival in the Holy City (1–3), the psalmist lauds Jerusalem as the goal of pilgrims and the seat of government (4f); he asks God's blessings upon it (6–9).

122, 6ff: *Peace: shalom,* the regular greeting in Hebrew; it is wider in meaning than the English word peace, and includes the idea of happiness, prosperity.

Ps 123: A supplication of the people. Protesting their loyal obedience to the Lord (1f), they beg him to have mercy on them in their humiliation (3f).

Ps 124: A hymn of thanksgiving in which the people acknowledge that without the Lord's help they would

have been utterly destroyed (1–5); they praise him, therefore, for having rescued them from their enemies (6–8).

124, 1: *Of David:* missing in some ancient sources.

124, 4f: *The waters:* a figure of affliction. Cf Pss 18, 5.17; 69, 2f.

Ps 125: A supplication in which the people, affirming their confidence in the Lord's protection (1f), pray that the reign of wickedness may end (3) and that the good may enjoy God's blessings (4f).

125, 1ff: Although Jerusalem itself is situated on a high hill, a rampart of still higher mountains surrounds it.

2 Mountains are round about
        Jerusalem;
    so the LORD is round about
        his people,
    both now and forever.

II

3 For the scepter of the wicked
        shall not remain
        upon the territory of the just,
    Lest the just put forth
        to wickedness their hands.

III

4 Do good, O LORD, to the good
        and to the upright of heart.
5 But such as turn aside to crooked
        ways
    may the LORD lead away with
        the evildoers!
    Peace be upon Israel!

PSALM 126

*The People's Prayer for Full
Restoration*

1 A song of ascents.

I

When the LORD brought back
        the captives of Zion,
    we were like men dreaming.
2 Then our mouth was filled with
        laughter,
    and our tongue with rejoicing.
    Then they said among the nations,
        "The LORD has done great
        things for them."
3 The LORD has done great things
        for us;
    we are glad indeed.

II

4 Restore our fortunes, O LORD,
    like the torrents in the
        southern desert.
5 Those that sow in tears
    shall reap rejoicing.

6 Although they go forth weeping,
    carrying the seed to be sown,
    They shall come back rejoicing,
    carrying their sheaves.

PSALM 127

*The Need of God's Blessing:
His Gift of Sons*

1 A song of ascents. Of Solomon.

I

Unless the LORD build the house,
    they labor in vain who build it.
Unless the LORD guard the city,
    in vain does the guard keep
        vigil.
2 It is vain for you to rise early,
    or put off your rest,
    You that eat hard-earned bread,
    for he gives to his beloved in
        sleep.

II

3 Behold, sons are a gift from the
        LORD;
    the fruit of the womb is a
        reward.
4 Like arrows in the hand of a
        warrior
    are the sons of one's youth.
5 Happy the man whose quiver is
        filled with them;
    they shall not be put to shame
        when they contend
    with enemies at the gate.

PSALM 128

The Happy Home of the Just Man

1 A song of ascents.

I

Happy are you who fear the
        LORD,
    who walk in his ways!
2 For you shall eat the fruit of
        your handiwork;
    happy shall you be, and favored.

3 Your wife shall be like a fruitful
        vine
    in the recesses of your home;
    Your children like olive plants
        around your table.
4 Behold, thus is the man blessed
    who fears the LORD.

II

5 The LORD bless you from Zion:
    may you see the prosperity of
        Jerusalem
    all the days of your life;
6 May you see your children's
        children.
    Peace be upon Israel!

PSALM 129

*Prayer for the Overthrow of
Israel's Foes*

1 A song of ascents.

I

Much have they oppressed me
        from my youth,
    let Israel say,
2 Much have they oppressed me
        from my youth;
    yet they have not prevailed
        against me.
3 Upon my back the plowers
        plowed;
    long did they make their
        furrows.
4 But the just LORD has severed
    the cords of the wicked.

II

5 May all be put to shame and fall
        back
    that hate Zion.
6 May they be like grass on the
        housetops,
    which withers before it is
        plucked;

Ps 126: Grateful for their happy return from exile
(1–3), the people beseech the Lord that he will prosper
their present struggle to rebuild their homeland (4–6).
Cf Ps 85.
    126, 1: *Like men dreaming:* the change from exile
to their own country was almost too good to be
believed. One can also understand, "like men restored to health."
    126, 4: As the infrequent rains cause the sudden
rush of waters through the dry and empty channels,
so may the Lord quickly restore the fortunes of the
exiles.
    Ps 127: Two short songs; the first (1f) stresses the
truth that without God's blessing all human endeavor
is futile, the second (3–5) congratulates the man whom
God has blessed with many children.

127, 2: Our Lord taught the same truth, that God's
blessings come to those who do not worry but trust
in his loving providence. Cf Mt 6, 25–34; Mk 4,
26–29; Lk 12, 22–31.
    127, 3: *Sons:* the word might also be rendered,
"children"; but boys were more welcome than girls
in an Israelite family.
    127, 5: *Enemies at the gate:* the sense is not "foes
besieging the walls of the city," but "adversaries in
the forum, in the court of justice." Local government
functioned in the large open space inside the city's
gate. The larger a man's family, the greater his
influence there. Cf Prv 31, 23.
    Ps 128: Like Ps 127, 3ff, this is a song celebrating
the blessings of family life. The psalmist congratulates the man to whom the Lord has given a fruitful

wife and sturdy children (1–4), and wishes him prosperity and long life (5f).
    128, 3: *Vine . . . olive plants:* merely for the pur-
pose of comparison; not to be understood as if these
plants grew inside a house. Cf Pss 52, 10; 92, 13ff.
    Ps 129: Bewailing the affliction that has so often
been Israel's lot (1–4), the people pray that their foes
may be brought to nought (5–8).
    129, 3: *Upon my back the plowers plowed:* Israel's
towns were changed into plowland. Some understand
the words to mean that Israel was scourged like a slave.
    129, 6f: The flat roofs of the houses in Palestine
were coated with a protective covering of clay; the
grass that sprouted in this clay after a heavy rain was
short-lived and worthless.

7 With which the reaper fills not
   his hand,
   nor the gatherer of sheaves
     his arms;
8 And those that pass by say not,
   "The blessing of the LORD be
     upon you!
   We bless you in the name of
     the LORD!"

PSALM 130

Prayer for Pardon and Mercy

1 A song of ascents.

I

Out of the depths I cry to you,
   O LORD;
   Lord, hear my voice!
2 Let your ears be attentive
   to my voice in supplication:

II

3 If you, O LORD, mark iniquities,
   Lord, who can stand?
4 But with you is forgiveness,
   that you may be revered.

III

5 I trust in the LORD;
   my soul trusts in his word.
6 My soul waits for the LORD
   more than sentinels wait for
     the dawn.

IV

More than sentinels wait for the
   dawn,
7   let Israel wait for the LORD,
For with the LORD is kindness
   and with him is plenteous
     redemption;
8 And he will redeem Israel
   from all their iniquities.

PSALM 131

Humble Trust in God

1 A song of ascents. Of David.

O LORD, my heart is not proud,
   nor are my eyes haughty;
I busy not myself with great
    things,
   nor with things too sublime
     for me.
2 Nay rather, I have stilled and
    quieted
   my soul like a weaned child.
Like a weaned child on its
    mother's lap.
   [so is my soul within me.]
3   O Israel, hope in the LORD,
   both now and forever.

PSALM 132

The Pact between David and the Lord

1 A song of ascents.

A

I

Remember, O LORD, for David
   all his anxious care:
2 How he swore to the LORD,
   vowed to the Mighty One of
     Jacob:
3 "I will not enter the house I
    live in,
   nor lie on the couch where I
     sleep;
4 I will give my eyes no sleep
   my eyelids no rest,
5 Till I find a place for the LORD,
   a dwelling for the Mighty One
     of Jacob."

II

6 Behold, we heard of it in
    Ephrathah;
   we found it in the fields of Jaar.

7 Let us enter into his dwelling,
   let us worship at his footstool.
8 Advance, O LORD, to your
    resting place
   you and the ark of your
     majesty.
9 May your priests be clothed
    with justice;
   let your faithful ones shout
     merrily for joy.
10 For the sake of David your
    servant,
   reject not the plea of your
     anointed.

B

I

11 The LORD swore to David
   a firm promise from which he
     will not withdraw:
  "Your own offspring
   I will set upon your throne;
12 If your sons keep my covenant
   and the decrees which I shall
     teach them,
  Their sons, too, forever
   shall sit upon your throne."
13 For the LORD has chosen Zion;
   he prefers her for his dwelling.

II

14 "Zion is my resting place forever;
   in her will I dwell, for I prefer
     her.
15 I will bless her with abundant
    provision,
   her poor I will fill with bread.
16 Her priests I will clothe with
    salvation,
   and her faithful ones shall
     shout merrily for joy.
17 In her will I make a horn to
    sprout forth for David;
   I will place a lamp for my
     anointed.

129, 8: Harvesters greeted one another with such blessings. Cf Ru 2, 4.

Ps 130: The sixth of the Penitential Psalms, the *De Profundis*, used in the liturgy of the Church as a prayer for the faithful departed. In deep sorrow the psalmist cries to the Lord (1f), begging pardon for his sins (3f); as he himself trusts in God's mercy (5-6b), so also should Israel wait in hope for the Lord's redemption (6c-8).

130, 1: *The depths:* of spiritual, not physical misery.

130, 4: *That you may be revered:* the thought of God's merciful forgiveness should lead one to seek his pardon and to fear offending him in the future. Cf Rom 2, 4.

130, 7f: The redemption of Israel from all their iniquities was achieved by Christ, the divine Redeemer. Cf Lk 2, 38.

Ps 131: A protestation of humility. The psalmist

asserts that he is free from all worldy ambition (1) and as simple as a child (2); he hopes that Israel will likewise have childlike confidence in the Lord (3).

Ps 132: A song reminding the people of the Lord's great promise to David that his descendants would always rule in Zion. It is similar to Ps 89 but differs from it in its lack of lamentation over present miseries. The psalmist first recalls how David vowed to build a new dwelling place for the Lord (1-5); he then recounts how the ark was brought to Zion (6-10). There follows the Lord's promise to David to bless his dynasty (11-13) and Zion, his capital (14-18).

132, 1: *All his anxious care:* to build the temple. Cf 2 Sm 7, 1ff; 1 Kgs 8, 17.

132, 2.5: *The Mighty One of Jacob:* one of the titles of the Lord. Cf Gn 49, 24; Is 49, 26; 60, 16.

132, 6: *Ephrathah:* Bethlehem, David's birthplace. Cf Ru 4, 11. *The fields of Jaar:* "Forestfield," the

same as Kiriath-jearim, "Forest-town," where the ark remained for several generations. Cf 1 Sm 7, 1f; 2 Sm 6, 2; 1 Chr 13, 5f.

132, 7: *His footstool:* the ark. Cf Ps 99, 5.

132, 10: *Your anointed:* the royal descendant of David, contemporaneous with the psalmist. According to some, this proves that the psalm is pre-exilic; according to others, the "anointed" of the Lord is Zerubbabel, the post-exilic descendant of David. Cf Ezr 3, 2; Hg 1, 1-2.23; Zec 4.

132, 17: *A horn to sprout forth for David:* a strong offspring of David. This refers pre-eminently to Christ, who is called a "sprout" of David by the prophets. Cf Jer 23, 5; 33, 15; Zec 3, 8; 6, 12. *I will place a lamp:* the ever-burning lamp in a house was a symbol of perpetual offspring; when a man died without descendants, his lamp was said to be put out. Cf 1 Kgs 11, 36; 15, 4; 2 Kgs 8, 19.

18 His enemies I will clothe with
shame,
but upon him my crown shall
shine."

PSALM 133

The Benefits of Brotherly Concord

1 A song of ascents. Of David.

Behold, how good it is, and
how pleasant,
where brethren dwell at one!
2 It is as when the precious
ointment upon the head
runs down over the beard, the
beard of Aaron,
till it runs down upon the
collar of his robe.
3 It is a dew like that of Hermon,
which comes down upon
the mountains of Zion;
For there the LORD has
pronounced his blessing,
life forever.

PSALM 134

*Exhortation to the Night Watch
to Bless the Lord*

1 A song of ascents.

Come, bless the LORD,
all you servants of the LORD
Who stand in the house of the
LORD
during the hours of night.
2 Lift up your hands toward the
sanctuary,
and bless the LORD.

3 May the LORD bless you from
Zion,
the maker of heaven and earth.

PSALM 135

*Praise of God, the Lord and
Benefactor of Israel*

1 Alleluia.

A

Praise the name of the LORD;
Praise, you servants of the
LORD
2 Who stand in the house of the
LORD,
in the courts of the house of
our God.
3 Praise the LORD, for the LORD
is good;
sing praise to his name, which
we love;
4 For the LORD has chosen Jacob
for himself,
Israel for his own possession.

B

I

5 For I know that the LORD is
great;
our Lord is greater than all
gods.
6 All that the LORD wills he does
in heaven and on earth,
in the seas and in all the
deeps.
7 He raises storm clouds from the
end of the earth;
with the lightning he makes
the rain;
he brings forth the winds
from his storehouse.

II

8 He smote the first-born in Egypt,
both of man and of beast.
9 He sent signs and wonders
into your midst, O Egypt,
against Pharaoh and against
all his servants.
10 He smote many nations
and slew mighty kings:
11 Sihon, king of the Amorites,
and Og, king of Bashan,
and all the kings of Canaan;

12 And he made their land a
heritage,
the heritage of Israel his
people.
13 Your name, O LORD, endures
forever;
LORD is your title through all
generations,
14 For the LORD defends his people,
and is merciful to his servants.

III

15 The idols of the nations are
silver and gold,
the handiwork of men.
16 They have mouths but speak
not;
they have eyes but see not;
17 They have ears but hear not,
nor is there breath in their
mouths.
18 Their makers shall be like them,
everyone that trusts in them.

C

19 House of Israel, bless the LORD,
house of Aaron, bless the
LORD,
20 House of Levi, bless the LORD;
you who fear the LORD, bless
the LORD.
21 Blessed from Zion be the LORD,
who dwells in Jerusalem.

PSALM 136

*Hymn of Thanksgiving for the
Everlasting Kindness
of the Lord*

1 Alleluia.

Give thanks to the LORD, for he
is good,
for his mercy endures forever;
2 Give thanks to the God of gods,
for his mercy endures forever;
3 Give thanks to the Lord of
lords,
for his mercy endures forever;

Ps 133: The psalmist rejoices in the compact settlement of the Israelite families as an evidence of God's blessing (1), just as the same divine blessing would be signified by the fragrant oil of anointing (2) used at the consecration of the high priest (Ex 30, 22–33), or by the rich dew (Gn 27, 27ff; Hos 14, 6; Jl 4, 17f) covering the mountain slopes round about Jerusalem (3). *Hermon* is the majestic snow-capped mountain at the north of the Holy Land. Its copious waters are the type of the divine blessing that fructifies the soil. Similarly, *Aaron* is the type for any high priest consecrated with the same precious oil. The *life forever* was understood in the first place of the preservation of earthly life; it is capable of a fuller application in the light of the Gospel. The similes used seem to suppose that the psalmist saw the returned exiles living in and about the Holy City,

crowning its mountaintop and spreading down over its slopes like a precious oil or a heaven-sent dew.
Ps 134: This short song seems to have been sung in the temple as an encouragement for the priests and Levites who were on duty there during the night (1f); they respond by blessing the people (3).
134, 1: *Servants of the Lord:* the priests and Levites. Cf Dt 10, 8; Pss 113, 1; 135, 1; Dn 3, 84f.
Ps 135: This hymn begins (1–4) and ends (19–21) with an exhortation to glorify God, who is the almighty Lord of creation (5–7) and the defender of his chosen people (8–14), whereas the pagan gods are lifeless idols (15–18). Many of the verses were borrowed from other psalms.
135, 1f: Very similar to Ps 134, 1.
135, 4: All nations belong to the Lord, but he has chosen Israel as his own in a special sense. Cf Ex 19,

5; Dt 7, 6; 14, 2; 26, 18; 32, 9.
135, 15–18: Almost identical with Ps 115, 4ff.8.
135, 19ff: Similar to Ps 118, 1–4.
Ps 136: This hymn has the form of a "litany," that is, each half-verse is followed by a refrain, the former probably sung by a soloist and the latter by the people. It seems fairly certain that at least the main section, vv 4–25, did not originally have this invariable refrain, which now interrupts the grammatical structure of the sentences. Besides the introductory and concluding invitations to give grateful praise (1–3.26), this hymn extols the Lord's greatness in creating the universe (4–9), as well as his goodness in bringing Israel to the Promised Land (10–22) and in having pity on the misery of the people (23–25).
136, 2: *The God of gods:* the supreme and only God.

I

4 Who alone does great wonders,
  for his mercy endures forever;
5 Who made the heavens in
    wisdom,
  for his mercy endures forever;
6 Who spread out the earth upon
    the waters,
  for his mercy endures forever;
7 Who made the great lights,
  for his mercy endures forever;
8 The sun to rule over the day,
  for his mercy endures forever;
9 The moon and the stars to rule
    over the night,
  for his mercy endures forever;

II

10 Who smote the Egyptians in their
    first-born,
  for his mercy endures forever;
11 And brought out Israel from
    their midst,
  for his mercy endures forever;
12 With a mighty hand and an
    outstretched arm,
  for his mercy endures forever;
13 Who split the Red Sea in twain,
  for his mercy endures forever;
14 And led Israel through its
    midst,
  for his mercy endures forever;
15 But swept Pharaoh and his army
    into the Red Sea,
  for his mercy endures forever;
16 Who led his people through the
    wilderness,
  for his mercy endures forever;
17 Who smote great kings,
  for his mercy endures forever;
18 And slew powerful kings,
  for his mercy endures forever;
19 Sihon, king of the Amorites,
  for his mercy endures forever;
20 And Og, king of Bashan,
  for his mercy endures forever;
21 And made their land a heritage,
  for his mercy endures forever;

22 The heritage of Israel his servant,
  for his mercy endures forever;

III

23 Who remembered us in our
    abjection,
  for his mercy endures forever;
24 And freed us from our foes,
  for his mercy endures forever;
25 Who gives food to all flesh,
  for his mercy endures forever.
26 Give thanks to the God of
    heaven,
  for his mercy endures forever.

PSALM 137

The Exile's Remembrance of Zion

I

1 By the streams of Babylon
    we sat and wept
    when we remembered Zion.
2 On the aspens of that land
    we hung up our harps,
3 Though there our captors asked
      of us
    the lyrics of our songs,
  And our despoilers urged us to
      be joyous:
    "Sing for us the songs of
      Zion!"

II

4 How could we sing a song of the
    LORD
    in a foreign land?
5 If I forget you, Jerusalem,
    may my right hand be
      forgotten!
6 May my tongue cleave to my
      palate
    if I remember you not,
  If I place not Jerusalem
    ahead of my joy.

III

7 Remember, O LORD, against the
    children of Edom,
    the day of Jerusalem,

When they said, "Raze it, raze it
    down to its foundations!"
8 O daughter of Babylon, you
      destroyer,
    happy the man who shall
      repay you
    the evil you have done us!
9 Happy the man who shall seize
    and smash
    your little ones against the
      rock!

PSALM 138

Hymn of a Grateful Heart
1 Of David.

I

I will give thanks to you, O
    LORD, with all my heart,
  [for you have heard the words
    of my mouth;]
  in the presence of the angels
    I will sing your praise;
2 I will worship at your holy
      temple
    and give thanks to your name,
  Because of your kindness and
      your truth;
    for you have made great
      above all things
    your name and your promise.
3 When I called, you answered
      me;
    you built up strength within
      me.

II

4 All the kings of the earth shall
    give thanks to you, O
      LORD,
    when they hear the words of
      your mouth;
5 And they shall sing of the ways
    of the LORD:
    "Great is the glory of the
      LORD."

136, 17–22: These verses occur in similar form but without the refrain in Ps 135, 10ff.
136, 23f: The reference seems to be to the Babylonian exile.
Ps 137: The psalmist, now apparently returned from exile, recalls how the Jews refused to sing for their captors (1–3) because they thought joyful songs out of harmony with their mournful remembrance of Zion (4–6); condign punishment is wished upon cruel Edom and Babylon (7–9).
137, 1: The streams of Babylon: the Euphrates and Tigris, with the numerous irrigation-canals which branched off from them.
137, 2: The aspens: not, "the willows," as the older versions generally rendered it; the Hebrew word

most probably signifies the populus euphraticus, the Mesopotamian aspen.
137, 7: The day of Jerusalem: the time when the Holy City was captured and destroyed by the Babylonians. In league with the latter were the Edomites, the southern neighbors and rivals of Judah. The prophets often threaten dire punishment to Edom for its hatred of Israel. Cf Is 34, 5–15; Jer 49, 7–22; Lam 4, 21f; Ez 25, 12ff; Am 1, 11f; Ob 1, 1–18.
137, 8: Daughter of Babylon: a Hebrew idiom for "city of Babylon."
137, 9: According to the ruthless custom of ancient warfare, children were indeed thus cruelly killed. Cf 2 Kgs 8, 12; Hos 9, 16. But it seems more probable that here the psalmist is personifying "the daughter of

Babylon" as a mother whose little ones are the adult citizens, not the infants, of the city. Cf Lk 19, 44.
Ps 138: Thanking God for having heard his prayer (1–3), the psalmist wishes that all the great ones of the earth might join him in his hymn of gratitude (4–6), for he is confident of the Lord's continual help (7f).
138, 1: The words in brackets are in the Greek version but not in the current Hebrew text. They are probably a variant of v 4b accidentally inserted here. The angels: in Hebrew, elohim, which is the word for "God," "gods," and sometimes "godlike beings," such as the angels. Cf Pss 8, 6; 97, 7. Some render, "In the face of the gods," that is, despite the false gods of the pagans.

6 The LORD is exalted, yet the
lowly he sees,
and the proud he knows from
afar.

III

7 Though I walk amid distress,
you preserve me;
against the anger of my
enemies you raise your
hand;
your right hand saves me.
8 The LORD will complete what he
has done for me;
your kindness, O LORD,
endures forever;
forsake not the work of your
hands.

PSALM 139

The All-knowing and Ever-present God

1 For the leader. A psalm of David.

I

O LORD, you have probed me
and you know me;
2 you know when I sit and when
I stand;
you understand my thoughts
from afar.
3 My journeys and my rest you
scrutinize,
with all my ways you are
familiar.
4 Even before a word is on my
tongue,
behold, O LORD, you know
the whole of it.
5 Behind me and before, you hem
me in
and rest your hand upon me.
6 Such knowledge is too wonderful
for me;
too lofty for me to attain.

II

7 Where can I go from your spirit?

from your presence where can
I flee?
8 If I go up to the heavens, you
are there;
if I sink to the nether world,
you are present there.
9 If I take the wings of the dawn,
if I settle at the farthest limits
of the sea,
10 Even there your hand shall
guide me,
and your right hand hold me
fast.
11 If I say, "Surely the darkness
shall hide me,
and night shall be my light"—
12 For your darkness itself is not
dark,
and night shines as the day.
[Darkness and light are the
same.]

III

13 Truly you have formed my
inmost being;
you knit me in my mother's
womb.
14 I give you thanks that I am
fearfully, wonderfully made;
wonderful are your works.
My soul also you knew full well;
15 nor was my frame unknown
to you
When I was made in secret,
when I was fashioned in the
depths of the earth.
16 Your eyes have seen my actions;
in your book they are all
written;
my days were limited before
one of them existed.
17 How weighty are your designs,
O God;
how vast the sum of them!
18 Were I to recount them, they
would outnumber the sands;
did I reach the end of them, I
should still be with you.

IV

19 If only you would destroy the
wicked, O God,
and the men of blood were to
depart from me!
20 Wickedly they invoke your
name;
your foes swear faithless oaths.
21 Do I not hate, O LORD, those
who hate you?
Those who rise up against you
do I not loathe?
22 With a deadly hatred I hate
them;
they are my enemies.
23 Probe me, O God, and know
my heart;
try me, and know my
thoughts;
24 See if my way is crooked,
and lead me in the way of old.

PSALM 140

Prayer for Deliverance from the Snares of the Wicked

1 For the leader. A psalm of David.

I

2 Deliver me, O LORD, from evil
men;
preserve me from violent men,
3 From those who devise evil in
their hearts,
and stir up wars every day.
4 They make their tongues sharp
as those of serpents;
the venom of asps is under
their lips.

II

5 Save me, O LORD, from the
hands of the wicked;
preserve me from violent men
Who plan to trip up my feet—
6 the proud who have hidden a
trap for me;

Ps 139: A hymn to God's omnipresence and omniscience, in the form of a meditation in which the
psalmist ponders the truths that the Lord sees and
knows him no matter where he may be (1–6); that
there is no escape from the all-seeing eye of God
(7–12); and that the divine Creator of man is also the
Author of his destiny (13–18). He therefore resolves
to abhor the wicked and to live sincerely in God's
sight (19–24). The current Hebrew text is rather
poorly preserved, and the interpretation of a few
passages is somewhat doubtful.
139, 2: *When I sit and when I stand:* in all human
activity.
139, 9: *Take the wings of the dawn:* go to the most
distant extremities of the east. *The farthest limits of*

the sea: the uttermost bounds of the west.
139, 12: *Darkness and light are the same:* as far as
God is concerned: an explanatory gloss on the two
preceding lines.
139, 15: *The depths of the earth:* figurative language
for "the womb"; stressing not so much the darkness
of the place as the hidden, mysterious nature of the
operations which occur there.
139, 16ff: The text of these three verses is obscure
in several places.
139, 18: *I should still be with you:* even though the
psalmist might reach the end of his own capacity for
understanding the divine attributes, the infinity of
God's nature would still stand before him as if he
had not even begun to comprehend it.

139, 24: *The way of old:* the manner of living of the
ancient patriarchs. Cf Jer 6, 16.
Ps 140: The psalmist beseeches God to rescue him
from his violent, treacherous foes (2–4); they lay a
trap for his life (5f), but he trusts in the Lord's
protection (7f). Therefore he prays that their evil
plans may recoil upon themselves (9–11), and that
God will render due justice to both the wicked and
the good (12–14).
140, 4: Similar metaphors for a wicked tongue are
used in Pss 52, 4; 55, 22; 58, 5.
140, 6: The same figure, taken from the custom of
a hunter laying a trap for his prey, occurs in Pss 9, 16;
31, 5; 35, 7; 57, 7; 64, 6. Cf Mt 22, 15; Lk 11, 54.

They have spread cords for a net;
　　by the wayside they have laid
　　　snares for me.
7 I say to the LORD, you are my
　　　God;
　　hearken, O LORD, to my
　　　voice in supplication.
8 O GOD, my Lord, my strength
　　　and my salvation;
　　you are my helmet in the day
　　　of battle!

III

9 Grant not, O LORD, the desires
　　　of the wicked;
　　further not their plans.
10 Those who surround me lift up
　　　their heads,
　　may the mischief which they
　　　threaten overwhelm them.
11 May he rain burning coals upon
　　　them;
　　may he cast them into the
　　　the depths, never to rise.

IV

12 A man of wicked tongue shall
　　　not abide in the land;
　　evil shall abruptly entrap the
　　　violent man.
13 I know that the LORD renders
　　　justice to the afflicted,
　　judgment to the poor.
14 Surely the just shall give thanks
　　　to your name:
　　the upright shall dwell in your
　　　presence.

PSALM 141

Prayer of a Just Man To Be Saved from Wickedness

1 A psalm of David.

I

O LORD, to you I call; hasten to
　　me;
　　hearken to my voice when I
　　　call upon you.
2 Let my prayer come like incense
　　before you;
　　the lifting up of my hands,
　　　like the evening sacrifice.

II

3 O LORD, set a watch before my
　　　mouth,
　　a guard at the door of my lips.
4 Let not my heart incline to the
　　　evil
　　of engaging in deeds of
　　　wickedness
　　With men who are evildoers;
　　and let me not partake of their
　　　dainties.
5 Let the just man strike me; that
　　　is kindness;
　　let him reprove me; it is oil
　　　for the head,
　　Which my head shall not refuse,
　　but I will still pray under
　　　these afflictions.
6 Their judges were cast down over
　　　the crag,
　　and they heard how pleasant
　　　were my words.
7 As when a plowman breaks
　　　furrows in the field,
　　so their bones are strewn by
　　　the edge of the nether world.

III

8 For toward you, O GOD, my
　　　Lord, my eyes are turned;
　　in you I take refuge; strip me
　　　not of life.
9 Keep me from the trap they
　　　have set for me,
　　and from the snares of
　　　evildoers.
10 Let all the wicked fall, each into
　　　his own net,
　　while I escape.

PSALM 142

Prayer of a Prisoner in Dire Straits

1 A *maskil* of David. A prayer when he was
　　in the cave.

I

2 With a loud voice I cry out to
　　the LORD;
　　with a loud voice I beseech
　　the LORD.

3 My complaint I pour out before
　　　him;
　　before him I bare my distress.
4 When my spirit is faint within
　　　me,
　　you know my path.

II

In the way along which I walk
　　they have hid a trap for me.
5 I look to the right to see,
　　but there is no one who pays
　　　me heed.
I have lost all means of escape;
　　there is no one who cares for
　　　my life.

III

6 I cry out to you, O LORD;
　　I say, "You are my refuge,
　　my portion in the land of the
　　　living."
7 Attend to my cry,
　　for I am brought low indeed.
Rescue me from my persecutors,
　　for they are too strong for me.
8 Lead me forth from prison,
　　that I may give thanks to
　　　your name.
The just shall gather around
　　me
　　when you have been good to
　　me.

PSALM 143

Prayer of a Penitent in Distress

1 A psalm of David.

I

O LORD, hear my prayer;
　　hearken to my pleading in
　　　your faithfulness;
　　in your justice answer me.
2 And enter not into judgment
　　with your servant,
　　for before you no living man
　　　is just.

Ps 141: After calling for divine aid in general (1f), the psalmist prays that he may not be led astray by the seductions of the wicked, whose end is destruction (3–7), and that their evil may harm only themselves (8–10).

141, 2: *Incense:* literally, "smoke," that is, the fragrant fumes which rose from the altar at the burning of sacrificial animals or of aromatic spices, including frankincense; also used in Rv 5, 8 as a symbol of prayer. *The lifting up of my hands:* the gesture of supplication. Cf Pss 28, 2; 63, 5; 77, 3; 88, 10; 119, 48; 134, 2; 143, 6.

141, 6f: The text of these two verses is very obscure, and their interpretation quite uncertain.

Ps 142: Imploring the Lord to behold his sad plight (2–4b), the psalmist tells how his enemies have hemmed him in (4c–5), and beseeches God to rescue him (6–8).

142, 1: *In the case:* cf 1 Sm 22, 1; 24, 1f; Ps 57, 1.

142, 8: *The just shall gather around me:* in the temple, when the psalmist offers up his thanksgiving sacrifice.

Ps 143: The seventh of the Penitential Psalms.

Pleading for divine assistance despite his sinfulness (1f), the psalmist describes his external and internal afflictions (3f) as he longs for the help which God has always offered his faithful servants (5f). He begs to be rescued from his enemies (7–9), and prays for God's saving guidance and the destruction of his foes (10–12).

143, 1f: Confident that God, in justice to his own promise, will answer his prayer, the psalmist admits that in strict justice to himself he does not deserve to be heard because of his sins.

II

3 For the enemy pursues me;
  he has crushed my life to the
    ground;
  he has left me dwelling in the
    dark, like those long dead.
4 And my spirit is faint within me,
  my heart within me is
    appalled.
5 I remember the days of old;
  I meditate on all your doings,
  the works of your hands I
    ponder.
6 I stretch out my hands to you;
  my soul thirsts for you like
    parched land.

III

7 Hasten to answer me, O LORD,
  for my spirit fails me.
  Hide not your face from me
    lest I become like those who
    go down into the pit.
8 At dawn let me hear of your
    kindness,
  for in you I trust.
  Show me the way in which I
    should walk,
  for to you I lift up my soul.
9 Rescue me from my enemies,
    O LORD,
  for in you I hope.

IV

10 Teach me to do your will,
  for you are my God.
  May your good spirit guide me
    on level ground.
11 For your name's sake, O LORD,
    preserve me;
  in your justice free me from
    distress,
12 And in your kindness destroy
    my enemies;
  bring to nought all my foes,
  for I am your servant.

PSALM 144

Prayer for Victory and Prosperity

1 Of David.

I

Blessed be the LORD, my rock,
  who trains my hands for
    battle, my fingers for war;
2 My refuge and my fortress,
  my stronghold, my deliverer,
  My shield, in whom I trust,
  who subdues peoples under
    me.

II

3 LORD, what is man, that you
    notice him;
  the son of man, that you take
    thought of him?
4 Man is like a breath;
  his days, like a passing
    shadow.
5 Incline your heavens, O LORD,
  and come down;
  touch the mountains, and they
    shall smoke;
6 Flash forth lightning, and put
    them to flight,
  shoot your arrows, and rout
    them;
7 Reach out your hand from on
    high—
  Deliver me and rescue me
    from many waters,
  from the hands of aliens,
8 Whose mouths swear false
    promises
  while their right hands
    are raised in perjury.

III

9 O God, I will sing a new song
    to you;
  with a ten-stringed lyre I will
    chant your praise,
10 You who give victory to kings,
  and deliver David, your
    servant.

11 From the evil sword deliver
    me;
  and rescue me from the
    hands of aliens,
  Whose mouths swear false
    promises
  while their right hands
    are raised in perjury.

IV

12 May our sons be like plants
  well-nurtured in their youth,
  Our daughters like wrought
    columns
  such as stand at the corners of
    the temple.
13 May our garners be full,
  affording every kind of store;
  May our sheep be in the
    thousands,
  and increase to myriads in our
    meadows;
14 may our oxen be well laden.
  May there be no breach in the
    walls, no exile,
  no outcry in our streets.
15 Happy the people for whom
    things are thus;
  happy the people whose God
    is the LORD.

PSALM 145

The Greatness and Goodness of God

1 Praise. Of David.

I will extol you, O my God and
    King,
  and I will bless your name
    forever and ever.
2 Every day will I bless you,
  and I will praise your name
    forever and ever.
3 Great is the LORD and highly to
    be praised;
  his greatness is unsearchable.
4 Generation after generation
  praises your works
  and proclaims your might.

143, 10: *On level ground:* some ancient sources read, "On a level path." Cf Pss 26, 12; 27, 11.
  Ps 144: Except for its final section, this psalm is made up almost entirely of verses borrowed from various other psalms; hence it is somewhat lacking in logical unity. The first section (1f) is a prayer of thanks for victory in war; the second (3–7a), a humble acknowledgment of man's nothingness and a supplication that God show forth his saving might; the third (9f), a promise of future thanksgiving; the

fourth (12–15), a wish for prosperity and peace. A slightly varying refrain, which contains a prayer for deliverance from treacherous foes, occurs after the second and third sections (7b–8, 11).
  144, 1f: Composed of phrases from Ps 18, 3.35.47f.
  144, 3: Very similar to Ps 8, 5.
  144, 4: Composed of phrases from Pss 39, 6; 102, 12.
  144, 5ff: Adapted in large part from Pss 18, 10.15.17; 104, 32.

144, 9f: Similar to Pss 18, 51; 33, 2f.
  144, 12: *Like wrought columns . . . of the temple:* well-formed, shapely. But the Hebrew text of these two lines is obscure, and the allusion is uncertain.
  Ps 145: An alphabetic psalm of which many of the phrases occur in similar form in other psalms or in other books of the Bible. The main thoughts of this hymn are concerned with God's sovereign majesty and loving providence.

5 They speak of the splendor of
    your glorious majesty
  and tell of your wondrous
    works.
6 They discourse of the power of
    your terrible deeds
  and declare your greatness.
7 They publish the fame of your
    abundant goodness
  and joyfully sing of your justice.
8 The LORD is gracious and
    merciful,
  slow to anger and of great
    kindness.
9 The LORD is good to all
  and compassionate toward all
    his works.

10 Let all your works give you
    thanks, O LORD,
  and let your faithful ones bless
    you.
11 Let them discourse of the glory
    of your kingdom
  and speak of your might,
12 Making known to men your
    might
  and the glorious splendor of
    your kingdom.
13 Your kingdom is a kingdom for
    all ages,
  and your dominion endures
    through all generations.

  The LORD is faithful in all his
    words
  and holy in all his works.
14 The LORD lifts up all who are
    falling
  and raises up all who are
    bowed down.
15 The eyes of all look hopefully
    to you,
  and you give them their food
    in due season;
16 You open your hand
  and satisfy the desire of every
    living thing.

17 The LORD is just in all his ways
  and holy in all his works.
18 The LORD is near to all who call
    upon him,
  to all who call upon him in
    truth.

19 He fulfills the desire of those
    who fear him,
  he hears their cry and saves
    them.
20 The LORD keeps all who love him,
  but all the wicked he will
    destroy.
21 May my mouth speak the praise
    of the LORD,
  and may all flesh bless his
    holy name
  forever and ever.

PSALM 146

Trust in God alone

1 Alleluia.

Praise the LORD, O my soul;
2   I will praise the LORD all my
      life;
    I will sing praise to my God
      while I live.

I

3 Put not your trust in princes,
  in man, in whom there is no
    salvation.
4 When his spirit departs he
    returns to his earth;
  on that day his plans perish.

II

5 Happy he whose help is the God
    of Jacob,
  whose hope is in the LORD,
    his God,
6 Who made heaven and earth,
  the sea and all that is in them;
  Who keeps faith forever,
7   secures justice for the
      oppressed,
    gives food to the hungry.
  The LORD sets captives free;
8   the LORD gives sight to the
      blind.
  The LORD raises up those that
    were bowed down;
  the LORD loves the just.
9 The LORD protects strangers;
  the fatherless and the widow
    he sustains,
  but the way of the wicked he
    thwarts.

10 The LORD shall reign forever;
  your God, O Zion, through all
    generations.   Alleluia.

PSALM 147

Zion's Grateful Praise to Her Bountiful Lord

I

1   Praise the LORD, for he is good;
    sing praise to our God, for he
      is gracious;
    it is fitting to praise him.
2 The LORD rebuilds Jerusalem;
  the dispersed of Israel he
    gathers.
3 He heals the brokenhearted
  and binds up their wounds.
4 He tells the number of the stars;
  he calls each by name.
5 Great is our Lord and mighty in
    power:
  to his wisdom there is no limit.
6 The LORD sustains the lowly;
  the wicked he casts to the
    ground.

II

7 Sing to the LORD with
    thanksgiving;
  sing praise with the harp to
    our God,
8 Who covers the heavens with
    clouds,
  who provides rain for the
    earth;
  Who makes grass sprout on the
    mountains
  and herbs for the service of
    men;
9 Who gives food to the cattle,
  and to the young ravens when
    they cry to him.
10 In the strength of the steed he
    delights not,
  nor is he pleased with the
    fleetness of men.
11 The LORD is pleased with those
    who fear him,
  with those who hope for his
    kindness.

Ps 146: A hymn in praise of the kindness and generosity of God. After a short introductory strophe (1f), the psalmist exposes the folly of trusting in merely human aid (3f), and then extols the goodness of God toward those who put their trust in him alone (5–10).

Ps 147: The Greek and Latin versions divide this psalm into two parts: Ps 146 (vv 1–11), Ps 147 (vv 12–20). The psalm sings the praises of God as the restorer of exiled Israel (1–6) who sustains the needy (7–11), and as the benefactor of Zion (12–20).

147, 8f: Just as the heavenly Father clothes the mountains with vegetation for the nourishment of man and beast, so does his loving providence feed the birds, especially the ravens, whose loud cawing is poetically taken as a cry to God for food. Cf Mt 6, 26–30.

147, 10f: Trust in his own natural strength makes a man proud and displeasing to God, who delights only in a humble confidence toward himself. Cf Pss 20, 8; 33, 16ff.

III

12 Glorify the LORD, O Jerusalem;
    praise your God, O Zion.
13 For he has strengthened the bars
        of your gates;
    he has blessed your children
        within you.
14 He has granted peace in your
        borders;
    with the best of wheat he
        fills you.
15 He sends forth his command to
        the earth;
    swiftly runs his word!
16 He spreads snow like wool;
    frost he strews like ashes.
17 He scatters his hail like crumbs;
    before his cold the waters
        freeze.
18 He sends his word and melts
        them;
    he lets his breeze blow and the
        waters run.
19 He has proclaimed his word to
        Jacob,
    his statutes and his
        ordinances to Israel.
20 He has not done thus for any
        other nation;
    his ordinances he has not
        made known to them.
        Alleluia.

PSALM 148

*Hymn of All Creation to the
Almighty Creator*

1 Alleluia.

I

Praise the LORD from the
    heavens,
    praise him in the heights;
2 Praise him, all you his angels,
    praise him, all you his hosts.
3 Praise him, sun and moon;
    praise him, all you shining
        stars.
4 Praise him, you highest heavens,
    and you waters above the
        heavens.

5 Let them praise the name of the
    LORD,
    for he commanded and they
        were created;
6 He established them forever and
        ever;
    he gave them a duty which
        shall not pass away.

II

7 Praise the LORD from the earth,
    you sea monsters and all
        depths;
8 Fire and hail, snow and mist,
    storm winds that fulfill his
        word;
9 You mountains and all you hills,
    you fruit trees and all you
        cedars;
10 You wild beasts and all tame
        animals,
    you creeping things and you
        winged fowl.

III

11 Let the kings of the earth and
        all peoples,
    the princes and all the judges
        of the earth;
12 Young men too, and maidens,
        old men and boys,
13 Praise the name of the LORD,
    for his name alone is exalted;
    His majesty is above earth and
        heaven,
14   and he has lifted up the horn
        of his people.
    Be this his praise from all his
        faithful ones,
    from the children of Israel, the
        people close to him.
        Alleluia.

PSALM 149

*Invitation to Glorify the Lord
with Song and Sword*

1 Alleluia.

I

Sing to the LORD a new song
    of praise in the assembly of
        the faithful.

2 Let Israel be glad in their maker,
    let the children of Zion rejoice
        in their king.
3 Let them praise his name in the
        festive dance,
    let them sing praise to him
        with timbrel and harp.
4 For the LORD loves his people,
    and he adorns the lowly with
        victory.
5 Let the faithful exult in glory;
    let them sing for joy upon
        their couches;
6   let the high praises of God be
        in their throats.

II

And let two-edged swords be in
    their hands:
7   to execute vengeance on the
        nations,
    punishments on the peoples;
8 To bind their kings with chains,
    their nobles with fetters of
        iron;
9 To execute on them the written
        sentence.
    This is the glory of all his
        faithful.   Alleluia.

PSALM 150

*Final Doxology with Full
Orchestra*

1 Alleluia.

Praise the LORD in his sanctuary,
    praise him in the firmament
        of his strength.
2 Praise him for his mighty deeds,
    praise him for his sovereign
        majesty.
3 Praise him with the blast of the
        trumpet,
    praise him with lyre and harp,
4 Praise him with timbrel and
        dance,
    praise him with strings and
        pipe.
5 Praise him with sounding cymbals,
    praise him with clanging
        cymbals.
6 Let everything that has breath
    praise the LORD!   Alleluia.

Ps 148: All creatures in the heavens (1–6) and on earth (7–10) are called upon to join in the hymn of praise that universal mankind, and especially Israel, should sing to the Lord of all (11–14).

148, 4: *Highest heavens:* literally, "the heavens of the heavens," that is, the space above the firmament, where the "upper waters" are stored. Cf Gn 1, 6ff; Dt 10, 14: 1 Kgs 8, 27; Ps 104, 3.13.

148, 14: *Lifted up the horn of his people:* restored

their power. Cf note on Ps 18, 3.

Ps 149: While the people are invited to praise the Lord with sacred music in the temple (1–6a), they stand with sword in hand for the defense of Zion (6b–9). Cf Neh 4, 16–23 (10–17); 1 Mc 4, 37f.54; 2 Mc 15, 26f.

149, 3: *The festive dance:* Cf Ex 15, 20; 2 Sm 6, 5.14.16.

Ps 150: As a grand finale, the psalmist calls upon

all the musical instruments of the temple service to join in the praise of the Lord; thus, the psalm serves as the closing doxology, not only to the Fifth Book of the Psalms, but to the whole Psalter.

150, 1: *Praise the Lord:* in Hebrew, *hallelu-yah,* which through the Greek and Latin versions has become our "Alleluia."

Proverbs

INTRODUCTION: THE VALUE OF WISDOM

Purpose of the Proverbs of Solomon

THE proverbs of Solomon, the son of David, king of Israel: 2 That men may appreciate wisdom and discipline, may understand words of intelligence; 3 May receive training in wise conduct, in what is right, just and honest; 4 That resourcefulness may be imparted to the simple, to the young man knowledge and discretion.

5 A wise man by hearing them will
    advance in learning,
an intelligent man will gain
    sound guidance,
6 That he may comprehend
    proverb and parable,
the words of the wise and
    their riddles.

7 The fear of the LORD is the
    beginning of knowledge;
wisdom and instruction fools
    despise.

The Path of the Wicked: Greed and Violence

8 Hear, my son, your father's
    instruction,
and reject not your mother's
    teaching;
9 A graceful diadem will they be
    for your head;
a torque for your neck.

10 My son, should sinners entice
    you,   11 and say,
"Come along with us!
Let us lie in wait for the honest
    man,
let us, unprovoked, set a trap
    for the innocent;
12 Let us swallow them up, as the
    nether world does, alive,
in the prime of life, like those
    who go down to the pit!
13 All kinds of precious wealth
    shall we gain,
we shall fill our houses with
    booty;
14 Cast in your lot with us,
    we shall all have one purse!"—

15 My son, walk not in the way
    with them,
hold back your foot from
    their path!
16 [For their feet run to evil,
    they hasten to shed blood.]

17 It is in vain that a net is spread
    before the eyes of any bird—
18 These men lie in wait for their
    own blood,
they set a trap for their own
    lives.
19 This is the fate of everyone
    greedy of loot:
unlawful gain takes away the
    life of him who acquires it.

Wisdom in Person Gives Warning

20 Wisdom cries aloud in the street,
    in the open squares she
    raises her voice;
21 Down the crowded ways she
    calls out,
at the city gates she utters her
    words:
22 "How long, you simple ones,
    will you love inanity,
23   how long will you turn away
    at my reproof?

1, 1–6: This prologue explains the purpose of the book: to educate the inexperienced in knowledge and right conduct, and to increase the learning of the wise man by proverbs, parables and riddles.
1, 2: *Discipline:* education or formation which dispels ignorance and corrects vice.
1, 4: *Simple:* immature and inexperienced, hence easily influenced for good or evil.

1, 7: *Fear of the Lord:* reverential fear and respect for God on account of his sovereignty, goodness and justice toward men. This is the foundation of religion.
1, 8–19: A warning against association with the greedy and the violent who seek to destroy the honest man and to steal his possessions (11–14). The trap which the wicked set for the innocent (11), in the end (19) takes away the life of the wicked themselves.

1, 17: Instructed by the wise man, the youth (of v 4) will recognize the invitation of the wicked (11–14) as a *net* spread before him, and he will thus, like the *bird*, be protected against falling into it.
1, 20–33: Wisdom is here personified; with divine authority she sets forth and proclaims the moral order, instructing and threatening (24–33) the multitudes in the streets and places of assembly.

Lo! I will pour out to you my
   spirit,
  I will acquaint you with my
    words.

24 "Because I called and you
    refused,
  I extended my hand and no
    one took notice;
25 Because you disdained all my
    counsel,
  and my reproof you ignored—
26 I, in my turn, will laugh at your
    doom;
  I will mock when terror
    overtakes you;
27 When terror comes upon you
    like a storm,
  and your doom approaches
    like a whirlwind;
  when distress and anguish
    befall you.

28 "Then they call me, but I
    answer not;
  they seek me, but find me not;
29 Because they hated knowledge,
  and chose not the fear of the
    LORD;
30 They ignored my counsel,
  they spurned all my reproof;
  And in their arrogance they
    preferred arrogance,
  and like fools they hated
    knowledge:

31 "Now they must eat the fruit of
    their own way,
  and with their own devices be
    glutted.
32 For the self-will of the simple
    kills them,
  the smugness of fools destroys
    them.
33 But he who obeys me dwells in
    security,
  in peace, without fear of
    harm."

The Blessings of Wisdom

2 My son, if you receive my words
   and treasure my commands,

2 Turning your ear to wisdom,
  inclining your heart to
   understanding;
3 Yes, if you call to intelligence,
  and to understanding raise
   your voice;
4 If you seek her like silver,
  and like hidden treasures
   search her out:
5 Then will you understand the
   fear of the LORD;
  the knowledge of God you
   will find;
6 For the LORD gives wisdom,
  from his mouth come
   knowledge and
   understanding;
7 He has counsel in store for the
   upright,
  he is the shield of those who
   walk honestly,
8 Guarding the paths of justice,
  protecting the way of his pious
   ones.

9 Then you will understand
   rectitude and justice,
  honesty, every good path;
10 For wisdom will enter your
   heart,
  knowledge will please your
   soul,
11 Discretion will watch over you,
  understanding will guard you;
12 Saving you from the way of evil
   men,
  from men of perverse speech,
13 Who leave the straight paths
  to walk in ways of darkness,
14 Who delight in doing evil,
  rejoice in perversity;
15 Whose ways are crooked,
  and devious their paths;

16 Saving you from the wife of
   another,
  from the adulteress with her
   smooth words,
17 Who forsakes the companions
   of her youth
  and forgets the pact with her
   God;

18 For her path sinks down to
   death,
  and her footsteps lead to the
   shades;
19 None who enter thereon come
   back again,
  or gain the paths of life.

20 Thus you may walk in the way
   of good men,
  and keep to the paths of the
   just.
21 For the upright will dwell in the
   land,
  the honest will remain in it;
22 But the wicked will be cut off
   from the land,
  the faithless will be rooted
   out of it.

Attitude toward the Lord

3 My son, forget not my teaching,
   keep in mind my commands;
2 For many days, and years of life,
  and peace, will they bring you.

3 Let not kindness and fidelity
   leave you;
  bind them around your neck;
4 Then will you win favor and
   good esteem
  before God and man.

5 Trust in the LORD with all your
   heart,
  on your own intelligence rely
   not;
6 In all your ways be mindful of
   him,
  and he will make straight
   your paths.

7 Be not wise in your own eyes,
  fear the LORD and turn away
   from evil;
8 This will mean health for your
   flesh
  and vigor for your bones.

9 Honor the LORD with your
   wealth,
  with first fruits of all your
   produce;

1, 28: Overtaken by doom, the foolish seek wisdom, but in vain because they do so too late. Cf Jn 7, 34; 8, 21.

1, 31: Sinners are punished by the bad fruits which their sins produce. Cf Wis 11, 16.

2—7: These chapters form an ordered discourse in seven "columns" of twenty-two verses each. Chapter 2 introduces the four topics about which the sage instructs his pupil: the service of God (3, 1–12.25–34), the search for wisdom (3, 13–24.35; 4, 1–9), the

avoidance of evil companions among men (4, 10–27; 5, 21–23), and among women (5, 1–20; 6, 20—7, 27). The last topic is treated at a length equal to the first three because the discourse is meant especially for youths (cf 1, 4).

2, 1–22: The search for wisdom (1–4) leads to the protection of God (5–8) and of wisdom herself (9ff; cf 1, 20–33) and to deliverance from evil men (12–15) and evil women (16–19), and so to lasting happiness (20ff).

2, 2f: *Wisdom, understanding, intelligence:* various names or aspects of the same gift.

3, 1–12: Many are the rewards for fidelity and trust in God, and for diffidence of self (1–8). Cf Dt 30, 20; Is 38, 19. The offering of material things for divine worship is blessed by an increase of such goods (9f). Even correction and chastisement are a mark of God's love and favor (11f).

10 Then will your barns be filled
      with grain,
   with new wine your vats will
      overflow.

11 The discipline of the LORD, my
      son, disdain not;
   spurn not his reproof;
12 For whom the LORD loves he
      reproves,
   and he chastises the son he
      favors.

The Value of Wisdom

13 Happy the man who finds
      wisdom,
   the man who gains
      understanding!
14 For her profit is better than
      profit in silver,
   and better than gold is her
      revenue;
15 She is more precious than corals,
   and none of your choice
      possessions can compare
      with her.

16 Long life is in her right hand,
   in her left are riches and
      honor;
17 Her ways are pleasant ways,
   and all her paths are peace;
18 She is a tree of life to those who
      grasp her,
   and he is happy who holds
      her fast.

19 The LORD by wisdom founded
      the earth,
   established the heavens by
      understanding;
20 By his knowledge the depths
      break open,
   and the clouds drop down
      dew.
21 My son, let not these slip out of
      your sight:
   keep advice and counsel in
      view;
22 So will they be life to your soul,
   and an adornment for your
      neck.

23 Then you may securely go your
      way;
   your foot will never stumble;
24 When you lie down, you need
      not be afraid,
   when you rest, your sleep will
      be sweet.
35 Honor is the possession of wise
      men,
   but fools inherit shame.

Attitude toward Fellow Men

25 Be not afraid of sudden terror,
   of the ruin of the wicked
      when it comes;
26 For the LORD will be your
      confidence,
   and will keep your foot from
      the snare.

27 Refuse no one the good on
      which he has a claim
   when it is in your power to do
      it for him.
28 Say not to your neighbor, "Go,
      and come again,
   tomorrow I will give," when
      you can give at once.

29 Plot no evil against your
      neighbor,
   against him who lives at peace
      with you.
30 Quarrel not with a man without
      cause,
   with one who has done you
      no harm.

31 Envy not the lawless man
   and choose none of his ways:
32 To the LORD the perverse man
      is an abomination,
   but with the upright is his
      friendship.

33 The curse of the LORD is on the
      house of the wicked,
   but the dwelling of the just
      he blesses;
34 When he is dealing with the
      arrogant, he is stern,
   but to the humble he shows
      kindness.

Wisdom: the Supreme Guide of Men

4 Hear, O children, a father's
      instruction,
   be attentive, that you may gain
      understanding!
2 Yes, excellent advice I give you;
   my teaching do not forsake.
3 When I was my father's child,
   frail, yet the darling of my
      mother,
4 He taught me, and said to me:
   "Let your heart hold fast my
      words:
   keep my commands, that you
      may live!
5 "Get wisdom, get understanding!
   Do not forget or turn aside
      from the words I utter.
6 Forsake her not, and she will
      preserve you;
   love her, and she will
      safeguard you;
7 The beginning of wisdom is: get
      wisdom;
   at the cost of all you have, get
      understanding.
8 Extol her, and she will exalt you;
   she will bring you honors if
      you embrace her;
9 She will put on your head a
      graceful diadem;
   a glorious crown will she
      bestow on you."

The Good and the Evil Way

10 Hear, my son, and receive my
      words,
   and the years of your life
      shall be many.
11 On the way of wisdom I direct
      you,
   I lead you on straightforward
      paths.
12 When you walk, your step will
      not be impeded,
   and should you run, you will
      not stumble.
13 Hold fast to instruction, never
      let her go;
   keep her, for she is your life.

3, 13–24: Wisdom, or understanding, is more valuable than silver and gold. Its fruit is long life, riches, honor and happiness (13–18). Even the creation of the universe and its adornment (Gn 1) were not done without wisdom (19f). It is the life of the soul and gives security in work and in repose (21–24).
3, 15: *Corals:* some precious stone may be intended.
3, 18: *A tree of life:* cf 11, 30; 13, 12; Gn 2, 9.

3, 20: For the Hebrews, *the depths* enclosed the great subterranean ocean; the rain and dew descended from the celestial ocean above the firmament; cf Gn 1, 6–10; Jb 26, 8.12; Pss 18, 16; 24, 2.
3, 25–34: Serving God with confidence in him (25f) requires serving one's neighbor through kindness (27f), peace with the good (29ff), no envy of the wicked (31), because the Lord's friendship and kindness are with the just; his curse is with the wicked.
3, 25: *The ruin of the wicked:* i.e., the ruin that

comes upon the wicked.
4, 1–9: The sage speaks as a father admonishing his children to secure wisdom at any cost.
4, 10–27: The way of wisdom leads directly to life (10–13); it is a light that grows brighter (18). The wise man is bound to shun (14–17) the dark and violent path of the wicked (19). Singleness of purpose and right conduct proceed from the heart of a wise man as from the source of life (23–26); they save him from destruction on evil paths (4, 27; 5, 21ff).

14 The path of the wicked enter
        not,
      walk not on the way of evil
        men;
15 Shun it, cross it not,
      turn aside from it, and pass on.
16 For they cannot rest unless they
        have done evil;
      to have made no one stumble
        steals away their sleep.
17 For they eat the bread of
        wickedness
      and drink the wine of violence.
19 The way of the wicked is like
        darkness;
      they know not on what they
        stumble.
18 But the path of the just is like
        shining light,
      that grows in brilliance till
        perfect day.

20 My son, to my words be
        attentive,
      to my sayings incline your ear;
21 Let them not slip out of your
        sight,
      keep them within your heart;
22 For they are life to those who
        find them,
      to man's whole being they are
        health.

23 With closest custody, guard your
        heart,
      for in it are the sources of life.
24 Put away from you dishonest
        talk,
      deceitful speech put far from
        you.
25 Let your eyes look straight
        ahead
      and your glance be directly
        forward.
26 Survey the path for your feet,
      and let all your ways be sure.
27 Turn neither to right nor to left,
      keep your foot far from evil.

Warning against Adultery

5 My son, to my wisdom be
        attentive,
      to my knowledge incline your
        ear,

2 That discretion may watch over
        you,
      and understanding may guard
        you.
3 The lips of an adulteress drip
        with honey,
      and her mouth is smoother
        than oil;
4 But in the end she is as bitter
        as wormwood,
      as sharp as a two-edged
        sword.
5 Her feet go down to death,
      to the nether world her steps
        attain;
6 Lest you see before you the road
        to life,
      her paths will ramble, you
        know not where.

7 So now, O children, listen to me,
      go not astray from the words
        of my mouth.
8 Keep your way far from her,
      approach not the door of her
        house,
9 Lest you give your honor to
        others,
      and your years to a merciless
        one;
10 Lest strangers have their fill of
        your wealth,
      your hard-won earnings go to
        an alien's house;
11 And you groan in the end,
      when your flesh and your body
        are consumed;
12 And you say, "Oh, why did I
        hate instruction,
      and my heart spurn reproof!
13 Why did I not listen to the
        voice of my teachers,
      nor to my instructors incline
        my ear!
14 I have all but come to utter
        ruin,
      condemned by the public
        assembly!"

15 Drink water from your own
        cistern,
      running water from your own
        well.

16 How may your water sources be
        dispersed abroad,
      streams of water in the streets?
17 Let your fountain be yours alone,
      not one shared with strangers;
18 And have joy of the wife of your
        youth,
19   your lovely hind, your graceful
        doe.
      Her love will invigorate you
        always,
      through her love you will
        flourish continually,
(6) 22 When you lie down she will
        watch over you,
      and when you wake, she will
        share your concerns;
      wherever you turn, she will
        guide you.
(5) 20 Why then, my son, should
        you go astray for another's
        wife
      and accept the embraces of an
        adulteress?

21 For each man's ways are plain to
        the LORD's sight;
      all their paths he surveys;
22 By his own iniquities the wicked
        man will be caught,
      in the meshes of his own sin
        he will be held fast;
23 He will die from lack of
        discipline,
      through the greatness of his
        folly he will be lost.

Miscellaneous Proverbs

6 My son, if you have become
        surety to your neighbor,
      given your hand in pledge to
        another,
2 You have been snared by the
        utterance of your lips,
      caught by the words of your
        mouth;
3 So do this, my son, to free
        yourself,
      since you have fallen into
        your neighbor's power:
      Go, hurry, stir up your neighbor!
4 Give no sleep to your eyes,
      nor slumber to your eyelids;

4, 18: *Till perfect day:* literally, "till the day is established"; this may refer to full daylight or to noonday.

5, 1-20: Understanding and discretion guard a man against the wiles of an adulteress, which lead astray and beget bitterness, bloodshed and death (1-6). They destroy honor, waste the years of life, despoil hard-earned wealth, consume the flesh, and

bring remorse in the end (7-14). Conjugal fidelity and love for one wife only bring happiness and security (15-20). Cf 6, 20—7, 27.

5, 9: *Honor:* the words "life" and "wealth" have also been read in this place. *A merciless one:* the offended husband; cf 6, 34f.

5, 19: *Lovely hind . . . graceful doe:* oriental symbols of feminine beauty and charm; cf Sg 2, 7.9.17.

5, 21-23: These verses are best read after 4, 27.

6, 1-19: These verses interrupt the discourse of chapters 2—7, which should be read apart from them; they contain four shorter proverbs akin to those in chapter 30.

6, 1: *Given your hand in pledge:* literally, "struck your hands"; this was probably the legal method for closing a contract.

5 Free yourself as a gazelle from
    the snare,
    or as a bird from the hand of
    the fowler.

6 Go to the ant, O sluggard,
    study her ways and learn
    wisdom;

7 For though she has no chief,
    no commander or ruler,

8 She procures her food in the
    summer,
    stores up her provisions in the
    harvest.

9 How long, O sluggard, will you
    rest?
    when will you rise from your
    sleep?

10 A little sleep, a little slumber,
    a little folding of the arms to
    rest—

11 Then will poverty come upon
    you like a highwayman,
    and want like an armed man.

12 A scoundrel, a villain, is he
    who deals in crooked talk.

13 He winks his eyes,
    shuffles his feet,
    makes signs with his fingers;

14 He has perversity in his heart,
    is always plotting evil,
    sows discord.

15 Therefore suddenly ruin comes
    upon him;
    in an instant he is crushed
    beyond cure.

16 There are six things the LORD
    hates,
    yes, seven are an abomination
    to him;

17 Haughty eyes, a lying tongue,
    and hands that shed innocent
    blood;

18 A heart that plots wicked
    schemes,
    feet that run swiftly to evil,

19 The false witness who utters lies,
    and he who sows discord
    among brothers.

Warning against Adultery

20 Observe, my son, your father's
    bidding,

and reject not your mother's
    teaching;

21 Keep them fastened over your
    heart always,
    put them around your neck;

23 For the bidding is a lamp, and
    the teaching a light,
    and a way to life are the
    reproofs of discipline;

24 To keep you from your
    neighbor's wife,
    from the smooth tongue of the
    adulteress.

25 Lust not in your heart after her
    beauty,
    let her not captivate you with
    her glance!

26 For the price of a loose woman
    may be scarcely a loaf of
    bread,
    But if she is married,
    she is a trap for your precious
    life.

27 Can a man take fire to his
    bosom,
    and his garments not be
    burned?

28 Or can a man walk on live coals,
    and his feet not be scorched?

29 So with him who goes in to his
    neighbor's wife—
    none who touches her shall go
    unpunished.

30 Men despise not the thief if he
    steals
    to satisfy his appetite when he
    is hungry;

31 Yet if he be caught he must pay
    back sevenfold;
    all the wealth of his house he
    may yield up.

32 But he who commits adultery is
    a fool;
    he who would destroy himself
    does it.

33 A degrading beating will he get,
    and his disgrace will not be
    wiped away;

34 For vindictive is the husband's
    wrath,
    he will have no pity on the
    day of vengeance;

35 He will not consider any
    restitution,
    nor be satisfied with the
    greatest gifts.

7 My son, keep my words,
    and treasure my commands.

2 Keep my commands and live,
    my teaching as the apple of
    your eye;

3 Bind them on your fingers,
    write them on the tablet of
    your heart.

4 Say to Wisdom, "You are my
    sister!"
    call Understanding, "Friend!"

5 That they may keep you from
    another's wife,
    from the adulteress with her
    smooth words.

6 For at the window of my house,
    through my lattice I looked
    out—

7 And I saw among the simple
    ones,
    I observed among the young
    men,
    a youth with no sense,

8 Going along the street near the
    corner,
    then walking in the direction
    of her house—

9 In the twilight, at dusk of day,
    at the time of the dark of
    night.

10 And lo! the woman comes to
    meet him,
    robed like a harlot, with
    secret designs—

11 She is fickle and unruly,
    in her home her feet cannot
    rest;

12 Now she is in the streets, now in
    the open squares,
    and at every corner she lurks
    in ambush—

13 When she seizes him, she
    kisses him,
    and with an impudent look
    says to him:

14 "I owed peace offerings,
    and today I have fulfilled my
    vows;

6, 10: This verse may be regarded as the sluggard's
reply or as a continuation of the remonstrance.
  6, 16–19: The seven vices symbolized for the most
part by bodily organs are pride, lying, murder,
intrigue, readiness to do evil, false witness, and the
stirring up of discord.
  6, 20—7, 27: Parental training and the love of

wisdom are an invaluable and constant help for the
young (6, 20–23; 7, 1–4). They are the best defense
against adultery (6, 24; 7, 5.24f), which involves the
guilty in many dangers and punishments (6, 26–35;
7, 6–26). Cf 5, 1–20).
  6, 26: Some interpret the verse in a progressive
sense, i.e., to satisfy the increasing demands of a

courtesan a man is reduced to poverty; if the woman
is married, even his very life is endangered.
  7, 14: "Peace offerings . . . vows": a portion of the
sacrifice reverted to the donor and had to be eaten
on the same day at a family festival (Lv 7, 11–15). In
this figure, the adulteress offers to share with the
foolish young man the deadly feast of her sensuality.

15 So I came out to meet you,
      to look for you, and I have
         found you!
16 With coverlets I have spread my
         couch,
      with brocaded cloths of
         Egyptian linen:
17 I have sprinkled my bed with
         myrrh,
      with aloes, and with
         cinnamon.

18 "Come, let us drink our fill of
         love,
      until morning, let us feast on
         love!
19 For my husband is not at home,
      he has gone on a long
         journey;
20 A bag of money he took with
         him,
      not till the full moon will he
         return home."

21 She wins him over by her
         repeated urging,
      with her smooth lips she leads
         him astray;
22 He follows her stupidly,
      like an ox that is led to
         slaughter;
   Like a stag that minces toward
         the net,
23   till an arrow pierces its liver;
   Like a bird that rushes into a
         snare,
      unaware that its life is at
         stake.

24 So now, O children, listen to me,
      be attentive to the words of
         my mouth!
25 Let not your heart turn to her
         ways,
      go not astray in her paths;
26 For many are those she has
         struck down dead,
      numerous, those she has slain.
27 Her house is made up of ways
         to the nether world,
      leading down into the
         chambers of death.

The Discourse of Wisdom

8 Does not Wisdom call,
      and Understanding raise her
         voice?
2 On the top of the heights along
         the road,
      at the crossroads she takes
         her stand;
3 By the gates at the approaches
         of the city,
      in the entryways she cries
         aloud:
4 "To you, O men, I call;
      my appeal is to the children
         of men.
5 You simple ones, gain resource,
      you fools, gain sense.

6 "Give heed! for noble things I
         speak;
      honesty opens my lips.
7 Yes, the truth my mouth
         recounts,
      but wickedness my lips abhor.
8 Sincere are all the words of my
         mouth,
      no one of them is wily or
         crooked;
9 All of them are plain to the
         man of intelligence,
      and right to those who attain
         knowledge.
10 Receive my instruction in
         preference to silver,
      and knowledge rather than
         choice gold.
11 [For Wisdom is better than
         corals,
      and no choice possessions can
         compare with her.]

12 "I, Wisdom, dwell with
         experience,
      and judicious knowledge I
         attain.
13 [The fear of the LORD is to hate
         evil;]
      Pride, arrogance, the evil way,
      and the perverse mouth I hate.
14 Mine are counsel and advice;
      Mine is strength; I am
         understanding.

15 By me kings reign,
      and lawgivers establish justice;
16 By me princes govern,
      and nobles; all the rulers of
         earth.

17 "Those who love me I also love,
      and those who seek me find
         me.
18 With me are riches and honor,
      enduring wealth and
         prosperity.
19 My fruit is better than gold, yes,
      than pure gold,
      and my revenue than choice
         silver.
20 On the way of duty I walk,
      along the paths of justice,
21 Granting wealth to those who
         love me,
      and filling their treasuries.

22 "The LORD begot me, the
         firstborn of his ways,
      the forerunner of his prodigies
         of long ago;
23 From of old I was poured forth,
      at the first, before the earth.
24 When there were no depths I
         was brought forth,
      when there were no fountains
         or springs of water;
25 Before the mountains were
         settled into place,
      before the hills, I was brought
         forth;
26 While as yet the earth and the
         fields were not made,
      nor the first clods of the world.

27 "When he established the
         heavens I was there,
      when he marked out the vault
         over the face of the deep;
28 When he made firm the skies
         above,
      when he fixed fast the
         foundations of the earth;
29 When he set for the sea its limit,
      so that the waters should not
         transgress his command;

8, 1–36: Wisdom is here personified as in 1, 20–33, to confirm the words of the teacher of wisdom. She exalts her grandeur and origin, and invites all (1–11) to be attentive to her salutary influence in human society (12–21), for she was privileged to be present at the creation of the world (22–31). Finally, she promises life and the favor of God to those who find her, death to those who despise her.

8, 5: *Simple ones . . . fools:* see note on 1, 4.

8, 7f: The truth and sincerity of wisdom are

absolute because they are divine. They can neither deceive nor tolerate deception. An intelligent man understands and accepts them.

8, 14: What is here predicated of wisdom is elsewhere attributed to God (Jb 12, 13–16).

8, 22–31: Wisdom is of divine origin. It is here represented as a being which existed before all things (22–26) and concurred with God when he planned and executed the creation of the universe, adorned it with beauty and variety, and established its wonderful

order (27–30). Here that plurality of divine Persons is foreshadowed which was afterward to be fully revealed when Wisdom in the Person of Jesus Christ became incarnate.

8, 23: *Poured forth:* the exact meaning of the Hebrew is uncertain; the expression must imply the equivalent of "born." The Hebrews liken the movement of air and of spirit to that of liquids.

8, 24–26: The formless mass from which God created the heavens and the earth; cf Gn 1, 1f; 2, 4ff.

30 Then was I beside him as his
    craftsman,
    and I was his delight day by
      day,
    Playing before him all the while,
31   playing on the surface of his
      earth;
    and I found delight in the
      sons of men.
32 "So now, O children, listen to
    me;
33   instruction and wisdom do not
    reject!
    Happy the man who obeys me,
    and happy those who keep
      my ways,
34 Happy the man watching daily
    at my gates,
    waiting at my doorposts;
35 For he who finds me finds life,
    and wins favor from the
      LORD;
36 But he who misses me harms
    himself;
    all who hate me love death."

The Two Banquets

9 Wisdom has built her house,
    she has set up her seven
      columns;
2 She has dressed her meat, mixed
    her wine,
    yes, she has spread her table.
3 She has sent out her maidens;
    she calls
    from the heights out over the
      city:
4 "Let whoever is simple turn in
    here;
    to him who lacks under-
      standing, I say,
5 Come, eat of my food,
    and drink of the wine I have
      mixed!
6 Forsake foolishness that you
    may live;
    advance in the way of
      understanding.
11 For by me your days will be
    multiplied
    and the years of your life
      increased."

7 He who corrects an arrogant
    man earns insult;
    and he who reproves a wicked
      man incurs opprobrium.
8 Reprove not an arrogant man,
    lest he hate you;
    reprove a wise man, and he
      will love you.
9 Instruct a wise man, and he
    becomes still wiser;
    teach a just man, and he
      advances in learning.

10 The beginning of wisdom is the
    fear of the LORD,
    and knowledge of the Holy
      One is understanding.
12 If you are wise, it is to your own
    advantage;
    and if you are arrogant, you
      alone shall bear it.

13 The woman Folly is fickle,
    she is inane, and knows
      nothing.
14 She sits at the door of her
    house
    upon a seat on the city heights,
15 Calling to passers-by
    as they go on their straight
      way:
16 "Let whoever is simple turn in
    here,
    or who lacks understanding;
    for to him I say,
17 Stolen water is sweet,
    and bread gotten secretly is
      pleasing!"
18 Little he knows that the shades
    are there,
    that in the depths of the nether
      world are her guests!

FIRST COLLECTION OF THE PROVERBS OF SOLOMON

10 The proverbs of Solomon:

A wise son makes his father
    glad,
    but a foolish son is a grief to
      his mother.

2 Ill-gotten treasures profit
    nothing,
    but virtue saves from death.
3 The LORD permits not the just to
    hunger,
    but the craving of the wicked
      he thwarts.
4 The slack hand impoverishes,
    but the hand of the diligent
      enriches.
5 A son who fills the granaries in
    summer is a credit;
    a son who slumbers during
      harvest, a disgrace.
6 Blessings are for the head of the
    just,
    but a rod for the back of the
      fool.
7 The memory of the just will be
    blessed,
    but the name of the wicked
      will rot.
8 A wise man heeds commands,
    but a prating fool will be
      overthrown.
9 He who walks honestly walks
    securely,
    but he whose ways are crooked
      will fare badly.
10 He who winks at a fault causes
    trouble,
    but he who frankly reproves
      promotes peace.
11 A fountain of life is the mouth
    of the just,
    but the mouth of the wicked
      conceals violence.
12 Hatred stirs up disputes,
    but love covers all offenses.
13 On the lips of the intelligent is
    found wisdom,
    [but the mouth of the wicked
      conceals violence].
14 Wise men store up knowledge,
    but the mouth of a fool is
      imminent ruin.

8, 30: *His craftsman:* furnishing God with the plan, as it were, for the creation of all things; cf. Jb 38, 1f; Wis 7, 22–8, 1. *I was his delight:* the ever-present object of God's complacency.

9, 1–6.13–18: Wisdom and folly are represented as matrons, each inviting people to her banquet. Wisdom offers the food and drink of divine doctrine and virtue which give life (1–6). Unstable and senseless folly furnishes the stolen bread and water of deceit and

vice which bring death to her guests.

9, 3: *She calls:* i.e., indirectly, through her maidens; but the text could also mean that wisdom herself publicly proclaims her invitation.

9, 17: The secrecy implies wrongdoing.

9, 18: The banquet chamber of folly is a tomb from which no one who enters it is released.

10, 1—22, 16: The varied contents of this first collection of Solomon's proverbs apply mostly to

individual life. Each of its three hundred and seventy-five proverbs is meant to be distinct from the others, developing one idea through contrasting parallelism in chapters 10—15, and a climactic treatment in 16—22.

10, 12: *Love covers all offenses:* a favorite maxim of the Apostles; cf 1 Cor 13, 7; Jas 5, 20; 1 Pt 4, 8; also Prv 17, 9.

15 The rich man's wealth is his
   strong city;
   the ruination of the lowly is
   their poverty.

16 The just man's recompense leads
   to life,
   the gains of the wicked, to sin.

17 A path to life is his who heeds
   admonition,
   but he who disregards reproof
   goes astray.

18 It is the lips of the liar that
   conceal hostility;
   but he who spreads
   accusations is a fool.

19 Where words are many, sin is not
   wanting;
   but he who restrains his lips
   does well.

20 Like choice silver is the just
   man's tongue;
   the heart of the wicked is of
   little worth.

21 The just man's lips nourish
   many,
   but fools die for want of
   sense.

22 It is the LORD's blessing that
   brings wealth,
   and no effort can substitute
   for it.

23 Crime is the entertainment of
   the fool;
   so is wisdom for the man of
   sense.

24 What the wicked man fears will
   befall him,
   but the desire of the just will
   be granted.

25 When the tempest passes, the
   wicked man is no more;
   but the just man is established
   forever.

26 As vinegar to the teeth, and
   smoke to the eyes,
   is the sluggard to those who
   use him as a messenger.

27 The fear of the LORD prolongs
   life,
   but the years of the wicked
   are brief.

28 The hope of the just brings
   them joy,
   but the expectation of the
   wicked comes to nought.

29 The LORD is a stronghold to him
   who walks honestly,
   but to evildoers, their
   downfall.

30 The just man will never be
   disturbed,
   but the wicked will not abide
   in the land.

31 The mouth of the just yields
   wisdom,
   but the perverse tongue will
   be cut off.

32 The lips of the just know how to
   please,
   but the mouth of the wicked,
   how to pervert.

11 False scales are an
   abomination to the
   LORD,
   but a full weight is his
   delight.

2 When pride comes, disgrace
   comes;
   but with the humble is wisdom.

3 The honesty of the upright
   guides them;
   the faithless are ruined by
   their duplicity.

4 Wealth is useless on the day of
   wrath,
   but virtue saves from death.

5 The honest man's virtue makes
   his way straight,
   but by his wickedness the
   wicked man falls.

6 The virtue of the upright saves
   them,
   but the faithless are caught in
   their own intrigue.

7 When a wicked man dies his
   hope perishes,
   and what is expected from
   strength comes to nought.

8 The just man escapes trouble,
   and the wicked man falls into
   it in his stead.

9 With his mouth the impious man
   would ruin his neighbor,
   but through their knowledge
   the just make their escape.

10 When the just prosper, the city
   rejoices;
   and when the wicked perish,
   there is jubilation.

11 Through the blessing of the
   righteous the city is exalted,
   but through the mouth of the
   wicked it is overthrown.

12 He who reviles his neighbor has
   no sense,
   but the intelligent man keeps
   silent.

13 A newsmonger reveals secrets,
   but a trustworthy man keeps
   a confidence.

14 For lack of guidance a people
   falls;
   security lies in many
   counselors.

15 He is in a bad way who becomes
   surety for another,
   but he who hates giving
   pledges is safe.

16 A gracious woman wins esteem,
   but she who hates virtue is
   covered with shame.

   [The slothful become
   impoverished,
   but the diligent gain wealth.]

17 A kindly man benefits himself,
   but a merciless man harms
   himself.

18 The wicked man makes empty
   profits,
   but he who sows virtue has a
   sure reward.

19 Virtue directs toward life,
   but he who pursues evil does
   so to his death.

20 The depraved in heart are an
   abomination to the LORD,
   but those who walk
   blamelessly are his delight.

21 Truly the evil man shall not go
   unpunished,
   but those who are just shall
   escape.

10, 15: The inspired author reflects upon the reality
of the power of money and the defeat of poverty,
without approving these things.

10, 22: The blessing of God rather than our own
industry crowns our efforts with success; cf Ps 127,
1f; Mt 6, 25–34.

11, 4: *Wealth . . . death:* not what a man is worth
but what he is, counts before God.

22 Like a golden ring in a swine's
     snout
        is a beautiful woman with a
        rebellious disposition.

23 The desire of the just ends only
     in good;
        the expectation of the wicked
        is wrath.

24 One man is lavish yet grows
     still richer;
        another is too sparing, yet
        is the poorer.

25 He who confers benefits will be
     amply enriched,
        and he who refreshes others
        will himself be refreshed.

26 Him who monopolizes grain, the
     people curse—
        but blessings upon the head of
        him who distributes it!

27 He who seeks the good
     commands favor,
        but he who pursues evil will
        have evil befall him.

28 He who trusts in his riches will
     fall,
        but like green leaves the just
        flourish.

29 He who upsets his household
     has empty air for a heritage;
        and the fool will become slave
        to the wise man.

30 The fruit of virtue is a tree of
     life,
        but violence takes lives away.

31 If the just man is punished on
     earth,
        how much more the wicked
        and the sinner!

12 He who loves correction
        loves knowledge,
     but he who hates reproof
        is stupid.

2 The good man wins favor from
     the LORD,
        but the schemer is condemned
        by him.

3 No man is built up by
     wickedness,
        but the root of the just will
        never be disturbed.

12, 14: Cf Mt 7, 17; Gal 6, 8.

4 A worthy wife is the crown of
     her husband,
        but a disgraceful one is like
        rot in his bones.

5 The plans of the just are
     legitimate;
        the designs of the wicked are
        deceitful.

6 The words of the wicked are a
     deadly ambush,
        but the speech of the upright
        saves them.

7 The wicked are overthrown and
     are no more,
        but the house of the just
        stands firm.

8 According to his good sense a
     man is praised,
        but one with a warped mind
        is despised.

9 Better a lowly man who supports
     himself
        than one of assumed
        importance who lacks bread.

10 The just man takes care of his
     beast,
        but the heart of the wicked is
        merciless.

11 He who tills his own land has
     food in plenty,
        but he who follows idle
        pursuits is a fool.

12 The stronghold of evil men will
     be demolished,
        but the root of the just is
        enduring.

13 In the sin of his lips the evil
     man is ensnared,
        but the just comes free of
        trouble.

14 From the fruit of his words a
     man has his fill of good
     things,
        and the work of his hands
        comes back to reward him.

15 The way of the fool seems right
     in his own eyes,
        but he who listens to advice
        is wise.

16 The fool immediately shows his
     anger,
        but the shrewd man passes
        over an insult.

17 He tells the truth who states
     what he is sure of,
        but a lying witness speaks
        deceitfully.

18 The prating of some men is like
     sword thrusts,
        but the tongue of the wise is
        healing.

19 Truthful lips endure forever,
        the lying tongue, for only a
        moment.

20 Deceit is in the hands of those
     who plot evil,
        but those who counsel peace
        have joy.

21 No harm befalls the just,
        but the wicked are
        overwhelmed with
        misfortune.

22 Lying lips are an abomination
     to the LORD,
        but those who are truthful
        are his delight.

23 A shrewd man conceals his
     knowledge,
        but the hearts of fools gush
        forth folly.

24 The diligent hand will govern,
        but the slothful will be
        enslaved.

25 Anxiety in a man's heart
     depresses it,
        but a kindly word makes it
        glad.

26 The just man surpasses his
     neighbor,
        but the way of the wicked
        leads them astray.

27 The slothful man catches not his
     prey.
        but the wealth of the diligent
        man is great.

28 In the path of justice there is
     life,
        but the abominable way leads
        to death.

13 A wise son loves correction,
        but the senseless one heeds
        no rebuke.

2 From the fruit of his words a
     man eats good things,
        but the treacherous one
        craves violence.

3 He who guards his mouth
  protects his life;
   to open wide one's lips brings
   downfall.

4 The soul of the sluggard craves
  in vain,
   but the diligent soul is amply
   satisfied.

5 Anything deceitful the just man
  hates,
   but the wicked brings shame
   and disgrace.

6 Virtue guards one who walks
  honestly,
   but the downfall of the
   wicked is sin.

7 One man pretends to be rich,
  yet has nothing;
   another pretends to be poor,
   yet has great wealth.

8 A man's riches serve as ransom
  for his life,
   but the poor man heeds no
   rebuke.

9 The light of the just shines
  gaily,
   but the lamp of the wicked
   goes out.

10 The stupid man sows discord
   by his insolence,
    but with those who take
    counsel is wisdom.

11 Wealth quickly gotten dwindles
   away,
    but amassed little by little, it
    grows.

12 Hope deferred makes the heart
   sick,
    but a wish fulfilled is a tree of
    life.

13 He who despises the word must
   pay for it,
    but he who reveres the
    commandment will be
    rewarded.

14 The teaching of the wise is a
   fountain of life,
    that a man may avoid the
    snares of death.

15 Good sense brings favor,
    but the way of the faithless is
    their ruin.

16 The shrewd man does everything
   with prudence,
    but the fool peddles folly.

17 A wicked messenger brings on
   disaster,
    but a trustworthy envoy is a
    healing remedy.

18 Poverty and shame befall the
   man who disregards
   correction,
    but he who heeds reproof is
    honored.

19 Lust indulged starves the soul,
    but fools hate to turn from
    evil.

20 Walk with wise men and you
   will become wise,
    but the companion of fools
    will fare badly.

21 Misfortune pursues sinners,
    but the just shall be
    recompensed with good.

22 The good man leaves an
   inheritance to his children's
   children,
    but the wealth of the sinner
    is stored up for the just.

23 A lawsuit devours the tillage of
   the poor,
    but some men perish for lack
    of a law court.

24 He who spares his rod hates his
   son,
    but he who loves him takes
    care to chastise him.

25 When the just man eats, his
   hunger is appeased;
    but the belly of the wicked
    suffers want.

14 Wisdom builds her house,
   but Folly tears hers down
   with her own hands.

2 He who walks uprightly fears the
  LORD,
   but he who is devious in his
   ways spurns him.

3 In the mouth of the fool is a
  rod for his back,
   but the lips of the wise
   preserve them.

4 When there are no oxen, the
  crib remains empty;
   but large crops come through
   the strength of the bull.

5 A truthful witness does not lie,
   but a false witness utters lies.

6 The senseless man seeks in vain
  for wisdom,
   but knowledge is easy to the
   man of intelligence.

7 To avoid the foolish man, take
  steps!
   But knowing lips one meets
   with by surprise.

8 The shrewd man's wisdom gives
  him knowledge of his way,
   but the folly of fools is their
   deception.

9 Guilt lodges in the tents of the
  arrogant,
   but favor in the house of the
   just.

10 The heart knows its own
   bitterness,
    and in its joy no one else
    shares.

11 The house of the wicked will be
   destroyed,
    but the tent of the upright
    will flourish.

12 Sometimes a way seems right to
   a man,
    but the end of it leads to death!

13 Even in laughter the heart may
   be sad,
    and the end of joy may be
    sorrow.

14 The scoundrel suffers the
   consequences of his ways,
    and the good man reaps the
    fruits of his paths.

15 The simpleton believes
   everything,
    but the shrewd man measures
    his steps.

16 The wise man is cautious and
   shuns evil;
    the fool is reckless and sure of
    himself.

17 The quick-tempered man makes
   a fool of himself,
    but the prudent man is at
    peace.

13, 9: *Light . . . lamp:* symbols of life and prosperity; cf 4, 18f.
13, 13: *Word:* advice, or God's law.

18 The adornment of simpletons is
   folly,
      but shrewd men gain the
      crown of knowledge.

19 Evil men must bow down
   before the good,
      and the wicked, at the gates of
      the just.

20 Even by his neighbor the poor
   man is hated,
      but the friends of the rich
      are many.

21 He sins who despises the
   hungry;
      but happy is he who is kind
      to the poor!

22 Do not those who plot evil go
   astray?
      But those intent on good gain
      kindness and constancy.

23 In all labor there is profit,
      but mere talk tends only to
      penury.

24 The crown of the wise is
   resourcefulness;
      the diadem of fools is folly.

25 The truthful witness saves lives,
      but he who utters lies is a
      betrayer.

26 In the fear of the LORD is a
   strong defense;
      even for one's children he will
      be a refuge.

27 The fear of the LORD is a
   fountain of life,
      that a man may avoid the
      snares of death.

28 In many subjects lies the glory
   of the king;
      but if his people are few, it is
      the prince's ruin.

29 The patient man shows much
   good sense,
      but the quick-tempered man
      displays folly at its height.

30 A tranquil mind gives life to the
   body,
      but jealousy rots the bones.

31 He who oppresses the poor
   blasphemes his Maker,
      but he who is kind to the
      needy glorifies him.

32 The wicked man is overthrown
   by his wickedness,
      but the just man finds a
      refuge in his honesty.

33 In the heart of the intelligent
   wisdom abides,
      but in the bosom of fools it is
      unknown.

34 Virtue exalts a nation,
      but sin is a people's disgrace.

35 The king favors the intelligent
   servant,
      but the worthless one incurs
      his wrath.

15 A mild answer calms wrath,
      but a harsh word stirs up
      anger.

2 The tongue of the wise pours
   out knowledge,
      but the mouth of fools spurts
      forth folly.

3 The eyes of the LORD are in
   every place,
      keeping watch on the evil and
      the good.

4 A soothing tongue is a tree of
   life,
      but a perverse one crushes the
      spirit.

5 The fool spurns his father's
   admonition,
      but prudent is he who heeds
      reproof.

6 In the house of the just there
   are ample resources,
      but the earnings of the wicked
      are in turmoil.

7 The lips of the wise disseminate
   knowledge,
      but the heart of fools is
      perverted.

8 The sacrifice of the wicked is an
   abomination to the LORD,
      but the prayer of the upright
      is his delight.

9 The way of the wicked is an
   abomination to the LORD,
      but he loves the man who
      pursues virtue.

10 Severe punishment is in store for
   the man who goes astray;
      he who hates reproof will die.

11 The nether world and the abyss
   lie open before the LORD;
      how much more the hearts of
      men!

12 The senseless man loves not to
   be reproved;
      to wise men he will not go.

13 A glad heart lights up the face,
      but by mental anguish the
      spirit is broken.

14 The mind of the intelligent
   man seeks knowledge,
      but the mouth of fools feeds
      on folly.

15 Every day is miserable for the
   depressed,
      but a lighthearted man has a
      continual feast.

16 Better a little with fear of the
   LORD
      than a great fortune with
      anxiety.

17 Better a dish of herbs where
   love is
      than a fatted ox and hatred
      with it.

18 An ill-tempered man stirs up
   strife,
      but a patient man allays
      discord.

19 The way of the sluggard is
   hemmed in as with thorns,
      but the path of the diligent
      is a highway.

20 A wise son makes his father
   glad,
      but a fool of a man despises
      his mother.

21 Folly is joy to the senseless man,
      but the man of understanding
      goes the straight way.

15, 11: *Nether world . . . abyss:* the abode of the
dead, signifying the profound obscurity which is open
nevertheless to the sight and power of God.
   15, 16f: Not the amount of temporal goods but the
virtue of their possessor makes them a source of
happiness.

22 Plans fail when there is no
    counsel,
    but they succeed when
    counselors are many.

23 There is joy for a man in his
    utterance;
    a word in season, how good
    it is!

24 The path of life leads the
    prudent man upward,
    that he may avoid the nether
    world below.

25 The LORD overturns the house
    of the proud,
    but he preserves intact the
    widow's landmark.

26 The wicked man's schemes are
    an abomination to the
    LORD,
    but the pure speak what is
    pleasing to him.

27 He who is greedy of gain brings
    ruin on his own house,
    but he who hates bribes will
    live.

28 The just man weighs well his
    utterance,
    but the mouth of the wicked
    pours out evil.

29 The LORD is far from the
    wicked,
    but the prayer of the just he
    hears.

30 A cheerful glance brings joy to
    the heart;
    good news invigorates the
    bones.

31 He who listens to salutary
    reproof
    will abide among the wise.

32 He who rejects admonition
    despises his own soul,
    but he who heeds reproof
    gains understanding.

33 The fear of the LORD is training
    for wisdom,
    and humility goes before
    honors.

16 Man may make plans in his
    heart,
    but what the tongue utters
    is from the LORD.

2 All the ways of a man may be
    pure in his own eyes,
    but it is the LORD who proves
    the spirit.

3 Entrust your works to the LORD,
    and your plans will succeed.

4 The LORD has made everything
    for his own ends,
    even the wicked for the evil
    day.

5 Every proud man is an
    abomination to the LORD;
    I assure you that he will not
    go unpunished.

6 By kindness and piety guilt is
    expiated,
    and by the fear of the LORD
    man avoids evil.

7 When the LORD is pleased with
    a man's ways,
    he makes even his enemies be
    at peace with him.

8 Better a little with virtue,
    than a large income with
    injustice.

9 In his mind a man plans his
    course,
    but the LORD directs his steps.

10 The king's lips are an oracle;
    no judgment he pronounces
    is false.

11 Balance and scales belong to
    the LORD;
    all the weights used with
    them are his concern.

12 Kings have a horror of
    wrongdoing,
    for by righteousness the
    throne endures.

13 The king takes delight in honest
    lips,
    and the man who speaks
    what is right he loves.

14 The king's wrath is like
    messengers of death,
    but a wise man can pacify it.

15 In the light of the king's
    countenance is life,
    and his favor is like a rain
    cloud in spring.

16 How much better to acquire
    wisdom than gold?
    To acquire understanding is
    more desirable than silver.

17 The path of the upright avoids
    misfortune;
    he who pays attention to his
    way safeguards his life.

18 Pride goes before disaster,
    and a haughty spirit before a
    fall.

19 It is better to be humble with
    the meek
    than to share plunder with the
    proud.

20 He who plans a thing will be
    successful;
    happy is he who trusts in the
    LORD!

21 The wise man is esteemed for his
    discernment,
    yet pleasing speech increases
    his persuasiveness.

22 Good sense is a fountain of life
    to its possessor,
    but folly brings chastisement
    on fools.

23 The mind of the wise man makes
    him eloquent,
    and augments the
    persuasiveness of his lips.

24 Pleasing words are a honeycomb,
    sweet to the taste and healthful
    to the body.

25 Sometimes a way seems right to
    a man,
    but the end of it leads to
    death!

26 The laborer's appetite labors for
    him,
    for his mouth urges him on.

27 A scoundrel is a furnace of evil,
    and on his lips there is a
    scorching fire.

16, 1: Words, like actions, often produce results
different from those which were planned.

16, 4: Even the wicked, in their punishment,
cannot escape glorifying God's justice.

16, 10: Decisions of supreme judicial authority
were presumed disinterested and correct.

28 An intriguer sows discord,
and a talebearer separates
bosom friends.

29 A lawless man allures his
neighbor,
and leads him into a way that
is not good.

30 He who winks his eye is plotting
trickery;
he who compresses his lips
has mischief ready.

31 Gray hair is a crown of glory;
it is gained by virtuous living.

32 A patient man is better than a
warrior,
and he who rules his temper,
than he who takes a city.

33 When the lot is cast into the lap,
its decision depends entirely
on the LORD.

17 Better a dry crust with peace
than a house full of feasting
with strife.

2 An intelligent servant will rule
over a worthless son,
and will share the inheritance
with the brothers.

3 The crucible for silver, and the
furnace for gold,
but the tester of hearts is the
LORD.

4 The evil man gives heed to
wicked lips,
and listens to falsehood from
a mischievous tongue.

5 He who mocks the poor
blasphemes his Maker;
he who is glad at calamity
will not go unpunished.

6 Grandchildren are the crown of
old men,
and the glory of children is
their parentage.

7 Fine words are out of place in
a fool;
how much more, lying words
in a noble!

8 A man who has a bribe to offer
rates it a magic stone;
at every turn it brings him
success.

9 He who covers up a misdeed
fosters friendship,
but he who gossips about it
separates friends.

10 A single reprimand does more
for a man of intelligence
than a hundred lashes for a
fool.

11 On rebellion alone is the wicked
man bent,
but a merciless messenger will
be sent against him.

12 Face a bear robbed of her cubs,
but never a fool in his folly!

13 If a man returns evil for good,
from his house evil will not
depart.

14 The start of strife is like the
opening of a dam;
therefore, check a quarrel
before it begins!

15 He who condones the wicked,
he who condemns the just,
are both an abomination to
the LORD.

16 Of what use in the fool's hand
are the means
to buy wisdom, since he has
no mind for it?

17 He who is a friend is always a
friend,
and a brother is born for the
time of stress.

18 Senseless is the man who gives
his hand in pledge,
who becomes surety for his
neighbor.

19 He who loves strife loves guilt;
he who builds his gate high
courts disaster.

20 He who is perverse in heart finds
no good,
and a double-tongued man
falls into trouble.

21 To be a fool's parent is grief for
a man;
the father of a numskull has
no joy.

22 A joyful heart is the health of
the body,
but a depressed spirit dries
up the bones.

23 The wicked man accepts a
concealed bribe
to pervert the course of justice.

24 The man of intelligence fixes his
gaze on wisdom,
but the eyes of a fool are on
the ends of the earth.

25 A foolish son is vexation to his
father,
and bitter sorrow to her who
bore him.

26 It is wrong to fine an
innocent man,
but beyond reason to scourge
princes.

27 He who spares his words is
truly wise,
and he who is chary of speech
is a man of intelligence.

28 Even a fool, if he keeps silent,
is considered wise:
if he closes his lips, intelligent.

18 In estrangement one seeks
pretexts:
with all persistence he picks
a quarrel.

2 The fool takes no delight in
understanding,
but rather in displaying what
he thinks.

3 With wickedness comes
contempt,
and with disgrace comes
scorn.

4 The words from a man's mouth
are deep waters,
but the source of wisdom is a
flowing brook.

5 It is not good to be partial to
the guilty,
and so to reject a rightful
claim.

16, 33: The favorable or unfavorable result of chance depends on God. Deciding strifes and doubts by lot was practiced by the ancient Hebrews; cf Ex

28, 15–30; Lv 16, 8; Jos 7, 14; 1 Sm 10, 20f.
17, 2: Intelligence and ability are esteemed more highly than nobility of blood.

17, 4: To justify his own evil ways, a wicked man judges evil of others. Cf Mt 7, 1–5.
17, 19: *Builds . . . high:* a symbol of arrogance.

6 The fool's lips lead him into
strife,
and his mouth provokes a
beating.

7 The fool's mouth is his ruin;
his lips are a snare to his life.

8 The words of a talebearer are
like dainty morsels
that sink into one's inmost
being.

9 The man who is slack in his
work
is own brother to the man
who is destructive.

10 The name of the LORD is a
strong tower;
the just man runs to it and is
safe.

11 The rich man's wealth is his
strong city;
he fancies it a high wall.

12 Before his downfall a man's
heart is haughty,
but humility goes before
honors.

13 He who answers before he
hears—
his is the folly and the shame.

14 A man's spirit sustains him in
infirmity—
but a broken spirit who can
bear?

15 The mind of the intelligent gains
knowledge,
and the ear of the wise seeks
knowledge.

16 A man's gift clears the way for
him,
and gains him access to great
men.

17 The man who pleads his case
first seems to be in the
right;
then his opponent comes and
puts him to the test.

18 The lot puts an end to disputes,
and is decisive in a controversy
between the mighty.

19 A brother is a better defense
than a strong city,
and a friend is like the bars
of a castle.

20 From the fruit of his mouth a
man has his fill;
with the yield of his lips he
sates himself.

21 Death and life are in the power
of the tongue;
those who make it a friend
shall eat its fruit.

22 He who finds a wife finds
happiness;
it is a favor he receives from
the LORD.

23 The poor man implores,
but the rich man answers
harshly.

24 Some friends bring ruin on us,
but a true friend is more
loyal than a brother.

19 Better a poor man who walks
in his integrity
than he who is crooked in
his ways and rich.

2 Without knowledge even zeal is
not good;
and he who acts hastily,
blunders.

3 A man's own folly upsets his
way,
but his heart is resentful
against the LORD.

4 Wealth adds many friends,
but the friend of the poor
man deserts him.

5 The false witness will not go
unpunished,
and he who utters lies will not
escape.

6 Many curry favor with a noble;
all are friends of the man who
has something to give.

7 All the poor man's brothers
hate him;
how much more do his
friends shun him!

8 He who gains intelligence is his
own best friend;
he who keeps understanding
will be successful.

9 The false witness will not go
unpunished,
and he who utters lies will
perish.

10 Luxury is not befitting a fool;
much less should a slave rule
over princes.

11 It is good sense in a man to be
slow to anger,
and it is his glory to overlook
an offense.

12 The king's wrath is like the
roaring of a lion,
but his favor, like dew on the
grass.

13 The foolish son is ruin to his
father,
and the nagging of a wife is a
persistent leak.

14 Home and possessions are an
inheritance from parents,
but a prudent wife is from the
LORD.

15 Laziness plunges a man into
deep sleep,
and the sluggard must go
hungry.

16 He who keeps the precept keeps
his life,
but the despiser of the word
will die.

17 He who has compassion on the
poor lends to the LORD,
and he will repay him for his
good deed.

18 Chastise your son, for in this
there is hope;
but do not desire his death.

19 The man of violent temper pays
the penalty;
even if you rescue him, you
will have it to do again.

20 Listen to counsel and receive
instruction,
that you may eventually
become wise.

18, 10f: Religion is a strong support and sure
refuge in the struggle of life. The rich foolishly rely
on their wealth for such support.

18, 12: Compare the Savior's words: "Whoever
exalts himself shall be humbled, but whoever
humbles himself shall be exalted" (Mt 23, 12).

18, 13: To speak without first listening is characteristic of a fool; cf 10, 14; Sir 11, 8.

18, 18: See note on 16, 33.

18, 20f: Everyone must accept the consequences,
of benefit or harm to himself, which his words produce.

19, 17: Cf Mt 25, 34–40.

21 Many are the plans in a man's
heart,
but it is the decision of the
LORD that endures.

22 From a man's greed comes his
shame;
rather be a poor man than a
liar.

23 The fear of the LORD is an aid
to life;
one eats and sleeps without
being visited by misfortune.

24 The sluggard loses his hand in
the dish;
he will not even lift it to his
mouth.

25 If you beat an arrogant man,
the simple learn a lesson;
if you rebuke an intelligent
man, he gains knowledge.

26 He who mistreats his father, or
drives away his mother,
is a worthless and disgraceful
son.

27 If a son ceases to hear
instruction,
he wanders from words of
knowledge.

28 An unprincipled witness
perverts justice,
and the mouth of the wicked
pours out iniquity.

29 Rods are prepared for the
arrogant,
and blows for the backs of
fools.

20 Wine is arrogant, strong
drink is riotous;
none who goes astray for
it is wise.

2 The dread of the king is as when
a lion roars;
he who incurs his anger
forfeits his life.

3 It is honorable for a man to
shun strife,
while every fool starts a
quarrel.

4 In seedtime the sluggard plows
not;
when he looks for the harvest,
it is not there.

5 The intention in the human
heart is like water far below
the surface,
but the man of intelligence
draws it forth.

6 Many are declared to be men
of virtue:
but who can find one worthy
of trust?

7 When a man walks in integrity
and justice,
happy are his children after
him!

8 A king seated on the throne of
judgment
dispels all evil with his glance.

9 Who can say, "I have made my
heart clean,
I am cleansed of my sin"?

10 Varying weights, varying
measures,
are both an abomination to
the LORD.

11 Even by his manners the child
betrays
whether his conduct is
innocent and right.

12 The ear that hears, and the eye
that sees—
the LORD has made them
both.

13 Love not sleep, lest you be
reduced to poverty;
eyes wide open mean abundant
food.

14 "Bad, bad!" says the buyer;
but once he has gone his
way, he boasts.

15 Like gold or a wealth of corals,
wise lips are a precious
ornament.

16 Take his garment who becomes
surety for another,
and for strangers yield it up!

17 The bread of deceit is sweet to a
man,
but afterward his mouth will
be filled with gravel.

18 Plans made after advice succeed;
so with wise guidance wage
your war.

19 A newsmonger reveals secrets;
so have nothing to do with a
babbler!

20 If one curses his father or
mother,
his lamp will go out at the
coming of darkness.

21 Possessions gained hastily at the
outset
will in the end not be blessed.

22 Say not, "I will repay evil!"
Trust in the LORD and he will
help you.

23 Varying weights are an
abomination to the LORD,
and false scales are not good.

24 Man's steps are from the LORD;
how, then, can a man
understand his way?

25 Rashly to pledge a sacred gift
is a trap for a man,
or to regret a vow once made.

26 A wise king winnows the wicked,
and threshes them under the
cartwheel.

27 A lamp from the LORD is the
breath of man;
it searches through all his
inmost being.

28 Kindness and piety safeguard
the king,
and he upholds his throne by
justice.

29 The glory of young men is their
strength,
and the dignity of old men is
gray hair.

30 Evil is cleansed away by bloody
lashes,
and a scourging to the inmost
being.

20, 9: Man can be free of sin only by the power of God. Cf 1 Kgs 8, 46ff; Jb 4, 17; 14, 4; Pss 51, 2ff; 130, 3f; Rom 3, 23f; 1 Jn 1, 8.
20, 14: What one wishes to buy is valued cheaply in order that it may be obtained at a low price; once purchased, it is deemed more valuable.
20, 16: Caution is again advised in the matter of becoming surety; cf 6, 1ff.
20, 20: *His lamp will go out*: misfortune, even death, awaits him; cf 13, 9; Ex 21, 17.
20, 24: Man is dependent upon God and cannot fully foresee his own course.
20, 25: This verse cautions against making vows without proper reflection; cf Dt 23, 22ff; Eccl 5, 4f.

21 Like a stream is the king's
heart in the hand of the
LORD;
wherever it pleases him, he
directs it.

2 All the ways of a man may be
right in his own eyes,
but it is the LORD who proves
hearts.

3 To do what is right and just
is more acceptable to the
LORD than sacrifice.

4 Haughty eyes and a proud
heart—
the tillage of the wicked is sin.

5 The plans of the diligent are
sure of profit,
but all rash haste leads
certainly to poverty.

6 He who makes a fortune by a
lying tongue
is chasing a bubble over
deadly snares.

7 The oppression of the wicked
will sweep them away,
because they refuse to do
what is right.

8 The way of the culprit is
crooked,
but the conduct of the
innocent is right.

9 It is better to dwell in a corner
of the housetop
than in a roomy house with
a quarrelsome woman.

10 The soul of the wicked man
desires evil;
his neighbor finds no pity in
his eyes.

11 When the arrogant man is
punished, the simple are the
wiser;
when the wise man is
instructed, he gains
knowledge.

12 The just man appraises the
house of the wicked:
there is one who brings down
the wicked to ruin.

13 He who shuts his ear to the cry
of the poor
will himself also call and not
be heard.

14 A secret gift allays anger,
and a concealed present,
violent wrath.

15 To practice justice is a joy for
the just,
but terror for evildoers.

16 The man who strays from the
way of good sense
will abide in the assembly of
the shades.

17 He who loves pleasure will
suffer want;
he who loves wine and
perfume will not be rich.

18 The wicked man serves as
ransom for the just,
and the faithless man for the
righteous.

19 It is better to dwell in a wilderness
than with a quarrelsome and
vexatious wife.

20 Precious treasure remains in the
house of the wise,
but the fool consumes it.

21 He who pursues justice and
kindness
will find life and honor.

22 The wise man storms a city of
the mighty,
and overthrows the stronghold
in which it trusts.

23 He who guards his mouth and
his tongue
keeps himself from trouble.

24 Arrogant is the name for the
man of overbearing pride
who acts with scornful
effrontery.

25 The sluggard's propensity slays
him,
for his hands refuse to work.

26 Some are consumed with avarice
all the day,
but the just man gives
unsparingly.

27 The sacrifice of the wicked is
an abomination,
the more so when they offer
it with a bad intention.

28 The false witness will perish,
but he who listens will finally
have his say.

29 The wicked man is brazenfaced,
but the upright man pays heed
to his ways.

30 There is no wisdom, no
understanding,
no counsel, against the
LORD.

31 The horse is equipped for the
day of battle,
but victory is the LORD's.

22 A good name is more
desirable than great
riches,
and high esteem, than
gold and silver.

2 Rich and poor have a common
bond:
the LORD is the maker of
them all.

3 The shrewd man perceives evil
and hides,
while simpletons continue on
and suffer the penalty.

4 The reward of humility and
fear of the LORD
is riches, honor and life.

5 Thorns and snares are on the
path of the crooked;
he who would safeguard his
life will shun them.

6 Train a boy in the way he
should go;
even when he is old, he will
not swerve from it.

7 The rich rule over the poor,
and the borrower is the slave
of the lender.

8 He who sows iniquity reaps
calamity,
and the rod destroys his
labors.

21, 3: External rites or sacrifices do not please God unless accompanied by internal worship and right moral conduct; cf 15, 8; 21, 27; Is 1, 11–15; Am 5, 22; Mal 1, 12.

21, 16: *Assembly of the shades:* cf note on Jb 26, 5.
21, 18: *Wicked . . . ransom for the just:* exemplified in the history of God's chosen people whom he ransomed from Egypt at the cost of the life of Pharaoh and his army (Ex 14, 23–31), and from Babylon by giving to Cyrus, the Persian conqueror, Egypt, Ethiopia and Seba, the richest lands of the world (Is 43, 1ff).

9 The kindly man will be blessed,
 for he gives of his sustenance
 to the poor.

10 Expel the arrogant man and
 discord goes out;
 strife and insult cease.

11 The LORD loves the pure of
 heart;
 the man of winning speech has
 the king for his friend.

12 The eyes of the LORD safeguard
 knowledge,
 but he defeats the projects of
 the faithless.

13 The sluggard says, "A lion is
 outside;
 in the streets I might be slain."

14 The mouth of the adulteress is a
 deep pit;
 he with whom the LORD is
 angry will fall into it.

15 Folly is close to the heart of a
 child,
 but the rod of discipline will
 drive it far from him.

16 He who oppresses the poor to
 enrich himself
 will yield up his gains to the
 rich as sheer loss.

SAYINGS OF THE WISE

17 The sayings of the wise:

 Incline your ear, and hear my
 words,
 and apply your heart to my
 doctrine;
18 For it will be well if you keep
 them in your bosom,
 if they all are ready on your
 lips.
19 That your trust may be in the
 LORD,
 I make known to you the
 words of Amen-em-Ope.
20 Have I not written for you the
 "Thirty,"
 with counsels and knowledge,

21 To teach you truly
 how to give a dependable
 report to one who sends
 you?

22 Injure not the poor because they
 are poor,
 nor crush the needy at the
 gate;
23 For the LORD will defend their
 cause,
 and will plunder the lives of
 those who plunder them.

24 Be not friendly with a
 hotheaded man,
 nor the companion of a
 wrathful man,
25 Lest you learn his ways,
 and get yourself into a snare.

26 Be not one of those who give
 their hand in pledge,
 of those who become surety
 for debts;
27 For if you have not the means
 to pay,
 your bed will be taken from
 under you.

28 Remove not the ancient
 landmark
 which your fathers set up.

29 You see a man skilled at his
 work?
 He will stand in the presence
 of kings;
 he will not stand in the
 presence of obscure men.

23 When you sit down to dine
 with a ruler,
 keep in mind who is
 before you;
2 And put a knife to your throat
 if you have a ravenous
 appetite.
3 Do not desire his delicacies;
 they are deceitful food.

4 Toil not to gain wealth,
 cease to be concerned about it;

5 While your glance flits to it, it
 is gone!
 for assuredly it grows wings,
 like the eagle that flies
 toward heaven.

6 Do not take food with a
 grudging man,
 and do not desire his dainties;
7 For in his greed he is like a
 storm.
 "Eat and drink," he says to
 you,
 though his heart is not with
 you;
8 The little you have eaten you
 will vomit up,
 and you will have wasted
 your agreeable words.

9 Speak not for the fool's hearing;
 he will despise the wisdom of
 your words.

10 Remove not the ancient
 landmark,
 nor invade the fields of
 orphans;
11 For their redeemer is strong;
 he will defend their cause
 against you.

12 Apply your heart to instruction,
 and your ears to words of
 knowledge.

13 Withhold not chastisement
 from a boy;
 if you beat him with the rod,
 he will not die.
14 Beat him with the rod,
 and you will save him from
 the nether world.

15 My son, if your heart be wise,
 my own heart also will
 rejoice;
16 And my inmost being will exult,
 when your lips speak what is
 right.

17 Let not your heart emulate
 sinners,
 but be zealous for the fear of
 the LORD always;

22, 13: To avoid the effort required for doing good, *the sluggard* exaggerates the difficulties that must be overcome.

22, 16: Money gained by exploiting the poor is in turn lost to those who are more wealthy.

22, 17—24, 22: This collection of proverbs, introduced as *sayings of the wise*, is given in the more intimate and personal form of an address to a pupil called the *son* and is arranged in strophes instead of couplets.

22, 17—23, 35: The maxims warn against: oppression of the poor and defenseless (22, 22f), anger (24f), giving surety for debts (26f), bad manners at a king's table (23, 1f), anxiety for riches (4f), a grudging host (6ff), intemperance in food and drink (19ff.29–35), and adultery (26ff). They exhort to: careful workmanship (22, 29), respect for the rights of orphans (23, 10f), correction of the young (13f), filial piety (15f.22–25), and fear of the LORD (17f).

22, 19f: *Amen-em-Ope:* an Egyptian scribe to whom is attributed a collection of maxims in *Thirty* chapters (v 20) composed for the instruction of his children and addressed to a young man who wishes to enter upon a career. The inspired editor of Proverbs does not translate these, but uses their materials in constructing a similar collection of proverbs.

23, 2: *Put a knife to your throat:* a metaphor for self-restraint.

18 For you will surely have a future,
    and your hope will not be cut
      off.

19 Hear, my son, and be wise,
    and guide your heart in the
      right way.
20 Consort not with winebibbers,
    nor with those who eat meat
      to excess;
21 For the drunkard and the
      glutton come to poverty,
    and torpor clothes a man in
      rags.

22 Listen to your father who begot
      you,
    and despise not your mother
      when she is old.
23 Get the truth, and sell it not—
    wisdom, instruction and
      understanding.
24 The father of a just man will
      exult with glee;
    he who begets a wise son will
      have joy in him.
25 Let your father and mother
      have joy;
    let her who bore you exult.

26 My son, give me your heart,
    and let your eyes keep to my
      ways.
27 For the harlot is a deep ditch,
    and the adulteress a narrow
      pit;
28 Yes, she lies in wait like a
      robber,
    and increases the faithless
      among men.

29 Who scream? Who shriek?
    Who have strife? Who have
      anxiety?
    Who have wounds for nothing?
    Who have black eyes?
30 Those who linger long over
      wine,
    those who engage in trials of
      blended wine.
31 Look not on the wine when it is
      red,
    when it sparkles in the glass.
    It goes down smoothly;

32 but in the end it bites like a
      serpent,
    or like a poisonous adder.
33 Your eyes behold strange sights,
    and your heart utters
      disordered thoughts;
34 You are like one now lying in
      the depths of the sea,
    now sprawled at the top of
      the mast.
35 "They struck me, but it pained
      me not;
    They beat me, but I felt it not;
    When shall I awake
      to seek wine once again?"

24 Be not emulous of evil men,
    and desire not to be with
      them;
2 For their hearts plot violence,
    and their lips speak of foul
      play.

3 By wisdom is a house built,
    by understanding is it made
      firm;
4 And by knowledge are its
      rooms filled
    with every precious and
      pleasing possession.

5 A wise man is more powerful
      than a strong man,
    and a man of knowledge than
      a man of might;
6 For it is by wise guidance that
      you wage your war,
    and the victory is due to a
      wealth of counselors.

7 For a fool, to be silent is
      wisdom;
    not to open his mouth at the
      gate.

8 He who plots evil doing—
    men call him an intriguer.
9 Beyond intrigue and folly and
      sin,
    it is arrogance that men find
      abominable.

10 If you remain indifferent in
      time of adversity,
    your strength will depart from
      you.

11 Rescue those who are being
      dragged to death,
    and from those tottering to
      execution withdraw not.
12 If you say, "I know not this
      man!"
    does not he who tests hearts
      perceive it?
    He who guards your life knows
      it,
    and he will repay each one
      according to his deeds.

13 If you eat honey, my son,
      because it is good,
    if virgin honey is sweet to
      your taste;
14 Such, you must know, is wisdom
      to your soul.
    If you find it, you will have a
      future,
    and your hope will not be
      cut off.

15 Lie not in wait against the home
      of the just man,
    ravage not his dwelling place;
16 For the just man falls seven
      times and rises again,
    but the wicked stumble to ruin.

17 Rejoice not when your enemy
      falls,
    and when he stumbles, let not
      your heart exult,
18 Lest the LORD see it, be
      displeased with you,
    and withdraw his wrath from
      your enemy.

19 Be not provoked with evildoers,
    nor envious of the wicked;
20 For the evil man has no future,
    the lamp of the wicked will
      be put out.

21 My son, fear the LORD and the
      king;
    have nothing to do with
      those who rebel against
      them;
22 For suddenly arises the
      destruction they send,
    and the ruin from either one,
      who can measure?

23, 29–35: A vivid description of the evil effects, physical and psychological, of drunkenness.

23, 35: Wine makes the drunkard insensible to bodily and moral harm. His one desire is to indulge again.

24, 1–22: These verses continue an exhortation to wisdom (vv 3–7,13f), and against: violence (1f), pride and intrigue (8f), callousness (10–12), injustice (15f),

joy in the failure of others (17f) or scandal at their success (19f), and rebellion against authority (21f).

24, 7: *At the gate:* of the city, where justice was administered and public affairs discussed; see note on Ru 4, 1. Cf also Pss 69, 13; 127, 5; Prv 22, 22; 31, 23.31.

24, 10: *Indifferent:* to those who suffer unjustly.

24, 11: *Rescue . . . death:* most probably refers to

the legal rescue of those unjustly condemned to death.

24, 16: *The just man* overcomes every misfortune which oppresses him. *Seven times:* i.e., an indefinite number; cf Mt 18, 21f; Lk 17, 4.

24, 21f: One owes obedience to God and to supreme civil authority (Mt 22, 21; Rom 13, 1ff; 1 Pt 2, 13f). The punishments for failure in either duty transcend the limits of private justice.

OTHER SAYINGS OF THE WISE

23 These also are sayings of the
wise:

To show partiality in judgment is
not good.
24 He who says to the wicked man,
"You are just"—
men will curse him, people
will denounce him;
25 But those who convict the
evildoer will fare well,
and on them will come the
blessing of prosperity.
26 He gives a kiss on the lips
who makes an honest reply.

27 Complete your outdoor tasks,
and arrange your work in the
field;
afterward you can establish
your house.

28 Be not a witness against your
neighbor without just cause,
thus committing folly with
your lips.

29 Say not, "As he did to me, so
will I do to him;
I will repay the man according
to his deeds."

30 I passed by the field of the
sluggard,
by the vineyard of the man
without sense;
31 And behold! it was all
overgrown with thistles;
its surface was covered with
nettles,
and its stone wall broken
down.
32 And as I gazed at it, I reflected;
I saw and learned the lesson:
33 A little sleep, a little slumber,
a little folding of the arms to
rest—
34 Then will poverty come upon
you like a highwayman,
and want like an armed man.

SECOND COLLECTION OF THE PROVERBS OF SOLOMON

25 These also are proverbs of
Solomon. The men
of Hezekiah, king of
Judah, transmitted them.

2 God has glory in what he
conceals,
kings have glory in what they
fathom.

3 As the heavens in height, and
the earth in depth,
the heart of kings is
unfathomable.

4 Remove the dross from silver,
and it comes forth perfectly
purified;
5 Remove the wicked from the
presence of the king,
and his throne is made firm
through righteousness.

6 Claim no honor in the king's
presence,
nor occupy the place of great
men;
7 For it is better that you be told,
"Come up closer!"
than that you be humbled before
the prince.

8 What your eyes have seen
bring not forth hastily against
an opponent;
For what will you do later on
when your neighbor puts you
to shame?
9 Discuss your case with your
neighbor,
but another man's secret do
not disclose;
10 Lest, hearing it, he reproach you,
and your ill repute cease not.

11 Like golden apples in silver
settings
are words spoken at the proper
time.

12 Like a golden earring, or a
necklace of fine gold,
is a wise reprover to an
obedient ear.

13 Like the coolness of snow in the
heat of the harvest
is a faithful messenger for the
one who sends him.
[He refreshes the soul of his
master.]

14 Like clouds and wind when no
rain follows
is the man who boastfully
promises what he never
gives.

15 By patience is a ruler persuaded,
and a soft tongue will break a
bone.

16 If you find honey, eat only
what you need,
lest you become glutted with
it and vomit it up.

17 Let your foot be seldom in
your neighbor's house,
lest he have more than
enough of you, and hate
you.

18 Like a club, or a sword, or a
sharp arrow,
is the man who bears false
witness against his neighbor.

19 Like an infected tooth or an
unsteady foot
is [dependence on] a faithless
man in time of trouble.

20 Like a moth in clothing, or a
maggot in wood,
sorrow gnaws at the human
heart,

21 If your enemy be hungry, give
him food to eat,
if he be thirsty, give him to
drink;
22 For live coals you will heap on
his head,
and the LORD will vindicate
you.

23 The north wind brings rain,
and a backbiting tongue an
angry countenance.

24, 23–34: This collection of sayings continues in
the same vein as the preceding: it instructs in fairness
(23–26) and preparation for the future (27); and warns
against vengeance (28f) and slothfulness (30–34).
24, 26: *He gives a kiss on the lips:* shows himself a
true friend.
24, 27: This verse is commonly interpreted as
advocating careful and practical preparation for
marriage.

24, 29: This verse indicates great progress from the
principle of the law of Talion (see note on Ex 21,
23ff) toward the teaching found in Rom 12, 17ff.
Cf also Prv 25, 21ff.
25, 1: *The men of Hezekiah:* literary men at the
royal court of Hezekiah who are represented as
transcribing the proverbs from other collections.
Hezekiah was a reformer of national religious life
(2 Chr 29, 25–30).

25, 6f: Compare the lesson on humility which was
taught by Christ (Lk 14, 7–11).
25, 21f: Charity is invaluable in resolving enmities
and restoring peace. *Live coals:* i.e., either remorse
and embarrassment for the harm done, or increased
punishment for refusing reconciliation. Cf Mt 5, 44;
Rom 12, 20.

24 It is better to dwell in a corner
   of the housetop
      than in a roomy house with
      a quarrelsome woman.

25 Like cool water to one faint
   from thirst
      is good news from a far
      country.

26 Like a trouble fountain or a
   polluted spring
      is a just man who gives way
      before the wicked.

27 To eat too much honey is not
   good;
      nor to seek honor after honor.

28 Like an open city with no
   defenses
      is the man with no check on
      his feelings.

26

Like snow in summer, or rain
   in harvest,
      honor for a fool is out of
      place.

2 Like the sparrow in its flitting,
      like the swallow in its flight,
   a curse uncalled-for arrives
      nowhere.

3 The whip for the horse, the
   bridle for the ass,
      and the rod for the back of
      fools.

4 Answer not the fool according
   to his folly,
      lest you too become like him.

5 Answer the fool according to
   his folly,
      lest he become wise in his
      own eyes.

6 He cuts off his feet, he drinks
   down violence,
      who sends messages by a fool.

7 A proverb in the mouth of a fool
   hangs limp, like crippled legs.

8 Like one who entangles the stone
   in the sling
      is he who gives honor to a
      fool.

9 Like a thorn stick brandished
      by the hand of a drunkard
   is a proverb in the mouth of
      fools.

10 Like an archer wounding all
   who pass by
      is he who hires a drunken fool.

11 As the dog returns to his vomit,
   so the fool repeats his folly.

12 You see a man wise in his own
   eyes?
      There is more hope for a fool
      than for him.

13 The sluggard says, "There is a
   lion in the street,
      a lion in the middle of the
      square!"

14 The door turns on its hinges,
   the sluggard, on his bed!

15 The sluggard loses his hand in
   the dish;
      he is too weary to lift it to
      his mouth.

16 The sluggard imagines himself
   wiser
      than seven men who answer
      with good sense.

17 Like the man who seizes a
   passing dog by the ears
      is he who meddles in a quarrel
      not his own.

18 Like a crazed archer
      scattering firebrands and
      deadly arrows

19 Is the man who deceives his
   neighbor,
      and then says, "I was only
      joking."

20 For lack of wood, the fire dies
   out;
      and when there is no
      talebearer, strife subsides.

21 What a bellows is to live coals,
      what wood is to fire,
   such is a contentious man in
      enkindling strife.

22 The words of a talebearer are
   like dainty morsels
      that sink into one's inmost
      being.

23 Like a glazed finish on
   earthenware
      are smooth lips with a
      wicked heart.

24 With his lips an enemy pretends,
      but in his inmost being he
      maintains deceit;

25 When he speaks graciously,
   trust him not,
      for seven abominations are in
      his heart.

26 A man may conceal hatred
      under dissimulation,
   but his malice will be
      revealed in the assembly.

27 He who digs a pit falls into it;
      and a stone comes back upon
      him who rolls it.

28 The lying tongue is its owner's
   enemy,
      and the flattering mouth
      works ruin.

27

Boast not of tomorrow,
   for you know not what
      any day may bring forth.

2 Let another praise you—not
   your own mouth;
      someone else—not your own
      lips.

3 Stone is heavy, and sand a
   burden,
      but a fool's provocation is
      heavier than both.

4 Anger is relentless, and wrath
   overwhelming—
      but before jealousy who can
      stand?

5 Better is an open rebuke
   than a love that remains
      hidden.

6 Wounds from a friend may be
   accepted as well meant,
      but the greetings of an enemy
      one prays against.

7 One who is full, tramples on
   virgin honey;
      but to the man who is hungry,
      any bitter thing is sweet.

25, 27: *Nor . . . honor after honor:* the text is
uncertain.
26, 1–28: Concrete images describe the vices of
fools (1–12), of sluggards (13–16), of meddlers (17–

19), of talebearers (20ff) and of flatterers (23–28).
26, 4f: There is no contradiction between these
two proverbs. In any answer the wise man gives he
must protect his own interest against the fool.

26, 7ff: The fool abuses whatever knowledge he
possesses.
26, 25: *Seven abominations:* many evil intentions.

8 Like a bird that is far from its
   nest
      is a man who is far from his
      home.

9 Perfume and incense gladden
   the heart,
      but by grief the soul is torn
      asunder.

10 Your own friend and your
   father's friend forsake not;
      but if ruin befalls you, enter
      not a kinsman's house.
      Better is a neighbor near at
      hand than a brother far
      away.

11 If you are wise, my son, you
   will gladden my heart,
      and I will be able to rebut
      him who taunts me.

12 The shrewd man perceives evil
   and hides;
      simpletons continue on and
      suffer the penalty.

13 Take his garment who becomes
   surety for another,
      and for the sake of a stranger,
      yield it up!

14 When one greets his neighbor
   with a loud voice in the
   early morning,
      a curse can be laid to his
      charge.

15 For a persistent leak on a rainy
   day
      the match is a quarrelsome
      woman.

16 He who keeps her stores up a
   stormwind;
      he cannot tell north from
      south.

17 As iron sharpens iron,
      so man sharpens his fellow
      man.

18 He who tends a fig tree eats its
   fruit,
      and he who is attentive to his
      master will be enriched.

19 As one face differs from another,
      so does one human heart
      from another.

20 The nether world and the abyss
   are never satisfied;
      so too the eyes of men.

21 As the crucible tests silver and
   the furnace gold,
      so a man is tested by the
      praise he receives.

22 Though you should pound the
   fool to bits
      with the pestle, amid the
      grits in a mortar,
      his folly would not go out of
      him.

23 Take good care of your flocks,
      give careful attention to your
      herds;

24 For wealth lasts not forever,
      nor even a crown from age to
      age.

25 When the grass is taken away
      and the aftergrowth appears,
      and the mountain greens are
      gathered in,

26 The lambs will provide you
   with clothing,
      and the goats will bring the
      price of a field,

27 And there will be ample goat's
   milk to supply you,
      [to supply your household,]
      and maintenance for your
      maidens.

28 The wicked man flees
      although no one
      pursues him;
      but the just man, like a
      lion, feels sure of
      himself.

2 If a land is rebellious, its
   princes will be many;
      but with a prudent man it
      knows security.

3 A rich man who oppresses the
   poor
      is like a devastating rain that
      leaves no food.

4 Those who abandon the law
      praise the wicked man,
      but those who keep the law
      war against him.

5 Evil men understand nothing of
   justice,
      but those who seek the LORD
      understand all.

6 Better a poor man who walks in
   his integrity
      than he who is crooked in his
      ways and rich.

7 He who keeps the law is a wise
   son,
      but the gluttons' companion
      disgraces his father.

8 He who increases his wealth by
   interest and overcharge
      gathers it for him who is kind
      to the poor.

9 When one turns away his ear
      from hearing the law,
      even his prayer is an
      abomination.

10 He who seduces the upright into
   an evil way
      will himself fall into his own
      pit.
      [And blameless men will gain
      prosperity.]

11 The rich man is wise in his own
   eyes,
      but a poor man who is
      intelligent sees through him.

12 When the just are triumphant,
      there is great jubilation;
      but when the wicked gain
      pre-eminence, people hide.

13 He who conceals his sins
      prospers not,
      but he who confesses and
      forsakes them obtains
      mercy.

14 Happy the man who is always
   on his guard;
      but he who hardens his heart
      will fall into evil.

15 Like a roaring lion or a
   ravenous bear
      is a wicked ruler over a poor
      people.

27, 13: See note on 20, 16.
   27, 14: The *loud voice* suggest hypocrisy in the
greeting.
   27, 23–27: The land of Palestine was very suitable
for flocks and herds, which formed the principal
source of wealth for their owners.

28, 2: The meaning of this poorly preserved verse
seems to be that frequent changes of rulers often
result from moral corruption and political disorder.
   28, 4: *The law:* religious and moral teaching.
   28, 8: *Interest and overcharge* were strictly forbidden in the old law among Israelites because it was

presumed that the borrower was in distress; cf Ex 22,
25; Lv 25, 35ff; Dt 23, 19; Ps 15, 5; Ez 18,8. Civil
and divine law will take the offender's wealth from
him.
   28, 9: Prayers offered in bad faith are displeasing
to God.

16 The less prudent the prince, the
    more his deeds oppress.
  He who hates ill-gotten gain
    prolongs his days.

17 Though a man burdened with
    human blood
  were to flee to the grave,
    none should support him.

18 He who walks uprightly is safe,
  but he whose ways are
    crooked falls into the pit.

19 He who cultivates his land will
    have plenty of food,
  but from idle pursuits a man
    has his fill of poverty.

20 The trustworthy man will be
    richly blessed;
  he who is in haste to grow
    rich will not go unpunished.

21 To show partiality is never good:
  for even a morsel of bread a
    man may do wrong.

22 The avaricious man is perturbed
    about his wealth,
  and he knows not when want
    will come upon him.

23 He who rebukes a man gets
    more thanks in the end
  than one with a flattering
    tongue.

24 He who defrauds father or
    mother and calls it no sin,
  is a partner of the brigand.

25 The greedy man stirs up
    disputes,
  but he who trusts in the
    Lord will prosper.

26 He who trusts in himself is a
    fool,
  but he who walks in wisdom
    is safe.

27 He who gives to the poor suffers
    no want,
  but he who ignores them gets
    many a curse.

28 When the wicked gain
    pre-eminence, other men
    hide;
  but at their fall the just
    flourish.

29 The man who remains
    stiff-necked and hates
    rebuke
  will be crushed suddenly
    beyond cure.

2 When the just prevail, the people
    rejoice;
  but when the wicked rule, the
    people groan.

3 He who loves wisdom makes his
    father glad,
  but he who consorts with
    harlots squanders his wealth.

4 By justice a king gives stability
    to the land;
  but he who imposes heavy
    taxes ruins it.

5 The man who flatters his
    neighbor
  is spreading a net under his
    feet.

6 The wicked man steps into a
    snare,
  but the just man runs on
    joyfully.

7 The just man has a care for the
    rights of the poor;
  the wicked man has no such
    concern.

8 Arrogant men set the city
    ablaze,
  but wise men calm the fury.

9 If a wise man disputes with a
    fool,
  he may rage or laugh but can
    have no peace.

10 Bloodthirsty men hate the
    honest man,
  but the upright show concern
    for his life.

11 The fool gives vent to all his
    anger;
  but by biding his time, the
    wise man calms it.

12 If a ruler listens to lying words,
  his servants all become
    wicked.

13 The poor and the oppressor have
    a common bond:
  the Lord gives light to the
    eyes of both.

14 If a king is zealous for the rights
    of the poor,
  his throne stands firm forever.

15 The rod of correction gives
    wisdom,
  but a boy left to his whims
    disgraces his mother.

16 When the wicked prevail, crime
    increases;
  but their downfall the just
    will behold.

17 Correct your son, and he will
    bring you comfort,
  and give delight to your soul.

18 Without prophecy the people
    became demoralized;
  but happy is he who keeps the
    law.

19 By words no servant can be
    trained;
  for he understands what is
    said, but obeys not.

20 Do you see a man hasty in his
    words?
  More can be hoped for from
    a fool!

21 If a man pampers his servant
    from childhood,
  he will turn out to be
    stubborn.

22 An ill-tempered man stirs up
    disputes,
  and a hotheaded man is the
    cause of many sins.

23 Man's pride causes his
    humiliation,
  but he who is humble of
    spirit obtains honor.

24 The accomplice of a thief is his
    own enemy:
  he hears himself put under a
    curse, yet discloses nothing.

25 The fear of man brings a snare,
  but he who trusts in the
    Lord is safe.

26 Many curry favor with the
    ruler,
  but the rights of each are
    from the Lord.

29, 13: God gives life to all classes of people;
cf 22, 2.

29, 24: *Is his own enemy:* because he not only
incurs guilt as an accomplice but, by his silence,

brings down on himself the curse invoked on the unknown guilty partner.

27 The evildoer is an abomination
    to the just,
  and he who walks uprightly
    is an abomination to the
    wicked.

THE WORDS OF AGUR

30 The words of Agur, son of
     Jakeh the Massaite:

  The pronouncement of mortal
    man: "I am not God;
  I am not God, that I should
    prevail.
2 Why, I am the most stupid of
    men,
  and have not even human
    intelligence;
3 Neither have I learned wisdom,
  nor have I the knowledge of
    the Holy One.
4 Who has gone up to heaven and
    come down again—
  who has cupped the wind in
    his hands?
  Who has bound up the waters
    in a cloak—
  who has marked out all the
    ends of the earth?
  What is his name, what is his
    son's name,
  if you know it?"
5 Every word of God is tested;
  he is a shield to those who
    take refuge in him.
6 Add nothing to his words,
  lest he reprove you, and you
    be exposed as a deceiver.

NUMERICAL PROVERBS

7 Two things I ask of you,
  deny them not to me before I
    die:
8 Put falsehood and lying far
    from me,
  give me neither poverty nor
    riches;
  [provide me only with the
    food I need;]
9 Lest, being full, I deny you,
  saying, "Who is the LORD?"

  Or, being in want, I steal,
  and profane the name of my
    God.

10 Slander not a servant to his
    master,
  lest he curse you, and you
    have to pay the penalty.

11 There is a group of people that
    curses its father,
  and blesses not its mother.
12 There is a group that is pure in
    its own eyes,
  yet is not purged of its filth.
13 There is a group—how haughty
    their eyes!
  how overbearing their glance!
14 There is a group whose incisors
    are swords,
  whose teeth are knives,
  Devouring the needy from the
    earth,
  and the poor from among
    men.

15 The two daughters of the leech
    are, "Give, Give."
  Three things are never satisfied,
    four never say, "Enough!"
16 The nether world, and the
    barren womb;
  the earth, that is never
    saturated with water,
  and fire, that never says,
    "Enough!"
17 The eye that mocks a father,
  or scorns an aged mother,
  Will be plucked out by the
    ravens in the valley;
  the young eagles will devour it.

18 Three things are too wonderful
    for me,
  yes, four I cannot understand:
19 The way of an eagle in the air,
  the way of a serpent upon a
    rock,
  The way of a ship on the high
    seas,
  and the way of a man with a
    maiden.

20 Such is the way of an adulterous
    woman:
  she eats, wipes her mouth,
  and says, "I have done no
    wrong."

21 Under three things the earth
    trembles,
  yes, under four it cannot bear
    up:
22 Under a slave when he becomes
    king,
  and a fool when he is glutted
    with food;
23 Under an odious woman when
    she is wed,
  and a maidservant when she
    displaces her mistress.

24 Four things are among the
    smallest on the earth.
  and yet are exceedingly wise:
25 Ants—a species not strong,
  yet they store up their food
    in the summer;
26 Rock-badgers—a species not
    mighty,
  yet they make their home in
    the crags;
27 Locusts—they have no king,
  yet they migrate all in array;
28 Lizards—you can catch them
    with your hands,
  yet they find their way into
    king's palaces.

29 Three things are stately in their
    stride,
  yes, four are stately in their
    carriage:
30 The lion, mightiest of beasts,
  who retreats before nothing;
31 The strutting cock, and the
    he-goat,
  and the king at the head of
    his people.

32 If you have foolishly been proud
  or presumptuous—put your
    hand on your mouth;

30, 1: *Agur:* an unknown person. *Massaite:* from
Massa in northern Arabia, elsewhere referred to as an
encampment of the Ishmaelites (Gn 25, 14). But the
word may not be intended as a place name; it might
signify "an oracle," "a prophecy."
  30, 1ff: Agur wishes to stress man's insignificance
when he is compared to God; cf Jb 38–39.
  30, 11–14: Perverted people are here classified as
unfilial (11), self-righteous (12), proud (13) and

rapacious (14).
  30, 15ff: *The two daughters . . . "Give, Give":* the
text is obscure but the sense esems to be that *the
leech* is unsatiable in its desire for blood, just as are
the nether world for victims, *the barren womb* for
offspring, the parched *earth* for water, and *fire* for
fuel (16).
  30, 18f: The soaring flight of the eagle, the mysterious movement upon a rock of the serpent which has

no feet, the path of the ship through the trackless
deep, and the marvelous procreation of human life
excite great wonderment.
  30, 20: This verse portrays the indifference of an
adulterous woman who thinks there is no trace of her
wicked act.
  30, 26: *Rock-badgers:* cf note to Ps 104, 18.
  30, 32f: The anger aroused by overwhelming pride
threatens an awesome punishment.

33 For the stirring of milk brings
    forth curds,
    and the stirring of anger
    brings forth blood.

THE WORDS OF LEMUEL

31 The words of Lemuel, king
    of Massa. The advice which
his mother gave him:

2 What, my son, my first-born!
    what, O son of my womb;
    what, O son of my vows!
3 Give not your vigor to women,
    nor your strength to those
    who ruin kings.
4 It is not for kings, O Lemuel,
    not for kings to drink wine;
    strong drink is not for
    princes!
5 Lest in drinking they forget
    what the law decrees,
    and violate the rights of all
    who are in need.
6 Give strong drink to one who is
    perishing,
    and wine to the sorely
    depressed;
7 When they drink they will
    forget their misery,
    and think no more of their
    burdens.
8 Open your mouth in behalf of
    the dumb,
    and for the rights of the
    destitute;

9 Open your mouth, decree what
    is just,
    defend the needy and the poor!

THE IDEAL WIFE

10 When one finds a worthy wife,
    her value is far beyond pearls.
11 Her husband, entrusting his
    heart to her,
    has an unfailing prize.
12 She bring him good, and not
    evil,
    all the days of her life.
13 She obtains wool and flax
    and makes cloth with skillful
    hands.
14 Like merchant ships,
    she secures her provisions
    from afar.
15 She rises while it is still night,
    and distributes food to her
    household.
16 She picks out a field to
    purchase;
    out of her earnings she plants
    a vineyard.
17 She is girt about with strength,
    and sturdy are her arms.
18 She enjoys the success of her
    dealings;
    at night her lamp is
    undimmed.
19 She puts her hands to the distaff,
    and her fingers ply the spindle.
20 She reaches out her hands to
    the poor,
    and extends her arms to the
    needy.

21 She fears not the snow for her
    household;
    all her charges are doubly
    clothed.
22 She makes her own coverlets;
    fine linen and purple are her
    clothing.
23 Her husband is prominent at the
    city gates
    as he sits with the elders of
    the land.
24 She makes garments and sells
    them,
    and stocks the merchants with
    belts.
25 She is clothed with strength and
    dignity,
    and she laughs at the days to
    come.
26 She opens her mouth in wisdom,
    and on her tongue is kindly
    counsel.
27 She watches the conduct of her
    household,
    and eats not her food in
    idleness.
28 Her children rise up and praise
    her;
    her husband, too, extols her:
29 "Many are the women of proven
    worth,
    but you have excelled them all."
30 Charm is deceptive and beauty
    fleeting;
    the woman who fears the
    LORD is to be praised.
31 Give her a reward of her labors,
    and let her works praise her
    at the city gates.

31, 12: *Good, and not evil:* i.e., prosperity, not
adversity.
31, 14: *Merchant:* literally, "Canaanite" (cf v 24),
probably because the merchant class had been

composed chiefly of Canaanites.
31, 18: *Her lamp is undimmed:* indicates abundance
of productive work and its accompanying prosperity;
cf 20, 20; Jb 18, 6.

31, 25: *Laughs at the day to come:* anticipates the
future with gladness free from anxiety.
31, 30: The true charm of the ideal wife is her
religious spirit, for she *fears the Lord:* cf note on 1, 7.

Ecclesiastes

Vanity of Toil without Profit

THE words of David's son, Qoheleth, king in Jerusalem: 2 Vanity of vanities, says Qoheleth, vanity of vanities! All things are vanity! 3 What profit has man from all the labor which he toils at under the sun? 4 One generation passes and another comes, but the world forever stays.

5 The sun rises and the sun goes
    down;
        then it presses on to the place
            where it rises.
6 Blowing now toward the south,
        then toward the north,
    the wind turns again and
        again, resuming its rounds.
7 All rivers go to the sea,
        yet never does the sea become
            full.
    To the place where they go,
        the rivers keep on going.
8 All speech is labored;
        there is nothing man can say.
    The eye is not satisfied with
        seeing
            nor is the ear filled with
                hearing.

9 What has been, that will be; what has been done, that will be done. Nothing is new under the sun. 10 Even the thing of which we say, "See, this is new!" has already existed in the ages that preceded us. 11 There is no remembrance of the men of old; nor of those to come will there be any remembrance among those who come after them.

QOHELETH'S INVESTIGATION OF LIFE

Twofold Introduction

12 I, Qoheleth, was king over Israel in Jerusalem, 13 and I applied my mind to search and investigate in wisdom all things that are done under the sun.

> A thankless task God has
>   appointed
>   for men to be busied about.

14 I have seen all things that are done under the sun, and behold, all is vanity and a chase after wind.

15 What is crooked cannot be made
        straight,
    and what is missing cannot be
        supplied.

16 Though I said to .myself, "Behold, I have become great and stored up wisdom beyond all who were before me in Jerusalem, and my mind has broad experience of wisdom and knowledge"; 17 yet when I applied my mind to know wisdom and knowledge, madness and folly, I learned that this also is a chase after wind.

18 For in much wisdom there is
        much sorrow,
    and he who stores up
        knowledge stores up grief.

Study of Pleasure-seeking

2 I said to myself, "Come, now, let me try you with pleasure and the enjoyment of good things." But behold, this too was vanity. 2 Of laughter I said: "Mad!" and of mirth: "What good does this do?" 3 I thought of beguiling my senses with wine, though my mind was concerned with wisdom, and of taking up folly, until I should understand what is best for men to do under the heavens during the limited days of their life.

1, 1: *Qoheleth:* see Introduction.
1, 2: *Vanity of vanities:* a Hebrew superlative expressing the supreme degree of futility and emptiness.
1, 3: *Under the sun:* used throughout this book to signify "on the earth."
1, 8: *All speech . . . man can say:* or "All things are wearisome beyond man's power to tell."
1, 11: Men remember nothing long, God never forgets.
1, 14: *Chase after wind:* futility, like an attempt to corral the winds. Cf Hos 12, 2. The versions understood "affliction of spirit." These words are used to conclude sections of the discourse, as far as 6, 9.
2, 1–11: The author here assumes the role of Solomon.
2, 3: *Though my mind . . . wisdom:* while indulging in pleasure the author hopes to discover wherein man's true happiness consists.

4 I undertook great works; I built myself houses and planted vineyards; 5 I made gardens and parks, and set out in them fruit trees of all sorts. 6 And I constructed for myself reservoirs to water a flourishing woodland. 7 I acquired male and female slaves, and slaves were born in my house. I also had growing herds of cattle and flocks of sheep, more than all who had been before me in Jerusalem. 8 I amassed for myself silver and gold, and the wealth of kings and provinces. I got for myself male and female singers and all human luxuries. 9 I became great, and I stored up more than all others before me in Jerusalem; my wisdom, too, stayed with me. 10 Nothing that my eyes desired did I deny them, nor did I deprive myself of any joy, but my heart rejoiced in the fruit of all my toil. This was my share for all my toil. 11 But when I turned to all the works that my hands had wrought, and to the toil at which I had taken such pains, behold! all was vanity and a chase after wind, with nothing gained under the sun. 12 For what will the man do who is to come after the king? What men have already done!

Study of Wisdom and Folly

I went on to the consideration of wisdom, madness and folly. 13 And I saw that wisdom has the advantage over folly as much as light has the advantage over darkness.

14 The wise man has eyes in his head,
　　but the fool walks in darkness.

Yet I knew that one lot befalls both of them. 15 So I said to myself, if the fool's lot is to befall me also, why then should I be wise? Where is the profit for me? And I concluded in my heart that this too is vanity. 16 Neither of the wise man nor of the fool will there be an abiding remembrance, for in days to come both will have been forgotten. How is it that the wise man dies as well as the fool! 17 Therefore I loathed life, since for

me the work that is done under the sun is evil; for all is vanity and a chase after wind.

Study of the Fruits of Toil To Others the Profits

18 And I detested all the fruits of my labor under the sun, because I must leave them to a man who is to come after me. 19 And who knows whether he will be a wise man or a fool? Yet he will have control over all the fruits of my wise labor under the sun. This also is vanity. 20 So my feelings turned to despair of all the fruits of my labor under the sun. 21 For here is a man who has labored with wisdom and knowledge and skill, and to another, who has not labored over it, he must leave his property. 22 This also is vanity and a great misfortune. For what profit comes to a man from all the toil and anxiety of heart with which he has labored under the sun? 23 All his days sorrow and grief are his occupation; even at night his mind is not at rest. This also is vanity.

24 There is nothing better for man than to eat and drink and provide himself with good things by his labors. Even this, I realized, is from the hand of God. 25 For who can eat or drink apart from him? 26 For to whatever man he sees fit he gives wisdom and knowledge and joy; but to the sinner he gives the task of gathering possessions to be given to whatever man God sees fit. This also is vanity and a chase after wind.

Man Cannot Hit on the Right Time to Act

3 There is an appointed time for everything,
　　and a time for every affair under the heavens.
2 A time to be born, and a time to die;
　　a time to plant, and a time to uproot the plant.
3 A time to kill, and a time to heal;
　　a time to tear down, and a time to build.

4 A time to weep, and a time to laugh;
　　a time to mourn, and a time to dance.
5 A time to scatter stones, and a time to gather them;
　　a time to embrace, and a time to be far from embraces.
6 A time to seek, and a time to lose;
　　a time to keep, and a time to cast away.
7 A time to rend, and a time to sew;
　　a time to be silent, and a time to speak.
8 A time to love, and a time to hate;
　　a time of war, and a time of peace.

9 What advantage has the worker from his toil 10 I have considered the task which God has appointed for men to be busied about. 11 He has made everything appropriate to its time, and has put the timeless into their hearts, without men's ever discovering, from beginning to end, the work which God has done. 12 I recognized that there is nothing better than to be glad and to do well during life. 13 For every man, moreover, to eat and drink and enjoy the fruit of all his labor is a gift of God. 14 I recognized that whatever God does will endure forever; there is no adding to it, or taking from it. Thus has God done that he may be revered. 15 What now is has already been; what is to be, already is; and God restores what would otherwise be displaced.

The Problem of Retribution

16 And still under the sun in the judgment place I saw wickedness, and in the seat of justice, iniquity. 17 And I said to myself, both the just and the wicked God will judge, since there is a time for every affair and on every work a judgment. 18 I said to myself: As for the children of men, it is God's way of testing them and of showing that they are in themselves like beasts. 19 For the lot of man and of beast is one lot, the

---

2, 24: Unrestrained indulgence is not advocated here, but legitimate pleasure and the cheerfulness it

begets.

3, 15: *God restores:* the meaning is probably that

God allows no part of his creation to drop out of existence.

one dies as well as the other. Both have the same life-breath, and man has no advantage over the beast; but all is vanity. 20 Both go to the same place; both were made from the dust, and to the dust they both return. 21 Who knows if the life-breath of the children of men goes upward and the life-breath of beasts goes earthward? 22 And I saw that there is nothing better for a man than to rejoice in his work; for this is his lot. Who will let him see what is to come after him?

Vanity of Toil

4 Again I considered all the oppressions that take place under the sun: the tears of the victims with none to comfort them! From the hand of their oppressors comes violence, and there is none to comfort them! 2 And those now dead, I declared more fortunate in death than are the living to be still alive. 3 And better off than both is the yet unborn, who has not seen the wicked work that is done under the sun. 4 Then I saw that all toil and skillful work is the rivalry of one man for another. This also is vanity and a chase after wind.

5 "The fool folds his arms
   and consumes his own
      flesh"—
6 Better is one handful with
   tranquility
      than two with toil and a chase
      after wind!

Companions and Successors

7 Again I found this vanity under the sun: 8 a solitary man with no companion; with neither son nor brother. Yet there is no end to all his toil, and riches do not satisfy his greed. "For whom do I toil and deprive myself of good things?" This also is vanity and a worthless task. 9 Two are better than one: they get a good wage for their labor. 10 If the one falls, the other will lift up his companion. Woe to the solitary man! For if he should fall, he

has no one to lift him up. 11 So also, if two sleep together, they keep each other warm. How can one alone keep warm? 12 Where a lone man may be overcome, two together can resist. A three-ply cord is not easily broken.

13 Better is a poor but wise youth than an old but foolish king who no longer knows caution; 14 for from a prison house one comes forth to rule, since even in his royalty he was poor at birth. 15 Then I saw all those who are to live and move about under the sun with the heir apparent who will succeed to his place. 16 There is no end to all these people, to all over whom he takes precedence; yet the later generations will not applaud him. This also is vanity and a chase after wind.

Vanity of Many Words

17 Guard your step when you go to the house of God. Let your approach be obedience, rather than the fools' offering of sacrifice; for they know not how to keep from doing evil. 1 Be not hasty in your utterance and let not your heart be quick to make a promise in God's presence. God is in heaven and you are on earth; therefore let your words be few.

2 For nightmares come with many
   cares,
      and a fool's utterance with
      many words.

3 When you make a vow to God, delay not its fulfillment. For God has no pleasure in fools; fulfill what you have vowed. 4 You had better not make a vow than make it and not fulfill it. 5 Let not your utterances make you guilty, and say not before his representative, "It was a mistake," lest God be angered by such words and destroy the works of your hands. 6 Rather, fear God!

Gain and Loss of Goods

7 If you see oppression of the poor, and violation of rights and justice in the realm, do not be shocked by the

fact, for the high official has another higher than he watching him and above these are others higher still—. 8 Yet an advantage for a country in every respect is a king for the arable land.

9 The covetous man is never satisfied with money, and the lover of wealth reaps no fruit from it; so this too is vanity. 10 Where there are great riches, there are also many to devour them. Of what use are they to the owner except to feast his eyes upon? 11 Sleep is sweet to the laboring man, whether he eats little or much, but the rich man's abundance allows him no sleep.

12 This is a grievous evil which I have seen under the sun: riches kept by their owner to his hurt. 13 Should the riches be lost through some misfortune, he may have a son when he is without means. 14 As he came forth from his mother's womb, naked as he came, having nothing from his labor that he can carry in his hand. 15 This too is a grievous evil, that he goes just as he came. What then does it profit him to toil for wind? 16 All the days of his life are passed in gloom and sorrow, under great vexation, sickness and wrath.

17 Here is what I recognize as good: it is well for a man to eat and drink and enjoy all the fruits of his labor under the sun during the limited days of the life which God gives him; for this is his lot. 18 Any man to whom God gives riches and property, and grants power to partake of them, so that he receives his lot and finds joy in the fruits of his toil, has a gift from God. 19 For he will hardly dwell on the shortness of his life, because God lets him busy himself with the joy of his heart.

Limited Worth of Enjoyment

6 There is another evil which I have seen under the sun, and it weighs heavily upon man: 2 there is the man to whom God gives riches and property and honor, so that he lacks none of all the things he craves; yet God does not grant him

---

4, 5: *Consumes his own flesh:* refuses to work for the necessities of life and consequently suffers hunger and impairs his bodily health.
4, 14: *Prison house:* probably his mother's womb, from which the king issues without possessions. Cf 5, 14.

4, 15: The king is no sooner dead than the people transfer their allegiance to his successor.
4, 17: *The fools' . . . sacrifice:* unacceptable to God because of their disobedience; cf 1 Sm 15, 22; Hos 6, 6.
5, 2: *Nightmares:* literally, "dreams."

5, 8: The wording of this verse has perhaps never been adequately explained.
5, 19: The meaning is that the joys of life, though temporary, keep a man from dwelling on the ills which afflict humanity.

power to partake of them, but a stranger devours them. This is vanity and a dire plague. 3 Should a man have a hundred children and live many years, no matter to what great age, still if he has not the full benefit of his goods, or if he is deprived of burial, of this man I proclaim that the child born dead is more fortunate than he. 4 Though it came in vain and goes into darkness and its name is enveloped in darkness; 5 though it has not seen or known the sun, yet the dead child is at rest rather than such a man. 6 Should he live twice a thousand years and not enjoy his goods, do not both go to the same place?

7 All man's toil is for his mouth, yet his desire is not fulfilled. 8 For what advantage has the wise man over the fool, or what advantage has the poor man in knowing how to conduct himself in life? 9 "What the eyes see is better than what the desires wander after." This also is vanity and a chase after wind.

QOHELETH'S CONCLUSIONS

10 Whatever is, was long ago given its name, and the nature of man is known, and that he cannot contend in judgment with one who is stronger than he. 11 For though there are many sayings that multiply vanity, what profit is there for a man? 12 For who knows what is good for a man in life, the limited days of his vain life (which God has made like a shadow)? Because—who is there to tell a man what will come after him under the sun?

A. *Man Cannot Find Out What is Good for Him to Do*

CRITIQUE OF SAGES ON THE DAY OF ADVERSITY

7 A good name is better than good ointment,
and the day of death than the the day of birth.

2 It is better to go to the house of mourning
than to the house of feasting,
For that is the end of every man,
and the living should take it to heart.
3 Sorrow is better than laughter,
because when the face is sad
the heart grows wiser.
4 The heart of the wise is in the house of mourning,
but the heart of fools is in the house of mirth.
5 It is better to hearken to the wise man's rebuke
than to hearken to the song of fools;
6 For as the crackling of thorns under a pot,
so is the fool's laughter.

This also is vanity,
7 For oppression can make a fool of a wise man,
and a bribe corrupts the heart.
8 Better is the end of speech than its beginning;
better is the patient spirit than the lofty spirit.
9 Do not in spirit become quickly discontented,
for discontent lodges in the bosom of a fool.

10 Do not say: How is it that former times were better than these? For it is not in wisdom that you ask about this.

11 Wisdom and an inheritance are good,
and an advantage to those that see the sun.

12 For the protection of wisdom is as the protection of money; and the advantage of knowledge is that wisdom preserves the life of its owner. 13 Consider the work of God. Who can make straight what he has made crooked? 14 On a good day enjoy good things, and on an evil day consider: Both the one and the other

God has made, so that man cannot find fault with him in anything.

CRITIQUE OF SAGES ON JUSTICE AND WICKEDNESS

15 I have seen all manner of things in my vain days: a just man perishing in his justice, and a wicked one surviving in his wickedness. 16 "Be not just to excess, and be not overwise, lest you be ruined. 17 Be not wicked to excess, and be not foolish. Why should you die before your time?" 18 It is good to hold to this rule, and not to let that one go; but he who fears God will win through at all events.

19 Wisdom is a better defense for the wise man than would be ten princes in the city, 20 yet there is no man on earth so just as to do good and never sin. 21 Do not give heed to every word that is spoken lest you hear your servant speaking ill of you, 22 for you know in your heart that you have many times spoken ill of others.

23 All these things I probed in wisdom. I said, "I will acquire wisdom"; but it was beyond me. 24 What exists is far-reaching; it is deep, very deep: who can find it out? 25 I turned my thought toward knowledge; I sought and pursued wisdom and reason, and I recognized that wickedness is foolish and folly is madness.

Critique of Sages on Women

26 More bitter than death I find the woman who is a hunter's trap, whose heart is a snare and whose hands are prison bonds. He who is pleasing to God will escape her, but the sinner will be entrapped by her. 27 Behold, this have I found, says Qoheleth, adding one thing to another that I might discover the answer 28 which my soul still seeks and has not found: One man out of a thousand have I come upon, but a woman among them all I have not found.

6, 3: A large family, a long life, an honorable burial, all were highly esteemed by the Hebrews, and it was considered a great misfortune to be deprived of them.

6, 6: *Same place:* the grave.

6, 7: *Mouth:* appetite, and therefore, body.

6, 9: *Better . . . wonder after:* the good that is present to us is better than that which is absent and, perhaps, unattainable.

6, 10: The one who is stronger than man is God.

7, 1: *Ointment:* applied to the child at birth; *a good name* remains even after death.

7, 16: St. Jerome explains the warning against excessive justice in reference to the self-righteous man who is so stern that he is never willing to forgive sin in others; cf vv 20ff.

7, 17: Untimely death was traditionally recognized as a divine punishment of the wicked; cf 1 Sm 2, 31–34; Jer 17, 11; Ps 55, 24; Prv 10, 27. This warning against presumptuous wickedness is not an

endorsement of any lesser degree of misconduct.

7, 18: *This rule . . . that one:* the sayings cited in vv 16f. Others refer *this* and *that* to riches and wisdom (cf 7, 12), justice and wisdom, or justice and wickedness. This last supposition makes the author's thought hard to follow.

7, 20: This is to be understood in the sense of Rom 5, 12. See note there.

7, 28: The author found sincerity rare among men, but among women still more rare.

29 Behold, only this have I found out: God made mankind straight, but men have had recourse to many calculations.

8 Who is like the wise man,
and who knows the
explanation of things?
A man's wisdom illumines his
face,
but an impudent look is
resented.

2 Observe the precept of the king, and in view of your oath to God, 3 be not hasty to withdraw from the king; do not join in with a base plot, for he does whatever he pleases, 4 because his word is sovereign, and who can say to him, "What are you doing?"

5 "He who keeps the commandment experiences no evil, and the wise man's heart knows times and judgments; 6 for there is a time and a judgment for everything"—Yet it is a great affliction for man 7 that he is ignorant of what is to come; for who will make known to him how it will be? 8 There is no man who is master of the breath of life so as to retain it, and none has mastery of the day of death. There is no exemption from the struggle, nor are the wicked saved by their wickedness. 9 All these things I considered and I applied my mind to every work that is done under the sun, while one man tyrannizes over another to his hurt.

The Problem of Retribution

10 Meanwhile I saw wicked men approach and enter; and as they left the sacred place, they were praised in the city for what they had done. This also is vanity. 11 Because the sentence against evildoers is not promptly executed, therefore the hearts of men are filled with the desire to commit evil— 12 because the sinner does evil a hundred times and survives. Though indeed I know that it shall be well with those who fear God, for

their reverence toward him; 13 and that it shall not be well with the wicked man, and he shall not prolong his shadowy days, for his lack of reverence toward God.

14 This is a vanity which occurs on earth: there are just men treated as though they had done evil and wicked men treated as though they had done justly. This, too, I say is vanity. 15 Therefore I commend mirth, because there is nothing good for man under the sun except eating and drinking and mirth: for this is the accompaniment of his toil during the limited days of the life which God gives him under the sun.

16 When I applied my heart to know wisdom and to observe what is done on earth, 17 I recognized that man is unable to find out all God's work that is done under the sun, even though neither by day nor by night do his eyes find rest in sleep. However much man toils in searching, he does not find it out; and even if the wise man says that he knows, he is unable to find it out.

B. *Man Does Not Know What is to Come*

9 All this I have kept in mind and recognized: the just, the wise, and their deeds are in the hand of God. Love from hatred man cannot tell; both appear equally vain, 2 in that there is the same lot for all, for the just and the wicked, for the good and the bad, for the clean and the unclean, for him who offers sacrifice and him who does not. As it is for the good man, so it is for the sinner; as it is for him who swears rashly, so it is for him who fears an oath. 3 Among all the things that happen under the sun, this is the worst, that things turn out the same for all. Hence the minds of men are filled with evil, and madness is in their hearts during life; and afterward they go to the dead.

4 Indeed, for any among the living there is hope; a live dog is better off than a dead lion. 5 For the living know that they are to die, but the

dead no longer know anything. There is no further recompense for them, because all memory of them is lost. 6 For them, love and hatred and rivalry have long since perished. They will never again have part in anything that is done under the sun.

7 Go, eat your bread with joy and drink your wine with a merry heart, because it is now that God favors your works. 8 At all times let your garments be white, and spare not the perfume for your head. 9 Enjoy life with the wife whom you love, all the days of the fleeting life that is granted you under the sun. This is your lot in life, for the toil of your labors under the sun. 10 Anything you can turn your hand to, do with what power you have; for there will be no work, nor reason, nor knowledge, nor wisdom in the nether world where you are going.

The Evil Time Not Known

11 Again I saw under the sun that the race is not won by the swift, nor the battle by the valiant, nor a livelihood by the wise, nor riches by the shrewd, nor favor by the experts; for a time of calamity comes to all alike. 12 Man no more knows his own time than fish taken in the fatal net, or birds trapped in the snare; like these children of men are caught when the evil time falls suddenly upon them.

13 On the other hand I saw this wise deed under the sun, which I thought sublime. 14 Against a small city with few men in it advanced a mighty king, who surrounded it and threw up great siegeworks about it. 15 But in the city lived a man who, though poor, was wise, and he delivered it through his wisdom. Yet no one remembered this poor man. 16 Though I had said, "Wisdom is better than force," yet the wisdom of the poor man is despised and his words go unheeded.

7, 29: *Calculations:* the many vain attempts and schemes of men to attain happiness by their own efforts.

8, 10: The text is obscure. The Latin has "wicked men buried, who, while still alive, were in the holy place and were praised in the city as if their works

were just."

8, 13: *Shadowy:* perhaps an addition here; cf 6, 12.
8, 15: See notes on 2, 24; 5, 19.
9, 1–10: These statements are based on a very imperfect concept of life beyond the grave. With Christian revelation about the future life came the only

satisfactory solution of the problem which so perplexed the author.
9, 1: *Love from hatred:* divine favor or disfavor.
9, 12: *His own time:* the time of death or sudden disaster.

17 "The quiet words of the wise are
      better heeded
   than the shout of a ruler of
      fools"—!

18 "A fly that dies can spoil the
      perfumer's ointment,
   and a single slip can ruin
      much that is good."

10 More weighty than wisdom
      or wealth is a little folly!

2 The wise man's understanding
      turns him to his right;
   the fool's understanding turns
      him to his left.

3 When the fool walks through the
street, in his lack of understanding he
calls everything foolish.

4 Should the anger of the ruler
burst upon you, forsake not your
place; for mildness abates great
offenses.

5 I have seen under the sun
another evil, like a mistake that proceeds from the ruler: 6 a fool put
in lofty position while the rich sit in
lowly places. 7 I have seen slaves
on horseback, while princes walked
on the ground like slaves.

8 He who digs a pit may fall into
      it,
   and he who breaks through a
      wall may be bitten by a
      serpent.

9 He who moves stones may be
      hurt by them,
   and he who chops wood is in
      danger from it.

10 If the iron becomes dull,
though at first he made easy progress, he must increase his efforts;
but the craftsman has the advantage
of his skill.

11 If the serpent bites because it has
      not been charmed,
   then there is no advantage for
      the charmer.

12 Words from the wise man's
      mouth win favor,
   but the fool's lips consume
      him.

13 The beginning of his words is
      folly,
   and the end of his talk is
      utter madness;

14 yet the fool multiplies words.
   Man knows not what is to come,
      for who can tell him what is
      to come after him?

15 When will the fool be weary of
      his labor,
   he who knows not the way to
      the city?

MAN DOES NOT KNOW WHAT
   EVIL WILL COME

16 Woe to you, O land, whose
      king was a servant,
   and whose princes dine in the
      morning!

17 Blessed are you, O land, whose
      king is of noble birth,
   and whose princes dine at the
      right time
   (for vigor and not in drinking
      bouts).

18 When hands are lazy, the rafters
      sag;
   when hands are slack, the
      house leaks.

19 Bread and oil call forth
      merriment
   and wine makes the living glad,
   but money answers for
      everything.

20 Even in your thoughts do not
      make light of the king,
   nor in the privacy of your
      bedroom revile the rich,
   Because the birds of the air may
      carry your voice,
   a winged creature may tell
      what you say.

11 Cast your bread upon the
      waters;
   after a long time you may
      find it again.

2 Make seven or eight portions;
   you know not what misfortune
      may come upon the earth.

MAN DOES NOT KNOW WHAT
   GOOD WILL COME

3 When the clouds are full,
   they pour out rain upon the
      earth.

Whether a tree falls to the south
      or to the north,
   wherever it falls, there shall it
      lie.

4 One who pays heed to the wind
      will not sow,
   and one who watches the
      clouds will never reap.

5 Just as you know not how the
      breath of life
   fashions the human frame in
      the mother's womb,
   So you know not the work of
      God
   which he is accomplishing in
      the universe.

6 In the morning sow your seed,
   and at evening let not your
      hand be idle:
   For you know not which of the
      two will be successful,
   or whether both alike will
      turn out well.

Poem on Youth and Old Age

7 Light is sweet! and it is pleasant
for the eyes to see the sun. 8 However many years a man may live, let
him, as he enjoys them all, remember
that the days of darkness will be
many. All that is to come is vanity.

9 Rejoice, O young man, while
      you are young
   and let your heart be glad in
      the days of your youth.
   Follow the ways of your heart,
      the vision of your eyes;
   Yet understand that as regards
      all this
   God will bring you to
      judgment.

10 Ward off grief from your heart
   and put away trouble from
      your presence,
   though the dawn of youth is
      fleeting.

12 Remember your Creator in
      the days of your youth,
   before the evil days come
   And the years approach of
      which you will say,
   I have no pleasure in them;

10, 2: It is doubtful whether the author is endorsing
either direction; cf Prv 4, 25ff.
10, 15: *He who . . . city:* perhaps a proverbial
expression for supreme stupidity.

11, 1: This may refer to a spirit of adventure in business or to generosity in almsgiving. *Waters:* of the ocean, which sometimes carry lost treasures to the shore.
11, 2: This verse refers either to almsgiving or to

the wisdom of not putting all one's cargo into a single
vessel.
11, 10: *Dawn . . . fleeting:* literally, "youth and the
dawn [of life] are vanity."

2 Before the sun is darkened,
    and the light, and the moon,
        and the stars,
    while the clouds return after
        the rain;
3 When the guardians of the
        house tremble,
    and the strong men are bent,
    And the grinders are idle
        because they are few,
    and they who look through
        the windows grow blind;
4 When the doors to the street are
        shut,
    and the sound of the mill is
        low;
    When one waits for the chirp of
        a bird;
    but all the daughters of song
        are suppressed;
5 And one fear heights,
    and perils in the street;

When the almond tree blooms,
    and the locust grows sluggish
    and the caper berry is without
        effect,
Because man goes to his lasting
        home,
    and mourners go about the
        streets;
6 Before the silver cord is
        snapped
    and the golden bowl is broken,
    And the pitcher is shattered
        at the spring,
    and the broken pulley falls
        into the well,
7 And the dust returns to the
        earth as it once was,
    and the life breath returns to
        God who gave it.

8 Vanity of vanities, says Qoheleth,
    all things are vanity!

Epilogue

9 Besides being wise, Qoheleth taught the people knowledge, and weighed, scrutinized and arranged many proverbs. 10 Qoheleth sought to find pleasing sayings, and to write down true sayings with precision. 11 The sayings of the wise are like goads; like fixed spikes are the topics given by one collector. 12 As to more than these, my son, beware. Of the making of many books there is no end, and in much study there is weariness for the flesh.

13 The last word, when all is heard: Fear God and keep his commandments, for this is man's all; 14 because God will bring to judgment every work, with all its hidden qualities, whether good or bad.

12, 2: *The sun . . . return:* the cloudy and rainy Palestinian winter, a natural symbol of old age.
  12, 3: *Guardians:* the arms; *strong men:* the legs; *grinders:* the teeth; *they who . . . windows:* the eyes.
  12, 4: *Doors:* the tightly compressed lips; *sound of the mill:* perhaps the sound of mastication; *daughters of song:* the voice.
  12, 5: *The almond tree blooms:* resembling the

white hair of age. *The locust . . . sluggish:* an image of the stiffness in movement of the aged. *The caper berry:* a stimulant for appetite.
  12, 6: *The golden bowl* suspended by *the silver cord* was a symbol of life; the snapping of the cord and the breaking of the bowl, a symbol of death. *The pitcher . . . the broken pulley:* another pair of metaphors for life and its ending.

12, 11: *Goads . . . one collector:* the *sayings* were stimulants to thought and also *spikes* or centers around which to group correlated pronouncements *of the wise.*
  12, 13: *Man's all:* St. Jerome explains: "Unto this is every man born, that, knowing his Maker, he may revere him in fear, honor, and the observance of his commandments."

Song of Songs

Love's Desires

THE song of songs by Solomon. *2B* Let him kiss me with kisses of his mouth! More delightful is your love than wine! 3 Your name spoken is a spreading perfume—that is why the maidens love you. 4 Draw me!—*D* We will follow you eagerly! *B* Bring me, O king, to your chambers.

D With you we rejoice and exult,
we extol your love; it is
beyond wine:
how rightly you are loved!

Love's Boast

5B I am as dark—but lovely,
O daughters of Jerusalem—
As the tents of Kedar,
as the curtains of Salma.

6 Do not stare at me because I
am swarthy,
because the sun has burned
me.
My brothers have been angry
with me;
they charged me with the
care of the vineyards:
my own vineyard I have not
cared for.

Love's Inquiry

7B Tell me, you whom my heart
loves,
where you pasture your
flock,
where you give them rest at
midday,
Lest I be found wandering
after the flocks of your
companions.

8G If you do not know,
O most beautiful among
women,
Follow the tracks of the flock
and pasture the young ones
near the shepherds' camps.

Love's Vision

9G To the steeds of Pharaoh's
chariots
would I liken you, my
beloved:

10 Your cheeks lovely in pendants,
your neck in jewels.

11 We will make pendants of gold
for you,
and silver ornaments.

Love's Union

12B For the king's banquet
my nard gives forth its
fragrance.

13 My lover is for me a sachet of
myrrh
to rest in my bosom.

14 My lover is for me a cluster of
henna
from the vineyards of
Engedi.

15G Ah, you are beautiful, my
beloved,
ah, you are beautiful; your
eyes are doves!

16B Ah, you are beautiful, my
lover—
yes, you are lovely.
Our couch, too, is verdant;

17 the beams of our house are
cedars,
our rafters, cypresses.

1, 2ff: The marginal letters indicate the speaker of the verses: *B*—Bride; *D*—Daughters of Jerusalem; *G*—Bridegroom. In vv 2–7 the bride and the daughters address the bridegroom who appears here as a king, but more often in the poem as a shepherd. King and shepherd are familiar figures of the Lord in the Sacred Scriptures, Cf Ps 23, 1; Is 40, 11; Jn 10, 1–16.

1, 5: *Daughters of Jerusalem:* the chorus whom the bride addresses and who ask her questions (5, 9; 6, 1), thus developing action within the poem. *Kedar:* a Syrian desert region whose name suggests blackness; tents were often made of black goat hair.

Curtains: tent coverings of *Salma,* a region close to Kedar.

1, 6: *Swarthy:* tanned by the sun from working in her brothers' vineyards. *My own vineyard:* the bride herself; cf 4, 14, where Israel is designated as the vineyard and the Lord is the Lover.

1, 7: Here and elsewhere in the Song (3, 1; 5, 8; 6, 1), the bride expresses her desire to be in the company of her lover. These verses point to a certain tension in the poem. Only at the end (8, 5ff) does mutual possession of the lovers become final.

1, 9ff: The bridegroom compares the girl's beauty

to the rich adornment of the royal chariot of Pharaoh.

1, 12: *Nard:* a precious perfume, a figure of the bride; cf 4, 14.

1, 13: *Myrrh:* produced from aromatic resin of balsam or roses.

1, 14: *Henna:* a plant which bears white scented flowers.

1, 15: *Doves:* suggesting innocence and charm.

1, 16f: Though the meeting place of the lovers is but a shepherd's hut of green branches, it becomes a palace with beams of cedar and rafters of cypress when adorned with their love.

2 I am a flower of Sharon,
a lily of the valley.

2G As a lily among thorns,
so is my beloved among
women.

3B As an apple tree among the
trees of the woods,
so is my lover among men.

I delight to rest in his shadow,
and his fruit is sweet to my
mouth.

4 He brings me into the banquet
hall
and his emblem over me is
love.

5 Strengthen me with raisin
cakes,
refresh me with apples,
for I am faint with love.

6 His left hand is under my
head
and his right arm embraces
me.

7 I adjure you, daughters of
Jerusalem,
by the gazelles and hinds of
the field,
Do not arouse, do not stir up
love
before its own time.

A Tryst in the Spring

8B Hark! my lover—here he
comes
springing across the
mountains,
leaping across the hills.

9 My lover is like a gazelle
or a young stag.
Here he stands behind our
wall,
gazing through the
windows,
peering through the lattices.

10 My lover speaks; he says to
me,
"Arise, my beloved, my
beautiful one,
and come!

11 "For see, the winter is past,
the rains are over and gone.

12 The flowers appear on the
earth,
the time of pruning the
vines has come,
and the song of the dove is
heard in our land.

13 The fig tree puts forth its figs,
and the vines, in bloom,
give forth fragrance.
Arise, my beloved, my
beautiful one,
and come!

14 "O my dove in the clefts of
the rock,
in the secret recesses of the
cliff,
Let me see you,
let me hear your voice,
For your voice is sweet,
and you are lovely."

15B Catch us the foxes, the little
foxes
that damage the vineyards;
for our vineyards are in
bloom!

16 My lover belongs to me and I
to him;
he browses among the lilies.

17 Until the day breathes cool
and the shadows lengthen,
roam, my lover,
Like a gazelle or a young stag
upon the mountains of
Bether.

Loss and Discovery

3B On my bed at night I sought
him
whom my heart loves—
I sought him but I did not
find him.

2 I will rise then and go about
the city;
in the streets and crossings
I will seek
Him whom my heart loves.
I sought him but I did not
find him.

3 The watchmen came upon me
as they made their rounds
of the city:
Have you seen him whom
my heart loves?

4 I had hardly left them
when I found him whom my
heart loves.
I took hold of him and would
not let him go
till I should bring him to the
home of my mother,
to the room of my parent.

5 I adjure you, daughters of
Jerusalem,
by the gazelles and hinds of
the field,
Do not arouse, do not stir up
love
before its own time.

Regal State of the Bridegroom

6D What is this coming up from
the desert,
like a column of smoke
Laden with myrrh, with
frankincense,
and with the perfume of
every exotic dust?

7 Ah, it is the litter of Solomon;
sixty valiant men surround
it,
of the valiant men of Israel:

8 All of them expert with the
sword,
skilled in battle,
Each with his sword at his
side
against danger in the watches
of the night.

9 King Solomon made himself
a carriage
of wood from Lebanon.

10 He made its columns of silver,
its roof of gold,
Its seat of purple cloth,
its framework inlaid with
ivory.

11 Daughters of Jerusalem, come
forth
and look upon King
Solomon

2, 1: *Flower of Sharon:* probably the narcissus, which grows in the fertile Plain of Sharon lying between Mount Carmel and Jaffa on the Mediterranean coast.

2, 4ff: *The banquet hall,* the sweet things of the table, the embrace of the bride and bridegroom express the delicacy of their affection and the intimacy of their love.

2, 7: *By the gazelles and hinds:* the swiftness of these animals and the luster and soft expression of their eyes are suggestive of love; cf Prv 5, 19.

2, 8ff: In this sudden change of scene, the bride pictures her lover hastening toward her dwelling until his voice is heard bidding her come to him.

2, 14: The bride is addressed as though she were a dove in a mountain fastness out of sight and reach.

2, 15: A snatch of song in answer to the request of v 14; cf 8, 13f. *Foxes:* all who threaten to disturb the

security of love symbolized by the vineyard; cf v 16.

2, 17: *Breathes cool:* in the evening when the sun is going down. Cf Gn 3, 8. *Bether:* a very obscure word; some interpret it in the sense of ruggedness; others, of spices; still others, of sacrifice (Gn 15, 10).

3, 1ff: See the parallel in 5, 2–8.

3, 6ff: The lover is portrayed as King Solomon, escorted by sixty armed men, coming in royal procession to meet his bride.

In the crown with which his
 mother has crowned him
on the day of his marriage,
on the day of the joy of his
 heart.

The Charms of the Beloved

4 *G* Ah, you are beautiful, my
 beloved,
 ah, you are beautiful!
Your eyes are doves
 behind your veil.
Your hair is like a flock of
 goats
 streaming down the
 mountains of Gilead.

2 Your teeth are like a flock of
 ewes to be shorn,
 which come up from the
 washing,
All of them big with twins,
 none of them thin and
 barren.

3 Your lips are like a scarlet
 strand;
 your mouth is lovely.
Your cheek is like a
 half-pomegranate
 behind your veil.

4 Your neck is like David's tower
 girt with battlements;
A thousand bucklers hang
 upon it,
 all the shields of valiant men.

5 Your breasts are like twin
 fawns,
 the young of a gazelle
 that browse among the lilies.

6 Until the day breathes cool
 and the shadows lengthen,
I will go to the mountain of
 myrrh,
 to the hills of incense.

7 You are all-beautiful, my
 beloved,
 and there is no blemish in
 you.

8 Come from Lebanon, my
 bride,
 come from Lebanon, come!

Descend from the top of
 Amana,
 from the top of Senir and
 Hermon,
From the haunts of lions,
 from the leopards'
 mountains.

9 You have ravished my heart,
 my sister, my bride;
 you have ravished my heart
 with one glance of your
 eyes,
 with one bead of your
 necklace.

10 How beautiful is your love,
 my sister, my bride,
 how much more delightful
 is your love than wine,
 and the fragrance of your
 ointments than all spices!

11 Your lips drip honey, my
 bride,
 sweetmeats and milk are
 under your tongue;
And the fragrance of your
 garments
 is the fragrance of Lebanon.

The Lover and his Garden

12 *G* You are an enclosed garden,
 my sister, my bride,
 an enclosed garden, a
 fountain sealed.

13 You are a park that puts
 forth pomegranates,
 with all choice fruits;

14 Nard and saffron, calamus
 and cinnamon,
 with all kinds of incense;
Myrrh and aloes,
 with all the finest spices.

15 You are a garden fountain, a
 well of water
 flowing fresh from Lebanon.

16 Arise, north wind! Come,
 south wind!
 blow upon my garden
 that its perfumes may spread
 abroad.

B Let my lover come to his
 garden
 and eat its choice fruits.

5 *G* I have come to my garden, my
 sister, my bride;
 I gather my myrrh and my
 spices,
I eat my honey and my
 sweetmeats,
 I drink my wine and my
 milk.

D Eat, friends; drink! Drink
 freely of love!

A Fruitless Search

2 *B* I was sleeping, but my heart
 kept vigil;
 I heard my lover knocking:
"Open to me, my sister, my
 beloved,
 my dove, my perfect one!
For my head is wet with dew,
 my locks with the moisture
 of the night."

3 I have taken off my robe,
 am I then to put it on?
I have bathed my feet,
 am I then to soil them?

4 My lover put his hand through
 the opening;
 my heart trembled within me,
 and I grew faint when he
 spoke.

5 I rose to open to my lover,
 with my hands dripping
 myrrh:
With my fingers dripping
 choice myrrh
 upon the fittings of the lock.

6 I opened to my lover—
 but my lover had departed,
 gone.
I sought him but I did not
 find him;
I called to him but he did not
 answer me.

4, 2: *Teeth:* praised for whiteness and regularity.

4, 3: *Pomegranate:* a fruit somewhat like an orange, with a firm skin and deep red color. The girl's cheek is compared, in roundness and tint, to a half-pomegranate.

4, 4: The ornaments about her neck are compared to the trophies on the city walls. Cf 1 Kgs 10, 10; 14, 26ff; Ez 27, 10.

4, 6: *Mountain of myrrh . . . hill of incense:* spoken figuratively of the bride; cf 8, 14.

4, 7: Cf St. Paul's description of the Church in Eph 5, 27. This verse is also applied to Our Lady, especi-

ally in the Liturgy of the feast of the Immaculate Conception.

4, 8: *Amana . . . Senir and Hermon:* these rugged heights symbolize obstacles that would separate the lovers; cf 2, 14.

4, 9: *Sister:* a term of endearment; it forms part of the conventional language of love used in this canticle.

4, 11: *Honey:* sweet words. Cf Prv 5, 3.

4, 12: *Enclosed garden . . . fountain sealed:* reserved for the bridegroom alone. The bride's fidelity is implied. Cf Prv 5, 15–19.

4, 14: These plants are all known for their sweet scent.

4, 16: The last two lines of the verse are spoken by the girl, inviting her lover to herself, the *garden*.

5, 1: *Eat, friends, drink!:* the lovers are encouraged to enjoy the delights of their love, symbol of Christ's union with the Church.

5, 2–8: A trial similar to that in 3, 1ff.

5, 3f: The bride's hesitation is due, not to levity, but to strong emotion.

5, 6: The disappearance of the lover seems to be a deliberate trial and test inflicted on the girl.

7　The watchmen came upon me
　　as they made their rounds
　　　of the city;
　They struck me, and wounded
　　me,
　and took my mantle from
　　me,
　　the guardians of the walls.

8　I adjure you, daughters of
　　Jerusalem,
　if you find my lover—
　What shall you tell him?—
　　that I am faint with love.

The Charms of the Lost Lover

9D　How does your lover differ
　　from any other,
　O most beautiful among
　　women?
　How does your lover differ
　　from any other,
　　that you adjure us so?

10B　My lover is radiant and ruddy;
　　he stands out among
　　　thousands.

11　His head is pure gold;
　　his locks are palm fronds,
　　black as the raven.

12　His eyes are like doves
　　beside running waters,
　His teeth would seem bathed
　　in milk,
　　and are set like jewels.

13　His cheeks are like beds of
　　spice
　with ripening aromatic
　　herbs.
　His lips are red blossoms;
　　they drip choice myrrh.

14　His arms are rods of gold
　　adorned with chrysolites.
　His body is a work of ivory
　　covered with sapphires.

15　His legs are columns of marble
　　resting on golden bases.
　His stature is like the trees on
　　Lebanon,
　　imposing as the cedars.

16　His mouth is sweetness itself;
　　he is all delight.

Such is my lover, and such
　　my friend,
　O daughters of Jerusalem.

Discovery

6D　Where has your lover gone,
　　O most beautiful among
　　　women?
　Where has your lover gone
　　that we may seek him with
　　　you?

2B　My lover has come down to
　　his garden,
　to the beds of spice,
　To browse in the garden
　　and to gather lilies.

3　My lover belongs to me and I
　　to him;
　　he browses among the lilies.

The Charms of the Beloved

4G　You are as beautiful as Tirzah,
　　my beloved,
　as lovely as Jerusalem,
　as awe-inspiring as bannered
　　troops.

5　Turn your eyes from me,
　　for they torment me.
　Your hair is like a flock of
　　goats
　streaming down from Gilead.

6　Your teeth are like a flock of
　　ewes
　which come up from the
　　washing,
　All of them big with twins,
　　none of them thin and
　　　barren.

7　Your cheek is like a
　　half-pomegranate
　behind your veil.

8　There are sixty queens, eighty
　　concubines,
　and maidens without
　　number—

9　One alone is my dove, my
　　perfect one,
　her mother's chosen,
　　the dear one of her parent.

The daughters saw her and
　　declared her fortunate,
　the queens and concubines,
　　and they sang her praises;

10D　Who is this that comes forth
　　like the dawn,
　as beautiful as the moon, as
　　resplendent as the sun,
　as awe-inspiring as bannered
　　troops?

Love's Meeting

11B　I came down to the nut
　　garden
　to look at the fresh growth
　　of the valley,
　To see if the vines were in
　　bloom.
　if the pomegranates had
　　blossomed.

12　Before I knew it, my heart had
　　made me
　the blessed one of my
　　kinswomen.

The Beauty of the Bride

7D　Turn, turn, O Shulammite,
　　turn, turn, that we may
　　look at you!

B　Why should you look at the
　　Shulammite
　as at the dance of the two
　　companies?

2D　How beautiful are your feet in
　　sandals,
　O prince's daughter!
　Your rounded thighs are like
　　jewels,
　the handiwork of an artist.

3　Your navel is a round bowl
　　that should never lack for
　　　mixed wine.
　Your body is a heap of wheat
　　encircled with lilies.

4　Your breasts are like twin
　　fawns,
　　the young of a gazelle.

5, 7: *The watchmen* do not know the reason for the girl's appearance in the city streets; cf 3, 2ff.

5, 10f: In answer to the question of v 9, the girl sings her lover's praises (vv 10–16). *Gold:* indicates how precious the lover is. *Palm fronds:* his thick, luxuriant growth of hair.

6, 1: The daughters of Jerusalem are won by this description of the lover and offer their aid in seeking him.

6, 2f: Determined to share her lover with no one, the girl refuses the aid offered by the daughters in seeking him. She implies that she had never really

lost him, for he *has come down to his garden.*

6, 4–9: The lover again celebrates her beauty. *Tirzah:* probably meaning "pleasant"; it was the early capital of the northern kingdom of Israel (1 Kgs 16).

6, 12: The text is obscure in Hebrew and in the ancient versions. The Vulgate reads: "I did not know; my soul disturbed me because of the chariots of Aminadab."

7, 1: *Shulammite:* so called either because the girl is considered to be from Shulam in the plain of Esdraelon (cf 1 Kgs 1, 3) or because the name may

mean "the peaceful one," and thus recall the name of Solomon. *As at the dance of the two companies:* the meaning is uncertain. The question in this verse could be construed as a refusal to dance; more probably, however, the girl accedes, as the following verses suggest.

7, 2–6: A flattering description of the girl's charms. *Rounded . . . jewels:* the meaning of these Hebrew words is not certain. *Wine* and *wheat* are symbolic of fertility; they are here associated with parts of the body which have a close relation to fruitfulness.

5 Your neck is like a tower of
          ivory.
     Your eyes are like the pools
          in Heshbon
     by the gate of Bath-rabbim.
     Your nose is like the tower on
          Lebanon
     that looks toward Damascus.
6 Your head rises like Carmel;
     your hair is like draperies of
          purple;
     a king is held captive in its
          tresses.

Love's Desires

7G How beautiful you are, how
          pleasing,
     my love, my delight!
8 Your very figure is like a palm
          tree.
     your breasts are like clusters.
9 I said: I will climb the palm
          tree,
     I will take hold of its
          branches.
     Now let your breasts be like
          clusters of the vine
     and the fragrance of your
          breath like apples,
10 And your mouth like an
          excellent wine—

Love's Union

B   that flows smoothly for my
          lover,
     spreading over the lips and
          the teeth.
11 I belong to my lover
     and for me he yearns.
12 Come, my lover, let us go
          forth to the fields
     and spend the night among
          the villages.
13 Let us go early to the
          vineyards, and see
     if the vines are in bloom,

If the buds have opened,
     if the pomegranates have
          blossomed;
     There will I give you my love.
14 The mandrakes give forth
          fragrance,
     and at our doors are all
          choice fruits;
     Both fresh and mellowed
          fruits, my lover,
     I have kept in store for you.

8 Oh, that you were my brother,
     nursed at my mother's
          breasts!
     If I met you out of doors, I
          would kiss you
     and none would taunt me.
2 I would lead you, bring you in
     to the home of my mother.
     There you would teach me to
          give you
     spiced wine to drink, and
          pomegranate juice.

3 His left hand is under my head
     and his right arm embraces
          me.
4 I adjure you, daughters of
          Jerusalem,
     by the gazelles and hinds of
          the field,
     Do not arouse, do not stir up
          love,
     before its own time.

Homecoming

5D Who is this coming up from
          the desert,
     leaning upon her lover?

G Under the apple tree I
          awakened you;
     it was there that your
          mother conceived you,
     it was there that your parent
          conceived.

True Love

6B Set me a seal on your heart,
     as a seal on your arm;
     For stern as death is love,
     relentless as the nether world
          is devotion;
     its flames are a blazing fire.
7 Deep waters cannot quench
          love,
     nor floods sweep it away.
     Were one to offer all he owns
          to purchase love,
     he would be roundly
          mocked.

Chastity and its Welcome

8 "Our sister is little
     and she has no breasts as yet.
     What shall we do for our
          sister
     when her courtship begins?
9 If she is a wall,
     we will build upon it a silver
          parapet;
     If she is a door,
     we will reinforce it with a
          cedar plank."

10 I am a wall,
     and my breasts are like
          towers.
     So now in his eyes I have
          become
     one to be welcomed.

The Bride and Her Dowry

11B Solomon had a vineyard at
          Baal-hamon;
     he gave over the vineyard to
          caretakers.
     For its fruit one would have
          to pay
     a thousand silver pieces.

7, 5: The comparison emphasizes the stateliness and whiteness of the neck, and the limpidity of the eyes. *Bath-rabbim:* a proper name which occurs only here; there was a city of Rabbah northeast of *Heshbon* in Transjordan. Cf Jer 49, 3.

7, 8f: *Palm tree:* a figure of stateliness. The bridegroom is eager to enjoy the possession of his bride.

7, 10: The bride delicately turns his compliment into an expression of the love and tenderness she feels for him.

7, 11–14: The girl's answer assures him of her affection and invites him to return with her to the rural delights which are associated with their love and which recall the meeting described in 6, 11f.

7, 14: *Mandrakes:* herbs believed to have power to arouse love and promote fertility; cf Gn 30, 14ff.

8, 5: The lovers are pictured walking homeward, enjoying the fulfillment of the desire which the girl expressed in vv 1f. The groom speaks of their first meeting.

8, 6f: *Seal:* this could be worn bound to the arm, as here, or suspended at the neck, or as a ring (Jer 22, 24). It was used for identification and signatures. *Stern . . . relentless:* in human experience, death and the nether world are inevitable, unrelenting; in the end they always triumph. Love, which is just as certain of its victory, matches its strength against the natural enemies of life; waters cannot extinguish it nor floods carry it away. It is more priceless than all riches.

8, 8ff: The bride affirms her chastity. In 8, 9 she quotes the course of action which her elder brothers

had decided on. While she is yet immature, they will shelter her in view of eventual marriage. If she is virtuous, she will be honored; if she is unchaste, she will be kept under strict vigilance. In reply to this she proclaims her virtue and boasts of having found welcome from her lover.

8, 11f: These enigmatic verses have been variously interpreted. In v 11 the girl alludes to a vineyard of great value which is compared to her own self in v 12. Her enormous dowry, *a thousand silver pieces,* is in keeping with her intrinsic worth. She has been the generous lover, giving herself and a dowry to her lover, referred to as *Solomon,* and also smaller gifts to her brothers, *the caretakers* (cf vv 8ff).

12 My vineyard is at my own
        disposal;
    the thousand pieces are for
        you, O Solomon,
    and two hundred for the
        caretakers of its fruit.

8, 13f: As in 2, 14f, her lover asks for a word or a
song and she replies in words similar to those found
in 2, 17.

Life Together

13G O garden-dweller,
        my friends are listening for
        your voice,
     let me hear it!

14B Be swift, my lover,
        like a gazelle or a young
        stag
     on the mountains of spices!

THE BOOK OF

Wisdom

THE REWARD OF JUSTICE

Exhortation to Justice, the Key to Life

LOVE justice, you who judge the earth; think of the Lord in goodness, and seek him in integrity of heart; 2 Because he is found by those who test him not, and he manifests himself to those who do not disbelieve him. 3 For perverse counsels separate a man from God, and his power, put to the proof, rebukes the foolhardy;

4 Because into a soul that plots evil wisdom enters not, nor dwells she in a body under debt of sin.

5 For the holy spirit of discipline flees deceit and withdraws from senseless counsels; and when injustice occurs it is rebuked.

6 For wisdom is a kindly spirit, yet she acquits not the blasphemer of his guilty lips;
Because God is the witness of his inmost self and the sure observer of his heart and the listener to his tongue.

7 For the spirit of the Lord fills the world, is all-embracing, and knows what man says.

8 Therefore no one who utters wicked things can go unnoticed, nor will chastising condemnation pass him by.

9 For the devices of the wicked man shall be scrutinized, and the sound of his words shall reach the Lord, for the chastisement of his transgressions;

10 Because a jealous ear hearkens to everything, and discordant grumblings are no secret.

11 Therefore guard against profitless grumbling, and from calumny withhold your tongues;
For a stealthy utterance does not go unpunished, and a lying mouth slays the soul.

12 Court not death by your erring way of life, nor draw to yourselves destruction by the works of your hands.

13 Because God did not make death, nor does he rejoice in the destruction of the living.

14 For he fashioned all things that they might have being; and the creatures of the world are wholesome,
And there is not a destructive drug among them nor any domain of the nether world on earth,

15 For justice is undying.

The Wicked Reject Immortality and Justice Alike

16 It was the wicked who with hands and words invited death, considered it a friend, and pined for it, and made a covenant with it,

---

1, 1: *Justice*: not merely the cardinal virtue of that name (cf 8, 7), but the universal moral quality which is the application of Wisdom to moral conduct.

1, 5: *Discipline*: here and elsewhere, another name for Wisdom; *injustice*: the opposite of the virtue in 1, 1.
1, 7: This verse is applied to the Holy Spirit in the liturgy at Pentecost.
1, 11: *Calumny*: speech against God and his providence is meant.

2 Because they deserve to be in
its possession,
they who said among
themselves, thinking not
aright:
"Brief and troublous is our
lifetime;
neither is there any remedy
for man's dying,
nor is anyone known to have
come back from the
nether world.

2 For haphazard were we born,
and hereafter we shall be as
though we had not been;
Because the breath in our
nostrils is a smoke
and reason is a spark at the
beating of our hearts,

3 And when this is quenched,
our body will be ashes
and our spirit will be poured
abroad like unresisting air.

4 Even our name will be forgotten
in time,
and no one will recall our
deeds.
So our life will pass away like
the traces of a cloud,
and will be dispersed like a
mist
Pursued by the sun's rays
and overpowered by its heat.

5 For our lifetime is the passing
of a shadow;
and our dying cannot be
deferred
because it is fixed with a
seal; and no one returns.

6 Come, therefore, let us enjoy
the good things that are real,
and use the freshness of
creation avidly.

7 Let us have our fill of costly
wine and perfumes,
and let no springtime
blossom pass us by;

8 let us crown ourselves with
rosebuds ere they wither.

9 Let no meadow be free from
our wantonness;
everywhere let us leave
tokens of our rejoicing,
for this our portion is, and
this our lot.

10 Let us oppress the needy just
man;
let us neither spare the widow
nor revere the old man for
his hair grown white with
time.

11 But let our strength be our norm
of justice;
for weakness proves itself
useless.

12 Let us beset the just one,
because he is obnoxious to
us;
he sets himself against our
doings,
Reproaches us for transgressions
of the law
and charges us with violations
of our training.

13 He professes to have knowledge
of God
and styles himself a child of
the Lord,

14 To us he is the censure of our
thoughts;
merely to see him is a
hardship for us,

15 Because his life is not like other
men's,
and different are his ways.

16 He judges us debased;
he holds aloof from our paths
as from things impure.
He calls blest the destiny of the
just
and boasts that God is his
Father.

17 Let us see whether his words be
true;
let us find out what will
happen to him.

18 For if the just one be the son of
God, he will defend him
and deliver him from the hand
of his foes.

19 With revilement and torture let
us put him to the test
that we may have proof of
his gentleness
and try his patience.

20 Let us condemn him to a
shameful death;
for according to his own
words, God will take care
of him."

21 These were their thoughts, but
they erred;
for their wickedness blinded
them,

22 And they knew not the hidden
counsels of God;
neither did they count on a
recompense of holiness
nor discern the innocent
souls' reward.

23 For God formed man to be
imperishable;
the image of his own nature
he made him.

24 But by the envy of the devil,
death entered the world,
and they who are in his
possession experience it.

The Hidden Counsels of God:

A. ON SUFFERING

3 But the souls of the just are in
the hand of God,
and no torment shall touch
them.

2 They seemed, in the view of
the foolish, to be dead;
and their passing away was
thought an affliction

3 and their going forth from us,
utter destruction.
But they are in peace.

4 For if before men, indeed, they
be punished,
yet is their hope full of
immortality;

5 Chastised a little, they shall be
greatly blessed,
because God tried them
and found them worthy of
himself.

6 As gold in the furnace, he
proved them,
and as sacrificial offerings he
took them to himself.

7 In the time of their visitation they
shall shine,
and shall dart about as sparks
through stubble;

8 They shall judge nations and
rule over peoples,
and the Lord shall be their
King forever.

2, 9: *Let no meadow . . . wantonness:* the extant Greek Mss have "Let none of us be without part in our wanton doings." Most Latin Mss have both forms of this line.
2, 12–20: Often applied to the Passion of our Lord; many have understood these verses as a direct prophecy. Cf. Mt 27, 41–44.
2, 12: *Law:* the law of Moses; *training* has the same meaning.
3, 1–8: Verses frequently applied to the martyrs.
3, 6: *Offerings:* the image is that of the holocaust, in which the victim is completely consumed by fire.

3, 7: *Visitation:* God's loving judgment of those who have been faithful to him; the same word is used in 14, 11 for the punishment of the wicked at God's final judgment. Cf also 3, 13, and *care,* 4, 15.

9 Those who trust in him shall
　　understand truth,
　and the faithful shall abide
　　with him in love:
　Because grace and mercy are
　　with his holy ones,
　and his care is with his elect.
10 But the wicked shall receive a
　　punishment to match their
　　thoughts,
　since they neglected justice
　　and forsook the Lord.
11 For he who despises wisdom
　　and instruction is doomed.
　Vain is their hope, fruitless are
　　their labors,
　and worthless are their works.
12 Their wives are foolish and their
　　children wicked;
　accursed is their brood.

B. ON CHILDLESSNESS

13 Yes, blessed is she who, childless
　　and undefiled,
　knew not transgression of the
　　marriage bed;
　she shall bear fruit at the
　　visitation of souls.
14 So also the eunuch whose hand
　　wrought no misdeed,
　who held no wicked thoughts
　　against the Lord—
　For he shall be given fidelity's
　　choice reward
　and a more gratifying heritage
　　in the Lord's temple.
15 For the fruit of noble struggles
　　is a glorious one;
　and unfailing is the root of
　　understanding.
16 But the children of adulterers
　　will remain without issue,
　and the progeny of an
　　unlawful bed will disappear.
17 For should they attain long life,
　　they will be held in no
　　esteem,
　and dishonored will their old
　　age be at last;
18 While should they die abruptly,
　　they have no hope
　nor comfort in the day of
　　scrutiny;
19 for dire is the end of the
　　wicked generation.

4 Better is childlessness with
　　virtue;
　for immortal is its memory:
　because both by God is it
　　acknowledged, and by men.
2 When it is present men imitate
　　it,
　and they long for it when it
　　is gone;
　And forever it marches crowned
　　in triumph,
　victorious in unsullied deeds
　　of valor.
3 But the numerous progeny of the
　　wicked shall be of no avail;
　their spurious offshoots shall
　　not strike deep root
　nor take firm hold.
4 For even though their branches
　　flourish for a time,
　they are unsteady and shall
　　be rocked by the wind
　and, by the violence of the
　　winds, uprooted;
5 Their twigs shall be broken off
　　untimely,
　and their fruit be useless,
　　unripe for eating,
　and fit for nothing.
6 For children born of lawless
　　unions
　give evidence of the
　　wickedness of their parents,
　when they are examined.

C. ON EARLY DEATH

7 But the just man, though he
　　die early, shall be at rest.
8 For the age that is honorable
　　comes not with the passing
　　of time,
　nor can it be measured in
　　terms of years.
9 Rather, understanding is the
　　hoary crown for men,
　and an unsullied life, the
　　attainment of old age.
10 He who pleased God was
　　loved;
　he who lived among sinners
　　was transported—
11 Snatched away, lest wickedness
　　pervert his mind
　or deceit beguile his soul;

12 For the witchery of paltry
　　things obscures what is right
　and the whirl of desire
　　transforms the innocent
　　mind.
13 Having become perfect in a
　　short while, he reached
　　the fullness of a long career;
14 　for his soul was pleasing to
　　the Lord,
　therefore he sped him out of
　　the midst of wickedness.
　But the people saw and did not
　　understand,
　nor did they take this into
　　account.
16 Yes, the just man dead
　　condemns the sinful who live,
　and youth swiftly completed
　　condemns the many years of
　　the wicked man grown old.
17 For they see the death of the
　　wise man
　and do not understand what
　　the Lord intended for him,
　or why he made him secure.
18 They see, and hold him in
　　contempt;
　but the Lord laughs them to
　　scorn.
19 And they shall afterward become
　　dishonored corpses
　and an unceasing mockery
　　among the dead.
　For he shall strike them down
　　speechless and prostrate
　and rock them to their
　　foundations;
　They shall be utterly laid waste
　　and shall be in grief
　and their memory shall perish.

The Final Judgment of the Wicked

20 Fearful shall they come, at the
　　counting up of their sins,
　and their lawless deeds shall
　　convict them to their face.

5 Then shall the just one with
　　great assurance confront
　his oppressors who set at
　　nought his labors.
2 Seeing this, they shall be shaken
　　with dreadful fear,
　and amazed at the
　　unlooked-for salvation.

3, 10: *To match their thoughts:* a fate as empty as that which they describe; cf 2, 1–5.
3, 13: *Visitation of souls:* that is, the last judgment. Cf 3, 7–9.
3, 14: *Fidelity's choice reward:* cf Is 56, 1–8. *More*

---

gratifying: better than sons and daughters; cf Is 56, 5.
4, 1: The Latin form of this line, "Oh, how fair is the chaste generation in its glory!" is a later adaptation, which is applied in the liturgy to the splendor of virginity.

4, 10f: There are allusions here to Enoch (Gn 5, 21–24), who was young by patriarchal standards, and to Lot (Gn 19, 10f; 2 Pt 2, 7f). Cf also Is 57, 1f.
4, 15, here omitted, repeats the last two lines of 3, 9.
4, 20: *Counting up:* the last judgment.

3 They shall say among
　　themselves, rueful
　and groaning through
　　anguish of spirit:
　"This is he whom once we held
　　as a laughingstock
4 　and as a type for mockery,
　　fools that we were!
　His life we accounted madness,
　　and his death dishonored.
5 See how he is accounted among
　　the sons of God;
　how his lot is with the saints!
6 We, then, have strayed from the
　　way of truth,
　and the light of justice did
　　not shine for us,
　and the sun did not rise for us.
7 We had our fill of the ways
　　of mischief and of ruin;
　we journeyed through
　　impassable deserts,
　but the way of the Lord we
　　knew not.
8 What did our pride avail us?
　What have wealth and its
　　boastfulness afforded us?
9 All of them passed like a shadow
　　and like a fleeting rumor;
10 Like a ship traversing the
　　heaving water,
　of which, when it has passed,
　　no trace can be found,
　no path of its keel in the
　　waves.
11 Or like a bird flying through
　　the air;
　no evidence of its course is to
　　be found—
　But the fluid air, lashed by the
　　beat of pinions,
　and cleft by the rushing force
　Of speeding wings, is traversed:
　　and afterward no mark of
　　passage can be found in it.
12 Or as, when an arrow has been
　　shot at a mark,
　the parted air straightway
　　flows together again
　so that none discerns the way
　　it went through—
13 Even so we, once born,
　　abruptly came to nought
　and held no sign of virtue to
　　display,
　but were consumed in our
　　wickedness."

―――――
6, 4: *Law:* that of Moses; cf v 10; 2, 12.
6, 10: *Response:* a suitable plea before the great
Judge. Cf Prv 22, 21; Job 31, 14; Hb 2, 1; Sir 8, 9.

14 Yes, the hope of the wicked is
　　like thistledown borne on
　　the wind,
　and like fine, tempest-driven
　　foam;
　Like smoke scattered by the wind,
　　and like the passing memory
　　of the nomad camping for
　　a single day.
15 But the just live forever,
　　and in the Lord is their
　　recompense,
　and the thought of them is
　　with the Most High.
16 Therefore shall they receive the
　　splendid crown,
　the beauteous diadem, from
　　the hand of the Lord—
　For he shall shelter them with
　　his right hand,
　and protect them with his arm.
17 He shall take his zeal for armor
　　and he shall arm creation to
　　requite the enemy;
18 He shall don justice for a
　　breastplate
　and shall wear sure judgment
　　for a helmet;
19 He shall take invincible
　　rectitude as a shield
20 　and whet his sudden anger
　　for a sword,
　And the universe shall war with
　　him against the foolhardy.
21 Well-aimed shafts of lightnings
　　shall go forth
　and from the clouds as from
　　a well-drawn bow shall
　　leap to the mark;
22 　and as from his sling,
　　wrathful hailstones shall be
　　hurled.
　The water of the sea shall be
　　enraged against them
　and the streams shall abruptly
　　overflow;
23 A mighty wind shall confront
　　them
　and a tempest winnow them
　　out;
　Thus lawlessness shall lay the
　　whole earth waste
　and evildoing overturn the
　　thrones of potentates.

Exhortation To Seek Wisdom

6 Hear, therefore, kings, and
　　understand;
　learn, you magistrates of the
　　earth's expanse!
2 Hearken, you who are in power
　　over the multitude
　and lord it over throngs of
　　peoples!
3 Because authority was given
　　you by the Lord
　and sovereignty by the Most
　　High,
　who shall probe your works
　　and scrutinize your
　　counsels!
4 Because, though you were
　　ministers of his kingdom,
　you judged not rightly,
　and did not keep the law,
　nor walk according to the
　　will of God,
5 Terribly and swiftly shall he
　　come against you,
　because judgment is stern for
　　the exalted—
6 For the lowly may be pardoned
　　out of mercy
　but the mighty shall be
　　mightily put to the test.
7 For the Lord of all shows no
　　partiality,
　nor does he fear greatness,
　Because he himself made the
　　great as well as the small,
　and he provides for all alike;
8 　but for those in power a
　　rigorous scrutiny impends.
9 To you, therefore, O princes,
　　are my words addressed
　that you may learn wisdom
　　and that you may not sin.
10 For those who keep the holy
　　precepts hallowed shall be
　　found holy,
　and those learned in them
　　will have ready a response.
11 Desire therefore my words;
　　long for them and you shall
　　be instructed.
12 Resplendent and unfading is
　　Wisdom,
　and she is readily perceived
　　by those who love her,
　and found by those who seek
　　her.
13 She hastens to make herself
　　known in anticipation of
　　men's desire;
14 　he who watches for her at
　　dawn shall not be
　　disappointed,
　for he shall find her sitting by
　　his gate.

15 For taking thought of her is
         the perfection of prudence,
      and he who for her sake
         keeps vigil shall quickly be
         free from care;
16 Because she makes her own
         rounds, seeking those
         worthy of her,
      and graciously appears to
         them in the ways,
      and meets them with all
         solicitude.
17 For the first step toward
         discipline is a very earnest
         desire for her;
      then, care for discipline is
         love of her;
18   love means the keeping of
         her laws;
      To observe her laws is the basis
         for incorruptibility;
19   and incorruptibility makes
         one close to God;
20   thus the desire for Wisdom
         leads up to a kingdom.
21 If, then, you find pleasure in
         throne and scepter,
      you princes of the peoples,
      honor Wisdom, that you
         may reign as kings forever.

PRAISE OF WISDOM BY SOLOMON

Introduction

22 Now what Wisdom is, and how
         she came to be, I shall
         relate;
      and I shall hide no secrets
         from you,
      But from the very beginning I
         shall search out
      and bring to light knowledge
         of her,
      nor shall I diverge from the
         truth.
23 Neither shall I admit consuming
         jealousy to my company,
      because that can have no
         fellowship with Wisdom.
24 A great number of wise men is
         the safety of the world,
      and a prudent king, the
         stability of his people;
25   so take instruction from my
         words, to your profit.

Solomon is Like All Other Men

7 I too am a mortal man, the
         same as all the rest,
      and a descendant of the first
         man formed of earth.
      And in my mother's womb I
         was molded into flesh
2   in a ten-months' period—
         body and blood,
      from the seed of man, and
      the pleasure that
         accompanies marriage.
3 And I too, when born, inhaled
         the common air,
      and fell upon the kindred
         earth;
      wailing, I uttered that first
         sound common to all.
4 In swaddling clothes and with
         constant care I was
         nurtured.
5 For no king has any different
         origin or birth,
6   but one is the entry into life
         for all; and in one same
         way they leave it.

Solomon Prayed and Wisdom and Riches Came to Him

7 Therefore I prayed, and
         prudence was given me;
      I pleaded, and the spirit of
         Wisdom came to me.
8 I preferred her to scepter and
         throne,
      And deemed riches nothing in
         comparison with her,
9   nor did I liken any priceless
         gem to her;
      Because all gold, in view of
         her, is a little sand,
      and before her, silver is to
         be accounted mire.
10 Beyond health and comeliness
         I loved her,
      And I chose to have her rather
         than the light,
      because the splendor of her
         never yields to sleep.
11 Yet all good things together
         came to me in her company,
      and countless riches at her
         hands;

12 And I rejoiced in them all,
         because Wisdom is their
         leader,
      though I had not known that
         she is the mother of these.

Solomon Prays for Help to Speak of Wisdom

13 Simply I learned about her,
         and ungrudgingly do I
         share—
      her riches I do not hide
         away;
14 For to men she is an unfailing
         treasure;
      those who gain this treasure
         win the friendship of God,
      to whom the gifts they have
         from discipline commend
         them.
15 Now God grant I speak
         suitably
      and value these endowments
         at their worth:
      For he is the guide of Wisdom
         and the director of the wise.
16 For both we and our words
         are in his hand,
      as well as all prudence and
         knowledge of crafts.
17 For he gave me sound
         knowledge of existing
         things,
      that I might know the
         organization of the universe
         and the force of its
         elements.
18 The beginning and the end and
         the midpoint of times,
      the changes in the sun's
         course and the variations
         of the seasons.
19 Cycles of years, positions
         of the stars,
20   natures of animals, tempers
         of beasts,
      Powers of the winds and
         thoughts of men,
      uses of plants and virtues of
         roots—
21 Such things as are hidden I
         learned, and such as are
         plain;
22   for Wisdom, the artificer of
         all, taught me.

7, 1: *First man formed of earth:* Adam. The author omits throughout the book the proper names of the characters in sacred history of whom he speaks; see

especially chapter 10.
7, 2: *In a ten-months' period:* thus the ancients

were accustomed to reckon the period of pregnancy.
7, 14: *Discipline:* cf note on 1, 5.

Nature and Incomparable Dignity of Wisdom

For in her is a spirit
    intelligent, holy, unique,
Manifold, subtle, agile,
    clear, unstained, certain,
Not baneful, loving the good,
    keen,
23   unhampered, beneficent,
        kindly,
Firm, secure, tranquil,
    all-powerful, all-seeing,
And pervading all spirits,
    though they be intelligent,
    pure and very subtle.
24 For Wisdom is mobile beyond
    all motion,
    and she penetrates and
    pervades all things by
    reason of her purity.
25 For she is an aura of the might
    of God
    and a pure effusion of the
    glory of the Almighty;
    therefore nought that is
    sullied enters into her.
26 For she is the refulgence of
    eternal light,
    the spotless mirror of the
    power of God,
    the image of his goodness.
27 And she, who is one, can do
    all things,
    and renews everything
    while herself perduring;
And passing into holy souls
    from age to age,
    she produces friends of God
    and prophets.
28 For there is nought God loves,
    be it not one who dwells
    with Wisdom.
29 For she is fairer than the sun
    and surpasses every
    constellation of the stars.
Compared to light, she takes
    precedence;
30   for that, indeed, night
        supplants,
    but wickedness prevails not
    over Wisdom.

8 Indeed, she reaches from end
    to end mightily
    and governs all things well.

Solomon Sought Wisdom, the Source of Blessings

2 Her I loved and sought after
    from my youth;
    I sought to take her for my
    bride
    and was enamored of her
    beauty.
3 She adds to nobility the
    splendor of companionship
    with God;
    even the Lord of all loved
    her.
4 For she is instructress in the
    understanding of God,
    the selector of his works.
5 And if riches be a desirable
    possession in life,
    what is more rich than
    Wisdom, who produces all
    things?
6 And if prudence renders service,
    who in the world is a better
    craftsman than she?
7 Or if one loves justice,
    the fruits of her works are
    virtues;
For she teaches moderation
    and prudence,
    justice and fortitude,
    and nothing in life is more
    useful for men than these.
8 Or again, if one yearns for
    copious learning,
    she knows the things of old,
    and infers those yet to come.
She understands the turns of
    phrases and the solutions
    of riddles;
    signs and wonders she knows
    in advance
    and the outcome of times and
    ages.

Solomon Sought Wisdom as His Counselor and Comfort

9 So I determined to take her to
    live with me,
    knowing that she would be
    my counselor while all was
    well,
    and my comfort in care and
    grief.

10 For her sake I should have
    glory among the masses,
    and esteem from the elders,
    though I be but a youth.
11 I should become keen in
    judgment,
    and should be a marvel before
    rulers.
12 They would abide my silence
    and attend my utterance;
    and as I spoke on further,
    they would place their hands
    upon their mouths.
13 For her sake I should have
    immortality
    and leave to those after me
    an everlasting memory.
14 I should govern peoples, and
    nations would be my
    subjects—
15   terrible princes, hearing of me,
        would be afraid;
    in the assembly I should
    appear noble, and in war
    courageous.
16 Within my dwelling, I should
    take my repose beside her;
For association with her
    involves no bitterness
    and living with her no grief,
    but rather joy and gladness.

Solomon Realizes that Wisdom is a Gift of God

17 Thinking thus within myself,
    and reflecting in my heart
That there is immortality in
    kinship with Wisdom,
18   and good pleasure in her
        friendship,
    and unfailing riches in the
    works of her hands,
And that in frequenting her
    society there is prudence,
    and fair renown in sharing
    her discourses,
    I went about seeking to take
    her for my own.
19 Now, I was a well-favored
    child,
    and I came by a noble nature;
20   or rather, being noble, I
        attained an unsullied body.

8, 1: *End to end:* from one end of the heavens to the other.
8, 7: *Moderation . . . fortitude:* what are now known as the cardinal virtues.
8, 12: *Hands upon their mouths:* an oft-mentioned sign of respect among the ancients for unanswerable wisdom; cf Jb 40, 4.
8, 19f: Here the sacred writer mentions first bodily, then spiritual, excellence. To make it plain that the latter is the governing factor in the harmonious development of the human person, he then reverses the order.

21 And knowing that I could not
   otherwise possess her except
   God gave it—
   and this, too, was prudence, to
   know whose is the gift—
   I went to the Lord and
   besought him,
   and said with all my heart:

Solomon's Prayer

9 God of my fathers, Lord of
   mercy,
   you who have made all things
   by your word
2 And in your wisdom have
   established man
   to rule the creatures produced
   by you,
3 To govern the world in holiness
   and justice,
   and to render judgment in
   integrity of heart:
4 Give me Wisdom, the attendant
   at your throne,
   and reject me not from
   among your children;
5 For I am your servant, the son
   of your handmaid,
   a man weak and short-lived
   and lacking in comprehension
   of judgment and of laws.
6 Indeed, though one be perfect
   among the sons of men,
   if Wisdom, who comes from
   you, be not with him,
   he shall be held in no esteem.
7 You have chosen me king over
   your people
   and magistrate for your sons
   and daughters.
8 You have bid me build a temple
   on your holy mountain
   and an altar in the city that is
   your dwelling place,
   a copy of the holy tabernacle
   which you had established
   from of old.
9 Now with you is Wisdom,
   who knows your works
   and was present when you
   made the world;
   Who understands what is
   pleasing in your eyes
   and what is conformable with
   your commands.

10 Send her forth from your holy
   heavens
   and from your glorious
   throne dispatch her
   That she may be with me and
   work with me,
   that I may know what is
   your pleasure.
11 For she knows and understands
   all things,
   and will guide me discreetly
   in my affairs
   and safeguard me by her glory;
12 Thus my deeds will be
   acceptable,
   and I shall judge your people
   justly
   and be worthy of my father's
   throne.
13 For what man knows God's
   counsel,
   or who can conceive what
   the Lord intends?
14 For the deliberations of mortals
   are timid,
   and unsure are our plans.
15 For the corruptible body
   burdens the soul
   and the earthen shelter
   weighs down the mind that
   has many concerns.
16 And scarce do we guess the
   things on earth,
   and what is within our grasp
   we find with difficulty;
   but when things are in
   heaven, who can search
   them out?
17 Or who ever knew your counsel,
   except you had given
   Wisdom
   and sent your holy spirit from
   on high?
18 And thus were the paths of
   those on earth made
   straight,
   and men learned what was
   your pleasure,
   and were saved by Wisdom.

Wisdom Preserves Her Followers

10 She preserved the first-formed
   father of the world
   when he alone had been
   created;

And she raised him up from his
   fall,
2 and gave him power to rule
   all things.
3 But when the unjust man
   withdrew from her in his
   anger,
   he perished through his
   fratricidal wrath.
4 When on his account the earth
   was flooded, Wisdom again
   saved it,
   piloting the just man on
   frailest wood.
5 She, when the nations were
   sunk in universal
   wickedness,
   knew the just man, kept
   him blameless before God,
   and preserved him resolute
   against pity for his child.
6 She delivered the just man from
   among the wicked who were
   being destroyed,
   when he fled as fire descended
   upon Pentapolis—
7 Where as a testimony to its
   wickedness,
   there yet remain a smoking
   desert,
   Plants bearing fruit that never
   ripens,
   and the tomb of a disbelieving
   soul, a standing pillar of
   salt.
8 For those who forsook Wisdom
   first were bereft of knowledge
   of the right,
   And then they left mankind a
   memorial of their folly—
   so that they could not even
   be hidden in their fall.
9 But Wisdom delivered from
   tribulations those who
   served her.
10 She, when the just man fled
   from this brother's anger,
   guided him in direct ways,
   Showed him the kingdom of
   God
   and gave him knowledge of
   holy things;
   She prospered him in his labors
   and made abundant the fruit
   of his works,

8, 21: *Possess her:* in the Latin, "be continent."
Though this verse has often been cited in connection
with the virtue of chastity, the original must certainly
mean "be possessed of Wisdom."
10, 1–21: This chapter prepares for the following
section (11, 2—19, 22) on the history of Israel in the

Exodus, by reviewing the dealings of Wisdom with
the patriarchs. It has a parallel in Sir 44–50; cf also
Wis 18, 9.
  10, 1f: Adam.
  10, 3: Cain.
  10, 4: Noah.

10, 5: Abraham.
10, 6: Lot. *Pentapolis:* the five cities, including
Sodom; cf Gn 14, 2.
10, 7: *Disbelieving soul:* Lot's wife; cf Gn 19, 26.
10, 10ff: Jacob.

11 Stood by him against the greed
of his defrauders,
and enriched him;
12 She preserved him from foes,
and secured him against
ambush,
And she gave him the prize
for his stern struggle
that he might know that
devotion to God is mightier
than all else.
13 She did not abandon the just
man when he was sold,
but delivered him from sin.
14 She went down with him into
the dungeon,
and did not desert him in his
bonds,
Until she brought him the
scepter of royalty
and authority over his
oppressors,
Showed those who had defamed
him false,
and gave him eternal glory.
15 The holy people and blameless
race—it was she
who delivered them from the
nation that oppressed them.
16 She entered the soul of the
Lord's servant,
and withstood fearsome kings
with signs and portents;
17 she gave the holy ones the
recompense of their labors,
Conducted them by a wondrous
road,
and became a shelter for them
by day
and a starry flame by night.
18 She took them across the Red
Sea
and brought them through
deep waters—
19 But their enemies she
overwhelmed,
and cast them up from the
bottom of the depths.
20 Therefore the just despoiled
the wicked;
and they sang, O Lord, your
holy name
and praised in unison your
conquering hand—

21 Because Wisdom opened the
mouths of the dumb,
and gave ready speech to
infants.

11 She made their affairs prosper
through the holy prophet.

SPECIAL PROVIDENCE OF GOD DURING THE EXODUS

Introduction

2 They journeyed through the
uninhabited desert,
and in solitudes they pitched
their tents;
3 they withstood enemies and
took vengeance on their
foes.
4 When they thirsted, they called
upon you,
and water was given them
from the sheer rock,
assuagement for their thirst
from the hard stone.
5 For by the things through which
their foes were punished
they in their need were
benefited.

First Example: Water Punishes the Egyptians and Benefits the Israelites

6 Instead of a spring, when the
perennial river
was troubled with impure
blood
7 as a rebuke to the decree
for the slaying of infants,
You gave them abundant water
in an unhoped-for way,
8 once you had shown by the
thirst they then had
how you punished their
adversaries.
9 For when they had been tried,
though only mildly
chastised,
they recognized how the
wicked, condemned in
anger, were being tormented.
11 Both those afar off and those
close by were afflicted:
10 the latter you tested,
admonishing them as a
father;

the former as a stern king
you probed and condemned.
12 For a twofold grief took hold of
them
and a groaning at the
remembrance of the ones
who had departed.
13 For when they heard that the
cause of their own
torments
was a benefit to these others,
they recognized the Lord.
14 Him who of old had been cast
out in exposure they
indeed mockingly rejected;
but in the end of events, they
marveled at him,
since their thirst proved
unlike that of the just.

Second Example: Animals Punish the Egyptians and Benefit the Israelites

15 And in return for their
senseless, wicked thoughts,
which misled them into
worshiping dumb serpents
and worthless insects,
You sent upon them swarms
of dumb creatures for
vengeance;
16 that they might recognize
that man is punished by
the very things through
which he sins.

Digression on God's Mercy

17 For not without means was
your almighty hand,
that had fashioned the
universe from formless
matter,
to send upon them a drove
of bears or fierce lions,
18 Or new-created, wrathful,
unknown beasts
to breathe forth fiery breath,
Or pour out roaring smoke,
or flash terrible sparks from
their eyes.
19 Not only could these attack and
completely destroy them;
even their frightful
appearance itself could slay.

10, 12: *Devotion to God:* in the Greek this signifies
"piety" or "religion," and is the equivalent of the
Hebrew "fear of the Lord"; cf Prv 1, 7.
10, 13f: Joseph.
10, 16: Moses.
10, 19: *Cast them up:* their bodies, on the shore.

11, 2ff: Few verses in these later chapters can be
fully understood without consulting the passages in
the Mosaic books which are indicated in the cross
references. The theme of this part of the book is
expressed in 11, 5, and is illustrated in the following
chapters by five examples drawn from Exodus events.

11, 6ff: *The perennial river:* the Nile; the contrast
is between the first plague of Egypt (Ex 7, 17–24) and
the water drawn from the rock in Horeb (Ex 17,
5–7; Nm 20, 8–11).
11, 15: *Dumb:* that is, irrational.

20 Even without these, they could
         have been killed at a single
         blast,
      pursued by retribution
      and winnowed out by your
         mighty spirit;
      But you have disposed all
         things by measure and
         number and weight.
21 For with you great strength
         abides always;
      who can resist the might of
         your arm?
22 Indeed, before you the whole
         universe is as a grain from
         a balance.
      or a drop of morning dew
         come down upon the earth.
23 But you have mercy on all,
         because you can do all
         things;
      and you overlook the sins of
         men that they may repent.
24 For you love all things that are
         and loathe nothing that you
         have made;
      for what you hated, you
         would not have fashioned.
25 And how could a thing remain,
         unless you willed it;
      or be preserved, had it not
         been called forth by you?
26 But you spare all things,
         because they are yours, O
         Lord and lover of souls,

12

      for your imperishable spirit
         is in all things!
2 Therefore you rebuke offenders
         little by little,
      warn them, and remind them
         of the sins they are
         committing,
      that they may abandon their
         wickedness and believe in
         you, O Lord!
3 For, truly, the ancient
         inhabitants of your holy
         land,
4 whom you hated for deeds
         most odious—
   Works of witchcraft and
         impious sacrifices;
5 a cannibal feast of human
         flesh
      and of blood, from the midst
         of . . .—

These merciless murderers of
         children,
6   and parents who took with
         their own hands defenseless
         lives,
   You willed to destroy by the
         hands of our fathers,
7   that the land that is dearest
         of all to you
      might receive a worthy
         colony of God's children.
8 But even these, as they were
         men, you spared,
      and sent wasps as forerunners
         of your army
      that they might exterminate
         them by degrees.
9 Not that you were without
         power to have the wicked
         vanquished in battle by the
         just,
      or wiped out at once by
         terrible beasts or by one
         decisive word;
10 But condemning them bit by
         bit, you gave them space
         for repentance.
   You were not unaware that their
         race was wicked
      and their malice ingrained,
   And that their dispositions
         would never change;
11   for they were a race accursed
         from the beginning.
   Neither out of fear for anyone
         did you grant amnesty for
         their sins.
12 For who can say to you,
         "What have you done?"
      or who can oppose your
         decree?
   Or when peoples perish, who
         can challenge you, their
         maker;
      or who can come into your
         presence as vindicator of
         unjust men?
13 For neither is there any god
         besides you who have the
         care of all,
      that you need show you have
         not unjustly condemned;
14 Nor can any king or prince
         confront you on behalf of
         those you have punished.

15 But as you are just, you govern
         all things justly;
      you regard it as unworthy of
         your power
      to punish one who has
         incurred no blame.
16 For your might is the source
         of justice;
      your mastery over all things
         makes you lenient to all.
17 For you show your might when
         the perfection of your
         power is disbelieved;
      and in those who know you,
         you rebuke temerity.
18 But though you are master of
         might, you judge with
         clemency,
      and with much lenience you
         govern us;
      for power, whenever you will,
         attends you.
19 And you taught your people, by
         these deeds,
      that those who are just must
         be kind;
   And you gave your sons good
         ground for hope
      that you would permit
         repentance for their sins.
20 For these were enemies of your
         servants, doomed to death;
      yet, while you punished them
         with such solicitude and
         pleading,
      granting time and opportunity
         to abandon wickedness,
21 With what exactitude you
         judged your sons,
      to whose fathers you gave the
         sworn covenants of goodly
         promises!
22 Us, therefore, you chastise, and
         our enemies with a thousand
         blows you punish,
      that we may think earnestly
         of your goodness when we
         judge,
      and, when being judged, may
         look for mercy.

Second Example Resumed

23 Hence those unjust also, who
         lived a life of folly,
      you tormented through their
         own abominations.

11, 22: *Grain from a balance:* a tiny particle used
for weighing on sensitive scales.
12, 5: *And of blood, from the midst of . . .:* this
line is obscure in the current Greek text and in all

extant translations. Either one or two words would
complete it. The horrible crimes here spoken of
(cf 14, 23) were not unheard of in the ancient pagan
world.

12, 17: The brunt of God's anger and vindictive
justice is borne by those who know him and yet
defy his authority and might. Cf 1, 2; 15, 2, but also
12, 27; 18, 13.

24 For they went far astray in the
      paths of error,
   taking for gods the worthless
      and disgusting among
      beasts,
   deceived like senseless infants.
25 Therefore as though upon
      unreasoning children,
   you sent your judgment on
      them as a mockery;
26 But they who took no heed of
      punishment which was but
      child's play
   were to experience a
      condemnation worthy of
      God.
27 For in the things through which
      they suffered distress,
   since they were tortured by
      the very things they deemed
      gods,
   They saw and recognized the
      true God
   whom before they had refused
      to know;
   with this, their final
      condemnation came upon
      them.

Digression on False Worship

A. NATURE WORSHIP

13 For all men were by nature
      foolish who were in
      ignorance of God,
   and who from the good things
      seen did not succeed in
      knowing him who is,
   and from studying the works
      did not discern the artisan;
2 But either fire, or wind, or the
      swift air,
   or the circuit of the stars, or
      the mighty water,
   or the luminaries of heaven,
      the governors of the world,
      they considered gods.
3 Now if out of joy in their beauty
      they thought them gods,
   let them know how far more
      excellent is the Lord than
      these;
   for the original source of
      beauty fashioned them.
4 Or if they were struck by their
      might and energy,

let them from these things
   realize how much more
   powerful is he who made
   them.
5 For from the greatness and the
      beauty of created things
   their original author, by
      analogy, is seen.
6 But yet, for these the blame is
      less;
   For they indeed have gone
      astray perhaps,
   though they seek God and
      wish to find him.
7 For they search busily among
      his works,
   but are distracted by what
      they see, because the things
      seen are fair.
8 But again, not even these are
      pardonable.
9 For if they so far succeeded in
      knowledge
   that they could speculate
      about the world,
   how did they not more
      quickly find its Lord?

B. IDOLATRY

10 But doomed are they, and in
      dead things are their hopes,
   who termed gods things
      made by human hands:
   Gold and silver, the product of
      art, and likenesses of
      beasts,
   or useless stone, the work of
      an ancient hand.

The Carpenter and Wooden Idols

11 A carpenter may saw out a
      suitable tree
   and skillfully scrape off all its
      bark,
   And deftly plying his art,
      produce something fit for
      daily use,
12   and use up the refuse from
      his handiwork in preparing
      his food, and have his fill;
13 Then the good-for-nothing
      refuse from these remnants,
   crooked wood grown full of
      knots,
   he takes and carves to occupy
      his spare time.

This wood he models with
   listless skill,
   and patterns it on the image
      of a man
14 or makes it resemble some
      worthless beast.
   When he has daubed it with red
      and crimsoned its surface
      with red stain,
   and daubed over every
      blemish in it,
15 He makes a fitting shrine for it
      and puts it on the wall,
   fastening it with a nail.
16 Thus lest it fall down he
      provides for it,
   knowing that it cannot help
      itself;
   for, truly, it is an image and
      needs help.
17 But when he prays about his
      goods or marriage or
      children,
   he is not ashamed to address
      the thing without a soul.
   And for vigor he invokes the
      powerless;
18   and for life he entreats the
      dead;
   And for aid he beseeches the
      wholly incompetent,
   and about travel, something
      that cannot even walk.
19 And for profit in business and
      success with his hands
   he asks facility of a thing
      with hands completely inert.

14 Again, one preparing for a
      voyage and about to
      traverse the wild waves
   cries out to wood more
      unsound than the boat that
      bears him.
2 For the urge for profits devised
      this latter,
   and Wisdom the artificer
      produced it.
3 But your providence, O Father!
      guides it,
   for you have furnished even
      in the sea a road,
   and through the waves a
      steady path,
4 Showing that you can save from
      any danger,
   so that even one without
      skill may embark.

13, 1: *Him who is:* the Hebrew sacred name of
God; cf Ex 3, 14.

13, 2: *Luminaries of heaven:* the Latin interprets,
"sun and moon"; *governors:* cf Gn 1, 16.

13, 6: *The blame is less:* the greater blame is
incurred by those mentioned in 13, 10 and 15, 14ff.

5 But you will that the products
    of your Wisdom be not idle;
    therefore men trust their
        lives even to frailest wood,
    and have been safe crossing
        the surge on a raft.
6 For of old, when the proud
        giants were being destroyed,
    the hope of the universe, who
        took refuge on a raft,
    left to the world a future
        for his race, under the
        guidance of your hand.
7 For blest is the wood through
        which justice comes about;
8 but the handmade idol is
        accursed, and its maker as
        well:
    he for having produced it,
        and it, because though
        corruptible, it was termed a
        god.
9 Equally odious to God are the
        evildoer and his evil deed;
10 and the thing made shall be
        punished with its contriver.
11 Therefore upon even the idols of
        the nations shall a
        visitation come,
    since they have become
        abominable amid God's
        works,
    Snares for the souls of men
    and a trap for the feet of the
        senseless.

The Origin and Evils of Idolatry

12 For the source of wantonness
        is the devising of idols;
    and their invention was a
        corruption of life.
13 For in the beginning they were
        not, nor shall they continue
        forever;
14 for by the vanity of men they
        came into the world,
    and therefore a sudden end is
        devised for them.
15 For a father, afflicted with
        untimely mourning,
    made an image of the child so
        quickly taken from him,
    And now honored as a god what
        was formerly a dead man
    and handed down to his
        subjects mysteries and
        sacrifices.

16 Then, in time, the impious
        practice gained strength and
        was observed as law,
    and graven things were
        worshiped by princely
        decrees.
17 Men who lived so far away
        that they could not honor
        him in his presence
    copied the appearance of the
        distant king
    And made a public image of
        him they wished to honor,
    out of zeal to flatter him
        when absent, as though
        present.
18 And to promote this observance
        among those to whom it
        was strange,
    the artisan's ambition
        provided a stimulus.
19 For he, mayhap in his
        determination to please the
        ruler,
    labored over the likeness to
        the best of his skill;
20 And the masses, drawn by the
        charm of the workmanship,
    soon thought he should be
        worshiped who shortly
        before was honored as a man.
21 And this became a snare for
        mankind,
    that men enslaved to either
        grief or tyranny
    conferred the incommunicable
        Name on stocks and stones.
22 Then it was not enough for
        them to err in their
        knowledge of God;
    but even though they live in
        a great war of ignorance,
    they call such evils peace.
23 For while they celebrate either
        child-slaying sacrifices or
        clandestine mysteries,
    or frenzied carousals in
        unheard-of rites,
24 They no longer safeguard either
        lives or pure wedlock;
    but each either waylays and
        kills his neighbor, or
        aggrieves him by adultery.
25 And all is confusion—blood
        and murder, theft and guile,
    corruption, faithlessness,
        turmoil, perjury,

26 Disturbance of good men,
        neglect of gratitude,
    besmirching of souls,
        unnatural lust,
    disorder in marriage, adultery
        and shamelessness.
27 For the worship of infamous idols
        is the reason and source and
        extremity of all evil.
28 For they either go mad with
        enjoyment, or prophesy lies,
    or live lawlessly or lightly
        forswear themselves.
29 For as their trust is in soulless
        idols,
    they expect no harm when
        they have sworn falsely.
30 But on both counts shall justice
        overtake them:
    because they thought ill of
        God and devoted themselves
        to idols,
    and because they deliberately
        swore false oaths, despising
        piety.
31 For not the might of those that
        are sworn by
    but the retribution of sinners
        ever follows upon the
        transgression of the wicked.

15 But you, our God, are good
        and true,
    slow to anger, and governing
        all with mercy.
2 For even if we sin, we are yours,
        and know your might;
    but we will not sin, knowing
        that we belong to you.
3 For to know you well is
        complete justice,
    and to know your might is
        the root of immortality.
4 For neither did the evil creation
        of men's fancy deceive us,
    nor the fruitless labor of
        painters,
    A form smeared with varied
        colors,
5 the sight of which arouses
        yearning in the senseless man,
    till he longs for the inanimate
        form of a dead image.
6 Lovers of evil things, and
        worthy of such hopes
    are they who make them and
        long for them and worship
        them.

14, 6: Noah.
14, 7: Often applied to the Cross of our Lord.

14, 30: *Piety:* the sanctity of oaths.
14, 31: Perjury is a form of deceit which calls for

punishment even though it be practiced in the name
of a lifeless idol.

The Potter and Clay Idols

7 For truly the potter, laboriously
    working the soft earth,
    molds for our service each
       several article:
    Both the vessels that serve for
       clean purposes
    and their opposites, all alike;
    As to what shall be the use of
       each vessel of either class
    the worker in clay is the
       judge.
8 And with misspent toil he molds
    a meaningless god from the
       selfsame clay;
    though he himself shortly
       before was made from the
       earth
    And after a little, is to go
       whence he was taken,
    when the life that was lent
       him is demanded back.
9 But his concern is not that he is
       to die
    nor that his span of life is
       brief;
    Rather, he vies with goldsmiths
       and silversmiths
    and emulates molders of
       bronze,
    and takes pride in modeling
       counterfeits.
10 Ashes his heart is! more
    worthless than earth is his
       hope,
    and more ignoble than clay
       his life;
11 Because he knew not the one
    who fashioned him,
    and breathed into him a
       quickening soul,
    and infused a vital spirit,
12 Instead, he esteemed our life a
    plaything,
    and our span of life a holiday
       for gain;
    "For one must," says he,
    "make profit every way, be
       it even out of evil."
13 For this man more than any
    knows that he is sinning,
    when out of earthen stuff he
       creates fragile vessels and
       idols alike.

14 But all quite senseless, and
    worse than childish in mind,
    are the enemies of your
       people who enslaved them.
15 For they esteemed all the idols
    of the nations gods,
    which have no use of the eyes
       for vision,
    nor nostrils to snuff the air,
    Nor ears to hear,
    nor fingers on their hands for
       feeling;
    even their feet are useless to
       walk with.
16 For a man made them;
    one whose spirit has been lent
       him fashioned them.
    For no man succeeds in
       fashioning a god like
       himself;
17 being mortal, he makes a
    dead thing with his lawless
       hands.
    For he is better than the things
       he worships;
    he at least lives, but never they.

Second Example Resumed

18 And besides, they worship the
    loathsome beasts—
    for compared as to folly, these
       are worse than the rest,
19 Nor for their looks are they
    good or desirable beasts,
    but they have escaped both
       the approval of God and
       his blessing.

16 Therefore they were fittingly
    punished by similar
       creatures,
    and were tormented by a
       swarm of insects.
2 Instead of this punishment,
    you benefited your people
    with a novel dish, the delight
       they craved,
    by providing quail for their
       food;
3 That those others, when they
    desired food,
    since the creatures sent to
       plague them were so
       loathsome,
    should be turned from even
       the craving of necessities,

    While these, after a brief period
       of privation,
    partook of a novel dish.
4 For upon those oppressors,
    inexorable want had to
       come;
    but these needed only be
       shown how their enemies
       were being tormented.
5 For when the dire venom of
    beasts came upon them
    and they were dying from the
       bite of crooked serpents,
    your anger endured not to
       the end.
6 But as a warning, for a short
    time they were terrorized,
    though they had a sign of
       salvation, to remind them
       of the precept of your Law.
7 For he who turned toward it
    was saved, not by what he
       saw,
    but by you, the savior of all.
8 And by this also you convinced
    our foes
    that you are he who delivers
       from all evil.
9 For the bites of locusts and of
    flies slew them,
    and no remedy was found to
       save their lives
    because they deserved to be
       punished by such means;
10 But not even the fangs of
    poisonous reptiles overcame
       your sons,
    for your mercy brought the
       antidote to heal them.
11 For as a reminder of your
    injunctions, they were stung,
    and swiftly they were saved,
    Lest they should fall into deep
       forgetfulness
    and become unresponsive to
       your beneficence.
12 For indeed, neither herb nor
    application cured them,
    but your all-healing word, O
       Lord!
13 For you have dominion over
    life and death;
    you lead down to the gates
       of the nether world, and
       lead back.

15, 18ff: The author here returns to the main theme of chapters 11–19, which was interrupted by the digression 13,1—15, 17.
15, 18: *For . . . rest:* this may mean that the

creatures worshiped by the Egyptians (e.g., crocodiles, serpents, scarabs, etc.) were more patently lacking in intelligence than the general run of beasts; cf 11, 15; 12, 24.

16, 1: *They:* the Egyptian idolaters.
16, 6: *Sign:* the brazen serpent; cf Nm 21, 9.

14 Man, however, slays in his
    malice,
    but when the spirit has come
      away, it does not return,
    nor can he bring back the
      soul once it is confined.
15 But your hand none can escape.

Third Example: A Rain of Manna for Israel instead of the Plague of Storms

16 For the wicked who refused to
    know you
    were punished by the might
      of your arm,
    Pursued by unwonted rains and
      hailstorms and unremitting
      downpours,
    and consumed by fire.
17 For against all expectation, in
    water which quenches
    anything,
    the fire grew more active;
    For the universe fights on behalf
      of the just.
18 For now the flame was tempered
    so that the beasts might not
      be burnt up that were sent
      upon the wicked,
    but that these might see and
      know they were struck by
      the judgment of God;
19 And again, even in the water,
    fire blazed beyond its
    strength
    so as to consume the produce
      of the wicked land.
20 Instead of this, you nourished
    your people with food of
    angels
    and furnished them bread
      from heaven, ready to hand,
      untoiled-for,
    endowed with all delights and
      conforming to every taste.
21 For this substance of yours
    revealed your sweetness
      toward your children,
    and serving the desire of him
      who received it,
    was blended to whatever
      flavor each one wished.
22 Yet snow and ice withstood fire
    and were not melted,
    that they might know that
      their enemies' fruits

Were consumed by a fire that
    blazed in the hail
    and flashed lightning in the rain.
23 But this fire, again, that the just
    might be nourished,
    forgot even its proper strength;
24 For your creation, serving you,
    its maker,
    grows tense for punishment
      against the wicked,
    but is relaxed in benefit for
      those who trust in you.
25 Therefore at that very time,
    transformed in all sorts
      of ways,
    it was serving your
      all-nourishing bounty
    according to what they
      needed and desired;
26 That your sons whom you loved
    might learn, O Lord,
    that it is not the various kinds
      of fruits that nourish man,
    but it is your word that
      preserves those who believe
      you!
27 For what was not destroyed by
    fire,
    when merely warmed by a
      momentary sunbeam,
    melted;
28 So that men might know that
    one must give you thanks
      before the sunrise,
    and turn to you at daybreak.
29 For the hope of the ingrate
    melts like a wintry frost
    and runs off like useless water.

Fourth Example: Darkness Afflicts the Egyptians While the Israelites Have Light

17 For great are your judgments,
    and hardly to be
    described;
    therefore the unruly souls
      were wrong.
2 For when the lawless thought
    to enslave the holy nation,
    shackled with darkness,
    fettered by the long night,
    they lay confined beneath
      their own roofs as exiles
      from the eternal providence.
3 For they who supposed their
    secret sins were hid
    under the dark veil of oblivion

Were scattered in fearful
    trembling,
    terrified by apparitions.
4 For not even their inner
    chambers kept them fearless,
    for crashing sounds on all
      sides terrified them,
    and mute phantoms with
      somber looks appeared.
5 No force, even of fire, was able
    to give light,
    nor did the flaming brilliance
      of the stars
    succeed in lighting up that
      gloomy night.
6 But only intermittent, fearful
    fires
    flashed through upon them;
    And in their terror they thought
      beholding these was worse
    than the times when that sight
      was no longer to be seen.
7 And mockeries of the magic art
    were in readiness,
    and a jeering reproof of their
      vaunted shrewdness.
8 For they who undertook to
    banish fears and terrors
      from the sick soul
    themselves sickened with a
      ridiculous fear.
9 For even though no monstrous
    thing frightened them,
    they shook at the passing of
      insects and the hissing of
      reptiles,
10 And perished trembling,
    reluctant to face even the air
      that they could nowhere
      escape.
11 For wickedness, of its nature
    cowardly, testifies in its
      own condemnation,
    and because of a distressed
      conscience, always
      magnifies misfortunes.
12 For fear is nought but the
    surrender of the helps that
      come from reason;
13 and the more one's
    expectation is of itself
    uncertain,
    the more one makes of not
      knowing the cause that
      brings on torment.
14 So they, during that night,
    powerless though it was,

16, 14: *Confined:* in the nether world, in limbo.
16, 22: *Snow and ice:* the manna; cf 16, 27; 19, 21.
17, 6: *Fires:* that is, lightnings.
17, 14: *Powerless:* the nether world, the home of
darkness, has no power against God, nor even against
such men as do not submit to it of themselves; cf 1, 14ff.

that had come upon them
from the recesses of a
powerless nether world,
while all sleeping the same sleep,

15 Were partly smitten by fearsome
apparitions
and partly stricken by their
soul's surrender;
for fear came upon them,
sudden and unexpected.

16 Thus, then, whoever was there fell
into that unbarred prison and
was kept confined.

17 For whether one was a farmer,
or a shepherd,
or a worker at tasks in the
wasteland,
Taken unawares, he served out
the inescapable sentence;

18   for all were bound by the one
bond of darkness.
And were it only the whistling
wind,
or the melodious song of birds
in the spreading branches,
Or the steady sound of rushing
water,

19   or the rude crash of
overthrown rocks,
Or the unseen gallop of
bounding animals,
or the roaring cry of the
fiercest beasts,
Or an echo resounding from
the hollow of the hills,
these sounds, inspiring terror,
paralyzed them.

20 For the whole world shone with
brilliant light
and continued its works
without interruption;

21 Over them alone was spread
oppressive night,
an image of the darkness
that next should come upon
them;
yet they were to themselves
more burdensome than the
darkness.

18 But your holy ones had very
great light;
And those others, who heard
their voices but did not see
their forms,
since now they themselves
had suffered, called them
blest;

2 And because they who formerly
had been wronged did not
harm them, they thanked
them,
and pleaded with them, for
the sake of the difference
between them.

3 Instead of this, you furnished
the flaming pillar
which was a guide on the
unknown way,
and the mild sun for an
honorable migration.

4 For those deserved to be
deprived of light and
imprisoned by darkness,
who had kept your sons
confined
through whom the
imperishable light of the
Law was to be given to the
world.

Fifth Example: Death of the Egyptian First-born; the Israelites Are Spared

5 When they determined to put
to death the infants of the
holy ones,
and when a single boy had
been cast forth but saved,
As a reproof you carried off
their multitude of sons
and made them perish all at
once in the mighty water.

6 That night was known
beforehand to our fathers,
that, with sure knowledge
of the oaths in which they
put their faith, they might
have courage.

7 Your people awaited
the salvation of the just and
the destruction of their foes.

8 For when you punished our
adversaries,
in this you glorified us whom
you had summoned.

9 For in secret the holy children
of the good were offering
sacrifice
and putting into effect with
one accord the divine
institution,
That your holy ones should
share alike the same good
things and dangers,

having previously sung the
praises of the fathers.

10 But the discordant cry of their
enemies responded,
and the piteous wail of
mourning for children was
borne to them.

11 And the slave was smitten with
the same retribution as his
master;
even the plebeian suffered the
same as the king.

12 And all alike by a single death
had countless dead;
For the living were not even
sufficient for the burial,
since at a single instant their
nobler offspring were
destroyed.

13 For though they disbelieved at
every turn on account of
sorceries,
at the destruction of the
first-born they
acknowledged that the
people was God's son.

14 For when peaceful stillness
compassed everything
and the night in its swift
course was half spent,

15 Your all-powerful word from
heaven's royal throne
bounded, a fierce warrior,
into the doomed land,

16   bearing the sharp sword of
your inexorable decree.
And as he alighted, he filled
every place with death;
he still reached to heaven,
while he stood upon the earth.

17 Then, forthwith, visions in horrible
dreams perturbed them
and unexpected fears assailed
them;

18 And cast half-dead, one here,
another there,
each was revealing the reason
for his dying.

19 For the dreams that disturbed
them had proclaimed this
beforehand,
lest they perish unaware of
why they suffered ill.

20 But the trial of death touched
at one time even the just,
and in the desert a plague
struck the multitude;

18, 2: *The difference between them:* God's distinctive manner of treating the Israelites and the Egyptians according to their respective merits.
18, 5: *Single boy:* Moses.

18, 9: *Praises of the fathers:* cf Sir 44–50; Wis 10.
18, 13: *People:* the Hebrews.

Yet not for long did the anger
　　last.
21 For the blameless man hastened
　　to be their champion,
　　bearing the weapon of his
　　　special office,
　　prayer and the propitiation of
　　　incense;
　He withstood the wrath and put
　　　a stop to the calamity,
　　showing that he was your
　　　servant.
22 And he overcame the bitterness
　　not by bodily strength, not by
　　　force of arms;
　But by word he overcame the
　　　smiter,
　　recalling the sworn covenants
　　　with their fathers.
23 For when corpses had already
　　fallen one on another in
　　　heaps,
　he stood in the midst and
　　checked the anger,
　　and cut off the way to the
　　　living.
24 For on his full-length robe was
　　the whole world,
　　and the glories of the fathers
　　were carved in four rows
　　　upon the stones,
　　and your grandeur was on the
　　　crown upon his head.
25 To these names the destroyer
　　yielded, and these he feared;
　　for the mere trial of anger
　　　was enough.

19 But the wicked, merciless wrath
　　assailed until the end.
　For he knew beforehand what
　　they were yet to do:
2 That though they themselves
　　had agreed to the departure
　　and had anxiously sent them
　　　on their way,
　　they would regret it and
　　　pursue them.
3 For while they were still engaged
　　in funeral rites
　　and were mourning at the
　　　burials of the dead,
　They adopted another senseless
　　plan;
　　and those whom they had
　　sent away with entreaty,
　　they pursued as fugitives.

4 For a compulsion suited to this
　　ending drew them on,
　　and made them forgetful of
　　what had befallen them,
　That they might fill out the
　　torments of their
　　　punishment,
5 and your people might
　　experience a glorious journey
　　while those others met an
　　extraordinary death.
6 For all creation, in its several
　　kinds, was being made over
　　　anew,
　　serving its natural laws,
　　that your children might be
　　preserved unharmed.
7 The cloud overshadowed their
　　camp;
　　and out of what had before
　　been water, dry land was
　　seen emerging:
　Out of the Red Sea an
　　unimpeded road,
　　and a grassy plain out of the
　　mighty flood.
8 Over this crossed the whole
　　nation sheltered by your
　　　hand,
　　after they beheld stupendous
　　wonders.
9 For they ranged about like horses,
　　and bounded about like lambs,
　　praising you, O Lord! their
　　　deliverer.
10 For they were still mindful of
　　what had happened in their
　　　sojourn:
　　how instead of the young of
　　animals the land brought
　　forth gnats,
　　and instead of fishes the river
　　swarmed with countless
　　　frogs.
11 And later they saw also a new
　　kind of bird
　　when, prompted by desire,
　　they asked for pleasant
　　　foods;
12 For to appease them quail
　　came to them from the sea.
13 And the punishments came upon
　　the sinners
　　only after forewarnings from
　　the violence of the
　　thunderbolts.

For they justly suffered for their
　　own misdeeds,
　　since indeed they treated
　　their guests with the more
　　grievous hatred.
14 For those others did not receive
　　unfamiliar visitors,
　　but these were enslaving
　　beneficent guests.
15 And not that only; but what
　　punishment was to be theirs
　　since they received strangers
　　unwillingly!
16 Yet these, after welcoming them
　　with festivities,
　　oppressed with awful toils
　　those who now shared with
　　them the same rights.
17 And they were struck with
　　blindness,
　　as those others had been at
　　the portals of the just—
　When, surrounded by yawning
　　darkness,
　　each sought the entrance of
　　his own gate.
18 For the elements, in variable
　　harmony among themselves,
　　like strings of the harp,
　　produce new melody,
　　while the flow of music
　　steadily persists.
　And this can be perceived
　　exactly from a review of
　　what took place.
19 For land creatures were changed
　　into water creatures,
　　and those that swam went
　　over on to the land.
20 Fire in water maintained its
　　own strength,
　　and water forgot its
　　quenching nature;
21 Flames, by contrast, neither
　　consumed the flesh
　　of the perishable animals
　　that went about in them,
　　nor melted the icelike,
　　quick-melting kind of
　　ambrosial food.
22 For every way, O Lord! you
　　magnified and glorified
　　your people;
　　unfailing, you stood by them
　　in every time and
　　circumstance.

18, 21: *Blameless man:* Aaron, acting according to
his office of high priest and intercessor.
　18, 22: *Smiter:* the destroying angel; cf v 25.
　18, 24: *Glories . . . grandeur:* the name of God and
the names of the tribes were inscribed on the high

priest's apparel.
　19, 1: *He:* i.e., God.
　19, 2: *Them:* the Hebrews.
　19, 3: *They:* the Egyptians.
　19, 5: *Glorious:* more precisely, "wondrous," but

the word reflects *glorified* in 18, 8 and 19, 22.
　19, 13: *More grievous:* than that of the people of
Sodom; cf Gn 19.
　19, 15: *Theirs:* the people of Sodom.

Sirach

(ECCLESIASTICUS)

Foreword

MANY important truths have been handed down to us through the law, the prophets, and the later authors; and for these the instruction and wisdom of Israel merit praise. Now, those who are familiar with these truths must not only understand them themselves but, as lovers of wisdom, be able, in speech and in writing, to help others less familiar. Such a one was my grandfather, Jesus, who, having devoted himself for a long time to the diligent study of the law, the prophets, and the rest of the books of our ancestors, and having developed a thorough familiarity with them, was moved to write something himself in the nature of instruction and wisdom, in order that those who love wisdom might, by acquainting themselves with what he too had written, make even greater progress in living in conformity with the divine law.

You therefore are now invited to read it in a spirit of attentive good will, with indulgence for any apparent failure on our part, despite earnest efforts, in the interpretation of particular passages. For words spoken originally in Hebrew are not as effective when they are translated into another language. That is true not only of this book but of the law itself, the prophets and the rest of the books, which differ no little when they are read in the original.

I arrived in Egypt in the thirty-eighth year of the reign of King Euergetes, and while there, I found a reproduction of our valuable teaching. I therefore considered myself in duty bound to devote some diligence and industry to the translation of this book. Many sleepless hours of close application have I devoted in the interval to finishing the book for publication, for the benefit of those living abroad who wish to acquire wisdom and are disposed to live their lives according to the standards of the law.

The law, the prophets and the rest of the books: the Sacred Scriptures of the Old Testament written before the time of Sirach, according to the threefold division of the present Hebrew Bible.

Thirty-eighth . . . Euergetes: 132 B.C. The reference is to Ptolemy VII, Physkon Euergetes II (170–163; 145–117 B.C.).

Reproduction . . . teaching: may refer to the Septuagint (Greek) translation of Hebrew wisdom writings predating Sirach.

THE WISDOM OF SIRACH

Praise of Wisdom

1 All wisdom comes from the LORD
   and with him it remains forever.
2 The sand of the seashore, the drops of rain,
   the days of eternity: who can number these?
3 Heaven's height, earth's breadth,
   the depths of the abyss: who can explore these?
4 Before all things else wisdom was created;
   and prudent understanding, from eternity.
5 To whom has wisdom's root been revealed?
   Who knows her subtleties?
6 There is but one, wise and truly awe-inspiring,
   seated upon his throne;
7 It is the LORD; he created her,
   has seen her and taken note of her.
8 He has poured her forth upon all his works,
   upon every living thing according to his bounty;
   he has lavished her upon his friends.

9 Fear of the LORD is glory and splendor,
   gladness and a festive crown.
10 Fear of the LORD warms the heart,
   giving gladness and joy and length of days.
11 He who fears the LORD will have a happy end;
   even on the day of his death he will be blessed.
12 The beginning of wisdom is fear of the LORD,
   which is formed with the faithful in the womb.
13 With devoted men was she created from of old,
   and with their children her beneficence abides.

14 Fullness of wisdom is fear of the LORD;
   she inebriates men with her fruits.
15 Her entire house she fills with choice foods,
   her granaries with her harvest.
16 Wisdom's garland is fear of the LORD,
   with blossoms of peace and perfect health.
17 Knowledge and full understanding she showers down;
   she heightens the glory of those who possess her.
18 The root of wisdom is fear of the LORD;
   her branches are length of days.

19 One cannot justify unjust anger;
   anger plunges a man to his downfall.
20 A patient man need stand firm but for a time,
   and then contentment comes back to him.
21 For a while he holds back his words,
   then the lips of many herald his wisdom.
22 Among wisdom's treasures is the paragon of prudence;
   but fear of the LORD is an abomination to the sinner.
23 If you desire wisdom, keep the commandments,
   and the LORD will bestow her upon you;
24 For fear of the LORD is wisdom and culture;
   loyal humility is his delight.
25 Be not faithless to the fear of the LORD,
   nor approach it with duplicity of heart.
26 Play not the hypocrite before men;
   over your lips keep watch.
27 Exalt not yourself lest you fall
   and bring upon you dishonor;

28 For then the LORD will reveal your secrets
   and publicly cast you down,
29 Because you approached the fear of the LORD
   with your heart full of guile.

Duties toward God

2 My son, when you come to serve the LORD,
   prepare yourself for trials.
2 Be sincere of heart and steadfast,
   undisturbed in time of adversity.
3 Cling to him, forsake him not;
   thus will your future be great.
4 Accept whatever befalls you,
   in crushing misfortune be patient;
5 For in fire gold is tested,
   and worthy men in the crucible of humiliation.
6 Trust God and he will help you;
   make straight your ways and hope in him.

7 You who fear the LORD, wait for his mercy,
   turn not away lest you fall.
8 You who fear the LORD, trust him,
   and your reward will not be lost.
9 You who fear the LORD, hope for good things,
   for lasting joy and mercy.
10 Study the generations long past and understand;
   has anyone hoped in the LORD and been disappointed?
   Has anyone persevered in his fear and been forsaken?
   has anyone called upon him and been rebuffed?
11 Compassionate and merciful is the LORD;
   he forgives sins, he saves in time of trouble.

1, 1–8: The Lord is the source and preserver of wisdom (1); he created her from eternity, *before all things else* (4–7); all his works reflect wisdom (2f.8).
1, 1: *Wisdom:* here the author speaks of true wisdom, namely God's external revelation of himself. Throughout the book he describes in great detail just what wisdom is; sometimes it is divine; sometimes it is a synonym for God's law; sometimes it is human. But the author makes clear that even human wisdom, properly understood, comes from God.

1, 9–18: Here are described the spiritual and temporal blessings that come during the lifetime of him who fears the Lord, i.e., practices true religion.
1, 9: *Fear of the Lord:* see note on Ps 111, 10.
1, 19–22: The disciple of wisdom shuns *unjust anger* which brings *downfall*. By patience and self-control he preserves calm, recovers *contentment*, and receives public praise. The sinner, on the contrary, despises the restraints which religion imposes.

1, 25–29: Infidelity to religion, or the use of it for any but the single purpose of serving God, is hypocrisy and self-exaltation, deserving of public disgrace.
2, 1–11: Serving God is not without its trials (1); moreover, it must be done with sincerity, steadfastness and fidelity (2f). Misfortune and humiliation merely purify man and prove his worth (4f). Patience and unwavering trust in God are always rewarded with the benefits of God's mercy and of *lasting joy* (6–11).

12 Woe to craven hearts and
       drooping hands,
   to the sinner who treads a
       double path!
13 Woe to the faint of heart who
       trust not,
   who therefore will have no
       shelter!
14 Woe to you who have lost hope!
   what will you do at the
       visitation of the LORD?
15 Those who fear the LORD
       disobey not his words;
   those who love him keep his
       ways.
16 Those who fear the LORD seek to
       please him,
   those who love him are filled
       with his law.
17 Those who fear the LORD
       prepare their hearts
   and humble themselves
       before him.

18 Let us fall into the hands of the
       LORD
   and not into the hands of
       men,
   For equal to his majesty
       is the mercy that he shows.

Duties toward Parents

3 Children, pay heed to a father's
       right;
   do so that you may live.
2 For the LORD sets a father in
       honor over his children;
   a mother's authority he
       confirms over her sons.
3 He who honors his father
       atones for sins;
4   he stores up riches who
       reveres his mother.
5 He who honors his father is
       gladdened by children,
   and when he prays he is
       heard.
6 He who reveres his father will
       live a long life;
   he obeys the LORD who brings
       comfort to his mother.

7 He who fears the LORD honors
       his father,
   and serves his parents as
       rulers.
8 In word and deed honor your
       father
   that his blessing may come
       upon you;
9 For a father's blessing gives a
       family firm roots,
   but a mother's curse uproots
       the growing plant.
10 Glory not in your father's
       shame,
   for his shame is no glory to
       you!
11 His father's honor is a man's
       glory;
   disgrace for her children, a
       mother's shame.
12 My son, take care of your
       father when he is old;
   grieve him not as long as he
       lives.
13 Even if his mind fail, be
       considerate with him;
   revile him not in the fullness
       of your strength.
14 For kindness to a father will
       not be forgotten,
   it will serve as a sin offering—
       it will take lasting root.
15 In time of tribulation it will be
       recalled to your advantage,
   like warmth upon frost it
       will melt away your sins.
16 A blasphemer is he who
       despises his father;
   accursed of his Creator, he
       who angers his mother.

Humility

17 My son, conduct your affairs
       with humility,
   and you will be loved more
       than a giver of gifts.
18 Humble yourself the more, the
       greater you are,
   and you will find favor with
       God.
19 For great is the power of God;
   by the humble he is glorified.

20 What is too sublime for you,
       seek not,
   into things beyond your
       strength search not.
21 What is committed to you,
       attend to;
   for what is hidden is not
       your concern.
22 With what is too much for you
       meddle not,
   when shown things beyond
       human understanding.
23 Their own opinion has misled
       many,
   and false reasoning
       unbalanced their judgment.
24 Where the pupil of the eye is
       missing, there is no light,
   and where there is no
       knowledge, there is no
       wisdom.

25 A stubborn man will fare badly
       in the end,
   and he who loves danger will
       perish in it.
26 A stubborn man will be
       burdened with sorrow;
   a sinner will heap sin upon
       sin.
27 For the affliction of the proud
       man there is no cure;
   he is the offshoot of an evil
       plant.
28 The mind of a sage appreciates
       proverbs,
   and an attentive ear is the
       wise man's joy.

Alms for the Poor

29 Water quenches a flaming fire,
   and alms atone for sins.
30 He who does a kindness is
       remembered afterward;
   when he falls, he finds a
       support.

4 My son, rob not the poor man
       of his livelihood;
   force not the eyes of the
       needy to turn away.
2 A hungry man grieve not,
   a needy man anger not;

2, 12–18: A warning to those who compromise
their religion in time of affliction; they fail in courage
and trust and therefore have no security (12ff). But
those who fear the Lord through obedience, reverence, love and humility find his *mercy equal to his
majesty* (15–18).
   3, 1–16: Besides the virtues that must characterize
our conduct toward God, special duties toward our
neighbor are enjoined, such as honor and respect
toward parents, with corresponding blessings (1–9).

Even to old and infirm parents this respect is due
(10–13); through it, the sins of children are pardoned
(14f). Failure to render respect is blasphemy and
merits a curse from God (16). Cf Ex 20, 12; Eph 6, 2f.
   3, 17–27: Humility gives a true estimate of self
(17ff). Through it a man performs duty, avoids what
is beyond his understanding and strength (20ff).
Pride, however, begets false greatness, misjudgment,
stubbornness, sorrow, affliction and perdition
(23–27).

3, 19: An alternate or additional line would read:
"For though many have been great in the course of
time, it is to the humble he reveals his secrets."
Cf Mt 11, 25f; 1 Cor 1, 26–29.
   3, 29—4, 10: Mercy and kindness toward those in
misfortune atone for sin and endear a man to God
and to his fellow men.
   4, 1: *Eyes of the needy:* when they look for help;
cf 18, 17.

3 Do not exasperate the
     downtrodden;
   delay not to give to the
     needy.
4 A beggar in distress do not
     reject;
   avert not your face from the
     poor.
5 From the needy turn not your
     eyes,
   give no man reason to curse
     you;
6 For if in the bitterness of his
     soul he curse you,
   his Creator will hear his
     prayer.
7 Endear yourself to the
     assembly;
   before a ruler bow your head.
8 Give a hearing to the poor man,
   and return his greeting with
     courtesy;
9 Deliver the oppressed from the
     hand of the oppressor;
   let not justice be repugnant
     to you.
10 To the fatherless be as a father,
    and help their mother as a
      husband would;
    Thus will you be like a son to
      the Most High,
    and he will be more tender to
      you than a mother.

The Rewards of Wisdom

11 Wisdom instructs her children
    and admonishes those who
      seek her.
12 He who loves her loves life;
    those who seek her out win
      her favor.
13 He who holds her fast inherits
      glory;
    wherever he dwells, the LORD
      bestows blessings.
14 Those who serve her serve
      the Holy One;
    those who love her the LORD
      loves.
15 He who obeys her judges
      nations;
    he who hearkens to her
      dwells in her inmost
      chambers.

16 If one trusts her, he will
      possess her;
    his descendants too will
      inherit her.
17 She walks with him as a stranger,
    and at first she puts him to
      the test;
    Fear and dread she brings upon
      him
    and tries him with her
      discipline;
    With her precepts she puts him
      to the proof,
    until his heart is fully with her.
18 Then she comes back to bring
      him happiness
    and reveal her secrets to him.
19 But if he fails her, she will
      abandon him
    and deliver him into the
      hands of despoilers.

Sincerity and Justice

20 Use your time well; guard
      yourself from evil,
    and bring upon yourself
      no shame.
21 There is a sense of shame laden
      with guilt,
    and a shame that merits
      honor and respect.
22 Show no favoritism to your
      own discredit;
    let no one intimidate you to
      your own downfall.
23 Refrain not from speaking at
      the proper time,
    and hide not away your
      wisdom;
24 For it is through speech that
      wisdom becomes known,
    and knowledge through the
      tongue's rejoinder.
25 Never gainsay the truth,
    and struggle not against the
      rushing stream.
26 Be not ashamed to acknowledge
      your guilt,
    but of your ignorance rather
      be ashamed.
27 Do not abase yourself before an
      impious man,
    nor refuse to do so before
      rulers.

28 Even to the death fight for truth,
    and the LORD your God will
      battle for you.
29 Be not surly in your speech,
    nor lazy and slack in your
      deeds.
30 Be not a lion at home,
    nor sly and suspicious at
      work.
31 Let not your hand be open to
      receive
    and clenched when it is time
      to give.

Against Presumption

5 Rely not on your wealth;
    say not: "I have the power."
2 Rely not on your strength
    in following the desires of
      your heart.
3 Say not: "Who can prevail
      against me?"
    for the LORD will exact the
      punishment.
4 Say not: "I have sinned, yet
      what has befallen me?"
    for the LORD bides his time.
5 Of forgiveness be not
      overconfident,
    adding sin upon sin.
6 Say not: "Great is his mercy;
      my many sins he will forgive."
7 For mercy and anger alike are
      with him;
    upon the wicked alights his
      wrath.
8 Delay not your conversion to
      the LORD,
    put it not off from day to
      day;
9 For suddenly his wrath flames
      forth;
    at the time of vengeance, you
      will be destroyed.
10 Rely not upon deceitful wealth,
    for it will be no help on the
      day of wrath.

Sincerity in Speech

11 Winnow not in every wind,
    and start not off in every
      direction.

4, 11–19: The Hebrew text presents wisdom speaking in the first person, as in ch 24. The precious fruits of wisdom: life, favor, glory, blessings, God's love, are intended to arouse desire for her (11–14). Her disciples are like priests (14) and judges (15), even partners who possess her for themselves and their descendants (16). They enjoy happiness and penetrate her profound secrets after surviving her tests (17f).

Those who fail her are abandoned to destruction (19).

4, 20–31: Besides the interior trials of discipline and precept, the disciple of wisdom is warned against external dangers to his sincerity and justice, namely evil, human respect (20f), compromise of liberty in speech and action (22–25), false shame, and ignorance (26). He must fight for the truth (28), and

avoid cynicism and laziness (29), and inconsistency in his conduct (30).

5, 1–10: The vices of the rich are pride and independence (1f), presumption (3), false security (4–7), and impenitence (8), which cannot escape the divine wrath (9f). Cf Prv 18, 23; 19, 1; 28, 6.

5, 11: A proverbial expression condemning inconstancy and advocating sincerity and honesty.

12 Be consistent in your thoughts;
   steadfast be your words.
13 Be swift to hear,
   but slow to answer.
14 If you have the knowledge,
     answer your neighbor;
   if not, put your hand over
     your mouth.
15 Honor and dishonor through
     talking!
   A man's tongue can be his
     downfall.
16 Be not called a detractor;
   Use not your tongue for
     calumny;
17 For shame has been created for
     the thief,
   and the reproach of his
     neighbor for the
     double-tongued.

6 Say nothing harmful, small or
     great;
   be not a foe instead of a
     friend;
   A bad name and disgrace will
     you acquire:
   "That for the evil man with
     double tongue!"

2 Fall not into the grip of desire,
   lest, like fire, it consume your
     strength;
3 Your leaves it will eat, your
     fruits destroy,
   and you will be left a dry
     tree,
4 For contumacious desire
     destroys its owner
   and makes him the sport of
     his enemies.

True Friendship

5 A kind mouth multiplies
     friends,
   and gracious lips prompt
     friendly greetings.
6 Let your acquaintances be many,
   but one in a thousand your
     confidant.
7 When you gain a friend, first
     test him,
   and be not too ready to trust
     him.

8 For one sort of friend is a
     friend when it suits him,
   but he will not be with you
     in time of distress.
9 Another is a friend who
     becomes an enemy,
   and tells of the quarrel to
     your shame.
10 Another is a friend, a boon
     companion,
   who will not be with you
     when sorrow comes.
11 When things go well, he is
     your other self,
   and lords it over your
     servants;
12 But if you are brought low, he
     turns against you
   and avoids meeting you.
13 Keep away from your enemies;
   be on your guard with your
     friends.
14 A faithful friend is a sturdy
     shelter;
   he who finds one finds a
     treasure.
15 A faithful friend is beyond price,
   no sum can balance his
     worth.
16 A faithful friend is a life-saving
     remedy,
   such as he who fears God
     finds;
17 For he who fears God behaves
     accordingly,
   and his friend will be like
     himself.

Blessings of Wisdom

18 My son, from your youth
     embrace discipline;
   thus will you find wisdom
     with graying hair.
19 As though plowing and sowing,
     draw close to her;
   then await her bountiful crops.
20 For in cultivating her you will
     labor but little,
   and soon you will eat of her
     fruits.
21 How irksome she is to the
     unruly!
   The fool cannot abide her.

22 She will be like a burdensome
     stone to test him,
   and he will not delay in
     casting her aside.
23 For discipline is like her name,
   she is not accessible to many.

24 Listen, my son, and heed my
     advice;
   refuse not my counsel.
25 Put your feet into her fetters,
   and your neck under her
     yoke.
26 Stoop your shoulders and carry
     her
   and be not irked at her
     bonds.
27 With all your soul draw close
     to her;
   with all your strength keep
     her ways.
28 Search her out, discover her;
   seek her and you will find
     her.
   Then when you have her,
   do not let her go;
29 Thus will you afterward find
     rest in her,
   and she will become your
     joy.
30 Her fetters will be your throne
     of majesty;
   her bonds, your purple cord.
31 You will wear her as your robe
     of glory,
   bear her as your splendid
     crown.

32 My son, if you wish, you can
     be taught;
   if you apply yourself, you
     will be shrewd.
33 If you are willing to listen, you
     will learn;
   if you give heed, you will be
     wise.
34 Frequent the company of the
     elders;
   whoever is wise, stay close
     to him.
35 Be eager to hear every godly
     discourse;
   let no wise saying escape
     you.

5, 12—6, 1: Proper use of the tongue requires constancy in speech (5, 12), prudence (13f), reserve (15), charity (6, 1), as well as the avoidance of detraction, *calumny* (16) and double talk, which bring shame and disgrace (5, 17; 6, 1).

6, 1: *"That . . . double tongue!"*: people will say this against the man whose deceitful tongue has brought him to disgrace.

6, 5–17: True friends are discerned not by prosperity (11) but through the trials of adversity: distress, quarrels (9), sorrow (10) and misfortune (12). Such friends are rare and their value is beyond estimation, a gift from God (14–17).

6, 18–37: The various figures in each of the three strophes urge the search for wisdom through patience (19–13), docility (32–37), and perseverance in trials

(25ff), promising rich rewards (28–31). Cf 4, 11–19.

6, 23: *Discipline (musar,* in the sense of wisdom) is a perfect homonym for *musar,* "removed, withdrawn"; thus the path of *discipline* is inaccessible to many.

6, 31: Some forms of the text speak also of the "yoke" of wisdom under the imagery of golden ornaments.

36 If you see a man of prudence,
      seek him out;
   let you feet wear away his
      doorstep!
37 Reflect on the precepts of the
      Lord,
   let his commandments be
      your constant meditation;
   Then he will enlighten your
      mind,
   and the wisdom you desire he
      will grant.

Conduct in Public Life

7 Do no evil, and evil will not
      overtake you;
2   avoid wickedness, and it will
      turn aside from you.
3 Sow not in the furrows of
      injustice,
   lest you harvest it sevenfold.
4 Seek not from the LORD
      authority,
   nor from the king a place of
      honor.
5 Parade not your justice before
      the Lord,
   and before the king flaunt
      not your wisdom.
6 Seek not to become a judge
   if you have not strength to
      root out crime,
   Or you will show favor to the
      ruler
   and mar your integrity.
7 Be guilty of no evil before the
      city's populace,
   nor disgrace yourself before
      the assembly .
8 Do not plot to repeat a sin;
   not even for one will you go
      unpunished.
9 Say not: "He will appreciate my
      many gifts;
   the Most High will accept my
      offerings."
10 Be not impatient in prayers,
   and neglect not the giving of
      alms.

11 Laugh not at an embittered
      man;
   be mindful of him who exalts
      and humbles.
12 Plot no mischief against your
      brother,
   nor against your friend and
      companion.
13 Delight not in telling lie after lie,
   for it never results in good.
14 Thrust not yourself into the
      deliberations of princes,
   and repeat not the words of
      your prayer.
15 Hate not laborious tasks,
   nor farming, which was
      ordained by the Most High.
16 Do not esteem yourself better
      than your fellows;
   remember, his wrath will not
      delay.
17 More and more, humble your
      pride;
   what awaits man is worms.

Duties of Family Life, Religion and Charity

18 Barter not a friend for money,
   nor a dear brother for the
      gold of Ophir.
19 Dismiss not a sensible wife;
   a gracious wife is more
      precious than corals.
20 Mistreat not a servant who
      faithfully serves,
   nor a laborer who devotes
      himself to his task.
21 Let a wise servant be dear to
      you as your own self;
   refuse him not his freedom.
22 If you have livestock, look after
      them;
   if they are dependable, keep
      them.
23 If you have sons, chastise them;
   bend their necks from
      childhood.
24 If you have daughters, keep them
      chaste,
   and be not indulgent to them.

25 Giving your daughter in marriage
      ends a great task;
   but give her to a worthy man.
26 If you have a wife, let her not
      seem odious to you;
   but where there is ill-feeling,
      trust her not.
27 With your whole heart honor
      your father;
   your mother's birthpangs
      forget not.
28 Remember, of these parents you
      were born;
   what can you give them for
      all they gave you?
29 With all your soul, fear God,
   revere his priests.
30 With all your strength, love
      your Creator,
   forsake not his ministers.
31 Honor God and respect the
      priest;
   give him his portion as you
      have been commanded:
   First fruits and contributions,
   due sacrifices and holy
      offerings.
32 To the poor man also extend
      your hand,
   that your blessing may be
      complete.
33 Be generous to all the living,
   and withhold not your
      kindness from the dead.
34 Avoid not those who weep,
   but mourn with those who
      mourn;
35 Neglect not to visit the sick —
   for these things you will be
      loved.
36 In whatever you do, remember
      your last days,
   and you will never sin.

Prudence in Dealing with Other Men

8 Contend not with an influential
      man,
   lest you fall into his power.

7, 1–17: In the conduct of social relations wisdom forbids *evil* and *injustice* (1ff), pride (5.15ff), ambition and human respect (4.6), public disorder (7), presumption and impatience toward God (9f), ridicule (11), *mischief* and deceit toward one's neighbor (8.12f).
7, 11: *Him who exalts and humbles:* God; cf 1 Sm 2, 7; Ps 75, 8; Lk 1, 52.
7, 14: *Repeat not . . . prayer:* brevity of speech in dealings with superiors and more especially with God is a sign of reverence and respect; cf Eccl 5, 1; Mt 6, 7.
7, 18–36: The duties of respect and appreciation, justice and kindness should characterize relations

toward members of the household (18–28), and also toward God and his priests (29ff), the poor and afflicted, the living and the dead (32–36).
7, 18: *Ophir* was the port, at present unidentified, to which the ships of Solomon sailed and from which they brought back gold and silver; cf note on Ps 44 (45), 10.
7, 21: After six years of service a Hebrew slave was entitled to freedom; cf Ex 21, 2; Dt 15, 12–15.
7, 23: *Bend their necks:* keep them from rebellious pride; so with the Greek. Cf 30, 12. The present Hebrew text, which is probably not original here, reads: "Choose wives for them while they are young."
7, 31: *First fruits . . . holy offerings:* cf Ex 29, 27;

Lv 7, 31–34; Nm 18, 8–20; Dt 18, 1–5.
7, 33: This seems to refer to the observances ordained toward the dead, that is, proper mourning and burial. Cf 2 Sm 21, 12ff; Tb 1, 20; 12, 12. When this verse is read in the light of later teaching, prayers for the souls of the deceased would also be recommended. Cf 2 Mc 12, 43ff.
8, 1–19: A prudent man will be circumspect, avoiding conflict with the powerful, the rich and insolent, the impious, the irascible, and with judges (1ff.10ff.14.16). He will seek friendship not with the undisciplined (4.12f) and the ruthless (15), nor with fools and strangers (17ff), but with the wise and the ancients of the people (8f).

2 Quarrel not with a rich man,
  lest he pay out the price of
      your downfall;
  For gold has dazzled many,
      and perverts the character of
      princes.
3 Dispute not with a man of
      railing speech,
  heap no wood upon his fire.
4 Be not too familiar with an
      unruly man,
  lest he speak ill of your
      forebears.
5 Shame not a repentant sinner;
  remember, we all are guilty.
6 Insult no man when he is old,
  for some of us, too, will grow
      old.
7 Rejoice not when a man dies;
  remember, we are all to die.
8 Spurn not the discourse of the
      wise,
  but acquaint yourself with
      their proverbs;
  From them you will acquire the
      training
      to serve in the presence of
      princes.
9 Reject not the tradition of old
      men
  which they have learned from
      their fathers;
  From it you will obtain the
      knowledge
      how to answer in time of
      need.
10 Kindle not the coals of a
      sinner,
  lest you be consumed in his
      flaming fire.
11 Let not the impious man
      intimidate you;
  it will set him in ambush
      against you.
12 Lend not to one more powerful
      than yourself;
  and whatever you lend, count
      it as lost.
13 Go not surety beyond your
      means;
  think any pledge a debt you
      must pay.

14 Contend not at law with a
      judge,
  for he will settle it according
      to his whim.
15 Travel not with a ruthless man,
  lest he weigh you down with
      calamity;
  For he will go his own way
      straight,
  and through his folly you will
      perish with him.
16 Provoke no quarrel with a
      quick-tempered man,
  nor ride with him through the
      desert,
  For bloodshed is nothing to
      him;
  when there is no one to help
      you, he will destroy you.
17 Take no counsel with a fool,
  for he can keep nothing to
      himself.
18 Before a stranger do nothing
      that should be kept secret,
  for you know not what it will
      engender.
19 Open your heart to no man,
  and banish not your
      happiness.

Advice concerning Women

9 Be not jealous of the wife of
      your bosom,
  lest you teach her to do evil
      against you.
2 Give no woman power over you
      to trample upon your
      dignity.
3 Be not intimate with a strange
      woman,
  lest you fall into her snares.
4 With a singing girl be not
      familiar,
  lest you be caught in her
      wiles.
5 Entertain no thoughts against a
      virgin,
  lest you be enmeshed in
      damages for her.
6 Give not yourself to harlots,
  lest you surrender your
      inheritance.

7 Gaze not about the lanes of the
      city
  and wander not through its
      squares;
8 Avert your eyes from a comely
      woman;
  gaze not upon the beauty of
      another's wife—
  Through woman's beauty many
      perish,
  for lust for it burns like fire.
9 With a married woman dine not,
  recline not at table to drink
      by her side,
  Lest your heart be drawn to her
  and you go down in blood to
      the grave.

Choice of Friends

10 Discard not an old friend,
  for the new one cannot equal
      him.
  A new friend is like new wine
  which you drink with pleasure
      only when it has aged.
11 Envy not a sinner's fame,
  for you know not what
      disaster awaits him.
12 Rejoice not at a proud man's
      success;
  remember he will not reach
      death unpunished.
13 Keep far from the man who has
      power to kill,
  and you will not be filled with
      the dread of death.
  But if you approach him,
      offend him not,
  lest he take away your life;
  Know that you are stepping
      among snares
  and walking over a net.
14 As best you can, take your
      neighbor's measure,
  and associate with the wise.
15 With the learned be intimate;
  let all your conversation be
      about the law of the Lord.
16 Have just men for your table
      companions;
  in the fear of God be your
      glory.

8, 5: *We are all guilty:* cf 1 Kgs 8, 46; 2 Chr 6, 36;
Eccl 7, 20; Rom 3, 9f; 1 Jn 1, 8.
8, 11: To give in to the wicked in one instance
becomes an occasion of sin for the future.
9, 1–9: Prudence and reserve in dealing with
women are the best defense of morality. To preserve
the liberty and dignity of his person and the integrity

of his possessions, a man must avoid jealousy toward
his own wife and familiarity toward all other women.
Cf 25, 12—26, 18.
9, 1: Unjust suspicions often engender hatred
between husband and wife and may prompt a wife to
commit those faults of which heretofore she had been
innocent.

9, 5: Cf Ex 22, 15f; Dt 22, 28f; Jb 31, 1.
9, 10–16: In social relations, adherence to *the law
of the Lord* should serve as a guide (15). Associate
with true friends (10), with the just and the learned
(14ff); avoid the company of the mighty and of
sinners doomed to punishment (11ff). Cf 8, 1–19.

Concerning Rulers

17 Skilled artisans are esteemed
　　for their deftness;
　　but the ruler of his people is
　　　the skilled sage.
18 Feared in the city is the man of
　　railing speech,
　　and he who talks rashly is
　　　hated.

10 A wise magistrate lends
　　　stability to his people,
　　and the government of a
　　　prudent man is well ordered.
2 As the people's judge, so are his
　　ministers;
　　as the head of a city, its
　　　inhabitants.
3 A wanton king destroys his
　　people,
　　but a city grows through the
　　　wisdom of its princes.
4 Sovereignty over the earth is in
　　the hand of God,
　　who raises up on it the man of
　　　the hour;
5 Sovereignty over every man is in
　　the hand of God,
　　who imparts his majesty to
　　　the ruler.

The Sin of Pride

6 No matter the wrong, do no
　　violence to your neighbor,
　　and do not walk the path of
　　　arrogance.
7 Odious to the Lord and to men
　　is arrogance,
　　and the sin of oppression
　　　they both hate.
8 Dominion is transferred from
　　one people to another
　　because of the violence of the
　　　arrogant.
9 Why are dust and ashes proud?
　　even during life man's body
　　　decays;
10 A slight illness—the doctor
　　jests,
　　a king today—tomorrow
　　　he is dead.
11 When a man dies, he inherits
　　corruption;
　　worms and gnats and maggots.

12 The beginning of pride is man's
　　stubbornness
　　in the withdrawing his heart
　　　from his Maker;
13 For pride is the reservoir of sin,
　　a source which runs over with
　　　vice;
　　Because of it God sends
　　　unheard-of afflictions
　　and brings men to utter ruin.
14 The thrones of the arrogant God
　　overturns
　　and establishes the lowly in
　　　their stead.
15 The roots of the proud God
　　plucks up,
　　to plant the humble in their
　　　place:
16 He breaks down their stem to
　　the level of the ground,
　　then digs their roots from the
　　　earth.
17 The traces of the proud God
　　sweeps away
　　and effaces the memory of
　　　them from the earth.
18 Insolence is not allotted to a
　　man,
　　nor stubborn anger to one
　　　born of woman.

True Glory

19 Whose offspring can be in honor?
　　Those of men.
　　Which offspring are in
　　　honor? Those who fear
　　　God.
　　Whose offspring can be in
　　　disgrace? Those of men.
　　Which offspring are in
　　　disgrace? Those who
　　　transgress the
　　　commandments.
20 Among brethren their leader is
　　in honor;
　　he who fears God is in honor
　　　among his people.
21 Be it tenant or wayfarer, alien
　　or pauper,
　　his glory is the fear of the
　　　LORD.
22 It is not just to despise a man
　　who is wise but poor,

nor proper to honor any
　　sinner.
23 The prince, the ruler, the
　　judge are in honor;
　　but none is greater than he
　　　who fears God.
24 When free men serve a prudent
　　slave,
　　the wise man does not
　　　complain.
25 Flaunt not your wisdom in
　　managing your affairs,
　　and boast not in your time of
　　　need.
26 Better the worker who has
　　plenty of everything
　　than the boaster who is
　　　without bread.

27 My son, with humility have
　　self-esteem;
　　prize yourself as you deserve.
28 Who will acquit him who
　　condemns himself?
　　who will honor him who
　　　discredits himself?
29 The poor man is honored for
　　his wisdom
　　as the rich man is honored for
　　　his wealth;
30 Honored in poverty, how much
　　more so in wealth!
　　Dishonored in wealth, in
　　　poverty how much the more!

11 The poor man's wisdom lifts
　　　his head high
　　and sets him among princes.
2 Praise not a man for his looks;
　　despise not a man for his
　　　appearance.
3 Least is the bee among winged
　　things,
　　but she reaps the choicest of
　　　all harvests.
4 Mock not the worn cloak
　　and jibe at no man's bitter day:
　　For strange are the works of the
　　　LORD,
　　hidden from men his deeds.
5 The oppressed often rise to a
　　throne,
　　and some that none would
　　　consider wear a crown.

9, 17—10, 5: Public office as conducted justly or
unjustly benefits or destroys the people, according to
the axiom, "as the prince, so the people." Cf Is 24, 2.
God, however, has sovereignty over both.

10, 6–18: Glory displayed through arrogance and
pride is false and displeasing to God and men,
because founded on *dust and ashes* (6–11). It is the
denial of the glory due to God, and therefore the

source of all sin (12f). Even the memory of the proud
is destroyed and God transfers their power to the
lowly (14–18).

10, 9f: The text is uncertain. Its general implication is that man deteriorates physically even while
alive: a slight illness today may be followed by death
tomorrow. The uncertainty of life leaves no room for
pride.

10, 19—11, 6: Regardless of social barriers, genuine honor among men comes from fear of the Lord
and a true estimate of self. The Lord exalts the lowly
and oppressed; transgressors of the *commandments*
merit dishonor and disgrace.

11, 5: Cf 1 Sm 2, 8; Ps 105, 17–22; Lk 1, 52.

6 The exalted often fall into utter
disgrace;
the honored are given into
enemy hands.

Moderation

7 Before investigating, find no fault;
examine first, then criticize.
8 Before hearing, answer not,
and interrupt no one in the
middle of his speech.
9 Dispute not about what is not
your concern;
in the strife of the arrogant
take no part.

10 My son, why increase your cares,
since he who is avid for
wealth will not be
blameless?
Even if you run after it, you will
never overtake it;
however you seek it, you will
not find it.
11 One may toil and struggle and
drive,
and fall short all the more.
12 Another goes his way a weakling
and a failure,
with little strength and great
misery—
Yet the eyes of the LORD look
favorably upon him;
he raises him free of the vile
dust,
13 Lifts up his head and exalts him
to the amazement of the
many.
14 Good and evil, life and death,
poverty and riches, are from
the LORD.
15 Wisdom and understanding and
knowledge of affairs,
love and virtuous paths are
from the LORD.
16 Error and darkness were formed
with sinners from their birth,
and evil grows old with
evildoers.
17 The Lord's gift remains with the
just;
his favor brings continued
success.

18 A man may become rich
through a miser's life,
and this is his allotted reward:
19 When he says: "I have found
rest,
now I will feast on my
possessions,"
He does not know how long it
will be
till he dies and leaves them to
others.

20 My son, hold fast to your duty,
busy yourself with it,
grow old while doing your
task.
21 Admire not how sinners live,
but trust in the LORD and
wait for his light;
For it is easy with the LORD
suddenly, in an instant, to
make a poor man rich.
22 God's blessing is the lot of the
just man,
and in due time his hopes
bear fruit.
23 Say not: "What do I need?
What further pleasure can be
mine?"
24 Say not: "I am independent.
What harm can come to me
now?"
25 The day of prosperity makes
one forget adversity;
the day of adversity makes
one forget prosperity.
26 For it is easy with the LORD on
the day of death
to repay man according to
his deeds.
27 A moment's affliction brings
forgetfulness of past
delights;
when a man dies, his life is
revealed.
28 Call no man happy before his
death,
for by how he ends, a man is
known.

Care in Choosing Friends

29 Bring not every man into your
house,

for many are the snares of
the crafty one;
30 Though he seem like a bird
confined in a cage,
yet like a spy he will pick
out the weak spots.
31 The talebearer turns good into
evil;
with a spark he sets many
coals afire.
32 The evil man lies in wait for
blood,
and plots against your
choicest possessions.
33 Avoid a wicked man, for he
breeds only evil,
lest you incur a lasting stain.
34 Lodge a stranger with you, and
he will subvert your course,
and make a stranger of you
to your own household.

12 If you do good, know for
whom you are doing it,
and your kindness will have
its effect.
2 Do good to the just man and
reward will be yours,
if not from him, from the LORD.
3 No good comes to him who
gives comfort to the
wicked,
nor is it an act of mercy that
he does.
4 Give to the good man, refuse
the sinner;
refresh the downtrodden, give
nothing to the proud man.
5 No arms for combat should you
give him,
lest he use them against
yourself;
6 With twofold evil you will meet
for every good deed you do
for him.
7 The Most High himself hates
sinners,
and upon the wicked he takes
vengeance.

8 In our prosperity we cannot
know new friends;
in adversity an enemy will
not remain concealed.

11, 7–25: Discretion regulates a man's conduct toward others and their affairs (7ff); as regards his own interests, a man should avoid solicitude for the passing external benefits of life and property (10–14.18f.21.23ff), and cultivate the lasting inward gifts of wisdom and virtue (15.17.20.22).
11, 14: Divine Providence ultimately governs the lives of men. *Evil*: misfortune and calamity sent by God either in punishment or as an incentive to

repentance or to greater virtue.
11, 15f: Some ancient witnesses omit these two verses.
11, 19: Cf the parable of the rich man, Lk 12, 16–21.
11, 26ff: Sirach, writing before Christian revelation, did not go beyond the hour of death to find full divine retribution.
12, 1–7: The limitations to the practice of charity

here reflected were removed by Christ, who requires that good be done even to enemies and to those who hate, persecute and calumniate us (Mt 5, 43–48).
12, 3ff: The author advises against generosity to those who would abuse it.
12, 8–18: Through adversity friends are distinguished from enemies; to trust the latter or permit them intimacy is to invite disaster. Cf note on 6, 5–17.

9 When a man is successful even
   his enemy is friendly;
   in adversity even his friend
   disappears.
10 Never trust your enemy,
   for his wickedness is like
   corrosion in bronze.
11 Even though he acts humbly
   and peaceably toward
   you,
   take care to be on your
   guard against him.
   Rub him as one polishes a
   brazen mirror,
   and you will find that there
   is still corrosion.
12 Let him not stand near you,
   lest he oust you and take
   your place.
   Let him not sit at your right
   hand,
   lest he then demand your
   seat,
   And in the end you appreciate
   my advice,
   when you groan with regret,
   as I warned you.

13 Who pities a snake charmer
   when he is bitten,
   or anyone who goes near a
   wild beast?
14 So is it with the companion of
   the proud man,
   who is involved in his sins:
15 While you stand firm, he makes
   no bold move;
   but if you slip, he cannot
   hold back.
16 With his lips an enemy speaks
   sweetly,
   but in his heart he schemes to
   plunge you into the abyss.
   Though your enemy has tears in
   his eyes,
   if given the chance, he will
   never have enough of your
   blood.
17 If evil comes upon you, you will
   find him at hand;
   feigning to help, he will trip
   you up,
18 Then he will nod his head and
   clap his hands
   and hiss repeatedly, and show
   his true face.

Caution regarding Associates

13 He who touches pitch
   blackens his hand;
   he who associates with an
   impious man learns his
   ways.
2 Bear no burden too heavy for
   you;
   go with no one greater or
   wealthier than yourself.
   How can the earthen pot go
   with the metal cauldron?
   When they knock together,
   the pot will be smashed:
3 The rich man does wrong and
   boasts of it,
   the poor man is wronged and
   begs forgiveness.
4 As long as the rich man can use
   you he will enslave you,
   but when you are exhausted,
   he will abandon you.
5 As long as you have anything he
   will speak fair words to
   you,
   and with smiles he will win
   your confidence;
6 When he needs something from
   you he will cajole you,
   then without regret he will
   impoverish you.
7 While it serves his purpose he
   will beguile you,
   then twice or three times he
   will terrify you;
   When later he sees you he will
   pass you by,
   and shake his head over you.
8 Guard against being
   presumptuous;
   be not as those who lack
   sense.
9 When invited by a man of
   influence, keep your
   distance;
   then he will urge you all the
   more.
10 Be not bold with him lest you
   be rebuffed,
   but keep not too far away
   lest you be forgotten.
11 Engage not freely in discussion
   with him,
   trust not his many words;
   For by prolonged talk he will
   test you,

and though smiling he will
   probe you.
12 Mercilessly he will make of you
   a laughingstock,
   and will not refrain from
   injury or chains.
13 Be on your guard and take care
   never to accompany men of
   violence.

14 Every living thing loves its own
   kind,
   every man a man like himself.
15 Every being is drawn to its own
   kind;
   with his own kind every man
   associates.
16 Is a wolf ever allied with a lamb?
   So it is with the sinner and
   the just.
17 Can there be peace between the
   hyena and the dog?
   Or between the rich and the
   poor can there be peace?
18 Lion's prey are the wild asses of
   the desert;
   so too the poor are feeding
   grounds for the rich.
19 A proud man abhors lowliness;
   so does the rich man abhor
   the poor.
20 When a rich man stumbles he is
   supported by a friend;
   when a poor man trips he is
   pushed down by a friend.
21 Many are the supporters for a
   rich man when he speaks;
   though what he says is odious,
   it wins approval.
   When a poor man speaks they
   make sport of him;
   he speaks wisely and no
   attention is paid him.
22 A rich man speaks and all are
   silent,
   his wisdom they extol to the
   clouds.
   A poor man speaks and they
   say: "Who is that?"
   If he slips they cast him down.
23 Wealth is good when there is
   no sin;
   but poverty is evil by the
   standards of the proud.
24 The heart of a man changes his
   countenance,
   either for good or for evil.

12, 11: *Brazen mirror:* see note on Ex 38, 8.
13, 1—14, 2: By means of various figures Sirach
indicates the practical impossibility of genuine and

sincere companionship between the poor and the
proud rich. He lays down the principle of associating
with equals (13, 15).

13, 17: The hostility between the dogs which
guard the flocks at night and the rapacious hyenas
is proverbial in Palestine.

25 The sign of a good heart is a
cheerful countenance;
withdrawn and perplexed is
the laborious schemer.

14

Happy the man whose
mouth brings him no
grief,
who is not stung by remorse
for sin.

2 Happy the man whose conscience
does not reproach him,
who has not lost hope.

The Use of Wealth

3 Wealth ill becomes the mean
man;
and to the miser, of what use
is gold?

4 What he denies himself he
collects for others,
and in his possessions a
stranger will revel.

5 To whom will he be generous
who is stingy with himself
and does not enjoy what is
his own?

6 None is more stingy than he
who is stingy with himself;
he punishes his own
miserliness.

7 If ever he is generous, it is by
mistake;
and in the end he displays his
greed.

8 In the miser's opinion his share
is too small;

9 he refuses his neighbor and
brings ruin on himself.

10 The miser's eye is rapacious for
bread,
but on his own table he sets
it stale.

11 My son, use freely whatever you
have
and enjoy it as best you can;

12 Remember that death does not
tarry,
nor have you been told the
grave's appointed time.

13 Before you die, be good to your
friend,
and give him a share in what
you possess.

14 Deprive not yourself of present
good things,
let no choice portion escape
you.

15 Will you not leave your riches
to others,
and your earnings to be divided
by lot?

16 Give, take, and treat yourself
well,
for in the nether world there
are no joys to seek.

17 All flesh grows old, like a
garment;
the age-old law is: All must
die.

18 As with the leaves that grow on
a vigorous tree:
one falls off and another
sprouts —
So with the generations of
flesh and blood:
one dies and another is born.

19 All man's works will perish in
decay,
and his handiwork will
follow after him.

The Search for Wisdom and Its Blessings

20 Happy the man who meditates
on wisdom,
and reflects on knowledge;

21 Who ponders her ways in his
heart,
and understands her paths;

22 Who pursues her like a scout,
and lies in wait at her entry
way;

23 Who peeps through her
windows,
and listens at her doors;

24 Who encamps near her house,
and fastens his tent pegs next
to her walls;

25 Who pitches his tent beside her,
and lives as her welcome
neighbor;

26 Who builds his nest in her
leafage,
and lodges in her branches;

27 Who takes shelter with her from
the heat,
and dwells in her home.

15

He who fears the LORD will
do this;
he who is practiced in the law
will come to wisdom.

2 Motherlike she will meet him,
like a young bride she will
embrace him,

3 Nourish him with the bread of
understanding,
and give him the water of
learning to drink.

4 He will lean upon her and not fall,
he will trust in her and not be
put to shame.

5 She will exalt him above his
fellows;
in the assembly she will make
him eloquent.

6 Joy and gladness he will find,
an everlasting name inherit.

7 Worthless men will not attain to
her,
haughty men will not behold
her.

8 Far from the impious is she,
not to be spoken of by liars.

9 Unseemly is praise on a
sinner's lips,
for it is not accorded to him
by God.

10 But praise is offered by the
wise man's tongue;
its rightful steward will
proclaim it.

Man's Free Will

11 Say not: "It was God's doing
that I fell away";
for what he hates he does not
do.

12 Say not: "It was he who set me
astray";
for he has no need of wicked
man.

13 Abominable wickedness the
LORD hates,
he does not let it befall those
who fear him.

14 When God, in the beginning,
created man,
he made him subject to his
own free choice.

15 If you choose you can keep the
commandments;
it is loyalty to do his will.

16 There are set before you fire
    and water;
  to whichever you choose,
    stretch forth your hand.
17 Before man are life and death,
    whichever he chooses shall be
    given him.
18 Immense is the wisdom of the
    LORD;
  he is mighty in power, and
    all-seeing.
19 The eyes of God see all he has
    made;
  he understands man's every
    deed.
20 No man does he command to
    sin,
  to none does he give strength
    for lies.

God's Punishment of Sinners

16 Desire not a brood of
      worthless children,
  nor rejoice in wicked
    offspring.
2 Many though they be, exult not
    in them
  if they have not the fear of
    the LORD.
3 Count not on their length of
    life,
  have no hope in their future.
  For one can be better than a
    thousand;
  rather die childless than have
    godless children!
4 Through one wise man can a
    city be peopled;
  through a clan of rebels it
    becomes desolate.
5 Many such things has my eye
    seen,
  even more than these has my
    ear heard.
6 Against a sinful band fire is
    enkindled,
  upon a godless people wrath
    flames out.
7 He forgave not the leaders of
    old
  who rebelled long ago in their
    might;

8 He spared not the neighbors of
    Lot
  whom he detested for their
    pride;
9 Nor did he spare the doomed
    people
  who were uprooted because of
    their sin;
10 Nor the six hundred thousand
    foot soldiers
  who perished for the impiety
    of their hearts.
11 And had there been but one
    stiffnecked man,
  it were a wonder had he gone
    unpunished.
  For mercy and anger alike are
    with him
  who remits and forgives,
    though on the wicked alights
    his wrath.
12 Great as his mercy is his
    punishment;
  he judges men, each
    according to his deeds.
13 A criminal does not escape with
    his plunder;
  a just man's hope God does
    not leave unfulfilled.
14 Whoever does good has his
    reward,
  which each receives according
    to his deeds.
15 Say not: "I am hidden from
    God;
  in heaven who remembers
    me?
  Among so many people I cannot
    be known;
  what am I in the world of
    spirits?
16 Behold, the heavens, the
    heaven of heavens,
  the earth and the abyss
    tremble at his visitation;
17 The roots of the mountains, the
    earth's foundations,
  at his mere glance, quiver and
    quake.
18 Of me, therefore, he will take
    no thought;
  with my ways who will
    concern himself?

19 If I sin, no eye will see me;
  if all in secret I am disloyal,
    who is to know?
20 Who tells him of just deeds
  and what could I expect for
    doing my duty?"
21 Such are the thoughts of senseless
    men,
  which only the foolish knave
    will think.

Divine Wisdom Seen in Creation

22 Hearken to me, my son, take
    my advice,
  apply your mind to my words,
23 While I propose measured
    wisdom,
  and impart accurate
    knowledge.
24 When at the first God created
    his works
  and, as he made them,
    assigned their tasks,
25 He ordered for all time what
    they were to do
  and their domains from
    generation to generation.
  They were not to hunger, nor
    grow weary,
  nor ever cease from their
    tasks.
26 Not one should ever crowd its
    neighbor,
  nor should they ever disobey
    his word.
27 Then the LORD looked upon the
    earth,
  and filled it with his blessings.
28 Its surface he covered with all
    manner of life
  which must return into it
    again.

17 The LORD from the earth
      created man,
  and in his own image he made
    him.
2 Limited days of life he gives
    him
  and makes him return to
    earth again.

16, 1–21: Sinful offspring are a great misfortune (1–4), for history and experience show how God punishes sin (5–10). He judges everyone according to his deeds (11ff); no one is hidden from him or escapes retribution at his hand (15–21).

16, 6: For Korah and his *band* (6a), see Nm 16, 35; Ps 106, 18; for the disgruntled Israelites (6b), Ps 78, 21f.

16, 7: *The leaders of old:* the "mighty men of old"

who were destroyed by the flood: Gn 6, 4; Wis 14, 6; Bar 3, 26ff.

16, 8: The people of Sodom and Gomorrah: Gn 19, 24f; Ez 16, 49f.

16, 9: The Canaanites: Ex 23, 23f.27–31; 33, 2; Dt 7, 1; Wis 12, 3.

16, 10: The Israelites who murmured against Moses: Nm 11, 20; 14, 12.22ff.

16, 22—17, 18: In harmony with Gn 1—2, the author describes God's wisdom in creating the universe and all things in it (22–28), endowing man with a moral nature, with wisdom and knowledge and freedom of will according to his own image (17, 1.6), so that man may govern the earth (3f), praise God's name (8), obey his law (9–12), and render to him an account of his deeds (18). Cf Pss 19; 104.

3 He endows man with a strength
of his own,
and with power over all
things else on earth.
4 He puts the fear of him in all
flesh,
and gives him rule over
beasts and birds.
5 He forms men's tongues and
eyes and ears,
and imparts to them an
understanding heart.
6 With wisdom and knowledge he
fills them;
good and evil he shows them.
7 He looks with favor upon their
hearts,
and shows them his glorious
works,
8 That they may describe the
wonders of his deeds
and praise his holy name.
9 He has set before them
knowledge,
a law of life as their
inheritance;
10 An everlasting covenant he has
made with them,
his commandments he has
revealed to them.
11 His majestic glory their eyes
beheld,
his glorious voice their ears
heard.
12 He says to them, "Avoid all evil";
each of them he gives precepts
about his fellow men.
13 Their ways are ever known to him,
they cannot be hidden from
his eyes.
14 Over every nation he places a
ruler,
but the LORD's own portion
is Israel.
15 All their actions are clear as the
sun to him,
his eyes are ever upon their
ways.
16 Their wickedness cannot be
hidden from him;
all of their sins are before the
LORD.

17 A man's goodness God
cherishes like a signet ring,
a man's virtue, like the apple
of his eye.
18 Later he will rise up and repay
them,
and requite each one of them
as they deserve.

Appeal for a Return to God

19 But to the penitent he provides
a way back,
he encourages those who are
losing hope!
20 Return to the LORD and give
up sin,
pray to him and make your
offenses few.
21 Turn again to the Most High
and away from sin,
hate intensely what he
loathes;
22 Who in the nether world can
glorify the Most High
in place of the living who
offer their praise?
23 No more can the dead give
praise than those who have
never lived;
they glorify the LORD who are
alive and well.
24 How great the mercy of the
LORD,
his forgiveness of those who
return to him!
25 The like cannot be found in men,
for not immortal is any son
of man.
26 Is anything brighter than the
sun? Yet it can be eclipsed.
How obscure then the
thoughts of flesh and
blood!
27 God watches over the hosts of
highest heaven,
while all men are dust and
ashes.

The Divine Power and Mercy

18 The Eternal is the judge of all
things without exception;
the LORD alone is just.

2 Whom has he made equal to
describing his works,
and who can probe his
mighty deeds?
3 Who can measure his majestic
power,
or exhaust the tale of his
mercies?
4 One cannot lessen, nor increase,
nor penetrate the wonders of
the LORD.
5 When a man ends he is only
beginning,
and when he stops he is still
bewildered.
6 What is man, of what worth is
he?
the good, the evil in him,
what are these?
7 The sum of a man's days is
great
if it reaches a hundred years:
8 Like a drop of sea water, like a
grain of sand,
so are these few years among
the days of eternity.
9 That is why the LORD is patient
with men
and showers upon them his
mercy.
10 He sees and understands that
their death is grievous,
and so he forgives them all
the more.
11 Man may be merciful to his
fellow man,
but the LORD's mercy reaches
all flesh,
12 Reproving, admonishing,
teaching,
as a shepherd guides his
flock;
13 Merciful to those who accept
his guidance,
who are diligent in his
precepts.

The Necessity of Prudence

14 My son, to your charity add no
reproach,
nor spoil any gift by harsh
words.

17, 10: *An everlasting covenant . . . his command-ments:* the various covenants which God entered into with mankind, e.g., Gn 2, 15ff; 17, 1–22; especially on Mount Sinai where the people saw God's glory and heard his voice (Ex 19, 16—24, 18).

17, 14: *Ruler:* this may refer to civil authority or to angels placed over nations as guardians; see note on Dt 32, 8 and the cross references above.

17, 19–27: Exhorting the sinner to return to God (19ff.24ff), the author implies that the Lord will

postpone death for a repentant sinner so that he may fulfill his destiny of praising God on earth (22f). In the light of Christian teaching, the gift of final penitence extends this divine purpose into life ever-lasting. See note on Ps 6, 6; cf also Ez 18, 23; 33. 11–16.

17, 26: *Obscure:* literally, evil; compare Gn 6, 5. Though moral fault is not excluded, the thought here is the inability to understand the merciful designs of God. Cf Wis 9, 14–18.

18, 1–13: Not only are God's justice and power beyond man's understanding (1–5), his mercy also is boundless and surpasses all human compassion (6–13).

18, 14–27: The practice of charity is an art which avoids every offense to the recipient (14–18). Prudence directs the changing circumstances of daily life toward the attainment of its reward *at the time of visitation,* i.e., the day of reckoning (19–27).

15 Like dew that abates a burning
    wind,
    so does a word improve a gift.
16 Sometimes the word means
    more than the gift;
    both are offered by a kindly
    man.
17 Only a fool upbraids before
    giving;
    a grudging gift wears out the
    expectant eyes.
18 Be informed before speaking;
    before sickness prepare the
    cure.
19 Before you are judged, seek
    merit for yourself,
    and at the time of visitation
    you will have a ransom.
20 Before you have fallen, humble
    yourself;
    when you have sinned, show
    repentance.
21 Delay not to forsake sins,
    neglect it not till you are in
    distress.
22 Let nothing prevent the prompt
    payment of your vows;
    wait not to fulfill them when
    you are dying.
23 Before making a vow have the
    means to fulfill it;
    be not one who tries the
    LORD.
24 Think of wrath and the day of
    death,
    the time of vengeance when
    he will hide his face.
25 Remember the time of hunger
    in the time of plenty,
    poverty and want in the day
    of wealth.
26 Between morning and evening
    the weather changes;
    before the LORD all things are
    fleeting.
27 A wise man is circumspect in
    all things;
    when sin is rife he keeps
    himself from wrongdoing.
28 Any learned man should make
    wisdom known,

and he who attains to her
    should declare her praise;
29 Those trained in her words
    must show their wisdom,
    dispensing sound proverbs
    like life-giving waters.

Self-Control

30 Go not after your lusts,
    but keep your desires in check.
31 If you satisfy your lustful
    appetites
    they will make you the sport
    of your enemies.
32 Have no joy in the pleasures of
    a moment
    which bring on poverty
    redoubled;
33 Become not a glutton and a
    winebibber
    with nothing in your purse.

19 He who does so grows no
    richer;
    he who wastes the little he has
    will be stripped bare.
2 Wine and women make the
    mind giddy,
    and the companion of harlots
    becomes reckless.
4 He who lightly trusts in them
    has no sense,
    and he who strays after them
    sins against his own life.
3 Rottenness and worms will
    possess him,
    for contumacious desire
    destroys its owner.

The Proper Use of Speech

5 He who gloats over evil will
    meet with evil,
    and he who repeats an evil
    report has no sense.
6 Never repeat gossip,
    and you will not be reviled.
7 Tell nothing to friend or foe;
    if you have a fault, reveal it
    not,
8 For he who hears it will hold it
    against you,
    and in time become your
    enemy.

9 Let anything you hear die
    within you;
    be assured it will not make
    you burst.
10 When a fool hears something,
    he is in labor,
    like a woman giving birth to
    a child.
11 Like an arrow lodged in a man's
    thigh
    is gossip in the breast of a
    fool.
12 Admonish your friend—he
    may not have done it;
    and if he did, that he may not
    do it again.
13 Admonish your neighbor—he
    may not have said it;
    and if he did, that he may not
    say it again.
14 Admonish your friend—often
    it may be slander;
    every story you must not
    believe.
15 Then, too, a man can slip and
    not mean it;
    who has not sinned with his
    tongue?
16 Admonish your neighbor before
    you break with him;
    thus will you fulfill the law of
    the Most High.

How To Recognize True Wisdom

17 All wisdom is fear of the LORD;
    perfect wisdom is the
    fulfillment of the law.
18 The knowledge of wickedness is
    not wisdom,
    nor is there prudence in the
    counsel of sinners.
19 There is a shrewdness that is
    detestable,
    while the simple man may be
    free from sin.
20 There are those with little
    understanding who fear
    God,
    and those of great intelligence
    who violate the law.

18, 19: *Merit . . . ransom:* almsgiving is often portrayed in the Bible as a means of approach to the forgiving mercy of God. Cf 3, 29f; 11f; Tb 12, 12f; Dn 4, 24; Lk 16, 9; Acts 10, 31.

18, 22f: The usual object of a vow in Old Testament times was the offering of a bloody sacrifice.

18, 28f: A general statement on the teaching of wisdom, serving either as a conclusion to the preceding section or as an introduction to the following one. The neighbors of the wise man are regarded as the

field into which he channels the waters of wisdom to encourage growth. Cf 24, 28–31.

18, 30—19, 4: Inordinate gratification of the senses makes a man unreasonable, the slave of passion, *the sport* of his *enemies.* In the end it destroys him physically and spiritually.

19, 5–16: An excellent commentary on the eighth commandment of the Decalogue, forbidding intemperance in speech through calumny, rash judgment and detraction (5f), and inculcating discreet silence

in defense of self and of neighbor (7–11). Justice requires that an accused neighbor be given a hearing and charity urges fraternal correction; both together fulfill *the law of the Most High* (12–16); cf Mt 7, 1f; 18, 15f.

19, 17–26: True and false wisdom as here described are synonymous with virtue and vice, with *the fulfillment of the law* and the violation of it.

21 There is a shrewdness keen but
      dishonest,
   which by duplicity wins a
      judgment.
22 There is the wicked man who
      is bowed in grief,
   but is full of guile within;
23 He bows his head and feigns
      not to hear,
   but when not observed, he
      will take advantage of you:
24 Even though his lack of strength
      keeps him from sinning,
   when he finds the opportunity,
      he will do harm.
25 One can tell a man by his
      appearance;
   a wise man is known as such
      when first met.
26 A man's attire, his hearty
      laughter and his gait,
   proclaim him for what he is.

Conduct of the Wise and the Foolish

20 An admonition can be
      inopportune,
   and a man may be wise to
      hold his peace.
2 It is much better to admonish
      than to lose one's temper,
   for one who admits his fault
      will be kept from disgrace.
3 Like a eunuch lusting for
      intimacy with a maiden
   is he who does right under
      compulsion.
4 One man is silent and is thought
      wise,
   another is talkative and is
      disliked.
5 One man is silent because he
      has nothing to say;
   another is silent, biding his time.
6 A wise man is silent till the
      right time comes,
   but a boastful fool ignores
      the proper time.
7 He who talks too much is
      detested;
   he who pretends to authority
      is hated.

8 Some misfortunes bring success;
   some things gained are a
      man's loss.
9 Some gifts do one no good,
   and some must be paid back
      double.
10 Humiliation can follow fame,
   while from obscurity a man
      can lift up his head.
11 A man may buy much for little,
   but pay for it seven times
      over.
12 A wise man makes himself
      popular by a few words,
   but fools pour forth their
      blandishments in vain.
13 A gift from a rogue will do you
      no good,
   for in his eyes one gift is
      equal to seven.
14 He gives little and criticizes
      often,
   and like a crier he shouts
      aloud.
   He lends today, he asks it back
      tomorrow;
   hateful indeed is such a man.
15 A fool has no friends,
   nor thanks for his generosity;
16 Those who eat his bread have
      an evil tongue.
   How many times they laugh
      him to scorn!
17 A fall to the ground is less
      sudden than a slip of the
      tongue;
   that is why the downfall of
      the wicked comes so
      quickly.
18 Insipid food is the untimely
      tale;
   the unruly are always ready
      to offer it.
19 A proverb when spoken by a
      fool is unwelcome,
   for he does not utter it at the
      proper time.
20 A man through want may be
      unable to sin,
   yet in this tranquility he
      cannot rest.

21 One may lose his life through
      shame,
   and perish through a fool's
      intimidation.
22 A man makes a promise to a
      friend out of shame,
   and has him for his enemy
      needlessly.
23 A lie is a foul blot in a man,
   yet it is constantly on the
      lips of the unruly.
24 Better a thief than an
      inveterate liar,
   yet both will suffer disgrace;
25 A liar's way leads to dishonor,
   his shame remains ever with
      him.

26 A wise man advances himself
      by his words,
   a prudent man pleases the
      great.
27 He who works his land has
      abundant crops,
   he who pleases the great is
      pardoned his faults.
28 Favors and gifts blind the eyes;
   like a muzzle over the mouth
      they silence reproof.
29 Hidden wisdom and unseen
      treasure—
   of what value is either?
30 Better the man who hides his
      folly
   than the one who hides his
      wisdom.

Sin Must be Avoided

21 My son, if you have sinned,
      do so no more,
   and for your past sins pray to
      be forgiven.
2 Flee from sin as from a serpent
      that will bite you if you go
      near it;
   Its teeth are lion's teeth,
   destroying the souls of men.
3 Every offense is a two-edged
      sword;
   when it cuts, there can be no
      healing.

20, 1–7: Wisdom indicates the proper times for speech and silence, that is, the occasions when the most benefit can be gained from them.
20, 3: The sense is that violence or force against a person can prevent an external act of sin or compel a good deed without eliminating the internal sin or desire of wrongdoing. Cf 20, 20.
20, 8–16: In a series of paradoxes the author indicates how much true and lasting values differ from apparent ones.

20, 9: *And some . . . double:* or perhaps, "but some are doubly precious."
20, 17–25: The ill-timed speech of *the wicked*, the *unruly* and *a fool* is repulsive (17ff); human respect exposes one to intimidation, rash promises and enmity (21f); lies bring dishonor and lasting disgrace (23ff).
20, 26–30: Unlike the fool who invites disaster through misuse of his tongue, the sage through prudent speech gains in honor and esteem among the

great (26f). He must beware, however, of accepting bribes, lest he share in evil through silence when he should reprove (28ff).
21, 1–10: Under various figures, the consequences of sin are described as destructive of wealth, and even of bodily life, and deserving of death and a place in the depths of the nether world (2ff.6a.8ff). Through prayer, forgiveness can be sought (1), and through fear of the Lord, repentance is achieved (1, 5.6b).

4 Violence and arrogance wipe out
    wealth;
      so too a proud man's home is
      destroyed.
5 Prayer from a poor man's lips
    is heard at once,
      and justice is quickly granted
      him.
6 He who hates correction walks
    the sinner's path,
      but he who fears the LORD
      repents in his heart.
7 Widely known is the boastful
    speaker,
      but the wise man knows his
      own faults.
8 He who builds his house with
    another's money
      is collecting stones for his
      funeral mound.
9 A band of criminals is like a
    bundle of tow;
      they will end in a flaming fire.
10 The path of sinners is smooth
    stones
      that end in the depths of the
      nether world.

The Wise and the Foolish Differ

11 He who keeps the law controls
    his impulses;
      he who is perfect in fear of the
      LORD has wisdom.
12 He can never be taught who is
    not shrewd,
      but one form of shrewdness is
      thoroughly bitter.
13 A wise man's knowledge wells
    up in a flood,
      and his counsel, like a living
      spring;
14 A fool's mind is like a broken
    jar—
      no knowledge at all can it
      hold.
15 When an intelligent man
    hears words of wisdom,
      he approves them and adds to
      them;

the wanton hears them with
    scorn
    and casts them behind his
    back.

16 A fool's chatter is like a load on
    a journey,
      but there is charm to be found
      upon the lips of the wise.
17 The views of a prudent man are
    sought in an assembly,
      and his words are considered
      with care.
18 Like a house in ruins is wisdom
    to a fool;
      the stupid man knows it only
      as inscrutable words.
19 Like fetters on the legs is learning
    to a fool,
      like a manacle on his right
      hand.
20 A fool raises his voice in
    laughter,
      but a prudent man at the
      most smiles gently.
21 Like a chain of gold is learning
    to a wise man,
      like a bracelet on his right arm.
22 The fool steps boldly into a
    house,
      while the well-bred man
      remains outside;
23 A boor peeps through the
    doorway of a house,
      but a cultured man keeps his
      glance cast down.
24 It is rude for one to listen at a
    door;
      a cultured man would be
      overwhelmed by the disgrace
      of it.
25 The lips of the impious talk of
    what is not their concern,
      but the words of the prudent
      are carefully weighed.
26 Fool's thoughts are in their
    mouths,
      wise men's words are in their
      hearts.

27 When a godless man curses his
    adversary,
      he really curses himself.
28 A slanderer besmirches himself,
    and is hated by his
    neighbors.

On Laziness and Foolishness

22 The sluggard is like a stone
    in the mud;
    everyone hisses at his
    disgrace.
2 The sluggard is like a lump of
    dung;
      whoever touches him wipes
      his hands.
3 An unruly child is a disgrace to
    its father;
      if it be a daughter, she brings
      him to poverty.
4 A thoughtful daughter becomes
    a treasure to her husband,
      a shameless one is her
      father's grief.
5 A hussy shames her father and
    her husband;
      by both she is despised.
6 Like a song in time of mourning
    is inopportune talk,
      but lashes and discipline are at
      all times wisdom.
7 Teaching a fool is like gluing a
    broken pot,
      or like disturbing a man in
      the depths of sleep;
8 He talks with a slumberer who
    talks with a fool,
      for when it is over, he will
      say, "What was that?"
9 Weep over the dead man, for
    his light has gone out;
      weep over the fool, for sense
      has left him.
10 Weep but a little over the dead
    man, for he is at rest;
      but worse than death is the
      life of a fool.
11 Seven days of mourning for the
    dead,
      but for the wicked fool a
      whole lifetime.

21, 10: *The path of sinners . . . nether world:* eternal retribution is not proposed in this reference. It became clearly revealed through the teaching of Christ; cf Mt 7, 13f; 25, 41–46; Lk 16, 19–31.

21, 11–28: The mind of the wise man is a fountain of knowledge (13.15); his will is trained to keep the law (11); his words are gracious, valued, carefully weighed, sincere (16f.25f); his conduct is respectful, cultured and restrained (20.22ff). The fool's mind is devoid of knowledge and impenetrable to it (12.14. 18f); his will rejects it (15); his talk is burdensome (16),

his laughter unrestrained (20), his conversation shallow and meddlesome (25f); his conduct is bold and rude (22ff); his abuse of others redounds on himself (27f).

21, 27: *Adversary:* this can be understood in the sense that, if a man curses one who led him into sin, he implicitly curses himself for having yielded to the sin; or in the sense that the enemy is the man's own sinful nature; or even in the sense that the enemy is the devil, since the Hebrew word used here is *satan.* Cf 1 Chr 21, 1; Zec 3, 2; 2 Pt 2, 12f; Jude 9.

22, 1–15: To Sirach, a lazy person and an unruly child are a cause of shame and disgrace; everyone wishes to be rid of them (1–5). A wicked fool is as senseless as a man asleep or dead, but the grief he causes others lasts a lifetime (7–11). He is like a brute, troublesome and intolerable (12–15).

22, 6: *Like a song . . . is . . . talk:* some understand *talk* in the sense of a rebuke unheeded by the unruly as a joyful song is out of place among mourners. Corporal punishment, however, is always effective.

12 Speak but seldom with the
    stupid man,
    be not the companion of a
       brute;
13 Beware of him lest you have
    trouble
    and be spattered when he
       shakes himself;
    Turn away from him and you
       will find rest
    and not be wearied by his
       lack of sense.
14 What is heavier than lead,
    and what is its name but
       "Fool"?
15 Sand and salt and an iron mass
    are easier to bear than a
       stupid man.

16 Masonry bonded with wooden
    beams
    is not loosened by an
       earthquake;
    Neither is a resolve constructed
    with careful deliberation
    shaken in a moment of fear.
17 A resolve that is backed by
    prudent understanding
    is like the polished surface of
       a smooth wall.
18 Small stones lying on an open
    height
    will not remain when the
       wind blows;
    Neither can a timid resolve
    based on foolish plans
    withstand fear of any kind.

The Preservation of Friendship

19 One who jabs the eye brings tears:
    he who pierces the heart
       bares its feelings.
20 He who throws stones at birds
    drives them away,
    and he who insults a friend
       breaks up the friendship.
21 Should you draw a sword against
    a friend,
    despair not, it can be undone.
22 Should you speak sharply to a
    friend,
    fear not, you can be reconciled.

But a contemptuous insult, a
    confidence broken,
    or a treacherous attack will
       drive away any friend.

23 Make fast friends with a man
    while he is poor;
    thus will you enjoy his
       prosperity with him.
    In time of trouble remain true
       to him,
    so as to share in his
       inheritance when it comes.
24 Before flames burst forth an
    oven smokes;
    so does abuse come before
       bloodshed.
25 From a friend in need of
    support
    no one need hide in shame;
26 But from him who brings harm
    to his friend
    all will stand aloof who hear
       of it.

Prayer

27 Who will set a guard over my
    mouth,
    and upon my lips an effective
       seal,
    That I may not fail through
       them,
    that my tongue may not
       destroy me?

23 LORD, Father and Master of
    my life,
    permit me not to fall by them!
2 Who will apply the lash to my
    thoughts,
    to my mind the rod of
       discipline,
    That my failings may not be
       spared,
    nor the sins of my heart
       overlooked;
3 Lest my failings increase,
    and my sins be multiplied;
    Lest I succumb to my foes,
    and my enemy rejoice over
       me?

4 LORD, Father and God of my
    life,
    abandon me not into their
       control!
5 A brazen look allow me not;
    ward off passion from my
       heart,
6 Let not the lustful cravings of
    the flesh master me,
    surrender me not to
       shameless desires.

The Proper Use of the Tongue

7 Give heed, my children, to the
    instruction that I pronounce,
    for he who keeps it will not
       be enslaved.
8 Through his lips is the sinner
    ensnared;
    the railer and the arrogant
       man fail thereby.
9 Let not your mouth form the
    habit of swearing,
    or becoming too familiar
       with the Holy Name.
10 Just as a slave that is
    constantly under scrutiny
    will not be without welts,
    So one who swears continually
    by the Holy Name
    will not remain free from
       sin.
11 A man who often swears heaps
    up his obligations;
    the scourge will never be far
       from his house.
    If he swears in error, he incurs
       guilt;
    if he neglects his obligation,
       his sin is doubly great.
    If he swears without reason he
    cannot be found just,
    and all his house will suffer
       affliction.
12 There are words which merit
    death;
    may they never be heard
       among Jacob's heirs.
    For all such words are foreign
       to the devout,
    who do not wallow in sin.

22, 16ff: A prudent mind firmly resolved is undisturbed by violent and conflicting thoughts,
whereas a foolish person is tossed about by the winds
of fear, like small stones whipped about by high
winds.
22, 19–26: As disputes and violence weaken
friendship, and disloyalty and abuse of confidence
destroy it utterly (99–22.24.26), so kindness to a poor
man in time of poverty and adversity builds up
friendship and merits a share in his prosperity and

inheritance (23.25).
22, 27—26, 6: The sage implores the divine assistance to preserve him through stern discipline from
sins of the tongue (22, 27; 23, 1); ignorance of mind
and weakness of will (2f); and inclinations of the
senses and the flesh, lest he fall into the hands of his
enemies, or become a prey of shameful desires (3–6).
23, 1: Lord, Father and Master of my life: these
words express the tender personal relationship
between the author's soul and God, the need of his

assistance, and the truth of his providence.
23, 7–15: A warning against sins of the tongue
through misuse of the Holy Name, thoughtless
swearing which involves obligation and incurs guilt
(7–11), blasphemy (12), talk that is coarse and
blundersome (13f), and the incorrigible habit of
abusive language (15).
23, 10: As a slave . . . under scrutiny, so is he who
calls on God to witness the truth of what he says.

13 Let not your mouth become
        used to coarse talk,
    for in it lies sinful matter.
14 Keep your father and mother in
        mind
    when you sit among the
        mighty,
    Lest in their presence you
        commit a blunder
    and disgrace your upbringing,
    By wishing you had never been
        born
    or cursing the day of your
        birth.
15 A man who has the habit of
        abusive language
    will never mature in character
        as long as he lives.

Sins of the Flesh

16 Two types of men multiply sins,
        a third draws down wrath;
    For burning passion is a
        blazing fire,
    not to be quenched till it
        burns itself out:
    A man given to sins of the
        flesh,
    who never stops until the fire
        breaks forth;
17 The rake to whom all bread is
        sweet
    and who is never through till
        he dies;
18 And the man who dishonors
        his marriage bed
    and says to himself, "Who can
        see me?
    Darkness surrounds me, walls
        hide me;
    no one sees me; why should I
        fear to sin?"
    Of the Most High he is not
        mindful,
19   fearing only the eyes of men;
    He does not understand that
        the eyes of the LORD,
    ten thousand times brighter
        than the sun,
    Observe every step a man takes
        and peer into hidden corners.

20 He who knows all things before
        they exist
    still knows them all after they
        are made.
21 Such a man will be punished in
        the streets of the city;
    when he least expects it, he
        will be apprehended.

22 So also with the woman who is
        unfaithful to her husband
    and offers as heir her son by a
        stranger.
23 First, she has disobeyed the law
        of the Most High;
    secondly, she has wronged her
        husband;
    Thirdly, in her wanton
        adultery
    she has borne children by
        another man.
24 Such a woman will be dragged
        before the assembly,
    and her punishment will
        extend to her children;
25 Her children will not take root;
        her branches will not bring
        forth fruit.
26 She will leave an accursed
        memory;
    her disgrace will never be
        blotted out.
27 Thus all who dwell on the earth
        shall know,
    and all who inhabit the world
        shall understand,
    That nothing is better than the
        fear of the LORD,
    nothing more salutary than to
        obey his commandments.

Praise of Wisdom

24 Wisdom sings her own
        praises,
    before her own people she
        proclaims her glory;
2 In the assembly of the Most
        High she opens her mouth,
    in the presence of his hosts
        she declares her worth:

3 "From the mouth of the Most
        High I came forth,
    and mistlike covered the
        earth.
4 In the highest heavens did I
        dwell,
    my throne on a pillar of
        cloud.
5 The vault of heaven I compassed
        alone,
    through the deep abyss I
        wandered.
6 Over waves of the sea, over all
        the land,
    over every people and nation
        I held sway.
7 Among all these I sought a
        resting place;
    in whose inheritance should I
        abide?

8 "Then the Creator of all gave
        me his command,
    and he who formed me chose
        the spot for my tent,
    Saying, 'In Jacob make your
        dwelling,
    in Israel your inheritance.'
9 Before all ages, in the beginning,
        he created me,
    and through all ages I shall
        not cease to be.
10 In the holy tent I ministered
        before him,
    and in Zion I fixed my
        abode.
11 Thus in the chosen city he has
        given me rest,
    in Jerusalem is my domain.
12 I have struck root among the
        glorious people,
    in the portion of the LORD,
        his heritage.

13 "Like a cedar on Lebanon I
        am raised aloft,
    like a cypress on Mount
        Hermon,
14 Like a palm tree in Engedi,
        like a rosebush in Jericho,

23, 16–27: From sins of the tongue the author
proceeds to treat of sins of the flesh and their dire
consequences. The passion of lust tyrannizes over its
victims and, like fire, consumes and utterly destroys
them (16f.22–26). The false security of the adulterer
serves but to aggravate his inevitable fate (18–21).
Only the fear of the Lord and observance of his
commandments can assure moral safety (27).
23, 16: *Two types . . . a third:* three kinds of
impurity, with increasing degrees of gravity: solitary
sins (16), fornication (17) and adultery (18–21).

23, 21: Cf Lv 20, 10; Dt 22, 22.
23, 23: The detailed evil of adultery includes
disobedience to God's law (Ex 20, 14), injustice to a
partner in marriage, and disgraceful offspring.
23, 24f: The judgment of *the assembly* determined
the illegitimacy of children born of adultery or
incest and excluded them from the "community of
the LORD" (Dt 23, 3). Cf Wis 3, 16–19; 4, 3–6.
24, 1–27: In this chapter Wisdom speaks in the
first person, describing her origin, her dwelling place
in Israel, and the reward she gives her followers. As

in Prv 8, Wisdom is described as a being who comes
from God and is distinct from him. While we do not
say with certainty that this description applies to a
personal being, it does foreshadow the beautiful
doctrine of the Word of God later developed in St.
John's Gospel (Jn 1, 1–14). In the liturgy this chapter
is applied to the Blessed Virgin because of her constant
and intimate association with Christ, the Incarnate
Wisdom.

Like a fair olive tree in the
field,
like a plane tree growing
beside the water.
15 Like cinnamon, or fragrant
balm, or precious myrrh,
I give forth perfume;
Like galbanum and onycha and
sweet spices,
like the odor of incense in
the holy place.
16 I spread out my branches like a
terebinth,
my branches so bright and so
graceful.
17 I bud forth delights like the
vine,
my blossoms become fruit
fair and rich.
18 Come to me, all you that yearn
for me,
and be filled with my fruits;
19 You will remember me as
sweeter than honey,
better to have than the
honeycomb.
20 He who eats of me will hunger
still,
he who drinks of me will
thirst for more;
21 He who obeys me will not be
put to shame,
he who serves me will never
fail."

22 All this is true of the book of
the Most High's covenant,
the law which Moses
commanded us
as an inheritance for the
community of Jacob.
23 It overflows, like the Pishon,
with wisdom—
like the Tigris in the days of
the new fruits.
24 It runs over, like the Euphrates,
with understanding,
like the Jordan at harvest
time.

25 It sparkles like the Nile with
knowledge,
like the Gihon at vintage time.
26 The first man never finished
comprehending wisdom,
nor will the last succeed in
fathoming her.
27 For deeper than the sea are her
thoughts;
her counsels, than the great
abyss.

28 Now I, like a rivulet from her
stream,
channeling the waters into a
garden,
29 Said to myself, "I will water my
plants,
my flower bed I will drench";
And suddenly this rivulet of
mine became a river,
then this stream of mine, a
sea.
30 Thus do I send my teachings
forth shining like the dawn,
to become known afar off.
31 Thus do I pour out instruction
like prophecy
and bestow it on generations
to come.

Those Who Are Worthy of Praise

25 With three things I am
delighted,
for they are pleasing to the
LORD and to men:
Harmony among brethren,
friendship among neighbors,
and the mutual love of
husband and wife.
2 Three kinds of men I hate;
their manner of life I loathe
indeed:
A proud pauper, a rich
dissembler,
and an old man lecherous in
his dotage.

3 What you have not saved in
your youth,
how will you acquire in your
old age?
4 How becoming to the gray-haired
is judgment,
and a knowledge of counsel
to those on in years!
5 How becoming to the aged is
wisdom,
understanding and prudence
to the venerable!
6 The crown of old men is wide
experience;
their glory, the fear of the LORD.
7 There are nine who come to my
mind as blessed,
a tenth whom my tongue
proclaims:
The man who finds joy in his
children,
and he who lives to see his
enemies' downfall.
8 Happy is he who dwells with a
sensible wife,
and he who plows not like a
donkey yoked with an ox.
Happy is he who sins not with
his tongue,
and he who serves not his
inferior.
9 Happy is he who finds a friend
and he who speaks to
attentive ears.
10 He who finds wisdom is great
indeed,
but not greater than he who
fears the LORD.
11 Fear of the LORD surpasses all
else,
its possessor is beyond
compare.

Wicked and Virtuous Women

12 Worst of all wounds is that of
the heart,
worst of all evils is that of a
woman.

24, 15: These substances were associated with worship, being mentioned in Ex 30, 22f.34 as the ingredients of the anointing oil and the sacred incense. Israel was a priestly nation.
24, 18: Compare the words of the Savior in Mt 11, 28ff.
24, 20: So pleasing is wisdom to man that, far from being satiated, he will always desire more.
24, 22: Here the author begins to speak once more, Wisdom having ended her discourse in the preceding verse. Wisdom and the law of Moses are now identified.
24, 25: *Gihon:* understood by some to have been a name for the Nile; cf Gn 2, 13.

24, 28–31: Spoken by the author. He had at first drawn a small portion of the water of wisdom for his own private benefit, but finding it so useful, he soon began to let others share in this boon by teaching them the lessons of wisdom.
25, 1–11: While praising brotherly love, love of neighbor, and conjugal love, the sage condemns their opposites in the arrogant pauper who despises his brother, the fraudulent rich man who cheats his neighbor, and the lecherous old man unfaithful to his wife (1f). This last, sensual from his youth, lacks the mature blessings of judgment and wisdom in old age (3–6), and the joy of a peaceful household, where honesty and dignity, friendship, wisdom and fear of

God prevail (7–11).
25, 8: *Like a donkey yoked with an ox:* incompatibility between husband and wife.
25, 12–25: Wickedness in a woman is most grievous, painful and bitter to her husband. Through it she becomes vengeful, dangerous and intolerable, jealous, talkative, intemperate and unchaste. Even her very appearance is changed (12–17). The worst of all evils, a source of grief, a snare and a disgrace to her husband, she depresses his mind, saddens and breaks his heart, destroys his strength (18–22). She must not be indulged but made obedient or punished (24f).

13 Worst of all sufferings is that
　　　from one's foes,
　　　worst of all vengeance is
　　　　that of one's enemies:
14 No poison worse than that of
　　　a serpent,
　　　no venom greater than that
　　　　of a woman.
15 With a dragon or a lion I
　　　would rather dwell
　　　than live with an evil woman.
16 Wickedness changes a woman's
　　　looks,
　　　and makes her sullen as a
　　　　female bear.
17 When her husband sits among
　　　his neighbors,
　　　a bitter sigh escapes him
　　　　unawares.
18 There is scarce any evil like
　　　that in a woman;
　　　may she fall to the lot of the
　　　　sinner!
19 Like a sandy hill to aged feet
　　　is a railing wife to a quiet
　　　　man.
20 Stumble not through woman's
　　　beauty,
　　　nor be greedy for her wealth;
21 The man is a slave, in disgrace
　　　and shame,
　　　when a wife supports her
　　　　husband.
22 Depressed mind, saddened face,
　　　broken heart—this from an
　　　　evil wife.
　　Feeble hands and quaking
　　　knees—
　　　from a wife who brings no
　　　　happiness to her husband.
23 In woman was sin's beginning,
　　　and because of her we all die.
24 Allow water no outlet,
　　　and be not indulgent to an
　　　　erring wife.
25 If she walks not by your side,
　　　cut her away from you.

26 Happy the husband of a
　　　good wife,
　　　twice-lengthened are his days;
2 A worthy wife brings joy to her
　　　husband,
　　　peaceful and full is his life.
3 A good wife is a generous gift
　　　bestowed upon him who fears
　　　　the LORD;
4 Be he rich or poor, his heart is
　　　content,
　　　and a smile is ever on his face.
5 There are three things at which
　　　my heart quakes,
　　　a fourth before which I
　　　　quail:
　　Though false charges in public,
　　　trial before all the people,
　　　and lying testimony are
　　　　harder to bear than death,
6 A jealous wife is heartache and
　　　mourning
　　　and a scourging tongue like
　　　　the other three.
7 A bad wife is a chafing yoke;
　　　he who marries her seizes a
　　　　scorpion.
8 A drunken wife arouses great
　　　anger,
　　　for she does not hide her
　　　　shame.
9 By her eyelids and her haughty
　　　stare
　　　an unchaste wife can be
　　　　recognized.
10 Keep a strict watch over an
　　　unruly wife,
　　　lest, finding an opportunity,
　　　　she make use of it;
11 Follow close if her eyes are
　　　bold,
　　　and be not surprised if she
　　　　betrays you:
12 As a thirsty traveler with eager
　　　mouth
　　　drinks from any water that he
　　　　finds,

So she settles down before
　　　every tent peg
　　　and opens her quiver for
　　　　every arrow.
13 A gracious wife delights her
　　　husband,
　　　her thoughtfulness puts flesh
　　　　on his bones;
14 A gift from the LORD is her
　　　governed speech,
　　　and her firm virtue is of
　　　　surpassing worth.
15 Choicest of blessings is a modest
　　　wife,
　　　priceless her chaste person.
16 Like the sun rising in the
　　　LORD's heavens,
　　　the beauty of a virtuous wife
　　　　is the radiance of her home.
17 Like the light which shines
　　　above the holy lampstand,
　　　are her beauty of face and
　　　　graceful figure.
18 Golden columns on silver bases
　　　are her shapely limbs and
　　　　steady feet.

Dangers to Integrity and Friendship
19 These two bring grief to my
　　　heart,
　　　and the third arouses my
　　　　horror:
　　A wealthy man reduced to
　　　want;
　　　illustrious men held in
　　　　contempt;
　　And the man who passes from
　　　justice to sin,
　　　for whom the LORD makes
　　　　ready the sword.
20 A merchant can hardly remain
　　　upright,
　　　nor a shopkeeper free from sin;
27 For the sake of profit many
　　　sin,
　　　and the struggle for wealth
　　　　blinds the eyes.

25, 23: According to the account in Gn 3 to which
Ben Sirach refers, sin, the cause of death, originated
in woman: Eve, the first human being to sin, induced
Adam to follow her example. But it is through Adam,
as head of the race, that original sin and its punishment of spiritual death are presented by St. Paul
(Rom 5) as having entered the world, to become the
occasion for the redemptive work of Christ our Lord.
　26, 1–4.13–18: *A good wife* is as a gift from God,
bringing *joy* and peace, happiness and contentment
to her husband (1–4) through *her thoughtfulness*,
reserve, modesty and chastity, *beauty*, grace and
virtue (13–18).
　26, 2: *Worthy:* gifted spiritually, mentally and
physically. Cf Prv 31, 10.
　26, 6–12: A repetition of the thought expressed
in 25, 12–25.

26, 17f: *The holy lampstand* and the *golden columns*
stood in the holy place of the ancient Tabernacle
(Ex 25, 31–40; 26, 32).
　26, 18: Among the additions found here in some
manuscripts are the following lines:

"My son, take care in the prime of life
　not to surrender your strength to strangers;
Single out from the land a goodly field
　and there with confidence sow the seed of your
　　increase;
So shall you have your offspring around you,
　and in confidence shall they grow up.

"Though a woman for hire be thought of as a
　trifle,
a married woman is a deadly snare for those
　who embrace her. [Cf Prv 6, 26.]

"A wife's complaint should be made in meekness,
　and show itself in a slight flush;
But a loud-mouthed, scolding wife
　is a trumpet signaling for battle:
Any human being who answers that challenge
　will spend his life amid the turbulence of war."

26, 20—27, 15: From proper conduct in family
life, the author proceeds to social morality, warning
especially against injustice in commerce (26, 20—27,
3), and perversity of speech in business (4–7). The
pursuit of *justice* in these matters is all the more meri-
torious as it is difficult (8ff). The discourses of the
devout are marked with wisdom, but the conversa-
tions of the wicked, with offense, swearing, *cursing*,
quarrels and even *bloodshed* (11–15).

2 Like a peg driven between
        fitted stones,
    between buying and selling
        sin is wedged in.
3 Unless you earnestly hold fast
        to the fear of the LORD,
    suddenly your house will be
        thrown down.
4 When a sieve is shaken, the
        husks appear;
    so do a man's faults when he
        speaks.
5 As the test of what the potter
        molds is in the furnace,
    so in his conversation is the
        test of a man.
6 The fruit of a tree shows the
        care it has had;
    so too does a man's speech
        disclose the bent of his
        mind.
7 Praise no man before he speaks,
    for it is then that men are
        tested.
8 If you strive after justice you
        will attain it,
    and put it on like a splendid
        robe.
9 Birds nest with their own kind,
    and fidelity comes to those
        who live by it.
10 As a lion crouches in wait for
        prey,
    so do sins for evildoers.
11 Ever wise are the discourses of
        the devout,
    but the godless man, like the
        moon, is inconstant.
12 Limit the time you spend
        among fools,
    but frequent the company of
        thoughtful men.
13 The conversation of the wicked
        is offensive,
    their laughter is wanton guilt.
14 Their oath-filled talk makes the
        hair stand on end,
    their brawls make one stop
        one's ears.
15 Wrangling among the haughty
        ends in bloodshed,
    their cursing is painful to
        hear.

16 He who betrays a secret cannot
        be trusted,

he will never find an intimate
        friend.
17 Cherish your friend, keep faith
        with him;
    but if you betray his
        confidence, follow him not;
18 For as an enemy might kill a
        man,
    you have killed your
        neighbor's friendship.
19 Like a bird released from the
        hand,
    you have let your friend go
        and cannot recapture him;
20 Follow him not, for he is far
        away,
    he has fled like a gazelle from
        the trap.
21 A wound can be bound up, and
        an insult forgiven,
    but he who betrays secrets
        does hopeless damage.

Malice, Anger and Vengeance

22 He who has shifty eyes plots
        mischief
    and no one can ward him
        off;
23 In your presence he uses
        honeyed talk,
    and admires your every word,
    But later he changes his tone
    and twists your words to
        your ruin.
24 There is nothing that I hate so
        much,
    and the LORD hates him as
        well.
25 As a stone falls back on him
        who throws it up,
    so a blow struck in treachery
        injures more than one.
26 As he who digs a pit falls into it,
    and he who lays a snare is
        caught in it,
27 Whoever does harm will be
        involved in it
    without knowing how it
        came upon him.

28 Mockery and abuse will be the
        lot of the proud,
    and vengeance lies in wait for
        them like a lion.

29 The trap seizes those who
        rejoice in pitfalls,
    and pain will consume them
        before they die;
30 Wrath and anger are hateful
        things,
    yet the sinner hugs them
        tight.

28 The vengeful will suffer the
        LORD's vengeance,
    for he remembers their sins in
        detail.
2 Forgive your neighbor's
        injustice;
    then when you pray, your own
        sins will be forgiven.
3 Should a man nourish anger
        against his fellows
    and expect healing from the
        LORD?
4 Should a man refuse mercy to
        his fellows,
    yet seek pardon for his own
        sins?
5 If he who is but flesh cherishes
        wrath,
    who will forgive his sins?
6 Remember your last days, set
        enmity aside;
    remember death and decay,
        and cease from sin!
7 Think of the commandments,
        hate not your neighbor;
    of the Most High's covenant,
        and overlook faults.

8 Avoid strife and your sins will
        be fewer,
    for a quarrelsome man
        kindles disputes,
9 Commits the sin of disrupting
        friendship
    and sows discord among those
        at peace.
10 The more wood, the greater the
        fire,
    the more underlying it, the
        fiercer the fight;
    The greater a man's strength,
        the sterner his anger,
    the greater his power, the
        greater his wrath.
11 Pitch and resin make fires
        flare up,
    and insistent quarrels provoke
        bloodshed.

27, 16—28, 11: Betrayal of *confidence* through in-
discretion destroys *friendship* and does irreparable
harm (16–21); cf 22, 22. False friendship based on
hypocrisy and deceit is hateful to God and man

(22ff); it soon becomes a victim of its own treachery
(25ff). The same fate awaits the malicious and
vengeful (27, 28—28, 1). They can obtain mercy and
forgiveness only by first forgiving their neighbor,

being mindful of death and of the commandments of
the Most High (28, 2–7). And they must avoid
quarrels and *strife* (8–11).

The Evil Tongue

12 If you blow upon a spark, it
    quickens into flame,
    if you spit on it, it dies out;
    yet both you do with your
    mouth!
13 Cursed be gossips and the
    double-tongued,
    for they destroy the peace of
    many.
14 A meddlesome tongue subverts
    many,
    and makes refugees among the
    peoples;
    It destroys walled cities,
    and overthrows powerful
    dynasties.
15 A meddlesome tongue can
    drive virtuous women from
    their homes
    and rob them of the fruit of
    their toil;
16 Whoever heeds it has no rest,
    nor can he dwell in peace.

17 A blow from a whip raises a
    welt,
    but a blow from the tongue
    smashes bones;
18 Many have fallen by the edge
    of the sword,
    but not as many as by the
    tongue.
19 Happy he who is sheltered from
    it,
    and has not endured its wrath;
    Who has not borne its yoke
    nor been fettered with its
    chains;
20 For its yoke is a yoke of iron
    and its chains are chains of
    bronze!
21 Dire is the death it inflicts,
    besides which even the
    nether world is a gain;
22 It will not take hold among the
    just
    nor scorch them in its flame,
23 But those who forsake the LORD
    will fall victims to it,
    as it burns among them
    unquenchably!
    It will hurl itself against them
    like a lion;

like a panther, it will tear
    them to pieces.
24 As you hedge round your
    vineyard with thorns,
    set barred doors over your
    mouth;
25 As you seal up your silver and
    gold,
    so balance and weigh your
    words.
26 Take care not to slip by your
    tongue
    and fall victim to your foe
    waiting in ambush.

Loans, Alms and Surety

29 He does a kindness who
    lends to his neighbor,
    and he fulfills the precepts
    who holds out a helping
    hand.
2 Lend to your neighbor in his
    hour of need,
    and pay back your neighbor
    when a loan falls due;
3 Keep your promise, be honest
    with him,
    and you will always come by
    what you need.
4 Many a man who asks for a
    loan
    adds to the burdens of those
    who help him;
5 When he borrows, he kisses the
    lender's hand
    and speaks with respect of his
    creditor's wealth;
    But when payment is due he
    disappoints him
    and says he is helpless to
    meet the claim.
6 If the lender is able to recover
    barely half,
    he considers this an
    achievement;
    If not, he is cheated of his wealth
    and acquires an enemy at no
    extra charge;
    With curses and insults the
    borrower pays him back,
    with abuse instead of honor.
7 Many refuse to lend, not out
    of meanness,
    but from fear of being cheated.

8 To a poor man, however, be
    generous;
    keep him not waiting for your
    alms;
9 Because of the precept, help the
    needy,
    and in their want, do not send
    them away empty-handed.

10 Spend your money for your
    brother and friend,
    and hide it not under a stone
    to perish;
11 Dispose of your treasure as the
    Most High commands,
    for that will profit you more
    than the gold.
12 Store up almsgiving in your
    treasure house,
    and it will save you from
    every evil;
13 Better than a stout shield and a
    sturdy spear
    it will fight for you against
    the foe.

14 A good man goes surety for his
    neighbor,
    and only the shameless
    would play him false;
15 Forget not the kindness of your
    backer,
    for he offers his very life for
    you.
16 The wicked turn a pledge on
    their behalf into misfortune,
    and the ingrate abandons his
    protector;
17 Going surety has ruined many
    prosperous men
    and tossed them about like
    waves of the sea,
18 Has exiled men of prominence
    and sent them wandering
    through foreign lands.
19 The sinner through surety comes
    to grief,
    and he who undertakes too
    much falls into lawsuits.
20 Go surety for your neighbor
    according to your means,
    but take care lest you fall
    thereby.

28, 12–26: Further treatment of sins of the tongue
and their havoc; cf 5, 12—6, 1; 19, 5–16; 20, 17–25;
23, 7–15. *Gossips and the double-tongued* destroy
domestic peace (12–16). The *whip, the sword, chains,*
even the nether world, are not so cruel as the suffering
inflicted by an evil tongue (17–21). Not *the just* but
those who forsake the Lord are *victims* of their evil

tongues (22f). Therefore, guard your mouth and
tongue as you would guard treasure against an
enemy (24ff).

29, 1–20: Some practical maxims concerning the
use of wealth. Give *to a poor man* (8f), lend to a needy
neighbor, but repay *when a loan falls due* lest the
lender's burden be increased (1–5) and his kindness

abused (6f); through charity build up defense against
evil (10–13). *Go surety for your neighbor according*
to your means, but take care (20) not to fall, for the
shameless play false and bring their protectors and
themselves to misfortune and ruin (14–19).

Frugality and Its Rewards

21 Life's prime needs are water,
　　　bread, and clothing,
　　a house, too, for decent
　　　privacy.
22 Better a poor man's fare under
　　　the shadow of one's own roof
　　than sumptuous banquets
　　　among strangers.
23 Be it little or much, be content
　　　with what you have,
　　and pay no heed to him who
　　　would disparage your home;
24 A miserable life it is to go from
　　　house to house,
　　for as a guest you dare not
　　　open your mouth.
25 The visitor has no thanks for
　　　filling the cups;
　　besides, you will hear these
　　　bitter words:
26 "Come here, stranger, set the
　　　table,
　　give me to eat the food you
　　　have!
27 Away, stranger, for one more
　　　worthy;
　　for my brother's visit I need
　　　the room!"
28 Painful things to a sensitive man
　　　are abuse at home and insults
　　　from his creditors.

The Training of Children

30 He who loves his son
　　　chastises him often,
　　that he may be his joy when
　　　he grows up.
2 He who disciplines his son will
　　　benefit from him,
　　and boast of him among his
　　　intimates.
3 He who educates his son makes
　　　his enemy jealous,
　　and shows his delight in him
　　　among his friends.
4 At the father's death, he will
　　　seem not dead,
　　since he leaves after him one
　　　like himself,

5 Whom he looks upon through
　　　life with joy,
　　and even in death, without
　　　regret:
6 The avenger he leaves against
　　　his foes,
　　and the one to repay his
　　　friends with kindness.

7 He who spoils his son will have
　　　wounds to bandage,
　　and will quake inwardly at
　　　every outcry.
8 A colt untamed turns out
　　　stubborn;
　　a son left to himself grows up
　　　unruly.
9 Pamper your child and he will
　　　be a terror for you,
　　indulge him and he will
　　　bring you grief.
10 Share not in his frivolity lest
　　　you share in his sorrow,
　　when finally your teeth are
　　　clenched in remorse.
11 Give him not his own way in
　　　his youth,
　　and close not your eyes to his
　　　follies.
12 Bend him to the yoke when he
　　　is young,
　　thrash his sides while he is
　　　still small,
　　Lest he become stubborn,
　　　disobey you,
　　and leave you disconsolate.
13 Discipline your son, make
　　　heavy his yoke,
　　lest his folly humiliate you.

Health of Soul and Body

14 Better a poor man strong and
　　　robust,
　　than a rich man with wasted
　　　frame.
15 More precious than gold is
　　　health and well-being,
　　contentment of spirit than
　　　coral.
16 No treasure greater than a
　　　healthy body;

no happiness, than a joyful
　　　heart!
17 Preferable is death to a bitter
　　　life,
　　unending sleep to constant
　　　illness.
18 Dainties set before one who
　　　cannot eat
　　are like the offerings placed
　　　before a tomb.
19 What good is an offering to an
　　　idol
　　that can neither taste nor
　　　smell?
20 So it is with the afflicted man
　　　who groans at the good things
　　　his eyes behold!

21 Do not give in to sadness,
　　　torment not yourself with
　　　brooding;
22 Gladness of heart is the very
　　　life of man,
　　cheerfulness prolongs his
　　　days.
23 Distract yourself, renew your
　　　courage,
　　drive resentment far away
　　　from you;
　　For worry has brought death
　　　to many,
　　nor is there aught to be
　　　gained from resentment.
24 Envy and anger shorten one's
　　　life,
　　worry brings on premature
　　　old age.
25 One who is cheerful and gay
　　　while at table
　　benefits from his food.

The Proper Attitude toward Riches

31 Keeping watch over riches
　　　wastes the flesh,
　　and care of wealth drives
　　　away rest.
2 Concern for one's livelihood
　　　banishes slumber;
　　more than a serious illness it
　　　disturbs repose.

29, 21–28: The man who provides his own basic *needs* of food, clothing and dwelling, and is content with what he has, preserves his freedom and self-respect (21ff). But if he lives as a guest, even among the rich, he exposes himself to insult and *abuse* (24–28).

30, 1–13: Sound discipline and careful education of children correct frivolity and stubbornness, prevent remorse and humiliation, and bring to parents lasting joy and delight, prestige among friends, jealousy of enemies, perpetuation and vindication of themselves through their offspring (1–6). Lack of

discipline and overindulgence of children bring *sorrow* and disappointment, *terror* and *grief* (7–13).

30, 14–25: Health of mind and body and joy of heart are judged more precious than wealth (14ff); bitterness, *constant illness* and affliction, more difficult to bear than *death* (17–20). Sadness, *resentment*, anxiety, *envy and anger shorten . . . life;* they should be dispelled by *cheerfulness* and *gladness of heart,* which help to prolong one's *days* (21–25).

30, 17: *Preferable is death . . . constant illness:* the true value of human suffering was revealed through

the passion and death of Christ. It serves as reparation for sin, and when united with Christ's suffering, as merit for eternal life.

31, 1–11: Solicitude for acquiring wealth and anxiety over preserving it disturb *repose* and easily lead to sin and ruin (1–7). Cf Mt 6, 25–34. A *rich man* who has not sinned or been seduced by wealth is worthy of praise (8–11).

31, 2: The Hebrew adds a verse that seems out of place here: "A faithful comrade drives away reproach, and the friend who keeps secrets is as dear as life."

3 The rich man labors to pile up
    wealth,
    and his only rest is wanton
        pleasure;
4 The poor man toils for a
    meager subsistence,
    and if ever he rests, he finds
        himself in want.
5 The lover of gold will not be
    free from sin,
    for he who pursues wealth is
        led astray by it.
6 Many have been ensnared by
    gold,
    though destruction lay before
        their eyes;
7 It is a stumbling block to those
    who are avid for it,
    a snare for every fool.

8 Happy the rich man found
    without fault,
    who turns not aside after
        gain!
9 Who is he, that we may praise
    him?
    he, of all his kindred, has
        done wonders,
10 For he has been tested by gold
    and come off safe,
    and this remains his glory;
    He could have sinned but did
        not,
    could have done evil but
        would not,
11 So that his possessions are
    secure,
    and the assembly recounts his
        praises.

Table Etiquette

12 If you are dining with a great
    man,
    bring not a greedy gullet to
        his table,
    Nor cry out, "How much food
        there is here!"
13   Remember that gluttony is
        evil.
    No creature is greedier than the
        eye:
    therefore it weeps for any
        cause.
15 Recognize that your neighbor
    feels as you do,

and keep in mind your own
    dislikes:
14 Toward what he eyes, do not
    put out a hand;
    nor reach when he does for
        the same dish.
16 Behave at table like a favored
    guest,
    and be not greedy, lest you
        be despised.
17 Be the first to stop, as befits
    good manners;
    gorge not yourself, lest you
        give offense.
18 If there are many with you at
    table,
    be not the first to reach out
        your hand.
19 Does not a little suffice for a
    well-bred man?
    When he lies down, it is
        without discomfort.
20 Distress and anguish and loss of
    sleep,
    and restless tossing for the
        glutton!
    Moderate eating ensures sound
        slumber
    and a clear mind next day on
        rising.
21 If perforce you have eaten too
    much,
    once you have emptied your
        stomach, you will have
        relief.

22 Listen to me, my son, and
    scorn me not;
    later you will find my advice
        good.
    In whatever you do, be
        moderate,
    and no sickness will befall you.
23 On a man generous with food,
    blessings are invoked,
    and this testimony to his
        goodness is lasting;
24 He who is miserly with food is
    denounced in public,
    and this testimony to his
        stinginess is lasting.
25 Let not wine-drinking be the
    proof of your strength,
    for wine has been the ruin of
        many.

26 As the furnace probes the work
    of the smith,
    so does wine the hearts of the
        insolent.
27 Wine is very life to man
    if taken in moderation.
    Does he really live who lacks
        the wine
    which was created for his
        joy?
28 Joy of heart, good cheer and
    merriment
    are wine drunk freely at the
        proper time.
29 Headache, bitterness and
    disgrace
    is wine drunk amid anger and
        strife.
30 More and more wine is a snare
    for the fool;
    it lessens his strength and
        multiplies his wounds.
31 Rebuke not your neighbor when
    wine is served,
    nor put him to shame while
        he is merry;
    Use no harsh words with him
    and distress him not in the
        presence of others.

32 If you are chosen to preside
    at dinner, be not puffed
        up,
    but with the guests be as one
        of themselves;
    Take care of them first before
        you sit down;
2   when you have fulfilled your
        duty, then take your place,
    To share in their joy
    and win praise for your
        hospitality.
3 Being older, you may talk; that
    is only your right,
    but temper your wisdom, not
    to disturb the singing.
4 When wine is present, do not
    pour out discourse,
    and flaunt not your wisdom
    at the wrong time.
5 Like a seal of carnelian in a
    setting of gold
    is a concert when wine is
        served.

31, 8ff: The Church in her liturgy applies this
passage to holy confessors of the Faith.
   31, 12—32, 13: A man observing etiquette at
table avoids greed and selfishness (31, 12f), is
considerate of a neighbor's likes and dislikes and
generous toward him (14f.23f), observes proper

manners (16ff), is *moderate* in *eating* and drinking
(19–22.25–30). A good host makes himself one with
his guests, is solicitous for them (32, 1f), provides
conversation and diversion (3–6), is modest in
speech (7f.10), is respectful of elders (9), polite in
comportment and grateful to God for his *favors* (11ff).

31, 21: *Emptied your stomach:* the practice of
induced vomiting, well-known among pagan Romans,
and less well-known among the Jews, seems to be
referred to here.

6 Like a gold mounting with an
      emerald seal
   is string music with delicious
      wine.
7 Young man, speak only when
      necessary,
   when they have asked you
      more than once;
8 Be brief, but say much in those
      few words,
   be like the wise man, taciturn.
9 When among your elders be not
      forward,
   and with officials be not too
      insistent.
10 Like the lightning that flashes
      before a storm
   is the esteem that shines on
      modesty.
11 When it is time to leave, tarry
      not;
   be off for home! There take
      your ease,
12 And there enjoy doing as you
      wish,
   but without sin or words of
      pride.
13 Above all, give praise to your
      Creator,
   who showers his favors upon
      you.

The Providence of God

14 He who would find God must
      accept discipline;
   he who seeks him obtains his
      request.
15 He who studies the law masters
      it,
   but the hypocrite finds it a
      trap.
16 His judgment is sound who fears
      the LORD;
   out of obscurity he draws
      forth a clear plan.
17 The sinner turns aside reproof
   and distorts the law to suit
      his purpose.
18 The thoughtful man will not
      neglect direction;
   the proud and insolent man is
      deterred by nothing.

19 Do nothing without counsel,
   and then you need have no
      regrets.
20 Go not on a way that is set
      with snares,
   and let not the same thing
      trip you twice.
21 Be not too sure even of smooth
      roads,
22 be careful on all your paths.
23 Whatever you do, be on your
      guard,
   for in this way you will keep
      the commandments.
24 He who keeps the law preserves
      himself;
   and he who trusts in the LORD
      shall not be put to shame.

33 No evil can harm the man
      who fears the LORD;
   through trials, again and
      again he is safe.
2 He who hates the law is without
      wisdom,
   and is tossed about like a
      boat in a storm.
3 The prudent man trusts in the
      word of the LORD,
   and the law is dependable for
      him as a divine oracle.
4 Prepare your words and you
      will be listened to;
   draw upon your training and
      then give your answer.

5 Like the wheel of a cart is the
      mind of a fool;
   his thoughts revolve in circles.
6 A fickle friend is like the stallion
      that neighs, no matter who the
      rider.
7 Why is one day more important
      than another,
   when it is the sun that lights
      up every day?
8 It is due to the LORD's wisdom
      that they differ;
   it is through him the seasons
      and feasts come and go.
9 Some he dignifies and sanctifies,
   and others he lists as ordinary
      days.

10 So too, all men are of clay,
   for from earth man was
      formed;
11 Yet with his great knowledge
   the LORD makes men unlike;
   in different paths he has them
      walk.
12 Some he blesses and makes
      great,
   some he sanctifies and draws
      to himself.
   Others he curses and brings low,
   and expels them from their
      place.
13 Like clay in the hands of a
      potter,
   to be molded according to his
      pleasure,
   So are men in the hands of
      their Creator,
   to be assigned by him their
      function.
14 As evil contrasts with good, and
      death with life,
   so are sinners in contrast with
      the just;
15 See now all the works of the
      Most High:
   they come in pairs, the one the
      opposite of the other.

16 Now I am the last to keep
      vigil,
   like a gleaner after the vintage;
17 Since by the LORD's blessing I
      have made progress
   till like a vintager I have
      filled my winepress,
18 I would inform you that not for
      myself only have I toiled,
   but for every seeker after
      wisdom.

Property and Servants

19 Listen to me, O leaders of the
      multitude;
   O rulers of the assembly,
      give ear!
20 Let neither son nor wife,
   neither brother nor friend,
   have power over you as long
      as you live.

32, 14—33, 4: God is shown to reveal himself
through the discipline of his law, a clear and safe
plan of life for the pious Jew of old. *Direction* and
counsel are aids in following it (14ff.18–24; 33, 1.3f.).
Sinners and hypocrites, hating *the law* or distorting
it, fail in wisdom and are devoid of security (32,
15.17f; 33, 2).
33, 3: *Oracle:* as the answer given through the
Urim and Thummim to the high priest is true, so the
law proves itself true to him who obeys it. Cf Ex 28,

30; Nm 27, 21.
33, 5–15: Contrasts observable in the physical
universe as well as in the moral order serve the
purposes of divine wisdom (5–9). All creatures are
like *clay . . . in the hands of their Creator*—the fool
and the wise man, the sinner, and the just (10–15).
This does not imply that man is created to be a sinner:
God is not the author of wickedness. Cf Jas 1, 13f.
33, 16ff: Here the author refers to himself as the
most recent of the writers who have endeavored to

present true wisdom to their readers.
33, 19–33: Public officials should reject every
influence that would restrict their freedom in the
management of their affairs. They must make their
own household subservient to them rather than be
subservient to it (19–24). Slaves are to be given *food*
and *work* and *correction* but never to be treated
unjustly (25–29). Great care should be taken of good
slaves (30–33).

21 While breath of life is still in
    you,
    let no man have dominion
      over you.
    Give not to another your
      wealth,
    lest then you have to plead
      with him;
22 Far better that your children
    plead with you
    than that you should look to
      their generosity.
23 Keep control over all your
    affairs;
    let no one tarnish your
      glory.
24 When your few days reach their
    limit,
    at the time of death distribute
      your inheritance.

25 Fodder and whip and loads for
    an ass;
    the yoke and harness and the
      rod of his master.
27 Food, correction and work for a
    slave;
    and for a wicked slave,
      punishment in the stocks.
26 Make a slave work and he will
    look for his rest;
    let his hands be idle and he
      will seek to be free.
28 Force him to work that he be
    not idle,
    for idleness is an apt teacher
      of mischief.
29 Put him to work, for that is
    what befits him;
    if he becomes unruly, load
      him with chains.
30 But never lord it over any
    human being,
    and do nothing unjust.
31 If you have but one slave,
    treat him like yourself,
    for you have acquired him
      with your life's blood;
32 If you have but one slave, deal
    with him as a brother,
    for you need him as you need
      your life:
33 If you mistreat him and he runs
    away,
    in what direction will you look
      for him?

Trust in the Lord and Not in Dreams

34 Empty and false are the
    hopes of the senseless,
and fools are borne aloft by
    dreams.
2 Like a man who catches at
    shadows or chases the wind,
    is the one who believes in
      dreams.
3 What is seen in dreams is to
    reality
    what the reflection of a face
      is to the face itself.
4 Can the unclean produce the
    clean?
    can the liar ever speak the
      truth?
5 Divination, omens and dreams
    all are unreal;
    what you already expect, the
      mind depicts.
6 Unless it be a vision specially
    sent by the Most High,
    fix not your heart on it;
7 For dreams have led many
    astray,
    and those who believed in
      them have perished.
8 The law is fulfilled without
    fail,
    and perfect wisdom is found
      in the mouth of the faithful
      man.

9 A man with training gains wide
    knowledge;
    a man of experience speaks
      sense.
10 One never put to the proof
    knows little,
    whereas with travel a man
      adds to his resourcefulness.
11 I have seen much in my travels,
    learned more than ever I
      could say.
12 Often I was in danger of death,
    but by these attainments I
      was saved.
13 Lively is the courage of those
    who fear the LORD,
    for they put their hope in
      their savior;
14 He who fears the LORD is never
    alarmed,

never afraid; for the LORD is
    his hope.
15 Happy the soul that fears the
    LORD!
    In whom does he trust, and
      who is his support?
16 The eyes of the LORD are upon
    those who love him;
    he is their mighty shield and
      strong support,
    A shelter from the heat, a shade
      from the noonday sun,
    a guard against stumbling,
    a help against falling.
17 He buoys up the spirits, brings
    a sparkle to the eyes,
    gives health and life and
      blessing.

True Worship of God

18 Tainted his gifts who offers in
    sacrifice ill-gotten goods!
    Mock presents from the
      lawless win not God's favor.
19 The Most High approves not the
    gifts of the godless,
    nor for their many sacrifices
      does he forgive their sins.
20 Like the man who slays a son
    in his father's presence
    is he who offers sacrifice from
      the possessions of the poor.
21 The bread of charity is life itself
    for the needy;
    he who withholds it is a man
      of blood.
22 He slays his neighbor who
    deprives him of his living:
    he sheds blood who denies
      the laborer his wages.

23 If one man builds up and
    another tears down,
    what do they gain but trouble?
24 If one man prays and another
    curses,
    whose voice will the LORD
      hear?
25 If a man again touches a corpse
    after he has bathed,
    what did he gain by the
      purification?
26 So with a man who fasts for
    his sins,
    but then goes and commits
      them again:

34, 1–17: Confidence placed in *dreams*, divinations and *omens* is false because they are devoid of reality (1–8). True confidence is founded on *knowledge* and *experience* (9–12), and above all on the fear of the Lord, with its accompanying blessings of divine assistance and protection (13–17).

34, 18–26: To be acts of true religion, sacrifice and penance must be accompanied by the proper moral dispositions. To offer to God goods taken from the poor (18–22), or to practice penance without interior reform, is a mockery, worthless in the sight of God (23–26). Cf Mt 15, 4–7; Mk 7, 9–13.

Who will hear his prayer,
and what has he gained by
his mortification?

35 To keep the law is a great
oblation,
and he who observes the
commandments sacrifices
a peace offering.
2 In works of charity one offers
fine flour,
and when he gives alms he
presents his sacrifice of
praise.
3 To refrain from evil pleases the
LORD,
and to avoid injustice is an
atonement.
4 Appear not before the LORD
empty-handed,
for all that you offer is in
fulfillment of the precepts.
5 The just man's offering enriches
the altar
and rises as a sweet odor
before the Most High.

6 The just man's sacrifice is most
pleasing,
nor will it ever be forgotten.
7 In generous spirit pay homage
to the LORD,
be not sparing of freewill
gifts.
8 With each contribution show a
cheerful countenance,
and pay your tithes in a
spirit of joy.
9 Give to the Most High as he has
given to you,
generously, according to your
means.

10 For the LORD is one who always
repays,
and he will give back to you
sevenfold.
11 But offer no bribes, these he
does not accept!
Trust not in sacrifice of the
fruits of extortion,
12 For he is a God of justice,
who knows no favorites.

13 Though not unduly partial
toward the weak,
yet he hears the cry of the
oppressed.
14 He is not deaf to the wail of
the orphan,
nor to the widow when she
pours out her complaint;
15 Do not the tears that stream
down her cheek
cry out against him that
causes them to fall?
16 He who serves God willingly is
heard;
his petition reaches the
heavens.
17 The prayer of the lowly pierces
the clouds;
it does not rest till it reaches
its goal,
18 Nor will it withdraw till the
Most High responds,
judges justly and affirms the
right.
19 God indeed will not delay,
and like a warrior, will not be
still
20 Till he breaks the backs of the
merciless
and wreaks vengeance upon
the proud;
21 Till he destroys the haughty
root and branch,
and smashes the scepter of
the wicked;
22 Till he requites mankind
according to its deeds,
and repays men according to
their thoughts;
23 Till he defends the cause of his
people,
and gladdens them by his
mercy.
24 Welcome is his mercy in time of
distress
as rain clouds in time of
drought.

A Prayer for God's People

36 Come to our aid, O God of
the universe,
and put all the nations in
dread of you!

2 Raise your hand against the
heathen,
that they may realize your
power.
3 As you have used us to show
them your holiness,
so now use them to show us
your glory.
4 Thus they will know, as we
know,
that there is no God but you.

5 Give new signs and work new
wonders;
show forth the splendor of
your right hand and arm;
6 Rouse your anger, pour out
wrath,
humble the enemy, scatter
the foe.
7 Hasten the day, bring on the
time;
9 crush the heads of the hostile
rulers.
8 Let raging fire consume the
fugitive,
and your people's oppressors
meet destruction.

10 Gather all the tribes of Jacob,
that they may inherit the land
as of old,
11 Show mercy to the people called
by your name;
Israel, whom you named your
first-born.
12 Take pity on your holy city,
Jerusalem, your dwelling
place.
13 Fill Zion with your majesty,
your temple with your glory.

14 Give evidence of your deeds of
old;
fulfill the prophecies spoken
in your name,
15 Reward those who have hoped
in you,
and let your prophets be
proved true.
16 Hear the prayer of your
servants,
for you are ever gracious to
your people;

35, 1–24: Keeping *the commandments* of the law
and avoiding *injustice* constitute sacrifice pleasing and
acceptable to God (1ff). Offerings also should be made
to him, cheerfully and *generously;* these he *repays . . .
sevenfold* (4–10). Extortion from widows and orphans
is injustice, which God quickly repays (11–18). Punishing the *proud* and the *merciless* and coming to the

aid of the distressed, he *requites* all *according to their
deeds* (19–24).
　35, 2: *Fine flour*, together with oil and frankincense,
was a prescribed offering to God; cf Lv 2, 1ff.
　35, 13: Cf Lv 19, 15.
　36, 1–17: Making an act of faith and hope in the
supreme Lord of the universe, the author begs God to

continue manifesting his *holiness* and *mercy* through
Israel, his people (1ff.10–13), and his *power* and
justice through the punishment of the nations (2.5–9),
that all the earth may acknowledge him *the eternal
God* (4.14–17).

17 Thus it will be known to the
     very ends of the earth
  that you are the eternal God.

Choice of Associates

18 The throat can swallow any
     food,
  yet some foods are more
     agreeable than others;
19 As the palate tests meat by its
     savor,
  so does a keen mind insincere
     words.
20 A deceitful character causes grief,
  but an experienced man can
     turn the tables on him.
21 Though any man may be
     accepted as a husband,
  yet one girl will be more
     suitable than another:
22 A woman's beauty makes her
     husband's face light up,
  for it surpasses all else that
     charms the eye;
23 And if, besides, her speech is
     kindly,
  his lot is beyond that of
     mortal men.
24 A wife is her husband's richest
     treasure,
  a helpmate, a steadying
     column.
25 A vineyard with no hedge will
     be overrun;
  a man with no wife becomes
     a homeless wanderer.
26 Who will trust an armed band
  that shifts from city to city?
27 Or a man who has no nest,
  but lodges where night
     overtakes him?

37 Every friend declares his
     friendship,
  but there are friends who are
     friends in name only.
 2 Is it not a sorrow unto death
  when your bosom companion
     becomes your enemy?
 3 "Alas, my companion! Why
     were you created
  to blanket the earth with
     deceit?"

 4 A false friend will share your
     joys,
  but in time of trouble he
     stands afar off.
 5 A true friend will fight with you
     against the foe,
  against your enemies he will
     be your shield-bearer.
 6 Forget not your comrade during
     the battle,
  and neglect him not when you
     distribute your spoils.

 7 Every counselor points out a
     way,
  but some counsel ways of
     their own;
 8 Be on the alert when one
     proffers advice,
  find out first of all what he
     wants.
  For he may be thinking of
     himself alone;
  why should the profit fall
     to him?
 9 He may tell you how good your
     way will be,
  and then stand by to watch
     your misfortune.
10 Seek no advice from one who
     regards you with hostility;
  from those who envy you,
     keep your intentions hidden.
11 Speak not to a woman about
     her rival,
  nor to a coward about war,
  to a merchant about business,
  to a buyer about value,
  to a miser about generosity,
  to a cruel man about mercy,
  to a lazy man about work,
  to a seasonal laborer about
     the harvest,
  to an idle slave about a great
     task:
  pay no attention to any
     advice they give.
12 Instead, associate with a religious
     man,
  who you are sure keeps the
     commandments;
  Who is like-minded with yourself
  and will feel for you if you fall.

13 Then, too, heed your own
     heart's counsel;
  for what have you that you
     can depend on more?
14 A man's conscience can tell him
     his situation
  better than seven watchmen
     in a lofty tower.
15 Most important of all, pray to
     God
  to set your feet in the path
     of truth.

Wisdom and Temperance

16 A word is the source of every
     deed;
  a thought, of every act.
17 The root of all conduct is the
     mind;
  four branches it shoots forth:
18 Good and evil, death and life,
  their absolute mistress is the
     tongue.
19 A man may be wise and benefit
     many,
  yet be of no use to himself.
20 Though a man may be wise,
  if his words are rejected
  he will be deprived of all
     enjoyment.
21 When a man is wise to his own
     advantage,
  the fruits of his knowledge
     are seen in his own person;
22 When a man is wise to his
     people's advantage,
  the fruits of his knowledge
     are enduring;
23 Limited are the days of one
     man's life,
  but the life of Israel is days
     without number.
24 One wise for himself has full
     enjoyment,
  and all who see him praise him;
25 One wise for his people wins a
     heritage of glory,
  and his name endures forever.

26 My son, while you are well,
     govern your appetite
  so that you allow it not what
     is bad for you;

36, 18—37, 15: In the choice of wife, friend or
associate, experience is a discerner of character
(18–21). *Beauty* and *kindly speech* make a woman
desirable as wife (22f). The good wife becomes *her
husband's richest treasure*, his *helpmate* in establishing
his household (24–27). *A true friend* fights for his
comrade and shares his spoils with him (37, 5f); a
false one deceives and abandons him in time of need

(1–4). A true counselor and associate should be
sought among those who keep the commandments,
not among those who break them and seek their own
advantage (7–12). In all things *pray to God* for light
and follow conscience (13ff).
  37, 16–25: Thoughts determine action. Wisdom is
the source of *good* and *life;* folly, of *evil* and *death*
(16ff). If the fruits of a man's wisdom benefit himself,

he may be praised in his own lifetime; if they benefit
his people, his praise endures after him, in their lives
(19–25).
  37, 26–30: Temperance and self-control should
govern a man's appetite for food, which is intended
not to destroy but to preserve life.

27 For not every food is good for
          everyone,
     nor is everything suited to
          every taste.
28 Be not drawn after every
          enjoyment,
     neither become a glutton for
          choice foods,
29 For sickness comes with
          overeating,
     and gluttony brings on
          biliousness.
30 Through lack of self-control
          many have died,
     but the abstemious man
          prolongs his life.

Sickness and Death

38 Hold the physician in honor,
          for he is essential to you,
     and God it was who
          established his profession.
2 From God the doctor has his
          wisdom,
     and the king provides for
          his sustenance.
3 His knowledge makes the
          doctor distinguished,
     and gives him access to those
          in authority.
4 God makes the earth yield
          healing herbs
     which the prudent man should
          not neglect.
5 Was not the water sweetened
          by a twig
     that men might learn his power?
6 He endows men with the
          knowledge
     to glory in his mighty works,
7 Through which the doctor
          eases pain
     and the druggist prepares his
          medicines;
8 Thus God's creative work
          continues without cease
     in its efficacy on the surface
          of the earth.

9 My son, when you are ill,
          delay not,
     but pray to God, who will
          heal you:

10 Flee wickedness; let your hands
          be just,
     cleanse your heart of every sin;
11 Offer your sweet-smelling
          oblation and petition,
     a rich offering according to
          your means.
12 Then give the doctor his place
          lest he leave; for you need
          him too.
13 There are times that give him
          an advantage,
14   and he too beseeches God
     That his diagnosis may be
          correct
     and his treatment bring about
          a cure.
15 He who is a sinner toward his
          Maker
     will be defiant toward the
          doctor.

16 My son, shed tears for one who
          is dead
     with wailing and bitter
          lament;
     As is only proper, prepare the
          body,
     absent not yourself from his
          burial:
17 Weeping bitterly, mourning fully,
     pay your tribute of sorrow,
          as he deserves,
18 One or two days, to prevent
          gossip;
     then compose yourself after
          your grief,
19 For grief can bring on an
          extremity
     and heartache destroy one's
          health.
20 Turn not your thoughts to him
          again;
     cease to recall him; think
          rather of the end.
21 Recall him not, for there is no
          hope of his return;
     it will not help him, but will
          do you harm.
22 Remember that his fate will also
          be yours;
     for him it was yesterday, for
          you today.

23 With the departed dead, let
          memory fade;
     rally your courage, once the
          soul has left.

Vocations of the Craftsman and the Scribe

24 The scribe's profession increases
          his wisdom;
     whoever is free from toil can
          become a wise man.
25 How can he become learned
          who guides the plow,
     who thrills in wielding the
          goad like a lance,
     Who guides the ox and urges on
          the bullock,
     and whose every concern is
          for cattle?
26 His care is for plowing furrows,
     and he keeps a watch on the
          beasts in the stalls.

27 So with every engraver and
          designer
     who, laboring night and day,
     Fashions carved seals,
     and whose concern is to vary
          the pattern.
     His care is to produce a vivid
          impression,
     and he keeps watch till he
          finishes his design.

28 So with the smith standing
          near his anvil,
     forging crude iron.
     The heat from the fire sears his
          flesh,
     yet he toils away in the
          furnace heat.
     The clang of the hammer deafens
          his ears,
     His eyes are fixed on the tool
          he is shaping.
     His care is to finish his work,
     and he keeps watch till he
          perfects it in detail.

29 So with the potter sitting at
          his labor,
     revolving the wheel with his
          feet.

38, 1–15: The profession of medicine comes from
God, who *makes the earth yield healing herbs* and
gives the physician knowledge of their virtue (1–8).
In illness the sick man should cleanse his soul from
sin and petition God for help through an offering of
sacrifice; the physician, too, does well to invoke God
that he may understand the illness and apply the
proper remedy (9–14). The sinner, in contrast, defies
both his Maker and the doctor (15).

38, 16–23: A period of mourning for the deceased
and care for their burial is becoming (16ff). But grief
should not be excessive, for it neither helps the dead,
who cannot return, nor fails to harm the living. The
mourner's own end will quickly follow, and the time
to prepare for it is now (19–23).
38, 24—39, 11: More excellent than the useful
service of craftsmen—farmer, engraver, smith, potter
(25–34)—is the profession of the scribe (24), who

studies and meditates on *the law of the Most High,*
seeks him in prayer of thanksgiving, petition and repentance for sin (39, 1.6f), *explores the wisdom* of the
past and present, travels abroad to observe the conduct of many peoples, and attends rulers and great
men. Through the spirit of understanding granted by
God, he will show forth his wisdom to the glory of
God's law, gaining renown for generations to come
(2–5.8–11).

He is always concerned for his
products,
and turns them out in quantity.
30 With his hands he molds the
clay,
and with his feet softens it.
His care is for proper coloring,
and he keeps watch on the
fire of his kiln.

31 All these men are skilled with
their hands,
each one an expert at his
own task;
32 Without them no city could be
lived in,
and wherever they stay, they
need not hunger.
33 They do not occupy the judge's
bench,
nor are they prominent in
the assembly;
They set forth no decisions or
judgments,
nor are they found among
the rulers;
34 Yet they maintain God's
ancient handiwork,
and their concern is for
exercise of their skill.

39 How different the man who
devotes himself
to the study of the law of the
Most High!
He explores the wisdom of the
men of old
and occupies himself with the
prophecies;
2 He treasures the discourses of
famous men,
and goes to the heart of
involved sayings;
3 He studies obscure parables,
and is busied with the hidden
meanings of the sages.
4 He is in attendance on the great,
and has entrance to the ruler.
5 He travels among the peoples
of foreign lands
to learn what is good and
evil among men.
6 His care is to seek the LORD,
his Maker,
to petition the Most High,

To open his lips in prayer,
to ask pardon for his sins.
Then, if it pleases the LORD
Almighty,
he will be filled with the
spirit of understanding;
He will pour forth his words of
wisdom
and in prayer give thanks to
the LORD,
7 Who will direct his knowledge
and his counsel,
as he meditates upon his
mysteries.
8 He will show the wisdom of
what he has learned
and glory in the law of the
LORD's covenant.
9 Many will praise his
understanding;
his fame can never be effaced;
Unfading will be his memory,
through all generations his
name will live;
10 Peoples will speak of his wisdom,
and in assembly sing his
praises.
11 While he lives he is one out of
a thousand,
and when he dies his renown
will not cease.

Praise of God the Creator

12 Once more I will set forth my
theme
to shine like the moon in
its fullness!
13 Listen, my faithful children:
open up your petals,
like roses planted near
running waters;
14 Send up the sweet odor of
incense,
break forth in blossoms like
the lily.
Send up the sweet odor of
your hymn of praise;
bless the LORD for all he has
done!
15 Proclaim the greatness of his
name,
loudly sing his praises,
With music on the harp and all
stringed instruments;
sing out with joy as you
proclaim:

16 The works of God are all of
them good;
in its own time every need is
supplied.
17 At his word the waters become
still as in a flask;
he had but to speak and the
reservoirs were made.
18 He has but to command and his
will is done;
nothing can limit his
achievement.
19 The works of all mankind are
present to him;
not a thing escapes his eye.
20 His gaze spans all the ages;
to him there is nothing
unexpected.
21 No cause then to say: "What
is the purpose of this?"
Everything is chosen to
satisfy a need.
22 His blessing overflows like the
Nile;
like the Euphrates it enriches
the surface of the earth.
23 Again, his wrath expels the
nations
and turns fertile land into a
salt marsh.
24 For the virtuous his paths are
level,
to the haughty they are steep;
25 Good things for the good he
provided from the
beginning,
but for the wicked good
things and bad.
26 Chief of all needs for human life
are water and fire, iron and
salt,
The heart of the wheat, milk
and honey,
the blood of the grape, and
oil, and cloth;
27 For the good all these are good,
but for the wicked they turn
out evil.
28 There are storm winds created
to punish,
which in their fury can
dislodge mountains;
When destruction must be, they
hurl all their force
and appease the anger of
their Maker.

39, 12–35: The sage invites his disciples to join him in joyfully proclaiming his favorite theme: *The works of God are all of them good; in its own time every need is supplied* (12–16.32–35). He describes God's omni- science, supreme power and wisdom, whereby all created things, good in themselves, are ever present to him, obey him, and fulfill their intended purpose (17–21), bringing blessing to the virtuous, but evil and punishment to the wicked who misuse them (22–31). Cf similar hymns of praise, 36, 1–17; 42, 15—43, 35.

29 In his treasury also, kept for the
    proper time,
  are fire and hail, famine,
    disease,
30 Ravenous beasts, scorpions,
    vipers,
  and the avenging sword to
    exterminate the wicked;
31 In doing his bidding they
    rejoice,
  in their assignments they
    disobey not his command.
32 So from the first I took my
    stand,
  and wrote down as my theme:
33 The works of God are all of
    them good;
  every need when it comes he
    fills.
34 No cause then to say: "This is
    not as good as that";
  for each shows its worth at
    the proper time.
35 So now with full joy of heart
    proclaim
  and bless the name of the
    Holy One.

Joys and Miseries of Life

40 A great anxiety has God
    allotted,
  and a heavy yoke, to the sons
    of men;
  From the day one leaves his
    mother's womb
  to the day he returns to the
    mother of all the living,
2 His thoughts, the fear in his
    heart,
  and his troubled forebodings
    till the day he dies—
3 Whether he sits on a lofty
    throne
  or grovels in dust and ashes,
4 Whether he bears a splendid
    crown
  or is wrapped in the coarsest
    of cloaks—
5 Are of wrath and envy, trouble
    and dread,
  terror of death, fury and
    strife.

Even when he lies on his bed
    to rest,
  his cares at night disturb his
    sleep.
6 So short is his rest it seems like
    none,
  till in his dreams he struggles
    as he did by day,
  Terrified by what his mind's
    eye sees,
  like a fugitive being pursued;
7 As he reaches safety, he wakes up
    astonished that there was
    nothing to fear.
8 So it is with all flesh, with man
    and with beast,
  but for sinners seven times
    more.
9 Plague and bloodshed, wrath
    and the sword,
  plunder and ruin, famine
    and death:
10 For the wicked, these were
    created evil,
  and it is they who bring
    on destruction.

11 All that is of earth returns to
    earth,
  and what is from above
    returns above.
12 All that comes from bribes or
    injustice will be wiped out,
  but loyalty remains for ages.
13 Wealth out of wickedness is
    like a wadi in spate:
  like a mighty stream with
    lightning and thunder,
14 Which, in its rising, rolls along
    the stones,
  but suddenly, once and for
    all, comes to an end.
15 The offshoot of violence will
    not flourish,
  for the root of the godless is
    on sheer rock;
16 Or they are like reeds on the
    riverbank,
  withered before all other
    plants;
17 But goodness will never be
    cut off,
  and justices endures forever.

Wealth or wages can make life
    sweet,
  but better than either is
    finding a treasure.
18 A child or a city will preserve
    one's name,
  but better than either,
    attaining wisdom.
19 Sheepfolds and orchards bring
    flourishing health;
  but better than either, a
    devoted wife;
20 Wine and music delight the soul,
  but better than either,
    conjugal love.
21 The flute and the harp offer
    sweet melody,
  but better than either, a voice
    that is true.
22 Charm and beauty delight the
    eye,
  but better than either, the
    flowers of the field.
23 A friend, a neighbor, are timely
    guides,
  but better than either, a
    prudent wife.
24 A brother, a helper, for times
    of stress;
  but better than either, charity
    that rescues.
25 Gold and silver make one's way
    secure,
  but better than either, sound
    judgment.
26 Wealth and vigor build up
    confidence,
  but better than either, fear
    of God.
  Fear of the LORD leaves nothing
    wanting;
  he who has it need seek no
    other support:
27 The fear of God is a paradise of
    blessings;
  its canopy, all that is glorious.

28 My son, live not the life of a
    beggar,
  better to die than to beg;
29 When one has to look to
    another's table,
  his life is not really a life.

40, 1–16: The former idyllic description of the universe is contrasted with the picture of the evils afflicting humanity. Every man, high or low, is burdened from birth to death with fears, anxieties and troubles, by day and often by night, the time appointed for rest (1–7). For sinners, the suffering is much greater (8ff). What they gained by violence and injustice is quickly destroyed; but *justice endures forever* (14ff).

40, 1: *Mother of all the living*: the earth from which man was taken. Cf Gn 2, 7; 2, 19f; Jb 1, 21; Ps 139, 15.
40, 11: *All that is of earth . . . returns above*: a reference to bodily mortality and to the divine origin of life from the Spirit of God. Cf 41, 10; Gn 2, 7; 3, 19; Jb 34, 14f; Pss 104, 29f; 146, 4; Eccl 12, 7. The Greek and the Latin render the second half of the verse: "all waters shall return to the sea."

40, 17–27: Of the many treasures making life sweet, such as *health*, children, friends, *music, vigor*, the best are called true *conjugal love, wisdom*, and, above all, *fear of God; cf* 25, 6–11.
40, 28ff: Among the Jews, beggary was considered degrading to human dignity; it was agreeable only to the shameless, who had lost their sense of honor. Cf 29, 22f.

His neighbor's delicacies bring
   revulsion of spirit
   to one who understands
   inward feelings:
30 In the mouth of the shameless
   man begging is sweet,
   but within him it burns like
   fire.

41 O death! how bitter the
      thought of you
   for the man at peace amid
      his possessions,
   For the man unruffled and
      always successful,
   who still can enjoy life's
      pleasures.
2 O death! how welcome your
      sentence
   to the weak man of failing
      strength,
   Tottering and always rebuffed,
      with no more sight, with
      vanished hope.
3 Fear not death's decree for you;
   remember, it embraces those
      before you, and those after.
4 Thus God has ordained for all
      flesh;
   why then should you reject
      the will of the Most High?
   Whether one has lived a
      thousand years, a hundred,
      or ten,
   in the nether world he has no
      claim on life.
5 A reprobate line are the
      children of sinners,
   and witless offspring are in the
      homes of the wicked.
6 Their dominion is lost to
      sinners' children,
   and reproach abides with
      their descendants.
7 Children curse their wicked father,
   for they suffer disgrace
      through him.
8 Woe to you, O sinful men,
   who forsake the law of the
      Most High.
9 If you have children, calamity
      will seize them;
   you will beget them only for
      groaning.

When you stumble, there is
   lasting joy;
   at death, you become a curse.
10 Whatever is of nought returns
      to nought,
   so too the godless from void
      to void.
11 Man's body is a fleeting thing,
   but a virtuous name will
      never be annihilated.
12 Have a care for your name, for
      it will stand by you
   better than precious treasures
      in the thousands;
13 The boon of life is for limited
      days,
   but a good name, for days
      without number.

True and False Shame

14 My children, heed my
      instruction about shame;
   judge of disgrace only
      according to my rules,
   For it is not always well to be
      ashamed,
   nor is it always the proper
      thing to blush:
15 Before father and mother be
      ashamed of immorality,
   before master and mistress,
      of falsehood;
16 Before prince and ruler, of flattery;
   before the public assembly,
      of crime;
17 Before friend and companion,
      of disloyalty,
   and of breaking an oath or
      agreement.
18 Be ashamed of theft from the
      people where you settle,
   and of stretching out your
      elbow when you dine;
19 Of refusing to give when asked,
   of defrauding another of his
      appointed share,
20 Of failing to return a greeting,
   and of rebuffing a friend;
21 Of gazing at a married woman,
   and of entertaining thoughts
      about another's wife;
   Of trifling with a servant girl
      you have,
   and of violating her couch;

22 Of using harsh words with
      friends,
   and of following up your
      gifts with insults;
23 Of repeating what you hear,
   and of betraying secrets—
24 These are the things you should
      rightly avoid as shameful
   if you would be looked upon
      by everyone with favor.

42 But of these things be not
      ashamed,
   lest you sin through human
      respect:
2 Of the law of the Most High
      and his precepts,
   or of the sentence to be
      passed upon the sinful;
3 Of sharing the expenses of a
      business or a journey,
   or of dividing an inheritance
      or property;
4 Of accuracy of scales and
      balances,
   or of tested measures and
      weights;
5 Of acquiring much or little,
   or of bargaining in dealing
      with a merchant;
   Of constant training of children,
   or of beating the sides of a
      disloyal servant;
6 Of a seal to keep an erring wife
      at home,
   or of a lock placed where
      there are many hands;
7 Of numbering every deposit,
   or of recording all that is
      given or received;
8 Of chastisement of the silly and
      the foolish,
   or of the aged and infirm
      answering for wanton
      conduct.
   Thus you will be truly cautious
   and recognized by all men as
      discreet.

A Father's care for his Daughter

9 A daughter is a treasure that
      keeps her father wakeful,
   and worry over her drives
      away rest:

Lest she pass her prime
unmarried,
or when she is married, lest
she be disliked;

10 While unmarried, lest she be
seduced,
or, as a wife, lest she prove
unfaithful;
Lest she conceive in her father's
home,
or be sterile in that of her
husband.

11 Keep a close watch on your
daughter,
lest she make you the sport
of your enemies,
A byword in the city, a reproach
among the people,
an object of derision in
public gatherings.
See that there is no lattice in
her room,
no place that overlooks the
approaches to the house.

12 Let her not parade her charms
before men,
or spend her time with married
women;

13 For just as moths come from
garments,
so harm to women comes
from women:

14 Better a man's harshness than a
woman's indulgence,
and a frightened daughter
than any disgrace.

The Works of God in Nature

15 Now will I recall God's works;
what I have seen, I will
describe.
At God's word were his works
brought into being;
they do his will as he has
ordained for them.

16 As the rising sun is clear to all,
so the glory of the LORD fills
all his works;

17 Yet even God's holy ones must
fail
in recounting the wonders of
the LORD,
Though God has given these,
his hosts, the strength
to stand firm before his glory.

18 He plumbs the depths and
penetrates the heart;

their innermost being he
understands.
The Most High possesses all
knowledge,
and sees from of old the
things that are to come:

19 He makes known the past and
the future,
and reveals the deepest
secrets.

20 No undertsanding does he lack;
no single thing escapes him.

21 Perennial is his almighty
wisdom;
he is from eternity one and
the same,

22 With nothing added, nothing
taken away;
no need of a counselor for
him!

23 How beautiful are all his works!
even to the spark and the
fleeting vision!

24 The universe lives and abides
forever;
to meet each need, each
creature is preserved.

25 All of them differ, one from
another,
yet none of them has he made
in vain,
For each in turn, as it comes, is
good;
can one ever see enough of
their splendor?

43 The clear vault of the sky
shines forth
like heaven itself, a vision of
glory.

2 The orb of the sun, resplendent
at its rising:
what a wonderful work of
the Most High!

3 At noon it seethes the surface
of the earth,
and who can bear its fiery
heat?

4 Like a blazing furnace of solid
metal,
it sets the mountains aflame
with its rays;
By its fiery darts the land is
consumed;
the eyes are dazzled by its
light.

5 Great indeed is the LORD who
made it,
at whose orders it urges on
its steeds.

6 The moon, too, that marks the
changing times,
governing the seasons, their
lasting sign,

7 By which we know the feast
days and fixed dates,
this light-giver which wanes in
its course:

8 As its name says, each month it
renews itself;
how wondrous in this change!

9 The beauty, the glory, of the
heavens are the stars
that adorn with their sparkling
the heights of God,

10 At whose command they keep
their place
and never relax in their vigils.
A weapon against the flood
waters stored on high,
lighting up the firmament by
its brilliance,

11 Behold the rainbow! Then bless
its Maker,
for majestic indeed is its
splendor;

12 It spans the heavens with its
glory,
this bow bent by the mighty
hand of God.

13 His rebuke marks out the path
for the lightning,
and speeds the arrows of his
judgment to their goal.

14 At it, the storehouse is opened,
and like vultures the clouds
hurry forth.

15 In his majesty he gives the storm
its power
and breaks off the hailstones.

16 The thunder of his voice makes
the earth writhe;
before his might the mountains
quake.

17 A word from him drives on the
south wind,
the angry north wind, the
hurricane and the storm.

18 He sprinkles the snow like
fluttering birds;
it comes to settle like swarms
of locusts.

42, 15—43, 35: These verses comprise a new section. In them the author contemplates God's power,
beauty and goodness as manifested in the mighty
work of creating and preserving the universe (42, 15ff.
23.25; 43, 1–27), his omniscience (42, 18ff), his perfect
wisdom (21f), his eternity (24), The conclusion is a
fervent hymn of praise (43, 28–35). Cf 16, 22—18, 13.

19 Its shining whiteness blinds the
    eyes,
    the mind is baffled by its
        steady fall.
20 He scatters frost like so much
    salt;
    it shines like blossoms on the
        thornbush.
21 Cold northern blasts he sends
    that turn the ponds to lumps
        of ice.
    He freezes over every body of
        water,
    and clothes each pool with a
        coat of mail.
22 When the mountain growth is
    scorched with heat,
    and the flowering plains as
        though by flames,
23 The dripping clouds restore
    them all,
    and the scattered dew enriches
        the parched land.
24 His is the plan that calms the
    deep,
    and plants the islands in the
        sea.
25 Those who go down to the sea
    tell part of its story,
    and when we hear them we
        are thunderstruck;
26 In it are his creatures,
    stupendous, amazing,
    all kinds of life, and the
        monsters of the deep.
27 For him each messenger
    succeeds,
    and at his bidding
        accomplishes his will.

28 More than this we need not add;
    let the last word be, he is all
        in all!
29 Let us praise him the more, since
    we cannot fathom him,
    for greater is he than all his
        works;
30 Awful indeed is the LORD's
    majesty,
    and wonderful is his power.
31 Lift up your voices to glorify
    the LORD,

though he is still beyond your
    power to praise;
32 Extol him with renewed strength,
    and weary not, though you
        cannot reach the end:
33 For who can see him and
    describe him?
    or who can praise him as he
        is?
34 Beyond these, many things lie
    hid;
    only a few of his works have
        we seen.
35 It is the LORD who has made
    all things,
    and to those who fear him he
        gives wisdom.

Praise of Israel's Great Ancestors

44 Now will I praise those
        godly men,
    our ancestors, each in his
        own time:
2 The abounding glory of the
    Most High's portion,
    his own part, since the days
        of old.
    Subduers of the land in kingly
        fashion,
    men of renown for their
        might,
3 Or counselors in their prudence,
    or seers of all things in
        prophecy;
4 Resolute princes of the folk,
    and governors with their
        staves;
    Authors skilled in composition,
    and forgers of epigrams with
        their spikes;
5 Composers of melodious psalms,
    or discoursers on lyric themes;
6 Stalwart men, solidly established
    and at peace in their own
        estates—
7 All these were glorious in their
    time,
    each illustrious in his day.
8 Some of them have left behind
    a name
    and men recount their
        praiseworthy deeds;

9 But of the others there is no
    memory,
    for when they ceased, they
        ceased.
    And they are as though they
        had not lived,
    they and their children after
        them.
10 Yet these also were godly men
    whose virtues have not been
        forgotten;
11 Their wealth remains in their
    families,
    their heritage with their
        descendants;
12 Through God's covenant with
    them their family endures,
    their posterity, for their sake.

13 And for all time their progeny
    will endure,
    their glory will never be
        blotted out;
14 Their bodies are peacefully laid
    away,
    but their name lives on and on.
15 At gatherings their wisdom is
    retold,
    and the assembly proclaims
        their praise.

The Early Patriarchs

16 [ENOCH walked with the LORD
    and was taken up,
    that succeeding generations
        might learn by his example.]
17 NOAH, found just and perfect,
    renewed the race in the time
        of devastation.
    Because of his worth there were
        survivors,
    and with a sign to him the
        deluge ended;
18 A lasting agreement was made
    with him,
    that never should all flesh be
        destroyed.
19 ABRAHAM, father of many
    peoples,
    kept his glory without stain:

43, 28: *All in all:* the perfections reflected in creation are found in a transcendent way in God, who
alone is their source.
44, 1—50, 24: As in the previous section God's
wisdom shone forth in the works of nature, so in these
chapters it is also revealed through the history of
God's peoples as seen in the lives of their patriarchs,
prophets, priests and rulers. The example of these
great men, whose virtues are here recalled, consti-

tutes a high point of the author's teaching and illustrates his belief in the canonical Scriptures.
44, 1–15: The reader is here introduced to those
men of Israel, later mentioned by name, who through
various achievements and beneficial social activities
have acquired great renown (1–8.14f); and also to
those who, though forgotten, endure through the
fruit of their *virtues* and through their families because of *God's covenant with them* (9–13).

44, 16: *Enoch:* because of his friendship with God
and also by reason of his unusual disappearance from
the earth, this prophet's renown was great among the
chosen people, particularly in the two centuries just
before the coming of Christ; cf Gn 5, 21–24; Heb 11,
5. The present verse is an expansion of the original
text; cf 49, 14.

20 He observed the precepts of the
　　Most High,
　　　and entered into an agreement
　　　　with him;
　　In his own flesh he incised the
　　　ordinance,
　　　and when tested he was found
　　　　loyal.
21 For this reason, God promised
　　him with an oath
　　　that in his descendants the
　　　　nations would be blessed,
　　That he would make numerous
　　　as the grains of dust,
　　　and exalt his posterity like the
　　　　stars;
　　That he would give them an
　　　inheritance from sea to sea,
　　　and from the River to the ends
　　　　of the earth.
22 And for ISAAC he renewed the
　　same promise
　　　because of Abraham, his
　　　　father.
　　The covenant with all his
　　　forebears was confirmed,
　　　and the blessing rested upon
　　　　the head of JACOB.
23 God acknowledged him as the
　　first-born,
　　　and gave him his inheritance.
　　He fixed the boundaries for his
　　　tribes,
　　　and their division into twelve.

Praise of Moses, Aaron and Phinehas

45 From him was to spring the
　　man
　　who won the favor of all:
　　Dear to God and men,
　　MOSES, whose memory is held
　　　in benediction.
2 God's honor devolved upon him,
　　and the Lord strengthened
　　　him with fearful powers;
3 God wrought swift miracles at
　　his words
　　　and sustained him in the
　　　　king's presence.

He gave him the commandments
　for his people,
　and revealed to him his glory.
4 For his trustworthiness and
　meekness
　　God selected him from all
　　　mankind;
5 He permitted him to hear his
　voice,
　　and led him into the cloud,
　Where, face to face, he gave
　　him the commandments,
　the law of life and
　　understanding,
　That he might teach his precepts
　　to Jacob,
　his judgments and decrees
　　to Israel.

6 He raised up also, like Moses in
　holiness,
　　his brother AARON, of the
　　　tribe of Levi.
7 He made him perpetual in his
　office
　　when he bestowed on him the
　　　priesthood of his people;
　He established him in honor
　　and crowned him with lofty
　　　majesty;
8 He clothed him with splendid
　apparel,
　　and adorned him with the
　　　glorious vestments:
　Breeches and tunic and robe
　　with pomegranates around the
　　　hem,
9 And a rustle of bells round
　about,
　　through whose pleasing sound
　　　at each step
　He would be heard within the
　　sanctuary,
　　and the children of his race
　　　would be remembered;
10 The sacred vestments of gold,
　　of violet,
　　and of crimson, wrought with
　　　embroidery;
　The breastpiece for decision,
　　the ephod and cincture

11 with scarlet yarn, the work
　　of the weaver;
　Precious stones with seal
　　engravings
　　in golden settings, the work
　　　of the jeweler,
　To commemorate in incised
　　letters
　　each of the tribes of Israel;
12 On his turban the diadem of
　gold,
　　its plate wrought with the
　　　insignia of holiness,
　Majestic, glorious, renowned for
　　splendor,
　　a delight to the eyes, beauty
　　　supreme.
13 Before him, no one was adorned
　with these,
　　nor may they ever be worn by
　　　any
　Except his sons and them alone,
　　generation after generation,
　　for all time.
14 His cereal offering is wholly burnt
　with the established sacrifice
　　twice each day;
15 For Moses ordained him
　and anointed him with the
　　holy oil,
　In a lasting covenant with him
　　and with his family, as
　　　permanent as the heavens,
　That he should serve God in his
　　priesthood
　　and bless his people in his
　　　name.
16 He chose him from all mankind
　to offer holocausts and choice
　　offerings,
　To burn sacrifices of sweet odor
　　for a memorial,
　　and to atone for the people of
　　　Israel.
17 He gave to him his laws,
　and authority to prescribe
　　and to judge:
　To teach the precepts to his
　　people,
　　and the ritual to the
　　　descendants of Israel.

44, 20: *In his own flesh . . . ordinance:* the covenant
of circumcision; cf Gn 17, 10–14. *And when tested . . .
loyal:* Abraham's willingness to sacrifice his son Isaac
at the Lord's command; cf Gn 22, 9–12.

44, 21: *The River:* the Euphrates; cf Gn 2, 14.

45, 1–5: *Moses* manifested God's power through
miracles (1ff), God's authority through the promulgation of the commandments and the law (5), and
God's mercy through the intimacy granted him by the
Lord for his own faithfulness and meekness (4f). The
very personification of the old covenant, Moses was
also a type of Christ, the prophet and Legislator of the

new; cf Dt 18, 15.

45, 2: *God's honor devolved upon him:* Moses was
actually God's substitute in dealing with Pharaoh,
hence God entrusted his own honor to Moses.

45, 5: *Face to face:* on God's intimacy with Moses,
see Ex 33, 11; Nm 12, 8. St. Paul alluded to this in
1 Cor 13, 12.

45, 6–21: The author here expresses his reverence
and esteem for the priesthood of the old covenant. He
recalls god's choice of *Aaron* and his sons for this
sublime office (6f), and describes in detail the beauty
of the high priest's vestments (8–13). He relates the

ordination of Aaron at the hands of Moses, his
brother (15), and describes the priestly functions, of
offering sacrifice to God (16), and of blessing (15),
teaching, governing and judging the people (17); the
inheritance of the high priest (20ff); the punishment
of those *families* who were *jealous* of Aaron (18f);
and the confirmation of the covenant of the priesthood
with Aaron's descendants through *Phinehas* (23ff).

45, 7: The *priesthood* of Aaron was superseded by
the priesthood of Christ; cf Heb 7, 18–28.

18 Men of other families were
       inflamed against him,
    were jealous of him in the
       desert,
    The followers of Dathan and
       Abiram,
    and the band of Korah in
       their defiance.
19 But the LORD saw this and
       became angry,
    he destroyed them in his
       burning wrath.
    He brought down upon them a
       miracle,
    and consumed them with his
       flaming fire.
20 Then he increased the glory of
       Aaron
    and bestowed upon him his
       inheritance:
    The sacred offerings he allotted
       to him,
    with the showbread as his
       portion;
21 The oblations of the LORD are
       his food,
    a gift to him and his
       descendants.
22 But he holds no land among
       the people
    nor shares with them their
       heritage;
    For the LORD himself is his
       portion,
    his inheritance in the midst
       of Israel.

23 PHINEHAS too, the son of
       Eleazar,
    was the courageous third of
       his line
    When, zealous for the God of all,
       he met the crisis of his people
    And, at the prompting of his
       noble heart,
    atoned for the children of
       Israel.
24 Therefore on him again God
       conferred the right,
    in a covenant of friendship,
       to provide for the sanctuary,
    So that he and his descendants
       should possess the high
       priesthood forever.

25 For even his covenant with
       David,
    the son of Jesse of the tribe
       of Judah,
    Was an individual heritage
       through one son alone;
    but the heritage of Aaron is
       for all his descendants.

26 And now bless the LORD
    who has crowned you with
       glory!
    May he grant you wisdom of
       heart
    to govern his people in justice,
    Lest their welfare should ever
       be forgotten,
    or your authority, throughout
       all time.

Joshua, Caleb and the Judges

46 Valiant leader was JOSHUA,
       son of Nun,
    assistant to Moses in the
       prophetic office,
    Formed to be, as his name
       implies,
    the great savior of God's
       chosen ones,
    To punish the enemy
       and to win the inheritance for
       Israel.
2 What glory was his when he
       raised his arm,
    to brandish his javelin against
       the city!
3 And who could withstand him
       when he fought the battles of
       the LORD?
4 Did he not by his power stop
       the sun,
    so that one day became two?
5 He called upon the Most High
       God
    when his enemies beset him on
       all sides,
    And God Most High gave
       answer to him
    in hailstones of tremendous
       power,
6 Which he rained down upon the
       hostile army
    till on the slope he destroyed
       the foe;

    That all the doomed nations
       might know
    that the LORD was watching
       over his people's battles.
    And because he was a devoted
       follower of God
7 and in Moses' lifetime showed
       himself loyal,
    He and CALEB, son of Jephunneh,
       when they opposed the rebel
       assembly,
    Averted God's anger from the
       people
    and suppressed the wicked
       complaint—
8 Because of this, they were the
       only two spared
    from the six hundred
       thousand infantry,
    To lead the people into their
       inheritance,
    the land flowing with milk
       and honey.
9 And the strength he gave to
       Caleb
    remained with him even in
       his old age
    Till he won his way onto the
       summits of the land;
    his family too received an
       inheritance,
10 That all the people of Jacob
       might know
    how good it is to be a devoted
       follower of the LORD.
11 The JUDGES, too, each one of
       them,
    whose hearts were not
       deceived,
    Who did not abandon God:
       may their memory be ever
       blessed,
12 Their bones return to life from
       their resting place,
    and their names receive fresh
       luster in their children!
13 Beloved of his people, dear to
       his Maker,
    dedicated from his mother's
       womb,
    Consecrated to the LORD as a
       prophet,
    was SAMUEL, the judge and
       priest.

46, 1–6: *Joshua*, whose name means "the Lord is savior" (1), was the instrument through which God delivered his people in miraculous ways (2–6) by destroying their enemies, whose land he gave to the Israelites as an *inheritance* (1).
46, 3: *The battles of the Lord:* cf Jos 6—10.
46, 7–10: *Caleb*, who with Joshua advised Moses and the people in the desert to conquer Canaan, des-

pite the counsel of their companion scouts and the rebellion of the people, merited to lead the Israelites of the succeeding generation into the Promised Land. Caleb in his old age received as his inheritance a portion of land which he himself had previously conquered; cf Jos 15, 13f.
46, 11–20: Of the *Judges* praised and blessed for their fidelity to God in opposing idolatry, *Samuel*, a

man of spotless integrity, was the greatest (11f.19). He was judge of the entire nation, and was also a prophet and priest who through his sacrificial offering obtained victory over the Philistines. He established the kingdom, anointed kings (13–18), and even after his death foretold the king's fate and *put an end to wickedness* (20).

At God's word he established
the kingdom
and anointed princes to rule
the people.
14 By the law of the LORD he
judged the nation,
when he visited the
encampments of Jacob.
15 As a trustworthy prophet he
was sought out
and his words proved him
true as a seer.
16 He, too, called upon God,
and offered him a suckling
lamb;
17 Then the LORD thundered forth
from heaven,
and the tremendous roar of
his voice was heard.
18 He brought low the rulers of the
enemy
and destroyed all the lords of
the Philistines.
19 When Samuel approached the
end of his life,
he testified before the LORD
and his anointed prince,
"No bribe or secret gift have I
taken from any man!"
and no one dared gainsay him.
20 Even when he lay buried, his
guidance was sought;
he made known to the king
his fate,
And from the grave he raised
his voice
as a prophet, to put an end
to wickedness.

Nathan, David and Solomon

47 After him came NATHAN
who served in the presence
of David.
2 Like the choice fat of the sacred
offerings,
so was DAVID in Israel.
3 He made sport of lions as
though they were kids,
and of bears, like lambs of
the flock.
4 As a youth he slew the giant
and wiped out the people's
disgrace,

When his hand let fly the
slingstone
that crushed the pride of
Goliath.
5 Since he called upon the Most
High God,
who gave strength to his
right arm
To defeat the skilled warrior
and raise up the might of his
people,
6 Therefore the women sang his
praises
and ascribed to him tens of
thousands.
When he assumed the royal
crown, he battled
7 and subdued the enemy on
every side.
He destroyed the hostile
Philistines
and shattered their power till
our own day.
8 With his every deed he offered
thanks
to God Most High, in words
of praise.
With his whole being he loved
his Maker
and daily had his praises sung;
9 He added beauty to the feasts
and solemnized the seasons of
each year
With string music before the
altar,
providing sweet melody for
the psalms
10 So that when the Holy Name
was praised,
before daybreak the sanctuary
would resound.
11 The LORD forgave him his sins
and exalted his strength
forever;
He conferred on him the rights
of royalty
and established his throne in
Israel.
12 Because of his merits he had as
his successor
a wise son, who lived in
security:

13 SOLOMON reigned during an era
of peace,
for God made tranquil all his
borders.
He built a house to the name of
God,
and established a lasting
sanctuary,
14 How wise you were when you
were young,
overflowing with instruction,
like the Nile in flood!
15 Your understanding covered the
whole earth,
and, like a sea, filled it with
knowledge.
16 Your fame reached distant
coasts,
and their peoples came to hear
you;
17 With song and story and riddle,
and with your answers, you
astounded the nations.
18 You were called by that
glorious name
which was conferred upon
Israel.
Gold you gathered like so much
iron,
you heaped up silver as though
it were lead;
19 But you abandoned yourself to
women
and gave them dominion over
your body.
20 You brought dishonor upon
your reputation,
shame upon your marriage,
Wrath upon your descendants,
and groaning upon your
domain;
21 Thus two governments came
into being,
when in Ephraim kingship
was usurped.
22 But God does not withdraw his
mercy,
nor permit even one of his
promises to fail.
He does not uproot the posterity
of his chosen one,
nor destroy the offspring of
his friend.

47, 1–11: *David,* a youthful and fearless warrior, the favorite of all Israel, by defeating *Goliath,* the boastful Philistine giant, removed *the people's disgrace* and greatly strengthened their power (1–7). *With his whole being he loved* and praised God, and his devotion to divine worship led him to develop liturgical cult. David fell into sin, but repenting, received pardon from God and the promise of an ever-

lasting kingdom (8–11).
47, 12–24: *Solomon,* son and successor of David, inherited peace through his father's conquests. He built the magnificent temple of Jerusalem (12f) and received from God the favor of unparalleled wisdom, through which he obtained great fame (14–17). Luxury and sensuality, however, brought disgrace upon him, and because of his oppressive burdens, he

disposed the kingdom for division after his death (19–21.23f). Nevertheless God did not withdraw his promise of establishing his throne in the descendants of David (22).
47, 18: Cf 2 Sm 12, 25, where Solomon is called Jedidiah, "beloved of the Lord." The same term is used of Israel in Jer 11, 15.

So he gave to Jacob a remnant,
    to David a root from his own
        family.
23 Solomon finally slept with his
        fathers,
    and left behind him one of
        his sons,
    Expansive in folly, limited in
        in sense,
    REHOBOAM, who by his policy
        made the people rebel;
    Until one arose who should not
        be remembered,
    the sinner who led Israel
        into sin,
    Who brought ruin to Ephraim
24   and caused them to be exiled
        from their land.

Elijah and Elisha

Their sinfulness grew more and
        more,
25   and they lent themselves to
        every evil,

48 Till like a fire there appeared
        the prophet
    whose words were as a
        flaming furnace.
2 Their staff of bread he shattered,
    in his zeal he reduced them to
        straits;
3 By God's word he shut up the
        heavens
    and three times brought down
        fire.
4 How awesome are you, ELIJAH!
    Whose glory is equal to yours?
5 You brought a dead man back
        to life
    from the nether world, by the
        will of the LORD.
6 You sent kings down to
        destruction,
    and nobles, from their beds
        of sickness.
7 You heard threats at Sinai,
    at Horeb avenging judgments.
8 You anointed kings who should
        inflict vengeance,
    and a prophet as your
        successor.

9 You were taken aloft in a
        whirlwind,
    in a chariot with fiery horses.
10 You are destined, it is written,
    in time to come
    to put an end to wrath before
        the day of the LORD,
    To turn back the hearts of
        fathers toward their sons,
    and to re-establish the tribes
        of Jacob.
11 Blessed is he who shall have
        seen you before he dies,
12   O Elijah, enveloped in the
        whirlwind!

Then ELISHA, filled with a
    twofold portion of his spirit,
    wrought many marvels by his
        mere word.
During his lifetime he feared
        no one,
    nor was any man able to
        intimidate his will.
13 Nothing was beyond his power;
    beneath him flesh was brought
        back into life.
14 In life he performed wonders,
    and after death, marvelous
        deeds.
15 Despite all this the people did
        not repent,
    nor did they give up their sins,
    Until they were rooted out of
        their land
    and scattered all over the earth.
    But Judah remained, a tiny
        people,
    with its rulers from the house
        of David.
16 Some of these did what was right,
    but the others were extremely
        sinful.

Hezekiah and Isaiah

17 HEZEKIAH fortified his city
    and had water brought into it;
    With iron tools he cut through
        the rock
    and he built reservoirs for
        water.

18 During his reign Sennacherib led
        an invasion,
    and sent his adjutant;
    He shook his fist at Zion
    and blasphemed God in his
        pride.
19 The people's hearts melted within
        them,
    and they were in anguish like
        that of childbirth.
20 But they called upon the Most
        High God
    and lifted up their hands to
        him;
    He heard the prayer they uttered,
    and saved them through
        ISAIAH.
21 God struck the camp of the
        Assyrians
    and routed them with a plague.
22 For Hezekiah did what was
        right
    and held fast to the paths of
        David,
    As ordered by the illustrious
        prophet
    Isaiah, who saw the truth in
        visions.
23 In his lifetime he turned back
        the sun
    and prolonged the life of the
        king.
24 By his powerful spirit he looked
        into the future
    and consoled the mourners of
        Zion;
25 He foretold what should be till
        the end of time,
    hidden things yet to be fulfilled.

Josiah and the Prophets

49 The name JOSIAH is like
        blended incense,
    made lasting by a skilled
        performer.
Precious is his memory, like
        honey to the taste,
    like music at a banquet.
2 For he grieved over our betrayals
    and destroyed the abominable
        idols.

47, 23: *Expansive:* the name *Rehoboam* means "the
people is expansive," that is, widespread. *The sinner:*
Jeroboam; cf 1 Kgs 12, 2.20.26–32.

47, 25—48, 11: The prophetic ministry of *Elijah*
amid widespread idolatry is here described as a judgment by fire (47, 25f). Through his preaching, miracles
and vengeance against God's enemies within and
without Israel, the prophet succeeded for a time in
destroying idols and in restoring faith and the worship of the true God (48, 2–8). His miraculous departure from this life gave rise to the belief that he did
not die but would return before the end of the world

to *put an end to wrath* and restore the tribes of Israel
(9ff). Cf Mt 17, 9–13.

48, 12–16: *Elisha* fearlessly continued the work of
his predecessor by numerous miracles (12ff), but the
obstinacy of the people eventually brought on the
destruction of the kingdom of Israel and the dispersion of its subjects. *Judah*, however, survived under
the rule of Davidic kings, both good and bad (15f).

48, 17–25: The fidelity, trust and courage of King
Hezekiah (17.22), the zeal of the prophet *Isaiah*, and
the prayer of the people (20) availed with God. The
Assyrian oppressors were routed (18f.21), the king's

life was prolonged, and consolations were granted
the people through Isaiah's prophecies concerning the
future (23ff), especially the coming of the Messiah and
the establishment of his kingdom; cf Is 7, 14; 9, 6f;
40–65.

49, 1–10: The author's praise of King *Josiah* (1–3),
of the prophets *Jeremiah* and *Ezekiel* and likewise the
minor prophets (7–10) derives from their spirit of
fidelity to the Lord and his law amid the infidelity of
kings and people (4ff.10).

3 He turned to God with his
      whole heart,
   and, though times were evil,
      he practiced virtue.
4 Except for David, Hezekiah and
      Josiah,
   they were all wicked;
   They abandoned the Law of the
      Most High,
   these kings of Judah, right to
      the very end.
5 So he gave over their power to
      others,
   their glory to a foolish foreign
      nation
6 Who burned the holy city
   and left its streets desolate,
7 As JEREMIAH had foretold; for
      they had treated him badly
   who even in the womb had
      made a prophet,
   To root out, pull down, and
      destroy,
   and then to build and plant.
8 EZEKIEL beheld the vision
   and described the different
      creatures of the chariot;
9 He also referred to JOB,
   who always persevered in the
      right path.
10 Then, too, the TWELVE
      PROPHETS—
   may their bones return to life
      from their resting place!—
   Gave new strength to Jacob
   and saved him by their faith
      and hope.

The Heroes after the Exile

11 How can we fittingly praise
      ZERUBBABEL,
   who was like a signet ring on
      God's right hand,
12 And Jeshua, Jozadak's son?
   In their time they built the
      house of God;
   They erected the holy temple,
      destined for everlasting glory.
13 Extolled be the memory of
      NEHEMIAH!
   He rebuilt our ruined walls,
   Restored our shattered defenses,
      and set up gates and bars.

The Earliest Patriarchs

14 Few on earth have been made
      the equal of ENOCH,
   for he was taken up bodily.
15 Was ever a man born like
      JOSEPH?
   Even his dead body was
      provided for.
16 Glorious, too, were SHEM and
      SETH and ENOS;
   but beyond that of any living
      being was the splendor of
      ADAM.

Simon, Son of Jochanan

50 The greatest among his
      brethren, the glory of his
      people,
   was SIMON the priest, son of
      Jochanan,
   In whose time the house of God
      was renovated,
   in whose days the temple was
      reinforced.
2 In his time also the wall was
      built
   with powerful turrets for the
      temple precincts;
3 In his time the reservoir was dug,
   the pool with a vastness like
      the sea's.
4 He protected his people against
      brigands
   and strengthened his city
      against the enemy.
5 How splendid he was as he
      appeared from the tent,
   as he came from within the
      veil!
6 Like a star shining among the
      clouds,
   like the full moon at the
      holyday season;
7 Like the sun shining upon the
      temple,
   like the rainbow appearing in
      the cloudy sky;
8 Like the blossoms on the
      branches in springtime,
   like a lily on the banks of a
      stream;

   Like the trees of Lebanon in
      summer,
9   like the fire of incense at the
      sacrifice;
   Like a vessel of beaten gold,
      studded with precious stones;
10 Like a luxuriant olive tree thick
      with fruit,
   like a cypress standing against
      the clouds;
11 Vested in his magnificent robes,
      and wearing his garments of
      splendor,
   As he ascended the glorious
      altar
   and lent majesty to the court
      of the sanctuary.

12 When he received the sundered
      victims from the priests
   while he stood before the
      sacrificial wood,
   His brethren ringed about like
      a garland,
   like a stand of cedars on
      Lebanon;
13 All the sons of Aaron in their
      dignity
   clustered around him like
      poplars,
   With the offerings to the LORD
      in their hands,
   in the presence of the whole
      assembly of Israel.
14 Once he had completed the
      services at the altar
   with the arranging of the
      sacrifices for the Most High,
15 And had stretched forth his hand
      for the cup,
   to offer blood of the grape,
   And poured it out at the foot
      of the altar,
   a sweet-smelling odor to the
      Most High God,
16 The sons of Aaron would sound
      a blast,
   the priests, on their trumpets
      of beaten metal;
   A blast to resound mightily
   as a reminder before the
      Most High.

49, 11ff: *Zerubbabel* and *Jeshua*, in rebuilding the temple, and *Nehemiah*, the governor, in repairing the walls of the Holy City also restored what these constructions signify, namely, religious worship and civil authority as prescribed in the law.
49, 14ff: The patriarchs here mentioned were glorious because of their spirit of religion, i.e., their profound reverence for God and obedience to him. *The splendor of Adam*, moreover, was due to his direct origin from God.

50, 1–21: The *son of Jochanan* here mentioned was Simon II, *in whose time* as high priest (219–196 B.C.) great works were accomplished for the benefit of public worship and welfare (1–4). The author, a contemporary of this high priest, describes in great detail and by numerous comparisons the impression of awful majesty received, the lofty joy aroused, at sight of the high priest fully vested entering the sanctuary, ascending the altar (6–11), and, in the presence of the whole assembly of Israel, encircled by assistant priests

bearing offerings, sacrificing the burnt offering on the Day of Atonement, while the trumpets blast and the people bow down in adoration of *the Most High* (12–17). The hymnody, the joyful shouts of the multitude, and finally the high priest's blessing, in which he pronounces—once only in the year, on this occasion—the holy name of Yahweh, climax the description of this most solemn Jewish liturgical function (18–21).

17 Then all the people with one
    accord
    would quickly fall prostrate
      to the ground
  In adoration before the Most
    High,
    before the Holy One of Israel.

18 Then hymns would re-echo,
    and over the throng sweet
      strains of praise resound.
19 All the people of the land
    would shout for joy,
    praying to the Merciful One,
  As the high priest completed
    the services at the altar
  by presenting to God the
    sacrifice due;
20 Then coming down he would
    raise his hands
  over all the congregation of
    Israel.
  The blessing of the LORD would
    be upon his lips,
  the name of the LORD would
    be his glory.
21 Then again the people would lie
    prostrate
  to receive from him the
    blessing of the Most High.

22 And now, bless the God of all,
    who has done wondrous
      things on earth;
  Who fosters men's growth from
    their mother's womb,
  and fashions them according
    to his will!
23 May he grant you joy of heart
    and may peace abide among
    you;
24 May his goodness toward us
    endure in Israel
  as long as the heavens are above.

Epilogue and Canticles

25 My whole being loathes two
    nations,
  the third is not even a people:

26 Those who live in Seir and
    Philistia,
  and the degenerate folk who
    dwell in Shechem.

27 Wise instruction, appropriate
    proverbs,
  I have written in this book,
  I, Jesus, son of Eleazar, son of
    Sirach,
  as they gushed forth from my
    heart's understanding.

28 Happy is the man who meditates
    upon these things,
  wise the man who takes them
    to heart!
29 If he puts them into practice,
    he can cope with anything,
  for the fear of the LORD is
    his lamp.

51 I give you thanks, O God of
    my father;
  I praise you, O God my
    savior!
  I will make known your name,
    refuge of my life;
2 you have been my helper
    against my adversaries.
  You have saved me from death,
    and kept back my body from
      the pit,
  From the clutches of the nether
    world you have snatched my
    feet;
3 you have delivered me, in your
    great mercy
  From the scourge of a
    slanderous tongue,
    and from lips that went over
      to falsehood;
  From the snare of those who
    watched my downfall,
    and from the power of those
      who sought my life;
  From many a danger you have
    saved me,

4 from flames that hemmed me
    in on every side;
  From the midst of unremitting
    fire,
5 from the deep belly of the
    nether world;
  From deceiving lips and painters
    of lies,
6 from the arrows of dishonest
    tongues.
  I was at the point of death,
    my soul was nearing the
      depths of the nether world;
7 I turned every way, but there
    was no one to help me,
  I looked for one to sustain me,
    but could find no one.
8 But then I remembered the
    mercies of the LORD,
    his kindness through ages past;
  For he saves those who take
    refuge in him,
    and rescues them from every
      evil.
9 So I raised my voice from the
    very earth,
    from the gates of the nether
      world, my cry.
10 I called out: O Lord, you are my
    father,
    you are my champion and my
      savior;
  Do not abandon me in time of
    trouble,
    in the midst of storms and
      dangers.
11 I will ever praise your name
    and be constant in my prayers
      to you.
  Thereupon the LORD heard my
    voice,
    he listened to my appeal;
12 He saved me from evil of every
    kind
    and preserved me in time of
      trouble.
  For this reason I thank him and
    I praise him;
    I bless the name of the LORD.

50, 22ff: Praise and thanksgiving are given to God for his wondrous works, and a blessing is invoked on man that he may enjoy peace and gladness of heart and the abiding goodness of the Most High.

50, 25f: The author's abhorrence of the pagan Edomites (Idumeans), Philistines and Samaritans can be understood in the light of Old Testament thinking, which does not always distinguish between hatred of evildoers and hatred of the evil they do.

50, 25: *Not even a people.*

50, 26: *Seir:* Mount Seir in the territory of the Edomites. *Shechem:* a city in Samaria.

50, 27ff: These verses contain the subscription of the author, *Jesus, son of Eleazar, son of Sirach,* to his

long and beautiful treatise on wisdom as applying to all of human life, integrating it under the direction of *the fear of the Lord.*

51, 1–12: A canticle of praise and thanks to God for delivering the author from slander, dangers, destruction, death, the nether world, and evil of every kind.

51, 12: After this verse the Hebrew text gives the litany of praise contained below. It is similar to Ps 136. Though not found in any versions, and therefore of doubtful authenticity, the litany seems from internal evidence to go back to the time of Sirach:

  Give thanks to the LORD, for he is good,
    for his mercy endures forever;

Give thanks to the God of glory,
  for his mercy endures forever;
Give thanks to the guardian of Israel,
  for his mercy endures forever;
Give thanks to the creator of the universe,
  for his mercy endures forever;
Give thanks to the redeemer of Israel,
  for his mercy endures forever;
Give thanks to him who gathers the dispersed of Israel,
  for his mercy endures forever;
Give thanks to him who builds his city and his sanctuary,
  for his mercy endures forever;

13 When I was young and innocent
     I sought wisdom.
14 She came to me in her beauty,
     and until the end I will
     cultivate her.
15 As the blossoms yielded to
     ripening grapes,
     the heart's joy,
   My feet keep to the level path
     because from earliest youth I
     was familiar with her.
16 In the short time I paid heed,
     I met with great instruction.
17 Since in this way I have profited,
     I will give my teacher grateful
     praise.
18 I became resolutely devoted to
     her—
     the good I persistently strove
     for.
19 I burned with desire for her,
     never turning back.
   I became preoccupied with her,
     never weary of extolling her.

20 For her I purified even the soles
     of my feet;
     in cleanness I attained her.
   At first acquaintance with her,
     I gained understanding
   such that I will never forsake
     her.
21 My whole being was stirred as I
     learned about her;
   therefore I have made her my
     prize possession.
22 The LORD has granted me my
     lips as a reward,
   and my tongue will declare
     his praises.

23 Come aside to me, you
     untutored,
   and take up lodging in the
     house of instruction;
24 How long will you be deprived
     of wisdom's food,
   how long will you endure
     such bitter thirst?

25 I open my mouth and speak
     of her:
   gain, at no cost, wisdom for
     yourselves.
26 Submit your neck to her yoke,
     that your mind may accept
     her teaching.
   For she is close to those who
     seek her,
   and the one who is in earnest
     finds her.
27 See for yourselves! I have
     labored only a little,
     but have found much.
28 Acquire but a little instruction;
     you will win silver and gold
     through her.
29 Let your spirits rejoice in the
     mercy of God,
     and be not ashamed to give
     him praise.
30 Work at your tasks in due season,
     and in his own time God will
     give you your reward.

Give thanks to him who makes a horn to sprout
     forth
   for the house of David, for his mercy endures
     forever;
Give thanks to him who has chosen for his priests
   the sons of Zadok, for his mercy endures
     forever;
Give thanks to the shield of Abraham,
   for his mercy endures forever;
Give thanks to the rock of Isaac,
   for his mercy endures forever;
Give thanks to the mighty one of Jacob,
   for his mercy endures forever;

Give thanks to him who has chosen Zion,
   for his mercy endures forever;
Give thanks to the king over kings of kings,
   for his mercy endures forever;
He has lifted up the horn of his people, be this his
   praise from all his faithful ones,
From the children of Israel, the people close to him.
   Alleluia! (Cf Ps 148, 14.)
51, 13–30: An alphabetic canticle describing: (a)
the approach to wisdom through prayer, persistent
study and instruction (13–17), purification from sin,

enlightenment and ardent desire; (b) the possession of
wisdom (18–22). The author concludes with an urgent
invitation to men to receive *instruction* in *wisdom* from
him, and to live by it, because wisdom gives herself *to
those who seek her* (23–26); and for their labor, God
will reward them in the end (27–30). Cf Mt 11, 28;
Eccl 12, 14.
   In the Greek of 13f there is an expression introducing Solomon as the speaker. This deviates from
the original author's intent. It reads: "Publicly, in my
prayer, facing the temple, I asked for her."

Isaiah

THE BOOK OF JUDGMENT

INDICTMENT OF ISRAEL AND JUDAH

Israel's Sinfulness

THE vision which Isaiah, son of Amoz, had concerning Judah and Jerusalem in the days of Uzziah, Jotham, Ahaz and Hezekiah, kings of Judah. 2 Hear, O heavens, and listen, O earth, for the LORD speaks: Sons have I raised and reared, but they have disowned me!

3 An ox knows its owner,
    and an ass, its master's manger;
But Israel does not know,
    my people has not understood.
4 Ah! sinful nation, people laden
    with wickedness,
    evil race, corrupt children!
They have forsaken the LORD,
    spurned the Holy One of
    Israel,
    apostatized.
5 Where would you yet be struck,
    you that rebel again and again?
The whole head is sick,
    the whole heart faint.
6 From the sole of the foot to the
    head
    there is no sound spot:
Wound and welt and gaping gash,
    not drained, or bandaged,
    or eased with salve.

7 Your country is waste,
    your cities burnt with fire;
Your land before your eyes
    strangers devour
    [a waste, like Sodom
      overthrown]—
8 And daughter Zion is left
    like a hut in a vineyard,
Like a shed in a melon patch,
    like a city blockaded.

9 Unless the LORD of hosts
    had left us a scanty remnant,
We had become as Sodom,
    we should be like Gomorrah.
10 Hear the word of the LORD,
    princes of Sodom!
Listen to the instruction of our
    God,
    people of Gomorrah!

11 What care I for the number of
    your sacrifices?
    says the LORD.
I have had enough of
    whole-burnt rams
    and fat of fatlings;
In the blood of calves, lambs
    and goats
    I find no pleasure.

12 When you come in to visit me,
    who asks these things of you?
13 Trample my courts no more!
    Bring no more worthless
    offerings;
    your incense is loathsome to
    me.
New moon and sabbath,
    calling of assemblies,
    octaves with wickedness:
    these I cannot bear.

1, 1: The title of the book: an editorial addition. *Isaiah:* meaning "the salvation of the Lord," or "The Lord is salvation." *Amoz:* not the minor prophet. *Judah:* the southern kingdom of the tribes of Judah and Benjamin. *Uzziah:* also called Azariah; cf 2 Kgs 15, 1; 2 Chr 26, 1.

1, 3: *Israel:* not the northern kingdom, as in 9, 11, exclusively, which Isaiah usually calls "Ephraim" from the tribe bordering on the southern kingdom,

but the entire chosen people; cf 8, 14.

1, 4: *Holy One of Israel:* a title used frequently by Isaiah, rarely by other writers.

1, 5–8: Sufferings inflicted upon God's people for their sins.

1, 8: *Daughter Zion:* Jerusalem. *Hut . . . shed:* for the shelter of watchmen and laborers.

1, 9: *Lord of hosts:* God, who is the Creator and Ruler of the heavenly armies of the angels, stars, etc.

Remnant: St. Paul uses this text in Rom 9, 29, where he speaks of God's saving mercy toward the Jews and Gentiles. *Sodom . . . Gomorrah:* cf Gn 19.

1, 11: *The number of your sacrifices:* however numerous, they are not acceptable without the right dispositions on the part of the worshipers.

1, 13: *Octaves with wickedness:* the solemnity of the feasts marred by evil deeds.

14 Your new moons and festivals
        I detest;
    they weigh me down, I tire
        of the load.
15 When you spread out your
        hands,
    I close my eyes to you;
    Though you pray the more,
        I will not listen.
    Your hands are full of blood!
16 Wash yourselves clean!
    Put away your misdeeds from
        before my eyes;
17   cease doing evil; learn to do
        good.
    Make justice your aim: redress
        the wronged,
        hear the orphan's plea, defend
        the widow.

18 Come now, let us set things
        right,
    says the LORD:
    Though your sins be like scarlet,
        they may become white as
        snow;
    Though they be crimson red,
        they may become white as
        wool.
19 If you are willing, and obey,
        you shall eat the good things
        of the land;
20 But if you refuse and resist,
        the sword shall consume you:
    for the mouth of the LORD has
        spoken!

21 How has she turned adulteress,
        the faithful city, so upright!
    Justice used to lodge within her,
        but now, murderers.
22 Your silver is turned to dross,
        your wine is mixed with water.
23 Your princes are rebels
        and comrades of thieves;
    Each one of them loves a bribe
        and looks for gifts.
    The fatherless they defend not,
        and the widow's plea does not
        reach them.
24 Now, therefore, says the Lord,
        the LORD of hosts, the Mighty
        One of Israel:

Ah! I will take vengeance on my
        foes
    and fully repay my enemies!
25 I will turn my hand against you,
        and refine your dross in the
        furnace,
    removing all your alloy.
26 I will restore your judges as at
        first,
    and your counselors as in the
        beginning;
    After that you shall be called
        city of justice, faithful city.

27 Zion shall be redeemed by
        judgment,
    and her repentant ones by
        justice.
28 Rebels and sinners alike shall
        be crushed,
    those who desert the LORD
        shall be consumed.
29 You shall be ashamed of the
        terebinths which you prized,
    and blush for the groves
        which you chose.
30 You shall become like a tree
        with falling leaves,
    like a garden that has no
        water.
31 The strong man shall turn to
        tow,
    and his work shall become a
        spark;
    Both shall burn together,
        and there shall be none to
        quench the flames.

Zion, the Messianic Capital

2 This is what Isaiah, son of
  Amoz, saw concerning Judah
and Jerusalem.

2   In days to come,
    The mountain of the LORD's
        house
        shall be established as the
        highest mountain
    and raised above the hills.
    All nations shall stream toward
        it;
3   many peoples shall come and
        say:

"Come, let us climb the LORD's
        mountain,
    to the house of the God of
        Jacob,
    That he may instruct us in his
        ways,
    and we may walk in his paths."
    For from Zion shall go forth
        instruction,
    and the word of the LORD
        from Jerusalem.
4 He shall judge between the
        nations,
    and impose terms on many
        peoples.
    They shall beat their swords
        into plowshares
    and their spears into pruning
        hooks;
    One nation shall not raise the
        sword against another,
    nor shall they train for war
        again.

5 O house of Jacob, come,
    let us walk in the light of the
        LORD!

The Lord's Judgment against Idols

6 You have abandoned your
        people,
    the house of Jacob,
    Because they are filled with
        fortunetellers
    and soothsayers, like the
        Philistines;
    they covenant with strangers.
7 Their land is full of silver and
        gold,
    and there is no end to their
        treasures;
    Their land is full of horses,
    and there is no end to their
        chariots.
8 Their land is full of idols;
    they worship the works of
        their hands,
    that which their fingers have
        made.
9 But man is abased,
    each one brought low.
    [Do not pardon them!]

1, 15: *Spread out your hands:* in prayer.
1, 21: A picture of Jerusalem, once so faithful to
God. Apostasy from the covenant is often likened by
the prophets to unfaithfulness to the marriage vow.
1, 27: This verse is the key to the whole Book of
Isaiah. Zion's defiant persistence in sin has demanded
a divine *judgment,* by which her survivors will be
cleansed and will return to God in *justice;* cf 40, 2.

1, 29: *Terebinths which you prized . . . groves which
you chose:* as popular shrines for idolatrous worship.
2, 1: An editorial addition introducing chapters 2–5.
2, 2–4: The Messianic destiny which ensures
Judah's later restoration. In the Messianic kingdom
the prophets generally see *the Lord's house* as the seat
of authority and the source of clear and certain
doctrine; also, its rule willingly accepted by all

peoples, maintained by spiritual sanctions, and tending to universal peace. This passage is found substantially unchanged in Mi 4, 1–3; it probably, although
not certainly, has Isaiah as its author.
2, 3: *Zion . . . Jerusalem:* types of the earthly center
of the Messianic kingdom.
2, 6: *Fortunetellers and soothsayers:* divination was
strictly forbidden; cf Dt 18, 9–14.

10 Get behind the rocks,
      hide in the dust,
   From the terror of the LORD
      and the splendor of his
         majesty!
11 The haughty eyes of man will
         be lowered,
      the arrogance of men will
         be abased,
      and the LORD alone will be
         exalted, on that day.
12 For the LORD of hosts will have
         his day
      against all that is proud and
         arrogant,
      all that is high, and it will be
         brought low;
13 Yes, against all the cedars of
         Lebanon
      and all the oaks of Bashan,
14 Against all the lofty mountains
      and all the high hills,
15 Against every lofty tower
      and every fortified wall,
16 Against all the ships of Tarshish
      and all stately vessels.
17 Human pride will be abased,
      the arrogance of men
         brought low,
   And the LORD alone will be
      exalted, on that day.

18   The idols will perish forever.

19 Men will go into caves in the
         rocks
      and into holes in the earth,
   From the terror of the LORD
      and the splendor of his
         majesty,
      when he arises to overawe the
         earth.

20 On that day men will throw to
the moles and the bats the idols of
silver and gold which they made for
worship.

21 They go into caverns in the
         rocks
      and into crevices in the cliffs,
   From the terror of the LORD
      and the splendor of his
         majesty,
      when he arises to overawe
         the earth.

22 As for you, let man alone,
      in whose nostrils is but a
         breath;
      for what is he worth?

Judgment of Judah and Jerusalem

3 The Lord, the LORD of hosts,
      shall take away from
         Jerusalem and from Judah
      support and prop [all supplies
         of bread and water]:
2 Hero and warrior,
      judge and prophet,
         fortuneteller and elder,
3 The captain of fifty and the
         nobleman,
      counselor, skilled magician,
         and expert charmer.
4 I will make striplings their
         princes;
      the fickle shall govern them,
5 And the people shall oppress
         one another,
      yes, every man his neighbor.
   The child shall be bold toward
         the elder,
      and the base toward the
         honorable.

6 When a man seizes his brother
      in his father's house, saying,
   "You have clothes! Be our
         ruler,
      and take in hand this ruin!"—
7   Then shall he answer in that
         day:
   "I will not undertake to cure
         this,
      when in my own house there
         is no bread or clothing!
   You shall not make me ruler
      of the people."

8 Jerusalem is crumbling, Judah is
         falling;
      for their speech and their
         deeds are before the LORD,
      a provocation in the sight of
         his majesty.
9 Their very look bears witness
         against them;
      their sin like Sodom they
         vaunt,
   They hide it not. Woe to them!
      they deal out evil to themselves.

10 Happy the just, for it will be well
         with them,
      the fruit of their works they
         will eat.
11 Woe to the wicked man! All
         goes ill,
      with the work of his hands he
         will be repaid.
12 My people—a babe in arms will
         be their tyrant,
      and women will rule them!
   O my people, your leaders
         mislead,
      they destroy the paths you
         should follow.

13 The LORD rises to accuse,
      standing to try his people.
14 The LORD enters into judgment
      with his people's elders and
         princes:
   It is you who have devoured the
         vineyard;
      the loot wrested from the poor
         is in your houses.
15 What do you mean by crushing
         my people,
      and grinding down the poor
         when they look to you?
      says the Lord, the GOD of
         hosts.

16 The LORD said:
   Because the daughters of Zion
         are haughty,
      and walk with necks
         outstretched
   Ogling and mincing as they go,
      their anklets tinkling with
         every step,
17 The Lord shall cover the scalps
         of Zion's daughters with
         scabs,
      and the LORD shall bare their
         heads.

18 On that day the Lord will do
away with the finery of the 19 anklets, sunbursts, and crescents; the
pendants, bracelets, 20 and veils;
the headdresses, bangles, cinctures,
perfume 21 boxes, and amulets;
the signet rings, and the nose rings;
22 the court dresses, wraps, cloaks,
and purses; 23 the mirrors, linen
tunics, turbans, and shawls.

2, 11: *That day:* the day of the Lord, a day of
retribution, often referred to, especially by the minor
prophets, and described in terms of natural phenomena: earthquake, fire, storm.
2, 13: *Lebanon:* Mount Lebanon in Syria, famed

for its cedars. *Bashan:* the wooded uplands east of the
Jordan River.
2, 16: *Tarshish:* cf note on Ps 48, 8.
3, 1–12: Anarchy will reign in Jerusalem and
Judah. In the prevailing desperation, even the most un-

worthy and the least qualified will be sought as rulers.
3, 17: *Bare their heads:* a mark of social disgrace;
cf Nm 5, 18.
3, 21: *Nose rings:* of gold, a feminine ornament in
the East; cf note on Gn 24, 22.

24 Instead of perfume there will be
        stench,
    instead of the girdle, a rope,
And for the coiffure, baldness;
    for the rich gown, a sackcloth
    skirt.
    Then, instead of beauty:
25 Your men will fall by the sword,
    and your champions, in war;
26 Her gates will lament and mourn,
    as the city sits desolate on the
    ground.

4 Seven women will take hold
        of one man
    on that day, saying:
    "We will eat our own food
    and wear our own clothing;
    Only let your name be given us,
    put an end to our disgrace!"

The Messianic Branch

2   On that day,
    The branch of the LORD will be
        luster and glory,
    and the fruit of the earth will
        be honor and splendor
    for the survivors of Israel.
3 He who remains in Zion
    and he that is left in Jerusalem
Will be called holy:
    every one marked down for
    life in Jerusalem.
4 When the Lord washes away
    the filth of the daughters of
        Zion,
    And purges Jerusalem's blood
        from her midst
    with a blast of searing
        judgment,
5 Then will the LORD create,
    over the whole site of Mount
        Zion
    and over her place of
        assembly,
    A smoking cloud by day
    and a light of flaming fire
        by night.
6 For over all, his glory will be
    shelter and protection:
    shade from the parching
        heat of day,
    refuge and cover from storm
    and rain.

The Vineyard Song

5 Let me now sing of my
        friend,
    my friend's song concerning
        his vineyard.
    My friend had a vineyard
    on a fertile hillside;
2 He spaded it, cleared it of
        stones,
    and planted the choicest vines;
Within it he built a watchtower,
    and hewed out a wine press.
Then he looked for the crop of
        grapes,
    but what it yielded was wild
    grapes.

3 Now, inhabitants of Jerusalem
    and men of Judah,
    judge between me and my
    vineyard:
4 What more was there to do for
        my vineyard
    that I had not done?
Why, when I looked for the
        crop of grapes,
    did it bring forth wild grapes?
5 Now, I will let you know
    what I mean to do to my
        vineyard:
    Take away its hedge, give it to
        grazing,
    break through its wall, let it
        be trampled!
6 Yes, I will make it a ruin:
    it shall not be pruned or hoed,
    but overgrown with thorns
        and briers;
    I will command the clouds
    not to send rain upon it.
7 The vineyard of the LORD of
        hosts is the house of Israel,
    and the men of Judah are his
        cherished plant;
He looked for judgment, but see,
        bloodshed!
    for justice, but hark, the
        outcry!

Doom of the Unjust

8 Woe to you who join house to
        house,
    who connect field with field,

Till no room remains, and you
    are left to dwell
    alone in the midst of the land!
9 In my hearing the LORD of hosts
        has sworn:
    Many houses shall be in ruins,
    large ones and fine, with no
        one to live in them.
10 Ten acres of vineyard
    shall yield but one liquid
        measure,
    And a homer of seed
    shall yield but an ephah.
17 Lambs shall graze there at
        pasture,
    and kids shall eat in the ruins
        of the rich.

11 Woe to those who demand
        strong drink
    as soon as they rise in the
        morning,
    And linger into the night
    while wine inflames them!
12 With harp and lyre, timbrel
        and flute,
    they feast on wine;
    But what the LORD does, they
        regard not,
    the work of his hands they
        see not.
13 Therefore my people go into
        exile,
    because they do not
        understand;
    Their nobles die of hunger,
    and their masses are parched
        with thirst.

14 Therefore the nether world
        enlarges its throat
    and opens its maw without
        limit;
    Down go their nobility and
        their masses,
    their throngs and their revelry.
15 Men shall be abased, each one
        brought low,
    and the eyes of the haughty
        lowered,
16 But the LORD of hosts shall be
        exalted by his judgment,
    and God the Holy shall be
        shown holy by his justice.

4, 1: *Seven women . . . one man:* the disproportion
of the sexes due to war leaves the female population
almost without male partners. The women are eager
to marry, not for support, but to avoid the disgrace
of being childless.
4, 2: *Branch of the Lord:* divine blessings in general, which later culminated in the Messiah; cf Jer 23,
5; Zec 3, 8; 6, 12.

4, 3: *Marked down for life:* in God's list of his
elect; cf Ex 32, 32.
5, 1: *My friend had a vineyard:* the Lord and his
chosen people.
5, 7: *Judgment . . . bloodshed . . . justice . . . outcry:*
in Hebrew, these adversative terms constitute a play
on words.

5, 8–10: Land-grabbers who unjustly acquire property will be impoverished instead of enriched.
5, 10: *Ten acres:* a field requiring ten days of
plowing by a yoke of oxen. *Liquid measure:* in Hebrew,
"a bath," i.e., about ten gallons. *Homer:* a dry
measure of about ten bushels. *Ephah:* a dry measure
of about one bushel.
5, 14: *Nether world:* cf note on Ps 6, 6.

18 Woe to those who tug at guilt
        with cords of perversity,
     and at sin as if with cart ropes!
19 To those who say, "Let him
        make haste
     and speed his work, that we
        may see it;
     On with the plan of the Holy
        One of Israel!
     let it come to pass, that we
        may know it!"
20 Woe to those who call evil
        good, and good evil,
     who change darkness into
        light, and light into
        darkness,
     who change bitter into sweet,
        and sweet into bitter!
21 Woe to those who are wise in
        their own sight,
     and prudent in their own
        esteem!
22 Woe to the champions at
        drinking wine,
     the valiant at mixing strong
        drink!
23 To those who acquit the guilty
        for bribes,
     and deprive the just man of
        his rights!
24 Therefore, as the tongue of fire
        licks up stubble,
     as dry grass shrivels in the flame,
     Even so their root shall become
        rotten
     and their blossom scatter like
        dust;
     For they have spurned the law
        of the LORD of hosts,
     and scorned the word of the
        Holy One of Israel.
25 Therefore the wrath of the LORD
        blazes against his people,
     he raises his hand to strike
        them;
     When the mountains quake,
        their corpses shall be like
        refuse in the streets.
     For all this, his wrath is not
        turned back,
     and his hand is still
        outstretched.

Invasion

26 He will give a signal to a far-
        off nation,
     and whistle to them from the
        ends of the earth;
     speedily and promptly will
        they come.
27 None of them will stumble with
        weariness,
     none will slumber and none
        will sleep.
     None will have his waist belt
        loose,
     nor the thong of his sandal
        broken.
28 Their arrows are sharp,
        and all their bows are bent.
     The hoofs of their horses seem
        like flint,
     and their chariot wheels like
        the hurricane.
29 Their roar is that of the lion,
        like the lion's whelps they
        roar;
     They growl and seize the prey,
        they carry it off and none will
        rescue it.
30 [They will roar over it, on that
        day,
     with a roaring like that of
        the sea.]

IMMANUEL PROPHECIES

Call of Isaiah

6 In the year King Uzziah died, I
     saw the Lord seated on a high
and lofty throne, with the train of his
garment filling the temple. 2 Seraphim were stationed above; each of
them had six wings: with two they
veiled their faces, with two they veiled
their feet, and with two they hovered
aloft.

3 "Holy, holy, holy is the LORD
of hosts!" they cried one to the other.
"All the earth is filled with his glory!"
4 At the sound of that cry, the frame
of the door shook and the house was
filled with smoke.

5 Then I said, "Woe is me, I am
doomed! For I am a man of unclean
lips, living among a people of unclean
lips; yet my eyes have seen the King,
the LORD of hosts!" 6 Then one of
the seraphim flew to me, holding an
ember which he had taken with tongs
from the altar.

7 He touched my mouth with it.
"See," he said, "now that this has
touched your lips, your wickedness
is removed, your sin purged."

8 Then I heard the voice of the
Lord saying, "Whom shall I send?
Who will go for us?" "Here I am,"
I said; " send me!" 9 And he re-
plied: Go and say to this people:

     Listen carefully, but you shall
        not understand!
     Look intently, but you shall
        know nothing!
10 You are to make the heart of
        this people sluggish,
     to dull their ears and close
        their eyes;
     Else their eyes will see, their
        ears hear,
     their heart understand,
     and they will turn and be
        healed.

11 "How long, O Lord?" I asked.
And he replied:

     Until the cities are desolate,
        without inhabitants,
     Houses, without a man,
        and the earth is a desolate
        waste.
12 Until the LORD removes men
        far away,
     and the land is abandoned
        more and more.
13 If there be still a tenth part in it,
        then this in turn shall be laid
        waste;
     As with a terebinth or an oak
        whose trunk remains when its
        leaves have fallen.
     [Holy offspring is the trunk.]

5, 26–30: A description of the invading Assyrian
army, God's instrument for punishing his people.

6, 1: *In the year King Uzziah died:* 742 B.C.

6, 1ff: *Temple:* the holy place, just in front of the
holy of holies. *Seraphim:* literally "the burning ones,"
are celestial beings who surround the throne of God.
Each has six wings. Reverence for the divine majesty
causes them to veil their faces with two wings; modesty, to veil their extremities in similar fashion;
alacrity in God's service, to extend two wings in

preparation for flight. *Holy, holy, holy:* God's perfect
interior holiness whose exterior manifestation is *his
glory.* These words are found in the Roman liturgy
just before the Canon of the Mass.

6, 4: *Smoke:* reminiscent of the clouds which surrounded God at Mount Sinai; cf Ex 19, 16–19; Dt 4,
11f.

6, 5: *Doomed:* it was popularly believed that to see
God would lead to one's death; cf Gn 32, 31; Ex 33,
20; Jg 13, 22.

6, 7: *Touched your lips:* Isaiah is thus symbolically
purified to be worthy of his vocation as God's prophet.
In the Roman liturgy, the celebrant at Mass makes reference to this incident just before he reads the Gospel.

6, 9f: The truth that the nation will remain impenitent is vividly foretold, as if its obstinacy would be
caused, instead of merely occasioned, by the prophet's
warning. Cf Mt 13, 13ff; Mk 4, 12; Lk 8, 10.

6, 12: Several limited deportations in the time of
Isaiah would later culminate in the Babylonian Exile.

Birth of Immanuel

7 In the days of Ahaz, king of Judah, son of Jotham, son of Uzziah, Rezin, king of Aram, and Pekah, king of Israel, son of Remaliah, went up to attack Jerusalem, but they were not able to conquer it. 2 When word came to the house of David that Aram was encamped in Ephraim, the heart of the king and the heart of the people trembled, as the trees of the forest tremble in the wind.

3 Then the LORD said to Isaiah: Go out to meet Ahaz, you and your son Shear-jashub, at the end of the conduit of the upper pool, on the highway of the fuller's field, 4 and say to him: Take care you remain tranquil and do not fear; let not your courage fail before these two stumps of smoldering brands [the blazing anger of Rezin and the Arameans, and of the son of Remaliah], 5 because of the mischief that Aram [Ephraim and the son of Remaliah] plots against you, saying, 6 "Let us go up and tear Judah asunder, make it our own by force, and appoint the son of Tabeel king there."

7 Thus says the Lord:
  This shall not stand, it shall
    not be!
8 Damascus is the capital of Aram,
  and Rezin the head of Damascus;
  Samaria is the capital of
    Ephraim,
  and Remaliah's son the head of
    Samaria.
9 But within sixty years and five,
  Ephraim shall be crushed, no
    longer a nation.
  Unless your faith is firm
    you shall not be firm!

10 Again the LORD spoke to Ahaz: 11 Ask for a sign from the LORD, your God; let it be deep as the nether world, or high as the sky! 12 But Ahaz answered, "I will not ask! I will not tempt the LORD!" 13 Then he said: Listen, O house of David! Is it not enough for you to weary men, must you also weary my God? 14 Therefore the Lord himself will give you this sign: the virgin shall be with child, and bear a son, and shall name him Immanuel. 15 He shall be living on curds and honey by the time he learns to reject the bad and choose the good. 16 For before the child learns to reject the bad and choose the good, the land of those two kings whom you dread shall be deserted.

17 The LORD shall bring upon you and your people and your father's house days worse than any since Ephraim seceded from Judah. [This means the king of Assyria.] 18 On that day

The LORD shall whistle
  for the fly that is in the
    farthest streams of Egypt,
  and for the bee in the land of
    Assyria.
19 All of them shall come and
    settle
  in the steep ravines and in the
    rocky clefts,
  on all thornbushes and in all
    pastures.

20 On that day the Lord shall shave with the razor hired from across the River [with the king of Assyria] the head, and the hair between the legs. It shall also shave off the beard.

21 On that day a man shall keep a heifer or a couple of sheep, 22 and from their abundant yield of milk he shall live on curds; curds and honey shall be the food of all who remain in the land. 23 On that day every place where there used to be a thousand vines, worth a thousand pieces of silver, shall be turned to briers and thorns. 24 Men shall go there with bow and arrows; for all the country shall be briers and thorns. 25 For fear of briers and thorns you shall not go upon any mountainside which used to be hoed with the mattock; they shall be grazing land for cattle and shall be trampled upon by sheep.

The Son of Isaiah

8 The LORD said to me: Take a large cylinder-seal, and inscribe on it in ordinary letters: "Belonging to Maher-shalal-hash-baz." 2 And I took reliable witnesses, Uriah the priest, and Zechariah, son of Jeberechiah. 3 Then I went to the prophetess and she conceived and bore a son. The LORD said to me: Name him Maher-shalal-hash-baz, 4 for before the child knows how to call his father or mother by name, the wealth of Damascus and the spoil of Samaria shall be carried off by the king of Assyria.

5 Again the Lord spoke to me:

6 Because this people has rejected
    the waters of Shiloah that
      flow gently,
  And melts with fear before the
      loftiness
    of Rezin and Remaliah's son,
7 Therefore the Lord raises
    against them

7, 1: *Days of Ahaz:* who ruled from 735 to 715 B.C. This attack against Jerusalem by the kings of *Aram* (Syria) and *Israel* was occasioned by Ahaz' refusal to enter with them into an anti-Assyrian alliance; cf 2 Kgs 16.

7, 3: *Shear-jashub:* this name means "a remnant will return."

7, 6: *Son of Tabeel:* an adherent of Jerusalem's enemies. His appointment would interrupt the lawful succession from David.

7, 9: *Within sixty years and five:* if the text is correct, its reference is unknown.

7, 11: *Deep . . . sky:* an extraordinary or miraculous sign that would prove God's firm will to save the royal house of David from its oppressors.

7, 12: *Tempt the Lord:* Ahaz expresses in this hypocritical way his preference for depending upon the might of Assyria rather than upon God.

7, 14: The *sign* proposed by Isaiah was concerned with the preservation of Judah in the midst of distress (cf 7, 15.17), but more especially with the fulfillment

of God's earlier promise to David (2 Sm 7, 12–16) in the coming of *Immanuel* (meaning, "With us is God") as the ideal king (cf 9, 5–6; 11, 1–5). The Church has always followed St. Matthew in seeing the transcendent fulfillment of this verse in Christ and his Virgin Mother. The prophet need not have known the full force latent in his own words; and some Catholic writers have sought a preliminary and partial fulfillment in the conception and birth of the future King Hezekiah, whose mother, at the time Isaiah spoke, would have been a young, unmarried woman (Hebrew, *almah*). The Holy Spirit was preparing, however, for another Nativity which alone could fulfill the divinely given terms of Immanuel's mission, and in which the perpetual virginity of the Mother of God was to fulfill also the words of this prophecy in the integral sense intended by the divine Wisdom.

7, 15: *Curds and honey:* the restricted diet of those who remain after devastation has changed the once fertile fields of Judah into grazing land; cf 7, 21–25.

7, 20: God will use the Assyrians *from across the River* (the Euphrates) as his instrument (*razor*) to inflict disgrace and suffering upon his people.

8, 1: *Ordinary letters:* easily read by all. *Maher-shalal-hash-baz:* a symbolic name to be given to another son of Isaiah (v 3); it means "quick spoils; speedy plunder," and describes what the Assyrians will do.

8, 2: *Reliable witnesses:* who would testify that Isaiah had indeed prophesied the future destruction. *Uriah the priest:* cf 2 Kgs 16, 10.

8, 3: *The prophetess:* wife of Isaiah.

8, 6ff: *This people:* Judah. *Waters of Shiloah:* the stream that flows into the pool of Shiloah in Jerusalem, its slow current symbolizing the silent, divine protection which Judah has rejected. God will therefore summon the mighty Assyrian army, symbolized by *the River* (Euphrates), to devastate Judah, which, however, will not be entirely destroyed, because it is the land of *Immanuel.*

the waters of the River, great
    and mighty
[the king of Assyria and all
    his power].
It shall rise above all its
    channels,
    and overflow all its banks;
8 It shall pass into Judah, and
    flood it all throughout:
up to the neck it shall reach;
It shall spread its wings
    the full width of your land,
    Immanuel!

9 Know, O peoples, and be
    appalled!
Give ear, all you distant
    lands!
Arm, but be crushed! Arm,
    but be crushed!
10 Form a plan, and it shall be
    thwarted;
    make a resolve, and it shall
    not be carried out,
    for "With us is God!"

Disciples of Isaiah

11 For thus said the LORD to me,
taking hold of me and warning me
not to walk in the way of this people:

12 Call not alliance what this
    people calls alliance,
    and fear not, nor stand in awe
    of what they fear.
13 But with the LORD of hosts
    make your alliance—
    for him be your fear and your
    awe.
14 Yet he shall be a snare, an
    obstacle and a stumbling
    stone
    to both the houses of Israel,
    A trap and a snare
    to those who dwell in
    Jerusalem;
15 And many among them shall
    stumble and fall,
    broken, snared, and captured.

16 The record is to be folded and
the sealed instruction kept among my

disciples.   17 For I will trust in the
LORD, who is hiding his face from
the house of Jacob; yes, I will wait
for him.   18 Look at me and the
children whom the LORD has given
me: we are signs and portents in
Israel from the LORD of hosts who
dwells on Mount Zion.   19 And
when they say to you, "Inquire of
mediums and fortunetellers (who
chirp and mutter!); should not a
people inquire of their gods, apply to
the dead on behalf of the living?"
20 —then this document will furnish
its instruction. That kind of thing
they will surely say.

The Prince of Peace

23 First he degraded the land of
Zebulun and the land of Naphtali;
but in the end he has glorified the
seaward road, the land west of the
Jordan, the District of the Gentiles.

Anguish has taken wing,
    dispelled is darkness:
    for there is no gloom where
    but now there was distress.
9 The people who walked in
    darkness
have seen a great light;
Upon those who dwelt in the
    land of gloom
    a light has shone.
2 You have brought them
    abundant joy
    and great rejoicing,
As they rejoice before you as at
    the harvest,
    as men make merry when
    dividing spoils.
3 For the yoke that burdened them,
    the pole on their shoulder,
And the rod of their taskmaster
    you have smashed, as on the
    day of Midian.
4 For every boot that tramped in
    battle,
    every cloak rolled in blood,
    will be burned as fuel for
    flames.

5 For a child is born to us, a son
    is given us;
    upon his shoulder dominion
    rests.
They name him Wonder-
    Counselor, God-Hero,
    Father-Forever, Prince of
    Peace.
6 His dominion is vast
    and forever peaceful,
From David's throne, and over
    his kingdom,
    which he confirms and sustains
By judgment and justice,
    both now and forever.
The zeal of the LORD of hosts
    will do this!

Fall of the Northern Kingdom

7 The Lord has sent word
    against Jacob,
    it falls upon Israel;
8 And all the people know it,
    Ephraim and those who dwell
    in Samaria,
    those who say in arrogance
    and pride of heart,
9 "Bricks have fallen,
    but we will build with cut
    stone;
Sycamores are felled,
    but we will replace them with
    cedars."
10 But the LORD raises up their
    foes against them
    and stirs up their enemies to
    action:
11 Aram on the east and the
    Philistines on the west
    devour Israel with open
    mouth.
For all this, his wrath is not
    turned back,
    and his hand is still
    outstretched!

12 The people do not turn to him
    who struck them,
    nor seek the LORD of hosts.

8, 10: The *plan* of Israel's enemies will be *thwarted* because, as the name "Immanuel" signifies, *With us is God.*

8, 16: *Kept among my disciples:* for preservation and transmission.

8, 18: *Signs:* Isaiah and his sons had symbolic names.

8, 19: *Chirp and mutter:* a mocking reference to the sounds uttered by necromancers, as if the dead were speaking; all such practices were forbidden.

8, 21f: These verses have been transported and

placed within 14, 25, which affords the context in which they can be understood.

8, 23: *Zebulun ... Naphtali:* northern Palestine, which was first to be attacked by the Assyrians; God, however, redeems it, as he redeems all his people. *Seaward road:* from Damascus, across southern Galilee to the Mediterranean Sea. *District of the Gentiles:* northern Galilee, inhabited by pagans; cf Jos 20, 7; Is 9, 1. Mt 4, 15f refers to this, since Jesus began his public mission in Galilee.

9, 5: *A child:* the Immanuel of Is 7, 14 and 8, 8; cf 11, 1.2.9. In Christian tradition and liturgy, this passage is used to refer to Christ. *Upon his shoulder dominion rests:* authority. *Wonder-Counselor:* remarkable for his wisdom and prudence. *God-hero:* a warrior and a defender of his people, like God himself. *Father-Forever:* ever devoted to his people. *Prince of Peace:* his reign will be characterized by peace.

9, 11: *Aram:* the Syrian kingdom, with its capital at Damascus.

13 So the LORD severs from Israel
    head and tail,
   palm branch and reed in one
    day.
14 [The elder and the noble are
    the head,
   the prophet who teaches
    falsehood is the tail.]
15 The leaders of this people
    mislead them
   and those to be led are
    engulfed.
16 For this reason, the Lord does
    not spare their young men,
   and their orphans and
    widows he does not pity;
   They are wholly profaned and
    sinful,
   and every mouth gives vent
    to folly.
   For all this, his wrath is not
    turned back,
   his hand is still outstretched!
17 For wickedness burns like fire,
    devouring brier and thorn;
   It kindles the forest thickets,
   which go up in columns of
    smoke.
18 At the wrath of the LORD of
    hosts the land quakes,
   and the people are like fuel
    for fire;
   No man spares his brother,
   each devours the flesh of his
    neighbor.
19 Though they hack on the right,
    they are hungry;
   though they eat on the left,
    they are not filled.
20 Manasseh devours Ephraim, and
    Ephraim Manasseh;
   together they turn on Judah.
   For all this, his wrath is not
    turned back,
   his hand is still outstretched!

Social Injustice

10 Woe to those who enact
    unjust statutes
   and who write oppressive
    decrees,
2 Depriving the needy of judgment
   and robbing my people's
    poor of their rights,
   Making widows their plunder,
   and orphans their prey!

3 What will you do on the day
    of punishment,
   when ruin comes from afar?
   To whom will you flee for help?
   Where will you leave your
    wealth,
4 Lest it sink beneath the captive
   or fall beneath the slain?
   For all this, his wrath is not
    turned back,
   his hand is still outstretched!

Assyria the Unconscious Instrument of God

5 Woe to Assyria! My rod in
    anger,
   my staff in wrath.
6 Against an impious nation I
    send him,
   and against a people under my
    wrath I order him
   To seize plunder, carry off loot,
   and tread them down like the
    mud of the streets.
7 But this is not what he intends,
   nor does he have this in mind;
   Rather, it is in his heart to destroy,
   to make an end of nations
    not a few.
8 "Are not my commanders all
    kings?" he says,
9   "Is not Calno like Carchemish,
   Or Hamath like Arpad,
   or Samaria like Damascus?
10 Just as my hand reached out to
    idolatrous kingdoms
   that had more images than
    Jerusalem and Samaria,
11 Just as I treated Samaria and
    her idols,
   shall I not do to Jerusalem
    and her graven images?"
12 [But when the Lord has brought
    to an end all his work
   on Mount Zion and in
    Jerusalem,
   I will punish the utterance
   of the King of Assyria's
    proud heart,
13 and the boastfulness of his
    haughty eyes. For he says:]

"By my own power I have done
    it,
   and by my wisdom, for I am
    shrewd.

   I have moved the boundaries of
    peoples,
   their treasures I have pillaged,
   and, like a giant, I have put
    down the enthroned.
14 My hand has seized like a nest
    the riches of nations;
   As one takes eggs left alone,
   so I took in all the earth;
   No one fluttered a wing,
   or opened a mouth, or
    chirped!"

15 Will the axe boast against him
    who hews with it?
   Will the saw exalt itself above
    him who wields it?
   As if a rod could sway him who
    lifts it,
   or a staff him who is not
    wood!
16 Therefore the Lord, the LORD
    of Hosts,
   will send among his fat ones
    leanness,
   And instead of his glory there
    will be kindling
   like the kindling of fire.
17 The Light of Israel will become
    a fire,
   Israel's Holy One a flame,
   That burns and consumes his
    briers
   and his thorns in a single day.
18 His splendid forests and
    orchards
   will be consumed, soul and
    body;
19 And the remnant of the trees in
    his forest
   will be so few,
   Like poles set up for signals,
   that any boy can record them.
20 On that day
   The remnant of Israel,
   the survivors of the house of
    Jacob,
   will no more lean upon him
    who struck them;
   But they will lean upon the
    LORD,
   the Holy One of Israel, in
    truth.
21 A remnant will return, the
    remnant of Jacob,
   to the mighty God.

9, 20: *Manasseh . . . Ephraim:* two of the leading
tribes of the northern kingdom.
   10, 6f: *Impious nation:* Israel. It was God's intention to use Assyria merely to punish, not to destroy,
his people.
   10, 9: *Calno . . . Damascus:* cities captured by the
Assyrians.
   10, 16: *His fat ones:* the strong men of the king
of Assyria.
   10, 21: *A remnant will return:* in Hebrew, *shear
jashub,* an allusion to the name of Isaiah's son, Shear-
jashub; cf 7, 3.

22 For though your people, O
    Israel,
    were like the sand of the sea,
    Only a remnant of them will
        return;
    their destruction is decreed
    as overwhelming justice
    demands.

23 Yes, the destruction he has decreed, the Lord, the GOD of hosts, will carry out within the whole land. 24 Therefore thus says the Lord, the GOD of hosts: O my people, who dwell in Zion, do not fear the Assyrian, though he strikes you with a rod, and raises his staff against you. 25 For only a brief moment more, and my anger shall be over; but them I will destroy in wrath. 26 Then the LORD of hosts will raise against them a scourge such as struck Midian at the rock of Oreb; and he will raise his staff over the sea as he did against Egypt. 27 On that day.

    His burden shall be taken from
        your shoulder.
    and his yoke shattered from
        your neck.

Sennacherib's Invasion

He has come up from the
    direction of Rimmon,
28 he has reached Aiath, passed
    through Migron,
    at Michmash his supplies are
    stored.
29 They cross the ravine:
    "We will spend the night at
        Geba."
    Rama is in terror,
    Gibeah of Saul has fled.
30 Cry and shriek, O daughter of
    Gallim!
    Hearken, Laishah! Answer
    her, Anathoth!
31 Madmenah is in flight,
    the inhabitants of Gebim seek
    refuge.
32 Even today he will halt at Nob,
    he will shake his first at the
        mount of daughter Zion,
    the hill of Jerusalem!

33 Behold, the Lord, the LORD of
    hosts,
    lops off the boughs with
    terrible violence;
    The tall of stature are felled,
    and the lofty ones brought
        low;
34 The forest thickets are felled
    with the axe,
    and Lebanon in its splendor
    falls.

The Rule of Immanuel

11 But a shoot shall sprout
      from the stump of Jesse,
    and from his roots a bud
    shall blossom.
2 The spirit of the LORD shall
    rest upon him:
    a spirit of wisdom and of
    understanding,
    A spirit of counsel and of
    strength,
    a spirit of knowledge and of
    fear of the LORD,
3   and his delight shall be the
    fear of the LORD.
    Not by appearance shall he
    judge,
    nor by hearsay shall he decide,
4 But he shall judge the poor
    with justice,
    and decide aright for the
    land's afflicted.
    He shall strike the ruthless with
    the rod of his mouth,
    and with the breath of his
    lips he shall slay the
    wicked.
5 Justice shall be the band around
    his waist,
    and faithfulness a belt upon
    his hips.

6 Then the wolf shall be a guest
    of the lamb,
    and the leopard shall lie
    down with the kid;
    The calf and the young lion
    shall browse together,
    with a little child to guide
    them.

7 The cow and the bear shall be
    neighbors,
    together their young shall rest;
    the lion shall eat hay like the ox.
8 The baby shall play by the
    cobra's den,
    and the child lay his hand on
    the adder's lair.
9 There shall be no harm or ruin
    on all my holy mountain;
    for the earth shall be filled
    with knowledge of the LORD,
    as water covers the sea.

Union of Ephraim and Judah

10   On that day,
    The root of Jesse,
    set up as a signal for the
    nations,
    The Gentiles shall seek out,
    for his dwelling shall be
    glorious.
11   On that day,
    The Lord shall again take it in
    hand
    to reclaim the remnant of his
    people
    that is left from Assyria and
    Egypt,
    Pathros, Ethiopia, and Elam,
    Shinar, Hamath, and the isles
    of the sea.
12 He shall raise a signal to the
    nations
    and gather the outcasts of
    Israel;
    The dispersed of Judah he shall
    assemble
    from the four corners of the
    earth.
13 The envy of Ephraim shall pass
    away,
    and the rivalry of Judah be
    removed;
    Ephraim shall not be jealous of
    Judah,
    and Judah shall not be
    hostile to Ephraim;
14 But they shall swoop down on
    the foothills
    of the Philistines to the west,
    together they shall plunder the
    Kedemites;

10, 27–32: A poetic description of the progress of the Assyrian army, advancing from the north through Judah to the gates of Jerusalem.

10, 32ff: Just when the enemy is about to capture Jerusalem, God intervenes and destroys the hostile army.

11, 1: *Jesse:* David's father. *Shoot . . . stump:* after the Babylonian Exile only a *stump* of the Davidic dynasty will remain; from it will arise the new *shoot,* the Messianic King.

11, 2f: The source of the traditional names of the gifts of the Holy Spirit. The Septuagint and the Vulgate read "piety" for *fear of the Lord* in its first occurrence, thus listing seven gifts.

11, 6–9: This picture of the idyllic harmony of paradise is a dramatic symbol of the universal peace and justice of Messianic times.

11, 11: *Pathros . . . sea:* where God's people lived in exile. *Pathros:* upper Egypt. *Elam:* east of Babylonia. *Shinar:* Babylonia. *Hamath:* on the Orontes River in Syria. *Isles:* or coastlands, in the Mediterranean.

11, 14: *Kedemites:* tribes in the Arabian Desert.

Edom and Moab shall be their
possessions,
and the Ammonites their
subjects.
15 The LORD shall dry up the
tongue of the Sea of Egypt,
and wave his hand over the
Euphrates in his fierce anger
And shatter it into seven
streamlets,
so that it can be crossed in
sandals.
16 There shall be a highway for the
remnant of his people
that is left from Assyria,
As there was for Israel
when he came up from the land
of Egypt.

Song of Thanksgiving

12 On that day, you will say:
I give you thanks, O LORD;
though you have been angry
with me,
your anger has abated, and
you have consoled me.
2 God indeed is my savior;
I am confident and unafraid.
My strength and my courage is
the LORD,
and he has been my savior.

3 With joy you will draw water
at the fountain of salvation,
4 and say on that day:
Give thanks to the LORD, acclaim
his name;
among the nations make
known his deeds,
proclaim how exalted is his
name.
5 Sing praise to the LORD for his
glorious achievement;
let this be known throughout
all the earth.
6 Shout with exultation, O city of
Zion,
for great in your midst
is the Holy One of Israel!

ORACLES AGAINST THE PAGAN NATIONS

Babylon

13 An oracle concerning Babylon;
a vision of Isaiah, son of Amoz.

2 Upon the bar mountains set up a
signal;
cry out to them,
Wave for them to enter
the gates of the volunteers.

3 I have commanded my dedicated
soldiers,
I have summoned my warriors,
eager and bold to carry out
my anger.
4 Listen! the rumble on the
mountains:
that of an immense throng!
Listen! the noise of kingdoms,
nations assembled!
The LORD of hosts is mustering
an army for battle.
5 They come from a far-off
country,
and from the end of the
heavens,
The LORD and the instruments of
his wrath,
to destroy all the land.

6 Howl, for the day of the LORD
is near;
as destruction from the
Almighty it comes.
7 Therefore all hands fall helpless,
the bows of the young men fall
from their hands.
Every man's heart melts 8 in
terror.
pangs and sorrows take hold
of them,
like a woman in labor they
writhe;
They look aghast at each other,
their faces aflame.

9 Lo, the day of the LORD comes
cruel, with wrath and burning
anger;
To lay waste the land
and destroy the sinners within
it!

10 The stars and constellations of
the heavens
send forth no light;
The sun is dark when it rises,
and the light of the moon does
not shine.

11 Thus I will punish the world for
its evil
and the wicked for their guilt.

I will put an end to the pride of
the arrogant,
the insolence of tyrants I will
humble.
12 I will make mortals more rare
than pure gold,
men, than gold of Ophir.
13 For this I will make the heavens
tremble
and the earth shall be shaken
from its place,
At the wrath of the LORD of hosts
on the day of his burning anger.

14 Like a hunted gazelle,
or a flock that no one gathers,
Every man shall turn to his
kindred
and flee to his own land.
15 Everyone who is caught shall be
run through;
to a man, they shall fall by the
sword.
16 Their infants shall be dashed to
pieces in their sight;
their houses shall be plundered
and their wives ravished.

17 I am stirring up against them the
Medes,
who think nothing of silver
and take no delight in gold.
18 The fruit of the womb they shall
not spare,
nor shall they have eyes of pity
for children.
19 And Babylon, the jewel of
kingdoms,
the glory and pride of the
Chaldeans,
Shall be overthrown by God
like Sodom and like Gomorrah.
20 She shall never be inhabited,
nor dwelt in, from age to age;
The Arab shall not pitch his tent
there,
nor shepherds couch their
flocks

11, 15: *Tongue . . . Egypt:* the body of water
between Egypt and Palestine.
12, 1–6: Israel's thanksgiving to the Lord, expressed in language like that of the Psalms.
13, 2: *To them:* the Medes (v 17) and Persians,
who would destroy Babylon. *Gates of the volunteers:*

the mustering places of Babylon's enemies for war
against her.
13, 3: *Dedicated soldiers:* in the sense that they
will wage a "holy war" and carry out God's plan.
13, 6ff: *Day of the Lord:* described often in pro-
phetical writings, it generally signified the coming of

the Lord in power and majesty to destroy his enemies
and inaugurate his kingdom. Here it refers to the
overthrow of Babylon. The figures used convey the
idea of horror and destruction. Read vv 6–8 with
vv 14–16.
13, 12: *Ophir:* cf note to Ps 45, 10.

21 But wildcats shall rest there
    and owls shall fill the houses;
There ostriches shall dwell,
    and satyrs shall dance.
22 Desert beasts shall howl in her
    castles,
    and jackals in her luxurious
    palaces.
Her time is near at hand
    and her days shall not be
    prolonged.

The King of Babylon

14 When the LORD has pity on Jacob and again chooses Israel and settles them on their own soil, the aliens will join them and be counted with the house of Jacob. 2 The house of Israel will take them and bring them along to its place, and possess them as male and female slaves on the Lord's soil, making captives of its captors and ruling over its oppressors. 3 On the day the LORD relieves you of sorrow and unrest and the hard service in which you have been enslaved, 4 you will take up this taunt-song against the king of Babylon.

  How the oppressor has reached
    his end!
    how the turmoil is stilled!
5 The LORD has broken the rod
    of the wicked,
    the staff of the tyrants
6 That struck the peoples in wrath
    relentless blows;
That beat down the nations in
    anger,
    with oppression unchecked.
7 The whole earth rests peacefully,
    song breaks forth;
8 The very cypresses rejoice over
    you,
    and the cedars of Lebanon:
"Now that you are laid to rest,
    there will be none to cut us
    down."

9 The nether world below is all
    astir
    preparing for your coming;
It awakens the shades to greet
    you,
    all the leaders of the earth;
It has the kings of all nations
    rise from their thrones.

10 All of them speak out
    and say to you,
  "You too have become weak like
    us,
    you are the same as we.
11 Down to the nether world your
    pomp is brought,
    the music of your harps.
The couch beneath you is the
    maggot,
    your covering, the worm."

12 How have you fallen from the
    heavens,
    O morning star, son of the
    dawn!
How are you cut down to the
    ground,
    you who mowed down the
    nations!
13 You said in your heart:
    "I will scale the heavens;
Above the stars of God
    I will set up my throne;
I will take my seat on the Mount
    of Assembly,
    in the recesses of the North.
14 I will ascend above the tops of the
    clouds;
    I will be like the Most High!"
15 Yet down to the nether world you
    go
    to the recesses of the pit!

16 When they see you they will
    stare,
    pondering over you:
"Is this the man who made the
    earth tremble,
    and kingdoms quake?
17 Who made the world a desert,
    razed its cities,
    and gave his captives no
    release?
18 All the kings of the nations lie in
    glory,
    each in his own tomb;
19 But you are cast forth without
    burial,
    loathsome and corrupt,
Clothed as those slain at
    sword-point,
    a trampled corpse.
Going down to the pavement of
    the pit,
20   you will never be one with
    them in the grave."

For you have ruined your land,
    you have slain your people!
Let him not be named forever,
    that scion of an evil race!
21 Make ready to slaughter his sons
    for the guilt of their fathers;
Lest they rise and possess the
    earth,
    and fill the breadth of the
    world with tyrants.

22 I will rise up against them, says the LORD of hosts, and cut off from Babylon name and remnant, progeny and offspring, says the LORD. 23 I will make it a haunt of hoot owls and a marshland; I will sweep it with the broom of destruction, says the LORD of hosts.

Assyria

24   The LORD of hosts has sworn:
    As I have resolved,
    so shall it be;
    As I have proposed,
    so shall it stand:
25 I will break the Assyrian in my
    land
    and trample him on my
    mountains;
(8) 21 He shall pass through it
    hard-pressed and hungry,
    and in his hunger he shall
    become enraged,
    and curse his king and his gods.
He shall look upward,
    but there shall be strict
    darkness
    without any dawn;
22 He shall gaze at the earth,
    but there shall be distress and
    darkness,
    with the light blacked out by
    its clouds.
(14) 25 Then his yoke shall be
    removed from them,
    and his burden from their
    shoulder.
26 This is the plan proposed for the
    whole earth,
    and this the hand outstretched
    over all nations.
27 The LORD of hosts has planned;
    who can thwart him?
His hand is stretched out;
    who can turn it back?

13, 21: *Satyrs*: in the popular mind, demons of goatlike form dwelling in ruins, symbols of immorality; cf Lv 17, 7.

14, 4–21: This *taunt-song*, or satire, is one of the finest in the Bible.
14, 12: *Morning star*: the king of Babylon. The

Vulgate has "Lucifer," a name applied by the Church Fathers to Satan.
14, 13: *Recesses of the North*: see note on Ps 48, 3.

Philistia

28 In the year that King Ahaz died, there came this oracle:

29 Rejoice not, O Philistia, not a
　　　man of you,
　　　that the rod which smote you
　　　　　is broken;
　　For out of the serpent's root
　　　　shall come an adder,
　　　its fruit shall be a flying
　　　　saraph.
30 In my pastures the poor shall eat,
　　　and the needy lie down in
　　　　safety;
　　But I will kill your root with
　　　　famine
　　　that shall slay even your
　　　　remnant.
31 Howl, O gate; cry out, O city!
　　Philistia, all of you melts
　　　　away!
　　For there comes a smoke from
　　　　the north,
　　　without a straggler in the ranks.
32 What will one answer the
　　　messenger of the nation?
　　"The LORD has established
　　　　Zion,
　　　and in her the afflicted of his
　　　　people find refuge."

Moab

15 Oracle on Moab:
　　Laid waste in a night,
　　Ar of Moab is destroyed;
　　Laid waste in a night,
　　Kir of Moab is destroyed.
2 Up goes daughter Dibon
　　to the high places to weep;
　　Over Nebo and over Medeba
　　　Moab wails.
　　Every head is shaved,
　　　every beard sheared off.
3 In the streets they wear sackcloth,
　　　lamenting and weeping;
　　On rooftops and in the squares
　　　everyone wails.
4 Heshbon and Elealeh cry out,
　　　they are heard as far as Jahaz.
　　At this the loins of Moab
　　　tremble,
　　his soul quivers within him;

5 The heart of Moab cries out,
　　his fugitives reach Zoar
　　[Eglath-shelishiyah].
　　The ascent of Luhith
　　　they climb weeping;
　　On the way to Horonaim
　　　they utter rending cries.
6 The waters of Nimrim
　　have become a waste;
　　The grass is withered,
　　　new growth is gone,
　　　nothing is green.
7 So now whatever they have
　　　acquired or stored away
　　they carry across the Gorge of
　　　the Poplars,
8 For the cry has gone round
　　the land of Moab;
　　As far as Eglaim the wailing,
　　　and to Beer-elim, the wail.
9 The waters of Dimon are filled
　　　with blood,
　　but I will bring still more upon
　　　Dimon:
　　Lions for those who are fleeing
　　　from Moab
　　and for those who remain in
　　　the land!

16 Send them forth, hugging the
　　　earth like reptiles,
　　from Sela across the desert,
　　to the mount of daughter Zion.
2 Like flushed birds,
　　like startled nestlings,
　　Are the daughters of Moab
　　at the fords of the Arnon.
3 Offer counsel, take their part:
　　at high noon let your shadow
　　　be like the night,
　　To hide the outcasts,
　　　to conceal the fugitives.
4 Let the outcasts of Moab live
　　with you,
　　be their shelter from the
　　　destroyer.
　　When the struggle is ended, the
　　　ruin complete,
　　and they have done with
　　　trampling the land,
5 A throne shall be set up in mercy,
　　and on it shall sit in fidelity
　　[in David's tent]

A judge upholding right
　　and prompt to do justice.
6 We have heard of the pride of
　　　Moab,
　　how very proud he is,
　　With his haughty, arrogant
　　　insolence
　　that his empty words do not
　　　match.
7 Therefore Moab wails for Moab,
　　　everywhere they wail;
　　For the raisin cakes of
　　　Kir-hareseth
　　they sigh, stricken with grief.
8 The terraced slopes of Heshbon
　　　languish,
　　the vines of Sibmah,
　　Whose clusters overpowered
　　　the lords of nations,
　　While they reached as far as
　　　Jazer
　　and scattered over the desert,
　　And whose branches spread
　　　forth
　　and extended over the sea.
9 Therefore I weep with Jazer
　　for the vines of Sibmah;
　　I water you with tears,
　　　Heshbon and Elealeh;
　　For on your summer fruits and
　　　harvests
　　the battle cry has fallen.
10 From the orchards are taken
　　　away
　　joy and gladness,
　　In the vineyards there is no
　　　singing,
　　no shout of joy;
　　In the wine presses no one treads
　　　grapes,
　　the vintage shout is stilled.
11 Therefore for Moab
　　my breast moans like a lyre,
　　and my heart for Kir-hareseth.
12 When Moab grows weary on the
　　　high places,
　　he shall enter his sanctuary to
　　　pray,
　　but it shall avail him nothing.

13 This is the word the LORD
spoke against Moab in times past.

14, 28: *The year that King Ahaz died:* 715 B.C.
14, 29: *Rod:* an Assyrian oppressor whose identity is uncertain. *Flying saraph:* a poisonous serpent, distinguished by its speedy movement; cf note on Nm 21, 6.
15, 2: *Every head . . . sheared off:* traditional signs of grief.
15, 9: There is in the Hebrew a play on words: *Dimon* and *dam,* the latter signifying "blood."

16, 2: *The Arnon:* principal river of Moab.
16, 3–5: Directed to Jerusalem, which should receive the suffering Moabites with mercy, as befits the city of David's family, who were partly descended from Ruth the Moabite.
16, 7–14: Moab had been prosperous; now it has become a desert.
16, 7: *Raisin cakes:* masses of dried compressed grapes used as food (cf 2 Sm 6, 19; 1 Chr 16, 3; Ct 2,

5), and also in pagan cult (Hos 3, 1).
16, 8: *Desert:* to the east. *Sea:* the Dead Sea.
16, 12: In vain do the Moabites appeal to their god Chemosh.
16, 13f: A prose application of the preceding poetic oracle against Moab (15, 1—16, 12); cf Jer 4, 8. *Like those of a hireling:* who fulfills his period of service according to the shortest manner of reckoning; cf 21, 16.

14 But now the LORD has spoken:
In three years, like those of a hireling,
the glory of Moab shall be degraded
despite all its great multitude; there
shall be a remnant, very small and
weak.

Damascus

17 Oracle on Damascus:
Lo, Damascus shall cease to
be a city
and become a ruin;
2 Her cities shall be forever
abandoned,
given over to flocks to lie in
undisturbed.
3 The fortress shall be lost to
Ephraim
and the kingdom to Damascus;
The remnant of Aram shall have
the same glory
as the Israelites,
says the LORD of hosts.
4   On that day
The glory of Jacob shall fade,
and his full body grow thin,
5 Like the reaper's mere armful of
stalks
when he gathers the standing
grain;
Or as when one gleans the ears
in the valley of Rephaim.
6 Only a scattering of grapes shall
be left!
As when an olive tree has been
beaten,
Two or three olives remain at the
the very top,
four or five on its fruitful
branches,
says the LORD, the God of
Israel.

7 On that day man shall look to his
maker,
his eyes turned toward the
Holy One of Israel.
8 He shall not look to the altars,
his handiwork,
nor shall he regard what his
fingers have made:
the sacred poles or the incense
stands.

9 On that day his strong cities shall
be
like those abandoned by the
Hivites and Amorites
When faced with the children of
Israel:
they shall be laid waste.
10 For you have forgotten God,
your savior,
and remembered not the Rock,
your strength.
Therefore, though you plant
your pagan plants
and set out your foreign vine
slips,
11 Though you make them grow the
day you plant them
and make your sprouts
blossom on the next morning,
The harvest shall disappear on the
day of the grievous blow,
the incurable blight.

12 Ah! the roaring of many peoples
that roar like the roar of the
seas!
The surging of nations
that surge like the surging of
mighty waves!
13 But God shall rebuke them,
and they shall flee far away;
Windswept, like chaff on the
mountains,
like tumbleweed in a storm.
14 In the evening, they spread
terror,
before morning, they are gone!
Such is the portion of those who
despoil us,
the lot of those who plunder us.

Ethiopia

18 Ah, land of buzzing insects,
beyond the rivers of
Ethiopia,
2 Sending ambassadors by sea,
in papyrus boats on the waters!
Go, swift messengers,
to a nation tall and bronzed,
To a people dreaded near and far,
a nation strong and
conquering,
whose land is washed by rivers.

3 All you who inhabit the world,
who dwells on earth,
When the signal is raised on the
mountain, look!
When the trumpet blows,
listen!
4 For thus says the LORD to me:
I will quietly look on from
where I dwell,
Like the glowing heat of
sunshine,
like a cloud of dew at harvest
time.
5 Before the vintage, when the
flowering is ended,
and the blooms are succeeded
by ripening grapes,
Then comes the cutting of
branches with pruning
hooks
and the discarding of the
lopped-off shoots.
6 They shall all be left to the
mountain birds of prey,
and to the beasts in the land;
The birds of prey shall summer
on them
and on them all the beasts of
the earth shall winter.

7 Then will gifts be brought to the
LORD of hosts from a people tall and
bronzed, from a people dreaded
near and far, a nation strong and
conquering, whose land is washed
by rivers—to Mount Zion where
dwells the name of the LORD of hosts.

Egypt

19 Oracle on Egypt:
See, the LORD is riding on a
swift cloud
on his way to Egypt;
The idols of Egypt tremble
before him,
the hearts of the Egyptians
melt within them.
2 I will rouse Egypt against Egypt:
brother will war against
brother,
Neighbor against neighbor,
city against city, kingdom
against kingdom.

17, 1: *Damascus:* capital of Syria, destroyed in 732 B.C.

17, 3: *Ephraim:* Israel, leagued with Syria against Assyria and Judah; destroyed in 721 B.C. *Aram:* Syria.

17, 5: *Valley of Rephaim:* a fertile plain to the southwest of Jerusalem; cf Jos 15, 8; 2 Sm 5, 18.

17, 6: Olives not easily picked by hand were knocked from the tree by means of a long stick; cf 24, 13.

17, 8: *Sacred poles:* see note on Ex 34, 13. *Incense stands:* small altars on which incense was burned in idolatrous worship; cf 27, 9; Lv 26, 30.

17, 10: *Pagan plants:* literally, "plants of delights," understood by some as planted in honor of the god of fertility.

17, 12f: *Many peoples:* the hordes that accompanied the invading Assyrians, whom God repels just as he vanquished the primeval waters of chaos; see

notes on Jb 3, 8; 7, 12; Ps 89, 11.

18, 1: *Land of buzzing insects:* the region of the Upper Nile where these multiplied with great rapidity.

18, 1f: *Papyrus boats:* light and serviceable vessels made of bundles of papyrus stalks and sealed with pitch. Egypt, ruled by a dynasty from *Ethiopia*, had invited Judah to join a coalition against Assyria, but Isaiah bade the *ambassadors* return to their own people.

3 The courage of the Egyptians
    ebbs away within them,
  and I will bring to nought
    their counsel;
  They shall consult idols and
    charmers,
    ghosts and spirits.
4 I will deliver Egypt
  into the power of a cruel
    master,
  A harsh king who shall rule over
    them,
  says the Lord, the LORD of
    hosts.
5 The water shall be drained from
    the sea,
  the river shall shrivel and dry up;
6 Its streams shall become foul,
  and the canals of Egypt shall
    dwindle and dry up.
  Reeds and rushes shall wither
    away,
7   and bulrushes on the bank of
    the Nile;
  All the sown land along the Nile
    shall dry up and blow away,
    and be no more.
8 The fishermen shall mourn and
    lament,
  all who cast hook in the Nile;
  Those who spread their nets in
    the water
    shall pine away.
9 The linen-workers shall be
    disappointed,
    the combers and weavers shall
    turn pale;
10 The spinners shall be crushed,
    all the hired laborers shall be
    despondent.

11 Utter fools are the princes of
    Zoan!
  the wisest of Pharaoh's
    advisers give stupid counsel.
  How can you say to Pharaoh,
  "I am a disciple of wise men,
    of ancient kings?"
12 Where then are your wise men?
  Let them tell you and make
    known
  What the LORD of hosts has
    planned
    against Egypt.

13 The princes of Zoan have become
    fools,
  the princes of Memphis have
    been deceived.
  The chiefs of her tribes
  have led Egypt astray.
14 The LORD has prepared among
    them
    a spirit of dizziness,
  And they have made Egypt
    stagger in whatever she does,
  as a drunkard staggers in his
    vomit.
15 Egypt shall have no work to do
    for head or tail, palm branch
    or reed.

16 On that day the Egyptians
shall be like women, trembling with
fear, because of the LORD of hosts
shaking his fist at them. 17 And
the land of Judah shall be a terror to
the Egyptians. Every time they
remember Judah, they shall stand
in dread because of the plan which
the LORD of hosts has in mind for
them.
18 On that day there shall be five
cities in the land of Egypt speaking
the language of Canaan and swearing
by the LORD of hosts; one shall be
called "City of the Sun."
19 On that day there shall be an
altar to the LORD in the land of
Egypt, and a sacred pillar to the
LORD near the boundary. 20 It
shall be a sign and a witness to the
LORD of hosts in the land of Egypt,
when they cry out to the LORD against
oppressors, and he sends them a
savior to defend and deliver them.
21 The LORD shall make himself
known to Egypt, and the Egyptians
shall know the LORD in that day;
they shall offer sacrifices and oblations, and fulfill the vows they make
to the LORD. 22 Although the LORD
shall smite Egypt severely, he shall
heal them; they shall turn to the
LORD and he shall be won over and
heal them.
23 On that day there shall be a
highway from Egypt to Assyria; the
Assyrians shall enter Egypt, and the
Egyptians enter Assyria, and Egypt
shall serve Assyria.
24 On that day Israel shall be a
third party with Egypt and Assyria, a
blessing in the midst of the land, 25
when the LORD of hosts blesses it:
"Blessed be my people Egypt, and
the work of my hands Assyria, and
my inheritance, Israel."

Captivity of Egypt and Ethiopia

20 In the year the general sent by
Sargon, king of Assyria, fought
against Ashdod and captured it, 2
the LORD gave a warning through
Isaiah, the son of Amoz: Go and
take off the sackcloth from your
waist, and remove the sandals from
your feet. This he did, walking naked
and barefoot. 3 Then the LORD
said: Just as my servant Isaiah has
gone naked and barefoot for three
years as a sign and portent against
Egypt and Ethiopia, 4 so shall the
king of Assyria lead away captives
from Egypt, and exiles from Ethiopia, young and old, naked and
barefoot, with buttocks uncovered
[the shame of Egypt]. 5 They shall
be dismayed and ashamed because of
Ethiopia, their hope, and because of
Egypt, their boast. 6 The inhabitants of this coastland shall say on
that day, "Look at our hope! We
have fled here for help and deliverance from the king of Assyria; where
can we flee now?"

Fall of Babylon

21 Oracle on the wastelands
    by the sea:
  Like whirlwinds sweeping in
    waves through the Negeb,
    there comes from the desert,
    from the fearful land,
2 A cruel sight, revealed to me:
    the traitor betrays,
    the despoiler spoils.
  "Go up, Elam; besiege, O
    Media;
    I will put an end to all
    groaning!"

19, 4: *Cruel master:* the king of Assyria.
19, 11.13: *Zoan,* later known as Tanis, and *Memphis* (in Hebrew *Noph*) were the key cities of the Nile Delta.
19, 15: *Head or tail, palm branch or reed:* the leaders or the people, cf 9, 13f.
19, 18: *Five cities:* colonies of Jews living together

and speaking their languages, Hebrew and Aramaic; cf Jer, chap. 43. *City of the Sun:* the meaning is uncertain, but the reference seems to be to the city known later as Heliopolis.
20, 2–6: The symbolic act of the prophet conveyed the idea that Assyria would lead captive the Egyptians and Ethiopians. The Judeans and their allies would

then realize the folly of having trusted in them.
21, 1: *Wastelands by the sea:* Babylonia. *Negeb:* the desert south of Judah.
21, 2: *Elam . . . Media:* nations which, under the leadership of Cyrus, captured Babylon in 538 B.C. *End to all groaning:* those who were captives of Baby-lon shall be freed.

3 Therefore my loins are filled with
     anguish,
   pangs have seized me like
     those of a woman in labor;
   I am too bewildered to hear,
   too dismayed to look.
4 My mind reels,
   shuddering assails me;
   My yearning for twilight
   has turned into dread.
5 They set the table,
   spread out the rugs;
   they eat, they drink.
   Rise up, O princes,
   oil the shield!

6 For thus says my Lord to me:
   Go, station a watchman,
   let him tell what he sees.
7 If he sees a chariot,
   a pair of horses,
   Someone riding an ass,
     someone riding a camel,
   Then let him pay heed,
     very close heed.
8 Then the watchman cried,
   "On the watchtower, O my Lord,
   I stand constantly by day;
   And I stay at my post
     through all the watches of the
     night.
9 Here he comes now:
   a single chariot,
     a pair of horses;
   He calls out and says,
   'Fallen, fallen is Babylon,
   And all the images of her gods
     are smashed to the ground.'"

10 O my people who have been
     threshed,
   beaten on my threshing floor!
   What I have heard
     from the LORD of hosts,
   The God of Israel,
   I have announced to you.

Edom

11 Oracle on Edom:
   They call to me from Seir,
   "Watchman, how much longer
     the night?
   Watchman, how much longer
     the night?"

12 The watchman replies,
   "Morning has come, and again
     night.
   If you will ask, ask; come
     back again."

Arabia

13 Oracle on Arabia:
   In the thicket in the nomad
     country spend the night,
   O caravans of Dedanites.
14 Meet the thirsty, bring them
     water;
   you who dwell in the land of
     Tema,
   greet the fugitives with bread.
15 They flee from the sword,
   from the whetted sword;
   From the taut bow,
   from the fury of battle.

16 For thus says the Lord to me: In
another year, like those of a hireling,
all the glory of Kedar shall come to
an end. 17 Few of Kedar's stalwart
archers shall remain, for the LORD,
the God of Israel, has spoken.

Jerusalem

22 Oracle of the Valley of
     Vision:
   What is the matter with you
     now, that you have gone up,
     all of you, to the housetops,
2 O city full of noise and chaos,
   O wanton town!
   Your slain are not slain with
     the sword,
   nor killed in battle.
3 All your leaders fled away
     together,
   fled afar off;
   All who were in you were
     captured together,
   captured without the use of a
     bow.
4 At this I say: Turn away from
     me,
   let me weep bitterly;
   Do not try to comfort me
   for the ruin of the daughter of
     my people.

5 It is a day of panic, rout and
     confusion,
   from the Lord, the GOD of
     hosts, in the Valley of Vision.
   Walls crash;
   they cry for help to the
     mountains.
6 Elam takes up the quivers,
   Aram mounts the horses,
   and Kir uncovers the shields.
7 Your choice valleys are filled
     with chariots,
   and horses are posted at the
     gates,
8 and shelter over Judah is
     removed.

   On that day you looked to the
weapons in the House of the Forest;
9 you saw that the breaches in the
City of David were many; you collected the water of the lower pool.
10 You numbered the houses of
Jerusalem, tearing some down to
strengthen the wall; 11 you made a
reservoir between the two walls for
the water of the old pool. But you did
not look to the city's Maker, nor did
you consider him who built it long
ago.

12 On that day the Lord,
   the GOD of hosts, called on you
   To weep and mourn,
   to shave your head and put on
     sackcloth.
13 But look! you feast and
     celebrate,
   you slaughter oxen and
     butcher sheep,
   You eat meat and drink wine:
   "Eat and drink, for tomorrow
     we die!"
14 This reaches the ears of the
     LORD of hosts—
   You shall not be pardoned
     this wickedness till you die,
   says the Lord, the GOD of hosts.

Shebna and Eliakim

15 Thus says the Lord, the GOD of
     hosts:
   Up, go to that official,
   Shebna, master of the palace,

21, 5: Babylon is destroyed while its leaders are feasting; cf Dn 5. Oil the shield: shields were oiled and greased so as to divert blows more easily.
21, 11f: Seir: another name for Edom. The Edomites ask the prophet how much longer they must suffer (the night of suffering); he answers ambiguously: "Liberation (morning) and further suffering (night)," but perhaps they will later receive a more encouraging answer (ask; come back again).
21, 13f: Arabia: that is, the nomad country. Dedanites: an Arab tribe associated with Edom and Tema, and living east of the Red Sea; cf Gn 10, 7; 25, 3; Jer 25, 23.
21, 16: Year . . . of a hireling: see note on 16, 14. Kedar: a nomad tribe in Arabia; cf 42, 11; 60, 7; Ps 120, 5.
22, 1-8: Valley of Vision: while the people live in revelry and disorder, the prophet foresees the impending doom of the city.
22, 6: Elam, Aram, Kir: all allies of Assyria. Kir: perhaps the same people referred to in Am 1, 5.
22, 8-11: Defense measures, in which the inhabi-tants of Jerusalem placed their trust instead of relying on God. House of the Forest: an armory built by Solomon; its columns of wood suggested the trees of a forest; cf 1 Kgs 7, 2; 10, 17.
22, 15: Shebna: referred to as the scribe in 36, 3.

16 Who has hewn for himself a
 sepulcher on a height
 and carved his tomb in the
 rock:
 "What are you doing here, and
  what people have you here,
 that here you have hewn for
  yourself a tomb?"
17 The LORD shall hurl you down
 headlong, mortal man!
 He shall grip you firmly
18 And roll you up and toss you
 like a ball
 into an open land
 To perish there, you and the
 chariots you glory in,
 you disgrace to your master's
 house!
19 I will thrust you from your
 office
 and pull you down from your
 station.

20 On that day I will summon my
 servant
 Eliakim, son of Hilkiah;
21 I will clothe him with your robe,
 and gird him with your sash,
 and give over to him your
 authority.
 He shall be a father to the
 inhabitants of Jerusalem,
 and to the house of Judah.
22 I will place the key of the
 House of David on his
 shoulder;
 when he opens, no one shall
 shut,
 when he shuts, no one shall
 open.
23 I will fix him like a peg in a
 sure spot,
 to be a place of honor for his
 family;
24 On him shall hang all the glory
 of his family:
 descendants and offspring,
 all the little dishes, from
 bowls to jugs.

25 On that day, says the LORD of
hosts, the peg fixed in a sure spot
shall give way, break off and fall, and
the weight that hung on it shall be
done away with; for the LORD has
spoken.

Tyre and Sidon

23 Oracle on Tyre:
 Wail, O ships of Tarshish,
 for your port is destroyed;
 From the land of the Kittim
 the news reaches them.
2 Silence! you who dwell on the
 coast,
 you merchants of Sidon,
 Whose messengers crossed the
 sea
3 over the deep waters.
 The grain of Shihor, the harvest
 of the Nile, was her revenue,
 and she the merchant among
 nations.
4 Shame, O Sidon, fortress on the
 sea,
 for the sea has spoken:
 "I have not been in labor, nor
 given birth,
 nor raised young men,
 nor reared virgins."
5 When it is heard in Egypt
 they shall be in anguish at the
 news of Tyre.
6 Pass over to Tarshish, wailing,
 you who dwell on the coast!
7 Is this your wanton city,
 whose origin is from of old,
 Whose feet have taken her
 to dwell in distant lands?
8 Who has planned such a thing
 against Tyre, the bestower of
 crowns,
 Whose merchants are princes,
 whose traders are the earth's
 honored men?
9 The LORD of hosts has planned
 it,
 to disgrace all pride of majesty,
 to degrade all the earth's
 honored men.
10 Cross to your own land,
 O ship of Tarshish;
 the harbor is no more.
11 His hand he stretches out over
 the sea,
 he shakes kingdoms;
The LORD has ordered the
 destruction
 of Canaan's strongholds.
12 You shall exult no more, he
 says,
 you who are now oppressed,
 virgin daughter Sidon.
 Arise, pass over to the Kittim,
 even there you shall find no
 rest.

13 [This people is the land of the
Chaldeans, not Assyria.]

 She whom the impious founded,
 setting up towers for her,
 Has had her castles destroyed,
 and has been turned into a
 ruin.
14 Lament, O ships of Tarshish,
 for your haven is destroyed.

15 On that day, Tyre shall be
forgotten for seventy years. With the
days of another king, at the end of
seventy years, it shall be for Tyre as
in the song about the harlot:

16 Take a harp, go about the city,
 O forgotten harlot;
 Pluck the strings skillfully, sing
 many songs,
 that they may remember you.

17 At the end of the seventy years
the LORD shall visit Tyre. She shall
return to her hire and deal with all
the world's kingdoms on the face of
the earth. 18 But her merchandise
and her hire shall be sacred to the
LORD. It shall not be stored up or laid
away, but from her merchandise
those who dwell before the LORD
shall eat their fill and clothe themselves in choice attire.

APOCALYPSE OF ISAIAH

Devastation of the World:
A Remnant Saved

24 Lo, the LORD empties the
 land and lays it waste;
 he turns it upside down,
 scattering its inhabitants:

22, 20: *Eliakim:* also referred to in 36, 3; he is described as loyal to God.
22, 22: *Key:* symbol of authority; cf Mt 16, 19; Rv 3, 7.
22, 24f: If Eliakim should anger God, he and his family (compared here to dishes, bowls and jugs) will suffer disaster.
23, 1–4.12ff: these verses refer to Sidon, vv 5–11 to Tyre.

23, 1: *Kittim:* Cyprus.
23, 3: *Shihor:* a synonym for the Nile.
23, 4: *The sea* brings to distant coasts the news that Sidon must disown her children; her people are dispersed.
23, 11: *Canaan's strongholds:* the fortresses of Phoenicia.
23, 13: The gloss here identifies *she whom the impious founded* with *the land of the Chaldeans.*

23, 15: *Seventy years:* a conventional period of time indicating simply a long disaster; cf Jer 25, 11 and 29, 10.
23, 18: Describes the conversion of Tyre.
24, 1–27, 13: This section, probably composed at a later date, contains oracles on the day of the Lord, combined with hymns of thanksgiving and of supplication.

2 Layman and priest alike,
    servant and master,
  The maid as her mistress,
    the buyer as the seller,
  The lender as the borrower,
    the creditor as the debtor.
3 The earth is utterly laid waste,
    utterly stripped,
  for the LORD has decreed this
    thing.
4 The earth mourns and fades,
    the world languishes and
    fades;
  both heaven and earth
    languish.
5 The earth is polluted because of
    its inhabitants,
  who have transgressed laws,
    violated statutes,
  broken the ancient covenant.
6 Therefore a curse devours the
    earth,
  and its inhabitants pay for
    their guilt;
  Therefore they who dwell on
    earth turn pale,
  and few men are left.
7 The wine mourns, the vine
    languishes,
  all the merry-hearted groan.
8 Stilled are the cheerful timbrels,
    ended the shouts of the
    jubilant,
  stilled is the cheerful harp.
9 They cannot sing and drink
    wine;
  strong drink is bitter to those
    who partake of it.
10 Broken down is the city of
    chaos,
  shut against entry, every
    house.
11 In the streets they cry out for
    lack of wine;
  all joy has disappeared
  and cheer has left the land.
12 In the city nothing remains but
    ruin;
  its gates are battered desolate.
13 Thus it is within the land,
    and among the peoples,
  As with an olive tree after it is
    beaten,
  as with a gleaning when the
    vintage is done.

14 These lift up their voice in
    acclaim;
  from the sea they proclaim
    the majesty of the LORD:
15 "For this, in the coastlands,
    give glory to the LORD!
  In the coastlands of the sea,
    to the name of the LORD, the
    God of Israel!"
16 From the end of the earth we
    hear songs:
  "Splendor to the Just One!"
  But I said, "I am wasted, wasted
    away.
  Woe is me! The traitors
    betray:
  with treachery have the
    traitors betrayed!
17 Terror, pit, and trap
    are upon you, inhabitant of
    the earth;
18 He who flees at the sound of
    terror
  will fall into the pit;
  He who climbs out of the pit
    will be caught in the trap.
  For the windows on high will be
    opened
  and the foundations of the
    earth will shake.
19 The earth will burst asunder,
    the earth will be shaken apart,
    the earth will be convulsed.
20 The earth will reel like a
    drunkard,
  and it will sway like a hut;
  Its rebellion will weigh it down,
    until it falls, never to rise
    again."

21 On that day the LORD will
    punish
  the host of the heavens in the
    heavens,
  and the kings of the earth on
    the earth.
22 They will be gathered together
    like prisoners into a pit;
  They will be shut up in a
    dungeon,
  and after many days they will
    be punished.
23 Then the moon will blush
    and the sun grow pale,

For the LORD of hosts will reign
    on Mount Zion and in
    Jerusalem,
  glorious in the sight of his elders.

25 O LORD, you are my God,
    I will extol you and praise
    your name;
  For you have fulfilled your
    wonderful plans of old,
    faithful and true.
2 For you have made the city a
    heap,
  the fortified city a ruin;
  The castle of the insolent is a
    city no more,
    nor ever to be rebuilt.
3 Therefore a strong people will
    honor you,
  fierce nations will fear you.
4 For you are a refuge to the poor,
    a refuge to the needy in
    distress;
  Shelter from the rain,
    shade from the heat.
  As with the cold rain,
5   as with the desert heat,
    even so you quell the uproar
    of the wanton.
6 On this mountain the LORD of
    hosts
  will provide for all peoples
  A feast of rich food and choice
    wines,
  juicy, rich food and pure,
    choice wines.
7 On this mountain he will destroy
    the veil that veils all peoples,
  The web that is woven over all
    nations;
8   he will destroy death forever.
  The Lord GOD will wipe away
    the tears from all faces;
  The reproach of his people he
    will remove
  from the whole earth; for the
    LORD has spoken.

9   On that day it will be said:
  "Behold our God, to whom we
    looked to save us!
  This is the LORD for whom we
    looked;
  let us rejoice and be glad that
    he has saved us!"

24, 5: *Ancient covenant:* God's commandments to
all mankind.
24, 10: *City of chaos:* a symbol of godlessness as
opposed to Jerusalem, the city of God.

24, 14: *These:* the saved.
24, 21: *Host of the heavens:* the stars, which were
regarded by the pagans as gods; cf Dt 4, 19; Jer 8, 2.
24, 23: *His elders:* the heavenly courtiers sur-

rounding the throne of God.
25, 1–8: Victory in Messianic times.
25, 6: *This mountain:* Zion, symbol of the heavenly
Jerusalem.

10 For the hand of the LORD will
       rest on this mountain,
   but Moab will be trodden
       down
   as a straw is trodden down in
       the mire.
11 He will stretch forth his hands
       in Moab
   as a swimmer extends his
       hands to swim;
   He will bring low their pride
   as his hands sweep over them.
12 The high-walled fortress he will
       raze,
   and strike it down level with
       the earth, with the very dust.

The Divine Vindicator

26 On that day they will sing this
       song in the land of Judah:

   "A strong city have we;
       he sets up walls and ramparts
       to protect us.
2 Open up the gates
       to let in a nation that is just,
       one that keeps faith.
3 A nation of firm purpose you
       keep in peace;
   in peace, for its trust in you."

4 Trust in the LORD forever!
       For the LORD is an eternal
       Rock.
5 He humbles those in high places,
       and the lofty city he brings
       down;
   He tumbles it to the ground,
       levels it with the dust.
6 It is trampled underfoot by the
       needy,
   by the footsteps of the poor.
7 The way of the just is smooth;
       the path of the just you make
       level.
8 Yes, for your way and your
       judgments, O LORD,
   we look to you;
   Your name and your title
       are the desire of our souls.
9 My soul yearns for you in the
       night,
   yes, my spirit within me keeps
       vigil for you;
   When your judgment dawns
       upon the earth,
   the world's inhabitants learn
       justice.

10 The wicked man, spared, does
       not learn justice;
   in an upright land he acts
       perversely,
   and sees not the majesty of
       the LORD.
11 O LORD, your hand is uplifted,
       but they behold it not;
   Let them be shamed when they
       see
   your zeal for your people:
   let the fire prepared for your
       enemies consume them.
12 O LORD, you mete out peace to
       us,
   for it is you who have
       accomplished all we have
       done.
13 O LORD, our God, other lords
       than you have ruled us;
   it is from you only that we
       can call upon your name.

14 Dead they are, they have no
       life,
   shades that cannot rise;
   For you have punished and
       destroyed them,
   and wiped out all memory of
       them.
15 You have increased the nation,
       O LORD,
   increased the nation to your
       own glory,
   and extended far all the
       borders of the land.
16 O LORD, oppressed by your
       punishment,
   we cried out in anguish under
       your chastising.
17 As a woman about to give birth
       writhes and cries out in her
       pains,
   so were we in your presence,
       O LORD.
18 We conceived and writhed in
       pain,
   giving birth to wind;
   Salvation we have not achieved
       for the earth,
   the inhabitants of the world
       cannot bring it forth.
19 But your dead shall live, their
       corpses shall rise;
   awake and sing, you who lie
       in the dust.

For your dew is a dew of light,
   and the land of shades gives
       birth.

Day of the Lord: Reward and Punishment

20 Go, my people, enter your
       chambers,
   and close your doors behind
       you;
   Hide yourselves for a brief
       moment,
   until the wrath is past.
21 See, the LORD goes forth from
       his place,
   to punish the wickedness of
       the earth's inhabitants;
   The earth will reveal the blood
       upon her,
   and no longer conceal her
       slain.

27 On that day,
   The LORD will punish with
       his sword
   that is cruel, great, and
       strong,
   Leviathan the fleeing serpent,
   Leviathan the coiled serpent;
   and he will slay the dragon
       that is in the sea.

2 On that day—
   The pleasant vineyard, sing
       about it!
3 I, the LORD, am its keeper,
       I water it every moment;
   Lest anyone harm it,
       night and day I guard it.
4 I am not angry,
       but if I were to find briers and
       thorns,
   In battle I should march against
       them;
   I should burn them all.
8 Expunging and expelling, I
       should strive against them,
   carrying them off with my
       cruel wind in time of storm.

6 In days to come Jacob shall
       take root,
   Israel shall sprout and
       blossom,
   covering all the world with
       fruit.

25, 10: *Moab:* symbol of God's enemies.
26, 19: This verse refers to the restoration of Israel

in Messianic times under the figure of the resurrection
of the dead; cf Ez, chap. 37.

27, 1: *Leviathan . . . dragon:* symbols of the forces
of evil which God vanquishes even as he overcame
primeval chaos; cf notes on Jb 3, 8; 7, 12.

7 Is he to be smitten as his smiter
     was smitten?
    or slain as his slayer was slain?
5 Or shall he cling to me for
    refuge?
    He must make peace with me;
    peace shall he make with me!
9 This, then, shall be the
    expiation of Jacob's guilt,
    this the whole fruit of the
    removal of his sin:
    He shall pulverize all the stones
    of the altars
    like pieces of chalk;
    no sacred poles or incense
    altars shall stand.

10 For the fortified city shall be
    desolate,
    an abandoned pasture, a
    forsaken wilderness,
    where calves shall browse and
    lie.
    Its boughs shall be destroyed,
11   its branches shall wither and
    be broken off,
    and women shall come to
    build a fire with them.
    This is not an understanding
    people;
    therefore their maker shall not
    spare them,
    nor shall he who formed them
    have mercy on them.

12   On that day,
    The LORD shall beat out the
    grain
    between the Euphrates and
    the Wadi of Egypt,
    and you shall be gleaned one
    by one, O sons of Israel.

13   On that day,
    A great trumpet shall blow,
    and the lost in the land of
    Assyria
    and the outcasts in the land of
    Egypt

Shall come and worship the
    LORD
    on the holy mountain, in
    Jerusalem.

THE LORD ALONE, ISRAEL'S AND JUDAH'S SALVATION

The Fate of Samaria

28 Woe to the majestic garland
    of the drunkard Ephraim,
to the fading blooms of his
    glorious beauty,
    on the head of him who is
    stupefied with wine.
2 Behold, the LORD has a strong
    one and a mighty,
    who, like a downpour of hail,
    a destructive storm,
    Like a flood of water, great and
    overflowing,
    levels to the ground with
    violence;
3 With feet that will trample
    the majestic garland of the
    drunkard Ephraim.
4 The fading blooms of his
    glorious beauty
    on the head of the fertile
    valley
    Will be like an early fig before
    summer:
    when a man sees it,
    he picks and swallows it at
    once.

5 On that day the LORD of hosts
    will be a glorious crown
    And a brilliant diadem
    to the remnant of his people,
6 A spirit of justice
    to him who sits in judgment,
    And strength to those
    who turn back the battle at
    the gate.

Against Judah

7 But these also stagger from wine
    and stumble from strong
    drink:

Priest and prophet stagger from
    strong drink,
    overpowered by wine;
    Led astray by strong drink,
    staggering in their visions,
    tottering when giving
    judgment.
8 Yes, all the tables
    are covered with filthy vomit,
    with no place left clean.
9 "To whom would he impart
    knowledge?
    To whom would he convey
    the message?
    To those just weaned from milk,
    those taken from the beast?
    10 For he says,
    'Command on command,
    command on command,
    rule on rule, rule on rule,
    here a little, there a little!'"
11 Yes, with stammering lips and
    in a strange language
    he will speak to this people
12   to whom he said:
    This is the resting place,
    give rest to the weary;
    Here is repose—
    but they would not listen.
13 So for them the word of the
    LORD shall be:
    "Command on command,
    command on command,
    Rule on rule, rule on rule,
    here a little, there a little!"
    So that when they walk, they
    stumble backward,
    broken, ensnared, and
    captured.

14 Therefore, hear the word of the
    LORD, you arrogant,
    who rule this people in
    Jerusalem:
15 Because you say, "We have
    made a covenant with death,
    and with the nether world we
    have made a pact;
    When the overwhelming scourge
    passes,
    it will not reach us;

27, 5.9: Israel will *make peace with* God and destroy all signs of idolatrous worship.

27, 7: God's people will not be treated as sternly as were their enemies.

27, 10f: *The fortified city:* symbol of the powers of evil; see note on 24, 10.

27, 12: *The Euphrates and the Wadi of Egypt:* the ideal borders of Israel; cf Gn 15, 18; 2 Kgs 24, 7.

27, 13: The triumph of God's people is described in eschatological language; they will gather in Jerusalem from *Assyria* and *Egypt.*

28, 1: *Ephraim:* the northern kingdom. Its capital, Samaria, was built upon a hill, suggestive of a *majestic garland* adorning the head of the drunken kingdom.

28, 2: *A strong one and a mighty:* Assyria.

28, 9f: The words of those who ridicule Isaiah. The Hebrew of v 10, by its very sound, conveys the idea of mocking imitation of what the prophet says, as though he spoke like a stammering child: *SAU LASAU, SAU LASAU, CAU LACAU, CAU LACAU, ZE'ER SHAM, ZE'ER SHAM.* But in v 13 God

repeats these words in deadly earnest, putting them in the mouth of the victorious pagan army.

28, 11: God will answer the mockers and defend Isaiah. *Strange language:* spoken by the invading army.

28, 15.18: *A covenant with death, and with the nether world:* an alliance with foreign powers, such as Egypt and Babylon, to prevent death and destruction. *Have made lies . . . a hiding place:* this confidence in human aid proves to be false and deceitful, incapable of averting the dreaded disaster. *Overwhelming scourge:* the flood of the Assyrian invasion; cf 8, 7f.

For we have made lies our
  refuge,
and in falsehood we have
  found a hiding place,"—

16   Therefore, thus says the
      Lord God:
  See, I am laying a stone
    in Zion,
  a stone that has been
    tested,
A precious cornerstone as
  a sure foundation;
  he who puts his faith in
    it shall not be shaken.

17   I will make of right a
      measuring line,
    of justice a level.—
Hail shall sweep away the refuge
  of lies,
  and waters shall flood the
    hiding place.

18 Your covenant with death shall
    be canceled
  and your pact with the nether
    world shall not stand.
When the overwhelming scourge
  passes,
  you shall be trampled down
    by it.

19 Whenever it passes, it shall take
    you;
  morning after morning it shall
    pass,
By day and by night;
  terror alone shall convey the
    message.

20 For the bed shall be too short
    to stretch out in,
  and the cover too narrow to
    wrap in.

21 For the Lord shall rise up as on
    Mount Perazim,
  bestir himself as in the valley
    of Gibeon,
To carry out his work, his
  singular work,
  to perform his deed, his
    strange deed.

22 Now, be arrogant no more
    lest your bonds be tightened,
For I have heard from the Lord,
  the God of hosts,

the destruction decreed for the
  whole earth.

23 Give ear and hear my voice,
    pay attention and listen to
    what I say:

24 Is the plowman forever plowing,
    always loosening and
    harrowing his land for
    planting?

25 When he has leveled the surface,
    does he not scatter gith and
    sow cumin,
  Put in wheat and barley,
    with spelt as its border?

26 He has learned this rule,
    instructed by his God.

27 Gith is not threshed with a sledge,
    nor does a cartwheel roll over
    cumin.
  But gith is beaten out with a staff,
    and cumin crushed for food
    with a rod.

28 No, he does not thresh it
    unendingly,
  nor does he crush it
    with his noisy cartwheels and
    horses.

29 This too comes from the Lord
    of hosts;
  wonderful is his counsel and
    great his wisdom.

The Fall of Jerusalem

29 Woe to Ariel, Ariel,
    the city where David
      encamped!
  Add year to year,
    let the feasts come round.

2 But I will bring distress upon
    Ariel,
  with mourning and grief.
  You shall be to me like Ariel,

3   I will encamp like David
    against you;
  I will encircle you with outposts
    and set up siege works against
    you.

4 Prostrate you shall speak from
    the earth,
  and from the base dust your
    words shall come.

Your voice shall be like a
  ghost's from the earth,
  and your words like chirping
    from the dust.

5 The horde of your arrogant
    shall be like fine dust,
  the horde of the tyrants like
    flying chaff.
Then suddenly, in an instant,

6   you shall be visited by the
    Lord of hosts,
With thunder, earthquake, and
  great noise,
  whirlwind, storm, and the
    flame of consuming fire.

7 Then like a dream,
    a vision in the night,
Shall be the horde of all the
  nations
  who war against Ariel
  with all the earthworks of her
    besiegers.

8 As when a hungry man dreams
    he is eating
  and awakens with an empty
    stomach,
Or when a thirsty man dreams
  he is drinking
  and awakens faint and dry,
So shall the horde of all the
  nations be,
  who make war against Zion.

Blindness and Perversity

9 Be irresolute, stupefied;
    blind yourselves and stay
    blind!
  Be drunk, but not from wine,
    stagger, but not from strong
    drink!

10 For the Lord has poured out
    on you
  a spirit of deep sleep.
He has shut your eyes [the
  prophets]
  and covered your heads [the
    seers].

11 For you the revelation of all
this has become like the words of a
sealed scroll. When it is handed to
one who can read, with the request,

28, 16: *A stone in Zion:* the true and *sure founda-tion* of salvation promised by God to the Davidic dynasty (cf 7, 13–16; 9, 1–6), which the Apostles saw fulfilled in Christ the universal Savior; cf 1 Pt 2, 6–8; Rom 9, 33; 10, 9ff. *Cornerstone:* the assurance of salvation rejected by Israel in the prophet's time, is reflected by the psalmist (Ps 118, 22) and fulfilled in the Person of Christ; cf Mt 21, 42; Lk 20, 17; Acts 4, 11; Rom 9.33; 1 Pt 2, 7.
28, 21: *Mount Perazim . . . valley of Gibeon:* where

David defeated the Philistines; cf 2 Sm 5, 20, 25; 1 Chr 14, 11.16.
28, 23–29: The practical variation of the farmer's work taught him by God reflects God's dealing with his people, wisely adapted to circumstances; he does not crush their weakness altogether; cf ch 29.
28, 25: *Gith . . . cumin:* herbs used in seasoning food. *Spelt:* a variety of wheat.
29, 1f: *Ariel:* variously interpreted to mean "lion of God" or "hearth (altar) of God," a poetic name for

Jerusalem; or perhaps to be read as Uru-el, "founda-tion of God," an archaic name for the Jebusite city of Jerusalem; *like* that *Ariel,* against which *David en-camped,* it will be besieged by God.
29, 4: *Chirping:* see note on 8, 19.
29, 7f: Just when the Assyrians think their capture of Jerusalem to be certain, the Lord will snatch victory from their hands and save his city.
29, 9–12: Jerusalem in her blindness refuses to believe God's revelation that she will be saved.

"Read this," he replies, "I cannot; it is sealed." 12 When it is handed to one who cannot read, with the request, "Read this," he replies, "I cannot read."

13 The Lord said:
Since this people draws near
   with words only
and honors me with their
   lips alone,
though their hearts are far
   from me,
And their reverence for me has
   become
routine observance of the
   precepts of men,
14 Therefore I will again deal with
   this people
in surprising and wondrous
   fashion:
The wisdom of its wise men
   shall perish
and the understanding of its
   prudent men be hid.
15 Woe to those who would hide
   their plans
too deep for the LORD!
Who work in the dark, saying,
   "Who sees us, or who knows
   us?"
16 Your perversity is as though the
   potter
were taken to be the clay:
As though what is made should
   say of its maker,
"He made me not!"
Or the vessel should say of the
   potter,
"He does not understand."

Redemption

17 But a very little while,
   and Lebanon shall be
      changed into an orchard,
   and the orchard be regarded
      as a forest!
18 On that day the deaf shall hear
   the words of a book;
And out of gloom and darkness,
   the eyes of the blind shall see.
19 The lowly will ever find joy in
   the LORD,
   and the poor rejoice in the
      Holy One of Israel.

20 For the tyrant will be no more
   and the arrogant will have
      gone;
All who are alert to do evil will
   be cut off,
21   those whose mere word
   condemns a man,
Who ensnare his defender at
   the gate,
   and leave the just man with
      an empty claim.
22 Therefore thus says the LORD,
   the God of the house of
      Jacob,
   who redeemed Abraham:
Now Jacob shall have nothing
   to be ashamed of,
   nor shall his face grow pale.
23 When his children see
   the work of my hands in his
      midst,
They shall keep my name holy;
   they shall reverence the Holy
      One of Jacob,
   and be in awe of the God of
      Israel.
24 Those who err in spirit shall
   acquire understanding,
   and those who find fault shall
      receive instruction.

Futile Alliance with Egypt

30 Woe to the rebellious
      children,
  says the LORD,
Who carry out plans that are
   not mine,
  who weave webs that are not
      inspired by me,
   adding sin upon sin.
2 They go down to Egypt,
   but my counsel they do not
      seek,
They find their strength in
   Pharaoh's protection
   and take refuge in Egypt's
      shadow;
3 Pharaoh's protection shall be
   your shame,
   and refuge in Egypt's shadow
      your disgrace.
4 When the princes are at Zoan
   and their messengers reach
      Hanes,

5 All shall be ashamed
   of a people that gain them
      nothing,
Neither help nor benefit,
   but only shame and reproach.

6 [Oracle on the Beasts of the Negeb]

Through the distressed and
   troubled land
   of the lioness and roaring
      lion,
   of the viper and flying saraph,
They carry their riches on the
   backs of asses
   and their treasures on the
      humps of camels
To a people good for nothing,
7   to Egypt whose help is futile
      and vain.
Therefore I call her
   "Rahab quelled."

8 Now come, write it on a tablet
   they can keep,
   inscribe it in a record;
That it may be in future days
   an eternal witness:
9 This is a rebellious people,
   deceitful children,
Children who refuse
   to obey the law of the LORD.
10 They say to the seers, "Have no
   visions";
   to the prophets, "Do not
      descry for us what is right;
   speak flatteries to us, conjure
      up illusions.
11 Out of the way! Out of our
   path!
Let us hear no more
   of the Holy One of Israel."

12 Therefore, thus says the Holy
   One of Israel:
Because you reject this word,
And put your trust in what is
   crooked and devious,
   and depend on it,
13 This guilt of yours shall be
   like a descending rift
Bulging out in a high wall
   whose crash comes suddenly,
   in an instant.
14 It crashes like a potter's jar
   smashed beyond rescue,

29, 17–24: The prophet presents God's plan of redemption in terms of unheard-of natural phenomena as if such changes in nature took place, e.g., the change of the cedars of Lebanon into an orchard (v 17).

29, 22: *Who redeemed Abraham:* by freeing him from the idolatry of his native land.
30, 6: *Flying saraph:* see note on Nm 21, 6.
30, 7: *Rahab:* Egypt, here as elsewhere (cf Ps 87, 4), is compared to the stormy, impetuous sea monster

(cf 51, 9; Jb 26, 12; Ps 89, 11), which yet, when asked for aid by Judah, becomes silent, *quelled.*
30, 8: Isaiah will write down his condemnation of the people so that (vv 12–18) its fulfillment may afterward be admitted.

And among its fragments
　　cannot be found
　　a sherd to scoop fire from the
　　　　hearth
　　or dip water from the cistern.

15 For thus said the Lord GOD,
　　　the Holy One of Israel:
　　By waiting and by calm you
　　　　shall be saved,
　　　in quiet and in trust your
　　　　strength lies.
　　But this you did not wish.
16 "No," you said,
　　　"Upon horses we will flee."
　　—Very well, flee!
　　"Upon swift steeds we will ride."
　　—Not so swift as your
　　　　pursuers.
17 A thousand shall tremble at the
　　　threat of one;
　　　if five threaten you, you shall
　　　　flee,
　　Until you are left like a flagstaff
　　　on the mountaintop,
　　like a flag on the hill.
18 Yet the LORD is waiting to show
　　　you favor,
　　　and he rises to pity you;
　　For the LORD is a God of justice:
　　　blessed are all who wait for
　　　　him!

19 O people of Zion, who dwell in
　　　Jerusalem,
　　no more will you weep;
　　He will be gracious to you
　　　when you cry out,
　　as soon as he hears he will
　　　answer you.
20 The Lord will give you the
　　　bread you need
　　　and the water for which you
　　　　thirst.
　　No longer will your Teacher
　　　hide himself,
　　but with your own eyes you
　　　shall see your Teacher,
21 While from behind, a voice
　　　shall sound in your ears:
　　"This is the way; walk in it,"
　　when you would turn to the
　　　right or to the left.
22 And you shall consider unclean
　　　your silver-plated idols
　　　and your gold-covered images;

You shall throw them away like
　　filthy rags
　　to which you say, "Begone!"

Zion's Future Prosperity

23 He will give rain for the seed
　　　that you sow in the ground,
　　And the wheat that the soil
　　　produces
　　　will be rich and abundant.
　　On that day your cattle will
　　　graze
　　　in spacious meadows;
24 The oxen and the asses that till
　　　the ground
　　　will eat silage tossed to them
　　with shovel and pitchfork.
25 Upon every high mountain and
　　　lofty hill
　　　there will be streams of
　　　　running water.
　　On the day of the great slaughter,
　　　when the towers fall,
26 The light of the moon will be
　　　like that of the sun
　　　and the light of the sun will
　　　　be seven times greater
　　[like the light of seven days].
　　On the day the LORD binds up
　　　the wounds of his people,
　　he will heal the bruises left by
　　　his blows.

Divine Judgment on Assyria

27 See the name of the LORD
　　　coming from afar
　　　in burning wrath, with
　　　　lowering clouds!
　　His lips are filled with fury,
　　　his tongue is like a consuming
　　　　fire;
28 His breath, like a flood in a
　　　ravine
　　　that reaches suddenly to the
　　　　neck,
　　Will winnow the nations with a
　　　destructive winnowing,
　　and with repeated winnowings
　　　will he battle against them
　　[and a bridle on the jaws of
　　　the peoples to send them
　　　astray].
30 The LORD will make his glorious
　　　voice heard,
　　　and let it be seen how his arm
　　　　descends

In raging fury and flame of
　　consuming fire,
　　in driving storm and hail.
31 When the LORD speaks, Assyria
　　　will be shattered,
　　　as he strikes with the rod;
32 While at every sweep of the rod
　　　which the LORD will bring
　　　　down on him in punishment,
29 You will sing
　　　as on a night when a feast is
　　　　observed,
　　And be merry of heart,
　　　as one marching along with a
　　　　flute
　　Toward the mountain of the
　　　LORD,
　　　toward the Rock of Israel,
　　accompanied by the timbrels
　　　and lyres.
33 For the pyre has long been ready,
　　　prepared for the king;
　　Broad and deep it is piled
　　　with dry grass and wood in
　　　　abundance,
　　And the breath of the LORD, like
　　　a stream of sulphur,
　　will set it afire.

Against the Egyptian Alliance

31 Woe to those who go down
　　　to Egypt for help,
　　　who depend upon horses;
　　Who put their trust in chariots
　　　because of their number,
　　　and in horsemen because of
　　　　their combined power,
　　But look not to the Holy One of
　　　Israel
　　　nor seek the LORD!
2 Yet he too is wise and will bring
　　　disaster;
　　　he will not turn from what he
　　　　has threatened to do.
　　He will rise up against the house
　　　of the wicked
　　　and against those who help
　　　　evildoers.
3 The Egyptians are men, not God,
　　　their horses are flesh, not
　　　　spirit;
　　When the LORD stretches forth
　　　his hand,
　　　the helper shall stumble, the
　　　　one helped shall fall,
　　and both of them shall perish
　　　together.

30, 20: *Teacher:* God, who in the past taught in a
veiled manner through his prophets, will in future
help them to understand his teaching clearly. This was

eminently true when the Son of God became Man.
30, 27–33: *God's punishment of Assyria. The name
of the Lord:* God himself; cf Ps 20, 2.

30, 29.33: *Pyre:* on which the corpse of the king of
Assyria is burned. This is the occasion of festal rejoicing for the Israelites, who are now free from his yoke.

4 Thus says the LORD to me:
As a lion or a lion cub
growling over its prey,
With a band of shepherds
assembled against it,
Is neither frightened by their
shouts
nor disturbed by their noise,
So shall the LORD of hosts
come down
to wage war upon the
mountain and hill of Zion.
5 Like hovering birds, so the
LORD of hosts
shall shield Jerusalem,
To protect and deliver,
to spare and rescue it.

6 Return, O children of Israel, to
him whom you have utterly deserted.
7 On that day each one of you shall
spurn his sinful idols of silver and
gold, which he made with his hands.

Downfall of Assyria

8 Assyria shall fall by a sword not
wielded by man,
no mortal sword shall devour
him;
He shall flee before the sword,
and his young men shall be
impressed as laborers.
9 He shall rush past his crag in
panic,
and his princes shall flee in
terror from his standard,
Says the LORD who has a fire in
Zion
and a furnace in Jerusalem.

The Kingdom of Justice

32 See, a king will reign justly
and princes will rule
rightly.
2 Each of them will be a shelter
from the wind,
a retreat from the rain.
They will be like streams of
water in a dry country,
like the shade of a great rock
in a parched land.
3 The eyes of those who see will
not be closed;
the ears of those who hear
will be attentive.

4 The flighty will become wise
and capable,
and the stutterers will speak
fluently and clearly.
5 No more will the fool be called
noble,
nor the trickster be considered
honorable.
6 For the fool speaks foolishly,
planning evil in his heart:
How to do wickedness,
to speak perversely against the
LORD,
To let the hungry go empty
and the thirsty be without
drink.
7 And the trickster uses wicked
trickery,
planning crimes:
How to ruin the poor with lies,
and the needy when they
plead their case.
8 But the noble man plans noble
things,
and by noble things he stands.

The Women of Jerusalem

9 O complacent ladies, rise up and
hear my voice,
overconfident women, give
heed to my words.
10 In a little more than a year
you overconfident ones will
be shaken;
The vintage will fail,
there will be no harvest.
11 Tremble, you who are
complacent!
Shudder, you who are
overconfident!
Strip yourselves bare,
with only a loincloth to cover
you.
12 Beat your breasts
for the pleasant fields, the
fruitful vine,
13 And the soil of my people,
overgrown with thorns and
briers;
For all the joyful houses,
the wanton city.
14 Yes, the castle will be forsaken,
the noisy city deserted;
19 Down it comes, as trees come
down in the forest!
The city will be utterly laid
low.

Hill and tower will become
wasteland forever
for wild asses to frolic in, and
flocks to pasture,
15 Until the spirit from on high
is poured out on us.

Then will the desert become an
orchard
and the orchard be regarded
as a forest.
16 Right will dwell in the desert
and justice abide in the
orchard.
17 Justice will bring about peace;
right will produce calm and
security.
18 My people will live in peaceful
country,
in secure dwellings and quiet
resting places.
20 Happy are you who sow beside
every stream,
and let the ox and the ass go
freely!

Overthrow of Assyria

33 Woe, O destroyer never
destroyed,
O traitor never betrayed!
When you finish destroying, you
will be destroyed;
when wearied with betraying,
you will be betrayed.
2 O LORD, have pity on us, for
you we wait.
Be our strength every morning,
our salvation in time of
trouble!
3 At the roaring sound, peoples
flee;
when you rise in your majesty,
nations are scattered.
4 Men gather spoil as caterpillars
are gathered up;
they rush upon it like the
onrush of locusts.
5 The LORD is exalted, enthroned
on high;
he fills Zion with right and
justice.
6 That which makes her seasons
lasting,
the riches that save her, are
wisdom and knowledge;
the fear of the LORD is her
treasure.

31,9: *Crag:* the king as the rallying point of the princes.
32,14.19: *The castle:* the citadel of Jerusalem.

Hill and tower: the fortified hill, in Hebrew *Ophel*, with its stronghold called "the great projecting tower" in Neh 3, 27.

32, 15–18.20: Extraordinary peace and prosperity will come to Israel under just rulers.

7 See, the men of Ariel cry out in
the streets,
the messengers of Shalem
weep bitterly.
8 The highways are desolate,
travelers have quit the paths,
Covenants are broken, their
terms are spurned;
yet no man gives it a thought.
9 The country languishes in
mourning,
Lebanon withers with shame;
Sharon is like the steppe,
Bashan and Carmel are
stripped bare.

10 Now will I rise up, says the
LORD,
now will I be exalted, now be
lifted up.
11 You conceive dry grass, bring
forth stubble;
my spirit shall consume you
like fire.
12 The peoples shall be as in a
limekiln,
like brushwood cut down for
burning in the fire.
13 Hear, you who are far off, what
I have done;
you who are near,
acknowledge my might.
14 On Zion sinners are in dread,
trembling grips the impious:
"Who of us can live with the
consuming fire?
who of us can live with the
everlasting flames?"
15 He who practices virtue and
speaks honestly,
who spurns what is gained by
oppression,
Brushing his hands free of
contact with a bribe,
stopping his ears lest he hear
of bloodshed,
closing his eyes lest he look on
evil—
16 He shall dwell on the heights,
his stronghold shall be the
rocky fastness,
his food and drink in steady
supply.

Restoration of Zion

17 Your eyes will see a king in his
splendor,

they will look upon a vast
land.
18 Your mind will dwell on the
terror:
"Where is he who counted,
where is he who weighed?
Where is he who counted the
towers?"
19 To the people of alien tongue
you will look no more,
the people of obscure speech,
stammering in a language not
understood.
20 Look to Zion, the city of our
festivals;
let your eyes see Jerusalem
as a quiet abode, a tent not
to be struck,
Whose pegs will never be pulled
up,
nor any of its ropes severed.
22 Indeed the LORD will be there
with us, majestic;
yes, the LORD our judge, the
LORD our lawgiver,
the LORD our king, he it is
who will save us.
21 In a place of rivers and wide
streams
on which no boat is rowed,
where no majestic ship
passes,
23 The rigging hangs slack;
it cannot hold the mast in
place,
nor keep the sail spread out.
Then the blind will divide great
spoils
and the lame will carry off
the loot.
24 No one who dwells there will
say, "I am sick";
the people who live there will
be forgiven their guilt.

THE LORD, ZION'S AVENGER

Judgment upon Edom

34 Come near, O nations, and
hear;
be attentive, O peoples!
Let the earth and what fills it
listen,
the world and all it produces.
2 The LORD is angry with all the
nations

and is wrathful against all their
host;
he has doomed them and
given them over to slaughter.
3 Their slain shall be cast out,
their corpses shall send up a
stench;
The mountains shall run with
their blood,
4 and all the hills shall rot;
The heavens shall be rolled up
like a scroll,
and all their host shall wither
away,
As the leaf wilts on the vine,
or as the fig withers on the
tree.

5 When my sword has drunk its
fill in the heavens,
lo, it shall come down in
judgment
upon Edom, a people I have
doomed.
6 The LORD has a sword filled
with blood,
greasy with fat,
With the blood of lambs and
goats,
with the fat of rams' kidneys;
For the LORD has a sacrifice in
Bozrah,
a great slaughter in the land
of Edom.
7 Wild oxen shall be struck down
with fatlings,
and bullocks with bulls;
Their land shall be soaked with
blood,
and their earth greasy with
fat.
8 For the LORD has a day of
vengeance,
a year of requital by Zion's
defender.
9 Edom's streams shall be changed
into pitch
and her earth into sulphur,
and her land shall become
burning pitch;
10 Night and day it shall not be
quenched,
its smoke shall rise forever.
From generation to generation
she shall lie waste,
never again shall anyone pass
through her.

33, 7: *Ariel . . . Shalem:* Jerusalem; cf 29, 1; Gn
14, 18.

33, 9: *Sharon:* the fertile plain near the Mediterranean.

33, 17: *King:* the Messianic king, or God; cf v 22.
33, 21.23: *Boat . . . majestic ship:* of a foreign
oppressor.

11 But the desert owl and hoot owl
  shall possess her,
  the screech owl and raven
  shall dwell in her.
The LORD will measure her with
  line and plummet
  to be an empty waste
  for satyrs to dwell in.

12 Her nobles shall be no more,
  nor shall kings be proclaimed
  there;
  all her princes are gone.
13 Her castles shall be overgrown
  with thorns,
  her fortresses with thistles
  and briers.
She shall become an abode for
  jackals
  and a haunt for ostriches.
14 Wildcats shall meet with desert
  beasts,
  satyrs shall call to one
  another;
There shall the lilith repose,
  and find for herself a place to
  rest.
15 There the hoot owl shall nest and
  lay eggs,
  hatch them out and gather
  them in her shadow;
There shall the kites assemble,
  none shall be missing its mate.

16 Look in the book of the LORD
  and read:
  No one of these shall be
  lacking,
For the mouth of the LORD has
  ordered it,
  and his spirit shall gather
  them there.
17 It is he who casts the lot for
  them,
  and with his hand he marks
  off their shares of her;
They shall possess her forever,
  and dwell there from
  generation to generation.

Israel's Deliverance

35 The desert and the parched
  land will exult;
  the steppe will rejoice and
  bloom.

2 They will bloom with abundant
  flowers,
  and rejoice with joyful song.
The glory of Lebanon will be
  given to them,
  the splendor of Carmel and
  Sharon;
They will see the glory of the
  LORD,
  the splendor of our God.
3 Strengthen the hands that are
  feeble,
  make firm the knees that are
  weak,
4 Say to those whose hearts are
  frightened:
  Be strong, fear not!
Here is your God,
  he comes with vindication;
With divine recompense
  he comes to save you.
5 Then will the eyes of the blind
  be opened,
  the ears of the deaf be cleared;
6 Then will the lame leap like a
  stag,
  then the tongue of the dumb
  will sing.

Streams will burst forth in the
  desert,
  and rivers in the steppe.
7 The burning sands will become
  pools,
  and the thirsty ground,
  springs of water;
The abode where jackals lurk
  will be a marsh for the reed
  and papyrus.
8 A highway will be there,
  called the holy way;
No one unclean may pass over
  it,
  nor fools go astray on it.
9 No lion will be there,
  nor beast of prey go up to be
  met upon it.
It is for those with a journey to
  make,
  and on it the redeemed will
  walk.
10 Those whom the LORD has
  ransomed will return

and enter Zion singing,
  crowned with everlasting joy;
They will meet with joy and
  gladness,
  sorrow and mourning will flee.

HISTORICAL APPENDIX

Invasion of Sennacherib

36 In the fourteenth year of King
Hezekiah, Sennacherib, king
of Assyria, went on an expedition
against all the fortified cities of
Judah and captured them. 2 From
Lachish the king of Assyria sent his
commander with a great army to
King Hezekiah in Jerusalem. When
he stopped at the conduit of the
upper pool, on the highway of the
fuller's field, 3 there came out to
him the master of the palace,
Eliakim, son of Hilkiah, and Shebna
the scribe, and the herald Joah, son
of Asaph. 4 The commander said
to them, "Tell King Hezekiah: Thus
says the great king, the king of
Assyria, 'On what do you base this
confidence of yours? 5 Do you
think mere words substitute for
strategy and might in war? On whom,
then, do you rely, that you rebel
against me? 6 This Egypt, the
staff on which you rely, is in fact a
broken reed which pierces the hand
of anyone who leans on it. That is
what Pharaoh, king of Egypt, is to all
who rely on him. 7 But if you say
to me: "We rely on the LORD, our
God," is not he the one whose high
places and altars Hezekiah removed,
commanding Judah and Jerusalem to
worship before this altar?'

8 "Now, make a wager with my
lord the king of Assyria: 'I will give
you two thousand horses, if you can
put riders on them.' 9 How then
can you repulse even one of the least
servants of my lord? And yet you
rely on Egypt for chariots and horsemen! 10 'Was it without the LORD's
will that I have come up to destroy
this land? The LORD said to me, "Go
up and destroy that land!"'"

34, 11: *Satyrs:* see note on 13, 21; cf 34, 14.
34, 14: *Lilith:* a female demon thought to roam
about the desert.
34, 16: *Book of the Lord:* God's list of all his
creatures; cf Ps 69, 29, "the book of the living";
Ps 139, 16, "your book."
35, 1–10: Similar to the description of the return

from the Exile, as found in chaps. 40–55.
36, 1—39, 8: Except for 38, 9–20, this historical
appendix describing the siege, etc., is paralleled in
2 Kgs 18, 13—20, 19, which, however, has certain
details proper to itself. The events are also recorded
in substantially the same way in the cuneiform
inscriptions of Sennacherib.

36, 7: The Assyrians pretend that Hezekiah's
removal of the *high places and altars* (illegal sanctuaries) was taken by the Lord as an insult. They declare
to Jerusalem's emissaries that the city therefore no
longer has a right to the Lord's protection and that
they are the ones who truly carry out his will (cf
v 10).

11 Then Eliakim and Shebna and Joah said to the commander, "Please speak to your servants in Aramaic; we understand it. Do not speak to us in Judean within earshot of the people who are on the wall."

12 But the commander replied, "Was it to you and your master that my lord sent me to speak these words? Was it not rather to the men sitting on the wall, who, with you, will have to eat their own excrement and drink their own urine?" 13 Then the commander stepped forward and cried out in a loud voice in Judean, "Listen to the words of the great king, the king of Assyria. 14 Thus says the king: 'Do not let Hezekiah deceive you, since he cannot deliver you. 15 Let not Hezekiah induce you to rely on the LORD, saying, "The LORD will surely save us; this city will not be handed over to the king of Assyria."' 16 Do not listen to Hezekiah, for the king of Assyria says: 'Make peace with me and surrender! Then each of you will eat of his own vine and of his own fig tree, and drink the water of his own cistern, 17 until I come to take you to a land like your own, a land of grain and wine, of bread and vineyards. 18 Do not let Hezekiah seduce you by saying, "The LORD will save us." Has any of the gods of the nations ever rescued his land from the hand of the king of Assyria? 19 Where are the gods of Hamath and Arpad? Where are the gods of Sepharvaim? Where are the gods of Samaria? Have they saved Samaria from my hand? 20 Which of all the gods of these lands ever rescued his land from my hand? Will the LORD then save Jerusalem from my hand?'" 21 But they remained silent and did not answer him one word, for the king had ordered them not to answer him.

22 Then the master of the palace, Eliakim, son of Hilkiah, Shebna the scribe, and the herald Joah, son of Asaph, came to Hezekiah with their garments torn, and reported to him what the commander had said.

37 When King Hezekiah heard this, he tore his garments, wrapped himself in sackcloth, and went into the temple of the LORD. 2 He sent Eliakim, the master of the palace, and Shebna, the scribe, and the elders of the priests, wrapped in sackcloth, to tell the prophet Isaiah, son of Amoz: 3 "Thus says Hezekiah: 'This is a day of distress, of rebuke, and of disgrace. Children are at the point of birth, but there is no strength to bring them forth. 4 Perhaps the LORD, your God, will hear the words of the commander, whom his master, the king of Assyria, sent to taunt the living God, and will rebuke him for the words which the LORD, your God, has heard. Send up a prayer for the remnant that is here.'"

5 When the servants of King Hezekiah had come to Isaiah, 6 he said to them: "Tell this to your master: 'Thus says the LORD: Do not be frightened by the words you have heard, with which the servants of the king of Assyria have blasphemed me. 7 I am about to put in him such a spirit that, when he hears a certain report, he will return to his own land, and there I will cause him to fall by the sword.'"

8 When the commander returned to Lachish and heard that the king of Assyria had left there, he found him besieging Libnah. 9 The king of Assyria heard a report that Tirhakah, king of Ethiopia, had come out to fight against him. Again he sent envoys to Hezekiah with this message: "Thus shall you say to Hezekiah, king of Judah: 10 'Do not let your God on whom you rely deceive you by saying that Jerusalem will not be handed over to the king of Assyria. 11 You yourself have heard what the kings of Assyria have done to all the countries: They doomed them! Will you, then, be saved? 12 Did the gods of the nations whom my fathers destroyed save them? Gozen, Haran, Rezeph, and the Edenites in Telassar? 13 Where is the king of Hamath, the king of Arpad, or a king of the cities of Sepharvaim, Hena or Ivvah?'"

14 Hezekiah took the letter from the hand of the messengers and read it; then he went up to the temple of the LORD, and spreading it out before him, 15 he prayed to the LORD: 16 "O LORD of hosts, God of Israel, enthroned upon the cherubim! You alone are God over all the kingdoms of the earth. You have made the heavens and the earth. 17 Incline your ear, O LORD, and listen! Open your eyes, O LORD, and see! Hear all the words of the letter that Sennacherib sent to taunt the living God. 18 Truly, O LORD, the kings of Assyria have laid waste all the nations and their lands, 19 and cast their gods into the fire; they destroyed them because they were not gods but the work of human hands, wood and stone. 20 Therefore, O LORD, our God, save us from his hand, that all the kingdoms of the earth may know that you, O LORD, alone are God."

Punishment of Sennacherib

21 Then Isaiah, son of Amoz, sent this message to Hezekiah; Thus says the LORD, the God of Israel: In answer to your prayer for help against Sennacherib, king of Assyria, 22 this is the word the LORD has spoken concerning him:

She despises you, laughs you to
　　scorn,
　　the virgin daughter Zion;
Behind you she wags her head,
　　daughter Jerusalem.
23 Whom have you insulted and
　　blasphemed,
　　against whom have you raised
　　　your voice
And lifted up your eyes on high?
　　Against the Holy One of
　　　Israel!
24 Through your servants you have
　　insulted the Lord:
　　You said, "With my many
　　　chariots
　　I climbed the mountain heights,
　　　the recesses of Lebanon;

36, 11: The Jewish emissaries ask that the conversation be carried on in *Aramaic*, not in *Judean*, for they fear the effect of the Assyrian claims upon the morale of the people.

37, 3: A proverbial expression. In the Bible the pangs of childbirth often typify extreme anguish; cf

13, 8; Jer 6, 24; Mi 4, 9f. In this instance there is reference to the desperate situation of Hezekiah from which he was scarcely able to free himself.

37, 9: *Tirhakah:* may have been general of the Egyptian army in 701 B.C.; later he became king, one of the Ethiopian dynasty of Egyptian kings (c. 690–

664 B.C.). Many consider that this account in Isaiah combines features of two originally distinct sieges of Jerusalem by Sennacherib.

37, 16: In contrast to the empty boasting of the Assyrians, Hezekiah proclaims the Lord as *God over all the kingdoms of the earth.*

I cut down its lofty cedars,
  its choice cypresses;
I reached the remotest heights,
  its forest park.
25 I dug wells and drank water in
    foreign lands;
  I dried up with the soles of
    my feet
  all the rivers of Egypt.

26 Have you not heard?
  Long ago I prepared it,
  From days of old I planned it,
    now I have brought it to pass:
  That you should reduce fortified
    cities
  into heaps of ruins,
27 While their inhabitants, shorn of
    power,
  are dismayed and ashamed,
  Becoming like the plants of the
    the field,
  like the green growth,
  like the scorched grass on the
    housetops.
28 I am aware whether you stand
    or sit;
  I know whether you come or
    go,
  and also your rage against me.
29 Because of your rage against me
    and your fury which has
    reached my ears,
  I will put my hook in your nose
    and my bit in your mouth,
    and make you return the way
      you came.

30 This shall be a sign for you:
    this year you shall eat the
      aftergrowth,
    next year, what grows of
      itself;
  But in the third year, sow and
      reap,
    plant vineyards and eat their
      fruit!
31 The remaining survivors of the
    house of Judah
  shall again strike root below
    and bear fruit above.

32 For out of Jerusalem shall come
    a remnant,
  and from Mount Zion,
    survivors.
  The zeal of the LORD of hosts
    shall do this.

33 Therefore, thus says the LORD
concerning the king of Assyria: He
shall not reach this city, nor shoot an
arrow at it, nor come before it with a
shield, nor cast up siegeworks against
it. 34 He shall return by the same
way he came, without entering the
city, says the LORD. 35 I will shield
and save this city for my own sake,
and for the sake of my servant
David.
36 The angel of the LORD went
forth and struck down one hundred
and eight-five thousand in the Assyrian camp. Early the next morning,
there they were, all the corpses of the
dead. 37 So Sennacherib, the king
of Assyria, broke camp and went
back home to Nineveh.
38 When he was worshiping in the
temple of his god Nisroch, his sons
Adrammelech and Sharezer slew him
with the sword and fled into the land
of Ararat. His son Esarhaddon
reigned in his stead.

Sickness and Recovery of
Hezekiah

38 In those days, when Hezekiah
was mortally ill, the prophet
Isaiah, son of Amoz, came and said
to him: "Thus says the LORD: Put
your house in order, for you are about
to die; you shall not recover." 2
Then Hezekiah turned his face to the
wall and prayed to the LORD: 3 "O
LORD, remember how faithfully and
wholeheartedly I conducted myself
in your presence, doing what was
pleasing to you!" And Hezekiah
wept bitterly.
4 Then the word of the LORD came
to Isaiah: 5 "Go, tell Hezekiah:
Thus says the LORD, the God of your

father David: I have heard your
prayer and seen your tears. I will heal
you: in three days you shall go up to
the LORD's temple; I will add fifteen
years to your life. 6 I will rescue
you and this city from the hand of the
king of Assyria; I will be a shield to
this city."
21 Isaiah then ordered a poultice
of figs to be taken and applied to the
boil, that he might recover. 22 Then
Hezekiah asked, "What is the sign
that I shall go up to the temple of the
LORD?"
7 [Isaiah answered:] "This will be
the sign for you from the LORD that
he will do what he has promised: 8
See, I will make the shadow cast by
the sun on the stairway to the terrace
of Ahaz go back the ten steps it has
advanced." So the sun came back the
ten steps it had advanced.

Hezekiah's Hymn of Thanksgiving

9 The song of Hezekiah, king of
Judah, after he had been sick and had
recovered from his illness:

10 Once I said,
  "In the noontime of life I
    must depart!
  To the gates of the nether world
    I shall be consigned
  for the rest of my years."
11 I said, "I shall see the LORD no
    more
  in the land of the living.
  No longer shall I behold my
    fellow men
  among those who dwell in the
    world."
12 My dwelling, like a shepherd's
    tent,
  is struck down and borne
    away from me;
  You have folded up my life,
    like a weaver
  who severs the last thread.
  Day and night you give me over
    to torment;

37, 30: *You:* Hezekiah. *A sign:* it is difficult to know the nature of this sign. Either it is merely a proverbial expression to signify that prosperity follows adversity, or it indicates that after two years the normal conditions of life will be resumed.

37, 36: The destruction of Sennacherib's army is also recorded by Herodotus, a Greek historian of the fifth century B.C. It was probably due to the bubonic plague, but the sacred author attributes it to its ultimate cause, God through his angel.

37, 38: The violent death of Sennacherib (681 B.C.) is also mentioned in non-biblical sources. It occurred

twenty years after his invasion of Judea.

38, 1—39, 8: The events of this section—sickness and recovery of Hezekiah, embassy of Merodach-baladan—point forward to Babylon (cc 40—66). They occurred prior to the events of 36, 1—37, 38, which point back to Assyria (1, 1—35, 10).

38, 1: *In those days:* a time prior to the siege of Jerusalem in 701 B.C.

38, 5: Since Hezekiah died in 687 B.C., this sickness of his seems to have been in 702 B.C., that is, *fifteen years* before.

38, 8: *Stairway to the terrace of Ahaz:* this inter-

pretation is based on a reading of the Hebrew text revised according to the Dead Sea Scroll of Isaiah; cf 2 Kgs 23, 12. Many translate the phrase as "steps of Ahaz" and understand this as referring to a sundial.

38, 10: *In the noontime of life:* long before the end of a full span of life; cf Pss 55, 24; 102, 25.

38, 11: *See the Lord:* go to the Temple and take part in its service.

38, 12: These two metaphors emphasize the suddenness and finality of death.

13 I cry out until the dawn.
    Like a lion he breaks all my
          bones;
    [day and night you give me
          over to torment].
14 Like a swallow I utter shrill cries;
    I moan like a dove.
    My eyes grow weak, gazing
          heavenward:
    O Lord, I am in straits; be my
          surety!

15 What am I to say or tell him?
    He has done it!
    I shall go on through all my
          years
    despite the bitterness of my
          soul.
16 Those live whom the LORD
          protects;
    yours . . . the life of my spirit.
    You have given me health and
          life;
17   thus is my bitterness
          transformed into peace.
    You have preserved my life
          from the pit of destruction,
    When you cast behind your back
          all my sins.

18 For it is not the nether world
          that gives you thanks,
    nor death that praises you;
    Neither do those who go down
          into the pit
    await your kindness.
19 The living, the living give you
          thanks,
    as I do today.
    Fathers declare to their sons,
    O God, your faithfulness.
20 The LORD is our savior;
    we shall sing to stringed
          instruments
    In the house of the LORD
    all the days of our life.

Embassy from Merodach-baladan

39 At that time when Merodach-
baladan, son of Baladan, king
of Babylon, heard that Hezekiah had
recovered from his sickness, he sent
letters and gifts to him. 2 Hezekiah
was pleased at this, and therefore
showed the messengers his treasury,
the silver and gold, the spices and fine
oil, his whole armory, and everything
that was in his storerooms; there was

nothing in his house or in his whole
realm that he did not show them.
3 Then Isaiah the prophet came
to King Hezekiah and asked him,
"What did these men say to you?
Where did they come from?" Hezekiah answered, "They came to me
from a distant land, from Babylon."
4 "What did they see in your house?"
he asked. Hezekiah replied, "They
saw everything in my house; there is
nothing in my storerooms that I did
not show them."
5 Then Isaiah said to Hezekiah,
"Hear the word of the LORD of
hosts: 6 Behold, the days shall
come when all that is in your house,
and everything that your fathers have
stored up until this day, shall be
carried off to Babylon; nothing shall
be left, says the LORD. 7 Some of
your own bodily descendants shall be
taken and made servants in the palace
of the king of Babylon." 8 Hezekiah replied to Isaiah, "The word of
the LORD which you have spoken is
favorable." For he thought, "There
will be peace and security in my
lifetime."

THE BOOK OF CONSOLATION

THE LORD'S GLORY IN ISRAEL'S LIBERATION

Promise of Salvation

40 Comfort, give comfort to my
          people,
    says your God.
2 Speak tenderly to Jerusalem,
    and proclaim to her
    that her service is at an end,
    her guilt is expiated;
    Indeed, she has received from
          the hand of the LORD
    double for all her sins.

3   A voice cries out:

In the desert prepare the way of
    the LORD!
Make straight in the wasteland
    a highway for our God!
4 Every valley shall be filled in,
    every mountain and hill shall
          be made low;
The rugged land shall be made
    a plain,
    the rough country, a broad
          valley.
5 Then the glory of the LORD

shall be revealed,
    and all mankind shall see it
          together;
    for the mouth of the LORD
    has spoken.

6 A voice says, "Cry out!"
    I answer, "What shall I cry
          out?"
    "All mankind is grass,
    and all their glory like the
          flower of the field.

38, 15: *What am I to say or tell him?:* a rhetorical
question, as if the poet were at a loss in giving fitting
expression to his gratitude; cf Ps 116, 12. *He has done
it:* accomplished the cure. *Despite the bitterness:*
even though the one praying was previously so
dejected.

38, 16: *Yours . . . the life of my spirit:* the current
Hebrew text is corrupt. The revised Latin psalter
renders it: "You have revived my soul."

38, 17: *You cast behind your back all my sins:*
figurative language to express the divine forgiveness

of sins, as if God no longer saw or cared about them.
This expression is ordinarily used of men forgetting
God; cf 1 Kgs 14, 9; Ez 23, 35; Ps 50, 17.

38, 18f: See note on Ps 6, 6.

39, 1: *Merodach-baladan:* twice king of Babylon,
probably from 721 to 710 B.C., and again for nine
months, in 704–703. This visit of his messengers,
certainly before 701, was in reality a political one.
Babylon hoped to lead an anti-Assyrian confederation composed of neighboring states.

39, 6: Because Judah preferred to follow a pro-

Babylonian policy, instead of trusting in God, it
would later be exiled to Babylon.

39, 8: *Favorable:* for the Exile would not occur in
his lifetime.

40, 2: *Service:* servitude and exile.

40, 3–5: The figurative language here describes the
actual return of the exiles from Babylon to Jerusalem.
It is the Lord who leads them; their road is made
easy for them. Mt 3, 3 and parallels see in these
verses a prophecy of the Baptist and Christ.

7 The grass withers, the flower
      wilts,
   when the breath of the LORD
      blows upon it.
   [So then, the people is the
      grass.]
8 Though the grass withers and
      the flower wilts,
   the word of our God stands
      forever."

9 Go up onto a high mountain,
      Zion, herald of glad tidings;
   Cry out at the top of your voice,
      Jerusalem, herald of good news!
   Fear not to cry out
      and say to the cities of Judah:
      Here is your God!
10 Here comes with power
      the Lord GOD,
   who rules by his strong arm;
   Here is his reward with him,
      his recompense before him.
11 Like a shepherd he feeds his
      flock;
   in his arms he gathers the
      lambs,
   Carrying them in his bosom,
      and leading the ewes with care.

Power of the Creator to Save
His People

12 Who has cupped in his hand the
      waters of the sea,
   and marked off the heavens
      with a span?
   Who has held in a measure the
      dust of the earth,
   weighed the mountains in
      scales
   and the hills in a balance?
13 Who has directed the spirit of
      the LORD,
   or has instructed him as his
      counselor?
14 Whom did he consult to gain
      knowledge?
   Who taught him the path of
      judgment,
   or showed him the way of
      understanding?
15 Behold, the nations count as a
      drop in the bucket,
   as dust on the scales;
   the coastlands weigh no more
      than powder.

16 Lebanon would not suffice for
      fuel,
   nor its animals be enough for
      holocausts.
17 Before him all the nations are
      as nought,
   as nothing and void he
      accounts them.
18 To whom can you liken God?
   With what equal can you
      confront him?
19 An idol, cast by a craftsman,
   which the smith plates with
      gold
   and fits with silver chains?
20 Mulberry wood, the choice
      portion
   which a skilled craftsman picks
      out for himself,
   Choosing timber that will not rot,
   to set up an idol that will not
      be unsteady?

(41) 6 One man helps another,
      one says to the other,
      "Keep on!"
   7 The craftsman encourages the
      goldsmith,
   the one who beats with the
      hammer, him who strikes
      on the anvil,
   He says the soldering is good,
      and he fastens it with nails to
      steady it.

(40) 21 Do you not know? Have
      you not heard?
   Was it not foretold you from
      the beginning?
   Have you not understood?
      Since the earth was founded
22 He sits enthroned above the
      vault of the earth,
   and its inhabitants are like
      grasshoppers;
   He stretches out the heavens
      like a veil,
   spreads them out like a tent
      to dwell in.
23 He brings princes to nought
   and makes the rulers of the
      earth as nothing.
24 Scarcely are they planted or
      sown,
   scarcely is their stem rooted
      in the earth,

When he breathes upon them
      and they wither,
   and the stormwind carries
      them away like straw.

25 To whom can you liken me as
      an equal?
   says the Holy One.
26 Lift up your eyes on high
   and see who has created these:
   He leads out their army and
      numbers them,
   calling them all by name.
   By his great might and the
      strength of his power
   not one of them is missing!
27 Why, O Jacob, do you say,
      and declare, O Israel,
   "My way is hidden from the
      LORD,
   and my right is disregarded
      by my God"?
28 Do you not know
   or have you not heard?
   The LORD is the eternal God,
      creator of the ends of the earth.
   He does not faint nor grow
      weary,
   and his knowledge is beyond
      scrutiny.
29 He gives strength to the fainting;
   for the weak he makes vigor
      abound.
30 Though young men faint and
      grow weary,
   and youths stagger and fall,
31 They that hope in the LORD will
      renew their strength,
   they will soar as with eagles'
      wings;
   They will run and not grow
      weary,
   walk and not grow faint.

The Liberator of Israel

41 Keep silence before me, O
      coastlands;
   you peoples, wait for my words!
   Let them draw near and speak;
   let us come together for
      judgment.

2 Who has stirred up from the
      East the champion of
      justice,
   and summoned him to be his
      attendant?

40, 12: *Span:* the distance between the extended
little finger and the thumb. *Measure:* literally,
"third"; here a small container.

40, 16: *Lebanon . . . fuel:* the famed cedars would
not be enough to keep the fires of sacrifice burning.

40, 26: *Created:* see note on Gn 1, 1. *By name:* for
he is their Creator.

40, 27f: God's people, here called *Jacob* and
Israel, must not give way to discouragement: their
Lord is the eternal God.

41, 1–4: It is generally agreed that these verses
describe the vocation and victory of Cyrus, whom the
Lord used as his instrument to redeem Israel.

41, 2: Cyrus is the *champion of justice* and God's
attendant.

To him he delivers the nations
and subdues the kings;
With his sword he reduces them
to dust,
with his bow, to driven straw.
3 He pursues them, passing on
without loss,
by a path his feet do not
even tread.
4 Who has performed these
deeds?
He who has called forth the
generations since the
beginning.
I, the LORD, am the first,
and with the last I will also be.
5 The coastlands see, and fear;
the ends of the earth tremble:
these things are near, they
come to pass.

8 But you, Israel, my servant,
Jacob, whom I have chosen,
offspring of Abraham my
friend—
9 You whom I have taken from
the ends of the earth
and summoned from its
far-off places,
You whom I have called my
servant,
whom I have chosen and will
not cast off—
10 Fear not, I am with you;
be not dismayed; I am your
God.
I will strengthen you, and help
you,
and uphold you with my right
hand of justice.

11 Yes, all shall be put to shame
and disgrace
who vent their anger against
you;
Those shall perish and come to
nought
who offer resistance.
12 You shall seek out, but shall not
find,
those who strive against you;
They shall be as nothing at all
who do battle with you.
13 For I am the LORD, your God,
who grasp your right hand;

It is I who say to you, "Fear not,
I will help you."
14 Fear not, O worm Jacob,
O maggot Israel;
I will help you, says the LORD;
your redeemer is the Holy
One of Israel.
15 I will make of you a threshing
sledge,
sharp, new, and double-edged,
To thresh the mountains and
crush them,
to make the hills like chaff.
16 When you winnow them, the
wind shall carry them off
and the storm shall scatter
them.
But you shall rejoice in the
LORD,
and glory in the Holy One of
Israel.

17 The afflicted and the needy seek
water in vain,
their tongues are parched with
thirst.
I, the LORD, will answer them;
I, the God of Israel, will not
forsake them.
18 I will open up rivers on the
bare heights,
and fountains in the broad
valleys;
I will turn the desert into a
marshland,
and the dry ground into
springs of water.
19 I will plant in the desert the
cedar,
acacia, myrtle, and olive;
I will set in the wasteland the
cypress,
together with the plane tree
and the pine,
20 That all may see and know,
observe and understand,
That the hand of the LORD has
done this,
the Holy One of Israel has
created it.

21 Present your case, says the
LORD;
bring forward your reasons,
says the King of Jacob.

22 Let them come near and foretell
to us
what it is that shall happen!
What are the things of long ago?
Tell us, that we may reflect
on them
And know their outcome;
or declare to us the things to
come!
23 Foretell the things that shall
come afterward,
that we may know that you
are gods!
Do something, good or evil,
that will put us in awe and in
fear.
24 Why, you are nothing and your
work is nought!
To choose you is an
abomination.

25 I have stirred up one from the
north, and he comes;
from the east I summon him
by name;
He shall trample the rulers down
like red earth,
as the potter treads the clay.
26 Who announced this from the
beginning, that we might
know;
beforehand, that we might say
it is true?
Not one of you foretold it, not
one spoke;
no one heard you say,
27 "The first news for Zion: they
are coming now,"
or, "For Jerusalem I will pick
out a bearer of the glad
tidings."
28 When I look, there is not one,
no one of them to give
counsel,
to make an answer when I
question them.
29 Ah, all of them are nothing,
their works are nought,
their idols are empty wind!

The Servant of the Lord

42 Here is my servant whom I
uphold,
my chosen one with whom
I am pleased,

41, 14: *Redeemer:* in Hebrew, "goel," one who
frees another from slavery and avenges his sufferings;
cf Lv 25, 48; Dt 19, 6.12.
41, 21–24: An indictment of idols.
41, 25: *I summon him:* Cyrus.

42, 1–4: *Servant:* there are three other "Servant-of-
the-Lord" oracles, 49, 1–7; 50, 4–11; 52, 13—53, 12.
Many identifications have been proposed, e.g.,
historical Israel, ideal Israel, an Old Testament
historical character before or during the lifetime of
the prophet, the prophet himself. The New Testament
and Christian tradition, however, have seen a fulfillment of these prophecies in Jesus Christ.

Upon whom I have put my
  spirit;
  he shall bring forth justice to
    the nations,
2 Not crying out, not shouting,
  not making his voice heard in
    the street.
3 A bruised reed he shall not
  break,
  and a smoldering wick he shall
    not quench,
4 Until he establishes justice on the
  earth;
  the coastlands will wait for his
    teaching.

5 Thus says God, the LORD,
  who created the heavens and
    stretched them out,
  who spreads out the earth
    with its crops,
Who gives breath to its people
  and spirit to those who walk
    on it:
6 I, the LORD, have called you
  for the victory of justice,
  I have grasped you by the
    hand;
I formed you, and set you
  as a covenant of the people,
  a light for the nations,
7 To open the eyes of the blind,
  to bring out prisoners from
    confinement,
  and from the dungeon, those
    who live in darkness.
8 I am the LORD, that is my name;
  my glory I give to no other,
  nor my praise to idols.
9 See, the earlier things have
  come to pass,
  new ones I now foretell;
Before they spring into being,
  I announce them to you.

The Salvation of Israel despite
its Sins

10 Sing to the LORD a new song,
  his praise from the end of the
    earth:
Let the sea and what fills it
  resound,
  the coastlands, and those who
    dwell in them.

11 Let the steppe and its cities cry
  out,
  the villages where Kedar
    dwells;
Let the inhabitants of Sela exult,
  and shout from the top of the
    mountains.
12 Let them give glory to the LORD,
  and utter his praise in the
    coastlands.

13 The LORD goes forth like a hero,
  like a warrior he stirs up his
    ardor;
He shouts out his battle cry,
  against his enemies he shows
    his might:
14 I have looked away, and kept
  silence,
  I have said nothing, holding
    myself in;
But now, I cry out as a woman
  in labor,
  gasping and panting.
15 I will lay waste mountains and
  hills,
  all their herbage I will dry up;
I will turn the rivers into
  marshes,
  and the marshes I will dry up.
16 I will lead the blind on their
  journey;
  by paths unknown I will
    guide them.
I will turn darkness into light
  before them,
  and make crooked ways
    straight.
These things I do for them,
  and I will not forsake them.
17 They shall be turned back in
  utter shame
  who trust in idols;
Who say to molten images,
  "You are our gods."
18 You who are deaf, listen,
  you who are blind, look and
    see!
19 Who is blind but my servant,
  or deaf like the messenger I
    send?
20 You see many things without
  taking note;
  your ears are open, but
    without hearing.

21 Though it pleased the LORD in
  his justice
  to make his law great and
    glorious,
22 This is a people despoiled and
  plundered,
  all of them trapped in holes,
    hidden away in prisons.
They are taken as booty, with no
  one to rescue them,
  as spoil, with no one to
    demand their return.

23 Who of you gives ear to this?
  Who listens and pays heed for
    the time to come?
24 Who was it that gave Jacob to
  be plundered,
  Israel to the despoilers?
Was it not the LORD, against
  whom we have sinned?
  In his ways they refused to
    walk,
  his law they disobeyed.
25 So he poured out wrath upon
  them,
  his anger, and the fury of
    battle;
It blazed round about them, yet
  they did not realize,
  it burned them, but they took
    it not to heart.

Promises of Redemption and
Restoration

43 But now, thus says the LORD,
  who created you, O Jacob,
  and formed you, O
    Israel:
Fear not, for I have redeemed
  you;
  I have called you by name:
    you are mine.
2 When you pass through the
  water, I will be with you;
  in the rivers you shall not
    drown.
When you walk through fire,
  you shall not be burned;
  the flames shall not consume
    you.
3 For I am the LORD, your God,
  the Holy One of Israel, your
    savior.

42, 3: A reference to the mercy of Christ.
42, 4: *Coastlands:* the lands of the Mediterranean. In the Old Testament the word often refers to the pagan lands of the west.

42, 11: *Kedar:* cf footnote to 21, 16. *Sela:* Petra, the capital of Edom.
42, 18–20: Because of their unbelief, the Lord rebukes his people, whom he calls his *servant,* his *messenger.*

42, 22: *A people:* Israel in exile.
42, 24: *Despoilers:* the Assyrians and Babylonians.
43, 3f: *Egypt . . . Ethiopia and Seba:* countries which God permitted the Persians to conquer in return for having given Israel its freedom.

I give Egypt as your ransom,
  Ethiopia and Seba in return
    for you.
4 Because you are precious in my
    eyes
  and glorious, and because I
    love you,
  I give men in return for you
  and peoples in exchange for
    your life.
5 Fear not, for I am with you;
  from the east I will bring back
    your descendants,
  from the west I will gather
    you.
6 I will say to the north: Give
    them up!
  and to the south: Hold not
    back!
  Bring back my sons from afar,
  and my daughters from the
    ends of the earth:
7 Everyone who is named as mine,
  whom I created for my glory,
  whom I formed and made.
8 Lead out the people who are
    blind though they have eyes,
  who are deaf though they
    have ears.

9 Let all the nations gather
    together,
  let the peoples assemble!
  Who among them could have
    revealed this,
  or foretold to us the earlier
    things?
  Let them produce witnesses to
    prove themselves right,
  that one may hear and say,
    "It is true!"
10 You are my witnesses, says the
    LORD,
  my servants whom I have
    chosen
  To know and believe in me
  and understand that it is I.
  Before me no god was formed,
  and after me there shall be
    none.

11 It is I, I the LORD;
  there is no savior but me.
12 It is I who foretold, I who saved;
  I made it known, not any
    strange god among you;

You are my witnesses, says the
    LORD.
  I am God,   13 yes, from
    eternity I am He;
  There is none who can deliver
    from my hand:
  who can countermand what I
    do?
14 Thus says the LORD, your
    redeemer,
  the Holy One of Israel:
  For your sakes I send to
    Babylon;
  I will lower all the bars,
  and the Chaldeans shall cry
    out in lamentation.
15 I am the LORD, your Holy One,
  the creator of Israel, your
    King.
16 Thus says the LORD,
  who opens a way in the sea
  and a path in the mighty
    waters,
17 Who leads out chariots and
    horsemen,
  a powerful army,
  Till they lie prostrate together,
    never to rise,
  snuffed out and quenched like
    a wick.

18 Remember not the events of the
    past,
  the things of long ago
    consider not;
19 See, I am doing something new!
  Now it springs forth, do you
    not perceive it?
  In the desert I make a way,
  in the wasteland, rivers.
20 Wild beasts honor me,
  jackals and ostriches,
  For I put water in the desert
  and rivers in the wasteland
    for my chosen people to
    drink,
21 The people whom I formed for
    myself,
  that they might announce my
    praise.

22 Yet you did not call upon me,
    O Jacob,
  for you grew weary of me, O
    Israel.

23 You did not bring me sheep for
    your holocausts,
  nor honor me with your
    sacrifices.
  I did not exact from you the
    service of offerings,
  nor weary you for
    frankincense.
24 You did not buy me sweet cane
    for money,
  nor fill me with the fat of
    your sacrifices;
  Instead, you burdened me with
    your sins,
  and wearied me with your
    crimes.
25 It is I, I, who wipe out,
  for my own sake, your
    offenses;
  your sins I remember no
    more.
26 Would you have me remember,
  have us come to trial?
  Speak up, prove your
    innocence!
27 Your first father sinned;
  your spokesmen rebelled
    against me
28 Till I repudiated the holy gates,
  put Jacob under the ban,
  and exposed Israel to scorn.

44 Hear then, O Jacob, my
    servant,
    Israel, whom I have chosen.
2 Thus, says the LORD who made
    you,
  your help, who formed you
    from the womb:
  Fear not, O Jacob, my servant,
  the darling whom I have
    chosen.
3 I will pour out water upon the
    thirsty ground,
  and streams upon the dry
    land;
  I will pour out my spirit upon
    your offspring,
  and my blessing upon your
    descendants.
4 They shall spring up amid the
    verdure
  like poplars beside the flowing
    waters.

43, 9: Only God can know and predict future events; cf 41, 1–5.21–29.

43, 14–17: The destruction of Babylon.

43, 18: No need to think solely of the past wonders of the exodus from Egypt; equally great is the exodus from Babylon.

43, 22–28: The reason for the liberation of the Israelites is not their fidelity but rather God's mercy.

43, 24: *Sewet cane:* a fragrant substance used in making incense and the sacred anointing oil; cf Ex 30, 23; Jer 6, 20.

43, 27: *First father:* Adam or Jacob, or collec-

tively "early ancestors." *Spokesmen:* leaders, priests, prophets.

44, 2: *The darling:* see note on Dt 32, 15; cf also Dt 33, 5.26.

5 One shall say, "I am the
    Lord's,"
    another shall be named after
      Jacob,
  And this one shall write on his
      hand, "The Lord's,"
    and Israel shall be his surname.

The True God and False Gods

6 Thus says the Lord, Israel's
    King
    and redeemer, the Lord of
      hosts:
  I am the first and I am the last;
    there is no God but me.
7 Who is like me? Let him stand
    up and speak,
    make it evident, and confront
      me with it.
  Who of old announced future
    events?
  Let them foretell to us the
    things to come.
8 Fear not, be not troubled:
    did I not announce and foretell
      it long ago?
  You are my witnesses! Is there
    a God
    or any Rock besides me?

9 Idol makers all amount to nothing, and their precious works are of no avail, as they themselves give witness. To their shame, they neither see nor know anything; and they are more deaf than men are. 10 Indeed, all the associates of anyone who forms a god, or casts an idol to no purpose, will be put to shame; 11 they will all assemble and stand forth, to be reduced to fear and shame. 12 The smith fashions an iron image, works it over the coals, shapes it with hammers, and forges it with his strong arm. He is hungry and weak, drinks no water and becomes exhausted. 13 The carpenter stretches a line and marks with a stylus the outline of an idol. He shapes it with a plane and measures it off with a compass, making it like a man in appearance and dignity, to occupy a shrine. 14 He cuts down cedars, takes a holm or an oak, and lays hold of other trees of the forest, which the Lord had planted and the rain made grow 15 to serve man for fuel. With a part of their wood he warms himself, or makes a fire for baking bread; but with another part he makes a god which he adores, an idol which he worships. 16 Half of it he burns in the fire, and on its embers he roasts his meat; he eats what he has roasted until he is full, and then warms himself and says, "Ah! I am warm, I feel the fire." 17 Of what remains he makes a god, his idol, and prostrate before it in worship, he implores it, "Rescue me, for you are my god."

18 The idols have neither knowledge nor reason; their eyes are coated so that they cannot see, and their hearts so that they cannot understand. 19 Yet he does not reflect, nor have the intelligence and sense to say, "Half of the wood I burned in the fire, and on its embers I baked bread and roasted meat which I ate. Shall I then make an abomination out of the rest, or worship a block of wood?" 20 He is chasing ashes—a thing that cannot save itself when the flame consumes it; yet he does not say, "Is not this thing in my right hand a fraud?"

21 Remember this, O Jacob,
    you, O Israel, who are my
      servant!
  I formed you to be a servant to
    me;
  O Israel, by me you shall
    never be forgotten:
22 I have brushed away your
    offenses like a cloud,
    your sins like a mist;
  return to me, for I have
    redeemed you.
23 Raise a glad cry, you heavens:
    the Lord has done this;
  shout, you depths of the
    earth.
  Break forth, you mountains,
    into song,
  you forest, with all your
    trees.

For the Lord, has redeemed
    Jacob,
  and shows his glory through
    Israel.

Cyrus, Anointed of the Lord, Liberator of Israel

24 Thus says the Lord, your
    redeemer,
    who formed you from the
      womb:
  I am the Lord, who made all
    things,
    who alone stretched out the
      heavens;
    when I spread out the earth,
    who was with me?
25 It is I who bring to nought the
    omens of liars,
    who make fools of diviners;
  I turn wise men back
    and make their knowledge
      foolish.
26 It is I who confirm the words of
    my servants,
  I carry out the plan
    announced by my
      messengers;
  I say to Jerusalem; Be inhabited;
    to the cities of Judah: Be
      rebuilt;
    I will raise up their ruins.
27 It is I who said to the deep: Be
    dry;
    I will dry up your wellsprings.
28 I say of Cyrus: My shepherd,
    who fulfills my every wish;
  He shall say of Jerusalem, "Let
    her be rebuilt,"
    and of the temple, "Let its
      foundations be laid."

45 Thus says the Lord to his
    anointed, Cyrus,
    whose right hand I grasp,
  Subduing nations before him,
    and making kings run in his
      service,
  Opening doors before him
    and leaving the gates unbarred:
2 I will go before you
    and level the mountains;
  Bronze doors I will shatter,
    and iron bars I will snap.

44, 5: *Write on his hand:* an allusion to the Babylonian custom of tatooing the owner's name on the hand of his slave; cf also Rv 13, 16.

44, 8: *Rock:* place of refuge; said of God in Dt 32, 4.18; 1 Sm 2, 2; etc.

44, 9–20: Satire on the makers and worshipers of idols.

44, 20: *Chasing ashes:* exerting efforts in vain; cf Hos 12, 2; Eccl 1, 14; 2, 11.17.

44, 28: *Cyrus:* king of Persia (559–529 B.C.) and conqueror of Babylon (538 B.C.), who liberated the Jews, permitting them to return to their native land and to rebuild Jerusalem and the Temple.

45, 1: *Anointed:* in Hebrew, *meshiah*, from which the word "Messiah" is derived; from its Greek translation, *Christos*, we have the name "Christ." Applied to kings, it originally referred only to those of Israel, but it is here given to *Cyrus* because he is the agent of the Lord.

45, 2: *Bronze doors:* of Babylon.

3 I will give you treasures out of
the darkness,
and riches that have been
hidden away,
That you may know that I am
the LORD,
the God of Israel, who calls
you by your name.

4 For the sake of Jacob, my
servant,
of Israel my chosen one,
I have called you by your name,
giving you a title, though you
knew me not.

5 I am the LORD and there is no
other,
there is no God besides me.
It is I who arm you, though you
know me not.

6 so that toward the rising and
the setting of the sun
men may know that there is
none besides me.
I am the LORD, there is no
other;

7 I form the light, and create
the darkness,
I make well-being and create
woe;
I, the LORD, do all these
things.

8 Let justice descend, O heavens,
like dew from above,
like gentle rain let the skies
drop it down.
Let the earth open and salvation
bud forth;
let justice also spring up!
I, the LORD, have created this.

9 Woe to him who contends with
his Maker;
a potsherd among potsherds
of the earth!
Dare the clay say to its modeler,
"What are you doing?"
or, "What you are making
has no hands"?

10 Woe to him who asks a father,
"What are you begetting?"
or a woman, "What are you
giving birth to?"

11 Thus, says the LORD,
the Holy One of Israel, his
maker:
You question me about my
children,
or prescribe the work of my
hands for me!

12 It was I who made the earth
and created mankind upon it;
It was my hands that stretched
out the heavens;
I gave the order to all their
host.

13 It was I who stirred up one for
the triumph of justice,
all his ways I make level.
He shall rebuild my city
and let my exiles go free
Without price or ransom,
says the LORD of hosts.

14　　Thus says the LORD:
The earnings of Egypt, the gain
of Ethiopia,
and the Sabeans, tall of
stature,
Shall come over to you and
belong to you;
they shall follow you, coming
in chains.
Before you they shall fall
prostrate,
saying in prayer:
"With you only is God, and
nowhere else;
the gods are nought.

15 Truly with you God is hidden,
the God of Israel, the savior!

16 Those are put to shame and
disgrace
who vent their anger against
him;
Those go in disgrace
who carve images.

17 Israel, you are saved by the LORD,
saved forever!
You shall never be put to shame
or disgrace
in future ages."

18　　For thus says the LORD,
The creator of the heavens,
who is God,

The designer and maker of the
earth
who established it,
Not creating it to be a waste,
but designing it to be lived in:
I am the LORD, and there is no
other.

19　I have not spoken from hiding
nor from some dark place of
the earth,
And I have not said to the
descendants of Jacob,
"Look for me in an empty
waste."
I, the LORD, promise justice,
I foretell what is right.

20 Come and assemble, gather
together,
you fugitives from among the
gentiles!
They are without knowledge who
bear wooden idols
and pray to gods that cannot
save.

21 Come here and declare
in counsel together:
Who announced this from the
beginning
and foretold it from of old?
Was it not I, the LORD,
besides whom there is no
other God?
There is no just and saving
God but me.

22 Turn to me and be safe,
all you ends of the earth,
for I am God; there is no
other!

23 By myself I swear,
uttering my just decree
and my unalterable word:
To me every knee shall bend;
by me every tongue shall
swear,

24 Saying, "Only in the LORD
are just deeds and power.
Before him in shame shall come
all who vent their anger
against him.

45, 6: The Gentiles will come to know the true
God; cf also vv 20–25.

45, 7: *Create woe:* God permits evil for the sake of
a greater good.

45, 8: The Vulgate rendering gives a more precise
Messianic sense to this verse, using "just one" and
"savior" in place of *justice* and *salvation.* The Advent
liturgy uses the Vulgate form, *Rorate coeli desuper*
. . . , to express the world's longing for the coming of
Christ.

45, 9: No one may challenge God's freedom of
action, exemplified here by the selection of Cyrus as
his anointed.

45, 13: *One:* Cyrus, called by God for the deliverance and restoration of Israel.

45, 14: *Egypt . . . Ethiopia . . . Sabeans:* the Egyptians and their allies who, when conquered by Cyrus,
are seen as acknowledging the God of Israel to be the
one true God; cf 43, 3.

45, 15: *God is hidden:* he dwells invisibly in the holy

of holies.

45, 18: *Waste:* an allusion to the beginning of
creation, when the earth was *waste and void* (Gn 1, 2),
the same Hebrew word, *tohu,* being used in both
passages. The further reference here is to Palestine,
which God wishes again to be inhabited by the
returning exiles.

45, 20: *Who bear wooden idols:* in their religious
processions. The gods of the pagans have feet but
cannot walk; cf Ps 115, 7; Bar 6, 25.

25 In the LORD shall be the
      vindication and the glory
   of all the descendants of
      Israel."

The Gods of Babylon

46 Bel bows down, Nebo stoops,
      their idols are upon beasts
      and cattle;
   They must be borne up on
      shoulders,
      carried as burdens by the
      weary.
2 They stoop and bow down
      together;
   unable to save those who bear
      them,
      they too go into captivity.

3 Hear me, O house of Jacob,
      all who remain of the house
      of Israel,
   My burden since your birth,
      whom I have carried from
      your infancy.
4 Even to your old age I am the
      same,
      even when your hair is gray I
      will bear you;
   It is I who have done this, I
      who will continue,
      and I who will carry you to
      safety.

5 Whom would you compare me
      with, as an equal,
      or match me against, as
      though we were alike?
6 There are those who pour out
      gold from a purse
      and weigh out silver on the
      scales;
   Then they hire a goldsmith to
      make it into a god
      before which they fall down
      in worship.
7 They lift it to their shoulders to
      carry;
      when they set it in place again,
      it stays,
      and does not move from the
      spot.
   Although they cry out to it, it
      cannot answer;
      it delivers no one from distress.

8 Remember this and be firm,
      bear it well in mind, you
      rebels;
      remember the former things,
      those long ago:
9 I am God, there is no other;
      I am God, there is none like
      me.
10 At the beginning I foretell the
      outcome;
      in advance, things not yet
      done.
   I say that my plan shall stand,
      I accomplish my every
      purpose.
11 I call from the east a bird of prey,
      from a distant land, one to
      carry out my plan.
   Yes, I have spoken, I will
      accomplish it;
      I have planned it, and I will
      do it.
12 Listen to me, you fainthearted,
      you who seem far from the
      victory of justice:
13 I am bringing on my justice, it
      is not far off,
      my salvation shall not tarry;
   I will put salvation within Zion,
      and give to Israel my glory.

The Fall of Babylon

47 Come down, sit in the dust,
      O virgin daughter Babylon;
   Sit on the ground, dethroned,
      O daughter of the Chaldeans.
   No longer shall you be called
      dainty and delicate.
2 Take the millstone and grind
      flour,
      remove your veil;
   Strip off your train, bare your
      legs,
      pass through the streams.
3 Your nakedness shall be
      uncovered
      and your shame be seen;
   I will take vengeance,
      I will yield to no entreaty,
      says our redeemer,
4 Whose name is the LORD of
      hosts,
      the Holy One of Israel.

5 Go into darkness and sit in
      silence,
      O daughter of the Chaldeans,

No longer shall you be called
      sovereign mistress of
      kingdoms.
6 Angry at my people,
      I profaned my inheritance,
   And I gave them into your
      hand;
      but you showed them no
      mercy,
   And upon old men
      you laid a very heavy yoke.
7 You said, "I shall remain
      always
      a sovereign mistress forever!"
   But you did not lay these things
      to heart,
      you disregarded their outcome.

8 Now hear this, voluptuous one,
      enthroned securely,
   Saying to yourself,
      "I, and no one else!
   I shall never be a widow,
      or suffer the loss of my
      children"—
9 Both these things shall come to
      you
      suddenly, in a single day:
   Complete bereavement and
      widowhood
      shall come upon you
   For your many sorceries
      and the great number of your
      spells;
10 Because you felt secure in your
      wickedness,
      and said, "No one sees me."

   Your wisdom and your
      knowledge
      led you astray,
   And you said to yourself,
      "I, and no one else!"
11 But upon you shall come evil
      you will not know how to
      predict;
   Disaster shall befall you
      which you cannot allay.
   Suddenly there shall come upon
      you
      ruin which you will not
      expect.
12 Keep up, now, your spells
      and your many sorceries.
   Perhaps you can make them
      avail,
      perhaps you can strike terror!

46, 1; *Bel . . . Nebo:* gods of Babylon; their complete helplessness is here contrasted with God's omnipotence.

46, 11: *From the east a bird of prey:* Cyrus; cf 41, 2–4.
47, 1–15: A taunt-song, mocking Babylon, once

queen of the nations, now made a slave girl.
47, 9.13.15: Babylon was known for its sorcery and astrology.

13 You wearied yourself with many
      consultations,
   at which you toiled from your
      youth;
   Let the astrologers stand forth
      to save you,
   the stargazers who forecast at
      each new moon
   what would happen to you.
14 Lo, they are like stubble,
   fire consumes them;
   They cannot save themselves
      from the spreading flames.
   This is no warming ember,
      no fire to sit before.
15 Thus do your wizards serve you
   with whom you have toiled
      from your youth;
   Each wanders his own way,
      with none to save you.

Exhortations to the Exiles

48 Hear this, O house of Jacob
         called by the name Israel,
      sprung from the stock of Judah,
   You who swear by the name of
      the LORD
   and invoke the God of Israel
   without sincerity or justice,
2 Though you are named after the
      holy city
   and rely on the God of Israel,
      whose name is the LORD of
      hosts.
3 Things of the past I foretold
      long ago,
   they went forth from my
      mouth, I let you hear of
      them;
   then suddenly I took action
      and they came to be.
4 Because I know that you are
      stubborn
   and that your neck is an iron
      sinew
   and your forehead bronze
5 I foretold them to you of old;
   before they took place I let
      you hear of them,
   That you might not say, "My
      idol did them,
   my statue, my molten image
      commanded them."
6 Now that you have heard, look
      at all this;
   must you not admit it?

From now on I announce new
      things to you,
   hidden events of which you
      knew not.
7 Now, not long ago, they are
      brought into being,
   and beforetime you did not
      hear of them,
   so that you cannot claim to
      have known them;
8 You neither heard nor knew,
      they did not reach your ears
      beforehand.
   Yes, I know you are utterly
      treacherous,
   a rebel you were called from
      birth.
9 For the sake of my name I
      restrain my anger,
   for the sake of my renown I
      hold it back from you,
   lest I should destroy you.
10 See, I have refined you like silver,
   tested you in the furnace of
      affliction.
11 For my sake, for my own sake,
      I do this;
   why should I suffer
      profanation?
   My glory I will not give to
      another.
12 Listen to me, Jacob,
   Israel, whom I named!
   I, it is I who am the first,
   and also the last am I.
13 Yes, my hand laid the
      foundations of the earth;
   my right hand spread out the
      heavens.
   When I call them,
      they stand forth at once.
14 All of you assemble and listen:
   Who among you foretold
      these things?
   The LORD's friend shall do his
      will
   against Babylon and the
      progeny of Chaldea.
15 I myself have spoken, I have
      called him,
   I have brought him, and his
      way succeeds!
16 Come near to me and hear this!
   Not from the beginning did I
      speak it in secret;

At the time it comes to pass, I
      am present:
   "Now the Lord GOD has
      sent me, and his spirit."
17 Thus says the LORD, your
      redeemer,
   the Holy One of Israel:
   I, the LORD, your God,
      teach you what is for your
      good,
   and lead you on the way you
      should go.
18 If you would hearken to my
      commandments,
   your prosperity would be like
      a river,
   and your vindication like the
      waves of the sea;
19 Your descendants would be like
      the sand,
   and those born of your stock
      like its grains,
   Their name never cut off
      or blotted out from my
      presence.
20 Go forth from Babylon, flee
      from Chaldea!
   With shouts of joy proclaim
      this, make it known;
   Publish it to the end of the
      earth, and say,
   "The LORD has redeemed his
      servant Jacob.
21 They did not thirst
   when he led them through
      dry lands;
   Water from the rock he set
      flowing for them;
   he cleft the rock, and waters
      welled forth."
22 [There is no peace for the wicked,
   says the LORD.]

EXPIATION OF SIN
SPIRITUAL LIBERATION OF ISRAEL

The Servant of the Lord

49 Hear me, O coastlands,
         listen, O distant peoples.
      The LORD called me from birth,
      from my mother's womb he
      gave me my name.
2 He made of me a sharp-edged
      sword
   and concealed me in the
      shadow of his arm.

He made me a polished arrow,
  in his quiver he hid me.
3 You are my servant, he said to
    me,
  Israel, through whom I show
    my glory.

4 Though I thought I had toiled
    in vain,
  and for nothing, uselessly,
    spent my strength,
  Yet my reward is with the
    LORD,
  my recompense is with my
    God.
5 For now the LORD has spoken
    who formed me as his servant
    from the womb,
  That Jacob may be brought
    back to him
  and Israel gathered to him;
  And I am made glorious in the
    sight of the LORD,
  and my God is now my
    strength!
6 It is too little, he says, for you
    to be my servant,
  to raise up the tribes of
    Jacob,
  and restore the survivors of
    Israel;
  I will make you a light to the
    nations,
  that my salvation may reach
    to the ends of the earth.
7 Thus says the LORD,
  the redeemer and the Holy
    One of Israel,
  To the one despised, whom the
    nations abhor,
  the slave of rulers:
  When kings see you, they shall
    stand up,
  and princes shall prostrate
    themselves
  Because of the LORD who is
    faithful,
  the Holy One of Israel who
    has chosen you.

The Liberation and Restoration of Zion

8   Thus says the LORD:
  In a time of favor I answer you,
    on the day of salvation I help
    you,

To restore the land
  and allot the desolate
    heritages,
9 Saying to the prisoners: Come
    out!
  To those in darkness: Show
    yourselves!
  Along the ways they shall find
    pasture,
  on every bare height shall their
    pastures be.
10 They shall not hunger or thirst,
  nor shall the scorching wind
    or the sun strike them;
  For he who pities them leads
    them
  and guides them beside
    springs of water.
11 I will cut a road through all my
    mountains,
  and make my highways level.
12 See, some shall come from afar,
  others from the north and the
    west,
  and some from the land of
    Syene.

13 Sing out, O heavens, and
    rejoice, O earth,
  break forth into song, you
    mountains.
  For the LORD comforts his
    people
  and shows mercy to his
    afflicted.

14 But Zion said, "The LORD has
    forsaken me;
  my Lord has forgotten me."
15 Can a mother forget her infant,
  be without tenderness for the
    child of her womb?
  Even should she forget,
  I will never forget you.
16 See, upon the palms of my hands
    I have written your name;
  your walls are ever before me.
17 Your rebuilders make haste,
  as those who tore you down
    and laid you waste
  go forth from you;
18 Look about and see,
  they are all gathering and
    coming to you.

As I live, says the LORD,
  you shall be arrayed with them
    all as with adornments,
  like a bride you shall fasten
    them on you.

19 Though you were waste and
    desolate,
  a land of ruins,
  Now you shall be too small for
    your inhabitants,
  while those who swallowed
    you up will be far away.
20 The children whom you had
    lost
  shall yet say to you,
  "This place is too small for me,
    make room for me to live in."
21 You shall ask yourself:
    "Who has borne me these?
  I was bereft and barren
    [exiled and repudiated];
  who has reared them?
  I was left all alone;
    where then do these come
    from?"

22   Thus says the Lord GOD:
  See, I will lift up my hand to
    the nations,
  and raise my signal to the
    peoples;
  They shall bring your sons in
    their arms,
  and your daughters shall be
    carried on their shoulders.
23 Kings shall be your foster
    fathers,
  their princesses your nurses;
  Bowing to the ground, they
    shall worship you
  and lick the dust at your feet.
  Then you shall know that I am
    the LORD,
  and those who hope in me
    shall never be disappointed.

24   Thus says the LORD:
  Can booty be taken from a
    warrior?
  or captives be rescued from a
    tyrant?
25 Yes, captives can be taken from
    a warrior,
  and booty be rescued from a
    tyrant;

49, 3: *Israel:* the Servant is identified with the people of Israel as their ideal representative; however, since vv 5f seem to distinguish the Servant from Israel, some regard the word *Israel* here as a gloss.

49, 6: The Servant's vocation will be not only the restoration of Israel but the conversion of the world; cf Lk 2, 32.

49, 12: *Syene:* now called Aswan, at the first

cataract of the Nile in southern Egypt.

49, 16: *Upon the palms ... name:* for continual remembrance; cf Ex 13, 9.16; Dt 6, 6–9.

Those who oppose you I will
 oppose,
 and your sons I will save.
26 I will make your oppressors eat
 their own flesh,
 and they shall be drunk with
 their own blood
 as with the juice of the grape.
All mankind shall know
 that I, the LORD, am your
 savior,
 your redeemer, the Mighty
 One of Jacob.

Salvation only through the Lord's Servant

50 Thus says the LORD:
 Where is the bill of divorce
 with which I dismissed your
 mother?
Or to which of my creditors
 have I sold you?
It was for your sins that you
 were sold,
 for your crimes that your
 mother was dismissed.

2 Why was no one there when I
 came?
 Why did no one answer when
 I called?
Is my hand too short to ransom?
 Have I not the strength to
 deliver?
Lo, with my rebuke I dry up the
 sea,
 I turn rivers into a desert;
Their fish rot for lack of water,
 and die of thirst.
3 I clothe the heavens in mourning,
 and make sackcloth their
 vesture.

4 The Lord GOD has given me
 a well-trained tongue,
That I might know how to
 speak to the weary
 a word that will rouse them.
Morning after morning
 he opens my ear that I may
 hear;
5 And I have not rebelled,
 have not turned back.

6 I gave my back to those who
 beat me,
 my cheeks to those who
 plucked my beard;
My face I did not shield
 from buffers and spitting.

7 The Lord GOD is my help,
 therefore I am not disgraced;
I have set my face like flint,
 knowing that I shall not be
 put to shame.
8 He is near who upholds my
 right;
 if anyone wishes to oppose me,
 let us appear together.
Who disputes my right?
 Let him confront me.
9 See, the Lord GOD is my help;
 who will prove me wrong?
Lo, they will all wear out like
 cloth,
 the moth will eat them up.

10 Who among you fears the LORD,
 heeds his servant's voice,
And walks in darkness
 without any light,
Trusting in the name of the
 LORD
 and relying on his God?
11 All of you kindle flames
 and carry about you fiery
 darts;
Walk by the light of your own
 fire
 and by the flares you have
 burnt!
This is your fate from my
 hand:
 you shall lie down in a place
 of pain.

Exhortation to Trust in the Lord

51 Listen to me, you who
 pursue justice,
 who seek the LORD;
Look to the rock from which
 you were hewn,
 to the pit from which you
 were quarried;
2 Look to Abraham, your father,
 and to Sarah, who gave you
 birth;

When he was but one I called
 him,
 I blessed him and made him
 many.
3 Yes, the LORD shall comfort
 Zion
 and have pity on all her ruins;
Her deserts he shall make like
 Eden,
 her wasteland like the garden
 of the LORD;
Joy and gladness shall be found
 in her,
 thanksgiving and the sound of
 song.

4 Be attentive to me, my people;
 my folk, give ear to me.
For law shall go forth from my
 presence,
 and my judgment, as the
 light of the peoples.
5 I will make my justice come
 speedily;
 my salvation shall go forth
 [and my arm shall judge the
 nations];
In me shall the coastlands hope,
 and my arm they shall await.

6 Raise your eyes to the heavens,
 and look at the earth below;
Though the heavens grow thin
 like smoke,
 the earth wears out like a
 garment
 and its inhabitants die like
 flies,
My salvation shall remain
 forever
 and my justice shall never be
 dismayed.
7 Hear me, you who know
 justice,
 you people who have my
 teaching at heart:
Fear not the reproach of men,
 be not dismayed at their
 revilings.
8 They shall be like a garment
 eaten by moths,
 like wool consumed by grubs;

50, 1: Responding to the people's complaint of utter abandonment by God, the prophet shows that their sins were responsible for their banishment. Since there was no bill of divorce, the bond between the Lord and his people still exists and he will ultimately save them.
50, 2: Israel's faith in God is weak; she does not answer his call, nor believe in his promises of deliverance.

50, 4–11: The third of the four "Servant-of-the-Lord" oracles; in vv 4–9 the Servant speaks; in vv 10f God reproves the people for not following the Servant.
50, 5: The Servant does not refuse the divine vocation.
50, 6: He willingly submits to insults and beatings. *Plucked my beard:* a grave insult.
50, 10f: Instead of trusting in the Lord and his

Servant, the people rely on their own devices, to their own destruction.
51, 1: *Rock . . . pit:* your glorious ancestry.
51, 4f: The conversion of the Gentiles.
51, 6: God's *salvation* and *justice* are eternal, in contrast to the impermanence of *the heavens* and *the earth:* cf Mt 24, 35.

But my justice shall remain
    forever
and my salvation, for all
    generations.

9 Awake, awake, put on strength,
    O arm of the LORD!
Awake as in the days of old,
    in ages long ago!
Was it not you who crushed
    Rahab,
    you who pierced the dragon?
10 Was it not you who dried up the
    sea,
    the waters of the great deep,
Who made the depths of the
    sea into a way
    for the redeemed to pass
    over?
11 Those whom the LORD has
    ransomed will return
    and enter Zion singing,
    crowned with everlasting joy;
They will meet with joy and
    gladness,
    sorrow and mourning will flee.

12 I, it is I who comfort you.
    Can you then fear mortal man,
    who is human only, to be
    looked upon as grass,
13 And forget the LORD, your
    maker,
    who stretched out the heavens
    and laid the foundations of
    the earth?
All the day you are in constant
    dread
    of the fury of the oppressor;
But when he sets himself to
    destroy,
    what is there of the
    oppressor's fury?

14 The oppressed shall soon be
    released;
    they shall not die and go down
    into the pit,
    nor shall they want for
    bread.
15 For I am the LORD, your God,
    who stirs up the sea so that
    its waves roar;
    the LORD of hosts by name.
16 I have put my words into your
    mouth
    and shielded you in the shadow
    of my hand,

I, who stretched out the heavens,
    who laid the foundations of
    the earth,
    who say to Zion: You are my
    people.

The Cup of the Lord

17 Awake, awake!
    Arise, O Jerusalem,
    You who drank at the LORD's
    hand
    the cup of his wrath;
    Who drained to the dregs
    the bowl of staggering!
18 She has no one to guide her
    of all the sons she bore;
    She has no one to grasp her by
    the hand,
    of all the sons she reared!—
19 Your misfortunes are double;
    who is there to condole with
    you?
    Desolation and destruction,
    famine and sword!
    Who is there to comfort you?
20 Your sons lie helpless
    at every street corner
    like antelopes in a net.
    They are filled with the wrath of
    the LORD,
    the rebuke of your God.

21 But now, hear this, O afflicted
    one,
    drunk, but not with wine,
22 Thus says the LORD, your
    Master,
    your God, who defends his
    people:
    See, I am taking from your hand
    the cup of staggering;
    The bowl of my wrath
    you shall no longer drink.
23 I will put it into the hands of
    your tormentors,
    those who ordered you
    to bow down, that they might
    walk over you,
    While you offered your back
    like the ground,
    like the street for them to
    walk on.

Let Zion Rejoice

52 Awake, awake!
    Put on your strength, O
    Zion;

Put on your glorious garments,
    O Jerusalem, holy city.
No longer shall the
    uncircumcised
    or the unclean enter you.
2 Shake off the dust,
    ascend to the throne,
    Jerusalem;
Loose the bonds from your
    neck,
    O captive daughter Zion!
3   For thus says the LORD:
You were sold for nothing,
    and without money you shall
    be redeemed.
4   Thus says the Lord GOD:
To Egypt in the beginning my
    people went down,
    to sojourn there;
Assyria, too, oppressed them
    for nought.
5 But now, what am I to do here?
    says the LORD.
My people have been taken
    away without redress;
    their rulers make a boast of
    it, says the LORD;
    all the day my name is
    constantly reviled.
6 Therefore on that day my people
    shall know my renown,
    that it is I who have foretold
    it. Here I am!
7 How beautiful upon the
    mountains
    are the feet of him who
    brings glad tidings,
Announcing peace, bearing good
    news,
    announcing salvation, and
    saying to Zion,
    "Your God is King!"
8 Hark! Your watchmen raise a
    cry,
    together they shout for joy,
For they see directly, before
    their eyes,
    the LORD restoring Zion.
9 Break out together in song,
    O ruins of Jerusalem!
For the Lord comforts his
    people,
    he redeems Jerusalem.
10 The LORD has bared his holy
    arm
    in the sight of all the nations;

51, 9: *Rahab:* see note on 30, 7. *The dragon:* see notes on 27, 1; Ps 74, 13.

51, 10: *Great deep:* another reference to the primeval chaos of Gn 1, 2.

52, 7–10: God leads his people back from Babylon to Zion, from whose ruined walls *watchmen . . . shout for joy;* cf Rom 10, 15.

All the ends of the earth will
    behold
        the salvation of our God.

11 Depart, depart, come forth
        from there,
    touch nothing unclean!
    Out from there! Purify yourselves,
        you who carry the vessels of
        the LORD.
12 Yet not in fearful haste will
        you come out,
    nor leave in headlong flight,
    For the LORD comes before you,
        and your rear guard is the
        God of Israel.

Suffering and Triumph of the Servant of the Lord

13 See, my servant shall prosper,
    he shall be raised high and
        greatly exalted.
14 Even as many were amazed at
        him—
    so marred was his look beyond
        that of man,
    and his appearance beyond
        that of mortals—
15 So shall he startle many nations,
    because of him kings shall
        stand speechless;
    For those who have not been
        told shall see,
    those who have not heard
        shall ponder it.

53 Who would believe what we
        have heard?
    To whom has the arm of
        the LORD been revealed?
2 He grew up like a sapling
        before him,
    like a shoot from the
        parched earth;
    There was in him no stately
        bearing to make us look at
        him,
    nor appearance that would
        attract us to him.
3 He was spurned and avoided by
        men,
    a man of suffering,
        accustomed to infirmity,

One of those from whom men
    hide their faces,
    spurned, and we held him in
        no esteem.

4 Yet it was our infirmities that
        he bore,
    our sufferings that he endured,
    While we thought of him as
        stricken,
    as one smitten by God and
        afflicted.
5 But he was pierced for our
        offenses,
    crushed for our sins;
    Upon him was the chastisement
        that makes us whole,
    by his stripes we were healed.
6 We had all gone astray like
        sheep,
    each following his own way;
    But the LORD laid upon him
        the guilt of us all.

7 Though he was harshly treated,
        he submitted
    and opened not his mouth;
    Like a lamb led to the slaughter
    or a sheep before the shearers,
        he was silent and opened not
        his mouth.
8 Oppressed and condemned, he
        was taken away,
    and who would have thought
        any more of his destiny?
    When he was cut off from the
        land of the living,
    and smitten for the sin of his
        people,
9 A grave was assigned him among
        the wicked
    and a burial place with
        evildoers,
    Though he had done no wrong
        nor spoken any falsehood.
10 [But the LORD was pleased
        to crush him in infirmity.]

If he gives his life as an offering
        for sin,
    he shall see his descendants
        in a long life,
    and the will of the LORD shall be
        accomplished through him.

11 Because of his affliction
    he shall see the light in fullness
        of days;
    Through his suffering, my
        servant shall justify many,
    and their guilt he shall bear.
12 Therefore I will give him his
        portion among the great,
    and he shall divide the spoils
        with the mighty,
    Because he surrendered himself
        to death
    and was counted among the
        wicked;
    And he shall take away the sins
        of many,
    and win pardon for their
        offenses.

The New Zion

54 Raise a glad cry, you barren
        one who did not bear,
    break forth in jubilant
        song, you who were not in
        labor,
    For more numerous are the
        children of the deserted
        wife
    than the children of her who
        has a husband,
    says the LORD.
2 Enlarge the space for your tent,
    spread out your tent cloths
        unsparingly;
    lengthen your ropes and make
        firm your stakes.
3 For you shall spread abroad to
        the right and to the left;
    Your descendants shall
        dispossess the nations
    and shall people the desolate
        cities.

4 Fear not, you shall not be put
        to shame;
    you need not blush, for you
        shall not be disgraced.
    The shame of your youth you
        shall forget,
    the reproach of your
        widowhood no longer
        remember.

52, 11: *From there:* from Babylon. *Vessels of the Lord:* taken to Babylon by Nebuchadnezzar, now carried back by the exiled priests returning in procession to Zion; cf Ezr 1, 7.

52, 13—53, 12: The last of the four "Servant-of-the-Lord" oracles. An extraordinary description of the sinless Servant, who by his voluntary suffering atones for the sins of his people, and saves them from just punishment at the hands of God. Only in Jesus

Christ is the prophecy perfectly fulfilled.

53, 2: Only God appreciated his Servant's true greatness.

53, 3: Because he suffered, he was regarded as a sinner and therefore as one to be *spurned*.

53, 4ff: He did indeed suffer but it was for the sins of mankind, and through his sufferings men are *healed*.

53, 10ff: Because he fulfilled the divine will by suffering for the sins of others, the Servant will be

rewarded by the Lord. *See the light:* enjoy happiness. This line may originally have read, "he shall drink and eat to the full"—at the thanksgiving sacrifice at which *he shall divide the spoils* (v 12).

54, 1: Jerusalem, pictured as a wife who had been *barren* and *deserted*, now suddenly finds herself with innumerable children (the returning exiles); cf Gal 4, 27 for the application of this text to the Church, the New Zion.

5 For he who has become your
    husband is your Maker;
  his name is the LORD of hosts;
Your redeemer is the Holy One
    of Israel,
  called God of all the earth.

6 The LORD calls you back,
  like a wife forsaken and
    grieved in spirit,
A wife married in youth and
    then cast off,
  says your God.
7 For a brief moment I abandoned
    you,
  but with great tenderness I
    will take you back.
8 In an outburst of wrath, for a
    moment
  I hid my face from you;
But with enduring love I take
    pity on you,
  says the LORD, your redeemer.

9 This is for me like the days of
    Noah,
  when I swore that the waters
    of Noah
  should never again deluge the
    earth;
So I have sworn not to be angry
    with you,
  or to rebuke you.
10 Though the mountains leave
    their place
  and the hills be shaken,
My love shall never leave you
  nor my covenant of peace be
    shaken,
  says the LORD, who has mercy
    on you.

11 O afflicted one, storm-battered
    and unconsoled,
  I lay your pavements in
    carnelians,
  and your foundations in
    sapphires;
12 I will make your battlements of
    rubies,
  your gates of carbuncles,
  and all your walls of precious
    stones.
13 All your sons shall be taught by
    the LORD,
  and great shall be the peace of
    your children.

14 In justice shall you be
    established,
  far from the fear of oppression,
  where destruction cannot come
    near you.
15 Should there be any attack, it
    shall not be of my making;
  whoever attacks you shall fall
    before you.
16 Lo, I have created the
    craftsman
  who blows on the burning
    coals
  and forges weapons as his
    work;
  It is I also who have created
    the destroyer to work havoc.
17 No weapon fashioned against
    you shall prevail;
  every tongue you shall prove
    false
  that launches an accusation
    against you.
This is the lot of the servants of
    the LORD,
  their vindication from me,
  says the LORD.

An Invitation to Grace

55 All you who are thirsty,
    come to the water!
You who have no money,
  come, receive grain and eat;
Come, without paying and
    without cost,
  drink wine and milk!
2 Why spend your money for
    what is not bread;
  your wages for what fails to
    satisfy?
Heed me, and you shall eat well,
  you shall delight in rich fare.
3 Come to me heedfully,
  listen, that you may have life.

I will renew with you the
    everlasting covenant,
  the benefits assured to David.
4 As I made him a witness to the
    peoples,
  a leader and commander of
    nations,
5 So shall you summon a nation
    you knew not,
  and nations that knew you not
    shall run to you,

Because of the LORD, your God,
  the Holy One of Israel, who
    has glorified you.

6 Seek the LORD while he may be
    found,
  call him while he is near.
7 Let the scoundrel forsake his
    way,
  and the wicked man his
    thoughts;
Let him turn to the LORD for
    mercy;
  to our God, who is generous
    in forgiving.
8 For my thoughts are not your
    thoughts,
  nor are your ways my ways,
    says the LORD.
9 As high as the heavens are above
    the earth,
  so high are my ways above
    your ways
  and my thoughts above your
    thoughts.

10 For just as from the heavens
    the rain and snow come down
And do not return there
  till they have watered the
    earth,
  making it fertile and fruitful,
Giving seed to him who sows
  and bread to him who eats,
11 So shall my word be
  that goes forth from my
    mouth;
It shall not return to me void,
  but shall do my will,
  achieving the end for which I
    sent it.

12 Yes, in joy you shall depart,
  in peace you shall be brought
    back;
Mountains and hills shall break
    out in song before you,
  and all the trees of the
    countryside shall clap their
    hands.
13 In place of the thornbush, the
    cypress shall grow,
  instead of nettles, the myrtle.
This shall be to the LORD's
    renown,
  an everlasting imperishable
    sign.

54, 5: *Redeemer:* cf note on 41, 14.
54, 11f: Cf Rv 21. *Afflicted one:* Jerusalem; *carnelians:* reddish quartz, hard and durable; *carbuncles:* another precious stone of red color.

55, 1ff: God's salvation is freely extended to his people and to all nations; through him will *the benefits assured to David* be renewed; cf 12, 3; Jn 7, 37.

55, 13: *Thornbush . . . nettles:* suggestive of the desert and therefore symbolic of suffering and hardship; *cypress, myrtle:* suggestive of fertile land and therefore symbolic of joy and strength.

RETURN OF THE FIRST CAPTIVES

The Lord's House Open to All

56 Thus says the LORD:
Observe what is right, do
what is just;
for my salvation is about to
come,
my justice, about to be
revealed.
2 Happy is the man who does this,
the son of man who holds to it;
Who keeps the sabbath free
from profanation,
and his hand from any
evildoing.
3 Let not the foreigner say,
when he would join himself
to the LORD,
"The LORD will surely exclude
me from his people";
Nor let the eunuch say,
"See, I am a dry tree."
4 For thus says the LORD:
To the eunuchs who observe my
sabbaths
and choose what pleases me
and hold fast to my covenant,
5 I will give, in my house
and within my walls, a
monument and a name
Better than sons and daughters;
an eternal, imperishable name
will I give them.

6 And the foreigners who join
themselves to the LORD,
ministering to him,
Loving the name of the LORD,
and becoming his servants—
All who keep the sabbath free
from profanation
and hold to my covenant,
7 Them I will bring to my holy
mountain
and make joyful in my house
of prayer;
Their holocausts and sacrifices
will be acceptable on my altar,
For my house shall be called
a house of prayer for all
peoples.

8 Thus says the Lord GOD,
who gathers the dispersed of
Israel:
Others will I gather to him
besides those already gathered.

Blind Leaders

9 All you wild beasts of the field,
come and eat,
all you beasts in the forest!
10 My watchmen are blind,
all of them unaware;
They are all dumb dogs,
they cannot bark;
Dreaming as they lie there,
loving their sleep.
11 They are relentless dogs,
they know not when they have
enough.
These are the shepherds
who know no discretion;
Each of them goes his own way,
every one of them to his own
gain:
12 "Come, I will fetch some wine;
let us carouse with strong
drink,
And tomorrow will be like
today,
or even greater."

57 The just man perishes,
but no one takes it to heart;
Devout men are swept away,
with no one giving it a
thought.
Though he is taken away from
the presence of evil,
the just man 2 enters into
peace;
There is rest on his couch
for the sincere,
straightforward man.

Faithless People

3 But you, draw near,
you sons of a sorceress,
adulterous, wanton race!
4 Of whom do you make sport,
at whom do you open wide
your mouth,
and put out your tongue?

Are you not rebellious children,
a worthless race;
5 You who are in heat among the
terebinths,
under every green tree;
You who immolate children in
the wadies,
behind the crevices in the cliffs?
6 Among the smooth stones of the
wady is your portion,
these are your lot;
To these you poured out
libations,
and brought offerings.
Should I decide not to punish
these things?
7 Upon a high and lofty mountain
you made your bed,
and there you went up to
offer sacrifice.
8 Behind the door and the
doorpost
you placed your indecent
symbol.
Deserting me, you spread out
your high, wide bed;
And of those whose embraces
you love
you carved the symbol and
gazed upon it
9 While you approached the king
with scented oil,
and multiplied your perfumes;
While you sent your
ambassadors far away,
down even to the nether
world.
10 Though worn out by your many
misdeeds,
you never said, "It is
hopeless";
New strength you found,
and so you did not weaken.
11 Of whom were you afraid?
Whom did you fear,
that you became false
And did not remember me
or give me any thought?
Was I to remain silent and
unseeing,
so that you would not have
me to fear?

56, 1–8: Participation in the future Messianic salvation is offered to all who believe in the Lord and keep his commandments, regardless of origin or social condition.

56, 3: Eunuchs had originally been excluded from the community of the Lord; cf Dt 23, 2; Wis 3, 14. *Dry tree:* unable to produce the fruit of offspring.

56, 5: *A monument and a name:* a memorial inscription to prevent oblivion for one who had no

children; cf 2 Sm 18, 18; Neh 7, 15; 13, 14.

56, 9—57, 13: This section is apparently pre-exilic, written in the manner of the older prophets who condemned the pagan rites of Baal worship.

56, 9: *Wild beasts:* foreign nations, which are invited to come and ravage Israel.

57, 6: *Smooth stones:* the Hebrew word for this expression has the same consonants as the word for "portion"; instead of making the Lord their portion

(cf Ps 16, 5), the people adored slabs of stone which they took from the streambeds in valleys and set up as idols; cf Jer 3, 9. Therefore, it is implied, they will be swept away as by a sudden torrent of waters carrying them down the rocky-bottomed gorge to destruction and death without burial.

57, 9: *The king:* the pagan god Moloch. *Ambassadors:* children sent to him through a sacrificial death.

12 I will expose your justice
   and your works;
13 They shall not help you when
   you cry out,
   nor save you in your distress.

   All these the wind shall carry off,
   the breeze shall bear away;
   But he who takes refuge in me
   shall inherit the land,
   and possess my holy mountain.

Comfort for the Afflicted

14 Build up, build up, prepare the
   way,
   remove the stumbling blocks
   from my people's path.
15 For thus says he who is high
   and exalted,
   living eternally, whose name
   is the Holy One:
   On high I dwell, and in holiness,
   and with the crushed and
   dejected in spirit,
   To revive the spirits of the
   dejected,
   to revive the hearts of the
   crushed.
16 I will not accuse forever,
   nor always be angry;
   For their spirits would faint
   before me,
   the souls that I have made.
17 Because of their wicked avarice
   I was angry,
   and struck them, hiding myself
   in wrath,
   as they went their own
   rebellious way.
18 I saw their ways,
   but I will heal them and lead
   them;
   I will give full comfort
   to them and to those who
   mourn for them,
19   I, the Creator, who gave them
   life.

   Peace, peace to the far and the
   near,
   says the LORD; and I will
   heal them.
20 But the wicked are like the
   tossing sea
   which cannot be calmed,
   And its waters cast up mud and
   filth.

21   No peace for the wicked!
   says my God.

True Fasting

58 Cry out full-throated and
   unsparingly,
   lift up your voice like a
   trumpet blast;
   Tell my people their
   wickedness,
   and the house of Jacob their
   sins.
2 They seek me day after day,
   and desire to know my ways,
   Like a nation that has done
   what is just
   and not abandoned the law of
   their God;
   They ask me to declare what is
   due them,
   pleased to gain access to God.
3 "Why do we fast, and you do
   not see it?
   afflict ourselves, and you take
   no note of it?"

   Lo, on your fast day you carry
   out your own pursuits,
   and drive all your laborers.
4 Yes, your fast ends in
   quarreling and fighting,
   striking with wicked claw.
   Would that today you might
   fast
   so as to make your voice
   heard on high!
5 Is this the manner of fasting I
   wish,
   of keeping a day of penance:
   That a man bow his head like
   a reed,
   and lie in sackcloth and ashes?
   Do you call this a fast,
   a day acceptable to the
   LORD?
6 This, rather, is the fasting that
   I wish:
   releasing those bound
   unjustly,
   untying the thongs of the
   yoke;
   Setting free the oppressed,
   breaking every yoke;
7 Sharing your bread with the
   hungry,
   sheltering the oppressed and
   the homeless;

   Clothing the naked when you
   see them,
   and not turning your back on
   your own.
8 Then your light shall break
   forth like the dawn,
   and your wound shall quickly
   be healed;
   Your vindication shall go before
   you,
   and the glory of the LORD
   shall be your rear guard.
9 Then you shall call, and the
   LORD will answer,
   you shall cry for help, and he
   will say: Here I am!
   If you remove from your midst
   oppression,
   false accusation and malicious
   speech;
10 If you bestow your bread on
   the hungry
   and satisfy the afflicted;
   Then light shall rise for you in
   the darkness,
   and the gloom shall become
   for you like midday;
11 Then the LORD will guide you
   always
   and give you plenty even on
   the parched land.
   He will renew your strength,
   and you shall be like a
   watered garden,
   like a spring whose water
   never fails.
12 The ancient ruins shall be
   rebuilt for your sake,
   and the foundations from
   ages past you shall raise up;
   "Repairer of the breach," they
   shall call you,
   "Restorer of ruined
   homesteads."

13 If you hold back your foot on
   the sabbath
   from following your own
   pursuits on my holy day;
   If you call the sabbath a delight,
   and the LORD's holy day
   honorable;
   If you honor it by not
   following your ways,
   seeking your own interests, or
   speaking with malice—

57, 12: *Justice:* here used ironically.
57, 13: *All these:* the wicked mentioned in 57, 3–10.

58, 1: This command is directed to the prophet.
58, 2–14: Merely external worship does not avail

with God; it must be joined to internal sincerity.

14 Then you shall delight in the
      LORD,
   and I will make you ride on
      the heights of the earth;
   I will nourish you with the
      heritage of Jacob, your
      father,
   for the mouth of the LORD
      has spoken.

Sin and Confession

59 Lo, the hand of the LORD is
         not too short to save,
      nor his ear too dull to hear.
2 Rather, it is your crimes
      that separate you from your
      God,
   It is your sins that make him
      hide his face
   so that he will not hear you.
3 For your hands are stained with
      blood,
      your fingers with guilt;
   Your lips speak falsehood,
      and your tongue utters deceit.
4 No one brings suit justly,
      no one pleads truthfully;
   They trust in emptiness and tell
      lies;
      they conceive mischief and
      bring forth malice.
5 They hatch adders' eggs,
      and weave spiders' webs:
   Whoever eats their eggs will die,
      if one of them is pressed, it
      will hatch as a viper;
6 Their webs cannot serve as
      clothing,
      nor can they cover themselves
      with their works.
   Their works are evil works,
      and deeds of violence come
      from their hands.
7 Their feet run to evil,
      and they are quick to shed
      innocent blood;
   Their thoughts are destructive
      thoughts,
      plunder and ruin are on their
      highways.
8 The way of peace they know not,
      and there is nothing that is
      right in their paths;

Their ways they have made
      crooked,
   whoever treads them knows
      no peace.
9 That is why right is far from us
      and justice does not reach us.
   We look for light, and lo,
      darkness;
      for brightness, but we walk in
      gloom!
10 Like blind men we grope along
      the wall,
   like people without eyes we
      feel our way.
   We stumble at midday as at
      dusk,
      in Stygian darkness, like the
      dead.
11 We all growl like bears,
      like doves we moan without
      ceasing.
   We look for right, but it is not
      there;
      for salvation, and it is far from
      us.
12 For our offenses before you are
      many,
      our sins bear witness against
      us.
   Yes, our offenses are present to
      us,
      and our crimes we know:
13 Transgressing, and denying the
      LORD,
      turning back from following
      our God,
   Threatening outrage, and
      apostasy,
      uttering words of falsehood
      the heart has conceived.
14 Right is repelled,
      and justice stands far off;
   For truth stumbles in the public
      square,
      uprightness cannot enter.
15 Honesty is lacking,
      and the man who turns from
      evil is despoiled.

The Redeemer in Zion

The LORD saw this, and was
      aggrieved
   that right did not exist.

16 He saw that there was no one,
      and was appalled that there
      was none to intervene;
   So his own arm brought about
      the victory,
      and his justice lent him its
      support.
17 He put on justice as his
      breastplate,
      salvation, as the helmet on
      his head;
   He clothed himself with
      garments of vengeance,
      wrapped himself in a mantle of
      zeal.
18 He repays his enemies their
      deserts,
      and requites his foes with
      wrath.

19 Those in the west shall fear the
      name of the LORD,
      and those in the east, his
      glory;
   For it shall come like a pent-up
      river
      which the breath of the LORD
      drives on.
20 He shall come to Zion a
      redeemer
      to those of Jacob who turn
      from sin, says the LORD.
21 This is the covenant with them
      which I myself have made,
      says the LORD:
   My spirit which is upon you
      and my words that I have put
      into your mouth
   Shall never leave your mouth,
      nor the mouths of your
      children
   Nor the mouths of your
      children's children
      from now on and forever,
      says the LORD.

Glory of the New Zion

60 Rise up in splendor! Your
         light has come,
      the glory of the Lord shines
      upon you.
2 See, darkness covers the earth,
      and thick clouds cover the
      peoples;

59, 4: *Emptiness:* things have no value.
59, 5f: A proverb signifying evil works—*adders'
eggs*—and useless devices—*spiders' webs;* the former
do positive harm to oneself and others, the latter

serve no useful purpose.
59, 9–15: Spoken by the people through the mouth
of the prophet.
60, 1–6: The Church makes use of these verses for

the Epistle of the Mass on the feast of Epiphany, for
she sees in them symbols of her universality.

But upon you the Lord shines,
and over you appears his
glory.
3 Nations shall walk by your
light,
and kings by your shining
radiance.
4 Raise your eyes and look about;
they all gather and come to
you:
Your sons come from afar,
and your daughters in the
arms of their nurses.

5 Then you shall be radiant at
what you see,
your heart shall throb and
overflow,
For the riches of the sea shall
be emptied out before you,
the wealth of nations shall be
brought to you.
6 Caravans of camels shall fill you,
dromedaries from Midian and
Ephah;
All from Sheba shall come
bearing gold and frankincense,
and proclaiming the praises of
the Lord.
7 All the flocks of Kedar shall be
gathered for you,
the rams of Nebaioth shall be
your sacrifices;
They will be acceptable offerings
on my altar,
and I will enhance the splendor
of my house.

8 What are these that fly along
like clouds,
like doves to their cotes?
9 All the vessels of the sea are
assembled,
with the ships of Tarshish in
the lead,
To bring your children from
afar
with their silver and gold,
In the name of the Lord, your
God,
the Holy One of Israel, who
has glorified you.

10 Foreigners shall rebuild your
walls,
and their kings shall be your
attendants;

Though I struck you in my
wrath,
yet in my good will I have
shown you mercy.
11 Your gates shall stand open
constantly;
day and night they shall not
be closed
But shall admit to you the
wealth of nations,
and their kings, in the
vanguard.
12 For the people or kingdom shall
perish
that does not serve you;
those nations shall be utterly
destroyed.
13 The glory of Lebanon shall
come to you:
the cypress, the plane and the
pine,
To bring beauty to my sanctuary,
and glory to the place where
I set my feet.
14 The children of your oppressors
shall come,
bowing low before you;
All those who despised you
shall fall prostrate at your
feet.
They shall call you "City of the
Lord,"
"Zion of the Holy One of
Israel."

15 Once you were forsaken,
hated and unvisited,
Now I will make you the pride
of the ages,
a joy to generation after
generation.
16 You shall suck the milk of
nations,
and be nursed at royal breasts;
You shall know that I, the
Lord, am your savior,
your redeemer, the mighty
one of Jacob.
17 In place of bronze I will bring
gold,
instead of iron, silver;
In place of wood, bronze,
instead of stones, iron;
I will appoint peace your
governor,
and justice your ruler.

18 No longer shall violence be
heard of in your land,
or plunder and ruin within
your boundaries.
You shall call your walls
"Salvation"
and your gates "Praise."
19 No longer shall the sun
be your light by day,
Nor the brightness of the moon
shine upon you at night;
The Lord shall be your light
forever,
your God shall be your glory.
20 No longer shall your sun go
down,
or your moon withdraw,
For the Lord will be your light
forever,
and the days of your mourning
shall be at an end.
21 Your people shall all be just,
they shall always possess the
land,
They, the bud of my planting,
my handiwork to show my
glory.
22 The smallest shall become a
thousand,
the youngest, a mighty nation;
I, the Lord, will swiftly
accomplish these things
when their time comes.

The Mission to the Afflicted

61 The spirit of the Lord God
is upon me,
because the Lord has anointed
me;
He has sent me to bring glad
tidings to the lowly,
to heal the brokenhearted,
To proclaim liberty to the
captives
and release to the prisoners,
2 To announce a year of favor
from the Lord
and a day of vindication by
our God,
to comfort all who mourn;
3 To place on those who mourn
in Zion
a diadem instead of ashes,
To give them oil of gladness in
place of mourning,
a glorious mantle instead of a
listless spirit.

60, 8f: *Like clouds, like doves:* the white sails of
the ships of Tarshish; cf note on Ps 48, 8.
60, 13: *Glory of Lebanon:* the cedars, together with

the cypress, the plane and the pine, all precious,
durable wood.

61, 1f: This was spoken by the prophet in regard

to the restoration of Zion, but quoted by Christ as
referring to his mission; cf Lk 4, 18f. *Year of favor . . .
day of vindication:* the time of God's salvation.

They will be called oaks of
    justice,
    planted by the LORD to show
    his glory.

The Reward of Israel

4 They shall rebuild the ancient
    ruins,
    the former wastes they shall
    raise up
And restore the ruined cities,
    desolate now for generations.
5 Strangers shall stand ready to
    pasture your flocks,
    foreigners shall be your
    farmers and vinedressers.
6 You yourselves shall be named
    priests of the LORD,
    ministers of our God you
    shall be called.
You shall eat the wealth of the
    nations
    and boast of riches from them.

7 Since their shame was double
    and disgrace and spittle were
    their portion,
They shall have a double
    inheritance in their land,
    everlasting joy shall be theirs.
8 For I, the LORD, love what is
    right,
    I hate robbery and injustice;
I will give them their
    recompense faithfully,
    a lasting covenant I will make
    with them.
9 Their descendants shall be
    renowned among the
    nations,
    and their offspring among the
    peoples;
All who see them shall
    acknowledge them
    as a race the LORD has blessed.

10 I rejoice heartily in the LORD,
    in my God is the joy of my
    soul;
For he has clothed me with a
    robe of salvation,
    and wrapped me in a mantle
    of justice,
Like a bridegroom adorned with
    a diadem,
    like a bride bedecked with
    her jewels.

11 As the earth brings forth its
    plants,
    and a garden makes its
    growth spring up,
So will the Lord GOD make
    justice and praise
    spring up before all the
    nations.

Jerusalem the Lord's Bride

62 For Zion's sake I will not be
    silent,
    for Jerusalem's sake I will
    not be quiet,
Until her vindication shines
    forth like the dawn
    and her victory like a burning
    torch.

2 Nations shall behold your
    vindication,
    and all kings your glory;
You shall be called by a new
    name
    pronounced by the mouth of
    the LORD.
3 You shall be a glorious crown
    in the hand of the LORD,
    a royal diadem held by your
    God.
4 No more shall men call you
    "Forsaken,"
    or your land "Desolate,"
But you shall be called "My
    Delight,"
    and your land "Espoused."
For the LORD delights in you,
    and makes your land his
    spouse.
5 As a young man marries a
    virgin,
    your Builder shall marry you;
And as a bridegroom rejoices
    in his bride
    so shall your God rejoice in
    you.

Restoration of Zion

6 Upon your walls, O Jerusalem,
    I have stationed watchmen;
Never, by day or by night,
    shall they be silent.
O you who are to remind the
    LORD,
    take no rest

7 And give no rest to him
    until he re-establishes
    Jerusalem
And makes of it
    the pride of the earth.

8 The LORD has sworn by his
    right hand
    and by his mighty arm:
No more will I give your grain
    as food to your enemies;
Nor shall foreigners drink your
    wine,
    for which you toiled.
9 But you who harvest the grain
    shall eat it,
    and you shall praise the LORD;
You who gather the grapes shall
    drink the wine
    in the courts of my sanctuary.
10 Pass through, pass through the
    gates,
    prepare the way for the
    people;
Build up, build up the
    highway,
    clear it of stones,
    raise up a standard over the
    nations.
11 See, the LORD proclaims
    to the ends of the earth:
Say to daughter Zion,
    your savior comes!
Here is his reward with him,
    his recompense before him.
12 They shall be called the holy
    people,
    the redeemed of the LORD,
And you shall be called
    "Frequented,"
    a city that is not forsaken.

Punishment of Edom

63 Who is this that comes from
    Edom,
    in crimsoned garments, from
    Bozrah—
This one arrayed in majesty,
    marching in the greatness of
    his strength?
"It is I, I who announce
    vindication,
    I who am mighty to save."
2 Why is your apparel red,
    and your garments like those
    of the wine presser?

62, 2: *New name:* figurative expression for a new state of happiness; cf Rv 2, 17; 3, 12.
62, 6f: *Remind the Lord . . . give no rest to him:* figuratively, as though to make certain that the Lord

will remember his pledge to Jerusalem. Cf Lk 11, 7f.
62, 10: The command is given to the workmen to begin the reconstruction of the city.

63, 1–6: In a dramatic dialogue between God and the prophet, the Lord is portrayed as the sole avenger of justice against his enemies.

3 "The wine press I have trodden
    alone,
    and of my people there was no
    one with me.
I trod them in my anger,
    and trampled them down in
    my wrath;
Their blood spurted on my
    garments;
    all my apparel I stained.
4 For the day of vengeance was in
    my heart,
    my year for redeeming was at
    hand.
5 I looked about, but there was
    no one to help,
    I was appalled that there was
    no one to lend support;
So my own arm brought about
    the victory
    and my own wrath lent me its
    support.
6 I trampled down the peoples in
    my anger,
    I crushed them in my wrath,
    and I let their blood run out
    upon the ground."

Prayer for the Return of God's Favor

7 The favors of the LORD I will
    recall,
    the glorious deeds of the
    LORD,
Because of all he has done for
    us;
    for he is good to the house of
    Israel,
He has favored us according to
    his mercy
    and his great kindness.

8 He said: They are indeed my
    people,
    children who are not disloyal;
So he became their savior
9   in their every affliction.
It was not a messenger or an
    angel,
    but he himself who saved
    them.
Because of his love and pity
    he redeemed them himself,
Lifting them and carrying them
    all the days of old.
10 But they rebelled, and grieved
    his holy spirit;

So he turned on them like an
    enemy,
    and fought against them.

11 Then they remembered the days
    of old
    and Moses, his servant;
Where is he who brought up
    out of the sea
    the shepherd of his flock?
Where is he who put his holy
    spirit
    in their midst;
12 Whose glorious arm
    was the guide at Moses'
    right;
Who divided the waters before
    them,
    winning for himself eternal
    renown;
13 Who led them without
    stumbling through the
    depths
    like horses in the open
    country,
14 Like cattle going down into the
    plain,
    the spirit of the LORD guiding
    them?
Thus you led your people,
    bringing glory to your name.

15 Look down from heaven and
    regard us
    from your holy and glorious
    palace!
Where is your zealous care and
    your might,
    your surge of pity and your
    mercy?
O Lord, hold not back,
16   for you are our father.
Were Abraham not to know us,
    nor Israel to acknowledge us,
You, LORD, are our father,
    our redeemer you are named
    forever.
17 Why do you let us wander, O
    LORD, from your ways,
    and harden our hearts so that
    we fear you not?
Return for the sake of your
    servants,
    the tribes of your heritage.
18 Why have the wicked invaded
    your holy place,

why have our enemies
    trampled your sanctuary?
19 Too long have we been like
    those you do not rule,
    who do not bear your name.

Oh, that you would rend the
    heavens and come down,
    with the mountains quaking
    before you,

64 As when brushwood is set
    ablaze,
    or fire makes the water boil!
Thus your name would be made
    known to your enemies
    and the nations would tremble
    before you,
2 While you wrought awesome
    deeds we could not hope for,
3 such as they had not heard of
    from of old.
No ear has ever heard, no eye
    ever seen,
    any God but you
    doing such deeds for those
    who wait for him.
4 Would that you might meet us
    doing right,
    that we were mindful of you
    in our ways!
Behold, you are angry, and we
    are sinful;
5 all of us have become like
    unclean men,
    all our good deeds are like
    polluted rags;
We have all withered like leaves,
    and our guilt carries us away
    like the wind.
6 There is none who calls upon
    your name,
    who rouses himself to cling
    to you;
For you have hidden your face
    from us
    and have delivered us up to
    our guilt.
7 Yet, O LORD, you are our father;
    we are the clay and you the
    potter:
    we are all the work of your
    hands.
8 Be not so very angry, LORD,
    keep not our guilt forever in
    mind;
    look upon us, who are all
    your people.

63, 7—64, 11: A prayer probably composed toward the end of the Exile, in which the prophet, after recalling God's blessings on Israel in its past history (63, 7–10), especially at the Exodus (11–14), begs the Lord to come once more to the aid of his people (63, 15—64, 3), who now humbly confess their sins (4–11).

9 Your holy cities have become
    a desert,
    Zion is a desert, Jerusalem a
      waste.
10 Our holy and glorious temple
    in which our fathers praised
      you
Has been burned with fire;
    all that was dear to us is laid
      waste.
11 Can you hold back, O LORD,
    after all this?
    Can you remain silent, and
      afflict us so severely?

Necessity of Punishment

65 I was ready to respond to
      those who asked me not,
    to be found by those who
      sought me not.
    I said: Here I am! Here I am!
    To a nation that did not call
      upon my name.

2 I have stretched out my hands
    all the day
    to a rebellious people,
Who walk in evil paths
    and follow their own thoughts,
3 People who provoke me
    continually, to my face,
Offering sacrifices in the groves
    and burning incense on bricks,
4 Living among the graves
    and spending the night in
      caverns,
Eating swine's flesh,
    with carrion broth in their
      dishes,
5 Crying out, "Hold back,
    do not touch me; I am too
      sacred for you!"

These things enkindle my wrath,
    a fire that burns all the day.
6 Lo, before me it stands written;
    I will not be quiet until I have
      paid in full
7 Your crimes and the crimes of
    your fathers as well,
    says the LORD.
Since they burned incense on the
      mountains,
    and disgraced me on the hills,

I will at once pour out in full
    measure
    their recompense into their
      laps.

Fate of the Good and the Bad in Israel

8 Thus says the LORD:
When the juice is pressed from
    grapes,
    men say, "Do not discard
      them,
    for there is still good in them";
Thus will I do with my servants:
    I will not discard them all;
9 From Jacob I will save offspring,
    from Judah, those who are to
      inherit my mountains;
My chosen ones shall inherit the
      land,
    my servants shall dwell there.
10 Sharon shall be a pasture for
    the flocks
    and the valley of Achor a
      resting place for the cattle
of my people who have sought
    me.

11 But you who forsake the LORD,
    forgetting my holy mountain,
You who spread a table for
    Fortune
    and fill cups of blended wine
      for Destiny,
12 You I will destine for the
    sword;
    you shall all go down in
      slaughter.
Since I called and you did not
    answer,
    I spoke and you did not
      listen,
But did what was evil in my
    sight
    and preferred things which
      displease me,
13 therefore thus says the Lord
    GOD:
Lo, my servants shall eat,
    but you shall go hungry;
My servants shall drink,
    but you shall be thirsty;
My servants shall rejoice,
    but you shall be put to shame;
14 My servants shall shout
    for joy of heart,

But you shall cry out for grief
    of heart
    and howl for anguish of spirit.
15 The Lord GOD shall slay you,
    and the name you leave
Shall be used by my chosen ones
    for cursing;
    but my servants shall be called
      by another name
16 By which he will be blessed
    on whom a blessing is invoked
      in the land.
He who takes an oath in the
    land
    shall swear by the God of
      truth;
For the hardships of the past
    shall be forgotten,
    and hidden from my eyes.

The World Renewed

17 Lo, I am about to create new
    heavens
    and a new earth;
The things of the past shall not
    be remembered
    or come to mind.
18 Instead, there shall always be
    rejoicing and happiness
    in what I create;
For I create Jerusalem to be a
    joy
    and its people to be a delight;
19 I will rejoice in Jerusalem
    and exult in my people.
No longer shall the sound of
    weeping be heard there,
    or the sound of crying;
20 No longer shall there be in it
    an infant who lives but a few
      days,
    or an old man who does not
      round out his full lifetime;
He dies a mere youth who
    reaches but a hundred years,
    and he who fails of a
      hundred shall be thought
      accursed.

21 They shall live in the houses
    they build,
    and eat the fruit of the
      vineyards they plant;
22 They shall not build houses for
    others to live in,
    or plant for others to eat.

65, 5: *I am too sacred for you:* the uncleanness of pork, obvious to a Semite, is what these people claim has made them sacred! The prophet ridicules them.

Some translate: "I will render you sacred," and understand this as referring to the concept of sacredness as something contagious.

65, 11f: *Destiny:* the Hebrew also has a play on the words *Destiny* and *destine; meni* and *manithi.*

As the years of a tree, so the
years of my people;
and my chosen ones shall long
enjoy
the produce of their hands.

23 They shall not toil in vain,
nor beget children for
sudden destruction;
For a race blessed by the LORD
are they and their offspring.

24 Before they call, I will answer;
while they are yet speaking, I
will hearken to them.

25 The wolf and the lamb shall
graze alike,
and the lion shall eat hay like
the ox
[but the serpent's food shall
be dust].
None shall hurt or destroy
on all my holy mountain,
says the LORD.

True and False Worship

66 Thus says the LORD:
The heavens are my throne,
the earth is my footstool.
What kind of house can you
build for me;
what is to be my resting
place?

2 My hand made all these things
when all of them came to be,
says the LORD.
This is the one whom I approve:
the lowly and afflicted man
who trembles at my word.

3 Merely slaughtering an ox is like
slaying a man;
sacrificing a lamb, like
breaking a dog's neck;
Bringing a cereal offering, like
offering swine's blood;
burning incense, like paying
homage to an idol.
Since these have chosen their
own ways
and taken pleasure in their
own abominations,

4 I in turn will choose ruthless
treatment for them
and bring upon them what
they fear.

Because, when I called, no one
answered,
when I spoke, no one
listened;
Because they did what was evil
in my sight,
and chose what gave me
displeasure,

5 Hear the word of the LORD,
you who tremble at his word:
Your brethren who, because of
my name,
hate and reject you, say,
"Let the LORD show his glory
that we may see your joy";
but they shall be put to
shame.

6 A sound of roaring from the
city,
a sound from the temple,
The sound of the LORD
repaying his enemies their
deserts!

Mother Zion

7 Before she comes to labor,
she gives birth;
Before the pains come upon her,
she safely delivers a male
child.

8 Who ever heard of such a thing,
or saw the like?
Can a country be brought forth
in one day,
or a nation be born in a
single moment?
Yet Zion is scarcely in labor
when she gives birth to her
children.

9 Shall I bring a mother to the
point of birth,
and yet not let her child be
born? says the LORD;
Or shall I who allow her to
conceive,
yet close her womb? says
your God.

10 Rejoice with Jerusalem and be
glad because of her,
all you who love her;
Exult, exult with her,
all you who were mourning
over her!

11 Oh, that you may suck fully
of the milk of her comfort,
That you may nurse with
delight
at her abundant breasts!

12 For thus says the LORD:
Lo, I will spread prosperity
over her like a river,
and the wealth of the nations
like an overflowing torrent.
As nurslings, you shall be
carried in her arms,
and fondled in her lap;

13 As a mother comforts her son,
so will I comfort you;
in Jerusalem you shall find
your comfort.

14 When you see this, your heart
shall rejoice,
and your bodies flourish like
the grass;
The LORD's power shall be
known to his servants,
but to his enemies, his wrath.

15 Lo, the LORD shall come in fire,
his chariots like the whirlwind,
To wreak his wrath with burning
heat
and his punishment with fiery
flames.

16 For the LORD shall judge all
mankind
by fire and sword,
and many shall be slain by
the LORD.

17 They who sanctify and purify
themselves to go to the groves, as
followers of one who stands within,
they who eat swine's flesh, loathsome
things and mice, shall all perish with
their deeds and their thoughts, says
the LORD.

Gathering of the Nations

18 I come to gather nations of
every language; they shall come and
see my glory. 19 I will set a sign
among them; from them I will send
fugitives to the nations: to Tarshish,
Put and Lud, Mosoch, Tubal and
Javan, to the distant coastlands that
have never heard of my fame, or seen

65, 25: See note on 11, 6–9.
66, 4f: Worship which is merely external is as evil
as though it were idolatry.
66, 7–9: The absence of labor in Zion's child-

bearing is a symbol of the joyful begetting of the new
people of God.
66, 18–21: God summons the neighboring nations
to Zion and from among them will send some to far

distant lands to proclaim his glory. *All your brethren:*
Jews in exile.

my glory; and they shall proclaim my glory among the nations. 20 They shall bring all your brethren from all the nations as an offering to the LORD, on horses and in chariots, in carts, upon mules and dromedaries, to Jerusalem, my holy mountain, says the LORD, just as the Israelites bring their offering to the house of the LORD in clean vessels. 21 Some of these I will take as priests and Levites, says the LORD.

***

66, 24: God's enemies lie dead outside the walls of the New Jerusalem; just as in the past, corpses, filth

Lasting Reward and Punishment

22 As the new heavens and the new earth
    which I will make
Shall endure before me, says the LORD,
    so shall your race and your name endure.
23 From one new moon to another,
    and from one sabbath to another,

***

and refuse lay in the Valley of Hennom outside the city, where huge fires were constantly burning; cf

All mankind shall come to worship
    before me, says the LORD.
24 They shall go out and see the corpses
    of the men who rebelled against me;
Their worm shall not die,
    nor their fire be extinguished,
    and they shall be abhorrent to all mankind.

***

Jos 15, 8; 2 Chr 28, 3; Mk 9, 45–48.

Jeremiah

ORACLES IN THE DAYS OF JOSIAH

THE words of Jeremiah, son of Hilkiah, of a priestly family in Anathoth, in the land of Benjamin. 2 The word of the LORD first came to him in the days of Josiah, son of Amon, king of Judah, in the thirteenth year of his reign, 3 and continued through the reign of Jehoiakim, son of Josiah, king of Judah, and until the downfall and exile of Jerusalem in the fifth month of the eleventh year of Zedekiah, son of Josiah, king of Judah.

Call of Jeremiah

4 The word of the LORD came to me thus:

5 Before I formed you in the
   womb I knew you,
   before you were born I
   dedicated you,
   a prophet to the nations I
   appointed you.
6 "Ah, Lord GOD!" I said,
   "I know not how to speak; I
   am too young."

7 But the LORD answered me,

Say not, "I am too young."
   To whomever I send you, you
   shall go;
   whatever I command you, you
   shall speak.

8 Have no fear before them,
   because I am with you to
   deliver you, says the LORD.

9 Then the LORD extended his hand
and touched my mouth, saying,

See, I place my words in your
   mouth!
10 This day I set you
    over nations and over
    kingdoms,
To root up and to tear down,
   to destroy and to demolish,
   to build and to plant.

11 The word of the LORD came to me with the question: What do you see, Jeremiah? "I see a branch of the watching-tree," I replied. 12 Then the LORD said to me: Well have you seen, for I am watching to fulfill my word. 13 A second time the word of the LORD came to me with the question: What do you see? "I see a boiling cauldron," I replied, "that appears from the north."

14 And from the north, said the LORD to me, evil will boil over upon all who dwell in the land.

15 Lo, I am summoning
   all the kingdoms of the
   north, says the LORD;
   Each king shall come and set up
   his throne
   at the gateways of Jerusalem,
   Opposite her walls all around
   and opposite all the cities of
   Judah.
16 I will pronounce my sentence
   against them
   for all their wickedness in
   forsaking me,
   And in burning incense to
   strange gods
   and adoring their own
   handiwork.

17 But do you gird your loins;
   stand up and tell them
   all that I command you.

1, 1: *Anathoth*: a village about three miles northeast of Jerusalem, where Solomon exiled Abiathar (1 Kgs 2, 26f); it is probable that Jeremiah belonged to the *priestly family* of Abiathar.
1, 3: *Until the downfall:* these words were originally prefixed as a title to a collection of Jeremiah's prophecies which lacked chapters 40–44. The new title in 40, 1 and the oracles that follow clearly show that Jeremiah continued to prophesy after the destruction of Jerusalem in 587 B.C.

1, 5: Jeremiah was destined to the office of prophet before his birth; cf Is 49, 1.5; Lk 1, 15; Gal 1, 15f. *I knew you:* I loved you and chose you. *I dedicated you:* I set you apart to be a prophet. Some Fathers and later theologians understand this to mean that Jeremiah was freed from original sin before his birth. The context does not justify this conclusion. *The nations:* the pagan neighbors of Judah, besides the great world powers—Assyria, Babylonia, Egypt— intimately associated with Judah's destiny.

1, 6: *I am too young:* Jeremiah's youth (he was less than thirty years old) must not be an obstacle to the responsibilities of the prophetic office; God will supply for his human defects (cf vv 7f).
1, 11: *The watching-tree:* the almond tree, which is the first to blossom in the springtime as though it had not slept. The Hebrew name contains a play on words with "I am watching."
1, 13: *Boiling cauldron . . . the north:* symbol of an invasion from the north; cf vv 14f.

Be not crushed on their account,
>as though I would leave you
>crushed before them;
18 For it is I this day
>who have made you a fortified
>city,
>A pillar of iron, a wall of brass,
>against the whole land:
>Against Judah's kings and
>princes,
>against its priests and people.
19 They will fight against you, but
>not prevail over you,
>for I am with you to deliver
>you, says the LORD.

Infidelity of Israel

2 This word of the LORD came to me: 2 Go, cry out this message for Jerusalem to hear!

I remember the devotion of your
>youth,
>how you loved me as a bride,
>Following me in the desert,
>in a land unsown.
3 Sacred to the LORD was Israel,
>the first fruits of his harvest;
>Should anyone presume to
>partake of them,
>evil would befall him, says
>the LORD.

4 Listen to the word of the
>LORD, O house of Jacob!
>All you clans of the house of
>Israel,
5 thus says the LORD:
>What fault did your fathers find
>in me
>that they withdrew from me,
>Went after empty idols,
>and became empty themselves?
6 They did not ask, "Where is the
>LORD
>who brought us up from the
>land of Egypt,
>Who led us through the desert,
>through a land of wastes and
>gullies,

Through a land of drought and
>darkness,
>through a land which no one
>crosses,
>where no man dwells?"
7 When I brought you into the
>garden land
>to eat its goodly fruits,
>You entered and defiled my
>land,
>you made my heritage
>loathsome.
8 The priests asked not,
>"Where is the LORD?"
>Those who dealt with the law
>knew me not;
>the shepherds rebelled against
>me.
>The prophets prophesied by Baal,
>and went after useless idols.
9 Therefore will I yet accuse you,
>says the LORD,
>and even your children's
>children I will accuse.
10 Pass over to the coasts of the
>Kittim and see,
>send to Kedar and carefully
>inquire:
>Where has the like of this
>been done?
11 Does any other nation change
>its gods?—
>yet they are not gods at all!
>But my people have changed
>their glory
>for useless things.
12 Be amazed at this, O heavens,
>and shudder with sheer
>horror, says the LORD.
13 Two evils have my people done:
>they have forsaken me,
>the source of living waters;
>They have dug themselves
>cisterns,
>broken cisterns, that hold no
>water.
14 Is Israel a slave, a bondman by
>birth?
>Why then has he become
>booty?

15 Against him lions roar
>full-throated cries.
>They have made his land a waste;
>his cities are charred ruins,
>without inhabitant.
16 Yes, the people of Memphis
>and Tahpanhes
>shave the crown of your head.
17 Has not the forsaking of the
>LORD, your God,
>done this to you?
18 And now, why go to Egypt,
>to drink the waters of the Nile?
>Why go to Assyria,
>to drink the waters of the
>Euphrates?
19 Your own wickedness chastises
>you,
>your own infidelities punish
>you.
>Know then, and see, how evil
>and bitter
>is your forsaking the LORD,
>your God,
>And showing no fear of me,
>says the Lord, the GOD of
>hosts.

20 Long ago you broke your yoke,
>you tore off your bonds.
>"I will not serve," you said.
>On every high hill, under every
>green tree,
>you gave yourself to harlotry.
21 I had planted you, a choice vine
>of fully tested stock;
>How could you turn out
>obnoxious to me,
>a spurious vine?
22 Though you scour it with soap,
>and use much lye,
>The stain of your guilt is still
>before me,
>says the Lord GOD.
23 How can you say, "I am not
>defiled,
>I have not gone after the
>Baals"?
>Consider your conduct in the
>Valley,
>recall what you have done:

2, 1–3, 5: These verses probably contain the earliest of Jeremiah's preachings. The covenant relationship, symbolized by the figure of a marriage, was frequently broken by Israel, seen here as an unfaithful wife unworthy of reconciliation with God (3, 1–5).
2, 2: *Devotion:* Israel's gratitude, fidelity, and love for God.
2, 3: *First fruits:* an offering to God which became his exclusive property, and could therefore not be put to profane use; cf Lv 22, 1.
2, 8: *Those who dealt with the law:* the priests.

The shepherds: the kings and nobles.
2, 10: *Kittim:* a Phoenician colony in Cyprus. *Kedar:* a nomad tribe of the Syrian desert. These two names represent West and East.
2, 14: *Bondman by birth:* a perpetual slave, different from the debt-slave, who was to be freed after six years; cf Ex 21, 2.
2, 16: *Memphis:* the capital of Lower Egypt. *Tehpanhes:* a frontier city of Egypt, east of the Delta. *Shave the crown of your head:* the spoliation of Judah at the hands of the Egyptians.
2, 18: *Egypt* and *Assyria* were the protecting

foreign powers favored by rival parties within Judah. The desire for such foreign alliances is a further desertion of the Lord, *the source of living waters* (v 13), in favor of the above-named powers, symbolized by the *Nile* and *the Euphrates* rivers.
2, 20: *Harlotry:* idolatry (because Israel is the bride of God).
2, 23: *The Valley:* of Ben-hinnom, south of Jerusalem, site of the infamous sanctuary of Topheth where children were sacrificed to Molech; cf 7, 31.

A frenzied she-camel, coursing
near and far,
24 breaking away toward the
desert,
Snuffing the wind in her ardor—
who can restrain her lust?
No beasts need tire themselves
seeking her;
in her mouth they will meet
her.

25 Stop wearing out your shoes
and parching your throat!
But you say, "No use! no!
I love these strangers,
and after them I must go."
26 As the thief is shamed when
caught,
so shall the house of Israel be
shamed:
They, their kings and their
princes,
their priests and their
prophets;
27 They who say to a piece of wood,
"You are my father,"
and to a stone, "You gave me
birth."
They turn to me their backs, not
their faces;
yet, in their time of trouble
they cry out,
"Rise up and save us!"
28 Where are the gods you made
for yourselves?
Let them rise up!
Will they save you in your
time of trouble?
For as numerous as your cities
are your gods, O Judah!
And as many as the streets of
Jerusalem
are the altars you have set up
for Baal.

29 How dare you still plead with
me?
You have all rebelled against
me, says the LORD.
30 In vain I struck your children;
the correction they did not
take.
Your sword devoured your
prophets
like a ravening lion.
31 You, of this generation,
take note of the word of the
Lord:

Have I been a desert to Israel,
a land of darkness?
Why do my people say, "We
have moved on.
we will come to you no
more"?
32 Does a virgin forget her
jewelry,
a bride her sash?
Yet my people have forgotten
me
days without number.

33 How well you pick your way
when seeking love!
You who, in your wickdness,
have gone by ways unclean!
34 You, on whose clothing there is
the life-blood of the innocent,
whom you found committing
no burglary;
35 Yet withal you say, "I am
innocent;
at least, his anger is turned
away from me."
Behold, I will judge you
on that word of yours, "I
have not sinned."
36 How very base you have become
in changing your course!
By Egypt will you be shamed,
as you were shamed by
Assyria.
37 From there also shall you go
away
with hands upon your head;
For the LORD has rejected those
in whom you trust,
with them you will have no
success.

3 If a man sends away his wife
and, after leaving him,
she marries another man,
Does the first husband come
back to her?
Would not the land be wholly
defiled?
But you have sinned with many
lovers,
and yet you would return to
me! says the LORD.

2 Lift your eyes to the heights,
and see,
where have men not lain with
you?

By the waysides you waited for
them
like an Arab in the desert.
You defiled the land
by your wicked harlotry.
3 Therefore the showers were
withheld,
the spring rain failed.
But because you have a harlot's
brow,
you refused to blush.
4 Even now do you not call me,
"My father,
you who are the bridegroom
of my youth"?
5 "Will he keep his wrath forever,
will he hold his grudge to
the end?"
This is what you say; yet you do
all the evil you can.

Judah and Israel

6 The LORD said to me in the days
of King Josiah: See now what
rebellious Israel has done! She has
gone up every high mountain, and
under every green tree she has played
the harlot. 7 And I thought, after
she has done all this she will return
to me. But she did not return. Then,
even though her traitor sister Judah
saw 8 that for all the adulteries
rebellious Israel had committed, I
put her away and gave her a bill of
divorce, nevertheless her traitor sister
Judah was not frightened; she too
went off and played the harlot. 9
Eager to sin, she polluted the land,
committing adultery with stone and
wood. 10 With all this, the traitor
sister Judah did not return to me
wholeheartedly, but insincerely, says
the LORD.

Restoration of Israel

11 Then the LORD said to me:
Rebel Israel is inwardly more just
than traitorous Judah. 12 Go, proclaim these words toward the north,
and say:

Return, rebel Israel, says the
LORD,
I will not remain angry with
you;

3, 1: Such remarriage of divorced spouses was
forbidden by Dt 24, 1–4. Under this figure the prophet sees the presumption of Judah, the unfaithful
spouse, who thinks she can return to the Lord after
uniting herself to other gods.

3, 2: *An Arab:* a marauding nomad who lay in wait
for caravans.

For I am merciful, says the
LORD,
  I will not continue my wrath
    forever.
13 Only know your guilt:
  how you rebelled against the
    LORD, your God,
  How you ran hither and yon to
    strangers
  [under every green tree]
  and would not listen to my
    voice, says the LORD.
14 Return, rebellious children, says
    the LORD,
  for I am your Master;
  I will take you, one from a city,
    two from a clan,
  and bring you to Zion.
15 I will appoint over you shepherds
    after my own heart,
  who will shepherd you wisely
    and prudently.
16 When you multiply and become
    fruitful in the land,
  says the LORD,
  They will in those days no
    longer say,
  "The ark of the covenant of
    the LORD!"
  They will no longer think of it,
    or remember it,
  or miss it, or make another.

17 At that time they will call
Jerusalem the LORD's throne; there
all nations will be gathered together
to honor the name of the LORD at
Jerusalem, and they will walk no
longer in their hardhearted wickedness. 18 In those days the house of
Judah will join the house of Israel;
together they will come from the
land of the north to the land which I
gave to your fathers as a heritage.

Conditions for Forgiveness

19 I had thought:
  How I should like to treat
    you as sons,
  And give you a pleasant land,
    a heritage most beautiful
      among the nations!

You would call me, "My
    Father," I thought,
  and never cease following me.
20 But like a woman faithless to her
    lover,
  even so have you been
    faithless to me,
  O house of Israel, says the
    LORD.
21 A cry is heard on the heights!
  the plaintive weeping of
    Israel's children,
  Because they have perverted
    their ways
  and forgotten the LORD, their
    God.
22 Return, rebellious children,
  and I will cure you of your
    rebelling.
  "Here we are, we now come to
    you
  because you are the LORD,
    our God.
23 Deceptive indeed are the hills,
  the thronging mountains;
  In the LORD, our God, alone
  is the salvation of Israel.
24 The shame-god has devoured
  our fathers' toil from our
    youth,
  Their sheep and their cattle,
  their sons and their daughters.
25 Let us lie down in our shame,
  let our disgrace cover us,
  for we have sinned against
    the LORD, our God,
  From our youth to this day, we
    and our fathers also;
  we listened not to the voice of
    the LORD, our God."

4 If you wish to return, O Israel,
    says the LORD,
  return to me.
  If you put your detestable things
    out of my sight,
  and do not stray,
2 Then you can swear, "As the
    LORD lives,"
  in truth, in judgment, and in
    justice;
  Then shall the nations use his
    name in blessing,
  and glory in him.

3 For to the men of Judah and to
Jerusalem, thus says the LORD:

  Till your untilled ground,
    sow not among thorns.
4 For the sake of the LORD, be
    circumcised,
  remove the foreskins of your
    hearts,
  O men of Judah and citizens
    of Jerusalem;
  Lest my anger break out like
    fire,
  and burn till none can quench
    it,
  because of your evil deeds.

The Invasion from the North

5 Proclaim it in Judah,
  make it heard in Jerusalem;
  Blow the trumpet through the
    land,
  summon the recruits!
  Say, "Fall in, let us march
  to the fortified cities."
6 Bear the standard to Zion,
  seek refuge without delay!
  Evil I bring from the north,
  and great destruction.
7 Up comes the lion from his lair,
  the destroyer of nations has
    set out,
  has left his place,
  To turn your land into
    desolation,
  till your cities lie waste and
    empty.
8 So gird yourselves with
    sackcloth,
  mourn and wail:
  "The blazing wrath of the LORD
  is not turned away from us."

9 In that day, says the LORD,
  The king will lose heart, and
    the princes;
  the priests will be amazed,
  and the prophets stunned.
10 "Alas! Lord GOD," they will say,
  "You only deceived us
  When you said: Peace shall be
    yours;
  for the sword touches our
    very soul."

3, 14–18: A remnant of Israel (14) will reunite with Judah (18). The elementary cult of the Lord represented by *the ark of the covenant* will now be replaced by a more deeply spiritual and universal alliance, symbolized by his throne in the ideal Jerusalem around which *all nations will be gathered together* (17).
3, 24: *Shame-god:* literally, shame, a term com

monly substituted for Baal, the Canaanite god with many local shrines.
4, 2: *As the Lord lives:* this oath, made sincerely, implies Israel's return to God and loyal adherence to him. Thus the ancient promises are fulfilled; cf Gn 12, 3; 18, 18; 22, 18; 26, 4; Ps 72, 17.
4, 4: The mere external rite of circumcision avails

nothing unless accompanied by the removal of blindness and obstinacy of heart; cf Rom 2, 25.29; 1 Cor 7, 19; Gal 5, 6; 6, 13.15.
4, 10: *You only deceived us:* the false prophets blame their deception on God; cf 14, 13–16.

11 At that time it will be said
    of this people and of
    Jerusalem,
    "From the glaring heights
        through the desert.
    a wind comes toward the
        daughter of my people."
    Not to winnow, not to cleanse,
12 does this wind from the
        heights come at my bidding;
    And I myself now pronounce
        sentence upon them.

13 See! like storm clouds he
        advances,
    like a hurricane his chariots;
    Swifter than eagles are his
        steeds:
    "Woe to us! we are ruined."
14 Cleanse your heart of evil, O
        Jerusalem,
    that you may be saved.
    How long must your pernicious
        thoughts
    lodge within you?
15 Listen! They proclaim it from
        Dan,
    from Mount Ephraim they
        announce destruction:
16 "Make this known to the
        nations,
    announce it to Jerusalem:
    The besiegers are coming from
        the distant land,
    shouting their war cry against
        the cities of Judah."
17 Like watchmen of the fields
        they surround her,
    for she has rebelled against
        me, says the LORD.
18 Your conduct, your misdeeds,
        have done this to you;
    how bitter is this disaster of
        yours,
    how it reaches to your very
        heart!

19 My breast! my breast! how I
        suffer!
    The walls of my heart!
    My heart beats wildly,
        I cannot be still;
    For I have heard the sound of
        the trumpet,
    the alarm of war.
20 Ruin after ruin is reported;
    the whole earth is laid waste.

In an instant my tents are
        ravaged;
    in a flash, my shelters.
21 How long must I see that signal,
    hear that trumpet sound!

22 Fools my people are,
        they know me not;
    Senseless children they are,
        having no understanding;
    They are wise in evil,
        but know not how to do good.
23 I looked at the earth, and it was
        waste and void;
    at the heavens, and their light
        had gone out!
24 I looked at the mountains, and
        they were trembling,
    and the hills were crumbling!
25 I looked and behold, there was
        no man;
    even the birds of the air had
        flown away!
26 I looked and behold, the garden
        land was a desert,
    with all its cities destroyed
    before the LORD, before his
        blazing wrath.

27   For thus says the LORD:
    Waste shall the whole land be;
        I will [not] wholly destroy it.
28 Because of this the earth shall
        mourn,
    the heavens above shall
        darken;
    I have spoken, I will not repent,
        I have resolved, I will not
        turn back.
29 At the shout of horseman and
        bowman
    each city takes to flight;
    They shrink into the thickets,
        they scale the rocks:
    All the cities are abandoned,
        and no one dwells in them.
30 You now who are doomed,
        what do you mean
    by putting on purple,
        bedecking yourself with gold,
    Shading your eyes with
        cosmetics,
    beautifying yourself in vain?
    Your lovers spurn you,
        they seek your life.
31 Yes, I hear the moaning, as of a
        woman in travail,
    like the anguish of a mother
        with her first child—

The cry of daughter Zion
        gasping,
    as she stretches forth her
        hands:
    "Ah, woe is me! I sink exhausted
        before the slayers!"

Universal Corruption

5 Roam the streets of Jerusalem,
    look about and observe,
    Search through her public places,
        to find even one
    Who lives uprightly
        and seeks to be faithful,
    and I will pardon her!
2 Though they say, "As the LORD
        lives,"
    they swear falsely.
3   O LORD, do your eyes not
        look for honesty?
    You struck them, but they did
        not cringe;
    you laid them low, but they
        refused correction;
    They set their faces harder than
        stone,
    and refused to return to you.
4 It is only the lowly, I thought,
        who are foolish;
    For they know not the way of
        the LORD,
    their duty to their God.
5 I will go to the great ones
        and speak with them;
    For they know the way of the
        LORD,
    their duty to their God.
    But, one and all, they had
        broken the yoke,
    torn off the harness.
6 Therefore lions from the forest
        slay them,
    wolves of the desert ravage
        them,
    Leopards keep watch round
        their cities:
    all who come out are torn to
        pieces
    For their many crimes
        and their numerous rebellions.

7 Why should I pardon you these
        things?
    Your sons have forsaken me,
        they swear by gods that are
        not.
    I fed them, but they committed
        adultery;
    to the harlot's house they
        throng.

4, 19ff: Probably the prophet's own anguish at the
coming destruction of Judah.

8 Lustful stallions they are,
  each neighs after another's
    wife.
9 Shall I not punish them for these
    things?
  says the LORD;
  On a nation such as this shall I
    not take vengeance?
10 Climb to her terraces, and
     ravage them,
   destroy them [not] wholly.
   Tear away her tendrils,
     they do not belong to the
       LORD.
11 For they have openly rebelled
     against me,
   both the house of Israel and
     the house of Judah,
   says the LORD.
12 They denied the LORD,
     saying, "Not he—
   No evil shall befall us,
     neither sword nor famine
       shall we see.
13 The prophets have become wind,
     and the word is not in them.
   May their threats be carried
     out against themselves!"

14 Now, for this that you have
     said,
   says the LORD, the God of
     hosts—
   Behold, I make my words
     in your mouth, a fire,
   And this people is the wood
     that it shall devour!—
15 Beware, I will bring against you
     a nation from afar,
   O house of Israel, says the
     LORD;
   A long-lived nation, an ancient
     nation,
   a people whose language you
     know not,
   whose speech you cannot
     understand.
16 Their quivers are like open
     graves;
   all of them are warriors.
17 They will devour your harvest
     and your bread,
   devour your sons and your
     daughters,
   Devour your sheep and cattle,
     devour your vines and fig
       trees;

They will beat flat with the
  sword
  the fortified city in which you
    trust.

18 Yet even in those days, says the
LORD, I will not wholly destroy you.
19 And when they ask, "Why has
the LORD done all these things to
us?" say to them, "As you have
forsaken me to serve strange gods
in your own land, so shall you serve
strangers in a land not your own."

20 Announce this to the house of
     Jacob,
   proclaim it in Judah:
21 Pay attention to this,
     foolish and senseless people
   Who have eyes and see not,
     who have ears and hear not.
22 Should you not fear me, says
     the LORD,
   should you not tremble before
     me?
   I made the sandy shore the
     sea's limit,
   which by eternal decree it
     may not overstep.
   Toss though it may, it is to no
     avail;
   though its billows roar, they
     cannot pass.
23 But this people's heart is
     stubborn and rebellious;
   they turn and go away,
24 And say not in their hearts,
     "Let us fear the LORD, our
       God,
   Who gives us rain
     early and late, in its time;
   Who watches for us
     over the appointed weeks of
       harvest."
25 Your crimes have prevented
     these things,
   your sins have turned back
     these blessings from you.
26 For there are among my people
     criminals;
   like fowlers they set traps,
     but it is men they catch.
27 Their houses are as full of
     treachery
   as a bird-cage is of birds;
   Therefore they grow powerful
     and rich,

28   fat and sleek.
   They go their wicked way;
     justice they do not defend
   By advancing the claim of the
     fatherless
   or judging the cause of the
     poor.
29 Shall I not punish these things?
     says the LORD;
   on a nation such as this shall
     I not take vengeance?
30 A shocking, horrible thing
     has happened in the land:
31 The prophets prophesy falsely,
     and the priests teach as they
       wish;
   Yet my people will have it so;
     what will you do when the end
       comes?

The Enemy at the Gates

6 Flee, sons of Benjamin,
    out of Jerusalem!
  Blow the trumpet in Tekoa,
    raise a signal over Beth-
      haccherem;
  For evil threatens from the
    north,
    and mighty destruction.
2 O lovely and delicate
    daughter Zion, you are
      ruined!
3 Against her, shepherds come
    with their flocks;
  all around, they pitch their
    tents,
  each one grazes his portion.
4 "Prepare for war against her,
    Up! let us rush upon her at
      midday!
  Alas! the day is waning,
    evening shadows lengthen;
5 Up! let us rush upon her by
    night,
    destroy her palaces!"

6   For thus says the LORD of
      hosts:
  Hew down her trees,
    throw up a siege mound
      against Juersalem.
  Woe to the city marked for
    punishment;
    nought but oppression within
      her!

5, 12: *They denied the Lord:* the people act as
though God does not exist and will not interfere.
5, 24: *Rain early and late:* autumn and spring

rains respectively. *Appointed weeks of harvest:* the
seven weeks between the Passover (Dt 16, 9f) and
Pentecost, during which it ordinarily did not rain.

6, 3: *Shepherds ... with their flocks:* foreign invaders with their armies.

---

7 As the well gushes out its
     waters,
   so she gushes out her
     wickedness.
Violence and destruction
     resound in her;
   ever before me are wounds
     and blows.
8 Be warned, O Jerusalem,
     lest I be estranged from you;
Lest I turn you into a desert,
   a land where no man dwells.

9 Thus says the LORD of hosts:
Glean, glean like a vine
   the remnant of Israel;
Pass your hand, like a vintager,
   repeatedly over the tendrils.
10 To whom shall I speak?
     whom shall I warn, and be
     heard?
See! their ears are uncircumcised,
   they cannot give heed;
See, the word of the LORD has
     become for them
   an object of scorn, which they
     will not have.
11 Therefore my wrath brims up
     within me,
   I am weary of holding it in;
I will pour it out upon the child
     in the street,
   upon the young men gathered
     together.
Yes, all will be taken, husband
     and wife,
   graybeard with ancient.
12 Their houses will fall to
     strangers,
   their fields and their wives
     as well;
For I will stretch forth my hand
     against those who dwell in
     this land, says the LORD.
13 Small and great alike, all are
     greedy for gain;
   prophet and priest, all
     practice fraud.
14 They would repair, as though it
     were nought,
   the injury to my people:
"Peace, peace!" they say,
   though there is no peace.
15 They are odious; they have
     done abominable things,

yet they are not at all
     ashamed,
   they know not how to blush.
Hence they shall be among those
     who fall;
   in their time of punishment
     they shall go down,
     says the LORD.

16 Thus says the LORD:
Stand beside the earliest roads,
   ask the pathways of old
Which is the way to good, and
     walk it;
   thus you will find rest for
     your souls.
But they said, "We will not
     walk it."
17 When I raised up watchmen for
     them:
"Hearken to the sound of the
     trumpet!"
   they said, "We will not
     hearken."
18 Therefore hear, O nations,
   and know, O earth,
   what I will do with them:
19 See, I bring evil upon this
     people,
   the fruit of their own schemes,
Because they heeded not my
     words,
   because they despised my law.
20 Of what use to me incense that
     comes from Sheba,
   or sweet cane from far-off
     lands?
Your holocausts find no favor
     with me,
   your sacrifices please me not.
21 Therefore, thus says the
     LORD:
See, I will place before this
     people
   obstacles to bring them down;
Fathers and sons alike,
   neighbors and friends shall
     perish.

22 Thus says the LORD:
See, a people comes from the
     land of the north,
   a great nation, roused from
     the ends of the earth.
23 Bow and javelin they wield;
   cruel and pitiless are they.

They sound like the roaring sea
   as they ride forth on steeds,
Each in his place, for battle
   against you, daughter Zion.
24 We hear the report of them;
   helpless fall our hands,
Anguish takes hold of us,
   throes like a mother's in
     childbirth.
25 Go not forth into the field,
   step not into the street,
Beware of the enemy's sword;
   terror on every side!
26 O daughter of my people, gird
     on sackcloth,
   roll in the ashes.
Mourn as for an only child
   with bitter wailing,
For sudden upon us
   comes the destroyer.

27 A tester among my people I
     have appointed you,
   to search and test their way.
28 Arch-rebels are they all,
   dealers in slander,
   all of them corrupt.
29 The bellows roars,
   the lead is consumed by the
     fire;
In vain has the smelter refined,
   the wicked are not drawn off.
30 "Silver rejected" they shall be
     called,
   for the LORD has rejected
     them.

ORACLES MOSTLY IN THE DAYS OF JEHOIAKIM

The Temple Sermon

7 The following message came to
Jeremiah from the LORD: 2
Stand at the gate of the house of the
LORD, and there proclaim this message: Hear the word of the LORD,
all you of Judah who enter these
gates to worship the LORD! 3 Thus
says the LORD of hosts, the God of
Israel: Reform your ways and your
deeds, so that I may remain with
you in this place. 4 Put not your
trust in the deceitful words: "This is
the temple of the LORD! The temple
of the LORD! The temple of the
LORD!" 5 Only if you thoroughly

6, 14: *As though it were nought:* the false assurance of well-being given by priest and prophet cannot
reduce the harm which universal materialism and
corruption have done to the people.

6, 16: *Earliest roads ... pathways of old:* history
and the lessons to be learned from it.
6, 17: *Watchmen:* the prophets who, like Jeremiah,
had upheld God's moral law.

7, 1–15: *The temple of the Lord* will not serve as a
place of refuge for the Jews against their enemies if
they fail to reform their evil ways.

reform your ways and your deeds; if each of you deals justly with his neighbor; 6 if you no longer oppress the resident alien, the orphan, and the widow; if you no longer shed innocent blood in this place, or follow strange gods to your own harm, 7 will I remain with you in this place, in the land which I gave your fathers long ago and forever.

8 But here you are, putting your trust in deceitful words to your own loss! 9 Are you to steal and murder, commit adultery and perjury, burn incense to Baal, go after strange gods that you know not, 10 and yet come to stand before me in this house which bears my name, and say: "We are safe; we can commit all these abominations again"? 11 Has this house which bears my name become in your eyes a den of thieves? I too see what is being done, says the LORD. 12 You may go to Shiloh, which I made the dwelling place of my name in the beginning. See what I did to it because of the wickedness of my people Israel. 13 And now, because you have committed all these misdeeds, says the LORD, because you did not listen, though I spoke to you untiringly; because you did not answer, though I called you, 14 I will do to this house named after me, in which you trust, and to this place which I gave to you and your fathers, just as I did to Shiloh. 15 I will cast you away from me, as I cast away all your brethren, all the offspring of Ephraim.

Abuses in Worship

16 You, now, do not intercede for this people; raise not in their behalf a pleading prayer! Do not urge me, for I will not listen to you. 17 Do you not see what they are doing in the cities of Judah, in the streets of Jerusalem? 18 The children gather wood, their fathers light the fire, and the women knead dough to make cakes for the queen of heaven, while libations are poured out to strange gods in order to hurt me. 19 Is it I whom they hurt, says the LORD; is it not rather themselves, to their own confusion? 20 See now, says the Lord GOD, my anger and my wrath will pour out upon this place, upon man and beast, upon the trees of the field and the fruits of the earth; it will burn without being quenched.

21 Thus says the LORD of hosts, the God of Israel: Heap your holocausts upon your sacrifices; eat up the flesh! 22 In speaking to your fathers on the day I brought them out of the land of Egypt, I gave them no command concerning holocaust or sacrifice. 23 This rather is what I commanded them: Listen to my voice; then I will be your God and you shall be my people. Walk in all the ways that I command you, so that you may prosper.

24 But they obeyed not, nor did they pay heed. They walked in the hardness of their evil hearts and turned their backs, not their faces, to me. 25 From the day that your fathers left the land of Egypt even to this day, I have sent you untiringly all my servants the prophets. 26 Yet they have not obeyed me nor paid heed; they have stiffened their necks and done worse than their fathers. 27 When you speak all these words to them, they will not listen to you either; when you call to them, they will not answer you. 28 Say to them: This is the nation which does not listen to the voice of the LORD, its God, or take correction. Faithfulness has disappeared; the word itself is banished from their speech.

29 Cut off your dedicated hair and
    throw it away!
  on the heights intone an
    elegy;
  For the LORD has rejected and
    cast off
  the generation that draws
    down his wrath.

30 The people of Judah have done what is evil in my eyes, says the LORD. They have defiled the house which bears my name by setting up in it their abominable idols. 31 In the Valley of Ben-hinnom they have built the high place of Topheth to immolate in fire their sons and daughters, such a thing as I never commanded or had in mind. 32 Therefore, beware! days will come, says the LORD, when Topheth and the Valley of Ben-hinnom will no longer be called such, but rather the Valley of Slaughter. For lack of space, Topheth will be a burial place. 33 The corpses of this people will be food for the birds of the sky and for the beasts of the field, which no one will drive away. 34 In the cities of Judah and in the streets of Jerusalem I will silence the cry of joy, the cry of gladness, the voice of the bridegroom and the voice of the bride; for the land will be 8 turned to rubble. 1 At that time, says the LORD, the bones of the kings and princes of Judah, the bones of the priests and the prophets, and the bones of the citizens of Jerusalem will be emptied out of their graves 2 and spread out before the sun and the moon and the whole army of heaven, which they loved and served, which they followed, consulted, and worshiped. They will not be gathered up for burial, but will lie like dung upon the ground. 3 Death will be preferred to life by all the survivors of this wicked race who remain in any of the places to which I banish them, says the LORD of hosts.

Israel's Conduct Incomprehensible

4   Tell them: Thus says the
      LORD:
    When someone falls, does he not
      rise again?
    if he goes astray, does he not
      turn back?
5 Why do these people rebel
    with obstinate resistance?

7, 6: *The resident alien:* specially protected by law; cf Ex 20, 10; Nm 9, 14; 15, 14; Dt 5, 14; 28, 43.

7, 12: *Shiloh:* original place of worship from the time of Joshua to that of Samuel. The sanctuary was later rejected by God and destroyed by the Philistines; cf 1 Sm 1, 9; 4, 3f; Ps 78, 60.68f.

7, 18: *Queen of heaven:* the Assyro–Babylonian Ishtar, goddess of fertility, whose worship was introduced under King Manasseh and was revived after Josiah's death. *Cakes* shaped like stars (Ishtar was identified with the planet Venus) were offered in her honor.

7, 22: *I gave them no command:* right conduct rather than mere external cult was God's will concerning his people (v 23).

7, 29: *Dedicated hair:* the unshorn hair of the nazirite, regarded as sacred because of a vow, temporary or permanent, to abstain from cutting or shaving the hair, from contact with a corpse, and from all products of the vine; cf Nm 6, 4–8. The cutting of this hair was a sign of extreme mourning.

8, 2: *Army of heaven:* the stars, worshiped by the pagan nations and even by the inhabitants of Jerusalem during the reigns of Manasseh and Amon.

Why do they cling to deceptive
 idols,
 refuse to turn back?
6 I listen closely:
 they speak what is not true;
No one repents of his
 wickedness,
 saying "What have I done!"
Everyone keeps on running his
 course,
 like a steed dashing into
 battle.
7 Even the stork in the air
 knows its seasons;
Turtledove, swallow and thrush
 observe their time of return,
But my people do not know
 the ordinance of the LORD.

8 How can you say, "We are wise,
 we have the law of the
 LORD"?
Why, that has been changed into
 falsehood
 by the lying pen of the scribes!
9 The wise are confounded,
 dismayed and ensnared;
Since they have rejected the
 word of the LORD,
 of what avail is their wisdom?

Shameless in Their Crimes

10 Therefore, I will give their wives
 to strangers,
 their fields to spoilers.
Small and great alike, all are
 greedy for gain,
 prophet and priest, all practice
 fraud.
11 They would repair, as though it
 were nought,
 the injury to the daughter of
 my people:
"Peace, peace!" they say,
 though there is no peace.
12 They are odious; they have
 done abominable things,
 yet they are not at all
 ashamed,
 they know not how to blush.
Hence they shall be among those
 who fall;
 in their time of punishment
 they shall go down,
 says the LORD.

Threats of Punishment

13 I will gather them all in, says
 the LORD:
 no grapes on the vine,
No figs on the fig trees,
 foliage withered!
14 Why do we remain here?
 Let us form ranks and enter
 the walled cities,
 to perish there;
For the LORD has wrought our
 destruction,
 he has given us poison to
 drink,
 because we have sinned
 against the LORD.
15 We wait for peace to no avail;
 for a time of healing, but
 terror comes instead.
16 From Dan is heard
 the snorting of his steeds;
The neighing of his stallions
 shakes the whole land.
They come devouring the land
 and all it contains,
 the city and those who dwell
 in it.
17 Yes, I will send against you
 poisonous snakes,
Against which no charm will
 work
 when they bite you, says the
 LORD.

The Prophet's Grief over the People's Suffering

18 My grief is incurable,
 my heart within me is faint.
19 Listen! the cry of the daughter
 of my people,
 far and wide in the land!
Is the LORD no longer in Zion,
 is her King no longer in her
 midst?
[Why do they provoke me with
 their idols,
 with their foreign nonentities?]
20 "The harvest has passed, the
 summer is at an end,
 and yet we are not safe!"
21 I am broken by the ruin of the
 daughter of my people.
 I am disconsolate; horror has
 seized me.

22 Is there no balm in Gilead,
 no physician there?
Why grows not new flesh
 over the wound of the
 daughter of my people?
23 Oh, that my head were a spring
 of water,
 my eyes a fountain of tears,
That I might weep day and night
 over the slain of the daughter
 of my people!

The Corruption of the People

9 Would that I had in the desert
 a travelers' lodge!
That I might leave my people
 and depart from them.
They are all adulterers,
 a faithless band.
2 They ready their tongues like
 a drawn bow;
 with lying, and not with truth,
 they hold forth in the land.
They go from evil to evil,
 but me they know not, says
 the LORD.
3 Be on your guard, everyone
 against his neighbor;
 put no trust in any brother.
Every brother apes Jacob, the
 supplanter,
 every friend is guilty of
 slander.
4 Each one deceives the other,
 no one speaks the truth.
They have accustomed their
 tongues to lying,
 and are perverse, and cannot
 repent.
5 Violence upon violence,
 deceit upon deceit:
They refuse to recognize me,
 says the LORD.

6 Therefore, thus says the
 LORD of hosts:
I will smelt them and test them;
 how else should I deal with
 their wickedness?
7 A murderous arrow is his
 tongue,
 his mouth utters deceit;
He speaks cordially with his
 friends,
 but in his heart he lays an
 ambush!

8, 8f: *Lying pen of the scribes:* because the interpretations and ordinances of the scribes ran counter to the *word of the Lord.*
8, 11: *Daughter of my people:* the people itself

personified as a woman.
8, 22: *Gilead:* noted for its healing balm but unable to heal the moral wound of the people.
9, 3: *Jacob, the supplanter:* in Hebrew, a play on

words. Jacob, as his name indicates ("he supplants"), deprived his brother Esau of his birthright; cf Gn 25, 26.33.

8 For these things, says the LORD,
    shall I not punish them?
On a nation such as this
    shall I not take vengeance?

Dirge over the Ravaged Land

9 Over the mountains, break out
    in cries of lamentation,
    over the pasture lands, intone
    a dirge:
They are scorched, and no man
    cross them,
    unheard is the bleat of the
    flock;
Birds of the air as well as beasts,
    all have fled, and are gone.
10 I will turn Jerusalem into a
    heap of ruins,
    a haunt of jackals;
The cities of Judah I will make
    into a waste,
    where no one dwells.

11 Who is so wise that he can understand this? Let him to whom the mouth of the LORD has spoken make it known:

    Why is the land ravaged,
      scorched like a wasteland
      untraversed?

12 The LORD answered: Because they have abandoned my law, which I set before them, and have not followed it or listened to my voice, 13 but followed rather the hardness of their hearts and the Baals, as their fathers had taught them; 14 therefore, thus says the LORD of hosts, the God of Israel: See now, I will give them wormwood to eat and poison to drink. 15 I will scatter them among nations whom neither they nor their fathers have known; I will send the sword to pursue them until I have completely destroyed them.

16   Thus says the LORD of hosts:
Attention! tell the wailing
    women to come,
    summon the best of them;
17 Let them come quickly
    and intone a dirge for us,
That our eyes may be wet with
    weeping,
    our cheeks run with tears.

18 The dirge is heard from Zion:
    Ruined we are, and greatly
      ashamed;
We must leave the land,
    give up our homes!
19 Hear, you women, the word of
    the LORD,
    let your ears receive his
      message.
Teach your daughters this dirge,
    and each other this lament.
20 Death has come up through our
    windows,
    has entered our palaces;
It cuts down the children in the
    street,
    young people in the squares.
21 The corpses of the slain
    lie like dung on a field,
Like sheaves behind the
    harvester,
    with no one to gather them.

True Glory

22   Thus says the LORD:
Let not the wise man glory in
    his wisdom,
    nor the strong man glory in
      his strength,
    nor the rich man glory in his
      riches;
23 But rather, let him who glories,
    glory in this,
    that in his prudence he knows
      me,
    Knows that I, the LORD, bring
      about kindness,
      justice and uprightness on the
      earth;
For with such am I pleased,
    says the LORD.

Circumcision Worthless

24 See, days are coming, says the LORD, when I will demand an account of all those circumcised in their flesh: 25 Egypt and Judah, Edom and the Ammonites, Moab and the desert dwellers who shave their temples. For all these nations, like the whole house of Israel, are uncircumcised in heart.

The Folly of Idolatry

10 Hear the word which the LORD speaks to you, O house of Israel. 2 Thus says the LORD:

Learn not the customs of the
    nations,
    and have no fear of the signs
      of the heavens,
    though the nations fear them.
3 For the cult idols of the nations
    are nothing,
    wood cut from the forest,
Wrought by craftsmen with the
    adze,
4   adorned with silver and gold.
With nails and hammers they
    are fastened,
    that they may not totter.
5 Like a scarecrow in a cucumber
    field are they,
    they cannot speak;
They must be carried about,
    for they cannot walk.
Fear them not, they can do no
    harm,
    neither is it in their power to
      do good.
6 No one is like you, O LORD,
    great are you,
    great and mighty is your
      name.
7 Who would not fear you,
    King of the nations,
    for it is your due!
Among all the wisest of the
    nations,
    and in all their domain,
    there is none like you.

8 One and all they are dumb and
    senseless,
    these idols they teach about
      are wooden:
9 Silver strips brought from
    Tarshish,
    and gold from Ophir,
The work of the craftsman
    and the handiwork of the
      smelter,
Clothed with violet and purple—
    all of them the work of
      artisans.

11 Thus shall you say of them: Let the gods that did not make heaven and earth perish from the earth, and from beneath these heavens!

10 The LORD is true God,
    he is the living God, the
      eternal King,

9, 25: *Desert dwellers . . . temples:* Arab tribesmen who cut off their hair and shaved their temples in honor of the pagan god Dushara. This was forbidden the Israelites (Lv 19, 27).

10, 2: *Signs of the heavens:* phenomena in the sky superstitiously regarded by the pagans as dire omens.

Before whose anger the earth
quakes,
whose wrath the nations
cannot endure:
12 He who made the earth by his
power,
established the world by his
wisdom,
and stretched out the heavens
by his skill.
13 When he thunders, the waters in
the heavens roar,
and he brings up clouds from
the end of the earth;
He makes the lightning flash in
the rain,
and releases stormwinds from
their chambers.
14 Every man is stupid, ignorant;
every artisan is put to shame
by his idol:
He has molded a fraud,
without breath of life.
15 Nothingness are they, a
ridiculous work;
they will perish in their time
of punishment.
16 Not like these is the portion of
Jacob:
he is the creator of all things;
Israel is his very own tribe,
LORD of hosts is his name.

Abandonment of Judah

17 Lift your bundle and leave the
land,
O city living in a state of siege!
18 For thus says the LORD:
Behold, this time
I will sling away the
inhabitants of the land;
I will hem them in,
that they may be taken.
19 Woe is me! I am undone,
my wound is incurable;
Yet I had thought:
if I make light of my wound,
I can bear it.
20 My tent is ruined,
all its cords are severed.
My sons have left me, they are
no more:
no one to pitch my tent,
no one to raise its curtains.
21 Yes, the shepherds were stupid
as cattle,
the LORD they sought not;
Therefore they had no success,
and all their flocks were
scattered.

22 Listen! a noise! it comes closer,
a great uproar from the
northern land:
To turn the cities of Judah
into a desert haunt of jackals.

Prayer of Jeremiah

23 You know, O LORD,
that man is not master of his
way;
Man's course is not within his
choice,
nor is it for him to direct his
step.
24 Punish us, O LORD, but with
equity,
not in anger, lest you have us
dwindle away.
25 Pour out your wrath on the
nations that know you not,
on the tribes that call not
upon your name;
For they have devoured Jacob
utterly,
and laid waste his dwelling.

Plea for Fidelity to the Covenant

11 The following message came
to Jeremiah from the LORD:
2 Speak to the men of Judah and
to the citizens of Jerusalem, 3 saying to them: Thus says the LORD, the
God of Israel: Cursed be the man
who does not observe the terms of
this covenant, 4 which I enjoined
upon your fathers the day I brought
them up out of the land of Egypt,
that iron foundry, saying: Listen to
my voice and do all that I command you. Then you shall be my
people, and I will be your God.
5 Thus I will fulfill the oath which
I swore to your fathers, to give them
a land flowing with milk and honey:
the one you have today. "Amen,
LORD," I answered.
6 Then the LORD said to me:
Proclaim all these words in the
cities of Judah and in the streets of
Jerusalem: Hear the words of this
covenant and obey them. 7 Urgently and constantly I warned your
fathers to obey my voice, from the
day I brought them up out of the
land of Egypt even to this day.
8 But they did not listen or give ear.
Each one followed the hardness of
his evil heart, till I brought upon

them all the threats of this covenant
which they had failed to observe as
I commanded them.
9 A conspiracy has been found,
the LORD said to me, among the
men of Judah and the citizens of
Jerusalem. 10 They have returned
to the crimes of their forefathers who
refused to obey my words. They also
have followed and served strange
gods; the covenant which I had made
with their fathers, the house of
Israel and the house of Judah have
broken. 11 Therefore, thus says
the LORD: See, I bring upon them
misfortune which they cannot escape.
Though they cry out to me, I will
not listen to them. 12 Then the
cities of Judah and the citizens of
Jerusalem will go and cry out to the
gods to which they have been
offering incense. But these gods will
give them no help whatever when
misfortune strikes.

13 For as numerous as your cities
are your gods, O Judah!
And as many as the streets of
Jerusalem
are the altars for offering
sacrifice to Baal.

14 Do not intercede on behalf of
this people, nor utter a plea for them.
I will not listen when they call to
me at the time of their misfortune.

Sacrifices of No Avail

15 What right has my beloved in
my house,
while she prepares her plots?
Can vows and sacred meat turn
away
your misfortune from you?
Will you still be jubilant
16 when you hear the great
invasion?
A spreading olive tree, goodly
to behold,
the LORD has named you;
Now he sets fire to it,
its branches burn.
17 The LORD of hosts who planted
you has decreed misfortune for you
because of the evil done by the house
of Israel and by the house of Judah,
who provoked me by sacrificing to
Baal.

The Plot against Jeremiah

18 I knew it because the LORD informed me; at that time you, O LORD, showed me their doings.

12
You would be in the right,
O LORD,
    if I should dispute with you;
    even so, I must discuss the
      case with you.
Why does the way of the godless
    prosper,
    why live all the treacherous
      in contentment?
2 You planted them; they have
    taken root,
    they keep on growing and
      bearing fruit.
You are upon their lips,
    but far from their inmost
      thoughts.
3 You, O Lord, know me, you
    see me,
    you have found that at heart
      I am with you.
Pick them out like sheep for the
    slaughter,
    set them apart for the day of
      carnage.
4 How long must the earth mourn,
    the green of the whole
      countryside wither?
For the wickedness of those who
    dwell in it
    beasts and birds disappear,
    because they say, "God does
      not see our ways."

5 If running against men has
    wearied you,
    how will you race against
      horses?
And if in a land of peace you
    fall headlong,
    what will you do in the
      thickets of the Jordan?

6 For even your own brothers, the members of your father's house, betray you; they have recruited a force against you. Do not believe them, even if they are friendly to you in their words.

(11) 19 Yet I, like a trusting lamb led to slaughter, had not realized that they were hatching plots against me: "Let us destroy the tree in its vigor; let us cut him off from the land of the living, so that his name will be spoken no more."

20 But, you, O LORD of hosts, O
    just Judge,
    searcher of mind and heart,
Let me witness the vengeance
    you take on them,
    for to you I have entrusted my
      cause!

21 Therefore, thus says the LORD concerning the men of Anathoth who seek your life, saying, "Do not prophesy in the name of the LORD; else you shall die by our hand." 22 Therefore, thus says the LORD of hosts: I am going to punish them. The young men shall die by the sword; their sons and daughters shall die by famine. 23 None shall be spared among them, for I will bring misfortune upon the men of Anathoth, the year of their punishment.

The Lord's Complaint

(12) 7 I abandon my house,
    cast off my heritage;
The beloved of my soul I deliver
    into the hand of her foes.
8 My heritage has turned on me
    like a lion in the jungle;
Because she has roared against
    me,
    I treat her as an enemy.
9 My heritage is a prey for hyenas,
    is surrounded by vultures;
Come, gather together, all you
    beasts of the field,
    come and eat!
10 Many shepherds have ravaged
    my vineyard,
    have trodden my heritage
      underfoot;
The portion that delighted me
    they have turned
    into a desert waste.
11 They have made it a mournful
    waste,
    desolate it lies before me,
Desolate, all the land,
    because no one takes it to
      heart.

12 Upon every desert height
    brigands have come up.
The LORD has a sword which
    consumes
    the land, from end to end:
    no peace for all mankind.
13 They have sown wheat and
    reaped thorns,
    they have tired themselves
      out to no purpose;
They recoil before their harvest,
    the flaming anger of the LORD.

Judah's Neighbors

14 Thus says the LORD against all my evil neighbors who plunder the heritage which I gave my people Israel as their own: See, I will pluck them up from their land; the house of Judah I will pluck up in their midst. 15 But after plucking them up, I will pity them again and bring them back, each to his heritage, each to his land. 16 And if they carefully learn my people's custom of swearing by my name, "As the LORD lives," they who formerly taught my people to swear by Baal shall be built up in the midst of my people. 17 But if they do not obey, I will uproot and destroy that nation entirely, says the LORD.

Judah's Corruption

13
The LORD said to me: Go buy yourself a linen loincloth; wear it on your lions, but do not put it in water. 2 I bought the loincloth, as the LORD commanded, and put it on. 3 A second time the word of the LORD came to me thus: 4 Take the loincloth which you bought and are wearing, and go now to the Parath; there hide it in a cleft of the rock. 5 Obedient to the LORD's command, I went to the Parath and buried the loincloth. 6 After a long interval, he said to me: Go now to the Parath and fetch the loincloth which I told you to hide there. 7 Again I went to the Parath, sought out and took the loincloth from the place where I had hid it. But it was rotted, good for nothing! 8 Then the message came

---

12, 3: Jeremiah does not seek private vengeance but the punishment of the wicked by the Lord; cf 20, 12. Nevertheless, the prophet's reaction to persecution shows the difference between the spirit of the Old Testament and the New.

12, 14: *My evil neighbors:* nations surrounding Israel, the land belonging to the Lord; cf Is 8, 8.
13, 1–11: This is probably a vision of the prophet symbolizing the religious corruption of Judah at the hands of the Babylonians, represented here by the

river *Parath*, the Euphrates; though a spring of the same name, northeast of Anathoth, may be directly meant.

to me from the LORD: 9 Thus says the LORD: So also I will allow the pride of Judah to rot, the great pride of Jerusalem. 10 This wicked people who refuse to obey my words, who walk in the stubbornness of their hearts, and follow strange gods to serve and adore them, shall be like this loincloth which is good for nothing. 11 For, as close as the loincloth clings to a man's loins, so had I made the whole house of Israel and the whole house of Judah cling to me, says the LORD; to be my people, my renown, my praise, my beauty. But they did not listen.

The Broken Wineflask

12 Now speak to them this word: Thus says the LORD, the God of Israel: Every wineflask is meant to be filled with wine. If they reply, "Do we not know that every wineflask is meant to be filled with wine?" 13 say to them: Thus says the LORD: Beware! I am filling with drunkenness all the inhabitants of this land, the kings who succeed to David's throne, the priests and prophets, and all the citizens of Jerusalem. 14 I will dash them against each other, fathers and sons together, says the LORD; I will show no compassion, I will not spare or pity, but will destroy them.

A Last Warning

15 Give ear, listen humbly,
      for the LORD speaks.
16 Give glory to the LORD, your
         God,
      before it grows dark;
   Before your feet stumble
      on darkening mountains;
   Before the light you look for
      turns to darkness,
      changes into black clouds.
17 If you do not listen to this in
         your pride,
      I will weep in secret many tears;
   My eyes will run with tears
      for the LORD's flock, led away
         to exile.

Exile

18 Say to the king and to the
         queen mother:
      come down from your throne;
   From your heads fall
      your magnificent crowns.

19 The cities of the Negeb are
         besieged,
      with no one to relieve them;
   All Judah is banished
      in universal exile.

Jerusalem's Disgrace

20 Lift up your eyes and see
      men coming from the north.
   Where is the flock entrusted to
         you,
      the sheep that were your
         glory?
21 What will you say when they
         place as rulers over you
      those whom you taught to be
         your lovers?
   Will not pangs seize you
      like those of a woman giving
         birth?
22 If you ask in your heart
      why these things befall you:
   For your great guilt your skirts
      are stripped away
      and you are violated.
23 Can the Ethiopian change his
         skin?
      the leopard his spots?
   As easily would you be able to
         do good,
      accustomed to evil as you are.
24 I will scatter them like chaff
      that flies
   when the desert wind blows.
25 This is your lot, the portion
      measured out to you
      from me, says the LORD.
   Because you have forgotten me,
      and trusted in the lying idol,
26 I now will strip off your skirts
         from you,
      so that your shame will
         appear.
27 Your adulteries, your neighings,
      your shameless prostitutions:
   On the hills in the highlands
      I see these horrible crimes of
         yours.
   Woe to you, Jerusalem, how
         long will it yet be
      before you become clean!

The Great Drought

14 The word of the LORD that came to Jeremiah concerning the drought:

2 Judah mourns,
      her gates are lifeless;

   Her people sink down in
         mourning:
      from Jerusalem ascends a cry
         of anguish.
3 The nobles send their servants
         for water,
      but when they come to the
         cisterns
   They find no water
      and return with empty jars.
   Ashamed, despairing, they cover
         their heads
4   because of the stricken soil;
   Because there is no rain in the
         land
      the farmers are ashamed, they
         cover their heads.
5 Even the hind in the field
      deserts her offspring
      because there is no grass.
6 The wild asses stand on the bare
         heights,
      gasping for breath like jackals;
   Their eyes grow dim,
      because there is no vegetation
         to be seen.

7 Even though our crimes bear
         witness against us,
      take action, O LORD, for the
         honor of your name—
   Even though our rebellions are
         many,
      though we have sinned against
         you.
8 O Hope of Israel, O LORD,
      our savior in time of need!
   Why should you be a stranger
      in this land,
      like a traveler who has stopped
         but for a night?
9 Why are you like a man
         dumbfounded,
      a champion who cannot save?
   You are in our midst, O LORD,
      your name we bear:
      do not forsake us!

10   Thus says the LORD of this
         people:
   They so love to wander
      that they do not spare their
         feet.
   The LORD has no pleasure in
         them;
      now he remembers their guilt,
      and will punish their sins.

11 Then the LORD said to me: Do not intercede for this people. 12 If they fast, I will not listen to their

supplication. If they offer holocausts or cereal offerings, I will not accept them. Rather, I will destroy them with the sword, famine, and pestilence.

13 Ah! Lord God, I replied, it is the prophets who say to them, "You shall not see the sword; famine shall not befall you. Indeed, I will give you lasting peace in this place."

14 Lies these prophets utter in my name, the Lord said to me. I did not send them; I gave them no command nor did I speak to them. Lying visions, foolish divination, dreams of their own imagination, they prophesy to you. 15 Therefore, thus says the Lord: Concerning the prophets who prophesy in my name, though I did not send them; who say, "Sword and famine shall not befall this land": by the sword and famine shall these prophets meet their end. 16 The people to whom they prophesy shall be cast out into the streets of Jerusalem by famine and the sword. No one shall bury them, their wives, their sons, or their daughters, for I will pour out upon them their own wickedness. 17 Speak to them this word:

Let my eyes stream with tears
   day and night, without rest,
Over the great destruction which
   overwhelms
     the virgin daughter of my
     people,
     over her incurable wound.
18 If I walk out into the field,
   look! those slain by the sword;
If I enter the city,
   look! those consumed by
   hunger.
Even the prophet and the priest
   forage in a land they know
   not.

19 Have you cast Judah off
   completely?
   Is Zion loathsome to you?
Why have you struck us a blow
   that cannot be healed?
We wait for peace, to no avail;
   for a time of healing, but
     terror comes instead.

15, 18: *A treacherous brook:* that dries up when its waters are needed. The prophet complains that he cannot rely on God with unfailing assurance of his assistance.

20 We recognize, O Lord, our
   wickedness,
   the guilt of our fathers;
   that we have sinned against
   you.
21 For your name's sake spurn us
   not,
   disgrace not the throne of your
   glory;
   remember your covenant
   with us, and break it not.
22 Among the nations' idols is
   there any that gives rain?
   Or can the mere heavens send
   showers?
Is it not you alone, O Lord
   our God, to whom we look?
   You alone have done all these
   things.

15 The Lord said to me: Even if Moses and Samuel stood before me, my heart would not turn toward this people. Send them away from me. 2 If they ask you where they should go, tell them, Thus says the Lord: Whoever is marked for death, to death; whoever is marked for the sword, to the sword; whoever is marked for famine, to famine; whoever is marked for captivity, to captivity. 3 Four kinds of scourge I have decreed against them, says the Lord: the sword to slay them; dogs to drag them about; the birds of the sky and the beasts of the earth to devour and destroy them. 4 And I will make them an object of horror to all the kingdoms of the earth because of what Manasseh, son of Hezekiah, king of Judah, did in Jerusalem.

Scene of Tragedy

5 Who will pity you, Jerusalem,
   who will console you?
Who will stop to ask
   about your welfare?
6 You have disowned me, says the
   Lord,
   turned your back upon me;
And so I stretched out my hand
   to destroy you,
   I was weary of sparing you.
7 I winnowed them with the fan
   in every city gate.
I destroyed my people through
   bereavement;
   they returned not from their
   evil ways.

8 Their widows were more
   numerous before me
   than the sands of the sea.
I brought against the mother
   of youths
   the spoiler at midday;
Suddenly I struck her
   with anguish and terror.
9 The mother of seven swoons
   away,
   gasping out her life;
Her sun sets in full day,
   she is disgraced, despairing.
Their survivors I will give to
   the sword
   before their enemies, says the
   Lord.

Jeremiah's Complaint

10 Woe to me, mother, that you
   gave me birth!
   a man of strife and contention
   to all the land!
I neither borrow nor lend,
   yet all curse me.
11 Tell me, Lord, have I not
   served you for their good?
   Have I not interceded with you
   in the time of misfortune and
   anguish?
15 You know I have.
Remember me, Lord, visit me,
   and avenge me on my
   persecutors.
Because of your long-suffering
   banish me not;
   know that for you I have
   borne insult.
16 When I found your words, I
   devoured them;
   they became my joy and the
   happiness of my heart,
Because I bore your name,
   O Lord, God of hosts.
17 I did not sit celebrating
   in the circle of merrymakers;
Under the weight of your hand
   I sat alone
   because you filled me with
   indignation.
18 Why is my pain continuous,
   my wound incurable, refusing
   to be healed?
You have indeed become for me
   a treacherous brook,
   whose waters do not abide!
19 Thus the Lord answered me:
If you repent, so that I restore
   you,
   in my presence you shall stand;

If you bring forth the precious
　　without the vile,
　　you shall be my mouthpiece.
Then it shall be they who turn
　　to you,
　　and you shall not turn to
　　them;
20 And I will make you toward
　　this people
　　a solid wall of brass.
Though they fight against you,
　　they shall not prevail,
For I am with you,
　　to deliver and rescue you,
　　says the LORD.
21 I will free you from the hand of
　　the wicked,
　　and rescue you from the
　　grasp of the violent.

Jeremiah's Life a Warning

16 This message came to me
from the LORD: 2 Do not
marry any woman; you shall not have
sons or daughters in this place,
3 for thus says the LORD concerning
the sons and daughters who will be
born in this place, the mothers who
will give them birth, the fathers who
will beget them in this land: 4 Of
deadly disease they shall die. Un-
lamented and unburied they will lie
like dung on the ground. Sword and
famine will make an end of them,
and their corpses will become food
for the birds of the sky and the
beasts of the field.

5 Go not into a house of mourning, the LORD continued: go not
there to lament or offer sympathy.
For I have withdrawn my friendship
from this people, says the LORD, my
kindness and my pity. 6 They shall
die, the great and the lowly, in this
land, and shall go unburied and un-
lamented. No one will gash himself
or shave his head for them. 7 They
will not break bread with the bereaved
to console them in their bereavement; they will not give them the
cup of consolation to drink over the
death of father or mother.

8 Enter not a house where people
are celebrating, to sit with them
eating and drinking. 9 For thus
says the LORD of hosts, the God of

Israel: Before your very eyes and
during your lifetime I will silence
from this place the cry of joy and
the cry of gladness, the voice of the
bridegroom and the voice of the
bride.

10 When you proclaim all these
words to this people and they ask
you: "Why has the LORD pronounced
all these great evils against us?
What is our crime? What sin have
we committed against the LORD, our
God?"— 11 you shall answer
them: It is because your fathers
have forsaken me, says the LORD,
and followed strange gods, which
they served and worshiped; but me
they have forsaken, and my law they
have not observed. 12 And you
have done worse than your fathers.
Here you are, every one of you,
walking in the hardness of his evil
heart instead of listening to me.
13 I will cast you out of this land
into a land that neither you nor your
fathers have known; there you can
serve strange gods day and night,
because I will not grant you my
mercy.

Return from Exile

14 However, days will surely come,
says the LORD, when it will no
longer be said, "As the LORD lives,
who brought the Israelites out of
Egypt"; 15 but rather, "As the
LORD lives, who brought the Israelites
out of the land of the north and out
of all the countries to which he had
banished them." I will bring them
back to the land which I gave their
fathers.

Double Punishment

16 Look! I will send many fishermen, says the LORD, to catch them.
After that, I will send many hunters
to hunt them out from every mountain and hill and from the clefts of
the rocks. 17 For my eyes are
upon all their ways; they are not
hidden from me, nor does their guilt
escape my view. 18 I will at once
repay them double for their crime
and their sin of profaning my land
with their detestable corpses of
idols, and filling my heritage with
their abominations.

Conversion of the Heathen

19 O LORD, my strength, my
　　fortress,
　　my refuge in the day of
　　distress!
To you will the nations come
　　from the ends of the earth,
　　and say,
"Mere frauds are the heritage
　　of our fathers,
　　empty idols of no use."
20 Can man make for himself
　　gods?
　　These are not gods.
21 Look, then: I will give them
　　knowledge;
　　this time I will leave them in
　　no doubt
Of my strength and my power:
　　they shall know that my name
　　is LORD.

The Sin of Judah and its Punishment

17 The sin of Judah is written
with an iron stylus,
Engraved with a diamond point
　　upon the tablets of their
　　hearts.

[And the horns of their altars, 2
when their sons remember their
altars and their sacred poles, beside
the green trees, on the high hills,
3 the peaks in the highland.]

Your wealth and all your
　　treasures
　　I will give as spoil.
In recompense for all your sins
　　throughout your borders,
4 You will relinquish your hold on
　　your heritage
　　which I have given you.
I will enslave you to your
　　enemies
　　in a land that you know not;
For a fire has been kindled by
　　my wrath
　　that will burn forever.

True Wisdom

5 Thus says the LORD:
Cursed is the man who trusts in
　　human beings,
　　who seeks his strength in
　　flesh,
　　whose heart turns away from
　　the LORD.

16, 6f: These verses refer to popular mourning
practices, sometimes connected with pagan superstition; cf Dt 14, 1f.

6 He is like a barren bush in the
　　desert
　　　that enjoys no change of season,
　But stands in a lava waste,
　　　a salt and empty earth.
7 Blessed is the man who trusts
　　in the LORD,
　　　whose hope is the LORD.
8 He is like a tree planted beside
　　the waters
　　　that stretches out its roots to
　　　the stream:
　It fears not the heat when it
　　comes,
　　　its leaves stay green;
　In the year of drought it shows
　　no distress,
　　　but still bears fruit.
9 More tortuous than all else is
　　the human heart,
　　　beyond remedy; who can
　　　understand it?
10 I, the LORD, alone probe the mind
　　and test the heart,
　To reward everyone according
　　to his ways,
　　　according to the merit of his
　　　deeds.
11 A partridge that mothers a
　　brood not her own
　　　is the man who acquires
　　　wealth unjustly:
　In midlife it will desert him;
　　　in the end he is only a fool.

The Source of Life

12 A throne of glory, exalted from
　　the beginning,
　　　such is our holy place.
13 O hope of Israel, O LORD!
　　all who forsake you shall be in
　　disgrace;
　The rebels in the land shall be
　　put to shame;
　　they have forsaken the source
　　of living waters
　　[the LORD].

Prayer for Vengeance

14 Heal me, LORD, that I may be
　　healed;
　　save me, that I may be saved,
　　for it is you whom I praise.
15 See how they say to me,
　　"Where is the word of the
　　LORD?
　Let it come to pass!"

16 Yet I did not press you to send
　　calamity;
　　the day without remedy I have
　　not desired.
　You know what passed my lips;
　　it is present before you.
17 Do not be my ruin,
　　you, my refuge in the day of
　　misfortune.
18 Let my persecutors, not me, be
　　confounded;
　　let them, not me, be broken.
　Bring upon them the day of
　　misfortune,
　　crush them with repeated
　　destruction.

Observance of the Sabbath

19 Thus said the LORD to me: Go,
stand at the Gate of Benjamin,
where the kings of Judah enter and
leave, and at the other gates of
Jerusalem. 20 There say to them:
Hear the word of the LORD, you
kings of Judah, and all Judah, and
all you citizens of Jerusalem who
enter these gates! 21 Thus says
the LORD: As you love your lives,
take care not to carry burdens on the
sabbath day, to bring them in
through the gates of Jerusalem.
22 Bring no burden from your
homes on the sabbath. Do no work
whatever, but keep holy the sabbath,
as I commanded your fathers, 23
though they did not listen or give
ear, but stiffened their necks so as
not to hear or take correction.
24 If you obey me wholeheartedly,
says the LORD, and carry no burden
through the gates of this city on the
sabbath, keeping the sabbath holy
and abstaining from all work on it,
25 then, through the gates of this
city, kings who sit upon the throne
of David will continue to enter,
riding in their chariots or upon their
horses, along with their princes, and
the men of Judah, and the citizens
of Jerusalem. This city will remain
inhabited forever. 26 To it people
will come from the cities of Judah
and the neighborhood of Jerusalem,
from the land of Benjamin and from
the foothills, from the hill country
and the Negeb, to bring holocausts
and sacrifices, cereal offerings and

incense and thank offerings to the
house of the LORD. 27 But if you
do not obey me and keep holy the
sabbath, if you carry burdens and
come through the gates of Jerusalem
on the sabbath, I will set unquenchable fire to its gates, which will
consume the palaces of Jerusalem.

The Potter's Vessel

18 This word came to Jeremiah
from the LORD: 2 Rise up,
be off to the potter's house; there I
will give you my message. 3 I
went down to the potter's house and
there he was, working at the wheel.
4 Whenever the object of clay
which he was making turned out
badly in his hand, he tried again,
making of the clay another object
of whatever sort he pleased. 5 Then
the word of the Lord came to me:
6 Can I not do to you, house of
Israel, as this potter has done? says
the LORD. Indeed, like clay in the
hand of the potter, so are you in
my hand, house of Israel. 7 Sometimes I threaten to uproot and tear
down and destroy a nation or a
kingdom. 8 But if that nation which
I have threatened turns from its
evil, I also repent of the evil which I
threatened to do. 9 Sometimes,
again, I promise to build up and
plant a nation or a kingdom.
10 But if that nation does what is
evil in my eyes, refusing to obey my
voice, I repent of the good with
which I promised to bless it.

11 And now, tell this to the men of
Judah and the citizens of Jerusalem:
Thus says the LORD: Take care! I
am fashioning evil against you and
making a plan. Return, each of
you, from his evil way; reform your
ways and your deeds. 12 But they
will say, "No use! We will follow
our own devices; each one of us
will behave according to the stubbornness of his evil heart!"

Judah's Apostasy Unnatural

13 Therefore thus says the LORD:
　Ask among the nations—
　　who has ever heard the like?
　Truly horrible things
　　has virgin Israel done!

17, 19: *The Gate of Benjamin:* probably the
northern gate of the temple area and city wall of
Jerusalem; cf 20, 2; 37, 12; 38, 7.

18, 1–12: The lesson of the potter is not that God
deals arbitrarily with his people, but that he is al-

mighty to destroy or restore, accordingly as they
disobey him or fulfill his plans.

14 Does the snow of Lebanon
      desert the rocky heights?
   Do the gushing waters dry up
      that flow fresh down the
      mountains?
15 Yet my people have forgotten
      me:
   they burn incense to a thing
      that does not exist.
   They stumble out of their ways,
      the paths of old,
   To travel on bypaths,
      not the beaten track.
16 Their land shall be turned into
      a desert,
   an object of lasting ridicule:
   All passers-by will be amazed,
      will shake their heads.
17 Like the east wind, I will scatter
      them
      before their enemies;
   I will show them my back, not
      my face,
      in their day of disaster.

Another Prayer for Vengeance

18 "Come," they said, "let us con-
trive a plot against Jeremiah. It will
not mean the loss of instruction from
the priests, nor of counsel from the
wise, nor of messages from the
prophets. And so, let us destroy him
by his own tongue; let us carefully
note his every word."

19 Heed me, O LORD,
      and listen to what my
         adversaries say.
20 Must good be repaid with evil
      that they should dig a pit to
         take my life?
   Remember that I stood before
      you
      to speak in their behalf,
      to turn away your wrath from
         them.
21 So now, deliver their children
      to famine,
   do away with them by the
      sword.
   Let their wives be made childless
      and widows;
   let their men die of pestilence,
      their young men be slain by
         the sword in battle.

22 May cries be heard from their
      homes,
   when suddenly you send
      plunderers against them.
   For they have dug a pit to
      capture me,
   they have hid snares for my
      feet;
23 But you, O LORD, know
      all their plans to slay me.
   Forgive not their crime,
      blot not out their sin in your
         sight!
   Let them go down before you,
      proceed against them in the
         time of your anger.

Symbol of the Potter's Flask

19 Thus said the LORD: Go, buy
a potter's earthen flask. Take
along some of the elders of the
people and of the priests, 2 and
go out toward the Valley of Ben-
hinnom, at the entrance of the
Potsherd Gate; there proclaim the
words which I will speak to you:
3 Listen to the word of the LORD,
kings of Judah and citizens of
Jerusalem: Thus says the LORD of
hosts, the God of Israel: I am going
to bring such evil upon this place
that all who hear of it will feel their
ears tingle. 4 This is because they
have forsaken me and alienated this
place by burning in it incense to
strange gods which neither they nor
their fathers knew; and the kings of
Judah have filled this place with the
blood of the innocent. 5 They have
built high places for Baal to immolate
their sons in fire as holocausts to
Baal: such a thing as I neither commanded nor spoke of, nor did it
ever enter my mind. 6 Therefore,
days will come, says the LORD, when
this place will no longer be called
Topheth, or the Valley of Ben-
hinnom, but rather, the Valley of
Slaughter. 7 In this place I will
foil the plan of Judah and Jerusalem;
I will make them fall by the sword
before their enemies, by the hand of
those that seek their lives. Their
corpses I will give as food to the

birds of the sky and the beasts of
the field. 8 I will make this city an
object of amazement and derision.
Because of all its wounds, every
passer-by will be amazed and will
catch his breath. 9 I will have them
eat the flesh of their sons and
daughters; they shall eat one another's
flesh during the strict siege by which
their enemies and those who seek
their lives will confine them.

10 And you shall break the flask
in the sight of the men who went
with you, 11 and say to them:
Thus says the LORD of hosts: Thus
will I smash this people and this city,
as one smashes a clay pot so that it
cannot be repaired. And Topheth
shall be a burial place, for lack of
place to bury elsewhere. 12 Thus
I will do to this place and to its
inhabitants, says the LORD; I will
make this city like Topheth. 13 And
the houses of Jerusalem and the
palaces of the kings of Judah shall
be defiled like the place of Topheth,
all the houses upon whose roofs they
burnt incense to the whole host of
heaven and poured out libations to
strange gods.

14 When Jeremiah returned from
Topheth, where the LORD had sent
him to prophesy, he stood in the
court of the house of God and said
to all the people: 15 Thus says the
LORD of hosts, the God of Israel:
I will surely bring upon this city all
the evil with which I threatened it,
because they have stiffened their
necks and have not obeyed my
words.

20 Jeremiah was heard prophesying these things by the
priest Pashhur, son of Immer, chief
officer in the house of the LORD.
2 So he had the prophet scourged
and placed in the stocks at the upper
Gate of Benjamin in the house of
the LORD. 3 The next morning,
after Pashhur had released Jeremiah
from the stocks, the prophet said to
him: Instead of Pashhur, the LORD
will name you "Terror on every

18, 14: *Lebanon:* here apparently including Mount
Hermon, whose snow-capped peak can be seen from
parts of Palestine all year round. The prophet contrasts the certainties of nature with Israel's unnatural desertion of the Lord for idols (v 15).

18, 21: In the Old Testament a man's family was

regarded as part of his personality, to be rewarded
or punished along with him; cf Jos 7, 24ff.

19, 2: *Potsherd Gate:* in the south wall of Jerusalem, through which potsherds and other refuse were
carried to the Valley of Ben-hinnom.

20, 1: *Chief officer in the house of the Lord:* head

of the temple police; cf 29, 26. By entering the
temple court (19, 14), Jeremiah had put himself under
Pashhur's jurisdiction.

20, 3: *Terror on every side:* Pashhur will share the
fate of doomed Jerusalem and will experience personally all that the people as a whole have had to endure.

side." 4 For thus says the LORD: Indeed, I will deliver you to terror, you and all your friends. Your own eyes shall see them fall by the sword of their enemies. All Judah I will deliver to the king of Babylon, who shall take them captive to Babylon or slay them with the sword. 5 All the wealth of this city, all it has toiled for and holds dear, all the treasures of the kings of Judah, I will give as plunder into the hands of their foes, who shall seize it and carry it away to Babylon. 6 You Pashhur, and all the members of your household shall go into exile. To Babylon you shall go, you and all your friends; there you shall die and be buried, because you have prophesied lies to them.

Jeremiah's Interior Crisis

7 You duped me, O LORD, and I
　　let myself be duped;
　you were too strong for me,
　　and you triumphed.
All the day I am an object of
　　laughter;
　everyone mocks me.
8 Whenever I speak, I must cry
　　out,
　violence and outrage is my
　　message;
The word of the LORD has
　　brought me
　derision and reproach all the
　　day.
9 I say to myself, I will not
　　mention him,
　I will speak in his name no
　　more.
But then it becomes like fire
　　burning in my heart,
　imprisoned in my bones;
I grow weary holding it in,
　I cannot endure it.
10 Yes, I hear the whisperings of
　　many:
　"Terror on every side!
　Denounce! let us denounce
　　him!"
All those who were my friends
　are on the watch for any
　　misstep of mine.

"Perhaps he will be trapped;
　then we can prevail,
　and take our vengeance on
　　him."
11 But the LORD is with me, like a
　　mighty champion:
　my persecutors will stumble,
　　they will not triumph.
In their failure they will be put
　　to utter shame,
　to lasting, unforgettable
　　confusion.
12 O LORD of hosts, you who test
　　the just,
　who probe mind and heart,
Let me witness the vengeance
　you take on them,
　for to you I have entrusted
　　my cause.
13 Sing to the LORD,
　praise the LORD,
For he has rescued the life of the
　poor
　from the power of the wicked!

14 Cursed be the day
　on which I was born!
May the day my mother gave
　me birth
　never be blessed!
15 Cursed be the man who brought
　　the news
　to my father, saying,
"A child, a son, has been born
　to you!"
　filling him with great joy.
16 Let that man be like the cities
　which the LORD relentlessly
　　overthrew;
Let him hear war cries in the
　　morning,
　battle alarms at noonday,
17　because he did not dispatch
　me in the womb!
Then my mother would have
　been my grave,
　her womb confining me
　forever.
18 Why did I come forth from the
　womb,
　to see sorrow and pain,
　to end my days in shame?

ORACLES IN THE LAST YEARS OF JERUSALEM

Fate of Zedekiah and Jerusalem

21 The message which came to Jeremiah from the LORD when King Zedekiah sent him Pashhur, son of Malchiah, and the priest Zephaniah, son of Maaseiah, with this request: 2 Inquire for us of the LORD, because Nebuchadnezzar, king of Babylon, is attacking us. Perhaps the LORD will deal with us according to all his wonderful works, so that he will withdraw from us. 3 But Jeremiah answered them: This is what you shall report to Zedekiah: 4 Thus says the LORD, the God of Israel: I will turn back in your hands the weapons with which you intend to fight the king of Babylon and the Chaldeans who besiege you outside the walls. These weapons I will pile up in the midst of this city, 5 and I myself will fight against you with outstretched hand and mighty arm, in anger, and wrath, and great rage! 6 I will strike the inhabitants of this city, both man and beast; they shall die in a great pestilence. 7 After that, says the LORD, I will hand over Zedekiah, king of Judah, and his ministers and the people in this city who survive pestilence, sword, and famine, into the hand of Nebuchadnezzar, king of Babylon, into the hands of their enemies and those who seek their lives. He shall strike them with the edge of the sword, without quarter, without pity or mercy. 8 And to this people you shall say: Thus says the LORD: See, I am giving you a choice between life and death. 9 Whoever remains in this city shall die by the sword or famine or pestilence. But whoever leaves and surrenders to the besieging Chaldeans shall live and have his life as booty. 10 For I have turned against this city, for its woe and not for its good, says the LORD. It shall be given into the power of the king of Babylon who shall burn it with fire.

20, 4: *Babylon:* mentioned here for the first time as the land of exile. The prophecy probably dates from after 605 B.C., when Nebuchadnezzar defeated Egypt and made the Chaldean empire dominant in Syria and Palestine.
　20, 7: *You duped me:* to be understood in the light of Jeremiah's intimate dealings with God; cf 15, 18.

20, 14–18: Deception, sorrow and terror have brought the prophet close to the point of despair; nevertheless he has expressed his utmost confidence in the triumph of God's will (vv 11ff); cf Jb 3, 3–12.
　21, 1: *Zedekiah:* brother of Jehoiakim, appointed king by Nebuchadnezzar after he had carried Jehoiachin away to captivity (2 Kgs 24, 17). *Pashhur:*

different from the one in 20, 1ff but also one of Jeremiah's enemies; cf 38, 1.4.
　21, 10: Jeremiah consistently pointed out the uselessness of resistance to Babylon, since the Lord had delivered Judah to Nebuchadnezzar (27, 6). Because of this the prophet was denounced and imprisoned as a traitor (37, 13f).

Oracles regarding the Kings

11 To the royal house of Judah:
Hear the word of the Lord,
    12 O house of David!
Thus says the Lord:
Each morning dispense justice,
    rescue the oppressed from the
        hand of the oppressor,
Lest my fury break out like fire
    which burns without being
        quenched,
    because of the evil of your
        deeds.
13 Beware! I am against you,
    Valley-site,
    Rock of the Plain, says the
        Lord.
    You who say, "Who will attack us,
        who can penetrate our
            retreats?"
14 I will punish you, says the Lord,
    as your deeds deserve!
    I will kindle a fire in its forest
        that shall devour all its
            surroundings.

22 The Lord told me this: Go down to the palace of the king of Judah and there deliver this message: 2 You shall say: Listen to the word of the Lord, king of Judah, who sit on the throne of David, you, your ministers, and your people that enter by these gates! 3 Thus says the Lord: Do what is right and just. Rescue the victim from the hand of his oppressor. Do not wrong or oppress the resident alien, the orphan, or the widow, and do not shed innocent blood in this place. 4 If you carry out these commands, kings who succeed to the throne of David will continue to enter the gates of this palace, riding in chariots or mounted on horses, with their ministers, and their

people. 5 But if you do not obey these commands, I swear by myself, says the Lord: this palace shall become rubble. 6 For thus says the Lord concerning the palace of the king of Judah:

Though you be to me like Gilead,
    like the peak of Lebanon,
I will turn you into a waste,
    a city uninhabited.
7 Against you I will send
    destroyers,
    each with his axe:
They shall cut down your choice
    cedars,
    and cast them into the fire.

8 Many people will pass by this city and ask one another: "Why has the Lord done this to so great a city?" 9 And the answer will be given: "Because they have deserted their covenant with the Lord, their God, by worshiping and serving strange gods."

Jehoahaz

10 Weep not for him who is dead,
    mourn not for him!
Weep rather for him who is
    going away;
    never again will he see
        the land of his birth.

11 Thus says the Lord concerning Shallum, son of Josiah, king of Judah, who succeeded his father as king. He has left this place never to return. 12 Rather, he shall die in the place where they exiled him; this land he shall not see again.

Jehoiakim

13 Woe to him who builds his
    house on wrong,
    his terraces on injustice;

Who works his neighbor without
    pay,
    and gives him no wages.
14 Who says, "I will build myself a
    spacious house,
    with airy rooms,"
Who cuts out windows for it,
    panels it with cedar,
    and paints it with vermillion.
15 Must you prove your rank
    among kings
    by competing with them in
        cedar?
Did not your father eat and
    drink?
He did what was right and just,
    and it went well with him.
16 Because he dispensed justice to
    the weak and the poor,
    it went well with him.
Is this not true knowledge of me?
    says the Lord.
17 But your eyes and heart are set
    on nothing
    except on your own gain,
On shedding innocent blood,
    on practicing oppression and
        extortion.

18 Therefore, thus says the Lord concerning Jehoiakim, son of Josiah, king of Judah:
They shall not lament him,
    "Alas! my brother"; "Alas!
        sister."
They shall not lament him,
    "Alas, Lord! alas, Majesty!"
19 The burial of an ass shall he be
    given,
    dragged forth and cast out
        beyond the gates of Jerusalem.

Jeconiah

20 Scale Lebanon and cry out,
    in Bashan lift up your voice;
Cry out from Abarim,
    for all your lovers are crushed.

21, 11–23, 8: This section contains an editor's collection of Jeremiah's oracles against the kings of Judah. They are placed in the chronological order of the kings, and are prefaced by the oracles against the kings of Judah in general (21, 11–22, 9).

21, 13: Valley-site, Rock of the Plain: Mount Zion, surrounded by valleys, was regarded by the royal house as impregnable. Despite this natural fortification, God shows derisively that it is no more than a rock rising from the plain, undefendable against the attack of his fury.

21, 14: Its forest: probably the royal palace, built of cedar wood; cf 22, 14; in 1 Kgs 7, 2 the armory of Solomon's palace is called "the house of the forest of Lebanon."

22, 6: Gilead . . . Lebanon: both were known for their trees; cf v 7.

22, 10: Him who is dead: Josiah. His successor,

Jehoahaz, who is going away, was deported by Pharaoh Neco to Egypt, where he died (2 Kgs 23, 33f).

22, 11: Shallum: Jehoahaz is called this only here. Presumably it was his name at birth, while Jehoiakim was his royal name.

22, 13: Without pay: either by forced labor in public works, or inasmuch as workers were defrauded of their hire. Despite the impoverishment caused in Judah by the payment of foreign tribute, Jehoiakim embarked on a program of lavish building in Jerusalem (v 14). Social injustice is the cause of much of the prophetic condemnation of the kings (v 17).

22, 15f: Josiah, the reforming king, prospered materially without oppressing his people; he embodied all the ideals of kingship.

22, 18: "Alas! my brother"; "Alas! sister": customary cries of mourning.

22, 19: The burial of an ass: no burial at all, except to be cast outside the city as refuse. This prophecy regards the popular feeling toward Jehoiakim rather than the actual circumstances of his burial. According to 2 Kgs 24, 5 he was buried with his fathers in Jerusalem. However, his grave may have been profaned by Nebuchadnezzar.

22, 20–23: The prophet first apostrophizes Jerusalem, which is bidden to scale Lebanon, Bashan, and Abarim, i.e., the highest surrounding mountains to the north, northeast, and southeast, to gaze on the ruin of its lovers, i.e., the false leaders of Judah, called its shepherds (22); cf 2, 8. The year is 597 B.C., after Nebuchadnezzar's deportation of Jehoiachin. Jerusalem still stands (23), apparently as secure as the heights of Lebanon, but destruction is to follow (cf v 6).

21 I spoke to you when you were
        secure,
    but you answered, "I will not
        listen."
    This has been your way from
        your youth,
    not to listen to my voice.
22 The wind shall shepherd all
        your shepherds,
    your lovers shall go into exile.
    Surely then you shall be ashamed
        and confounded
    because of all your wickedness.
23 You who dwell on Lebanon,
        who nest in the cedars,
    How you shall groan when
        pains come upon you,
    like the pangs of a woman in
        travail!

24 As I live, says the LORD, if
you, Coniah, son of Jehoiakim, king
of Judah, are a signet ring on my
right hand, I will snatch you from it.
25 I will deliver you into the hands
of those who seek your life; the
hands of those whom you fear; the
hands of Nebuchadnezzar, king of
Babylon, and the Chaldeans. 26 I
will cast you out, you and the mother
who bore you, into a different land
from the one you were born in; and
there you shall die. 27 Neither of
them shall come back to the land for
which they yearn.

28 Is this man Coniah a vessel
        despised, to be broken up,
    an instrument that no one
        wants?
    Why are he and his descendants
        cast out,
    why thrown into a land they
        know not?
29 O land, land, land,
        hear the word of the LORD—
30   Thus says the LORD:
    Write this man down as one
        childless,

who will never thrive in his
    lifetime!
No descendant of his shall
    achieve
a seat on the throne of David
    as ruler again over Judah.

Messianic Reign

23 Woe to the shepherds who
    mislead and scatter the flock
of my pasture, says the LORD.
2 Therefore, thus says the LORD, the
God of Israel, against the shepherds
who shepherd my people: You have
scattered my sheep and driven them
away. You have not cared for them,
but I will take care to punish your
evil deeds. 3 I myself will gather
the remnant of my flock from all the
lands to which I have driven them
and bring them back to their
meadow; there they shall increase
and multiply. 4 I will appoint shepherds for them who will shepherd
them so that they need no longer
fear and tremble; and none shall be
missing, says the LORD.

5 Behold, the days are coming,
        says the LORD,
    when I will raise up a righteous
        shoot to David;
    As king he shall reign and govern
        wisely,
    he shall do what is just and
        right in the land.
6 In his days Judah shall be saved,
    Israel shall dwell in security.
    This is the name they give him:
    "The LORD our justice."

7 Therefore, the days will come,
says the LORD, when they shall no
longer say, "As the LORD lives, who
brought the Israelites out of the land
of Egypt"; 8 but rather, "As the
LORD lives, who brought the descendants of the house of Israel up
from the land of the north"—and

from all the lands to which I banished
them; they shall again live on their
own land.

The False Prophets

9   Concerning the prophets:
    My heart within me is broken,
        my bones all tremble;
    I am like a man who is drunk,
        overcome by wine,
    Because of the LORD,
        because of his holy words.
10 With adulterers the land is
        filled;
    on their account the land
        mourns,
    the pasture ranges are seared.
    Theirs is an evil course,
        theirs is unjust power.
11 Both prophet and priest are
        godless!
    In my very house I find their
        wickedness,
    says the LORD.
12 Hence their way shall become
        for them
    slippery ground.
    In the darkness they shall lose
        their footing,
    and fall headlong;
    Evil I will bring upon them:
        the year of their punishment,
    says the LORD.
13 Among Samaria's prophets
    I saw unseemly deeds:
    They prophesied by Baal
    and led my people Israel
        astray.
14 But among Jerusalem's prophets
    I saw deeds still more
        shocking:
    Adultery, living in lies,
        siding with the wicked,
    so that no one turns from
        evil;
    To me they are all like Sodom,
        its citizens like Gomorrah.

22, 24: *Coniah:* a shortened form of Jeconiah, the
name which Jeremiah gives the king called elsewhere in
the Bible Jehoiachin. *A signet ring:* the seal used by
important men—in a sense, their most valuable
possession—mounted in a ring worn constantly on
the hand. The Lord says that even were Jehoiachin
such a precious possession, he would reject him.
The words in vv 24–30 date from the short three-
month reign of Jehoiachin, before he was carried
away by Nebuchadnezzar.

22, 26: *You and the mother who bore you:* the queen
mother held a special position in the monarchy of
Judah, and in the Books of Kings she is invariably
mentioned by name along with the king (1 Kgs 15, 2;
2 Kgs 18, 2). Jehoiachin did indeed die in Babylon.

22, 30: *Childless:* Jehoiachin is so considered because none of his descendants will be king. From the
Book of Ezekiel, who dates his oracles according to
Jehoiachin's fictitious regnal years, it is evident that
the people expected Jehoiachin to return. The above
prophecy of Jeremiah was uttered to dispel this hope
(28, 4). Of the seven sons born to Jehoiachin in exile,
none became king. His grandson Zerubbabel presided
for a time over the Jewish community after the return
from exile, but not as king.

23, 1–8: With the false rulers who have governed
his people the Lord contrasts himself, the Good
Shepherd, who will in the times of restoration appoint
worthy rulers (1–4). A Messianic king will arise from
the line of David who will rule over Judah and Israel

with the justice of the Lord, fulfilling all the kingly
ideals (5f). *"The Lord our justice"* is probably an
ironic wordplay on the name of the weak King
Zedekiah ("The Lord is justice"); the Messianic
king will be in reality what Zedekiah's name falsely
proclaims him. The final verses, 7–8, were probably
added during the exile.

23, 9–40: After the collection of oracles against
the kings, the editor of the book placed this collection
of oracles against the false prophets. With them are
associated the priests, for both have betrayed their
trust as instructors in the religion of the Lord; cf
2, 8; 4, 9; 6, 13f.

15 Therefore, thus says the LORD of hosts against the prophets:

Behold, I will give them
wormwood to eat,
and poison to drink;
For from Jerusalem's prophets
ungodliness has gone forth
into the whole land.

16 Thus says the LORD of hosts:
Listen not to the words of your
prophets,
who fill you with emptiness;
Visions of their own fancy they
speak,
not from the mouth of the
LORD.
17 They say to those who despise
the word of the LORD,
"Peace shall be yours";
And to everyone who walks in
hardness of heart,
"No evil shall overtake you."
18 Now, who has stood in the
council of the LORD,
to see him and to hear his
word?
Who has heeded his word, so
as to announce it?
19 See, the storm of the LORD!
His wrath breaks forth
In a whirling storm
that bursts upon the heads of
the wicked.
20 The anger of the LORD shall
not abate
until he has done and fulfilled
what he has determined in his
heart.
When the time comes,
you shall fully understand.
21 I did not send these prophets,
yet they ran;
I did not speak to them,
yet they prophesied.
22 Had they stood in my council,
and did they but proclaim to
my people my words,
They would have brought them
back from evil ways
and from their wicked deeds.

23 Am I a God near at hand only,
says the LORD,
and not a God far off?
24 Can a man hide in secret
without my seeing him? says
the LORD.
Do I not fill
both heaven and earth? says
the LORD.

25 I have heard the prophets who prophesy lies in my name say, "I had a dream! I had a dream!" 26 How long will this continue? Is my name in the hearts of the prophets who prophesy lies and their own deceitful fancies? 27 By their dreams which they recount to each other, they think to make my people forget my name, just as their fathers forgot my name for Baal. 28 Let the prophet who has a dream recount his dream; let him who has my word speak my word truthfully!

What has straw to do with the
wheat?
says the LORD.
29 Is not my word like fire, says
the LORD,
like a hammer shattering
rocks?

30 Therefore I am against the prophets, says the LORD, who steal my words from each other. 31 Yes, I am against the prophets, says the LORD, who borrow speeches to pronounce oracles. 32 Yes, I am against the prophets who prophesy lying dreams, says the LORD, and who lead my people astray by recounting their lies and by their empty boasting. From me they have no mission or command, and they do this people no good at all, says the LORD.

33 And when this people, or a prophet or a priest asks you, "What is the burden of the LORD?" you shall answer, "You are the burden, and I cast you off, says the LORD." 34 If a prophet or a priest or anyone else mentions "the burden of the

LORD," I will punish that man and his house. 35 Thus you shall ask, when speaking to one another, "What answer did the LORD give?" or, "What did the LORD say?" 36 But the burden of the LORD you shall mention no more. For each man his own word becomes the burden so that you pervert the words of the living God, the LORD of hosts, our God. 37 Thus shall you ask the prophet, "What answer did the LORD give?" or, "What did the LORD say?" 38 But if you ask about "the burden of the LORD," then thus says the LORD: Because you use this phrase, "the burden of the LORD," though I forbade you to use it, 39 therefore I will lift you on high and cast you from my presence, you and the city which I gave to you and your fathers. 40 And I will bring upon you eternal reproach, eternal, unforgettable shame.

The Two Baskets of Figs

24 The LORD showed me two baskets of figs placed before the temple of the LORD.—This was after Nebuchadnezzar, king of Babylon, had exiled from Jerusalem Jeconiah, son of Jehoiakim, king of Judah, and the princes of Judah, the artisans and the skilled workers, and brought them to Babylon.— 2 One basket contained excellent figs, the early-ripening kind. But the other basket contained very bad figs, so bad they could not be eaten. 3 Then the LORD said to me: What do you see, Jeremiah? "Figs," I replied; "the good ones are very good, but the bad ones very bad, so bad they cannot be eaten." 4 Thereupon this word of the LORD came to me: 5 Thus says the LORD, the God of Israel: Like these good figs, even so will I regard with favor Judah's exiles whom I sent away from this place into the land of the Chaldeans. 6 I will look after them for their good, and bring them back to this land, to build them up, not to tear

23, 17–20. Not only are the false prophets personally immoral, but they encourage immorality by prophesying good of those who do evil. The true prophet, on the other hand, sees the inevitable consequences of sin.
23, 23: *Near at hand only . . . far off:* God knows not merely the present but also the future.
23, 28f: *Straw . . . wheat:* such is the contrast between false and true prophecy. True prophecy is

like fire (cf 5, 14; 20, 9), producing violent results (v 29); Jeremiah's own life is a testimony of this.
23, 33–40: A wordplay on *maśśā'*, which means both oracle (usually of woe) and burden. In 34ff it appears that the word *maśśā'* itself is forbidden the people in the meaning of a divine oracle. Doubtless this was because of some association unknown to us. In Hos 2, 18 it is forbidden to call God "Baal"

("master"), because of the association of this title with the Canaanite god.
24, 1–10: Jeremiah, like Ezekiel, saw that no good could be expected from the people who had been left in Judah under Zedekiah or who had fled into Egypt; good was to be hoped for only from those who would pass through the purifying experience of the exile to form the new Israel.

them down; to plant them, not to pluck them out. 7 I will give them a heart with which to understand that I am the LORD. They shall be my people and I will be their God, for they shall return to me with their whole heart. 8 And like the figs that are bad, so bad they cannot be eaten—yes, thus says the LORD— even so will I treat Zedekiah, king of Judah, and his princes, the remnant of Jerusalem remaining in this land and those who have settled in the land of Egypt. 9 I will make them an object of horror to all the kingdoms of the earth, a reproach and a byword, a taunt and a curse, in all the places to which I will drive them. 10 I will send upon them the sword, famine, and pestilence, until they have disappeared from the land which I gave them and their fathers.

Seventy Years of Exile

25 The word that came to Jeremiah concerning all the people of Judah, in the fourth year of Jehoiakim, son of Josiah, king of Judah (the first year of Nebuchadnezzar, king of Babylon). 2 This word the prophet Jeremiah spoke to all the people of Judah and all the citizens of Jerusalem: 3 Since the thirteenth year of Josiah, son of Amon, king of Judah, to this day—these three and twenty years—the word of the LORD has come to me and I spoke to you untiringly, but you would not listen. 4 Though you refused to listen or pay heed, the LORD has sent you without fail all his servants the prophets 5 with this message: Turn back, each of you, from your evil way and from your evil deeds; then you shall remain in the land which the LORD gave you and your fathers, from of old and forever. 6 Do not follow strange gods to serve and adore them, lest you provoke me with your handiwork, and I bring evil upon you. 7 But you would not listen to me, says the LORD, and so you provoked me with your handi-

work to your own harm. 8 Hence, thus says the LORD of hosts: Since you would not listen to my words, 9 lo! I will send for and fetch all the tribes of the north, says the LORD (and I will send to Nebuchadnezzar, king of Babylon, my servant); I will bring them against this land, against its inhabitants, and against all these neighboring nations. I will doom them, making them an object of horror, of ridicule, of everlasting reproach. 10 Among them I will bring to an end the song of joy and the song of gladness, the voice of the bridegroom and the voice of the bride, the sound of the millstone and the light of the lamp. 11 This whole land shall be a ruin and a desert. Seventy years these nations shall be enslaved to the king of Babylon; 12 but when the seventy years have elapsed, I will punish the king of Babylon and the nation and the land of the Chaldeans for their guilt, says the LORD. Their land I will turn into everlasting desert. 13 Against that land I will fulfill all the words I have spoken against it [all that is written in this book, which Jeremiah prophesied against all the nations]. 14 They also shall be enslaved to great nations and mighty kings, and thus I will repay them according to their own deeds and according to their own handiwork.

The Cup of Judgment on the Nations

15 For thus said the LORD, the God of Israel, to me: Take this cup of foaming wine from my hand, and have all the nations to whom I will send you drink it. 16 They shall drink, and be convulsed, and go mad, because of the sword I will send among them. 17 I took the cup from the hand of the LORD and gave drink to all the nations to which the LORD sent me: 18 [Jerusalem, the cities of Judah, her kings and her princes, to make them a

ruin and a desert, an object of ridicule and cursing, as they are today;] 19 Pharaoh, king of Egypt, and his servants, his princes, all the people under him, native 20 and foreign; all the kings of the land of Uz; all the kings of the land of the Philistines: Ashkelon, Gaza, Ekron, and the remnant of Ashdod; 21 Edom, Moab, and the Ammonites; 22 all the kings of Tyre, of Sidon, and of the shores beyond the sea; 23 Dedan and Tema and Buz, all the desert dwellers who shave their temples; 24 [all the kings of Arabia;] 25 all the kings of Zimri, of Elam, of the Medes; 26 all the kings of the north, near and far, one after the other; all the kingdoms upon the face of the earth [and after them the king of Sheshach shall drink].

27 Tell them: Thus says the LORD of hosts, the God of Israel: Drink! become drunk and vomit; fall, never to rise, before the sword that I will send among you! 28 If they refuse to take the cup from your hand and drink, say to them: Thus says the LORD of hosts: You must drink! 29 For since with this city, which is called by my name, I begin to inflict evil, how can you possibly be spared? You shall not be spared! I will call down the sword upon all who inhabit the earth, says the LORD of hosts.

30 Prophesy against them all these things and say to them:

The LORD roars from on high,
　from his holy dwelling he
　　raises his voice;
Mightily he roars over the range,
　a shout like that of vintagers
　　over the grapes.
31 To all who inhabit the earth to
　its very ends
　the uproar spreads;
For the LORD has an indictment
　against the nations,
　he is to pass judgment upon
　　all mankind:

25, 1-14: *The fourth year of Jehoiakim:* 605 B.C. Officially, *the first year of Nebuchadnezzar* began the following year; but as early as his victory over Egypt at Carchemish in 605, Nebuchadnezzar was the dominant power in the Near East, in whom Jeremiah now saw the fulfillment of his prophecy of the enemy to come from the north (cf 1, 13; 6, 22ff). In vv 11f occurs for the first time the prophecy of the seventy years' exile; cf 29, 10. This Jeremiah

intends as a round number, to signify that the present generation must die out.

25, 15ff: Jeremiah is a prophet to the nations (cf 1, 5) as well as to his own people. All the nations mentioned here appear again in the more extensive collection of Jeremiah's oracles against the nations in chapters 46-51.

25, 20: *Uz:* the homeland of Job, in Edomite or Arabian territory.

25, 22: *The shores beyond the sea:* Phoenician commercial colonies planted throughout the Mediterranean world.

25, 23: *Dedan and Tema and Buz:* North Arabian tribes.

25, 26: *Sheshach:* Babylon. The word is formed from *bābēl* by substituting letters of the Hebrew alphabet in inverse order.

The godless shall be given to the
  sword,
    says the LORD.
32 Thus says the LORD of hosts:
  Lo! calamity stalks
    from nation to nation;
  A great storm is unleashed
    from the ends of the earth.

33 On that day, those whom the
LORD has slain will be strewn from
one end of the earth to the other.
None will mourn them, none will
gather them for burial; they shall lie
like dung on the field.

34 Howl, you shepherds, and wail!
  roll in the dust, leaders of the
    flock!
  The time for your slaughter has
    come;
  like choice rams you shall fall.
35 There is no flight for the
    shepherds,
  no escape for the leaders of
    the flock.
36 Listen! Wailing from the
    shepherds,
  howling by the leaders of the
    flock!
  For the LORD lays waste their
    grazing place,
37 desolate lie the peaceful
    pastures;
38 The lion leaves his lair,
  and their land is made
    desolate
  By the sweeping sword,
    by the burning wrath of the
      LORD.

Jeremiah Threatened with Death

26 In the beginning of the reign
of Jehoiakim, son of Josiah,
king of Judah, this message came
from the LORD: 2 Thus says the
LORD: Stand in the court of the
house of the LORD and speak to the
people of all the cities of Judah who
come to worship in the house of the
LORD; whatever I command you, tell
them, and omit nothing. 3 Perhaps
they will listen and turn back, each
from his evil way, so that I may
repent of the evil I have planned to

inflict upon them for their evil deeds.
4 Say to them: Thus says the LORD:
If you disobey me, not living according to the law I placed before you 5
and not listening to the words of my
servants the prophets, whom I send
you constantly though you do not
obey them, 6 I will treat this house
like Shiloh, and make this the city
which all the nations of the earth
shall refer to when cursing another.

7 Now the priests, the prophets,
and all the people heard Jeremiah
speak these words in the house of the
LORD. 8 When Jeremiah finished
speaking all that the LORD bade him
speak to all the people, the priests
and prophets laid hold of him,
crying, "You must be put to death!
9 Why do you prophesy in the name
of the LORD: 'This house shall be like
Shiloh,' and 'This city shall be
desolate and deserted'?" And all the
people gathered about Jeremiah in
the house of the LORD.

10 When the princes of Judah were
informed of these things, they came
up from the king's palace to the
house of the LORD and held court at
the New Gate of the house of the
LORD. 11 The priests and prophets
said to the princes and to all the
people, "This man deserves death;
he has prophesied against this city,
as you have heard with your own
ears." 12 Jeremiah gave this answer to the princes and all the people:
"It was the LORD who sent me to
prophesy against this house and city
all that you have heard. 13 Now,
therefore, reform your ways and
your deeds; listen to the voice of the
LORD your God, so that the LORD
will repent of the evil with which he
threatens you. 14 As for me, I am
in your hands; do with me what
you think good and right. 15 But
mark well: if you put me to death,
it is innocent blood you bring on
yourselves, on this city and its
citizens. For in truth it was the LORD
who sent me to you, to speak all
these things for you to hear."

16 Thereupon the princes and all

the people said to the priests and the
prophets, "This man does not deserve
death; it is in the name of the LORD,
our God, that he speaks to us." 17
At this, some of the elders of the land
came forward and said to all the
people assembled, 18 "Micah of
Moresheth used to prophesy in the
days of Hezekiah, king of Judah,
and he told all the people of Judah:
Thus says the LORD of hosts:

  Zion shall become a plowed
    field,
  Jerusalem a heap of ruins,
    and the temple mount a forest
      ridge.

19 Did Hezekiah, king of Judah,
and all Judah condemn him to
death? Did they not rather fear the
LORD and entreat the favor of the
LORD, so that he repented of the evil
with which he had threatened them?
But we are on the point of committing this great evil to our own
undoing."

The Fate of Uriah

20 There was another man who
prophesied in the name of the LORD,
Uriah, son of Shemaiah, from
Kiriath-jearim; he prophesied the
same things against this city and
land as Jeremiah did. 21 When
King Jehoiakim and all his officers
and princes were informed of his
words, the king sought to kill him.
But Uriah heard of it and fled in fear
to Egypt. 22 Thereupon King
Jehoiakim sent Elnathan, son of
Achbor, and others with him into
Egypt 23 to bring Uriah back to
the king, who had him slain by the
sword and his corpse cast into the
common grave. 24 But Ahikam,
son of Shaphan, protected Jeremiah,
so that he was not handed over to the
people to be put to death.

Serve Babylon or Perish

27 [In the beginning of the reign
of Jehoiakim, son of Josiah,
king of Judah,] . . . this message
came to Jeremiah from the LORD: 2

26, 1: *The beginning of the reign:* a technical
expression for the time between a king's accession
to the throne and the beginning of his first official
(calendar) year as king. Jehoiakim's first regnal year
was 608 B.C.
26, 18: *Micah of Moresheth:* the prophet Micah,
who appears among the canonical minor prophets
(cf Mi 1, 1).

26, 24: *Ahikam, son of Shaphan:* one of Josiah's
officials (2 Kgs 22, 12) and father of Gedaliah, Jeremiah's friend, who was governor of Judah after
Zedekiah's deportation (cf 39, 14; 40, 5ff).
27, 1—29, 32: A special collection of Jeremiah's
prophecies dealing with false prophets. From stylistic
peculiarities, quite evident in the Hebrew, it is plain
that these three chapters once existed independently

of the other prophecies of Jeremiah.
27, 1: [*In the beginning of the reign of Jehoiakim . . .
Judah*]: this gloss cannot be correct because according
to 28, 1 the time is the fourth year of Zedekiah,
594 B.C., the occasion of an embassy of the neighboring states (v 3), doubtless for the purpose of laying
plans against Nebuchadnezzar.

Thus said the LORD to me: Make for yourself bands and yoke bars and put them over your shoulders. 3 Send to the kings of Edom, of Moab, of the Ammonites, of Tyre, and of Sidon, through the ambassadors who have come to Jerusalem to Zedekiah, king of Judah, 4 and charge them thus: Tell your masters: Thus says the LORD of hosts, the God of Israel: 5 It was I who made the earth, and man and beast on the face of the earth, by my great power, with my outstretched arm; and I can give them to whomever I think fit. 6 Now I have given all these lands into the hand of Nebuchadnezzar, king of Babylon, my servant; even the beasts of the field I have given him for his use. 7 All nations shall serve him and his son and his grandson, until the time of his land, too, shall come. Then it in turn shall serve great nations and mighty kings. 8 Meanwhile, if any nation or kingdom will not serve Nebuchadnezzar, king of Babylon, or will not bend its neck under the yoke of the king of Babylon, I will punish that nation with sword, famine, and pestilence, says the LORD, until I give them into his hand.

9 You, however, must not listen to your prophets, to your diviners and dreamers, to your soothsayers and sorcerers, who say to you, "You need not serve the king of Babylon." 10 For they prophesy lies to you, in order to drive you far from your land, to make me banish you so that you will perish. 11 The people that submits its neck to the yoke of the king of Babylon to serve him I will leave in peace on its own land, says the LORD, to till it and dwell in it.

12 To Zedekiah, king of Judah, I spoke the same words: Submit your necks to the yoke of the king of Babylon; serve him and his people, so that you may live. 13 Why should you and your people die by sword, famine, and pestilence, with which the LORD has threatened the nation that will not serve the king of Babylon? 14 Do not listen to the words of those prophets who say,

"You need not serve the king of Babylon," for they prophesy lies to you. 15 I did not send them, says the LORD, but they prophesy falsely in my name, with the result that I must banish you, and you will perish, you and the prophets who are prophesying to you.

16 To the priests and to all the people I spoke as follows: Thus says the LORD: Do not listen to the words of your prophets who prophesy to you: "The vessels of the house of the LORD will be brought back from Babylon soon now," for they prophesy lies to you. 17 Do not listen to them! Serve the king of Babylon that you may live; else this city will become a heap of ruins. 18 If they were prophets, if the word of the LORD were with them, they would intercede with the LORD of hosts, that the vessels which remain in the house of the LORD and in the palace of the king of Judah and in Jerusalem might not be taken to Babylon. 19 For thus says the LORD of hosts concerning the pillars, the bronze sea, the stands, and the rest of the vessels that remain in this city, 20 which Nebuchadnezzar, king of Babylon, did not take when he exiled Jeconiah, son of Jehoiakim, king of Judah, from Jerusalem to Babylon, along with all the nobles of Judah and Jerusalem — 21 yes, thus says the LORD of hosts, the God of Israel, concerning the vessels that remain in the house of the LORD, in the palace of the king of Judah, and in Jerusalem: 22 To Babylon they shall be brought, and there they shall remain, until the day I look for them, says the LORD; then I will bring them back and restore them to this place.

The Two Yokes

28 That same year, in [the beginning of] the reign of Zedekiah, king of Judah, in the fifth month of the fourth year, the prophet Hananiah, son of Azzur, from Gibeon, said to me in the house of the LORD in the presence of the priests and all the people: 2 "Thus says the LORD

of hosts, the God of Israel: 'I will break the yoke of the king of Babylon. 3 Within two years I will restore to this place all the vessels of the temple of the LORD which Nebuchadnezzar, king of Babylon, took away from this place to Babylon. 4 And I will bring back to this place Jeconiah, son of Jehoiakim, king of Judah, and all the exiles of Judah who went to Babylon,' says the LORD, 'for I will break the yoke of the king of Babylon.'"

5 The prophet Jeremiah answered the prophet Hananiah in the presence of the priests and all the people assembled in the house of the LORD, 6 and said: Amen! thus may the LORD do! May he fulfill the things you have prophesied by bringing the vessels of the house of the LORD and all the exiles back from Babylon to this place! 7 But now, listen to what I am about to state in your hearing and the hearing of all the people. 8 From of old, the prophets who were before you and me prophesied war, woe, and pestilence against many lands and mighty kingdoms. 9 But the prophet who prophesies peace is recognized as truly sent by the LORD only when his prophetic prediction is fulfilled.

10 Thereupon the prophet Hananiah took the yoke from the neck of the prophet Jeremiah, broke it, 11 and said in the presence of all the people: "Thus says the LORD: 'Even so, within two years I will break the yoke of Nebuchadnezzar, king of Babylon, from off the neck of all the nations.'" At that, the prophet Jeremiah went away.

12 Some time after the prophet Hananiah had broken the yoke from off the neck of the prophet Jeremiah, the word of the LORD came to Jeremiah: 13 Go tell Hananiah this: Thus says the LORD: By breaking a wooden yoke, you forge an iron yoke! 14 For thus says the LORD of hosts, the God of Israel: A yoke of iron I will place on the necks of all these nations serving Nebuchadnezzar, king of Babylon, and they shall serve him; even the beasts of the field I give him.

27, 9: *Your prophets:* seers and diviners served the Gentile kings as the professional prophets served the kings of Judah.

27, 19–22: This prophecy was fulfilled after Zedekiah's disastrous defeat; cf 2 Kgs 25, 13ff.

15 To the prophet Hananiah the prophet Jeremiah said: Hear this, Hananiah! The LORD has not sent you, and you have raised false confidence in this people. 16 For this, says the LORD, I will dispatch you from the face of the earth; this very year you shall die, because you have preached rebellion against the LORD. 17 That same year, in the seventh month, Hananiah the prophet died.

Letter to the Exiles in Babylon

29 This is the contents of the letter which the prophet Jeremiah sent from Jerusalem to the remaining elders among the exiles, to the priests, the prophets, and all the people who were exiled by Nebuchadnezzar from Jerusalem to Babylon. 2 This was after King Jeconiah and the queen mother, the courtiers, the princes of Judah and Jerusalem, the artisans and the skilled workmen had left Jerusalem. 3 Delivered in Babylon by Elasah, son of Shaphan, and by Gemariah, son of Hilkiah, whom Zedekiah, king of Judah, sent to the king of Babylon, the letter read:

4 Thus says the LORD of hosts, the God of Israel, to all the exiles whom I exiled from Jerusalem to Babylon: 5 Build houses to dwell in; plant gardens, and eat their fruits. 6 Take wives and beget sons and daughters; find wives for your sons and give your daughters husbands, so that they may bear sons and daughters. There you must increase in number, not decrease. 7 Promote the welfare of the city to which I have exiled you; pray for it to the LORD, for upon its welfare depends your own.

10 Thus says the LORD: Only after seventy years have elapsed for Babylon will I visit you and fulfill for you my promise to bring you back to this place. 11 For I know well the plans I have in mind for you, says the LORD, plans for your welfare, not for woe! plans to give you a future full of hope. 12 When you call me, when you go to pray to me, I will listen to you. 13 When you look for me, you will find me. Yes, when you seek me with all your heart, 14 you will find me with you, says the LORD, and I will change your lot; I will gather you together from all the nations and all the places to which I have banished you, says the LORD, and bring you back to the place from which I have exiled you.

16 Thus says the LORD concerning the king who sits on David's throne, and all the people who remain in this city, your brethren who did not go with you into exile; 17 thus says the LORD of hosts: I am sending against them sword, famine and pestilence. I will make them like rotten figs, too bad to be eaten. 18 I will pursue them with sword, famine, and pestilence, and make them an object of horror to all the kingdoms of the earth, of malediction, astonishment, ridicule, and reproach to all the nations among which I will banish them. 19 For they did not listen to my words, says the LORD, though I kept sending them my servants the prophets, only to have them go unheeded, says the LORD.

20 You, now, listen to the word of the LORD, all you exiles whom I sent away from Jerusalem to Babylon. 15 As for your saying, "The LORD has raised up for us prophets here in Babylon"— 8 thus says the LORD of hosts, the God of Israel: Do not let yourselves be deceived by the prophets and diviners who are among you; do not listen to those among you who dream dreams. 9 For they prophesy lies to you in my name; I did not send them, says the LORD. 21 This is what the LORD of hosts, the God of Israel, has to say about those who prophesy lies to you in my name, Ahab, son of Kolaiah, and Zedekiah, son of Maaseiah: I am handing them over to Nebuchadnezzar, king of Babylon, who will slay them before your eyes. 22 All the exiles of Judah in Babylon will pattern a curse after them: "May the LORD make you like Zedekiah and Ahab, whom the king of Babylon roasted in the flames." 23 For they are criminals in Israel, committing adultery with their neighbors' wives, and alleging in my name things I did not command. I know, I am witness, says the LORD.

The False Prophet Shemaiah

24 Say this to Shemaiah, the Nehelamite: 25 Thus says the LORD of hosts, the God of Israel: Because you sent letters on your own authority to all the people of Jerusalem, to all the priests and to Zephaniah, the priest, son of Maaseiah, with this message: 26 "The LORD has appointed you priest in place of the priest Jehoiada, so that there may be police officers in the house of the LORD, to take action against all madmen and those who pose as prophets, by putting them into the stocks or the pillory. 27 Why, then, do you not rebuke Jeremiah of Anathoth who poses as a prophet among you? 28 For he sent us in Babylon this message: It will be a long time; build houses to live in; plant gardens and eat their fruits. . . ."

29 When the priest Zephaniah read this letter to the prophet, 30 the word of the LORD came to Jeremiah: 31 Send the message to all the exiles: Thus says the LORD concerning Shemaiah, the Nehelamite: Because Shemaiah prophesies to you without a mission from me, and raises false confidence, 32 says the LORD, I will therefore punish Shemaiah, the Nehelamite, and his offspring. None of them shall survive among this people to see the good I will do to this people, says the LORD, because he preached rebellion against the LORD.

The Restoration

30 The following message came to Jeremiah from the LORD: 2 Thus says the LORD, the God of

---

29, 3: *Elasah:* possibly the brother of Ahikam (cf 26, 24). *Gemariah:* perhaps the son of the high priest Hilkiah; cf 2 Kgs 22, 4. Zedekiah had dispatched these men to Nebuchadnezzar for some other purpose, possibly the payment of tribute, but Jeremiah took advantage of their mission to send his letter by them.

29, 26–29: The words of Jeremiah to the false prophet Shemaiah are not fully preserved in the current Hebrew text, as is seen in the incomplete sentence of this translation (vv 25–28). In his letter to Zephaniah Shemaiah reminds him of his authority, as Pashhur's successor, to imprison Jeremiah. Zephaniah, however, merely reads the letter to Jeremiah but does not imprison him.

30, 1—31, 40: These two chapters do not belong chronologically to those that precede or follow. They contain mainly oracles of salvation which Jeremiah originally uttered on behalf of the conquered remnants of the northern kingdom; then, after Judah began to share Samaria's fate, the oracles were extended to include Judah. Their composition is to be placed early in Jeremiah's ministry, probably after the fall of Nineveh (612 B.C.), when Josiah assumed power over the North; cf 2 Kgs 23, 15ff.

Israel: Write all the words I have spoken to you in a book. 3 For behold, the days will come, says the LORD, when I will change the lot of my people (of Israel and Judah, says the LORD), and bring them back to the land which I gave to their fathers; they shall have it as their possession.

4 These are the words which the LORD spoke to Israel and to Judah: 5 thus says the LORD:

A cry of dismay we hear;
    fear reigns, not peace.
6 Inquire, and see:
    since when do men bear
        children?
Why, then, do I see all these men,
    with their hands on their loins
    like women in childbirth?
Why have all their faces turned
    deathly pale?
7 How mighty is that day—
    none like it!
A time of distress for Jacob,
    though he shall be saved from
        it.

8 On that day, says the LORD of hosts, "I will break his yoke from off your necks and snap your bonds." Strangers shall no longer enslave them; 9 instead, they shall serve the LORD, their God, and David, their king, whom I will raise up for them.

10 But you, my servant Jacob,
    fear not, says the LORD,
    be not dismayed, O Israel!
Behold, I will deliver you from
    the far-off land,
    your descendants, from their
        land of exile;
Jacob shall again find rest,
    shall be tranquil and
        undisturbed.
11   for I am with you, says the
            LORD, to deliver you.
I will make an end of all the
        nations
    among which I have scattered
        you;
    but of you I will not make an
        end.

I will chastise you as you
        deserve,
    I will not let you go
        unpunished.

12   For thus says the LORD:
Incurable is your wound,
    grievous your bruise;
13 There is none to plead your
        cause,
    no remedy for your running
        sore,
    no healing for you.
14 All your lovers have forgotten
        you,
    they do not seek you.
I struck you as an enemy would
        strike,
    punished you cruelly;
15 Why cry out over your wound?
    your pain is without relief.
Because of your great guilt,
    your numerous sins,
    I have done this to you.

16 Yet all who devour you shall be
        devoured,
    all your enemies shall go
        into exile.
All who plunder you shall be
        plundered,
    all who pillage you I will
        hand over to pillage.
17 For I will restore you to health;
    of your wounds I will heal
        you, says the LORD.
"The outcast" they have called
        you,
    "with no avenger."

18   Thus says the LORD:
See! I will restore the tents of
        Jacob,
    his dwellings I will pity;
City shall be rebuilt upon hill,
    and palace restored as it was.
19 From them will resound songs
        of praise,
    the laughter of happy men.
I will make them not few, but
        many;
    they will not be tiny, for I
        will glorify them.

20 His sons shall be as of old,
    his assembly before me shall
        stand firm;
    I will punish all his
        oppressors.
21 His leader shall be one of his
        own,
    and his rulers shall come
        from his kin.
When I summon him, he shall
        approach me;
    how else should one take the
        deadly risk
    of approaching me? says the
        LORD.
22 You shall be my people,
    and I will be your God.

23 See, the storm of the LORD!
    His wrath breaks forth
In a whirling storm
    that bursts upon the heads of
        the wicked.
24 The anger of the LORD will not
        abate
    until he has done and fulfilled
    what he has determined in his
        heart.
When the time comes,
    you will fully understand.

Good News of the Return

31 At that time, says the LORD,
        I will be the God of all the
            tribes of Israel,
        and they shall be my people.
2   Thus says the LORD:
The people that escaped the
        sword
    have found favor in the desert.
As Israel comes forward to be
        given his rest,
3   the LORD appears to him
            from afar:
With age-old love I have loved
        you;
    so I have kept my mercy
        toward you.
4 Again I will restore you, and
        you shall be rebuilt,
    O virgin Israel;
Carrying your festive
        tambourines,
    you shall go forth dancing
        with the merrymakers.

30, 9: *David, their king:* the Messianic king of the Davidic line, often called David by the prophets; cf Ez 34, 23f; 37, 24f; Hos 3, 5.

30, 21: *His leader:* probably not the Messianic king, but simply any one of the rulers of the restored Israel, who will no longer be foreigners, and with

whom the Lord will be on terms of intimacy, as with the whole people. *The deadly risk of approaching me:* to approach God unsummoned brings death; cf Lv 16, 1f.

31, 2: *The people that escaped the sword:* the exiles who were not killed but deported; they *have found*

favor in the desert, across which they were driven into captivity. The prophet alludes to the first desert wandering of Israel (Ex 16ff), in which the people found the Lord. *His rest:* the land of promise. The perfect fulfillment of this promised rest is found only in the New Testament (Heb., chapters 3 and 4).

5 Again you shall plant vineyards
    on the mountains of Samaria;
    those who plant them shall
      enjoy the fruits.
6 Yes, a day will come when the
    watchmen
    will call out on Mount
    Ephraim:
    "Rise up, let us go to Zion,
    to the LORD, our God."

The Road of Return

7   For thus says the LORD:
    Shout with joy for Jacob,
    exult at the head of the nations;
    proclaim your praise and say:
    The LORD has delivered his
      people,
      the remnant of Israel.
8 Behold, I will bring them back
    from the land of the north;
    I will gather them from the ends
      of the world,
    with the blind and the lame
      in their midst,
    The mothers and those with child;
    they shall return as an
      immense throng.
9 They departed in tears,
    but I will console them and
      guide them;
    I will lead them to brooks of
      water,
    on a level road, so that none
      shall stumble.
    For I am a father to Israel,
    Ephraim is my first-born.
10 Hear the word of the LORD,
    O nations,
    proclaim it on distant coasts,
    and say:
    He who scattered Israel, now
      gathers them together,
    he guards them as a shepherd
      his flock.
11 The LORD shall ransom Jacob,
    he shall redeem him from the
      hand of his conqueror.
12 Shouting, they shall mount
    the heights of Zion,
    they shall come streaming to
    the LORD's blessings:

The grain, the wine, and the oil,
    the sheep and the oxen;
    They themselves shall be like
      watered gardens,
    never again shall they
      languish.
13 Then the virgins shall make
      merry and dance,
    and young men and old as
      well.
    I will turn their mourning into
      joy,
    I will console and gladden
      them after their sorrows.
14 I will lavish choice portions
    upon the priests,
    and my people shall be filled
      with my blessings,
    says the LORD.

End of Rachel's Mourning

15   Thus says the LORD:
    In Ramah is heard the sound of
      moaning,
    of bitter weeping!
    Rachel mourns her children,
    she refuses to be consoled
    because her children are no
      more.
16   Thus says the LORD:
    Cease your cries of mourning,
    wipe the tears from your eyes.
    The sorrow you have shown
      shall have its reward,
    says the LORD,
    they shall return from the
      enemy's land.
17 There is hope for your future,
    says the LORD;
    Your sons shall return to
      their own borders.

18 I hear, I hear Ephraim pleading:
    You chastised me, and I am
      chastened;
    I was an untamed calf.
    If you allow me, I will return,
    for you are the LORD, my
      God.
19 I turn in repentance;
    I have come to myself, I
      strike my breast;

I blush with shame,
    I bear the disgrace of my
      youth.
20 Is Ephraim not my favored son,
    the child in whom I delight?
    Often as I threaten him,
    I still remember him with
      favor;
    My heart stirs for him,
    I must show him mercy, says
      the LORD.

Summons to Return Home

21 Set up road markers,
    put up guideposts;
    Turn your attention to the
      highway,
    the road by which you went.
    Turn back, O virgin Israel,
    turn back to these your cities.
22 How long will you continue to
      stray,
    rebellious daughter?
    The LORD has created a new
      thing upon the earth:
    the woman must encompass
      the man with devotion.

23 Thus says the LORD of hosts, the God of Israel: When I change their lot in the land of Judah and her cities, they shall again repeat this greeting: "May the LORD bless you, holy mountain, abode of justice!" 24 Judah and all her cities, the farmers and those who lead the flock, shall dwell there together. 25 For I will refresh the weary soul; every soul that languishes I will replenish. 26 Upon this I awoke and opened my eyes; but my sleep was sweet to me.

27 The days are coming, says the LORD, when I will seed the house of Israel and the house of Judah with the seed of man and the seed of beast. 28 As I once watched over them to uproot and pull down, to destroy, to ruin, and to harm, so I will watch over them to build and to

---

31, 15: *Ramah:* a village about five miles north of Jerusalem, where Rachel was buried (1 Sm 10, 2). *Rachel:* said to mourn for her children since she was the ancestress of Ephraim, the chief of the northern tribes. Mt 2, 18 applies this verse to the slaughter of the innocents by Herod.

31, 22: *The woman must encompass the man:* the words "with devotion," not in the Hebrew, are added for the sense. No fully satisfactory explanation has been given this text. Among the more probable are

these: (a) Formerly the man (the Lord) encompassed the woman (Israel) with mercy and devotion; now in the spiritual religion of Israel which will follow on the restoration, this order will be reversed. (b) So secure will Israel be after the restoration that women will no longer need the natural protection of their husbands, but even weak women can protect men. (c) St. Jerome in his commentary on this verse understood it of Mary's virginal conception of Christ. "The Lord has created a new thing on earth; without seed of

man, without carnal union and conception, 'a woman will encompass a man' within her womb—One who, though he will later appear to advance in wisdom and age through the stages of infancy and childhood, yet, while confined for the usual number of months in his mother's womb, will already be perfect man."

31, 26: *I awoke . . . sweet to me:* probably said by the prophet himself.

plant, says the LORD. 29 In those days they shall no longer say,

"The fathers ate unripe grapes,
and the children's teeth are
set on edge,"

30 but through his own fault only shall anyone die: the teeth of him who eats the unripe grapes shall be set on edge.

The New Covenant

31 The days are coming, says the LORD, when I will make a new covenant with the house of Israel and the house of Judah. 32 It will not be like the covenant I made with their fathers the day I took them by the hand to lead them forth from the land of Egypt; for they broke my covenant, and I had to show myself their master, says the LORD. 33 But this is the covenant which I will make with the house of Israel after those days, says the LORD. I will place my law within them, and write it upon their hearts; I will be their God, and they shall be my people. 34 No longer will they have need to teach their friends and kinsmen how to know the LORD. All, from least to greatest, shall know me, says the LORD, for I will forgive their evildoing and remember their sin no more.

Certainty of God's Promise

35　Thus says the LORD,
He who gives the sun to light the
day,
moon and stars to light the
night;
Who stirs up the sea till its
waves roar,
whose name is LORD of hosts:
36 If ever these natural laws give way
in spite of me, says the LORD,

Then shall the race of Israel
cease
as a nation before me
forever.
37　Thus says the LORD:
If the heavens on high can be
measured,
or the foundations below the
earth be sounded,
Then will I cast off the whole
race of Israel
because of all they have done,
says the LORD.

Rebuilding of Jerusalem

38 The days are coming, says the LORD, when the city shall be rebuilt as the LORD's, from the Tower of Hananel to the Corner Gate. 39 The measuring line shall be stretched from there straight to the hill Gareb and then turn to Goah. 40 The whole valley of corpses and ashes, all the slopes toward the Kidron Valley, as far as the corner of the Horse Gate at the east, shall be holy to the LORD. Never again shall the city be rooted up or thrown down.

Pledge of Restoration

32 This message came to Jeremiah from the LORD in the tenth year of Zedekiah, king of Judah, the eighteenth year of Nebuchadnezzar. 2 At that time the army of the king of Babylon was besieging Jerusalem, and the prophet Jeremiah was imprisoned in the quarters of the guard, at the king's palace. 3 Zedekiah, king of Judah, had imprisoned him there, remonstrating: "How dare you prophesy: Thus says the LORD: I am handing over this city to the king of Babylon, who will capture it. 4 Neither shall Zedekiah, king of Judah, escape the hands of the Chaldeans; rather shall

he be handed over to the king of Babylon. They shall meet and speak face to face, 5 and Zedekiah shall be taken to Babylon. There he shall remain, until I attend to him, says the LORD; in fighting the Chaldeans, you cannot win!"

6 This message came to me from the LORD, said Jeremiah: 7 Hanamel, son of your uncle Shallum, will come to you with the offer: "Buy for yourself my field in Anathoth, since you, as nearest relative, have the first right of purchase." 8 Then, as the LORD foretold, Hanamel, my uncle's son, came to me to the quarters of the guard and said, "Please buy my field in Anathoth, in the district of Benjamin; as nearest relative, you have the first claim to possess it; make it yours." I knew this was what the LORD meant, 9 so I bought the field in Anathoth from my cousin Hanamel, paying him the money, seventeen silver shekels.

10 When I had written and sealed the deed, called witnesses and weighed out the silver on the scales, 11 I accepted the deed of purchase, both the sealed copy, containing title and conditions, and the open one. 12 This deed of purchase I gave to Baruch, son of Neriah, son of Mahseiah, in the presence of my cousin Hanamel and of the witnesses who had signed the deed, and before all the men of Judah who happened to be in the quarters of the guard.

13 In their presence I gave Baruch this charge: 14 Thus says the LORD of hosts, the God of Israel: Take these deeds, both the sealed and the open deed of purchase, and put them in an earthen jar, so that they can be kept there a long time. 15 For thus

---

31, 29: "The fathers . . . on edge": a proverb used in Israel, expressing the idea that children suffer for the sins of their parents (cf Ex 18, 2). The Israel of the restoration will be characterized instead by personal responsibility and retribution for one's acts (v 30; cf vv 31-34).

31, 31-34: The new covenant to be made with Israel is a common theme of the prophets, beginning with Hosea. According to Jeremiah, the qualities of the new covenant that make it different from the old are: (a) It will not be broken, but will last forever; (b) Its law will be written in the heart, not merely on tablets of stone; (c) The knowledge of God will be so generally shown forth in the life of the people that it will no longer be necessary to put it into words of instruction. In the fullest sense, this prophecy was fulfilled only through the work of Jesus Christ; cf Lk 22, 20; 1 Cor 11, 25.

31, 38: From the Tower of Hananel to the Corner Gate: from the northeast to the northwest.

31, 40: Valley of corpses and ashes: the Valley of Ben-hinnom, which joins the Kidron at the southeast of ancient Jerusalem. The Horse Gate: in the eastern city wall, at the southeast corner of the temple area.

32, 1: The tenth year of Zedekiah: 588 B.C. The eighteenth year of Nebuchadnezzar, dating his reign from his victory at Carchemish; see note on 25, 1-14.

32, 1-44: This chapter recounts a prophecy "in action." At the Lord's command, Jeremiah fulfills his family duty to purchase the land of his cousin, carrying out all the legal forms, including records, to testify that Judah will be restored and that the life of the past will be resumed.

32, 6-9: Jeremiah's imprisonment by the weak-

willed Zedekiah was a technical custody that did not deprive him of all freedom of action. The siege maintained by the Chaldeans (v 2) was only now beginning (v 24), and could be by-passed by individual persons going to and fro between Jerusalem and nearby Anathoth.

32, 7: The first right of purchase: the obligation of the closest relative to redeem the property of one in economic distress, so that the ancestral land might remain within the family (Lv 25, 25-28); see note on Ru 2, 20.

32, 11: The sealed copy . . . and the open one: the legal deed of sale was written on a scroll, which was then rolled up and sealed; about it was rolled another scroll, left unsealed, containing a copy or a summary of the first.

32, 14: In an earthen jar: the first of the Dead Sea Scrolls were found in such a jar.

says the LORD of hosts, the God of Israel: Houses and fields and vineyards shall again be bought in this land.

16 After giving the deed of purchase to Baruch, son of Neriah, I prayed thus to the LORD: 17 Ah, Lord GOD, you have made heaven and earth by your great might, with your outstretched arm; nothing is impossible to you. 18 You continue your kindness through a thousand generations; and you repay the fathers' guilt, even into the lap of their sons who follow them. O God, great and mighty, whose name is LORD of hosts, 19 great in counsel, mighty in deed, whose eyes are open to all the ways of men, giving to each according to his ways, according to the fruit of his deeds: 20 you have wrought signs and wonders in the land of Egypt and to this day, both in Israel and among all other men, until now you have gained renown. 21 With strong hand and outstretched arm you brought your people Israel out of the land of Egypt amid signs and wonders and great terror. 22 This land you gave them, as you had promised their fathers under oath, a land flowing with milk and honey. 23 They entered and took possession of it, but they did not listen to your voice; by your law they did not live, and what you commanded they failed to do. Hence you let all these evils befall them. 24 See, the siegeworks have arrived at this city to breach it; the city will be handed over to the Chaldeans who are attacking it, amid sword, famine, and pestilence. What you threatened has happened, you see it yourself; 25 and yet you tell me, O Lord GOD: Buy the field with money, call in witnesses. But the city has already been handed over to the Chaldeans!

26 Then this word of the LORD came to Jeremiah: 27 I am the LORD, the God of all mankind! Is anything impossible to me? 28 This now is what the LORD says: I will hand over this city to the Chaldeans, for Nebuchadnezzar, king of Babylon, to take. 29 The Chal-

deans who are attacking it shall enter this city and set fire to it, burning it and its houses, on the roofs of which incense was burned to Baal and libations were poured out to strange gods as a provocation to me. 30 The Israelites and the Judeans from their youth have done only what is evil in my eyes; the Israelites did nothing but provoke me with the works of their hands, says the LORD. 31 From the day it was built to this day, this city has excited my anger and wrath, 32 so that I must put it out of my sight for all the wickedness the Israelites and Judeans, with their kings and their princes, their priests and their prophets, the men of Judah and the citizens of Jerusalem, have done to provoke me. 33 They turned their backs to me, not their faces; though I kept teaching them, they would not listen to my correction. 34 They defiled the house named after me by the horrid idols they set up in it. 35 They built high places to Baal in the Valley of Ben-hinnom, and immolated their sons and daughters to Molech, bringing sin upon Judah; this I never commanded them, nor did it even enter my mind that they should practice such abominations.

36 Now, therefore, thus says the LORD, the God of Israel, concerning this city, which as you say is handed over to the king of Babylon amid sword, famine, and pestilence: Behold, 37 I will gather them together from all the lands to which in anger, wrath, and great rage I banish them; I will bring them back to this place and settle them here in safety. 38 They shall be my people, and I will be their God. 39 One heart and one way I will give them, that they may fear me always, to their own good and that of their children after them. 40 I will make with them an eternal covenant, never to cease doing good to them; into their hearts I will put the fear of me, that they may never depart from me. 41 I will take delight in doing good to them: I will replant them firmly in this land, with all my heart and soul.

42 For thus says the LORD: Just as I brought upon this people all

this great evil, so I will bring upon them all the good I promise them. 43 Fields shall again be bought in this land, which you call a desert, without man or beast, handed over to the Chaldeans. 44 Fields shall be bought with money, deeds written and sealed, and witnesses shall be used in the land of Benjamin, in the suburbs of Jerusalem, in the cities of Judah and of the hill country, in the cities of the foothills and of the Negeb, when I change their lot, says the LORD.

Restoration of Jerusalem

33 The word of the LORD came to Jeremiah a second time while he was still imprisoned in the quarters of the guard: 2 Thus says the LORD who made the earth and gave it form and firmness, whose name is LORD: 3 Call to me, and I will answer you; I will tell to you things great beyond reach of your knowledge. 4 Thus says the LORD, the God of Israel, concerning the houses of this city and the palaces of Judah's kings, which are being destroyed in the face of siegeworks and the sword: 5 men come to battle the Chaldeans, and these houses will be filled with the corpses of those whom I slay in my anger and wrath, when I hide my face from this city for all their wickedness.

6 Behold, I will treat and assuage the city's wounds; I will heal them, and reveal to them an abundance of lasting peace. 7 I will change the lot of Judah and the lot of Israel, and rebuild them as of old. 8 I will cleanse them of all the guilt they incurred by sinning against me; all their offenses by which they sinned and rebelled against me, I will forgive. 9 Then Jerusalem shall be my joy, my praise, my glory, before all the nations of the earth, as they hear of all the good I will do among them. They shall be in fear and trembling over all the peaceful benefits I will give her.

10 Thus says the LORD: In this place of which you say, "How desolate it is, without man, without beast!" and in the cities of Judah, in the streets of Jerusalem that are now deserted, without man, without citizen, without beast, there shall yet

---

32, 35: *Molech:* the god to whom human sacrifice was offered in the Valley of Ben-hinnom. Here, as in 19, 5, he is given the name *Baal;* see note on Lv 18, 21.

be heard 11 the cry of joy, the cry of gladness, the voice of the bridegroom, the voice of the bride, the sound of those who bring thank offerings to the house of the LORD, singing, "Give thanks to the LORD of hosts, for the LORD is good; his mercy endures forever." For I will restore this country as of old, says the LORD.

12 Thus says the LORD of hosts: In this place, now desolate, without man or beast, and in all its cities there shall again be sheepfolds for the shepherds to couch their flocks. 13 In the cities of the hill country, of the foothills, and of the Negeb, in the land of Benjamin and the suburbs of Jerusalem, and in the cities of Judah, flocks will again pass under the hands of the one who counts them, says the LORD.

14 The days are coming, says the LORD, when I will fulfill the promise I made to the house of Israel and Judah. 15 In those days, in that time, I will raise up for David a just shoot; he shall do what is right and just in the land. 16 In those days Judah shall be safe and Jerusalem shall dwell secure; this is what they shall call her: "The LORD our justice." 17 For thus says the LORD: Never shall David lack a successor on the throne of the house of Israel, 18 nor shall priests of Levi ever be lacking, to offer holocausts before me, to burn cereal offerings, and to sacrifice victims.

This word of the LORD also came to Jeremiah: 19 Thus says the LORD: 20 If you can break my covenant with day, and my covenant with night, so that day and night no longer alternate in sequence, 21 then can my covenant with my servant David also be broken, so that he will not have a son to be king upon his throne, and my covenant with the priests of Levi who minister to me. 22 Like the

host of heaven which cannot be numbered, and the sands of the sea which cannot be counted, I will multiply the descendants of my servant David and the Levites who minister to me.

23 This word of the LORD came to Jeremiah: 24 Have you not noticed what these people are saying: "The LORD has rejected the two tribes which he had chosen"? They spurn my people as if it were no longer a nation in their eyes. 25 Thus says the LORD: When I have no covenant with day and night, and have given no laws to heaven and earth, 26 then too will I reject the descendants of Jacob and of my servant David, so as not to take from his descendants rulers for the race of Abraham, Isaac, and Jacob. For I will change their lot and show them mercy.

FALL OF JERUSALEM

Fate of Zedekiah

34 This word came to Jeremiah from the LORD while Nebuchadnezzar, king of Babylon, and his armies and the earth's kingdoms subject to him, as well as the other peoples, were all attacking Jerusalem and all her cities: 2 Thus says the LORD, the God of Israel: Go to Zedekiah, king of Judah, and tell him: Thus says the LORD: I am handing this city over to the king of Babylon; he will destroy it with fire. 3 Neither shall you escape his hand; rather you will be captured and fall into his hands. You shall see the king of Babylon and speak to him face to face. Then you shall be taken to Babylon.

4 But if you obey the word of the LORD, Zedekiah, king of Judah, then, says the LORD to you, you shall not die by the sword. 5 You shall die in peace, and they will lament you as their lord, and burn spices for

your burial as they did for your fathers, the kings who preceded you from the first; it is I who make this promise, says the LORD.

6 The prophet Jeremiah told all these things to Zedekiah, king of Judah, in Jerusalem, 7 while the armies of the king of Babylon were attacking Jerusalem and the remaining cities of Judah, Lachish, and Azekah, since these alone were left of the fortified cities of Judah.

The Pact Broken

8 This is the word that came to Jeremiah from the LORD after King Zedekiah had made an agreement with all the people in Jerusalem to issue an edict of emancipation. 9 Everyone was to free his Hebrew slaves, male and female, so that no one should hold a man of Judah, his brother, in slavery. 10 All the princes and the others who entered the agreement consented to set free their male and female servants, so that they should be slaves no longer. But though they agreed and freed them, 11 afterward they took back their male and female slaves whom they had set free and again forced them into service.

12 Then this word of the LORD came to Jeremiah: 13 Thus says the LORD, the God of Israel: The day I brought your fathers out of the land of Egypt, out of the place where they were slaves, I made this covenant with them: 14 Every seventh year each of you shall set free his Hebrew brother who has sold himself to you; six years he shall serve you, but then you shall let him go free. Your fathers, however, did not heed me or obey me. 15 Today you indeed repented and did what is right in my eyes by proclaiming the emancipation of your brethren and making an agreement before me in the house that is named after me. 16 But then you

---

33, 14–26: This is the longest continuous passage in the Book of Jeremiah that is lacking in the Greek. It appears to be the postexilic composition of an inspired writer who used parts of the prophecies of Jeremiah—often, however, in a sense different from the prophet's. The prediction of an eternal Davidic dynasty (14–17) to fulfill the prophecy of Nathan (2 Sm 7, 11–16), and of a perpetual priesthood and sacrifice (18), was not to be realized in the restoration of the Jewish nation. It finds its fulfillment only in Jesus of Nazareth, who combined with his Messianic

Davidic kingship an eternal priesthood; cf Heb 6, 20; 7, 24f.

34, 7: *Lachish and Azekah:* fortress towns to the southwest of Jerusalem which Nebuchadnezzar besieged to prevent help coming to Jerusalem from Egypt. Between 1935 and 1938, archaeologists found at Lachish several letters written on pottery fragments which date from 598 or 588 B.C., and which mention both Lachish and Azekah.

34, 8–22: While the Chaldean siege of Jerusalem was in progress, the citizens of Jerusalem made a

covenant at Zedekiah's instigation to free their brother Judeans who were in slavery. Doubtless this was both to provide additional free defenders for the city and to offer reparation for past violations of the law, according to which Hebrew slaves were to serve no longer than six years (Dt 15, 12–15). But when the siege was temporarily lifted, probably because of the help promised by Pharaoh Hophra (cf 37, 5), the inhabitants of Jerusalem broke the covenant and once more pressed their brethren into slavery (v 11).

changed your mind and profaned my name by taking back your male and female slaves to whom you had given their freedom; you forced them once more into slavery. 17 Therefore, thus says the LORD: You did not obey me by proclaiming your neighbors and kinsmen free. I now proclaim you free, says the LORD, for the sword, famine, and pestilence. I will make you an object of horror to all the kingdoms of the earth. 18 The men who violated my covenant and did not observe the terms of the agreement which they made before me, I will make like the calf which they cut in two, between whose two parts they passed. 19 The princes of Judah and of Jerusalem, the courtiers, the priests, and the common people, who passed between the parts of the calf, 20 I will hand over, all of them, to their enemies, to those who seek their lives: their corpses shall be food for the birds of the air and the beasts of the field.

21 Zedekiah, too, king of Judah, and his princes, I will hand over to their enemies, to those who seek their lives, to the soldiers of the king of Babylon who have at present withdrawn from you. 22 I will give the command, says the LORD, and bring them back to this city. They shall attack and capture it, and destroy it with fire; the cities of Judah I will turn into a desert where no man dwells.

The Faithful Rechabites

35 This word came to Jeremiah from the LORD in the days of Jehoiakim, son of Josiah, king of Judah: 2 Approach the Rechabites and speak to them; bring them into the house of the LORD, to one of the rooms, and give them wine to drink. 3 So I went and brought Jaazaniah, son of Jeremiah, son of Habazziniah, his brothers and all his sons, the whole company of the Rechabites, 4 into the house of the LORD, to the room of the sons of Hanan, son of Igdaliah, the man of God, next to the princes' room, above the room of Maaseiah, son of Shallum, keeper of the doorway. 5 I set before these Rechabite men bowls full of wine and offered them cups to drink the wine.

6 "We do not drink wine," they said to me: "Jonadab, Rechab's son, our father, forbade us in these words: 'Neither you nor your children shall ever drink wine. 7 Build no house and sow no seed; neither plant nor own a vineyard. You shall dwell in tents all your life, so that you may live long on the earth where you are wayfarers.' 8 Now we have heeded Jonadab, Rechab's son, our father, in all his prohibitions. All our lives we have not drunk wine, neither we, nor our wives, nor our sons, nor our daughters. 9 We build no houses to live in; we own no vineyards or fields or crops, 10 and we live in tents; we obediently do everything our father Jonadab commanded us. 11 But when Nebuchadnezzar, king of Babylon, invaded this land, we decided to come into Jerusalem to escape the army of the Chaldeans and the army of Aram; that is why we are now living in Jerusalem."

12 Then this word of the LORD came to Jeremiah: 13 Thus says the LORD of hosts, the God of Israel: Go, say to the men of Judah and to the citizens of Jerusalem: Will you not take correction and obey my words? says the LORD. 14 The advice of Jonadab, Rechab's son, by which he forbade his children to drink wine, has been followed: to this day they have not drunk it; they obeyed their father's command. Me, however, you have not obeyed, although I spoke to you untiringly and insistently. 15 I kept sending you all my servants the prophets, telling you to turn back, all of you, from your evil way; to reform your conduct, and not follow strange gods or serve them, if you would remain on the land which I gave you and your fathers; but you did not heed me or obey me. 16 Yes, the children of Jonadab, Rechab's son, observed the command which their father laid on them; but this people does not obey me! 17 Now, therefore, says the LORD God of hosts, the God of Israel: I will bring upon Judah and all the citizens of Jerusalem every evil that I threatened; because when I spoke they did not obey, when I called they did not answer.

18 But to the company of the Rechabites Jeremiah said: Thus says the LORD of hosts, the God of Israel: Since you have obeyed the command of Jonadab, your father, kept all his commands and done everything he commanded you, 19 thus therefore says the LORD of hosts, the God of Israel: Never shall there fail to be a descendant of Jonadab, Rechab's son, standing in my service.

Baruch Writes the Prophecies of Jeremiah

36 In the fourth year of Jehoiakim, son of Josiah, king of Judah, this word came to Jeremiah from the LORD: 2 Take a scroll and write on it all the words I have spoken to you against Israel, Judah, and all the nations, from the day I first spoke to you, in the days of Josiah, until today. 3 Perhaps, when the house of Judah hears all the evil I have in mind to do to them, they will turn back each from his evil way, so that I may forgive their wickedness and their sin. 4 So Jeremiah called Baruch, son of Neriah, who wrote down on a scroll, as Jeremiah dictated, all the words which the LORD had spoken to him.

9 In the ninth month, in the fifth year of Jehoiakim, son of Josiah, king of Judah, a fast to placate the LORD was proclaimed for all the people of Jerusalem and all who

---

34, 18f: As the Bible (Gn 15, 10–17) and also contemporary inscriptions make clear, agreements were sometimes ratified by walking between the divided pieces of animals while the contracting parties invoked on themselves a fate similar to that of the slaughtered beast if they should fail to keep their word. *The agreement:* that mentioned in vv 10.15.

35, 2: *The Rechabites:* reactionaries who believed that the Lord could not be well served except by maintaining the original nomadic conditions of Israel's life. Without sharing their convictions, the prophet holds up their fidelity to their ideals as an example to put to shame his faithless countrymen. *In the days of Jehoiakim:* probably in 599 or 598 B.C.

35, 4: *The sons of Hanan:* probably the disciples of this *man of God* or prophet. *Maaseiah:* possibly the father of the priest Zephaniah (29, 25; 37, 3). *Keeper of the doorway:* a priestly function of responsibility; cf 52, 24.

35, 6: *Jonadab:* a contemporary of King Jehu; cf 2 Kgs 10, 15ff.

35, 11: *The army of Aram:* Nebuchadnezzar enlisted the help of Judah's foreign neighbors in his assault on Jerusalem.

came from Judah's cities to Jerusalem. 5 Then Jeremiah charged Baruch: I cannot go to the house of the LORD; I am prevented from doing so. 6 Do you go on the fast day and read publicly in the LORD's house the LORD's words from the scroll you wrote at my dictation; read them also to all the men of Judah who come up from their cities. 7 Perhaps they will lay their supplication before the LORD and will all turn back from their evil way; for great is the fury of anger with which the LORD has threatened this people.

8 Baruch, son of Neriah, did everything the prophet Jeremiah commanded; from the book-scroll he read the LORD's words in the LORD's house. 10 It was in the room of Gemariah, son of the scribe Shaphan, in the upper court of the LORD's house, at the entrance of the New Temple-Gate, that Baruch publicly read the words of Jeremiah from his book.

11 Now Micaiah, son of Gemariah, son of Shaphan, heard all the words of the LORD read from the book. 12 So he went down to the king's palace, into the scribe's chamber, where the princes were just then in session: Elishama, the scribe, Delaiah, son of Shemaiah, Elnathan, son of Achbor, Gemariah, son of Shaphan, Zedekiah, son of Hananiah, and the other princes. 13 To them Micaiah reported all that he had heard Baruch read publicly from his book. 14 Thereupon the princes sent Jehudi, son of Nethaniah, son of Shelemiah, son of Cushi, to Baruch with the order: "Come, and bring with you the scroll you read publicly to the people." Scroll in hand, Baruch, son of Neriah, went to them. 15 "Sit down," they said to him, "and read it to us." Baruch read it to them, 16 and when they heard all its words, they were frightened and said to one another, "We must certainly tell the king all these things." 17 Then they asked

Baruch: "Tell us, please, how you came to write down all these words." 18 "Jeremiah dictated all these words to me," Baruch answered them, "and I wrote them down with ink in the book." 19 At this the princes said to Baruch, "Go into hiding, you and Jeremiah; let no one know where you are."

20 Leaving the scroll in safe-keeping in the room of Elishama the scribe, they entered the room where the king was. When they told him everything that had happened, 21 he sent Jehudi to fetch the scroll. Jehudi brought it from the room of Elishama the scribe, and read it to the king and to all the princes who were in attendance on the king. 22 Now the king was sitting in his winter house, since it was the ninth month, and fire was burning in a brazier before him. 23 Each time Jehudi finished reading three or four columns, the king would cut off the piece with a scribe's knife and cast it into the fire in the brazier, until the entire roll was consumed in the fire. 24 Hearing all these words did not frighten the king and his ministers or cause them to rend their garments. 25 And though Elnathan, Delaiah, and Gemariah urged the king not to burn the scroll, he would not listen to them, 26 but commanded Jerahmeel, a royal prince, and Seraiah, son of Azriel, and Shelemiah, son of Abdeel, to arrest Baruch, the secretary, and the prophet Jeremiah. But the LORD kept them concealed.

27 This word of the LORD came to Jeremiah, after the king burned the scroll with the text Jeremiah had dictated to Baruch: 28 Take another scroll, and write on it everything that the first scroll contained, which Jehoiakim, king of Judah, burned up. 29 And against Jehoiakim, king of Judah, say this: Thus says the LORD: You burned that scroll, saying, "Why did you write on it: Babylon's king shall surely come and lay waste this land and empty it of

man and beast?" 30 The LORD now says of Jehoiakim, king of Judah: No descendant of his shall succeed to David's throne; his corpse shall be cast out, exposed to the heat of day, to the cold of night. 31 I will punish him and his descendants and his ministers for their wickedness; against them and the citizens of Jerusalem and the men of Judah I will fulfill all the threats of evil which went unheeded.

32 Jeremiah took another scroll, and gave it to his secretary, Baruch, son of Neriah; he wrote on it at Jeremiah's dictation all the words contained in the book which Jehoiakim, king of Judah, had burned in the fire, and many others of the same kind in addition.

Jeremiah in the Dungeon

37 Coniah, son of Jehoiakim, was succeeded by king Zedekiah, son of Josiah; he was made king over the land of Judah by Nebuchadnezzar, king of Babylon. 2 Neither he, nor his ministers, nor the people of the land would listen to the words of the LORD spoken by Jeremiah the prophet. 3 Yet King Zedekiah sent Jehucal, son of Shelemiah, and Zephaniah, son of Maaseiah the priest, to the prophet Jeremiah with this request: "Pray to the LORD, our God, for us." 4 At this time Jeremiah had not yet been put into prison; he still came and went freely among the people. 5 Also, Pharaoh's army had set out from Egypt, and when the Chaldeans who were besieging Jerusalem heard this report they marched away from the city.

6 This word of the LORD then came to the prophet Jeremiah: 7 Thus says the LORD, the God of Israel: Give this answer to the king of Judah who sent you to me to consult me: Pharaoh's army which has set out to help you will return to its own land, Egypt. 8 The Chaldeans shall return to the fight

---

36, 5: *I am prevented:* probably because of his temple sermon (7, 1–15), or because of temporary ritual uncleanness.

36, 10: *Gemariah:* member of a family friendly to Jeremiah, which had rights to a room in the fortress of the temple gateway overlooking the court of the temple; from a window in this room Baruch read

Jeremiah's prophetic sermon to the people.

36, 12: *The scribe's chamber:* the office of the royal secretary.

36, 23: *A scribe's knife:* used to sharpen the reeds which were employed as pens.

36, 30: Jehoiakim's son Jehoiachin was named king, but reigned only three months; he was known

better for his thirty-seven-year exile in Babylon. *His corpse shall be cast out:* see note on 22, 19.

37, 4: *Put into prison:* as described in 32, 1ff. Chronologically, the present episode follows 34, 1–7.

37, 5: *Pharaoh's army:* the force sent by Pharaoh Hophra which caused the Chaldeans momentarily to lift the siege of Jerusalem (cf 34, 21).

against this city; they shall capture it and destroy it with fire.

9 Thus says the LORD: Do not deceive yourselves with the thought that the Chaldeans will leave you for good, because they shall not leave! 10 Even if you were to defeat the whole Chaldean army now attacking you, and only the wounded remained, each in his tent, these would rise up and destroy the city with fire.

11 When the Chaldean army lifted the siege of Jerusalem at the threat of the army of Pharaoh, 12 Jeremiah set out from Jerusalem for the district of Benjamin, to take part with his family in the division of an inheritance. 13 But when he reached the Gate of Benjamin, he met the captain of the guard, a man named Irijah, son of Shelemiah, son of Hananiah; he seized the prophet Jeremiah, saying, "You are deserting to the Chaldeans!" 14 "That is a lie!" Jeremiah answered, "I am not deserting to the Chaldeans." Without listening, Irijah kept Jeremiah in custody and brought him to the princes.

15 The princes were enraged, and had Jeremiah beaten and thrown into prison in the house of Jonathan the scribe, which they were using as a jail. 16 And so Jeremiah entered the vaulted dungeon, where he remained a long time.

17 Once King Zedekiah had him brought to his palace and he asked him secretly whether there was any message from the LORD. Yes! Jeremiah answered: You shall be handed over to the king of Babylon. 18 Jeremiah then asked King Zedekiah: In what have I wronged you, or you ministers, or this people, that you should put me in prison? 19 And where are your own prophets now, 20 who prophesied to you that the king of Babylon would not attack you or this land? Hear now, my lord king, and grant my petition: do not send me back into the house of Jonathan the scribe, or I shall die there.

21 King Zedekiah ordered that Jeremiah be confined in the quarters of the guard, and given a loaf of bread each day from the baker's shop until all the bread in the city was eaten up. Thus Jeremiah remained in the quarters of the guard.

Jeremiah in the Miry Cistern

38 Shephatiah, son of Mattan, Gedaliah, son of Pashhur, Jucal son of Shelemiah, and Pashhur, son of Malchiah, heard Jeremiah speaking these words to all the people: 2 Thus says the LORD: He who remains in this city shall die by sword, or famine, or pestilence; but he who goes out to the Chaldeans shall live; his life shall be spared him as booty, and he shall live. 3 Thus says the LORD: This city shall certainly be handed over to the army of the king of Babylon; he shall capture it.

4 "This man ought to be put to death," the princes said to the king; "he demoralizes the soldiers who are left in this city, and all the people, by speaking such things to them; he is not interested in the welfare of our people, but in their ruin." 5 King Zedekiah answered: "He is in your power"; for the king could do nothing with them. 6 And so they took Jeremiah and threw him into the cistern of Prince Malchiah, which was in the quarters of the guard, letting him down with ropes. There was no water in the cistern, only mud, and Jeremiah sank into the mud.

7 Now Ebed-melech, a Cushite, a courtier in the king's palace, heard that they had put Jeremiah into the cistern. The king happened just then to be at the Gate of Benjamin, 8 and Ebed-melech went there from the palace and said to him, 9 "My lord king, these men have been at fault in all they have done to the prophet Jeremiah, casting him into the cistern. He will die of famine on the spot, for there is no more food in the city." 10 Then the king ordered Ebed-melech the Cushite to take three men along with him, and draw the prophet Jeremiah out of the cistern before he should die. 11 Ebed-melech took the men along with him, and went first to the linen closet in the palace, from which he took some old, tattered rags; these he sent down to Jeremiah in the cistern, with ropes. 12 Then he said to Jeremiah: "Put the old, tattered rags between your armpits and the ropes." Jeremiah did so, 13 and they drew him up with the ropes out of the cistern. But Jeremiah remained in the quarters of the guard.

14 Once King Zedekiah summoned the prophet Jeremiah to come to him at the third entrance to the house of the LORD. "I have a question to ask you," the king said to Jeremiah; "hide nothing from me." Jeremiah answered Zedekiah: 15 If I tell you anything, you will have me killed, will you not? If I counsel you, you will not listen to me! 16 But King Zedekiah swore to Jeremiah secretly: "As the LORD lives who gave us the breath of life, I will not kill you; nor will I hand you over to these men who seek your life."

17 Thereupon Jeremiah said to Zedekiah: Thus says the LORD God of hosts, the God of Israel: If you surrender to the princes of Babylon's king, you shall have your life; this city shall not be destroyed with fire, and you and your family shall live. 18 But if you do not surrender to the princes of Babylon's king, this city shall fall into the hands of the Chaldeans, who shall destroy it with fire, and you shall not escape their hands.

19 King Zedekiah, however, said to Jeremiah, "I am afraid of the men of Judah who have deserted to the Chaldeans; I may be handed over to them, and they will mistreat me." 20 You will not be handed over, Jeremiah answered. Please obey the voice of the LORD and do as I tell you; then it shall go well with you, and your life shall be spared. 21 But if you refuse to surrender, this is what the LORD shows me: 22 All the women left in the house of Judah's king shall be brought out

---

38, 1: Jeremiah enjoyed sufficient liberty *in the quarters of the guard* (37, 21) to speak to the people; cf 32, 6–9. *Gedaliah, son of Pashhur:* the latter is possibly the Pashhur of 20, 1. *Pashhur, son of Mal-* chiah: mentioned in 21, 1.

38, 4: *He demoralizes the soldiers:* literally, "he weakens their hands." One of the Lachish ostraca (see note on 34, 7) uses the same expression of the prince in Jerusalem.

38, 7: *A Cushite:* an Ethiopian. Ebed-melech evidently held a position of some authority at court.

to the princes of Babylon's king, and they shall taunt you thus:

"They betrayed you, outdid you,
    your good friends!
Now that your feet are stuck in
    the mud,
    they slink away."

23 All your wives and sons shall be led forth to the Chaldeans, and you shall not escape their hands; you shall be handed over to the king of Babylon, and this city shall be destroyed with fire.

24 Then Zedekiah said to Jeremiah, "Let no one know about this conversation, or you shall die. 25 If the princes hear I spoke to you, if they come and ask you, 'Tell us what you said to the king; do not hide it from us, or we will kill you,' or 'What did the king say to you?' 26 give them this answer: 'I petitioned the king not to send me back to Jonathan's house to die there.'" 27 When all the princes came to Jeremiah, they questioned him, and he answered them in the very words the king had commanded. They said no more to him, for nothing had been heard of the earlier conversation. 28 Thus Jeremiah stayed in the quarters of the guard till the day Jerusalem was taken.

Jeremiah and Gedaliah

39 When Jerusalem was taken.... In the tenth month of the ninth year of Zedekiah, king of Judah, Nebuchadnezzar, king of Babylon, and all his army marched against Jerusalem and besieged it. 2 On the ninth day of the fourth month, in the eleventh year of Zedekiah, a breach was made in the city's defenses. 3 All the princes of the king of Babylon came and occupied the middle gate: Nergal-sharezer, of Simmagir, the chief officer, Nebushazban, the high dignitary, and all the other princes of the king of Babylon.... 4 When Zedekiah, king of Judah, saw them, he and all his warriors fled by night, leaving the city on the Royal Garden Road through the gate between the two walls. He went in the direction of the Arabah, 5 but the Chaldean army pursued them, and overtook and captured Zedekiah in the desert near Jericho. He was brought to Riblah, in the land of Hamath, where Nebuchadnezzar, king of Babylon pronounced sentence upon him. 6 As Zedekiah looked on, his sons were slain at Riblah by order of the king of Babylon, who slew also all the nobles of Judah. 7 He then blinded Zedekiah and bound him in chains to bring him to Babylon.

8 The Chaldeans set fire to the king's palace and the houses of the people, and demolished the walls of Jerusalem. 9 Nebuzaradan, chief of the bodyguard, deported to Babylon the rest of the people left in the city, those who had deserted to him, and the rest of the workmen. 10 But some of the poor who had no property were left in the land of Judah by Nebuzaradan, chief of the bodyguard, and were given at the same time vineyards and farms.

11 Concerning Jeremiah, Nebuchadnezzar, king of Babylon, gave the following orders through Nebuzaradan, chief of the bodyguard: 12 "Take him and look after him; let no harm befall him, but treat him as he himself requests." 13 Thereupon Nebuzaradan, chief of the bodyguard, and Nebushazban, the high dignitary, and Nergal-sharezer, the chief officer, and all the nobles of the king of Babylon, 14 had Jeremiah taken out of the quarters of the guard, and entrusted to Gedaliah, son of Ahikam, son of Shaphan, to be brought home. And so he remained among the people.

A Word of Comfort for Ebed-melech

15 While Jeremiah was still imprisoned in the quarters of the guard, the word of the LORD came to him: 16 Go, tell this to Ebed-melech the Cushite: Thus says the LORD of hosts, the God of Israel: Behold, I am now fulfilling the words I spoke against this city, for evil and not for good; and this before your very eyes. 17 But on that day I will rescue you, says the LORD; you shall not be handed over to the men of whom you are afraid. 18 I will make certain that you escape and do not fall by the sword. Your life shall be spared as booty, because you trusted in me, says the LORD.

Jeremiah Still in Judah

40 This word came to Jeremiah from the LORD, after Nebuzaradan, captain of the bodyguard, had released him in Ramah, where he had found him a prisoner in chains, among the captives of Jerusalem and Judah who were being exiled to Babylon. 2 When the captain of the bodyguard took charge of Jeremiah, he said to him, "The LORD, your God, foretold the ruin of this place. 3 Now he has brought about in deed what he threatened; because you sinned against the LORD and did not obey his voice, this fate has befallen you. 4 And now, I am freeing you today from the fetters that bind your hands; if it seems good to you to come with me to Babylon, you may come: I will look after you well. But if it does not please you to come to Babylon, you need not come. See, the whole land is before you; go wherever you think good and proper"; 5 and then, before he left — "or go to Gedaliah, son of Ahikam, son of Shaphan, whom the king of Babylon has appointed ruler over the cities of Judah; stay with him among the people, or go wherever you please." The captain of the bodyguard gave him food and gifts and let him go. 6 Jeremiah went to Gedaliah, son of Ahikam, in Mizpah, and stayed with him among the people left in the land.

39, 1: *The tenth month of the ninth year:* the month Tebet (mid-December to mid-January) of the year 589/8 B.C.

39, 2: *The ninth day of the fourth month, in the eleventh year:* in July of 587 B.C.

39, 4: *The Royal Garden Road:* along the southeast side of the city; the royal garden was in the Kidron Valley. *The gate between the two walls:* the southern-most city gate, at the end of the Tyropoean valley. *The Arabah:* the Jordan valley. Zedekiah was attempting to escape across the Jordan when he was captured near Jericho.

39, 5: *Riblah:* Nebuchadnezzar's headquarters in Syria, which had also been used by Pharaoh Neco (2 Kgs 23, 33).

40, 1: *This word:* actually, no further word of the Lord is recorded until 42, 7ff. This is a title affixed to the following chapters after they were attached to an earlier form of the book ending with chapter 39.

40, 6: *Mizpah:* some five miles northwest of Jerusalem, where Israel chose its first king (1 Sm 10, 17–24). Presumably Jerusalem had been damaged too much by the Chaldean conquest to remain a seat of government.

7 When the army leaders who were still in the field with all their men heard that the king of Babylon had given Gedaliah, son of Ahikam, charge of the land, of men, women, and children, and of those poor who had not been led captive to Babylon, 8 they came with their men to Gedaliah in Mizpah: Ishmael, son of Nethaniah; Johanan, son of Kareah; Seraiah, son of Tanhumeth; the sons of Ephai of Netopha; and Jezaniah of Beth-maacah. 9 Gedaliah, son of Ahikam, son of Shaphan, adjured them and their men not to be afraid to serve the Chaldeans: to stay in the land and submit to the king of Babylon, for their own welfare, 10 saying that he himself would remain in Mizpah, as their intermediary with the Chaldeans who should come to them. They were to collect the wine, the fruit, and the oil, to store them in jars, and to settle in the cities they occupied. 11 When the people of Judah in Moab, those among the Ammonites, those in Edom, and those in all other lands heard that the king of Babylon had left a remnant in Judah, and had appointed over them Gedaliah, son of Ahikam, son of Shaphan, 12 they all returned to the land of Judah from the places to which they had scattered. They went to Gedaliah at Mizpah and had a rich harvest of wine and fruit.

Assassination of Gedaliah

13 Now Johanan, son of Kareah, and all the leaders of the armies in the field came to Gedaliah in Mizpah 14 and asked him whether he did not know that Baalis, the king of the Ammonites, had sent Ishmael, son of Nethaniah, to assassinate him. 15 But Gedaliah, son of Ahikam, would not believe them. Then Johanan, son of Kareah, said secretly to Gedaliah in Mizpah: "Let me go and kill Ishmael, son of Nethaniah; no one will know it. Why should he be allowed to kill you? All the Jews who have now rallied to you will be dispersed and the remnant of Judah

will perish." 16 Nevertheless, Gedaliah, son of Ahikam, answered Johanan, son of Kareah, "You shall do nothing of the kind; you have lied about Ishmael."

41 In the seventh month Ishmael, son of Nethaniah, son of Elishama, of royal descent, one of the king's nobles, came with ten men to Gedaliah, son of Ahikam, at Mizpah. And while they were together at table in Mizpah, 2 Ishmael, son of Nethaniah, and the ten who were with him, rose up and attacked with swords Gedaliah, son of Ahikam, son of Shaphan, whom the king of Babylon had made ruler over the land; and they killed him. 3 Ishmael also slew all the men of Judah of military age who were with Gedaliah and the Chaldean soldiers who were there.

4 The second day after the murder of Gedaliah, before anyone knew of it, 5 eighty men with beards shaved off, clothes in rags, and with gashes on their bodies came from Shechem, Shiloh, and Samaria, bringing food offerings and incense for the house of the LORD. 6 Ishmael, son of Nethaniah, went out from Mizpah to meet them, weeping as he went. 7 "Come to Gedaliah, son of Ahikam," he said as he met them. When they were once inside the city, Ishmael, son of Nethaniah, and his men slew them and threw them into the cistern. 8 But there were ten among them who pleaded with Ishmael: "Do not kill us; we have stores buried in the field: wheat and barley, oil and honey." And so he spared them and did not kill them, as he had killed their companions. 9 The cistern into which Ishmael threw all the corpses of the men he had killed was the large one made by King Asa to defend himself against Baasha, king of Israel; this cistern Ishmael, son of Nethaniah, filled with the slain.

10 Ishmael, son of Nethaniah, led away the remnant of the people left in Mizpah and the princesses, whom Nebuzaradan, captain of the body-

guard, had confided to Gedaliah, son of Ahikam. With these captives, Ishmael, son of Nethaniah, set out to make his way to the Ammonites.

Flight to Egypt

11 But when Johanan, son of Kareah, and the other army leaders with him heard of the crimes Ishmael, son of Nethaniah, had committed, 12 they took all their men and set out to attack Ishmael, son of Nethaniah. They overtook him at the Great Waters in Gibeon. 13 At the sight of Johanan, son of Kareah, and the other army leaders, the people who were Ishmael's captives rejoiced. 14 All of those whom Ishmael had brought away from Mizpah went over to Johanan, son of Kareah. 15 But Ishmael, son of Nethaniah, escaped from Johanan and fled to the Ammonites with eight men. 16 Then Johanan, son of Kareah, and all his army leaders took charge of the remnant of the people, both the soldiers and the women and children with their guardians, whom Ishmael, son of Nethaniah, had brought away from Mizpah after he killed Gedaliah, son of Ahikam. From Gibeon, 17 they retreated to the lodging place of Chimham near Bethlehem, where they stopped, intending to flee into Egypt. 18 They were afraid of the Chaldeans, because Ishmael, son of Nethaniah, had slain Gedaliah, son of Ahikam, whom the king of Babylon had made ruler in the land of Judah.

42 Then all the army leaders, Johanan, son of Kareah, Azariah, son of Hoshaiah, and all the people, high and low, approached the prophet Jeremiah 2 and said, "Grant our petition; pray for us to the LORD, your God, for all this remnant. We are now few who once were many, as you well see. 3 Let the LORD, your God, show us what way we should take and what we should do." 4 Very well! the prophet Jeremiah answered them: I will

---

40, 8: *Jezaniah:* the seal ring of a high official of this name was discovered in 1932 at the site usually identified with Mizpah, Tell en-Nsabe.

40, 14: *The Ammonites:* they resented the survival of their ancient enemy, Judah. *Ishmael:* their willing

tool, who doubtless aspired to rule over Judah himself, as he was of the house of David; cf 41, 1.

41, 10: *The princesses:* of the royal house of Judah. They had not been deported to Babylon with the men of this house.

41, 12: *Gibeon:* today called El-Jib; it is northwest of Jerusalem. The most recent excavations have revealed the extensive dimensions of the city spring and well, called here *the Great Waters;* cf 2 Sm 2, 12ff.

pray to the LORD, your God, as you desire; whatever the LORD answers you, I will tell you; I will withhold nothing from you. 5 And they said to Jeremiah, "May the LORD be our witness: we will truly and faithfully follow all the instructions the LORD, your God, will send us. 6 Whether it is pleasant or difficult, we will obey the command of the LORD, our God, to whom we are sending you, so that it will go well with us for obeying the command of the LORD, our God."

7 Ten days passed before the word of the LORD came to Jeremiah. 8 Then he called Johanan, son of Kareah, his army leaders, and all the people, high and low, 9 and said to them: Thus says the LORD, the God of Israel, to whom you sent me to offer your prayer: 10 If you remain quietly in this land I will build you up, and not tear you down; I will plant you, not uproot you; for I regret the evil I have done you. 11 Do not fear the king of Babylon, before whom you are now afraid; do not fear him, says the LORD, for I am with you to save you, to rescue you from his power. 12 I will grant you mercy, so that he will be sorry for you and let you return to your land. 13 But if you disobey the voice of the LORD, your God, and decide not to remain in this land, 14 saying, "No, we will go to Egypt, where we will see no more of war, hear the trumpet alarm no longer, nor hunger for bread; there we will live"; 15 then listen to the word of the LORD, remnant of Judah: Thus says the LORD of hosts, the God of Israel: If you are determined to go to Egypt, when you arrive there to stay, 16 the sword you fear shall reach you in the land of Egypt; the hunger you dread shall cling to you no less in Egypt, and there you shall die. 17 All those men who determine to go to Egypt to stay, shall die by the sword, famine, and pestilence; not one shall survive or escape the evil that I will bring upon them. 18 For thus says the LORD of hosts, the God of Israel: Just as my furious anger was poured out

upon the citizens of Jerusalem, so shall my anger be poured out on you when you reach Egypt. You shall become an example of malediction and horror, a curse and a reproach, and you shall never see this place again.

19 It is the LORD who has spoken to you, remnant of Judah; do not go to Egypt! You can never say that I did not warn you this day. 20 At the cost of your lives you have deceived me, sending me to the LORD, your God, saying, "Pray for us to the LORD, our God; make known to us all that the LORD, our God, shall say, and we will do it." 21 Today I proclaim his message, but you obey the voice of the LORD, your God, in nothing that he has commissioned me to make known to you. 22 Have no doubt of this, you shall die by the sword, famine, and pestilence in the place where you wish to go and settle.

43 When Jeremiah finished speaking to the people all these words of the LORD, their God, with which the LORD had sent him to them, 2 Azariah, son of Hoshaiah, Johanan, son of Kareah, and all the insolent men shouted to Jeremiah: "You lie; it was not the LORD, our God, who sent you to tell us not to go to Egypt to settle. 3 It is Baruch, son of Neriah, who stirs you up against us, to hand us over to the Chaldeans to be killed or exiled to Babylon."

4 Johanan, son of Kareah, and the rest of the leaders and the people did not obey the LORD's command to stay in the land of Judah. 5 Instead, Johanan, son of Kareah, and all the army leaders took along the whole remnant of Judah that had been dispersed among the nations and had returned thence to dwell again in the land of Judah: 6 men, women, and children, the princesses and everyone whom Nebuzaradan, captain of the bodyguard, had entrusted to Gedaliah, son of Ahikam, son of Shaphan; also Jeremiah, the prophet, and Baruch, son of Neriah. 7 Against the LORD's

command they went to Egypt, and arrived at Tahpanhes. . . .

Jeremiah in Egypt

8 This word of the LORD came to Jeremiah in Tahpanhes: 9 Take with you large stones and sink them in mortar in the brickyard at the entrance to the royal building in Tahpanhes, while the men of Judah look on, 10 and then say to them: Thus says the LORD of hosts, the God of Israel: I will send for my servant Nebuchadnezzar, king of Babylon, and bring him here. He will set his throne upon these stones which I, Jeremiah, have sunk, and stretch his canopy over them. 11 He shall come and strike the land of Egypt: with death, whoever is marked for death; with exile, everyone destined for exile; with the sword, all who are intended for the sword. 12 He shall set fire to the temples of Egypt's gods, and burn the gods or carry them off. As a shepherd delouses his cloak, he shall delouse the land of Egypt and depart victorious. 13 He shall smash the obelisks of the temple of the sun in the land of Egypt and destroy with fire the temples of the Egyptian gods.

44 This word came to Jeremiah for all the people of Judah who were living in Egypt, at Migdol, Tahpanhes, and Memphis, and in Upper Egypt: 2 Thus says the LORD of hosts, the God of Israel: You have seen all the evil I brought on Jerusalem and the other cities of Judah. Today they are ruins and uninhabited, 3 because of the evil they did to provoke me, going after strange gods, serving them and sacrificing to them, gods which neither they, nor you, nor your fathers knew. 4 Though I kept sending to you all my servants the prophets, with the plea not to commit this horrible deed which I hate, 5 they would not listen or accept the warning to turn away from the evil of sacrificing to strange gods. 6 Therefore the fury of my anger poured forth in flame over the cities

---

43, 9: *The royal building:* residence of the Egyptian governor.
44, 2–30: Chronologically, this is the last of

Jeremiah's prophecies to his countrymen. The narrative leaves him an old man nearing seventy,

rejected by his people. According to tradition, he was murdered in Egypt by fellow Judeans.

of Judah and the streets of Jerusalem, so that they became the ruinous waste they are today.

7 Now thus says the LORD God of hosts, the God of Israel: Why do you inflict so great an evil upon yourselves? Will you root out from Judah man and wife, child and nursling, and not leave yourselves even a remnant? 8 Will you go on provoking me by the works of your hands, by sacrificing to strange gods here in the land of Egypt where you have come to live? Will you be rooted out and become a curse and a disgrace among all the nations of the earth? 9 Have you forgotten the evil deeds which your fathers, and the kings of Judah and their wives, and you yourselves and your wives have done in the land of Judah and the streets of Jerusalem? 10 To this day they have not been crushed; they do not fear or follow the law and the statutes which I set before you and your fathers.

11 Hence, thus says the LORD of hosts, the God of Israel: I have determined evil against you; and I will uproot all Judah. 12 I will take away the remnant of Judah who insisted on coming to dwell in Egypt, so that they shall be wholly destroyed. In the land of Egypt they shall fall by the sword or be consumed by hunger. High and low, they shall die by the sword, or by hunger, and become an example of malediction, a horror, a curse and a reproach. 13 Thus will I punish those who live in Egypt, just as I punished Jerusalem with sword, hunger, and pestilence. None of the remnant of Judah that have come to settle in the land of Egypt shall escape or survive. 14 None shall return to the land of Judah, though they yearn to return and live there. Only scattered refugees shall return.

15 From all the men who knew that their wives were burning incense to strange gods, from all the women who were present in the immense crowd, and from all the people who lived in Lower and Upper Egypt,

Jeremiah received this answer: 16 "We will not listen to what you say in the name of the LORD. 17 Rather will we continue doing what we had proposed; we will burn incense to the queen of heaven and pour out libations to her, as we and our fathers, our kings and princes have done in the cities of Judah and the streets of Jerusalem. Then we had enough food to eat and we were well off; we suffered no misfortune. 18 But since we stopped burning incense to the queen of heaven and pouring out libations to her, we are in need of everything and are being destroyed by the sword and by hunger. 19 And when we burned incense to the queen of heaven and poured out libations to her, was it without our husbands' consent that we baked for her cakes in her image and poured out libations to her?"

20 To all the people, men and women, who gave him this answer, Jeremiah said: 21 Was it not this that the LORD remembered and brought to mind, that you burned incense in the cities of Judah and the streets of Jerusalem: you, your fathers, your kings and princes, and the people generally? 22 The LORD could no longer bear your evil deeds, the horrible things which you were doing; and so your land became a waste, a desert, a thing accursed and without inhabitants, as it is today. 23 Because you burned incense and sinned against the LORD, not obeying the voice of the LORD, not living by his law, his statutes, and his decrees, this evil has befallen you at the present day.

24 Jeremiah said further to all the people, including the women: Hear the word of the LORD, all you Judeans in the land of Egypt: 25 Thus says the LORD of hosts, the God of Israel: You and your wives have stated your intentions, and kept them in fact: "We will continue to fulfill the vows we have made to burn incense to the queen of heaven and to pour out libations to her." Very well! keep your vows, carry out

your resolutions! 26 But listen then to the word of the LORD, all you people of Judah who live in Egypt; I swear by my own great name, says the LORD, in the whole land of Egypt no man of Judah shall henceforth pronounce my name, saying, "As the Lord GOD lives." 27 I am watching over them to do evil, not good. All the men of Judah in Egypt shall perish by the sword or famine until they are utterly destroyed. 28 Those who escape the sword to return from the land of Egypt to the land of Judah shall be few in number. The whole remnant of Judah who came to settle in Egypt shall know whose word stands, mine or theirs.

29 That you may know how surely my threats of punishment for you shall be fulfilled, this shall be a sign to you, says the LORD, that I will punish you in this place. 30 Thus says the LORD: See! I will hand over Pharaoh Hophra, king of Egypt, to his enemies, to those who seek his life, just as I handed over Zedekiah, king of Judah, to his enemy and mortal foe, Nebuchadnezzar, king of Babylon.

A Message to Baruch

45 This is the message that the prophet Jeremiah gave to Baruch, son of Neriah, when he wrote in a book the prophecies that Jeremiah dictated in the fourth year of Jehoiakim, son of Josiah, king of Judah: 2 Thus says the LORD, God of Israel, to you, Baruch, 3 because you said, "Alas! the LORD adds grief to my pain; I am weary from groaning, and can find no rest": 4 say this to him, says the LORD: What I have built, I am tearing down; what I have planted, I am uprooting: even the whole land. 5 And do you seek great things for yourself? Seek them not! I am bringing evil on all mankind, says the LORD, but your life I will leave you as booty, wherever you may go.

44, 30: *Hophra:* killed by his own people. The ruler of Egypt at the time of its conquest by Nebuchadnezzar was Hophra's successor Amasis, who was also slain by his enemies.

45, 1–5: At the conclusion of his narrative, Baruch appends a prophecy given him personally by Jeremiah when he first wrote down Jeremiah's words (cf chap. 36). The future revealed by the prophet had

depressed Baruch; this prophecy was to assure him of his personal safety, while repeating the Lord's determination to destroy Judah.

ORACLES AGAINST THE NATIONS

46 This is the word of the LORD that came to the prophet Jeremiah against the nations.

Against Egypt

2 Concerning Egypt. Against the army of Pharaoh Neco, king of Egypt, which was defeated at Carchemish on the Euphrates by Nebuchadnezzar, king of Babylon, in the fourth year of Jehoiakim, son of Josiah, king of Judah:

3 Prepare shield and buckler!
　　march to battle!
4 Harness the horses,
　　mount, charioteers!
Fall in with your helmets;
　　polish your spears, put on
　　　your breastplates.
5 What do I see?
　　With broken ranks
They fall back;
　　their heroes are routed,
They flee headlong
　　without making a stand.
Terror on every side,
　　says the LORD!
6 The swift cannot flee,
　　nor the hero escape:
There in the north, on the
　　Euphrates' bank,
they stumble and fall.

7 Who is this that surges forward
　　like the Nile,
　　like rivers of billowing waters?
8 Egypt surges like the Nile,
　　like rivers of billowing waters.
"I will surge forward," he says,
　　and cover the earth,
　　destroying the city and its
　　　people.
9 Forward, horses!
　　drive madly, chariots!
Set out, warriors,
　　Cush and Put, bearing your
　　　shields,
　　Men of Lud, stretching your
　　　bows!"

10 But this is the day of the Lord
　　GOD of hosts,
　　a day of vengeance, vengeance
　　　on his foes!
The sword devours, is sated,
　　drunk with their blood:
for the Lord GOD of hosts
　　holds a slaughter feast
in the northland, on the
　　Euphrates.

11 Go up to Gilead, and take balm,
　　O virgin daughter Egypt!
No use to multiply remedies;
　　for you there is no cure.
12 The nations hear of your shame,
　　your cries fill the earth.
Warrior trips over warrior,
　　both fall together.

13 The message which the LORD gave to the prophet Jeremiah concerning the advance of Nebuchadnezzar, king of Babylon, to attack the land of Egypt:

14 Announce it in Egypt, publish it
　　in Migdol,
　　proclaim it in Memphis and
　　　Tahpanhes!
Say: Take your stand, prepare
　　yourselves,
　　the sword has already
　　devoured your neighbors.
15 Why has Apis fled,
　　your mighty one failed to
　　　stand?
The LORD thrust him down;
16 　he stumbled repeatedly, and
　　　fell.
They said one to another,
　　"Up! let us return to our own
　　　people,
To the land of our birth,
　　away from the destroying
　　　sword."

17 Call Pharaoh, king of Egypt,
　　by the name
　　"The noise that let its time
　　　go by."
18 As I live, says the King
　　whose name is LORD of hosts,

Like Tabor among the
　　mountains he shall come,
　　like Carmel above the sea.
19 Pack your baggage for exile,
　　capital city of daughter Egypt;
Memphis shall become a desert,
　　an empty ruin.

20 Egypt is a pretty heifer,
　　from the north a horsefly
　　lights upon her.
21 The mercenaries in her ranks
　　are like fatted calves;
They too turn and flee together,
　　stand not their ground,
When the day of their ruin
　　comes upon them,
　　the time of their punishment.
22 She sounds like a retreating
　　reptile!
　　Yes, they come in force;
　　like woodchoppers, they
　　attack her with axes.
23 They cut down her forest, says
　　the LORD,
　　impenetrable though it be;
More numerous than locusts,
　　they cannot be counted.
24 Disgraced is daughter Egypt,
　　handed over to the people
　　of the north.

25 The LORD of hosts, the God of Israel, has said: See! I will punish Amon of Thebes, and Egypt, her gods and her kings, Pharaoh, and those who trust in him. 26 I will hand them over to those who seek their lives, to Nebuchadnezzar, king of Babylon, and his ministers. But later on Egypt shall be inhabited again, as in times past, says the LORD.

27 But you, my servant Jacob,
　　fear not;
be not dismayed, O Israel.
Behold, I will deliver you from
　　the far-off land,
　　your descendants, from their
　　land of exile.
Jacob shall again find rest,
　　shall be tranquil and
　　undisturbed.

46—51: In these chapters most of Jeremiah's oracles against the foreign nations have been gathered together and placed at the end of his book; in the Greek text they appear with the other oracles against the nations, in chap. 25. In general, they are in chronological order: 46, 1—49, 33, from the fourth year of Jehoiakim; 49, 34-39, at the beginning of Zedekiah's reign; 50, 1—51, 64, from the fourth year of Zedekiah.

46, 2: *Carchemish on the Euphrates:* the western terminus of the Mesopotamian trade route, where Nebuchadnezzar defeated Neco in 605 B.C., thus gaining undisputed control of Syria and Palestine.
46, 13: In 601 B.C. Nebuchadnezzar advanced against Egypt and even entered the country, but finally had to withdraw to Syria.
46, 15: *Apis:* the chief god of Memphis, venerated in the form of a black bull.

46, 17: *"The noise . . . go by":* in Hebrew there is wordplay here on the name Hophra, who still made a pretense of power though his career was at an end.
46, 18: *Tabor . . . Carmel:* outstanding mountains of Palestine, symbols of strength, to which Nebuchadnezzar is compared.
46, 25: *Amon:* the sun-god worshiped at Thebes, in Upper Egypt.

28 You, my servant Jacob, never
        fear, says the LORD,
     for I am with you;
   I will make an end of all the
        nations
     to which I have driven you,
   But of you I will not make an
        end:
     I will chastise you as you
        deserve,
     I will not let you go
        unpunished.

Against the Philistines

47 This is the word that came
        from the LORD to the prophet
Jeremiah concerning the Philistines,
before Pharaoh attacked Gaza: 2
Thus says the LORD:

   Behold: waters are rising from
        the north,
     a torrent in flood;
   It shall flood the land and all
        that is in it,
     the cities and their people.
   All the people of the land
     set up a wailing cry.
3 They hear the stamping hooves
        of his steeds,
     the rattling chariots, the
        rumbling wheels.
   Fathers turn not to save their
        children;
     their hands fall helpless
4 Because of the day which has
        come
     to ruin all the Philistines,
   And cut off from Tyre and
        Sidon
     the last of their allies.
   Yes, the LORD is destroying
        the Philistines,
     the remnant from the coasts
        of Caphtor.
5 Gaza is shaved bald,
     Ashkelon is reduced to silence;
   Ashdod, the remnant of their
        strength,
     how long will you gash
        yourself?
6 Alas, sword of the LORD!
     how long till you find rest?
   Return into your scabbard;
     stop, be still!

7 How can it find rest
     when the LORD has
        commanded it?
   Against Ashkelon and the
        seashore
     he has appointed it.

Against Moab

48 Concerning Moab, thus says
        the LORD of hosts, the God of
Israel:

   Woe to Nebo, it is laid waste;
     Kiriathaim is disgraced and
        captured,
   Disgraced and overthrown is the
        stronghold:
2   Moab's glory is no more.
   Evil they plan against Heshbon:
     "Come, let us put an end to
        her as a people."
   You, too, Madmen, shall be
        reduced to silence;
     behind you stalks the sword.
3 Listen! a cry from Horonaim
     of ruin and great destruction!
4 Moab is crushed,
     their outcry is heard in Zoar.
5 The ascent of Luhith
     they climb weeping;
   On the descent to Horonaim
     the cry of destruction is heard.
6 "Flee, save your lives,
     to survive like the wild ass
        in the desert!"
7 Because you trusted in your
        works and your treasures,
     you also shall be captured.
   Chemosh shall go into exile,
     his priests and princes with
        him.
8 The destroyer comes upon every
        city,
     not a city escapes;
   Ruined is the valley,
     wasted the plain, as the LORD
        has said.
9 Set up a memorial for Moab,
     for it is an utter wasteland;
   Its cities are turned into ruins
     where no one dwells.
10 [Cursed be he who does the
        LORD's work remissly,
     cursed he who holds back
        his sword from blood.]

11 Moab has been tranquil from
        his youth,
     has rested upon his lees;
   He was not poured from one
        flask to another,
     he went not into exile.
   Thus he kept his taste,
     and his scent was not lost.

12 Hence, the days shall come,
says the LORD, when I will send him
coopers to run him over; they shall
empty his flasks and break his jars.
13 Chemosh shall disappoint Moab,
as Israel was disappointed by Bethel
in which they trusted.

14 How can you say, "We are
        heroes,
     men valiant in war"?
15 The ravager of Moab and his
        cities advances,
     the flower of his youth goes
        down to be slaughtered,
     says the King, the LORD of
        hosts by name.
16 Near at hand is Moab's ruin,
     his disaster hastens apace.
17 Mourn for him, all you his
        neighbors,
     all you who knew him well!
   Say: How the strong staff is
        broken,
     the glorious rod!
18 Come down from glory, sit on
        the ground,
     you that dwell in Dibon;
   Moab's ravager has come up
        against you,
     he has ruined your
        strongholds.
19 Stand by the wayside, watch
        closely,
     you that dwell in Aroer;
   Ask the man who flees, the
        woman who tries to escape:
     say to them, "What has
        happened?"
20 Moab is disgraced, yes,
        destroyed,
     howl and cry out;
   Publish it at the Arnon,
     Moab is ruined!

21 For judgment has come on the
land of the plateau: on Holon,

47, 2–7: This prophecy was fulfilled in 605/4 B.C.
47, 4: *Tyre and Sidon:* Phoenician cities associated
commercially with the Philistines, and enemies of
Nebuchadnezzar; cf 27, 1–4. Nebuchadnezzar
carried out a thirteen-year siege of Tyre which was
only partially successful. *Caphtor:* probably the
island of Crete, the traditional place of origin of the
Philistines; cf Am 9, 7.
47, 5: Of the ancient Philistine cities, neither Gath
nor Ekron (25, 20) is mentioned in this period of
waning independence of the seacoast.
47, 6: Words of the Philistines.
48, 1–47: Moab was one of the Israelites' bitterest
enemies. According to Flavius Josephus, Moab and
Ammon were conquered by Nebuchadnezzar in his
twenty-third year, 582 B.C., five years after the
destruction of Jerusalem.
48, 7: *Chemosh:* chief god of the Moabites.

Jahzah, and Mephaath, 22 on Dibon, Nebo, and Beth-diblathaim, 23 on Kariathaim, Beth-gamul, and Beth-meon, 24 on Kerioth and on Bozrah: on all the cities of Moab, far and near.

25 Moab's strength is broken,
    his might is shattered, says
        the LORD.

26 Because he boasted against the LORD, make Moab drunk so that he retches and vomits, and he too becomes a laughingstock. 27 Is Israel a laughingstock to you? Was she caught among thieves, that you shake your head whenever you speak of her?

28 Leave the cities, dwell in the
        crags,
    you that dwell in Moab.
Be like a dove that nests
    out of reach on the edge of a
        chasm.
29 We have heard of the pride of
        Moab,
    pride beyond bounds:
His loftiness, his pride, his
        scorn,
    his insolence of heart.
30 I know, says the LORD, his
        arrogance;
    liar in boast, liar in deed.
31 And so I wail over Moab,
    over all Moab I cry,
    over the men of Kir-heres I
        moan.
32 More than for Jazer I weep over
        you,
    vineyard of Sibmah.
Your tendrils trailed down to
        the sea,
    as far as Jazer they stretched.
Upon your harvest, upon your
        vintage,
    the ravager has fallen.
33 Joy and jubilation are at an end
    in the fruit gardens of the
        land of Moab.
I drain the wine from the wine
        vats,
    the treader treads no more,
    the vintage shout is stilled.

34 The cry of Heshbon and Elealeh is heard as far as Jahaz; they call from Zoar to Horonaim,

and to Eglath-shelishiyah, for even the waters of Nimrim turn into a desert. 35 I will leave no one in Moab, says the LORD, to offer a holocaust on the high place, or to burn incense to his gods. 36 Hence the wail of flutes for Moab is in my heart; for the men of Kir-heres the wail of flutes is in my heart: the wealth they acquired has perished. 37 Every head has been made bald, every beard shaved; every hand is gashed, and the loins of all are clothed in sackcloth. 38 On every roof of Moab and in all his squares there is mourning; I have shattered Moab like a pot that no one wants, says the LORD. 39 How terror seizes Moab, and wailing! How he turns his back in shame! Moab has become a laughingstock and a horror to all his neighbors! 40 For thus says the LORD:

Behold, like an eagle he soars,
    spreads his wings over Moab.
41 Cities are taken,
    strongholds seized:
On that day the hearts of
        Moab's heroes
    are like the heart of a woman
        in travail.
42 Moab shall be destroyed, no
        more a people,
    because he boasted against
        the LORD.
43 Terror, pit, and trap be upon
        you,
    people of Moab, says the
        LORD.
44 He who flees from the terror
    falls into the pit;
He who climbs from the pit
    is caught in the trap;
For I will bring these things
        upon Moab
    in the year of their
        punishment, says the LORD.
45 In Heshbon's shadow stop
        short
    the exhausted refugees;
For fire breaks forth from
        Heshbon,
    and a blaze from the house
        of Sihon:
It consumes the brow of Moab,
    the skull of the noisemakers.

46 Woe to you, O Moab,
    you are ruined, O people of
        Chemosh!
Your sons are taken into exile,
    your daughters into captivity.
47 But I will change the lot of
        Moab
    in the days to come, says the
        LORD.

Thus far the judgment on Moab.

Against the Ammonites

49 Concerning the Ammonites,
    thus says the LORD:
Has Israel no sons?
    has he no heir?
Why then has Milcom
    disinherited Gad,
    why have his people settled
        in Gad's cities?
2 But the days are coming, says
        the LORD,
    when against Rabbah of the
        Ammonites
I will sound the battle alarm;
    She shall become a mound of
        ruins,
    and her daughter cities shall
        be destroyed by fire.
Israel shall inherit those who
    disinherited her,
    says the LORD.
3 Howl, Heshbon, for the ravager
        approaches,
    shriek, daughters of Rabbah!
Put on sackcloth and mourn,
    run to and fro, gashing
        yourselves;
For Milcom goes into exile
    along with his priests and
        captains.
4 Why do you glory in your
        strength,
    your ebbing strength,
        rebellious daughter?
You who trust in your treasures,
        saying,
    "Who can come against me?"
5 I am bringing terror upon you,
    says the Lord GOD of hosts,
    from all round about you;
You shall be scattered, each man
    in headlong flight,
    with no one to rally the
        fugitives.

49, 1: *Milcom:* chief god of the Ammonites. The Transjordan tribe of Gad bordered on Ammon, and after the collapse of the northern kingdom the

Ammonites occupied its territory.
49, 2: *Rabbah of the Ammonites:* or Rabbath-Ammon, capital of the Ammonite kingdom. The

modern Amman is the capital of the kingdom of Jordan.

6 But afterward I will change the
　　lot
　　of the Ammonites, says the
　　LORD.

Against Edom

7 Concerning Edom, thus says the
LORD of hosts:

Is there no more wisdom in
　　Teman,
　has counsel perished from the
　　prudent,
　has their wisdom become
　　corrupt?
8 Flee, retreat, hide in deep holes,
　you who live in Dedan:
For I will bring destruction
　　upon Esau
　when I come to punish him.
9 If vintagers came upon you,
　they would leave no gleanings;
If thieves by night,
　they would destroy as they
　　pleased.
10 So I myself will strip Esau;
I will uncover his retreats so
　　that he cannot hide.
He is ruined: sons, and brothers,
　and neighbors, so that he is
　　no more.
11 Leave your orphans behind, I
　will keep them alive;
　your widows, let them trust
　　in me.

12 For thus says the LORD: Even
those not sentenced to drink the cup
must drink it! Shall you then go
unpunished? You shall not go
unpunished; you shall surely drink
it. 13 By my own self I have sworn,
says the LORD: Bozrah shall become
an object of horror and a disgrace,
a desolation and a curse; she and
all her cities shall become ruins
forever.

14 I have heard a report from the
　　LORD,
　a herald has been sent among
　　the nations:
　Gather together, move against
　　her,
　rise up for battle.

15 Small will I make you among
　　the nations,
　despised among men!
16 The terror you spread beguiled
　　you,
　and your presumption of
　　heart;
You that live in rocky crags,
　that hold the heights of the
　　hill:
Though you build your nest
　high as the eagle,
　from there I will drag you
　　down, says the LORD.

17 Edom shall become an object
of horror. Every passer-by shall be
appalled and catch his breath at all
her wounds. 18 As when Sodom,
Gomorrah, and their neighbors were
overthrown, says the LORD, not a
man shall dwell there: no one shall
visit there.

19 As when a lion comes up from
　　the thicket of Jordan
　to the permanent feeding
　　grounds,
So I, in an instant, will drive
　men off;
　and whom I choose I will
　　establish there!
For who is like me? who can
　call me to account?
What shepherd can stand
　against me?
20 Therefore, hear the counsel of
　　the LORD,
　which he has taken against
　　Edom;
Hear the plans he has made
　against those that live in
　　Teman:
They shall be dragged away,
　even the smallest sheep,
　their own pasture shall be
　　aghast because of them.
21 At the noise of their fall the
　　earth quakes,
　to the Red Sea the outcry is
　　heard!
22 See! like an eagle he soars aloft,
　and spreads his wings over
　　Bozrah;

On that day the hearts of
　Edom's heroes shall be
like the heart of a woman in
　travail.

Against Damascus

Concerning Damascus.

23 Hamath and Arpad are covered
　　with shame,
　they have heard bad news;
Worried, they toss like the sea
　which cannot rest.
24 Damascus is weakened, she
　　turns to flee,
　panic has seized her.
Distress and pangs take hold of
　　her,
　like those of a woman in
　　travail.
25 How can the city of glory be
　　forsaken,
　the town of delight!
26 But now her young men shall
　　fall in her streets,
　and all her warriors shall be
　　stilled.
On that day, says the LORD
　of hosts,
27 I will set fire to the wall of
　　Damascus,
　and it shall devour the palaces
　　of Ben-hadad.

Against Arabia

28 Of Kedar and the kingdoms of
Hazor, defeated by Nebuchadnez-
zar, king of Babylon, thus says the
LORD:

Rise up, attack Kedar,
　ravage the Easterners.
29 Their tents and herds shall be
　　taken away,
　their tent curtains and all
　　their goods;
Their camels they shall carry off
　for themselves,
　and shout from upon them,
　　"Terror on every side!"
30 Flee! leave your homes, hide in
　　deep holes,
　you that live in Hazor, says
　　the LORD;

49, 7–22: *Edom:* this implacable enemy from ancient times profited from Judah's downfall; cf Ob 11f.

49, 7: *Teman:* a district of Edom, used here for the whole country; it was famous for its wise men; cf Jb 2, 11.

49, 8: *Esau:* Jacob's brother, the traditional ancestor of the Edomites; cf Gn 36.

49, 13: *Bozrah:* capital of Edom, southeast of the Dead Sea.

49, 23: *Hamath and Arpad:* independent Aramean states to the north of Damascus; the invasion is con-

ceived as coming from the north. The situation is of the eighth century B.C. Cf Is 10, 9ff.

49, 27: *The palaces of Ben-hadad:* the royal palaces in Damascus, where at least three kings bore this name; cf 1 Kgs 15, 18; 20.

For counsel has been taken
against you,
a plan has been formed
against you
[Nebuchadnezzar, king of
Babylon].
31 Rise up! set out against a
nation that is at peace,
that lives secure, says the LORD,
That has no gates or bars,
and dwells alone.
32 Their camels shall be your booty,
their many herds your spoil;
I will scatter to the winds those
who shave their temples,
from all sides I will bring ruin
upon them,
says the LORD.
33 Hazor shall become a haunt of
jackals,
a desert forever,
Where no man lives,
no human being stays.

Against Elam

34 The following word of the
LORD against Elam came to the
prophet Jeremiah at the beginning of
the reign of Zedekiah, king of Judah:
35 Thus says the LORD of hosts

Behold, I will break the bow of
Elam,
the mainstay of their might.
36 I will bring upon Elam the four
winds
from the four ends of the
heavens:
I will scatter them to all these
winds, till there is no nation
to which the outcasts of Elam
shall not come.
37 I will break Elam before their
foes,
before those who seek their
life;
I will bring evil upon them,
my burning wrath, says the
LORD.
I will send the sword to pursue
them
until I have completely made
an end of them;

38 My throne I will set up in Elam
and destroy from there king
and princes,
says the LORD.
39 But in the days to come I will
change
the lot of Elam, says the LORD.

The First Prophecy against Babylon

50 The word which the LORD
spoke against Babylon, against
the land of the Chaldeans, through
the prophet Jeremiah:

2 Announce and publish it among
the nations;
publish it, hide it not, but say:
Babylon is taken, Bel confounded,
Merodach shattered;
her images are put to shame,
her idols shattered.
3 A people from the north
advances against her
to turn her land into a desert,
So that no one shall live there,
because man and beast have
fled away.
4 In those days, at that time, says
the LORD,
the men of Israel and of
Judah shall come,
Weeping as they come, to seek
the LORD, their God;
5 to their goal in Zion they
shall ask the way.
"Come, let us join ourselves to
the LORD
with covenant everlasting,
never to be forgotten."
6 Lost sheep were my people,
their shepherds misled them,
straggling on the mountains;
From mountain to hill they
wandered,
losing the way to their fold.
7 Whoever came upon them
devoured them,
and their enemies said,
"We incur no guilt,
Because they sinned against the
LORD,
the hope of their fathers,
their abode of justice."

8 Flee from Babylon, leave the
land of the Chaldeans,
be like the rams at the head
of the flock.
9 See, I am stirring up against
Babylon
a band of great nations from
the north;
from there they advance, and
she shall be taken.
Their arrows are arrows of the
skilled warrior;
none shall return without effect.
10 Chaldea shall be their plunder,
and all her plunderers shall
be enriched, says the LORD.
11 Yes, rejoice and exult,
you that plunder my portion;
Frisk like calves on the green,
snort like stallions!
12 Your mother shall be sorely
put to shame,
she that bore you shall be
abashed;
See, the last of the nations,
a desert, dry and waste.
13 Because of the LORD's wrath
she shall be empty,
and become a total desert;
Everyone who passes by Babylon
will be appalled
and catch his breath, at all
her wounds.
14 Take your posts encircling
Babylon,
you who bend the bow;
Shoot at her, spare not your
arrows,
15 raise the war cry against her
on all sides.
She surrenders, her bastions fall,
her walls are torn down:
Vengeance of the LORD is this!
Take revenge on her,
as she has done, do to her;
for she sinned against the
LORD.
16 Cut off from Babylon the sower
and him who wields the sickle
in harvest time!
Before the destroying sword,
each of them turns to his own
people,
everyone flees to his own land.

49, 34: *Elam:* the ancient kingdom to the east of
Babylonia.
50, 1—51, 58: a collection of miscellaneous prophecies against Babylon which now stands as the
introduction to the story in 51, 59–64. The Greek text
of 50, 1 omits *through the prophet Jeremiah*, and it is

in fact likely that these oracles are not Jeremiah's, but
were composed by other inspired writers after the fall
of Jerusalem, who may have used some of Jeremiah's
texts. Babylon fell to the Persians in 538 B.C.
50, 2: *Bel:* originally the name of the god of
Nippur in Mesopotamia, then identified with *Mero-*

dach (Marduk), chief god of Babylon.
50, 15: *Her walls are torn down:* the prophet is not
predicting the details of Babylon's downfall, but
describing such a downfall in conventional language.
Actually, Babylon was surrendered peaceably, without destruction.

17 A stray sheep was Israel
 that lions pursued;
Formerly the king of Assyria
 devoured her,
 now Nebuchadnezzar of
  Babylon gnaws her bones.

18 Therefore, thus says the LORD of
hosts, the God of Israel:

I will punish the king of Babylon
 and his land,
 as once I punished the king
  of Assyria;
19 But I will bring back Israel to
 her fold,
 to feed on Carmel and Bashan,
And on Mount Ephraim and
 Gilead,
 till she has her fill.

20 In those days, at that time, says
the LORD:

They shall seek Israel's guilt, but
 it shall be no more,
 and Judah's sins, but these shall
 no longer be found;
 for I will forgive the remnant I
 preserve.

21 Attack the land of Merathaim,
 and those who live in Pekod;
Slaughter and doom them, says
 the LORD,
 do all I have commanded you.
22 Battle alarm in the land,
 dire destruction!
23 How has the hammer of the
 whole earth
 been broken and shattered!
What an object of horror
 Babylon has become among
 the nations!
24 You ensnared yourself, and
 were caught,
 O Babylon, before you knew it!
You were discovered and seized,
 because you challenged the
 LORD.
25 The LORD opens his armory
 and brings forth the weapons
 of his wrath;
For the Lord GOD of hosts has
 work to do
 in the land of the Chaldeans.

26 Come upon her from every side,
 open her granaries,
Pile up her goods in heaps and
 doom it,
 leave not a remnant.
27 Slay all her oxen,
 let them go down to the
 slaughter;
Woe to them! their day has come,
 the time of their punishment.
28 Listen! the fugitives, the
 escaped
 from the land of Babylon:
They announce in Zion
 the vengeance of the LORD,
 our God.
29 Call up against Babylon archers,
 all who bend the bow;
Encamp around her,
 let no one escape.
Repay her for her deeds;
 as she has done, do to her,
For she insulted the LORD,
 the Holy One of Israel.
30 Therefore her young men shall
 fall in her streets,
 all her warriors shall perish
 on that day,
 says the LORD.

31 I am against you, man of
 insolence,
 says the Lord GOD of hosts;
For your day has come,
 the time for me to punish you.
32 Insolence stumbles and falls;
 there is no one to raise him up.
I will kindle in his cities a fire
 that shall devour everything
 around him.
33 Thus says the LORD of hosts:
Oppressed are the men of Israel,
 and with them the men of
 Judah;
All their captors hold them fast
 and refuse to let them go.
34 Strong is their avenger,
 whose name is LORD of hosts;
He will defend their cause with
 success,
 and give rest to the earth,
 but unrest to those who live
 in Babylon.

35 A sword upon the Chaldeans,
 says the LORD,
 upon Babylon's people, her
 princes and wise men!
36 A sword upon the soothsayers,
 that they may become fools!

A sword upon her warriors,
 that they may tremble;
37 A sword upon her motley throng,
 that they may become women!
A sword upon her treasures,
 that they may be plundered;
38 A sword upon her waters,
 that they may dry up!
For it is a land of idols,
 and they shall be made frantic
 by fearful things.
39 Hence, wildcats and desert beasts
 shall dwell there,
 and ostriches shall occupy it;
Never again shall it be peopled,
 or lived in,
 from age to age.
40 As when God overturned Sodom
 and Gomorrah, with their
 neighbors, says the LORD,
Not a man shall dwell there,
 no human being shall tarry
 there.

41 See! a people comes from the
 north,
 a great nation, and mighty kings
 roused from the ends of the
 earth.
42 Bow and javelin they wield,
 cruel and pitiless are they;
They sound like the roaring sea,
 as they ride forth on steeds,
Each in his place for battle
 against you, daughter Babylon.
43 The king of Babylon hears news
 of them,
 and helpless fall his hands;
Anguish seizes him,
 throes like a mother's in
 childbirth.
44 As when a lion comes up from
 the Jordan's thicket
 to the permanent feeding
 grounds,
So I, in one instant, will drive
 them off,
 and whom I choose I will
 establish there;
For who is like me? who calls
 me to account?
 what shepherd can stand
 against me?
45 Therefore hear the counsel of
 the LORD
 which he has taken against
 Babylon;
Hear the plans he has made
 against the land of the
 Chaldeans:

50, 21: *Merathaim*, "twice bitter," and *Pekod*,
"punishment," are here symbolic terms for Babylonia,
though probably they suggest also the names of
regions in that country.

They shall be dragged away,
  even the smallest sheep;
  their own pasture shall be
  aghast because of them.
46 At the cry "Babylon is
  captured!" the earth quakes;
  the outcry is heard among the
  nations.

The Second Prophecy against Babylon

51 Thus says the LORD:
  See! I rouse against Babylon,
    and against those who live in
      Chaldea,
    a destroying wind.
2 Against Babylon I will send
    winnowers
  to winnow her and lay waste
    her land;
  They shall besiege her from all
    sides
  on the day of affliction.
3 Let the bowman draw his bow,
    and flaunt his coat of mail;
  Spare not her young men,
    doom her entire army.
4 The slain shall fall in the land
    of Chaldea,
  the transfixed, in her streets;
5 For Israel and Judah are not
    widowed
  of their God, the LORD of
    hosts,
  And the Chaldean land is full
    of guilt
  to be punished by the Holy
    One of Israel.

6 Flee out of Babylon;
  let each one save his life,
    perish not for her guilt;
  This is a time of vengeance for
    the LORD,
  he pays her her due.
7 Babylon was a golden cup in
    the hand of the LORD
  which made the whole earth
    drunk;
  The nations drank its wine,
    with this they have become
      mad.
8 Babylon suddenly falls and is
    crushed:
  howl over her!
  Bring balm for her wounds,
    in case she can be healed.

9 "We have tried to heal Babylon,
    but she cannot be healed.
  Leave her, let us go, each to
    his own land."
  Her judgment reaches heaven,
    it touches the clouds.
10 The LORD has brought to light
    our just cause;
  come, let us tell in Zion
  what the LORD, our God, has
    done.

11 Sharpen the arrows,
    fill the quivers;
  The LORD has stirred up the
    spirit of Media's kings;
  Babylon he is resolved to
    destroy.
  Yes, it is the vengeance of the
    LORD,
  vengeance for his temple.
12 Against the walls of Babylon
    raise a signal,
  make strong the watch;
  Post sentries,
    arrange ambushes!
  For the LORD has planned and
    he will carry out
  his threat against the
    inhabitants of Babylon.
13 You who dwell by mighty waters,
    rich in treasure,
  Your end has come,
    the term at which you shall
      be cut off!

14 The LORD of hosts has sworn
    by himself:
  I will fill you with men as
    numerous as locusts,
  who shall raise over you the
    vintage shout!
15 He has sworn who made the
    earth by his power,
  and established the world by
    his wisdom,
  and stretched out the heavens
    by his skill.
16 When he thunders, the waters in
    the heavens roar,
  and he brings up clouds from
    the end of the earth;
  He makes the lightning flash
    in the rain,
  and releases stormwinds from
    their chambers.

17 Every man is stupid, ignorant;
  every artisan is put to shame
    by his idol:
  He molded a fraud,
    without breath of life.
18 Nothingness are they, a
    ridiculous work,
  that will perish in their time
    of punishment.
19 Not like these is the portion of
    Jacob,
  he is the creator of all things;
  Israel is his very own tribe,
  LORD of hosts is his name.

20 You are my hammer,
    my weapon for war;
  With you I shatter nations,
    with you I destroy kingdoms.
21 With you I shatter horse and
    rider,
  with you I shatter chariot
    and driver.
22 With you I shatter man and
    wife,
  with you I shatter old and
    young,
  with you I shatter youth and
    maiden.
23 With you I shatter the shepherd
    and his flock,
  with you I shatter the farmer
    and his team,
  with you I shatter satraps
    and prefects.
24 Thus will I repay Babylon,
  and all who live in Chaldea
  All the evil they did to Zion,
    as you shall see with your
      own eyes, says the LORD.

25 Beware! I am against you,
    destroying mountain,
  destroyer of the entire earth,
    says the LORD;
  I will stretch forth my hand
    against you,
  roll you down over the cliffs,
  and make you a burnt
    mountain:
26 They will not take from you a
    cornerstone,
  or a foundation stone;
  Ruins forever shall you be,
    says the LORD.

51, 11: *Media's kings:* the Medes dwelt with the Persians in the land now known as Iran. At the time these words were written the Medes were the dominant people of the two, but within a short time the Persians had gained the ascendancy.

27 Raise a signal on the earth,
    blow the trumpet among the
      nations;
 Dedicate peoples to war
    against her,
    summon against her the
      kingdoms,
      Ararat, Minni, and Ashkenaz;
 Appoint recruiting officers
    against her,
    send up horses like bristling
      locusts.
28 Dedicate people to war against
    her:
    the king of Media,
 Its governors and all its prefects,
    every land in his domain.
29 The earth quakes and writhes,
    the LORD's plan against
      Babylon is carried out,
 Turning the land of Babylon
    into a desert where no one lives.
30 Babylon's warriors have ceased
    to fight,
    they remain in their
      strongholds;
 Dried up is their strength,
    they have become women.
 Burned are their homes,
    and broken their bars.
31 One runner meets another,
    herald meets herald,
 Telling the king of Babylon
    that all his city is taken.
32 The fords have been seized,
    and the fortresses set on fire,
    while warriors are in panic.

33 For thus says the LORD of hosts,
the God of Israel:

    Daughter Babylon is like a
      threshing floor
    at the time it is trodden;
 Yet a little while,
    and the harvest time will
      come for her.
34 He has consumed me, routed me,
    [Nebuchadnezzar, king of
      Babylon,]
    he has left me as an empty
      vessel;
 He has swallowed me like a
    dragon:
    filled his belly with my
      delights, and cast me out.

51, 27: *Ararat, Minni, and Ashkenaz:* regions or
people in what is now Armenia, subject at this time
to Media.
   51, 34f: *Me, my:* refers to Jerusalem.

35 My torn flesh be upon Babylon,
    says the city on Zion;
 My blood upon the people of
    Chaldea,
    says Jerusalem.
36   But now, thus says the LORD:
 Surely I will defend your cause,
    I will avenge you;
 I will dry up her sea,
    and drain her fountain.
37 Babylon shall become a heap
    of ruins,
    a haunt of jackals;
 A place of horror and ridicule,
    where no one lives.
38 They all roar like lions,
    growl like lion cubs.
39 When they are parched, I will
    set a drink before them
    to make them drunk, that they
      may be overcome
    with perpetual sleep, never
      to awaken, says the LORD.

40 I will bring them down like
    lambs to the slaughter,
    like rams and goats.
41 How has she been seized,
    made captive,
    the glory of the whole world!
 What a horror has Babylon
    become among nations:
42   against Babylon the sea rises,
    she is overwhelmed by the
      roaring waves!
43 Her cities have become a desert,
    parched and arid land
 Where no man lives,
    and no one passes through.
44 I will punish Bel in Babylon,
    and make him disgorge what
      he swallowed;
    peoples shall stream to him
      no more.
 The wall of Babylon falls!
45   Leave her, my people, let
    each one save himself
    from the burning wrath of
      the LORD.

46 Be not discouraged for fear of
rumors spread in the land; this year
the rumor comes, then violence in the
land, tyrant against tyrant. 47 But
behold, the days are coming when
I will punish the idols of Babylon;
her whole land shall be put to shame,
and all her slain shall lie fallen within
her. 48 Then heaven, and earth,
and everything in them shall shout
over Babylon with joy, when the

destroyers come against her from the
north, says the LORD. 49 Babylon,
too, must fall, O slain of Israel, as at
the hands of Babylon have fallen the
slain of all the earth.

50 You who have escaped the
    sword,
    go on, stand not still;
 Remember the LORD from afar,
    let Jerusalem come to your
      minds.
51 We are ashamed because we
    have heard taunts,
    confusion covers our faces;
    strangers have entered
    the holy places of the house
      of the LORD.
52 But behold, the days are
    coming, says the LORD,
    when I will punish her idols,
    and in her whole land the
      wounded will groan.
53 Though Babylon scale the
    heavens,
    and make her strong heights
      inaccessible,
    destroyers from me shall reach
      her, says the LORD.
54 Hear! loud cries from Babylon,
    dire destruction from the land
      of the Chaldeans;
55 For the LORD lays Babylon waste,
    stills her loud cry,
 Though her waves were roaring
    like mighty waters,
    and their clamor was heard
      afar.
56 For the destroyer comes upon
    her, [Babylon,]
    her heroes are captured, their
      bows broken;
 The LORD is a God who requites,
    he will surely repay.

57 I will make her princes and her
wise men drunk, her governors, her
prefects, and her warriors, so that
they sleep an eternal sleep, never to
awaken, says the King, whose name
is the LORD of hosts. 58 Thus says
the LORD of hosts:

    The walls of spacious Babylon
      shall be leveled utterly;
    her lofty gates shall be
      destroyed by fire.
 The toil of the nations is for
    nothing;
    for the flames the peoples
      weary themselves.

The Prophecy Sent to Babylon

59 This was the errand given by the prophet Jeremiah to Seraiah, son of Neriah, son of Mahseiah, when he went to Babylon for the king in the fourth year of the reign of Zedekiah; Seraiah was chief quartermaster. 60 Jeremiah had written all the misfortune that was to befall Babylon in a single book: all these words that were written against Babylon. 61 And Jeremiah said to Seraiah: When you reach Babylon, see that you read aloud all these words, 62 and then say: "O LORD, you yourself threatened to destroy this place, so that neither man nor beast should dwell in it, since it would remain an everlasting desert." 63 When you have finished reading this book, tie a stone to it and throw it in the Euphrates, 64 and say: Thus shall Babylon sink. Never shall she rise, because of the evil I am bringing upon her. [To "weary themselves" are the words of Jeremiah.]

HISTORICAL APPENDIX

Capture of Jerusalem

52 Zedekiah was twenty-one years old when he became king, and he reigned eleven years in Jerusalem. His mother's name was Hamutal, daughter of Jeremiah of Libnah. 2 He did what was evil in the eyes of the LORD, just as Jehoiakim had done. 3 Indeed, what was done in Jerusalem and in Judah so angered the LORD that he cast them out from his presence.

Zedekiah rebelled against the king of Babylon. 4 In the tenth month of the ninth year of his reign, on the tenth day of the month, Nebuchadnezzar, king of Babylon, and his whole army advanced against Jerusalem, encamped around it, and built siege walls on every side. 5 The siege of the city continued until the eleventh year of King Zedekiah.

6 On the ninth day of the fourth month, when famine had gripped the city and the people had no more bread, 7 the city walls were breached. Then all the soldiers took to flight and left the city by night through the gate between the two walls which was near the king's garden. With the Chaldeans surrounding the city, they went in the direction of the Arabah. 8 But the Chaldean army pursued the king and overtook Zedekiah in the desert near Jericho, while his whole army fled from him.

9 The king, therefore, was arrested and brought to Riblah, in the land of Hamath, to the king of Babylon, who pronounced sentence on him. 10 As Zedekiah looked on, the king of Babylon slew his sons as well as all the princes of Judah at Riblah. 11 Then he blinded Zedekiah, bound him with fetters, and had him brought to Babylon and kept in prison until the day of his death.

Destruction of Jerusalem

12 On the tenth day of the fifth month (this was in the nineteenth year of Nebuchadnezzar, king of Babylon), Nebuzaradan, captain of the bodyguard, came to Jerusalem as the representative of the king of Babylon. 13 He burned the house of the LORD, the palace of the king, and all the houses of Jerusalem; every large building he destroyed with fire. 14 And the Chaldean troops who were with the captain of the guard tore down all the walls that surrounded Jerusalem.

15 Then Nebuzaradan, captain of the guard, led into exile the rest of the people left in the city, and those who had deserted to the king of Babylon, and the rest of the artisans. 16 But some of the country's poor, Nebuzaradan, captain of the guard, left behind as vinedressers and farmers.

17 The bronze pillars that belonged to the house of the LORD, and the wheeled carts and the bronze sea in the house of the LORD, the Chaldeans broke into pieces; they carried away all the bronze to Babylon. 18 They took also the pots, the shovels, the snuffers, the bowls, the pans, and all the bronze vessels used for service. 19 The basins also, the fire holders, the bowls, the pots, the lampstands, the pans, the sacrificial bowls which were of gold or silver, these too the captain of the guard carried off, 20 as well as the two pillars, the one sea, and the twelve oxen of bronze under the sea, and the wheeled carts which King Solomon had made for the house of the LORD. The bronze of all these furnishings could not be weighed.

21 Each of the pillars was eighteen cubits high and twelve cubits in diameter; each was four fingers thick, and hollow inside. 22 A bronze capital five cubits high surmounted the one pillar, and a network with pomegranates encircled the capital, all of brass; and so for the other pillar. The pomegranates ... 23 there were ninety-six pomegranates. There were a hundred pomegranates, all around the network.

24 The captain of the guard also took Seraiah, the high priest, Zephaniah, the second priest, and the three keepers of the entry. 25 And from the city he took one courtier, a commander of soldiers, and seven men in the personal service of the king who were present in the city, and the scribe of the army commander who mustered the people of the land, and sixty of the common people who were in the city. 26 The captain of the guard, Nebuzaradan, arrested these and brought them to the king of Babylon at Riblah, 27 who had them struck down and put to death in Riblah, in the land of Hamath.

51, 59: *Seraiah:* the brother of Baruch; cf 32, 12. *The king:* Zedekiah. Perhaps Seraiah went to Babylon to explain away the presence of foreign ambassadors in Jerusalem that same year; cf 27, 3.

51, 60: Jeremiah prophesied against Babylon, even as he foretold Judah's release from Babylon's power (3, 14–18; 32, 15; 33, 6–9.12f); but his *book* against Babylon was thrown in the Euphrates (v 63). The preceding oracles were composed by later writers; see note on 50, 1—51, 58.

51, 64: *To "weary themselves" are the words of Jeremiah:* an editorial remark concerning the end of v 58.

52, 1–34: This supplement to the Book of Jeremiah was taken by the final editor from 2 Kgs 24, 18—25, 30 and placed here in order to show the fulfillment of Jeremiah's prophecies. In part this repeats the history given in Jer 39—41; the history of Gedaliah in 2 Kgs 25, 22–26, however, has not been reproduced here.

52, 4: *In the tenth month of the ninth year of his reign, on the tenth day of the month:* January 15, 588 B.C. Cf 39, 1.

52, 12: *On the tenth day of the fifth month ... nineteenth year:* the tenth of Ab—July/August in 587 B.C.

Thus was Judah exiled from her land.　28 This is the number of the people whom Nebuchadnezzar led away captive: in his seventh year, three thousand and twenty-three people of Judah;　29 in the eighteenth year of Nebuchadnezzar, eight hundred and thirty-two persons from Jerusalem;　30 in the twenty-third year of Nebuchadnezzar, Nebuzaradan, captain of the guard, exiled seven hundred and forty-five people of Judah: four thousand six hundred persons in all.

Favor Shown to Jehoiachin

31 In the thirty-seventh year of the exile of Jehoiachin, king of Judah, on the twenty-fifth day of the twelfth month, Evil-merodach, king of Babylon, in the inaugural year of his reign, took up the case of Jehoiachin, king of Judah, and released him from prison.　32 He spoke kindly to him and gave him a throne higher than that of the other kings who were with him in Babylon.　33 Jehoiachin took off his prison garb and ate at the king's table as long as he lived.　34 The allowance given him by the king of Babylon was a perpetual allowance, in fixed daily amounts, all the days of his life until the day of his death.

52, 28–30: These verses are missing in the Greek text and have not been taken from 2 Kgs 25, but from some other source using a different system of chronology. Besides the deportations of 598 and 587 B.C., mention is made here of a final one that took place in the year 582/1, possibly as a sequel to the murder of Gedaliah, cf 41, 2.

52, 31–34: In the year 561/60 B.C., Jehoiachin was released from prison by Nebuchadnezzar's successor Awel-Marduk (Evil-merodach), who reigned only two years. Babylonian records confirm the fact that Jehoiachin and his family were supported at public expense.

52, 32: *The other kings:* who had also been brought as captives to Babylon.

Lamentations

Jerusalem Abandoned and Disgraced

HOW lonely she is now, the once crowded city! Widowed is she who was mistress over nations; The princess among the provinces has been made a toiling slave. 2 Bitterly she weeps at night, tears upon her cheeks, With not one to console her of all her dear ones;

Her friends have all betrayed her
and become her enemies.

3 Judah has fled into exile
from oppression and cruel
slavery;
Yet where she lives among the
nations
she finds no place to rest:
All her persecutors come upon
her
where she is narrowly confined.

4 The roads to Zion mourn
for lack of pilgrims going to
her feasts;
All her gateways are deserted,
her priests groan,
Her virgins sigh;
she is in bitter grief.

5 Her foes are uppermost,
her enemies are at ease;
The LORD has punished her
for her many sins.
Her little ones have gone away,
captive before the foe.

6 Gone from daughter Zion
is all her glory:

Her princes, like rams
that find no pasture,
Have gone off without strength
before their captors.

7 Jerusalem is mindful of the days
of her wretched homelessness,
When her people fell into
enemy hands,
and she had no one to help
her;
When her foes gloated over her,
laughed at her ruin.

8 Through the sin of which she is
guilty,
Jerusalem is defiled;
All who esteemed her think her
vile
now that they see her
nakedness;
She herself groans
and turns away.

9 Her filth is on her skirt;
she gave no thought how she
would end.
Astounding is her downfall,
with no one to console her.
Look, O LORD, upon her misery,
for the enemy has triumphed!

10 The foe stretched out his hand
to all her treasures;
She has seen those nations
enter her sanctuary
Whom you forbade to come
into your assembly.

11 All her people groan,
searching for bread;
They give their treasures for
food,
to retain the breath of life.
"Look, O LORD, and see
how worthless I have become!

12 "Come, all you who pass by
the way,
look and see
Whether there is any suffering
like my suffering,
which has been dealt me
When the LORD afflicted me
on the day of his blazing
wrath.

13 "From on high he sent fire
down into my very frame;
He spread a net for my feet,
and overthrew me.
He left me desolate,
in pain all the day.

1, 1–22: In this poem the poet first describes Jerusalem's miserable state after the destruction wrought by the Chaldeans (vv 1–11a); in v 11b the city itself takes up the lament.

713

14 "He has kept watch over my sins;
    by his hand they have been
      plaited:
They have settled about my neck,
    he has brought my strength
      to its knees;
The Lord has delivered me into
      their grip,
I am unable to rise.

15 "All the mighty ones in my
      midst
    the Lord has cast away;
He summoned an army against
      me
    to crush my young men;
The LORD has trodden in the
      wine press
    virgin daughter Judah.

16 "At this I weep,
    my eyes run with tears:
Far from me are all who could
      console me,
    any who might revive me;
My sons were reduced to silence
    when the enemy prevailed."

17 Zion stretched out her hands,
    but there was no one to
      console her;
The LORD gave orders against
      Jacob
    for his neighbors to be his foes;
Jerusalem has become in their
      midst
    a thing unclean.

18 "The LORD is just;
    I had defied his command.
Listen, all you peoples,
    and behold my suffering:
My maidens and my youths
    have gone into captivity.

19 "I cried out to my lovers,
    but they failed me.
My priests and my elders
    perished in the city;
Where they sought food for
      themselves,
    they found it not.

20 "Look, O LORD, upon my
      distress:
    all within me is in ferment,
My heart recoils within me
    from my monstrous rebellion.

In the streets the sword bereaves,
    at home death stalks.

21 "Give heed to my groaning;
    there is no one to console me.
All my enemies rejoice at my
      misfortune:
    it is you who have wrought it.
Bring on the day you have
      proclaimed,
    that they may be even as I.

22 "Let all their evil come before
      you;
    deal with them
As you have dealt with me
    for all my sins;
My groans are many,
    and I am sick at heart."

The Lord's Wrath against Zion

2 How the Lord in his wrath
    has detested daughter Zion!
He has cast down from heaven
      to earth
    the glory of Israel,
Unmindful of his footstool
    on the day of his wrath.

2 The Lord has consumed without
      pity
    all the dwellings of Jacob;
He has torn down in his anger
    the fortresses of daughter
      Judah;
He has brought to the ground
    in dishonor
    her king and her princes.

3 He broke off, in fiery wrath,
    the horn that was Israel's
      whole strength;
He withheld the support of his
      right hand
    when the enemy approached;
He blazed up in Jacob like a
      flaming fire
    devouring all about it.

4 Like an enemy he made taut
    his bow;
    with his arrows in his right
      hand
He took his stand as a foe,
    and slew
    all on whom the eye doted;

Over the tent of daughter Zion
    he poured out his wrath like fire.

5 The Lord has become an enemy,
    he has consumed Israel:
Consumed all her castles
    and destroyed her fortresses;
For daughter Judah he has
      multiplied
    moaning and groaning.

6 He has demolished his shelter
    like a garden booth,
    he has destroyed his dwelling;
In Zion the LORD has made
    feast and sabbath to be
      forgotten;
He has scorned in fierce wrath
    both king and priest.

7 The Lord has disowned his altar,
    rejected his sanctuary;
The walls of her towers
    he has handed over to the
      enemy,
Who shout in the house of the
      LORD
    as on a feast day.

8 The LORD marked for
      destruction
    the wall of daughter Zion:
He stretched out the measuring
      line;
    his hand brought ruin, yet
      he did not relent—
He brought grief on wall and
      rampart
    till both succumbed.

9 Sunk into the ground are her
      gates;
    he has removed and broken
      her bars.
Her king and her princes are
    among the pagans;
    priestly instruction is wanting.
And her prophets have not
      received
    any vision from the LORD.

10 On the ground in silence sit
    the old men of daughter Zion;
They strew dust on their heads
    and gird themselves with
      sackcloth;
The maidens of Jerusalem
    bow their heads to the ground.

1, 14: *They have been plaited . . . my neck:* the sins of the people have been bound together and laid as a yoke on their back; cf Mt 23, 4.

1, 19: *My lovers:* Zion's foreign allies, who failed to help her, as the prophets had warned.

1, 22: Zion fully acknowledges her guilt and the justness of divine punishment; nevertheless, she pleads that her enemies also be punished for their guilt.

2, 1: *The glory of Israel:* the temple. *His footstool:* the ark of the covenant (1 Chr 28, 2; Ps 99, 5; 132, 7); or again, the temple (Ez 43, 7).

2, 3: *Horn:* symbol of power and strength; cf 2, 17;

1 Sm 2, 10; Lk 1, 69; etc.

2, 8: *The measuring line:* used not only in building, but in deciding what must be destroyed; cf Is 34, 11; 2 Kgs 21, 13.

2, 10: *They strew dust:* as a sign of penance; cf Jb 2, 12.

11 Worn out from weeping are
      my eyes,
   within me all is in ferment;
   My gall is poured out on the
      ground
   because of the downfall of the
      daughter of my people,
   As child and infant faint away
      in the open spaces of the town.

12 They ask their mothers,
      "Where is the cereal?"—in vain,
   As they faint away like the
      wounded
      in the streets of the city,
   And breathe their last
      in their mothers' arms.

13 To what can I liken or
      compare you,
      O daughter Jerusalem?
   What example can I show you
      for your comfort,
      virgin daughter Zion?
   For great as the sea is your
      downfall;
      who can heal you?

14 Your prophets had for you
      false and specious visions;
   They did not lay bare your guilt,
      to avert your fate;
   They beheld for you in vision
      false and misleading portents.

15 All who pass by
      clap their hands at you;
   They hiss and wag their heads
      over daughter Jerusalem:
   "Is this the all-beautiful city,
      the joy of the whole earth?"

16 All your enemies
      open their mouths against you;
   They hiss and gnash their teeth.
      They say, "We have devoured
         her.
   This at last is the day we
      hoped for;
      we have lived to see it!"

17 The LORD has done as he
      decreed:
      he has fulfilled the threat
   He set forth from days of old;
      he has destroyed and had no
         pity,
   Letting the enemy gloat over you
      and exalting the horn of your
         foes.

18 Cry out to the Lord;
      moan, O daughter Zion!
   Let your tears flow like a torrent
      day and night;
   Let there be no respite for you,
      no repose for your eyes.

19 Rise up, shrill in the night,
      at the beginning of every watch;
   Pour out your heart like water
      in the presence of the Lord;
   Lift up your hands to him
      for the lives of your little ones
   [Who faint from hunger
      at the corner of every street].

20 "Look, O LORD, and consider:
      whom have you ever treated
         thus?
   Must women eat their offspring,
      their well-formed children?
   Are priest and prophet to be slain
      in the sanctuary of the LORD?

21 "Dead in the dust of the streets
      lie young and old;
   My maidens and young men
      have fallen by the sword;
   You have slain on the day of
      your wrath,
      slaughtered without pity.

22 "You summoned as for a feast
      day
      terrors against me from all
         sides;
   There was not, on the day of
      your wrath,
      either fugitive or survivor;
   Those whom I bore and reared
      my enemy has utterly
         destroyed."

Sufferings of the Prophet and
His People

3 I am a man who knows affliction
      from the rod of his anger,
2 One whom he has led and
      forced to walk
      in darkness, not in the light;
3 Against me alone he brings
      back his hand
      again and again all the day.

4 He has worn away my flesh and
      my skin,
      he has broken my bones;
5 He has beset me round about
      with poverty and weariness;

6 He has left me to dwell in the
      dark
      like those long dead.

7 He has hemmed me in with no
      escape
      and weighed me down with
         chains;
8 Even when I cry out for help,
      he stops my prayer;
9 He has blocked my ways with
      fitted stones,
      and turned my paths aside.

10 A lurking bear he has been to me,
      a lion in ambush!
11 He deranged my ways, set me
      astray,
      left me desolate.
12 He bent his bow, and set me up
      as the target for his arrow.

13 He pierces my sides
      with shafts from his quiver.
14 I have become a laughingstock
      for all nations,
      their taunt all the day long;
15 He has sated me with bitter food,
      made me drink my fill of
         wormwood.

16 He has broken my teeth with
      gravel,
      pressed my face in the dust;
17 My soul is deprived of peace,
      I have forgotten what
         happiness is;
18 I tell myself my future is lost,
      all that I hoped for from the
         LORD.

19 The thought of my homeless
      poverty
      is wormwood and gall;
20 Remembering it over and over
      leaves my soul downcast
         within me.
21 But I will call this to mind,
      as my reason to have hope:

22 The favors of the LORD are not
      exhausted,
      his mercies are not spent;
23 They are renewed each morning,
      so great is his faithfulness.
24 My portion is the LORD, says
      my soul;
      therefore will I hope in him.

2, 11: *My gall is poured out on the ground:* I am
afflicted with bitter sorrow; cf Jb 16, 13.

2, 20: *Must women eat their offspring:* extreme

famine in a besieged city sometimes led to this form
of cannibalism; cf 4, 10; 2 Kgs 6, 28f; Bar 2, 3;
Ez 5, 10.

3, 1–21: The author identifies Zion's sufferings
with his own.

25 Good is the LORD to one who
        waits for him,
        to the soul that seeks him;
26 It is good to hope in silence
        for the saving help of the LORD.
27 It is good for a man to bear
        the yoke from his youth.

28 Let him sit alone and in silence,
        when it is laid upon him.
29 Let him put his mouth to the dust;
        there may yet be hope.
30 Let him offer his cheek to be
        struck,
        let him be filled with disgrace.

31 For the Lord's rejection
        does not last forever;
32 Though he punishes, he takes
        pity,
        in the abundance of his
        mercies;
33 He has no joy in afflicting
        or grieving the sons of men.

34 When anyone tramples underfoot
        all the prisoners in the land,
35 When he distorts men's rights
        in the very sight of the
        Most High,
36 When he pressed a crooked claim,
        the Lord does not look on
        unconcerned.

37 Who commands, so that it
        comes to pass,
        except the Lord ordains it;
38 Except it proceeds from the
        mouth of the Most High,
        whether the thing be good or
        bad!
39 Why should any living man
        complain,
        any mortal, in the face of
        his sins?

40 Let us search and examine
        our ways
        that we may return to the
        LORD!
41 Let us reach out our hearts
        toward God in heaven!
42 We have sinned and rebelled;
        you have not forgiven us.

43 You veiled yourself in wrath
        and pursued us,
        you slew us and took no pity;
44 You wrapped yourself in a cloud
        which prayer could not pierce.

45 You have made us offscourings
        and refuse
        among the nations.
46 All our enemies
        have opened their mouths
        against us;
47 Terror and the pit have been
        our lot,
        desolation and destruction;
48 My eyes run with streams of
        water
        over the downfall of the
        daughter of my people.

49 My eyes flow without ceasing,
        there is no respite,
50 Till the LORD from heaven
        looks down and sees.
51 My eyes torment my soul
        at the sight of all the
        daughters of my city.

52 Those who were my enemies
        without cause
        hunted me down like a bird;
53 They struck me down alive in
        the pit,
        and sealed me in with a stone.
54 The waters flowed over my head,
        and I said, "I am lost!"

55 I called upon your name,
        O LORD,
        from the bottom of the pit;
56 You heard me call,
        "Let not your ear
        be deaf to my cry for help!"
57 You came to my aid when I
        called to you;
        you said, "Have no fear!"

58 You defended me in mortal
        danger,
        you redeemed my life.
59 You see, O LORD, how I am
        wronged;
        do me justice!
60 You see all their vindictiveness,
        all their plots against me.

61 You hear their insults, O LORD,
        [all their plots against me],
62 The whispered murmurings of
        my foes,
        against me all the day;
63 Whether they sit or stand,
        see, I am their taunt song.

64 Requite them as they deserve,
        O LORD,
        according to their deeds;
65 Give them hardness of heart,
        as your curse upon them;
66 Pursue them in wrath and
        destroy them
        from under your heavens!

Miseries of the Besieged City

4 How tarnished is the gold,
        how changed the noble metal;
   How the sacred stones lie strewn
        at every street corner!

2 Zion's precious sons,
        fine gold their counterpart,
   Now worth no more than
        earthen jars
        made by the hands of a potter!

3 Even the jackals bare their
        breasts
        and suckle their young;
   The daughter of my people has
        become as cruel
        as the ostrich in the desert.

4 The tongue of the suckling cleaves
        to the roof of its mouth in
        thirst;
   The babes cry for food,
        but there is no one to give it
        to them.

5 Those accustomed to dainty food
        perish in the streets;
   Those brought up in purple
        now cling to the ash heaps.

6 The punishment of the daughter
        of my people
        is greater than the penalty of
        Sodom,
   Which was overthrown in an
        instant
        without the turning of a hand.

7 Brighter than snow were her
        princes,
        whiter than milk,
   More ruddy than coral,
        more precious than sapphire.

8 Now their appearance is blacker
        than soot,
        they are unrecognized on the
        streets;
   Their skin shrinks on their bones,
        as dry as wood.

3, 27: *To bear the yoke:* to do God's will; cf. Jer 2, 20.

3, 29: *Let him put his mouth to the dust:* in humble submission; cf Ps 72, 9.

4, 3: *Cruel as the ostrich:* see note on Jb 39, 14ff. Jerusalem, in her distress, has abandoned her children.

9 Better for those who perish by
    the sword
      than for those who die of
      hunger,
  Who waste away, as though
      pierced through,
      lacking the fruits of the field!

10 The hands of compassionate
    women
      boiled their own children,
  To serve them as mourners' food
      in the downfall of the daughter
      of my people.

11 The LORD has spent his anger,
      poured out his blazing wrath;
  He has kindled a fire in Zion
      that has consumed her
      foundations.

12 The kings of the earth did not
    believe,
      nor any of the world's
      inhabitants,
  That enemy or foe could enter
      the gates of Jerusalem.

13 Because of the sins of her
    prophets
      and the crimes of her priests,
  Who shed in her midst
      the blood of the just!—

14 They staggered blindly in the
    streets,
      soiled with blood,
  So that people could not touch
      even their garments:

15 "Away, you unclean!" they
    cried to them,
      "Away, away, do not draw
      near!"
  If they left and wandered
      among the nations,
      nowhere could they remain.

16 The LORD himself has dispersed
    them,
      he regards them no more;
  He does not receive the priests
      with favor,
      nor show kindness to the elders.

17 Our eyes ever wasted away,
      looking in vain for aid;
  From our watchtower we
      watched
      for a nation that could not
      save us.

18 Men dogged our steps
      so that we could not walk in
      our streets;
  Our end drew near, and came;
      our time had expired.

19 Our pursuers were swifter
      than eagles in the air,
  They harassed us on the
      mountains
      and waylaid us in the desert.

20 The anointed one of the LORD,
      our breath of life,
      was caught in their snares,
  He in whose shadow we thought
      we could live on among the
      nations.

21 Though you rejoice and are
      glad, O daughter Edom,
      you who dwell in the land
      of Uz,
  To you also shall the cup be
      passed;
      you shall become drunk and
      naked.

22 Your chastisement is completed,
      O daughter Zion,
      he will not prolong your exile;
  But your wickedness, O daughter
      Edom, he will punish,
      he will lay bare your sins.

The Prophet's Lament and Supplication

5 Remember, O LORD, what has
    befallen us,
      look, and see our disgrace:
2 Our inherited lands have been
      turned over to strangers,
      our homes to foreigners.
3 We have become orphans,
      fatherless;
      widowed are our mothers.
4 The water we drink we must buy,
      for our own wood we must pay.
5 On our necks is the yoke of
      those who drive us;
      we are worn out, but
      allowed no rest.

6 To Egypt we submitted,
      and to Assyria, to fill our
      need of bread.
7 Our fathers, who sinned, are
      no more;
      but we bear their guilt.
8 Slaves rule over us;
      there is no one to rescue us
      from their hands.
9 At the peril of our lives we
      bring in our sustenance,
      in the face of the desert heat;
10 Our skin is shriveled up, as
      though by a furnace,
      with the searing blasts of
      famine.

11 The wives in Zion were ravished
      by the enemy,
      the maidens in the cities of
      Judah;
12 Princes were gibbeted by them,
      elders shown no respect.
13 The youths carry the millstones,
      boys stagger under their
      loads of wood;
14 The old men have abandoned
      the gate,
      the young men their music.

15 The joy of our hearts has ceased,
      our dance has turned into
      mourning;

4, 13ff: The priests and the false prophets lulled the people into an illusory security (Jer 2, 8; 5, 31; 6, 13; etc.), condoning and entering into their crimes so that they themselves became unclean.
4, 17: A nation: Egypt, which failed to give effective aid against Babylon.
4, 20: Our breath of life: the king. This is a royal epithet borrowed from Egyptian usage, while the anointed one of the Lord is Israelite. After the disaster of 598 B.C. (2 Kgs 24, 1–17), Jerusalem could have hoped to live in peace amidst her neighbors; but they

(vv 21f) as well as Babylon turned against her to ensure her total devastation in 587 B.C.
4, 21: Uz: see note on Jer 25, 20.
5, 6: In its state of abjection, Judah was forced to depend on its traditional enemies to the west and the east for subsistence. Mesopotamia is here called by the name it had long borne, Assyria, though in these times the power of the Assyrians had been superseded by that of the Chaldeans.
5, 7: Our fathers: collective responsibility, for good and for evil, was recognized in the Old Testament; cf

Jer 31, 29. But the present generation is also personally guilty of sin (v 16).
5, 8: Administrations imposed by foreign powers were notoriously corrupt and inept. The Hebrew word for "slave" is the same as that used for an official (servant of the ruler); the author doubtless intends the double meaning here.
5, 14: The gate: the place of assembly, where city decisions were made and judgment given by the elders and other notables; see note on Ru 4, 1.

16 The garlands have fallen from
    our heads:
  woe to us, for we have sinned!
17 Over this our hearts are sick,
  at this our eyes grow dim:
18 That Mount Zion should be
    desolate,
  with jackals roaming there!

19 You, O LORD, are enthroned
    forever;
  your throne stands from age
    to age.
20 Why, then, should you forget
    us,
  abandon us so long a time?

21 Lead us back to you, O LORD,
  that we may be restored:
  give us anew such days as we
    had of old.
22 For now you have indeed
    rejected us,
  and in full measure turned
    your wrath against us.

PRAYER OF THE EXILES

Meeting in Babylon

NOW these are the words of the scroll which Baruch, son of Neriah, son of Mahseiah, son of Zedekiah, son of Hasadiah, son of Hilkiah, wrote in Babylon, 2 in the fifth year [on the seventh day of the month, at the time when the Chaldeans took Jerusalem and burnt it with fire]. 3 And Baruch read the words of this scroll for Jeconiah, son of Jehoiakim, king of Judah, to hear it, as well as all the people who came to the reading: 4 the nobles, the kings' sons, the elders, and the whole people, small and great alike—all who lived in Babylon by the river Sud.

5 They wept and fasted and prayed before the Lord, 6 and collected such funds as each could furnish. 7 These they sent to Jerusalem, to Jehoiakim, son of Hilkiah, son of Shallum, the priest, and to the priests and the whole people who were with him in Jerusalem. 8 [This was when he received the vessels of the house of the Lord that had been removed from the temple, to restore them to the land of Judah, on the tenth of Sivan. These silver vessels Zedekiah, son of Josiah, king of Judah, had had made 9 after Nebuchadnezzar, king of Babylon, carried off Jeconiah, and the princes, and the skilled workers, and the nobles, and the people of the land from Jerusalem, as captives, and brought them to Babylon.]

10 Their message was: "We send you funds, with which you are to procure holocausts, sin offerings, and frankincense, and to prepare cereal offerings; offer these on the altar of the Lord our God, 11 and pray for the life of Nebuchadnezzar, king of Babylon, and that of Belshazzar, his son, that their lifetimes may equal the duration of the heavens above the earth; 12 and that the Lord may give us strength, and light to our eyes, that we may live under the protective shadow of Nebuchadnezzar, king of Babylon, and that of Belshazzar, his son, and serve them long, finding favor in their sight.

Confession of Guilt

13 "Pray for us also to the Lord, our God; for we have sinned against the Lord, our God, and the wrath and anger of the Lord have not yet been withdrawn from us at the present day. 14 And read out publicly this scroll which we send you, in the house of the Lord, on the feast day and during the days of assembly: 15 "Justice is with the Lord, our God; and we today are flushed with shame, we men of Judah and citizens of Jerusalem, 16 that we, with our kings and rulers and priests and prophets, and with our fathers, 17 have sinned in the Lord's sight 18 and disobeyed him. We have neither heeded the voice of the Lord, our God, nor followed the precepts which the Lord set before us. 19 From the time the Lord led our fathers out of the land of Egypt until the present day, we have been disobedient to the Lord, our God, and only too ready to disregard his voice. 20 And the evils and the curse which the Lord enjoined upon Moses, his

---

1, 2: *In the fifth year on the seventh day of the month:* Jerusalem fell on the seventh day of the fifth month; cf 2 Kgs 25, 8; Jer 52, 12. Either the text read originally "the fifth month," or it refers to the observance of an anniversary of the fall of Jerusalem in 587 B.C.

1, 4: *The river Sud:* one of the Babylonian canals, not otherwise identified. In ancient non-Biblical

Hebrew fragments discovered in 1952, there is reference to a river "Sur" in a similar context.

1, 8f: *He:* possibly Baruch; less likely *Jehoiakim . . . the priest* (v 7), a member of the high-priestly family not mentioned elsewhere. The *silver vessels* here described are distinct from the vessels referred to in 2 Kgs 25, 14 and Ezr 1, 7ff. The author of this note may have thought of the *fifth year* (v 1) of Zedekiah,

in view of Jer 28, 1; 29, 1ff. A "fifth year," again with no month mentioned, is given in Ez 1, 2 for the inaugural vision of Ezekiel's prophetic career.

1, 11: *Nebuchadnezzar . . . Belshazzar, his son:* as in Dn 5, 1f. Later Jewish tradition seems to have simplified the history of the past by making the last Chaldean ruler of Babylon the son of the conqueror of Jerusalem.

servant, at the time he led our fathers forth from the land of Egypt to give us the land flowing with milk and honey, cling to us even today. 21 For we did not heed the voice of the Lord, our God, in all the words of the prophets whom he sent us, 22 but each one of us went off after the devices of our own wicked hearts, served other gods, and did evil in the sight of the Lord, our God.

2 "And the Lord fulfilled the warning he had uttered against us: against our judges, who governed Israel, against our kings and princes, and against the men of Israel and Judah. 2 He brought down upon us evils so great that there has not been done anywhere under heaven what has been done in Jerusalem, as was written in the law of Moses: 3 that one after another of us should eat the flesh of his son or of his daughter. 4 He has made us subject to all the kingdoms round about us, a reproach and a horror among all the nations round about to which the Lord has scattered us. 5 We are brought low, not raised up, because we sinned against the Lord, our God, not heeding his voice.

6 "Justice is with the Lord, our God; and we, like our fathers, are flushed with shame even today. 7 All the evils of which the Lord had warned us have come upon us; 8 and we did not plead before the Lord, or turn, each from the figments of his evil heart. 9 And the Lord kept watch over the evils, and brought them home to us; for the Lord is just in all the works he commanded us to do, 10 but we did not heed his voice, or follow the precepts of the Lord which he set before us.

Prayer for Deliverance

11 "And now, Lord, God of Israel, you who led your people out of the land of Egypt with your mighty hand, with signs and wonders and great might, and with your upraised arm, so that you have made for yourself a name till the present day: 12 we have sinned, been impious, and violated, O Lord, our God, all your

statutes. 13 Let your anger be withdrawn from us, for we are left few in number among the nations to which you scattered us. 14 Hear, O Lord, our prayer of supplication, and deliver us for your own sake: grant us favor in the presence of our captors, 15 that the whole earth may know that you are the Lord, our God, and that Israel and his descendants bear your name. 16 O Lord, look down from your holy dwelling and take thought of us; turn, O Lord, your ear to hear us. 17 Look directly at us, and behold: it is not the dead in the nether world, whose spirits have been taken from within them, who will give glory and vindication to the Lord. 18 He whose soul is deeply grieved, who walks bowed and feeble, with failing eyes and famished soul, will declare your glory and justice, Lord!

19 "Not on the just deeds of our fathers and our kings do we base our plea for mercy in your sight, O Lord, our God. 20 You have brought your wrath and anger down upon us, as you had warned us through your servants the prophets: 21 'Thus says the Lord: Bend your shoulders to the service of the king of Babylon, that you may continue in the land 22 I gave your fathers: for if you do not hear the Lord's voice so as to serve the king of Babylon,

23 I will make to cease from the cities of Judah
and from the streets of Jerusalem
The sounds of joy and the sounds of gladness,
the voice of the bridegroom and the voice of the bride;
And all the land shall be deserted,
without inhabitants.'

24 But we did not heed your voice, or serve the king of Babylon, and you fulfilled the threats you had made through your servants the prophets, to have the bones of our kings and the bones of our fathers brought out from their burial places. 25 And indeed, they lie exposed to the heat of day and the frost of night.

They died in dire anguish, by hunger and the sword and plague. 26 And you reduced the house which bears your name to what it is today, for the wickedness of the kingdom of Israel and the kingdom of Judah.

God's Promises Recalled

27 "But with us, O Lord, our God, you have dealt in all your clemency and in all your great mercy. 28 This was your warning through your servant Moses, the day you ordered him to write down your law in the presence of the Israelites: 29 If you do not heed my voice, surely this great and numerous throng will dwindle away among the nations to which I will scatter them. 30 For I know they will not heed me, because they are a stiff-necked people. But in the land of their captivity they shall have a change of heart; 31 they shall know that I, the Lord, am their God. I will give them hearts, and heedful ears; 32 and they shall praise me in the land of their captivity, and shall invoke my name. 33 Then they shall turn back from their stiff-necked stubbornness, and from their evil deeds, because they shall remember the fate of their fathers who sinned against the Lord. 34 And I will bring them back to the land which with my oath I promised to their fathers, to Abraham, Isaac and Jacob; and they shall rule it. I will make them increase; they shall not then diminish. 35 And I will establish for them, as an eternal covenant, that I will be their God, and they shall be my people; and I will not again remove my people Israel from the land I gave them.

3 "Lord Almighty, God of Israel, afflicted souls and dismayed spirits call to you. 2 Hear, O Lord, for you are a God of mercy; and have mercy on us, who have sinned against you: 3 for you are enthroned forever, while we are perishing forever. 4 Lord Almighty, God of Israel, hear the prayer of Israel's few, the sons of those who sinned against you; they did not heed the voice of the Lord, their God, and the evils cling

---

2, 3: *One after another of us should eat:* see note on Lam 2, 20.

2, 25: *They lie exposed:* probably an allusion to Jer 36, 30; see note on Jer 22, 19.

2, 26: *The house which bears your name:* the temple of Jerusalem. *What it is today:* during the exile it lay in ruins.

to us.   5 Remember at this time not the misdeeds of our fathers, but your own hand and name: 6 for you are the Lord our God; and you, O Lord, we will praise!   7 For this, you put into our hearts the fear of you: that we may call upon your name, and praise you in our captivity, when we have removed from our hearts all the wickedness of our fathers who sinned against you.   8 Behold us today in our captivity, where you scattered us, a reproach, a curse, and a requital for all the misdeeds of our fathers, who withdrew from the Lord, our God."

PRAISE OF WISDOM IN THE LAW OF MOSES

9 Hear, O Israel, the
   commandments of life:
   listen, and know prudence!
10 How is it, Israel,
   that you are in the land of
     your foes,
   grown old in a foreign land,
   Defiled with the dead,
11   accounted with those destined
    for the nether world?
12 You have forsaken the fountain
   of wisdom!
13   Had you walked in the way
    of God,
   you would have dwelt in
    enduring peace.
14 Learn where prudence is,
   where strength, where
    understanding;
   That you may know also
   where are length of days, and
    life,
   where light of the eyes, and
    peace.

15 Who has found the place of
   wisdom,
   who has entered into her
    treasures?
16 Where are the rulers of the
   nations,
   they who lorded it over the
    wild beasts of the earth,
17   and made sport of the birds
    of the heavens:
   They who heaped up the silver
   and the gold in which men
    trust;

of whose possessions there
   was no end?
18 They schemed anxiously for
   money,
   but there is no trace of their
    work:
19 They have vanished down into
   the nether world,
   and others have risen up in
    their stead.

20 Later generations have seen the
   light,
   have dwelt in the land,
   But the way to understanding
    they have not known,
21   they have not perceived her
    paths, or reached her;
   their offspring were far from
    the way to her.
22 She has not been heard of in
   Canaan,
   nor seen in Teman.
23 The sons of Hagar who seek
   knowledge on earth,
   the merchants of Midian and
    Teman,
   the phrasemakers seeking
    knowledge,
   These have not known the way
    to wisdom,
   nor have they her paths in
    mind.

24 O Israel, how vast is the house
   of God,
   how broad the scope of his
    dominion:
25 Vast and endless,
   high and immeasurable!
26 In it were born the giants,
   renowned at the first,
   stalwarts, skilled in war.
27 Not these did God choose,
   nor did he give them the way
    of understanding;
28 They perished for lack of
   prudence,
   perished through their folly.
29 Who has gone up to the
   heavens and taken her,
   or brought her down from
    the clouds?
30 Who has crossed the sea and
   found her,
   bearing her away rather than
    choice gold?

31 None know the way to her,
   nor has any understood her
    paths.

32 Yet he who knows all things
   knows her;
   he has probed her by his
    knowledge—
   He who established the earth
    for all time,
   and filled it with four-footed
    beasts;
33 He who dismisses the light, and
   it departs,
   calls it, and it obeys him
    trembling;
34 Before whom the stars at their
   posts
   shine and rejoice;
35 When he calls them, they
   answer, "Here we are!"
   shining with joy for their
    Maker.
36 Such is our God;
   no other is to be compared
    to him:
37 He has traced out all the way
   of understanding,
   and has given her to Jacob,
    his servant,
   to Israel, his beloved son.

38 Since then she has appeared on
   earth,
   and moved among men.
4 She is the book of the precepts
   of God,
   the law that endures forever;
   All who cling to her will live,
   but those will die who forsake
    her.
2 Turn, O Jacob, and receive her:
   walk by her light toward
    splendor.
3 Give not your glory to another,
   your privileges to an alien race.
4 Blessed are we, O Israel;
   for what pleases God is
    known to us!

JERUSALEM BEWAILS AND CONSOLES HER CAPTIVE CHILDREN

5 Fear not, my people!
   Remember, Israel,
6 You were sold to the nations
   not for your destruction;

3, 22f: Despite the renown for wisdom of the peoples of *Canaan* or Phoenicia (Ez 28, 3f), of *Teman*

(Jer 49, 7), of *the sons of Hagar* or the Arabians, they did not possess true wisdom, which is found only in

the law of God.
3, 24: *The house of God:* here, the created universe.

It was because you angered God
   that you were handed over to
   your foes.
7 For you provoked your Maker
   with sacrifices to demons, to
   no-gods;
8 You forsook the Eternal God
   who nourished you,
   and you grieved Jerusalem
   who fostered you.
9 She indeed saw coming upon you
   the anger of God; and she said:

"Hear, you neighbors of Zion!
   God has brought great
   mourning upon me,
10 For I have seen the captivity
   that the Eternal God has
   brought
   upon my sons and daughters.
11 With joy I fostered them;
   but with mourning and
   lament I let them go.
12 Let no one gloat over me, a
   widow,
   bereft of many:
For the sins of my children I
   am left desolate,
   because they turned from the
   law of God,
13   and did not acknowledge his
   statutes;
In the ways of God's commandments they did not walk,
   nor did they tread the
   disciplined paths of his
   justice.
14 "Let Zion's neighbors come,
   to take note of the captivity
   of my sons and daughters,
   brought upon them by the
   Eternal God.
15 He has brought against them a
   nation from afar,
   a nation ruthless and of alien
   speech,
That has neither reverence for age
   nor tenderness for childhood;
16 They have led away this widow's
   cherished sons,
   have left me solitary, without
   daughters.
17 What can I do to help you?
18   He who has brought this evil
   upon you
   must himself deliver you from
   your enemies' hands.

19 Farewell, my children, farewell:
   I am left desolate.
20 I have taken off the garment of
   peace,
   have put on sackcloth for my
   prayer of supplication,
   and while I live I will cry out
   to the Eternal God.

21 "Fear not, my children; call
   upon God,
   who will deliver you from
   oppression at enemy hands.
22 I have trusted in the Eternal
   God for your welfare,
   and joy has come to me from
   the Holy One
Because of the mercy that will
   swiftly reach you
   from your eternal savior.
23 With mourning and lament I
   sent you forth,
   but God will give you back
   to me
   with enduring gladness and joy.
24 As Zion's neighbors lately saw
   you taken captive,
   so shall they soon see God's
   salvation come to you,
   with great glory and the
   splendor of the Eternal God.

25 "My children, bear patiently
   the anger
   that has come from God upon
   you;
Your enemies have persecuted
   you,
   and you will soon see their
   destruction
   and trample upon their necks.
26 My pampered children have
   trodden rough roads,
   carried off by their enemies
   like sheep in a raid.
27 Fear not my children; call out
   to God!
   He who brought this upon
   you will remember you.
28 As your hearts have been
   disposed to stray from God,
   turn now ten times the more
   to seek him;
29 For he who has brought
   disaster upon you
   will, in saving you, bring you
   back enduring joy."

JERUSALEM CONSOLED: THE CAPTIVITY ABOUT TO END

30 Fear not, Jerusalem!
   He who gave you your name
   is your encouragement.
31 Fearful are those who harmed you,
   who rejoiced at your downfall;
32 Fearful are the cities where your
   children were enslaved,
   fearful the city that took your
   sons.
33 As that city rejoiced at your
   collapse,
   and made merry at your
   downfall,
   so shall she grieve over her
   own desolation.
34 I will take from her the joyous
   throngs,
   and her exultation shall be
   turned to mourning:
35 For fire shall come upon her
   from the Eternal God, for a
   long time,
   and demons shall dwell in her
   from that time on.
36 Look to the east, Jerusalem!
   behold the joy that comes to
   you from God.
37 Here come your sons whom
   you once let go,
   gathered in from the east and
   from the west
By the word of the Holy One,
   rejoicing in the glory of God.

5 Jerusalem, take off your robe of
   mourning and misery;
   put on the splendor of glory
   from God forever:
2 Wrapped in the cloak of justice
   from God,
   bear on your head the mitre
   that displays the glory of the
   eternal name.
3 For God will show all the
   earth your splendor:
4   you will be named by God
   forever
   the peace of justice, the glory
   of God's worship.
5 Up, Jerusalem! stand upon the
   heights;
   look to the east and see your
   children

4, 25: *Trample upon their necks:* love of enemies was not an Old Testament ideal. The Babylonians are considered here, however, to be God's enemies as well as Israel's.

4, 35: Deserts and desolate places were looked upon as the special habitations of *demons;* Tb 8, 3; Lk 11, 24.

Gathered from the east and the
west
at the word of the Holy One,
rejoicing that they are
remembered by God.
6 Led away on foot by their
enemies they left you:
but God will bring them
back to you
borne aloft in glory as on
royal thrones.
7 For God has commanded
that every lofty mountain be
made low,
And that the age-old depths
and gorges
be filled to level ground,
that Israel may advance
secure in the glory of God.
8 The forests and every fragrant
kind of tree
have overshadowed Israel at
God's command;
9 For God is leading Israel in joy
by the light of his glory,
with his mercy and justice for
company.

THE LETTER OF JEREMIAH AGAINST IDOLATRY

6 A copy of the letter which Jeremiah sent to those who were being led captive to Babylon by the king of the Babylonians, to convey to them what God had commanded him.

For the sins you committed before God, you are being led captive to Babylon by Nebuchadnezzar, king of the Babylonians. 2 When you reach Babylon you will be there many years, a period seven generations long; after which I will bring you back from there in peace. 3 And now in Babylon you will see borne upon men's shoulders gods of silver and gold and wood, which cast fear upon the pagans. 4 Take care that you yourselves do not imitate their alien example and stand in fear of them, 5 when you see the crowd before them and behind worshiping them. Rather, say in your hearts, "You, O Lord, are to be worshiped!"; 6 for

my angel is with you, and he is the custodian of your lives.

7 Their tongues are smoothed by woodworkers; they are covered with gold and silver—but they are a fraud, and cannot speak. 8 People bring gold, as to a maiden in love with ornament, 9 and furnish crowns for the heads of their gods. Then sometimes the priests take the silver and gold from their gods and spend it on themselves, 10 or give part of it to the harlots on the terrace. They trick them out in garments like men, these golds of silver and gold and wood; 11 but though they are wrapped in purple clothing, they are not safe from corrosion or insects. 12 They wipe their faces clean of the house dust which is thick upon them. 13 Each has a scepter, like the human ruler of a district; but none does away with those that offend against it. 14 Each has in its right hand an axe or dagger, but it cannot save itself from war or pillage. Thus it is known they are not gods; do not fear them.

15 As useless as one's broken tools 16 are their gods, set up in their houses; their eyes are full of dust from the feet of those who enter. 17 Their courtyards are walled in like those of a man brought to execution for a crime against the king; the priests reinforce their houses with gates and bars and bolts, lest they be carried off by robbers. 18 They light more lamps for them than for themselves, yet not one of these can they see. 19 They are like any beam in the house; it is said their hearts are eaten away. Though the insects out of the ground consume them and their garments, they do not feel it. 20 Their faces are blackened by the smoke of the house. 21 Bats and swallows alight on their bodies and on their heads; and cats as well as birds. 22 Know, therefore, that they are not gods, and do not fear them.

23 Despite the gold that covers them for adornment, unless someone wipes away the corrosion, they do

not shine; nor did they feel anything when they were molded. 24 They are bought at any price, and there is no spirit in them. 25 Having no feet, they are carried on men's shoulders, displaying their shame to all; and those who worship them are put to confusion 26 because, if they fall to the ground, the worshipers must raise them up. They neither move of themselves if one sets them upright, nor come upright if they fall; but one puts gifts beside them as beside the dead. 27 Their priests resell their sacrifices for their own advantage. Even their wives cure parts of the meat, but do not share it with the poor and the weak; 28 the menstruous and women in childbed handle their sacrifices. Knowing from this that they are not gods, do not fear them.

29 How can they be called gods? For women bring the offerings to these gods of silver and gold and wood; 30 and in their temples the priests squat with torn tunic and with shaven hair and beard, and with their heads uncovered. 31 They shout and wail before their gods as others do at a funeral banquet. 32 The priests take some of their clothing and put it on their wives and children. 33 Whether they are treated well or ill by anyone, they cannot requite it; they can neither set up a king nor remove him. 34 Similarly, they cannot give anyone riches or coppers; if one fails to fulfill a vow to them, they cannot exact it of him. 35 They neither save a man from death, nor deliver the weak from the strong. 36 To no blind man do they restore his sight, nor do they save any man in an emergency. 37 They neither pity the widow nor benefit the orphan. 38 These gilded and silvered wooden statues are like stones from the mountains; and their worshipers will be put to shame. 39 How then can it be thought or claimed that they are gods? 40 Even the Chaldeans themselves have no respect for them; for when they see a deaf mute, incapable of

---

6, 2: *Seven generations*: possibly an indication of the date of this composition by an author writing for his contemporaries for whom the conditions of the Exile were still realities. He has multiplied the *seventy years* of Jer 29, 10 by three or four.

6, 10: *Harlots on the terrace*: cult prostitutes, common in the idolatrous religions of the Gentiles.
6, 27–31: From the point of view of Jewish ritual law, the practices named here were grotesque and depraved; cf Lv 12, 2ff; 15, 19–23.

6, 33–39: All that the gods cannot do, the true God does; cf 1 Sm 2, 7; Dt 23, 22; Pss 68, 6; 146, 7–9; Is 35, 4f.
6, 40: *Bel*: cf note on Jer 50, 2.

speech, they bring forward Bel and ask the god to make noise, as though the man could understand; 41 and they are themselves unable to reflect and abandon these gods, for they have no sense. 42 And their women, girt with cords, sit by the roads, burning chaff for incense; 43 and whenever one of them is drawn aside by some passerby who lies with her, she mocks her neighbor who has not been dignified as she has, and has not had her cord broken. 44 All that takes place around these gods is a fraud: how then can it be thought or claimed that they are gods?

45 They are produced by wood-workers and goldsmiths, and they are nothing else than what these crafts-men wish them to be. 46 Even those who produce them are not long-lived; 47 how then can what they have produced be gods? They have left frauds and opprobrium to their successors. 48 For when war or disaster comes upon them, the priests deliberate among themselves where they can hide with them. 49 How then can one not know that these are no-gods, which do not save themselves either from war or from disaster? 50 They are wooden, gilded and silvered; they will later be known for frauds. To all peoples and kings it will be clear that they are not gods, but human handiwork; and that God's work is not in them.

51 Who does not know that they are not gods? 52 They set no king over the land, nor do they give men rain. 53 They neither vindicate their own rights, nor do they recover what is unjustly taken, for they are unable; 54 they are like crows between heaven and earth. For when fire breaks out in the temple of these wooden or gilded or silvered gods, though the priests flee and are safe, they themselves are burnt up in the fire like beams. 55 They cannot resist a king, or enemy forces. 56 How then can it be admitted or thought that they are gods?

They are safe from neither thieves nor bandits, these wooden and silvered and gilded gods; 57 those who seize them strip off the gold and the silver, and go away with the clothing that was on them, and they cannot help themselves. 58 How much better to be a king displaying his valor, or a handy tool in a house, the joy of its owner, than these false gods; or the door of a house, that keeps safe those who are within, rather than these false gods; or a wooden post in a palace, rather than these false gods! 59 The sun and moon and stars are bright, and obedient in the service for which they are sent. 60 Likewise the lightning, when it flashes, is a goodly sight; and the same wind blows over all the land. 61 The clouds, too, when com-

manded by God to proceed across the whole world, fulfill the order; 62 and fire, sent from on high to burn up the mountains and the forests, does what has been commanded. But these false gods are not their equal, whether in beauty or in power; 63 so that it is unthinkable, and cannot be claimed, that they are gods. They can neither execute judgment, nor benefit man. 64 Know, therefore, that they are not gods, and do not fear them.

65 Kings they neither curse nor bless. 66 They show the nations no signs in the heavens, nor are they brilliant like the sun, nor shining like the moon. 67 The beasts which can help themselves by fleeing to shelter are better than they are. 68 Thus in no way is it clear to us that they are gods; so do not fear them. 69 For like a scarecrow in a cucumber patch, that is no protection, are their wooden, gilded, silvered gods. 70 Just like a thornbush in a garden on which perches every kind of bird, or like a corpse hurled into darkness, are their silvered and gilded wooden gods. 71 From the rotting of the purple and the linen upon them, it can be known that they are not gods; they themselves will in the end be consumed, and be a disgrace in the land. 72 The better for the just man who has no idols: he shall be far from disgrace!

6, 42f: This seems to refer to the obligation of Babylonian women to serve once in their lives as cult prostitutes. The unbroken cord was a sign that this duty had not yet been fulfilled. *Chaff:* burnt as an aphrodisiac or for use in erotic rites.

Ezekiel

CALL OF THE PROPHET

The Vision: God on the Cherubim

IN the thirtieth year, on the fifth day of the fourth month, while I was among the exiles by the river Chebar, the heavens opened, and I saw divine visions.— 2 On the fifth day of the month, the fifth year, that is, of King Jehoiachin's exile, 3 the word of the LORD came to the priest Ezekiel, the son of Buzi, in the land of the Chaldeans by the river Chebar.— There the hand of the LORD came upon me.

4 As I looked, a stormwind came from the North, a huge cloud with flashing fire [enveloped in brightness], from the midst of which [the midst of the fire] something gleamed like electrum. 5 Within it were figures resembling four living creatures that looked like this: their form was human, 6 but each had four faces and four wings, 7 and their legs went straight down; the soles of their feet were round. They sparkled with a gleam like burnished bronze.

10 Their faces were like this: each of the four had the face of a man, but on the right side was the face of a lion, and on the left side the face of an ox, and finally each had the face of an eagle. 9 Their faces [and their wings] looked out on all their four sides; they did not turn when they moved, but each went straight forward. 12 [Each went straight forward; wherever the spirit wished to go, there they went; they did not turn when they moved.]

8 Human hands were under their wings, and the wings of one touched those of another. 11 Each had two wings spread out above so that they touched one another's, while the other two wings of each covered his body. 13 In among the living creatures something like burning coals of fire could be seen; they seemed like torches, moving to and fro among the living creatures. The fire gleamed, and from it came forth flashes of lightning.

15 As I looked at the living creatures, I saw wheels on the ground, one beside each of the four living creatures. 16 The wheels had the sparkling appearance of chrysolite, and all four of them looked the same: they were constructed as though one wheel were within another. 17 They could move in any of the four directions they faced, without veering as they moved. 18 The four of them had rims, and I saw that their rims were full of eyes all around. 19 When the living creatures moved, the wheels moved with them; and when the living creatures were raised from the ground, the wheels also were raised. 20 Wherever the spirit wished to go, there the wheels went, and they were raised together with the living creatures; for the spirit of the living creatures was in the wheels.

22 Over the heads of the living creatures, something like a firmament could be seen, seeming like glittering crystal, stretched straight out above their heads. 23 Beneath the firmament their wings were stretched out, one toward the other. [Each of them had two covering his body.] 24 Then I heard the sounds of their wings, like the roaring of mighty

---

1, 1: *The thirtieth year*, which corresponds to the fifth year of exile (v 2), has never been satisfactorily explained; possibly it refers to the prophet's age. *The river Chebar:* probably a canal near Nippur, southeast of Babylon, one of the sites on which the Jewish exiles were settled.

1, 2: *The fifth day of the* fourth *month, the fifth year:* July 31, 593 B.C.: cf v 1.
1, 4: *The North:* the abode of God; see notes on Jb 37, 22; Ps 48, 3. *Electrum:* an alloy of gold and silver, used here for some undetermined bright metal.
1, 5: *Four living creatures:* identified as cherubim in 10, 20f.
1, 10—22: Note the changed order of the verses and the omission of the textually uncertain verses 14 and 21. Such changes also occur elsewhere in this book.
1, 22f.26: This symbolic description of God's throne is similar to that in Ex 24, 9f.

waters, like the voice of the Almighty. When they moved, the sound of the tumult was like the din of an army. [And when they stood still, they lowered their wings.]

26 Above the firmament over their heads something like a throne could be seen, looking like sapphire. Upon it was seated, up above, one who had the appearance of a man. 27 Upward from what resembled his waist I saw what gleamed like electrum; downward from what resembled his waist I saw what looked like fire; he was surrounded with splendor. 28 Like the bow which appears in the clouds on a rainy day was the splendor that surrounded him. Such was the vision of the likeness of the glory of the LORD.

Eating of the Scroll

2 When I had seen it, I fell upon my face and heard a voice that said to me Son of man stand up! I wish to speak with you. 2 As he spoke to me, spirit entered into me and set me on my feet, and I heard the one who was speaking 3 say to me: Son of man, I am sending you to the Israelites, rebels who have rebelled against me; they and their fathers have revolted against me to this very day. 4 Hard of face and obstinate of heart are they to whom I am sending you. But you shall say to them: Thus says the Lord GOD! 5 And whether they heed or resist— for they are a rebellious house—they shall know that a prophet has been among them. 6 But as for you, son of man, fear neither them nor their words when they contradict you and reject you, and when you sit on scorpions. Neither fear their words nor be dismayed at their looks, for they are a rebellious house. 7 [But speak my words to them, whether they heed or resist, for they are rebellious.] 8 As for you, son of man, obey me when I speak to you: be not rebellious like this house of rebellion,

but open your mouth and eat what I shall give you.

9 It was then I saw a hand stretched out to me, in which was a written scroll 10 which he unrolled before me. It was covered with writing front and back, and written on it was: Lamentation and wailing and woe!

3 He said to me: Son of man, eat what is before you; eat this scroll, then go, speak to the house of Israel. 2 So I opened my mouth and he gave me the scroll to eat. 3 Son of man, he then said to me, feed your belly and fill your stomach with this scroll I am giving you. I ate it, and it was as sweet as honey in my mouth. He said: 4 Son of man, go now to the house of Israel, and speak my words to them.

5 Not to a people with difficult speech and barbarous language am I sending you, 6 nor to the many peoples [with difficult speech and barbarous language] whose words you cannot understand. If I were to send you to these, they would listen to you; 7 but the house of Israel will refuse to listen to you, since they will not listen to me. For the whole house of Israel is stubborn of brow and obstinate in heart. 8 But I will make your face as hard as theirs, and your brow as stubborn as theirs, 9 like diamond, harder than flint. Fear them not, nor be dismayed at their looks, for they are a rebellious house.

10 Son of man, he said to me, take into your heart all my words that I speak to you; hear them well. 11 Now go to the exiles, to your countrymen, and say to them: Thus says the Lord GOD!—whether they heed or resist!

12 Then spirit lifted me up, and I heard behind me the noise of a loud rumbling as the glory of the LORD rose from its place: 13 the noise made by the wings of the living creatures striking one another, and

by the wheels alongside them, a loud rumbling. 14 The spirit which had lifted me up seized me, and I went off spiritually stirred, while the hand of the LORD rested heavily upon me. 15 Thus I came to the exiles who lived at Tel-abib by the river Chebar, and for seven days I sat among them distraught.

The Prophet as Watchman

17 Thus the word of the LORD came to me: Son of man, I have appointed you a watchman for the house of Israel. When you hear a word from my mouth, you shall warn them for me.

18 If I say to the wicked man, You shall surely die; and you do not warn him or speak out to dissuade him from his wicked conduct so that he may live: that wicked man shall die for his sin, but I will hold you responsible for his death. 19 If, on the other hand, you have warned the wicked man, yet he has not turned away from his evil nor from his wicked conduct, then he shall die for his sin, but you shall save your life.

20 If a virtuous man turns away from virtue and does wrong when I place a stumbling block before him, he shall die. He shall die for his sin, and his virtuous deeds shall not be remembered; but I will hold you responsible for his death if you did not warn him. 21 When, on the other hand, you have warned a virtuous man not to sin, and he has in fact not sinned, he shall surely live because of the warning, and you shall save your own life.

Ezekiel's Dumbness

22 The hand of the LORD came upon me, and he said to me: Get up and go out into the plain, where I will speak with you. 23 So I got up and went out into the plain, and I saw that the glory of the LORD was in that place, like the glory I had seen by the river Chebar. I fell prone, 24 but

---

1, 26: *One who had the appearance of a man:* God appearing in human form (v 28); cf Ex 33, 18–23.

2, 1: *Son of man:* a formal way of saying simply "man"; God's habitual way of addressing the prophet throughout this book. Probably the title is used to emphasize the separation of the divine and the human.

2, 2: *Spirit:* vital power, coming from God, which enables the prophet to hear the word of God; cf 8, 3; 9, 24; 11, 1.

2, 6: *When you sit on scorpions:* the prophet must be prepared for the bitterest opposition.

3, 3: *As sweet as honey:* though the prophet must foretell terrible things, the word of God is sweet to him who receives it.

3, 12: *The Glory of the Lord:* the divine presence, manifested here in visible form.

3, 15: *Tel-abib:* one of the sites where the exiles were settled, probably near Nippur.

3, 17–21: This passage refers to one of the prophet's

most characteristic qualities. It was placed here by an editor, though it properly belongs to a later stage in Ezekiel's ministry; cf chapter 33.

3, 22–27: This passage also belongs to a later period, with 24, 25ff and 33, 21f, during the time of the final siege of Jerusalem, when Ezekiel's prophecies consisted mainly of symbolic actions rather than words.

then spirit entered into me and set me on my feet, and he spoke with me.

He said to me: Go shut yourself up in your house. 25 [As for you, son of man, they will put cords upon you and bind you with them, so you cannot go out among them.] 26 I will make your tongue stick to your palate so that you will be dumb and unable to rebuke them for being a rebellious house. 27 Only when I speak with you and open your mouth, shall you say to them: Thus says the Lord GOD! Let him heed who will, and let him resist who will, for they are a rebellious house.

BEFORE THE SIEGE OF JERUSALEM

Acts Symbolic of Siege and Exile

16 At the end of seven days . . . :
4 As for you, son of man, take a clay tablet; lay it in front of you, and draw on it a city [Jerusalem]. 2 Raise a siege against it: build a tower, lay out a ramp, pitch camps, and set up battering rams all around. 3 Then take an iron griddle and set it up as an iron wall between you and the city. Fix your gaze on it: it shall be in the state of siege, and you shall besiege it. This shall be a sign for the house of Israel. 4 Then you shall lie on your left side, while I place the sins of the house of Israel upon you. As many days as you lie thus, you shall bear their sins. 5 For the years of their sins I allot you the same number of days, three hundred and ninety, during which you will bear the sins of the house of Israel. 6 When you finish this, you are to lie down again, but on your right side, and bear the sins of the house of Judah forty days; one day for each year I have allotted you. 7 Fixing your gaze on the siege of Jerusalem, with bared arm you shall prophesy against it. 8 See, I will bind you with cords so that you cannot turn from one side to the

other until you have completed the days of your siege.

9 Again, take wheat and barley, and beans and lentils, and millet and spelt; put them in a single vessel and make bread out of them. Eat it for as many days as you lie upon your side, three hundred and ninety. 10 The food you eat shall be twenty shekels a day by weight; each day the same. 11 And the water you drink shall be the sixth of a hin by measure; each day the same. 16 Then he said to me: Son of man, I am breaking the staff of bread in Jerusalem. They shall eat bread which they have weighed out anxiously, and they shall drink water which they have measured out fearfully, 17 so that, owing to the scarcity of bread and water, everyone shall be filled with terror and waste away because of his sins.

12 For your food you must bake barley loaves over human excrement in their sight, said the LORD. 13 Thus the Israelites shall eat their food unclean among the nations where I scatter them. 14 "Oh no, Lord GOD!" I protested. "Never have I been made unclean, and from my youth till now, never have I eaten carrion flesh or that torn by wild beasts; never has any unclean meat entered my mouth." 15 Very well, he replied, I allow you cow's dung in place of human excrement; bake your bread on that.

5 As for you, son of man, take a sharp sword and use it like a barber's razor, passing it over your head and beard. Then take a set of scales and divide the hair you have cut. 2 Burn a third in the fire, within the city, when the days of your siege are completed; place another third around the city and strike it with the sword; the final third strew in the wind, and pursue it with the sword. 3 [But of the last take a small number and tie them in the hem of your garment. 4 Then take

some of these and throw them in the midst of the fire and burn them.]

Say to the house of Israel: 5 Thus says the Lord GOD: This is Jerusalem! In the midst of the nations I placed her, surrounded by foreign countries. 6 But she rebelled against my ordinances more wickedly than the nations, and against my statutes more than the foreign countries surrounding her; she has spurned my ordinances and has not lived by my statutes. 7 Therefore thus says the Lord GOD: Because you have been more rebellious than the nations surrounding you, not living by my statutes nor fulfilling my ordinances, but acting according to the ordinances of the surrounding nations; 8 therefore thus says the Lord GOD: See, I am coming at you! I will inflict punishments in your midst while the nations look on. 9 Because of all your abominations I will do with you what I have never done before, the like of which I will never do again. 10 This means that fathers within you shall eat sons, and sons shall eat fathers. I will inflict punishments upon you and scatter all that remain of your people in every direction.

11 Therefore, as I live, says the Lord GOD, because you have defiled my sanctuary with all your detestable abominations, I swear to cut you down. I will not look upon you with pity nor have mercy. 12 A third of your people shall die of pestilence and perish of hunger within you; another third shall fall by the sword all around you; and a third I will scatter in every direction, and I will pursue them with the sword. 16 When I loose against you the cruel, destructive arrows of hunger, I will break your staff of bread; 17 I will send famine against you and wild beasts that shall rob you of your children. Pestilence and bloodshed shall stalk through you, and I will bring the sword upon you. I, the LORD have spoken!

3, 26: *Dumb:* unwilling to speak to the people in exile while Jerusalem was being besieged; cf 24, 27.
3, 16: *At the end of seven days . . . :* the incomplete sentence probably contained some such words as "the word of the Lord came to me." For *seven days,* see v 15.
4, 5f: *Three hundred and ninety* days . . . *forty days:* symbolically representing the respective lengths of the periods of exile of northern Israelites and Judahites. Northern Israel had already fallen to Assyria in

722 B.C. The letters in the Hebrew phrase for *the days of your siege* (v 8), each of which has its own numerical value, add up to three hundred and ninety. Forty years represent one generation.
4, 7: *Bared arm:* a symbol of unrestrained power.
4, 9–17: This action represents the scarcity of food during the siege of Jerusalem, and the consequent need to eat whatever is at hand. *Twenty shekels:* about nine ounces. *The sixth of a hin:* about one quart.
4, 16: *Breaking the staff of bread:* reducing the

supply of bread which sustains the life of man as the walking staff sustains the traveler on his journey, cf 5, 16; 14, 13; Lv 26, 26; Ps 105, 16; Is 3, 1.
5, 2: *The city:* the one drawn on the tablet.
5, 8: *I am coming at you:* an expression borrowed from the language of warfare in which enemies attacked one another with the sword. *You* in vv 8–17 is Jerusalem.
5, 10: *Fathers . . . shall eat sons, and sons . . . fathers:* see note on Lam 2, 20.

13 Thus shall my anger spend itself, and I will wreak my fury upon them till I am appeased; they shall know that I, the LORD, have spoken in my jealousy when I spend my fury upon them. 14 I will make you a waste and a reproach among the nations that surround you, which every passer-by may see. 15 When I execute judgment upon you in anger and fury and with furious chastisements, you shall be a reproach and an object of scorn, a terrible warning to the nations that surround you. I, the LORD, have spoken!

Against the Mountains of Israel

6 Thus the word of the LORD came to me: 2 Son of man, turn toward the mountains of Israel, and prophesy against them: 3 Mountains of Israel, hear the word of the Lord GOD. Thus says the Lord GOD [to the mountains and hills, the ravines and valleys]: See, I am bringing a sword against you, and I will destroy your high places. 4 Your altars shall be laid waste, your incense stands shall be broken, and I will cast down your slain ones before your idols; 5 I will scatter their bones all around your altars. 6 In all your dwelling places cities shall be made desolate and high places laid waste, so that your altars will be made desolate and laid waste, your idols broken and removed, and your incense stands smashed to bits. 7 [The slain shall fall in your midst, and you shall know that I am the LORD. 8 I have warned you.]

When some of your people have escaped to other nations from the sword, and have scattered over the foreign lands, 9 then those who have escaped will remember me among the nations to which they have been exiled, after I have broken their adulterous heart that turned away from me [and their eyes which lusted after idols]. They shall loathe themselves because of their evil deeds, all their abominations. 10 Then they shall know that it was not in vain

that I, the LORD, threatened to inflict this calamity upon them.

11 Thus says the Lord GOD: Clap your hands, stamp your feet, and cry "Alas!" because of all the abominations of the house of Israel, for which they shall fall by the sword, by famine, and by pestilence. 12 He that is far off shall die of pestilence, he that is near shall fall by the sword, and he that is besieged shall perish by famine; so will I spend my fury upon them. 13 Then shall they know that I am the LORD, when their slain shall lie amid their idols, all about their altars, on every high hill and mountaintop, beneath every green tree and leafy oak, wherever they offered appeasing odors to any of their gods. 14 I will stretch out my hand against them, and wherever they live I will make the land a desolate waste, from the desert to Riblah; thus shall they know that I am the LORD.

The End Has Come

7 Thus the word of the LORD came to me: 2 Son of man, now say: Thus says the Lord GOD to the land of Israel: An end! The end has come upon the four corners of the land! 3 Now the end is upon you; I will unleash my anger against you and judge you according to your conduct and lay upon you the consequences of all your abominations. 4 I will not look upon you with pity nor have mercy; I will bring your conduct down upon you, and the consequences of your abominations shall be in your midst; then shall you know that I am the LORD.

5 Thus says the Lord GOD: Disaster upon disaster! See it coming! 6 An end is coming, the end is coming upon you! See it coming! 7 The climax has come for you who dwell in the land! The time has come, near is the day: a time of consternation, not of rejoicing. 8 Soon now I will pour out my fury upon you and spend my anger upon you; I will judge you according to your conduct and lay upon you the consequences of all your abominations. 9 I will

not look upon you with pity nor have mercy; I will deal with you according to your conduct, and the consequences of your abominations shall be in your midst; then shall you know that it is I, the LORD, who strike.

10 See, the day of the LORD! See, the end is coming! Lawlessness is in full bloom, insolence flourishes, 11 violence has risen to support wickedness. It shall not be long in coming, nor shall it delay. 12 The time has come, the day dawns. Let not the buyer rejoice nor the seller mourn, for wrath shall be upon all the throng. 13 The seller shall not regain what he sold as long as he lives, for wrath shall be upon all the throng. Because of his sins, no one shall preserve his life. 14 They shall sound the trumpet and make everything ready, yet no one shall go to war, for my wrath is upon all the throng.

15 The sword is outside; pestilence and hunger are within. He that is in the country shall die by the sword; pestilence and famine shall devour those in the city. 16 Even those who escape and flee to the mountains like the doves of the valleys—I will put them all to death, each one for his own sins. 17 All their hands shall be limp, and all their knees shall run with water. 18 They shall put on sackcloth, and horror shall cover them; shame shall be on all their faces and baldness on all their heads. 19 They shall fling their silver into the streets, and their gold shall be considered refuse. Their silver and gold cannot save them on the day of the LORD's wrath. They shall not be allowed to satisfy their craving or fill their bellies, for this has been the occasion of their sin. 20 In the beauty of their ornaments they put their pride: they made of them their abominable images [their idols]. For this reason I make them refuse. 21 I will hand them over as booty to foreigners, to be spoiled and defiled by the wicked of the earth. 22 I will turn away my face from them, and my treasure shall be profaned: robbers shall enter and profane it.

6, 3: *High places:* the sanctuaries on the mountaintops where illegal worship, whether of the Lord or of Canaanite deities, was performed.

6, 5: *Scatter their bones . . . altars:* dead men's bones defiled a place; cf 2 Kgs 23, 14.

6, 11: *Clap your hands, stamp your feet:* here

evidently signs of mourning; in 25, 6, signs of joy.

6, 13: *Every green tree and leafy oak:* sacred groves had a long history in Palestine as places of worship; cf Dt 12, 2; note on Gn 12, 6.

6, 14: *From the desert to Riblah:* the whole land, from the far south to the far north.

7, 12f: Mundane affairs will cease to have any meaning in view of the disaster that is to come.

7, 18: *Baldness:* shaving the head was a sign of mourning.

7, 22: *My treasure:* the temple of Jerusalem.

23 They shall wreak slaughter, for the land is filled with bloodshed and the city full of violence. 24 I will bring in the worst of the nations, who shall take possession of their houses. I will put an end to their proud strength, and their sanctuaries shall be profaned. 25 When anguish comes they shall seek peace, but there will be none. 26 There shall be disaster after disaster, rumor after rumor. Prophetic vision shall fade; instruction shall be lacking to the priest, and counsel to the elders, 27 while the prince shall be enveloped in terror, and the hands of the common people shall tremble. I will deal with them according to their conduct, and according to their judgments I will judge them; thus they shall know that I am the LORD.

Vision of Abominations in the Temple

8 3 Spirit lifted me up in the air and brought me in divine visions to Jerusalem, to the entrance of the north gate, where stood the statue of jealousy which stirs up jealousy. 5 He said to me: Son of man, look toward the north! I looked toward the north and saw northward of the gate the altar of the statue of jealousy. 6 Son of man, he asked me, do you see what they are doing? Do you see the great abominations that the house of Israel is practicing here, so that I must depart from my sanctuary? But you shall see still greater abominations!

7 Then he brought me to the entrance of the court, where I saw there was a hole in the wall. 8 Son of man, he ordered, dig through the wall. I dug through the wall and saw a door. 9 Enter, he said to me, and see the abominable evils which they are doing here. 10 I entered and saw that all around upon the wall

were pictured the figures of all kinds of creeping things and loathsome beasts [all the idols of the house of Israel]. 11 Before these stood seventy of the elders of the house of Israel, among whom stood Jaazaniah, son of Shaphan, each of them with his censer in his hand, and the fragrance of the incense was rising upward. 12 Then he said to me: Do you see, son of man, what each of these elders of the house of Israel is doing in his idol room? They think: "The LORD cannot see us; the LORD has forsaken the land." 13 He continued: You shall see still greater abominations that they are practicing.

14 Then he brought me to the entrance of the north gate of the temple, and I saw sitting there the women who were weeping for Tammuz. 15 Then he said to me: Do you see this, son of man? You shall see other abominations, greater than these!

16 Then he brought me into the inner court of the LORD's house, and there at the door of the LORD's temple, between the vestibule and the altar, were about twenty-five men with their backs to the LORD's temple and their faces toward the east; they were bowing down to the sun. 17 Do you see, son of man? he asked me. Is it such a trivial matter for the house of Judah to do the abominable things they have done here—for they have filled the land with violence, and again and again they have provoked me—that now they must also put the branch to my nose? 18 Therefore I in turn will act furiously: I will not look upon them with pity nor will I show mercy.

Slaughter of the Idolaters

9 Then he cried loud for me to hear: Come, you scourges of the city! 2 With that I saw six men coming from the direction of the upper gate

which faces the north, each with a destroying weapon in his hand. In their midst was a man dressed in linen, with a writer's case at his waist. They entered and stood beside the bronze altar. 3 Then he called to the man dressed in linen with the writer's case at his waist, 4 saying to him: Pass through the city [through Jerusalem] and mark an X on the foreheads of those who moan and groan over all the abominations that are practiced within it. 5 To the others I heard him say: Pass through the city after him and strike! Do not look on them with pity nor show any mercy! 6 Old men, youths and maidens, women and children—wipe them out! But do not touch any marked with the X; begin at my sanctuary. So they began with the men [the elders] who were in front of the temple. 7 Defile the temple, he said to them, and fill the courts with the slain; then go out and strike in the city.

8 As they began to strike, I was left alone. I fell prone, crying out, "Alas, Lord GOD! Will you destroy all that is left of Israel when you pour out your fury on Jerusalem?" 9 He answered me: The sins of the house of Israel are great beyond measure; the land is filled with bloodshed, the city with lawlessness. They think that the LORD has forsaken the land, that he does not see them. 10 I, however, will not look upon them with pity, nor show any mercy. I will bring down their conduct upon their heads.

11 Then I saw the man dressed in linen with the writing case at his waist make his report: "I have done as you ordered."

(11) 24 Spirit lifted me up and brought me back to the exiles in Chaldea [in a vision, by God's spirit]. Then the vision I had seen left me, 25 and I told the exiles everything the LORD had shown me.

8, 3: *The statue of jealousy which stirs up jealousy:* the statue which provokes the Lord's jealousy for his honor. This was probably the statue of the goddess Asherah erected by the wicked King Manasseh (cf 2 Kgs 21, 7; 2 Chr 33, 7.15). Though it had been removed by King Josiah (2 Kgs 23, 6), it had no doubt been set up again in the repaganizing of Jerusalem that followed on Josiah's death.

8, 5: *He:* an angel accompanies Ezekiel in these visions and represents the voice of the Lord; cf 40, 3f.

8, 10: *Creeping things and loathsome beasts:*

probably Egyptian deities, which were represented in animal form. During the last days of Jerusalem King Zedekiah was allied with Egypt, trusting in it for protection against the Chaldeans.

8, 14: *Weeping for Tammuz:* the withering of trees and plants in autumn was thought to be due to the descent of Tammuz, the Babylonian god of fertility, to the nether world of the dead; this descent was bewailed by the women.

8, 16: *Bowing down to the sun:* sun worship had been made an important part of Judahite idolatry by the impious kings; cf 2 Kgs 23, 11.

8, 17: *Put the branch to my nose:* the meaning is uncertain. Perhaps it refers to an Egyptian practice imported into Judah: the Egyptian sun god Re is pictured with a vine branch at his nose, signifying the transfer of creative power (divine breath) to living things. Such rites were abominable to the Lord.

9, 4: Ezekiel is pre-eminently the prophet of personal retribution; the innocent inhabitants of Jerusalem are to be spared when the idolatrous are punished. *An X:* literally, the Hebrew letter taw, which had the form of a cross.

God's Glory Leaves Jerusalem

(8) 1 On the fifth day of the month, in the sixth year, as I was sitting in my house, and the elders of Judah sat before me, the hand of the Lord GOD fell upon me there. 2 I looked up and saw a form that looked like a man. Downward from what seemed to be his waist, there was fire; from his waist upward there seemed to be a brightness like the sheen of electrum. He stretched out what appeared to be a hand and seized me by the hair of my head. . . .

4 I saw there the glory of the God of Israel, like the vision I had seen in the plain. The cherubim were station-

10 ed to the right of the temple; 20 these were the living creatures I had seen beneath the God of Israel by the river Chebar, whom I now recognized to be cherubim. 21 Each had four faces and four wings; something like human hands were under their wings. 22 Their faces looked just like those I had seen by the river Chebar; each one went straight forward. 14 Each had four faces: the first face was that of an ox, the second that of a man, the third that of a lion, and the fourth that of an eagle. 15 Such were the living creatures I had seen by the river Chebar.

9 I also saw four wheels beside them, one wheel beside each cherub; the wheels appeared to have the luster of chrysolite stone. 10 All four of them seemed to be made the same, as though there were a wheel within a wheel. 11 When they moved, they went in any one of their four directions without veering as they moved; for in whichever direction they were faced, they went straight towards it without veering as they moved. 12 The rims of the four wheels were full of eyes all around. 13 I heard the wheels given the name "wheelwork." 16 When the cherubim moved, the wheels went beside them; when the cherubim lifted their wings to rise from the earth even then the wheels did not leave their sides. 17 When

they stood still, the wheels stood still; when they rose, the wheels rose with them; for the living creatures' spirit was in them.

1 I looked and saw in the firmament above the cherubim what appeared to be sapphire stone; something like a throne could be seen upon it. 2 He said to the man dressed in linen: Go within the wheelwork under the cherubim; fill both your hands with burning coals from among the cherubim, then scatter them over the city. As I looked on, he entered.

The glory of the God of Israel had gone up from the cherubim, upon which it had been, to the threshold of the temple. 3 As the man entered, the cloud filled the inner court, 4 and the glory of the LORD rose from over the cherubim to the threshold of the temple; the temple was filled with the cloud, and all the court was bright with the glory of the LORD. 5 The noise of the wings of the cherubim could be heard as far as the outer court; it was like the voice of God the Almighty when he speaks.

6 When he had commanded the man dressed in linen to take fire from within the wheelwork, among the cherubim, the man entered and stood by one of the wheels. 7 Thereupon its cherub stretched out his hand toward the fire that was among the cherubim. He took up some of it and put it in the hands of the one dressed in linen, who took it and came out. 8 [Something like human hands could be seen under the wings of the cherubim.]

18 Then the glory of the LORD left the threshold of the temple and rested upon the cherubim. 19 These lifted their wings, and I saw them rise from the earth, the wheels rising along with them. They stood at the entrance of the eastern gate of the LORD's house, and the glory of the

11 God of Israel was up above them. 22 Then the cherubim lifted their wings, and the wheels went along with them, while up above

them was the glory of the God of Israel. 23 And the glory of the LORD rose from the city and took a stand on the mountain which is to the east of the city.

Judgment of the Princes

1 Spirit lifted me up and brought me to the east gate of the temple. At the entrance of the gate I saw twenty-five men, among whom were Jaazaniah, son of Azzur, and Pelatiah, son of Benaiah, princes of the people. 2 The LORD said to me: Son of man, these are the men who are planning evil and giving wicked counsel in this city. 3 "Shall we not," they say, "be building houses soon? The city is the kettle, and we are the meat." 4 Therefore prophesy against them, son of man, prophesy! 5 Then the spirit of the LORD fell upon me, and he told me to say: Thus says the LORD: This is the way you talk, house of Israel, and what you are plotting I well know. 6 You have slain many in this city and have filled its streets with your slain. 7 Therefore thus says the Lord GOD: Your slain whom you have placed within it, they are the meat, and the city is the kettle; but you I will take out of it. 8 You fear the sword, but the sword I will bring upon you, says the Lord GOD. 9 I will bring you out of the city, and hand you over to foreigners, and inflict punishments upon you. 10 By the sword you shall fall; at the boundaries of Israel I will judge you; thus you shall know that I am the LORD. 11 The city shall not be a kettle for you, nor shall you be the meat within it. At the boundaries of Israel I will judge you, 12 and you shall know that I am the LORD, by whose statutes you have not lived, and whose ordinances you have not kept; rather, you have acted according to the ordinances of the nations around you.

13 While I was prophesying, Pelatiah, the son of Benaiah, died. I fell prone and cried out in a loud voice:

8, 1–11, 25: In these chapters of the current Hebrew text, several visions involving the temple of Jerusalem were combined to form a single continuous vision. The redistribution of verses in this translation is an attempt to separate the original visions.

8, 1: *The fifth day of the sixth month, in the sixth year:* September 17, 592 B.C.

8, 2: The dots suppose the omission of some words describing the prophet's being transported in his visions to the court of the temple.

10, 2: The *burning coals* within the wheelwork under God's throne, a sign of the divine presence (cf 28, 14; Ps 18, 13), symbolize the judgment to be visited on the city.

11, 3: These words reflect the false confidence of the inhabitants of Jerusalem in the face of the Chaldean invasion. Jerusalem, they think, is like an iron kettle protecting the meat within it from harm; but cf 24, 3–6.

"Alas, Lord GOD! will you utterly wipe out what remains of Israel?"

Restoration of the Exiles

14 Thus the word of the LORD came to me: 15 Son of man, it is about your kinsmen, your fellow exiles, and the whole house of Israel that the inhabitants of Jerusalem say, "They are far away from the LORD; to us the land of Israel has been given as our possession." 16 Therefore say: Thus says the Lord GOD: Though I have removed them far among the nations and scattered them over foreign countries—and was for a while their only sanctuary in the countries to which they had gone— 17 I will gather you from the nations and assemble you from the countries over which you have been scattered, and I will restore to you the land of Israel. 18 They shall return to it and remove from it all its detestable abominations. 19 I will give them a new heart and put a new spirit within them; I will remove the stony heart from their bodies, and replace it with a natural heart, 20 so that they will live according to my statutes, and observe and carry out my ordinances; thus they shall be my people and I will be their God. 21 But as for those whose hearts are devoted to their detestable abominations, I will bring down their conduct upon their heads, say the Lord GOD.

Acts Symbolic of the Exile

12 Thus the word of the LORD came to me: 2 Son of man, you live in the midst of a rebellious house; they have eyes to see but do not see, and ears to hear but do not hear, for they are a rebellious house. 3 Now, son of man, during the day while they are looking on, prepare your baggage as though for exile, and again while they are looking on, migrate from where you live to another place; perhaps they will see that they are a rebellious house. 4 You shall bring out your baggage like an exile in the daytime while

they are looking on, you shall go out like one of those driven into exile; 5 while they look on, dig a hole in the wall and pass through it; 6 while they look on, shoulder the burden and set out in darkness; cover your face that you may not see the land, for I have made you a sign for the house of Israel.

7 I did as I was told. During the day I brought out my baggage as though it were that of an exile, and at evening I dug a hole through the wall with my hand and, while they looked on, set out in darkness, shouldering my burden.

8 Then, in the morning, the word of the LORD came to me: 9 Son of man, did not the house of Israel, that rebellious house, ask you what you were doing? 10 Tell them: Thus says the Lord GOD: This oracle concerns Jerusalem and the whole house of Israel within it. 11 I am a sign for you: as I have done, so shall it be done to them; as captives they shall go into exile. 12 The prince who is among them shall shoulder his burden and set out in darkness, going through a hole that he has dug in the wall, and covering his face lest he be seen by anyone. 13 But I will spread my net over him, and he shall be taken in my snare. I will bring him to Babylon, into the land of the Chaldeans—but he shall not see it— and there he shall die. 14 All his retinue, his aides, and his troops I will scatter in every direction, and pursue them with the sword. 15 Then shall they know that I am the LORD, when I disperse them among the nations and scatter them over foreign lands. 16 Yet I will leave a few of them to escape the sword, famine and pestilence, so that they may tell of all their abominations among the nations to which they will come; thus they shall know that I am the LORD.

17 Thus the word of the LORD came to me: 18 Son of man, eat your bread trembling, and drink your water shaking with anxiety. 19 Then say to the people of the land:

Thus says the Lord GOD of the inhabitants of Jerusalem [to the land of Israel]: They shall eat their bread in anxiety and drink their water in horror, that their land be emptied of the violence of all its inhabitants that now fills it. 20 Inhabited cities shall be in ruins, and the land shall be a waste; thus you shall know that I am the LORD.

Prophecy Ridiculed

21 Thus the word of the LORD came to me: 22 Son of man, what is this proverb that you have in the land of Israel: "The days drag on, and no vision ever comes to anything"? 23 Say to them therefore: Thus says the Lord GOD: I will put an end to this proverb; they shall never quote it again in Israel. Rather, say to them: The days are at hand, and also the fulfillment of every vision. 25 Whatever I speak is final, and it shall be done without further delay. In your days, rebellious house, whatever I speak I will bring about, says the Lord GOD.

24 There shall no longer be any false visions or deceitful divinations within the house of Israel, because it is I, the LORD, who will speak.

26 Thus the word of the LORD came to me: 27 Son of man, listen to the house of Israel saying, "The vision he sees is a long way off; he prophesies of the distant future!" 28 Say to them therefore: Thus says the Lord GOD: None of my words shall be delayed any longer; whatever I speak is final, and it shall be done, says the Lord GOD.

Against the Prophets of Peace

13 Thus the word of the LORD came to me: 2 Son of man, prophesy against the prophets of Israel, prophesy! Say to those who prophesy their own thought: Hear the word of the LORD: 5 You did not step into the breach, nor did you build a wall about the house of Israel that would stand firm against attack on the day of the LORD. 7 Was not the vision you saw false, and your

---

11, 15–21: Like Jeremiah (cf chapter 29), Ezekiel knows that no reform is to be expected from the men of Judah who remained in Palestine; but the exiles will be the ones to form the new Israel. The new,

spiritual covenant will replace the former covenant; cf Jer 24, 7.
12, 5: *Dig a hole in the wall:* the exiles are to leave Jerusalem through the broken walls of the ruined city.
12, 13: *But he shall not see it:* Zedekiah was

blinded by Nebuchadnezzar before being deported to Babylonia; cf 2 Kgs 25, 7.
12, 22.27: These words were used against Ezekiel because of the apparent failure of his prophecies; cf Jer 20, 7ff.

divination lying? 8 Therefore thus says the Lord GOD: Because you have spoken falsehood and have seen lying visions, therefore see! I am coming at you, says the Lord GOD.

10 For the very reason that they led my people astray, saying, "Peace!" when there was no peace, and that, as one built a wall, they would cover it with whitewash, 11 say then to the whitewashers: I will bring down a flooding rain; hailstones shall fall, and a stormwind shall break out. 12 And when the wall has fallen, will you not be asked: Where is the whitewash you spread on?

13 Therefore thus says the Lord GOD: In my fury I will let loose stormwinds; because of my anger there shall be a flooding rain, and hailstones shall fall with destructive wrath. 14 I will tear down the wall that you have whitewashed and level it to the ground, laying bare its foundations. When it falls, you shall be crushed beneath it; thus you shall know that I am the LORD. 15 When I have spent my fury on the wall and its whitewashers, I tell you there shall be no wall, nor shall there be whitewashers— 16 those prophets of Israel who prophesied to Jerusalem and saw for it visions of peace when there was no peace, says the Lord GOD.

Against False Prophets in Chaldea

3 Thus says the Lord GOD: Woe to those prophets who are fools, who follow their own spirit and have seen no vision. 4 Like foxes among ruins are your prophets, O Israel! 6 Their visions are false and their divination lying. They say, "Thus says the LORD!" though the LORD did not send them; then they wait for him to fulfill their word! 9 But I will stretch out my hand against the prophets who have false visions and who foretell lies. They shall not belong to the community of my people, nor be recorded in the register of the house of Israel, nor enter the

land of Israel; thus you shall know that I am the LORD.

Against False Prophetesses

17 Now, son of man, turn toward the daughters of your people who prophesy their own thoughts; against these, prophesy: Thus says the Lord GOD: 22 Because you have disheartened the upright man with lies when I did not wish him grieved, and have encouraged the wicked man not to turn from his evil conduct and save his life; 23 therefore you shall no longer see false visions and practice divination, but I will rescue my people from your power. Thus you shall know that I am the LORD.

Against Sorceresses

18 Woe to those who sew bands for everyone's wrists and make veils for every size of head so as to entrap their owners. Do you think to entrap the lives of my people, yet keep yourselves alive? 19 You dishonor me before my people with handfuls of barley and crumbs of bread, killing those who should not die and keeping alive those who should not live, lying to my people who willingly hear lies. 20 Therefore thus says the Lord GOD: See! I am coming at those bands of yours in which you entrap men's lives: I will tear them from their arms and set free those you have caught. 21 I will tear off your veils and rescue my people from your power, so that they shall no longer be prey to your hands. Thus you shall know that I am the LORD.

Prophecy Useless for Idolaters

14 When certain elders of Israel came and sat down before me, 2 the word of the LORD came to me: 3 Son of man, these men have the memory of their idols fresh in their hearts, and they keep the occasion of their sin before them. Why should I allow myself to be consulted by them? 4 Therefore speak with them, and say to them: Thus says the Lord GOD: If

anyone of the house of Israel, holding the memory of his idols in his heart and keeping the occasion of his sin before him, has recourse to a prophet, I, the LORD, will be his answer in person because of his many idols. 5 Thus would I bring back to their senses the house of Israel, who have become estranged from me through all their idols.

6 Therefore say to the house of Israel: Thus says the Lord GOD: Return and be converted from your idols; turn yourselves away from all your abominations. 7 For if anyone of the house of Israel or any alien resident in Israel is estranged from me, and holds the memory of his idols in his heart and keeps the occasion of his sin before him, yet asks a prophet to consult me for him, I, the LORD, will be his answer in person. 8 I will turn against that man, and make him an example and a byword. I will cut him off from the midst of my people. Thus you shall know that I am the LORD.

9 As for the prophet, if he is beguiled into speaking a word, I, the LORD, shall have beguiled that prophet; I will stretch out my hand against him and root him out of my people Israel. 10 Each shall receive punishment for his sin, the inquirer and the prophet shall be punished alike, 11 so that the house of Israel may no longer stray from me and may no longer be defiled by all their sins. Thus they shall be my people, and I will be their God, says the Lord GOD.

Personal Responsibility

12 Thus the word of the LORD came to me: 13 Son of man, when a land sins against me by breaking faith, I stretch out my hand against it and break its staff of bread, I let famine loose upon it and cut off from it both man and beast; 14 and even if these three men were in it, Noah, Daniel, and Job, they could only save themselves by their virtue, says

---

13, 10: To the confidence which the people had in their defenses against the Chaldeans, the false prophets contributed the illusion of security by predictions of peace, like men who whitewash a wall rather than allow its defects to be seen.
13, 18: *Sew bands . . . make veils:* magical practices believed to give to the sorceresses power over those on whom they placed these objects.

13, 19: *Handfuls of barley and crumbs of bread:* used in divination and forecasting the future.
14, 9: *I, the Lord, shall have beguiled that prophet:* the ancient Israelites attributed to God every action, good or evil; cf 1 Sm 18, 10; 2 Sm 24, 1ff. We would say, rather, that God permitted this deceit.
14, 12–23: The doctrine of personal responsibility before God was not new (cf 3, 16–21; 18; 33, 1–20);

but it had not been emphasized by the prophets before the Exile, who mostly predicted national retribution and called for national repentance.
14, 14: *Noah, Daniel, and Job:* proverbially virtuous men. The Daniel named here may be the traditional just judge of the ancient past, celebrated in Canaanite literature, who is possibly reflected in Dn 13, but is not the hero of Dn 1–12.

the Lord GOD. 15 If I were to cause wild beasts to prowl the land, depopulating it so that it became a waste, traversed by none because of the wild beasts, 16 and these three men were in it, as I live, says the Lord GOD, I swear they could save neither sons nor daughters; they alone would be saved, and the land would be a waste. 17 Or if I brought the sword upon this country, commanding the sword to pass through the land cutting off from it man and beast, 18 and these three men were in it, as I live, says the Lord GOD, they would be unable to save either sons or daughters; they alone would be saved. 19 Or if I were to send pestilence into this land, pouring out upon it my bloodthirsty fury, cutting off from it man and beast, 20 even if Noah, Daniel, and Job were in it, as I live, says the Lord GOD, I swear that they could save neither son nor daughter; they would save only themselves by their virtue.

21 Thus says the Lord GOD: Even though I send Jerusalem my four cruel punishments, the sword, famine wild beasts, and pestilence, to cut off from it man and beast, 22 still some survivors shall be left in it who will bring out sons and daughters; when they come out to you, you shall see their conduct and their actions and be consoled regarding the evil I have brought on Jerusalem [all that I have brought upon it]. 23 They shall console you when you see their conduct and actions, for you shall then know that it was not without reason that I did to it what I did, says the Lord GOD.

Parable of the Vine

15 Thus the word of the LORD came to me: 2 Son of man, what makes the wood of the vine better than any other wood? That branch among the trees of the forest! 3 Can you use its wood to make anything worthwhile? Can you make even a peg from it, to hang on it any kind of vessel? 4 If you throw it on the fire as fuel and the fire devours

both ends and even the middle is scorched, is it still good for anything? 5 Why, even when it was whole it was good for nothing; how much less, when the fire has devoured and scorched it, can it be used for anything! 6 Therefore, thus says the Lord GOD: Like the wood of the vine among the trees of the forest, which I have destined as fuel for the fire, do I make the inhabitants of Jerusalem. 7 I will set my face against them; they have escaped from the fire, but the fire shall devour them. Thus you shall know that I am the LORD, when I turn my face against them. 8 I will make the land a waste, because they have broken faith, says the Lord GOD.

The Faithless Spouse

16 Thus the word of the LORD came to me: 2 Son of man, make known to Jerusalem her abominations: 3 Thus says the Lord GOD to Jerusalem: By origin and birth you are of the land of Canaan; your father was an Amorite and your mother a Hittite. 4 As for your birth, the day you were born your navel cord was not cut; you were neither washed with water nor anointed, nor were you rubbed with salt, nor swathed in swaddling clothes. 5 No one looked on you with pity or compassion to do any of these things for you. Rather, you were thrown out on the ground as something loathsome, the day you were born.

6 Then I passed by and saw you weltering in your blood. I said to you: Live in your blood 7 and grow like a plant in the field. You grew and developed, you came to the age of puberty; your breasts were formed, your hair had grown, but you were still stark naked. 8 Again I passed by you and saw that you were now old enough for love. So I spread the corner of my cloak over you to cover your nakedness; I swore an oath to you and entered into a covenant with you; you became mine, says the Lord GOD. 9 Then I bathed you with water, washed away your blood, and

anointed you with oil. 10 I clothed you with an embroidered gown, put sandals of fine leather on your feet; I gave you a fine linen sash and silk robes to wear. 11 I adorned you with jewelry: I put bracelets on your arms, a necklace about your neck, 12 a ring in your nose, pendants in your ears, and a glorious diadem upon your head. 13 Thus you were adorned with gold and silver; your garments were of fine linen, silk and embroidered cloth. Fine flour, honey, and oil were your food. You were exceedingly beautiful, with the dignity of a queen. 14 You were renowned among the nations for your beauty, perfect as it was, because of my splendor which I had bestowed on you, says the Lord GOD.

15 But you were captivated by your own beauty, you used your renown to make yourself a harlot, and you lavished your harlotry on every passerby, whose own you became. 16 You took some of your gowns and made for yourself gaudy high places, where you played the harlot. . . . 17 You took the splendid gold and silver ornaments that I had given you and made for yourself male images, with which also you played the harlot. 18 You took your embroidered gowns to cover them; my oil and my incense you set before them; 19 the food that I had given you, the fine flour, the oil, and the honey with which I fed you, you set before them as an appeasing odor, says the Lord GOD. 20 The sons and daughters you had borne me you took and offered as sacrifices to be devoured by them! Was it not enough that you had become a harlot? 21 You slaughtered and immolated my children to them, making them pass through fire. 22 And through all your abominations and harlotries you remembered nothing of when you were a girl, stark naked and weltering in your blood.

23 Then after all your evildoing— woe, woe to you! says the Lord GOD — 24 you raised for yourself a platform and a dais in every public place. 25 At every street corner

16, 3f: By origin and birth . . . Canaan . . . Amorite . . . Hittite: the inhabitants of Jerusalem and Judah absorbed not only pre-Israelite racial strains, but also many elements of the country's pagan cult and customs.
16, 8: I spread the corner of my cloak over you to

cover your nakedness: and also to signify the intention of marriage; cf Ru 3, 9.
16, 16: Fine robes were used to cover a couch for harlotry; cf Prv 7, 16f. In the allegory of this chapter the viewpoint often shifts from the figure (harlotry) to the reality (idolatry).

16, 20f: Human sacrifice was introduced under Judah's impious kings; cf 2 Kgs 16, 3; 17, 17; Jer 7, 31.
16, 24: A platform and a dais: associated with ritual prostitution, which the Israelites borrowed from Canaanite practice.

you built a dais for yourself to use your beauty obscenely, spreading your legs for every passer-by, playing the harlot countless times. 26 You played the harlot with the Egyptians, your lustful neighbors, so many times that I was provoked to anger. 27 Therefore I stretched out my hand against you, I diminished your allowance and delivered you over to the will of your enemies, the Philistines, who revolted at your lewd conduct. 28 You also played the harlot with the Assyrians, because you were not satisfied; and after playing the harlot with them, you were still not satisfied. 29 Again and again you played the harlot, now going to Chaldea, the land of the traders; but despite this, you were still not satisfied.

30 How wild your lust! says the Lord GOD, that you did all these things, acting like a shameless prostitute, 31 building your platform at every street corner and erecting your dais in every public place! Yet you were unlike a prostitute, since you disdained payment. 32 The adulterous wife receives, instead of her husband, payment. 33 All harlots receive gifts. But you rather bestowed your gifts on all your lovers, bribing them to come to you from all sides for your harlotry. 34 Thus in your harlotry you were different from all other women. No one sought you out for prostitution. Since you gave payment instead of receiving it, how different you were!

35 Therefore, harlot, hear the word of the LORD! 36 Thus says the Lord GOD: Because you poured out your lust and revealed your nakedness in your harlotry with your lovers and abominable idols, and because you sacrificed the lifeblood of your children to them, 37 I will now gather together all your lovers whom you tried to please, whether you loved them or loved them not; I will gather them against you from all sides and expose you naked for them to see. 38 I will inflict on you the sentence of adulteresses and murderesses; I will wreak fury and jealousy upon you. 39 I will hand you over to them to tear down your platform and de-

molish your dais; they shall strip you of your garments and take away your splendid ornaments, leaving you stark naked. 40 They shall lead an assembly against you to stone you and hack you with their swords. 41 They shall burn your apartments with fire and inflict punishments on you while many women look on. Thus I will put an end to your harlotry, and you shall never again give payment. 42 When I have wreaked my fury upon you I will cease to be jealous of you, I will be quiet and no longer vexed. 43 Because you did not remember what happened when you were a girl, but enraged me with all these things, therefore in return I am bringing down your conduct upon your head, says the Lord GOD. For did you not add lewdness to the rest of your abominable deeds?

44 See, everyone who is fond of proverbs will say of you, 'Like mother, like daughter.' 45 Yes, you are the true daughter of the mother who spurned her husband and children, and you are a true sister to those who spurned their husbands and children—your mother was a Hittite and your father an Amorite. 46 Your elder sister was Samaria with her daughters, living to the north of you; and your younger sister, living to the south of you, was Sodom with her daughters. 47 Yet not only in their ways did you walk, and act as abominably as they did; in a very short time you became more corrupt in all your ways than they. 48 As I live, says the Lord GOD, I swear that your sister Sodom, with her daughters, has not done as you and your daughters have done! 49 And look at the guilt of your sister Sodom: she and her daughters were proud, sated with food, complacent in their prosperity, and they gave no help to the poor and needy. 50 Rather, they became haughty and committed abominable crimes in my presence; then, as you have seen, I removed them. 51 Samaria did not commit half your sins! You have done more abominable things than they, and have even made your sisters appear just, with all the abominable deeds

you have done. 52 You, then, bear your shame; you are an argument in favor of your sisters! In view of your sinful deeds, more abominable than theirs, they appear just in comparison with you. Blush for shame, and bear the shame of having made your sisters appear just.

53 I will restore their fortunes, the fortune of Sodom and her daughters and of Samaria and her daughters, [and I will restore your fortune along with them], 54 that you may bear your shame and be disgraced for all the comfort you brought them. 55 Yes, your sisters, Sodom and her daughters, Samaria and her daughters, shall return to their former state [you and your daughters shall return to your former state]. 56 Was not your sister Sodom kept in bad repute by you while you felt proud of yourself, 57 before your wickedness became evident? Now you are like her, reproached by the Edomites and all your neighbors, despised on all sides by the Philistines. 58 The penalty of your lewdness and your abominations—you must bear it all, says the LORD.

59 For thus speaks the Lord GOD: I will deal with you according to what you have done, you who despised your oath, breaking a covenant. 60 Yet I will remember the covenant I made with you when you were a girl, and I will set up an everlasting covenant with you. 61 Then you shall remember your conduct and be ashamed when I take your sisters, those older and younger than you, and give them to you as daughters, even though I am not bound by my covenant with you. 62 For I will re-establish my covenant with you, that you may know that I am the LORD, 63 that you may remember and be covered with confusion, and that you may be utterly silenced for shame when I pardon you for all you have done, says the Lord GOD.

The Eagles and the Vine

17 Thus the word of the LORD came to me: 2 Son of man, propose a riddle, and speak this

---

16, 45: *True daughter of the mother:* Jerusalem has followed in the footsteps of its heathen forebears; cf v 3.

16, 46: *Your elder sister was Samaria:* Samaria can be called an elder sister in view of the relatively greater importance of the northern kingdom, Israel,

during most of Old Testament history. Also, the relatively insignificant Sodom of ancient history can be called *your younger sister.*

proverb to the house of Israel: 3
Thus speaks the Lord GOD:

The great eagle, with great
     wings, with long pinions,
     with thick plumage, many-
     hued, came to Lebanon.
He took the crest of the cedar,
4   tearing off its topmost branch,
And brought it to a land of
     tradesmen,
     set it in a city of merchants.
5 Then he took some seed of the
     land,
     and planted it in a seedbed;
A shoot by plentiful waters,
     like a willow he placed it,
6 To sprout and grow up a vine,
     dense and low-lying,
Its branches turned toward him,
     its roots lying under him.
Thus it became a vine, produced
     branches and put forth
     shoots.
7 But there was another great
     eagle,
     great of wing, rich in plumage;
To him this vine bent its roots,
     sent out its branches,
That he might water it more
     freely
     than the bed where it was
     planted.
8 In a fertile field by plentiful
     waters it was planted,
     to grow branches, bear fruit,
     and become a majestic vine.

9 Say: Thus says the Lord GOD:
Can it prosper? Will he not rather
tear it out by the roots and strip off
its fruit, so that all its green growth
will wither when he pulls it up by the
roots? [No need of a mighty arm or
many people to do this.] 10 True,
it is planted, but will it prosper? Will
it not rather wither, when touched
by the east wind, in the bed where it
grew?
11 Thus the word of the LORD
came to me: 12 Son of man, say
now to the rebellious house: Do you
not understand what this means? It
is this: The king of Babylon came to
Jerusalem and took away its king
and princes with him to Babylon.

13 Then he selected a man of the
royal line with whom he made a
covenant, binding him under oath,
while removing the nobles of the land,
14 so that the kingdom would
remain a modest one, without aspirations, and would keep his covenant and obey him. 15 But this man
rebelled against him, sending envoys
to Egypt to obtain horses and a great
army. Can he prosper? Can he who
does such things escape? Can he
break a covenant and still go free?
16 As I live, says the Lord GOD, in
the home of the king who set him up
to rule, whose oath he spurned, whose
covenant with him he broke, there in
Babylon I swear he shall die! 17
When ramps are cast up and siege
towers are built for the destruction of
many lives, he shall not be saved in
the conflict by Pharaoh with a great
army and numerous troops. 18 He
spurned his oath, breaking his covenant. Though he gave his hand in
pledge, he did all these things. He
shall not escape!
19 Therefore say: Thus says the
Lord GOD: As I live, my oath which
he spurned, my covenant which he
broke, I swear to bring down upon
his head. 20 I will spread my net
over him, and he shall be taken in my
snare. I will bring him to Babylon
and enter into judgment with him
there over his breaking faith with me.
21 All the crack troops among his
forces shall fall by the sword, and the
survivors shall be scattered in every
direction. Thus you shall know that I,
the LORD, have spoken.
22 Therefore say: Thus says the
Lord GOD:

I, too, will take from the crest
     of the cedar,
     from its topmost branches
     tear off a tender shoot,
And plant it on a high and lofty
     mountain;
23   on the mountain heights
     of Israel I will plant it.
It shall put forth branches
     and bear fruit,
     and become a majestic cedar.

Birds of every kind shall dwell
     beneath it,
     every winged thing in the
     shade of its boughs.
24 And all the trees of the field
     shall know
     that I, the LORD,
Bring low the high tree,
     lift high the lowly tree,
Wither up the green tree,
     and make the withered tree
     bloom.

As I, the LORD, have spoken, so will
I do.

Personal Responsibility

18 Thus the word of the LORD
came to me: Son of man, 2
what is the meaning of this proverb
that you recite in the land of Israel:

"Fathers have eaten green
     grapes,
     thus their children's teeth
     are on edge"?

3 As I live says the Lord GOD: I
swear that there shall no longer be
anyone among you who will repeat
this proverb in Israel. 4 For all lives
are mine; the life of the father is like
the life of the son, both are mine;
only the one who sins shall die.
5 If a man is virtuous—if he does
what is right and just, 6 if he does
not eat on the mountains, nor raise
his eyes to the idols of the house of
Israel; if he does not defile his
neighbor's wife, nor have relations
with a woman in her menstrual period;
7 if he oppresses no one, gives back
the pledge received for a debt,
commits no robbery; if he gives food
to the hungry and clothes the naked;
8 if he does not lend at interest nor
exact usury; if he holds off from
evildoing, judges fairly between a
man and his opponent; 9 if he
lives by my statutes and is careful to
observe my ordinances, that man is
virtuous—he shall surely live, says
the Lord GOD.
10 But if he begets a son who is a
thief, a murderer, or who does any

17, 11–21: These verses explain the foregoing allegory. In 597 B.C. Nebuchadnezzar removed King Jehoiachin and took him into exile; in his place he set Zedekiah, Jehoiachin's uncle, on the throne and received from him the oath of loyalty. But Zedekiah was beguiled into rebellion by Pharoah Hophra of

Egypt, and thereby merited punishment; cf 2 Kgs 24, 10–25, 7.
17, 22f: *I, too, will take from the crest of the cedar . . . plant it:* the Lord will restore Israel under a Messianic king from the same Davidic dynasty.
18, 2: *Fathers . . . on edge:* a proverb by which the

people claimed that they were being punished for their ancestors' sins rather than for their own; cf Jer 31, 29.
18, 6: *Eat on the mountains:* partake of ritual meals at the heathen high places.

of these things 11 (though the father does none of them), a son who eats on the mountains, defiles the wife of his neighbor, 12 oppresses the poor and needy, commits robbery, does not give back a pledge, raises his eyes to idols, does abominable things, 13 lends at interest and exacts usury—this son certainly shall not live. Because he practiced all these abominations, he shall surely die; his death shall be his own fault.

14 On the other hand, if a man begets a son who, seeing all the sins his father commits, yet fears and does not imitate him; 15 a son who does nor eat on the mountains, or raise his eyes to the idols of the house of Israel, or defile his neighbor's wife; 16 who does not oppress anyone, or exact a pledge, or commit robbery; who gives his food to the hungry and clothes the naked; 17 who holds off from evildoing, accepts no interest or usury, but keeps my ordinances and lives by my statutes—this one shall not die for the sins of his father, but shall surely live. 18 Only the father, since he violated rights, and robbed, and did what was not good among his people, shall in truth die for his sins. 19 You ask: "Why is not the son charged with the guilt of his father?" Because the son has done what is right and just, and has been careful to observe all my statutes, he shall surely live. 20 Only the one who sins shall die. The son shall not be charged with the guilt of his father, nor shall the father be charged with the guilt of his son. The virtuous man's virtue shall be his own, as the wicked man's wickedness shall be his.

21 But if the wicked man turns away from all the sins he committed, if he keeps all my statutes and does what is right and just, he shall surely live, he shall not die. 22 None of the crimes he committed shall be remembered against him; he shall live because of the virtue he has practiced. 23 Do I indeed derive any pleasure from the death of the wicked? says the Lord GOD. Do I not rather rejoice when he turns from his evil way that he may live?

24 And if the virtuous man turns from the path of virtue to do evil, the same kind of abominable things that the wicked man does, can he do this and still live? None of his virtuous deeds shall be remembered, because he has broken faith and committed sin; because of this, he shall die. 25 You say, "The LORD's way is not fair!" Hear now, house of Israel: Is it my way that is unfair, or rather, are not your ways unfair? 26 When a virtuous man turns away from virtue to commit iniquity, and dies, it is because of the iniquity he committed that he must die. 27 But if a wicked man, turning from the wickedness he has committed, does what is right and just, he shall preserve his life; 28 since he has turned away from all the sins which he committed, he shall surely live, he shall not die. 29 And yet the house of Israel says, "The LORD's way is not fair!" Is it my way that is not fair, house of Israel, or rather, is it not that your ways are not fair?

30 Therefore I will judge you, house of Israel, each one according to his ways, says the Lord GOD. Turn and be converted from all your crimes, that they may be no cause of guilt for you. 31 Cast away from you all the crimes you have committed, and make for yourselves a new heart and a new spirit. Why should you die, O house of Israel? 32 For I have no pleasure in the death of anyone who dies, says the Lord GOD. Return and live!

19 As for you, son of man, raise a lamentation over the prince of Israel:

Allegory of the Lions

2 What a lioness was your mother,
    a lion of lions!
Among young lions she couched
    to rear her whelps.
3 One whelp she raised up,
    a young lion he became;
He learned to seize prey,
    men he devoured;
4 Then nations raised cries
    against him,
    in their pit he was caught;

They took him away with hooks
    to the land of Egypt.
5 Then she saw that in vain she
    had waited,
    her hope was destroyed.
She took another of her whelps,
    him she made a young lion.
6 He prowled among the lions,
    a young lion he became;
He learned to seize prey,
    men he devoured;
7 He ravaged their strongholds,
    their cities he wasted.
The land and all in it were
    appalled
    at the noise of his roar.
8 Nations laid out against him
    snares all about him;
They spread their net to take him,
    in their pit he was caught.
9 They put him in a cage and
    took him away
    to the king of Babylon,
So that his voice would not
    be heard
    on the mountains of Israel.

Allegory of the Vine Branch

10 Your mother was like a vine
    planted by the water;
Fruitful and branchy was she
    because of the abundant
    water.
11 One strong branch she put out
    as a royal scepter.
Stately was her height
    amid the dense foliage;
Notably tall was she
    with her many clusters.
12 But she was torn up in fury
    and flung to the ground;
The east wind withered her up,
    her fruit was torn off;
Then her strong branch
    withered up,
    fire devoured it.
13 So now she is planted in the
    desert,
    in a land dry and parched,
14 For fire came out of the branch
    and devoured her shoots;
She is now without a strong
    branch,
    a ruler's scepter.

This is a lamentation and serves as a
    lamentation.

19, 2-9: The meaning of this allegory is uncertain. Probably the two *young lions* are Jehoahaz and Zedekiah, sons of the same mother, who were deport-ed to Egypt and Babylonia respectively. Cf 2 Kgs 23, 31, 31-34; 24, 18ff.

19, 10-14: *A vine:* Judah. *One strong branch:* the Davidic king.

Israel's History of Infidelity

20 In the seventh year, on the tenth day of the fifth month, some of the elders of Israel came to consult the LORD and sat down before me. 2 Then the word of the LORD came to me: 3 Son of man, speak with the elders of Israel and say to them: Thus says the Lord GOD: Have you come to consult me? As I live! I swear I will not allow myself to be consulted by you, says the Lord GOD.

4 Will you judge them? Will you judge, son of man? Make known to them the abominations of their ancestors 5 in these words: Thus speaks the Lord GOD: The day I chose Israel, I swore to the descendants of the house of Jacob; in the land of Egypt I revealed myself to them and swore: I am the LORD, your God. 6 That day I swore to bring them out of the land of Egypt to the land I had scouted for them, a land flowing with milk and honey, a jewel among all lands. 7 Then I said to them: Throw away, each of you, the detestable things that have held your eyes; do not defile yourselves with the idols of Egypt: I am the LORD, your God.

8 But they rebelled against me and refused to listen to me; none of them threw away the detestable things that had held their eyes, they did not abandon the idols of Egypt. Then I thought of pouring out my fury on them and spending my anger on them there in the land of Egypt; 9 but I acted for my name's sake, that it should not be profaned in the sight of the nations among whom they were, in whose presence I had made myself known to them, revealing that I would bring them out of the land of Egypt. 10 Therefore I led them out of the land of Egypt and brought them into the desert. 11 Then I gave them my statutes and made known to them that my ordinances, which everyone must keep, to have life through them. 12 I also gave them my sabbaths to be a sign between me and them, to show that it

was I, the LORD, who made them holy.

13 But the house of Israel rebelled against me in the desert. They did not observe my statutes, and they despised my ordinances that bring life to those who keep them. My sabbaths, too, they desecrated grievously. Then I thought of pouring out my fury on them in the desert to put an end to them, 14 but I acted for my name's sake, that it should not be profaned in the sight of the nations in whose presence I had brought them out. 15 Nevertheless I swore to them in the desert not to bring them to the land I had given them, a land flowing with milk and honey, a jewel among all lands. 16 So much were their hearts devoted to their idols, they had not lived by my statutes, but despised my ordinances and desecrated my sabbaths. 17 But I looked on them with pity, not wanting to destroy them, so I did not put an end to them in the desert.

18 Then I said to their children in the desert: Do not observe the statutes of your parents or keep their ordinances; do not defile yourselves with their idols. 19 I am the LORD, your God: observe my statutes and be careful to keep my ordinances; 20 keep holy my sabbaths, as a sign between me and you to show that I am the LORD, your God. 21 But their children rebelled against me: they did not observe my statutes or keep my ordinances that bring life to those who observe them, and my sabbaths they desecrated. Then I thought of pouring out my fury on them, of spending my anger on them in the desert; 22 but I stayed my hand, acting for my name's sake, lest it be profaned in the sight of the nations in whose presence I brought them out. 23 Nevertheless I swore to them in the desert that I would disperse them among the nations and scatter them over foreign lands; 24 for they did not keep my ordinances, but despised my statutes and desecrated my sabbaths, with eyes only for the idols of their fathers. 25 Therefore I gave them statutes that were not good, and

ordinances through which they could not live. 26 I let them become defiled by their gifts, by their immolation of every first-born, so as to make them an object of horror.

27 Therefore speak to the house of Israel, son of man, and tell them: Thus says the Lord GOD: In this way also your fathers blasphemed me, breaking faith with me: 28 when I had brought them to the land I had sworn to give them, and they saw all its high hills and leafy trees, there they offered their sacrifices [there they brought their offensive offerings], there they set up appeasing odors, and there they poured out their libations. 29 I asked them: To what sort of high place do you betake yourselves?—and so they call it a high place even to the present day. 30 Therefore say to the house of Israel: Thus says the Lord GOD: will you defile yourselves like your fathers? Will you lust after their detestable idols? 31 By offering your gifts, by making your children pass through the fire, you defile yourselves with all your idols even to this day. Shall I let myself be consulted by you, house of Israel? As I live! says the Lord GOD: I swear I will not let myself be consulted by you.

32 What you are thinking of shall never happen: "We shall be like the nations, like the peoples of foreign lands, serving wood and stone." 33 As I live, says the Lord GOD, with a mighty hand and outstretched arm, with poured-out wrath, I swear I will be king over you! 34 With a mighty hand and outstretched arm, with poured-out wrath, I will bring you out from the nations and gather you from the countries over which you are scattered; 35 then I will lead you to the desert of the peoples, where I will enter into judgment with you face to face. 36 Just as I entered into judgment with your fathers in the desert of the land of Egypt, so will I enter into judgment with you, says the Lord GOD. 37 I will count you with the staff and bring back but a small number. 38 I will separate from you those who have rebelled

---

20, 1: *The seventh year, on the tenth day of the fifth month:* August 14, 591 B.C.

20, 25f: *I gave them statutes that were not good:* the Lord permitted them to adopt pagan practices,

including the abominable sacrifice of their newborn infants, which could only merit their destruction. See note on 14, 9.

20, 35–38: Exile in the pagan lands will serve the

same purpose as the desert journey after the Exodus from Egypt: the rebellious will be eliminated, and only a remnant survive.

and transgressed against me; from the land where they sojourned as aliens I will bring them out, but they shall not return to the land of Israel. Thus you shall know that I am the LORD.

39 As for you, house of Israel, thus says the Lord GOD: Come, each one of you, destroy your idols! Then listen to me, and never again profane my holy name with your gifts and your idols. 40 For on my holy mountain, on the mountain height of Israel, says the Lord GOD, there the whole house of Israel without exception shall worship me; there I will accept them, and there I will claim your tributes and the first fruits of your offerings, and all that you dedicate. 41 As a pleasing odor I will accept you, when I have brought you from among the nations and gathered you out of the countries over which you were scattered; and by means of you I will manifest my holiness in the sight of the nations. 42 Thus you shall know that I am the LORD, when I bring you back to the land of Israel, the land which I swore to give to your fathers. 43 There you shall recall your conduct and all the deeds by which you defiled yourselves; and you shall loathe yourselves because of all the evil things you did. 44 And you shall know that I am the LORD when I deal with you thus, for my name's sake, and not according to your evil conduct and corrupt actions, O house of Israel, says the Lord GOD.

The Sword of the Lord

21 Thus the word of the Lord came to me: 2 Son of man, look southward, preach against the south, and prophesy against the forest of the southern land. 3 Hear the word of the LORD! you shall say to the southern forest. Thus says the Lord GOD: See! I am kindling a fire in you that shall devour all trees, the green as well as the dry. The blazing flame shall not be quenched, but

from south to north every face shall be scorched by it. 4 Everyone shall see that I, the LORD, have kindled it, and it shall not be quenched.

5 But I said, "Alas! Lord GOD, they say to me, 'Is not this the one who is forever spinning parables?'" 6 Then the word of the LORD came to me: 7 Son of man, look toward Jerusalem, preach against their sanctuary, and prophesy against the land of Israel, 8 saying to the land of Israel: Thus says the LORD: See! I am coming at you; I will draw my sword from its sheath and cut off from you the virtuous and the wicked. 9 Thus my sword shall leave its sheath against everyone from south to north, 10 and everyone shall know that I, the LORD, have drawn my sword from its sheath, and it shall not be sheathed again.

Act Symbolic of the City's Fall

11 As for you, son of man, groan! with shattered strength groan bitterly while they look on. 12 And when they ask you, "Why are you groaning?", you shall say: Because of a report; when it comes every heart shall fail, every hand shall fall helpless, every spirit shall be daunted, and every knee shall run with water. See, it is coming, it is here! says the Lord GOD.

Song of the Sword

13 Thus the word of the LORD came to me: 14 Son of man, prophesy! say: Thus says the LORD:

A sword, a sword has been
      sharpened,
    a sword, a sword has been
      burnished:
15 To work slaughter has it been
      sharpened,
    to flash lightning has it been
      burnished.
    Why should I now withdraw it?
    You have spurned the rod
      and every judgment!

16 I have given it over to the
      burnisher
    that he might hold it in his
      hand,
    A sword sharpened and
      burnished
    to be put in the hand of a
      slayer.
17 Cry out and wail, son of man,
    for it is destined for my people;
    It is for all the princes of Israel,
    victims of the sword with my
      people.

Therefore, slap your thigh, 18 for the sword has been tested; and why should it not be so? says the Lord GOD, since you have spurned the rod.

19 As for you, son of man,
      prophesy,
    brushing one hand against
      the other:
    While the sword is doubled and
      tripled,
    this sword of slaughter,
    This great sword of slaughter
    which threatnes all around,
20 That every heart may tremble;
    for many will be the fallen.
    At all their gates
    I have appointed the sword
      for slaughter,
    Fashioned to flash lightning,
    burnished for slaughter.
21 Cleave to the right! destroy!
    to the left! wherever your
      edge is turned.

22 Then I, too, shall brush one hand against the other and wreak my fury. I, the LORD, have spoken.

Nebuchadnezzar at the Crossroads

23 Thus the word of the LORD came to me: 24 Son of man, make for yourself two roads over which the sword of the king of Babylon can come. Both roads shall lead out from the same land. Then put a signpost at the head of each road, 25 so that the sword can come to Rabbah of the Ammonites or to Judah's capital, Jerusalem. 26 For at the fork where the two roads divide stands the king

---

21, 2ff: The southern kingdom, Judah, is likened to a forest about to be burned; cf Jer 21, 14.

21, 8: *Cut off from you the virtuous and the wicked:* a more complete devastation of Jerusalem than that described in 9, 6.

21, 12: *A report:* the news of the fall of Jerusalem; cf 33, 21f.

21, 18: *Slap your thigh:* a gesture signifying grief and dread.

21, 22: *Brush one hand against the other:* a gesture signifying the rejection of responsibility; cf 22, 13; Nm 24, 10.

21, 26: Three forms of divination are mentioned: *arrow* divination, consisting in the use of differently

marked arrows extracted or shaken from a case at random; the consultation of the *teraphim* or household idols; and *liver* divination, scrutiny of the configurations of the livers of newly slaughtered animals, a common form of divination in Mesopotamia.

of Babylon, divining; he has shaken the arrows, inquired of the teraphim, inspected the liver. 27 In his right hand is the divining arrow marked "Jerusalem," bidding him to give the order for slaying, to raise his voice in the battle cry to post battering-rams at the gates, to cast up a ramp, to build a siege tower. 28 In their eyes this is but a lying oracle; yet they are bound by the oaths they have sworn, and the arrow taken in hand marks their guilt.

29 Therefore thus says the Lord GOD: Because you have drawn attention to your guilt, with your crimes laid bare and your sinfulness in all your wicked deeds revealed (because attention has been drawn to you), you shall be taken in hand. 30 And as for you, depraved and wicked prince of Israel, whose day is coming when your life of crime will be ended, 31 thus says the Lord GOD: Off with the turban and away with the crown! Nothing shall be as it was! Up with the low and down with the high! 32 Twisted, twisted, twisted will I leave it; it shall not be the same until he comes who has the claim against the city; and to him I will hand it over.

Against the Ammonites

33 As for you, son of man, prophesy: Thus says the Lord GOD against the Ammonites and their insults: A sword, a sword is drawn for slaughter, burnished to consume and to flash lightning, 34 because you planned with false visions and lying divinations to lay it on the necks of depraved and wicked men whose day has come when their crimes are at an end. 35 Return it to its sheath! In the place where you were created, in the land of your origin, I will judge you. 36 I will pour out my indignation upon you, breathing my fiery wrath upon you; I will hand you over to ravaging men, artisans of destruction. 37 You shall be fuel for the fire, your blood shall flow throughout the land. You shall not be remembered, for I, the LORD, have spoken.

Crimes of Jerusalem

22 Thus the word of the LORD came to me: 2 You, son of man, would you judge, would you judge the bloody city? Then make known all her abominations, 3 and say: Thus says the Lord GOD: Woe to the city which sheds blood within herself so that her time has come, and which has made idols for her own defilement. 4 By the blood which you shed you have made guilty, and with the idols you made you have become defiled; you have brought on your day, so that the end of your years has come. Therefore I make you an object of scorn to the nations and a laughingstock to all foreign lands. 5 Those near you and those far off shall deride you because of your foul reputation and your great perversity. 6 See! the princes of Israel, family by family, are in you only for bloodshed. 7 Within you, father and mother are despised; in your midst, they extort from the resident alien; within you, they oppress orphans and widows. 8 What is holy to me you have spurned, and my sabbaths you have desecrated. 9 There are those in you who slander to cause bloodshed; within you are those who feast on the mountains; in your midst are those who do lewd things. 10 In you are those who uncover the nakedness of their fathers, and in you those who coerce women in their menstrual period. 11 There are those in you who do abominable things with the wives of their neighbors, men who defile their daughters-in-law by incest, men who coerce their sisters, the daughters of their own fathers. 12 There are those in you who take bribes to shed blood. You exact interest and usury; you despoil your neighbors violently; and me you have forgotten, says the Lord GOD.

13 See, I am brushing one hand against the other because of the unjust profits you have made and because of the bloodshed in your midst. 14 Can your heart remain firm, will your hands be strong, in the days when I deal with you? I,

the LORD, have spoken, and I will act. 15 I will disperse you among the nations and scatter you over foreign lands, so that I may purge your uncleanness. 16 In you I will allow myself to be profaned in the eyes of the nations; thus you shall know that I am the LORD.

17 Thus the word of the LORD came to me: 18 Son of man, the house of Israel has become dross for me. All of them are bronze and tin, iron and lead [in the midst of a furnace]: dross from silver have they become. 19 Therefore thus says the Lord GOD: Because all of you have become dross, therefore I must gather you together within Jerusalem. 20 Just as silver, bronze, iron, lead, and tin are gathered into a furnace and smelted in the roaring flames, so I will gather you together in my furious wrath, put you in, and smelt you. 21 When I have assembled you, I will blast you with the fire of my anger and smelt you with it. 22 You shall be smelted by it just as silver is smelted in a furnace. Thus you shall know that I, the LORD, have poured out my fury on you.

23 Thus the word of the LORD came to me: 24 Son of man, say to her: You are a land unrained on [that is, not rained on] at the time of my fury. 25 Her princes are like roaring lions that tear prey; they devour people, seizing their wealth and precious things, and make widows of many within her. 26 Her priests violate my law and profane what is holy to me; they do not distinguish between the sacred and the profane, nor teach the difference between the unclean and the clean; they pay no attention to my sabbaths, so that I have been profaned in their midst. 27 Her nobles within her are like wolves that tear prey, shedding blood and destroying lives to get unjust gain. 28 Her prophets cover them with whitewash, pretending to visions that are false and performing lying divinations, saying, "Thus says the Lord GOD," although the LORD has not spoken. 29 The people of the land practice extortion and

---

21, 27f: An *arrow marked "Jerusalem"* is picked out, which *marks* the guilt of the city's inhabitants for having broken their oath of allegiance to Nebuchadnezzar.

21, 33–37: In the preceding section Nebuchadnezzar is represented as deciding whether to attack Jerusalem or Rabbath-Ammon. As it happened, Jerusalem was chosen for attack; later, however, the

Chaldeans also invaded Ammon. The present oracle against Ammon is inserted here, rather than in chapters 25–32, in order to complement the oracle against Jerusalem.

commit robbery; they afflict the poor and the needy, and oppress the resident alien without justice. 30 Thus I have searched among them for someone who could build a wall or stand in the breach before me to keep me from destroying the land; but I found no one. 31 Therefore I have poured out my fury upon them; with my fiery wrath I have consumed them; I have brought down their conduct upon their heads says the Lord God.

The Two Sisters

23 Thus the word of the Lord came to me: 2 Son of man, there were two women, daughters of the same mother, 3 who even as young girls played the harlot in Egypt. There the Egyptians caressed their bosoms and fondled their virginal breasts. 4 Oholah was the name of the elder, and the name of her sister was Oholibah. They became mine and bore sons and daughters. [As for their names: Samaria is Oholah and Jerusalem is Oholibah.] 5 Oholah became a harlot faithless to me; she lusted after her lovers, the Assyrians, warriors 6 dressed in purple, governors and officers all of them attractive young men, knights mounted on horses. 7 Thus she gave herself as a harlot to them, to all the elite of the Assyrians, and she defiled herself with all those for whom she lusted [with all their idols]. 8 She did not give up the harlotry which she had begun in Egypt, when they had lain with her as a young girl, fondling her virginal breasts and pouring out their impurities on her.

9 Therefore I handed her over to her lovers, the Assyrians for whom she had lusted. 10 They exposed her nakedness, her sons and daughters they took away, and herself they slew with the sword. Thus she became a byword for women, for they punished her grievously.

11 Though her sister Oholibah saw all this, her lust was more depraved than her sister's, and she outdid her in harlotry. 12 She too lusted after the Assyrians, governors and officers, warriors impeccably clothed, knights mounted on horses, all of them attractive young men. 13 I saw that she had defiled herself. Both had gone down the same path, 14 yet she went further in her harlotry. When she saw men drawn on the wall, the images of Chaldeans drawn with vermillion, 15 with sashes girded about their waists, flowing turbans on their heads, all looking like chariot warriors, the portraits of Babylonians, natives of Chaldea, 16 she lusted for them; no sooner had she set eyes on them than she sent messengers to them in Chaldea. 17 Then the Babylonians came to her, to the love couch, and defiled her with their intercourse. As soon as she was defiled by them, she became disgusted with them. 18 Her harlotry was discovered and her shame was revealed, and I became disgusted with her as I had become disgusted with her sister. 19 But she played the harlot all the more, recalling the days of her girlhood, when she had been a harlot in the land of Egypt. 20 She lusted for the lechers of Egypt, whose members are like that of an ass, and whose heat is like that of stallions.

21 You yearned for the lewdness of your girlhood, when the Egyptians fondled your breasts, caressing your bosom. 22 Therefore, Oholibah, thus says the Lord God: I will now stir up your lovers against you, those with whom you are disgusted, and I will bring them against you from every side: 23 the men of Babylon and all of Chaldea, Pekod, Shoa and Koa, along with all those of Assyria, attractive young men, all of them governors and officers, charioteers and warriors, all of them horsemen. 24 They shall come against you from the north with chariots and wagons and many peoples. Shields, bucklers, and helmets they shall array against you everywhere. 25 I will leave it to them to judge, and they will judge you by their own ordinances. I will let loose my jealousy against you, so that they shall deal with you in fury, cutting off your nose and ears; and what is left of you shall fall by the sword. They shall take away your sons and daughters, and what is left of you shall be devoured by fire. 26 They shall strip off your clothes and seize your splendid ornaments. 27 I will put an end to your lewdness and to the harlotry you began in Egypt; you shall no longer look toward it, nor shall you remember Egypt again.

28 For thus says the Lord God: I am now handing you over to those whom you hate, to those who fill you with disgust. 29 They shall deal with you in hatred, seizing all that you have worked for and leaving you stark naked, so that your indecent nakedness is exposed. Your lewdness and harlotry 30 have brought these things upon you, because you played the harlot with the nations by defiling yourself with their idols. 31 Because you followed in the path of your sister, I will hand you her cup. 32 Thus says the Lord God:

> The cup of your sister you shall
> 　drink,
> 　　so wide and deep, which
> 　　　holds so much,
> 33 Filled with destruction and
> 　grief,
> 　　a cup of dismay, the cup of
> 　　your sister.

34 You shall drain it dry, and gnaw at the very sherds of the cup, and you shall tear out your breasts; for I have spoken, says the Lord God. 35 Therefore thus says the Lord God: Because you have forgotten me and cast me behind your back, it is for you to bear the penalty of your lewdness and harlotry.

36 Then the Lord said to me: Son of man, would you judge Oholah and Oholibah? Then make known to them their abominations. 37 For they committed adultery, and blood is on their hands. They committed adultery with their idols; to feed them they immolated the children they had borne me. 38 [This, too, they did to me: they defiled my sanctuary and desecrated my sabbaths. 39 On the very day they slew their children for their idols, they entered my sanctuary to desecrate it. Thus

---

23, 4: *Oholah . . . Oholibah:* symbolic names. The first, standing for Samaria, may be read to mean "her own tent"; the latter, standing for Jerusalem, means

"my tent is in her." The references seem to be the schismatic temple and cult of the Lord in Samaria, as opposed to their authentic counterpart in Jerusalem.

23, 23: *Pekod, Shoa and Koa:* peoples living about the Tigris, part of "greater Babylonia."

they acted within my house.] 40 Moreover, they sent for men who had to come from afar, to whom messengers were sent. And so they came—and for them you bathed yourself, painted your eyes, and put on ornaments. 41 You sat on a couch prepared for them, with a table spread before it, on which you had set my incense and oil. 42 Then was heard the shout of a carefree mob in the city, and these were men brought in from the desert, who put bracelets on the women's arms and splendid diadems on their heads. 43 So I said: "Oh, this woman jaded with adulteries! Now they will commit whoredom with her, and as for her. . . ." 44 And indeed they did come to her as men to a harlot. Thus they came to Oholah and Oholibah, the lewd women. 45 But just men shall punish them with the sentence meted out to adulteresses and murderesses, for they have committed adultery, and blood is on their hands. 46 Thus says the Lord GOD: Summon an assembly against them, and deliver them over to terror and plunder. 47 The assembly shall stone them and hack them to pieces with their swords. They shall slay their sons and daughters, and burn their houses with fire. 48 Thus I will put an end to lewdness in the land, and all the women will be warned not to imitate your lewdness. 49 They shall inflict on you the penalty of your lewdness, and you shall pay for your sins of idolatry. Thus you shall know that I am the LORD.

Allegory of the Pot

24 On the tenth day of the tenth month, in the ninth year, the word of the LORD came to me: 2 Son of man, write down this date today, for this very day the king of Babylon has invested Jerusalem. 3 Propose this parable to the rebellious house: Thus says the Lord GOD:

Set up the pot, set it up,
    then pour in some water.

4 Put in it pieces of meat,
    all good pieces: thigh and
        shoulder;
Fill it with the choicest joints
5   taken from the pick of the
        flock.
Then pile the wood beneath it;
    bring to a boil these pieces
    and the joints that are in it.
6 Take out its pieces, one by one,
    without casting lots for it.

Therefore, thus says the Lord GOD: Woe to the bloody city a pot containing rust, whose rust has not been removed. 7 For the blood she shed is in her midst: she poured it on the bare rock; she did not pour it on the earth, to be covered with dust. 8 To work up my wrath, to excite my vengeance, she put blood on the bare rock, not to be covered. 9 Therefore, thus says the Lord GOD:

I, too, will heap up a great
    bonfire,
10   piling on wood and kindling
        the fire,
Till the meat has been cooked,
    till the broth has boiled.

11 Then I will set the pot empty on the coals till its metal glows red hot, till the impurities in it melt, and its rust disappears. 12 Yet not even with fire will its great rust be removed. 13 Because you have sullied youself with lewdness when I would have purified you, and you refused to be purified of your uncleanness, therefore you shall not be purified until I wreak my fury on you. 14 I, the LORD, have spoken; it is coming, for I will bring it about without fail. I will not have pity nor repent. By your conduct and your deeds you shall be judged, says the Lord GOD.

Symbol of the Destruction of the Temple

15 Thus the word of the LORD came to me: 16 Son of man, by a sudden blow I am taking away from you the delight of your eyes, but do not mourn or weep or shed any tears.

17 Groan in silence, make no lament for the dead, bind on your turban, put your sandals on your feet, do not cover your beard, and do not eat the customary bread. 18 That evening my wife died, and the next morning I did as I had been commanded. 19 Then the people asked me, "Will you not tell us what all these things that you are doing mean for us?" I therefore spoke to the people that morning, 20 saying to them: Thus the word of the LORD came to me: 21 Say to the house of Israel: Thus says the Lord GOD: I will now desecrate my sanctuary, the stronghold of your pride, the delight of your eyes, the desire of your soul. The sons and daughters you left behind shall fall by the sword. 24 Ezekiel shall be a sign for you: all that he did you shall do when it happens. Thus you shall know that I am the LORD. 22 You shall do as I have done, not covering your beards nor eating the customary bread. 23 Your turbans shall remain on your heads, your sandals on your feet. You shall not mourn or weep, but you shall rot away because of your sins and groan one to another.

End of Ezekiel's Dumbness

25 As for you, son of man, truly, on the day I take away from them their bulwark, their glorious joy, the delight of their eyes, the desire of their soul, and the pride of their hearts, their sons and daughters, 26 that day the fugitive will come to you, that you may hear it for yourself; 27 that day your mouth shall be opened and you shall be dumb no longer. Thus you shall be a sign to them, and they shall know that I am the LORD.

PROPHECIES AGAINST FOREIGN NATIONS

Against Ammon

25 Thus the word of the LORD came to me: 2 Son of man, turn toward the Ammonites and prophesy against them. 3 Say to

---

23, 40: *Men who had come from afar:* ambassadors from Assyria and Babylon. Alliances with these countries aided in the corruption of both Israel and Judah.

24, 1: *The tenth day of the tenth month, in the ninth year:* January 15, 588 B.C. The same date is given in Jer 52, 4.

24, 3ff: This present comparison of the inhabitants of Jerusalem to meat boiled in a pot symbolizes their punishment rather than their supposed protection as in 11, 3.

24, 7: *Blood . . . to be covered with dust:* since blood was sacred to God, it had to be covered with earth (Lv 17, 13); the blood of a murdered man that was left uncovered cried to heaven for vengeance; cf Jb 16, 18; Gn 4, 10.

24, 17: *The customary bread:* eaten as a mourning observance; cf Jer 16, 7. The other gestures here forbidden were also popular mourning customs.

24, 22f: The fall of the city will be so sudden and final that the exiles will have no time to go into mourning.

the Ammonites: Hear the word of the LORD! Thus says the Lord GOD: Because you cried out your joy over the desecration of my sanctuary, the devastation of the land of Israel, and the exile of the house of Judah, 4 therefore I will deliver you into the possession of the Easterners. They shall set up their encampments among you and pitch their tents; they shall eat your fruits and drink your milk. 5 I will make Rabbah a pasture for camels, and the villages of the Ammonites a resting place for flocks. Thus you shall know that I am the LORD.

6 For thus says the Lord GOD: Because you clapped your hands and stamped your feet, rejoicing most maliciously in your heart over the land of Israel, 7 therefore I will stretch out my hand against you. I will make you plunder for the nations, I will cut you off from the peoples, and remove you from the lands. I will destroy you, and thus you shall know that I am the LORD.

Against Moab

8 Thus says the Lord GOD: Because Moab said, "See! the house of Judah is like all other nations," 9 therefore I will clear the shoulder of Moab totally of its cities, the jewels of the land: Beth-jesimoth, Baalmeon, and Kiriathaim. 10 I will hand her over, along with the Ammonites, into the possession of the Easterners, that she may not be remembered among the peoples. 11 Thus I will execute judgment upon Moab, that they may know that I am the LORD.

Against Edom

12 Thus says the Lord GOD: Because Edom has taken vengeance on the house of Judah and has made itself grievously guilty by taking vengeance on them, 13 therefore thus says the Lord GOD: I will stretch out my hand against Edom and cut off from it man and beast. I will make it a waste from Teman to Dedan; they shall fall by the sword. 14 My vengeance upon Edom I will

entrust to my people Israel, who will deal with Edom in accordance with my anger and my fury; thus they shall know my vengeance, says the Lord GOD.

Against the Philistines

15 Thus says the Lord GOD: Because the Philistines have acted revengefully, and have taken vengeance with destructive malice in their hearts, with an undying enmity, 16 therefore thus says the Lord GOD: See! I am stretching out my hand against the Philistines; I will cut off the Cherethites and wipe out the remnant on the seacoast. 17 I will execute great acts of vengeance on them, punishing them furiously. Thus they shall know that I am the LORD, when I wreak my vengeance on them.

Against the City of Tyre

26 On the first day of the . . . month in the eleventh year, the word of the LORD came to me: 2 Son of man, because of what Tyre said to Jerusalem:

"Aha! it is broken, the gateway
  to the peoples;
  now that it is ruined, its
  wealth reverts to me!"
3 therefore thus says the Lord
  GOD:
See! I am coming at you, Tyre;
  I will churn up against you
  many nations,
  even as the sea churns up its
  waves;
4 They shall destroy the walls of
  Tyre
  and raze her towers.
I will scrape the ground from
  her
  and leave her a bare rock;
5 She shall be a drying place for
  nets
  in the midst of the sea.

I have spoken, says the Lord GOD: and she shall be booty for the nations. 6 And her daughters on the mainland shall be slaughtered by the sword; thus they shall know that I am the LORD.

7 For thus says the Lord GOD: I am now bringing up against Tyre from the north Nebuchadnezzar the king of Babylon, the king of kings, with horses and chariots, with cavalry and a great and mighty army.

8 Your daughters on the mainland
  he shall slay with the sword;
He shall place a siege tower
  against you,
  cast up a ramp about you,
  and raise his shields against
  you.
9 He shall pound your walls with
  battering-rams
  and break down your towers
  with his weapons.
10 The surge of his horses shall
  cover you with dust,
  amid the noise of steeds,
  of wheels and of chariots.
Your walls shall shake as he
  enters your gates,
  even as one enters a city
  that is breached.
11 With the hoofs of his horses
  he shall trample all your
  streets;
Your people he shall slay by
  the sword;
  your mighty pillars he shall
  pull to the ground.
12 Your wealth shall be plundered,
  your merchandise pillaged;
Your walls shall be torn down,
  your precious houses
  demolished;
Your stones, your timber, and
  your clay
  shall be cast into the sea.
13 I will put an end to the noise
  of your songs,
  and the sound of your lyres
  shall be heard no more.
14 I will make you a bare rock;
  a drying place for nets shall
  you be.

Never shall you be rebuilt, for I have spoken, says the Lord GOD.

15 Thus says the Lord GOD to Tyre: At the noise of your fall, at the groaning of the wounded, when the sword slays in your midst, shall not the isles quake? 16 All the princes

---

25, 4: *The Easterners:* nomadic tribes to the east of Ammon and Moab.
25, 9: *The shoulder of Moab:* the edge of the Moabite plateau.

25, 16: *Cherethites:* a people forming part of the Philistine nation; cf Zep 2, 5.
26, 4f: *A bare rock:* the Tyre of Ezekiel's time was situated on a rocky island just off the Phoenician

coast; it was not until the time of Alexander the Great that it was connected by a causeway to the mainland.
26, 6: *Her daughters:* tributary towns and villages on the mainland.

of the sea shall step down from their thrones, lay aside their robes, and strip off their embroidered garments. They shall be clothed in mourning and, sitting on the ground, they shall tremble at every moment and be horrified at you. 17 Then they shall utter a lament over you:

How have you perished, gone
    from the seas,
    city most prized!
Once she was mighty on the sea,
    she and her dwellers,
Who spread terror into all
    that dwelt by the sea.
18 On this, the day of your fall,
    the islands quake!

The isles in the sea are terrified at your passing.
19 For thus says the Lord GOD: When I make you a city desolate like cities that are no longer inhabited, when I churn up the abyss against you, and its mighty waters cover you, 20 then I will thrust you down with those who descend into the pit, those of the bygone age; and I will make you dwell in the nether lands, in the everlasting ruins, with those who go down to the pit, so that you may never return to take your place in the land of the living. 21 I will make you a devastation, and you shall be no more; you shall be sought, but never again found, says the Lord GOD.

The Ship Tyre

27 Thus the word of the LORD came to me: 2 As for you, son of man, utter a lament over Tyre, 3 and say to Tyre that is situated at the approaches of the sea, that brought the trade of the peoples to many a coastland: Thus says the Lord GOD:

Tyre, you said, "I am a ship,
    perfect in beauty."
4 In the midst of the sea your
    builders placed you,
    perfected your beauty.
5 With cypress from Senir they
    built for you
    all of your decks;

Cedar from Lebanon they took
    to make you a mast;
6 From the highest oaks of
    Bashan
    they made your oars;
Your bridge they made of
    cypress wood
    from the coasts of Kittim.
7 Fine embroidered linen from
    Egypt
    became your sail [to serve
    you as a banner].
Purple and scarlet from the
    coasts of Elishah
    covered your cabin.
8 Citizens of Sidon and Arvad
    served as your oarsmen;
Skilled men of Zemer were in
    you
    to be your mariners;
9 The elders and experts of Gebal
    were in you
    to caulk your seams.

Every ship and sailor on the sea came to you to carry trade. 10 Persia and Lud and Put were in your army as warriors; shield and helmet they hung upon you, increasing your splendor. 11 The men of Arvad were all about your walls, and the Gamadites were in your towers; they hung their bucklers all around on your walls, and made perfect your beauty. 12 Tarshish traded with you, so great was your wealth, exchanging silver, iron, tin and lead for your wares. 13 Javan, Tubal, and Meshech were also traders with you, exchanging slaves and articles of bronze for your goods. 14 From Beth-togarmah horses, steeds, and mules were exchanged for your wares. 15 The Rhodanites trafficked with you; many coastlands traded with you; ivory tusks and ebony wood they gave you for payment. 16 Edom traded with you, so many were your products, exchanging garnets, purple, embroidered cloth, fine linen, coral, and rubies for your wares. 17 Judah and the land of Israel trafficked with you, exchanging Minnith wheat, figs, honey, oil, and balm for your goods. 18 Damascus traded with you, so great was your wealth, exchanging

Helbon wine and Zahar wool. 19 Javan exchanged wrought iron, cassia and aromatic cane from Uzal for your wares. 20 Dedan traded with you for riding gear. 21 The trade of Arabia and of all the sheikhs of Kedar belonged to you; they dealt in lambs, rams, and goats. 22 The merchants of Sheba and Raamah also traded with you, exchanging for your wares the very choicest spices, all kinds of precious stones, and gold. 23 Haran, Canneh, and Eden, the merchants of Sheba, Asshur, and Chilmad 24 traded with you, marketing with you rich garments, violet mantles, embroidered cloth, vari-colored carpets, and firmly woven cords. 25 Ships of Tarshish journeyed for you in your merchandising.

You were full and heavily laden
    in the heart of the sea.
26 Through the deep waters your
    oarsmen
    brought you home,
But the east wind smashed you
    in the heart of the sea.
27 Your wealth, your goods, your
    wares,
    your sailors, and your crew,

[the caulkers of your seams, those who traded for your goods, all your warriors who were in you, and all the great crowd within you]

Sank into the heart of the sea
    on the day of your shipwreck.
28 Hearing the shouts of your
    mariners,
    the shores begin to quake.
29 Down from their ships
    come all who ply the oar;
The sailors, all the mariners
    of the sea,
    stand on the shore,
30 Making their voice heard on
    your behalf,
    shouting bitter cries,
Strewing dust on their heads,
    rolling in the ashes.
31 For you they shave their heads
    and put on sackcloth,
For you they weep in anguish,
    with bitter lament.

26, 20: *Those who descend into the pit:* the dead, pictured as dwelling in a place or cave of darkness.
27, 5: *Senir:* another name for Mount Hermon; cf Dt 3, 9.

27, 6: *Bashan:* northern Transjordan, which, like Lebanon, was noted for its great forests. *Kittim:* probably Cyprus.
27, 7: *Elishah:* probably another term for Cyprus.

27, 8f: *Sidon ... Arvad ... Zemer ... Gebal:* Phoenician cities in Tyre's orbit of influence; the last-named is the classical Byblos.

32 In their mourning they utter a
      lament over you;
    thus they wail over you:
    Who was ever destroyed like
      Tyre
    in the midst of the sea?
33 With your goods which you
      drew from the seas
    you filled many peoples;
    With your great wealth and
      merchandise
    you enriched the kings of
      the earth.
34 Now you are wrecked in the sea,
      in the watery depths;
    Your wares and all your crew
    have gone down with you.
35 All who dwell on the coastlands
      are aghast over you,
    Their kings are terrified,
      their faces convulsed.
36 The traders among the peoples
      now hiss at you;
    You have become a horror,
      and you shall be no more.

The Prince of Tyre

28 Thus the word of the LORD
      came to me: 2 Son of man,
say to the prince of Tyre: Thus says
the Lord GOD:

    Because you are haughty of
      heart,
      you say, "A god am I!
    I occupy a godly throne
      in the heart of the sea!"—
    And yet you are a man, and not
      a god,
      however you may think
        yourself like a god.
3 Oh yes, you are wiser than
      Daniel,
    there is no secret that is
      beyond you.
4 By your wisdom and your
      intelligence
    you have made riches for
      yourself;
    You have put gold and silver
      into your treasuries.
5 By your great wisdom applied
      to your trading
    you have heaped up your
      riches;
    your heart has grown haughty
      from your riches—

6 therefore thus says the Lord
      GOD:
    Because you have thought
      yourself
    to have the mind of a god,
7 Therefore I will bring against
      you
    foreigners, the most bar-
      barous of nations.
    They shall draw their swords
    against your beauteous
      wisdom,
    they shall run them through
      your splendid apparel.
8 They shall thrust you down to
      the pit, there to die
    a bloodied corpse, in the
      heart of the sea.
9 Will you then say, "I am a
      god!"
    when you face your
      murderers?
    No, you are a man, not a god,
    handed over to those who
      will slay you.
10 You shall die the death of the
      uncircumcised
    at the hands of foreigners,
    for I have spoken,
    says the Lord GOD.

11 Thus the word of the LORD
came to me: 12 Son of man, utter
a lament over the king of Tyre, saying
to him: Thus says the Lord GOD:

    You were stamped with the
      seal of perfection,
    of complete wisdom and
      perfect beauty.
13 In Eden, the garden of God,
      you were,
    and every precious stone was
      your covering
[carnelian, topaz, and beryl, chrysolite, onyx, and jasper, sapphire, garnet, and emerald];
    Of gold your pendants and
      jewels
    were made, on the day you
      were created.
14 With the Cherub I placed you;
    you were on the holy
      mountain of God,
    walking among the fiery
      stones.

15 Blameless you were in your
      conduct
    from the day you were
      created,
    Until evil was found in you,
16 the result of your far-flung
      trade;
    violence was your business,
      and you sinned.
    Then I banned you from the
      mountain of God;
    the Cherub drove you from
      among the fiery stones.
17 You became haughty of heart
      because of your beauty;
    for the sake of splendor
      you debased your wisdom.
    I cast you to the earth, so great
      was your guilt;
    I made you a spectacle in the
      sight of kings.
18 Because of your great guilt,
      your sinful trade,
    I have profaned your
      sanctuaries,
    And I have brought out fire
      from your midst
    which will devour you.
    I have reduced you to dust
      on the earth
    in the sight of all who should
      see you.
19 Among the peoples, all who
      knew you
    stand aghast at you;
    You have become a horror,
      you shall be no more.

Against Sidon

20 Thus the word of the LORD
came to me: 21 Son of man, look
toward Sidon, and prophesy against
it: 22 Thus says the Lord GOD:
See! I am coming at you, Sidon; I
will be glorified in your midst. Then
they shall know that I am the LORD,
when I inflict punishments upon it
and use it to manifest my holiness.

23 Into it I will send pestilence,
    and blood shall flow in its
      streets.
    Within it shall fall those slain
    by the sword that comes
      against it from every side.

Thus they shall know that I am the
the LORD.   24 Sidon shall no longer

28, 3: *Wiser than Daniel:* see note on 14, 14.
28, 12–19: This picture of Tyre and its fall recalls
images of the earthly paradise portraying the creation

of man in perfection and his fall (Gn, chapters
2–3).
28, 14: *The holy mountain of God:* the residence of

God was sometimes designated as a mountain; cf Is
14, 13. *The fiery stones:* associated with the divine
presence; cf 1, 13; Ps 18, 13.

be a tearing thorn for the house of Israel, a brier that scratches them more than all the others about them who despise them; thus they shall know that I am the LORD.

25 Thus says the Lord GOD: When I gather the house of Israel from the peoples among whom they are scattered, then I will manifest my holiness through them in the sight of the nations. Then they shall live on their land which I gave to my servant Jacob; 26 they shall live on it in security, building houses and planting vineyards. They shall dwell secure while I inflict punishments on all their neighbors who despised them; thus they shall know that I, the LORD, am their God.

Egypt the Crocodile

29 On the twelfth day of the tenth month in the tenth year, the word of the LORD came to me: 2 Son of man, set your face against Pharaoh, king of Egypt, and prophesy against him and against all Egypt. 3 Say this to him: Thus says the Lord GOD:

See! I am coming at you,
    Pharaoh,
    king of Egypt,
Great crouching monster
    amidst your Niles;
Who say, "The Niles are mine;
    it is I who made them!"

4 I will put hooks in your jaws and make the fish of your Niles stick to your scales, then draw you up from the midst of your Niles along with all the fish of your Niles sticking to your scales.

5 I will cast you into the desert,
    you and all the fish of your
        Niles;
You shall fall upon the open
        field,
    you shall not be taken up or
        buried;

To the beasts of the earth and
    the birds of the air
I give you as food,
6 That all who dwell in Egypt
    may know
    that I am the LORD.
Because you have been a reed
        staff
    for the house of Israel:
7 When they held you in hand,
    you splintered,
    throwing every shoulder out
        of joint;
When they leaned on you, you
        broke,
    bringing each one of them
        down headlong;

8 therefore thus says the Lord GOD: See! I will bring the sword against you, and cut off from you both man and beast. 9 The land of Egypt shall become a desolate waste; thus they shall know that I am the LORD. Because you said, "The Niles are mine; it is I who made them," 10 therefore see! I am coming at you and against your Niles; I will make the land of Egypt a waste and a desolation from Migdol to Syene, and even to the frontier of Ethiopia. 11 No foot of man or beast shall pass through it; they shall not pass through it, and it will be uninhabited for forty years. 12 I will make the land of Egypt the most desolate of lands, and its cities shall be the most deserted of cities for forty years; and I will scatter the Egyptians among the nations and strew them over foreign lands. 13 Yet thus says the Lord GOD: At the end of forty years I will gather the Egyptians from the peoples among whom they are scattered, 14 and I will restore Egypt's fortune, bringing them back to the land of Pathros, the land of their origin, where it will be the lowliest 15 of kingdoms, never more to set itself above the nations. I will make them few, that they may not dominate the nations. 16 No longer shall they be for the house of Israel

to trust in, but the living reminder of its guilt for having turned to follow after them. Thus they shall know that I am the LORD.

The Wages of Nebuchadnezzar

17 On the first day of the first month in the twenty-seventh year, the word of the LORD came to me: 18 Son of man, Nebuchadnezzar, the king of Babylon, has led his army in an exhausting campaign against Tyre. Their heads became bald and their shoulders were galled; but neither he nor his army received any wages from Tyre for the campaign he led against it. 19 Therefore thus says the Lord GOD: I am now giving the land of Egypt to Nebuchadnezzar, king of Babylon. He shall carry off its riches, plundering and pillaging it for the wages of his soldiers, 20 who did it for me; as payment for his toil I have given him the land of Egypt, says the Lord GOD.

21 On that day I will make a horn sprout for the house of Israel, and I will cause you to speak out in their midst; thus they shall know that I am the LORD.

The Day of the Lord against Egypt

30 Thus the word of the LORD came to me: 2 Son of man, speak this prophecy: Thus says the Lord GOD: Cry, Oh, the day! 3 for near is the day, near is the day of the LORD; a day of clouds, doomsday for the nations shall it be. 4 Then a sword shall come upon Egypt, and anguish shall be in Ethiopia, when the slain fall in Egypt, when her riches are seized and her foundations are overthrown. 5 Ethiopia, Put, Lud, all Arabia, Libya, and people of the allied territory shall fall by the sword with them. 6 Those who support Egypt shall fall, and down shall come her proud strength; from Migdol to Syene they shall fall there by the sword, says

---

29, 1: *The twelfth day of the tenth month in the tenth year:* January 7, 587 B.C. The siege of Jerusalem had begun a year earlier; cf 24, 1.

29, 2: Egypt was allied with Judah against the Chaldeans.

29, 3: *Niles:* the many rivulets of the Nile as it branches out into the Delta.

29, 10: *From Migdol to Syene:* from the northern

to the southern extremity of Egypt. *Syene* is the modern Assuan.

29, 14: *Pathros, the land of their origin:* upper Egypt, that is, southern Egypt, where the Egyptians were thought to have originated; Is 11, 11; Jer 44, 1.15.

29, 17: *The first day of the first month in the twenty-seventh year:* April 26, 571 B.C. This is the latest date attached to any prophecy in Ezekiel.

29, 18 f: The fulfillment of Ezekiel's prophecy against Tyre (chapters 26–28) was a thirteen-year siege of the city by Nebuchadnezzar (587–574 B.C.). Tyre seems to have been taken, but its resources were exhausted and the booty was small. Therefore Ezekiel now prophesies that Nebuchadnezzar will collect his *wages* as God's instrument in the punishment of Tyre, by plundering Egypt.

the Lord GOD. 7 She shall be the most devastated of lands, and her cities shall be the most desolate of all. 8 Then they shall know that I am the LORD, when I set fire to Egypt and when all who help her are broken. 9 On that day messengers shall hasten forth at my command to terrify unsuspecting Ethiopia; they shall be in anguish on the day of Egypt, which is surely coming.

10 Thus says the Lord GOD: I will put an end to the throngs of Egypt by the hand of Nebuchadnezzar, king of Babylon. 11 He and his people with him, the most ruthless of nations, shall be brought in to devastate the land. They shall draw their swords against Egypt, and fill the land with the slain. 12 I will turn the Niles into dry land and sell the land over to the power of the wicked. The land and everything in it I will hand over to foreigners to devastate. I, the LORD, have spoken.

13 Thus says the Lord GOD: I will put an end to the great ones of Memphis and the princes of the land of Egypt, that they may be no more. I will cast fear into the land of Egypt, and devastate Pathros. 14 I will set fire to Zoan, and inflict punishments on Thebes. 15 I will pour out my wrath on Pelusium, Egypt's stronghold, and cut down the crowds in Memphis. 16 I will set fire to Egypt; Syene shall writhe in anguish; Thebes shall be breached and its walls shall be demolished. 17 The young men of On and of Pibeseth shall fall by the sword, and the cities themselves shall go into captivity. 18 In Tehaphnehes the day shall be darkened when I break the scepter of Egypt. Her haughty pride shall cease from her, clouds shall cover her, and her daughters shall go into captivity. 19 Thus will I inflict punishments on Egypt, that they may know that I am the LORD.

Pharaoh's Broken Arm

20 On the seventh day of the first month in the eleventh year, the word of the LORD came to me: 21 Son of man, I have broken the arm of Pharaoh, the king of Egypt, and see, it has not been bound up with bandages and healing remedies that it may be strong enough to hold the sword. 22 Therefore thus says the Lord GOD: See! I am coming at Pharaoh, the king of Egypt. I will break his strong arm, so that the sword drops from his hand. 23 I will scatter the Egyptians among the nations and strew them over foreign lands. 24 But I will strengthen the arms of the king of Babylon, and put my sword in his hand, which he will bring against Egypt so as to plunder and pillage it. 25 [I will make the arms of the king of Babylon strong, but the arms of Pharaoh shall drop.] Then they shall know that I am the LORD, when I put my sword in the hand of the king of Babylon for him to wield against the land of Egypt. 26 [I will scatter the Egyptians among the nations and strew them over foreign lands.] Thus they shall know that I am the LORD.

Allegory of the Cypress

31 On the first day of the third month in the eleventh year, the word of the LORD came to me: 2 Son of man, say to Pharaoh, the king of Egypt, and to his hordes: What are you like in your greatness?

3 Behold, a cypress [cedar] in
      Lebanon,
   beautiful of branch, lofty of
      stature,
   amid the very clouds lifted its
      crest.
4 Waters made it grow, the abyss
      made it flourish,
   sending its rivers round where
      it was planted,
   turning its streams to all the
      trees of the field.
5 Thus it grew taller than every
      other tree of the field,
   and longer of branch because
      of the abundant water.

6 In its boughs nested all the
      birds of the air,
   under its branches all beasts of
      the field gave birth,
   in its shade dwelt numerous
      peoples of every race.
7 It became beautiful and stately
      in its spread of foliage,
   for its roots were turned
      toward abundant water.
8 The cedars in the garden of God
      were not its equal,
   nor could the fir trees match
      its boughs,
   Neither were the plane trees
      like it for branches;
   no tree in the garden of God
      matched its beauty.
9 I made it beautiful, with much
      foliage,
   the envy of all Eden's trees in
      the garden of God.

10 Therefore thus says the Lord GOD: Because it became lofty in stature, raising its crest among the clouds, and because it became proud in heart at its height, 11 I have handed it over to the mightiest of the nations, which has dealt with it in keeping with its wickedness. I humiliated it. 12 Foreigners, the most ruthless of the nations, cut it down and left it on the mountains. Its foliage was brought low in all the valleys, its branches lay broken in all the ravines of the land, and all the peoples of the land withdrew from its shade, abandoning it.

13 On its fallen trunk rested all the
      birds of the air,
   and by its branches were all
      the beasts of the field.

14 Thus no tree may grow lofty in stature or raise its crest among the clouds; no tree fed by water may stand by itself in its loftiness.

   For all of them are destined for
      death,
      for the land below,
   For the company of mortals,
      those who go down into the
      pit.

---

15 Thus says the Lord GOD: On the day he went down to the nether world I made the abyss close up over him; I stopped its streams so that the deep waters were held back. I cast gloom over Lebanon because of him, so that all the trees in the land drooped on his account. 16 At the crash of his fall I made the nations rock, when I cast him down to the nether world with those who go down into the pit. In the land below, all Eden's trees were consoled, Lebanon's choice and best, all that were fed by water. 17 They too have come down with him to the nether world, to those slain by the sword; those who dwelt in his shade are dispersed among the nations. 18 Which was your equal in glory or size among the trees of Eden? Yet you have been brought down with the trees of Eden to the land below. You shall lie with the uncircumcised, with those slain by the sword. Such are Pharaoh and all his hordes, says the Lord GOD.

Dirge over Pharaoh

32 On the first day of the twelfth month in the twelfth year, the word of the LORD came to me: 2 Son of man, utter a lament over Pharaoh, the king of Egypt, saying to him: Lion of the nations, you are destroyed.

You were like a monster in the sea,
spouting in your streams,
Stirring the water with your feet and churning its streams.

3 Thus says the Lord GOD:

I will spread my net over you [with a host of many nations], and draw you up in my seine.
4 I will leave you on the land; on the open field I will cast you.
I will have all the birds of the air alight on you,
and all the beasts of the earth eat their fill of you.
5 I will leave your flesh on the mountains,
and fill the valleys with your carcass.

6 I will water the land with what flows from you,
and the river beds shall be filled with your blood.
7 When I snuff you out I will cover the heavens,
and all their stars I will darken;
The sun I will cover with clouds, and the moon shall not give its light.
8 All the shining lights in the heavens
I will darken on your account,
And I will spread darkness over your land,
says the Lord GOD.

9 I will grieve the hearts of many peoples when I lead you captive among the nations, to lands which you do not know. 10 Many peoples shall be appalled at you, and their kings shall shudder over you in horror when they see me brandish my sword, and on the day of your downfall every one of them shall continuously tremble for his own life. 11 For thus says the Lord GOD: The sword of the king of Babylon shall come upon you.

12 I will cut down your horde with the blades of warriors,
all of them the most ruthless of the nations;
They shall lay waste the glory of Egypt,
and all her hordes shall be destroyed.
13 I will have all of her animals perish
beside her abundant waters;
The foot of man shall stir them no longer,
nor shall the hoof of beast disturb them.
14 Then will I make their waters clear,
and their streams flow like oil, says the Lord GOD.

15 When I turn Egypt into a waste, the land shall be devastated of all that is in it; when I strike all who live there, they shall know that I am the LORD. 16 This is a dirge, and it shall be sung: the daughters of the nations shall chant it; over Egypt and all its hordes shall they chant it, says the Lord GOD.

Dirge over Egypt

17 On the fifteenth day of the first month in the twelfth year, the word of the LORD came to me: 18 Son of man, lament over the throngs of Egypt, for the mighty nations have thrust them down to the bottom of the earth, with those who go down into the pit. 20 In the midst of those slain by the sword shall they fall, and place shall be made with them for all their hordes. Then from the midst of the nether world, the mighty warriors shall speak to Egypt: 19 "Whom do you excel in beauty? 21 Come down, you and your allies, lie with the uncircumcised, with those slain by the sword."

22 There is Assyria with all her company, all of them slain, 23 whose graves have been made in the recesses of the pit; her company is around Egypt's grave, all of them slain, fallen by the sword, who spread terror in the land of the living. 24 There is Elam with all her throng about Egypt's grave, all of them slain, fallen by the sword: they have gone down uncircumcised to the bottom of the earth, who spread their terror in the land of the living, and they bear their disgrace with those who go down into the pit; 25 in the midst of the slain they are placed. 26 There are Meshech and Tubal and all their throng about her grave, all of them uncircumcised, slain by the sword, for they spread their terror in the land of the living.

27 They do not lie with the mighty men fallen of old, who went down to the nether world with their weapons of war, whose swords were placed under their heads and whose shields were laid over their bones, though the mighty men caused terror in the land of the living. 28 But in the midst of the uncircumcised shall you lie, with those slain by the sword.

29 There are Edom, her kings, and all her princes, who despite their might have been placed with those

---

32, 1: *The first day of the twelfth month in the twelfth year:* March 3, 585 B.C.

32, 27: *The mighty men fallen of old:* the semi-legendary heroes of the prehistoric past, who were

thought to have once dominated the world; cf Is 14, 9.

slain by the sword; with the uncircumcised they lie, and with those who go down into the pit. 30 There are all the princes of the north and all the Sidonians, who have gone down with the slain, because of the terror their might inspired; they lie uncircumcised with those slain by the sword and bear their disgrace with those who go down to the pit. 31 When Pharaoh sees these, he shall be comforted for all his hordes slain by the sword—Pharaoh and all his army, says the Lord GOD. 32 Since he spread his terror in the land of the living, therefore is he laid to rest among the uncircumcised, with those slain by the sword—Pharaoh and all his hordes, says the Lord GOD.

SALVATION FOR ISRAEL

The Prophet a Watchman

33 Thus the word of the LORD came to me: 2 Son of man, speak thus to your countrymen: When I bring the sword against a country, and the people of this country select one of their number to be their watchman, 3 and the watchman, seeing the sword coming against the country, blows the trumpet to warn the people, 4 anyone hearing but not heeding the warning of the trumpet and therefore slain by the sword that comes against him, shall be responsible for his own death. 5 He heard the trumpet blast yet refused to take warning; he is responsible for his own death, for had he taken warning he would have escaped with his life. 6 But if the watchman sees the sword coming and fails to blow the warning trumpet, so that the sword comes and takes anyone, I will hold the watchman responsible for that person's death, even though that person is taken because of his own sin.

7 You, son of man, I have appointed watchman for the house of Israel; when you hear me say anything, you shall warn them for me. 8 If I tell the wicked man that he shall surely die, and you do not speak

out to dissuade the wicked man from his way, he [the wicked man] shall die for his guilt, but I will hold you responsible for his death. 9 But if you warn the wicked man, trying to turn him from his way, and he refuses to turn from his way, he shall die for his guilt, but you shall save yourself.

Individual Retribution

10 As for you, son of man, speak to the house of Israel: You people say, "Our crimes and our sins weigh us down; we are rotting away because of them. How can we survive?" 11 Answer them: As I live, says the Lord GOD, I swear I take no pleasure in the death of the wicked man, but rather in the wicked man's conversion, that he may live. Turn, turn from your evil ways! Why should you die, O house of Israel?

12 As for you, son of man, tell your countrymen: The virtue which a man has practiced will not save him on the day that he sins; neither will the wickedness that a man has done bring about his downfall on the day that he turns from his wickedness [nor can the virtuous man, when he sins, remain alive]. 13 Though I say to the virtuous man that he shall surely live, if he then presumes on his virtue and does wrong, none of his virtuous deeds shall be remembered; because of the wrong he has done, he shall die. 14 And though I say to the wicked man that he shall surely die, if he turns away from his sin and does what is right and just, 15 giving back pledges, restoring stolen goods, living by the statutes that bring life, and doing no wrong, he shall surely live, he shall not die. 16 None of the sins he committed shall be held against him; he has done what is right and just, he shall surely live.

17 Yet your countrymen say, "The way of the LORD is not fair!"; but it is their way that is not fair. 18 When a virtuous man turns away from what is right and does wrong, he shall die for it. 19 But when a

wicked man turns away from wickedness and does what is right and just, because of this he shall live. 20 And still you say, "The way of the LORD is not fair!"? I will judge every one of you according to his ways, O house of Israel.

The Fugitive from Jerusalem

21 On the fifth day of the tenth month, in the twelfth year of our exile, the fugitive came to me from Jerusalem and said, "The city is taken!" 22 The hand of the LORD had come upon me the evening before the fugitive arrived, and he opened my mouth when the fugitive reached me in the morning. My mouth was opened, and I was dumb no longer.

The Survivors in Judah

23 Thus the word of the LORD came to me: 24 Son of man, they who live in the ruins on the land of Israel reason thus: "Abraham, though but a single individual, received possession of the land; we, therefore, being many, have as permanent possession the land that has been given to us." 25 Give them this answer: Thus says the Lord GOD: You eat on the mountains, you raise your eyes to your idols, you shed blood—yet you would keep possession of the land? 26 You rely on your sword, you do abominable things, each one of you defiles his neighbor's wife—yet you would keep possession of the land? 27 Tell them this: Thus says the Lord GOD: As I live, those who are in the ruins I swear shall fall by the sword; those who are in the open field I have given to the wild beasts for food; and those who are in fastnesses and in caves shall die by the plague. 28 I will make the land a desolate waste, so that its proud strength will come to an end, and the mountains of Israel shall be so desolate that no one will cross them. 29 Thus they shall know that I am the LORD, when I make the land a desolate waste because of all the abominable things they have done.

33, 21f: January 8, 585 B.C According to Jeremiah (39, 2), Jerusalem was taken in July, 587. Some MSS read "eleventh" for twelfth year (January, 586); even so, there was ample time between the fall of Jerusalem and the arrival of the fugitive from that

city to journey to Babylon. However, this is the fugitive sent to fulfill the promise of 24, 25.27, the eyewitness who would release Ezekiel from his dumbness; cf 2, 26f.

33, 23–29: News brought by the fugitive fur-

nished the occasion of this prophecy. Like Jeremiah, Ezekiel rejects the idea that the survivors in Judah have any claim to the land. The new Israel is to be formed from the exiles.

The Prophet's False Popularity

30 As for you, son of man, your countrymen are talking about you along the walls and in the doorways of houses. They say to one another, "Come and hear the latest word that comes from the LORD." 31 My people come to you as people always do; they sit down before you and hear your words, but they will not obey them, for lies are on their lips and their desires are fixed on dishonest gain. 32 For them you are only a ballad singer, with a pleasant voice and a clever touch. They listen to your words, but they will not obey them. 33 But when it comes—and it is surely coming!—they shall know that there was a prophet among them.

Parable of the Shepherds

34 Thus the word of the LORD came to me: 2 Son of man, prophesy against the shepherds of Israel, in these words prophesy to them [to the shepherds]: Thus says the Lord GOD: Woe to the shepherds of Israel who have been pasturing themselves! Should not shepherds, rather, pasture sheep? 3 You have fed off their milk, worn their wool, and slaughtered the fatlings, but the sheep you have not pastured. 4 You did not strengthen the weak nor heal the sick nor bind up the injured. You did not bring back the strayed nor seek the lost, but you lorded it over them harshly and brutally. 5 So they were scattered for lack of a shepherd, and became food for all the wild beasts. My sheep were scattered 6 and wandered over all the mountains and high hills; my sheep were scattered over the whole earth, with no one to look after them or to search for them.

7 Therefore, shepherds, hear the word of the LORD: 8 As I live, says the Lord GOD, because my sheep have been given over to pillage, and because my sheep have become food for every wild beast, for lack of a shepherd; because my shepherds did not look after my sheep, but

pastured themselves and did not pasture my sheep; 9 because of this, shepherds, hear the word of the LORD: 10 Thus says the Lord GOD: I swear I am coming against these shepherds. I will claim my sheep from them and put a stop to their shepherding my sheep so that they may no longer pasture themselves. I will save my sheep, that they may no longer be food for their mouths.

11 For thus says the Lord GOD: I myself will look after and tend my sheep. 12 As a shepherd tends his flock when he finds himself among his scattered sheep, so will I tend my sheep. I will rescue them from every place where they were scattered when it was cloudy and dark. 13 I will lead them out from among the peoples and gather them from the foreign lands; I will bring them back to their own country and pasture them upon the mountains of Israel [in the land's ravines and all its inhabited places]. 14 In good pastures will I pasture them, and on the mountain heights of Israel shall be their grazing ground. There they shall lie down on good grazing ground, and in rich pastures shall they be pastured on the mountains of Israel. 15 I myself will pasture my sheep; I myself will give them rest, says the Lord GOD. 16 The lost I will seek out, the strayed I will bring back, the injured I will bind up, the sick I will heal [but the sleek and the strong I will destroy], shepherding them rightly.

Separation of the Sheep

17 As for you, my sheep, says the Lord GOD, I will judge between one sheep and another, between rams and goats. 18 Was it not enough for you to graze on the best pasture, that you had to trample the rest of your pastures with your feet? Was it not enough for you to drink the clearest water, that you had to foul the remainder with your feet? 19 Thus my sheep had to graze on what your feet had trampled and drink what your feet had fouled. 20 Therefore

thus says the Lord GOD: Now will I judge between the fat and the lean sheep. 21 Because you push with side and shoulder, and butt all the weak sheep with your horns until you have driven them out, 22 I will save my sheep so that they may no longer be despoiled, and I will judge between one sheep and another. 23 I will appoint one shepherd over them to pasture them, my servant David; he shall pasture them and be their shepherd. 24 I, the LORD, will be their God, and my servant David shall be prince among them. I, the LORD, have spoken.

25 I will make a covenant of peace with them, and rid the country of ravenous beasts, that they may dwell securely in the desert and sleep in the forests. 26 I will place them about my hill, sending rain in due season, rains that shall be a blessing to them. 27 The trees of the field shall bear their fruits, and the land its crops, and they shall dwell securely on their own soil. Thus they shall know that I am the LORD when I break the bonds of their yoke and free them from the power of those who enslaved them. 28 They shall no longer be despoiled by the nations or devoured by beasts of the earth, but shall dwell secure, with no one to frighten them. 29 I will prepare for them peaceful fields for planting; they shall no longer be carried off by famine in the land, or bear the reproaches of the nations. 30 Thus they shall know that I, the LORD, am their God, and they are my people, the house of Israel, says the Lord GOD. 31 [You, my sheep, you are the sheep of my pasture, and I am your God, says the Lord GOD.]

Against Edom

35 Thus the word of the LORD came to me: 2 Son of man, set your face against Mount Seir, and prophesy against it. 3 Say to it: Thus says the Lord GOD: See! I am coming at you, Mount Seir. I will stretch out my hand against you and make you a desolate waste. 4 Your

---

33, 30: The fulfillment of Ezekiel's prophecies about Jerusalem was responsible for this temporary enthusiasm among the unstable people.
34, 2: *The shepherds of Israel:* the leaders of the people.

34, 23: *One shepherd . . . my servant David:* a Messianic Davidic king who will rule over the restored Israel (vv 25–31) in the name of the Lord.
35, 1–15: After the fall of Jerusalem, Edom

assisted the Chaldeans in devastating the land and subduing the population, and ended by occupying part of Judah's former territory. For this reason these oracles against Edom are found in the context of the city's fall.

cities I will turn into ruins, and you shall be a waste; thus you shall know that I am the LORD.

5 Because you never let die your hatred for the Israelites, whom you delivered over to the power of the sword at the time of their trouble, when their crimes came to an end, 6 therefore, as I live, says the Lord GOD, you have been guilty of blood, and blood, I swear, shall pursue you. 7 I will make Mount Seir a desolate waste, and cut off from it any traveler. 8 With the slain I will fill your hills, your valleys, and all your ravines [in them the slain shall fall by the sword]: 9 desolate will I make you forever, and leave your cities without inhabitants; thus you shall know that I am the LORD.

10 Because you said: The two nations and the two lands have become mine: we shall possess them— although the LORD was there— 11 therefore, as I live, says the Lord GOD, I will deal with you according to your anger and your envy which you have exercised [in your hatred] against them. I will make myself known among you when I judge you, 12 and you shall know that I am the LORD.

I have heard all the contemptuous things you have uttered against the mountains of Israel: "They are desolate, they have been given us to devour." 13 I have heard the insolent and wild words you have spoken against me. 14 Thus says the Lord GOD: Just as you rejoiced over my land because it was desolate, so will I do to you. 15 In keeping with your glee over the devastation of the inheritance of the house of Israel, so will I treat you. A waste shall you be, Mount Seir, you and the whole of Edom. Thus they shall know that I am the LORD.

Regeneration of the Land

36 As for you, son of man, prophesy to the mountains of Israel: Mountains of Israel, hear the word of the LORD! 2 Thus says the Lord GOD: Because the enemy has said of you, "Ha! the everlasting heights have become our possession"

3 [therefore prophesy in these words: Thus says the Lord GOD:]; because you have been ridiculed and despised on all sides for having become a possession for the rest of the nations, and have become a byword and a popular jeer; 4 therefore, mountains of Israel, hear the word of the LORD: [Thus says the Lord GOD to the mountains and hills, the ravines and valleys, the desolate ruins and abandoned cities, which have been given over to the pillage and mockery of the remaining nations round about; 5 therefore thus says the Lord GOD:] Truly, with burning jealousy I speak against the rest of the nations [and against all of Edom] who with wholehearted joy and utter contempt have considered my land their possession to be delivered over to plunder. 6 [Therefore, prophesy concerning the land of Israel, and say to the mountains and hills, the ravines and valleys: Thus says the Lord GOD:] With jealous fury I speak, because you have borne the reproach of the nations. 7 Therefore do I solemnly swear that your neighboring nations shall bear their own reproach.

8 As for you, mountains of Israel, you shall grow branches and bear fruit for my people Israel, for they shall soon return. 9 See, I come to you, it is to you that I turn; you will be tilled and sown, 10 and I will settle crowds of men upon you, the whole house of Israel; cities shall be repeopled, and ruins rebuilt. 11 I will settle crowds of men and beasts upon you, to multiply and be fruitful. I will repeople you as in the past, and be more generous to you than in the beginning; thus you shall know that I am the LORD.

12 [My people Israel are the ones whom I will have walk upon you; they shall take possession of you, and you shall be their heritage. Never again shall you rob them of their children.]

13 Thus says the Lord GOD: Because they have said of you, "You are a land that devours men, and you rob your people of their children"; 14 therefore, never again shall you

devour men or rob your people of their children, says the Lord GOD. 15 No more will I permit you to hear the reproach of nations, or bear insults from peoples, or rob your people of their children, says the Lord GOD.

Regeneration of the People

16 Thus the word of the LORD came to me: 17 Son of man, when the house of Israel lived in their land, they defiled it by their conduct and deeds. In my sight their conduct was like the defilement of a menstruous woman. 18 Therefore I poured out my fury upon them [because of the blood which they poured out on the ground, and because they defiled it with idols]. 19 I scattered them among the nations, dispersing them over foreign lands; according to their conduct and deeds I judged them. 20 But when they came among the nations [wherever they came], they served to profane my holy name, because it was said of them: "These are the people of the LORD, yet they had to leave their land." 21 So I have relented because of my holy name which the house of Israel profaned among the nations where they came. 22 Therefore say to the house of Israel: Thus says the Lord GOD: Not for your sakes do I act, house of Israel, but for the sake of my holy name which you profaned among the nations to which you came. 23 I will prove the holiness of my great name, profaned among the nations, in whose midst you have profaned it. Thus the nations shall know that I am the LORD, says the Lord GOD, when in their sight I prove my holiness through you. 24 For I will take you away from among the nations, gather you from all the foreign lands, and bring you back to your own land. 25 I will sprinkle clean water upon you to cleanse you from all your impurities, and from all your idols I will cleanse you. 26 I will give you a new heart and place a new spirit within you, taking from your bodies your stony hearts and giving you natural hearts. 27 I will put my spirit within you and make you live by my statutes, careful to

---

35, 10: *The two nations and the two lands:* the superseded kingdoms of Israel and Judah and their

territories.

36, 13: *A land that devours men:* destroys its own

population, as could be seen in its disastrous political history.

observe my decrees. 28 You shall live in the land I gave your fathers; you shall be my people, and I will be your God. 29 I will save you from all your impurities; I will order the grain to be abundant, and I will not send famine against you. 30 I will increase the fruit on your trees and the crops in your fields; thus you shall no longer bear among the nations the reproach of famine. 31 Then you shall remember your evil conduct, and that your deeds were not good; you shall loathe yourselves for your sins and your abominations. 32 Not for your sakes do I act, says the Lord GOD—let this be known to you! Be ashamed and abashed because of your conduct, O house of Israel.

33 Thus says the Lord GOD: When I purify you from all your crimes, I will repeople the cities, and the ruins shall be rebuilt; 34 the desolate land shall be tilled, which was formerly a wasteland exposed to the gaze of every passer-by. 35 "This desolate land has been made into a garden of Eden," they shall say. "The cities that were in ruins, laid waste, and destroyed are now repeopled and fortified." 36 Thus the neighboring nations that remain shall know that I, the LORD, have rebuilt what was destroyed and replanted what was desolate. I, the LORD, have promised, and I will do it.

37 Thus says the Lord GOD: This also I will be persuaded to do for the house of Israel: to multiply them like sheep. 38 As with sacrificial sheep, the sheep of Jerusalem on its feast days, the cities which were in ruins shall be filled with flocks of men; thus they shall know that I am the LORD.

Vision of the Dry Bones

37 The hand of the LORD came upon me, and he led me out in the spirit of the LORD and set me in the center of the plain, which was now filled with bones. 2 He made me walk among them in every direction so that I saw how many they were on the surface of the plain. How dry they were! 3 He asked me: Son of man, can these bones come to life? "Lord GOD," I answered, "you alone know that." 4 Then he said to me: Prophesy over these bones, and say to them: Dry bones, hear the word of the LORD! 5 Thus says the Lord GOD to these bones: See! I will bring spirit into you, that you may come to life. 6 I will put sinews upon you, make flesh grow over you, cover you with skin, and put spirit in you so that you may come to life and know that I am the LORD. 7 I prophesied as I had been told, and even as I was prophesying I heard a noise; it was a rattling as the bones came together, bone joining bone. 8 I saw the sinews and the flesh come upon them, and the skin cover them, but there was no spirit in them. 9 Then he said to me: Prophesy to the spirit, prophesy, son of man, and say to the spirit: Thus says the Lord GOD: From the four winds come, O spirit, and breathe into these slain that they may come to life. 10 I prophesied as he told me, and the spirit came into them; they came alive and stood upright, a vast army. 11 Then he said to me: Son of man, these bones are the whole house of Israel. They have been saying, "Our bones are dried up, our hope is lost, and we are cut off." 12 Therefore, prophesy and say to them: Thus says the Lord GOD: O my people, I will open your graves and have you rise from them, and bring you back to the land of Israel. 13 Then you shall know that I am the LORD, when I open your graves and have you rise from them, O my people! 14 I will put my spirit in you that you may live, and I will settle you upon your land; thus you shall know that I am the LORD. I have promised, and I will do it, says the LORD.

The Two Sticks

15 Thus the word of the LORD came to me: 16 Now, son of man, take a single stick, and write on it: Judah and those Israelites who are associated with him. Then take another stick and write on it: Joseph [the stick of Ephraim] and all the house of Israel associated with him. 17 Then join the two sticks together, so that they form one stick in your hand. 18 When your countrymen ask you, "Will you not tell us what you mean by all this?", 19 answer them: Thus says the Lord GOD: [I will take the stick of Joseph, which is in the hand of Ephraim, and of the tribes of Israel associated with him, and I will join to it the stick of Judah, making them a single stick; they shall be one in my hand. 20 The sticks on which you write you shall hold up before them to see. 21 Tell them: Thus speaks the Lord GOD:] I will take the Israelites from among the nations to which they have come, and gather them from all sides to bring them back to their land. 22 I will make them one nation upon the land, in the mountains of Israel, and there shall be one prince for them all. Never again shall they be two nations, and never again shall they be divided into two kingdoms.

23 No longer shall they defile themselves with their idols, their abominations, and all their transgressions. I will deliver them from all their sins of apostasy, and cleanse them so that they may be my people and I may be their God. 24 My servant David shall be prince over them, and there shall be one shepherd for them all; they shall live by my statutes and carefully observe my decrees. 25 They shall live on the land which I gave to my servant Jacob, the land where their fathers lived; they shall live on it forever, they, and their children, and their children's children, with my servant David their prince forever. 26 I will make with them a covenant of peace; it shall be an everlasting covenant with them, and I will multiply them, and put my sanctuary among them forever. 27 My dwelling shall be with them; I will be their God, and they shall be my people. 28 Thus the nations shall know that it is I, the LORD, who make Israel holy, when my sanctuary shall be set up among them forever.

37, 1–14: This vision is a prediction of the restoration of Israel under the figure of a resurrection from the dead; it is not concerned with doctrine of resurrection itself.

37, 15–22: The symbolic action of joining two sticks into one signifies the future union of Israel and Judah under one Messianic king.

First Prophecy against Gog

38 Thus the word of the LORD came to me: 2 Son of man, turn toward Gog [the land of Magog], the chief prince of Meshech and Tubal, and prophesy against him: 3 Thus says the Lord GOD: See! I am coming at you, Gog, chief prince of Meshech and Tubal. 4 I will lead you forth with all your army, horses and riders all handsomely outfitted, a great horde with bucklers and shields, all of them carrying swords: 5 Persia, Cush, and Put with them [all with shields and helmets], 6 Gomer with all its troops, Beth-togarmah from the recesses of the north with all its troops, many peoples with you. 7 Prepare yourself, be ready, you and all your horde assembled about you, and be at my disposal. 8 After many days you will be mustered [in the last years you will come] against a nation which has survived the sword, which has been assembled from many peoples [on the mountains of Israel which were long a ruin], which has been brought forth from among the peoples and all of whom now dwell in security. 9 You shall come up like a sudden storm, advancing like a cloud to cover the earth, you and all your troops and the many peoples with you.

10 Thus says the Lord GOD: At that time thoughts shall arise in your mind, and you shall devise an evil scheme: 11 "I will go up against a land of open villages and attack the peaceful people who are living in security, all of them living without walls, having neither bars nor gates, 12 to plunder and pillage, turning my hand against the ruins that were repeopled and against a people gathered from the nations, a people concerned with cattle and goods, who dwell at the navel of the earth." 13 Sheba and Dedan, the merchants of Tarshish and all her young lions shall ask you: "Is it for plunder that you have come? Is it for pillage

that you have summoned your horde, to carry off silver and gold, to take away cattle and goods, to seize much plunder?"

17 Thus says the Lord GOD: It is of you that I spoke in ancient times through my servants, the prophets of Israel, who prophesied in those days that I would bring you against them. 18 But on that day, the day when Gog invades the land of Israel, says the Lord GOD, my fury shall be aroused. In my anger 19 and in my jealousy, in my fiery wrath, I swear: On that day there shall be a great shaking upon the land of Israel. 20 Before me shall tremble the fish of the sea and the birds of the air, the beasts of the field and all the reptiles that crawl upon the ground, and all men who are on the land. Mountains shall be overturned, and cliffs shall tumble, and every wall shall fall to the ground. 21 Against him I will summon every terror, says the Lord GOD, every man's sword against his brother. I will hold judgment with him in pestilence and bloodshed; 22 flooding rain and hailstones, fire and brimstone, I will rain upon him, upon his troops, and upon the many peoples with him. 23 I will prove my greatness and holiness and make myself known in the sight of many nations; thus they shall know that I am the LORD.

Second Prophecy against Gog

14 Therefore prophesy, son of man, and say to Gog: Thus says the Lord GOD: When my people Israel are dwelling in security, will you not bestir yourself 15 and come from your home in the recesses of the north, you and many peoples with you, all mounted on horses, a great horde and a mighty army? 16 You shall come up against my people Israel like a cloud covering the land. In the last days I will bring you against my land, that the nations may know of me, when in their sight I prove my holiness through you, O Gog.

Third Prophecy against Gog

39 Now, son of man, prophesy against Gog in these words: Thus says the Lord GOD: See! I am coming at you, Gog, chief prince of Meshech and Tubal. 2 I will turn you about, I will urge you on, and I will make you come up from the recesses of the north; I will lead you against the mountains of Israel. 3 Then I will strike the bow from your left hand, and make the arrows drop from your right. 4 Upon the mountains of Israel you shall fall, you and all your troops and the peoples who are with you. To birds of prey of every kind and to the wild beasts I am giving you to be eaten. 5 On the open field you shall fall, for I have decreed it, says the Lord GOD.

6 I will send fire upon Magog and upon those who live securely in the coastlands; thus they shall know that I am the LORD. 7 I will make my holy name known among my people Israel; I will no longer allow my holy name to be profaned. Thus the nations shall know that I am the LORD, the Holy One in Israel. 8 Yes, it is coming and shall be fulfilled, says the Lord GOD. This is the day I have decreed.

9 Then shall those who live in the cities of Israel go out and burn weapons: [shields and bucklers,] bows and arrows, clubs and lances; for seven years they shall make fires with them. 10 They shall not have to bring in wood from the fields or cut it down in the forests, for they shall make fires with the weapons. Thus they shall plunder those who plundered them and pillage those who pillaged them, says the Lord GOD.

11 On that day I will give Gog for his tomb a well-known place in Israel, the valley of Abarim east of the sea [it is blocked to travelers]. Gog shall be buried there with all his horde, and it shall be named "Valley of Hamon-gog." 12 To purify the land, the house of Israel shall need

---

38, 1—39, 20: These three oracles against Gog may refer either to a specific foreign invasion in the future, or to the apocalyptic struggle between good and evil at the end of time. By some they are ascribed to a later author than Ezekiel, who lived after the Exile and the return to Palestine.
38, 2: *Gog:* the name is almost certainly a symbolic one taken from that of Gyges, king of Lydia, whether

or not the prophet has a specific person in mind. The gloss *Magog* may be an Akkadian expression, *mat-Gog,* "the land of Gog." *Meshech and Tubal,* as well as *Gomer and Beth-togarmath* (v 6), were countries around the Black Sea, the northernmost countries known to the Hebrews: *the north* (cf also v 15) was the traditional direction from which invasion was expected; cf Jer 1, 13ff.

38, 12: *Who dwell at the navel of the earth:* the people of Israel (cf v 18; also 5, 5). Many ancient peoples spoke of their own homelands as "the navel," that is, the center of the earth.
39, 11: *The valley of Abarim:* in the Abarim mountains, east of the Jordan. *Hamon-gog:* means "the horde of Gog."

seven months to bury them. 13 All the people of the land shall bury them and gain renown for it, when I reveal my glory, says the Lord GOD. 14 Men shall be permanently employed to pass through the land burying those who lie unburied, so as to purify the land. For seven months they shall keep searching. 15 When they pass through, should they see a human bone, let them put up a marker beside it, until others have buried it in the Valley of Hamongog. 16 [Also the name of the city shall be Hamonah.] Thus the land shall be purified.

17 As for you, son of man, says the Lord GOD, say to birds of every kind and to all the wild beasts: Come together, from all sides gather for the slaughter I am about to provide for you, a great slaughter on the mountains of Israel: you shall have flesh to eat and blood to drink. 18 You shall eat the flesh of warriors and drink the blood of the princes of the land [rams, lambs, and goats, bullocks, fatlings of Bashan, all of them]. 19 From the slaughter which I will provide for you, you shall eat fat until you are filled and drink blood until you are drunk. 20 You shall be filled at my table with horses and riders, with warriors and soldiers of every kind, says the Lord GOD.

Israel's Return

21 Thus I will display my glory among the nations, and all the nations shall see the judgment I have executed and the hand I have laid upon them. 22 From that day forward the house of Israel shall know that I am the LORD, their God. 23 The nations shall know that because of its sins the house of Israel went into exile; for they transgressed against me, and I hid my face from them and handed them over to their foes, so that all of them fell by the sword. 24 According to their uncleanness and their transgressions I dealt with them, hiding my face from them.

25 Therefore, thus says the Lord GOD: Now I will restore the fortunes of Jacob and have pity on the whole house of Israel, and I will be jealous for my holy name. 26 They shall forget their disgrace and all the times they broke faith with me, when they live in security on their land with no one to frighten them. 27 When I bring them back from among the peoples, I will gather them from the lands of their enemies, and will prove my holiness through them in the sight of many nations. 28 Thus they shall know that I, the LORD, am their God, since I who exiled them among the nations, will gather them back on their land, not leaving any of them behind. 29 No longer will I hide my face from them, for I have poured out my spirit upon the house of Israel, says the Lord GOD.

THE NEW ISRAEL

The New Temple

The Man with a Measure

40 On the tenth day of the month beginning the twenty-fifth year of our exile, fourteen years after the city was taken, that very day the hand of the LORD came upon me and brought me 2 in divine visions to the land of Israel, where he set me down on a very high mountain. On it there seemed to be a city being built before me. 3 When he had brought me there, all at once I saw a man whose appearance was that of bronze; he was standing in the gate, holding a linen cord and a measuring rod. 4 The man said to me, "Son of man, look carefully and listen intently, and pay strict attention to all that I will show you, for you have been brought here so that I might show it to you. Tell the house of Israel all that you see." 5 [Then I saw an outer wall that completely surrounded the temple. The man was holding a measuring rod six cubits long, each cubit being a cubit and a handbreadth; he

measured the width and the height of the structure, each of which were found to be one rod.]

The East Gate

6 Then he went to the gate which faced the east, climbed its steps, and measured the gate's threshold, which was found to be a rod wide. 7 The cells were a rod long and a rod wide, and the pilasters between the cells measured five cubits. The threshold of the gate adjoining the vestibule of the gate toward the inside measured one rod. 8 He measured the vestibule of the gate, 9 which was eight cubits, and its pilasters, which were two cubits. The vestibule of the gate was toward the inside. 10 The cells of the east gate were three on either side, of equal size, and the pilasters on either side were also of equal size. 11 He measured the gate's entrance, which was ten cubits wide, while the width of the gate's passage itself was thirteen cubits. 12 The border before each of the cells on both sides was one cubit; the cells themselves were six cubits on either side, from opening to opening. 13 He measured the gate from the back wall of one cell to the back wall of the cell on the opposite side: the width was twenty-five cubits. 14 He measured the vestibule, which was twenty-five cubits. The pilasters adjoining the court on either side were six cubits. 15 The length of the gate from the front entrance to the front of the vestibule on the inside was fifty cubits. 16 Within the gateway on both sides there were splayed windows let into the cells [and into their pilasters]; likewise, within the vestibule on both sides there were windows. The pilasters were decorated with palms.

The Outer Court

17 Then he brought me to the outer court, where there were chambers and a pavement. The pavement was laid all around the court, and the

40, 1—48, 35: This lengthy vision of the new Israel is dated (40, 1) April 28, 573 B.C. It is largely concerned with the new temple and the prescriptions to govern it, but other details of the restored commonwealth are included, forming a kind of program for the future. The literary form of the vision has been aptly termed "utopian": it is plain that the prophet did not expect a literal fulfillment of much of what he described. The passage doubtless underwent suc-

cessive additions, both from the prophet and from later inspired writers.
40, 5: A cubit and a handbreadth: the ordinary cubit consisted of six handbreadths; the great cubit, of seven. In measuring the temple, a rod six great cubits long was used. The ordinary cubit was about one and a half feet, or, more exactly, 17.5 inches; the large cubit, 20.4 inches.
40, 6-16: The east gate, leading into the outer

court of the temple, is described more fully than the north and south gates, which, however, were of the same dimensions. On the west side of the outer court there was a large building instead of a gate (41, 12).
40, 17: The outer court: the court outside the temple area proper, which had its own inner court (vv 28-37).

chambers, which were on the pavement, were thirty in number. 18 The pavement lay alongside the gates, as wide as the gates were long; this was the lower pavement. 19 He measured the width of the court from the front of the lower gate to the front of the inner gate; it was one hundred cubits between them.

The North Gate

Then he proceeded north, 20 where, on the outer court, there was a gate facing north, whose length and width he measured. 21 Its cells, three on either side, its pilasters, and its vestibule had the same measurements as those of the first gate; it was fifty cubits long and twenty-five cubits wide. 22 Its windows, the windows of its vestibule, and its palm decorations were of the same proportions as those of the gate facing the east. Seven steps led up to it, and its vestibule was toward the inside. 23 The inner court had a gate opposite the north gate, just as at the east gate; he measured one hundred cubits from one gate to the other.

The South Gate

24 Then he led me south, to where there was a southern gate, whose cells, pilasters, and vestibule he measured; they were the same size as the others. 25 The gate and its vestibule had windows on both sides, like the other windows. It was fifty cubits long and twenty-five cubits wide. 26 It was ascended by seven steps; its vestibule was toward the inside; and it was decorated with palms here and there on its pilasters. 27 The inner court also had a southern gate; from gate to gate he measured one hundred cubits.

Gates of the Inner Court

28 Then he brought me to the inner court by the south gate, where he measured the south gate. Its dimensions were the same as the others; 29 its cells, its pilasters, and its vestibule were the same size

as the others. The gate and its vestibule had windows on both sides; and it was fifty cubits long and twenty-five cubits wide. 31 But its vestibule was toward the outer court; palms were on its pilasters, and it had a stairway of eight steps. 32 Then he brought me to the gate facing the east, where he measured the gate, whose dimensions were found to be the same. 33 Its cells, its pilasters, and its vestibule were the same size as the others; the gate and its vestibule had windows on both sides; it was fifty cubits long and twenty-five cubits wide. 34 But its vestibule was toward the outer court; palms were on its pilasters here and there, and it had a stairway of eight steps. 35 Then he brought me to the north gate, where he measured the dimensions 36 of its cells, its pilasters, and its vestibule, and found them the same. The gate and its vestibule had windows on both sides; it was fifty cubits long and twenty-five cubits wide. 37 Its vestibule was toward the outer court; palms were on its pilasters here and there, and it had a stairway of eight steps.

Side Rooms

38 There was a chamber opening off the vestibule of the gate, where the holocausts were rinsed. 39 In the vestibule of the gate there were two tables on either side, on which were slaughtered the sin offerings and guilt offerings. 40 Along the wall of the vestibule, but outside, near the entrance of the north gate, were two tables, and on the other side of the vestibule of the gate there were two tables. 41 There were four tables on either side of the gate [eight tables], on which the sacrifices were slaughtered. 42 There were four tables for holocausts, made of cut stone, one and a half cubits long, one and a half cubits wide, and one cubit high. 43 The ledges, a handbreadth wide, were set on the inside all around, and on them were laid the instruments with which the holocausts were slaughtered. On the

tables themselves the flesh was laid. 44 He then led me to the inner court where there were two chambers, one beside the north gate, facing south, and the other beside the south gate, facing north. 45 He said to me, "This chamber which faces south is for the priests who have charge of the temple, 46 and the chamber which faces north is for the priests who have charge of the altar. These are the Zadokites, the only Levites who may come near to minister to the LORD." 47 Then he measured the court, which was a hundred cubits long and a hundred cubits wide, a perfect square. The altar stood in front of the temple.

The Temple Building

48 Then he brought me into the vestibule of the temple and measured the pilasters on each side, which were five cubits. The width of the doorway was fourteen cubits, and the side walls on either side of the door measured three cubits. 49 The vestibule was twenty cubits wide and twelve cubits deep; ten steps led up to it, and there were columns by the pilasters, one on either side.

41 Then he brought me to the nave and measured the pilasters, which were six cubits thick on either side. 2 The width of the entrance was ten cubits, and the walls at either side of it measured five cubits each. He measured the length of the nave, which was found to be forty cubits, while its width was twenty.

3 Then he went in beyond and measured the pilasters flanking that entrance, which were two cubits; the width of the entrance was six cubits, and the walls at either side of it extended seven cubits each. 4 He measured the space beyond the nave, twenty cubits long and twenty cubits wide, and said to me, "This is the holy of holies."

5 Then he measured the wall of the temple, which was six cubits thick; the side chambers, which extended all the way around the temple, had a

---

40, 28–37: The gates leading into the inner court of the temple area correspond to the gates leading into the outer court, with the exception that their vestibules are on the outer rather than the inner side.

40, 46: *The Zadokites:* descendants of the priestly line of Zadok; cf 2 Sm 15, 24–29; 1 Kgs 1, 32ff; 2, 35.
40, 48—41, 15: The description of Ezekiel's visionary temple closely follows the description of the temple of Solomon (1 Kgs 6).

40, 49—41, 4: *Vestibule . . . nave . . . holy of holies:* the three divisions of the temple building in progressing order of sanctity. The last is called "the inner sanctuary" in 1 Kgs 6.

width of four cubits. 6 There were thirty side chambers built one above the other in three stories, and there were offsets in the outside wall of the temple that enclosed the side chambers; these served as supports, so that there were no supports in the temple wall proper. 7 There was a broad circular passageway that led upward to the side chambers, for the temple was enclosed all the way around and all the way upward; therefore the temple had a broad way running upward so that one could pass from the lowest to the middle and the highest story. 8 About the temple was a raised pavement completely enclosing it—the foundations of the side chambers—a full rod of six cubits in extent. 9 The width of the outside wall which enclosed the side chambers was five cubits. Between the side chambers of the temple 10 and the chambers of the court was an open space twenty cubits wide going all around the temple. 11 The side chambers had entrances to the open space, one entrance on the north and another on the south. The width of the wall surrounding the open space was five cubits. 12 The building fronting the free area on the west side was seventy cubits front to back; the wall of the building was five cubits thick all around, and it measured ninety cubits from side to side. 13 He measured the temple, which was one hundred cubits long. The free area, together with the building and its walls, was a hundred cubits in length. 14 The façade of the temple, along with the free area, on the east side, was one hundred cubits wide. 15 He measured the building which lay the length of the free area and behind it, and together with its walls on both sides it was one hundred cubits.

Interior of the Temple

16 The inner nave and the outer vestibule were paneled with precious wood all around, covered from the ground to the windows. There were splayed windows with trellises about them [facing the threshold]. 17 As high as the lintel of the door, even into the interior part of the temple as well as outside, on every wall on every side in both the inner and outer rooms were carved 18 the figures of cherubim and palmtrees: a palmtree between every two cherubim. Each cherub had two faces: 19 a man's face looking at a palmtree on one side, and a lion's face looking at a palmtree on the other; thus they were figured on every side throughout the whole temple. 20 From the ground to the lintel of the door the cherubim and palmtrees were carved on the walls. 21 The way into the nave was a square doorframe. In front of the holy place was something that looked like 22 a wooden altar, three cubits in height, two cubits long, and two cubits wide. It had corners, and its base and sides were of wood. He said to me, "This is the table which is before the LORD." 23 The nave had a double door, and also the holy place had 24 a double door. Each door had two movable leaves; two leaves were on one doorjamb and two on the other. 25 Carved upon them [on the doors of the nave] were cherubim and palmtrees, like those carved on the walls. Before the vestibule outside was a wooden lattice. 26 There were splayed windows [and palmtrees] on both side walls of the vestibule, and the side chambers of the temple. . . .

Other Structures

42 Then he led me north to the outer court, bringing me to some chambers on the north that lay across the free area and which were also across from the building. 2 Their length was a hundred cubits on the north side, and they were fifty cubits wide. 3 Across the twenty cubits of the inner court and the pavement of the outer court, there were three parallel rows of them on different levels. 4 In front of the chambers, to the inside, was a walk ten cubits broad and a wall of one cubit; but the entrances of the chambers were on the north. 5 The outermost chambers were the lowest, for the system of levels set them at a level lower than the closest chambers and those in between; 6 for they were in three rows and had no foundations to conform with the foundations of the courts, therefore they were on a lower terrace of the ground than the closest and the middle chambers. 7 On the far side there was a wall running parallel to the chambers along the outer court; its length before these chambers was fifty cubits, 8 for the length of the chambers belonging to the outer court was fifty cubits, but along its entire length the wall measured one hundred cubits. 9 Below these chambers there was the way in from the east, so that one could enter from the outer court 10 where the wall of the court began.

To the south along the side of the free area and the building there were also chambers, 11 before which was a passage. These looked like the chambers to the north, just as long and just as wide, with the same exits and plan and entrances. 12 Below the chambers to the south there was an entrance at the beginning of the way which led to the back wall, by which one could enter from the east. 13 He said to me, "The north and south chambers which border on the free area are the sanctuary chambers; here the priests who draw near to the LORD shall eat the most sacred meals, and here they shall keep the most sacred offerings: cereal offerings, sin offerings, and guilt offerings; for it is a holy place. 14 When the priests have once entered, they shall not leave the holy place for the outer court until they have left here the clothing in which they ministered, for it is holy. They shall put on other garments, and then approach the place destined for the people."

Measuring the Outer Court

15 When he had finished measuring the inner temple area, he brought me out by way of the gate which faces east and measured all the limits of the court. 16 He measured the east side: five hundred cubits by his

---

41, 12: *The building:* the function of this structure lying behind the temple is never specified.
41, 22: *A wooden altar:* the altar of incense, stand-

ing in the nave at the entrance to the holy of holies.
42, 5f: The three rows of identical chambers, since they rested on different ground levels, neces-

sarily had roofs on correspondingly different levels.
42, 13: The function of these chambers is explained again in 46, 19f.

measuring rod. 17 Then he turned and measured the north side: five hundred cubits by the measuring rod. He turned 18 to the south and measured five hundred cubits by the measuring rod. 19 Then he turned to the west and measured five hundred cubits by the measuring rod. 20 Thus he measured it in the four directions, five hundred cubits long and five hundred cubits wide. It was surrounded by a wall, to separate the sacred from the profane.

Restoration of the Temple

The Return of the Lord

43 Then he led me to the gate which faces the east, 2 and there I saw the glory of the God of Israel coming from the east. I heard a sound like the roaring of many waters, and the earth shone with his glory. 3 The vision was like that which I had seen when he came to destroy the city, and like that which I had seen by the river Chebar. I fell prone 4 as the glory of the LORD entered the temple by way of the gate which faces the east, 5 but spirit lifted me up and brought me to the inner court. And I saw that the temple was filled with the glory of the LORD. 6 Then I heard someone speaking to me from the temple, while the man stood beside me. 7 The voice said to me: Son of man, this is where my throne shall be, this is where I will set the soles of my feet; here I will dwell among the Israelites forever. Never again shall they and their kings profane my holy name with their harlotries and with the corpses of their kings [their high places]. 8 When they placed their threshold against my threshold and their doorpost next to mine, so that only a wall was between us, they profaned my holy name by their abominable deeds; therefore I consumed them in my wrath. 9 From now on they shall put far from me their harlotry and the corpses of their kings, and I will dwell in their midst forever.

The Law of the Temple

10 As for you, son of man, describe the temple to the house of Israel [that they may be ashamed of their sins], both its measurements and its design; 11 [and if they are ashamed of all that they have done,] make known to them the form and design of the temple, its exits and entrances, all its statutes and laws; write these down for them to see, that they may carefully observe all its laws and statutes. 12 This is the law of the temple: its whole surrounding area on the mountain top shall be most sacred.

The Altar

13 These were the measurements of the altar in cubits of one cubit plus a handbreadth. Its base was one cubit high and one cubit deep, with a rim around its edge of one span. The height of the altar itself was as follows: 14 from its base at the bottom up to the lower ledge it was two cubits high, and this ledge was one cubit deep; from the lower to the upper ledge it was four cubits high, and this ledge also was one cubit deep; 15 the hearth of the altar was four cubits high, and extending from the top of the hearth were the four horns of the altar. 16 The hearth was a square: twelve cubits long and twelve cubits wide. 17 The upper ledge was also a square: fourteen cubits long and fourteen cubits wide. The lower ledge, likewise a square, was sixteen cubits long and sixteen cubits wide, with a half-cubit rim surrounding it. And there was a base of one cubit all around. The steps of the altar face the east.

18 Then he said to me: Son of man, thus says the Lord GOD: These are the statutes for the altar when it is set up for the offering of holocausts upon it and for the sprinkling of blood against it. 19 Give a young bull as a sin offering to the priests, the Levites who are of the line of Zadok, who draw near me to minister to me, says the Lord GOD.

20 Take some of its blood and put it on the four horns of the altar, and on the four corners of the ledge, and on the rim all around. Thus you shall purify it and make atonement for it. 21 Then take the bull of the sin offering, which is to be burnt in a designated part of the temple, outside the sanctuary. 22 On the second day present an unblemished he-goat as a sin offering, to purify the altar as was done with the bull. 23 When you have finished the purification, bring an unblemished young bull and an unblemished ram from the flock, 24 and present them before the LORD; the priests shall strew salt on them and offer them to the LORD as holocausts. 25 Daily for seven days you shall offer a he-goat as a sin offering, and a young bull and a ram from the flock, all unblemished, shall be offered 26 for seven days. Thus atonement shall be made for the altar, and it shall be purified and dedicated. 27 And when these days are over, from the eighth day on, the priests shall offer your holocausts and peace offerings on the altar. Then I will accept you, says the Lord GOD.

The Closed Gate

44 Then he brought me back to the outer gate of the sanctuary, facing the east; but it was closed. 2 He said to me: This gate is to remain closed; it is not to be opened for anyone to enter by it; since the LORD, the God of Israel, has entered by it, it shall remain closed. 3 Only the prince may sit down in it to eat his meal in the presence of the LORD. He must enter by way of the vestibule of the gate, and leave by the same way.

The New Law

Admission to the Temple

4 Then he brought me by way of of the north gate to the façade of the temple, and when I looked I saw the glory of the LORD filling the LORD's temple, and I fell prone. 5 Then he said to me: Son of man, pay strict

---

43, 8: *They placed their threshold against my threshold:* the pre-exilic temple and the royal palace belonged to the same complex of buildings, and this physical proximity was reflected in the use made of the temple by kings like Ahaz and Manasseh, who treated it as their private chapel for pagan rites. In the new Israel the temple is free, even physically, from civil jurisdiction; cf 45, 7f.

43, 13: *The altar:* of holocausts, standing in the inner court of the temple area; cf 40, 47.

44, 3: The prince stands at the eastern gate of the inner court while his sacrifice is offered up (46, 2); he then goes to the vestibule of the outer court, there to partake of his sacrificial meal. The closed outer gate on the eastern side signifies that the Lord has entered the temple permanently, not to depart again.

attention, look carefully, and listen intently to all that I will tell you about the statues and laws of the Lord's temple; be attentive in regard to those who are to be admitted to the temple and all those who are to be excluded from the sanctuary. 6 Say to that rebellious house, the house of Israel: Thus says the Lord God: Enough of all these abominations of yours, O house of Israel! 7 You have admitted foreigners, uncircumcised both in heart and flesh, to my sanctuary to profane it when you offered me food, fat, and blood; thus you have broken my covenant by all your abominations. 8 Instead of caring for the service of my temple, you have appointed such as these to serve me in my sanctuary in your stead. 9 Thus says the Lord God: No foreigners, uncircumcised in heart and in flesh, shall ever enter my sanctuary; none of the foreigners who live among the Israelites.

Levites

10 But as for the Levites who departed from me when Israel strayed from me to pursue their idols, they shall bear the consequences of their sin. 11 They shall serve in my sanctuary as gatekeepers and temple servants; they shall slaughter the holocausts and the sacrifices for the people, and they shall stand before the people to minister for them. 12 Because they used to minister for them before their idols, and became an occasion of sin to the house of Israel, therefore I have sworn an oath against them, says the Lord God: they shall bear the consequences of their sin. 13 They shall no longer draw near me to serve as my priests, nor shall they touch any of my sacred things, or the most sacred things. Thus they shall bear their disgrace because of all their abominable deeds. 14 But I will set them to the service of the temple, for all its work and for everything that is to be done in it.

Priests

15 As for the Levitical priests, however, the Zadokites who cared for my sanctuary when the Israelites strayed from me, they shall draw near me to minister to me, and they shall stand before me to offer me fat and blood, says the Lord God. 16 It is they who shall enter my sanctuary, they who shall approach my table to minister to me, and they who shall carry out my service. 17 Whenever they enter the gates of the inner court, they shall wear linen garments; they shall not put on anything woolen when they minister at the gates of the inner court or within the temple. 18 They shall have linen turbans on their heads and linen drawers on their loins; they shall not gird themselves with anything that causes sweat. 19 When they are to go out to the people in the outer court, they shall take off the garments in which they ministered and leave them in the chambers of the sanctuary, putting on other garments; thus they will not transmit holiness to the people with their garments.

20 They shall not shave their heads nor let their hair hang loose, but they shall keep their hair carefully trimmed. 21 No priest shall drink wine when he is to enter the inner court. 22 They shall not take for their wives either widows or divorced women, but only virgins of the race of Israel; however, they may marry women who are the widows of priests. 23 They shall teach my people to distinguish between the sacred and the profane, and make known to them the difference between the clean and the unclean. 24 In capital cases they shall stand as judges, judging them according to my decrees. They shall observe my laws and statutes on all my festivals, and keep my sabbaths holy.

25 They shall not make themselves unclean by coming near any dead person, unless it be their father,

mother, son, daughter, brother, or maiden sister, for these they may make themselves unclean. 26 After a priest has been cleansed, he must wait an additional seven days, 27 and on the day he enters the inner court to minister in the sanctuary, he shall present his sin offering, says the Lord God. 28 They shall have no inheritance, for I am their inheritance; you shall give them no property in Israel, for I am their property. 29 They shall eat the cereal offering, the sin offering, and the guilt offering; whatever is under the ban in Israel shall be theirs. 30 All the choicest first fruits of every kind, and all the best of your offerings of every kind, shall belong to the priests; likewise the best of your dough you shall give to the priests to bring a blessing down upon your house. 31 The priests shall not eat anything, whether flesh or fowl, that has died of itself or has been killed by wild beasts.

The Sacred Tract

45 When you apportion the land into inheritances, you shall set apart a sacred tract of land for the Lord, twenty-five thousand cubits long and twenty thousand wide; its whole area shall be sacred. 2 Of this land a square plot, five hundred cubits, surrounded by a free space of fifty cubits, shall be assigned to the sanctuary. 3 Also from this sector measure off a strip, twenty-five thousand cubits long and ten thousand wide, within which shall be the sanctuary, the holy of holies. 4 This shall be the sacred part of the land belonging to the priests, the ministers of the sanctuary, who draw near to minister to the Lord; it shall be a place for their homes and pasture land for their cattle. 5 Also there shall be a strip twenty-five thousand cubits long and ten thousand wide as property for the Levites, the ministers of the temple, that they may have cities to live in. 6 As property of the City you shall designate a strip five thousand cubits

---

44, 7ff: In the pre-exilic temple various menial services had been performed by foreigners; cf Jos 9, 22-27. In the new temple the Levites will perform these services (vv 10-14).
44, 10-14: Levites other than the Zadokite priesthood of Jerusalem had performed priestly functions at the various sanctuaries and high places in

Israel and Judah, where the worship of the Lord had often been corrupted with pagan elements. The demotion of the Levites to menial service in the temple was enforced in the actual restoration after the Exile, and explains why relatively few Levites were willing to return; cf Ezr 8, 15ff.
44, 19: *Thus they will not transmit holiness to the*

people: holiness was thought of as something physical, as though it were communicable, and therefore not to be brought in contact with unconsecrated persons.
44, 29: *Under the ban:* dedicated to the Lord, withdrawn from profane use.

wide and twenty-five thousand long, parallel to the sacred tract; this shall belong to the whole house of Israel. 7 The prince shall have a section bordering on both sides of the combined sacred tract and City property, extending westward on the western side and eastward on the eastern side, corresponding in length to one of the tribal portions from the western boundary to the eastern boundary 8 of the land. This shall be his property in Israel, so that the princes of Israel will no longer oppress my people, but will leave the land to the house of Israel according to their tribes.

Weights and Measures

9 Thus says the Lord GOD: Enough, you princes of Israel! Put away violence and oppression, and do what is right and just! Stop evicting my people! says the Lord GOD. 10 You shall have honest scales, an honest ephah, and an honest liquid measure. 11 The ephah and the liquid measure shall be of the same size: the liquid measure equal to a tenth of a homer, and the ephah equal to a tenth of a homer; by the homer they shall be determined. 12 The shekel shall be twenty gerahs. Twenty shekels, twenty-five shekels, plus fifteen shekels shall be your mina.

Offerings

13 These are the offerings you shall make: one sixth of an ephah from each homer of wheat, and one sixth of an ephah from each homer of barley. 14 The regulation for oil: for every measure of oil, a tenth of a measure, computed by the kor of ten liquid measures [or a homer, for ten liquid measures make a homer]. 15 One sheep from the flock for every two hundred from the pasturate of Israel, for sacrifice—holocausts and peace offerings and atonement sacrifices, says the Lord GOD. 16 All the people of the land shall be bound to this offering [for the prince in Israel]. 17 It shall be the duty of the prince to provide the holocausts,

cereal offerings, and libations on the feasts, new moons, and sabbaths, on all the festivals of the house of Israel. He shall offer the sin offerings, cereal offerings, holocausts, and peace offerings, to make atonement on behalf of the house of Israel.

The Passover

18 Thus says the Lord GOD: On the first day of the first month you shall use an unblemished young bull as a sacrifice to purify the sanctuary. 19 Then the priest shall take some of the blood from the sin offering and put it on the doorposts of the temple, on the four corners of the ledge of the altar, and on the doorposts of the gates of the inner court. 20 You shall repeat this on the first day of the seventh month for those who have sinned through inadvertence or ignorance; thus you shall make atonement for the temple. 21 On the fourteenth day of the first month you shall observe the feast of the Passover; for seven days unleavened bread is to be eaten. 22 On that day the prince shall offer on his own behalf, and on behalf of all the people of the land, a bull as a sin offering. 23 On each of the seven days of the feast he shall offer as a holocaust to the LORD seven bulls and seven rams without blemish, and as a sin offering he shall offer one male goat each day. 24 As a cereal offering he shall offer one ephah for each bull and one ephah for each ram; and he shall offer one hin of oil for each ephah.

The Feast of Booths

25 On the fifteenth day of the seventh month, the feast day, and for seven days, he shall perform the same rites, making the same sin offerings, the same holocausts, the same cereal offerings and offerings of oil.

Sabbaths

46 Thus says the Lord GOD: The gate toward the east of the inner court shall remain closed

throughout the six working days, but on the sabbath and on the day of the new moon it shall be open. 2 The prince shall enter from outside by way of the vestibule of the gate and remain standing at the doorpost of the gate; then while the priests offer his holocauts and peace offerings, he shall worship at the threshold of the gate and then leave; the gate shall not be closed until evening. 3 The people of the land shall worship before the LORD at the door of this gate on the sabbaths and new moons. 4 The holocausts which the prince presents to the LORD on the sabbath shall consist of six unblemished lambs and an unblemished ram 5 together with a cereal offering of one ephah for the ram, whatever he pleases for the lambs, and a hin of oil for each ephah. 6 On the day of the new moon he shall provide an unblemished young bull, also six lambs and a ram without blemish, 7 with a cereal offering of one ephah for the bull and one for the ram, for the lambs as much as he has at hand, and for each ephah a hin of oil.

Ritual Laws

8 The prince shall always enter and depart by the vestibule of the gate. 9 When the people of the land enter the presence of the LORD to worship on the festivals, if they enter by the north gate they shall leave by the south gate, and if they enter by the south gate they shall leave by the north gate; no one shall return by the gate through which he has entered, but he shall leave by the opposite gate. 10 The prince shall be in their midst when they enter, and he shall also leave with them. 11 On the feasts and festivals the cereal offering shall be an ephah for a bull, an ephah for a ram, but for the lambs as much as one pleases, and a hin of oil with each ephah. 12 When the prince makes a freewill offering to the LORD, whether holocausts or peace offerings, the eastern gate shall be opened for him, and he

45, 9–12: Besides the land monopoly fostered by royal greed and collusion with the wealthy (Mi 2, 2; Is 3, 12–15; 5, 8–10), one grave social evil of pre-exilic Israel was dishonesty in business; cf Hos 12, 8; Am 8, 5. *Ephah:* a dry measure; *liquid measure:* in Hebrew "a bath," standardized according to the *homer* (a dry measure of about 10 bushels, or 80

gallons). In v 12 reference is made to the change in value of the *mina:* before the Exile it was valued at 50 shekels, but afterward, in imitation of Babylonian practice, the 60-shekel mina was adopted. The shekel was a unit of weight slightly less than half an ounce. As a monetary unit, the value obviously differ-

ed greatly, depending on whether it was a gold or a silver shekel.
45, 14: *Kor:* both a liquid and a dry measure, corresponding to the homer.
45, 24: *Hin:* a sixth part of the liquid measure called a bath.

shall offer his holocausts or his peace offerings as on the sabbath; then he shall leave, and the gate shall be closed after his departure. 13 He shall offer as a daily holocaust to the LORD an unblemished yearling lamb; this he shall offer every morning. 14 With it every morning he shall provide as a cereal offering one sixth of an ephah, with a third of a hin of oil to moisten the fine flour. This cereal offering to the LORD is mandatory with the established holocaust. 15 The lamb, the cereal offering, and the oil are to be offered every morning as an established holocaust.

The Prince and the Land

16 Thus says the Lord GOD: If the prince makes a gift of part of his inheritance to any of his sons, it shall belong to his sons; that property is theirs by inheritance. 17 But if he makes a gift of part of his inheritance to one of his servants, it shall belong to the latter only until the year of release, when it shall revert to the prince. Only the inheritance given to his sons is permanent. 18 The prince shall not seize any part of the inheritance of the people by evicting them from their property. He shall provide an inheritance for his sons from his own property, so that none of my people will be driven from their property.

The Temple Kitchens

19 Then he brought me by the entrance which is on the side of the gate to the chambers [of the sanctuary, reserved to the priests] which face the north. There, at their west end, I saw a place, 20 concerning which he said to me, "Here the priests cook the guilt offerings and the sin offerings, and bake the cereal offerings, so that they do not have to take them into the outer court at the risk of transmitting holiness to the people." 21 Then he led me into the outer court and had me pass around the four corners of the court, and I saw that in each corner there was another

court: 22 in the four corners of the court, minor courts, forty cubits long and thirty wide, all four of them the same size. 23 A wall of stones surrounded each of the four, and hearths were built beneath the stones all the way around. 24 He said to me, "These are the kitchens where the temple ministers cook the sacrifices of the people."

The Wonderful Stream

47 Then he brought me back to the entrance of the temple, and I saw water flowing out from beneath the threshold of the temple toward the east, for the façade of the temple was toward the east; the water flowed down from the southern side of the temple, south of the altar. 2 He led me outside by the north gate, and around to the outer gate facing the east, where I saw water trickling from the southern side. 3 Then when he had walked off to the east with a measuring cord in his hand, he measured off a thousand cubits and had me wade through the water, which was ankle-deep. 4 He measured off another thousand and once more had me wade through the water, which was now knee-deep. Again he measured off a thousand and had me wade; the water was up to my waist. 5 Once more he measured off a thousand, but there was now a river through which I could not wade; for the water had risen so high it had become a river that could not be crossed except by swimming. 6 He asked me, "Have you seen this, son of man?" Then he brought me to the bank of the river, where he had me sit. 7 Along the bank of the river I saw very many trees on both sides. 8 He said to me, "This water flows into the eastern district down upon the Arabah, and empties into the sea, the salt waters, which it makes fresh. 9 Wherever the river flows, every sort of living creature that can multiply shall live, and there shall be abundant fish, for wherever this water comes the sea shall be

made fresh. 10 Fishermen shall be standing along it from En-gedi to En-eglaim, spreading their nets there. Its kinds of fish shall be like those of the Great Sea, very numerous. 11 Only its marshes and swamps shall not be made fresh; they shall be left for salt. 12 Along both banks of the river, fruit trees of every kind shall grow; their leaves shall not fade, nor their fruit fail. Every month they shall bear fresh fruit, for they shall be watered by the flow from the sanctuary. Their fruit shall serve for food, and their leaves for medicine."

THE NEW ISRAEL

Boundaries of the Land

13 Thus says the Lord GOD: These are the boundaries within which you shall apportion the land among the twelve tribes of Israel [Joseph having two portions]. 14 All of you shall have a like portion in this land which I swore to give to your fathers, that it might fall to you as your inheritance. 15 This is the boundary of the land on the north side: from the Great Sea in the direction of Hethlon, past Labo of Hamath, to Zedad, 16 Berothah, and Sibraim, along the frontiers of Hamath and Damascus, to Hazar-enon which is on the border of the Hauran. 17 Thus the border shall extend from the sea to Hazar-enon, with the frontier of Hamath and Damascus to the north. This is the northern boundary. 18 The eastern boundary: between the Hauran—toward Damascus—and Gilead on the one side, and the land of Israel on the other side, the Jordan shall form the boundary down to the eastern sea as far as Tamar. This is the eastern boundary. 19 The southern boundary: from Tamar to the waters of Meribath-kadesh, thence to the Wadi of Egypt, and on to the Great Sea. This is the southern boundary. 20 The western boundary: the Great Sea forms the boundary up to a point parallel to Labo of Hamath. This is the western boundary.

46, 17: *The year of release:* the jubilee year; cf Lv 25, 23–55.

47, 1–12: The wonderful and superabundant stream flowing from the temple, restoring to fertility traditionally arid ground, is symbolic of the return

of the conditions of primeval paradise; cf Gn 2, 10–14. Water signifies great blessings, just as dryness signifies a curse; cf 26, 5.14.

47, 10: *From En-gedi to En-eglaim:* the former was about halfway down the western shore of the Dead

Sea, the latter may have been at its northern extremity.

47, 13–20: These boundaries of the restored Israel correspond to those of the Davidic kingdom at its fullest extent, the so-called "ideal boundaries" of the promised land; cf Nm 34, 3–12.

The Northern Portions

21 You shall distribute this land among yourselves according to the tribes of Israel. 22 You shall allot it as inheritances for yourselves and for the aliens resident in your midst who have bred children among you. The latter shall be to you like native Israelites; along with you they shall receive inheritances among the tribes of Israel. 23 In whatever tribe the alien may be resident, there you shall assign him his inheritance, says the Lord GOD.

48 This is the list of the tribes. Dan: at the northern extremity, adjoining Hamath, all along from the approaches to Hethlon through Labo of Hamath to Hazarenon, on the northerly border with Damascus, with his possession reaching from the eastern to the western boundary. 2 Asher: on the frontier of Dan, from the eastern to the western boundary. 3 Naphtali: on the frontier of Asher, from the eastern to the western boundary. 4 Manasseh: on the frontier of Naphtali, from the eastern to the western boundary. 5 Ephraim: on the frontier of Manasseh, from the eastern to the western boundary. 6 Reuben: on the frontier of Ephraim, from the eastern to the western boundary. 7 Judah: on the frontier of Reuben, from the eastern to the western boundary.

The Sacred Tract

8 On the frontier of Judah, from the eastern to the western boundary there shall be the tract which you shall set apart, twenty-five thousand cubits from north to south, and as wide as one of the tribal portions from the eastern to the western boundary. In the center of the tract shall be the sanctuary. 9 The tract that you set aside for the LORD shall be twenty-five thousand cubits across by twenty thousand north and south. 10 In this sacred tract the priests shall have twenty-five thousand cubits on the north, ten thousand on the west, ten thousand on the east, and twenty-five thousand on the south; and the sanctuary of the LORD shall be in its center. 11 The consecrated priests, the Zadokites, who fulfilled my service and did not stray along with the Israelites as the Levites did, 12 shall have within this tract of land their own most sacred domain, next to the territory of the Levites. 13 The Levites shall have a territory corresponding to that of the priests, twenty-five thousand cubits by ten thousand. The whole tract shall be twenty-five thousand cubits across and twenty thousand north and south. 14 They may not sell or exchange or alienate this, the best part of the land, for it is sacred to the LORD. 15 The remaining five thousand cubits along the twenty-five-thousand-cubit line are profane land, assigned to the City for dwellings and pasture; the City shall be at their center. 16 These are the dimensions of the City: the north side, forty-five hundred cubits; the south side, forty-five hundred cubits; the east side, forty-five hundred cubits; and the west side, forty-five hundred cubits. 17 The pasture lands of the City shall extend north two hundred and fifty cubits, south two hundred and fifty cubits, east two hundred and fifty cubits, and west two hundred and fifty cubits. 18 There shall remain an area along the sacred tract, ten thousand cubits to the east and ten thousand to the west, whose produce shall provide food for the workers of the City. 19 The workers in the City shall be taken from all the tribes of Israel. 20 The entire tract shall be twenty-five thousand by twenty-five thousand cubits; as a perfect square you shall set apart the sacred tract together with the City property.

21 The remainder shall belong to the prince: the land on both sides of the sacred tract and the City property, extending along the twenty-five-thousand-cubit line eastward to the eastern boundary, and westward along the twenty-five-thousand-cubit line to the western boundary, a territory parallel with the tribal portions for the prince. The sacred tract and the sanctuary of the temple shall be in the middle. 22 Thus, except for the property of the Levites and the City property, which lie in the midst of the prince's property, the territory between the portions of Judah and of Benjamin shall belong to the prince.

The Southern Portions

23 These are the remaining tribes. Benjamin: from the eastern to the western boundary. Simeon: 24 on the frontier of Benjamin, from the eastern to the western boundary. 25 Issachar: on the frontier of Simeon, from the eastern to the western boundary. 26 Zebulun: on the frontier of Issachar, from the eastern to the western boundary. 27 Gad: on the frontier of Zebulun, from the eastern to the western boundary. 28 Along the frontier of Gad shall be the southern boundary, which shall extend from Tamar to the waters of Meribath-kadesh, and from there to the Wadi of Egypt, and on to the Great Sea. 29 Such is the land which you shall apportion as inheritances among the tribes of Israel, and these are their portions, says the Lord GOD.

The Gates of the City

30 These are the exits of the City, the gates of which are named after the tribes of Israel. On the north side, measuring forty-five hundred cubits, 31 there shall be three gates: the gates of Reuben, the gate of Judah, and the gate of Levi. 32 On the east side, measuring forty-five hundred cubits, there shall be three gates: the gate of Joseph, the gate of Benjamin, and the gate of Dan. 33 On the south side, measuring forty-five hundred cubits, there shall be three gates: the gate of Simeon, the gate of Issachar, and the gate of Zebulun. 34 On the west side, measuring forty-five hundred cubits, there shall be three gates: the gate of Gad, the gate of Asher, and the gate of Naphtali. 35 The perimeter of the City is eighteen thousand cubits. The name of the City shall henceforth be "The LORD is here."

48, 1–29: This distribution of the land among the tribes does not correspond to the geographical realities of Palestine. It is a description of the ideal order, like that in 47, 1–12.

Daniel

DANIEL AND THE KINGS OF BABYLON

The Food Test

IN the third year of the reign of Jehoiakim, king of Judah, King Nebuchadnezzar of Babylon came and laid siege to Jerusalem. 2 The Lord handed over to him Jehoiakim, king of Judah, and some of the vessels of the temple of God, which he carried off to the land of Shinar, and placed in the temple treasury of his god.

3 The king told Ashpenaz, his chief chamberlain, to bring in some of the Israelites of royal blood and of the nobility, 4 young men without any defect, handsome, intelligent and wise, quick to learn, and prudent in judgment, such as could take their place in the king's palace; they were to be taught the language and literature of the Chaldeans; 5 after three years' training they were to enter the king's service. The king allotted them a daily portion of food and wine from the royal table. 6 Among these were men of Judah: Daniel, Hananiah, Mishael, and Azariah. 7 The chief chamberlain changed their names: Daniel to Belteshazzar, Hananiah to Shadrach, Mishael to Meshach, and Azariah to Abednego.

8 But Daniel was resolved not to defile himself with the king's food or wine; so he begged the chief chamberlain to spare him this defilement. 9 Though God had given Daniel the favor and sympathy of the chief chamberlain, 10 he nevertheless said to Daniel, "I am afraid of my lord the king; it is he who allotted your food and drink. If he sees that you look wretched by comparison with the other young men of your age, you will endanger my life with the king." 11 Then Daniel said to the steward whom the chief chamberlain had put in charge of Daniel, Hananiah, Mishael, and Azariah, 12 "Please test your servants for ten days. Give us vegetables to eat and water to drink. 13 Then see how we look in comparison with the other young men who eat from the royal table, and treat your servants according to what you see." 14 He acceded to this request, and tested them for ten days; 15 after ten days they looked healthier and better fed than any of the young men who ate from the royal table. 16 So the steward continued to take away the food and wine they were to receive, and gave them vegetables.

17 To these four young men God gave knowledge and proficiency in all literature and science, and to Daniel the understanding of all visions and dreams. 18 At the end of the time the king had specified for their preparation, the chief chamberlain brought them before Nebuchadnezzar. 19 When the king had spoken with all of them, none was found equal to Daniel, Hananiah, Mishael, and Azariah; and so they entered the king's service. 20 In any question of wisdom or prudence which the king put to them, he found them ten times better than all the magicians and enchanters in his kingdom. 21 Daniel remained there until the first year of King Cyrus.

1, 2: *Shinar:* ancient name for Babylonia, a deliberate archaism in this text; cf Gn 10, 10; 11, 2.

1, 7: The young men are given Babylonian names as a sign of their adoption by the king.

1, 8: *This defilement:* the bread, meat, and wine of the Gentiles, which were unclean (Hos 9, 3; Tb 1, 12; Jdt 10, 5; 12, 1f) because they might have been offered to idols or prepared over firewood taken from a sacred grove. Only raw vegetables and water were safe from this danger (v 12).

1, 21: *The first year of King Cyrus:* the year of this Persian king's conquest of Babylon, 539/8 B.C.

The King's Dream

2 In the second year of his reign, King Nebuchadnezzar had a dream which left his spirit no rest and robbed him of his sleep. 2 So he ordered that the magicians, enchanters, sorcerers, and Chaldeans be summoned to interpret the dream for him. When they came and presented themselves to the king, 3 he said to them, "I had a dream which will allow my spirit no rest until I know what it means." 4 The Chaldeans answered the king [Aramaic]: "O king, live forever! Tell your servants the dream and we will give its meaning." 5 The king answered the Chaldeans, "This is what I have decided: unless you tell me the dream and its meaning, you shall be cut to pieces and your houses destroyed. 6 But if you tell me the dream and its meaning, you shall receive from me gifts and presents and great honors. Now tell me the dream and its meaning."

7 Again they answered, "Let the king tell his servants the dream and we will give its meaning." 8 But the king replied: "I know for certain that you are bargaining for time, since you know what I have decided. 9 If you do not tell me the dream, there can be but one decree for you. You have framed a false and deceitful interpretation to present me with till the crisis is past. Tell me the dream, therefore, that I may be sure that you can also give its correct interpretation."

10 The Chaldeans answered the king: "There is not a man on earth who can do what you ask, O king; never has any king, however great and mighty, asked such a thing of any magician, enchanter, or Chaldean. 11 What you demand, O king, is too difficult; there is no one who can tell it to the king except the gods who do not dwell among men." 12 At this the king became violently angry and ordered all the wise men of Babylon

to be put to death. 13 When the decree was issued that the wise men should be slain, Daniel and his companions were also sought out.

14 Then Daniel prudently took counsel with Arioch, the captain of the king's guard, who had set out to kill the wise men of Babylon: 15 "O officer of the king," he asked, "what is the reason for this harsh order from the king?" When Arioch told him, 16 Daniel went and asked for time from the king, that he might give him the interpretation.

17 Daniel went home and informed his companions Hananiah, Mishael, and Azariah, 18 that they might implore the mercy of the God of heaven in regard to this mystery, so that Daniel and his companions might not perish with the rest of the wise men of Babylon. 19 During the night the mystery was revealed to Daniel in a vision, and he blessed the God of heaven:

20 "Blessed be the name of God
　　forever and ever,
　for wisdom and power are his.
21 He causes the changes of the
　　times and seasons,
　makes kings and unmakes them.
　He gives wisdom to the wise
　and knowledge to those who
　　understand.
22 He reveals deep and hidden things
　and knows what is in the
　　darkness,
　for the light dwells with him.
23 To you, O God of my fathers,
　I give thanks and praise,
　because you have given me
　　wisdom and power.
　Now you have shown me what
　　we asked of you,
　you have made known to us
　　the king's dream."

24 So Daniel went to Arioch, whom the king had appointed to destroy the wise men of Babylon, and said to him, "Do not put the wise men of Babylon to death. Bring me

before the king, and I will tell him the interpretation of the dream." Arioch quickly brought Daniel to the king and said, 25 "I have found a man among the Judean captives who can give the interpretation to the king." 26 The king asked Daniel, whose name was Belteshazzar, "Can you tell me the dream that I had, and its meaning?" 27 In the king's presence Daniel made this reply:

"The mystery about which the king has inquired, the wise men, enchanters, magicians, and astrologers could not explain to the king. 28 But there is a God in heaven who reveals mysteries, and he has shown King Nebuchadnezzar what is to happen in days to come; this was the dream you saw as you lay in bed. 29 To you in your bed there came thoughts about what should happen in the future, and he who reveals mysteries showed you what is to be. 30 To me also this mystery has been revealed; not that I am wiser than any other living person, but in order that its meaning may be made known to the king, that you may understand the thoughts in your own mind.

31 "In your vision, O king, you saw a statue, very large and exceedingly bright, terrifying in appearance as it stood before you. 32 The head of the statue was pure gold, its chest and arms were silver, its belly and thighs bronze, 33 the legs iron, its feet partly iron and partly tile. 34 While you looked at the statue, a stone which was hewn from a mountain without a hand being put to it, struck its iron and tile feet, breaking them in pieces. 35 The iron, tile, bronze, silver, and gold all crumbled at once, fine as the chaff on the threshing floor in summer, and the wind blew them away without leaving a trace. But the stone that struck the statue became a great mountain and filled the whole earth.

36 "This was the dream; the interpretation we shall also give in the

---

2, 1–49: The chronology of v 1 is in conflict with that of 1, 5.18, and in v 25 Daniel appears to be introduced to the king for the first time. It seems that the story of this chapter was originally entirely independent of chapter 1, and later retouched slightly to fit its present setting.

2, 2: *Chaldeans:* here probably astrologers, who were so associated with the Chaldeans in the Hebrew mind that in the later language they are sometimes simply called by the name of that people.

2, 4: *Aramaic:* from 2, 4 to 7, 28 the text of Daniel is in Aramaic, not Hebrew, as indicated by this gloss.

2, 33: *Partly tile:* terra cotta tile was much in use among the Babylonians for decoration and for actual construction.

2, 36–45: The four successive kingdoms in this apocalyptic perspective are the Babylonian (gold), the Median (silver), the Persian (bronze), and the Hellenistic (iron). The last, after Alexander's death, was divided among his generals (vv 41f). The two

resulting kingdoms, which most affected the Jews, were the dynasty of the Ptolemies in Egypt and that of the Seleucids in Syria, who tried in vain, by war and through intermarriage, to restore the unity of Alexander's empire (v 43). The stone hewn from the mountain is the Messianic kingdom awaited by the Jews (vv 44f). Our Lord made this image personal to himself; cf Lk 20, 17f.

king's presence. 37 You, O king, are the king of kings; to you the God of heaven has given dominion and strength, power and glory; 38 men, wild beasts, and birds of the air, wherever they may dwell, he has handed over to you, making you ruler over them all; you are the head of gold. 39 Another kingdom shall take your place, inferior to yours, then a third kingdom, of bronze, which shall rule over the whole earth. 40 There shall be a fourth kingdom, strong as iron; it shall break in pieces and subdue all these others, just as iron breaks in pieces and crushes everything else. 41 The feet and toes you saw, partly of potter's tile and partly of iron, mean that it shall be a divided kingdom, but yet have some of the hardness of iron. As you saw the iron mixed with clay tile, 42 and the toes partly iron and partly tile, the kingdom shall be partly strong and partly fragile. 43 The iron mixed with clay tile means that they shall seal their alliances by intermarriage, but they shall not stay united, any more than iron mixes with clay. 44 In the lifetime of those kings the God of heaven will set up a kingdom that shall never be destroyed or delivered up to another people; rather, it shall break in pieces all these kingdoms and put an end to them, and it shall stand forever. 45 That is the meaning of the stone you saw hewn from the mountain without a hand being put to it, which broke in pieces the tile, iron, bronze, silver, and gold. The great God has revealed to the king what shall be in the future; this is exactly what you dreamed, and its meaning is sure."

46 Then King Nebuchadnezzar fell down and worshiped Daniel and ordered sacrifice and incense offered to him. 47 To Daniel the king said, "Truly your God is the God of gods and Lord of kings and a revealer of mysteries; that is why you were able to reveal this mystery." 48 He advanced Daniel to a high post, gave him many generous presents, made him ruler of the whole province of Babylon and chief prefect over all the wise men of Babylon. 49 At Daniel's request the king made Shadrach, Meshach, and Abednego administrators of the province of Babylon, while Daniel himself remained at the king's court.

The Fiery Furnace

3 King Nebuchadnezzar had a golden statue made, sixty cubits high and six cubits wide, which he set up in the plain of Dura in the province of Babylon. 2 He then ordered the satraps, prefects, and governors, the counselors, treasurers, judges, magistrates and all the officials of the provinces to be summoned to the dedication of the statue which he had set up. 3 The satraps, prefects, and governors, the counselors, treasurers, judges, and magistrates and all the officials of the provinces, all these came together for the dedication and stood before the statue which King Nebuchadnezzar had set up. 4 A herald cried out: "Nations and peoples of every language, when you hear the sound of the trumpet, flute, lyre, harp, psaltery, bagpipe, and all the other musical instruments, 5 you are ordered to fall down and worship the golden statue which King Nebuchadnezzar has set up. 6 Whoever does not fall down and worship shall be instantly cast into a white-hot furnace." 7 Therefore, as soon as they heard the sound of the trumpet, flute, lyre, harp, psaltery, bagpipe, and all the other musical instruments, the nations and peoples of every language all fell down and worshiped the golden statue which King Nebuchadnezzar had set up.

8 At that point, some of the Chaldeans came and accused the Jews 9 to King Nebuchadnezzar: "O king, live forever! 10 O king, you issued a decree that everyone who heard the sound of the trumpet, flute, lyre, harp, psaltery, bagpipe, and all the other musical instruments should fall down and worship the golden statue; 11 whoever did not was to be cast into a white-hot furnace. 12 There are certain Jews whom you have made administrators of the province of Babylon: Shadrach, Meshach, Abednego; these men, O king, have paid no attention to you; they will not serve your god or worship the golden statue which you set up."

13 Nebuchadnezzar flew into a rage and sent for Shadrach, Meshach, and Abednego, who were promptly brought before the king. 14 King Nebuchadnezzar questioned them: "Is it true, Shadrach, Meshach, and Abednego, that you will not serve my god, or worship the golden statue that I set up? 15 Be ready now to fall down and worship the statue I had made, whenever you hear the sound of the trumpet, flute, lyre, harp, psaltery, bagpipe, and all the other musical instruments; otherwise, you shall be instantly cast into the white-hot furnace; and who is the God that can deliver you out of my hands? 16 Shadrach, Meshach, and Abednego answered King Nebuchadnezzar, "There is no need for us to defend ourselves before you in this matter. 17 If our God, whom we serve, can save us from the white-hot furnace and from your hands, O king, may he save us! 18 But even if he will not, know, O king, that we will not serve your god or worship the golden statue which you set up."

19 Nebuchadnezzar's face became livid with utter rage against Shadrach, Meshach, and Abednego. He ordered the furnace to be heated seven times more than usual 20 and had some of the strongest men in his army bind Shadrach, Meshach, and Abednego and cast them into the white-hot furnace. 21 They were bound and cast into the white-hot furnace with their coats, hats, shoes, and other garments, 22 for the king's order was urgent. So huge a fire was kindled in the furnace that the flames devoured the men who threw Shadrach, Meshach, and Abednego into it. 23 But these three fell, bound, into the midst of the white-hot furnace.

3, 1: *Dura:* several places in Babylonia bore this name. Probably the present reference is to one a few miles south of Babylon. Colossi of the type mentioned here were not uncommon in antiquity; a cubit was seventeen and a half inches.

3, 2: *Satraps:* the Persian major governors.
3, 4: *Psaltery:* a harplike instrument.
3, 6: Death by fire was not unknown as a punishment in Babylonia; cf Jer 29, 22.

3, 17: *If our God . . . can save us:* the youths do not question the efficacy of the divine power, but whether it will be exercised (v 18).

24 They walked about in the flames, singing to God and blessing the Lord. 25 In the fire Azariah stood up and prayed aloud:

26 "Blessed are you, and praiseworthy,
    O Lord, the God of our fathers,
    and glorious forever is your name.
27 For you are just in all you have done;
    all your deeds are faultless,
    all your ways right,
    and all your judgments proper.
28 You have executed proper judgments
    in all that you have brought upon us
    and upon Jerusalem, the holy city of our fathers.
    By a proper judgment you have done all this
    because of our sins;
29 For we have sinned and transgressed
    by departing from you,
    and we have done every kind of evil.
30 Your commandments we have not heeded or observed,
    nor have we done as you ordered us for our good.
31 Therefore all you have brought upon us,
    all you have done to us,
    you have done by a proper judgment.
32 You have handed us over to our enemies,
    lawless and hateful rebels;
    to an unjust king, the worst in all the world.
33 Now we cannot open our mouths;
    we, your servants, who revere you,
    have become a shame and a reproach.
34 For your name's sake, do not deliver us up forever,
    or make void your covenant.
35 Do not take away your mercy from us,
    for the sake of Abraham, your beloved,

Isaac your servant, and Israel your holy one,
36 To whom you promised to multiply their offspring
    like the stars of heaven,
    or the sand on the shore of the sea.
37 For we are reduced, O Lord, beyond any other nation,
    brought low everywhere in the world this day
    because of our sins.
38 We have in our day no prince, prophet, or leader,
    no holocaust, sacrifice, oblation, or incense,
    no place to offer first fruits, to find favor with you.
39 But with contrite heart and humble spirit
    let us be received;
40 As though it were holocausts of rams and bullocks,
    or thousands of fat lambs,
    So let our sacrifice be in your presence today
    as we follow you unreservedly;
    for those who trust in you cannot be put to shame.
41 And now we follow you with our whole heart,
    we fear you and we pray to you.
42 Do not let us be put to shame, but deal with us in your kindness and great mercy.
43 Deliver us by your wonders, and bring glory to your name, O Lord:
44 Let all those be routed who inflict evils on your servants;
    Let them be shamed and powerless,
    and their strength broken;
45 Let them know that you alone are the Lord God,
    glorious over the whole world."

46 Now the king's men who had thrown them in continued to stoke the furnace with brimstone, pitch, tow, and faggots. 47 The flames rose forty-nine cubits above the furnace, 48 and spread out, burning the Chaldeans nearby. 49 But

the angel of the Lord went down into the furnace with Azariah and his companions, drove the fiery flames out of the furnace, 50 and made the inside of the furnace as though a dew-laden breeze were blowing through it. The fire in no way touched them or caused them pain or harm. 51 Then these three in the furnace with one voice sang, glorifying and blessing God:

52 "Blessed are you, O Lord, the God of our fathers,
    praiseworthy and exalted above all forever;
    And blessed is your holy and glorious name,
    praiseworthy and exalted above all for all ages.
53 Blessed are you in the temple of your holy glory,
    praiseworthy and glorious above all forever.
54 Blessed are you on the throne of your kingdom,
    praiseworthy and exalted above all forever.
55 Blessed are you who look into the depths
    from your throne upon the cherubim,
    praiseworthy and exalted above all forever.
56 Blessed are you in the firmament of heaven,
    praiseworthy and glorious forever.
57 Bless the Lord, all you works of the Lord,
    praise and exalt him above all forever.
58 Angels of the Lord, bless the Lord,
    praise and exalt him above all forever.
59 You heavens, bless the Lord,
    praise and exalt him above all forever.
60 All you waters above the heavens, bless the Lord,
    praise and exalt him above all forever.
61 All you hosts of the Lord, bless the Lord;
    praise and exalt him above all forever.

3, 24–90: These verses are inspired additions to the Aramaic text of Daniel, translated from the Greek form of the book. They were originally composed in Hebrew or Aramaic, which has not been preserved. The Church has always regarded them as part of the canonical Scriptures.

62 Sun and moon, bless the Lord;
    praise and exalt him above all
      forever.

63 Stars of heaven, bless the Lord;
    praise and exalt him above all
      forever.

64 Every shower and dew, bless the
      Lord;
    praise and exalt him above all
      forever.

65 All you winds, bless the Lord;
    praise and exalt him above all
      forever.

66 Fire and heat, bless the Lord;
    praise and exalt him above all
      forever.

67 [Cold and chill, bless the Lord;
    praise and exalt him above all
      forever.

68 Dew and rain, bless the Lord;
    praise and exalt him above all
      forever.]

69 Frost and chill, bless the Lord;
    praise and exalt him above all
      forever.

70 Ice and snow, bless the Lord;
    praise and exalt him above all
      forever.

71 Nights and days, bless the
      Lord;
    praise and exalt him above all
      forever.

72 Light and darkness, bless the
      Lord;
    praise and exalt him above all
      forever.

73 Lightnings and clouds, bless the
      Lord;
    praise and exalt him above all
      forever.

74 Let the earth bless the Lord,
    praise and exalt him above all
      forever.

75 Mountains and hills, bless the
      Lord;
    praise and exalt him above all
      forever.

76 Everything growing from the
      earth, bless the Lord;
    praise and exalt him above all
      forever.

77 You springs, bless the Lord;
    praise and exalt him above all
      forever.

78 Seas and rivers, bless the Lord;
    praise and exalt him above all
      forever.

79 You dolphins and all water
      creatures, bless the Lord;
    praise and exalt him above all
      forever.

80 All you birds of the air, bless
      the Lord;
    praise and exalt him above all
      forever.

81 All you beasts, wild and tame,
      bless the Lord;
    praise and exalt him above all
      forever.

82 You sons of men, bless the Lord;
    praise and exalt him above all
      forever.

83 O Israel, bless the Lord;
    praise and exalt him above all
      forever.

84 Priests of the Lord, bless the
      Lord;
    praise and exalt him above all
      forever.

85 Servants of the Lord, bless the
      Lord;
    praise and exalt him above all
      forever.

86 Spirits and souls of the just,
      bless the Lord;
    praise and exalt him above all
      forever.

87 Holy men of humble heart, bless
      the Lord;
    praise and exalt him above all
      forever.

88 Hananiah, Azariah, Mishael,
      bless the Lord;
    praise and exalt him above all
      forever.

  For he has delivered us from the
      nether world,
  and saved us from the power
      of death;
  He has freed us from the raging
      flame
  and delivered us from the fire.

89 Give thanks to the Lord, for he
      is good,
    for his mercy endures forever.

90 Bless the God of gods, all you
      who fear the Lord;
    praise him and give him
      thanks,
    because his mercy endures
      forever."

Hearing them sing, and astonished
at seeing them alive,   91 King Neb-

uchadnezzar rose in haste and asked
his nobles, "Did we not cast three
men bound into the fire?" "Assuredly, O king," they answered. 92
"But," he replied, "I see four men
unfettered and unhurt, walking in the
fire, and the fourth looks like a son
of God."   93 Then Nebuchadnezzar
came to the opening of the white-hot
furnace and called to Shadrach,
Meshach, and Abednego: "Servants
of the most high God, come out."
Thereupon Shadrach, Meshach, and
Abednego came out of the fire.   94
When the satraps, prefects, governors, and nobles of the king came
together, they saw that the fire had
had no power over the bodies of
these men; not a hair of their heads
had been singed, nor were their
garments altered; there was not even
a smell of fire about them. 95
Nebuchadnezzar exclaimed, "Blessed
be the God of Shadrach, Meshach,
and Abednego, who sent his angel to
deliver the servants that trusted in
him; they disobeyed the royal command and yielded their bodies rather
than serve or worship any god except their own God. 96 Therefore
I decree for nations and peoples of
every language that whoever blasphemes the God of Shadrach, Meshach, and Abednego shall be cut to
pieces and his house destroyed. For
there is no other God who can rescue
like this." 97 Then the king promoted Shadrach, Meshach, and
Abednego in the province of Babylon.

Vision of the Great Tree

98 King Nebuchadnezzar to the
nations and peoples of every language, wherever they dwell on earth:
abundant peace! 99 It has seemed
good to me to publish the signs and
wonders which the most high God
has accomplished in my regard.

100 How great are his signs, how
      mighty his wonders;
    his kingdom is an everlasting
      kingdom,
    and his dominion endures
      through all generations.

3, 92: *A son of God:* an angel; cf Jb 1, 6.
3, 98—4, 34: This section has the form of a letter
written by Nebuchadnezzar to his subjects.

3, 99: *The most high God:* the Jews, especially in
the diaspora, used this title to distinguish their God
from those of the pagans. On the lips of a polytheist

(so also in v 93) it was merely the title of another
god. It was an ancient divine name used in Canaan; cf
Gn 14, 18.

4 I, Nebuchadnezzar, was at home in my palace, content and prosperous. 2 I had a terrifying dream as I lay in bed, and the images and the visions of my mind frightened me. 3 So I issued a decree that all the wise men of Babylon should be brought before me to give the interpretation of the dream. 4 When the magicians, enchanters, Chaldeans, and astrologers had come in, I related the dream before them; but none of them could tell me its meaning. 5 Finally there came before me Daniel, whose name is Belteshazzar after the name of my god, and in whom is the spirit of the holy God. I repeated the dream to him: 6 "Belteshazzar, chief of the magicians, I know that the spirit of the holy God is in you and no mystery is too difficult for you; tell me the meaning of the visions that I saw in my dream.

7 "These were the visions I saw while in bed: I saw a tree of great height at the center of the world. 8 It was large and strong, with its top touching the heavens, and it could be seen to the ends of the earth. 9 Its leaves were beautiful and its fruit abundant, providing food for all. Under it the wild beasts found shade, in its branches the birds of the air nested; all men ate of it. 10 In the vision I saw while in bed, a holy sentinel came down from heaven, 11 and cried out:

"'Cut down the tree and lop off
      its branches,
  strip off its leaves and scatter
      its fruit;
  let the beasts flee its shade,
      and the birds its branches.
12 But leave in the earth its stump
      and roots,
  fettered with iron and bronze,
      in the grass of the field.
  Let him be bathed with the dew
      of heaven;

his lot be to eat, among
      beasts, the grass of the earth.
13 Let his mind be changed from
      the human;
  let him be given the sense of a
      beast,
  till seven years pass over him.
14 By decree of the sentinels is this
      decided,
  by order of the holy ones, this
      sentence;
  That all who live may know
      that the Most High rules over
      the kingdom of men:
  He can give it to whom he will,
      or set over it the lowliest of
      men.'

15 "This is the dream that I, King Nebuchadnezzar, had. Now, Belteshazzar, tell me its meaning. Although none of the wise men in my kingdom can tell me the meaning, you can, because the spirit of the holy God is in you."

16 Then Daniel, whose name was Belteshazzar, was appalled for a while, terrified by his thoughts. "Belteshazzar," the king said to him, "let not the dream or its meaning terrify you." 17 "My lord," Belteshazzar replied, "this dream should be for your enemies, and its meaning for your foes. The large, strong tree that you saw, with its top touching the heavens, that could be seen by the whole earth, 18 which had beautiful foliage and abundant fruit, providing food for all, under which the wild beasts lived, and in whose branches the birds of the air dwelt— 19 you are that tree, O king, large and strong! Your majesty has become so great as to touch the heavens, and your rule extends over the whole earth. 20 As for the king's vision of a holy sentinel that came down from heaven and proclaimed: 'Cut down the tree and destroy it, but leave in the earth its stump and roots, fettered with iron and bronze in the

grass of the field; let him be bathed with the dew of heaven, and let his lot be among wild beasts till seven years pass over him'—21 this is its meaning, O king; this is the sentence which the Most High has passed upon my lord king: 22 You shall be cast out from among men and dwell with wild beasts; you shall be given grass to eat like an ox and be bathed with the dew of heaven; seven years shall pass over you, until you know that the Most High rules over the kingdom of men and gives it to whom he will. 23 The command that the stump and roots of the tree are to be left means that your kingdom shall be preserved for you, once you have learned it is heaven that rules. 24 Therefore, O king, take my advice; atone for your sins by good deeds, and for your misdeeds by kindness to the poor; then your prosperity will be long."

25 All this happened to King Nebuchadnezzar. 26 Twelve months later, as he was walking on the roof of the royal palace in Babylon, 27 the king said, "Babylon the great! Was it not I, with my great strength, who built it as a royal residence for my splendor and majesty?" 28 While these words were still on the king's lips, a voice spoke from heaven, "It has been decreed for you, King Nebuchadnezzar, that your kingdom is taken from you! 29 You shall be cast out from among men, and shall dwell with wild beasts; you shall be given grass to eat like an ox, and seven years shall pass over you, until you learn that the Most High rules over the kingdom of men and gives it to whom he will." 30 At once this was fulfilled. Nebuchadnezzar was cast out from among men, he ate grass like an ox, and his body was bathed with the dew of heaven, until his hair grew like the feathers of an eagle, and his nails like the claws of a bird.

4, 5: *After the name of my god:* Belteshazzar, the Babylonian name given to Daniel at the king's orders (1, 7), is Balatsu-ussur, "protect his life." In the king's intention, this would be an abbreviation for *Bel-balatsu-ussur.* It would thus include an appeal to the god Bel, originally the name of the city god of Nippur, and later identified with Marduk, the chief god of Babylon. Daniel's use of the name would refer the prayer rather than to the true God.

4, 10: *A holy sentinel:* an angel. This term is found in the Bible only in this chapter of Daniel, but it is

common in later Jewish literature.

4, 11ff: As the tree is Nebuchadnezzar (v 19), the description passes from metaphor to the reality.

4, 17: *"This dream...for your foes":* Daniel speaks as a courtier.

4, 22: The description is of a form of insanity called lycanthropy, in which the patient acts like a wolf.

4, 24: A classic Scriptural text for the efficacy of good works.

4, 27: The words attributed to the king are similar

to the boastings in the royal inscriptions by which the Mesopotamian kings testified to their mighty works.

4, 30ff: There is no certainty of any such thing happening to Nebuchadnezzar as is described here. Some scholars think that the Nebuchadnezzar of this chapter is actually Nabonidus, the father of Belshazzar, who was mysteriously absent from Babylon for a number of years. The Biblical author's chief interest was not in the historicity of this popular tale, but in the object lesson it contained for the proud "divine" kings of the Seleucid dynasty.

31 When this period was over, I, Nebuchadnezzar, raised my eyes to heaven; my reason was restored to me, and I blessed the Most High, I praised and glorified him who lives forever:

His dominion is an everlasting
      dominion,
   and his kingdom endures
      through all generations.
32 All who live on the earth are
      counted as nothing;
   he does as he pleases with the
      powers of heaven
   as well as with those who live
      on the earth.
There is no one who can stay
      his hand
   or say to him, "What have
      you done?"

33 At the same time my reason returned to me, and for the glory of my kingdom, my majesty and my splendor returned to me. My nobles and lords sought me out; I was restored to my kingdom, and became much greater than before. 34 Therefore, I, Nebuchadnezzar, now praise and exalt and glorify the King of heaven, because all his works are right and his ways just; and those who walk in pride he is able to humble.

The Writing on the Wall

5 King Belshazzar gave a great banquet for a thousand of his lords, with whom he drank. 2 Under the influence of the wine, he ordered the gold and silver vessels which Nebuchadnezzar, his father, had taken from the temple in Jerusalem, to be brought in so that the king, his lords, his wives and his entertainers might drink from them. 3 When the gold and silver vessels taken from the house of God in Jerusalem had been brought in, and while the king, his lords, his wives and his entertainers were drinking 4 wine from them, they praised their gods of gold and silver, bronze and iron, wood and stone.

5 Suddenly, opposite the lampstand, the fingers of a human hand appeared, writing on the plaster of the wall in the king's palace. When the king saw the wrist and hand that wrote, 6 his face blanched; his thoughts terrified him, his hip joints shook, and his knees knocked. 7 The king shouted for the enchanters, Chaldeans, and astrologers to be brought in. "Whoever reads this writing and tells me what it means," he said to the wise men of Babylon, "shall be clothed in purple, wear a golden collar about his neck, and be third in the government of the kingdom." 8 But though all the king's wise men came in, none of them could either read the writing or tell the king what it meant. 9 Then King Belshazzar was greatly terrified; his face went ashen, and his lords were thrown into confusion.

10 When the queen heard of the discussion between the king and his lords, she entered the banquet hall and said, "O king, live forever! Be not troubled in mind, nor look so pale! 11 There is a man in your kingdom in whom is the spirit of the holy God; during the lifetime of your father he was seen to have brilliant knowledge and god-like wisdom. In fact, King Nebuchadnezzar, your father, made him chief of the magicians, enchanters, Chaldeans, and astrologers, 12 because of the extraordinary mind possessed by this Daniel, whom the king named Belteshazzar. He knew and understood how to interpret dreams, explain enigmas, and solve difficulties. Now therefore, summon Daniel to tell you what this means."

13 Then Daniel was brought into the presence of the king. The king asked him, "Are you the Daniel, the Jewish exile, whom my father, the king, brought from Judah? 14 I have heard that the spirit of God is in you, that you possess brilliant knowledge and extraordinary wisdom. 15 Now, the wise men and enchanters were brought in to me to read this writing and tell me its meaning, but they could not say what the words meant. 16 But I have heard that you can interpret dreams and solve difficulties; if you are able to read the writing and tell me what it means, you shall be clothed in purple, wear a gold collar about your neck, and be third in the government of the kingdom."

17 Daniel answered the king: "You may keep your gifts, or give your presents to someone else; but the writing I will read for you, O king, and tell you what it means. 18 The Most High God gave your father Nebuchadnezzar a great kingdom and glorious majesty. 19 Because he made him so great, the nations and peoples of every language dreaded and feared him. Whomever he wished, he killed or let live; whomever he wished, he exalted or humbled. 20 But when his heart became proud and his spirit hardened by insolence, he was put down from his royal throne and deprived of his glory; 21 he was cast out from among men and was made insensate as a beast; he lived with wild asses, and ate grass like an ox; his body was bathed with the dew of heaven, until he learned that the Most High God rules over the kingdom of men and appoints over it whom he will. 22 You, his son, Belshazzar, have not humbled your heart, though you knew all this; 23 you have rebelled against the Lord of heaven. You had the vessels of his temple brought before you, so that you and your nobles, your wives and your entertainers, might drink wine from them; and you praised the gods of silver and gold, bronze and iron, wood and stone, that neither see nor hear nor have intelligence. But the God in whose hand is your life breath and the whole course of your life, you did not glorify. 24 By him were the wrist and hand sent, and the writing set down.

25 "This is the writing that was inscribed: MENE, TEKEL, and PERES. These words mean: 26 MENE, God has numbered your kingdom and put an end to it; 27 TEKEL, you have been weighed on the scales and found wanting; 28 PERES, your kingdom

---

5, 1: *King Belshazzar:* Belshazzar was actually the crown prince, but he had been given royal authority in Babylon by his father Nabonidus.

5, 2: *Nebuchadnezzar, his father:* several kings of Babylon intervened between Nebuchadnezzar and Belshazzar. Either the term *father* is used here in the broad sense of "remote predecessor," or the name *Nebuchadnezzar* is used for "Nabonidus."

5, 25: *Mene, Tekel, and Peres:* these seem to be the Aramaic names of weights and monetary values: the mina, the shekel (the sixtieth part of a mina), and the parsu (a half-mina).

5, 26ff: Daniel interprets these three terms by a play on the words: *Mene,* connected with the verb meaning to number; *Tekel,* with the verb meaning to weigh; *Peres,* with the verb meaning to divide. There is also a play on the last term with the word for Persians.

has been divided and given to the Medes and Persians."

29 Then by order of Belshazzar they clothed Daniel in purple, with a gold collar about his neck, and proclaimed him third in the government of the kingdom. 30 The same night Belshazzar, the Chaldean king, was slain; 1 and Darius the Mede succeeded to the kingdom at the age of sixty-two.

In The Lion's Den

2 Darius decided to appoint over his entire kingdom one hundred and twenty satraps, to safeguard his interests; 3 these were accountable to three supervisors, one of whom was Daniel. 4 Daniel outshone all the supervisors and satraps because an extraordinary spirit was in him, and the king thought of giving him authority over the entire kingdom. 5 Therefore the supervisors and satraps tried to find grounds for accusation against Daniel as regards the administration. But they could accuse him of no wrongdoing; because he was trustworthy, no fault of neglect or misconduct was to be found in him. 6 Then these men said to themselves, "We shall find no grounds for accusation against this Daniel unless by way of the law of his God." 7 So these supervisors and satraps went thronging to the king and said to him, "King Darius, live forever! 8 All the supervisors of the kingdom, the prefects, satraps, nobles, and governors are agreed that the following prohibition ought to be put in force by royal decree: no one is to address any petition to god or man for thirty days, except to you, O king; otherwise he shall be cast into a den of lions. 9 Now, O king, issue the prohibition over your signature, immutable and irrevocable under Mede and Persian law." 10 So King Darius signed the prohibition and made it law.

11 Even after Daniel heard that this law had been signed, he continued his custom of going home to kneel in prayer and give thanks to his God in the upper chamber three times a day, with the windows open toward Jerusalem. 12 So these men rushed in and found Daniel praying and pleading before his God. 13 Then they went to remind the king about the prohibition: "Did you not decree, O king, that no one is to address a petition to god or man for thirty days, except to you, O king; otherwise he shall be cast into a den of lions?" The king answered them, "The decree is absolute, irrevocable under the Mede and Persian law." 14 To this they replied, "Daniel, the Jewish exile, has paid no attention to you, O king, or to the decree you issued; three times a day he offers his prayer." 15 The king was deeply grieved at this news and he made up his mind to save Daniel; he worked till sunset to rescue him. 16 But these men insisted. "Keep in mind, O king," they said, "that under the Mede and Persian law every royal prohibition or decree is irrevocable." 17 So the king ordered Daniel to be brought and cast into the lions' den. To Daniel he said, "May your God, whom you serve so constantly, save you." 18 To forestall any tampering, the king sealed with his own ring and the rings of the lords the stone that had been brought to block the opening of the den.

19 Then the king returned to his palace for the night; he refused to eat and he dismissed the entertainers. Since sleep was impossible for him, 20 the king rose very early the next morning and hastened to the lions' den. 21 As he drew near, he cried out to Daniel sorrowfully, "O Daniel, servant of the living God, has the God whom you serve so constantly been able to save you from the lions?" 22 Daniel answered the

king: "O king, live forever! 23 My God has sent his angel and closed the lions' mouths so that they have not hurt me. For I have been found innocent before him; neither to you have I done any harm, O king!" 24 This gave the king great joy. At his order David was removed from the den, unhurt because he trusted in his God. 25 The king then ordered the men who had accused Daniel, along with their children and their wives, to be cast into the lions' den. Before they reached the bottom of the den, the lions overpowered them and crushed all their bones.

26 Then King Darius wrote to the nations and peoples of every language, wherever they dwell on the earth: "All peace to you! 27 I decree that throughout my royal domain the God of Daniel is to be reverenced and feared:

> "For he is the living God,
>   enduring forever;
> his kingdom shall not be
>   destroyed,
> and his dominion shall be
>   without end.
28 He is a deliverer and savior,
>   working signs and wonders in
>   heaven and on earth,
> and he delivered Daniel from
>   the lions' power."

29 So Daniel fared well during the reign of Darius and the reign of Cyrus the Persian.

DANIEL'S VISIONS

Vision of the Four Beasts

7 In the first year of King Belshazzar of Babylon, Daniel had a dream as he lay in bed, and was terrified by the visions of his mind. Then he wrote down the dream; the account began: 2 In the vision I saw during the night, suddenly the four winds of heaven stirred up the

6, 1: *Darius the Mede:* unknown in profane history. The Median kingdom had already been conquered by Cyrus the Persian, and it was Cyrus who captured Babylon. Evidently the author of Daniel has deliberately adopted an apocalyptic view of history, derived from prophecy (cf Is 13, 17f; Jer 51, 11.28ff), according to which the Medes formed the second of four world kingdoms preceding the Messianic times; see note on 2, 36-45. The character of Darius the Mede has probably been modeled on that of the Persian King Darius the Great (522-486 B.C.), the second successor of Cyrus.

6, 9: *Immutable and irrevocable:* the passages in Est 1, 19 and 8, 8 also refer to the immutability of Medo-Persian laws. The historian Diodorus Siculus indicates that such a concept existed in the time of Darius III (335-331 B.C.), the last of the Persian kings. Cf vv 13.16.
6, 17: *The lions' den:* a pit too deep to be easily scaled; its opening was blocked with a stone (v 18).
7, 1-27: The significance of this vision is the same as that of Nebuchadnezzar's dream in chapter 2; see note on 2, 36-45. To the four succeeding world kingdoms, Babylonian, Median, Persian, and Greek,

is opposed the Messianic kingdom of the people of God. The imagery of this chapter has been used extensively in the Revelation of St. John, where it is applied to the Roman empire, the persecutor of the Church.
7, 2: *The great sea:* the primordial ocean beneath the earth, according to primitive cosmology (Gn 7, 11; 49, 25). This was thought to contain various monsters (Is 27, 1; Jb 7, 12), and in particular mythological monsters symbolizing the chaos which God had vanquished in ancient times (Jb 9, 13: 26, 13; etc.).

great sea, 3 from which emerged four immense beasts, each different from the others. 4 The first was like a lion, but with eagle's wings. While I watched, the wings were plucked; it was raised from the ground to stand on two feet like a man, and given a human mind. 5 The second was like a bear; it was raised up on one side, and among the teeth in its mouth were three tusks. It was given the order, "Up, devour much flesh." 6 After this I looked and saw another beast, like a leopard; on its back were four wings like those of a bird, and it had four heads. To this beast dominion was given. 7 After this, in the visions of the night I saw the fourth beast, different from all the others, terrifying, horrible, and of extraordinary strength; it had great iron teeth with which it devoured and crushed, and what was left it trampled with its feet. 8 I was considering the ten horns it had, when suddenly another, a little horn, sprang out of their midst, and three of the previous horns were torn away to make room for it. This horn had eyes like a man, and a mouth that spoke arrogantly. 9 As I watched,

Thrones were set up
and the Ancient One took his
throne.
His clothing was snow bright,
and the hair on his head as
white as wool;
His throne was flames of fire,
with wheels of burning fire.
10 A surging stream of fire
flowed out from where he sat;
Thousands upon thousands were
ministering to him,
and myriads upon myriads
attended him.

The court was convened, and the books were opened. 11 I watched, then, from the first of the arrogant

words which the horn spoke, until the beast was slain and its body thrown into the fire to be burnt up. 12 The other beasts, which also lost their dominion, were granted a prolongation of life for a time and a season. 13 As the visions during the night continued, I saw

One like a son of man coming,
on the clouds of heaven;
When he reached the Ancient
One
and was presented before him,
14 He received dominion, glory,
and kingship;
nations and peoples of every
language serve him.
His dominion is an everlasting
dominion
that shall not be taken away,
his kingship shall not be
destroyed.

15 I, Daniel, found my spirit anguished within its sheath of flesh, and I was terrified by the visions of my mind. 16 I approached one of those present and asked him what all this meant in truth; in answer, he made known to me the meaning of the things; 17 "These four great beasts stand for four kingdoms which shall arise on the earth. 18 But the holy ones of the Most High shall receive the kingship, to possess it forever and ever." 19 But I wished to make certain about the fourth beast, so very terrible and different from the others, devouring and crushing with its iron teeth and bronze claws, and trampling with its feet what was left; 20 about the ten horns on its head, and the other one that sprang up, before which three horns fell; about the horn with the eyes and the mouth that spoke arrogantly, which appeared greater than its fellows. 21 For, as I watched, that horn made war

against the holy ones and was victorious 22 until the Ancient One arrived; judgment was pronounced in favor of the holy ones of the Most High, and the time came when the holy ones possessed the kingdom. 23 He answered me thus:

"The fourth beast shall be a
fourth kingdom on earth,
different from all the others;
It shall devour the whole earth,
beat it down, and crush it.
24 The ten horns shall be ten
kings
rising out of that kingdom;
another shall rise up after
them,
Different from those before
him,
who shall lay low three kings.
25 He shall speak against the
Most High
and oppress the holy ones of
the Most High,
thinking to change the feast
days and the law.
They shall be handed over to
him
for a year, two years, and a
half-year.
26 But when the court is convened,
and his power is taken away
by final and absolute
destruction,
27 Then the kingship and dominion
and majesty
of all the kingdoms under the
heavens
shall be given to the holy
people of the Most High,
Whose kingdom shall be
everlasting:
all dominions shall serve and
obey him."

28 The report concluded: I, Daniel, was greatly terrified by my thoughts, and my face blanched, but I kept the matter to myself.

7, 4: The representation of the Babylonian empire as a winged lion, a common motif in Babylonian art, symbolizes the bestial power hostile to God. The two wings that *were plucked* represent Nebuchadnezzar and Belshazzar. *On two feet like a man . . . a human mind:* contrasts with what is said in 4, 13.30.

7, 5: *A bear:* represents the Median empire, its *three tusks* symbolizing its destructive nature; hence, the command: *"Up, devour much flesh."*

7, 6: *A leopard:* used to symbolize the swiftness with which Cyrus the Persian established his kingdom. *Four heads:* corresponding to the four Persian kings of 11, 2.

7, 7f: Alexander's empire was *different from all the others* in that it was Western rather than Oriental in

inspiration. The *ten horns* represent the kings of the Seleucid dynasty, the only part of the Hellenistic empire that concerned the author. The *little horn* is Antiochus IV Epiphanes (175–163 B.C.), the worst of the Seleucid kings, who usurped the throne.

7, 9f: A vision of the heavenly throne of God (*the Ancient One*), who sits in judgment (symbolized by *fire*) over the nations. Some of the details of the vision, depicting the divine majesty and omnipotence, are to be found in Ez 1.

7, 13f: *One like a son of man:* in contrast to the worldly kingdoms opposed to God, which appear as beasts, the glorified people of God that will form his kingdom on earth is represented in human form (v 18). Just as our Lord applied the figure of the stone

hewn from the mountain to himself (2, 36–45), he also made the title "Son of Man" his most characteristic way of referring to himself, as the One in whom and through whom the salvation of God's people came to be realized.

7, 25: The reference is to the persecutions of Antiochus IV and his attempt to force the Jews to give up their customs and to adopt Hellenistic ways (1 Mc 1, 33f). *A year, two years, and a half-year:* an indefinite, evil period of time. As seven is the Jewish "perfect" number, half of it signifies great imperfection. Actually, this corresponds fairly accurately to the duration of Antiochus' persecution.

7, 28: This verse ends the Aramaic part of the Book of Daniel.

Vision of the Ram and He-goat

8 After this first vision, I, Daniel, had another, in the third year of the reign of King Belshazzar. 2 In my vision I saw myself in the fortress of Susa in the province of Elam; I was beside the river Ulai. 3 I looked up and saw standing by the river a ram with two great horns, the one larger and newer than the other. 4 I saw the ram butting toward the west, north, and south. No beast could withstand it or be rescued from its power; it did what it pleased and became very powerful.

5 As I was reflecting, a he-goat with a prominent horn on its forehead suddenly came from the west across the whole earth without touching the ground. 6 It approached the two-horned ram I had seen standing by the river, and rushed toward it with savage force.

7 I saw it attack the ram with furious blows when they met, and break both its horns. It threw the ram, which had not the force to withstand it, to the ground, and trampled upon it; and no one could rescue it from its power.

8 The he-goat became very powerful, but at the height of its power the great horn was shattered, and in its place came up four others, facing the four winds of heaven. 9 Out of one of them came a little horn which kept growing toward the south, the east, and the glorious country. 10 Its power extended to the host of heaven so that it cast down to earth some of the host and some of the stars and trampled on them. 11 It boasted even against the prince of the host, from whom it removed the daily sacrifice, and whose sanctuary it cast down, 12 as well as the host, while sin replaced the daily sacrifice. It cast

truth to the ground, and was succeeding in its undertaking.

13 I heard a holy one speaking, and another said to whichever one it was that spoke, "How long shall the events of this vision last concerning the daily sacrifice, the desolating sin which is placed there, the sanctuary, and the trampled host?" 14 He answered him, "For two thousand three hundred evenings and mornings; then the sanctuary shall be purified."

15 While I, Daniel, sought the meaning of the vision I had seen, a manlike figure stood before me, 16 and on the Ulai I heard a human voice that cried out, "Gabriel, explain the vision to this man." 17 When he came near where I was standing, I fell prostrate in terror. But he said to me, "Understand, son of man, that the vision refers to the end time." 18 As he spoke to me, I fell forward in a faint; he touched me and made me stand up. 19 "I will show you," he said, "what is to happen later in the period of wrath; for at the appointed time, there will be an end.

20 "The two-horned ram you saw represents the kings of the Medes and Persians. 21 The he-goat is the king of the Greeks, and the great horn on its forehead is the first king. 22 The four that rose in its place when it was broken are four kingdoms that will issue from his nation, but without his strength.

23 "After their reign,
        when sinners have reached
            their measure,
    There shall arise a king,
            impudent
        and skilled in intrigue.
24 He shall be strong and powerful,
        bring about fearful ruin,
        and succeed in his undertaking.

He shall destroy powerful
        peoples;
25   his cunning shall be against
            the holy ones,
        his treacherous conduct shall
            succeed.
    He shall be proud of heart
        and destroy many by stealth.
    But when he rises against the
            prince of princes,
        he shall be broken without a
            hand being raised.
26 The vision of the evenings and
            the mornings
        is true, as spoken;
    Do you, however, keep this
            vision undisclosed,
        because the days are to be
            many."

27 I, Daniel, was weak and ill for some days; then I arose and took care of the king's affairs. But I was appalled at the vision, which I could not understand.

Gabriel and the Seventy Weeks

9 It was the first year that Darius, son of Ahasuerus, of the race of the Medes, reigned over the kingdom of the Chaldeans; 2 in the first year of his reign I, Daniel, tried to understand in the Scriptures the counting of the years of which the LORD spoke to the prophet Jeremiah: that for the ruins of Jerusalem seventy years must be fulfilled.

3 I turned to the Lord God, pleading in earnest prayer, with fasting, sackcloth, and ashes. 4 I prayed to the LORD, my God, and confessed, "Ah, Lord, great and awesome God, you who keep your merciful covenant toward those who love you and observe your commandments! 5 We have sinned, been wicked and done evil; we have rebelled and departed from your commandments and your laws. 6 We have not

---

8, 1–27: This vision repeats the major part of the preceding one, though in a more explicit fashion. As explained in vv 20ff, *the two-horned ram* represents the combined kingdom of the Medes and Persians, destroyed by Alexander's Hellenistic empire originating in the west. Once again the author is interested only in the Seleucid dynasty, which emerged from the dissolution of Alexander's empire after his death in 323 B.C.

8, 2: *The fortress of Susa:* the royal palace of the Persian kings in the ancient territory of Elam, east of Babylonia. *The river Ulai:* a canal along the northern side of Susa.

8, 9: *A little horn,* as in chapter 7, is Antiochus IV. *The glorious country:* Palestine.

8, 10ff: *The host of heaven:* ordinarily meaning the stars, here refers to the people of God; cf 12, 3. *The prince of the host:* God himself, with whose holy religion Antiochus interfered (1 Mc 1, 45).

8, 13: *The desolating sin:* the Hebrew contains a wordplay (*shomen*) on the name Baal Shamen ("lord of the heavens," the Greek Zeus Olympios), referring to the statue with which Antiochus profaned the temple of Jerusalem (2 Mc 6, 2).

8, 16: The angel Gabriel is mentioned here for the first time in the Bible. There is wordplay in the preceding verse on *geber—manlike figure.*

8, 17: *The end time:* the day of the Lord, when God sits in judgment on his enemies (v 19).

9, 1: *Darius:* see the note on 6, 1.

9, 2: *Seventy years:* the prophet Jeremiah (25, 11; 29, 10) prophesied a Babylonian captivity of seventy years, a round number signifying the complete passing away of the existing generation. Jeremiah's prophecy was fulfilled in the capture of Babylon by Cyrus and the subsequent return of the Jews to Palestine. However, the author of Daniel, living during the persecution of Antiochus, sees the conditions of the Exile still existing; therefore in his meditation he extends Jeremiah's number to seventy weeks of years (v 24), i.e., seven times seventy years, to characterize the Jewish victory over the Seleucids as the ultimate fulfillment of the prophecy.

obeyed your servants the prophets, who spoke in your name to our kings, our princes, our fathers, and all the people of the land. 7 Justice, O Lord, is on your side; we are shamefaced even to this day: the men of Judah, the residents of Jerusalem, and all Israel, near and far, in all the countries to which you have scattered them because of their treachery toward you. 8 O LORD, we are shamefaced, like our kings, our princes, and our fathers, for having sinned against you. 9 But yours, O Lord, our God, are compassion and forgiveness! Yet we rebelled against you 10 and paid no heed to your command, O LORD, our God, to live by the law you gave us through your servants the prophets. 11 Because all Israel transgressed your law and went astray, not heeding your voice, the sworn malediction, recorded in the law of Moses, the servant of God, was poured out over us for our sins. 12 You carried out the threats you spoke against us and against those who governed us, by bringing upon us in Jerusalem the greatest calamity that has ever occurred under heaven. 13 As it is written in the law of Moses, this calamity came full upon us. As we did not appease the LORD, our God, by turning back from our wickedness and recognizing his constancy, 14 so the LORD kept watch over the calamity and brought it upon us. You, O LORD, our God, are just in all that you have done, for we did not listen to your voice.

15 "Now, O Lord, our God, who led your people out of the land of Egypt with a strong hand, and made a name for yourself even to this day, we have sinned, we are guilty. 16 O Lord, in keeping with all your just deeds, let your anger and your wrath be turned away from your city Jerusalem, your holy mountain. On account of our sins and the crimes of our fathers, Jerusalem and your people have become the reproach of all our neighbors. 17 Hear, therefore, O God, the prayer and petition of your servant; and for your own sake, O Lord, let your face shine upon your desolate sanctuary. 18 Give ear, O my God, and listen; open your eyes and see our ruins and the city which bears your name. When we present our petition before you, we rely not on our just deeds, but on your great mercy. 19 O Lord, hear! O Lord, pardon! O Lord, be attentive and act without delay, for your own sake, O my God, because this city and your people bear your name!"

20 I was still occupied with my prayer, confessing my sin and the sin of my people Israel, presenting my petition to the LORD, my God, on behalf of his holy mountain— 21 I was still occupied with this prayer, when Gabriel, the one whom I had seen before in vision, came to me in rapid flight at the time of the evening sacrifice. 22 He instructed me in these words: "Daniel, I have now come to give you understanding. 23 When you began your petition, an answer was given which I have come to announce, because you are beloved. Therefore, mark the answer and understand the vision.

24 "Seventy weeks are decreed
  for your people and for you
    holy city:
Then transgression will stop and
  sin will end,
  guilt will be expiated,

Everlasting justice will be
  introduced,
  vision and prophecy ratified,
and a most holy will be
  anointed.
25   Know and understand this:
From the utterance of the word
  that Jerusalem was to be
    rebuilt
Until one who is anointed and a
  leader,
  there shall be seven weeks.
During sixty-two weeks
  it shall be rebuilt,
With streets and trenches,
  in time of affliction.
26 After the sixty-two weeks
  an anointed shall be cut down
  when he does not possess the
    city;
And the people of a leader who
  will come
  shall destroy the sanctuary.
Then the end shall come like a
  torrent;
  until the end there shall be war,
  the desolation that is decreed.
27 For one week he shall make
  a firm compact with the many;
Half the week
  he shall abolish sacrifice and
    oblation;
On the temple wing shall be the
  horrible abomination
  until the ruin that is decreed
  is poured out upon the
    horror."

Vision of the Hellenistic Wars

10 In the third year of Cyrus, king of Persia, a revelation was given to Daniel, who had been named Belteshazzar. The revelation was certain: a great war; he understood it from the vision. 2 In those days, I, Daniel, mourned three full

---

9, 13: *As it is written:* the first time that this formula of Scriptural citation is used in the Bible. The reference (v 11) is to the sanctions of Lv 26, 14ff; Dt 28, 15ff.

9, 21: *At the time of the evening sacrifice:* between three and four in the afternoon.

9, 24: *Seventy weeks:* i.e., of years. Just as Jeremiah's seventy years was an approximation (see note on v 2), the four hundred and ninety years here is not to be taken literally. Similarly, the distribution of the "weeks" in the following verses indicates only relative proportions of the total figure. *A most holy:* an expression used almost always of an object, the altar or the temple, but once (1 Chr 23, 13) of Aaron the high priest. The author sees the definitive establishment of the kingdom of God, realized in the reconsecration of the temple after Antiochus' desecration, or personified in the holy community (like the Son of Man of chapter 7). The Fathers of the Church

almost unanimously understood the reference to be to Christ, the final realization of the prophecy.

9, 25: *From the utterance . . . to be rebuilt:* from the time of Jeremiah's prophecy. *One . . . anointed and a leader:* either Cyrus, who was called the anointed of the LORD to end the Exile (Is 45, 1), or the high priest Joshua who presided over the rebuilding of the altar of sacrifice after the Exile (Ezr 3, 2). *Seven weeks:* forty-nine years, an approximation of the time of the Exile. *During sixty-two weeks . . . rebuilt:* a period of 434 years, roughly approximating the interval between the rebuilding of Jerusalem after the Exile and the beginning of the Seleucid persecution.

9, 26: *An anointed:* doubtless the high priest Onias III, murdered in 171 B.C., from which the author dates the beginning of the persecution. Onias was in exile when he was killed. *A leader:* Antiochus IV.

9, 27: *One week:* the final phase of the period in view, the time of Antiochus' persecution; *he* is Antiochus himself. *The many:* the faithless Jews who allied themselves with the heathen; cf 1 Mc 1, 11ff. *Half the week:* three and a half years; see note on 7, 25. The temple was desecrated by Antiochus from 167 to 165 B.C. *The temple wing:* probably the main portal. *The horrible abomination:* see note on 8, 13. Perhaps an inscription was placed on the portal of the temple dedicating it to the Olympian Zeus. Our Lord referred to this passage in his own prediction of the destruction of Jerusalem (Mt 24, 15).

10, 1—12, 13: This final vision repeats some of the material contained in the others. It is concerned with history of the worldly kingdoms from the time of Cyrus to the defeat of the tyrant Antiochus.

10, 2: *Mourned:* perhaps the author intends to recall the interruption in the rebuilding of the temple, which occurred during this time (Ezr 4, 1–4).

weeks. 3 I ate no savory food, I took no meat or wine, and I did not anoint myself at all until the end of the three weeks.

4 On the twenty-fourth day of the first month I was on the bank of the great river, the Tigris. 5 As I looked up, I saw a man dressed in linen with a belt of fine gold around his waist. 6 His body was like chrysolite, his face shone like lightning, his eyes were like fiery torches, his arms and feet looked like burnished bronze, and his voice sounded like the roar of a multitude. 7 I alone, Daniel, saw the vision; but great fear seized the men who were with me; they fled and hid themselves, although they did not see the vision. 8 So I was left alone, seeing this great vision. No strength remained in me; I turned the color of death and was powerless. 9 When I heard the sound of his voice, I fell face forward in a faint.

10 But then a hand touched me, raising me to my hands and knees. 11 "Daniel, beloved," he said to me, "understand the words which I am speaking to you; stand up, for my mission now is to you." When he said this to me, I stood up trembling. 12 "Fear not, Daniel," he continued; "from the first day you made up your mind to acquire understanding and humble yourself before God, your prayer was heard. Because of it I started out, 13 but the prince of the kingdom of Persia stood in my way for twenty-one days, until finally Michael, one of the chief princes, came to help me. I left him there with the prince of the kings of Persia, 14 and came to make you understand what shall happen to your people in the days to come; for there is yet a vision concerning those days."

15 While he was speaking thus to me, I fell forward and kept silent. 16 Then something like a man's hand touched my lips; I opened my mouth and said to the one facing me, "My lord, I was seized with pangs at the vision and I was powerless. 17 How can my lord's servant speak with you, my lord? For now no strength or even breath is left in me." 18 The one who looked like a man touched me again and strengthened me, saying, 19 "Fear not, beloved, you are safe; take courage and be strong." 20 When he spoke to me, I grew strong and said, "Speak, my lord, for you have strengthened me." "Do you know," he asked, "why I have come to you? Soon I must fight the prince of Persia again. When I leave, the prince of Greece will come; 21 but I shall tell you what is written in the truthful book. No one supports me against all these except Michael, your prince,

11 1 standing as a reinforcement and a bulwark for me. 2 Now I shall tell you the truth.

"Three kings of Persia are yet to come; and a fourth shall acquire the greatest riches of all. Strengthened by his riches, he shall rouse all the kingdom of Greece. 3 But a powerful king shall appear and rule with great might, doing as he pleases. 4 No sooner shall he appear than his kingdom shall be broken and divided in the four directions under heaven; but not among his descendants or in keeping with his mighty rule, for his kingdom shall be torn to pieces and belong to others than they.

5 "The king of the south shall grow strong, but one of his princes shall grow stronger still and govern a domain greater than his. 6 After some years they shall become allies: the daughter of the king of the south shall come to the king of the north in the interest of peace. But her bid for power shall fail: and her line shall not be recognized, and she shall be given up, together with those who brought her, her son and her husband. But later 7 a descendant of her line shall succeed to his rank, and shall come against the rampart and enter the stronghold of the king of the north, and conquer them. 8 Even their gods, with their molten images and their precious vessels of silver and gold, he shall carry away as booty into Egypt. For years he shall have nothing to do with the king of the north. 9 Then the latter shall invade the land of the king of the south, and return to his own country.

10 "But his sons shall prepare and assemble a great armed host, which shall advance like a flood, then withdraw. When it returns and surges around the stronghold, 11 the king of the south, provoked, shall go out to fight against the king of the north, whose great host shall make a stand but shall be given into his hand and be carried off. 12 In the pride of his heart, he shall lay low tens of thousands, but he shall not triumph. 13 For the king of the north shall raise another army, greater than before; after some years he shall attack with this large army and great resources. 14 In those times many shall resist the king of the south, and outlaws of your people shall rise up in fulfillment of vision, but they fail. 15 When the king of the north comes, he shall set up siegeworks and take the fortified city by storm. The power of the south shall not withstand him, and not even his picked troops shall have the strength to resist. 16 He shall attack him and do as he pleases, with no one to withstand him. He shall stop in the glorious land, dealing destruction. 17 He shall set himself to penetrate the entire strength of his kingdom. He shall conclude an agreement with him and give him a daughter in marriage in order to destroy the kingdom, but this shall not succeed in his favor. 18 He shall turn to the coastland and take many, but a leader shall put an end to his shameful conduct, so that he cannot renew

---

10, 4: *The first month:* the month Nisan (mid-March to mid-April).

10, 5f: The heavenly person of the vision is probably the angel Gabriel, as in 9, 21. *Chrysolite:* or topaz, a yellowish precious stone.

10, 13: *The prince of the kingdom of Persia:* the guardian angel of Persia. The later Judaism ascribed protecting angels to various groups of human society, often as little more than personifications. *Michael:* the angel who is the protector of God's

people (v 21).

11, 2-4: The *three kings of Persia* who follow Cyrus are uncertain, since there were more than three Persian kings between Cyrus and the dissolution of the kingdom. The *fourth* is doubtless Xerxes I (486–465 B.C.), the great campaigner against Greece. The *powerful king* is Alexander the Great, who ended the Persian empire by his victory at Issus in 333 B.C.

11, 5-45: These verses describe the dynastic histories of the Ptolemies in Egypt (*the king of the south*) and the Seleucids in Syria (*the king of the north*), the two divisions of the Hellenistic empire that were of interest to the author (v 6). In vv 10–20 is described the struggle between the two kingdoms for the control of Palestine, in which the Seleucids were eventually victorious. The reference in v 20 is to Seleucus IV, who sent Heliodorus to plunder the temple treasure in Jerusalem (2 Mc 3). Finally, vv 21–45 describe the career of Antiochus IV and his persecution, in details that have been seen above.

it against him. 19 He shall turn to the strongholds of his own land, but shall stumble and fall, to be found no more. 20 In his stead one shall arise who will send a tax collector through the glorious kingdom, but he shall soon be destroyed, though not in conflict or in battle.

21 "There shall rise in his place a despicable person, to whom the royal insignia shall not be given. By stealth and fraud he shall seize the kingdom. 22 Armed might shall be completely overwhelmed by him and crushed, and even the prince of the covenant. 23 After allying with him, he shall treacherously rise to power with a small party. 24 By stealth he shall enter prosperous provinces and do that which his fathers or grandfathers never did; he shall distribute spoil, booty, and riches among them and devise plots against their strongholds; but only for a time. 25 He shall call on his strength and cleverness to meet the king of the south with a great army; the king of the south shall prepare for battle with a very large and strong army, but he shall not succeed because of the plots devised against him. 26 Even his table companions shall seek to destroy him, his army shall be overwhelmed, and many shall fall slain. 27 The two kings, resolved on evil, shall sit at table together and exchange lies, but they shall have no success, because the appointed end is not yet.

28 "He shall turn back toward his land with great riches, his mind set against the holy covenant; he shall arrange matters and return to his land. 29 At the time appointed he shall come again to the south, but this time it shall not be as before. 30 When ships of the Kittim confront him, he shall lose heart and retreat. Then he shall direct his rage and energy against the holy covenant; those who forsake it he shall once more single out. 31 Armed forces shall move at his command and defile the sanctuary stronghold, abolishing the daily sacrifice and setting up the horrible abomination. 32 By his deceit he shall make some who were disloyal to the covenant apostatize; but those who remain loyal to their God shall take strong action. 33 The nation's wise men shall instruct the many; though for a time they will become victims of the sword, of flames, exile, and plunder. 34 When they fall, few people shall help them, but many shall join them out of treachery. 35 Of the wise men, some shall fall, so that the rest may be tested, refined, and purified, until the end time which is still appointed to come.

36 "The king shall do as he pleases, exalting himself and making himself greater than any god; he shall utter dreadful blasphemies against the God of gods. He shall prosper only till divine wrath is ready, for what is determined must take place. 37 He shall have no regard for the gods of his ancestors or for the one in whom women delight; for no god shall he have regard, because he shall make himself greater than all. 38 Instead, he shall give glory to the god of strongholds; a god unknown to his fathers he shall glorify with gold, silver, precious stones, and other treasures. 39 To defend the strongholds he shall station a people of a foreign god. Whoever acknowledges him he shall provide with abundant honor; he shall make them rule over the many and distribute the land as a reward.

40 "At the appointed time the king of the south shall come to grips with him, but the king of the north shall overwhelm him with chariots and horsemen and a great fleet, passing through the countries like a flood. 41 He shall enter the glorious land and many shall fall, except Edom, Moab, and the chief part of Ammon, which shall escape from his power. 42 He shall extend his power over the countries, and not even the land of Egypt shall escape. 43 He shall control the riches of gold and silver and all the treasures of Egypt; Libya and Ethiopia shall be in his train. 44 When news from the east and the north terrifies him, he shall set out with great fury to slay and to doom many. 45 He shall pitch the tents of his royal pavilion between the sea and the glorious holy mountain, but he shall come to his end with none to help him.

12 "At that time there shall arise
Michael, the great prince,
guardian of your people;
It shall be a time unsurpassed in
distress
since nations began until that
time.
At that time your people shall
escape,
everyone who is found written
in the book.
2 Many of those who sleep
in the dust of the earth shall
awake;
Some shall live forever,
others shall be an everlasting
horror and disgrace.
3 But the wise shall shine brightly
like the splendor of the
firmament,
And those who lead the many
to justice
shall be like the stars forever.

4 "As for you, Daniel, keep secret the message and seal the book until the end time; many shall fall away and evil shall increase."

5 I, Daniel, looked and saw two others, one standing on either bank of the river. 6 One of them said to the man clothed in linen, who was upstream, "How long shall it be to the end of these appalling things?" 7 The man clothed in linen, who was upstream, lifted his right and left hands to heaven; and I heard him swear by him who lives forever that it should be for a year, two years, a half-year; and that, when the power of the destroyer of the holy people was brought to an end, all these things should end. 8 I heard, but I

11, 30: *Kittim:* originally this word meant Cypriots or other island dwellers. Here it means the Romans, who forced Antiochus to withdraw from Egypt during his second campaign there.

11, 36–39: Instead of venerating Apollo, one of *the gods of his ancestors,* Antiochus venerated, and even identified himself with, Zeus Olympios, whom the Romans equated with the god of their fortress in Rome, Jupiter Capitolinus, *the god of strongholds.*

12, 1: *Written in the book:* the book of God's predestination.

12, 2: The first Israelites who have fallen (11, 33ff) *shall awake,* that is, rise to *live forever.* A resurrection of the wicked as in later, Christian teaching (Jn 5, 28f) is implied here if the *others* are included in the *many;* but cf Is 66, 24.

12, 7: *A year, two years, a half year:* see note on 7, 25. The author's perspective is the end of Antiochus, and beyond, the final consummation of all things.

did not understand; so I asked, "My lord, what follows this?" 9 "Go, Daniel," he said, "because the words are to be kept secret and sealed until the end time. 10 Many shall be refined, purified, and tested, but the wicked shall prove wicked; none of them shall have understanding, but the wise shall have it. 11 From the time that the daily sacrifice is abolished and the horrible abomination is set up, there shall be one thousand two hundred and ninety days. 12 Blessed is the man who has patience and perseveres until the one thousand three hundred and thirty-five days. 13 Go, take your rest, you shall rise for your reward at the end of days."

APPENDIX

Susanna's Virtue

13 In Babylon there lived a man named Joakim, 2 who married a very beautiful and God-fearing woman, Susanna, the daughter of Hilkiah; 3 her pious parents had trained their daughter according to the law of Moses. 4 Joakim was very rich; he had a garden near his house, and the Jews had recourse to him often because he was the most respected of them all.

5 That year, two elders of the people were appointed judges, of whom the Lord said, "Wickedness has come out of Babylon: from the elders who were to govern the people as judges." 6 These men, to whom all brought their cases, frequented the house of Joakim. 7 When the people left at noon, Susanna used to enter her husband's garden for a walk. 8 When the old men saw her enter every day for her walk, they began to lust for her. 9 They suppressed their consciences; they would not allow their eyes to look to heaven, and did not keep in mind just judgments. 10 Though both were enamored of her, they did not tell each other their trouble, 11 for they were ashamed to reveal their lustful desire to have her. 12 Day by day they watched eagerly for her. 13 One day they said to each other,

"Let us be off for home, it is time for lunch." So they went out and parted; 14 but both turned back, and when they met again, they asked each other the reason. They admitted their lust, and then they agreed to look for an occasion when they could meet her alone.

15 One day, while they were waiting for the right moment, she entered the garden as usual, with two maids only. She decided to bathe, for the weather was warm. 16 Nobody else was there except the two elders, who had hidden themselves and were watching her. 17 "Bring me oil and soap," she said to the maids, "and shut the garden doors while I bathe." 18 They did as she said; they shut the garden doors and left by the side gate to fetch what she had ordered, unaware that the elders were hidden inside.

19 As soon as the maids had left, the two old men got up and hurried to her. 20 "Look," they said, "the garden doors are shut, and no one can see us; give in to our desire, and lie with us. 21 If you refuse, we will testify against you that you dismissed your maids because a young man was here with you." 22 "I am completely trapped," Susanna groaned. "If I yield, it will be my death; if I refuse, I cannot escape your power. 23 Yet it is better for me to fall into your power without guilt than to sin before the Lord." 24 Then Susanna shrieked, and the old men also shouted at her, 25 as one of them ran to open the garden doors. 26 When the people in the house heard the cries from the garden, they rushed in by the side gate to see what had happened to her. 27 At the accusations by the old men, the servants felt very much ashamed, for never had any such thing been said about Susanna.

28 When the people came to her husband Joakim the next day, the two wicked elders also came, fully determined to put Susanna to death. Before all the people they ordered: 29 "Send for Susanna, the daughter of Hilkiah, the wife of Joakim." When she was sent for, 30 she

came with her parents, children and all her relatives. 31 Susanna, very delicate and beautiful, 32 was veiled; but those wicked men ordered her to uncover her face so as to sate themselves with her beauty. 33 All her relatives and the onlookers were weeping.

34 In the midst of the people the two elders rose up and laid their hands on her head. 35 Through her tears she looked up to heaven, for she trusted in the Lord wholeheartedly. 36 The elders made this accusation: "As we were walking in the garden alone, this woman entered with two girls and shut the doors of the garden, dismissing the girls. 37 A young man, who was hidden there, came and lay with her. 38 When we, in a corner of the garden, saw this crime, we ran toward them. 39 We saw them lying together, but the man we could not hold, because he was stronger than we; he opened the doors and ran off. 40 Then we seized this one and asked who the young man was, 41 but she refused to tell us. We testify to this." The assembly believed them, since they were elders and judges of the people, and they condemned her to death.

42 But Susanna cried aloud: "O eternal God you know what is hidden and are aware of all things before they come to be: 43 you know that they have testified falsely against me. Here I am about to die, though I have done none of the things with which these wicked men have charged me."

44 The Lord heard her prayer. 45 As she was being led to execution, God stirred up the holy spirit of a young boy named Daniel, 46 and he cried aloud: "I will have no part in the death of this woman." 47 All the people turned and asked him, "What is this you are saying?" 48 He stood in their midst and continued, "Are you such fools, O Israelites! To condemn a woman of Israel without examination and without clear evidence? 49 Return to court, for they have testified falsely against her."

13, 1—14, 42: The short stories in these two chapters may have originally been about some other Daniel or Daniels than the hero of the main part of the book. They exist now only in Greek, but probably were first composed in Hebrew or Aramaic. They are excluded from the Jewish canon of Scripture, but the Church has always included them among the inspired writings.

50 Then all the people returned in haste. To Daniel the elders said, "Come sit with us and inform us, since God has given you the prestige of old age." 51 But he replied, "Separate these two far from one another that I may examine them."

52 After they were separated one from the other, he called one of them and said: "How you have grown evil with age! Now have your past sins come to term: 53 passing unjust sentences, condemning the innocent, and freeing the guilty, although the Lord says, 'The innocent and the just you shall not put to death.' 54 Now, then, if you were a witness, tell me under what tree you saw them together." 55 "Under a mastic tree," he answered. "Your fine lie has cost you your head," said Daniel; "for the angel of God shall receive the sentence from him and split you in two." 56 Putting him to one side, he ordered the other one to be brought. "Offspring of Canaan, not of Judah," Daniel said to him, "beauty has seduced you, lust has subverted your conscience. 57 This is how you acted with the daughters of Israel, and in their fear they yielded to you; but a daughter of Judah did not tolerate your wickedness. 58 Now, then, tell me under what tree you surprised them together." 59 "Under an oak," he said. "Your fine lie has cost you also your head," said Daniel; "for the angel of God waits with a sword to cut you in two so as to make an end to you both."

60 The whole assembly cried aloud, blessing God who saves those that hope in him. 61 They rose up against the two elders, for by their own words Daniel had convicted them of perjury. According to the law of Moses, they inflicted on them the penalty they had plotted to impose on their neighbor: 62 they put them to death. Thus was innocent blood spared that day.

63 Helcia and his wife praised God for their daughter Susanna, as did Joakim her husband and all her relatives, because she was found innocent of any shameful deed. 64 And from that day onward Daniel was greatly esteemed by the people.

Bel and the Dragon

14 After King Astyages was laid with his fathers, Cyrus the Persian succeeded to his kingdom. 2 Daniel was the king's favorite and was held in higher esteem than any of the friends of the king. 3 The Babylonians had an idol called Bel, and every day they provided for it six barrels of fine flour, forty sheep, and six measures of wine. 4 The king worshiped it and went every day to adore it; but Daniel adored only his God. 5 When the king asked him, "Why do you not adore Bel?" Daniel replied, "Because I worship not idols made with hands, but only the living God who made heaven and earth and has dominion over all mankind." 6 Then the king continued, "You do not think Bel is a living god? Do you not see how much he eats and drinks every day?" 7 Daniel began to laugh. "Do not be deceived, O king," he said; "it is only clay inside and bronze outside; it has never taken any food or drink." 8 Enraged, the king called his priests and said to them, "Unless you tell me who it is that consumes these provisions, you shall die. 9 But if you can show that Bel consumes them, Daniel shall die for blaspheming Bel." Daniel said to the king, "Let it be as you say!" 10 There were seventy priests of Bel, besides their wives and children.

When the king went with Daniel into the temple of Bel, 11 the priests of Bel said, "See, we are going to leave. Do you, O king, set out the food and prepare the wine; then shut the door and seal it with your ring. 12 If you do not find that Bel has eaten it all when you return in the morning, we are to die; otherwise Daniel shall die for his lies against us." 13 They were not perturbed because under the table they had made a secret entrance through which they always came in to consume the food. 14 After they departed the king set the food before Bel, while Daniel ordered his servants to bring some ashes, which they scattered through the whole temple; the king alone was present. Then they went outside, sealed the closed door with the king's ring, and departed. 15 The priests entered that night as usual, with their wives and children, and they ate and drank everything.

16 Early the next morning, the king came with Daniel. 17 "Are the seals unbroken, Daniel?" he asked. And Daniel answered, "They are unbroken, O king." 18 As soon as he had opened the door, the king looked at the table and cried aloud, "Great you are, O Bel; there is no trickery in you." 19 But Daniel laughed and kept the king from entering. "Look at the floor," he said; "whose footprints are these?" 20 "I see the footprints of men, women, and children!" said the king. 21 The angry king arrested the priests, their wives, and their children. They showed him the secret door by which they used to enter to consume what was on the table. 22 He put them to death, and handed Bel over to Daniel, who destroyed it and its temple.

23 There was a great dragon which the Babylonians worshiped. 24 "Look!" said the king to Daniel, "you cannot deny that this is a living god, so adore it." 25 But Daniel answered, "I adore the Lord, my God, for he is the living God. 26 Give me permission, O king, and I will kill this dragon without sword or club." "I give you permission," the king said. 27 Then Daniel took some pitch, fat, and hair; these he boiled together and made into cakes. He put them into the mouth of the dragon, and when the dragon ate them, he burst asunder. "This," he said, "is what you worshiped."

28 When the Babylonians heard this, they were angry and turned

---

13, 55–59: The contrast between the *mastic tree*, which is small, and the majestic *oak* emphasizes the contradiction between the statements of the two elders. In the Greek text there is a play on words between the names of these two trees and the mortal punishment decreed by Daniel for the elders.

13, 57: Besides the evident moral intent of this story, it appears to have served the purpose of contrasting the northern and the southern kingdoms, Israel and Judah in favor of the latter.

14, 1: *King Astyages:* the last of the Median kings, defeated by Cyrus in 550 B.C. This story preserves the fiction of a successive Median and Persian rule of Babylon.

14, 2: This verse in the Septuagint Greek text reads: "There was once a priest, Daniel by name, the son of Abal, a favorite of the king of Babylon." This may represent an earlier form of the story, before it was attached to the Book of Daniel.

14, 3: *Bel:* see the note on 4, 5.

against the king. "The king has become a Jew," they said; "he has destroyed Bel, killed the dragon, and put the priests to death." 29 They went to the king and demanded: "Hand Daniel over to us, or we will kill you and your family." 30 When he saw himself threatened with violence, the king was forced to hand Daniel over to them. 31 They threw Daniel into a lions' den, where he remained six days. 32 In the den were seven lions, and two carcasses and two sheep had been given to them daily. But now they were given nothing, so that they would devour Daniel.

33 In Judea there was a prophet, Habakkuk; he mixed some bread in a bowl with the stew he had boiled, and was going to bring it to the reapers in the field, 34 when an angel of the Lord told him, "Take the lunch you have to Daniel in the lions' den at Babylon." 35 But Habakkuk answered, "Babylon, sir, I have never seen, and I do not know the den!" 36 The angel of the Lord seized him by the crown of his head and carried him by the hair; with the speed of the wind, he set him down in Babylon above the den. 37 "Daniel, Daniel," cried Habakkuk, "take the lunch God has sent you." 38 "You

have remembered me, O God," said Daniel; "you have not forsaken those who love you." 39 While Daniel began to eat, the angel of the Lord at once brought Habakkuk back to his own place.

40 On the seventh day the king came to mourn for Daniel. As he came to the den and looked in, there was Daniel, sitting there! 41 The king cried aloud, "You are great, O Lord, the God of Daniel, and there is no other besides you!" 42 Daniel he took out, but those who had tried to destroy him he threw into the den, and they were devoured in a moment before his eyes.

Hosea

THE PROPHET'S MARRIAGE AND ITS LESSON

Marriage with an Unfaithful Wife

THE word of the LORD that came to Hosea, the son of Beeri, in the days of Uzziah, Jotham, Ahaz, Hezekiah, kings of Judah, and in the days of Jeroboam, son of Joash, king of Israel. 2 In the beginning of the LORD's speaking to Hosea, the LORD said to Hosea:

Go, take a harlot wife and
  harlot's children,
for the land gives itself to
  harlotry,
  turning away from the LORD.

3 So he went and took Gomer, the daughter of Diblaim; and she conceived and bore him a son. 4 Then the LORD said to him:

Give him the name Jezreel,
  for in a little while
I will punish the house of Jehu
  for the bloodshed at Jezreel
And bring an end to the
  kingdom
  of the house of Israel;
5 On that day I will break the
  bow of Israel
  in the valley of Jezreel.

6 When she conceived again and bore a daughter, the LORD said to him:

Give her the name Lo-ruhama;
I no longer feel pity for the
  house of Israel:
  rather, I abhor them utterly.

7 Yet for the house of Judah I
  feel pity;
  I will save them by the LORD,
    their God;
But I will not save them by war,
  by sword or bow, by horses
    or horsemen.

8 After she weaned Lo-ruhama, she conceived and bore a son. 9 Then the LORD said:

Give him the name Lo-ammi,
  for you are not my people,
  and I will not be your God.

Israel's Punishment and Restoration

2 4 Protest against your mother,
    protest!
  for she is not my wife,
  and I am not her husband.
Let her remove her harlotry
  from before her,
  her adultery from between
    her breasts,
5 Or I will strip her naked,
  leaving her as on the day of
    her birth;
I will make her like the desert,
  reduce her to an arid land,
  and slay her with thirst.

1—3: This section is ordinarily thought to be biographical, the prophet's personal tragedy figuring as the relation of God to his people Israel. Hosea's marriage to a harlot wife represents Israel's infidelity to her Lord; hence the symbolic names of the children (1, 4–9). In 2, 4–25 the Lord protests this infidelity and decrees its consequences, but promises restoration in return for amendment; his punishments are medicinal. In chapter 3 Hosea once more takes back his wife, but only conditionally, signifying God's long-suffering love for Israel and hope for her return.
1, 2: *A harlot wife:* this does not necessarily mean that Gomer was a harlot when Hosea married her; the verse describes the event in its final consequences.
1, 4: *Jezreel:* the strategic valley in northern

Israel where *Jehu* brought the dynasty of Omri to an end through bloodshed (2 Kgs 9–10). Jeroboam II was the last king but one of the house of Jehu; the prophecy in this verse was fulfilled by the murder of his son, who reigned only six months (2 Kgs 15, 8–10).
1, 6: *Lo-ruhama:* "she is not pitied." The "pity" that is here withheld from Israel is God's gratuitous love which inspires his beneficent acts.
1, 7: The terrible punishments announced by the prophets were so fully realized that later generations made a point of recalling the same prophets' messages of consolation also, even though it meant taking these words from another context. Thus, an editor placed the words of 2, 1ff after the repudiation of Israel in 1, 9; here the more natural order has been restored.

The present verse is another example of the same thing. In addition, it may be the work of a later hand, dating from a time when the prophecies of Hosea were circulated in the south, after the dissolution of the northern kingdom that he had prophesied. The second part of the verse emphasizes the power of the Lord, who needs no human agents to fulfill his will. It may refer to the deliverance of Jerusalem from the siege of Sennacherib (2 Kgs 19, 35ff).
1, 9: *Lo-ammi:* "not my people."
2, 4: The Lord speaks of Israel, still using the example of Hosea's wife.
2, 5: *I will strip her naked:* contemporary documents indicate that this was a conventional punishment for adultery.

6 I will have no pity on her
        children,
    for they are the children of
        harlotry.
7 Yes, their mother has played
        the harlot;
    she that conceived them has
        acted shamefully.
    "I will go after my lovers," she
        said,
    "who give me my bread and
        my water,
    my wool and my flax, my oil
        and my drink."

10 Since she has not known
        that it was I who gave her
        the grain, the wine, and the oil,
    And her abundance of silver,
        and of gold, which they used
        for Baal,
11 Therefore I will take back my
        grain in its time,
    and my wine in its season;
    I will snatch away my wool and
        my flax,
    with which she covers her
        nakedness.
12 So now I will lay bare her shame
        before the eyes of her lovers,
    and no one can deliver her
        out of my hand.
13 I will bring an end to all her joy,
        her feasts, her new moons, her
        sabbaths,
    and all her solemnities.
14 I will lay waste her vines and fig
        trees,
    of which she said, "These are
        the hire
    my lovers have given me";
    I will turn them into rank growth
    and wild beasts shall devour
        them.
15 I will punish her for the days of
        the Baals,
    for whom she burnt incense

While she decked herself out
    with her rings and her
        jewels,
    and, in going after her lovers,
    forget me, says the LORD.

8 Therefore, I will hedge in her
        way with thorns
    and erect a wall against her,
    so that she cannot find her
        paths.
9 If she runs after her lovers,
        she shall not overtake them;
    if she looks for them she shall
        not find them.
    Then she shall say,
    "I will go back to my first
        husband,
    for it was better with me then
        than now."

16 So I will allure her;
    I will lead her into the desert
    and speak to her heart.
17 From there I will give her the
        vineyards she had,
    and the valley of Achor as a
        door of hope.
    She shall respond there as in the
        days of her youth,
    when she came up from the
        land of Egypt.

18   On that day, says the LORD,
    She shall call me "My husband,"
    and never again "My baal."
19 Then will I remove from her
        mouth the names of the
        Baals,
    so that they shall no longer be
        invoked.
20 I will make a covenant for them
        on that day,
    with the beasts of the field,
    With the birds of the air,
    and with the things that crawl
        on the ground.

Bow and sword and war
    I will destroy from the land,
    and I will let them take their
        rest in security.

21 I will espouse you to me
        forever:
    I will espouse you in right
        and in justice,
    in love and in mercy;
22 I will espouse you in fidelity,
    and you shall know the LORD.
23 On that day I will respond, says
        the LORD;
    I will respond to the heavens,
    and they shall respond to the
        earth;
24 The earth shall respond to the
        grain, and wine, and oil,
    and these shall respond to
        Jezreel.
25 I will sow him for myself in the
        land,
    and I will have pity on
        Lo-ruhama.
    I will say to Lo-ammi, "You
        are my people,"
    and he shall say, "My God!"

Triumph of Love

3 Again the LORD said to me:
    Give your love to a woman
        beloved of a paramour, an
        adulteress;
    Even as the LORD loves the
        people of Israel,
    though they turn to other gods
    and are fond of raisin cakes.

2 So I bought her for fifteen pieces
of silver and a homer and a lethech
of barley.   3 Then I said to her:

    "Many days you shall wait for
        me;
    you shall not play the harlot
    Or belong to any man;
    I in turn will wait for you."

2, 7: *My lovers:* the local fertility deities to whom, rather than to the Lord (v 10), the unfaithful Israelites attributed the produce of the land.

2, 8f: The crop failures, blight, etc., sent by the Lord (vv 11–14) have as their purpose to make Israel see the folly of her ways.

2, 15: *The days of the Baals:* ritual observances held in various local shrines in honor of Baal.

2, 16f: Israel's journey in the desert represents for Hosea the time of Israel's fidelity, before it was corrupted by the ways of Canaan; cf Jer 2, 2–7; Am 5, 25. Thus, he pictures a restoration in terms of a new entry into the promised land.

2, 18: *My baal:* the word means "lord, master." It was commonly used by women of their husbands, but it is to be shunned as a title for the Lord because of its association with the pagan god Baal. Probably

it had been so used by many Israelites, who saw little if any difference between the worship of the Lord and the worship of Baal.

2, 21f: The Lord will once more espouse Israel; the qualities ascribed to the renewed people are the bridal gift (cf Gn 24, 53) with which he will endow it. *In right and in justice:* two terms dear to Hosea, used by him especially to condemn the popular social injustice and corruption of the legal processes. Here they mean right conduct in general. *Love:* one of the most characteristic words of Hosea's prophecy. It means a dutiful love, based on a social relation; here it refers to the covenant between God and his people. It is a love fulfilled by the performance of mutual obligations. *Mercy:* from the same root as the word translated *pity* in 1, 6; cf v. 25. *And you shall know the Lord:* another characteristic expression of Hosea;

cf 4, 1; 5, 4; 6, 3.6. It means not an abstract but a practical knowledge, i.e., acknowledgment of his will, obedience to his law.

3, 1–5: Hosea is instructed to take Gomer back, redeeming her from her paramours. On condition of her amendment, she will be restored to her former position of wife. This in turn signifies God's enduring love for his people. He will put the people through a period of trial—the dissolution of the kingdom—in order that they may return to him wholeheartedly.

3, 1: *Raisin cakes:* offerings to the fertility goddess Ashera, the female counterpart of Baal; cf Jer 7, 18; 44, 19.

3, 2: *Homer:* about ten bushels. *Lethech:* a half-homer.

4 For the people of Israel shall
　　　remain many days
　　without king or prince,
　Without sacrifice or sacred
　　　pillar,
　　without ephod or household
　　　idols.
5 Then the people of Israel shall
　　turn back
　　and seek the LORD, their God,
　　and David, their king;
　They shall come trembling to
　　　the LORD
　　and to his bounty, in the last
　　　days.

(2) 1 The number of the Israelites
　　shall be like the sand of the
　　　sea,
　　which can be neither measured
　　　nor counted.
　Whereas they were called,
　　"Lo-ammi,"
　They shall be called,
　　"Children of the living God."
2 Then the people of Judah and of
　　Israel
　　shall be gathered together;
　They shall appoint for
　　themselves one head
　　and come up from other
　　　lands,
　for great shall be the day of
　　Jezreel.
3 Say to your brothers, "Ammi,"
　　and to your sisters, "Ruhama."

ISRAEL'S GUILT AND PUNISHMENT

Crimes of Israel

4 Hear the word of the LORD, O
　　people of Israel,
　for the LORD has a grievance
　　against the inhabitants of the
　　　land:
　There is no fidelity, no mercy,
　　no knowledge of God in the
　　　land.

2 False swearing, lying, murder,
　　stealing and adultery!
　in their lawlessness, bloodshed
　　follows bloodshed.
3 Therefore the land mourns,
　　and everything that dwells
　　in it languishes:
　The beast of the field,
　　the birds of the air,
　　and even the fish of the sea
　　perish.

Guilt of the Priests

4 But let no one protest, let no
　　one complain;
　with you is my grievance, O
　　priests!
5 You shall stumble in the day,
　　and the prophets shall stumble
　　with you at night;
　I will destroy your mother.
6 My people perish for want of
　　knowledge!
　Since you have rejected
　　knowledge,
　I will reject you from my
　　priesthood;
　Since you have ignored the law
　　of your God,
　I will also ignore your sons.
7 One and all they sin against me,
　　exchanging their glory for
　　shame.
8 They feed on the sin of my
　　people,
　　and are greedy for their guilt.
9 The priest shall fare no better
　　than the people:
　I will punish them for their
　　ways,
　　and repay them for their
　　deeds.
10 They shall eat but not be
　　satisfied,
　they shall play the harlot but
　　not increase,
　Because they have abandoned
　　the LORD
11　to practice harlotry.

Old wine and new
　deprive my people of
　　understanding.
12 They consult their piece of wood,
　　and their wand makes
　　pronouncements for them,
　For the spirit of harlotry has
　　led them astray;
　they commit harlotry,
　　forsaking their God.
13 On the mountaintops they offer
　　sacrifice
　　and on the hills they burn
　　incense,
　Beneath oak and poplar and
　　terebinth,
　　because of their pleasant shade.
　That is why your daughters play
　　the harlot,
　　and your daughters-in-law
　　are adulteresses.
14 Am I then to punish your
　　daughters for their harlotry,
　　your daughters-in-law for their
　　adultery?
　You yourselves consort with
　　harlots,
　　and with prostitutes you offer
　　sacrifice!
　So must a people without
　　understanding come to ruin.

15 Though you play the harlot,
　　O Israel,
　　let not Judah become guilty!
　Come not to Gilgal,
　　nor up to Beth-aven,
　　to swear, "As the Lord lives!"
16 For Israel is as stubborn as a
　　heifer;
　　will the LORD now give them
　　broad pastures
　　as though they were lambs?
17 Ephraim is an associate of idols,
　　let him alone!
18 When their carousing is over,
　　they give themselves to harlotry;
　　in their arrogance they love
　　shame.

3, 4: *Sacred pillar:* the stone massebah, originally perhaps a phallic symbol, representing Baal. These were also used, with another signification, in Israelite worship; see notes on Gn 28, 18; Ex 34, 13. *Ephod:* an instrument used in consulting the deity; cf 1 Sm 23, 6–12; 30, 7; see notes on Ex 28, 6.15-30. *Household idols:* images regarded as the tutelary deities of the household; cf Gn 31, 19; Jgs 17, 5; 18, 14.17f.
3, 5: *David their king:* the Messianic king of the Davidic line who will restore the kingdom of God's people; cf Jer 23, 5; Ez 34, 23f. *The last days:* the Messianic age.
2, 1–3: These verses continue the conditional promise of restoration made in 3, 1–5, reversing the

dire predictions of chapter 1; the symbolic names now become names of honor: *Jezreel,* "God sows"; *Ammi,* "my people"; *Ruhama,* "she is pitied."
4, 4ff: Hosea is particularly severe with the *priests* in the northern kingdom, who had led the way in the general apostasy from God's law. The *prophets* here associated with the priests (v 5) were doubtless cult prophets, who were often unworthy of their pretended calling; cf Jer 2, 8; 4, 9f; 6, 13f; 23, 9–40.
4, 12: *Wood . . . wand:* an idol used in divination.
4, 14: *With prostitutes you offer sacrifice:* the ritual prostitution practiced at the Canaanite shrines was introduced even into sanctuaries dedicated to the Lord. In comparison, the adultery that had become

common in Israel was a far less reprehensible crime.
4, 15: *Gilgal:* not the Gilgal of the south (Jos 4, 19f), but a sanctuary north of Bethel where there was an association of cult prophets (2 Kgs 2, 1ff; 4, 38). *Beth-aven:* literally, "house of iniquity," Hosea's nickname for Bethel, or a scribal substitute for Bethel, "house of god," in this context. Bethel was one of the royal shrines of Israel, where there was a schismatic public worship of the Lord; cf 1 Kgs 12, 26–30.
4, 17: *Ephraim:* the heartland of the northern kingdom. During the latter part of Hosea's prophetic career, Ephraim was all that remained of Israel after the Assyrians had overrun Transjordan and Galilee.

19 The wind has bound them up in
    its pinions;
    they shall have only shame
      from their altars.

Guilt of the Leaders

5 Hear this, O priests,
    Pay attention, O house of
      Israel,
    O household of the king, give
      ear!
    It is you who are called to
      judgment.
    For you have become a snare
      at Mizpah,
    and a net spread upon Tabor.
2 In their perversity they have
    sunk into wickedness,
    and I am rejected by them all.

3 I know Ephraim,
    and Israel is not hidden from
      me;
    Now Ephraim has played the
      harlot,
    Israel is defiled.
4 Their deeds do not allow them
    to return to their God;
    For the spirit of harlotry is in
      them,
    and they do not recognize
      the LORD.

5 The arrogance of Israel bears
    witness against him;
    Ephraim stumbles in his guilt,
    and Judah stumbles with them.
6 With their flocks and their herds
    they shall go
    to seek the LORD, but they
      shall not find him;
    he has withdrawn himself
      from them.
7 They have been untrue to the
      LORD,
    for they have begotten
      illegitimate children;
    Now shall the new moon devour
      them
    together with their fields.

Political Upheavals

8 Blow the horn in Gibeah,
    the trumpet in Ramah!
    Sound the alarm in Beth-aven:
      "Look behind you, O
        Benjamin!"
9 Ephraim shall become a waste
    on the day of chastisement:
    Against the tribes of Israel
      I announce what is sure to be.
10 The princes of Judah have
      become
    like those who move a
      boundary line;
    Upon them I will pour out
      my wrath like water.

11 Is Ephraim maltreated, his
    rights violated?
    No, he has willingly gone
      after filth!
12 I am like a moth for Ephraim,
    like maggots for the house of
      Judah.
13 When Ephraim saw his infirmity,
    and Judah his sore,
    Ephraim went to Assyria,
    and Judah sent to the great
      king.
    But he cannot heal you
      nor take away your sore.
14 For I am like a lion to Ephraim,
    like a young lion to the house
      of Judah;
    It is I who rend the prey and
      depart,
    I carry it away and no one
      can save it from me.

Insincere Conversion

15 I will go back to my place
    until they pay for their guilt
    and seek my presence.

In their affliction, they shall look
    for me:
6   "Come, let us return to the
      LORD,

For it is he who has rent, but
    he will heal us;
    he has struck us, but he will
      bind our wounds.
2 He will revive us after two days;
    on the third day he will raise
      us up,
    to live in his presence.
3 Let us know, let us strive to
    know the LORD;
    as certain as the dawn is his
      coming,
    and his judgment shines forth
      like the light of day!
    He will come to us like the rain,
    like spring rain that waters the
      earth."

4 What can I do with you,
    Ephraim?
    What can I do with you, Judah?
    Your piety is like a morning
      cloud,
    like the dew that early passes
      away.
5 For this reason I smote them
    through the prophets,
    I slew them by the words of
      my mouth;
6 For it is love that I desire, not
    sacrifice,
    and knowledge of God rather
      than holocausts.
7 But they, in their land, violated
    the covenant;
    there they were untrue to me.

8 Gilead is a city of evildoers,
    tracked with blood.
9 As brigands ambush a man,
    a band of priests slay on the
      way to Shechem,
    committing monstrous crime.
10 In the house of Israel I have seen
    a horrible thing:
    there harlotry is found in
      Ephraim,
    Israel is defiled.
11 For you also, O Judah,
    a harvest has been appointed.

4, 19: The Israelites shall be carried from their country as by a whirlwind. To this their idolatry has brought them.

5, 1: *Mizpah:* probably the Mizpah in Transjordan is meant; cf Jos 11, 8. *Tabor:* the mountain that dominates the valley of Jezreel.

5, 8–14: This passage refers to the Syro–Ephraimite war of 735-734 B.C., when a coalition of Arameans and Israelites attempted to dethrone the king of Judah. Judah repulsed the attempt with the aid of Assyria, and the latter devastated both Aram and Israel; cf 2 Kgs 16, 5–9. Hosea condemns both Israel and Judah for the war.

5, 8: A vision of invasion from *Gibeah* and *Ramah* in northern Judah, into Israel.

5, 10: *Like those that move a boundary line:* comparison of the invaders to a classic case of social injustice; cf Dt 19, 14; 27, 17; Prv 23, 10f.

5, 11: *Gone after filth:* by allying himself with Aram.

5, 12: *Moth . . . maggots:* internal corruption will work the Lord's punishment on both Israel and Judah.

5, 13: *Ephraim went . . . the great king:* in 738 B.C. the Israelite King Manahem had to pay tribute to the Assyrian king Tiglath-pileser III, whose vassal he became (2 Kgs 15, 19f). Under the threat of the

Syro-Ephraimite invasion King Ahaz of Judah also submitted himself and his country to Tiglath-pileser (2 Kgs 16, 7–9). "The great king" was the title used by the Assyrian kings.

5, 15: The Lord withdraws himself from Israel, hoping for its repentance.

6, 2: *After two days; on the third day:* after a short lapse of time.

6, 4: *Piety:* the word is translated "love" in 2, 21 and in v 6 below.

6, 11: *Harvest:* when the land will reap the consequences of its sins.

7 When I would bring about the restoration of my people, when I would heal Israel, The guilt of Ephraim stands out, the wickedness of Samaria; They practice falsehood, thieves break in, bandits plunder abroad.

2 Yet they do not remind themselves that I remember all their wickedness. Even now their crimes surround them, present to my sight.

Failure of the Monarchy

3 In their wickedness they regale the king, the princes too, with their deceits.

4 They are all kindled to wrath like a blazing oven, Whose fire the baker desists from stirring once the dough is kneaded until it has risen.

5 On the day of our king, the princes are overcome with the heat of wine. He extends his hand among dissemblers;

6 the plotters approach with hearts like ovens. All the night their anger sleeps; in the morning it flares like a blazing fire.

7 They are all heated like ovens, and consume their rulers. All their kings have fallen; none of them calls upon me.

Foreign Alliances

8 Ephraim mingles with the nations, Ephraim is a hearth cake unturned.

9 Strangers have sapped his strength, but he takes no notice of it;

Of gray hairs, too, there is a sprinkling, but he takes no notice of it.

10 The arrogance of Israel bears witness against him; yet they do not return to the LORD, their God, nor seek him, for all that.

11 Ephraim is like a dove, silly and senseless; They call upon Egypt, they go to Assyria.

12 Even as they go I will spread my net around them, like birds in the air I will bring them down. In an instant I will send them captive from their land.

Perversity of Israel

13 Woe to them, they have strayed from me! Ruin to them, they have sinned against me! Though I wished to redeem them, they spoke lies against me.

14 They have not cried to me from their hearts when they wailed upon their beds; For wheat and wine they lacerated themselves, while they rebelled against me.

15 Though I trained and strengthened their arms, yet they devised evil against me.

16 They have again become useless, like a treacherous bow. Their princes shall fall by the sword because of the insolence of their tongues; thus they shall be mocked in the land of Egypt.

8 A trumpet to your lips, You who watch over the house of the LORD!

Since they have violated my covenant, and sinned against my law,

2 While to me they cry out, "O God of Israel, we know you!"

3 The men of Israel have thrown away what is good; the enemy shall pursue them.

4 They made kings, but not by my authority; they established princes, but without my approval. With their silver and gold they made idols for themselves, to their own destruction.

5 Cast away your calf, O Samaria! my wrath is kindled against them; How long will they be unable to attain innocence in Israel?

6 The work of an artisan, no god at all, Destined for the flames— such is the calf of Samaria!

7 When they sow the wind, they shall reap the whirlwind; The stalk of grain that forms no ear can yield no flour; Even if it could, strangers would swallow it.

8 Israel is swallowed up; he is now among the nations a thing of no value.

9 They went up to Assyria— a wild ass off on its own— Ephraim bargained for lovers.

10 Even though they bargain with the nations, I will now gather an army; King and princes shall shortly succumb under the burden.

11 When Ephraim made many altars to expiate sin, his altars became occasions of sin.

7, 3–7: This passage refers to the dynastic upheavals of Israel's declining days. Between the death of Jeroboam II and the fall of Samaria to the Assyrians, a matter of some twenty-five years, there were four separate dynasties on the throne and as many murdered kings. The prophet compares the Israelite nobles who were inflamed with passion to an overheated oven that consumes what it is supposed to bake; thus the land consumes its kings. *Regale:* with wine (v 5). Like fire smoldering through the night and blazing up in the morning, the sleeping anger of plotters soon breaks out in open rebellion; the succession of night and morning suggest the short

reigns of the various kings of this troubled period.

7, 8: *A hearth cake unturned:* burnt on one side, half baked on the other, and therefore useless. Israel's decline in power is ascribed to its disastrous meddling in the power politics of the neighboring nations.

7, 14: *They lacerated themselves:* a common oriental practice in prayers of earnest impetration (1 Kgs 18, 28); the practice was forbidden in Israelite religion (Lv 19, 28; Dt 14, 1).

8, 4–6: Israel's monarchy and separate sanctuary are here associated, as in 1 Kgs 12, 20–33; both were the result of rebellion against the divinely approved Davidic dynasty and the Jerusalem temple with the

ark of the covenant. The calf image set up by Jeroboam I in the royal shrines prevented Israel from attaining *innocence* (vv 5f).

8, 11: The very multiplicity of sanctuaries throughout the land was a danger to the purity of worship. The local shrines were speedily assimilated to the cult places used by the Canaanites, and the Lord was identified with the god Baal worshiped there. Thus the Deuteronomic writers, influenced by prophetic ideas, ended by restricting sacrificial worship to the one temple in Jerusalem.

12 Though I write for him my
      many ordinances,
   they are considered as a
      stranger's.
13 Though they offer sacrifice,
      immolate flesh and eat it,
      the LORD is not pleased with
         them.
   He shall still remember their guilt
      and punish their sins;
   they shall return to Egypt.
14 Israel has forgotten his maker
      and built palaces.
   Judah, too, has fortified many
      cities;
   but I will send fire upon his
      cities,
   to devour their castles.

Exile without Worship

9 Rejoice not, O Israel,
      exult not like the nations!
   For you have been unfaithful
      to your God,
      loving a harlot's hire
      upon every threshing floor.
2 Threshing floor and wine press
      shall not nourish them,
   the new wine shall fail them.

3 They shall not dwell in the
      LORD's land;
   Ephraim shall return to Egypt,
   and in Assyria they shall eat
      unclean food.
4 They shall not pour libations of
      wine to the LORD,
   or proffer their sacrifices
      before him.
   Theirs will be like mourners'
      bread,
   that makes unclean all who
      eat of it;
   Such food as they have shall be
      for themselves;
   it cannot enter the house of
      the LORD.

5 What will you do on the festival
      day,
   the day of the LORD's feast?
6 When they go from the ruins,
   Egypt shall gather them in,
      Memphis shall bury them.

   Weeds shall overgrow their
      silver treasures,
   and thorns invade their tents.

The Prophet Ridiculed

7 They have come, the days of
      punishment!
   they have come, the days of
      recompense!
   Let Israel know it!
      "The prophet is a fool,
      the man of the spirit is mad!"
   Because your iniquity is great,
      great, too, is your hostility.

8 A prophet is Ephraim's
      watchman with God,
   yet a fowler's snare is on all
      his ways,
   hostility in the house of his
      God.
9 They have sunk to the depths
      of corruption,
   as in the days of Gibeah;
   He shall remember their iniquity
   and punish their sins.

Crime of Baal-peor

10 Like grapes in the desert,
      I found Israel;
   Like the first fruits of the fig
      tree in its prime,
   I considered your fathers.
   When they came to Baal-peor
      and consecrated themselves
      to the Shame,
   they became as abhorrent as
      the thing they loved.
11 The glory of Ephraim flies away
      like a bird:
   no birth, no carrying in the
      womb, no conception.
   Were they to bear children,
   I would slay the darlings of
      their womb.
12 Even though they bring up their
      children,
   I will make them childless,
      till not one is left.
   Woe to them
      when I turn away from them!

13 Ephraim, as I saw, was like
      Tyre,
   planted in a beauteous spot;
   But Ephraim shall bring out
      his children to the slayer.
14 Give them, O LORD!
      give them what?
   Give them an unfruitful womb,
      and dry breasts!

Crime of Gilgal

15 All their wickedness is in Gilgal;
   yes, there they incurred my
      hatred.
   Because of their wicked deeds
   I will drive them out of my
      house.
   I will love them no longer;
      all their princes are rebels.
16 Ephraim is stricken,
      their root is dried up;
   they shall bear no fruit.
17 My God will disown them
   because they have not listened
      to him;
   they shall be wanderers among
      the nations.

Punishment of Idolatry

10 Israel is a luxuriant vine
      whose fruit matches its
         growth.
   The more abundant his fruit,
      the more altars he built;
   The more productive his land,
      the more sacred pillars he set
         up.
2 Their heart is false,
      now they pay for their guilt;
   God shall break down their
      altars
   and destroy their sacred
      pillars.
3 If they would say,
      "We have no king"—
   Since they do not fear the LORD,
      what can the king do for them?
4 Nothing but make promises,
      swear false oaths, and make
         alliances,
   While justice grows wild
      like wormwood in a plowed
         field!

9, 1f: *Upon every threshing floor:* an allusion to harvest festivals in honor of Baal, to whom the Israelites had attributed the fertility of the land; cf 2, 7.

9, 4: *Mourners' bread:* bread eaten at funeral rites; cf Dt 26, 13f. Contact with a corpse made a person ritually unclean, together with everything he touched. Such bread could not be offered to the Lord.

9, 5: *The Lord's feast:* doubtless the autumn feast of Booths, the most important of the Israelite public celebrations; cf Lv 23, 34.

9, 9: *The days of Gibeah:* a reference to the outrage committed at Gibeah in the days of the Judges (Jgs 19, 22–30).

9, 10: At *Baal-peor* (Nm 25, 1–5) the Israelites consecrated themselves to Baal, here called *the Shame.*

9, 14: *An unfruitful womb:* this appears to be a reversal of the ancient blessing of Joseph contained in Gn 49, 25f, in which the increase, hence fruitfulness,

promised to the patriarch is even signified by the name of his son Ephraim, on whose descendants the prophet now invokes the curse of extinction.

9, 15: *Gilgal:* see note on 4, 15.

10, 1: *Sacred pillars:* see note on 3, 4.

10, 4: *Justice . . . like wormwood:* the administration of justice, which should have been the mainstay of the people, has in corrupt hands become another instrument of oppression; cf Am 6, 13.

5 The inhabitants of Samaria fear
for the calf of Beth-aven;
The people mourn for it
and the priests wail over it,
because the glory has departed
from it.
6 It too shall be carried to Assyria,
as an offering to the great
king.
Ephraim shall be taken into
captivity,
Israel be shamed by his
schemes.
7 The king of Samaria shall
disappear,
like foam upon the waters.
8 The high places of Aven shall
be destroyed,
the sin of Israel;
thorns and thistles shall
overgrow their altars.
Then they shall cry out to the
mountains, "Cover us!"
and to the hills, "Fall upon us!"

9 Since the days of Gibeah
you have sinned, O Israel.
There they took their stand;
war was not to reach them in
Gibeah.
10 Against the wanton people I
came
and I chastised them;
I gathered troops against them
when I chastised them for
their two crimes.

Time To Seek the Lord

11 Ephraim was a trained heifer,
willing to thresh;
I myself laid a yoke
upon her fair neck;
Ephraim was to be harnessed,
Judah was to plow,
Jacob was to break his
furrows:
12 "Sow for yourselves justice,
reap the fruit of piety;
Break up for yourselves a new
field,
for it is time to seek the LORD,
till he come and rain down
justice upon you."

13 But you have cultivated
wickedness,
reaped perversity,
and eaten the fruit of falsehood.

Because you have trusted in your
chariots,
and in your many warriors,
14 Turmoil shall break out among
your tribes
and all your fortresses shall
be ravaged
As Salman ravaged Beth-arbel
in time of war,
smashing mothers and their
children.
15 So shall it be done to you,
Bethel,
because of your utter
wickedness:
At dawn the king of Israel
shall perish utterly.

When Israel Was a Child

11 When Israel was a child I
loved him,
out of Egypt I called my son.
2 The more I called them,
the farther they went from me,
Sacrificing to the Baals
and burning incense to idols.
3 Yet it was I who taught
Ephraim to walk,
who took them in my arms;
4 I drew them with human cords,
with bands of love;
I fostered them like one
who raises an infant to his
cheeks;
Yet, though I stooped to feed
my child,
they did not know that I was
their healer.

5 He shall return to the land of
Egypt,
and Assyria shall be his king;
6 The sword shall begin with his
cities
and end by consuming his
solitudes.
Because they refused to repent,
their own counsels shall
devour them.

7 His people are in suspense
about returning to him;
and God, though in unison
they cry out to him,
shall not raise them up.

End of the Exile

8 How could I give you up, O
Ephraim,
or deliver you up, O Israel?
How could I treat you as Admah,
or make you like Zeboiim?
My heart is overwhelmed,
my pity is stirred.
9 I will not give vent to my
blazing anger,
I will not destroy Ephraim
again;
For I am God and not man,
the Holy One present among
you;
I will not let the flames
consume you.

10 They shall follow the LORD,
who roars like a lion;
When he roars,
his sons shall come frightened
from the west,
11 Out of Egypt they shall come
trembling, like sparrows,
from the land of Assyria, like
doves;
And I will resettle them in their
homes,
says the LORD.

Infidelity of Israel

12 Ephraim has surrounded me
with lies,
the house of Israel, with
deceit;
Judah is still rebellious against
God,
against the Holy One, who is
faithful.
2 Ephraim chases the wind,
ever pursuing the gale.
His lies and falsehoods are
many:
he comes to terms with
Assyria,
and carries oil to Egypt.

10, 5: *The calf of Beth-aven:* see notes on 4, 15; 8, 4ff.
10, 10: *Their two crimes:* possibly the outrage described in Jgs 19 is conceived as a double crime, of adultery and murder. Or the prophet regards the proclamation of the monarchy (cf 1 Sm 10, 23f) as a crime.
10, 14: *As Salman ravaged Beth-arbel:* allusion to an invasion not otherwise mentioned in the Bible.

Salman may have been the Moabite king of this name mentioned in an inscription of Tiglath-pileser III. There were several Beth-arbels in Palestine; this one was probably in Transjordan.
11, 1: *Out of Egypt:* Hosea, like most of the prophets, dates the real beginning of Israel from the time of Moses and the Exodus. Mt 2, 15 applies this text to the return of the Christ Child from Egypt.

11, 4: *I drew them . . . with bands of love:* not forcing them like draft animals, but drawing them with kindness and affection.
11, 8: *Admah . . . Zeboiim:* cities destroyed with Sodom and Gomorrah (Dt 29, 22).
12, 2: *He comes . . . Egypt:* allusion to the commercial and military pacts with the great powers, consistently condemned by the prophets as derogatory of the Lord's claim on his people.

3 The LORD has a grievance
      against Israel:
   he shall punish Jacob for his
      conduct,
   for his deeds he shall repay him.
4 In the womb he supplanted his
      brother,
   and as a man he contended
      with God;
5 He contended with the angel
      and triumphed,
   entreating him with tears.
   At Bethel he met God
   and there he spoke with him:
6 The LORD, the God of hosts,
   the LORD is his name!
7 You shall return by the help of
      your God,
   if you remain loyal and do
      right
   and always hope in your God.

8 A merchant who holds a false
      balance,
   who loves to defraud!
9 Though Ephraim says,
   "How rich I have become;
   I have made a fortune!"
   All his gain shall not suffice him
   for the guilt of his sin.
10 I am the LORD, your God,
   since the land of Egypt;
   I will again have you live in tents,
   as in that appointed time.
11 I granted many visions
   and spoke to the prophets,
   through whom I set forth
      examples.
12 In Gilead is falsehood, they have
   come to nought,
   in Gilead they sacrifice to
      bullocks;
   Their altars are like heaps of
      stones
   in the furrows of the field.
13 When Jacob fled to the land of
      Aram,
   he served for a wife;
   for a wife Israel tended sheep.
14 By a prophet the LORD brought
   Israel out of Egypt,
   and by a prophet they were
      protected.

15 Ephraim has exasperated his
      LORD;
   therefore he shall cast his
      blood-guilt upon him
   and repay him for his
      outrage.

13 Ephraim's word caused fear,
      for he was exalted in Israel;
   but he sinned through Baal
      and died.

Punishment for Ingratitude

2 Now they continue to sin,
   making for themselves molten
      images,
   Silver idols according to their
      fancy,
   all of them the work of
      artisans.
   "To these," they say, "offer
      sacrifice."
   Men kiss calves!
3 Therefore, they shall be like a
   morning cloud
   or like the dew that early
      passes away,
   Like chaff storm-driven from
      the threshing floor
   or like smoke out of the
      window.

4 I am the LORD, your God,
   since the land of Egypt;
   You know no God besides me,
   and there is no savior but me.
5 I fed you in the desert,
   in the torrid land.
6 They ate their fill;
   when filled, they became
      proud of heart
   and forgot me.

7 Therefore, I will be like a lion
   to them,
   like a panther by the road I
   will keep watch.
8 I will attack them like a bear
   robbed of its young,
   and tear their hearts from
      their breasts;
   I will devour them on the spot
   like a lion,
   as though a wild beast were
   to rend them.

9 Your destruction, O Israel!
   who is there to help you?
10 Where now is your king,
   that he may rescue you in all
      your cities?
   And your rulers, of whom you
      said,
   "Give me a king and
      princes"?
11 I give you a king in my anger,
   and I take him away in my
      wrath.

12 The guilt of Israel is wrapped
      up,
   his sin is stored away.
13 The birth pangs shall come for
      him,
   but he shall be an unwise
      child;
   For when it is time he shall not
      present himself
   where children break forth.
14 Shall I deliver them from the
      power of the nether world?
   shall I redeem them from
      death?
   Where are your plagues, O
      death!
   where is your sting, O nether
      world!
   My eyes are closed to
      compassion.

15 Though he be fruitful among
      his fellows,
   an east wind shall come,
   a wind from the LORD,
   rising from the desert,
   That shall dry up his spring,
   and leave his fountain dry.
   It shall loot his land
   of every precious thing.

14 Samaria shall expiate her
      guilt,
   for she has rebelled against
      her God.
   They shall fall by the sword,
   their little ones shall be dashed
      to pieces,
   their expectant mothers shall
      be ripped open.

12, 3-7: Contemporary Israel and the Israel represented by its ancestor Jacob (Israel) are here alternated, a splendid example of the Hebrew concept of "corporate personality" or easy transition from the individual to the community of which he is a part. Hosea recalls the history of Jacob as it now appears in Genesis, but with some differences of detail and order.

12, 14: *A prophet:* Moses.

13, 11: *I give you a king . . . in my wrath:* the Lord punishes the people of the northern kingdom by giving them incompetent kings who are soon deposed.

13, 13: Israel's sin is such as to warrant its destruction (v 12), because it refuses to do penance. It will therefore perish as surely as the unborn child

which dies in its mother's body because it does not properly employ the only way to safety.

13, 14: *Shall . . . nether world:* a vigorous affirmation of the Lord's determination to destroy Israel. St. Paul cites these words in a different sense (1 Cor 15, 54f), that of the ultimate victory of life over death in the resurrection of the body on the last day, wrought through the merits of Christ's passion and resurrection.

Sincere Conversion

2 Return, O Israel, to the LORD,
    your God;
    you have collapsed through
      your guilt.
3 Take with you words,
    and return to the LORD;
    Say to him, "Forgive all iniquity,
    and receive what is good, that
      we may render
    as offerings the bullocks from
      our stalls.
4 Assyria will not save us,
    nor shall we have horses to
      mount;
    We shall say no more, 'Our god,'
    to the work of our hands;
    for in you the orphan finds
      compassion."

14, 10: A later addition in the style of the wisdom literature.

5 I will heal their defection,
    I will love them freely;
    for my wrath is turned away
      from them.
6 I will be like the dew for
      Israel:
    he shall blossom like the lily;
    He shall strike root like the
      Lebanon cedar,
7 and put forth his shoots.
    His splendor shall be like the
      olive tree
    and his fragrance like the
      Lebanon cedar.
8 Again they shall dwell in his
      shade
    and raise grain;
    They shall blossom like the vine,
    and his fame shall be like
      the wine of Lebanon.

9 Ephraim! What more has he to
      do with idols?
    I have humbled him, but I
      will prosper him.
    "I am like a verdant cypress
      tree"—
    Because of me you bear fruit!

*　*　*

10 Let him who is wise understand
      these things;
    let him who is prudent know
      them.
    Straight are the paths of the
      LORD,
    in them the just walk,
    but sinners stumble in them.

Joel

The Land Invaded

THE word of the LORD which came to Joel, the son of Pethuel. 2 Hear this, you elders! Pay attention, all you who dwell in the land! Has the like of this happened in your days, or in the days of your fathers? 3 Tell it to your children, and your children to their children, and their children to the next generation.

4 What the cutter left,
    the locust swarm has eaten;
What the locust swarm left,
    the grasshopper has eaten;
And what the grasshopper left,
    the devourer has eaten.

5 Wake up, you drunkards, and
    weep;
    wail, all you drinkers of wine,
Because the juice of the grape
    will be withheld from your
    mouths.
6 For a people has invaded my
    land,
    mighty and without number;
His teeth are the teeth of a lion,
    and his molars those of a
    lioness.
7 He has laid waste my vine,
    and blighted my fig tree;
He has stripped it, sheared off
    its bark;
    its branches are made white.

8 Lament like a virgin girt with
    sackcloth
    for the spouse of her youth.

9 Abolished are offering and
    libation
    from the house of the LORD;
In mourning are the priests,
    the ministers of the LORD.
10 The field is ravaged,
    the earth mourns,
Because the grain is ravaged,
    the must has failed,
    the oil languishes.

11 Be appalled, you husbandmen!
    wail, you vinedressers!
Over the wheat and the barley,
    because the harvest of the field
    has perished.
12 The vine has dried up,
    the fig tree is withered;
The pomegranate, the date
    palm also, and the apple,
all the trees of the field are
    dried up;
Yes, joy has withered away
    from among mankind.

Call to Penance

13 Gird yourselves and weep, O
    priests!
    wail, O ministers of the altar!
Come, spend the night in
    sackcloth,
    O ministers of my God!
The house of your God is
    deprived
    of offering and libation.
14 Proclaim a fast,
    call an assembly;
Gather the elders,
    all who dwell in the land,
Into the house of the LORD,
    your God,
    and cry to the LORD!

15 Alas, the day!
    for near is the day of the LORD,
    and it comes as ruin from the
    Almighty.
16 From before our very eyes
    has not the food been cut off;
And from the house of our God,
    joy and gladness?
17 The seed lies shriveled under its
    clods;
    the stores are destroyed,
The barns are broken down,
    for the grain has failed.
18 How the beasts groan!
    The herds of cattle are
    bewildered!

1, 4: *Cutter . . . locust . . . grasshopper . . . devourer:* these names refer to various species of locusts: they can only be approximate.

1, 6: *A people:* the locusts compared to an invading army.

Because they have no pasturage,
even the flocks of sheep have
perished.

19 To you, O Lord, I cry!
for fire has devoured the
pastures of the plain,
and flame has enkindled all the
trees of the field.
20 Even the beasts of the field
cry out to you;
For the streams of water are
dried up,
and fire has devoured the
pastures of the plain.

The Day of the Lord

2 Blow the trumpet in Zion,
sound the alarm on my holy
mountain!
Let all who dwell in the land
tremble,
for the day of the Lord is
coming;
2 Yes, it is near, a day of darkness and of gloom,
a day of clouds and
somberness!
Like dawn spreading over the
mountains,
a people numerous and
mighty!
Their like has not been from
of old,
nor will it be after them,
even to the years of distant
generations.
3 Before them a fire devours,
and after them a flame
enkindles;
Like the garden of Eden is the
land before them,
and after them a desert waste;
from them there is no escape.

4 Their appearance is that of
horses;
like steeds they run.
5 As with the rumble of chariots
they leap on the mountaintops;
As with the crackling of a fiery
flame
devouring stubble;
Like a mighty people
arrayed for battle.

6 Before them peoples are in
torment,
every face blanches.

7 Like warriors they run,
like soldiers they scale the
wall;
They advance, each in his own
lane,
without swerving from their
paths.
8 No one crowds another,
each advances in his own
track;
Though they fall into the
ditches,
they are not checked.

9 They assault the city,
they run upon the wall,
they climb into the houses;
In at the windows
they come like thieves.
10 Before them the earth trembles,
the heavens shake;
The sun and the moon are
darkened,
and the stars withhold their
brightness.

11 The Lord raises his voice
at the head of his army;
For immense indeed is his
camp,
yes, mighty, and it does his
bidding.
For great is the day of the Lord,
and exceedingly terrible; who
can bear it?
12 Yet even now, says the Lord,
return to me with your whole
heart,
with fasting, and weeping,
and mourning;
13 Rend your hearts, not your
garments,
and return to the Lord, your
God.
For gracious and merciful is he,
slow to anger, rich in
kindness,
and relenting in punishment.
14 Perhaps he will again relent
and leave behind him a
blessing,
Offerings and libations
for the Lord, your God.

15 Blow the trumpet in Zion!
proclaim a fast,
call an assembly;
16 Gather the people,
notify the congregation;
Assemble the elders,
gather the children
and the infants at the breast;
Let the bridegroom quit his
room,
and the bride her chamber.
17 Between the porch and the altar
let the priests, the ministers of
the Lord, weep,
And say, "Spare, O Lord, your
people,
and make not your heritage
a reproach,
with the nations ruling over
them!
Why should they say among the
peoples,
'Where is their God?'"

Blessings for God's People

18 Then the Lord was stirred to
concern for his land and took pity on
his people. 19 The Lord answered
and said to his people:

See, I will send you
grain, and wine, and oil,
and you shall be filled with
them;
No more will I make you
a reproach among the
nations.
20 No, the northerner I will
remove far from you,
and drive him out into a land
arid and waste,
With his van toward the eastern
sea,
and his rear toward the
western sea;
And his foulness shall go up,
and his stench shall go up.

21 Fear not, O land!
exult and rejoice!
for the Lord has done great
things.
22 Fear not, beasts of the field!
for the pastures of the plain
are green;
The tree bears its fruit,
the fig tree and the vine give
their yield.

2, 17: The priests stood in the open space between the outdoor altar of holocausts and the temple building, facing the latter in order thereby to look toward

God present in the holy of holies.
2, 20: *The northerner:* the locusts, that are compared to an invading army, which in Palestine came

from the north; cf Jer 1, 14f; 4, 6; Ez 26, 7; 38, 6.15.

23 And do you, O children of Zion,
　　exult
　　　and rejoice in the LORD, your
　　　　God!
　　He has given you the teacher
　　　of justice:
　　　he has made the rain come
　　　　down for you,
　　　the early and the late rain as
　　　　before.
24 The threshing floors shall be full
　　of grain
　　and the vats shall overflow
　　　with wine and oil.

25 And I will repay you for the years
　　which the locust has eaten,
　　The grasshopper, the devourer,
　　　and the cutter,
　　　my great army which I sent
　　　　among you.
26 You shall eat and be filled,
　　and shall praise the name of
　　　the LORD, your God,
　　Because he has dealt
　　　wondrously with you;
　　my people shall nevermore
　　　be put to shame.
27 And you know that I am in the
　　midst of Israel;
　　I am the LORD, your God,
　　　and there is no other;
　　my people shall nevermore
　　　be put to shame.

3 Then afterward I will pour out
　　my spirit upon all mankind.
　　Your sons and daughters shall
　　　prophesy,
　　　your old men shall dream
　　　　dreams,
　　　your young men shall see
　　　　visions;
　2 Even upon the servants and the
　　handmaids,
　　　in those days, I will pour out
　　　　my spirit.

　3 And I will work wonders in the
　　heavens and on the earth,
　　blood, fire and columns of
　　　smoke;

4 The sun will be turned to
　　darkness,
　　and the moon to blood,
　　At the coming of the Day of the
　　　LORD,
　　the great and terrible day.
5 Then everyone shall be rescued
　　who calls on the name of the
　　　LORD;
　　For on Mount Zion there shall
　　　be a remnant,
　　as the LORD has said,
　　And in Jerusalem survivors
　　whom the LORD shall call.

Judgment upon the Nations

4 Yes, in those days, and at that
　　time,
　　when I would restore the
　　　fortunes
　　of Judah and Jerusalem,
2 I will assemble all the nations
　　and bring them down to the
　　　Valley of Jehoshaphat,
　　And I will enter into judgment
　　　with them there
　　on behalf of my people and
　　　my inheritance, Israel;
　　Because they have scattered
　　　them among the nations,
　　and divided my land.
3 Over my people they have cast
　　lots;
　　they gave a boy for a harlot,
　　and sold a girl for the wine
　　　they drank.

4 Moreover, what are you to me,
Tyre and Sidon, and all the regions of
Philistia? Would you take vengeance
upon me by some action? But if you
do take action against me, swiftly,
speedily, I will return your deed upon
your own head. 5 You took my
silver and my gold, and brought my
precious treasures into your temples!
6 You sold the people of Judah and
Jerusalem to the Greeks, removing
them far from their own country! 7
See, I will rouse them from the place
into which you have sold them, and

I will return your deed upon your
own head. 8 I will sell your sons
and your daughters to the people
of Judah, who shall sell them to the
Sabeans, a nation far off. Indeed, the
LORD has spoken.

9 Declare this among the nations:
　　proclaim a war,
　　rouse the warriors to arms!
　　Let all the soldiers
　　report and march!
10 Beat your plowshares into
　　swords,
　　and your pruning hooks into
　　　spears;
　　let the weak man say,
　　"I am a warrior!"
11 Hasten and come, all you
　　neighboring peoples,
　　assemble there!
　　[Bring down, O Lord, your
　　　warriors!]
12 Let the nations bestir
　　themselves and come up
　　to the Valley of Jehoshaphat;
　　For there will I sit in judgment
　　upon all the neighboring
　　　nations.

13 Apply the sickle,
　　for the harvest is ripe;
　　Come and tread,
　　for the wine press is full;
　　The vats overflow,
　　for great is their malice.
14 Crowd upon crowd
　　in the valley of decision;
　　For near is the day of the LORD
　　in the valley of decision.
15 Sun and moon are darkened,
　　and the stars withhold their
　　　brightness.
16 The LORD roars from Zion,
　　and from Jerusalem raises his
　　　voice;
　　The heavens and the earth quake,
　　but the LORD is a refuge to
　　　his people,
　　a stronghold to the men of
　　　Israel.

2, 23: *The teacher of justice:* the rain sent by God
to show his fidelity to his promises, and to teach his
people to be faithful to his commandments; cf Dt 11,
14. There is also a play on words here between the
Hebrew word *moreh* (teacher) and the Hebrew word
yoreh (the early rain). The expression likewise has a
Messianic connotation; cf Is 30, 20. The founder of
the Essene sect of Qumran (second century B.C.) was
known as "The Teacher of Justice."

3, 1f: *I will pour out my spirit:* in the Old Testament
the *spirit* is the gift of God bestowed on those acting

as his agents. The promise of the spirit is quoted by
St. Peter in Acts 2, 17–21 as fulfilled in an eminent
way by the gift of the Holy Spirit, the Third Person of
the Blessed Trinity, bestowed on the Apostles.

4, 2: *Valley of Jehoshaphat:* a symbolic name of the
place of final judgment (v 14). The name Jehoshaphat
signifies "Yahweh judges." This place has been
popularly identified with the Kidron Valley.

4, 8: *Sabeans:* a south Arabian people known for
their commerce.

4, 10: This imagery is used in the reverse sense in

Is 2, 4; Mi 4, 3. Here the warlike weapons are made in
response to God's summons to armies which he
selected to expel forever the unlawful invaders from
the land of his chosen people.

4, 11: *Warriors:* the angels; cf Zec 14, 5.

4, 13: Because of their numerous crimes, the nations
are ripe for punishment. The use of warlike weapons
against them at harvest time is likened to the onslaught on the fields
and vines at harvest time.

Salvation for God's Elect

17 Then shall you know that I, the
LORD, am your God,
dwelling on Zion, my holy
mountain;
Jerusalem shall be holy,
and strangers shall pass
through her no more.
18 And then, on that day,
the mountains shall drip new
wine,

and the hills shall flow with
milk;
And the channels of Judah
shall flow with water:
A fountain shall issue from the
house of the LORD,
to water the Valley of
Shittim.
19 Egypt shall be a waste,
and Edom a desert waste,

Because of violence done to the
people of Judah,
because they shed innocent
blood in their land.
20 But Judah shall abide forever,
and Jerusalem for all generations.
21 I will avenge their blood,
and not leave it unpunished.
The LORD dwells in Zion.

4, 18: *The Valley of Shittim,* or "the ravine of the acacia trees": perhaps a part of the Kidron Valley southeast of Jerusalem; the prophetic picture of a stream of water flowing from a fountain in the temple of Jerusalem is to be found in Ez 47, 1. The Shittim east of the Jordan (see note on Nm 25, 1) is hardly referred to here.

JUDGMENT OF THE NATIONS

THE words of Amos, a shepherd from Tekoa, which he received in vision concerning Israel, in the days of Uzziah, king of Judah, and in the days of Jeroboam, son of Joash, king of Israel, two years before the earthquake: 2 The LORD will roar from Zion, and from Jerusalem raise his voice:
The pastures of the shepherds
    will languish,
and the summit of Carmel
    wither.

Aram

3   Thus says the LORD:
For three crimes of Damascus,
    and for four,
I will not revoke my word;
Because they threshed Gilead
    with sledges of iron,
4 I will send fire upon the house
    of Hazael,
to devour the castles of
    Benhadad.
5 I will break the bar of
    Damascus;
I will root out those who live
    in the Valley of Aven,
And the sceptered ruler of Beth-
    eden;

the people of Aram shall be
    exiled to Kir,
says the LORD.

Philistia

6   Thus says the LORD:
For three crimes of Gaza, and
    for four,
I will not revoke my word;
Because they took captive
    whole groups
    to hand over to Edom,
7 I will send fire upon the wall of
    Gaza,
    to devour her castles;
8 I will root out those who live in
    Ashdod,
and the sceptered ruler of
    Ashkelon;
I will turn my hand against
    Ekron,
and the last of the Philistines
    shall perish,
says the Lord GOD.

Tyre

9   Thus says the LORD:
For three crimes of Tyre, and
    for four,
I will not revoke my word;
Because they delivered whole
    groups captive to Edom,
and did not remember the
    pact of brotherhood,
10 I will send fire upon the wall of
    Tyre,
    to devour her castles.

Edom

11   Thus says the LORD:
For three crimes of Edom, and
    for four,
I will not revoke my word;
Because he pursued his brother
    with the sword,
    choking up all pity;
Because he persisted in his anger
    and kept his wrath to the end,

1, 1: *The earthquake:* which according to Hebrew tradition marked the crime of Uzziah when he attempted to offer incense in the temple (2 Chr 26, 16–21). Zechariah mentions it several centuries later (Zec 14, 5).

1, 3: *For three crimes . . . four:* crime after crime, an indefinite number; cf 1, 6. The series of judgments on the foreign nations shows that the Lord demands the observance of the moral order everywhere; Israel and Judah, despite their privileged position, are no exception. *I will not revoke my word:* God will not

withdraw his threat of punishment against each of these nations. *They threshed Gilead:* the people of Aram under King Hazael had devastated Gilead; cf 2 Kgs 10, 32f.

1, 4: *Fire:* devastation caused by the Assyrians (1, 7.10.12.14; 2, 2.5); cf 1 Sm 15, 18. *Hazael* and *Benhadad:* kings of the Arameans whose capital was *Damascus* (v 5); they fought against Israel (2 Kgs 13, 3), and had long occupied the region of Gilead (v 3) in Transjordan.

1, 5: *Bar of Damascus:* the beam securing the main

gate of the city against invaders, symbol of its defenses. *Valley of Aven* ("vale of wickedness") and *Beth-eden* ("house of pleasure"): Aramean territory from southwest to northeast.

1, 9: *Pact of brotherhood:* Hiram of Tyre had made a pact with Solomon and called him brother (1 Kgs 5, 12; 9, 13).

1, 11: *Pursued his brother:* the Edomites were descended from Esau, the brother of Jacob (Gn 25—27); nevertheless they constantly nourished enmity against Jacob's descendants, the Israelites.

12 I will send fire upon Teman,
    and it will devour the castles
       of Bozrah.

Ammon

13   Thus says the LORD:
  For three crimes of the
       Ammonites, and for four,
    I will not revoke my word;
  Because they ripped open
       expectant mothers in
       Gilead,
    while extending their territory,
14 I will kindle a fire upon the wall
       of Rabbah,
    and it will devour her castles
  Amid clamor on the day of
       battle
    and stormwind in a time of
       tempest.
15 Their king shall go into
       captivity,
    he and his princes with him,
       says the LORD.

Moab

2   Thus says the LORD:
  For three crimes of Moab, and
       for four,
    I will not revoke my word;
  Because he burned to ashes
       the bones of Edom's king,
2 I will send fire upon Moab,
    to devour the castles of
       Kerioth;
  Moab shall meet death amid
       uproar
    and shouts and trumpet blasts.
3 I will root out the judge from
       her midst,
    and her princes I will slay
       with him, says the LORD.

Judah

4   Thus says the LORD:
  For three crimes of Judah, and
       for four,
    I will not revoke my word;
  Because they spurned the law
       of the LORD,
    and did not keep his statutes;

Because the lies which their
       fathers followed
    have led them astray,
5 I will send fire upon Judah,
    to devour the castles of
       Jerusalem.

Israel

6   Thus says the LORD:
  For three crimes of Israel, and
       for four,
    I will not revoke my word;
  Because they sell the just man
       for silver,
    and the poor man for a pair
       of sandals.
7 They trample the heads of the
       weak
    into the dust of the earth,
    and force the lowly out of the
       way.
Son and father go to the same
       prostitute,
    profaning my holy name.
8 Upon garments taken in pledge
    they recline beside any altar;
  And the wine of those who have
       been fined
    they drink in the house of
       their god.
9 Yet it was I who destroyed the
       Amorites before them,
  who were as tall as the cedars,
    and as strong as the oak trees.
  I destroyed their fruit above,
    and their roots beneath.
10 It was I who brought you up
       from the land of Egypt,
    and who led you through the
       desert for forty years,
    to occupy the land of the
       Amorites:
11 I who raised up prophets among
       your sons,
    and nazirites among your
       young men.
  Is this not so, O men of Israel?
    says the LORD.
12 But you gave the nazirites wine
       to drink,
    and commanded the prophets
       not to prophesy.

13 Beware, I will crush you into
       the ground
    as a wagon crushes when
       laden with sheaves.
14 Flight shall perish from the
       swift,
    and the strong man shall not
       retain his strength;
  The warrior shall not save his
       life,
15   nor the bowman stand his
       ground;
  The swift of foot shall not
       escape,
    nor the horseman save his
       life.
16 And the most stouthearted of
       warriors
    shall flee naked on that day,
       says the LORD.

WORDS AND WOES FOR ISRAEL

First Word

3 Hear this word, O men of Israel,
that the LORD pronounces over
you, over the whole family that I
brought up from the land of Egypt:

2 You alone have I favored,
    more than all the families of
       the earth;
  Therefore I will punish you
    for all your crimes.

3 Do two walk together
    unless they have agreed?
4 Does a lion roar in the forest
    when it has no prey?
  Does a young lion cry out from
       its den
    unless it has seized something?
5 Is a bird brought to earth by a
       snare
    when there is no lure for it?
  Does a snare spring up from the
       ground
    without catching anything?
6 If the trumpet sounds in a city,
    will the people not be
       frightened?
  If evil befalls a city,
    has not the LORD caused it?

1, 12: *Teman and Bozrah:* two of the chief cities in Edom; cf Jer 49, 20.

1, 14: *Rabbah:* now called Amman, the modern capital of the Hashemite Kingdom of Jordan.

2, 1: Here the prophet stresses the gravity of Moab's violation of the Semitic custom of providing honorable burial for the dead.

2, 4: *The lies:* false gods, who exist only in the mind of their worshipers. The crimes of Judah are infidelity and idolatry, in contrast to the sins for which the

surrounding nations are judged.

2, 6: *A pair of sandals:* indicating how cheaply the rich regarded the poor.

2, 6–13: The detailed crimes of Israel are placed in strong contrast with the benefits with which the Lord favored his people.

2, 8: *Upon garments . . . any altar:* usurers kept the garments taken as pledges from the poor; but instead of restoring them to their owners before nightfall (Ex 22, 25; Dt 24, 12), they used them in

idolatrous worship. *Wine . . . their god:* under the guise of a religious ceremony they drink the wine obtained through unjust fines.

2, 11: *Nazirites:* see note on Nm 6, 1ff.

3, 2: God's choice of Israel brought its own responsibility.

3, 6: The sufferings which sinful man experiences through the permissive will of God are presented here, as elsewhere in the Old Testament, simply as caused by the Lord.

7 Indeed, the Lord GOD does
      nothing
   without revealing his plan
   to his servants, the prophets.

8 The lion roars—
   who will not be afraid!
   The Lord GOD speaks—
   who will not prophesy!

9 Proclaim this in the castles of
      Ashdod,
   in the castles of the land of
      Egypt:
   "Gather about the mountain of
      Samaria,
   and see the great disorders
      within her,
   the oppression in her midst."
10 For they know not how to do
      what is right,
   says the LORD,
   Storing up in their castles
   what they have extorted and
      robbed.
11   Therefore, thus says the Lord
      GOD:
   An enemy shall surround the
      land,
   and strip you of your strength,
   and pillage your castles.

12 Thus says the LORD:
   As the shepherd snatches from
      the mouth of the lion
   a pair of legs or the tip of an
      ear of his sheep,
   So the Israelites who dwell in
      Samaria shall escape
   with the corner of a couch or
      a piece of a cot.

   13 Hear and bear witness against
the house of Jacob, says the Lord
GOD, the God of hosts:

14 On the day when I punish Israel
      for his crimes,
   I will visit also the altars of
      Bethel:
   The horns of the altar shall be
      broken off
   and fall to the ground.
15 Then will I strike the winter
      house
   and the summer house;

The ivory apartments shall be
      ruined,
   and their many rooms shall
      be no more,
   says the LORD.

Second Word

4 Hear this word, women of the
      mountain of Samaria,
   you cows of Bashan,
   You who oppress the weak
   and abuse the needy;
   Who say to your lords,
   "Bring drink for us!"
2 The Lord GOD has sworn by
      his holiness:
   Truly the days are coming
      upon you
   When they shall drag you away
      with hooks,
   the last of you with fish-
      hooks;
3 You shall go out through the
      breached walls
   each by the most direct way,
   And you shall be cast into the
      mire,
   says the LORD.

4 Come to Bethel and sin,
   to Gilgal, and sin the more;
   Each morning bring your
      sacrifices,
   every third day, your tithes;
5 Burn leavened food as a
      thanksgiving sacrifice,
   proclaim publicly your freewill
      offerings,
   For so you love to do, O men
      of Israel,
   says the Lord GOD.

6 Though I have made your teeth
      clean of food in all your cities,
   and have made bread scarce in
      all your dwellings,
   Yet you returned not to me,
   says the LORD.

7 Though I also withheld the rain
      from you
   when the harvest was still
      three months away;
   I sent rain upon one city
   but not upon another;

One field was watered by rain,
   but another without rain
      dried up;
8 Though two or three cities
      staggered to one city
   for water that did not quench
      their thirst;
   Yet you returned not to me,
   says the LORD.

9 I struck you with blight and
      searing wind;
   your many gardens and
      vineyards,
   your fig trees and olive trees
   the locust devoured;
   Yet you returned not to me,
   says the LORD.

10 I sent you a pestilence like that
      of Egypt,
   and with the sword I slew
      your young men;
   Your horses I let be captured,
   to your nostrils I brought
   the stench of your camps;
   Yet you returned not to me,
   says the LORD.

11 I brought upon you such
      upheaval
   as when God overthrew
      Sodom and Gomorrah:
   you were like a brand
   plucked from the fire;
   Yet you returned not to me,
   says the LORD.

12 So now I will deal with you in
      my own way, O Israel!
   and since I will deal thus
      with you,
   prepare to meet your God,
   O Israel:
13 Him who formed the mountains,
   and created the wind,
   and declares to man his
      thoughts;
   Who made the dawn and the
      darkness,
   and strides upon the heights
      of the earth:
   The LORD, the God of hosts
   by name.

3, 9: *Israel's southern neighbors*, beyond Judah,
are invited by the prophetic orator to witness the
moral disorders of God's people.
   3, 15: *Ivory apartments*: rooms containing furniture inlaid in ivory, similar to the pieces discovered in
the excavations at Samaria.

4, 1: *Bashan*: the region east of the Sea of Galilee,
famous for its rich pasture and fattened herds, to
which Amos likens the indolent women of Samaria.
   4, 4f: This invitation to the sanctuaries of the
northern kingdom is ironical. Pilgrimages to the
shrines of *Bethel* and *Gilgal* were the more displeasing

to God because they were contary to his will and
ineffective toward improvement of morals.
   4, 10: *Pestilence like that of Egypt*: plagues were
well known in Egypt; cf Dt 7, 15; 28, 27.60. *Stench
of your camps*: caused by the unburied bodies.

Third Word

5 Hear this word which I utter
over you,
a lament, O house of Israel:
2 She is fallen, to rise no more,
the virgin Israel;
She lies abandoned upon her
land,
with no one to raise her up.

3   For thus says the Lord GOD:
The city that marched out with
a thousand
shall be left with a hundred,
Another that marched out with
a hundred
shall be left with ten,
of the house of Israel.

4 For thus says the LORD
to the house of Israel:
Seek me, that you may live,
5   but do not seek Bethel;
Do not come to Gilgal,
and do not cross to
Beer-sheba.
For Gilgal shall be led into
exile,
and Bethel shall become
nought.
6 Seek the LORD, that you may
live,
lest he come upon the house
of Joseph like a fire
That shall consume, with none
to quench it
for the house of Israel:
8 He who made the Pleiades and
Orion,
who turns darkness into dawn,
and darkens day into night;
Who summons the waters of the
sea,
and pours them out upon the
surface of the earth;
9 Who flashes destruction upon
the strong,
and brings ruin upon the
fortress;
whose name is LORD.

First Woe

7 Woe to those who turn
judgment to wormwood
and cast justice to the
ground!
10 They hate him who reproves at
the gate
and abhor him who speaks the
truth.
11 Therefore, because you have
trampled upon the weak
and exacted of them levies of
grain,
Though you have built houses
of hewn stone,
you shall not live in them!
Though you have planted choice
vineyards,
you shall not drink their
wine!

12 Yes, I know how many are your
crimes,
how grievous your sins:
Oppressing the just, accepting
bribes,
repelling the needy at the gate!
13 Therefore the prudent man is
silent at this time,
for it is an evil time.

14 Seek good and not evil,
that you may live;
Then truly will the LORD, the
God of hosts,
be with you as you claim!
15 Hate evil and love good,
and let justice prevail at the
gate;
Then it may be that the LORD,
the God of hosts,
will have pity on the remnant
of Joseph.

16 Therefore, thus says the LORD,
the God of hosts, the Lord:
In every square there shall be
lamentation,
and in every street they shall
cry, Alas! Alas!

They shall summon the farmers
to wail
and professional mourners to
lament,
17 And in every vineyard there shall
be lamentation
when I pass through your
midst, says the LORD.

Second Woe

18 Woe to those who yearn for the
day of the LORD!
What will this day of the
LORD mean for you?
Darkness and not light!
19 As if a man were to flee from a
lion,
and a bear should meet him;
Or as if on entering his house
he were to rest his hand
against the wall,
and a snake should bite him.
20 Will not the day of the LORD
be darkness and not light,
gloom without any brightness?

21 I hate, I spurn your feasts,
I take no pleasure in your
solemnities;
22 Your cereal offerings I will not
accept,
nor consider your stall-fed
peace offerings.
23 Away with your noisy songs!
I will not listen to the
melodies of your harps.
But if you would offer me
holocausts,
24 then let justice surge like water,
and goodness like an unfailing
stream.
25 Did you bring me sacrifices and
offerings
for forty years in the desert,
O house of Israel?
26 You will carry away Sakkuth,
your king,
and Kaiwan, your star god,
the images that you have
made for yourselves;

5, 6: *House of Joseph*: the kingdom of Israel or northern kingdom, the chief tribes of which were descended from Ephraim and Manasseh, the sons of Joseph; cf 5, 15; 6, 6.

5, 10: *At the gate*: see note on Ps 127, 5.

5, 18: *Day of the Lord*: a technical expression which in earliest times referred to God's special intervention in human affairs. Through it his power and justice triumphed in his people. The present passage is the first instance in which it means a day of punishment of sinners. During the Exile it assumed the meaning of a time when God would avenge Israel against her oppressors and bring about her restoration (Jer 50, 27; Ez 30, 3ff). Still later it came to mean the day of final judgment of the world when the good will be rewarded and the wicked punished (Mal 3, 19ff; Jl 2, 1ff; Zep 1, 14ff).

5, 21–27: The Lord condemns, not ritual worship in itself, but the cult whose exterior rites and solemnity have no relation to interior morality and justice. The Israelites falsely worshiped him as neighboring nations adored Baal or Chamos, deities which were thought to protect their respective peoples against their enemies in return for ritual observances, without any relation to right conduct.

5, 25: The meaning is not certain; according to some, the idea is that during the forty years' wandering in the desert the simple, rudimentary worship of God was accompanied by the practice of justice, in contrast to the elaborate ritual unaccompanied by works of justice in the prophet's time.

5, 26: *Sakkuth . . . star god*: although the text is uncertain, it seems quite probable that reference is made to the Assyrian deities, Sakkuth, god of war and light, and Kaiwan, the planet Saturn. The people will go into exile, from which these gods have been unable to save them.

27 For I will exile you beyond
Damascus,
say I, the LORD, the God of
hosts by name.

Third Woe

6 Woe to the complacent in Zion,
to the overconfident on the
mount of Samaria,
Leaders of a nation favored
from the first,
to whom the people of Israel
have recourse!
2 Pass over to Calneh and see,
go from there to Hamath
the great,
and down to Gath of the
Philistines!
Are you better than these
kingdoms,
or is your territory wider than
theirs?
3 You would put off the evil day,
yet you hasten the reign of
violence!
4 Lying upon beds of ivory,
stretched comfortably on
their couches,
They eat lambs taken from the
flock,
and calves from the stall!
5 Improvising to the music of the
harp,
like David, they devise their
own accompaniment.
6 They drink wine from bowls
and anoint themselves with
the best oils;
yet they are not made ill by
the collapse of Joseph!
7 Therefore, now they shall be the
first to go into exile,
and their wanton revelry shall
be done away with.
8 The Lord GOD has sworn by
his very self,
say I, the LORD, the God of
hosts:
I abhor the pride of Jacob,
I hate his castles,
and I give over the city with
everything in it;

9 Should there remain ten men
in a single house, these shall
die.
10 Only a few shall be left
to carry the dead out of the
houses;
If one says to a man inside a
house,
"Is anyone with you?"
and he answers, "No one,"
Then he shall say, "Silence!"
for no one must mention the
name of the LORD.
11 Indeed, the LORD has given the
command
to shatter the great house to
bits,
and reduce the small house
to rubble.
12 Can horses run across a cliff?
or can one plow the sea with
oxen?
Yet you have turned judgment
into gall,
and the fruit of justice into
wormwood.
13 You rejoice in Lodebar,
and say, "Have we not, by
our own strength,
seized for ourselves Karnaim?"
14 Beware, I am raising up against
you, O house of Israel,
say I, the LORD, the God of
hosts,
A nation that shall oppress you
from Labo of Hamath even
to the Wadi Arabah.

SYMBOLIC VISIONS:
THREATS AND PROMISES

Vision of the Locusts

7 This is what the LORD God showed me: He was forming a locust
swarm when the late growth began
to come up (the late growth after the
king's mowing). 2 While they were
eating all the grass in the land, I said:

Forgive, O Lord GOD!
How can Jacob stand?
He is so small!

3 And the LORD repented of this.
"It shall not be," said the Lord GOD.

Vision of Fire

4 Then the Lord GOD showed me
this: he called for a judgment by fire.
It had devoured the great abyss, and
was consuming the land, 5 when
I said:

Cease, O Lord GOD!
How can Jacob stand?
He is so small!

6 The LORD repented of this.
"This also shall not be," said the
Lord GOD.

Vision of the Plummet

7 Then the Lord GOD showed me
this: he was standing by a wall,
plummet in hand. 8 The LORD
asked me, "What do you see, Amos?"
And when I answered, "A plummet,"
the LORD said:

See, I will lay the plummet
in the midst of my people
Israel;
I will forgive them no longer.
9 The high places of Isaac shall
be laid waste,
and the sanctuaries of Israel
made desolate;
I will attack the house of
Jeroboam with the sword.

Amos and Amaziah

10 Amaziah, the priest of Bethel,
sent word to Jeroboam, king of
Israel: "Amos has conspired against
you here within Israel; the country
cannot endure all his words. 11
For this is what Amos says:

Jeroboam shall die by the
sword,
and Israel shall surely be
exiled from its land."

12 To Amos, Amaziah said: "Off
with you, visionary, flee to the land
of Judah! There earn your bread by
prophesying, 13 but never again
prophesy in Bethel; for it is the

6, 1–7: The luxury of the people in Samaria will be punished by exile. They failed to learn the lesson from *Calneh, Hamath* and *Gath* at the approach of the powerful and warlike Assyrians.
6, 1: *The complacent in Zion . . . the overconfident . . . of Samaria:* the proud and self-interested rulers of Judah and Israel.
6, 12: *Can horses . . . oxen?:* one cannot change

the course of nature, as the Israelites attempted to do by their sins of injustice.
6, 13: *Lodebar . . . Karnaim:* in Transjordan; they had been captured by the Israelites. Perhaps it is in irony that reference is made to these two cities, for the root of the first suggests "nothing" and that of the second, "horns" or "strength."
6, 14: *A nation:* Assyria.

7, 1: *The king's mowing:* the first mowing, a portion of which was payable to the king as a tax.
7, 4: *Fire:* understood by many as a burning drought.
7, 7: *Plummet in hand:* signifying that God is about to withdraw his mercy from his people and that the nation is to be measured for destruction.

king's sanctuary and a royal temple."
14 Amos answered Amaziah, "I was
no prophet, nor have I belonged to
a company of prophets; I was a
shepherd and a dresser of sycamores.
15 The LORD took me from following the flock, and said to me, Go,
prophesy to my people Israel. 16
Now hear the word of the LORD!"

You say: prophesy not against
    Israel,
preach not against the house
    of Isaac.
17   Now thus says the LORD:
Your wife shall be made a
    harlot in the city,
and your sons and daughters
    shall fall by the sword;
Your land shall be divided by
    measuring line,
and you yourself shall die in
    an unclean land;
Israel shall be exiled from its
    land.

Vision of the Fruit Basket

8 This is what the Lord GOD
showed me: a basket of ripe fruit.
2 "What do you see, Amos?" he
asked. I answered, "A basket of ripe
fruit." Then the LORD said to me:

The time is ripe to have done
    with my people Israel;
I will forgive them no longer.
3 The temple songs shall become
    wailings on that day,
says the Lord GOD.
Many shall be the corpses,
    strewn everywhere.—Silence!

Against Greed

4 Hear this, you who trample
    upon the needy
and destroy the poor of the
    land!
5 "When will the new moon be
    over," you ask,
"that we may sell our grain,
and the sabbath, that we may
    display the wheat?
We will diminish the ephah,
    add to the shekel,
and fix our scales for cheating!

6 We will buy the lowly man for
    silver,
and the poor man for a pair
    of sandals;
even the refuse of the wheat
    we will sell!"

7 The LORD has sworn by the
    pride of Jacob:
Never will I forget a thing
    they have done!
8 Shall not the land tremble
    because of this,
and all who dwell in it mourn,
While it rises up and tosses like
    the Nile,
and settles back like the river
    of Egypt?

9 On that day, says the Lord GOD,
    I will make the sun set at
    midday
and cover the earth with
    darkness in broad daylight.
10 I will turn your feasts into
    mourning
and all your songs into
    lamentations.
I will cover the loins of all with
    sackcloth
and make every head bald.
I will make them mourn as for
    an only son,
and bring their day to a bitter
    end.

11 Yes, days are coming, says the
    Lord GOD,
when I will send famine upon
    the land:
Not a famine of bread, or thirst
    for water,
but for hearing the word of
    the LORD
12 Then shall they wander from
    sea to sea
and rove from the north to
    the east
In search of the word of the
    LORD,
but they shall not find it.
13 On that day, fair virgins and
    young men
shall faint from thirst;

14 Those who swear by the shame-
    ful idol of Samaria,
"By the life of your god,
    O Dan!"
"By the life of your love, O
    Beer-sheba!"
those shall fall, never to rise
    again.

Vision of the Altar

9 I saw the Lord standing beside
the altar, and he said:

Strike the bases, so that the
    doorjambs totter
till you break them off on the
    heads of them all!
Those who are left I will slay
    with the sword;
not one shall flee,
no survivor shall escape.
2 Though they break through to
    the nether world,
even from there my hand
    shall bring them out;
Though they climb to the
    heavens,
I will bring them down;
3 Though they hide on the
    summit of Carmel,
there too I will hunt them out
    and take them away;
Though they hide from my gaze
    in the bottom of the sea,
I will command the serpent
    there to bite them;
4 Though they are led into
    captivity by their enemies,
there will I command the
    sword to slay them.
I will fix my gaze upon them
    for evil, and not for good,
5 I, the Lord GOD of hosts.
I melt the earth with my touch,
    so that all who dwell on it
    mourn,
While it all rises up like the Nile,
    and settles back like the river
    of Egypt;
6 I have built heaven, my upper
    chamber,
and established my vault over
    the earth;

7, 14f: Amos denies that he belonged to the class
of professional prophets; his vocation is due to the
personal intervention of the Lord.

8, 5: *Ephah:* a standard of measure; a little more
than a bushel.

8, 7: *The pride of Jacob:* the sinful pride detested
by God (6, 8), in contrast to God himself, who is the

true Pride of Jacob.

8, 8: The figure is based on the annual flooding of
the river Nile.

8, 14: *Dan* and *Beer-sheba,* the extreme northern
and southern limits of the country, where idolatrous
worship was offered.

9, 1–8: There will be no escape from God's

punishment, symbolized here by the destruction of a
building, probably the schismatic temple at Bethel.

9, 3: *Serpent:* the sea monster of familiar legend,
subdued by God at the time of creation and lurking
still in the ocean depths; cf Ps 89, 10f.

I summon the waters of the sea
    and pour them out upon the
      surface of the earth,
      I, the LORD by name.

7 Are you not like the Ethiopians
      to me,
    O men of Israel, says the
      LORD?
    Did I not bring the Israelites
      from the land of Egypt
    As I brought the Philistines
      from Caphtor
    and the Arameans from Kir?
8 The eyes of the Lord GOD are
      on this sinful kingdom:
    I will destroy it from off the
      face of the earth.

Epilogue: Messianic Perspective

But I will not destroy the house
    of Jacob completely,
    says the LORD.

9 For see, I have given the
    command
    to sift the house of Israel
      among all the nations,
    As one sifts with a sieve,
      letting no pebble fall to the
      ground.
10 By the sword shall all sinners
      among my people die,
    those who say, "Evil will not
      reach or overtake us."
11 On that day I will raise up
      the fallen hut of David;
    I will wall up its breaches,
      raise up its ruins,
      and rebuild it as in the days
      of old,
12 That they may conquer what is
      left of Edom
    and all the nations that shall
      bear my name,
    say I, the LORD, who will do
      this.
13 Yes, days are coming,
    says the LORD,

When the plowman shall
    overtake the reaper,
    and the vintager, him who
      sows the seed;
The juices of grapes shall drip
    down the mountains,
    and all the hills shall run with
      it.
14 I will bring about the restora-
      tion of my people Israel;
    they shall rebuild and inhabit
      their ruined cities,
Plant vineyards and drink the
    wine,
    set out gardens and eat the
      fruits.
15 I will plant them upon their
      own ground;
    never again shall they be
      plucked
From the land I have given
    them,
    say I, the LORD, your God.

9, 7: *The Ethiopians . . . the Philistines . . . the Arameans:* by nature Israel is not different from any other nation. It was not because of any merit on Israel's part that God delivered them from Egypt. *Caphtor:* the island of Crete.

9, 11f: In Acts 15, 15ff St. James interprets this passage in a Messianic sense. *Fallen hut:* the kingdom. *The nations that shall bear my name:* the Gentile peoples who shall be converted to the Lord, that is, conquered by him, and therefore shall bear his name.

Obadiah

Title and Theme

THE vision of Obadiah. [Thus says the Lord GOD:] Of Edom we have heard a message from the LORD, and a herald has been sent among the nations: "Up! let us go to war against him!" 2 See, I make you small among the nations; you are held in dire contempt.

Edom Shall Perish

3 The pride of your heart has
  deceived you:
  you who dwell in the clefts
  of the rock,
  whose abode is in the heights,
Who say in your heart,
  "Who will bring me down to
  earth?"
4 Though you go as high as the
  eagle,
  and your nest be set among
  the stars,
From there will I bring you down,
  says the LORD.
5 If thieves came to you, if
  robbers by night,
  how could you be thus
  destroyed:
  would they not steal merely
  till they had enough?
If vintagers came to you,
  would they not leave some
  gleanings?
6 How they search Esau,
  seek out his hiding places!
7 To the border they drive you—
  all your allies;

They deceive you, they
  overpower you—
  those at peace with you;
Those who eat your bread
  lay snares beneath you:
  There is no understanding in
  him!
8 Shall I not, says the LORD, on
  that day
  make the wise men disappear
  from Edom,
  and understanding from the
  mount of Esau?
9 Your warriors, O Teman, shall
  be crushed,
  till all on Mount Esau are
  destroyed.

The Cause

10 Because of violence to your
  brother Jacob,
  disgrace shall cover you
  and you shall be destroyed
  forever.
11 On the day when you stood by,
  on the day when aliens
  carried off his possessions,

And strangers entered his gates
  and cast lots over Jerusalem,
  you too were one of them.
12 Gaze not upon the day of your
  brother,
  the day of his disaster;
Exult not over the children of
  Judah
  on the day of their ruin;
Speak not haughtily
  on the day of distress!
13 Enter not the gate of my people
  on the day of their calamity;
Gaze not, you at least, upon his
  misfortune
  on the day of his calamity;
Lay not hands upon his
  possessions
  on the day of his calamity!
14 Stand not at the crossroads
  to slay his refugees;
Betray not his fugitives
  on the day of distress!

Judgment upon the Nations

15 For near is the day of the LORD
  for all the nations!

5: Something of value may escape the robber, and the vintager always leaves something for the gleaners, but God's devastation of Edom will be complete.
7: *There is no understanding in him:* Edom's faithless allies assure one another that he does not have sense enough to be able to defend himself.

8: *The wise men:* Edom was proverbial for its wise men; cf Jer 49, 7.
9: *Teman:* one of the names used for the land southeast of Palestine, here synonymous with Edom. *Esau:* here used as the name of the land.
10: *Your brother Jacob:* Esau, also called Edom,

and Jacob, the father of Judah, were the sons of Isaac (Gn 25, 24ff).
11: After the devastation of Judah, Edom occupied the southern part of its territory. Edomites also joined the invading Chaldean forces (13) and assisted them in capturing the people of Judah (14).

As you have done, so shall it be
     done to you,
     your deed shall come back
     upon your own head;
16 As you have drunk upon my
     holy mountain,
     so shall all the nations drink
     continually.
   Yes, they shall drink and
     swallow,
     and shall become as though
     they had not been.

Judah Shall Be Restored

17 But on Mount Zion there shall
     be a portion saved;
     the mountain shall be holy,

And the house of Jacob shall
     take possession
     of those that dispossessed them.
18 The house of Jacob shall be a fire,
     and the house of Joseph a
     flame;
   The house of Esau shall be
     stubble,
     and they shall set them ablaze
     and devour them;
   Then none shall survive of the
     house of Esau,
     for the LORD has spoken.
19 They shall occupy the Negeb,
     the mount of Esau,
     and the foothills of the
     Philistines;

And they shall occupy the lands
     of Ephraim
     and the lands of Samaria,
   And Benjamin shall occupy Gilead.
20 The captives of this host of the
     children of Israel
     shall occupy the Canaanite
     land as far as Zarephath,
   And the captives of Jerusalem
     who are in Sepharad
     shall occupy the cities of the
     Negeb.
21 And saviors shall ascend Mount
     Zion
     to rule the mount of Esau,
     and the kingship shall be the
     LORD's.

16: *As you have drunk:* the Lord addresses the people of Judah. As the people of Jerusalem have drunk the cup of retribution, so shall the nations, and especially Edom (18), suffer punishment. This metaphorical use of drinking the cup of God's wrath is common in the Bible; cf Jb 21, 20; Is 19, 14; Jer 25, 15f.

17ff: The Israelites shall be restored and shall occupy the lands of those who oppressed them. The survivors of Judah shall be rejoined by the returned exiles from northern Israel.

20: *Zarephath:* a town in Phoenica, north of Tyre; cf 1 Kgs 17, 10. Ezekiel's ideal boundaries of the new

Israel (47, 13ff) extend farther north. *Sepharad:* probably Sardis in western Asia Minor. The later rabbis thought it to be Spain.

21: *Saviors:* the victorious Israelites who will rule over their enemies after the fashion of the ancient Judges; cf Jgs 3, 9.15.31; 10, 1.

Jonah

The First Mission

THIS is the word of the LORD that came to Jonah, son of Amittai: 2 "Set out for the great city of Nineveh, and preach against it; their wickedness has come up before me." 3 But Jonah made ready to flee to Tarshish away from the LORD. He went to Joppa, found a ship going to Tarshish, paid the fare, and went aboard to journey with them to Tarshish, away from the LORD.

4 The LORD, however, hurled a violent wind upon the sea, and in the furious tempest that arose the ship was on the point of breaking up. 5 Then the mariners became frightened and each one cried to his god. To lighten the ship for themselves, they threw its cargo into the sea. Meanwhile, Jonah had gone down into the hold of the ship, and lay there fast asleep. 6 The captain came to him and said, "What are you doing asleep? Rise up, call upon your God! Perhaps God will be mindful of us so that we may not perish."

7 Then they said to one another, "Come, let us cast lots to find out on whose account we have met with this misfortune." So they cast lots, and thus singled out Jonah. 8 "Tell us," they said, "what is your business? Where do you come from? What is your country, and to what people do you belong?" 9 "I am a Hebrew," Jonah answered them; "I worship the LORD, the God of heaven, who made the sea and the dry land."

10 Now the men were seized with great fear and said to him, "How could you do such a thing!"—They knew that he was fleeing from the LORD, because he had told them.— 11 "What shall we do with you," they asked, "that the sea may quiet down for us?" For the sea was growing more and more turbulent. 12 Jonah said to them, "Pick me up and throw me into the sea, that it may quiet down for you; since I know it is because of me that this violent storm has come upon you."

13 Still the men rowed hard to regain the land, but they could not, for the sea grew ever more turbulent. 14 Then they cried to the LORD: "We beseech you, O LORD, let us not perish for taking this man's life; do not charge us with shedding innocent blood, for you, LORD, have done as you saw fit." 15 Then they took Jonah and threw him into the sea, and the sea's raging abated. 16 Struck with great fear of the LORD, the men offered sacrifice and made vows to him.

2 But the LORD sent a large fish, that swallowed Jonah; and he remained in the belly of the fish three days and three nights. 2 From the belly of the fish Jonah said this prayer to the LORD, his God:

Psalm of Thanksgiving

3 Out of my distress I called to
    the LORD,
    and he answered me;
From the midst of the nether
    world I cried for help,
    and you heard my voice.
4 For you cast me into the deep,
    into the heart of the sea,
    and the flood enveloped me;
All your breakers and your
    billows
    passed over me.
5 Then I said, "I am banished
    from your sight!
    yet would I again look upon
    your holy temple."

1, 1: *Jonah, son of Amittai:* a prophet of this name lived at the time of Jeroboam II (786–746 B.C.).
1, 3: *Tarshish:* identified by many with Tartessus, an ancient Phoenician colony in southwest Spain; precise identification with any particular Phoenician center in the western Mediterranean is uncertain. To the Hebrews it stood for the far west.

1, 14: Since it has pleased the Lord to punish Jonah, the mariners ask that in ridding themselves of him they be not charged with the crime of murder.

6 The waters swirled about me,
　　threatening my life;
　the abyss enveloped me;
　seaweed clung about my head.
7 Down I went to the roots of
　　the mountains;
　the bars of the nether world
　　were closing behind me
　　forever,
　But you brought up my life
　　from the pit,
　O Lord, my God.
8 When my soul fainted within
　　me,
　I remembered the Lord;
　My prayer reached you
　　in your holy temple.
9 Those who worship vain idols
　　forsake their source of mercy.
10 But I, with resounding praise,
　　will sacrifice to you;
　What I have vowed I will pay:
　　deliverance is from the Lord.

11 Then the Lord commanded the
fish to spew Jonah upon the shore.

Conversion of Nineveh

3 The word of the Lord came to
Jonah a second time: 2 "Set
out for the great city of Nineveh, and
announce to it the message that I will
tell you." 3 So Jonah made ready
and went to Nineveh, according to
the Lord's bidding. Now Nineveh
was an enormously large city; it took
three days to go through it. 4
Jonah began his journey through the
city, and had gone but a single day's
walk announcing, "Forty days more
and Nineveh shall be destroyed," 5
when the people of Nineveh believed
God; they proclaimed a fast and all
of them, great and small, put on
sackcloth.
6 When the news reached the king
of Nineveh, he rose from his throne,
laid aside his robe, covered himself
with sackcloth, and sat in the ashes.
7 Then he had this proclaimed
throughout Nineveh, by decree of the
king and his nobles: "Neither man
nor beast, neither cattle nor sheep,
shall taste anything; they shall not
eat, nor shall they drink water. 8
Man and beast shall be covered with
sackcloth and call loudly to God;
every man shall turn from his evil
way and from the violence he has in
hand. 9 Who knows, God may
relent and forgive, and withhold his
blazing wrath, so that we shall not
perish." 10 When God saw by their
actions how they turned from their
evil way, he repented of the evil that
he had threatened to do to them; he
did not carry it out.

Jonah's Anger: God's Reproof

4 But this was greatly displeasing
to Jonah, and he became angry.
2 "I beseech you, Lord," he prayed,
"is not this what I said while I was
still in my own country? This is why
I fled at first to Tarshish. I knew that
you are a gracious and merciful God,
slow to anger, rich in clemency,
loathe to punish. 3 And now, Lord,
please take my life from me; for it
is better for me to die than to live."
4 But the Lord asked, "Have you
reason to be angry?"
5 Jonah then left the city for a
place to the east of it, where he built
himself a hut and waited under it in
the shade, to see what would happen
to the city. 6 And when the Lord
God provided a gourd plant, that
grew up over Jonah's head, giving
shade that relieved him of any dis-
comfort, Jonah was very happy over
the plant. 7 But the next morning
at dawn God sent a worm which
attacked the plant, so that it withered.
8 And when the sun arose, God sent
a burning east wind; and the sun
beat upon Jonah's head till he became
faint. Then he asked for death, saying,
"I would be better off dead than
alive."
9 But God said to Jonah, "Have
you reason to be angry over the
plant?" "I have reason to be angry,"
Jonah answered, "angry enough to
die." 10 Then the Lord said, "You
are concerned over the plant which
cost you no labor and which you
did not raise; it came up in one night
and in one night it perished. 11
And should I not be concerned over
Nineveh, the great city, in which
there are more than a hundred and
twenty thousand persons who cannot
distinguish their right hand from their
left, not to mention the many cattle?"

3, 4: *Shall be destroyed:* the Hebrew expression
reminds the reader of the "overthrowing" of the
wicked cities, Sodom and Gomorrah, by a special act
of God.

3, 8: *Beast . . . sackcloth:* the animals carried the
signs of this repentance, as on occasions of joy they
bore garlands.

4, 1: *He became angry:* because of his narrowly

nationalistic vindictiveness, Jonah did not wish the
Lord to forgive the Ninevites.

4, 6: *Gourd plant:* the Hebrew word, *kikayon* means
here a wide-leafed plant of the cucumber or castor-
bean variety.

4, 10f: Jonah is selfish in bemoaning his personal
loss of a shady gourd plant without any concern over
the threat of loss of life to the Ninevites through the

destruction of their city. If God in his kindness provided the plant for his prophet without the latter's
effort or merit, how much more is he disposed to show
love and mercy toward all men, Jew and Gentile, when
they repent of their sins and implore his pardon!
God's providence is also shown here to extend even
to animals

Micah

PUNISHMENT OF ISRAEL'S SINS

Divine Judgment

THE word of the LORD which came to Micah of Moresheth in the days of Jotham, Ahaz, and Hezekiah, kings of Judah: that is, the vision he received concerning Samaria and Jerusalem. 2 HEAR, O PEOPLES, all of you, give heed, O earth, and all that fills you! Let the

Lord GOD be witness
against you,
the Lord from his holy temple!

3 For see, the LORD comes forth
from his place,
he descends and treads upon
the heights of the earth.
4 The mountains melt under him
and the valleys split open,
Like wax before the fire,
like water poured down a
slope.

5 For the crime of Jacob all this
comes to pass,
and for the sins of the house
of Israel.
What is the crime of Jacob?
Is it not Samaria?
And what is the sin of the house
of Judah?
Is it not Jerusalem?
6 I will make Samaria a stone
heap in the field,
a place to plant for vineyards;

I will throw down into the
valley her stones,
and lay bare her foundations.

7 All her idols shall be broken to
pieces,
all her wages shall be burned
in the fire,
and all her statues I will
destroy.
As the wages of a harlot they
were gathered,
and to the wages of a harlot
shall they return.

8 For this reason I lament and
wail,
I go barefoot and naked;
I utter lamentation like the
jackals,
and mourning like the
ostriches.
9 There is no remedy for the blow
she has been struck;
rather, it has come even to
Judah,

It reaches to the gate of my
people,
even to Jerusalem.

10 Publish it not in Gath,
weep not at all;
In Beth-leaphrah
roll in the dust.
11 Pass by,
you who dwell in Shaphir!
The inhabitants of Zaanan
come not forth from their city.
The lamentation of Beth-ezel
finds in you its grounds.
12 How can the inhabitants of
Maroth
hope for good?
For evil has come down from
the LORD
to the gate of Jerusalem.

13 Harness steeds to the chariots,
O inhabitants of Lachish;
Lachish, the beginning of sin
for daughter Zion,
Because there were in you
the crimes of Israel.

1, 2: *His holy temple:* God's heavenly temple; the
prophet pictures a theophany (3f).
1, 7: The comparison of the unfaithful people with
a prostitute, first found in Hosea, is frequent with the
prophets; probably ritual prostitution is meant; cf
Am 2, 7f; Hos 4, 14.
1, 10–15: The Judean cities here named were in the
vicinity of Moresheth, the region with which Micah
was most familiar. They were to experience divine
chastisement. In the Hebrew, wordplays on the names
of these cities abound. The text is partly obscure.

14 Therefore you shall give parting
      gifts
   to Moresheth-gath;
   Beth-achzib is a deception
   to the kings of Israel.
15 Yet must I bring to you the
      the conqueror,
   O inhabitants of Mareshah;
   Even to Adullam shall go
   the glory of Israel.

16 Make yourself bald, pluck out
      your hair,
   for the children whom you
      cherish;
   Let your baldness be as the
      eagle's,
   because they are exiled from
      you.

Social Evils

2 Woe to those who plan iniquity,
   and work out evil on their
      couches;
   In the morning light they
      accomplish it
   when it lies within their
      power.
2 They covet fields, and seize
      them;
   houses, and they take them;
   They cheat an owner of his
      house,
   a man of his inheritance.

3 Therefore thus says the LORD:
   Behold, I am planning against
      this race an evil
   from which you shall not
      withdraw your necks;
   Nor shall you walk with head
      high,
   for it will be a time of evil.

4 On that day a satire shall be
      sung over you,
   and there shall be a plaintive
      chant:
   "Our ruin is complete,
   our fields are portioned out
      among our captors,

   The fields of my people are
      measured out,
   and no one can get them
      back!"
5 Thus you shall have no one
   to mark out boundaries by
      lot
   in the assembly of the LORD.

6 "Preach not," they preach,
   "let them not preach of these
      things!"
   The shame will not withdraw.
7 How can it be said, O house of
      Jacob,
   "Is the LORD short of patience,
   or are such his deeds?"
   Do not my words promise good
   to him who walks uprightly?

8 But of late my people has risen
      up as an enemy:
   you have stripped off the
      mantle covering the tunic
   Of those who go their way in
      confidence,
   as though it were spoils of
      war.
9 The women of my people you
      drive out
   from their pleasant houses;
   From their children you take
      away
   forever the honor I gave them.
10 "Up! Be off,
   this is no place to rest";
   For any trifle you exact
   a crippling pledge.

11 If one, acting on impulse, should
      make the futile claim:
   "I pour you wine and strong
      drink as my prophesy,"
   then he would be the prophet
   of this people.
12 I will gather you, O Jacob, each
      and every one,
   I will assemble all the remnant
      of Israel;
   I will group them like a flock in
      the fold,

   like a herd in the midst of its
      corral;
   they shall not be thrown into
      panic by men.
13 With a leader to break the path
   they shall burst open the gate
      and go out through it;
   Their king shall go through
      before them,
   and the LORD at their head.

Downfall of Present Leaders

3 And I said:
   Hear, you leaders of Jacob,
   rulers of the house of Israel!
   Is it not your duty to know what
      is right,
2 You who hate what is good,
      and love evil?
   You who tear their skin from
      them,
   and their flesh from their
      bones!
3 They eat the flesh of my people,
   and flay their skin from them,
   and break their bones.
   They chop them in pieces like
      flesh in a kettle,
   and like meat in a caldron
4 When they cry to the LORD,
   he shall not answer them;
   Rather shall he hide his face
      from them at that time,
   because of the evil they have
      done.

5 Thus says the LORD regarding
      the prophets
   who lead my people astray;
   Who, when their teeth have
      something to bite,
      announce peace,
   But when one fails to put
      something in their mouth,
   proclaim war against him.
6 Therefore you shall have night,
      not vision,
   darkness, not divination;
   The sun shall go down upon the
      prophets,
   and the day shall be dark for
      them.

1, 16: Shaving the head was a sign of mourning; cf Is 3, 24; Am 8, 10.
2, 2: Land monopoly, also denounced by Isaiah, was a chronic vice in Judah. To protect the poor against it, a man's *inheritance*, his ancestral property, was supposed to be inviolate; cf 1 Kgs 21, 1–4; but the wealthy in their greed were enslaving men for their debts and depriving them of their land.
2, 5: To mark out boundaries by lot: an allusion to the initial distribution of the land of Palestine among the Israelites; cf Jos 13–21. The appropriate punish-
ment of those greedy for land will be the loss of their land to their enemies (v 4), a loss that will be irrevoc-able.
2, 6f: The words in quotation marks are the protestations of the people against the prophet's predictions of doom.
2, 9: The honor I gave them: their dignity as free Israelites.
2, 10: A crippling pledge: Israelite law forbade exacting pledges for loans that would work hardship on the borrower (Ex 22, 25f; Dt 24, 6.10–13.17); but
the law was habitually violated.
2, 12f: This Messianic passage concerning the restoration after the Babylonian Exile seems out of place here and is probably a later addition.
3, 5–8: Almost all the prophetic books contain oracles against the false prophets. Here Micah accuses them of prophesying for venal motives and determining the prophecy by the price that is paid them; he contrasts his own disinterested preaching of the word of God.

7 Then shall the seers be put to
        shame,
    and the diviners confounded;
  They shall cover their lips, all
        of them,
    because there is no answer
        from God.
8 But as for me, I am filled with
        power,
    with the spirit of the LORD,
    with authority and with might;
  To declare to Jacob his crimes
    and to Israel his sins.

9 Hear this, you leaders of the
        house of Jacob,
    you rulers of the house of
        Israel!
  You who abhor what is just,
    and pervert all that is right;
10 Who build up Zion with
        bloodshed,
    and Jerusalem with
        wickedness!
11 Her leaders render judgment
        for a bribe,
    her priests give decisions for
        a salary,
    her prophets divine for money,
  While they rely on the LORD,
        saying,
    "Is not the LORD in the midst
        of us?
    No evil can come upon us!"
12 Therefore, because of you,
    Zion shall be plowed like a
        field,
    and Jerusalem reduced to
        rubble,
  And the mount of the temple
    to a forest ridge.

THE NEW ISRAEL

The People To Be Restored

4 In days to come
    the mount of the LORD's
        house
  Shall be established higher than
        the mountains;
    it shall rise above the hills,
  And peoples shall stream to it:
2   Many nations shall come, and
        say,

"Come, let us climb the mount
        of the LORD,
    to the house of the God of
        Jacob,
  That he may instruct us in his
        ways,
    that we may walk in his paths."
  For from Zion shall go forth
        instruction,
    and the word of the LORD
        from Jerusalem.
3 He shall judge between many
        peoples
    and impose terms on strong
        and distant nations;
  They shall beat their swords
        into plowshares,
    and their spears into pruning
        hooks;
  One nation shall not raise the
        sword against another,
    nor shall they train for war
        again.
4 Every man shall sit under his
        own vine
    or under his own fig tree,
        undisturbed;
    for the mouth of the LORD of
        hosts has spoken.
5 For all the peoples walk
    each in the name of its god,
  But we will walk in the name of
        the LORD,
    our God, forever and ever.

6 On that day, says the LORD,
    I will gather the lame,
  And I will assemble the outcasts,
    and those whom I have
        afflicted.
7 I will make of the lame a
        remnant,
    and of those driven far off a
        strong nation;
  And the LORD shall be king
    over them on Mount Zion,
    from now on forever.
8 And you, O Magdal-eder,
    hillock of daughter Zion!
  Unto you shall it come:
    the former dominion shall be
        restored,
    the kingdom of daughter
        Jerusalem.

9 Now why do you cry out so?
    Are you without a king?
    Or has your counselor
        perished,
  That you are seized with pains
    like a woman in travail?
10 Writhe in pain, grow faint,
    O daughter Zion,
    like a woman in travail;
  For now shall you go forth from
        the city
    and dwell in the fields;
  To Babylon shall you go,
    there shall you be rescued.
  There shall the LORD redeem you
    from the hand of your enemies.

11 How many nations are gathered
        against you!
    They say, "Let her be profaned,
    let our eyes see Zion's
        downfall!"
12 But they know not the thoughts
        of the LORD,
    nor understand his counsel,
  When he has gathered them
    like sheaves on the threshing
        floor.
13 Arise and thresh, O daughter
        Zion;
    your horn I will make iron
  And your hoofs bronze,
    that you may crush many
        peoples;
  You shall devote their spoils to
        the LORD,
    and their riches to the Lord
        of the whole earth.

Restoration through the Messiah

14 Now fence yourself in, Bat-gader!
    "They have laid siege against
        us!"
  With the rod they strike on the
        cheek
    the ruler of Israel.

5 But you, Bethlehem-Ephrathah
    too small to be among the
        clans of Judah,
  From you shall come forth for
        me
    one who is to be ruler in
        Israel;

4, 1ff: See note on Is 2, 2ff.
4, 8: *Magdal-eder:* "tower of the flock," an ancient place name (cf Gn 35, 21), here used symbolically of Jerusalem.
4, 10: *For now . . . your enemies:* probably a later addition to the text, when the prediction of exile had been fulfilled in the Babylonian captivity. The prophet

sees the Exile as the means whereby God will purify and restore his people.
4, 14: *Bat-gader:* "fenced-in maiden," another symbolic name for Jerusalem, then under siege from the Assyrians.
5, 1: In contrast to Bat-gader (4, 14), where *the ruler of Israel,* the reigning king, is in peril of his life

from the Assyrians, is the tiny city and clan of *Bethlehem-Ephrathah,* from which comes the ancient Davidic dynasty (*whose origin is from of old, from ancient times*) with its Messianic king, *one who is to be ruler in Israel.*

Whose origin is from of old,
  from ancient times.
2 (Therefore the Lord will give
    them up, until the time
  when she who is to give birth
    has borne,
And the rest of his brethren
    shall return
  to the children of Israel.)
3 He shall stand firm and shepherd
    his flock
  by the strength of the LORD,
  in the majestic name of the
    LORD, his God;
And they shall remain, for now
    his greatness
  shall reach to the ends of the
    earth;
4   he shall be peace.

If Assyria invades our country
  and treads upon our land,
We shall raise against it seven
    shepherds,
  eight men of royal rank;
5 And they shall tend the land of
    Assyria with the sword,
  and the land of Nimrod with
    the drawn sword;
And we shall be delivered from
    Assyria,
  if it invades our land
  and treads upon our borders.

6 The remnant of Jacob shall be
  in the midst of many peoples,
Like dew coming from the
    LORD,
  like raindrops on the grass,
Which wait for no man,
  nor tarry for the sons of men.
7 And the remnant of Jacob shall
    be among the nations,
  in the midst of many peoples,
Like a lion among beasts of the
    forest,
  like a young lion among
    flocks of sheep;

When it passes through, it
    tramples
  and tears, and there is none to
    deliver.
8 Your hand shall be lifted above
    your foes,
  and all your enemies shall be
    destroyed.

9   On that day, says the LORD,
I will destroy the horses from
    your midst
  and ruin your chariots;
10 I will demolish the cities of your
    land
  and tear down all your
    fortresses.
11 I will abolish the means of
    divination from your use,
  and there shall no longer be
    soothsayers among you.
12 I will abolish your carved images
    and the sacred pillars from
    your midst;
And you shall no longer adore
  the works of your hands.
13 I will tear out the sacred poles
    from your midst,
  and destroy your cities.
14 I will wreak vengeance in anger
    and wrath
  upon the nations that have not
    hearkened.

ADMONITION

Accusation and Answer

6 Hear, then, what the LORD says:
Arise, present your plea before
    the mountains,
  and let the hills hear your
    voice!
2 Hear, O mountains, the plea of
    the LORD,
  pay attention, O foundations of
    the earth!
For the LORD has a plea against
    his people,
  and he enters into trial with
    Israel.

3 O my people, what have I done to
    you,
  or how have I wearied you?
    Answer me!
4 For I brought you up from the
    land of Egypt,
  from the place of slavery I
    released you;
And I sent before you Moses,
    Aaron, and Miriam.
5 My people, remember what
    Moab's King Balak planned,
  and how Balaam, the son of
    Beor, answered him
  . . . from Shittim to Gilgal,
  that you may know the just
    deeds of the LORD.

6 With what shall I come before the
    LORD,
  and bow before God most high?
Shall I come before him with
    holocausts,
  with calves a year old?
7 Will the LORD be pleased with
    thousands of rams,
  with myriad streams of oil?
Shall I give my first-born for my
    crime,
  the fruit of my body for the sin
    of my soul?
8 You have been told, O man, what
    is good,
  and what the LORD requires of
    you:
Only to do the right and to love
    goodness,
  and to walk humbly with your
    God.

9 Hark! the LORD cries to the city.
  [It is wisdom to fear your
    name!]
  Hear, O tribe and city council,
12 You whose rich men are full of
    violence,
  whose inhabitants speak
    falsehood
  with deceitful tongues in their
    heads!

5, 2: *She who is to give birth:* the mother of the Messiah: cf Is 7, 14.

5, 4f: This passage, expressing confidence in Judah's ability to deliver itself from Assyria, is in contrast with the preceding Messianic oracle, which ascribes deliverance to the Lord and his agent. Some believe that here the prophet is quoting the words of the defiant men of Judah. The *shepherds* and *men of royal rank* are one and the same: warriors capable of routing Assyria. The same kind of numerical progression is used by Amos (1, 3), and elsewhere in the Bible.

5, 5: *Nimrod:* the legendary ancestor of the Mesopotamians; cf Gn 10, 10ff.

5, 9-13: Part of the Messianic restoration will

consist in the removal of everything that has drawn Israel away from the Lord; this includes not only the objects of false worship, but also the armaments in which the idolators had trusted.

5, 12f: *Sacred pillars . . . sacred poles:* see note on Ex 34, 13.

6, 5: *From Shittim to Gilgal:* from the east to the west side of the Jordan; the events described in Jos 3-5 are meant. The text is defective; however, it is evident that this verse continues the remembrance of God's deeds of mercy to Israel, beginning with the Exodus (v 4) and extending to the conquest, deeds which have provoked so little response from his people.

6, 6ff: The people ask how they shall worship the Lord, proposing the various forms of sacrifice. The prophet replies that sacrifice avails nothing without the true spirit of religion. This is one of the best expressions of the prophetic teaching on religion, the preparation for such New Testament passages as Jas 1, 27.

6, 7: *Shall I give my first-born:* through Canaanite influence the abominable practice of human sacrifice had been introduced under impious kings (cf 2 Kgs 16, 3; 21, 6).

6, 9: *The city:* Jerusalem as the embodiment of the crimes of the entire land.

10 Am I to bear any longer criminal
      hoarding
      and the meager ephah that is
      accursed?
11 Shall I acquit criminal balances,
      bags of false weights?

13 Rather I will begin to strike you
      with devastation because of
      your sins.
15 You shall sow, yet not reap,
      tread out the olive, yet pour no
      oil,
      and the grapes, yet drink no
      wine.
14 You shall eat, without being
      satisfied,
      food that will leave you empty;
   What you acquire, you cannot
      save;
      what you do save, I will deliver
      up to the sword.
16 You have kept the decrees of
      Omri,
      and all the works of the house
      of Ahab,
      and you have walked in their
      counsels;
   Therefore I will deliver you up to
      ruin,
      and your citizens to derision;
      and you shall bear the reproach
      of the nations.

Condemnation and Prayer

7 Alas! I am as when the fruit is
      gathered,
      as when the vines have been
      gleaned;
   There is no cluster to eat,
      no early fig that I crave.
2 The faithful are gone from the
      earth,
      among men the upright are no
      more!
   They all lie in wait to shed blood,
      each one ensnares the other.
3 Their hands succeed at evil;
      the prince makes demands,
   The judge is had for a price,
   The great man speaks as he
      pleases,

4 The best of them is like a brier,
      the most upright like a thorn
      hedge.

   The day announced by your
      watchmen!
      your punishment has come;
      now is the time of your con-
      fusion.
5 Put no trust in a friend,
      have no confidence in a com-
      panion;
   Against her who lies in your
      bosom
      guard the portals of your
      mouth.
6 For the son dishonors his father,
      the daughter rises up against
      her mother,
   The daughter-in-law against her
      mother-in-law,
      and a man's enemies are those
      of his household.
7 But as for me, I will look to the
      LORD,
      I will put my trust in God my
      savior;
      my God will hear me!
8 Rejoice not over me, O my
      enemy!
      though I have fallen, I will
      arise;
      though I sit in darkness, the
      LORD is my light.
9 The wrath of the LORD I will
      endure
      because I have sinned against
      him,
   Until he takes up my cause,
      and establishes my right.
   He will bring me forth to the light;
      I will see his justice.
10 When my enemy sees this,
      shame shall cover her:
   She who said to me,
      "Where is the LORD, thy God?"
   My eyes shall see her downfall;
      now shall she be trampled
      underfoot,
      like the mire in the streets.
11 It is the day for building your
      walls;
      on that day the boundary shall
      be taken away.

12 It is the day; and they shall come
      to you
      from Assyria and from Egypt,
   From Tyre even to the River,
      from sea to sea, and from
      mountain to mountain;
13 And the land shall be a waste
      because of its citizens,
      as a result of their deeds.

14 Shepherd your people with your
      staff,
      the flock of your inheritance,
   That dwells apart in a woodland,
      in the midst of Carmel.
   Let them feed in Bashan and
      Gilead,
      as in the days of old;
15 As in the days when you came
      from the land of Egypt,
      show us wonderful signs.

16 The nations shall behold and be
      put to shame,
      in spite of all their strength;
   They shall put their hands over
      their mouths;
      their ears shall become deaf.
17 They shall lick the dust like the
      serpent,
      like reptiles on the ground;
   They shall come quaking from
      their fastnesses,
      trembling in fear of you [the
      LORD, our God].
18 Who is there like you, the God
      who removes guilt
      and pardons sin for the
      remnant of his inheritance;
   Who does not persist in anger
      forever,
      but delights rather in clemency,
19 And will again have compassion
      on us,
      treading underfoot out guilt?
   You will cast into the depths of
      the sea
      all our sins;
20 You will show faithfulness to
      Jacob,
      and grace to Abraham,
   As you have sworn to our
      fathers
      from days of old.

6, 16: Judah has followed the example of the northern kingdom epitomized in the semipaganism of
Omri and his son Ahab (1 Kgs 16, 25-34), copying
both the corrupted worship and the social injustice of
their reigns.

7, 5f: Corresponding to the widespread civil
corruption and apostasy from religion is the break-

down of normal human and family relations.

7, 8ff: The unnamed enemy of Judah mentioned in
these verses may be Assyria or one of the neighboring
countries, such as Edom, which stood by to profit at
Judah's downfall.

7, 11ff: This prophecy of restoration and repopula-
tion of the promised land by the Jews now in exile

appears to be from the period after the destruction of
Jerusalem by the Chaldeans (587 B.C.).

7, 14–17: This prayer appears to be from the time
after the return from exile (537 B.C.), when the people,
few in number, possessed only a fragment of their
former land, and were surrounded by hostile nations.

Nahum

The Lord's Coming in Judgment

ORACLE about Nineveh. The book of the vision of Nahum of Elkosh. 2 A jealous and avenging God is the Lord, an avenger is the Lord, and angry; The Lord brings vengeance on his adversaries, and lays up wrath for his enemies; 3 The Lord is slow to anger,

yet great in power,
and the Lord never leaves the
guilty unpunished.
In hurricane and tempest is his
path,
and clouds are the dust at his
feet;
4 He rebukes the sea and leaves it
dry,
and all the rivers he dries up.
Withered are Bashan and Carmel,
and the bloom of Lebanon
fades;
5 The mountains quake before him,
and the hills dissolve;
The earth is laid waste before him,
the world and all who dwell in
it.
6 Before his wrath, who can stand
firm,
and who can face his blazing
anger?
His fury is poured out like fire,
and the rocks are rent asunder
before him.
7 The Lord is good,
a refuge on the day of distress;

He takes care of those who have
recourse to him,
8   when the flood rages;
He makes an end of his
opponents,
and his enemies he pursues with
darkness.

9 What are you imputing to the
Lord?
It is he who will make an end!
The enemy shall not rise a
second time;
10 As when a tangle of thornbushes
is set aflame,
like dry stubble, they shall be
utterly consumed.
12 For, says the Lord,
be they ever so many and so
vigorous,
still they shall be mown down
and disappear.
Though I have humbled you,
I will humble you no more.
13 Now will I break his yoke from
off you,
and burst asunder your bonds.

11 From you he came
who devised evil against the
Lord,
the scoundrel planner.

14 The Lord has commanded
regarding you:
no descendant shall come to
bear your name;
From your temple I will abolish
the carved and the molten
image;
I will make your grave a
mockery.

2 See, upon the mountains there
advances
the bearer of good news,
announcing peace!
Celebrate your feasts, O Judah,
fulfill your vows!
For nevermore shall you be
invaded
by the scoundrel; he is
completely destroyed.

1, 2–8: A poem written in the style of the alphabetic psalms; cf Pss 9A; 25; 111; 119. Here,
however, most of the verses beginning with the letters
of the second half of the alphabet are not preserved.
1, 2: *A jealous . . . God:* see note on Ex 20, 5.
1, 4: *Bashan, Carmel* and *Lebanon* were famous for
their forests.

1, 6f: The coming of God in judgment has two
aspects: to those who oppose him it will be un-
bearable; to *those who have recourse to him* it will
bring strength and consolation.
1, 9: *What are you imputing to the Lord?:* the people
of Judah are asked what they think God has in
mind.

1, 12f: *They:* the enemies of Judah. *You:* Judah.
His yoke: the dominion of the Assyrian king over
Judah.
1, 11: *From you . . . the scoundrel planner:* addressed to Nineveh, the capital city of Sennacherib,
king of Assyria, who besieged Jerusalem c. 700 B.C.
1, 14: *You:* the king of Assyria.

3 The LORD will restore the vine of
    Jacob,
        the pride of Israel,
  Though ravagers have ravaged
    them
        and ruined the tendrils.

The Fall of Nineveh

2 The hammer comes up against
    you;
        guard the rampart,
  Keep watch on the road, gird
    your loins,
        marshal all your strength!
4 The shields of his warriors are
    crimsoned,
        the soldiers colored in scarlet;
  Fiery steel are the chariots
        on the day of his mustering.
  The horses are frenzied;
5   the chariots dash madly through
        the streets
  And wheel in the squares,
        looking like firebrands,
        flashing like lightning bolts.
6 His picked troops are called,
        ranks break at their charge;
  To the wall they rush,
        the mantelet is set up.
7 The river gates are opened,
        the palace shudders.
8 Its mistress is led forth captive,
        and her handmaids, under
        guard,
  Moaning like doves,
        beating their breasts.
9 Nineveh is like a pool
        whose waters escape;
  "Stop! Stop!"
        but none turns back.
10 "Plunder the silver, plunder the
        gold!"
  There is no end to the treasure,
        to their wealth in precious
        things of every kind!

11 Emptiness, desolation, waste;
        melting hearts and trembling
        knees,
  Writhing in every frame,
        every face blanched!
12 Where is the lions' cave,
        the young lions' den,

Where the lion went in and out,
        and the cub, with no one to
        disturb them?
13 The lion snatched enough for his
        cubs,
        and strangled for his lionesses;
  He filled his dens with prey,
        and his caves with plunder.
14 I come against you,
        says the LORD of hosts;
  I will consume in smoke your
        chariots,
        and the sword shall devour
        your young lions;
  Your preying on the land I will
        bring to an end,
        the cry of your lionesses shall
        be heard no more.

Ruin Imminent and Inevitable

3 Woe to the bloody city, all lies,
    full of plunder, whose looting
        never stops!
2 The crack of the whip, the
        rumbling sound of wheels;
        horses a-gallop, chariots
        bounding,
3 Cavalry charging,
  The flame of the sword, the flash
        of the spear,
        the many slain, the heaping
        corpses,
        the endless bodies to stumble
        upon!
4 For the many debaucheries of the
        harlot,
        fair and charming, a mistress of
        witchcraft,
  Who enslaved nations with her
        harlotries,
        and peoples by her witchcraft:
5 I am come against you,
        and I will strip your skirt from
        you;
  I will show your nakedness to the
        nations,
        to the kingdoms your shame!
6 I will cast filth upon you,
        disgrace you and put you to
        shame;
7 Till everyone who sees you runs
        from you, saying,

"Nineveh is destroyed; who
        can pity her?
  Where can one find any to
        console her?"

8 Are you better than No-amon
        that was set among the streams,
  Surrounded by waters,
        with the flood for her rampart
        and water her wall?
9 Ethiopia was her strength, and
        Egypt,
        and others without end;
  Put and the Libyans were her
        auxiliaries.
10 Yet even she went captive into
        exile,
        even her little ones were dashed
        to pieces
        at the corner of every street;
  For her nobles they cast lots,
        and all her great men were put
        into chains.
11 You, too, shall drink of this till
        you faint away;
        you, too, shall seek a refuge
        from the foe.
12 All your fortresses are but fig
        trees,
        bearing early figs
  That fall, when shaken,
        into the hungry mouth.
13 See, the troops are women in your
        midst;
        to your foes the gates of your
        land are open wide,
        fire has consumed their bars.
14 Draw water for the siege,
        strengthen your fortresses;
  Go down into the mud and tread
        the clay,
        take hold of the brick mold!
15 There the fire shall consume you,
        the sword shall cut you down.

  Multiply like the grasshoppers,
        multiply like the locusts!
16 Make your couriers more num-
        erous than the stars,
17   your garrisons as many as
        grasshoppers,
  And your scribes as locust swarms
        gathered on the rubble fences
        on a cold day!

2, 2: *The hammer comes up against you:* the enemy
is about to crush Nineveh.
  2, 6: *Mantelet:* a movable shelter protecting the
besiegers.
  2, 8: *Mistress . . . and her handmaids:* either the
queen of Nineveh with the ladies of her court, or the

statue of Ishtar, Nineveh's chief goddess, with her
temple prostitutes.
  2, 12: *The lion:* the king of Assyria.
  3, 5f: The punishment of adulteresses.
  3, 8: *No-amon:* No was the Egyptian name of the
capital of Upper Egypt, called Thebes by the Greeks;

its tutelary deity was Amon. This great city was
destroyed by the Assyrians in 663 B.C.
  3, 14: An ironic exhortation to prepare the city for
a futile defense. *Go down . . . brick mold:* make bricks
for the city walls.

Yet when the sun warms them,
  the grasshoppers will spread
    their wings and fly,
and vanish, no one knows
    where.
18 Alas! how your shepherds slumber, O king of Assyria,
  your nobles have gone to rest;
Your people are scattered upon
    the mountains,
  with none to gather them.
19 There is no healing for your hurt,
your wound is mortal.
All who hear this news of you
  clap their hands over you;
For who has not been
    overwhelmed,
  steadily, by your malice?

Habakkuk

The Prophet's Complaint and Its Answer

THE oracle which Habakkuk THE PROPHET received in vision. 2 How long, O LORD? I cry for help but you do not listen! I cry out to you, "Violence!" but you do not intervene. 3 Why do you let me see ruin; why must I look at misery? Destruction and violence

are before me;
there is strife, and clamorous
discord.
4 This is why the law is benumbed,
and judgment is never rendered:
Because the wicked circumvent
the just;
this is why judgment comes
forth perverted.

5 Look over the nations and see,
and be utterly amazed!
For a work is being done in your
days
that you would not have
believed, were it told.
6 For see, I am raising up Chaldea,
that bitter and unruly people,
That marches the breadth of the
land
to take dwellings not his own.
7 Terrible and dreadful is he,
from himself derive his law and
his majesty.

8 Swifter than leopards are his
horses,
and keener than wolves at
evening.
His horses prance,
his horsemen come from afar:
They fly like the eagle hastening
to devour;
9 each comes for the rapine,
Their combined onset is that of a
stormwind
that heaps up captives like
sand.
10 He scoffs at kings,
and princes are his
laughingstock;
He laughs at any fortress,
heaps up a ramp, and conquers
it.
11 Then he veers like the wind and is
gone—
this culprit who makes his own
strength his god!

12 Are you not from eternity, O
LORD,
my holy God, immortal?
O LORD, you have marked him
for judgment,
O Rock, you have readied him
for punishment!
13 Too pure are your eyes to look
upon evil,
and the sight of misery you
cannot endure.
Why, then, do you gaze on the
faithless in silence
while the wicked man devours
one more just than himself?
14 You have made man like the fish
of the sea,
like creeping things without a
ruler.
15 He brings them all up with his
hook,
he hauls them away with his
net,

1, 2–4: Traditionally, these verses have been taken as the prophet's complaint against the internal evils of Judah; the language used is that employed by Amos, Isaiah, and Jeremiah to condemn the social abuses of their day. In vv 5ff the Lord answers this complaint by indicating the Chaldean empire as his instrument for punishing his people for these sins.

1, 5: *Look over the nations and see:* after Nebuchadnezzar's defeat of Egypt in 605 B.C., there could be little doubt that it was the Chaldean ambition to dominate the entire Near East.

1, 8: *Wolves at evening:* the wolf is apparently thought of as more rabid and vicious in the evening when setting out for prey (Jer 5, 6; Zep 3, 3).

1, 11: *Veers like the wind:* the conquests of the ancient Near East were mainly raiding expeditions to collect tribute. As far as administration of conquered territories was concerned, both the Assyrians and Chaldeans were usually content to install friendly rulers and then depart. *This culprit:* though the Chaldeans were used by God as the agents of his punishment, this did not diminish their own guilt as ruthless marauders.

1, 12—2, 1: It is generally thought that this complaint is directed against the Chaldeans and their

terrible destruction. But it may well be a continuation of 1, 2–4, against the wicked Judahites who have merited God's punishment.

1, 12: *O Rock:* an ancient title celebrating the Lord's power; cf Ps 18, 32.

1, 15: The *he* of this and the following verses, to whom is attributed such extensive evil and the destruction of many peoples, may be the wicked of Judah embodied in King Jehoiakim, ally of the powerful Pharaoh Neco of Egypt; the devastation wrought by Jehoiakim and Neco together is condemned.

He gathers them in his seine;
and so he rejoices and exults.
16 Therefore he sacrifices to his net,
and burns incense to his seine;
For thanks to them his portion is
generous,
and his repast sumptuous.
17 Shall he, then, keep on brandishing his sword
to slay peoples without mercy?

2 I will stand at my guard post,
and station myself upon the
rampart,
And keep watch to see what he
will say to me,
and what answer he will give to
my complaint.

2 Then the LORD answered me and
said:
Write down the vision
Clearly upon the tablets,
so that one can read it readily.
3 For the vision still has its time,
presses on to fulfillment, and
will not disappoint;
If it delays, wait for it,
it will surely come, it will not
be late.

4 The rash man has no integrity;
but the just man, because of his
faith, shall live.
Wealth, too, is treacherous:
the proud, unstable man—
5 He who opens wide his throat
like the nether world,
and is insatiable as death,
Who gathers to himself all the
nations,
and rallies to himself all the
peoples—
6 Shall not all these take up a
taunt against him,
satire and epigrams about him,
to say:

Woe to him who stores up what is
not his:
how long can it last!

he loads himself down with
debts.
7 Shall not your creditors rise
suddenly?
Shall not they who make you
tremble awake?
You shall become their spoil!
8 Because you despoiled many
peoples
all the rest of the nations shall
despoil you;
Because of men's blood shed,
and violence done to the land,
to the city and to all who dwell
in it.

9 Woe to him who pursues evil gain
for his household,
setting his nest on high
to escape the reach of
misfortune!
10 You have devised shame for your
household,
cutting off many peoples,
forfeiting your own life:
11 For the stone in the wall shall cry
out,
and the beam in the woodwork
shall answer it!

12 Woe to him who builds a city by
bloodshed,
and establishes a town by
wickedness!
13 Is not this from the LORD of hosts:
peoples toil for the flames,
and nations grow weary for
nought!
14 But the earth shall be filled
with the knowledge of the
LORD's glory
as water covers the sea.

15 Woe to you who give your
neighbors
a flood of your wrath to drink,
and make them drunk, till their
nakedness is seen!

16 You are filled with shame instead
of glory;
drink, you too, and stagger!
On you shall revert the cup from
the LORD's right hand,
and utter shame on your glory.
17 For the violence done to Lebanon
shall cover you,
and the destruction of the
beasts shall terrify you;
Because of men's blood shed,
and violence done to the land,
to the city and to all who dwell
in it.

19 Woe to him who says to wood,
"Awake!"
to dumb stone, "Arise!"
Can such a thing give oracles?
See, it is overlaid with gold and
silver,
but there is no life breath in it.
18 Of what avail is the carved image,
that its maker should carve it?
Or the molten image and lying
oracle,
that its very maker should
trust in it,
and make dumb idols?
20 But the LORD is in his holy
temple;
silence before him, all the
earth!

Canticle
Prayer of Habakkuk, the prophet.
To a plaintive tune.

3 O LORD, I have heard your
renown,
and feared, O LORD, your work.
In the course of the years revive
it,
in the course of the years make
it known;
in your wrath remember
compassion!

3 God comes from Teman,
the Holy One from Mount
Paran.

1, 16: *He sacrifices to his net:* in v 15 the wicked ruler in question is represented as catching men in a net. This verse alludes to some rite involving the sacrificial veneration of the weapons of war.
2, 4: *The just man, because of his faith, shall live:* the faith which here enables the virtuous man to survive the impending doom is both a confident belief in God's justice, and patience in awaiting its execution. St. Paul quotes these words (Rom 1, 17; Gal 3, 11; Heb 10, 38) to confirm his teaching that man receives justification and supernatural life through faith in Christ.
2, 11f: The palaces, built at the expense of gross injustice (vv 6–10), call down vengeance on their

builders. This is typical prophetic language for the condemnation of social crimes within Israel and Judah.
2, 13: *Peoples toil for the flames:* they build only to have fire consume their work, when they build contrary to God's will.
2, 17: *The violence done to Lebanon:* the spoliation of the cedar forests of Lebanon, used in lavish building projects by the great conquerors; cf Is 14, 8; 37, 24. *The destruction of the beasts:* the killing off of the wild animals through excessive hunting by the same conquerors; cf Bar 3, 16.
2, 18–20: Idolatrous worship is here shown to be folly by contrasting man-made idols with the majesty

of the one true God.
3, 1: A later liturgical rubric. So also the end of v 19.
3, 2: *In the course of the years revive it:* renew today your wondrous deeds of the past.
3, 3: *Teman:* a region in Edom. *Mount Paran:* in the territory of Edom, or the northern part of the Sinaitic peninsula. The Lord is represented as coming from Sinai, where he had appeared to Moses and given Israel the covenant and the law.
3, 3–15: Cf the theophanies in Dt 33, 2f; Jgs 5, 4f; Pss 18, 8–16; 68, 8f; 77, 17–21; 97, 1–5; Na 1, 3–6, etc. Conventional language is employed to describe the appearance of the Lord, as in Ex 19, 16–19.

Covered are the heavens with his
　　glory,
　　and with his praise the earth is
　　　filled.
4 His splendor spreads like the
　　light;
　　rays shine forth from beside
　　　him,
　　where his power is concealed.
5 Before him goes pestilence,
　　and the plague follows in his
　　　steps.
6 He pauses to survey the earth;
　　his look makes the nations
　　　tremble.
　The eternal mountains are shat-
　　tered,
　　the age-old hills bow low
　　along his ancient ways.

7 I see the tents of Cushan
　　collapse;
　　trembling are the pavilions of
　　　the land of Midian.
8 Is your anger against the streams,
　　O Lord?
　　Is your wrath against the
　　　streams,
　　your rage against the sea,

That you drive the steeds
　　of your victorious chariot?
9 Bared and ready is your bow,
　　filled with arrows is your
　　　quiver.
　Into streams you split the earth;
10　at sight of you the mountains
　　　tremble.
　A torrent of rain descends;
　　the ocean gives forth its roar.
　The sun forgets to rise,
11　the moon remains in its shelter,
　At the light of your flying arrows,
　　at the gleam of your flashing
　　　spear.

12 In wrath you bestride the earth,
　　in fury you trample the nations.
13 You come forth to save your
　　people,
　　to save your anointed one.
　You crush the heads of the
　　wicked,
　　you lay bare their bases at the
　　　neck.
14 You pierce with your shafts the
　　heads of their princes
　　whose boast would be of
　　　devouring
　　the wretched in their lair.

15 You tread the sea with your
　　steeds
　　amid the churning of the deep
　　　waters.
16 I hear, and my body trembles;
　　at the sound, my lips quiver.
　Decay invades my bones,
　　my legs tremble beneath me.
　I await the day of distress
　　that will come upon the people
　　　who attack us.

17 For though the fig tree blossom
　　not
　　nor fruit be on the vines,
　Though the yield of the olive fail
　　and the terraces produce no
　　　nourishment,
　Though the flocks disappear from
　　the fold
　　and there be no herd in the
　　　stalls,
18 Yet will I rejoice in the Lord
　　and exult in my saving God.
19 God, my Lord, is my strength;
　　he makes my feet swift as those
　　　of hinds
　　and enables me to go upon the
　　　heights.

For the leader; with stringed instruments.

3, 13: *Your anointed one:* the theocratic king, the
head of God's people.

Zephaniah

The Day of the Lord: A Day of Doom

THE word of the LORD which came to Zephaniah, the son of Cushi, the son of Gedaliah, the son of Amariah, the son of Hezekiah, in the days of Josiah, the son of Amon, king of Judah. 2 I will completely sweep away all things from the face of the earth, says the LORD.

3 I will sweep away man and beast,
  I will sweep away the birds of
    the sky,
  and the fishes of the sea.
I will overthrow the wicked;
  I will destroy mankind
  from the face of the earth, says
    the LORD.
4 I will stretch out my hand against
    Judah,
  and against all the inhabitants
    of Jerusalem;
I will destroy from this place the
    last vestige of Baal,
  the very names of his priests,
5 And those who adore the host of
    heaven on the roofs,
  with those who adore the LORD
  but swear by Milcom;
6 And those who have fallen away
    from the LORD,
  and those who do not seek the
    LORD.

7 Silence in the presence of the
    Lord GOD!
  for near is the day of the LORD,

Yes, the LORD has prepared a
    slaughter feast,
  he has consecrated his guests.
8 On the day of the LORD's
    slaughter feast
I will punish the princes, and the
    king's sons,
  and all that dress in foreign
    apparel.
9 I will punish, on that day,
  all who leap over the
    threshold,
Who fill the house of their master
  with violence and deceit.
10 On that day, says the LORD,
A cry will be heard from the Fish
    Gate,
  a wail from the New Quarter,
  loud crashing from the hills.
11 Wail, O inhabitants of the
    Mortar!
  for all the merchants will be
    destroyed,
  all who weigh out silver, done
    away with.
12 At that time I will explore
  Jerusalem with lamps;

I will punish the men who
  thicken on their lees,
Who say in their hearts,
  "Neither good nor evil can the
    LORD do."
13 Their wealth shall be given to
    pillage
  and their houses to devastation;
They will build houses, but shall
    not dwell in them,
  plant vineyards, but not drink
    their wine.
14 Near is the great day of the
    LORD,
  near and very swiftly coming;
Hark, the day of the LORD!
  bitter, then, the warrior's cry.
15 A day of wrath is that day
  a day of anguish and distress,
A day of destruction and
    desolation,
  a day of darkness and gloom,
A day of thick black clouds,
16 a day of trumpet blasts and
    battle alarm
  Against fortified cities,
  against battlements on high.

1, 5: *The host of heaven:* the stars, the worship of which was introduced into Judah by the Assyrians. *Milcom:* the god of the Ammonites; cf 1 Kgs 11, 5.7.33; 2 Kgs 23, 13.
1, 7: *He has consecrated his guests:* God has prepared those whom he has invited to share as

soldiers in the booty, or as beast and bird scavengers of carrion, on the day of slaughter. Cf Jer 46, 10; Ez 39, 17.
1, 9: *Leap over the threshold:* the reference is to a superstitious custom of the pagans, witnessed to at least in regard to the worship of Dagon (1 Sm 5, 5).

1, 10f: *The New Quarter . . . the Mortar:* sections of Jerusalem (cf 2 Kgs 22, 14).
1, 12: *The men who thicken on their lees:* those who are overconfident because, like bottles of wine in which the sediment has settled to the bottom, they have remained at peace and undisturbed for a long time.

17 I will hem men in
      till they walk like the blind,
   because they have sinned
      against the LORD;
   And their blood shall be poured
      out like dust,
      and their brains like dung.
18 Neither their silver nor their gold
      shall be able to save them
      on the day of the LORD's
         wrath,
   When in the fire of his jealousy
      all the earth shall be consumed.
   For he shall make an end, yes, a
      sudden end,
      of all who live on the earth.

The Day of the Lord: A Day of Judgment

2 Gather, gather yourselves
      together,
      O nation without shame!
2 Before you are driven away,
      like chaff that passes on;
   Before there comes upon you
      the blazing anger of the LORD:
   Before there comes upon you
      the day of the LORD's anger.
3 Seek the LORD, all you humble of
      the earth,
      who have observed his law;
   Seek justice, seek humility;
      perhaps you may be sheltered
      on the day of the LORD's anger.
4 For Gaza shall be forsaken,
      and Ashkelon shall be a waste,
   Ashdod they shall drive out at
      midday,
      and Ekron shall be uprooted.
5 Woe to you who dwell by the
      seacoast,
      to the Cretan folk!
   The word of the LORD is against
      you,
   I will humble you, land of the
      Philistines,
   and leave you to perish without
      an inhabitant!
6 The coastland of the Cretans
      shall become
      fields for shepherds, and folds
      for flocks.
7 The coast shall belong
      to the remnant of the house of
         Judah;
      by the sea they shall pasture.

In the houses of Ashkelon at
      evening
   they shall couch their flocks,
   For the LORD their God shall
      visit them,
   and bring about their
      restoration.

8 I have heard the revilings
      uttered by Moab,
   and the insults of the
      Ammonites,
   When they reviled my people
      and made boasts against their
      territory.
9 Therefore, as I live, says the
      LORD of hosts,
      the God of Israel,
   Moab shall become like Sodom,
      the land of Ammon like
         Gomorrah:
   A field of nettles and a salt pit
      and a waste forever.
   The remnant of my people shall
      plunder them,
      the survivors of my nation
      dispossess them.
10 Such shall be the requital of their
      pride,
   because they reviled and
      boasted against
      the people of the LORD of hosts.
11 The LORD shall inspire them with
      fear
   when he makes all the gods of
      earth to waste away;
   Then, each from its own place,
      all the coastlands of the nations
      shall adore him.

12 You too, O Cushites,
   shall be slain by the sword of
      the LORD.
13 He will stretch out his hand
      against the north,
      to destroy Assyria;
   He will make Nineveh a waste,
      dry as the desert.
14 In her midst shall settle in droves
      all the wild life of the hollows;
   The screech owl and the desert
      owl
      shall roost in her columns;
   Their call shall resound from the
      window,
      the raven's croak from the
      doorway.

15 Is this the exultant city
      that dwelt secure;
   That told herself,
      "There is no other than I!"
   How has she become a waste,
      a lair for wild beasts?
   Whoever passes by her
      hisses, and shakes his fist!

Reproach and Promise for Jerusalem

3 Woe to the city, rebellious and
      polluted,
      to the tyrannical city!
2 She hears no voice,
      accepts no correction;
   In the LORD she has not trusted,
      to her God she has not drawn
      near.
3 Her princes in her midst
      are roaring lions;
   Her judges are wolves of the night
      that have had no bones to
      gnaw by morning.
4 Her prophets are insolent,
      treacherous men;
   Her priests profane what is holy,
      and do violence to the law.
5 The LORD within her is just,
      who does no wrong;
   Morning after morning he renders
      judgment
      unfailingly, at dawn.

6 I have destroyed nations,
      their battlements are laid waste;
   I have made their streets deserted,
      with no one passing through;
   Their cities are devastated,
      with no man dwelling in them.
7 I said, "Surely now you will fear
      me,
      you will accept correction";
   She should not fail to see
      all I have visited upon her.
   Yet all the more eagerly have they
      done
      all their corrupt deeds.
8 Therefore, wait for me, says the
      LORD,
      against the day when I arise as
      accuser;
   For it is my decision to gather
      together the nations,
      to assemble the kingdoms,

2, 1: *Nation without shame:* Judah.
2, 4: *Gaza . . . Ashkelon . . . Ashdod . . . Ekron:* four of the five cities of the Philistine confederation. The fifth city, Gath is not mentioned, perhaps because

it was already destroyed.
2, 5: *Cretan folk:* the Philistines, who came from Crete; see note on Dt 2, 23.

2, 12: *Cushites:* the Egyptians, at this time under a Cushite or Ethiopian dynasty.
2, 15: *The exultant city:* Nineveh.

In order to pour out upon them
   my wrath,
  all my blazing anger;
For in the fire of my jealousy
  shall all the earth be consumed.

9 For then I will change and purify
  the lips of the peoples,
  That they all may call upon the
   name of the LORD,
   to serve him with one accord;
10 From beyond the rivers of Ethiopia
  and as far as the recesses of the
   North,
  they shall bring me offerings.

11   On that day
You need not be ashamed
  of all your deeds,
   your rebellious actions against
   me;
For then will I remove from your
  midst
  the proud braggarts,
And you shall no longer exalt
  yourself
  on my holy mountain.
12 But I will leave as a remnant in
  your midst
  a people humble and lowly,

Who shall take refuge in the name
  of the LORD:
13   the remnant of Israel.
They shall do no wrong
  and speak no lies;
Nor shall there be found in their
  mouths
  a deceitful tongue;
They shall pasture and couch
  their flocks
  with none to disturb them.

14 Shout for joy, O daughter Zion!
  sing joyfully, O Israel!
Be glad and exult with all your
  heart,
  O daughter Jerusalem!
15 The LORD has removed the
  judgment against you,
  he has turned away your
  enemies;
The King of Israel, the LORD, is
  in your midst,
  you have no further misfortune to fear.
16 On that day, it shall be said to
  Jerusalem:
Fear not, O Zion, be not
  discouraged!
17 The LORD, your God, is in your
  midst,
  a mighty savior;

He will rejoice over you with
  gladness,
  and renew you in his love,
He will sing joyfully because of
  you,
18   as one sings at festivals.

I will remove disaster from among
  you,
  so that none may recount your
  disgrace.
19 Yes, at that time I will deal
  with all who oppress you:
I will save the lame,
  and assemble the outcasts;
I will give them praise and renown
  in all the earth, when I bring
  about their restoration.
20 At that time I will bring you
  home,
  and at that time I will gather
  you;
For I will give you renown and
  praise,
  among all the peoples of the
  earth,
When I bring about your restoration
  before your very eyes, says the
  LORD.

Haggai

Exhortation To Rebuild the Temple of the Lord

ON the first day of the sixth month in the second year of King Darius, the word of the LORD came through the prophet Haggai to the governor of Judah, Zerubbabel, son of Shealtiel, and to the high priest Joshua, son of Jehozadak: 2 Thus says the LORD of hosts: This people says: "Not now has the time come to rebuild the house of the LORD." 3 (Then this word of the LORD came through Haggai, the prophet:) 4 Is it time for you to dwell in your own paneled houses, while this house lies in ruins?

5 Now thus says the LORD of hosts:
　　Consider your ways!
6 You have sown much, but have
　　brought in little;
　　you have eaten, but have not
　　been satisfied;
　You have drunk, but have not
　　been exhilarated;
　have clothed yourselves, but
　　not been warmed;
　And he who earned wages
　　earned them for a bag with
　　holes in it.

7　　Thus says the LORD of hosts:
　Consider your ways!
8 Go up into the hill country;
　　bring timber, and build the
　　house
　That I may take pleasure in it
　　and receive my glory, says the
　　LORD.

9 You expected much, but it came
　　to little;
　and what you brought home,
　　I blew away.

　For what cause? says the LORD
　　of hosts.
　Because my house lies in ruins,
　　while each of you hurries to his
　　own house.
10 Therefore the heavens withheld
　　from you their dew,
　　and the earth her crops.
11 And I called for a drought
　　upon the land and upon the
　　mountains;
　Upon the grain, and upon the
　　wine, and upon the oil,
　　and upon all that the ground
　　brings forth;
　Upon men and upon beasts,
　　and upon all that is produced by
　　hand.

12 Then Zerubbabel, son of Shealtiel, and the high priest Joshua, son of Jehozadak, and all the remnant of the people listened to the voice of the LORD, their God, and to the words of the prophet Haggai, because the LORD, their God, had sent him, and

the people feared because of the LORD. 13 And the LORD's messenger, Haggai, proclaimed to the people as the message of the LORD: I am with you, says the LORD.

14 Then the LORD stirred up the spirit of the governor of Judah, Zerubbabel, son of Shealtiel, and the spirit of the high priest Joshua, son of Jehozadak, and the spirit of all the remnant of the people, so that they came and set to work on the house of the LORD of hosts, their God, 15 on the twenty-fourth day of the sixth month.

Future Glory of the New Temple

2 In the second year of King Darius, on the twenty-first day of the seventh month, the word of the LORD came through the prophet Haggai: 2 Tell this to the governor of Judah, Zerubbabel, son of Shealtiel, and to the high priest Joshua, son of Jehozadak, and to the remnant of the people:

3 Who is left among you
　　that saw this house in its
　　former glory?

1, 1: *The sixth month in the second year:* August/September in 520 B.C.

1, 4: The luxury of the homes of the wealthy with their *paneled houses* contrasts sadly with the ruined state of the Lord's *house.*

1, 12: *The remnant of the people:* a technical term in Haggai and Zechariah for the returned exiles.

And how do you see it now?
  Does it not seem like nothing
    in your eyes?
4 But now take courage, Zerub-
    babel, says the LORD,
  and take courage, Joshua, high
    priest, son of Jehozadak,
  And take courage, all you people
    of the land
    says the LORD, and work!
  For I am with you, says the
    LORD of hosts.
5 This is the pact that I made with
    you
  when you came out of Egypt,
  And my spirit continues in your
    midst;
    do not fear!

6   For thus says the LORD of hosts:
  One moment yet, a little while,
    and I will shake the heavens
      and the earth,
      the sea and the dry land.
7 I will shake all the nations,
    and the treasures of all the
      nations will come in,
  And I will fill this house with
    glory,
    says the LORD of hosts.
8 Mine is the silver and mine the
    gold
    says the LORD of hosts.
9 Greater will be the future glory
    of this house
    than the former, says the LORD
      of hosts;
  And in this place I will give peace,
    says the LORD of hosts!

Offerings of the Unclean Rejected

10 On the twenty-fourth day of the
ninth month, in the second year of
King Darius, the word of the LORD
came to the prophet Haggai: 11
Thus says the LORD of hosts: Ask
the priests for a decision: 12 If a
man carries sanctified flesh in the
fold of his garment and the fold
touches bread, or pottage, or wine,
or oil, or any other food, do they
become sanctified? "No," the priests
answered. 13 Then Haggai said:
If a person unclean from contact
with a corpse touches any of these,
do they become unclean? The priests
answered, "They become unclean."
14 Then Haggai continued:

  So is this people, and so is this
    nation
  in my sight, says the LORD:
  And so are all the works of
    their hands;
    and what they offer there is
      unclean.

Promise of Immediate Blessings

15 But now, consider from this
day forward. Before there was a
stone laid upon a stone in the temple
of the LORD,   16 how did you fare?

  When one went to a heap of
    grain for twenty measures,
    it would yield but ten;
  When another went to the vat
    to draw fifty measures,
    there would be but twenty.
17 I struck you in all the works
    of your hands
    with blight, searing wind, and
      hail,
    yet you did not return to me,
      says the LORD.

18 [Consider from this day forward: from the twenty-fourth day of
the ninth month. From the day on
which the temple of the LORD was
founded, consider!]

19 Indeed, the seed has not
    sprouted,
  nor have the vine, the fig, the
    pomegranate
  and the olive tree yet borne.
  From this day, I will bless!

Pledge to Zerubbabel

20 The message of the LORD came
a second time to Haggai on the
twenty-fourth day of the month:
21 Tell this to Zerubbabel, the governor of Judah:

  I will shake the heavens and the
    earth;
22 I will overthrow the thrones of
    kingdoms,
    destroy the power of the
      kingdoms of the nations.
  I will overthrow the chariots
    and their riders,
    and the riders with their
      horses
    shall go down by one
      another's sword.
23 On that day, says the LORD of
    hosts,
  I will take you, Zerubbabel,
    son of Shealtiel, my servant,
      says the LORD,
  And I will set you as a signet
    ring;
    for I have chosen you, says
      the LORD of hosts.

2, 6–9: From the later period of Ezekiel's preaching
onward, the temple became, as here, one of the
dominant Messianic themes. *Greater will be the future
glory of this house than the former:* because Christ will
enter it.
2, 12ff: According to the ritual concepts of the
Jews, uncleanness was more contagious than sacredness. Inasmuch as the people were unclean, their
offerings became unclean (Nm 19, 22).
2, 15–19: This prophecy is intimately linked with
chapter 1, and should be read with it.
2, 18: *The ninth month:* the ordinal *ninth* has been
copied incorrectly from 2, 10. This note clearly
concerns the *twenty-fourth day of the sixth month,*
on which the temple of the Lord was founded (1,
15).
2, 20: *The month:* probably again the sixth month,
as in 1, 15 and 2, 18; see note on the latter.
2, 23: This promise to Zerubbabel, reversing the
punishment of his grandfather (Jer 22, 24), is a continuation of the Messianic hope; cf Zec 6, 11f.

Zechariah

Necessity of Conversion

IN the second year of Darius, in the eighth month, the word of the LORD came to the prophet Zechariah, son of Berechiah, son of Iddo: 2 The LORD was indeed angry with your fathers.... 3 and say to them: Thus says the LORD of hosts: Return to me, says the LORD of hosts, and I will return to you, says the LORD of hosts. 4 Be not like your fathers whom the former prophets warned: Thus says the LORD of hosts: Turn from your evil ways and from your wicked deeds. But they would not listen or pay attention to me, says the LORD. 5 Your fathers, where are they? And the prophets, can they live forever? 6 But my words and my decrees, which I entrusted to my servants the prophets, did not these overtake your fathers? Then they repented and admitted: "The LORD of hosts has treated us according to our ways and deeds, just as he had determined he would."

The Four Horsemen

7 In the second year of Darius, on the twenty-fourth day of Sabat, the eleventh month, the word of the LORD came to the prophet Zechariah, son of Berechiah, son of Iddo, in the following way: 8 I had a vision during the night. There appeared the driver of a red horse, standing among myrtle trees in a shady place, and behind him were red, sorrel, and white horses. 9 Then I asked, "What are these, my lord?"; and the angel who spoke with me answered me, "I will show you what these are." 10 The man who was standing among the myrtle trees spoke up and said, "These are they whom the LORD has sent to patrol the earth." 11 And they answered the angel of the LORD who was standing among the myrtle trees and said, "We have patrolled the earth; see, the whole earth is tranquil and at rest!"

12 Then the angel of the LORD spoke out and said, "O LORD of hosts, how long will you be without mercy for Jerusalem and the cities of Judah that have felt your anger these seventy years?" 13 To the angel who spoke with me, the LORD replied with comforting words.

14 And the angel who spoke with me said to me, Proclaim: Thus says the LORD of hosts: I am deeply moved for the sake of Jerusalem and Zion, 15 and I am exceedingly angry with the complacent nations; whereas I was but a little angry, they added to the harm. 16 Therefore, says the LORD: I will turn to Jerusalem in mercy; my house shall be built in it, says the LORD of hosts, and a measuring line shall be stretched over Jerusalem. 17 Proclaim further: Thus says the LORD of hosts: My cities shall again overflow with prosperity; the LORD will again comfort Zion, and again choose Jerusalem.

Four Horns and Four Blacksmiths

2 I raised my eyes and looked: there were four horns. 2 Then I asked the angel who spoke with me what these were. He answered me, "These are the horns that scattered Judah and Israel and Jerusalem."

3 Then the LORD showed me four blacksmiths. And I asked, "What are these coming to do?" 4 And he said, "Here are the horns that scattered Judah, so that no man raised his

---

1, 1: *The second year...eighth month:* October/November, 520 B.C.

1, 7: *The second year...eleventh month:* January/February, 519 B.C.

1, 8–11: *The driver of a red horse:* apparently distinct from *the man,* or *angel of the Lord... standing among the myrtle trees,* who spoke with the prophet. The four horsemen are sent by God to the four corners of the earth (2, 10), to see if the whole earth is at peace.

1, 12: *These seventy years:* see note on Jer 25, 1–14.

1, 15: *The complacent nations:* the neighbors of Judah, especially Edom, which enjoyed their present prosperity and security at Judah's expense.

1, 16: *Measuring line:* not for devastation, as in Is 34, 11, but for reconstruction.

2, 1–4: *Four horns:* symbolic of the hostile forces which, from the four corners of the earth, invaded and devastated *the land of Judah. Four blacksmiths:* the powers used by God to destroy these enemies of his people.

head any more; but these have come to terrify them: to cast down the horns of the nations that raised their horns to scatter the land of Judah."

The New Jerusalem

5 Again I raised my eyes and looked: there was a man with a measuring line in his hand. 6 "Where are you going?" I asked. "To measure Jerusalem," he answered; "to see how great is its width and how great its length." 7 Then the angel who spoke with me advanced, and another angel came out to meet him 8 and said to him, "Run tell this to that young man: People will live in Jerusalem as though in open country, because of the multitude of men and beasts in her midst. 9 But I will be for her an encircling wall of fire, says the LORD, and I will be the glory in her midst."

10 Up, up! Flee from the land of the north, says the LORD; for I scatter you to the four winds of heaven, says the LORD. 11 Up, escape to Zion! you who dwell in daughter Babylon. 12 For thus said the LORD of hosts (after he had already sent me) concerning the nations that have plundered you: Whoever touches you touches the apple of my eye. 13 See, I wave my hand over them; they become plunder for their slaves. Thus you shall know that the LORD of hosts has sent me.

14. Sing and rejoice, O daughter Zion! See, I am coming to dwell among you, says the LORD. 15 Many nations shall join themselves to the LORD on that day, and they shall be his people, and he will dwell among you, and you shall know that the LORD of hosts has sent me to you. 16 The LORD will possess Judah as his portion in the holy land, and he will again choose Jerusalem. 17 Silence, all mankind, in the presence

of the LORD! for he stirs forth from his holy dwelling.

Joshua the High Priest

3 Then he showed me Joshua the high priest standing before the angel of the LORD, while Satan stood at his right hand to accuse him. 2 And the angel of the LORD said to Satan, "May the LORD rebuke you, Satan; may the LORD who has chosen Jerusalem rebuke you! Is not this man a brand snatched from the fire?"

3 Now Joshua was standing before the angel, clad in filthy garments. 4 He spoke and said to those who were standing before him, "Take off his filthy garments, and clothe him in festal garments." 5 He also said, "Put a clean miter on his head." And they put a clean miter on his head and clothed him with the garments. Then the angel of the LORD, standing, said, "See, I have taken away your guilt."

6 The angel of the LORD then gave Joshua this assurance:

7 "Thus says the LORD of hosts: If you walk in my ways and heed my charge, you shall judge my house and keep my courts, and I will give you access among those standing here. 8 Listen, O Joshua, high priest! You and your associates who sit before you are men of good omen. Yes, I will bring my servant the Shoot. 9 Look at the stone that I have placed before Joshua, one stone with seven facets. I will engrave its inscription, says the LORD of hosts, and I will take away the guilt of the land in one day. 10 On that day, says the LORD of hosts, you will invite one another under your vines and fig trees."

4 Then I said to the angel who spoke with me, "What are these things, my lord?" 5 And the angel who spoke with me replied, "Do you not know what these things are?"

"No, my lord," I answered. 6 Then he said to me, "This is the LORD's message to Zerubbabel: Not by an army, nor by might, but by my spirit, says the LORD of hosts. 7 What are you, O great mountain? Before Zerubbabel you are but a plain. He shall bring out the capstone amid exclamations of 'Hail, Hail' to it."

8 This word of the LORD then came to me: 9 The hands of Zerubbabel have laid the foundations of this house, and his hands shall finish it; then you shall know that the LORD of hosts has sent me to you. 10 For even they who were scornful on that day of small beginnings shall rejoice to see the select stone in the hands of Zerubbabel. These seven facets are the eyes of the LORD that range over the whole earth.

The Lampstand

1 Then the angel who spoke with me returned and awakened me, like a man awakened from his sleep. 2 "What do you see?" he asked me. "I see a lampstand all of gold, with a bowl at the top," I replied; "on it are seven lamps with their tubes, 3 and beside it are two olive trees, one on the right and the other on the left." I then asked him, 11 "What are these two olive trees at each side of the lampstand?" 12 And again I asked, "What are the two olive tufts which freely pour out fresh oil through the two golden channels?" 13 "Do you not know what these are?" he said to me. "No, my lord," I answered him. 14 He said, "These are the two anointed who stand by the LORD of the whole earth."

The Flying Scroll

5 Then I raised my eyes again and saw a scroll flying. 2 "What do you see?" he asked me. I answered, "I see a scroll flying; it is twenty cubits long and ten cubits wide."

2, 8: *That young man:* the angel or *man with a measuring line* of v 5.
2, 10: *The land of the north:* Babylonia (v 11).
3, 3: *Filthy garments:* symbolic of mourning for the dead, or of national catastrophe, and implying acknowledgement of guilt (v 5).
3, 8: *Men of good omen:* the restoration of the priesthood is a sign of the coming of the Messianic times. *My servant the Shoot:* identified, in the earliest form of 6, 11f as the prophet composed it, with Zerubbabel, direct descendant of King David and rebuilder of the temple; and, as such, a type of the Messiah; cf Jer 23, 5.

3, 9: *One stone with seven facets:* apparently the same as *the select stone* of 4, 10, which seems to be a precious gem. The *seven facets* are explained in 4, 10 as signifying the Lord's vigilance over the world. *I will engrave its inscription:* the same Hebrew verb for *engrave* is used in Ex 28, 9.11 in regard to the inscriptions on the twelve precious stones of the priestly breastpiece.
4, 7: *Great mountain:* figure of the obstacles confronting Zerubbabel in building the temple. *A plain:* figure of the ease with which he will overcome these obstacles.
4, 1ff.11–14: *The two anointed:* literally "the two

sons of oil," Joshua, the anointed high priest, and Zerubbabel, the anointed prince. Just as the two olive trees in this imagery supply the sacred seven-branched lampstand (Ex 25, 31–40) with oil (v 12), so these two men, in ministering to the community, *stand by* (serve) *the Lord.*
5, 1–4: The enormous scroll, thirty feet by fifteen (the dimensions in length and breadth of the portico of Solomon's temple, 1 Kgs 6, 3), contains a list of maledictions on sinners, similar to that in Dt 27, 15–26. The *thief* and the *perjurer* represent all sinners, who are expelled from the holy community.

Then he said to me: 3 "This is the curse which is to go forth over the whole earth; in accordance with it shall every thief be swept away, and in accordance with it shall every perjurer be expelled from here. 4 I will send it forth, says the LORD of hosts, and it shall come into the house of the thief, or into the house of him who perjures himself with my name; it shall lodge within his house, consuming it, timber and stones."

The Flying Bushel

5 Then the angel who spoke with me came forward and said to me, "Raise your eyes and see what is this that comes forth."

6 "What is it?" I asked. And he answered, "This is a bushel container coming. This is their guilt in all the land." 7 Then a leaden cover was lifted, and there was a woman sitting inside the bushel. 8 "This is Wickedness," he said; and he thrust her inside the bushel, pushing the leaden cover into the opening. 9 Then I raised my eyes and saw two women coming forth with a wind ruffling their wings, for they had wings like the wings of a stork. 10 As they lifted up the bushel into the air, I said to the angel who spoke with me, "Where are they taking the bushel?" 11 He replied, "To build a temple for it in the land of Shinar; when the temple is ready, they will deposit it there in its place."

Four Chariots

6 Again I raised my eyes and saw four chariots coming out from between two mountains; and the mountains were of bronze. 2 The first chariot had red horses, the second chariot black horses, 3 the third chariot white horses, and the fourth chariot spotted horses—all of them strong horses 4 I asked the angel who spoke with me, "What are these, my lord?" 5 The angel said to me in reply, "These are the four winds of the heavens, which are coming forth after being reviewed by the Lord of all the earth." 6 The chariot with the black horses was turning toward the land of the north, the red and the white horses went after them, and the spotted ones went toward the land of the south. 7 As these strong horses emerged, eager to set about patrolling the earth, he said, "Go, patrol the earth!" Then, as they patrolled the earth, 8 he called out to me and said, "See, they that go forth to the land of the north will make my spirit rest in the land of the north."

The Coronation

9 This word of the LORD then came to me: 10 Take from the returned captives Heldai, Tobijah, Jedaiah; and go the same day to the house of Josiah, son of Zephaniah (these had come from Babylon). 11 Silver and gold you shall take, and make a crown; place it on the head of [Joshua, son of Jehozadak, the high priest] Zerubbabel. 12 And say to him: Thus says the LORD of hosts: Here is a man whose name is Shoot, and where he is he shall sprout, and he shall build the temple of the LORD. 13 Yes, he shall build the temple of the LORD, and taking up the royal insignia, he shall sit as ruler upon his throne. The priest shall be at his right hand, and between the two of them there shall be friendly understanding. 14 The crown itself shall be a memorial offering in the temple of the LORD in favor of Heldai, Tobijah, Jedaiah, and the son of Zephaniah. 15 And they who are from afar shall come and build the temple of the LORD, and you shall know that the LORD of hosts has sent me to you. And if you heed carefully the voice of the LORD your God. . . .

True Fasting

7 In the fourth year of Darius the king [the word of the LORD came to Zechariah], on the fourth day of Chislev, the ninth month, Bethelsarezer sent Regemmelech and his men to implore favor of the Lord 3 and to ask the priests of the house of the LORD of hosts, and the prophets, "Must I mourn and abstain in the fifth month as I have been doing these many years?" 4 Thereupon this word of the LORD of hosts came to me: 5 Say to all the people of the land and to the priests: When you fasted and mourned in the fifth and in the seventh month these seventy years, was it really for me that you fasted? 6 And when you were eating and drinking, was it not for yourselves that you ate, and for yourselves that you drank? 7 Were not these the words which the LORD spoke through the former prophets, when Jerusalem and the surrounding cities were inhabited and at peace, when the Negeb and the foothills were inhabited? 8 [This word of the LORD came to Zechariah: 9 Thus says the LORD of hosts:] Render true judgment, and show kindness and compassion toward each other. 10 Do not oppress the widow or the orphan, the alien or the poor; do not plot evil against one another in your hearts. 11 But they refused to listen; they stubbornly turned their backs and stopped their ears so as not to hear. 12 And they made their hearts diamond-hard so as not to hear the teaching and the message that the LORD of hosts had sent by his spirit through the former prophets. 13 Then the LORD of hosts in his great anger said that, as they had not listened when he called, so he would not listen when they called, 14 but would scatter them with a whirlwind among all the nations that they did not know. Thus the land was left desolate after them with no one traveling to and fro; they made the pleasant land into a desert.

In the Days of the Messiah

8 This word of the LORD of hosts came: 2 Thus says the LORD of hosts:

5, 5–11: *The woman sealed in the bushel container* is a figure of the general corruption of the people of Judah. She is removed from the Holy Land and transported to *Shinar:* that is, Babylonia, where a dwelling is being prepared for her; this is a symbol of the reign of *Wickedness* in pagan lands, contrasted with the reign of holiness in the Lord's dwelling on Mount Zion.

6, 1–18: The *four chariots* represent the angelic hosts sent by the Lord to the four ends of the earth. The chariot with the *black horses* brings the *spirit,* i.e., anger of the Lord against the land of the north, Babylonia.

6, 11: *Make a crown; place it on the head of* [*Joshua, son of Jehozadak, the high priest*] *Zerubbabel:* According to the current Hebrew text, Joshua the high priest is to be crowned. However, since the crown is a sign of royalty, the original text must have had the name of Zerubbabel here, not that of Joshua. In 3, 8 Joshua is a different man from the one called *the Shoot,* and in v 12 it is upon *the Shoot* that the crown is to be placed.

7, 1: *The fourth year of Darius . . . the fourth day of Chislev, the ninth month:* November, 518 B.C.

I am intensely jealous for Zion,
stirred to jealous wrath for
her.
3 Thus says the LORD:
I will return to Zion,
and I will dwell within
Jerusalem;
Jerusalem shall be called the
faithful city,
and the mountain of the
LORD of hosts,
the holy mountain.

4 Thus says the LORD of hosts:
Old men and old women, each with
staff in hand because of old age, shall
again sit in the streets of Jerusalem.
5 The city shall be filled with boys
and girls in her streets. 6 Thus says
the LORD of hosts: Even if this should
seem impossible in the eyes of the
remnant of this people, shall it in
those days be impossible in my eyes
also, says the LORD of hosts? 7
Thus says the LORD of hosts: Lo, I
will rescue my people from the land
of the rising sun, and from the land
of the setting sun. 8 I will bring
them back to dwell within Jerusalem.
They shall be my people, and I will be
their God, with faithfulness and
justice.
9 Thus says the LORD of hosts:
Let your hands be strong, you who
in these days hear these words
spoken by the prophets on the day
when the foundation of the house of
the LORD of hosts was laid for the
building of the temple. 10 For
before those days there were no
wages for men, or hire for beasts;
those who came and went had no
security from the enemy, for I set
every man against his neighbor. 11
But now I will not deal with the
remnant of this people as in former
days, says the LORD of hosts, 12 for
it is the seedtime of peace: the vine
shall yield its fruit, the land shall bear
its crops, and the heavens shall give
their dew; all these things I will have
the remnant of the people possess.
13 Just as you were a curse among

the nations, O house of Judah and
house of Israel, so will I save you
that you may be a blessing; do not
fear, but let your hands be strong.
14 Thus says the LORD of hosts:
As I determined to harm you when
your fathers provoked me to wrath,
says the LORD of hosts, and I did not
relent, 15 so again in these days I
have determined to favor Jerusalem
and the house of Judah; do not fear!
16 These are the things you should
do: Speak the truth to one another;
let there be honesty and peace in the
judgments at your gates, 17 and let
none of you plot evil against another
in his heart, nor love a false oath.
For all these things I hate, says the
LORD.
18 This word of the LORD of hosts
came to me: 19 Thus says the LORD
of hosts: The fast days of the fourth,
the fifth, the seventh, and the tenth
months shall become occasions of
joy and gladness, cheerful festivals
for the house of Judah; only love
faithfulness and peace. 20 Thus says
the LORD of hosts: There shall yet
come peoples, the inhabitants of
many cities; 21 and the inhabitants
of one city shall approach those of
another, and say, "Come! let us go to
implore the favor of the LORD"; and,
"I too will go to seek the LORD." 22
Many peoples and strong nations
shall come to seek the LORD of hosts
in Jerusalem and to implore the favor
of the LORD. 23 Thus says the
LORD of hosts: In those days ten men
of every nationality, speaking different tongues, shall take hold, yes, take
hold of every Jew by the edge of his
garment and say, "Let us go with you,
for we have heard that God is with
you."

Invasion by the Lord

9 An oracle:
The word of the LORD is upon
the land of Hadrach,
and Damascus is its resting
place,

For the cities of Aram are the
LORD's,
as are all the tribes of Israel,
2 Hamath also, on its border,
Tyre too, and Sidon, however
wise they be.
3 Tyre built herself a stronghold,
and heaped up silver like dust,
and gold like the mire of the
streets.
4 Lo, the LORD will strip her of
her possessions,
and smite her power on the
sea,
and she shall be devoured by
fire.
5 Ashkelon shall see it and be
afraid;
Gaza also: she shall be in
great anguish;
Ekron, too, for her hope shall
come to nought.
The king shall disappear from
Gaza,
and Ashkelon shall not be
inhabited,
6 and the baseborn shall occupy
Ashdod.
I will destroy the pride of the
Philistine
7 and take from his mouth his
bloody meat,
and his abominations from
between his teeth:
He also shall become a remnant
for our God,
and shall be like a family in
Judah,
and Ekron shall be like the
Jebusites.
8 I will encamp by my house as
a guard
that none may pass to and fro;
No oppressor shall pass over
them again,
for now I have regard for their
affliction.

Restoration under the Messiah

9 Rejoice heartily, O daughter
Zion,
shout for joy, O daughter
Jerusalem!

8, 19: The fast day of *the fourth* month recalled the
fall of Jerusalem in June, 587 B.C. (2 Kgs 25, 3f); that
of *the fifth* month, the burning of the temple by
Nebuzaradan in July of the same year (2 Kgs 25, 8f);
that of *the seventh* month, the murder of Gedaliah in
September of the same year (Jer 41, 1f); that of *the
tenth* month, the beginning of the final siege of
Jerusalem in January, 588 B.C. (2 Kgs 25, 1).
9, 1–8: Divine judgment is about to fall on the

surrounding hostile peoples: *Aram* (Syria), including the cities of *Hadrach* and *Damascus;* Phoenicia,
with its cities of *Tyre* and *Sidon;* Philistia, with its
cities of *Ashkelon, Gaza, Ekron,* and *Ashdod.*
9, 6: *The baseborn:* people of mixed ancestry.
9, 7: *Remnant:* see note on Hg 1, 12. The *Jebusites:*
the pre-Israelite inhabitants of Jerusalem, conquered
by David and incorporated into Israel.
9, 8: *My house:* the Holy Land; cf Hos 8, 1; 9, 15;

Jer 12, 7.
9, 9: The Messiah will come, not as a conquering
warrior, but in lowliness and peace. Not like the last
kings of Judah, who rode in chariots and on horses
(Jer 17, 25; 22, 4), but like the princes of old (Gn 49,
11; Jgs 5, 10; 10, 4), the Messiah will ride on an ass.
The Evangelists see a literal fulfillment of this prophecy
in the Savior's triumphant entry into Jerusalem (Mt
21, 4f; Jn 12, 14f).

See, your king shall come to
  you;
    a just savior is he,
Meek, and riding on an ass,
  on a colt, the foal of an ass.
10 He shall banish the chariot from
  Ephraim,
    and the horse from Jerusalem;
The warrior's bow shall be
  banished,
    and he shall proclaim peace
    to the nations.
His dominion shall be from
  sea to sea,
    and from the River to the
    ends of the earth.
11 As for you, for the blood of
  your covenant with me,
    I will bring forth your
    prisoners from the dungeon.
12 In the return to the fortress
  of the waiting prisoners,
This very day, I will return you
  double for your exile.
13 For I will bend Judah as my bow,
  I will arm myself with
  Ephraim;
I will arouse your sons, O Zion,
  [against your sons, O Yavan,]
    and I will use you as a
    warrior's sword.

14 The LORD shall appear over
  them,
    and his arrow shall shoot
    forth as lightning;
The Lord GOD shall sound the
  trumpet,
    and come in a storm from
    the south.
15 The LORD of hosts shall be a
  shield over them,
    they shall overcome sling
    stones
    and trample them underfoot;
They shall drink blood like
  wine,
    till they are filled with it like
    libation bowls,
    like the corners of the altar.
16 And the LORD, their God, shall
  save them on that day,
    his people, like a flock.
For they are the jewels in a
  crown
    raised aloft over his land.

17 For what wealth is theirs, and
  what beauty!
    grain that makes the youths
    flourish,
    and new wine, the maidens!

The New Order of Things

10 Ask of the LORD rain in the
  spring season!
    It is the LORD who makes the
    storm clouds.
And sends men the pouring
  rain;
    for everyone, grassy fields.
2 For the teraphim speak nonsense,
    the diviners have false visions:
Deceitful dreams they tell,
  empty comfort they offer.
This is why they wander like
  sheep,
    wretched: they have no
    shepherd.
3 My wrath is kindled against the
  shepherds,
    and I will punish the leaders;
For the LORD of hosts will visit
  his flock,
    the house of Judah,
    and make them his stately
    war horse.

4 From him shall come leader
  and chief,
    from him warrior's bow and
    every officer.
5 They shall all be warriors,
  trampling the mire of the
  streets in battle;
They shall wage war because
  the LORD is with them,
    and shall put the horsemen
    to rout.
6 I will strengthen the house of
  Judah,
    the house of Joseph I will
    save;
I will bring them back, because
  I have mercy on them,
    they shall be as though I had
    never cast them off,
    for I am the LORD, their God,
    and I will hear them.
7 Then Ephraim shall be valiant
  men,

and their hearts shall be
  cheered as by wine.
Their children shall see it and
  be glad,
    their hearts shall rejoice in
    in the LORD.

8 I will whistle for them to come
  together,
    and when I redeem them
    they will be as numerous as
    before.
9 I sowed them among the nations,
  yet in distant lands they
  remember me;
    they shall rear their children
    and return.
10 I will bring them back from the
  land of Egypt,
    and gather them from Assyria.
I will bring them into Gilead
  and into Lebanon,
    but these shall not suffice
    them;
11 I will cross over to Egypt
  and smite the waves of the sea
    and all the depths of the Nile
    shall be dried up.
The pride of Assyria shall be
  cast down,
    and the scepter of Egypt
    taken away.
12 I will strengthen them in the
  LORD,
    and they shall walk in his
    name, says the LORD.

11 Open your doors, O Lebanon,
  that the fire may devour
  your cedars!
2 Wail, you cypress trees,
  for the cedars are fallen,
    the mighty have been
    despoiled.
Wail, you oaks of Bashan,
  for the impenetrable forest is
  cut down!
3 Hark! the wailing of the
  shepherds,
    their glory has been ruined.
Hark! the roaring of the young
  lions,
    the jungle of the Jordan is
    laid waste.

9, 10: *The River:* the Euphrates; see note on Ps
72, 8.
  9, 11: *The blood of your covenant with me:* the
covenant between the Lord and Israel sealed with

sacrificial blood (Ex 24, 8).
  9, 12: *The waiting prisoners:* the exiles awaiting the
return to their country, where they will receive a
double compensation for the double punishment they

had suffered; cf Is 40, 2; 61, 7.
  10, 2: *Teraphim:* household idols, used for divination; cf Gn 31, 19.34f; Jgs 17, 5; 18, 17f.20; Ez 21, 26;
Hos 3, 4.

Allegory of the Shepherds

4 Thus said the LORD my God: Shepherd the flock to be slaughtered. 5 For they who buy them slay them with impunity; while those who sell them say, "Blessed be the LORD, I have become rich!" Even their own shepherds do not feel for them. 6 (Nor shall I spare the inhabitants of the earth any more, says the LORD. Yes, I will deliver each of them into the power of his neighbor, or into the power of his king; they shall crush the earth, and I will not deliver it out of their power.)

7 So I became the shepherd of the flock to be slaughtered for the sheep merchants. I took two staffs, one of which I called "Favor," and the other, "Bonds," and I fed the flock. 8 In a single month I did away with the three shepherds. I wearied of them, and they behaved badly toward me. 9 "I will not feed you," I said. "What is to die, let it die; what is to perish, let it perish, and let those that are left devour one another's flesh."

10 Then I took my staff "Favor" and snapped it asunder, breaking off the covenant which I had made with all peoples; 11 that day it was broken off. The sheep merchants who were watching me understood that this was the word of the LORD. 12 I said to them, "If it seems good to you, give me my wages; but if not, let it go." And they counted out my wages, thirty pieces of silver. 13 But the Lord said to me, "Throw it in the treasury, the handsome price at which they valued me." So I took the thirty pieces of silver and threw them into the treasury in the house of the LORD.

14 Then I snapped asunder my other staff, "Bonds," breaking off the brotherhood between Judah and Israel.

15 The LORD said to me: This time take the gear of the foolish shepherd. 16 For I will raise up a shepherd in the land who will take no note of those that perish, nor seek the strays, nor heal the injured, nor feel what survives—he will eat the flesh of the fat ones and tear off their hoofs!

17 Woe to my foolish shepherd
    who forsakes the flock!
May the sword fall upon his arm
    and upon his right eye;
Let his arm wither away entirely,
    and his right eye be blind
    forever!

Jerusalem God's Instrument

12 An oracle: the word of the LORD concerning Israel. Thus says the LORD, who spreads out the heavens, lays the foundations of the earth, and forms the spirit of man within him: 2 See, I will make Jerusalem a bowl to stupefy all peoples round about. [Judah will be besieged, even Jerusalem.] 3 On that day I will make Jerusalem a weighty stone for all peoples. All who attempt to lift it shall injure themselves badly, and all the nations of the earth shall be gathered against her. 4 On that day, says the LORD, I will strike every horse with fright, and its rider with madness. I will strike blind all the horses of the peoples, but upon the house of Judah I will open my eyes, 5 and the princes of Judah shall say to themselves, "The inhabitants of Jerusalem have their strength in the LORD of hosts, their God." 6 On that day I will make the princes of Judah like a brazier of fire in the woodland, and like a burning torch among sheaves, and they shall devour right and left all the surrounding peoples; but Jerusalem shall still abide on its own site. 7 The LORD shall save the tents of

Judah first, that the glory of the house of David and the glory of the inhabitants of Jerusalem may not be exalted over Judah. 8 On that day, the LORD will shield the inhabitants of Jerusalem, and the weakling among them shall be like David on that day, and the house of David godlike, like an angel of the LORD before them. 9 On that day I will seek the destruction of all nations that come against Jerusalem.

Messianic Jerusalem

10 I will pour out on the house of David and on the inhabitants of Jerusalem a spirit of grace and petition; and they shall look on him whom they have thrust through, and they shall mourn for him as one mourns for an only son, and they shall grieve over him as one grieves over a first-born.

11 On that day the mourning in Jerusalem shall be as great as the mourning of Hadadrimmon in the plain of Megiddo.

12 And the land shall mourn, each family apart: the family of the house of David, and their wives; the family of the house of Nathan, and their wives; 13 the family of the house of Levi, and their wives; the family of Shemei, and their wives; 14 and all the rest of the families, each family apart, and the wives apart.

The End of Falsehood

13 On that day there shall be open to the house of David and to the inhabitants of Jerusalem, a fountain to purify from sin and uncleanness. 2 On that day, says the LORD of hosts, I will destroy the names of the idols from the land, so that they shall be mentioned no more; I will also take away the prophets and the spirit of uncleanness from the land. 3 If a man still prophesies,

---

11, 4–17: In this allegory the prophet becomes the good shepherd of God's flock, which is being slaughtered; he is the defender of the people exploited by bad rulers. *The three shepherds*, rulers in general, are to destroy one another in a short time (*a single month*). The service of the good shepherd is contemptuously valued at *thirty pieces of silver*, the legal indemnity (Ex 21, 32) for a gored slave. The prophet is thus a type of Christ, whose mission of salvation to his people was appraised by the Sanhedrists, the false shepherds, at the same base price (Mt 26, 14ff). In the case of the prophet as well as of Christ (Mt 27, 5), the money is thrown into the temple treasury, i.e., paid to God, showing thereby how shamefully

his divine love and care are requited.

12, 1–9: Under the image of the deliverance of Judah and Jerusalem from invading enemies, the prophet foretells the ultimate victory of God's people in the Messianic age.

12, 10: The divine blessings (*a spirit of grace and petition*) will be poured out on God's people through the intervention of an unnamed sufferer (*him whom they have thrust through*), similar to the Servant of the Lord in Is 52, 13—53, 12. In Jn 19, 37 the Evangelist sees in this passage a prophecy fulfilled in the piercing of Christ's side.

12, 11: The mourning for the pierced victim in Jerusalem is compared to a lamentation *in the plain*

of Megiddo apparently over a certain personage called *Hadadrimmon*. The reference is no longer clear. Both *Hadad* and *Rimmon* were names of the Semitic storm god, often identified with the god Baal. Some see here a reference to the annual mourning by the pagans over the death of the fertility god. According to others, *Hadadrimmon* is the name of a place near Megiddo, and the reference would then be to the mourning over the death of King Josiah, who was killed in battle there; cf Chr 35, 22–25.

13, 1: *A fountain to purify from sin:* in contrast to the lustral water used in ritual purification; cf Nm 19, 9.13.20; 31, 23. The Lord himself is the *fountain* of living water (Jer 2, 13); cf Is 12, 2ff.

his parents, father and mother, shall say to him, "You shall not live, because you have spoken a lie in the name of the LORD." When he prophesies, his parents, father and mother, shall thrust him through.

4 On that day, every prophet shall be ashamed to prophesy his vision, neither shall he assume the hairy mantle to mislead, 5 but he shall say, "I am no prophet, I am a tiller of the soil, for I have owned land since my youth." 6 And if anyone asks him, "What are these wounds on your chest?" he shall answer, "With these I was wounded in the house of my dear ones."

The Song of the Sword

7 Awake, O sword, against my
    shepherd,
    against the man who is my
      associate,
    says the LORD of hosts.
Strike the shepherd
    that the sheep may be dis-
      persed,
    and I will turn my hand
      against the little ones.
8 In all the land, says the LORD,
    two thirds of them shall be
      cut off and perish,
    and one third shall be left.
9 I will bring the one third
      through fire,
    and I will refine them as silver
      is refined,
    and I will test them as gold is
      tested.
They shall call upon my name,
    and I will hear them.
I will say, "They are my people,"
    and they shall say, "The LORD
      is my God."

The Fight for Jerusalem

14 Lo, a day shall come for the LORD when the spoils shall be divided in your midst. 2 And I will gather all the nations against Jerusalem for battle: the city shall be taken, houses plundered, women ravished; half of the city shall go into exile, but the rest of the people shall not be removed from the city. 3 Then the LORD shall go forth and fight against those nations, fighting as on a day of battle. 4 That day his feet shall rest upon the Mount of Olives, which is opposite Jerusalem to the east. The Mount of Olives shall be cleft in two from east to west by a very deep valley, and half of the mountain shall move to the north and half of it to the south. 5 And the valley of the LORD's mountain shall be filled up when the valley of those two mountains reaches its edge; it shall be filled up as it was filled up by the earthquake in the days of King Uzziah of Judah. Then the LORD, my God, shall come, and all his holy ones with him.

6 On that day there shall no longer be cold or frost. 7 There shall be one continuous day, known to the LORD, not day and night, for in the evening time there shall be light.

8 On that day, living waters shall flow from Jerusalem, half to the eastern sea, and half to the western sea, and it shall be so in summer and in winter. 9 The LORD shall become king over the whole earth; on that day the LORD shall be the only one, and his name the only one.

10 And from Geba to Rimmon in the Negeb, all the land shall turn into a plain; but Jerusalem shall remain exalted in its place. From the Gate of Benjamin to the place of the First Gate, to the Corner Gate; and from the Tower of Hananel to the king's wine presses, 11 they shall occupy her. Never again shall she be doomed; Jerusalem shall abide in security.

12 And this shall be the plague with which the LORD shall strike all the nations that have fought against Jerusalem: their flesh shall rot while they stand upon their feet, and their eyes shall rot in their sockets, and their tongues shall rot in their mouths. 13 On that day there shall be among them a great tumult from the LORD: every man shall seize the hand of his neighbor, and the hand of each shall be raised against that of his neighbor. 14 Judah also shall fight against Jerusalem. The riches of all the surrounding nations shall be gathered together, gold, silver, and garments, in great abundance.

15 Similar to this plague shall be the plague upon the horses, mules, camels, asses, and upon all the beasts that are in those camps.

16 All who are left of all the nations that came against Jerusalem shall come up year after year to worship the King, the LORD of hosts, and to celebrate the feast of Booths. 17 If any of the families of the earth does not come up to Jerusalem to worship the King, the LORD of hosts, no rain shall fall upon them. 18 And if the family of Egypt does not come up, or enter, upon them shall fall the plague which the LORD will inflict upon all the nations that do not come up to celebrate the feast of Booths. 19 This shall be the punishment of Egypt, and the punishment of all the nations that do not come up to celebrate the feast of Booths.

20 On that day there shall be upon the bells of the horses, "Holy to the LORD." The pots in the house of the LORD shall be as the libation bowls before the altar. 21 And every pot in Jerusalem and in Judah shall be holy to the LORD of hosts; and all who come to sacrifice shall take them and cook in them. On that day there shall no longer be any merchant in the house of the LORD of hosts.

13, 4: *Hairy mantle:* worn by prophets as a mark of their calling; cf 2 Kgs 1, 8; Mt 3, 4.

13, 6: *Wounds on your chest:* literally, "wounds between your hands." The false prophets, like the prophet of Baal (1 Kgs 18, 28), apparently inflicted wounds on themselves; to defend himself against the accusation of being a false prophet, a man will deny having inflicted wounds on himself and say instead that he received them at home, "*in the house of my dear ones.*" In the liturgy this text is applied to Christ in an accommodated sense.

13, 7: When the shepherd is killed, the sheep are scattered. In Mt 26, 31 the Evangelist quotes from this verse, in somewhat different form, the words, *I will smite the shepherd, and the sheep of the flock will be scattered,* as said by Christ shortly before his arrest in the Garden of Olives and the flight of the Apostles.

14, 1–21: An apocalyptic description of the Day of the Lord, in which Jerusalem, the figure of God's elect, after much suffering (siege: vv 1ff; riot: v 13; plague: vv 12.15), is rescued by the Lord (vv 4f) and given great blessings (vv 6–11.14.16–21).

Malachi

Israel preferred to Edom

AN oracle. The word of the LORD to Israel through Malachi. 2 I have loved you, says the LORD; but you say, "How have you loved us?" 3 Was not Esau Jacob's brother? says the LORD: yet I loved Jacob, but hated Esau; I made his mountains a waste, his heritage a desert for jackals.

4 If Edom says, "We have been
      crushed
   but we will rebuild the ruins,"
Thus says the LORD of hosts:
   They indeed may build, but
      I will tear down,
   And they shall be called the
      land of guilt,
   the people with whom the
      LORD is angry forever.
5 Your own eyes shall see it, and
      you will say,
   "Great is the LORD, even
      beyond the land of Israel."

Sins of the Priests and Levites

6 A son honors his father,
   and a servant fears his master;
If then I am a father,
   where is the honor due to me?
And if I am a master,
   where is the reverence due to
      me?—
So says the LORD of hosts to
      to you, O priests,
   who despise his name.

But you ask, "How have we
   despised your name?"
7 By offering polluted food on my
      altar!
Then you ask, "How have we
   polluted it?"
   By saying the table of the
      LORD may be slighted!
8 When you offer a blind animal
   for sacrifice,
   is this not evil?
When you offer the lame or the
   sick,
   is it not evil?
Present it to your governor;
   see if he will accept it,
   or welcome you, says the
      LORD of hosts.
9 So now if you implore God for
   mercy on us,
   when you have done the like
Will he welcome any of you?
   says the LORD of hosts.

10 Oh, that one among you would
   shut the temple gates
   to keep you from kindling fire
   on my altar in vain!

I have no pleasure in you, says
   the LORD of hosts;
   neither will I accept any
      sacrifice from your hands,
11 For from the rising of the sun,
   even to its setting,
   my name is great among the
      nations;
And everywhere they bring
   sacrifice to my name,
   and a pure offering;
For great is my name among
   the nations,
   says the LORD of hosts.
12 But you behave profanely
   toward me by thinking
   the LORD's table and its
      offering may be polluted,
   and its food slighted.
13 You also say, "What a burden!"
   and you scorn it, says the
      LORD of hosts;
You bring in what you seize,
   or the lame, or the sick;
   yes, you bring it as a sacrifice.
Shall I accept it from your
   hands?
   says the LORD.

1, 3ff: The thought passes from the person *Esau* to his descendants, *Edom*, and from the person *Jacob* to his descendants, *Israel. Loved:* preferred; *hated:* rejected; cf Gn 25, 21ff. St Paul uses this passage as an example of God's freedom of choice in calling the Gentiles to the faith (Rom 9, 13).

1, 8: The offering in sacrifice of a *lame, sick* or *blind animal* was forbidden in the law (Lv 22, 17–25, Dt 17, 1).

1, 10f: The imperfect sacrifices offered without sincerity by the people of Judah are displeasing to the Lord. He will rather be pleased with the offerings of the Gentile nations throughout the world (*from the rising of the sun, even to its setting*), which anticipate the *pure offering* to be sacrificed in Messianic times, the universal Sacrifice of the Mass, as we are told by the Council of Trent.

14 Cursed is the deceiver, who has
       in his flock a male,
    but under his vow sacrifices
       to the LORD a gelding;
    For a great King am I, says the
       LORD of hosts,
    and my name will be feared
       among the nations.

2 And now, O priests, this
       commandment is for you:
    If you do not listen,
2 And if you do not lay it to
       heart,
    to give glory to my name,
       says the LORD of hosts,
    I will send a curse upon you
    and of your blessing I will
       make a curse.
    Yes, I have already cursed it,
       because you do not lay it to
       heart.
3 Lo, I will deprive you of the
       shoulder
    and I will strew dung in your
       faces,
    The dung of your feasts,
       and you will be carried off
       with it.
4 Then you will know that I sent
       you this commandment
    because I have a covenant
       with Levi,
    says the LORD of hosts.
5 My covenant with him was one
       of life and peace;
    fear I put in him, and he
       feared me,
    and stood in awe of my name.
6 True doctrine was in his mouth,
    and no dishonesty was found
       upon his lips;
    He walked with me in integrity
       and uprightness,
    and turned many away from
       evil.
7 For the lips of the priest are to
       keep knowledge,
    and instruction is to be sought
       from his mouth,
    because he is the messenger
       of the LORD of hosts.

8 But you have turned aside from
       the way,
    and have caused many to
       falter by your instruction;
    You have made void the coven-
       ant of Levi,
    says the LORD of hosts.
9 I, therefore, have made you
       contemptible
    and base before all the people,
    Since you do not keep my ways,
    but show partiality in your
       decisions.

Sins of the People

10 Have we not all the one Father?
    Has not the one God created
       us?
    Why then do we break faith
       with each other,
    violating the covenant of our
       fathers?
11 Judah has broken faith; an
       abominable thing
    has been done in Jerusalem.
    Judah has profaned the temple
       which the LORD loves,
    and has married an idolatrous
       woman.
12 May the LORD cut off from the
       man who does this
    both witness and advocate out
       of the tents of Jacob,
    and anyone to offer sacrifice
       to the LORD of hosts!

13 This also you do: the altar of
       the LORD you cover
    with tears, weeping and groan-
       ing,
    Because he no longer regards
       your sacrifice
    nor accepts it favorably from
       your hand;
14 And you say, "Why is it?"—
    Because the LORD is witness
    between you and the wife of
       your youth,
    With whom you have broken
       faith
    though she is your companion,
       your betrothed wife.

15 Did he not make one being,
       with flesh and spirit:
    and what does that one
       require but godly offspring?
    You must then safeguard life
       that is your own,
    and not break faith with the
       wife of your youth.
16 For I hate divorce,
       says the LORD, the God of
       Israel,
    And covering one's garment with
       injustice,
       says the LORD of hosts;
    You must then safeguard life
       that is your own,
    and not break faith.

17 You have wearied the LORD
       with your words,
    yet you say, "How have we
       wearied him?"
    By your saying, "Every evildoer
       is good in the sight of the
       LORD,
    And he is pleased with him";
    or else, "Where is the just
       God?"

The Messenger of the Covenant

3 Lo, I am sending my messenger
       to prepare the way before me;
    And suddenly there will come
       to the temple
    the LORD whom you seek,
    And the messenger of the
       covenant whom you desire.
    Yes, he is coming, says the
       LORD of hosts.
2 But who will endure the day of
       his coming?
    And who can stand when he
       appears?
    For he is like the refiner's fire,
       or like the fuller's lye.
3 he will sit refining and purifying
       [silver],
    and he will purify the sons of
       Levi,
    Refining them like gold or like
       silver
    that they may offer due
       sacrifice to the LORD.

2, 3: *I will deprive you of the shoulder:* this part
of a sacrificial animal, allotted by the law (Dt 18, 3)
to the priests, will be withheld from them.
2, 10-16: Intermarriage of Israelites with foreigners
was forbidden according to Dt 7, 1–4. After the Exile
this law was strictly enforced (Ezr 9–10). Foreign
marriages are here portrayed as a violation of the

covenant (v 10), which made the sacrifices offered by
the offenders unacceptable to God (v 13). They were
all the more reprehensible when accompanied by the
divorce of Israelite wives (vv 14ff). This gradual
return to the primitive ideal of the indissolubility of
marriage was fully realized in New Testament times
through the teaching of Christ; cf Mt 19, 3–12.

3, 1: *My messenger . . . before me:* in v 23 this
messenger is called Elijah. In Mt 11, 10 these words
are quoted by Christ as referring to John the Baptist,
who prepared the way for the coming of the Savior;
cf Mt 3, 1ff.11f; 17, 11ff; Mk 1, 2–8; Lk 3, 2–18;
Jn 1, 31–34.

4 Then the sacrifice of Judah and
     Jerusalem
     will please the LORD,
   as in the days of old, as in
     years gone by.
5 I will draw near to you for
     judgment,
   and I will be swift to bear
     witness
   Against the sorcerers, adulterers,
     and perjurers,
   those who defraud the hired
     man of his wages,
   Against those who defraud
     widows and orphans;
   those who turn aside the
     stranger,
   and those who do not fear me,
   says the LORD of hosts.

6 Surely I, the LORD, do not
     change,
   nor do you cease to be sons
     of Jacob.
7 Since the days of your fathers
     you have turned aside
   from my statutes, and have
     not kept them.
   Return to me, and I will return
     to you,
   says the LORD of hosts.
   Yet you say, "How must we
     return?"
8 Dare a man rob God? Yet you
     are robbing me!
   And you say, "How do we rob
     you?"
   In tithes and in offerings!
9 You are indeed accursed,
   for you, the whole nation,
     rob me.
10 Bring the whole tithe
     into the storehouse,
   That there may be food in my
     house,
   and try me in this, says the
     LORD of hosts:

Shall I not open for you the
     floodgates of heaven,
   to pour down blessing upon
     you without measure?
11 For your sake I will forbid the
     locust
   to destroy your crops;
   And the vine in the field will
     not be barren,
   says the LORD of hosts.
12 Then all nations will call you
     blessed,
   for you will be a delightful
     land,
   says the LORD of hosts.

13 You have defiled me in word,
     says the LORD,
   yet you ask, "What have we
     spoken against you?"
14 You have said, "It is vain to
     serve God,
   and what do we profit by
     keeping his command,
   And going about in penitential
     dress
   in awe of the LORD of hosts?
15 Rather must we call the proud
     blessed;
   for indeed evildoers prosper,
   and even tempt God with
     impunity."
16 Then they who fear the LORD
     spoke with one another,
   and the LORD listened
     attentively;
   And a record book was written
     before him
   of those who fear the LORD
   and trust in his name.
17 And they shall be mine, says
     the LORD of hosts,
   my own special possession,
   on the day I take action.
   And I will have compassion on
     them,
   as a man has compassion on
     his son who serves him.

18 Then you will again see the
     distinction
   between the just and the
     wicked;
   Between him who serves God,
   and him who does not serve
     him.
19 For lo, the day is coming,
     blazing like an oven,
   when all the proud and all
     evildoers will be stubble,
   And the day that is coming will
     set them on fire,
   leaving them neither root nor
     branch,
   says the LORD of hosts.
20 But for you who fear my name,
     there will arise
   the sun of justice with its
     healing rays;
   And you will gambol like calves
     out of the stall
21   and tread down the wicked;
   They will become ashes under
     the soles of your feet,
   on the day I take action, says
     the LORD of hosts.

22 Remember the law of Moses my
     servant,
   which I enjoined upon him
     on Horeb,
   The statutes and ordinances
     for all Israel.
23 Lo, I will send you
     Elijah, the prophet,
   Before the day of the LORD
     comes,
   the great and terrible day,
24 To turn the hearts of the fathers
     to their children,
   and the hearts of the children
     to their fathers,
   Lest I come and strike
     the land with doom.

   Lo, I will send you
     Elijah, the prophet,
   Before the day of the LORD comes,
     the great and terrible day.

3, 6f: God is faithful to his promises. He will not
abandon the Israelites, who are still his people.
3, 10: *Storehouse:* the temple treasury.
3, 16: *Record book:* see note on Ex 32, 32.
3, 23: *Elijah:* described in 2 Kgs 2, 11 as taken

heavenward in a fiery chariot. Here his return to earth
seems to be foretold. Jewish tradition has interpreted
this literally; Christ declares it to be fulfilled in the
coming of John the Baptist (Mt 17, 10–13).

3, 24: The words in fine print, a repetition of a
v 23a-d, have been added by the scribes so that the
collection of the twelve minor prophets will not end
with the threat of doom.

The Tree of Jesse

THE TREE OF JESSE, from the Psalter of Queen Ingeburge (c.1200)

Iɴ ᴛʜᴇ ᴇɪɢʜᴛʜ ᴄᴇɴᴛᴜʀʏ before the birth of Christ, the prophet Isaiah foretold the nature and virtues of the Messiah, the just king who was to rule in the golden age of peace and unity. He was to come from the stock of David and he would manifest the virtues that had marked the great kings and patriarchs—the intellect of Solomon, the courage and integrity of David, the perseverance and dedication of Moses, Jacob, and Abraham:

"... a shoot shall sprout from the stump of Jesse,
  and from his roots a bud shall blossom.
The spirit of the Lord shall rest upon him:
  a spirit of wisdom and understanding,
A spirit of counsel and of strength,
  a spirit of knowledge and of fear of the
    Lord,
  and his delight shall be the fear of the
    Lord" (Is 11,1-3).

The artists of the Middle Ages drew upon this text of Isaiah for one of their most powerful and effective themes, the Tree of Jesse, a representation of the genealogy of Christ which illustrated the continuity between the Testaments and outlined the Davidic descent of the Messiah.

The Fathers and the medieval theologians were unanimous in interpreting the prophecy of Isaiah: the shoot was the Virgin Mary, the bud or flower was Jesus Christ.

Tradition does not speak of Jesse himself, who seems almost mysterious in his insignificance; one interpretation is that he is chosen for the beginning of this epic genealogy only because of the great contrast that results between the progenitor of the line and its culmination.

This was the tradition that guided the artist when the subject first became popular, in the first half of the twelfth century.

THE TREE OF JESSE

The first notable example is attributed to the Abbot Suger (1081-1151), a versatile genius who was regent of France when Louis VII went off to lead the Second Crusade and who won the title of "Father of His Country."

In 1144 Abbot Suger commissioned a stained glass window with the Jesse theme for his Abbey of St. Denis, near Paris. Suger's window was broken up in the course of time, but a version of it was installed in Chartres Cathedral (1150), and this survives intact.

In the Chartres window—regarded by many as the best work ever produced in stained glass—Jesse, the father of David, is pictured deep asleep in the night of the Old Testament, the gloom about him lit by a single lamp swinging above his head. From this sleeping figure a great tree (or vine) grows, and along the rising trunk are shown a number of the kings of Judah in whom the line of David was continued. The Chartres tree, like other early examples, pictures only a few kings, but in later times as many as fifty ancestors of Christ were represented.

Above the kings comes Mary and, finally, Christ, the Messiah, about whom flutter seven doves, the gifts of the Holy Spirit foretold by Isaiah. Along the branches, on either side of the trunk, stand the prophets, who preached through the ages the coming of the flower from the shoot of Jesse, sustaining the hope of the Messiah in generation after generation.

The Chartres Jesse Tree is on a monumental scale (25 feet high by 9 wide) and other early windows are of similar proportions. However, the theme soon appeared in smaller forms—in sculpture, wood carvings, tapestries, frescoes, and enamels, as well as miniatures in bibles, psalters, and breviaries. Jesse Trees became a commonplace element in the portals of churches and later (15th cent.) in predellas and choir stalls.

One of the finest miniature paintings of a Jesse Tree is found in the Psalter of Queen Ingeburge (c. 1200). The small size of the page has required the ultimate in condensation, and the kings of Judah are here reduced to two. The miniature versions often turn to folklore and fantasy. The *Holkham Bible Picture Book*, the work of an Anglo-Norman artist, has touches of Druidic lore in one tree, and in another introduces three sets of ancestors into the genealogy—twelve with Abraham, twelve more with Jesse, and another thirteen with Manasseh. The tree in this latter version stems from the side of Abraham, not from Jesse.

Between the first significant emergence of the Jesse Tree and its decline toward the end of the sixteenth century, there were inevitably many extreme variations, but the form developed for Abbot Suger generally prevailed, the only common deviation being that, in the thirteenth century, with the growing devotion to Mary, she is sometimes found at the topmost branch, holding the Divine Infant in her arms.

THE TREE OF JESSE, by Brother Placid, O.S.B., St. John's Abbey, Collegeville, Minn. A modern interpretation of this theme, with only the essential details but with full respect for the traditional contents of the subject.

The
NEW TESTAMENT

THE GOSPEL ACCORDING TO

Matthew

PROLOGUE: THE COMING OF THE SAVIOR

Genealogy of Jesus

A FAMILY record of Jesus Christ, son of David, son of Abraham. 2 Abraham was the father of Isaac, Isaac the father of Jacob, Jacob the father of Judah and his brothers.

3 Judah was the father of Perez and Zerah, whose mother was Tamar.
Perez was the father of Hezron,
Hezron the father of Ram.
4 Ram was the father of Amminadab,
Amminadab the father of Nahshon,
Nahshon the father of Salmon.
5 Salmon was the father of Boaz,
whose mother was Rahab,
Boaz was the father of Obed,
whose mother was Ruth.
Obed was the father of Jesse,
6 Jesse the father of King David.
David was the father of Solomon,
whose mother had been the wife of Uriah.
7 Solomon was the father of Rehoboam,
Rehoboam the father of Abijah,
Abijah the father of Asa.
8 Asa was the father of Jehoshaphat,
Jehoshaphat the father of Joram,
Joram the father of Uzziah.
9 Uzziah was the father of Jotham,
Jotham the father of Ahaz,
Ahaz the father of Hezekiah.
10 Hezekiah was the father of Manasseh,
Manasseh the father of Amos,
Amos the father of Josiah.
11 Josiah became the father of Jechoniah and his brothers at the time of the Babylonian exile.
12 After the Babylonian exile Jechoniah was the father of Shealtiel,
Shealtiel the father of Zerubbabel.
13 Zerubbabel was the father of Abiud,
Abiud the father of Eliakim,
Eliakim the father of Azor.
14 Azor was the father of Zadok,
Zadok the father of Achim,

1, 1: *A family record of Jesus Christ:* the Greek may also be taken to mean "book of the history of the origin of Jesus Christ." In this sense the opening verse is a title for the whole gospel, which then begins with the genealogy of Christ; cf Gn 2, 4. *Jesus:* the Greek and Latin form of the late Hebrew and Aramaic name *Jeshua*, meaning "The Lord is salvation." *Christ:* in v 17 and elsewhere, a title from the Greek *Christos* which translates the Hebrew *Mashiah*, "Anointed One," applied to the expected representative of God

on earth. Matthew in v 1 uses "Jesus Christ" as a proper name, as was customary in later Christian circles; cf Jn 1, 17; Phil 2, 11.
1, 2–17: The genealogy points out Jesus' Davidic lineage through Joseph who, however, is called "the husband of Mary" (1, 16), not the father of Jesus. In 1, 18–25, the evangelist explains the reason for the foster paternity of Joseph. The genealogy recalls the messianic hope of Israel by alluding to the divine promises to the patriarchs (2) and to David (6); cf 2

Sm 7, 12–16. It places this hope in the context of Israel's sinfulness by allusion to David's murder of Uriah (6), and also to the Babylonian captivity (11). The constant repetition of the term "was the father of," literally "begot," implies the continuous presence of God in Israel sustaining the faith and hope of the people. For the implication of the divine presence in the Greek term, cf 1 Cor 4, 15; Gal 4, 24.

Achim the father of Eliud.
15 Eliud was the father of Eleazar,
Eleazar the father of Matthan,
Matthan the father of Jacob.
16 Jacob was the father of Joseph
the husband of Mary.
It was of her that Jesus who is
called the Messiah was
born.
17 Thus the total number of
generations is:
from Abraham to David,
fourteen generations;
from David to the Babylonian
captivity, fourteen
generations;
from the Babylonian captivity
to the Messiah, fourteen
generations.

The Birth of Jesus

18 Now this is how the birth of
Jesus Christ came about. When his
mother Mary was engaged to Joseph,
but before they lived together, she
was found with child through the
power of the Holy Spirit. 19 Joseph
her husband, an upright man unwilling to expose her to the law,
decided to divorce her quietly.
20 Such was his intention when
suddenly the angel of the Lord appeared in a dream and said to him:
"Joseph, son of David, have no fear
about taking Mary as your wife.
It is by the Holy Spirit that she has
conceived this child. 21 She is to
have a son and you are to name him
Jesus because he will save his people
from their sins." 22 All this happened to fulfill what the Lord had
said through the prophet:

23 "The virgin shall be with child
and give birth to a son,
and they shall call him
Emmanuel,"

a name which means "God is with
us." 24 When Joseph awoke he
did as the angel of the Lord had
directed him and received her into
his home as his wife. 25 He had no
relations with her at any time before
she bore a son, whom he named
Jesus.

The Astrologers

2 After Jesus' birth in Bethlehem
of Judea during the reign of King
Herod, astrologers from the east
arrived one day in Jerusalem 2 inquiring, "Where is the newborn king
of the Jews? We observed his star at
its rising and have come to pay him
homage." 3 At this news King
Herod became greatly disturbed, and
with him all Jerusalem. 4 Summoning all of the chief priests and
scribes of the people, he inquired of
them where the Messiah was to be
born. 5 "In Bethlehem of Judea,"
they informed him. "Here is what
the prophet has written:

6 'And you, Bethlehem, land of
Judah,
are by no means least among
the princes of Judah,
since from you shall come a
ruler
who is to shepherd my people
Israel.'"

7 Herod called the astrologers aside
and found out from them the exact
time of the star's appearance. 8
Then he sent them to Bethlehem,
after having instructed them: "Go
and get detailed information about
the child. When you have found
him, report your findings to me so
that I may go and offer him homage
too."

9 After their audience with the
king, they set out. The star which
they had observed at its rising went
ahead of them until it came to a
standstill over the place where the
child was. 10 They were overjoyed
at seeing the star, 11 and on
entering the house, found the child
with Mary his mother. They prostrated themselves and did him
homage. Then they opened their
coffers and presented him with
gifts of gold, frankincense, and
myrrh.

12 They received a message in a
dream not to return to Herod, so
they went back to their own country
by another route.

1, 17: The genealogy is artificially constructed out
of three groups of fourteen names each, taken principally from Genesis, Ruth, 1 Chronicles and 2
Kings. The list of names beginning with Abiud in
1, 13 is unknown to the Old Testament. The number
14 is undoubtedly a mnemonic device, perhaps chosen
because the numerical value of the three letters of
David's name (DVD) yields in Hebrew the sum of 14.
1, 18-25: The evangelist shows that Jesus was
introduced into the Davidic line through the divine
choice of Joseph as his legal father. Throughout the
public ministry of Jesus it was understandably the
common opinion that Joseph was the natural father
of Jesus; cf Mt 13, 55; Jn 6, 42.
1, 18: Mary was engaged to Joseph: they were
living in a state of espousal which usually lasted one
year in Galilee.
1, 19: A common opinion from the time of the
Church Fathers ascribes to Joseph the fear that Mary's
child was a consequence of adultery. The evangelist
depicts Joseph in a dilemma: he feels it would not be
honorable for him to assume the paternity of the
child in view of the requirements of "justice" under
Mosaic law; but at the same time he realizes that even
a private divorce in the presence of only a few
witnesses would eventually expose Mary to the
popular suspicion of adultery.
1, 20f: To what extent the angelic visitation of
Joseph through a dream is reality or popular description surrounding the divine message to him is subject
to discussion. In either case the evangelist makes it
abundantly clear to his readers that Joseph accepted
Mary as his wife, together with the child, because he

saw the will of God expressed in the circumstances.
He will save his people from their sins: the child will
not be a warrior-king overcoming the enemies of
Israel, but will free the people from sin.
1, 22f: This is a prophetic reinterpretation of Is
7, 14, in the light of the facts Matthew has outlined:
the virginal conception of Jesus, his Davidic messianic role in a spiritual sense, Joseph's legal paternity,
and the unique presence of God in Jesus, which the
church of the evangelist's time had to come to understand as his divinity. All these things about Jesus that
were faintly traced in Is 7, 14 are now seen by Matthew
to be fully brought to light as God's plan.
1, 25: He had no relations with her at any time
before: the evangelist emphasizes the virginity of the
mother of Jesus from the moment of his conception
to his birth. He does not concern himself here with
the period that followed the birth of Jesus, but merely
wishes to show that Joseph fully respected the legal
character of the paternity imposed on him by the
divine will. Moreover, the New Testament makes no
mention anywhere of children of Joseph and Mary.
2, 1-25: The episodes which follow the explanation
of Jesus' Davidic origin through the legal paternity of
Joseph raise the question: Do we have here a historical composition with theological overtones or a
theological composition resting on a broad historical
basis? The latter supposition finds support in the
typology of the second chapter of Matthew, which
parallels Jesus with Israel and Moses in a way that
suggests an influence of extra-biblical Jewish religious
traditions.
2, 1: King Herod: called "the Great" because of

his political astuteness and his achievements in
building, which included the temple in Jerusalem.
In 40 B.C. the Roman senate appointed him king of
Judea. From then on Herod succeeded in extending
his rule to other parts of Palestine. Since Herod is
known to have died in 4 B.C., scholars assign 7 or 6
B.C. as the actual date of the birth of Jesus; cf Mt
2, 16. Astrologers from the east: the various personages
designated by the Greek term magoi did not include
kings. Many think that the allusion is to learned men
from Babylon who had contact with Jewish messianism; cf Dn 2, 2.
2, 5f: The citation combines Mi 5, 1 and 2 Sm
5, 2. It emphasizes the fulfillment of Old Testament
prophecy concerning Bethlehem, the birthplace of
Jesus. For the expression of a current opinion that the
Messiah was to come from Bethlehem, cf Jn 7, 42.
2, 9f: The action of the star implies that in the
evangelist's thought it is a supernatural phenomenon. It is a symbol of faith leading the Gentiles to
the discovery of Jesus as their king and savior; cf 2
Pt 1, 19.
2, 11: The house: Matthew's tradition of the
astrologers' visit to a house is unrelated to the place of
Jesus' birth as reported in Luke 2, 12. Gold, frankincense and myrrh: such gifts were customary in the
Orient as signs of homage. The association of 2, 11
with Ps 72, 10f occasioned the mistaken supposition
that the astrologers were kings. For the Old Testament oracles concerning the Gentiles' homage to
Yahweh, cf Nm 24, 17; Is 49, 23; 60, 5f.

The Flight into Egypt

13 After they had left, the angel of the Lord suddenly appeared in a dream to Joseph with the command: "Get up, take the child and his mother, and flee to Egypt. Stay there until I tell you otherwise. Herod is searching for the child to destroy him." 14 Joseph got up and took the child and his mother and left that night for Egypt. 15 He stayed there until the death of Herod, to fulfill what the Lord had said through the prophet:

"Out of Egypt I have called my
    son."

The Innocents

16 Once Herod realized that he had been deceived by the astrologers, he became furious. He ordered the massacre of all the boys two years old and under in Bethlehem and its environs, making his calculations on the basis of the date he had learned from the astrologers. 17 What was said through Jeremiah the prophet was then fulfilled:

18 "A cry was heard at Ramah,
    sobbing and loud lamentation:
Rachel bewailing her children;
    no comfort for her, since they
    are no more."

The Return to Nazareth

19 But after Herod's death, the angel of the Lord appeared in a dream to Joseph in Egypt 20 with the command: "Get up, take the child and his mother, and set out for the land of Israel. Those who had designs on the life of the child are dead." 21 He got up, took the child and his mother, and returned to the land of Israel. 22 He heard, however, that Archelaus had succeeded his father Herod as king of Judea, and he was afraid to go back there. Instead, because of a warning received in a dream, Joseph went to the region of Galilee. 23 There he settled in a town called Nazareth. In this way what was said through the prophets was fulfilled:

"He shall be called a Nazorean."

PROMULGATION OF THE REIGN OF GOD

John the Baptizer

3 When John the Baptizer made his appearance as a preacher in the desert of Judea, this was his theme: 2 "Reform your lives! The reign of God is at hand." 3 It was of him that the prophet Isaiah had spoken when he said:

"A herald's voice in the desert:
'Prepare the way of the Lord,
make straight his paths.'"

4 John was clothed in a garment of camel's hair, and wore a leather belt around his waist. Grasshoppers and wild honey were his food. 5 At that time Jerusalem, all Judea, and the whole region around the Jordan were going out to him. 6 They were being baptized by him in the Jordan River as they confessed their sins.

7 When he saw that many of the Pharisees and Sadducees were stepping forward for this bath, he said to them: "You brood of vipers! Who told you to flee from the wrath to come? 8 Give some evidence that you mean to reform. 9 Do not pride yourselves on the claim, 'Abraham is our father.' I tell you, God can raise up children to Abraham from these very stones. 10 Even now the ax is laid to the root of the tree. Every tree that is not fruitful will be cut down and thrown into the fire. 11 I baptize you in water for the sake of reform, but the one who will follow me is more powerful than I. I am not even fit to carry his sandals. He it is who will baptize you in the Holy Spirit and fire. 12 His winnowing-fan is in his hand. He will clear the threshing floor and gather his grain into the barn, but the chaff he will burn in unquenchable fire."

The Baptism of Jesus

13 Later Jesus, coming from Galilee, appeared before John at the Jordan to be baptized by him. 14 John tried to refuse him with the protest, "I should be baptized by you, yet you come to me!" 15 Jesus answered: "Give in for now. We must do this if we would fulfill all of God's demands." So John gave in. 16 After Jesus was baptized, he came directly out of the water. Suddenly the sky opened and he saw the Spirit of God descend like a dove and hover over him. 17 With that, a voice from the heavens said, "This is my beloved Son. My favor rests on him."

2, 13: *Flee to Egypt:* from the time of the Maccabees, Egypt had been a customary place of refuge. An earlier example is Jeroboam's flight to Egypt (1 Kgs 11, 40).

2, 15: The citation of Hos 11, 1, relates Jesus to Israel. Just as God called Israel out of Egypt to create a people peculiarly his own, so he called Jesus out of Egypt into the land of Israel to accomplish his purpose of creating the new Israel and people of God. The story of the flight into Egypt illustrates the divine concealment of the child so that he might fulfill his role as head of the new Israel.

2, 17f: The plaint over the massacre is not ascribed to the people of Bethlehem but figuratively to Rachel bewailing Israel's exile (Jer 31, 15f). She is comforted by a promise of restoration. A note of consolation seems implied in Matthew's citation, which views the massacre of infants as a guarantee of God's action to create the new people of God through Jesus; cf Rv 6, 9ff.

2, 22: *Archelaus:* i.e., "leader of the people," a son of Herod the Great and brother of Herod Antipas;

see note on Acts 4, 27. He ruled as ethnarch of Judea, Samaria and Idumea from 4 B.C. to A.D. 6, when he was deposed by the Emperor Augustus.

2, 23: *He shall be called a Nazorean:* unidentifiable in any Old Testament passage. Jesus' residence in Galilee amid a mixed population of Jews and Gentiles is viewed as a providential indication of his messianic mission to the Gentiles; cf Is 66, 18f; Am 9, 11f.

3, 1–17: This narrative is concerned with the prophetic message and person of John (1–5), his baptism (6), his critique of the Pharisees and Sadducees (7–10), his message concerning Jesus (11f), and his baptism of Jesus, with its theological significance (13–17).

3, 2: *Reform your lives!:* on the notion of repentance, see note on Acts 2, 38. *The reign of God is at hand:* literally, "the kingdom of heaven." "Heaven" is a conventional expression which avoids using the divine name. The term invokes God's sovereign authority over the human race. It announces that a new intervention of God is beginning in history which

invites Israel to accept the prophetic manifestation of his will through the Baptizer.

3, 4: The Baptizer's garb recalls that of Elijah in 2 Kgs 1, 8: Jesus speaks of the Baptizer as Elijah who *has already come* (Mt 17, 10ff; Mk 9, 10ff); cf Mal 3, 24.

3, 7–10: John's criticism of the Pharisees and Sadducees implies that they have come to receive baptism for the purpose of gaining popular favor rather than to exercise their religious leadership in a national program of true reform. Matthew sees the Christian community to be the true *children of Abraham* who fulfill the Baptizer's prophetic words (v 10).

3, 11f: The baptism of John prepares for the purifying action *in the Holy Spirit and fire* which Jesus will effect; cf Is 1, 25; Zec 13, 9; Mal 3, 2. Refusal of this baptism of Jesus leads to a final judgment of condemnation *in unquenchable fire;* cf Is 34, 8ff; Jer 7, 20.

3, 13–17: For the theological significance of this account of Jesus' baptism, see note on Mk 1, 9ff.

The Temptation

4 Then Jesus was led into the desert by the Spirit to be tempted by the devil. 2 He fasted forty days and forty nights, and afterward was hungry. 3 The tempter approached and said to him, "If you are the Son of God, command these stones to turn into bread." 4 Jesus replied, "Scripture has it:

'Not on bread alone is man to live
but on every utterance that comes from the mouth of God.'"

5 Next the devil took him to the holy city, set him on the parapet of the temple, 6 and said, "If you are the Son of God, throw yourself down. Scripture has it:

'He will bid his angels take care of you;
with their hands they will support you
that you may never stumble on a stone.'"

7 Jesus answered him, "Scripture also has it:

'You shall not put the Lord your God to the test.'"

8 The devil then took him up a very high mountain and displayed before him all the kingdoms of the world in their magnificence, promising, 9 "All these will I bestow on you if you prostrate yourself in homage before me." 10 At this, Jesus said to him, "Away with you, Satan! Scripture has it:

'You shall do homage to the Lord your God;

him alone shall you adore.'"

11 At that the devil left him, and angels came and waited on him.

Jesus in Capernaum

12 When Jesus heard that John had been arrested, he withdrew to Galilee. 13 He left Nazareth and went down to live in Capernaum by the sea near the territory of Zebulun and Naphtali, 14 to fulfill what had been said through Isaiah the prophet:

15 "Land of Zebulun, land of Naphtali
along the sea beyond the Jordan, heathen Galilee:
16 a people living in darkness has seen a great light.
On those who inhabit a land overshadowed by death, light has arisen."

17 From that time on Jesus began to proclaim this theme: "Reform your lives! The kingdom of heaven is at hand."

The First Disciples Called

18 As he was walking along the Sea of Galilee he watched two brothers, Simon now known as Peter, and his brother Andrew, casting a net into the sea. They were fishermen. 19 He said to them, "Come after me and I will make you fishers of men." 20 They immediately abandoned their nets and became his followers. 21 He walked along farther and caught sight of two other brothers, James, Zebedee's son, and his brother John. They too were in their boat,

getting their nets in order with their father, Zebedee. 22 He called them, and immediately they abandoned boat and father to follow him.

The Mission of Preaching

23 Jesus toured all of Galilee. He taught in their synagogues, proclaimed the good news of the kingdom, and cured the people of every disease and illness. 24 As a consequence of this, his reputation traveled the length of Syria. They carried to him all those afflicted with various diseases and racked with pain: the possessed, the lunatics, the paralyzed. He cured them all. 25 The great crowds that followed him came from Galilee, the Ten Cities, Jerusalem and Judea, and from across the Jordan.

5 When he saw the crowds he went up on the mountainside. After he had sat down his disciples gathered around him, 2 and he began to teach them:

The Beatitudes

3 "How blest are the poor in spirit: the reign of God is theirs.
Blest too are the sorrowing; they shall be consoled.
[Blest are the lowly; they shall inherit the land.]
6 Blest are they who hunger and thirst for holiness;
they shall have their fill.
7 Blest are they who show mercy; mercy shall be theirs.
8 Blest are the single-hearted for they shall see God.

4, 1–11: An introduction to the gospel proper; see note on Mk 1, 12f. Some regard the account as a Christian reflection on Jesus' messianic role: he refuses to use his miraculous power simply to relieve human need (3f), or to satisfy requests of unbelievers (5ff); he disdains a messianic role (8ff) that would be purely political in its implications. The central theme is the obedience of Jesus to God as he is known through the Old Testament.
4, 3: *If you are the son of God:* in the sense of the messianic king of Ps 2.
4, 4: A citation of Dt 8, 3, signifying that the miracles of the Exodus were signs of God's religious, rather than physical, care of Israel.
4, 6f: The tempter here applies to the Messiah verse 11 of Psalm 91 dealing with God's protection of the just. Jesus' reply (Dt 6, 16) teaches that miracles are not to be demanded of God as evidence of his care of man.
4, 10: The citation expresses the basic attitude of worship which every man should have toward God.

4, 12–17: The gospel proper begins here with a summary introduction to the Galilean ministry: the Baptizer is arrested by Herod Antipas (12); Jesus makes Capernaum the center of his activity (13) and preaching (17). The citation from Is 9, 1f identifies the ministry of Jesus as fulfilling the prophecy of the restoration of the northern kingdom, destroyed by the Assyrians in 721 B.C.
4, 17: See note on 3, 2.
4, 19: To be *fishers of men* requires abandonment of former means of livelihood in order to preach the kingdom of God and testify to its arrival in the name of Jesus; cf 10, 1f. It may be assumed that this complete dedication was accomplished only gradually.
5, 3–12: The beatitudes announce religious happiness for the *anawim*, i.e., those who lack material goods and stand in need of the spiritual blessings promised by Christ; cf Dt 24, 14; Ps 37, 14; 40, 18; Is 61, 1. This happiness is to reach its fulfillment through Christ. Recognition of the *anawim* contrasts with the religious thought of the time which regarded human

affliction and sorrow as the punishment of personal sin. For the Christian attitude toward the poor and afflicted, cf Mt 25, 34–46; Jas 2, 15f; 1 Jn 4, 20.
5, 7: Matthew fashions the Sermon on the Mount from the sayings of Jesus concerning Moses and the law. Luke's corresponding Sermon on the Plain (6, 17–49) is differently arranged. A key factor is that Jesus came not to abolish but to fulfill the law and the prophets. Jesus makes greater demands on men than did the law of Moses; but he bestows the justice needed for meeting these demands (Rom 8, 1–11), and his disciples are bound to respond to the divine gift (5, 20; 7, 21.24–27). Though concerned with the relationship between God and the individual, the social implications of the Sermon on the Mount are evident.
5, 8: *The single-hearted:* those who serve God loyally for his own sake and not primarily out of self-interest.

9 Blest too the peacemakers; they
    shall be called sons of God.
10 Blest are those persecuted for
    holiness' sake; the reign of
    God is theirs.
11 Blest are you when they insult
    you and persecute you and
    utter every kind of slander
    against you because of me.
12 Be glad and rejoice, for your
    reward is great in heaven;
    they persecuted the prophets
    before you in the very same
    way.

The Disciples

13 "You are the salt of the earth.
But what if salt goes flat? How can
you restore its flavor? Then it is good
for nothing but to be thrown out and
trampled underfoot.
14 "You are the light of the
world. A city set on a hill cannot be
hidden. 15 Men do not light a
lamp and then put it under a bushel
basket. They set it on a stand where
it gives light to all in the house.
16 In the same way, your light must
shine before men so that they may
see goodness in your acts and give
praise to your heavenly Father.

The Old Law and the New

17 "Do not think that I have come
to abolish the law and the prophets.
I have come, not to abolish them, but
to fulfill them. 18 Of this much I
assure you: until heaven and earth
pass away, not the smallest letter of
the law, not the smallest part of a
letter, shall be done away with until
it all comes true. 19 That is why
whoever breaks the least significant
of these commands and teaches
others to do so shall be called least
in the kingdom of God. Whoever
fulfills and teaches these commands
shall be great in the kingdom of
God. 20 I tell you, unless your
holiness surpasses that of the scribes

and Pharisees you shall not enter the
kingdom of God.

Against Anger

21 "You have heard the commandment imposed on your forefathers. 'You shall not commit
murder; every murderer shall be
liable to judgment.' 22 What I say
to you is: everyone who grows angry
with his brother shall be liable to
judgment; any man who uses abusive
language toward his brother shall be
answerable to the Sanhedrin, and if
he holds him in contempt he risks
the fires of Gehenna. 23 If you
bring your gift to the altar and there
recall that your brother has anything
against you, 24 leave your gift at
the altar, go first to be reconciled
with your brother, and then come
and offer your gift. 25 Lose no
time; settle with your opponent
while on your way to court with him.
Otherwise your opponent may hand
you over to the judge, who will hand
you over to the guard, who will
throw you into prison. 26 I warn
you, you will not be released until
you have paid the last penny.

Occasions of Impurity

27 "You have heard the commandment, 'You shall not commit
adultery.' 28 What I say to you is:
anyone who looks lustfully at a
woman has already committed adultery with her in his thoughts. 29 If
your right eye is your trouble, gouge
it out and throw it away! Better to
lose part of your body than to have it
all cast into Gehenna. 30 Again, if
your right hand is your trouble, cut
it off and throw it away! Better to
lose part of your body than to have
it all cast into Gehenna.

Divorce

31 "It was also said, 'Whenever a
man divorces his wife, he must give

her a decree of divorce.' 32 What I
say to you is: everyone who divorces
his wife—lewd conduct is a separate
case—forces her to commit adultery.
The man who marries a divorced
woman likewise commits adultery.

On Oaths

33 "You have heard the commandment imposed on your forefathers, 'Do not take a false oath;
rather, make good to the Lord all
your pledges.' 34 What I tell you is:
do not swear at all. Do not swear by
heaven (it is God's throne), 35 nor
by the earth (it is his footstool), nor
by Jerusalem (it is the city of the
great King); 36 do not swear by
your head (you cannot make a
single hair white or black). 37 Say,
'Yes' when you mean 'Yes' and 'No'
when you mean 'No'. Anything
beyond that is from the evil one.

New Law of Retaliation

38 "You have heard the commandment, 'An eye for an eye, a
tooth for a tooth.' 39 But what I
say to you is: offer no resistance to
injury. When a person strikes you
on the right cheek, turn and offer him
the other. 40 If anyone wants to go
to law over your shirt, hand him
your coat as well. 41 Should anyone press you into service for one
mile, go with him two miles. 42
Give to the man who begs from you.
Do not turn your back on the
borrower.

Love of Enemies

43 "You have heard the commandment, 'You shall love your
countryman but hate your enemy.'
44 My command to you is: love
your enemies, pray for your persecutors. 45 This will prove that you
are sons of your heavenly Father, for
his sun rises on the bad and the good,
he rains on the just and the unjust.

5, 9: *The peacemakers:* those whose lives promote
harmony within the human community (1 Thes 5, 14)
as contrasted with those who foster strife through
violence for personal advantage.
5, 10: *For holiness' sake:* fidelity to the divine
precepts through which holiness is attained is
deepened by the test of persecution.
5, 13–16: The disciples of Jesus, despite reproach
and persecution (11f), make the human community
valuable in God's eyes (*salt of the earth*) and enlighten
the world with *the light* of God's prophetic word,
which they preach by word and example (16).
5, 17–20: Jesus' teaching does not reject the old

law and the prophets; instead, it illumines the
meaning God intended the Old Testament ultimately
to have (17). Disregard of even the slightest detail of
the law means failure to secure that fullness of the
kingdom of God (19) which those achieve who both
teach and fulfill the law. In contrast, the false justice
of the Pharisees, their lack of true interior holiness,
will exclude them from the kingdom (20).
5, 27–32: Women are to be accorded the respect
due to their persons as children of the same God as
men. The deeper implications of the divine law are seen
to prohibit, not merely indecent actions against
the religious dignity of the human person, but impure

thoughts and desires as well. Jesus here repudiates the
norm contained in Dt 24, 1 which allows a husband to
dismiss his wife with a written decree of divorce
for the purpose of remarriage. See note on Mt 19, 3–8.
5, 33–37: In the ordinary conduct of human
affairs, personal trustworthiness should be such that
the invocation of the divine name as evidence of
truth is altogether unnecessary.
5, 43–48: As God invites the unjust to respond to
him through the evidence of his love, so the disciples
of Jesus must be the bearers of the same love toward
their enemies.

46 If you love those who love you, what merit is there in that? Do not tax collectors do as much? 47 And if you greet your brothers only, what is so praiseworthy about that? Do not pagans do as much? 48 In a word, you must be made perfect as your heavenly Father is perfect.

Purity of Intention

6 "Be on guard against performing religious acts for people to see. Otherwise expect no recompense from your heavenly Father. 2 When you give alms, for example, do not blow a horn before you in synagogues and streets like hypocrites looking for applause. You can be sure of this much, they are already repaid. 3 In giving alms you are not to let your left hand know what your right hand is doing. 4 Keep your deeds of mercy secret, and your Father who sees in secret will repay you.

Prayer

5 "When you are praying, do not behave like the hypocrites who love to stand and pray in synagogues or on street corners in order to be noticed. I give you my word, they are already repaid. 6 Whenever you pray, go to your room, close your door, and pray to your Father in private. Then your Father, who sees what no man sees, will repay you. 7 In your prayer do not rattle on like the pagans. They think they will win a hearing by the sheer multiplication of words. 8 Do not imitate them. Your Father knows what you need before you ask him. 9 This is how you are to pray:

'Our Father in heaven,
hallowed be your name,
10 your kingdom come,
your will be done
on earth as it is in heaven.
11 Give us today our daily bread,
12 and forgive us the wrong we
have done
as we forgive those who wrong
us.

13 Subject us not to the trial
but deliver us from the evil one.'

14 "If you forgive the faults of others, your heavenly Father will forgive you yours. 15 If you do not forgive others, neither will your Father forgive you.

Fasting

16 "When you fast, you are not to look glum as the hypocrites do. They change the appearance of their faces so that others may see they are fasting. I assure you, they are already repaid. 17 When you fast, see to it that you groom your hair and wash your face. 18 In that way no one can see you are fasting but your Father who is hidden; and your Father who sees what is hidden will repay you.

True Riches

19 "Do not lay up for yourselves an earthly treasure. Moths and rust corrode; thieves break in and steal. 20 Make it your practice instead to store up heavenly treasure, which neither moths nor rust corrode nor thieves break in and steal. 21 Remember, where your treasure is, there your heart is also. 22 The eye is the body's lamp. If your eyes are good, your body will be filled with light; 23 if your eyes are bad, your body will be in darkness. And if your light is darkness, how deep will the darkness be! 24 No man can serve two masters. He will either hate one and love the other or be attentive to one and despise the other. You cannot give yourself to God and money. 25 I warn you, then: do not worry about your livelihood, what you are to eat or drink or use for clothing. Is not life more than food? Is not the body more valuable than clothes? 26 "Look at the birds in the sky. They do not sow or reap, they gather nothing into barns; yet your heavenly Father feeds them. Are not you more important than they? 27 Which of you by worrying can add a moment

to his life-span? 28 As for clothes, why be concerned? Learn a lesson from the way the wild flowers grow. They do not work; they do not spin. 29 Yet I assure you, not even Solomon in all his splendor was arrayed like one of these. 30 If God can clothe in such splendor the grass of the field, which blooms today and is thrown on the fire tomorrow, will he not provide much more for you, O weak in faith! 31 Stop worrying, then, over questions like, 'What are we to eat, or what are we to drink, or what are we to wear?' 32 The unbelievers are always running after these things. Your heavenly Father knows all that you need. 33 Seek first his kingship over you, his way of holiness, and all these things will be given you besides. Enough, then, of worrying about tomorrow. Let tomorrow take care of itself. Today has troubles enough of its own.

Avoiding Judgment

7 "If you want to avoid judgment, stop passing judgment. 2 Your verdict on others will be the verdict passed on you. The measure with which you measure will be used to measure you. 3 Why look at the speck in your brother's eye when you miss the plank in your own? 4 How can you say to your brother, 'Let me take that speck out of your eye,' while all the time the plank remains in your own? 5 You hypocrite! Remove the plank from your own eye first; then you will see clearly to take the speck from your brother's eye.

6 "Do not give what is holy to dogs or toss your pearls before swine. They will trample them under foot, at best, and perhaps even tear you to shreds.

The Power of Prayer

7 "Ask, and you will receive. Seek, and you will find. Knock, and it will be opened to you. 8 For the

---

5, 48: The perfection of the Father is revealed in his redemptive love of mankind, cf Jn 3, 16; I Jn 4, 9ff. For an application of the principle, cf 1 Cor 8, 7–11.
6, 1–6.16ff: To be of value in the eyes of God, religious duties, public and private, must be performed for the single-hearted purpose of serving God, and not for human esteem.
6, 19ff: A concluding parable to confirm Jesus'

teaching on the true service of God; recompense for good works is to be expected from him alone.
6, 22f: A person with proper vision can easily direct the movements of his body. In a similar way, one who makes use of the prophetic vision of Christ can direct his way to God.
7, 1–5: Judgments of condemnation upon one's neighbor and refusal to pardon him entail loss of

God's pardon for one's own sins.
7, 6: The teaching of the gospel will be rejected by some precisely because it is holy, and those who teach it will themselves be subjected to attack.
7, 7–11: The persevering prayer of sinful humanity receives a divine response because of the generosity of God.

one who asks, receives. The one who seeks, finds. The one who knocks, enters. 9 Would one of you hand his son a stone when he asks for a loaf, 10 or a poisonous snake when he asks for a fish? 11 If you, with all your sins, know how to give your children what is good, how much more will your heavenly Father give good things to anyone who asks him!

The Golden Rule

12 "Treat others the way you would have them treat you: this sums up the law and the prophets.

13 "Enter through the narrow gate. The gate that leads to damnation is wide, the road is clear, and many choose to travel it. 14 But how narrow is the gate that leads to life, how rough the road, and how few there are who find it!

15 "Be on your guard against false prophets, who come to you in sheep's clothing but underneath are wolves on the prowl. 16 You will know them by their deeds. Do you ever pick grapes from thornbushes, or figs from prickly plants? Never! 17 Any sound tree bears good fruit, while a decayed tree bears bad fruit. 18 A sound tree cannot bear bad fruit any more than a decayed tree can bear good fruit. 19 Every tree that does not bear good fruit is cut down and thrown into the fire. 20 You can tell a tree by its fruit. 21 None of those who cry out, 'Lord, Lord,' will enter the kingdom of God but only the one who does the will of my Father in heaven. 22 When that day comes, many will plead with me, 'Lord, Lord, have we not prophesied in your name? Have we not exorcised demons by its power? Did we not do many miracles in your name as well?' 23 Then I will declare to them solemnly, 'I never knew you. Out of my sight, you evildoers!'

Conclusion of the Sermon

24 "Anyone who hears my words and puts them into practice is like the wise man who built his house on rock. 25 When the rainy season set in, the torrents came and the winds blew and buffeted his house. It did not collapse; it had been solidly set on rock. 26 Anyone who hears my words but does not put them into practice is like the foolish man who built his house on sandy ground. 27 The rains fell, the torrents came, the winds blew and lashed against his house. It collapsed under all this and was completely ruined."

28 Jesus finished this discourse and left the crowds spellbound at his teaching. 29 The reason was that he taught with authority and not like their scribes.

PREACHING THE REIGN OF GOD

The Leper

8 When he came down from the mountain, great crowds followed him. 2 Suddenly a leper came forward and did him homage, saying to him, "Sir, if you will to do so, you can cure me." 3 Jesus stretched out his hand and touched him and said, "I do will it. Be cured." Immediately the man's leprosy disappeared. 4 Then Jesus said to him: "See to it that you tell no one. Go and show yourself to the priest and offer the gift Moses prescribed. That should be the proof they need."

The Centurion's Servant

5 As Jesus entered Capernaum, a centurion approached him with this request: 6 "Sir, my serving boy is at home in bed paralyzed, suffering painfully." 7 He said to him, "I will come and cure him." 8 "Sir," the centurion said in reply, "I am not worthy to have you under my roof. Just give an order and my boy will get better. 9 I am a man under authority myself and I have troops assigned to me. If I give one man the order, 'Dismissed,' off he goes. If I say to another, 'Come here,' he comes. If I tell my slave, 'Do this,' he does it." 10 Jesus showed amazement on hearing this and remarked to his followers, "I assure you, I have never found this much faith in Israel. 11 Mark what I say! Many will come from the east and the west and will find a place at the banquet in the kingdom of God with Abraham, Isaac, and Jacob, 12 while the natural heirs of the kingdom will be driven out into the dark. Wailing will be heard there, and the grinding of teeth." 13 To the centurion Jesus said, "Go home. It shall be done because you trusted." That very moment the boy got better.

Peter's Mother-in-law

14 Jesus entered Peter's house and found Peter's mother-in-law in bed with a fever. 15 He took her by the hand and the fever left her. She got up at once and began to wait on him.

Other Miracles

16 As evening drew on, they brought him many who were possessed. He expelled the spirits by a simple command and cured all who were afflicted, 17 thereby fulfilling what had been said through Isaiah the prophet:

"It was our infirmities he bore,
our sufferings he endured."

Conditions for Following Jesus

18 Seeing the people crowd around him, Jesus gave orders to cross to the other shore. 19 A scribe approached him and said, "Teacher, wherever you go I will come after you."

7, 12: An isolated saying introduced to show that the moral teaching concerning neighbor in the reign of God is the golden rule of true fraternal charity.

7, 13–27: A series of parables warning that only through the good works outlined in the Sermon does man find the way of life that leads to the happiness God has in store for him.

7, 28: A general formula used in Matthew at the conclusion of the five collections of the sayings of Jesus (11, 1; 13, 53; 19, 1; 26, 1).

7, 29—9, 38: By means of miracle narratives and other events, Matthew portrays Jesus' unique power in word and action. Jesus uses the twofold charism of miracles and prophecy in behalf of the people to invite them to accept the new sovereign rule of God which he proclaims (8, 16-22; 9, 13.36). The miracle accounts appear in groups of three (8, 1–15; 8, 23—9, 8; 9, 18–34). Other incidents and comments are interspersed between these groupings.

8, 4: See note on Mk 1, 40-45.

8, 10ff: The great trust of the centurion consisted in his honest acceptance of the religious authority of Jesus, displayed in curing the sick. Jesus' comment invites his contemporaries to match the centurion's trust.

8, 17: Matthew sees in Jesus the true servant of Yahweh (Is 53, 4), whose miraculous healings are the external sign of the redemption which Jesus was now accomplishing as he bore, i.e., "took upon himself," our infirmities, i.e., "our sins," to free us from them.

20 Jesus said to him, "The foxes have lairs, the birds in the sky have nests, but the Son of Man has nowhere to lay his head." 21 Another, a disciple, said to him, "Lord, let me go and bury my father first." 22 But Jesus told him, "Follow me, and let the dead bury their dead."

Storm on the Lake

23 He got into the boat and his disciples followed him. 24 Without warning a violent storm came up on the lake, and the boat began to be swamped by the waves. 25 Jesus was sleeping soundly, so they made their way toward him and woke him: "Lord, save us!" 26 He said to them: "Where is your courage? How little faith you have!" Then he stood up and took the winds and the sea to task. Complete calm ensued; 27 the men were dumbfounded. "What sort of man is this," they said, "that even the winds and the sea obey him?"

Expulsion of the Demons in Gadara

28 As he approached the Gadarene boundary, he encountered two men coming out of the tombs. They were possessed by demons and were so savage that no one could travel along that road. 29 With a sudden shriek they cried: "Why meddle with us, Son of God? Have you come to torture us before the appointed time?" 30 Some distance away a large herd of swine was feeding. 31 The demons kept appealing to him, "If you expel us, send us into the herd of swine." 32 He answered, "Out with you!" At that they came forth and entered the swine. The whole herd went rushing down the bluff into the sea and were drowned. 33 The swineherds took to their heels, and upon their arrival in the town related everything that had happened, including the story about the two possessed men. 34 The upshot was that the entire town came out to meet Jesus. When they caught sight of him, they begged him to leave their neighborhood.

A Paralytic at Capernaum

9 Then he reentered the boat, made the crossing, and came back to his own town. 2 There the people at once brought to him a paralyzed man lying on a mat. When Jesus saw their faith he said to the paralytic, "Have courage, son, your sins are forgiven." 3 At that some of the scribes said to themselves, "The man blasphemes." 4 Jesus was aware of what they were thinking and said: "Why do you harbor evil thoughts? 5 Which is less trouble to say, 'Your sins are forgiven' or 'Stand up and walk'? 6 To help you realize that the Son of Man has authority on earth to forgive sins"— he then said to the paralyzed man— "Stand up! Roll up your mat, and go home." 7 The man stood up and went toward his home. 8 At the sight, a feeling of awe came over the crowd, and they praised God for giving such authority to men.

Call of Matthew

9 As he moved on, Jesus saw a man named Matthew at his post where taxes were collected. He said to him, "Follow me." Matthew got up and followed him. 10 Now it happened that, while Jesus was at table in Matthew's home, many tax collectors and those known as sinners came to join Jesus and his disciples at dinner. 11 The Pharisees saw this and complained to his disciples, "What reason can the Teacher have for eating with tax collectors and those who disregard the law?" 12 Overhearing the remark, he said: "People who are in good health do not need a doctor; sick people do. 13 Go and learn the meaning of the words, 'It is mercy I desire and not sacrifice.' I have come to call, not the self-righteous, but sinners."

The Question of Fasting

14 Later on, John's disciples came to him with the objection, "Why is it that while we and the Pharisees fast, your disciples do not?" Jesus said to them: 15 "How can wedding guests go in mourning so long as the groom is with them? When the day comes that the groom is taken away, then they will fast. 16 Nobody sews a piece of unshrunken cloth on an old cloak; the very thing he has used to cover the hole will pull, and the rip only get worse. 17 People do not pour new wine into old wineskins. If they do, the skins burst, the wine spills out, and the skins are ruined. No, they pour new wine into new wineskins, and in that way both are preserved."

A Dead Girl; a Woman with a Hemorrhage

18 Before Jesus had finished speaking to them, a synagogue leader came up, did him reverence, and said: "My daughter has just died. Please come and lay your hand on her and she will come back to life." 19 Jesus stood up and fol-

---

8, 20: *Son of Man:* an enigmatic title of Christ used in the gospels and in Acts 7, 56. Jesus is reported as using it frequently of himself; it was well adapted to his purpose of both veiling and revealing his person and mission. On the one hand, it simply meant "man" (Ez 2, 1) and emphasized the lowliness of the human condition (Mt 8, 20; 11, 19; 20, 28), especially in Christ's humiliation and death (17, 22). On the other hand, it expressed the triumph of Jesus' resurrection (17, 9), his return to glory (24, 30; Dn 7, 13), and his second coming as judge of the world (25, 31).

At his trial before the Sanhedrin, Jesus is described as using the title *Son of Man* in a well-defined religious sense (26, 64). Though he stood before his accusers an innocent victim, charged with blasphemy and condemned to die, he prophesied his vindication and future glory, *seated at the right hand of the Power*, i.e. God, not merely as man but as Lord (Dn 7, 13; Mk 14, 62).

Jewish apocalyptic literature (1 Enoch, 2 Ezra, 2 Baruch) employed the title to describe a unique religious personage endowed with extraordinary spiritual power, who would receive the kingdom from God at the end of time. Early Christian communities held this title in reverence because it reminded them of Jesus' awareness of his double destiny, of humiliation and of glory, in which the Christian community also shares (Mt 24, 30f).

8, 22: Jesus has subordinated family ties to the needs of his mission of salvation (8, 20). He requires the same sacrifice of those called to share this mission with him, when other members of the family can perform the deeds of filial piety. These latter are *dead* only in the sense that they have not received the divine call to separate themselves from family responsibility in order to preach the gospel of the kingdom. They can, however, be Jesus' disciples in another sense.

8, 29: *Son of God:* see note on Mk 3, 12. *Before the appointed time:* a phrase peculiar to Matthew in this account. Even in pagan territory the demons already feel the threat of Jesus before the destruction of Satan's power at the end of the world (1 Cor 15, 24f)

9, 8: *Such authority to men:* the principal issue of Jesus' authority here is the power to forgive sins. Matthew's use of the plural *men* suggests the power of the Christian community to forgive sins in Jesus' name; cf Acts 2, 38; Jas 5, 16.

9, 13: Jesus' association with tax collectors and violators of the law is conformable to his teaching about the need of repentance (4, 17). He cites Hos 6, 6 to show that love of neighbor gives value to sacrifices offered as evidence of love of God.

9, 14–17: Jesus' presence among men during his public ministry is comparable to that of a bridegroom during the marriage feast. The time of fasting is temporarily set aside until after Jesus' death to bring about those changes in the human person required for assimilating the new doctrinal ideas.

9, 18–26: See note on Mk 5, 21–43.

lowed him, and his disciples did the same. 20 As they were going, a woman who had suffered from hemorrhages for twelve years came up behind him and touched the tassel on his cloak. 21 "If only I can touch his cloak," she thought, "I shall get well." 22 Jesus turned around and saw her and said, "Courage, daughter! Your faith has restored you to health." That very moment the woman got well.

23 When Jesus arrived at the synagogue leader's house and saw the flute players and the crowd who were making a din, he said, 24 "Leave, all of you! The little girl is not dead. She is asleep." At this they began to ridicule him. 25 When the crowd had been put out he entered and took her by the hand, and the little girl got up. 26 News of this circulated throughout the district.

Two Blind Men

27 As Jesus moved on from there, two blind men came after him crying out, "Son of David, have pity on us!" 28 When he got to the house, the blind men caught up with him. Jesus said to them, "Are you confident I can do this?" "Yes, Lord," they told him. 29 At that he touched their eyes and said; "Because of your faith it shall be done to you"; 30 and they recovered their sight. Then Jesus warned them sternly, "See to it that no one knows of this." 31 But they went off and spread word of him through the whole area.

A Possessed Mute

32 As they were leaving, suddenly some people brought him a mute who was possessed by a demon. 33 Once the demon was expelled the mute began to speak, to the great surprise of the crowds. "Nothing like this has ever been seen in Israel!" they exclaimed. 34 But the Pharisees were saying, "He casts out demons through the prince of demons."

Mission of the Twelve

35 Jesus continued his tour of all the towns and villages. He taught in their synagogues, he proclaimed the good news of God's reign, and he cured every sickness and disease. 36 At the sight of the crowds, his heart was moved with pity. They were lying prostrate from exhaustion, like sheep without a shepherd. 37 He said to his disciples: "The harvest is good but laborers are scarce. Beg the harvest master 38 to send out laborers to gather his harvest."

10 Then he summoned his twelve disciples and gave them authority to expel unclean spirits and to cure sickness and disease of every kind. 2 The names of the twelve apostles are these: first Simon, now known as Peter, and his brother Andrew; James, Zebedee's son, and his brother John; 3 Philip and Bartholomew, Thomas and Matthew the tax collector; James, son of Alphaeus, and Thaddaeus; 4 Simon the Zealot Party member, and Judas Iscariot, who betrayed him. 5 Jesus sent these men on mission as the Twelve, after giving them the following instructions:

"Do not visit pagan territory and do not enter a Samaritan town. 6 Go instead after the lost sheep of the house of Israel. 7 As you go, make this announcement: 'The reign of God is at hand!' 8 Cure the sick, raise the dead, heal the leprous, expel demons. The gift you have received, give as a gift. 9 Provide yourselves with neither gold nor silver nor copper in your belts; 10 no traveling bag, no change of shirt, no sandals, no walking staff. The workman, after all, is worth his keep.

11 "Look for a worthy person in every town or village you come to and stay with him until you leave. 12 As you enter his home bless it. 13 If the home is deserving, your blessing will descend on it. If it is not, your blessing will return to you. 14 If anyone does not receive you or listen to what you have to say, leave that house or town, and once outside it shake its dust from your feet. 15 I assure you, it will go easier for the region of Sodom and Gomorrah on the day of judgment than it will for that town.

16 "What I am doing is sending you out like sheep among wolves. You must be clever as snakes and innocent as doves. 17 Be on your guard with respect to others. They will hale you into court, they will flog you in their synagogues. 18 You will be brought to trial before rulers and kings, to give witness before them and before the Gentiles on my account. 19 When they hand you over, do not worry about what you will say or how you will say it. When the hour comes, you will be given what you are to say. 20 You yourselves will not be the speakers; the Spirit of your Father will be speaking in you.

21 "Brother will hand over brother to death, and the father his child; children will turn against parents and have them put to death. 22 You will be hated by all on account of me. But whoever holds out till the end will escape death. 23 When they persecute you in one town, flee to the next. I solemnly assure you, you will not have covered the towns of Israel before the Son of Man comes.

24 "No pupil outranks his teacher, no slave his master. 25 The pupil should be glad to become like his teacher, the slave like his master. If they call the head of the house Beelzebul, how much more the members of his household! 26 Do not let them intimidate you. Nothing is concealed that will not be revealed, and nothing hidden that will not become known. 27 What I tell you in

---

9, 27-31: See note on Mk 10, 46-52.

9, 35—10, 1: Having preached and ministered widely in Galilee, Jesus sees the people's need for prophetic leadership; cf Nm 27, 17. He therefore expands his missionary activity by conferring his own powers on certain of his disciples.

10, 2-33: These verses, which conserve Jesus' instructions to his disciples for their missionary activity, constitute a norm for all Christian missioners.

Certain of his prophecies are incorporated into the discourse because they reflected the church's experience (10, 17-21); cf 2 Cor 11, 23ff; Acts 5, 40; 24, 1-23.

10, 12f: The blessing referred to is a wish of peace. The blessing, once invoked, is considered to continue to exist. An undeserving household will not receive it; therefore it returns and benefits the one who uttered it.

10, 23: The missioners are not to risk their lives unnecessarily. *You will not have covered . . . the Son of Man comes:* Jesus implies, not that he expects the parousia (see note on 1 Thes 4, 13-18) and God's final judgment before the termination of his disciples' mission, but rather that the divine plan of Israel's salvation will not be completed before the parousia because of hostility.

darkness, speak in the light. What you hear in private, proclaim from the housetops.

28 "Do not fear those who deprive the body of life but cannot destroy the soul. Rather, fear him who can destroy both body and soul in Gehenna. 29 Are not two sparrows sold for next to nothing? Yet not a single sparrow falls to the ground without your Father's consent. 30 As for you, every hair of your head has been counted; 31 so do not be afraid of anything. You are worth more than an entire flock of sparrows. 32 Whoever acknowledges me before men I will acknowledge before my Father in heaven. 33 Whoever disowns me before men I will disown before my Father in heaven.

34 "Do not suppose that my mission on earth is to spread peace. My mission is to spread, not peace, but division. 35 I have come to set a man at odds with his father, a daughter with her mother, a daughter in-law with her mother-in-law; 36 in short, to make a man's enemies those of his own household. 37 Whoever loves father or mother, son or daughter, more than me is not worthy of me. 38 He who will not take up his cross and come after me is not worthy of me. 39 He who seeks only himself brings himself to ruin, whereas he who brings himself to nought for me discovers who he is.

40 "He who welcomes you welcomes me, and he who welcomes me welcomes him who sent me. 41 He who welcomes a prophet because he bears the name of prophet receives a prophet's reward; he who welcomes a holy man because he is known to be holy receives a holy man's reward. 42 And I promise you that whoever gives a cup of cold water to one of these lowly ones because he is a disciple will not want for his reward."

11 When Jesus had finished instructing his twelve disciples,

he left that locality to teach and preach in their towns.

MYSTERY OF THE REIGN OF HEAVEN

The Baptizer's Deputation

2 Now John in prison heard about the works Christ was performing, and sent a message by his disciples to ask him, 3 "Are you 'He who is to come' or do we look for another?" 4 In reply, Jesus said to them: "Go back and report to John what you hear and see: 5 the blind recover their sight, cripples walk, lepers are cured, the deaf hear, dead men are raised to life, and the poor have the good news preached to them. 6 Blest is the man who finds no stumbling block in me."

Christ's Witness to John

7 As the messengers set off, Jesus began to speak to the crowds about John: "What did you go out to the wasteland to see—a reed swaying in the wind? 8 Tell me, what did you go out to see—someone luxuriously dressed? Remember, those who dress luxuriously are to be found in royal palaces. 9 Why then did you go out—to see a prophet? A prophet indeed, and something more! 10 It is about this man that Scripture says,

'I send my messenger ahead of you
to prepare your way before you.'

11 "I solemnly assure you, history has not known a man born of woman greater than John the Baptizer. Yet the least born into the Kingdom of God is greater than he. 12 From John the Baptizer's time until now the kingdom of God has suffered violence, and the violent take it by force. 13 All the prophets as well as the law spoke prophetically until John. 14 If you are prepared to accept it, he is Elijah, the one who

was certain to come. 15 Heed carefully what you hear!

The Wayward Children

16 "What comparison can I use to describe this breed? They are like children squatting in the town squares, calling to their playmates:

17 'We piped you a tune but you
        did not dance!
    We sang you a dirge but you
        did not wail!'

18 In other words, John appeared neither eating nor drinking, and people say, 'He is mad!' 19 The Son of Man appeared eating and drinking, and they say, 'This one is a glutton and drunkard, a lover of tax collectors and those outside the law!' Yet time will prove where wisdom lies."

The Impenitent Towns

20 He began to reproach the towns where most of his miracles had been worked, with their failure to reform: 21 "It will go ill with you, Chorazin! And just as ill with you, Bethsaida! If the miracles worked in you had taken place in Tyre and Sidon, they would have reformed in sackcloth and ashes long ago. 22 I assure you, it will go easier for Tyre and Sidon than for you on the day of judgment. 23 As for you, Capernaum,

'Are you to be exalted to the
        skies?
    You shall go down to the realm
        of death!'

If the miracles worked in you had taken place in Sodom, it would be standing today. 24 I assure you, it will go easier for Sodom than for you on the day of judgment."

Jesus and His Father

25 On one occasion Jesus spoke thus: "Father, Lord of heaven and

11, 2—12, 50: Jesus' messianic role is questioned and rejected. John sends a query to Jesus about his role (11, 2–6). Jesus himself comments on the resistance to his message in certain key cities of Galilee (11, 20–24). The scribes and Pharisees, and even Jesus' relatives, are hostile to him (12, 1–50).

11, 3: John is puzzled because Jesus continues to appeal for repentance rather than inflict final divine punishment on the unrepentant; cf Mt 3, 12.

11, 7–15: In this collection of sayings Jesus eulogizes the strength of John the Baptizer's religious convictions, the austerity of his life (7f) and his

unique prophetic role as the messianic precursor (9–15).

11, 11: Greater than he: the disciples benefit from Jesus' prophetic light, which surpasses that of John.

11, 12: A highly enigmatic saying—probably so because of isolation from its original historical context. It contrasts Jesus' message of renewal through repentance and the faith that leads to admission into God's kingdom, with the false messianism of the "holy war" advocated, e.g., by the Zealots and the sectaries of Qumran.

11, 19: Time will prove where wisdom lies: neither

the austere preaching and penance of John the Baptizer nor the gentle persuasion of Jesus elicits the good will of unbelievers. God's wisdom triumphs over them in the end.

11, 20–24: Sayings of Jesus, uttered perhaps during his preaching in these cities, and summarized here. They are directed against those who fail to recognize the presence of God in Jesus so as to avoid repentance.

earth, to you I offer praise; for what you have hidden from the learned and the clever you have revealed to the merest children. 26 Father, it is true. You have graciously willed it so. 27 Everything has been given over to me by my Father. No one knows the Son but the Father, and no one knows the Father but the Son—and anyone to whom the Son wishes to reveal him.

28 "Come to me, all you who are weary and find life burdensome, and I will refresh you. 29 Take my yoke upon your shoulders and learn from me, for I am gentle and humble of heart. Your souls will find rest, 30 for my yoke is easy and my burden light."

The Disciples and the Sabbath

12 Once on a sabbath Jesus walked through the standing grain. His disciples felt hungry, so they began to pull off the heads of grain and eat them. 2 When the Pharisees spied this, they protested: "See here! Your disciples are doing what is not permitted on the sabbath." 3 He replied: "Have you not read what David did when he and his men were hungry, 4 how he entered God's house and ate the holy bread, a thing forbidden to him and his men or anyone other than priests? 5 Have you not read in the law how the priests on temple duty can break the sabbath rest without incurring guilt? 6 I assure you, there is something greater than the temple here. 7 If you understood the meaning of the text, 'It is mercy I desire and not sacrifice,' you would not have condemned these innocent men. 8 The

Son of Man is indeed Lord of the sabbath."

A Man with a Shriveled Hand

9 He left that place and went into their synagogue. 10 A man with a shriveled hand happened to be there, and they put this question to Jesus, hoping to bring an accusation against him: "Is it lawful to work a cure on the sabbath?" 11 He said in response: "Suppose one of you has a sheep and it falls into a pit on the sabbath. Will he not take hold of it and pull it out? 12 Well, think how much more precious a human being is than a sheep. Clearly, good deeds may be performed on the sabbath."

13 To the man he said, "Stretch out your hand." He did so, and it was perfectly restored; it became as sound as the other. 14 When the Pharisees were outside they began to plot against him to find a way to destroy him. 15 Jesus was aware of this, and so he withdrew from that place.

The Mercy of Jesus

Many people followed him and he cured them all, 16 though he sternly ordered them not to make public what he had done. 17 This was to fulfill what had been said through Isaiah the prophet:

18 "Here is my servant whom I
     have chosen,
   my loved one in whom I delight.
   I will endow him with my spirit
   and he will proclaim justice to
     the Gentiles.
19 He will not contend or cry out,

nor will his voice be heard in the
     streets.
20 The bruised reed he will not
     crush;
   the smoldering wick he will not
     quench
   until judgment is made
     victorious.
21 In his name, the Gentiles will
     find hope."

Blasphemy of the Pharisees

22 A possessed man who was brought to him was blind and mute. He cured the man so that he could speak and see. 23 All in the crowd were astonished. "Might this not be David's son?" they asked. 24 When the Pharisees heard this, they charged, "This man can expel demons only with the help of Beelzebul, the prince of demons." 25 Knowing their thoughts, he said to them: "A kingdom torn by strife is headed for its downfall. A town or household split into factions cannot last for long. 26 If Satan is expelling Satan, he must be torn by dissension. How, then, can his dominion last? 27 If I expel demons with Beelzebul's help, by whose help do your people expel them? Let them be the ones to judge you. 28 But if it is by the Spirit of God that I expel demons, then the reign of God has overtaken you.

29 "How can anyone enter a strong man's house and make off with his property unless he first ties him securely? Only then can he rob his house. 30 He who is not with me is against me, and he who does not gather with me scatters. 31 "That, I assure you, is why

---

11, 27: This verse has a Johannine ring in thought and style (Jn 3, 16f; 5, 19–23) and uses as introduction a saying of the risen Christ (Mt 28, 18). Only God the Father fully comprehends Jesus' mission, and only Jesus fully understands God's saving plan which he gradually unveils to men. This saying may have originated in the instruction of the risen Lord; cf Acts 1, 3.
11, 28: *Who are weary . . . burdensome:* a probable allusion to the moral and legal prescriptions of rabbinic Judaism, which needed to be balanced by prophetic vision in order to give joy and peaceful expectancy to the Mosaic tradition.
11, 29: *Your souls will find rest:* through acceptance of the gospel teaching which satisfies the longings of those who are wearied by the burdens of life.
12, 3–6: Jesus responds to the objection of the Pharisees: if they hold so rigidly to their interpretation of the law, they should be critical of David's action (1 Sm 21, 1–6), and also that of the priests who on the sabbath prepare the offerings of the lambs (Nm 28, 9f). If these violations of the law in the temple, God's dwelling, are above criticism, neither should Jesus be

criticized, for God is present in him as is manifested through his miracles; cf Jn 10, 38.
12, 8: See note on Mk 2, 28.
12, 10: *Is it lawful to work a cure on the sabbath:* curing on the sabbath was a frequent issue against Jesus in the gospels and one of considerable tension between him and the religious authorities (Jn 7, 23f). The basis of this altercation is not entirely clear. The sabbath healings did not accord with the teaching of the rabbis on the limited degree of aid to be given the sick or injured on that day. It seems, however, from the complete gospel that the issue was more complex than one of mere legalism. The healings produced clamorous crowds and processions of other sick persons (Lk 13, 14), which greatly disturbed the sabbath rest. At times Jesus overrode the sabbath restrictions (Jn 5, 18), challenged the authority of the scribes and Pharisees, and thoroughly involved them in his message. They had no choice but to take a stand, whether favorable or hostile, to Jesus.
12, 15–21: Jesus shows no inclination to counteract the hostility of the Pharisees by any action on his part, such as enlisting popular support against them.

Instead he withdraws *from that place,* even orders those cured *not to make public what he had done.* The free citation of Is 42, 1–4 is a reflection of the meekness of Jesus, the harbinger of the divine mercy to Jews and Gentiles.
12, 24–29: To the Pharisees' charge that Jesus performs exorcisms by a pact with Satan, he replies by showing that the objection lacks common sense (25f), overlooks the tradition of exorcistic power in Israel (27), and refuses to acknowledge, in the person and teaching of Christ, the new reign of God, capable of destroying Satan's power (28f).
12, 31f: The Pharisees are said to attribute Jesus' exorcisms to satanic power and thus to deny the unique presence of God in Jesus. They thereby assign his entire work and teaching to an evil principle, making it anti-God. This is the *blasphemy against the Spirit that will not be forgiven,* because it negates the evidence of God's saving action in history. However, misidentifications of Jesus' teaching and misconceptions of his Person due to human error or prejudice will be forgiven (Act 9, 4f; I Tm 1, 13).

every sin, every blasphemy, will be forgiven men, but blasphemy against the Spirit will not be forgiven. 32 Whoever says anything against the Son of Man will be forgiven, but whoever says anything against the Holy Spirit will not be forgiven, either in this age or in the age to come. 33 Declare a tree good and its fruit good or declare a tree rotten and its fruit rotten, one or the other, for you can tell a tree by its fruit. 34 How can you utter anything good, you brood of vipers, when you are so evil? The mouth speaks whatever fills the mind. 35 A good man produces good from his store of goodness; an evil man produces evil from his evil store. 36 I assure you, on judgment day people will be held accountable for every unguarded word they speak. 37 By your words you will be acquitted, and by your words you will be condemned."

The Sign of Jonah

38 Some of the scribes and Pharisees then spoke up, saying, "Teacher, we want to see you work some signs." 39 He answered: "An evil and unfaithful age is eager for a sign! No sign will be given it but that of the prophet Jonah. 40 Just as Jonah spent three days and three nights in the belly of the whale, so will the Son of Man spend three days and three nights in the bowels of the earth. 41 At the judgment, the citizens of Nineveh will rise with the present generation and be the ones to condemn it. At the preaching of Jonah they reformed their lives; but you have a greater than Jonah here. 42 At the judgment, the queen of the South will rise with the present generation and be the one to condemn it. She came from the farthest corner of the earth to listen to the wisdom of Solomon; but you have a greater than Solomon here.

43 "When the unclean spirit departs from a man, it roams through arid wastes searching for a place of rest and finding none. 44 Then it says, 'I will go back where I came from,' and returns to find the dwelling unoccupied, though swept and tidied now. 45 Off it goes again to bring back with it this time seven spirits more evil than itself. They move in and settle there. Thus the last state of that man becomes worse than the first. And that is how it will be with this evil generation."

Jesus and His Family

46 He was still addressing the crowds when his mother and his brothers appeared outside to speak with him. 47 Someone said to him, "Your mother and your brothers are standing out there and they wish to speak to you." 48 He said to the one who had told him, "Who is my mother? Who are my brothers?" 49 Then, extending his hand toward his disciples, he said, 50 "There are my mother and my brothers. Whoever does the will of my heavenly Father is brother and sister and mother to me."

13 That same day, on leaving the house, Jesus sat down by the lakeshore. 2 Such great crowds gathered around him that he went and took his seat in a boat while the crowd stood along the shore. 3 He addressed them at length in parables, speaking in this fashion:

Parable of the Seed

4 "One day a farmer went out sowing. Part of what he sowed landed on a footpath, where birds came and ate it up. 5 Part of it fell on rocky ground, where it had little soil. It sprouted at once since the soil had no depth, 6 but when the sun rose and scorched it, it began to wither

for lack of roots. 7 Again, part of the seed fell among thorns, which grew up and choked it. 8 Part of it, finally, landed on good soil and yielded grain a hundred- or sixty- or thirtyfold. 9 Let everyone heed what he hears!"

10 When the disciples got near him, they asked him, "Why do you speak to them in parables?" 11 He answered: "To you has been given a knowledge of the mysteries of the reign of God, but it has not been given to the others. 12 To the man who has, more will be given until he grows rich; the man who has not, will lose what little he has. 13 "I use parables when I speak to them because they look but do not see, they listen but do not hear or understand. 14 Isaiah's prophecy is fulfilled in them which says:

'Listen as you will, you shall not
    understand,
look intently as you will, you
    shall not see.
15 Sluggish indeed is this people's
    heart.
They have scarcely heard with
    their ears,
they have firmly closed their eyes;
otherwise they might see with
    their eyes,
and hear with their ears,
and understand with their hearts,
and turn back to me,
and I should heal them.'

16 "But blest are your eyes because they see and blest are your ears because they hear. 17 I assure you, many a prophet and many a saint longed to see what you see but did not see it, to hear what you hear but did not hear it.

18 "Mark well, then, the parable of the sower. 19 The seed along the path is the man who hears the message about God's reign without understanding it. The evil one ap-

---

12, 33–37: Those who charge that Jesus is in league with Satan reflect a basic evil in themselves that can be cured only by a radical renewal of faith and love.

12, 38ff: A current opinion in Judaism (Jn 7, 31) was that the Messiah would perform a unique kind of miracle. This view was not supported by the Old Testament but was apparently adhered to in circles of apocalyptic thought. The only additional sign to be given the faithless is that of Jesus' death and resurrection, typified by the story of Jonah in the belly of the fish. The allusion to Jesus' resurrection could not have been grasped by his audience at the time.

12, 41f: The sayings insist that Jesus' message of repentance has been more forcefully presented than in the preaching of Jonah and that his teaching shows greater divine wisdom than the perceptions of Solomon.

12, 43ff: The religious history of man is a repetitious interchange of good and evil. The sayings warn that the option for evil can reach the point of taking full possession of a man.

12, 46–50: See note on Mk 3, 20–35.

13, 1–53: The main theme of this collection of parables is the mystery of the reign or kingship of God, a plan hidden in God and only incompletely

manifested to men (10–17.34f); cf Eph 3, 4ff. The teaching of Jesus reveals that it is God who introduces his reign into history (3–9), intangibly brings it to fruition among men through his power (31ff), and will perfect it in his own good time (24–30). A secondary theme encourages adherence to Jesus' teaching despite hardships (18–23), and acceptance of God's toleration of evil (36–43.47–50). It places the reign proclaimed by Jesus above all the things in human existence which men hold dear (44ff).

13, 10–15: Precisely because the prophetic message is understandable, it can be, and frequently is, rejected (cf Is 6, 9f).

proaches him to steal away what was sown in his mind. 20 The seed that fell on patches of rock is the man who hears the message and at first receives it with joy. 21 But he has no roots, so he lasts only for a time. When some setback or persecution involving the message occurs, he soon falters. 22 What was sown among briers is the man who hears the message, but then worldly anxiety and the lure of money choke it off. Such a one produces no yield. 23 But what was sown on good soil is the man who hears the message and takes it in. He it is who bears a yield of a hundred- or sixty- or thirtyfold."

The Weeds

24 He proposed to them another parable: "The reign of God may be likened to a man who sowed good seed in his field. 25 While everyone was asleep, his enemy came and sowed weeds through his wheat, and then made off. 26 When the crop began to mature and yield grain, the weeds made their appearance as well. 27 The owner's slaves came to him and said, 'Sir, did you not sow good seed in your field? Where are the weeds coming from?' 28 He answered, 'I see an enemy's hand in this.' His slaves said to him, 'Do you want us to go out and pull them up?' 29 'No,' he replied, 'pull up the weeds and you might take the wheat along with them. 30 Let them grow together until harvest; then at harvest time I will order the harvesters, First collect the weeds and bundle them up to burn, then gather the wheat into my barn.'"

The Mustard Seed and the Leaven

31 He proposed still another parable: "The reign of God is like a mustard seed which someone took and sowed in his field. 32 It is the smallest seed of all, yet when full-grown it is the largest of plants. It becomes so big a shrub that the birds of the sky come and build their nests in its branches."

33 He offered them still another image: "The reign of God is like yeast which a woman took and kneaded into three measures of flour. Eventually the whole mass of dough began to rise." 34 All these lessons Jesus taught the crowds in the form of parables. He spoke to them in parables only, 35 to fulfill what had been said through the prophet:

"I will open my mouth in parables,
I will announce what has lain hidden since the creation of the world."

36 Then, dismissing the crowds, he went home. His disciples came to him with the request, "Explain to us the parable of the weeds in the field." 37 He said in answer: "The farmer sowing good seed is the Son of Man; 38 the field is the world, the good seed the citizens of the kingdom. The weeds are the followers of the evil one 39 and the enemy who sowed them is the devil. The harvest is the end of the world, while the harvesters are the angels. 40 Just as weeds are collected and burned, so will it be at the end of the world. 41 The Son of Man will dispatch his angels to collect from his kingdom all who draw others to apostasy, and all evildoers. 42 The angels will hurl them into the fiery furnace where they will wail and grind their teeth. 43 Then the saints will shine like the sun in their Father's kingdom. Let everyone heed what he hears!

The Treasure and the Pearl

44 "The reign of God is like a buried treasure which a man found in a field. He hid it again, and rejoicing at his find went and sold all he had and bought that field. 45 Or again, the kingdom of heaven is like a merchant's search for fine pearls. 46 When he found one really valuable pearl, he went back and put up for sale all that he had and bought it.

Parable of the Net

47 "The reign of God is also like a dragnet thrown into the lake, which collected all sorts of things. 48 When it was full they hauled it ashore and sat down to put what was worthwhile into containers. What was useless they threw away. 49 That is how it will be at the end of the world. Angels will go out and separate the wicked from the just 50 and hurl the wicked into the fiery furnace, where they will wail and grind their teeth.

51 "Have you understood all this?" "Yes," they answered; 52 to which he replied, "Every scribe who is learned in the reign of God is like the head of a household who can bring from his storeroom both the new and the old."

53 When Jesus had finished these parables, he moved on from that district.

THE REIGN BECOME CHURCH

Jesus at Nazareth

54 Jesus next went to his native place and spent his time teaching them in their synagogue. They were filled with amazement, and said to one another, "Where did this man get such wisdom and miraculous powers? 55 Isn't this the carpenter's son? Isn't Mary known to be his mother and James, Joseph, Simon, and Judas his brothers? 56 Aren't his sisters our neighbors? Where did he get all this?" 57 They found him altogether too much for them. Jesus said to them, "No prophet is without honor except in his

---

13, 51f: Jesus' teaching on the mystery of the kingdom of God is a prophetic development of the doctrine of the Old Testament requiring spiritual discernment for its acceptance; cf 1 Cor 2, 10–16.

13, 53—19, 1: The main purpose in this section of the gospel is to place the Person of Jesus at the very center of the mystery of the reign of God. Beginning with the rejection of Jesus at Nazareth and the execution of John (13, 53—14, 12), the evangelist alludes to the eucharistic mystery in the accounts of the multiplication of the loaves (14, 19; 15, 36), and of the walking on the water (14, 22–33); reports the doctrinal conflict between Jesus and the religious authorities (15, 1–20); raises again the question of the sign of Jonah (16, 1–4; see note on 12, 38ff), later explained to mean the passion, death and resurrection of Jesus (16, 21ff) which must occur before the reign of God reaches a new stage (16, 28). This is the message of the transfiguration (17, 5). A second purpose of the evangelist is to pattern the life of the Christian community after the model-life of Jesus (18, 1–35). This discourse takes its cue from Jesus' role as Servant of Yahweh (Is 42, 1) alluded to in 17, 5. Under the imagery of children, Jesus' disciples are identified with the *anawim*, who are so profoundly changed that they place the service of God entirely above personal gain; cf 2 Cor 11, 7. These members of the Christian community enjoy the divine favor, which will pursue them should they fall as a result of the entrapments set out for them by others (18, 5–14). This is to be borne in mind if the discipline of the gospel is to be enforced on those members who have deviated from it (18, 15f). If completely recalcitrant, they are to be cut off from the community; if repentant, they may be reinstated because of the limitless forgiveness within the community (18, 17–34).

13, 55: See note on Mk 6, 1–6.

native place, indeed in his own house." 58 And he did not work many miracles there because of their lack of faith.

Death of the Baptizer

14 On one occasion Herod the tetrarch, having heard of Jesus' reputation, 2 exclaimed to his courtiers, "This man is John the Baptizer—it is he in person, raised from the dead; that is why such miraculous powers are at work in him!" 3 Recall that Herod had had John arrested, put in chains, and imprisoned on account of Herodias, the wife of his brother Philip. 4 That was because John had told him, "It is not right for you to live with her." 5 Herod wanted to kill John but was afraid of the people, who regarded him as a prophet. 6 Then on Herod's birthday Herodias' daughter performed a dance before the court which delighted Herod so much 7 that he swore he would grant her anything she asked for. 8 Prompted by her mother she said, "Bring me the head of John the Baptizer on a platter." 9 The king immediately had his misgivings, but because of his oath and the guests who were present he gave orders that the request be granted. 10 He sent the order to have John beheaded in prison. 11 John's head was brought in on a platter and given to the girl, who took it to her mother. 12 Later his disciples presented themselves to carry his body away and bury it. Afterward, they came and informed Jesus.

Jesus Feeds Five Thousand

13 When Jesus heard this, he withdrew by boat from there to a deserted place by himself. The crowds heard of it and followed him on foot from the towns. 14 When he disembarked and saw the vast throng, his heart was moved with pity, and he cured their sick. 15 As evening drew on, his disciples came to him

with the suggestion: "This is a deserted place and it is already late. Dismiss the crowds so that they may go to the villages and buy some food for themselves." 16 Jesus said to them: "There is no need for them to disperse. Give them something to eat yourselves." 17 "We have nothing here," they replied, "but five loaves and a couple of fish." 18 "Bring them here," he said. 19 Then he ordered the crowds to sit down on the grass. He took the five loaves and two fish, looked up to heaven, blessed and broke them and gave the loaves to the disciples, who in turn gave them to the people. 20 All those present ate their fill. The fragments remaining, when gathered up, filled twelve baskets. 21 Those who ate were about five thousand, not counting women and children.

Jesus Walks on the Water

22 Immediately afterward, while dismissing the crowds, Jesus insisted that his disciples get into the boat and precede him to the other side. 23 When he had sent them away, he went up on the mountain by himself to pray, 24 remaining there alone as evening drew on. Meanwhile the boat, already several hundred yards out from shore, was being tossed about in the waves raised by strong head winds. 25 At about three in the morning, he came walking toward them on the lake. 26 When the disciples saw him walking on the water, they were terrified. "It is a ghost!" they said, and in their fear they began to cry out. 27 Jesus hastened to reassure them: "Get hold of yourselves! It is I. Do not be afraid!" 28 Peter spoke up and said, "Lord, if it is really you, tell me to come to you across the water." 29 "Come!" he said. So Peter got out of the boat and began to walk on the water, moving towards Jesus. 30 But when he perceived how strong the wind was, becoming frightened, he began to sink and cried out, "Lord,

save me!" 31 Jesus at once stretched out his hand and caught him. "How little faith you have!" he exclaimed. "Why did you falter?" 32 Once they had climbed into the boat, the wind died down. 33 Those who were in the boat showed him reverence, declaring, "Beyond doubt you are the Son of God!"

Other Miracles

34 After making the crossing they reached the shore at Gennesaret; 35 and when the men of that place recognized him they spread the word throughout the region. People brought him all the afflicted, 36 with the plea that he let them do no more than touch the tassel of his cloak. As many as touched it were fully restored to health.

Jesus and the Pharisees

15 Pharisees and scribes from Jerusalem approached Jesus with the question: 2 "Why do your disciples act contrary to the tradition of our ancestors? They do not wash their hands, for example, before eating a meal." 3 In reply he said to them: "Why do you for your part act contrary to the commandment of God for the sake of your 'tradition'? 4 For instance, God has said, 'Honor your father and your mother,' and 'Whoever curses father or mother shall be put to death.' 5 Yet you declare, 'Whoever says to his father or his mother, Any support you might have had from me is dedicated to God, 6 need not honor his father or his mother.' This means that for the sake of your tradition you have nullified God's word.

7 "You hypocrites! How accurately did Isaiah prophesy about you when he said:

8 'This people pays me lip service but their heart is far from me.
9 They do me empty reverence, making dogmas out of human precepts.'"

14, 19: The rite of blessing and distribution anticipates the Last Supper.
14, 22–33: See note on Mk 6, 45–52.
14, 28–31: These verses are proper to Matthew. Peter, who exercised the leading role among the Twelve through the decision of Christ (16, 18; Acts 1, 15), had also to find his salvation in Jesus.
14, 33: *Beyond doubt you are the Son of God:* during the mortal life of Jesus, his divine nature was

concealed. The confession therefore cannot be taken as evidence that the disciples comprehended Jesus' divine status at this time (Phil 2, 5–8). In the Old Testament the term "son" of God is applied to those who enjoy God's favor (Ex 4, 23; Ps 2, 7). However, the confession may be the evangelist's retrojection of the post-Easter faith into the time of Jesus' ministry; cf Mt 16, 16.
15, 5f: Property dedicated by vow was considered

sacred, and therefore not to be claimed by parents for their support. But since ownership of the property was still retained, the vow and its effect became a mere figment of law and a means of escape from the duty of filial piety. However, rabbinic evidence suggests that such was not the ordinary teaching of the rabbis.

10 He summoned the crowd and said to them: "Give ear and try to understand it. 11 It is not what goes into a man's mouth that makes him impure; it is what comes out of his mouth." 12 His disciples approached him and said, "Do you realize the Pharisees were scandalized when they heard your pronouncement?" 13 "Every planting not put down by my heavenly Father will be uprooted," he replied. 14 "Let them go their way; they are blind leaders of the blind. If one blind man leads another, both will end in a pit." 15 Then Peter spoke up to say, "Explain the parable to us." 16 "Are you, too, still incapable of understanding?" he asked. 17 "Do you not see that everything that enters the mouth passes into the stomach and is discharged into the latrine, 18 but what comes out of the mouth originates in the mind? It is things like these that make a man impure. 19 From the mind stem evil designs—murder, adulterous conduct, fornication, stealing, false witness, blasphemy. 20 These are the things that make a man impure. As for eating with unwashed hands— that makes no man impure."

The Canaanite Woman

21 Then Jesus left that place and withdrew to the district of Tyre and Sidon. 22 It happened that a Canaanite woman living in that locality presented herself, crying out to him, "Lord, Son of David, have pity on me! My daughter is terribly troubled by a demon." 23 He gave her no word of response. His disciples came up and began to entreat him, "Get rid of her. She keeps shouting after us." 24 "My mission is only to the lost sheep of the house of Israel," Jesus replied. 25 She came forward then and did him homage with the plea, "Help me, Lord!" 26 But he answered, "It is not right to take the food of sons and daughters and throw it to the dogs." 27 "Please, Lord," she insisted, "even the dogs eat the leavings that fall from their masters' tables." 28 Jesus then said in reply, "Woman, you have great faith! Your wish will come to pass." That very moment her daughter got better.

Jesus Heals the Suffering

29 Jesus left that place and passed along the Sea of Galilee. He went up onto the mountainside and sat down there. 30 Large crowds of people came to him bringing with them cripples, the deformed, the blind, the mute, and many others besides. They laid them at his feet and he cured them. 31 The result was great astonishment in the crowds as they beheld the mute speaking, the deformed made sound, cripples walking about, and the blind seeing. They glorified the God of Israel.

Jesus Feeds Four Thousand

32 Jesus called his disciples to him and said: "My heart is moved with pity for the crowd. By now they have been with me three days, and have nothing to eat. I do not wish to send them away hungry, for fear they may collapse on the way." 33 His disciples said to him, "How could we ever get enough bread in this deserted spot to satisfy such a crowd?" 34 But Jesus asked them, "How many loaves of bread do you have?" "Seven," they replied, "and a few small fish." 35 The he directed the crowd to seat themselves on the ground. 36 He took the seven loaves and the fish, and after giving thanks he broke them and gave them to the disciples, who in turn gave them to the crowds. 37 All ate until they were full. When they gathered up the fragments left over, these filled seven hampers. 38 The people who were fed numbered four thousand, apart from women and children.

39 Then, after he had dismissed the crowds, he got into the boat and went to the district of Magadan.

The Pharisees and Sadducees

16 The Pharisees and Sadducees came along, and as a test asked him to show them some sign in the sky. 2 He gave them this reply: ["In the evening you say, 'Red sky at night, the day will be bright'; 3 but in the morning, 'Sky red and gloomy, the day will be stormy.' If you know how to interpret the look of the sky, can you not read the signs of the times?] 4 An evil, faithless age is eager for a sign, but no sign will be given it except that of Jonah." With that he left them abruptly.

The Leaven of the Pharisees

5 The disciples discovered when they arrived at the other side that they had forgotten to bring any bread along. 6 When Jesus said to them, "Be on the lookout against the yeast of the Pharisees and Sadducees," 7 they could think only, "This is because we have brought no bread." 8 Jesus knew their thoughts and said, "Why do you suppose it is because you have no bread? How weak your faith is! 9 Do you still not understand? Do you not remember the five loaves among five thousand and how many baskets-full you picked up? 10 Or the seven loaves among four thousand and how many hampers-full you retrieved? 11 Why is it you do not see that I was not speaking about bread at all but warning you against the yeast of the Pharisees?" 12 They finally realized he was not issuing a warning against yeast [used for bread] but against the Pharisees' and Sadducees' teaching.

Peter the Rock

13 When Jesus came to the neighborhood of Caesarea Philippi, he asked his disciples this question: "Who do people say that the Son of Man is?" 14 They replied, "Some say John the Baptizer, others Elijah, still others Jeremiah or one of the prophets." 15 "And you," he said to them, "who do you say that I am?" 16 "You are the Messiah," Simon

---

15, 10f: Before God, human guilt or innocence stems from deliberate human decision, not from any (presumed) evil in material creation. How difficult it was to change this mentality of Jesus' contemporaries is evident from Acts 10, 9–16.
15, 21–28: See note on Mk 7, 24–30.

15, 32–38: See note on Mk 8, 1–9.
16, 16–20: To the tradition of Peter's confession at Caesarea Philippi (Mk 8, 27–30), Matthew adds the doctrine of the divinity of Christ, together with Jesus' prophecy that he will successfully build a new Israel, i.e., the church, upon Peter. Considering the

unresolved dispute among the Twelve as to who was the greatest (Mt 20, 20–24), it is probable that this prophecy as a whole was made by the risen Christ (Jn 21, 15ff). The importance of the prophecy is seen from the fact that Matthew conserves it three decades after Peter's martyrdom, when his leadership of the

Peter answered, "the Son of the living God!" 17 Jesus replied, "Blest are you, Simon son of John! No mere man has revealed this to you, but my heavenly Father. 18 I for my part declare to you, you are 'Rock,' and on this rock I will build my church, and the jaws of death shall not prevail against it. 19 I will entrust to you the keys of the kingdom of heaven. Whatever you declare bound on earth shall be bound in heaven; whatever you declare loosed on earth shall be loosed in heaven." 20 Then he strictly ordered his disciples not to tell anyone that he was the Messiah.

First Prophecy of Passion and Resurrection

21 From then on Jesus [the Messiah] started to indicate to his disciples that he must go to Jerusalem and suffer greatly there at the hands of the elders, the chief priests, and the scribes, and be put to death, and raised up on the third day. 22 At this, Peter took him aside and began to remonstrate with him. "May you be spared, Master! God forbid that any such thing ever happen to you!" 23 Jesus turned on Peter and said, "Get out of my sight, you satan! You are trying to make me trip and fall. You are not judging by God's standards but by man's."

Doctrine of the Cross

24 Jesus then said to his disciples: "If a man wishes to come after me, he must deny his very self, take up his cross, and begin to follow in my footsteps. 25 Whoever would save his life will lose it, but whoever loses his life for my sake will find it. 26 What profit would a man show if he were to gain the whole world

and destroy himself in the process? What can a man offer in exchange for his very self? 27 The Son of Man will come with his Father's glory accompanied by his angels. When he does, he will repay each man according to his conduct. 28 I assure you, among those standing here there are some who will not experience death before they see the Son of Man come in his kingship."

Jesus Transfigured

17 Six days later Jesus took Peter, James, and his brother John and led them up on a high mountain by themselves. 2 He was transfigured before their eyes. His face became as dazzling as the sun, his clothes as radiant as light. 3 Suddenly Moses and Elijah appeared to them conversing with him. 4 Then Peter said to Jesus, "Lord, how good that we are here! With your permission I will erect three booths here, one for you, one for Moses, and one for Elijah." 5 He was still speaking when suddenly a bright cloud overshadowed them. Out of the cloud came a voice which said, "This is my beloved Son on whom my favor rests. Listen to him." 6 When they heard this the disciples fell forward on the ground, overcome with fear. 7 Jesus came toward them and laying his hand on them, said, "Get up! Do not be afraid." 8 When they looked up they did not see anyone but Jesus.

The Coming of Elijah

9 As they were coming down the mountainside Jesus commanded them, "Do not tell anyone of the vision until the Son of Man rises from the dead." 10 The disciples put this question to him: "Why do

the scribes claim that Elijah must come first?" 11 In reply he said: "Elijah is indeed coming, and he will restore everything. 12 I assure you, though that Elijah has already come, but they did not recognize him and they did as they pleased with him. The Son of Man will suffer at their hands in the same way." 13 The disciples then realized that he had been speaking to them about John the Baptizer.

The Possessed Boy

14 As they approached the crowd, a man came up to him and knelt before him. 15 "Lord," he said, "take pity on my son, who is demented and in a serious condition. For example, he often falls into the fire and frequently into the water. 16 I have brought him to your disciples but they could not cure him." 17 In reply Jesus said: "What an unbelieving and perverse lot you are! How long must I remain with you? How long can I endure you? Bring him here to me!" 18 Then Jesus reprimanded him, and the demon came out of him. That very moment the boy was cured.

19 The disciples approached Jesus at that point and asked him privately, "Why could we not expel it?" 20 "Because you have so little trust," he told them. "I assure you, if you had faith the size of a mustard seed, you would be able to say to this mountain, 'Move from here to there,' and it would move. Nothing would be impossible for you. 21 [This kind does not leave but by prayer and fasting.]"

Second Prophecy of the Passion

22 When they met again in Galilee, Jesus said to them, "The Son of Man

---

Jerusalem community is already a thing of the past. In Matthew, the building of the new Israel on Peter pertains to Jesus' own role in the mystery of the reign of God that has appeared in history; see notes on 13, 1–53; 13, 53—19, 1. Jesus cannot begin to build his church upon Peter until after his death and resurrection (16, 21ff). For Matthew, Jesus' building of the new people of God upon Peter is a continuing reality for the Christian community of his time.

16, 17: Jesus' messianic identity and divinity cannot be truly known from human reason, but only from God's revelation (1 Cor 12, 3).

16, 18: You are "Rock": the Greek petros and its Aramaic equivalent kepha, "rock" is here conferred on Simon as a personal name to indicate his role as the firm foundation on which Jesus builds his church. The jaws of death: literally, "the gates of Sheol" (Nm 16, 33), i.e., death's realm, here used to signify

the power or force of evil responsible first for physical then for spiritual death. The new people of God will overcome both forms of death to achieve the glorious entrance into the final kingdom (Rv 20, 4ff).

16, 19: I will entrust . . . kingdom of heaven: i.e., spiritual power to be exercised over the life of God's people, in contrast to the previously mentioned "gates," i.e., the evil power of death that would not prevail against the church. Simon Peter is the keeper of the keys, the one who has power to open and to close, to "bind" and to "loose," to allow and to forbid; cf Is 22, 22. The exercise of this responsibility is here compared to the disciplinary and doctrinal authority of the rabbis who in Jesus' time interpreted the Old Testament for the faith and life of the people. The exact nature of the extraordinary power here conferred became clear through the historical development of the Christian community in terms of the

primacy of Peter, i.e., his supreme authority in teaching, governing and sanctifying the people of God.

16, 24ff: See note on Mk 8, 34—9, 1.

16, 27f: These two sayings seem to refer to distinct phases of the kingdom of God: the reign of Christ in and through the new Christian community, with its orientation through faith to the second coming of Christ (27); and the eschatological kingdom of the Father, to be inaugurated when the Son of Man comes in glory at the end of time (28). See note on Mk 9, 1; Acts 1, 11.

17, 1–8: See note on Mk 9, 2–8.

17, 9: Misunderstanding the necessity of the passion, they are not to reveal the vision until after Jesus' resurrection.

17, 14–20: See note on Mk 9, 14–29.

is going to be delivered into the hands of men 23 who will put him to death, and he will be raised up on the third day." At these words they were overwhelmed with grief.

Paying the Temple Tax

24 When they entered Capernaum, the collectors of the temple tax approached Peter and said, "Does your master not pay the temple tax?" 25 "Of course he does," Peter replied. Then Jesus on entering the house asked, without giving him time to speak: "What is your opinion, Simon? Do the kings of the world take tax or toll from their sons, or from foreigners?" 26 When he replied, "From foreigners," Jesus observed: "Then their sons are exempt. 27 But for fear of disedifying them go to the lake, throw in a line, and take out the first fish you catch. Open its mouth and you will discover there a coin worth twice the temple tax. Take it and give it to them for you and me."

Against Ambition

18 Just then the disciples came up to Jesus with the question, "Who is of greatest importance in the kingdom of God?" 2 He called a little child over and stood him in their midst 3 and said: "I assure you, unless you change and become like little children, you will not enter the kingdom of God. 4 Whoever makes himself lowly, becoming like this child, is of greatest importance in that heavenly reign.

Avoiding Scandal

5 "Whoever welcomes one such child for my sake welcomes me. 6 On the other hand, it would be better for anyone who leads astray one of these little ones who believe in me, to be drowned by a millstone around his neck, in the depths of the sea. 7 What terrible things will come on the world through scandal! It is inevitable that scandal should occur. Nonetheless, woe to that man through whom scandal comes! 8 If

your hand or foot is your undoing, cut it off and throw it from you! Better to enter life maimed or crippled than be thrown with two hands or feet into endless fire. 9 If your eye is your downfall, gouge it out and cast it from you! Better to enter life with one eye than be thrown with both into fiery Gehenna.

The Straying Sheep

10 "See that you never despise one of these little ones. I assure you, their angels in heaven constantly behold my heavenly Father's face. 12 What is your thought on this: A man owns a hundred sheep and one of them wanders away; will he not leave the ninety-nine out on the hills and go in search of the stray? 13 If he succeeds in finding it, believe me he is happier about this one than about the ninety-nine that did not wander away. 14 Just so, it is no part of your heavenly Father's plan that a single one of these little ones shall ever come to grief.

Fraternal Correction

15 "If your brother should commit some wrong against you, go and point out his fault, but keep it between the two of you. If he listens to you, you have won your brother over. 16 If he does not listen, summon another, so that every case may stand on the word of two or three witnesses. 17 If he ignores them, refer it to the church. If he ignores even the church, then treat him as you would a Gentile or a tax collector. 18 I assure you, whatever you declare bound on earth shall be held bound in heaven, and whatever you declare loosed on earth shall be held loosed in heaven.

The Power of United Prayer

19 "Again I tell you, if two of you join your voices on earth to pray for anything whatever, it shall be granted you by my Father in heaven. 20 Where two or three are gathered in my name, there am I in their midst."

The Merciless Official

21 Then Peter came up and asked him, "Lord, when my brother wrongs me, how often must I forgive him? Seven times?" 22 "No," Jesus replied, "not seven times; I say, seventy times seven times. 23 That is why the reign of God may be said to be like a king who decided to settle accounts with his officials. 24 When he began his auditing, one was brought in who owed him a huge amount. 25 As he had no way of paying it, his master ordered him to be sold, along with his wife, his children, and all his property, in payment of the debt. 26 At that the official prostrated himself in homage and said, 'My lord, be patient with me and I will pay you back in full.' 27 Moved with pity, the master let the official go and wrote off the debt. 28 But when that same official went out he met a fellow servant who owed him a mere fraction of what he himself owed. He seized him and throttled him. 'Pay back what you owe,' he demanded. 29 His fellow servant dropped to his knees and began to plead with him, 'Just give me time and I will pay you back in full.' 30 But he would hear none of it. Instead, he had him put in jail until he paid back what he owed. 31 When his fellow servants saw what had happened they were badly shaken, and went to their master to report the whole incident. 32 His master sent for him and said, 'You worthless wretch! I canceled your entire debt when you pleaded with me. 33 Should you not have dealt mercifully with your fellow servant, as I dealt with you?' 34 Then in anger the master handed him over to the torturers until he paid back all that he owed. 35 My heavenly Father will treat you in exactly the same way unless each of you forgives his brother from his heart."

19 When Jesus had finished this discourse, he left Galilee and came to the district of Judea across

---

18, 11: Omitted here with many MSS.

18, 15–18: Note the transition from fraternal correction to the further action (17) of delivering the obstinate sinner to the authority of the church. Exclusion and readmission of such a one is a function of the power of binding and loosing which belongs to the Christian community. There is no concrete

evidence as to how the communities of New Testament times exercised this power.

19, 3–8: The Pharisees wish to force Jesus to take sides on the question of divorce for the purpose of remarriage. (The stringent position at the time was that of the school of Shammai, while leniency was advocated by the school of Hillel.) In reply, Jesus

proclaims the indissolubility of marriage, citing Gn 1, 27 and 2, 24. He declares this scriptural doctrine to be God's ultimate intent for marriage in human society, explaining that the divorce granted in the Old Testament was due to the stubbornness of the Jews, i.e., to their cultural *mores*, which God in his wisdom chose to leave unenlightened. *Let no man* the Jordan. 2 Great crowds followed him and he cured them there.

FIRST STEPS IN ESTABLISHING GOD'S REIGN

The Question of Divorce

3 Some Pharisees came up to him and said, to test him, "May a man divorce his wife for any reason whatever?" 4 He replied, "Have you not read that at the beginning the Creator made them male and female 5 and declared, 'For this reason a man shall leave his father and mother and cling to his wife, and the two shall become as one'? 6 Thus they are no longer two but one flesh. Therefore, let no man separate what God has joined." 7 They said to him, "Then why did Moses command divorce and the promulgation of a divorce decree?" 8 "Because of your stubbornness Moses let you divorce your wives," he replied; "but at the beginning it was not that way. 9 I now say to you, whoever divorces his wife (lewd conduct is a separate case) and marries another commits adultery, and the man who marries a divorced woman commits adultery."

10 His disciples said to him, "If that is the case between man and wife, it is better not to marry." 11 He said, "Not everyone can accept this teaching, only those to whom it is given to do so. 12 Some men are incapable of sexual activity from birth; some have been deliberately made so; and some there are who have freely renounced sex for the sake of God's reign. Let him accept this teaching who can."

Jesus Blesses the Children

13 At one point, children were brought to him so that he could place his hands on them in prayer. The disciples began to scold them, 14 but Jesus said, "Let the children come to me. Do not hinder them. The kingdom of God belongs to such as these." 15 And he laid his hands on their heads before he left that place.

The Danger of Riches

16 Another time a man came up to him and said, "Teacher, what good must I do to possess everlasting life?" 17 He answered, "Why do you question me about what is good? There is One who is good. If you wish to enter into life, keep the commandments." 18 "Which ones?" he asked. Jesus replied, "'You shall not kill'; 'You shall not commit adultery'; 'You shall not steal'; 'You shall not bear false witness'; 19 'Honor your father and your mother'; and 'Love your neighbor as yourself.'" 20 The young man said to him, "I have kept all these; what do I need to do further?" 21 Jesus told him, "If you seek perfection, go, sell your possessions, and give to the poor. You will then have treasure in heaven. Afterward come back and follow me." 22 Hearing these words, the young man went away sad, for his possessions were many.

23 Jesus said to his disciples: "I assure you, only with difficulty will a rich man enter into the kingdom of God. 24 I repeat what I said: it is easier for a camel to pass through a needle's eye than for a rich man to enter the kingdom of God." 25 When the disciples heard this they were completely overwhelmed, and exclaimed, "Then who can be saved?" 26 Jesus looked at them and said, "For man it is impossible; but for God all things are possible."

27 Then it was Peter's turn to say to him: "Here we have put everything aside to follow you. What can we expect from it?" 28 Jesus said to them: "I give you my solemn word, in the new age when the Son of Man takes his seat upon a throne befitting his glory, you who have followed me shall likewise take your places on twelve thrones to judge the twelve tribes of Israel. 29 Moreover, everyone who has given up home, brothers or sisters, father or mother, wife or children or property for my sake will receive many times as much and inherit everlasting life. 30 Many who are first shall come last, and the last shall come first.

The Laborers in the Vineyards

20 "The reign of God is like the case of the owner of an estate who went out at dawn to hire workmen for his vineyard. 2 After reaching an agreement with them for the usual daily wage, he sent them out to his vineyard. 3 He came out about midmorning and saw other men standing around the marketplace without work, 4 so he said to them, 'You too go along to my vineyard and I will pay you whatever is fair.' 5 At that they went away. He came out again around noon and midafternoon and did the same. 6 Finally, going out in late afternoon he found still others standing around. To these he said, 'Why have you been standing here idle all day?' 7 'No one has hired us,' they told him. He said, 'You go to the vineyard too.' 8 When evening came the owner of the vineyard said to his foreman, 'Call the workmen and give them their pay, but begin with the last group and end with the first.' 9 When those hired late in the afternoon came up they received a full day's pay, 10 and

---

separate what God has joined: not by mere legislation, for neither civil law, nor social custom, nor mutual consent forges the unbreakable bond, but rather the divine involvement in the union of marriage. The citation of Gn 2, 24 indicates that in the divine "joining together," God ratifies the mutual love of persons; their sexual union serves as a pledge of exclusive fidelity to each other; cf Mk 10, 2–12; Lk 16, 18; 1 Cor 7, 10f. For reflection on the theological implications of the Lord's new teaching, cf Eph 5, 21–33.

19, 9: Lewd conduct is a separate case: literally "except for porneia," i.e., immorality, fornication, even incest. A growing number of scholars consider this to refer to Christians who, prior to their conversion, had married within the prohibited degree of

blood relationship as stated in Lv 18, 6–18. The same position seems to be taken in Acts 15, 20. As it stands, however, this Matthean clause of exception and that of 5, 32 cannot easily be reconciled with the absolute prohibition of divorce repeated in Mk 10, 11f and Lk 16, 18. Whatever may have been the situation prevailing among the Christians for whom Matthew wrote, the more stringent understanding of Jesus' words prevailed throughout the church.

19, 12: This verse is proper to Matthew. While there is no consensus on its meaning, some exegetes understand it to refer to voluntary and perpetual celibacy for members of the Christian community who wish to dedicate themselves completely to the kingdom of God; cf Mt 13, 44ff; 19, 29.

19, 13ff: Children were the symbol Jesus used for

the anawim, the poor in spirit or the lowly, within the Christian community; see note on 5, 3–12. Like the apostles, these have surrendered personal possessions (16–30) for total dedication to his ministry.

19, 16: See note on Mk 10, 17f.

19, 21: The young man is invited to join the anawim.

19, 23–26: Jesus' contemporaries consider wealth a sign of divine favor. When he denies this and shows that wealth can even obstruct the spiritual perception of his message, the disciples conclude that virtually no one can be saved. Jesus replies that the rich as well as the poor are dependent on God for their salvation.

19, 27–30: Voluntary renunciation of home, property and relatives for the sake of Christ will evoke the divine generosity in this life and in the next.

when the first group appeared they supposed they would get more; 11 yet they received the same daily wage. Thereupon they complained to the owner, 12 'This last group did only an hour's work, but you have put them on the same basis as us who have worked a full day in the scorching heat.' 13 'My friend,' he said to one in reply, 'I do you no injustice. You agreed on the usual wage, did you not? 14 Take your pay and go home. I intend to give this man who was hired last the same pay as you. 15 I am free to do as I please with my money, am I not? Or are you envious because I am generous?' 16 Thus the last shall be first and the first shall be last."

Third Prophecy: Passion and Resurrection

17 As Jesus was starting to go up to Jerusalem, he took the Twelve aside on the road and said to them: 18 "We are going up to Jerusalem now. There the Son of Man will be handed over to the chief priests and scribes, who will condemn him to death. 19 They will turn him over to the Gentiles, to be made sport of and flogged and crucified. But on the third day he will be raised up."

The Mother of James and John

20 The mother of Zebedee's sons came up to him accompanied by her sons, to do him homage and ask of him a favor. 21 "What is it you want?" he said. She answered, "Promise me that these sons of mine will sit, one at your right hand and the other at your left, in your kingdom." 22 In reply Jesus said, "You do not know what you are asking. Can you drink of the cup I am to drink of?" "We can," they said. 23 He told them, "From the cup I drink of, you shall drink. But sitting at my right hand or my left is not mine to give. That is for those to whom it has been reserved by my Father." 24 The other ten, on hearing this, be-

came indignant at the two brothers. 25 Jesus then called them together and said: "You know how those who exercise authority among the Gentiles lord it over them; their great ones make their importance felt. 26 It cannot be like that with you. Anyone among you who aspires to greatness must serve the rest, 27 and whoever wants to rank first among you must serve the needs of all. 28 Such is the case with the Son of Man who has come, not to be served by others, but to serve, to give his own life as a ransom for the many."

The Two Blind Men at Jericho

29 As they were leaving Jericho a large crowd followed him, 30 and suddenly two blind men sitting by the roadside, who heard that Jesus was passing by, began to shout, "Lord, Son of David, have pity on us!" 31 The crowd began to scold them in an effort to reduce them to silence, but they only shouted the louder, "Lord, Son of David, have pity on us!" 32 Jesus then stopped and called out to them, "What do you want me to do for you?" 33 "Lord," they told him, "open our eyes!" 34 Moved with compassion, Jesus touched their eyes, and immediately they could see; and they became his followers.

Triumphal Entry into Jerusalem

21 As they drew near Jerusalem, entering Bethphage on the Mount of Olives, Jesus sent off two disciples 2 with the instructions: "Go into the village straight ahead of you and you will immediately find an ass tethered and her colt with her. Untie them and lead them back to me. 3 If anyone says a word to you, say, 'The Master needs them.' Then he will let them go at once." 4 This came about to fulfil what was said through the prophet:

5 "Tell the daughter of Zion,
   Your king comes to you without
      display

astride an ass, astride a colt,
   the foal of a beast of burden."

6 So the disciples went off and did what Jesus had ordered; 7 they brought the ass and the colt and laid their cloaks on them, and he mounted. 8 The huge crowd spread their cloaks on the road, while some began to cut branches from the trees and lay them along his path. 9 The groups preceding him as well as those following kept crying out:

"Hosanna to the Son of David!
Blessed is he who comes in the
      name of the Lord!
Hosanna in the highest!"

10 As he entered Jerusalem the whole city was stirred to its depths, demanding, "Who is this?" 11 And the crowd kept answering, "This is the prophet Jesus from Nazareth in Galilee."

Cleaning out the Temple

12 Jesus entered the temple precincts and drove out all those engaged there in buying and selling. He overturned the money changers' tables and the stalls of the dove-sellers, 13 saying to them: "Scripture has it,

'My house shall be called a
   house of prayer,'

but you are turning it into a den of thieves." 14 The blind and the lame came to him inside the temple area and he cured them. 15 The chief priests and the scribes became indignant when they observed the wonders he worked, and how the children were shouting out in the temple precincts, "Hosanna to the Son of David!" 16 "Do you hear what they are saying?" they asked him. Jesus said to them, "Of course I do! Did you never read this:

'From the speech of infants and
   children
you have framed a hymn of
   praise'?"

20, 1-34: A development of the thought of 19, 30: God requires service of his followers while reserving to himself the modes and occasions of his generosity (1-16). He makes the same requirement of Jesus himself (17ff) and of his apostles (20-28), without indicating what will be the nature of God's generous return. The cure of the blind men (29-34) shows that Jesus is still the servant of men as he proceeds to his

death in Jerusalem.
21, 1-11: See note on Mk 11, 1-11.
21, 5: A free citation of Is 62, 11 and Zec 9, 9 indicating that Jesus entered Jerusalem as king of peace, riding, not the horse, symbol of the conqueror (Jer 22, 4), but the ass, the work beast of the poor.
21, 9: A citation of Ps 118, 25f used for the purpose of acknowledging Jesus to be the Messiah and son of

David. See note on Mk 11, 1-11. *Hosanna* (the Hebrew *Hôsî' ah-nnā*, literally "Do save!"): meant here as an acclamation or shout of praise honoring Jesus as the Savior.
21, 12-22: See notes on Mk 11, 15-19 and on 11, 12ff, in that order.

17 With that he left them and went out of the city to Bethany, where he spent the night.

Jesus Curses a Fig Tree

18 At dawn, as Jesus was returning to the city, he felt hungry. 19 Seeing a fig tree by the roadside he went over to it, but found nothing there except leaves. He said to it, "Never again shall you produce fruit!"; and it withered up instantly. 20 The disciples were dumbfounded when they saw this. They asked, "Why did the fig tree wither up so quickly?" 21 Jesus said: "Believe me, if you trust and do not falter, not only will you do what I did to the fig tree, but if you say to this mountain, 'Be lifted up and thrown into the sea,' even that will happen. 22 You will receive all that you pray for, provided you have faith."

The Authority of Jesus

23 After Jesus had entered the temple precincts, and while he was teaching, the chief priests and elders of the people came up to him and said: "On what authority are you doing these things? Who has given you this power?" 24 Jesus answered: "I too will ask a question. If you answer it for me, then I will tell you on what authority I do the things I do. 25 What was the origin of John's baptism? Was it divine or merely human?" They thought to themselves, "If we say 'divine,' he will ask us, 'Then why did you not put faith in it?'; 26 while if we say, 'merely human,' we shall have reason to fear the people, who all regard John as a prophet." 27 So their answer to Jesus was, "We do not know." He said in turn, "Then neither will I tell you on what authority I do the things I do.

Parable of the Two Sons

28 "What do you think of this case? There was a man who had two sons. He approached the elder and said, 'Son, go out and work in the vineyard today.' 29 The son replied, 'I am on my way, sir'; but he never went. 30 Then the man came to his second son and said the same thing. This son said in reply, 'No, I will not'; but afterward he regretted it and went. 31 Which of the two did what the father wanted?" They said, "The second." Jesus said to them, "Let me make it clear that tax collectors and prostitutes are entering the kingdom of God before you. 32 When John came preaching a way of holiness, you put no faith in him; but the tax collectors and the prostitutes did believe in him. Yet even when you saw that, you did not repent and believe in him.

Parable of the Tenants

33 "Listen to another parable. There was a property owner who planted a vineyard, put a hedge around it, dug out a vat, and erected a tower. Then he leased it out to tenant farmers and went on a journey. 34 When vintage time arrived he dispatched his slaves to the tenants to obtain his share of the grapes. 35 The tenants responded by seizing the slaves. They beat one, killed another, and stoned a third. 36 A second time he dispatched even more slaves than before, but they treated them the same way. 37 Finally he sent his son to them, thinking, 'They will respect my son.' 38 When they saw the son, the tenants said to one another, 'Here is the one who will inherit everything. Let us kill him and then we shall have his inheritance!' 39 With that they seized him, dragged him outside the vineyard, and killed him. 40 What do you suppose the owner of the vineyard will do to those tenants when he comes?" 41 They replied, "He will bring that wicked crowd to a bad end and lease his vineyard out to others who will see to it that he has grapes at vintage time." 42 Jesus said to them, "Did you never read in the Scriptures,

'The stone which the builders rejected
has become the keystone of the structure.
It was the Lord who did this
and we find it marvelous to behold'?

43 For this reason, I tell you, the kingdom of God will be taken away from you and given to a nation that will yield a rich harvest. 44 [The man who falls upon that stone will be smashed to bits; and he on whom it falls will be crushed.]"

45 When the chief priests and the Pharisees heard these parables, they realized he was speaking about them. 46 Although they sought to arrest him, they had reason to fear the crowds who regarded him as a prophet.

The Wedding Banquet

22 Jesus began to address them, once more using parables. 2 "The reign of God may be likened to a king who gave a wedding banquet for his son. 3 He dispatched his servants to summon the invited guests to the wedding, but they refused to come. 4 A second time he sent other servants, saying: 'Tell those who are invited, See, I have my dinner prepared! My bullocks and corn-fed cattle are killed; everything is ready. Come to the feast.' 5 Some ignored the invitation and went their way, one to his farm, another to his business. 6 The rest laid hold of his servants, insulted them, and killed them. 7 At this the king grew furious and sent his army to destroy those murderers and burn their city. 8 Then he said to his servants: 'The banquet is ready, but those who were invited were unfit to come. 9 That is why you must go out to the byroads and invite to the wedding anyone you come upon.' 10 The servants then went out into the byroads and rounded up everyone they met, bad as well as good. This filled the wedding hall with banqueters.

11 "When the king came in to meet the guests, however, he caught sight of a man not properly dressed for a wedding feast. 12 'My friend,' he said, 'how is it you came in here not properly dressed?' The man had nothing to say. 13 The king then said to the attendants, 'Bind him hand and foot and throw him out into the night to wail and grind his teeth.' 14 The invited are many, the elect are few."

22, 14: The failure of Israel to accept Jesus' prophetic message deserved the punishment of deprivation—a warning of divine judgment against Christians who fail to live according to their faith.

Paying Tax to the Emperor

15 Then the Pharisees went off and began to plot how they might trap Jesus in speech. 16 They sent their disciples to him, accompanied by Herodian sympathizers, who said: "Teacher, we know you are a truthful man and teach God's way sincerely. You court no one's favor and do not act out of human respect. 17 Give us your opinion, then, in this case. Is it lawful to pay tax to the emperor or not?" 18 Jesus recognized their bad faith and said to them, "Why are you trying to trip me up, you hypocrites? 19 Show me the coin used for the tax." When they handed him a small Roman coin 20 he asked them, "Whose head is this, and whose inscription?" 21 "Caesar's," they replied. At that he said to them, "Then give to Caesar what is Caesar's, but give to God what is God's." 22 Taken aback by this reply, they went off and left him.

The Sadducees and the Resurrection

23 That same day some Sadducees, who hold there is no resurrection, came to him with a question: 24 "Teacher, Moses declared, 'If a man dies without children, his brother must take the wife and produce offspring for his brother.' 25 Once there were seven brothers. The eldest died after marrying, and since he had no children, left his wife to his brother. 26 The same thing happened to the second, the third, and so on, down to the seventh. 27 Last of all the woman died too. 28 At the resurrection, whose wife will she be, since all seven of them married her?" 29 Jesus replied: "You are badly misled because you fail to understand the Scriptures and the power of God. 30 When people rise from the dead, they neither marry nor are given in marriage but live like angels in heaven. 31 As to the fact that the dead are raised, have you not read what God said to you,

32 'I am the God of Abraham, the God of Isaac, the God of Jacob'? He is the God of the living, not of the dead." 33 The crowds who listened were spellbound by his teaching.

The Great Commandment

34 When the Pharisees heard that he had silenced the Sadducees, they assembled in a body; 35 and one of them, a lawyer, in an attempt to trip him up, asked him, 36 "Teacher, which commandment of the law is the greatest?" 37 Jesus said to him:

"'You shall love the Lord your God
with your whole heart,
with your whole soul,
and with all your mind.'

38 This is the greatest and first commandment. 39 The second is like it:

'You shall love your neighbor
as yourself.'

40 On these two commandments the whole law is based, and the prophets as well."

The Son of David

41 In turn Jesus put a question to the assembled Pharisees, 42 "What is your opinion about the Messiah? Whose son is he?" "David's," they answered. He said to them, 43 "Then how is it that David under the Spirit's influence calls him 'lord,' as he does:

44 'The Lord said to my lord, Sit
at my right hand,
until I humble your enemies
beneath your feet'?

45 If David calls him 'lord,' how can he be his son?" 46 No one could give him an answer; therefore no one dared, from that day on, to ask him any questions.

Hypocrisy of the Scribes and Pharisees

23 Then Jesus told the crowds and his disciples: 2 "The scribes and the Pharisees have succeeded Moses as teachers; 3 therefore, do everything and observe everything they tell you. But do not follow their example. 4 Their words are bold but their deeds are few. They bind up heavy loads, hard to carry, to lay on other men's shoulders, while they themselves will not lift a finger to budge them. 5 All their works are performed to be seen. They widen their phylacteries and wear huge tassels. 6 They are fond of places of honor at banquets and the front seats in synagogues, 7 of marks of respect in public and of being called 'Rabbi.' 8 As to you, avoid the title 'Rabbi.' One among you is your teacher, the rest are learners. 9 Do not call anyone on earth your father. Only one is your father, the One in heaven. 10 Avoid being called teachers. Only one is your teacher, the Messiah. 11 The greatest among you will be the one who serves the rest. 12 Whoever exalts himself shall be humbled, but whoever humbles himself shall be exalted.

13 "Woe to you scribes and Pharisees, you frauds! You shut the doors of the kingdom of God in men's faces, neither entering yourselves nor admitting those who are trying to enter. 15 Woe to you scribes and Pharisees, you frauds! You travel over sea and land to make a single convert, but once he is converted you make a devil of him twice as wicked as yourselves. 16 It is an evil day for you, blind guides! You declare, 'If a man swears by the temple it means nothing, but if he swears by the gold of the temple he is obligated.' 17 Blind fools! Which is more important, the gold or the temple which makes it sacred? 18 Again you declare, 'If a man swears by the altar it means nothing, but if he swears by the gift on the altar he is obligated.' 19 How blind you are! Which is more important, the offering or the altar which makes the offering sacred? 20 The man who swears by the altar is swearing by it and by everything on it. 21 The

---

23, 1–36: These strong criticisms of the scribes and Pharisees are found also in Mk 12, 38ff. The collection of them in Matthew is probably explained by a hostility that had developed between Judaism and Christianity. See note on Acts 8, 3. It may also be

that some members of the Judaeo-Christian communities still adhered to certain ideas and practices of the Pharisees which are here reprobated.

23, 8ff: Typical hyperbolic speech of the time. It does not reject authority in principle, but authori-

tarianism; not the use of titles, but the failure to acknowledge that authority exists to serve God, his anointed One, and one's neighbor.

23, 14: Omitted here with many MSS.

man who swears by the temple is swearing by it and by him who dwells there. 22 The man who swears by heaven is swearing by God's throne and by him who is seated on that throne. 23 Woe to you scribes and Pharisees, you frauds! You pay tithes on mint and herbs and seeds while neglecting the weightier matters of the law, justice and mercy and good faith. It is these you should have practiced, without neglecting the others.

24 "Blind guides! You strain out the gnat and swallow the camel! 25 Woe to you scribes and Pharisees, you frauds! You cleanse the outside of cup and dish, and leave the inside filled with loot and lust! 26 Blind Pharisee! First cleanse the inside of the cup so that its outside may be clean. 27 Woe to you scribes and Pharisees, you frauds! You are like white-washed tombs, beautiful to look at on the outside but inside full of filth and dead men's bones. 28 Thus you present to view a holy exterior while hypocrisy and evil fill you within. 29 Woe to you scribes and Pharisees, you frauds! You erect tombs for the prophets and decorate the monuments of the saints. 30 You say, 'Had we lived in our forefathers' time we would not have joined them in shedding the prophets' blood.' 31 Thus you show that you are the sons of the prophets' murderers. 32 Now it is your turn: fill up the vessel measured out by your forefathers. 33 Vipers' nest! Brood of serpents! How can you escape condemnation to Gehenna? 34 For this reason I shall send you prophets and wise men and scribes. Some you will kill and crucify, others you will flog in your synagogues and hunt down from city to city; 35 until retribution overtakes you for all the blood of the just ones shed on earth, from the blood of holy Abel to the blood of Zechariah son of Barachiah, whom you murdered between the temple building and the altar. 36 All this, I assure you, will be the fate of the present generation. 37 O Jerusalem, Jerusalem, murderess of prophets and stoner of those who were sent to you! How often have I yearned to gather your children, as a mother bird gathers her young under

her wings, but you refused me. 38 Recall the saying, 'You will find your temple deserted.' 39 I tell you, you will not see me from this time on until you declare, 'Blessed is he who comes in the name of the Lord!'"

Beginning of Calamities

24 Jesus left the temple precincts then, and his disciples came up and pointed out to him the buildings of the temple area. 2 His comment was: "Do you see all these buildings? I assure you, not one stone will be left on another—it will all be torn down." 3 While he was seated on the Mount of Olives, his disciples came up to him privately and said: "Tell us, when will all this occur? What will be the sign of your coming and the end of the world?" 4 In reply Jesus said to them: "Be on guard! Let no one mislead you. 5 Many will come attempting to impersonate me. 'I am the Messiah!' they will claim, and they will deceive many. 6 You will hear of wars and rumors of wars. Do not be alarmed. Such things are bound to happen, but that is not yet the end. 7 Nation will rise against nation, one kingdom against another. There will be famine and pestilence and earthquakes in many places. 8 These are the early stages of the birth pangs. 9 They will hand you over to torture and kill you. 10 Indeed, you will be hated by all nations on my account. Many will falter then, betraying and hating one another. 11 False prophets will rise in great numbers to mislead many. 12 Because of the increase of evil, the love of most will grow cold. 13 The man who holds out to the end, however, is the one who will see salvation. 14 This good news of the kingdom will be proclaimed throughout the world as a witness to all the nations. Only after that will the end come.

The Final Test

15 "When you see the abominable and destructive thing which the prophet Daniel foretold standing on holy ground (let the reader take note!), 16 those in Judea must flee to the mountains. 17 If a man is on the roof terrace, he must not come

down to get anything out of his house. 18 If a man is in the field, he must not turn back to pick up his cloak. 19 It will be hard on pregnant or nursing mothers in those days. 20 Keep praying that you will not have to flee in winter or on a sabbath, 21 for those days will be more filled with anguish than any from the beginning of the world until now or in all ages to come. 22 Indeed, if the period had not been shortened, not a human being would be saved. For the sake of the chosen, however, the days will be shortened. 23 If anyone tells you at that time, 'Look, the Messiah is here,' or 'He is there,' do not believe it. 24 False messiahs and false prophets will appear, performing signs and wonders so great as to mislead even the chosen if that were possible. 25 Remember, I have told you all about it beforehand; 26 so if they tell you, 'Look, he is in the desert,' do not go out there; or 'He is in the innermost rooms,' do not believe it. 27 As the lightening from the east flashes to the west, so will the coming of the Son of Man be. 28 Where the carcass lies, there the vultures gather.

Coming of the Son of Man

29 "Immediately after the stress of that period, 'the sun will be darkened, the moon will not shed her light, the stars will fall from the sky, and the hosts of heaven will be shaken loose.' 30 Then the sign of the Son of Man will appear in the sky, and 'all the clans of earth will strike their breasts' as they see 'the Son of Man coming on the clouds of heaven' with power and great glory. 31 He will dispatch his angels 'with a mighty trumpet blast, and they will assemble his chosen from the four winds, from one end of the heavens to the other.' 32 From the fig tree learn a lesson. When its branch grows tender and sprouts leaves, you realize that summer is near. 33 Likewise, when you see all these things happening, you will know that he is near, standing at your door. 34 I assure you, the present generation will not pass away until all this takes place.

24, 1–51: See note on Mk 13, 1–37.

35 The heavens and the earth will pass away but my words will not pass.

The Need for Watchfulness

36 "As for the exact day or hour, no one knows it, neither the angels in heaven nor the Son, but the Father only. 37 The coming of the Son of Man will repeat what happened in Noah's time. 38 In the days before the flood people were eating and drinking, marrying and being married, right up to the day Noah entered the ark. 39 They were totally unconcerned until the flood came and destroyed them. So will it be at the coming of the Son of Man. 40 Two men will be out in the field; one will be taken and one will be left. 41 Two women will be grinding meal; one will be taken and one will be left. 42 Stay awake, therefore! You cannot know the day your Lord is coming.

43 "Be sure of this: if the owner of the house knew when the thief was coming he would keep a watchful eye and not allow his house to be broken into. 44 You must be prepared in the same way. The Son of Man is coming at the time you least expect. 45 Who is the faithful, farsighted servant whom the master has put in charge of his household to dispense food at need? 46 Happy that servant whom his master discovers at work on his return! 47 I assure you, he will put him in charge of all his property. 48 But if the servant is worthless and tells himself, 'My master is a long time in coming,' 49 and begins to beat his fellow servants, to eat and drink with drunkards, 50 that man's master will return when he is not ready and least expects him. 51 He will punish him severely and settle with him as is done with hypocrites. There will be wailing then and grinding of teeth.

Parable of the Ten Virgins

25 "The reign of God can be likened to ten bridesmaids who took their torches and went out to welcome the groom. 2 Five of them were foolish, while the other five were sensible. 3 The foolish ones, in taking their torches, brought no oil along, 4 but the sensible ones took flasks of oil as well as their torches. 5 The groom delayed his coming, so they all began to nod, then to fall asleep. 6 At midnight someone shouted, 'The groom is here! Come out and greet him!' 7 At the outcry all the virgins woke up and got their torches ready. 8 The foolish ones said to the sensible, 'Give us some of your oil. Our torches are going out.' 9 But the sensible ones replied, 'No, there may not be enough for you and us. You had better go to the dealers and buy yourselves some.' 10 While they went off to buy it the groom arrived, and the ones who were ready went in to the wedding with him. Then the door was barred. 11 Later the other bridesmaids came back. 'Master, master!' they cried. 'Open the door for us,' 12 But he answered, 'I tell you, I do not know you.' 13 The moral is: keep your eyes open, for you know not the day or the hour.

Parable of the Silver Pieces

14 "The case of a man who was going on a journey is similar. He called in his servants and handed his funds over to them according to each man's abilities. 15 To one he disbursed five thousand silver pieces, to a second two thousand, and to a third a thousand. Then he went away. 16 Immediately the man who received the five thousand went to invest it and made another five. 17 In the same way, the man who received the two thousand doubled his figure. 18 The man who received the thousand went off instead and dug a hole in the ground, where he buried his master's money. 19 After a long absence, the master of those servants came home and settled accounts with them. 20 The man who had received the five thousand came forward bringing the additional five. 'My lord,' he said, 'you let me have five thousand. See, I have made five thousand more.' 21 His master said to him, 'Well done! You are an industrious and reliable servant. Since you were dependable in a small matter I will put you in charge of larger affairs. Come, share your master's joy!' 22 The man who had received the two thousand then stepped forward. 'My lord,' he said, 'you entrusted me with two thousand and I have made two thousand more.' 23 His master said to him, 'Cleverly done! You too are an industrious and reliable servant. Since you were dependable in a small matter I will put you in charge of larger affairs. Come, share your master's joy!'

24 "Finally the man who had received the thousand stepped forward. 'My lord,' he said, 'I knew you were a hard man. You reap where you did not sow and gather where you did not scatter, 25 so out of fear I went off and buried your thousand silver pieces in the ground. Here is your money back.' 26 His master exclaimed: 'You worthless, lazy lout! You know I reap where I did not sow and gather where I did not scatter. 27 All the more reason to deposit my money with the bankers, so that on my return I could have had it back with interest. 28 You, there! Take the thousand away from him and give it to the man with the ten thousand. 29 Those who have, will get more until they grow rich, while those who have not, will lose even the little they have. 30 Throw this worthless servant into the darkness outside, where he can wail and grind his teeth.

The Last Judgment

31 "When the Son of Man comes in his glory, escorted by all the angels of heaven, he will sit upon his royal throne, 32 and all the nations will be assembled before him. Then he will separate them into two groups, as a shepherd separates sheep from goats. 33 The sheep he will place on his right hand, the goats on his left. 34 The king will say to those on his right: 'Come. You have my Father's blessing! Inherit the kingdom prepared for you from the creation of the world. 35 For I was

25, 1–46: The parables teach that the Christian community is to be ever ready to meet the Lord at his second coming (1–13); to function with a sense of personal responsibility for divine gifts received (14–30); and to be constantly aware of the primacy of love of neighbor (31–46).

hungry and you gave me food, I was thirsty and you gave me drink. I was a stranger and you welcomed me, 36 naked and you clothed me. I was ill and you comforted me, in prison and you came to visit me.' 37 Then the just will ask him: 'Lord, when did we see you hungry and feed you or see you thirsty and give you drink? 38 When did we welcome you away from home or clothe you in your nakedness? 39 When did we visit you when you were ill or in prison?' 40 The king will answer them: 'I assure you, as often as you did it for one of my least brothers, you did it for me.'

41 "Then he will say to those on his left: 'Out of my sight, you condemned, into that everlasting fire prepared for the devil and his angels! 42 I was hungry and you gave me no food, I was thirsty and you gave me no drink. 43 I was away from home and you gave me no welcome, naked and you gave me no clothing. I was ill and in prison and you did not come to comfort me.' 44 Then they in turn will ask: 'Lord, when did we see you hungry or thirsty or away from home or naked or ill or in prison and not attend you in your needs?' 45 He will answer them: 'I assure you, as often as you neglected to do it to one of these least ones, you neglected to do it to me.' 46 These will go off to eternal punishment and the just to eternal life."

Epilogue

26 Now when Jesus had finished all these discourses, he declared to his disciples, 2 "You know that in two days' time it will be Passover, and that the Son of Man is to be handed over to be crucified."

THE PASSION AND RESURRECTION

The Conspiracy

3 At that time the chief priests and elders of the people were assembled in the palace of the high priest, whose name was Caiaphas. 4 They plotted to arrest Jesus by some trick and kill him; 5 but they said, "Not during the festival, for fear of a riot among the people."

The Anointing at Bethany

6 While Jesus was in Bethany at the house of Simon the leper, 7 a woman carrying a jar of costly perfume came up to him at table and began to pour it on his head. 8 When the disciples saw this they grew indignant, protesting: "What is the point of such extravagance? 9 This could have been sold for a good price and the money given to the poor." 10 Jesus became aware of this and said to them: "Why do you criticize the woman? It is a good deed she has done for me. 11 The poor you will always have with you but you will not always have me. 12 By pouring this perfume on my body, she has contributed toward my burial preparation. 13 I assure you, wherever the good news is proclaimed throughout the world, what she did will be spoken of as her memorial."

14 Then one of the Twelve whose name was Judas Iscariot went off to the chief priests 15 and said, "What are you willing to give me if I hand him over to you?" They paid him thirty pieces of silver, 16 and from that time on he kept looking for an opportunity to hand him over.

Passover Preparation

17 On the first day of the feast of Unleavened Bread, the disciples came up to Jesus and said, "Where do you wish us to prepare the Passover supper for you?" 18 He said, "Go to this man in the city and tell him, 'The Teacher says, My appointed time draws near. I am to celebrate the Passover with my disciples in your house.'"

19 The disciples then did as Jesus had ordered, and prepared the Passover supper.

The Betrayer

20 When it grew dark he reclined at table with the Twelve. 21 In the course of the meal he said, "I assure you, one of you is about to betray me." 22 Distressed at this, they began to say to him one after another, "Surely it is not I, Lord?" 23 He replied: "The man who has dipped his hand into the dish with me is the one who will hand me over.

24 The Son of Man is departing, as Scripture says of him, but woe to that man by whom the Son of Man is betrayed. Better for him if he had never been born."

25 Then Judas, his betrayer, spoke: "Surely it is not I, Rabbi?" Jesus answered, "It is you who have said it."

The Holy Eucharist

26 During the meal Jesus took bread, blessed it, broke it, and gave it to his disciples. "Take this and eat it," he said, "this is my body." 27 Then he took the cup, gave thanks, and gave it to them. "All of you must drink from it," he said, 28 for this is my blood, the blood of the covenant, to be poured out in behalf of many for the forgiveness of sins. 29 I tell you, I will not drink this fruit of the vine from now until the day when I drink it new with you in my Father's reign." 30 Then, after singing songs of praise, they walked out to the Mount of Olives.

Peter's Denial Foretold

31 Jesus then said to them, "Tonight your faith in me will be shaken, for Scripture has it:

'I will strike the shepherd
and the sheep of the flock will
be dispersed.'

32 But after I am raised up, I will go to Galilee ahead of you." 33 Peter responded, "Though all may have their faith in you shaken, mine will never be shaken!" 34 Jesus said to him, "I give you my word, before the cock crows tonight you will deny me three times." 35 Peter replied, "Even though I have to die with you, I will never disown you." And all the other disciples said the same.

The Agony in the Garden

36 Then Jesus went with them to a place called Gethsemani. He said to his disciples, "Stay here while I go over there and pray." 37 He took along Peter and Zebedee's two sons, and began to experience sorrow and distress. Then he said to them, 38 "My heart is nearly broken with sorrow. Remain here and stay awake

26, 1–75: See note on Mk 14, 1—15, 57.

with me." 39 He advanced a little and fell prostrate in prayer. "My Father, if it is possible, let this cup pass me by. Still, let it be as you would have it, not as I." 40 When he returned to his disciples, he found them asleep. He said to Peter, "So you could not stay awake with me for even an hour? 41 Be on guard, and pray that you may not undergo the test. The spirit is willing but nature is weak." 42 Withdrawing a second time, he began to pray: "My Father, if this cannot pass me by without my drinking it, your will be done!" 43 Once more, on his return, he found them asleep; they could not keep their eyes open. 44 He left them again, withdrew somewhat, and began to pray a third time, saying the same words as before. 45 Finally he returned to his disciples and said to them: "Sleep on now. Enjoy your rest! The hour is on us when the Son of Man is to be handed over to the power of evil men. 46 Get up! Let us be on our way! See, my betrayer is here."

Jesus Arrested

47 While he was still speaking, Judas, one of the Twelve, arrived accompanied by a great crowd with swords and clubs. They had been sent by the chief priests and elders of the people. 48 His betrayer had arranged to give them a signal, saying, "The man I shall embrace is the one; take hold of him." 49 He immediately went over to Jesus, said to him, "Peace Rabbi," and embraced him. 50 Jesus answered, "Friend, do what you are here for!" At that moment they stepped forward to lay hands on Jesus, and arrested him. 51 Suddenly one of those who accompanied Jesus put his hand to his sword, drew it, and slashed at the high priest's servant, cutting off his ear. 52 Jesus said to him: "Put back your sword where it belongs. Those who use the sword are sooner or later destroyed by it. 53 Do you not suppose I can call on my Father to provide at a moment's notice more than twelve legions of angels? 54 But then how would the Scriptures be fulfilled which say it must happen this way?"

55 At that very time Jesus said to the crowd: "Am I a brigand, that you have come armed with swords and clubs to arrest me? From day to day I sat teaching in the temple precincts, yet you never arrested me. 56 Nonetheless, all this has happened in fulfillment of the writings of the prophets." Then all the disciples deserted him and fled.

Jesus before the Sanhedrin

57 Those who had apprehended Jesus led him off to Caiaphas the high priest, where the scribes and elders were convened. 58 Peter kept following him at a distance as far as the high priest's residence. Going inside, he sat down with the guards to see the outcome. 59 The chief priests, with the whole Sanhedrin, were busy trying to obtain false testimony against Jesus so that they might put him to death. 60 They discovered none, despite the many false witnesses who took the stand. Finally two came forward 61 who stated: "This man has declared, 'I can destroy God's sanctuary and rebuild it in three days,'" 62 The high priest rose to his feet and addressed him: "Have you no answer to the testimony leveled against you?" 63 But Jesus remained silent. The high priest then said to him: "I order you to tell us under oath before the living God whether you are the Messiah, the Son of God." 64 Jesus answered: "It is you who say it. But I tell you this: Soon you will see the Son of Man seated at the right hand of the Power and coming on the clouds of heaven." 65 At this the high priest tore his robes: "He has blasphemed! What further need have we of witnesses? 66 Remember, you heard the blasphemy. What is your verdict?" They answered, "He deserves death!" 67 Then they began to spit in his face and hit him. Others slapped him, saying: 68 "Play the prophet for us, Messiah! Who struck you?"

Peter's Denial

69 Peter was sitting in the courtyard when one of the serving girls came over to him and said, "You too were with Jesus the Galilean." 70 He denied it in front of everyone: "I do not know what you are talking about!" 71 When he went out to the gate another girl saw him and said to those nearby, "This man was with Jesus the Nazorean." 72 Again he denied it with an oath: "I do not know the man!" 73 A little while later some bystanders came over to Peter and said, "You are certainly one of them! Even your accent gives you away!" 74 At that he began cursing, and swore, "I do not even know the man!" Just then a cock began to crow 75 and Peter remembered the prediction Jesus had made: "Before the cock crows, you will deny me three times." He went out and began to weep bitterly.

27 At daybreak all the chief priests and elders of the people took formal action against Jesus to put him to death. 2 They bound him and led him away to be handed over to the procurator Pilate.

The End of Judas

3 Then Judas, who had handed him over, seeing that Jesus had been condemned, began to regret his action deeply. He took the thirty pieces of silver back to the chief priests and elders and said, 4 "I did wrong to deliver up an innocent man!" They retorted, "What is that to us? It is your affair!" 5 So Judas flung the money into the temple and left. He went off and hanged himself. 6 The chief priests picked up the silver, observing, "It is not right to deposit this in the temple treasury since it is blood money." 7 After consultation, they used it to buy the potter's field as a cemetery for foreigners. 8 That is why that field, even today, is called Blood Field. 9 On that occasion, what was said through Jeremiah the prophet was fulfilled:

27, 3–10: The tragic death of Judas is elsewhere related only in Acts 1, 18; see note. Despite differences in the accounts, there is agreement in essentials: a plot of land near Jerusalem, popularly called the "Field of Blood," was purchased with the money Judas received for betraying Jesus, and the traitor died an infamous death. Matthew's free citation of Jer 18, 2f; 19, 1f; 32, 6–15 and Zec 11, 13 shows that he regards Judas' death as a divine judgment.

"They took the thirty pieces of silver, the value of a man with a price on his head, a price set by the Israelites, 10 and they paid it out for the potter's field just as the Lord had commanded me."

Jesus before Pilate

11 Jesus was arraigned before the procurator who questioned him: "Are you the king of the Jews?" Jesus responded, *As you say.* 12 Yet when he was accused by the chief priests and elders, he had made no reply. 13 Then Pilate said to him, "Surely you hear how many charges they bring against you?" 14 He did not answer him on a single count, much to the procurator's surprise.

15 Now on the occasion of a festival the procurator was accustomed to release one prisoner, whom the crowd would designate. 16 They had at the time a notorious prisoner named Barabbas. 17 Since they were already assembled, Pilate said to them, "Which one do you wish me to release for you, Barabbas or Jesus the so-called Messiah?" 18 He knew, of course, that it was out of jealousy that they had handed him over.

19 While he was still presiding on the bench, his wife sent him a message: "Do not interfere in the case of that holy man. I had a dream about him today which has greatly upset me."

20 Meanwhile, the chief priests and elders convinced the crowds that they should ask for Barabbas and have Jesus put to death. 21 So when the procurator asked them, "Which one do you wish me to release for you?" they said, "Barabbas." 22 Pilate said to them, "Then what am I to do with Jesus, the so-called Messiah?" "Crucify him!" they all cried. 23 He said, "Why, what crime has he committed?" But they only shouted the louder, "Crucify him!" 24 Pilate finally realized that he was making no impression and that a riot was breaking out instead. He called for water and

washed his hands in front of the crowd, declaring as he did so, "I am innocent of the blood of this just man. The responsibility is yours." 25 The whole people said in reply, "Let his blood be on us and on our children." 26 At that, he released Barabbas to them. Jesus, however, he first had scourged; then he handed him over to be crucified.

The Crowning with Thorns

27 The procurator's soldiers took Jesus inside the praetorium and collected the whole cohort around him. 28 They stripped off his clothes and wrapped him in a scarlet military cloak. 29 Weaving a crown out of thorns they fixed it on his head, and stuck a reed in his right hand. Then they began to mock him by dropping to their knees before him, saying, "All hail, king of the Jews!" 30 They also spat at him. Afterward they took hold of the reed and kept striking him on the head. 31 Finally, when they had finished making a fool of him, they stripped him of the cloak, dressed him in his own clothes, and led him off to crucifixion.

The Way of the Cross

32 On their way out they met a Cyrenian named Simon. This man they pressed into service to carry the cross. 33 Upon arriving at a site called Golgotha (a name which means Skull Place), 34 they gave him a drink of wine flavored with gall, which he tasted but refused to drink.

The Crucifixion

35 When they had crucified him, they divided his clothes among them by casting lots; 36 then they sat down there and kept watch over him. 37 Above his head they had put the charge against him in writing: "THIS IS JESUS, KING OF THE JEWS." 38 Two insurgents were crucified along with him, one at his right and one at his left. 39 People going by kept insulting him, tossing their

heads 40 and saying: "So you are the one who was going to destroy the temple and rebuild it in three days! Save yourself, why don't you? Come down off that cross if you are God's Son!" 41 The chief priests, the scribes, and the elders also joined in the jeering: 42 "He saved others but he cannot save himself! So he is the king of Israel! Let's see him come down from that cross and then we will believe in him. 43 He relied on God; let God rescue him now if he wants to. After all, he claimed, 'I am God's Son.'" 44 The insurgents who had been crucified with him kept taunting him in the same way.

The Death of Jesus

45 From noon onward, there was darkness over the whole land until midafternoon. 46 Then toward midafternoon Jesus cried out in a loud tone, *"Eli, Eli, lema sabachthani?"*, that is, "My God, my God, why have you forsaken me?" 47 This made some of the bystanders who heard it remark, "He is invoking Elijah!" 48 Immediately one of them ran off and got a sponge. He soaked it in cheap wine, and sticking it on the reed, tried to make him drink. 49 Meanwhile the rest said, "Leave him alone. Let's see whether Elijah comes to his rescue." 50 Once again Jesus cried out in a loud voice, and then gave up his spirit.

51 Suddenly the curtain of the sanctuary was torn in two from top to bottom. 52 The earth quaked, boulders split, tombs opened. 53 Many bodies of saints who had fallen asleep were raised. After Jesus' resurrection they came forth from their tombs and entered the holy city and appeared to many. 54 The centurion and his men who were keeping watch over Jesus were terror-stricken at seeing the earthquake and all that was happening, and said, "Clearly this was the Son of God!"

55 Many women were present looking on from a distance. They had

---

27, 19f: This passage is proper to Matthew. The episode concerning Pilate's wife accords with evidence that women sometimes intervened in the political affairs of the Roman world. Her concern is for the welfare of her husband rather than of Jesus;

for this reason she does not wish Pilate to become involved in the religious affairs of the Jews.

27, 25: *Let his blood be on us and on our children:* probably the evangelist's commentary on the responsibility for Jesus' death; cf Jer 51, 35.

27, 51ff: The tearing of the sanctuary veil between the holy place and the holy of holies symbolizes a break with the past; the other phenomena portend the resurrection of all men, the final cosmic event of human history; cf Is 13, 9f; 34, 4; Dn 12, 2; Jl 2, 10.

followed Jesus from Galilee to attend to his needs. 56 Among them were Mary Magdalene, and Mary the mother of James and Joseph, and the mother of Zebedee's sons.

The Burial

57 When evening fell, a wealthy man from Arimathea arrived, Joseph by name. He was another of Jesus' disciples, 58 and had gone to request the body of Jesus. Thereupon Pilate issued an order for its release. 59 Taking the body, Joseph wrapped it in fresh linen 60 and laid it in his own new tomb which had been hewn from a formation of rock. Then he rolled a huge stone across the entrance of the tomb and went away. 61 But Mary Magdalene and the other Mary remained sitting there, facing the tomb.

Precautions of the Chief Priests

62 The next day, the one following the Day of Preparation, the chief priests and the Pharisees called at Pilate's residence. 63 "Sir," they said, "we have recalled that that impostor while he was still alive made the claim, 'After three days I will rise.' 64 You should issue an order having the tomb kept under surveillance until the third day. Otherwise his disciples may go and steal him and tell the people, 'He has been raised from the dead!' This final imposture would be worse than the first." 65 Pilate told them, "You have a guard. Go and secure the tomb as best you can." 66 So they went and kept it under surveillance of the guard, after fixing a seal to the stone.

The Women at the Tomb

28 After the sabbath, as the first day of the week was dawning, Mary Magdalene came with the other Mary to inspect the tomb. 2 Suddenly there was a mighty earthquake, as the angel of the Lord descended from heaven. He came to the stone, rolled it back, and sat on it. 3 In appearance he resembled a flash of lightning while his garments were as dazzling as snow. 4 The guards grew paralyzed with fear of him and fell down like dead men. 5 Then the angel spoke, addressing the women: "Do not be frightened. I know you are looking for Jesus the crucified, 6 but he is not here. He has been raised, exactly as he promised. Come and see the place where he was laid. 7 Then go quickly and tell his disciples: 'He has been raised from the dead and now goes ahead of you to Galilee, where you will see him.' That is the message I have for you."

8 They hurried away from the tomb half-overjoyed, half-fearful, and ran to carry the good news to his disciples. 9 Suddenly, without warning, Jesus stood before them and said, "Peace!" The women came up and embraced his feet and did him homage. 10 At this Jesus said to them, "Do not be afraid! Go and carry the news to my brothers that they are to go to Galilee, where they will see me."

Tale of the Guards and Chief Priests

11 As the women were returning, some of the guard went into the city and reported to the chief priests all that had happened. 12 They, in turn, convened with the elders and worked out their strategy, giving the soldiers a large bribe 13 with the instructions: "You are to say, 'His disciples came during the night and stole him while we were asleep.' 14 If any word of this gets to the procurator, we will straighten it out with him and keep you out of trouble." 15 The soldiers pocketed the money and did as they had been instructed. This is the story that circulates among the Jews to this very day.

Commission of the Apostles

16 The eleven disciples made their way to Galilee, to the mountain to which Jesus had summoned them. 17 At the sight of him, those who had entertained doubts fell down in homage. 18 Jesus came forward and addressed them in these words:

"Full authority has been given to me
both in heaven and on earth;
19 go, therefore, and make disciples of all the nations.
Baptize them in the name
'of the Father,
and of the Son,
and of the Holy Spirit.'
20 Teach them to carry out everything I have commanded you.
And know that I am with you always, until the end of the world!"

27, 62–66: This account is proper to Matthew. It is thought to have originated among Judaeo-Christians in response to a Jewish allegation that Jesus' disciples had stolen the body. Matthew wishes to emphasize the supernatural character of Jesus' departure from the tomb, to which there was no human witness; cf 28, 2ff.

28, 1–20: See note on Lk 24, 1–53.

28, 11–15: The chief priests and elders are not concerned with the resurrection itself, which they simply deem impossible, but with the repercussions on the people of the apostolic preaching concerning the resurrection.

28, 16: The tradition of Jesus' appearance to his disciples in Galilee is also reflected in Jn 21, 1–23.

28, 17: *Those who had entertained doubts:* literally, "but some doubted"; probably a summary allusion to the initial doubts of the disciples over the reality of the resurrection; cf Lk 24, 22ff.38; Jn 20, 27. The resurrection narratives are characterized by a condensed description of events.

28, 19: *Go, therefore, and make . . . the nations:* some regard these words as an interpretation of Jesus' final instructions in the light of the church's early change from a mission to the Jews to one in behalf of the Gentiles; see Introduction to Acts.

Baptize them . . . Holy Spirit: The baptismal formula reflects the church's gradual understanding of God as three Persons (Acts 2, 38; 2 Cor 13, 13).

28, 20: The apostles are to teach the world not merely the doctrine of the resurrection but the historical teaching of Jesus. This the evangelist Matthew obviously considers to be contained in the gospel he has written. *I am with you always:* The power of the risen Christ (18) will ever sustain those whom he has commissioned to preach the "good news" of salvation to the world.

THE GOSPEL ACCORDING TO

PROLOGUE: PREPARATION FOR THE MINISTRY OF JESUS

John the Baptizer

HERE begins the gospel of Jesus Christ, the Son of God. 2 In Isaiah the prophet it is written: "I send my messenger before you to prepare your way: 3 a herald's voice in the desert, crying, 'Make ready the way of the Lord, clear him a straight path.'"

4 Thus it was that John the Baptizer appeared in the desert, proclaiming a baptism of repentance which led to the forgiveness of sins. 5 All the Judean countryside and the people of Jerusalem went out to him in great numbers. They were being baptized by him in the Jordan River as they confessed their sins. 6 John was clothed in camel's hair, and wore a leather belt around his waist. His food was grasshoppers and wild honey. 7 The theme of his preaching was: "One more powerful than I is to come after me. I am not fit to stoop and untie his sandal straps. 8 I have baptized you in water; he will baptize you in the Holy Spirit."

The Baptism of Jesus

9 During that time, Jesus came from Nazareth in Galilee and was baptized in the Jordan by John. 10 Immediately on coming up out of the water he saw the sky rent in two and the Spirit descending on him like a dove. 11 Then a voice came from the heavens: "You are my beloved Son. On you my favor rests."

The Temptation

12 At that point the Spirit sent him out toward the desert. 13 He stayed in the wasteland forty days, put to the test there by Satan. He was with the wild beasts, and angels waited on him.

1, 1: This verse is probably the title of the entire gospel, which Mark regards as the account of Jesus' ministry of redemption. Several important early manuscripts lack the phrase *Son of God;* its authenticity, however, is accepted by most modern scholars.

1, 2f: Portions of Exodus (23, 20), Malachi (3, 1) and Isaiah (40, 3) are combined here; cf Mt 11, 10; Lk 7, 26. Mark mentions only Isaiah.

1, 3f: The historical concept of God's fulfillment of prophecy is the same as in Matthew. See note on Mt 3, 1. On repentance, see note on Acts 2, 38.

1, 5: See note on Mt 3, 11f. *They confessed their sins:* whether the confession was explicit and individual or general and collective is not determinable from the text.

1, 6: *Clothed in camel's hair . . . waist:* see note on Mt 3, 4.

1, 7f: Here the figure of Jesus is kept foremost in the Baptizer's preaching. He is the *One more powerful* who *is to come.* Matthew (3, 7–10) and Luke (3, 7–14) add elements of warning against those who hear the invitation to repentance and fail to heed it.

1, 9ff: The synoptic gospels concentrate on the baptism of Jesus, while the fourth gospel (Jn 1, 24–37) is concerned with the role of the Baptizer in identifying Jesus as the One who is to come. The synoptics ascribe directly to God the Father the identification of Jesus as "Servant of Yahweh." The dove is the symbol of the Holy Spirit (Mk 1, 10), derived perhaps from the image of the creative spirit of God hovering over the waters (Gn 1, 2). The intimation is that Jesus, possessor of the Spirit, is the creator of the new people of God. The occasion of Jesus' baptism is the response to the prayer in Is 64, 1 for the heavens to open and rain down messianic salvation (1, 10). The designation of Jesus as God's Son reflects the early Christian usage of Ps 2, 7, which sees the sonship there spoken of prophetically fulfilled in Jesus' resurrection.

1, 12f: Jesus, possessor of the Spirit, is directed irresistibly to a confrontation with Satan over the course of forty days. Both angels and wild beasts are present. Though the sense of the imagery is uncertain, some evidence in New Testament times shows demons symbolized by wild beasts. Following the extra-biblical Jewish literary tradition of holy men subjected to temptation, Mark depicts Jesus as the faithful servant of Yahweh, loyal to God in his time of trial (Heb 2, 14–18). The temptation narrative expresses, in terms of a drama, Jesus' ministry, passion and death as a conflict with satanic power.

THE MYSTERY OF JESUS

Call of the First Disciples

14 After John's arrest, Jesus appeared in Galilee proclaiming the good news of God· 15 "This is the time of fulfillment. The reign of God is at hand! Reform your lives and believe in the gospel!"

16 As he made his way along the Sea of Galilee, he observed Simon and his brother Andrew casting their nets into the sea; they were fishermen. 17 Jesus said to them, "Come after me; I will make you fishers of men." 18 They immediately abandoned their nets and became his followers. 19 Proceeding a little further along, he caught sight of James, Zebedee's son, and his brother John. They too were in their boat putting their nets in order. He summoned them on the spot. 20 They abandoned their father Zebedee, who was in the boat with the hired men, and went off in his company. 21 Shortly afterward they came to Capernaum, and on the sabbath he entered the synagogue and began to teach. 22 The people were spellbound by his teaching because he taught with authority, and not like the scribes.

Cure of a Demoniac

23 There appeared in their synagogue a man with an unclean spirit that shrieked: 24 "What do you want of us, Jesus of Nazareth? Have you come to destroy us? I know who you are—the holy One of God!" 25 Jesus rebuked him sharply: "Be quiet! Come out of the man!" 26 At that the unclean spirit convulsed the man violently and with a loud shriek came out of him. 27 All who looked on were amazed. They began to ask one another: "What does this mean? A completely new

teaching in a spirit of authority! He gives orders to unclean spirits and they obey!" 28 From that point on his reputation spread throughout the surrounding region of Galilee.

Peter's Mother-in-law

29 Immediately upon leaving the synagogue, he entered the house of Simon and Andrew with James and John. 30 Simon's mother-in-law lay ill with a fever, and the first thing they did was to tell him about her. 31 He went over to her and grasped her hand and helped her up, and the fever left her. She immediately began to wait on them.

Other Miracles

32 After sunset, as evening drew on, they brought him all who were ill, and those possessed by demons. 33 Before long the whole town was gathered outside the door. 34 Those whom he cured, who were variously afflicted, were many, and so were the demons he expelled. But he would not permit the demons to speak, because they knew him. 35 Rising early the next morning, he went off to a lonely place in the desert; there he was absorbed in prayer. 36 Simon and his companions managed to track him down, and 37 when they found him, they told him, "Everybody is looking for you!" 38 He said to them: "Let us move on to the neighboring villages so that I may proclaim the good news there also. That is what I have come to do." So he went into their synagogues preaching the good news and expelling demons throughout the whole of Galilee.

A Leper

40 A leper approached him with a request, kneeling down as he

addressed him: "If you will to do so, you can cure me." 41 Moved with pity, Jesus stretched out his hand, touched him, and said: "I will do it. Be cured." 42 The leprosy left him then and there, and he was cured. 43 Jesus gave him a stern warning and sent him on his way. 44 "Not a word to anyone, now," he said. "Go off and present yourself to the priest and offer for your cure what Moses prescribed. That should be a proof for them." 45 The man went off and began to proclaim the whole matter freely, making the story public. As a result of this, it was no longer possible for Jesus to enter a town openly. He stayed in desert places; yet people kept coming to him from all sides.

A Paralytic at Capernaum

2 He came back to Capernaum after a lapse of several days and word got around that he was at home. 2 At that they began to gather in great numbers. There was no longer any room for them, even around the door. 3 While he was delivering God's word to them, some people arrived bringing a paralyzed man to him. The four who carried him 4 were unable to bring him to Jesus because of the crowd, so they began to open the roof over the spot where Jesus was. When they had made a hole, they let down the mat on which the paralytic was lying. 5 When Jesus saw their faith, he said to the paralyzed man, "My son, your sins are forgiven." 6 Now some of the scribes were sitting there asking themselves: 7 "Why does the man talk in that way? He commits blasphemy! Who can fogive sins except God alone?" 8 Jesus was immediately aware of their reasoning,

---

1, 14f: *Jesus appeared . . . the good news of God:* a summary statement concerning Jesus' preaching, to introduce his public ministry. *This is the time of fulfillment:* the period in human history appointed by God for making good his messianic promises. *The reign of God is at hand:* see note on Mt 3, 1. Though some scholars maintain that Jesus proclaimed the kingdom as imminent but not yet arrived it is more probable that he announced it as actually arrived yet awaiting future development. *Reform your lives:* see note on Acts 2, 38.

1, 16–20: See note on Mt 4, 19.

1, 21f: The people realize that Jesus presents himself as a prophet who does not depend on rabbinic tradition for his teaching.

1, 23–28: This account of exorcism is the first of four such narratives in Mark (5, 1–20; 7, 24–30;

9, 14–27). The gospel also contains several allusions to Jesus' numerous exorcisms (1, 34.39; 3, 11f), and records a debate between Jesus and the scribes over their meaning (3, 22–30). Matthew and Luke present some of the same traditional accounts as Mark but add no new ones. Note that Jesus neither declares diabolical "possession" to be a phenomenon in Israel nor contests any affirmation of the presence of diabolic beings. When the scribes accuse Jesus of performing exorcisms by the power of Satan, they imply that there are diabolic manifestations among the sick brought to Jesus. Apart from the case of the Syro-Phoenician woman's daughter (see note on 7, 24–30), nowhere is Jesus asked precisely to perform an exorcism.

1, 34: *Because they knew him:* probably the knowledge which the demons had about Jesus is to be

understood in the broad sense, i.e., they were reported as having recognized Jesus as their enemy without having specific knowledge of his actual identity.

1, 40–45: For the various forms of skin disease, cf Lv 13, 1–50 and the note on Lv 13, 2ff. Jesus shows concern for the proper interpretation of his miracles. He assumes that the priests will perceive the messianic significance of the miracle. On the "messianic secret" involved in this narrative, see note on 8, 27–30.

2, 1–12: Besides his power over demonic spirits and physical illness, Jesus manifests his power to forgive sins. This miracle story constitutes a transition to the conflict narratives which follow. Once Christians believed in the divinity of Jesus after his resurrection, they realized that he forgave sins through the power he had conferred on the community; cf Mt 9, 8.

though they kept it to themselves, and he said to them: "Why do you harbor these thoughts? 9 Which is easier, to say to the paralytic, 'Your sins are forgiven,' or to say, 'Stand up, pick up your mat, and walk again'? 10 That you may know that the Son of Man has authority on earth to forgive sins" (he said to the paralyzed man), 11 "I command you: Stand up! Pick up your mat and go home." 12 The man stood and picked up his mat and went outside in the sight of everyone. They were awestruck; all gave praise to God, saying, "We have never seen anything like this!"

The Call of Levi

13 Another time, while he went walking along the lakeshore, people kept coming to him in crowds and he taught them. 14 As he moved on he saw Levi the son of Alphaeus at his tax collector's post, and said to him, "Follow me." Levi got up and became his follower. 15 While Jesus was reclining to eat in Levi's house, many tax collectors and those known as sinners joined him and his disciples at dinner. The number of those who followed him was large. 16 When the scribes who belonged to the Pharisee party saw that he was eating with tax collectors and offenders against the law, they complained to his disciples, "Why does he eat with such as these?" 17 Overhearing the remark, Jesus said to them, "People who are healthy do not need a doctor; sick people do. I have come to call sinners, not the self-righteous."

The Question of Fasting

18 Now John's disciples and the Pharisees were accustomed to fast. People came to Jesus with the objection, "Why do John's disciples and those of the Pharisees fast while yours do not?" 19 Jesus replied: "How can the guests at a wedding fast as long as the groom is still among them? So long as the groom stays with them, they cannot fast. 20 The day will come, however, when the groom will be taken away from them; on that day they will fast. 21 No one sews a patch of unshrunken cloth on an old cloak. If he should do so, the very thing he has used to cover the hole would pull away—the new from the old—and the tear would get worse. 22 Similarly, no man pours new wine into old wineskins. If he does so, the wine will burst the skins and both wine and skins will be lost. No, new wine is poured into new skins."

The Disciples and the Sabbath

23 It happened that he was walking through standing grain on the sabbath, and his disciples began to pull off heads of grain as they went along. 24 At this the Pharisees protested: "Look! Why do they do a thing not permitted on the sabbath?" 25 He said to them: "Have you never read what David did when he was in need and he and his men were hungry? 26 How he entered God's house in the days of Abiathar the high priest and ate the holy bread which only the priests were permitted to eat? He even gave it to his men." 27 Then he said to them: "The sabbath was made for man, not man for the sabbath. 28 That is why the Son of Man is lord even of the sabbath."

A Man with a Withered Hand

3 He returned to the synagogue where there was a man whose hand had shriveled up. 2 They kept an eye on Jesus to see whether he would heal him on the sabbath, hoping to be able to bring an accusation against him. 3 He addressed the man with the shriveled hand: "Stand up here in front!" 4 Then he said to them: "Is it permitted to do a good deed on the sabbath—or an evil one? To preserve life—or to destroy it?" At this they remained silent. 5 He looked around at them with anger, for he was deeply grieved that they had closed their minds against him. Then he said to the man, "Stretch out your hand." The man did so and his hand was perfectly restored. 6 When the Pharisees went outside, they immediately began to plot with the Herodians how they might destroy him.

The Mercy of Jesus

7 Jesus withdrew toward the lake with his disciples. A great crowd followed him from Galilee, 8 and an equally great multitude came to him from Judea, Jerusalem, Idumea, Transjordan, and the neighborhood of Tyre and Sidon, because they had heard what he had done. 9 In view of their numbers, he told his disciples to have a fishing boat ready for him so that he could avoid the press of the crowd against him. 10 Because he had cured many, all who had afflictions kept pushing toward him to touch him. 11 Unclean spirits would catch sight of him, fling themselves down at his feet, and shout, "You are the Son of God!", 12 while he kept ordering them sternly not to reveal who he was.

Choice of the Twelve

13 He then went up the mountain and summoned the men he himself had decided on, who came and joined him. 14 He named twelve as his companions whom he would send to preach the good news; 15 they were likewise to have authority to expel demons. 16 He appointed the Twelve as follows: 17 Simon to whom he gave the name Peter; James, son of Zebedee; and John, the brother of James (he gave these two the name Boanerges, or "sons of thunder"); 18 Andrew, Philip,

---

2, 15ff: See note on Mt 9, 13.
2, 18–22: See note on Mt 9, 14–17.
2, 23–27: See note on Mt 12, 3–6.
2, 28: This statement seems to be an editorial addition to teach that the early Christian community's freedom from Jewish sabbath regulations relies on the authority of Jesus, now fully vindicated by his resurrection and ascension. On the title *Son of Man*, see note on 8, 31ff.
3, 1–6: See note on Mt 12, 10.

3, 12: Jesus refuses to receive witness concerning his identity from evil spirits. Since this identity can be known only from divine revelation, Mark does not ascribe true knowledge of Jesus to evil spirits. See note on Mt 16, 17.
3, 13–19: Within the circle of Jesus' disciples, the Twelve were given a privileged position. They alone were present with Jesus at the Last Supper (14, 17). Later they exercised leadership over the primitive community in Jerusalem (Acts 1, 26; 2, 14; 5, 20f),

and were responsible for the information about Jesus that developed into the gospel tradition (Acts 6, 2.4).
3, 20–35: Reactions to the person and teaching of Jesus are varied: the crowds are favorable to him (1, 27.37.45; 2, 15; 3, 8); the scribes and Pharisees are increasingly hostile (2, 13—3, 6); his relatives are unbelieving (3, 20f). Faith in Jesus' prophetic word creates a relationship superior to that between himself and his relatives.

Bartholomew, Matthew, Thomas, James son of Alphaeus; Thaddaeus, Simon of the Zealot party, 19 and Judas Iscariot, who betrayed him.

Blasphemy of the Scribes

20 He returned to the house with them and again the crowd assembled, making it impossible for them to get any food whatever. 21 When his family heard of this they came to take charge of him, saying, "He is out of his mind"; 22 while the scribes who arrived from Jerusalem asserted, "He is possessed by Beelzebul," and "He expels demons with the help of the prince of demons." 23 Summoning them, he then began to speak to them by way of examples: "How can Satan expel Satan? 24 If a kingdom is torn by civil strife, that kingdom cannot last. 25 If a household is divided according to loyalties, that household will not survive. 26 Similarly, if Satan has suffered mutiny in his ranks and is torn by dissension, he cannot endure; he is finished. 27 No one can enter a strong man's house and despoil his property unless he has first put him under restraint. Only then can he plunder his house.

28 "I give you my word, every sin will be forgiven mankind and all the blasphemies men utter, 29 but whoever blasphemes against the Holy Spirit will never be forgiven. He carries the guilt of his sin without end." 30 He spoke thus because they had said, "He is possessed by an unclean spirit."

Jesus and His Family

31 His mother and his brothers arrived, and as they stood outside they sent word to him to come out. 32 The crowd seated around him told him, "Your mother and your brothers and sisters are outside asking for you." 33 He said in reply, "Who are my mother and my brothers?" 34 And gazing around him at those seated in the circle he continued, "These are my mother and my brothers. 35 Whoever does the will of God is brother and sister and mother to me."

Parable of the Seed

4 On another occasion he began to teach beside the lake. Such a huge crowd gathered around him that he went and sat in a boat on the water, while the crowd remained on the shore nearby. 2 He began to instruct them at great length, by the use of parables, and in the course of his teaching said: 3 "Listen carefully to this. A farmer went out sowing. 4 Some of what he sowed landed on the footpath, where the birds came along and ate it. 5 Some of the seed landed on rocky ground where it had little soil; it sprouted immediately because the soil had no depth. 6 Then, when the sun rose and scorched it, it began to wither for lack of roots. 7 Again, some landed among thorns, which grew up and choked it off, and there was no yield of grain. 8 Some seed, finally, landed on good soil and yielded grain that sprang up to produce at a rate of thirty- and sixty- and a hundredfold." 9 Having spoken this parable, he added: "Let him who has ears to hear me, hear!"

10 Now when he was away from the crowd, those present with the Twelve questioned him about the parables. 11 He told them: "To you the mystery of the reign of God has been confided. To the others outside it is all presented in parables. 12 so that they will look intently and not see, listen carefully and not understand, lest perhaps they repent and be forgiven."

13 He said to them: "You do not understand this parable? How then are you going to understand other figures like it? 14 What the sower is sowing is the word. 15 Those on the path are the ones to whom, as soon as they hear the word, Satan comes to carry off what was sown in them. 16 Similarly, those sown on rocky ground are people who on listening to the word accept it joyfully at the outset. 17 Begin rootless, they last only a while. When some pressure or persecution overtakes them because of the word, they falter. 18 Those sown among thorns are another class. They have listened to the word, 19 but anxieties over life's demands, and the desire for wealth, and cravings of other sorts come to choke it off; it bears no yield. 20 But those sown on good soil are the ones who listen to the word, take it to heart, and yield at thirty- and sixty- and a hundredfold."

Purpose of this Teaching

21 He said to them: "Is a lamp acquired to be put under a bushel basket or hidden under a bed? Is it not meant to be put on a stand? 22 Things are hidden only to be revealed at a later time; they are covered so as to be brought out into the open. 23 Let him who has ears to hear me, hear!" 24 He said to them another time: "Listen carefully to what you hear. In the measure you give you shall receive, and more besides. 25 To those who have, more will be given; from those who have not, what little they have will be taken away."

Seed Grows of Itself

26 He also said: "This is how it is with the reign of God. A man scatters seed on the ground. 27 He goes to bed and gets up day after day. Through it all the seed sprouts and grows without his knowing how it happens. 28 The soil produces of itself first the blade, then the ear, finally the ripe wheat in the ear. 29

4, 1–34: See note on Mt 13, 1–53 for the sense of the parables of the sower, the mustard seed, and the leaven.

4, 10ff: In Mt 13, 10, attention centers on the method of teaching in parables. Jesus gives the same response here as he gave there. The light shed by the parables on the reign of God, though real, is far from complete. For the disciples, well-disposed to accept the teaching, questions are answered; not so for the crowds, ill-prepared at this time to abandon their false preconceptions. Thus Mark indicates a gradual

unveiling of the mystery, beginning with the parables and continuing as a slow realization on the part of hearers that the traditional conceptions about God's reign were false and contrary to his plan; cf Mt 13, 33. Divine wisdom is described as justified in this procedure in terms of Is 6, 9f.

4, 21–25: These sayings, found in other contexts as well (Mt 5, 15; 7, 2; 10, 26; 13, 12), are here presented as commentary on the revelation of the reign of God. Jesus' teaching in parables begins this revelation (21); time and events will make it more

clear (22). Acceptance of the original light gives promise of more in the future (24). Conversely, rejection of that light results in greater obscurity and misunderstanding (25).

4, 26–29: This parable is found only in Mark. Through the ministry of Jesus, God's sovereign rule over men is made manifest. It comes without warning; it is destined to spread throughout the world and to continue for the length of time set by God.

When the crop is ready he 'wields the sickle, for the time is ripe for harvest.'"

The Mustard Seed

30 He went on to say: "What comparison shall we use for the reign of God? What image will help to present it? 31 It is like mustard seed which, when planted in the soil, is the smallest of all the earth's seeds, 32 yet once it is sown, springs up to become the largest of shrubs, with branches big enough for the birds of the sky to build nests in its shade." 33 By means of many such parables he taught them the message in a way they could understand. 34 To them he spoke only by way of parable, while he kept explaining things privately to his disciples.

The Storm on the Sea

35 That day as evening drew on he said to them, "Let us cross over to the farther shore." 36 Leaving the crowd, they took him away in the boat in which he was sitting, while the other boats accompanied him. 37 It happened that a bad squall blew up. The waves were breaking over the boat and it began to ship water badly. 38 Jesus was in the stern through it all, sound asleep on a cushion. They finally woke him and said to him, "Teacher, does it not matter to you that we are going to drown?" 39 He awoke and rebuked the wind and said to the sea: "Quiet! Be still!" The wind fell off and everything grew calm. 40 Then he said to them, "Why are you so terrified? Why are you lacking in faith?" 41 A great awe overcame them at this. They kept saying to one another, "Who can this be that the wind and sea obey him?"

Expulsion of the Devils in Gerasa

5 They came to Gerasene territory on the other side of the lake. 2 As he got out of the boat, he was immediately met by a man from the tombs who had an unclean spirit. 3 The man had taken refuge among the tombs; he could no longer be restrained even with a chain. 4 In fact, he had frequently been secured with handcuffs and chains, but had pulled the chains apart and smashed the fetters. No one had proved strong enough to tame him. 5 Uninterruptedly night and day, amid the tombs and on the hillsides, he screamed and gashed himself with stones. 6 Catching sight of Jesus at a distance, he ran up and did him homage, 7 shrieking in a loud voice, "Why meddle with me, Jesus, Son of God Most High? I implore you in God's name, do not torture me!" 8 (Jesus had been saying to him, "Unclean spirit, come out of the man!") 9 "What is your name?" Jesus asked him. "Legion is my name," he answered. "There are hundreds of us." 10 He pleaded hard with Jesus not to drive them away from that neighborhood.

11 It happened that a large herd of swine was feeding there on the slope of the mountain. 12 "Send us into the swine," they begged him. "Let us enter them." 13 He gave the word, and with it the unclean spirits came out and entered the swine. The herd of about two thousand went rushing down the bluff into the lake, where they began to drown. 14 The swineherds ran off and brought the news to field and village, and the people came to see what had happened. 15 As they approached Jesus, they caught sight of the man who had been possessed by Legion sitting fully clothed and perfectly sane, and they were seized with fear. 16 The spectators explained what had happened to the possessed man, and told them about the swine. 17 Before long they were begging him to go away from their district. 18 As Jesus was getting into the boat, the man who had been possessed was pressing to accompany him. 19 Jesus did not grant his request, but told him instead: "Go home to your family and make it clear to them how much the Lord in his mercy has done for you." 20 At that the man went off and began to proclaim throughout the Ten Cities what Jesus had done for him. They were all amazed at what they heard.

The Daughter of Jairus; the Woman with a Hemorrhage

21 Now when Jesus had crossed back to the other side again in the boat, a large crowd gathered around him and he stayed close to the lake. 22 One of the officials of the synagogue, a man named Jairus, came near. Seeing Jesus, he fell at his feet 23 and made this earnest appeal: "My little daughter is critically ill. Please come and lay your hands on her so that she may get well and live." 24 The two went off together and a large crowd followed, pushing against Jesus.

25 There was a woman in the area who had been afflicted with a hemorrhage for a dozen years. 26 She had received treatment at the hands of doctors of every sort and exhausted her savings in the process, yet she got no relief; on the contrary, she only grew worse. 27 She had heard about Jesus and came up behind him in the crowd and put her hand to his cloak. 28 "If I just touch his clothing," she thought, "I shall get well." 29 Immediately her flow of blood dried up and the feeling that she was cured of her affliction ran through her whole body. 30 Jesus was conscious at once that healing power had gone out from him. Wheeling about in the crowd, he began to ask, "Who touched my clothing?" 31 His disciples said to him, "You can see how this crowd hems you in, yet you ask, 'Who touched me?' 32 Despite this, he kept looking around to see the woman who had done it. 33 Fearful and beginning to tremble now as she realized what had

---

4, 33f: See note on 4, 10ff.

4, 35–41: The sequence of action in this event is rearranged in Mt 8, 23–27 to teach the Christian community what great trust in Jesus it must have in time of peril. In Mark, the disciples' panic is reflected in their reproachful question to Jesus. He in return interprets the event for them as showing the need for absolute confidence in him.

5, 21–43: This narrative is significant for Christology. Jesus knows that a cure has occurred in favor of someone who touched him; he does not know the person's identity (30). Informed of the death of Jairus' daughter, he decides his course of action from the development of events; he recognizes in them the divine will to raise the girl to life (35f). His assertion, *The child is not dead. She is asleep*, leaves the girl's condition unclear (38), so that he can more easily prohibit the witnesses from speaking of the event as an unmistakable manifestation of his power to raise the dead (43).

happened, the woman came and fell in front of him and told him the whole truth. 34 He said to her, "Daughter, it is your faith that has cured you. Go in peace and be free of this illness."

35 He had not finished speaking when people from the official's house arrived saying, "Your daughter is dead. Why bother the Teacher further?" 36 Jesus disregarded the report that had been brought and said to the official: "Fear is useless. What is needed is trust." 37 He would not permit anyone to follow him except Peter, James, and James's brother John. 38 As they approached the house of the synagogue leader, Jesus was struck by the noise of people wailing and crying loudly on all sides. 39 He entered and said to them: "Why do you make this din with your wailing? The child is not dead. She is asleep." 40 At this they began to ridicule him. Then he put them all out.

Jesus took the child's father and mother and his own companions and entered the room where the child lay. 41 Taking her hand he said to her, "Talitha, koum," which means, "Little girl, get up." 42 The girl, a child of twelve, stood up immediately and began to walk around. At this the family's astonishment knew no bounds. 43 He enjoined them strictly not to let anyone know about it, and told them to give her something to eat.

Jesus at Nazareth

6 He departed from there and returned to his own part of the country followed by his disciples. 2 When the sabbath came he began to teach in the synagogue in a way that kept his large audience amazed. They said: "Where did he get all this? What kind of wisdom is he endowed with? How is it that such miraculous deeds are accomplished by his hands? 3 Is this not the carpenter, the son of Mary, a brother of James and Joses and Judas and Simon? Are not his sisters our neighbors here?" They found him too much for them. 4

Jesus' response to all this was: "No prophet is without honor except in his native place, among his own kindred, and in his own house." 5 He could work no miracle there, apart from curing a few who were sick by laying hands on them, 6 so much did their lack of faith distress him. He made the rounds of the neighboring villages instead, and spent his time teaching.

Mission of the Twelve

7 Jesus summoned the Twelve and began to send them out two by two, giving them authority over unclean spirits. 8 He instructed them to take nothing on the journey but a walking stick—no food, no traveling bag, not a coin in the purses in their belts. 9 They were, however, to wear sandals. "Do not bring a second tunic," he said, 10 and added: "Whatever house you find yourself in, stay there until you leave the locality. 11 If any place will not receive you or hear you, shake its dust from your feet in testimony against them as you leave." 12 With that they went off, preaching the need of repentance. 13 They expelled many demons, anointed the sick with oil, and worked many cures.

Death of the Baptizer

14 King Herod came to hear of Jesus, for his reputation had become widespread and people were saying, "John the Baptizer has been raised from the dead; that is why such miraculous powers are at work in him." 15 Others were saying, "He is Elijah"; still others, "He is a prophet equal to any of the prophets." 16 On hearing of Jesus, Herod exclaimed, "John, whose head I had cut off, has been raised up!" 17 Herod was the one who had ordered John arrested, chained, and imprisoned on account of Herodias, the wife of his brother Philip, whom he had married. 18 That was because John had told Herod, "It is not right for you to live with your brother's wife." 19 Herodias harbored a grudge against him for this

and wanted to kill him but was unable to do so. 20 Herod feared John, knowing him to be an upright and holy man, and kept him in custody. When he heard him speak he was very much disturbed; yet he felt the attraction of his words. 21 Herodias had her chance one day when Herod held a birthday dinner for his court circle, military officers, and the leading men of Galilee. 22 Herodias' own daughter came in at one point and performed a dance which delighted Herod and his guests. The king told the girl, "Ask for anything you want and I will give it to you." 23 He went so far as to swear to her: "I will grant you whatever you ask, even to half my kingdom!" 24 She went out and said to her mother, "What shall I ask for?" The mother answered, "The head of John the Baptizer." 25 At that the girl hurried back to the king's presence and made her request: "I want you to give me, at once, the head of John the Baptizer on a platter." 26 The king bitterly regretted the request; yet because of his oath and the presence of the guests, he did not want to refuse her. 27 He promptly dispatched an executioner, ordering him to bring back the Baptizer's head. 28 The man went and beheaded John in the prison. He brought in the head on a platter and gave it to the girl, and the girl gave it to her mother. 29 Later, when his disciples heard about this, they came and carried his body away and laid it in a tomb.

Return of the Disciples

30 The apostles returned to Jesus and reported to him all that they had done and what they had taught. 31 He said to them, "Come by yourselves to an out-of-the-way place and rest a little." People were coming and going in great numbers, making it impossible for them to so much as eat. 32 So Jesus and the apostles went off in the boat by themselves to a deserted place. 33 People saw them leaving, and many got to know about it. People from all the towns

---

6, 1–6: The townsmen of Jesus were not disposed to believe in him because he had not first exercised his power of miracles in their midst (2f). *Is this not the carpenter . . . our neighbors here?*: some manuscripts have, "Is this not the carpenter's son?" The question

about the brothers of Jesus and *his sisters* (3) cannot easily be decided on linguistic grounds. Greek-speaking Semites used the terms *adelphos* and *adelphē*, not only in the ordinary sense of blood brother and sister, but also for nephew, niece, half-brother, half-

sister, and cousin. The question of meaning here would not have arisen but for the faith of the church in Mary's perpetual virginity.

hastened on foot to the place, arriving ahead of them.

Jesus Feeds Five Thousand

34 Upon disembarking Jesus saw a vast crowd. He pitied them, for they were like sheep without a shepherd; and he began to teach them at great length. 35 It was now getting late and his disciples came to him with a suggestion: "This is a deserted place and it is already late. 36 Why do you not dismiss them so that they can go to the crossroads and villages around here and buy themselves something to eat?" 37 "You give them something to eat," Jesus replied. At that they said, "Are we to go and spend two hundred days' wages for bread to feed them?" 38 "How many loaves have you?" Jesus asked. "Go and see." When they learned the number they answered, "Five, and two fish." 39 He told them to make the people sit down on the green grass in groups or parties. 40 The people took their places in hundreds and fifties, neatly arranged like flower beds. 41 Then, taking the five loaves and the two fish, Jesus raised his eyes to heaven, pronounced a blessing, broke the loaves, and gave them to the disciples to distribute. He divided the two fish among all of them 42 and they ate until they had their fill. 43 They gathered up enough leftovers to fill twelve baskets, besides what remained of the fish. 44 Those who had eaten the loaves numbered five thousand men.

Jesus Walks on the Water

45 Immediately afterward he insisted that his disciples get into the boat and precede him to the other side toward Bethsaida, while he dismissed the crowd. 46 When he had taken leave of them, he went off to the mountain to pray. 47 As evening drew on, the boat was far out on the lake while he was alone on the land. 48 Then, seeing them tossed about as they tried to row with the wind against them, he came walking toward them on the water; the time was between three and six in the morning. He meant to pass them by. 49 When they saw him walking on the lake, they thought it was a ghost and they began to cry out. 50 They had all seen him and were terrified. He hastened to reassure them: "Get hold of yourselves! It is I. Do not be afraid!" 51 He got into the boat with them and the wind died down. They were taken aback by these happenings, 52 for they had not understood about the loaves. On the contrary, their minds were completely closed to the meaning of the events.

Other Miracles

53 After making the crossing they came ashore at Gennesaret, and tied up there. 54 As they were leaving the boat people immediately recognized him. 55 The crowds scurried about the adjacent area and began to bring in the sick on bedrolls to the place where they heard he was. 56 Wherever he put in an appearance, in villages, in towns, or at crossroads, they laid the sick in the market places and begged him to let them touch just the tassel of his cloak. All who touched him got well.

Jesus and the Pharisees

7 The Pharisees and some of the experts in the law who had come from Jerusalem gathered around him. 2 They had observed a few of his disciples eating meals without having purified—that is to say, washed—their hands. 3 The Pharisees, and in fact all Jews, cling to the custom of their ancestors and never eat without scrupulously washing their hands. 4 Moreover, they never eat anything from the market without first sprinkling it. There are many other traditions they observe—for example, the washing of cups and jugs and kettles. 5 So the Pharisees and the scribes questioned him: "Why do your disciples not follow the tradition of our ancestors, but instead take food without purifying their hands?" 6 He said to them: "How accurately Isaiah prophesied about you hypocrites when he wrote,

'This people pays me lip service
but their heart is far from me.
7 Empty is the reverence they do me
because they teach as dogmas
mere human precepts.'

8 You disregard God's commandment and cling to what is human tradition."

9 He went on to say: "You have made a fine art of setting aside God's commandment in the interests of keeping your traditions! 10 For example, Moses said, 'Honor your father and your mother'; and in another place, 'Whoever curses father or mother shall be put to death.' 11 Yet you declare, 'If a person says to his father or mother, Any support you might have had from me is *korban*' (that is, dedicated to God), 12 you allow him to do nothing more for his father or mother. 13 That is the way you nullify God's word in favor of the traditions you have handed on. And you have many other such practices besides." 14 He summoned the crowd again and said to them: "Hear me, all of you, and try to understand. 15 Nothing that enters a man from outside can make him impure; that which comes out of him, and only that, constitutes impurity. 16 Let everyone heed what he hears!"

17 When he got home, away from the crowd, his disciples questioned him about the proverb. 18 "Are you, too, incapable of understanding?" he asked them. "Do you not see that nothing that enters a man from outside can make him impure? 19 It does not penetrate his being, but enters his stomach only and passes into the latrine." Thus did

---

6, 45–52: Mt 14, 22–33 and Jn 6, 15–21, as well as Mark, place the event of Jesus' walking on the sea after the miracle of the loaves and fish. The disciples would not have been so astonished at it had they understood the meaning of the multiplication of the loaves (51f). But contrast Matthew's conclusion in 14, 33.

6, 53–56: This summary statement conveys the popular faith in Jesus. *Came ashore at Gennesaret:* in

Jn 6, 24 the name of the place is Capernaum, an apparent indication of two traditions underlying the account.

7, 1–23: The reference to ceremonial washings (2ff) reflects, no doubt, the opposition of the early Christian communities to them. Jesus is described as criticizing the overconcern of the scribes and Pharisees for their traditions to the neglect of the command-

ments enunciated in the Scriptures (6ff); see note on Mt 15, 5f. Even among Gentile Christians scruples existed concerning the moral implications supposedly inherent in the eating of certain foods (Rom 14, 2f.6), a fact that accounts for the editorial observation in Mk 7, 19.

he render all foods clean. 20 He went on: "What emerges from within a man, that and nothing else is what makes him impure. 21 Wicked designs come from the deep recesses of the heart: acts of fornication, theft, murder, 22 adulterous conduct, greed, maliciousness, deceit, sensuality, envy, blasphemy, arrogance, an obtuse spirit. 23 All these evils come from within and render a man impure."

A Canaanite Woman

24 From that place he went off to the territory of Tyre and Sidon. He retired to a certain house and wanted no one to recognize him; however, he could not escape notice. 25 Soon a woman, whose small daughter had an unclean spirit, heard about him. She approached him and crouched at his feet. 26 The woman who was a Greek—a Syro-Phoenician by birth—began to beg him to expel the demon from her daughter. 27 He told her: "Let the sons of the household satisfy themselves at table first. It is not right to take the food of the children and throw it to the dogs." 28 "Please, Lord," she replied, "even the dogs under the table eat the family's leavings." 29 Then he said to her, "For such a reply, be off now! The demon has already left your daughter." 30 When she got home, she found the child lying in bed and the demon gone.

Healing of a Deaf-mute

31 He then left Tyrian territory and returned by way of Sidon to the Sea of Galilee, into the district of the Ten Cities. 32 Some people brought him a deaf man who had a speech impediment and begged him to lay his hand on him. 33 Jesus took him off by himself away from the crowd. He put his fingers into the man's ears and, spitting, touched his tongue; 34 then he looked up to heaven and emitted a groan. He said to him, *"Ephphatha!"* (that is, "Be opened!"). 35 At once the man's ears were opened; he was freed from the impediment, and began to speak plainly. 36 Then he enjoined them strictly not to tell anyone; but the more he ordered them not to, the more they proclaimed it. 37 Their amazement went beyond all bounds: "He has done everything well! He makes the deaf hear and the mute speak!"

Jesus Feeds Four Thousand

8 At about that time another large crowd assembled, and they were without anything to eat. He called the disciples over to him and said: 2 "My heart is moved with pity for the crowd. By now they have been with me three days and have nothing to eat. 3 If I send them home hungry, they will collapse on the way. Some of them have come a great distance." 4 His disciples replied, "How can anyone give these people sufficient bread in this deserted spot?" 5 Still he asked them, "How many loaves do you have?" "Seven," they replied. 6 Then he directed the crowd to take their places on the ground. Taking the seven loaves he gave thanks, broke them, and gave them to his disciples to distribute, and they handed them out to the crowd. 7 They also had a few small fish; asking a blessing on the fish, he told them to distribute these also. 8 The people in the crowd ate until they had their fill; then they gathered up seven wicker baskets of leftovers. 9 Those who had eaten numbered about four thousand.

10 He dismissed them and got into the boat with his disciples to go to the neighborhood of Dalmanutha.

The Pharisees Ask a Sign

11 The Pharisees came forward and began to argue with him. They were looking for some heavenly sign from him as a test. 12 With a sigh from the depths of his spirit he said, "Why does this age seek a sign? I assure you, no such sign will be given it!" 13 Then he left them, got into the boat again, and went off to the other shore.

The Leaven of the Pharisees

14 They had forgotten to bring any bread along; except for one loaf they had none with them in the boat. 15 So when he instructed them, "Keep your eyes open! Be on your guard against the yeast of the Pharisees and the yeast of Herod," 16 they concluded among themselves that it was because they had no bread. 17 Aware of this he said to them, "Why do you suppose that it is because you have no bread? Do you still not see or comprehend? Are your minds completely blinded? 18 Have you eyes but no sight? Ears but no hearing? 19 Do you remember when I broke the five loaves for the five thousand, how many baskets of fragments you gathered up?" They answered, "Twelve." 20 When I broke the seven loaves for the four thousand, how many full hampers of fragments did you collect?" They answered, "Seven." 21 He said to them again, "Do you still not understand?"

A Blind Man at Bethsaida

22 When they arrived at Bethsaida, some people brought him a blind man and begged him to touch

---

7, 24–30: The Syro-Phoenician woman ascribes her daughter's illness to an evil spirit. The mind of the time was inclined to attribute the more baffling sicknesses to satanic power. Without contesting the woman's assertion, Jesus pronounces the curing word in the same terms: *The demon has already left your daughter.*

Jewish authors sometimes used the term "dogs" of Gentiles to express their scorn of paganism. Because the woman's subtle response acknowledges her dependence on the God of Israel, whom Jesus represents, he cures her daughter.

7, 31–37: The actions attributed to Jesus (33f) were used by healers of the time, who considered them effective in themselves. With Jesus, however, they have a sacramental purpose inasmuch as they

are effective by his power through his relation to the Father; cf Jn 11, 41; 17, 1.

8, 1–9: Many scholars regard this as a second version of the one multiplication of loaves, set in a Gentile context because of the eucharistic significance which the early Christian communities saw in it. Note that in this account Jesus' initiative in feeding the crowd is emphasized; the disciples appear helpless except in dependence on him (2ff).

8, 11f: The Pharisees object that the miracles wrought by Jesus are unsatisfactory as proof of the arrival of God's reign. This is comparable to the complaint in Jn 6, 30f. Jesus replies that a request for a sign which originates in human distrust will not be provided.

8, 15: *Be on your guard against the yeast . . . of*

Herod: Mt 16, 12 explains the leaven as the teaching of the religious authorities; Lk 12, 1 takes it to symbolize their hypocrisy. In the light of Mk 8, 11f, the reference here is to their deep-seated hostility toward Jesus, which for different reasons Herod also shares.

8, 22–26: Jesus' actions and the gradual cure of the blind man probably have the same purpose as in the case of the deaf man; see note on 7, 31–37. Some authors regard the cure as an intended symbol of the gradual enlightenment of the disciples concerning the difference between Jesus' teaching and the views of the authorities.

him. 23 Jesus took the blind man's hand and led him outside the village. Putting spittle on his eyes he laid his hands on him and asked, "Can you see anything?" 24 The man opened his eyes and said, "I can see people but they look like walking trees!" 25 Then a second time Jesus laid hands on his eyes, and he saw perfectly; his sight was restored and he could see everything clearly. 26 Jesus sent him home with the admonition, "Do not even go into the village."

THE MYSTERY BEGINS TO BE REVEALED

The Messiah

27 Then Jesus and his disciples set out for the villages around Caesarea Philippi. On the way he asked his disciples this question: "Who do people say that I am?" 28 They replied, "Some, John the Baptizer, others, Elijah, still others, one of the prophets." 29 "And you," he went on to ask, "who do you say that I am?" Peter answered him, "You are the Messiah!" 30 Then he gave them strict orders not to tell anyone about him.

First Teaching of the Paschal Event

31 He began to teach them that the Son of Man had to suffer much, be rejected by the elders, the chief priests, and the scribes, be put to death, and rise three days later. 32 He said these things quite openly. Peter then took him aside and began to remonstrate with him. 33 At this he turned around and, eyeing the disciples, reprimanded Peter: "Get out of my sight, you satan!

You are not judging by God's standards but by man's!"

The Doctrine of the Cross

34 He summoned the crowd with his disciples and said to them: "If a man wishes to come after me, he must deny his very self, take up his cross, and follow in my steps. 35 Whoever would preserve his life will lose it, but whoever loses his life for my sake and the gospel's will preserve it. 36 What profit does a man show who gains the whole world and destroys himself in the process? 37 What can a man offer in exchange for his life? 38 If anyone in this faithless and corrupt age is ashamed of me and my doctrine, the Son of Man will be ashamed of him when he comes with the holy angels in his Father's glory."

9 He also said to them: "I assure you, among those standing here there are some who will not taste death until they see the reign of God established in power."

Jesus Transfigured

2 Six days later, Jesus took Peter, James, and John off by themselves with him and led them up a high mountain. He was transfigured before their eyes 3 and his clothes became dazzlingly white—whiter than the work of any bleacher could make them. 4 Elijah appeared to them along with Moses; the two were in conversation with Jesus. 5 Then Peter spoke to Jesus: "Rabbi, how good it is for us to be here! Let us erect three booths on this site, one for you, one for Moses, and one for Elijah." 6 He hardly knew what to say, for they were all overcome with awe. 7 A cloud came, overshadow-

ing them, and out of the cloud a voice: "This is my Son, my beloved. Listen to him." 8 Suddenly looking around they no longer saw anyone with them—only Jesus.

On the Coming of Elijah

9 As they were coming down the mountain, he strictly enjoined them not to tell anyone what they had seen, before the Son of Man had risen from the dead. 10 They kept this word of his to themselves, though they continued to discuss what "to rise from the dead" meant. 11 Finally they put to him this question: "Why do the scribes claim that Elijah must come first?" 12 He told them: "Elijah will indeed come first and restore everything. Yet why does Scripture say of the Son of Man that he must suffer much and be despised? 13 Let me assure you, Elijah has already come. They did entirely as they pleased with him, as the Scriptures say of him."

A Possessed Boy

14 As they approached the disciples, they saw a large crowd standing around, and scribes in lively discussion with them. 15 Immediately on catching sight of Jesus, the whole crowd was overcome with awe. They ran up to greet him. 16 He asked them, "What are you discussing among yourselves?" 17 "Teacher," a man in the crowd replied, "I have brought my son to you because he is possessed by a mute spirit. 18 Whenever it seizes him it throws him down; he foams at the mouth and grinds his teeth and becomes rigid. Just now I asked your disciples to expel him, but they were unable to do so." 19 He replied by saying to the crowd,

8, 27–30: This episode marks a turning point in Mark's portrait of Jesus in his public ministry. Varieties of popular opinion concerning him concur in regarding him as a prophet. The disciples, by contrast, believe him to be the Messiah. He is described as acknowledging this identification, but prohibits them from making his messianic office known.
8, 31ff: Son of Man: an enigmatic title. Jewish apocryphal tradition (I Enoch, 4 Ezra, 2 Baruch) uses it to describe a unique religious personage, a messiah with extraordinary spiritual endowments. Jesus' use of it seems to derive from Ez 2, where it is a title of humility, and Dn 7, 13f, where it indicates a clearly messianic figure. It expresses for him his twofold destiny, of suffering (8, 31; 9, 11.31; 10, 33; 12, 31; 14, 21) and of glory (8, 38; 12, 36; 14, 62). Peter, along with the other disciples, fails (despite his

confession) to grasp the association of suffering and death with the office of Messiah.
8, 34—9, 1: Mt 16, 24–28 and Lk 9, 23–27 place these sayings in the same context as Mark, namely, Peter's messianic confession and Jesus' rebuke to Peter and the disciples in the prophecy of the passion. Mark and Luke apply the doctrine of the cross to Christians in general. The disciples are instructed to sacrifice even life itself to follow Jesus (34). To strengthen their waning confidence, Jesus foretells that some of them will live to see the arrival of the reign of God in power (9, 1).
9, 2–8: The synoptic gospels place the transfiguration of Jesus six days after the first prediction of his passion and death and his instruction to rebuke the disciples on the doctrine of the cross (Mt 17, 1–8; Lk 9, 28–36). Thus it counterbalances the prediction of the passion

by affording certain of the disciples' insight into the divine glory which he possessed. His glory will overcome his death and that of his disciples; cf 2 Pt 1, 16ff; 2 Cor 3, 18. The heavenly voice (6) prepares the disciples to understand that in the divine plan Jesus must die ignominiously before his messianic glory is made manifest; cf Lk 24, 25ff. The appearance of Moses and Elijah indicates that the purpose of both the law and the prophets was to prepare for Christ.
9, 14–29: The disciples' failure to effect a cure seems to reflect unfavorably on Jesus (14–18). In response, he exposes their lack of trust in God (19) and scores their neglect of prayer, i.e., of the conscious reliance on God's power when acting in Jesus' name. Mark and Matthew (17, 14–18) concur on this point; Luke (9, 37–43) centers attention on Jesus' sovereign power.

"What an unbelieving lot you are! How long must I remain with you? How long can I endure you? Bring him to me." 20 When they did so the spirit caught sight of Jesus and immediately threw the boy into convulsions. As he fell to the ground he began to roll around and foam at the mouth. 21 Then Jesus questioned the father: "How long has this been happening to him?" "From childhood," the father replied. 22 "Often it throws him into fire and into water. You would think it would kill him. If out of the kindness of your heart you can do anything to help us, please do!" 23 Jesus said, "'If you can'? Everything is possible to a man who trusts." 24 The boy's father immediately exclaimed, "I do believe! Help my lack of trust!" 25 Jesus, on seeing a crowd rapidly gathering, reprimanded the unclean spirit by saying to him, "Mute and deaf spirit, I command you: Get out of him and never enter him again!" 26 Shouting, and throwing the boy into convulsions, it came out of him; the boy became like a corpse, which caused many to say, "He is dead." 27 But Jesus took him by the hand and helped him to his feet. 28 When Jesus arrived at the house his disciples began to ask him privately, "Why is it that we could not expel it?" 29 He told them, "This kind you can drive out only by prayer."

Second Teaching: Passion and Resurrection

30 They left that district and began a journey through Galilee, but he did not want anyone to know about it. 31 He was teaching his disciples in this vein: "The Son of Man is going to be delivered into the hands of men who will put him to death; three days after his death he will rise." 32 Though they failed to understand his words, they were afraid to question him.

THE FULL REVELATION OF THE MYSTERY

Against Ambition and Envy

33 They returned to Capernaum and Jesus, once inside the house, began to ask them, "What were you discussing on the way home?" 34 At this they fell silent, for on the way they had been arguing about who was the most important. 35 So he sat down and called the Twelve around him and said, "If anyone wishes to rank first, he must remain the last one of all and the servant of all." 36 Then he took a little child, stood him in their midst, and putting his arms around him, said to them, 37 "Whoever welcomes a child such as this for my sake welcomes me. And whoever welcomes me welcomes, not me, but him who sent me."

38 John said to him, "Teacher, we saw a man using your name to expel demons and we tried to stop him because he is not of our company." 39 Jesus said in reply: "Do not try to stop him. No man who performs a miracle using my name can at the same time speak ill of me. 40 Anyone who is not against us is with us. 41 Any man who gives you a drink of water because you belong to Christ will not, I assure you, go without his reward. 42 But it would be better if anyone who leads astray one of these simple believers were to be plunged in the sea with a great millstone fastened around his neck.

43 "If your hand is your difficulty, cut it off! Better for you to enter life maimed than to keep both hands and enter Gehenna with its unquenchable fire. 45 If your foot is your undoing, cut it off! Better for you to enter life crippled than to be thrown into Gehenna with both feet. 47 If your eye is your downfall, tear it out! Better for you to enter the kingdom of God with one eye than to be thrown with both eyes into Gehenna, 48 where 'the worm dies not and the fire is never extinguished.'

49 Everyone will be salted with fire 50 Salt is excellent in its place; but if salt becomes tasteless, how can you season it? Keep salt in your hearts and you will be at peace with one another."

10 From there he moved on to the districts of Judea and across the Jordan. Once more crowds gathered around him, and as usual he began to teach them.

The Question of Divorce

2 Then some Pharisees came up and as a test began to ask him whether it was permissible for a husband to divorce his wife. 3 In reply he said, "What command did Moses give you?" 4 They answered, "Moses permitted divorce and the writing of a decree of divorce." 5 But Jesus told them: "He wrote that commandment for you because of your stubbornness. 6 At the beginning of creation God made them male and female; 7 for this reason a man shall leave his father and mother 8 and the two shall become as one. They are no longer two but one flesh. 9 Therefore let no man separate what God has joined." 10 Back in the house again, the disciples began to question him about this. 11 He told them, "Whoever divorces his wife and marries another commits adultery against her; 12 and the woman who divorces her husband and marries another commits adultery."

Jesus Blesses the Children

13 People were bringing their little children to him to have him touch them, but the disciples were scolding them for this. 14 Jesus became indignant when he noticed it and said to them: "Let the children come to me and do not hinder them. It is to just such as these that the kingdom of God belongs. 15 I assure you that whoever does not accept the reign of God like a little

---

9, 30ff: Although the disciples heard Jesus' new prediction concerning his passion, they failed to accept its truth because they did not understand his messianic role.

9, 33–37: The evangelist probably intends this incident and the sayings that follow as a commentary on the disciples' lack of understanding (9, 32). Their role in Jesus' work is one of service, especially to the poor and lowly. For this concept of the child, see note on Mt 19, 13ff.

9, 38–41: Jesus warns against jealously and intolerance toward good works, such as exorcism, performed in his name by those whose faith is imperfect. The saying in 9, 40 is a broad principle of the divine tolerance: God repays men for the smallest courtesies they show to those who teach in Jesus' name.

9, 42–50: A collection of Jesus' sayings, rather loosely connected. Vv 44 and 46 are omitted here as additions to the text taken from v 48 and a modified

citation of Is 66, 24. The concluding sayings in vv 49f probably allude to the sacrifices required for loyal adherence to the teaching of Jesus. For the imagery of salt, cf Lv 2, 13 and note.

9, 44.46: Not found in many manuscripts.

10, 1–12: See notes on Mt 19, 3–8 and 19, 9.

10, 13–16: See note on Mt 19, 13ff.

child shall not take part in it." 16 Then he embraced them and blessed them, placing his hands on them.

The Danger of Riches

17 As he was setting out on a journey a man came running up, knelt down before him and asked, "Good Teacher, what must I do to share in everlasting life?" 18 Jesus answered, "Why do you call me good? No one is good but God alone. 19 You know the commandments:

'You shall not kill;
You shall not commit adultery;
You shall not steal;
You shall not bear false witness;
You shall not defraud;
Honor your father and your
    mother.'"

20 He replied, "Teacher, I have kept all these since my childhood." 21 Then Jesus looked at him with love and told him, "There is one thing more you must do. Go and sell what you have and give to the poor; you will then have treasure in heaven. After that, come and follow me." 22 At these words the man's face fell. He went away sad, for he had many possessions. 23 Jesus looked around and said to his disciples, "How hard it is for the rich to enter the kingdom of God!" 24 The disciples could only marvel at his words. So Jesus repeated what he had said: "My sons, how hard it is to enter the kingdom of God! 25 It is easier for a camel to pass through a needle's eye than for a rich man to enter the kingdom of God." 26 They were completely overwhelmed at this, and exclaimed to one another, "Then who can be saved?" 27 Jesus fixed his gaze on them and said, "For man it is impossible but not for God. With God all things are possible."

28 Peter was moved to say to him:

"We have put aside everything to follow you!" 29 Jesus answered: "I give you my word, there is no one who has given up home, brothers or sisters, mother or father, children or property, for me and for the gospel 30 who will not receive in this present age a hundred times as many homes, brothers and sisters, mothers, children and property—and persecution besides—and in the age to come, everlasting life. 31 Many who are first shall come last, and the last shall come first."

Third Teaching: Passion and Resurrection

32 The disciples were on the road going up to Jerusalem, with Jesus walking in the lead. Their mood was one of wonderment, while that of those who followed was fear. Taking the Twelve aside once more, he began to tell them what was going to happen to him. 33 "We are on our way up to Jerusalem, where the Son of Man will be handed over to the chief priests and the scribes. 34 They will condemn him to death and hand him over to the Gentiles, who will mock him and spit at him, flog him, and finally kill him. But three days later he will rise."

Ambition of James and John

35 Zebedee's sons, James and John, approached him. "Teacher," they said, "we want you to grant our request." 36 "What is it?" he asked. 37 They replied, "See to it that we sit, one at your right and the other at your left, when you come into your glory." 38 Jesus told them, "You do not know what you are asking. Can you drink the cup I shall drink or be baptized in the same bath of pain as I?" 39 "We can," they told him. Jesus said in response, "From the cup I drink of you shall

drink; the bath I am immersed in you shall share. 40 But as for sitting at my right or my left, that is not mine to give; it is for those to whom it has been reserved." 41 The other ten, on hearing this, became indignant at James and John. 42 Jesus called them together and said to them: "You know how among the Gentiles those who seem to exercise authority lord it over them; their great ones make their importance felt. 43 It cannot be like that with you. Anyone among you who aspires to greatness must serve the rest; 44 whoever wants to rank first among you must serve the needs of all. 45 The Son of Man has not come to be served but to serve—to give his life in ransom for the many."

The Blind Bartimaeus

46 They came to Jericho next, and as he was leaving that place with his disciples and a sizable crowd, there was a blind beggar Bartimaeus ("son of Timaeus") sitting by the roadside. 47 On hearing that it was Jesus of Nazareth, he began to call out, "Jesus, Son of David, have pity on me!" 48 Many people were scolding him to make him keep quiet, but he shouted all the louder, "Son of David, have pity on me!" 49 Then Jesus stopped and said, "Call him over." So they called the blind man over, telling him as they did so, "You have nothing to fear from him! Get up! He is calling you!" 50 He threw aside his cloak, jumped up and came to Jesus. 51 Jesus asked him, "What do you want me to do for you?" "Rabboni," the blind man said, "I want to see." 52 Jesus said in reply, "Be on your way. Your faith has healed you." Immediately he received his sight and started to follow him up the road.

10, 17f: Jesus' repudiation of the term "good" is probably in response to the man's implication that Jesus will reveal to him the secret of eternal life. What Jesus requires of the man is not necessarily congenial to his ideas. The remainder of the story in vv 19–22 bears out the point.

10, 23–27: See note on Mt 19, 23–26.

10, 28–31: See note on Mt 19, 27–30.

10, 32ff: The disciples are apprehensive because Jesus, after prophesying his execution in Jerusalem, now proceeds deliberately to confront it (Lk 9, 51; Jn 11, 16). No doubt the prophecies in the synoptic tradition about the passion of Christ have been

schematized through the influence of the event of the crucifixion. There seems to be no question, however, that frequent repetition of a passion prophecy by Jesus was part of the original tradition.

10, 35–45: If Mark has placed this narrative in its actual historical context (cf Mt 20, 20), the petition of James and John becomes dramatic: they declare themselves ready to risk death with Jesus provided he will guarantee to them the highest positions in the kingdom. While accepting their pledge to suffer with him, Jesus observes that it lies beyond his personal authority to make such concessions (35–40). If not in its actual historical context, the petition of

James and John has been placed here by the evangelist to align the sacrifices required of disciples with the personal sacrifice made by Jesus. Whatever authority the disciples exercise is to be viewed, like the authority of Jesus (v 45), in terms of service to others rather than as a sign of personal eminence (42ff).

10, 46–52: The synoptic gospels locate this event at Jericho on Jesus' last journey to Jerusalem (Mt 20, 29–34; Lk 18, 35–43). The blind man, unaffected by what he heard of Jesus' lowly condition, accords him the messianic title, "Son of David." He requests a cure in order that he may see Jesus. On this basis his sight is restored.

Triumphal Entry into Jerusalem

11 Then, as they neared Bethphage and Bethany on the Mount of Olives, close to Jerusalem, he sent off two of his disciples 2 with the instruction: "Go to the village straight ahead of you, and as soon as you enter it you will find tethered there a colt on which no one has ridden. Untie it and bring it back. 3 If anyone says to you, 'Why are you doing that?' say, 'The Master needs it but he will send it back here at once.'" 4 So they went off, and finding a colt tethered out on the street near a gate, they untied it. 5 Some of the bystanders said to them, "What do you mean by untying that colt?" 6 They answered as Jesus had told them to, and the men let them take it. 7 They brought the colt to Jesus and threw their cloaks across its back, and he sat on it. 8 Many people spread their cloaks on the road, while others spread reeds which they had cut in the fields. 9 Those preceding as well as those who followed cried out:

"Hosanna!
Blessed is he who comes in the
     name of the Lord!
10 Blessed is the reign of our
     father David to come!
Hosanna in the highest!"

11 He entered Jerusalem and went into the temple precincts. He inspected everything there, but since it was already late in the afternoon, he went out to Bethany accompanied by the Twelve.

Jesus Curses a Fig Tree

12 The next day when they were leaving Bethany he felt hungry. 13 Observing a fig tree some distance off, covered with foliage, he went over to it to see if he could find anything on it. When he reached it he found nothing but leaves; it was not the time for figs. 14 Then addressing it he said, "Never again shall anyone eat of your fruit!" His disciples heard all this.

Cleansing of the Temple

15 When they reached Jerusalem he entered the temple precincts and began to drive out those who were engaged in buying and selling. He overturned the money-changers' tables and the stalls of the men selling doves; moreover, 16 he would not permit anyone to carry things through the temple area. 17 Then he began to teach them: "Does not Scripture have it,

'My house shall be called a
     house of prayer for all
     peoples'—?

but you have turned it into a den of thieves." 18 The chief priests and the scribes heard of this and began to look for a way to destroy him. They were at the same time afraid of him because the whole crowd was under the spell of his teaching. 19 When the evening drew on, Jesus and his disciples went out of the city. 20 Early next morning, as they were walking along, they saw the fig tree withered to its roots. 21 Peter remembered and said to him, "Rabbi, look! The fig tree you cursed has withered up." 22 In reply Jesus told them: "Put your trust in God. 23 I solemnly assure you, whoever says to this mountain, 'Be lifted up and thrown into the sea,' and has no inner doubts but believes that what he says will happen, shall have it done for him. 24 I give you my word, if you are ready to believe that you will receive whatever you ask for in prayer, it shall be done for you. 25 When you stand to pray, forgive anyone against whom you have a grievance so that your heavenly Father may in turn forgive you your faults."

The Authority of Jesus

27 They returned once more to Jerusalem. As he was walking in the temple precincts the chief priests, the scribes, and the elders approached him 28 and said to him, "On what authority are you doing these things? Who has given you the power to do them?" 29 Jesus said to them, "I will ask you a question. If you give me an answer, I will tell you on what authority I do the things I do. 30 Tell me, was John's baptism of divine origin or merely from men?" 31 They thought to themselves, "If we say 'divine,' he will ask, 'Then why did you not put faith in it?' 32 But can we say, 'merely human'?" (They had reason to fear the people, who all regarded John as a true prophet.) 33 So their answer to Jesus was, "We do not know." In turn, Jesus said to them, "Then neither will I tell you on what authority I do the things I do."

Parable of the Tenants

12 He began to address them once more in parables: "A man planted a vineyard, put a hedge around it, dug out a vat, and erected a tower. Then he released it to tenant farmers and went on a journey. 2 In due time he dispatched a man in his service to the tenants to obtain from them his share of produce from the vineyard. 3 But they seized him, beat him, and sent him off empty-handed. 4 The second time he sent them another servant; him too they beat over the head and treated shamefully. 5 He sent yet another and they killed him.

11, 1–11: The nature of Jesus' entry into Jerusalem is not entirely clear in the synoptic tradition. In Jn 12, 12f the popular excitement upon his arrival in the city is associated with his raising of Lazarus to life (Jn 12, 18). This explains the acclaim Jesus receives on entering the city. In Mk 11, 9f the greeting Jesus receives stops short of proclaiming him Messiah. He is greeted rather as the prophet of the coming messianic kingdom; cf Mt 21, 11. Matthew introduces the notion of fulfillment of Old Testament prophecy (Zec 9, 9).

11, 12ff: Jesus' search for fruit on the fig tree recalls the prophets' earlier use of this image to designate Israel; cf Jer 8, 13; Ez 17, 24; Jl 1, 7; Hos 9, 10. Cursing the fig tree is a parable in action

representing Christ's judgment on barren Israel for failing to receive his teaching.

11, 15–19: The expulsion of the buyers and sellers from the temple does not seem to be properly understood if regarded simply as an objection to the practice within the temple precincts, for it was fairly well controlled by the religious authorities. The key to an understanding of the incident is the citation of Is 56, 7 and Jer 7, 11. Both prophets objected that the worship in the temple was not consistent with true conversion. Jesus' action is a symbol of God's judgment against the abuses of his temple, due to the priests' failure to instruct the people in the meaning of temple worship.

11, 26: Omitted with many MSS.

11, 27—12, 27: For a similar series of conflicts see Mk 2, 1—3, 6. The parable of the vineyard tenants (Mt 21, 33–46; Lk 20, 9–19) indicates Jesus' self-awareness of his unique divine sonship (12, 1–12) His superior wisdom sees no conflict between Roman taxation and Israel's worship of God (12, 13–17). His prophetic insight exposes the specious arguments against resurrection of the dead adduced by the Sadducees, who fail to understand that the messianic promises benefit here and hereafter all who have hoped in God (12, 18–27).

So too with many others: some they beat; some they killed. 6 He still had one to send—the son whom he loved. He sent him to them as a last resort, thinking, 'They will have to respect my son.' 7 But those tenants said to one another, 'Here is the one who will inherit everything. Come, let us kill him, and the inheritance will be ours.' 8 Then they seized and killed him and dragged him outside the vineyard. 9 What do you suppose the owner of the vineyard will do? He will come and destroy those tenants and turn his vineyard over to others. 10 Are you not familiar with this passage of Scripture:

'The stone rejected by the
    builders
  has become the keystone of
    the structure.
11 It was the Lord who did it
  and we find it marvelous to
    behold'?"

12 They wanted to arrest him at this, yet they had reason to fear the crowd. (They knew well enough that he meant the parable for them.) Finally they left him and went off.

Tribute to the Emperor

13 They next sent some Pharisees and Herodians after him to catch him in his speech. 14 The two groups came and said to him: "Teacher, we know you are a truthful man, unconcerned about anyone's opinion. It is evident you do not act out of human respect but teach God's way of life sincerely. Is it lawful to pay the tax to the emperor or not? Are we to pay or not to pay?" 15 Knowing their hypocrisy he said to them, "Why are you trying to trip me up? Bring me a coin and let me see it." 16 When they brought one, he said to them, "Whose head is this and whose inscription is it?" "Caesar's," they told him. 17 At that Jesus said to them, "Give to Caesar what is Caesar's but give to God what is God's." Their amazement at him knew no bounds.

The Sadducees and the Resurrection

18 Then some Sadducees who hold there is no resurrection came to him with a question: 19 "Teacher, we were left this in writing by Moses: 'If anyone's brother dies leaving a wife but no child, his brother must take the wife and produce offspring for his brother.' 20 There were these seven brothers. The eldest took a wife and died, leaving no children. 21 The second took the woman, and he too died childless. The same thing happened to the third; 22 in fact none of the seven left any children behind. Last of all, the woman also died. 23 At the resurrection, when they all come back to life, whose wife will she be? All seven married her." 24 Jesus said: "You are badly misled, because you fail to understand the Scriptures or the power of God. 25 When people rise from the dead, they neither marry nor are given in marriage but live like angels in heaven. 26 As to the raising of the dead, have you not read in the book of Moses, in the passage about the burning bush, how God told him,

'I am the God of Abraham, the
    God of Isaac, the God of
    Jacob'?

27 He is the God of the living, not of the dead. You are very much mistaken."

The Great Commandment

28 One of the scribes came up, and when he heard them arguing he realized how skillfully Jesus answered them. He decided to ask him, "Which is the first of all the commandments?" 29 Jesus replied: "This is the first:

'Hear, O Israel! The Lord our
    God is Lord alone!
30 Therefore you shall love the
    Lord your God
with all your heart,
with all your soul,
with all your mind,
and with all your strength.'

31 This is the second,

'You shall love your neighbor as
    yourself.'

There is no other commandment greater than these." 32 The scribe said to him: "Excellent, Teacher! You are right in saying, 'He is the One, there is no other than he.' 33 Yes, 'to love him with all our heart, with all our thoughts and with all our strength, and to love our neighbor as ourselves' is worth more than any burnt offering or sacrifice." 34 Jesus approved the insight of this answer and told him, "You are not far from the reign of God." And no one had the courage to ask him any more questions.

The Son of David

35 As Jesus was teaching in the temple precincts he went on to say: "How can the scribes claim, 'The Messiah is David's son'? 36 David himself, inspired by the Holy Spirit, said,

'The Lord said to my Lord: Sit
  at my right hand until I
  make your enemies your
    footstool.'

37 If David himself addresses him as 'Lord,' in what sense can he be his son?" The majority of the crowd heard this with delight.

Hypocrisy of the Opponents of Jesus

38 In the course of his teaching he said: "Be on guard against the scribes, who like to parade around in their robes and accept marks of respect in public, 39 front seats in the synagogues, and places of honor at banquets. 40 These men devour the savings of widows and recite long prayers for appearance' sake; it is they who will receive the severest sentence."

The Widow's Mite

41 Taking a seat opposite the treasury, he observed the crowd putting the money into the collection

---

12, 35–44: Jesus questions the claim of the scribes about the Davidic descent of the Messiah, not to deny it (Mt 1, 1; Acts 2, 20.34; Rom 1, 3; 2 Tm 2, 8), but to imply that he is more than this. His superiority derives from his transcendent origin (35ff), to which David himself attested when he addressed the Messiah with the name reserved for Yahweh (Ps 110, 1).

Jesus was pained by the scribes' abuse of religious position (38ff). At the same time he was deeply sympathetic toward the religious generosity of the poor (41–44).

box. Many of the wealthy put in sizable amounts; 42 but one poor widow came and put in two small copper coins worth a few cents. 43 He called his disciples over and told them: "I want you to observe that this poor widow contributed more than all the others who donated to the treasury. 44 They gave from their surplus wealth, but she gave from her want, all that she had to live on."

Questions about the Temple

13 As he was making his way out of the temple area, one of his disciples said to him, "Teacher, look at the huge blocks of stone and the enormous buildings!" 2 Jesus said to him, "You see these great buildings? Not one stone will be left upon another—all will be torn down." 3 While he was seated on the Mount of Olives facing the temple, Peter, James, John, and Andrew began to question him privately. 4 "Tell us, when will this occur? What will be the sign that all this is coming to an end?"

Beginning of the Calamities

5 Jesus began his discourse: "Be on your guard. Let no one mislead you. 6 Any number will come attempting to impersonate me. 'I am he,' they will claim, and will lead many astray. 7 When you hear about wars and threats of war, do not yield to panic. Such things are bound to happen, but this is not yet the end. 8 Nation will rise against nation, one kingdom against another. There will be earthquakes in various places and there will be famine. This is but the onset of the pains of labor. 9 Be constantly on your guard. They will hand you over to the courts. You will be beaten in synagogues. You will be arraigned before governors and kings on my account and

have to testify to your faith before them. 10 But the good news must first be proclaimed to all the Gentiles. 11 When men take you off into custody, do not worry beforehand about what to say. In that hour, say what you are inspired to say. It will not be yourselves speaking but the Holy Spirit. 12 Brother will hand over brother for execution and likewise the father his child; children will turn against their parents and have them put to death. 13 Because of my name, you will be hated by everyone. Nonetheless, the man who holds out till the end is the one who will come through safe.

The Supreme Tribulation

14 "When you see the abominable and destructive presence standing where it should not be—let the reader take note!—those in Judea must flee to the mountains. 15 If a man is on the roof terrace, he must not come down or enter his house to get anything out of it. 16 If a man is in the field, he must not turn back to pick up his cloak. 17 It will go badly with pregnant and nursing women in those days. 18 Keep praying that none of this happens in winter. 19 Those times will be more distressful than any between God's work of creation and now, and for all time to come. 20 Indeed, had the Lord not shortened the period, not a person would be saved. But for the sake of those he has chosen, he has shortened the days. 21 If anyone tells you at that time, 'Look, the Messiah is here!' 'Look, he is there!' —do not believe it. 22 False Messiahs and false prophets will appear performing signs and wonders to mislead, if it were possible, even the chosen. 23 So be constantly on guard! I have told you about it beforehand.

Last Act of the Drama

24 "During that period after trials of every sort the sun will be darkened, the moon will not shed its light, 25 stars will fall out of the skies, and the heavenly hosts will be shaken. 26 Then men will see the Son of Man coming in the clouds with great power and glory. 27 He will dispatch his angels and assemble his chosen from the four winds, from the farthest bounds of earth and sky. 28 Learn a lesson from the fig tree. Once the sap of its branches runs high and it begins to sprout leaves, you know that summer is near. 29 In the same way, when you see these things happening, you will know that he is near, even at the door. 30 I assure you, this generation will not pass away until all these things take place. 31 The heavens and the earth will pass away but my words will not pass.

Need for Watchfulness

32 "As to the exact day or hour, no one knows it, neither the angels in heaven nor even the Son, but only the Father. 33 Be constantly on the watch! Stay awake! You do not know when the appointed time will come. 34 It is like a man traveling abroad. He leaves home and places his servants in charge, each with his own task; and he orders the man at the gate to watch with a sharp eye. 35 Look around you! You do not know when the master of the house is coming, whether at dusk, at midnight, when the cock crows, or at early dawn. 36 Do not let him come suddenly and catch you asleep. 37 What I say to you, I say to all: Be on guard!"

The Official Decision

14 The feasts of Passover and Unleavened Bread were to be observed in two days' time, and

---

13, 1–37: This chapter and its parallels (Mt 24, 1–44; Lk 21, 5–36) express the principal New Testament thought on the second coming of Christ; cf 1 Thes 4, 3–18 and note. Each of the three evangelists in his own way relates the second coming to Jesus' prophecy of the destruction of Jerusalem. The *abominable and destructive presence* (Dn 9, 27), i.e., the profanation of the temple by the Roman power, will be the sign of imminent destruction. Jesus urges flight from Jerusalem rather than defense of the city through misguided messianic hope (14–23). Intervention will only occur after the destruction (24–27), which itself is to occur before the end of the first Christian genera-

tion (28–31). No one but the Father knows the precise time, nor that of Jesus' second coming (32), hence the necessity of constant vigilance (33–37). The chronological proximity of the second coming and the destruction of the temple is not determined (2–27). Luke sets the second coming at a later date, in *the times of the Gentiles* (Lk 21, 24).

14, 1—15, 47: In this solemn narrative the principal facts of the sufferings and death of Jesus are interwoven with implications of their religious significance. The facts include: a plan to arrest Jesus secretly and thus prevent tumult (1ff); facilitation of the plan through Judas' betrayal (10f); the arrest of Jesus

(43–47); inquest before the Sanhedrin and indictment for blasphemy (55–64); transfer to Pilate's court and the insinuation of political sedition (15, 1–5); official and popular demand for Jesus' condemnation and crucifixion; Pilate's consent under pressure (15, 6–15); the mockery, scourging and crucifixion (15, 15–27); death on the cross (15, 29–39); and burial by Joseph of Arimathea (15, 42–47).

Jesus is described as interpreting the events of his passion as follows: the anointing at Bethany as a preparation for his death (14, 3–9); his celebration of the Passover (12–16) as the inauguration of a new and lasting covenant in which his body and blood are therefore the chief priests and scribes began to look for a way to arrest him by some trick and kill him. 2 Yet they pointed out, "Not during the festival, or the people may riot."

The Anointing at Bethany

3 When Jesus was in Bethany reclining at table in the house of Simon the leper, a woman entered carrying an alabaster jar of perfume made from expensive aromatic nard. Breaking the jar, she began to pour the perfume on his head. 4 Some were saying to themselves indignantly: "What is the point of this extravagant waste of perfume? 5 It could have been sold for over three hundred silver pieces and the money given to the poor." They were infuriated at her. 6 But Jesus said: "Let her alone. Why do you criticize her? She has done me a kindness. 7 The poor you will always have with you and you can be generous to them whenever you wish, but you will not always have me. 8 She has done what she could. By perfuming my body she is anticipating its preparation for burial. 9 I assure you, wherever the good news is proclaimed throughout the world, what she has done will be told in her memory."

The Betrayal

10 Then Judas Iscariot, one of the Twelve, went off to the chief priests to hand Jesus over to them. 11 Hearing what he had to say, they were jubilant and promised to give him money. He for his part kept looking for an opportune way to hand him over.

Passover Preparation

12 On the first day of Unleavened Bread, when it was customary to sacrifice the paschal lamb, his disciples said to him, "Where do you wish us to go to prepare the Passover supper for you?" 13 He sent two of his disciples with these instructions: "Go into the city and you will come upon a man carrying a water jar. Follow him. 14 Whatever house he enters, say to the owner, 'The Teacher asks, Where is my guest room where I may eat the Passover with my disciples?' 15 Then he will show you an upstairs room, spacious, furnished, and all in order. That is the place you are to get ready for us." 16 The disciples went off. When they reached the city they found it was just as he had told them, and they prepared the Passover supper.

The Betrayer

17 As it grew dark he arrived with the Twelve. 18 They reclined at table, and in the course of the meal Jesus said, "I give you my word, one of you is about to betray me, yes, one who is eating with me." 19 They began to say to him sorrowfully, one by one, "Surely not I!" 20 He said, "It is one of the Twelve—a man who dips into the dish with me. 21 The Son of Man is going the way the Scripture tells of him. Still, accursed be that man by whom the Son of Man is betrayed. It were better for him had he never been born."

The Holy Eucharist

22 During the meal he took bread, blessed and broke it, and gave it to them. "Take this," he said, "this is my body." 23 He likewise took a cup, gave thanks and passed it to them, and they all drank from it. 24 He said to them: "This is my blood, the blood of the covenant, to be poured out on behalf of many. 25 I solemnly assure you, I will never again drink of the fruit of the vine until the day when I drink it new in the reign of God."

26 After singing songs of praise, they walked out to the Mount of Olives.

Peter's Denial Foretold

27 Jesus then said to them: "Your faith in me shall be shaken, for Scripture has it,

'I will strike the shepherd
and the sheep will be dispersed.'

28 But after I am raised up, I will go to Galilee ahead of you." 29 Peter said to him, "Even though all are shaken in faith, it will not be that way with me." 30 Jesus answered, "I give you my assurance, this very night before the cock crows twice, you will deny me three times." 31 But Peter kept reasserting vehemently, "Even if I have to die with you, I will not deny you." They all said the same.

The Agony in the Garden

32 They went then to a place named Gethsemani. "Sit down here while I pray," he said to his disciples; 33 at the same time he took along with him Peter, James, and John. 34 Then he began to be filled with fear and distress. He said to them, "My heart is filled with sorrow to the point of death. Remain here and stay awake." 35 He advanced a little and fell to the ground, praying that if it were possible this hour might pass him by. 36 He kept saying, *Abba* (O Father), you have the power to do all things. Take this cup away from me. But let it be as you would have it, not as I." 37 When he returned he found them asleep. He said to Peter, "Asleep, Simon? You could not stay awake for even an hour? 38 Be on guard and pray that you may not be put to the test. The spirit is willing but nature is weak." 39 Going back again he began to pray in the same words. 40 Once again he found them asleep on his return. They could not keep their eyes open, nor did they know what to say to him. 41 He returned a third time and said to them, "Still sleeping? Still taking your ease? It will have to do. The hour is on us. You will see that the Son of Man is to be handed over to the clutches of evil men. 42 Rouse yourselves and come along. See! My betrayer is near."

---

to be shared in the form of bread and wine, symbols of his passion and death (22ff). He prophesies Peter's denial and the apostles' desertion and subsequent reunion (26ff). Jesus declares his acceptance of the passion to be in conformity with his Father's will (32–42), and confesses his awareness of what was foretold by the Scriptures concerning him (48f). He refuses to throw himself on the mercy of Pilate (15, 2–5) and rejects the drug that would cloud his mind to the reality of the crucifixion (36). He prays Psalm 22 from the cross (34). The Roman centurion's tribute to Jesus' courage (39) is actually a concluding Marcan confession of faith, put on Gentile lips.

The religious cast of the Marcan passion narrative derives from the consistent theme of fulfillment of prophecy, even concerning the conduct of Jesus' disciples. Though complete in itself, this narrative is closely joined to the account of Jesus' ministry. One single item remains to be fulfilled: the prophecy of his future vindication (14, 62).

Jesus Arrested

43 Even while he was still speaking, Judas, one of the Twelve, made his appearance accompanied by a crowd with swords and clubs; these people had been sent by the chief priests, the scribes, and the elders. 44 The betrayer had arranged a signal for them, saying, "The man I shall embrace is the one; arrest him and lead him away, taking every precaution." 45 He then went directly over to him and said, "Rabbi!" and embraced him. 46 At this, they laid hands on him and arrested him. 47 One of the bystanders drew his sword and struck the high priest's slave, cutting off his ear. 48 Addressing himself to them, Jesus said: "You have come out to arrest me armed with swords and clubs as if against a brigand. 49 I was within your reach daily, teaching in the temple precincts, yet you never arrested me. But now, so that the Scriptures may be fulfilled . . ." 50 With that, all deserted him and fled. 51 There was a young man following him who was covered by nothing but a linen cloth. As they seized him 52 he left the cloth behind and ran off naked.

Jesus before the Sanhedrin

53 Then they led Jesus off to the high priest, and all the chief priests, the elders and the scribes came together. 54 Peter followed him at a distance right into the high priest's courtyard, where he found a seat with the temple guard and began to warm himself at the fire. 55 The chief priests with the whole Sanhedrin were busy soliciting testimony against Jesus that would lead to his death, but they could not find any. 56 Many spoke against him falsely under oath but their testimony did not agree. 57 Some, for instance, on taking the stand, testified falsely by alleging, 58 "We heard him declare, 'I will destroy this temple made by human hands,' and 'In three days I will construct another not made by human hands.'" 59 Even so, their testimony did not agree.

60 The high priest rose to his feet before the court and began to interrogate Jesus: "Have you no answer to what these men testify against you?" 61 But Jesus remained silent; he made no reply. Once again the high priest interrogated him: "Are you the Messiah, the Son of the Blessed One?" 62 Then Jesus answered: "I am; and you will see the Son of Man seated at the right hand of the Power and coming with the clouds of heaven." 63 At that the high priest tore his robes and said: "What further need do we have of witnesses? 64 You have heard the blasphemy. What is your verdict?" They all concurred in the verdict "guilty," with its sentence of death. 65 Some of them then began to spit on him. They blindfolded him and hit him, saying, "Play the prophet!" while the officers manhandled him.

Peter's Denial

66 While Peter was down in the courtyard, one of the servant girls of the high priest came along. 67 When she noticed Peter warming himself, she looked at him more closely and said, "You too were with Jesus of Nazareth." 68 But he denied it: "I do not know what you are talking about! What are you getting at?" Then he went out into the gateway. [At that moment a cock crowed.] 69 The servant girl, keeping an eye on him, started again to tell the bystanders, "This man is one of them." 70 Once again he denied it. A little later the bystanders said to Peter once more, "You are certainly one of them! You are a Galilean, are you not?" 71 He began to curse, and to swear, "I do not even know the man you are talking about!" 72 Just then a second cockcrow was heard and Peter recalled the prediction Jesus had made to him, "Before the cock crows twice you will deny me three times." He broke down and began to cry.

Jesus before Pilate

15 As soon as it was daybreak the chief priests, with the elders and scribes (that is, the whole Sanhedrin), reached a decision. They bound Jesus, led him away, and handed him over to Pilate. 2 Pilate interrogated him: "Are you the king of the Jews?" "You are the one who is saying it," Jesus replied. 3 The chief priests, meanwhile, brought many accusations against him. 4 Pilate interrogated him again: "Surely you have some answer? See how many accusations they are leveling against you." 5 But greatly to Pilate's surprise, Jesus made no further response.

6 Now on the occasion of a festival he would release for them one prisoner—any man they asked for. 7 There was a prisoner named Barabbas jailed along with the rebels who had committed murder in the uprising. 8 When the crowd came up to press their demand that he honor the custom, 9 Pilate rejoined, "Do you want me to release the king of the Jews for you?" 10 He was aware, of course, that it was out of jealously that the chief priests had handed him over. 11 Meanwhile, the chief priests incited the crowd to have him release Barabbas instead. 12 Pilate again asked them, "What am I to do with the man you call the king of the Jews?" 13 They shouted back, "Crucify him!" 14 Pilate protested, "Why? What crime has he committed?" They only shouted the louder, "Crucify him!" 15 So Pilate, who wished to satisfy the crowd, released Barabbas to them; and after he had had Jesus scourged, he handed him over to be crucified.

The Crowning with Thorns

16 The soldiers now led Jesus away into the hall known as the praetorium; at the same time they assembled the whole cohort. 17 They dressed him in royal purple, then wove a crown of thorns and put it on him, 18 and began to salute him, "All hail! King of the Jews!" 19 Continually striking Jesus on the head with a reed and spitting at him, they genuflected before him and pretended to pay him homage. 20 When they had finished mocking him, they stripped him of the purple, dressed him in his own clothes, and led him out to crucify him.

The Way of the Cross: the Crucifixion

21 A man named Simon of Cyrene, the father of Alexander and Rufus, was coming in from the fields, and they pressed him into service to carry the cross. 22 When they brought Jesus to the site of Golgotha (which means "Skull Place"), 23 they tried to give him wine drugged with myrrh, but he would not take it. 24 Then they crucified him and divided up his garments by rolling dice for them to see what each should take. 25 It was about nine in the morning when they crucified him. 26 The inscription proclaiming his offense read, "THE KING OF THE JEWS."

27 With him they crucified two insurgents, one at his right and one at his left. 29 People going by kept insulting him, tossing their heads and saying, "Ha, ha! So you were going to destroy the temple and rebuild it in three days! 30 Save yourself now by coming down from the cross!" 31 The chief priests and the scribes also joined in and jeered: "He saved others but he cannot save himself! 32 Let the 'Messiah,' the 'king of Israel,' come down from that cross here and now so that we can see it and believe in him!" The men who had been crucified with him likewise kept taunting him.

Death of Jesus

33 When noon came, darkness fell on the whole countryside and lasted until midafternoon. 34 At that time Jesus cried in a loud voice, *"Eloi, Eloi, lama sabachthani?"* which means, "My God, my God, why have you forsaken me?" 35 A few of the bystanders who heard it remarked, "Listen! He is calling on Elijah!" 36 Someone ran off, and soaking a sponge in sour wine, stuck it on a reed to try to make him drink. The man said, "Now let's see whether Elijah comes to take him down."

37 Then Jesus, uttering a loud cry, breathed his last. 38 At that moment the curtain in the sanctuary was torn in two from top to bottom. 39 The centurion who stood guard over him, on seeing the manner of his death, declared, "Clearly this man was the Son of God!" 40 There were also women present looking on from a distance. Among them were Mary Magdalene, Mary the Mother of James the younger and Joses, and Salome. 41 These women had followed Jesus when he was in Galilee and attended to his needs. There were also many others who had come up with him to Jerusalem.

The Burial

42 As it grew dark (it was Preparation Day, that is, the eve of the sabbath), 43 Joseph from Arimathea arrived—a distinguished member of the Sanhedrin. He was another who looked forward to the reign of God. He was bold enough to seek an audience with Pilate and urgently requested the body of Jesus. 44 Pilate was surprised that Jesus should have died so soon. He summoned the centurion and inquired whether Jesus was already dead. 45 Learning from him that he was dead, Pilate released the corpse to Joseph. 46 Then, having bought a linen shroud, Joseph took him down, wrapped him in the linen, and laid him in a tomb which had been cut out of rock. Finally he rolled a stone across the entrance of the tomb. 47 Meanwhile, Mary Magdalene and Mary the mother of Joses observed where he had been laid.

The Women at the Tomb

16 When the sabbath was over, Mary Madalene, Mary the mother of James, and Salome bought perfumed oils with which they intended to go and anoint Jesus. 2 Very early, just after sunrise, on the first day of the week they came to the tomb. 3 They were saying to one another, "Who will roll back the stone for us from the entrance to the tomb?" 4 When they looked, they found that the stone had been rolled back. (It was a huge one.) 5 On entering the tomb they saw a young man sitting at the right, dressed in a white robe. 6 This frightened them thoroughly, but he reassured them: "You need not be amazed! You are looking for Jesus of Nazareth, the one who was crucified. He has been raised up; he is not here. See the place where they laid him. 7 Go now and tell his disciples and Peter, 'He is going ahead of you to Galilee, where you will see him just as he told you.'" 8 They made their way out and fled from the tomb bewildered and trembling; and because of their great fear, they said nothing to anyone.

The Longer Ending: 16, 9–20

9 Jesus rose from the dead early on the first day of the week. He first appeared to Mary Magdalene, out of whom he had cast seven demons. 10 She went to announce the good news to his followers, who were now grieving and weeping. 11 But when they heard that he was alive and had been seen by her, they refused to believe it. 12 Later on, as two of them were walking along on their way to the country, he was revealed to them completely changed in appearance. 13 These men retraced their steps and announced the good news to the others; but the others put no more faith in them than in Mary Magdalene. 14 Finally, as they were at table, Jesus was revealed to the Eleven. He took them to task for their disbelief and their stubbornness, since they put no faith in those who had seen him after he had been raised.

Then he told them: 15 "Go into the whole world and proclaim the good news to all creation. 16 The

---

15, 28: Omitted with many MSS.

16, 1–8: The purpose of this narrative is to show, in the mystery of Jesus' resurrection, the fulfillment of Jesus' prophecy before the Sanhedrin. The women find the tomb empty and an angel stationed there announces to them what has happened: *He has been raised up; he is not here.* They are told to proclaim the news to Peter and the disciples in order to prepare

them for a reunion with him. Mark's composition of the gospel ends at 16, 8 with the women silenced by the mystery. This abrupt termination causes many to believe that the original ending of this gospel may have been lost. See note on vv 9–20.

16, 9–20: This passage, termed "the longer ending" to the Marcan gospel by comparison with a much briefer conclusion found in some less important

manuscripts, has traditionally been accepted as an inspired part of the gospel. Early citations of it by the Fathers indicate that it was composed in the first century, although vocabulary and style argue strongly that it was written by someone other than Mark. It is a general résumé of the material concerning the appearances of the risen Jesus, reflecting, in particular, traditions found in Luke (24) and John (20).

man who believes in it and accepts baptism will be saved; the man who refuses to believe in it will be condemned. 17 Signs like these will accompany those who have professed their faith: they will use my name to expel demons, they will speak entirely new languages, 18 they will be able to handle serpents, they will be able to drink deadly poison without harm, and the sick upon whom they lay their hands will recover." 19 Then, after speaking to them, the Lord Jesus was taken up into heaven and took his seat at God's right hand. 20 The Eleven went forth and preached everywhere. The Lord continued to work with them throughout and confirm the message through the signs which accompanied them.

The Shorter Ending*

They promptly reported to Peter and his companions all that had been announced to them. Later on it was through them that Jesus himself sent out from east to west the sacred and immortal proclamation of eternal salvation.

The Freer Logion†

They offered this excuse: "This lawless and faithless age is under Satan, who does not allow what is unclean and dominated by spirits to grasp the true power of God. Therefore," they said to Christ, "reveal your just authority now." Christ replied: "The measure of the years of Satan's power has been fulfilled, but other terrible things are imminent. Yet it was for the sake of sinners that I was handed over to death, that they might return to the truth and sin no more, and inherit the spiritual and immortal glory of justification in heaven."

* Found after Mark 16, 8 before the Longer Ending, in some late Greek manuscripts as well as some ancient versions.

† Found after Mark 16, 14 in a fourth–fifth century manuscript preserved in the Freer Gallery of Art, Washington, D. C. This ending was known to St. Jerome.

THE GOSPEL ACCORDING TO

Luke

Preface

MANY have undertaken to compile a narrative of the events which have been fulfilled in our midst, 2 precisely as those events were transmitted to us by the original eyewitnesses and ministers of the word. 3 I too have carefully traced the whole sequence of events from the beginning, and have decided to set it in writing for you, Theophilus, 4 so that Your Excellency may see how reliable the instruction was that you received.

THE INFANCY NARRATIVE

Announcement of the Birth of John

5 In the days of Herod, king of Judea, there was a priest named Zechariah of the priestly class of Abijah; his wife was a descendant of Aaron named Elizabeth. 6 Both were just in the eyes of God, blamelessly following all the commandments and ordinances of the Lord. 7 They were childless, for Elizabeth was sterile; moreover, both were advanced in years.

8 Once, when it was the turn of Zechariah's class and he was fulfilling his functions as a priest before God, 9 it fell to him by lot according to priestly usage to enter the sanctuary of the Lord and offer incense. 10 While the full assembly of people was praying outside at the incense hour, 11 an angel of the Lord appeared to him, standing at the right of the altar of incense. 12 Zechariah was deeply disturbed upon seeing him, and overcome by fear.

13 The angel said to him: "Do not be frightened, Zechariah; your prayer has been heard. Your wife Elizabeth shall bear a son whom you shall name John. 14 Joy and gladness will be yours, and many will rejoice at his birth; 15 for he will be great in the eyes of the Lord. He will never drink wine or strong drink, and he will be filled with the Holy Spirit from his mother's womb. 16 Many of the sons of Israel will he bring back to the Lord their God. 17 God himself will go before him, in the spirit and power of Elijah, to turn the hearts of fathers to their children and the rebellious to the wisdom of the just, and to prepare for the Lord a people well-disposed."

18 Zechariah said to the angel: "How am I to know this? I am an old man; my wife too is advanced in age." 19 The angel replied: "I am Gabriel, who stand in attendance before God. I was sent to speak to you and bring you this good news. 20 But now you will be mute—unable to speak—until the day these things take place, because you have not

---

1, 5—2, 52: Beneath the simple beauty of Luke's infancy narrative there lies a remarkable depth of theological reflection. It centers about the similarity and the contrast between the religious mission of John the Baptizer and that of Jesus. By presenting the parallel announcements of their conception and birth (1, 5–25; 1, 26–38; 1, 57f; 2, 1–20) and the parallel narratives of their circumcision (1, 59–63; 2, 21), to which are added prophecies concerning the unique religious importance of Jesus (2, 22–40), the evangelist brings into sharp focus the transcendence of Jesus' person and mission over John's.

This parallelism in literary structure, along with the pervading use of Old Testament passages and ideas, conveys the basically theological character of the infancy gospel.

Mary is presented as the virgin divinely chosen in Israel to be the mother of Jesus and to experience the mystery and the spiritual benefits of his redemptive mission (1, 34–38.42.45–55; 2, 19.35.51). She is the prefiguration of the life and destiny of the Christian community.

1, 20: Though Zechariah's punishment is usually thought to have been due to unbelief in the angelic message concerning the child's conception, the sign he was asking for (1, 18) may have been some proof within his own lifetime of the child's future prophetic role.

trusted my words. They will all come true in due season." 21 Meanwhile, the people were waiting for Zechariah, wondering at his delay in the temple. 22 When he finally came out he was unable to speak to them, and they realized that he had seen a vision inside. He kept making signs to them, for he remained speechless.

23 Then, when his time of priestly service was over, he went home.

24 Afterward, his wife Elizabeth conceived. She went into seclusion for five months, saying: 25 "In these days the Lord is acting on my behalf; he has seen fit to remove my reproach among men."

Announcement of the Birth of Jesus

26 In the sixth month, the angel Gabriel was sent from God to a town of Galilee named Nazareth, 27 to a virgin betrothed to a man named Joseph, of the house of David. The virgin's name was Mary. 28 Upon arriving, the angel said to her: "Rejoice, O highly favored daughter! The Lord is with you. Blessed are you among women." 29 She was deeply troubled by his words, and wondered what his greeting meant. 30 The angel went on to say to her: "Do not fear, Mary. You have found favor with God. 31 You shall conceive and bear a son and give him the name Jesus. 32 Great will be his dignity and he will be called Son of the Most High. The Lord God will give him the throne of David his father. He will rule over the house of Jacob forever 33 and his reign will be without end."

34 Mary said to the angel, "How can this be since I do not know man?" 35 The angel answered her: "The Holy Spirit will come upon you and the power of the Most High will overshadow you; hence, the holy offspring to be born will be called Son of God. 36 Know that Elizabeth

your kinswoman has conceived a son in her old age; she who was thought to be sterile is now in her sixth month, 37 for nothing is impossible with God."

38 Mary said: "I am the servant of the Lord. Let it be done to me as you say." With that the angel left her.

The Visit

39 Thereupon Mary set out, proceeding in haste into the hill country to a town of Judah, 40 where she entered Zechariah's house and greeted Elizabeth. 41 When Elizabeth heard Mary's greeting, the baby leapt in her womb. Elizabeth was filled with the Holy Spirit 42 and cried out in a loud voice: "Blest are you among women and blest is the fruit of your womb. 43 But who am I that the mother of my Lord should come to me? 44 The moment your greeting sounded in my ears, the baby leapt in my womb for joy. 45 Blest is she who trusted that the Lord's words to her would be fulfilled."

Mary's Canticle

46 Then Mary said:

"My being proclaims the
    greatness of the Lord,
47   my spirit finds joy in God my
    savior,
48 For he has looked upon his
    servant in her lowliness;
    all ages to come shall call me
    blessed.
49 God who is mighty has done
    great things for me,
    holy is his name;
50 His mercy is from age to age
    on those who fear him.

51 He has shown might with his
    arm;
    he has confused the proud in
    their inmost thoughts.
52 He has deposed the mighty from
    their thrones

and raised the lowly to high
    places.
53 The hungry he has given every
    good thing,
    while the rich he has sent
    empty away.
54 He has upheld Israel his servant,
    ever mindful of his mercy;
55 Even as he promised our fathers,
    promised Abraham and his
    descendants forever."

56 Mary remained with Elizabeth about three months and then returned home.

57 When Elizabeth's time for delivery arrived, she gave birth to a son. 58 Her neighbors and relatives, upon hearing that the Lord had extended his mercy to her, rejoiced with her. 59 When they assembled for the circumcision of the child on the eighth day, they intended to name him after his father Zechariah. 60 At this his mother intervened, saying, "No, he is to be called John." 61 They pointed out to her, "None of your relatives has this name." 62 Then, using signs, they asked the father what he wished him to be called.

63 He signaled for a writing tablet and wrote the words, "His name is John." This astonished them all. 64 At that moment his mouth was opened and his tongue loosed, and he began to speak in praise of God.

65 Fear descended on all in the neighborhood; throughout the hill country of Judea these happenings began to be recounted to the last detail. 66 All who heard stored these things up in their hearts, saying, "What will this child be?" and, "Was not the hand of the Lord upon him?"

Zechariah's Canticle

67 Then Zechariah his father, filled with the Holy Spirit, uttered this prophecy:

1, 28: *Highly favored daughter:* Mary is to be the recipient of the divine favor, i.e., of the sanctifying power of God, in view of her office of mother of the Messiah, which the angel announces to her.

1, 30–34: The angel's message to Mary (30f) shows a certain similarity to the announcements made to some sterile women of the Old Testament who by God's intervention became the mothers of personages illustrious in salvation history: Sarah, mother of Isaac (Gn 17, 16.19); Samson's mother (Jgs 13, 2f);

Hannah, mother of Samuel (1 Sm 1, 9–20). Mary, however, who is betrothed but not yet married (27), cannot be called sterile. Her question, then, directs itself precisely to the issue of divine favor in her case (30–33). How is she to know that the child she is now to conceive will be the Son of the Most High?

1, 34: *I do not know man:* i.e., as husband. Scholars generally explain this verse as a literary form emphasizing the faith of the first-century church in the virginal conception and birth of the Messiah.

1, 35ff: The overshadowing of Mary recalls the cloud that covered with glory the Meeting Tent (Ex 40, 34f) and the temple of the Lord (1 Kgs 8, 10; Hg 2, 7). The descent of the Holy Spirit upon her, the designation of her child as Son of God, are further signs of God's favor. As a divine pledge of this, she is informed of the approaching maternity of her aged and hitherto sterile cousin Elizabeth.

68 "Blessed be the Lord the God of
  Israel
    because he has visited and
    ransomed his people.
69 He has raised a horn of saving
    strength for us
    in the house of David his
    servant,
70 As he promised through the
    mouths of his holy ones,
    the prophets of ancient times:
71 Salvation from our enemies
    and from the hands of all our
    foes.
72 He has dealt mercifully with our
    fathers
    and remembered the holy
    covenant he made,
73 The oath he swore to Abraham
    our father he would grant
    us:
74   that, rid of fear and delivered
    from the enemy,
75 We should serve him devoutly
    and through all our days
    be holy in his sight.
76 And you, O child, shall be called
    prophet of the Most High;
    For you shall go before the Lord
    to prepare straight paths for
    him,
77 Giving his people a knowledge
    of salvation
    in freedom from their sins.
78 All this is the work of the kind-
    ness of our God;
    he, the Dayspring, shall visit
    us in his mercy
79 To shine on those who sit in
    darkness and in the shadow
    of death,
    to guide our feet into the way
    of peace."

80 The child grew up and matured
in spirit. He lived in the desert until
the day when he made his public
appearance in Israel.

Birth of Jesus

2 In those days Caesar Augustus
published a decree ordering a
census of the whole world. 2 This
first census took place while Quirinius

was governor of Syria. 3 Everyone
went to register, each to his own
town. 4 And so Joseph went from
the town of Nazareth in Galilee to
Judea, to David's town of Bethlehem—because he was of the house
and lineage of David— 5 to register with Mary, his espoused wife,
who was with child.
6 While they were there the days
of her confinement were completed
7 She gave birth to her first-born son
and wrapped him in swaddling
clothes and laid him in a manger, because there was no room for them in
the place where travelers lodged.

The Shepherds

8 There were shepherds in that
locality, living in the fields and keeping night watch by turns over their
flocks. 9 The angel of the Lord
appeared to them as the glory of the
Lord shone around them, and they
were very much afraid. 10 The
angel said to them: "You have
nothing to fear! I come to proclaim
good news to you—tidings of great
joy to be shared by the whole people.
11 This day in David's city a savior
has been born to you, the Messiah
and Lord. 12 Let this be a sign to
you: in a manger you will find an
infant wrapped in swaddling clothes."
13 Suddenly, there was with the
angel a multitude of the heavenly
host, praising God and saying,

14 "Glory to God in high heaven,
    peace on earth to those on
    whom his favor rests."

15 When the angels had returned
to heaven, the shepherds said to one
another: "Let us go over to Bethlehem and see this event which the
Lord has made known to us." 16
They went in haste and found Mary
and Joseph, and the baby lying in the
manger; 17 once they saw, they
understood what had been told them
concerning this child. 18 All who
heard of it were astonished at the
report given them by the shepherds.

19 Mary treasured all these things
and reflected on them in her heart.
20 The shepherds returned, glorifying and praising God for all they had
heard and seen, in accord with what
had been told them.

Circumcision of Jesus

21 When the eighth day arrived
for his circumcision, the name Jesus
was given the child, the name the
angel had given him before he was
conceived.

Presentation in the Temple

22 When the day came to purify
them according to the law of Moses,
the couple brought him up to Jerusalem so that he could be presented to
the Lord, 23 for it is written in the
law of the Lord, "Every first-born
male shall be consecrated to the
Lord." 24 They came to offer in
sacrifice "a pair of turtledoves or two
young pigeons," in accord with the
dictate in the law of the Lord.

25 There lived in Jerusalem at the
time a certain man named Simeon.
He was just and pious, and awaited
the consolation of Israel, and the
Holy Spirit was upon him. 26 It
was revealed to him by the Holy
Spirit that he would not experience
death until he had seen the Anointed
of the Lord. 27 He came to the
temple now, inspired by the Spirit;
and when the parents brought in the
child Jesus to perform for him the
customary ritual of the law, 28 he
took him in his arms and blessed God
in these words:

29 "Now, Master, you can dismiss
    your servant in peace;
    you have fulfilled your word.
30 For my eyes have witnessed your
    , saving deed
31   displayed for all the peoples to
    see:
32 A revealing light to the Gentiles,
    the glory of your people
    Israel."

33 The child's father and mother

2, 1–5: Luke introduces the census to explain the
time of Jesus' birth at Bethlehem. Scholars interpret
inscriptions found near Tivoli in 1764, and at Antioch
in Pisidia in 1912, to point to Cyrinus as governor of
Syria between the years 10 and 8 B.C. The census may
well have been inaugurated by him and hence named
after him, even if continued and completed under
Saturninus, his successor (8–6 B.C.).

2, 7: *Her first-born son:* a reference to the preferen-
tial status of the eldest son rather than an implication
of subsequent offspring. In Israel the rights of primogeniture—authority, responsibility, succession—
accrued to the first-born. He was considered holy; he
belonged to God (Ex 13, 1f.14f; 22, 28; 34, 19f) and
had to be redeemed, i.e., ransomed by an offering of
five shekels made to the sanctuary (Nm 3, 47f; 18, 5f).

2, 14: *Those on whom his favor rests:* an illusion to
the mystery of divine election that bestows the gift of
faith upon people of divine choice. To these, the
messianic mission of Jesus also brings a special gift of
peace, the restored friendship between God and man.

were marveling at what was being said about him. 34 Simeon blessed them and said to Mary his mother: "This child is destined to be the downfall and the rise of many in Israel, a sign that will be opposed— 35 and you yourself shall be pierced with a sword—so that the thoughts of many hearts may be laid bare."

The Prophetess

36 There was also a certain prophetess, Anna by name, daughter of Phanuel of the tribe of Asher. She had seen many days, having lived seven years with her husband after her marriage 37 and then as a widow until she was eighty-four. She was constantly in the temple, worshipping day and night in fasting and prayer. 38 Coming on the scene at this moment, she gave thanks to God and talked about the child to all who looked forward to the deliverance of Jerusalem.

39 When the pair had fulfilled all the prescriptions of the law of the Lord, they returned to Galilee and their own town of Nazareth. 40 The child grew in size and strength, filled with wisdom, and the grace of God was upon him.

The Finding in the Temple

41 His parents used to go every year to Jerusalem for the feast of the Passover, 42 and when he was twelve they went up for the celebration as was their custom. 43 As they were returning at the end of the feast, the child Jesus remained behind unknown to his parents. 44 Thinking he was in the party, they continued their journey for a day, looking for him among their relatives and acquaintances.

45 Not finding him, they returned to Jerusalem in search of him. 46 On the third day they came upon him in the temple sitting in the midst of the teachers, listening to them and asking them questions. 47 All who heard him were amazed at his intelligence and his answers. 48 When his parents saw him they

were astonished, and his mother said to him: "Son, why have you done this to us? You see that your father and I have been searching for you in sorrow." 49 He said to them: "Why did you search for me? Did you not know I had to be in my Father's house?" 50 But they did not grasp what he said to them.

51 He went down with them then, and came to Nazareth, and was obedient to them. His mother meanwhile kept all these things in memory. 52 Jesus, for his part, progressed steadily in wisdom and age and grace before God and men.

PREPARATION FOR THE PUBLIC MINISTRY

John the Baptizer

3 In the fifteenth year of the rule of Tiberius Caesar, when Pontius Pilate was procurator of Judea, Herod tetrarch of Galilee, Philip his brother tetrarch of the region of Ituraea and Trachonitis, and Lysanias tetrarch of Abilene, 2 during the high-priesthood of Annas and Caiaphas, the word of God was spoken to John son of Zechariah in the desert. 3 He went about the entire region of the Jordan proclaiming a baptism of repentance which led to the forgiveness of sins, 4 as is written in the book of the words of Isaiah the prophet:

"A herald's voice in the desert, crying,
'Make ready the way of the Lord,
Clear him a straight path.
5 Every valley shall be filled
And every mountain and hill shall be leveled.
The windings shall be made straight
And the rough ways smooth,
6 And all mankind shall see the salvation of God.'"

7 He would say to the crowds that came out to be baptized by him: "You brood of vipers! Who told you

to flee from the wrath to come? 8 Give some evidence that you mean to reform. Do not begin by saying to yourselves, 'Abraham is our father.' I tell you, God can raise up children to Abraham from these stones. 9 Even now the ax is laid to the root of the tree. Every tree that is not fruitful will be cut down and thrown into the fire."

10 The crowds asked him, "What ought we to do?" 11 In reply he said, "Let the man with two coats give to him who has none. The man who has food should do the same."

12 Tax collectors also came to be baptized, and they said to him, "Teacher, what are we to do?" 13 He answered them, "Exact nothing over and above your fixed amount."

14 Soldiers likewise asked him, "What about us?" He told them, "Don't bully anyone. Denounce no one falsely. Be content with your pay."

15 The people were full of anticipation, wondering in their hearts whether John might be the Messiah. 16 John answered them all by saying: "I am baptizing you in water, but there is one to come who is mightier than I. I am not fit to loosen his sandal strap. He will baptize you in the Holy Spirit and in fire. 17 His winnowing-fan is in his hand to clear his threshing floor and gather the wheat into his granary; but the chaff he will burn in unquenchable fire." 18 Using exhortations of this sort, he preached the good news to the people.

19 Herod the tetrarch was censured by John on the subject of Herodias, his brother's wife, and for all his other crimes. 20 He added to his guilt by shutting John up in prison.

Baptism of Jesus

21 When all the people were baptized, and Jesus was at prayer after likewise being baptized, the skies opened 22 and the Holy Spirit descended on him in visible form like a dove. A voice from heaven was heard

---

3, 1: *In the fifteenth year . . . Caesar:* this chronological datum enables scholars to calculate that John the Baptizer began his mission sometime between A.D. 27 and 29.

3, 2–18: See the notes on the verses in Mt 3, 1–17.

The Lucan account of the Baptizer's mission gives examples which clarify the meaning of repentance (3, 10–14).

3, 15: This popular conception concerning John the Baptizer closely resembles that in John 1, 20.25.

3, 21f: See note on Mk 1, 9ff.

3, 23–38: Luke traces the genealogy of Jesus to Adam in order to identify Jesus with all humanity; Matthew (1, 1–16) traces it to Abraham to identify Jesus with Israel.

to say: "You are my beloved Son. On you my favor rests."

Genealogy of Jesus

23 When Jesus began his work he was about thirty years of age, being—so it was supposed—the son of Joseph, son of Heli, 24 son of Matthat, son of Levi, son of Melchi, son of Jannai, son of Joseph, 25 son of Mattathias, son of Amos, son of Nahum, son of Esli, son of Naggai, 26 son of Maath, son of Mattathias, son of Semein, son of Josech, son of Joda, 27 son of Joanan, son of Rhesa, son of Zerubbabel, son of Shealtiel, son of Neri, 28 son of Melchi, son of Addi, son of Cosam, son of Elmadam, son of Er, 29 son of Joshua, son of Eliezer, son of Jorim, son of Matthat, son of Levi, 30 son of Simeon, son of Judah, son of Joseph, son of Jonam, son of Eliakim, 31 son of Melea, son of Menna, son of Mattatha, son of Nathan, son of David, 32 son of Jesse, son of Obed, son of Boaz, son of Sala, son of Nahshon, 33 son of Amminadab, son of Admin, son of Arni, son of Hezron, son of Perez, son of Judah, 34 son of Jacob, son of Isaac, son of Abraham, son of Terah, son of Nahor, 35 son of Serug, son of Reu, son of Peleg, son of Eber, son of Shelah, 36 son of Cainan, son of Arphaxad, son of Shem, son of Noah, son of Lamech, 37 son of Methuselah, son of Enoch, son of Jared, son of Mahalaleel, son of Cainan, 38 son of Enos, son of Seth, son of Adam, son of God.

Temptation in the Desert

4 Jesus, full of the Holy Spirit, then returned from the Jordan and was conducted by the Spirit into the desert 2 for forty days, where he was tempted by the devil. During that time he ate nothing, and at the end of it he was hungry. 3 The devil said to him, "If you are the Son of God, command this stone to turn into bread." 4 Jesus answered him, "Scripture has it, 'Not on bread alone shall man live.'"

5 Then the devil took him up higher and showed him all the kingdoms of the world in a single instant. 6 He said to him, "I will give you all this power and the glory of these kingdoms; the power has been given to me and I give it to whomever I wish. 7 Prostrate yourself in homage before me, and it shall all be yours." 8 In reply, Jesus said to him, "Scripture has it,

'You shall do homage to the
     Lord your God;
   him alone shall you adore.'"

9 Then the devil led him to Jerusalem, set him on the parapet of the temple, and said to him, "If you are the Son of God, throw yourself down from here, 10 for Scripture has it,

'He will bid his angels watch over
     you';

11 and again,

'With their hands they will
     support you,
  that you may never stumble
     on a stone.'"

12 Jesus said to him in reply, "It also says, 'You shall not put the Lord your God to the test.'"
13 When the devil had finished all the tempting he left him, to await another opportunity.

THE MINISTRY IN GALILEE

Beginning of Preaching

14 Jesus returned in the power of the Spirit to Galilee, and his reputation spread throughout the region. 15 He was teaching in their synagogues, and all were loud in his praise.
16 He came to Nazareth where he had been reared, and entering the synagogue on the sabbath as he was in the habit of doing, he stood up to do the reading. 17 When the book of the prophet Isaiah was handed him, he unrolled the scroll and found the passage where it was written:

18 "The spirit of the Lord is upon
     me;

therefore he has anointed me.
He has sent me to bring glad
     tidings to the poor,
  to proclaim liberty to captives,
Recovery of sight to the blind
     and release to prisoners,
19 To announce a year of favor
     from the Lord."

20 Rolling up the scroll he gave it back to the assistant and sat down. All in the synagogue had their eyes fixed on him. 21 Then he began by saying to them, "Today this Scripture passage is fulfilled in your hearing." 22 All who were present spoke favorably of him; they marveled at the appealing discourse which came from his lips. They also asked, "Is not this Joseph's son?"
23 He said to them, "You will doubtless quote me the proverb, 'Physician, heal yourself,' and say, 'Do here in your own country the things we have heard you have done in Capernaum.' 24 But in fact," he went on, "no prophet gains acceptance in his native place. 25 Indeed, let me remind you, there were many widows in Israel in the days of Elijah when the heavens remained closed for three and a half years and a great famine spread over the land. 26 It was to none of these that Elijah was sent, but to a widow of Zarephath near Sidon. 27 Recall, too, the many lepers in Israel in the time of Elisha the prophet; yet not one was cured except Naaman the Syrian."
28 At these words the whole audience in the synagogue was filled with indignation. 29 They rose up and expelled him from the town, leading him to the brow of the hill on which it was built and intending to hurl him over the edge. 30 But he went straight through their midst and walked away.

Jesus teaches in Capernaum

31 He then went down to Capernaum, a town of Galilee, where he began instructing them on the sabbath day. 32 They were spell-bound by his teaching, for his words had authority.

4, 1–13: See note on Mt 4, 1–11.

4, 14–30: After noting Jesus' initial popularity throughout Galilee, Luke combines, into a single scene laid at Nazareth, the favorable reception given

his announcement of the arrival of the messianic era (16–22), the objections to him which Jesus senses in the attitude of his townsmen (23–27; see note on Mk 6, 1–6), and their personal attack on him for refusing

to work many miracles for them because of their lack of faith (28ff). Luke intends the entire scene to be prophetic of the ultimate rejection of Jesus by his contemporaries.

Cure of a Demoniac

33 In the synagogue there was a man with an unclean spirit, who shrieked in a loud voice: 34 "Leave us alone! What do you want of us, Jesus of Nazareth? Have you come to destroy us? I know who you are: the Holy One of God." 35 Jesus said to him sharply, "Be quiet! Come out of him." At that, the demon threw him to the ground before everyone's eyes and came out of him without doing him any harm. 36 All were struck with astonishment, and they began saying to one another: "What is there about his speech? He commands the unclean spirits with authority and power, and they leave." 37 His renown kept spreading through the surrounding country.

38 Leaving the synagogue, he entered the house of Simon. Simon's mother-in-law was in the grip of a severe fever, and they interceded with him for her 39 He stood over her and addressed himself to the fever, and it left her. She got up immediately and waited on them.

40 At sunset all who had people sick with a variety of diseases took them to him, and he laid hands on each of them and cured them. 41 Demons departed from many, crying out as they did so, "You are the son of God!" He rebuked them and did not allow them to speak because they knew that he was the Messiah.

42 The next morning he left the town and set out into the open country. The crowds went in search of him, and when they found him they tried to keep him from leaving them. 43 But he said to them, "To other towns I must announce the good news of the reign of God, because that is why I was sent." 44 And he continued to preach in the synagogues of Judea.

Call of the First Disciples

5 As he stood by the Lake of Gennesaret, and the crowd pressed in on him to hear the word of God, 2 he saw two boats moored by the side of the lake; the fishermen had disembarked and were washing their nets. 3 He got into one of the boats, the one belonging to Simon, and asked him to pull out a short distance from the shore; then, remaining seated, he continued to teach the crowds from the boat. 4 When he had finished speaking he said to Simon, "Put out into deep water and lower your nets for a catch." 5 Simon answered, "Master, we have been hard at it all night long and have caught nothing; but if you say so, I will lower the nets." 6 Upon doing this they caught such a great number of fish that their nets were at the breaking point. 7 They signaled to their mates in the other boat to come and help them. These came, and together they filled the two boats until they nearly sank.

8 At the sight of this, Simon Peter fell at the knees of Jesus saying, "Leave me, Lord. I am a sinful man." 9 For indeed, amazement at the catch they had made seized him and all his shipmates, 10 as well as James and John, Zebedee's sons, who were partners with Simon. Jesus said to Simon, "Do not be afraid. From now on you will be catching men." 11 With that they brought their boats to land, left everything, and became his followers.

Cure of a Leper

12 On one occasion in a certain town, a man full of leprosy came to him. Seeing Jesus, he bowed down to the ground and said to him, "Lord, if you will to do so, you can cure me." 13 Jesus stretched out his hand to touch him and said, "I do will it. Be cured." Immediately the leprosy left him. 14 Jesus then instructed the man: "Tell no one, but go and show yourself to the priest. Offer for your healing what Moses prescribed; that should be a proof for them." 15 His reputation spread more and more, and great crowds gathered to hear him and to be cured of their maladies. 16 He often retired to deserted places and prayed.

A Paralyzed Man Cured

17 One day Jesus was teaching, and the power of the Lord made him heal. Sitting close by were Pharisees and teachers of the law who had come from every village of Galilee and from Judea and Jerusalem. 18 Some men came along carrying a paralytic on a mat. They were trying to bring him in and lay him before Jesus; 19 but they found no way of getting him through because of the crowd, so they went up on the roof. There they let him down with his mat through the tiles into the middle of the crowd before Jesus. 20 Seeing their faith, Jesus said, "My friend, your sins are forgiven you."

21 The scribes and the Pharisees began a discussion, saying: "Who is this man who utters blasphemies? Who can forgive sins but God alone?" 22 Jesus, however, knew their reasoning and answered them by saying: "Why do you harbor these thoughts? 23 Which is easier: to say, 'Your sins are forgiven you,' or to say, 'Get up and walk'? 24 In any case, to make it clear to you that the Son of Man has authority on earth to forgive sins"—he then addressed the paralyzed man: "I say to you, get up! Take your mat with you, and return to your house."

25 At once the man stood erect before them. He picked up the mat he had been lying on and went home praising God. 26 At this they were all seized with astonishment. Full of awe, they gave praise to God, saying, "We have seen incredible things today!"

The Call of Levi

27 Afterward he went out and saw a tax collector named Levi sitting at his customs post. He said to him, "Follow me." 28 Leaving everything behind, Levi stood up and became his follower. 29 After that Levi gave a great reception for Jesus in his house, in which he was joined by a large crowd of tax collectors and others at dinner. 30 The Pharisees and the scribes of their party said to his disciples, "Why do you eat and drink with tax collectors and nonobservers of the law?" 31 Jesus said to them, "The healthy do not

---

4, 33–37: See note on Mk 1, 23–28.

5, 1–11: This scene of the miraculous catch of fish parallels the call of the disciples in Mt 4, 18–22; Mk 1, 16–20. Probably it is related to the miraculous catch after the resurrection, mentioned in Jn 21, 1–8, to which it bears a certain affinity. The final mandate which the risen Christ gave Simon Peter and the other disciples is here anticipated by Luke in an account which portrays Simon's leadership of the disciples and their role of continuing the spiritual mission of Jesus.

5, 12ff: see note on Mk 1, 40–45.

5, 17–26: see note on Mk 2, 1–12.

need a doctor; sick people do. 32 I have not come to invite the self-righteous to a change of heart, but sinners."

The Question of Fasting

33 They said to him: "John's disciples fast frequently and offer prayers; the disciples of the Pharisees do the same. Yours, on the contrary, eat and drink freely." 34 Jesus replied: "Can you make guests of the groom fast while the groom is still with them? 35 But when the days come that the groom is removed from their midst, they will surely fast in those days."

36 He then proposed to them this figure: "No one tears a piece from a new coat to patch an old one. If he does, he will only tear the new coat, and the piece taken from it will not match the old. 37 Moreover, no one pours new wine into old wine-skins. Should he do so, the new wine will burst the old skins, the wine will spill out, and the skins will be lost. 38 New wine should be poured into fresh skins. 39 No one, after drinking old wine, wants new. He says, 'I find the old wine better.'"

The Disciples and the Sabbath

6 Once on a sabbath Jesus was walking through the standing grain. His disciples were pulling off grain-heads, shelling them with their hands, and eating them. 2 Some of the Pharisees asked, "Why are you doing what is prohibited on the sabbath?" 3 Jesus said to them: "Have you not read what David did when he and his men were hungry— 4 how he entered God's house and took and ate the holy bread and gave it to his men, even though only priests are allowed to eat it?" 5 Then he said to them, "The Son of Man is Lord even of the sabbath."

6 On another sabbath he came to teach in a synagogue where there was a man whose right hand was withered. 7 The scribes and Pharisees were on the watch to see if he

would perform a cure on the sabbath so that they could find a charge against him. 8 He knew their thoughts, however, and said to the man whose hand was withered, "Get up and stand here in front." The man rose and remained standing. 9 Jesus said to them, "I ask you, is it lawful to do good on the sabbath— or evil? To preserve life—or destroy it?" 10 He looked around at them all and said to the man, "Stretch out your hand." The man did so and his hand was perfectly restored.

11 At this they became frenzied and began asking one another what could be done to Jesus.

Choice of the Twelve

12 Then he went out to the mountain to pray, spending the night in communion with God. 13 At day-break he called his disciples and selected twelve of them to be his apostles: 14 Simon, to whom he gave the name Peter, and Andrew his brother, James and John, Philip and Bartholomew, 15 Matthew and Thomas, James son of Alphaeus, and Simon called the Zealot, 16 Judas son of James, and Judas Iscariot, who turned traitor.

The Great Discourse

17 Coming down the mountain with them, he stopped at a level stretch where there were many of his disciples; a large crowd of people was with them from all Judea and Jerusalem and the coast of Tyre and Sidon, 18 people who came to hear him and be healed of their diseases. Those who were troubled with un-clean spirits were cured; 19 indeed, the whole crowd was trying to touch him because power went out from him which cured all. 20 Then, raising his eyes to his disciples, he said:

　"Blest are you poor; the reign
　　of God is yours.
21 Blest are you who hunger; you
　　shall be filled.

　Blest are you who are weeping;
　　you shall laugh.

22 "Blest shall you be when men hate you, when they ostracize you and insult you and proscribe your name as evil because of the Son of Man. 23 On the day they do so, rejoice and exult, for your reward shall be great in heaven. Thus it was that their fathers treated the prophets.

24 "But woe to you rich, for your
　　consolation is now.
25 Woe to you who are full; you
　　shall go hungry.
　Woe to you who laugh now;
　　you shall weep in your
　　grief.

26 "Woe to you when all speak well of you. Their fathers treated the false prophets in just this way.

Love of One's Enemy

27 "To you who hear me, I say: Love your enemies, do good to those who hate you; 28 bless those who curse you and pray for those who maltreat you. 29 When someone slaps you on one cheek, turn and give him the other; when someone takes your coat, let him have your shirt as well. 30 Give to all who beg from you. When a man takes what is yours, do not demand it back. 31 Do to others what you would have them do to you. 32 If you love those who love you, what credit is that to you? Even sinners love those who love them, 33 If you do good to those who do good to you, how can you claim any credit? Sinners do as much. 34 If you lend to those from whom you expect repayment, what merit is there in it for you? Even sinners lend to sinners, expecting to be repaid in full.

35 "Love your enemy and do good; lend without expecting repay-ment. Then will your recompense be great. You will rightly be called sons of the Most High, since he himself is good to the ungrateful and the wicked. 36 "Be compassionate, as your

---

5, 33–39: See note on Mt 9, 14–17.
6, 1–5: See note on Mt 12, 3–6.
6, 6–11: See note on Mt 12, 10.
6, 12–16: See note on Mk 3, 13–19.
6, 20–49: The Lucan Sermon on the Plain charac-terizes the Christian as distinctive for his poverty (20–23), cautious against the dangers of wealth (24f),

loving toward his enemy (27–38), critical of himself (39–45), and obedient to the teaching of Jesus (46–49). It is reasonable to assume that this Lucan arrange-ment of Jesus' teaching was addressed to the econo-mically deprived and politically threatened Christian communities of Asia Minor and Greece. It thus possesses a special poignancy, born of Luke's faith

in the inevitable victory of the Christian message in a hostile environment, provided Christians accept their poverty in the spirit of Christ and endeavor to con-quer their persecutors by the love they show them. The sermon seems to intimate a relevance between the actual situation of the Christian communities it addresses and the teaching of Jesus.

Father is compassionate. 37 Do not judge, and you will not be judged. Do not condemn, and you will not be condemned. Pardon, and you shall be pardoned. 38 Give, and it shall be given to you. Good measure pressed down, shaken together, running over, will they pour into the fold of your garment. For the measure you measure with will be measured back to you."

39 He also used images in speaking to them: "Can a blind man act as guide to a blind man? Will they not both fall into a ditch? 40 A student is not above his teacher; but every student when he has finished his studies will be on a par with his teacher.

41 "Why look at the speck in your brother's eye when you miss the plank in your own? 42 How can you say to your brother, 'Brother, let me remove the speck from your eye,' yet fail yourself to see the plank lodged in your own? Hypocrite, remove the plank from your own eye first; then you will see clearly enough to remove the speck from your brother's eye.

43 'A good tree does not produce decayed fruit any more than a decayed tree produces good fruit. 44 Each tree is known by its yield. Figs are not taken from thornbushes, nor grapes picked from brambles. 45 A good man produces goodness from the good in his heart; an evil man produces evil out of his store of evil. Each man speaks from his heart's abundance. 46 Why do you call me 'Lord, Lord,' and not put into practice what I teach you? 47 Any man who desires to come to me will hear my words and put them into practice. I will show you with whom he is to be compared. 48 He may be likened to the man who, in building a house, dug deeply and laid the foundation on a rock. When the floods came the torrent rushed in on that house, but failed to shake it because of its solid foundation. 49 On the other hand, anyone who has heard my words but not put them into practice is like the man who

built his house on the ground without any foundation. When the torrent rushed upon it, it immediately fell in and was completely destroyed."

Cure of the Centurion's Servant

7 When he had finished this discourse in the hearing of the people, he entered Capernaum. 2 A centurion had a servant he held in high regard, who was at that moment sick to the point of death. 3 When he heard about Jesus he sent some Jewish elders to him, asking him to come and save the life of his servant.

4 Upon approaching Jesus they petitioned him earnestly. 5 "He deserves this favor from you," they said, "because he loves our people, and even built our synagogue for us." 6 Jesus set out with them. When he was only a short distance from the house, the centurion sent friends to tell him: "Sir, do not trouble yourself, for I am not worthy to have you enter my house. 7 That is why I did not presume to come to you myself. Just give the order and my servant will be cured. 8 I too am a man who knows the meaning of an order, having soldiers under my command. I say to one, 'On your way,' and off he goes; to another, 'Come here,' and he comes; to my slave, 'Do this,' and he does it." 9 Jesus showed amazement on hearing this, and turned to the crowd which was following him to say, "I tell you, I have never found so much faith among the Israelites." 10 When the deputation returned to the house, they found the servant in perfect health.

The Widow's Son

11 Soon afterward he went to a town called Naim, and his disciples and a large crowd accompanied him. 12 As he approached the gate of the town a dead man was being carried out, the only son of a widowed mother. A considerable crowd of townsfolk were with her. 13 The Lord was moved with pity upon seeing her and said to her, "Do not cry." 14 Then he stepped forward

and touched the litter; at this, the bearers halted. He said, "Young man, I bid you get up." 15 The dead man sat up and began to speak. Then Jesus gave him back to his mother. 16 Fear seized them all and they began to praise God. "A great prophet has risen among us," they said; and, "God has visited his people." 17 This was the report that spread about him throughout Judea and the surrounding country.

Jesus' Testimony

18 The disciples of John brought their teacher word of all these happenings. 19 Summoning two of them, John sent them to ask the Lord, "Are you 'He who is to come' or are we to expect someone else?" 20 When the men came to him they said, "John the Baptizer sends us to you with this question: 'Are you "He who is to come" or do we look for someone else?'" 21 (At that time he was curing many of their diseases, afflictions, and evil spirits; he also restored sight to many who were blind.) 22 Jesus gave this response: "Go and report to John what you have seen and heard. The blind recover their sight, cripples walk, lepers are cured, the deaf hear, dead men are raised to life, and the poor have the good news preached to them. 23 Blest is that man who finds no stumbling block in me."

24 When the messengers of John had set off, Jesus began to speak about him to the crowds. "What did you go out to see in the desert—a reed swayed by the wind? 25 What, really, did you go out to see—someone dressed luxuriously? Remember, those who dress in luxury and eat in splendor are to be found in royal palaces. 26 Then what did you go out to see—a prophet? He is that, I assure you, and something more. 27 This is the man of whom Scripture says,

'I send my messenger ahead of you
to prepare your way before you.'

28 I assure you, there is no man born

7, 1–10: The placement of this event after the Sermon on the Plain (6, 46–49) serves as an example of that practical acknowledgment of Jesus' authority which is recommended at the conclusion of the sermon.

7, 11–17: This account of the raising to life of the widow's son prepares for Jesus' response about his ministry, made to the inquiring disciples of John the Baptizer (20.22). The observation in 7, 15, *Jesus gave*

him back to his mother relates the mission of Jesus to that of Elijah (1 Kgs 17, 23).
7, 18–23: See note on Mt 11, 3.
7, 24–35: See notes on Mt 11, 7–15; 11, 11; 11, 19.

of woman greater than John. Yet the least born into the kingdom of God is greater than he."

John's Baptism

29 The entire populace that had heard Jesus, even the tax collectors, gave praise to God, for they had received from John the baptismal bath he administered. 30 The Pharisees and the lawyers, on the other hand, by failing to receive his baptism defeated God's plan in their regard.

Christ's Verdict

31 "What comparison can I use for the men of today? What are they like? 32 They are like children squatting in the city squares and calling to their playmates,

'We piped you a tune but you
did not dance,
We sang you a dirge but you did
not wail.'

33 I mean that John the Baptizer came neither eating bread nor drinking wine, and you say, 'He is mad!' 34 The Son of Man came and he both ate and drank, and you say, 'Here is a glutton and a drunkard, a friend of tax collectors and sinners!' 35 God's wisdom is vindicated by all who accept it."

The Penitent Woman

36 There was a certain Pharisee who invited Jesus to dine with him. Jesus went to the Pharisee's home and reclined to eat. 37 A woman known in the town to be a sinner learned that he was dining in the Pharisee's home. She brought in a vase of perfumed oil 38 and stood behind him at his feet, weeping so that her tears fell upon his feet. Then she wiped them with her hair, kissing them and perfuming them with the oil. 39 When his host, the Pharisee, saw this, he said to himself, "If this man were a prophet, he would know who and what sort of woman this is that touches him—that she is a sinner." 40 In answer to his thoughts, Jesus said to him, "Simon, I have some-

thing to propose to you." "Teacher," he said, "speak."

41 "Two men owed money to a certain money-lender; one owed a total of five hundred coins, the other fifty. 42 Since neither was able to repay, he wrote off both debts. Which of them was more grateful to him?" 43 Simon answered, "He, I presume, to whom he remitted the larger sum." Jesus said to him, "You are right."

44 Turning then to the woman, he said to Simon: "You see this woman? I came to your home and you provided me with no water for my feet. She has washed my feet with her tears and wiped them with her hair. 45 You gave me no kiss, but she has not ceased kissing my feet since I entered. You did not anoint my head with oil, but she has anointed my feet with perfume. 47 I tell you, that is why her many sins are forgiven—because of her great love. Little is forgiven the one whose love is small."

48 He said to her then, "Your sins are forgiven"; 49 at which his fellow guests began to ask among themselves, "Who is this that he even forgives sins?" 50 Meanwhile he said to the woman, "Your faith has been your salvation. Now go in peace."

The Women Who Served

8 After this he journeyed through towns and villages preaching and proclaiming the good news of the kingdom of God. The Twelve accompanied him, 2 and also some women who had been cured of evil spirits and maladies: Mary called the Magdalene, from whom seven devils had gone out, 3 Joanna, the wife of Herod's steward Chuza, Susanna, and many others who were assisting them out of their means.

Parable of the Sower

4 A large crowd was gathering, with people resorting to him from one town after another. He spoke to them in a parable: 5 "A farmer

went out to sow some seed. In the sowing, some fell on the footpath where it was walked on and the birds of the air ate it up. 6 Some fell on rocky ground, sprouted up, then withered through lack of moisture. 7 Some fell among briers, and the thorns growing up with it stifled it. 8 But some fell on good soil, grew up, and yielded grain a hundredfold."

As he said this he exclaimed: "Let everyone who has ears attend to what he has heard." 9 His disciples began asking him what the meaning of this parable might be. 10 He replied, "To you the mysteries of the reign of God have been confided, but to the rest in parables that,

'Seeing they may not perceive,
and hearing they may not understand.'

11 This is the meaning of the parable. The seed is the word of God. 12 Those on the footpath are people who hear, but the devil comes and takes the word out of their hearts lest they believe and be saved. 13 Those on the rocky ground are the ones who, when they hear the word, receive it with joy. They have no root; they believe for a while, but fall away in time of temptation. 14 The seed fallen among briers are those who hear, but their progress is stifled by the cares and riches and pleasures of life and they do not mature. 15 The seed on good ground are those who hear the word in a spirit of openness, retain it, and bear fruit through perseverance.

Parable of the Lamp

16 "No one lights a lamp and puts it under a bushel basket or under a bed; he puts it on a lampstand so that whoever comes in can see it. 17 There is nothing hidden that will not be exposed, nothing concealed that will not be known and brought to light. 18 Take heed, therefore, how you hear: to the man who has, more will be given; and he who has not, will lose even the little he thinks he has."

7, 36–50: Jesus admits both the gravity of the woman's sins and the relative justice of Simon. But he points out her superiority to the Pharisee, for she expresses the love that stems from repentance, whereas Simon's pride prevents him from acknowledging his real, though lesser, sinfulness.

8, 1ff: Luke notes Jesus' acceptance of the aid of women during his ministry. The evangelist probably also has in mind their contributions to the early Christian communities.
8, 4–15: On the meaning of the parable of the sower and its explanation, see the note on Mt 13, 1–53.

8, 19ff: This passage is to be understood in the light of Luke's theological conception of the mother of Jesus as the figure or type of the Christian community. She acquiesces fully, as the Christian should, to the mystery of God's word; cf 1, 38.

True Kindred of Jesus

19 His mother and brothers came to be with him, but they could not reach him because of the crowd. 20 He was told, "Your mother and your brothers are standing outside and they wish to see you." 21 He told them in reply, "My mother and my brothers are those who hear the word of God and act upon it."

Calming of the Tempest

22 One day he got into a boat with his disciples and said to them, "Let us cross over to the far side of the lake." So they set out, 23 and as they sailed he slept. A windstorm descended on the lake, and they began to ship water and to be in danger. 24 They came to awaken him, saying, "Master, master, we are lost!" He awoke and rebuked the wind and the tumultuous waves. The waves subsided and it grew calm. 25 Then he asked them, "Where is your faith?" Filled with fear and admiration, they said to one another, "What sort of man can this be who commands even the winds and the sea and they obey him?"

The Gerasene Demoniac

26 They sailed to the country of the Gerasenes, which is opposite Galilee. 27 When he came to land, he was met by a man from the town who was possessed by demons. For a long time he had not worn any clothes; he did not live in a house, but among the tombstones. 28 On seeing Jesus he began to shriek; then he fell at his feet and exclaimed at the top of his voice, "Jesus, Son of God Most High, why do you meddle with me? Do not torment me, I beg you." 29 By now Jesus was ordering the unclean spirit to come out of the man. This spirit had taken hold of him many a time. The man used to be tied with chains and fetters, but he would break his bonds and the demon would drive him into places of solitude. 30 "What is your name?" Jesus demanded. "Legion," he answered, because the demons who had entered him were many. 31 They pleaded with him not to order them back to the abyss. 32 It happened that a large herd of swine was feeding nearby on the hillside, and the demons asked him to permit them to enter the swine. This he granted. 33 The demons then came out of the man and entered the swine, and the herd charged down the bluff into the lake, where they drowned.

34 When the swineherds saw what had happened, they took to their heels and brought the news to the town and country roundabout. 35 The people went out to see for themselves what had happened. Coming on Jesus, they found the man from whom the devils had departed sitting at his feet dressed and in his full senses; this sight terrified them. 36 They were told by witnesses how the possessed man had been cured. 37 Shortly afterward, the entire population of the Gerasene territory asked Jesus to leave their neighborhood, for a great fear had seized them; so he got into the boat and went back across the lake.

38 The man from whom the devils had departed asked to come with him, 39 but he sent him away with the words, "Go back home and recount all that God has done for you." The man went all through the town making public what Jesus had done for him.

Jairus' Child; a Hemorrhage Victim

40 On his return, Jesus was welcomed by the crowd; indeed, they were all waiting for him. 41 A man named Jairus, who was chief of the synagogue, came up and fell at Jesus' feet, begging that he come to his home 42 because his only daughter, a girl of about twelve, was dying. As Jesus went, the crowds almost crushed him. 43 A woman with a hemorrhage of twelve years' duration, incurable at any doctor's hands, 44 came up behind him and touched the tassel on his cloak. Immediately her bleeding stopped. 45 Jesus asked, "Who touched me?" Everyone disclaimed doing it, while Peter said, "Lord, the crowds are milling and pressing around you!" 46 Jesus insisted, "Someone touched me; I know that power has gone forth from me." 47 When the woman saw that her act had not gone unnoticed, she came forward trembling. Falling at his feet, she related before the whole assemblage why she had touched him and how she had been instantly cured. 48 Jesus said to her, "Daughter, it is your faith that has cured you. Now go in peace."

49 He was still speaking when a man came from the ruler's house with the announcement, "Your daughter is dead; do not bother the Teacher further." 50 Jesus heard this, and his response was: "Fear is useless; what is needed is trust and her life will be spared." 51 Once he had arrived at the house, he permitted no one to enter with him except Peter, John, James, and the child's parents. 52 While everyone wept and lamented her, he said, "Stop crying for she is not dead but asleep." 53 They laughed at him, being certain she was dead. 54 He took her by the hand and spoke these words: "Get up, child." 55 The breath of life returned to her and she got up immediately; whereupon he told them to give her something to eat. 56 Her parents were astounded, but he ordered them not to tell anyone what had happened.

Mission of the Twelve

9 Jesus now called the Twelve together and gave them power and authority to overcome all demons and to cure diseases. 2 He sent them forth to proclaim the reign of God and heal the afflicted. 3 Jesus advised them: "Take nothing for the journey, neither walking staff nor traveling bag; no bread, no money. No one is to have two coats. 4 Stay at whatever house you enter and proceed from there. 5 When people will not receive you, leave that town and shake its dust from your feet as a testimony against them." 6 So they set out and went from village to village, spreading the good news everywhere and curing diseases.

Herod Learns of Jesus

7 Herod the tetrarch heard of all that was happening and was perplexed, for some were saying, "John

---

8, 22–25: See note on Mk 4, 35–41.
8, 26–39: See note on Mk 1, 23–28 concerning the exorcisms performed by Jesus.
8, 40–56: See note on Mk 5, 21–43.

has been raised from the dead"; 8 others, "Elijah has appeared"; and still others, "One of the prophets of old has risen." 9 But Herod said, "John I beheaded. Who is this man about whom I hear all these reports?" He was very curious to see him.

Multiplication of the Loaves

10 The apostles on their return related to Jesus all they had accomplished. Taking them with him, he retired to a town called Bethsaida, 11 but the crowds found this out and followed him. He received them and spoke to them of the reign of God, and he healed all who were in need of healing.

12 As sunset approached the Twelve came and said to him, "Dismiss the crowd so that they can go into the villages and farms in the neighborhood and find themselves lodging and food, for this is certainly an out-of-the-way place." 13 He answered them, "Why do you not give them something to eat yourselves?" They replied, "We have nothing but five loaves and two fish. Or shall we ourselves go and buy food for all these people?" 14 (There were about five thousand men.) Jesus said to his disciples, "Have them sit down in groups of fifty or so." 15 They followed his instructions and got them all seated. 16 Then, taking the five loaves and the two fish, Jesus raised his eyes to heaven, pronounced a blessing over them, broke them, and gave them to his disciples for distribution to the crowd. 17 They all ate until they had enough. What they had left, over and above, filled twelve baskets.

Peter's Profession of Faith

18 One day when Jesus was praying in seclusion and his disciples were with him, he put the question to them, "Who do the crowds say that I am?" "John the Baptizer," 19 they replied, "and some say Elijah, while others claim that one of the prophets of old has returned from the dead." 20 "But you—who do

you say that I am?" he asked them. Peter said in reply, "The Messiah of God." 21 He strictly forbade them to tell this to anyone. 22 "The Son of Man," he said, "must first endure many sufferings, be rejected by the elders, the high priests and the scribes, and be put to death, and then be raised up on the third day."

Conditions of Discipleship

23 Jesus said to all: "Whoever wishes to be my follower must deny his very self, take up his cross each day, and follow in my steps. 24 Whoever would save his life will lose it, and whoever loses his life for my sake will save it. 25 What profit does he show who gains the whole world and destroys himself in the process? 26 If a man is ashamed of me and my doctrine, the Son of Man will be ashamed of him when he comes in his glory and that of his Father and his holy angels. 27 I assure you, there are some standing here who will not taste death until they see the reign of God."

Jesus Transfigured

28 About eight days after saying this he took Peter, John and James, and went up onto a mountain to pray. 29 While he was praying, his face changed in appearance and his clothes became dazzlingly white. 30 Suddenly two men were talking with him—Moses and Elijah. 31 They appeared in glory and spoke of his passage, which he was about to fulfill in Jerusalem. 32 Peter and those with him had fallen into a deep sleep; but awakening, they saw his glory and likewise saw the two men who were standing with him. 33 When these were leaving, Peter said to Jesus: "Master, how good it is for us to be here. Let us set up three booths, one for you, one for Moses, and one for Elijah." (He did not really know what he was saying.) 34 While he was speaking, a cloud came and overshadowed them, and the disciples grew fearful as the others entered it. 35 Then from the

cloud came a voice which said, "This is my Son, my Chosen One. Listen to him." 36 When the voice fell silent, Jesus was there alone. The disciples kept quiet, telling nothing of what they had seen at that time to anyone.

A Possessed Boy

37 The following day they came down from the mountain and a large crowd met them. 38 Suddenly a man from the crowd exclaimed: "Teacher, I beg you to look at my son; he is my only child. 39 A spirit takes possession of him and with a sudden cry throws him into a convulsion and makes him foam at the mouth, then abandons him in his shattered condition. 40 I asked your disciples to cast out the spirit but they could not." 41 Jesus said in reply: "What an unbelieving and perverse lot you are! How long must I remain with you? How long can I endure you? Bring your son here to me." 42 As he was being brought, the spirit threw him into convulsions on the ground. 43 Jesus then rebuked the unclean spirit, cured the boy, and restored him to his father. 44 And all who saw it marveled at the greatness of God.

Second Prediction of the Passion

In the midst of their amazement at all that he was doing, Jesus said to his disciples: "Pay close attention to what I tell you: the Son of Man must be delivered into the hands of men." 45 They failed, however, to understand this warning; its meaning was so concelaed from them they did not grasp it at all, and they were afraid to question him about the matter.

Against Ambition

46 A discussion arose among them as to which of them was the greatest. 47 Jesus, who knew their thoughts, took a little child and placed it beside him, 48 after which he said to them, "Whoever welcomes this little child on my account welcomes me, and whoever welcomes me welcomes

9, 18–22: Luke omits reference to Caesarea Philippi (Mt 16, 13; Mk 8, 27) as the locale of Peter's confession. This is because his chief interest in the event centers upon Jesus' awareness of his messianic identity in his onward movement toward Jerusalem

(not away from it) to achieve the climax of his mission through the passion and resurrection.
9, 23–27: See note on Mk 8, 34—9, 1.
9, 28–36: See note on Mk 9, 2–8. Lk 9, 31 explicitly associates the transfiguration with Jesus' passion and

resurrection.
9, 37–43: See note on Mk 9, 14–29.
9, 44f: See note on Mk 9, 30ff.
9, 46ff: See note on Mk 9, 33–37.

him who sent me; for the least one among you is the greatest."

49 It was John who said, "Master, we saw a man using your name to expel demons, and we tried to stop him because he is not of our company." 50 Jesus told him in reply, "Do not stop him, for any man who is not against you is on your side."

THE JOURNEY THROUGH PEREA

Samaritan Inhospitality

51 As the time approached when he was to be taken from this world, he firmly resolved to proceed toward Jerusalem, and sent messengers on ahead of him. 52 These entered a Samaritan town to prepare for his passing through, 53 but the Samaritans would not welcome him because he was on his way to Jerusalem. 54 When his disciples James and John saw this, they said, "Lord, would you not have us call down fire from heaven to destroy them?" 55 He turned toward them only to reprimand them. 56 Then they set off for another town.

The Apostles' Requirements

57 As they were making their way along, someone said to him, "I will be your follower wherever you go." 58 Jesus said to him, "The foxes have lairs, the birds of the sky have nests, but the Son of Man has nowhere to lay his head." 59 To another he said, "Come after me." The man replied, "Let me bury my father first." 60 Jesus said to him, "Let the dead bury their dead; come away and proclaim the kingdom of God." 61 Yet another said to him, "I will be your follower, Lord, but first let me take leave of my people at home." 62 Jesus answered him, "Whoever puts his hand to the plow but keeps looking back is unfit for the reign of God."

Mission of the Seventy-two

10 After this, the Lord appointed a further seventy-two and sent them in pairs before him to every town and place he intended to visit. 2 He said to them: "The harvest is rich but the workers are few; therefore ask the harvest-master to send workers to his harvest. 3 Be on your way, and remember: I am sending you as lambs in the midst of wolves. 4 Do not carry a walking staff or traveling bag; wear no sandals and greet no one along the way. 5 On entering any house, first say, 'Peace to this house.' 6 If there is a peaceable man there, your peace will rest on him; if not, it will come back to you. 7 Stay in the one house eating and drinking what they have, for the laborer is worth his wage. Do not move from house to house.

8 "Into whatever city you go, after they welcome you, eat what they set before you, 9 and cure the sick there. Say to them, 'The reign of God is at hand.' 10 If the people of any town you enter do not welcome you, go into its streets and say, 11 'We shake the dust of this town from our feet as testimony against you. But know that the reign of God is near.' 12 I assure you, on that day the fate of Sodom will be less severe than that of such a town. 13 It will go ill with you, Chorazin! And just as ill with you, Bethsaida! If the miracles worked in your midst had occurred in Tyre and Sidon, they would long ago have reformed in sackcloth and ashes. 14 It will go easier on the day of Judgment for Tyre and Sidon than for you. 15 And as for you, Capernaum, 'Are you to be exalted to the skies? You shall be hurled down to the realm of death!'

16 "He who hears you, hears me. He who rejects you, rejects me. And he who rejects me, rejects him who sent me."

17 The seventy-two returned in jubilation saying, "Master, even the demons are subject to us in your name." 18 He said in reply: "I watched Satan fall from the sky like lightning. 19 See what I have done; I have given you power to tread on snakes and scorpions and all the forces of the enemy, and nothing shall ever injure you. 20 Nevertheless, do not rejoice so much in the fact that the devils are subject to you as that your names are inscribed in heaven."

Hymn of Praise

21 At that moment Jesus rejoiced in the Holy Spirit and said: "I offer you praise, O Father, Lord of heaven and earth, because what you have hidden from the learned and the clever you have revealed to the merest children.

"Yes, Father, you have graciously willed it so. 22 Everything has been given over to me by my Father. No one knows the Son except the Father and no one knows the Father except the Son—and anyone to whom the Son wishes to reveal him."

Privilege of the Disciples

23 Turning to his disciples he said to them privately: "Blest are the eyes that see what you see. 24 I tell you, many prophets and kings wished to see what you see but did not see it, and to hear what you hear but did not hear it."

The Good Samaritan

25 On one occasion a lawyer stood up to pose him this problem: "Teacher, what must I do to inherit everlasting life?" 26 Jesus answered him: "What is written in the law? How do you read it?" 27 He replied:

"You shall love the Lord your
     God
  with all your heart,
  with all your soul,
  with all your strength,
  and with all your mind;
  and your neighbor as yourself."

9, 49f: See note on Mk 9, 38–41.

9, 51—18, 14: This section, composed mainly of sayings, parables and incidents found only in Luke, is derived from special sources at Luke's disposal and has come to be called "the great insertion." The evangelist presents these things within the framework of a geographical theme of Jesus' last journey to Jerusalem (9, 53.57; 10, 1; 13, 22.33; 17, 11). The several incidents recounted show the superior wisdom

of Jesus, e.g., his response to the lawyer concerning the way to eternal life (10, 25–28), and his defense of healing on the sabbath (13, 10–17; 14, 1–6).

The principal themes of Jesus' teaching in this section concern the sacrifices required for discipleship (9, 57–62); God's action in history directing the gospel message to the simple ones (10, 21); reliance on persevering prayer (11, 1–13; 18, 1–8); the supreme value of man's response to God's word (10, 38–42;

11, 27f); the gravity of the refusal to repent (11, 29–32; 13, 1–5); the sinfulness of hypocrisy (11, 37—12, 3); the threat to salvation presented by material wealth (12, 13–34; 16, 1–15.19–31); constant readiness for divine judgment (12, 35–48.54–59; 13, 6–9.22–30; 14, 16–24; 17, 20–37); and the bestowal of the divine mercy upon sinners (15, 3–32).

28 Jesus said, "You have answered correctly. Do this and you shall live." 29 But because he wished to justify himself he said to Jesus, "And who is my neighbor?" 30 Jesus replied: "There was a man going down from Jerusalem to Jericho who fell prey to robbers. They stripped him, beat him, and then went off leaving him half-dead. 31 A priest happened to be going down the same road; he saw him but continued on. 32 Likewise there was a Levite who came the same way; he saw him and went on. 33 But a Samaritan who was journeying along came on him and was moved to pity at the sight. 34 He approached him and dressed his wounds, pouring in oil and wine. He then hoisted him on his own beast and brought him to an inn, where he cared for him. 35 The next day he took out two silver pieces and gave them to the innkeeper with the request: 'Look after him, and if there is any further expense I will repay you on my way back.'

36 "Which of these three, in your opinion, was neighbor to the man who fell in with the robbers?" 37 The answer came, "The one who treated him with compassion." Jesus said to him, "Then go and do the same."

Martha and Mary

38 On their journey Jesus entered a village where a woman named Martha welcomed him to her home. 39 She had a sister named Mary, who seated herself at the Lord's feet and listened to his words. 40 Martha, who was busy with all the details of hospitality, came to him and said, "Lord, are you not concerned that my sister has left me to do the household tasks all alone? Tell her to help me."

41 The Lord in reply said to her: "Martha, Martha, you are anxious and upset about many things; 42 one thing only is required. Mary has chosen the better portion and she shall not be deprived of it."

The Our Father

11 One day he was praying in a certain place. When he had finished, one of his disciples asked him, "Lord, teach us to pray, as John taught his disciples." 2 He said to them, "When you pray, say:

"Father,
hallowed be your name,
your kingdom come.
3 Give us each day our daily
bread.
4 Forgive us our sins
for we too forgive all who do us
wrong;
and subject us not to the trial.'"

Two Parables on Prayer

5 Jesus said to them: "If one of you knows someone who comes to him in the middle of the night and says to him, 'Friend, lend me three loaves, 6 for a friend of mine has come in from a journey and I have nothing to offer him'; 7 and he from inside should reply, 'Leave me alone. The door is shut now and my children and I are in bed. I cannot get up to look after your needs'— 8 I tell you, even though he does not get up and take care of the man because of friendship, he will do so because of his persistence, and give him as much as he needs.

9 "So I say to you, 'Ask and you shall receive; seek and you shall find; knock and it shall be opened to you.' 10 "For whoever asks, receives; whoever seeks, finds; whoever knocks, is admitted. 11 What father among you will give his son a snake if he asks for a fish, 12 or hand him a scorpion if he asks for an egg? 13 If you, with all your sins, know how to give your children good things, how much more will the heavenly Father give the Holy Spirit to those who ask him."

Jesus and Beelzebul

14 Jesus was casting out a devil which was mute, and when the devil was cast out the dumb man spoke. The crowds were amazed at this. 15 Some of them said, "It is by Beelzebul, the prince of devils, that he casts out devils." 16 Others, to test him, were demanding of him a sign from heaven.

17 Because he knew their thoughts, he said to them: "Every kingdom divided against itself is laid waste. Any house torn by dissension falls.

18 If Satan is divided against himself, how can his kingdom last?—since you say it is by Beelzebul that I cast out devils. 19 If I cast out devils by Beelzebul, by whom do your people cast them out? In such case, let them act as your judges. 20 But if it is by the finger of God that I cast out devils, then the reign of God is upon you.

21 "When a strong man fully armed guards his courtyard, his possessions go undisturbed. 22 But when someone stronger than he comes and overpowers him, such a one carries off the arms on which he was relying and divides the spoils. 23 He who is not with me is against me, and he who does not gather with me scatters.

24 "When an unclean spirit has gone out of a man, it wanders through arid wastes searching for a resting-place; failing to find one, it says, 'I will go back to where I came from.' 25 It then returns, to find the house swept and tidied. 26 Next it goes out and returns with seven other spirits far worse than itself, who enter in and dwell there. The result is that the last state of the man is worse than the first."

True Happiness

27 While he was saying this a woman from the crowd called out, "Blest is the womb that bore you and the breasts that nursed you!" 28 "Rather," he replied, "blest are they who hear the word of God and keep it."

The Sign of Jonah

29 While the crowds pressed around him he began to speak to them in these words: "This is an evil age. It seeks a sign. But no sign will be given it except the sign of Jonah. 30 Just as Jonah was a sign for the Ninevites, so will the Son of Man be a sign for the present age. 31 The queen of the South will rise at the judgment along with the men of this generation, and she will condemn them. She came from the farthest corner of the world to listen to the wisdom of Solomon, but you have a greater than Solomon here. 32 At

the judgment, the citizens of Nineveh will rise along with the present generation, and they will condemn it. For at the preaching of Jonah they reformed, but you have a greater than Jonah here.

Parable of the Lamp

33 "One who lights a lamp does not put it in the cellar or under a bushel basket, but rather on a lampstand, so that they who come in may see the light. 34 The eye is the lamp of your body. When your eyesight is sound, your whole body is lighted up, but when your eyesight is bad, your body is in darkness. 35 Take care, then, that your light is not darkness. 36 If your whole body is lighted up and not partly in darkness, it will be as fully illumined as when a lamp shines brightly for you."

Hypocrisy of Pharisees and Lawyers

37 As he was speaking, a Pharisee invited him to dine at his house. He entered and reclined at table. 38 Seeing this, the Pharisee was surprised that he had not first performed the ablutions prescribed before eating. 39 The Lord said to him: "You Pharisees! You cleanse the outside of cup and dish, but within you are filled with rapaciousness and evil. 40 Fools! Did not he who made the outside make the inside too? But if you give what you have as alms, all will be wiped clean for you. 42 Woe to you Pharisees! You pay tithes on mint and rue and all the garden plants, while neglecting justice and the love of God. These are the things you should practice, without omitting the others. 43 Woe to you Pharisees! You love the front seats in synagogues and marks of respect in public. 44 Woe to you! You are like hidden tombs over which men walk unawares."

45 In reply one of the lawyers said to him, "Teacher, in speaking this way you insult us too." 46 Jesus answered: "Woe to you lawyers also! You lay impossible burdens on men but will not lift a finger to lighten them. 47 Woe to you! You build the tombs of the prophets, but it was your fathers who murdered them. 48 You show that you stand behind the deeds of your fathers: they committed the murders and you erect the tombs. 49 That is why the wisdom of God has said, 'I will send them prophets and apostles, and some of these they will persecute and kill'; 50 so that this generation will have to account for the blood of all the prophets shed since the foundation of the world. 51 Their guilt stretches from the blood of Abel to the blood of Zechariah, who met his death between the altar and the sanctuary! Yes, I tell you, this generation will have to account for it. 52 Woe to you lawyers! You have taken away the key of knowledge. You yourselves have not gained access, yet you have stopped those who wished to enter!"

53 After he had left this gathering, the scribes and Pharisees began to manifest fierce hostility to him and to make him speak on a multitude of questions, 54 setting traps to catch him in his speech.

Courage under Persecution

12 Meanwhile a crowd of thousands had gathered, so dense that they were treading on one another. He began to speak first to his disciples: "Be on guard against the yeast of the Pharisees, which is hypocrisy. 2 There is nothing concealed that will not be revealed, nothing hidden that will not be made known. 3 Everything you have said in the dark will be heard in the daylight; what you have whispered in locked rooms will be proclaimed from the rooftops.

4 "I say to you who are my friends: Do not be afraid of those who kill the body and can do no more. 5 I will show you whom you ought to fear. Fear him who has power to cast into Gehenna after he has killed. Yes, I tell you, fear him. 6 Are not five sparrows sold for a few pennies? Yet not one of them is neglected by God. 7 In very truth, even the hairs of your head are counted! Fear nothing, then. You are worth more than a flock of sparrows.

8 "I tell you, whoever acknowledges me before men—the Son of Man will acknowledge him before the angels of God. 9 But the man who has disowned me in the presence of men will be disowned in the presence of the angels of God. 10 Anyone who speaks against the Son of Man will be forgiven, but whoever blasphemes the Holy Spirit will never be forgiven. 11 When they bring you before synagogues, rulers and authorities, do not worry about how to defend yourselves or what to say. 12 The Holy Spirit will teach you at that moment all that should be said."

Trust in God, Not in Possessions

13 Someone in the crowd said to him, "Teacher, tell my brother to give me my share of our inheritance." 14 He replied, "Friend, who has set me up as your judge or arbiter?" 15 Then he said to the crowd, "Avoid greed in all its forms. A man may be wealthy, but his possessions do not guarantee him life."

16 He told them a parable in these words: "There was a rich man who had a good harvest. 17 'What shall I do?' he asked himself. 'I have no place to store my harvest. 18 I know!' he said. 'I will pull down my grain bins and build larger ones. All my grain and my goods will go there. 19 Then I will say to myself: You have blessings in reserve for years to come. Relax! Eat heartily, drink well. Enjoy yourself.' 20 But God said to him, 'You fool! This very night your life shall be required of you. To whom will all this piled-up wealth of yours go?' 21 That is the way it works with the man who grows rich for himself instead of growing rich in the sight of God."

Dependence on Providence

22 He said to his disciples: "That is why I warn you, Do not be concerned for your life, what you are to eat, or for your body, what you are to wear. 23 Life is more important than food and the body more than clothing. 24 Consider the ravens: they do not sow, they do not reap, they have neither cellar nor barn— yet God feeds them. How much more important you are than the birds! 25 Which of you by worrying can add a moment to his life-span? 26 If the smallest things are beyond your

power, why be anxious about the rest?

27 "Or take the lilies: they do not spin, they do not weave; but I tell you, Solomon in all his splendor was not arrayed like any one of them. 28 If God clothes in such splendor the grass of the field, which grows today and is thrown on the fire tomorrow, how much more will he provide for you, O weak in faith!' 29 It is not for you to be in search of what you are to eat or drink. Stop worrying. 30 The unbelievers of this world are always running after these things. Your Father knows that you need such things. 31 Seek out instead his kingship over you, and the rest will follow in turn.

The Heart's Treasure

32 "Do not live in fear, little flock. It has pleased your Father to give you the kingdom. 33 Sell what you have and give alms. Get purses for yourselves that do not wear out, a never-failing treasure with the Lord which no thief comes near nor any moth destroys. 34 Wherever your treasure lies, there your heart will be.

Preparedness for the Master's Return

35 "Let your belts be fastened around your waists and your lamps be burning ready. 36 Be like men awaiting their master's return from a wedding, so that when he arrives and knocks, you will open for him without delay. 37 It will go well with those servants whom the master finds wide-awake on his return. I tell you, he will put on an apron, seat them at table, and proceed to wait on them. 38 Should he happen to come at midnight or before sunrise and find them prepared, it will go well with them. 39 You know as well as I that if the head of the house knew when the thief was coming he would not let him break into his house. 40 Be on guard, therefore. The Son of Man will come when you least expect him."

41 Peter said, "Do you intend this parable for us, Lord, or do you mean it for everyone?" 42 The Lord said, "Who in your opinion is that faithful, farsighted steward whom the master will set over his servants to dispense their ration of grain in season? 43 That servant is fortunate whom his master finds busy when he returns. 44 Assuredly, his master will put him in charge of all his property. 45 But if the servant says to himself, 'My master is taking his time about coming,' and begins to abuse the housemen and servant girls, to eat and drink and get drunk, 46 that servant's master will come back on a day when he does not expect him, at a time he does not know. He will punish him severely and rank him among those undeserving of trust. 47 The slave who knew his master's wishes but did not prepare to fulfill them will get a severe beating, 48 whereas the one who did not know them and who nonetheless deserved to be flogged will get off with fewer stripes. When much has been given a man, much will be required of him. More will be asked of a man to whom more has been entrusted.

49 'I have come to light a fire on the earth. How I wish the blaze were ignited! 50 I have a baptism to receive. What anguish I feel till it is over! 51 Do you think I have come to establish peace on the earth? I assure you, the contrary is true; I have come for division. 52 From now on, a household of five will be divided three against two and two against three; 53 father will be split against son and son against father, mother against daughter and daughter against mother, mother-in-law against daughter-in-law, daughter-in-law against mother-in-law.'"

Signs of the Times

54 He said to the crowds: "When you see a cloud rising in the west, you say immediately that rain is coming—and so it does. 55 When the wind blows from the south, you say it is going to be hot—and so it is. 56 You hypocrites! If you can interpret the portents of earth and sky, why can you not interpret the present time? 57 Tell me, why do you not judge for yourselves what is just? 58 When you are going with your opponent to appear before a magistrate, try to settle with him on the way lest he turn you over to the judge, and the judge deliver you up to the jailer, and the jailer throw you into prison. 59 I warn you, you will not be released from there until you have paid the last penny."

Providential Calls to Penance

13 At that time, some were present who told him about the Galileans whose blood Pilate had mixed with their sacrifices. 2 He said in reply: "Do you think that these Galileans were the greatest sinners in Galilee just because they suffered this? 3 By no means! But I tell you, you will all come to the same end unless you reform. 4 Or take those eighteen who were killed by a falling tower in Siloam. Do you think they were more guilty than anyone else who lived in Jerusalem? 5 Certainly not! But I tell you, you will all come to the same end unless you reform."

The Barren Fig Tree

6 Jesus spoke this parable: "A man had a fig tree growing in his vineyard, and he came out looking for fruit on it but did not find any. 7 He said to the vinedresser, 'Look here! For three years now I have come in search of fruit on this fig tree and found none. Cut it down. Why should it clutter up the ground?' 8 In answer, the man said, 'Sir, leave it another year, while I hoe around it and manure it; 9 then perhaps it will bear fruit. If not, it shall be cut down.'"

A Sabbath Cure

10 On a sabbath day he was teaching in one of the synagogues. 11 There was a woman there who for eighteen years had been possessed by a spirit which drained her strength. She was badly stooped—quite incapable of standing erect. 12 When Jesus saw her, he called her to him and said, "Woman, you are free of your infirmity." 13 He laid his hand on her, and immediately she stood up straight and began thanking God.

14 The Chief of the synagogue, indignant that Jesus should have healed on the sabbath, said to the congregation, "There are six days for working. Come on those days to be cured, not on the sabbath." 15 The

Lord said in reply, "O you hypocrites! Which of you does not let his ox or ass out of the stall on the sabbath to water it? 16 Should not this daughter of Abraham here who has been in the bondage of Satan for eighteen years have been released from her shackles on the sabbath?" 17 At these words, his opponents were covered with confusion; meanwhile, everyone else rejoiced at the marvels Jesus was accomplishing.

Parable of the Mustard Seed

18 Then he said: "What does the reign of God resemble? To what shall I liken it? 19 It is like mustard seed which a man took and planted in his garden. It grew and became a large shrub and the birds of the air nested in its branches."

Parable of the Yeast

20 He went on: "To what shall I compare the reign of God? 21 It is like yeast which a woman took to knead into three measures of flour until the whole mass of dough began to rise."

The Narrow Door

22 He went through cities and towns teaching—all the while making his way toward Jerusalem. 23 Someone asked him, "Lord, are they few in number who are to be saved?" 24 He replied: "Try to come in through the narrow door. Many, I tell you, will try to enter and be unable. 25 When once the master of the house has risen to lock the door and you stand outside knocking and saying, 'Sir, open for us,' he will say in reply, 'I do not know where you come from.' 26 Then you will begin to say, 'We ate and drank in your company. You taught in our streets.' 27 But he will answer, 'I tell you, I do not know where you come from. Away from me, you evildoers!'

28 "There will be wailing and grinding of teeth when you see Abraham, Isaac, Jacob, and all the prophets safe in the kingdom of God, and you yourselves rejected. 29 People will come from the east and the west, from the north and the south, and will take their place at the feast in the kingdom of God. 30 Some who are last will be first and some who are first will be last."

Herod the Fox

31 It was then that certain Pharisees came to him. "Go on your way!" they said. "Leave this place! Herod is trying to kill you." 32 His answer was: "Go tell that fox, 'Today and tomorrow I cast out devils and perform cures, and on the third day my purpose is accomplished. 33 For all that, I must proceed on course today, tomorrow, and the day after, since no prophet can be allowed to die anywhere except in Jerusalem.'

Apostrophe to Jerusalem

34 "O Jerusalem, Jerusalem, you slay the prophets and stone those who are sent to you! How often have I wanted to gather your children together as a mother bird collects her young under her wings, and you refused me! 35 Your temple will be abandoned. I say to you, you shall not see me until the time comes when you say, 'Blessed is he who comes in the name of the Lord.'"

Cure and a Lesson in Humility

14 When Jesus came on a sabbath to eat a meal in the house of one of the leading Pharisees, they observed him closely. 2 Directly in front of him was a man who suffered from dropsy. 3 Jesus asked the lawyers and the Pharisees, "Is it lawful to cure on the sabbath or not?" 4 At this they kept silent. He took the man, healed him, and sent him on his way. 5 Then he addressed himself to them: "If one of you has a son or an ox and he falls into a pit, will he not immediately rescue him on the sabbath day?" 6 This they could not answer.

7 He went on to address a parable to the guests, noticing how they were trying to get the places of honor at the table: 8 "When you are invited by someone to a wedding party, do not sit in the place of honor in case some greater dignitary has been invited. 9 Then the host might come and say to you, 'Make room for this man,' and you would have to proceed shamefacedly to the lowest place. 10 What you should do when you have been invited is go and sit in the lowest place, so that when your host approaches you he will say, 'My friend, come up higher.' This will win you the esteem of your fellow guests. 11 For everyone who exalts himself shall be humbled and he who humbles himself shall be exalted."

The Poor

12 He said to the one who had invited him: "Whenever you give a lunch or dinner, do not invite your friends or brothers or relatives or wealthy neighbours. They might invite you in return and thus repay you. 13 No, when you have a reception, invite beggars and the crippled, the lame and the blind. 14 You should be pleased that they cannot repay you, for you will be repaid in the resurrection of the just." 15 At these words one in the party said to him, "Happy is he who eats bread in the kingdom of God." 16 Jesus responded: "A man was giving a large dinner and he invited many. 17 At dinner time he sent his servant to say to those invited, 'Come along, everything is ready now.' 18 But they began to excuse themselves, one and all. The first one said to the servant, 'I have bought some land and must go out and inspect it. Please excuse me.' 19 Another said, 'I have bought five yoke of oxen and I am going out to test them. Please excuse me.' 20 A third said, 'I am newly married and so I cannot come.' 21 The servant returning reported all this to his master. The master of the house grew angry at the account. He said to his servant, 'Go out quickly into the streets and alleys of the town and bring in the poor and the crippled, the blind and the lame.' 22 The servant reported, after some time, 'Your orders have been carried out, my lord, and there is still room.' 23 The master then said to the servant, 'Go out into the highways and along the hedgerows and force them to come in. I want my house to be full, 24 but I tell you that not one of those invited shall taste a morsel of my dinner.'"

25 On one occasion when a great crowd was with him, he turned to them and said, 26 "If anyone

comes to me without turning his back on his father and mother, his wife and his children, his brothers and sisters, indeed his very self, he cannot be my follower. 27 Anyone who does not take up his cross and follow me cannot be my disciple. 28 If one of you decides to build a tower, will he not first sit down and calculate the outlay to see if he has enough money to complete the project? 29 He will do that for fear of laying the foundation and then not being able to complete the work; for all who saw it would jeer at him, 30 saying, 'That man began to build what he could not finish.'

31 "Or if a king is about to march on another king to do battle with him, will he not sit down first and consider whether, with ten thousand men, he can withstand an enemy coming against him with twenty thousand? 32 If he cannot, he will send a delegation while the enemy is still at a distance, asking for terms of peace. 33 In the same way, none of you can be my disciple if he does not renounce all his possessions. 34 Salt is good, but if salt loses its flavor what good is it for seasoning? 35 It is fit for neither the soil nor the manure heap; it has to be thrown away. Let him who hears this, heed it."

Parable of Divine Mercy

15 The tax collectors and sinners were all gathering around to hear him, 2 at which the Pharisees and the scribes murmured, "This man welcomes sinners and eats with them." 3 Then he addressed this parable to them: 4 "Who among you, if he has a hundred sheep and loses one of them, does not leave the ninety-nine in the wasteland and follow the lost one until he finds it? 5 And when he finds it, he puts it on his shoulders in jubilation. 6 Once arrived home, he invites friends and neighbors in and says to them, 'Rejoice with me because I have found my lost sheep.' 7 I tell you, there will likewise be more joy in heaven over one repentant sinner than over ninety-nine righteous people who have no need to repent.

8 "What woman, if she has ten silver pieces and loses one, does not light a lamp and sweep the house in a

diligent search until she has retrieved what she lost? 9 And when she finds it, she calls in her friends and neighbors to say, 'Rejoice with me! I have found the silver piece I lost.' 10 I tell you, there will be the same kind of joy before the angels of God over one repentant sinner.''

The Prodigal Son

11 Jesus said to them: "A man had two sons. 12 The younger of them said to his father, 'Father, give me the share of the estate that is coming to me.' So the father divided up the property. 13 Some days later this younger son collected all his belongings and went off to a distant land, where he squandered his money on dissolute living. 14 After he had spent everything, a great famine broke out in that country and he was in dire need. 15 So he attached himself to one of the propertied class of the place, who sent him to his farm to take care of the pigs. 16 He longed to fill his belly with the husks that were fodder for the pigs, but no one made a move to give him anything, 17 Coming to his senses at last, he said: 'How many hired hands at my father's place have more than enough to eat, while here I am starving! 18 I will break away and return to my father, and say to him, Father, I have sinned against God and against you; I no longer deserve to be called your son. 19 Treat me like one of your hired hands.' 20 With that he set off for his father's house. While he was still a long way off, his father caught sight of him and was deeply moved. He ran out to meet him, threw his arms around his neck, and kissed him. 21 The son said to him, 'Father, I have sinned against God and against you; I no longer deserve to be called your son.' 22 The father said to his servants: 'Quick! bring out the finest robe and put it on him; put a ring on his finger and shoes on his feet. 23 Take the fatted calf and kill it. Let us eat and celebrate 24 because this son of mine was dead and has come back to life. He was lost and is found.' Then the celebration began.

25 "Meanwhile the elder son was out on the land. As he neared the

house on his way home, he heard the sound of music and dancing. 26 He called one of the servants and asked him the reason for the dancing and the music. The servant answered, 'Your brother is home, and your father has killed the fatted calf because he has him back in good health.' 28 The son grew angry at this and would not go in; but his father came out and began to plead with him.

29 "He said to his father in reply: 'For years now I have slaved for you. I never disobeyed one of your orders, yet you never gave me so much as a kid goat to celebrate with my friends. 30 Then, when this son of yours returns after having gone through your property with loose women, you kill the fatted calf for him.'

31 "'My son,' replied the father, 'you are with me always, and everything I have is yours. 32 But we had to celebrate and rejoice! This brother of yours was dead, and has come back to life. He was lost, and is found.'"

The Wily Manager

16 Another time he said to his disciples: "A rich man had a manager who was reported to him for dissipating his property. 2 He summoned him and said, 'What is this I hear about you? Give me an account of your service, for it is about to come to an end.' 3 The manager thought to himself, 'What shall I do next? My employer is sure to dismiss me. I cannot dig ditches. I am ashamed to go begging. 4 I have it! Here is a way to make sure that people will take me into their homes when I am let go.'

5 "So he called in each of his master's debtors, and said to the first, 'How much do you owe my master?' 6 The man replied, 'A hundred jars of oil.' The manager said, 'Take your invoice, sit down quickly, and make it fifty.' 7 Then he said to a second, 'How much do you owe?' The answer came, 'A hundred measures of wheat,' and the manager said, 'Take your invoice and make it eighty.'

8 "The owner then gave his devious employee credit for being

enterprising! Why? Because the worldly take more initiative than the other-worldly when it comes to dealing with their own kind.

Right Use of Money

9 "What I say to you is this: Make friends for yourselves through your use of this world's goods, so that when they fail you, a lasting reception will be yours. 10 If you can trust a man in little things, you can also trust him in greater; while anyone unjust in a slight matter is also unjust in greater. 11 If you cannot be trusted with elusive wealth, who will trust you with lasting? 12 And if you have not been trustworthy with someone else's money, who will give you what is your own?

13 "No servant can serve two masters. Either he will hate the one and love the other or be attentive to the one and despise the other. You cannot give yourself to God and money." 14 The Pharisees, who were avaricious men, heard all this and began to deride him. 15 He said to them: "You justify yourselves in the eyes of men, but God reads your hearts. What man thinks important, God holds in contempt.

The Law

16 "The law and the prophets were in force until John. From his time on, the good news of God's kingdom has been proclaimed, and people of every sort are forcing their way in. 17 It is easier for the heavens and the earth to pass away than for a single stroke of a letter of the law to pass. 18 Everyone who divorces his wife and marries another commits adultery. The man who marries a woman divorced from her husband likewise commits adultery.

The Rich Man and Lazarus

19 "Once there was a rich man who dressed in purple and linen and feasted splendidly every day. 20 At his gate lay a beggar named Lazarus who was covered with sores. 21 Lazarus longed to eat the scraps that fell from the rich man's table. The dogs even came and licked his sores. 22 Eventually the beggar died. He was carried by angels to the bosom of Abraham. The rich man likewise died and was buried. 23 From the abode of the dead where he was in torment, he raised his eyes and saw Abraham afar off, and Lazarus resting in his bosom.

24 "He called out, 'Father Abraham, have pity on me. Send Lazarus to dip the tip of his finger in water to refresh my tongue, for I am tortured in these flames.' 25 'My child,' replied Abraham, 'remember that you were well off in your lifetime, while Lazarus was in misery. Now he has found consolation here, but you have found torment. 26 And that is not all. Between you and us there is fixed a great abyss, so that those who might wish to cross from here to you cannot do so, nor can anyone cross from your side to us.'

27 "'Father, I ask you, then,' the rich man said, 'send him to my father's house 28 where I have five brothers. Let him be a warning to them so that they may not end in this place of torment.' 29 Abraham answered, 'They have Moses and the prophets. Let them hear them.' 30 'No, Father Abraham,' replied the rich man. 'But if someone would only go to them from the dead, then they would repent.' 31 Abraham said to him, 'If they do not listen to Moses and the prophets, they will not be convinced even if one should rise from the dead.'"

Four Sayings of Jesus

17 He said to his disciples: "Scandals will inevitably arise, but woe to him through whom they come. 2 He would be better off thrown into the sea with a millstone around his neck than giving scandal to one of these little ones.

3 "Be on your guard. If your brother does wrong, correct him; if he repents, forgive him. 4 If he sins against you seven times a day, and seven times a day turns back to you saying, 'I am sorry,' forgive him."

5 The apostles said to the Lord, "Increase our faith," 6 and he answered: "If you had faith the size of a mustard seed, you could say to this sycamore, 'Be uprooted and transplanted into the sea,' and it would obey you.

7 "If one of you had a servant plowing or herding sheep and he came in from the fields, would you say to him, 'Come and sit down at table'? 8 Would you not rather say, 'Prepare my supper. Put on your apron and wait on me while I eat and drink. You can eat and drink afterward'? 9 Would he be grateful to the servant who was only carrying out his orders? 10 It is quite the same with you who hear me. When you have done all you have been commanded to do, say, 'We are useless servants. We have done no more than our duty.'"

Ten Lepers

11 On his journey to Jerusalem he passed along the borders of Samaria and Galilee. 12 As he was entering a village, ten lepers met him. Keeping their distance, 13 they raised their voices and said, "Jesus, Master, have pity on us!" 14 When he saw them, he responded, "Go and show yourselves to the priests." 15 On their way there they were cured. 15 One of them, realizing that he had been cured, came back praising God in a loud voice. 16 He threw himself on his face at the feet of Jesus and spoke his praises. This man was a Samaritan. 17 Jesus took the occasion to say, "Were not all ten made whole? Where are the other nine? 18 Was there no one to return and give thanks to God except this foreigner?" 19 He said to the man, "Stand up and go your way; your faith has been your salvation."

Coming of the Reign of God

20 Once, on being asked by the Pharisees when the reign of God would come, he replied: "You cannot tell by careful watching when the reign of God will come. 21 Neither is it a matter of reporting that it is 'here' or 'there'. The reign of God is already in your midst."

Day of the Son of Man

22 He said to the disciples: "A time will come when you will long to see one day of the Son of Man but will not see it. 23 They will tell you he is to be found in this place or that. Do not go running about excitedly. 24 The Son of Man in his day will be like the lightning that flashes from

one end of the sky to the other. 25 First, however, he must suffer much and be rejected by the present age. 26 As it was in the days of Noah, so it will be in the days of the Son of Man. 27 They ate and drank, they took husbands and wives, right up to the day Noah entered the ark—and when the flood came, it destroyed them all. 28 It was much the same in the days of Lot: they ate and drank, they bought and sold, they built and planted. 29 But on the day Lot left Sodom, fire and brimstone rained down from heaven and destroyed them all.

30 "It will be like that on the day the Son of Man is revealed. 31 On that day, if a man is on the rooftop and his belongings are in the house, he should not go down to get them; neither should the man in the field return home. 32 Remember Lot's wife. 33 Whoever tries to preserve his life will lose it; whoever loses it will keep it. 34 I tell you, on that night there will be two men in one bed; one will be taken and the other left. 35 Two women will be grinding grain together; one will be taken and the other left." 37 "Where, Lord?" they asked him, and he answered, "Wherever the carcass is, there will the vultures gather."

The Corrupt Judge

18 He told them a parable on the necessity of praying always and not losing heart: 2 "Once there was a judge in a certain city who respected neither God nor man. 3 A widow in that city kept coming to him saying, 'Give me my rights against my opponent.' 4 For a time he refused, but finally he thought, 'I care little for God or man, 5 but this widow is wearing me out. I am going to settle in her favor or she will end by doing me violence.'" 6 The Lord said, "Listen to what the corrupt judge has to say. 7 Will not God then do justice to his chosen who call out to him day and night? Will he delay long over them, do you suppose? 8 I tell you, he will give them swift justice. But

when the Son of Man comes, will he find any faith on the earth?"

The Pharisee and the Tax Collector

9 He then spoke this parable addressed to those who believed in their own self-righteousness while holding everyone else in contempt: 10 "Two men went up to the temple to pray; one was a Pharisee, the other a tax collector. 11 The Pharisee with head unbowed prayed in this fashion: 'I give you thanks, O God, that I am not like the rest of men—grasping, crooked, adulterous —or even like this tax collector. 12 I fast twice a week. I pay tithes on all I possess.' 13 The other man, however, kept his distance, not even daring to raise his eyes to heaven. All he did was beat his breast and say, 'O God, be merciful to me, a sinner.' 14 Believe me, this man went home from the temple justified but the other did not. For everyone who exalts himself shall be humbled while he who humbles himself shall be exalted."

Jesus and the Children; a Rich Man

15 They even brought babies to be touched by him. When the disciples saw this, they scolded them roundly; 16 but Jesus called for the children, saying: "Let the little children come to me. Do not shut them off. The reign of God belongs to such as these. 17 Trust me when I tell you that whoever does not accept the kingdom of God as a child will not enter into it."

18 One of the ruling class asked him then, "Good teacher, what must I do to share in everlasting life?" 19 Jesus said to him, "Why call me 'good'? None is good but God alone. 20 You know the commandments:

"You shall not commit adultery.
You shall not kill.
You shall not steal.
You shall not bear dishonest witness.
Honor your father and your mother."

21 He replied, "I have kept all these since I was a boy." 22 When Jesus heard this he said to him: "There is one thing further you must do. Sell all you have and give to the poor. You will have treasure in heaven. Then come and follow me." 23 On hearing this he grew melancholy, for he was a very rich man. 24 When Jesus observed this he said: "How hard it will be for the rich to go into the kingdom of God! 25 Indeed, it is easier for a camel to go through a needle's eye than for a rich man to enter the kingdom of heaven."

26 His listeners asked him, "Who, then, can be saved?" 27 to which he replied, "Things that are impossible for men are possible for God." 28 Peter said, "We have left all we own to become your followers." 29 His answer was; "I solemnly assure you, there is no one who has left home or wife or brothers, parents or children, for the sake of the kingdom of God 30 who will not receive a plentiful return in this age and life everlasting in the age to come."

31 Taking the Twelve aside, he said to them: "We must now go up to Jerusalem so that all that was written by the prophets concerning the Son of Man may be accomplished. 32 He will be delivered up to the Gentiles. He will be mocked and outraged and spat upon. 33 They will scourge him and put him to death, and on the third day he will rise again."

34 They understood nothing of this. His utterance remained obscure to them, and they did not grasp his meaning.

35 As he drew near Jericho a blind man sat at the side of the road begging. 36 Hearing a crowd go by the man asked, "What is that?" 37 The answer came that Jesus of Nazareth was passing by. 38 He shouted out, "Jesus, Son of David, have pity on me!" 39 Those in the lead sternly ordered him to be quiet, but he cried out all the more, "Son of David, have pity on me!" 40 Jesus halted and ordered that he be brought to him. When he had come close,

---

17, 36: Omitted here with many MSS.
18, 15ff: See note on Mt 19, 13ff.
18, 18–21: See note on Mk 10, 17f.

18, 24–27: See note on Mt 19, 23–26.
18, 28ff: See note on Mt 19, 27–30.
18, 31–34: See note on Mk 10, 32ff.

18, 35–43: See note on Mk 10, 46–52.

Jesus asked him, 41 "What do you want me to do for you?" "Lord," he answered, "I want to see." 42 Jesus said to him, "Receive your sight. Your faith has healed you." 43 At that very moment he was given his sight and began to follow him, giving God the glory. All the people witnessed it and they too gave praise to God.

Zacchaeus the Tax Collector

19 Entering Jericho, he passed through the city. There was a man there named Zacchaeus, the chief tax collector and a wealthy man. 3 He was trying to see what Jesus was like, but being small of stature, was unable to do so because of the crowd. 4 He first ran on in front, then climbed a sycamore tree which was along Jesus' route, in order to see him. 5 When Jesus came to the spot he looked up and said, "Zacchaeus, hurry down. I mean to stay at your house today." 6 He quickly descended, and welcomed him with delight. 7 When this was observed, everyone began to murmur, "He has gone to a sinner's house as a guest." 8 Zacchaeus stood his ground and said to the Lord: "I give half my belongings, Lord, to the poor. If I have defrauded anyone in the least, I pay him back fourfold." 9 Jesus said to him: "Today salvation has come to this house, for this is what it means to be a son of Abraham. 10 The Son of Man has come to search out and save what was lost."

Parable of the Sums of Money

11 While they were listening to these things he went on to tell a parable, because he was near Jerusalem where they thought that the reign of God was about to appear. 12 He said: "A man of noble birth went to a faraway country to become its king, and then return. 13 He summoned ten of his servants and gave them sums of ten units each,

saying to them, 'Invest this until I get back.' 14 But his fellow citizens despised him, and they immediately sent a deputation after him with instructions to say, 'We will not have this man rule over us.' 15 He returned, however, crowned as king. Then he sent for the servants to whom he had given the money, to learn what profit each had made. 16 The first presented himself and said, 'Lord, the sum you gave me has earned you another ten.' 'Good man!' he replied. 'You showed yourself capable in a small matter. For that you can take over ten villages.' 18 The second came and said, 'Your investment, my lord, has netted you five.' 19 His word to him was, 'Take over five villages.' 20 The third came in and said: 'Here is your money, my lord, which I hid for safekeeping. 21 You see, I was afraid of you because you are a hard man. You withdraw what you never deposited. You reap what you never sowed.' 22 To him the king said: 'You worthless lout! I intend to judge you on your own evidence. You knew I was a hard man, withdrawing what I never deposited, reaping what I never sowed! 23 Why, then, did you not put my money out on loan, so that on my return I could get it back with interest?' 24 He said to those standing around, 'Take from him what he has, and give it to the man with the ten.' 25 'Yes, but he already has ten,' they said. 26 He responded with, 'The moral is: whoever has will be given more, but the one who has not will lose the little he has. 27 Now about those enemies of mine who do not want me to be king, bring them in and slay them in my presence.'"

THE JERUSALEM MINISTRY

Messianic Entry into Jerusalem

28 Having spoken thus he went ahead with his ascent to Jerusalem.

29 As he approached Bethphage and Bethany on the mount called Olivet, he sent two of the disciples 30 with these instructions: "Go into the village straight ahead of you. Upon entering it you will find an ass tied there which no one has yet ridden. Untie it and lead it back. 31 If anyone should ask you, 'Why are you untying the beast?' say, 'The Master has need of it.'"

32 They departed on their errand and found things just as he had said. 33 As they untied the ass, its owners said to them, "Why are you doing that?" 34 They explained that the Master needed it. 35 Then they led the animal to Jesus, and laying their cloaks on it, helped him mount. 36 They spread their cloaks on the roadway as he moved along; 37 and on his approach to the descent from Mount Olivet, the entire crowd of disciples began to rejoice and praise God loudly for the display of power they had seen, 38 saying:

> "Blessed be he who comes as king
> in the name of the Lord!
> Peace in heaven
> and glory in the highest!"

39 Some of the Pharisees in the crowd said to him, "Teacher, rebuke your disciples." 40 He replied, "If they were to keep silence, I tell you the very stones would cry out."

Lamentation for Jerusalem

41 Coming within sight of the city, he wept over it and said: 42 "If only you had known the path to peace this day; but you have completely lost it from view! 43 Days will come upon you when your enemies encircle you with a rampart, hem you in, and press you hard from every side. 44 They will wipe you out, you and your children within your walls, and leave not a stone on a stone within you, because you failed to recognize the time of your visitation."

19, 11–27: The parable of the sums of money presents two principal ideas: 1) Jesus is the Messiah-king; he understands this office to be a religious one despite the opposition of his contemporaries (19, 12–15). The reign of God is actually present in his person and teaching. 2) In exercising his messianic kingship Jesus demands the response of men to the gifts of God. The kingdom will appear in its permanent form

when Christ renders the final judgement on humanity's response to him (19, 15–27).

19, 28–38: See note on Mk 11, 1–11.

19, 41–44: This lamentation over Jerusalem implies that Jesus has previously visited the city in his public ministry, a fact that is brought out only in John (2, 13; 5, 1; 7, 10.14; 10, 22; 12, 12).

Here the thought of the impending destruction of

Jerusalem because of its refusal to accept the Messiah is contrasted with the city's potentiality as the principal center of the Christian message. Jerusalem became that center for only a short time, as the Acts attest (9, 31; 12, 1–5); the city was destroyed in A.D. 70. The allusions here are drawn from Jeremiah: v 42 (Jer 6, 8.10.14); v 43 (Jer 6, 6); v 44 (Jer 6, 2.11.17. 21).

The Traders Expelled

45 Then he entered the temple and began ejecting the traders 46 saying:"Scripture has it,

'My house is meant for a house
of prayer' but you have made
it 'a den of thieves.'"

47 He was teaching in the temple area from day to day. The chief priests and scribes meanwhile were looking for a way to destroy him, as were the leaders of the people, 48 but they had no idea how to achieve it, for indeed the entire populace was listening to him and hanging on his words.

The Authority of Jesus

20 One day when he was teaching the people in the temple and proclaiming the good news, the high priests and Pharisees, accompanied by the elders, approached him 2 with the question, "Tell us, by what authority do you do these things? In other words, who has authorized you?" 3 He replied,"Let me put a question for you to answer: 4 Did the baptism of John come from God or from men?" 5 They held a brief conference during which someone said, "If we answer, 'From God,' he will say, 'Then why do you not believe in it?'; 6 whereas if we say, 'From men,' the people will stone us, so convinced are they that John was a prophet." 7 They ended by replying they did not know where it came from. 8 Jesus said to them, "In that case, neither will I tell you by whose authority I act."

Parable of the Tenants

9 He then began to tell the people the following parable: "A man planted a vineyard, leased it to tenant farmers, and went away for a long time. 10 At vintage time he sent a servant to the tenant farmers to receive his share of the crop from them; but they beat him and sent him away empty-handed. 11 He sent a second servant whom they also beat. Him too they sent away empty-handed, after treating him shamefully. 12 He sent still a third, whom they likewise maltreated before driving him away. 13 The owner of the vineyard asked himself, 'What am I to do now? Perhaps if I send the son I love, they will respect him.' 14 "But when the tenant farmers saw the son, they reflected, 'This is the heir. Let us kill him so that the inheritance will be ours.' 15 With that, they dragged him outside the vineyard and killed him. What fate do you suppose the owner of the vineyard has in store for them? 16 I will tell you. He will make an end to those tenant farmers and give the vineyard to others."

17 When they heard this they said, "God forbid!" He looked directly at them and said,"What do the Scriptures mean when they say,

'The stone which the builders
rejected has become the
keystone of the structure'?

18 The man who falls on that stone will be smashed to pieces. It will make dust of anyone on whom it falls." 19 At these words the scribes and high priests tried to get their hands on him, but they were afraid of the people. They were well aware that he had told the parable with them in mind.

Tribute to the Emperor

20 Waiting their chance, they sent spies to him in the guise of honest men to trap him in speech, so that they might then hand him over to the office and authority of the procurator. 21 They put to him this problem: "Teacher, we know that your words and your doctrine are completely forthright, that you are no respecter of persons but teach the way of God in truth. 22 May we pay tax to the emperor or not?" Realizing their duplicity he said, 24 "Show me a coin. Whose head is this? Whose inscription do you read?" "Caesar's," they replied, 25 to which he said, "Then give to Caesar what is Caesar's, but give to God what is God's." 26 They were unable to trap him publicly in speech. His answer completely disconcerted them and reduced them to silence.

Resurrection of the Dead

27 Some Sadducees came forward (the ones who claim there is no resurrection) 28 to pose this problem to him: "Master, Moses prescribed that if a man's brother dies leaving a wife and no child, the brother should marry the widow and raise posterity to his brother. 29 Now there were seven brothers. 30 The first one married and died childless. 31 Next, the second brother married the widow, then the third, and so on. All seven died without leaving her any children. 32 Finally the widow herself died. 33 At the resurrection, whose wife will she be? Remember, seven married her."

34 Jesus said to them:"The children of this age marry and are given in marriage, 35 but those judged worthy of a place in the age to come and of resurrection from the dead do not. 36 They become like angels and are no longer liable to death. Sons of the resurrection, they are sons of God. 37 Moses in the passage about the bush showed that the dead rise again when he called the Lord the God of Abraham, and the God of Isaac, and the God of Jacob. 38 God is not the God of the dead but of the living. All are alive for him."

39 Some of the scribes responded, "Well said, Teacher." 40 They did not dare ask him anything else.

Jesus, Son and Lord of David

41 Jesus then said to them:"How can they say that the Messiah is the son of David? 42 Does not David himself say in the psalms,

'The Lord said to my lord: Sit
at my right hand
43 while I make your enemies your
footstool'?

44 Now if David accords him the title 'lord,' how can he be his son?"

The Scribes Condemned

45 In the hearing of all the people, Jesus said to his disciples: 46 "Beware of the scribes, who like to parade around in their robes, and love marks of respect in public, front seats in synagogues, and places of honor at banquets. 47 These men are going through the savings of widows while they recite long prayers

19, 45f: See note on Mk 11, 15–19.　　　20, 1–40: See note on Mk 11, 27—12, 27.　　　20, 41—21, 4: See note on Mk 12, 35–44.

to keep up appearances. The heavier sentence will be theirs."

The Widow's Mite

21 He glanced up and saw the rich putting their offerings into the treasury, 2 and also a poor widow putting in two copper coins. At that he said: 3 "I assure you, this poor widow has put in more than all the rest. 4 They make contributions out of their surplus, but she from her want has given what she could not afford—every penny she had to live on."

The Cataclysm To Come

5 Some were speaking of how the temple was adorned with precious stones and votive offerings. 6 He said, "These things you are contemplating—the day will come when not one stone will be left on another, but it will all be torn down." 7 They asked him, "When will this be, Teacher? And what will be the sign that it is going to happen?" 8 He said, "Take care not to be misled. Many will come in my name saying, 'I am he' and 'The time is at hand.' Do not follow them. 9 Neither must you be perturbed when you hear of wars and insurrections. These things are bound to happen first, but the end does not follow immediately."

10 He said to them further: "Nation will rise against nation and kingdom against kingdom. 11 There will be great earthquakes, plagues and famines in various places—and in the sky fearful omens and great signs. 12 But·before any of this, they will manhandle and persecute you, summoning you to synagogues and prisons, bringing you to trial before kings and governors, all because of my name. 13 You will be brought to give witness on account of it. 14 I bid you resolve not to worry about your defense beforehand, 15 for I will give you words and a wisdom which none of your adversaries can take excep-

tion to or contradict. 16 You will be delivered up even by your parents, brothers, relatives and friends, and some of you will be put to death. 17 All will hate you because of me, 18 yet not a hair of your head will be harmed. 19 By patient endurance you will save your lives.

Siege and Fall of Jerusalem

20 "When you see Jerusalem encircled by soldiers, know that its devastation is near. 21 Those in Judea at the time must flee to the mountains; those in the heart of the city must escape it; those in the country must not return. 22 These indeed will be days of retribution, when all that is written must be fulfilled.

23 "The women who are pregnant or nursing at the breast will fare badly in those days! The distress in the land and the wrath against this people will be great. 24 The people will fall before the sword; they will be led captive in the midst of the Gentiles. Jerusalem will be trampled by the Gentiles, until the times of the Gentiles are fulfilled.

Coming of the Son of Man

25 "There will be signs in the sun, the moon and the stars. On the earth, nations will be in anguish, distraught at the roaring of the sea and the waves. 26 Men will die of fright in anticipation of what is coming upon the earth. The powers in the heavens will be shaken. 27 After that, men will see the Son of Man coming on a cloud with great power and glory. When these things begin to happen, stand up straight and raise your heads, for your ransom is near at hand."

Parable of the Fig Tree

29 Then he told them a parable: "Notice the fig tree, or any other tree. 30 You observe them when they are budding, and know for yourselves that summer is near. 31

Likewise when you see all the things happening of which I speak, know that the reign of God is near. 32 Let me tell you this: the present generation will not pass away until all this takes place. 33 The heavens and the earth will pass away, but my words will not pass.

34 "Be on guard lest your spirits become blotted with indulgence and drunkenness and worldly cares. The great day will suddenly close in on you like a trap. 35 The day I speak of will come upon all who dwell on the face of the earth. 36 So be on the watch. Pray constantly for the strength to escape whatever is in prospect, and to stand secure before the Son of Man."

Last Days of Jesus

37 He would teach in the temple by day, and leave the city to spend the night on the Mount of Olives. 38 At daybreak all the people came to hear him in the temple.

THE PASSION OF JESUS

The Council and the Betrayal

22 The feast of unleavened bread known as the Passover was drawing near, 2 and the high priests and scribes began to look for some way to dispose of him; but they were afraid of the people. 3 Then Satan took possession of Judas, the one called Iscariot, a member of the Twelve. 4 He went off to confer with the chief priests and officers about a way to hand him over to them. 5 They were delighted, and agreed to give him money. 6 He accepted, then kept looking for an opportunity to hand him over without creating a disturbance.

The Passover Preparation

7 The day of Unleavened Bread arrived on which it was appointed to sacrifice the paschal lamb. 8 Accordingly, Jesus sent Peter and John off with the instruction, "Go and

---

21, 5–36: See note on Mk 13, 1–37.

22, 1—23, 56: Certain features of this narrative of the passion of Jesus are distinctive of Luke. There are omissions: the flight of the disciples at the arrest of Jesus (Mk 14, 50ff), the false witnesses (Mk 14, 55–59), which many consider a Marcan insertion into traditional materials, the mistreatment at the hands of the Roman soldiery (Mk 15, 16–20), the offering of a

narcotic to Jesus before the crucifixion (Mk 15, 23), and the praying of Psalm 22 from the cross (Mk 15, 34ff).

Additions found in Luke include: the elements of Jesus' farewell address at the Last Supper (22, 15.25–30.35–38); reference to the angel at the agony, which heightens the religious solemnity of the scene (22, 43); Jesus' look at Peter after his denial (22, 61); the

appearance of Jesus before Herod (23, 6–11); his conversation with the women of Jerusalem (23, 27–31); and his words from the cross (23, 34.43.46).

Luke depicts Jesus throughout his passion as the innocent victim (23, 4.14.22.47) of satanic activity (22, 3), who forgives his enemies (22, 51; 23, 34) and accepts his suffering and death as the will of his Father (23, 46).

prepare our Passover supper for us." 9 They asked him, "Where do you want us to get it ready?" 10 He explained to them: "Just as you enter the city, you will come upon a man carrying a water jar. Follow him into the house he enters, and say to the owner, 11 'The Teacher asks you: Do you have a guest room where I may eat the Passover with my disciples?' 12 That man will show you an upstairs room, spacious and furnished. It is there you are to prepare." 13 They went off and found everything just as he had said; and accordingly they prepared the Passover supper.

The Holy Eucharist

14 When the hour arrived, he took his place at table, and the apostles with him. 15 He said to them: "I have greatly desired to eat this Passover with you before I suffer. 16 I tell you, I will not eat again until it is fulfilled in the kingdom of God."

17 Then taking a cup he offered a blessing in thanks and said: "Take this and divide it among you; 18 I tell you, from now on I will not drink of the fruit of the vine until the coming of the reign of God."

19 Then, taking bread and giving thanks, he broke it and gave it to them, saying: "This is my body to be given for you. Do this as a remembrance of me." 20 He did the same with the cup after eating, saying as he did so: "This cup is the new covenant in my blood, which will be shed for you.

The Betrayer

21 "And yet the hand of my betrayer is with me at this table. 22 The Son of Man is following out his appointed course, but woe to that man by whom he is betrayed." 23 Then they began to dispute among themselves as to which of them would do such a deed.

Who is Greatest?

24 A dispute arose among them about who should be regarded as the greatest. 25 He said: "Earthly kings lord it over their people. Those who exercise authority over them are called their benefactors. 26 Yet it cannot be that way with you. Let the greater among you be as the junior, the leader as the servant. 27 Who, in fact, is the greater—he who reclines at table or he who serves the meal? Is it not the one who reclines at table? Yet I am in your midst as the one who serves you. 28 You are the ones who have stood loyally by me in my temptations. 29 I for my part assign to you the dominion my Father has assigned to me. 30 In my kingdom you will eat and drink at my table, and you will sit on thrones judging the twelve tribes of Israel.

Peter's Denials Foretold

31 "Simon, Simon! Remember that Satan has asked for you, to sift you all like wheat. 32 But I have prayed for you that your faith may never fail. You in turn must strengthen your brothers." 33 "Lord," he said to him, "at your side I am prepared to face imprisonment and death itself." 34 Jesus replied, "I tell you, Peter, the cock will not crow today until you have three times denied that you know me."

35 He asked them, "When I sent you on mission without purse or traveling bag or sandals, were you in need of anything?" "Not a thing," they replied. 36 He said to them: "Now, however, the man who has a purse must carry it; the same with the traveling bag. And the man without a sword must sell his coat and buy one. 37 It is written in Scripture,

'He was counted among the wicked,'

and this, I tell you, must come to be fulfilled in me. All that has to do with me approaches its climax." 38 They said, "Lord, here are two swords!" He answered, "Enough."

The Agony in the Garden

39 Then he went out and made his way, as was his custom, to the Mount of Olives; his disciples accompanied him. 40 On reaching the place he said to them, "Pray that you may not be put to the test." 41 He withdrew from them about a stone's throw, then went down on his knees and prayed in these words: 42 "Father, if it is your will, take this cup from me; yet not my will but yours be done." 43 An angel then appeared to him from heaven to strengthen him. 44 In his anguish he prayed with all the greater intensity, and his sweat became like drops of blood falling to the ground. 45 Then he rose from prayer and came to his disciples, only to find them asleep, exhausted with grief. 46 He said to them, "Why are you sleeping? Wake up, and pray that you may not be subjected to the trial."

Jesus Arrested

47 While he was still speaking a crowd came, led by the man named Judas, one of the Twelve. He approached Jesus to embrace him. 48 Jesus said to him, "Judas, would you betray the Son of Man with a kiss?" 49 When the companions of Jesus saw what was going to happen, they said, "Lord, shall we use the sword?" 50 One of them went so far as to strike the high priest's servant and cut off his right ear. 51 Jesus said in answer to their question, "Enough!" Then he touched the ear and healed the man. 52 But to those who had come out against him—the chief priests, the chiefs of the temple guard, and the ancients—Jesus said, "Am I a criminal that you come out after me armed with swords and clubs? 53 When I was with you day after day in the temple you never raised a hand against me. But this is your hour—the triumph of darkness!"

Peter's Denial

54 They led him away under arrest and brought him to the house of the high priest, while Peter followed at a distance. 55 Later they lighted a fire in the middle of the courtyard and were sitting beside it, and Peter sat among them. 56 A servant girl saw him sitting in the light of the fire. She gazed at him intently, then said, 57 "This man was with him." He denied the fact, saying, "Woman, I do not know him." 58 A little while later someone else saw

---

22, 28: *My temptations:* both from Satan (4, 13) and from the enemies of Jesus who served the purposes of Satan.

him and said, "You are one of them too." But Peter said, "No, sir, not I!" 59 About an hour after that another spoke more insistently: "This man was certainly with him, for he is a Galilean." 60 Peter responded, "My friend, I do not know what you are talking about." At the very moment he was saying this, a rooster crowed. 61 The Lord turned around and looked at Peter, and Peter remembered the word that the Lord had spoken to him, "Before the rooster crows today you will deny me three times." 62 He went out and wept bitterly.

Jesus before the Sanhedrin

63 Meanwhile the men guarding Jesus amused themselves at his expense. 64 They blindfolded him first, slapped him, and then taunted him: "Play the prophet; which one struck you?" 65 And they directed many other insulting words at him.

66 At daybreak, the elders of the people, the chief priests, and the scribes assembled again. Once they had brought him before their council, they said, "Tell us, are you the Messiah?" 67 He replied, "If I tell you, you will not believe me, 68 and if I question you, you will not answer. 69 This much only will I say: 'From now on, the Son of Man will have his seat at the right hand of the Power of God.'" 70 "So you are the Son of God?" they asked in chorus. He answered, "It is you who say I am." 71 They said, "What need have we of witnesses? We have heard it from his own mouth."

Jesus before Pilate

23 Then the entire assembly rose up and led him before Pilate. 2 They started his prosecution by saying, "We found this man subverting our nation, opposing the payment of taxes to Caesar, and calling himself the Messiah, a king." 3 Pilate asked him, "Are you the king of the Jews?" He answered, "That is your term." 4 Pilate reported to the chief priests and the crowds, "I do not find a case against this man." 5 But they insisted, "He stirs up the people by his teaching throughout the whole of Judea, from Galilee,

where he began, to this very place." 6 On hearing this Pilate asked if the man was a Galilean; 7 and when he learned that he was under Herod's jurisdiction, he sent him to Herod, who also happened to be in Jerusalem at the time.

8 Herod was extremely pleased to see Jesus. From the reports about him he had wanted for a long time to see him, and he was hoping to see him work some miracle. 9 He questioned Jesus at considerable length, but Jesus made no answer. 10 The chief priests and scribes were at hand to accuse him vehemently. 11 Herod and his guards then treated him with contempt and insult, after which they put a magnificent robe on him and sent him back to Pilate. 12 Herod and Pilate, who had previously been set against each other, became friends from that day.

Jesus Again before Pilate

13 Pilate then called together the chief priests, the ruling class, and the people, 14 and said to them: "You have brought this man before me as one who subverts the people. I have examined him in your presence and have no charge against him arising from your allegations. 15 Neither has Herod, who therefore has sent him back to us; obviously this man has done nothing that calls for death. 16 Therefore I mean to release him, once I have taught him a lesson." 18 The whole crowd cried out, "Away with this man; release Barabbas for us!" 19 This Barabbas had been thrown in prison for causing an uprising in the city, and for murder. 20 Pilate addressed them again, for he wanted Jesus to be the one he released.

21 But they shouted back, "Crucify him, crucify him!" 22 He said to them for the third time, "What wrong is this man guilty of? I have not discovered anything about him that calls for the death penalty. I will therefore chastise him and release him." 23 But they demanded with loud cries that he be crucified, and their shouts increased in violence. 24 Pilate then decreed that what they demanded should be done. 25 He released the one they asked for, who had been thrown in prison for

insurrection and murder, and delivered Jesus up to their wishes.

The Way of the Cross

26 As they led him away, they laid hold of one Simon the Cyrenean who was coming in from the fields. They put a crossbeam on Simon's shoulder for him to carry along behind Jesus. 27 A great crowd of people followed him, including women who beat their breasts and lamented over him. 28 Jesus turned to them and said: "Daughters of Jerusalem, do not weep for me. Weep for yourselves and for your children. 29 The days are coming when they will say, 'Happy are the sterile, the wombs that never bore and the breasts that never nursed.' 30 Then they will begin saying to the mountains, 'Fall on us,' and to the hills, 'Cover us.' 31 If they do these things in the green wood, what will happen in the dry?"

The Crucifixion

32 Two others who were criminals were led along with him to be crucified. 33 When they came to Skull Place, as it was called, they crucified him there and the criminals as well, one on his right and the other on his left. 34 [Jesus said, "Father, forgive them; they do not know what they are doing."] They divided his garments, rolling dice for them.

35 The people stood there watching, and the leaders kept jeering at him, saying, "He saved others; let him save himself if he is the Messiah of God, the chosen one." 36 The soldiers also made fun of him, coming forward to offer him their sour wine 37 and saying, "If you are the king of the Jews, save yourself." 38 There was an inscription over his head:

"THIS IS THE KING OF THE JEWS."

39 One of the criminals hanging in crucifixion blasphemed him: "Aren't you the Messiah? Then save yourself and us." 40 But the other one rebuked him: "Have you no fear of God, seeing you are under the same sentence? 41 We deserve it, after all. We are only paying the price for

23, 17: Omit with some MSS. Others read: "At the festival time he had to release a prisoner to them."

what we've done, but this man has done nothing wrong." 42 He then said, "Jesus, remember me when you enter upon your reign." 43 And Jesus replied, "I assure you: this day you will be with me in paradise."

Jesus Dies on the Cross

44 It was now around midday, and darkness came over the whole land until midafternoon with an eclipse of the sun. 45 The curtain in the sanctuary was torn in two. 46 Jesus uttered a loud cry and said,

"Father, into your hands I commend my spirit."

After he said this, he expired. 47 The centurion, upon seeing what had happened, gave glory to God by saying, "Surely this was an innocent man." 48 When the crowd which had assembled for this spectacle saw what had happened, they went home beating their breasts. 49 All his friends and the women who had accompanied him from Galilee were standing at a distance watching everything.

The Burial

50 There was a man named Joseph, an upright and holy member of the Sanhedrin, 51 who had not been associated with their plan or their action. He was from Arimathea, a Jewish town, and he looked expectantly for the reign of God. 52 This man approached Pilate with a request for Jesus' body. 53 He took it down, wrapped it in fine linen, and laid it in a tomb hewn out of the rock, in which no one had yet been buried. 54 That was the Day of Preparation, and the sabbath was about to begin. 55 The women who had come with him from Galilee followed along behind. They saw the

tomb and how his body was buried. 56 Then they went home to prepare spices and perfumes. They observed the sabbath as a day of rest, in accordance with the law.

APPEARANCES AFTER THE RESURRECTION

The Women at the Tomb

24 On the first day of the week, at dawn, the women came to the tomb bringing the spices they had prepared. 2 They found the stone rolled back from the tomb; 3 but when they entered the tomb, they did not find the body of the Lord Jesus. 4 While they were still at a loss over what to think of this, two men in dazzling garments stood beside them. 5 Terrified, the women bowed to the ground. The men said to them: "Why do you search for the Living One among the dead? 6 He is not here; he has been raised up. Remember what he said to you while he was still in Galilee— 7 that the Son of Man must be delivered into the hands of sinful men, and be crucified, and on the third day rise again." 8 With this reminder, his words came back to them.

9 On their return from the tomb, they told all these things to the Eleven and the others. 10 The women were Mary of Magdala, Joanna, and Mary the mother of James. The other women with them also told the apostles, 11 but the story seemed like nonsense and they refused to believe them. 12 Peter, however, got up and ran to the tomb. He stooped down but could see nothing but the wrappings. So he went away full of amazement at what had occurred.

Emmaus

13 Two of them that same day

were making their way to a village named Emmaus seven miles distant from Jerusalem, 14 discussing as they went all that had happened. 15 In the course of their lively exchange, Jesus approached and began to walk along with them. 16 However, they were restrained from recognizing him. 17 He said to them, "What are you discussing as you go your way?" 18 They halted, in distress, and one of them, Cleopas by name, asked him, "Are you the only resident of Jerusalem who does not know the things that went on there these past few days?" 19 He said to them, "What things?" They said: "All those that had to do with Jesus of Nazareth, a prophet powerful in word and deed in the eyes of God and all the people; 20 how our chief priests and leaders delivered him up to be condemned to death, and crucified him. 21 We were hoping that he was the one who would set Israel free. Besides all this, today, the third day since these things happened, 22 some women of our group have just brought us some astonishing news. They were at the tomb before dawn 23 and failed to find his body, but returned with the tale that they had seen a vision of angels who declared he was alive. 24 Some of our number went to the tomb and found it to be just as the women said; but him they did not see."

25 Then he said to them, "What little sense you have! How slow you are to believe all that the prophets have announced! 26 Did not the Messiah have to undergo all this so as to enter into his glory?" 27 Beginning, then, with Moses and all the prophets, he interpreted for them every passage of Scripture which referred to him. 28 By now they were near the village to which they were going, and he acted as if he were

---

24, 1–53: The resurrection narratives in the gospels do not derive directly from the primitive stage when the apostolic testimony was as yet unchallenged by the unbeliever. They reflect a somewhat later period, when the average Christian was aware of the unbeliever's principal counter-arguments against the doctrine of the resurrection; namely, that Jesus' disciples had removed his body from the tomb, or that they were victims of visionary or other objectively unreal experiences. The gospels and the tradition that preceded them carefully interwove the data of the resurrection with the replies to these arguments, so that Christians might remain in peaceful possession of their faith.

The narratives, then, begin with the account of the

women's visit to the tomb—no doubt to make clear that up to this point the male disciples of Jesus had not come near the tomb (1–8). The reaction of the disciples to the women's report reveals that they did not anticipate Jesus' immediate resurrection (10f), much less think of creating a resurrection myth by removal of the body. The stress on the incredulity of the disciples (11.25.41; cf Mt 28, 17; Jn 20, 24–29) depicts them as men not easily convinced of the resurrection event: *They thought they were seeing a ghost* (37). But their experience of his presence for the duration of meals (42f; cf Jn 20, 9–13), and their conversation with him in which they recognized that his earlier teaching actually culminated in these new circumstances (44; cf Jn 20, 21; 21, 15ff), required

the acceptance of the one before them as Jesus of Nazareth, who had returned to life after undergoing the reality of death.

The greater problem of the disciples in accepting the fact of the resurrection was, no doubt, its messianic implications. These new and unanticipated concepts presented an extraordinary challenge to the faith of Israel, a point that Luke's resurrection narrative is careful to make (25ff. 44–47). In addition to the apologetic response to the denials of the resurrection, Luke (44–49), like Matthew (28, 19f) and John (20, 21ff), incorporates into his gospel the instructions of the risen Jesus concerning the mission of the disciples and of the Christian community.

going farther.   29 But they pressed him: "Stay with us. It is nearly evening—the day is practically over." So he went in to stay with them.

30 When he had seated himself with them to eat, he took bread, pronounced the blessing, then broke the bread and began to distribute it to them.   31 With that their eyes were opened and they recognized him; whereupon he vanished from their sight.   32 They said to one another, "Were not our hearts burning inside us as he talked to us on the road and explained the Scriptures to us?"   33 They got up immediately and returned to Jerusalem, where they found the Eleven and the rest of the company assembled. They were greeted with, 34 "The Lord has been raised! It is true! He has appeared to Simon."   35 Then they recounted what had happened on the road and how they had come to know him in the breaking of bread.

Jesus Appears to the Eleven

36 While they were still speaking about all this, he himself stood in their midst [and said to them, "Peace to you."].   37 In their panic and fright they thought they were seeing a ghost.   38 He said to them, "Why are you disturbed? Why do such ideas cross your mind? 39 Look at my hands and my feet; it is really I. Touch me, and see that a ghost does not have flesh and bones as I do."   40 As he said this he showed them his hands and feet.   41 They were still incredulous for sheer joy and wonder, so he said to them, "Have you anything here to eat?"   42 They gave him a piece of cooked fish, 43 which he took and ate in their presence.   44 Then he said to them, "Recall those words I spoke to you when I was still with you: everything written about me in the law of Moses and the prophets and psalms had to be fulfilled."   45 Then he opened their minds to the understanding of the Scriptures.

46 He said to them: "Thus it is written that the Messiah must suffer and rise from the dead on the third day.   47 In his name, penance for the remission of sins is to be preached to all the nations, beginning at Jerusalem.   48 You are witnesses of this.   49 See, I send down upon you the promise of my father. Remain here in the city until you are clothed with power from on high."

The Ascension

50 Then he led them out near Bethany, and with hands upraised, blessed them.   51 As he blessed, he left them, and was taken up to heaven.   52 They fell down to do him reverence, then returned to Jerusalem filled with joy.   53 There they were to be found in the temple constantly, speaking the praises of God.

THE GOSPEL ACCORDING TO

PROLOGUE

IN the beginning was the Word; the Word was in God's presence, and the Word was God. 2 He was present to God in the beginning. 3 Through him all things came into being, and apart from him nothing came to be. 4 Whatever came to be in him, found life, life for the light of men.

5 The light shines on in darkness,
a darkness that did not overcome it.

6 There was a man named John sent by God, 7 who came as a witness to testify to the light, so that through him all men might believe— 8 but only to testify to the light, for he himself was not the light. 9 The real light which gives light to every man was coming into the world.

10 He was in the world,
and through him the world was made,
yet the world did not know who he was.

11 To his own he came,
yet his own did not accept him.

12 Any who did accept him
he empowered to become
children of God.

These are they who believe in his name— 13 who were begotten not by blood, nor by carnal desire, nor by man's willing it, but by God.

14 The Word became flesh
and made his dwelling among us,
and we have seen his glory:
the glory of an only Son coming
from the Father,
filled with enduring love.

15 John testified to him by proclaiming: "This is he of whom I said, 'The one who comes after me ranks ahead of me, for he was before me.'"

1, 1–18: The Prologue is a hymn, formally poetic in style—perhaps originally an independent composition and only later adapted and edited to serve as an overture to the gospel. Its closest parallel is found in the christological hymns in Col 1, 15–20; Phil 2, 6–11; I Tm 3, 16. The Roman writer Pliny (A.D. 111) mentions the Christians of Asia Minor as singing hymns to Christ as a god. Commentators are divided on whether the initial reference to the earthly ministry of Jesus Christ is in 1, 9 or 1, 14.
1, 1: *In the beginning:* these, the first words of Gn 1, 1, serve as the Hebrew title of that book. Here, however, they introduce the two verses describing the situation before creation. *Was:* three times in the first verse this verb is used of the Word. First, it indicates timeless existence; next, relationship to the Father; finally, identity with God.
1, 3f: In the Clementine Vulgate, the words *whatever came to be* are put at the end of v 3: "*Apart from him,* nothing came into being which came to be. In him was life, etc." The best evidence favors the division given above. *Found life:* literally "was life."
1, 3: The creation was through the Word and in the Word; cf Col 1, 16.
1, 5: *Overcome:* if this translation is accepted,

hostility between darkness and light is indicated, perhaps a reference to the sin of Gn 3. Other possible translations—"grasp," "comprehend," "receive"— are preferred by those who regard the verse as referring to the ministry of Jesus.
1, 6ff: These are more prosaic than the other verses of the Prologue, and their content is intrusive, separating 5 from 9 or 10. Vv 6ff, perhaps including 9, are to be regarded as a parenthetical addition by the Johannine editor of the hymn. For him, the reference to the ministry of Jesus came after 6ff.
1, 9: The earlier versions make *every man* (instead of *the light*) the subject of *coming into the world.*
1, 11: *His own:* in 11a, a neuter expression, probably meaning his own country, the Holy Land; in 11b, *his own* is masculine, and refers to Israel or to the Jews.
1, 12f: *Empowered:* or "gave authority." *These are they who believe in his name,* etc.: many regard these verses as part of the final edition rather than of the original hymn.
1, 13: *Who were begotten:* some minor textual witnesses and some early Fathers read "he who was begotten"—a reference to Jesus. This is probably a free adaptation of the text to illustrate the virgin birth.

Not by blood . . . desire: no human agency, male or female, begets God's children. That is done through baptism and the Holy Spirit; cf 3, 5.
1, 14: *Made his dwelling:* literally, "set up his tent, or tabernacle." In the Exodus the tabernacle or tent of meeting was the site of God's dwelling among men (Ex 25, 8f); now that site is the Word-made-flesh. *Glory:* the glory of God (the visible manifestation of his majesty in power), which once filled the tabernacle (Ex 40, 34) and the temple (1 Kgs 8, 10f.27), is now centered in Jesus. *Filled with enduring love:* It is not clear whether *filled* modifies *glory* or *Word* or only *Son.* The two words *love* and *enduring* (often translated "grace and truth") represent two Old Testament terms used to describe the dealings of the God of the covenant with Israel (Ex 34, 6): *love* signifying God's love in choosing Israel and his steadfast expression of that love in the covenant; *enduring* signifying his faithfulness to his covenant promises. Jesus is a new manifestation of God's covenant, *enduring love,* replacing the old; cf v 16.
1, 15: This verse, of the same nature as 6ff, seems to be drawn from v 30; it interrupts vv 14 and 16, which belong together.

---

16 Of his fullness
we have all had a share—
love following upon love.

17 For while the law was given
through Moses, this enduring love
came through Jesus Christ. 18 No
one has ever seen God. It is God the
only Son, ever at the Father's side,
who has revealed him.

THE BOOK OF SIGNS

Testimony for John to the Envoys

19 The testimony John gave when
the Jews sent priests and Levites from
Jerusalem to ask, "Who are you?"
20 was the direct statement, "I am
not the Messiah." 21 They questioned him further, "Who, then?
Elijah?" "I am not Elijah," he
answered. "Are you the Prophet?"
"No," he replied.

22 Finally they said to him: "Tell
us who you are, so that we can give
some answer to those who sent us.
What do you have to say for yourself?" 23 He said, quoting the
prophet Isaiah, "I am

'a voice in the desert, crying out:
Make straight the way of the
Lord!'"

24 Those whom the Pharisees had
sent 25 proceeded to question him
further: "If you are not the Messiah,
nor Elijah, nor the Prophet, why do
you baptize?" 26 John answered
them: "I baptize with water. There is
one among you whom you do not
recognize— 27 the one who is to

come after me—the strap of whose
sandal I am not worthy to unfasten."
28 This happened in Bethany,
across the Jordan, where John was
baptizing.

His Testimony to Jesus

29 The next day, when John
caught sight of Jesus coming toward
him, he exclaimed:

"Look! There is the Lamb of
God
who takes away the sin of the
world!

30 It is he of whom I said:

'After me is to come a man
who ranks ahead of me,
because he was before me.'

31 I confess I did not recognize him,
though the very reason I came baptizing with water was that he might be
revealed to Israel."
32 John gave this testimony also:

"I saw the Spirit descend
like a dove from the sky,
and it came to rest on him.

33 But I did not recognize him.
The one who sent me to baptize with
water told me, 'When you see the
Spirit descend and rest on someone,
it is he who is to baptize with the
Holy Spirit.' 34 Now I have seen
for myself and have testified, 'This is
God's chosen One.'"

The First Disciples

35 The next day John was there
again with two of his disciples.

36 As he watched Jesus walk by he
said, "Look! There is the Lamb of
God!" 37 The two disciples heard
what he said, and followed Jesus.
38 When Jesus turned around and
noticed them following him, he asked
them, "What are you looking for?"
They said to him, "Rabbi (which
means Teacher), where do you stay?"
"Come and see," he answered. 39
So they went to see where he was
lodged, and stayed with him that
day. (It was about four in the
afternoon.)

40 One of the two who had followed him after hearing John was
Simon Peter's brother Andrew. 41
The first thing he did was seek out
his brother Simon and tell him, "We
have found the Messiah!" (This
term means the Anointed.) 42 He
brought him to Jesus, who looked at
him and said, "You are Simon, son
of John; your name shall be Cephas
(which is rendered Peter)."

43 The next day he wanted to set
out for Galilee, but first he came
upon Philip. "Follow me," Jesus
said to him. 44 Now Philip was
from Bethsaida, the same town as
Andrew and Peter. 45 Philip sought
out Nathanael and told him, "We
have found the one Moses spoke of
in the law—the prophets too—
Jesus, son of Joseph, from Nazareth."
46 Nathanael's response to that was,
"Can anything good come from
Nazareth?" and Philip replied,
"Come, see for yourself." 47 When
Jesus saw Nathanael coming toward

1, 16: *Love following upon love:* the endless accumu-
lation of God's goodness in Jesus. Other possible
translations are: "love in place of love"—the love
manifested in Jesus replacing the love manifested in
Moses (cf 1, 17)—and "love for love"—our love
corresponding to Jesus' love.
1, 17f: Many commentators regard these verses
as explanation rather than part of the pre-Prologue
hymn. *God the only Son:* other MSS read "the Son,
the only one" or "the only Son." *Ever at the Father's
side:* literally, "in [to] the bosom of the Father."
1, 19: *The Jews:* throughout most of the gospel,
with the notable exception of chapters 11 and 12, the
"Jews" are not the Jewish people as such. They are
the hostile authorities, the Pharisees and Sadducees,
particularly those in Jerusalem, who refuse to believe
in Jesus. The use of the term reflects the atmosphere
at the end of the first century, when polemics expressed the hostility between the synagogue, and the
church.
1, 21: *"Elijah?" "I am not":* the Baptizer himself
did not claim to be Elijah returned to earth; with
greater insight, Jesus (Mt 11, 14) explained the Baptizer's career as fulfilling the rôle Malachi (4, 5)
attributed to Elijah. *The Prophet:* probably the prophet
like Moses of Dt 18, 15; cf Acts 3, 22.
1, 24: *Those whom the Pharisees had sent:* it would
be very unusual for the priestly and levitical envoys

of v 19 to have been of the Pharisees' party rather than
that of the Sadducees. Some would translate: "There
were some Pharisees sent," or "Some of the Pharisees'
party were sent." If the latter translation is correct,
the evangelist has simplified party distinctions, since
the Sadducees were no longer important in the late
first century.
1, 28: *Bethany, across the Jordan:* this is not the
Bethany near Jerusalem (11, 18); the actual site is
unknown. "Bethabara" ("place of crossing over") is
read by the Old Syriac, and Origen accepted it as the
correct reading.
1, 29: *The Lamb of God:* perhaps, for the Baptizer
this meant the great apocalyptic lamb who would
destroy evil in the world (Rv 17, 14). The evangelist
may see a reference to the paschal lamb, and/or to the
suffering servant led like a lamb to the slaughter as an
offering for sin (Is 53, 7.10).
1, 30: *He was before me:* preexistence is a Johannine theme (1, 1; 8, 58; 17, 5).
1, 32: John the Evangelist does not actually describe the baptism of Jesus, but the occasion of the
vision narrated here is almost certainly to be understood as the baptism.
1, 34: *God's chosen One:* the better Greek MSS
have "God's Son." The heavenly voice in the synoptic
gospels proclaims: "This is my beloved Son" (Mt 3,
17; Mk 1, 11; Lk 3, 22). It is difficult to see why

scribes would change "God's Son" to "God's chosen
One," and easy to see why for harmonizing and
theological purposes a change in the opposite direction
would be made. *Chosen One* is probably a reference
to the Servant of Yahweh (Is 42, 1).
1, 37: *Two disciples:* one is Andrew (v 40); the
other, unnamed here, is traditionally identified as
John, son of Zebedee. See note on 13, 23.
1, 39: *Four in the afternoon:* literally, the tenth
hour. The evangelists seem to use the Roman method
of reckoning time; the hours from sunrise (6 A.M.) are
counted as the daylight hours. Some suggest that it
was a Friday afternoon; the next day, beginning at
sunset, would be the sabbath, which was why they
stayed with him.
1, 41: The reading of *first* is uncertain: our interpretation follows the best MSS, including the early
papyri. *The Messiah:* the actual Aramaic word *meshiha*
—"anointed one"—appears in the Greek as the
transliterated *messias* here and in 4, 25. Elsewhere the
Greek translation *christos* is used.
1, 43: The subject of the first two verbs is not
clear: grammatically it could be Peter, but logically it
is probably Jesus.
1, 47: *A true Israelite:* Jacob was the first to bear
the name "Israel" (Gn 22, 28ff), but Jacob was a man
of guile (Gn 27, 35).

him, he remarked: "This man is a true Israelite. There is no guile in him." "How do you know me?" 48 Nathanael asked him. "Before Philip called you," Jesus answered, "I saw you under the fig tree." 49 "Rabbi," said Nathanael, "you are the Son of God; you are the king of Israel." 50 Jesus responded. 'Do you believe just because I told you I saw you under the fig tree? You will see much greater things than that."

51 He went on to tell them, "I solemnly assure you, you shall see the sky opened and the angels of God ascending and descending on the Son of Man."

The Wedding at Cana

2 On the third day there was a wedding at Cana in Galilee, and the mother of Jesus was there. 2 Jesus and his disciples had likewise been invited to the celebration. 3 At a certain point the wine ran out, and Jesus' mother told him, "They have no more wine." 4 Jesus replied, "Woman, how does this concern of yours involve me? My hour has not yet come." 5 His mother instructed those waiting on table, "Do whatever he tells you." 6 As prescribed for Jewish ceremonial washings, there were at hand six stone water jars, each one holding fifteen to twenty-five gallons. 7 "Fill those jars with water," Jesus ordered, at which they filled them to the brim. 8 "Now," he said, "draw some out and take it to the waiter in charge." They did as he instructed them. 9 The waiter in charge tasted the water made wine, without knowing where it had come from; only the waiters knew, since they had drawn the water. Then the waiter in charge called the groom over 10 and remarked to him: "People usually serve the choice wine first; then when the guests have been drinking awhile, a lesser vintage. What you have done is keep the choice wine until now." 11 Jesus performed this first of his signs at Cana in Galilee. Thus did he reveal his glory, and his disciples believed in him.

12 After this he went down to Capernaum, along with his mother and brothers [and his disciples] but they stayed there only a few days.

Cleansing of the Temple

13 As the Jewish Passover was near, Jesus went up to Jerusalem. 14 In the temple precincts he came upon people engaged in selling oxen, sheep and doves, and others seated changing coins. 15 He made a [kind of] whip of cords and drove sheep and oxen alike, out of the temple area, and knocked over the money-changers' tables, spilling their coins. 16 He told those who were selling doves: "Get them out of here! Stop turning my Father's house into a marketplace!" 17 His disciples recalled the words of Scripture: "Zeal for your house consumes me."

18 At this the Jews responded, "What sign can you show us authorizing you to do these things?" 19 "Destroy this temple," was Jesus' answer, "and in three days I will raise it up." 20 They retorted, "This temple took forty-six years to build, and you are going to 'raise it up in three days!'" 21 Actually he was talking about the temple of his body. 22 Only after Jesus had been raised from the dead did his disciples recall that he had said this, and come to believe the Scripture and the word he had spoken.

23 While he was in Jerusalem during the Passover festival, many believed in his name, for they could see the signs he was performing. 24 For his part, Jesus would not trust himself to them because he knew them all. 25 He needed no one to give him testimony about human nature. He was well aware of what was in man's heart.

Nicodemus

3 A certain Pharisee named Nicodemus, a member of the Jewish Sanhedrin, 2 came to him at night. "Rabbi," he said, "we know you are a teacher come from God, for no man can perform signs and wonders such as you perform unless God is with him." 3 Jesus gave him this answer:

"I solemnly assure you,
no one can see the reign of God
unless he is begotten from
    above."

4 "How can a man be born again once he is old?" retorted Nicodemus. "Can he return to his mother's womb and be born over again?" 5 Jesus replied:

"I solemnly assure you,
no one can enter into God's
    kingdom
without being begotten of water
    and Spirit.

1, 50f: *You will see . . . :* these verses may be a play on the name "Israel," which was popularly interpreted as "a man who sees God." There may be a reference in v 51 to Jacob's ladder (Gn 28, 12). *I solemnly assure you:* literally, "Amen, amen." The double "amen" is characteristic of John.

2, 4: *Woman:* this form of address, normally given by Jesus to the women he encountered during his ministry (Mt 15, 28; Lk 13, 12) is entirely courteous. However, there is no attestation of a son's use of "woman," without any qualification, to address his mother; and so some commentators suggest a symbolic meaning. Mary is again called "woman" in 19, 26, and the mother of the Messiah in Rv 12, 1–5 is described as "a woman clothed with the sun." Is there symbolic reference to Eve, "the woman" of Genesis? *How does this concern of yours involve me?*: literally, "What is this to me and to you?"—a Hebrew expression; e.g., 2 Kgs 3, 13, where it denies the speaker's involvement in a project proposed by another. *My hour has not yet come:* the translation of this as a question ("Has not my hour now come?") is quite unlikely from a comparison with 7, 6–30. The *hour* is the hour of

Jesus' passion, death, resurrection and ascension (13, 1).

2, 6: *Fifteen to twenty-five gallons:* literally, "two or three measures"; the measure in question was of eight or nine gallons.

2, 8: *Waiter in charge:* it is not clear if the official is a majordomo, or a friend of the family who acted as master of ceremonies; see Sir 32, 1.

2, 12: This transitional verse may be a harmonization with the synoptic tradition in Lk 4, 31 and Mt 4, 13. There are many textual variants.

2, 13: *Passover:* this is the first Passover mentioned in John; a second is mentioned in 6, 4, a third in 13, 1. If these chronological indications are to be taken literally, they point to a ministry of at least two years.

2, 14ff: This is almost certainly the same cleansing the other gospels place in the last days of Jesus' life (Mt, on the day Jesus entered Jerusalem; Mk, on the next day). The order of events in the gospel narratives is often determined by theological motives rather than by chronological data.

2, 15: *Sheep and oxen:* in John the cleansing is a more violent attack on the temple, because the animals necessary for sacrifice are expelled.

2, 19: This saying is reported by the false witnesses in the synoptic account of Jesus' trial before Caiaphas (Mk 14, 58; Mt 26, 61); see also Mk 15, 29; Acts 6, 14. According to John, Jesus says that it is the Jewish authorities themselves who will destroy the temple; the false witnesses say that Jesus threatened to destroy it.

3, 3: *Begotten:* the Greek verb can mean "born" from a female principle, or "begotten" by a male principle. As in 1, 13, John primarily means it as "begotten," though many early versions translate it as "born" or even, with heightened baptismal symbolism, "reborn." *From above:* the Greek term *anothen* means both "again" and "from above." V 31 below shows that Jesus means it as "from above," but Nicodemus misunderstands. (A misunderstanding that brings out Jesus' teaching is a common literary device in John.)

3, 5: The Council of Trent declared that *water* here is not a metaphor but means real water. This passage has had an important role in baptismal theology.

6 Flesh begets flesh,
   Spirit begets spirit.
7 Do not be surprised that I tell
   you
   you must all be begotten from
     above.
8 The wind blows where it will.
   You hear the sound it makes
   but you do not know where it
     comes from, or where it
     goes.
   So it is with everyone begotten
     of the Spirit."

9 "How can such a thing happen?"
asked Nicodemus. 10 Jesus responded: "You hold the office of
teacher of Israel and still you do not
understand these matters?

11 "I solemnly assure you,
   we are talking about what we
     know,
   we are testifying to what we
     have seen,
   but you do not accept our
     testimony.
12 If you do not believe
   when I tell you about earthly
     things,
   how are you to believe
   when I tell you about those of
     heaven?
13 No one has gone up to heaven
   except the One who came down
     from there—
   the Son of Man [who is in
     heaven].
14 Just as Moses lifted up the
     serpent in the desert,
   so must the Son of Man be
     lifted up,
15 that all who believe
   may have eternal life in him.
16 Yes, God so loved the world
   that he gave his only Son,
   that whoever believes in him
     may not die
   but may have eternal life.

17 God did not send the Son into
     the world
   to condemn the world,
   but that the world might be
     saved through him.
18 Whoever believes in him avoids
     condemnation,
   but whoever does not believe is
     already condemned
   for not believing in the name of
     God's only Son.
19 The judgment of condemnation
     is this:
   the light came into the world,
   but men loved darkness rather
     than light
   because their deeds were wicked.
20 Everyone who practices evil
   hates the light;
   he does not come near it
   for fear his deeds will be exposed.
21 But he who acts in truth
   comes into the light,
   to make clear
   that his deeds are done in God."

Final Witness of the Baptizer

22 Later on, Jesus and his disciples came into Judean territory, and
he spent some time with them there
baptizing. 23 John too was baptizing at Aenon near Salim where
water was plentiful, and people kept
coming to be baptized. 24 (John
of course, had not yet been thrown
into prison.) 25 A controversy
about purification arose between
John's disciples and a certain Jew.
26 So they came to John, saying,
"Rabbi, the man who was with you
across the Jordan—the one about
whom you have been testifying—
is baptizing now, and everyone
is flocking to him." 27 John
answered:

"No one can lay hold on
  anything

unless it is given him from on
  high.

28 You yourselves are witnesses to
the fact that I said: 'I am not the
Messiah; I am sent before him.'

29 "It is the groom who has the
     bride.
   The groom's best man
   waits there listening for him
   and is overjoyed to hear his
     voice.
   That is my joy, and it is
     complete.
30 He must increase,
   while I must decrease.

Discourse Concluded

31 "The One who comes from
     above is above all;
   the one who is of the earth is
     earthly,
   and he speaks on an earthly
     plane.
   The One who comes from
     heaven [who is above all]
32 testifies to what he has seen and
     heard,
   but no one accepts his testimony.
33 Whoever does accept this
     testimony
   certifies that God is truthful.
34 For the One whom God has
     sent
   speaks the words of God;
   he does not ration his gift of the
     Spirit.
35 The Father loves the Son
   and has given everything over
     to him.
36 "Whoever believes in the Son
   has life eternal.
   Whoever disobeys the Son
   will not see life,
   but must endure the wrath of
     God."

3, 8: *Wind:* the Greek word *pneuma* means both "wind" and "spirit." We can see from the context that John is playing on the double meaning, with wind as the primary comparison.

3, 13: *Has gone up to heaven:* the seeming reference to the ascension in the past tense is difficult, but tenses in John seem to be somewhat timeless; see 8, 58. *Who is in heaven:* if this is a true reading, it may be compared to 1, 18.

3, 14: *Lifted up:* the first of three references (8, 28; 12, 32) to the "lifting up" of Jesus the Son of Man: i.e., in crucifixion, resurrection, and ascension. These are comparable to the three references to the passion and resurrection in the synoptics (Mk 8, 31; 9, 30; 10, 31).

3, 15: This might be translated "that everyone who

believes in him may have eternal life." *Eternal life,* used here for the first time in John, stresses the quality of the life rather than its duration.

3, 16: *Gave:* a reference to both the incarnation and the death of Jesus; cf Rom 8, 32.

3, 17ff: *Condemn . . . judgment:* the same Greek root is involved, and it has both shades of meaning. Jesus' coming provokes judgment; his purpose is to save, but some condemn themselves by turning from the light.

3, 19: John stresses that judgment is not only a matter of the future but is partially realized here and now.

3, 22: *Baptizing:* that after his baptism Jesus conducted a baptizing ministry is not mentioned by the synoptics; cf 4, 2.

3, 23: *Aenon near Salim:* uncertain site, either in the upper Jordan valley or in Samaria.

3, 25: *Controversy:* perhaps this dispute concerned the relative value of the two baptisms or the value of baptism vs. Jewish purifications (2, 6).

3, 27: *No one:* it is more likely that this refers to Jesus than to the Baptizer.

3, 29: *Groom's best man:* the one who arranged the wedding and acted as go-between for groom and bride.

3, 31–36: It is uncertain whether these words are spoken by the Baptizer, by Jesus, or by the evangelist. Perhaps an originally independent discourse of Jesus has been brought here by way of comment on the two preceding scenes of ch 3. *His gift:* it is uncertain to whom the "his" refers: to God or to Jesus.

4 Now when Jesus learned that the Pharisees had heard that he was winning over and baptizing more disciples than John 2 (in fact, however, it was not Jesus himself who baptized, but his disciples), 3 he left Judea and started back for Galilee again.

The Samaritan Woman

4 He had to pass through Samaria, 5 and his journey brought him to a Samaritan town named Shechem near the plot of land which Jacob had given to his son Joseph. 6 This was the site of Jacob's well. Jesus, tired from his journey, sat down at the well.

The hour was about noon. 7 When a Samaritan woman came to draw water, Jesus said to her, "Give me a drink." 8 (His disciples had gone off to the town to buy provisions.) 9 The Samaritan woman said to him, "You are a Jew. How can you ask me, a Samaritan and a woman, for a drink?" (Recall that Jews have nothing to do with Samaritans.) 10 Jesus replied:

"If only you recognized God's gift,
and who it is that is asking you for a drink,
you would have asked him instead,
and he would have given you living water."

11 "Sir," she challenged him, "you do not have a bucket and this well is deep. Where do you expect to get this flowing water? 12 Surely you do not pretend to be greater than our ancestor Jacob, who gave us this well and drank from it with his sons and his flocks?" 13 Jesus replied:

"Everyone who drinks this water will be thirsty again.

14 But whoever drinks the water I give him
will never be thirsty;
no, the water I give
shall become a fountain within him,
leaping up to provide eternal life."

15 The woman said to him, "Give me this water, sir, so that I shall not grow thirsty and have to keep coming here to draw water." 16 He said to her, "Go, call your husband, and then come back here." 17 "I have no husband," replied the woman. "You are right in saying you have no husband!" Jesus exclaimed. 18 "The fact is, you have had five, and the man you are living with now is not your husband. What you said is true."

19 "Sir," answered the woman, "I can see you are a prophet. 20 Our ancestors worshiped on this mountain, but you people claim that Jerusalem is the place where men ought to worship God." 21 Jesus told her:

"Believe me, woman,
an hour is coming
when you will worship the Father
neither on this mountain
nor in Jerusalem.
22 You people worship what you do not understand,
while we understand what we worship;
after all, salvation is from the Jews.
23 Yet an hour is coming, and is already here,
when authentic worshipers will worship the Father in Spirit and truth.
Indeed, it is just such worshipers the Father seeks.
24 God is Spirit,
and those who worship him must worship in Spirit and truth."

25 The woman said to him: "I know there is a Messiah coming." (This term means Anointed.) "When he comes, he will tell us everything." 26 Jesus replied, "I who speak to you am he."

27 His disciples, returning at this point, were surprised that Jesus was speaking with a woman. No one put a question, however, such as "What do you want of him?" or "Why are you talking with her?" 28 The woman then left her water jar and went off into the town. She said to the people: 29 "Come and see someone who told me everything I ever did! Could this not be the Messiah?" 30 At that they set out from the town to meet him.

31 Meanwhile the disciples were urging him, "Rabbi, eat something." 32 But he told them:

"I have food to eat
of which you do not know."

33 At this the disciples said to one another, "Do you suppose that someone has brought him something to eat?" 34 Jesus explained to them:

"Doing the will of him who sent me
and bringing his work to completion
is my food.
35 Do you not have a saying:
'Four months more
and it will be harvest!'?
Listen to what I say:
Open your eyes and see!
The fields are shining for harvest!
36 The reaper already collects his wages
and gathers a yield for eternal life,
that sower and reaper may rejoice together.

4, 2: An editorial refinement on 3, 22, perhaps against followers of the Baptizer in the late first century who exalted the Baptizer above Jesus.

4, 5f: Shechem: most MSS have Sychar which St. Jerome identifies with Shechem. He may be correct in saying that copyists mistakenly put "Sychar" for "Shechem." Jacob's well (unmentioned in the Old Testament) is the well of Shechem. The town is situated in the valley between Mounts Gerizim and Ebal; cf Dt 27; Jos 3, 30.

4, 9: Samaritan women were regarded as ritually impure, and therefore Jews were forbidden to drink from any vessel they had handled.

4, 10f: Living water: Jesus is speaking of the water of life; the woman thinks of flowing water, so much more desirable than stale cistern water. This is a typical example of Johannine use of a hearer's misunderstanding; cf note on 3, 3.

4, 19: Sir: the original word (used also in v 11) means either "Sir" or "Lord"; here the latter term may be more appropriate if the woman is moving toward faith.

4, 20: The Samaritans included among the ten commandments the obligation to worship on Mount Gerizim. It was an ancient holy place. "Ebal" is probably an anti-Samaritan Jewish emendation of "Gerizim"; cf Dt 27, 4.

4, 23: In Spirit and truth: this is not a reference to an interior worship within man's spirit. The Spirit is the Spirit of truth (14, 16f), the Spirit given by God which reveals truth and raises up man to worship God on the appropriate level. This idea presupposes the "begetting by Spirit" in 3, 5.

4, 25: The expectations of the Samaritans are expressed here in more familiar Jewish terminology. They did not expect a messianic king of the house of David but a prophet like Moses (Dt 18, 15).

4, 35: This is probably a proverb rather than a real time indication; cf Mt 9, 37f.

4, 36: Already: it is possible that this word belongs at the end of v 35.

37 Here we have the saying verified: 'One man sows; another reaps.'
38 I sent you to reap what you had not worked for. Others have done the labor, and you have come into their gain.''

39 Many Samaritans from that town believed in him on the strength of the woman's word of testimony: "He told me everything I ever did." 40 The result was that, when these Samaritans came to him, they begged him to stay with them awhile. So he stayed there two days, 41 and through his own spoken word many more came to faith. 42 As they told the woman: "No longer does our faith depend on your story. We have heard for ourselves, and we know that this really is the Savior of the world."

Return to Galilee

43 When the two days were over, he left for Galilee. 44 (Jesus himself had testified that no one esteems a prophet in his own country.) 45 When he arrived in Galilee, the people there welcomed him. They themselves had been at the feast and had seen all that he had done in Jerusalem on that occasion.

Second Sign at Cana

46 He went to Cana in Galilee once more, where he had made the water wine. At Capernaum there happened to be a royal official whose son was ill. 47 When he heard that Jesus had come back from Judea to Galilee, he went to him and begged him to come down and restore health

to his son, who was near death. 48 Jesus replied, "Unless you people see signs and wonders, you do not believe." 49 "Sir," the royal official pleaded with him, "come down before my child dies." 50 Jesus told him, "Return home. Your son will live." The man put his trust in the word Jesus spoke to him, and started for home.

51 He was on his way there when his servants met him with the news that his boy was going to live. 52 When he asked them at what time the boy had shown improvement, they told him, "The fever left him yesterday afternoon about one." 53 It was at that very hour, the father realized, that Jesus had told him, "Your son is going to live." He and his whole household thereupon became believers. 54 This was the second sign that Jesus performed on returning from Judea to Galilee.

Cure on a Sabbath Feast

5 Later, on the occasion of a Jewish feast, Jesus went up to Jerusalem. 2 Now in Jerusalem by the Sheep Pool there is a place with the Hebrew name Bethesda. Its five porticoes 3 were crowded with sick people lying there blind, lame or disabled [4] [waiting for the movement of the water]. 5 There was one man who had been sick for thirty-eight years. 6 Jesus, who knew he had been sick a long time, said when he saw him lying there, "Do you want to be healed?" 7 "Sir," the sick man answered, "I do not have anyone to plunge me into the pool once the water has been stirred up. By the time I get there,

someone else has gone in ahead of me." 8 Jesus said to him, "Stand up! Pick up your mat and walk!" 9 The man was immediately cured; he picked up his mat and began to walk.

The day was a sabbath. 10 Consequently, some of the Jews began telling the man who had been cured, "It is the sabbath, and you are not allowed to carry that mat around." 11 He explained: "It was the man who cured me who told me, 'Pick up your mat and walk.'" 12 "This person who told you to pick it up and walk," they asked, "who is he?" 13 The man who had been restored to health had no idea who it was. The crowd in that place was so great that Jesus had been able to slip away.

14 Later on, Jesus found him in the temple precincts and said to him: "Remember, now, you have been cured. Give up your sins so that something worse may not overtake you." 15 The man went off and informed the Jews that Jesus was the one who had cured him.

Discourse on His Sabbath Work

16 It was because Jesus did things such as this on the sabbath that they began to persecute him. 17 But he had an answer for them:

"My Father is at work until now, and I am at work as well."

18 The reason why the Jews were even more determined to kill him was that he not only was breaking the sabbath but, worse still, was speaking

---

4, 44: The parenthetical verse is probably the reminiscence of a tradition similar to that in Mk 6, 4.

4, 46–52: The story of the royal official's son is probably a third version of the story of the centurion's boy (Mt 8, 5–13) or servant (Lk 7, 1–10) found in slightly different forms in the synoptic tradition. The variants are inconsequential details, of the sort that could arise in oral tradition.

4, 50f.53: *Live:* this theme of life will be commented on by Jesus in 5, 21ff.

4, 53: The author ends a section by referring back to its beginning (2, 11).

5, 1: This was probably not a winter feast or the people would not have been in open porticoes. The reference later in the discourse to Moses (5, 45f) leads some scholars to think that the feast was Pentecost (fifty days after Passover; the feast of the giving of the law to Moses on Sinai). Another suggestion is Passover. All that John emphasizes is that it was a sabbath.

5, 2: Another possible translation is "Now in Jerusalem, by the Sheep [Gate], there is a pool with

the Hebrew name Bethesda." The name of the region was given to the pool as well. Variants of *Bethesda* are "Bethsaida" and "Be(t)zatha." This pool with its five porticoes has been excavated in recent years in the area northeast of the temple.

5, 3: Some good Western MSS, including St. Jerome's Vulgate, have the additional phrase [waiting for the movement of the water]. We may conclude from v 7 that there was an intermittent spring in the pool that bubbled up occasionally. People attributed a curative value to the turbulence produced by the spring.

5, 4: Toward the end of the second century in the West, and among the fourth-century Greek Fathers, there is knowledge of an additional verse: "For [from time to time] an angel of the Lord used to come down into the pool; and the water was stirred up, so the first one to get in [after the bubbling of the water] was healed of whatever sickness he had had." The appearance of the angel is probably a popular explanation of the turbulence and the healing powers attributed to it. The verse is missing in our best early Greek

witnesses, and the earliest versions; it is not to be found in St. Jerome's original Vulgate. The vocabulary of the verse is markedly non-Johannine.

5, 10: Carrying a sleeping mat on the sabbath was specifically forbidden in rabbinic law.

5, 14: *Give up your sins:* Jesus never draws a one-to-one connection between sin and sickness or misfortune; cf Jn 9, 3; Lk 12, 1–5. Nevertheless he regards sickness as part of the evil introduced into the world by sin, and his mission is to destroy the kingdom of evil in all its forms (Mk 2, 8–11).

5, 17: The sabbath observance was based on God's resting after six days of creation, but the Jewish theologians were perfectly aware that divine providence remained active on the sabbath, keeping all things in existence. It was obvious that on the sabbath God gave life in birth and took it away in death. Jesus is claiming the same right to work as the Father, and, in the discourse that follows, the same power over life and death.

of God as his own Father, thereby making himself God's equal.

The Work of the Son

19 This was Jesus' answer:

"I solemnly assure you,
the Son cannot do anything by
    himself—
he can do only what he sees the
    Father doing.
For whatever the Father does,
the Son does likewise.
20 For the Father loves the Son
and everything the Father does he
    shows him.
Yes, to your great wonderment,
he will show him even greater
    works than these.
21 Indeed, just as the Father raises
    the dead and grants life,
so the Son grants life to those to
    whom he wishes.
22 The Father himself judges no
    one,
but has assigned all judgment to
    the Son,
23 so that all men may honor the
    Son
just as they honor the Father.
He who refuses to honor the Son
refuses to honor the Father who
    sent him.
24 I solemnly assure you,
the man who hears my word
and has faith in him who sent
    me
possesses eternal life.
He does not come under
    condemnation,
but has passed from death to
    life.
25 I solemnly assure you,
an hour is coming, has indeed
    come,
when the dead shall hear the
    voice of the Son of God,
and those who have heeded it
    shall live.
26 Indeed, just as the Father
    possesses life in himself,
so has he granted it to the Son
    to have life in himself.

27 The Father has given over to
    him power to pass judgment
because he is Son of Man;
28 no need for you to be surprised
    at this,
for an hour is coming
in which all those in their tombs
shall hear his voice and come
    forth.
29 Those who have done right shall
    rise to live;
the evildoers shall rise to be
    damned.
30 I cannot do anything of myself.
I judge as I hear,
and my judgment is honest
because I am not seeking my
    own will
but the will of him who sent me.

Witnesses to Jesus

31 "If I witness on my own behalf,
you cannot verify my testimony;
32 but there is another who is
    testifying on my behalf,
and the testimony he renders me
I know can be verified.
33 You have sent to John,
who has testified to the truth.
34 (Not that I myself accept such
    human testimony—
I refer to these things only for
your salvation.)
35 He was the lamp, set aflame and
    burning bright,
and for a while you exulted
    willingly in his light.
36 Yet I have testimony greater
    than John's,
namely, the works the Father
    has given me to accomplish.
These very works which I
    perform
testify on my behalf
that the Father has sent me.
37 Moreover, the Father who sent
    me
has himself given testimony on
    my behalf.
His voice you have never heard,
his form you have never seen,
38 neither do you have his word
    abiding in your hearts

because you do not believe
the One he has sent.
39 Search the Scriptures
in which you think you have
    eternal life—
they also testify on my behalf.
40 Yet you are unwilling to come
    to me
to possess that life.

Unbelief of Jesus' Hearers

41 "It is not that I accept human
    praise—
42 it is simply that I know you,
and you do not have the love of
    God in your hearts.
43 I have come in my Father's
    name,
yet you do not accept me.
But let someone come in his
    own name
and him you will accept.
44 How can people like you believe,
when you accept praise from
    one another
yet do not seek the glory that
    comes from the One [God]?
45 Do not imagine that I will be
    your accuser before the
    Father;
the one to accuse you is Moses
on whom you have set your
    hopes.
46 If you believed Moses
you would then believe me,
for it was about me that he
    wrote.
47 But if you do not believe what
    he wrote,
how can you believe what I say?"

Multiplication of the Loaves at Passover

6 Later on, Jesus crossed the Sea of Galilee [to the shore] of Tiberias; 2 a vast crowd kept following him because they saw the signs he was performing for the sick. 3 Jesus then went up the mountain and sat down there with his disciples. 4 The Jewish feast of Passover was near; 5 when Jesus looked up and caught sight of a vast crowd coming

---

5, 32: *Another:* this is generally understood to be the Father who in four different ways gives testimony to Jesus, as indicated in the verse groupings 33f; 36; 37f; 39f.

5, 35: *Lamp:* this may reflect the description of Elijah in Sir 48, 1.

5, 39: *Search:* this may be a statement: "You

search the Scriptures because you think [them] to have eternal life."

5, 41: *Praise:* the same Greek word means "praise" (from men) and "glory" (from God). There will be a play on this in v 44.

6, 1: *Of Tiberias:* if the bracketed clause is omitted, "Tiberias" stands in awkward apposition as another

name of the lake. It was only considerably later than Jesus' time that this name was given to the lake, since the city of Tiberias was completed only just before Jesus' ministry. If the clause is left in, then the multiplication took place near Tiberias.

6, 5ff: The Gospels of John and Luke have only one account of a multiplication of loaves and fish; Mark and Matthew have two accounts.

toward him, he said to Philip, "Where shall we buy bread for these people to eat?" 6 (He knew well what he intended to do but he asked this to test Philip's response.) 7 Philip replied, "Not even with two hundred days' wages could we buy loaves enough to give each of them a mouthful!"

8 One of Jesus' disciples, Andrew, Simon Peter's brother, remarked to him, 9 "There is a lad here who has five barley loaves and a couple of dried fish, but what good is that for so many?" 10 Jesus said, "Get the people to recline." Even though the men numbered about five thousand, there was plenty of grass for them to find a place on the ground. 11 Jesus then took the loaves of bread, gave thanks, and passed them around to those reclining there; he did the same with the dried fish, as much as they wanted. 12 When they had had enough, he told his disciples, "Gather up the crusts that are left over so that nothing will go to waste." 13 At this, they gathered twelve baskets full of pieces left over by those who had been fed with the five barley loaves.

14 When the people saw the sign he had performed they began to say, "This is undoubtedly the Prophet who is to come into the world." 15 At that, Jesus realized that they would come and carry him off to make him king, so he fled back to the mountain alone.

Walking on the Sea

16 As evening drew on, his disciples came down to the lake. 17 They embarked, intending to cross the lake toward Capernaum. By this time it was dark, and Jesus had still not joined them; 18 moreover, with a strong wind blowing, the sea was becoming rough. 19 Finally, when they had rowed three or four miles, they sighted Jesus approaching the boat, walking on the water. They were frightened, 20 but he told them, "It is I; do not be afraid." 21 They wanted to take him into the boat, but suddenly it came aground on the shore they had been approaching.

22 The crowd remained on the other side of the lake. The next day they realized that there had been only one boat there and that Jesus had not left in it with his disciples; rather, they had set out by themselves. 23 Then some boats came out from Tiberias near the place where they had eaten the bread after the Lord had given thanks. 24 Once the crowd saw that neither Jesus nor his disciples were there, they too embarked in the boats and went to Capernaum looking for Jesus.

Discourse on the Bread of Life

25 When they found him on the other side of the lake, they said to him, "Rabbi, when did you come here?" 26 Jesus answered them:

"I assure you,
you are not looking for me
　　because you have seen signs
but because you have eaten your
　　fill of the loaves.
27 You should not be working for
　　perishable food
but for food that remains unto
　　life eternal,
food which the Son of Man will
　　give you;
it is on him that God the Father
　　has set his seal."

28 At this they said to him, "What must we do to perform the works of God?" 29 Jesus replied:

"This is the work of God:
have faith in the One whom he
　　sent."

30 "So that we can put faith in you," they asked him, "what sign are you going to perform for us to see? What is the 'work' you do? 31 Our ancestors had manna to eat in the desert; according to Scripture, 'He gave them bread from the heavens to eat.'" 32 Jesus said to them:

"I solemnly assure you,
　　it was not Moses who gave you
　　　　bread from the heavens;
　　it is my Father who gives you
　　　　the real heavenly bread.
33 God's bread comes down from
　　heaven
　　and gives life to the world."

34 "Sir, give us this bread always," they besought him.

35 Jesus explained to them:

"I myself am the bread of life.
　No one who comes to me shall
　　　ever be hungry,
　no one who believes in me shall
　　　ever thirst.
36 But as I told you—
　though you have seen me, you
　　　still do not believe.
37 All that the Father gives me
　　　shall come to me;
　no one who comes will I ever
　　　reject,
38 because it is not to do my own
　　　will
　that I have come down from
　　　heaven,
　but to do the will of him who
　　　sent me.
39 It is the will of him who sent me
　that I should lose nothing of
　　　what he has given me;
　rather, that I should raise it up
　　　on the last day.
40 Indeed, this is the will of my
　　　Father,
　that everyone who looks upon
　　　the Son
　and believes in him
　shall have eternal life."

6, 14: *The Prophet*: probably the prophet like Moses (see note on 1, 21). Jesus, like Moses, had fed the people miraculously.

6, 19: *Walking on the water*: the Greek would permit a translation "on the seashore" or "by the sea." This would eliminate the miraculous from the story and leave it pointless. In Mt 14, 24–25, it is quite clear that Jesus walked upon the sea.

6, 20: *It is I*: literally, "I am"—perhaps the expression intended to connote divinity; see note on 8, 24.

6, 21: It is not clear whether Jesus got into the boat, or whether the sudden arrival at the shore is presented as miraculous. Possibly both are intended.

6, 22ff: These verses have many variants in the manuscripts and are awkward and somewhat illogical. Were all five thousand transported? There may be several forms of the account combined in our present readings.

6, 23: *From Tiberias near the place*: it is not clear whether Tiberias is near the place or the boats came near to the place; cf v 1 and the note there.

6, 31: There is evidence that the Jews believed the miracle of the manna would be repeated in the last days; hence their challenge to discover whether these were the last days.

6, 33: *God's bread comes down*: the Greek is ambiguous for it literally reads, "God's bread is that which [or he who] comes down," etc.

6, 35: What does Jesus mean by "the bread of life"? Because of the emphasis on believing and teaching in vv 35–50, most scholars today think of the bread in these verses as primarily a figurative reference to Jesus' revelation or teaching. There may well be a secondary reference to the Eucharist. In vv 51–58, however, the eucharistic theme comes to the fore. Many, then, place a break in the discourse between vv 50 and 51.

6, 37.39: *All that . . . nothing*: for a reason not totally clear, the evangelist uses the neuter in these verses. Some think it is a grammatical peculiarity with no special significance; others see it as a reading indicative of universality.

Him I will raise up on the last
   day."

41 At this the Jews started to murmur
in protest because he claimed, "I am
the bread that came down from
heaven." 42 They kept saying: "Is
this not Jesus, the son of Joseph?
Do we not know his father and
mother? How can he claim to have
come down from heaven?"

43 "Stop your murmuring," Jesus
told them.

44 "No one can come to me
   unless the Father who sent me
      draws him;
   I will raise him up on the last
      day.
45 It is written in the prophets:
   'They shall all be taught by God.'
   Everyone who has heard the
      Father
   and learned from him
   comes to me.
46 Not that anyone has seen the
      Father—
   only the one who is from God
   has seen the Father.
47 Let me firmly assure you,
   he who believes has eternal life.
48 I am the bread of life.
49 Your ancestors ate manna in the
      desert, but they died.
50 This is the bread that comes
      down from heaven
   for a man to eat and never die.
51 I myself am the living bread
   come down from heaven.
   If anyone eats this bread
   he shall live forever;
   the bread I will give
   is my flesh, for the life of the
      world."

52 At this the Jews quarreled
among themselves, saying, "How
can he give us his flesh to eat?"
53 Thereupon Jesus said to them:

   "Let me solemnly assure you,

if you do not eat the flesh of the
      Son of Man
   and drink his blood,
   you have no life in you.
54 He who feeds on my flesh
   and drinks my blood
   has life eternal,
   and I will raise him up on the
      last day.
55 For my flesh is real food
   and my blood real drink.
56 The man who feeds on my
      flesh
   and drinks my blood
   remains in me, and I in him.
57 Just as the Father who has life
      sent me
   and I have life because of the
      Father,
   so the man who feeds on me
   will have life because of me.
58 This is the bread that came
      down from heaven.
   Unlike your ancestors who ate
      and died nonetheless,
   the man who feeds on this bread
   shall live forever."

59 He said this in a synagogue
instruction at Capernaum.

Effect of the Discourse

60 After hearing his words, many
of his disciples remarked, "This sort
of talk is hard to endure! How can
anyone take it seriously?" 61 Jesus
was fully aware that his disciples were
murmuring in protest at what he had
said. "Does it shake your faith?" he
asked them.

62 "What, then, if you were to see
      the Son of Man
   ascend to where he was
      before . . . ?
63 It is the spirit that gives life;
   the flesh is useless.
   The words I spoke to you
   are spirit and life.

64 Yet among you there are some
   who do not believe."

(Jesus knew from the start, of course,
the ones who refused to believe, and
the one who would hand him over.)
65 He went on to say:

   "This is why I have told you
   that no one can come to me
   unless it is granted him by the
      Father."

66 From this time on, many of his
disciples broke away and would not
remain in his company any longer.
67 Jesus then said to the Twelve,
"Do you want to leave me too?"
68 Simon Peter answered him, "Lord
to whom shall we go? You have the
words of eternal life. 69 We have
come to believe; we are convinced
that you are God's holy one."

70 Jesus replied, "Did I not choose
the Twelve of you myself? Yet one
of you is a devil." 71 (He was
talking about Judas, son of Simon
the Iscariot, who, though one of the
Twelve, was going to hand Jesus
over.)

Feast of Booths

7 After this, Jesus moved about
   within Galilee. He had decided
not to travel in Judea because some
of the Jews were looking for a chance
to kill him. 2 However, as the
Jewish feast of Booths drew near,
3 his brothers had this to say: "You
ought to leave here and go to Judea
so that your disciples there may see
the works you are performing. 4
No one who wishes to be known publicly keeps his actions hidden. If you
are going to do things like these, you
may as well display yourself to the
world at large." 5 (As a matter of
fact, not even his brothers had
much confidence in him.) 6 Jesus
answered them:

6, 51: The last two lines of 51 may be compared to
the Lucan eucharistic formula (22, 19): "This [bread]
is my body which is given for you."

6, 54–58: *Feeds:* the verb that John uses in these
verses is not the regular verb "to eat," but a very
realistic verb with a rather crude connotation of
"munch, gnaw." This may be part of John's emphasis
on the reality of the flesh and blood of Jesus; cf v 55.

6, 57: *Because of me:* this can mean either "from
me" (as the source) or "for my sake" (as the reason).

6, 60ff: These verses seem to refer more to the
themes of vv 35–50, than to those of vv 51–58.

6, 62: This unfinished conditional sentence is

obscure. Probably there is a reference to vv 49–51.
Jesus claims to be *the bread that comes down from
heaven;* this claim provokes incredulity (v 60); and so
Jesus asks what will be said when he goes up to
heaven.

6, 63: *Spirit . . . flesh:* probably not a reference to
the eucharistic flesh of Jesus but to the supernatural
and the natural, as in 3, 6.

6, 65: *I have told:* presumably, this is a reference to
v 44 combined with v 37.

6, 71: Here and in 13, 2.26, it is not entirely clear
whether Iscariot (man from Kerioth?) modifies *Judas*
or *Simon.*

7, 2: *Booths:* the autumn harvest feast lasting eight
days, during which the people lived in huts. This was
looked on as a reminiscence of their ancestors' life in
tents in the desert after the Exodus. The Hebrew name
for this festival and its booths is Sukkoth.

7, 3: *Brothers:* these relatives are never portrayed
as disciples until after the resurrection (Acts 1, 14).
Mt 13, 55 and Mk 6, 3 give the names of four of them.

7, 6: *Time:* a synonym for "hour" (see 2, 4), the
period of Jesus' death and resurrection. The Christian
reader of the gospel understands the theological play
on words: this feast does not yet mark the time of
Jesus' glorification; he will not die at this time.

"It is not yet the right time for
   me,
whereas the time is always right
   for you.
7 The world is incapable of hating
   you,
but it does hate me
because of the evidence I bring
   against it
that what it does is evil.

8 Go up yourselves to the festival.
I am not going up to this festival
because the time is not yet ripe for
me." 9 Having said this, he stayed
on in Galilee. 10 However, once
his brothers had gone up to the
festival he too went up, but as if in
secret and not for all to see.

11 During the festival, naturally,
the Jews were looking for him,
asking, "Where is that troublemaker?" 12 Among the crowds
there was much guarded debate
about him. Some maintained, "He
is a good man," while others kept
saying, "Not at all—he is only misleading the crowd!" 13 No one
dared talk openly about him, however, for fear of the Jews.

First Episode

14 The feast was half over by the
time Jesus went into the temple area
and began to teach. 15 The Jews
were filled with amazement and said,
"How did this man get his education
when he had no teacher?" 16 This
was Jesus' answer:

"My doctrine is not my own;
it comes from him who sent me.
17 Any man who chooses to do his
   will
will know about this doctrine—
namely, whether it comes from
   God
or is simply spoken on my own.
18 Whoever speaks on his own
is bent on self-glorification.

The man who seeks glory for
   him who sent him is
   truthful;
there is no dishonesty in his
   heart.
19 Moses has given you the law,
   has he not?
Yet not one of you keeps it.
Why do you look for a chance
   to kill me?"

20 "You are mad!" the crowd retorted. "Who wants to kill you?"
21 Jesus answered:

"I have performed a single work
and you profess astonishment
   over it.
22 Moses gave you circumcision
(though it did not originate with
   Moses but with the
   patriarchs).
And so, even on a sabbath you
   circumcise a man.
23 If a man can be circumcised on
   the sabbath
to prevent a violation of Mosaic
   law,
how is it you are angry with me
for curing a whole man on the
   sabbath?
24 Stop judging by appearances
and make an honest judgment."

25 This led some of the people of
Jerusalem to remark: "Is this not
the one they want to kill? 26 Here
he is speaking in public and they
don't say a word to him! Perhaps even
the authorities have decided that
this is the Messiah. 27 Still, we know
where this man is from. When the
Messiah comes, no one is supposed
to know his origins."

28 At this, Jesus, who was teaching
in the temple area, cried out:

"So you know me,
and you know my origins?
The truth is, I have not come of
   myself.
I was sent by One who has the
   right to send,

and him you do not know.
29 I know him
because it is from him I come:
   he sent me."

30 At this they tried to seize him, but
no one laid a finger on him because his
hour had not yet come. 31 Many
in the crowd came to believe in him.
They kept saying, "When the Messiah
comes, can he be expected to perform
more signs than this man?" 32
The Pharisees overheard this debate
about him among the crowd, and the
chief priests and Pharisees together
sent temple guards to arrest him.

33 Jesus then said to them:

"Only a little while longer am I
   to be with you,
then I am going away to him
   who sent me.
34 You will look for me, but you
   will not find me;
where I am you cannot come."

35 This caused the Jews to exclaim
among themselves: "Where does he
intend to go that we will not find him?
Surely he is not going off to the
Diaspora among the Greeks, to
teach them? 36 What does he
mean by saying, 'You will look for
me, but you will not find me,' and,
'Where I am you cannot come'?"

Second Episode

37 On the last and greatest day of
the festival, Jesus stood up and cried
out:

"If anyone thirsts, let him come
   to me;
38 let him drink who believes in me.
Scripture has it:
'From within him rivers of
   living water shall flow.'"

39 (Here he was referring to the
Spirit, whom those that came to
believe in him were to receive. There
was, of course, no Spirit as yet, since
Jesus had not yet been glorified.)

7, 8: *I am not going up:* another play on words.
"Go up" refers to his elevation in crucifixion,
resurrection, and ascension; cf 20, 17.

7, 15: *Education:* literally, "How does he know
letters . . ." Children were taught to read and write
by means of the Scriptures. But here more than Jesus'
literacy is being discussed; the people are wondering
how he can teach like a rabbi. Rabbis were trained by
other rabbis and used to quote their teachers.

7, 20: *Mad:* literally, "You have a demon." The
insane were thought to possess or be possessed by a
demonical spirit. One has to determine from the con-

text whether the charge in our terms is one of insanity
or of possession.

7, 26: *Authorities:* the Sanhedrin members; the
same term is used to describe Nicodemus (3, 1).

7, 35: *Diaspora:* the Jews living outside Palestine.
Greeks: probably refers to the Gentiles in the
Mediterranean area; cf 12, 20.

7, 37f: *Last and greatest day:* probably the seventh
day, since the eighth was a day of rest after the feast.
There is some MS evidence for the omission of
greatest as a copyist's clarification.
The translation given makes Christ the source of

the living water. Another reading is possible which
makes the believer himself the source; in that case a
period is placed after *drink* and what remains becomes an independent sentence, "He who believes in
me, etc. *Scripture has it* is not an exact citation of any
passage. Perhaps the reference is to the rock that
Moses tapped during the Exodus. *From within him:*
literally, "from his belly."

7, 39: *No spirit as yet:* in relation to the Christian,
the sending of the Spirit was not to take place until
Jesus' death, resurrection, and ascension; cf 20, 22.

40 Some in the crowd who heard these words began to say, "This must be the Prophet." 41 Others were claiming, "He is the Messiah." But an objection was raised: "Surely the Messiah is not to come from Galilee? 42 Does not Scripture say that the Messiah, being of David's family, is to come from Bethlehem, the village where David lived?" 43 In this fashion the crowd was sharply divided over him. 44 Some of them even wanted to apprehend him. However, no one laid hands on him.

45 When the temple guards came back, the chief priests and Pharisees asked them, "Why did you not bring him in?" 46 "No man ever spoke like that before," the guards replied. "Do not tell us you too have been taken in!" 47 the Pharisees retorted. 48 "You do not see any of the Sanhedrin believing in him, do you? Or the Pharisees? 49 Only this lot, that knows nothing about the law—and they are lost anyway!" 50 One of their own number, Nicodemus (the man who had come to him), spoke up to say, 51 "Since when does our law condemn any man without first hearing him and knowing the facts?" 52 "Do not tell us you are a Galilean too," they taunted him. "Look it up. You will not find the Prophet coming from Galilee."

The Adulteress

53 [Then each went off to his own
8 house, 1 while Jesus went out to the Mount of Olives. 2 At daybreak he reappeared in the temple area; and when the people started coming to him, he sat down and began to teach them. 3 The scribes and the Pharisees led a woman forward who had been caught in adultery. They made her stand there in front of everyone. 4 "Teacher," they said to him, "this woman has been caught in the act of adultery. 5 In the law, Moses ordered such women to be stoned. What do you have to say about the case?" 6 (They were posing this question to trap him, so that they could have something to accuse him of.) Jesus bent down and started tracing on the ground with his finger. 7 When they persisted in their questioning, he straightened up and said to them, "Let the man among you who has no sin be the first to cast a stone at her." 8 A second time he bent down and wrote on the ground. 9 Then the audience drifted away one by one, beginning with the elders. This left him alone with the woman, who continued to stand there before him. Jesus finally straightened up and said to her, "Woman, where did they all disappear to? Has no one condemned you?" 11 "No one, sir," she answered. Jesus said, "Nor do I condemn you. You may go. But from now on, avoid this sin."]

Third Episode

12 Jesus spoke to them once again:

"I am the light of the world.
No follower of mine shall ever
    walk in darkness;
no, he shall possess the light of
    life."

13 This caused the Pharisees to break in with: "You are your own witness. Such testimony cannot be valid." 14 Jesus answered:

"What if I am my own witness?
My testimony is valid
    nonetheless,
because I know where I came
    from
and where I am going;
you know neither the one nor
    the other.
15 You pass judgment according to
    appearances
but I pass judgment on no man.
16 Even if I do judge,
that judgment of mine is valid
because I am not alone:

I have at my side the One who
    sent me [the Father].
17 It is laid down in your law
    that evidence given by two
        persons is valid.
18 I am one of those testifying in
    my behalf,
    the Father who sent me is the
        other."

19 They pressed him: "And where is this 'Father' of yours?" Jesus replied:

"You know neither me nor my
    Father.
If you knew me, you would
    know my Father too."

20 He spoke these words while teaching at the temple treasury. Still, he went unapprehended, because his hour had not yet come.

Warning to Unbelievers

21 Again he said to them:

"I am going away. You will
    look for me
but you will die in your sins.
Where I am going you cannot
    come."

22 At this some of the Jews began to ask, "Does he mean he will kill himself when he claims, 'Where I am going you cannot come'?" 23 He went on:

"You belong to what is below;
I belong to what is above.
You belong to this world—
a world which cannot hold me.
24 That is why I said you would
    die in your sins.
You will surely die in your sins
unless you come to believe that
    I AM."

25 "Who are you, then?" they asked him. Jesus answered:

"What I have been telling you
    from the beginning.
26 I could say much about you in
    condemnation,
but no, I only tell the world

7, 53ff: The story of the adulteress is missing from the best early Greek MSS. Where it does appear, it is found in different places in different MSS; here; or after 7, 36; or at the end of this gospel; or after Lk 21, 38. It seems to have been preserved largely in Western and Latin circles. There are many non-Johannine features in the language, and there are also many doubtful readings. It appears in Jerome's Vulgate. However, it is certainly out of place here; it fits better with the general situation in Lk 21, 38. The Catholic Church accepts it as inspired Scripture.

8, 6: *Tracing*: or "writing" or "recording"; whether Jesus was writing something meaningful is not clear.

8, 15: *Appearances*: literally, "according to the flesh."

8, 16: The last line is literally, "but I and the One who sent me [the Father]."

8, 24.28: *I AM*, an expression which late Jewish tradition understands as a name for God; cf 8, 58.

8, 25: *What I have been telling you from the beginning*: this is a very unclear verse and several other translations are possible: (I am) "what I say to you"; "How is it that I speak to you at all?" The earliest attested reading (Bodmer Papyrus P66) has, "I told you at the beginning what I am also telling you (now)."

what I have heard from him,
the truthful One who sent me."

27 They did not grasp that he was speaking to them of the Father. 28 Jesus continued:

"When you lift up the Son of
     Man,
you will come to realize that I
     AM
and that I do nothing by myself.
I say only what the Father has
     taught me.
29 The One who sent me is with me.
He has not deserted me
since I always do what pleases
     him."

30 Because he spoke this way, many came to believe in him.

Jesus and Abraham

31 Jesus then went on to say to those Jews who believed in him:

"If you live according to my
     teaching,
you are truly my disciples;
32 then you will know the truth,
and the truth will set you free."

33 "We are descendants of Abraham," was their answer. "Never have we been slaves to anyone. What do you mean by saying, 'You will be free'?" 34 Jesus answered them:

"I give you my assurance,
everyone who lives in sin
is the slave of sin.
35 (No slave has a permanent place
     in the family,
but the son has a place there
     forever.)
36 That is why, if the son frees you,
you will really be free.
37 I realize you are of Abraham's
     stock.
Nonetheless, you are trying to
     kill me
because my word finds no
     hearing among you.
38 I tell what I have seen in the
     Father's presence;

you do what you have heard
     from your father."

39 They retorted, "Our father is Abraham." Jesus told them:

"If you were Abraham's children,
you would be following
     Abraham's example.
40 The fact is, you are trying to
     kill me,
a man who has told you the
     truth
which I have heard from God.
Abraham did nothing like that.
41 Indeed you are doing your
     father's works!"

They cried, "We are no illegitimate breed! We have but one father and that is God himself," 42 Jesus answered:

"Were God your father
you would love me,
for I came forth from God, and
     am here.
I did not come of my own will;
it was he who sent me.
43 Why do you not understand
     what I say?
It is because you cannot bear to
     hear my word.
44 The father you spring from is the
     devil,
and willingly you carry out his
     wishes.
He brought death to man from
     the beginning,
and has never based himself on
     truth;
the truth is not in him.
Lying speech
is his native tongue;
he is a liar and the father of lies.
45 But because I deal in the truth,
you give me no credence.
46 Can any one of you convict me
     of sin?
If I am telling the truth,
why do you not believe me?
47 Whoever is of God
hears every word God speaks.
The reason you do not hear

is that you are not of God."

48 The Jews answered, "Are we not right, after all, in saying you are a Samaritan, and possessed besides?" 49 Jesus replied:

"I am not possessed.
However, I revere my Father,
while you fail to respect me.
50 I seek no glory for myself;
there is one who seeks it, and it
     is he who judges.
51 I solemnly assure you,
if a man is true to my word
he shall never see death."

52 "Now we are sure you are possessed," the Jews retorted. "Abraham is dead. The prophets are dead. Yet you claim, 'A man shall never know death if he keeps my word.' 53 Surely you do not pretend to be greater than our father Abraham, who died! Or the prophets, who died! Whom do you make yourself out to be?" 54 Jesus answered:

"If I glorify myself,
that glory comes to nothing.
He who gives me glory is the
     Father,
the very one you claim for your
     God,
55 even though you do not know
     him.
But I know him.
Were I to say I do not know
     him,
I would be no better than you
     —a liar!
Yes, I know him well,
and I keep his word.
56 Your father Abraham rejoiced
that he might see my day.
He saw it and was glad."

57 At this the Jews objected: "You are not yet fifty! How can you have seen Abraham?" 58 Jesus answered them:

"I solemnly declare it:

before Abraham came to be, I
     AM."

8, 37: *Finds no hearing:* or "finds no place in you"; "does not continue in you"; "takes no hold in you."

8, 38: The translation given in the text understands the second part of the verse to be a sarcastic reference to the descent of the Jews from their father, the devil. There are good grounds, however, for another translation in which (as in the first part of the verse) *father* means God: "you should do what you have heard from the Father."

8, 40: Nowhere else in the New Testament is Jesus

described as *a man* in this broad sense. Probably the phrase is a Semitic expression for "someone."

8, 41: *Illegitimate:* literally, "of fornication"; in the Old Testament, fornication signifies the worship of false gods.

8, 44: *The father of lies:* literally, "of him [i.e., the liar]" or "of it [i.e., the lie]."

8, 48: *Samaritan:* the Samaritans were noted for an interest in magical powers; see Simon Magus in Acts 7, 14–24.

8, 56: *He saw it:* presumably this is a reference to the birth of Jacob (Israel), which was the beginning of the fulfillment of the promises concerning Abraham's seed; see Gn 17, 7 and 21, 6. But there may also be a reference to a popular Jewish tradition that Abraham saw all of his descendants.

8, 57: There is equally good evidence for reading: "How can Abraham have seen you?"

59 At that they picked up rocks to throw at Jesus, but he hid himself and slipped out of the temple precincts.

The Man Born Blind

9 As he walked along, he saw a man who had been blind from birth. 2 His disciples asked him, "Rabbi, was it his sin or that of his parents that caused him to be born blind?" 3 "Neither," answered Jesus:

"It was no sin, either of this
  man
or of his parents.
Rather, it was to let God's
  works show forth in him.
4 We must do the deeds of him
  who sent me
while it is day.
The night comes on
when no one can work.
5 While I am in the world
I am the light of the world."

6 With that Jesus spat on the ground, made mud with his saliva, and smeared the man's eyes with the mud. 7 Then he told him, "Go, wash in the pool of Siloam." (This name means "One who has been sent.") So the man went off and washed, and came back able to see.

8 His neighbors and the people who had been accustomed to see him begging began to ask, "Isn't this the fellow who used to sit and beg?" 9 Some were claiming it was he; others maintained it was not but someone who looked like him. The man himself said, "I am the one." 10 They said to him then, "How were your eyes opened?" 11 He answered: "That man they call Jesus made mud and smeared it on my eyes, telling me to go to Siloam and wash. When I did go and wash, I was able to see." 12 "Where is he?" they asked. He replied, "I have no idea."

13 Next, they took the man who had been born blind to the Pharisees. 14 (Note that it was on a sabbath that Jesus had made the mud paste and opened his eyes.) 15 The Pharisees, in turn, began to inquire how he had recovered his sight. He told them, "He put mud on my eyes. I washed it off, and now I can see." 16 This prompted some of the Pharisees to assert, "This man cannot be from God because he does not keep the sabbath." Others objected, "If a man is a sinner, how can he perform signs like these?" They were sharply divided over him. 17 Then they addressed the blind man again: "Since it was your eyes he opened, what do you have to say about him?" "He is a prophet," he replied.

18 The Jews refused to believe that he had really been born blind and had begun to see, until they summoned the parents of this man who now could see. 19 "Is this your son?" they asked, "and if so, do you attest that he was blind at birth? How do you account for the fact that now he can see?" 20 The parents answered: "We know this is our son, and we know he was blind at birth. 21 But how he can see now, or who opened his eyes, we have no idea. Ask him. He is old enough to speak for himself." 22 (His parents answered in this fashion because they were afraid of the Jews, who had already agreed among themselves that anyone who acknowledged Jesus as the Messiah would be put out of the synagogue. 23 That was why his parents said, "He is of age—ask him.")

24 A second time they summoned the man who had been born blind and said to him, "Give glory to God! First of all, we know this man is a sinner." 25 "I would not know whether he is a sinner or not," he answered. "I know this much: I was blind before; now I can see." 26 They persisted: "Just what did he do

to you? How did he open your eyes?" 27 "I have told you once, but you would not listen to me," he answered them. "Why do you want to hear it all over again? Do not tell me you want to become his disciples too?" 28 They retorted scornfully: "You are the one who is that man's disciple. We are disciples of Moses. 29 We know that God spoke to Moses, but we have no idea where this man comes from." 30 He came back at them: "Well, this is news! You do not know where he comes from, yet he opened my eyes. 31 We know that God does not hear sinners, but that if someone is devout and obeys his will, he listens to him. 32 It is unheard of that anyone ever gave sight to a person blind from birth. 33 If this man were not from God, he could never have done such a thing." 34 "What!" they exclaimed, "You are steeped in sin from your birth, and you are giving us lectures?" With that they threw him out bodily.

35 When Jesus heard of his expulsion, he sought him out and asked him, "Do you believe in the Son of Man?" 36 He answered, "Who is he, sir, that I may believe in him?" 37 "You have seen him," Jesus replied. "He is speaking to you now." 38 ["I do believe, Lord," he said, and bowed down to worship him. 39 Then Jesus said:]

"I came into this world to
  divide it,
to make the sightless see
and the seeing blind."

40 Some of the Pharisees around him picked this up, saying, "You are not calling us blind, ar　you?" 41 To which Jesus replied:

"If you were blind
there would be no sin in that.
'But we see,' you say,
and your sin remains.

9, 1: It is difficult to be certain where or when this scene took place. The similarity of 9, 5 and 8, 12 may indicate that the scene is also part of the "Booths" setting. The next time indication is in 10, 22, three months after the feast of Booths. The evangelist may have given to this story a secondary baptismal symbolism by stressing that the man was born blind and was healed by the waters of the pool (v 7).

9, 7: One who has been sent: a reference to Jesus, sent by the Father.
9, 14: In using spittle, and in kneading mud, Jesus had broken the sabbath rules laid down by the scribes.
9, 22f: This parenthetical explanation seems to envisage a situation during the writer's lifetime after Jesus' ministry. Rejection from the synagogue of those Jews who confessed Jesus as the Messiah seems to have

begun in the late eighties, when the curse against the minim or heretics was introduced.
9, 24: Give glory to God: this oath formula before taking testimony is attested in Jos 7, 19.
9, 38: This verse, omitted in important MSS, may be an addition from a baptismal liturgy.

The Good Shepherd

10 "Truly I assure you:
Whoever does not enter the
   sheepfold through the gate
but climbs in some other way
is a thief and a marauder.
2 The one who enters through the
   gate
is shepherd of the sheep;
3 the keeper opens the gate for
   him.
The sheep hear his voice
as he calls his own by name
and leads them out.
4 When he has brought out [all]
   those that are his,
he walks in front of them,
and the sheep follow him
because they recognize his voice.
5 They will not follow a stranger;
such a one they will flee,
because they do not recognize a
   stranger's voice."

6 Even though Jesus used this
figure with them, they did not grasp
what he was trying to tell them.
7 He therefore said [to them again]:

"My solemn word is this:
I am the sheepgate.
8 All who came before me
were thieves and marauders
whom the sheep did not heed.
9 "I am the gate.
Whoever enters through me
will be safe.
He will go in and out,
and find pasture.
10 The thief comes
only to steal and slaughter and
   destroy.
I came that they might have life
and have it to the full.
11 I am the good shepherd;
the good shepherd lays down
   his life for the sheep.
12 The hired hand—who is no
   shepherd

nor owner of the sheep—
catches sight of the wolf coming
and runs away, leaving the
   sheep
to be snatched and scattered by
   the wolf.
13 That is because he works for
   pay;
he has no concern for the sheep.
14 "I am the good shepherd.
I know my sheep
and my sheep know me
15 in the same way that the Father
   knows me
and I know the Father;
for these sheep I will give my
   life.
16 I have other sheep
that do not belong to this fold.
I must lead them, too,
and they shall hear my voice.
There shall be one flock then,
   one shepherd.
17 The Father loves me for this:
that I lay down my life
to take it up again.
18 No one takes it from me;
I lay it down freely.
I have power to lay it down,
and I have power to take it up
   again.
This command I received from
   my Father."

19 Because of these words, the Jews
were sharply divided once more.
20 Many were claiming: "He is
possessed by a devil—out of his
mind! Why pay any attention
to him?" 21 Others maintained:
"These are not the words of a
madman. Surely a devil cannot open
the eyes of the blind!"

Feast of the Dedication

22 It was winter, and the time
came for the feast of the Dedication
in Jerusalem.   23 Jesus was walking

in the temple area, in Solomon's
Portico,   24 when the Jews gathered
around him and said, "How long
are you going to keep us in suspense?
If you really are the Messiah, tell
us so in plain words." 25 Jesus
answered:

"I did tell you, but you do not
   believe.
The works I do in my Father's
   name
give witness in my favor,
26 but you refuse to believe
because you are not my sheep.
27 My sheep hear my voice.
I know them,
and they follow me.
28 I give them eternal life,
and they shall never perish.
No one shall snatch them out of
   my hand.
29 My Father is greater than all, in
   what he has given me,
and there is no snatching out of
   his hand.
30 The Father and I are one."

31 When some of the Jews again
reached for rocks to stone him,
32 Jesus protested to them, "Many
good deeds have I shown you from
the Father. For which of these do you
stone me?"   33 "It is not for any
'good deed' that we are stoning you,"
the Jews retorted, "but for blaspheming.
You who are only a man are
making yourself God." 34 Jesus
answered:

"Is it not written in your law,
'I have said, You are gods'?
35 If it calls those men gods
to whom God's word was
   addressed—
and Scripture cannot lose its
   force—
36 do you claim that I blasphemed
when, as he whom the Father
   consecrated

10, 1: The exact time when these parables were
spoken is difficult to determine—whether at the feast
of Booths, as in chapters 7–9, or at the feast of the
Dedication, as in 10, 22; but they continue the theme
of attack on the Pharisees that ends chapter 9.

10, 6: *Figure:* John uses a different word for
illustrative speech than the "parable" of the synoptics,
but the idea is the same.

10, 7–10: In 7f, the figure is of a gate for the
shepherd to come to the sheep; in 9f, of a gate for the
sheep to *go in and out.*

10, 11.14: The normal Greek word for *good* does
not occur here. Were not the expression *good shepherd*
traditional, it might be preferable to translate "model"
or "noble" shepherd.

10, 16: *Other sheep:* the Gentiles, God's dispersed

children destined to be gathered into one (11, 52).
One flock: St. Jerome in the Vulgate translates "one
fold," but there is no evidence in Greek or Latin to
support this reading. Translating the Greek word as
"sheep-herd" would bring out the wordplay involved
as the Greek terms for "flock" and "shepherd" are as
much alike as "sheep-herd" and "shepherd."

10, 22: *Feast of the Dedication:* held in December,
three months after the feast of Booths (7, 2), to celebrate the Maccabees' rededication of the altar and
reconsecration of the temple in 164 B.C., after their
desecration by the Syrians (1 Mc 4, 36.59). Under its
Hebrew name, Hanukkah, this feast is still a regular
part of Jewish religious observance.

10, 23: *Solomon's Portico:* was on the east side of
the temple area and would offer protection from the

cold winds sweeping in from the desert.

10, 24: *Keep us in suspense:* the literal translation
of the words is "How long will you take away our
life?" Cf 11, 48ff.

10, 29: The textual evidence for the first clause is
very divided; it may also be translated: "As for the
Father, what he has given me is greater than all."

10, 34: This is a reference to the judges who, since
they exercised the divine prerogative to judge (Dt
1, 17), were called "gods"; cf Ex 21, 6, besides Ps
82, 6 from which the quotation comes.

10, 36: *Consecrated:* may be a reference to the
theme of the Hanukkah feast; see note on 10, 22. In
place of the rededicated temple altar, Jesus is consecrated by the Father.

and sent into the world,
I said, 'I am God's Son'?
37 If I do not perform my Father's works,
put no faith in me.
38 But if I do perform them,
even though you put no faith in me,
put faith in these works,
so as to realize what it means
that the Father is in me
and I in him."

39 At these words they again tried to arrest him, but he eluded their grasp.

Return to the Jordan

40 Then he went back across the Jordan to the place where John had been baptizing earlier, and while he stayed there 41 many people came to him. "John may never have performed a sign," they commented, "but whatever John said about this man was true." 42 In that place, many came to believe in him.

The Raising of Lazarus

11 There was a certain man named Lazarus who was sick. He was from Bethany, the village of Mary and her sister Martha. 2 (This Mary whose brother Lazarus was sick was the one who anointed the Lord with perfume and dried his feet with her hair.) 3 The sisters sent word to Jesus to inform him, "Lord, the one you love is sick." 4 Upon hearing this, Jesus said:

"This sickness is not to end in death;
rather it is for God's glory,
that through it the Son of God
may be glorified."

5 Jesus loved Martha and her sister and Lazarus very much. 6 Yet, after hearing that Lazarus was sick, he stayed on where he was for two days more. 7 Finally he said to his disciples, "Let us go back to Judea." 8 "Rabbi," protested the disciples, "with the Jews only recently trying to stone you, you are going back up there again?" 9 Jesus answered:

"Are there not twelve hours of daylight?
if a man goes walking by day
he does not stumble
because he sees the world
bathed in light.
10 But if he goes walking at night
he will stumble
since there is no light in him."

11 After uttering these words, he added, "Our beloved Lazarus has fallen asleep, but I am going there to wake him." 12 At this the disciples objected, "Lord, if he is asleep his life will be saved." 13 Jesus had been speaking about his death, but they thought he meant sleep in the sense of slumber. 14 Finally Jesus said plainly: "Lazarus is dead. 15 For your sakes I am glad I was not there, that you may come to believe. In any event, let us go to him." 16 Then Thomas (the name means "Twin") said to his fellow disciples, "Let us go along, to die with him."

17 When Jesus arrived at Bethany he found that Lazarus had already been in the tomb four days. 18 The village was not far from Jerusalem—just under two miles— 19 and many Jewish people had come out to console Martha and Mary over their brother. 20 When Martha heard that Jesus was coming, she went to meet him, while Mary sat at home. 21 Martha said to Jesus, "Lord, if you had been here, my brother would never have died. 22 Even now, I am sure that God will give you whatever you ask of him." 23 "Your brother will rise again," Jesus assured her. 24 "I know he will rise again," Martha replied, "in the resurrection on the last day." 25 Jesus told her:

"I am the resurrection and the life:
26 whoever believes in me,
though he should die, will come to life;
and whoever is alive and believes in me
will never die.

Do you believe this?" 27 "Yes, Lord," she replied. "I have come to believe that you are the Messiah, the Son of God: he who is to come into the world."

28 When she had said this she went back and called her sister Mary. "The Teacher is here, asking for you," she whispered. 29 As soon as Mary heard this, she got up and started out in his direction. 30 (Actually Jesus had not yet come into the village but was still at the spot where Martha had met him.) 31 The Jews who were in the house with Mary consoling her saw her get up quickly and go out, so they followed her, thinking she was going to the tomb to weep there. 32 When Mary came to the place where Jesus was, seeing him, she fell at his feet and said to him, "Lord, if you had been here my brother would never have died." 33 When Jesus saw her weeping, and the Jews who had accompanied her also weeping, he was troubled in spirit, moved by the deepest emotions. 34 "Where have you laid him?" he asked. "Lord, come and see," they said. 35 Jesus began to weep, 36 which caused the Jews to remark, "See how much he loved him!" 37 But some said, "He opened the eyes of that blind man. Why could not he have done something to stop this man from dying?" 38 Once again troubled in spirit, Jesus approached the tomb.

It was a cave with a stone laid across it. 39 "Take away the stone," Jesus directed. Martha, the dead man's sister, said to him, "Lord, it has been four days now; surely there will be a stench!" 40 Jesus replied, "Did I not assure you that if you believed you would see the glory of God displayed?" 41 They then took

---

11, 1: *Bethany:* a town near Jerusalem (v 18), distinct from Bethany in the Transjordan (1, 28). Among the synoptics, only Luke (10, 38) writes of Mary and Martha, but he locates the scene involving them in the journey from Galilee toward Jerusalem.
11, 10: *No light in him:* the ancient Palestinians

apparently did not grasp clearly the entry of light *through* the eye, but seem to have thought of it as being *in* the eye: cf Lk 11, 34; Mt 6, 23.
11, 16: *The name means "Twin":* or "Thomas, the one called Didymus." "Thomas" is derived from the Hebrew word for twin; "Didymus," a Greek personal

name of the time, from the Greek word for twin.
11, 33: *He was troubled in spirit . . . deepest emotions:* probably signifies that Jesus was angry, perhaps at the lack of faith or at the presence of evil (death).

away the stone and Jesus looked upward and said:

"Father, I thank you for having heard me.
42 I know that you always hear me but I have said this for the sake of the crowd, that they may believe that you sent me."

43 Having said this, he called loudly, "Lazarus, come out!" 44 The dead man came out, bound hand and foot with linen strips, his face wrapped in a cloth. "Untie him," Jesus told them, "and let him go free."

Session of the Sanhedrin

45 This caused many of the Jews who had come to visit Mary, and had seen what Jesus did, to put their faith in him. 46 Some others, however, went to the Pharisees and reported what Jesus had done. 47 The result was that the chief priests and the Pharisees called a meeting of the Sanhedrin. "What are we to do," they said, "with this man performing all sorts of signs? 48 If we let him go on like this, the whole world will believe in him. Then the Romans will come in and sweep away our sanctuary and our nation." 49 One of their number named Caiaphas, who was high priest that year, addressed them at this point: "You have no understanding whatever! 50 Can you not see that it is better for you to have one man die [for the people] than to have the whole nation destroyed?" 51 (He did not say this on his own. It was rather as high priest for that year that he prophesied that Jesus would die for the nation— 52 and not for this nation only, but to gather into one all the dispersed children of God.)

53 From that day onward there was a plan afoot to kill him. 54 In consequence, Jesus no longer moved about freely in Jewish circles. He withdrew instead to a town called Ephraim in the region near the desert, where he stayed with his disciples.

The Last Passover

55 The Jewish Passover was near, which meant that many people from the country went up to Jerusalem for Passover purification. 56 They were on the lookout for Jesus, various people in the temple vicinity saying to each other, "What do you think? Is he likely to come for the feast?" 57 (The chief priests and the Pharisees had given orders that anyone who knew where he was should report it, so that they could apprehend him.)

Anointing at Bethany

12 Six days before Passover Jesus came to Bethany, the village of Lazarus whom Jesus had raised from the dead. 2 There they gave him a banquet, at which Martha served. Lazarus was one of those at table with him. 3 Mary brought a pound of costly perfume made from genuine aromatic nard, with which she anointed Jesus' feet. Then she dried his feet with her hair, and the house was filled with the ointment's fragrance. 4 Judas Iscariot, one of his disciples (the one about to hand him over), protested: 5 "Why was not this perfume sold? It could have brought three hundred silver pieces, and the money have been given to the poor." 6 (He did not say this out of concern for the poor, but because he was a thief. He held the purse, and used to help himself to what was deposited there.) 7 To this Jesus replied: "Leave her alone. Let her

keep it against the day they prepare me for burial. 8 The poor you always have with you, but me you will not always have."

9 The great crowd of Jews discovered he was there and came out, not only because of Jesus but also to see Lazarus whom he had raised from the dead. 10 The fact was, the chief priests planned to kill Lazarus too, 11 because many Jews were going over to Jesus and believing in him on account of Lazarus.

Entry into Jerusalem

12 The next day the great crowd that had come for the feast heard that Jesus was to enter Jerusalem, 13 so they got palm branches and came out to meet him. They kept shouting:

"Hosanna!
Blessed is he who comes in the name of the Lord!
Blessed is the King of Israel!"

14 Jesus found a donkey and mounted it, in accord with Scripture:

15 "Fear not, O daughter of Zion! Your king approaches you on a donkey's colt."

16 (At first, the disciples did not understand all this, but after Jesus was glorified they recalled that the people had done to him precisely what had been written about him.)

17 The crowd that was present when he called Lazarus out of the tomb and raised him from the dead kept testifying to it. 18 The crowd came out to meet him because they heard he had performed this sign. 19 The Pharisees remarked to one another, "See, there is nothing you can do! The whole world has run after him."

11, 47: *What are we to do?:* could be the rhetorical "Why are we doing nothing?"

11, 49: *That year:* emphasizes the conjunction of the office and the year. The Jews attributed a gift of prophecy, sometimes unconscious, to the high priest.

11, 50: *For the people:* this phrase is omitted in some impressive patristic witnesses, and may be a gloss. If it is original, Caiaphas meant "in place of the people"; but in v 51, John takes it to mean "on behalf of."

11, 54: Ephraim is usually located about twelve miles northeast of Jerusalem, as the mountains descend into the Jordan valley.

12, 1ff: This is probably the same scene of anointing that we find in Mk 14, 3-9. The anointing reported in Lk 7, 36-38 is part of a different scene.

Details from these various episodes may have become interchanged.

12, 3: *Perfume made from genuine aromatic nard:* this phrase, found also in Mk 14, 3, is of uncertain meaning.

12, 5: *Silver pieces:* literally, "denarii." A denarius is a day's wage in Mt 20, 2.

12, 7: An obscure verse. It could be taken to mean that Mary was to keep the perfume for Jesus' future burial, though Mk 14, 8 and Jn 19, 39 seem to rule out a future reference. The present scene probably represents Jesus' embalming in a figurative sense.

12, 9: The expression *the great crowd,* here and in v 12, is even more awkward in Greek than in English; many textual witnesses have smoothed it out by omitting the article. It seems to have the function of

uniting the crowd of the entry scene with the witnesses of the Lazarus miracle.

12, 13: See Psalm 118, 25f, and the note there on *Hosanna.*

12, 17f: There seem to be two different crowds in these verses. There are good witnesses to the text which have another reading for v 17: "Then the crowd that was with him began to testify that he had called Lazarus out of the tomb and raised him from the dead."

12, 19: *The whole world:* the sense is that everyone is following Jesus, but John has an ironic play on *world;* he alludes to the universality of salvation (3, 17; 4, 42).

The Coming of Jesus' Hour

20 Among those who had come up to worship at the feast were some Greeks. 21 They approached Philip, who was from Bethsaida in Galilee, and put this request to him: "Sir, we should like to see Jesus." 22 Philip went to tell Andrew; Philip and Andrew in turn came to inform Jesus. 23 Jesus answered them:

"The hour has come
for the Son of Man to be
glorified.
24 I solemnly assure you,
unless the grain of wheat falls
to the earth and dies,
it remains just a grain of wheat
But if it dies,
it produces much fruit.
25 The man who loves his life
loses it,
while the man who hates his
life in this world
preserves it to life eternal.
26 If anyone would serve me,
let him follow me;
where I am,
there will my servant be.
If anyone who serves me,
him the Father will honor.
27 My soul is troubled now,
yet what should I say—
Father, save me from this hour?
But it was for this that I came
to this hour.
28 Father, glorify your name!"

Then a voice came from the sky:

"I have glorified it,
and will glorify it again."

29 When the crowd of bystanders heard the voice, they said it was thunder. Others maintained, "An angel was speaking to him." 30 Jesus answered, "That voice did not come for my sake, but for yours.

31 "Now has judgment come upon
this world,
now will this world's prince be
driven out,
32 and I—once I am lifted up from
earth—
will draw all men to myself."

33 (This statement indicated the sort of death he had to die.) 34 The crowd objected to his words: "We have heard it said in the law that the Messiah is to remain forever. How can you claim that the Son of Man must be lifted up? Just who is this 'Son of Man'?" 35 Jesus answered:

"The light is among you only a
little longer.
Walk while you still have it
or darkness will come over you.
The man who walks in the dark
does not know where he is going.
36 While you have the light,
keep faith in the light;
thus you will become sons of
light."

After this utterance, Jesus left them and went into hiding.

Evaluation of the Ministry

37 Despite his many signs performed in their presence, they refused to believe in him. 38 This was to fulfill the word of the prophet Isaiah:

"Lord, who has believed what
has reached our ears?
To whom has the might of the
Lord been revealed?"

39 The reason they could not believe was that, as Isaiah says elsewhere:

40 "He has blinded their eyes,
and numbed their hearts,
lest they see
or comprehend,
or have a change of heart—
and I should heal them."

41 Isaiah uttered these words because he had seen Jesus' glory, and it was of him he spoke.
42 There were many, even among the Sanhedrin, who believed in him; but they refused to admit it because of the Pharisees, for fear they might be ejected from the synagogue. 43 They preferred the praise of men to the glory of God.

Summary Proclamation

44 Jesus proclaimed aloud:
"Whoever puts faith in me
believes not so much in me
as in him who sent me;
45 and whoever looks on me
is seeing him who sent me.
46 I have come to the world as its
light,
to keep anyone who believes in
me
from remaining in the dark.
47 If anyone hears my words and
does not keep them,
I am not the one to condemn
him,
for I did not come to condemn
the world
but to save it.
48 Whoever rejects me and does
not accept my words
already has his judge,
namely, the word I have
spoken—
it is that which will condemn
him on the last day.
49 For I have not spoken on my
own;
no, the Father who sent me
has commanded me
what to say and how to speak.
50 Since I know that his commandment means eternal life,
whatever I say
is spoken just as he instructed
me."

THE BOOK OF GLORY

The Washing of the Feet

13 Before the feast of Passover, Jesus realized that the hour had come for him to pass from this world to the Father. He had loved his own in this world, and would show his love for them to the end. 2 The devil had already induced Judas, son of Simon Iscariot, to hand

---

12, 20: *Greeks:* not used here in a nationalistic sense. These are Gentile proselytes to Judaism; cf 7, 35.
12, 24: *It remains just a grain of wheat:* literally, "it remains alone."
12, 25: *His life:* the Greek word *psyche* refers to a man's natural life. It does not mean "soul," for Hebrew anthropology did not postulate body/soul dualism in the way that is familiar to us.
12, 34: There is no passage in the Old Testament that states precisely that *the Messiah is to remain forever.* Perhaps the closest is Ps 89, 37.
12,38 ff: John gives a historical explanation of Jewish disbelief, not a psychological one. The Old Testament had to be fulfilled in the New; the disbelief that met Isaiah's message was a foreshadowing of the disbelief that Jesus encountered. In 12, 42 and also in 3, 20, we see that there is no negation of freedom.
13, 2: *Induced:* literally, "The devil put into the heart that Judas should hand him over." It is uncertain into whose heart, Judas' or the devil's?

him over; and so, during the supper, 3 Jesus—fully aware that he had come from God and was going to God, the Father who had handed everything over to him— 4 rose from the meal and took off his cloak. He picked up a towel and tied it around himself. 5 Then he poured water into a basin and began to wash his disciples' feet and dry them with the towel he had around him. 6 Thus he came to Simon Peter, who said to him, "Lord, are you going to wash my feet?" 7 Jesus answered, "You may not realize now what I am doing, but later you will understand." 8 Peter replied, "You shall never wash my feet!" "If I do not wash you," Jesus answered, "you will have no share in my heritage." 9 "Lord," Simon Peter said to him, "then not only my feet, but my hands and head as well." 10 Jesus told him, "The man who has bathed has no need to wash [except for his feet]; he is entirely cleansed, just as you are; though not all." 11 (The reason he said, "Not all are washed clean," was that he knew his betrayer.)

12 After he had washed their feet, he put his cloak back on and reclined at table once more. He said to them:

"Do you understand what I
    just did for you?
13 You address me as 'Teacher'
    and 'Lord,'
and fittingly enough,
    for that is what I am.
14 But if I washed your feet—
I who am Teacher and Lord—
then you must wash each other's
    feet.
15 What I just did was to give you
    an example:
as I have done, so you must do.
16 I solemnly assure you,
    no slave is greater than his
        master;
    no messenger outranks the one
        who sent him.
17 Once you know all these things,

blest will you be if you put
    them into practice.

Role of Judas

18 "What I say is not said of all,
for I know the kind of men I
    chose.
My purpose here is the
    fulfillment of Scripture:
'He who partook of bread with
    me
has raised his heel against me.'
19 I tell you this now, before it
    takes place,
so that when it takes place you
    may believe
that I AM.
20 I solemnly assure you,
he who accepts anyone I send
accepts me,
and in accepting me
accepts him who sent me."

21 After saying this, Jesus grew deeply troubled. He went on to give this testimony:

"I tell you solemnly,
one of you will betray me."

22 The disciples looked at one another, puzzled as to whom he could mean. 23 One of them, the disciple whom Jesus loved, reclined close to him as they ate. 24 Simon Peter signaled him to ask Jesus whom he meant. 25 He leaned back against Jesus' chest and said to him, "Lord, who is he?" 26 Jesus answered, "The one to whom I give the bit of food I dip in the dish." He dipped the morsel, then took it and gave it to Judas, son of Simon Iscariot. 27 Immediately after, Satan entered his heart. Jesus addressed himself to him: "Be quick about what you are to do." 28 (Naturally, none of those reclining at table understood why Jesus said this to him. 29 A few had the idea that, since Judas held the common purse, Jesus was telling him to buy what was needed for the feast, or to give something to the poor.) 30 No sooner

had Judas eaten the morsel than he went out. It was night.

31 Once Judas had left, Jesus said:

"Now is the Son of Man
    glorified
and God is glorified in him.
32 [If God has been glorified in
    him,]
God will, in turn, glorify him in
    himself,
and will glorify him soon.
33 My children, I am not to be
    with you much longer.
You will look for me,
but I say to you now
what I once said to the Jews:
'Where I am going, you cannot
    come.'
34 I give you a new commandment:
Love one another.
Such as my love has been for
    you,
so must your love be for each
    other.
35 This is how all will know you
    for my disciples:
your love for one another."

Peter's Denial Predicted

36 "Lord," Simon Peter said to him, "Where do you mean to go?" Jesus answered:

"I am going where you cannot
    follow me now;
later on you shall come after
    me."

37 "Lord," Peter said to him, "why can I not follow you now? I will lay down my life for you!" 38 "You will lay down your life for me, will you?" Jesus answered. "I tell you truly, the cock will not crow before you have three times disowned me!

Last Discourse

14 "Do not let your hearts be
    troubled.
Have faith in God
and faith in me.

13, 5: *Basin*: the exact vessel is not certain, but it was used for washing, perhaps by pouring, in which case the translation should be "pitcher."

13, 10: *Bathed*: many have suggested that this passage is a symbolic reference to baptism. The Greek root involved is used in baptismal contexts in 1 Cor 6, 11; Eph 5, 26; Ti 3, 5; Heb 10, 22. The washing of the feet was connected with Baptism in early Christian liturgy.

13, 16: *Messenger*: the Greek has *apostolos*, the

only occurrence of the term in John. It is not used in the technical sense here.

13, 23: *The disciple whom Jesus loved* is mentioned in 19, 26; 20, 2; 21, 7. A disciple, called *another disciple* or *the other disciple*, is mentioned in 18, 15 and 20, 2; and in the latter reference he is identified with the disciple whom Jesus loved. There is also an unnamed disciple in 1, 35–40. It has been traditional to identify the disciple thus variously referred to as St. John.

13, 31–38: These verses form an introduction to the last discourse of Jesus, which runs through chapters 14–17. In it John has collected Jesus' words to *his own* (cf 13, 1). There are indications that several speeches have been fused together, e.g., in 14, 31 and 17, 1.

13, 32: *God will . . . glorify him in himself*: the concluding word probably refers to the Father rather than to Jesus; cf 17, 5.21.

2 In my Father's house there are
    many dwelling places;
  otherwise, how could I have told
    you
  that I was going to prepare a
    place for you?
3 I am indeed going to prepare a
    place for you,
  and then I shall come back to
    take you with me,
  that where I am you also may
    be.
4 You know the way that leads
    where I go."

5 "Lord," said Thomas, "we do not
know where you are going. How can
we know the way?" 6 Jesus told
him:

  "I am the way, and the truth,
    and the life;
  no one comes to the Father but
    through me.
7 If you really knew me, you
    would know my Father
    also.
  From this point on you know
    him; you have seen him."

8 "Lord," Philip said to him,
"show us the Father and that will be
enough for us." 9 "Philip," Jesus
replied, "after I have been with you
all this time, you still do not know
me?

  "Whoever has seen me has seen
    the Father.
  How can you say, 'Show us the
    Father'?
10 Do you not believe that I am
    in the Father
  and the Father is in me?
  The words I speak are not
    spoken of myself;
  it is the Father who lives in me
    accomplishing his works.
11 Believe me that I am in the
    Father
  and the Father is in me,

or else, believe because of the
    works I do.
12 I solemnly assure you,
  the man who has faith in me
  will do the works I do,
  and greater far than these.
  Why? Because I go to the
    Father,
13 and whatever you ask in my
    name
  I will do,
  so as to glorify the Father in
    the Son.
14 Anything you ask me in my
    name
  I will do.
15 If you love me
  and obey the commands I give
    you,
16 I will ask the Father
  and he will give you another
    Paraclete—
  to be with you always:
17 the Spirit of truth,
  whom the world cannot accept,
  since it neither sees him nor
    recognizes him;
  but you can recognize him
  because he remains with you
  and will be within you.
18 I will not leave you orphaned;
  I will come back to you.
19 A little while now and the world
    will see me no more;
  but you see me
  as one who has life, and you
    will have life.
20 On that day you will know
  that I am in my Father,
  and you in me, and I in you.
21 He who obeys the command-
    ments he has from me
  is the man who loves me;
  and he who loves me will be
    loved by my Father.
  I too will love him
  and reveal myself to him."

22 Judas (not Judas Iscariot) said to
him, "Lord, why is it that you will

reveal yourself to us and not to the
world?"   23 Jesus answered:

  "Anyone who loves me
  will be true to my word,
  and my Father will love him;
  we will come to him
  and make our dwelling place
    with him.
24 He who does not love me does
    not keep my words.
  Yet the word you hear is not
    mine;
  it comes from the Father who
    sent me.
25 This much have I told you while
    I was still with you;
26 the Paraclete, the Holy Spirit
  whom the Father will send in
    my name,
  will instruct you in everything,
  and remind you of all that I
    told you.
27 'Peace' is my farewell to you,
  my peace is my gift to you;
  I do not give it to you as the
    world gives peace.
  Do not be distressed or fearful.
28 You have heard me say,
  'I go away for a while, and I
    come back to you.'
  If you truly loved me
  you would rejoice to have me
    go to the Father,
  for the Father is greater than I.
29 I tell you this now, before it
    takes place,
  so that when it takes place you
    may believe.
30 I shall not go on speaking to
    you longer;
  the Prince of this world is at
    hand.
  He has no hold on me,
31 but the world must know that I
    love the Father
  and do as the Father has
    commanded me.
  Come, then! Let us be on our
    way.

14, 2: A number of MSS omit *that* in this sentence, thus giving different inflections of meaning to the verse, with three distinct statements in it.

14, 7: An alternative reading is: "If you know me, then you know my Father also." The form in the text above is a rebuke akin to 8, 19.

14, 15: There is attestation for several other readings of this verse: "If you love me, keep my commandments" or "If you love me, you will keep my commandments."

14, 16: *Another Paraclete:* evidently Jesus is the first Paraclete; see 1 Jn 2, 2, where Jesus is a Paraclete

in the sense of heavenly intercessor. However, this verse could be translated: "another, a Paraclete." The Johannine term *paraclete* derived from Greek legal terminology is used secularly for a defense attorney, a spokesman, an intercessor, although none of these terms fits precisely in John. The Paraclete in John is a teacher, a witness to Jesus, and a prosecutor of the world. He represents the continued presence on earth of the Jesus who has returned to the Father.

14, 17: The Greek word for "Spirit" is neuter, and while we use personal pronouns in English ("he," "his," "him"), most Greek MSS employ "it."

14, 19: The last part can be made a separate sentence: "Because I have life, you also will have life."

14, 22: *Not Judas Iscariot:* other readings are "Judas the Cananean" and "Judas Thomas." Perhaps the original had simply "Judas." There is a Judas son of James in the Lucan lists of the Twelve (Lk 6, 16; Acts 1, 13), but there is no corresponding name in the Matthean or Marcan lists.

14, 27: *Peace:* Jesus gives to his disciples the traditional Hebrew salutation "Shalom"; but his *shalom* is a gift of salvation and not a conventional word of farewell, as it is among other men.

The Vine and the Branches

15 "I am the true vine
and my Father is the
vinegrower.

2 He prunes away
every barren branch,
but the fruitful ones
he trims clean
to increase their yield.

3 You are clean already,
thanks to the word I have
spoken to you.

4 Live on in me, as I do in you.
No more than a branch can
bear fruit of itself
apart from the vine,
can you bear fruit
apart from me.

5 I am the vine, you are the
branches.
He who lives in me and I in him,
will produce abundantly,
for apart from me you can do
nothing.

6 A man who does not live in me
is like a withered, rejected
branch,
picked up to be thrown in the
fire and burnt.

7 If you live in me,
and my words stay part of you,
you may ask what you will—
it will be done for you.

8 My Father has been glorified
in your bearing much fruit
and becoming my disciples.

A Disciple's Love

9 "As the Father has loved me,
so I have loved you.
Live on in my love.

10 You will live in my love
if you keep my commandments,
even as I have kept my Father's
commandments,
and live in his love.

11 All this I tell you

that my joy may be yours
and your joy may be complete.

12 This is my commandment:
love one another
as I have loved you.

13 There is no greater love than
this:
to lay down one's life for one's
friends.

14 You are my friends
if you do what I command you.

15 I no longer speak of you as
slaves,
for a slave does not know what
his master is about.
Instead, I call you friends,
since I have made known to
you all that I heard from
my Father.

16 It was not you who chose me,
it was I who chose you
to go forth and bear fruit.
Your fruit must endure,
so that all you ask the Father
in my name
he will give you.

17 The command I give you is this,
that you love one another.

The World's Hate

18 "If you find that the world hates
you,
know it has hated me before you.

19 If you belonged to the world,
it would love you as its own;
the reason it hates you
is that you do not belong to the
world
But I chose you out of the
world.

20 Remember what I told you:
no slave is greater than his
master.
They will harry you
as they harried me.
They will respect your words
as much as they respected mine.

21 All this they will do to you
because of my name,
for they know nothing of him
who sent me.

22 If I had not come to them and
spoken to them,
they would not be guilty of sin;
now, however, their sin cannot
be excused.

23 To hate me is to hate my Father.

24 Had I not performed such
works among them
as no one has ever done before,
they would not be guilty of sin;
but as it is, they have seen,
and they go on hating me and
my Father.

25 However, this only fulfills the
text in their law:
'They hated me without cause.'

26 When the Paraclete comes,
the Spirit of truth who comes
from the Father—
and whom I myself will send
from the Father—
he will bear witness on my
behalf.

27 You must bear witness as well,
for you have been with me from
the beginning.

16 "I have told you all this
to keep your faith from being
shaken.

2 Not only will they expel you
from synagogues;
a time will come
when anyone who puts you to
death
will claim to be serving God!

3 All this they will do [to you]
because they knew neither the
Father nor me.

4 But I have told you these things
that when their hour comes
you may remember my telling
you of them.

15, 1: In the Bible Israel is spoken of as a vineyard (Is 5, 1–7; Mt 21, 33–46) and as a vine (Jer 2, 21). The identification of the vine as the son of man in Ps 80, 16, and Wisdom's description of herself as a vine in Sir 24, 17, are important background for Jesus' use of this figure as a self-description. In the synoptic account of the institution of the Eucharist at the Last Supper, we hear of "the fruit of the vine" (Mk 12, 25). The Didache refers to the eucharistic cup as "the holy vine of David your servant revealed through Jesus Christ." Consequently there may be secondary eucharistic symbolism here.

15, 2: *Prunes away . . . trims clean:* in Greek there is a play on two related verbs, *airein* and *kathairein*.

15, 4–7: *Live on in . . . live in . . . stay part of:* these all represent the same Greek expression for "remain in."

15, 13: *For one's friends:* in 9–13a, the words for love are related to the Greek *agapan*. In 13b–15, the words for love are related to the Greek *philein*. For John, the two roots are synonymous and mean "to love." The word *philos* in vv 13ff, is here translated "friend."

15, 18: The section 15, 18—16, 4 has numerous parallels with predictions of persecution made by Jesus in the synoptic gospels—especially with Mt 10, 17–25.

15, 20: *What I told you:* a reference to 13, 16.

15, 21: *Because of my name:* the idea of persecution because of Jesus' name is frequent in the New Testament (Mt 10, 22; 24, 9; Acts 9, 14). For John, association with Jesus' name implies union with Jesus.

15, 22.24: Jesus' words (*spoken*) and deeds (*works performed*) are the great motives of credibility.

They have seen . . . go on hating: probably means they have seen his works and still have hated; but the Greek can be read: "have seen both me and my Father and still have hated both me and my Father."

15, 25: *Law:* a larger concept than the Pentateuch, for the reference is to Ps 35, 19 or 69, 5. See notes on 10, 34; 12, 34.

15, 26: *Comes from the Father:* refers to the mission of the Spirit to men, not to the eternal procession of the Spirit. Compare 14, 26, where the Father, not Jesus, is said to send the Spirit.

15, 27: *You . . . as well:* this witness of the disciples is not different or distinct from that of the Paraclete; rather, it exteriorizes the Paraclete's internal witness.

16, 2: *Time* is literally "hour"—not "the hour" of Jesus but the period of persecution.

Jesus' Departure; Coming of the Paraclete

"I did not speak of this with
    you from the beginning
because I was with you.
5 Now that I go back to him who
    sent me,
not one of you asks me, 'Where
    are you going?'
6 Because I have had all this to
    say to you,
you are overcome with grief.
7 Yet I tell you the sober truth:
It is much better for you that I
    go.
If I fail to go,
the Paraclete will never come to
    you,
whereas if I go,
I will send him to you.
8 When he comes,
he will prove the world wrong
    about sin,
about justice,
about condemnation.
9 About sin—
in that they refuse to believe in
    me;
10 about justice—
from the fact that I go to the
    Father
and you can see me no more;
11 about condemnation—
for the prince of this world has
    been condemned.
12 I have much more to tell you,
but you cannot bear it now.
13 When he comes, however,
being the Spirit of truth
he will guide you to all truth.
He will not speak on his own,
but will speak only what he
    hears,
and will announce to you the
    things to come.
14 In doing this he will give glory
    to me,
because he will have received
    from me

what he will announce to you.
15 All that the Father has belongs
    to me.
That is why I said that what he
    will announce to you
he will have from me.
16 Within a short time you will
    lose sight of me,
but soon after that you shall see
    me again."

The Return of Jesus

17 At this, some of his disciples
asked one another: "What can he
mean, 'Within a short time you will
lose sight of me, but soon after that
you will see me'? And did he not say
that he is going back to the Father?"
18 They kept asking: "What does he
mean by this 'short time'? We do not
know what he is talking about."
19 Since Jesus was aware that they
wanted to question him, he said:
"You are asking one another about
my saying, 'Within a short time you
will lose sight of me, but soon after
that you will see me.'

20 "I tell you truly:
you will weep and mourn
while the world rejoices;
you will grieve for a time,
but your grief will be turned
    to joy.
21 When a woman is in labor
she is sad that her time has
    come.
When she has borne her child,
she no longer remembers her
    pain
for joy that a man has been born
    into the world.
22 In the same way, you are sad
    for a time,
but I shall see you again;
then your hearts will rejoice
with a joy no one can take from
    you.
23 On that day you will have no
    questions to ask me.

I give you my assurance,
whatever you ask the Father,
he will give you in my name.
24 Until now you have not asked
    for anything in my name.
Ask and you shall receive,
that your joy may be full.
25 I have spoken these things to
    you in veiled language.
A time will come when I shall
    no longer do so,
but shall tell you about the
    Father in plain speech.
26 On that day you will ask in my
    name
and I do not say that I will
    petition the Father for you.
27 The Father already loves you,
because you have loved me
and have believed that I came
    from God.
28 [I did indeed come from the
    Father;]
I came into the world.
Now I am leaving the world
to go to the Father."

29 "At last you are speaking
plainly," his disciples exclaimed,
"without talking in veiled language!
30 We are convinced that you know
everything. There is no need for
anyone to ask you questions. We do
indeed believe you came from God."
31 Jesus answered them:

"Do you really believe?
32 An hour is coming—has indeed
    already come—
when you will be scattered and
    each will go his way,
leaving me quite alone.
(Yet I can never be alone;
the Father is with me.)
33 I tell you all this
that in me you may find peace.
You will suffer in the world.
But take courage!
I have overcome the world."

16, 5: *Not one of you asks me:* the difficulty of reconciling this with Simon Peter's question in 13, 36 and Thomas' words in 14, 5, strengthens the supposition that the last discourse has been made up of several collections of Johannine material.

16, 8–11: These verses illustrate the forensic character of the Paraclete's role: in the forum of the disciples' conscience he prosecutes the world. He leads believers to see (a) that the basic sin of men was and is their refusal to believe in Jesus; (b) that, although Jesus was found guilty and apparently died in disgrace, in reality justice has triumphed, for Jesus has returned to his Father; (c) finally, that it is the prince of this world, Satan, who has been condemned through Jesus' death (12, 32).

16, 13: *Announce to you the things to come:* this is not necessarily a reference to new future predictions; the Greek verb is used in Daniel for interpretation, in relation to the present and the future, of what has already happened. The Paraclete makes Jesus' message continually relevant for each generation.

16, 17: The disciples are puzzled by the contrast between their seeing Jesus soon again (v 16) and his return to the Father (v 10), presumably to stay.

16, 20: Jesus does not discuss the *short time* mentioned in v 18, but the contrast between sorrow and joy implicit in v 16. The *grief* of this verse and the *pain* of the next are the same Greek word as the *grief* of v 6 The promise of joy will be fulfilled in 20, 20.

16, 23: Having no questions to ask is a matter of

seeking or not seeking understanding. "Ask and you shall receive" is a matter of petitioning.

16, 25: *In veiled language:* may be a reference to the parabolic comparisons of the vine and the branches (15, 1–16) and the woman in labor (16, 21).

16, 30: The reference is seemingly to the fact that Jesus could anticipate their question in v 19. The disciples naively think they have the full understanding that is the climax of "the hour" of Jesus' death, resurrection and ascension (v 25), but the only part of the hour that is at hand for them is their share in the passion (v 32).

Completion of Jesus' Work

17 After he had spoken these words, Jesus looked up to heaven and said:

"Father, the hour has come!
Give glory to your Son
that your Son may give glory to
you,
2 inasmuch as you have given him
authority over all mankind,
that he may bestow eternal life
on those you gave him.
3 (Eternal life is this:
to know you, the only true God,
and him whom you have sent,
Jesus Christ.)
4 I have given you glory on earth
by finishing the work you gave
me to do.
5 Do you now, Father, give me
glory at your side,
a glory I had with you before
the world began.
6 I have made your name known
to those you gave me out of the
world.
These men you gave me were
yours;
they have kept your word.
7 Now they realize
that all that you gave me comes
from you.
8 I entrusted to them
the message you entrusted to me,
and they received it.
They have known that in truth I
came from you,
they have believed it was you
who sent me.

Prayer for the Disciples

9 "For these I pray—
not for the world
but for these you have given me,
for they are really yours.
10 (Just as all that belongs to me
is yours,

so all that belongs to you is
mine.)
It is in them that I have been
glorified.
11 I am in the world no more,
but these are in the world
as I come to you.
O Father most holy,
protect them with your name
which you have given me,
[that they may be one, even as
we are one].
12 As long as I was with them,
I guarded them with your name
which you gave me.
I kept careful watch,
and not one of them was lost,
none but him who was destined
to be lost—
in fulfillment of Scripture.
13 Now, however, I come to you;
I say all this while I am still in
the world
that they may share my joy
completely.
14 I gave them your word,
and the world has hated them
for it;
they do not belong to the world
[any more than I belong to the
world].
15 I do not ask you to take them
out of the world,
but to guard them from the evil
one.
16 They are not of the world,
any more than I belong to the
world.
17 Consecrate them by means of
truth—
'Your word is truth.'
18 As you have sent me into the
world,
so I have sent them into the
world;
19 I consecrate myself for their
sakes now,

that they may be consecrated in
truth.

Prayer for All Believers

20 "I do not pray for them alone.
I pray also for those who will
believe in me through their
word,
21 that all may be one
as you, Father, are in me, and I
in you;
I pray that they may be [one] in
us,
that the world may believe that
you sent me.
22 I have given them the glory you
gave me
that they may be one, as we are
one—
23 I living in them, you living in
me—
that their unity may be complete.
So shall the world know that
you sent me,
and that you loved them as you
loved me.
24 Father,
all those you gave me
I would have in my company
where I am,
to see this glory of mine
which is your gift to me,
because of the love you bore me
before the world began.
25 Just Father,
the world has not known you,
but I have known you;
and these men have known that
you sent me.
26 To them I have revealed your
name,
and I will continue to reveal it
so that your love for me may
live in them,
and I may live in them."

17, 1–26: Since the sixteenth century this part of the last discourse has been called the "high priestly prayer" of Jesus. Here his words are addressed directly to the Father rather than to the disciples, who only overhear. Although still in the world (v 13), Jesus looks on his earthly ministry as a thing of the past (vv 4,12). Whereas Jesus has hitherto stated that the disciples could not follow him (13, 33.36), now he wishes them to be with him in union with the Father (vv 12ff). He is crossing the threshold of eternity.

17, 1: The action of looking up to heaven and the address *Father* are typical of Jesus at prayer; cf 11, 41.

17, 2: Another possible interpretation is to treat the first line of the verse as parenthetical and the second as an appositive to the clause that ends v 1:

that your Son may give glory to you (*inasmuch . . . mankind*), *that he may bestow eternal life. . . .*

17, 3: This verse was clearly added in the editing of the gospel, for Jesus would hardly have referred to himself as Jesus Christ.

17, 6: *I have made your name known:* perhaps the name is *I AM;* cf 8, 24.28.58; 13, 19.

17, 11: *Protect them with your name which you have given me:* here and in the next verse, some witnesses read: "Protect with your name those whom you have given to me."

17, 12: *Scripture:* Jn 13, 18 cites Ps 41, 10.

17, 15: Note the resemblance to the petition of the Our Father "deliver us from the evil one." Both probably refer to the devil rather than to abstract evil.

17, 17: *"Your word is truth":* seemingly a citation from the Greek form of Ps 119, 142, as found in Codex Sinaiticus.

17, 21: For other Johannine passages on unity, see 10, 16; 11, 52. The world (21.23) is once more to be challenged by the mission of the disciples and given the opportunity of self-judgment inasmuch as it will either accept or reject Jesus.

17, 24: *Where I am:* Jesus prays for the believers ultimately to join him in heaven. Then they will not see his glory as in a mirror but clearly (2 Cor 3, 18; 1 Jn 3, 2).

17, 26: *Will continue to reveal:* through the Paraclete.

Jesus Arrested

18 After this discourse, Jesus went out with his disciples across the Kidron Valley. There was a garden there, and he and his disciples entered it. 2 The place was familiar to Judas as well (the one who was to hand him over) because Jesus had often met there with his disciples. 3 Judas took the cohort as well as guards supplied by the chief priests and the Pharisees, and came there with lanterns, torches and weapons. 4 Jesus, aware of all that would happen to him, stepped forward and said to them, "Who is it you want?" 5 "Jesus the Nazorean," they replied. "I am he," he answered. (Now Judas, the one who was to hand him over, was there with them.) 6 As Jesus said to them, "I am he," they retreated slightly and fell to the ground. 7 Jesus put the question to them again, "Who is it you want?" "Jesus the Nazorean," they repeated. 8 "I have told you, I am he," Jesus said. "If I am the one you want, let these men go." 9 (This was to fulfill what he had said, "I have not lost one of those you gave me.")

10 Then Simon Peter, who had a sword, drew it and struck the slave of the high priest, severing his right ear. (The slave's name was Malchus.) 11 At that Jesus said to Peter, "Put your sword back in its sheath. Am I not to drink the cup the Father has given me?"

12 Then the soldiers of the cohort, their tribune, and the Jewish guards arrested Jesus and bound him. 13 They led him first to Annas, the father-in-law of Caiaphas who was high priest that year. 14 (It was Caiaphas who had proposed to the Jews the advantage of having one man die for the people.)

Peter's First Denial

15 Simon Peter, in company with another disciple, kept following Jesus closely. This disciple, who was known to the high priest, stayed with Jesus as far as the high priest's courtyard, 16 while Peter was left standing at the gate. The disciple known to the high priest came out and spoke to the woman at the gate, and then brought Peter in. 17 This servant girl who kept the gate said to Peter, "Are you not one of this man's followers?" "Not I," he replied.

18 Now the night was cold, and the servants and the guards who were standing around had made a charcoal fire to warm themselves by. Peter joined them and stood there warming himself.

The Inquiry before Annas

19 The high priest questioned Jesus, first about his disciples, 20 then about his teaching. Jesus answered by saying:

"I have spoken publicly to any
    who would listen.
I always taught in a synagogue
    or in the temple area
where all the Jews come together.
There was nothing secret about
    anything I said.
21 Why do you question me?

Question those who heard me when I spoke. It should be obvious that they will know what I said." 22 At this reply, one of the guards who was standing nearby gave Jesus a sharp blow on the face. "Is that the way to answer the high priest?" he said. 23 Jesus replied, "If I said anything wrong produce the evidence, but if I spoke the truth why hit me?" 24 Annas next sent him, bound, to the high priest Caiaphas.

The Further Denials

25 All through this, Simon Peter had been standing there warming himself. They said to him, "Are you not a disciple of his?" He denied it and said, "I am not!" 26 "But did I not see you with him in the garden?" insisted one of the high priest's slaves—as it happened, a relative of the man whose ear Peter had severed. 27 Peter denied it again. At that moment a cock began to crow.

The Trial before Pilate

28 At daybreak they brought Jesus from Caiaphas to the praetorium. They did not enter the praetorium themselves, for they had to avoid ritual impurity if they were to eat the Passover supper. 29 Pilate came out to them. "What accusation do you bring against this man?" he demanded. 30 "If he were not a criminal," they retorted, "we would certainly not have handed him over to you." 31 At this Pilate said, "Why do you not take him and pass judgment on him according to your

---

18, 1–13: John does not mention the agony in the garden and the kiss of Judas, nor does he identify the place as Gethsemani or the Mount of Olives.

18, 1: *Jesus went out:* see 14, 31, where it seems he is leaving the supper room. *Kidron Valley:* literally, "the winter-flowing Kidron"; this wadi has water only during the winter rains.

18, 3: *Cohort:* seems to refer to Roman troops, the full cohort of 600 soldiers or the maniple of 200 under their tribune (v 12). In this case John is hinting at Roman collusion in the action against Jesus before he was brought to Pilate.

18, 5: *Nazorean:* The form found in Matthew is here used in preference to the *Nazarene* of Mark. *I am he:* this *Ego eimi* may be intended by the evangelist as an expression of divinity; see note on 8, 24. John sets the confusion of the arresting party against the background of Jesus' divine majesty.

18, 9: The citation may refer to 17, 12; 6, 39; or 10, 28.

18, 10: Only John gives the names of the two antagonists; both John and Luke mention the right ear.

18, 11: The theme of the cup is found in the synoptic account of the agony (Mk 14, 36) and parallels.

18, 13: *Annas:* only John mentions an inquiry before Annas, who is presumably the *high priest* of vv 16 and 19. Patriarch of a family of high priests, he had been deposed by the Romans in A.D. 15; but since, according to Jewish law, the office was for life, Annas may still have been the legitimate high priest in the eyes of many. Luke (3, 2) and Acts (4, 6) mention him in terms of high priesthood. There have been many attempts by scribes and commentators to rearrange or interpret the verses of John so that Caiaphas does the interrogating. It may be said with reasonable certainty that this night time interrogation before Annas is not the same as the trial before Caiaphas placed by Matthew and Mark at night and by Luke in the morning.

18, 15: *Courtyard:* the Greek word can mean this or "palace."

18, 15f: *Another disciple:* many scholars identify him with *the other disciple* of 20, 2, who is the beloved disciple; see note on 13, 23. But how would a Galilean fisherman be *known to the high priest*? An early (but unlikely) tradition has it that John was himself a priest. See note on 19, 25 for John's possible relation to Mary, who had priestly relatives.

18, 20: *I always taught . . . in the temple area:* in the synoptics a similar statement appears in the garden scene (Mk 14, 49).

18, 24: *Caiaphas:* John may leave room here for the trial before Caiaphas not narrated by him but dealt with in the synoptic gospels. Details paralleling those of the synoptic trial are scattered throughout John.

18, 27: Cockrow was the third Roman division of the night lasting from 12 to 3 a.m.

18, 28: *Daybreak:* literally, "the early hour," or fourth Roman division of the night, 3 to 6 a.m.; here presumably about 6 a.m. *Praetorium:* the residence of the Roman governor in Jerusalem was either the Herodian palace on the western hill or the fortress Antonia near the temple. *The Passover supper:* the synoptic gospels give the impression that the Thursday night supper was the Passover meal (Mk 14, 12); for John that meal is still to be eaten Friday night.

18, 31: *We may not put anyone to death:* only John gives this reason for their bringing Jesus to Pilate. Jewish sources are not clear on the competence of the Sanhedrin at this period to sentence and to execute for political crimes.

law?" "We may not put anyone to death," the Jews answered. 32 (This was to fulfill what Jesus had said indicating the sort of death he had to die.)

33 Pilate went back into the praetorium and summoned Jesus. "Are you the King of the Jews?" he asked him. 34 Jesus answered, "Are you saying this on your own, or have others been telling you about me?" 35 "I am no Jew!" Pilate retorted. "It is your own people and the chief priests who have handed you over to me. What have you done?" 36 Jesus answered:

> "My kingdom does not belong
>   to this world.
> If my kingdom were of this
>   world,
> my subjects would be fighting
> to save me from being handed
>   over to the Jews.
> As it is, my kingdom is not
>   here."

37 At this Pilate said to him, "So, then, you are a king?" Jesus replied:

> "It is you who say I am a
>   king.
> The reason I was born,
> the reason why I came into the
>   world,
> is to testify to the truth.
> Anyone committed to the truth
>   hears my voice."

38 "Truth!" said Pilate, "What does that mean?"

After this remark, Pilate went out again to the Jews and said to them: "Speaking for myself, I find no case

against this man. 39 Recall your custom whereby I release someone to you at Passover time. Do you want me to release to you the king of the Jews?" 40 They shouted back, "We want Barabbas, not this one!" (Barabbas was an insurrectionist.)

19 Pilate's next move was to take Jesus and have him scourged. 2 The soldiers then wove a crown of thorns and fixed it on his head, throwing around his shoulders a cloak of royal purple. 3 Repeatedly they came up to him and said, "All hail, king of the Jews!" slapping his face as they did so.

4 Pilate went out a second time and said to the crowd: "Observe what I do. I am going to bring him out to you to make you realize that I find no case [against him]." 5 When Jesus came out wearing the crown of thorns and the purple cloak, Pilate said to them, "Look at the man!" 6 As soon as the chief priests and the temple guards saw him they shouted, "Crucify him! Crucify him!" Pilate said, "Take him and crucify him yourselves; I find no case against him." 7 "We have our law," the Jews responded, "and according to that law he must die because he made himself God's Son." 8 When Pilate heard this kind of talk, he was more afraid than ever.

9 Going back into the praetorium, he said to Jesus, "Where do you come from?" Jesus would not give him any answer. 10 "Do you refuse to speak to me?" Pilate asked him. "Do you not know that I have

the power to release you and the power to crucify you?" 11 Jesus answered:

> "You would have no power
>   over me whatever
> unless it were given you from
>   above.
> That is why he who handed me
>   over to you
> is guilty of the greater sin."

12 After this, Pilate was eager to release him, but the Jews shouted, "If you free this man you are no 'Friend of Caesar.' Anyone who makes himself a king becomes Caesar's rival." 13 Pilate heard what they were saying, then brought Jesus outside and took a seat on a judge's bench at the place called the Stone Pavement—Gabbatha in Hebrew. 14 (It was the Preparation Day for Passover, and the hour was about noon.) He said to the Jews, "Look at your king!" 15 At this they shouted, "Away with him! Away with him! Crucify him!" "What!" Pilate exclaimed. "Shall I crucify your king?" The chief priests replied, "We have no king but Caesar." 16 In the end, Pilate handed Jesus over to be crucified.

Crucifixion and Death

17 Jesus was led away, and carrying the cross by himself, went out to what is called the Place of the Skull (in Hebrew, Golgotha). 18 There they crucified him, and two others with him: one on either side, Jesus in the middle. 19 Pilate had an inscription placed on the cross which read,

---

18, 32: The Jewish punishment for blasphemy was stoning (Lv 24, 16). In coming to the Romans to ensure that Jesus would be crucified, the Jewish authorities fulfilled his prophecy that he would be lifted up; cf 12, 32f.

18, 37: It is you who say I am a king: see Mt 26, 64 for a similar response to the high priest. It is a reluctant affirmative, equaling "Yes, but the terminology is yours."

18, 39: This privilege connected with Passover is not clearly attested outside the gospels.

18, 40: Insurrectionist: a guerrilla warrior fighting both for nationalistic aims and for gain, Barabbas had been arrested for murder in a recent insurrection (Mk 15, 7).

19, 1: Luke places the mockery of Jesus at the midpoint in the trial when Jesus was sent to Herod. Mark and Matthew place the scourging and mockery at the end of the trial after the sentence of death. Scourging was an integral part of the crucifixion penalty.

19, 7: Made himself God's Son: this question was

not raised in John's account of the Jewish interrogation of Jesus as it was in the synoptic account. Nevertheless, see 5, 18; 8, 53; 10, 36.

19, 12: 'Friend of Caesar': a technical Roman term of honor.

19, 13: Took a seat: many scholars think this should be translated transitively, "sat him down." In John's thought, Jesus is the real judge of men, and they suggest that John portrays him seated on the judgment bench. We find this tradition in the second century. Stone Pavement: under the fortress Antonia, one of the conjectured locations of the praetorium, a tremendous stone pavement has been uncovered. The Aramaic word Gabbatha probably means "ridge, elevation."

19, 14: Preparation Day for Passover: the synoptics describe this as Friday (Mk 15, 42). Noon: Mk 15, 25 has Jesus crucified "at the third hour," which means either 9 a.m. or the period from 9 to 12. Noon, the time when, according to John, Jesus was sentenced to death, was the hour at which the priests began to slaughter Passover lambs in the temple; see Jn 1, 29.

19, 16: In the end, Pilate handed Jesus over: according to the sequence this would seem to mean "handed him over to the chief priests." Lk 23, 25 has a similar ambiguity. There is a polemic tendency in the later gospels to place the guilt of the crucifixion solely on the Jewish authorities and to excuse the Romans from blame. Actually, John later mentions the Roman soldiers, and it was to these soldiers that Pilate handed Jesus over.

19, 17: Carrying the cross by himself: this is a different picture from that of the synoptics, especially Lk 23, 26, where Simon of Cyrene is made to bear the cross, walking behind Jesus. In John's theology Jesus remained master of his destiny (10, 18). Place of the Skull: the Latin word for skull is Calvaria; hence "Cavalry." Golgotha is actually an Aramaic rather than a Hebrew word.

19, 19: The inscription or "title," found here in its technical form appears with slightly different words in each of the four gospels. Only John mentions its polyglot character and Pilate's role in keeping the title unchanged.

JESUS THE NAZOREAN
THE KING OF THE JEWS

20 This inscription, in Hebrew, Latin, and Greek, was read by many of the Jews, since the place where Jesus was crucified was near the city. 21 The chief priests of the Jews tried to tell Pilate, "You should not have written, 'The King of the Jews.' Write instead, 'This man claimed to be King of the Jews.'" 22 Pilate answered, "What I have written, I have written."

23 After the soldiers had crucified Jesus they took his garments and divided them four ways, one for each soldier. There was also his tunic, but this tunic was woven in one piece from top to bottom and had no seam. 24 They said to each other, "We should not tear it. Let us throw dice to see who gets it." (The purpose of this was to have the Scripture fulfilled:

"They divided my garments
    among them;
for my clothing they cast lots.")

And this was what the soldiers did.

25 Near the cross of Jesus there stood his mother, his mother's sister, Mary the wife of Clopas, and Mary Magdalene. 26 Seeing his mother there with the disciple whom he loved, Jesus said to his mother, "Woman, there is your son." 27 In turn he said to the disciple, "There is your mother." From that hour onward, the disciple took her into his care.

28 After that, Jesus, realizing that everything was now finished, said to fulfill the Scripture, "I am thirsty." 29 There was a jar there, full of common wine. They stuck a sponge soaked in this wine on some hyssop and raised it to his lips. 30 When Jesus took the wine, he said, "Now it is finished." Then he bowed his head, and delivered over his spirit.

The Blood and Water

31 Since it was the Preparation Day, the Jews did not want to have the bodies left on the cross during the sabbath, for that sabbath was a solemn feast day. They asked Pilate that the legs be broken and the bodies be taken away. 32 Accordingly, the soldiers came and broke the legs of the men crucified with Jesus, first of the one, then of the other. 33 When they came to Jesus and saw that he was already dead, they did not break his legs. 34 One of the soldiers thrust a lance into his side, and immediately blood and water flowed out. 35 (This testimony has been given by an eyewitness, and his testimony is true. He tells what he knows, so that you may believe.) 36 These events took place for the fulfillment of Scripture:

"Break none of his bones."

37 There is still another Scripture passage which says:

"They shall look on him whom
    they have pierced."

Burial

38 Afterward, Joseph of Arimathea, a disciple of Jesus (although a secret one for fear of the Jews), asked Pilate's permission to remove Jesus' body. Pilate granted it, so they came and took the body away. 39 Nicodemus (the man who had first come to Jesus at night) likewise came, bringing a mixture of myrrh and aloes which weighed about a hundred pounds. 40 They took Jesus' body, and in accordance with Jewish burial custom bound it up in wrappings of cloth with perfumed oils. 41 In the place where he had been crucified there was a garden, and in the garden a new tomb in which no one had ever been buried. 42 Because of the Jewish Preparation Day they buried Jesus there, for the tomb was close at hand.

Peter and the Disciple

20 Early in the morning on the first day of the week, while it was still dark, Mary Magdalene came to the tomb. 2 She saw that the stone had been moved away, so she ran off to Simon Peter and the other disciple (the one Jesus loved) and told them, "The Lord has been taken from the tomb! We don't know where they have put him!" 3 At that, Peter and the other disciple started out on their way toward the tomb. 4 They were running side by side, but then the other disciple outran Peter and reached the tomb first. 5 He did not enter but bent down to peer in, and saw the wrappings lying on the ground. 6 Presently, Simon Peter came along behind him and entered

---

19, 23: Perhaps this seamless tunic is meant to recall the tunic of the high priest which Josephus (*Antiquities* III, 8, 4) says was without seam. Rv 1, 13 shows Jesus in priestly robes. The synoptics do not have the details about Jesus' garments.

19, 25: It is not clear whether three of four women are meant (i.e., whether *Mary the wife of Clopas* is or is not in apposition with *his mother's sister*); the Syriac tradition has four women. Only John mentions the mother of Jesus. The synoptics have a group of women *at a distance* from the cross (Mk 15, 40). If *his mother's sister* is not *Mary the wife of Clopas*, is she to be identified with *Salome* of the synoptic account? Salome was the mother of James and John, the sons of Zebedee; and thus these two disciples would have been Jesus' cousins.

19, 26f: This scene is to be read in the light of the Cana story in chapter 2. The presence of the mother of Jesus, the use of *woman*, and the mention of the *hour*, are elements of both scenes. Now that the hour has come, Mary (a symbol of the church?) is given a role as the mother of Christians (personified by the beloved disciple).

19, 28: *The Scripture:* it is not certain whether the fulfillment is in the scene of 25–27, or in the *I am*

thirsty of 28. If the latter, Pss 69, 22 and 22, 16 deserve consideration.

19, 29: *Common wine:* John does not mention the drugged wine, a narcotic which Jesus refused as the crucifixion began (Mk 15, 25), but only this final gesture of kindness at the end (Mk 15, 36). Hyssop, a small plant, is scarcely suitable for carrying a sponge (Mark mentions a reed) and may be a symbolic reference to the hyssop used to put the blood of the paschal lamb on the doorpost of the Hebrews (Ex 12, 22).

19, 30: *Delivered over his spirit:* it is awkward in English to preserve the possible double nuance of dying (giving up the last breath or spirit) and that of passing on the Holy Spirit; see 7, 39, which connects the giving of the Spirit with Jesus' glorious return to the Father.

19, 34f: John probably emphasizes these verses to show the reality of Jesus' death, against the Docetic heretics. In the blood and water there may also be a symbolic reference to the Eucharist and Baptism.

19, 35: *He tells:* it is not certain from the Greek that this *he* is the *eyewitness* of the first part of the sentence.

19, 36: The scriptural reference is probably to Ex

12, 46 (Nm 9, 12), which has directions for dealing with the Passover lamb. That Jesus is the Paschal Lamb is a Johannine theme, and thus at the end of the gospel we are called back to 1, 29. There may also be a reference to Ps 34, 21, describing God's safeguarding of an innocent man.

19, 37: John cites Zec 12, 10 (also cited in Rv 1, 7) but not exactly according to either the standard Hebrew reading or the Greek Old Testament. There was a Jewish tradition of uncertain date that this text referred to the Messiah.

19, 38–42: In the first three gospels there is no embalming on Friday. In Matthew and Luke the women come to the tomb on Sunday morning precisely to anoint Jesus.

20, 1: *Still dark:* according to Mark the sun had risen, and Matthew speaks of the first rays of light.

20, 3–10: The basic narrative is told of Peter alone in Lk 24, 12, a verse missing in important MSS and which may be borrowed from tradition similar to John. Lk 24, 24 also generally reflects this story.

20, 6–8: There was some special feature about the state of the burial wrappings that caused the beloved disciple to believe. Some suggest that Jesus had passed through them without their being unrolled.

the tomb. He observed the wrappings on the ground   7 and saw the piece of cloth which had covered the head not lying with the wrappings, but rolled up in a place by itself.   8 Then the disciple who had arrived first at the tomb went in. He saw and believed.   9 (Remember, as yet they did not understand the Scripture that Jesus had to rise from the dead.)   10 With this, the disciples went back home.

Mary Magdalene

11 Meanwhile, Mary stood weeping beside the tomb. Even as she wept, she stooped to peer inside, 12 and there she saw two angels in dazzling robes. One was seated at the head and the other at the foot of the place where Jesus' body had lain.   13 "Woman," they asked her, "why are you weeping?" She answered them, "Because the Lord has been taken away, and I do not know where they have put him."   14 She had no sooner said this than she turned around and caught sight of Jesus standing there. But she did not know him.   15 "Woman," he asked her, "why are you weeping? Who is it you are looking for?" She supposed he was the gardener, so she said, "Sir, if you are the one who carried him off, tell me where you have laid him and I will take him away."   16 Jesus said to her, "Mary!" She turned to him and said [in Hebrew], "Rabbouni!" (meaning "Teacher").   17 Jesus then said: "Do not cling to me, for

I have not yet ascended to the Father. Rather, go to my brothers and tell them, 'I am ascending to my Father and your Father, to my God and your God!'"   18 Mary Magdalene went to the disciples. "I have seen the Lord!" she announced. Then she reported what he had said to her.

Appearance to the Disciples

19 On the evening of that first day of the week, even though the disciples had locked the doors of the place where they were for fear of the Jews, Jesus came and stood before them. "Peace be with you," he said. 20 When he had said this, he showed them his hands and his side. At the sight of the Lord the disciples rejoiced. 21 "Peace be with you," he said again.

"As the Father has sent me,
so I send you."

22 Then he breathed on them and said:

"Receive the Holy Spirit.
23 If you forgive men's sins,
they are forgiven them;
if you hold them bound,
they are held bound."

Thomas

24 It happened that one of the Twelve, Thomas (the name means "Twin"), was absent when Jesus came.   25 The other disciples kept telling him: "We have seen the Lord!" His answer was, "I will never believe it

without probing the nailprints in his hands, without putting my finger in the nailmarks and my hand into his side."

26 A week later, the disciples were once more in the room, and this time Thomas was with them. Despite the locked doors, Jesus came and stood before them. "Peace be with you," he said;   27 then, to Thomas: "Take your finger and examine my hands. Put your hand into my side. Do not persist in your unbelief, but believe!"   28 Thomas said in response, "My Lord and my God!" 29 Jesus then said to him:

"You became a believer because
you saw me.
Blest are they who have not seen
and have believed."

Conclusion

30 Jesus performed many other signs as well—signs not recorded here—in the presence of his disciples. 31 But these have been recorded to help you believe that Jesus is the Messiah, the Son of God, so that through this faith you may have life in his name.

APPENDIX:
THE RESURRECTION APPEARANCE
IN GALILEE

The Fishermen

21 Later, at the sea of Tiberias, Jesus showed himself to the disciples [once again]. This is how

---

20, 9: Probably a general reference to the Scriptures is intended, as in Lk 24, 26 and 1 Cor 15, 4. Some individual Old Testament passages suggested are Ps 16, 10; Hos 6, 2; Jon 1, 17; 2, 1.

20, 17: *Do not cling to me:* literally "Don't keep touching me." See Mt 28, 9, where the women take hold of his feet. *I have not yet ascended:* for John and many of the New Testament writers, the ascension in the theological sense of going to the Father to be glorified took place with the resurrection as one action. This scene in John dramatizes such an understanding, for by Easter night Jesus is glorified and can give the Spirit. Therefore his ascension takes place immediately after he has talked to Mary. In such a view, the ascension after forty days described in Acts 1, 1–11 would be simply the termination of earthly appearances. *My Father and your Father:* this echoes Ru 1, 16, *Your people shall be my people, and your God my God.* The Father of Jesus will now become the Father of the disciples because, once ascended, Jesus can give them the Spirit that comes from the Father and beget them as God's children (3, 5). That is why he calls them *my brothers.*

20, 19: *The disciples:* by implication from v 24, this means ten of the Twelve. Lk 24, 33 mentions a larger group; Mk 16, 14 refers to the Eleven. Pre-

sumably they are in Jerusalem; see Lk 24, 33. The "upper room" is first mentioned in Acts 1, 13, as the place to which the Eleven came forty days later, after Jesus' final departure. *Peace be with you:* although this could be an ordinary greeting, John intends here to echo 14, 27. The theme of rejoicing in v 20 echoes 16, 22.

20, 20: *Hands and . . . side:* Lk 24, 39f mentions "hands and feet"; cf Ps 22, 17.

20, 21: By means of this sending, the Eleven were made *apostles,* that is, "those sent"; cf 17, 18. A solemn mission or "sending" is also the subject of the post-resurrection appearances to the Eleven in Mt 28, 19; Lk 24, 47; Mk 16, 15.

20, 22: According to the Second Council of Constantinople, the Spirit was truly given here and the breathing on the disciples was not merely symbolic. This action recalls Gn 2, 7, where God breathed on man and gave him the natural spirit or life-force; in John it is the life-source for supernatural life that is given. The apostles are recreated as new men, sons of God. The further giving of the Spirit in chapter 2 of Acts is a more public charism for the church.

20, 23: The Council of Trent defined that the power to forgive sins given here is the same power exercised in the Sacrament of Penance. See Mt 16, 19 and 18,

18. *If you hold them bound, they are held bound;* the reference of *they, them,* not wholly clear in the Greek, is more probably to *sins* than to *men.*

20, 28: The Second Council of Constantinople defined that this confession of Thomas referred to Christ and was not simply an expression of glory to God the Father. *Lord* and *God* are two Old Testament titles of God (Ps 35, 23).

20, 30f: These verses are clearly a conclusion to the gospel.

20, 31: See 1 Jn 5, 13: *To help you believe:* it is difficult to determine whether the Greek should be read "that you may continue to believe" (i.e., the readers are Christians) or "that you may come to believe" (i.e., perhaps the readers are non-Christians).

21, 1–23: There are many non-Johannine peculiarities in this chapter, some suggesting Lucan Greek style; yet there are many Johannine features as well. Perhaps the tradition was ultimately derived from John but preserved by some disciple other than the writer of the rest of the gospel. The appearances narrated seem to be independent of those in chapter 20. Even if a later addition, the chapter was added before publication of the gospel, for it appears in all MSS.

the appearance took place. 2 Assembled were Simon Peter, Thomas ("the Twin"), Nathanael (from Cana in Galilee), Zebedee's sons, and two other disciples. 3 Simon Peter said to them, "I am going out to fish." "We will join you," they replied, and went off to get into their boat. All through the night they caught nothing. 4 Just after daybreak Jesus was standing on the shore, though none of the disciples knew it was Jesus. 5 He said to them, "Children, have you caught anything to eat?" "Not a thing," they answered. 6 "Cast your net off to the starboard side," he suggested, "and you will find something." So they made a cast, and took so many fish they could not haul the net in. 7 Then the disciple Jesus loved cried out to Peter, "It is the Lord!" On hearing it was the Lord, Simon Peter threw on some clothes—he was stripped—and jumped into the water.

8 Meanwhile the other disciples came in the boat, towing the net full of fish. Actually they were not far from land—no more than a hundred yards.

9 When they landed, they saw a charcoal fire there with a fish laid on it and some bread. 10 "Bring some of the fish you just caught," Jesus told them. 11 Simon Peter went aboard and hauled ashore the net loaded with sizable fish—one hundred fifty-three of them! In spite of the great number, the net was not torn.

12 "Come and eat your meal," Jesus told them. Not one of the disciples presumed to inquire, "Who are you?" for they knew it was the Lord. 13 Jesus came over, took the bread and gave it to them, and did the same with the fish. 14 This marked the third time that Jesus appeared to the disciples after being raised from the dead.

Peter the Shepherd

15 When they had eaten their meal, Jesus said to Simon Peter, "Simon, son of John, do you love me more than these?" "Yes, Lord," he said, "you know that I love you." At which Jesus said, "Feed my lambs."

16 A second time he put his question, "Simon, son of John, do you love me?" "Yes, Lord," Peter said, "you know that I love you." Jesus replied, "Tend my sheep."

17 A third time Jesus asked him, "Simon, son of John, do you love me?" Peter was hurt because he had asked a third time, "Do you love me?" So he said to him: "Lord, you know everything. You know well that I love you." Jesus said to him, "Feed my sheep.

18 "I tell you solemnly:
as a young man
you fastened your belt
and went about as you pleased;
but when you are older
you will stretch out your hands,
and another will tie you fast

and carry you off against your will."

19 (What he said indicated the sort of death by which Peter was to glorify God.) When Jesus had finished speaking he said to him, "Follow me."

The Beloved Disciple

20 Peter turned around at that, and noticed that the disciple whom Jesus loved was following (the one who had leaned against Jesus' chest during the supper and said, "Lord, which one will hand you over?"). 21 Seeing him, Peter was prompted to ask Jesus, "But Lord, what about him?" 22 "Suppose I want him to stay until I come," Jesus replied, "how does that concern you? Your business is to follow me." 23 This is how the report spread among the brothers that this disciple was not going to die. Jesus never told him, as a matter of fact, that the disciple was not going to die; all he said was, "Suppose I want him to stay until I come [how does that concern you]?"

Conclusion

24 It is this same disciple who is the witness to these things; it is he who wrote them down and his testimony, we know, is true. 25 There are still many other things that Jesus did, yet if they were written about in detail, I doubt there would be room enough in the entire world to hold the books to record them.

21, 2: *Zebedee's sons:* the only mention by name of James and John in this gospel. Perhaps the phrase was inserted to identify the *two other disciples.* The anonymity of the latter phrase is more Johannine (1, 35).
21, 3–6: This may be a variant of Luke's account of the catch of fish (5, 1–11), which he joined with the call of the first disciples.
21, 9.12f: It is strange that Jesus already has fish since none have yet been brought ashore. This meal may have had eucharistic significance for early Christians since v 13 recalls John 6, 11, which uses the vocabulary of Jesus' action at the Last Supper.
21, 11: The exact number, 153, is probably meant to have a symbolic meaning, perhaps in relation to the apostles' mission to catch men. The net which was not torn *may* represent the church.

21, 12: *Not one . . . presumed:* is Jesus' appearance strange to them? See Lk 24, 16; Mk 16, 12; Jn 20, 14.
21, 14: This verse connects chapters 20 and 21.
21, 15ff: In these three verses there is a remarkable variety of synonyms: two different Greek verbs for *love;* two verbs for *feed/tend;* two or three nouns for *sheep;* two verbs for *know.* Apparently there is no difference of meaning. The First Vatican Council cited this verse in defining that the risen Jesus gave Peter the jurisdiction of supreme shepherd and ruler over the whole flock.
21, 15: *More than these:* probably "more than these disciples do" rather than "more than you love these things [fishing, etc.]."
21, 18: A figurative reference to the crucifixion of Peter.
21, 23: This whole scene takes on more significance

if the disciple is already dead. The death of the apostolic generation caused problems in the church because of a belief that Jesus was to have returned first. Loss of faith sometimes resulted; cf 2 Pt 3, 4.
21, 24: *Who wrote them down:* this does not necessarily mean he wrote them with his own hand. The same expression is used in 19, 9 of Pilate, who certainly did not write the inscription himself. *We know:* it is probably not the beloved disciple of v 7 who speaks here as *we.*

The Acts

OF THE APOSTLES

PROLOGUE

Jesus' Final Instructions and Ascension

IN my first account, Theophilus, I dealt with all that Jesus did and taught 2 until the day he was taken up to heaven, having first instructed the apostles he had chosen through the Holy Spirit. 3 In the time after his suffering he showed them in many convincing ways that he was alive, appearing to them over the course of forty days and speaking to them about the reign of God. 4 On one occasion when he met with them, he told them not to leave Jerusalem: "Wait, rather, for the fulfillment of my Father's promise, of which you have heard me speak. 5 John baptized with water, but within a few days you will be baptized with the Holy Spirit."

6 While they were with him they asked, "Lord, are you going to restore the rule to Israel now?" 7 His answer was: "The exact time it is not yours to know. The Father has reserved that to himself. 8 You will receive power when the Holy Spirit comes down on you; then you are to be my witnesses in Jerusalem, throughout Judea and Samaria, yes, even to the ends of the earth." 9 No sooner had he said this than he was lifted up before their eyes in a cloud which took him from their sight.

10 They were still gazing up into the heavens when two men dressed in white stood beside them. 11 "Men of Galilee," they said, "why do you stand here looking up at the skies? This Jesus who has been taken from you will return, just as you saw him go up into the heavens."

12 After that they returned to Jerusalem from the mount called Olivet near Jerusalem—a mere sabbath's journey away. 13 Entering the city, they went to the upstairs room where they were staying: Peter

---

1, 1–26: This introductory material connects Acts with Luke's gospel (1, 1f); shows that the apostles were instructed by the risen Jesus (1, 3ff); points out that the parousia or renewed presence of Jesus will occur as certainly as his resurrection occurred (1, 6–11); and lists the members of the Twelve, stressing their role as a body of divinely mandated witnesses to his life, teaching, and resurrection (1, 12–26).

1, 3: *In many convincing ways:* the meaning of the Greek is that the apostles received evidence of Jesus' resurrection decisive enough to eliminate doubt from their minds (Lk 24, 36–49). This divinely offered proof, however, entailed more than an appeal to human reason. It included prophetic illumination which rendered the apostles certain that the appearances of the risen Christ were actions of God mani-

festing himself to their human experience. *Appearing to them over the course of forty days:* Christian tradition considered especially sacred the interval in which the appearances and instructions of the risen Jesus occurred, and expressed it therefore in terms of the sacred number forty; cf Dt 8, 2.

According to John (20, 17), the ascension of Jesus to the kingdom of his Father took place on the day of his resurrection. Luke writes from a different perspective and speaks of a visible ascension of Jesus after forty days. For John, the ascension means primarily the risen Jesus' new existence with the Father, and the appearances are those of the risen and ascended One. For Luke, the ascension marks the end of the appearances of Jesus except for the extraordinary appearance to Paul.

1, 4: *My Father's promise:* the Holy Spirit, as is

clear from 1, 5. This gift of the Spirit formed part of the instructions of the risen Jesus on the kingdom of God, of which Luke speaks in 1, 3. Probably this instruction is the source of the material on the Holy Spirit in Jn 15, 26f and 16, 7–15.

1, 7: This verse echoes the tradition that the precise time of the parousia is not revealed to men; cf Mk 13, 32; 1 Thes 5, 1ff.

1, 9: Comparison of this verse with Lk 24, 51 suggests that there were several visible ascensions of the risen Christ. Mt 28, 16–20 raises the possibility of a similar visible ascension of Christ in Galilee. The visible ascension accorded with the cosmological conception of the time that held the sky to be a solid vault above which was God's throne. On other occasions, Jesus simply vanished; cf Lk 24, 31. A visible ascension is not described in Jn 20, 17.

and John and James and Andrew; Philip and Thomas, Bartholomew and Matthew; James son of Alpheus; Simon, the Zealot party member, and Judas son of James. 14 Together they devoted themselves to constant prayer. There were some women in their company, and Mary the mother of Jesus, and his brothers.

THE COMMUNITY IN JERUSALEM FINDS MATURITY IN THE SPIRIT

Matthias Chosen

15 At one point during those days, Peter stood up in the center of the brothers; there must have been a hundred and twenty gathered together. 16 "Brothers," he said, "the saying in the Scripture uttered long ago by the Holy Spirit through the mouth of David was destined to be fulfilled in Judas, the one who guided those that arrested Jesus. 17 He was one of our number and he had been given a share in this ministry of ours. 18 "That individual bought a piece of land with his unjust gains, and fell headlong upon it. His body burst wide open, all his entrails spilling out. 19 This event came to be known by the inhabitants of Jerusalem, who named the property Field of Blood—'Akeldama' in their own language. 20 'It is written in the Book of Psalms,

'Let his encampment be desolate. May no one dwell on it.'

And again,

'May another take his office.'

21 It is entirely fitting, therefore, that one of those who was of our company while the Lord Jesus moved among us, 22 from the baptism of John until the day he was taken up from us, should be named as witness with us to his resurrection." 23 At that they nominated two, Joseph (called Barsabbas, also known as Justus) and Matthias. 24 Then they prayed: "O Lord, you read the hearts of men. Make known to us which of these two you choose 25 for this apostolic ministry, replacing Judas, who deserted the cause and went the way he was destined to go." 26 They then drew lots between the two men. The choice fell to Matthias, who was added to the eleven apostles.

Descent of the Holy Spirit

2 When the day of Pentecost came it found them gathered in one place. 2 Suddenly from up in the sky there came a noise like a strong, driving wind which was heard all through the house where they were seated. 3 Tongues as of fire appeared, which parted and came to rest on each of them. 4 All were filled with the Holy Spirit. They began to express themselves in foreign tongues and make bold proclamation as the Spirit prompted them.

5 Staying in Jerusalem at the time were devout Jews of every nation under heaven. 6 These heard the sound, and assembled in a large crowd. They were much confused because each one heard these men speaking his own language. 7 The whole occurrence astonished them. They asked in utter amazement, "Are not all of these men who are speaking Galileans? 8 How is it that each of us hears them in his native tongue? 9 We are Parthians, Medes, and Elamites. We live in Mesopotamia, Judea and Cappadocia, Pontus, the province of Asia, 10 Phrygia and Pamphylia, Egypt, and the regions of Libya around Cyrene. There are even visitors from Rome— 11 all Jews, or those who have come over to Judaism; Cretans and Arabs too. Yet each of us hears them speaking in his own tongue about the marvels God has accomplished." 12 They were dumbfounded, and could make nothing at all of what had happened. "What does this mean?" they asked one another, 13 while a few remarked with a sneer, "They have had too much new wine!"

Peter's Discourse

14 Peter stood up with the Eleven, raised his voice, and addressed them: "You who are Jews, indeed all of you staying in Jerusalem! Listen to

---

1, 18: Luke records a popular tradition on the death of Judas that seems to differ from that of Mt 27, 5, according to which Judas hanged himself. Here, though the text is not entirely clear, Judas is depicted as purchasing a piece of property with the betrayal money and being killed on it in a fall.

1, 26: The need for replacing Judas so as to restore the apostolic college to the number of twelve was probably dictated by the symbolism of the number. It recalled the twelve tribes from which all Israelites were thought to be descended, and indicated that the messianic teaching about Jesus was to be directed first to the whole of Israel.

2, 2: From up in the sky there came a noise like a strong, driving wind: the wind and the Holy Spirit are associated in Jn 3, 8. The sound of a great rush of wind would aptly presage a new action of God in the history of salvation.

2, 1–41: Luke's pentecostal narrative consists of an introduction (2, 1–13), a speech ascribed to Peter declaring the resurrection of Jesus and its messianic significance (2, 14–36), and a favorable response from the audience (2, 39ff). It is likely that the narrative telescopes events that took place over a period of time and on a less dramatic scale. The Twelve were not originally in a position to proclaim publicly the messianic office of Jesus without incurring immediate reprisal from those religious authorities in Jerusalem who had encompassed Jesus' death precisely to stem the rising tide in his favor; cf Jn 11, 47f. Once the

"new covenant" had acquired many adherents, public teaching could more easily be undertaken. In any case, these reflections point up Luke's emphasis on the Holy Spirit. He is at pains to show that Christianity cannot be accounted a mere religious sect within Judaism that developed its own brand of messianism. On the contrary, it declared itself from the beginning as originating in the inspiration and under the impulsion of God.

2, 3: Tongues as of fire: see Ex 19, 18, where fire symbolizes the presence of God to initiate the covenant on Sinai. Here the Holy Spirit acts upon the apostles, preparing them to proclaim the new covenant with its unique gift of the Spirit (2, 38).

2, 4: To express themselves in foreign tongues: ecstatic prayer in praise of God; cf 2, 11.

2, 6–13: The multitude receives the charism of interpretation of tongues (1 Cor 12, 10). The question of the meaning of this charism is raised. To some of the hearers, however, the language is unintelligible, and they conclude the apostles are drunk. Luke may have in mind here the varying reactions to the gift in the early Christian communities; cf 1 Cor 14, 22–25.

2, 14–36: The first of six discourses in Acts (see 3, 12–26; 4, 8–12; 5, 29–32; 10, 34–43; 13, 16–41) dealing with the substance of Christian messianism, the resurrection of Jesus and its messianic import. Five of these are attributed to Peter, the final one to Paul. In 1 Cor 15, 11 Paul refers to the apostolic

teaching on the death and resurrection of Jesus as "the preaching" or "proclamation". Hence modern scholars term these discourses in Acts the "kerygma", the Greek word for proclamation.

In the present discourse, Peter appeals to the religious faith of the audience and presents himself as one in possession of certain religious information given him by God together with the ability to interpret it. This is called a prophetic announcement. The following chief points are made:

(1) The ecstatic prayer is due to the influence of the Spirit, which the prophet Joel foretold would be especially active in messianic times (16–21); (2) the crucifixion of Jesus of Nazareth, a man publicly known in Jerusalem because of his miracle-working, was an integral part of God's saving plan, as God has indicated by raising him from the dead (22ff); (3) the prophetic understanding of the Old Testament reveals that the resurrection and ascension of the Messiah was God's actual saving plan (25–35); (4) the true meaning of the death, resurrection and ascension of Jesus is that he is the divinely enthroned messianic King of Israel (36), bestowing the gift of the Spirit upon all who accept him as Savior (38).

The prophetic character of the kerygmatic discourses in Acts explains why they do not include accounts of the appearances of Jesus. Only to one who accepts the prophetic announcement of Jesus' resurrection will acccounts of his subsequent appearances convey any meaning.

what I have to say. 15 You must realize that these men are not drunk, as you seem to think. It is only nine in the morning! 16 No, it is what Joel the prophet spoke of:

17 'It shall come to pass in the last
    days, says God,
    that I wil pour out a portion
       of my spirit on all mankind:
    Your sons and daughters shall
       prophesy,
    your young men shall see
       visions
    and your old men shall dream
       dreams.
18 Yes, even on my servants and
       handmaids
    I will pour out a portion of
       my spirit in those days,
    and they shall prophesy.
19 I will work wonders in the
       heavens above
    and signs on the earth below:
       blood, fire, and a cloud of
       smoke.
20 The sun shall be turned to
       darkness and the moon to
       blood
    before the coming of that
       great and glorious day of
       the Lord.
21 Then shall everyone be saved
       who calls on the name of
       the Lord.'

22 "Men of Israel, listen to me! Jesus the Nazorean was a man whom God sent to you with miracles, wonders, and signs as his credentials. These God worked through him in your midst, as you well know. 23 He was delivered up by the set purpose and plan of God; you even made use of the pagans to crucify and kill him. 24 God freed him from death's bitter pangs, however, and raised him up again, for it was impossible that death should keep its hold on him. 25 David says of him:

'I have set the Lord ever before
    me,
    with him at my right hand I
       shall not be disturbed.
26 My heart has been glad and my
       tongue has rejoiced,
    my body will live on in hope,
27 for you will not abandon my
       soul to the nether world,
    nor will you suffer your
       faithful one to undergo
       corruption.
28 You have shown me the paths
       of life;
    you will fill me with joy in
       your presence.'

29 Brothers, I can speak confidently to you about our father David. He died and was buried, and his grave is in our midst to this day. 30 He was a prophet and knew that God had sworn to him that one of his descendants would sit upon his throne. 31 He said that he was not abandoned to the nether world, nor did his body undergo corruption, thus proclaiming beforehand the resurrection of the Messiah. 32 This is the Jesus God has raised up, and we are his witnesses. 33 Exalted at God's right hand, he first received the promised Holy Spirit from the Father, then poured this Spirit out on us. This is what you now see and hear. 34 David did not go up to heaven, yet David says,

'The Lord said to my Lord,
    Sit at my right hand
35   until I make your enemies
       your footstool.'

36 Therefore let the whole house of Israel know beyond any doubt that God has made both Lord and Messiah this Jesus whom you crucified."

37 When they heard this, they were deeply shaken. They asked Peter and the other apostles, "What are we to do, brothers?" 38 Peter answered: "You must reform and be baptized, each one of you, in the name of Jesus Christ, that your sins may be forgiven; then you will receive the gift of the Holy Spirit. 39 It was to you and your children that the promise was made, and to all those still far off whom the Lord our God calls."

40 In support of his testimony he used many other arguments, and kept urging, "Save yourselves from this generation which has gone astray." 41 Those who accepted his message were baptized; some three thousand were added that day.

Communal Life

42 They devoted themselves to the apostles' instruction and the communal life, to the breaking of bread and the prayers. 43 A reverent fear overtook them all, for many wonders and signs were performed by the apostles. 44 Those who believed shared all things in common; 45 they would sell their property and goods, dividing everything on the basis of each one's need. 46 They went to the temple area together every day, while in their homes they broke bread. With exultant and sincere hearts they took their meals in common, 47 praising God and winning the approval of all the people. Day by day the Lord added to their number those who were being saved.

Cure of a Cripple

3 Once, when Peter and John were going up to the temple for prayer at the three o'clock hour, 2 a man

---

2, 38: *You must reform and be baptized:* repentance is a positive concept, a change of heart toward God reflected in the actual goodness of one's own life. It is in accord with the apostolic teaching derived from Jesus (2, 42) and ultimately recorded in the four gospels. Jesus made use of baptism at the beginning of his ministry (Jn 3, 22; 4, 2), but according to the synoptic evangelists abandoned the practice after the arrest of the Baptizer. Matthew tells us (28, 19) that the sacramental usage of baptism was an instruction given to the apostles by the risen Christ. Jesus spoke of this new baptism to Nicodemus (Jn 3, 5).

2, 42–47: The first of three summary passages (see 4, 32–37 and 5, 12–16) which outline, somewhat ideally, the chief characteristics of the Jerusalem community: adherence to the teachings of the Twelve concerning repentance; the centering of its religious life in the eucharistic liturgy (42); a system of distribution of goods that led wealthier Christians to sell their possessions when the needs of the community's poor required it (44 and note on 4, 32—5, 11); continued attendance at the Temple, since in this initial stage there was little or no thought of dividing lines between Judaism and Christianity.

2, 47: *Those who were being saved:* not that Christians are absolutely saved, but rather that to those who believe in Christ God directly reveals his saving action in their behalf. If Christians are not saved, it is because of their failure to respond to God's saving action; cf Rom 8, 1.

3, 1—4, 31: This section presents a series of related events: the dramatic cure of a lame beggar (3, 1–10) produces a large audience for the kerygmatic discourse of Peter (3, 11–26). The Sadducees, taking exception to the doctrine of resurrection, have Peter, John, and apparently the beggar as well arrested (4, 1–4) and brought to trial before the Sanhedrin. The issue concerns the authority on which Peter and John publicly teach religious doctrine in the temple (5ff). Peter replies with a brief summary of the kerygma, implying that his authority is prophetic (8–12). The court warns the apostles to abandon their practice of invoking prophetic authority in the name of Jesus (13–18). When Peter and John reply that the prophetic role cannot be abandoned to satisfy the objections of men, the court nevertheless releases them, afraid to do otherwise since the beggar, lame from birth and over forty years old, is a well-known figure in Jerusalem and the facts of his cure are common property (19–22). The narrative concludes with a prayer of the Christian community imploring divine aid against threats of persecution (23–31).

crippled from birth was being carried in. They would bring him every day and put him at the temple gate called "the Beautiful" to beg from the people as they entered. 3 When he saw Peter and John on their way in, he begged them for an alms. 4 Peter fixed his gaze on the man; so did John. "Look at us!" Peter said. 5 The cripple gave them his whole attention, hoping to get something. 6 Then Peter said: "I have neither silver nor gold, but what I have I give you! In the name of Jesus Christ the Nazorean, walk!" 7 Then Peter took him by the right hand and pulled him up. Immediately the beggar's feet and ankles became strong; 8 he jumped up, stood for a moment, then began to walk around. He went into the temple with them—walking, jumping about, and praising God. 9 When the people saw him moving and giving praise to God, 10 they recognized him as that beggar who used to sit at the Beautiful Gate of the temple. They were struck with astonishment —utterly stupefied at what had happened to him.

Peter's Discourse

11 As the man stood there clinging to Peter and John, the whole crowd rushed over to them excitedly in Solomon's Portico. 12 When Peter saw this, he addressed the people as follows: "Fellow Israelites, why does this surprise you? Why do you stare at us as if we had made this man walk by some power or holiness of our own? 13 The God of Abraham, of Isaac, and of Jacob, the God of our fathers, has glorified his Servant Jesus, whom you handed

over and disowned in Pilate's presence when Pilate was ready to release him. 14 You disowned the Holy and Just One and preferred instead to be granted the release of a murderer. 15 You put to death the Author of life. But God raised him from the dead, and we are his witnesses. 16 It is his name, and trust in this name, that has strengthened the limbs of this man whom you see and know well. Such faith has given him perfect health, as all of you can observe.

17 "Yet I know, my brothers, that you acted out of ignorance, just as your leaders did. 18 God has brought to fulfillment by this means what he announced long ago through all the prophets: that his Messiah would suffer. 19 Therefore, reform your lives! Turn to God, that your sins may be wiped away! 20 Thus may a season of refreshment be granted you by the Lord when he sends you Jesus, already designated as your Messiah. 21 Jesus must remain in heaven until the time of universal restoration which God spoke of long ago through his holy prophets. 22 For Moses said: "'The Lord God will raise up for you a prophet like me from among your own kinsmen: you shall listen to him in everything he says to you. 23 Anyone who does not listen to that prophet shall be ruthlessly cut off from the people.'

24 "Moreover, all the prophets who have spoken, from Samuel onward, have announced the events of these days. 25 You are the children of those prophets, you are the heirs of the covenant God made with your fathers when he said to Abra-

ham, 'In your offspring, all the families of the earth shall be blessed.' 26 When God raised up his servant, he sent him to you first to bless you by turning you from your evil ways."

4 While Peter and John were still addressing the crowd, the priests, the captain of the temple guard, and the Sadducees came up to them, 2 angry because they were teaching the people and proclaiming the resurrection of the dead in the person of Jesus. 3 It was evening by now, so they arrested them and put them in jail for the night. 4 Despite this, many of those who had heard the speech believed; the number of the men came to about five thousand.

Before the Sanhedrin

5 When the leaders, the elders, and the scribes assembled the next day in Jerusalem, 6 Annas the high priest, Caiaphas, John, Alexander, and all who were of the high-priestly class were there. 7 They brought Peter and John before them and began the interrogation in this fashion: "By what power or in whose name have men of your stripe done this?"

8 Then Peter, filled with the Holy Spirit, spoke up: "Leaders of the people! Elders! 9 If we must answer today for a good deed done to a cripple and explain how he was restored to health, 10 then you and all the people of Israel must realize that it was done in the name of Jesus Christ the Nazorean whom you crucified and whom God raised from the dead. In the power of that name this man stands before you perfectly sound. 11 This Jesus is

---

3, 1: *Prayer at the three o'clock hour:* when the evening sacrifice was offered in the temple; cf Ex 29, 38f.

3, 6–10: The miracle has a dramatic cast; it symbolizes the saving power of Christ and leads the beggar to enter the temple, where he hears Peter's proclamation of salvation through Jesus.

3, 13: *Servant:* the Greek word can be rendered "son" or even "child" here and also in 3, 26; 4, 25 (applied to David); 4, 27–30. Scholars are of the opinion, however, that the original concept reflected in the word identified Jesus in the early apostolic preaching with the suffering Servant of the Lord of Is 52, 13–53, 12. *Has glorified:* through the resurrection and ascension of Jesus, God reversed the judgment against him on the occasion of his trial.

3, 14: *The Holy and Just One:* a characterization of Jesus as Messiah, emphasizing his sinlessness and extraordinary religious dignity, which are placed in sharp contrast with the guilt of those who rejected him in favor of Barabbas; Mt 27, 15–23.

3, 15: *The author of life:* the source of the messianic benefits for Israel.

3, 17: *You acted out of ignorance, just as your leaders did:* even those actually responsible for the execution of Jesus were unaware of his messianic dignity.

3, 18: *Through all the prophets:* Christian prophetic insight into the Old Testament saw the crucifixion and death of Jesus as the main burden of messianic prophecy. The Jews themselves did not anticipate a suffering Messiah; they usually understood the Servant Song in Is 52, 13–53, 12 to signify their own suffering as a people (as most Jews still do to the present day).

3, 20: *Thus may a season of refreshment be granted you:* an allusion to the parousia or second coming of Christ, judged to be imminent in the apostolic age. This reference to its nearness is the only explicit one in Acts; see note on 5, 1–11.

3, 22: A loose citation of Dt 18, 15, which teaches that the Israelites are to learn the will of Yahweh from

no one but their prophets. At the time of Jesus the Jews expected a unique prophet to come in fulfillment of this text (Jn 1, 21; 6, 14; 7, 40). Early Christianity understood this tradition and text as applying to Jesus, and used them especially in defense of the divergence of Christian teaching from traditional Judaism.

4, 1: *The priests, the captain of the temple guard, and the Sadducees:* the priests performed the temple liturgy. The officer of the temple, a Levite, was in charge of the temple guard. The Sadducees, a party within Judaism at this time, rejected those doctrines (among them bodily resurrection) which they believed alien to the ancient Mosaic religion. The Sadducees were drawn from priestly families and the lay aristocracy.

4, 11: Early Christianity applied this citation from Ps 118, 22 to Jesus; cf Mark 12, 10; 1 Pt 2, 7.

'the stone rejected by you the builders which has become the cornerstone.' 12 There is no salvation in anyone else, for there is no other name in the whole world given to men by which we are to be saved."

13 Observing the self-assurance of Peter and John, and realizing that the speakers were uneducated men of no standing, the questioners were amazed. Then they recognized these men as having been with Jesus. 14 When they saw the man who had been cured standing there with them, they could think of nothing to say, 15 so they ordered them out of the court while they held a consultation. "What shall we do with these men? 16 Everyone who lives in Jerusalem knows what a remarkable show of power took place through them. We cannot deny it. 17 To stop this from spreading further among the people we must give them a stern warning never to mention that man's name to anyone again." 18 So they called them back and made it clear that under no circumstances were they to speak the name of Jesus or teach about him. 19 Peter and John answered, "Judge for yourselves whether it is right in God's sight for us to obey you rather than God. 20 Surely we cannot help speaking of what we have heard and seen." 21 At that point they were dismissed with further warnings. The court could find no way to punish them because of the people, all of whom were praising God for what had happened. 22 The fact was, the man thus miraculously cured was more than forty years of age.

Thanksgiving

23 After being released, the two went back to their own people and told them what the priests and elders had said. 24 All raised their voices in prayer to God on hearing the story: "Sovereign Lord, who made heaven and earth and sea and all that is in them, 25 you have said by the Holy Spirit through the lips of our father David your servant:

'Why did the Gentiles rage,
    the peoples conspire in folly?
26 The kings of the earth were
    aligned,
    the princes gathered together
    against the Lord and
        against his anointed.'

27 Indeed, they gathered in this very city against your holy Servant, Jesus, whom you anointed—Herod and Pontius Pilate in league with the Gentiles and the peoples of Israel. 28 They have brought about the very things which in your powerful providence you planned long ago. 29 But now, O Lord, look at the threats they are leveling against us. Grant to your servants, even as they speak your words, complete assurance 30 by stretching forth your hand in cures and signs and wonders to be worked in the name of Jesus, your holy Servant."

31 The place where they were gathered shook as they prayed. They were filled with the Holy Spirit and continued to speak God's word with confidence.

Life of the Christians

32 The community of believers were of one heart and one mind.

None of them ever claimed anything as his own; rather, everything was held in common. 33 With power the apostles bore witness to the resurrection of the Lord Jesus, and great respect was paid to them all; 34 nor was there anyone needy among them, for all who owned property or houses sold them and donated the proceeds. 35 They used to lay them at the feet of the apostles to be distributed to everyone according to his need.

36 There was a certain Levite from Cyprus named Joseph, to whom the apostles gave the name Barnabas (meaning "son of encouragement"). 37 He sold a farm that he owned and made a donation of the money, laying it at the apostles' feet.

Ananias and Sapphira

5 Another man named Ananias and his wife Sapphira likewise sold a piece of property. 2 With the connivance of his wife he put aside a part of the proceeds for himself; the rest he took and laid at the feet of the apostles. 3 Peter exclaimed: "Ananias, why have you let Satan fill your heart so as to make you lie to the Holy Spirit and keep for yourself some of the proceeds from that field? 4 Was it not yours so long as it remained unsold? Even when you sold it, was not the money still yours? How could you ever concoct such a scheme? You have lied not to men but to God!" 5 At the sound of these words, Ananias fell dead. Great fear came upon all who later heard of it. 6 Some of the young men came forward, wrapped up the body, and carried it out for

---

4, 24–30: An example of the type of prayer common in the early Christian community. After invoking God as Creator (4, 24) it cites the messianic Psalm 2, 1f, much favored in early Christianity, to recall men's impotence against God's designs (4, 25f), as exemplified by the resurrection of Jesus, which frustrated the actions of Herod and Pilate against him (4, 27f). It then appeals to the members of the community for courage to proclaim the Christian kerygma in a hostile world and pleads for divine aid through the bestowal of the charism to perform physical cures (4, 29f).

4, 27: *Herod:* Herod Antipas, ruler of Galilee and Perea from 4 B.C. to A.D. 39, who executed John the Baptizer, and before whom Jesus was arraigned; cf Lk 23, 6–12.

4, 31: *The place . . . shook:* the earthquake is used as a sign of the divine presence in Ex 19, 18; Is 6, 4. Here the shaking of the building symbolizes God's favorable response to prayer. Luke may have had an additional reason for using the symbol in

this sense the fact that it was familiar to the Hellenistic world. Ovid and Virgil also employ it.

4, 32–37: This is a second summary characterization of the Jerusalem community (see note on 2, 42–47). It highlights the system of the distribution of goods, and introduces Barnabas, who figures later in Acts as the friend and companion of Paul, and who, as noted here (v 37), endeared himself to the community by a donation of money through the sale of property. Careful examination of Luke's statements on *everything in common* indicates that: (1) members of the community were free to dispose of their property or to retain it as they saw fit; (2) donation of property or of money accruing from its sale was not a condition of membership in the community; and (3) the holding of property *in common* meant that the poor of the community were cared for through the substantial donations of the wealthier members.

5, 1–11: The peculiarities latent in this narrative afford the basis of its proper interpretation. The harsh treatment meted out to Ananias (3f) does not

accord with Luke's portrait of the love operative within the community; cf 2, 44–47. This harshness becomes even more painfully evident when Sapphira is not informed of her husband's death, or of the fact that their deceit has been discovered (7f); neither of them is given that opportunity for repentance which lies at the heart of the teaching of the Christian community (2, 38).

Their sin did not consist in the withholding of part of the money, even deceitfully, but in their deception of the community. The true nature of this deceit is revealed in the light of the early Christian expectation of the parousia; cf Acts 3, 20; 1 Thes 4, 13–17. Their gift supposedly symbolized their complete confidence in the proximity of Christ's final coming, which rendered earthly possessions unimportant. (For a similar line of thought, cf 1 Cor 7, 29ff.) Their deaths are ascribed to a lie to the Holy Spirit (3–9). i.e., they accepted the honor accorded them by the community for their apparent faith in the proximate parousia but in reality they were not deserving of it.

burial. 7 Three hours later Ananias' wife came in, unaware of what had happened. 8 Peter said to her, "Tell me, did you sell that piece of property for such and such an amount?" She answered, "Yes, that was the sum." 9 Peter replied, "How could you two scheme to put the Spirit of the Lord to the test? The footsteps of the men who have just buried your husband can be heard at the door. They stand ready to carry you out too." 10 With that, she fell dead at his feet. The young men came in, found her dead, and carried her out for burial beside her husband. 11 Great fear came on the whole church and on all who heard of it.

Signs and Wonders

12 Through the hands of the apostles, many signs and wonders occurred among the people. By mutual agreement they used to meet in Solomon's Portico. 13 No one else dared to join them, despite the fact that the people held them in great esteem. 14 Nevertheless more and more believers, men and women in great numbers, were continually added to the Lord. 15 The people carried the sick into the streets and laid them on cots and mattresses, so that when Peter passed by at least his shadow might fall on one or another of them. 16 Crowds from the towns around Jerusalem would gather, too, bringing their sick and those who were troubled by unclean spirits, all of whom were cured.

Second Trial before the Sanhedrin

17 The high priest and all his supporters (that is, the party of the Sadducees), filled with jealousy, 18 arrested the apostles and threw them into the public jail. 19 During the night, however, an angel of the Lord opened the gates of the jail, led them forth, and said, 20 "Go out

now and take your place in the temple precincts and preach to the people all about this new life." 21 Accordingly they went into the temple at dawn and resumed their teaching.

When the high priest and his supporters arrived they convoked the Sanhedrin, the full council of the elders of Israel. They sent word to the jail that the prisoners were to be brought in. 22 But when the temple guard got to the jail they could not find them, 23 and hurried back with the report, "We found the jail securely locked and the guards at their posts outside the gates, but when we opened it we found no one inside."

24 On hearing this report, the captain of the temple guard and the high priests did not know what to make of the affair. 25 Someone then came up to them, pointing out, "Look, there! Those men you put in jail are standing over there in the temple, teaching the people." 26 At that, the captain went off with the guard and brought them in, but without any show of force, for fear of being stoned by the crowd. 27 When they had led them in and made them stand before the Sanhedrin, the high priest began the interrogation in this way: 28 "We gave you strict orders not to teach about that name, yet you have filled Jerusalem with your teaching and are determined to make us responsible for that man's blood." 29 To this, Peter and the apostles replied: "Better for us to obey God than men! 30 The God of our fathers has raised up Jesus whom you put to death, hanging him on a tree. 31 He whom God has exalted at his right hand as ruler and savior is to bring repentance to Israel and forgiveness of sins. 32 We testify to this. So too does the Holy Spirit, whom God has given to those that obey him."

33 When the Sanhedrin heard this, they were stung to fury and wanted to kill them. 34 Then a member of the Sanhedrin stood up, a Pharisee named Gamaliel, a teacher of the law highly regarded by all the people. He had the accused ordered out of court for a few minutes, 35 and then said to the assembly, "Fellow Israelites, think twice about what you are going to do with these men. 36 Not long ago a certain Theudas came on the scene and tried to pass himself off as someone of importance. About four hundred men joined him. However he was killed, and all those who had been so easily convinced by him were disbanded. In the end it came to nothing. 37 Next came Judas the Galilean at the time of the census. He too built up quite a following, but likewise died, and all his followers were dispersed. 38 The present case is similar. My advice is that you have nothing to do with these men. Let them alone. If their purpose or activity is human in its origins, it will destroy itself. 39 If, on the other hand, it comes from God, you will not be able to destroy them without fighting God himself."

This speech persuaded them. 40 In spite of it, however, the Sanhedrin called in the apostles and had them whipped. They ordered them not to speak again about the name of Jesus, and afterward dismissed them. 41 The apostles for their part left the Sanhedrin full of joy that they had been judged worthy of ill-treatment for the sake of the Name. 42 Day after day, both in the temple and at home, they never stopped teaching and proclaiming the good news of Jesus the Messiah.

SPREAD OF THE CHURCH THROUGH
PERSECUTION IN JERUSALEM

The Need of Assistants

6 In those days, as the number of disciples grew, the ones who spoke Greek complained that their

---

5, 12–16: This, the third summary portrait of the Jerusalem community, underscores the Twelve as its bulwark, especially because of their charismatic power to heal the sick; cf 2, 42–47; 4, 32–37.

5, 17–42: A second action against the community is taken by the Sanhedrin in the arrest and trial of the Twelve; cf 4, 1ff. The motive is the jealousy of the religious authorities over the popularity of the apostles (17), who are now charged with defiance of the Sanhedrin's previous order to them to abandon their prophetic role (28; cf 4, 18). In this crisis the

apostles are favored by a miraculous release from prison (18–24). (For similar incidents involving Peter and Paul, cf 12, 6–11; 16, 25–29.) The real significance of such an event, however, would be manifest only to men of faith, not to unbelievers; since the Sanhedrin had already judged the Twelve to be unauthentic prophets, it could disregard reports of their miracles. When the Twelve immediately resumed public teaching, the Sanhedrin determined to invoke upon them the penalty of death (5, 33) prescribed in Dt 13, 6–10. Gamaliel's advice against this course

finally prevailed, but it did not save the Twelve from the punishment of scourging (5, 40f), in a last endeavor to shake their conviction of their prophetic mission.

6, 1–11: An example of the solution of conflicts within the Christian community. It is probable that the seven men assigned to this duty from among the Hellenist Christians, i.e., Jews from the diaspora, already possessed standing in the community as catechists, a role later ascribed to Stephen (8ff) and Philip (8, 5).

widows were being neglected in the daily distribution of food, as compared with the widows of those who spoke Hebrew. 2 The Twelve assembled the community of the disciples and said, "It is not right for us to neglect the word of God in order to wait on the tables. 3 Look around among your own number, brothers, for seven men acknowledged to be deeply spiritual and prudent, and we shall appoint them to this task. 4 This will permit us to concentrate on prayer and the ministry of the word." 5 The proposal was unanimously accepted by the community. Following this they selected Stephen, a man filled with faith and the Holy Spirit; Philip, Prochorus, Nicanor, Timon, Parmenas, and Nicolaus of Antioch, who had been a convert to Judaism. 6 They presented these men to the apostles, who first prayed over them and then imposed hands on them.

7 The word of God continued to spread, while at the same time the number of the disciples in Jerusalem enormously increased. There were many priests among those who embraced the faith.

Stephen Accused

8 The Stephen already spoken of was a man filled with grace and power, who worked great wonders and signs among the people. 9 Certain members of the so-called "Synagogue of Roman Freedmen" (that is, the Jews from Cyrene, Alexandria, Cilicia and Asia) would undertake to engage Stephen in debate, 10 but they proved no match for the wisdom and spirit with which he spoke. 11 They persuaded some of the men to make

the charge that they had heard him speaking blasphemies against Moses and God, 12 and in this way they incited the people, the elders, and the scribes. All together they confronted him, seized him, and led him off to the Sanhedrin. 13 There they brought in false witnesses, who said: "This man never stops making statements against the holy place and the law. 14 We have heard him claim that Jesus the Nazorean will destroy this place and change the customs which Moses handed down to us." 15 The members of the Sanhedrin who sat there stared at him intently. Throughout, Stephen's face seemed like that of an angel.

Stephen's Discourse

7 The high priest asked whether the charges were true. 2 To this Stephen replied: "My brothers! Fathers! Listen to me. The God of glory appeared to our father Abraham when he was still in Mesopotamia and before he settled in Haran. 3 God said to him, Leave your country and your kinsfolk, and go to the land I will show you. 4 So he left the land of the Chaldeans and settled in Haran. After his father died, God made him move from there to this land where you now dwell. 5 God did not give him any of it as his heritage, not even a foot of land, but he promised to give it to him and his descendants after him as a possession—although he had no child. 6 These are the words God used: Abraham's posterity will be strangers in a foreign land, and they will be subject to slavery and oppressed four hundred years. 7 But I will judge that nation which

they serve, God said, and after that they will worship me in this place.

8 "God then made a covenant of circumcision with him, and Abraham, who had become the father of Isaac, circumcised him on the eighth day. Isaac did the same for Jacob, and Jacob for the twelve patriarchs. 9 Out of envy, the patriarchs sold Joseph into slavery in Egypt, 10 but God was with him and rescued him from all his tribulations. He granted him favor and wisdom in the court of the Pharaoh, king of Egypt, and made him the governor of Egypt and of the Pharaoh's entire household. 11 When famine and great trial came upon Egypt and Canaan, our fathers could find no sustenance. 12 Hearing that there was grain in Egypt, Jacob sent our fathers there on a first mission. 13 The second time, Joseph made himself known to his brothers, and his family ties became known to the Pharaoh. 14 Then Joseph sent for his father Jacob, inviting him and all his kinsfolk—seventy-five persons in all. 15 Jacob went down to Egypt and died there, as did our fathers. 16 Their remains were transferred to Shechem and placed in the tomb which Abraham had bought with silver from the sons of Hamor at Shechem.

17 "When the time drew near for the fulfillment of the promise made by God to Abraham, our people in Egypt grew more and more numerous, 18 until a new king came to power in Egypt, who knew not Joseph. 19 This one dealt craftily with our people and oppressed them. He forced our fathers to abandon their infants to exposure so that the people would not survive.

6, 2.4: The essential function of the Twelve is the "service of the word", i.e., development of the kerygma by formulation of the teachings of Jesus. This became the material that went into the formation of the gospels.

6, 6: They ... imposed hands on them: the customary Jewish way of designating a person for a task and invoking upon him the divine blessing and power to perform it.

6, 8—8, 1: The summary statement (6, 7) on the progress of the Jerusalem community, illustrated by the conversion of the priests, is followed by a lengthy narrative regarding Stephen. Stephen's defense is not a response to the charges made against him, but takes the form of a discourse that reviews the fortunes of God's word to Israel and leads to a prophetic declaration: a plea for the hearing of that word as announced by Christ and now possessed by the Christian community.

The charges that Stephen depreciated the importance of the temple and the Mosaic law and elevated Jesus to a stature above Moses (6, 13f) were in fact true. Before a non-Christian audience such as the Sanhedrin, no defense against them was possible. With Stephen, who thus perceived the fuller implications of the teaching of Jesus, the differences between Judaism and Christianity began to appear. Luke's account of Stephen's martyrdom and its aftermath shows how the major impetus behind the Christian movement passed from Jerusalem, where temple and law prevailed, to Antioch in Syria, where these influences were less pressing.

6, 13: False witnesses: here and in his account of Stephen's execution (7, 54—60), Luke parallels the martyrdom of Stephen with the death of Jesus.

6, 14: Will destroy this place and change the customs: a possible indication that Stephen and other members of the community had begun to reflect upon

the religious significance of Christ's prophecy concerning the destruction of the temple (Mk 13, 1f) and upon his attitude toward the law: cf Mk 2, 18—3, 6.

7, 2: God ... appeared to ... Abraham ... in Mesopotamia: the first of a number of minor discrepancies between the data of the Old Testament and the data of Stephen's discourse. According to Gn 12, 1 God first spoke to Abraham in Haran. The main discrepancies are these: In 7, 16 it is said that Jacob was buried in Shechem, whereas Gn 50, 13 says he was buried at Hebron; in the same verse it is said that the tomb was purchased by Abraham, but in Gn 33, 19 and Jos 24, 32 the purchase is attributed to Jacob himself. The exactitude of detail achievable by modern scholarship was not a concern of ancient writers—who in any case were dealing with a variety of biblical and extra-biblical traditions.

20 "It was at this time that Moses was born. He proved to be an exceedingly handsome child. For the first three months he was reared in his father's house, 21 but afterward he was abandoned, and Pharaoh's daughter adopted him and brought him up as her own son. 22 Moses was educated in all the lore of Egypt. He was a man powerful in word and deed. 23 When he was forty, he decided to visit his kinsmen, the Israelites. 24 Upon seeing one of them maltreated, he went to his aid and avenged the victim by slaying the Egyptian. 25 He assumed that his kinsmen would understand that God was using him to bring them deliverance; but they did not. 26 He appeared the next day while some of them were fighting, and tried to reconcile them by saying: 'Friends, you are blood brothers. Why are you trying to hurt each other?' 27 At that, the man who was wronging his neighbor pushed Moses aside. 'And who has appointed you ruler and judge over us?' he said. 28 'Are you thinking of killing me as you killed the Egyptian yesterday?' 29 On hearing this, Moses fled. He took up his residence as an alien in the land of Midian, where he became the father of two sons.

30 "Forty years later an angel appeared to him in the desert near Mount Sinai in the flame of a burning thornbush. 31 When Moses saw it, he marveled at the sight. As he drew near to observe it carefully, the voice of the Lord was heard: 32 'I am the God of your fathers, the God of Abraham, of Isaac, and of Jacob.' Moses began to tremble and dared look no more. 33 The Lord said to him: 'Remove the sandals from your feet, for the place where you stand is holy ground. 34 I have witnessed the affliction of my people in Egypt and have heard their groaning, and I have come down to rescue them. Come now, I will send you into Egypt.'

35 "This very Moses whom they had rejected with the words, 'Who has appointed you ruler and judge?', was the one whom God, through the angel appearing to him in the thornbush, sent to be their ruler and deliverer. 36 It was he who led them forth, all the while performing wonders and signs in the land of Egypt, in the Red Sea, and for forty years in the desert. 37 This Moses is the one who said to the Israelites, 'God will raise up for you from among your kinsmen a prophet like me.' 38 In that desert assembly, it was he who was in conversation with the angel on Mount Sinai and with our fathers; he too received the oracles of life to pass on to you. 39 He it was whom our fathers would not obey; rather, they thrust him aside and longed to return to Egypt. 40 'Make us gods that will be our leaders,' they said to Aaron. 'As for that Moses who brought us out of the land of Egypt, we have no idea what has happened to him.' 41 It was then that they fashioned the calf and offered sacrifice to the idol, and had a festive celebration over the product of their own hands. 42 But God turned away from them and abandoned them to the worship of the galaxies in the heavens. So we find it written in the Book of the Prophets:

'Did you bring me sacrifices
    and offerings
  for forty years in the desert,
    O house of Israel?
43 Not at all! You took along the
    tent of Moloch
  and the star of the god
    Rephan,
  the images you had made for
    your cult.
For that I will exile you
    beyond Babylon.'

44 "Our fathers in the desert had the meeting tent as God prescribed it when he spoke to Moses, ordering him to make it according to the pattern he had seen. 45 The next generation of our fathers inherited it. Under Joshua, they brought it into the land during the conquest of those peoples whom God drove out to make room for our fathers. So it was until the time of David, 46 who found favor with God and begged that he might find a dwelling place for the house of Jacob. 47 It was Solomon, however, who constructed the building for that house. 48 Yet the Most High does not dwell in buildings made by human hands, for as the prophet says:

49 'The heavens are my throne,
    the earth is my footstool;
  What kind of house can you
    build me?
    asks the Lord.
  What is my resting-place to
    be like?
50 Did not my hand make all
    these things?'

Conclusion

51 "You stiff-necked people, uncircumcised in heart and ears, you are always opposing the Holy Spirit just as your fathers did before you. 52 Was there ever any prophet whom your fathers did not persecute? In their day, they put to death those who foretold the coming of the Just One; now you in your turn have become his betrayers and murderers. 53 You who received the law through the ministry of angels have not observed it."

Stephen's Martyrdom

54 Those who listened to his words were stung to the heart; they ground their teeth in anger at him. 55 Stephen meanwhile, filled with the Holy Spirit, looked to the sky above and saw the glory of God, and Jesus standing at God's right hand. 56 "Look!" he exclaimed, "I see an opening in the sky, and the Son of Man standing at God's right hand." 57 The onlookers were shouting aloud, holding their hands over their ears as they did so. Then they rushed at him as one man, 58 dragged him out of the city, and began to stone him. The witnesses meanwhile were piling their cloaks at the feet of a young man named Saul. 59 As Stephen was being stoned he could be heard praying,

---

7, 55: *Stephen . . . saw . . . Jesus standing at God's right hand:* whether this statement is intended to introduce the description of a vision, or is a dramatized version of Stephen's expression of faith in Christ, is of less importance than the meaning Luke attaches to it for his Christian reader. Stephen affirms to the Sanhedrin that the prophecy Jesus made before them has been fulfilled (Mk 14, 62).

7, 57: *Holding their hands over their ears:* Stephen's declaration, like that of Jesus, is a scandal to the court, which regards it as blasphemy.
7, 59f: Compare Lk 23, 34.46.

"Lord Jesus receive my spirit." 60 He fell to his knees and cried out in a loud voice, "Lord, do not hold this sin against them." And with that he died.

The Church Persecuted

8 Saul, for his part, concurred in the act of killing. That day saw the beginning of a great persecution of the church in Jerusalem. All except the apostles scattered throughout the countryside of Judea and Samaria. 2 Devout men buried Stephen, bewailing him loudly as they did so. 3 After that, Saul began to harass the church. He entered house after house, dragged men and women out, and threw them into jail.

THE COMMUNITY CARRIES THE MESSAGE TO SAMARIA, SYRIA AND CYPRUS

Philip in Samaria

4 The members of the church who had been dispersed went about preaching the word. 5 Philip, for example, went down to the town of Samaria and there proclaimed the Messiah. 6 Without exception, the crowds that heard Philip and saw the miracles he performed attended closely to what he had to say. 7 There were many who had unclean spirits, which came out shrieking loudly. Many others were paralytics or cripples, and these were cured. 8 The rejoicing in that town rose to fever pitch.

Simon Magus

9 A certain man named Simon had been practicing magic in the town and holding the Samaritans spellbound. He passed himself off as someone of great importance. 10 People from every rank of society were paying attention to him. "He is the power of the great God," they said. 11 Those who followed him had been under the spell of his magic over a long period; 12 but once they began to believe in the good news that Philip preached about the kingdom of God and the name of Jesus Christ, men and women alike accepted baptism. 13 Even Simon believed. He was baptized like the rest and became a devoted follower of Philip. He watched the signs and the great miracles as they occurred, and was quite carried away.

14 When the apostles in Jerusalem heard that Samaria had accepted the word of God, they sent Peter and John to them. 15 The two went down to these people and prayed that they might receive the Holy Spirit. 16 It had not as yet come down upon any of them since they had only been baptized in the name of the Lord Jesus. 17 The pair upon arriving imposed hands on them and they received the Holy Spirit. 18 Simon observed that it was through the laying on of hands that the apostles conferred the Spirit, and he made them an offer of money 19 with the request, "Give me that power too, so that if I place my hands on anyone he will receive the Holy Spirit."

20 Peter said in answer: "May you and your money rot—thinking that God's gift can be bought! 21 You can have no portion or lot in this affair. Your heart is not steadfastly set on God. 22 Reform your evil ways. Pray that the Lord may pardon you for thinking the way you have. 23 I see you poisoned with gall and caught in the grip of sin." 24 Simon responded, "I need the prayers of all of you to the Lord, so that what you have just said may never happen to me."

25 After giving their testimony and proclaiming the word of the Lord, they went back to Jerusalem bringing the good news to many villages of Samaria on the way.

Philip and the Ethiopian

26 An angel of the Lord then addressed himself to Philip: "Head south toward the road which goes from Jerusalem to Gaza, the desert route." Philip began the journey. 27 It happened that an Ethiopian eunuch, a court official in charge of the entire treasury of Candace (a name meaning queen) of the Ethiopians, had come on a pilgrimage to Jerusalem and was returning home. 28 He was sitting in the carriage reading the prophet Isaiah. 29 The Spirit said to Philip, "Go and catch up with that carriage." 30 Philip ran ahead and heard the man reading the prophet Isaiah. He said to him, "Do you really grasp what you are reading?" 31 "How can I," the man replied, "unless someone explains it to me?" With that, he invited Philip to get in and sit down beside him. 32 This was the passage of Scripture he was reading:

"Like a sheep he was led to the
　　slaughter,
　like a lamb before its shearer
　　he was silent
　and opened not his mouth.
33 In his humiliation he was
　　deprived of justice.
　Who will ever speak of his
　　posterity,

8, 1–40: Some idea of the severity of the persecution that now breaks out against the Jerusalem community can be gathered from Acts 22, 4 and 26, 9ff. Luke, however, concentrates on the fortunes of the word of God among men, indicating how the dispersal of the Jerusalem community resulted in the conversion of the Samaritans (8, 4–17.25). His narrative is further expanded to include the account of Philip's acceptance of a Gentile from Ethiopia (8, 26–39).

8, 1: *All except the apostles scattered:* this observation leads some modern scholars to conclude that the persecution was limited to the Hellenist Christians, and that the Judaeo-Christians were not molested. Whatever the facts, it appears that the Twelve took no public stand regarding Stephen's position, choosing, instead, to await the development of events.

8, 3: *Saul began to harass the church:* like Stephen, Saul was able to perceive that the Christian movement contained the seeds of serious doctrinal divergence from Judaism. A pupil of Gamaliel (22, 3), and totally dedicated to the law as the way of salvation (Gal 1, 13f), Saul accepted the task of crushing the Christian movement, at least insofar as it detracted from the importance of the temple and the law. His vehement opposition to Christianity reveals how difficult it was for a Jew of his time to accept a messianism that differed so greatly from the general expectation.

8, 9–13. 18–24: Sorcerers were well known in the ancient world. Probably the incident involving Simon and his altercation with Peter is introduced to show that the miraculous charisms possessed by members of the Christian community (8, 6f) were not to be confused with the magic of sorcerers.

8, 25: Stephen's insistence that the presence of God was not confined to the temple in Jerusalem (7, 48f) is now fully accepted by the apostles as a result of the success of Philip in Samaria.

8, 26–40: In the account of the conversion of the Ethiopian eunuch, Luke adduces additional evidence to show that the spread of Christianity outside the confines of Judaism itself was in accord with the plan of God. He does not make clear whether the Ethiopian was originally a convert to Judaism or, as is more probable, a "God-fearer" (10, 1), i.e., one who accepted Jewish monotheism and ethic and attended the synagogue but did not consider himself bound by other regulations. The story of his conversion to Christianity is given a strong supernatural cast by the introduction of an angel (8, 26), instruction from the Holy Spirit (8, 29), and the strange removal of Philip from the scene (8, 38).

8, 30–34: Philip is brought alongside the carriage at the very moment when the Ethiopian is pondering the meaning of Is 53, 7f, a passage which Christianity, from its earliest origins, has understood of Jesus; cf note on 3, 13.

for he is deprived of his life
on earth?"

34 The eunuch said to Philip, "Tell
me, if you will, of whom the prophet
says this—himself or someone else?"
35 Philip launched out with this
Scripture passage as his starting
point, telling him the good news of
Jesus. 36 As they moved along the
road they came to some water, and
the eunuch said, 37 "Look, there
is some water right there. What is to
keep me from being baptized?"
38 He ordered the carriage stopped,
and Philip went down into the water
with the eunuch and baptized him.
39 When they came out of the water,
the Spirit of the Lord snatched Philip
away and the eunuch saw him no
more. Nevertheless, the man went
on his way rejoicing. 40 Philip
found himself at Azotus next, and he
went about announcing the good news
in all the towns until he reached
Caesarea.

The Vocation of Saul

9 Saul, still breathing murderous
threats against the Lord's disciples, went to the high priest 2
and asked him for letters to the
synagogues in Damascus which
would empower him to arrest and
bring to Jerusalem anyone he might
find, man or woman, living according
to the new way. 3 As he traveled
along and was approaching Damascus, a light from the sky suddenly
flashed about him. 4 He fell to the
ground and at the same time heard a
voice saying, "Saul, Saul, why do
you persecute me?" 5 "Who are
you, sir?" he asked. The voice
answered, "I am Jesus, the one you
are persecuting. 6 Get up and go
into the city, where you will be told
what to do." 7 The men who were
traveling with him stood there
speechless. They had heard the voice

but could see no one. 8 Saul got
up from the ground unable to see,
even though his eyes were open.
They had to take him by the hand
and lead him into Damascus. 9
For three days he continued blind,
during which time he neither ate nor
drank.

Saul's Baptism

10 There was a disciple in Damas-
cus named Ananias to whom the
Lord had appeared in a vision.
"Ananias!" he said. "Here I am,
Lord," came the answer. 11 The
Lord said to him, "Go at once to
Straight Street, and at the house of
Judas ask for a certain Saul of
Tarsus. 12 He is there praying."
(Saul saw in a vision a man named
Ananias coming to him and placing
his hands on him so that he might
recover his sight.) 13 But Ananias
protested: "Lord, I have heard from
many sources about this man and all
the harm he has done to your holy
people in Jerusalem. 14 He is here
now with authorization from the chief
priests to arrest any who invoke your
name." 15 The Lord said to him:
"You must go! This man is the
instrument I have chosen to bring
my name to the Gentiles and their
kings and to the people of Israel.
16 I myself shall indicate to him how
much he will have to suffer for my
name." 17 With that Ananias left.
When he entered the house he laid
his hands on Saul and said, "Saul,
my brother, I have been sent by the
Lord Jesus who appeared to you on
the way here, to help you recover
your sight and be filled with the Holy
Spirit." 18 Immediately something
like scales fell from his eyes and he
regained his sight. He got up and was
baptized, 19 and his strength returned to him after he had taken
food.

Saul Preaches in Damascus

Saul stayed some time with the
disciples in Damascus, 20 and soon
began to proclaim in the synagogues
that Jesus was the Son of God. 21
Any who heard it were greatly taken
aback. They kept saying: "Isn't this
the man who worked such havoc in
Jerusalem among those who invoke
this name? Did he not come here
purposely to apprehend such people
and bring them before the chief
priests?"
22 Saul for his part grew steadily
more powerful, and reduced the
Jewish community of Damascus to
silence with his proofs that this
Jesus was the Messiah.

Saul Visits Jerusalem

23 After quite some time had
passed, certain Jews conspired to kill
Saul, 24 but their plot came to his
attention. They went so far as to
keep close watch on the city gates
day and night in an attempt to do
away with him. 25 Some of his
disciples, therefore, took him along
the wall one night and lowered him
to the ground, using ropes and a
hamper. 26 When he arrived back
in Jerusalem he tried to join the
disciples there; but it turned out that
they were all afraid of him. They
even refused to believe that he was a
disciple. 27 Then Barnabas took
him in charge and introduced him
to the apostles. He explained to
them how on his journey Saul had
seen the Lord, who had conversed
with him, and how Saul had been
speaking out fearlessly in the name
of Jesus at Damascus. 28 Saul
stayed on with them, moving freely
about Jerusalem and expressing himself quite openly in the name of the
Lord. 29 He even addressed the
Greek-speaking Jews and debated
with them. They for their part

9, 1–19: This is the first of three accounts of Paul's
conversion (see 22, 3–16 and 26, 2–18), with some
differences of detail. Paul's experience was not
visionary but was precipitated by the actual appearance
of Jesus, as he insists in 1 Cor 15, 8. The words of
Jesus, "Saul, Saul, why do you persecute me?",
related by Luke with no variation in all three accounts,
exerted a profound and lasting influence on the
thought of Paul. Under the impulsion of this experience he gradually developed his understanding of
justification by faith (see Epistles to Galatians and
Romans), and of the identification of the Christian
community with Jesus Christ; cf Col 1, 18.
9, 2: The new way: an early name for Christian

discipleship; cf 16, 17; 18, 26; 19, 9.23; 24, 14.22.
The term, no doubt Christian in origin, expresses the
idea that Christian discipleship is the culmination of
God's revelation to men and of men's relationship
to God.
9, 8: Unable to see: a temporary blindness (9, 18)
miraculous in origin, symbolizing the religious
blindness of Saul as persecutor.
9, 15: To bring my name to the Gentiles: only
gradually was the significance of this prophecy
realized by Paul as the church was compelled to turn
its attention more and more to the Gentiles.
9, 19–30: This is the brief résumé of Paul's initial
experience as an apostolic preacher, though that

aspect of his career did not begin immediately upon
his conversion (Gal 1, 17). At first he found himself
in the position of being both a turncoat to the Jews
and an enigma to the Christian community of
Jerusalem. His acceptance by the latter was finally
brought about through his friendship with Barnabas.
9, 20: The Son of God: to be understood in the sense
of "the Christ" in 9, 22; cf Acts 13, 33 citing Ps 2, 7
in this sense. Perhaps Luke chooses this expression
here because, for Paul and Christians generally, the
title "Son of God" soon became the one most ex-
pressive of Jesus' true dignity; cf 1 Thes 1, 10; Rom
1, 2ff.

responded by trying to kill him. 30 When the brothers learned of this, some of them took him down to Caesarea and sent him off to Tarsus.

The Church at Peace

31 Meanwhile, throughout all Judea, Galilee, and Samaria the church was at peace. It was being built up and was making steady progress in the fear of the Lord; at the same time it enjoyed the increased consolation of the Holy Spirit.

Peter Visits Lydda and Joppa

32 Once when Peter was making numerous journeys, he went—among other places—to God's holy people living in Lydda. 33 There he found a man named Aeneas, a paralytic who had been bedridden for eight years. 34 Peter said to him, "Aeneas, Jesus Christ cures you! Get up and make your bed." The man got up at once. 35 All the inhabitants of Lydda and Sharon, upon seeing him, were converted to the Lord.

36 Now in Joppa there was a certain woman convert named Tabitha (in Greek Dorcas, meaning a gazelle). Her life was marked by constant good deeds and acts of charity. 37 At about that time she fell ill and died. They washed her body and laid it out in an upstairs room. 38 Since Lydda was near Joppa, the disciples, who had heard that Peter was there, sent two men to him with the urgent request, "Please come over to us without delay." 39 Peter set out with them as they asked. Upon his arrival they took him upstairs to the room. All the widows came to him in tears and showed him the various garments Dorcas had made when she was still with them. 40 Peter first made everyone go outside; then he knelt down and prayed. Turning to the dead body, he said, "Tabitha, stand up." She opened her eyes, then looked at Peter and sat up. 41 He gave her his hand and helped her to her feet. The next thing he did was to call in those who were believers and the widows to show them that she was still alive. 42 This became known all over Joppa, and because of it, many came to believe in the Lord. 43 Thus it happened that Peter stayed on in Joppa for a considerable time at the house of Simon, a tanner of leather.

The Vision of Cornelius

10 Now in Caesarea there was a centurion named Cornelius, of the Roman cohort Italica, who was religious and God-fearing. The same was true of his whole household. 2 He was in the habit of giving generously to the people and he constantly prayed to God. One afternoon at about three he had a vision in which he clearly saw a messenger of God coming toward him and calling, "Cornelius!" 4 He stared at the sight and said in fear, "What is it, sir?" The answer came: "Your prayers and your generosity have risen in God's sight, and because of them he has remembered you. 5 Send some men to Joppa and summon a certain Simon, known as Peter. 6 He is a guest of Simon the leather-tanner whose house stands by the sea." 7 When the messenger who spoke these words had disappeared, he called two servants and a devout soldier from among those whom he could trust. 8 He explained every-thing to them and dispatched them to Joppa.

Peter's Vision

9 About noontime the next day, as the men were traveling along and approaching the city, Peter went up to the roof terrace to pray. 10 He became hungry and asked for some food, and while it was being pre-pared he fell into a trance. 11 He saw the sky open and an object come down that looked like a big canvas. It was lowered to the ground by its four corners. 12 Inside it were all the earth's four-legged creatures and reptiles and birds of the sky. 13 A voice said to him: "Get up, Peter! Slaughter, then eat." 14 He answered: "Sir, it is un-thinkable! I have never eaten any-thing unclean or impure in my life." 15 The voice was heard a second time: "What God has purified you are not to call unclean." 16 This happened three times; then the object was snatched up into the sky. 17 While Peter was trying to make out the meaning of the vision he had had, the men sent by Cornelius arrived at the gate asking for the house of Simon. 18 They called out to inquire whether Simon Peter was a guest there. 19 Peter was still pondering the vision when the Spirit said to him: "There are two men in search of you. 20 Go downstairs and set out with them unhesitatingly, for it is I who sent them." 21 Peter went down to the men and said, "I am the man you are looking for. What brought you here?" 22 They answered: "The centurion Cornelius, who is an upright and God-fearing man, well thought of in the whole Jewish community, has been instructed by a holy messenger to summon you to his house. There he is to hear what you

---

9, 31–43: In the context of the period of peace enjoyed by the community through the cessation of Paul's activities against it, Luke introduces two traditions concerning the miraculous powers of Peter. The towns of Lydda, Sharon and Joppa were populated by both Jews and Gentiles, and their Christian communities may well have been mixed. No particular motive for the cure of Aeneas is assigned, though it is not said that he was a Christian prior to the cure. The actual motive for the raising of Tabitha may have been the expectation of the parousia; in view of her unique charity, the community apparently found it hard to understand her death before this event had occurred.

9, 43: The fact that Peter lodged with a tanner

would have been significant to both Gentile and Judaeo-Christians, for Judaism considered the tanning occupation unclean.

10, 1–48: The narrative centers on the conversion of Cornelius, a Gentile and a "God-fearer." See note on 8, 26–40). Luke considers the event of great importance, as is evident from his long treatment of it. The incident is again related in 11, 1–18 and alluded to in 15, 7ff. The narrative divides itself easily into a series of distinct episodes, concluding with Peter's presentation of the Christian kerygma (34–43), and a pentecostal experience undergone by Cornelius' household preceding their reception of baptism (44–48).

10, 7: A devout soldier: by using this adjective

Luke probably intends to classify him as a "God-fearer." The point is that Cornelius is careful to select a soldier who will respect his account of the apparition.

10, 9–16: The vision is intended to prepare Peter to share the food of Cornelius' household without qualms of conscience (10, 48). The necessity of such instruction to Peter reveals that at first not even the apostles fully grasped the implications of Jesus' teaching on the law. The initial insight belongs to Stephen.

10, 17–23: The arrival of the Gentile emissaries with their account of the angelic apparition illuminates Peter's vision: he is to be prepared to admit Gentiles into the Christian community.

have to say." 23 With that, Peter invited them in and treated them as guests.

Peter in Caesarea

The next day he went off with them, accompanied by some of the brothers from Joppa. 24 The following day, he arrived in Caesarea. Cornelius, who was expecting them, had called in his relatives and close friends. 25 As Peter entered, Cornelius went to meet him, dropped to his knees before him and bowed low. 26 Peter said as he helped him to his feet, "Get up! I am only a man myself." 27 Peter then went in, talking with him all the while. He found many people assembled there, and 28 he began speaking to them thus: "You must know that it is not proper for a Jew to associate with a Gentile or to have dealings with him. But God has made it clear to me that no one should call any man unclean or impure. 29 That is why I have come in response to your summons without raising any objection. I should, of course, like to know why you summoned me." 30 Cornelius replied: "Just three days ago at this very hour, namely three o'clock, I was praying at home when a man in dazzling robes stood before me. 31 'Cornelius,' he said, 'your prayer has been heard and your generosity remembered in God's presence. 32 Send someone to Joppa to invite Simon known as Peter to come here. He is a guest in the house of Simon the leather-tanner, by the sea.' 33 I sent for you immediately, and you have been kind enough to come. All of us stand before God at this moment to hear whatever directives the Lord has given you."

Peter's Discourse

34 Peter proceeded to address them in these words: "I begin to see how true it is that God shows no partiality. 35 Rather, the man of any nation who fears God and acts uprightly is acceptable to him. 36 This is the message he has sent to the sons of Israel, the good news of peace proclaimed through Jesus Christ who is the Lord of all. 37 I take it you know what had been reported all over Judea about Jesus of Nazareth, beginning in Galilee with the baptism John preached; 38 of the way God anointed him with the Holy Spirit and power. He went about doing good works and healing all who were in the grip of the devil, and God was with him. 39 We are witnesses to all that he did in the land of the Jews and in Jerusalem. 40 They killed him, finally, hanging him on a tree, only to have God raise him up on the third day and grant that he be seen, 41 not by all, but only by such witnesses as had been chosen beforehand by God—by us who ate and drank with him after he rose from the dead. 42 He commissioned us to preach to the people and to bear witness that he is the one set apart by God as judge of the living and the dead. 43 To him all the prophets testify, saying that everyone who believes in him has forgiveness of sins through his name."

Baptism of Cornelius

44 Peter had not finished these words when the Holy Spirit descended upon all who were listening to Peter's message. 45 The circumcised believers who had accompanied Peter were surprised that the gift of the Holy Spirit should have been poured out on the Gentiles also, 46 whom they could hear speaking in tongues and glorifying God. Peter put the question at that point: 47 "What can stop these people who have received the Holy Spirit, even as we have, from being baptized with water?" 48 So he gave orders that they be baptized in the name of Jesus Christ. After this was done, they asked him to stay with them for a few days.

The Call of the Gentiles Explained

11 All through Judea the apostles and the brothers heard that Gentiles, too, had accepted the word of God. 2 As a result, when Peter went up to Jerusalem some among the circumcised took issue with him, saying, 3 "You entered the house of uncircumcised men and ate with them." 4 Peter then explained the whole affair to them step by step from the beginning: 5 "I was at prayer in the city of Joppa when, in a trance, I saw a vision. An object like a big canvas came down; it was lowered down to me from the sky by its four corners. 6 As I stared at it I could make out four-legged creatures of the earth, wild beasts and reptiles, and birds of the sky. 7 I listened as a voice said to me, 'Get up, Peter! Slaughter, then eat.' 8 I replied: 'Not for a moment, sir! Nothing unclean or impure has ever entered my mouth!' 9 A second time the voice from the heavens spoke out: 'What God has purified you are not to call unclean.' 10 This happened three times; then the canvas with everything in it was drawn up again into the sky.

11 "Immediately after that, the

10, 24ff: So impressed is Cornelius with the apparition that he invites close personal friends to support him in his confrontation with Peter. But his understanding of the personage he is about to meet is not devoid of superstition. For a similar experience of Paul and Barnabas, see 14, 10–17.

10, 28: Peter now fully understands the meaning of his vision; see note on 10, 17–23.

10, 34f: God shows no partiality: the revelation of his choice of Israel to be the people of God did not mean he withheld the divine favor from other men.

10, 37: You know what has been reported all over Judea about Jesus of Nazareth: God's revelation of his plan for the destiny of mankind through Israel culminated in Jesus of Nazareth. Consequently, the ministry of Jesus is an integral part of God's revelation. This viewpoint explains why the early Christian

communities were interested in conserving the historical substance of the ministry of Jesus, a tradition leading to the production of the four gospels.

10, 39: We are witnesses: the apostolic testimony was not restricted to the resurrection of Jesus but also included his historical ministry. This witness, however, was theological in character: the Twelve, divinely mandated as prophets, were empowered to interpret his sayings and deeds in the light of his redemptive death and resurrection. The meaning of these words and deeds was to be made clear to the developing Christian community as the bearer of the word of salvation; cf 1, 21–26.

10, 42: As judge of the living and the dead: the apostolic preaching to the Jews appealed to their messianic hope, while the appeal to the Gentiles stressed the coming divine judgment; cf 1 Thes 1, 10.

11, 1–18: Scholars differ regarding the historical realities behind this narrative and Luke's purpose in utilizing them. Simply understood, the narrative indicates the following:

(1) The Judaeo-Christians of Jerusalem were scandalized to learn of Peter's sojourn in the house of the Gentile Cornelius; (2) nonetheless they had to accept the divine directions given to both Peter and Cornelius; (3) they concluded that the setting aside of the legal barriers between Jew and Gentile was an exceptional ordinance of God in this one case to indicate that the apostolic kerygma was also to be directed to the Gentiles. As yet, the Jerusalem Christians were unwilling to accept mixed communities.

three men who had been sent to me from Caesarea came to the house where we were staying. 12 The Spirit instructed me to accompany them without hesitation. These six brothers came along with me, and we entered the man's house. 13 He informed us that he had seen an angel standing in his house and that the angel had said: 'Send someone to Joppa and fetch Simon, known also as Peter. 14 In the light of what he will tell you, you shall be saved, and all your household.' 15 As I began to address them the Holy Spirit came upon them, just as it had upon us at the beginning. 16 Then I remembered what the Lord had said: 'John baptized with water but you will be baptized with the Holy Spirit.' 17 If God was giving them the same gift he gave us when we first believed in the Lord Jesus Christ, who was I to interfere with him?' 18 When they heard this they stopped objecting, and instead began to glorify God in these words: "If this be so, then God has granted life-giving repentance even to the Gentiles."

The Church Established at Antioch

19 Those in the community who had been dispersed by the persecution that arose because of Stephen went as far as Phoenicia, Cyprus and Antioch, making the message known to none but Jews. 20 However, some men of Cyprus and Cyrene among them who had come to Antioch began to talk even to the Greeks, announcing the good news of the Lord Jesus to them. 21 The hand of the Lord was with them and a great number of them believed and were converted to the Lord. 22 News of this eventually reached the ears of the church in Jerusalem,

resulting in Barnabas' being sent to Antioch. 23 On his arrival he rejoiced to see the evidence of God's favor. He encouraged them all to remain firm in their commitment to the Lord, 24 since he himself was a good man filled with the Holy Spirit and faith. Thereby large numbers were added to the Lord. 25 Then Barnabas went off to Tarsus to look for Saul; 26 once he had found him, he brought him back to Antioch. For a whole year they met with the church and instructed great numbers. It was in Antioch that the disciples were called Christians for the first time.

Prediction of Agabus

27 At about that time, certain prophets came down from Jerusalem to Antioch. 28 One of them named Agabus was inspired to stand up and proclaim that there was going to be a severe famine all over the world. (It did in fact occur while Claudius was emperor.) 29 This made the disciples determine to set something aside, each according to his means, and send it to the relief of the brothers who lived in Judea. 30 They did this, dispatching it to the presbyters in the care of Barnabas and Saul.

Herod Persecutes the Church

12 During that period, King Herod started to harass some of the members of the church. 2 He beheaded James the brother of John, 3 and when he saw that this pleased certain of the Jews, he took Peter into custody too. 4 During the feast of Unleavened Bread he had him arrested and thrown into prison, with four squads of soldiers to guard him. Herod intended to bring him before the people after the Passover. 5 Peter was thus detained in prison,

while the church prayed fervently to God on his behalf. 6 During the night before Herod was to bring him to trial, Peter was sleeping between two soldiers, fastened with double chains, while guards kept watch at the door. 7 Suddenly an angel of the Lord stood nearby and light shone in the cell. He tapped Peter on the side and woke him. "Hurry, get up!" he said. With that, the chains dropped from Peter's wrists. 8 The angel said, "Put on your belt and your sandals!" This he did. Then the angel told him, "Now put on your cloak and follow me."

9 Peter followed him out, but with no clear realization that this was taking place through the angel's help. The whole thing seemed to him a mirage. 10 They passed the first guard, then the second, and finally came to the iron gate leading out to the city, which opened for them of itself. They emerged and made their way down a narrow alley, when suddenly the angel left him. 11 Peter had recovered his senses by this time, and said, "Now I know for certain that the Lord has sent his angel to rescue me from Herod's clutches and from all that the Jews hoped for."

12 After coming to realize this, he went to the house of Mary the mother of John (also known as Mark), where many others were gathered in prayer. 13 Peter knocked at the door and a maid named Rhoda came to answer it. 14 On recognizing his voice she was so overjoyed that she did not stop to open the door, but ran in and announced that Peter was outside. 15 "You're out of your wits," they said to her, but she insisted it was true. All they could say was, "It must be his angel." 16 Through all this, Peter kept on knocking. They finally opened the door and were astonished to see him.

11, 12: *These six brothers:* companions from the Christian community of Joppa; cf 10, 23.

11, 19–26: The Judaeo-Christian antipathy to the mixed community was reflected by the early missioners generally. The few among them who entertained a different view succeeded in introducing Gentiles into the community at Antioch (in Syria). When the disconcerted Jerusalem community sent Barnabas to investigate, he was so favorably impressed by what he observed that he persuaded his friend Saul to participate in the Antioch experiment. The venture was successful; within a year, members of the mixed community in Antioch had acquired the new name of "Christians."

11, 27–30: It is not clear whether the prophets from Jerusalem came to Antioch to request help in view of the coming famine or whether they received this insight during their visit there. The former supposition seems more likely. Suetonius and Tacitus speak of famines during the reign of Claudius (A.D. 41–54), while the Jewish historian Josephus records a famine in Judea in A.D. 46–48. Luke is interested, rather, in showing the charity of the Antiochean community toward the Judaeo-Christians of Jerusalem despite their differences on mixed communities.

12, 1–19: Herod Agrippa ruled Judea A.D. 41–44. While Luke does not assign a motive for his execution of James and his intended execution of Peter, the

broad background lies in Herod's policy of conciliating his Jewish subjects. The Judaeo-Christians had lost the popularity they had had in Jerusalem (2, 47), perhaps because of suspicions against them traceable to the teaching of Stephen. The account of Peter's escape derives from his subjective visionary experience, making him aware essentially of what was happening to him. Exactly how divine power effected the release is not possible to determine. The events related in this narrative are probably to be dated before the occurrence of the famine mentioned in 11, 27–30.

17 He motioned to them to be quiet, and explained how the Lord had brought him out of prison. "Report this to James and the brothers," he said, then left them to go off to another place. 18 At daybreak confusion broke out among the soldiers, who did not know what had happened to Peter. 19 Herod then initiated a search for him. When it proved unsuccessful, he had the guards tried and executed. Shortly after this, Herod left Judea to spend some time in Caesarea.

Herod's Death

20 Herod had long been infuriated by the people of Tyre and Sidon, who now by common consent came before him in his court. They won over his royal chamberlain Blastus and attempted to placate him, because their country was supplied with food from the king's territory. 21 On an appointed day Herod, arrayed in royal robes, took his seat on the rostrum and publicly addressed them. 22 The assembled crowd shouted back, "This is the voice of a god, not a man!" 23 The angel of the Lord struck Herod down at once because he did not ascribe the honor to God, and he died eaten by worms.

24 Meanwhile, the word of the Lord continued to spread and increase.

MISSION OF BARNABAS AND SAUL

25 Barnabas and Saul returned to Jerusalem upon completing the relief mission, taking with them John Mark.

13 There were in the church at Antioch certain prophets and teachers: Barnabas, Symeon known as Niger, Lucius of Cyrene, Manaen (who had been brought up with Herod the tetrarch), and Saul. 2 On one occasion, while they were engaged in the liturgy of the Lord and were fasting, the Holy Spirit spoke to them: "Set apart Barnabas and Saul for me to do the work for which I have called them." 3 Then, after they had fasted and prayed, they imposed hands on them and sent them off.

First Mission Begins in Cyprus

4 These two, sent forth by the Holy Spirit, went down to the port of Seleucia and set sail from there for Cyprus. 5 On their arrival in Salamis they proclaimed the word of God in the Jewish synagogues, John accompanying them as an assistant. 6 They traveled over the whole island as far as Paphos, where they came across a Jewish magician named Bar-Jesus who posed as a prophet. 7 He was attached to the court of the proconsular governor Sergius Paulus, a man of intelligence who had summoned Barnabas and Saul and was anxious to hear the word of God. 8 But Elymas—"the magician," for that is what his name means—opposed them and sought to turn the governor away from the faith. 9 Saul (also known as Paul) was filled with the Holy Spirit; he stared at him 10 and exclaimed: "You are an imposter and a thoroughgoing fraud, you son of Satan and enemy of all that is right! Will you never stop trying to make crooked the straight paths of the Lord? 11 The Lord's hand is upon you even now! For a time you shall be blind, unable so much as to see the sun." At once a misty darkness came over him, and he groped about for someone to lead him by the hand. 12 When the governor saw what had happened, he believed, so impressed was he by the teaching about the Lord.

Arrival at Antioch in Pisidia

13 From Paphos, Paul and his companions put out to sea and sailed to Perga in Pamphylia. There John left them and returned to Jerusalem. 14 They continued to travel on from Perga and came to Antioch in Pisidia. On the sabbath day they entered the synagogue and sat down. 15 After the reading of the law and of the prophets, the leading men of the synagogue sent this message to them: "Brothers, if you have any exhortation to address to the people, please speak up."

Preaching in the Synagogue

16 So Paul arose, motioned to them for silence, and began: "Fellow Israelites and you others who reverence our God, listen to what I have to say! 17 The God of the people Israel once chose our fathers. He made this people great during their sojourn in the land of Egypt, and with an outstretched arm he led them out of it. 18 For forty years he put up with them in the desert: then he destroyed seven nations in the land of Canaan to give them that country as their heritage 20 at the end of some four hundred and fifty years. Later on he set up judges to rule them until the time of the prophet Samuel. 21 When they asked for a king, God gave them Saul son of Kish, of the tribe of Benjamin, who ruled for forty years. 22 Then God removed him and raised up David as their king; on his behalf God testi-

12, 17: He . . . left them to go off to another place: the conjecture that Peter left for Rome at this time has nothing to recommend it. His chief responsibility was still the leadership of the Judaeo-Christian communities in Palestine: Gal 2, 7. The concept of the great missionary effort of the church was yet to come; cf 13, 1ff.

12, 20–23: Josephus gives a similar account of Herod's death. Early Christian tradition considered the manner of it to be a divine punishment upon his evil life. See 2 Kgs 19, 35 for the figure of the angel of the Lord in such a context.

13, 1ff: The impulse for the first missionary effort in Asia Minor is ascribed to the prophets of the Antiochean community, under the inspiration of the Holy Spirit. The thinking behind the mission was perhaps that if the Jews of the diaspora could be converted as successfully as had been the case at Antioch, the Jews of Palestine would eventually lose their hostility toward Christian messianism.

13, 4—14, 27: The key event in Luke's account of the first missionary journey is the experience of Paul and Barnabas at Pisidian Antioch (14–52). The Christian kerygma proclaimed by Paul in the synagogue was favorably received. Some Jews and "God-fearers" were effectively converted (42f—see note on 8, 26–40), and the congregation at large asked the missionaries to speak again on the following sabbath. By that time, however, the appearance of a large number of Gentiles from the city had so disconcerted the Jews that they became hostile toward the apostles (44f). Thus the Jews of Pisidian Antioch proved no less opposed to the mixed community than the Judaeo-Christians of Jerusalem. As long as Paul refused to incorporate the Gentiles into Judaism as the condition for their acceptance of Christ, the Jews

continued to regard Christian messianism as destructive of their religious traditions and their culture. This fear of theirs appears in all three accounts of Paul's missionary journeys in Acts, the Jews of Iconium (14, 1f) and Beroea (17, 11) being notable exceptions.

13, 6: A Jewish magician named Bar-Jesus who posed as a prophet: again Luke takes the opportunity to dissociate Christianity from the magical arts of the time (7–11); cf 8, 18–24.

13, 11f: The temporary blindness symbolized the falsity of the man's teaching.

13, 13: There John left them: it has been conjectured that John Mark objected to Paul's ascendancy over his cousin Barnabas, but it is more likely that the rugged country and alien culture had made Mark homesick for Jerusalem; cf 12, 12.

fied, 'I have found David son of Jesse to be a man after my own heart who will fulfill my every wish.'

23 "According to his promise, God has brought forth from this man's descendants Jesus, a savior for Israel. 24 John heralded the coming of Jesus by proclaiming a baptism of repentance to all the people of Israel. 25 As John's career was coming to an end, he would say, 'What you suppose me to be I am not. Rather, look for the one who comes after me. I am not worthy to unfasten the sandals on his feet.' 26 My brothers, children of the family of Abraham and you others who reverence our God, it was to us that this message of salvation was sent forth. 27 The inhabitants of Jerusalem and their rulers failed to recognize him, and in condemning him they fulfilled the words of the prophets which we read sabbath after sabbath. 28 Even though they found no charge against him which deserved death, they begged Pilate to have him executed. 29 Once they had thus brought about all that had been written of him, they took him down from the tree and laid him in a tomb. 30 Yet God raised him from the dead, 31 and for many days thereafter Jesus appeared to those who had come up with him from Galilee to Jerusalem. These are the witnesses now before the people.

32 "We ourselves announce to you the good news that what God promised our fathers 33 he has fulfilled for us, their children, in raising up Jesus, according to what is written in the second psalm, 'You are my son; this day I have begotten you.' 34 As a proof that the one whom he raised from the dead would never again see the decay of death, God declared, 'I will give you the benefits assured to David under the covenant.' 35 That is why he said in still another place, 'You will not suffer your faithful one to undergo corruption.' 36 Now David, after he had spent a lifetime in carrying

out God's will, fell asleep and joined his fathers, thereby undergoing corruption. 37 But the one whom God has raised up did not undergo corruption. 38 You must realize, my brothers, that it is through him that the forgiveness of sins is being proclaimed to you, including the remission of all those charges you could never be acquitted of under the law of Moses. 39 In him, every believer is acquitted. 40 Have a care, then, lest what was said by the prophets be realized in you: 41 'Look on in amazement, you cynics, then disappear! For I am doing a deed in your days which you never would have believed even if you had been told.'"

42 As they were leaving, the people invited them to speak on this subject again on the following sabbath. 43 When the congregation finally broke up, many Jews and devout Jewish converts followed Paul and Barnabas, who spoke to them and urged them to hold fast to the grace of God.

Address to the Gentiles

44 The following sabbath, almost the entire city gathered to hear the word of God. 45 When the Jews saw the crowds, they became very jealous and countered with violent abuse whatever Paul said. 46 Paul and Barnabas spoke out fearlessly, nonetheless: "The word of God has to be declared to you first of all; but since you reject it and thus convict yourselves as unworthy of everlasting life, we now turn to the Gentiles. 47 For thus were we instructed by the Lord: 'I have made you a light to the nations, a means of salvation to the ends of the earth.'" 48 The Gentiles were delighted when they heard this and responded to the word of the Lord with praise. All who were destined for life everlasting believed in it. 49 Thus the word of the Lord was carried throughout that area.

50 But some of the Jews stirred up their influential women sympa-

thizers and the leading men of the town, and in that way got a persecution started against Paul and Barnabas. The Jews finally expelled them from their territory. 51 So the two shook the dust from their feet in protest and went on to Iconium. 52 The disciples could not but be filled with joy and the Holy Spirit.

Preaching at Iconium

14 In Iconium likewise, they entered the Jewish synagogue and spoke in such a way as to convince a good number of Jews and Greeks. 2 But the Jews who remained unconvinced stirred up the Gentiles and poisoned their minds against the brothers. 3 Paul and Barnabas spent considerable time there and spoke out fearlessly, in complete reliance on the Lord. He, for his part, confirmed the message with his grace and caused signs and wonders to be done at their hands. 4 Most of the townspeople were divided over them, some siding with the Jews and others with the apostles. 5 A move was made by Gentiles and Jews, together with their leaders, to abuse and stone them. 6 When Paul and Barnabas learned of this, they fled to the Lycaonian towns of Lystra and Derbe and to the surrounding country, 7 where they continued to proclaim the good news.

A Cure in Lystra

8 At Lystra there was a man who was lame from birth; he used to sit crippled, never having walked in his life. 9 On one occasion he was listening to Paul preaching, and Paul looked directly at him and saw that he had the faith to be saved. 10 He called out to him in a loud voice, "Stand up! On your feet!" The man jumped up and began to walk around. 11 When the crowds saw what Paul had done, they cried out in Lycaonian, "Gods have come to us in the form of men!" 12 They named Barnabas Zeus; Paul they called Hermes, since he was the spokesman. 13 Even the priest of

---

13, 31: *These are his witnesses now before the people:* the prophetic rule of the Twelve concerning Jesus; see note on 10, 39.

13, 38: *Including the remission of all those charges you could never be acquitted of under the law of Moses:* a doctrinal statement of justification by faith, par-

ticularly appropriate to Paul; see note on 9, 1–19.

13, 46: *Unworthy of everlasting life:* the refusal to believe frustrates God's plan for his chosen people; however, no adverse judgment is made here concerning their ultimate destiny.

14, 8–17: In an effort to convince his hearers that

the divine power works through his word, Paul cures the cripple. However, the pagan tradition of the occasional appearance of gods among men leads the people astray in interpreting the miracle. The incident reveals the cultural difficulties with which the church had to cope.

the temple of Zeus, which stood outside the town, brought oxen and garlands to the gates because he wished to offer sacrifice to them with the crowds.

14 When the apostles Barnabas and Paul heard of this, they tore their garments and rushed out into the crowd. 15 "Friends, why do you do this?" they shouted frantically. "We are only men, human like you. We are bringing you the good news that will convert you from just such follies as these to the living God, 'the one who made heaven and earth and the sea and all that is in them.' 16 In past ages he let the Gentiles go their way. 17 Yet in bestowing his benefits, he has not hidden himself completely, without a clue, From the heavens he sends down rain and rich harvests; your spirits he fills with food and delight." 18 Yet even with a speech such as this, they could scarcely stop the crowds from offering sacrifice to them.

End of the First Mission

19 Just at that point, some Jews from Antioch and Iconium arrived and won the people over. They stoned Paul and dragged him out of the town, leaving him there for dead. 20 His disciples quickly formed a circle about him, and before long he got up and went back into the town. The next day he left with Barnabas for Derbe. 21 After they had proclaimed the good news in that town and made numerous disciples, they retraced their steps to Lystra and Iconium first, then to Antioch. 22 They gave their disciples reassurances, and encouraged

them to persevere in the faith with this instruction: "We must undergo many trials if we are to enter into the reign of God." 23 In each church they installed presbyters and, with prayer and fasting, commended them to the Lord in whom they had put their faith.

Return to Antioch

24 Then they passed through Pisidia and came to Pamphylia. 25 After preaching the message in Perga, they went down to Attalia. 26 From there they sailed back to Antioch, where they had first been commended to the favor of God for the task they had now completed. 27 On their arrival, they called the congregation together and related all that God had helped them accomplish, and how he had opened the door of faith to the Gentiles. 28 Then they spent some time there with the disciples.

Council of Jerusalem

15 Some men came down to Antioch from Judea and began to teach the brothers: "Unless you are circumcised according to Mosaic practice, you cannot be saved." 2 This created dissension and much controversy between them and Paul and Barnabas. Finally it was decided that Paul, Barnabas, and some others should go up to see the apostles and presbyters in Jerusalem about this question.

3 The church saw them off and they made their way through Phoenicia and Samaria, telling everyone about the conversion of the Gentiles as they went. Their story caused great joy among the brothers.

4 When they arrived in Jerusalem they were welcomed by that church, as well as by the apostles and the presbyters, to whom they reported all that God had helped them accomplish. 5 Some of the converted Pharisees then got up and demanded that such Gentiles be circumcised and told to keep the Mosaic law.

6 The apostles and the presbyters accordingly convened to look into the matter. 7 After much discussion, Peter took the floor and said to them: "Brothers, you know well enough that from the early days God selected me from your number to be the one from whose lips the Gentiles would hear the message of the gospel and believe. 8 God, who reads the hearts of men, showed his approval by granting the Holy Spirit to them just as he did to us. 9 He made no distinction between them and us, but purified their hearts by means of faith also. 10 Why, then, do you put God to the test by trying to place on the shoulders of these converts a yoke which neither we nor our fathers were able to bear? 11 Our belief is rather that we are saved by the favor of the Lord Jesus and so are they." 12 At that the whole assembly fell silent. They listened to Barnabas and Paul as the two described all the signs and wonders God had worked among the Gentiles through them.

James on Dietary Law

13 When they concluded their presentation, James spoke up: "Brothers, listen to me. 14 Symeon has told you how God first concerned himself with taking from among the Gentiles a people to bear his name.

14, 23: *In each church they installed presbyters:* the communities are given their own religious leaders. Seemingly (cf Jas 5, 14), a part of their task is the performance of liturgical rites, especially the liturgy of the Eucharist; cf 2, 42. Paul's caution in organizing the communities is shown by the fact that they receive presbyters only after a period of testing.

14, 26: The report of the missioners to the church at Antioch was not wholly encouraging. The attempt to create mixed communities after the Antiochean model had been essentially a failure; cf 13, 46.50f; 14, 2.4f.19. On the other hand, the receptivity among the Gentiles offered hope for the future.

15, 1–5: When some of the converted Pharisees of Jerusalem discover the results of the first missionary journey of Paul, they conclude that their worst fears over the Antiochean experiment of the mixed community have been realized. They urge that the lesson to be learned from Paul's failure to convert the Jews of the diaspora is that the Gentiles must be taught to adopt the religious traditions of Judaism, for only in

this way will it be possible for the Jews of the diaspora to form a common church with the Gentiles.

15, 6–12: This gathering is probably the same as that recalled by Paul in Gal 2, 1–10. Note that in 15, 2 it is only the apostles and presbyters, a small group, with whom Paul and Barnabas are to meet. Here Luke gives the meeting a public character because he wishes to emphasize its doctrinal significance for the entire world; cf v 22.

15, 7ff: Paul's refusal to impose the Mosaic law on the Gentile Christians is supported by Peter on the ground that within his own experience God bestowed the Holy Spirit upon Cornelius and his household without preconditions concerning the adoption of the Mosaic law; cf 10, 44–47.

15, 10: A devout Jew considered the law a blessing. For the Christian, however, who understood that in his regard its observance was not a condition for receiving the divine benefits, such observance could be only a burden; cf Gal 4, 31.

15, 11: In support of Paul, Peter formulates the

fundamental meaning of the gospel: that all mankind is invited to be saved through faith in the salvific power of Christ; personal observance of the divine law is man's necessary response to God's saving action, though not the cause of it.

15 13–35: Some scholars think that this apostolic decree requested by James, the immediate leader of the Jerusalem community, derives from another historical occasion than the meeting in question. This seems to be the case if the meeting is the same as the one related in Galatians 2, 1–10. According to that account, nothing was imposed upon Gentile Christians in respect to Mosaic law; whereas the decree instructs Gentile Christians of mixed communities to abstain from meats offered to idols and from blood-meats, and to avoid marriage within forbidden degrees of kindred (Lv 18), all of which practices were especially abhorrent to Jews.

15, 14: *Symeon:* Simon Peter; cf 15, 7.

15 The words of the prophets agree with this, where it says in Scripture, 16 'Hereafter I will return and rebuild the fallen hut of David: from its ruins I will rebuild it and set it up again, 17 so that all the rest of mankind and all the nations that bear my name may seek out the Lord. 18 Thus says the Lord who accomplishes these things known to him from of old.' 19 It is my judgment, therefore, that we ought not to cause God's Gentile converts any difficulties. 20 We should merely write to them to abstain from anything contaminated by idols, from illicit sexual union, from the meat of strangled animals, and from eating blood. 21 After all, for generations now Moses has been proclaimed in every town and has been read aloud in the synagogues on every sabbath."

Letter of the Apostles

22 It was resolved by the apostles and the presbyters, in agreement with the whole Jerusalem church, that representatives be chosen from among their number and sent to Antioch along with Paul and Barnabas. Those chosen were leading men of the community, Judas, known as Barsabbas, and Silas. 23 They were to deliver this letter:

"The apostles and the presbyters, your brothers, send greetings to the brothers of Gentile origin in Antioch, Syria, and Cilicia. 24 We have heard that some of our number without any instructions from us have upset you with their discussions and disturbed your peace of mind. 25 Therefore we have unanimously resolved to choose representatives and send them to you, along with our beloved Barnabas and Paul, 26 who have dedicated themselves to the cause of our Lord Jesus Christ.

27 Those whom we are sending you are Judas and Silas, who will convey this message by word of mouth: 28 'It is the decision of the Holy Spirit, and ours too, not to lay on you any burden beyond that which is strictly necessary, 29 namely, to abstain from meat sacrificed to idols, from blood, from the meat of strangled animals, and from illicit sexual union. You will be well advised to avoid these things. Farewell.'"

Delegates to Antioch

30 Thus were the representatives sent on their way to Antioch; and upon their arrival there they called the assembly together to deliver the letter. 31 When it was read there was great delight at the encouragement it gave. 32 Judas and Silas, who were themselves prophets, strengthened the community and gave them reassurance in a long discourse. 33 After passing some time there, they were sent back with greetings from the brothers to those who had commissioned them. 35 Paul and Barnabas continued in Antioch, along with many others, teaching and preaching the word of the Lord.

PAUL'S MISSION TO THE GENTILES

Paul and Barnabas Separate

36 After a certain time Paul said to Barnabas, "Let us go back now and see how the brothers are getting on in each of the towns where we proclaimed the word of the Lord." 37 Barnabas wanted to take along John, called Mark. 37 But Paul insisted that, as he had deserted them at Pamphylia, refusing to join them on that mission, he was not fit to be taken along now. 39 The disagreement which ensued was so sharp that the two separated. Barnabas took Mark along with him and sailed for Cyprus.

40 Paul, for his part, chose Silas to accompany him on his journey, and in this he was commended by the brothers to the favor of the Lord. 41 He traveled throughout Syria and Cilicia, giving the churches there renewed assurance.

In Lycaonia: Timothy

16 Paul arrived first at Derbe; next he came to Lystra, where there was a disciple named Timothy, whose mother was Jewish and a believer, and whose father was a Greek. 2 Since the brothers in Lystra and Iconium spoke highly of him, 3 Paul was anxious to have him come along on the journey. Paul had him circumcised because of the Jews of that region, for they knew that it was only his father who was Greek. 4 As they made their way from town to town, they transmitted to the people for observance the decisions which the apostles and presbyters had made in Jerusalem.

5 Through all this, the congregations grew stronger in faith and daily increased in numbers.

Through Asia Minor

6 They next traveled through Phrygia and Galatian territory, because they had been prevented by the Holy Spirit from preaching the message in the province of Asia. 7 When they came to Mysia they tried to go on into Bithynia, but again the Spirit of Jesus would not allow them. 8 Crossing through Mysia instead, they came down to Troas. 9 There one night Paul had a vision. A man of Macedonia stood before him and invited him, "Come over to Macedonia and help us." 10 After this vision, we immedi-

---

15, 34: Certain codices add: "But Silas decided to remain there"; however, the verse is omitted in the Greek manuscripts.

15, 36—18, 22: This continuous narrative recounts Paul's second missionary journey. On the internal evidence of the Lucan account it lasted about three years. Paul first visited the communities he had established on his first journey (16, 1–5), then pushed on into Macedonia, where he established communities at Philippi, Thessalonica and Beroea (16, 6—17, 15). To escape the hostility of the Jews of Thessalonica he left for Greece, and while resident in Athens attempted, without success, to establish an effective Christian community there. From Athens he proceeded to Corinth, and after a stay of a year and a half, re-turned to Antioch by way of Ephesus and Jerusalem (17, 16—18, 22). Luke's narrative is colorful and lively. He does not concern himself with the structure or statistics of the communities but aims to show the general progress of the gospel in the Gentile world, as well as its continued failure to take root in the Jewish community.

16, 3: Paul had him circumcised: in order that Timothy might be able to socialize with the Jews and so perform a ministry among them. Paul did not object to the Judaeo-Christians' adherence to the law out of custom, as was the case in Palestine. But he insisted that the law could not be imposed on the Gentiles. Paul himself lived in accordance with the law, or as exempt from the law, according to par-ticular circumstances; cf 1 Cor 9, 19–23.

16, 6: The prohibition may have come through one of Paul's companions endowed with a prophetic charism; cf 11, 27f.

16, 10–17: This is the first of the so-called "we-sections" in Acts, where Luke writes as one of Paul's companions. The other passages are 20, 5–15; 21, 1–18; 27, 1–28, 16. Scholars debate whether Luke may not have used the first person plural simply as a literary device to lend color to the narrative. It is more probable, however, that the "we" includes Luke or another companion of Paul whose data Luke used as a source.

ately made efforts to get across to Macedonia, concluding that God summoned us to proclaim the good news there.

Into Europe

11 We put out to sea from Troas and set a course straight for Samothrace, and the next day on to Neapolis; 12 from there we went to Philippi, a leading city in the district of Macedonia and a Roman colony. 13 We spent some time in that city. Once, on the sabbath, we went outside the city gate to the bank of the river, where we thought there would be a place of prayer. We sat down and spoke to the women who were gathered there. 14 One who listened was a woman named Lydia, a dealer in purple goods from the town of Thyatira. She already reverenced God, and the Lord opened her heart to accept what Paul was saying. 15 After she and her household had been baptized, she extended us an invitation: "If you are convinced that I believe in the Lord, come and stay at my house." She managed to prevail on us.

Philippi: Imprisonment

16 It was while we were on our way out of the place of prayer that we met a slave girl who had a clairvoyant spirit. She used to bring substantial profit to her masters by fortune-telling. 17 The girl began to follow Paul and the rest of us shouting, "These men are servants of the Most High God; they will make known to you a way of salvation." 18 She did this for several days until finally Paul became annoyed, turned around, and said to the spirit, "In the name of Jesus Christ I command you, come out of her!" Then and there the spirit left her.

19 When her masters saw that their source of profit was gone, they seized Paul and Silas and dragged them into the main square before the local authorities. 20 They turned them over to the magistrates

with this complaint: "These men are agitators disturbing the peace of our city! Furthermore, they are Jews, 21 which means they advocate customs which are not lawful for us Romans to adopt or practice." 22 The crowd joined in the attack on them, and the magistrates stripped them and ordered them to be flogged. 23 After receiving many lashes they were thrown into prison, and the jailer was given instructions to guard them well. 24 Upon receipt of these instructions he put them in maximum security, going so far as to chain their feet to a stake.

The Earthquake

25 About midnight, while Paul and Silas were praying and singing hymns to God as their fellow prisoners listened, 26 a severe earthquake suddenly shook the place, rocking the prison to its foundations. Immediately all the doors flew open and everyone's chains were pulled loose. 27 The jailer woke up to see the prison gates wide open. Thinking that the prisoners had escaped, he drew his sword to kill himself; 28 but Paul shouted to him: "Do not harm yourself! We are all still here." 29 The jailer called for a light, then rushed in and fell trembling at the feet of Paul and Silas. 30 After a brief interval he led them out and said, "Men, what must I do to be saved?" 31 Their answer was, "Believe in the Lord Jesus and you will be saved, and all your household." 32 They proceeded to announce the word of God to him and to everyone in his house. 33 At that late hour of the night he took them in and bathed their wounds; then he and his whole household were baptized. 34 He led them up into his house, spread a table before them, and joyfully celebrated with his whole family his newfound faith in God.

Release from Prison

35 When it was day, the magistrates dispatched officers with orders to let these men go. 36 The jailer

conveyed this information to Paul: "The magistrates have sent orders that you are to be released. Get started, now. On your way!" 37 Paul's response to this was, "They flogged us in public without even a trial, then they threw us into jail, although we are Roman citizens! Now they want to smuggle us out in secret. Not a bit of it! Let them come into the prison and escort us out." 38 The officers reported this to the magistrates, who were immediately alarmed at hearing they were Roman citizens. 39 They came along and tried to quiet them; then they escorted them out with the request that they leave the city. 40 Once outside the prison, however, the two first made their way to Lydia's house, where they saw and encouraged the brothers; afterward they departed.

Problems at Thessalonica

17 Paul and Silas took the road through Amphipolis and Apollonia and came to Thessalonica, where there was a Jewish synagogue. 2 Following his usual custom, Paul joined the people there and conducted discussions with them about the Scriptures for three sabbaths. 3 He explained many things, showing that the Messiah had to suffer and rise from the dead: "This Jesus I am telling you about is the Messiah!" 4 Some of the Jews were convinced and threw in their lot with Paul and Silas. So, too, did a great number of Greeks sympathetic to Judaism, and numerous prominent women.

5 This only aroused the resentment of the Jews, however, who engaged loafers from the public square to form a mob and start a riot in the town. They marched on the house of Jason in an attempt to bring Paul and Silas before the people's assembly. 6 When they could not find them there, they dragged Jason himself and some of the brothers to the town magistrates, shouting: "These men have been creating a

---

16, 11–40: The church at Philippi became a sufficiently flourishing community for Paul to honor it with one of his letters. Judging, however, from Luke's account of Paul's vicissitudes in the city, his personal success was minimal. Evidently the community grew considerably after his departure and,

as is clear from Paul's letter to them, he reserved his greatest affection for the Christians of Philippi.
16, 22: Apparently the attack on Paul and Silas was so violent that they were unable to invoke their Roman citizenship to avoid the scourging; cf 16, 37f.
16, 25f: The earthquake seems to have been a

visionary experience that accompanied the opening of the doors and the unfastening of the chains. It is otherwise difficult to see why the jailer was so impressed; cf 16, 27–34.

disturbance all over the place. 7 Now they come here and Jason has taken them in. To a man, they disregard the Emperor's decrees and claim instead that a certain Jesus is king." 8 In this way they stirred up the crowd. When the town's magistrates heard the whole story 9 they released Jason and the others on bail.

Paul in Beroea

10 As soon as it was night, the brothers sent Paul and Silas off to Beroea. On their arrival, they went to the Jewish synagogue. 11 Its members were better disposed than those in Thessalonica, and welcomed the message with great enthusiasm. Each day they studied the Scriptures to see whether these things were so. 12 Many of them came to believe, as did numerous influential Greek women and men. 13 But when the Jews of Thessalonica learned that the word of God had been proclaimed by Paul in Beroea also, they hurried there to cause a commotion and stir up the crowds. 14 The brothers sent Paul off directly on his way to the sea, while Silas and Timothy stayed behind. 15 Paul was taken as far as Athens by his escort, who then returned with instructions for Silas and Timothy to join him as soon as possible.

Paul at Athens

16 While Paul was waiting for them in Athens, he grew exasperated at the sight of idols everywhere in the city. 17 In the synagogue he used to hold discussions with the Jews and those sympathetic to Judaism, as well as daily debates in the public square with ordinary passers-by. 18 Epicurean and Stoic philosophers disputed with him, some of them asking, "What is this magpie trying to say to us?" Others commented, "He sounds like a promoter of foreign gods," because he was heard

to speak of "Jesus" and "the resurrection." 19 They then led him off the Areopagus, saying, "We are curious to know what this new teaching is that you propose. 20 You are introducing subjects unfamiliar to us and we should like to know what it is all about." 21 (Indeed, all Athenian citizens, as well as the foreigners who live there, love nothing more than to tell about or listen to something new.)

Paul's Discourse

22 Then Paul stood up in the Areopagus and delivered this address: "Men of Athens, I note that in every respect you are scrupulously religious. 23 As I walked around looking at your shrines, I even discovered an altar inscribed, 'To a God Unknown.' Now, what you are thus worshiping in ignorance I intend to make known to you. 24 For the God who made the world and all that is in it, the Lord of heaven and earth, does not dwell in sanctuaries made by human hands; 25 nor does he receive man's service as if he were in need of it. Rather, it is he who gives to all life and breath and everything else. 26 From one stock he made every nation of mankind to dwell on the face of the earth. It is he who set limits to their epochs and fixed the boundaries of their regions. 27 They were to seek God, yes to grope for him and perhaps eventually to find him—though he is not really far from any one of us. 28 'In him we live and move and have our being,' as some of your own poets have put it, 'for we too are his offspring.' 29 If we are in fact God's offspring, we ought not to think of divinity as something like a statue of gold or silver or stone, a product of man's genius and his art. 30 God may well have overlooked bygone periods when men did not know him; but now he calls on all men everywhere to reform their lives.

31 He has set the day on which he is going to 'judge the world with justice' through a man he has appointed—one whom he has endorsed in the sight of all by raising him from the dead."

32 When they heard about the raising of the dead, some sneered, while others said, "We must hear you on the topic some other time." 33 At that point, Paul left them. 34 A few did join him, however, to become believers. Among these were Dionysius, a member of the court of the Areopagus, a woman named Damaris, and a few others.

Paul Founds the Church in Corinth

18 After that, Paul left Athens and went to Corinth. 2 There he found a Jew named Aquila, a native of Pontus recently arrived from Italy with his wife Priscilla. An edict of Claudius had ordered all Jews to leave Rome. 3 Paul went to visit the pair, whose trade he had in common with them. He took up lodgings with them and they worked together as tentmakers. 4 Every sabbath, in the synagogue, Paul led discussions in which he persuaded certain Jews and Greeks.

5 When Silas and Timothy came down from Macedonia, Paul was absorbed in preaching and giving evidence to the Jews that Jesus was the Messiah. 6 When they opposed him and insulted him, he would shake out his garments in protest and say to them: "Your blood be on your own heads. I am not to blame! From now on, I will turn to the Gentiles."

7 Later, Paul withdrew and went to the house of a Gentile named Titus Justus, who reverenced God; his house was next door to the synagogue. 8 A leading man of the synagogue, Crispus, along with his whole household, put his faith in the Lord. Many of the Corinthians, too,

---

17, 7: *A certain Jesus is king:* a distortion into a political sense of the apostolic proclamation of Jesus' religious kingship.

17, 20f: According to ancient writers the Athenians' interest in novel ideas was proverbial.

17, 22-31: Paul's discourse appeals to the Greek world's belief in divinity as responsible for the origin and existence of the universe. It contests the common belief in a multiplicity of gods supposedly exerting their powers through their images (idol-worship).

It acknowledges (17, 27) that mankind's attempt to understand God is one of the most anxious of all its endeavors. It declares, further, that the divine being is the judge of mankind, and concludes by hinting that the apostle has information on the latter subject concerning a man who God raised from the dead and who is to be the judge of all men. The speech reflects sympathy with pagan religiosity, handles the subject of idol-worship gently, and appeals for a new examination of divinity, not from the standpoint of

creation but from the standpoint of judgment. It is possible that Luke intends to show in the whole incident the difficulties of the learned men of the time in accepting the Christian message; cf 17, 32ff; 1 Cor 1, 26f.

18, 2: *Aquila . . . with his wife Priscilla:* if this couple were not already Christians they soon became such; cf 18, 26. According to 1 Cor 16, 19 their home became a Christian meeting place.

who heard Paul believed and were baptized. 9 One night in a vision the Lord said to Paul: "Do not be afraid. Go on speaking and do not be silenced, 10 for I am with you. No one will attack you or harm you. There are many of my people in this city." 11 Paul ended by settling there for a year and a half, teaching them the word of God.

Paul Accused before Gallio

12 During Gallio's proconsulship in Achaia, the Jews rose in a body against Paul and brought him before the bench. 13 "This fellow," they charged, "is influencing people to worship God in ways that are against the law." 14 Paul was about to speak in self-defense when Gallio said to the Jews: "If it were a crime or a serious fraud, I would give you Jews a patient and reasonable hearing. 15 But since this is a dispute about terminology and titles and your own law, you must see to it yourselves. I refuse to judge such matters." 16 With that, he dismissed them from the court. 17 Then they all pounced on Sosthenes, a leading man of the synagogue, and beat him in full view of the bench; but Gallio paid no attention to it.

Return to Antioch

18 Paul stayed on in Corinth for quite a while; but eventually he took leave of the brothers and sailed for Syria, in the company of Priscilla and Aquila. At the port of Cenchreae he shaved his head because of a vow he had taken. 19 When they landed at Ephesus, he left Priscilla and Aquila behind and entered the synagogue to hold discussions with the Jews. 20 They asked him to stay on longer but he declined. 21 As he said goodbye he gave them his promise, "God willing, I will come back to you again." Then he set sail from Ephesus. 22 On landing at Caesarea, he went up and paid his

respects to the congregation, and then went down to Antioch.

23 After spending some time there he set out again, traveling systematically through the Galatian country and Phrygia to reassure all his disciples.

The Orator Apollos

24 A Jew named Apollos, a native of Alexandria and a man of eloquence, arrived by ship at Ephesus. He was both an authority on Scripture 25 and instructed in the new way of the Lord. Apollos was a man full of spiritual fervor. He spoke and taught accurately about Jesus, although he knew only of John's baptism. 26 He too began to express himself fearlessly in the synagogue. When Priscilla and Aquila heard him, they took him home and explained to him God's new way in greater detail. 27 He wanted to go on to Achaia, and so the brothers encouraged him by writing the disciples there to welcome him. When he arrived, he greatly strengthened those who, through God's favor, had become believers. 28 He was vigorous in his public refutation of the Jewish party as he went about establishing from the Scriptures that Jesus is the Messiah.

Paul in Ephesus

19 While Apollos was in Corinth, Paul passed through the interior of the country and came to Ephesus. There he found some disciples 2 to whom he put the question, "Did you receive the Holy Spirit when you became believers?" They answered, "We have not so much as heard that there is a Holy Spirit." 3 "Well, how were you baptized?" he persisted. They replied, "With the baptism of John." 4 Paul then explained, "John's baptism was a baptism of repentance. He used to tell the people about the one who would come after him in

whom they were to believe—that is Jesus." 5 When they heard this, they were baptized in the name of the Lord Jesus. 6 As Paul laid his hands on them, the Holy Spirit came down on them and they began to speak in tongues and to utter prophecies. 7 There were in the company about twelve men in all.

8 Paul entered the synagogue, and over a period of three months debated fearlessly, with persuasive arguments, about the kingdom of God. 9 When some in their obstinacy would not believe, but chose to speak ill of the new way in the presence of the assembly, Paul simply left them. He took his disciples with him, and after that held his discussions from day to day in the lecture hall of Tyrannus. 10 This continued for two years, with the result that all the inhabitants of the province of Asia, Jews and Greeks alike, heard the word of the Lord. 11 Meanwhile, God worked extraordinary miracles at the hands of Paul. 12 When handkerchiefs or cloths which had touched his skin were applied to the sick, their diseases were cured and evil spirits departed from them.

The Jewish Exorcists

13 Some itinerant Jewish exorcists once tried to invoke the name of the Lord Jesus over those who were possessed by evil spirits, saying, "I adjure you by the Jesus whom Paul preaches." 14 Another time, when the seven sons of Sceva, a Jewish high priest, were doing this, 15 the evil spirit answered, "Jesus I recognize, Paul I know; but who are you?" 16 Then the man with the evil spirit sprang at them and overpowered them all. He dealt with them so violently that they fled from his house naked and bruised. 17 When this became known to the Jews and Greeks living in Ephesus, fear fell upon all, and the name of the Lord

---

18, 23—21, 16: Luke's account of Paul's third missionary journey devotes itself mainly to his work at Ephesus (19, 1—20, 1) and to his farewell address to the elders of this community (20, 17—35). Throughout the narrative runs a theme reflecting a certain restlessness and uneasiness on Paul's part. He has a growing conviction that the Spirit bids him return to Jerusalem and prepare to go to Rome (19, 21). He senses that imprisonment and suffering will be his lot in Jerusalem (20, 22f) and that he has paid his

last visit to the Ephesian community (20, 25). Arriving at Tyre, on the Phoenician coast, he is warned by Christian prophets not to proceed to Jerusalem (21, 4). When he reaches Caesarea on the way to Jerusalem, another Christian prophet utters the same warning (21, 10f).

18, 24f: Apollos became a celebrated Christian preacher in the Corinthian community; 1 Cor 1, 12; 3, 5. He made use of the teaching of Jesus but placed it in the context of John's baptism of repentance.

Since the teaching of Jesus was already known in an oral form to Apollos, it seems evident that the Christian communities likewise possessed this teaching.

19, 1–4: Upon his arrival in Ephesus Paul discovers other men at the same religious stage as Apollos, though they seem to have considered themselves followers of Christ, not of the Baptizer.

19, 6: A pentecostal experience at Ephesus.

Jesus came to be held in great reverence. 18 Many who had become believers came forward and openly confessed their former practices. 19 A number who had been dealing in magic even collected their books and burned them in public. When the value of these was assessed, it came to fifty thousand silver pieces.

20 Thus did the word of the Lord continue to spread with influence and power.

Future Plans

21 When all this was concluded, Paul made up his mind to travel through Macedonia and Achaia again, and then go on to Jerusalem. "Once I have been there," he said, "I must visit Rome too." 22 So he sent two of his assistants, Timothy and Erastus, into Macedonia ahead of him, while he himself stayed on for a time in Asia.

Riot of the Silversmiths

23 At about that time a serious disturbance broke out concerning the new way. 24 There was a silversmith named Demetrius who made miniature shrines of Artemis and brought in no little work for his craftsmen. 25 He called a meeting of these men and other workers in the same craft. "Men," he said, "you know that our prosperity depends on this work. 26 But as you can see and hear for yourselves, not only at Ephesus but throughout most of the province of Asia, this Paul has persuaded great numbers of people to change their religion. He tells them that man-made gods are no gods at all. 27 The danger grows, not only that our trade will be discredited, but even that the temple of the great goddess Artemis will count for nothing. In fact, she whom Asia and all the world revere may soon be stripped of her magnificence."

28 When they heard this speech, they were overcome with fury and began to shout, "Long live Artemis of Ephesus!" 29 Before long, confusion spread throughout the city. People rushed together to the theater and dragged in Gaius and Arist-

archus, Paul's traveling companions from Macedonia. 30 Paul wanted to go before this gathering but his disciples would not let him. 31 Even some of the Asiarchs who were friends of Paul sent word to him advising him not to venture into the theater. 32 Meanwhile, various people were shouting all sorts of things, with the whole assembly in chaos and the majority not even knowing why they had come together. 33 Some brought out of the crowd Alexander, as the Jews pushed him forward. He motioned for silence, indicating that he wanted to explain something to the gathering. 34 But when they recognized that he was a Jew, they started to chant in unison, "Long live Artemis of Ephesus!" and kept shouting for about two hours.

35 Finally the town clerk quieted the mob. "Citizens of Ephesus," he said, "what man is there who does not know that Ephesus is the custodian of the temple of the great Artemis, and of her image which fell from the sky? 36 Since this is beyond question, you must calm yourselves and not do anything rash. 37 These men whom you have brought here are not temple-robbers. They have not insulted our goddess. 38 If Demetrius and his fellow craftsmen want to bring charges against anyone, there are courts in session for that. There are proconsuls. Let the parties argue their case. 39 If there is any further matter you want to investigate, it ought to be settled in the lawful assembly. 40 As it is, we run the risk of being accused of rioting because of today's conduct. We have no valid excuse for this wild demonstration." These words of his broke up the meeting.

Paul Departs for Greece

20 When the disturbance was over, Paul brought his disciples together to encourage them. Then he said goodbye and set out on his journey to Macedonia. 2 He traveled throughout its regions, providing as he went many words of

encouragement for the Christians there. Finally he arrived in Greece, 3 where he stayed for three months. As he was on the point of embarking for Syria, a plot was hatched against him by certain Jews; so he decided to return by way of Macedonia.

Return to Troas

4 Accompanying him were Sopater, son of Pyrrhus, from Beroea; Aristarchus and Secundus from Thessalonica; Gaius from Derbe; Timothy; Tychicus and Trophimus from Asia. 5 These companions went on ahead and waited for us in Troas. 6 We ourselves set sail from Philippi as soon as the festival of Unleavened Bread was over. Five days later we joined them in Troas, where we spent a week.

Eutychus Restored to Life

7 On the first day of the week, when we gathered for the breaking of bread, Paul preached to them. Because he intended to leave the next day, he kept on speaking until midnight. 8 As it happened, there were many lamps in the upstairs room where we were assembled. Paul talked on and on, and 9 a certain young lad named Eutychus who was sitting on the window-sill became drowsier and drowsier. He finally went sound asleep, and fell from the third story to the ground. When they picked him up he was dead. 10 Paul hurried down immediately and threw himself on him, clutching the boy to himself. "Don't be alarmed!" he said to them. "There is life in him." 11 Afterward, Paul went upstairs again, broke bread, and ate. Then he talked for a long while—until his departure at dawn. 12 To the great comfort of the people, they were able to take the boy away alive.

Journey to Miletus

13 We ourselves went on ahead to the ship and set sail for Assos, where we were to pick Paul up. This was the arrangement he had made, since his plan was to travel overland. 14 When he met us at Assos we took him aboard and sailed to Mitylene.

20, 7: *The first day of the week:* the day after the sabbath, apparently chosen originally by the Jerusalem community for the celebration of the liturgy of the

Eucharist in order to relate it to the resurrection of Christ. Thus, in view of the sacramental presence of

Christ in the Eucharist, the liturgy of the Eucharist was an anticipated parousia; cf 1 Cor 10, 16.

15 From there we took off the next day, and reached a point opposite Chios; on the second day we crossed to Samos, and on the day after that we put in at Miletus. 16 Paul had decided to sail past Ephesus so as not to lose time in Asia, for he was eager to get to Jerusalem by the feast of Pentecost if at all possible.

Address to the Miletus Presbyters

17 Paul sent word from Miletus to Ephesus, summoning the presbyters of that church. 18 When they came to him he delivered this address: "You know how I lived among you from the first day I set foot in the province of Asia— 19 how I served the Lord in humility through the sorrows and trials that came my way from the plottings of certain Jews. 20 Never did I shrink from telling you what was for your own good, or from teaching you in public or in private. 21 With Jews and Greeks alike I insisted solemnly on repentance before God and on faith in our Lord Jesus. 22 But now, as you see, I am on my way to Jerusalem compelled by the Spirit and not knowing what will happen to me there— 23 except that the Holy Spirit has been warning me from city to city that chains and hardships await me. 24 I put no value on my life if only I can finish my race and complete the service to which I have been assigned by the Lord Jesus, bearing witness to the gospel of God's grace. 25 I know as I speak these words that none of you among whom I went about preaching the kingdom will ever see my face again. 26 Therefore I solemnly declare this day that I take the blame for no man's conscience, 27 for I have never shrunk from announcing to you God's design in its entirety. 28 "Keep watch over yourselves, and over the whole flock the Holy Spirit has given you to guard. Shepherd the church of God, which he has acquired at the price of his

own blood. 29 I know that when I am gone, savage wolves will come among you who will not spare the flock. 30 From your own number, men will present themselves distorting the truth and leading astray any who follow them. 31 Be on guard, therefore. Do not forget that for three years, night and day, I never ceased warning you individually even to the point of tears. 32 I commend you now to the Lord, and to that gracious word of his which can enlarge you, and give you a share among all who are consecrated to him. 33 Never did I set my heart on anyone's silver or gold or envy the way he dressed. 34 You yourselves know that these hands of mine have served both my needs and those of my companions. 35 I have always pointed out to you that it is by such hard work that you must help the weak. You need to recall the words of the Lord Jesus himself, who said, 'There is more happiness in giving than receiving.'"

36 After this discourse, Paul knelt down with them all and prayed. 37 They began to weep without restraint, throwing their arms around him and kissing him, 38 for they were deeply distressed to hear that they would never see his face again. Then they escorted him to the ship.

Arrival in Tyre

21 When we had finally taken leave of them, we put out to sea and sailed straight to Cos. On the following day we came to Rhodes and went on from there to Patara. 2 When we found a ship bound for Phoenicia, we boarded it and sailed off. 3 We caught sight of Cyprus but passed it by on our left as we continued on toward Syria. Finally we put in at Tyre, where the ship had to unload cargo.

4 We looked for the disciples there and stayed with them for a week. Under the Spirit's prompting, they tried to tell Paul that he should not go up to Jerusalem; 5 but to no

purpose. Then, when our time was up, we continued our journey. All of them—wives and children included—came out of the city to see us off, and we knelt down on the beach and prayed. After we had said goodbye to one another, 6 we boarded the ship and they returned home.

At Ptolemais and Caesarea

7 Continuing our voyage from Tyre, we put in at Ptolemais, where we greeted the brothers and spent the day with them. 8 The next day we pushed on and came to Caesarea. There we entered the home of Philip the evangelist, one of the Seven, with whom we stayed. 9 This man had four unmarried daughters gifted with prophecy. 10 During our few days' stay, a prophet named Agabus arrived from Judea. 11 He came up to us, and taking Paul's belt, tied his hands and feet with it. Then he said, "Thus says the Holy Spirit: 'This is how the Jews in Jerusalem will bind the owner of this belt and hand him over to the Gentiles.'" 12 Upon hearing this, both we ourselves and the people of Caesarea urged Paul not to proceed to Jerusalem. 13 He answered with a question: "Why are you crying and breaking my heart in this way? For the name of the Lord Jesus I am prepared, not only for imprisonment, but for death, in Jerusalem." 14 Since he would not be dissuaded, we said nothing further except, "The Lord's will be done."

PAUL THE PRISONER BEARS WITNESS TO THE RESURRECTION

Paul and James in Jerusalem

15 At the conclusion of our stay, we got ready and started up toward Jerusalem. 16 Some of the disciples from Caesarea came along to escort us to the house of Mnason, a Cypriot and an early disciple, with

---

20, 16–35: Apparently Paul was aware of difficulties in the Christian communities at Ephesus and neighboring areas, and felt that he would be long detained if he undertook to deal with them himself. He determined to remind the presbyters of the communities of their responsibility, calling them together for this purpose at Miletus, about thirty miles from

Ephesus. Paul's moving discourse reminds them of his apostolic activity in their area and stresses his total dedication to the gospel (18–21); it describes his reaction to his presentiment that he is about to suffer for the gospel (22–27), and admonishes them to guard their communities against the teaching of false prophets, who he feels sure will arise upon his

departure (20ff). He concludes by citing a saying of Jesus (35) not recorded in the gospel tradition but known to them. To the extent that Luke may be responsible for the discourse in this form, he portrays Paul as the model leader of the Christian community.

21, 8: One of the Seven: see note on 6, 1–11.

whom we were to stay. 17 On our arrival in Jerusalem, the brothers there gave us a warm welcome. 18 The next day, Paul and the rest of us paid a visit to James in the presence of all the presbyters. 19 Paul first greeted them, and then described in detail all that God had accomplished among the Gentiles through his ministry. 20 When they heard it they praised God, and said to Paul:

"You see brother, how many thousands of Jews have come to believe, all of them staunch defenders of the law. 21 Yet they have been informed that you teach the Jews who live among the Gentiles to abandon Moses, to give up the circumcision of their children, and to renounce their customs. 22 What are we to do about your coming, of which they are sure to hear? 23 Please do as we tell you. There are four men among us who have made a vow. 24 Take them along with you and join with them in their rite of purification; pay the fee for the shaving of their heads. In that way, everyone will know that there is nothing in what they have been told about you, but that you follow the law yourself with due observance. 25 As for the Gentile converts, we sent them a letter with our decision that they were merely to avoid meat sacrificed to idols, blood, the flesh of strangled animals, and illicit sexual union."

26 Accordingly, Paul gathered the men together and went through the rite of purification with them the next day. Then he entered the temple precincts to give notice of the day when the period of purification would be over, at which time the offering was to be made for each of them.

Riot in the Temple

27 The seven-day period was nearing completion when some Jews from the province of Asia recognized Paul in the temple precincts and began to stir up the whole crowd there. They seized him, 28 shouting: "Fellow Israelites, help us! This is the man who is spreading his teaching everywhere against our people, our law, and this sanctuary. He has even brought Greeks into the temple area and thus profaned this sacred place." 29 They had seen Trophimus, an Ephesian, with him in the city earlier, so they now assumed that Paul had brought him into the temple.

30 Before long the whole city was in turmoil. People came running from all sides. They seized Paul, dragged him outside the temple, and immediately closed its gates. 31 Attempts were being made on his life when a report reached the commander of the cohort that all Jerusalem was rioting. 32 Immediately the commander took his soldiers and centurions and charged down on the rioters. As soon as the crowd caught sight of him and the soldiers, they stopped assaulting Paul. 33 Then, when the commander arrived on the scene, he arrested Paul and had him bound with double irons. He tried to find out who he was and what he had been doing, 34 but different people in the crowd shouted out different answers.

The commander could not get at the truth because of the uproar, so he ordered Paul to be led away to headquarters. 35 When Paul reached the steps, he actually had to be carried up by the soldiers because of the violence of the mob. 36 A crowd of people was following along shouting, "Kill him! Kill him!" 37 Just as Paul was about to be led into the headquarters, he said to the commander, "May I say something to you?" "So you know Greek!" the commander exclaimed. 38 "Aren't you that Egyptian who caused the riot some time ago and led a band of four thousand cutthroats out into the desert?" 39 Paul replied, "I am a Jew, a citizen of Tarsus in Cilicia—no mean city; I beg you, let me address these people." 40 With his permission Paul then stood on the steps and motioned the people to silence. A great hush fell on them as he began to speak to them in Hebrew.

Discourse to the Crowd

22 "My brothers and fathers, listen to what I have to say to you in my defense." 2 When they heard him addressing them in Hebrew, they grew quieter still. He went on: 3 "I am a Jew, born in Tarsus in Cilicia, but I was brought up in this city. Here I sat at the feet of Gamaliel and was educated strictly in the law of our fathers. I was a staunch defender of God, just as all of you are today. 4 Furthermore I persecuted this new way to the point of death. I arrested and imprisoned both men and women.

5 "On this point the high priest and the whole council of elders can bear me witness, for it was from them that I received letters to our brother Jews in Damascus. I set out with the intention of bringing the prisoners I would arrest back to Jerusalem for punishment. 6 As I was traveling along, approaching Damascus around noon, a great light from the sky suddenly flashed all about me. 7 I fell to the ground and heard a voice say to me, 'Saul, Saul, why do you persecute me?' 8 I answered, 'Who are you, sir?' He said to me, 'I am Jesus the Nazorean whom you are persecuting.' 9 My companions saw the light but did not hear the voice speaking to me. 10 'What is it I must do, sir?' I asked, and the Lord replied, 'Get up and go into Damascus. There you will be told about everything you are destined to

21, 17–26: The leaders of the Judaeo-Christians of Jerusalem inform Paul that the Jews there believe he has encouraged the Jews of the diaspora to abandon the Mosaic law. In reality, Paul had no objection to the retention of the law, according to custom, by the Judaeo-Christians of Jerusalem, and left the Jews of the diaspora who accepted Christian messianism free to follow the same practice. Perhaps this misunderstanding of Paul's position was supported by the fact that some Judaeo-Christians of the diaspora had abandoned the law.

21, 23f: The leaders of the community suggest that Paul, on behalf of four members of the Jerusalem community, make the customary payment for the sacrifices offered at the termination of the nazirite vow; cf Nm 6, 1–21. Since Paul himself had once made this vow (18, 18), his respect for the law would be on public record.
21, 25: The allusion to the apostolic decree (15, 13–29) was probably introduced here by Luke to remind his readers that the Gentile Christians themselves were asked to respect certain Jewish practices deriving

from the law. Paul was not being asked to violate his conscience.
21, 40: In Hebrew: more precisely, "Aramaic," which at this time was the Semitic tongue in common use. This indicates that Paul's audience was principally composed of native-born Palestinian Jews.
22, 6–16: See note on 9, 1–19.

do.' 11 But since I could not see because of the brilliance of the light, I had to be taken by the hand and led into Damascus by my companions.

12 "A certain Ananias, a devout observer of the law and well spoken of by all the Jews who lived there, 13 came and stood by me. 'Saul, my brother,' he said, 'recover your sight.' In that instant I regained my sight and looked at him. 14 The next thing he said was, 'The God of our fathers long ago designated you to know his will, to look upon the Just One, and to hear the sound of his voice; 15 before all men you are to be his witness to what you have seen and heard. 16 Why delay, then? Be baptized at once and wash away your sins as you call upon his name.'

17 "Upon my return to Jerusalem I was praying in the court of the temple, where I fell into a trance 18 and saw Jesus speaking to me. 'You must make haste,' he said. 'Leave Jerusalem at once because they will not accept your testimony about me.' 19 I answered: 'Lord, it is because they know that I imprisoned those who believed in you and flogged them in every synagogue. 20 While the blood of your witness Stephen was being shed, I stood by and approved it. I even guarded the cloaks of those who killed him!' 21 With that he said to me: 'Be on your way. I mean to send you far from here, among the Gentiles.'"

Paul Imprisoned

22 Up to this point in his speech the crowd had been listening to Paul, but now they began to shout, "Kill him! Rid the earth of the likes of him! He isn't worthy to live!" 23 They yelled and waved their cloaks and flung dirt through the air. 24 At that display, the commander directed Paul to be brought inside the headquarters. He issued orders that he be examined under the lash to find out why they made such an outcry against him. 25 No sooner

had they bound Paul than he said to the centurion who was standing by, "Is it legal to flog a Roman citizen without a trial?" 26 On hearing this, the centurion ran to the commander and demanded, "Do you realize what you are doing? This man is a Roman citizen!" 27 The commander rushed in and asked Paul, "Is it true? Are you a Roman citizen?" "I am," Paul answered. 28 The commander then observed, "It cost me quite a sum to get my citizenship." "Ah," said Paul, "but I am a citizen by birth!" 29 At these words, those who were about to interrogate him backed away. The commander became alarmed because he realized that in restraining Paul he had restrained a citizen of Rome.

Paul Before the Sanhedrin

30 The next day the commander released Paul from prison, intending to look carefully into the charge which the Jews were bringing against him. He summoned the chief priests and the whole Sanhedrin to a meeting; then he brought Paul down and made him stand before them.

23 Paul gazed intently at the Sanhedrin. Then he said, "Brothers, to this day I have lived my life with a clear conscience before God." 2 At that, the high priest Ananias ordered his attendants to strike Paul on the mouth. 3 Paul said to him in rebuttal: "You are the one God will strike, you whitewashed wall! You sit there judging men according to the law, yet you violate the law yourself by ordering me to be struck!" 4 At this the attendants protested, "How dare you insult God's high priest?" 5 Paul answered: "My brothers, I did not know that he was the high priest. Indeed, Scripture has it, 'You shall not curse a prince of your people!'"

6 Paul, it should be noted, was aware that some of them were Sadducees and some Pharisees. Con-

sequently he spoke out before the Sanhedrin: "Brothers, I am a Pharisee and was born a Pharisee. I find myself on trial now because of my hope in the resurrection of the dead." 7 At these words, a dispute arose between Pharisees and Sadducees which divided the whole assembly. 8 (The Sadducees, of course, maintain that there is no resurrection and that there are neither angels nor spirits, while the Pharisees believe in all these things.) 9 A loud uproar ensued. Finally, some scribes of the Pharisee party arose and declared emphatically: "We do not find this man guilty of any crime. If a spirit or an angel has spoken to him. . . ." 10 At this, the dispute grew worse and the commander feared they would tear Paul to pieces. He therefore ordered his troops to go down and rescue Paul from their midst and take him back to headquarters. 11 That night the Lord appeared at Paul's side and said: "Keep up your courage! Just as you have given testimony to me here in Jerusalem, so must you do in Rome."

Transfer to Caesarea

12 When it was day, certain Jews formed a conspiracy in which they bound themselves by oath not to eat or drink until they had killed Paul. 13 (There were more than forty of them who took the oath together.) 14 They then went to the chief priests and the elders and said: "We have bound ourselves by oath to touch no food until we kill Paul. 15 Now, together with the Sanhedrin you must suggest to the commander that he have Paul brought down to you on the pretext that you would like to examine his case more carefully. We are prepared to kill him before he gets there." 16 The son of Paul's sister heard about the plot, and when he did so he came to headquarters. They allowed him to enter, and he told Paul about it. 17 Paul then called for one of the centurions, to whom he said, "Take

---

22, 21: Paul endeavors to explain that his position on the law has not been identical with that of his audience because it has been his prophetic mission to preach to the Gentiles, to whom the law was not addressed and who had no faith in it as a way of salvation.

22, 22: Paul's suggestion that his prophetic mission

to the Gentiles did not involve his imposing the law on them provokes the same opposition as occurred in Pisidian Antioch (13, 45f).

22, 25: A Roman citizen could not be punished unless legally condemned. The tribune considers it his duty to be assured that Paul is not a seditionist.

23, 5: This was probably not said in sarcasm. Paul

withdraws the epithet *whitewashed wall* when he is reminded of the rule in Ex 22, 27.

23, 11: The occurrence of the vision of Christ suggests that Paul's experiences may have placed him in a state of depression.

this young man to the commander; he has something to report to him." 18 The centurion took him in charge and led him to the commander, with the explanation, "The prisoner Paul called me and asked me to bring you this boy, who has something to tell you." 19 The commander took him by the hand and drew him aside to ask privately, "What do you have to report?" 20 The boy replied: "The Jews have agreed among themselves to ask you tomorrow to have Paul brought down to the Sanhedrin, on the pretext that they want to question him more carefully. 21 But don't be fooled by them. More than forty of them are lying in wait; they have bound themselves by oath not to eat or drink until they kill him. They are all ready now, waiting only for your consent." 22 The commander sent the boy away with the order, "Don't tell anyone that you gave me this information."

23 Then the commander summoned two of his centurions and said to them, "Get ready to leave for Caesarea by nine o'clock tonight, with two hundred infantrymen, seventy cavalrymen, and two hundred spearmen. 24 Also provide horses for Paul's journey, so that you may give him safe conduct to Felix the governor." 25 He then wrote the governor a letter to this effect:

26 "Claudius Lysias sends greetings to His Excellency Felix, Governor. 27 Here is a man whom the Jews seized and were about to murder. When I learned that he was a Roman citizen, I intervened with my troops and rescued him. I then had him brought before the Sanhedrin, 28 hoping to determine what their charge against him was. 29 I subsequently discovered that he was accused in matters of their own law and was in no way guilty of anything deserving death or imprisonment. 30 When I later came to be informed of a plot against this man's life, I decided at once to send him to you.

I have also instructed his accusers to take the matter up with you."

31 According to their orders, the infantry took Paul and escorted him that night as far as Antipatris. 32 The next day they returned to headquarters, leaving it to the cavalry to go on with him. 33 When the cavalrymen arrived in Caesarea, they delivered the letter to the governor and brought Paul before him. 34 The governor, upon reading the letter, asked Paul what province he came from, only to learn he was from Cilicia. 35 "I shall hear your case," he said, "when your accusers arrive." Then he ordered Paul to be kept under guard in Herod's praetorium.

Trial before Felix

24 Five days later, the high priest Ananias came down to Caesarea with some of the elders and an attorney named Tertullus. They presented their case against Paul to the governor. 2 Following Paul's summons to the bar, Tertullus began his prosecution by addressing Felix: "Your Excellency, through your efforts we enjoy great peace. Many improvements have been made in this nation through your provident care. 3 Therefore we must always and everywhere acknowledge our deep gratitude to you. 4 But now, lest I impose on your time unduly, I beg your indulgence for a brief hearing of our case. 5 We have found that this man is a troublemaker who stirs up sedition among the Jews all over the world. He is a ringleader of the sect of Nazoreans. 6 He even tried to desecrate our temple, but we apprehended him in time. 8 Feel free now to question him about all this and learn for yourself why we are accusing him." 9 The Jews supported this indictment and maintained that these were the facts.

10 The governor then gestured to Paul, who replied as follows: "I know that you have been a judge over this nation for many years. I am

thus encouraged to make my defense before you, 11 since you are in a position to understand. Not more than twelve days have passed since I went to Jerusalem to worship there. 12 Neither in the temple area, nor in the synagogue, nor anywhere else in the city, did my accusers find me debating with anyone or inciting a mob. 13 They cannot substantiate the charges they are making against me. 14 I admit to you that it is according to the new way—which they call a sect—that I worship the God of our fathers. At the same time, I believe all that is written in the law and the prophets, 15 and I have the same hope in God as these men have that there is to be a resurrection of the good and the wicked alike. 16 In this regard I too always strive to keep my conscience clear before God and man.

17 "After several years' absence, I had come to bring alms to my own people and to make my offerings. 18 That is what I was doing when they found me in the temple court completing the rites of purification without any crowd around me or any disturbance. 19 Certain Jews from the province of Asia are the ones who found me. These are the men who should be here before you to make whatever charge they have against me. 20 Let those who are here declare what crime they found me guilty of when I stood before the Sanhedrin, 21 unless it was what I called out as I stood in their presence: 'I am on trial before you today because of the resurrection of the dead.'"

Captivity at Caesarea

22 Felix was rather well informed about the new way, and when he heard these words he adjourned the trial, saying merely, "I will decide the case when Lysias the commander arrives." 23 He gave orders to the centurion that Paul was to be kept in custody but allowed some freedom,

---

23, 26–30: The letter emphasizes the fact that Paul is a Roman citizen and asserts the lack of evidence that he is guilty of a crime against the empire. The tone of the letter implies that the commander became initially involved in Paul's case because of his Roman citizenship, but this is not an exact description of what really happened; cf 21, 31–33; 22, 25ff.

24, 5f: The charges leveled against Paul accurately reflect the portrait formed of him among the Jews.
24, 6b–7: This portion is not found in the best Greek MSS.
24, 11ff: Whereas the lawyer Tertullus referred to Paul's activities on his missionary journeys, the apostle narrowed the charges down to the riot

connected with the incident in the temple; cf 21, 27–30; 24, 17–20.
24, 22: *Rather well informed about the new way:* he probably had learned from talking to Christians that Christianity posed no threat to the empire. He may have kept Paul in custody simply to forestall fresh trouble in Jerusalem.

and that no one was to prevent his friends from seeing to his wants.

24 A few days later Felix came with his Jewish wife Drusilla, and sent for Paul to hear him speak about faith in Christ Jesus. 25 As Paul talked on about uprightness, continence, and the coming judgment, Felix became frightened. Before long he exclaimed: "That's enough for now! You can go. I'll send for you again when I find the time." 26 At the same time, he hoped he would be offered a bribe by Paul, so he used to send for him frequently to converse with him.

27 Two years passed, following which Felix was succeeded by Porcius Festus. The latter wanted to ingratiate himself with the Jews, so he left Paul in prison.

Appeal to the Emperor

25 Three days after Festus had arrived in the province, he went up from Caesarea to Jerusalem. 2 There the Jewish chief priests and the leaders presented him with their case against Paul, 3 requesting that he favor them rather than Paul, and urging Festus to send him to Jerusalem. Their plot was to kill him on the way. 4 But Festus answered that Paul was being kept in custody at Caesarea, and that he himself would be returning there soon. 5 "Your leading men can come down with me," he said, "and if this man is at fault, they can prosecute him there."

6 After spending eight or ten days in Jerusalem, Festus went down to Caesarea. On the following day he took his seat on the bench and ordered Paul to be brought in. 7 When Paul appeared, the Jews who had come down from Jerusalem surrounded him and leveled many serious charges against him, none of which they were able to prove. 8 Paul's defense was, "I have committed no crime either against the law of the Jews or against the temple

or against the emperor." 9 But Festus, wishing to please the Jewish people, asked Paul, "Are you willing to go up to Jerusalem and stand trial before me there on these charges?" 10 Paul answered: "I stand before the imperial bench; that is where I must be tried. I have done the Jews no wrong, as you yourself realize. 11 If I am guilty, if I have committed a crime deserving death, I do not seek to escape that penalty. But if there is nothing to the charges these men bring against me, no one has a right to hand me over to them. I appeal to the emperor!" 12 Thereupon Festus conferred with his council and finally declared: "You have appealed to the emperor. To the emperor you shall go."

Agrippa Invited To Hear Paul

13 A few days later King Agrippa and Bernice arrived in Caesarea and paid Festus a courtesy call. 14 Since they were to spend several days there, Festus referred Paul's case to the king. "There is a prisoner here," he said, "whom Felix left behind in custody. 15 While I was in Jerusalem the chief priests and the elders of the Jews presented their case against this man and demanded his condemnation. 16 I replied that it was not the Roman practice to hand an accused man over before he had been confronted with his accusers and given a chance to defend himself against their charges. 17 When they came here with me, I did not delay the matter. The very next day I took my seat on the bench and ordered the man brought in. 18 His accusers surrounded him but they did not charge him with any of the crimes I expected. 19 Instead they differed with him over issues in their own religion, and about a certain Jesus who had died but who Paul claimed is alive. 20 Not knowing how to decide the case, I asked whether the prisoner was willing to go to Jerusalem and stand trial there on these

charges. 21 Paul appealed to be kept here until there could be an imperial investigation of his case, so I issued orders that he be kept in custody until I could send him to the emperor."

22 Agrippa said to Festus, "I too should like to hear this man." "Tomorrow you shall hear him," replied Festus. 23 So the next day Agrippa and Bernice came with great pomp and entered the audience chamber in the company of military officers and prominent men of the city. At Festus' command Paul was brought in. 24 The governor began to speak: "King Agrippa and all you who are here present with us, look at this man! The whole Jewish community, both here and in Jerusalem, has appealed to me about him, clamoring that he should live no more. 25 But I did not find that he had done anything deserving of death, so when he appealed to His Majesty the Emperor, I determined to send him on. 26 The trouble is, I have nothing definite to write about him to our sovereign. That is why I have brought him before all of you, and in particular before you, King Agrippa, that from this investigation I may have something to set down in his regard. 27 It seems to me a senseless procedure to send on a prisoner without indicating the charges against him."

Agrippa Hears Paul

26 Agrippa now spoke to Paul: "You have permission to state your case." So Paul stretched out his hand and began his defense.

2 "Many charges have been leveled against me by the Jews, King Agrippa. I count myself fortunate to be able to make my defense today in your presence, 3 especially since you are expert in all the various Jewish customs and disputes. I beg you to listen to me patiently.

4 "The way I have lived since my youth, and the life I have led among

---

24, 24f: The way of Christian discipleship greatly disquiets Felix, who has entered into an adulterous marriage with Drusilla, daughter of Herod Agrippa I.

24, 26: As time passed Felix began to hope that Paul would be willing to leave the country under Roman protection, which he would be prepared to arrange in exchange for a bribe.

25, 2: Even after two years the animosity toward Paul in Jerusalem has not subsided; cf 24, 27.

25, 11f: Paul uses his right as a Roman citizen to appeal his case to the jurisdiction of the emperor (Nero, c A.D. 60). This move broke the deadlock between Roman protective custody of Paul and the plan of his enemies to kill him; cf 25, 3.

25, 13: *King Agrippa and Bernice:* brother and sister, children of Herod Agrippa I whose activities against the Jerusalem community are mentioned in 12, 1-19. Agrippa was a petty ruler over small areas

in northern Palestine and some villages in Perea.

25, 27: Festus' difficulty of lacking a charge against Paul from the Roman jurisdiction is not solved by Agrippa; cf 26, 31f. One solution open to the governor would have been a statement similar to Lysias's letter (23, 26-30) with the addition of Paul's appeal to the emperor.

my own people from the beginning and later at Jerusalem, is well known to all Jews. 5 They have been acquainted with me for a long time and can testify, if they wish, to my life lived as a Pharisee, the strictest sect of our religion. 6 But today I stand trial because of my hope in the promise made by God to our fathers. 7 The twelve tribes of our people fervently worship God day and night in the hope that they will see that promise fulfilled. It is because of this hope, Your Majesty, that I stand accused by the Jews. 8 Let me ask why you, above all, who are Jews, should find it hard to believe that God raises dead men to life.

9 "For my part, I once thought it my duty to oppose the name of Jesus the Nazorean in every way possible. 10 That is just what I did in Jerusalem. With the authority I received from the chief priests, I sent many of God's holy people to prison. When they were to be put to death I cast my vote against them. 11 Many a time, in synagogue after synagogue, I compelled them by force to blaspheme. Indeed, so wild was my fury against them that I pursued them even to foreign cities.

12 "On one such occasion I was traveling toward Damascus armed with the authority and commission of the chief priests. 13 On this journey, Your Majesty, I saw a light more brilliant than the sun shining in the sky at midday. It surrounded me and those who were traveling with me. 14 All of us fell to the ground and I heard a voice saying to me in Hebrew, 'Saul, Saul, why do you persecute me? It is hard for you to kick against the goad.' 15 I said, at that, 'Who are you, sir?' and the Lord answered: 'I am that Jesus whom you are persecuting. 16 Get up now and stand on your feet. I have appeared to you to designate you as my servant and as a witness to what you have seen of me and what you will see of me. 17 I have delivered you from this people and from the nations, 18 to open the eyes of those to whom I am sending

you, to turn them from darkness to light and from the dominion of Satan to God; that through their faith in me they may obtain the forgiveness of their sins and a portion among God's people.'

19 "King Agrippa, I could not disobey that heavenly vision. 20 I preached a message of reform and of conversion to God, first to the people of Damascus, then to the people of Jerusalem and all the country of Judea; yes, even to the Gentiles. I urged them to act in conformity with their change of heart. 21 That is why the Jews seized me in the temple court and tried to murder me. 22 But I have had God's help to this very day, and so I stand here to testify to great and small alike. Nothing that I say differs from what the prophets and Moses foretold: 23 namely, that the Messiah must suffer, and that, as the first to rise from the dead, he will proclaim light to our people and to the Gentiles."

Reactions to Paul's Speech

24 As Paul went on defending himself in this way, Festus interrupted with a shout, "Paul, you are mad! And your great learning is driving me mad!" 25 "No, Your Excellency," answered Paul, "I am not mad. The message I proclaim is the sober truth. 26 The king here is well acquainted with these matters. Before him I can speak freely. I am convinced that none of this escapes him—after all, it did not take place in a dark corner! 27 Do you believe the prophets, King Agrippa? I am sure you do." 28 At this, Agrippa said, "A little more, Paul, and you will make a Christian out of me!" 29 Paul replied, "Whether little more or much more, I would to God that not only you but all who listen to me today might become what I am—without these chains!"

30 Then the king rose, and with him the governor and Bernice and the rest of the company. 31 After they had left the chamber, they talked matters over among themselves and admitted, "This man is doing

nothing that deserves death or imprisonment." 32 Agrippa further remarked to Festus, "He could have been set at liberty if he had not appealed to the emperor!"

Departure for Rome

27 When it was decided that we were to sail for Italy, Paul and some other prisoners were handed over to a centurion named Julius from the cohort known as Augusta. 2 We boarded a ship from Adramyttium bound for ports in the province of Asia, and set sail. With us was a Macedonian, Aristarchus of Thessalonica. 3 The following day we put in at Sidon, where Julius kindly allowed Paul to visit some friends who cared for his needs. 4 Then, putting out from Sidon, we sailed around the sheltered side of Cyprus because of strong headwinds. 5 We crossed the open sea off the coast of Cilicia and Pamphylia, and came to Myra in Lycia.

Storm and Shipwreck

6 There the centurion discovered an Alexandrian vessel bound for Italy, and he ordered us aboard. 7 For many days we made little headway, arriving at Cnidus only with difficulty. Since the winds would not permit us to continue our course, we sailed for Salmone and the shelter of Crete. 8 Again with difficulty we moved along the coast to a place called Fair Havens, near the town of Lasea.

9 Much time had now gone by. The autumn fast was over, and with the lateness of the year sailing had become hazardous. It was then that Paul uttered this warning: 10 "Men, I can see that this voyage is bound to meet with disaster and heavy loss, not only to ship and cargo, but to our own lives as well." 11 However, the centurion preferred listening to the pilot and the shipowner to listening to Paul. 12 Since the harbor was not fit to pass the winter in, the majority preferred to put out to sea, in the hope of making Phoenix and spending the

26, 9–18: See note on 9, 1–19.
26, 31: In recording the episode of Paul's appearance before Agrippa, Luke wishes to show that when Paul's case was judged impartially, no grounds for legal action against him were found.

27, 1—28, 15: Here Luke has written a stirring account of adventure on the high seas, incidentally to his main purpose of showing how well Paul got along with his captors and how his prophetic influence ultimately saved the lives of all on board. The

recital also establishes the existence of Christian communities in Puteoli and Rome.

winter there. This was a Cretan port exposed on the southwest and the northwest. 13 When a gentle south wind began to blow, they thought they had what they were looking for, so they weighed anchor and proceeded, hugging the coast of Crete. 14 It was not long before a hurricane struck, the kind called a "northeaster." 15 Since the ship was caught up in it and could not head into the wind, we yielded and ran before it. 16 We passed under the lee of a small island named Cauda and only with difficulty were we able to gain control of the ship's boat. 17 They hoisted it aboard and then made use of cables to brace the ship itself. Because of their fear that they would be driven on the reef of Syrtis, they lowered the small anchor used for moving the ship, and the ship was carried along. 18 We were being pounded by the storm so violently that the next day some of the cargo was thrown over the side. 19 On the third day they deliberately threw even the ship's gear overboard. 20 For many days neither the sun nor the stars were to be seen, so savagely did the storm rage. Toward the end, we abandoned any hope of survival.

21 All hands had gone without food for a long time when Paul stood up among them and said: "Men, you should have taken my advice and not set sail from Crete. Then you would not have incurred this disastrous loss. 22 I urge you now to keep up your courage. None among you will be lost—only the ship. 23 Last night a messenger of the God whose man I am and whom I serve, stood by me. 24 'Do not be afraid, Paul,' he said. 'You are destined to appear before the emperor. Therefore, as a favor to you, God has granted safety to all who are sailing with you.' 25 So keep up your courage, men. I trust in God that it will all work out just as I have been told, 26 though we still have to face shipwreck on some island."

27 It was the fourteenth night of the storm, and we were still being driven across the Ionian Sea, when toward midnight the sailors began to suspect that land was near. 28 They took a sounding and found a depth of twenty fathoms: after sailing on a short distance they again took a sounding and found it to be fifteen. 29 For fear that we should be dashed against some rocky coast, then dropped four anchors from the stern and prayed for daylight. 30 Then the sailors tried to abandon ship. Pretending that they were going to run out anchors from the bow of the ship, they let the ship's boat down into the sea. 31 Paul alerted the centurion and the soldiers to this: "If these men do not stay with the ship, you have no chance to survive." 32 At this, the soldiers cut the ropes and let the boat drift.

33 At dawn Paul urged all on board to take some food: "For fourteen days you have been in constant suspense; you have gone hungry—eaten nothing. 34 Now I urge you to take some food, which will give you strength to survive. Not one of you shall lose a hair of his head." 35 When he had said this he took some bread, gave thanks to God before all of them, broke it, and began to eat. 36 This gave them new courage, and they too had something to eat. 37 (In all, there were two hundred and seventy-six of us on board.) 38 When they had had enough to eat, they lightened the ship further by throwing the wheat overboard.

39 With the coming of daylight, they did not recognize the land they saw. They could make out a bay with a sandy beach, however, so they planned to run the ship aground on it if possible. 40 They cut loose the anchors and abandoned them to the sea. At the same time they untied the guy-ropes of the rudders, hoisted the foresail into the wind, and made for the beach; 41 but the ship hit a sandbar and ran aground. The bow stuck fast and could not be budged, while the stern was shattered by the pounding of the sea. 42 The soldiers thought at first of killing the prisoners so that none might swim away and escape; 43 but because the centurion was anxious to save Paul, he opposed their plan. Instead, he ordered those who could swim to jump overboard first and make for land. 44 The rest were to follow, on planks, or on other debris from the ship. In this way all came safely ashore.

Winter in Malta

28 Once on shore, we learned that the island was called Malta. 2 The natives showed us extraordinary kindness by lighting a fire and gathering us all around it, for it had begun to rain and was growing cold. 3 Paul had just fed the fire with a bundle of brushwood he had collected, when a poisonous snake, escaping from the heat, fastened itself on his hand. 4 At the sight of the snake hanging from his hand, the natives said to one another, "This man must really be a murderer if, after his escape from the sea, Justice will not let him live." 5 But Paul shook the snake off into the fire and suffered no ill effects from the bite. 6 They expected to see him swell up or suddenly fall dead. After waiting for quite some time, however, and seeing nothing unusual happen to him, they changed their minds and began to say that he was a god.

7 In the vicinity of that place was the estate of Publius, the chief figure on the island. He took us in and gave us kind hospitality for three days. 8 It happened that Publius' father was sick in bed, laid up with chronic fever and dysentery. Paul went in to see the man and, praying, laid his hands on him and cured him. 9 After this happened, the rest of the sick on the island began to come to Paul and they too were healed. 10 They paid us much honor, and when we eventually set sail they brought us provisions for our needs.

Arrival at Rome

11 Three months later we set sail in a ship which had passed the winter at the island. It was an Alexandrian vessel with the "Heavenly Twins" as its figurehead. 12 We put in at Syracuse and spent three days there. 13 Then we sailed around the toe and arrived at Rhegium. A day later a south wind began to blow, which enabled us to reach Puteoli in two days. 14 Here we found some of the brothers, who urged us to stay on with them for a week.

This is how we finally came to

Rome. 15 Certain brothers from Rome who heard about us came out as far as the Forum of Appius and the Three Taverns to meet us. When Paul saw them, he thanked God and took fresh courage. 16 Upon our entry into Rome, Paul was allowed to take a lodging of his own, although a soldier was assigned to keep guard over him.

Testimony to Roman Jews

17 Three days later Paul invited the prominent men of the Jewish community to visit him. When they had gathered he said: "My brothers, I have done nothing against our people or our ancestral customs; yet in Jerusalem I was handed over to the Romans as a prisoner. 18 The Romans tried my case and wanted to release me because they found nothing against me deserving of death. 19 When the Jews objected, I was forced to appeal to the emperor, though I had no cause to make accusations against my own people. 20 This is the reason, then, why I have asked to see you and speak with you. I wear these chains solely because I share the hope of Israel."

21 They replied: "We have had no letters from Judea about you, nor have any of the brothers arrived with a report or rumor to your discredit. 22 For our part, we are anxious to hear you present your views. We know very well that this sect is denounced everywhere."

23 With that, they arranged a day with him and came to his lodgings in great numbers. From morning to evening he laid the case before them, bearing witness to the reign of God among men. He sought to convince them about Jesus by appealing to the law of Moses and the prophets. 24 Some, indeed, were convinced by what he said; others would not believe.

25 Without reaching any agreement among themselves, they began to leave. Then Paul added one final word: "The Holy Spirit stated it well when he said to your fathers through the prophet Isaiah:

26　　　'Go to this people and say:
　　You may listen carefully yet
　　　　you will never understand;
　　you may look intently yet
　　　　you will never see.
27　The mind of this people has
　　　　grown sluggish.
　　They have scarcely used their
　　　　ears to listen;
　　　their eyes they have closed,
　　Lest they should see with their
　　　　eyes,
　　　hear with their ears,
　　　understand with their minds,
　　And repent;
　　　and I should have to heal
　　　　them.'

28 Now you must realize that this salvation of God has been transmitted to the Gentiles—who will heed it!"

Summary

30 For two full years Paul stayed on in his rented lodgings, welcoming all who came to him. 31 With full assurance, and without any hindrance whatever, he preached the reign of God and taught about the Lord Jesus Christ.

28, 16: The mild form of custody in which Paul is detained reflects, perhaps, the arrangements made for him by Festus; cf 25, 27.

28, 17–22: Paul's first act in Rome is to learn from the leaders of the Jewish community whether the Jews of Jerusalem plan to pursue their case against him before the Roman jurisdiction. He is informed that no such plan is afoot, but that the Jews of Rome have heard the Christian teaching denounced. Paul's offer to explain it to them is readily accepted.

28, 23–28: Some critics of Acts have expressed doubt that these meetings between Paul and the leading Jews of Rome took place; they incline to the view that Luke here created ideal scenes to show the final separation between Judaism and Christianity. The scenes, however, are historically plausible: Paul would naturally have been concerned that the Christian community of Rome be not embarrassed by charges against it if he were brought to trial; while the Jews of Rome stood to gain from an explanation of the new doctrines by a trained rabbi. The citation from Isaiah is probably introduced by Luke, who uses the unbelief of Israel as typical of the difficulty men meet when confronted with the prophetic word of God.

28, 29: This verse is not found in the Greek manuscripts.

28, 30f: Many attempts have been made to explain what seems to be the abrupt ending of Luke's Acts of the Apostles. The author has Paul still in detention, though he intimates a bright outcome for his case. Perhaps the most satisfactory explanation is that Luke does not regard the subsequent missionary activity of Paul or his martyrdom as necessary for his account of the origin and development of the church.

THE EPISTLE OF PAUL TO THE

Romans

INTRODUCTION

Greetings

GREETINGS from Paul, a servant of Christ Jesus, called to be an apostle and set apart to proclaim the gospel of God 2 which he promised long ago through his prophets, as the holy Scriptures record— 3 the gospel concerning his Son, who was descended from David according to the flesh 4 but was made Son of God in power according to the spirit of holiness, by his resurrection from the dead: Jesus Christ our Lord. 5 Through him we have been favored with apostleship, that we may spread his name and bring to obedient faith all the Gentiles, 6 among whom are you who have been called to belong to Jesus Christ.

7 To all in Rome, beloved of God and called to holiness, grace and peace from God our Father and the Lord Jesus Christ.

Paul and the Romans

8 First of all, I give thanks to my God through Jesus Christ for all of you because your faith is heralded throughout the world. 9 The God I worship in the spirit by preaching the gospel of his Son will bear witness that I constantly mention you in prayer, 10 always pleading that somehow by God's will I may at last find my way clear to visit you. 11 For I long to see you and share with you some spiritual gift to strengthen you— 12 rather, what I wish is that we may be mutually encouraged by our common faith. 13 My brothers, I want you to know that I have often planned to visit you (though up to now I have been kept from it) in order to do some fruitful work among you, as I have among the other Gentiles. 14 I am under obligation to Greeks and non-Greeks, to learned and unintelligent alike. 15 That is why I am eager to preach the gospel to you Romans as well.

God's Power for Salvation

16 I am not ashamed of the gospel. It is the power of God leading everyone who believes in it to salvation, the Jew first, then the Greek. 17 For in the gospel is revealed the justice of God which begins and ends with faith; as Scripture says, "The just man shall live by faith."

1, 1–7: The address follows the epistolary style of Paul's time, naming the sender and the addressees and extending good wishes (1.7). Paul proclaims the Christian faith in the humanity of Jesus (v 3) and in his divine sanctifying power (v 4).

1, 4: *Was made Son of God in power:* other possible translations are "was declared" or "proclaimed the powerful Son of God." *By his resurrection from the dead:* the resurrection made Jesus a "life-giving spirit" (1 Cor 15, 45), able to communicate the Spirit to those who believe in him. This is the power which he now exercises as exalted Son of God.

1, 5: Paul recalls his apostolic office, implying that the Romans know something of his history.

1, 16f: The principal theme of the letter is salvation through faith. *I am not ashamed of the gospel:* a reminder of the criticism which Jews and Gentiles leveled against the doctrine of the crucified Savior; cf 1 Cor 1, 23f. Paul affirms, however, that it is precisely through the crucifixion and resurrection of Jesus that God chose to manifest his saving will and power. The apostle appeals through Jesus and his teaching for a faith to be held by all the world.

1, 17: *In the gospel is revealed the justice of God*

which begins and ends with faith: the gospel is concerned with Jesus, in whom God has made known his saving presence and justice in history. Through Jesus, God offers the gift of faith, which makes his saving action effective in man. It manifests God's supremacy over man and his destiny, and likewise moves man to respond to the divine generosity. Faith makes clear the purpose and meaning of the Old Testament, revealing through the history of Israel the inability of man to effect his salvation in terms of covenant law.

Punishment of Idolatry

18 The wrath of God is being revealed from heaven against the irreligious and perverse spirit of men who, in this perversity of theirs, hinder the truth. 19 In fact, whatever can be known about God is clear to them; he himself made it so. 20 Since the creation of the world, invisible realities, God's eternal power and divinity, have become visible, recognized through the things he has made. Therefore these men are inexcusable. 21 They certainly had knowledge of God, yet they did not glorify him as God or give him thanks; they stultified themselves through speculating to no purpose, and their senseless hearts were darkened. 22 They claimed to be wise, but turned into fools instead; 23 they exchanged the glory of the immortal God for images representing mortal man, birds, beasts, and snakes. 24 In consequence, God delivered them up in their lusts to unclean practices; they engaged in the mutual degradation of their bodies, 25 these men who exchanged the truth of God for a lie and worshiped and served the creature rather than the Creator— blessed be he forever, amen! 26 God therefore delivered them up to disgraceful passions. Their women exchanged natural intercourse for unnatural, 27 and the men gave up natural intercourse with women and burned with lust for one another. Men did shameful things with men, and thus received in their own persons the penalty for their perversity. 28 They did not see fit to acknowledge God, so God delivered them up to their own depraved sense to do what is unseemly. 29 They are filled with every kind of wickedness: maliciousness, greed, ill will, envy, murder, bickering, deceit, craftiness. They are gossips 30 and slanderers, they hate God, are insolent, haughty,

boastful, ingenious in their wrongdoing and rebellious toward their parents. 31 One sees in them men without conscience, without loyalty, without affection, without pity. 32 They know God's just decree that all who do such things deserve death; yet they not only do them but approve them in others.

God's Just Judgment

2 That is why every one of you who judges another is inexcusable. By your judgment you convict yourself, since you do the very same things. 2 "We know that God's judgment on men who do such things is just." 3 Do you suppose, then, that you will escape his judgment, you who condemn these things in others yet do them yourself? 4 Or do you presume on his kindness and forbearance? Do you not know that God's kindness is an invitation to you to repent? 5 In spite of this, your hard and impenitent heart is storing up retribution for that day of wrath when the just judgment of God will be revealed, 6 when he will repay every man for what he has done: 7 eternal life to those who strive for glory, honor, and immortality by patiently doing right; 8 wrath and fury to those who selfishly disobey the truth and obey wickedness. 9 Yes, affliction and anguish will come upon every man who has done evil, the Jew first, then the Greek. 10 But there will be glory, honor, and peace for everyone who has done good, likewise the Jew first, then the Greek. 11 With God there is no favoritism.

Judgment by the Interior Law

12 Sinners who do not have the law will perish without reference to it; sinners bound by the law will be judged in accordance with it. 13 For it is not those who hear the law who are just in the sight of God; it is

those who keep it who will be declared just. 14 When Gentiles who do not have the law keep it as by instinct, these men although without the law serve as a law for themselves. 15 They show that the demands of the law are written in their hearts. Their conscience bears witness together with that law, and their thoughts will accuse or defend them 16 on the day when, in accordance with the gospel I preach, God will pass judgment on the secrets of men through Christ Jesus.

Judgment by the Mosaic Law

17 Let us suppose you bear the name of "Jew" and rely firmly on the law and pride yourself on God. 18 Instructed by the law, you know his will and are able to make sound judgments on disputed points. 19 You feel certain that you can guide the blind and enlighten those in darkness, 20 that you can discipline the foolish and teach the simple, because in the law you have at hand a clear pattern of knowledge and truth. 21 Now then, teacher of others, are you failing to teach yourself? You who preach against stealing, do you steal? 22 You who forbid adultery, do you commit adultery? You who abhor idols, do you rob temples? 23 You who pride yourself on the law, do you dishonor God by breaking the law? 24 As Scripture says, "On your account the name of God is held in contempt among the Gentiles."

25 Circumcision, to be sure, has value if you observe the law, but if you break it you might as well be uncircumcised! 26 Again, if an uncircumcised person keeps the precepts of the law, will he not be considered circumcised? 27 If a man who is uncircumcised keeps the law, he will pass judgment on you who, with your written law and circumcision, break it. 28 Appearance

---

1, 18–32: The conversion of the Gentiles through the gospel preaching constituted the divine indictment against paganism, which error had benighted and moral depravity had corrupted. It was the evil will of the pagan world that provoked the divine anger and abandonment (v 18). Contrary to nature itself which provides evidence of God's existence, power, and divinity through creation (19f), pagan society misread the evidence, fashioned gods of its own that could not exert any moral restraint, and freely indulged its perverse desires through every kind of wickedness (21– 32; cf Wis 13, 1–14, 31).

2, 1—3, 9: The key to this passage is in the final verse: *We have already brought the charge against Jews and Greeks alike that they are under the domination of sin.* This judgment is based on the doctrine of universal salvation through the redemptive death of Christ. The Jew cannot condemn the sins of Gentiles without implicitly condemning himself (2, 1–11). He cannot reasonably demand from them the standard of conduct inculcated in the Old Testament since God did not address its revelation to them. Rather, God gave the Gentile the law of reason and conscience by which he was to be judged (2, 12–16). Not mere pos-

session of the law by Jew or Gentile, but observance of it, is evidence of virtue (2, 17–29). Paul responds to the objection that his teaching on the sinfulness of all humanity detracts from the religious privileges of Israel, by stressing that the Jew always remained the vehicle of God's revelation despite his sins. His privileges depend, not on his own attainments, but on the fidelity of God (3, 1–4).

does not make a Jew. True circumcision is not a sign in the flesh. 29 He is a real Jew who is one inwardly, and true circumcision is of the heart; its source is the spirit, not the letter. Such a one receives his praise, not from men, but from God.

Answers to Objections

3 What is the advantage, then, of being a Jew, and what value is there in circumcision? 2 The answer is, much in every respect. First of all, the Jews were entrusted with the words of God. 3 You may ask, what if some of them have not believed? Will not their unbelief put an end to God's faithfulness? 4 Of course not! God must be proved true even though every man be proved a liar, so that, as Scripture says,

"You shall be vindicated in what you say,
　and win out when you are judged."

5 But if our wrongdoing provides proof of God's justice, what are we to say? "Is not God unjust when he inflicts punishment?" (I speak in a merely human way.) 6 Assuredly not! If that were so, how could God judge the world? 7 Another question: If my falsehood brings to light God's truth and thus promotes his glory, why must I be condemned as a sinner? 8 Or why may we not do evil that good may come of it? This is the very thing that some slanderously accuse us of teaching; but they will get what they deserve.

Universal Bondage of Sin

9 Well, then, do we find ourselves in a position of superiority? Not entirely. We have already brought the charge against Jews and Greeks alike that they are under the domination of sin. 10 It is as Scripture says:

"There is no just man, not even one;

11　there is no one who understands,
　　no one in search of God.
12 All have taken the wrong course,
　　all alike have become worthless;
　　not one of them acts uprightly, no, not one.
13 Their throats are open tombs;
　　they use their tongues to deceive;
　　The venom of asps lies behind their lips.
14　Their mouths are full of curses and bitterness.
15 Swiftly run their feet to shed blood;
16　ruin and misery strew their course.
17 The path of peace is unknown to them;
18　the fear of God is not before their eyes."

19 We know that everything the law says is addressed to those who are under its authority. This means that every mouth is silenced and the whole world stands convicted before God, 20 since no one will be justified in God's sight through observance of the law; the law does nothing but point out what is sinful.

SALVATION THROUGH FAITH IN CHRIST

Justice apart from the Law

21 But now the justice of God has been manifested apart from the law, even though both law and prophets bear witness to it— 22 that justice of God which works through faith in Jesus Christ for all who believe. 23 All men have sinned and are deprived of the glory of God. 24 All men are now undeservedly wrought in Christ Jesus. 25 Through his blood, God made him the means of expiation for all who believe. He did so to manifest his own justice, for the sake of remitting sins committed in the past— 26 to manifest his justice in the present, by

way of forbearance, so that he might be just and might justify those who believe in Jesus.

27 What occasion is there then for boasting? It is ruled out. By what law, the law of works? Not at all! By the law of faith. 28 For we hold that a man is justified by faith apart from observance of the law. 29 Does God belong to the Jews alone? Is he not also the God of the Gentiles? Yes, of the Gentiles too. 30 It is the same God who justifies the circumcised and the uncircumcised on the basis of faith. 31 Are we then abolishing the law by means of faith? Not at all! On the contrary, we are confirming the law.

Abraham Justified by Faith

4 What, then, shall we say of Abraham, our ancestor according to the flesh? 2 Certainly if Abraham was justified by his deeds, he has grounds for boasting, but not in God's view; 3 for what does Scripture say? "Abraham believed God, and it was credited to him as justice." 4 Now, when a man works, his wages are not regarded as a favor but as his due. 5 But when a man does nothing, yet believes in him who justifies the sinful, his faith is credited as justice. 6 Thus David congratulates the man to whom God credits justice without requiring deeds:

7 "Blest are they whose iniquities are forgiven,
　　whose sins are covered over.
8 Blest is the man to whom the Lord imputes no guilt."

9 Does this blessedness apply only to the circumcised, or to the uncircumcised as well? For we say that Abraham's faith was "credited as justice." 10 What were the circumstances in which it was credited? Was it after he was circumcised or before? It was before. 11 In fact, he received the sign of circumcision as a seal attesting to the justice received through faith while he was still uncircumcised. Thus he was to be the

---

3, 21–31: *The justice of God* is his mercy whereby he declares guilty man innocent and makes him so. He does this, not as a result of the law, but *apart from it* (v 21); not because of any merit of man, but through forgiveness of his sins (v 24), in virtue of *the redemption wrought in Christ Jesus* for all who believe (22. 24f). No man can boast of his own holiness, since it is

God's free gift (v 27), both to the Jew who practices circumcision out of faith, and to the Gentile who accepts faith without the Old Testament religious culture symbolized by circumcision (29f).
3, 31: *We are confirming the law:* placing it in its proper perspective. The Old Testament law, unable to effect salvation, was observed out of the motive of

faith. Now, through the revelation of Christ, the importance of faith is manifest.
4, 1–25: This is an expanded treatment of the significance of Abraham's faith, which Paul discusses in Gal 3, 6–18; see notes there.

father of all the uncircumcised who believe, so that for them too faith might be credited as justice, 12 as well as the father of those circumcised, who are not merely so but who follow the path of faith which Abraham walked while still uncircumcised.

Inheritance through Faith

13 Certainly the promise made to Abraham and his descendants that they would inherit the world did not depend on the law; it was made in view of the justice that comes from faith. 14 If only those who observe the law are heirs, then faith becomes an empty word and the promise loses its meaning. 15 Indeed, the law serves only to bring down wrath, for where there is no law there is no transgression. 16 Hence, all depends on faith, everything is grace. Thus the promise holds true for all Abraham's descendants, not only for those who have the law but for all who have his faith. He is father of us all, 17 which is why Scripture says, "I have made you father of many nations." Yes, he is our father in the sight of God in whom he believed, the God who restores the dead to life and calls into being those things which had not been. 18 Hoping against hope, Abraham believed and so became the father of many nations, just as it was once told him, "Numerous as this shall your descendants be." 19 Without growing weak in faith he thought of his own body, which was as good as dead (for he was nearly a hundred years old), and of the dead womb of Sarah. 20 Yet he never questioned or doubted God's promise; rather, he was strengthened in faith and gave glory to God, 21 fully persuaded that God could do whatever he had promised. 22 Thus his faith was credited to him as justice.

23 The words, "It was credited to him," were not written with him alone in view; 24 they were intended for us too. For our faith will be credited to us also if we believe in him who raised Jesus our Lord from the dead, 25 the Jesus who was handed over to death for our sins and raised up for our justification.

Faith, Hope, and Love

5 Now that we have been justified by faith, we are at peace with God through our Lord Jesus Christ. 2 Through him we have gained access by faith to the grace in which we now stand, and we boast of our hope for the glory of God. 3 But not only that—we even boast of our afflictions! We know that affliction makes for endurance, 4 and endurance for tested virtue, and tested virtue for hope. 5 And this hope will not leave us disappointed, because the love of God has been poured out in our hearts through the Holy Spirit who has been given to us. 6 At the appointed time, when we were still powerless, Christ died for us godless men. 7 It is rare that anyone should lay down his life for a just man, though it is barely possible that for a good man someone may have the courage to die. 8 It is precisely in this that God proves his love for us: that while we were still sinners, Christ died for us. 9 Now that we have been justified by his blood, it is all the more certain that we shall be saved by him from God's wrath. 10 For if, when we were God's enemies, we were reconciled to him by the death of his Son, it is all the more certain that we who have been reconciled will be saved by his life. 11 Not only that; we go so far as to make God our boast through our Lord Jesus Christ, through whom we have now received reconciliation.

Mankind's Sin through Adam

12 Therefore, just as through one man sin entered the world and with sin death, death thus coming to all men inasmuch as all sinned— 13 before the law there was sin in the world, even though sin is not imputed when there is no law— 14 I say, from Adam to Moses death reigned, even over those who had not sinned by breaking a precept as did Adam, that type of the man to come.

Grace and Life through Christ

15 But the gift is not like the offense. For if by the offense of the one man all died, much more did the grace of God and the gracious gift of the one man, Jesus Christ, abound for all. 16 The gift is entirely different from the sin committed by the one man. In the first case, sentence followed upon one offense and brought condemnation, but in the second, the gift came after many offenses and brought acquittal. 17 If death began its reign through one man because of his offense, much more shall those who receive the overflowing grace and gift of justice live and reign through the one man, Jesus Christ.

18 To sum up, then: just as a single offense brought condemnation to all men, a single righteous act brought all men acquittal and life. 19 Just as through one man's disobedience all became sinners, so through one man's obedience all shall become just.

Purpose of the Law

20 The law came in order to increase offenses; but despite the increase of sin, grace has far surpassed it, 21 so that, as sin reigned through death, grace may reign by way of justice leading to eternal life, through Jesus Christ our Lord.

JUSTIFICATION AND THE CHRISTIAN LIFE

Death to Sin, Life in God

6 What, then, are we to say? "Let us continue in sin that grace may abound"? 2 Certainly not! How

5, 1–5: A development of the doctrine of justification by faith. It is God who effects man's justification through Christ. This gives the believer a firm confidence in his salvation (5, 1f). The hardships of life should merely teach him patience and strengthen his hope (3f), which will not disappoint him because the Holy Spirit dwells in his heart and infuses into it God's love (v 5).

5, 12–21: Paul reflects on the sin of Adam (Gn 3, 1–13) in the light of the redemptive mystery of Christ. Sin, i.e., man's guilt before God which merited the punishment of death and loss of grace, began with Adam and infected the entire human race (v 12). Through the Old Testament law the sinfulness of mankind, operative from the beginning (v 13), became abundantly manifest (v 20). The judgments in 5, 12ff are based on the mystery of man's redemption through the death of Christ. Paul contrasts the divergent effects of Adam and of Christ on the human race (15–21) to show the culmination in Christ of what is revealed concerning man's condition and destiny.

6, 1–11: Paul denies that sin calls forth the grace of God; it is rather the divine generosity that is the source of the gift of grace (3, 22; cf note on Mk 1, 9ff). Grace is bestowed at baptism and produces a true renewal. It makes the baptized person capable of responding effectively to the dictates of his conscience concerning faith and life. This renewal is the prelude to the Christian's bodily resurrection and admission to eternal life (5, 21).

can we who died to sin go on living in it? 3 Are you not aware that we who were baptized into Christ Jesus were baptized into his death? 4 Through baptism into his death we were buried with him, so that, just as Christ was raised from the dead by the glory of the Father, we too might live a new life. 5 If we have been united with him through likeness to his death, so shall we be through a like resurrection. 6 This we know: our old self was crucified with him so that the sinful body might be destroyed and we might be slaves to sin no longer. 7 A man who is dead has been freed from sin. 8 If we have died with Christ, we believe that we are also to live with him. 9 We know that Christ, once raised from the dead, will never die again; death has no more power over him. 10 His death was death to sin, once for all; his life is life for God. 11 In the same way, you must consider yourselves dead to sin but alive for God in Christ Jesus.

12 Do not, therefore, let sin rule your mortal body and make you obey its lusts; 13 no more shall you offer the members of your body to sin as weapons for evil. Rather, offer yourselves to God as men who have come back from the dead to life, and your bodies to God as weapons for justice. 14 Sin will no longer have power over you; you are now under grace, not under the law.

15 What does all this lead to? Just because we are not under the law but under grace, are we free to sin? By no means! 16 You must realize that, when you offer yourselves to someone as obedient slaves, you are the slaves of the one you obey, whether yours is the slavery of sin, which leads to death, or of obedience, which leads to justice. 17 Thanks be to God, though once you were slaves of sin, you sincerely obeyed that rule of teaching which was imparted to you; 18 freed from your sin, you became

slaves of justice. 19 (I use the following example from human affairs because of your weak human nature.) Just as formerly you enslaved your bodies to impurity and licentiousness for their degradation, make them now the servants of justice for their sanctification. 20 When you were slaves of sin, you had freedom from justice. 21 What benefit did you then enjoy? Things you are now ashamed of, all of them tending toward death. 22 But now that you are freed from sin and have become slaves of God, your benefit is sanctification as you tend toward eternal life. 23 The wages of sin is death, but the gift of God is eternal life in Christ Jesus our Lord.

Freedom from the Law

7 Are you not aware, my brothers (I am speaking to men who know what law is), that the law has power over a man only so long as he lives? 2 For example, a married woman is bound to her husband by law while he lives, but if he dies she is released from the law regarding husbands. 3 She will be called an adulteress if, while her husband is still alive, she gives herself to another. But if her husband dies she is freed from that law, and does not commit adultery by consorting with another man. 4 In the same way, my brothers, you died to the law through the body of Christ, that you might belong to that Other who was raised from the dead, so that we might bear fruit for God. 5 When we were in the flesh, the sinful passions roused by the law worked in our members and we bore fruit for death. 6 Now we have been released from the law—for we have died to what bound us—and we serve in the new spirit, not the antiquated letter.

Knowledge of Sin through the Law

7 What follows from what I have

said? That the law is the same as sin? Certainly not! Yet it was only through the law that I came to know sin. I should never have known what evil desire was unless the law had said, "You shall not covet." 8 Sin seized that opportunity; it used the commandment to rouse in me every kind of evil desire. Without law sin is dead, 9 and at first I lived without law. Then the commandment came; with it sin came to life, 10 and I died. The commandment that should have led to life brought me death. 11 Sin found its opportunity and used the commandment: first to deceive me, then to kill me. 12 Yet the law is holy and the commandment is holy and just and good.

Sin and Death

13 Did this good thing then become death for me? Not that either! Rather, sin, in order to be seen clearly as sin, used what was good to bring about my death. It did so that, by misusing the commandment, sin might go to the limit of sinfulness. 14 We know that the law is spiritual, whereas I am weak flesh sold into the slavery of sin. 15 I cannot even understand my own actions. I do not do what I want to do but what I hate. 16 When I act against my own will, by that very fact I agree that the law is good. 17 This indicates that it is not I who do it but sin which resides in me. 18 I know that no good dwells in me, that is, in my flesh; the desire to do right is there but not the power. 19 What happens is that I do, not the good I will to do, but the evil I do not intend. 20 But if I do what is against my will, it is not I who do it, but sin which dwells in me. 21 This means that even though I want to do what is right, a law that leads to wrongdoing is always ready at hand. 22 My inner self agrees with the law of God, 23 but I see in my body's members another law at war with the law of

---

6, 12–19: While the Christian remains in this mortal life, the power of sin in him is not fully overcome; his personal effort under the influence of grace is required to surmount the weakness remaining in him.

6, 20–23: The two ways of life, intrinsically opposed, produce opposite results: false *freedom from justice* brings enslavement to sin and the punishment of death; freedom from sin begets sanctification and *eternal life in Christ Jesus.*

7, 1–6: Paul reflects upon the fact that the Christian

has a different understanding of the law because of his faith in Christ. Law binds the living, not the dead, as exemplified in marriage, which binds in life but is dissolved through death. Similarly the Christian, who through baptism has died with Christ to sin, is freed from the law that occasioned sin and its punishment of death. Having risen with Christ, he is joined to him in newness of life so as to *bear fruit for God.*

7, 7–12: The apostle defends himself against the charge of identifying law with sin. Sin does not exist

in law but rather in man, whose sinful inclinations are not overcome by the mere proclamation of law.

7, 13–25: The man who does not experience the justifying grace of God recognizes a rift between his reasoned desire for the goodness of the law and his actual performance contrary to the law. These two are found to be basically opposed. Unable to free himself from the slavery of sin and the power of death, he can only be rescued from defeat in the conflict by the power of God's grace working through Jesus Christ.

my mind; this makes me the prisoner of the law of sin in my members. 24 What a wretched man I am! Who can free me from this body under the power of death? 25 All praise to God, through Jesus Christ our Lord! So with my mind I serve the law of God but with my flesh the law of sin.

The Flesh and the Spirit

8 There is no condemnation now for those who are in Christ Jesus. 2 The law of the spirit, the spirit of life in Christ Jesus, has freed you from the law of sin and death. 3 The law was powerless because of its weakening by the flesh. Then God sent his son in the likeness of sinful flesh as a sin offering, thereby condemning sin in the flesh, 4 so that the just demands of the law might be fulfilled in us who live, not according to the flesh, but according to the spirit. 5 Those who live according to the flesh are intent on the things of the flesh, those who live according to the spirit, on those of the spirit. 6 The tendency of the flesh is toward death but that of the spirit toward life and peace. 7 The flesh in its tendency is at enmity with God; it is not subject to God's law. Indeed, it cannot be; 8 those who are in the flesh cannot please God. 9 But you are not in the flesh; you are in the spirit, since the Spirit of God dwells in you. If anyone does not have the Spirit of Christ, he does not belong to Christ. 10 If Christ is in you, the body is dead because of sin, while the spirit lives because of justice. 11 If the Spirit of him who raised Jesus from the dead dwells in you, then he who raised Christ from the dead will bring your mortal bodies to life also, through his Spirit dwelling in you. 12 We are debtors, then, my brothers—but not to the flesh, so that we should live according to the flesh. 13 If you live according to the flesh, you will die; but if by the spirit you put to death the evil deeds of the body, you will live.

Sons of God through Adoption

14 All who are led by the Spirit of God are sons of God. 15 You did not receive a spirit of slavery leading you back into fear, but a spirit of adoption through which we cry out, "Abba!" (that is, "Father"). 16 The Spirit himself gives witness with our spirit that we are children of God. 17 But if we are children, we are heirs as well: heirs of God, heirs with Christ, if only we suffer with him so as to be glorified with him.

Destiny of Glory

18 I consider the sufferings of the present to be as nothing compared with the glory to be revealed in us. 19 Indeed, the whole created world eagerly awaits the revelation of the sons of God. 20 Creation was made subject to futility, not of its own accord but by him who once subjected it; yet not without hope, 21 because the world itself will be freed from its slavery to corruption and share in the glorious freedom of the children of God. 22 Yes, we know that all creation groans and is in agony even until now. 23 Not only that, but we ourselves, although we have the Spirit as first fruits, groan inwardly while we await the redemption of our bodies. 24 In hope we were saved. But hope is not hope if its object is seen; how is it possible for one to hope for what he sees? 25 And hoping for what we cannot see means awaiting it with patient endurance. 26 The Spirit too helps us in our weakness, for we do not know how to pray as we ought; but the Spirit himself makes intercession for us with groanings that cannot be expressed in speech. 27 He who searches hearts knows what the Spirit means, for the Spirit intercedes for the saints as God himself wills.

God's Love for Man

28 We know that God makes all things work together for the good of those who have been called according to his decree. 29 Those whom he foreknew he predestined to share the image of his Son, that the Son might be the first-born of many brothers. 30 Those he predestined he likewise called; those he called he also justified; and those he justified he in turn glorified. 31 What shall we say after that? If God is for us, who can be against us? 32 Is it possible that he who did not spare his own Son but handed him over for the sake of us all will not grant us all things besides? 33 Who shall bring a charge against God's chosen ones? God, who justifies? 34 Who shall condemn them? Christ Jesus, who died or rather was raised up, who is at the right hand of God and who intercedes for us?

Indomitable Love for Christ

35 Who will separate us from the love of Christ? Trial, or distress, or persecution, or hunger, or nakedness, or danger, or the sword? 36 As Scripture says: "For your sake we are being slain all the day long; we are looked upon as sheep to be slaughtered." 37 Yet in all this we are more than conquerors because of him who has loved us. 38 For I am certain that neither death nor life, neither angels nor principalities, neither the present nor the future, nor powers, 39 neither height nor depth nor any other creature, will be able to separate us from the love of God that comes to us in Christ Jesus, our Lord.

8, 1–13: This is a reflection on the redemptive work of Christ mentioned in 7, 25. The Christian is freed from God's judgment of condemnation by reason of Christ's death for the sins of humanity (1–4). With *the just demands of the law* thus fulfilled, he must live now, not *according to the flesh, . . . at enmity with God,* threatened with death, but *according to the spirit* which dwells in him and leads to *life and peace* (5–17).
8, 14–17: The Christian, by reason of the Spirit's presence within him, enjoys not only new life but also a new relationship to God, that of adopted son and heir through Christ, whose sufferings and glory he shares.
8, 18–27: The glory which the believer is destined to share with Christ far exceeds the sufferings of the present life. Paul considers the created world to be linked to human destiny through its solidarity with man. As it shares in man's penalty of corruption through sin, so also it will share in his benefits of redemption and future glory (19ff). At present both must suffer until they achieve through hope and patient endurance the full harvest of the Spirit's presence, of which they now possess the first fruits or guarantee.
8, 28ff: These verses outline the Christian vocation as it was designed by God: *to share the image of his Son, that the Son might be the first-born of many brothers.* In terms of God's initiative, the call in its totality consists in the exercise of the divine foreknowledge, God's predetermination, God's gift of the call, his sanctification and glorification of the Christian. Thus all that happens to one who loves God is directed by God toward the achievement of that *good* which is likeness to God's Son through grace and glory.
8, 31–39: The all-conquering power of God's love has overcome every obstacle to man's salvation and every threat of his separation from God. That power manifested itself fully when God delivered up to death even his own Son for our salvation. Through him, the Christian can overcome all his afflictions and trials.

ISRAEL'S PRESENT REJECTION

Grief for the Jews

9 I speak the truth in Christ: I do not lie. My conscience bears me witness in the Holy Spirit 2 that there is great grief and constant pain in my heart. 3 Indeed, I could even wish to be separated from Christ for the sake of my brothers, my kinsmen 4 the Israelites. Theirs were the adoption, the glory, the covenants, the law-giving, the worship, and the promises; 5 theirs were the patriarchs, and from them came the Messiah (I speak of his human origins). Blessed forever be God who is over all! Amen.

God's Free Choice

6 Not that God's word has failed. For not all Israelites are true Israelites 7 nor are all Abraham's descendants his children, but as Scripture says, "Through Isaac shall your descendants be called." 8 That means that it is not the children of the flesh who are the children of God; it is the children of the promise who are to be considered descendants. 9 And this was the promise: "I will return at this time, and Sarah shall have a son." 10 Not only that; for when Rebecca had conceived twin children by one man, our father Isaac— 11 while they were yet unborn and had done neither good nor evil, in order that God's decree might stand fast 12 "not by works but by the favor of him who calls"—God said to her, "The older shall serve the younger." 13 It is just as Scripture says, "I have loved Jacob and hated Esau." 14 What are we to say, then? That God is unjust? Not at all! 15 He says to Moses, "I will show mercy to whomever I choose; I will have pity on whomever I wish." 16 So it is not a question of man's willing or doing but of God's mercy. 17 Scripture says to Pharaoh, "This is why I raised you up: that through you I might show my power, and my name might be proclaimed throughout all the earth." 18 In other words, God has mercy on whom he wishes, and whom he wishes he makes obdurate.

19 You will say to me, "Why, then, does he find fault? For who can oppose his will?" 20 Friend, who are you to answer God back? Does something molded say to its molder, "Why did you make me like this?" 21 Does not a potter have the right to make from the same lump of clay one vessel for a lofty purpose and another for a humble one? 22 What if God, wishing to show his wrath and make known his power, has endured with much patience vessels fit for wrath, 23 ready to be destroyed, in order to make known the riches of his glory toward the vessels for mercy which he prepared for glory— 24 I am speaking about us whom he called, not only from among the Jews, but from among the Gentiles.

Witness of the Old Testament

25 As it says in the Book of Hosea: "Those who were not my people I will call 'my people,' and those who were not loved I will call 'Beloved'; 26 in the very place where it was said to them, 'You are not my people,' they shall be called sons of the living God." 27 Isaiah cries out, referring to Israel, "Though the number of the Israelites should be as the sands of the sea, only the remnant will be saved, 28 for quickly and decisively will the Lord execute sentence upon the earth." 29 It is just as Isaiah predicted: "Unless the Lord of hosts had left us a remnant, we should have become as Sodom, we should be like Gomorrah."

Israel's Unbelief

30 How, then, shall we put it? That the Gentiles, who were not seeking justice, attained it—the justice which comes from faith— 31 while Israel, seeking a law from which justice would come, did not arrive at that law? 32 And why did it not? Because justice comes from faith, not from works. They stumbled over the stumbling stone, 33 as Scripture says: "Behold, I am placing in Zion a stone to make men stumble and a rock to make them fall; but he who believes in him will not be put to shame."

10 Brothers, my heart's desire, my prayer to God for the Israelites, is that they may be saved. 2 Indeed, I can testify that they are zealous for God though their zeal is unenlightened. 3 Unaware of God's justice and seeking to establish their own, they did not subject themselves to the justice of God. 4 Christ is the end of the law. Through him, justice comes to everyone who believes. 5 Moses writes of the justice that comes from the law, "The one who observes the law shall live by it." 6 But of the justice that comes from faith he says, "Do not say in your heart, 'Who shall go up into heaven?' (that is, to bring Christ down), 7 or 'Who shall go down

---

9, 1—11, 36: Israel's unbelief and its rejection of Jesus as Savior astonished and puzzled Christians. It constituted a serious theological problem for them in view of God's specific preparation of Israel for the advent of the Messiah. Paul addresses himself here to the essential question of how the divine plan could be frustrated by Israel's unbelief.

9, 1–5: The apostle speaks in strong terms of the depth of his grief over the unbelief of his own people. He would willingly undergo a curse himself for the sake of them and their coming to the knowledge of Christ (v 3; cf Lv 27, 28f). His love of them derives from God's choice of them and the spiritual benefits he bestowed on them (4f).

9, 6–13: Israel's unbelief reflects the mystery of the divine election that was always operative within it. Mere natural descent from Abraham did not ensure the full possession of the divine gifts; it was God's sovereign prerogative to bestow this fullness upon, or

to withhold it from, whomsoever he wished; cf Mt 3, 9; Jn 3, 3f. The choice of Jacob over Esau is a case in point.

9, 14–18: The principle of divine election does not mean that God is unfair in his dealings with men. Rather, he reveals in this way that the gift of faith is the enactment of his mercy (v 16). God raised up Moses to display his mercy and Pharaoh to display his severity in punishing those who obstinately oppose him.

9, 19–29: The apostle responds to the objection that if God rules over faith through the principle of divine election, he cannot then accuse the unbelieving man of sin (v 19). For Paul, this objection is in the last analysis a manifestation of human insolence, and his "answer" is less an explanation of God's ways than the rejection of an argument which places man on the level of God.

9, 30–33: In the conversion of the Gentiles, and by

contrast, of relatively few Jews, the Old Testament prophecies are seen to be fulfilled; cf 9, 25–29. Israel placed an unbalanced overemphasis on the literal observance of the law and was thus unwilling to accept the doctrine of justification by faith; the Gentiles were more open to this doctrine because to them the very idea of justification was new.

10, 1–4: Despite Israel's unbelief in Christ, Paul does not abandon hope for its salvation (v 1). Israel misunderstood the true nature of salvation (v 3), but retained its faith in God (v 4).

10, 5–13: In the past, Israel was promised particular benefits for observance of the law (v 5), but in Christ the law has been fulfilled (4f). It is faith in Jesus which is the source of God's saving action for Jew and Gentile alike (6–13).

into the abyss?' (that is, to bring Christ up from the dead)." 8 What is it he does say? "The word is near you, on your lips and in your heart" (that is, the word of faith which we preach). 9 For if you confess with your lips that Jesus is Lord, and believe in your heart that God raised him from the dead, you will be saved. 10 Faith in the heart leads to justification, confession on the lips to salvation. 11 Scripture says, "No one who believes in him will be put to shame." 12 Here there is no difference between Jew and Greek; all have the same Lord, rich in mercy toward all who call upon him. 13 "Everyone who calls on the name of the Lord will be saved."

14 But how shall they call on him in whom they have not believed? And how can they believe unless they have heard of him? And how can they hear unless there is someone to preach? 15 And how can men preach unless they are sent? Scripture says, "How beautiful are the feet of those who announce good news!" 16 But not all have believed the gospel. Isaiah asks, "Lord, who has believed what he has heard from us?" 17 Faith, then, comes through hearing, and what is heard is the word of Christ. 18 I ask you, have they not heard? Certainly they have, for "their voice has sounded over the whole earth, and their words to the limits of the world." 19 I put the question again, did Israel really not understand? First of all, Moses says, "I will make you jealous of those who are not even a nation; with a senseless nation I will make you angry." 20 Then Isaiah says boldly, "I was found by those who were not seeking me; to those who were not looking for me I revealed myself." 21 But of Israel he says, "All day long I stretched out my hands to an unbelieving and contentious people."

Partial Rejection of Israel

11 I ask, then, has God rejected his people? Of course not! I myself am an Israelite, descended from Abraham, of the tribe of Benjamin. 2 No, God has not rejected his people whom he foreknew. Do you not know what Scripture says about Elijah, how he pleaded with God against Israel? 3 "Lord, they have killed your prophets, they have torn down your altars; I alone am left and they are seeking my life." 4 How does God answer him? "I have left for myself seven thousand men who have not bowed the knee to Baal." 5 Just so, in the present time there is a remnant chosen by the grace of God. 6 But if the choice is by grace, it is not because of their works—otherwise grace would not be grace. 7 What then are we to say? Just this: Israel did not obtain what she was seeking, but those who were chosen did. 8 The rest became blind, as Scripture says: "God gave them a spirit of stupor; blind eyes and deaf ears, and it is so to this day." 9 David says: "Let their table become a snare and a trap, a stumbling stone and a retribution; 10 let their eyes be darkened so that they may not see. Bow down their back forever."

Israel's Fall the Gentiles' Salvation

11 I further ask, does their stumbling mean that they are forever fallen? Not at all! Rather, by their transgression salvation has come to the Gentiles to stir Israel to envy. 12 But if their transgression and their diminishing have meant riches for the Gentile world, how much more their full number! 13 I say this now to you Gentiles: Inasmuch as I am the apostle of the Gentiles, I glory in my ministry, 14 trying to rouse my fellow Jews to envy and save some of them. 15 For if their rejection has meant

reconciliation for the world, what will their acceptance mean? Nothing less than life from the dead! 16 If the first fruits are consecrated, so too is the whole mass of dough, and if the root is consecrated, so too are the branches. 17 If some of the branches were cut off and you, a branch of the wild olive tree, have been grafted in among the others and have come to share in the rich root of the olive, do not boast against the branches. 18 If you do boast, remember that you do not support the root; the root supports you. 19 You will say, "Branches were cut off that I might be grafted in." 20 Well and good. They were cut off because of unbelief and you are there because of faith. 21 Do not be haughty on that account, but fearful. If God did not spare the natural branches, he will certainly not spare you.

22 Consider the kindness and the severity of God—severity toward those who fell, kindness toward you, provided you remain in his kindness; if you do not, you too will be cut off. 23 And if the Jews do not remain in their unbelief they will be grafted back on, for God is able to do this. 24 If you were cut off from the natural wild olive and, contrary to nature, were grafted into the cultivated olive, so much the more will they who belong to it by nature be grafted into their own olive tree.

Israel's Final Conversion

25 Brothers, I do not want you to be ignorant of this mystery lest you be conceited: blindness has come upon part of Israel until the full number of Gentiles enter in, and then all Israel will be saved. 26 As Scripture says: "Out of Zion will come the deliverer who shall remove all impiety from Jacob; 27 and this is the covenant I will make with them when I take away their sins." 28 In respect to the gospel, the Jews

---

10, 14–21: The gospel has been sufficiently proclaimed to Israel, which has adequately understood it, but, as in the past, has not accepted the prophetic message; cf Acts 7, 51ff.

11, 1–10: Though Israel has been unfaithful to the prophetic message of the gospel (10, 14–21), God remains faithful to Israel. Proof of the divine fidelity lies in the existence of the Judaeo-Christians like Paul himself. The unbelieving Jews have been blinded by the Christian teaching concerning the Messiah.

11, 11–15: The unbelief of Israel has paved the way for the preaching of the gospel to the Gentiles and for their easier acceptance of it outside the context of Jewish culture. In God's design it should follow that Israel's ultimate acceptance of the gospel message will benefit the world even more than its original unbelief.

11, 16–24: Israel remains holy in the eyes of God and stands as a witness to the faith of the Old Testament because of the *first fruits which are consecrated*,

---

i.e., the converted remnant, and the *root* which *is consecrated*, i.e., the patriarchs (v 16). The Jews' failure to believe in Christ is a warning to Gentile Christians to be on guard lest they themselves fail through loss of faith.

11, 25–32: In God's design, Israel's unbelief is being utilized to grant the light of faith to the Gentiles. Meanwhile, Israel remains dear to God, still the object of his special providence, the mystery of which will one day be revealed.

are enemies of God for your sake; in respect to the election, they are beloved by him because of the patriarchs. 29 God's gifts and his call are irrevocable.

Triumph of God's Mercy

30 Just as you were once disobedient to God and now have received mercy through their disobedience, 31 so they have become disobedient—since God wished to show you mercy—that they too may receive mercy. 32 God has imprisoned all in disobedience that he might have mercy on all.

33 How deep are the riches and the wisdom and the knowledge of God! How inscrutable his judgments, how unsearchable his ways! 34 For "who has known the mind of the Lord? Or who has been his counselor? 35 Who has given him anything so as to deserve return?" 36 For from him and through him and for him all things are. To him be glory forever. Amen.

THE DUTIES OF CHRISTIANS

Sacrifice of Body and Mind

12 And now, brothers, I beg you through the mercy of God to offer your bodies as a living sacrifice holy and acceptable to God, your spiritual worship. 2 Do not conform yourselves to this age but be transformed by the renewal of your mind, so that you may judge what is God's will, what is good, pleasing and perfect.

Many Members in One Body

3 Thus, in virtue of the favor given to me, I warn each of you not to think more highly of himself than he ought. Let him estimate himself soberly, in keeping with the measure of faith that God has apportioned him. 4 Just as each of us has one body with many members, and not all the members have the same function, 5 so too we, though many, are one body in Christ and individually members one of another. 6

We have gifts that differ according to the favor bestowed on each of us. One's gift may be prophecy; its use should be in proportion to his faith. 7 It may be the gift of ministry; it should be used for service. One who is a teacher should use his gift for teaching; 8 one with the power of exhortation should exhort. He who gives alms should do so generously; he who rules should exercise his authority with care; he who performs works of mercy should do so cheerfully.

Fraternal Charity

9 Your love must be sincere. Detest what is evil, cling to what is good. 10 Love one another with the affection of brothers. Anticipate each other in showing respect. 11 Do not grow slack but be fervent in spirit; he whom you serve is the Lord. 12 Rejoice in hope, be patient under trial, persevere in prayer. 13 Look on the needs of the saints as your own; be generous in offering hospitality. 14 Bless your persecutors; bless and do not curse them. 15 Rejoice with those who rejoice, weep with those who weep. 16 Have the same attitude toward all. Put away ambitious thoughts and associate with those who are lowly. Do not be wise in your own estimation. 17 Never repay injury with injury. See that your conduct is honorable in the eyes of all. 18 If possible, live peaceably with everyone. 19 Beloved, do not avenge yourselves; leave that to God's wrath, for it is written: "'Vengeance is mine; I will repay,' says the Lord." 20 But "if your enemy is hungry, feed him; if he is thirsty, give him something to drink; by doing this you will heap burning coals upon his head." 21 Do not be conquered by evil but conquer evil with good.

Obedience to Authority

13 Let everyone obey the authorities that are over him, for there is no authority except from God, and all authority that exists is

established by God. 2 As a consequence, the man who opposes authority rebels against the ordinance of God; those who resist thus shall draw condemnation down upon themselves. 3 Rulers cause no fear when a man does what is right but only when his conduct is evil. Do you wish to be free from the fear of authority? Do what is right and you will gain its approval, 4 for the ruler is God's servant to work for your good. Only if you do wrong ought you to be afraid. It is not without purpose that the ruler carries the sword; he is God's servant, to inflict his avenging wrath upon the wrongdoer. 5 You must obey, then, not only to escape punishment but also for conscience' sake. You pay taxes for the same reason, 6 magistrates being God's ministers who devote themselves to his service with unremitting care. 7 Pay each one his due: taxes to whom taxes are due; toll to whom toll is due; respect and honor to everyone who deserves them.

Love Fulfills the Law

8 Owe no debt to anyone except the debt that binds us to love one another. He who loves his neighbor has fulfilled the law. 9 The commandments, "You shall not commit adultery; you shall not murder; you shall not steal; you shall not covet," and any other commandment there may be are all summed up in this, "You shall love your neighbor as yourself." 10 Love never wrongs the neighbor, hence love is the fulfillment of the law.

Christian Use of Time

11 Take care to do all these things, for you know the time in which we are living. It is now the hour for you to wake from sleep, for our salvation is closer than when we first accepted the faith. 12 The night is far spent; the day draws near. Let us cast off deeds of darkness and put on the armor of light. 13 Let us live honorably as in daylight; not in

11, 33–36: This final reflection celebrates the wisdom of God's plan of salvation. As Paul has indicated throughout these chapters, both Jew and Gentile, despite the religious recalcitrance of each, have received the gift of faith. Thus the divine plan of salvation has become open and comprehensible to the whole human race.

12, 1—13, 14: This moral teaching expresses the necessary response to the gift of justification through faith. It is the Christian's personal sacrificial way of serving God (12, 1f). It consists in the humble use of one's gifts for the benefit of the community (12, 3–13); it is marked by love of enemies (12, 14–21), and by the acceptance of legitimate civil authority (13, 1–7).

The commandments of the Mosaic covenant (Ex 20, 13–17) remain its norm, and the hope of salvation in Christ its incentive (13, 11–14).

carousing and drunkenness, not in sexual excess and lust, not in quarreling and jealousy. 14 Rather, put on the Lord Jesus Christ and make no provision for the desires of the flesh.

To Live and Die for Christ

14 Extend a kind welcome to those who are weak in faith. Do not enter into disputes with them. 2 A man of sound faith knows he can eat anything, while one who is weak in faith eats only vegetables. 3 The man who will eat anything must not ridicule him who abstains from certain foods; the man who abstains must not sit in judgment on him who eats. After all, God himself has made him welcome. 4 Who are you to pass judgment on another's servant? His master alone can judge whether he stands or falls. And stand he will, for the Lord is able to make him stand. 5 One man regards this day as better than that; someone else considers all days alike. Each should be certain of his own conscience. 6 The man who observes the day does so to honor the Lord. The man who eats does so to honor the Lord, and he gives thanks to God. The man who does not eat abstains to honor the Lord, and he too gives thanks to God. 7 None of us lives as his own master and none of us dies as his own master. 8 While we live we are responsible to the Lord, and when we die we die as his servants. Both in life and in death we are the Lord's. 9 That is why Christ died and came to life again, that he might be Lord of both the dead and the living. 10 But you, how can you sit in judgment on your brother? Or you, how can you look down on your brother? We shall all have to appear before the judgment seat of God. 11 It is written, "As surely as I live, says the Lord, every knee shall bend before me and every tongue shall give praise to God."

Peace and Joy in the Holy Spirit

12 Every one of us will have to give an account of himself before God. 13 Therefore we must no longer pass judgment on one another.

Instead, you should resolve to put no stumbling block or hindrance in your brother's way. 14 I know with certainty on the authority of the Lord Jesus that nothing is unclean in itself; it is only when a man thinks something unclean that it becomes so for him. 15 If, then, your brother feels remorse for the food he has eaten, you have ceased to follow the rule of love. You must not let the food you eat bring to ruin him for whom Christ died; 16 neither may you allow your privilege to become an occasion for blasphemy. 17 The kingdom of God is not a matter of eating or drinking, but of justice, peace, and the joy that is given by the Holy Spirit. 18 Whoever serves Christ in this way pleases God and wins the esteem of men. 19 Let us, then, make it our aim to work for peace and to strengthen one another.

20 Take care not to destroy God's work for the sake of something to eat. True, all foods are clean; but it is wrong for a man to eat when the food offends his conscience. 21 You would be acting nobly if you abstained from eating meat, or drinking wine, or anything else that offers your brother an occasion for stumbling or scandal, or that weakens him in any way. 22 Use the faith you have as your rule of life in the sight of God. Happy the man whose conscience does not condemn what he has chosen to do! 23 But if a man eats when his conscience has misgivings about eating, he is already condemned, because he is not acting in accordance with what he believes. Whatever does not accord with one's belief is sinful.

Patience and Self-denial

15 We who are strong in faith should be patient with the scruples of those whose faith is weak; we must not be selfish. 2 Each should please his neighbor so as to do him good by building up his spirit. 3 Thus, in accord with Scripture, Christ did not please himself: "The reproaches they uttered against you fell on me." 4 Everything written before our time was written

for our instruction, that we might derive hope from the lessons of patience and the words of encouragement in the Scriptures. 5 May God, the source of all patience and encouragement, enable you to live in perfect harmony with one another according to the spirit of Christ Jesus, 6 so that with one heart and voice you may glorify God, the Father of our Lord Jesus Christ.

God's Fidelity and Mercy

7 Accept one another, then, as Christ accepted you, for the glory of God. 8 Yes, I affirm that Christ became the servant of the Jews because of God's faithfulness in fulfilling the promises to the patriarchs, 9 whereas the Gentiles glorify God because of his mercy. As Scripture has it, "Therefore I will praise you among the Gentiles and I will sing to your name." 10 Again, "Rejoice, O Gentiles, with his people." 11 And, "Praise the Lord, all you Gentiles and sing his glory, all you peoples." 12 Once more, Isaiah says, "The root of Jesse will appear, he who will rise up to rule the Gentiles; in him the Gentiles will find hope." 13 So may God, the source of hope, fill you with all joy and peace in believing so that through the power of the Holy Spirit you may have hope in abundance.

CONCLUSION

Apostle of the Gentiles

14 I am convinced, my brothers, that you are filled with goodness, that you have complete knowledge, and that you are able to give advice to one another. 15 Yet I have written to you rather boldly in parts of this letter by way of reminder. I take this liberty because God has given me the grace 16 to be a minister of Christ Jesus among the Gentiles, with the priestly duty of preaching the gospel of God so that the Gentiles may be offered up as a pleasing sacrifice, consecrated by the Holy Spirit. 17 This means I can take glory in Christ Jesus for the work I have done for God. 18 I will not

---

14, 1—15, 6: Paul applies the principle of love of neighbor to a certain conflict existing within the Roman community over clean and unclean foods.

Although he acknowledges that in principle no food is a source of moral contamination (14, 14), he recommends that the consciences of Christians who

are scrupulous in this regard be respected by other Christians (14, 21).

dare to speak of anything except what Christ has done through me to win the Gentiles to obedience by word and deed, 19 with mighty signs and marvels, by the power of God's Spirit. As a result, I have completed preaching the gospel of Christ from Jerusalem all the way around to Illyria. 20 It has been a point of honor with me never to preach in places where Christ's name was already known, for I did not want to build on a foundation laid by another 21 but rather to fulfill the words of Scripture, "They who received no word of him will see him, and they who have never heard will understand."

Paul's Plans; Need for Prayers

22 That is why I have so often been hindered from visiting you. 23 Now I have no more work to do in these regions, and I continue to cherish the desire to visit you which I have had for many years. 24 As soon as I can set out for Spain, I hope to see you in passing; I trust that you will send me on my journey only after I have had the joy of being with you for a little while. 25 Just now I am leaving for Jerusalem to bring assistance to the saints. 26 Macedonia and Achaia have kindly decided to make a contribution for those in need among the saints in Jerusalem. 27 They did so of their own accord, yet they are also under obligation. For if the Gentiles have shared in the spiritual blessings of the Jews, they ought to contribute to their temporal needs in return. 28 When I have finished my task and have safely handed over this contribution to them, I shall set out for Spain, passing through your midst on the way. 29 I am certain that when I do visit you, I shall come with Christ's full blessing.

30 I beg you, brothers, for the sake of our Lord Jesus Christ and the love of the Spirit, join me in the struggle by your prayers to God on my behalf. 31 Pray that I may be kept safe from the unbelievers in Judea, and that the offerings I bring to Jerusalem may be well received by the saints there; 32 so that, God willing, I may come to you with joy and be refreshed in spirit by your company. 33 May the God of peace be with you all. Amen.

Phoebe Commended

16 I commend to you our sister Phoebe, who is a deaconess of the church of Cenchreae. 2 Please welcome her in the Lord, as saints should. If she needs help in anything, give it to her, for she herself has been of help to many, including myself.

Paul's Greetings

3 Give my greetings to Prisca and Aquila; they were my fellow workers in the service of Christ Jesus 4 and even risked their lives for the sake of mine. Not only I but all the churches of the Gentiles are grateful to them. 5 Remember me also to the congregation that meets in their house. Greetings to my beloved Epaenetus; he is the first offering that Asia made to Christ. 6 My greetings to Mary, who has worked hard for you, 7 and to Andronicus and Junias, my kinsmen and fellow prisoners; they are outstanding apostles, and they were in Christ even before I was. 8 Greetings to Ampliatus, who is dear to me in the Lord; 9 to Urbanus, our fellow worker in the service of Christ; and to my beloved Stachys. 10 Greetings to Apelles, who proved himself in Christ's service, and to all who belong to the household of Aristobulus. 11 Greetings to my kinsman Herodion and to the members of the household of Narcissus who are in the Lord. 12 Greetings, too, to Tryphaena and Tryphosa, who have worked hard for the Lord; and also to dear Persis, who has labored long in the Lord's service. 13 Greetings to Rufus, a chosen servant of the Lord, and to his mother, who has been a mother to me as well. 14 Greetings to Asyncritus, Phlegon, Hermes, Patrobas, Hermas, and the brothers who are with them; 15 to Philologus and Julia, to Nereus and his sister, to Olympas, and all the saints who are with them. 16 Greet one another with a holy kiss. All the churches of Christ send you greetings.

Against Dissenters

17 Brothers, I beg you to be on the watch against those who cause dissension and scandal, contrary to the teaching you have received. Avoid their company. 18 Such men serve, not Christ our Lord, but their own bellies, and they deceive the simple-minded with smooth and flattering speech. 19 Your obedience is known to all, and so I am delighted with you. I want you to be wise in regard to what is good and innocent of all evil. 20 Then the God of peace will quickly crush Satan under your feet. May the grace of our Lord Jesus Christ be with you.

Greetings from Corinth

21 Timothy, my fellow worker, sends you his greetings; so, too, do my kinsmen Lucius, Jason, and Sosipater. 22 I, Tertius, who have written this letter, send you my greetings in the Lord. 23 Greetings also from Gaius, who is host to me and to the whole church. 24 Erastus, the city treasurer, and our brother Quartus wish to be remembered to you.

Doxology

25 Now to him who is able to strengthen you in the gospel which I proclaim when I preach Jesus Christ, the gospel which reveals the mystery hidden for many ages 26 but now manifested through the writings of the prophets, and, at the command of the eternal God, made known to all the Gentiles that they may believe and obey— 27 to him, the God who alone is wise, may glory be given through Jesus Christ unto endless ages. Amen.

16, 1–23: Some authorities regard these verses as a later addition to Paul's letter, but in general the evidence favors the view that they were included in the original.

16, 25: *The gospel which reveals the mystery hidden for many ages:* justification and salvation through faith, with all the implications for Jew and Gentile that Paul has developed in this letter.

THE FIRST EPISTLE OF PAUL TO THE

INTRODUCTION

Greeting to the Church

AUL, called by God's will to be an apostle of Christ Jesus, and Sosthenes our brother, 2 send greetings to the church of God which is in Corinth; to you who have been consecrated in Christ Jesus and called to be a holy people, as to all those who, wherever they may be, call on the name of our Lord Jesus Christ, their Lord and ours. 3 Grace and peace from God our Father and the Lord Jesus Christ.

Thanksgiving

4 I continually thank my God for you because of the favor he has bestowed on you in Christ Jesus, 5 in whom you have been richly endowed with every gift of speech and knowledge. 6 Likewise, the witness I bore to Christ has been so confirmed among you 7 that you lack no spiritual gift as you wait for the revelation of our Lord Jesus Christ. 8 He will strengthen you to the end, so that you will be blameless on the day of our Lord Jesus [Christ]. 9 God is faithful, and it was he who called you to fellowship with his Son, Jesus Christ our Lord.

CONDEMNATION OF DISORDERS IN THE CORINTHIAN CHURCH

Factions

10 I beg you, brothers, in the name of our Lord Jesus Christ, to agree in what you say. Let there be no factions; rather, be united in mind and judgment. 11 I have been informed, my brothers, by certain members of Chloe's household that you are quarreling among yourselves. 12 This is what I mean: One of you will say, "I belong to Paul," another, "I belong to Apollos," still another, "Cephas has my allegiance," and the fourth, "I belong to Christ." 13 Has Christ, then, been divided into parts? Was it Paul who was crucified for you? Was it in Paul's name that you were baptized? 14 Thank God, I baptized none of you except Crispus and Gaius, 15 so there are none who can say that you were baptized in my name. 16 Oh, and I baptized the household of Stephanas. Beyond that, I am not aware of having baptized anyone else. 17 For Christ did not send me to baptize, but to preach the gospel—not with worldy "wisdom," however, lest the cross of Christ be rendered void of its meaning!

The Wisdom and Folly of the Cross

18 The message of the cross is complete absurdity to those who are headed for ruin, but to us who are

1, 1–9: After the customary salutation (1ff), Paul commends the Christian community of Corinth (4–7), and reminds its members of their expectation of Christ's second coming (8f; cf note on 1 Thes 4, 13–18).

1, 10–16: The presence in the community of factions due to particular attachments to Paul, Apollos,

and Cephas (the reference to Christ may well be ironically intended) is an indication both of the enthusiasm for the newfound faith and the imperfect understanding of it among some of the Corinthians. We can merely conjecture about the divisions and the groups to which the apostle refers.

1, 17–25: From the allusions here to *wisdom* (17)

and the *wise* (19), it seems the Christians mentioned in v 12 were attempting unsuccessfully to align their faith with the philosophies of the day. Paul points out that the Christian message of redemption through the crucifixion of Christ (17f) lies outside the ken of philosophical speculation. It is God, not man, who controls human destiny beyond this life.

experiencing salvation it is the power of God. 19 Scripture says,

"I will destroy the wisdom of
　　the wise,
　　and thwart the cleverness of
　　　the clever."

20 Where is the wise man to be found? Where the scribe? Where is the master of worldly argument? Has not God turned the wisdom of this world into folly? 21 Since, in God's wisdom, the world did not come to know him through "wisdom," it pleased God to save those who believe through the absurdity of the preaching of the gospel. 22 Yes, Jews demand "signs" and Greeks look for "wisdom," 23 but we preach Christ crucified—a stumbling block to Jews, and an absurdity to Gentiles; 24 but to those who are called, Jews and Greeks alike, Christ the power of God and the wisdom of God. 25 For God's folly is wiser than men, and his weakness more powerful than men.

The Case of the Corinthians

26 Brothers, you are among those called. Consider your situation. Not many of you are wise, as men account wisdom; not many are influential; and surely not many are well-born. 27 God chose those whom the world considers absurd to shame the wise; he singled out the weak of this world to shame the strong. 28 He chose the world's lowborn and despised, those who count for nothing, to reduce to nothing those who were something; 29 so that mankind can do no boasting before God. 30 God it is who has given you life in Christ Jesus. He has made him our wisdom and also our justice, our sanctification, and our redemption. 31 This is just as you find it written, "Let him who would boast, boast in the Lord."

Paul's Preaching

2 As for myself, brothers, when I came to you I did not come proclaiming God's testimony with any particular eloquence or "wisdom." 2 No, I determined that while I was with you I would speak of nothing but Jesus Christ and him crucified. 3 When I came among you it was in weakness and fear, and with much trepidation. 4 My message and my preaching had none of the persuasive force of "wise" argumentation, but the convincing power of the Spirit. 5 As a consequence, your faith rests not on the wisdom of men but on the power of God.

True Wisdom

6 There is, to be sure, a certain wisdom which we express among the spiritually mature. It is not a wisdom of this age, however, nor of the rulers of this age, who are men headed for destruction. 7 No, what we utter is God's wisdom: a mysterious, a hidden wisdom. God planned it before all ages for our glory. 8 None of the rulers of this age knew the mystery; if they had known it, they would never have crucified the Lord of glory. 9 Of this wisdom it is written:

"Eye has not seen, ear has not
　　heard,
　　nor has it so much as dawned
　　　on man
　　what God has prepared for
　　　those who love him."

10 Yet God has revealed this wisdom to us through the Spirit. The Spirit scrutinizes all matters, even the deep things of God. 11 Who, for example, knows a man's innermost self but the man's own spirit within him? Similarly, no one knows what lies at the depths of God but the Spirit of God. 12 The Spirit we have received is not the world's spirit but God's

Spirit, helping us to recognize the gifts he has given us. 13 We speak of these, not in words of human wisdom but in words taught by the Spirit, thus interpreting spiritual things in spiritual terms. 14 The natural man does not accept what is taught by the Spirit of God. For him, that is absurdity. He cannot come to know such teaching because it must be appraised in a spiritual way. 15 The spiritual man, on the other hand, can appraise everything, though he himself can be appraised by no one. 16 For, "Who has known the mind of the Lord so as to instruct him?" But we have the mind of Christ.

Immaturity of the Corinthians

3 Brothers, the trouble was that I could not talk to you as spiritual men but only as men of flesh, as infants in Christ. 2 I fed you with milk, and did not give you solid food because you were not ready for it, You are not ready for it even now, 3 being still very much in a natural condition. For as long as there are jealousy and quarrels among you, are you not of the flesh? And is not your behavior that of ordinary men? 4 When someone says, "I belong to Paul," and someone else, "I belong to Apollos," is it not clear that you are still at the human level?

The Office of God's Ministers

5 After all, who is Apollos? And who is Paul? Simply ministers through whom you became believers, each of them doing only what the Lord assigned him. 6 I planted the seed and Apollos watered it, but God made it grow. 7 This means that neither he who plants nor he who waters is of any special account, only God, who gives the growth. 8 He who plants and he who waters work to the same end. Each will receive

1, 19: Is 29, 14.
1, 26–31: God's choice of the foolish, the weak, the lowborn and the despised among the Corinthians to bestow on them the gift of faith in Christ, while shaming the wise and the strong of this world and reducing to nothing those who were something, is a sign that man receives life and attains to God in Christ Jesus, not by his own effort, but by God's act.
2, 1–5: In Paul's preaching at Corinth, he proclaimed the crucified Jesus as God's message of salvation to mankind. He is not denying here that he employed human eloquence, but rather pointing out that he presented himself as a man commissioned by

God; cf Gal 4, 14. Thus the Corinthians believed in the gospel message on God's authority rather than on its intrinsic appeal to human reason.
2, 6–9: The Christian message is rightly termed a "wisdom," but a God-given wisdom pertaining to man's ultimate destiny through God's power. It is completely unknown to the rulers and great minds of the world (v 8).
2, 9: Is 64, 3.
2, 10–16: Just as the individual is the only one cognizant of his own thoughts, which he alone can reveal, so it is with God and his plans for the salvation of humanity (10f). The Christian message expresses

the secret thoughts, not of men, but of God (12f). It applies those thoughts to the innermost recesses of the mind and soul of man. By his acceptance or rejection of the gospel, a person shows himself to be affected or unaffected by the presence of God in the gospel (14ff).
3, 1–9: Here Paul seems to address himself to those who were more impressed by Apollos' preaching than by his own. His teaching had to be elementary, since it was the Corinthians' first confrontation with the demands of the Christian message. However, comparison between Apollos and himself is irrelevant, for they performed different tasks for the community, whose actual success was due to the presence of God.

his wages in proportion to his toil. 9 We are God's co-workers, while you are his cultivation, his building.

The Work of God's Ministers

10 Thanks to the favor God showed me I laid a foundation as a wise master-builder might do, and now someone else is building upon it. Everyone, however, must be careful how he builds. 11 No one can lay a foundation other than the one that has been laid, namely Jesus Christ. 12 If different ones build on this foundation with gold, silver, precious stones, wood, hay or straw, 13 the work of each will be made clear. The Day will disclose it. That day will make its appearance with fire, and fire will test the quality of each man's work. 14 If the building a man has raised on this foundation still stands, he will receive his recompense; 15 if a man's building burns, he will suffer loss. He himself will be saved, but only as one fleeing through fire.

16 Are you not aware that you are the temple of God, and that the Spirit of God dwells in you? 17 If anyone destroys God's temple, God will destroy him. For the temple of God is holy, and you are that temple.

18 Let no one delude himself. If any one of you thinks he is wise in a worldly way, he had better become a fool. In that way he will really be wise, 19 for the wisdom of this world is absurdity with God. Scripture says, "He catches the wise in their craftiness"; 20 and again, "The Lord knows how empty are the thoughts of the wise." 21 Let there be no boasting about men. All things are yours, 22 whether it be Paul, or Apollos, or Cephas, or the world, or life, or death, or the present, or the future: all these are yours, 23 and you are Christ's, and Christ is God's.

Christ Judges His Ministers

4 Men should regard us as servants of Christ and administrators of the mysteries of God. 2 The first requirement of an administrator is that he prove trustworthy. 3 It matters little to me whether you or any human court pass judgment on me. I do not even pass judgment on myself. 4 Mind you, I have nothing on my conscience. But that does not mean that I am declaring myself innocent. 5 The Lord is the one to judge me, so stop passing judgment before the time of his return. He will bring to light what is hidden in darkness and manifest the intentions of hearts. At that time, everyone will receive his praise from God.

Corinthians Contrasted with Apostles

6 Brothers, I have applied all this to myself and Apollos by way of example for your benefit. May you learn from us not to go beyond what is set down, so that none of you will grow self-important by reason of his association with one person rather than another. 7 Who confers any distinction on you? Name something you have that you have not received. If, then, you have received it, why are you boasting as if it were your own? 8 At the moment you are completely satisfied. You have grown rich! You have launched upon your reign with no help from us. Would that you had really begun to reign, that we might be reigning with you! 9 As I see it, God has put us apostles at the end of the line, like men doomed to die in the arena. We have become a spectacle to the universe, to angels and men alike. 10 We are fools on Christ's account. Ah, but in Christ you are wise! We are the weak ones, you the strong! They honor you, while they sneer at us! 11 Up to this very hour we go hungry and thirsty, poorly clad, roughly treated, wandering about homeless. 12 We work hard at manual labor. When we are insulted we respond with a blessing. Persecution comes our way; we bear it patiently. 13 We are slandered, and we try conciliation. We have become the world's refuse, the scum of all; that is the present state of affairs.

14 I am writing you in this way not to shame you but to admonish you as my beloved children. 15 Granted you have ten thousand guardians in Christ, you have only one father. It was I who begot you in Christ Jesus through my preaching of the gospel. 16 I beg you, then, be imitators of me. 17 This is why I have sent you Timothy, my beloved and faithful son in the Lord. He will remind you of my ways in Christ, just as I teach them in all the churches.

18 Some have grown full of self-importance, thinking that I will not come to you. 19 But I shall come to you soon, the Lord willing, and find out, not what they say, but what they can do. 20 The kingdom of God does not consist in talk but in power. 21 Which do you prefer, that I come to you with a rod, or with love and a gentle spirit?

MORAL DISORDERS

An Incestuous Man

5 It is actually reported that there is lewd conduct among you of a kind not even found among the

---

3, 10–15: Paul's work was to found the community on Christ (10f). The work of others for the spiritual good of the community is to be evaluated in terms of enhancing faith in Christ, and of this, God is ultimately the judge (12–15).

3, 16f: *You are the temple of God . . . dwells in you:* God's Spirit sanctifies the Christian community, making it a fit abode for God. *If anyone destroys . . . God will destroy him:* the sudden vehemence seems strange in the context. Some scholars believe Paul has in mind those guilty of corrupting the community morally; cf 5, 1–13; 6, 12–20. However, he may now wish to stress the importance of the Christian teacher's work (10–15), since he previously subordinated this role (5–19) to the effective action of God.

3, 18–23: The Corinthians will prove themselves fools, no better than "the wise" of this world, if they continue *boasting about men.* But since through their faith they belong to Christ, and through him to God, all things, *life* and *death* themselves, can assist them in attaining their end.

4, 1–5: Paul and his associates are to be regarded as assistants and managers in God's household, charged with administering the mysteries in complete dependence upon him. It is his truth which they preach and his interests which they serve. Therefore they are accountable only to him, not to the judgments of men.

4, 6–13: The example of Paul and Apollos is offered as a norm or pattern of conduct for the Corinthians. The sufferings of the apostles, their humiliations and lowly condition, contrast sharply with the self-satisfaction and boastfulness of the Corinthians. And yet all the benefits the latter enjoy are gifts from God, and, as such, should preclude their boasting as if they had not received them.

4, 14–21: Paul tempers his severity by reminding them that, as the founder of their community, he has a certain right to display his feelings. Moreover, he reserves the further right to confront personally in the future those who may remain recalcitrant.

5, 1–13: Two deviations of the community are considered here: the toleration of the incestuous union of a man with his stepmother (1–8); and the misunderstanding of Paul's admonition against associating with fellow Christians guilty of sexual immorality (9–13). In the first case, Paul (impelled perhaps by his belief in the imminence of the parousia) recommends the ecclesial penalty of separating the offender from the unity of the faithful and handing him over to Satan, i.e., for medicinal punishment through bodily affliction, even death (1 Tm 1, 20), so that the incestuous relationship may be destroyed and the path to repentance and reunion laid open.

pagans—a man living with his father's wife. 2 Still you continue to be self-satisfied, instead of grieving, and getting rid of the offender! 3 As for me, though absent in body I am present in spirit, and have already passed sentence in the name of our Lord Jesus Christ on the man who did this deed. 4 United in spirit with you and empowered by our Lord Jesus, 5 I hand him over to Satan for the destruction of his flesh, so that his spirit may be saved on the day of the Lord.

6 This boasting of yours is an ugly thing. Do you not know that a little yeast has its effect all through the dough? 7 Get rid of the old yeast to make of yourselves fresh dough, unleavened loaves, as it were; Christ our Passover has been sacrificed. 8 Let us celebrate the feast not with the old yeast, that of corruption and wickedness, but with the unleavened bread of sincerity and truth.

9 I wrote you in my letter not to associate with immoral persons. 10 I was not speaking of association with immoral people in this world, or the covetous or thieves or idolaters. 11 To avoid them, you would have to leave the world! What I really wrote about was your not associating with anyone who bears the title "brother" if he is immoral, covetous, an idolater, an abusive person, a drunkard, or a thief. It is clear that you must not eat with such a man. 12 What business is it of mine to judge outsiders? Is it not those inside the community you must judge? 13 God will judge the others. "Expel the wicked man from your midst."

Lawsuits before Pagans

6 How can anyone with a case against another dare bring it for judgment to the wicked and not to God's holy people? 2 Do you not know that the believers will judge the

world? If the judgment of the world is to be yours, are you to be thought unworthy of judging in minor matters? 3 Do you not know that we are to judge angels? Surely, then, we are up to deciding everyday affairs. 4 If you have such matters to decide, do you accept as judges those who have no standing in the church? 5 I say this in an attempt to shame you. Can it be that there is no one among you wise enough to settle a case between one member of the church and another? 6 Must brother drag brother into court, and before unbelievers at that? 7 Why, the very fact that you have lawsuits against one another is disastrous for you. Why not put up with injustice, and let yourselves be cheated? 8 Instead, you yourselves injure and cheat your very own brothers. 9 Can you not realize that the unholy will not fall heir to the kingdom of God? Do not deceive yourselves: no fornicators, idolaters, or adulterers, no sodomites, 10 thieves, misers, or drunkards, no slanderers or robbers will inherit God's kingdom. 11 And such were some of you; but you have been washed, consecrated, justified in the name of our Lord Jesus Christ and in the Spirit of our God.

Against Sexual Immorality

12 "Everything is lawful for me" —but that does not mean that everything is good for me. "Everything is lawful for me"—but I will not let myself be enslaved by anything. 13 "Food is for the stomach and the stomach for food, and God will do away with them both in the end"— but the body is not for immorality; it is for the Lord, and the Lord is for the body. 14 God, who raised up the Lord, will raise us also by his power.

15 Do you not see that your bodies are members of Christ?

Would you have me take Christ's members and make them the members of a prostitute? God forbid! 16 Can you not see that the man who is joined to a prostitute becomes one body with her? Scripture says, "The two shall become one flesh." 17 But whoever is joined to the Lord becomes one spirit with him. 18 Shun lewd conduct. Every other sin a man commits is outside his body, but the fornicator sins against his own body. 19 You must know that your body is a temple of the Holy Spirit, who is within—the Spirit you have received from God. You are not your own. 20 You have been purchased, and at a price. So glorify God in your body.

Advice to the Married

7 Now for the matters you wrote about. A man is better off having no relations with a woman. 2 But to avoid immorality, every man should have his own wife and every woman her own husband. 3 The husband should fulfill his conjugal obligations toward his wife, the wife hers toward her husband. 4 A wife does not belong to herself but to her husband; equally, a husband does not belong to himself but to his wife. 5 Do not deprive one another, unless perhaps by mutual consent for a time, to devote yourselves to prayer. Then return to one another, that Satan may not tempt you through your lack of self-control. 6 I say this by way of concession, not as a command. 7 Given my preference, I should like you to be as I am. Still, each one has his own gift from God, one this and another that.

Advice to the Unmarried

8 To those not married and to widows I have this to say: It would be well if they remain as they are, even as I do myself; 9 but if they cannot exercise self-control, they should marry. It is better to marry

---

6, 1–8: The apostle expresses his dismay that the image of mutual charity among Christians is being tarnished by their lawsuits in Roman courts. This is all the more deplorable since Christians are to share with Christ the judgment of the world, and ought therefore to be capable of settling one another's minor cases within the society of believers; cf Dn 7, 22.27.

6, 9–20: Paul insists that the Christian give evidence of the reality of his faith in Christ by living

according to a high moral standard. The gravity of the sins mentioned in vv 9f can be gauged from the fact that they exclude the offender from inheriting the kingdom of God. In 6, 12–20 the fornication referred to is probably that of religious prostitution, an accepted part of pagan culture in Rome.

7, 1–11: Paul's teaching concerning marriage and the celibate state is placed in the framework of the second coming of Christ (26.28f); see note on 1 Thes 4, 13–18. The apostle commends sexual asceticism in

marriage provided it is agreed to by both parties, spiritually motivated, and not carried beyond either party's limits of control (1–7). The existing practice within the community of widows and widowers remaining unmarried is also commended, without, however, any implication against the freedom to remarry should sexual attraction prove irresistible. Christ's teaching against divorce and remarriage must be strictly adhered to in marriages between Christians; cf Mk 10, 9.

than to be on fire. 10 To those now married, however, I give this command (though it is not mine; it is the Lord's): a wife must not separate from her husband. 11 If she does separate, she must either remain single or become reconciled to him again. Similarly, a husband must not divorce his wife.

Obligation of the Believing Partner

12 As for the other matters, although I know of nothing the Lord has said, I say: If any brother has a wife who is an unbeliever but is willing to live with him, he must not divorce her. 13 And if any woman has a husband who is an unbeliever but is willing to live with her, she must not divorce him. 14 The unbelieving husband is consecrated by his believing wife; the unbelieving wife is consecrated by her believing husband. If it were otherwise, your children should be unclean; but as it is, they are holy.

15 If the unbeliever wishes to separate, however, let him do so. The believing husband or wife is not bound in such cases. God has called you to live in peace. 16 Wife, how do you know that you will not save your husband; or you, husband, that you will not save your wife?

No Change To Be Sought

17 The general rule is that each one should lead the life the Lord has assigned him, continuing as he was when the Lord called him. This is the rule I give in all the churches. 18 Was someone called after he had been circumcised? He should not try to hide his circumcision. Did the call come to another who had never been circumcised? He is not to be circumcised. 19 Circumcision counts for nothing, and its lack makes no difference either. What matters is keeping God's commandments. 20

Everyone ought to continue as he was when he was called. 21 Were you a slave when your call came? Give it no thought. Even supposing you could go free, you would be better off making the most of your slavery. 22 The slave called in the Lord is a freedman of the Lord, just as the freeman who has been called is a slave of Christ. 23 You have been bought at a price! Do not enslave yourselves to men. 24 Brothers, each of you should continue before God in the condition of life that was his when he was called.

The State of Virginity

25 With respect to virgins, I have not received any commandment from the Lord, but I give my opinion as one who is trustworthy, thanks to the Lord's mercy. 26 It is this: In the present time of stress it seems good to me for a person to continue as he is. 27 Are you bound to a wife? Then do not seek your freedom. Are you free of a wife? If so, do not go in search of one. 28 Should you marry, however, you will not be committing sin. Neither does a virgin commit a sin if she marries. But such people will have trials in this life, and these I should like to spare you.

29 I tell you, brothers, the time is short. From now on those with wives should live as though they had none; 30 those who weep should live as though they were not weeping, and those who rejoice as though they were not rejoicing; buyers should conduct themselves as though they owned nothing, 31 and those who make use of the world as though they were not using it, for the world as we know it is passing away.

32 I should like you to be free of all worries. The unmarried man is busy with the Lord's affairs, concerned with pleasing the Lord; 33 but the married man is busy with this

world's demands and occupied with pleasing his wife. This means he is divided. 34 The virgin—indeed, any unmarried woman—is concerned with things of the Lord, in pursuit of holiness in body and spirit. The married woman, on the other hand, has the cares of this world to absorb her and is concerned with pleasing her husband. 35 I am going into this with you for your own good. I have no desire to place restrictions on you, but I do want to promote what is good, what will help you to devote yourselves entirely to the Lord.

A Question of Marriage

36 If anyone thinks he is behaving dishonorably toward his virgin because a critical moment has come and it seems that something should be done, let him do as he wishes. He commits no sin if there is a marriage. 37 The man, however, who stands firm in his resolve, who while without constraint and free to carry out his will makes up his mind to keep his virgin, also acts rightly. 38 To sum up: the man who marries his virgin, acts fittingly; the one who does not, will do better.

Widows

39 A wife is bound to her husband as long as he lives. If her husband dies she is free to marry, but on one condition, that it be in the Lord. 40 She will be happier, though, in my opinion, if she stays unmarried. I am persuaded that in this I have the Spirit of God.

Meats Offered to Idols

8 Now about meats that have been offered to idols. Of course we all "know" about that. But whereas "knowledge" inflates, love up-builds. 2 If a man thinks he knows something, that means he has never really known it as he ought. 3 But if anyone loves God, that man is known by

---

7, 12–16: In the case of marriage between Christians and non-Christians, there must be no divorce as long as the unbelieving partner is willing to live peacefully with the Christian spouse (12f). But if the non-believer wishes to separate, or refuses to live peacefully with the Christian, the latter is no longer bound (15f).

7, 17–24: A degree of importance is attached to the circumstances that basically condition one's life at the time of conversion. Normally, everyone, whether Jew or Gentile, slave or free, should expect to retain his particular state.

7, 25–31: The above principle of retention of one's state applies also to both the unmarried and the married because, in the light of the second coming of Christ, it is not the state that is important but rather the use of it in a spirit of sacrifice, i.e., as though not using it. In this way all things are made subservient to the supreme end of preparedness for Christ's coming in judgment.

7, 32–35: Those who were unmarried at the time of conversion should realize that their celibate state relieves them of the responsibilities of marriage and family, and the resulting involvement in wordly affairs.

They are more free to engage directly in the service of the Lord (32ff). This does not, however, contradict the individual's freedom to marry (v 35; cf 7, 8f.28).

7, 36ff: These verses may mean either that a) a man living chastely with a virgin may marry her; or b) a father may give his daughter in marriage, or a guardian his ward. However, dedicated celibacy and virginity anticipate the life of glory after the resurrection, when marriage will no longer exist; cf Mt 22, 30.

7, 39f: Widows who choose to remarry should prefer Christian husbands.

8, 1–13: See note on Romans 14, 1—15, 6.

him. 4 So, then, about this matter of eating meats that have been offered to idols: we know that an idol is really nothing, and that there is no God but one. 5 Even though there are so-called gods in the heavens and on the earth—there are, to be sure, many such "gods" and "lords"— 6 for us there is one God, the Father, from whom all things come and for whom we live; and one Lord Jesus Christ, through whom everything was made and through whom we live.

Practical Rules

7 Not all, of course, possess this "knowledge." Because some were so recently devoted to idols, they eat meat, fully aware that it has been sacrificed, and because their conscience is weak, it is defiled by the eating. 8 Now food does not bring us closer to God. We suffer no loss through failing to eat, and we gain no favor by eating. 9 Take care, however, lest in exercising your right you become an occasion of sin to the weak. 10 If someone sees you, with your "knowledge," reclining at table in the temple of an idol, may not his conscience in its weak state be influenced to the point that he eats the idol-offering? 11 Because of your "knowledge" the weak one perishes, that brother for whom Christ died. 12 When you sin thus against your brothers and wound their weak consciences, you are sinning against Christ. 13 Therefore, if food causes my brother to sin I will never eat meat again, so that I may not be an occasion of sin to him.

Paul's Rights as an Apostle

9 Am I not free? Am I not an apostle? Have I not seen Jesus our Lord? And are you not my work in the Lord? 2 Although I may not be an apostle for others, I certainly am one for you. You are the very seal of my apostolate in the Lord.

3 My defense against those who criticize me is this: 4 Do we not have the right to eat and drink? 5 Do we not have the right to marry a believing woman like the rest of the apostles and the brothers of the Lord and Cephas? 6 Is it only myself and Barnabas who are forced to work for a living? What soldier in the field pays for his rations? 7 Who plants a vineyard and does not eat of its yield? What shepherd does not nourish himself with the milk of his flock? 8 You may think the reasons I am giving are merely human ones, but does not the law itself speak of these things? It is written in the law of Moses, "You shall not muzzle an ox while it treads out grain." 9 Is God concerned here for oxen, 10 or does he not rather say this for our sakes? You can be sure it was written for us, for the plowman should plow in hope and the harvester expect a share in the grain. 11 If we have sown for you in the spirit, is it too much to expect a material harvest from you? 12 If others have this right over you, is not our right even greater? But we have not used this right. On the contrary, we put up with all sorts of hardships so as not to place any obstacle in the way of the gospel of Christ. 13 Do you not realize that those who work in the temple are supported by the temple, and those who minister at the altar share the offerings of the altar? 14 Likewise the Lord himself ordered that those who preach the gospel should live by the gospel.

Reason for Not Using Rights

15 As for me, I have not used any of these rights, nor do I write this now to see to it that anything should be done for me. I would rather die than let anyone rob me of my boast! 16 Yet preaching the gospel is not the subject of a boast; I am under compulsion and have no choice. I am ruined if I do not preach it! 17 If I do it willingly, I have my recompense; if unwillingly, 18 I am nonetheless entrusted with a charge. And this recompense of mine? It is simply this, that when preaching I offer the gospel free of charge and do not make full use of the authority the gospel gives me.

All Things to All Men

19 Although I am not bound to anyone, I made myself the slave of all so as to win over as many as possible. 20 I became like a Jew to the Jews in order to win the Jews. To those bound by the law I became like one who is bound (although in fact I am not bound by it), that I might win those bound by the law. 21 To those not subject to the law I became like one not subject to it (not that I am free from the law of God, for I am subject to the law of Christ), that I might win those not subject to the law. 22 To the weak I became a weak person with a view to winning the weak. I have made myself all things to all men in order to save at least some of them. 23 In fact, I do all that I do for the sake of the gospel in the hope of having a share in its blessings.

24 You know that while all the runners in the stadium take part in the race, the award goes to one man. In that case, run so as to win! 25 Athletes deny themselves all sorts of things. They do this to win a crown of leaves that withers, but we a crown that is imperishable. 26 I do not run like a man who loses sight of the finish line. I do not fight as if I were shadowboxing. 27 What I do is discipline my own body and master it, for fear that after having preached to others I myself should be rejected.

Against Over-confidence

10 Brothers, I want you to remember this: our fathers were all under the cloud and all passed through the sea; 2 by the cloud and the sea all of them were bap-

---

9, 1–23: Behind this passage lies some objection within the Corinthian community to Paul's apostolic role. Since he does not accept material support from the community or make use of a woman servant, like the other apostles, he is apparently not to be considered their equal. Paul replies that he is quite aware of his right to do these things, but that he has made a free, personal decision not to exercise this right. He feels that his preaching of the gospel is a duty laid upon him by God, which he must fulfill by presenting the gospel to men as gratuitously as God gave it to him (15–18). He cannot be accused of pride, for his apostolic life is proof that he has conquered his pride; he adapts himself to the customary observances of the law when residing among Judaeo-Christians, and to its non-observance when he shares the life of Gentile Christians (19–23).

10, 1–13: Paul approaches the question of participation in the sacrificial worship of pagan temples (14–22) by invoking Old Testament traditions from the history of Israel in the desert, especially Israel's forbidden worship of the golden calf (Ex 32, 1–29). Christians, in their turn, possess the spiritual gifts of God but this does not free them from the danger of yielding to temptation.

tized into Moses. 3 All ate the same spiritual food. 4 All drank the same spiritual drink (they drank from the spiritual rock that was following them, and the rock was Christ), 5 yet we know that God was not pleased with most of them, for "they were struck down in the desert."

6 These things happened as an example to keep us from wicked desires such as theirs. 7 Do not become idolaters, as some of them did. Scripture says, "The people sat down to eat and drink, and arose to take their pleasure." 8 Let us not indulge in lewdness as some of them did, so that in one day twenty-three thousand perished. 9 Let us not test the Lord as some of them did, only to be destroyed by snakes. 10 Nor are you to grumble as some of them did, to be killed by the destroying angel. 11 The things that happened to them serve as an example. They have been written as a warning to us, upon whom the end of the ages has come. 12 For all these reasons, let anyone who thinks he is standing upright watch out lest he fall! 13 No test has been sent you that does not come to all men. Besides, God keeps his promise. He will not let you be tested beyond your strength. Along with the test he will give you a way out of it so that you may be able to endure it.

The Eucharist versus Pagan Sacrifices

14 I am telling you, whom I love, to shun the worship of idols, 15 and I address you as one addresses sensible people. You may judge for yourselves what I am saying. 16 Is not the cup of blessing we bless a sharing in the blood of Christ? And is not the bread we break a sharing in the body of Christ? 17 Because the loaf of bread is one, we, many though we are, are one body, for we all partake of the one loaf.

18 Look at Israel according to the flesh and see if those who eat the sacrifices do not share in the altar! 19 What am I saying—that meat offered to an idol is really offered to that idol, or that an idol is a reality? 20 No, I mean that the Gentiles sacrifice to demons and not to God, and I do not want you to become sharers with demons. 21 You cannot drink the cup of the Lord and also the cup of demons. You cannot partake of the table of the Lord and likewise the table of demons. 22 Do we mean to provoke the Lord to jealous anger? Surely we are not stronger than he!

Concerning Idol Offerings

23 "All things are lawful," but not all are advantageous. "All things are lawful"—which does not mean that everything is constructive. 24 No man should seek his own interest but rather that of his neighbor. 25 Eat whatever is sold in the market without raising any question of conscience. 26 "The earth and its fullness are the Lord's." 27 If an unbeliever invites you to his table and you want to go, eat whatever is placed before you, without raising any question of conscience. 28 But if someone should say to you, "This was offered in idol worship," do not eat it, both for the sake of the one who called attention to it and on account of the conscience issue— 29 not your own conscience but your neighbor's. You may ask, Why should my liberty be restricted by another man's conscience? 30 And why is it, if I partake thankfully, that I should be blamed for the food over which I gave thanks?

Conclusion

31 The fact is that whether you eat or drink—whatever you do—you should do all for the glory of God. 32 Give no offense to Jew or Greek or to the church of God, 33 just as I try to please all in any way I can by seeking, not my own advantage, but that of the many, that they may be saved.

11

1 Imitate me as I imitate Christ.

CONDUCT AT PUBLIC WORSHIP

Headdress of Women

2 I praise you because you always remember me and are holding fast to the traditions just as I handed them on to you. 3 I want you to know that the head of every man is Christ; the head of a woman is her husband; and the head of Christ is the Father. 4 Any man who prays or prophesies with his head covered brings shame upon his head. 5 Similarly, any woman who prays or prophesies with her head uncovered brings shame upon her head. It is as if she had had her head shaved. 6 Indeed, if a woman will not wear a veil, she ought to cut off her hair. If it is shameful for a woman to have her hair cut off or her head shaved, it is clear that she ought to wear a veil. 7 A man, on the other hand, ought not to cover his head, because he is the image of God and the reflection of his glory. 8 Woman, in turn, is the reflection of man's glory. Man was not made from woman but woman from man. 9 Neither was man created for woman but woman for man. 10 For this reason a woman ought to have a sign of submission on her head, because of the angels. 11 Yet, in the Lord, woman is not independent of man nor man independent of woman. 12 In the same way that woman was made from man, so man is born of woman; and all is from God. 13 I will let you judge for yourselves. Is it proper for a woman to pray to God unveiled? 14 Does not nature itself teach you that it is dishonorable for a man to wear his hair long, while the long hair of a woman is her glory? 15 Her hair has been given her for a covering. 16 If anyone wants to argue about this, remember that neither we nor the churches of God recognize any other usage.

10, 14–22: Paul repudiates idol-worship on the ground of the meaning of the Eucharist: it is the Christian sacrifice that effects union with the living Christ. Although the pagan sacrifices aim at a union with the gods, in the light of Christian teaching they are seen to serve only the cause of evil.

10, 23—11, 1: See note on Romans 14, 1—15, 6.

11, 2–16: The apostle regards the independence of the Corinthian women who participate in worship with unveiled heads as a lack of humility, since a woman's veil is regarded as a sign of dependence on the authority of her husband. Paul's argument is based on his view of nature and on propriety, i.e., the custom of the earliest Christian communities.

The Lord's Supper

17 What I now have to say is not said in praise, because your meetings are not profitable but harmful. 18 First of all, I hear that when you gather for a meeting there are divisions among you, and I am inclined to believe it. 19 There may even have to be factions among you for the tried and true to stand out clearly. 20 When you assemble it is not to eat the Lord's Supper, 21 for everyone is in haste to eat his own supper. One person goes hungry while another gets drunk. 22 Do you not have homes where you can eat and drink? Would you show contempt for the church of God, and embarrass those who have nothing? What can I say to you? Shall I praise you? Certainly not in this matter!

23 I received from the Lord what I handed on to you, namely, that the Lord Jesus on the night in which he was betrayed took bread, 24 and after he had given thanks, broke it and said, "This is my body, which is for you. Do this in remembrance of me." 25 In the same way, after the supper, he took the cup, saying, "This cup is the new covenant in my blood. Do this, whenever you drink it, in remembrance of me." 26 Every time, then, you eat this bread and drink this cup, you proclaim the death of the Lord until he comes! 27 This means that whoever eats the bread or drinks the cup of the Lord unworthily sins against the body and blood of the Lord. 28 A man should examine himself first; only then should he eat of the bread and drink of the cup. 29 He who eats and drinks without recognizing the body eats and drinks a judgment on himself. 30 That is why many among you are sick and infirm, and why so many are dying. 31 If we were to examine ourselves, we would not be falling under judgment in this way; 32 but since it is the Lord who judges us, he chastens us to keep us from being condemned with the rest of the world. 33 Therefore, my brothers, when you assemble for the meal, wait for one another. 34 If anyone is hungry let him eat at home, so that your assembly may not deserve condemnation. As for other matters, I shall give instructions when I come.

SPIRITUAL GIFTS

Variety and Unity

12 Now, brothers, I do not want to leave you in ignorance about spiritual gifts. 2 You know that when you were pagans you were led astray to mute idols, as impulse drove you. 3 That is why I tell you that nobody who speaks in the Spirit of God ever says, "Cursed be Jesus." And no one can say: "Jesus is Lord," except in the Holy Spirit.

4 There are different gifts but the same Spirit; 5 there are different ministries but the same Lord; 6 there are different works but the same God who accomplishes all of them in everyone. 7 To each person the manifestation of the Spirit is given for the common good. 8 To one the Spirit gives wisdom in discourse, to another the power to express knowledge. 9 Through the Spirit one receives faith; by the same Spirit another is given the gift of healing, 10 and still another miraculous powers. Prophecy is given to one; to another power to distinguish one spirit from another. One receives the gift of tongues, another that of interpreting the tongues. 11 But it is one and the same Spirit who produces all these gifts, distributing them to each as he wills.

Analogy of the Body

12 The body is one and has many members, but all the members, many though they are, are one body; 13 and so it is with Christ. It was in one Spirit that all of us, whether Jew or Greek, slave or free, were baptized into one body. All of us have been given to drink of the one Spirit. 14 Now the body is not one member, it is many. 15 If the foot should say, "Because I am not a hand I do not belong to the body," would it then no longer belong to the body? 16 If the ear should say, "Because I am not an eye I do not belong to the body," would it then no longer belong to the body? 17 If the body were all eye, what would happen to our hearing? If it were all ear, what would happen to our smelling? 18 As it is, God has set each member of the body in the place he wanted it to be. 19 If all the members were alike, where would the body be? 20 There are, indeed, many different members, but one body. 21 The eye cannot say to the hand, "I do not need you," any more than the head can say to the feet, "I do not need you." 22 Even those members of the body which seem less important are in fact indispensable. 23 We honor the members we consider less honorable by clothing them with greater care, 24 thus bestowing on the less presentable a propriety which the more presentable already have. God has so constructed the body as to give greater honor to the lowly members, 25 that there may be no dissension in the body, but that all the members may be concerned for one another. 26 If one member suffers, all the members suffer with it; if one member is honored, all the members share its joy.

The One Body of Christ

27 You, then, are the body of Christ. Every one of you is a member of it. 28 Furthermore, God has set up in the church first apostles, second prophets, third teachers, then

---

11, 17–34: Paul concerns himself with the proper celebration of the eucharistic liturgy (33f). He has become aware that at the agape preceding the celebration of the Eucharist, the mutual charity of sharing food and companionship is being violated through discrimination against the needy (21f). Moreover, even drunkenness has not been unknown (21). In this earliest written account of the Lord's Supper Paul emphasizes its sacrificial aspect, i.e., the proclamation of Jesus' death in atonement for sin (23–26). Participation in this mystery requires a clean conscience (27ff). Abuse of the mystery on the part of some is the cause of their punishment through illness and death (30ff).

12, 1—14, 40: Here Paul speaks of special spiritual gifts (charisms) enabling individuals to exercise an office or function within the community. He provides a list of charisms in 12, 8ff (cf Rom 12, 6ff; Eph 4, 11) which he wishes to be recognized as a manifestation of the presence of the Holy Spirit (3–11), each contributing in its own way to the good of the whole community (12–30). (Paul does not value the charisms for their own sake, since Christian love is the only enduring gift of God; cf 12, 31—13, 13). Corinthians may lawfully desire to possess the charisms, but they should aspire especially to the gift of prophecy (probably, the gift of directing the community in new situations, and of revealing what could not otherwise be known; cf 14, 3.30; Acts 13, 1f). The apostle criticizes the overstressing of the gift of tongues (probably ecstatic utterances requiring an interpreter; cf 14, 1–25), and directs that this gift be employed only when an interpreter is present. At the assembly no more than three persons, not including women, are to act on the basis of a charism (26–40).

miracle workers, healers, assistants, administrators, and those who speak in tongues. 29 Are all apostles? Are all prophets? Are all teachers? Do all work miracles 30 or have the gift of healing? Do all speak in tongues, all have the gift of interpretation of tongues? 31 Set your hearts on the greater gifts.

Excellence of the Gift of Love

13 Now I will show you the way which surpasses all the others. 1 If I speak with human tongues and angelic as well, but do not have love, I am a noisy gong, a clanging cymbal. 2 If I have the gift of prophecy and, with full knowledge, comprehend all mysteries, if I have faith great enough to move mountains, but have not love, I am nothing. 3 If I give everything I have to feed the poor and hand over my body to be burned, but have not love, I gain nothing.

4 Love is patient; love is kind. Love is not jealous, it does not put on airs, it is not snobbish. Love is never rude, it is not self-seeking, it is not prone to anger; neither does it brood over injuries. 6 Love does not rejoice in what is wrong but rejoices with the truth. 7 There is no limit to love's forbearance, to its trust, its hope, its power to endure.

8 Love never fails. Prophecies will cease, tongues will be silent, knowledge will pass away. 9 Our knowledge is imperfect and our prophesying is imperfect. 10 When the perfect comes, the imperfect will pass away. 11 When I was a child I used to talk like a child, think like a child, reason like a child. When I became a man I put childish ways aside. 12 Now we see indistinctly, as in a mirror; then we shall see face to face. My knowledge is imperfect now; then I shall know even as I am known. 13 There are in the end three things that last: faith, hope, and love, and the greatest of these is love.

Gift of Prophecy

14 Seek eagerly after love. Set your hearts on spiritual gifts— above all, the gift of prophecy. 2 A man who speaks in a tongue is talking not to men but to God. No

one understands him, because he utters mysteries in the Spirit. 3 The prophet, on the other hand, speaks to men for their upbuilding, their encouragement, their consolation. 4 He who speaks in a tongue builds up himself, but he who prophesies builds up the church. 5 I should like it if all of you spoke in tongues, but I much prefer that you prophesy. The prophet is greater than one who speaks in tongues, unless the speaker can also interpret for the upbuilding of the church.

Interpretation of Tongues

6 Just suppose, brothers, that I should come to you speaking in tongues. What good will I do you if my speech does not have some revelation, or knowledge, or prophecy, or instruction for you? 7 Even in the case of lifeless things which produce a sound, such as a flute or a harp, how will anyone know what is being played if there is no distinction among the notes? 8 If the bugle's sound is uncertain, who will get ready for battle? 9 Similarly, if you do not utter intelligible speech because you are speaking in a tongue, how will anyone know what you are saying? You will be talking to the air. 10 There are many different languages in the world and all are marked by sound; 11 but if I do not know the meaning, I shall be a foreigner to the speaker and he a foreigner to me. 12 Since you have set your hearts on spiritual gifts, try to be rich in those that build up the church.

13 This means that the man who speaks in a tongue should pray for the gift of interpretation. 14 If I pray in a tongue my spirit is at prayer but my mind contributes nothing. 15 What is my point here? I want to pray with my spirit, and also to pray with my mind. I want to sing with my spirit and with my mind as well. 16 If your praise of God is solely with the spirit, how will the one who does not comprehend be able to say "Amen" to your thanksgiving? He will not know what you are saying. 17 You will be uttering praise very well indeed, but the other man will not be helped. 18 Thank God, I speak in tongues more than

any of you, 19 but in the church I would rather say five intelligible words to instruct others than ten thousand words in a tongue.

Function of These Gifts

20 Brothers, do not be childish in your outlook. Be like children as far as evil is concerned, but in mind be mature. 21 It is written in the law, "In strange tongues and in alien speech I will speak to this people, and even so they will not heed me, says the Lord." 22 The gift of tongues is a sign, not for those who believe but for those who do not believe, while prophecy is not for those who are without faith but for those who have faith. 23 If the uninitiated or unbelievers should come in when the whole church is assembled and everyone is speaking in tongues, would they not say that you are out of your minds? 24 But if an unbeliever or an uninitiate enters while all are uttering prophecy, he will be taken to task by all and called to account by all, and the secret of his heart will be laid bare. Falling prostrate, he will worship God, crying out, "God is truly among you."

Rules of Order

26 What do we propose, brothers? When you assemble, one has a psalm, another some instruction to give, still another a revelation to share; one speaks in a tongue, another interprets. All well and good, so long as everything is done with a constructive purpose. 27 If any are going to talk in tongues let it be at most two or three, each in turn, with another to interpret what they are saying. 28 But if there is no one to interpret, there should be silence in the assembly, each one speaking only to himself and to God. 29 Let no more than two or three prophets speak, and let the rest judge the worth of what they say. 30 If another, sitting by, should happen to receive a revelation, the first ones should then keep quiet. 31 You can all speak your prophecies, but one by one, so that all may be instructed and encouraged. 32 The spirits of the prophets are under the prophet's control, 33 since God is

---

13, 1–13: See notes on 1 John 4, 7—5, 45.

a God, not of confusion, but of peace.

34 According to the rule observed in all the assemblies of believers, women should keep silent in such gatherings. They may not speak. Rather, as the law states, submissiveness is indicated for them. 35 If they want to learn anything, they should ask their husbands at home. It is a disgrace when a woman speaks in the assembly. 36 Did the preaching of God's word originate with you? Are you the only ones to whom it has come?

37 If anyone thinks he is a prophet or a man of the Spirit, he should know that what I have written you is the Lord's commandment. 38 If anyone ignores it, he in turn should be ignored. 39 Set your hearts on prophecy, my brothers, and do not forbid those who speak in tongues, 40 but make sure that everything is done properly and in order.

THE RESURRECTION

Christ's Resurrection

15 Brothers, I want to remind you of the gospel I preached to you, which you received and in which you stand firm. 2 You are being saved by it at this very moment if you hold fast to it as I preached it to you. Otherwise you have believed in vain. 3 I handed on to you first of all what I myself received, that Christ died for our sins in accordance with the Scriptures; 4 that he was buried and, in accordance with the Scriptures, rose on the third day; 5 that he was seen by Cephas, then by the Twelve. 6 After that he was seen by five hundred brothers at once, most of whom are still alive, although some have fallen asleep. 7 Next he was seen by James; then by all the apostles. 8 Last of all he was seen by me, as one born out of the normal course. 9 I am the least of the apostles; in fact, because I persecuted the church of God, I do not even

deserve the name. 10 But by God's favor I am what I am. This favor of his to me has not proved fruitless. Indeed, I have worked harder than all the others, not on my own but through the favor of God. 11 In any case, whether it be I or they, this is what we preach and this is what you believed.

The Resurrection and Faith

12 Tell me, if Christ is preached as raised from the dead, how is it that some of you say there is no resurrection of the dead? 13 If there is no resurrection of the dead, Christ himself has not been raised. 14 And if Christ has not been raised, our preaching is void of content and your faith is empty too. 15 Indeed, we should then be exposed as false witnesses of God, for we have borne witness before him that he raised up Christ; but he certainly did not raise him up if the dead are not raised. 16 Why? Because if the dead are not raised, then Christ was not raised; 17 and if Christ was not raised, your faith is worthless. You are still in your sins, 18 and those who have fallen asleep in Christ are the deadest of the dead. 19 If our hopes in Christ are limited to this life only, we are the most pitiable of men.

Christ, the First Fruits

20 But as it is, Christ is now raised from the dead, the first fruits of those who have fallen asleep. 21 Death came through a man; hence the resurrection of the dead comes through a man also. 22 Just as in Adam all die, so in Christ all will come to life again, 23 but each one in proper order: Christ the first fruits and then, at his coming, all those who belong to him. 24 After that will come the end, when, after having destroyed every sovereignty, authority, and power, he will hand over the kingdom to God the Father. 25 Christ must reign until God has put all enemies under his feet, 26 and

the last enemy to be destroyed is death. 27 Scripture reads that God "has placed all things under his feet." But when it says that everything has been made subject, it is clear that he who has made everything subject to Christ is excluded. 28 When, finally, all has been subjected to the Son, he will then subject himself to the One who made all things subject to him, so that God may be all in all.

Practical Faith

29 If the dead are not raised, what about those who have themselves baptized on behalf of the dead? If the raising of the dead is not a reality, why be baptized on their behalf? 30 And why are we continually putting ourselves in danger? 31 I swear to you, brothers, by the very pride you take in me, which I cherish in Christ Jesus our Lord, that I face death every day. 32 If I fought those beasts at Ephesus for purely human motives, what profit was there for me? If the dead are not raised, "Let us eat and drink, for tomorrow we die!" 33 Do not be led astray any longer. "Bad company corrupts good morals." Return to reason, as you ought, and stop sinning. 34 Some of you are quite ignorant of God; I say it to your shame.

Manner of the Resurrection

35 Perhaps someone will say, "How are the dead to be raised up? What kind of body will they have?" 36 A nonsensical question! The seed you sow does not germinate unless it dies. 37 When you sow, you do not sow the full-blown plant, but a kernel of wheat or some other grain. God gives body to it as he pleases— 38 to each seed its own fruition. 39 Not all bodily nature is the same. Men have one kind of body, animals another. Birds are of their kind, fish are of theirs. 40 There are heavenly bodies and there are earthly bodies. The splendor of the heavenly bodies is one thing, that of the earthly

---

15, 1–58: This exposition of the Christian doctrine of the resurrection of the dead in Christ was prompted by the belief among some of the Corinthians that the resurrection of the body was impossible (12, 35), though apparently they did not deny the resurrection of Christ (v 12). Paul takes up the issue by listing the divinely appointed witnesses to the resurrection (1–11). He develops its significance as revealing God's plan to raise the dead (12–28), belief in which has been a basic Christian incentive. It encourages the apostles in the face of the hardships of their ministry, and has even occasioned the practice in Corinth of baptism on behalf of the dead (29–34). Those who reject the doctrine of resurrection because of the fact of bodily corruption fail to understand the mystery of God's creative activity, which provides the kind of body suited to the new life after death (35–49). The risen body of man will be a body so changed by the power of God as to be immortal (50–53). Christ died for sin, which is the cause of man's death (Gn 3, 19); he rose from the dead to be the cause of man's resurrection (54–58).

another. 41 The sun has a splendor of its own, so has the moon, and the stars have theirs. Even among the stars, one differs from another in brightness. 42 So it is with the resurrection of the dead. What is sown in the earth is subject to decay, what rises is incorruptible. 43 What is sown is ignoble, what rises is glorious. Weakness is sown, strength rises up. 44 A natural body is put down and a spiritual body comes up.

The Natural and the Spiritual Body

45 If there is a natural body, be sure there is also a spiritual body. Scripture has it that Adam, the first man, became a living soul; the last Adam has become a life-giving spirit. 46 Take note, the spiritual was not first; first came the natural and after that the spiritual. 47 The first man was of earth, formed from dust, the second is from heaven. 48 Earthly men are like the man of earth, heavenly men are like the man of heaven. 49 Just as we resemble the man from earth, so shall we bear the likeness of the man from heaven.

Glorification of the Body

50 This is what I mean, brothers: flesh and blood cannot inherit the kingdom of God; no more can corruption inherit incorruption. 51 Now I am going to tell you a mystery. Not all of us shall fall asleep, but all of us are to be changed— 52 in an instant, in the twinkling of an eye, at the sound of the last trumpet. The trumpet will sound and the dead will be raised incorruptible, and we shall be changed. 53 This corruptible body must be clothed with incorruptibility, this

mortal body with immortality. 54 When the corruptible frame takes on incorruptibility and the mortal immortality, then will the saying of Scripture be fulfilled: "Death is swallowed up in victory." 55 "O death, where is your victory? O death, where is your sting?" 56 The sting of death is sin, and sin gets its power from the law. 57 But thanks be to God who has given us the victory through our Lord Jesus Christ. 58 Be steadfast and persevering, my beloved brothers, fully engaged in the work of the Lord. You know that your toil is not in vain when it is done in the Lord.

The Collection

16 About the collection for the saints, follow the instructions I gave the churches of Galatia. 2 On the first day of each week everyone should put aside whatever he has been able to save, so that the collection will not have to be taken up after I arrive. 3 When I come I shall give letters of introduction to those whom you have chosen to take your gift to Jerusalem. 4 If it seems fitting that I should go myself, they will accompany me.

Paul's Plans

5 I shall come to you after I have passed through Macedonia. 6 If it is at all possible, I should like to remain with you for some time—even to spend the winter with you—that you may provide me with what I need for the rest of my journey. 7 I do not want to see you just in passing. I hope to spend some time with you, if the Lord permits. 8 I intend to stay in Ephesus until Pentecost. 9 A door has been opened wide for my

work, but at the same time there are many opposed. 10 If Timothy should come, be sure to put him at ease among you. He does the Lord's work just as I do, 11 so let no one treat him disdainfully. Rather, help him come to me by sending him on his way in peace. I am expecting him with the brothers. 12 As for our brother Apollos, I urged him strongly to go to you with the brothers, but he did not wish to go at this time. He will go when circumstances are more favorable.

Directions and Greetings

13 Be on your guard, stand firm in the faith, and act like men. 14 In a word, be strong. Do everything with love. 15 You know that the household of Stephanas is the first fruits of Achaia and is devoted to the service of the saints. 16 I urge you to serve under such men and under everyone who cooperates and toils with them. 17 I was very happy at the arrival of Stephanas, Fortunatus, and Achaicus, because they made up for your absence. 18 They have refreshed my spirit as they did yours. You should recognize the worth of such men.

19 The churches of Asia send you greetings. Aquila and Prisca, together with the assembly that meets in their house, send you cordial greetings in the Lord. 20 All the brothers greet you. Greet one another with a holy kiss.

21 It is I, Paul, who send you this greeting in my own hand. 22 If anyone does not love the Lord, let a curse be upon him. O Lord, come! 23 The favor of the Lord Jesus be with you. 24 My love to all of you in Christ Jesus.

16, 1: This collection taken up for the poor Christians of Jerusalem is elsewhere referred to (Acts 24, 17; Rom 15, 26ff; 2 Cor 8, 1—9, 15; Gal 2, 10). Paul is especially interested in it as an opportunity to break down the barriers between Jew and Gentile.

16, 22: *O Lord, come!: Maranatha:* an Aramaic expression, reflected also in Rv 22, 20, probably used in the Christian liturgy of the time. It may be read as a prayer for the arrival of the second coming of Christ: *Marana tha,* "Lord, come"; or as an expres-

sion of hope in the proximity of the parousia, *Maran atha,* "The Lord is coming." See note on 1 Thes 4, 13—18.

THE SECOND EPISTLE OF PAUL TO THE

Corinthians

Greeting to the Church

PAUL, by God's will an apostle of Jesus Christ, and Timothy his brother, to the church of God that is at Corinth and to all the holy ones of the church who live in Achaia. 2 Grace and peace from God our Father and the Lord Jesus Christ.

Thanksgiving after Affliction

3 Praised be God, the Father of our Lord Jesus Christ, the Father of mercies, and the God of all consolation! 4 He comforts us in all our afflictions and thus enables us to comfort those who are in trouble, with the same consolation we have received from him. 5 As we have shared much in the suffering of Christ, so through Christ do we share abundantly in his consolation. 6 If we are afflicted it is for your encouragement and salvation, and when we are consoled it is for your consolation, so that you may endure patiently the same sufferings we endure. 7 Our hope for you is firm because we know that just as you share in the sufferings, so you will share in the consolation.

8 Brothers, we do not wish to leave you in the dark about the trouble we had in Asia; we were crushed beyond our strength, even to the point of despairing of life. 9 We were left to feel like men condemned to death so that we might trust, not in ourselves, but in God who raises the dead. 10 He rescued us from that danger of death and will continue to do so. We have put our hope in him who will never cease to deliver us. 11 But you must help us with your prayers, so that on our behalf God may be thanked for the gift granted us through the prayers of so many.

Paul's Sincerity

12 Conscience gives testimony to the boast that in our behavior toward all and especially toward you we have always acted from God-given holiness and candor; this has been prompted, not by debased human wisdom, but by God's goodness. 13 We never write anything that you cannot read and understand. I hope that, just as you know us to a certain degree already, you will in time come to know us well, 14 and will recognize that we shall be your boast, and you ours, on the day of our Lord Jesus.

15 Confident as I am about this, I wanted to visit you first so that a double grace might be yours. 16 I planned to visit you, both on my way to Macedonia and on my return, that I might receive your help on my journey to Judea. 17 Do you suppose that in making those plans I was acting insincerely? Or that my plans are so determined by self-interest that I change my mind from one minute to the next? 18 As God keeps his word, I declare that my word to you is not "yes" one minute and "no"

1, 1f: See note on Rom 1, 1–7.
1, 3–11: Paul gives thanks to God, as he informs the Corinthians that he has been relieved of the serious troubles he experienced in the province of Asia Minor, and is now at peace. The community was evidently aware of the apostle's difficulties, but their nature is now unknown.

1, 5: The sufferings of Paul are identified with those of Christ, for whom they are endured; the consolation he receives is shared with the Christians at Corinth.
1, 12—2, 4: Paul answers the criticism leveled against him for having twice planned and twice failed to visit the Corinthians (1, 15f). He denies that

his original plan failed for any but apostolic reasons (1, 17–22), namely, lack of favorable circumstances to discharge his office peaceably. Instead of visiting the Corinthians he sent them a severe letter which caused them distress (2, 3; cf 7, 8), for it was weighted with his own anguish over the situation in their community (2, 4).

the next. Jesus Christ, 19 whom Silvanus, Timothy, and I preached to you as Son of God, was not alternately "yes" and "no"; he was never anything but "yes." 20 Whatever promises God has made have been fulfilled in him; therefore it is through him that we address our Amen to God when we worship together. 21 God is the one who firmly establishes us along with you in Christ; it is he who anointed us 22 and has sealed us, thereby depositing the first payment, the Spirit in our hearts.

23 I call on God as my witness that it was out of consideration for you that I did not come to Corinth again. 24 Domineering over your faith is not my purpose. I prefer to work with you toward your happiness. As regards faith, you are standing firm. 1 I did decide, however, not to visit you again in painful circumstances. 2 For if I cause you pain, who can make me happy again but the ones I grieved? 3 I wrote as I did so that when I come I may not be saddened by those who should rejoice my heart. I know you all well enough to be convinced that my happiness is yours. 4 That is why I wrote you in great sorrow and anguish, with copious tears—not to make you sad but to help you realize the great love I bear you.

Forgiveness for the Offender

5 If anyone has given offense he has hurt not only me, but in some measure, to say no more, every one of you. 6 The punishment already inflicted by the majority on such a one is enough; 7 you should now relent and support him so that he may not be crushed by too great a weight of sorrow. 8 I therefore beg you to reaffirm your love for him. 9 The reason I wrote you was to test you and learn whether you are obedient in all matters. 10 If you forgive a man anything, so do I. Any forgiving I have done has been for

your sakes and, before Christ, 11 to prevent Satan—whose guile we know too well—from outwitting us.

Paul's Anxiety and Relief

12 When I came to Troas to preach the gospel of Christ, the door of opportunity was opened wide for me by the Lord. 13 Yet I was inwardly troubled because I did not find my brother Titus there. So I said good-bye to them and went off to Macedonia. 14 Thanks be to God, who unfailingly leads us on in Christ's triumphal train, and employs us to diffuse the fragrance of his knowledge everywhere! 15 We are an aroma of Christ for God's sake, both among those who are being saved and those on the way to destruction; 16 to the latter an odor dealing death, to the former a breath bringing life. 17 We at least are not like so many who trade on the word of God. We speak in Christ's name, pure in motivation, conscious of having been sent by God and of standing in his presence.

Ministers of the New Covenant

3 Am I beginning to speak well of myself again? Or do I need letters of recommendation to you or from you as others might? 2 You are my letter, known and read by all men, written on your hearts. 3 Clearly you are a letter of Christ which I have delivered, a letter written not with ink but by the Spirit of the living God, not on tablets of stone but on tablets of flesh in the heart.

4 This great confidence in God is ours, through Christ. 5 It is not that we are entitled of ourselves to take credit for anything. Our sole credit is from God, 6 who has made us qualified ministers of a new covenant, a covenant not of a written law but of spirit. The written law kills, but the Spirit gives life.

7 If the ministry of death, carved in writing on stone, was inaugurated with such glory that the Israelites

could not look on Moses' face because of the glory that shone on it (even though it was a fading glory), 8 how much greater will be the glory of the ministry of the Spirit? 9 If the ministry of the covenant that condemned had glory, greater by far is the glory of the ministry that justifies. 10 Indeed, when you compare that limited glory with this surpassing glory, the former should be declared no glory at all. 11 If what was destined to pass away was given in glory, greater by far is the glory that endures.

12 Our hope being such, we speak with full confidence. 13 We are not like Moses, who used to hide his face with a veil so that the Israelites could not see the final fading of that glory. 14 Their minds, of course, were dulled. To this very day, when the old covenant is read the veil remains unlifted; it is only in Christ that it is taken away. 15 Even now, when Moses is read a veil covers their understanding. 16 "But whenever he turns to the Lord, the veil is removed." 17 The Lord is the Spirit, and where the Spirit of the Lord is, there is freedom. 18 All of us, gazing on the Lord's glory with unveiled faces, are being transformed from glory to glory into his very image by the Lord who is the Spirit.

Treasure in Earthen Vessels

4 Because we possess this ministry through God's mercy, we do not give in to discouragement. 2 Rather, we repudiate shameful, underhanded practices. We do not resort to trickery or falsify the word of God. We proclaim the truth openly and commend ourselves to every man's conscience before God. 3 If our gospel can be called "veiled" in any sense, it is such only for those who are headed toward destruction. 4 Their unbelieving minds have been blinded by the god of the present age so that they do not see the splendor of the gospel showing fourth the

---

1, 22: *First payment:* on full messianic benefits; cf Eph 1, 13f.

2, 5–11: Some scholars believe that the person alluded to here rejected Paul's authority, thereby scandalizing many in the community. It is clear that these latter took action against him, and the apostle now recommends that the punishment be terminated.

2, 14—4, 18: Paul wishes to convince the Corinthians that his actions toward them were motivated, not by selfish reasons, but by apostolic concern. This leads him to a series of reflections on the apostolic office: his effectiveness as an apostle derives from Christ (2, 14–17); his achievements are supported by the Holy Spirit (3, 1ff); his qualifications for the

apostolate are gifts of God; and his ministry of the justifying power of God is superior to that of the Mosaic covenant (3, 4–11). The apostle knows that his work is to result in the permanent presence of Christ among men through the power of the Holy Spirit (3, 13–18).

glory of Christ, the image of God. 5 It is not ourselves we preach but Christ Jesus as Lord, and ourselves as your servants for Jesus' sake. 6 For God, who said, "Let light shine out of darkness," has shone in our hearts, that we in turn might make known the glory of God shining on the face of Christ. 7 This treasure we possess in earthen vessels to make it clear that its surpassing power comes from God and not from us. 8 We are afflicted in every way possible, but we are not crushed; full of doubts, we never despair. 9 We are persecuted but never abandoned; we are struck down but never destroyed. 10 Continually we carry about in our bodies the dying of Jesus, so that in our bodies the life of Jesus may also be revealed. 11 While we live we are constantly being delivered to death for Jesus' sake, so that the life of Jesus may be revealed in our mortal flesh. 12 Death is at work in us, but life in you. 13 We have that spirit of faith of which the Scripture says, "Because I believed, I spoke out." We believe and so we speak, 14 knowing that he who raised up the Lord Jesus will raise us up along with Jesus and place both us and you in his presence. 15 Indeed, everything is ordered to your benefit, so that the grace bestowed in abundance may bring greater glory to God because they who give thanks are many.

Living by Faith

16 We do not lose heart, because our inner being is renewed each day even though our body is being destroyed at the same time. 17 The present burden of our trial is light enough, and earns for us an eternal weight of glory beyond all comparison. 18 We do not fix our gaze on what is seen but on what is unseen.

What is seen is transitory; what is unseen lasts forever.

5 Indeed, we know that when the earthly tent in which we dwell is destroyed we have a dwelling provided for us by God, a dwelling in the heavens, not made by hands but to last forever. 2 We groan while we are here, even as we yearn to have our heavenly habitation envelop us. 3 This it will, provided we are found clothed and not naked. 4 While we live in our present tent we groan; we are weighed down because we do not wish to be stripped naked but rather to have the heavenly dwelling envelop us, so that what is mortal may be absorbed by life. 5 God has fashioned us for this very thing and has given us the spirit as a pledge of it.

6 Therefore we continue to be confident. We know that while we dwell in the body we are away from the Lord. 7 We walk by faith, not by sight. 8 I repeat, we are full of confidence and would much rather be away from the body and at home with the Lord. 9 This being so, we make it our aim to please him whether we are with him or away from him. 10 The lives of all of us are to be revealed before the tribunal of Christ so that each one may receive his recompense, good or bad, according to his life in the body.

Ministry of Reconciliation

11 Standing in awe of the Lord we try to persuade men, but what we are is known to God. I hope that it is also known to you in your consciences. 12 We shall not begin to recommend ourselves to you again, but we are giving you an opportunity to boast about us so that you may have something to say to those who take pride in external appearances, and

not in what lies in the heart. 13 Indeed, if we are every caught up out of ourselves, God is the reason; and when we are brought back to our senses, it is for your sakes. 14 The love of Christ impels us who have reached the conviction that since one died for all, all died. 15 He died for all so that those who live might live no longer for themselves, but for him who for their sakes died and was raised up.

16 Because of this we no longer look on anyone in terms of mere human judgment. If at one time we so regarded Christ, we no longer know him by this standard. 17 This means that if anyone is in Christ, he is a new creation. The old order has passed away; now all is new! 18 All this has been done by God, who has reconciled us to himself through Christ and has given us the ministry of reconciliation. 19 I mean that God, in Christ, was reconciling the world to himself, not counting men's transgressions against them, and that he has entrusted the message of reconciliation to us. 20 This makes us ambassadors for Christ, God as it were appealing through us. We implore you, in Christ's name: be reconciled to God! 21 For our sakes God made him who did not know sin to be sin, so that in him we might become the very holiness of God.

6 As your fellow workers we beg you not to receive the grace of God in vain. 2 For he says, "In an acceptable time I have heard you; on a day of salvation I have helped you." Now is the acceptable time! Now is the day of salvation! 3 We avoid giving anyone offense, so that our ministry may not be blamed. 4 On the contrary, in all that we do we strive to present ourselves as minis-

---

4, 1–6: The power of the gospel is divine; the apostle, therefore, has no need to modify it to make it acceptable to men (1f). It is men who blind themselves to the light of Christ (3–6).

4, 7–12: The apostle's sufferings reenact the life of Jesus, both as a sign and as an instrument of the divine life he ministers to men.

4, 13f: Paul lives through faith in his own future resurrection and that of his fellow Christians. *He . . . will raise us up:* this may imply that Paul did not expect to be alive at the parousia; cf 1 Cor 15, 51–55.

4, 16ff: Though the apostle's physical forces are being spent. his soul is renewed daily through living the Christ life and meriting that transformation of soul and body after death in which transitory realities

are exchanged for those that are eternal; cf 1 Cor 15, 42ff.

5, 6–9: Paul comforts himself with the thought that his present existence is in a sense an exile from Christ, whereas death brings life with Christ through the possession of heavenly glory.

5, 11–6, 14: Paul trusts that his dispositions, known to God, may also be recognized by the Corinthians whom he serves, so that they in turn can answer his critics (5, 11f). In his dealings with people, he is motivated by love for Christ (5, 14). To delve into his past might reveal that he once entertained mistaken ideas about the Savior (5, 16). This may be the meaning of looking upon Christ *in terms of mere human judgment.* But the apostle, like other Christians

is also a new man; reconciled to God through Christ, he is given the special mission of serving as Christ's ambassador, the essential purpose of his own personal renewal by God (5, 17–21). His mission is to appeal to men to accept God's salvation in Christ (6, 1f), a task he tries to perform with the greatest possible discretion. The attempt nevertheless produces personal hardships and social upheavals, even though all that he strives to offer is God's word and power (6, 3–10). In conclusion, Paul asks of the Corinthians that they be as open to him in acceptance of his ministry as he has been frank and loving toward them (6, 11ff; cf 7, 2).

ters of God, acting with patient endurance amid trials, difficulties, distresses, 5 beatings, imprisonments, and riots; as men familiar with hard work, sleepless nights, and fastings; 6 conducting ourselves with innocence, knowledge, and patience, in the Holy Spirit, in sincere love; 7 as men with the message of truth and the power of God; wielding the weapons of righteousness with right hand and left, 8 whether honored or dishonored, spoken of well or ill. We are called imposters, yet we are truthful; 9 nobodies who in fact are well known; dead, yet here we are, alive; punished, but not put to death; 10 sorrowful, though we are always rejoicing; poor, yet we enrich many. We seem to have nothing, yet everything is ours!

11 Men of Corinth, we have spoken to you frankly, opening our hearts wide to you. 12 There is no lack of room for you in us; the narrowness is in you. 13 In fair exchange, then (I speak as a father to his children), open wide your hearts!

The Temple of the Living God

14 Do not yoke yourselves in a mismatch with unbelievers. After all what do righteousness and lawlessness have in common, or what fellowship can light have with darkness? 15 What accord is there between Christ and Belial, what common lot between believer and unbeliever? 16 Tell me what agreement there is between the temple of God and idols. You are the temple of the living God, just as God has said:

"I will dwell with them and
　　walk among them.
I will be their God
and they shall be my people.
17 Therefore, 'Come out from
　　among them
and separate yourselves from
　　them,' says the Lord;
and touch nothing unclean.

18 I will welcome you and be a
　　father to you
and you will be my sons and
　　daughters,'
says the Lord Almighty."

7 Since we have these promises, beloved, let us purify ourselves from every defilement of flesh and spirit, and in the fear of God strive to fulfill our consecration perfectly.

Joy over Repentance

2 Make room for us in your hearts! We have injured no one, we have corrupted no one, we have cheated no one. 3 I do not condemn you. I have already said that you are in our hearts, even to the sharing of death and life together. 4 I speak to you with utter frankness and boast much about you. I am filled with consolation, and despite my many afflictions my joy knows no bounds.

5 When I arrived in Macedonia I was restless and exhausted. I was under all kinds of stress—quarrels with others and fears within myself. 6 But God, who gives heart to those who are low in spirit, gave me strength with the arrival of Titus. 7 This he did, not only by his arrival but by the reinforcement Titus had already received from you; for he reported your longing, your grief, and your ardent concern for me, so that my joy is greater still. 8 If I saddened you by my letter I have no regrets. Or if I did feel some regret (because I understand that the letter caused you grief for a time), 9 I am happy once again; not because you were saddened, but because your sadness led to repentence. You were filled with a sorrow that came from God; thus you did not suffer any loss from us. 10 Indeed, sorrow for God's sake produces a repentance without regrets, leading to salvation, whereas worldly sorrow brings death. 11 Just look at the fruit of this sorrow which stems from God. What a

measure of holy zeal it has brought you, not to speak of readiness to defend yourselves! What indignation, fear, and longing! What ardent desire to restore the balance of justice! In every way you have displayed your innocence in this matter. 12 Therefore, my writing to you was not intended for the man who had given the offense or for the one offended, but to make plain in the sight of God the devotion you have for us. 13 This done, we are comforted.

Beyond this consolation, we have rejoiced even more at the joy of Titus because his mind has been set at rest by all of you. 14 For though I had boasted to him about you, I was not put to shame. Rather, just as everything I ever said to you was true, so my boasting to Titus has been proved equally true. 15 His heart embraces you with an expanding love as he recalls the obedience you showed to God when you received him in fear and trembling. 16 I rejoice because I trust you utterly.

Liberal Giving

8 Brothers, I should like you to know of the grace of God conferred on the churches of Macedonia. 2 In the midst of severe trial their overflowing joy and deep poverty have produced an abundant generosity. 3 According to their means—indeed I can testify even beyond their means—and voluntarily, 4 they begged us insistently for the favor of sharing in this service to members of the church. 5 Beyond our hopes they first gave themselves to God and then to us by the will of God. 6 That is why I have exhorted Titus, who had already begun this work of charity among you, to bring it to successful completion: 7 that just as you are rich in every respect, in faith and discourse, in knowledge, in total concern, and in the love we bear you, so may you abound in this charity.

6, 14—7, 1: It is difficult to account for this passage in the present context. It has similarities with the Qumran literature, and may be an excerpt of a lost Pauline epistle.

7, 5–16: Paul resumes the thought from which he had digressed in 2, 13, completing the account of his meeting with Titus to discuss the community's reaction to his severe letter; see note on 1, 12—2, 4. He expresses genuine satisfaction over the steps they

have taken to correct what he had found objectionable in their conduct. The joy of Titus over their response to the apostles admonitions pleases Paul all the more and justifies his complete trust in them.

8, 1—9, 15: See note on 1 Corinthians 16, 1 concerning the collection spoken of here. No doubt the conflicts in Corinth to which this letter alludes were responsible for delaying this collection (8, 10). Paul here presents certain motives to the community for

completing it: they are to emulate the generosity of the Macedonians (8, 1–5) and imitate the poverty of Christ (8, 9); they too may at some time need the charity of others (8, 14). Paul plans to visit them and convey the generous fruit of their charity to the community in Jerusalem. Not only will it supply the needs of that church; it will be the cause of their giving thanks and glory to God and of obtaining God's favor for themselves (9, 6–15).

8 I am not giving an order but simply testing your generous love against the concern which others show. 9 You are well acquainted with the favor shown you by our Lord Jesus Christ: how for your sake he made himself poor though he was rich, so that you might become rich by his poverty. 10 I am about to give you some advice on this matter of rich and poor. It will help you who began this good work last year, not only to carry it through, but to do so willingly. 11 Carry it through now to a successful completion, so that your ready resolve may be matched by giving according to your means. 12 The willingness to give should accord with one's means, not go beyond them. 13 The relief of others ought not to impoverish you; there should be a certain equality. 14 Your plenty at the present time should supply their needs so that their surplus may one day supply your need, with equality as the result. 15 It is written, "He who gathered much had no excess and he who gathered little had no lack."

Titus and His Companions

16 Thanks be to God, who has put an equal zeal for you in the heart of Titus! 17 Not only did he welcome our appeal, but being very eager he has gone to you freely. 18 We have sent along with him that brother whom all the churches praise for his preaching of the gospel. 19 He has been appointed our traveling companion by the churches, as we willingly carry on this work of charity for the glory of the Lord. 20 There is one thing I wish to avoid, namely any blame over my handling of this generous collection. 21 We are concerned not only for God's approval but also for the good esteem of men. 22 We have sent along that brother whose eagerness has been proved to us in many ways. He is now more eager than ever for this work because of his great trust in you. 23 As for Titus, he is my companion and fellow worker in

your behalf; our brothers too are apostles of the churches, the glory of Christ. 24 Therefore, show these men the proof of your love, and why we boast about you, for all the churches to see.

The Offering for the Saints

9 There is really no need for me to write you about this collection for the members of the church. 2 I already know your willingness, and boast about you to the Macedonians with respect to it, saying that Achaia has been ready since last year. Your zeal has stirred up most of them. 3 I nonetheless send the brothers so that our claims for you in this regard may not be shown empty. I do so that you may be ready, as I have been saying you are, 4 lest any Macedonians come with me and find you unready; then I should be put to shame—to say nothing of you—for having had this trust. 5 I have thought it necessary to exhort the brothers to go to you and arrange in advance for the bountiful gift you have already promised. It should be ready as a gracious gift, not as an exaction.

6 Let me say this much: He who sows sparingly will reap sparingly, and he who sows bountifully will reap bountifully. 7 Everyone must give according to what he has inwardly decided; not sadly, not grudgingly, for God loves a cheerful giver. 8 God can multiply his favors among you so that you may always have enough of everything and even a surplus for good works, 9 as it is written:

"He scattered abroad and gave
　　to the poor,
　his justice endures forever."

10 He who supplies seed for the sower and bread for the eater will provide in abundance; he will multiply the seed you sow and increase your generous yield. 11 In every way your liberality is enriched; through us it results in thanks offered to God. 12 The administering of this public benefit not only supplies

the needs of the members of the church but also overflows in much gratitude to God. 13 Because of your praiseworthy service they are glorifying God for your obedient faith in the gospel of Christ, and for your generosity in sharing with them and with all. 14 They pray for you longingly because of the surpassing grace God has given you. 15 Thanks be to God for his indescribable gift!

Paul Defends His Ministry

10 I, Paul, exhort you by the meekness and kindness of Christ, I who (you say) when present in your midst am lowly, but when absent am bold toward you. 2 I beg you that when I am there, I may not have to act boldly, with that assurance I might dare to use courageously against certain ones who accuse us of weak human behavior. 3 We do indeed live in the body but we do not wage war with human resources. 4 The weapons of our warfare are not merely human. They possess God's power for the destruction of strongholds. 5 We demolish sophistries and every proud pretension that raises itself against the knowledge of God; we likewise bring every thought into captivity to make it obedient to Christ. 6 We are ready to punish disobedience in anyone else once your own obedience is perfect.

7 You view things superficially. If anyone is convinced that he belongs to Christ, let him reflect on this: he may belong to Christ but just as much do we. 8 If I find I must make a few further claims about the power the Lord has given us for your upbuilding and not for your destruction, this will not embarass me in the least. 9 At the same time, I do not wish to intimidate you with my letters. 10 His letters, they say, are severe and forceful, but when he is here in person he is unimpressive and his word makes no great impact. 11 Well, let such people give this some thought, that what we are by word,

---

10, 1–18: Since Paul's previous tone of gentleness changes in chapters 10 through 13 to one of aggressive criticism, some scholars conclude that these chapters belong to a lost Pauline epistle, probably the severe letter; see note on 2 Corinthians 7, 5–16. The

background to these chapters is the criticism directed against Paul by people whom he names *super-apostles* (11, 5; 12, 11). He appeals to the community to take the proper steps to safeguard his authority; otherwise he will exercise it personally and fully (10, 1–11). He

observes that the disturbers of the community are self-praisers, boasting of work which not they, but others, have accomplished. To be approved requires recommendation by God, not by oneself (10, 12–18).

in the letters during our absence, that we mean to be in action when we are present.

12 We are not so bold, of course, as to classify or compare ourselves with certain people who recommend themselves. Since people like that are their own appraisers, comparing themselves with one another, they only demonstrate their ignorance. 13 When we make claims we will not go over the mark but will stay within the bounds the God of moderation has set for us—leading us to you. 14 We are not overreaching ourselves, as we should be doing if we had not bothered to come to you. But indeed we did get as far as you with the gospel of Christ. 15 We do not boast immoderately of the work of others; we hope that as your faith grows our influence may also grow among you and overflow. 16 Following the rule laid down for us, we hope to preach the gospel even beyond your borders without having to boast of work already done by another in his allotted territory. 17 "Let him who would boast, boast in the Lord." 18 It is not the man who recommends himself who is approved but the man whom the Lord recommends.

Paul and the False Apostles

11 You must endure a little of my folly. Put up with me, I beg you! 2 I am jealous of you with the jealousy of God himself, since I have given you in marriage to one husband, presenting you as a chaste virgin to Christ. 3 My fear is that, just as the serpent seduced Eve by his cunning, your thoughts may be corrupted and you may fall away from your sincere and complete devotion to Christ. 4 I say this because when someone comes preaching another Jesus than the one we preached, or when you receive a different spirit than the one you have received, or a gospel other than the gospel you accepted, you seem to endure it quite well. 5 I consider myself inferior to the "super-apostles"

in nothing. 6 I may be unskilled in speech but I know that I am not lacking in knowledge. We have made this evident to you in every conceivable way.

7 Could I have done wrong when I preached the gospel of God to you free of charge, humbling myself with a view to exalting you? 8 I robbed other churches, I accepted support from them in order to minister to you. 9 When I was with you and in want I was a burden to none of you, for the brothers who came from Macedonia supplied my needs. In every way possible I kept myself from being burdensome to you, and I shall continue to do so. 10 I swear by the Christ who is in me that this boast of mine will not cease in the regions of Achaia! 11 Why? Because I do not love you? God knows I do. 12 What I am doing I shall continue to do, depriving at every turn those who look for a chance to say that in their much-vaunted ministry they work on the same terms as we do. 13 Such men are false apostles. They practice deceit in their disguise as apostles of Christ. 14 And little wonder! For even Satan disguises himself as an angel of light. 15 It comes as no surprise that his ministers disguise themselves as ministers of the justice of God. But their end will correspond to their deeds.

Paul's Sufferings as an Apostle

16 I repeat: let no one think me foolish. But if you do, then accept me as a fool all the way and let me do a little boasting. 17 What I am about to say in this self-assured boasting, I speak not as the Lord desires but after the manner of a fool. 18 Since many are bragging about their human distinctions, I too will boast. 19 Being wise yourselves, you gladly put up with fools. 20 You even put up with those who exploit you, who impse upon you and put on airs, with those who slap your face. 21 To my shame I must confess that we have been too weak to do such things. But

what anyone else dares to claim—I speak with absolute foolishness now —I, too, will dare. 22 Are they Hebrews? So am I! Are they Israelites? So am I! Are they the seed of Abraham? So am I! 23 Are they ministers of Christ? Now I am really talking like a fool—I am more: with my many more labors and imprisonments, with far worse beatings and frequent brushes with death. 24 Five times at the hands of the Jews I received forty lashes less one; 25 three times I was beaten with rods; I was stoned once, shipwrecked three times; I passed a day and a night on the sea. 26 I traveled continually, endangered by floods, robbers, my own people, the Gentiles; imperiled in the city, in the desert, at sea, by false brothers; 27 enduring labor, hardship, many sleepless nights; in hunger and thirst and frequent fastings, in cold and nakedness. 28 Leaving other sufferings unmentioned, there is that daily tension pressing on me, my anxiety for all the churches. 29 Who is weak that I am not affected by it? Who is scandalized that I am not aflame with indignation? 30 If I must boast, I will make a point of my weaknesses. 31 The God and Father of the Lord Jesus knows— blessed be he forever—that I do not lie. 32 In Damascus the ethnarch of King Aretas was keeping a close watch on the city in order to arrest me, 33 but I was lowered in a basket through a window in the wall and escaped his hands.

Visions and Revelations

12 I must go on boasting, however useless it may be, and speak of visions and revelations of the Lord. 2 I know a man in Christ who, fourteen years ago, whether he was in or outside his body I cannot say, only God can say—a man who was snatched up to the third heaven. 3 I know that this man—whether in or outside his body I do not know, God knows— 4 was snatched up to Paradise to hear words which

11, 1–15: Paul sees in the work of the *super-apostles* a threat to the purity of the gospel as he preached it to Corinthians (1–6). He regards his own selflessness in the ministry as worthy of a hearing against the conduct of those whom he now designates as false apostles (7–15).

11, 16—12, 10: Since the false apostles have thrilled the community with accounts of their achievements, Paul will boast of his sufferings and humiliations (16–33). If they seek from Paul evidence of unique religious experiences, his have been so extraordinary as to be incapable of expression in

words (12, 1–5). To keep him humble despite his unique visions, God gave Paul a special affliction, *a thorn in the flesh* (12, 7)—whether a disease or a spiritual affliction is not certain (12, 7–10). If his phrase is an echo of Nm 33, 55 or Ez 28, 24, the thorn is the "super-apostles."

cannot be uttered, words which no man may speak. 5 About this man I will boast; but I will do no boasting about myself unless it be about my weaknesses. 6 And even if I were to boast it would not be folly in me because I would only be telling the truth.

7 But I refrain, lest anyone think more of me than what he sees in me or hears from my lips. As to the extraordinary revelations, in order that I might not become conceited I was given a thorn in the flesh, an angel of Satan to beat me and keep me from getting proud. 8 Three times I begged the Lord that this might leave me. 9 He said to me, "My grace is enough for you, for in weakness power reaches perfection." And so I willingly boast of my weaknesses instead, that the power of Christ may rest upon me.

10 Therefore I am content with weakness, with mistreatment, with distress, with persecutions and difficulties for the sake of Christ; for when I am powerless, it is then that I am strong.

Concern for the Corinthian Church

11 What a fool I have become! You have driven me to it. You are the ones who should have been commending me. Even though I am nothing, I am no way inferior to the "super-apostles." 12 Indeed, I have performed among you with great patience the signs that show the apostle, signs and wonders and deeds of power. 13 In what way are you inferior to the other churches except in this, that I was no burden to you? Forgive me this injustice! 14 This is the third time that I am about to visit you, and I am not going to burden you; for I do not want what you have, I only want you. Children should not save up for their parents, but parents for children. 15 I will gladly spend myself and be spent for your sakes. If I love you too much, will I be loved the less for that? 16 Granted that I did not burden you—but being crafty, you say, I caught you by guile. 17 Did I ever take advantage of you through any of the men I sent to you? 18 I urged Titus to go to you, and I sent the other brother with him. Did Titus take advantage of you in any way? Did we not act in the one spirit, walk in the same footsteps?

19 Do you think throughout this recital that I am defending myself to you? Before God I tell you, in Christ, I have done everything to build you up, my dear ones. 20 I fear that when I come I may not find you to my liking, nor may you find me to yours. I fear I may find discord, jealousy, outbursts of anger, selfish ambitions, slander and gossip, self-importance, disorder. 21 I fear that when I come again my God may humiliate me before you, and I may have to mourn over the many who sinned earlier and have not repented of the uncleanness, fornication, and sensuality they practiced.

Final Warnings

13 This is the third time I shall be coming to you. "A judicial fact shall be established only on the testimony of two or three witnesses." 2 I said before when I was there the second time—and I repeat it now in my absence—to those who sinned before and to all the rest, that if I come again I shall not spare you. 3 You are, after all, looking for a proof of the Christ who speaks in me. He is not weak in dealing with you, but is powerful in you. 4 It is true he was crucified out of weakness, but he lives by the power of God. We too are weak in him, but we live with him by God's power in us. 5 Test yourselves to see whether you are living in faith; examine yourselves. Perhaps you yourselves do not realize that Christ Jesus is in you—unless, of course, you have failed the challenge. 6 I hope you will understand that we have not failed. 7 We pray God that you may do no evil—not in order that we may appear approved but simply that you may do what is good, even though we may seem to have failed. 8 We cannot do anything against the truth, but only for the sake of the truth. 9 We even rejoice when we are weak and you are strong. Our prayer is that you may be built up to completion.

Farewell

10 I am writing in this way while away from you, so that when I am with you I may not have to exercise with severity the authority the Lord has given me—authority to build up rather than to destroy. 11 And now, brothers, I must say good-bye. Mend your ways. Encourage one another. Live in harmony and peace, and the God of love and peace will be with you. 12 Greet one another with a holy kiss. All the holy ones send greetings to you. 13 The grace of the Lord Jesus Christ, and the love of God, and the fellowship of the Holy Spirit be with you all!

12, 11–21: Paul recalls to the minds of the Corinthians the kind of apostle he showed himself in their midst (11–15). He indicates the absurdity of the false apostles' suggestions that he and Titus took no support from the community in order to gain control of it more easily (16ff). His aim has been, not to defend himself, but to keep the community faithful to the teaching of Christ (19ff).

13, 1–10: The apostle's final appeal is that the community correct the evils within it through an examination of its own conscience. This will preclude the disagreeable necessity of his taking severe action against them.

THE EPISTLE OF PAUL TO THE

INTRODUCTION

Greetings

AUL, an apostle sent, not by men or by any man, but by Jesus Christ and God his Father who raised him from the dead— 2 I and my brothers who are with me send greetings to the churches in Galatia. 3 We wish you the favor and peace of God our Father and of the Lord Jesus Christ, 4 who gave himself for our sins, to rescue us from the present evil age, as our God and Father willed— 5 to him be glory for endless ages. Amen.

Reproof for Disloyalty

6 I am amazed that you are so soon deserting him who called you in accord with his gracious design in Christ, and are going over to another gospel. 7 But there is no other. Some who wish to alter the gospel of Christ must have confused you. 8 For if even we, or an angel from heaven, should preach to you a gospel not in accord with the one we delivered to you, let a curse be upon him! 9 I repeat what I have just said: if anyone preaches a gospel to you other than the one you received, let a curse be upon him!

10 Whom would you say I am trying to please at this point—men or God? Is this how I seek to ingratiate myself with men? If I were trying to win man's approval, I would surely not be serving Christ!

PAUL'S DEFENSE OF HIS AUTHORITY AND DOCTRINE

Called by Christ

11 I assure you, brothers, the gospel I proclaimed to you is no mere human invention. 12 I did not receive it from any man, nor was I schooled in it. It came by revelation from Jesus Christ. 13 You have heard, I know, the story of my former way of life in Judaism. You know that I went to extremes in persecuting the church of God and

1, 1–5: Together with his customary greeting (see note on Rom 1, 1–7), Paul abruptly introduces the two main topics of the epistle: the authenticity of his apostolic office (1ff) and the doctrine of justification through faith rather than through observance of the law. Alluding to the Judaizers, i.e., Judaeo-Christians who have attempted to introduce traditional Jewish observances into the Galatian churches (Cf. 2, 4), he reminds the Galatians of his direct appointment to the office of apostle by Christ (v 1). He reaffirms what he had previously preached to them, that Christ's sacrificial death alone saves from sin (v 4).

1, 6–10: To impress upon the Galatians the doctrinal seriousness of their inclination to combine the practices of Judaism as saving acts with their faith in Christ, Paul calls this teaching *another gospel*, i.e., a doctrine of salvation substantially different from authentic Christian teaching (v 6), and declares that the Judaeo-Christians responsible for introducing it into the Galatian communities are to be condemned (v 9). The Judaizers have alleged that Paul originally refrained from teaching the Galatians the practices of Judaism in order to win them over more easily; the charge is now refuted, for he has made it clear that he will not compromise even with his fellow Jewish-Christians (v 10).

1, 11–24: *The gospel I proclaimed:* this is shown to be the common possession of all the apostles in-cluding himself (see note on v 4). It was an understanding of the meaning of Christ's death in the order of salvation, divinely granted to Paul (11f), which led him to surrender his early career in Judaism (13f). Once he received this understanding of Christ and the apostolic office, he deemed it unnecessary to confer with the other apostles. Instead he went into retirement for a time (15ff). When, three years later, he spent two weeks with Peter in Jerusalem, he did not compare his understanding of Christ with that of the other apostles (18f). He is speaking truthfully, for the Judaeo-Christian churches near Jerusalem also recognized that he had abandoned Judaism for Christ as the way of salvation (20–24).

tried to destroy it; 14 I made progress in Jewish observance far beyond most of my contemporaries, in my excess of zeal to live out all the traditions of my ancestors.

15 But the time came when he who had set me apart before I was born and called me by his favor 16 chose to reveal his Son to me, that I might spread among the Gentiles the good tidings concerning him. Immediately, without seeking human advisers 17 or even going to Jerusalem to see those who were apostles before me, I went off to Arabia; later I returned to Damascus. 18 Three years after that I went up to Jerusalem to get to know Cephas, with whom I stayed fifteen days. 19 I did not meet any other apostles except James, the brother of the Lord. 20 I declare before God that what I have just written is true.

21 Thereafter I entered the regions of Syria and Cilicia. 22 The communities of Christ in Judea had no idea what I looked like; 23 they had only heard that "he who was formerly persecuting us is now preaching the faith he tried to destroy," 24 and they gave glory to God on my account.

The Council of Jerusalem

2 Then, after fourteen years, I went up to Jerusalem again with Barnabas, this time taking Titus with me. 2 I went prompted by a revelation, and I laid out for their scrutiny the gospel as I present it to the Gentiles—all this in private conference with the leaders, to make sure the course I was pursuing, or had

pursued, was not useless. 3 Not even Titus, who was with me, was ordered to undergo circumcision, despite his being a Greek. 4 Certain false claimants to the title of brother were smuggled in; they wormed their way into the group to spy on the freedom we enjoy in Christ Jesus and thereby to make slaves of us, but 5 we did not submit to them for a moment. We resisted so that the truth of the gospel might survive intact for your benefit.

6 Those who were regarded as important, however (and it makes no difference to me how prominent they were—God plays no favorites), made me add nothing.

7 On the contrary, recognizing that I had been entrusted with the gospel for the uncircumcised, just as Peter was for the circumcised 8 (for he who worked through Peter as his apostle among the Jews had been at work in me for the Gentiles), 9 and recognizing, too, the favor bestowed on me, those who were the acknowledged pillars, James, Cephas, and John, gave Barnabas and me the handclasp of fellowship, signifying that we should go to the Gentiles as they to the Jews. 10 The only stipulation was that we should be mindful of the poor—the one thing that I was making every effort to do.

Peter and the Judaizers

11 When Cephas came to Antioch I directly withstood him, because he was clearly in the wrong. 12 He had been taking his meals with the Gentiles before others came who were

from James. But when they arrived he drew back to avoid trouble with those who were circumcised. 13 The rest of the Jews joined in his dissembling, till even Barnabas was swept away by their pretense. 14 As soon as I observed that they were not being straightforward about the truth of the gospel, I had this to say to Cephas in the presence of all: "If you who are a Jew are living according to Gentile ways rather than Jewish, by what logic do you force the Gentiles to adopt Jewish ways?"

Paul's Basic Teaching

15 We are Jews by birth, not sinners of Gentile origin. 16 Nevertheless, knowing that a man is not justified by legal observance but by faith in Jesus Christ, we too have believed in him in order to be justified by faith in Jesus Christ, not by observance of the law; for by works of the law no one will be justified. 17 But if, in seeking to be justified in Christ, we are shown to be sinners, does that mean that Christ is encouraging sin? Unthinkable! 18 If, however, I were to build up the very things I had demolished, I should then indeed be a transgressor. 19 It was through the law that I died to the law, to live for God. I have been crucified with Christ, 20 and the life I live now is not my own; Christ is living in me. I still live my human life, but it is a life of faith in the Son of God, who loved me and gave himself for me. 21 I will not treat God's gracious gift as pointless. If justice is available through the law, then Christ died to no purpose!

2, 1–10: The *private conference with the leaders* is probably the same described by Luke in Acts 15; see note on Acts 15, 6–12. The first time Paul discussed the nature of the Christian gospel with other apostles was some fourteen years after his conversion (v 1), and then in consequence of a prophetic inspiration (v 2). The misgivings about Paul entertained at that time did not pertain to his doctrine, but probably to his persistence in establishing Christian communities among the Gentiles despite Jewish opposition (v 2; cf Acts 13, 13f.27). When it was suggested by Judaeo-Christians who opposed him that the Gentile Christian Titus be circumcised so as to display Paul's respect for Judaism, he refused to comply lest such a concession be turned against him (2, 3ff). James, Cephas, and John, far from objecting to his stand, even conceded that he possessed a God-given mission to the Gentiles, just as Peter was founder and leader of the Judaeo-Christian communities of Palestine. It was agreed then that Gentile Christians would not adopt the practices of Judaism, even though the

Judaeo-Christian communities continued to retain them for cultural reasons (6–9). Paul readily acceded to the idea of organizing a collection among the Gentile communities for the poor Christians of Jerusalem (v 10), for he saw in it an occasion to develop unity of faith despite the prevailing diversity of culture; cf 2 Cor 9, 13.

2, 11–14: This incident, which probably occurred after the meeting of 2, 1–10, is more understandable if the policy then arrived at was not publicly promulgated to the Judaeo-Christians of Jerusalem (see note on Acts 15, 6–12). When Peter realized that sharing the agape-meal (see note on 1 Cor 11, 17–34) with Gentile Christians wounded the sensibilities of Judaeo-Christians, he abandoned the practice out of deference to their presence (11f). Other Judaeo-Christians in Antioch followed suit, thereby placing in jeopardy the unity of the Antiochean church (v 13). Paul publicly criticized Peter's conduct because it implied that, although in theory the Judaeo-Christian could eat with Gentile Christians, in practice the

Gentile Christian should not eat with Judaeo-Christians (v 14).

2, 15–21: Although the Judaeo-Christian enjoys a certain religious privilege by birth (v 15), he knows that he is not justified by the Mosaic law but by faith in Christ (v 16). If he insists on his privilege as a Jew (vv 11–14), he implies that Christ has misled him (a probable sense of v 17), and that he has sinned in abandoning his privilege by accepting Christ (v 18). The Judaeo-Christian, like Paul, knows that his privileged position occasioned his transgression of the law and revealed him to be a sinner in need of the redemptive death of Christ (v 19). Therefore, disregarding his privileged status as Jew, he values only the new condition received from Christ, the source of his holiness (v 20). He seeks no privileged status in the Christian community—*I will not treat God's gracious gift as pointless* (v 21)—lest his justification seem to come from the law and not from the sacrifice of Christ.

CHRISTIAN FAITH AND LIBERTY

Justification through Faith

3 You senseless Galatians! Who has cast a spell over you—you before whose eyes Jesus Christ was displayed to view upon his cross? 2 I want to learn only one thing from you: how did you receive the Spirit? Was it through observance of the law or through faith in what you heard? 3 How could you be so stupid? After beginning in the spirit, are you now to end in the flesh? 4 Have you had such remarkable experiences all to no purpose—if indeed they were to no purpose? 5 Is it because you observe the law or because you have faith in what you heard that God lavishes the Spirit on you and works wonders in your midst? 6 Consider the case of Abraham: he "believed God, and it was credited to him as justice." 7 This means that those who believe are sons of Abraham. 8 Because Scripture saw in advance that God's way of justifying the Gentiles would be through faith, it foretold this good news to Abraham: "All nations shall be blessed in you." 9 Thus it is that all who believe are blessed along with Abraham, the man of faith.

No Justification from the Law

10 All who depend on observance of the law, on the other hand, are under a curse. It is written, "Cursed is he who does not abide by everything written in the book of the law and carrry it out." 11 It should be obvious that no one is justified in God's sight by the law, for "the just man shall live by faith." 12 But the law does not depend on faith. Its terms are: "Whoever does these things shall live by them." 13 Christ has delivered us from the power of the law's curse by himself becoming a curse for us, as it is written: "Accursed is anyone who is hanged on a tree." 14 This has happened so that through Christ Jesus the blessing bestowed on Abraham might descend on the Gentiles in Christ Jesus, thereby making it possible for us to receive the promised Spirit through faith.

Promise Not Nullified by the Law

15 Brothers, let me give you an everyday example. You cannot add anything to a man's will or set it aside once it is legally validated. 16 There were promises spoken to Abraham and to his "descendant." Scripture does not say "and to your descendants," as if it applied to many, but as if it applied only to one, "and to your descendant"; that is, to Christ. 17 My point is this: a covenant formally ratified by God is not set aside as invalid by any law that came into being four hundred and thirty years later, nor is its promise nullified. 18 Clearly, if one's inheritance comes through the law, it is no longer conferred in virtue of the promise. Yet it was by way of promise that God granted Abraham his privilege.

True Function of the Law

19 What is the relevance of the law, in such case? It was given in view of transgressions and promulgated by angels, at the hands of a mediator; it was to be valid only until that descendant or offspring came to whom the promise had been given. 20 Now, there can be no mediator when only one person is involved; and God is one. 21 Does this mean that the law is opposed to the promises [of God]? Again, unthinkable! If the law that was given was such that it could impart life, then justice would be a consequence of the law. 22 In fact, however, Scripture has locked all things in under the constraint of sin. Why? So that the promise might be fulfilled in those who believe, in consequence of faith in Jesus Christ.

The Benefit of Faith

23 Before faith came we were under the constraint of the law, locked in until the faith that was coming should be revealed. 24 In other words, the law was our monitor until Christ came to bring about our justification through faith. 25 But now that faith is here, we are no longer in the monitor's charge. 26 Each one of you is a son of God because of your faith in Christ Jesus. 27 All of you who have been baptized into Christ have clothed yourselves with him. 28 There does not exist among you Jew or Greek, slave or freeman, male or female. All are one in Christ Jesus. 29 Furthermore, if you belong to Christ you are the descendants of Abraham, which means you inherit all that was promised.

3, 1–5: Paul suggests that the Galatians must be under an evil spell to have forgotten the redemptive meaning of Jesus' crucifixion (v 1). He asks them to recall the reason for their conversion: the reception of the Spirit, not the works of the law (2–5).

3, 6–9: Probably in response to the argument of the Judaizers that if a Christian wishes to benefit fully from the promises made to Abraham he should embrace Judaism, Paul cites Gn 15, 6 to the effect that Abraham won God's favor because of his faith. Christians too have already won God's favor through their faith in Christ; cf 3, 2–5. They therefore may expect the fullness of the benefits promised Abraham for the Gentile nations (7–9).

3, 10–14: To seek salvation through observance of the law is to subject oneself to divine retribution (v 10), for the law is not the source of justification (v 11). It is associated with justification only if it is observed through faith (v 12). Christ removed the threat of divine retribution which came with non-observance of the law (v 13) in order that the Gentiles might receive through faith the blessings promised to Abraham on their behalf. Thus they are freed of the continual threat of divine punishment (v 14).

3, 15–18: The example of the promise to Abraham derives its force from a certain continuity in the divine plan of salvation. Abraham, on whom the law that came only centuries later was not imposed, is the type of figure of God's gift of salvation to the Gentiles as well as to Israel. Hence to impose the law upon men as a means of salvation would be to deface the image of Abraham in Genesis as the spiritual father of all nations; cf Gn 12, 3.

3, 19–22: Though not the source of justification and salvation (3, 11), the Mosaic law fulfilled the purpose of revealing through Israel's history, illumined by the sacrifice of Christ, the sinfulness of all humanity (v 19; cf Rom 3, 9–20). Through the coming of Christ, this divine revelation is now fully grasped by those who believe in him (v 22). The fact that the law was delivered through Moses as mediator indicates that the law is not the fulfillment of the promise to Abraham concerning the Gentiles (v 19; cf Gn 12, 3). It is God alone who fulfills this promise of his for their salvation (v 20; cf Rom 3, 24). He could have imposed a law upon man that would justify him through its observance (v 21); instead he used the Mosaic law to reveal the sinfulness of man, and thus prepare him for salvation from sin through faith in Christ (v 22).

3, 23–39: Paul here summarizes his previous thought. The purpose of the Mosaic law was to keep man aware of his own sinfulness—locked in—that he might realize his need of justification through an act of God accepted in faith (v 23). The value of the law lay in its role of leading to an understanding of the absolute necessity of faith in Christ (v 24). This having been accomplished, its function is fulfilled (v 25). The Galatian Christians, whether Jew or Gentile, slave or free, men or women, all walk the same path of salvation through faith in Christ. In this they are the true descendants of Abraham, the man of faith (23–29).

Free Sons of God in Christ

4 Brothers: as long as a designated heir is not of age his condition is no different from that of a slave, even though in name he is master of all his possessions; 2 for he is under the supervision of guardians and administrators until the time set by his father. 3 In the same way, while we were not yet of age we were like slaves subordinated to the elements of the world; 4 but when the designated time had come, God sent forth his Son born of a woman, born under the law, 5 to deliver from the law those who were subjected to it, so that we might receive our status as adopted sons. 6 The proof that you are sons is the fact that God has sent forth into our hearts the spirit of his Son which cries out "Abba!" ("Father!") 7 You are no longer a slave but a son! And the fact that you are a son makes you an heir, by God's design.

No Return to Slavery

8 In the past, when you did not acknowledge God, you served as slaves to gods who are not really divine. 9 Now that you have come to know God—or rather, have been known by him—how can you return to those powerless, worthless, natural elements to which you seem willing to enslave yourselves once more? 10 You even go so far as to keep the ceremonial observance of days and months, seasons and years! 11 I fear for you; all my efforts with you may have been wasted.

Former Devotions of the Galatians

12 I beg you, brothers, to become like me as I became like you. (Understand, you have not done me any wrong.) 13 You are aware that it was a bodily ailment that first occasioned my bringing you the gospel. 14 My physical condition was a challenge which you did not despise or brush aside in disgust. On the contrary, you took me to yourselves as an angel of God, even as if I had been Christ Jesus! 15 What has happened to your openhearted spirit? I can testify on your behalf that if it were possible you would have plucked out your eyes and given them to me. 16 Have I become your enemy just because I tell you the truth?

17 The people I have referred to are not courting your favor in any generous spirit. What they really want is to exclude you so that you may court their favor. 18 It would be well for you to be courted for the right reasons at all times, and not only when I happen to be with you. 19 You are my children, and you put me back in labor pains until Christ is formed in you. 20 If only I could be with you now and speak to you differently! You have me at a complete loss!

Allegory on Freedom

21 You who want to be subject to the law, tell me: do you know what the law has to say? 22 There it is written that Abraham had two sons, one by the slave girl, the other by his freeborn wife. 23 The son of the slave girl had been begotten in the course of nature, but the son of the free woman was the fruit of the promise. 24 All this is an allegory: the two women stand for the two covenants. One is from Mount Sinai, and brought forth children to slavery: this is Hagar. 25 The mountain Sinai [Hagar] is in Arabia and corresponds to the Jerusalem of our time, which is likewise in slavery with her children. 26 But the Jerusalem on high is freeborn, and it is she who is our mother. 27 That is why Scripture says:

"Rejoice, you barren one who
			bear no children;
break into song, you stranger
			to the pains of childbirth!
For many are the children of
			the wife deserted—
far more than of her who has
			a husband!"

28 You, my brothers, are children of the promise, as Isaac was. 29 But just as in those days the son born in nature's course persecuted the one whose birth was in the realm of spirit, so do we find it now. 30 What does Scripture say on the point? "Cast out slave girl and son together; for the slave girl's son shall never be an heir on equal terms with the son" of the one born free.

31 Therefore, my brothers, we are not children of a slave girl but of a mother who is free.

EXHORTATION TO CHRISTIAN LIVING

Basic Import of Faith

5 It was for liberty that Christ freed us. So stand firm, and do not take on yourselves the yoke of slavery a second time! 2 Pay close attention to me, Paul, when I tell you that if you have yourselves circumcised, Christ will be of no use to you! 3 I point out once more to all who receive circumcision that they are bound to the law in its entirety. 4 Any of you who seek your justification in the law have severed yourselves from Christ and fallen from God's favor! 5 It is in the spirit that we eagerly await the justification we hope for, and only faith can yield it. 6 In Christ Jesus neither circumcision nor the lack of it counts for anything; only faith, which expresses itself through love.

4, 1–7: Paul draws on the culture of the time to indicate to the Galatians their status in the history of salvation. They have reached a point in the religious history of humanity comparable to the state of a child in a Roman family who has attained his majority. From that moment he enjoys the goods, rights and privileges of an adult (1–3). The Galatians have been freed through Christ from the tutelage of the law, which kept humanity conscious of its slavery to sin. As a result they have experienced the power of the Holy Spirit, who has recreated them as God's sons and enabled them to live their lives according to the sense and spirit of this new relationship (4–7).

4, 8–11: Referring to the conversion of the Galatians, Paul presses his argument against their adoption of practices of the law by showing that, if they were to accept Judaism as a partial principle of salvation, it would be no less futile than to return to polytheism.
4, 12–20: The apostle appeals to their personal loyalty to him through whom Christ was formed in them.
4, 21–31: Paul creates an allegory out of the story of Sarah and Hagar (Gn 21, 8–21; cf Gn 16, 1–16). The two women represent two covenants: Hagar, the slave girl, represents the covenant of Sinai. The

children of this covenant are sons of Abraham *begotten in the course of nature.* By the covenant of Sinai they were enslaved to the law like Hagar's offspring, who were born into slavery. Sarah, the freewoman, represents the covenant made by God with Abraham. The children of this covenant, also sons of Abraham, are *the fruit of the promise.* Like the offspring of Sarah, born to freedom, these are free from the slavery of the Mosaic law.

Against Being Misled

7 You were progressing so very well; who diverted you from the path of truth? 8 Such enticement does not come from him who calls you. 9 "A little yeast can affect the entire dough." 10 I trust that, in the Lord, you will not adopt a different view. May condemnation fall on whoever it is that is unsettling you! 11 As for me, brothers, if I am still preaching circumcision, why do the attacks on me continue? If I were, the cross would be a stumbling block no more. 12 Would that those who are troubling you might go the whole way, and castrate themselves!

Proper Use of Freedom

13 My brothers, remember that you have been called to live in freedom—but not a freedom that gives free rein to the flesh. Out of love, place yourselves at one another's service. 14 The whole law has found its fulfillment in this one saying: "You shall love your neighbor as yourself." 15 If you go on biting and tearing one another to pieces, take care! You will end up in mutual destruction!

16 My point is that you should live in accord with the spirit and you will not yield to the cravings of the flesh. 17 The flesh lusts against the spirit and the spirit against the flesh; the two are directly opposed. This is why you do not do what your will intends. 18 If you are guided by the spirit, you are not under the law. 19 It is obvious what proceeds from the flesh: lewd conduct, im-

purity, licentiousness, 20 idolatry, sorcery, hostilities, bickering, jealousy, outbursts of rage, selfish rivalries, dissensions, factions, 21 envy, drunkenness, orgies, and the like. I warn you, as I have warned you before: those who do such things will not inherit the kingdom of God!

22 In contrast, the fruit of the spirit is love, joy, peace, patient endurance, kindness, generosity, faith, 23 mildness, and chastity. Against such there is no law! 24 Those who belong to Christ Jesus have crucified their flesh with its passions and desires. 25 Since we live by the spirit, let us follow the spirit's lead. 26 Let us never be boastful, or challenging, or jealous toward one another.

The Demands of Conscience

6 My brothers, if someone is detected in sin, you who live by the spirit should gently set him right, each of you trying to avoid falling into temptation himself. 2 Help carry one another's burdens; in that way you will fulfill the law of Christ. 3 If anyone thinks he amounts to something, when in fact he is nothing, he is only deceiving himself. 4 Each man should look to his conduct; if he has reason to boast of anything, it will be because the achievement is his and not another's. 5 Everyone should bear his own responsibility.

6 The man instructed in the word should share all he has with his instructor. 7 Make no mistake about it, no one makes a fool of God!

A man will reap only what he sows. 8 If he sows in the field of the flesh, he will reap a harvest of corruption; but if his seed-ground is the spirit, he will reap everlasting life. 9 Let us not grow weary of doing good; if we do not relax our efforts, in due time we shall reap our harvest. 10 While we have the opportunity, let us do good to all men—especially those of the household of the faith.

CONCLUSION

The Cross, Our True Boast

11 See, I write to you in my own large handwriting! 12 Those who are trying to force you to be circumcised are making a play for human approval—with an eye to escaping persecution for the cross of Christ. 13 The very ones who accept circumcision do not follow the law themselves. They want you to be circumcised only that they may boast about your bodily observance.

14 May I never boast of anything but the cross of our Lord Jesus Christ! Through it, the world has been crucified to me and I to the world. 15 It means nothing whether one is circumcised or not. All that matters is that one is created anew. 16 Peace and mercy on all who follow this rule of life, and on the Israel of God.

17 Henceforth, let no man trouble me, for I bear the brand marks of Jesus in my body.

18 Brothers, may the favor of our Lord Jesus Christ be with your spirit. Amen.

5, 7–12: A strongly worded appeal that they will reject the teachers who are misleading them.

5, 13–26: Since the teaching of the Judaizers has apparently provoked dissension within the community, Paul urges upon all the Christian law of love

of neighbor (13ff). He forestalls the accusation that his doctrine of justification by faith opens the way to a life of moral irresponsibility (16–26).

6, 11–18: Paul asserts that the Judaizers wish the Gentile Christians to observe the laws of Judaism

only in order that they themselves may escape persecution by the Jews. He observes that he already bears the scars of such persecution, but this has not prevented him from reaffirming the true doctrine in the present epistle.

THE EPISTLE OF PAUL TO THE

Greeting

PAUL, by the will of God an apostle of Jesus Christ, to the holy ones [at Ephesus], believers in Christ Jesus. 2 Grace and peace to you from God our Father and the Lord Jesus Christ.

The Father's Plan of Salvation

3 Praised be the God and the Father of our Lord Jesus Christ who has bestowed on us in Christ every spiritual blessing in the heavens! 4 God chose us in him before the world began, to be holy and blameless in his sight, to be full of love; 5 he likewise predestined us through Christ Jesus to be his adopted sons—such was his will and pleasure— 6 that all might praise the glorious favor he has bestowed on us in his beloved.

Fulfillment through Christ

7 It is in Christ and through his blood that we have been redeemed and our sins forgiven, 8 so immeasurably generous is God's favor to us. 9 God has given us the wisdom to understand fully the mystery, the plan he was pleased to decree in Christ, 10 to be carried out in the fullness of time: namely, to bring all things in the heavens and on earth into one under Christ's headship.

Blessing for Jew and Gentile

11 In him we were chosen; for in the decree of God, who administers everything according to his will and counsel, we were predestined 12 to praise his glory by being the first to hope in Christ. 13 In him you too were chosen; when you heard the glad tidings of salvation, the word of truth, and believed in it, you were sealed with the Holy Spirit who had been promised. 14 He is the pledge of our inheritance, the first payment against the full redemption of a people God has made his own, to praise his glory.

Fulfillment in the Church

15 For my part, from the time I first heard of your faith in the Lord Jesus and your love for all the members of the church, 16 I have never stopped thanking God for you and recommending you in my prayers. 17 May the God of our Lord Jesus Christ, the Father of glory, grant you a spirit of wisdom and insight to know him clearly. 18 May he enlighten your innermost vision that you may know the great hope to which he has called you, the

---

1, 3–14: This prayer of thanksgiving, similar in its opening words to Colossians 1, 12, is better understood if the later verses also (Col 1, 15–20) are taken into consideration. The exalted Christology of the second passage of Colossians is at one with this prayer which reflects upon the divine plan of salvation centering in Christ and revealed to Christians as fully at work in themselves. The spiritual blessings the Christian communities have received through Christ (v 3) are gratefully enumerated: the call to faith and holiness (v 4; cf Rom 3, 30); the gift of divine adop-

tive sonship establishing a unique spiritual relationship with God the Father through Christ (v 5; cf Rom 8, 14–17); the liberation from sin through Christ's sacrificial death (v 7); the revelation of God's plan of salvation in Christ (v 9; cf Rom 16, 25; Eph 3, 3f); the gift of faith in Christ bestowed upon Jews (11f); and finally, the same gift granted to Gentiles (v 13). In the christological faith of the Christian communities the apostle sees the predetermined plan of God (4.11) to bring all creation under the final rule of Christ (v 10). The Christian community has the

initial understanding of the gifts God has so freely given to men for the sake of Christ (6.8f), which all humanity will eventually possess.

1, 15–23: Paul prays that the blessings of the faith imparted by God the Father (v 3) to the Ephesians will be strengthened in them through the message of the gospel (1, 17ff). Those blessings are to be measured by his power in establishing the sovereignty of Christ over all other creatures (1, 20f) and in appointing him head of the church (1, 22f). For the allusion to angelic spirits, see the note on Colossians 1, 15.20.

wealth of his glorious heritage to be distributed among the members of the church, 19 and the immeasurable scope of his power in us who believe. It is like the strength 20 he showed in raising Christ from the dead and seating him at his right hand in heaven, 21 high above every principality, power, virtue, and domination, and every name that can be given in this age or in the age to come.

22 He has put all things under Christ's feet and has made him, thus exalted, head of the church, 23 which is his body: the fullness of him who fills the universe in all its parts.

Generosity of God's Plan

2 You were dead because of your sins and offenses, 2 as you gave allegiance to the present age and to the prince of the air, that spirit who is even now at work among the rebellious. 3 All of us were once of their company; we lived at the level of the flesh, following every whim and fancy, and so by nature deserved God's wrath like the rest. 4 But God is rich in mercy; because of his great love for us 5 he brought us to life with Christ when we were dead in sin. By this favor you were saved. 6 Both with and in Christ Jesus he raised us up and gave us a place in the heavens, 7 that in the ages to come he might display the great wealth of his favor, manifested by his kindness to us in Christ Jesus. 8 I repeat, it is owing to his favor that salvation is yours through faith. This is not your own doing, it is God's gift; 9 neither is it a reward for anything you have accomplished, so let no one pride himself on it. 10 We are truly his handiwork, created in

Christ Jesus to lead the life of good deeds which God prepared for us in advance.

All United in Christ

11 You men of Gentile stock— called "uncircumcised" by those who, in virtue of a hand-executed rite on their flesh, call themselves "circumcised"—remember 12 that, in former times, you had no part in Christ and were excluded from the community of Israel. You were strangers to the covenant and its promise; you were without hope and without God in the world. 13 But now in Christ Jesus you who once were far off have been brought near through the blood of Christ. 14 It is he who is our peace, and who made the two of us one by breaking down the barrier of hostility that kept us apart. 15 In his own flesh he abolished the law with its commands and precepts, to create in himself one new man from us who had been two and to make peace, 16 reconciling both of us to God in one body through his cross, which put that enmity to death. 17 He came and "announced the good news of peace to you who were far off, and to those who were near"; 18 through him we both have access in one Spirit to the Father.

19 This means that you are strangers and aliens no longer. No, you are fellow citizens of the saints and members of the household of God. 20 You form a building which rises on the foundation of the apostles and prophets, with Christ Jesus himself as the capstone. 21 Through him the whole structure is fitted together and takes shape as a holy temple in the Lord; 22 in him you are being built into this

temple, to become a dwelling place for God in the Spirit.

Commission To Preach God's Plan

3 2 I am sure you have heard of the ministry which God in his goodness gave me in your regard. 1 That is why to me, Paul, a prisoner for Christ Jesus on behalf of you Gentiles, 3 God's secret plan as I have briefly described it was revealed. 4 When you read what I have said, you will realize that I know what I am talking about in speaking of the mystery of Christ, 5 unknown to men in former ages but now revealed by the Spirit to the holy apostles and prophets. 6 It is no less than this: in Christ Jesus the Gentiles are now co-heirs with the Jews, members of the same body and sharers of the promise through the preaching of the gospel.

Mission to the Gentiles

7 Through the gift God in his goodness bestowed on me by the exercise of his power, I became a minister of the gospel. 8 To me, the least of all believers, was given the grace to preach to the Gentiles the unfathomable riches of Christ 9 and to enlighten all men on the mysterious design which for ages was hidden in God, the Creator of all. 10 Now, therefore, through the church, God's manifold wisdom is made known to the principalities and powers of heaven, 11 in accord with his age-old purpose, carried out in Christ Jesus our Lord. 12 In Christ and through faith in him we can speak freely to God, drawing near him with confidence. 13 Hence, I beg you not to be disheartened by the trials I endure for you; they are your glory.

2, 1–10: The recipients of Paul's letter have experienced in their redemption from sin, the effect of Christ's supremacy (1f), the power of which overcame the evil force of demons. (In Jewish thought these were considered to dwell in the air.) Both Jew and Gentile have experienced, through Christ, God's generosity, his free gift of salvation which already marks them for a heavenly destiny (3–6). In Christ, God reveals the wealth of his kindness (v 7), saving men through faith and not by any works of their own (8f). Christians are a newly created people in Christ, fashioned by God for a new life of goodness (v 10).

2, 11–22: The Gentiles were without Israel's messianic expectation, without the various covenants God made with Israel, without hope of salvation and knowledge of the true God (11f); but through Christ, all these religious barriers between Jew and Gentile

have been transcended (13f) by the abolition of the Mosaic covenant-law (v 15) for the sake of uniting Jew and Gentile into a single religious community (15ff), imbued with the same Holy Spirit and worshiping the same Father (v 18). The Gentiles are now within the pale of God's revelation (v 19) as it derives from the apostles, assisted by those endowed with the prophetic charism, the preachers of Christ (v 20; cf Acts 8, 4f; 1 Cor 12, 28). With Christ as the capstone (v 20), they are being built into the holy temple of God's people where the divine presence dwells (21f).

3, 1: *A prisoner for Christ Jesus:* see the Introduction.

3, 1–13: Paul reflects on his mission to the Gentiles. He alludes to his conversion and appointment to the apostolic office (2f) and observes that his own apostolic experience, as well as that of the other

apostles and charismatic prophets in the church (4f), has deepened his understanding of God's plan of salvation in Christ. Paul is the special herald (v 7) of a new revelation to the world (v 6): that the divine plan includes the Gentiles in the spiritual benefits promised to Israel. Not only does he enjoy this unique apostolic role, but he also has been given the task of explaining to all men the divine plan of salvation (8f). Through the church, God's plan of salvation in Christ becomes manifest to angelic beings (v 10), a plan which God had kept hidden from all creatures (v 11). The fulfillment of the plan in Christ gives the whole church more confidence in God (v 12). The readers of this epistle are also encouraged to greater confidence despite Paul's imprisonment (v 13).

Prayer for the Readers

14 That is why I kneel before the Father 15 from whom every family in heaven and on earth takes its name; 16 and I pray that he will bestow on you gifts in keeping with the riches of his glory. May he strengthen you inwardly through the working of his Spirit. 17 May Christ dwell in your hearts through faith, and may charity be the root and foundation of your life. 18 Thus you will be able to grasp fully, with all the holy ones, the breadth and length and height and depth of Christ's love, 19 and experience this love which surpasses all knowledge, so that you may attain to the fullness of God himself.

20 To him whose power now at work in us can do immeasurably more than we ask or imagine— 21 to him be glory in the church and in Christ Jesus through all generations, world without end. Amen.

Unity in the Mystical Body

4 I plead with you, then, as a prisoner for the Lord, to live a life worthy of the calling you have received, 2 with perfect humility, meekness, and patience, bearing with one another lovingly. 3 Make every effort to preserve the unity which has the Spirit as its origin and peace as its binding force. 4 There is but one body and one Spirit, just as there is but one hope given all of you by your call. 5 There is one Lord, one faith, one baptism; 6 one God and Father of all, who is over all, and works through all, and is in all.

Diversity of Graces

7 Each of us has received God's favor in the measure in which Christ bestows it. 8 Thus you find Scripture saying:

"When he ascended on high, he took a host of captives

and gave gifts to men."

9 "He ascended"—what does this mean but that he had first descended into the lower regions of the earth? 10 He who descended is the very one who ascended high above the heavens, that he might fill all men with his gifts.

11 It is he who gave apostles, prophets, evangelists, pastors and teachers 12 in roles of service for the faithful to build up the body of Christ, 13 till we become one in faith and the knowledge of God's Son, and form that perfect man who is Christ come to full stature.

14 Let us, then, be children no longer, tossed here and there, carried about by every wind of doctrine that originates in human trickery and skill in proposing error. 15 Rather, let us profess the truth in love and grow to the full maturity of Christ the head. 16 Through him the whole body grows, and with the proper functioning of the members joined firmly together by each supporting ligament, builds itself up in love.

Renewal in Christ

17 I declare and solemnly attest in the Lord that you must no longer live as the pagans do—their minds empty, 18 their understanding darkened. They are estranged from a life in God because of their ignorance and their resistance; 19 without remorse they have abandoned themselves to lust and the indulgence of every sort of lewd conduct. 20 That is not what you learned when you learned Christ! 21 I am supposing, of course, that he has been preached and taught to you in accord with the truth that is in Jesus: 22 namely, that you must lay aside your former way of life and the old self which deteriorates through illusion and desire, 23 and acquire

a fresh, spiritual way of thinking. 24 You must put on that new man created in God's image, whose justice and holiness are born of truth.

Vices To Be Avoided

25 See to it, then, that you put an end to lying; let everyone speak the truth to his neighbor, for we are members of one another. 26 If you are angry, let it be without sin. The sun must not go down on your wrath; 27 do not give the devil a chance to work on you. 28 The man who has been stealing must steal no longer; rather, let him work with his hands at honest labor so that he will have something to share with those in need. 29 Never let evil talk pass your lips; say only the good things men need to hear, things that will really help them. 30 Do nothing to sadden the Holy Spirit with whom you were sealed against the day of redemption. 31 Get rid of all bitterness, all passion and anger, harsh words, slander, and malice of every kind. 32 In place of these, be kind to one another, compassionate, and mutually forgiving, just as God has forgiven you in Christ.

5 Be imitators of God as his dear children. 2 Follow the way of love, even as Christ loved you. He gave himself for us as an offering to God, a gift of pleasing fragrance.

3 As for lewd conduct or promiscuousness or lust of any sort, let them not even be mentioned among you; your holiness forbids this. 4 Nor should there be any obscene, silly, or suggestive talk; all that is out of place. 5 Instead, give thanks. Make no mistake about this: no fornicator, no unclean or lustful person—in effect an idolater—has any inheritance in the kingdom of Christ and of God. 6 Let no one deceive you with worthless arguments. These are sins that bring God's wrath

---

3, 14–21: The apostle prays that those he is addressing may, like the rest of the church, deepen their understanding of God's plan of salvation in Christ. It is a plan which affects the whole universe: this is the sense of *the breadth and length and height and depth* (v 18). The apostle prays further that they may receive the redemptive love of Christ for them and be completely immersed in the mystery of Christ in God (14–19). The prayer concludes with a doxology to God the Father (20f).
4, 1–16: A general plea for unity in the churches. Christians have been fashioned through the Spirit

into a single harmonious religious community (*one body*), distinguished by a single Lord in contrast to the many gods of the pagan world, and by one way of salvation through faith, brought out especially by the significance of baptism (1–6; cf Rom 6, 1–11). But Christian unity is more than adherence to a common belief. It works itself out functionally through Christ's gifts to individuals to rule and teach so as to make the community ever more Christlike (11–16). This teaching on Christ as the source of the charisms is introduced by a citation of Psalm 68, 18 which depicts Yahweh triumphantly leading Israel to

salvation in Jerusalem. It is here understood of Christ, the God-man, head of the church; through his redemptive death, resurrection and ascension he has become the source of the church's spiritual gifts. The "descent" of Christ (9f) refers more probably to the incarnation than to Christ's presence after his death in the abode of the dead.
4, 17—5, 20: For similar exhortations to a morally good life in response to God's gift of faith, see notes on Romans 12, 1—13, 14 and Galatians 5, 13–26.

down on the disobedient; 7 therefore have nothing to do with them.

Duty To Live in the Light

8 There was a time when you were darkness, but now you are light in the Lord. Well, then, live as children of light. 9 Light produces every kind of goodness and justice and truth. 10 Be correct in your judgment of what pleases the Lord. 11 Take no part in vain deeds done in darkness; rather, condemn them. 12 It is shameful even to mention the things these people do in secret; 13 but when such deeds are condemned they are seen in the light of day, and all that then appears is light. 14 That is why we read:

"Awake, O sleeper,
　　arise from the dead,
　　and Christ will give you
　　　light."

15 Keep careful watch over your conduct. Do not act like fools, but like thoughtful men. 16 Make the most of the present opportunity, for these are evil days. 17 Do not continue in ignorance, but try to discern the will of the Lord. 18 Avoid getting drunk on wine; that leads to debauchery. Be filled with the Spirit, 19 addressing one another in psalms and hymns and inspired songs. Sing praise to the Lord with all your hearts. 20 Give thanks to God the Father always and for everything in the name of our Lord Jesus Christ. 21 Defer to one another out of reverence for Christ.

Christian Wives and Husbands

22 Wives should be submissive to their husbands as if to the Lord 23 because the husband is head of his wife just as Christ is head of his body the church, as well as its savior. 24 As the church submits to Christ, so wives should submit to their husbands in everything.

25 Husbands, love your wives, as Christ loved the church. He gave himself up for her 26 to make her holy, purifying her in the bath of water by the power of the word, 27 to present to himself a glorious church, holy and immaculate, without stain or wrinkle or anything of that sort. 28 Husbands should love their wives as they do their own bodies. He who loves his wife loves himself. 29 Observe that no one ever hates his own flesh; no, he nourishes it and takes care of it as Christ cares for the church— 30 for we are members of his body.

31 "For this reason a man shall
　　leave his father and mother,
　　and shall cling to his wife,
　　and the two shall be made
　　　into one."

32 This is a great foreshadowing; I mean that it refers to Christ and the church. 33 In any case, each one should love his wife as he loves himself, the wife for her part showing respect for her husband.

Children and Parents

6 Children, obey your parents in the Lord, for that is what is expected of you. 2 "Honor your father and mother" is the first commandment to carry a promise with it— 3 "that it may go well with you, and that you may have long life on the earth."
4 Fathers, do not anger your children. Bring them up with the training and instruction befitting the Lord.

Slaves and Masters

5 Slaves, obey your human masters with the reverence, the awe, and the sincerity you owe to Christ. 6 Do not render service for appearance only and to please men, but do God's will with your whole heart as

slaves of Christ. 7 Give your service willingly, doing it for the Lord rather than men. 8 You know that each one, whether slave or free, will be repaid by the Lord for whatever good he does.
9 Masters, act in a similar way toward your slaves. Stop threatening them. Remember that you and they have a Master in heaven who plays no favorites.

Christian Warfare

10 Finally, draw your strength from the Lord and his mighty power. 11 Put on the armor of God so that you may be able to stand firm against the tactics of the devil. 12 Our battle is not against human forces but against the principalities and powers, the rulers of this world of darkness, the evil spirits in regions above. 13 You must put on the armor of God if you are to resist on the evil day; do all that your duty requires, and hold your ground. 14 Stand fast, with the truth as the belt around your waist, justice as your breastplate, 15 and zeal to propagate the gospel of peace as your footgear. 16 In all circumstances hold faith up before you as your shield; it will help you extinguish the fiery darts of the evil one. 17 Take the helmet of salvation and the sword of the spirit, the word of God.

Assiduous Prayer

18 At every opportunity pray in the Spirit, using prayers and petitions of every sort. Pray constantly and attentively for all in the holy company. 19 Pray for me that God may put his word on my lips, that I may courageously make known the mystery of the gospel— 20 that mystery for which I am an ambassador in chains. Pray that I may have courage to proclaim it as I ought.

5, 21–33: The apostle exhorts married Christians to a strong mutual love. Holding with Genesis 2, 24 that marriage is a divine institution (v 31), he sees Christian marriage as taking on a new meaning symbolic of the intimate relationship of love between Christ and the church. The wife should serve her husband in the same spirit as that of the church's service to Christ (22ff), and the husband should care for his

wife with the devotion of Christ to the church (25–30). In his conclusion Paul gives to the Genesis passage its highest meaning in the light of the union of Christ and the church, of which Christlike loyalty and devotion in Christian marriage is a clear reflection (31ff).

6, 1–9: See note on Colossians 3, 18—4, 1.

6, 10–20: A general exhortation to courage and

prayer. Drawing upon the imagery and ideas of Isaiah 11, 5; 59, 16ff and Wisdom 5, 17–23, Paul describes the Christian in terms of the dress and equipment of the Roman soldier. He observes, however, that the Christian's readiness for combat is not directed against men but against the spiritual powers of evil (10–17). Observe the unique importance he places on prayer (18ff).

Conclusion

21 Tychicus, my dear brother and faithful minister in the Lord, will keep you informed as to how I am and what I was doing. 22 I have sent him to you for the very purpose of giving you news about me for your hearts' consolation.

23 May God the Father and the Lord Jesus Christ grant the brothers peace and love and faith. 24 Grace be with all who love our Lord Jesus Christ with unfailing love.

6, 21–24: Tychicus is the bearer of the letter. On the assumption that Ephesians was addressed to several Christian communities (see the Introduction), it is understandable that no greetings to individual members of these communities should have been included in it.

THE EPISTLE OF PAUL TO THE

Philippians

Greetings

PAUL and Timothy, servants of Christ Jesus, to all the holy ones at Philippi, with their bishops and deacons in Christ Jesus. 2 Grace and peace be yours from God our Father and from the Lord Jesus Christ!

THE EXAMPLE OF PAUL

Gratitude and Hope

3 I give thanks to my God every time I think of you— 4 which is constantly, in every prayer I utter— rejoicing, as I plead on your behalf, 5 at the way you have all continually helped promote the gospel from the very first day.

6 I am sure of this much: that he who has begun the good work in you will carry it through to completion, right up to the day of Christ Jesus. 7 It is only right that I should entertain such expectations in your regard since I hold all of you dear—you who, to a man, are sharers of my gracious lot when I lie in prison or am summoned to defend the solid grounds on which the gospel rests. 8 God himself can testify how much I long for each of you with the affection of Christ Jesus! 9 My prayer is that your love may more and more abound, both in understanding and wealth of experience, 10 so that with a clear conscience and blameless conduct you may learn to value the things that really matter, up to the very day of Christ. 11 It is my wish that you may be found rich in the harvest of justice which Jesus Christ has ripened in you, to the glory and praise of God.

The Spreading Gospel

12 My brothers, I want you to know that my situation has worked out to the furtherance of the gospel. 13 My imprisonment in Christ's cause has become well known throughout the praetorium here, and to others as well; 14 most of my brothers in Christ, taking courage from my chains, have been further emboldened to speak the word of God fearlessly. 15 It is true, some preach Christ from motives of envy and rivalry, but others do so out of good will. 16 Some act from unaffected love, aware that my circumstances provide an opportunity to defend the gospel's cause; 17 others promote Christ, not from pure motives but as an intrigue against me, thinking that it will make my imprisonment even harsher.

18 What of it? All that matters is that in any and every way, whether

1, 1f: See note on Romans 1, 1–7. *Bishops and deacons:* literally, "overseers and assistants." This structure of the Christian community is similar to that found in the Pastoral Epistles.

1, 3–11: The Philippians' devotion to their faith and to Paul made them his pride and joy. Here he is possibly alluding to their monetary gifts (5f; cf 4, 14ff), and surely to their sufferings for the faith (1, 29f), and he expresses his conviction that the characteristics thus manifested are evidence of the community's preparation for the Lord's parousia (5f). He feels keenly (v 8) their concern for his apostolic work, which has created a special relationship between them and himself (v 7). He prays that the love they have shown for him may also affect other phases of their lives so as to prepare them perfectly for the parousia (9ff; see note on 1 Thes 4, 13–18).

1, 12–26: Knowing their concern for his apostolate, Paul informs the Philippians of the positive effect his imprisonment has had upon the spread of the gospel (12ff). He notes, however, that some Christian preachers have been hostile to him personally (15f), a fact that pains him until he recalls that in any case Christ is being made known (v 18) and that his own pain will contribute to his salvation (v 19). Facing the possibility of a death sentence, he reflects that for him both life and death take their meaning from Christ (20f). In life he can bear witness to him (v 22), in death, which he prefers as the outcome of his imprisonment, he will be finally united to him (v 23). But the Philippians' need of him makes him confident that he will be released from his imprisonment (24ff).

from specious motives or genuine ones, Christ is being proclaimed! That is what brings me joy. Indeed, I shall continue to rejoice, 19 in the conviction that this will turn out to my salvation, thanks to your prayers and the support I receive from the Spirit of Jesus Christ. 20 I firmly trust and anticipate that I shall never be put to shame for my hopes; I have full confidence that now as always Christ will be exalted through me, whether I live or die. 21 For, to me, "life" means Christ; hence dying is so much gain. 22 If, on the other hand, I am to go on living in the flesh, that means productive toil for me—and I do not know which to prefer. 23 I am strongly attracted by both: I long to be freed from this life and to be with Christ, for that is the far better thing; 24 yet it is more urgent that I remain alive for your sakes. 25 This fills me with confidence that I will stay with you, and persevere with you all, for your joy and your progress in the faith. 26 My being with you once again should make you even prouder of me in Christ.

PLEAS FOR CHRISTIAN HEROISM

Courage in Professing the Faith

27 Conduct yourselves, then, in a way worthy of the gospel of Christ. If you do, whether I come and see you myself or hear about your behavior from a distance, it will be clear that you are standing firm in unity of spirit and exerting yourselves with one accord for the faith of the gospel. 28 Do not be intimidated by your opponents in any situation. Their opposition foreshadows downfall for them, but

salvation for you. All this is as God intends, 29 for it is your special privilege to take Christ's part—not only to believe in him but also to suffer for him. 30 Yours is the same struggle as mine, the one in which you formerly saw me engaged and now hear that I am caught up in.

Imitating Christ's Humility

2 In the name of the encouragement you owe me in Christ, in the name of the solace that love can give, of fellowship in spirit, compassion, and pity, I beg you: 2 make my joy complete by your unanimity, possessing the one love, united in spirit and ideals. 3 Never act out of rivalry or conceit; rather, let all parties think humbly of others as superior to themselves, 4 each of you looking to others' interests rather than his own. 5 Your attitude must be that of Christ:

6 Though he was in the form of God,
  he did not deem equality with God
  something to be grasped at.
7 Rather, he emptied himself
  and took the form of a slave,
  being born in the likeness of men.
He was known to be of human estate,
8 and it was thus that he humbled himself,
  obediently accepting even death,
  death on a cross!
9 Because of this,
  God highly exalted him
  and bestowed on him the name
  above every other name,

10 So that at Jesus' name
  every knee must bend
  in the heavens, on the earth,
  and under the earth,
11 and every tongue proclaim
  to the glory of God the Father:
  JESUS CHRIST IS LORD!

Innocence of the Children of God

12 So then, my dearly beloved, obedient as always to my urging, work with anxious concern to achieve your salvation, not only when I happen to be with you but all the more now that I am absent. 13 It is God who, in his good will toward you, begets in you any measure of desire or achievement. 14 In everything you do, act without grumbling or arguing; 15 prove yourselves innocent and straightforward, children of God beyond reproach in the midst of a twisted and depraved generation—among whom you shine like the stars in the sky 16 while holding fast to the word of life. As I look to the Day of Christ, you give me cause to boast that I did not run the race in vain or work to no purpose. 17 Even if my life is to be poured out as a libation over the sacrificial service of your faith, I am glad of it and rejoice with all of you. 18 May you be glad on the same score, and rejoice with me!

PAUL'S ASSISTANTS AND PLANS

Timothy

19 I hope, in the Lord Jesus, 6 to send Timothy to you very soon, that I may derive courage from learning how things go with you. 20 I have no one quite like him for

---

1, 27–30: He encourages them to hold fast, in the face of opposition, to their faith in the gospel.

2, 1–11: This passage is composed of two parts: introductory exhortations pleading for unity in the Philippian church and for the elimination of differences that are harmful to the community (1–4); and a panegyric hymn (6–11) which reflects the self-effacement of Christ, the model for Christian service (v 5). The hymn begins by invoking Christian faith in Jesus' divinity (*Though he was in the form of God*), and by recalling that, paradoxically, his divinity was concealed throughout his mortal life (v 6). Divesting himself of his divine prerogatives, not indeed of the divinity itself but of the state of glory rightfully his, and assuming the role of a servant, he presented himself simply as a man (v 7; cf Is 52, 13–53; 42, 1). Having fully accepted the human condition, he followed it in obedience to the Father even to death on a cross (v 8). The Father responded by raising him from the dead and placing him at his right hand. The

resurrection and ascension are the theological sense of *hypsoun*, the Greek verb used; cf also Acts 2, 33. God endowed him with his own name (v 9), so that the name JESUS (Saviour) would be identified in the knowledge of every creature with the very same name (*kyrios*, "Lord") that is addressed to God the Father (2, 10f).

2, 12–18: Paul exhorts his readers further through a reminder that the goal of their endeavors within the community is their salvation (v 12); this is the whole purpose of the divine activity within them (v 13). Consequently, all complaints and disputes harmful to the community should be avoided so that the Philippians may be a shining light to pagans everywhere (14f). They should transmit to the world the life of the gospel and thus become a source of pride for him at the parousia (v 16). If they achieve this, he can rejoice in the sufferings of his imprisonment and they in turn can be happy because of his joy (17f).

2, 19–3, 1: To show his concern for the Philip-

pians, Paul announces his intention of sending them his most trusted assistant in his apostolate—Timothy, whom they already know (cf Acts 16, 1–15). If Paul is released, as he anticipates, he himself plans a visit to them (19–24). He commends Epaphroditus, whom they had sent to aid him in his imprisonment. He is relieved that Epaphroditus' recovery from a critical illness spares him, Paul, the sorrow of a death in the midst of this display of the Philippians' charity; indicating that as soon as Epaphroditus is well enough to make the journey, he will return to them (25–30). 3, 1 seems to be the beginning of a conclusion to the letter, interrupted by Paul's second thought of adding a strong warning against the teaching of the Judaizers (see notes on Gal 1, 1–5 and 1, 6–10). Some scholars think the verse implies a previous letter to the Philippians, now lost.

genuine interest in whatever concerns you. 21 Everyone is busy seeking his own interests rather than those of Christ Jesus. 22 You know from experience what Timothy's qualities are, how he was like a son at his father's side serving the gospel along with me. 23 I hope to send him as soon as I see how things go with me. 24 In fact, I am confident in the Lord that I myself will be coming soon.

Epaphroditus

25 I have decided, too, that I must send you Epaphroditus, my brother, co-worker, and comrade in arms, whom you sent to take care of my needs. 26 He has been longing for all of you, and was distressed that you heard about his illness. 27 He was, in fact, sick to the point of death, but God took pity on him; not just on him, I should say, but on me, too, so as to spare me one sorrow after another. 28 I have been especially eager to send him so that you may renew your joy on seeing him, and my own anxieties may be lessened. 29 Welcome him joyously in the Lord and hold men like him in esteem, 30 for he came near to death for the sake of Christ's work. He risked his life in an effort to render me those services you could not render.

CHRISTIAN DEDICATION

Breaking with the Past

3 For the rest, my brothers, rejoice in the Lord. I find writing you these things no burden, and for you it is a safeguard.
2 Beware of unbelieving dogs. Watch out for workers of evil. Be on guard against those who mutilate.

3 It is we who are the circumcision, who worship in the spirit of God and glory in Christ Jesus rather than putting our trust in the flesh— 4 though I can be confident even there. If anyone thinks he has a right to put his trust in external evidence, all the more can I! 5 I was circumcised on the eighth day, being of the stock of Israel and the tribe of Benjamin, a Hebrew of Hebrew origins; in legal observance I was a Pharisee, 6 and so zealous that I persecuted the church. I was above reproach when it came to justice based on the law.

7 But those things I used to consider gain I have now reappraised as loss in the light of Christ. 8 I have come to rate all as loss in the light of the surpassing knowledge of my Lord Jesus Christ. For his sake I have forfeited everything; I have accounted all else rubbish so that Christ may be my wealth 9 and I may be in him, not having any justice of my own based on observance of the law. The justice I possess is that which comes through faith in Christ. It has its origin in God and is based on faith. 10 I wish to know Christ and the power flowing from his resurrection; likewise to know how to share in his sufferings by being formed into the pattern of his death. 11 Thus do I hope that I may arrive at resurrection from the dead.

12 It is not that I have reached it yet, or have already finished my course; but I am racing to grasp the prize if possible, since I have been grasped by Christ [Jesus]. 13 Brothers, I do not think of myself as having reached the finish line. I give no thought to what lies behind but push on to what is ahead. 14 My entire attention is on the finish line as I run toward the prize to which God

calls me—life on high in Christ Jesus. 15 All of us who are spiritually mature must have this attitude. If you see it another way, God will clarify the difficulty for you. 16 It is important that we continue on our course, no matter what stage we have reached.

Christ Our Goal

17 Be imitators of me, my brothers. Take as your guide those who follow the example that we set. 18 Unfortunately, many go about in a way which shows them to be enemies of the cross of Christ. I have often said this to you before; this time I say it with tears. 19 Such as these will end in disaster! Their god is their belly and their glory is in their shame. I am talking about those who are set upon the things of this world. 20 As you well know, we have our citizenship in heaven; it is from there that we eagerly await the coming of our Savior, the Lord Jesus Christ. 21 He will give a new form to this lowly body of ours and remake it according to the pattern of his glorified body, by his power to subject everything to himself.

EXHORTATIONS TO VIRTUE

Christian Concord

4 For these reasons, my brothers, you whom I so love and long for, you who are my joy and my crown, continue, my dear ones, to stand firm in the Lord. 2 I plead with Evodia just as I do with Syntyche: come to some mutual understanding in the Lord. 3 Yes, and I ask you, too, my dependable fellow worker, to go to their aid; they have struggled at my side in promoting the gospel,

---

3, 2–4, 1: The Judaizers are called *unbelieving dogs* (the customary Jewish term at the time for Gentiles, here applied ironically) and *workers of evil*. Their urging of the religious rite of circumcision upon Christians is regarded as mutilation (v 2). The apostle declares that Christians, who possess the true worship prefigured by circumcision, have no need of this religious rite (v 3). He offers himself an example of one reared in the Jewish tradition of circumcision and the law, which he thought it his duty to defend by persecuting the Christian communities (4ff). Because of his faith in Christ he has now abandoned this religious tradition of salvation (7f). He relies solely on Christ for his justice before God, not on his own efforts to observe the law (v 9). He conforms his life to the sufferings of Christ, that he may know him alone, and experience bodily resurrection through

him (10f). This adherence to Christ in faith does not mean that Paul has already ensured his own salvation by arriving at perfect spiritual maturity (v 12). He strives for still greater perfection, mindful of the meaning of God's call in Christ (13f).
Paul's prayer is that God may correct the Philippians if their attitude in this regard is different, though he sincerely believes they have no need except to make still greater progress (15f). His way and that of his followers are the model for their study (v 17). He mourns for those in the Christian community who fail to perceive that salvation lies in the cross of Christ, not in food regulations or circumcision (18f). Salvation does not lie in the body but in Christ, who at his second coming, will transform the body (20f). Paul begs the Philippians, in terms of great affection, to adhere firmly to what he has taught (4, 1).

4, 2–9: The apostle appeals personally to these two women to reconcile their differences (v 2) and adds a further appeal to *syzygos* to aid them in achieving a reconciliation. This word means "comrade, yoke-fellow," and may be a proper name, though no evidence has been found of its use as such (v 3). Paul wishes the Philippians to be a model community, marked by a joy that will have its effect also upon non-Christians (4f). Mindful of the possible nearness of the parousia (see note on 1 Thes 4, 13–18), the Philippians are not to be overly concerned about their troubles but instead are to resolve them in prayer (5f). Thus they will always be at peace (v 7). Their thoughts and lives should reflect only what is true, pure, admirable, virtuous or worthy of praise, as exemplified by his own life among them (8f).

along with Clement and the others who have labored with me, whose names are in the book of life.

Joy and Peace

4 Rejoice in the Lord always! I say it again. Rejoice! 5 Everyone should see how unselfish you are. The Lord is near. 6 Dismiss all anxiety from your minds. Present your needs to God in every form of prayer and in petitions full of gratitude. 7 Then God's own peace, which is beyond all understanding, will stand guard over your hearts and minds, in Christ Jesus.

8 Finally, my brothers, your thoughts should be wholly directed to all that is true, all that deserves respect, all that is honest, pure, admirable, decent, virtuous, or worthy of praise. 9 Live according to what you have learned and accepted, what you have heard me say and seen me do. Then will the God of peace be with you.

Generosity

10 It gave me great joy in the Lord that your concern for me bore fruit once more. You had been concerned all along, of course, but lacked the opportunity to show it. 11 I do not say this because I am in want, for whatever the situation I find myself in I have learned to be self-sufficient. 12 I am experienced in being brought low, yet I know what it is to have an abundance. I have learned how to cope with every circumstance—how to eat well or go hungry, to be well provided for or do without. 13 In him who is the source of my strength I have strength for everything.

14 Nonetheless, it was kind of you to want to share in my hardships. 15 You yourselves know, my dear Philippians, that at the start of my evangelizing, when I left Macedonia, not a single congregation except yourselves shared with me by giving me something for what it had received. 16 Even when I was at Thessalonica you sent something for my needs, not once but twice. 17 It is not that I am eager for the gift; rather, my concern is for the ever-growing balance in your account. 18 Herewith is my receipt, which says that I have been fully paid and more. I am well supplied because of what I received from you through Epaphroditus, a fragrant offering, a sacrifice acceptable and pleasing to God.

19 My God in turn will supply your needs fully, in a way worthy of his magnificent riches in Christ Jesus. 20 All glory to our God and Father for unending ages! Amen.

Farewell

21 Give my greetings in Christ Jesus to every member of the church. My brothers here send you theirs, 22 as do all those who believe, particularly those in Caesar's service. 23 May the favor of the Lord Jesus Christ be with your spirit. Amen.

4, 10–20: Paul thanks the Philippians for their monetary contribution, brought by Epaphroditus (v 18). He accepts it gratefully, though not because he needs the money, for with God's help he always manages to provide for his wants (10–13); rather, he appreciates their sharing with him, noting that they are the only community from which he has taken such a gift (14ff). His joy in accepting the gift, more than he actually needed, comes from his certainty that God will reward their charity by fulfilling all their needs in turn (17–20).

4, 21ff: The final greetings, extended to all the members of the Philippian community individually, come not only from Paul but also from the Christians of the place where the letter originated (see Introduction).

THE EPISTLE OF PAUL TO THE

Colossians

INTRODUCTION

GREETING

PAUL, an apostle of Christ Jesus by the will of God, and Timothy our brother, 2 to the holy ones at Colossae, faithful brothers in Christ. May God our Father give you grace and peace.

Thanksgiving

3 We always give thanks to God, the Father of our Lord Jesus Christ, in our prayers for you 4 because we have heard of your faith in Christ Jesus and the love you bear toward all the saints—moved as you are by the hope held in store for you in heaven. 5 You heard of this hope through the message of truth, the gospel, 6 which has come to you, has borne fruit, and has continued to grow in your midst, as it has everywhere in the world. This has been the case from the day you first heard it and comprehended God's gracious 7 intention through the instructions of Epaphras, our

dear fellow slave, who represents us as a faithful minister of Christ. 8 He it was who told us of your love in the Spirit.

Prayer for Continued Progress

9 Ever since we heard this we have been praying for you unceasingly and asking that you may attain full knowledge of his will through perfect wisdom and spiritual insight. 10 Then you will lead a life worthy of the Lord and pleasing to him in every way. You will multiply good works of every sort and grow in the knowledge of God. 11 By the might of his glory you will be endowed with the strength

needed to stand fast, even to endure joyfully whatever may come, 12 giving thanks to the Father for having made you worthy to share the lot of the saints in light. 13 He rescued us from the power of darkness and brought us into the kingdom of his beloved Son. 14 Through him we have redemption, the forgiveness of our sins.

THE PREEMINENCE OF CHRIST

Fullness and Reconciliation

15 He is the image of the invisible God, the first-born of all creatures. 16 In him everything in heaven and on earth was created, things visible

---

1, 1f: For the epistolary form used by Paul at the beginning of his letters, see note on Romans 1, 1–7. The apostle frequently designates the members of the Christian community as *holy ones* (literally, "saints"), a term that includes the Old Testament idea of the people of God, and now expresses a relation to Christ. They have been called by God to union with Christ and have experienced the spiritual benefits of this union. The awareness of it helps them to be *faithful brothers in Christ*, i.e., dedicated to the tasks implied in their calling.
1, 3–8: Recalling his prayers for them and the deeply satisfying account of them he has received, the

apostle congratulates the Colossians upon their acceptance of Christ and their faithful efforts to live his gospel (3ff). For their encouragement he mentions the success of the gospel elsewhere (v 6), and assures them that his knowledge of their community is accurate since he has been in personal contact with Epaphras, their presumed founder (7f).
1, 9–14: Moved by Epaphras' account, the apostle has prayed fervently for the Colossians that their response to the gospel may bring the fullest knowledge of God's will, *through perfect wisdom and spiritual insight* (v 9; cf 3, 10). He expects a mutual interaction between their life according to the gospel

and this knowledge (v 10), which will reveal the power of God's presence among them, inspire them to courage and calm determination (v 11), and result in grateful love of the Father for his saving gifts (v 12). For he conquers the power of evil over men by offering them the power of his Son, who is his love in person (v 13) and has already forgiven their sins (v 10).
1, 15–20: Scholars raise the question whether Paul may not have adapted these verses from a Christian hymn or a Hellenistic wisdom poem. Whatever the case, the passage with all its lyricism is probably Paul's. Its exalted Christology synthesizes

and invisible, whether thrones or dominations, principalities or powers; all were created through him, and for him. 17 He is before all else that is. In him everything continues in being. 18 It is he who is head of the body, the church; he who is the beginning, the first-born of the dead, so that primacy may be his in everything. 19 It pleased God to make absolute fullness reside in him 20 and, by means of him, to reconcile everything in his person, both on earth and in the heavens, making peace through the blood of his cross. 21 You yourselves were once alienated from him; you nourished hostility in your hearts because of your evil deeds. 22 But now Christ has achieved reconciliation for you in his mortal body by dying, so as to present you to God holy, free of reproach and blame. 23 But you must hold fast to faith, be firmly grounded and steadfast in it, unshaken in the hope promised you by the gospel you have heard. It is the gospel which has been announced to every creature under heaven, and I, Paul, am its servant.

The Mystery: Christ in Us

24 Even now I find my joy in the suffering I endure for you. In my own flesh I fill up what is lacking in the sufferings of Christ for the sake of his body, the church. 25 I became

a minister of this church through the commission God gave me to preach among you his word in its fullness, 26 that mystery hidden from ages and generations past but now revealed to his holy ones. 27 God has willed to make known to them the glory beyond price which this mystery brings to the Gentiles—the mystery of Christ in you, your hope of glory. 28 This is the Christ we proclaim while we admonish all men and teach them in the full measure of wisdom, hoping to make every man complete in Christ. 29 For this I work and struggle, impelled by that energy of his which is so powerful a force within me.

2 I want you to know how hard I am struggling for you and for the Laodiceans and the many others who have never seen me in the flesh. 2 I wish their hearts to be strengthened and themselves to be closely united in love, enriched with full assurance by their knowledge of the mystery of God—namely Christ— 3 in whom every treasure of wisdom and knowledge is hidden.

WARNINGS AGAINST FALSE TEACHERS

A General Admonition

4 I tell you all this so that no one may delude you with specious arguments. 5 I may be absent in body but I am with you in spirit, happy to

see good order among you and the firmness of your faith in Christ. 6 Continue, therefore, to live in Christ Jesus the Lord, in the spirit in which you received him. 7 Be rooted in him and built up in him, growing ever stronger in faith, as you were taught, and overflowing with gratitude. 8 See to it that no one deceives you through any empty, seductive philosophy that follows mere human traditions, a philosophy based on cosmic powers rather than on Christ.

Sovereign Role of Christ

9 In Christ the fullness of deity resides in bodily form. Yours is a share of this fullness, in him 10 who is the head of every principality and power. 11 You were also circumcised in him, not with the circumcision administered by hand but with Christ's circumcision which strips off the carnal body completely. 12 In baptism you were not only buried with him but also raised to life with him because you believed in the power of God who raised him from the dead. 13 Even when you were dead in sin and your flesh was uncircumcised, God gave you new life in company with Christ. He pardoned all our sins. 14 He canceled the bond that stood against us with all its claims, snatching it up and nailing it to the cross. 15 Thus did God disarm the principalities

---

the growing awareness in New Testament times of Christ as man, Son of God, king and judge of the world, endowed with divine redemptive power, and containing in himself the fullness of that effective presence of God among men which was first manifested in the Old Testament (cf Jn 1, 1–18). Whereas man is patterned after the image of God, being given a certain likeness to him (Gn 1, 26f), Christ is the actual likeness of God. Through faith, the remote reality of the Deity is rendered discernibly present in him and comprehensible to men. *He is the image of the invisible God* (v 15), in the sense that as a person he is supreme in every way over all creation. Christ's supremacy requires not only that nothing appear in creation except in relation to him but also that he himself share in the creation of all things (v 16). Such is his supremacy that he existed before creation came into being. It is to him that creation owes all that it has been, is, and will be (v 17).

Christ cannot be anything but supreme over the church, which in any case is unthinkable and unrealizable without him (his *body*). Furthermore, because of his supremacy he was the first to be raised by God from the dead; and his resurrection placed him in full possession of headship over the community which he brought into being (v 18). Since, as is clear from Christ's role in creation (v 16), the cosmos is dependent on him (v 19), his death upon the cross has its effect on the whole of creation without exception, pacifying it and uniting it to God (v 20). Paul's clear exposition of the supremacy of Christ

was occasioned by the Colossians' difficulties concerning the relationship of angelic spirits to the world (see Introduction).

1, 21ff: Paul reminds them that they have experienced the reconciling effect of Christ's death, and appeals to them to adhere firmly to him as their only conciliator with God.

1, 24f—2.5: As the community at Colossae is not personally known to Paul (see Introduction), he here invests his recommendations with greater authority by presenting a brief sketch of his apostolic ministry and sufferings as they reflect those of Christ in behalf of the church (v 24). The preaching of God's word (v 25) manifests the divine will to sanctify the Gentiles (v 26) by revealing God's saving presence among them in Christ (v 27). It teaches men the God-given wisdom about Christ (v 28), whose power works mightily in the apostle (v 29). Even in those communities which do not know him personally (2, 1), he can increase their perception of God in Christ, unite the faithful more firmly in love, and so bring spiritual comfort to them (v 2). He hopes that his apostolic authority will make the Colossians perceive more readily the defects in the teaching of others who have sought to delude them (4f).

2, 6—3, 4: The Colossians are admonished to adhere to the gospel as it was first preached to them (v 6), steeping themselves in it with grateful hearts (v 7). They must reject religious teachings originating in any source except the gospel (v 8) because in Christ alone will they have access to the divinity (v 9). So

fully has he enlightened them that they need no other source of religious knowledge or virtue (v 10). They do not require circumcision (v 11), for in baptism their whole being has been affected by Christ (v 12) through forgiveness of sin and restoration to a new life (v 13; cf Rom 6, 1–11).

On the cross Christ canceled the bond that stood against us, with all its claims; i.e., he eliminated the law (cf Eph 2, 15), which men could not observe—and which could not save them. He forgave sins against the law (v 14), and exposed as false and misleading (v 15) all other powers which offer salvation to men. Therefore the Colossians are not to judge food and drink or the keeping of religious festivals according to the rule of other religious powers, including angelic spirits (16ff), for they thereby risk severing themselves from Christ (v 19). If, when they accepted the gospel, they believed in Christ as their Savior, they must be convinced that their salvation cannot be achieved by appeasing ruling spirits through dietary practices, or through a wisdom gained simply in virtue of harsh asceticism (20–23). By retaining the message of the gospel that the risen, living Christ is the source of their salvation, they will be free from false religious evaluations of the things of the world (3, 1f). The Colossians, it is true, will not have the personal satisfaction that material religious practices offer. They have died to these; but one day they will live with Christ in the presence of God (3f).

and powers. He made a public show of them and, leading them off captive, triumphed in the person of Christ.

Practices contrary to Faith

16 No one is free, therefore, to pass judgment on you in terms of what you eat or drink or what you do on yearly or monthly feasts, or on the sabbath. 17 All these were but a shadow of things to come; the reality is the body of Christ. 18 Let no one rob you of your prize by insisting on servility in the worship of angels. Such a one takes his stand on his own experience; he is inflated with empty pride by his human reflections 19 when he should be in close touch with the head. The whole body, mutually supported and upheld by joints and sinews, achieves a growth from this source which comes from God.

20 If with Christ you have died to cosmic forces, why should you be bound by rules that say, 21 "Do not handle! Do not taste! Do not touch!" as though you were still living a life bounded by this world? Such prescriptions deal with things that perish in their use. They are based on merely human precepts and doctrines. 23 While these make a certain show of wisdom in their affected piety, humility, and bodily austerity, their chief effect is that they indulge men's pride.

THE IDEAL CHRISTIAN LIFE IN THE WORLD

Mystical Death and Resurrection

3 Since you have been raised up in company with Christ, set your heart on what pertains to higher realms where Christ is seated at God's right hand. 2 Be intent on things above rather than on things of earth. 3 After all, you have died! Your life is hidden now with Christ in God. 4 When Christ our life appears, then you shall appear with him in glory.

Renunciation of Vices

5 Put to death whatever in your nature is rooted in earth: fornication, uncleanness, passion, evil desires, and that lust which is idolatry. 6 These are the sins which provoke God's wrath. 7 Your own conduct was once of this sort, when these sins were your very life. 8 You must put that aside now: all the anger and quick temper, the malice, the insults, the foul language. 9 Stop lying to one another. What you have done is put aside your old self with its past deeds 10 and put on a new man, one who grows in knowledge as he is formed anew in the image of his Creator. 11 There is no Greek or Jew here, circumcised or uncircumcised, foreigner, Scythian, slave, or freeman. Rather, Christ is everything in all of you.

The Practice of Virtues

12 Because you are God's chosen ones, holy and beloved, clothe yourselves with heartfelt mercy, with kindness, humility, meekness, and patience. 13 Bear with one another; forgive whatever grievances you have against one another. 14 Forgive as the Lord has forgiven you. Over all these virtues put on love, which binds the rest together and makes them perfect. 15 Christ's peace must reign in your hearts, since as members of the one body you have been called to that peace. Dedicate yourselves to thankfulness. 16 Let the word of Christ, rich as it is, dwell in you. In wisdom made perfect, instruct and admonish one another. Sing gratefully to God from your hearts in psalms, hymns, and inspired songs. 17 Whatever you do, whether in speech or in action, do it in the name of the Lord Jesus. Give thanks to God the Father through him.

The Christian Family

18 You who are wives, be submissive to your husbands. This is your duty in the Lord. 19 Hus-

bands, love your wives. Avoid any bitterness toward them. 20 You children, obey your parents in everything as the acceptable way in the Lord. 21 And fathers, do not nag your children lest they lose heart.

Slaves and Masters

22 To slaves I say, obey your human masters perfectly, not with the purpose of attracting attention and pleasing men but in all sincerity and out of reverence for the Lord. 23 Whatever you do, work at it with your whole being. 24 Do it for the Lord rather than for men, since you know full well you will receive an inheritance from him as your reward. 25 Be slaves of Christ the Lord. Whoever acts unjustly will be repaid for the wrong he has done. No favoritism will be shown.

4 You slaveowners, deal justly and fairly with your slaves, realizing that you too have a master in heaven.

Prayer and Apostolic Spirit

2 Pray perseveringly, be attentive to prayer, and pray in a spirit of thanksgiving. 3 Pray for us, too, that God may provide us with an opening to proclaim the mystery of Christ, for which I am a prisoner. 4 Pray that I may speak it clearly, as I must. 5 Be prudent in dealing with outsiders; make the most of every opportunity. 6 Let your speech be always gracious and in good taste, and strive to respond properly to all who address you.

CONCLUSION

Tychicus and Onesimus

7 Tychicus, our dear brother, our faithful minister and fellow slave in the Lord, will give you all the news about me. 8 I am sending him to you for this purpose, and to comfort your hearts. 9 With him is Onesimus, our dear and faithful brother, who is one of you. They will tell you all that has happened here.

3, 5–17: In lieu of false asceticism and superstitious festivals, the apostle reminds the Colossians of the moral life that is to characterize their response to God through Christ. He urges their participation in the liturgical hymns and prayers that center upon God's plan of salvation in Christ (16f).

3, 18–4, 18: After general recommendations which connect family life and the social condition of slavery with the service of Christ (3, 18–4, 1), Paul requests prayers for himself, especially in view of his imprisonment (2f), and recommends friendly relations and meaningful discussions of Christian teaching

with non-Christians (5f). He concludes with greetings and information concerning various Christians known to the Colossians (7–18).

From Paul's Co-workers

10 Aristarchus, who is a prisoner along with me, sends you greetings. So does Mark, the cousin of Barnabas. You have received instructions about him: if he comes to you, make him welcome. 11 Jesus known also as Justus sends greetings. These are the only circumcised ones among those who working with me for the kingdom of God. They have been a great comfort to me. 12 Epaphras, who is one of you, sends greetings. He is a servant of Christ Jesus who is always pleading earnestly in prayer that you stand firm, that you be perfect and have full conviction about whatever pertains to God's will. 13 I can certainly testify how solicitous he is for you and for those at Laodicea and Hierapolis. 14 Luke, our dear physician, sends you greetings. So does Demas.

A Message for the Laodiceans

15 Give our best wishes to the brothers at Laodicea and to Nymphas and the assembly that meets at his house. 16 Once this letter has been read to you, see that it is read in the assembly of the Laodiceans as well, and that you yourselves read the letter that is coming from Laodicea. 17 To Archippus say, "Take care to discharge the ministry you have received in the Lord."

18 This greeting is from Paul—in my own hand! Remember my chains. Grace be with you.

4, 16: The reference is perhaps to a letter Paul wrote to be read in a number of Christian communities in the area of the Lycus Valley, that eventually became known as the letter to the Ephesians (see Ephesians Introduction).

THE FIRST EPISTLE OF PAUL TO THE

Thessalonians

INTRODUCTION

GREETING

PAUL, Silvanus, and Timothy, to the church of the Thessalonians who belong to God the Father and the Lord Jesus Christ. Grace and peace be yours. 2 We keep thanking God for all of you and we remember you in our prayers 3 for we constantly are mindful before our God and Father,

A Model for Believers

of the way you are proving your faith, and laboring in love, and showing constancy of hope in our Lord Jesus Christ. 4 We know, too, brothers beloved of God, how you were chosen. 5 Our preaching of the gospel proved not a mere matter of words for you but one of power; it was carried on in the Holy Spirit and out of complete conviction. You know as well as we do what we proved to be like when, while still among you, we acted on your behalf. 6 You, in turn, became imitators of us and of the Lord, receiving the word despite great trials, with the joy that comes from the Holy Spirit. 7 Thus you became a model for all the believers of Macedonia and Achaia. 8 The word of the Lord has echoed forth from you resoundingly. This is true not only in Macedonia and Achaia; throughout every region your faith in God is celebrated, which makes it needless for us to say anything more. 9 The people of those parts are reporting what kind of reception we had from you, and how you turned to God from idols, to serve him who is the living and true God 10 and to await from heaven the Son he raised from the dead—Jesus, who delivers us from the wrath to come.

RELATIONS WITH THE THESSALONIANS

Paul's Sincerity

2 You know well enough, brothers, that our coming among you was not without effect. 2 Fresh from the humiliation we had suffered at Philippi—about which you know—we drew courage from our God to preach his good tidings to you in the face of great opposition. 3 The exhortation we deliver does not spring from deceit or impure motives or any sort of trickery; 4 rather, having met the test imposed on us by God, as men entrusted with the good tidings, we speak like those who strive to please God, "the tester of our hearts," rather than men.

5 We were not guilty, as you well know, of flattering words or greed under any pretext, as God is our witness! 6 Neither did we seek glory from men, you or any others, 7 even though we could have insisted on our own importance as apostles of Christ.

1, 1: For Paul's use of the conventional epistolary form, see note on Romans 1, 1–7.

1, 2–10: The apostle expresses his satisfaction that the three principal Christian characteristics, faith, hope and love, are at work in the Thessalonian community (2f). Unhesitatingly he places its members among those specially beloved and chosen by God (v 4); recalling that his preaching of the gospel to them was not received as a mere intellectual exercise but had made a strong actual impact on their lives (v 5) which not even the opposition of unbelievers could dispel (v 6). Their faith has been an inspiration to Christians elsewhere (7f), who have been impressed especially by the Thessalonians' complete abandonment of idolatry for the worship of the true God, and by their profound orientation toward the second coming of Jesus (9f).

2, 1–12: Paul had experienced such great opposition in Thessalonica that he had to be secretly escorted from the city (Acts 17, 1–10). It is probably the memory of this which underlies the present words recalling his selflessness in preaching the gospel to them (1–7), his affection for them (8f), and the pleasant relationships he established with them (10ff).

On the contrary, while we were among you we were as gentle as any nursing mother fondling her little ones. 8 So well disposed were we to you, in fact, that we wanted to share with you not only God's tidings but our very lives, so dear had you become to us. 9 You must recall, brothers, our efforts and our toil: how we worked day and night all the time we preached God's good tidings to you in order not to impose on you in any way. 10 You are witnesses, as is God himself, of how upright, just, and irreproachable our conduct was toward you who are believers. 11 You likewise know how we exhorted every one of you, as a father does his children— 12 how we encouraged and pleaded with you to make your lives worthy of the God who calls you to his kingship and glory. 13 That is why we thank God constantly that in receiving his message from us you took it, not as the word of men, but as it truly is, the word of God at work within you who believe.

Partnership in Suffering

14 Brothers, you have been made like the churches of God in Judea which are in Christ Jesus. You suffered the same treatment from your fellow countrymen as they did from the Jews 15 who killed the Lord Jesus and the prophets, and persecuted us. Displeasing to God and hostile to all mankind, 16 they try to keep us from preaching salvation to the Gentiles. All this time they have been "filling up their quota of sins," but the wrath has descended upon them at last.

17 Brothers, when we were orphaned by separation from you for a time—in sight, not in mind—we were seized with the greatest longing to see you. 18 So we tried to come to you—I, Paul, tried more than once—but Satan blocked the way. 19 Who, after all, if not you, will be our hope or joy, or the crown we exult in, before our Lord Jesus Christ at his coming? 20 You are our boast and our delight.

Mission of Timothy

3 That is why, when we could endure it no longer, we decided to remain alone at Athens 2 and send you Timothy. He is our brother and God's fellow worker in preaching the gospel of Christ, and so we sent him to strengthen and encourage you in regard to your faith 3 lest any one of you be shaken by these trials. You know well enough that such trials are our common lot. 4 When we were still with you, we used to warn you that we would undergo trial; now it has happened, and you know what we meant. 5 That is why I sent to find out about your faith when I could stand the suspense no longer, fearing that the tempter had put you to the test and all our labor might have gone for nothing. 6 But now, brothers, since Timothy has returned to us from you reporting the good news of your faith and love, and telling us that you constantly remember us and are as desirous to see us as we are to see you, 7 we have been much consoled by your faith throughout our distress and trial— 8 so much so that we shall continue to flourish only if you stand firm in the Lord!

Plea for Growth in Holiness

9 What thanks can we give to God for all the joy we feel in his presence because of you, 10 as we ask him fervently night and day that we may see you face to face and remedy any shortcomings in your faith? 11 May God himself, who is our Father, and our Lord Jesus make our path to you a straight one! 12 And may the Lord increase you and make you overflow with love for one another and for all, even as our love does for you. 13 May he strengthen your hearts, making them blameless and holy before our God and Father at the coming of our Lord Jesus with all his holy ones.

Chastity and Charity

4 Now, my brothers, we beg and exhort you in the Lord Jesus that, even as you learned from us how to conduct yourselves in a way pleasing to God—which you are indeed doing—so you must learn to make still greater progress. 2 You know the instructions we gave you in the Lord Jesus. 3 It is God's will that you grow in holiness: that you abstain from immorality, 4 each of you guarding his member in sanctity and honor, 5 not in passionate desire as do the Gentiles who know not God; 6 and that each refrain from overreaching or cheating his brother in the matter at hand; for the Lord is an avenger of all such things, as we once indicated to you by our testimony. 7 God has not called us to immorality but to holiness; hence, 8 whoever rejects these instructions rejects, not man, but God who sends his Holy Spirit upon you.

9 As regards brotherly love, there is no need for me to write you. God himself has taught you to love one another, 10 and this you are doing with respect to all the brothers throughout Macedonia. Yet we exhort you to even greater progress, brothers. 11 Make it a point of honor to remain at peace and attend to your own affairs. Work with your hands as we directed you to do, 12 so that you will give good example to outsiders and want for nothing.

2, 13–16: The apostle is grateful because the Thessalonians accepted his preaching as a message from God and not as a mere human communication (v 13). This perception has enabled them, as well as the Judaeo-Christians of Jerusalem, to be steadfast in the face of persecution (v 14). Paul condemns the active Jewish opposition to the gospel, branding it as sinful and worthy of divine punishment (15f).

2, 17–20: Twice had Paul made an effort to visit the community at Thessalonica, only to be "blocked by Satan"—an expression which probably refers to the situation in Thessalonica itself; cf 3, 5.

3, 1–10: Troubled by the lack of news concerning the Thessalonians, Paul had sent Timothy to them as his representative. Timothy's report was reassuring (6ff) except as regards certain possible *shortcomings* in their faith (v 10). Paul is probably dealing with these defects concretely in chapters 4 and 5 of the epistle.

3, 11ff: The theme of this prayer is solidarity: between Paul and the Thessalonian Christians (his prospective visit); among themselves; between them and all men (Christian love); and between them and God (holiness).

4, 1–12: To conserve their holiness they are to recall what the apostle taught them in the name of Christ at the time of their conversion (1f). Fornication and all sexual misconduct are to be avoided (3–6), in consideration of the truth that God sanctifies his faithful by the presence of the Holy Spirit (7f). They have heeded Christ's message of love of neighbor and should improve it within the community (9f). He urges that they concern themselves with their own affairs, each laboring faithfully to earn his own living and all presenting a good example to the outside world (11f; cf 5, 14; 2 Thes 3, 10ff).

THE LORD'S SECOND COMING

Witnessed by the Dead

13 We would have you be clear about those who sleep in death, brothers; otherwise you might yield to grief, like those who have no hope. 14 For if we believe that Jesus died and rose, God will bring forth with him from the dead those also who have fallen asleep believing in him. 15 We say to you, as if the Lord himself had said it, that we who live, who survive until his coming, will in no way have an advantage over those who have fallen asleep. 16 No, the Lord himself will come down from heaven at the word of command, at the sound of the archangel's voice and God's trumpet; and those who have died in Christ will rise first. 17 Then we, the living, the survivors, will be caught up with them in the clouds to meet the Lord in the air. Thenceforth we shall be with the Lord unceasingly. 18 Console one another with this message.

The Need for Preparation

5 As regards specific times and moments, brothers, we do not need to write you; 2 you know very well that the day of the Lord is coming like the thief in the night. 3 Just when people are saying, "Peace and security," ruin will fall on them with the suddenness of pains overtaking a woman in labor, and there will be no escape. 4 You are not in the dark, brothers, that the day should catch you off guard, like a thief. 5 No, all of you are children of light and of the day. We belong neither to darkness nor to night; 6 therefore let us not be asleep like the rest, but awake and sober! 7 Sleepers sleep by night and drunkards drink by night. 8 We who live by day must be alert, putting on faith and love as a breastplate and the hope of salvation as a helmet. 9 God has not destined us for wrath but for acquiring salvation through our Lord Jesus Christ. 10 He died for us, that all of us, whether awake or asleep, together might live with him. 11 Therefore, comfort and upbuild one another, as indeed you are doing.

Christian Conduct

12 We beg you, brothers, respect those among you whose task it is to exercise authority in the Lord and admonish you; 13 esteem them with the greatest love because of their work. Remain at peace with one another. 14 We exhort you to admonish the unruly; cheer the fainthearted; support the weak; be patient toward all. 15 See that no one returns evil to any other; always seek one another's good and, for that matter, the good of all.

16 Rejoice always, 17 never cease praying, 18 render constant thanks; such is God's will for you in Christ Jesus.

19 Do not stifle the Spirit. 20 Do not despise prophecies. 21 Test everything; retain what is good. 22 Avoid any semblance of evil.

Blessing and Greeting

23 May the God of peace make you perfect in holiness. May he preserve you whole and entire, spirit, soul, and body, irreproachable at the coming of our Lord Jesus Christ. 24 He who calls us is trustworthy, therefore he will do it.

25 Brothers, pray for us too.

26 Greet all the brothers with a holy embrace. 27 I adjure you by the Lord that this letter be read to them all.

28 May the grace of our Lord Jesus Christ be with you.

4, 13–18: Here Paul takes up the practice among the Thessalonians of mourning excessively for their dead (v 13), a reaction deriving from the stress placed by the community on the proximity of the parousia; cf 1, 10. The apostle reminds them of the Christian doctrine of the resurrection of the dead in Christ (v 14). On the basis of Christ's teaching, he affirms that the resurrection of the dead is to precede the second coming. Those who are alive at the time of the latter will not have the advantage over the dead of being the first witnesses to it (v 15), for the Lord will first command the dead to rise (v 16); the living will then join them and both groups will be witnesses of the parousia (v 17); this and the preceding verse reflect the traditional apocalyptic imagery for an act of God). The doctrine spoken of here is to be recalled when future bereavements overtake the community (v 18). Since Paul does not know the time of the parousia (5, 2; Mt 24, 43) he aligns himself with the Thessalonians (we . . . who survive, v 15) in the hope of living until that day, i.e., within the first Christian generation. In his mind such a possibility seems not to have been excluded by the teaching of Jesus himself.

5, 1–11: Paul does not wish his criticism of the Thessalonians' grief over their dead to de-emphasize the doctrine of the parousia itself; he commends the importance they accord it and its influence over their lives. They know how unexpected, sudden, and certain it will be (1ff); therefore they are to live in constant anticipation of it, for it will determine their salvation (4–11).

5, 12–22: Respect and love are due to those who hold positions of authority in the community (12f); possibly the presbyters are meant; cf Acts 14, 23. It is the duty of all to reprove and strengthen those who fail in their Christian duty and to show patience toward non-believers, especially by quenching the spirit of revenge (14f). The spirit of joy, prayer, and thanksgiving must prevail (16ff). Due respect is to be shown to the charism of prophecy, but its authentic presence is not to be admitted uncritically (19ff), as evil may make its entrance even by this door (v 22).

5, 23ff: The burden of the apostle's prayer is the sanctification of the community (cf 3, 13—4, 12) in preparation for the second coming of Christ.

5, 27: The public reading of the Pauline letters is the method to be employed for insuring their acceptance by the Christian assembly as the word of God.

THE SECOND EPISTLE OF PAUL TO THE

INTRODUCTION

GREETING

PAUL, Silvanus, and Timothy, to the church of the Thessalonians who belong to God our Father and the Lord Jesus Christ. 2 Grace and peace be yours from God the Father and the Lord Jesus Christ. 3 It is no more than right that we thank God unceasingly for you, brothers, because your

Praise for the Church at Thessalonica

faith grows apace and your mutual love increases; 4 so much so that in God's communities we can boast of your constancy and your faith in persecution and trial. You endure these 5 as an expression of God's just judgment, in order to be found worthy of his kingdom—it is for his kingdom you suffer— 6 even if strict justice would require that God visit hardships on those who visit them on you. 7 He will provide relief to you who are sorely tried, as well as to us, when the Lord Jesus is revealed

from heaven with his mighty angels; 8 when "with flaming power he will inflict punishment on those who do not acknowledge God nor heed" the good news of our Lord Jesus. 9 Such as these will suffer the penalty of eternal ruin apart from the presence of the Lord and the glory of his might 10 on the Day when he comes, to be glorified in his holy ones and adored by all who have believed—for you already have our witness to you.

Prayer for Their Progress

11 We pray for you always that

our God may make you worthy of his call, and fulfill by his power every honest intention and work of faith. 12 In this way the name of our Lord Jesus may be glorified in you and you in him, in accord with the gracious gift of our God and of the Lord Jesus Christ.

THE LORD'S SECOND COMING

Adversary Restrained

2 On the question of the coming of our Lord Jesus Christ and our being gathered to him, we beg you, brothers, 2 not to be so easily

1, 1f: On the address and greeting, see note on Romans 1, 1–7.

1, 3–12: The Thessalonian community is encouraged to stand fast under the severe trial they are experiencing (3ff). *God's just judgment* will bring relief to the afflicted as well as punishment to the persecutors (6–10). The harassment of the community seems to have intensified during the interval between the writing of 1 and 2 Thessalonians; cf 1 Thes 2, 14ff. This plight may well have contributed to the notion that the parousia was near. Paul considers this question in 2, 1–12.

2, 1–12: Though the parousia is certain (v 1), the Thessalonians are not to expect it to occur at almost

any time in the immediate future. No appeal to an utterance of a self-styled prophet, or to any supposed letter of Paul justifies such an expectation (v 2). They should not allow themselves to be duped into this way of thinking, for a religious apostasy is destined to precede the Lord's second coming. It will be embodied in *the man of lawlessness*, a personage totally dedicated to evil, *that son of perdition* marked for eternal doom (vv 3f); cf Jn 17, 12. In the epistles of John he is usually identified with the antichrist (1 Jn 2, 18.22; 4, 3; 2 Jn 7). He will be anti-God and will himself lay claim to divine honors (v 4).

During Paul's stay at Thessalonica (Acts 17, 1–9) he instructed the people on this subject (v 5). Now

he wishes to add that there is a restraining power which prevents the man of lawlessness from coming into his own (v 6). *The secret force of lawlessness*, though *already at work*, is held down now by a restraining power (v 7), the nature of which Paul does not explain. While the restraint continues, the parousia cannot occur; but when it is removed, *the lawless one* will make his appearance accompanied by all the panoply of satanic power (vv 8f). He will bring some to ruin (v 10), but is destined to be destroyed by Jesus' coming (v 8). God acts toward the impious in such a way as to allow them to become confirmed in evil (v 11; cf Rom 1, 24f) through their deliberate rejection of the truth (v 12).

agitated or terrified, whether by an oracular utterance, or rumor, or a letter alleged to be ours, into believing that the day of the Lord is here.

3 Let no one seduce you, no matter how. Since the mass apostasy has not yet occurred nor the man of lawlessness been revealed—that son of perdition 4 and adversary who exalts himself above every so-called god proposed for worship, he who seats himself in God's temple and even declares himself to be God— 5 do you not remember how I used to tell you about these things when I was still with you? 6 You know what restrains him until he shall be revealed in his own time. 7 The secret force of lawlessness is already at work, mind you, but there is one who holds him back until that restrainer shall be taken from the scene. 8 Thereupon the lawless one will be revealed, and the Lord Jesus will destroy him with the breath of his mouth and annihilate him by manifesting his own presence. 9 This lawless one will appear as part of the workings of Satan, accompanied by all the power and signs and wonders at the disposal of falsehood— 10 by every seduction the wicked can devise for those destined to ruin because they have not opened their hearts to the truth in order to be saved. 11 Therefore God is sending upon them a perverse spirit which leads them to give credence to falsehood, 12 so that all who have not believed the truth but have delighted in evildoing will be condemned.

Encouraging Words

13 We are bound to thank God for you always, beloved brothers in the Lord, because you are the first fruits of those whom God has chosen for salvation, in holiness of spirit and fidelity to truth. 14 He called you through our preaching of the good news so that you might achieve the glory of our Lord Jesus Christ.

15 Therefore, brothers, stand firm. Hold fast to the traditions you received from us, either by our word or by letter. 16 May our Lord Jesus Christ himself, may God our Father who loved us and in his mercy gave us eternal consolation and hope, 17 console your hearts and strengthen them for every good work and word.

EXHORTATION

Request for Prayers

3 For the rest, brothers, pray for us that the word of the Lord may make progress and be hailed by many others, even as it has been by you. 2 Pray that we may be delivered from confused and evil men. For not every man has faith, but 3 the Lord keeps faith; he it is who will strengthen you and guard you against the evil one. 4 In the Lord we are confident that you are doing and will continue to do whatever we enjoin. 5 May the Lord rule your hearts in the love of God and the constancy of Christ.

Dealing with the Idle

6 We command you, brothers, in the name of the Lord Jesus Christ, to avoid any brother who wanders from the straight path and does not follow the tradition you received from us. 7 You know how you ought to imitate us. We did not live lives of disorder when we were among you, nor depend on anyone for food. 8 Rather, we worked day and night, laboring to the point of exhaustion so as not to impose on any of you. 9 Not that we had no claim on you, but that we might present ourselves as an example for you to imitate. 10 Indeed, when we were with you we used to lay down the rule that anyone who would not work should not eat.

11 We hear that some of you are unruly, not keeping busy but acting like busybodies. 12 We enjoin all such, and we urge them strongly in the Lord Jesus Christ, to earn the food they eat by working quietly.

13 You must never grow weary of doing what is right, brothers.

14 If anyone will not obey our injunction, delivered through this letter, single him out to be ostracized that he may be ashamed of his conduct. 15 But do not treat him like an enemy; rather, correct him as you would a brother.

Final Blessing and Greeting

16 May he who is the Lord of peace give you continued peace in every possible way. The Lord be with you all.

17 This greeting is in my own hand —Paul's. I append this signature to every letter I write.

18 May the grace of our Lord Jesus Christ be with you all.

2, 13–17: The Christian faithful are on the path of salvation. They have received, through the medium of Paul's preaching, the divine gift of sanctification that flows from faith in the gospel (v 13); it is the first step toward ultimate participation in Christ's glory (v 14). They are not to depart from the instructions given them at the time of their conversion (cf Acts 17, 1–9) nor from those contained in Paul's previous letter (1 Thes 2:15). The apostle's prayer is that God may comfort and strengthen them as they strive to live out the gospel in their own lives (16f).

3, 1–5: Paul requests that his preaching of the gospel may continue to be successful (v 1), and he himself may be free from hindrance by the wicked (v 2). He is confident that the Lord will preserve the faith of the community (v 3) and help them to carry out faithfully all that has been enjoined upon them (v 4). A second prayer reminds them that the goal of their efforts is to love God through patient acceptance of trials, inspired by the example of Christ (v 5).

3, 6–15: Some members of the community, whether in good or bad faith, have ceased to work for a living; they claim to regard money as useless in view of the imminence of the parousia (cf 2, 1–12), and consequently depend upon others for sustenance (8.10). This result of their false expectation has posed a perplexing problem to the charitable of the community. Stringent measures are to be taken against them: avoidance of voluntary association with them (v 6); refusal to support them gratuitously (v 10); and a gradual but firm exclusion of them from the community (v 14).

3, 17: The apostle takes up the pen himself, evidence that he normally engaged a secretary in the composition of his epistles. Out of fear of possible forgeries composed in his name (2 Thes 2, 2), he points to the unusually large Greek letters that characterize his handwriting.

THE FIRST EPISTLE OF PAUL TO

Timothy

PAUL, an apostle of Christ Jesus by command of God our saviour and Christ Jesus our hope, 2 to Timothy, my own true child in faith. May grace, mercy, and peace be yours from God the Father and Christ Jesus our Lord. 3 I repeat the directions I gave you when I was on my way to

On Holding Fast to Sound Doctrine

Macedonia: stay on in Ephesus in order to warn certain people there against teaching false doctrines 4 and busying themselves with interminable myths and genealogies, which promote idle speculations rather than that training in faith which God requires.

5 What we are aiming at in this warning is the love that springs from a pure heart, a good conscience, and sincere faith. 6 Some people have neglected these and instead have turned to meaningless talk, 7 wanting to be teachers of the law but actually not understanding the words they are using, much less the matters they discuss with such assurance.

8 We know that the law is good, provided one uses it in the way law is supposed to be used— 9 that is, with the understanding that it is aimed, not at good men but at the lawless and unruly, the irreligious and the sinful, the wicked and the godless, men who kill their fathers or mothers, murderers, 10 fornicators, sexual perverts, kidnapers, liars, perjurers, and those who in other ways flout the sound teaching 11 that pertains to the glorious gospel of God—blessed be he—with whom I have been entrusted.

12 I thank Christ Jesus our Lord, who has strengthened me, that he has made me his servant and judged me faithful. 13 I was once a blasphemer, a persecutor, a man filled with arrogance; but because I did not know what I was doing in my unbelief, I have been treated mercifully, 14 and the grace of our Lord has been granted me in overflowing measure, along with the faith and love which are in Christ Jesus. 15 You can depend on this as worthy of full acceptance: that Christ Jesus came into the world to save sinners. Of these I myself am the worst. 16 But on that very account I was dealt with mercifully, so that in me, as an extreme case, Jesus Christ might display all his patience, and that I might become an example to those who would later have faith in him and gain everlasting life. 17 To the King of ages, the immortal, the invisible, the only God, be honor and glory forever and ever! Amen.

18 I have a solemn charge to give

1, 1f: For Pauline use of the conventional epistolary form, see note on Romans 1, 1–7.

1, 3–7: Here Timothy's initial task in Ephesus (cf Acts 20, 17–35) is outlined: to suppress the idle religious speculations, probably about Old Testament figures (3f), which do not contribute to the development of love within the community (v 5) but rather encourage others to similar useless conjectures (1, 6f).

1, 8–11: Those responsible for the empty surmises which are to be suppressed by Timothy do not present the Old Testament from the Christian viewpoint. The Christian values the Old Testament, not as a system of law, but as the first stage in God's revelation

of his saving plan, which is brought to fulfillment in the good news of salvation through faith in Jesus Christ.

1, 12–17: Present gratitude for the Christian apostleship leads to a recalling of the earlier time when Paul was a fierce persecutor of the Christian communities (cf Acts 26, 9ff), until his conversion by intervention of the divine mercy. This and his subsequent apostolic experience testify to the saving purpose of Jesus' incarnation. The fact of his former ignorance of the truth has not kept the apostle from regarding himself as having been the worst of sinners (v 15). Yet he was chosen to be an apostle, that God might manifest his firm will to save sinful humanity

through Jesus Christ (v 16). The recounting of so great a mystery of mercy leads to a spontaneous outpouring of adoration (v 17).

1, 18ff: Timothy is to be mindful of his calling, which is here compared to that of Barnabas and Saul; cf Acts 13, 1ff. Such is probably the sense of the allusion to *the prophecies* (v 18). His task is not to yield, whether in doctrine or in conduct, to erroneous opinions, taking warning from what has already happened at Ephesus in the case of Hymenaeus and Alexander (19f). For the error of Hymenaeus, cf 2 Tm 2, 17f.

you, Timothy, my child. This charge is in accordance with the prophecies made in your regard, 19 and I give it to you so that under the inspiration of these prophecies you may fight the good fight and hold fast to faith and a good conscience. Some men, by rejecting the guidance of conscience, have made shipwreck of their faith, 20 among them Hymenaeus and Alexander; these I have turned over to Satan so that they may learn not to blaspheme.

Conduct of Men and Women

2 First of all, I urge that petitions, prayers, intercessions, and thanksgivings be offered for all men, 2 especially for kings and those in authority, that we may be able to lead undisturbed and tranquil lives in perfect piety and dignity. 3 Prayer of this kind is good, and God our savior is pleased with it, 4 for he wants all men to be saved and come to know the truth. 5 And the truth is this:

"God is one.
One also is the mediator
    between God and men,
    the man Christ Jesus,
6 who gave himself as a ransom
    for all."

This truth was attested at the fitting time. 7 I have been made its herald and apostle (believe me, I am not lying but speak the truth), the teacher of the nations in the true faith.

8 It is my wish, then, that in every place the men shall offer prayers with blameless hands held aloft and be free from anger and dissension. 9 Similarly, the women must deport themselves properly. They should dress modestly and quietly, and not be decked out in fancy hair styles, gold ornaments, pearls, or costly clothing; 10 rather, as becomes women who profess to be religious, their adornment should be good deeds. 11 A woman must listen in silence and be completely submissive. 12 I do not permit a woman to act as teacher, or in any way to have authority over a man; she must be quiet. 13 For Adam was created first, Eve afterward; 14 moreover, it was not Adam who was deceived but the woman. It was she who was led astray and fell into sin. 15 She will be saved through childbearing, provided she continues in faith and love and holiness—her chastity, of course, being taken for granted.

Qualifications of Various Ministers

3 You can depend on this: whoever wants to be a bishop aspires to a noble task. 2 A bishop must be irreproachable, married only once, of even temper, self-controlled, modest, and hospitable. He should be a good teacher. 3 He must not be addicted to drink. He ought not to be contentious but, rather, gentle, a man of peace. Nor can he be someone who loves money. 4 He must be a good manager of his own household, keeping his children under control without sacrificing his dignity; 5 for if a man does not know how to manage his own house, how can he take care of the church of God? 6 He should not be a new convert, lest he become conceited and thus incur the punishment once meted out to the devil. 7 He must also be well thought of by those outside the church, to ensure that he does not fall into disgrace and the devil's trap. 8 In the same way, deacons must be serious, straightforward, and truthful. They may not overindulge in drink or give in to greed. 9 They must hold fast to the divinely revealed faith with a clear conscience. 10 They should be put on probation first; then, if there is nothing against them, thay may serve as deacons. 11 The women, similarly, should be serious, not slanderous gossips. They should be temperate and entirely trustworthy. 12 Deacons may be married but once and must be good managers of their children and their households. 13 Those who serve well as deacons gain a worthy place for themselves and much assurance in their faith in Christ Jesus.

14 Although I hope to visit you soon, I am writing you about these matters 15 so that if I should be delayed you will know what kind of conduct befits a member of God's household, the church of the living God, the pillar and bulwark of truth. 16 Wonderful, indeed, is the mystery of our faith, as we say in professing it:

"He was manifested in the flesh,
    vindicated in the Spirit;
Seen by the angels;
    preached among the Gentiles,
Believed in throughout the
    world,
    taken up into glory."

2, 1–8: This marked insistence that the liturgical prayer of the community concern itself with the needs of all men, whether Christian or not, and especially of those in authority, may imply that a disposition existed at Ephesus to refuse prayer for pagans. In actuality, such prayer aids the community to achieve peaceful relationships with non-Christians (v 2) and contributes to their salvation, since it derives its value from the presence within the community of Christ who is the one and only Savior of all men (3–6). The vital apostolic mission to the Gentiles concerning Christ's purpose of the universal salvation should be reflected in the prayer of the community (v 7), which should be unmarred by internal dissension (v 8); cf Mt 5, 23ff.

2, 9–13: At the liturgical assembly the dress of women should be appropriate to the occasion (v 9); their chief adornment is to be their reputation for good works (v 10). Women are not to take part in the charismatic activity of the assembly (11f; cf 1 Cor 14, 34); their conduct there should not reflect authority but the role of man's helpmate (v 13; cf Gn 2, 18), thus reversing the relationship of Eve to Adam (v 14; cf Gn 3, 6f). As long as women perform their role as wives and mothers in faith and love, their salvation is assured (v 15).

3, 1–7: The passage begins by commending those who aspire to the office of bishop within the community (v 1), and proceeds to list the qualifications required: personal stability and graciousness; talent for teaching (v 2); moderation in habits and temperament (v 3); managerial ability (v 4), and experience in Christian living (3, 5f). Moreover the candidate's life before his conversion should provide no grounds for the charge that he did not previously practice what he now preaches.

3, 8–13: Deacons, besides possessing the virtue of moderation (v 8), are to be outstanding for their faith (v 9) and well respected within the community (v 10). Women in this same role (cf Rom 16, 1) must be of serious mien, temperate, and dedicated, and not given to malicious talebearing (v 11). Deacons must have shown stability in marriage and have a good record as family men (v 12), for such experience prepares them well for the exercise of their ministry in behalf of the community (v 13).

3, 14ff: Lest there be some delay in the visit planned for the near future to Timothy at Ephesus, the present letter is being sent on ahead to arm and enlighten him in his task of preserving sound Christian conduct in the Ephesian church (14f). The care he must exercise over this community is required by the profound nature of Christianity. It centers in Christ, preexistent but appearing in human flesh; the goodness of his mortal existence was verified by the Holy Spirit; the mystery of his Person was revealed to the angels, announced to the Gentiles, and accepted by them in faith. He himself was returned (through his resurrection and ascension) to the divine glory that is properly his (v 16). This passage apparently includes part of a liturgical hymn used among the Christian communities in and around Ephesus, and directed against the cult of Artemis.

False Asceticism

4 The Spirit distinctly says that in later times some will turn away from the faith and will heed deceitful spirits and things taught by demons 2 through plausible liars—men with seared consciences 3 who forbid marriage and require abstinence from foods which God created to be received with thanksgiving by believers who know the truth. 4 Everything God created is good; nothing is to be rejected when it is received with thanksgiving, 5 for it is made holy by God's word and by prayer.

Counsel to Timothy

6 If you put these instructions before the brotherhood you will be a good servant of Christ Jesus, reared in the words of faith and the sound doctrine you have faithfully followed. 7 Have nothing to do with profane myths or old wives' tales. Train yourself for the life of piety, 8 for while physical training is to some extent valuable, the discipline of religion is incalculably more so, with its promise of life here and hereafter. 9 You can depend on this as worthy of complete acceptance.

10 This explains why we work and struggle as we do; our hopes are fixed on the living God who is the savior of all men, but especially of those who believe.

11 Such are the things you must urge and teach. 12 Let no one look down on you because of your youth, but be a continuing example of love, faith, and purity to believers. 13 Until I arrive, devote yourself to the reading of Scripture, to preaching and teaching. 14 Do not neglect the gift you received when, as a result of prophecy, the presbyters

laid their hands on you. 15 Attend to your duties; let them absorb you, so that everyone may see your progress. 16 Watch yourself and watch your teaching. Persevere at both tasks. By doing so you will bring to salvation yourself and all who hear you.

5 Never censure an older man, but appeal to him as to a father. You should treat younger men as brothers, 2 older women as mothers, and younger women as sisters, with absolute purity.

Rules for Widows

3 Honor the claims of widows who are real widows—that is, who are alone and bereft. 4 If a widow has any children or grandchildren, let these learn that piety begins at home and that they should fittingly support their parents and grandparents; this is the way God wants it to be. 5 The real widow, left destitute, is one who has set her hope on God and continues night and day in supplications and prayers. 6 A widow who gives herself up to selfish indulgence, however, leads a life of living death.

7 Make the following rules about widows, so that no one may incur blame. 8 If anyone does not provide for his own relatives and especially for members of his immediate family, he has denied the faith; he is worse than an unbeliever. 9 To be on the church's roll of widows, a widow should be not less than sixty years of age. She must have been married only once. 10 Her good character will be attested to by her good deeds. Has she brought up children? Has she been hospitable to strangers? Has she

washed the feet of Christian visitors? Has she given help to those in distress? In a word, has she been eager to do every possible good work?

11 Refuse to enroll the younger widows, for when their passions estrange them from Christ they will want to marry. 12 This will bring them condemnation for breaking their first pledge. 13 Besides, they learn to be ladies of leisure, who go about from house to house—becoming not only time-wasters but gossips and busybodies as well, talking about things they ought not. 14 That is why I should like to see the younger ones marry, have children, keep house, and in general give our enemies no occasion to speak ill of us. 15 Already, some have turned away to follow Satan. 16 If a woman church member has relatives who are widows, she must assist them. She should not let them become a burden to the church, which ought to be free to give help to the widows who are really in need.

17 Presbyters who do well as leaders deserve to be paid double, especially those whose work is preaching and teaching. 18 The Scripture says, "You shall not put a muzzle on an ox when he is threshing the grain," and also, "The worker deserves his wages."

19 Pay no attention to an accusation against a presbyter unless it is supported by two or three witnesses. 20 The ones who do commit sin, however, are to be publicly reprimanded, so that the rest may fear to offend. 21 I charge you before God, Christ Jesus, and the chosen angels: apply these rules without prejudice, act with complete impartiality! 22 Never lay hands

---

4, 1–11: Doctrinal deviations within the church from the true Christian message have been prophesied though the origin of the prophecy is not specified (1f); cf Acts 20, 29f. The letter warns against a false asceticism which prohibits marriage and regards certain foodstuffs as morally contaminating (v 3). Timothy is urged to reiterate the Christian teaching that neither salvation nor damnation is to be found in material creation (4–8). Man is saved only by the action of God (9ff).

4, 12–16: Timothy is urged to preach and teach with confidence, relying on the gifts and the mission that God has bestowed on him.

5, 1–16: After a few words of general advice based on common sense (1f), the letter takes up, in its several aspects, the subject of widows. The first responsibility for their care belongs to the family

circle, not to the Christian community as such (3f.16). The widow left without the aid of relatives may benefit the community by her prayer, and the community should consider her material sustenance its responsibility (5f). Widows who wish to work directly for the Christian community should not be accepted unless they are well beyond the probability of marriage, i.e., sixty years of age, married only once, and with a reputation for good works (9f). Younger widows are apt to be troublesome and should be encouraged to remarry (11–15).

5, 17–25: The function of *presbyters* is not exactly the same as that of the "episkopos," *bishop* (3, 1); in fact, the relation of the two at the time of this epistle is obscure. The pastorals seem to reflect a transitional stage that developed into the monarchical episcopate of the second century (v 17). The pres-

byters possess the responsibility of preaching and teaching, for which functions they are supported by the community (5, 17f). The realization that their position subjects them to adverse criticism is implied in the direction to Timothy (19f) to make sure of the truth of any accusation against them before public reproof is given. He must be as objective as possible in weighing charges against presbyters (v 21), learning from his experience to take care in selecting them (v 22) and to judge prudently any criticism of them. The letter now sounds an informal note of personal concern in its advice to Timothy not to take his task so strenuously that he even avoids table wine (v 23). Judgment concerning the fitness of candidates to serve as presbyters is easy with persons of open conduct, more difficult and prolonged with those of greater reserve (24f).

hastily on anyone, or you may be sharing in the misdeeds of others. Keep yourself pure.

23 Stop drinking water only. Take a little wine for the good of your stomach, and because of your frequent illnesses.

24 Some men's sins are flagrant and cry out for judgment now, while other men's sins will appear only later. 25 Similarly, some good deeds stand out clearly as such; even inconspicuous ones cannot be hidden forever.

6 All under the yoke of slavery must regard their masters as worthy of full respect; otherwise the name of God and the church's teaching suffer abuse. 2 Those slaves whose masters are brothers in the faith must not take liberties with them on that account. They must perform their tasks even more faithfully, since those who will profit from their work are believers and beloved brothers. These are the things you must teach and preach. 3 Whoever teaches in any other way, not holding to the sound doctrines of our Lord Jesus Christ and the teaching proper to true religion, 4 should be recognized as both conceited and ignorant, a sick man in his passion for polemics and controversy. From these come envy, dissension, slander, evil suspicions— 5 in a word, the bickering of men with twisted minds who have lost all sense of truth. Such men value religion only as a means of personal gain. 6 There is, of course, great gain in religion—provided one is content with a sufficiency. 7 We brought nothing into this world, nor have we the power to take anything out. 8 If we have food and clothing we have all that we need. 9 Those who want to be rich are falling into temptation and a trap. They are letting themselves be captured by foolish and harmful desires which drag men down to ruin and destruction. 10 The love of money is the root of all evil. Some men in their passion for it have strayed from the faith, and have come to grief amid great pain.

11 Man of God that you are, flee from all this. Instead, seek after integrity, piety, faith, love, steadfastness, and a gentle spirit. 12 Fight the good fight of faith. Take firm hold on the everlasting life to which you were called when, in the presence of many witnesses, you made your noble profession of faith. 13 Before God, who gives life to all, and before Christ Jesus, who in bearing witness made his noble profession before Pontius Pilate, 14 I charge you to keep God's command without blame or reproach until our Lord Jesus Christ shall appear. 15 This appearance God will bring to pass at his chosen time. He is the blessed and only ruler, the King of kings and Lord of lords 16 who alone has immortality and who dwells in unapproachable light, whom no human being has ever seen or can see. To him be honor and everlasting rule! Amen.

17 Tell those who are rich in this world's goods not to be proud, and not to rely on so uncertain a thing as wealth. Let them trust in the God who provides us richly with all things for our use. 18 Charge them to do good, to be rich in good works and generous, sharing what they have. 19 Thus will they build a secure foundation for the future, for receiving that life which is life indeed.

20 O Timothy, guard what has been committed to you. Stay clear of worldly, idle talk and the contradictions of what is falsely called knowledge. 21 In laying claim to such knowledge, some men have missed the goal of faith. Grace be with you.

6, 1f: Domestic relationships derive supernatural value from the Christian faith.

6, 3–10: Timothy is exhorted to maintain steadfastly the position outlined in this letter, not allowing himself to be pressured into any other course. He must realize that false teachers can be discerned by their pride, envy, quarrelsomeness, and their greed for material gain.

6, 11–16: Timothy's position demands total dedication to God and faultless witness to Christ (11–14) operating from an awareness, through faith, of the coming revelation of Jesus as King, Lord, and God (15f).

6, 17ff: Timothy is directed to instruct the rich, advising them to make good use of their wealth by aiding the poor.

6, 20f: The final words reflect the chief concern of this letter: that Timothy take every means to preserve the traditional Christian faith.

THE SECOND EPISTLE OF PAUL TO

Timothy

 PAUL, by the will of God an apostle of Christ Jesus sent to proclaim the promise of life in him,   2 to Timothy, my child whom I love. May grace, mercy, and peace from God the Father and from Christ Jesus our Lord be with you.

Thanksgiving and Prayer

3 I thank God, the God of my forefathers whom I worship with a clear conscience, whenever I remember you in my prayers—as indeed I do constantly, night and day. 4 Recalling your tears when we parted, I yearn to see you again. That would make my happiness complete.   5 I find myself thinking of your sincere faith—faith which first belonged to your grandmother Lois and to your mother Eunice, and which (I am confident) you also have.

Exhortation to Faithfulness

6 For this reason, I remind you to stir into flame the gift of God bestowed when my hands were laid on you. 7 The Spirit God has given us is no cowardly spirit, but rather one that makes us strong, loving, and wise.   8 Therefore, never be ashamed of your testimony to our Lord, nor of me, a prisoner for his sake; but with the strength which comes from God bear your share of the hardship which the gospel entails.

9 God has saved us and has called us to a holy life, not because of any merit of ours but according to his own design—the grace held out to us in Christ Jesus before the world began   10 but now made manifest through the appearance of our Savior. He has robbed death of its power and has brought life and immortality into clear light through the gospel.   11 In the service of this gospel I have been appointed preacher and apostle and teacher,   12 and for its sake I undergo present hardships. But I am not ashamed, for I know him in whom I have believed, and I am confident that he is able to guard what has been entrusted to me until that Day.   13 Take as a model of sound teaching what you have heard me say, in faith and love in Christ Jesus. 14 Guard the rich deposit of faith with the help of the Holy Spirit who dwells within us.

15 You know that all in Asia, including even Phygelus and Hermogenes, have turned their backs on me.   16 May the Lord have mercy on the family of Onesiphorus, because he has often given me new heart and has not been ashamed of me, even in my chains.   17 When he was in Rome, he sought me out earnestly and found me.   18 When he stands before the Lord on the great Day, may the Lord grant him mercy! And the many services he has performed for Christ in Ephesus you know even better than I.

1, 1f: For the formula of address and greeting, see note on Romans 1, 1–7. *The promise of life in him:* which God grants to men through union with Christ in faith and love; cf Col 3, 4; 1 Tm 4, 8.

1, 4f: Purportedly written from prison in Rome (1, 8; 4, 6ff) shortly before the writer's death, the letter recalls the earlier sorrowful parting from Timothy, commending him for his faith and expressing the longing to see him again.

1, 6: *The gift of God bestowed when my hands were laid on you:* the grace of ordination, signified by the laying on of hands; cf 1 Tm 4, 14.

1, 8: *Never be ashamed of your testimony to our Lord:* i.e., of preaching and suffering for the sake of the gospel.

1, 9f: Redemption from sin and the call to holiness of life are not won by personal deeds but gratuitously bestowed through the incarnation according to God's eternal plan; cf Eph 1, 4.

1, 12: *He is able to guard . . . until that Day:* the deposit of faith (or, less likely, the reward of Christian ministry) until the second coming of Christ.

1, 15: Keen disappointment is expressed, here and later (4, 16), that the Christians of the province of Asia, especially Phygelus and Hermogenes, should have *abandoned* the writer and done nothing to defend his *case* in court.

1, 16ff: *The family of Onesiphorus, because he . . . even in my chains:* Onesiphorus seems to have died before this letter was written. His family is mentioned twice (v 16 and 4, 19), though it was Onesiphorus himself who was helpful to Paul in prison and rendered much service to the community of Ephesus (16ff). Because the apostle complains of abandonment by *all in Asia* during his second imprisonment and trial, the assistance of Onesiphorus is understood as having been given to Paul during his first Roman imprisonment (A.D. 61–63).

184

The Gospel versus Empty Fables

2 So you, my son, must be strong in the grace which is ours in Christ Jesus. 2 The things which you have heard from me through many witnesses you must hand on to trustworthy men who will be able to teach others. 3 Bear hardship along with me as a good soldier of Christ Jesus. 4 No soldier becomes entangled in the affairs of civilian life; he avoids this in order to please his commanding officer. 5 Similarly, if one takes part in an athletic contest, he cannot receive the winner's crown unless he has kept the rules. 6 The hardworking farmer is the one who should have the first share of the crop. 7 Reflect on what I am saying, for the Lord will make my meaning fully clear.

8 Remember that Jesus Christ, a descendant of David, was raised from the dead. 9 This is the gospel I preach; in preaching it I suffer as a criminal, even to the point of being thrown into chains—but there is no chaining the word of God! 10 Therefore I bear with all of this for the sake of those whom God has chosen, in order that they may obtain the salvation to be found in Christ Jesus and with it eternal glory.

11 You can depend on this:

If we have died with him
    we shall also live with him;
12 If we hold out to the end
    we shall also reign with him.

But if we deny him he will deny us. 13 If we are unfaithful he will still remain faithful, for he cannot deny himself.

14 Keep reminding people of these things and charge them before God to stop disputing about mere words.

This does no good and can be the ruin of those who listen. 15 Try hard to make yourself worthy of God's approval, a workman who has no cause to be ashamed, following a straight course in preaching the truth. 16 Avoid worldly, idle talk, for those who indulge in it become more and more godless, 17 and the influence of their talk will spread like the plague. This is the case with Hymenaeus and Philetus, 18 who have gone far wide of the truth in saying that the resurrection has already taken place. 19 They are upsetting some people's faith. But the foundation God has laid stands firm. It bears this inscription: "The Lord knows those who are his"; and, "Let everyone who professes the name of the Lord abandon evil."

20 In every large household there are vessels not only of gold and silver but also of wood and clay, some for distinguished and others for common use. 21 The lesson is that if a person will but cleanse himself of evil things he may be a distinguished vessel, dedicated and useful to the master of the house and ready for every noble service. 22 So, turn from youthful passions and pursue integrity, faith, love, and peace, along with those who call on the Lord in purity of heart. 23 Have nothing to do with senseless, ignorant disputations. As you well know, they only breed quarrels, 24 and the servant of the Lord must not be quarrelsome but must be kindly toward all. He must be an apt teacher, patiently and 25 gently correcting those who contradict him, in the hope always that God will enable them to repent and know the truth. 26 Thus, taken captive by God to do his will, they shall escape the devil's trap.

Against False Teachers

3 Do not forget this: there will be terrible times in the last days. 2 Men will be lovers of self and of money, proud, arrogant, abusive, disobedient to their parents, ungrateful, profane, 3 inhuman, implacable, slanderous, licentious, brutal, hating the good. 4 They will be treacherous, reckless, pompous, lovers of pleasure rather than of God 5 as they make a pretense of religion but negate its power. Stay clear of them. 6 It is such as these who worm their way into homes and make captives of silly women burdened with sins and driven by desires of many kinds, 7 always learning but never able to reach a knowledge of the truth. 8 Just as Jannes and Jambres opposed Moses, so these men also oppose the truth; with perverted minds they falsify the faith. 9 But they will not get very far; as with those two men, the stupidity of these will be plain for all to see.

Paul's Example and Teaching

10 You have followed closely my teaching and my conduct. You have observed my resolution, fidelity, patience, love, and endurance, 11 through persecutions and sufferings in Antioch, Iconium, and Lystra. You know what persecutions I have had to bear, and you know how the Lord saved me from them all. 12 Anyone who wants to live a godly life in Christ Jesus can expect to be persecuted. 13 But all the while evil men and charlatans will go from bad to worse, deceiving others, themselves deceived. 14 You, for your part, must remain faithful to what you have learned and believed, because you know who your teachers were. 15 Likewise, from your in-

---

2, 1–7: This passage manifests a characteristic deep concern for safeguarding the deposit of faith and faithfully transmitting it through *trustworthy men* (1f; cf 1, 14; 1 Tm 6, 20; Ti 1, 9). Comparisons to the soldier's loyalty, the athlete's fidelity, and the farmer's arduous work as the price of reward (4ff) emphasize the need of singleness of purpose in preaching the word, even at the cost of hardship, for the sake of Christ (v 3).
2, 8–13: Through baptism, Christians die spiritually with Christ and *live with him* in the hope of reigning with him forever, but not without giving witness to him through suffering in the present life, even as the apostle has been imprisoned for preaching the gospel (v 9). His sufferings are helpful to the elect in attaining

salvation and glory in Christ (v 10), who will reward the faithful and disown the unfaithful (12f).
2, 14–19: For those who dispute about mere words (cf 2, 23f) and indulge in irreligious talk to the detriment of their listeners (14.16–19), see note on 1 Tm 1, 3f. *Hymenaeus and Philetus* (v 17), while accepting the Christian's mystical death and resurrection in Christ through baptism, deny the resurrection of the body and eternal glory.
2, 22: *Those who call on the Lord*: those who believe in Christ and worship him as Lord, i.e., Christians (Acts 9, 14ff.20f; Rom 10, 12f).
3, 1–9: The moral depravity and false teachings of men that will prevail in the last days are already at work (1–5). Frivolous and superficial women too,

devoid of the true spirit of religion, will be easy victims of those who pervert them by falsifying the truth (6ff), just as Jannes and Jambres, the magicians of Egypt (Ex 7, 11f.22), discredited the truth in Moses' time.
3, 15ff: The Scriptures are the source of wisdom, i.e., of belief in and loving fulfillment of God's word revealed in Christ, through whom man finds salvation. *All Scripture is inspired of God:* has God as his principal author, with the writer as the human collaborator. Thus the Scriptures are the word of God in human language. *Useful for teaching . . . every good work:* because as God's word the Scriptures share his divine authority. It is exercised through those who are the ministers of the word.

fancy you have known the sacred Scriptures, the source of the wisdom which through faith in Jesus Christ leads to salvation. 16 All Scripture is inspired of God and is useful for teaching—for reproof, correction, and training in holiness 17 so that the man of God may be fully competent and equipped for every good work.

Apostolic Charge

4 In the presence of God and of Christ Jesus, who is coming to judge the living and the dead, and by his appearing and his kingly power, 2 I charge you to preach the word, to stay with this task whether convenient or inconvenient—correcting, reproving, appealing—constantly teaching and never losing patience. 3 For the time will come when people will not tolerate sound doctrine, but, following their own desires, will surround themselves with teachers who tickle their ears. 4 They will stop listening to the truth and will wander off to fables. 5 As for you, be steady and self-possessed; put up with hardship, perform your work as an evangelist, fulfill your ministry.

Reward for Fidelity

6 I for my part am already being poured out like a libation. The time of my dissolution is near. 7 I have fought the good fight, I have finished the race, I have kept the faith. 8 From now on a merited crown awaits me; on that Day the Lord, just judge that he is, will award it to me—and not only to me, but to all who have looked for his appearing with eager longing.

Paul's Loneliness

9 Do your best to join me soon, 10 for Demas, enamored of the present world, has left me and gone to Thessalonica. Crescens has gone to Galatia and Titus to Dalmatia. 11 I have no one with me but Luke. Get Mark and bring him with you, for he can be of great service to me. 12 Tychicus I have sent to Ephesus. 13 When you come, bring the cloak I left in Troas with Carpus, and the books, especially the parchments.

Comfort in Trial

14 Alexander the coppersmith did me a great deal of harm; the Lord will repay him according to his deeds. 15 Meanwhile, you too had better be on guard, for he has strongly resisted our preaching. 16 At the first hearing of my case in court, no one took my part. In fact, everyone abandoned me. 17 May it not be held against them! But the Lord stood by my side and gave me strength, so that through me the preaching task might be completed and all the nations might hear the gospel. That is how I was saved from the lion's jaws. 18 The Lord will continue to rescue me from all attempts to do me harm and will bring me safe to his heavenly kingdom. To him be glory forever and ever. Amen.

Greetings

19 Greet Prisca and Aquila and and the family of Onesiphorus. 20 Erastus has stayed in Corinth, while Trophimus I had to leave ill at Miletus. 21 Get here before winter if you can. Eubulus, Pudens, Linus, Claudia, and all the brothers send greetings.

22 The Lord be with your spirit. Grace be with you.

4, 1–5: The gravity of the obligation incumbent on Timothy to preach the word can be gauged from the solemn adjuration: *in the presence of God*, and of Christ coming as universal judge *and by his appearing and his kingly power* (v 1). Patience, courage, constancy, and endurance are required despite the opposition, hostility, indifference, and defection of many to whom the truth has been preached (2–5).

4, 6: The apostle recognizes his death through martyrdom to be imminent. He regards it, like the death of Christ, as an act of worship in which his blood will be poured out in sacrifice; cf Ex 29, 40.

4, 7: *I have fought the good fight, I have finished the race:* at the close of his life Paul could testify to the accomplishment of what Christ himself had foretold concerning him at the time of his conversion: *I myself shall indicate to him how much he will have to suffer for my name* (Acts 9, 16). *I have kept the faith:* preserved the true teaching concerning Christ, both in his personal adherence to it, and in his ministry.

4, 8: When the world is judged at the parousia all who have eagerly *looked for his appearing*, i.e., lived according to his teaching, will be rewarded. A *merited crown:* a reference to the laurel wreath placed on the heads of conquerors and winners of various contests; cf 2, 5; 1 Cor 9, 25.

4, 10–13: *Demas* either abandoned the work of the ministry for worldly affairs or, perhaps, gave up the faith itself (v 10). *Luke* may have accompanied Paul on part of his second and third missionary journeys (Acts 16, 10–18; 20, 5–21, 19). *Mark*, once rejected by Paul (Acts 13, 13; 15, 39–40), is now to render him *great service* (v 11); cf Col 4, 10; Phlm 24. *Tychicus I have sent to Ephesus:* see Eph 6, 21; cf also Acts 20, 4; Col 4, 7 (12f).

4, 14–18: *Alexander:* an opponent of Paul's preaching (14f), perhaps the same who is mentioned in 1 Tm 1, 20. Despite Paul's abandonment by his friends in the province of Asia (cf 1, 15f), the divine assistance brought this first trial to a successful issue—

---

even to the point of making the gospel message known to those who participated in or witnessed the trial (16f). Though Paul was not released from prison, he was made ready for the *heavenly kingdom* (v 18).

4, 19–22: *Prisca and Aquila* assisted Paul in his ministry in Corinth (Acts 18, 2f) and Ephesus (Acts 18, 19.26; 1 Cor 16, 19). They risked death to save his life, and all the Gentile communities are indebted to them (Rom 16, 3ff), (v 19). *Erastus:* treasurer of the city of Corinth (Rom 16, 23); cf also Acts 19, 22. *Trophimus:* from the province of Asia, who accompanied Paul from Greece to Troas (Acts 20, 4f). *Linus:* possibly to be identified with Linus, the supposed successor of Peter as Bishop of Rome. *Claudia:* in the Constitutio apostolica 7.46, 17–19, she is called mother of Linus, Bishop of Rome.

THE EPISTLE OF PAUL TO

INTRODUCTION

Greeting

AUL, a servant of God, sent as an apostle of Jesus Christ for the sake of the faith of those whom God has chosen, and to promote their knowledge of the truth as our religion embodies it, 2 in the hope of that eternal life which God, who cannot lie, promised in endless ages past. 3 This he has now manifested in his own good time as his word, in the preaching entrusted to me by the command of God our Savior. 4 Paul to Titus, my own true child in our common faith: May grace and peace from God our Father, and Christ Jesus our Savior, be with you.

PASTORAL CHARGE

Qualities of a Presbyter

5 My purpose in leaving you in Crete was that you might accomplish what had been left undone, especially the appointment of presbyters in every town. As I instructed you, 6 a presbyter must be irreproachable, married only once, the father of children who are believers and are known not to be wild and insubordinate. 7 The bishop as God's steward must be blameless. He may not be self-willed or arrogant, a drunkard, a violent or greedy man. 8 He should, on the contrary, be hospitable and a lover of goodness; steady, just, holy, and self-controlled. 9 In his teaching he must hold fast to the authentic message, so that he will be able to encourage men to follow sound doctrine and to refute those who contradict it. 10 There are many irresponsible teachers, especially from among the Jewish converts—men who are empty talkers and deceivers. 11 These must be silenced. They are upsetting whole families by teaching things they have no right to teach—and all for sordid gain! 12 A man of Crete, one of their own prophets, has testified,

"Cretans have ever been liars,
    beasts, and lazy gluttons,"
and that is the simple truth!

13 Admonish them sharply, in an attempt to keep them close to sound faith, 14 and unaffected by Jewish myths or rules invented by men who have swerved from the truth. 15 To the clean all things are clean, but to those defiled unbelievers nothing is clean. Their very minds and consciences are tainted. 16 They claim to "know God," but by their actions they deny that he exists. They

1, 1–4: On the epistolary form, see note on Romans 1, 1–7. The apostolate is the divinely appointed mission to lead others to the true faith, and through it to eternal salvation (1ff).

1, 5–9: This instruction on the selection and appointment of presbyters, substantially identical in 1 Timothy 3, 1–7 (see note), was aimed at strengthening the authority of Titus by apostolic mandate; cf 2, 15. In Titus 1, 6f and Acts 20, 17.28 the terms *episkopos* and *presbyteros* ("bishop" and "presbyter") refer to the same persons. As they did not exercise the functions reserved to the apostle Paul and his legates, such as Timothy and Titus, they were not bishops in the later sense familiar to us.

1, 10–16: This adverse criticism of the defects within the community is directed especially against certain Judaeo-Christians, who busy themselves with useless speculations over persons mentioned in the Old Testament and insist on the observance of Jewish ritual purity regulations, thereby *upsetting whole families by teaching things they have no right to teach;* cf 3, 9; 1 Tm 1, 3–10; 4, 1–10; 6, 3–10. One of Titus' main tasks in Crete is to become acquainted with the national character of the Cretans and thereby learn to cope with its deficiencies (cf 1, 12, the citation from the sixth-century B.C. Cretan poet Epimenides).

are disgusting—intractable and thoroughly incapable of any decent action.

TEACHING THE CHRISTIAN LIFE

Various Counsels

2 As for yourself, let your speech be consistent with sound doctrine. 2 Tell the older men that they must be temperate, serious-minded, and self-controlled; likewise sound in the faith, loving, and steadfast. 3 Similarly, the older women must behave in ways that befit those who belong to God. They must not be slanderous gossips or slaves to drink. By their good example they must teach 4 the younger women to love their husbands and children 5 to be sensible, chaste, busy at home, kindly, submissive to their husbands. Thus the word of God will not fall into disrepute. 6 Tell the young men to keep themselves completely under control— 7 nor may you yourself fail to set them good example. Your teaching must have the integrity of serious, 8 sound words to which no one can take exception. If it does, no opponent will be able to find anything bad to say about us, and hostility will yield to shame.

9 Slaves are to be submissive to their masters. They should try to please them in every way, not contradicting them 10 nor stealing from them, but expressing a constant fidelity by their conduct, so as to adorn in every way possible the doctrine of God our Savior.

Transforming of Life

11 The grace of God has appeared, offering salvation to all men. 12 It trains us to reject godless ways and worldly desires, and live temperately, justly, and devoutly in this age 13 as we await our blessed hope, the appearing of the glory of the Great God and of our Savior Christ Jesus. 14 It was he who sacrificed himself for us, to redeem us from all unrighteousness and to cleanse for himself a people of his own, eager to do what is right.

15 These are the things you are to say. Make our appeals and corrections with the authority of command. Let no one look down on you.

3 Remind people to be loyally subject to the government and its officials, to obey the laws, to be ready to take on any honest employment. 2 Tell them not to speak evil of anyone or be quarrelsome. They must be forbearing and display a perfect courtesy toward all men. 3 We ourselves were once foolish, disobedient, and far from true faith; we were the slaves of our passions and of pleasures of various kinds. We went our way in malice and envy, hateful ourselves and hating one another. 4 But when the kindness and love of God our savior appeared, 5 he saved us; not because of any righteous deeds we had done, but because of his mercy. He saved us through the baptism of new birth and renewal by the Holy Spirit. 6 This Spirit he lavished on us through

Jesus Christ our Savior, 7 that we might be justified by his grace and become heirs, in hope, of eternal life. 8 You can depend on this to be true.

Advice to Titus

I want you to lay great weight on the things I have been saying, so that those who have committed themselves to God may be careful to do what is right. This is what is good and advantageous for men. 9 See to it that you abstain from stupid arguments and genealogies, and from all controversies and quarrels about the law. They are useless and have no point. 10 Warn a heretic once and then a second time; after that, have nothing to do with him. 11 You must recognize such a person as perverted and sinful; he stands self-condemned.

Directives, Greetings and Blessing

12 When I send Artemas to you, or perhaps Tychicus, hurry to me at Nicopolis; I have decided to spend the winter there. 13 Speed Zenas the lawyer and Apollos on their journey, having first seen to it that they have everything they need. 14 Let our people devote themselves to honest work in order to take care of their needs, so that they may be in position to live fruitful lives.

15 All who are with me send their greetings. Greet those who love us in the faith.

May grace be with you all!

2, 11–15: The moving force in the moral improvement outlined in 2, 1–10 is to be the constant appeal to God's revelation of salvation in Christ, with its demand for transformation of life.
3, 1–7: The spiritual renewal of the Cretans, signi-fied in God's merciful gift of baptism (4–7), should be reflected in their improved attitude toward civil authority and in their Christian relationship with all (1ff).
3, 8–11: In matters of good conduct and religious doctrine Titus is to show himself uncompromising.
3, 12–15: Artemas or Tychicus (2 Tm 4, 12) is to replace Titus, who will join Paul in his winter sojourn at Nicopolis in Epirus, on the western coast of Greece. Titus will no doubt report on his efforts in Crete, and perhaps also assist in preaching the gospel.

THE EPISTLE OF PAUL TO

Philemon

Greeting

PAUL, a prisoner of Christ Jesus, and Timothy our brother, to our beloved friend and fellow worker Philemon, 2 to Apphia our sister, to our fellow soldier Archippus, and to the church that meets in your house. 3 Grace to you and peace from God our Father and from the Lord Jesus Christ.

Philemon's Faith and Charity

4 I thank God always, my brother, as I commend you in my prayers, 5 for I keep hearing of your love and faith toward the Lord Jesus and all God's people. 6 And my prayer is that your sharing of the faith with others may enable you to know all the good which is ours in Christ. 7 I find great joy and comfort in your love, because through you the hearts of God's people have been refreshed.

Plea for Onesimus

8 Therefore, although I feel that I have every right to command you to do what ought to be done, 9 I prefer to appeal in the name of love. Yes, I, Paul, ambassador of Christ and now a prisoner for him, 10 appeal to you for my child, whom I have begotten during my imprisonment. 11 He has become in truth Onesimus [Useful], for he who was formerly useless to you is now useful indeed both to you and to me. 12 It is he I am sending to you—and that means I am sending my heart!

13 I had wanted to keep him with me, that he might serve me in your place while I am in prison for the gospel; 14 but I did not want to do anything without your consent, that kindness might not be forced on you but might be freely bestowed. 15 Perhaps he was separated from you for a while for this reason: that you might possess him forever, 16 no longer as a slave but as more than a slave, a beloved brother, especially dear to me; and how much more than a brother to you, since now you will know him both as a man and in the Lord.

17 If then you regard me as a partner, welcome him as you would me. 18 If he has done you an injury or owes you anything, charge it to me. 19 I, Paul, write this in my own hand: I agree to pay—not to mention that you owe me your very self! 20 You see, brother, I want to make you "useful" to me in the Lord. Refresh this heart of mine in Christ.

Farewell Blessing

21 Confident of your compliance, I write you, knowing that you will do more than I say. 22 And get a room ready for me; I hope that through your prayers I shall be restored to you.

23 Epaphras, my fellow prisoner in Christ Jesus, greets you, 24 as do Mark, Aristarchus, Demas, and Luke, my fellow workers.

25 The grace of our Lord Jesus Christ be with your spirit.

1ff: It is the prisoner and friend appealing, rather than the apostle commanding with authority, who greets Philemon, Apphia, Archippus, and the assembly that meets in Philemon's house.

4–7: Philemon's faith in and love for the Lord and the people of God who he refreshes have urged him to share these blessings with others (5.7). Paul prays that as a result Philemon himself will benefit by a deepening knowledge and appreciation of the endless good they possess in common in possessing Christ (4.6).

10–22: *Appeal to you for my child:* Onesimus, Philemon's runaway slave, whom Paul the prisoner converted to the Christian faith (v 10), and whom he now asks Philemon to recieve back as *a beloved brother* (16f), rather than as a slave liable to punishment for theft and damage and for escape (18). The name Onesimus means "useful" or profitable. Paul realizes that his convert has shown himself "useless" by his previous conduct; but he is confident that Onesimus will now live up to his name and be useful both to Philemon and to Paul himself (11.20). He would even prefer to have the service of Onesimus for the work of the ministry, but recognizes Philemon's prior right (13ff).

23f: *Epaphras:* a Colossian who founded the church in Colossae (Col 1, 7) and perhaps also in Laodicea and Hierapolis (Col 2, 1; 4, 12f). *Aristarchus:* a native of Thessalonica and fellow worker of Paul (Acts 19, 29; 20, 4; 27, 2). For Mark, Demas, and Luke, see 2 Timothy 4, 10–13 and note.

THE EPISTLE TO THE

Hebrews

INTRODUCTION

IN times past, God spoke in fragmentary and varied ways to our fathers through the prophets; 2 in this, the final age, he has spoken to us through his Son, whom he has made heir of all things and through whom he first created the universe. 3 This Son is the reflection of the Father's glory, the exact representation of the Father's being, and he sustains all things by his powerful word. When he had cleansed us from our sins, he took his seat at the right hand of the Majesty in heaven, 4 as far superior to the angels as the name he has inherited is superior to theirs.

THE SON HIGHER THAN THE ANGELS

Messianic Enthronement

5 To which of the angels did God ever say,

"You are my son; today I have begotten you"?

Or again,

"I will be his father, and he shall be my son"?

6 And again, when he leads his first-born into the world, he says,

"Let all the angels of God worship him."

7 Of the angels he says,

"He makes his angels winds, and his ministers flaming fire";

8 but of the Son,

"Your throne, O God, stands forever and ever; a righteous scepter is the scepter of your kingdom. 9 You have loved justice and hated wickedness, therefore God, your God, has anointed you with the oil of gladness above your fellow kings."

10 And,

"Lord, of old you established the earth, and the heavens are the work of your hands. 11 They will perish, but you remain; all of them will grow old like a garment. 12 You will roll them up like a cloak. like a garment they will be changed. But you are the same, and your years will have no end."

13 To which of the angels has God ever said,

"Sit at my right hand till I make your enemies your footstool"?

14 Are they not all ministering

1, 1-4: The letter opens with a reflection on the climax of God's revelation to mankind in his Son (v 3). The divine communication with men was initiated and maintained during Old Testament times through chosen men, the prophets (v 1). But now in messianic times, the final period of man's religious history, God the Son, creator and end of all things, is the communicator with men (v 2). He is the perfect and *exact representation of the Father's being*—even

to the divine creative power—who entered human existence to destroy the power of sin. After accomplishing this he returned, through his resurrection and ascension, to his natural place with the Father (v 3). No creature, not even angels, can match the unique dignity of his Person (v 4).

1, 5-14: The citations from the psalms in v 5 (Ps 2, 7) and v 13 (Ps 110, 1) were traditionally used of Jesus' messianic sonship (cf Acts 13, 33) through

his resurrection and ascension (cf Acts 2, 33ff); those in v 8 (Ps 45, 6f) and vv 10ff (Ps 102, 25ff) are concerned with his divine kingship and his creative function. The author states that, in the Christian understanding of Christ, the Old Testament elevates him above the angels. At best the angels can only be servants at the disposal of the creator (v 7, citing Ps 104, 4) and consequently they are *sent to serve those who are to inherit salvation* (v 14).

spirits, sent to serve those who are to inherit salvation?

Exhortation to Faithfulness

2 In view of this, we must attend all the more to what we have heard, lest we drift away. 2 For if the word spoken through angels stood unchanged, and all transgression and disobedience received its due punishment, 3 how shall we escape if we ignore a salvation as great as ours? Announced first by the Lord, it was confirmed to us by those who had heard him. 4 God then gave witness to it by signs, miracles, varied acts of power, and distribution of the gifts of the Holy Spirit as he willed.

Exhaltation through Abasement

5 For he did not make the world to come—that world of which we speak—subject to angels. 6 Somewhere this is testified to, in the passage that says:

"What is man that you should
    be mindful of him,
  or the son of man that you
    should care for him?
7 You made him for a little while
  lower than the angels;
  you crowned him with glory
    and honor,
8 and put all things under
  his feet."

In subjecting all things to him, God left nothing unsubjected. At present we do not see all things thus subject, 9 but we do see Jesus crowned with glory and honor because he suffered death: Jesus, who was made for a little while lower than the angels, that through God's gracious will he might taste death for the sake of all men. 10 Indeed, it was fitting that

when bringing many sons to glory God, for whom and through whom all things exist, should make their leader in the work of salvation perfect through suffering. 11 He who consecrates and those who are consecrated have one and the same Father. Therefore he is not ashamed to call them brothers, 12 saying,

"I will announce your name to
  my brothers,
  I will sing your praise in the
    midst of the assembly";
13 and,

"I will put my trust in him";
and again,

"Here am I, and the children
  God has given me!"

14 Now, since the children are men of blood and flesh, Jesus likewise had a full share in ours, that by his death he might rob the devil, the prince of death, of his power, 15 and free those who through fear of death had been slaves their whole life long. 16 Surely he did not come to help angels, but rather the children of Abraham; 17 therefore he had to become like his brothers in every way, that he might be a merciful and faithful high priest before God on their behalf, to expiate the sins of the people. 18 Since he was himself tested through what he suffered, he is able to help those who are tempted.

JESUS, FAITHFUL AND COMPASSIONATE HIGH PRIEST

Jesus Superior to Moses

3 Therefore, holy brothers who share a heavenly calling, fix your eyes on Jesus, the apostle and high priest whom we acknowledge in

faith, 2 who was faithful to him who appointed him. Moses, too, "was faithful in all God's household," 3 but Jesus is more worthy of honor than he, as the founder of a house is more honorable than the house itself. 4 Every house is founded by someone, but God is the founder of all. 5 Moses "was faithful in all God's household" as a servant charged with the task of witnessing to what would be spoken; 6 but Christ was faithful as the Son placed over God's house. It is we who are that house if we hold fast to our confidence and the hope of which we boast.

Israel's Infidelity, a Warning

7 Wherefore, as the Holy Spirit says:

"Today, if you should hear his
  voice,
8 harden not your hearts as at
    the revolt
  in the day of testing in the
    desert,
9 When your fathers tested and
  tried me,
10 and saw my works for forty
    years.
Because of this I was angered
  with that generation
  and I said, 'They have always
    been of erring heart,
  and have never known my
    ways.'
11 "Thus I swore in my anger,
  'They shall never enter into
    my rest.'"

12 Take care, my brothers, lest any of you have an evil and unfaithful spirit and fall from the living God. 13 Encourage one another daily while it is still "today," so that no one grows hardened by the deceit of

---

2, 1–4: The absolute supremacy of Christ should greatly strengthen Christians against abandoning their faith (v 1). If according to Jewish tradition (Gal 3, 19), angels played the role of intermediaries for the Mosaic covenant, the violation of which was divinely punished (v 2), an even severer punishment awaits those who knowingly neglect the salvation offered in Christ's own word, proclaimed by witnesses whom God appointed (Lk 1, 1f; Acts 1, 21f) and confirmed by divine power through *signs* and *miracles* (3f).

2, 5–18: The humanity and the suffering of Jesus do not constitute a valid reason for relinquishing the Christian faith. The thought of the psalmist (Ps 8, 4ff in the Septuagint) concerning man's glory and splendor despite his subordination to the angels (6f) is perfectly reflected in the history of Jesus, who lived a truly human existence during his mortal life but is

now in full possession of the divine kingly glory (v 9). It was altogether fitting that God should direct him along the path of suffering (v 10), since in the spirit of the Old Testament (Ps 22, 22; Is 8, 17f) he identified himself entirely with those for whom he obtained sanctification (11–15). He deliberately allied himself with the descendants of Abraham (v 16) in order to function as an authentic high priest, expiating the sins of the people (v 17) as one who experienced the same tests as they (v 18).

3, 1–6: Christians must have full confidence in Jesus, whom their faith recognizes as the one sent by God (*the apostle*) to be the high priest of the Christian community (v 1). Like Moses, the leader of the people of Israel, Jesus was faithful to the task assigned to him (v 2). Moses, however, was faithful *in* the house of God, i.e., he was himself but a member of God's chosen people (3ff), whereas Jesus possesses the

fidelity of God's Son *over* the new people of God (v 6).

3, 7–4, 11: The author appeals for steadfastness of faith in Jesus. Citing the Old Testament warning (Ps 95, 7–11) against hardness of heart, i.e., practical disregard of the divine message (7–11), he urges the community to watchfulness and mutual encouragement (12ff). They are to remember the example of Israel's revolt in the desert which cost a whole generation the loss of the promised land (15–19; cf Nm 14, 20–29). The promised land, designated here under the concept of *rest*, is the author's symbol for final union with Christ. He concludes his appeal, developing the idea that his Christian audience is experiencing a test of faith similar to that of Israel in the desert, and one which could have the same unfortunate results (4, 1–11).

sin. 14 We have become partners of Christ if only we maintain to the end that confidence with which we began. 15 When Scripture says,

"Today, if you should hear his voice,
harden not your hearts as at the revolt,"

16 who were those that revolted when they heard that voice? Was it not all whom Moses had led out of Egypt? 17 With whom was God angry for forty years? Was it not those who had sinned, whose corpses fell in the desert? 18 To whom but to the disobedient did he swear that they would not enter into his rest? 19 We see, moreover, that it was their unbelief that kept them from entering.

4 Therefore, while the promise of entrance into his rest still holds, we ought to be fearful of disobeying lest any one of you be judged to have lost his chance of entering. 2 We have indeed heard the good news, as they did. But the word which they heard did not profit them, for they did not receive it in faith. 3 It is we who have believed who enter into the rest, just as God said:

"Thus I swore in my anger,
'They shall never enter into my rest.'"

Yet God's work was finished when he created the world, 4 for in reference to the seventh day Scripture somewhere says, "And God rested from all his work on the seventh day"; 5 and again, in the place we have referred to, God says, "They shall never enter into my rest." 6 Therefore, since it remains for some to enter, and those to whom it was first announced did not because of unbelief, 7 God once more set a day, "today," when long afterward

he spoke through David the words we have quoted:

"Today, if you should hear his voice,
harden not your hearts."

8 Now if Joshua had led them into the place of rest, God would not have spoken afterward of another day. 9 Therefore a sabbath rest still remains for the people of God. 10 And he who enters into God's rest, rests from his own work as God did from his. 11 Let us strive to enter into that rest, so that no one may fall, in imitation of the example of Israel's unbelief.

12 Indeed, God's word is living and effective, sharper than any two-edged sword. It penetrates and divides soul and spirit, joints and marrow; it judges the reflections and thoughts of the heart. 13 Nothing is concealed from him; all lies bare and exposed to the eyes of him to whom we must render an account.

Jesus, Compassionate High Priest

14 Since then, we have a great high priest who has passed through the heavens, Jesus, the Son of God, let us hold fast to our profession of faith. 15 For we do not have a high priest who is unable to sympathize with our weakness, but one who was tempted in every way that we are, yet never sinned. 16 So let us confidently approach the throne of grace to receive mercy and favor and to find help in the time of need.

5 Every high priest is taken from among men and made their representative before God, to offer gifts and sacrifices for sins. 2 He is able to deal patiently with erring sinners, for he himself is beset by weakness 3 and so must make sin offerings for himself as well as for the

people. 4 One does not take this honor on his own initiative, but only when called by God as Aaron was. 5 Even Christ did not glorify himself with the office of high priest; he received it from the One who said to him,

"You are my son;
today I have begotten you";

6 just as he says in another place,

"You are a priest forever,
according to the order of Melchizedek."

7 In the days when he was in the flesh, he offered prayers and supplications with loud cries and tears to God, who was able to save him from death, and he was heard because of his reverence. 8 Son though he was, he learned obedience from what he suffered; 9 and when perfected, he became the source of eternal salvation for all who obey him, 10 designated by God as high priest according to the order of Melchizedek.

JESUS' ETERNAL PRIESTHOOD AND ETERNAL SACRIFICE

Exhortation to Spiritual Renewal

11 About this we have much to say, and it is difficult to explain, for you have become deaf. 12 Although by this time you should be teaching others, you need to have someone teach you again the basic elements of the oracles of God; you need milk, not solid food. 13 Everyone whose food is milk alone is ignorant of the word that sanctifies, for he is a child. 14 Solid food is for the mature, for those whose faculties are trained by practice to distinguish good from evil.

6 Let us, then, go beyond the initial teaching about Christ and advance to maturity, not laying the

---

4, 12–15: The word of God, i.e., the divine message of salvation in Jesus, lays open to God man's real intentions and purposes in this life (v 12) so that there is no escaping the manifestation of his conscience (v 13). But the Christian who holds fast to his faith in Jesus as high priest (v 14; 2, 17) need have no fear even of his own weakness (16), for his appeal is to a high priest who understands the human condition from his own experience of suffering and temptation, sin excepted (v 15).

5, 1–10: The true humanity of Jesus (see note on 2, 5–18) makes him a more rather than a less effective high priest to the Christian community. In Old

Testament tradition the high priest was identified with the people, guilty of personal sin just as they were (1ff). Even so, the office was of divine appointment (v 4), as was also the case with the sinless (4, 15) Christ (v 5). For v. 6, see note on Ps 110,4. Although Jesus was Son of God, he was destined as man to learn obedience by accepting the suffering which he had to endure (v 8). Because of his perfection through this experience of human suffering he is the cause of salvation for all (v 9), a *high priest according to the order of Melchizedek* (v 10; cf 7, 3).

5, 11–14: By way of preparation for his reflections on the priesthood of Christ, in chapter 7, the author

deliberately arouses his audience by provocation, observing that they are not really prepared to assimilate advanced theological reflection.

6, 1–8: The author judges that the community's faith will benefit more from profound theological reflection than from a repetition of traditional catechesis (1ff). He will make no effort to address himself to apostates, for their very hostility to the Christian message cuts them off completely from Christ (4–8).

foundation all over again: repentance from dead works, faith in God, 2 instruction about baptisms and laying-on of hands, resurrection of the dead, and eternal judgment. 3 And, God permitting, we shall advance!

4 For when men have once been enlightened and have tasted the heavenly gift and become sharers in the Holy Spirit, 5 when they have tasted the good word of God and the powers of the age to come, 6 and then have fallen away, it is impossible to make them repent again, since they are crucifying the Son of God for themselves and holding him up to contempt. 7 Ground which drinks in the rain falling on it again and again, and brings forth vegetation useful to those for whom it is cultivated, receives the blessing of God. 8 But if it bears thorns and thistles, it is worthless; it is soon cursed, and finally is burned.

9 Beloved, even though we speak in this way, we are persuaded of better things in your regard, things pointing to your salvation. 10 God is not unjust; he will not forget your work and the love you have shown him by your service, past and present, to his holy people. 11 Our desire is that each of you show the same zeal till the end, fully assured of that for which you hope. 12 Do not grow lazy, but imitate those who, through faith and patience, are inheriting the promises.

13 When God made his promise to Abraham, he swore by himself, having no one greater to swear by, 14 and said, "I will indeed bless you, and multiply you." 15 And so, after patient waiting, Abraham ob-

tained what God had promised. 16 Men swear by someone greater than themselves; an oath gives firmness to a promise and puts an end to all argument. 17 God, wishing to give the heirs of his promise even clearer evidence that his purpose would not change, guaranteed it by oath, 18 so that, by two things that are unchangeable, in which he could not lie, we who have taken refuge in him might be strongly encouraged to seize the hope which is placed before us. 19 Like a sure and firm anchor, that hope extends beyond the veil 20 through which Jesus, our forerunner, has entered on our behalf, being made high priest forever according to the order of Melchizedek.

Melchizedek a Type of Christ

7 This Melchizedek, king of Salem and priest of the Most High God, met Abraham returning from his defeat of the kings and blessed him. 2 And Abraham apportioned to him one tenth of all his booty. His name means "king of justice"; he was also king of Salem, that is, "king of peace." 3 Without father, mother or ancestry, without beginning of days or end of life, like the Son of God he remains a priest forever.

4 See the greatness of this man to whom Abraham the patriarch gave one tenth of his booty! 5 The law provides that the priests of the tribe of Levi should receive tithes from the people, their brother Israelites, even though all of them are descendants of Abraham; 6 but Melchizedek, who was not of their ancestry, received tithes of Abraham and blessed him who had received God's promises. 7 It is indisputable that

a lesser person is blessed by a greater. 8 And whereas men subject to death receive tithes, Scripture testifies that this man lives on. 9 Levi, who receives tithes, was, so to speak, tithed in the person of his father, 10 for he was still in his father's loins when Melchizedek met Abraham.

11 If then, perfection had been achieved through the levitical priesthood (on the basis of which the people received the law), what need would there have been to appoint a priest according to the order of Melchizedek, instead of choosing a priest according to the order of Aaron? 12 When there is a change of priesthood, there is necessarily a change of law. 13 Now he of whom these things are said was of a different tribe, none of whose members ever officiated at the altar. 14 It is clear that our Lord rose from the tribe of Judah, regarding which Moses said nothing about priests. 15 The matter is clearer still if another priest is appointed according to the likeness of Melchizedek: 16 one who has become a priest, not in virtue of a law expressed in a commandment concerning physical descent, but in virtue of the power of a life which cannot be destroyed. 17 Scripture testifies: "You are a priest forever according to the order of Melchizedek."

18 The former commandment has been annulled because of its weakness and uselessness, 19 for the law brought nothing to perfection. But a better hope has supervened, and through it we draw near to God. 20 This has been confirmed by an oath. The priests of the old covenant became priests without an oath,

---

6, 9–20: To balance his criticism of the community (1ff.9), the author expresses his confidence that its members are living truly Christian lives, and that God will justly reward their efforts (v 10). He is concerned especially about their persevering (11f), and cites in this regard the achievement of Abraham, who relied on God's promise and on God's oath (13–18; cf Gn 22, 16). The author proposes to them a firm anchor of Christian hope, the high priesthood of Christ now living with God (19f).

7, 1ff: Recalling the meeting between Melchizedek and Abraham described in Genesis 14, 17–20, the author enhances the significance of this priest by providing the etymological meaning of his name and that of the city over which he ruled (v 2). Since Genesis gives no information on the parentage or the death of Melchizedek, he is seen here as a type of Christ, representing a priesthood that is unique and eternal (v 3).

7, 4–10: The tithe which Abraham gave to Mel-

chizedek (v 4), a practice later followed by the levitical priesthood (v 5), was a gift (v 6) acknowledging a certain superiority in Melchizedek, the foreign priest (v 7). This is further indicated by the fact that the institution of the levitical priesthood was sustained by hereditary succession in the tribe of Levi, whereas the absence of any mention of Melchizedek's death in Genesis implies that his personal priesthood is permanent (v 8). The levitical priesthood itself, through Abraham, its ancestor, paid tithes to Melchizedek, thus acknowledging the superiority of his priesthood over its own (9f).

7, 11–14: The levitical priesthood was not typified by the priesthood of Melchizedek, for Psalm 110, 4 speaks of a priesthood of a new order, the order of Melchizedek, to arise in messianic times (v 11). Since the levitical priesthood served the Mosaic law, a new priesthood (v 12) would not come into being without a change in the law itself. Thus Jesus was not associated with the Old Testament priesthood, for he was a

descendant of the tribe of Judah, which had never exercised the priesthood (13f).

7, 15–19: Jesus does not exercise a priesthood through family lineage but through his immortal existence (15f), fulfilling Psalm 110, 4 (v 17; cf 7, 3). Thus he abolishes forever both the levitical priesthood and the law it serves, because neither could effectively sanctify men (v 18) by leading them into direct communication with God (v 19).

7, 20–25: As was the case with the promise to Abraham (6, 13)—but not with the levitical priesthood—the eternal priesthood of the order of Melchizedek was confirmed by God's oath (20f); cf Ps 110, 4. Thus Jesus becomes the guarantee of a permanent covenant (v 22) that does not require a succession of priests as did the levitical priesthood (v 23), because his high priesthood is eternal and unchangeable (v 24). Jesus, therefore, is able to save all who draw near to God through him since he is their everliving intercessor (v 25).

21 unlike Jesus to whom God said:

"The Lord has sworn, and he
    will not repent:
    'You are a priest forever,
        according to the order of
            Melchizedek.'"

22 Thus has Jesus become the guarantee of a better covenant. 23 Under the old covenant there were many priests because they were prevented by death from remaining in office; 24 but Jesus, because he remains forever, has a priesthood which does not pass away. 25 Therefore he is always able to save those who approach God through him, since he forever lives to make intercession for them.

26 It was fitting that we should have such a high priest: holy, innocent, undefiled, separated from sinners, higher than the heavens. 27 Unlike the other high priests, he has no need to offer sacrifice day after day, first for his own sins and then for those of the people; he did that once for all when he offered himself. 28 For the law sets up as high priests men who are weak, but the word of the oath which came after the law appoints as priest the Son, made perfect forever.

The Heavenly Priesthood of Jesus

8 The main point in what we are saying is this: we have such a high priest, who has taken his seat at the right hand of the throne of the Majesty in heaven, 2 minister of the sanctuary and of that true tabernacle set up, not by man, but by the Lord. 3 Now every high priest is appointed to offer gifts and sacrifices; hence the necessity for this one to have something to offer.

4 If he were on earth he would not be a priest, for there are priests already offering the gifts which the law prescribes. 5 They offer worship in a sanctuary which is only a copy and shadow of the heavenly one, for Moses, when about to erect the tabernacle, was warned, "See that you make everything according to the pattern shown you on the mountain." 6 Jesus has obtained a more excellent ministry now, just as he is mediator of a better covenant founded on better promises.

The Old and the New Covenants

7 If that first covenant had been faultless, there would have been no place for a second one. 8 But God, finding fault with them, says:

"Days are coming, says the Lord,
    when I will make a new
        covenant with the house
            of Israel
    and with the house of Judah.
9 It will not be like the covenant
    I made with their fathers
    the day I took them by the
        hand
    to lead them forth from the
        land of Egypt;
For they broke my covenant
    and I grew weary of them,
        says the Lord.
10 But this is the covenant I will
        make with the house of
            Israel
    after those days, says the
        Lord:
I will place my laws in their
        minds
    and I will write them upon
        their hearts;
I will be their God
    and they shall be my people.

11 And they shall not teach their
        fellow citizens
    or their brothers, saying,
        'Know the Lord,'
    for all shall know me, from
        least to greatest.
12 I will forgive their evildoing,
    and their sins I will remember
        no more."

13 When he says, "a new covenant," he declares the first one obsolete. And what has become obsolete and has grown old is close to disappearing.

The Worship of the Old Covenant

9 The first covenant had regulations for worship and an earthly sanctuary. 2 For a tabernacle was constructed, the outer one, in which were the lampstand, the table, and the showbread; this was called the holy place. 3 Behind the second veil was the tabernacle called the holy of holies, 4 in which were the golden altar of incense and the ark of the covenant entirely covered with gold. In the ark were the golden jar containing the manna, the rod of Aaron which had blossomed, and the tablets of the covenant. 5 Above the ark were the cherubim of glory overshadowing the place of expiation. We cannot speak now of each of these in detail. 6 These were the arrangements for worship. In performing their service the priests used to go into the outer tabernacle constantly, 7 but only the high priest went into the inner one, and that but once a year, with the blood which he offered for himself and for the sins of the people. 8 The Holy Spirit was showing thereby that while the first tabernacle was still standing, the way into the sanctuary

---

7, 26–28: Jesus is precisely the high priest whom mankind requires, holy and sinless, installed far above humanity (v 26); one having no need to offer his sacrifice daily for the sins of men, but making a single offering of himself (v 27) once and for all. The law could only appoint high priests with human limitations, but the fulfillment of God's oath regarding the priesthood of Melchizedek (Ps 110, 4) makes the Son of God the perfect priest forever (v 28).

8, 1–5: The Christian community has in Jesus the kind of high priest described in 7, 26ff. In virtue of his ascension Jesus has taken his place at God's right hand in accordance with Psalm 110, 1 (v 1), where he presides over the heavenly sanctuary established by God himself (v 2). Like every high priest, he has his offering to make (v 3; cf 9, 12.14), but it differs from that of the levitical priesthood in which he had no

share (v 4), and which was in any case but a shadowy reflection of the true offering in the heavenly sanctuary (v 5).

8, 6–13: Jesus' ministry in the heavenly sanctuary is that of mediator of a superior covenant which accomplishes what it signifies (v 6). Since the first covenant was deficient in this respect, it had to be replaced (v 7), as Jeremiah (31, 31–34) had prophesied (8–12). Even in the time of Jeremiah, the first covenant was antiquated (v 13).

9, 1–14: The regulations for worship under the old covenant permitted all the priests to enter the holy place (2, 6), but only the high priest to enter the holy of holies and then only once a year (3ff.7). The description of the sanctuary and its furnishing is taken essentially from Exodus 25–26. This exclusion of the people from the holy of holies signified that

they were not allowed to stand in God's presence (v 8) because their offerings and sacrifices, which were merely symbols of their need of spiritual renewal (v 10), could not obtain forgiveness of their sins (v 9). But Christ, the high priest of the spiritual blessings foreshadowed in the Old Testament sanctuary, has actually entered the true sanctuary of heaven that is not of man's making (v 11). His place there is permanent, and his offering is his own blood which won man's eternal redemption (v 12). If the sacrifice of animals could bestow legal purification (v 13), how much more effective is the blood of the sinless, divine Christ who spontaneously offered himself to purge man of his sins and to render him fit for the service of God (v 14)!

had not yet been revealed. 9 This is a symbol of the present time, in which gifts and sacrifices are offered that can never make perfect the conscience of the worshiper, 10 but can only cleanse in matters of food and drink and various ritual washings: regulations concerning the flesh, imposed until the time of the new order.

The Sacrifice of Jesus

11 But when Christ came as high priest of the good things which have come to be, he entered once for all into the sanctuary, passing through the greater and more perfect tabernacle not made by hands, that is, not belonging to this creation. 12 He entered, not with the blood of goats and calves, but with his own blood, and achieved eternal redemption. 13 For if the blood of goats and bulls and the sprinkling of a heifer's ashes can sanctify those who are defiled so that their flesh is cleansed, 14 how much more will the blood of Christ, who through the eternal spirit offered himself unblemished to God, cleanse our consciences from dead works to worship the living God!

15 This is why he is mediator of a new covenant: since his death has taken place for deliverance from transgressions committed under the first covenant, those who are called may receive the promised eternal inheritance. 16 Where there is a testament, it is necessary that the death of the testator be confirmed. 17 For a testament comes into force only in the case of death; it has no force while the testator is alive. 18 Hence, not even the first covenant was inaugurated without blood. 19 When Moses had read all the

commandments of the law to the people, he took the blood of goats and calves, together with water and crimson wool and hyssop, and sprinkled the book and all the people 20 saying, "This is the blood of the covenant which God has enjoined upon you." 21 He also sprinkled the tabernacle and all the vessels of worship with blood. 22 According to the law almost everything is purified by blood, and without the shedding of blood there is no forgiveness.

23 It was necessary that the copies of the heavenly models be purified in this way, but the heavenly realities themselves called for better sacrifices. 24 For Christ did not enter into a sanctuary made by hands, a mere copy of the true one; he entered heaven itself that he might appear before God now on our behalf. 25 Not that he might offer himself there again and again, as the high priest enters year after year into the sanctuary with blood that is not his own; 26 if that were so, he would have had to suffer death over and over from the creation of the world. But now he has appeared at the end of the ages to take away sins once for all by his sacrifice. 27 Just as it is appointed that men die once, and after death be judged, 28 so Christ was offered up once to take away the sins of many; he will appear a second time not to take away sin but to bring salvation to those who eagerly await him.

One Sacrifice instead of Many

10 Since the law had only a shadow of the good things to come, and no real image of them, it was never able to perfect the worshipers by the same sacrifices offered

continually year after year. 2 Were matters otherwise, the priests would have stopped offering them, for the worshipers, once cleansed, would have had no sin on their conscience. 3 But through those sacrifices there came only a yearly recalling of sins, 4 because it is impossible for the blood of bulls and goats to take sins away. 5 Wherefore, on coming into the world, Jesus said:

"Sacrifice and offering you did not desire,
but a body you have prepared for me;
6 Holocausts and sin offerings you took no delight in.
7 Then I said, 'As is written of me in the book,
I have come to do your will, O God.'"

8 First he says,

"Sacrifices and offerings, holocausts and sin offerings, you neither desired nor delighted in."

(These are offered according to the prescriptions of the law.) 9 Then he says,

"I have come to do your will."

In other words, he takes away the first covenant to establish the second. 10 By this "will," we have been sanctified through the offering of the body of Jesus Christ once for all. 11 Every other priest stands ministering day by day, and offering again and again those same sacrifices which can never take away sins. 12 But Jesus offered one sacrifice for sins and took his seat forever at the right hand of God; 13 now he waits until his enemies are placed beneath his feet. 14 By one offering

9, 15–28: Jesus' role as mediator of the new covenant resulted in his death, which freed men from the sins committed under the Mosaic covenant and made them instead inheritors of the benefits of the new covenant (v 15). This effect of his work follows the human pattern whereby a last will and testament becomes effective only with the death of the testator (16f). The Mosaic covenant was also associated with death, for Moses made use of blood to seal the pact between God and the people (18–21). In Old Testament tradition guilt could normally not be remitted without the use of blood (v 22; cf Lv 17, 11). Since inevitably the blood of animals became a cleansing symbol among Old Testament prefigurations, it was necessary that the realities foreshadowed be brought into being by a shedding of blood that was infinitely more effective by reason of its worth (v 23). Christ did

not simply prefigure the heavenly realities (v 24) by performing an annual sacrifice with a blood not his own (v 25), but offered the single sacrifice of himself as the final annulment of sin (v 26). Just as death is the unrepeatable act which ends man's life, so Christ's offering of himself for all men is the unrepeatable sacrifice which has once and for all achieved redemption (27).

10, 1–10: Christian faith now realizes that the Old Testament sacrifices did not effect the spiritual benefits to come, but only prefigured them (v 1). For if the sacrifices actually effected the forgiveness of sin, there would have been no reason for their constant repetition (v 2). They were rather a continual reminder of the people's sins (v 3). It is not reasonable to suppose that human sins could be removed by the blood of animal sacrifices (v 4). Christ, therefore, is here shown

to understand his mission in terms of Psalm 40, 6ff, cited according to the Septuagint (5–7). Jesus acknowledged that the Old Testament sacrifices did not remit the sins of the people and so, perceiving the will of God, offered his own body for this purpose (8ff).

10, 11–18: Whereas the levitical priesthood offered daily sacrifices that were ineffectual in remitting sin (v 11), Jesus offered a single sacrifice which won him a permanent place at God's right hand. There he has only to await the final outcome of his work (12f; cf Ps 110, 1). Thus he has brought into being in his own person the new covenant prophesied by Jeremiah (31, 33f) which has rendered meaningless all other offerings for sin (14–18).

he has forever perfected those who are being sanctified. 15 The Holy Spirit attests this to us, for after saying,

16 "This is the covenant I will
      make with them
      after those days, says the
          Lord:
  I will put my laws in their
      hearts
      and I will write them on their
      minds,"

17 he also says,

"Their sins and their
      transgressions
  I will remember no more."

18 Once these have been forgiven, there is no further offering for sin.

Recalling the Past

19 Brothers, since the blood of Jesus assures our entrance into the sanctuary 20 by the new and living path he has opened up for us through the veil (the "veil" meaning his flesh), 21 and since we have a great priest who is over the house of God, 22 let us draw near in utter sincerity and absolute confidence, our hearts sprinkled clean from the evil which lay on our conscience and our bodies washed in pure water. 23 Let us hold unswervingly to our profession which gives us hope, for he who made the promise deserves our trust. 24 We must consider how to rouse each other to love and good deeds. 25 We should not absent ourselves from the assembly, as some do, but encourage one another; and this all the more because you see that the Day draws near. 26 If we sin willfully after receiving the truth, there remains for

us no further sacrifice for sin— 27 only a fearful expectation of judgment and a flaming fire to consume the adversaries of God. 28 Anyone who rejects the law of Moses is put to death without mercy on the testimony of two or three witnesses. 29 Do you not suppose that a much worse punishment is due the man who disdains the Son of God, thinks the covenant-blood by which he was sanctified to be ordinary, and insults the Spirit of grace? 30 We know who said,

"Vengeance is mine; I will
      repay,"
and

"The Lord will judge his people."

31 It is a fearful thing to fall into the hands of the living God.

32 Recall the days gone by when, after you had been enlightened, you endured a great contest of suffering. 33 At times you were publicly exposed to insult and trial; at other times you associated yourselves with those who were being so dealt with. 34 You even joined in the sufferings of those who were in prison and joyfully assented to the confiscation of your goods, knowing that you had better and more permanent possessions. 35 Do not, then, surrender your confidence; it will have great reward. 36 You need patience to do God's will and receive what he has promised.

37 For, just a brief moment,
      and he who is to come will
          come; he will not delay.
38 My just man will live by faith,
      and if he draws back
      I take no pleasure in him.

39 We are not among those who

draw back and perish, but among those who have faith and live.

EXAMPLES, DISCIPLINE
DISOBEDIENCE

Faith of the Ancients

11 Faith is confident assurance concerning what we hope for, and conviction about things we do not see. 2 Because of faith the men of old were approved by God. 3 Through faith we perceive that the worlds were created by the word of God, and that what is visible came into being through the invisible. 4 By faith Abel offered God a sacrifice greater than Cain's. Because of this he was attested to be just, God himself having borne witness to him on account of his gifts; therefore, although Abel is dead, he still speaks. 5 By faith Enoch was taken away without dying, and "he was seen no more because God took him." Scripture testifies that, before he was taken up, he was pleasing to God— 6 but without faith, it is impossible to please him. Anyone who comes to God must believe that he exists, and that he rewards those who seek him. 7 By faith Noah, warned about things not yet seen, revered God and built an ark that his household might be saved. He thereby condemned the world and inherited the justice which comes through faith. 8 By faith Abraham obeyed when he was called, and went forth to the place he was to receive as a heritage; he went forth, moreover, not knowing where he was going. 9 By faith he sojourned in the promised land as in a foreign country, dwelling in tents with Isaac and Jacob, heirs of the same promise; 10 for he was looking forward to the

---

10, 19–39: Practical consequences from these reflections on the priesthood and the sacrifice of Christ should make it clear that Christians may now have direct and confident access to God through the person of Jesus (19f), who rules God's house as high priest (v 21). They should approach God with sincerity and faith, in the knowledge that through baptism their sins have been remitted (v 22), reminding themselves of the hope they expressed in Christ at that event (v 23). They are to encourage one another to Christian love and activity (v 24), not refusing, no matter what the reason, to participate in in the community's assembly especially in view of the parousia (v 25; cf 1 Thes 4, 13–18). If refusal to participate in the assembly indicates rejection of Christ, no sacrifice exists to obtain forgiveness for so great a sin (v 26); only the dreadful judgment of God remains (v 27). For if violation of the Mosaic law could be punished by death, how much worse will be

the punishment of those who have turned their backs on Christ by despising his sacrifice and disregarding the gifts of the Holy Spirit (28f)! Judgment belongs to the Lord, and he enacts it by his living presence (30f). There was a time when the spirit of their community caused them to welcome and share their sufferings (32ff). To revitalize that spirit is to share in the courage of the Old Testament prophets (cf Is 26, 20; Hab 2, 3f), the kind of courage that must distinguish the faith of the Christian (35–39).

11, 1–40: This chapter draws upon the people and events of the Old Testament to paint an inspiring portrait of religious faith, firm and unyielding in the face of any obstacles that confront it. In the opinion of some authorities, these pages rank among the most eloquent and lofty to be found in the Bible. They expand the author's theme, broached in 6, 12, to which he now returns (10, 39).

The material of the chapter is consistently de-

veloped. Verses 3–7 draw upon the first nine chapters of Genesis; 8–22, upon the period of the patriarchs; 23–31, upon the time of Moses; 32–38, upon the history of the judges, the prophets and the Maccabean martyrs. The author gives the most extensive description of faith provided in the New Testament, though his interest does not lie in a technical, theological definition. In view of the needs of his audience he describes what authentic faith does, not what it is in itself. Through faith God guarantees the blessings to be hoped for from him, providing evidence in the gift of faith that what he promises will eventually come to pass (v 1). Because they accepted in faith God's guarantee of the future, the biblical personages discussed in 3–38 were themselves commended by God (v 2). Christians have even greater reason to remain firm in faith, since they, unlike the Old Testament men of faith, have perceived the beginning of God's fulfillment of his messianic promises (39f).

city with foundations, whose designer and maker is God. 11 By faith Sarah received power to conceive though she was past the age, for she thought that the One who had made the promise was worthy of trust. 12 As a result of this faith, there came forth from one man, who was himself as good as dead, descendants as numerous as the stars in the sky and the sands of the seashore.

13 All of these died in faith. They did not obtain what had been promised but saw and saluted it from afar. By acknowledging themselves to be strangers and foreigners on the earth, 14 they showed that they were seeking a homeland. 15 If they had been thinking back to the place from which they had come, they would have had the opportunity of returning there. 16 But they were searching for a better, a heavenly home. Wherefore God is not ashamed to be called their God, for he has prepared a city for them. 17 By faith Abraham, when put to the test, offered up Isaac; he who had received the promises was ready to sacrifice his only son, 18 of whom it was said, "Through Isaac shall your descendants be called." 19 He reasoned that God was able to raise from the dead, and so he received Isaac back as a symbol. 20 By faith Isaac invoked for Jacob and Esau blessings that were still to be.

21 By faith Jacob, when dying, blessed each of the sons of Joseph, and worshiped God, leaning on the head of his staff. 22 By faith Joseph, near the end of his life, spoke of the Exodus of the Israelites, and gave instructions about his burial. 23 By faith Moses' parents hid him for three months after his birth, thereby disregarding the king's edict, because they saw that he was a beautiful child.

24 By faith Moses, when he had grown up, refused to be known as the son of Pharaoh's daughter; 25 he wished to be ill-treated along with God's people rather than enjoy the fleeting rewards of sin. 26 Moses considered the reproach borne by God's Anointed greater riches than the treasures of Egypt, for he was looking to the reward. 27 By faith he left Egypt, not fearing the king's wrath, for he persevered as if he were looking on the invisible God. 28 By faith he kept the Passover and sprinkled the lamb's blood, that the destroying angel might not touch the first-born of Israel. 29 By faith the Israelites crossed the Red Sea as if it were dry land, but when the Egyptians attempted the same thing they were drowned. 30 Because of Israel's faith, the walls of Jericho fell after being encircled for seven days. 31 By faith Rahab the harlot escaped from being destroyed with the unbelievers, for she had peacefully received the spies.

32 What more shall I recount? I have not time to tell of Gideon, Barak, Samson, Jephthah, of David and Samuel and the prophets, 33 who by faith conquered kingdoms, did what was just, obtained the promises; they broke the jaws of lions, 34 put out raging fires, escaped the devouring sword; though weak they were made powerful, became strong in battle, and turned back foreign invaders. 35 Women received back their dead through resurrection. Others were tortured and would not receive deliverance, in order to obtain a better resurrection. 36 Still others endured mockery, scourging, even chains and imprisonment. 37 They were stoned, sawed in two, put to death at sword's point; they went about garbed in the skins of sheep or goats, needy, afflicted, tormented. 38 The world was not worthy of them. They wandered about in deserts and on mountains, they dwelt in caves and in holes of the earth. 39 Yet despite the fact that all of these were approved because of their faith, they did not obtain what had been promised. 40 God had made a better plan, a plan which included us. Without us, they were not to be made perfect.

God's Treatment of His Sons

12 Therefore, since we for our part are surrounded by this cloud of witnesses, let us lay aside every encumbrance of sin which clings to us and persevere in running the race which lies ahead; 2 let us keep our eyes fixed on Jesus, who inspires and perfects our faith. For the sake of the joy which lay before him he endured the cross, heedless of its shame. He has taken his seat at the right of the throne of God. 3 Remember how he endured the opposition of sinners; hence do not grow despondent or abandon the struggle. 4 In your fight against sin you have not yet resisted to the point of shedding blood. 5 Moreover, you have forgotten the encouraging words addressed to you as sons:

"My sons, do not disdain the discipline of the Lord
nor lose heart when he reproves you;
6 For whom the Lord loves, he disciplines;
he scourges every son he receives."

7 Endure your trials as the discipline of God, who deals with you as sons. For what son is there whom his father does not discipline? 8 If you do not know the discipline of sons, you are not sons but bastards. 9 If we respected our earthly fathers who corrected us, should we not all the more submit to the Father of spirits, and live? 10 They disciplined us as seemed right to them, to prepare us for the short span of mortal life; but God does so for our true profit, that we may share his holiness. 11 At the time it is administered, all discipline seems a cause for grief and not for joy, but later it brings forth the fruit of peace and justice to those who are trained in its school. 12 So strengthen your drooping hands and your weak knees. 13 Make straight the paths you walk on, that your halting limbs may not be dislocated but healed.

12, 1-4: Christian life is to be inspired not only by the Old Testament men of faith (v 1), but above all by Jesus. As the architect of Christian faith, he had himself to endure the cross before receiving the glory of his triumph (v 2). Reflection on his sufferings should give his followers courage to continue the struggle, if necessary even to the shedding of blood (3f).

12, 5-13: Christians should regard their own sufferings as the affectionate correction of the Lord, who loves them as a father loves his children.

Penalties of Disobedience

14 Strive for peace with all men, and for that holiness without which no one can see the Lord. 15 See to it that no man falls away from the grace of God; that no bitter root springs up through which many may become defiled; 16 that there be among you no fornicator or godless person like Esau, who sold his birthright for a meal. 17 You know that afterward he wanted to inherit his father's blessing, but he was rejected because he had no opportunity to alter his choice, even though he sought the blessing with tears.

18 You have not drawn near to an untouchable mountain and a blazing fire, nor gloomy darkness and storm 19 and trumpet blast, a voice speaking words such that those who heard begged that they be not addressed to them, 20 for they could not bear to hear the command: "If even an animal touches the mountain, it must be stoned to death." 21 Indeed, so fearful was the spectacle that Moses said, "I am terrified and trembling." 22 No, you have drawn near to Mount Zion and the city of the living God, the heavenly Jerusalem, to myriads of angels in festal gathering, 23 to the assembly of the first-born enrolled in heaven, to God the judge of all, to the spirits of just men made perfect, 24 to Jesus, the mediator of a new covenant, and to the sprinkled blood which speaks more eloquently than that of Abel.

25 Do not refuse to hear him who speaks. For if the Israelites did not escape punishment when they refused to listen as God spoke to them on earth, how much greater punishment will be ours if we turn away from him who speaks from heaven! 26 His voice then shook the earth, but

now he has promised, "I will once more shake not only earth but heaven!" 27 And that "once more" shows that shaken, created things will pass away, so that only what is unshaken may remain. 28 Wherefore, we who are receiving the unshakable kingdom should hold fast to God's grace, through which we may offer worship acceptable to him in reverence and awe. 29 For our God is a consuming fire.

FINAL EXHORTATION, BLESSING, GREETINGS

13 Love your fellow Christians always. 2 Do not neglect to show hospitality, for by that means some have entertained angels without knowing it. 3 Be as mindful of prisoners as if you were sharing their imprisonment, and of the ill-treated as of yourselves, for you may yet suffer as they do. 4 Let marriage be honored in every way and the marriage bed be kept undefiled, for God will judge fornicators and adulterers. 5 Do not love money but be content with what you have, for God has said, "I will never desert you, nor will I forsake you." 6 Thus we may say with confidence:

"The Lord is my helper,
  I will not be afraid;
What can man do to me?"

7 Remember your leaders who spoke the word of God to you; consider how their lives ended, and imitate their faith. 8 Jesus Christ is the same yesterday, today, and forever. 9 Do not be carried away by all kinds of strange teaching. It is good to have our hearts strengthened by the grace of God and not by foods which are useless to those who take them as a standard for living. 10 We have an altar from which

those who serve the tabernacle have no right to eat. 11 The bodies of the animals whose blood is brought into the sanctuary by the high priest as a sin offering are burned outside the camp. 12 Therefore Jesus died outside the gate, to sanctify the people by his own blood. 13 Let us go to him outside the camp, bearing the insult which he bore. 14 For here we have no lasting city; we are seeking one which is to come. 15 Through him let us continually offer God a sacrifice of praise, that is, the fruit of lips which acknowledge his name.

16 Do not neglect good deeds and generosity; God is pleased by sacrifices of that kind. 17 Obey your leaders and submit to them, for they keep watch over you as men who must render an account. So act that they may fulfill their task with joy, not with sorrow, for that would be harmful to you. 18 Pray for us; we are confident that we have a good conscience, wishing, as we do, to act rightly in every respect. 19 I especially ask your prayers that I may be restored to you very soon.

20 May the God of peace, who brought up from the dead the great Shepherd of the sheep by the blood of the eternal covenant, Jesus our Lord, 21 furnish you with all that is good, that you may do his will. Through Jesus Christ may he carry out in you all that is pleasing to him. To Christ be glory forever! Amen.

22 My brothers, I beg you to bear with this word of encouragement, for I have written to you rather briefly. 23 I must let you know that our brother Timothy has been set free. If he is able to join me soon, he will be with me when I see you. 24 Greetings to all your leaders, and to all the people of God. 25 Grace be with you all.

12, 14–17: The example of Esau's conduct should warn the community against apostasy from Christ.

12, 18–29: As a final appeal for adherence to Christian teaching, the two covenants, of Moses and of Christ, are compared. The Mosaic covenant is shown to have originated in fear of God and threats of divine punishment (18–21). The covenant in Christ gives men direct access to God (v 22), makes them members of the Christian community, God's sons, a sanctified people (v 23) who have Jesus as mediator to speak for them (v 24). Not to heed the voice of the risen Christ is a sin more grave by far than the rejection of the word of Moses (25ff). Though men fall

away, God's kingdom in Christ will remain, and his justice will punish those guilty of deserting it (28f).

13, 1–16: After recommendations on social and moral matters (1–6), the letter turns to doctrinal issues. The fact that the original leaders are dead should not cause the recipients of this letter to lose their faith (v 7), for Christ still lives and he remains always the same (v 8). They must not rely on their personal sanctification on regulations concerning foods (v 9), nor should they entertain the notion that Judaism and Christianity can be intermingled (v 10; cf note on Gal 2, 11–14; 15–21). As Jesus died separated from his own people, so must the Christian

community remain apart from the religious doctrines of Judaism (11–14). Christ must be the heart and center of the community (15–16).

13, 17ff: Recommending obedience to the leaders of the community, the author observes that he has done his best not to give cause for objection to himself.

13, 20–25: The letter concludes with a prayer (20f); a final request for the acceptance of its message (v 22); casual information regarding Timothy; and general greetings (23ff).

THE EPISTLE OF

James

ENDURANCE

O the twelve tribes in the dispersion, James, a servant of God and of the Lord Jesus Christ, sends greeting. 2 My brothers, count it pure joy when you are involved in every sort of trial. 3 Realize that when your faith is tested this makes for endurance. 4 Let endurance come to its perfection so that you may be fully mature and lacking in nothing.

Prayer for Wisdom

5 If any of you is without wisdom, let him ask it from the God who gives generously and ungrudgingly to all, and it will be given him. 6 Yet he must ask in faith, never doubting, for the doubter is like the surf tossed and driven by the wind. 7 A man of this sort, devious and erratic in all that he does, 8 must not expect to receive anything from the Lord.

Humility

9 Let the brother in humble circumstances take pride in his emi-nence 10 and the rich man be proud of his lowliness, for he will disappear "like the flower of the field." 11 When the sun comes up with its scorching heat it parches the meadow, the field flowers droop, and with that the meadow's loveliness is gone. Just so will the rich man wither away amid his many projects.

Temptation

12 Happy the man who holds out to the end through trial! Once he has been proved, he will receive the crown of life the Lord has promised to those who love him. 13 No one who is tempted is free to say, "I am being tempted by God." Surely God, who is beyond the grasp of evil, tempts no one. 14 Rather, the tug and lure of his own passion tempts every man. 15 Once passion has conceived, it gives birth to sin, and when sin reaches maturity it begets death.

Response to God's Gift

16 Make no mistake about this, my dear brothers. 17 Every worth-while gift, every genuine benefit comes from above, descending from the Father of the heavenly lumi-naries, who cannot change and who is never shadowed over. 18 He wills to bring us to birth with a word spoken in truth so that we may be a kind of first fruits of his creatures.

1, 1: *James, servant of God and of the Lord Jesus Christ:* a declaration of authority for instructing the Christian communities; cf Rom 1, 1. On the identity of the author, see the Introduction.

1, 2: *Count it pure joy . . . every sort of trial:* a frequent teaching of the New Testament derived from the words and sufferings of Christ (Mt 5, 10ff; Jn 10, 11; 15, 12f; Acts 5, 41).

1, 3–8: The gradation of testing, endurance and perfection indicate the manner of achieving spiritual maturity and full preparedness for the coming of Christ (3f; cf Rom 5, 3ff; 1 Pt 1, 6f). To sustain trials, to achieve endurance and perfection, require wisdom which God readily grants to believing petitioners but withholds from those who doubt (5–8; cf Sir 4, 7).

1, 9ff: From the religious standpoint, the lot of the poor and the lowly as opposed to that of the proud rich is, here and elsewhere in the epistle, found to have value in inverse ratio to circumstance (2, 5.13; 4, 10.13–16; 5, 1–6).

1, 12: *The crown of life:* the ultimate and eternal reward for fidelity and perseverance in following the law of Christ; cf Rom 8, 28; 2 Tm 4, 8; 1 Pt 5, 4; Rv 2, 10.

1, 13ff: It is contrary to the nature of God for him to be the author of man's temptation (v 13). In the genesis of sin, man is first beguiled by passion (v 14), then gives his consent, which in turn begets the act of sin. As sin grows, it incurs the ultimate penalty of death (v 15).

1, 18: *He wills to bring us to birth . . . truth:* acceptance of the gospel message constitutes a new birth and makes the recipient the first fruits of a new creation; cf Jn 3, 5f; Rom 8, 23.

19 Keep this in mind, dear brothers.

Let every man be quick to hear, slow to speak, slow to anger; 20 for a man's anger does not fulfill God's justice. 21 Strip away all that is filthy, every vicious excess. Humbly welcome the word that has taken root in you, with its power to save you. 22 Act on this word. If all you do is listen to it, you are deceiving yourselves.

23 A man who listens to God's word but does not put it into practice is like a man who looks into a mirror at the face he was born with; 24 he looks at himself, then goes off and promptly forgets what he looked like. 25 There is, on the other hand, the man who peers into freedom's ideal law and abides by it. He is no forgetful listener, but one who carries out the law in practice. Happy will this man be in whatever he does.

26 If a man who does not control his tongue imagines that he is devout, he is self-deceived; his worship is pointless. 27 Looking after orphans and widows in their distress and keeping oneself unspotted by the world make for pure worship without stain before our God and Father.

Against Favoritism

2 My brothers, your faith in our Lord Jesus Christ glorified must not allow of favoritism. 2 Suppose there should come into your assembly a man fashionably dressed, with gold rings on his fingers, and at the same time a poor man in shabby clothes. 3 Suppose further that you were to take notice of the well-dressed man and say, "Sit right here, please," whereas you were to say to the poor man, "You can stand!" or "Sit over there by my footrest." 4 Have you not in a case like this discriminated in your hearts? Have you not set yourselves up as judges who hand down corrupt decisions?

5 Listen, dear brothers. Did not God choose those who are poor in the eyes of the world to be rich in faith and heirs of the kingdom he promised to those who love him? 6 Yet you treated the poor man shamefully. Are not the rich exploiting you? They are the ones who hale you into the courts 7 and who blaspheme that noble name which has made you God's own.

8 You are acting rightly, however, if you fulfill the law of the kingdom. Scripture has it, "You shall love your neighbor as yourself." 9 But if you show favoritism, you commit sin and are convicted by the law as transgressors. 10 Whoever falls into sin on one point of the law, even though he keeps the entire remainder, has become guilty on all counts. 11 For he who said, "You shall not commit adultery," also said, "You shall not kill." If therefore you do not commit adultery but do commit murder, you have become a transgressor of the law.

12 Always speak and act as men destined for judgment under the law of freedom. 13 Merciless is the judgment on the man who had not shown mercy; but mercy triumphs over judgment.

Faith and Good Works

14 My brothers, what good is it to profess faith without practicing it? Such faith has no power to save one, has it? 15 If a brother or sister has nothing to wear and no food for the day, 16 and you say to them, "Goodbye and good luck! Keep warm and well fed," but do not meet their bodily needs, what good is that? 17 So it is with the faith that does nothing in practice. It is thoroughly lifeless.

18 To such a person one might say, "You have faith and I have works— is that it?" Show me your faith without works, and I will show you the faith that underlies my works! 19 Do you believe that God is one? You are quite right. The demons believe that, and shudder. 20 Do you want proof, you ignoramus, that without works faith is idle? 21 Was not our father Abraham justified by his works when he offered his son Isaac on the altar? 22 There you see proof that faith was both assisting his works and implemented by his works. 23 You also see how the Scripture was fulfilled which says, "Abraham believed God, and it was credited to him as justice"; for this he received the title "God's friend."

24 You must perceive that a person is justified by his works and not by faith alone. 25 Rahab the harlot will illustrate the point. Was she not justified by her works when she harbored the messengers and sent them out by a different route? 26 Be assured, then, that faith without works is as dead as a body without breath.

Restraining the Tongue

3 Not many of you should become teachers, my brothers; you should realize that those of us who do so will be called to the stricter account. 2 All of us fall short in many respects. If a person is without fault in speech he is a man in the fullest sense, because he can control his entire body. 3 When we put bits into the mouths of horses to make them obey us, we guide the rest of their bodies. 4 It is the same with ships: however large they are, and despite the fact that they are driven by fierce winds, they are directed by very small rudders on whatever course the steersman's impulse may

---

1, 19–25: To *be quick to hear* the gospel is to accept it readily and to act in conformity with it, removing from one's soul whatever opposes it so that it may take root and effect salvation (19–22). To listen to and not practice the gospel message is to misunderstand religion (23f). Only conformity of life to the ideal law of true freedom brings happiness (v 25).

1, 26: For control of the tongue, see note on 3, 1–12.

1, 27: *Orphans and widows:* the defenseless and oppressed; cf Acts 6, 1ff.

2, 1–13: In the Christian community there must be no discrimination against the poor, or favoritism toward the rich based on a mistaken exaltation of status or wealth (2ff); cf Mt 23, 6. Divine favor rather consists in God's promises, his election, and his rewards elicited by man's faith and response to his love (v 5); cf Mt 5, 3; 11, 5; 1 Cor 1, 17–29. The impious rich who oppress the poor dishonor the name of Christ. By violating the law of love of neighbor, they offend against the whole law (6f.9ff). On the other hand, abiding consciousness of the final judgment helps the faithful to fulfill the whole law (v 12).

2, 14–26: The theme of these verses is the relationship of faith and good works. Neither can merit salvation without the other, as even the demons, who believe that God exists (v 19), can testify (14–20).

The faith that justified Abraham was accompanied by his willingness, at the divine behest, to sacrifice his son Isaac (21ff). A living faith works through love, as opposed to a dead faith that lacks good works (24.26).

3, 1–12: The use and abuse of the important role of teaching in the church are here (v 1) related to the good or bad use of the tongue (9–12), the instrument through which teaching was chiefly conveyed; cf Sir 5, 13–6, 1; 28, 12–26. The bit and the rudder are figures of the tongue's control (2ff), just as the spark and destroying flames portray the evils of unbridled speech. The tongue is *a whole universe of malice,* a defiler of the body (v 6), *a restless evil, full of deadly poison* (5–8).

select. 5 The tongue is something like that. It is a small member, yet it makes great pretensions.

See how tiny the spark is that sets a huge forest ablaze! 6 The tongue is such a flame. It exists among our members as a whole universe of malice. The tongue defiles the entire body. Its flames encircle our course from birth, and its fire is kindled by hell. 7 Every form of life, four-footed or winged, crawling or swimming, can be tamed, and has been tamed, by mankind; 8 the tongue no man can tame. It is a restless evil, full of deadly poison. 9 We use it to say, "Praised be the Lord and Father"; then we use it to curse men, though they are made in the likeness of God. 10 Blessing and curse come out of the same mouth. This ought not to be, my brothers! 11 Does a spring gush forth fresh water and foul from the same outlet? 12 A fig tree, brothers, cannot produce olives, or a grapevine figs; no more can a brackish source yield fresh water.

True Wisdom

13 If one of you is wise and understanding, let him show this in practice through a humility filled with good sense. 14 Should you instead nurse bitter jealousy and selfish ambition in your hearts, at least refrain from arrogant and false claims against the truth. 15 Wisdom like this does not come from above. It is earthbound, a kind of animal, even devilish, cunning. 16 Where there are jealousy and strife, there also are inconstancy and all kinds of vile behavior. 17 Wisdom from above, by contrast, is first of all innocent. It is also peaceable, lenient, docile, rich in sympathy and the kindly deeds that are its fruits, impartial and sincere. 18 The har-vest of justice is sown in peace for those who cultivate peace.

Worldly Desires

4 Where do the conflicts and disputes among you originate? Is it not your inner cravings that make war within your members? 2 What you desire you do not obtain, and so you resort to murder. You envy and you cannot acquire, so you quarrel and fight. You do not obtain because you do not ask. 3 You ask and you do not receive because you ask wrongly, with a view to squandering what you receive on your pleasures. 4 O you unfaithful ones, are you not aware that love of the world is enmity to God? A man is marked out as God's enemy if he chooses to be the world's friend. 5 Do you suppose it is to no purpose that Scripture says, "The spirit he has implanted in us tends toward jealousy"? 6 Yet he bestows a greater gift, for the sake of which it is written,

"God resists the proud
　but bestows his favor on the
　lowly."

7 Therefore submit to God; resist the devil and he will take flight. 8 Draw close to God, and he will draw close to you. Cleanse your hands, you sinners; purify your hearts, you backsliders. 9 Begin to lament, to mourn, and to weep; let your laughter be turned into mourning and your joy into sorrow. 10 Be humbled in the sight of the Lord and he will raise you on high.

Judging One's Fellows

11 Do not, my brothers, speak ill of one another. The one who speaks ill of his brother or judges his brother is speaking against the law. It is the law he judges. If, however, you judge the law you are no ob-server of the law, you are its judge. 12 There is but one Lawgiver and Judge, one who can save and destroy. Who then are you to judge your neighbor?

Against Presumption

13 Come now, you who say, "Today or tomorrow we shall go to such and such a town, spend a year there, trade, and come off with a profit!" 14 You have no idea what kind of life will be yours tomorrow. You are a vapor that appears briefly and vanishes. 15 Instead of saying, "If the Lord wills it, we shall live to do this or that," 16 all you can do is make arrogant and pretentious claims. All such boasting is repre-hensible. 17 When a man knows the right thing to do and does not do it, he sins.

Warning to the Rich

5 As for you, you rich, weep and wail over your impending miseries. 2 Your wealth has rotted, your fine wardrobe has grown moth-eaten, 3 your gold and silver have corroded, and their corrosion shall be a testimony against you; it will devour your flesh like a fire. See what you have stored up for yourselves against the last days. 4 Here, crying aloud, are the wages you withheld from the farmhands who harvested your fields. The shouts of the harvesters have reached the ears of the Lord of hosts. 5 You lived in wanton luxury on the earth; you fattened yourselves for the day of slaughter. 6 You condemned, even killed, the just man; he does not resist you.

Patience

7 Be patient, therefore, my brothers, until the coming of the Lord. See how the farmer awaits the

---

3, 13–18: This discussion on true wisdom is related to the previous reflection on the role of the teacher as one who is in control of his speech. The qualities of the wise man endowed from above (15, 17f) are: innocence, peace, docility, sincerity, impartiality, sympathy and kindly deeds (cf Gal 5, 22f): all this in contrast to earthbound wisdom with its cunning, jealousy, strife, inconstancy, arrogance and endless variety of vile behavior (14ff); cf 2 Cor 12, 20.

4, 1–12: The concern here is with the origin of conflicts in the Christian community. These are occasioned by misuse of the tongue (cf 3, 2–16), and false wisdom shown by *love of the world* which *is*

enmity to God (v 4). Further, the conflicts are bound up with failure to pray properly (cf Mt 7, 7–11; Jn 6, 33)—that is, not petitioning God at all or using his kindness only for the petitioner's pleasure (2f). In contrast, the proper dispositions are submission to God, repentance, humility and resistance to evil (7–10).

4, 13–17: The uncertainty of life (v 14), its complete dependence on God, the necessity of submitting to his will (v 15), all help man to know and to do *the right* (v 17). To disregard this standard is to live arrogantly and presumptuously (v 16), i.e., without God. This is sin (v 17).

5, 1–6: Continuing with the theme of the transitory character of life on earth, the epistle traces the impending ruin of the godless. It denounces the unjust rich, whose victims cry to heaven for judgment on their exploiters (4ff). The decay and corrosion of the costly garments and metals, which here signalize *wealth*, prove them worthless and portend the destruction of their possessors (2f).

5, 7–11: Those oppressed by the unjust rich are reminded of the need for patience, both in bearing the sufferings of human life (v 9) and in their expectation of the coming of the Lord. It is then that they will receive their reward (7f.10f; cf Heb 10, 25; 1 Jn 2, 18).

precious yield of the soil. He looks forward to it patiently while the soil receives the winter and the spring rains. 8 You too, must be patient. Steady your hearts, because the coming of the Lord is at hand. 9 Do not grumble against one another, my brothers, lest you be condemned. See! The judge stands at the gate. 10 As your models in suffering hardship and in patience, brothers, take the prophets who spoke in the name of the Lord. 11 Those who have endured we call blessed. You have heard of the steadfastness of Job, and have seen what the Lord, who is compassionate and merciful, did in the end.

12 Above all else, my brothers, you must not swear an oath, any oath at all, either "by heaven" or "by earth." Rather, let it be "yes" if you mean yes and "no" if you mean no. In this way you will not incur condemnation.

Anointing and Prayer

13 If anyone among you is suffering hardship, he must pray. If a person is in good spirits, he should sing a hymn of praise. 14 Is there anyone sick among you? He should ask for the presbyters of the church. They in turn are to pray over him, anointing him with oil in the Name [of the Lord]. 15 This prayer uttered in faith will reclaim the one who is ill, and the Lord will restore him to health. If he has committed any sins, forgiveness will be his.

16 Hence, declare your sins to one another, and pray for one another, that you may find healing.

The fervent petition of a holy man is powerful indeed. 17 Elijah was only a man like us, yet he prayed earnestly that it would not rain and no rain fell on the land for three years and six months. 18 When he prayed again, the sky burst forth with rain and the land produced its crop.

19 My brothers, the case may arise among you of someone straying from the truth, and of another bringing him back. 20 Remember this: the person who brings a sinner back from his way will save his soul from death and cancel a multitude of sins.

5, 12: This is a threat of condemnation for the abuse of an oath; cf Mt 5, 33–37. *By heaven* and *by earth* were substitutes for the original form of an oath, to circumvent its binding force, and to avoid pronouncing the holy name of Yahweh; cf Ex 22, 10.

5, 14: *Is there anyone sick . . . Lord:* in case of the serious, even if not extreme, illness of a member of the community, *he should ask for the presbyters,* i.e., those who have authority in the church (Acts 15, 2.22f; 1 Tm 5, 17; Ti 1, 5). *They . . . are to pray over him* (cf Sir 38, 9), *anointing him with oil:* oil was used for medicinal purposes in oriental medicine (cf Is 1, 6; Lk 10, 34). In Mark 6, 13 it is also the medium through which miraculous healing is effected *in the name of the Lord,* i.e., by the power of Jesus Christ.

5, 15: *This prayer uttered in faith . . . to health:* though other passages in James speak of saving or salvation in reference to the soul (1, 21; 2, 14; 4, 12; 5, 20), here the reference is to bodily health: *the Lord will restore him to health,* literally "raise him up" (Mk 1, 31; 9, 27). *If he has committed any sins, forgiveness will be his.* In the public ministry of Jesus, bodily cures and forgiveness of sins are often closely related (Mt 9, 1–8; Mk 2, 1–12; Jn 5, 14). The Council of Trent (Sess. 14) declared the Anointing of the Sick to be a sacrament "instituted by Christ our Lord and promulgated by blessed James the apostle."

5, 16ff: *Declare sins:* as a sign of repentance (cf Lv 5, 5; Ps 31, 5; Ezr 9, 6–15; Mt 3, 6; Acts 19, 18); *to one another:* probably in connection with liturgical prayer to make the public confession more efficacious, as witness the *Didache. Pray for one another:* cf Col 3, 4; 1 Thes 5, 25; Heb 13, 18.

5, 19f: This passage is reminiscent of the parable of the Good Shepherd (Lk 15, 3–7).

5, 20: *Will save his soul from death:* the soul of the sinner will be saved from eternal condemnation.

THE FIRST EPISTLE OF

Peter

GREETING

 ETER, an apostle of Jesus Christ, to those who live as strangers scattered throughout Pontus, Galatia, Cappadocia, Asia, and Bithynia; to men chosen 2 according to the foreknowledge of God the Father, consecrated by the Spirit to a life of obedience to Jesus Christ and purification with his blood. Favor and peace be yours in abundance.

Thanksgiving

3 Praised be the God and Father
of our Lord Jesus Christ,
he who in his great mercy
gave us new birth;
a birth unto hope which draws
  its life
from the resurrection of Jesus
  Christ from the dead;
4 a birth to an imperishable
  inheritance,
incapable of fading or defilement,
which is kept in heaven for you
5 who are guarded with God's
  power through faith;

a birth to a salvation which
  stands ready
to be revealed in the last days.

6 There is cause for rejoicing here. You may for a time have to suffer the distress of many trials; 7 but this is so that your faith, which is more precious than the passing splendor of fire-tried gold, may by its genuineness lead to praise, glory and honor when Jesus Christ appears. 8 Although you have never seen him, you love him, and without seeing you now believe in him, and rejoice with inexpressible joy touched with glory 9 because you are achieving faith's goal, your salvation. 10 This is the salvation which the prophets carefully searched out and examined. They prophesied the divine favor that was destined to be yours. 11 They investigated the times and the circumstances which the Spirit of Christ within them was pointing to, for he predicted the sufferings destined for Christ and the glories that would follow. 12 They knew by revelation that they were providing, not for themselves but for you, what has now been proclaimed to you by those who preach the gospel to you, in the power of the Holy Spirit sent from heaven. Into these matters angels long to search.

Filial Obedience and Fear

13 So gird the loins of your

1, 1f: The introductory formula names Peter as the writer (see Introduction). He is Simon, son of John (Mt 16, 18; Jn 21, 15ff), whom Christ called Cephas, meaning Peter, "rock" (Jn 1, 42): an apostle (Mt 10, 2) and fellow elder (1 Pt 5, 1). In his office of apostle he addresses himself to the Gentile converts of Asia Minor. Their privileged status of a *chosen, consecrated,* and *purified* people makes them worthy of God's peace and favor. In contrast is their actual existence as pilgrims and strangers, scattered among pagans, far from their true country.

1, 3ff: A prayer of praise and thanksgiving to God who bestows the gift of new life and hope that derive from the resurrection of his Son. It contains the promise, not of an earthly land, but of *an imperishable inheritance . . . in heaven,* for those *guarded with God's power through faith,* and it is *to be revealed in the last days.*

1, 6–9: As the glory of Christ's resurrection was preceded by his sufferings and death, the new life of faith which it bestows is to be subjected to *many trials* (v 6) while achieving its goal: the glory of the fullness of salvation (v 9) at the coming of Christ (v 8).

1, 10ff: *The Spirit of Christ* (v 11) is here shown to have been present in both the prophets and the apostles: in the prophets moving them to search out, examine, investigate, and predict the divine favor of salvation that was to come (v 10); in the apostles impelling them to preach the fulfillment of salvation in the mystery of Christ's sufferings and glory (v 12).

1, 13–25: These verses are concerned with the call of God's people to holiness and to fraternal love by reason of their relationship with him, a covenant sealed with the blood of his Son.

1, 13: *Gird the loins of your understanding:* a figure reminiscent of the rite of Passover when the Israelites were in flight from their oppressors (Ex 12, 11), and suggesting also the vigilance of the Christian people in expectation of the second coming of Christ (Lk 12, 35f).

understanding; live soberly; set all your hope on the gift to be conferred on you when Jesus Christ appears. 14 As obedient sons, do not yield to the desires that once shaped you in your ignorance. 15 Rather, become holy yourselves in every aspect of your conduct, after the likeness of the holy One who called you; 16 remember, Scripture says, "Be holy, for I am holy." 17 In prayer you call upon a Father who judges each one justly on the basis of his actions. Since this is so, conduct yourselves reverently during your sojourn in a strange land. 18 Realize that you were delivered from the futile way of life your fathers handed on to you, not by any diminishable sum of silver or gold, 19 but by Christ's blood beyond all price: the blood of a spotless, unblemished lamb 20 chosen before the world's foundation and revealed for your sake in these last days. 21 It is through him that you are believers in God, the God who raised him from the dead and gave him glory. Your faith and hope, then, are centered in God.

Brotherly Love

22 By obedience to the truth you have purified yourselves for a genuine love of your brothers; therefore, love one another constantly from the heart. 23 Your rebirth has come, not from a destructible but from an indestructible seed, through the living and enduring word of God. 24 For,

"All mankind is grass

and the glory of men is like the flower of the field.
The grass withers, the flower wilts,
but the word of the Lord endures forever."

25 Now this "word" is the gospel which was preached to you.

Growth in Holiness

2 So strip away everything vicious, everything deceitful; pretenses, jealousies, and disparaging remarks of any kind. 2 Be as eager for milk as newborn babies—pure milk of the spirit to make you grow unto salvation, 3 now that you have tasted that the Lord is good.

4 Come to him, a living stone, rejected by men but approved, nonetheless, and precious in God's eyes. 5 You too are living stones, built as an edifice of spirit, into a holy priesthood, offering spiritual sacrifices acceptable to God through Jesus Christ. 6 For Scripture has it:

"See, I am laying a cornerstone in Zion,
an approved stone, and precious. He who puts his faith in it shall not be shaken."

7 The stone is of value for you who have faith. For those without faith, it is rather,

"A stone which the builders rejected
that became a cornerstone."

8 It is likewise "an obstacle and a stumbling stone." Those who stumble and fall are the disbelievers in God's

word; it belongs to their destiny to do so.

9 You, however, are "a chosen race, a royal priesthood, a holy nation, a people he claims for his own to proclaim the glorious works" of the One who called you from darkness into his marvelous light. 10 Once you were no people, but now you are God's people; once there was no mercy for you, but now you have found mercy.

Good Example

11 Beloved, you are strangers and in exile; hence I urge you not to indulge your carnal desires. By their nature they wage war on the soul. 12 Though the pagans may slander you as troublemakers, conduct yourselves blamelessly among them. By observing your good works they may give glory to God on the day of visitation.

For the Citizen

13 Because of the Lord, be obedient to every human institution, whether to the emperor as sovereign 14 or to the governors he commissions for the punishment of criminals and the recognition of the upright. 15 Such obedience is the will of God. You must silence the ignorant talk of foolish men by your good behavior. 16 Live as free men, but do not use your freedom as a cloak for vice. In a word, live as servants of God. 17 You must esteem the person of every man. Foster love for the brothers, reverence for God, respect for the emperor.

1, 14–17: The *ignorance* here referred to (v 14) was their former lack of knowledge of God, leading inevitably to godless conduct; holiness (15f), on the contrary, is the result of their call to the knowledge and love of God as the *Father who judges each one justly* (v 17).

1, 18f: The deliverance or ransom of Israel foretold by Isaiah (52, 3) is here fulfilled in behalf of the Christian people at the cost of the blood (i.e., the life) of the spotless lamb (Is 53, 7.10; Rom 3, 24f; 1 Cor 6, 20; cf Ex 12, 5).

1, 23ff: The rebirth of Christians (v 23) derives from Christ, the *indestructible seed* effecting a new and lasting existence in those who accept the gospel (24f), and making them brothers with the duty of loving one another (v 22).

2, 1ff: Growth *unto salvation* (v 2) is here considered negatively, as a stripping away of all that is contrary to the new life received from Christ; and positively, as the taking of the *pure milk*, i.e., the nourishment which the newly baptized *have tasted* and found *good* (1f).

2, 4–8: *Come to him:* to Christ, *a living stone, rejected by men but approved* by God because of his death and resurrection (v 4). Believers joined by the

Spirit (1 Cor 3, 16) to Christ the *cornerstone* (v 7) themselves become *living stones* and constitute the spiritual edifice of the Christian community. They are a *holy priesthood* whose function is to offer *spiritual sacrifices acceptable to God through Jesus Christ* (5f). To unbelievers, Christ is *an obstacle and a stumbling stone* on which they are destined to fall (v 8); cf Rom 11, 11.

2, 9: The prerogatives of ancient Israel here mentioned are now more fully and fittingly applied to the Christian people: *a chosen race* (cf Is 44, 1ff) indicates their divine election (Eph 1, 4ff); *a royal priesthood* (cf *a kingdom of priests*, Ex 19, 6) to serve and worship God in Christ, thus continuing the priestly functions of his life, passion, and resurrection; *a holy nation* (Ex 19, 6) reserved for God; *a people he claims for his own* (cf Mal 3, 17) in virtue of their baptism into his death and resurrection. This transcends all natural and national divisions, and unites the people into one community to glorify him who led them from the darkness of paganism to the light of faith in Christ. From being "no people," deprived of all mercy, they have become the very people of God, the chosen recipients of his mercy; cf Hos 1, 9; 2, 25.

2, 11–3, 12: After explaining the doctrinal basis

for the Christian community, the letter traces its practical applications in terms of the virtues that should prevail in all the social relationships of the members of the community: good example to pagan neighbors (2, 11f); respect for human authority (2, 13–17); obedience, patience, and endurance of hardship in domestic relations (2, 18–25); Christian behavior of husbands and wives (3, 1–7); mutual charity (3, 8–12).

2, 11: *You are strangers and in exile:* no longer signifying absence from one's native land (Gn 23, 4), this denotes rather their estrangement from this world during their earthly pilgrimage in search of the city *which is to come* (Heb 13, 14).

2, 13: *Be obedient to every human institution:* the text could also mean, though less probably, "every human creature." This obedience is enjoined *because of the Lord*, i.e., it conforms to his will (v 15).

2, 16f: *Live as free men . . . vice:* the freedom of the Christian is that which derives from right order, i.e., service of God and *reverence* toward him, besides *esteem* for *every man* (v 17).

For the Slave

18 You household slaves, obey your masters with all deference, not only the good and reasonable ones but even those who are harsh. 19 When a man can suffer injustice and endure hardship through his awareness of God's presence, this is the work of grace in him. 20 If you do wrong and get beaten for it, what credit can you claim? But if you put up with suffering for doing what is right, this is acceptable in God's eyes. 21 It was for this you were called, since Christ suffered for you in just this way and left you an example, to have you follow in his footsteps. 22 He did no wrong; no deceit was found in his mouth. 23 When he was insulted, he returned no insult. When he was made to suffer, he did not counter with threats. Instead, he delivered himself up to the One who judges justly. 24 In his own body he brought your sins to the cross, so that all of us, dead to sin, could live in accord with God's will. By his wounds you were healed. 25 At one time you were straying like sheep, but now you have returned to the shepherd, the guardian of your souls.

For Wife and Husband

3 You married women must obey your husbands, so that any of them who do not believe in the word of the gospel may be won over apart from preaching, through their wives' conduct. 2 They have only to observe the reverent purity of your way of life. 3 The affection of an elaborate hairdress, the wearing of golden jewelry, or the donning of rich robes is not for you. 4 Your adornment is rather the hidden character of the heart, expressed in the unfading beauty of a calm and gentle disposition. This is precious in God's eyes. 5 The holy women of past ages used to adorn themselves in this way, reliant on God and obedient to their husbands— 6 for example, Sarah, who was subject to Abraham and called him her master. You are her children when you do what is right and let no fears alarm you.

7 You husbands, too, must show consideration for those who share your lives. Treat women with respect as the weaker sex, heirs just as much as you to the gracious gift of life. If you do so, nothing will keep your prayers from being answered.

In Christian Charity

8 In summary, then, all of you should be like-minded, sympathetic, loving toward one another, kindly disposed, and humble. 9 Do not return evil for evil or insult for insult. Return a blessing instead. This you have been called to do, that you may receive a blessing as your inheritance.
10 "He who cares for life
　　and wants to see prosperous
　　　days
　　must keep his tongue from evil
　　and his lips from uttering deceit.
11 He must turn from evil and do
　　good,
　　seek peace and follow after it,
12 because the Lord has eyes for
　　the just
　　and ears for their cry;
　　but against evildoers the Lord
　　sets his face."

In Christian Suffering

13 Who indeed can harm you if you are committed deeply to doing what is right? 14 Even if you should have to suffer for justice' sake, happy will you be. "Fear not and do not stand in awe of what this people fears." 15 Venerate the Lord, that is, Christ, in your hearts. Should anyone ask you the reason for this hope of yours, be ever ready to reply, 16 but speak gently and respectfully. Keep your conscience clear, so that, whenever you are defamed, those who libel your way of life in Christ may be disappointed. 17 If it should be God's will that you suffer, it is better to do so for good deeds than for evil ones.

18 This is why Christ died for sins once for all, a just man for the sake of the unjust: so that he could lead you to God. He was put to death insofar as fleshly existence goes, but was given life in the realm of the spirit. 19 It was in the spirit also that he went to preach to the spirits in prison. 20 They had disobeyed as long ago as Noah's day, while God patiently waited until the ark was built. At that time, a few persons, eight in all, escaped in the ark through the water. 21 You are now saved by a baptismal bath which corresponds to this exactly. This baptism is no removal of physical stain, but the pledge to God of an irreproachable conscience through the resurrection of Jesus Christ. 22 He went to heaven and is at God's right hand, with angels, rulers, and powers subjected to him.

In Christian Faithfulness

4 Since Christ suffered in the flesh, you must arm yourselves with his outlook. He who has suffered in the flesh has broken with sin. 2 You are not to spend what remains of your earthly life on human desires but on the will of God. 3 Already you have devoted enough time to what the pagans enjoy, living lives of

---

2, 18–25: The author's concern for *household slaves* was not aimed at overthrowing the institution of slavery, but was meant rather to indicate how those in servitude should accept it through the power of grace as a means of imitating the suffering Christ. They are reminded that his willing endurance of insult, suffering, and death delivered men from the bondage of sin and won for them the freedom of living according to God's will; cf Is 53, 1–12; Gal 3, 13.

2, 25: *The shepherd, the guardian of your souls:* the familiar shepherd-and-flock figures express the care, vigilance, and love of God for his people in the Old Testament (Ps 23; Is 23, 3f; 40, 11; Ez 34, 11–16), and of Christ for all men in the New (Mt 18, 10–14; Lk 15, 3–6; Jn 10, 11; Heb 13, 20). In Acts (20, 28), St. Paul calls the elders of the church of Ephesus, shepherds and guardians of the flock.

3, 1–7: This passage outlines, on the one hand, the marital duties of wives: reverence, chaste conduct, and obedience to their husbands; and on the other, the love and consideration husbands owe their wives (cf Eph 5, 21–28). At the same time, attention is called to the opportunity of wives for winning over their pagan husbands to belief in the gospel by their own Christian conduct. In imitation of the pious women of the past, they are to cultivate the virtues of the interior life instead of indulging in the display of robes and jewelry. The fulfillment of these duties by husbands and wives is the surest guarantee of God's response to their prayers.

3, 8–12: To the proper ordering of Christian life in its various aspects as described in 2, 11–3, 9 there is promised the blessing expressed in Psalm 34, 13–17. In the Old Testament, this referred to the temporal benefits of longevity and prosperity; in the New, it refers to eternal life.

3, 13–22: This exposition, centering on verse 17, runs as follows: By his suffering and death Christ the just One saved the unjust (v 18); by his resurrection he acquired the new life in the spirit, which he communicates to believers through the baptismal bath that cleanses their consciences from sin. As the ark saved Noah's family, so baptism saves sinners from the flood waters that would destroy them (19–22). Hence they need not share the fear of sinners; they should rather rejoice in suffering because of their hope in Christ. Thus their innocence disappoints their accusers (13–16; Mt 10, 28; Rom 8, 35–39).

3, 19: There are various interpretations of this verse. It probably refers to the risen Christ making known to imprisoned souls his victory over sin and death as he passed into his glory.

4, 1–6: Willingness to suffer with Christ equips the Christian with the power to conquer sin. Christ is here portrayed as the judge to whom those guilty of pagan vices must render an account; cf Jn 5, 22–27; Acts 10, 42; 2 Tm 4, 1.

debauchery, evil desires, drunkenness, orgies, carousing, and wanton idolatry. 4 It is no wonder that those blasphemers are surprised when you do not plunge into the same swamp of profligacy as they. 5 They shall give an accounting to him who stands ready to judge the living and the dead. 6 The reason the gospel was preached even to the dead was that, although condemned in the flesh in the eyes of men, they might live in the spirit in the eyes of God.

Mutual Charity

7 The consummation of all is close at hand. Therefore do not be perturbed; remain calm so that you will be able to pray. 8 Above all, let your love for one another be constant, for love covers a multitude of sins. 9 Be mutually hospitable without complaining. 10 As generous distributors of God's manifold grace, put your gifts at the service of one another, each in the measure he has received. 11 The one who speaks is to deliver God's message. The one who serves is to do it with the strength provided by God. Thus, in all of you God is to be glorified through Jesus Christ: to him be glory and dominion throughout the ages. Amen.

Blessings of Persecution

12 Do not be surprised, beloved, that a trial by fire is occurring in your midst. It is a test for you, but it should not catch you off guard. 13 Rejoice instead, insofar as you share Christ's sufferings. When his glory is revealed, you will rejoice exultantly. 14 Happy are you when you are insulted for the sake of Christ, for then God's Spirit in its glory has come to rest on you. 15 See to it that none of you suffers for being a murderer, a thief, a malefactor, or a destroyer of another's rights. 16 If anyone suffers for being a Christian, however, he ought not to be ashamed. He should rather glorify God in virtue of that name. 17 The season of judgment has begun, and begun with God's own household. If it begins this way with us, what must be the end for those who refuse obedience to the gospel of God? 18 And if the just man is saved only with difficulty, what is to become of the godless and the sinner? 19 Accordingly, let those who suffer as God's will requires continue in good deeds, and entrust their lives to a faithful Creator.

For the Ministry

5 To the elders among you I, a fellow elder, a witness of Christ's sufferings and sharer in the glory that is to be revealed, make this appeal. 2 God's flock is in your midst; give it a shepherd's care. Watch over it willingly as God would have you do, not under constraint; and not for shameful profit either, but generously. 3 Be examples to the flock, not lording it over those assigned to you, 4 so that when the chief Shepherd appears you will win for yourselves the unfading crown of glory.

Counsel to the Laity

5 In the same way, you younger men must be obedient to the elders. In your relations with one another, clothe yourselves with humility, because God "is stern with the arrogant but to the humble he shows kindness." 6 Bow humbly under God's mighty hand, so that in due time he may lift you high. 7 Cast all your cares on him because he cares for you. 8 Stay sober and alert. Your opponent the devil is prowling like a roaring lion looking for someone to devour. 9 Resist him, solid in your faith, realizing that the brotherhood of believers is undergoing the same sufferings throughout the world. 10 The God of all grace, who called you to his everlasting glory in Christ, will himself restore, confirm, strengthen, and establish those who have suffered a little while. 11 Dominion be his throughout the ages! Amen.

Farewell

12 I am writing briefly through Silvanus, whom I take to be a faithful brother to you. Herewith are expressed my encouragement and my testimony that this is the true grace of God. Be steadfast in it. 13 The church that is in Babylon, chosen together with you, sends you greeting, as does Mark my son. 14 Greet one another with the embrace of true love. Peace to all of you who are in Christ.

4, 6: *The gospel was preached even to the dead:* i.e., the benefits of salvation were brought to Christians now dead by the followers of Christ before 1 Peter was written. They continue to live in the spirit through Christ; cf Rom 8, 11; 1 Thes 4, 13ff.

4, 7–11: The author outlines the means to be used in preparing for *the consummation of all* at the parousia (7): calmness, prayer, and constant love for one another through unfeigned hospitality and the generous love of one's gifts for the glory of God and of Christ (8–11); cf Lk 21, 34ff; 1 Cor 7, 29ff; Jas 5, 7–12.

4, 8: *Love covers a multitude of sins:* a favorite maxim of the apostles, based on Proverbs 10, 12. Fraternal love will overcome such evils as occur (cf Lk 7, 47; Jas 5, 20).

4, 11: *God is to be glorified . . . throughout the ages. Amen:* this doxology concludes the portion of 1 Peter begun in 1, 3. The source of the letter here used seems to have been a sermon of exhortation on the sacrament of baptism, to which numerous references are made.

4, 12–19: A trial of suffering faces the followers of Christ (12). If it is inflicted on them for the sake of his name, i.e., because of their being Christians (16), they are to rejoice in thus sharing the sufferings of the Christ whose glorification they will also share (13f;

cf Rom 8, 17). If the trial is inflicted because of sins and misdeeds (v 15), the present judgment, though severe even for those of *God's own household,* is but the beginning of punishment for those *who refuse obedience to the gospel of God* (17f). The watchword is perseverance in the good and trust in God's fidelity (19).

4, 12: *A trial by fire:* severe affliction—in the form of slander (2, 12), insult (4, 14), and persecution from pagan neighbors; cf 3, 14.17.

4, 14: *God's Spirit in its glory has come to rest on you:* the Spirit both strengthens Christians to endure suffering and then glorifies them because they suffer for Christ; even as the glorification of Christ consisted, not only in his resurrection and ascension, but in his passion as well (Jn 13, 31f).

5, 1: *Elders:* "presbyteroi"—those to whom the task, both of governing the faithful and of conducting worship for them, was entrusted; cf 1 Tm 5, 17f; Ti 1, 5.7f; Jas 5, 14. Peter, here called *a fellow elder,* nevertheless admonishes the others as one exercising authority over them.

5, 2ff: In imitation of Christ, *the chief Shepherd,* those charged with the pastoral office are to shepherd the flock by their care, by their solicitude for what pertains to doctrine and discipline, and by their example. They are to render this service, *not under*

constraint, and not for shameful profit, nor to lord it over the flock, but out of generosity and kindness, as God would have them do, thus meriting *the unfading crown of glory;* cf Acts 20, 17–31 and note on 2, 25.

5, 5–11: The laity are to be obedient toward the elders, and to show humility toward one another and complete trust in God's loving care (5ff). By sobriety, alertness, and firm faith, they must ward off the evil one who seeks to destroy their souls. Their sufferings are shared with Christians everywhere (8ff). As a reward for their faith and trust in God, they will be strengthened and attain to *everlasting glory in Christ* (10).

5, 8: *Your opponent the devil . . . someone to devour:* the synonymous Greek terms "antidikos" (*opponent*) and "diabolos" (*accuser*) are used to designate those who persecute Christians. In the manner of Satan they prowl *like a roaring lion* seeking to destroy their victims (Ps 22, 14).

5, 12ff: *Sylvanus:* Paul's companion (2 Cor 1, 19; 1 Thes 1, 1; 2 Thes 1, 1). *This is the true grace of God:* a possible reference to the trials which the Christians were enduring, regarded from the standpoint of their salutary effects. *Babylon:* Rome which, like ancient Babylon, conquered Jerusalem and destroyed its temple. *Mark my son:* cf Acts 12, 25; 13, 5; Col 4, 10.

THE SECOND EPISTLE OF

GREETING

SIMEON Peter, servant and apostle of Jesus Christ, to those who have been given a faith like ours in the justifying power of our God and Saviour Jesus Christ: 2 may grace be yours and peace in abundance through your knowledge of God and of Jesus, our Lord.

Christian Virtue

3 That divine power of his has freely bestowed on us everything necessary for a life of genuine piety, through knowledge of him who called us by his own glory and power. 4 By virtue of them he has bestowed on us the great and precious things he promised, so that through these you who have fled a world corrupted by lust might become sharers of the divine nature. 5 This is reason enough for you to make every effort to undergird your virtue with faith, your discernment with virtue, 6 and your self-control with discern-ment. This self-control, in turn, should lead to perseverance, and perseverance to piety, 7 and piety to care for your brother, and care for your brother, to love.

8 Qualities like these, made increasingly your own, are by no means ineffectual; they bear fruit in true knowledge of our Lord Jesus Christ. 9 Any man who lacks these qualities is shortsighted to the point of blindness. He forgets the cleansing of his long-past sins. 10 Be solicitous to make your call and election permanent, brothers; surely those who do so will never be lost. 11 On the contrary, your entry into the everlasting kingdom of our Lord and Savior Jesus Christ will be richly provided for.

Witness to Christ

12 I intend to recall these things to you constantly, even though you already understand and are firmly rooted in the truth you possess. 13 I consider it my duty, as long as I live, to prompt you with this reminder. 14 I know, by the indications our Lord Jesus Christ has given me, how close is the day when I must fold my tent. 15 I shall press to have you recall these things frequently after my

---

1, 1: *Simeon Peter, servant and apostle of Jesus Christ:* on the question of authorship of 2 Peter see the Introduction. *To those who have been given a faith . . . Jesus Christ:* it is *the justifying power* of Jesus, *God and Savior,* which causes the faith of the apostles and of succeeding believers to be one and the same.

1, 3f: Christian life in its fullness is a gift of divine power to those who are called. This power effects in them a knowledge of Christ and fulfills the divine promises in their regard, making them sharers of the divine nature, safe from a *world corrupted by lust;* cf 1, 2.8; 3, 18; Jn 17, 22; Rom 8, 14–17; 1 Jn 3, 2.

1, 5–9: Note the climactic gradation of qualities. beginning with faith and leading to the fullness of Christian life which is love (5–7); cf Rom 5, 3ff; 10, 14f. Their fruit is the knowledge of Christ (v 8) referred to in 1, 3; their absence is spiritual blindness (v 9).

1, 10f: Perseverance in the Christian vocation is the best preventative against losing it and the safest provision for attaining its goal, entrance *into the everlasting kingdom,* identified here as the *kingdom of our Lord and Savior Jesus Christ.*

1, 12–19: Alive to his responsibility even when faced with the proximity of death, the apostle be-queaths to his readers a perpetual reminder of the teachings of the faith (12–15) and of the certainty of Christ's coming in power (v 16). As motives for belief in the parousia, he offers the prophetic message of Scripture and also his own testimony as eyewitness to the transfiguration of Christ in glory and majesty, confirmed by the voice of God the Father (18–22). These serve as a shining light amid the darkness to those preparing for the parousia. The value of continual reminders and repeated instructions, for preserving the truths of the faith and the historic facts surrounding them, is insisted on in the New Testament (12f.15; 3, 1f; 1 Cor 11, 2; 15, 1).

departure. 16 It was not by way of cleverly concocted myths that we taught you about the coming in power of our Lord Jesus Christ, 17 for we were eyewitnesses of his sovereign majesty. He received glory and praise from God the Father when that unique declaration came to him out of the majestic splendor: "This is my beloved Son, on whom my favor rests." 18 We ourselves heard this said from heaven while we were in his company on the holy mountain. 19 Besides, we possess the prophetic message as something altogether reliable. Keep your attention closely fixed on it, as you would on a lamp shining in a dark place until the first streaks of dawn appear and the morning star rises in your hearts.

The Nature of Prophecy

20 First you must understand this: there is no prophecy contained in Scripture which is a personal interpretation. 21 Prophecy has never been put forward by man's willing it. It is rather that men impelled by the Holy Spirit have spoken under God's influence.

False Teachers

2 In times past there were false prophets among God's people, and among you also there will be false teachers who will smuggle in pernicious heresies. They will go so far as to deny the Master who acquired them for his own, thereby bringing on themselves swift disaster. 2 Their lustful ways will lure many away. Through them, the true way will be made subject to contempt.

Warning from the Past

3 They will deceive you with fabricated tales, in a spirit of greed. Their condemnation has not lain idle all this time, however; their destruction is not asleep. 4 Did God spare even the angels who sinned? He did not! He held them captive in Tartarus —consigned them to pits of darkness, to be guarded until judgment. 5 Nor did he spare the ancient world —even though he preserved Noah as a preacher of holiness, with seven others, when he brought down the flood on that godless earth. 6 He blanketed the cities of Sodom and Gomorrah in ashes and condemned them to destruction, thereby showing what would happen in the future to the godless. 7 He did deliver Lot, however, a just man oppressed by the conduct of men unprincipled in their lusts. 8 (Day after day that just one, good as he was, felt himself tormented by seeing and hearing about the lawless deeds of those among whom he lived.) 9 The Lord, indeed, knows how to rescue devout men from trial, and how to continue the punishment of the wicked up to the day of judgment.

Punishment of Evildoers

10 He knows, especially, how to treat those who live for the flesh in their desire for whatever corrupts, and who despise authority. These bold and arrogant men have no qualms whatever about reviling celestial beings, 11 on whom angels, though greater than men in strength and power, pass no opprobrious sentence in the Lord's presence. 12 These men pour abuse on things of which they are ignorant. They act like creatures of instinct, brute animals born to be caught and destroyed. Because of their decadence they too will be destroyed, suffering the reward of their wickedness. 13 Thinking daytime revelry a delight, they are stain and defilement as they share your feasts in a spirit of seduction. 14 Constantly on the lookout for a woman, theirs is a never-ending search for sin. They lure the weaker types. Their hearts are trained in greed. An accursed lot are they! 15 They have abandoned the straight road and wandered off on the path taken by Balaam, son of Beor. He was a man attracted to dishonest gain, 16 but he was rebuked for his evildoing. A mute beast spoke with a human voice to restrain the prophet's madness.

17 These men are waterless springs, mists whipped by the gale. The darkest gloom has been reserved for them. 18 They talk empty bombast while baiting their hooks with passion, with the lustful ways of the flesh, to catch those who have just come free of a life of errors. 19 They promise them freedom though they themselves are slaves of corruption—for surely anyone is the slave of that by which he has been overcome. 20 When men have fled a polluted world by recognizing the Lord and Savior Jesus Christ, and then are caught up and overcome in pollution once more, their last condition is worse than their first. 21 It would have been better for them not to have recognized the road to holiness than to have turned their backs on the holy law handed on to them, once they had known it. 22 How well the proverb fits them: "The dog returns to its vomit," and, "A sow bathes by wallowing in the mire."

2, 1–22: This account of the false teachers and evildoers and the dire punishments which threaten them finds a parallel in Jude 4–13. The present passage is generally considered by scholars to be dependent on Jude, despite modifications and omissions.

2, 1ff: The pattern of false teaching in the Old Testament recurs in apostolic times among the people of the New, and will be repeated (10–22) before the final cataclysm at the end of the world (Mt 24, 11). It is accompanied by denial of faith in Christ, immorality, scandal, and contempt for the way of salvation.

2, 3–9: *Their condemnation . . .; their destruction is not asleep:* the interventions of the divine chastisement are exemplified in the case of the rebellious angels (v 4; Jude 6), the deluge (v 6; Jude 7), and the destruction of Sodom and Gomorrah.

2, 4: *Tartarus:* a term borrowed from Greek mythology to indicate the infernal regions, *pits of darkness* where sinners, especially fallen angels, are punished.

2, 5: The deluge is described as marking the end of *the ancient world* and the beginning of the new. Noah, the preacher of holiness, is the type of new life initiated through Christian baptism and made conformable to God's sanctity (1 Pt 3, 20f).

2, 6: The destruction of the cities of Sodom and Gomorrah stands for all time as a warning of punishment of sin. The association of this catastrophe with that of the deluge is also found in Wisdom 10, 4ff and in Christ's prediction concerning the signs of the coming of the kingdom of God (Lk 17, 26–29).

2, 10–22: These verses portray in detail the conduct of the false teachers. They are slaves of the flesh and its passions; they despise true sovereignty, that of Christ and his church (v 10); they even revile the *celestial beings* considered to be fallen angels (cf 2, 4) in comparison to the angels in 2, 11. Abusive in their ignorance, imitating brute animals in their irrationality, decadent in their instincts, they deserve, like animals, *to be caught and destroyed* (v 12). In their day-long revelries they seduce others (v 13), even those who *have just come free of a life of errors* (v 18), making their new condition of return to corruption and rejection of Christ worse than the first (18–22). In their greed they abandon righteousness, like Balaam of old, for the sake of material gain (14ff).

Christ Will Come in Judgment

3 I am writing you this second letter, dear friends, intending them both as reminders urging you to sincerity of outlook. 2 Recall the teaching delivered long ago by the holy prophets, as well as the new command of the Lord and Savior preached to you by the apostles.

3 Note this first of all: in the last days, mocking, sneering men who are ruled by their passions will arrive on the scene. 4 They will ask: "Where is that promised coming of his? Our forefathers have been laid to rest, but everything stays just as it was when the world was created." 5 In believing this, they do not take into account that of old there were heavens and an earth drawn out of the waters and standing between the waters, all brought into being by the word of God. 6 By water that world was then destroyed; it was overwhelmed by the deluge. 7 The present heavens and earth are reserved by God's word for fire; they are kept for the day of judgment, the day when godless men will be destroyed.

8 This point must not be overlooked, dear friends. In the Lord's eyes, one day is as a thousand years and a thousand years are as a day. 9 The Lord does not delay in keeping his promise—though some consider it "delay." Rather, he shows you generous patience, since he wants none to perish but all to come to repentance. 10 The Day of the Lord will come like a thief, and on that day the heavens will vanish with a roar; the elements will be destroyed by fire, and the earth and all its deeds will be made manifest.

11 Since everything is to be destroyed in this way, what sort of men must you not be! How holy in your conduct and devotion, 12 looking for the coming of the day of God and trying to hasten it! Because of it, the heavens will be destroyed in flames and the elements will melt away in a blaze. 13 What we await are new heavens and a new earth where, according to his promise, the justice of God will reside.

Preparation for the Coming

14 So, beloved, while waiting for this, make every effort to be found without stain or defilement, and at peace in his sight. 15 Consider that our Lord's patience is directed toward salvation. Paul, our beloved brother, wrote you this in the spirit of wisdom that is his, 16 dealing with these matters as he does in all his letters. There are certain passages in them hard to understand. The ignorant and the unstable distort them (just as they do the rest of Scripture) to their own ruin.

17 You are forewarned, beloved brothers. Be on your guard lest you be led astray by the error of the wicked, and forfeit the security you enjoy. 18 Grow rather in grace, and in the knowledge of our Lord and Savior Jesus Christ. Glory be to him now and to the day of eternity! Amen.

3, 1–4: The false teachers not only flout Christian morality (cf Jude 18f), they also deny the second coming of Christ and eternal retribution. They seek to justify their licentiousness, arguing that the promised return of Christ has not been realized and the world is the same, no better than it was before (3f). The author wishes to strengthen the faithful against the pernicious error by reminding them of the instruction in his letters (1 and 2 Peter), and of the teaching of the prophets and of Christ, conveyed through the apostles (1f); cf 1 Pt 1, 10ff; 16–21; Eph 2, 20.

3, 4: *Our forefathers have been laid to rest:* the death of the apostolic fathers indicates a date after that time for the composition of 2 Peter.

3, 5–10: The scoffers' objection (v 4) is refuted by showing that the power of God's word, which called the world into being, also destroyed it by the waters of a flood, and will destroy it again by fire on the day of judgment (5ff). The delay of the Lord is not an indication of failure to fulfill his word but rather of his *generous patience* in giving time for repentance before the final judgment (8ff; 1 Thes 5, 2). The new

Testament writers used the deluge as a figure of eschatalogical events; cf Mt 24, 37ff; Lk 17, 26f. The effect of Christian baptism is compared to the radical action of fire which purifies metal of dross. For Old Testament examples of God's judgment described by the imagery of fire, see Is 66, 15f; Mi 1, 4; Dn 7, 9ff; Zep 1, 18; 3, 8; Ps 97, 3. Acceptance of the truths of faith does not require acceptance of the popular imagery used to describe them.

3, 9: *He shows you generous patience:* the long-suffering of God is a sign of his mercy toward man, who is so slow to change. God wills all men to be saved and to come to the knowledge of the truth; cf Wis 11, 23–26; Ez 18, 23; 33, 11; Rom 11, 32; 1 Tm 2, 4.

3, 11–15: The coming of Christ and the judgment of the world are the doctrinal bases here and elsewhere in the New Testament for the moral exhortation to preparedness through vigilance and a virtuous life (Mt 24, 42.51; Lk 12, 40; 1 Thes 5, 1–11; Jude 20f).

3, 12: *Trying to hasten it:* i.e., the Day of God, by advancing his kingdom through holiness of life; cf v 9.

3, 13: *New heavens and a new earth:* the fulfillment of the divine promises after the Day of judgment will have passed and the universe will be transformed by the reign of perfect justice; cf Is 65, 17; 66, 22; Acts 3, 21; Rom 8, 19ff; Rv 21, 1.

3, 15f: The teachings of this epistle—the Lord's salvific will toward mankind (Rom 2, 4; 9, 22f; 1 Cor 1, 7f); preparedness for the judgment (Eph 1, 4–14; 4, 30; 5, 5.14ff; Col 1, 22ff); the coming of Christ (1 Thes 4, 16f; 1 Cor 15, 23.52)—are further confirmed by the letters of Paul. He is called here *our beloved brother,* i.e., a fellow apostle of Peter, after whom this letter is named.

The rest of Scripture: the sacred writings inspired by the Holy Spirit to regulate the religious life of the people. The writings of Paul are thus recognized as having the same quality and authority as the books of the Old Testament.

3, 17f: To avoid the danger of error and loss of security, the faithful are exhorted to persevere in the principles of the Christian life through growth *in the knowledge* of Christ. The final doxology recalls that of 1 Pt 4, 11.

THE FIRST EPISTLE OF

John

PROLOGUE

THIS is what we proclaim to you: what was from the beginning, what we have heard, what we have seen with our eyes, what we have looked upon and our hands have touched—we speak of the word of life. 2 (This life became visible; we have seen and bear witness to it, and we

proclaim to you the eternal life
that was present to the Father
and became visible to us.)
3 What we have seen and heard
we proclaim in turn to you
so that you may share life with us.
This fellowship of ours is with
the Father
and with his Son, Jesus Christ.
4 Indeed, our purpose in writing
you this
is that our joy may be complete.

The Light of God
5 Here, then, is the message
we have heard from him
and announce to you:

that God is light;
in him there is no darkness.

Claims of False Teachers
6 If we say, "We have fellowship
with him,"
while continuing to walk in
darkness,
we are liars and do not act in
truth.
7 But if we walk in light,
as he is in the light,
we have fellowship with one
another,
and the blood of his Son Jesus
cleanses us from all sin.

8 If we say, "We are free of the
guilt of sin,"
we deceive ourselves; the truth
is not to be found in us.
9 But if we acknowledge our sins,
he who is just can be trusted
to forgive our sins
and cleanse us from every
wrong.
10 If we say, "We have never
sinned,"
we make him a liar
and his word finds no place
in us.
2 MY LITTLE ONES,
I am writing this to keep you
from sin.

1, 1–4: There is a striking parallel between this prologue and that of the gospel of John (1, 1–16). The substance of the apostles' teaching is their experience of the historic Christ and the witness they bear to him (v 1; cf Jn 1, 7f.15). He is *the word of life* (v 1; cf Jn 1, 4), *eternal life that was present to the Father and became visible* to the apostles (v 2; cf Jn 1, 1.14). The purpose of their teaching is to share that *life*, called *fellowship . . . with the Father and with his Son Jesus Christ*, with those who receive their witness (v 3; Jn 1, 14.16), and thus to make the joy of the apostles complete (v 4).
1, 5ff: *Light* is to be understood here as truth and goodness; *darkness*, as error and depravity; cf Jn 3, 19ff; 17, 17; Eph 5, 8f; 1 Thes 5, 5. To walk in light or darkness is to live according to truth or error, not merely intellectual but moral as well; that is, in accordance with, or contrary to, God's will. Thus, fellowship with God (v 6) and with one another (v 7) consists in a life according to truth and goodness as found in God and in Christ, their source. This is made possible through the redemptive work of Christ, who cleanses us from our sins; cf Jn 8, 12; 12, 35f.
1, 8ff: One is never entirely free from sin. To claim the contrary would be self-deception and would even contradict divine revelation (v 10; cf 1 Kgs 8, 46; Prv 24, 16). There is the continual possibility of sin's recurrence. Forgiveness and deliverance from sin through Christ are assured provided the sin is acknowledged through repentance. Such acknowledgment refers probably to a rite of confession; cf Mt 16, 19; 18, 18; Jn 20, 23; Jas 5, 16.
2, 1f: Believers are here addressed as *little ones* (v 1), elsewhere as *children* (2, 18) or *dearly beloved* (2, 7), to express the pastoral love and devotion of the apostles toward those entrusted to their care; cf Jn 13, 33; 21, 5; 1 Cor 4, 15; Gal 4, 19. After exhorting Christians to keep free from sin, the author returns to the thought of 1, 9: the assurance of forgiveness of sin through the power of Christ's intercession. *He is an offering for our sins:* literally, "propitiation," i.e., a permanent office exercised by Christ on behalf of sinners.

But if anyone should sin,
we have, in the presence of the
  Father,
Jesus Christ, an intercessor
  who is just.
2 He is an offering for our sins,
and not for our sins only,
but for those of the whole
  world.

Keeping the Commandments

3 The way we can be sure of our
  knowledge of him
is to keep his commandments.
4 The man who claims, "I have
  known him,"
without keeping his
  commandments,
is a liar; in such a one there is
  no truth.
5 But whoever keeps his word
truly has the love of God made
  perfect in him.
The way we can be sure we are
  in union with him
6 is for the man who claims to
  abide in him
to conduct himself just as he did.
7 Dearly beloved,
it is no new commandment that
  I write to you,
but an old one which you had
  from the start.
The commandment, now old, is
  the word you have already
  heard.
8 On second thought, the
  commandment that I write
  you is new,
as it is realized in him and you,
for the darkness is over
and the real light begins to
  shine.

9 The man who claims to be in
  light,
hating his brother all the while,
is in darkness even now.
10 The man who continues in the
  light is the one who loves
  his brother;
there is nothing in him to cause
  a fall.
11 But the man who hates his
  brother is in darkness.
He walks in shadows,
not knowing where he is going,
since the dark has blinded his
  eyes.

Members of the Community

12 Little ones, I address you,
for through his Name your sins
  have been forgiven.
13 Fathers, I address you,
for you have known him who is
  from the beginning.
Young men, I address you,
for you have conquered the
  evil one.
14 I address you, children,
for you have known the Father.
I address you, fathers,
for you have known him who is
  from the beginning.
I address you, young men,
for you are strong,
and the word of God remains
  in you,
and you have conquered the
  evil one.

Against the World

15 Have no love for the world,
nor the things that the world
  affords.
If anyone loves the world,

the Father's love has no place in
  him,
16 for nothing that the world
  affords
comes from the Father.
Carnal allurements,
enticements for the eye,
the life of empty show—
all these are from the world.
17 And the world with its
  seductions is passing away
but the man who does God's
  will
endures forever.

Against Antichrists

18 Children, it is the final hour;
just as you heard that the
  antichrist was coming,
so now many such antichrists
  have appeared.
This makes us certain that it is
  the final hour.
19 It was from our ranks that they
  took their leave—
not that they really belonged
  to us;
for if they had belonged to us,
they would have stayed with us.
It only served to show that
  none of them was ours.
20 But you have the anointing that
  comes from the Holy One,
so that all knowledge is yours.
21 My reason for having written
  you
is not that you do not know
  the truth
but that you do,
and that no lie has anything in
  common with the truth.
22 Who is the liar?
He who denies that Jesus is the
  Christ.

2, 3–6: *The way we can be sure of our knowledge . . . commandments:* not mere intellectual knowledge of Christ but a life conformable to the divine will revealed to mankind through his teaching and example (v 6; cf Jn 14, 21–24; 17, 3). Thus *love of God is made perfect* (v 5) and those who live in this manner abide in Christ (v 6) and achieve union with him; cf 3, 2f. Disparity between moral life and doctrinal teaching was the error of the Gnostics.

2, 7–11: The law of fraternal charity is based on human nature itself and is confirmed by the divine positive command to the Israelites (Lv 19, 18). Through Christ, however, a new and higher relationship with neighbor (vv 8.10) is achieved as a result of the new relationship in which as sons of God (cf Jn 1, 12) and brothers of Christ (Lk 8.21). Note here and elsewhere the characteristic Johannine polemic in which a positive assertion is further emphasized by the negative statement of its opposite (9ff).

2, 12–17: The Christian community, which has experienced the grace of God through forgiveness of sin and knowledge of Christ, i.e., practice of the faith,

is thereby armed against *the evil one* and protected from the world with its allurements; cf 3, 7–10; 5, 18f.

2, 15: *The World:* men subject to sin and therefore hostile toward God. Love of the world and love of God are mutually exclusive; cf Jas 4, 4.

2, 16: *Carnal allurements:* inordinate desire for sensuality (cf Eph 2, 3; 1 Pt 2, 11; 2 Pt 2, 10.18); *enticements for the eye:* avarice; the eyes are regarded as the windows of the soul (cf Jb 31, 1; Ez 23, 12–17; Mt 5, 27ff); *the life of empty show:* ostentation, pride and arrogance, independence of God, in the temporal existence of man.

2, 18: *The final hour:* the time between the first and second coming of Christ. *The antichrist:* the opponent or adversary of Christ; one who denies *the Father and the Son* (v 22). The term is found in 1 and 2 John; cf Mt 24, 23f; Mk 3, 21f. Paul calls him *the man of lawlessness, the son of perdition and adversary* (2 Thes 2, 3.8; cf Rv 13; 17, 7–14). Matthew, Mark, and Revelation seem to refer to a collectivity of persons. *Many such antichrists have appeared:* the reference is to all the false teachers who afflict the church in *the final hour.* The early Christian community was

familiar with this doctrine and expected an early return or second coming of Christ.

2, 19: *If they had belonged to us, . . . stayed with us:* the antichrists, apostate teachers, have always lacked the true spirit of the community of God's people.

2, 20f.27: *The anointing that comes from the Holy One:* the Spirit of God which the faithful received. It preserves them against the errors of the antichrists. The *Holy One* may refer to Christ, whose name (*Christos,* "anointed one") and mission are in a real sense shared by his followers. *All knowledge is yours:* one of the gifts of the Holy Spirit (Is 11, 2) by which the faithful could distinguish truth from falsehood (Jn 16, 13ff). The author's purpose is to reassure rather than instruct (v 21), because his readers have already received knowledge through their anointing (v 27).

2, 22f: To deny the Son is to deny the Father since only in and through the Son has God fully revealed his fatherhood; cf Mt 11, 27; Lk 10, 22; Jn 5, 23; 10, 30; Jn 14. 7.9.

He is the antichrist,
denying the Father and the
    Son.
23 Anyone who denies the Son
has no claim on the Father,
but he who acknowledges the
    Son
can claim the Father as well.

Life for God's Anointed

24 As for you,
let what you heard from the
    beginning
remain in your hearts.
If what you heard from the
    beginning
does remain in your hearts,
then you in turn will remain in
    the Son and in the Father.
25 He himself made us a promise
and the promise is no less than
    this:
eternal life.
26 I have written you these things
about those who try to deceive
    you.
27 As for you,
the anointing you received from
    him
remains in your hearts.
This means you have no need
for anyone to teach you.
Rather, as his anointing teaches
    you about all things
and is true—free from any lie—
remain in him
as that anointing taught you.

Children of God

28 Remain in him now, little ones,
so that, when he reveals himself,
we may be fully confident
and not retreat in shame at his
    coming.
29 If you consider the holiness that
    is his,
you can be sure that everyone
    who acts in holiness
has been begotten by him.

3 SEE WHAT LOVE the Father has
    bestowed on us
in letting us be called children
    of God!
Yet that is what we are.
The reason the world does not
    recognize us
is that it never recognized the
    Son.
2 Dearly beloved,
we are God's children now;
what we shall later be has not
    yet come to light.
We know that when it comes
    to light
we shall be like him,
for we shall see him as he is.
3 Everyone who has this hope
    based on him
keeps himself pure, as he is
    pure.

Avoiding Sin

4 Everyone who sins acts
    lawlessly,
for sin is lawlessness.
5 You know well that the reason
    he revealed himself
was to take away sins;
in him there is nothing sinful.
6 The man who remains in him
    does not sin,
The man who sins has not seen
    him
or known him.
7 Little ones,
let no one deceive you;
the man who acts in holiness is
    holy indeed,
even as the Son is holy.
8 The man who sins belongs to
    the devil,
because the devil is a sinner
    from the beginning.
It was to destroy the devil's
    works
that the Son of God revealed
    himself.
9 No one begotten of God acts
    sinfully

because he remains of God's
    stock;
he cannot sin
because he is begotten of God.
10 That is the way to see who are
    God's children,
and who are the devil's.
No one whose actions are
    unholy belongs to God,
nor anyone who fails to love his
    brother.

Keeping the Commandments

11 This, remember, is the message
you heard from the beginning:
we should love one another.
12 We should not follow the example
    of Cain
who belonged to the evil one
and killed his brother.
Why did he kill him?
Because his own deeds were
    wicked
while his brother's were just.
13 No need, then, brothers, to be
    surprised
if the world hates you.
14 That we have passed from death
    to life we know
because we love the brothers.
The man who does not love is
    among the living dead.
15 Anyone who hates his brother is
    a murderer,
and you know that eternal life
abides in no murderer's heart.
16 The way we came to understand
    love
was that he laid down his life
    for us;
we too must lay down our lives
    for our brothers.
17 I ask you, how can God's love
    survive in a man
who has enough of this world's
    goods
yet closes his heart to his
    brother
when he sees him in need?
18 Little children,

2, 25: *The promise is no less than this: eternal life:* the only passage of the Johannine writings in which *eternal life* has the exclusively eschatological sense of the life of glory, the object of Christian hope and striving. Elsewhere the term is invariably used of the present life of grace leading to glory.

2, 28f: A renewed exhortation to Christians to *remain* in Christ, i.e., to live the Christ-life and thus enjoy the assurance of acceptance by him at his second coming. The verses prepare them for the transition to the theme of their divine sonship and the duties flowing from it: *Everyone who acts in holiness has been begotten by him.*

3, 1ff: The greatest proof of God's love for men is the gift of his Son, through whom they are not only called, but are in reality, God's sons; cf Jn 3, 16. This condition is true of their present life and, in the fullest sense, of the life to come when the divine filiation will result in their being like God and in seeing him *as he is.* They prepare for it by leading a life like that of God's Son, keeping themselves *pure, as he is pure* (v 3). Since the world never recognized the Father in the Son, neither will it recognize those who are children of the Father.

3, 4–10: The two contrary states, of sin and of holiness, are shown here in their intrinsic opposition.

Release from sin establishes union and fellowship with Christ; adherence to sin, fellowship with the devil, who is *a sinner from the beginning.* Thus virtue and sin are the two opposite characteristics for distinguishing the children of God from the children of the devil.

3, 4: *Lawlessness:* hostility toward God and rejection of Christ, the standard of holiness.

3, 11–24: The virtue of charity, even to the point of giving up one's life for his neighbor as Christ did (v 16), is the fulfillment of the commandments (22ff), the guarantee of life and union with God through the presence of the Spirit (21.24).

let us love in deed and in truth
and not merely talk about it.
19 This is our way of knowing we
　　are committed to the truth
and are at peace before him
20 no matter what our consciences
　　may charge us with;
for God is greater than our
　　hearts
and all is known to him.
21 Beloved,
if our consciences have nothing
　　to charge us with,
we can be sure that God is with
　　us
22 and that we will receive at his
　　hands
whatever we ask.
Why? Because we are keeping
　　his commandments
and doing what is pleasing in
　　his sight.
23 His commandment is this:
we are to believe in the name of
　　his Son, Jesus Christ,
and are to love one another as
　　he commanded us.
24 Those who keep his
　　commandments remain in
　　him
and he in them.
And this is how we know that
　　he remains in us:
from the Spirit that he gave us.

Testing the Spirits

4 BELOVED,
do not trust every spirit,
but put the spirits to a test
to see if they belong to God,
because many false prophets
　　have appeared in the world.
2 This is how you can recognize
　　God's Spirit:
every spirit that acknowledges
　　Jesus Christ come in the
　　flesh
belongs to God,
3 while every spirit that fails to
　　acknowledge him

does not belong to God.
Such is the spirit of the
　　antichrist
which, as you have heard, is to
　　come;
in fact, it is in the world already.
4 You are of God, you little ones,
and thus you have conquered
　　the false prophets.
For there is One greater in you
than there is in the world.
5 Those others belong to the
　　world;
that is why theirs is the language
　　of the world
and why the world listens to
　　them.
6 We belong to God
and anyone who has knowledge
　　of God gives us a hearing,
while anyone who is not of God
　　refuses to hear us.
Thus do we distinguish the spirit
　　of truth
from the spirit of deception.

God's Love and Ours

7 Beloved,
let us love one another
because love is of God;
everyone who loves is begotten
　　of God
and has knowledge of God.
8 The man without love has
　　known nothing of God,
for God is love.
9 God's love was revealed in our
　　midst in this way:
he sent his only Son to the
　　world
that we might have life through
　　him.
10 Love, then, consists in this:
not that we have loved God,
but that he has loved us
and has sent his Son as an
　　offering for our sins.
11 Beloved,
if God has loved us so,

we must have the same love for
　　one another.
12 No one has ever seen God.
Yet if we love one another
God dwells in us,
and his love is brought to
　　perfection in us.
13 The way we know we remain in
　　him
and he in us
is that he has given us of his
　　Spirit.
14 We have seen for ourselves, and
　　can testify,
that the Father has sent the Son
　　as savior of the world.
15 When anyone acknowledges
　　that Jesus is the Son of
　　God,
God dwells in him
and he in God.
16 We have come to know and to
　　believe in the love God has
　　for us.

God is love,
and he who abides in love
abides in God,
and God in him.
17 Our love is brought to perfection
　　in this,
that we should have confidence
　　on the day of judgment;
for our relation to this world is
　　just like his.
18 Love has no room for fear;
rather, perfect love casts out all
　　fear.
And since fear has to do with
　　punishment,
love is not yet perfect in one
　　who is afraid.

19 We, for our part, love
because he first loved us.
20 If anyone says, "My love is
　　fixed on God,"
yet hates his brother,
he is a liar.

4, 1–6: Delusion and deception are invariably possible in matters of spiritual phenomena. Discernment between a true and false spirit of prophecy depends on acceptance or rejection of sound doctrine; cf 1 Cor 12, 3.10. Thus, acknowledgment or denial of the central truth of Christianity, the incarnation of Jesus Christ, the Son of God, is proof of whether one belongs to God or to antichrist (1ff). A power greater than that of the world abides in those who belong to God and who heed the teaching of the apostles (2.6). It conquers the false prophets (v 4) who belong to the world, speak its language and receive its attention (v 5; cf 2, 12–17.22–27).

4, 7–21: These verses explain the nature of love as revealed by God and accepted by man through faith.
4, 7f: *Love is of God:* therefore one who loves shows that he is begotten of God. *God is love:* love is his very being. To love God is to know him and to share his life.
4, 9: *God's love . . . in this way:* the revelation of God's being consists in sending the Son of his love *to the world* as our Savior (cf v 14) that *we might have life through him;* cf Jn 3, 16.
4, 10: *Love . . . consists in this: not that we have loved God but that he has loved us:* man has not

merited God's love. It has been given freely and its value consists in sharing and continuing that love which is in God; cf v 19. *He . . . has sent his Son as an offering for our sins:* an act of his mercy and forgiveness manifested through the death of Christ; cf 2, 2. This is the motive of our love for one another.
4, 11f: Through love for one another we can be certain that *God dwells in us* and brings *his love . . . to perfection* in us. Thus we are able to "see," i.e., to know, the invisible God.

One who has no love for the
brother he has seen
cannot love the God he has not
seen.
21 The commandment we have
from him is this:
whoever loves God must also
love his brother.

5 EVERYONE WHO BELIEVES that
Jesus is the Christ
has been begotten of God.
Now, everyone who loves the
father
loves the child he has begotten.
2 We can be sure that we love
God's children
when we love God
and do what he has commanded.
3 The love of God consists in
this:
that we keep his
commandments—
and his commandments are not
burdensome.
4 Everyone begotten of God
conquers the world,
and the power that has
conquered the world
is this faith of ours.
5 Who, then, is conqueror of the
world?
The one who believes that Jesus
is the Son of God.

6 Jesus Christ it is who came
through water and blood—

not in water only,
but in water and in blood.
It is the Spirit who testifies to
this,
and the Spirit is truth.
7 Thus there are three that testify,
8 the Spirit and the water and the
blood—
and these three are of one
accord.
9 Do we not accept human
testimony?
The testimony of God is much
greater:
it is the testimony God has
given
on his own Son's behalf.
10 Whoever believes in the Son of
God
possesses that testimony within
his heart.
Whoever does not believe God
has made God a liar
by refusing to believe in the
testimony
he has given on his own Son's
behalf.
11 The testimony is this:
God gave us eternal life,
and this life is in his Son.
12 Whoever possesses the Son
possesses life;
whoever does not possess the
Son of God
does not possess life.

13 I have written this to you to

make you realize that you possess
eternal life—you who believe in the
name of the Son of God.

Prayer for Sinners

14 We have this confidence in
God: that he hears us whenever we
ask for anything according to his
will. 15 And since we know that
he hears us whenever we ask, we
know that what we have asked him
for is ours. 16 Anyone who sees
his brother sinning, if the sin is not
deadly, should petition God, and
thus life will be given to the sinner.
This is only for those whose sin is not
deadly. There is such a thing as a
deadly sin; I do not say that one
should pray about that. 17 True,
all wrongdoing is sin, but not all sin
is deadly.

18 We know that no one begotten
of God commits sin; rather, God
protects the one begotten by him,
and so the evil one cannot touch him.
19 We know that we belong to God,
while the whole world is under the
evil one. 20 We know, too, that
the Son of God has come and has
given us discernment to recognize
the One who is true. And we are in
the One who is true, for we are in his
Son Jesus Christ. He is the true God
and eternal life.

21 My little children, be on your
guard against idols.

5, 1–5: To become a child of God it is necessary to
believe in the divine sonship of Jesus Christ, the only-
begotten Son of the Father. It is through him that we
receive our sonship. The proof of love for God consists in keeping his commandments (cf 2, 3–6; 3, 24),
the greatest of which, after love for God, is love of the
brethren, i.e., those begotten of God; cf 4, 21; Mt
22, 37–40; Mk 12, 30f; Lk 10, 27f. Practical faith of
this kind confers a power that conquers the world of
evil, even as Christ overcame the world (Jn 16, 33).
5, 6: *Jesus Christ it is who came through water and
blood:* references to the divine sonship of the Father's testimony: *This is my
beloved Son* (Mt 3, 17) when Jesus was baptized in the
waters of the Jordan, and to Jesus' office of Savior
through the shedding of his blood on the cross (Jn
19, 34).
5, 7ff: The testimony to Christ, the Son of God
and Savior (v 5), is confirmed by divine witness,
greater by far than the two legally required human

witnesses (Dt 17, 6) to substantiate truth; cf Jn 8, 17f.
There is probably a symbolic reference here to baptism and the Eucharist whose existence and efficacy,
like that of all the sacraments, derive from the death
of Christ; cf Jn 19, 34.
5, 10: Through man's belief in the divine sonship
of Christ, God dwells in man through Christ. Thus he
becomes the witness to this truth. Unbelief in the
divine sonship of Jesus means rejecting the divine
testimony, thereby making God the author of a
lie.
5, 11f: By accepting Christ as Son of God through
faith, we receive Christ himself who becomes in us
the source of eternal life.
5, 13: This summary of the epistle recalls the
epilogue of the gospel of John (20, 30f).
5, 14f: The intimate relationship between God and
those begotten of him creates in his children conformity to the divine will which gives them confident

assurance of receiving what they ask for; cf 2, 28;
4, 17; 3, 21f.
5, 16f: The prayer of Christians for their erring
brethren is in conformity to the will of God, who in
turn will restore life to the sinners. *Deadly sin:*
probably apostasy or final impenitence.
5, 18–21: The epistle concludes with the solemn
reaffirmation and summary of the great truths contained therein as well as the false doctrines which
these truths condemn. There is again the sharp antithesis between, on the one hand, God, his Son, and
those begotten of God through faith, and on the other,
the evil one and the world of those enslaved by him.
The Son reveals the God of truth in himself and in
those who accept him. He conquers the evil one, and
by dwelling in his followers and giving them eternal
life, preserves them from the sin of the world and
from the *idols* of false teachings that threaten the
Christian community.

THE SECOND EPISTLE OF

THE ELDER to a lady who is elect and to her children. In truth I love each of you—and not only I but also all those who have come to know the truth. 2 This love is based on the truth that abides in us and will be with us forever. 3 In truth and love, then, we shall have grace, mercy, and peace from God the Father and from Jesus Christ, Son of the Father.

4 It has given me great joy to find some of your children walking in the path of truth, just as we were commanded by the Father. 5 But now, my Lady, I would make this request of you (not as if I were writing you some new commandment; rather, it is a commandment we have had from the start): let us love one another. 6 This love involves our walking according to the commandments, and as you have heard from the beginning, the commandment is the way in which you should walk.

7 Many deceitful men have gone out into the world, men who do not acknowledge Jesus Christ as coming in the flesh. Such is the deceitful one! This is the antichrist! 8 Look out that you yourselves do not lose what you have worked for; you must receive your reward in full. 9 Anyone who is so "progressive" that he does not remain rooted in the teaching of Christ does not possess God; while anyone who remains rooted in the teaching possesses both the Father and the Son. 10 If anyone comes to you who does not bring this teaching, do not receive him into your house; do not even greet him, 11 for whoever greets him shares in the evil he does.

12 While there is much more that I could write you, I do not intend to put it down on paper; instead, I hope to visit you and talk with you face to face, so that our joy may be full.

13 The children of your elect sister send you their greetings.

1: *A lady who is elect:* the adjective *elect* ("chosen by God") is applied to Christians at the beginning of some other New Testament epistles (1 Pt 1, 1f; Ti 1, 1). In 1 Peter 5, 13, a Christian community (in Rome under the name of *Babylon*) is referred to as *chosen together with you* (the Christians of the dispersion; 1 Pt 1, 1). *The truth:* the revelation of God in Jesus, which Christians accept through faith.

3: *Grace, mercy, and peace:* like 1 and 2 Tm, this letter adds *mercy* to the *grace and peace* salutation that is common in the Pauline letters. *Son of the Father:* this title embodies the substance of the entire New Testament, and close variations of it occur; cf, e.g., Jn 1, 14.18; 3, 35; 5, 20. However, the precise wording used here is not found elsewhere in the New Testament. It is echoed in the hymn "Glory to God" of the Roman Mass.

4: *To find some of your children:* those whom he met. There is no necessary indication that others were not *walking in the path* of truth, literally "walking in truth": a Semitic expression used in Johannine writing to describe a way of living in which the Christian faith comes to expression. *Commanded:* either the commandment of brotherly love is meant (Jn 13, 34; 15, 12; 1 Jn 2, 7–11; 4, 21), or the twofold commandment of love and of orthodox belief about Jesus Christ (1 Jn 3, 23). Love is stressed in 2 Jn 4ff, belief in 7ff.

7: *Such is the deceitful one:* another title of antichrist and of those associated with antichrist; cf 1 Jn 2, 18f.22; 4, 2f.

8: *We:* it is not certain whether this means the elder (3 Jn 9f.12) or the Christians as above in vv 2–4. Many MSS have "you."

9: *Anyone who is so "progressive":* literally "Everyone who moves ahead." The elder does not condemn all theological development but only that which departs from Jesus' teaching.

10f: The attitude inculcated here reflects the life-and-death struggle between Christianity and Docetism at the end of the first century. To imitate this attitude in the changed circumstances of our own times would be to misuse Scripture and to fail to understand its time-conditioned aspect. The love that the elder inculcates above (5f) requires in our times that we extend kindness to one another in a divided Christianity.

12: *Our joy:* other textual witnesses read "your joy."

13: *Your elect sister:* the community where the elder resides.

THE THIRD EPISTLE OF

John

THE ELDER to the beloved Gaius, whom indeed I love. 2 Beloved, I hope you are in good health—may you thrive in all other ways as you do in the spirit. 3 For it has given me great joy to have the brothers bear witness to how truly you walk in the path of truth. 4 Nothing delights me more than to hear that my children are walking in this path.

5 Beloved, you demonstrate fidelity by all that you do for the brothers even though they are strangers; 6 indeed, they have testified to your love before the church. And you will do a good thing if, in a way that pleases God, you help them to continue their journey. 7 It was for the sake of the Name that they set out, and they are accepting nothing from the pagans. 8 Therefore, we owe it to such men to support them and thus to have our share in the work of truth.

9 I did write to the church; but Diotrephes, who enjoys being their leader, ignores us. 10 Therefore, if I come I will speak publicly of what he is doing in spreading evil nonsense about us. And that is not all. Not only does he refuse to welcome the brothers himself but he even hinders those who wish to do so and expels them from the church!

11 Beloved, do not imitate what is evil but what is good. Whoever does what is good belongs to God; whoever does what is evil has never seen God. 12 Demetrius is one who gets a good testimonial from all, even from truth itself. We give our testimonial as well, and you know that our testimony is true.

13 There is much more that I had in mind to write you, but I do not wish to write it out with pen and ink. 14 Rather, I hope to see you soon, when we can talk face to face.

15 Peace be with you. The beloved here send you their greetings; greet the beloved there, each by name.

1: *Gaius:* although influential, he does not seem to have had an office in the community. He is referred to as one of the elder's spiritual children (v 4); whether this means he was converted by the elder, or simply that he accepted the elder's leadership, is uncertain. Gaius is called *beloved,* a frequent form of address for fellow Christians in New Testament epistolary literature.

3: *The brothers:* a designation of fellow Christians; cf Jn 21, 23. In this letter it refers to Christians who have been on a missionary enterprise, visiting Gaius and receiving hospitality from him, even though they had been previously unknown to him (v 5).

5: *Demonstrate fidelity by all that you do:* literally, "Whatever work you do for the brothers, you are doing something faithful." Gaius' hospitality is a manifestation of his true Christian faith.

6: *Help them to continue:* besides asking for maintenance for the missionaries while they are in Gaius' community, the elder asks him to equip them for their further travels.

7: *The Name:* Jesus, referred to in this manner in the New Testament (Acts 5, 41) and in later Christian works. *Accepting nothing:* not expecting support from the pagans to whom they preach the gospel, in contrast to some of the devotees of pagan gods who were constantly begging money.

9: *I did write:* a letter probably destroyed by Diotrephes. *Enjoys being their leader:* the elder does not deny that Diotrephes is the leader of the community but implicitly criticizes his ambition to be independent of the elder's influence.

10: *Spreading evil nonsense:* probably Diotrephes is accusing the elder of dictatorial interference in the community on account of his sending the missionaries.

11: *What is evil:* Gaius should not be influenced by Diotrephes but should maintain his previous policy of hospitality.

12: *Testimonial:* because of the danger of heretical teachers (2 Jn), strange missionaries needed recommendation from someone who could vouch for them; cf 2 Cor 3, 1; Rom 16, 1f; Col 4, 7f. *From truth itself:* refers probably to the way Demetrius lived this external witness to the truth that was in him (2 Jn 2).

15: *Beloved:* The Greek word *philos* in the Johannine vocabulary is probably a synonym for *agapetos,* "beloved," which appears in vv 1, 2, 5 and 11. Every Christian was a *philos* of Jesus and of every other Christian: "I no longer speak of you as slaves, . . . Instead I call you friends (*philous*)," i.e., beloved (Jn 15, 15). See note on Jn 15, 13.

THE EPISTLE OF

GREETING

JUDE, a servant of Jesus Christ and brother of James, to those who have been called by God; who have found love in God the Father and have been guarded safely in Jesus Christ. 2 May mercy, peace, and love be yours in ever greater measure.

Exhortation to Steadfastness

3 I was already fully intent on writing you, beloved, about the salvation we share. But now I feel obliged to write and encourage you to fight hard for the faith delivered once for all to the saints. 4 Certain individuals have recently wormed their way into your midst, godless types, long ago destined for the condemnation I shall describe. They pervert the gracious gift of our God to sexual excess and deny Jesus Christ, our only master and Lord.

Against False Teachers

5 I wish to remind you of certain things, even though you may already be very well aware of them. The Lord first rescued his people from the land of Egypt but later destroyed those who refused to believe. 6 There were angels, too, who did not keep to their own domain, who deserted their dwelling place. These the Lord has kept in perpetual bondage, shrouded in murky darkness against the judgment of the great day. 7 Sodom, Gomorrah, and the towns thereabout indulged in lust, just as those angels did; they practiced unnatural vice. They are set before us to dissuade us, as they undergo a punishment of eternal fire.

8 Similarly, these visionaries pollute the flesh; they spurn God's dominion and revile the angelic beings. 9 Even the archangel Michael, when his case with the devil was being judged—a dispute over Moses' body—did not venture to charge him with blasphemy. He simply said, "May the Lord punish you." 10 These people, however, not only revile what they have no knowledge of but are corrupted through the very things they know by instinct, like brute animals. 11 So much the worse for them! They have taken the road Cain took. They have abandoned themselves to Balaam's error for pay, and like Korah they

---

1f: *Jude, . . . brother of James:* for the identity of the author of this letter, see the Introduction. *To those who have been called by God:* the vocation to the Christian faith is God's free gift to those whom he loves and whom he safely protects in Christ until the Lord's second coming.

3f: *The salvation we share:* the teachings of the Christian faith *delivered once for all to the saints:* i.e., handed down in their entirety and accepted by the Christian community. They are not to be perverted by heterodoxy; cf 1 Cor 3, 11; 15, 1; Gal 1, 6–19; 1Tm 1, 3; 6, 3. *Certain individuals . . . destined for the condemnation:* false teachers within the community who deny Christ as Lord and Savior and seduce the people by advocating sexual lawlessness. Their punishment is already foreshadowed in Old Testament

examples of unfaithful ones among the angels and among God's people (5ff). There is also reference here to the apocryphal Book of Enoch (14f), which was highly regarded in the early centuries of the Christian era.

5: *Destroyed those who refused to believe:* see note on Nm 14, 28f.

6: See note on Gn 6, 1–4; cf also 2 Pt 2, 4–6.

7: *Sodom, Gomorrah:* frequently used in the Scriptures as examples of sin and punishment; cf Is 1, 9; Jer 50, 40; Lam 4, 6; Ez 16, 56; Mt 10, 15; 11, 24; Lk 17, 29. See note on Gn 19, 25.

8: *Visionaries:* victims of hallucination, or self-authorized prophets of revelation (cf 2 Pt 2, 10.18) who distort and debase Christian revelation to the detriment of the community.

Revile the angelic beings: i.e., probably by attributing their own disorders to the angels whom they invoke as their patrons.

9: *The archangel Michael . . . blasphemy:* an apparent reference to the story concerning the dispute between Michael and the devil over Moses' body, as described in the apocryphal *Assumption of Moses.* If Michael did not accuse even the devil but left the judgment of him to God, how much less should men presume to revile the angels! Michael was regarded as the protector of ancient Israel and of the new Israel, the church; cf Rv 12, 7; Dan 10, 13.20f; 13, 1ff.

11: *Cain . . . Balaam . . . Korah:* examples of rebellious leaders and of the punishments their conduct incurred; cf Gn 4, 8–16; Nm 16, 1–35; 31, 16.

perish in rebellion. 12 These men are blotches on your Christian banquets. They join your solemn feasts without shame and only look after themselves. They are blown on the wind like clouds that bring no rain. Like trees at the year's end they bear no fruit, being dead and up-rooted. 13 They are wild ocean waves, splashing their shameless deeds abroad like foam, or shooting stars for whom the thick gloom of darkness has been reserved forever. 14 It was about these that Enoch, who was of the seventh generation descended from Adam, prophesied when he said, "See, the Lord has come with his countless holy ones about him   15 to pass judgment on all men, indicting the godless for every evil deed they have done, and

convicting those godless sinners of every harsh word they have uttered against him."

16 These men are grumblers and whiners. They live by their passions, uttering bombast. Whenever it is expedient, they resort to flattery. 17 Remember, beloved, all of you, the prophetic words of the apostles of our Lord Jesus Christ; 18 how they kept telling you, "In the last days there will be impostors living by their godless passions." 19 These sensualists, devoid of the Spirit, are causing divisions among you.

Christian Admonitions

20 But you, beloved, grow strong in your holy faith through prayer in

the Holy Spirit. 21 Persevere in God's love, and welcome the mercy of our Lord Jesus Christ which leads to life eternal. 22 Correct those who are confused; the others you must rescue, snatching them from the fire. 23 Even with those you pity, be on your guard; abhor so much as their flesh-stained clothing.

Doxology

24 There is One who can protect you from a fall and make you stand unblemished and exultant in the presence of his glory. 25 Glory be to this only God our savior, through Jesus Christ our Lord. Majesty, too, be his, might and power from ages past, now and for ages to come. Amen.

12f: *Blotches on your Christian banquets:* scandalous conduct in connection with the eucharistic celebrations (cf 2 Pt 2, 13) which in apostolic times were associated with a community meal; cf Acts 2, 46; 1 Cor 11, 20-34.

Clouds that bring no rain; trees . . . dead and uprooted; wild ocean waves; shooting stars: empty display of force and beauty and splendor devoid of any genuine source to sustain them. Shooting stars were considered by the ancients to forebode catastrophe. Here they symbolize Christians who have withdrawn far from God as they plunge into exterior darkness; cf Enoch 18-21.

14f: A reference to Enoch (1, 9). For the descrip-

tion of Christ the universal judge of mankind, surrounded by his angels, cf Dn 7, 10; Mt 25, 21; Heb 12, 22.

17ff: The prophetic utterance of the apostles concerning the last days are repeated here to help Christians prepare themselves for the struggle against the enemies of their faith.

18: *In the last days . . . godless passions:* the substance rather than the direct quotation of the many New Testament passages, such as Mk 13, 22; Acts 20, 30; 1 Tm 4, 1ff; 2 Pt 3, 3. *The last* refers not to the immanent proximity of the second coming of Christ, as thought by many in the early Christian community, but to various stages in messianic times.

20f: These verses contain the trinitarian doctrine: God (the Father) who loves us, *the Holy Spirit* who prays in us, and *our Lord Jesus Christ* who *leads* us to *life eternal.* They also sum up the Christian life in terms of the theological virtues (faith, hope, charity) and the practice of prayer.

24f: *There is One who can protect you:* God through Jesus Christ. The purpose of the epistle is brought back into focus at its conclusion: perseverance of Christians in the faith amid the many evils that threaten to destroy it; cf 1 Pt 3, 17f. Verse 25 contains an illustrious New Testament doxology; cf also Rom 16, 27; Eph 3, 20; 1 Pt 4, 11; 2 Pt 3, 18.

THE BOOK OF

PROLOGUE

THIS is the revelation God gave to Jesus Christ, that he might show his servants what must happen very soon. He made it known by sending his angel to his servant John, 2 who in reporting all he saw bears witness to the word of God and the testimony of Jesus Christ. 3 Happy is the man who reads this prophetic message, and happy are those who hear it and heed what is written in it, for the appointed time is near!

LETTERS TO THE CHURCHES OF ASIA

Greeting

4 To the seven churches in the province of Asia: John wishes you grace and peace—from him who is and who was and who is to come, and from the seven spirits before his throne, 5 and from Jesus Christ the faithful witness, the first-born from the dead and ruler of the kings of earth. To him who loves us and freed us from our sins by his own blood, 6 who has made us a royal nation of priests in the service of his God and Father—to him be glory and power forever and ever! Amen.

7 See, he comes amid the clouds!
Every eye shall see him,
even of those who pierced him.
All the peoples of the earth
shall lament him bitterly.
So it is to be! Amen!

8 The Lord God says, "I am the Alpha and the Omega, the One who is and who was and who is to come, the Almighty!"

First Vision

9 I, John, your brother, who share with you the distress and the kingly reign and the endurance we have in Jesus, found myself on the island called Patmos because I proclaimed God's word and bore witness to Jesus. 10 On the Lord's Day I was caught up in ecstasy, and I heard behind me a piercing voice like the sound of a trumpet, 11 which said, "Write on a scroll what you now see and send it to the seven churches: to Ephesus, Smyrna, Pergamum, Thyatira, Sardis, Philadelphia, and Laodicea." 12 I turned around to see whose voice it was that spoke to me. When I did so I saw seven lampstands of gold, 13 and among the lampstands One like a Son of Man wearing an ankle-length robe, with a sash of gold about his breast. 14 The hair of his head was as white as snow-white wool and his eyes blazed

---

1, 3: *Happy is the man:* the first of seven beatitudes in this book; the others are in 14, 13; 16, 15; 19, 9; 20, 6; 22, 7.14. *Those who hear it:* in the liturgical assembly. *The appointed time:* when Jesus will return in glory; cf 1, 7; 3, 11; 22, 7.10.12.20.

1, 4: *Seven churches . . . Asia:* in western Asia Minor (modern Turkey). These representative churches are mentioned by name in 1, 11; each is the recipient of a message (2, 1—3, 22). *Seven* is the biblical number suggesting fullness and completeness;

thus John is writing for the whole church.

1, 5: *Freed us:* other ancient MSS read "washed us."

1, 8: *The Alpha and the Omega:* the first and last letters of the Greek alphabet. In 22, 13 the same words occur, together with the expressions *the First and the Last, the beginning and the End;* cf 1, 17; 2, 8; 21, 6; Is 44, 6.

1, 9: *Island called Patmos:* in the Aegean Sea, southwest of Ephesus.

1, 10: *The Lord's day:* Sunday.

1, 12–16: A symbolic description of Christ in glory; cf Introduction.

1, 13: *Son of Man:* see note on Mt 8, 20. *Ankle-length robe:* Christ is priest; cf Ex 28, 4; 29, 5. *Sash of gold:* Christ is king; cf 1 Mc 10, 89; 11, 58.

1, 14: *Hair . . . white as snow-white wool:* Christ is eternal (v 18; Dn 7, 9). *His eyes blazed like fire:* Christ is omniscient; cf 2, 23; Ps 7, 10; Jer 17, 10.

like fire. 15 His feet gleamed like polished brass refined in a furnace, and his voice sounded like the roar of rushing waters. 16 In his right hand he held seven stars. A sharp, two-edged sword came out of his mouth, and his face shone like the sun at its brightest.

17 When I caught sight of him I fell down at his feet as though dead. He touched me with his right hand and said: "There is nothing to fear. I am the First and the Last 18 and the One who lives. Once I was dead but now I live—forever and ever. I hold the keys of death and the nether world. 19 Write down, therefore, whatever you see in visions—what you see now and will see in time to come. 20 This is the secret meaning of the seven stars you saw in my right hand, and of the seven lampstands of gold: the seven stars are the presiding spirits of the seven churches, and the seven lampstands are the seven churches.

To Ephesus

2 "To the presiding spirit of the church in Ephesus, write this:

"'The One who holds the seven stars in his right hand and walks among the seven lampstands of gold has this to say: 2 I know your deeds, your labors, and your patient endurance. I know you cannot tolerate wicked men; you have tested those self-styled apostles who are nothing of the sort, and discovered that they are impostors. 3 You are patient and endure hardship for my cause. Moreover, you do not become discouraged. 4 I hold this against you, though: you have turned aside from your early love.

5 Keep firmly in mind the heights from which you have fallen. Repent, and return to your former deeds. If you do not repent I will come to you and remove your lampstand from its place. 6 But you have this much in your favor: you detest the practices of the Nicolaitans, just as I do.

7 "'Let him who has ears heed the Spirit's word to the churches! I will see to it that the victor eats from the tree of life which grows in the garden of God.'

To Smyrna

8 "To the presiding spirit of the church in Smyrna, write this:

"'The First and the Last who once died but now lives has this to say: 9 I know of your tribulation and your poverty, even though you are rich. I know the slander you endure from self-styled Jews who are nothing other than members of Satan's assembly. 10 Have no fear of the sufferings to come. The devil will indeed cast some of you into prison to put you to the test; you will be tried over a period of ten days. Remain faithful until death and I will give you the crown of life.

11 "'Let him who has ears heed the Spirit's word to the churches! The victor shall never be harmed by the second death.'

To Pergamum

12 "To the presiding spirit of the church in Pergamum, write this:

"'The One with the sharp, two-edged sword has this to say: 13 I know you live in the very place where Satan's throne is erected; and I know

you hold fast to my name and have not denied the faith you have in me, not even at the time when Antipas, my faithful witness, was martyred in your city where Satan has his home. 14 Nevertheless I hold a few matters against you: there are some among you who follow the teaching of Balaam, who instructed Balak to throw a stumbling block in the way of the Israelites by tempting them to eat food sacrificed to idols and to practice fornication. 15 Yes, you too have those among you who hold to the teaching of the Nicolaitans. 16 Therefore repent! If you do not, I will come to you soon and fight against them with the sword of my mouth.

17 "'Let him who has ears heed the Spirit's word to the churches! To the victor I will give the hidden manna; I will also give him a white stone upon which is inscribed a new name, to be known only by him who receives it.'

To Thyatira

18 "To the presiding spirit of the church in Thyatira, write this:

"'The Son of God, whose eyes blaze like fire and whose feet gleam like polished brass, has this to say: 19 I know your deeds—your love and faith and service—as well as your patient endurance; I know also that your efforts of recent times are greater than ever. 20 Nevertheless I hold this against you: you tolerate a Jezebel—that self-styled prophetess who seduces my servants by teaching them to practice lewdness and to eat food sacrificed to idols. 21 I have given her a chance to repent but she

---

1, 15: *His feet . . . furnace:* Christ is immutable; cf Ez 1, 27; Dn 10, 6. *His voice . . . waters:* Christ speaks with divine authority; cf Ez 1, 24.
1, 16: *A sharp, two-edged sword:* the word of God (Eph 6, 17; Heb 4, 12), which will destroy unrepentant sinners (2, 16; 19, 15). *His face . . . brightest:* the divine majesty of Christ; cf 21, 23; Is 60, 19.
1, 17: It was an Old Testament belief that for sinful man to see God was to die (Ex 19, 21; 33, 20; Is 6, 5).
1, 18: *Nether world:* the abode of the dead (20, 13).
1, 20: *Presiding spirits:* literally, angels. Angels were thought to be in charge of the physical world (7, 1; 16, 5), as well as of nations (Dn 10, 13; 12, 1), communities (the seven churches), and individuals (Mt 18, 10; Acts 12, 15).
2, 1–3, 22: Each of the seven letters follows the same pattern: address; description of the exalted Christ; blame and/or praise for the church addressed; threat and/or admonition; final exhortation and

promise to all Christians.
2, 1: *Ephesus:* capital of the Roman province of Asia. *Walks among the seven lampstands:* Christ is always present in the church; see note on 1, 4.
2, 2: *Self-styled apostles . . . impostors:* unauthorized and perverse missionaries; cf Acts 20, 29f.
2, 6: *Nicolaitans:* perhaps the impostors of v 2; see note on vv 14f.
2, 7: *The tree of life . . . garden of God:* reference to the tree in the primeval paradise (Gn 2, 9); cf 22, 2.14.19.
2, 8: *Smyrna:* modern Izmir, north of Ephesus.
2, 9f: The church in Smyrna was materially poor but spiritually rich. Accusations made by Jews occasioned the persecution of Christians; cf Acts 14, 2.19; 17, 5.13.
2, 11: *The second death:* when sinners will receive their final punishment (20, 6.14f; 21, 8).
2, 12: *Pergamum:* modern Bergama, north of Smyrna.

2, 13: *Satan's throne:* reference to emperor worship and other pagan practices that flourished in the city.
2, 14f: Like Balaam, the biblical prototype of religious compromisers (Nm 25, 1ff; 31, 16; 2 Pt 2, 15; Jude 11), the Nicolaitans in Pergamum and Ephesus (v 6) accommodated their Christian faith to paganism. They misused the law of liberty enunciated by St. Paul (1 Cor 9, 19–23).
2, 17: *The hidden manna:* the food of life; cf Ps 78, 24f. *White stone:* symbol of victory and joy; cf 3. 4f. *New name:* reference to the Christian's rebirth in Christ; cf 3, 12; 19, 12; Is 62, 2; 65, 15.
2, 18: *Thyatira:* modern Akhisar, southeast of Pergamum.
2, 20: The scheming and treacherous Jezebel of old (1 Kgs 21, 1–14; 2 Kgs 9, 22.30–34) introduced pagan customs into the religion of Israel; this new Jezebel was doing the same to Christianity.

refuses to turn from her lewdness. 22 I mean to cast her down on a bed of pain; her companions in sin I will plunge into intense suffering unless they repent of their sins with her, 23 and her children I will put to death. Thus shall all the churches come to know that I am the searcher of hearts and minds, and that I will give each of you what your conduct deserves. 24 And now I address myself to you others in Thyatira who do not uphold this teaching and know nothing of the so-called "deep secrets" of Satan; on you I place no further burden. 25 In any case, hold fast to what you have until I come.

26 "'To the one who wins the victory, who keeps to my ways till the end, I will give authority over the nations—the same authority I received from my Father. 27 He shall rule them with a rod of iron and shatter them like crockery; and 28 I will give him the morning star.

29 "'Let him who has ears heed the Spirit's word to the churches!'

To Sardis

3 "To the presiding spirit of the church in Sardis, write this:

"'The One who holds the seven spirits of God, the seven stars, has this to say: I know your conduct; I know the reputation you have of being alive, when in fact you are dead! 2 Wake up, and strengthen what remains before it dies. I find that the sum of your deeds is less than complete in the sight of my God. 3 Call to mind how you accepted what you heard; keep to it, and repent. If you do not rouse yourselves I will come upon you like a thief, at a time you cannot know. 4 I realize that you have in Sardis a few persons who have not soiled their garments; these shall walk with me in white because they are worthy.

5 "'The victor shall go clothed in white. I will never erase his name from the book of the living, but will acknowledge him in the presence of my Father and his angels.

6 "'Let him who has ears heed the Spirit's word to the churches!'

To Philadelphia

7 "To the presiding spirit of the church in Philadelphia, write this:

"'The holy One, the true,
     who wields David's key,
     who opens and no one can
          close,
     who closes and no one can
          open,

has this to say:

8 "'I know of your deeds; that is why I have left an open door before you which no one can close. I know that your strength is limited; yet you have held fast to my word and have not denied my name. 9 I mean to make some of Satan's assembly, those self-styled Jews who are not really Jews but frauds, come and fall down at your feet; they will learn of my love for you in that way. 10 Because you have kept my plea to stand fast, I will keep you safe in the time of trial which is coming on the whole world, to test all men on earth. 11 I am coming soon. Hold fast to what you have lest someone rob you of your crown.

12 "'I will make the victor a pillar in the temple of my God and he shall never leave it. I will inscribe on him the name of my God and the name of the city of my God, the new Jerusalem which he will send down from heaven, and my own name which is new.

13 "'Let him who has ears heed the Spirit's word to the churches!'

To Laodicea

14 "To the presiding spirit of the church in Laodicea, write this:

"'The Amen, the faithful Witness and true, the Source of God's creation, has this to say: 15 I know your deeds; I know you are neither hot nor cold. How I wish you were one or the other—hot or cold! 16 But because you are lukewarm, neither hot nor cold, I will spew you out of my mouth! 17 You keep saying, "I am so rich and secure that I want for nothing." Little do you realize how wretched you are, how pitiable and poor, how blind and naked! 18 Take my advice. Buy from me gold refined by fire if you would be truly rich. Buy white garments in which to be clothed, if the shame of your nakedness is to be covered. Buy ointment to smear on your eyes, if you would see once more. 19 Whoever is dear to me I reprove and chastise. Be earnest about it, therefore. Repent!

20 "'Here I stand, knocking at the door. If anyone hears me calling and opens the door, I will enter his house and have supper with him, and he with me. 21 I will give the victor the right to sit with me on my throne, as I myself won the victory and took my seat beside my Father on his throne.

22 "'Let him who has ears heed the Spirit's word to the churches.'"

PREPARATION FOR THE DAY OF THE LORD

Vision of Heavenly Worship

4 After this I had another vision: above me there was an open door to heaven, and I heard the

---

2, 24: The so-called "deep secrets" of Satan: a scathing reference to the perverse teaching of the Nicolaitans (v 15).

2, 26ff: The Christian who perseveres in faith will share in Christ's messianic authority and victory over death, symbolized by the morning star (22, 16); cf Ps 2, 8f.

3, 1f: Sardis, south and east of Thyatira, is reproached for the feverish activity of its Christians (the reputation you have of being alive), since such activity could not substitute for a living faith.

3, 4f: In white: the sign of victory and joy; see note on 2, 17. The book of the living: where the names of the redeemed are kept (21, 27); cf 13, 8; 17, 8; 20, 12.15; Phil 4, 3; Dn 12, 1. They will be acknowledged by Christ in heaven (Mt 10, 32).

3, 7: Philadelphia, modern Alaşehir, southeast of Sardis. Destroyed by earthquake in A.D. 17 and rebuilt with money from the Emperor Tiberius, the city was renamed Neocaesarea, "New Caesar City." David's key: to the heavenly City of David, the new Jerusalem (v 12), over which Christ has supreme authority; cf Is 22, 22.

3, 8: An open door: opportunities for sharing and proclaiming the faith; cf 1 Cor 16, 19; 2 Cor 2, 12.

3, 12: A pillar: allusion to the rebuilding of the city; see note on v 7. New Jerusalem: described in 21, 10—22, 5.

3, 14: Laodicea, southeast of Philadelphia, was a wealthy commercial center. The Amen: a divine title applied to Christ; cf Is 65, 16; 2 Cor 1. 20. Source of

God's creation: a concept found also in Jn 1, 3; Col 1, 16f; Heb 1, 2; cf Wis 9, 1f.

3, 15f: Halfhearted commitment to the faith is nauseating to Christ.

3, 17: Material well-being occasioned spiritual bankruptcy.

3, 18: Gold . . . fire: God's grace. White garments: symbol of an upright life (the city was noted for its black woolen cloth). Ointment . . . eyes: to remove spiritual blindness (one of the city's exports was eye ointment).

3, 20: Christ invites all men to the Messianic banquet in heaven (Lk 14, 15; 22, 30); cf Is 25, 6.

4, 1: The ancients viewed heaven as a solid vault, entered by way of actual doors.

trumpetlike voice which had spoken to me before. It said, "Come up here and I will show you what must take place in time to come." 2 At once I was caught up in ecstasy. A throne was standing there in heaven, and on the throne was seated One 3 whose appearance had a gemlike sparkle as of jasper and carnelian. Around the throne was a rainbow as brilliant as emerald. 4 Surrounding this throne were twenty-four other thrones upon which were seated twenty-four elders; they were clothed in white garments and had crowns of gold on their heads. 5 From the throne came flashes of lightning and peals of thunder; before it burned seven flaming torches, the seven spirits of God. 6 The floor around the throne was like a sea of glass that was crystal-clear.

At the very center, around the throne itself, stood four living creatures covered with eyes front and back. 7 The first creature resembled a lion, the second an ox; the third had the face of a man, while the fourth looked like an eagle in flight. 8 Each of the four living creatures had six wings and eyes all over, inside and out.

Day and night, without pause, they sing:

"Holy, holy, holy, is the Lord
     God Almighty,
   He who was, and who is, and
     who is to come!"

9 Whenever these creatures give glory and honor and praise to the One seated on the throne, who lives forever and ever, 10 the twenty-four elders fall down before the One seated on the throne, and worship him who lives forever and ever. They throw down their crowns before the throne and sing:

11 "O Lord our God, you are
     worthy

to receive glory and honor
     and power!
For you have created all things;
   by your will they came to be
     and were made!"

The Scroll and the Lamb

5 In the right hand of the One who sat on the throne I saw a scroll. It had writing on both sides and was sealed with seven seals. 2 Then I saw a mighty angel who proclaimed in a loud voice: "Who is worthy to open the scroll and break its seals?" 3 But no one in heaven or on earth or under the earth could be found to open the scroll or examine its contents. 4 I wept bitterly because no one could be found worthy to open or examine the scroll. 5 One of the elders said to me: "Do not weep. The Lion of the tribe of Judah, the Root of David, has won the right by his victory to open the scroll with the seven seals."

6 Then, between the throne with the four living creatures and the elders, I saw a Lamb standing, a Lamb that had been slain. He had seven horns and seven eyes; these eyes are the seven spirits of God, sent to all parts of the world. 7 The Lamb came and received the scroll from the right hand of the One who sat on the throne. 8 When he had taken the scroll, the four living creatures and the twenty-four elders fell down before the Lamb. Along with their harps, the elders were holding vessels of gold filled with aromatic spices, which were the prayers of God's holy people. 9 This is the new hymn they sang:

"Worthy are you to receive the
     scroll
   and break open its seals,
   for you were slain.
With your blood you purchased
     for God
   men of every race and tongue,
   of every people and nation.

10 You made of them a kingdom,
   and priests to serve our God,
   and they shall reign on the
     earth."

11 As my vision continued, I heard the voices of many angels who surrounded the throne and the living creatures and the elders. They were countless in number, thousands and tens of thousands, 12 and they all cried out:

"Worthy is the Lamb that was
     slain
   to receive power and riches,
     wisdom and strength,
   honor and glory and praise!"

13 Then I heard the voices of every creature in heaven and on earth and under the earth and in the sea; everything in the universe cried aloud:

"To the One seated on the
     throne, and to the Lamb,
   be praise and honor, glory
     and might,
   forever and ever!"

14 The four living creatures answered, "Amen," and the elders fell down and worshiped.

The First Six Seals

6 Then I watched while the Lamb broke open the first of the seven seals, and I heard one of the four living creatures cry out in a voice like thunder, "Come forward!" 2 To my surprise I saw a white horse; its rider had a bow, and he was given a crown. He rode forth victorious, to conquer yet again.

3 When the Lamb broke open the second seal, I heard the second living creature cry out, "Come forward!" 4 Another horse came forth, a red one. Its rider was given power to rob the earth of peace by allowing men to slaughter one another. For this he was given a huge sword.

4, 2–8: Much of the imagery here is taken from Ez 1 and 10.
4, 4: *Twenty-four elders:* representing the twelve tribes of Israel and the twelve apostles; cf 21, 12ff.
4, 5: *Flashes of lightning and peals of thunder:* as in other descriptions of God's appearances or activity (8, 5; 11, 19; 16, 18; Ex 19, 16; Ez 1, 13).
4, 6ff: *A sea of glass . . . crystal-clear:* image adapted from Ez 1, 22–26. *Four living creatures:* symbols taken from Ez 1, 5–21; they are identified as cherubim in Ez 10, 20. *Covered with eyes:* suggesting

God's knowledge and concern. *Six wings:* like the seraphim of Is 6, 2.
5, 1: *A scroll:* containing the list of afflictions reserved for sinful men; cf Ez 2, 9f. *Sealed with seven seals:* totally hidden from all but God. Only the Lamb (vv 7ff) has the right to carry out the divine plan.
5, 5: *The Lion of the tribe of Judah, the Root of David:* messianic titles applied to Christ (22, 16; Gn 49, 9; Is 11, 1.10).
5, 6: Christ is the Paschal Lamb without blemish, whose blood saved the new Israel from sin and death

(Jn 1, 29.36; 1 Pt 1, 18f; Acts 8, 32); cf Ex 12; Is 53, 7. *Seven horns and seven eyes:* Christ has the fullness (see note on 1, 4) of power and knowledge. *Seven spirits:* as in 1, 4 and 4, 5.
6, 1–8: Each of the four horsemen symbolizes a particular woe connected with war and destruction. The imagery is adapted from Zec 1, 8ff; 6, 1–8.
6, 2: *White horse . . . bow:* symbolizing the Parthians on the eastern border of the Roman empire. Expert in the use of the bow, they constantly harassed the Romans.
6, 4: *Huge sword:* symbol of war and violence.

5 When the Lamb broke open the third seal, I heard the third living creature cry out, "Come forward!" This time I saw a black horse, the rider of which held a pair of scales in his hand. 6 I heard what seemed to be a voice coming from in among the four living creatures. It said: "A day's pay for a ration of wheat and the same for three of barley! But spare the olive oil and the wine!"

7 When the Lamb broke open the fourth seal, I heard the voice of the fourth living creature cry out, "Come forward!" 8 Now I saw a horse sickly green in color. Its rider was named Death, and the nether world was in his train. These four were given authority over one quarter of the earth, to kill with sword and famine and plague and the wild beasts of the earth.

9 When the Lamb broke open the fifth seal, I saw under the altar the spirits of those who had been martyred because of the witness they bore to the word of God. 10 They cried out at the top of their voices: "How long will it be, O Master, holy and true, before you judge our cause and avenge our blood among the inhabitants of the earth?" 11 Each of the martyrs was given a long white robe, and they were told to be patient a little while longer until the quota was filled of their fellow servants and brothers to be slain, as they had been.

12 When I saw the Lamb break open the sixth seal, there was a violent earthquake; the sun turned black as a goat's-hair tentcloth and the moon grew red as blood. 13 The stars in the sky fell crashing to earth like figs shaken loose by a mighty wind. 14 Then the sky disappeared as if it were a scroll being rolled up; every mountain and island was uprooted from its base. 15 The kings of the earth, the nobles and those in command, the wealthy and

powerful, the slave and the free—all hid themselves in caves and mountain crags. 16 They cried out to the mountains and rocks, "Fall on us! Hide us from the face of the One who sits on the throne and from the wrath of the Lamb! 17 The great day of their vengeance has come. Who can withstand it?"

Sealing of the Thousands

7 After this I saw four angels standing at the four corners of the earth; they held in check the earth's four winds so that no wind blew on land or sea or through any tree. 2 I saw another angel come up from the east holding the seal of the living God. He cried out at the top of his voice to the four angels who were given power to ravage the land and the sea, 3 "Do no harm to the land or the sea or the trees until we imprint this seal on the foreheads of the servants of our God." 4 I heard the number of those who were so marked—one hundred and forty-four thousand from every tribe of Israel: 5 twelve thousand from the tribe of Judah, twelve thousand from the tribe of Reuben, twelve thousand from the tribe of Gad, 6 twelve thousand from the tribe of Asher, twelve thousand from the tribe of Naphtali, twelve thousand from the tribe of Manasseh, 7 twelve thousand from the tribe of Simeon, twelve thousand from the tribe of Levi, twelve thousand from the tribe of Issachar, 8 twelve thousand from the tribe of Zebulun, twelve thousand from the tribe of Joseph, and twelve thousand from the tribe of Benjamin.

Triumph of the Elect

9 After this I saw before me a huge crowd which no one could count from every nation and race, people and tongue. They stood before the throne and the Lamb, dressed in long

white robes and holding palm branches in their hands. 10 They cried out in a loud voice, "Salvation is from our God, who is seated on the throne, and from the Lamb!" 11 All the angels who were standing around the throne and the elders and the four living creatures fell down before the throne to worship God. They said: 12 "Amen! Praise and glory, wisdom and thanksgiving and honor, power and might, to our God forever and ever. Amen!"

13 Then one of the elders asked me, "Who are these people all dressed in white? And where have they come from?" 14 I said to him, "Sir, you should know better than I." He then told me, "These are the ones who have survived the great period of trial; they have washed their robes and made them white in the blood of the Lamb.

15 "It was this that brought them
　　before God's throne:
　　day and night they minister to
　　　him in his temple;
　he who sits on the throne will
　　give them shelter.
16 Never again shall they know
　　hunger or thirst,
　　nor shall the sun or its heat
　　　beat down on them,
17 　for the Lamb on the throne
　　　will shepherd them.
He will lead them to springs of
　　life-giving water,
　and God will wipe every tear
　　from their eyes."

The Seven Trumpets

8 When the Lamb broke open the seventh seal, there was silence in heaven for about half an hour. 2 Then, as I watched, the seven angels who minister in God's presence were given seven trumpets.

The Gold Censer

3 Another angel came in holding a censer of gold. He took his place

---

6, 5: *Black horse:* symbol of famine, the usual accompaniment of war in antiquity.

6, 6: *A day's pay:* literally, "denarius," a silver coin. Famine brought about the rationing of supplies, and the prices were exorbitant. *Barley:* food of the poor.

6, 8: *Sickly green:* symbol of death.

6, 12ff: Symbolic rather than literal description of the cosmic upheavals attending the Day of the Lord, when the martyrs' prayer for vindication (v 10) would be answered; cf Mt 24, 29; Am 8, 8f; Is 34, 4; Jl 2, 10, 3, 3f.

7, 1–17: Two scenes precede the breaking of the seventh seal. In the first (vv 1–8), the elect receive *the seal of the living God;* cf Ez 9, 4ff. The second scene (vv 9–17) portrays the victorious martyrs before God's throne.

7, 4–8: *One hundred and forty-four thousand:* the square of twelve (the number of Israel's tribes) multiplied by a thousand, symbolic of the new Israel that embraces men *from every nation and race, people and tongue* (v 9); cf Gal 6, 16; Jas 1, 1.

7, 9: *Long white robes . . . palm branches:* symbols of joy and victory; see note on 3, 4f.

7, 14: *Great period of trial:* fierce persecution by the Romans; cf Introduction.

7, 17: *Life-giving water:* God's grace, which flows from Christ (21, 6; 22, 1.17; Jn 4, 10.14).

8, 1: *Silence in heaven:* as in Zep 1, 7, a prelude to the eschatological woes that are to follow.

8, 2: The breaking of the seventh seal brings not one, but seven, symbolic disasters, each to be announced by the blowing of a trumpet (8, 6ff); see note on 6, 12ff.

at the altar of incense and was given large amounts of incense to deposit on the altar of gold in front of the throne, together with the prayers of all God's holy ones. 4 From the angel's hand the smoke of the incense went up before God, and with it the prayers of God's people. 5 Then the angel took the censer, filled it with live coals from the altar, and hurled it down to the earth. Peals of thunder and flashes of lightning followed, and the earth trembled.

First Four Trumpets

6 The seven angels with the seven trumpets made ready to blow them.

7 When the first angel blew his trumpet, there came hail and then fire mixed with blood, which was hurled down to the earth. A third of the land was scorched, along with a third of the trees and every green plant.

8 When the second angel blew his trumpet, something like a huge mountain all in flames was cast into the sea. 9 A third of the sea turned to blood, a third of the creatures living in the sea died, and a third of the ships were wrecked.

10 When the third angel blew his trumpet, a huge star burning like a torch crashed down from the sky. It fell on a third of the rivers and the springs. The star's name was "Wormwood" because a third part of all the water turned to wormwood. Many people died from this polluted water.

12 When the fourth angel blew his trumpet, a third of the sun, a third of the moon, and a third of the stars were hit hard enough to be plunged into darkness. The day lost a third of its light, as did the night.

13 As my vision continued, I heard an eagle flying in mid-heaven cry out in a loud voice, "Woe, woe, and again woe to the inhabitants of earth from the trumpet blasts the other three angels are about to blow!"

The Fifth Trumpet

9 Then the fifth angel blew his trumpet, and I saw a star fall from the sky to the earth. The star was given the key to the shaft of the abyss; 2 he opened it and smoke poured out of the shaft like smoke from an enormous furnace. The sun and the air were darkened by the smoke from the shaft. 3 Out of the smoke, onto the land, came locusts as powerful as scorpions in their sting. 4 The locusts were commanded to do no harm to the grass in the land or to any plant or tree but only to those men who had not the seal of God on their foreheads. 5 The locusts were not allowed to kill them but only to torture them for five months; the pain they inflicted was like that of a scorpion's sting. 6 During that time these men will seek death but will not find it; they will yearn to die but death will escape them.

7 In appearance the locusts were like horses equipped for battle. On their heads they wore something like gold crowns; their faces were like men's faces 8 but they had hair like women's hair. Their teeth were the teeth of lions, 9 their chests like iron breastplates. Their wings made a sound like the roar of many chariots and horses charging into battle. 10 They had tails with stingers like scorpions; in their tails was enough venom to harm men for five months. 11 Acting as their king was the angel in charge of the abyss, whose name in Hebrew is Abaddon and in Greek Apollyon.

The Sixth Trumpet

12 The first woe is past, but beware! There are two more to come. 13 Then the sixth angel blew his trumpet, and I heard a voice coming from between the horns of the altar of gold in God's presence. 14 It said to the sixth angel, who was

still holding his trumpet, "Release the four angels who are tied up on the banks of the great river Euphrates!" 15 So the four angels were released; this was precisely the hour, the day, the month, and the year for which they had been prepared, to kill a third of mankind. 16 Their cavalry troops, whose count I heard, were two hundred million in number—a number I heard myself. 17 Now, in my vision, this is how I saw the horses and their riders. The breastplates they wore were fiery red, deep blue, and pale yellow. The horses' heads were like heads of lions, and out of their mouths came fire and sulphur and smoke. 18 By these three plagues—the smoke and sulphur and fire which shot out of their mouths—a third of mankind was slain. 19 The deadly power of the horses was not only in their mouths but in their tails; for their tails were like snakes with heads poised to strike.

20 That part of mankind which escaped the plagues did not repent of the idols they had made. They did not give up the worship of demons, or of gods made from gold and silver, from bronze and stone and wood, which cannot see or hear or walk. 21 Neither did they repent of their murders or their sorcery, their fornication or their thefts.

Angel with the Scroll

10 Then I saw another mighty angel come down from heaven wrapped in a cloud, with a rainbow about his head; his face shone like the sun and his legs like pillars of fire. 2 In his hand he held a little scroll which had been opened. He placed his right foot on the sea and his left foot on the land, 3 and then gave a loud cry like the roar of a lion. When he cried out, the seven thunders raised their voices too. 4 I was about to start writing when the seven

---

8, 7: This woe resembles the seventh plague of Egypt (Ex 9, 23f); cf Jl 3, 3.

8, 8–11: The background of these two woes is the first plague of Egypt (Ex 7, 20f).

8, 11: *Wormwood:* a bitter plant symbolizing the punishment God inflicts on the ungodly; cf Jer 9, 12ff; 23, 15.

8, 13: *Woe, woe and again woe:* each of the three woes pronounced by the angel represents a separate disaster; cf 9, 12; 11, 14. The final woe, released by the seventh trumpet blast, includes the plagues of chapter 16.

9, 1: *A star:* an angel. *The abyss:* where Satan and the fallen angels are kept for a thousand years, to be cast afterward into the pool of fire (20, 7–10).

9, 2–6: This woe combines elements from the eighth and ninth plagues of Egypt (Ex 10, 12–15.21ff); cf Jl 1, 4—2, 10.

9, 11: *Abaddon:* destruction or ruin. *Apollyon:* destroyer.

9, 13–19: The sixth woe is a symbolic invasion by the Parthians living east of the Euphrates; see note on 6, 2. At the appointed time (v 15), the frightful horses act as God's agents of judgment. The imaginative

details are not to be taken literally; see Introduction and note on 6, 12ff.

9, 20: *The idols they had made:* literally, the works of their hands.

10, 1–11. 14: An interlude in two scenes (10, 1–11 and 11, 1–14) precedes the sounding of the seventh trumpet; cf 7, 1–17.

10, 3f: *The seven thunders:* God's voice announcing judgment and doom; cf Ps 29, 3–9.

thunders spoke, but I heard a voice from heaven say, "Seal up what the seven thunders have spoken and do not write it down!" 5 Then the angel whom I saw standing on the sea and on the land raised his right hand to heaven 6 and took an oath by the One who lives forever and ever, who created heaven and earth and sea along with everything in them: "There shall be no more delay. 7 When the time comes for the seventh angel to blow his trumpet, the mysterious plan of God, which he announced to his servants the prophets, shall be accomplished in full."

8 Then the voice which I heard from heaven spoke to me again and said, "Go, take the open scroll from the hand of the angel standing on the sea and on the land." 9 I went up to the angel and said to him, "Give me the little scroll." He said to me, "Here, take it and eat it! It will be sour in your stomach, but in your mouth it will taste as sweet as honey." 10 I took the little scroll from the angel's hand and ate it. In my mouth it tasted as sweet as honey, but when I swallowed it my stomach turned sour. 11 Then someone said to me, "You must prophesy again for many peoples and nations, languages and kings."

The Two Witnesses

11 Someone gave me a measuring rod and said: "Come and take the measurements of God's temple and altar, and count those who worship there. 2 Exclude the outer court of the temple, however; do not measure it, for it has been handed over to the Gentiles, who will crush the holy city for forty-two months.

3 I will commission my two witnesses to prophesy for those twelve hundred and sixty days, dressed in sackcloth."

4 These are the two olive trees and the two lampstands which stand in the presence of the Lord of the earth. 5 If anyone tries to harm them, fire will come out of the mouths of these witnesses to devour their enemies. Anyone attempting to harm them will surely be slain in this way. 6 These witnesses have power to close up the sky so that no rain will fall during the time of their mission. They also have power to turn water into blood and to afflict the earth at will with any kind of plague.

7 When they have finished giving their testimony, the wild beast that comes up from the abyss will wage war against them and conquer and kill them. 8 Their corpses will lie in the streets of the great city, which has the symbolic name "Sodom" or "Egypt," where also their Lord was crucified. 9 Men from every people and race, language and nation, stare at their corpses for three and a half days but refuse to bury them. 10 The earth's inhabitants gloat over them and in their merriment exchange gifts, because these two prophets harassed everyone on earth. 11 But after the three and a half days, the breath of life which comes from God returned to them. When they stood on their feet sheer terror gripped those who saw them. 12 The two prophets heard a loud voice from heaven say to them, "Come up here!" So they went up to heaven in a cloud as their enemies looked on. 13 At that moment there was a violent earthquake and a tenth of the city fell in ruins. Seven thousand

persons were killed during the earthquake; the rest were so terrified that they worshiped the God of heaven.

14 The second woe is past, but beware! The third is coming very soon.

The Seventh Trumpet

15 Then the seventh angel blew his trumpet. Loud voices in heaven cried out, "The kingdom of the world now belongs to our Lord and to his anointed One, and he shall reign forever and ever." 16 The twenty-four elders who were enthroned in God's presence fell down to worship God 17 and said:

"We praise you, the Lord God Almighty
  who is and who was.
You have assumed your great power,
  you have begun your reign.
18 The nations have raged in anger,
  but then came your day of wrath
  and the moment to judge the dead:
The time to reward your
  servants the prophets
  and the holy ones who revere you,
  the great and the small alike;
The time to destroy those who
  lay the earth waste."

19 Then God's temple in heaven opened and in the temple could be seen the ark of his covenant. There were flashes of lightning and peals of thunder, an earthquake, a violent hailstorm.

The Woman and the Dragon

12 A great sign appeared in the sky, a woman clothed with the

---

10, 6: *Heaven and earth and sea:* the three parts of the universe.

10, 7: *The mysterious plan of God:* the end of the present age, when the forces of evil will be put down (17, 1—19, 4.11–21; 20, 7–10; cf 2 Thes 2, 6–12; Rom 16, 25f) and the establishment of the reign of God, when all creation will be made anew (21, 1—22, 5).

10, 9f: The little scroll was sweet because it predicted the final victory of God's holy people; it was sour because it also announced the sufferings they are to endure; cf Ez 3, 1ff.

10, 11: This further prophecy is contained in chapters 12–22.

11, 1: The temple and altar symbolize the new Israel; see note on 7, 4–8. The worshipers represent Christians; cf Ez 40, 3—42, 20; 47, 1–12; Zec 2, 5f. The measuring of the temple suggests that God will preserve the faithful remnant who continue true to Christ (14, 1–5); cf Is 4, 2f.

11, 2: *The outer court:* The court of the Gentiles.

Crush . . . forty-two months: the duration of the vicious persecution of the Jews by Antiochus IV Epiphanes (Dn 7, 25; 12, 7). This persecution of three and a half years (1260 days: v 3; 12, 6) became the prototype of periods of trial for God's people; cf Lk 4, 25; Jas 5, 17. The reference here is to the persecution by the Romans; cf Introduction.

11, 3f: The two witnesses who are *dressed in sackcloth,* symbolizing lamentation and repentance, are perhaps the apostles Peter and Paul, who represent all Christian martyrs. *The two olive trees and the two lampstands:* the martyrs who stand *in the presence of the Lord.* The imagery is taken from Zec 4, 1–3.11–14, where the olive trees refer to Joshua and Zerubbabel.

11, 5f: These details are derived from stories of Moses, who turned *water into blood* (Ex 7, 17–20), and of Elijah, who called down fire from heaven (1 Kgs 18, 36–40; 2 Kgs 1, 10) and closed up the sky (1 Kgs 17, 1).

11, 7: *The wild beast . . . from the abyss:* the Roman emperor Nero, who symbolizes the forces of evil, or

the Antichrist (13, 1.8; 17, 8); cf Introduction; Dn 7, 2–8.11f.19–22.

11, 8: *"Sodom" or "Egypt":* symbols of immorality and oppression of God's people; cf Ex 1, 11–14; Is 1, 10. *Where also their Lord was crucified:* not the geographical, but the symbolic, Jerusalem which rejects God and his witnesses—Rome, called Babylon in chapters 16–19; see note on 17, 9 and Introduction.

11, 9–12: Over the martyrdom (v 7) of the two witnesses, now called prophets, the ungodly rejoice *for three and a half days,* a symbolic period of time; see note on v 2. Afterward they go in triumph to heaven, as did Elijah (2 Kgs 2, 11).

11, 15–19: The seventh trumpet proclaims the coming of God's reign; see note on 10, 7.

12, 1f.4–6: The woman adorned with the sun, the moon, and the stars symbolizes God's people in the Old and the New Testament; cf Gn 37, 9f. The Israel of old gave birth to the Messiah (v 5) and then became the new Israel, the church, which suffers persecution by the dragon (vv 6.13–17).

sun, with the moon under her feet, and on her head a crown of twelve stars. 2 Because she was with child, she wailed aloud in pain as she labored to give birth. 3 Then another sign appeared in the sky: it was a huge dragon, flaming red, with seven heads and ten horns; on his heads were seven diadems. 4 His tail swept a third of the stars from the sky and hurled them down to the earth. Then the dragon stood before the woman about to give birth, ready to devour her child when it should be born. 5 She gave birth to a son—a boy destined to shepherd all the nations with an iron rod. Her child was caught up to God and to his throne. 6 The woman herself fled into the desert, where a special place had been prepared for her by God; there she was taken care of for twelve hundred and sixty days.

7 Then war broke out in heaven; Michael and his angels battled against the dragon. Although the dragon and his angels fought back, 8 they were overpowered and lost their place in heaven. 9 The huge dragon, the ancient serpent known as the devil or Satan, the seducer of the whole world, was driven out; he was hurled down to earth and his minions with him.

10 Then I heard a loud voice in heaven say:

"Now have salvation and power
    come,
  the reign of our God and the
    authority of his Anointed
    One.
For the accuser of our brothers
    is cast out,
  who night and day accused
    them before our God.
11 They defeated him by the blood
    of the Lamb

and by the word of their
    testimony;
  love for life did not deter
    them from death.
12 So rejoice, you heavens,
    and you that dwell therein!
But woe to you, earth and sea,
    for the devil has come down
      upon you!
His fury knows no limits,
    for he knows his time is
      short."

13 When the dragon saw that he had been cast down to the earth, he pursued the woman who had given birth to the boy. 14 But the woman was given the wings of a gigantic eagle so that she could fly off to her place in the desert, where, far from the serpent, she could be taken care of for a year and for two and a half years more. 15 The serpent, however, spewed a torrent of water out of his mouth to search out the woman and sweep her away. 16 The earth then came to the woman's rescue by opening its mouth and swallowing the flood which the dragon spewed out of his mouth. 17 Enraged at her escape, the dragon went off to make war on the rest of her offspring, on those who keep God's commandments and give witness to Jesus. He took up his position by the shore of the sea.

The First Beast

13 Then I saw a wild beast come out of the sea with ten horns and seven heads; on its horns were ten diadems and on its heads blasphemous names. 2 The beast I saw was like a leopard, but it had paws like a bear and the mouth of a lion.

The dragon gave it his own power and throne, together with great authority. 3 I noticed that one of the beast's heads seemed to have been mortally wounded, but this mortal wound was healed. In wonderment, the whole world followed after the beast. 4 Men worshiped the dragon for giving his authority to the beast; they also worshiped the beast and said, "Who can compare with the beast, or come forward to fight against it?"

5 The beast was given a mouth for uttering proud boasts and blasphemies, but the authority it received was to last only forty-two months. 6 It began to hurl blasphemies against God, reviling him and the members of his heavenly household as well. 7 The beast was allowed to wage war against God's people and conquer them. It was likewise granted authority over every race and people, language and nation. 8 The beast will be worshiped by all those inhabitants of earth who did not have their names written at the world's beginning in the book of the living, which belongs to the Lamb who was slain.

9 Let him who has ears heed these words! 10 If one is destined for captivity, into captivity he goes! If one is destined to be slain by the sword, by the sword he will be slain! Such is the faithful endurance that distinguishes God's holy people.

The Second Beast

11 Then I saw another wild beast come up out of the earth; it had two horns like a ram and it spoke like a dragon. 12 It used the authority of the first beast to promote its interests by making the world and

---

12, 2: Because of Eve's sin, the woman gives birth in distress and pain (Gn 3, 16).

12, 3: *Huge dragon:* symbol of the forces of evil (v 9).

12, 5: *Shepherd . . . iron rod:* fulfilled in 19, 15; cf Ps 2, 9. *Was snatched up to God:* a reference to Christ's ascension.

12, 6: God protects the persecuted church; see note on 11, 2.

12, 7: *Michael:* the archangel, guardian and champion of Israel; cf Dn 10, 13.21; 12, 1; Jude 9.

12, 9: *The ancient serpent who seduced Eve* (Gn 3, 1–6), mother of mankind; cf 20, 2; Eph 6, 12.

12, 10: *The accuser:* the meaning of the Hebrew word "Satan," found in v 9; Jb 1—2; Zec 3, 1; and 1 Chr 21, 1.

12, 14: *Gigantic eagle:* symbol of the power and

swiftness of divine help; cf Ex 19, 4; Dt 32, 11; Is 40, 13.

12, 15: The serpent is depicted as the sea monster; cf 13, 1; Is 27, 1; Ez 32, 2; Ps 74, 13.

12, 17: Though the church is protected by God's special providence (v 16), the individual Christian is to expect persecution and suffering.

13, 1–8: This wild beast, combining features of the four beasts in Dn 7, 2–28, symbolizes the Roman empire; the seven heads represent the emperors; see notes on 17, 9f.12ff.

13, 2: Satan (12, 9), the prince of this world (Jn 12, 31), commissioned the beast to persecute the church (vv 5ff).

13, 3: This is perhaps a reference to the popular legend that Nero would come back to life and rule again after his death (which occurred in A.D. 68 from

a self-inflicted wound in the throat); cf v 14; 17, 8. Domitian (A.D. 81–96) embodied all the cruelty and impiety of Nero; cf Introduction.

13, 4: *Worshiped the dragon:* allusion to emperor worship, which Domitian insisted upon and ruthlessly enforced.

13, 5f: Domitian, like Antiochus IV (Dn 7, 8.11.25), demanded that he be called by divine titles such as "our lord and god" and "Jupiter"; see note on 11, 2.

13, 11–17: The second beast is described in terms of the false prophets; cf 16, 13; 19, 20; 20, 10; they accompany the false messiahs (the first beast) foretold by Jesus (Mt 24, 24; Mk 13, 22; 2 Thes 2, 9); cf Dt 13, 2ff. Christians had either to worship the emperor and his image or to suffer martyrdom.

all its inhabitants worship the first beast, whose mortal wound had been healed. 13 It performed great prodigies; it could even make fire come down from heaven to earth as men looked on. 14. Because of the prodigies it was allowed to perform by authority of the first beast, it led astray the earth's inhabitants, telling them to make an idol in honor of the beast that had been wounded by the sword and yet lived. 15 The second wild beast was then permitted to give life to the beast's image, so that the image had the power of speech and of putting to death anyone who refused to worship it. 16 It forced all men, small and great, rich and poor, slave and free, to accept a stamped image on their right hand or their forehead. Moreover, it did not allow a man to buy or sell anything 17 unless he was first marked with the name of the beast or with the number that stood for its name.

18 A certain wisdom is needed here; with a little ingenuity anyone can calculate the number of the beast, for it is a number that stands for a certain man. The man's number is six hundred sixty-six.

Companions of the Lamb

14 Then the Lamb appeared in my vision. He was standing on Mount Zion, and with him were the hundred and forty-four thousand who had his name and the name of his Father written on their foreheads. 2 I heard a sound from heaven which resembled the roaring of the deep, or loud peals of thunder; the sound I heard was like the melody of harpists playing on their harps. 3 They were singing a new hymn before the throne, in the presence of the four living creatures and the elders. This hymn no one could

learn except the hundred and forty-four thousand who had been ransomed from the world. 4 These are men who have never been defiled by immorality with women. They are pure and follow the Lamb wherever he goes. They have been ransomed as the first fruits of mankind for God and the Lamb. 5 On their lips no deceit has been found; they are indeed without flaw.

The Three Angels

6 Then I saw another angel flying in mid-heaven, the herald of everlasting good news to the whole world, to every nation and race, language and people. 7 He said in a loud voice: "Honor God and give him glory, for his time has come to sit in judgment. Worship the Creator of heaven and earth, the Creator of the sea and the springs."

8 A second angel followed and cried out:

"Fallen, fallen is Babylon the
great,
  which made all the nations
  drink
  the poisoned wine of her
  lewdness!"

9 A third angel followed the others and said in a loud voice: "If anyone worships the beast or its image, or accepts its mark on his forehead or hand, 10 he too will drink the wine of God's wrath, poured full strength into the cup of his anger. He will be tormented in burning sulphur before the holy angels and before the Lamb, and the smoke of their torment shall rise forever and ever. 11 There shall be no relief day or night for those who worship the beast or its image or accept the mark of its name." 12 This is what sustains the holy

ones, who keep the commandments of God and their faith in Jesus.

13 I heard a voice from heaven say to me: "Write this down: Happy now are the dead who die in the Lord!" The Spirit added, "Yes, they shall find rest from their labors, for their good works accompany them."

The Harvest of the Earth

14 Then, as I watched, a white cloud appeared, and on the cloud sat One like a Son of Man wearing a gold crown on his head and holding a sharp sickle in his hand. 15 Another angel came out of the temple and in a loud voice cried out to him who sat on the cloud, "Use your sickle and cut down the harvest, for now is the time to reap; the earth's harvest is fully ripe." 16 So the one sitting on the cloud wielded his sickle over all the earth and reaped the earth's harvest.

17 Then out of the temple in heaven came another angel, who likewise held a sharp sickle. 18 A second angel, who was in charge of the fire at the altar of incense, cried out in a loud voice to the one who held the sharp sickle, "Use your sharp sickle and gather the grapes from the vines of the earth, for the clusters are ripe." 19 So the angel wielded his sickle over the earth and gathered the grapes of the earth. He threw them into the huge winepress of God's wrath. 20 The winepress was trodden outside the city, and so much blood poured out of the winepress that for two hundred miles around, it reached as high as a horse's bridle.

The Seven Last Plagues

15 I saw in heaven another sign, great and awe-inspiring: seven angels holding the seven final plagues

---

13, 18: Each of the letters of the alphabet in Hebrew as well as in Greek has a numerical value. Many possible combinations of letters will add up to the total *six hundred sixty-six*, and many candidates have been nominated for this infamous number. The most likely, however, is the emperor Caesar Nero (see note on v 3), whose name in Hebrew letters gives the required sum. Nero personifies the emperors who viciously persecuted the church.

14, 1: *Mount Zion:* Jerusalem, the traditional place where the true remnant, the Israel of faith, is to be gathered together in the messianic reign of Christ; cf 2 Kgs 19, 30f; Mi 4, 6ff; Ob 17; Jl 3, 5; Zep 3, 12–20. *His name . . . foreheads:* in contrast to the pagans who were marked with the name or number of the beast (13, 17); cf note on 7, 4–8.

14, 4: *Pure:* literally, virgins, because they never indulged in any idolatrous practices, which are considered to be adultery and fornication (2, 14f.20ff; 17, 1–7; cf Ez 16, 1–58; ch 23).

14, 5: *No deceit:* because they did not deny Christ or do homage to the beast.

14, 6: *Everlasting good news:* that God's eternal reign is about to begin; see note on 10, 7.

14, 8: This verse anticipates the lengthy dirge over Babylon (Rome) in chapter 18.

14, 10f: *The wine of God's wrath:* image taken from Is 51, 17; Jer 25, 15f; 49, 12; 51, 7; Ez 23, 31–34. Eternal punishment in the fiery pool of burning sulphur is also reserved for the devil, the beast, and the false prophet (19, 20; 20, 10; 21, 8).

14, 12f: In addition to *faith in Jesus* John insists

upon the necessity and value of *good works*, as in 2, 23; 20, 12f; 22, 12; see note on 1, 3.

14, 14–20: The cutting down of the harvest as well as the gathering and treading of the grapes symbolize the doom of the ungodly which will come (19, 11–21); cf Jl 4, 12f; Is 63, 1–6.

14, 20: *Two hundred miles:* literally, 1600 stadia. The stadion, a Greek unit of measurement, was about 607 feet in length.

15, 1–4: A vision of the victorious martyrs precedes the vision of woe in 15, 5—16, 21; cf 7, 9–12.

which would bring God's wrath to a climax.

2 I then saw something like a sea of glass mingled with fire. On the sea of glass were standing those who had won the victory over the beast and its image, and also the number that signified its name. They were holding the harps used in worshiping God, 3 and they sang the song of Moses, the servant of God, and the song of the Lamb:

"Mighty and wonderful are
        your works,
    Lord God Almighty!
Righteous and true are your
        ways,
    O King of the nations!
4 Who would dare refuse you
        honor,
    or the glory due your name,
        O Lord?
Since you alone are holy,
    all nations shall come
    and worship in your presence.
Your mighty deeds are clearly
        seen."

5 After this I had another vision. The heavenly sanctuary which is the tent of witness opened up, 6 and out of it came the seven angels holding the seven plagues. The angels were dressed in pure white linen, each with a sash of gold about his breast. 7 One of the four living creatures gave to the seven angels seven golden bowls filled with the wrath of the God who lives forever and ever. 8 Then the sanctuary became so filled with the smoke which arose from God's glory and might that no one could enter it until the seven plagues of the seven angels had come to an end.

The Seven Bowls

16 I heard a mighty voice from the sanctuary say to the seven angels, "Go and pour out upon the earth the seven bowls of God's wrath!"

2 The first angel went out, and when he poured out his bowl on the earth, severe and festering boils broke out on the men who had accepted the mark of the beast or worshiped its image.

3 The second angel poured out his bowl on the sea. The sea turned to blood like that of a corpse, and every creature living in the sea died.

4 The third angel poured out his bowl on the rivers and springs. These also turned to blood. 5 Then I heard the angel in charge of the waters cry out:

"You are just, O holy One
    who is and who was,
    in passing this sentence!
6 To those who shed the blood of
        saints and prophets,
    you have given blood to
        drink;
    they deserve it."

7 Then I heard the altar cry out:

"Yes, Lord God Almighty,
    your judgments are true and
        just!"

8 The fourth angel poured out his bowl on the sun. He was commissioned to burn men with fire. 9 Those who were scorched by the intense heat blasphemed the name of God who had power to send these plagues, but they did not repent or give him due honor.

10 The fifth angel poured out his bowl on the throne of the beast. Its kingdom was plunged into darkness; men bit their tongues in pain 11 and blasphemed the God of heaven because of their suffering and their boils. But they did not turn away from their wicked deeds.

12 The sixth angel poured out his bowl on the great river Euphrates. Its water was dried up to prepare the way for the kings of the East. 13 I saw three unclean spirits like frogs come from the mouth of the dragon, from the mouth of the beast, and from the mouth of the false prophet; 14 these spirits were devils who worked prodigies. They went out to assemble all the kings of the earth for battle on the great day of God the Almighty. 15 (Be on your guard! I come like a thief. Happy the man who stays wide awake and fully clothed for fear of going naked and exposed for all to see!) 16 The devils then assembled the kings in a place called in Hebrew "Armageddon."

17 Finally, the seventh angel poured out his bowl upon the empty air. From the throne in the sanctuary came a loud voice which said, "It is finished!" 18 There followed lightning flashes and peals of thunder, then a violent earthquake. Such was its violence that there has never been one like it in all the time men have lived on the earth. 19 The great city was split into three parts, and the other Gentile cities also fell. God remembered Babylon the great, giving her the cup filled with the blazing wine of his wrath. 20 Every island fled and mountains disappeared. 21 Giant hailstones like huge weights came crashing down on mankind from the sky, and men blasphemed God for the plague of hailstones, because this plague was so severe.

PUNISHMENT OF BABYLON

Babylon the Great

17 Then one of the seven angels who were holding the seven bowls came to me and said: "Come, I will show you the judgment in store for the great harlot who sits by the waters of the deep. 2 The kings of the earth have committed fornication with her, and the earth's inhabitants

---

15, 3: *The song of Moses:* which Moses and the Israelites sang after their escape from the oppression of Egypt (Ex 15, 1–19). The martyrs have escaped from the oppression of the devil.

15, 5: *The tent of witness:* the name of the meeting tent in the Greek text of Ex 40.

16, 1–21: These seven bowls, like the seven seals (6, 1–17; 8, 1) and the seven trumpets (8, 2—9, 21; 11, 15–19), bring on a succession of disasters modeled in part on the plagues of Egypt (Ex 7—12); see note on 6, 12ff.

16, 2: Like the sixth Egyptian plague (Ex 9, 8–11).

16, 3f: *Like the first Egyptian plague* (Ex 7, 20f). The same woe followed the blowing of the second trumpet (8, 8f).

16, 10: *The throne of the beast:* symbol of the forces of evil. *Darkness:* like the ninth Egyptian plague (Ex 10, 21ff); cf 9, 2.

16, 12: *The kings of the East:* Parthians; see notes on 6, 2 and 17, 12ff.

16, 15: *Like a thief:* as in 3, 3; cf Mt 24, 42ff; 1 Thes 5, 2. *Happy:* see note on 1, 3. *Fully clothed:* see note on 3, 18.

16, 16: *Armageddon:* "Mountain of Megiddo."

Since Megiddo was the scene of many decisive battles in antiquity (Jgs 5, 19f; 2 Kgs 9, 27; 2 Chr 35, 20–24), the town became the symbol of the final disastrous rout of the forces of evil; see note on v 19.

16, 19: *The great city:* Rome and the empire.

16, 20f: See note on 6, 12ff. *Hailstones:* as in the seventh Egyptian plague (Ex 9, 23f); cf 8, 7.

17, 1–6: Babylon, *a symbolic name* (v 5) of Rome, is graphically described as *the great harlot.*

17, 2: *Fornication . . . lewdness:* see note on 14, 4. The pagan kings subject to Rome adopted the cult of the emperor.

have grown drunk on the wine of her lewdness." 3 The angel then carried me away in spirit to a desolate place where I saw a woman seated on a scarlet beast which was covered with blasphemous names. This beast had seven heads and ten horns. 4 The woman was dressed in purple and scarlet and adorned with gold and pearls and other jewels. In her hand she held a gold cup that was filled with the abominable and sordid deeds of her lewdness. 5 On her forehead was written a symbolic name, "Babylon the great, mother of harlots and all the world's abominations." 6 I saw that the woman was drunk with the blood of God's holy ones and the blood of those martyred for their faith in Jesus.

The Meaning of Beast and Harlot

When I saw her I was greatly astonished. 7 The angel said to me: "Why are you so taken aback? I will explain to you the symbolism of the woman and of the seven-headed and ten-horned beast carrying her. 8 The beast you saw existed once but now exists no longer. It will come up from the abyss once more before going to final ruin. All the men of the earth whose names have not been written in the book of the living from the creation of the world shall be amazed when they see the beast, for it existed once and now exists no longer, and yet it will exist again. 9 Here is the clue for one who possesses wisdom! The seven heads are seven hills on which the woman sits enthroned. They are also seven kings: 10 five have already fallen, one lives now, and the last has not yet come; but when he does come he will remain only a short while. 11 The beast which existed once but now exists no longer, even though it is an eighth king, is really one of the seven and is on its way to ruin. 12 The ten horns you saw represent ten kings who have not yet been

crowned; they will possess royal authority along with the beast, but only for an hour. 13 Then they will come to agreement and bestow their power and authority on the beast. 14 They will fight against the Lamb but the Lamb will conquer them, for he is the Lord of lords and the King of kings; victorious, too, will be his followers—the ones who were called: the chosen and the faithful."

15 The angel then said to me: "The waters on which you saw the harlot enthroned are large numbers of peoples and nations and tongues. 16 The ten horns you saw on the beast will turn against the harlot with hatred; they will strip off her finery and leave her naked; they will devour her flesh and set her on fire. 17 For God has put it into their minds to carry out his plan, by making them agree to bestow their sovereignty on the beast until his will is accomplished. 18 The woman you saw is the great city which has sovereignty over the kings of the earth."

The Fall of Babylon

18 After this I saw another angel coming down from heaven. His authority was so great that all the earth was lighted up by his glory. 2 He cried out in a strong voice:

"Fallen, fallen is Babylon the
    great!
She has become a dwelling
    place for demons.
She is a cage for every unclean
    spirit,
a cage for every filthy and
    disgusting bird;
3 For she has made all the
    nations drink
the poisoned wine of her
    lewdness.
The kings of the earth
    committed fornication with
    her,

and the world's merchants
    grew rich from her
    wealth and wantonness."

4 Then I heard another voice from heaven say:

"Depart from her, my people,
    for fear of sinning with her
    and sharing the plagues
    inflicted on her!
5 For her sins have piled up as
    high as heaven,
    and God keeps count of her
    crimes.
6 Pay her back as she has paid
    others;
    pay her double for her deeds!
Pour into her cup twice the
    amount she concocted!
7   In proportion to her boasting
        and sensuality,
    repay her in torment and
        grief!
For she said to herself,
    'I sit enthroned as a queen.
No widow am I,
    and never will I go into
        mourning!'
8 Therefore her plagues will come
        all at once,
    death and mourning and
        famine.
She shall be consumed by fire,
    for mighty is the Lord God
        who condemns her."

9 The kings of the earth who committed fornication with her and wallowed in her sensuality will weep and lament over her when they see the smoke arise as she burns. 10 They will keep their distance for fear of the punishment inflicted on her, and will say:

"Alas, alas, great city that you
        are,
    Babylon the mighty!
In a single hour your doom
        has come!"

11 The merchants of the world will weep and mourn over her too,

---

17, 3: *Scarlet beast:* see note on 13, 1–8. *Blasphemous names:* divine titles assumed by the Roman emperors; see note on 13, 5f.
17, 4: Reference to the great wealth of Rome.
17, 8: Allusion to the belief that the dead Nero would return to power (v 11); see note on 13, 3.
17, 9: *Seven hills:* of Rome.
17, 10: There is little agreement as to the identity of the Roman emperors alluded to here. The number *seven* (v 9) suggests that all the emperors are meant; see note on 1, 4.

17, 11: *The beast:* Nero; see note on v 8.
17, 12ff: *Ten kings . . . not yet . . . crowned:* perhaps Parthian satraps who are to accompany the revived Nero (*the beast*) in his march on Rome to regain power; see note on 13, 3. In 19, 11ff, *the Lamb* and *his followers* will conquer them.
17, 16ff: The ten pagan kings (v 12) unwittingly fulfill God's will against *the harlot* Rome, *the great city;* cf Ez 16, 37.
18, 1—19, 4: A stirring dirge over the fall of Babylon-Rome. The perspective is prophetic—as if

the fall of Rome had already taken place. The imagery here, as elsewhere in this book, is not to be taken literally. The vindictiveness of some of the language is meant to portray symbolically the inexorable demands of God's holiness and justice.
18, 3.24: Rome is condemned for *her lewdness,* symbol of idolatry (see note on 14, 4), and for persecuting the church; cf 19, 2.
18, 11: Ironically, the merchants weep not for Babylon-Rome, but for their lost markets; cf Ez 27, 36.

for there will be no more market for their imports— 12 their cargoes of gold and silver, precious stones and pearls; fine linen and purple garments, silk and scarlet cloth; fragrant wood of every kind, all sorts of ivory pieces and expensive wooden furniture; bronze, iron and marble; 13 cinnamon and amomum, perfumes, myrrh and frankincense; wine and olive oil, fine flour and grain; cattle and sheep, horses and carriages; slaves and human lives.

14 "The fruit your appetite craved
    has deserted you.
  All your luxury and splendor are
    gone;
      you shall never find them
        again!"

15 The merchants who deal in these goods, who grew rich from business with the city, will keep their distance for fear of the punishment inflicted on her. Weeping and mourning, 16 they cry out:

"Alas, alas, the great city,
    dressed in fine linen
    and purple and scarlet,
  Adorned all in gold
    and jewels and pearls!
17 In a single hour
    this great wealth has been
      destroyed!"

Every captain and navigator, all sailors and seafaring men, then stood at a distance 18 and cried out when they saw the smoke go up as the city burned to the ground: "What city could have compared with this great one!" 19 They poured dust on their heads and cried out, weeping and mourning:

"Alas, alas, the great city,
    in which all shipowners grew
      rich
  from their profitable trade
    with her!
  In a single hour
    her destruction has come
      about!"

20 Rejoice over her, you heavens, you saints, apostles and prophets!

For God has exacted punishment from her on your account.

21 A powerful angel picked up a stone like a huge millstone and hurled it into the sea and said:

"Babylon the great city
    shall be cast down like this,
      with violence,
  and nevermore be found!
22 No tunes of harpists and
      minstrels,
  of flutists and trumpeters,
    shall ever again be heard in
      you!
  No craftsmen in any trade
    shall ever again be found in
      you!
  No sound of the millstone
    shall ever again be heard in
      you!
23 No light from a burning lamp
    shall ever again shine out in
      you!
  No voices of bride and groom
    shall ever again be heard in
      you!
  Because your merchants were
    the world's nobility,
  you led all nations astray by
    your sorcery.

24 "In her was found the blood of prophets and saints and of all who were slain on the earth."

19 After this I heard what sounded like the loud song of a great assembly in heaven. They were singing:

"Alleluia!
  Salvation, glory and might
    belong to our God,
2   for his judgments are true
      and just!
  He has condemned the great
      harlot
  who corrupted the earth with
    her harlotry.
  He has avenged the blood of his
      servants
  which was shed by her hand."

3 Once more they sang "Alleluia!" And as the smoke began to rise from

her forever and ever, the four and twenty elders and the four living creatures fell down and worshiped God seated on the throne and sang, "Amen! Alleluia!"

Song of Victory

5 A voice coming from the throne cried out:

"Praise our God, all you his
      servants,
  the small and the great, who
    revere him!"

6 Then I heard what sounded like the shouts of a great crowd, or the roaring of the deep, or mighty peals of thunder, as they cried:

"Alleluia!
  The Lord is king,
    our God, the Almighty!
7 Let us rejoice and be glad,
    and give him glory!
  For this is the wedding day of
    the Lamb,
  his bride has prepared herself
    for the wedding.
8 She has been given a dress to
      wear
  made of finest linen, brilliant
    white."

(The linen dress is the virtuous deeds of God's saints.)

9 The angel then said to me: "Write this down: Happy are they who have been invited to the wedding feast of the Lamb." The angel continued, "These words are true; they come from God." 10 I fell at his feet to worship him, but he said to me, "No, get up! I am merely a fellow servant with you and your brothers who give witness to Jesus. Worship God alone. The prophetic spirit proves itself by witnessing to Jesus."

DESTRUCTION OF PAGAN NATIONS

The King of Kings

11 The heavens were opened, and as I looked on, a white horse appeared; its rider was called "The

---

19, 7: *The wedding day of the Lamb:* symbol of God's reign about to begin (21, 1–22, 5); see note on 10, 7. *His bride:* the church (2 Cor 11, 2; Eph 5, 22–27). Marriage is one of the biblical metaphors used to describe the covenant relationship between God and his people (Hos 2, 16–22; Is 54, 5f; 62, 5; Ez 16, 6–

14). Hence, idolatry and apostasy are viewed as adultery and prostitution (Hos 2, 4–15; Ez 16, 15–63); see note on 14, 4.
19, 8: See note on 14, 12f.
19, 9: *Happy:* see note on 1, 3.
19, 10: *The prophetic spirit . . . Jesus:* As the

prophets were inspired to proclaim God's word, so the Christian is called to give witness to the Word of God (v 13) made flesh; cf 1, 2; 6, 9; 12, 17.
19, 11–16: Symbolic description of the exalted Christ (1, 13–16), who, together with the armies of heaven, overcomes the beast and its followers (17, 14).

Faithful and True." Justice is his standard in passing judgment and in waging war. 12 His eyes blazed like fire, and on his head were many diadems. Inscribed on his person was a name known to no one but himself. 13 He wore a cloak that had been dipped in blood, and his name was the Word of God. 14 The armies of heaven were behind him riding white horses and dressed in fine linen, pure and white. 15 Out of his mouth came a sharp sword for striking down the nations. He will shepherd them with an iron rod; it is he who will tread out in the winepress the blazing wrath of God the Almighty. 16 A name was written on the part of the cloak that covered his thigh: "King of kings and Lord of lords."

17 Next I saw an angel standing on the sun. He cried out in a loud voice to all the birds flying in midheaven: "Come! Gather together for the great feast God has prepared for you! 18 You are to eat the flesh of kings, of commanders and warriors, of horses and their riders; the flesh of all men, the free and the slave, the small and the great." 19 Then I saw the beast and the kings of the earth, and the armies they had mustered to do battle with the One riding the horse, and with his army. 20 The beast was captured along with the false prophet who performed in its presence the prodigies that led men astray, making them accept the mark of the beast and worship its image. Both were hurled down alive into the fiery pool of burning sulphur. 21 The rest were slain by the sword which came out of the mouth of the One who rode the horse, and all the birds gorged themselves on the flesh of the slain.

Thousand-Year Reign

20 Then I saw an angel come down from heaven, holding the key to the abyss and a huge chain in his hand. 2 He seized the dragon, the ancient serpent, who is the devil or Satan, and chained him up for a thousand years. 3 The angel hurled him into the abyss, which he closed and sealed over him. He did this so that the dragon might not lead the nations astray until the thousand years are over. After this, the dragon is to be released for a short time.

4 Then I saw some thrones. Those who were sitting on them were empowered to pass judgment. I also saw the spirits of those who had been beheaded for their witness to Jesus and the word of God, those who had never worshiped the beast or its image nor accepted its mark on their foreheads or their hands. They came to life again and reigned with Christ for a thousand years. 5 The others who were dead did not come to life till the thousand years were over. This is the first resurrection; 6 happy and holy are they who share in the first resurrection! The second death will have no claim on them; they shall serve God and Christ as priests, and shall reign with him for a thousand years.

7 When the thousand years are over, Satan will be released from his prison. 8 He will go out to seduce the nations in all four corners of the earth, and muster for war the troops of Gog and Magog, numerous as the sands of the sea. 9 They invaded the whole country and surrounded the beloved city where God's people were encamped; but fire came down from heaven and devoured them. 10 The devil who led them astray

was hurled into the pool of burning sulphur, where the beast and the false prophet had also been thrown. There they will be tortured day and night, forever and ever.

The Last Judgment

11 Next I saw a large white throne and the One who sat on it. The earth and the sky fled from his presence until they could no longer be seen. 12 I saw the dead, the great and the lowly, standing before the throne. Lastly, among the scrolls, the book of the living was opened. The dead were judged according to their conduct as recorded on the scrolls. 13 The sea gave up its dead; then death and the nether world gave up their dead. Each person was judged according to his conduct. 14 Then death and the nether world were hurled into the pool of fire, which is the second death; 15 anyone whose name was not found inscribed in the book of the living was hurled into this pool of fire.

NEW CREATION

New Heavens and New Earth

21 Then I saw new heavens and a new earth. The former heavens and the former earth had passed away, and the sea was no longer. 2 I also saw a new Jerusalem, the holy city, coming down out of heaven from God, beautiful as a bride prepared to meet her husband. 3 I heard a loud voice from the throne cry out: "This is God's dwelling among men. He shall dwell with them and they shall be his people and he shall be their God who is always with them. 4 He shall wipe every tear from their eyes, and

---

19, 12: *A name . . . no one but himself:* in Semitic thought, the name conveyed the reality of the person; cf Mt 11, 27; Lk 10, 22.

19, 13: *Had been dipped in:* other ancient MSS read "had been sprinkled with"; cf v 15. *The Word of God:* Christ is the revelation of the Father (Jn 1, 1.14; 1 Jn 2, 14).

19, 15: The treading of *the winepress* is a prophetic symbol used to describe the destruction of God's enemies (Is 63, 1–6; Jl 4, 13).

19, 17f.21: Gruesome imagery borrowed from Ez 39, 4.17–20.

19, 20: *Beast . . . false prophet:* see notes on chapter 13. *The fiery pool . . . sulphur:* symbol of hell (14, 10; 20, 10.14f), different from the abyss; see note on 9, 1.

20, 1–6: Like the other numerical values in this book, *the thousand years* are not to be taken literally;

they symbolize the long period of time between the chaining up of Satan (a symbol for Christ's resurrection-victory over death and the forces of evil) and the end of the world. During this time God's people share in the glorious reign of God which is present to them in virtue of their baptism-victory over death and sin (Rom 6, 1–8; Jn 5, 24f; 16, 33; 1 Jn 3, 14; Eph 2, 1).

20, 1: *Abyss:* see note on 9. 1.

20, 2: *Dragon . . . serpent . . . Satan:* see notes on 12, 3.9f.15.

20, 4: *Beast . . . mark:* see chapter 13 and its notes.

20, 6: *Happy:* see note on 1, 3. *Second death:* see note on 2, 11. *Priests:* as in 1, 6; 5, 10; 22, 3; cf 1 Pt 2, 9.

20, 7–10: A description of the symbolic battle to take place when Satan is released at the end of time, *when the thousand years are over;* see note on vv 1–6.

20, 8: *Gog and Magog:* symbols of all pagan nations; the names are taken from Ez 38, 1—39, 20.

20, 9: *The whole country:* Palestine. *The beloved city:* Jerusalem; see note on 14, 1.

20, 12: *The book of the living:* see note on 3, 4f. *Judged . . . scrolls:* see note on 14, 12f.

20, 13: *The nether world:* see note on 1, 18.

20, 14: *Second death:* see note on 2, 11.

21, 1—22, 5: A description of God's eternal kingdom in heaven under the symbols of new heavens and a new earth (Is 65, 17–25; 66, 22).

21, 2: *New Jerusalem . . . bride:* symbol of the church (Gal 4, 26); see note on 19, 7.

21, 3f: Language taken from Ez 37, 27; Is 8, 8; 25, 8; 35, 10; cf 7, 17.

there shall be no more death or mourning, crying out or pain, for the former world has passed away."

5 The One who sat on the throne said to me, "See, I make all things new!" Then he said, "Write these matters down, for the words are trustworthy and true!" 6 He went on to say: "These words are already fulfilled! I am the Alpha and the Omega, the Beginning and the End. To anyone who thirsts I will give to drink without cost from the spring of life-giving water. 7 He who wins the victory shall inherit these gifts; I will be his God and he shall be my son. 8 As for the cowards and traitors to the faith, the depraved and murderers, the fornicators and sorcerers, the idol-worshipers and deceivers of every sort—their lot is the fiery pool of burning sulphur, the second death!"

The New Jerusalem

9 One of the seven angels who held the seven bowls filled with the seven last plagues came and said to me, "Come, I will show you the woman who is the bride of the Lamb." 10 He carried me away in spirit to the top of a very high mountain and showed me the holy city Jerusalem coming down out of heaven from God. 11 It gleamed with the splendor of God. The city had the radiance of a precious jewel that sparkled like a diamond. 12 Its wall, massive and high, had twelve gates at which twelve angels were stationed. Twelve names were written on the gates, the names of the twelve tribes of Israel. 13 There were three gates facing east, three north, three south, and three west. 14 The wall of the city had twelve courses of stones as its foundation, on which were written the names of the twelve apostles of the Lamb.

15 The one who spoke to me held a rod of gold for measuring the city, its gates, and its wall. 16 The city is perfectly square, its length and its width being the same. He measured the city with a rod and found it twelve thousand furlongs in length, in width, and in height. 17 Its wall measured a hundred and forty-four cubits in height by the unit of measurement the angel used. 18 The wall was constructed of jasper; the city was of pure gold, crystal-clear. 19 The foundation of the city wall was ornate with precious stones of every sort: the first course of stones was jasper, the second sapphire, the third chalcedony, the fourth emerald, 20 the fifth sardonyx, the sixth carnelian, the seventh chrysolite, the eighth beryl, the ninth topaz, the tenth chrysoprase, the eleventh hyacinth, and the twelfth amethyst. 21 The twelve gates were twelve pearls, each made of a single pearl; and the streets of the city were of pure gold, transparent as glass.

I saw no temple in the city. 22 The Lord, God the Almighty, is its temple—he and the Lamb. 23 The city had no need of sun or moon, for the glory of God gave it light, and its lamp was the Lamb. 24 The nations shall walk by its light; to it the kings of the earth shall bring their treasures. 25 During the day its gates shall never be shut, and there shall be no night. 26 The treasures and wealth of the nations shall be brought there, 27 but nothing profane shall enter it, nor anyone who is a liar or has done a detestable act. Only those shall enter whose names are inscribed in the book of the living kept by the Lamb.

22 The angel then showed me the river of life-giving water, clear as crystal, which issued from the throne of God and of the Lamb 2 and flowed down the middle of the streets. On either side of the river grew the trees of life which produce fruit twelve times a year, once each month; their leaves serve as medicine for the nations. 3 Nothing deserving a curse shall be found there. The throne of God and of the Lamb shall be there, and his servants shall serve him faithfully. 4 They shall see him face to face and bear his name on their foreheads. 5 The night shall be no more. They will need no light from lamps or the sun, for the Lord God shall give them light, and they shall reign forever.

EPILOGUE

6 The angel said to me: "These words are trustworthy and true; the Lord, the God of prophetic spirits, has sent his angel to show his servants what must happen very soon."

7 "Remember, I am coming soon! Happy the man who heeds the prophetic message of this book!"

8 It is I, John, who heard and saw all these things, and when I heard and saw them I fell down to worship at the feet of the angel who showed them to me. 9 But he said to me: "No, get up! I am merely a fellow servant with you and your brothers the prophets and those who heed the message of this book. Worship God alone!"

10 Then someone said to me: "Do not seal up the prophetic words of this book, for the appointed time is near! 11 Let the wicked continue in their wicked ways, the depraved in their depravity! The virtuous

---

21, 5: *The One . . . on the throne:* God himself; cf 4, 1–11.

21, 6: *These words . . . fulfilled:* God's reign has already begun; see note on 20, 1–6. *Alpha and . . . Omega:* see note on 1, 8. *Life-giving water:* see note on 7, 17.

21, 7: *The victory:* over the forces of evil; see the conclusions of the seven letters (2, 7.11.17.26; 3, 5.12.21). *He shall be my son:* the victorious Christian enjoys divine sonship by adoption (Gal 4, 4–7; Rom 8, 14–17); see note on 2, 26ff.

21, 8: *Cowards:* their conviction is so weak that they deny Christ in time of trial and become *traitors. Second death:* see note on 2, 11.

21, 9–22, 5: Symbolic description of the new Jerusalem, the church. Most of the images are

borrowed from Ez 40–48.

21, 9: *The woman . . . bride of the Lamb:* the church (v 2), the new Jerusalem (v 10).

21, 14: *Courses of stones . . . apostles:* cf Eph 2, 19f.

21, 15ff: The city is shaped like a gigantic cube, a symbol of perfection (cf 1 Kgs 6, 19f). The measurements of the city and its wall are multiples of the symbolic number twelve; see note on 7, 4–8. *Twelve thousand furlongs:* literally, 12,000 stades, about 1500 miles; see note on 14, 20. The cubit was about 18 inches.

21, 18–21: The gold and precious gems symbolize the beauty and excellence of the church; cf Ex 28, 15–21; Is 54, 11f; Tb 13, 16f.

21, 22: Christ is present throughout the church;

hence, no temple is needed as an earthly dwelling for God; cf Mt 18, 20; 28, 20; Jn 4, 21.

21, 23: *Lamp . . . Lamb:* cf Jn 8, 12.

21, 24–27: All men of good will are welcome in the church; cf Is 60, 1.3.5.11. *The book of the living:* see note on 3, 4f.

22, 1.17: *Life-giving water:* see note on 7, 17.

22, 2: *The tree of life:* cf v 14; see note on 2, 7. *Fruit . . . medicine:* cf Ez 47, 12.

22, 4: *See him face to face:* cf Mt 5, 8; 1 Cor 13, 12; 1 Jn 3, 2.

22, 7.12.20: *I am coming soon:* Christ is the speaker; see note on 1, 3.

22, 7.14: *Happy:* see note on 1, 3.

22, 10: *The appointed time:* see note on 1, 3.

must live on in their virtue and the holy ones in their holiness!

12 "Remember, I am coming soon! I bring with me the reward that will be given to each man as his conduct deserves. 13 I am the Alpha and the Omega, the First and the Last, the Beginning and the End! 14 Happy are they who wash their robes so as to have free access to the tree of life and enter the city through its gates! 15 Outside are the dogs and sorcerers, the fornicators and murderers, the idol-worshipers and all who love falsehood.

16 "It is I, Jesus, who have sent my angel to give you this testimony about the churches. I am the Root and Offspring of David, the Morning Star shining bright."

17 The Spirit and the Bride say, "Come!" Let him who hears answer, "Come!" Let him who is thirsty come forward; let all who desire it accept the gift of life-giving water.

18 I myself give witness to all who hear the prophetic words of this book. If anyone adds to these words, God will visit him with all the plagues described herein! 19 If anyone takes from the words of this prophetic book, God will take away his share in the tree of life and the holy city described here!

20 The One who gives this testimony says, "Yes, I am coming soon!" Amen! Come, Lord Jesus!

21 The grace of the Lord Jesus be with you all. Amen!

22, 13: Christ applies to himself the words used by God in 1, 8.

22, 14: *The city:* heavenly Jerusalem; see note on 21, 2.

22, 16: *The Root . . . of David:* see note on 5, 5. *Morning star:* see note on 2, 26ff

22, 17: *Bride:* the church; see note on 21, 2.

22, 20: *Come, Lord Jesus:* a liturgical refrain, similar to the Aramaic expression *Marana tha*, "Our Lord, come!" in 1 Cor 16, 22. It was a prayer for the coming of Christ in glory at the parousia; see note on 1, 3.

CONSTITUTION ON DIVINE REVELATION

Preface

1. Hearing the word of God with reverence and proclaiming it with faith, the sacred synod takes its direction from these words of St. John: "We proclaim to you the eternal life that was present to the Father and became visible to us. What we have seen and heard we proclaim in turn to you so that you may share life with us. This fellowship of ours is with the Father and with his Son, Jesus Christ" (I John 1:2-3). Therefore, following in the footsteps of the Council of Trent and of the First Vatican Council, this present council wishes to set forth authentic doctrine on divine revelation and how it is handed on, so that by hearing the message of salvation the whole world may believe, by believing it may hope, and by hoping it may love.

REVELATION ITSELF

2. In His goodness and wisdom God chose to reveal Himself and to make known to us the hidden purpose of His will (see Eph. 1:9) by which through Christ, the Word made flesh, man might in the Holy Spirit have access to the Father and come to share in the divine nature (see Eph. 2:18, 2 Peter 1:4). Through this revelation, therefore, the invisible God (see Col. 1:15; 1 Tim. 1:17) out of the abundance of His love speaks to men as friends (see Ex. 33:11; John 15:14-15) and lives among them (see Bar. 3:38), so that He may invite and take them into fellowship with Himself. This plan of revelation is realized by deeds and words having an inner unity: the deeds wrought by God in the history of salvation manifest and confirm the teaching and realities signified by the words, while the words proclaim the deeds and clarify the mystery contained in them. By this revelation then, the deepest truth about God and the salvation of man shines out for our sake in Christ, who is both the mediator and the fulness of all revelation.

3. God, who through the Word creates all things (see John, 1:3) and keeps them in existence, gives men an enduring witness to Himself in created realities (see Rom. 1:19-20). Planning to make known the way of heavenly salvation, He went further and from the start manifested Himself to our first parents. Then after their fall His promise of redemption aroused in them the hope of being saved (see Gen. 3:15) and from that time on He ceaselessly kept the human race in His care, to give eternal life to those who perseveringly do good in search of salvation (see Rom. 2:6-7). Then, at the time He had appointed He called Abraham in order to make of him a great nation (see Gen. 12:2). Through the patriarchs, and after them through Moses and the prophets, He taught this people to acknowledge Himself the one living and true God, provident father and just judge, and to wait for the Savior promised by Him, and in this manner prepared the way for the Gospel down through the centuries.

4. Then, after speaking in many and varied ways through the prophets, "in this, the final age, he has spoken to us through his Son" (Heb. 1:2). For he sent His Son, the eternal Word, who enlightens all men, so that He might dwell among men and tell them of the innermost being of God (see John 1:1-18). Jesus Christ, therefore, the Word made flesh, was sent as "a man to men." He "speaks the words of God" (John 3:34), and completes the work of salvation which His Father gave Him to do (see John 5:36, 17:4). To see Jesus is to see His Father (John 14:9). For this reason Jesus perfected revelation by fulfilling it through His whole work of making Himself present and manifesting Himself: through His words and deeds, His signs and wonders, but especially through His death and glorious resurrection from the dead and final sending of the Spirit of truth. Moreover He confirmed with divine testimony what revelation proclaimed, that God is with us to free us from the darkness of sin and death, and to raise us up to life eternal.

The Christian dispensation, therefore, as the new and definitive covenant, will never pass away and we now await no further new public revelation before the glorious manifestation of our Lord Jesus Christ (see I Tim. 6:14 and Titus 2:13).

5. "The obedience of faith" (Rom. 16:26; see 1:5; 2 Cor. 10:5-6) is to be given to God who reveals, an obedience by which man commits his whole self freely to God, offering "full submission of intellect and will to God who reveals," and freely assenting to the truth revealed by Him. To make this act of faith, the grace of God and the interior help of the Holy Spirit must precede and assist, moving the heart and turning it to God, opening the eyes of the mind and giving "joy and ease to everyone in assenting to the truth and believing it." To bring about an ever deeper understanding of revelation the same Holy Spirit constantly brings faith to completion by His gifts.

6. Through divine revelation, God chose to show forth and communicate Himself and the eternal decisions of His will regarding the salvation of men. That is to say, He chose to share with them those divine treasures which totally transcend the understanding of the human mind.

This sacred synod has affirmed, God, the beginning and end of all things, can be known with certainty from created reality by the light of human reason (see Rom. 1:20); but teaches that it is through His revelation that those religious truths which are by their nature accessible to human reason can be known by all men with ease, with solid certitude and with no trace of error, even in this present state of the human race.

HANDING ON DIVINE REVELATION

7. In His gracious goodness, God has seen to it that what He had revealed for the salvation of all nations would abide perpetually in its full integrity and be handed on to all generations. Therefore Christ the Lord in whom the full revelation of the supreme God is brought to completion (see II Cor. 1:20; 3:13; 4:6), commissioned the Apostles to preach to all men that Gospel which is the source of all saving truth and moral teaching, and to impart to them heavenly gifts. This Gospel had been promised in former times through the prophets, and Christ Himself had fulfilled it and promulgated it with His lips. This commission was faithfully fulfilled by the Apostles who, by their oral preaching, by example, and by observances handed on what they had received from the lips of Christ, from living with Him, and from what He did, or what they had learned through the prompting of the Holy Spirit. The commission was fulfilled, too, by those Apostles and apostolic men who under the inspiration of the same Holy Spirit committed the

message of salvation to writing.

But in order to keep the Gospel forever whole and alive within the Church, the Apostles left bishops as their successors, "handing over" to them "the authority to teach in their own place." This sacred tradition, therefore, and Sacred Scripture of both the Old and New Testaments are like a mirror in which the pilgrim Church on earth looks at God, from whom she has received everything, until she is brought finally to see Him as He is, face to face (see I John 3:2).

8. And so the apostolic preaching, which is expressed in a special way in the inspired books, was to be preserved by an unending succession of preachers until the end of time. Therefore the Apostles, handing on what they themselves had received, warn the faithful to hold fast to the traditions which they have learned either by word of mouth or by letter (see 2 Thess. 2:15), and to fight in defense of the faith handed on once and for all (see Jud. 3). Now what was handed on by the Apostles includes everything which contributes toward the holiness of life and increase in faith of the people of God; and so the Church, in her teaching, life and worship, perpetuates and hands on to all generations all that she herself is, all that she believes.

This tradition which comes from the Apostles develops in the Church with the help of the Holy Spirit. For there is a growth in the understanding of the realities and the words which have been handed down. This happens through the contemplation and study made by believers, who treasure these things in their hearts (see Luke, 2:19, 51) through a penetrating understanding of the spiritual realities which they experience, and through the preaching of those who have received through episcopal succession the sure gift of truth. For as the centuries succeed one another, the Church constantly moves forward toward the fulness of divine truth until the words of God reach their complete fulfillment in her.

The words of the holy fathers witness to the presence of this living tradition, whose wealth is poured into the practice and life of the believing and praying Church. Through the same tradition the Church's full canon of the sacred books is known, and the sacred writings themselves are more profoundly understood and unceasingly made active in her; and thus God, who spoke of old, uninterruptedly converses with the bride of His beloved Son; and the Holy Spirit, through whom the living voice of the Gospel resounds in the Church, and

through her, in the world, leads unto all truth those who believe and makes the word of Christ dwell abundantly in them (see Col. 3:16).

9. Hence there exists a close connection and communication between sacred tradition and sacred Scripture. For both of them, flowing from the same divine wellspring, in a certain way merge into a unity and tend toward the same end. For Sacred Scripture is the word of God inasmuch as it is consigned to writing under the inspiration of the divine Spirit, while sacred tradition takes the word of God entrusted by Christ the Lord and the Holy Spirit to the Apostles, and hands it on to their successors in its full purity, so that led by the light of the Spirit of truth, they may in proclaiming it preserve this word of God faithfully, explain it, and make it more widely known. Consequently it is not from Sacred Scripture alone that the Church draws her certainty about everything which has been revealed. Therefore both sacred tradition and Sacred Scripture are to be accepted and venerated with the same sense of loyalty and reverence.

10. Sacred tradition and sacred Scripture form one sacred deposit of the word of God, committed to the Church. Holding fast to this deposit the entire holy people united with their shepherds remain always steadfast in the teaching of the Apostles, in the common life, in the breaking of the bread and in prayers (see Acts 2, 42, Greek text), so that holding to, practicing and professing the heritage of the faith, it becomes on the part of the bishops and faithful a single common effort.

But the task of authentically interpreting the word of God, whether written or handed on, has been entrusted exclusively to the living teaching office of the Church, whose authority is exercised in the name of Jesus Christ. This teaching office is not above the word of God, but serves it, teaching only what has been handed on, listening to it devoutly, guarding it scrupulously and explaining it faithfully in accord with a divine commission and with the help of the Holy Spirit; it draws from this one deposit of faith everything which it presents for belief as divinely revealed.

It is clear, therefore, that sacred tradition, sacred Scripture and the teaching authority of the Church, in accord with God's most wise design, are so linked and joined together that one cannot stand without the others, and that all together and each in its own way under the action of the one Holy Spirit contribute effectively to the salvation of souls.

SACRED SCRIPTURE, ITS INSPIRING AND DIVINE INTERPRETATION

11. Those divinely revealed realities which are contained and presented in sacred Scripture have been committed to writing under the inspiration of the Holy Spirit. For holy mother Church, relying on the belief of the Apostles (see John, 20:31; 2 Tim. 3:16; 2 Peter 1:19-20, 3:15-16), holds that the books of both the Old and New Testaments in their entirety, with all their parts, are sacred and canonical because written under the inspiration of the Holy Spirit, they have God as their author and have been handed on as such to the Church herself. In composing the sacred books, God chose men and while employed by Him they made use of their powers and abilities, so that with Him acting in them and through them, they, as true authors, consigned to writing everything and only those things which He wanted.

Therefore since everything asserted by the inspired authors or sacred writers must be held to be asserted by the Holy Spirit, it follows that the books of Scripture must be acknowledged as teaching solidly, faithfully and withour error that truth which God wanted put into the sacred writings for the sake of our salvation. Therefore "all Scripture is inspired of God and is useful for teaching—for reproof, correction, and training in holiness so that the man of God may be fully competent and equipped for every good work" (2 Tim. 3:16-17, Greek text).

12. However, since God speaks in sacred Scripture through men in human fashion, the interpreter of sacred Scripture, in order to see clearly what God wanted to communicate to us, should carefully investigate what meaning the sacred writers really intended, and what God wanted to manifest by means of their words.

To search out the intention of the sacred writers, attention should be given, among other things, to "literary forms." For truth is set forth and expressed differently in texts which are variously historical, prophetic, poetic, or of other forms of discourse. The interpreter must investigate what meaning the sacred writer intended to express and actually expressed in particular circumstances by using contemporary literary forms in accordance with the situation of his own time and culture. For the correct understanding of what the sacred author wanted to assert, due attention must be paid to the customary and characteristic styles of feeling, speaking and narrating which prevailed at the time of the sacred writer, and to the patterns men normally employed at that period in their everyday dealings with one another.

But, since holy Scripture must be read and interpreted in the same spirit in which it was written, no less serious attention must be given to the content and unity of the whole of Scripture if the meaning of the sacred texts is to be correctly worked out. The living tradition of the whole Church must be taken into account along with the harmony which exists between elements of the faith. It is the task of exegetes to work according to these rules toward a better understanding and explanation of the meaning of sacred Scripture, so that through preparatory study the judgment of the Church may mature. For all of what has been said about the way of interpreting Scripture is subject finally to the judgment of the Church, which carries out the divine commission and ministry of guarding and interpreting the word of God.

13. In sacred Scripture, therefore, while the truth and holiness of God always remains intact, the marvelous "condescension" of eternal wisdom is clearly shown, "that we may learn the gentle kindness of God, which words cannot express, and how far He has gone in adapting His language with thoughtful concern for our weak human nature." For the words of God, expressed in human language, have been made like human discourse, just as the word of the eternal Father, when He took to Himself the flesh of human weakness, was in every way made like men.

THE OLD TESTAMENT

14. In carefully planning and preparing the salvation of the whole human race the God of infinite love, by a special dispensation, chose for Himself a people to whom He would entrust His promises. First He entered into a covenant with Abraham (see Gen. 15:18) and, through Moses, with the people of Israel (see Ex. 24:8). To this people which He had acquired for Himself, He so manifested Himself through words and deeds as the one true and living God that Israel came to know by experience the ways of God with men. Then, too, when God Himself spoke to them through the mouth of the prophets, Israel daily gained a deeper and clearer understanding of His ways and made them more widely known among the nations (see Ps. 21:29; 95:1-3; Is. 2:1-5; Jer. 3:17). The plan of salvation foretold by the sacred authors, recounted and explained by them, is found as the

true word of God in the books of the Old Testament: these books, therefore, written under divine inspiration, remain permanently valuable. "Everything written before our time was written for our instruction, that we might derive hope from the lessons of patience and the words of encouragement in the Scriptures" (Rom. 15:4).

15. The principal purpose to which the plan of the old covenant was directed was to prepare for the coming of Christ, the redeemer of all and of the messianic kingdom, to announce this coming by prophecy (see Luke 24:44, John 5:39; 1 Peter 1:10), and to indicate its meaning through various types (see I Cor. 10:12). Now the books of the Old Testament, in accordance with the state of mankind before the time of salvation established by Christ, reveal to all men the knowledge of God and of man and the ways in which God, just and merciful, deals with men. These books, though they also contain some things which are incomplete and temporary, nevertheless show us true divine pedagogy. These same books, then, give expression to a lively sense of God, contain a store of sublime teachings about God, sound wisdom about human life, and a wonderful treasury of prayers, and in them the mystery of our salvation is present in a hidden way. Christians should receive them with reverence.

16. God, the inspirer and author of both Testaments, wisely arranged that the New Testament be hidden in the Old and the Old be made manifest in the New. For, though Christ established the new covenant in His blood (see Luke 22:20; 1 Cor. 11:25), still the books of the Old Testament with all their parts, caught up into the proclamation of the Gospel, acquire and show forth their full meaning in the New Testament (see Matt. 5:17; Luke 24:27; Rom. 16:25-26; 2 Cor. 14:16) and in turn shed light on it and explain it.

THE NEW TESTAMENT

17. The word of God, which is the power of God for the salvation of all who believe (see Rom. 1:16), is set forth and shows its power in a most excellent way in the writings of the New Testament. For when the fulness of time arrived (see Gal. 4:4), the Word was made flesh and dwelt among us in His fulness of graces and truth (see John 1:14). Christ established the kingdom of God on earth, manifested His Father and Himself by deeds and words, and completed His work by His death, resurrection and glorious Ascension and by the

sending of the Holy Spirit. Having been lifted up from the earth, He draws all men to Himself (see John 12:32, Greek text), He who alone has the words of eternal life (see John 6:68). This mystery had not been manifested to other generations as it was now revealed to His holy Apostles and prophets in the Holy Spirit (see Eph. 3:4-6, Greek text), so that they might preach the Gospel, stir up faith in Jesus, Christ and Lord, and gather together the Church. Now the writings of the New Testament stand as a perpetual and divine witness to these realities.

18. It is common knowledge that among all the Scriptures, even those of the New Testament, the Gospels have a special preeminence, and rightly so, for they are the principal witness for the life and teaching of the incarnate Word, our savior.

The Church has always and everywhere held and continues to hold that the four Gospels are of apostolic origin. For what the Apostles preached in fulfillment of the commission of Christ, afterwards they themselves and apostolic men, under the inspiration of the divine Spirit, handed on to us in writing: the foundation of faith, namely, the fourfold Gospel, according to Matthew, Mark, Luke and John.

19. Holy Mother Church has firmly and with absolute constancy held, and continues to hold, that the four Gospels just named, whose historical character the Church unhesitatingly asserts, faithfully hand on what Jesus Christ, while living among men, really did and taught for their eternal salvation until the day He was taken up into heaven (see Acts 1:1). Indeed, after the ascension of the Lord the Apostles handed on to their hearers what He had said and done. This they did with that clearer understanding which they enjoyed after they had been instructed by the glorious events of Christ's life and taught by the light of the Spirit of truth. The sacred authors wrote the four Gospels, selecting some things from the many which had been handed on by word of mouth or in writing, reducing some of them to a synthesis, explaining some things in view of the situation of their churches, and preserving the form of proclamation but always in such fashion that they told us the honest truth about Jesus. For their intention in writing was that either from their own memory and recollections, or from the witness of those who themselves were "The original eyewitnesses and ministers of the word" we might know "the truth" concerning those

matters about which we have been instructed (see Luke 1:2-4).

20. Besides the four Gospels, the canon of the New Testament also contains the epistles of St. Paul and other apostolic writings, composed under the inspiration of the Holy Spirit, by which according to the wise plan of God, those matters which concern Christ the Lord are confirmed, His true teaching is more and more fully stated, the saving power of the divine work of Christ is preached, the story is told of the beginnings of the Church and its marvelous growth, and its glorious fulfillment is foretold.

For the Lord Jesus was with His apostles as He had promised (see Matt. 28:20) and sent them the advocate Spirit who would lead them into the fulness of truth (see John 16:13).

SACRED SCRIPTURE
IN THE LIFE OF THE CHURCH

21. The Church has always venerated the divine Scriptures just as she venerates the body of the Lord, since, especially in the sacred liturgy, she unceasingly receives and offers to the faithful the bread of life from the table both of God's word and of Christ's body. She has always maintained them, and continues to do so, together with sacred tradition, as the supreme rule of faith, since, as inspired by God and committed once and for all to writing, they impart the word of God Himself without change, and make the voice of the Holy Spirit resound in the words of the prophets and Apostles. Therefore, like the Christian religion itself, all the preaching of the Church must be nourished and regulated by sacred Scripture. For in the sacred books, the Father who is in heaven meets His children with great love and speaks with them; and the force and power in the word of God is so great that it stands as the support and energy of the Church, the strength of faith for her sons, the food of the soul, the pure and everlasting source of spiritual life. Consequently these words are perfectly applicable to sacred Scripture: "Indeed, God's word is living and active" (Heb. 4:12) and it "can enlarge you, and give you a share among all who are consecrated to him" (Acts 20:32; see I Thess. 2:13).

22. Easy access to sacred Scripture should be provided for all the Christian faithful. That is why the Church from the very beginning accepted as her own that very ancient Greek translation of the Old Testament which is called the septuagint; and she has always given a place of honor to other Eastern translations and Latin ones, especially the Latin translation known as the vulgate. But since the word of God should be accessible at all times, the Church by her authority and with maternal concern sees to it that suitable and correct translations are made into different languages, especially from the original texts of the sacred books. And should the opportunity arise and the Church authorities approve, if these translations are produced in cooperation with the separated brethren as well, all Christians will be able to use them.

23. The bride of the incarnate Word, the Church taught by the Holy Spirit, is concerned to move ahead toward a deeper understanding of the sacred Scriptures so that she may increasingly feed her sons with the divine words. Therefore, she also encourages the study of the holy Fathers of both East and West and of sacred liturgies. Catholic exegetes then and other students of sacred theology, working diligently together and using appropriate means, should devote their energies, under the watchful care of the sacred teaching office of the Church, to an exploration and exposition of the divine writings. This should be so done that as many ministers of the divine word as possible will be able effectively to provide the nourishment of the Scriptures for the people of God, to enlighten their minds, strengthen their wills, and set men's hearts on fire with the love of God. The sacred synod encourages the sons of the Church and Biblical scholars to continue energetically, following the mind of the Church, with the work they have so well begun, with a constant renewal of vigor.

24. Sacred theology rests on the written word of God, together with sacred tradition, as its primary and perpetual foundation. By scrutinizing in the light of faith all truth stored up in the mystery of Christ, theology is most powerfully strengthened and constantly rejuvenated by that word. For the sacred Scriptures contain the word of God and since they are inspired really are the word of God; and so the study of the sacred page is, as it were, the soul of sacred theology. By the same word of Scripture the ministry of the word also, that is, pastoral preaching, catechetics and all Christian instruction, in which the liturgical homily must hold the foremost place, is nourished in a healthy way and flourishes in a holy way.

25. Therefore, all the clergy must hold fast to the sacred Scriptures through diligent sacred reading and careful study, especially the priests of Christ and others, such as deacons and catechists who are legitimately active in the ministry of the word. This is to be done so that none of them will become "an empty preacher of the word of God outwardly, who is not a listener to it inwardly" since they must share the abundant wealth of the divine word with the faithful committed to them, especially in the sacred liturgy. The sacred synod also earnestly and especially urges all the Christian faithful, especially Religious, to learn by frequent reading of the divine Scriptures the "surpassing knowledge" of Jesus Christ (Phil. 3:8). "For ignorance of the Scriptures is ignorance of Christ." Therefore, they should gladly put themselves in touch with the sacred text itself, whether it be through the liturgy, rich in the divine word, or through devotional reading, or through instructions suitable for the purpose and other aids which, in our time, with approval and active support of the shepherds of the Church, are commendably spread everywhere. And let them remember that prayer should accompany the reading of sacred Scripture, so that God and man may talk together; for "we speak to Him when we pray; we hear Him when we read the divine saying."

It devolves on sacred bishops "who have the apostolic teaching" to give the faithful entrusted to them suitable instruction in the right use of the divine books, especially the New Testament and above all the Gospels. This can be done through translations of the sacred texts, which are to be provided with the necessary and really adequate explanations so that the children of the Church may safely and profitably become conversant with the sacred Scriptures and be penetrated with their spirit.

Furthermore, editions of the sacred Scriptures, provided with suitable footnotes, should be prepared also for the use of non-Christians and adapted to their situation. Both pastors of souls and Christians generally should see to the wise distribution of these in one way or another.

26. In this way, therefore, through the reading and study of the sacred books "the word of the Lord may make progress and be hailed" (2 Thess. 3:1) and the treasure of revelation, entrusted to the Church, may more and more fill the hearts of men. Just as the life of the Church is strengthened through more frequent celebration of the Eucharistic mystery, similarly we may hope for a new stimulus for the life of the Spirit from a growing reverence for the word of God, which "stands forever" (Is. 40:8; see I Peter 1:23-25).